Contents

D0123085

Preface to the Third Edition

More than two decades have passed since the creation of "Quality Control Handbook" (First Edition 1951) as a reference work for managers, supervisors, and engineers in industry. The intervening years have seen a gratifying acceptance of the Handbook. This response has been international in scope, extending to multiple foreign translations of both the first and second editions.

These same years have also witnessed a remarkable transformation of the quality function in industry. From a minor, obscure activity, usually relegated to the lowest levels of organization, it has emerged as a major industrial function which increasingly commands the attention of leaders of the national economy. There is hardly a day when quality is not "news" in the national press. Often it is front page news: product safety, reliability of defense weapons, product recalls, lawsuits based on product failures. None of us had foreseen, several decades ago, that the quality function might grow so explosively in importance.

The industrial enterprises have reacted to this growth of the quality function not only by enlarging the breadth of the quality manager's job (increasingly he holds the rank of vice-president); the reaction has also included new organization forms which provide broad participation in the quality function by all departments. Common examples of such participation are design reviews, Material Review Boards, Product Safety Committees, quality improvement programs, and still other interdepartmental forms, along with an emerging interest in corporate quality policies and goals. This increased participation by all departments makes clear that a handbook devoted to quality control should reflect the interests of all departments of the enterprise and should provide an array of quality control knowhow suitable for reference by all managers and specialists.

In response to this "remarkable transformation" of the quality function, "Quality Control Handbook" has likewise undergone a revolutionary set of changes:

1. The third edition has grown in several ways:
There are now 52 Sections (chapters) vs. 39 in the second edition.
The number of authors has grown to 42 (from 26).
The size of the book has grown to 1,800 pages (from 1,200).

2. An important area of growth has been in the business and managerial subject matter, as exemplified by the emergence of whole Sections devoted to: Quality and Income, Quality Costs, Motivation, Upper Management and Quality, Support Operations, Service Industries.

3. A series of eight coordinated Sections has been prepared in a way which follows the product during its natural life cycle: New-Product Quality, Manufacturing Planning, Vendor Quality, Production of Quality, Inspection and Test, Measurement, Marketing of Quality, and Field Performance. This series typifies the broad view taken of the entire quality function as a service to the enterprise and to society generally.

4. The number of "industry" Sections has grown to 20 (from 13). Included in this growth are nonmanufacturing activities such as Support Operations and Service Industries.

5. The international nature of quality activities has been recognized by the creation of two Sections devoted to the special problems of Quality and the National Culture. Correspondingly, the Handbook includes, for the first time, contributions from non-American authors—five of them.

6. The statistical Sections have been reorganized to expand on advanced techniques while retaining the basics in more succinct form.

7. Even the "same" Sections differ extensively from their predecessors. For example, the Section on New-Product Quality is now heavily involved with reliability, maintainability, design for safety, etc., all on a scale well beyond that prevailing in prior editions.

The resulting larger third edition, with its higher density of contents, also complicates the reader's problems of finding what he is looking for. To this end, new Sections are provided on How to Use the Handbook and on Basic Concepts. New charts and diagrams have been added, as well as new tabular organization of text material, all to permit more and more recognition "at a glance" of complex interrelationships in the subject matter. Finally, a shocking number of man-hours has been devoted to making that vital Handbook tool, the Index, serve as a swift, sure guide to the contents.

Although the primary use of the Handbook has been as a reference work, there has been a substantial added use as a training text. In my judgment, this added usage was the result of a vacuum in textbooks. The available textbooks on quality control were (virtually without exception) oriented exclusively to statistical methodology. To secure the benefits of a broader base of subject matter, some professors and instructors turned to the Handbook and used it as a broad-based textbook.

To fill this vacuum in textbooks, I prepared "Quality Planning and Analysis" (in collaboration with Dr. F. M. Gryna, Jr.). This book, published in 1970 (McGraw-Hill Book Company), is keyed to "Quality Control Handbook." With the publication of the third edition of the Handbook, "Quality Planning and Analysis" will be revised to key its references to the third edition. "Quality Planning and Analysis" has met with good adoption among Universities, Technical Colleges, Professional Societies, and in-house training programs. In addition, it has been translated, or is in process of translation, into Hungarian, Japanese, Polish, Romanian, Serbo-Croatian, and Spanish.

Also keyed to the Handbook has been my course on Management of Quality Control. This course (whose origins go back to 1928) has evolved into a well-documented full week's training course which (along with some shorter derivatives) has been conducted over 200 times, in over 25 countries on all continents. Over 10,000 managers and engineers — a significant proportion of the current generation of managers and quality specialists — have undergone this training.

The expanded size and complexity of the third edition have enlarged the editorial burdens as well. The task of revision, both in man-hours and in calendar months, has considerably exceeded that of the second edition. As a result, I am deeply indebted to the Associate Editors who have helped me shoulder this burden.

Dr. Frank M. Gryna, Jr., who had been Associate Editor for the second edition, has again edited the statistical Sections into a coordinated whole, while continuing his role as author. Richard S. Bingham, Jr., who had been a contributor to the second edition, has expanded his role to that of Asso-ciate Editor for the "Industry" Sections, while coauthoring no fewer than four Sections. In addition, both Associate Editors have participated fully in planning the revision, and have provided critiques of *all* outlines and manuscripts. Collectively, these activities have constituted a formidable undertaking for busy men.

Another debt is owed to the authors — managers, educators, and special-ists — who took time from full schedules to share their knowledge and experience with their international counterparts. These contributions are the very heart of the Handbook. Supporting these authors are the numer-ous secretaries, staff members, and librarians (as well as family members) who assisted in the exacting preparation of the technical manuscripts. All of us deeply appreciate the dedication behind this essential support.

I am indebted to the Literary Executor of the late Sir Ronald A. Fisher, F.R.S., to Dr. Frank Yates, F.R.S., and to Oliver and Boyd, Edinburgh, for permission to reprint Table III from their book "Statistical Tables for Biological, Agricultural and Medical Research."

Dr. Gryna acknowledges the help of Mrs. Willie Luscher and Mrs. Marion Nelson, who carried his principal secretarial burdens. Messrs. Joseph Tsiakals, Thomas Hudock, and P. Natarajan were most helpful in perform-ing calculations, preparing illustrations, and handling other details. He owes a special thanks to his wife Dee and to Wendy, Derek, and Gary for their patience and encouragement.

Mr. Bingham acknowledges the teamwork exhibited by the authors of the Industry Sections, and their achievement in meeting the challenge of reflecting current effective practice while insisting on excellence in the examples cited. He also acknowledges the admirable secretarial and editorial assistance provided by Ms. C. Virnig and M. McIntosh, respectively. To his favorite proofreader and critic, his wife Edith, his thanks for "tremendous support and understanding."

Finally, I am privileged once again to acknowledge the material assistance and moral support of Mrs. J. M. Juran. For nearly half a century she has collaborated with me in the preparation of manuscripts for 12 books and hundreds of papers for publication. It has been a performance beyond the call of duty.

J. M. Juran

Section **1**

How to Use the Handbook

J. M. JURAN

INTRODUCTION

This is a reference book for all who are involved with "fitness for use" of products and services. "All who are involved" includes:

The various departmental functions, e.g., product development, purchasing, manufacture, inspection, sales, field service

The various levels of management, from top executives through foremen

The various staff specialties associated with policies, objectives, planning, organizing, and improving and controlling quality

Practitioners in a variety of industries and processes, e.g., chemical, metallurgical, mechanical, electronic, job shop, service, etc.

It is a mistake to assume that the sole purpose of the book is to serve the needs of quality managers and quality specialists. The purpose of the book is to serve the entire quality function, and this includes participation from every major department of the organization.

While there is a great deal of know-how in this book, it takes skill and a bit of determination to learn how to find and make use of it. This first Section of the book has therefore been designed to help the reader to find and apply those contents of the Handbook which relate to the problem at hand.

USES OF THE HANDBOOK

Practitioners make a wide variety of uses of the "Quality Control Handbook." A survey conducted as part of the planning for the Third Edition showed that usage is dominated by the following principal motives:

1. To study the narrative material as an aid to solving problems
2. To find structured answers in tables, charts, formulas, etc.
3. To review for specific self-training
4. To secure material for the teaching or training of others

Beyond these four most frequent uses, there is a longer list of less frequent uses:

To review for personal briefing prior to attending a meeting
To cross-check one's approach to tackling a problem
As references for instructors and students during training courses
To indoctrinate the boss
To train new employees
To help sell ideas to others, based on (1) the information in the Handbook and (2) the authoritative status of the Handbook[1]

Usage appears to be more frequent during times of change, e.g., while developing new programs, working on new contracts and projects, reassigning functions, or trying out new ideas.

Irrespective of intended use, the information is very likely there. The problem for the practitioner becomes one of (1) knowing where to find it and (2) adapting the information to his specific needs.

ORGANIZATION OF THE HANDBOOK

Knowing "where to find it" starts with understanding how the Handbook is structured. The Handbook consists of several broad groupings, outlined below, of quality control know-how.

Managing the Quality Function   This Management Group of Handbook Sections (i.e., chapters) is devoted to the attainment of quality in *any* industry, product, or process. Some of the Sections in this group follow the "management sequence" as applied to the quality function: policy formation, goal setting, planning, organizing, manning, motivation, etc. Other Sections of this Management Group follow the "product progression sequence": new-product development, purchasing, manufacture, test, marketing, field service, etc. Still other Sections deal with broad problems of a coordinating nature, e.g., quality costs and quality improvement. Collectively, the Management Group consists of 21 Sections (Sections 3 through 21, plus 48 and 48A), and constitutes about half of the contents of the Handbook.

Statistical Methods   This Statistical Group shows how to make use of most of the statistical tools which are available for controlling and improving quality. This group is made up of the following:

1. Sections 22 through 28, each of which deals with one or more of these statistical tools
2. The Glossary of Symbols (Appendix I)
3. The supplemental statistical tables and charts (Appendix II)

Collectively, the Statistical Group makes up about 20% of the Handbook.

Industries and Processes   This Industry Group summarizes how quality is attained and maintained in each of a number of leading industries. These may be product-based (e.g., Household Appliances) or process-based (e.g., Metal Fabricating). This group (Sections 29 through 47) constitutes about 30% of the Handbook.

With one exception, these three groups make up the "know-how" contents of the Handbook. That exception is Section 2, Basic Concepts. In Section 2, a number of the most widely used "universal" concepts in the quality function (e.g., Control, Reliability, The Pareto Principle, Consumerism) are explained in detail. The purpose of creating a special Section for explaining these concepts is twofold:

1. To avoid what would otherwise be numerous duplicate explanations throughout the Handbook. Wherever one of these basic concept terms is used outside of Section 2, the explanation consists of a reference to Section 2.

---

[1] Also to impress visitors by the presence of an authoritative book on one's desk!

2. To make the explanation without the bias of attachment to some specialized use of the concept.

HOW TO FIND IT

There are three main roads for locating information in the Handbook:
1. Tables of Contents
2. The Index
3. Cross-references

In addition, there are supplemental devices to aid in securing elaboration.

Note that the Handbook follows *a dual system of numbering,* consisting of the Section number followed by page number, figure number, or table number. For example, page number 16-7 is the seventh page in Section 16. Figure or table number 12-4 is in Section 12, and it is the fourth figure or table in that Section.

Tables of Contents   There is a hierarchy of these. At the top is the list of 52 *Section headings,* each of which describes, in the broadest terms, the contents of that Section.

Next there is the *list of contents* that appears on the first page of each Section. Each item in any Section's list of contents becomes a *major heading* within that Section.

Next, under each of these major headings, there may be one or more *minor headings,* each descriptive of its bundle of contents. Some of these bundles may be broken down still further by alphabetic or numeric lists of subtopics.

In a good many cases, it will suffice merely to follow the hierarchy of tables of contents to find the information sought. In many other cases it will not. For such cases, an alternative approach is to use the Index.

Use of the Index   A great deal of effort has gone into preparing the Index so that, through it, the reader can locate *all* the Handbook material bearing on his subject. For example, the topic "self-control" is one of the "basic concepts" explained in Section 2. In addition, the concept of self-control is found in other Sections (e.g., 9, Manufacturing Planning; 11, Production of Quality; 18, Motivation, etc.). The Index entry for "self-control" assembles *all* these uses of the self-control concept and shows the numbers of the pages on which they may be found.

The fact that information about a single topic is found in more than one Section (and even in many Sections) gives rise to criticisms of the organization of the Handbook; i.e., Why can't all the information on one subject be brought together in one place? The answer is that we require multiple and interconnected uses of knowledge, and hence these multiple appearances cannot be avoided. In fact, what must be done to minimize duplication is to make one and only one exhaustive explanation at some logical place and then to use cross-referencing elsewhere. In a sense, all the information on one subject *is* brought together—in the Index.

Some key words and phrases may be explained in several places in the Handbook. However, there is always one passage which constitutes the major explanation or definition. In the Index, the word "defined" is used to identify this major definition, for example, "Evolutionary Operation, defined."

The Index also serves to assemble all case examples or applications under one heading for easy reference. For example, Section 16 deals with the general approach to quality improvement and includes numerous examples of the application of this approach. However, additional examples are found in other Sections, notably Sections 29 through 46. The Index enables the reader to find these additional examples readily, since the page numbers are given.

Cross-References   The Handbook makes extensive use of cross-references in order to (1) guide the reader to further information on his subject and (2) avoid duplicate explanations of the same subject matter. The reader should regard these cross-references, wherever they occur, as extensions of the text.

Cross-referencing is to either (1) specific major headings in various Sections or (2) specific figure numbers or table numbers. Cross-referencing may be done in the text or by way of footnotes. Either way, study of the referenced material will provide further illumination.

A Note on Abbreviations. Abbreviations of names of organizations are usually used only after the full name has previously been spelled out, e.g., American Society for Quality Control (ASQC). In any case, all such abbreviations are listed and defined in the Index.

Main Road and Side Roads   The text of the Handbook emphasizes the "main road" of quality control know-how, i.e., the comparatively limited number of usual situations which nevertheless occupy the bulk of the time and attention of practitioners. Beyond the main road are numerous "side roads," i.e., less usual situations which are quite diverse and which require special solutions.

(The term "side road" is not used in any derogatory sense. The practitioner who faces an unusual problem must nevertheless find a solution for it.)

As to these side roads, the Handbook text, while not complete, nevertheless points the reader to available solutions. This is done in several ways:

Citations. The Handbook cites numerous papers, books, and other bibliographic references. In most cases these citations also indicate the nature of the special contribution made by the work cited in order to help the reader to decide whether he should go to the original source for elaboration.

Footnotes. In addition to serving the conventional purposes, some of the footnotes provide some side-road discussion as well. Being related to the less usual situations, these side-road discussions are given in footnotes rather than in the main text.

Special Bibliographies. Some Sections provide supplemental lists of bibliographical material for further reference. The editors have attempted to restrict the contents of these lists to items which (1) bear directly on the subject matter discussed in the text or (2) are of uncommon interest to the practitioner.

Literature Search. Papers, books, and other references cited in the Handbook contain further references which can be hunted up for further study. Use can be made of available abstracting and indexing services. A broad abstracting service in the engineering field is Engineering Index, Inc., 347 E. 47 St., New York, N.Y. 10017. A specialized abstracting service in quality control and applied statistics is Executive Sciences Institute, Inc., Whippany, New Jersey. In addition, various other specialized abstracting services are available on such subjects as reliability, statistical methods, research and development, etc.[2]

In searching the literature, the practitioner is well advised to make use of librarians. To an astonishing degree, library specialists have devised tools for locating literature on any designated subject: special bibliographies, abstracting services, indexes by subject and author, etc. Librarians are trained in the use of these tools, and they maintain an effective communication network among themselves.

Author Contact. The written book or paper is usually a condensation of the author's knowledge; i.e., what he wrote is derived from material which is one or two orders of magnitude more voluminous than the published work. In some cases it is worthwhile to contact the author to discover whether he is willing to elaborate on what he wrote. Most authors have no objection to being contacted, and some of

---

[2] For a list of some of these services, plus related discussion, see Glenn, William A., The Role of Technical Information Services in Education for Quality Control and Reliability Engineers, *Industrial Quality Control,* pp. 645–647, June 1967.

these contacts lead not only to more information but also to visits and enduring collaboration.

Other Sources.   Resourceful men are able to find still other sources of information relating to the problem at hand.   They contact the editors of journals to discover which companies have faced similar problems, so that they may contact these companies.   They contact vendors and customers to learn if competitors have found solutions.   They attend meetings—such as courses, seminars, and conferences of professional societies—at which there is discussion of the problem.   There is hardly a problem faced by any practitioner which has not already been actively studied by his contemporaries.

ADAPTING TO USE

In many cases a practitioner is faced with adapting, to his special situation, knowledge derived from a totally different technology, i.e., industry, product, process. Making this transition requires that he identify the commonality, i.e., the common principle to which both his special situation and the derived knowledge correspond.

Often the commonality is managerial in nature and is comparatively easy to grasp. For example, the concept of self-control[3] is a management universal and is applicable to any person in the company.

Commonality of a statistical nature is even easier to grasp, since so much information is reduced to formulas which are indifferent to the nature of the technology involved.

Even in technological matters, it is possible to identify commonalities despite great outward differences.   For example, the concept of "anatomy of the process" is used as a basis for manufacturing planning, the approach to planning being strongly influenced by the nature of the process.[4]   In like manner, the approaches used to make quality improvements by discovering the causes of defects have been classified into specific categories which exhibit a great deal of commonality despite wide differences in technology.[5]

In all these situations, the challenge to the practitioner is to establish a linkage between his own situation and that from which the know-how was derived.   This linkage he must establish by discovering the commonality which makes them both members of one species.

A final aspect of adapting to use is that of cultural resistance to technological change.   This is usually the main obstacle.   See, for extensive discussion, Section 7, under Administration of the Quality Staff Specialty: Introducing Change.   See also J. M. Juran, "Managerial Breakthrough," McGraw-Hill Book Company, 1964, Chapter 9, Resistance to Change—Cultural Patterns.

[3] See Section 2, under Self-Control.
[4] See Section 9, under Responsibility for Manufacturing Planning: Anatomy of the Process.
[5] See Section 2, under The Universal Sequence for Breakthrough.   See also Section 16 generally.

Basic Concepts

J. M. JURAN

BASIC CONCEPTS: GENERAL

Any widespread discipline must identify and clarify the universal concepts which underlie its very existence as a discipline. In addition, it must evolve and standardize the key words and phrases through which the practitioners of the discipline can communicate with each other.

The quality function has taken some steps to identify and clarify these concepts and to prepare some glossaries of terms.[1] Because these have not been widely adopted (or even circulated), there is great difficulty in reaching a meeting of the minds when practitioners convene to solve problems.

[1] A major glossary of terms is the European Organization for Quality Control (EOQC) "Glossary of Terms Used in Quality Control." This compilation lists 398 terms and defines them in English. In addition, the compilation shows, for 14 other languages (13 European plus Arabic), the equivalents of these 398 terms (but not equivalent definitions). This glossary (3d ed., 1972) was prepared by the Glossary Committee of EOQC. Available from European Organization for Quality Control, P.O. Box 1976, Rotterdam 3005, Netherlands.

A glossary of terms and definitions relating mainly to reliability is contained in the "Handbook Reliability Engineering," NAVAIR 00-66-502, NAVORD OD-41146, pp. A1-2 to A1-13, published (1964, rev. 1968) by the direction of the Commander, Naval Air Systems Command, and the Commander, Naval Ordnance Systems Command, Washington, D.C.

The purpose of this Section is to define those concepts which are recognized as the principal universals in the quality function. These universals are identified and explained in that terminology which appears to have gained wide acceptance. In those cases where alternative terms have gained a significant following, these alternatives are also presented.

Some of these concepts are utilized in so many Sections of the Handbook that the main exposition is made here in Section 2. In such cases, cross-reference is made to this exposition in other Sections. Thereby, duplication of material is minimized.

Other concepts, while also universal, receive their main exposition elsewhere in the Handbook. In such cases, the present Section 2 gives only a brief definition and then makes reference to the broader exposition which appears elsewhere.

There are also numerous words and phrases which are used in special meanings not found in common dictionaries. Definitions for such words or phrases are given wherever they appear or through cross-reference. In addition, the Index identifies, for each such word or phrase, the location of the principal definition.

The reader is urged to keep in mind that differences in meanings of key words and phrases are a frequent source of confusion. The question "Just what do you mean by that word?" is especially important in those cases where someone else is drawing an "illogical" conclusion from the identical set of facts. Such outward differences in conclusions are seldom the result of illogical reasoning. More usually they are the result of logical reasoning from different concepts or premises.

FITNESS FOR USE

Of all concepts in the quality function (and in this Handbook), none is so far-reaching or vital as "fitness for use."

All human institutions (industrial companies, schools, hospitals, churches, governments) are engaged in providing products or services to human beings. This relationship is constructive only if the goods and services respond to the overall needs of the user in price, delivery date, and fitness for use. If the goods and services do respond to these overall needs, they are said to possess marketability or salability.

Among these overall needs, the extent to which the product successfully serves the purposes of the user, during usage, is called its "fitness for use." This concept of fitness for use, popularly called by such names as "quality," is a universal concept, applicable to all goods and services.

Fitness for use is determined by those features of the product which the user can recognize as beneficial to him, e.g., fresh baked *taste* of bread, clear *reception* of radio programs, *timeliness* of bus service, *life* of shoes, *beauty* of a painting, *status* of a club membership. Fitness for use is judged *as seen by the user,* not by the manufacturer, merchant, or repair shop.

Fitness for use is the resultant of some well-known parameters. These are discussed below, under Parameters of Fitness for Use.

As yet there is no standard, agreed-upon term to designate the concept of fitness for the user. Some decades ago the term "quality" had wide acceptance for this purpose. However, this term was weakened by the "reliability movement." In their zeal to be organized independently of the Quality Managers, the Reliability Engineers contended that product performance over a period of time was something different from the popular concept of "quality." These contentions were accepted in enough companies to weaken the term "quality" as an overall designation.[2] The creation, by the Reliability Engineers, of the term "quality and reliability" was an ex-

---

[2] This weakening took place among the industry managers and engineers but not among the general public. In those countries which have made "quality and reliability" a theme for national propaganda, the situation may be otherwise.

pression of their urge to emphasize a new specialty. Then, as more and more "abilities" came into prominence, the idea of creating long phrases by stringing together numerous added "abilities" (e.g., maintainability, producibility) was discarded as too cumbersome.[3] (The phrase "quality and reliability" may have been in a decline ever since.) Instead, totally new terms were created. Of these, the term "system effectiveness" has met with response among military, space, and complex system users.[4] Other terms have been "product performance" and "product effectiveness."

It would be most desirable to agree upon on a single short phrase to designate fitness for use in all situations. The word "system" is too elaborate for the bulk of the economy, e.g., food, clothing, shelter. The word "product" fails to include the service industries. Serious consideration should be given to a word not in common use, so as to avoid the reflexes and vested interests associated with words already in use.[5]

CUSTOMERS, USERS, AND CONSUMERS

A *customer* is one who buys from another. The purchase may be for the purpose of resale, in which case the customer is commonly a merchant of some sort. Alternatively, the purchase may be for use, in which case the customer is also a *user*. The purchaser of services is often called a *client*.

A *user* is one who receives the intended benefit of the product. The user may *consume* the product (e.g., burning of fuel or wearing out of a machine), or he may perform further processing to create a different product for sale.

Individuals and families who consume goods for personal purposes are commonly called *consumers*. Terms such as *consumerism* and organizations created to protect the interests of consumers refer to such individuals and families. In most organizations, usage is usually by some individual for the benefit of the organization, e.g., the machinist running a lathe, the stenographer operating a typewriter, the soldier firing a rifle.

The interests of manufacturers, merchants, and repair shops differ importantly from those of users and consumers. These differences are discussed in Section 4, under Contrast in Views: User and Manufacturer.

PRODUCTS AND SERVICES

To the economist there are *products* (e.g., milk, automobiles), and *services* (e.g., haircuts, lodging, electric power). The user is interested only in services, even though he may seem to buy products. He buys milk but really wants nourishment. He buys an automobile but really wants transportation, convenience, status.

The "service" industries commonly sell directly to consumers without the intervention of merchants. Through the resulting direct feedback, these industries become well sensitized to the concept of "fitness for use." (See Section 47.)

In contrast, manufacturing companies, particularly those who make consumer products, do most of their selling through an intermediate chain of merchants.

[3] For a tongue-in-cheek analysis, see Juran, J. M., A Visit to Complex Systems, Inc., *Industrial Quality Control*, pp. 37–40, January 1962.

[4] See, for example, "Final Report of Task Group II—Prediction-Measurement (Concepts, Task Analysis, Principles of Model Construction)," Weapons System Effectiveness Industry Advisory Committee, U.S. Air Force Systems Command, 1965.

[5] An interesting nomination is the word "ophelimity." The literal meaning is "power to give satisfaction," with a connotation that economic satisfaction is involved. The word is derived from the Greek "ophelimos," which means helpful, useful. (Private communication from Mr. Henry H. Schmalz, Quality Manager, Zenith Radio Corporation.)

Lacking as direct a feedback from users, these manufacturers tend to emphasize conformance to product specification rather than fitness for use. (See below.)

Products may be "hardware" (e.g., a computer) or "software" (e.g., a computer program). Sometimes the software rather than the hardware is the real product. For example, a product-development contract provides for delivery of a model plus the associated design data. The real product in such a case is the design data.

QUALITY CHARACTERISTIC

The basic building block on which fitness for use is built is the *quality characteristic*. Any feature (property, attribute, etc.) of the products, materials, or processes which is needed to achieve fitness for use is a quality characteristic. These characteristics exist in several subspecies:

Technological, e.g., hardness, inductance, acidity
Psychological, e.g., taste, beauty, status
Time-oriented, e.g., reliability, maintainability
Contractual, e.g., guarantee provisions
Ethical, e.g., courtesy of sales personnel, honesty of service shops

The concept of "quality characteristics" is as old as the human species (the entire biological world is responsive to the concept). However, there has been a long-range trend to quantify these characteristics. Technological characteristics, notably properties of materials, were extensively quantified beginning several centuries ago with the accelerated growth of instrumentation. The twentieth century has seen a similar movement to quantify the remaining types of characteristics.

Service industry quality characteristics, while including all of the above sub-species, are dominated by the psychological and ethical. In addition, the service industries generally regard promptness of service as a quality characteristic, whereas the manufacturing industries generally do not. Instead, manufacturing companies regard promptness (i.e., timely delivery of products to customers in accordance with promised date) as a parameter very different from "quality." The distinction is so sharp that there is a separate organization (Production Control) to set standards for delivery time (schedules), to measure performance, and to stimulate compliance.

PARAMETERS OF FITNESS FOR USE

Quality characteristics can readily be classified into several useful categories or parameters of fitness for use. This classification helps us to understand the nature and interrelation of the major economic forces involved and to define more precisely the needs of the user. The resulting major parameters are:

Quality of design
Quality of conformance
The "abilities"
Field service

The nature of these parameters is discussed below. Their interrelation then follows under the heading Interrelation among Parameters.

It is quite important to distinguish clearly among these parameters, as some very similar terms mean very different things. In a meeting of managers, if one asks for a show of hands on the questions "Does higher quality cost more?" and "Does higher quality cost less?" some will answer it costs more; others will answer it costs less. All are correct. Some have in mind quality of design, for which "higher" quality (i.e., greater fitness for use) commonly costs more. Others have in mind quality of conformance, for which "higher" quality (i.e., fewer defects) commonly costs less.

Because the unqualified word "quality" has multiple meanings, it is risky to use it in unqualified form. In the above example, though the same word ("quality") was used, one group of managers would literally not know what the other group was talking about.

QUALITY OF DESIGN: GRADE

All human beings exhibit certain basic needs, e.g., for nourishment and shelter. The industrial society elaborates these basic needs to include many others, e.g., transportation, communication. In addition, the human species has exhibited a timeless, powerful urge for control over the forces of nature, for security, for comfort, for artistic achievement, and for just more of everything.

While these human wants are almost universally aggressive, the human individuals (and human organizations) vary widely in their purchasing power or affluence. The resulting imbalance between a high level of human wants and a variable level of human affluence has led to the creation or recognition of different *levels of excellence* of products and services. For example, transportation may take place via a public bus, a private Volkswagen, a private Rolls-Royce, a private jet airplane. Each of these levels is called a "grade." A difference in grade is a difference in "quality of design," i.e., design to meet a human need (transportation in the example given).

"Grade" is a nontechnical term. It is widely used and understood by the public to mean a certain level of quality, which relates also to a level of fitness for use and a level of affluence.

"Quality of design" is a technical term. It can be regarded as a composite of three separate steps in a common progression of activities:

1. Identification of what constitutes fitness for use to the user

Curiously, there is no widely used term to describe this activity. Because the identification is the result of market research, the effectiveness of the activity might be termed "quality of market research."[6,7]

2. Choice of a concept of product or service to be responsive to the identified needs of the user

Masing[8] uses the term "quality of concept" to designate the extent to which the intended features of the product (the product concept) respond to the actual market needs. Haussmann[9] appears to use the term "quality of project." Grant and Bell[10] use the term "quality of design" in the sense of "degree of excellence of the design objective" (i.e., grade).

3. Translation of the chosen product concept into a detailed set of specifications which, if faithfully executed, will then meet the users' needs.

[6] See Haussmann, U., Quality, Effectiveness and Economic Quality Control (Qualität, Rentabilität und wirtschaftliche Qualitätskontrolle), *Qualitätskontrolle*, vol. 12, no. 6, pp. 66–72, June 1967. Haussmann tends to create "stages" of activity based on the functional departments involved. His categories (subject to translation difficulty) appear to include all three of the listed elements of quality of design.

[7] See also Chove, J., Quality and Manufacture of Industrial Products (La qualité et l'élaboration des produits industriels), *Bulletin de l'AFCIQ*, vol. 3, no. 2, pp. 49–58, 1967. Chove recognizes three levels of activity as contributing to design:
1. The level of use
2. The level of definition of function
3. The level of technical specification

[8] Masing, Walter, Quality Assurance—The Managerial Viewpoint, *Quality* (EOQC journal) Winter 1966.

[9] Haussmann, op. cit.

[10] Grant, Eugene L., and Lawrence F. Bell, Some Comments on the Semantics of Quality and Reliability, *Industrial Quality Control*, pp. 14–17, May 1961.

Grant and Bell[11] use the term "quality of specifications" to describe the extent to which the actual design specifications conform to the needs of fitness for use for the grade.

The total progression composed of these three activities is usually called "quality of design." Such is the designation in this Handbook. Under the terminology quoted above, quality of design may be said to consist of:

Quality of market research
Quality of concept
Quality of specification

Other terms seen in the literature (as synonymous with quality of design) include "degree of excellence," "design adequacy," "design capability," "design compatibility" (with the environment).

QUALITY OF CONFORMANCE

The design must reflect the needs of fitness for use, and the product must also conform to the design. The extent to which the product does conform to the design is called "quality of conformance." This term is widely accepted. Alternative terms are "quality of manufacture," "quality of production," "quality of product."

Quality of conformance is the resultant of numerous variables: machines, tools, supervision, workmanship, etc. Sections 11 and 12 are extensively concerned with this parameter.

THE "ABILITIES"

For products which are promptly consumed (e.g., food, fuel), the parameters of quality of design and quality of conformance are largely sufficient to determine fitness for use. For long-lived products, some new time-oriented factors come into play: Availability, Reliability, and Maintainability. These abilities are closely interrelated and are vital to fitness for use.[12]

Availability Continuity of life in the industrial society depends absolutely on the continuity of service from sources of energy, communication, transport, water, etc.[13] To provide this continuity, much effort has been devoted to discovering how to minimize the failure rates of products and how to restore service promptly in case of failure. One element of this effort has been to recognize continuity of service as a parameter of fitness for use and to set up to measure it. The name given to this parameter is "availability." It is time-related and is measured by the extent to which the user can secure service when he wants it.

A product is said to be available when it is in an operative state. The total time in the operative state (also called uptime) is the sum of the time spent (1) in active use and (2) in standby state.

The total time in the nonoperative state (also called downtime) is the sum of the time spent (3) under active repair (i.e., diagnosis and remedy), and (4) waiting for spare parts, paper work, etc.[14]

[11] Grant and Bell, *op. cit.*
[12] Still other "abilities" which have been nominated as useful parameters include:
Usability, which is a measure of the extent to which the design is convenient and foolproof for use.
Producibility (or manufacturability), which is a measure of the extent to which the design can be readily produced with existing machinery and processes. (This parameter has little direct relation to fitness for use.)
[13] For an elaboration of this concept, see Juran, J. M., Mobilizing for the 1970's, *Quality Progress,* August 1969.
[14] See Section 8, Fig. 8-11a and associated discussion.

Availability is expressed mathematically by the ratio:

$$\frac{uptime}{uptime + downtime}$$

In equivalent terminology, availability is also expressed by the ratio:

$$\frac{mean\ time\ between\ failures\ (MTBF)}{MTBF + mean\ time\ to\ repair\ (MTTR)}$$

Other terms used as equivalents of availability are "operational readiness" and "percent uptime."[15]

Reliability   If products never failed, availability would be 100%. However, products do fail, so that an essential subparameter of availability is freedom from failure, for which the accepted technical term is "reliability." The classic definition is "the probability of a product performing without failure a specified function under given conditions for a specified period of time."[16]

Architects and designers have for millennia tried to design structures and products for long life. What is now new is the movement to *quantify* reliability. It is a movement similar to, and probably as important as, the movement several centuries ago to quantify properties of materials. Once we are able to quantify reliability, we can more scientifically do many other things about reliability: predict, apportion, plan, achieve, test, control, improve.[17]

The probability of performing without failure can be converted readily to other measures, such as mean time between failures (MTBF), failure rate, etc. For simple systems the calculations are comparatively simple. However, for complex systems they become extremely complex. This has given rise to a huge literature on the methods for quantifying reliability.

Reliability is determined largely by the quality of design. The attainable reliability inherent in the design is called "intrinsic reliability." However, the achieved reliability is usually less than this due to unanticipated environments during use, lapses in quality of conformance, inadequacies in maintenance, etc.

The term "operational reliability" is sometimes used to distinguish attained reliability from intrinsic reliability.

Reliability is not to be confused with conformance to product specification (as evidenced by test of conformance) or even with reliability estimates based on life tests in the laboratory. The evaluation of achieved reliability requires actual use of product over a period of time plus collection and interpretation of data on performance and failures during that time.

Maintainability   The need for continuity of service has also stimulated much effort to improve the maintenance of long-life products. This maintenance takes place in two major ways:

1. Preventive or scheduled maintenance consisting of tests and checkouts to detect potential failures, scheduled servicing (e.g., lubrication), and planned overhauls plus replacement of worn or failure-prone parts

2. Unscheduled maintenance consisting of restoring service in the event of failure

The term "maintainability" has been adopted as an expression of the ease with which maintenance can be conducted.

Attempts to quantify maintainability soon encounter the fact that multiple measures are involved. Maintenance requires not only time but also manpower, spare

---

[15] See also Section 8, under Maintainability Concepts and Terms.

[16] "Reliability of Military Electronic Equipment," report by Advisory Group on Reliability of Electronic Equipment, Office of the Assistant Secretary of Defense (R&D), June 1957. (The historic AGREE report.)

[17] For extensive discussion on methodology, see Section 8, under Reliability in New-Product Design.

parts, expendable supplies, and other costs. Hence multiple measures of maintenance have been developed to correspond to these multiple factors. Of these measures, those that are time-oriented are regarded as most important, because so much human activity remains disturbed until service is restored.

The measures of maintainability actually in use include:

Mean time to repair (MTTR).
Probability of restoring service in the time period specified.
Mean time for scheduled maintenance (this is often subdivided between the inspecting and the servicing).

An emerging practice is to establish standards for the various repetitive time-consuming elements of maintenance.[18]

Effectiveness of maintenance is strongly influenced by the supporting technology: design for easy access and modular replacement at the users' premises, special instruments for easy diagnosis of causes of failure, special repair tools, technical information about the product and its use. Providing this supporting technology is generally regarded as a part of the subject matter of maintainability.

Effectiveness of maintenance is also strongly influenced by the availability of spare parts, sometimes called "logistical support." Providing this logistical support is regarded by some practitioners as part of the subject matter of maintainability.[19]

Terminology associated with maintainability is still in a state of evolution. Some practitioners separate maintainability into two categories: (1) the ease of conducting scheduled inspections and servicing, called serviceability, and (2) the ease of restoring service after failure, called "repairability."

FIELD SERVICE

The foregoing parameters are influenced mainly by what goes on prior to sale of the product to the user. Following the sale, the user's ability to secure continuity of service depends largely on some service organization which should:

1. Provide clear, unequivocal service contracts
2. Establish adequate repair equipment capacity and supplies of spare parts
3. Recruit and train a service force competent to diagnose and remedy failures
4. Provide prompt response to service calls
5. Conduct its affairs with courtesy and integrity[20]

The parameter which includes these after-sale service needs of the user is known variously as "field service," "customer service," "sales service," or just "service." The department supplying these needs is usually called "Customer Service." (This terminology has yet to be standardized.) The usual distinguishing features of this parameter are that:

It relates to activities which are carried on after sale rather than before sale[21]
It is performed by organizations regarded as service industries rather than manufacturing
It includes extensive contractual and informal contact directly with the user

Field service constitutes an underdeveloped segment of industrial activity, especially for small users. The large user has the economic justification and technological resources to create a captive repair shop from which he can secure good maintenance. Alternatively, he may contract out the repair work, in which case he has the

---

[18] See also Section 15, under Field Performance Measures.
[19] See Section 8, under Maintainability in New-Product Design.
[20] For an extensive discussion, see Section 15, under Field Service.
[21] The French term is "après vente," meaning, literally, "after sale."

technological capability for supervising the outside shop and the economic muscle to demand and receive good service.   The small user (consumer) lacks both technological and economic muscle and hence must rely heavily on the competence and integrity of independent service shops, of whom too many are not possessed of either competence or integrity.   (See Section 15.)

INTERRELATION AMONG PARAMETERS

The foregoing parameters can be sketched out in the form of a "tree" which helps bring out the interrelation (Figure 2-1).   There are numerous ways of subdividing these parameters, structuring the resulting trees, and setting up models for evaluation.[22]

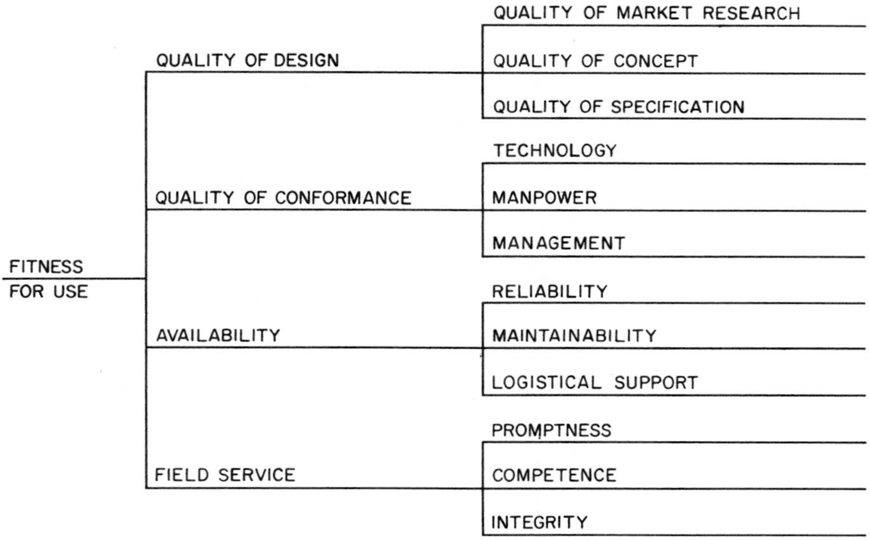

		QUALITY OF MARKET RESEARCH
	QUALITY OF DESIGN	QUALITY OF CONCEPT
		QUALITY OF SPECIFICATION
		TECHNOLOGY
	QUALITY OF CONFORMANCE	MANPOWER
		MANAGEMENT
FITNESS FOR USE		RELIABILITY
	AVAILABILITY	MAINTAINABILITY
		LOGISTICAL SUPPORT
		PROMPTNESS
	FIELD SERVICE	COMPETENCE
		INTEGRITY

Fig. 2-1   Interrelation among parameters.

As evaluations are prepared, it becomes easier to institute trade-offs, e.g., improve quality of design to reduce failure rates or to shorten repair time.   Some of the economics of trade-off are discussed in Section 4, under Life Cycle Costing.   Design aspects are discussed in Section 8, under Managerial Methods for Launching New Products.

SPECIFICATIONS AS SUBSTITUTES FOR KNOWLEDGE OF FITNESS FOR USE

In primitive societies there is little need for formal specifications.   Producer and consumer are often the same person, e.g., food gatherer, farmer, hunter.   Alternatively, they are different persons but they live in the same village and conduct their

---

[22] Welker, Everett L., Definition of Various Elements within the System Effectiveness Concept, *Proceedings Twelfth Annual Symposium on Reliability,* IEEE, pp. 149–161, 1966.   See also McCracken, Charles, *Probabilistic Model for Weapon System Performance,* Operations Research Society of America, Twenty-ninth Annual Meeting, 1966.

business in the village marketplace. They trade in products which are familiar to both and which are available then and there for inspection. When the purchased product turns out to be not fit for use, this knowledge can be communicated promptly from consumer to producer. With such short feedback loops, a producer is well provided with the knowledge needed to achieve fitness for use despite the absence of written specifications.

In the industrial societies, fitness for use cannot be achieved by such simple collaboration. For any one product, the activities of design, production, sale, use, etc., are carried out by numerous persons employed in various companies and widely dispersed geographically. In complex products the part time or full time of hundreds of individuals may contribute to the final result. Of these numerous individuals, only a few are so situated that they can understand how their contribution affects the

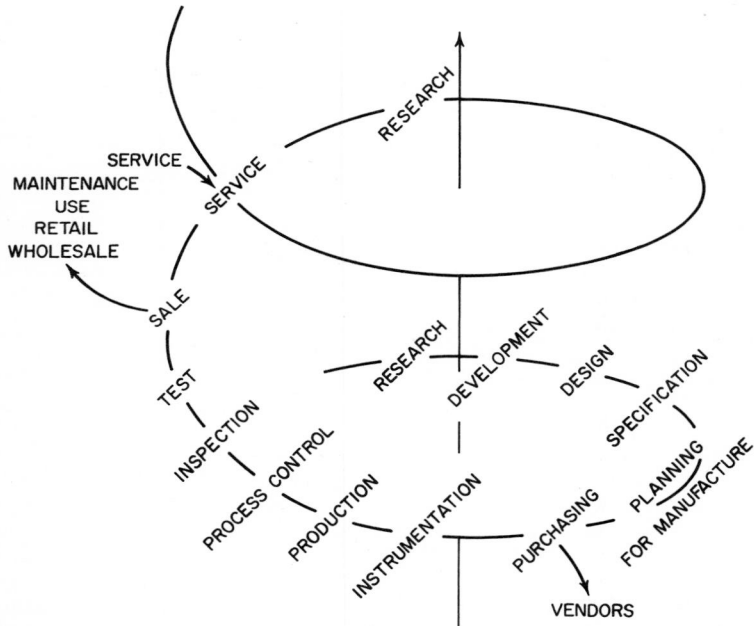

Fig. 2-2 The spiral of progress in quality.

real goal, which is fitness for use. In consequence, it is necessary to provide these individuals with a substitute goal, i.e., specifications. Subspecies of specifications (e.g., for materials, processes, products, test, maintenance, etc.) are available for every activity which contributes to fitness for use.

QUALITY FUNCTION

Achievement of fitness for use involves the performance of a number of separate deeds or activities in a logical progression. The principal activities in this progression are depicted in the Spiral of Progress, Figure 2-2. A turn of the spiral of progress starts with product research and development to create an improvement in fitness for use.   At the end of that turn, the experience of use creates a new idea, which starts a new turn of the spiral for further improvement.

Figure 2-2 makes clear that the activities needed to achieve fitness for use are scattered among many persons in many specialized departments.   Some of these are in-house.   Others are not—they are a part of vendor companies, merchant companies, user companies, consumer families.   In the companies, the specialized departments are also concerned with other functions, e.g., cost, delivery, personnel, technology.   Being concerned with multiple functions, the departments have multiple goals as well.   A major problem of modern industry is how to orchestrate the widely scattered activities which collectively constitute the quality function.   (See Section 7, Organization for Quality.)

The quality function is the entire collection of activities through which we achieve fitness for use, no matter where these activities are performed.

The term "quality function" is by no means standardized.   Until the twentieth century, the very concept of a quality function was obscure.

CONTROL

Much human energy is properly devoted to adherence to standards, which is a form of preventing adverse change.   Biologically this consists of maintaining the body temperature, the blood count, etc.   Industrially it takes the form of meeting standards: delivery according to schedule, expenses according to budget, quality according to specification.   The *process* through which we establish and meet standards is commonly called "control."   This process consists of a universal series of steps which, when applied to problems of quality, can be listed as follows:

1. Choosing the control subject, i.e., selecting what is to be regulated
2. Choosing a unit of measure
3. Setting a standard value, i.e., specifying the quality characteristic
4. Creating a sensing device which can measure the characteristic in terms of the unit of measure
5. Conducting actual measurement
6. Interpreting the difference between actual and standard
7. Decision making and acting on the difference[23]

The foregoing series of steps is the regulatory process by which we control anything; i.e., if you know how to control, you can control anything.[24]

The above definition of "control" as a process is very different from the meaning given in European countries to a word of the same pronunciation.   The European word, spelled variously as "control," "controle," "Kontrola," "Kontroll," or (Cyrillic) "КОНТРОЛ," is used in the narrow sense of product inspection.

QUALITY CONTROL

When the universal regulatory process (see Control, above) is applied to problems of product quality, it is often called "quality control."   This term also has other meanings, and it is essential to distinguish these from each other.   In this Handbook:

Quality control is the regulatory process through which we measure actual quality performance, compare it with standards, and act on the difference.

---

[23] The mechanism which carries out this universal series of steps is the feedback loop.   See Section 6, Figure 6-4 and associated discussion, under Planning for Control.

[24] For an extensive discussion of this universal process, see Juran, J. M., "Managerial Breakthrough," McGraw-Hill Book Company, New York, 1964, Chapters 12 through 20.

The other meanings of "quality control" include:

1. A part of the regulatory process, e.g., product inspection.

2. The name of a department which is devoted full-time to the quality function. In this usage, the term is capitalized, i.e., Quality Control.[25]

3. The tools, skills, or techniques through which some or all of the quality function is carried out.

The term "quality control" has had a short but lively history. Early in the twentieth century, it began to be used as a synonym for "defect prevention" (in contrast to the widely prevailing after-the-fact inspection).[26] However, during the 1940s and 1950s there was a wave of enthusiasm (and overenthusiasm) for the use of statistical methods in quality control. The proponents of this movement coined the phrase "Statistical Quality Control" (SQC) and publicized it so widely that many managers gained the impression that quality control consisted of the use of statistical methods in industry. A consequence was that the SQC movement weakened the use of "quality control" as an accepted term for the regulatory process.

In the late 1950s there arose a countermovement aimed at deemphasizing the limited approach of SQC and restoring the concept that a broad collection of tools is needed for regulation, of which statistical methods is but one. Various new terms were coined as labels for this countermovement, and some were well publicized, e.g., "Total Quality Control."[27]

During the 1960s, two additional movements helped to confuse the terminology. One of these was the trend to quantify reliability and related concepts. The advocates of this movement proposed to their companies the creation of Reliability Engineering departments which would be independent of the then existing Quality Managers. As part of their argument, these advocates contended that quality control as a regulatory process, and Quality Control as a regulatory department, had been limited in scope to "time zero" parameters. This contention was accepted in enough companies to undermine seriously the use of "quality control" as a comprehensive term for the regulatory process.

Additional confusion was created by the "motivational" programs of the 1960s. These programs, often called "Zero Defects" and undertaken (mainly) by government contractors, attained wide national publicity under a theory that adequate motivation will eliminate defects. (See Section 18, under The Formal Motivational Campaign.) One effect was again to undermine the prevailing terminology, since the terms used as names for the motivational programs received wider publicity.

It would be helpful to agree on a single term for the regulatory process. However, it would be difficult to secure such agreement. Most men tend to structure their glossary in a way which affirms their beliefs on organization structure, on priority of technique, etc. There have been enough instances in which choice of terminology was decisive in settling jurisdictional disputes to cause men to use terminology as a weapon in such contests. It is not merely a matter of aggression; there are many sincere human beings who feel that broadly standardized terminology is a detriment to their company needs (or personal aspirations) and that therefore new, local terminology must be coined to respond to these needs.

[25] For discussion on this point, see Juran, J. M., Activities and Labels; Functions and Names, *Industrial Quality Control,* pp. 248–250, November 1967.

[26] According to Bicking, C. A. (The Technical Aspects of Quality Control, *Industrial Quality Control,* March 1958), the term "control of quality" was first used in a paper by G. S. Radford (The Control of Quality, *Industrial Management,* vol. 54, p. 100, 1917). Radford's book, "The Control of Quality of Manufacturing" (Ronald Press Company, New York, 1922), is probably the first book in the field.

[27] Feigenbaum, A. V., "Total Quality Control," McGraw-Hill Book Company, New York, 1961.

SELF-CONTROL

When work is organized in a way which enables a person to have full mastery over the attainment of planned results, that person is said to be in a state of self-control and can properly be held responsible for the results. Self-control is a universal concept, being applicable to the General Manager responsible for running a company division at a profit; the plant manager responsible for meeting the various goals set for that plant; the machinist running a lathe, etc.

Before a person can be in a state of self-control, several fundamental criteria must be met. He must be provided with:

1. Knowledge of what he is *supposed to do,* i.e., the budgeted profit, the schedule, the specification.

2. Knowledge of what he *is doing,* i.e., the actual profit, the delivery rate, the extent of conformance to specification.

3. Means for *regulating* what he is doing in the event that he is failing to meet the goals. These means must always include the *authority* to regulate and the *ability* to regulate either by *(a)* varying the process under the person's authority or *(b)* varying the person's own conduct.

If *all* the foregoing parameters have been met, the person is said to be in a state of self-control and can properly be held responsible for any deficiencies in performance. If *any* of the parameters has not been met, the person is not in a state of control, and, to the extent of the deficiency, cannot properly be held responsible.

The application of the concept of self-control can be seen in great detail in Section 11, under Concept of Operator Self-Control, *et seq.*

SPORADIC TROUBLES: TROUBLESHOOTING

All continuing performances are subject to variation. Some of these variations are nonsignificant[28] and are ignored or deferred as to corrective action. Other variations are so significant that they trigger the alarm signals of the control system. These significant variations are a form of sporadic departure from standard, and demand that the personnel responsible for control heed the alarm signals and take steps to restore the status quo by (1) discovering which process changes created the symptoms responsible for triggering the alarm signal and (2) removing the causes of the changes.

Figure 2-3 shows a typical performance history embodying a sporadic departure from standard.

The sequence of events used to restore the status quo is known variously as "troubleshooting," "firefighting," etc. It constitutes an essential human activity and happens often enough to suggest that those who are responsible for meeting standards should be trained in the techniques of troubleshooting.[29]

CHRONIC TROUBLES: BREAKTHROUGH

In any system of control, the standard level of performance is also the goal. Implicit in this concept is the assumption that it is not economical (or even possible with known technology) to improve on the standard level.

Nevertheless, managers know that what used to be standard levels have often

---

[28] Significance may be either statistical or economic or both. For a discussion of statistical significance, see Section 22, under Tests of Hypotheses. Economic significance is influential in establishing the order of priority of corrective actions to be taken.

[29] For a discussion of troubleshooting as applied to Production, see Section 11, under Troubleshooting.

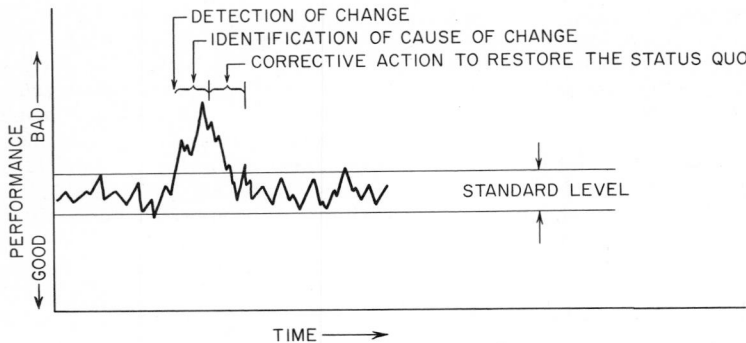

Fig. 2-3 Holding the status quo. *(From J. M. Juran, "Managerial Breakthrough," McGraw-Hill Book Company, 1964, p. 7.)*

been made obsolete through improvements achieved by determined men.   The process of achieving such improvements differs remarkably from the control process, since at the very outset the standard level is itself regarded as the wrong level of performance.   The difference between the (old) standard level and a proposed new level is regarded as a "chronic disease," for which a remedy can be found by determined men.   When a new, superior level of performance is attained as the result of such human determination, it is called "breakthrough."

Figure 2-4 shows graphically the breakthrough concept of improving on standard performance.

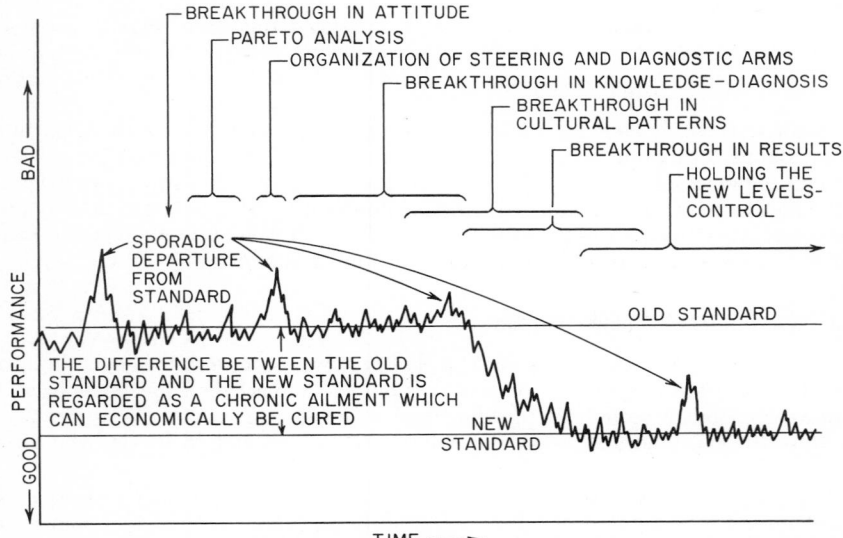

Fig. 2-4 Breakthrough. *(From J. M. Juran, "Managerial Breakthrough," McGraw-Hill Book Company, 1964, p. 7.)*

Some breakthrough forms differ in nature from that charted in Figure 2-4.   In many processes, reduction in process variation to a degree never previously attained can constitute a much-desired breakthrough.

Table 2-1 lists the major contrasts between sporadic and chronic problems as applied to shop defects.[30]

TABLE 2-1   Distinction between Sporadic and Chronic Defects

Aspect	Nature of sporadic defects	Nature of chronic defects
Tangible economic loss	Minor	Major
Extent of irritations caused	Substantial. Sudden nature of trouble attracts supervisory attention	Small. Continuing nature of trouble leads all concerned to accept it as unavoidable
Type of solution required	Restore the status quo	Change the status quo
Type of data needed	Simple data showing trend of quality with respect to one or two variables such as time or lot number	Complex data showing relation of quality to numerous variables
Plan for collecting data	Routine	Specially designed
Data collected	By inspectors in the usual course of their work	Often through special experimental procedures
Frequency of analysis	Very frequent. May require review every hour or every lot	Infrequent. Data may be accumulated for several months before analysis is made
Analysis made by.	People on the factory floor such as the production supervisor	Technical personnel
Type of analysis.	Usually simple	Possibly intricate. May require correlation study, analysis of variance, etc.
Action by whom	Usually by personnel on the factory floor	Usually by some department other than production

THE UNIVERSAL SEQUENCE FOR BREAKTHROUGH

An improvement is called a "breakthrough" if it meets two essential criteria:

1. The new (superior) level of performance has never previously been attained; it sets a new record.

2. The change is the result of human determination to set a new record; it is not the result of luck.   Man, not chance, is the master.

Analysis of the anatomy of achieved breakthroughs discloses that there is a universal series of steps to be followed:

1. Proving that breakthrough is needed and creating an attitude which is favorable for embarking on a program to attain this breakthrough

2. Identifying the vital few projects which justify the effort for improvement (See the Pareto principle, below.)

3. Organizing to secure the new knowledge needed to take effective action through providing the means for:

    a. Guiding and coordinating work on the projects

    b. Conducting the detailed study and analysis

---

[30] For an extensive discussion of the distinction between sporadic and chronic problems, see Juran, J. M., "Managerial Breakthrough," McGraw-Hill Book Company, New York, 1964, Chapter 1, Breakthrough and Control, A Contrast.

4. Actual conduct of the analysis or diagnosis
5. Dealing with the cultural resistance to the indicated technological changes
6. Taking action to institute the improvement
7. Instituting the necessary controls to hold the new level of performance[31]

The individual steps in this sequence are extensively exemplified and elaborated in Section 16, Improvement of Quality. Dealing with cultural resistance to technological change is elaborated in Section 7, under Introducing Change.

THE NATURE OF IMPROVEMENT

There are several ways in which tomorrow's quality performance is made to be superior to today's performance:

1. Troubleshooting to eliminate today's *sporadic* problems so that we restore the normal state of control, or status quo. This activity is defined above and is discussed extensively in Sections 11, 12, and 23.

2. Breakthrough, i.e., going from today's level of performance to a superior level by eliminating *chronic* causes of poor performance (or by removing chronic obstacles to better performance). The most extensive discussion of application of breakthrough is in Section 16, Improvement of Quality.

3. Planning, i.e., launching new products, processes, etc., in a way which avoids the creation of new chronic problems and which minimizes the appearance of sporadic problems. The planning process is extensively discussed in Sections 6, 8, 9, and 12 and is incidentally discussed in most other Sections.

THE PARETO PRINCIPLE

Managers are well aware that the numerous situations and problems they face are unequal in importance. In marketing, 20% of the customers (the "key" customers) account for over 80% of the sales. In purchasing, a few percent of the purchase orders account for the bulk of the dollars of purchase. In personnel relations, a few percent of the employees account for most of the absenteeism. In inventory control, a few percent of the catalog items account for most of the dollar inventory.[32] In cost analysis, roughly 20% of the parts contain 80% of the factory costs; the basic function of a product accounts for 80% of the cost, while the secondary functions account for only 20% of the cost.[33] In quality control, the bulk of the field failures, downtime, shop scrap, rework, sorting, and other quality costs are traceable to a vital few field failure modes, shop defects, products, components, processes, vendors, designs, operators, etc.

This phenomenon is not limited to industrial management. In human affairs generally, a few percent of the people own most of the wealth; a few countries account for most of the world's population. The principle extends to biological and other natural phenomena; e.g., a few percent of the biological species account for the bulk of the animal population; one planet contains the bulk of the mass of the solar system.

What runs through all these phenomena is the principle of the "vital few and the trivial many." A vital few members of the assortment account for most of the total

---

[31] For a detailed exposition, see Juran, J. M., "Managerial Breakthrough," McGraw-Hill Book Company, New York, 1964, Chapters 2 through 11.

[32] This is the basis of the so-called "ABC principle" of inventory control. See Prince, T. R., "Information Systems for Management Planning and Control" (rev. ed.), Richard D. Irwin, Inc., Homewood, Ill., 1970, p. 237.

[33] Mudge, Arthur E., "Value Engineering," McGraw-Hill Book Company, New York, 1971, p. 56.

effect. The bulk of the members (the trivial many) account for very little of the total effect. [34]

Many years ago, the author became aware that this phenomenon of vital few and trivial many was a universal. During the late 1940s he gave it the name "the Pareto principle," and this name has endured. [35]

A major use of the Pareto principle is in the design of quality improvement programs. Here the principle has so wide an application that no intelligent approach to quality improvement is possible without it. Improvement can be justified only for the *vital few projects*. It is these projects which contain the bulk of the opportunity for improvement in failure rates, quality costs, downtime, process yields, etc.

The vital few projects are identified through a "Pareto analysis." In its most basic form, this consists of a listing of the contributions to the problem in the order of their importance. For example, Table 2-2 is a listing of the work of 15 weavers in a textile department. The weavers are shown in an order reflecting the extent to which they produced imperfect product during that month.

TABLE 2-2   Pareto Analysis of Weaving Imperfects

Weaver	Defective yardage	Percent of all defective yardage	Cumulative defective yardage	Cumulative percent
A	106	33	106	33
B	81	25	187	58
C	51	16	238	74
D	21	6	259	80
E	14	4	273	84
F	13	4	286	88
G	9	3	295	91
H	8	2	303	93
J	5	2	308	95
K	3	1	311	96
L	3	1	314	97
M	3	1	317	98
N	2	1	319	99
P	2	1	321	100
Q	2	1	323	100

[34] For an extensive discussion, see Juran, J. M., "Managerial Breakthrough," McGraw-Hill Book Company, New York, 1964, Chapter 4, The Pareto Principle.

[35] Historical note by J. M. Juran: It was a mistake to name it the Pareto principle. Vilfredo Pareto, an Italian economist (1848–1923), had studied the distribution of wealth and had quantified the extent of inequality or nonuniformity of this distribution. However, he had not generalized this concept of unequal distribution to other fields. To make matters worse, the cumulative "Pareto" curves first published in the First Edition of the "Quality Control Handbook" should have been identified with M. O. Lorenz, who had used such curves to depict concentration of wealth in graphic form. (M. O. Lorenz, Methods of Measuring the Concentration of Wealth, *American Statistical Association Publication*, vol. 9, pp. 200–219, 1904–1905.)

To set the record straight:

1. Numerous men, over the centuries, have observed the existence of the phenomenon of vital few and trivial many as it applied to their local sphere of activity.

2. Pareto observed this phenomenon as applied to the distribution of wealth and advanced the theory of a logarithmic law of income distribution to fit the phenomenon.

3. Lorenz developed a form of cumulative curve to depict the distribution of wealth graphically.

(Footnote continued on page 2-18)

It is seen that there are striking differences in the extent of imperfects. Weaver A accounted for 106 imperfect yards, or 33% of all the imperfects, whereas several other weavers had less than 1% of the imperfects.

When the data are accumulated (right-hand columns of Table 2-2), it is at once evident that three of the weavers (the vital few) account for 74% of the total imperfect yardage. In contrast, the lowest 10 weavers (the trivial many) account for only 16% of the imperfect yardage.

A common graphic presentation of the data of Table 2-2 is shown in Figure 2-5. The chart shows two curves: (1) a frequency histogram of the imperfects by weaver

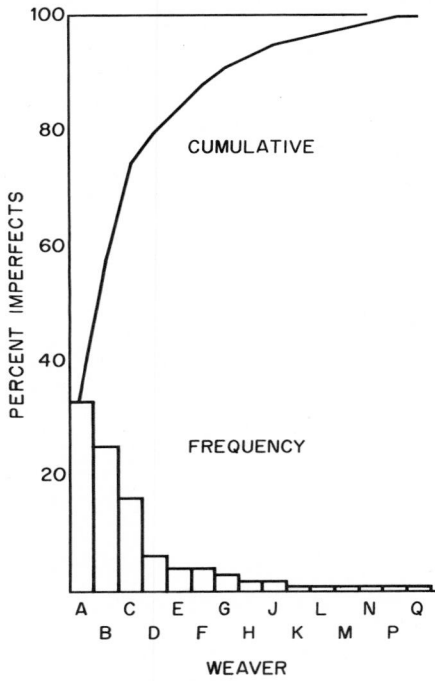

Fig. 2-5   Pareto analysis of weaving imperfects.

and (2) a cumulative frequency histogram of the type traceable to Lorenz (see historical note by J. M. Juran, footnote 35).

A useful variation in charting is seen in Figure 2-6, which makes more clear the relationship of the individual contributions to the cumulative totals.[36]

(Footnote continued from page 2-17)

4. Juran was (seemingly) the first to identify the phenomenon of the vital few and trivial many as a universal, applicable to many fields.

5. Juran applied the name "the Pareto principle" to this universal. Juran also coined the phrase "vital few and trivial many" and applied the Lorenz curves to depict this universal in graphic form.

(See also Juran, J. M., Pareto, Lorenz, Cournot, Bernoulli, Juran, and Others, *Industrial Quality Control*, October 1960, p. 25.)

[36] For added examples, see Peck, F. A., Concentrate on the Few, *Quality Progress*, pp. 21–23, March 1969.

The foregoing listing of weavers is an example of a Pareto analysis in its most rudimentary form, i.e., by production operator. The analysis may be also made in a variety of other ways, i.e., by types of defect, types of product, types of process, vendor, machine, work shift, date of manufacture, etc. (For actual examples, see Section 16, under Pareto Analysis.) The attempt is to find that maldistribution for which the fewest potential projects would provide the greatest potential for improvement.

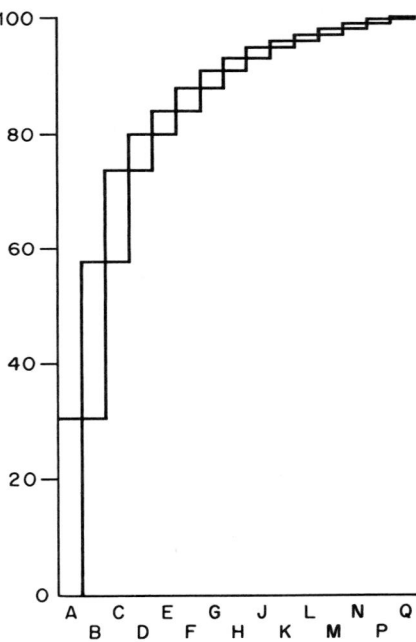

Fig. 2-6 Alternative Pareto diagram.

A more sophisticated form of analysis is by matrix. Table 2-3 shows an analysis of quality losses for machine shop scrap during a three-month period, using product classes on one axis and material composition on the other axis. The matrix makes clear at once that the scrap is dominated by product class A using material composition Y.

Examples of application of the Pareto principle are found throughout the Handbook, with a concentration in Section 16.

TABLE 2-3   Pareto Analysis by Matrix — Machine Shop Scrap ($000)

Material composition	Product classes				
	A	B	C	D	Total
X	1	1	4	1	7
Y	24	2	2	—	28
Z	2	—	—	—	2
Totals	27	3	6	1	37

THE DIAGNOSTIC AND REMEDIAL JOURNEYS

The activities known as defect prevention, quality improvement, quality cost reduction, troubleshooting, etc., all have their origin in an awareness of the undue presence of defects and a determination to do something about it. Once this determination has been made, the ability to take remedial action depends largely on the successful completion of two "journeys"—diagnostic and remedial.

The diagnostic journey consists of:

1. Study of the symptoms surrounding the defects to serve as a basis for theorizing about causes

2. Theorizing on the causes of these symptoms

3. Analysis and experiment to establish the true causes

The remedial journey normally begins when the true causes are known. It consists of:

4. Proposals of alternatives for remedy

5. Selection and application of remedy

6. Provision to hold the gains

Successful completion of these two journeys is aided considerably by a clear understanding of just what is meant by each of the key steps involved. A good starting point is to define some critical terms and to clarify some essential concepts.

A *defect* is any state of unfitness for use, or nonconformance to specification, e.g., oversize, low mean time between failures, poor appearance.

A *problem* is a potential task resulting from the existence of defects. The defects may be so minor that nothing will be done. At the other extreme, the defects may constitute so significant a problem that an organized approach will be structured for solution.

A *project* is a problem selected for solution through an organized approach of diagnosis and remedy.

A *symptom* is an observable phenomenon arising from and accompanying a defect. Sometimes, but not always, the same word is used both as a defect description and as a symptom description, e.g., "open circuit." More usually, a defect will have multiple symptoms, e.g., "insufficient torque" may include the symptoms of vibration, overheating, erratic function, etc.

A *theory* is an unproved assertion as to reasons for the existence of defects and symptoms. Usually multiple theories are advanced to explain the presence of the observed phenomena.

A *cause* is a proved reason for the existence of the defect. Often there are multiple causes, in which case they follow the Pareto principle, i.e., one or two causes will dominate all the rest.

A *dominant cause* is a major contributor to the existence of defects and one which must be remedied before there can be an adequate solution.

Diagnosis is the process of studying symptoms, taking and analyzing data, conducting experiments to test theories, and establishing relationships between causes and effects.

A *remedy* is a change which can successfully eliminate or neutralize a cause of defects. Usually, there are multiple proposals for remedy, and the remedial process must choose from the alternatives. In some cases, remedy takes place without knowledge of causes; e.g., take back the defective unit and give the customer a new one; cut away the rotten spot on the apple.[37]

---

[37] The medical profession also faces a need for precise definition of terms in diagnosis and remedy. It is useful to look sideways at some of its terminology, being mindful that their definitions are not fully applicable to industrial problems.

A *disease* is an abnormality in the functioning of an organism, e.g., smallpox. A *symptom*

Of these two journeys, the diagnostic is the main source of confusion. The reason for this is in part organizational. For sporadic defects—i.e., troubleshooting—the responsibility for diagnosis is usually clear. For chronic defects this responsibility is sometimes not clear, with the result that no one makes the diagnostic journey.

However, the main source of confusion is in concepts and terminology. In particular, managers tend to do the following:

1. Confuse symptom with cause. For example, internal scrap data sheets often have a column headed "cause," under which are listed such terms as "undersize," "broken," etc. The word "cause" is used in the sense of "reason for scrapping." However, such usage leads managers to assume that the cause of the defects is really known and that hence no diagnosis is needed—only remedy.

2. Confuse theory with cause. In discussing causes of defects, it is common for numerous theories to be advanced earnestly and even heatedly. "I *know* this is the cause." What the advocate means is that he personally is convinced. However, he lacks the data which can convince his colleagues in the face of all those other competing theories. Actually, until the diagnosis is complete, it is not known which is the dominant cause. In addition, since many theories had been advanced, only a small minority of the theories turn out to be decisive in the solution. (What all chronic defects have in common is that we don't *know* the causes. Lacking this knowledge, the defect goes on and on, which is what makes it chronic.)

For chronic defects, the diagnostic and remedial journeys are a part of a more comprehensive improvement program. This is discussed in Section 16, under Organizing for Improvement and other headings.

BUSINESS, MANAGEMENT, AND TECHNOLOGY

The activities needed to achieve fitness for use (Figure 2-2) can also be classified in terms of the basic disciplines employed. Three of these are of major concern:

1. *Business or entrepreneurship.* This is concerned with taking the risks associated with doing business at all and with the circumstances under which risks are taken. It includes judging the economic climate, choosing which markets to enter, financing the enterprise, taking specific investment risks, etc.

2. *Management.* This is the process through which people are mobilized to achieve designated goals. The process consists of a universal sequence of activities:

   a. Establishing the broad principles which are to guide action. These principles are, in this book, referred to as "policies." (See Section 3.)

   b. Establishing the quantitative goals or targets for performance. These goals are, in this book, referred to as "objectives." (See Section 3.)

   c. Defining the list and timetable of deeds which need to be done in order to carry out the objectives. Defining the list of deeds is, in this book, referred to as "planning." (See Section 6.)

   d. Defining the organization posts, i.e., jobs which need to be set up so that the planning will be executed. These jobs are known, collectively, as the "organization structure." The process of setting them up is known as "organizing." (See Section 7.)

---

is one of the outward evidences of a disease, e.g., fever. (Diseases have multiple symptoms.) A *syndrome* is that group of symptoms which uniquely points to a specific disease. *Diagnosis* is the analysis of symptoms to identify the disease which exhibits them. *Cause* is the proved active agent producing the abnormality. *Remedy* is the treatment process for neutralizing or eliminating the effect of the active agent.

e. Selecting and training people to man these jobs. This process is known as "manning." (See Section 17.)

f. Stimulating people to meet the objectives. This is known as "motivating." (See Section 18.)

g. Reviewing results against objectives and acting on the differences. This is known as "controlling." (See, for example, Section 21.)

The leaders of this sequence of activities are generically called "managers." What distinguishes the manager from other individuals is the fact that he must secure results through the efforts of other people.

3. *Technology.* This is concerned with harnessing the forces and materials of nature for the benefit of man. Technological quality matters include designs, specifications, processes, instruments, tests, failure analyses.

Many quality problems are traceable to the fact that top managers live in the world of business and management, whereas the quality specialists live in the world of technology.[38] The higher a man climbs the hierarchical ladder, the more time he devotes to business and managerial problems. (See Section 17, Figure 17-1 and associated discussion.) Top management's attention to quality activities is almost exclusively devoted to managerial matters. When we ask a company president "What does the word 'quality' mean to you?" he usually answers in business terminology, e.g., "Quality is what we sell. It's what our customers want. Our reputation is built on quality." Seldom is the answer in technological terms, e.g., tolerances, control charts, gage laboratories, etc.

These same differences are evident in the setting of quality goals and in planning to meet those goals. Company goals and plans are usually in business and managerial terms, whereas departmental goals and plans are usually in technological terms.

In this Handbook, the Sections dealing with business and management make little distinction as to industry involved, since these two disciplines apply to all industries with little variation in application. This commonality in the business and management aspects of quality extends to the industry Sections as well. In consequence, despite the great differences in technology among the industry Sections, they exhibit extensive commonality due to the need for adhering to common business and management principles.

CONSUMERISM

Large industrial buyers are commonly well able to protect themselves on matters of quality. They employ knowledgeable purchasing specialists who are backed up by competent engineers and supporting laboratories. They also have substantial economic bargaining power. Armed with this economic power and with the knowledge of how to use it, they are able to deal successfully with the sellers of goods and services on matters of fitness for use. Their complaints receive serious consideration, as do their ideas for quality and cost improvement. They can secure good repair service both within and outside the guarantee. Often they have an in-house repair service under their direct command.

In contrast, a small user (e.g., the housewife, the householder) has none of these protections. Lacking knowledge of the technology, he must secure his product knowledge largely from the advertising. Lacking knowledge of the inherent costs, he must rely on competition in the marketplace to keep the prices down. Lacking the personal competence to effect repairs, he must rely on the dubious competence, promptness, and integrity of independent repair shops. Lacking economic muscle,

---

[38] For elaboration, see Juran, J. M., The Two Worlds of Quality Control, *Industrial Quality Control,* pp. 238–244, November 1964.

he is sometimes brushed off when he complains about misleading advertising, product failures, or poor field service.

While the individual consumer has little economic muscle, the number of these consumers is very large. In consequence, their potential collective power is also very large once it is mobilized toward a common objective.

The movement to mobilize the collective strength of consumers is called "consumerism." The leadership of this movement comes from an assortment of sources: reformers, journalists, politicians, independent laboratories, labor unions, consumer cooperatives, industrialists. The 1960s saw the first major evidences that it might be feasible to mobilize consumers into an organized force in the economy. The implications for the future are profound.[39]

The detailed implications of consumerism, along with steps in progress to deal with the movement, are discussed in Section 4, under Consumerism.

QUALITY ASSURANCE

The ultimate responsibility for product fitness for use rests with the top managers, who are accountable to the directors, owners, regulators, public, etc., for the performance of the company. These top managers can and do delegate to subordinate managers the responsibility for carrying out those activities which make up the quality function. However, they may not delegate the accountability.

Historically, the top managers have guarded themselves against unpleasant quality surprises by making delegations to trusted subordinates, supplemental personal observation, studying reports from staff specialists, etc. Collectively, these methods were adequate to provide top managers with confidence in the conduct of the quality function.

More recently, as the quality function has become remarkably more important, there has emerged the concept that the top managers need an added source of confidence—formal, independent evidence to the effect that all is well with the quality function.

A parallel can be seen in the finance function. This function has always been regarded as critical, since a serious failure could bankrupt the company. In consequence, top managers, owners, bankers, regulators, tax collectors, etc., have long made use of independent sources of confidence. A major form has been the "independent financial audit," which provides assurance that:

1. The system of accounting is such that, if followed, it will correctly reflect the financial condition of the company

2. The system is actually being followed

The types of evidence being used to provide formal quality assurance include the "quality equivalent" of the financial audit. (See Section 21, under Quality Audit.) In addition, there are various other types of evidence. These are discussed in Section 21, under Quality Assurance.

The activity of supplying this added confidence to top managers (and to others concerned) is usually called "quality assurance." As used in this Handbook:

Quality assurance is the activity of providing, to all concerned, the evidence needed to establish confidence[40] *that the quality function is being performed adequately.*

While such is the meaning given in this Handbook, the term "quality assurance" has other meanings as well. Practitioners are well advised to understand these mul-

---

[39] For an extensive discussion, see Juran, J. M., Consumerism and Product Quality, *Quality Progress*, pp. 18–27, July 1970.

[40] This is not to be confused with "statistical confidence," which has a special meaning.

tiple meanings, since confusion on this important term can lead to serious misunderstandings. The added meanings include the following:

1. The name of the department which provides formal quality assurance as defined above. In such usage, the term is capitalized, i.e., Quality Assurance. This meaning of the term gives little trouble.

2. A new, more glamorous name for the activity of quality control as defined in Quality Control, above. Any renaming of an activity without changing its content is a sure step toward confusion. (An earlier example was that of renaming the activity of "inspection" by the term "quality control.")

3. A broad list of activities closely bound up with the quality function, i.e., quality planning, control, coordination, assurance, analysis, etc. Many United States companies have structured their organizations in a way which makes a centralized department responsible for conducting such a broad list of activities.[41] In such cases it is quite appropriate to coin new names in order to distinguish the new, broader list of activities from the former, narrow list. Failing this, retaining the old name conceals the change.[42]

4. The name of the department which carries out this broad list of activities. This uses the capitalized "Quality Assurance" and involves the same problems as (3) above.[43]

A WISTFUL POSTSCRIPT ON TERMINOLOGY

Communication in the quality function is seriously handicapped by the lack of standardization of terminology. One must cope not only with multiple terms for the same concepts but also with single terms that have multiple meanings.

It would be wonderful if all managers and practitioners were to standardize on the terminology used to describe concepts, deeds, and meanings. Such a paradise is far away, since there are some very active obstacles to standardization. These obstacles are mainly the following:

The differences in the technology, dialect, and cultural history of the various industries

The rapidly changing ingredients of fitness for use

The deliberate efforts of human beings to create and use terminology to secure benefits for their organizations and for themselves

The prime need is to discover the realities under the labels, i.e., the deeds, activities, or things which the other fellow is talking about. Once these are understood, accurate communication can take place whether the labels are agreed on or not. In contrast, if communication is purely through labels, it is easy to be deluded into believing there is an understanding despite the fact that each of the parties literally does not know what the other fellow is talking about.

[41] See Section 7, Table 7-2 and associated discussion, under Evolution of the Quality Control Hierarchy. See also Organization for Assurance under the same heading.

[42] For elaboration, see Juran, J. M., Activities and Labels; Functions and Names, *Industrial Quality Control*, pp. 248–250, November 1967.

[43] For further discussion, see Juran, *ibid.*

Section **3**

Quality Policies and Objectives

J. M. JURAN

THE NEED FOR QUALITY POLICIES

All organizations have in mind (or in writing) some principles, creeds, beliefs, etc., which are their broad guides to managerial conduct. These guides rest on a phil-. osophical and ethical base. They concern important issues, are the result of much reflection, and are intended to have long life, i.e., to act as a stabilizer. In this Handbook such principles, etc., are designated as *policies*.[1]

In tiny organizations where one man makes all the decisions, these guides to conduct are literally "in mind." The one man operates in accordance with his unwritten code of conduct. Anyone who wants to discover that code must deduce it from the observed deeds.

For example, the master of a small shop adheres to the (unwritten) policy of making good on any defects in his products. The townspeople discover this policy from his deeds and "publish" the policy by word-of-mouth.

As organizations grow, more and more managers are engaged in making significant decisions. These decisions affect numerous people inside and out of the organization, including the managers themselves. Unless there is consistency in these decisions, there is *no predictability;* neither insiders nor outsiders know what to expect. An impersonal way of creating this predictability is to think through, write down, and publish the policies which then become the basis for consistent conduct.

---

[1] The word "policy" is not standardized as to meaning. In many companies the organization charts and the procedures for control are assembled into a manual which is called the "policy manual" or "policy and procedures manual."

SUBJECT MATTER OF QUALITY POLICIES

The most common form of quality policy statement is a brief declaration such as the following:

It is the policy of the company to provide products and services of a quality that meets the initial and continuing needs and expectations of customers in relation to the price paid and to the nature of competitive offerings, and in doing so, to be the leader in product quality reputation.[2]

It is the policy of the corporation that its products shall meet all specified and implied standards of performance, reliability and quality.[3]

No one quarrels with such statements. However, they are regarded by most managers as too vague to provide guides for conduct. (Hence the name "motherhood" policies; i.e., everyone is in favor of motherhood.) To be useful, quality policies should provide specific guides to action for specific, important matters. Such guides help the insiders understand what is expected of them and the outsiders understand what to expect from the company managers.

For example, in vendor relations there is much debate on whether the buyer should provide technical assistance to vendors and whether there should be exchange visits between the buyers' and vendors' engineers to see the respective processes. In the Johnson & Johnson written policy on vendor relations, the following are included among the company's responsibilities to its vendors:

5. To place, whenever possible, the facilities of our research, development, and technical services at the disposal of our suppliers in order to help them with any problems they may encounter in supplying materials to our specifications and to aid them in developing better means for production and quality improvement.

6. To encourage exchange visiting by our suppliers' technical personnel and our technical personnel to observe our respective plant operations, thereby promoting a better understanding of mutual problems and objectives.[4]

Such published statements make clear, both to the company's managers and to the vendor's managers, the relationship to be established.[5]

Fundamental Policy Subjects   Choice of subject matter for quality policies is made to measure for each company. However, some matters are so fundamental and have such wide application that they should be considered by any company which is about to prepare written quality policy. These fundamental topics include the following:

What level of clientele constitutes the company's market? (This bears directly on choice of quality of design or grade.)

Is the company to strive for quality leadership, competitiveness, or adequacy?

Is the company selling standard products or is it selling a service in which the product is one of the ingredients of sale? (This affects the emphasis on conformance to specifications versus fitness for use.)

Is the company to market its products on the basis of high reliability at higher initial price or lower reliability at lower initial price?

Should the effort be to optimize users' costs or manufacturers' costs?

Should the "abilities" (reliability, maintainability, etc.) be quantified?

[2,3] These examples are from companies who have published them for internal use.

[4] Quoted through courtesy of Johnson & Johnson, New Brunswick, N.J.

[5] The Johnson & Johnson vendor relations policy ("Principles of Good Source Relations") includes a list of 20 responsibilities of the company to its vendors and 10 responsibilities of the vendors to the company.

Should the company rely for its controls on systems or on men?

Should quality planning be done by staff or line people?

Should the vendor be put on the team?

Should top management actively participate in quality planning and assurance, or should it delegate this to someone else?

Corporate and Divisional Policies   As the company grows to an extent which involves it in multiple markets and products, it becomes evident that no one set of quality policies can fit all company activities.   This problem is solved by creating several levels of quality policy.

One of these levels is corporate quality policy, which consists of the following:

1. A statement of those policies which are companywide in their effect and hence binding on all company organization units.   This corporate policy statement usually sets out:

> The purpose of writing and publishing quality policies
>
> A brief statement of corporate intent as to quality (the "motherhood" statement)
>
> The minimal actions to be taken by company Divisions with respect to quality (see below)
>
> Interdivisional relationships concerning quality
>
> Quality standards policies for overlapping markets
>
> Definition of responsibility for implementing quality policies
>
> Provision for corporate audit of compliance with quality policies
>
> Relationship of quality policies to other company policies

2. A delegation of authority to subordinate company organization units (usually the "profit centers" known as "Divisions") to establish subsidiary quality policies appropriate to their needs.   This delegation is needed because the Divisions are commonly engaged in different businesses—each involving different markets, laws, traditions, technology, etc.—which require different policies.

In making the delegation, the corporation usually imposes some mandatory minimal requirements for Divisional action.   In large companies it is typical to require the Divisions to:

> Prepare a formal plan for quality assurance, including minimal contents such as formal systems for design reviews, vendor qualification, process control, inspection and test, and field feedback.
>
> Publish a quality manual which includes the formal plans, the definitions of responsibility, the organization charts, the procedures, etc.
>
> Conduct audits to determine the extent to which the plans are adequate and are being carried out.   (Copies of the audit reports are required to be submitted to the Corporate offices.)

Aside from Divisional policies, quality policies may be prepared for functional organization units or for programmed activities.   For example, one company developed the following policies to guide its reliability programs:

> The program must cover all phases from development through usage.
>
> Funding should be determined during the proposal stage.
>
> The program should be written and should specify responsibility, procedures, and schedules.
>
> The program should include controls to measure and report progress.
>
> The program should include suppliers as well as inside departments.[6]

[6] Derived from Gryna, F. M., Jr., Total Quality Control through Reliability, *1960 Convention Transactions,* ASQC, pp. 295–301.

Governmental organizations commonly make extensive use of published quality policies.   For example, the well-known MIL-Q-9858A ("Quality Program Requirements") includes numerous quality policy provisions.   The long-range planning done by these same organizations also tends to reduce policies to writing.   One military Quality Assurance organization enunciated the following quality policies:

Encompass all phases—procurement, storage, usage.
Aim to prevent defects.
Avoid duplicating contractors' work.
Retain final decisions on acceptability.
Use performance in service as the ultimate measure.[7]

Industry Quality Policies   In some industry situations, the number of companies involved makes it difficult for one or several companies to provide industry leadership in quality policies.   In such cases the need may be to establish quality policies at the industry level.   This is done through an industry committee, operating under the sponsorship of the industry Association.[8]

Once industry policies are agreed on and published, there remains a problem of assuring compliance.   The industry Association is seldom able or willing to apply sanctions to violators.   However, the very fact of having made the policies clear, plus the attendant publicity, is a useful force toward securing compliance.   The consumer is better able to take his case to the press or to the regulatory bodies.   In addition, the competitors and the industry Association are better able to apply pressures.

FORMULATION OF QUALITY POLICIES

The key managers must participate in the formulation of quality policies.   (The vendor relations policy of Johnson & Johnson, quoted above, required review by all functions of the company.)   Since the chief executive must approve all policies, he requires that the departments affected review them beforehand.   In addition, since policy formation is undertaken only for major questions, a policy always affects several company functions.   The two examples given below show that quality affects company income and company costs.

The first example comes from the late Alfred P. Sloan, Jr., who followed some specific business policies with respect to quality.   Sloan's policy was "Quality competition against products below a certain price tag, and price competition against products above that price tag."[9]

The second example is the famous plaque on the grounds of the Newport News Shipbuilding & Dry Dock Company, which reads "We will build good ships—at a profit if we can, at a loss if we must—but always good ships."

The "Right" Policies   Managers often wonder whether the "right" policies can be found somewhere in the literature.   The answer is that there are no "right" policies other than for a few rather obvious questions.   Instead, policy decisions must be made to measure.   Each company is unique in its history, management, and state of development.   The deliberating managers must identify that uniqueness and structure their policies to fit it.

---

[7] Derived from Fouch, George E., "Second Annual NAVSHIPS Quality Assurance Seminar," Virginia Beach, Va., 1967.

[8] For an example see Sec. 43, under Specifications: Test Standardization.

[9] Sloan, Alfred P., Jr., "My Years With General Motors," Doubleday and Company, Garden City, N.Y., 1964, p. 67.

In addition, the managers must watch the horizon. Policies are stable from one year to the next but not from one decade to the next. Just during the two decades from 1950 to 1970, the following truly massive forces emerged:

A "population explosion" of consumer products with a resulting spectacle of millions of consumers owning and depending for day-to-day health and convenience on products they are unable to repair or even understand ("Life behind the quality dikes")

A public awakening to the problems of pollution, many of which have their origin in the operation of manufactured products

An erosion of traditional manufacturers' defenses in matters of safety and product liability

The emergence of very complex apparatus—aerospace systems, automated factories, defense systems, computers

A consumerism movement directed at protecting the small user from misleading advertising and from failures without recourse

A growing invasion of government regulation not only in the traditional fields of human health and safety but also consumer economics, i.e., integrity of guarantee, product labeling, etc.

Every single one of these changes is a revolutionary challenge to the existing order and requires a revolutionary response.[10]

The Policy Formulating Process   The *process* of formulating policies requires that the key managers have the opportunity for participation but without the burden of performing the detailed staff work. One way to do this is to assign to a specialist the job of securing from these key managers:

1. Their nominations for what should be the subject matter contained in quality policies

2. Their judgment as to what should be the direction of the company with respect to these subjects

Through this method it is possible to discover the consensus among these key managers for the various subjects. A draft prepared in the light of this consensus then contains the basis for a meeting of the minds, even on abstract matters.

For example, in one company it became important to establish a policy on a number of quality matters including the elusive question of quality leadership. The man assigned to interview the key managers included in his questions a choice of quality leadership levels, i.e., should the company aim to be:

1. The recognized quality leader of the industry ("sole leadership")

2. One of the top group of companies ("shared leadership")

3. Competitive with the average of the industry ("respectability")

4. Adequate as to quality so as to secure minimal costs and charge minimal prices ("adequacy")

The 26 managers interviewed opted as follows:

Sole leadership	3
Shared leadership	22
Respectability	1
Adequacy	0

This consensus resolved a long-standing debate.

Publication of Policies   Until the 1960s, examples of published quality policy were rare. Those which were published were usually the result of requirements by gov-

---

[10] For elaboration, see Juran, J. M., Mobilizing for the 1970's, *Quality Progress,* August 1969. Also, Juran, J. M., Consumerism and Product Quality, *Quality Progress,* July 1970.

ernment agencies that their contractors prepare written quality manuals for review and approval.

The trend to use of written quality policy has been accelerated by major forces such as are exemplified under The "Right" Policies, above. While the resulting written quality policies have been published mainly for internal use, the need for broader publication is evident from these same forces.[11] It is likely that the trend to the use of written quality policy will continue and accelerate further.

There are important advantages to written policy:

1. It forces those concerned to think out their problem to a depth never before achieved. "Before you can write it down, you must first think it out."

2. It establishes legitimacy and can be communicated in an authoritative, uniform manner.

3. It provides a basis for management by agreed policies rather than by crisis or opportunism.

4. It permits practice to be audited against that policy.

ADHERENCE TO POLICIES

Before a policy is published, it is well to face realistically the question, "Do we intend to adhere to this policy?" If there is doubt about this, the policy should not be published.

In the long run, insiders and outsiders alike draw their conclusions about company policy from the deeds. If the company's products continue to show innovation, observers conclude that the company has a policy of design leadership. If the company adjusts quality complaints promptly and fairly, the observers conclude that the company has a policy of ethical dealing on quality.[12,13]

If, in addition, there is a written policy and it conforms to the deeds, the written policy gains credibility. If, however, the written policy says one thing and the deeds say something else, what is believed is the deeds. Not only does the written policy lose its credibility but other pronouncements of the company become suspect as well.

So important is the need for adherence to published policy that most companies establish audits to provide a feedback on how well the policies are being followed.

QUALITY OBJECTIVES

Many organizations achieve their results through establishing specific, attainable goals and then attaining them. These goals, when defined and quantified so as to serve as a basis for planning, are known as *objectives.*

The concept of "management by objectives" is widespread. Under this concept, managers participate in establishing objectives which are then reduced to writing and become the basis of planning for results. This practice has been growing because clearly defined objectives:

Help to unify the thinking of the managers
Have the power within themselves to stimulate action

---

[11] One of the industry responses to the consumerism criticism of the 1960s was to formulate and publicize policies on redress associated with guarantees on long-life apparatus, e.g., "hot lines" to some company official.

[12] One observer has pointed out that quality and service are the most visible of the company's activities and hence the major base on which the company's image is built. See Ely, Clair G., The Corporate Image—Shadow or Substance, *The Management Review,* November 1961.

[13] See also, Section 14, under Warranty of Quality.

Are a necessary prerequisite to operating on a planned basis rather than from crisis to crisis

Permit a subsequent comparison of performance against objective

Objectives in the quality function may be either for:
1. Breakthrough,[14] e.g., to reduce scrap to 2.5% by the end of 19--
2. Control, e.g., to hold scrap to its present level of 3.0% during 19--

The most important single decision in setting objectives is whether to go for a breakthrough or to hold the status quo.

Objectives for Breakthrough   There are many reasons why managers create objectives for breakthrough.[15] Among the more usual are the facts that:

1. They wish to attain or hold quality leadership. (Even to hold quality leadership requires continuing breakthrough because competitors are ever closing the gap.) They may launch innovative product designs, offer superior service, provide more complete technical assistance, etc.

2. They have identified some opportunities to improve income through superior fitness for use. For example, a company improved the reliability of its products and found from field studies that the users' costs of maintenance, and especially of downtime, were sharply reduced thereby. In consequence, the company was able to increase its prices without losing customers.

3. They are losing share of market through lack of competitiveness. For example, a company making abrasive cloth found that although its products met specification, the users' "cost per hundred pieces polished" was greater than when using competitive cloth.

4. They have too many field troubles—failures, complaints, returns—and wish to reduce these as well as cutting the external costs resulting from guarantee charges, investigation expense, product discounts, etc. Solution may require new test programs, product redesign, training manuals for users, etc.

5. They have identified some projects which offer internal cost-reduction opportunities, e.g., improvement of process yields or reduction of scrap, rework, inspection, or testing.

6. They have a poor image with customers, vendors, the public, or other group of outsiders.

7. There is internal dissension and the need to improve motivation and morale.

Objectives for breakthrough are not limited to "hardware," or to things which can be counted, e.g., income, cost. Objectives for breakthrough can include projects such as a reliability training program for designers, a vendor rating plan, a complaint · investigation manual, a reorganization of the quality control staff, or a new executive report on quality.

Objectives for Control   Managers have many reasons for *avoiding* breakthrough. In such cases the objectives are to hold the status quo, i.e., maintain control at present levels. The more usual reasons for choosing control in specific situations are that:

1. The managers believe that improvement is uneconomic; i.e., the cost of trying for breakthrough would not be recovered.

2. Present performance is competitive. Many managers regard "the market" as a sound standard since it embodies the breakthrough efforts of competitors.

3. There are few alarm signals—e.g., few complaints or internal flareups—to suggest the need for breakthrough.

4. There is need for breakthrough but it is not timely to undertake breakthrough

[14] See Section 2, under Breakthrough.
[15] See generally Section 16, especially under Proof of the Need for a Program.

because *(a)* there has been no agreement on the specific projects to be tackled or *(b)* the climate for quality breakthrough is unfavorable (e.g., too many other programs going; some key manager is not convinced; the breakthrough would require risky technological research).

The more usual objectives for control include holding the materials, processes, and products to specification; holding the field failures, complaints, returns, and other external performance measures to current levels; holding costs of inspection, test, scrap, rework, and other internal costs to current levels; holding the gains achieved by recent breakthrough projects.

Interrelation of Objectives   The interrelation between objectives for breakthrough and control may be seen in the following extract from the quarterly report of a Quality Control Department:

Review and Preview

For the past 2½ years the principal activity of the Quality Control Department has been defect prevention projects.   For each of these projects the department has turned up new facts which have provided the basis for scrap reduction by the plant supervision.   By and large, the plant supervisors have saved about five dollars in scrap for every dollar of analysis.

This rate of return is slowing up, for several reasons:

1. The more fruitful projects were tackled first, leaving the projects of less yield, and the marginal projects, to be dealt with later.

2. For each project it has been necessary to establish a "rear guard" of controls to hold the gains made.   The time required to do this has reduced the time available for improvement projects.

3. It has been necessary to reexamine activities such as inspection and gage maintenance, as well as to set up new activities such as product audit of outgoing products and process audit of Production practices.[16]

The above example makes clear that there is continuing shifting of the pattern of objectives.   When successful breakthroughs are made, the need for holding the gains requires that an objective for control follow the objective for breakthrough.   Correspondingly, a preoccupation with control ends up in obsolescence and requires a breakthrough to become competitive again.

ESTABLISHING QUALITY OBJECTIVES

In small organizations the chief executive can determine what the quality needs are by personal observation of deeds and by direct contact with people; he can then set quality objectives accordingly.   In large organizations this personal contact is no longer feasible.   Unless some substitute for this personal contact is worked out, the leadership for setting quality objectives passes from the chief executive to the department heads.   The resulting quality objectives then tend to be departmental rather than corporate in character.

Reactions from numerous middle managers[17] tend to establish that:

1. Most companies have quality objectives, but most often these are not in written form.

2. Objectives for improving field performance are more common than objectives for improving internal performance, e.g., process yields.

3. Objectives for internal control are established not by upper management but by middle managers (Quality Control, Technical, Manufacture).

Identifying Potential Objectives   As an alternative to the personal leadership of the chief executive, a large company can create an interdepartmental mechanism to

[16] Consulting experience of J. M. Juran.
[17] Feedbacks to J. M. Juran during conduct of his course on Management of Quality Control in numerous countries.

identify potential objectives, estimate their economic and other results, and secure for them a priority in the program for action.

Quality objectives can be identified[18] from a variety of inputs such as the following:

Pareto analysis[19] of repetitive external alarm signals (field failures, complaints, returns, etc.)

Pareto analysis of repetitive internal alarm signals (scrap, rework, sorting, 100% test, etc.)

Proposals from key insiders—managers, supervisors, professionals, union stewards

Proposals from suggestion schemes

Field study of users' needs, costs

Data on performance of products versus competitors (from users and from laboratory tests)

Comments of key people outside the company (customers, vendors, journalists, critics)

Findings and comments of government regulators, independent laboratories, reformers

Some of these inputs can be derived from regular company reports. Others just float around inside and outside the company and must be retrieved. Still others require an organized effort specially created to secure the information.

Analysis and use of these inputs requires, as in formulating policies, an organization mechanism which gives to the managers the opportunity for participation in setting objectives without the burden of performing the detailed staff work. To carry this out, quality control engineers and other staff specialists are assigned the job of analyzing the available inputs and of creating any essential missing inputs. These analyses point to potential projects which are then proposed. The proposals are reviewed by managers at progressively higher organization levels. At each level there is summary and consolidation until the corporate level is reached. The foregoing process, when formalized, is similar to that used in preparing the annual financial budget. (See Section 6, under Annual Quality Program.)

Quantifying Objectives An objective is unlikely to receive high priority unless it is quantified. All managers have multiple objectives for which they are later held to account. In this accounting, the quantified objectives usually receive more attention than vague objectives since there is less room for debate on what has actually happened. With this in mind, advocates of specific objectives should get them quantified to increase the likelihood that they will actually be met.[20]

Typical statements of quantification are as follows:

Nature of objective	Quantified statement
Product improvement	To market a fail-safe rotor by June 30
Training	To conduct a 20-hour reliability training course for all designers during 19__
Procedural change	To put the quality report system on the computer by the end of 19__
Cost control	To hold the cost of inspection and test at 4.3% of manufacturing cost during 19__
Cost reduction	To cut rework to $1.60 per unit during 19__
Field performance	To increase MTBF to 3,500 hours during 19__

[18] See also Section 16, under Identifying the Projects.
[19] See Section 2, under The Pareto Principle.
[20] See also Section 16, under Securing Management Approval.

Objectives have even more meaning if they include a statement of the detailed deeds to be performed along with the quantified result of those deeds. Generally, however, these deeds, along with lower-level objectives, are identified in the planning process. (See Section 6.)

The vague objective is at its worst during attempts to introduce undefined programs under the guise of "objectives." Familiar examples have been statistical quality control, operations research, total quality control, zero defects, etc. None of these terms had a standardized dictionary meaning. Unless care is taken to define what these programs mean in terms of objectives, plans, and responsibilities, only the advocates know what the program means.

Establishing Priorities for Objectives[21]   Objectives for control meet little resistance —too little. In many companies there is not enough challenge to the comfort of the predictable present order. However, there are also some difficult questions of discovering when the economic limit of improvement has been reached. (See Section 5, under Discovering the Optimum.)

Objectives for breakthrough arouse a good deal of debate. When reviewed at progressively higher and higher levels, they face competition for the available manpower, facilities, and funds. This competition exists not only among quality objectives but also between quality objectives and other objectives.

Competition among quality objectives is resolved by consideration of several aids for setting priorities:

1. Status in the Pareto analysis.[22] The analysis quantifies the amounts at stake and shows which symptom costs the most, which is second, etc. This ranking carries much weight but is not conclusive.

2. Estimate of return on investment.[23] For some objectives the investment needed to realize their benefits is so high that it does not pay; i.e., other objectives are more attractive because they return the investment sooner.

3. State of the art. For most objectives the technology of solution is known. For others it is not, and these involve the risks associated with conducting a research to discover the new technology needed for solution.

4. Climate for improvement. Objectives for breakthrough compete not only with each other but also with broad objectives for control, with departmental objectives, and especially with the personal aspirations of key managers in specific divisions, functions, and product lines. Some of these key managers create an unfavorable climate for breakthrough, and this fact is considered in setting the priorities.

5. Subjective judgment. Intangible factors such as employee morale or customer goodwill are dominant in some objectives. Setting priorities for such intangibles becomes a matter of subjective judgment.

6. "Jury of opinion." In some companies the need for subjective managerial judgment is recognized by providing an organized approach to collecting those judgments. All nominated projects are written out, one to an index card. Each key manager is asked to rank each card in the deck in his order of priority. The composite of these rankings is then worked up as an aid to agreeing on priorities.

Upper Management Views: Languages in the Company   In the upper management levels, quality objectives face competition from other objectives. Some of the criteria for setting priorities remain as in the lower levels, e.g., return on investment. However, the climate of thinking at top management level is strongly biased with respect to three vital criteria:

1. Breakthrough versus control. Top managers prefer objectives for break-

---

[21] See also Section 16, under Identifying the Projects: Priority Rating.

[22] See Section 16, especially Tables 16-2 through 16-5.

[23] See Sec. 16, Table 16-6 and associated discussion.

through over objectives for holding the status quo. The former is the key to the long-range progress of the company, and top management has prime responsibility for this leadership. In contrast, control is concerned with meeting short-range targets, which top management tries to delegate to the lower levels.

2. Business and management versus technology. Top managers exhibit a bias for projects of a business or management nature: growth, share of market, organization, manager development, motivation. Technology is often one of the means for meeting business objectives, but many top managers have little understanding of technology.

3. Language of money or things. The company contains two common languages.[24,25] (See Figure 3-1.)

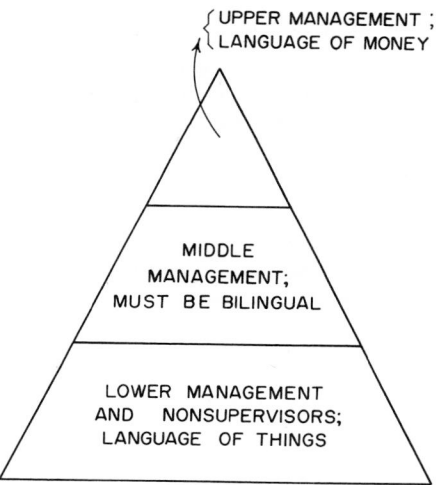

UPPER MANAGEMENT ;
LANGUAGE OF MONEY

MIDDLE
MANAGEMENT;
MUST BE BILINGUAL

LOWER MANAGEMENT
AND NONSUPERVISORS;
LANGUAGE OF THINGS

Fig. 3-1 Common languages in the company.

At the bottom of the company (i.e., nonsupervisors, foremen) the language is in terms of "things." Anyone who wishes to communicate with these levels must talk about tons, meters, kilowatts, man-hours, units of product.

At the top of the company the common language is money, i.e., sales, profits, investment, return on investment, etc. Only through use of such a common language are the top managers able to make useful decisions about alternative courses of action.[26]

In such a state of affairs, the middle managers and professionals *must be bilingual.* They must be able to talk to the people at the bottom in the language of things. They must also be able to talk to the top management in the language of money. Failing this, they jeopardize their objectives in the competition against those middle managers who are bilingual.

[24] There are also numerous local dialects peculiar to various functions, e.g., accounting, market research, quality control. These dialects are understood by the local professionals and by few others.

[25] See also Section 16, under Securing Management Approval.

[26] This common language of money applies to top managers in socialistic as well as capitalistic countries. (Personal observation of J. M. Juran.)

When objectives meet all three of the above criteria simultaneously, their odds are optimal. In addition, middle managers who have a record of proposing objectives which regularly meet these criteria are looked upon as exhibiting one of the necessary capacities for upper management posts.

The participation of the top management, while necessary to legitimize the objectives, is not enough to get them achieved. An objective to reduce scrap by 20% has little meaning until the deeds which must be performed in the various departments to bring about such a result have been identified. In turn, identifying the deeds and getting men to be responsible for doing them requires participation by middle and lower management. The mechanism for this is the planning process, and it is described in Section 6. Through this process, the short list of company objectives expands into a long list of departmental objectives plus associated needs and deeds.

POLICIES AND OBJECTIVES: HOLY GROUND?

In many companies there is little initiative from lower or middle management to propose policies or objectives. In some cases this is the result of an unfavorable climate created by previous or present top managements. In other cases there is lack of awareness by middle management that their proposals are an expected and useful contribution. Some of this lack of awareness is the result of a mistaken belief that company objectives, and especially policies, are "holy ground." The belief stems from reasoning as follows: since only top management can approve company policies, only top management can venture on such ground.

In most companies this reasoning is not well founded. The road to final approval of broad policies and objectives is somewhat as follows:

Activities in formulating policies and objectives	Usual roles	
	Middle management	Upper management
Identify need and nominate	X	X
Draft proposal.	X	
Review.		X
Redraft.	X	
Review.		X
Approve		X

It is evident that middle management has a very real role to play.

Section **4**

Quality and Income

J. M. JURAN

QUALITY AND ECONOMICS

"Quality" affects the industrial company's economics in two major ways:

1. The effect on *costs*. (Here "quality" is used mainly in the sense of conformance to specification.) This relationship is discussed in Section 5.

2. The effect on *income*.[1] (Here "quality" is used mainly in the sense of fitness for use.) This is discussed in two Sections. The present Section discusses the
forces through which quality affects income, and the means available for quantifying
these effects. Section 14, Marketing of Quality, discusses the business steps which
the company takes to secure income through quality.

---

[1] "Income," as used here, means the revenues received by the company and not the net income, or profit.

While quality specialists have made extensive studies of the effect of quality on costs, they have done little to study the effect of quality on income.[2] This is the more surprising since the latter usually has more influence on the company's economics than the former. A consequence of this imbalance is the opportunity presented for creative and imaginative invention of new ways to study the effect of quality on income.

MAJOR ECONOMIC INFLUENCES

The ability of an industrial company to secure income is strongly influenced by the economic climate and by the cultural habits which the various economies have evolved. These overriding influences affect product quality as well as other elements of commerce.

National Affluence and Organization   The form of a nation's economy and its degree of affluence strongly influence the approach to its quality problems.

Subsistence Economies. In such economies the numerous impoverished users have little choice but to devote their income to basic human needs. Their protection against poor quality is derived more from collective political power than from their collective economic power. Most of the world's population remains in a state of subsistence economy.

Planned Economies. In all countries there are some socialized industries, i.e., government monopolies for specific products or services. In some countries the entire economy is so organized. These monopolies limit the choice of the user to those qualities which result from the national planning and its execution. For elaboration, see Section 48A.

Shortages and Surpluses. In all economies, a shortage of goods (a "sellers' market") results in a relaxing of quality standards. Because the demand for goods exceeds the supply, users take what they can get (and bid up the price to boot). In contrast, a buyers' market results in a tightening of quality standards.

Life Behind the Quality Dikes   In the twentieth century, for the first time in human history, great masses of human beings placed their safety, health, and even their daily well-being behind numerous protective dikes of quality control. For example:

The daily safety and health of the common man now depend absolutely on the quality of manufactured products: drugs, food, aircraft, automobiles, elevators, tunnels, bridges, etc.

The very continuity of our daily lives is built around the continuity of numerous vital services: power, transport, communication, water, waste removal and many others. We have structured our society on the premise that these services will continue without interruption. A major power failure paralyzes the lives of millions of people.[3]

Not only individuals but also nations and their economies live dangerously behind the dikes of quality control. National productivity relies on automated processes. National defense relies on complex weaponry. The national income depends on the marketability of products. The growth of the national economy is keyed to the reliability of its systems for energy, communication, transport, etc.

In such situations, users (whether individuals or nations) are willing to pay for good dikes.

Voluntary Obsolescence   As customers acquire affluence, the industrial companies increasingly bring out new products and new models of old products and urge prospective users to buy. Many of the users who buy these new models do so while

---

[2] See in this connection Juran, J. M., Quality and Profit, *Industrial Quality Control,* p. 48 *et seq.,* July 1967.

[3] These quotations and the associated discussion are derived from Juran, J. M., *Mobilizing for the 1970's, Quality Progress,* August 1969.

possessing older models which are still in working order. This practice is regarded by some economists and reformers as a reprehensible economic waste.[4]

In their efforts to put an end to this waste, the reformers have attacked the industrial companies who bring out these new models and who promote their sale. Using the term "planned obsolescence," the reformers imply (and state outright) that the large companies, by their clever new models and their powerful sales promotion, break down the resistance of the users. Under this theory, the responsibility for the waste lies with the industrial companies who create the new models.

In the experience and judgment of the author, this theory of planned obsolescence is mostly nonsense. The simple fact, obvious both to manufacturers and consumers, is that *the consumer makes the decision* (of whether to discard the old product and buy the new). Periodically this fact is dramatized by some massive failure.

For example, in March 1971, E. I. Du Pont de Nemours & Co., Inc. (Du Pont) announced its plans to discontinue the manufacture and sale of "Corfam," a synthetic material invented to compete with leather for shoe uppers (and other applications). Corfam, though costly, possessed excellent properties for shoe uppers: durability, ease of care, shape retention, scuff resistance, water repellency, and ability to "breathe." Although Du Pont became a major supplier of shoe upper materials, it withdrew from the business because Corfam "never attained sufficient sales volume to show a profit."

Industry observers felt that the high durability of Corfam was an irrelevant property due to rapid style obsolescence; i.e., the life of the shoes was determined not by the inherent technological properties but by style obsolescence. Du Pont's investment in Corfam may have exceeded $100 million.

In the Corfam case, a large corporation undertook a program which was antagonistic to obsolescence, but the users decided against it. In a miscalculation involving an even larger investment, the Ford Motor Company's Edsel automobile failed to gain consumer acceptance despite possessing numerous innovations and being promoted by an extensive marketing campaign.

Involuntary Obsolescence Quite a different situation is the case in which long-life products contain components which will not last for the life of the product. The life of these components is determined by the manufacturer. As a result, even though the user decides to have the failed component replaced (to keep the product in service), *the manufacturer makes the real decision* because his design determines the life of the component.[5]

This situation is at its worst when the original manufacturer has designed the product in such a way that the supplies, spare parts, etc., are nonstandard, so that, in effect, the sole source for these needs is the original manufacturer. In such a situation, the user is locked in to a single source of supply. Collectively, these cases have lent themselves to a good deal of abuse and have contributed to the consumerism movement.

CONTRAST IN VIEWS: USER AND MANUFACTURER

Industrial companies derive their income from the users[6] of their products. (The actual sale may be directly to users or to intermediate agents, e.g., merchants, repair shops.)

---

[4] Whether this "waste" is a good thing or a bad thing for the economy is a question largely outside the scope of this Handbook.

[5] For elaboration, see Juran, J. M., Consumerism and Product Quality, *Quality Progress,* July 1970.

[6] For elaboration on the meanings of some of the key words used here, see Section 2, under Customers, Users, and Consumers.

With respect to quality and costs, the views of these users are quite different from those of manufacturers. Table 4-1 summarizes the main differences. Because the views of users so greatly influence company income, it is necessary for manufacturers to understand these differences and to use this understanding in establishing their quality policies and objectives.

TABLE 4-1   Contrasting Views: Users and Manufacturers

Aspects of quality and cost	Principal views of the user	Principal views of the manufacturer
Subject matter of the sales contract	A service needed by the user	A product made by the manufacturer
Definition of quality	Fitness for use on arrival	Conformance to specification on test
Cost	Cost of usage, including: Original price Operation costs Maintenance Downtime Depreciation Loss on resale	Manufacturers' quality costs
Responsibility for keeping in service	Over the entire useful life	During the guarantee period
Spare parts	A necessary evil	A profitable business

Products versus Services[7]   The user's prime interest is in *services,* not in products. These services cover a wide range of human needs: nourishment, shelter, transport, status, etc. To a large degree, *products* are essential or helpful in providing these services.

The user has options as to how he will contract to secure the services he needs. In the case of transportation, for example, the user may

1. Buy a product, e.g., bicycle, automobile, boat
2. Rent a product, e.g., hire a drive-it-yourself automobile
3. Buy the service only, e.g., a bus ride

Because human wants are very complex, the products needed to supply services also become complex. The vehicles made to supply transportation also supply status, comfort, safety, etc.

Some manufacturers are quite aware that the user is interested in his service needs, not in the manufacturer's product. Such manufacturers do their advertising and promotion accordingly. For example:

Manufacturer's product	*Emphasis of the sales propaganda*
Grinding wheels	Metal removal
Nuts and bolts	Fastening systems
Toothpaste	Clean teeth, sweet breath, improved social life
Aluminum siding	Maintenance-free exteriors

However, there remain many, many manufacturers whose orientation is to products. In the extreme cases this can lead to outright extinction of the company.[8]

---

[7] See also Section 2, under Products and Services.

[8] Two hairnet manufacturers were in competition. They devoted much energy to improving the qualities of the product and to strengthening their marketing techniques. They were both made extinct when someone developed a hair spray which gave the user a better way of holding her hair in place. (Private communication to J. M. Juran.)

In less extreme cases this narrow orientation shuts off the view of business opportunities which would become clear if seen from the service viewpoint.[9]

Definition of Quality To the user, quality is fitness for use, not conformance to specification.[10] The ultimate user seldom knows what is in the specifications. His evaluation of quality is based on whether the product is fit for use on delivery to him and on whether it continues to be fit for use.

In contrast, many manufacturers, while aware of the importance of fitness for use, put great emphasis on conformance to specification at the time of final test (which is really a simulation of use). The operations of packing, transport, storage, etc., often do not receive the rigorous quality planning and control applied to the operations of fabricating the product. In like manner, the field performance after the guarantee period receives little attention compared to performance during the guarantee period.

Cost of Usage[11] For each form of usage, the user incurs a cost:

Type of usage	Cost incurred
Purchase of service only, e.g., the bus ride	The admission fee, the ticket, etc.
Rent of a product to secure service from it	The rent
Purchase of a product to secure service from it	Original cost plus upkeep

When the user purchases a long-life product, his cost of usage is properly figured over the useful life of that product and is a composite of:
1. The original price paid for the product
2. Operation costs, e.g., energy, consumable supplies
3. Maintenance costs, e.g., repair labor, spare parts
4. Downtime resulting from product failures
5. Depreciation of the product value due to wearing out and obsolescence
6. Loss on resale or trade-in

Because of long-standing emphasis on original price,[12] industry practice in recognizing the other elements of cost of usage is only beginning to emerge. In consequence, manufacturing companies optimize their own costs[13] and not the user's costs. This leads to a number of suboptimizations. The manufacturer optimizes manufacturing costs. The merchant optimizes his marketing costs. The maintenance shop optimizes its repair costs. These various suboptimizations do not necessarily optimize the user's costs. In some cases, as in the supply of spare parts, they can be antagonistic to the user's costs.

What is emerging is a new concept of cost of usage which optimizes the user's costs of obtaining the services he wants. There are various approaches to this: "life cycle costing," contracts based on actual product usage, incentives to manufacturers based on cost of usage, etc. These approaches are discussed below under Life Cycle Costing *et seq.*

[9] For elaboration, see the widely read article by Theodore Levitt entitled Marketing Myopia. (*Harvard Business Review,* July–August 1960.) See also Section 14, under Discovering Market Opportunities.

[10] For a detailed definition, see Section 2, under Fitness for Use.

[11] A note on terminology. There is no generally accepted term to cover cost of usage in all of its forms (purchase of service only, rent of a product, purchase of a product). The term "price" applies to all forms, but in the case of purchase of a product, "price" is commonly understood to mean only the original price. "Life cycle cost" (see below) applies only to usage growing out of purchase of long-lived products. The author has employed the term "cost of usage" despite the possibility of confusion with "cost of operation."

[12] See Life Cycle Costing, later in this Section.

[13] See Section 5 for the systematic approach to optimizing quality costs.

Continuity of Service   The user's needs are for availability of service over the useful life of the product. The manufacturer's active responsibility is with the guarantee period, which is normally in the range of 5 to 10% of the useful life of the product. However, the economy is poorly organized to help the user during the long nonguarantee period. The resulting frustrations have infuriated many users and have driven them to personalize the blame. (The high visibility of the large manufacturing companies has made them an obvious target.) In addition, the users have turned to new leadership—e.g., legislators, reformers—in an effort to find solutions. The growth of the consumerism movement has clearly been aided by these frustrations.

Spare Parts   As summarized in Table 4-1, the user regards spare parts (and associated repair time, downtime, etc.) as a necessary evil, whereas the manufacturer usually regards spare parts as a profitable part of his business. The situation leaves the manufacturers open to the charge of "planned obsolescence" i.e., deliberately putting out short-life components in products so as to be able to sell the spare parts. The charge is valid in some cases but mostly not, for several reasons:

a. They don't know how to increase the life, e.g., automotive spark plugs.

b. They know how, but to do so would deteriorate something else, e.g., a harsher ride from tires and shock absorbers.

c. They know how, but it would clearly be a waste for the user, e.g., women's dress shoes, where style changes rather than technology decide the useful life.

d. They know how, and the result would be a long range cost reduction for the user. However, the tradition of emphasizing original price stands in the way. . . .[14]

Opportunities for Manufacturers[15]   The contrasts in the views of the user versus manufacturer present opportunities to manufacturers who can find new ways to bridge this gap. The needs are to:

Discover the problems, economics, and needs of the user

Evaluate the effect of the present product on the user's needs

Revise the product or redesign the system the better to meet the user's needs (sometimes this is done jointly with the user)[16]

The process for making discoveries of the user's situation is described in Section 14, under Market Research.

The failure of manufacturers to bridge the gap between their views and those of the users has been a major factor in stimulating the rise of other forces in the economy which offer to help bridge the gap: government agencies, industry associations, consumer organizations, standardization bodies, etc.

DEGREES OF USER KNOWLEDGE

As societies develop affluence, users develop options through which they can influence the income of manufacturers. The users can spend or withhold (other than for subsistence). They can exercise a choice among competing services and prod-

[14] Juran, J. M., Consumerism and Product Quality, *Quality Progress,* pp. 18–27, July 1970.

[15] See generally Juran, J. M., Quality and Income, *Proceedings, International Conference on Quality Control,* JUSE, pp. 161–163, 1969.

[16] An example relating to automobile maintenance is seen in the advertisement of a major manufacturer claiming eight ways of reducing users' service costs through electronic ignition, solid-state voltage regulator, and superior filters. Each of the eight claims is based on quantified frequency of service versus that required by competitors' products (*The New York Times,* p. 27 Oct. 17, 1972).

ucts.[17]   However, these choices are limited by the extent of user knowledge of the interrelated factors of fitness for use, cost of usage, and delivery date.

Table 4-2 summarizes the extent of customer knowledge and strength in the

TABLE 4-2   Customer Influences on Quality

Aspects of the problem	Original equipment manufacturers (OEM)	Dealers and repair shops	Consumers
Makeup of the market	A few very large customers	Some large customers plus many smaller ones	Very many very small customers
Economic strength of any one customer	Very large, cannot be ignored	Modest or low	Negligible
Technological strength of customer	Very high; has engineers and laboratories	Low or nil	Nil; requires technical assistance
Political strength of customer	Modest or low	Low to nil	Variable, but can be very great collectively
Fitness for use is judged mainly by	Qualification testing	Absence of consumer complaints	Successful usage
Quality specifications dominated by	Customers	Manufacturer	Manufacturer
Use of incoming inspection	Extensive test for conformance to specification	Low or nil for dealers; in-use tests by repair shops	In-use test
Collection and analysis of failure data	Good to fair	Poor to nil	Poor to nil

marketplace as related to product quality matters.   The broad conclusions which can be drawn from Table 4-2 are as follows:

1. Original equipment manufacturers (OEM) can protect themselves through their technological and/or economic power as much as through contract provisions.

2. Merchants and repair shops must rely mainly on contract provisions supplemented by some economic power.

3. Small users have very limited knowledge and protection.   The situation of the small user requires some elaboration.

Fitness for Use   With few exceptions, small users are devoid of understanding of the technological nature of the product.   The user does have sensory recognition of some aspects of fitness for use: the bread smells fresh-baked, the radio set has clear reception, the shoes are good-looking.   Beyond such sensory judgments, and especially concerning the long-life performance of the product, the small user must rely mainly on prior personal experience with the manufacturer or merchant.   Lacking such prior experience, the small user must choose from the propaganda of competing manufacturers plus other available inputs (neighbors, merchants, independent laboratories, etc.).

To the extent that the user does understand fitness for use, the effect on the manufacturer's income is somewhat as follows:

---

[17] As affluence grows, so does the breadth of competition.   The breakfast cereal of Company A competes with that of Companies B, C, etc.   However, all of them compete with bacon and eggs.

As seen by the user, product or service is	Resulting income to the producer is
Not fit for use	None, or in immediate jeopardy
Fit for use but noticeably inferior to competitive products	Low due to need for lowering prices
Fit for use and competitive	At market prices
Noticeably superior to competitive products	High due to premium prices or greater share of market

In the foregoing, the terms "fitness for use," "inferior," "competitive," and "superior" all relate to the situation *as seen by the user.* (The foregoing table is valid as applied to both large customers and small users.)

Cost of Usage versus Price   For short-lived products the original price is closely correlated with cost of usage. All customers, including small users, can readily understand the cost implications in such cases.[18]

For long-life products, the cost of usage involves multiple factors, as shown in Table 4-1 and the associated discussion. In such cases the original price can readily be a minority factor in cost of usage. In consequence, if the user's cost of usage is to be optimized, means must be found to quantify the remaining factors which contribute to cost of usage. This concept has been given the name "life cycle costing" and is applicable to both industrial and consumer products. (See below, under the respective headings.)

QUALITY AND PRICE

Quality differences can be translated into price differences provided that:

1. The difference can be explained to the user
2. The user regards the difference as a form of superior fitness for use

Even with industrial users, there may be difficulty in translating quality superiority into price differentials. For example, a company making standard power tools improved the reliability of the tools, but the marketing manager resisted increasing the prices on the ground that they were standard tools and that he would lose share of market if he raised prices.[19] A field study disclosed that the high-reliability tools greatly reduced the costs of the (industrial) users in maintenance and especially in downtime. This information then became the means of convincing users to accept a price increase (of $500,000 per year).

What appear to be standard commodities can also exhibit important quality differences which influence pricing. Blough[20] noted that structural steels have progressively changed in quality so that the user gets greater value per ton.

The price differential the user is willing to pay is based not on the manufacturers' costs but on the value to the user. On critical matters these differentials can be very high. Professional men who are at the top of their field command fees which may be several times those of their less distinguished colleagues. Brand-named drugs,

[18] Installment purchases are baffling to some users, since they involve two very different matters: (1) cost of product and (2) cost of credit. The cost of credit is beyond the scope of this Section, as are matters such as "unit pricing" (e.g., if boxes contain $13\frac{1}{2}$ ounces each and sell at two for 79 cents, what is the price per ounce?).

[19] Marketing managers have no hesitancy in using price differentials for special products versus standard products. However, they resist price differentials for quality differences within standard products. In contrast, they are highly skilled in establishing price differentials for nonquality differences. "If the steaks are alike, sell the sizzle." It is quite common for identical products to command prices that are up to 10 or 20% higher where they are sold under opulent rather than plain circumstances. (A surprising number of consumers carry the conviction that the higher-priced product must also be the better product.)

[20] Roger Blough, quoted in *Fortune,* p. 139, January 1965.

clinically tested and produced (usually) by leading manufacturers, command a considerable price differential over generic equivalents that are not clinically tested and are made (usually) by "unknown" manufacturers. Copies made by the pioneering dry-process copier using uncoated papers are priced well above the inherent costs.[21]

Most actual structuring of price in relation to quality is done by adopting the market price for the grade in accordance with the principle of "standard product, market price." The manufacturer who is convinced by study that his product line is above standard as seen by the user may adjust his prices accordingly.

MacGowan[22] reported such a study. He compared his company's product lines with competitors' for both quality and price. In making the comparison he used two concepts:

1. A "percentage of desirability" determined by comparing the quality of design of his products with that of competitors
2. A "competitive price index" determined by dividing the price ratio by the percentage of desirability

Based on this study, he made price changes in about 60% of the products, mainly to raise them.

A quality superiority may be converted either into higher price or higher share of market. The latter gains higher sales volume and still higher profit due to the nature of the break-even chart (see below, under Quality and Share of Market). The former gains a rise in total sales in proportion to the price increase (assuming no change in share of market). However, profit rises spectacularly, since the entire increase is profit.

The "Bundled" Price   Many "products" are sold at a price which is really a "bundle" containing the cost of both products and services. The bundled price can apply to short-lived as well as to long-lived products.

For example, specialty chemicals are usually sold on a basis of providing technical assistance to the user. The manufacturer (1) prescribes the chemical which meets the user's needs and (2) fills the prescription. The pricing is "bundled" on a per-pound basis, without showing how much of the price is for material and how much for technical service.

Similar bundled prices are seen in long-life products which involve technical assistance not only before sale but after sale as well.

Bundled prices are an advantage to the manufacturer as long as the "product" remains a specialty and requires the associated technical services. However, if wide use of the specialty products results in standardization, the need for the technical services diminishes. In such cases it is common for competitors to offer the standard product at lower prices but without the technical services. This is a form of "unbundling" the price.[23]

QUALITY AND SHARE OF MARKET

Once a product is actively on the market, it attains a "share of market," i.e., a proportion of all sales by all manufacturers for that type of product.[24] This attained share

---

[21] Perhaps the extreme of differentials is found in works of art by recognized masters.

[22] MacGowan, T. G., Competitive Pricing, *National Industrial Conference Board Studies in Business Policies,* no. 84, 1957.

[23] The growth of the discount house is due in part to unbundling the prices of the department stores by eliminating services, including some related to quality.

[24] Companies are commonly well organized to measure their own sales. To measure competitors' sales, there are available various statistical sources and market research services. Details of all this are beyond the scope of this Handbook.

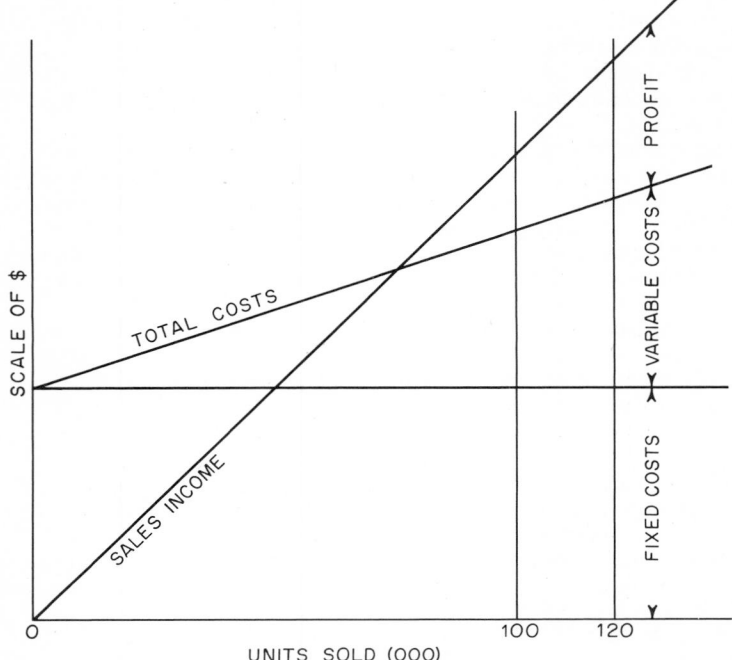

Fig. 4-1   Break-even chart.

of market is of great economic importance.   As share of market rises, so does volume of sales.   However, profit rises even faster due to the nature of the break-even chart (Figure 4-1).

In Figure 4-1, an increase of 20% in sales creates an increase of 50% in profit since no increase in "constant" costs is involved.   (Actually, constant costs do vary with volume, but not at all in proportion.)   There is little risk involved in such an increase, since the technology, production facilities, market, etc., are already in existence and of proved effectiveness.   In contrast, to increase sales by creating a new product line involves much investment in market research, technology, facilities, and manpower. In addition, the venture is far more risky than greater share of market in an existing product line.   In this way, a dollar of sales gained through a quality superiority is commonly much more valuable than a dollar of sales gained through investment in a new venture.

Most forms of product superiority can be used to attain added share of market even though the "inferior" product is fit for use.   For example, a manufacturer of antifriction bearings had refined his processes to such an extent that his products were more precise than those of his competitors.   As it happened, the competitors' products were entirely fit for use, so no price differential was feasible.   Nevertheless, the fact of greater precision was a forceful selling tool and resulted in increased share of market.

In the case of consumer products, even a small product difference can be translated into an increased share of market if the consumers are adequately sensitized.[25]

---

[25] Even when there is no product difference, the shares of market can differ remarkably solely due to differences in marketing skills.

For example, a manufacturer of candy-coated chocolates seized on the fact that his product did not create chocolate smudge marks on consumers' hands. He dramatized this in television advertisements by contrasting the appearance of children's hands after eating his and competitors' (uncoated) chocolate. His share of market rose dramatically.

Consumer Preference and Share of Market The willingness of the consumer to respond to qualities and to differences he can sense has resulted in much study to:

1. Develop objective methods for measuring consumer preference and other forms of consumer response. A large body of literature is now available setting out the types of sensory tests, the methods for conducting them, and the interpretation of the resulting data. (See Section 12, under Sensory Testing.)

2. Use these methods to aid in making decisions. While much of this application has been for process control and product acceptance decisions (see Section 12), there is a growing use of these methods for market testing, product development, advertising, and marketing of products.[26]

For some products it is easy to secure a measure of consumer preference through "forced choice" test. For example, a table is set up in a department store and passersby are invited to taste two cups of coffee, A and B, and to express their preference. Pairs of swatches of carpet may be shown to panels of potential buyers with the request that they indicate their preferences. For comparatively simple consumer products, these preference tests can secure good data on consumer preference. In turn, these data can be used to make sound marketing decisions.[27]

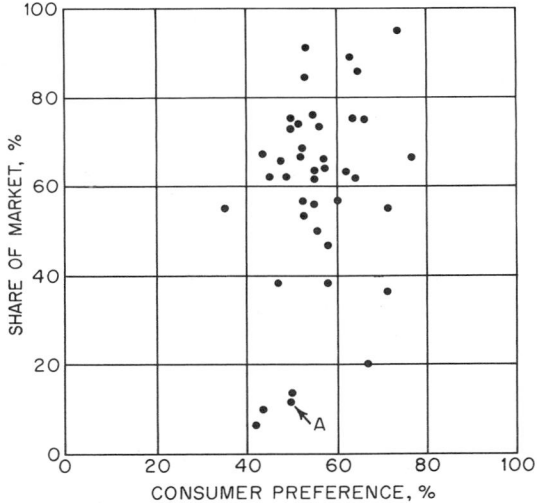

Fig. 4-2 Consumer preference versus share of market.

The value of consumer preference data is greatly multiplied through correlation with data on share of market. Figure 4-2 shows such a correlation for 41 different

[26] See, for example, Kuehn, Alfred L., and Ralph L. Day, Strategy of Product Quality, *Harvard Business Review*, pp. 100–110, November–December 1962.

[27] In interpreting preference data, care must be taken to avoid some traps. The fact that one product has a minority consumer preference does not necessarily mean that it is disliked. Most consumers may prefer licorice flavor to ginger, but a minority may definitely prefer ginger to licorice. For an elaboration, see Kuehn and Day, op. cit.

packaged consumer products. This was an uncommonly important analysis and deserves careful study.[28]

Each dot on Figure 4-2 represents a type of product sold on supermarket shelves. It competes there with other products for shelf space. The competing products sell for identical prices and are packaged in identically sized boxes containing identical amounts of product. What may influence the housewife are:

1. the marketing skills, i.e., attractiveness of the package, the appeal of the prior advertising, the reputation of the manufacturer, etc.

2. the contents of the package as judged by her senses and usage, which may cause the housewife to prefer A to B.

On Figure 4-2 the horizontal scale shows consumer preference over the leading competitor as determined by statistically sound preference testing. The vertical scale shows the share of market versus the leading competitor, considering the two as constituting 100%.

It is evident that in no instance did any product exhibit a consumer preference below 25% (or above 75%). This phenomenon is undoubtedly related to the fact that a consumer quality preference above 75% means that the product is so superior that three users out of four can detect that superiority. Since all other factors are essentially equal, the product which is so overwhelmingly preferred takes over the entire market while its competition disappears.

In contrast to the vacant areas on the horizontal scale of consumer preference, the vertical scale of share of market has data along the entire spectrum. One product (marked A on Figure 4-2) lies squarely on the 50% consumer preference line, which probably means (under forced choice testing) that the users are guessing as to whether they prefer that product or its competition. Yet this product has only 10% share of market and its competitor 90%. Not only that, this inequality in share of market has persisted for years. The reason is that the 90% company had pioneered in that product, acquired a "prior franchise," and retained its position through good promotion thereafter.

The conclusion is that when competing products are quite similar in consumer preference, any effect of such small quality differentials is obscured by the effect of the marketing skills. In consequence, it is logical to conclude that when quality preferences are clearly evident to the user, such quality differences are decisive in share of market, all other things being equal. When quality preferences are slight, the decisive factor in share of market is the marketing skills.

As a corollary, it appears that companies are well advised to undertake quality improvements which will result in either (1) bringing them from a clearly weak to an acceptable preference or (2) bringing them from an acceptable preference to a clearly dominant preference. However, companies are not well advised to undertake quality improvements which will merely move them from one acceptable level to another, since the dominant role in share of market in such cases is played by the marketing skills.

It is easy for technologists to conclude that what they regard as important in the product is also of prime concern to the user. In the carpet industry, the engineers devote much effort to improving wear qualities and other technological aspects of fitness for use. However, a market survey established that consumers' reasons for selecting carpets were primarily sensory, i.e.,

Color	56%
Pattern	20%

[28] Juran, J. M., A Note on Economics of Quality, *Industrial Quality Control*, pp. 20–23, February 1959. The study involved consumer products. Data were available showing, for each of the 41 products, (1) the percent of consumer preference, on blindfold tests, against competing brands and (2) the share of market based on actual sales versus competing brands. (Consulting experience of J. M. Juran.)

Other sensory   6%

Non-sensory   18%[29]

For more complex consumer products it would seem feasible, in theory, to study the relation of quality to share of market by securing quantitive data on (1) actual changes in buying patterns of consumers and (2) states of quality which may have brought about these changes.

In practice, it is soon discovered that such data are difficult to acquire and that it is also very difficult to conclude, in any one instance, why the purchase was of model A rather than B. What does emerge are some "demographic" patterns, i.e., age of buyers, size of family, etc., which favor model A rather than B. In addition, there emerge some "negatives" i.e., what *not* to do.[30]

Industrial Products and Share of Market Industrial products are sold much more on technological performance than on sensory qualities. However, the principle of preference is still present, and there is need to find ways of relating quality to customer preference and to share of market.

One approach is that of sales analysis, as described in Section 14, under Analysis of Available Market Quality Information: Decline of Sales. For the vital few large accounts, such analyses can be made individually. For the numerous small accounts, sampling is adequate.

Another approach is to analyze the company's performance during its bidding for contracts. The practice of competitive bidding is widespread. Most government agencies are required by law to secure competitive bids before awarding large contracts. Industrial companies require their purchasing agents to do the same. The usual factors of price, delivery date, and quality enter the bidding process, as do the marketing skills. Quality includes the usual parameters of fitness for use plus the important factor of quality reputation of the manufacturer.

The ratio of awards received to bids made is of great significance. The volume of sales and profit depends importantly on this ratio. In addition, the cost of preparing bids is substantial; for large systems the cost of bid preparation is itself large. Finally, the ratio affects the morale of the men involved. (Members of a winning team fight their competitors; members of a losing team fight each other.)

It is feasible to analyze the record of prior bids in an effort to improve the award percentage. Table 4-3 shows such an analysis involving 20 unsuccessful bids. Quality of design was a major contributor in the pattern. From knowledge of the users' specific objections to the designs and other users' preferences in successful bids, the needed remedies emerged much more clearly than was evident merely from the memory of the managers involved.

QUALITY REPUTATION

A positive quality reputation, whether for consumer products or for capital goods, is of the highest value.

Most consumers are unable to understand the morass of technological detail involved in product designs. Even less are they able to test conformance to that design. Instead, they are driven to rely on their senses, which can detect only the evidence of lack of fitness for use, i.e., service failure or obvious deterioration.

In addition, the consumer can sense still another phenomenon — the record of performance of the manufacturer's products. Where this record is good, the consumer

---

[29] Private communication to J. M. Juran.

[30] In another proposed type of analysis, frequency of failure is compared for (1) automobile buyers who remained loyal to their previous manufacturer and (2) buyers who switched to a new manufacturer. From the data an "annoyance index" is determined. See Nevitt, P. J., Reliability as a Design Criterion, *Quality Engineer*, pp. 43–48, 60, March–April 1967.

TABLE 4-3   Analysis of Unsuccessful Bids

Contract proposal	Bid not accepted due to				
	Quality of design	Product price	Installation price*	Reciprocal buying	Other
A 1	...	X	X	...	X
A 2	...	...	XX	...	...
A 3	XX	X	...	...	...
A 4	XX	...	X	...	...
A 5	XX	...	...	...	...
A 6	XX	...	...	...	...
A 7	...	XX	...	...	...
A 8	...	XX	...	...	...
A 9	...	...	XX	...	...
A 10	...	...	XX	...	...
B 1	X	...	X	...	...
B 2	...	...	...	XX	...
B 3	...	...	...	XX	...
B 4	...	...	...	XX	...
B 5	...	X	X	...	...
B 6	...	X	XX	...	...
B 7	XX	...	...	...	...
B 8	...	X	X	...	...
B 9	...	...	...	X	...
B 10	X	X	X	...	...
Totals	7	8	10 (of 14)	4	1

X = Contributing reason
XX = Main reason
*Only 14 bids were made for installation.

learns to rely on that manufacturer. Such is the enduring basis for a quality reputation. The consumer learns to use this reputation as a bridge across all that morass of technological detail.

Manufacturers are well aware of the value of a quality reputation. Now and then this value is dramatized by some catastrophic failure. For example, a Japanese dairy products manufacturer once had 70% of the Japanese market in powdered milk for babies. A ghastly error resulted in the death of many infants and illness for thousands. The share of market soon dropped to less than 10%. Fifteen years later it had gone back up to 35%, but the former leadership had still not been regained.[31]

In some cases the quality reputation is built not around a specific company but around an association of companies. In that event this association adopts and publicizes some mark or symbol.[32] The quality reputation becomes identified with this symbol, and the association goes to great lengths to protect this reputation.

The medieval guilds imposed strict specifications and quality controls on their members, including "export" (i.e., beyond the city) controls on the finished goods.[33] Such export controls are common in some industrial countries today.[34]

[31] *Business Week*, pp. 44 and 45, June 20, 1970.

[32] See Section 14, under Labeling: Brand Labeling.

[33] For some interesting examples, see Lerner, F., Quality Control in Pre-Industrial Times, *CIBA Review*, pp. 2–15, 1968/4.

[34] See Section 48, especially under Quality Control in Developing Countries; see also below, Government Regulation of Quality: Export Controls.

The quality reputation of the Swiss watch industry has been an industry (and national) asset for centuries. The very term "Swiss watch" has been internationally identified with precision. When Japanese watches showed up strongly in the Geneva horological competition of 1969, the entire country was concerned.[35]

Companies which make a broad line of products find that the reputation derived from one line helps or hinders sales of other product lines.[36]

The quality reputation affects industrial and government buyers as well. When all other things are equal (and even when they are not), the buyer derives an important personal protection from a record which shows the prudence of having dealt with manufacturers of known rather than unknown quality reputation.

The great importance of good quality suggests that companies should take positive steps to achieve it. (See Quality Leadership, below.)

Quality Leadership   In many product lines, one of the competing brands is generally regarded as the quality leader. This leadership is the result of an original quality superiority which gains what marketers call a "prior franchise." Once gained, this franchise can be maintained through continuing product improvement and effective market promotion.

So important is quality leadership that marketing managers choose it in preference to all other elements of marketability. A survey of 125 senior marketing executives[37] as to their first preference for their own product superiority showed the following:

Form of product superiority	Percent of marketing executives giving first preference to this form
Superior quality	40
Lower price (or better value)	17
More features, options, or uses.	12
All other	31

Policy on Leadership.   Companies trying to attain quality leadership may choose one of two main approaches:

1. Let nature take its course. In this approach, companies apply their best efforts, confident that in time these efforts will be recognized.

2. Help nature out by adopting a positive policy, i.e., establish leadership as a formal goal and then set out to reach that goal.

Those who decide to make quality leadership a formal goal soon find that they must answer also the question, "Leadership in what?" Quality leadership can exist in any of the multiple aspects of fitness for use, but the structure of the company will differ significantly depending on which aspect is chosen.

If quality leadership is to consist of	The company must emphasize
Superior quality of design	Product development, systems development
Superior quality of conformance	Manufacturing quality controls
Availability	Reliability and maintainability programs
Guarantees, field service	Field service capability

While all these aspects of fitness for use are interrelated, it is unusual for any one company to attain recognized leadership in all of them. (See, in this connection,

---

[35] *Time,* pp. 58 and 59, April 20, 1970.

[36] One large manufacturer advertised widely the case of an industrialist who bought a computer from his company, having been influenced to do so by the reliability of his household refrigerator which had been bought from the same firm 36 years earlier and was still running.

[37] Hopkins, David S., and Earl L. Bailey, New Product Pressures, *The Conference Board Record,* pp. 16–24, June 1971.

the quality policy of Alfred P. Sloan, Jr., in Section 3, under Formulation of Quality Policies.)

Once quality leadership has been established as a formal project, it becomes the subject of quality planning in the same manner as any other project (see Section 6).

LIFE CYCLE COSTING

The concept of cost of usage goes under various names, one of these being the term "life cycle costing" popularized in military contracting.[38]   Under this concept, the various elements of cost of usage (Table 4-1) are quantified in order to enable the users and manufacturers to improve their decision making in ways which will optimize the user's cost of usage.

Other terms which have been coined to express cost of usage include "cost of ownership," "mission cost," "cost effectiveness," etc.   Examples of units of measure include:

Mission cost for engineered systems[39]
Cost per operating hour of aircraft engines[40]
Cost per hour of satellite life[41]
Launch vehicles per 100 million dollars[42]

TABLE 4-4   Life Cycle Costing: Capital Goods ($000)

Elements of cost	Bidding company		
	X	Y	Z
Original price..................	42	60	47
Maintenance over life of product			
Labor	129	116	84
Spare parts	40	30	20
Paper work	12	18	12
Operation costs (power, supplies).....	235	225	245
Inventory management...........	60	45	30
Training	8	8	8
Downtime....................	80	100	70
Total life cycle costs.............	606	602	516

SOURCE: Adapted from *Business Week*, May 13, 1967.

[38] Military experience had indicated that *annual* maintenance costs ran from two to more than twenty times the original equipment costs.   See E. F. Dertinger, Funding Reliability Programs, *Proceedings Ninth National Symposium on Reliability and Quality Control*, 1963, IEEE, pp. 16–33.   See also Stroop, Paul D., Quality Control Impact on Military Hardware, *Industrial Quality Control*, pp. 298–304, December 1964.

[39] Darnell, P. S., Some Economic Concepts Underlying Reliability Engineering, *Transactions, 3rd Annual Quality Control—Reliability Conference*, Long Island Section ASQC, Hofstra University, pp. 11–23, 1964.

[40] Madden, John I., Cost-Effectiveness Maximum Times for Aircraft Engines, *Proceedings, 1966 Annual Symposium on Reliability*, IEEE, pp. 118–124.

[41] Myers, R. H., Predicting the Reliability of Satellite Systems, *Industrial Quality Control*, February 1964.

[42] Winlund, E. S., Cost-Effectiveness Analysis for Optimal Reliability and Maintainability, *Proceedings, 11th National Symposium on Reliability and Quality Control*, IEEE, pp. 107–114, 1964.

Application to Capital Goods Table 4-4 is a model showing the bids of three manufacturers for supplying a capital goods system to a user. The breakdown shows also how the costs of operation and maintenance differ among the three proposals. These differences show that in this case the system with the lowest original price results in the highest cost of usage.

Models such as Table 4-4 dramatize the need for putting the emphasis on the cost of usage rather than on the original price. In turn, this emphasis makes it easier to direct attention to two major opportunities for reducing the cost of usage:

1. Conduct the bidding based on the life cycle cost rather than on the original price.

2. Restudy the original design and the other contributions to the life cycle cost, and then, through trade offs among parameters, reduce the total.

TABLE 4-5   Cost versus Reliability

MTBF*	R&D costs*	Total operational costs*	Total program costs*
0.10	0.425	4.03	4.45
0.25	0.635	1.92	2.56
0.50	0.800	1.21	2.01
0.75	1.00	0.98	1.98
1.00	1.15	0.86	2.01
1.50	1.35	0.73	2.08
2.00	1.50	0.68	2.18
2.50	1.61	0.64	2.25

* Normalized

Common to all these models is the principle that improving the original design to increase reliability, maintainability, etc., reduces the operating and maintenance costs. However, the time comes when the incremental costs of still further design improvements are so great that the resulting reduction in cost of usage is too small to justify the superior design. An example is seen in the missile guidance computer (MGC).[43] In that program several levels of reliability were considered. Estimates were prepared for the costs of achieving these levels of reliability as well as for the resulting operational and total costs. These estimates are shown in Table 4-5, and the data are graphed in Figure 4-3. The nature of the minimum is clearly evident.

Competing systems may differ radically in their basic concept. In one example, four different system design approaches were evaluated for dealing with failure (in service) of a helicopter power unit:

1. Remove the failed unit and replace with a new unit. Return the failed unit to a repair depot for overhaul.

2. Remove the power unit under a scheduled replacement program (even if there has been no failure). Replace with a new unit and send the replaced unit to the repair depot for overhaul.

3. Design the power unit under a modular concept so that, in case of field failure, only the failed module is replaced.

4. Design the power unit to be thrown away in case of failure.

[43] Colandene, B. T., Program Costs vs. Reliability, *10th Annual Symposium on Reliability & Quality Control,* IEEE, pp. 386–394, 1964.

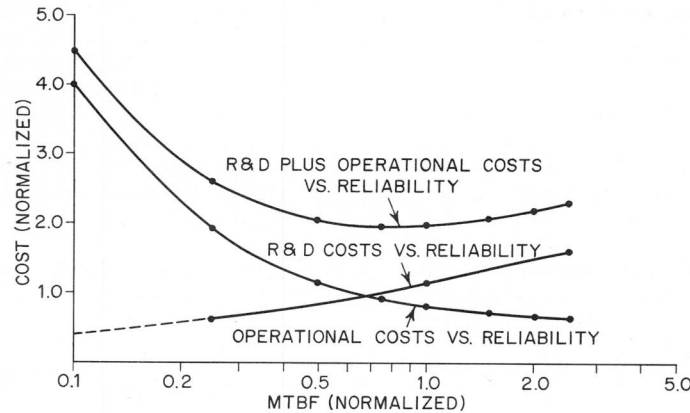

Fig. 4-3   Cost versus reliability.

These alternatives have different life cycle costs and present different problems of field inventory.[44]

Application to Consumer Products   The cost of usage concept applies also to consumer products.[45] Table 4-6 is based on studies of a number of types of long-life apparatus and shows that for such products the life cycle cost runs from about two to five times the original cost.[46]

TABLE 4-6   Life Cycle Costing: Consumer Products

Product	Original price	Operation plus maintenance	Total	Ratio, life cycle cost to original price
Room air conditioner	$200	$465	$665	3.3
Dishwasher	245	372	617	2.5
Freezer	165	628	793	4.8
Range, electric	175	591	766	4.4
Range, gas	180	150	330	1.9
Refrigerator	230	561	791	3.5
TV (black & white)	200	305	505	2.5
TV (color)	560	526	1086	1.9
Washing machine	235	617	852	3.6

When solid-state electronics were developed for home entertainment purposes, the manufacturers sold the new products despite higher original prices. It was known that 80% of service calls on the older circuitry were for changing electron tubes. In consequence, the manufacturers raised the warranties up to five years on the parts, instead of the 90 days prevailing on tube sets. (Elimination of the warm-up time was, of course, a feature the user could sense personally.)

[44] Gallagher, B. M., and W. H. Knobloch, Helicopter Auxiliary Power Unit Cost of Ownership, *17th Annual Symposium on Reliability,* IEEE, pp. 285–291, 1971.

[45] The late comedian Ed Wynn is said to have worn the same $3.50 shoes through his long career in vaudeville, radio, and television. They cost him $3,000 in repairs.

[46] Gryna, F. M., Jr., User Costs of Poor Quality, doctoral dissertation, 1970. (Available from F. M. Gryna, Jr., Bradley University, Peoria, Ill.)

More usually, the concept of consumer cost of usage runs into very severe problems of application.   They include:

1. Setting up the needed data banks (see below)
2. Overcoming some deep-seated cultural resistance (see below)
3. Administering numerous small long-life contracts, which is inherently a costly process
4. Solving the problems of multiple ownership

The most notable example of the last problem is passenger automobiles, which, in the United States, usually go through multiple ownership before being scrapped. Even under short-term guarantees, the transfer of ownership creates severe problems of administering guarantee contracts.   Existing practice usually imposes a charge for transfer of short-term guarantees between successive owners.   For contracts over the useful life of the product, this problem would become considerably more complicated.

The "trade-in" problem is already an asserted reason for keeping some design improvements off the market.   During the 1960s, a solid-state distributor mechanism was developed for use in automobiles.   This device would give failure-free performance for the life of the car and would save the user about $40 in out-of-pocket repairs and maintenance at an increase of $80 in the original price. [47]   When downtime, inconvenience, and risk of inflated repair bills are added in, the solid-state device, if available as an option, would very likely attract a clientele.   However, the original buyer whose practice is to trade in after one or two years would derive little benefit from his added original cost and might fail to recover this cost during trade-in.

Data Banks   To make the life cycle costing concept effective requires knowledge of failure rates, downtime, repair costs, and other aspects of cost of usage.   Lacking such data, the parties lack a solid basis for their negotiations.

Sometimes a conventional study of quality costs [48] will provide the entering wedge for examining cost of usage.

A large printing company made such a study of its quality costs.   The largest single item was press downtime, amounting to $404,000 or 23% of the total of $1,725,000 for all quality costs. [49]

Another such analysis by an airline (British European Airways) provided estimates of cost per hour of delay for aircraft, as follows:

Comet $650
Trident $900
Vanguard. $670

For all fleets the total came to $8.4 million per year. [50]

Large users who are attracted to the concept of cost of usage will find in short order that the data banks are a prerequisite to widespread use of the concept. Actually, these data are needed anyway as part of the means for good operation and maintenance of technological systems.   Manufacturers who need such cost of usage data can obtain them by collaboration with users.   If necessary, arrangements can be made to buy the data.   (See Section 14, under Analysis of Available Market Quality Information.)

[47] Private communication to J. M. Juran.
[48] See Section 5.
[49] For elaboration, see Section 5, Table 5-2 and associated discussion.
[50] Rossiter, H. G., The State of Affairs in Civil Airlines, *Journal Royal Aeronautical Society,* pp. 394–396, March 1966.

For consumer products, the data banks on cost of usage are more difficult to organize. Manufacturers usually do have good feedback on repair labor and spare parts used during the guarantee period but not on cost of downtime and other nonreimbursible costs. Beyond the guarantee period, all data are sparse. To collect all these missing data and structure them into well-organized data banks is a substantial market research problem.

An example of such a research study is the Federal Highway Administration study *Cost of Operating an Automobile.* [51] The complexity of the study is indicated from the broad categories of costs involved (costs are in cents per mile).

TABLE 4-7   Cost of Operating an Automobile

	Size of automobile		
Cost factor	Standard	Compact	Subcompact
Original vehicle depreciation	4.4	2.7	2.1
Maintenance, accessories, parts and tires.	2.6	2.2	2.1
Gasoline and oil (excluding taxes)	2.1	1.8	1.4
Garage, parking, and tolls	1.8	1.8	1.8
Insurance	1.4	1.3	1.2
Federal and state taxes	1.3	1.0	0.8
Total	13.6	10.8	9.4

In the absence of good data banks, there is also a risk of overreaction to dramatic instances of failure. Numerous cases have been cited in which some defect in a "minor" component was responsible for a huge loss. For example, a failure of a $25 fuel valve lost a missile and damaged a launch site for a total bill of about $22 million. [52] The loss of a $3.7 million jet aircraft was traced to the omission of a cotter pin in a bolted assembly. [53] Commonly such instances take place despite the fact that there already exist quality control and other programs for which huge sums have been spent. (For complex military and space systems, the cost of quality is of the order of magnitude of 10 to 25% of the system budget.)

The cases where the failure cost was many thousand times the value of the guilty component make grim reading, but it does not follow that the spending of a trivial amount would have avoided the failure. In such systems, many thousands of components, processes, operators, etc., are involved, resulting in myriads of permutations for potential failure. Since it is not known which of these permutations will actually result in catastrophic failure, it follows that a program of extra effort would need to extend over many thousands of permutations and hence would in itself be very costly.

Cultural Resistance   For thousands of years, buyers and sellers, whether house-

---

[51] Available from the Superintendent of Documents, U.S. Government Printing Office, Washington, D.C.

[52] Estes, Howell M., Reliability Today—and Tomorrow, *10th National Symposium on Reliability and Quality Control,* IEEE, Keynote address, 1964.

[53] Stroop, *op. cit.*

wives or managers, have emphasized the original price of the product. For short-life products this was and still is a very logical emphasis. For long-life products, life cycle costs are often a better basis for negotiation. However, the long-standing habit of emphasizing original price is now deeply rooted in the industrial culture. To illustrate:

Product designers have long been urged to come up with designs which can feature low original cost and price. The personal progress of designers is influenced by their ability to respond to these criteria.

Sales managers and purchasing agents have built their know-how and skills around negotiating the original price. A change to life cycle costing demands a considerable shift in knowledge and a different set of skills.[54]

Two kinds of money are involved—capital budgets and operating expenses—with differences in levels of management approval, accounting practices, and tax implications. Cost of usage runs to several times the face value of original-price-of-product contracts and has an impact on all these variables.[55]

Company and government regulations on competitive bidding have long been oriented to original cost. (Government use of life cycle costing has required some new legislation.) As awards are made based on life cycle costs, those who submit the lowest bids for the equipment are able to muster support for their position.

The laws of contract are well worked out as applied to original price contracts, but they are only in evolution as applied to life cycle costing contracts, which thereby contain many unknowns.

Very likely the most deeply rooted habits are those of the small user. He keeps no records of cost of usage and tends to underestimate the amount.[56] For many less-than-affluent consumers, the whole question is obscured by the fact that they lack the capital needed even for the original price and hence must borrow part of it.

Obviously, makers of consumer goods cannot abandon marketing on original price when such is the cultural pattern. What they can do is to experiment by offering some optional models designed for lower cost of usage as a means of gaining experience and time for the day when life cycle costing comes into wide use.

Makers of industrial products also face cultural resistance in trying to use life cycle costing as a business opportunity. However, with good data they can make out a persuasive case and strike responsive chords in men who see in these data a way to further the interests of their company and themselves.

GOVERNMENT REGULATION OF QUALITY

From time immemorial, "governments" have established and enforced standards of quality. Some of these governments have been political—national, provincial, local. Others have been nonpolitical: Professional Societies, Industry Associations, Standardization Organizations, Independent Laboratories, etc. Whether through delegation of political power or through long custom, these governing bodies have

[54] The fact that the Quality Control specialists concentrated their studies on manufacturers' costs rather than on cost of usage is very like attributable to cultural resistance. See Juran, J. M., Whose Quality Costs? *Industrial Quality Control*, pp. 82 and 83, August 1965.

[55] The Model in Table 4-4 includes both capital and operating expenditures, which affect financial results in different ways. One method of analysis for such projects is "Return on Investment" (ROI). Under the ROI concept, the depreciation, interest, and other charges associated with capital expenditures are quantified to make possible a computation of percent return on investment. This return can then be compared with competing projects. See for example, Kaufman, Robert J., Life Cycle Costing: Decision Making Tool for Capital Equipment Acquisitions, *Journal of Purchasing*, pp. 16–31, August 1969.

[56] Gryna, *op. cit.*

attained a status which enables them to carry out programs of regulation as discussed below.

Bases for Regulation   Regulation of quality has evolved to serve some very selective, limited purposes:

Metrology.   All organized human activity, and especially technological activity, involves standardized units of measure for time, mass, and other fundamental constants.   So basic are these standards that they are now international in scope.

Interchangeability.   A second level of standards has brought order out of chaos in such day-to-day matters as household voltages and interchangeability of myriads of the bits and pieces of an industrial society.   Compliance is an economic necessity.

Technological Definition.   A third array of standards has been prepared to define numerous materials, processes, products, tests, etc.   These standards are developed by committees drawn from the various interested segments of society.   While compliance is usually voluntary, the economic imperatives result in a high degree of acceptance and use of these standards.

Beyond the foregoing bases, which are all related to standardization and encounter little resistance to compliance, there are other bases which involve enforcement as well as standardization.[57]

Safety and Health of the Citizenry.   The main emphasis of political government regulation has been at this level.   There are laws which prescribe and enforce safety standards for building construction, oceangoing ships, mines, aircraft, bridges, and many other structures.   Other laws are aimed at hazards which have their origins in fire, food, drugs, dangerous chemicals, etc.   Still other laws regulate who may perform certain activities essential to public safety and health, e.g., licensing of professional engineers, physicians, airline pilots.   (Some of the standards for safety are established and enforced by nonpolitical government.)

Safety and Health of the State.   In addition to protecting their military safety, governments have developed standards and regulation to protect their economic health.   Integrity of the coinage is one example.   (Political governments have a monopoly on the right to debase the currency.)   Laws regulating the quality of exports are of ancient origin and are for the purpose of protecting the national quality reputation from the carelessness or greed of individual manufacturers.   (See Export Control, below.)   In those cases where the government is a purchaser (defense weapons, public utility facilities) the basis of government regulation includes the normal rights of a purchaser to ascertain fitness for use.

Economics of the Citizenry.   This category of government regulation is highly controversial in the market-based societies.   Some of the resistance is on ideological grounds — the competitive marketplace is asserted to be a far better regulator than a government bureau.   Other resistance is based on the known deficiencies of the administration of government regulation (see below).   Some of the growth of this category of regulation is stimulated by the consumerism movement (see below).

The Plan of Regulation   Once it has been determined that there shall be regulation in some new matter involving quality, the approach follows a well-beaten path.   The sequence of events listed below, while described in the language of regulation by political government, applies to nonpolitical government as well.

The Statute.   An enabling act, defines the purpose of the regulation and especially the products or services to be regulated.   It establishes the "rules of the game" and creates an agency to administer the act.

The Administrator.   He is given powers to establish standards and to see that

---

[57] The broad definition of standardization is "the establishment, by authority, custom or general consent of a rule or model to be followed." Coonley, Howard, and P. G. Agnew, "The Role of Standards in a System of Free Enterprise," American National Standards Institute, New York.

they are enforced. To this end he is armed with the means for making awards and applying sanctions on matters of great importance to the regulated industries.

The Standards. The administrator has the power to set standards and may exercise this power by adopting existing industry standards. These standards are not limited to products; they may deal with materials, processes, tests, descriptive literature, advertising, qualifications of personnel, etc.

Test Laboratories. The administrator has the power to establish criteria to be used for judging the qualifications of "independent" test laboratories. Once these criteria are established, he also may have the power to issue certificates of qualification to laboratories which meet the criteria. In some cases he has the power to establish his own test laboratories.

Test and Evaluation. Here there is great variation. For some undertakings prior test and evaluation are a prerequisite to the right to market, e.g., new drug applications (see Section 32) or plans for the operation and maintenance of a new fleet of airplanes. Some agencies put much stress on surveillance, i.e., review of the manufacturer's control plan and his adherence to that plan. Other agencies emphasize final product sampling and test.

The Seal or Mark. Regulated products are frequently required to display a seal or mark to attest to the fact of compliance with the regulations. Where the regulating agency does the actual testing, it affixes this mark, e.g., government meat inspectors physically stamp the carcasses.[58]

More usually, the agency does not test and stamp the product. Instead, it determines, by test, that the product design is adequate. It also determines, by surveillance, that the manufacturer's system of control is adequate. Having made these determinations, it authorizes the manufacturer to affix the seal or mark. The statutes always provide for penalties for unauthorized use of the mark.

Sanctions. The regulatory agency has wide powers of enforcement, such as the right to:

Investigate product failures and user complaints
Inspect the manufacturer's processes and system of controls
Test products in all stages of distribution
Recall products already sold to users
Revoke the manufacturer's right to sell, or to apply the mark
Inform users of deficiencies
Issue cease and desist orders

Export Controls   Government regulation is widely used in many countries to control the quality of exported products. Usually these controls apply only to a selected list of products which are regarded as significantly affecting the economy of the country. For countries heavily involved in exports, the list of products controlled becomes formidable. Administration of the controls is commonly by a department of the Ministry of Foreign Trade.

For example, under the Japanese Export Inspection Law, certain classes of products (representing the bulk of exports) may not be shipped out of the country unless they meet export standards. During the 1960s a total of 39 independent laboratories employing over 4,500 people carried out these controls under the general supervision of government agencies. The laboratories are supported by fees collected for exercising the controls.[59]

While some of the products under export control are critical to safety and health,

---

[58] The British Hallmark was established in the year 1300 to assure the integrity of gold and silver products. Government assay offices test the product and stamp it with symbols showing fineness of gold or silver, the symbol of the assaying office, and the year of the test.

[59] "Quality Control in Japan," Published by Japan Trade Center, New York.

most of them are not. For these noncritical products, the controls are mandatory for a different reason—to protect the foreign trade of the country from being damaged by careless or unscrupulous manufacturers.

Noncritical Domestic Products   Government controls on quality are also applied to products which are neither critical to human safety nor exported. Mandatory forms of these controls, i.e., full regulation, are extensive in Eastern European countries (see Section 48A) and in some developing countries (see Section 48). Elsewhere, mandatory government control of these products is seldom used.

Where the control is mandatory, the procedure used follows that discussed under The Plan of Regulation, above.

More usually, the controls on these products are *voluntary* and follow a procedure quite different from that used for mandatory controls. See Section 14, under Labeling.

Some Realities of Government Regulation   The proliferation of government regulation of quality has resulted in the creation of new agencies that are pioneering in new fields with inexperienced personnel and untested procedures. In addition, these agencies are subjected to severe pressures from critics: reformers, legislators, journalists, industrial companies. Some of these critics are powerfully based and use this power to make reckless attacks on the regulatory agencies. Until the agencies can stabilize their operations and achieve a position of respect, they have no choice but to adapt to some of these pressures.

Proposals to remedy the more usual failings of regulatory agencies include the following:

Regulate fitness for use, not conformance to specification.
Concentrate on the vital few qualities.
Concentrate on the "bad guys" i.e., the persistent violators.
Use surveillance, not retest.
Publish scoreboards of what progress is being made toward fitness for use.
Avoid taking over industry's basic responsibility for achieving fitness for use.[60]

Effect of Strict Enforcement.   The distinction between conformance to specification and fitness for use is widely observed by industrial companies but not by regulatory agencies. When the specification has the force of law, the regulators, especially in new agencies, tend to make a "federal case" out of any nonconformance. If, as sometimes happens, the regulatory agency adopts some of the standards prevailing in the industry, the result is a shock due to the new level of strict enforcement on matters which do not affect fitness for use. *The change in level of enforcement becomes a tightening of standards.*

A contributing factor may be that the standard was needlessly tight in the first place and had then been rationalized by loose enforcement. Yet the tight values remained on the books and became the basis for the strict enforcement.[61]

CONSUMER TEST SERVICES

The widening gap in product knowledge between manufacturer and consumer has given added stimulus to the old concept of the independent product label. Under this concept, a competent laboratory makes an expert, independent evaluation of the

---

[60] For elaboration see Juran, J. M., Consumerism and Product Quality, *Quality Progress,* July 1970.
[61] For some other aspects of government regulation of quality, see Section 14, under Advertising of Quality and under Warranty of Quality. See also the cases discussed in Section 12, under Quality Planning: Extent of Planning.

product so that the consumer can obtain the added, unbiased information he needs to make sound judgments about quality of product.

Adequate consumer test services involve professionals and skilled technicians, well-equipped test laboratories, acquisition of products for test, and dissemination of the resulting information. Financing of all these needs becomes so severe a problem that the method of financing determines the organization form and the policies of the test service.

Consumer-financed Tests   In this form the test laboratory derives its income by publication of test results, usually in the form of a monthly journal plus an annual compendium. Consumers are urged to subscribe to the journal on the ground that they will save money by acquiring superior knowledge of product values thereby. The advertising by the test laboratory stresses the question, "Would you pay $100 for an appliance when independent tests show that a $75 appliance is just as good?"

In their operation, these consumer-financed test laboratories buy and test competitive products, evaluate their failures and their fitness for use, compare these evaluations with the product prices, and rate the products according to some scale of relative value, e.g., best value, good value, poor value. The ratings, test result summaries, description of tests conducted, etc., are published in the journals. Manufacturers play no role in the testing and evaluation, although they may be consulted on market information. In addition, manufacturers are not permitted to quote the ratings, test results, or other material in the journals.

It is seen that the service offered to consumers consists of:

1. Laboratory test results which are commonly objective and unbiased.

2. Judgments of values which are subjective and carry a risk of bias, i.e., the stress of the advertising (showing the consumer that lower-priced products are as good as higher-priced products) creates a bias against higher-priced products. More importantly, the judgments are not necessarily typical of consumer judgments.

Despite the obvious problems of financing a test service out of numerous small subscription prices, there are many such services in existence in affluent and even developing countries.[62,63]

Manufacturer-financed Tests   In this form, the income of the test service is derived from fees paid by manufacturers who seek the mark (seal, label) of the testing service as an aid to marketing the product. These test services vary widely in their purpose and especially in their objectivity.

Mandatory Marks.   An obvious example is the mark needed for export of products from those countries which impose controls of export quality. The laboratories are financed out of fees paid by the exporters, and the exporter must pay the fees if he wishes to market his products abroad.

Closely related is the example of Underwriters' Laboratories, Inc. (UL). Historically created by the National Board of Fire Underwriters to aid in fire prevention, UL (now independent) is involved in the general field of fire protection, burglary protection, hazardous chemicals, and still other matters of safety. Its activities include:

Developing and publishing standards for materials, products, and systems.

---

[62] See *Consumers Directory,* 1969, International Organization of Consumer Unions, The Hague, Holland.

[63] For example, in the Netherlands, a government-financed Consumer Contact Board provides money for independent product testing and advises the government as to needed legislation. Through collaboration with consumer organizations and labor unions, a monthly television program is used to disseminate product quality information (including data on named brands) as well as other forms of information useful to consumers. The influence of these television programs is profound, having resulted in some company bankruptcies and some crash programs to redesign products.

Testing manufacturers' products for compliance with these standards (or with other recognized standards).

Awarding the UL mark to products which comply. This is known as "listing" the products.

Numerous other laboratories are similarly involved in safety matters, e.g., steam boilers, marine safety.

In some of these safety categories it is unlawful to market the products without the certificate of the testing service. In other cases it is lawful, but the testing is mandatory for economic reasons, e.g., the insurance companies will demand extraordinarily high premiums or will not provide insurance at all. Because of these legal or economic imperatives, the laboratories (which often have achieved a status that confers a monopoly for that type of testing) are generally able to support themselves out of the fees paid for testing.

Voluntary Marks. These forms of testing service are built around the same elements as the mandatory mark:

1. Developing and publishing standards
2. Testing products for conformance
3. Awarding a mark to conforming products

The distinguishing feature of the voluntary mark[64] is that the manufacturer is under no compelling legal (e.g., export control) or economic (e.g., insurance) imperative to obtain the mark. Lacking these imperatives, the manufacturer is interested in the mark solely as a device for competitive marketing. Understandably, the manufacturers vary in their views of the value of the mark. Generally, the powerful companies tend to feel that their own brand or mark[65] carries greater prestige than that of the testing laboratory and that the independent mark has value only for less prestigious companies.

In some countries the voluntary mark is offered by organizations whose independent status is beyond question since they are the official national standardization bodies, e.g., Japan Standards Association or the French AFNOR. Companies that wish to use the JIS mark (Japan Industrial Standards) or the NF mark (Normale Français) must first submit their products to independent test and must pay for these tests. If the products qualify, the manufacturers are granted the right to use the mark.

Government-subsidized Tests   In this form, neither the consumer nor the manufacturer pays for the standardization and testing, the concept being that the costs should be borne by the public generally. The concept is widely used in the Eastern European countries.

An example in a market-based country was the Teltag scheme administered by the British Consumer Council.[66] Under this scheme, the Council, in consultation with interested groups, decided what data were needed by consumers for various consumer products. The Teltags were designed to provide these needed data on the basis of tests and verifications made by the Council. See Figure 4-4.

Any manufacturer could then voluntarily apply for a license to use the tags on his products. To secure the license, he had to submit his product, factory operations, and plan of quality control to examination by the Council. If the license was issued, the manufacturer could attach the Teltags to his product and could refer to the fact of certification in his advertising. The Council derived its income partly from

---

[64] For a discussion, see Riordan, John J., and Joseph A. Greenwood, A Program for the Control and Assurance of Quality, *Quality* (EOQC Journal), vol. 8, no. 1, pp. 13–16, Spring 1964.

[65] See, in this connection, Section 14, under Labeling.

[66] The Consumer Council was a nonprofit organization qualified under Board of Trade regulations governing independent laboratories. (Under British law, Certification Trade Marks approved by the Board of Trade are issued only to nontrading organizations.)

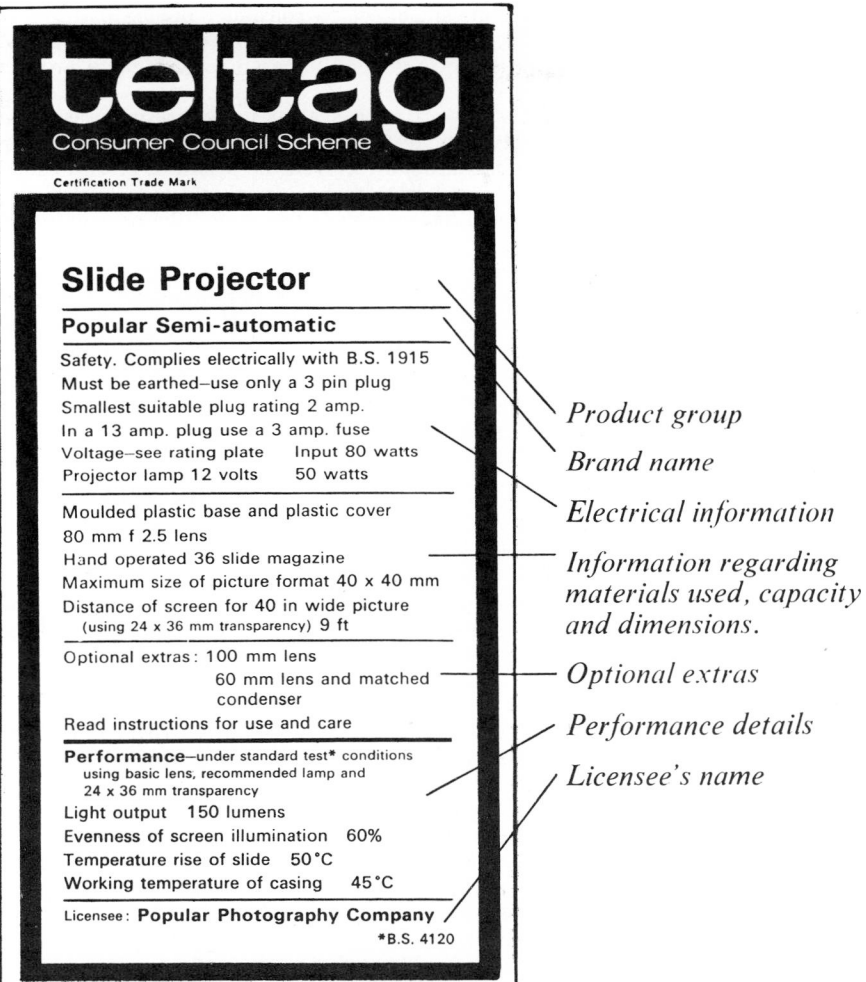

Fig. 4-4 British "Teltag."

license fees and sale of the tags but largely from a government subsidy.   When the government withdrew the subsidy, the scheme was no longer financially viable. [67]

During 1969, an American merchant, Federated Department Stores, Inc., undertook a project in its Lazarus store (Columbus, Ohio) to determine consumer reaction to a form of Buying Guide Tag similar to the Teltag of the British Consumer Council. The experiment was conducted in the company's Lazarus store located in downtown Columbus, Ohio.   The conclusions were essentially that (within the limited experi-

---

[67] Reliance on subsidies creates its own problems for any testing service, since the service must ever justify the renewal of its subsidies before legislators who have their own views of the mission of such a laboratory.

ment conducted) there was no significant effect on consumer buying patterns or product return patterns. However, the sales personnel benefited because the added point of sale information enabled them to give customers more complete product information.[68]

Standards for Consumer Products   Award of a seal or mark presupposes some standard against which the product can be tested on an objective basis.[69] Providing such standards for consumer products has not received the priorities given to standards for metrology, basic materials, and other technological and industrial needs. However, the consumerism movement has very likely stimulated the pace of developing these standards. Industry Associations especially have been stimulated to undertake more of this type of activity.

A continuing need for consumer standards is in the definition of key words! When the same word has both a technical meaning and a common dictionary meaning, this difference may become critical in consumer products. For example, one measure of the quality of watches has been the number of jewels. When some manufacturers began to include nonfunctional jewels to provide a basis for labeling the watch to imply higher quality, it became necessary to create a precise definition of what constitutes a jewel. (International Standards Organization Recommendation R1112 – 1969.)

In like manner, an attempt to redefine "bourbon" soon runs into vested interests. During the 1930s the government definition of bourbon included a stipulation that the whisky be stored in *new* charred-oak barrels. Anything stored in *used* barrels could not be labeled as bourbon when bottled. When some distillers proposed abolition of the requirement for new barrels, the proposal was resisted not only by other distillers but also by the cooperage industry which makes the barrels. The contention was that such a change would virtually wipe out an industry employing about 25,000 workers.

A serious limitation on creating standards for consumer products is the pace of product obsolescence versus the time required to set standards. Usually, it takes years to evolve a standard due to the need for securing a broad base of agreement.[70] For comparatively stable subjects such as metrology or basic materials and tests, these standards, once approved, will have a very long life. However, for consumer products the life is limited by the rate of obsolescence, and for many products the life of the standard becomes so short as to raise serious questions about the economics of doing it at all.

A further problem in standards for consumer products is that the traditional emphasis of the standardization bodies has been on quality of design. The resulting tests and marks have also emphasized quality of design.

However, many of the consumer problems are traceable to deficiencies with respect to other parameters—quality of conformance, the "abilities," quality of field service.[71] The test laboratories have generally not been involved in these matters and have only recently begun to respond to them.

Generally the laboratories are not able to certify quality of conformance. Many of the certification agreements do contain language authorizing the laboratories to sample the flow or production or to visit the manufacturing premises for surveil-

[68] Buying Guide Tag Pilot Program, Federated Department Stores, Washington, D.C.

[69] The American standard for procedures for certifications to the public requires, as a prerequisite, a standard developed by an appropriate body. See Standard Z34.1 – 1947, American National Standards Institute (ANSI), New York.

[70] Also, the lack of short-term economic reward tends to give low industrial priority to such standards work.

[71] See generally Juran, J. M., Consumerism and Product Quality, *Quality Progress,* July 1970.

lance. In practice, the authority is seldom used because the tradition and the fee structure are against it.

In the case of the "abilities," we are only in the first stages of being able to use the concept of a mark. Standards are either in rudimentary form or nonexistent. The ratios between laboratory test results and usage results are similarly in early stages of development.

In post-sale service, the situation is at its worst. Here the laboratory and its equipment are academic matters in relation to the problem, since the standards needed are for the competence, promptness, and integrity of the service organizations.

The Standardization Organizations.   There are many of these, but those of greatest importance to consumers are:

1. Leading manufacturers and merchants, whose standards exert wide influence on vendors and competitors

2. Industry bodies such as the American Gas Association or the Association of Home Appliance Manufacturers[72]

3. Professional organizations such as the American Society for Testing and Materials or the Society of Automotive Engineers

4. Independent agencies such as Underwriters' Laboratories, Inc.

5. The American National Standards Institute (ANSI), which is a recognized clearinghouse for committees engaged in setting national standards and is the official publisher of the approved standards

6. The National Bureau of Standards, the government agency which establishes and maintains standards for metrology

Objectivity of Test Services   Unless the testing service is objective, the consumer may be misled by the very organization on which he thought he could rely. The criteria for objectivity include:

Financial Independence.   This requires that the income of the test service be unrelated to the test results. The best form of this independence exists when the income is derived from sources other than the manufacturer whose products are under test. Failing this, the payments by the manufacturer should be solely for the test service and in no way contingent on the test results.

One example of failure to meet these criteria is the organization which carries on the dual activities of (1) conducting a labeling scheme based on product test and approval and (2) publishing a journal of general circulation in which manufacturers who apply for the label must also be advertisers in the journal.

In such arrangements, the risk of conflict of interest is very high, and consumers should be cautious about giving credence to such marks.

Organizational Independence.   The personnel of the test service should not be subordinate to the companies whose products are undergoing test.

Objective Standards.   In the absence of standards, the test facility is placed in the position of simultaneously setting standards and testing conformance. Long experience has confirmed the need for separating these very different functions.

Technological Capability.   This obvious need includes a qualified professional staff, appropriate test equipment, and competent management. Whether the managers should judge these capabilities of their own organization is open to serious question.

So important is the question of objectivity that in cases of mandated testing it is usual to write into the statute the need for defining criteria for what constitutes an appropriate laboratory. The administrator of the act is then responsible for determining qualifications of laboratories against these criteria.

---

[72] See Section 43 for some details of operation.

Information Types It is seen that, aside from the various forms of financing and organization used to provide test services to consumers, the types of information also vary. The principal forms are:

1. Comparative data on competitive products for *(a)* price and *(b)* fitness for use, plus a judgment of comparative value. In this form, the information is also a recommendation for action.

2. Comparative data on competitive products for conformance to standard. In this form, the consumer is thrown on his own to discover competitive prices and to make a judgment on comparative fitness. For many consumers, it is a considerable burden to provide this added information.

3. Evidence of single product conformance to standard (through the seal or mark). Here the consumer is largely asked to equate the standard with fitness for use and to use other means to discover competitive differences and competitive prices.

While conformance to standard serves many useful purposes to industrial buyers, it is very doubtful that this information, by itself, is of great intrinsic value to the consumer. For him the optimum information consists of comparative data on fitness for use plus comparative data on cost of usage.

CONSUMERISM

"Consumerism" is the name given to the movement which emerged during the 1960s as a response to numerous consumer grievances. These grievances included quality complaints which were concentrated in three main areas:[73, 74]

Misrepresentation of product quality
Product failures
Inability to get satisfaction when products do fail

The huge array of individual complaints responsible for this consumer unrest had never been analyzed objectively to discover the vital few causes, to learn whether the situation was getting better or worse, and to determine whether broad programs of action were in order. Instead, individual investigators conducted and published researches and pseudoresearches on various aspects of the problems of consumers. Generally these publications dramatized selected instances of asserted company and industry responsibility for consumer troubles and then generalized from these instances to make public attacks on the competence and integrity of the companies.

The published attacks were successful in attracting a large following among the public, the press, and the legislators. Lacking scoreboards and other accepted indexes, the companies and industries were unable to make a successful defense, so that they lost the initiative for action. The resulting vacuum attracted numerous contenders for leadership of the consumerism movement: government agencies, politicians, social reformers, consumer advocates ("consumerists"), consumer associations, standardization organizations, independent test laboratories, and still others. A serious risk arose that a bargaining agent would intervene between industrial companies and their customers.

This competition for leadership of the consumerism movement has stimulated numerous proposals for remedy of consumer problems despite lack of agreement on

---

[73] For a broad discussion, see Juran, J. M., Consumerism and Product Quality, *Quality Progress,* July 1970.

[74] There were also numerous other complaints on matters not commonly regarded as quality problems: deceptive pricing, cost of credit, some forms of environmental pollution, etc.

the causes and despite lack of knowledge of the costs.[75]   Some of these proposals deal with prevention before the fact; others deal with remedy after the fact.

Prevention Proposals   These are aimed at eliminating the causes of consumer problems at their source or at giving the consumer sufficient added information to enable him to judge beforehand whether he is about to buy trouble.

Data Banks on Products.   This proposal would involve the creation of quality information centers.   These would collect data on actual product performance, quality failures, consumer complaints, and other evidences relating to product fitness for use.   The data bank would process the data and publish the results, so that consumers could inform themselves on the quality performance of competing products before making their purchases.

Under the concept, industrial companies would be required to disclose their test data, complaint data, etc., to the data bank.   The bank would also collect data from users as to product performance, service effectiveness, company response to failures, etc.   In addition, the bank would acquire data from any other sources which had useful data to contribute, e.g., government regulatory agencies.[76]

A long-standing parallel for such data banks is the finance (credit) data bank of Dun & Bradstreet, Inc.   The use of vendor rating plans (see Section 10) is to the same effect.   While in the free market economies there has been much resistance to identifying product quality data with manufacturers and merchants, the likelihood is that this resistance will be eroded.[77]

Data Banks on Business Practices.   Many consumer complaints are traceable to company business practices, e.g., evasiveness in meeting the provisions of the guarantee rather than product failures in the technological sense.   There is a school of thought which contends that the Pareto principle holds here, i.e., that a comparatively few companies engage in those business practices which create the bulk of the consumer problems.[78]   If this view is sound, a data bank on company business practices would serve to identify the vital few "bad guys" and aid in removing their influence.

The organizations known as Better Business Bureaus (BBB) have been a step in the direction of creating such data banks.   The BBB receives consumer complaints (among others) on unethical business practices, and endeavors as an ombudsman (see below) to get these practices changed.   When a citizen calls the BBB, he is able to learn whether the company under inquiry has a record of complaints lodged against it.

As in the case of product data banks, there exists a cultural resistance to publicizing the names of companies.   Even highly ethical companies exhibit such resistance, one major reason being the belief that the information will be seized on by publicists, muckrakers, and political demagogues to make unwarranted attacks and smears. (On the record, there is much evidence to support this belief.)

Independent Certification.   Advocates of this concept propose that there be

---

[75] The mandated safety devices for automobiles were responsible for adding about $100 cost per car in the United States or an annual cost to consumers of about $1 billion per annum.   At the time these devices were mandated, it was not known how many lives, if any, would be saved thereby.   See Juran, J. M., Product Safety, *Quality Progress,* pp. 30–32, July 1972.

[76] See in this connection Section 14, under Analysis of Available Market Quality Information.

[77] When the Insurance Institute for Highway Safety (IIHS) conducted crash tests of automobiles at various speeds, it publicized widely the dollars of damage done for each of the models tested.   See, for example, Hassett, John J., Auto Insurance Industry Speaks, *Quality Assurance,* pp. 44, 45, and 58, September 1970.

[78] The author shares this view.

established independent boards and laboratories to pass on the adequacy of products before they are allowed to be sold to the public. These proposals would make mandatory, for consumer products generally, the procedures now used to control the quality of food, drugs, exports (in some countries), etc. Generally, the market-based economies have avoided such mandatory independent certification and have relied on the competitive forces of the marketplace to contest for the favor of the consumers, in quality as well as in other matters. In contrast, the planned economies, as exemplified by the Soviet Union, have gone heavily into the setting of standards for consumer products and the use of independent laboratories to enforce compliance to these standards (which have the force of law).[79]

The proposed detailed plans for independent certification follow the Plan of Regulation discussed under Government Regulation of Quality, above, though modified by some of the techniques discussed under Consumer Test Services.[80]

Remedy after the Fact   A second category of proposals of consumerists centers on remedies for consumers who encounter frustration in getting satisfaction following product failures, misrepresentation, etc. These proposals all involve intervention of some third party to aid in settling disputes. The main forms are discussed below.

The Ombudsman. This is a Swedish word used to designate an official whose job is to receive citizens' complaints and to help them secure action from the government bureaucracy. The ombudsman is familiar with government organization channels and is able to find the government official who has the authority or the duty to act. The ombudsman has no authority to compel action, but he has the power to publicize failures to act.

The concept of the ombudsman can be applied readily to problems in product quality. Some companies have created an in-house ombudsman and have publicized his name and telephone number. Consumers can phone him (free of charge) to air grievances and to secure information.

Another form is the industry ombudsman. An example is the Major Appliance Consumer Action Panel (a group of independent consumer experts) created by the Association of Home Appliance Manufacturers to receive complaints from consumers who have not been able to secure satisfaction locally. (See Section 43, under Prognosis.)

Still another form is the Joint Industry–Consumer Complaint Board. Examples are the government-funded boards which mediate and adjudicate consumer disputes in some Scandinavian industries. The boards have no power to enforce their awards other than publicity given to unsatisfied awards. Yet they have met with wide acceptance by and cooperation from the businessmen.

The concept of the ombudsman is fundamentally sound, and it should be considered seriously by companies and industries. The concept is also attractive to various nonindustrial people as a device for service to the public. Some newspapers provide an ombudsman service as part of their department of Letters to the Editor. (Such a service extends, of course, far beyond problems of quality.) In addition, the ombudsman concept is being employed by various advocates in the consumerism movement, some of whom use it incidentally as a device for publicized attacks on industrial companies.

Arbitration   A major background reason for consumerism is the high cost of lawsuits. Unless the amount at stake is substantial, the consumer cannot use the law courts, i.e., the cost of the suit would be far higher than the amount of the claim.

[79] For elaboration, see Section 48A.

[80] For some sweeping proposals, see, as an example, Final Report of the National Commission on Product Safety, Chapter 12. (Available from the U.S. Government Printing Office, Washington, D.C., 20402.)

All this is maddeningly frustrating to consumers who know very well that their claim is valid. An alternative to the prohibitive costs of the law courts is the concept of arbitration in various forms. These include the following:

Community-type Centers. An example is the Neighborhood Consumer Information Center of the District of Columbia, which operates in low-income communities. Its functions include consumer education, complaint investigation, and mediation. Arbitration is available through arrangement with the American Arbitration Association's Community Dispute Center. The merchant's willingness to agree to arbitration is stimulated through the background risk of legal action by the neighborhood legal service attorneys.

Special Arbitration Panels. Experiments are under way to provide local arbitration panels, either as an adjunct of the Better Business Bureau or as specialized panels for a specific industry, e.g., television repairs.

Underlying these and other arbitration approaches is the awareness that for many consumer complaints nothing short of third-party intervention will provide a solution. The legal remedy, available in theory, is too costly in practice. Simpler forms of adjudication appear to be feasible, using the pressures of the industry and the threat of publicity to secure compliance to the awards.[81]

Punitive Legislation. Some consumerists urge that legislation be enacted which will remove the relative immunity that manufacturers and merchants have from lawsuits over consumer complaints (i.e., the cost of the suit is too large in relation to the amount of damage). The proposals for such legislation include:

1. "Class action suits," under which one consumer can bring a lawsuit on behalf of all consumers who assertedly have been damaged

2. Authorization for governments to file suits on behalf of consumers

3. Punitive damages or fines as punishment

Some consumer organizations, individual reformers, and government officials are strong advocates of punitive legislation.

Consumer Organizations   These exist in a wide variety of forms. Some are product- or service-oriented, e.g., automotive safety, truth in lending. Others are adjuncts of broader organizations, e.g., departments of test laboratories, labor unions, or farm cooperatives. Still others are specially organized to deal broadly with consumer problems. In addition, there are broader federations, national and international, which endeavor to find ways of improving the collected strength of all local and specialized consumer groups.

Government Agencies. These exist at national, state, and local levels of government. All invite consumers to bring unresolved complaints to them as well as to report instances of business malpractice. These complaints aid the agency in identifying widespread problems, which, in turn, become the basis for:

1. Conducting investigations in depth

2. Proposing new legislation

3. Issuing new administrative regulations

The agencies also try to help the complaining consumers, either in an ombudsman role or by threat of legal action.

Testing Organizations. These offer to the consumer a form of independent product knowledge, either through:

1. A combination of product standard plus test of conformance and a label or seal attesting to conformance

2. A test of fitness for use plus a judgment of value

See Consumer Test Services, above, for details of these approaches.

---

[81] For an excellent, extensive discussion, see Jones, Mary Gardner, Wanted: A New System for Solving Consumer Grievances, *The Arbitration Journal,* vol. 25, no. 4, pp. 234–248, 1971.

Other Organizations.   These consist of miscellaneous groups organized for consumer education, lobbying, and "exposing."   Many are one-man enterprises of mixed stature and integrity.   Collectively, their effect is not known, and with rare exceptions it is probably not significant.

PERFECTIONISM

The human being exhibits an instinctive drive for precision, beauty, and perfection. When unrestrained by economics, this drive has created the art treasures of the ages. In the arts and in esthetics, this timeless human instinct still prevails.

In the industrial society there are many situations in which this urge for perfection coincides with technological needs.   In food and drug preparation, certain organisms must be completely eliminated or they will multiply and create health hazards. Nuclear reactors, underground mines, aircraft, and other structures susceptible to catastrophic destruction of life require a determined pursuit of perfection to minimize dangers to human safety.   So does the mass production of hazardous products.

However, there are numerous other situations in which the pursuit of perfection is antagonistic to society, since it consumes materials and energy without adding to fitness for use, either technologically or esthetically.   This wasteful activity is termed "perfectionism."   It can be found among all parameters of fitness for use.

Perfectionism in Quality of Design.   This is often called "overdesign."   Common examples are:

Long life for products which will become obsolete before they wear out.   (See the Corfam case under Voluntary Obsolescence, above.)

Costly finishes on nonvisible surfaces.[82]

Tolerances or features added beyond the needs of fitness for use.[83,84]   (The military budget reviewers call this "gold-plating.")

Some cases of overdesign are not simple matters of yes or no.   For example, in television reception there are "fringe areas" which give poor reception with conventional circuit design.   For such areas, supplemental circuitry is needed to attain good quality of image.   However, this extra circuitry is for most areas an overdesign and a waste.   The alternative of designing an attachment to be used only in fringe areas creates other problems, since these attachments must be installed under nonfactory conditions.

It is best to prevent overdesign during design review, while the design is still fluid. Those who understand the economics of manufacture, marketing, usage, and maintenance can then challenge any design features which do not contribute to fitness for use and which therefore will add to costs without adding to income.   Some systems of design review provide for classification of characteristics, e.g., essential, desirable, unessential.[85]   The unessential then become candidates for removal on the ground of perfectionism.[86]

[82] The company which wants to avoid such waste may on occasion be driven into it by shortsighted competitors.   Some marketers seize on a perfectionist refinement not possessed by competitive products and sensitize the users to the existence of the refinement.   The effect may be to force the entire industry to do the same, thus making the waste universal.

[83] Some of this reflects the pride of the designer, i.e., he exhibits the instinctive human urge for beauty.   In other cases he is endeavoring to demonstrate his virtuosity as a designer.   In still other cases he simply lacks the information on costs.

[84] An obvious example is the high grade of finish applied to many nonessential surfaces of watches, i.e., nonfunctional surfaces never seen by the user.

[85] See, for example, Reeves, T. G., Specification Review—A Key to Value Improvement, *Electrical Manufacturing,* pp. 100–102, November 1958.

[86] Overdesign is also one of the targets of Value Analysis.   See Section 16, under Value Analysis.

Perfectionism in Quality of Conformance.   Typical examples are:

Insistence on conformance to specification despite longstanding successful use of nonconforming product

Setting of appearance standards to levels beyond those sensed by users[87]

Tightening process tolerances because a process is regularly more precise than specification[88]

Generally, perfectionism in quality of conformance can be held in check by separating two decisions which are all too often confounded: (1) the decision on whether product conforms to specification and (2) the decision on whether nonconforming product is fit for use.   While decision (1) should be delegated to the inspectors at the bottom of the hierarchy, decision (2) usually should not.[89]

Perfectionism in the "Abilities."   Some of the examples encountered are these:

"Worst case" designs in which provision is made to anticipate the worst combination of adverse conditions which might converge to cause a failure, even when the odds against such a combination are fantastically high

Use of unduly large factors of safety

Use of high-duty or high-precision components for products which will be subjected to conventional usage

Because such instances have their origin in design, the remedies are through design reviews such as are discussed above under Perfectionism in Quality of Design.

Perfectionism in Field Service.   To date there has been little of this; more commonly the service has been inadequate.

Perfectionism by Government Regulators.   There is an uncomfortable degree of this, though with more experience the practice may moderate.   Forms of this practice include:

Tightening product tolerances because a new instrument permits a new level of precise measurement, e.g., tolerances for penicillin contamination and for particles in ophthalmic ointments.

Tightening product tolerances because processes are regularly more precise than specification.

Removing products from the market in the absence of evidence of unfitness for use.   For example, cyclamates used as artificial sweeteners were removed from the market although at the time there was literally no case known of any human being who had been damaged by the cyclamates.

Some of this perfectionism is undoubtedly influenced by the pressures to which regulators are subjected from reformers, special pleaders, and zealots.   Public officials cannot readily defend themselves against all such pressures.

The Perfectionists.   It is possible to categorize the people most often contributing to perfectionism, and the more usual forms in which their proposals are presented.   Table 4-8 shows this relationship.

Those who advocate perfectionism often do so with the best intentions and always

---

[87] Such cases are legion.   See Section 12, under Sensory Qualities.

[88] Some quality managers tend to pursue this form of perfectionism.   In one course on Management of Quality Control, the following case was put to 50 quality managers from different companies:

A product with tolerances of $\pm 10\%$ for a certain quality has demonstrated a record of fitness for use.   However, the process can hold a tolerance of $\pm 5\%$.   Should the product tolerance be tightened?   Of the 34 responses there were: Yes—7; No—27.

[89] See Section 12, under Judgment of Fitness for Use.

TABLE 4-8   Perfectionists

Basis for perfectionism	Usual guilty parties
"Superiority" which does not add to fitness for use	Top management, marketing managers
Urge to comply with the specification despite clear evidence of fitness for use	Government regulators, industrial quality managers
Belief that tighter specifications assure greater fitness for use	Researchers; designers; theoreticians
Belief that humans can be motivated to make no errors	Enthusiasts and fanatics behind misguided motivational programs
Contention that failure to conform is proof of unfitness for use	Reformers, politicians, journalists, publicity seekers
Adverse publicity given to isolated failures	Muckrakers, publicity seekers

for reasons which seem logical to them.   The resulting proposals are nevertheless of no benefit to users for one of several common reasons:

The added perfection has no value to the user.   (The advocate is not aware of this.)

The added perfection has value to the user, but not enough to make up for the added cost.   (The advocate is unaware of the extent of the costs involved.)

The added perfection is proposed not to benefit the user but to protect the personal position of the advocate (e.g., he has responsibility for conformance but not for cost), or to make a hero of the advocate in the eyes of some bloc.

The weaknesses of these proposals are all related back to costs: ignorance of the costs, no responsibility for costs, indifference to costs due to preoccupation with

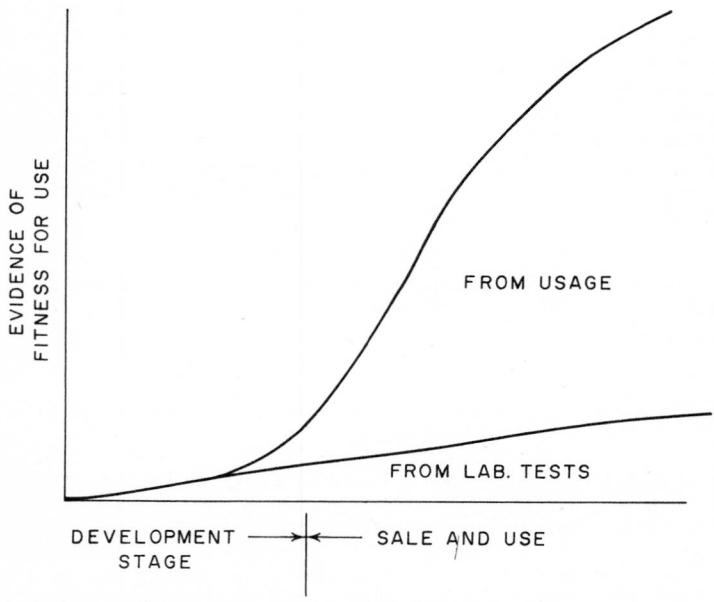

Fig. 4-5   Successful usage as evidence of fitness for use.

something else. Those who do have responsibility for the costs must quantify them and then dramatize the results in order to provide the best challenge.

Defenses against Perfectionism   There are several of these: quantifying the economics, dramatizing the feedback of fitness for use, use of the concept that "the customer is right."

Quantifying the Economics.   A major defense against perfectionism is to quantify and dramatize the costs. Precision, reliability, or conformance can always be improved, but the cost of improvement rises spectacularly as we approach perfection. The model for this relationship is shown in Section 5, Figure 5-2. As we approach perfection, the costs rise to infinity. Somewhere before infinity is what the economists call the point of diminishing returns.

Figure 5-2 is not merely a theoretical model. It is feasible to quantify the parameters by securing the key facts and applying estimates of costs. For example, in one improvement project it was estimated that it would be worth $100 to remove 1 pound of weight from a component. However, closer analysis showed that removing the first 0.9 pound cost only $10, whereas removing the last 0.1 pound cost $90, or $900 per pound.[90]

In the case of improvement of quality of conformance, the model of Figure 5-2 can be quantified based on some of the quality cost parameters. See Section 5, under Discovering the Optimum, especially Figure 5-3.

Dramatizing Fitness for Use.   The model of evidence of fitness for use is shown in Figure 4-5. Originally, evidence of fitness for use is derived from product development and test information. Then, as the product is marketed, new evidence comes from the marketplace in the form of repeat orders, absence of complaints, absence of orders for spare parts, etc. This growing feedback should be embodied into the decision-making process, e.g., material review board decisions, deviation practices, design changes.

"The Customer Is Right."   Use can also be made of the concept that "the customer is right," not only as to things he can sense but also as to things he cannot sense.[91]

[90] Heller, E. D., Cost Analysis in Product Design, *Journal of Value Engineering,* September 1962.

[91] See Section 12, under Sensory Qualities. See also Juran, J. M., Is Your Product Too Fussy? *Factory Management and Maintenance,* pp. 125–128, August 1952.

Section **5**

Quality Costs

DANIEL M. LUNDVALL

President, Telecommunications Industries, Inc.

Copiague, New York

J. M. JURAN

EVOLUTION OF THE QUALITY COST CONCEPT

Industry makes wide use of the concept of identifying the costs needed to carry out the various functions—e.g., Marketing, Production—of an enterprise. Prior to the 1950s this concept had been applied to the costs of inspection but not to the broader quality function, i.e., the activities needed to achieve fitness for use as depicted in Section 2, Figure 2-2. The costs of the quality function were widely scattered throughout various accounts in the company's books. Some of these costs were clearly defined and quantified; others not.

During the 1950s the new Statistical Quality Control Departments found that they could no longer "sell" their programs solely on enthusiasm for the statistical tools. A new approach was needed based on the language of management—i.e., money.[1]

[1] See Section 16, under Securing Management Approval.

5-1

This need for a new approach was first met by the concept of "Gold in the Mine." This was defined as the "total of avoidable costs of quality."[2] Behind the concept was the implication that costs resulting from defects were a gold mine in which profitable digging could be done. This concept became widely used to demonstrate that programs for defect reduction could be carried out at a good return on investment in staff manpower.

As the staff quality specialists made use of the concept of Gold in the Mine, they became better informed on three matters importantly concerned with the quality cost concept:

1. The nature of the company's accounting system. It became evident that the existing charts of accounts and systems for presenting cost summaries did not meet the needs of the quality function.

2. The concept of identifying all the costs associated with the quality function so that summaries could be prepared paralleling those available for other functions.

3. The concept of an *optimum* for quality costs.

The urge to measure quality costs came not only from the staff quality specialists but from outside the company as well. These outside forces included:

1. The increasing costs of achieving fitness for use due to more complex products, greater precision, higher reliability, etc. It is probable that the order of magnitude of quality costs, as a national figure, lies between 5 and 10% of company sales. These are enormous sums of money.

2. The initiative of the federal government. As government contracts changed from cost plus fixed fee to fixed fee (or cost plus incentive fee), all costs, including quality costs, came under closer scrutiny. In due course the government quality program requirements included provisions making mandatory the identification and use of quality cost data (e.g., MIL-Q-9858A, section 3.6).

3. Growth of long-life products. As these products came into wide use, it became evident that maintenance due to unreliability greatly exceeded original costs. This relationship gave impetus to the concept of reliability programs which would improve original reliability at higher initial cost in order to reduce the lifetime costs.[3]

4. A consequence of (2) and (3) above was the evolution of separate quotations for reliability programs and separation of quality cost budgets in preparation of bids on government contracts.

These external forces together with the internal activities of the quality staff specialists combined to advance the concept of identifying all costs associated with the quality function so that these costs could be measured, improved, and controlled. The emerging publications, committee studies, seminars, etc., helped to disseminate the concept further.[4]

THE PHASED PROGRAM

Companies that undertake a quality cost program soon must face the question, "What are we trying to accomplish?" Generally, two schools of thought have existed as to the purposes of these programs:

---

[2] The first elaboration of this concept was published in 1951 in the First Edition of this Handbook. The total "Gold in the Mine" was to be evaluated by answering the question "What costs would disappear if all defects disappeared?" The First Edition listed 12 categories of avoidable quality costs, along with definitions and examples.

[3] See Section 4, under Life Cycle Costing. Note that Section 4 deals with users' costs whereas the present Section deals with manufacturers' costs.

[4] One such study was by the Quality Cost Committee of the American Society for Quality Control. See "Quality Costs—What and How," 1967, available from the Society.

1. To estimate the quality costs as a "one shot" study, with a view of using the information to justify a program of quality improvement and quality cost reduction

2. To measure quality costs and to publish the results as a continuing scoreboard, in the expectation that the new knowledge will stimulate managers to take appropriate action

What is emerging is an awareness that these two schools of thought are interrelated and that a quality cost program actually consists of three phases which naturally merge into each other. Table 5-1 shows these three phases and their interrelation.

TABLE 5-1   Phases in Quality Cost Programs

	Selling phase	Project phase	Control phase
Objectives of the phases	To justify launching a program of quality improvement and cost reduction.	To observe and stimulate progress during the improvement program	To hold gains made during the improvement program and to provide data for continuing control of quality costs
Sources of information	Estimates made by QC specialists, supplemented by Accounting data	Accounting data supplemented by estimates made by QC specialists	Accounting data
Information published by	Quality Control	Quality Control, with verification by Accounting	Accounting, with charting and commentary by Quality Control
Frequency of publication	One-time or infrequently, e.g., annually	At least annually; sometimes monthly	Monthly or quarterly

The three phases of quality cost study are directly related to the "breakthrough" concept as discussed in Section 2 and depicted in Figure 2-4. Figure 5-1 shows this relationship in simplified form.

In the left-hand portion of Figure 5-1, the first or "selling" phase of the quality cost study serves to identify the existence of a chronic quality cost situation which could economically be improved.

In the middle portion of the diagram, the second or "project," phase of the quality cost study serves to observe progress during the improvement program.

In the right-hand portion of the diagram, the need is to hold the gains made; hence the third or "control" phase of the quality cost program provides the data needed for control at the new (improved) level.

QUALITY COST CATEGORIES

Reducing the quality cost concept to practice requires first that there be a clear identification of just what costs are to be considered as falling within the broad term "quality costs." Some ready criteria can be established for what is to be *included,* e.g., all costs which would disappear if there were no defects. However, it is difficult to define what should be *excluded.*

For example, the work of product design includes choice of product tolerances, which certainly influences fitness for use. Yet no widely used list of quality cost categories includes this aspect of product design. Neither do such lists include the work involved in purchasing quality materials, production to quality standards,

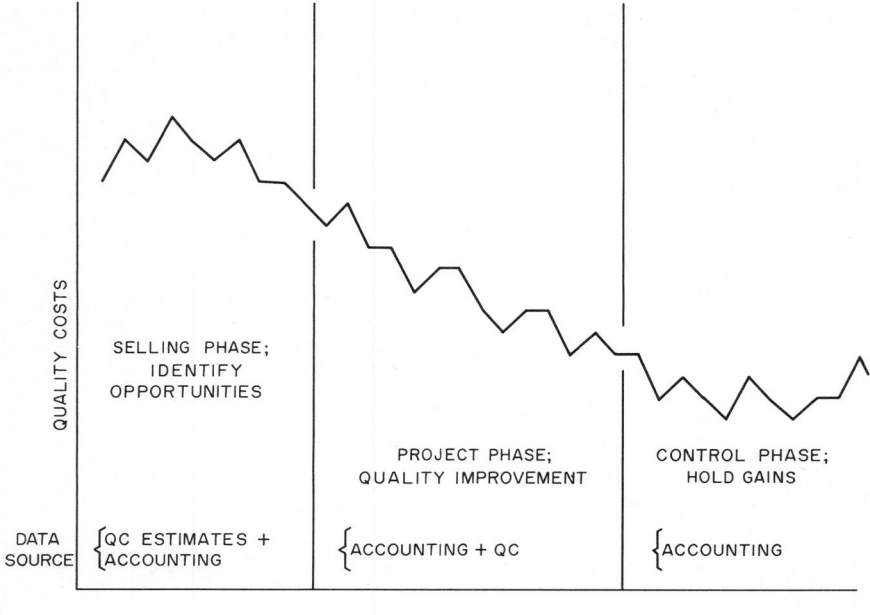

Fig. 5-1 Schematic of phases in quality cost programs.

marketing the product based on its qualities, etc. All such categories of costs are regarded as belonging to the respective functions of design, purchasing, production, and marketing.

However, the discussions of what to include in quality costs have resulted in a fairly standardized set of "core" categories. These have been tested extensively over a wide variety of industries and have proved to be well suited for the purpose. The core categories and their usual definitions are as follows:

Internal Failure Costs   These are costs which would disappear if no defects existed in the product prior to shipment to the customer. They include:

Scrap.   The net loss in labor and material[5] resulting from defectives which cannot economically be repaired or used.

Rework.   The cost of correcting defectives to make them fit for use. Sometimes this category is broadened to include extra operations created to solve an epidemic of defects, or special piece rates provided for a similar purpose.

Retest.   The cost of reinspection and retest of products which have undergone rework or other revision.

Downtime.   The cost of idle facilities resulting from defects (e.g., printing press down due to paper breaks, aircraft idle due to unreliability). In some industries this category is very large and hence is quantified. In most companies, this is ignored.

Yield Losses.   The cost of process yields lower than might be attainable by improved controls. Includes "overfill" of containers (going to customers) due to variability in filling and measuring equipment.

---

[5] See, in this connection, Avoidable and Unavoidable Costs, below.

Disposition.   The effort required to determine whether nonconforming products are usable and to make final disposition.   Includes the time of individuals and material review boards, no matter what the department of origin of the men involved, e.g., a designer preparing a deviation authorization.

External Failure Costs   These costs also would disappear if there were no defects. They are distinguished from the internal failure costs by the fact that the defects are found after shipment to the customer.   They include:

Complaint Adjustment.   All costs of investigation and adjustment of justified complaints attributable to defective product or installation.

Returned Material.   All costs associated with receipt and replacement of defective product returned from the field.

Warranty Charges.   All costs involved in service to customers under warranty contracts.

Allowances.   Costs of concessions made to customers due to substandard products being accepted by the customer as is.   Includes loss in income due to downgrading products for sale as seconds.

Appraisal Costs   These are the costs incurred to discover the condition of the product, mainly during the "first time through."   The costs include:

Incoming Material Inspection.   The cost of determining the quality of vendor-made products, whether by inspection on receipt, by inspection at the source, or by surveillance methods.

Inspection and Test.   The costs of checking the conformance of the product throughout its progression in the factory, including final acceptance, and check of packing and shipping.   Includes life, environmental, and reliability tests.   Also includes testing done at the customer's premises prior to turning the product over to the customer.   (It is usual to keep separate subaccounts for inspection, laboratory testing, and field testing.)   In collecting these costs, what is decisive is the kind of work done and not the department name (i.e., the work may be done by chemists in a Technical Department laboratory, by sorters in the Production Department, by testers in the Inspection Department, or by outside services engaged for the purpose of testing).

Maintaining Accuracy of Test Equipment.   Includes the cost of operating the system that keeps the measuring instruments and equipment in calibration.

Materials and Services Consumed.   Includes the costs of products consumed through destructive tests, materials consumed (e.g., x-ray film), and services (e.g., electric power) where significant.

Evaluation of Stocks.   Includes the costs of testing products in field storage or in stock to evaluate degradation.

Prevention Costs   These costs are incurred to keep failure and appraisal costs to a minimum.   The usual categories are as follows:

Quality Planning.   This includes the broad array of activities which collectively create the overall quality plan, the inspection plan, the reliability plan, the data system, and the numerous specialized plans.   It includes also preparation of the manuals and procedures needed to communicate these plans to all concerned.

As in the case of inspection and test, some of this work may be done by personnel who are not on the payroll of a department called Quality Control.   The decisive criterion is again the type of work, not the name of the department performing the work.

New-Products Review.   Includes preparation of bid proposals, evaluation of new designs, preparation of test and experimental programs, and other quality activities associated with the launching of new designs.

Training.   The costs of preparing training programs for attaining and improving quality performance, no matter which department is to be the recipient of the training.   Includes the cost of conducting formal training programs as well.

Process Control. Includes that part of process control which is conducted to achieve fitness for use, as distinguished from achieving productivity, safety, etc. (Separating these is often difficult.)

Quality Data Acquisition and Analysis. This is the work of running the quality data system to acquire continuing data on quality performance. It includes analysis of these data to identify the quality troubles, to sound the alarms, stimulate study, etc.

Quality Reporting. Includes the work of summarizing and publishing quality information to the middle and upper management.

Improvement Projects. Includes the work of structuring and carrying out programs for breakthrough to new levels of performance, i.e., defect prevention programs, motivation programs, etc.

SECURING THE COST FIGURES

When a company first undertakes to identify and measure quality costs, it soon finds that "the books are not kept that way." The exceptions occur in those cases where the plan of departmental organization happens to coincide with the quality cost category, e.g., product inspection by the Inspection Department. In such cases, the accountant has some ready-made data to offer, since his budgets and his cost keeping are invariably structured along departmental organization lines. In addition, some accountants have structured separate accounts for some nondepartmental cost categories, e.g., scrap, guarantee charges. Where these categories form separate accounts, such accounts may likewise fit readily into the quality cost program.

At this point the road forks, and the problem of measuring the costs differs considerably depending on whether the measurement is to provide information for (1) a "one shot" study to estimate the potential for improvement (This is the first phase of quality cost programs)[6] or (2) a continuing scoreboard to serve the third phase.

The one-shot study collects its cost data from widely different sources:

1. From established accounts, as in the common cases of inspection costs or guarantee charges.

2. From analysis of the ingredients of established accounts. For example, an account consists of the cost of customers' returns. However, these returns are made for two different reasons: defective product and surplus product. The accountant's subaccounts usually permit a ready analysis so that the quality costs can be separated from nonquality costs.

3. From basic accounting records. For example, some Production Department employees are engaged full-time in product inspection. By securing their names and then using payroll department records, it is feasible to summarize this contribution to quality costs.

4. By estimate. For example, the Process Development Department engages in some activities which are classified as quality costs, but the personnel do not separate their time charges in a way which permits an evaluation of these costs. The departmental supervisor is asked to work up an estimate based on work sampling or by judging the proportions of time spent by various men on the quality cost activity.

5. By creating temporary records. For example, several Production operators spend part of their time repairing defective product. No records are available to show how this time has been divided in the past. The men are asked to keep records for a four-week period, and the results are used to create an estimate.

A quality cost study prepared in such a mixture of ways does not satisfy the accountants. (To the accountant, the word "estimate" is a dirty word.) However,

[6] See The Phased Program, above.

the mixture is entirely satisfactory for a one-shot study to identify opportunities or projects for improvement. Managers frequently make decisions based on estimate of the facts or on incomplete facts. Cost estimates which may be off the mark by 10 or 20% seldom affect the managerial decision of whether to tackle a project or not.

In the second phase and especially in the third phase, when the quality costs are to serve as a continuing scoreboard, the situation is different. Now the need is to structure the scorekeeping so that it will not lead to endless argument about the validity of the estimates. This requires a restructuring of the accounts and is discussed below under the heading The Continuing Scoreboard.

AVOIDABLE AND UNAVOIDABLE QUALITY COSTS

In most companies the total of the quality costs is a very large sum of money, often larger than the company's profits. Since such a sum attracts attention, it becomes important to avoid overstating it. Otherwise the overstatement is attacked, and any valid proposed program may be jeopardized due to an unnecessary exaggeration.

Inclusion of Nonquality Costs. The most usual form of overstatement of quality costs is to include nonquality costs in with the quality costs. For example, the term "scrap" as used by the Quality Control people means products which are so defective as to be beyond salvage and hence are to be junked. However, the term "scrap" as used by the accountant may refer to all material sold by weight to the junk man. These sales include not only scrap as defined by Quality Control but also lathe turnings, trim removed from coils of sheet metal, and skeleton scrap from the pressroom. Similarly, the accountant's "loss" due to poor yields may include not only Quality Control's category of spoiled batches but also kettle residues which are washed away during cleaning between batches. Care should be taken to separate such nonquality costs out of the totals so that attention will be directed to the main issue.

Implication of "Zero Defects." A second form of overstatement arises from presenting quality costs with the implication that they could be reduced to zero and that hence the total of quality costs is avoidable. This is simply not so. There is an optimum level of quality costs, and this optimum is decidedly not zero. (See Discovering the Optimum, below.)

This form of overstatement can be avoided by identifying the potential projects and estimating the amount which might economically be gained by an improvement program. (See Section 16, Table 16-6 for the essential format.)

Avoidable Costs Hidden in Standards. Avoidable costs can also be *under*stated. A widespread form of this is present in companies which are too deeply preoccupied with variances. In such cases there are true quality costs which are included in the standards and are thereby *disguised as unavoidable*. For example, a process may for years have operated at a yield of 90% good product. No one has been able to reduce the 10% defective, so over the years the accountants have revised the standards to include the effect of the "regular" 10% defectives. Hence the alarm signals ring only when the 10% is exceeded. In such cases the cost of the 10% defectives is properly a part of the quality costs (and a likely project for improvement).

In similar manner, product designs which are unduly precise may require continuing quality costs in the form of sorting and rework. These quality costs are avoidable in the sense that the undue precision is not needed. To the same effect is perfectionism in inspection standards, in tolerable percent defective, and in similar criteria.[7]

---

[7] For added examples, along with some approaches used in analysis and improvement, see Norquist, Warren R., Improve Material Utilization—Engineer Your Scrap Accounts, *Industrial Quality Control,* pp. 2–4, May 1962.

PRESENTATION TO UPPER MANAGEMENT

The first phase of quality cost presentation is for the purpose of convincing upper management to support a program of improvement. To carry such conviction, quality specialists have made use of the following principles in their presentations:

1. Establish that quality costs are of a size and nature sufficient to attract upper management attention. This is done by presenting simple summaries of the total quality costs and of the main elements which build up these summaries.

Table 5-2 shows a simple presentation of quality costs for a large printing company.[8] The size of the total (as well as the size of the major components) is obviously sufficient to attract upper management attention.

TABLE 5-2   Quality Costs: Printing Company ($000)

Losses due to quality failures	
Press downtime.	404
Correction of typos	309
Bindery waste.	74
Plate revision	40
Cover-making waste	56
Customer complaint remakes	41
Total.	924
Appraisal expenses	
Proofreading.	709
Other checking and inspection	62
Total.	771
Prevention expenses	
Quality improvement project	20
Quality planning	10
Total.	30
Total quality costs	1,725

2. Identify some of the likely opportunities for making improvements. This may be done in several ways:

a. Single out individual cost elements which look like they have potential, and dramatize them. For example, Table 5-2 points out three obvious projects.

b. Prepare a matrix to show the concentration of quality costs. Table 5-3 shows such a matrix, in which product types are listed vertically and defect types are listed horizontally. (Numerous other combinations can be used for structuring these matrixes.) Managers find such matrix presentations to be helpful in setting priorities for projects.

c. Prepare a Pareto analysis to show which elements of quality cost are the vital few and which the trivial many. This analysis is in extensive international use and has wide appeal to managers. For a discussion of the concept, see Section 2, under The Pareto Principle. For examples of application, see Section 16, under Pareto Analysis.

d. Prepare the "return on investment" estimates for specific projects identified by the Pareto analysis. These estimates involve the potential improvement and the analytical effort required to discover causes and to point to remedies. See Section 16, Table 16-6 for the usual format.

[8] Consulting practice of L. A. Seder.

e. Prepare and present the quality cost summary by cost categories. The right-hand column of figures in Table 5-4 is an example of such a summary and is discussed below.

TABLE 5-3   Matrix of Quality Costs

Type	Trim	Visual defects*	Caliper	Tear	Porosity	All other causes	Total
A	$27,000	$ 9,400	None†	$ 16,200	$43,000	$36,400	$132,000
B	12,000	3,300	None†	61,200	5,800	13,700	96,000
C	9,500	7,800	$38,000	3,100	7,400	6,200	72,000
D	8,200	10,300	None†	9,000	29,700	10,800	68,000
E	5,400	10,800	None†	24,600	None†	6,200	47,000
F	5,100	4,900	3,900	1,600	3,300	14,200	33,000
Total	$67,200	$46,500	$41,900	$115,700	$89,200	$87,500	$448,000

* Slime spots, holes, wrinkles, etc.
† Not a specified requirement for this type.

Interpreting the Quality Cost Summaries   Managers can learn a good deal from study of the size and interrelation of the quality costs in the various cost categories. In the example of Table 5-4, the following becomes evident from a brief study:

1. The total quality costs for the year are $3,755,000, which is obviously a top management problem.

TABLE 5-4   Example of Quality Cost Data*

Cost categories	Quality Costs ($000) by Quarters				
	I	II	III	IV	Year
QC engineering	5	5	5	5	20
Tool maintenance	4	5	4	4	17
Gage control	3	3	3	3	12
Other.	1	1	1	1	4
Total prevention	13	14	13	13	53
Inspection	66	72	51	66	255
Test.	24	30	10	18	82
Test materials.	12	22	12	27	73
Vendor inspection.	8	9	6	8	31
Other.	21	20	19	22	82
Total appraisal	131	153	98	141	523
Rework	74	98	55	69	296
Spoilage.	58	20	30	35	143
Other internal failure	24	30	22	26	102
Total internal failure	156	148	107	130	541
Complaints and other external failure	601	51	668	1,318	2,638
Total failure costs	757	199	775	1,448	3,179
Grand total	901	366	886	1,602	3,755

* General Electric Co.

2. The failure costs of $3,179,000 are 85% of all quality costs. Hence any real improvement must come primarily from reduction of failure costs.

3. Complaint costs of $2,638,000 are 83% of failure costs. Hence any major reduction in failure costs must come from reducing complaint costs.

4. Failure costs are six times as large as appraisal costs. Very likely, any reduction in appraisal costs must be preceded by reduction in failure costs.

5. Prevention costs are only about 1 percent of total quality costs. This seems ridiculously low.

Structuring the Improvement Program   This program is inseparable from the broader subject of Quality Improvement, which is the subject of Section 16. The reader should examine the topics of that Section, which expounds in detail the methods used to secure quality improvement and the associated cost improvement.

MEASURING PROGRESS IN QUALITY COST REDUCTION

As the quality cost program moves from the "selling" phase into the "project" phase, the managers look for reports which can tell them:

1. The progress being made on specific projects for improvement. Of course, the men actively involved in guiding such projects (the "steering arms") know very well what is going on with respect to the projects they are guiding. However, other managers also need information on the progress being made on these same projects. This need is met by a newsletter or similar report showing, for each project,

    a. What action has been taken since the last report

    b. What remains to be done

    c. Whose turn it is to act next, what he is to do, and the schedule for doing it

2. In addition to following progress on the individual projects, many managers want to see the resulting overall effect on the summaries of quality costs, in total and for the main categories. The steps taken to prepare periodic reports on this progress are also the first steps taken in evolution of the system of control reports for quality costs.

Implications of the Shift from Selling Phase to the Project Phase   As the progress reports are prepared and issued, it soon becomes evident that the estimating used so freely during the selling phase of the program is not adequate for the project phase. Now the figures are being used not solely to justify the original program but increasingly to measure how well the managers are carrying out the improvement projects. These managers are not willing to be judged by estimates, and they demand greater precision in the figures.

To attain this greater precision, especially on failure costs, often requires changes in data recording practices and in accounting practices. A frequent discovery is that the shop or field personnel have not been making out the paper work or have been doing it so incompletely that the data are of poor quality. Sometimes this tightening up of the recording procedure results in a "rise" in reported failure costs, merely because prior costs were understated.

Overhauling these practices usually requires redesign of data forms to simplify and improve the data recording. The personnel must be retrained and must be motivated to provide good records. (Failure to make out the scrap tickets does not conceal the losses; they show up at the end of the year as inventory shrinkages. However, the failure to make out the tickets greatly complicates the problem of discovering the causes of the losses.) In some cases the responsibility for recording must be changed, e.g., instead of asking the 500 production operators to make out scrap tickets, the job may be given to the 25 inspectors.

The accounting practices always require some revision in the chart of accounts. In addition, there may be need for a new system of code numbers, new "pricing" to state more completely the losses being incurred, separation of blanket variances into their components, etc. [9]

[9] See, for an example, Boruta, Roman E., *Application of Quality Cost System at Chrysler,* *15th Annual Greater Detroit Forum,* Ann Arbor, Mich., Sept. 10. 1960.

Table 5-4 shows a typical format for reporting progress during the early stages of quality cost reduction. As time goes on and the project phase moves into the control phase, the reporting format changes considerably. A main reason is that the responsibility for gathering and publishing the figures meanwhile shifts from the Quality Control department to the Accounting department. When Accounting takes over this responsibility, it makes a number of revisions in charts of accounts and in report format to harmonize the quality cost report with other reports it issues. These revisions are discussed below, under The Control Scoreboard.

DISCOVERING THE OPTIMUM

When quality cost summaries are first presented to managers, one of the usual questions is: "What are the right quality costs?" The managers are looking for a standard ("par") against which to compare their actual costs so that they may make a judgment on whether there is need to structure a program of improvement. As the project phase progresses, there arises an added need to know "What is par?" Without such knowledge, managers cannot be sure when the project phase is terminating and when the control phase is becoming dominant. If there is a premature conclusion that the control phase has already been reached, the standards for control will be too loose and will be used to perpetuate some continuing, avoidable losses. If there is a delayed conclusion, the project work will be directed into unprofitable channels, i.e., the cures will cost more than the diseases.

Companies discover the level of optimum quality costs by using the following main methods:

1. By securing data on "market" quality costs
2. By using their regular budgetary process
3. By establishing ratios for quality cost categories

Market Data on Quality Costs   In this approach the source of information on "What is par?" is "What are the quality costs of other companies?" To date, it has not been possible to secure good guidelines from this source.[10] It is known generally that there is wide variation among *industries*. In simple, low-tolerance industries, the quality costs can run under 2% of sales. In extreme cases (high precision, complexity, and reliability) the quality costs can run to over 25% of sales.[11]

Periodically a within-industry survey is conducted. Such surveys have repeatedly shown that even within a single industry, there are wide variations in quality costs from one company to another. The surveys do not disclose whether these variations are due to differences in systems of accounting, in organization structure, in management effectiveness, etc. In consequence, these surveys have failed to provide useful guides to action, either as to the total of quality costs or as to the ratios of the various major categories to the total. Such information as is available on these ratios indicates that:

Failure costs generally run at several times the appraisal costs in the consumer products industries.

Prevention costs commonly run under 10% of all quality costs.

However, these ratios vary widely among companies, and again there is a lack of useful guidelines.

The Budgetary Process   Companies have long controlled various elements of quality costs through the regular budgetary process. Budgets for inspection costs are in

---

[10] An occasional exception arises in bidding, where there is opportunity to learn of competing bids on quality costs, e.g., reliability programs, test programs.

[11] The editor (Juran) has seen cases, e.g., some biological drugs, in which the testing costs alone exceed the production costs.

universal use, often based on engineered standards.[12] In similar manner, prevention costs, which consist almost entirely of personnel costs, have long been budgeted, though the standards are usually based on history.

Budgeting is also done for some failure costs, but the standards are based almost entirely on past history. As a result, many companies have watched not the costs but the variances from those costs. This has tended to perpetuate bad levels of performance, since no alarm signals sound when current costs are no worse than prior costs.

The weaknesses in the budgetary process are not merely in the use of dubious historical standards. Even more significant is the fact that budgeting the various elements of quality cost does not succeed in optimizing the total. The elements are interrelated, and this fact is utilized in the approach of optimizing quality costs based on the ratios for the various cost categories.

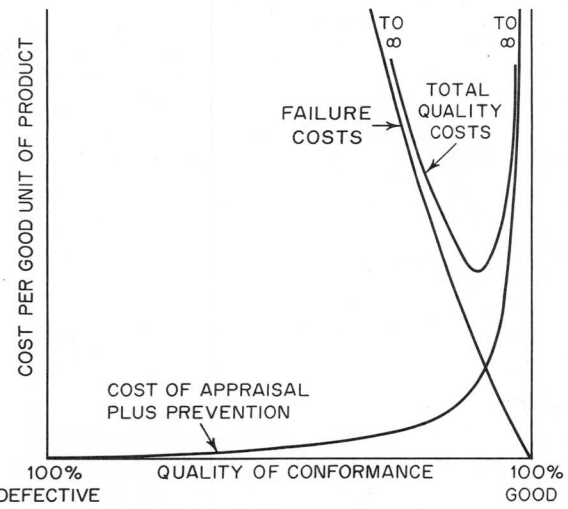

Fig. 5-2 Model for optimum quality costs.

Ratios for Quality Cost Categories A third approach to discovering the optimum is through analysis of the interrelationships among the cost categories. The basic model for this concept is seen in Figure 5-2. This model shows the principal quality costs which enter the achievement of fitness for use. They consist of:

1. The costs of appraisal and prevention. When these costs are zero, the product is 100% defective (left-hand boundary of Figure 5-2). To improve conformance, prevention and appraisal costs are increased until perfection is approached. Here the prevention costs rise asymptotically, becoming infinite at 100% conformance.

2. The failure costs due to the existence of defects. At the right-hand boundary of Figure 5-2 the product is 100% good. Hence there are no defects and zero failure costs. As nonconformance sets in, failure costs rise until, at 100% nonconformance (the left hand boundary of the chart), the product is 100% defective. At this point none of the units are good, and the failure costs *per good unit* become infinite, i.e., the denominator of the fraction is zero.

[12] See Section 12, under Budgeting for Inspection.

The curve of total quality costs (Figure 5-2) is seen to have a minimum.[13] This minimum is not merely a philosophical concept; *the minimum has practical meaning and application.*

The application of the model (Figure 5-2) is seen in Figure 5-3, which divides the total quality cost curve into three zones.   These zones can usually be identified from the prevailing ratios of the quality costs in the principal categories, as follows:

Quality Improvement Zone.   This is the left-hand portion of Figure 5-3.   The usual distinguishing features are that failure costs constitute over 70% of the total quality costs, while prevention costs are under 10% of the total.   In such cases,

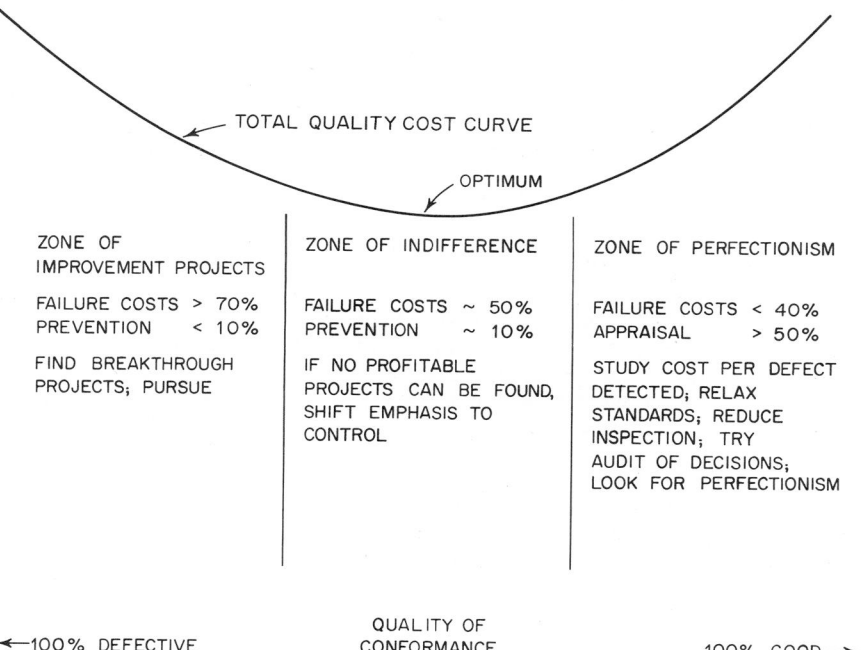

ZONE OF IMPROVEMENT PROJECTS	ZONE OF INDIFFERENCE	ZONE OF PERFECTIONISM
FAILURE COSTS > 70% PREVENTION < 10%	FAILURE COSTS ~ 50% PREVENTION ~ 10%	FAILURE COSTS < 40% APPRAISAL > 50%
FIND BREAKTHROUGH PROJECTS; PURSUE	IF NO PROFITABLE PROJECTS CAN BE FOUND, SHIFT EMPHASIS TO CONTROL	STUDY COST PER DEFECT DETECTED; RELAX STANDARDS; REDUCE INSPECTION; TRY AUDIT OF DECISIONS; LOOK FOR PERFECTIONISM

◄—100% DEFECTIVE   QUALITY OF CONFORMANCE   100% GOOD —►

Fig. 5-3   Optimum segment of quality cost model.

experience has shown that there are profitable improvement projects waiting to be pursued.[14]

Perfectionism Zone.   This is the right-hand zone of Figure 5-3 and is usually characterized by the fact that appraisal costs exceed failure costs.   In such cases it is usual to find, on closer study, that perfectionism[15] has set in.   Now the improvement

[13] The basic manufacturing costs—i.e., material, labor, facilities, etc.—are also part of the cost of achieving fitness for use.   However, these costs are constant irrespective of quality of conformance, e.g., the amount of material originally entering a unit of product is the same whether or not the unit turns out to be good.   Hence the curve of basic manufacturing costs is a horizontal line and does not affect the left-to-right location of the total quality cost curve. As a corollary, the left-to-right location of the optimum (enlarged in Figure 5-3) is not affected by the basic manufacturing costs.

[14] See Section 16 for the approach used.

[15] See Section 4, under Perfectionism.

projects consist of discovering and removing the undue costs of perfectionism. This may be done by programs such as:

1. Studying the cost of detecting defects compared to the damage done if they are not detected

For example, a company had long engaged in detailed inspection for quality characteristic X. The detail inspection had been originated at a time when defect X was widespread. Meanwhile over the years, the process had been improved to a point where defect X was a rare occurrence—only 15 per million. However, the detail inspection went on and on. A study showed that it was costing the company about $2.80 to find each defect X. Yet the sales price of the product was under 5 cents each.

2. Reviewing the quality standards to see if they are realistic in relation to fitness for use

3. Seeing if it is feasible to reduce inspection through use of process capability and preserving the order[16]

4. Considering the feasibility of audit of decisions[17] to reduce inspection costs

Indifference Zone. This is the central zone of Figure 5-2. In this zone the optimum has been reached or approximated and hence the problem has become one of control—how to hold this optimum level. Generally, the indifference zone is characterized by the fact that about half the quality costs are failure costs, while prevention costs are about 10% of all quality costs.[18]

Optimizing the Categories It is evident from the foregoing that optimizing the total quality costs is not solely a matter of optimizing each category. There is interaction among the categories, and this relationship is critical. However, there are also some guidelines relative to the individual categories:

1. Failure costs are at their optimum when we are unable to identify profitable projects for reducing them.

2. Appraisal costs are at their optimum when (a) failure costs have been brought down to optimum, (b) we are unable to identify profitable projects for further reducing appraisal costs, and (c) we have established good work methods and standards for inspection and test and are meeting those standards.

3. Prevention costs are at their optimum when (a) the bulk of prevention work is being directed to authorized improvement projects, (b) prevention work itself has been subject to analysis for improvement,[19] and (c) the nonproject prevention work is controlled by sound budgeting.

Quality Costs and Company Costs In striving to reduce quality costs, care must be taken not to increase total costs. This can take place when nonquality costs are increased disproportionally to reduce quality costs. All projects should keep in mind the entire array of costs. Reduction of quality costs is not an end in itself; it is a means to the end of improving the overall company economics.[20]

---

[16] See Section 12, under How Much Inspection?

[17] See Section 11, under Product Acceptance by Operators; also Section 10, under Audit of Decisions.

[18] Note by the Editor (Juran). The model of Figure 5-2, and the concept of the three zones associated with the optimum (Figure 5-3) were original with Juran during the late 1920s and the 1930s. The concepts very likely had occurred independently to other investigators as well.

The idea of quantifying the quality cost ratios applicable to the three zones appears to have originated with L. A. Seder during the 1960s.

[19] Improvement projects to reduce cost of prevention include procedures improvement, elimination of obsolete reports, and more economic documentation. See in this connection Holguin, Rene, Do You Know What Cost Reduction Can Do for You? *Quality Progress,* pp. 22–24, January 1968.

[20] For an example, see the metal cutting case in Section 16, under Diagnosis through Experiment; Input Skills.

A common problem in balancing quality costs and nonquality costs arises in the interrelation between productivity and quality. For example, in a composing room, one operator was 20% slower than the average, so that his annual production cost was $728 above average. However, he also made fewer errors, and the effect of this greater precision was to save $1,714 annually in quality costs.[21]

Still other cases involve the question of where is the most economic place to find a defect. A company which purchased electronic components and assembled them into consumer products was incurring rework because of occasional electrical failures in one type of component. Under the pressure of a drive on quality costs, the assembly manager insisted that the components be detail-tested at incoming inspection. The result was a reduction of failure costs of $450 per year in the Assembly Department at an increase in appraisal costs of $3,900 per year in the Incoming Inspection Department.[22]

THE CONTROL SCOREBOARD

As the quality cost program succeeds in reducing quality costs to a point approaching the optimum, it enters the control phase. In this phase the need is to set standards and budgets which reflect the attainable quality costs and to establish a continuing scoreboard on how actual quality costs compare to these budgets.

In contrast to the use of estimates and other shortcuts which are adequate in the selling phase, the continuing scoreboard must be based on a formal system of data collection carried out in full collaboration with the Accounting Department. Failing this, there will arise continuing problems due to the presence of multiple systems of cost accounting, multiple demands on line departments for cost data, conflicts in summaries presented in cost reports, and jurisdictional disputes over presentation of cost data to management.

To collect and use cost data systematically requires:

A list or chart of accounts against which charges of all sorts can be made, e.g., salaries, scrap, downtime, etc.

A system of record keeping to enable the charges to be collected for data processing

A plan for summarizing the data in ways which will simplify managerial interpretation

Establishment of bases for comparison, plus standards and budgets

Publication of the results in a form convenient for managerial control

Chart of Accounts The company's man-hours, materials, machines, tools, etc., are used for "regular" work which does not contribute to quality costs and also for "extra" work which does contribute to quality costs. The human beings involved need clear, simple means for classifying these uses of materials and facilities. They also need guidelines for classifying their working time. The language used to describe the quality cost category is sometimes an adequate guideline for these classifications. More usually, it is necessary to redefine the quality cost categories into terms which are directly applicable to the activities performed or guided by the employees.

For example, Inspection and Test is a quality cost category. However, for subclassification purposes and to assist in identifying avoidable quality costs, it may be necessary to create several accounts, e.g.:

---

[21] From Van der Burg, A. R., *Kwaliteits-en Kwantiteitskosten* (Costs of Quality and Quantity), *Sigma*, vol. 8, no. 1, pp. 3–4, 1962 (in Dutch).

[22] Personal communication to J. M. Juran.

Sampling inspection to determine lot conformance to specification
Sorting of nonconforming lots
Reinspection of repaired product
Inspection of field returns

Where the full time of individuals is devoted to a single quality cost category, the definition of the account may be simply a rephrasing of that job description or even the job title.[23] Some companies prepare a full list of quality control "work elements" which then become modular definitions for multiple purposes, including for quality cost accounts.[24]

Material and facilities usage likewise requires careful breakdown to separate quality costs from other costs. Vendor-caused costs must be kept separate from in-house costs. Material junked due to obsolescence must be kept out of quality costs. Concessions to customers for "sales policy" reasons must be kept separate from adjustments due to service failures. These examples can be multiplied.

Generally, it is the responsibility of Quality Control to identify what quality cost elements are needed and to define them sufficiently so that the resulting data collection will meet the needs of the quality cost concept. Generally, it is the responsibility of Accounting to work out the means for quantifying the amount of money associated with each of these accounts. However, carrying out these responsibilities requires extensive participation from the line departments to assure that the essential data are provided at minimal cost and at minimal inconvenience to daily operations.

The decision of what accounts to create is special to each company. However, within any industry there is much commonality among companies. For example, in the aerospace industry the quality costs needed during research and development are very high. Hence a number of separate quality categories are used which have little application to other industries.[25] Generally, the larger the organization, the larger the number of accounts and the greater their variety.

The Illusion of Totality. It is possible to go too far in assuring that *all* quality costs are included in the picture. This is known as pursuit of the "illusion of totality." For example, good tool maintenance clearly contributes to good quality. It also contributes to high productivity, low production costs, and prompt delivery. There have been some heated discussions on whether tool maintenance should or should not be classified as a quality cost, and there is room for a difference of opinion. However, it does not really matter very much. So long as tool maintenance is consistently omitted (or included), the scoreboard will remain consistent. The opportunities for improvement can still be identified whether tool maintenance is included or excluded.

Data Collection System[26] The data collection system provides the essential ingredients through which the various quality costs are charged to the proper accounts,

---

[23] Such is the approach used, in part, in "Quality Costs—What and How," American Society for Quality Control, 1967.

[24] See Section 7, under Quality Control Work Elements. For a good example, see Purcell, Warren R., Quality Cost Control, *Industrial Quality Control,* pp. 22–26, May 1962.

[25] See Pierce, R. J., and R. E. Beames, A Matter of Management—Quality Costs for Missile and Space Products, *ASQC Technical Conference Transactions,* pp. 99–108, 1965. The authors list 65 accounts for the industry generally. Even more extensive is the list of 191 accounts in *"Quality Cost Analysis Implementation Handbook, A Report to the Air Force Systems Command,"* project no. 65-43. (This is available from the U.S. Government Printing Office, Washington, D.C. 20402.) Both references note that no one company will need to use all the accounts.

[26] See generally Sections 19 and 20 on the approach to quality data systems.

priced out, and prepared for data processing. A basic step is to provide code numbers to facilitate data recording on the source documents. These code numbers (often devised in mnemonic order) also greatly simplify the subsequent data processing.[27] Code numbers are assigned to the accounts, departments, products, components, operations, dates, machine classes, types of defects, job orders, vendors, customers, operators, etc. Choice of the input codes decides absolutely the extent of detail which is available for subsequent analysis.

The source record may be a time card, material requisition, inspection report, scrap ticket, repair ticket, field service report, complaint report, Material Review Board report, etc. It may be designed for manual processing,[28] electronic data processing,[29] and still other methods. The data processing may make use of master decks of cards which convert the "natural" data such as man-hours or units of product into money equivalents. Data processing equipment now includes computers at high levels of sophistication. For example, in one steel company, standards are available for the cost per pound of each type of product at each of the various stages of processing. These standards are stored in the computer. When a given weight of steel is rejected at a given stage of processing, the computer finds the proper standard and evaluates the cost of the rejection.[30]

Summarizing the Data   There are multiple ways of summarizing the quality cost data, and these serve multiple purposes. The published reports consist of combinations of such summaries, the most basic being:

1. By product, process, component, defect type, or other likely defect concentration pattern. Such summaries make it easy to conduct the Pareto analysis to find the vital few contributors to quality costs.[31] The data processing equipment can be programmed to prepare the data tabulations based on their money ranking.

2. By organizational responsibility. Such summaries are by division, department, or similar organization unit, which is then identified with the cognizant manager or supervisor. These summaries are in the nature of personal scoreboards for the men involved and provide essential feedback on current or recent performance.

3. By quality cost category. These summaries assist in updating the relationships among categories, which are an index of the phase status of the quality cost program. In addition, the total of costs and trends for each category has significance in its own right.

4. By time. Summaries of cost data by calendar periods become the input to the time series reports and charts which are used to observe trends and progress.

5. By project. Here the purpose is to monitor the progress of the project as well as to compare actual costs with budget.[32]

Bases for Comparison   When managers use a scoreboard for quality costs, they are not content to look at the gross dollar figures. They want, in addition, to compare the quality costs with some base which is a measure or an *index of the opportunity for creating quality costs.* The usual indexes of quality costs are as follows:

[27] See, for example, Weis, A. E., Quality Control Reporting System, *Quality Progress,* pp. 21–24, May 1968.

[28] See, for example, Moburg, Keith W., Defect Management by Exception, *ASQC Technical Conference Transactions,* pp. 685–690, 1968.

[29] See, for example, Barrabee, James M., The Development of a Scrap Cost Program, *Industrial Quality Control,* pp. 342–345, January 1965.

[30] Dunn, David S., Rapid Feedback of Quality Failure Costs in the Specialty Steel Industry, *ASQC Technical Conference Transactions,* pp. 211–215, 1968. See also, in general, Section 20.

[31] See Barrabee, *op. cit.*

[32] See, for example, Judelson, Perry J., Estimating Quality Control Engineering Costs for Proposals, *Industrial Quality Control,* pp. 253–255, November 1967.

1. Per hour of direct production labor. This is an old, durable measure. "Direct production hours" is a useful short-range measure of activity. In addition, it is a measure which is promptly available and widely used for other indexes.[33]

2. Per dollar of direct production labor. By using an index of dollars divided by dollars, the money inflation factor tends to be neutralized. In virtually all plants, a figure on dollars of direct production labor is readily available from the accountants.

3. Per dollar of standard manufacturing cost.[34] This is an extension of (2) by adding in the cost of materials and of factory overheads. This index tends to have greater stability than (2), since it is not as strongly affected by automation.

4. Per dollar of processing cost (also called "per dollar of value added"). This index is favored for making comparisons among plants which differ widely in the ratio of materials cost to processing cost.[35] (Generally, quality costs correlate more closely with processing costs than with material costs.)

5. Per dollar of sales.[36] This index has an appeal to members of higher management, who are close observers of sales trends. However, the index has an inherent weakness, i.e., the sales dollar includes marketing expenses, general overhead, and profit, whereas the cost dollar includes none of these.

6. Per unit of product. Where the product line exhibits much internal similarity, a common unit may suffice for the entire line, e.g., per ton of steel, per motor vehicle. However, where the product line has inherent dissimilarity, the index may be in the form of dollars of quality cost per equivalent unit of product, e.g., per 1,000 pounds of air frame or per 1,000 electrical connections.

As reports are published, managers learn to interpret the significance of the figures against the various potential indexes. From this experience, the most useful indexes are agreed on, and these become the accepted bases for comparison. In addition, the urge to establish standards and budgets leads to use of the agreed indexes as bases for establishing standards for quality costs and for budgeting of quality costs.

Publication   Published reports on quality costs take three major forms (1) tabular, (2) graphic, and (3) narrative.

Tabular Reports.   Table 5-5 shows a conventional format for tabular reports. The quality cost categories are listed, along with subtotals and totals. In addition, data are shown for the comparison bases used, and the resulting ratios of quality costs to bases are shown as well.[37]

---

[33] The hours here may be standard production hours rather than actual hours. See Weis, *op. cit.* Weis also makes use of a concept of "opportunities to fail," i.e., the number of operations performed per piece times the number of pieces produced.

[34] See, for example, Bicking, Charles A., Cost and Value Aspects of Quality Control, *Industrial Quality Control,* pp. 306–308, December 1967.

[35] For an example, see Calahan, Richard C., Quality Cost Control in a Multifactory Organization, *Transactions Conference on Quality Control, Metropolitan Section,* ASQC, Sept. 11, 1964.

[36] For an example of use of quality costs as a percent of sales in a very large international company, see Groocock, J. M., Quality Control in ITT (Europe), *ASQC Technical Conference,* 1970. (Presented, but not in published preconference Transactions.) See also Ladue, Harold J., Quality Loss Reporting—An Effective Management Tool, *Industrial Quality Control,* pp. 293–296, December 1965.

[37] See, for example, Purcell, *op. cit.,* in which three ratios are part of the quality cost scoreboard:
Internal quality costs to cost of manufacture
Warranty costs to sales
Total quality costs to sales

TABLE 5-5 Quality Cost Report: Tabular Format

	This Month	
	Dollars	Percent of total
Prevention costs		
Quality Control Administration		
Quality Control Engineering . . . . . :		
Other quality planning		
Training		
Total Prevention.		
Appraisal costs		
Inspection		
Test		
Vendor control.		
Measurement control		
Materials consumed		
Product quality audits.		
Total appraisal		
Internal failure costs		
Scrap		
Repair, rework.		
Vendor losses.		
Failure analysis		
Total internal		
External failure costs		
Failures — manufacturing.		
Failures — engineering.		
Failures — sales.		
Warranty charges.		
Failure analysis		
Total external.		
Total quality costs		
Bases		
Direct labor.		
Conversion cost		
Sales.		
Ratios		
Internal to direct labor		
Internal to conversion.		
Total to sales		

Usually these tabular reports show this month's quality costs in dollars and as a percent of the total. In addition, they may show the corresponding figures for year to date. If budgets have been set, the budgeted figures and variances will be shown.

Graphic Reports. Graphic presentation is the second major format used for quality cost reporting, and permits wide variation in technique. In these charts, the horizontal scale represents time, usually months or quarters. The vertical scale may consist of:

1. Dollars of quality cost (Figure 5-4). This is the common language of upper management and hence has strong appeal for this group. For trend purposes this form has some built-in weaknesses, since the figures are influenced by variations in volume of business and by the effect of money inflation. To offset these effects, use may be made of a second chart showing on the vertical scale:

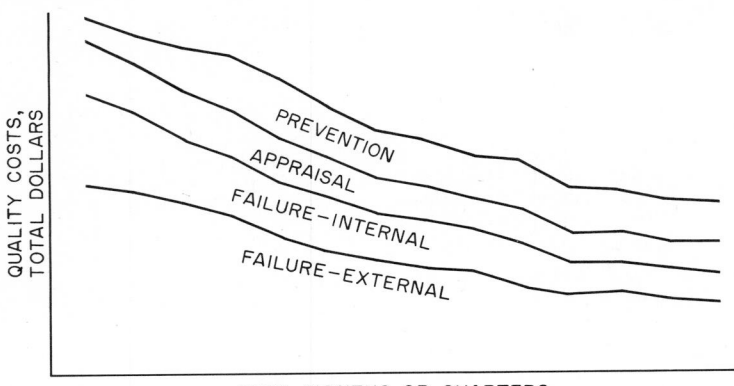

Fig. 5-4   Graphic report, quality cost in dollars.

2. Index of quality cost (Figure 5-5).   Some indexes, e.g., quality cost per dollar of sales, largely eliminate the effect of money inflation as well as the effect of variations in the volume of business.

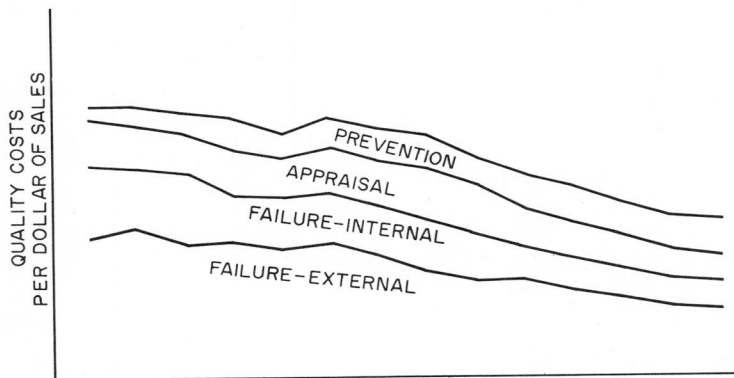

Fig. 5-5   Graphic report, ratio of quality cost to sales.

3. Ratio to total quality costs (Figure 5-6).   In this chart,[38] 100% of all quality costs is a horizontal line, so that the categories show only as percentages of the total. The trend of the ratios is easier to judge from such a chart than from (1) or (2).[39]

Narrative Reports.   These are usually for reporting on the status of projects. They also identify future potential projects by bringing up to date the matrixes discussed above and by revising the Pareto analyses.

[38] From Brisac, A., G. Oistrach, and O. Yanez, Quality Cost Data in Three Spanish Automotive Companies, *Quality* (EOQC Journal), vol. 15, no. 4, pp. 99–104, Winter 1971.

[39] For an actual example of use of both (2) and (3) for the same company, see Quality Must Be Expressed in Terms of Earnings, Costs, Profits, *Quality Assurance,* p. 14, December 1970.

Responsibility for Publication. This is best divided between Accounting and Quality Control. The basic cost data collection and data processing commonly are better done by Accounting. Such an approach uses the extensive experience of the company's experts in this field, avoids jurisdictional disputes, and adds to the credibility of the figures. (Upper management generally looks to Accounting for unbiased financial figures.)

Publication of tabular reports based solely on cost figures is again best done by Accounting, though other departments, and especially Quality Control, should participate actively in the design of the format and in the selection of bases for com-

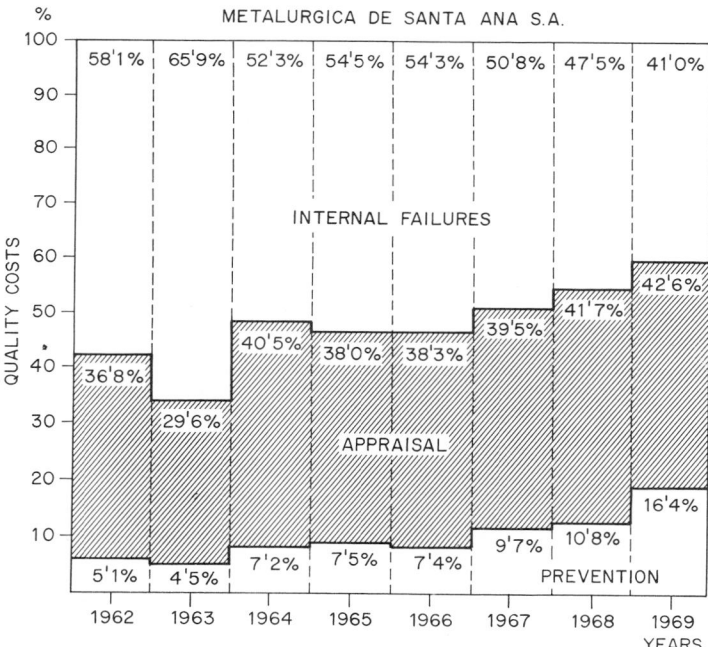

Fig. 5-6 Graphic report, interrelation of quality cost categories.

parison. In contrast, Quality Control is best equipped, by experience and professional know-how, to prepare and publish the graphic reports of trends and to provide the supplementary interpretation.

For example, guarantee charges are not synchronous with sales, and special provisions are needed to avoid errors in reading trends. (See Section 43, under Quality Assurance: Quality Costs; also Figure 43-7.)

Distribution List. All levels of management receive quality cost reports, but they do not all receive the same thing. Summaries are prepared for each level of responsibility, and these can be programmed and interfaced so that the same basic data provide ultimate inputs to all. For an example, see Figure 21-3.

Frequency of Reports. The frequency varies with the level of management. For upper management, reports are usually quarterly or monthly. For the lowest levels, some reporting may be weekly. Improvement reports are issued infrequently, i.e., quarterly or so, because the projects move slowly. However, the minutes of meetings provide interim information.

Transfers of Charges In some companies an effort is made to use some or all of the quality costs as a basis for transfer of charges between departments; i.e., if Department A's mistake caused Department B to incur extra charges, the amount of these extra charges will be transferred to the account of Department A. The success of such an approach depends largely on whether the company supervisors possess the means (personal skills, support from staff specialists) to diagnose the causes of the defects and to provide remedies. Lacking these means, the situation will simply go on and on. The solution will not be through some basic remedy but by an increase in budget on the grounds that, since it goes on and on, it must be unavoidable.

ESTIMATING QUALITY COSTS FOR BID PROPOSALS

A special use of quality cost data is to prepare estimates for bid purposes. In any case, the bidding company needs good data on which to structure the estimates. In addition, there has been an increasing tendency for government agencies to call for separate estimates of quality costs.

Major categories of quality costs in such estimates include:

Reliability programs as discussed in detail in Sec. 8.
Development of test equipment and test procedures
Documentation and data systems appropriate to the needs of the contract
Quality Control Engineering activities[40]

---

[40] For a detailed list, see Judelson, *op. cit.*

Section **6**

Quality Planning

RICHARD J. PIERCE

Quality Systems Consultant, Reentry and Environmental Systems Division,
General Electric Company

THE PLANNING CONCEPT

The term "quality planning," as used in this Handbook, refers to the process of preparing to achieve quality objectives. There is no such thing as planning in the abstract; planning is done only to meet objectives. Once clear objectives have been defined, planning can commence. The end result of planning is a list of deeds to be done, identification of those who are to do them, a timetable, and still other "elements of planning." The planning is complete when the operating forces have been put in a state of readiness for execution of the plan.

All major quality objectives are interdepartmental in nature. For such objectives, the quality planning must likewise be interdepartmental and must therefore be coordinated. Such coordinated quality planning is the subject of this Section.

There are also departmental quality objectives. For these, the quality planning can be carried out in the departments which perform the specialized activities of the Spiral of Quality (Section 2, Figure 2-2). Such departmental planning is discussed in other Sections of this Handbook.

Quality objectives exhibit great variation in nature and scope. They may be for breakthrough or for control.[1] They can be departmental, companywide, or intercompany in scope. They can deal with matters of great importance or with numerous trivia. The resulting permutations of kind and scope of quality objectives call for a corresponding assortment of quality plans. Table 6-1 lists the more usual quality objectives and the types of quality plans which have been evolved in response to the various types of objectives.

It is evident from Table 6-1 that there are many subspecies of plans. As will be

---

[1] See generally Section 3, under Quality Objectives.

TABLE 6-1   Types of Quality Plans

Objectives for breakthrough	Associated forms of quality planning	Discussed under
A. Numerous small projects for change	Multiple use procedures, plus departmental planning	Routine Projects for Change
B. Few, major projects for change	Special, supplemental planning, e.g., committee, project engineer, high-level coordination	Major Project Planning
C. Mixture of important and routine projects	A plus B, plus "switching mechanism"	Spectrum of Projects
D. Launching major new products	Similar to B	New-Product Planning
E. Major reliability programs	Similar to B	The Reliability Program, Section 8
F. Complex intercompany projects	Special "program management" organization	Multidivision and Intercompany Quality Planning
G. Adaptation to future needs and major economic forces	Long-range and short-range companywide quality planning	The Annual Quality Program
Objectives for control		
H. Meeting broad quality goals and budgets	Control process	Planning for Control; also The Annual Quality Program
I. Orderly conduct of numerous day-to-day departmental quality activities	Multiple use control procedures plus departmental planning	The Quality Control Manual; also in various "departmental" sections of this Handbook
J. Review of adequacy of control system and execution	Audit plans	Provision for Audit; also Section 21

seen, these subspecies differ widely in responsibility for the active work of planning and for the coordination. In addition, there is wide variation in the extent of formality needed.

The topics which follow elaborate on the manner in which the principal types of quality plans are designed to respond to the objectives served by these plans. The first group of topics deals with plans associated with projects for change. The second group of topics deals with plans associated with projects for control.

MAJOR PROJECT PLANNING

To launch a new project usually requires participation from multiple company departments. For example, processing a new customer order requires varying degrees of participation from all departments around the Spiral of Quality (Section 2, Figure 2-2). When the new project is only a small modification of existing practice, there is little real change to be digested. In such cases the departments affected can, through departmental planning, digest the change successfully. For these small changes the main coordination effort can be an overall procedure governing introduction of change.

However, when the new project is a major company undertaking, it becomes risky to rely on departmental planning even when there is a governing procedure. In some companies, the health of the enterprise depends largely on the results attained in several major projects. Even in companies whose business rests on a base of numerous small orders, there are usually a few large projects which carry considerable influence. Either way, a failure in a large or critical project becomes a significant blow to the company's health.

For such key projects companies are understandably unwilling to leave the planning to conventional procedures. Instead, the companies create special organization machinery to provide tailor-made planning for each key project. The special organization forms used usually consist of a combination of the following:

1. A committee or team of managers to guide the project
2. A project engineer from an existing department to carry out the details of planning, reporting, expediting, etc.
3. A project department specially created to guide the project

The larger and more elaborate the project, the greater is the need to create a special department for project planning.

When use is made of the project engineer or project manager, he is always given the responsibility for:

1. Drafting the plan and securing the approval of the departments involved
2. Following progress and reporting results
3. Sounding the alarm when the project runs into trouble
4. Expediting the work of all departments and stimulating progress

In some cases the assignment to the project department goes beyond planning and coordination. It may include control of the funding as well as functions such as product development or manufacturing planning. In such cases engineers from the "regular" departments are assigned to the project department for the duration of the project. These engineers are under the direction of the project manager as to the priority of the work to be performed, but they continue to receive professional guidance from their "regular" department on matters concerning the technological disciplines involved (e.g., solid-state circuitry, machine design, aerodynamics, etc.).

Project groups may include quality control engineers, reliability engineers, and other quality specialists. In such cases, they carry out, within the project group, their usual tasks of design review, study of process capability, inspection and test planning, etc.

The model for project planning consists of a universal sequence of activities, as follows:

1. Breakdown of the objective into logical, convenient subobjectives, each to be carried out by some identifiable department. Often these subobjectives are grouped together to constitute a stage or phase of progress. These subdivisions simplify the shifts of responsibility which must parallel the progression from one department to another. Figure 6-1 exemplifies the stage concept as used by a leading manufacturer.[2]
2. Definition of the deeds to be done.
3. Assignment of responsibilities for doing these deeds.
4. Establishment of milestones and schedules.
5. Description of methods and procedures.
6. Provision of facilities, instruments, equipment, and space.
7. Selection and training of people.
8. Provision for measurement and reporting of results for control.
9. Provision for audit.

The detailed planning is usually summarized in the form of a diagram showing

---

[2] See Juran, J. M., "Managerial Breakthrough," McGraw-Hill Book Company, New York, 1964, p. 210.

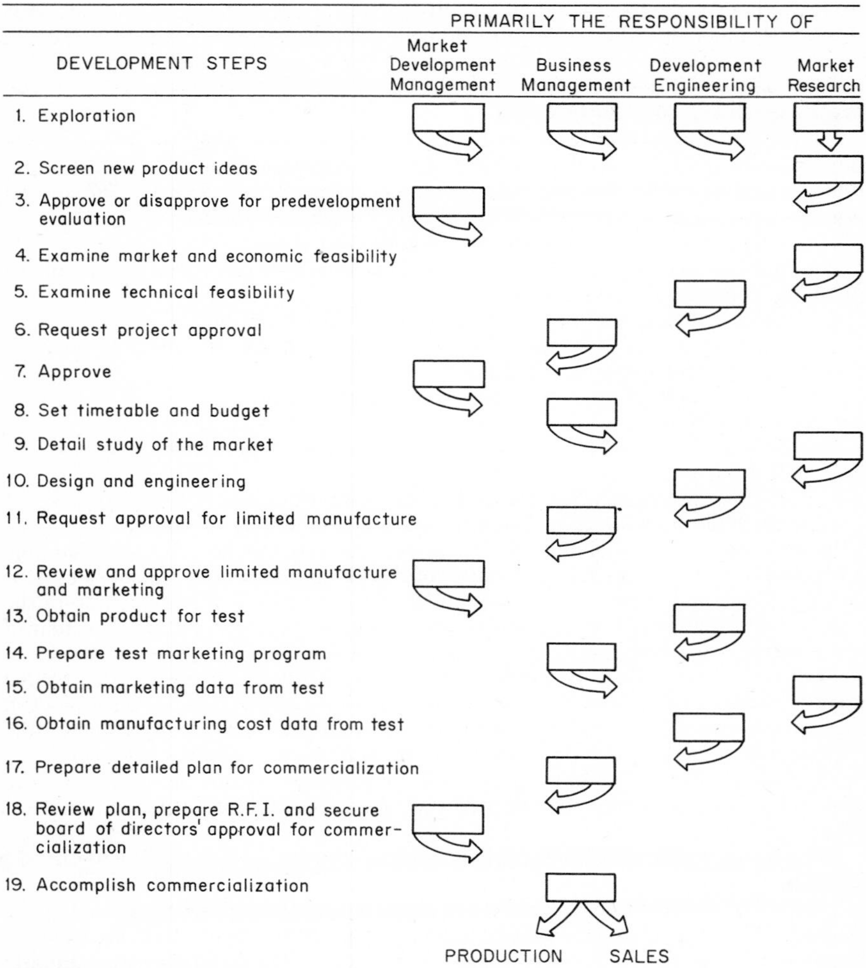

DEVELOPMENT STEPS	PRIMARILY THE RESPONSIBILITY OF			
	Market Development Management	Business Management	Development Engineering	Market Research
1. Exploration				
2. Screen new product ideas				
3. Approve or disapprove for predevelopment evaluation				
4. Examine market and economic feasibility				
5. Examine technical feasibility				
6. Request project approval				
7. Approve				
8. Set timetable and budget				
9. Detail study of the market				
10. Design and engineering				
11. Request approval for limited manufacture				
12. Review and approve limited manufacture and marketing				
13. Obtain product for test				
14. Prepare test marketing program				
15. Obtain marketing data from test				
16. Obtain manufacturing cost data from test				
17. Prepare detailed plan for commercialization				
18. Review plan, prepare R.F.I. and secure board of directors' approval for commercialization				
19. Accomplish commercialization				

PRODUCTION   SALES

Fig. 6-1 Kaiser stage system.

the tasks to be done, identifying those who are to perform the tasks, and setting up the timetable for completion.   Figure 6-2 is an example of such a diagram.[3]

Making this model effective requires that there be agreement among the top managers as to where the responsibilities for performing the work lie.   This requires that "work" be subdivided into segments small enough to be clearly identifiable. Table 6-2 is an example of a responsibilities matrix created to show:

Areas of responsibility
Departments accepting responsibility
Degree of responsibility, whether primary (R) or contributing (C)

[3] Courtesy Allis Chalmers Manufacturing Company.

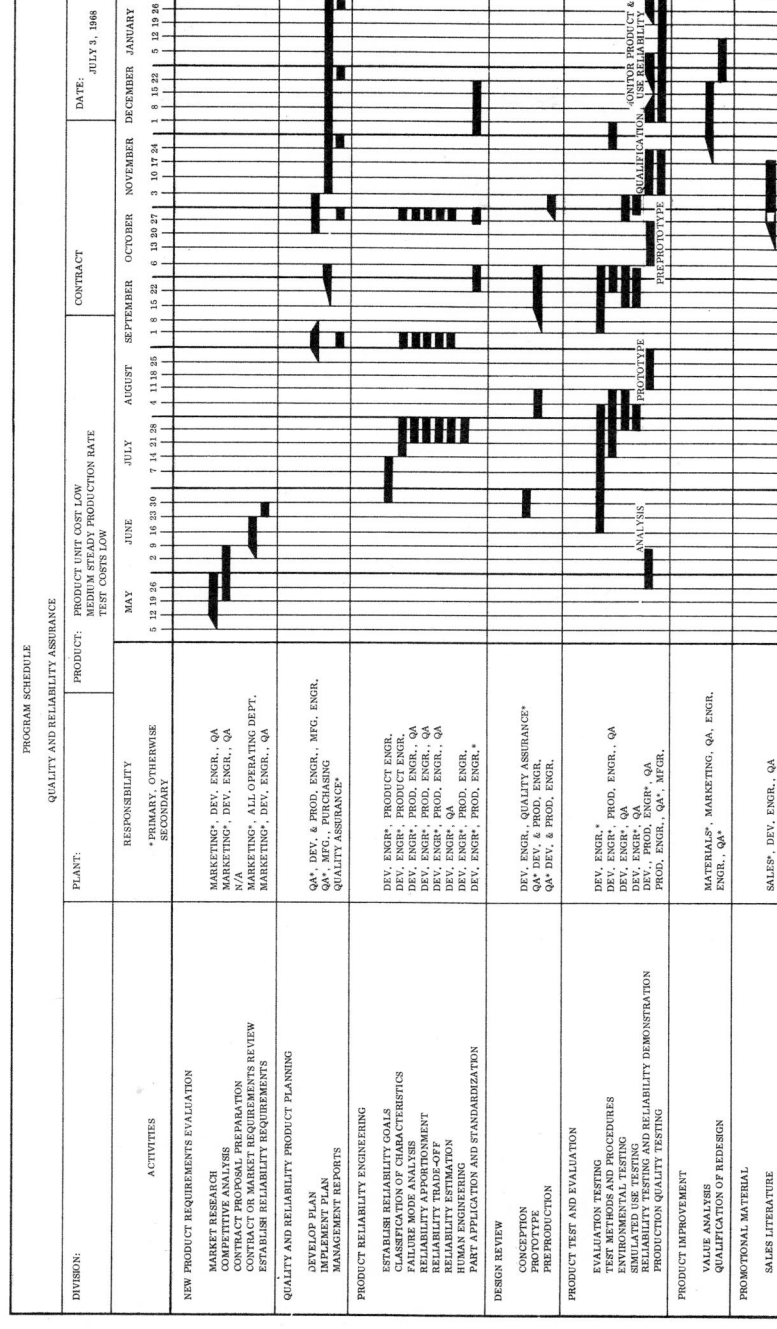

Fig. 6-2 Program schedule, Allis Chalmers Manufacturing Company.

TABLE 6-2   Responsibilities Matrix

There exist primary responsibilities (R) and contributing responsibilities (C) for product quality. These responsibilities are defined in the matrix below:

Areas of responsibility	Gen. mgr.	Mktg.	Prog. mgr.	Eng.	Mfg.	QC& Test	Finance
Product Quality Level for Business	R	C	C			C	
Initiate Program Plan, Schedules, and Budgets		C	R	C	C	C	C
Issue Work Statement		R	C				
Customer Quality Requirements		C	R	C		C	
Prepare Quality Plan						R	
Establish Engineering Standards				R			
Establish Quality Standards						R	
Establish Product Design Capability			C	R			
Provide Reliability Apportionment			C	R			
Prepare Design Specifications			C	R	C	C	
Perform Design Review			C	R	C	C	
Accomplish Make/Buy Decision			C	C	R	C	C
Provide Drawing and Change Control			C	R	C	C	
Implement Production Process Designs					R		
Implement New Design Control by Reviewing Engineering and Manufacturing Designs against: Quality Standards			C	C	C	R	
Engineering Standards			C	R	C	C	
Configuration Definition			C	R			
Produce Product to Design Specifications					R		
Configuration Verification						R	
Implement Incoming Material Control			C	C	C	R	
Design Major Items of Test Equipment Which Require Significant Design Effort				R		C	
Design All Other Test Equipment and Fixtures and Procure All Test Equipment and Fixtures for QC&T, Plant and Field Use. Provide QC Requirements for Engineering Designs					C	R	

"Projects" as used in the foregoing refers to *any* major identifiable change requiring interdepartmental action. Some of these projects, e.g., new-product planning, are discussed in this Section. Other projects, e.g., quality improvement, are discussed in other sections of the Handbook.

NEW-PRODUCT PLANNING

In launching a major new product, the quality function is all-pervasive; it involves all departments around the Spiral (Section 2, Figure 2-2). In addition, the growing emphasis on long life and reliability has demanded that the quality planning encompass the entire life cycle of the product, from "cradle to grave."

Cradle-to-grave quality planning involves:

1. An understanding of the company's business policies, the users' quality requirements, and the concept of fitness for use.

2. A listing of the major activities or deeds which must be performed, whether inside the company or outside, in order to achieve fitness for use. In very large projects the number of these deeds is so great that resort is had to the phase or stage system to provide a first breakdown of the project. These phases are designed to terminate either (1) when a major department has concluded its creative work, e.g., market research, or (2) when a major activity, e.g., prototype design, is sufficiently complete to permit a review of results and a decision on whether to go on with the next phase.

Figure 6-3 identifies 15 phases of the life cycle of a new product and also shows, in flow-diagram form, some of the movement of information associated with the various phases.[4] The flow-chart format is useful for showing the orderly succession of activities needed to achieve fitness for use. It also simplifies the necessary assignment of responsibilities and the identification of needs for coordination and feedback.

3. A detailed breakdown of the activities and deeds to be performed during each phase. Table 6-3 is a summary of the quality activities usually associated with various phases in the new-product life cycle.[5]

4. A timetable showing when tasks are to be started and finished. Figure 6-2 shows such a timetable in Gantt chart form. In some projects the timetable is elaborated into PERT and critical path diagrams to quantify bottleneck activities and to plan accordingly.

5. Assignment of responsibility to make clear who is to do which tasks. Table 6-2 is a portion of a responsibilities matrix for various phases of new-product planning.

6. Controls which will assure that the tasks are completed, and on time. The project managers and project engineers play a major role in this control activity by observing actual performance and by sounding the alarms when the plan is in jeopardy.

Figure 6-2 exemplifies the planning deeds, responsibilities, and schedules as applied to product reliability. There are, of course, many other deeds to be performed in launching a new product, e.g., manufacturing planning, test planning,

---

[4] Courtesy General Electric Company.

[5] Table 6-3 is a composite of many published lists. It has drawn heavily on the paper of Dr. Alfredo Bar entitled "Quality Planning in the Domestic Appliance Industry," presented at the European Organization for Quality Control Conference, Madrid, 1968. Other lists are available, some in considerable detail. See, for example, Jaworski, Chester S., Pre-Production Planning Pays Off on Complex Equipment, *Evaluation Engineering,* pp. 62–64, March–April 1968.

For some examples in practice, see in this Handbook Section 43, under Preproduction Activities; also Section 42, under Product Planning.

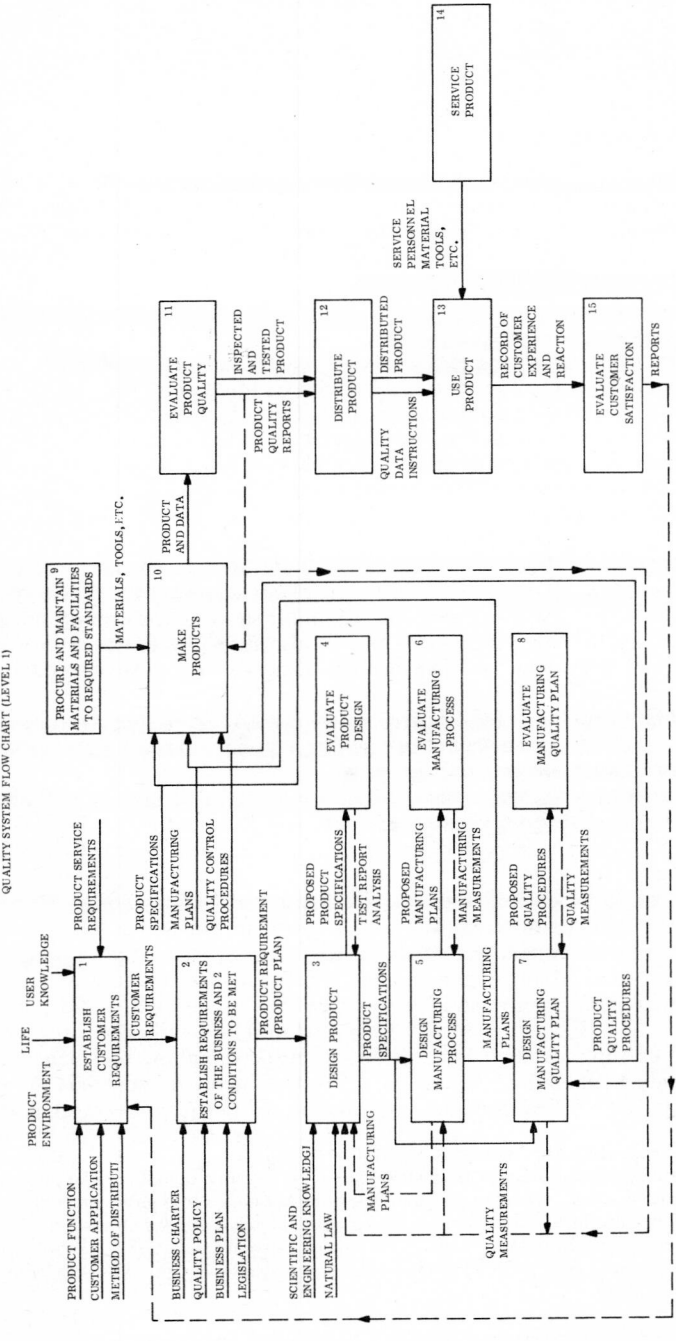

Fig. 6-3 Life cycle of a new product.

TABLE 6-3   Quality Planning Activities for New Product Phases

Phase	Quality planning activities
Market Research	Analysis of customer complaints, returns, service troubles, and other evidences of dissatisfaction Study of competitive product quality Study of user needs, for opportunities to improve income through quality (see Sections 4 and 14)
Product Concept	Review for conformance to customer needs
Prototype Design	Design review for fitness for use; reliability planning
Prototype Construction, Test	Qualification test (environment, life, reliability); confirm fitness for use; define performance of product, components; define life, reliability, service call rate
Production Design	Design review for tolerancing, producibility, maintainability; improvement studies; packaging analysis; warranty planning
Pilot Production	Material specification, vendor qualification, process selection, process capability, instrumentation, process control planning, inspection planning, work methods, training, data feedback planning
Production	Data feedback for improvement, control; quality cost studies; other improvement studies
Usage, Service, Maintenance	Performance feedback on reliability, maintainability, warranty; failure analysis

field service, user maintenance, vendor relations. In cradle-to-grave planning the detailed tasks needed are identified in advance and are assigned as to responsibility, timetable, budget, etc., in the original coordinated planning. In this Handbook these detailed tasks are discussed in the specialized Sections, e.g., 8, New-Product Quality; 9, Manufacturing Planning; 10, Vendor Quality; etc.

ROUTINE PROJECTS FOR CHANGE

An example of this category of objectives is the procession of customer orders calling for nonstandard products from manufacturers of (say) paint or gears. Any such order calls for a color or configuration not available as standard product. The "special" order is acted on sequentially by various departments around the Spiral (Section 2, Figure 2-2) in accordance with a prefabricated plan.

This plan is contained in a written procedure which defines the results to be achieved or the actions to be taken by each of the departments in the chain of progression of the customer order. In this way the procedure serves as a repetitive use plan and as an impersonal coordinator. Usually the departmental planning needed to achieve the specified results is left to the individual departments to work out for themselves. However, in those cases where departmental discretion must be limited (to avoid damaging company performance), the procedure includes some departmental planning as well.

The manual of procedure, as an impersonal coordinator of multiple departmental actions, has wide application in quality planning, e.g., processing design changes, purchase of instruments, processing of quality complaints. All such applications serve the useful purpose of coordinating numerous routine interdepartmental projects without taking up the time of the managers. However, while the coordination per se is economic, the blind use of the manual of procedure can lead to difficulty in two major ways:

1. For nonroutine projects, adherence to the manual fails to recognize that some-

thing is unusual and deals with it in a usual way. The unusual feature may consist of such things as:

A time schedule not attainable by routine progression through the series of departments
A quality requirement more demanding than the routine product
A critical interface with the work of outside organizations
Penalty or incentive clauses on performance

For such nonroutine projects it is common to assign a project engineer (various titles are used) to supply added coordination and stimulus to aid in meeting the special needs. The project engineer is a shepherd for the project. He understands its peculiarities, alerts the departments as to the special needs, helps them to anticipate problems, observes and reports progress, expedites and sounds the alarm in case of trouble.

2. For projects which require only part of the procedure, the cost of following the manual can become excessive. See below, under Spectrum of Projects.

The approach used to prepare manuals of procedure is discussed below, under The Quality Control Manual.

SPECTRUM OF PROJECTS

Using the procedure manual is an economical way to plan projects which follow a common pattern. Once prepared, the standard procedure can be used over and over again for project after project. This repetitive use is justified as long as the projects follow the usual pattern around which the procedure was designed. However, virtually all companies are involved with a spectrum of projects like this:

1. The normal projects for which the standard planning procedure is designed.
2. The major projects for which the procedure manual is insufficient. Such projects require individual, tailor-made planning (see Major Project Planning, above).
3. Still other projects for which the standard procedure is too much.

For example, a company designing and making instruments to customer order uses a procedure to plan the product design, purchasing, manufacture, test, etc. However, some orders are "special" in minor ways, e.g., the customer wants a standard instrument but with a special color for the front panel. If the procedure is followed blindly, the "regular" departments will go through the steps of estimating, product design, design review, issuance of drawings, preparing purchase orders and manufacturing process sheets, etc. However, a more economical way is for one "jack-of-all trades" to interpret the order, purchase the material with petty cash, fabricate the panel with general-use tools, and assemble it to a standard instrument. Where such special orders are numerous, the jack-of-all-trades concept is actually followed. A special order department is created and put in charge of a manager who is personally competent to do design, purchase, production, etc. The time for getting out the orders then becomes far less than it would be if the full routine were followed, and the cost is lower because some of the costly steps are bypassed.

Still another method of approach is to create more than one standard planning procedure. For example, the Department of Defense applies MIL-Q-9858A for large contracts requiring a comprehensive quality program. However, for smaller contracts involving production only, a different plan, MIL-I-45208A, may be invoked. In this plan the emphasis is on inspection rather than on cradle-to-grave planning.

Dealing with a full spectrum of projects also requires a "switching" mechanism for choosing the form of planning which best fits each project. There are several such mechanisms in common use:

1. A committee which reviews projects before they are approved for work and which chooses the planning mechanism.

2. An individual designated to be the "switching station." Depending on the nature of the business, the individual may be a part of Sales Planning, Estimating, Production Control, or still other departments.

3. Limits established impersonally, by dollar size of the project. These limits are based on past experience and serve as a guide to the choice of planning to be used.

Finally, it is common to find that there is a good deal of informal recognition of the spectrum of projects. Major or critical projects are assigned to top-level committees or to senior project managers. Standard or less than standard projects are delegated further down in the organization. Coordinating groups—such as design review boards or material review boards—meet with full membership to go over major projects but leave the rest to a subcommittee or an individual to process. Even in departmental planning, critical work is assigned to people with proved capability for doing the job.

PLANNING FOR CONTROL: GENERAL

Control is the process through which we prevent change or retain the status quo.[6] In this Handbook, planning for control is discussed under three main subjects:

1. The universal principles and tools through which all control is exercised. This is discussed below under Planning for Control: The Universals.

2. Those control systems which are interdepartmental or companywide in scope. These are discussed later in this Section.

3. Those control systems which are departmental in nature, for example, control during manufacture. Such control systems are discussed in the respective departmental Sections of the Handbook.

PLANNING FOR CONTROL: THE UNIVERSALS

The control process operates through a universal mechanism known as "the feedback loop" (Figure 6-4). The nucleus of this loop is the control subject—the variable which we are trying to regulate.

In the operation of the feedback loop, a standard is set as the intended value of the control subject. A sensor is designed to measure the actual value (performance). A collator compares actual with standard. When actual differs from standard by an amount greater than a predetermined tolerance, the loop is closed, setting into motion the means for restoring the status quo.[7] The loop being universal, "If you know how to control, you can control anything."

The Control Subject. At the technological level there are enormous numbers of control subjects: quality characteristics of components, processes, units, subsystems, systems; elements of documentation; myriads of measurements. Control over these huge numbers can nevertheless be accomplished by relatively few human beings through use of the "control pyramid."[8]

At the managerial level, the control subjects are few in number, but now each

[6] For an elaboration of this definition, see Section 2, Basic Concepts, under Control.

[7] For an exhaustive discussion, see Juran, J. M. "Managerial Breakthrough," McGraw-Hill Book Company, New York, 1964, pp. 181–344.

[8] See Juran, *op. cit.,* pp. 188 and 189.

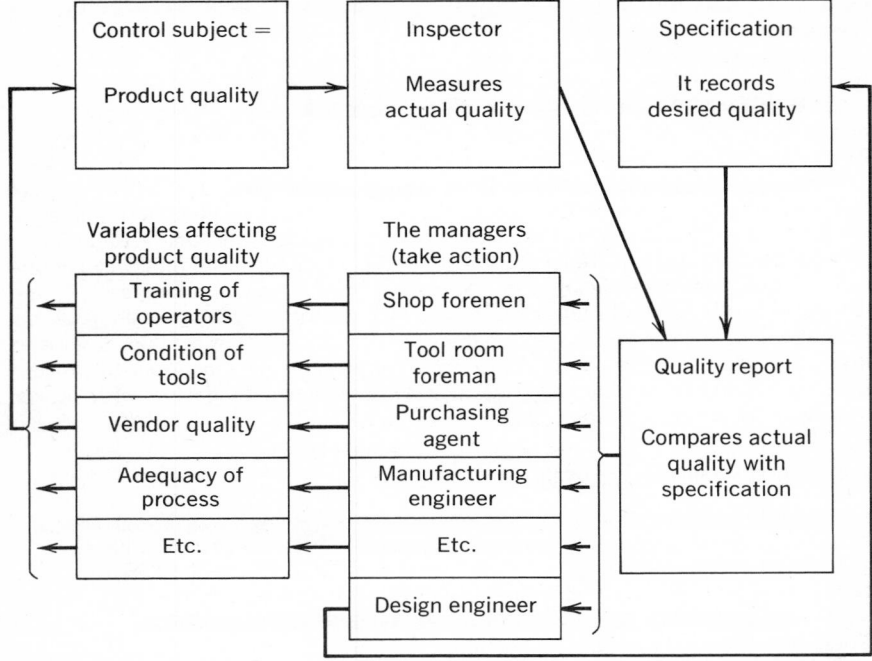

Fig. 6-4 Feedback loop.

becomes quite important. These managerial control subjects (fitness for use, quality costs, etc.) are discussed in Section 21, under the heading Executive Reports.

In applying the feedback loop, managers make use of some well-known control tools:

Flow Diagram.   Figure 6-5 shows the progression of events through which electron tubes are manufactured. Multiple departments are involved, in combination with multiple operations, inspections, storages, tests, etc. While departmental supervisors, working in isolation, could plan in a way which would achieve conformance to departmental specifications, the collective results would not optimize company performance. In consequence, it is good practice for some staff specialist to prepare a flow diagram for the entire progression from materials to finished product. This diagram (Figure 6-5) enables each supervisor to see what goes on before and after his operations. When these supervisors are then convened to discuss planning for control of electron tube manufacture, the flow diagram helps them arrive at a plan which optimizes company performance.

The flow-diagram concept can be applied to the entire progression of the product[9] from "cradle to grave" or to any segment of this progression. For example, Figure 6-5 is the flow diagram merely for production and test of the electron tube. It does not include other segments such as product development, marketing, field service.[10]

[9] For some examples, see the flow diagrams in Sections 33, 39, and 42.

[10] For some experience with use of standard symbols for flow diagrams, see Veen, B., Standardization of Flow Charts for Process Quality Control Systems, *Quality* (EOQC Journal), vol. 15, no. 2, pp. 35–39, 1971.

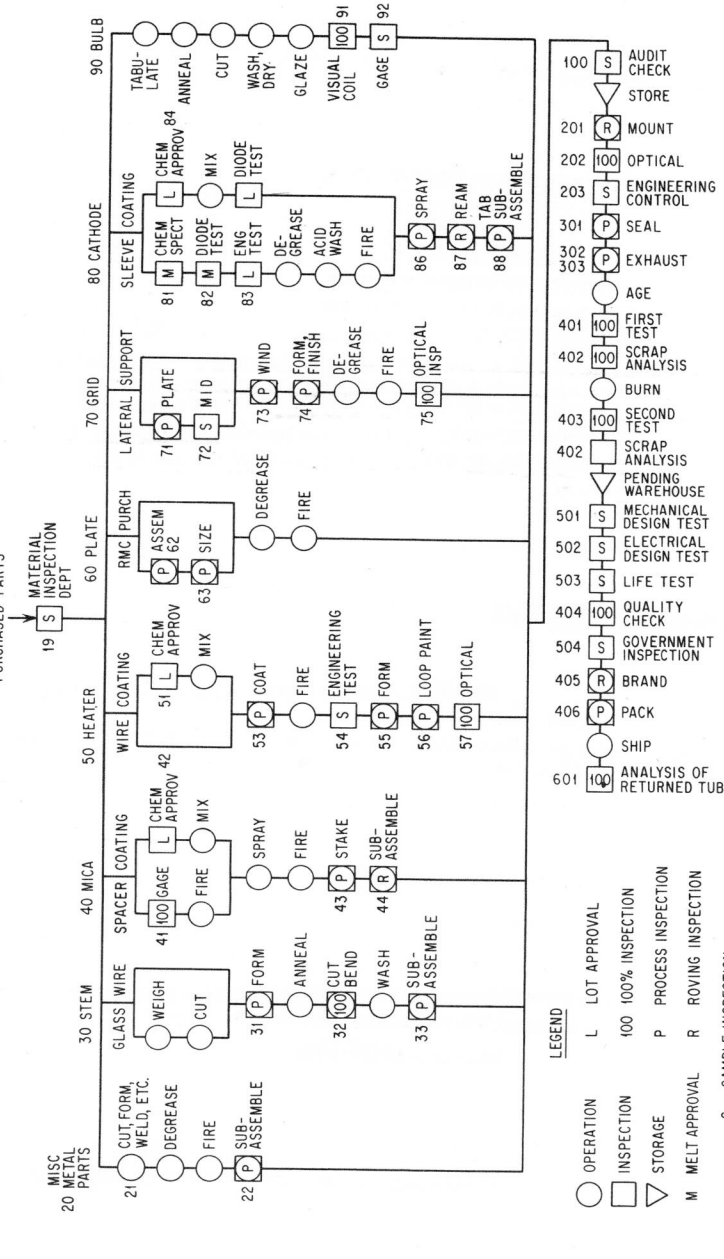

Fig. 6-5 Flow diagram, electron tubes.

The Control Station. The control process is carried out in a limited number of areas or control stations. These control stations carry out the work needed to close the feedback loop for a selected list of control subjects. Examination of numerous control stations soon discloses that they are usually located in one of several principal ways:

1. At changes of jurisdiction, to protect the recipients: between stages of major projects (e.g., design review); at movement of production between companies or between major departments; prior to delivery to finished goods store or to the customer.

2. Before embarking on an irreversible path: setup approval before production; product approval before completing a costly operation, e.g., laboratory test before pouring a heat of steel; product approval before diffusion of a uniform stream.

3. After creation of a critical quality.

4. At dominant process variables, i.e., the vital few.

5. At natural "windows," for economical control.

Definition of Work: Criteria. For each control station, there must be defined what work needs to be done to achieve control: what characteristics to measure, with what instrument; what data to record; what standards to use for comparison; what deviations to allow; what action to take in the event the standard is not being met. This definition of work should include provision of some essential criteria: seriousness classification of defects; sample sizes; standards for characteristics not covered by specifications. In some situations the people at the control station are qualified, by knowledge of fitness for use, to determine these criteria for themselves. More usually, they lack this knowledge and hence are not qualified to establish the criteria. However, if the managers fail to provide the criteria, then, by default, the criteria must be set by people not qualified to do so.[11]

Definition of Responsibility. Usually there are several people associated with each control station. For example, in a factory department, the work of control is shared by setup men, operators, patrol inspectors, bench inspectors, supervisors, engineers, and still others. The need for clear definition is evident in the frequent question "Who is responsible for quality?"

This question cannot be answered in the form stated. Instead, the question must be restated to identify deeds, actions, decisions. It *is* possible to answer the question "Who is responsible for making this decision (or taking this action)?" For an example of the approach to definition of responsibility for specific decisions and actions, see Section 11, under Quality Responsibilities on the Factory Floor.

Information Feedback. Those who are to take action need information to tell them what action to take. Some of this information comes from personal observation of the conditions at the control station. Other information comes from instrumentation, from verbal briefings, from records and reports. The choice of information feedback is tailored to the situation at hand.

Provision for Audit. The final tool in the control kit is the audit which is made to assure that all other tools are being used as intended. There are multiple levels of this audit, and they are discussed in Section 21, under Quality Audit *et seq.*

THE ANNUAL QUALITY PROGRAM

It is only in recent decades that the quality function has emerged as a major industrial or company function. So important a function now requires top management

---

[11] For some elaboration and examples, see Section 12, under Inspection Planning and under Visual Quality Characteristics.

leadership, but the leadership of the quality function has traditionally been dele-gated to middle managers. (In many companies there has not even been a clear delegation—the leadership has been vague.) To break with tradition so as to give the leadership of the quality function to top management requires the creation of new management tools. Of these new tools, the annual quality program gives promise of enabling top management to participate in the formation of quality policies, plans, and goals and thereby to give leadership to the quality function.

Financial Analogy The annual quality program bears a marked similarity to the annual financial budget, a device which enables top management to participate in the formation of financial policies, objectives, and plans and thereby to give leadership to the finance function.[12] Because of this similarity, a good approach to evolving an annual quality program is to study the process used in preparing the annual financial budget. The precedents already set for the latter will likely be-come effective for the former.

Commonly, the budgetary process exhibits the following major elements:
1. Long-range programming to simplify preparation of the annual budget.
2. Broad estimate by top management of acceptable goals for the year ahead.
3. Appointment of a coordinator (the budget officer). His duties include:
    a. Preparation of a standard format to facilitate collecting the data from all departments on a uniform basis
    b. Assisting and coaching all departments in preparation of their departmental budgets
    c. Summarizing the departmental budgets for review by higher and higher levels until the final review by top management
    d. Publishing the final approved budget
    e. Reporting the results attained against budget

Long-range Programming Logically, long-range quality programming[13] should pre-cede preparation of the annual quality program. The long-range program does not lead directly to action; i.e., the company departments do not take their orders from the long-range program. However, the long-range program helps the managers to unify their thinking on what needs to be done for the years ahead and thus becomes a major input to the annual program. The two types of programs are related as follows:

The long-range program (1) identifies the challenges and opportunities of the future, (2) outlines the broad responses needed, and (3) concludes where we want to be with respect to quality in the long range.

The annual short-range program (1) evaluates where we are now with respect to quality, (2) establishes the goals to be reached a year from now, and (3) spells out the steps needed to reach those goals.[14]

To accomplish long-range quality programming, the managers:

Study the trends taking place in the company, the industry, the economy

---

[12] For an elaboration of this thesis, see Juran, J. M., The Two Worlds of Quality Control, *Industrial Quality Control,* November pp. 238–244, 1964; also Juran, J. M., Mobilizing for the 1970's, *Quality Progress,* pp. 8–17, August 1969.

[13] In the discussion which follows, the term "program" is used in the sense of including policies, objectives, plans, and other elements of a broad approach for defining what needs to be done and how to do it. The term "plan" is given the narrower meaning of the "process for preparing to achieve quality objectives."

[14] In large companies, long-range and annual programs are often made up for each auton-omous division or profit center as well as for the corporation. In the so-called "conglomerates," the divisions have little in common and quality programming is limited to the divisions.

Look into the future to identify the major forces which are coming over the horizon

Reach conclusions or assumptions as to the threats and opportunities ahead

Define the broad directions to be taken and goals to be reached by the company as a response to these threats and opportunities

For example, one such look into the future[15] suggested that the decade ahead required the following pattern of responses:

Emphasis on fitness for use rather than on conformance to specification

Optimizing costs of the user rather than costs of the manufacturer

Study of effect of quality on income rather than studying only the effect of quality on costs

Restraint on the forces of perfectionism

Straightening out the confusion on motivation for quality

Training of all departments in the use of tools for achieving quality rather than restricting such training to Quality Control Departments

Reexamination of long-standing practices on organization for quality

Putting the vendors on the team

Revising the approach to launching new products

Dealing with the growing trend to government regulation of quality

Dealing with the growth of product liability

Providing for top management participation in quality planning and assurance

TABLE 6-4   Some Considerations Common to Most Quality Programs

The company's status
    Business policies and objectives
    Management processes
    Extent of training
    Level of motivation
    Quality costs
Forces in the economy
    Government regulation
    Evolving legislation
    Product liability
Trends in the industry
    Consumer attitudes
    Customer complaint data
    Costs to the user
    Competitive product features
    Product warranties
    Licenses
State of technology
    New materials, processes
    New manufacturing and measurement concepts and equipment
    New scientific breakthroughs

Although some of the considerations are common to most industries (Table 6-4), each enterprise faces the job of examining its own situation and arriving at its own tailor-made list.

Most long-range quality programming is informal or intuitive. However, there is value in formalizing this process. The formality requires that the managers re-

[15] Juran, J. M., Mobilizing for the 1970's, *Quality Progress,* August 1969.

duce to writing their assumptions about the future. These assumptions can then be challenged by the "jury" of managers to reduce the risk of error inherent in the biases of individuals. For example, the Defense Contract Administration Services (DCAS) made the following assumptions[16] in structuring one of their long-range programs:

1. Department of Defense spending will remain in the range of $70 billion (per annum).

2. Computer technology and management science techniques will expand within DCAS.

3. New processes, techniques, products and materials will be developed.

4. Consumer demand for better quality will cause industry to assume a greater role in product reliability.

5. Government/industry programs will increase in popularity and become more effective instruments of coordination.

Having agreed on the assumptions, it became easier to agree on the long-range responses needed. For example, DCAS assumption number three was considered to require responses as follows: (1) Additional skills will be required to support these developments and (2) further training of DCAS employees will be required at all levels.

Annual Programming. The final result of the long-range program is definition of the objectives to be reached some years hence. In contrast, the final result of the annual quality program is definition of the objectives to be reached during the next year, along with plans for meeting these objectives. (The annual program logically includes objectives for both breakthrough and control.)

In its most useful form for securing top management participation, the annual quality program emphasizes those quality objectives which can improve income and reduce costs. Objectives for improving income[17] include such matters as:

1. Superior quality of design, e.g., easier installation, greater operating convenience, lower operating cost

2. Superior availability, e.g., lower failure rates, easier maintainability

3. Superior postsale service

4. Superiority over competitors as an aid to bidding for new business

Objectives for reducing costs[18] are closely related to improving quality of conformance, and they involve reduction in costs due to scrap, rework, complaints, returns, inspection, test, etc.

Still other objectives may relate to essential aspects of management performance, e.g., organization design, manpower development, systems and procedures, etc.

Commonly the objectives are established with an eye on where we are now. In consequence, the annual programming includes a review of the current year's performance. This review provides a measure of the length of the journey to the long range goals, and makes it easier to decide how much of that journey should be taken during the year ahead.

Once the goals and the subgoals have been established, the planning proceeds in the manner described elsewhere in this Section. Planning for improvement is centered on each project. Planning for control is centered on each control subject.

Ideally, the evolution of the annual quality program follows the approach used in budgeting, as noted in the finance function analogy above. A coordinator (commonly from the Quality Control department) does the following:

Prepares a standard format to aid in structuring the departmental programs

---

[16] Private communication, Glenn J. Soares to J. M. Juran, October 1970.

[17] See generally Section 4, Quality and Income.

[18] See generally Section 5, Quality Costs.

Assists and coaches the departments during their programming

Summarizes the departmental programs for review by higher and higher levels of management

Publishes the final approved program

Reports results achieved against program

Because the annual quality program is a recent development, it is to be expected that there will be awkwardness during the first several years of evolution. Moreover, since the format for such programs has not yet been standardized, the pioneering companies will be forced to improvise and invent as they progress. As more and more case histories are published, companies will be able to take advantage of the inventions of the pioneers. For example, a common objective in annual quality programs is reduction of quality costs. A published example[19] of format for quality cost reduction is seen in the "flag" chart of Komatsu Manufacturing Co. (Figure 6-6). The chart shows the program for reducing failure costs. The company's costs are broken down by contributing department, and a reduction goal is set for each so that the company goal can be met thereby. The Komatsu flag chart concept can be generalized to cover any instance of quality objectives in which the company goal is broken down to divisional, departmental, etc., goals to constitute a cohesive pyramid.[20]

The annual quality program should be distinguished from the collection of multiple use plans contained in the Quality Control Manual (see below). Like any set of statutes and ordinances, the manual, once enacted, remains relatively static. It does not tell the managers what products to launch and what products to eliminate. It does not decide what levels of quality to attain or what quality costs to attack. To establish these and other goals, managers use different tools, and the annual quality program is one of them. Table 6-5 summarizes the contrast between the annual quality program and the Quality Control Manual.

The annual quality program should also be distinguished from the annual budget. In a sense, the former is a specialized segment of the latter. Many of the inputs are common to both, as are those outputs which are expressed in the language of money. In addition, the time for preparing the two is logically simultaneous.

However, the conventional financial budget is devoid of information on quality policies, goals, plans. It makes no provision for optimizing quality costs or for otherwise optimizing quality performance. It has no means for reflecting goals which cannot be expressed in the common language of money. In consequence, while it may be desirable to work both up simultaneously, there are compelling reasons for ending up with two separate programs.

MULTIDIVISION AND INTERCOMPANY QUALITY PLANNING

Quality planning involving multiple companies has grown remarkably during the twentieth century due to a combination of events: expanding use of subcontracting, growth of international trade, growth of multinational companies, etc. The result-

---

[19] Kogure, Masao, On the Systems Approach in Japan's Quality Control, *Annual Technical Conference Transactions,* ASQC, pp. 429–439, 1970; also *Reports of Statistical Applications Research,* JUSE, vol. 17, no. 3, pp. 54–69, 1970.

[20] During the 1960s a number of Japanese companies undertook annual (and even semi-annual) quality planning under the name "President's Audit." For a discussion, See Mizuno, S. Quality Systems in Japan, *Reports of Statistical Application Research,* JUSE, vol. 15, no. 1, 1968 (in English). For other examples see *Proceedings, International Conference on Quality Control,* JUSE, Tokyo, 1969.

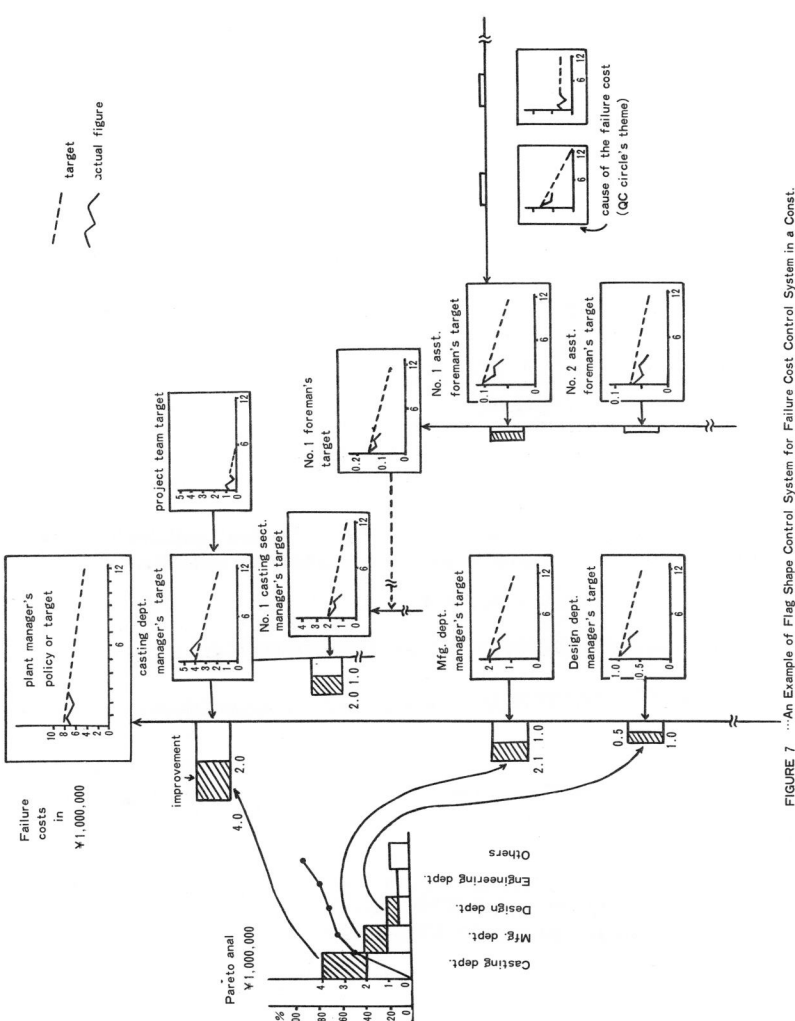

FIGURE 7 ···An Example of Flag Shape Control System for Failure Cost Control System in a Const. Equipm't Mfg. Co.

Fig. 6-6 Flag chart, Komatsu Manufacturing Company.

TABLE 6-5 Contrast—Annual Quality Program with Quality Control Manual

Annual Quality Program	Quality Control Manual
Concerned with policies, goals, plans, both for breakthrough and control	Concerned with plans only, mainly for control
Spells out goals to be met and results to be achieved, at all levels	Spells out the process to be followed in performing work
Is authoritative in defining what work has legitimacy	Not authoritative on what is to be done; only on how to do work authorized by programs or budgets
Measure of effectiveness is whether goals have been met	Measure of effectiveness is whether procedures have been followed
Requires annual revision due to old goals having been met, new needs waiting to be met, and close coupling with annual financial budgeting	Remains fairly static, but requires periodic maintenance

ing patterns of quality planning are greatly influenced by the nature of the basic relationships among the companies involved.

Domestic Subsidiaries or Autonomous Divisions.   In some cases there are compelling reasons for careful joint planning among such divisions because:

The divisions sell in overlapping markets, requiring standardization of the finished product and, as a consequence, of the product and process specifications as well.

The divisions "buy" materials and components from each other, requiring a vendor relations type of joint quality planning.

The corporate image of each division is affected by the conduct of every other division.

Where such "compelling reasons" prevail, it is usual to create a corporate staff quality control office to stimulate the necessary joint quality planning.   The elements of planning depend on the precise interfaces of the divisions but usually include:

Joint establishment of product and process specifications, test methods, and other technological and managerial interfaces of quality planning

Audit, by the corporate staff, of execution against plan

One large multidivisional company created a special Review Board to assist the corporation in responding to quality needs and in making the "external publics" aware of these responses.   The Review Board made use of available corporate staff efforts in order to:

Evaluate the quality expectations of the external publics

Provide awareness of these expectations to the cognizant corporate people

Provide corporate effort to stimulate appropriate responses

Measure product quality against evolving legislative standards and identify needs for corporate response

Provide counsel to corporate managers
Provide means for organized response
Review product and service performance
Demonstrate to the external publics the corporation's concern and action

Multinational Companies.   The usual pattern is that a corporation in one country controls subsidiaries in other countries through ownership or joint ventures.   Some of these relationships exhibit a need for joint quality planning similar to that required for domestic subsidiaries and divisions.   The methods of planning are quite similar, but there are differences:
The language, laws, customs, and cultural patterns differ from country to country, and the planning must be flexible enough to accommodate these differences.
Because of these international differences, the quality coordination office is often a part of the International Division rather than a part of the corporate quality control office.
Subcontracting.   The joint quality planning needed when one company buys more than just standard commodities from another is discussed extensively in Section 10, Vendor Relations.
Program Management.   This term describes the form of management used when a "complex system" is to be produced by the joint efforts of multiple companies. See Section 44, Complex Systems.
International Contracting.   Some of these relationships are similar to subcontracting and involve a conventional vendor relationship, but with the complications of language, laws, customs, etc.   In such cases the quality planning must open up to take account of these differences.   Numerous failures are traceable to "simple" misunderstandings which caused otherwise sound quality control planning to fail.
Among the most complex international relations are those involving a high technology product which is to be engineered and built from technology and components assembled from companies in several different countries.[21]   The planners must be quite as skilled and experienced in international communication as in the tools of quality planning.
Conglomerates.   This term refers to companies whose subsidiaries do not exhibit a commonality in markets, technology, facilities, etc.   In such cases there is no "compelling reason" for joint quality planning and the conglomerates do not organize for it.   Some do maintain a corporate quality control office, but in such cases the role is mainly that of consulting.[22]

FORMALITY IN QUALITY PLANNING

In tiny companies all planning is informal.   With growth in size and complexity, the planning becomes formalized for some well-known reasons:

To force the people involved to think it through
To convert solved problems into recorded knowledge so as to avoid the need for solving them over and over again
To optimize company performance rather than departmental performance
To provide legitimacy and authority for the deeds needed to execute the plans
To make responsibility clear and to create the conditions of self-control
To provide coordination for interdepartmental action

[21] For an example, see Biedenbender, R. E. and R. H. Rockwell, NATO Quality Control Standards, *Journal of Quality Technology*, pp. 159–167, July 1972.
[22] For a general discussion of the role of the corporate quality control office, see Section 7, under The Corporate Quality Manager.

To improve communication and to provide consistency and predictability in carrying out repetitive tasks; to guard against drift to undesirable practices

To provide training and reference material for new people

To provide an authoritative reference in the event of conflicts

To provide criteria for audit of execution against authorized practices

An important impetus to formalized quality planning has been provided by the actions of the Department of Defense (DoD) in shifting its emphasis from incoming inspection to vendor surveillance. In making this shift, DoD required that contractors, in addition to making the product:

Prepare a formal plan for control of quality

Provide objective evidence that the plan has been followed

Both these requirements (the formal plan and the objective evidence) forced contractors to expand their formality. Most of this added formality was then recognized by them to be good business practice, and this recognition stimulated extension of formality of quality planning to nonmilitary business as well.

Models of formal quality planning are now available for study. Of these, the best known is MIL-Q-9858A, the Department of Defense "Quality Program Requirements."[23] Many company quality planning approaches are derived from this military specification. A far more rigorous specification is the National Aeronautics and Space Administration's NHB 5300.4 (1B) "Quality Program Provisions for Aeronautical and Space System Contractors."[24]

Industrial examples of formal quality planning are mainly contained in the quality control manuals of industrial companies. These are numerous but are commonly published solely for internal use. However, a generalization of these plans appears under the heading The Quality Control Manual, below.

Within any company, the type of formal planning developed is strongly influenced by size, tradition, organization form, etc. In consequence, these plans exhibit special features which are appropriate to the culture in which they evolved. For example, under the General Electric Company's concept of "Total Quality Control," there are defined four primary areas of quality control activity: new design, incoming material, product, and special process studies. Also defined are ten subsystems of quality function. The interrelation of these subdivisions is seen in Figure 6-7. The instruction manuals, the training programs, and the organization design are all in harmony with these concepts.

In the case of untried products or processes, it is well to delay formalizing until good progress has been made in developing the best practice. Formality tends to stabilize practices at the then existing level.

It is also possible to overextend formal quality planning, and some of this has happened, both in government and in industry. Overextension takes various forms. Some plans are developed in unnecessary detail. Requirements for records and certificates are extended beyond the need of proving fitness for use. Formal systems, such as control charts or PERT, are applied on a wholesale basis instead of a selective basis.

Such overextensions commonly result from a combination of the following:

Staff enthusiasm for applying new techniques which show promise or have already demonstrated their usefulness in selected situations

---

[23] Available from the Naval Publications and Forms Center, 5801 Tabor Ave., Philadelphia Pa. 19120.

[24] Available from Superintendent of Documents, U.S. Government Printing Office, Washington, D.C. 20402.

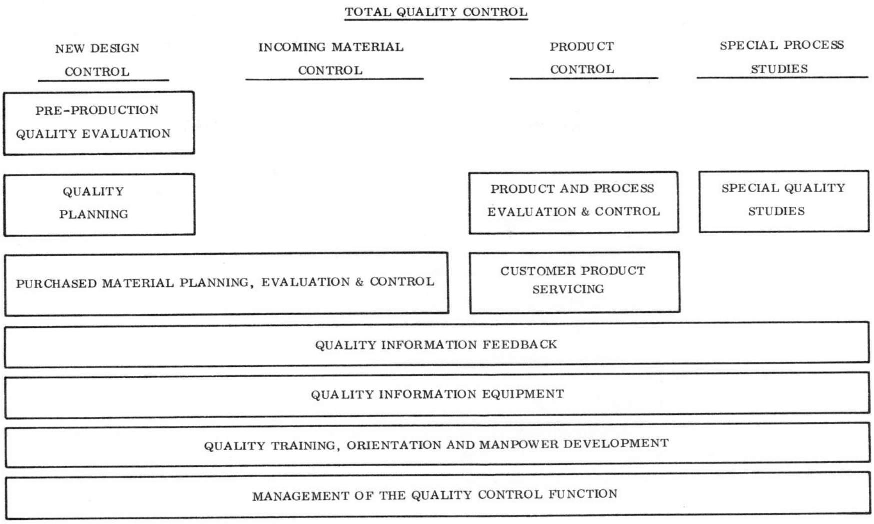

TOTAL QUALITY CONTROL

NEW DESIGN CONTROL	INCOMING MATERIAL CONTROL	PRODUCT CONTROL	SPECIAL PROCESS STUDIES

PRE-PRODUCTION
QUALITY EVALUATION

QUALITY PLANNING		PRODUCT AND PROCESS EVALUATION & CONTROL	SPECIAL QUALITY STUDIES

PURCHASED MATERIAL PLANNING, EVALUATION & CONTROL	CUSTOMER PRODUCT SERVICING

QUALITY INFORMATION FEEDBACK

QUALITY INFORMATION EQUIPMENT

QUALITY TRAINING, ORIENTATION AND MANPOWER DEVELOPMENT

MANAGEMENT OF THE QUALITY CONTROL FUNCTION

SOURCE: THE GENERAL ELECTRIC COMPANY

Fig. 6-7 Interrelation, General Electric Company quality planning subsystems.

Ample budgets in a time of growth

Inability of line managers to provide adequate evaluation due to unfamiliarity with the new techniques

Of course, as experience is gained, the challenge to overextension becomes more forceful. However, the excesses have meanwhile taken root and are difficult to pull out. It may be necessary to wait for a period of tight budgets to make a successful challenge to the entrenched overextensions.

THE QUALITY CONTROL MANUAL

A great deal of quality planning is done with the aid of formal, interdepartmental, multiple-use plans also called quality *systems* or *procedures*.[25] Such procedures are thought out, written out, formally approved, and published to become the authorized, legitimate way of conducting the company's affairs.

The subject matter of these interdepartmental quality plans ranges over the entire spectrum of the activities through which companies achieve fitness for use. These plans are often published collectively in a document known as the Quality Control Manual. This is an authoritative collection of written procedures setting out how to

[25] The terms "method" and "routine" also refer to multiple use plans, but with a connotation of departmental activities to be carried out at the bottom of the company hierarchy. Single-use plans, tailor-made to fit specific projects, are called "project plans." "Practice" usually refers to informal plans. The terminology is not yet standardized.

perform the various tasks through which the company makes its products fit for use. Such manuals are seldom needed in very small companies since the few people involved have much personal knowledge of fitness for use and the employees receive personal supervision direct from top management. As companies grow in size and complexity, most employees lose their personal knowledge of fitness for use and this personal supervision direct from top management. These losses must be made up somehow. The quality control manual becomes the principal means of making up these losses.[26]

The manual is organized into modular sections, each dealing with some aspect of the quality function. There are several groups of these sections.

General Sections. These usually include:

1. A message from the General Manager, the delegations made, the signatures which confer legitimacy
2. The stated purpose of the manual, the intended use, how to use it.
3. Table of contents
4. The company's quality policies
5. Organization charts and responsibility tables pertinent to the quality function
6. Authorized distribution list for copies of the manual
7. Provision for keeping the manual up to date, e.g., annual review, provision for audit
8. Glossary of terms used, definitions, reference sources
9. Index

Managerial Sections. These are quite similar from one company to another. They include procedures covering:

Marketing activities: Review of quotations for new business, estimate of quality costs for new contracts, competitive quality evaluation, customer quality surveys

New-product introduction: Product development, design reviews, prototype construction and test, specifications and drawings, qualification testing, reliability and maintainability activities, configuration and engineering change control, other aspects of "cradle-to-grave" planning

Manufacturing quality planning: Producibility analysis, equipment specification and procurement, prove-in of processes, pilot production runs

Vendor quality control: Qualifying new vendors, vendor surveys, purchase agreements, vendor assistance and service, incoming inspection and test, nonconforming vendor material, vendor rating

Inspection and test: In-process control, final inspection and test, visual and other sensory standards.

Measuring equipment: Design, specification, procurement, checkout, calibration, maintenance of accuracy

Nonconforming material: Identification, segregation, Material Review Board, corrective action

Postmanufacture: Identification, packing, storage, transport, uncrating, installation and check-out

Usage and field service: Service instructions, tools and equipment, usage, evaluation of use, field failure analysis, complaint analysis, customer returns, warranty administration, spare parts ordering, stocking, inventory

Quality assurance: Rating of outgoing product, audit of plans, audit of execution versus plans

Quality costs: Classification, collection, summary, reporting

---

[26] The detailed purposes behind formalizing the plans and procedures are set out under the heading Formality in Quality Planning, above.

Defect prevention: Project identification, diagnosis of causes, prevention

Quality motivation: Product information, exhibits, error cause removal suggestion, analysis of operator error causes, remedy

Manpower: Recruitment, selection, training, qualification

Statistical methodology: Process capability studies, sampling tables, control charts, other statistical tools

Data systems (recording, summary, analysis, reporting) covering all the foregoing activities

Technological Sections. These deal with the numerous materials, processes, components, products, tests, etc., which are special to the company. Usually these sections are intradepartmental in nature, and often the publications are not in the company manual but in separate departmental manuals.

Evolution of the Manual. The predecessors of an organized manual are a wide assortment of memoranda, instructions, marked prints, and other bits of information. These have multiple origins and end up in desk drawers, filing cabinets, people's heads, and wastebaskets. As these things multiply, so does the job of finding authoritative information. Finally a state is reached where the company concludes that a more orderly approach is needed.

The moving force for the first quality control manual is usually the Quality Control Manager. In consequence, the first manual also tends to be mainly departmental in nature and to emphasize procedures for improving the effectiveness of the Quality Control Department rather than for optimizing company performance. However, as evolution proceeds, the manual tends to expand into all activities which affect fitness for use.[27]

For some companies, the decisive factor in moving from a narrow- to a broad-based manual has been a determined customer, notably the military. The following provision in MIL-Q-9858A is pertinent:

3.3 Work Instructions. The quality program shall insure that all work affecting quality . . . shall be prescribed in clear and complete documented instructions. . . .

Department of Defense criteria for a quality manual are implied in Handbook H50 (formerly H110), "Evaluation of a Contractor's Quality Program."[28] This handbook refers to MIL-Q-9585A, "Quality Program Requirements," from which the above paragraph is pertinent.

National Aeronautics and Space Administration criteria for quality manuals appear in NHB 5300.4 (1B) "Quality Program Provisions for Aeronautical and Space System Contractors"[29] (formerly NPC 200-2).

As the company grows and breaks up into divisions which are themselves autonomous businesses, the bulk of the procedures are contained in divisional manuals. However, there evolves a corporate quality control manual which contains corporate quality policies, corporate organization, interdivisional quality procedures, and other matters of a corporate or interdivisional nature.

---

[27] For some case examples of evolution of a quality manual see Holmes, J., Quality Manuals, *Quality,* pp. 102–105, Winter 1968. also Erhardt, C. C., How to Prepare a Quality Control Manual, *Industrial Quality Control,* pp. 349–352, January 1965. For a discussion of format, see Fleischhauer, F. W., Quality Writing for QA People, *Quality Assurance,* pp. 32–34, June 1966.

[28] Superintendent of Documents, U.S. Government Printing Office, Washington, D.C. 20402.

[29] Superintendent of Documents, U.S. Government Printing Office, Washington, D.C. 20402.

(Departmental procedures or manuals are not discussed in the foregoing. Instead, they are treated in the specialized Sections of this Handbook.)

How to distribute the quality control manual is a tailor-made decision. Where the manual becomes bulky, it is common to prepare tables showing which departments are to be on the mailing list for which section. It is common practice to provide vendors with that part of the manual dealing with vendor relations. Many companies who sell to a few large customers follow the practice of dressing up certain sections of the manual and giving copies to these customers (and prospective customers) as a sales promotion device.

PROVISION FOR AUDIT

Any well-designed plan includes provisions for reviewing results to see whether the execution follows the plan. Sometimes these provisions are written into the plans themselves; e.g., the quality control manual may stipulate that there shall be an annual review of execution versus plan. More usually, there is a separate "plan" for audit, sometimes informal, sometimes formal.

On examination, the term "audit" turns out to have multiple meanings. Applied to quality planning, two of these meanings are vital:

1. Audit to see if the quality plans are adequate to achieve the quality goals of the company

2. Audit to see if the execution follows the plans

These are discussed in Section 21, under the headings Audit of Quality Plans and Audit of Execution versus Plan.

WHO PLANS?

Responsibility for planning must be distinguished from responsibility for execution, i.e., carrying out the tasks listed in the plan. Table 6-2 and Figure 6-2 are examples of allocation of responsibility for execution. In contrast, Table 6-6 is an example of responsibility for planning.

It is evident from Table 6-6 and from Figure 2-2 (the Spiral) that all departments contribute to quality planning. These departmental contributions remain even when the company grows in size and complexity. The change that takes place is the emergence of company or divisional[30] specialists and specialist departments to do the work of drafting the plan, coordinating, publishing, etc.

The presence of two sets of planners (departmental and company) requires careful management to channel the potential competition into useful directions. The various planners represent departments which possess different skills, are subject to different forces, and pursue different priorities as to the list of parameters to be optimized. These differences logically lead to contesting views among the planners.

To orchestrate these departmental plans into a harmonious whole, use is made of several concepts and tools:

1. Responsibilities for planning, execution, and audit are clearly separated so that the "line" departments retain exclusive jurisdiction over the activity most im-

---

[30] In the "civilian" industries, the term "division" designates a subcompany profit center which has a continuing life based on a continuing product line. In the aerospace and defense industries, a subcompany profit center is often specially created for a specific program or project and will have a life concurrent with the life of the project. The resulting "division" will be given a degree of autonomy comparable to the civilian division, including its own Quality Control organization.

TABLE 6-6 Who Plans?

Subject matter of quality planning	Collect information; draft plan	Review, modify, coordinate†	Final approval	Publish, maintain
Procedures for routine projects*	Procedures specialists; quality specialists	Line department managers, Quality Manager, Procedures Manager	General Manager	Procedures Department
Major projects for change (includes new major product planning)	Project engineers	Line department managers; Project Manager	General Manager	Project Management Department
Reliability	Reliability engineers or project engineers	Line department managers, Quality Manager, Project Manager	General Manager	Reliability Engineering Department or Project Management Department
Annual quality program	Quality control engineers; line departments	Line department managers, Quality Manager, upper management	Top management	Quality Control Department
Quality Control Manual	Quality control engineers	Line department managers, Quality Manager	General Manager	Quality Control Department

* These procedures commonly include other functions in addition to quality.
† For elaboration on alternatives to coordination, see Sec. 7, under Coordination of the Quality Function.

portant to them, i.e., the execution of the plans. This is accomplished by the following table of delegation:

Activity	Line department	Staff-level department
Prepare quality plan........	X	X
Execute plan	X	...
Audit execution vs. plan	...	X

2. Detailed tables of responsibility are prepared to show the primary and contributing responsibilities of all departments. Table 6-2 is an example of such a table in the form of a matrix of activities and departments.

3. Upper management participates in the reviews, not only to provide the benefit of its experience and authority but also to foster a spirit of mutual confidence and emphasis on company goals rather than departmental goals. Through its participation, upper management also identifies any need for clearing up questions of responsibility.

Within limits, the contests among planners are highly productive. In advocating their views, the contesting parties make use of creativity and ingenuity which can be harnessed for the common good. The end result of such contests should be not an answer to "Who is right?" but an optimum for fitness for use.

The departmental planners, as specialists in essential skills and tools, bring to the planning meetings the knowledge of what is feasible in these specialties. The staff-level planners have the role of orchestrating or coordinating for the common good the work of the departmental planners. Being human, the men have honest differences of opinion about what constitutes the common good. However, in a climate of mutual confidence, fostered by the upper management, these differences of opinion can be turned to constructive purposes.

TOOLS FOR QUALITY PLANNERS

Quality planners have evolved numerous tools through which the planning becomes economical as well as effective. Some of the major tools (e.g., the annual quality program, the quality control manual) are discussed as major topics in this Section. Other quality planning tools are discussed in the departmental sections of the Handbook, e.g., design review (Section 8), process capability evaluation (Section 9), vendor surveys (Section 10), quality cost analysis (Section 5), etc.

There are also some universal planning tools which have wide application for breakthrough or control and sometimes for both. Most of these are discussed or exemplified in the present section:

The phase or stage concept for planning.

Pareto analysis to identify the vital few projects or whatever. (See also Section 2, under The Pareto Principle.)

Return on investment analysis to compare the cost of solving a problem with the value of the solution.

Responsibilities matrix for organization planning, e.g., Table 6-2.

The feedback loop for control, e.g., Figure 6-4.

The flow diagram, e.g., Figure 6-5.

The concept of control stations.

Seriousness classification (see Section 12).

Gantt charts, PERT and other tools for controlling the timetable. The Gantt chart

(e.g., Figure 6-2) features equally spaced vertical lines, each space representing three units of measure:
  a. A calendar of equal time units (hours, weeks, etc.)
  b. Equal quantities of *scheduled* work, e.g., pieces, tons, percent completion
  c. Equal quantities of *actual* work [31]

PERT (Program Evaluation Review Technique) goes a step further by evaluating the alternative routes available for completing the project, determining the "critical path," and structuring reviews to keep a close watch on the critical aspects of progress. [32]

A final, fundamental tool is the factual approach. This is the concept of creating factual data to improve decision making. To quote: ". . . who is to take on the role of quality specialist should grasp fully the importance of the factual approach. He becomes an advocate of change in an environment where he may be the least experienced as to the technology. The factual approach is his major tool for raising him to a state of equality in contributing to the problem at hand." [33]

[31] See Juran, J. M., "Managerial Breakthrough," McGraw-Hill Book Company, New York, 1964, pp. 321, 322.

[32] Stilian, Gabriel N., and others, *PERT*, American Management Association, 1962. See also King, Harley L., PERT as Related to Quality Management, *Industrial Quality Control*, pp. 196–197, October 1965.

[33] Juran, J. M., and F. M. Gryna, Jr., "Quality Planning and Analysis," McGraw-Hill Book Company, New York, 1960, p. 15.

Section 7

Organization

J. M. JURAN

INTRODUCTION

Organizing is part of the planning process and is an essential tool for getting work done by human beings. Applied to achieving fitness for use, organizing consists of:

1. Identifying the quality activities or tasks which need to be performed around the Spiral. (See Section 2, Figure 2-2.)

2. Assigning responsibility for performing these activities, whether to internal departments or to outside agencies.

3. Dividing the total work pile up into logical[1] parcels of work, called "jobs."

---

[1] The criteria for what is "logical" will be developed shortly. One universal criterion is that the job contain a collection of duties (in amount and kind) so chosen that it is readily feasible to recruit or train people to perform that collection of duties.

7-1

4. Defining the responsibilities and authorities associated with each job.

5. Defining the relationships of each job to other jobs. These relationships include:

    a. The hierarchical relationships, i.e., the chain of command.

    b. The communication and coordination patterns through which interdepartmental quality activities are coordinated to carry out specific purposes. Since these purposes are multiple, the coordination patterns are likewise multiple.

6. "Orchestrating" the work of internal departments and outside agencies so that the company's quality mission is carried out in an optimum manner.

In this Section, the emphasis is on the overall company organization, not on departmental organization. The latter is dealt with in the departmental sections of the Handbook, e.g., Vendor Relations (Section 10), Inspection and Test (Section 12). However, this Section does deal with the problems of organizing the "staff" quality departments, since none of the departmental Sections is devoted to these problems.

The word "organization" is used to denote two very different aspects of getting work done by human beings:

1. The *structure* resulting from the process in items 1 through 6, above. This is often called the "organization structure" and is discussed in the present Section.

2. The people who "inhabit" the structure. They are often called "manpower" or personnel. The process of making this manpower effective is discussed in Sections 17 and 18.

Organization planners make extensive use of well-known tools, chiefly:

1. The job description, which lists the responsibilities and authorities of a job and its relationships to other jobs. See, for example, Section 17, Figure 17-4.

2. The organization chart, which shows how the lines of authority and responsibility flow from one job to another. See, for example, Section 12, Figures 12-11 through 12-18.

3. The responsibility matrix, showing the interrelation of jobs in interdepartmental activities. See, for example, Section 6, Figure 6-2 and Table 6-2. See also Section 9, Table 9-1.

QUALITY CONTROL WORK ELEMENTS AND JOBS

Achieving fitness for use requires the performance of numerous quality-oriented tasks or quality control "work elements." The Spiral (Section 2, Figure 2-2) makes it evident that many departments inside the company (and agencies outside the company) participate in achieving fitness for use. This participation necessarily requires that they perform quality-oriented tasks.

The List of Elements   A fundamental part of organizing for quality is the identification of the essential quality control work elements and the assignment of clear responsibility for getting them done. The list which follows sets out those principal elements which (in the United States) are usually assigned to departments oriented full-time to the quality function.[2] Because the elements are so numerous, they have been grouped by categories.

1. *Top Management Administration*

Develop company quality policies and major quality objectives.

Develop the overall company quality plan for meeting major objectives.

Design the organization structure needed to carry out the plan.

Design the system of product quality rating, audits, surveillance, and summarized reports needed to provide quality assurance to management.

---

[2] The remaining quality control work elements are discussed in detail in those Sections which deal with the functions performed by the respective departments.

Carry out the program of quality assurance and report the findings to management.

2. *Launching New Products*

Study customer needs for all parameters of fitness for use.

Review past performance of similar products to identify chronic difficulties in manufacture, test, and usage.

Conduct reliability analysis. (This is a whole array of work elements: reliability apportionment, prediction, etc.)

Conduct design review for various purposes: economics of manufacture, maintainability, etc.

Establish environmental test programs to evaluate materials, processes, products.

Conduct inspections and tests of prototypes.

Estimate quality costs for bid proposals and for new designs.

3. *Vendor Relations*

Prepare vendor quality relations manual, including policies, methods, procedures.

Prepare plan for conducting vendor quality relations.

Conduct surveillance and analysis to judge quality competence of prospective vendors.

Assist vendors through seriousness classifications, measurement cross-checks, etc.

Conduct inspection and test of vendor shipments; provide feedback of data.

Rate vendor performance.

4. *Process Control*

Prepare the process control plan for Production as well as for Inspection: choice of control stations, definition of control activities to be conducted at each station, criteria to be used, data feedback systems, etc.

Determine capabilities of processes; disseminate information to all concerned.

Conduct process inspection and surveillance.

Investigate causes of out-of-control conditions; follow to secure corrective action.

Rate performance of production operators where appropriate.

5. *Inspection and Test*

Design the inspection and test plan; choose control stations; define work to be done at each station.

Prepare supplementary standards and criteria as needed, e.g., standards for sensory qualities; standardize test procedures.

Prepare inspection manuals, systems, procedures.

Prepare inspection job specifications; recruit, select and train inspectors.

Conduct inspections and tests in accordance with the plan.

Investigate causes of sporadic defects; report findings; follow up for corrective action.

Initiate action to dispose of nonconforming product.

Prepare and report summaries of results of inspection in appropriate ways: by product, by component, by process, by department responsible, by operator, etc.

Provide for measurement of inspector accuracy.

6. *Metrology*

Design gages, instruments, and test equipment.

Construct or buy measuring equipment.

Maintain calibration of measuring equipment.

Design and administer systems for ensuring maintenance of precision of measuring equipment.

7. *Customer Relations*

Test finished products; evaluate fitness for use.

Evaluate effect of activities which follow final product testing: packing, shipping, transport, storage.

Analyze customer complaints and returns; recommend corrective action.

Survey customers' activities to evaluate service needs, experiences with products, quality costs; secure customers' evaluation of fitness for use versus competing products; discover the opportunities presented.

Analyze competitor product in relation to own product and to fitness for use.

Study economics of quality guarantees; recommend needed revisions.

Design certification plans for assistance to customers.

8. *Special Analysis, Audit, and Consulting*

Conduct analysis of quality costs.

Provide analysis of causes of chronic defects for defect prevention programs.

Coordinate programs of quality motivation.

Provide consulting service on use of statistical methods in design of experiments, analysis of data, sampling plans, reliability analysis, etc.

Design and conduct training programs in various specialties related to quality: quality costs, statistical methods, reliability, inspection, etc.

Published lists of quality control work elements are usually limited to brief statements of each element. However, some lists provide good elaboration of what is meant by the brief statements.[3] The list published by the American Society for Quality Control[4] is oriented to a concept of a "profession" of Quality Control Engineering, and this orientation has influenced the choice of elements to enter the list.

Assignment of Responsibility   The work elements may be assigned to several categories of organization units.

1. *"Non-QC" Departments.*   For example:

Work element	Assigned to
Choose design tolerance	Design
Measure product to see if the production process is under control	Production
Remedy field failures under warranty	Service
Decide whether to conduct a quality improvement program	Upper Management

2. *"Line" Quality Control Departments.*   An example is the task of inspection and test, which is so time-consuming that many people are assigned to it full-time; i.e., the job consists of one task.

3. *"Staff" Quality Control Departments.*   These tasks are mainly of a planning and analysis nature. In the United States, they are usually assigned to full-time quality specialists, e.g., quality control engineers.

4. *Outside Agencies.*   Still other quality-oriented tasks are assigned to be performed by vendors, users, service shops, and others.

Whether these elements are assigned to non-QC departments depends largely on:

1. The extent to which these departments have been trained (or are willing to be trained) to perform the work elements.

2. The prior record of initiative or resistance of these departments in responding to new ways.

3. The traditions with respect to separating planning from execution and use of staff versus line. These traditions have a built-in momentum and vary remarkably among companies, industries, and nations.

4. The volume of the work. As the company grows in size and complexity, the staff departments tend to proliferate.

[3] See, for example, Purcell, Warren R., Quality Cost Control, *Industrial Quality Control*, pp. 22–26, May 1962.

[4] The Basic Work Elements of Quality Control Engineering, *American Society for Quality Control*, 1961.

Structuring Jobs   A job is the "bundle of work" assigned to one person.   The bundle may consist of various mixtures of work elements, as for example:

When the contents of the bundle of work consists:	*The resulting job is called:*
Solely of a single quality control work element, e.g., inspection, test	Inspector, Tester, etc.
Solely of multiple quality control work elements	Quality Control Engineer, Reliability Engineer, etc.
Mainly of non-QC elements plus a minority of quality control work elements	Designer, Production Operator, etc.

While jobs are structured with a view toward stability and toward fitting into a career pattern (see Section 17), the elements which make up the job are not stable. The advance of technology creates new elements and makes old ones obsolete. In addition, elements are frequently transferred from one job to another.[5]   A test which once could be performed only by specialists in a laboratory may be turned over to production operators due to the advent of a simplified instrument.   The task of computing mean time between failures, once performed by reliability engineers, may be turned over, following a training program, to designers.

Because of the mobility and mortality of work elements, there are constant discussions on how to make the assignment.   For example, the work element "Design test equipment" might logically be assigned to a line manager (inspection supervisor), an existing staff specialty (quality control engineer), or a new staff specialty (test equipment engineer).   The choice depends as much on the record of each department in carrying out its assignments to date as on organization theory.   Managers tend to give assignments to men who have demonstrated that they get results. As a corollary, managers do not assign new duties to men whose record is mediocre, no matter how "logical" it would look on the organization chart.   If necessary, related duties will be divided, new departments will be created, and organization charts will be distorted rather than giving important new duties to men who have a record of poor performance.

A further problem in assignment of quality control work elements is competition among staff departments.   This problem is discussed below, under Staff Quality Control Departments.

EVOLUTION OF THE QUALITY CONTROL HIERARCHY

Any major industrial function acquires recognition in the form of status on the organization chart and leadership from a member of the management team.   During the twentieth century, the quality function attained this status through an evolution which is still in progress.

Organization for Inspection   The first major step in this evolution was the formation of the Central Inspection Department.   Section 12, under Organization for Inspection and Test, describes this step in some detail.   It consisted mainly of creation of a hierarchy of inspection supervisors to direct the work of the scattered inspectors. These supervisors headed up to the new post of Chief Inspector, as did auxiliary

---

[5] Ford Motor Company makes use of modular definitions of "quality control functions" as the building blocks for organization structure.   There are over a hundred of these numbered activities which collectively define the work needed to achieve quality control.   Aside from their use in defining the activities themselves, the modules are ingeniously used in design of organization.   The responsibilities for a department consist merely of a listing of the numbers of those activity modules which have been assigned to that department.

activities such as the measurement laboratory and the disposition of nonconforming products.

Creation of the Inspection Department required also an answer to the question, "To whom should the Chief Inspector report?" The usual solution was to make him responsible to the Factory Manager (see Section 12, Figure 12-12), though there were variations in detail (Figures 12-15 and 12-16).

In the United States, the concept of the central Inspection Department was widely adopted in the two decades following World War I. By the early 1940s, the majority of industrial companies had adopted this concept.

Organization for Prevention   World War II required that industry make a drastic shift from civilian to military production. Many companies encountered problems in meeting delivery schedules, and a major obstacle was failure to meet quality specifications. It became dramatically evident that what was missing was the means for preventing defects from happening in the first place.

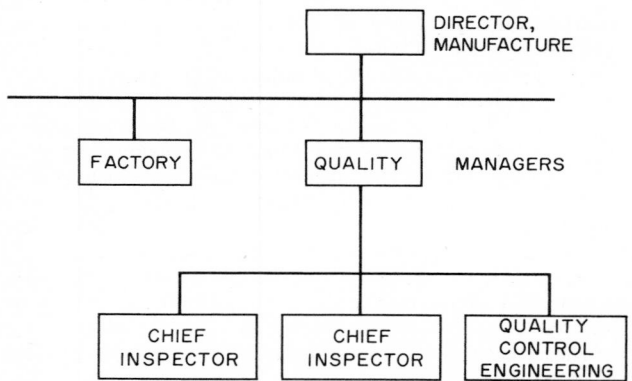

Fig. 7-1   Organization for prevention, mechanical and electronic industries.

Quality Control Engineering. After some experimentation, there emerged, in the 1950s, a new department created to conduct quality planning and analysis, especially for defect prevention. This department came to be known as Quality Control Engineering.[6]

It became necessary to locate the new department somewhere on the organization tree. To do this, there was created a new post of Quality Manager (or Quality Control Manager) to which the Chief Inspector, the new department (Quality Control Engineering), and the associated services now reported.[7] Figure 7-1 shows the resulting organization chart. This was the majority organization form adopted in the mechanical and electronic industries.

The process industries evolved differently. In these industries, inspection for nonfunctional qualities (e.g., appearance) had commonly been done by inspectors responsible to the Production Department. However, the functional testing and the process controls had commonly been done by a laboratory which was responsible to

[6] Many of these departments were created during a period of great enthusiasm for statistical methodology as a means for solving quality problems, and their names reflected this, e.g., Statistical Quality Control Department. When this enthusiasm went to excesses, it was necessary to rename such departments.

[7] For a case history, see Dale, Everett H., Effective Reorganization of the Inspection Function, *15th Annual Convention Transactions,* ASQC, pp. 537-545, 1961.

the Technical Department.   In consequence, when the new departments of Quality Control Engineering were created in the process industries, they were located in the Technical Department, the precise location being either (1) reporting to the Manager of Process Development (see Figure 7-2) or (2) reporting to a newly created post of Quality Manager, to whom also reported the traditional Laboratory (see Figure 7-3).

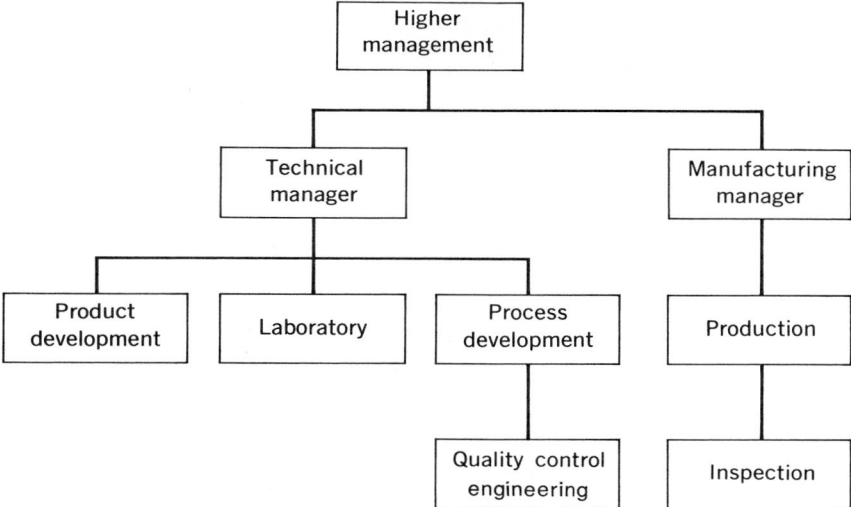

Fig. 7-2   Organization form, process industries.

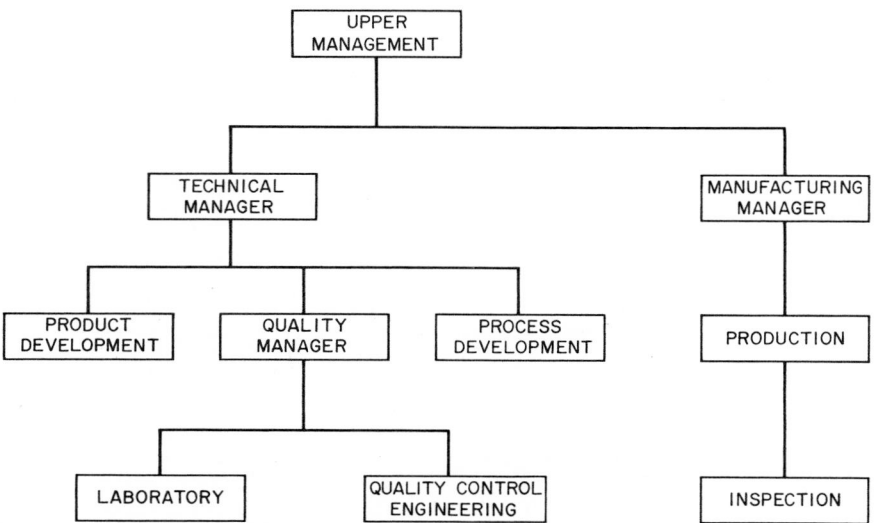

Fig. 7-3   Alternative organization form, process industries.

Reliability Engineering.   During the 1950s a number of companies were faced with new problems of designing and building complex systems to levels of reliability well beyond usual practice.   Traditional approaches to product development and design soon proved inadequate—the field failure rates were unacceptable.   One consequence was the rise of a new type of specialist known as a "Reliability Engineer."   These engineers recommended that a separate department be created for them, and the managers usually accepted this recommendation.   The activities of this department and its internal organization forms are discussed below, under Staff Quality Control Departments—Reliability Engineering.

Several alternatives were tried for locating the work of reliability engineering on

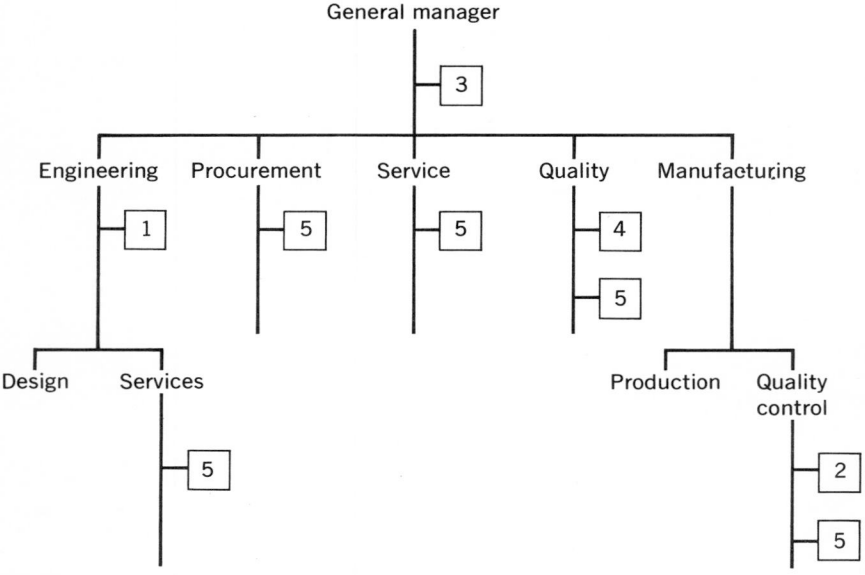

Fig. 7-4   Organization alternatives for location of reliability engineering.

the organization chart.   Figure 7-4 shows these alternatives graphically.   Table 7-1 shows the comparative advantages and disadvantages of these organization forms.[8]

Organization for Assurance   The term "assurance" is used here in the limited sense of determining with confidence that the company's quality mission is being well carried out.   For a more extended discussion of the meanings of "quality assurance," see Section 2, under Quality Assurance.   See also Section 21, under Quality Assurance—General.

The managers of small enterprises secured this assurance from personal contact, e.g., personal examination of the products and processes.   As the enterprises grew,

[8] For a good discussion on grouping reliability activities into logical categories, see Management Aspects of Reliability, *Industrial Quality Control,* July 1967, pp. 34–36.   This is a document developed by a committee of the International Electrotechnical Commission.   See also Sternberg, Alexander, Basic Tools of Reliability, *Journal of the Electronics Division,* ASQC, pp. 15–20, June 1965.   See also Barr, Phil I., and James Rusk, Jr., *Effectiveness Planning for Reliability Programs: 1964 Western Region Conference,* ASQC, pp. 165–174.

TABLE 7-1   Reliability Engineering Organization Forms—Advantages and Disadvantages*

Organization Form	Advantages	Disadvantages
1. Reporting to director of engineering	Easy to coordinate with design activities	Difficult to coordinate with manufacturing and quality control activities
2. Reporting to quality control manager	Easy to coordinate with manufacturing quality problems	Difficult to coordinate with design activities (often not accepted by designers)
3. Reporting to general manager	Can influence policy formation and objectives for reliability and quality control	Receives little effective supervision; too far removed from the action level, especially in large organizations
4. Separate major company department	On policy making and goal setting level; can influence work along entire "spiral." Simplifies coordination among quality specialists	Difficult to coordinate with work of line departments unless they have been well trained in the specialties
5. Decentralized among line departments, coordinated by a separate quality staff department	Access to policy making and goal setting in all departments; access to department heads for dealing with unreliable products; greater likelihood of acceptance by line departments	Difficult to coordinate the scattered reliability activities into a coherent plan; risk that specialists will be assigned to sporadic rather than chronic problems

* From J. M. Juran and F. M. Gryna Jr., "Quality Planning and Analysis," McGraw Hill Book Company, New York, 1970, p. 157.

this personal contact was delegated to intermediate supervisors and to inspectors, thereby depriving the upper managers of "assurance through personal observation." For many years, the upper managers derived their assurance from their confidence in these supervisors and inspectors, but without creating a substitute for the former "independent" assurance (through personal observation). However, it became progressively evident that some form of independent assurance was essential, so a search began for new forms of such assurance.

One form of such assurance now in wide use requires prior preparation of detailed quality plans plus subsequent reviews and audits to establish that (1) the plans are adequate, and (2) the plans are being followed.[9]   The organization structure through which this is accomplished is as follows:

Activities	Line departments	Staff quality departments	
		Quality planning	Quality assurance
Prepare the quality plans	X	X	. . .
Execute the plans.	X	. . .	. . .
Audit to see whether the execution follows the plans.	. . .	. . .	X

[9] For a detailed discussion of the approach to quality assurance, see Section 21, under Quality Assurance: General *et seq.*

Use of this plan of delegation retains for the line departments the full command of their personnel while providing for independent reviews of plans and execution.

Where to locate the assurance job[10] on the organization chart has been debated exhaustively, mainly on the question of "independence." Ideally, those engaged in providing quality assurance should not be subordinate to any manager whose work is itself under review. In theory, this requires that the assurance job should report to the General Manager. In practice, such an arrangement means that the assurance job receives no supervision. In consequence, the usual practice is to make the assurance job subordinate to the Quality Manager (Figure 7-5).

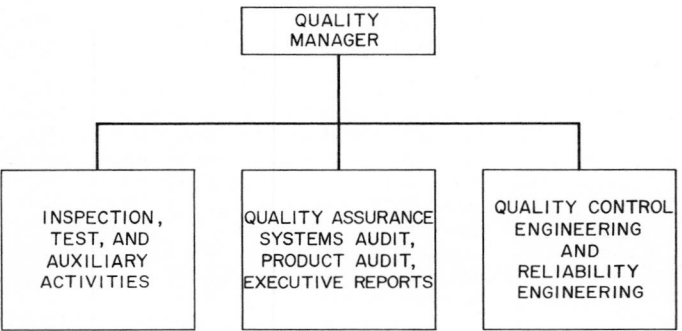

Fig. 7-5 Organization location for quality assurance.

Only a very small staff is needed to provide assurance (that the quality plan is adequate and is being followed). However, if the word "assurance" is used in its broader meanings (see Section 21, under Quality Assurance: General), the staff can increase considerably.

The Broad-based Quality Control Department While a department called "Quality Control" (or Quality and Reliability, Quality Assurance, etc.) is found in all but very small companies, the job assigned to these departments varies remarkably from one company to another. Table 7-2 lists, in the approximate historical sequence of evolution, the activities which may be assigned to such departments. Table 7-2 also indicates whether the usual responsibility of the Quality Control Department is one of command, analysis, planning, coordination, etc.

In those cases where virtually the entire list of these activities is assigned to a broad-based Quality Control Department, the departmental organization is arranged in a manner similar to that shown in Figure 7-6.

The broader the base of the Quality Control Department, the higher is its stature on the organization chart. A department such as is depicted in Figure 7-6 commonly reports to the General Manager of the company or the Division. In such cases the head of the department carries an important title, e.g., Vice President for Quality, Director of Quality, etc. More usually, these departments are more narrowly based, in which case they report to one of the vice presidents (usually, Manufacture or Technical). A usual title for the heads of such departments is Quality Manager.[11]

[10] The term "assurance job" is used here as a label for the department assigned to provide quality assurance. A reasonable title would be "Quality Assurance Department." However, some organizations use this title to designate the entire full-time central department concerned with all aspects of the quality function. See Section 2, under Quality Assurance.

[11] For an elaboration of the role of this manager, see Section 17, under Quality Managers.

TABLE 7-2   Activities Assigned to Quality Control Departments

Activity	Usual responsibility	See Section
Product inspection; Final; Process; Vendor	Command	12
Measurement control	Command	13
Field complaint analysis	Analysis	15
Quality planning	Coordination	6
Inspection planning	Command	12
Statistical methodology	Consulting; analysis	22–28
Process control	Planning; assurance	11
Defect prevention programs	Planning; coordination	16
Analysis of causes of defects	Analysis; consulting	16
Vendor surveillance	Planning; assurance	10
Quality cost analysis	Planning; analysis	5
New product reviews; reliability; other abilities	Analysis; consulting	6, 8
Motivational programs	Planning; coordination	18
Assurance	Planning; analysis	21
In process of evolution		
Quality policies and objectives	Coordination	3
Annual quality program	Analysis; coordination	6
Organization studies	Analysis; coordination	7
Customer viewpoint; Consumerism; Product liability	Analysis; coordination	4, 14
Quality income studies	Analysis	4, 14
Executive reports	Analysis; coordination	21
Inspection by operators	Analysis; audit	11
Government controls on quality	Coordination	4
Training for quality—all levels, functions	Planning; coordination	17

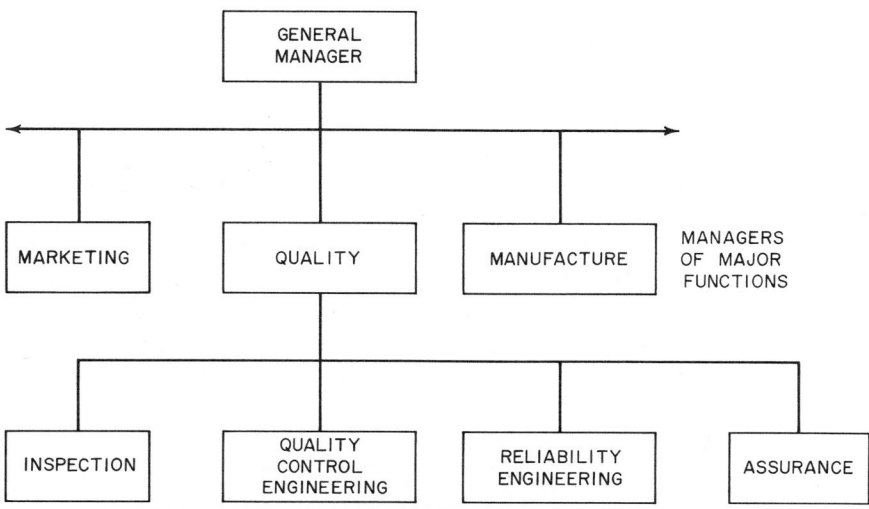

Fig. 7-6   Organization of broad-based Quality Control Department.

Nomenclature It is evident from the foregoing that the activities carried out by the department central to the quality function have varied over the years and that the evolutionary process is likely still going on. In such situations it is difficult to standardize on a name for the department, since a static name does not reflect the dynamic changes in responsibility. The human drive for status has added to the confusion, since departmental titles are coined to derive status as well as to describe the activities performed.

The result has been a continuing change in the nomenclature used to designate the central department: Inspection, Quality Control, Quality and Reliability, Quality Assurance. In some companies it is not possible to discover, from the nomenclature, what the activities of the department are. Instead, it is necessary to make this discovery from the deeds being performed.

Loose use of nomenclature inevitably causes confusion among several overlapping concepts requiring terminology:

The deeds (or the work elements) needed to achieve fitness for use
The names of these deeds
The titles of the men who perform these deeds
The names of the departments to which these men are assigned

Only as these very different concepts are clearly designated can the nomenclature serve its intended purpose of conveying complex ideas through simple wording.[12]

THE QUALITY CONTROL HIERARCHY IN PRACTICE

The structure of the quality control hierarchy varies considerably with the size of the organization, the geographical locations[13] of its component units, the nature of the product, etc. Several of the more usual situations are listed below, along with the associated hierarchical structure.

The One-Location Profit Center In its simplest form, the Quality Control Department serves as one of the functional departments in a moderate-sized company operating in a single location as a single "profit center," i.e., only the General Manager has true profit responsibility.

As companies grow and grow, this functional form becomes unwieldy. In its place there evolve a number of autonomous Divisions. Each of these Divisions conducts a significant segment of the company's business. Each is relatively independent of other Divisions (by virtue of differences in product line, market area, etc.). Each reports to a General Manager who is given responsibility for the profit performance of the Division and who is also given the command over those personnel whose activities determine whether the Division profit goals are met.

This concept of the autonomy of the Division is decisive as to the divisional organization for quality. The divisional General Manager is given command over his own quality control personnel, since these do strongly influence the Division's performance. In consequence, each Division has a Division Quality Manager who is responsible to the Division General Manager, either directly or through an intermediate official.

Single-Plant Organization Where the company or Division is housed in one location, it is convenient and usual to give the Quality Control Department command

---

[12] See in this connection Juran, J. M., Activities and Labels; Functions and Names, *Industrial Quality Control*, pp. 248–250, November 1967; see also Section 2, under A Wistful Postscript on Terminology.

[13] For added discussion on hierarchical structure, as used in other countries, see Sections 48 and 48A.

over the inspectors and the support activities. The Quality Manager is regularly on the scene and is available for day-to-day participation in questions of product quality. There can be debate over whether he should command the inspectors, but there is no effective debate on whether day-to-day decisions are being held up due to an absentee Quality Manager.

Multiple-Plant Organization In many profit centers (companies or autonomous Divisions of companies) the work of manufacture is conducted in multiple plants, each physically separated from the rest. Being physically separated, each plant is equipped with its own laboratory for conducting process control and product acceptance. There has been much debate over whether these laboratories should be responsible to:

1. The local plant manager. Advocates of this plan point to the need of giving the plant manager the authority for making day-to-day decisions without intervention by nonresident managers.

2. The headquarters (company or divisional) Quality Manager. Advocates of this plan are concerned that a plant manager faced with meeting today's delivery and cost standards will do so at a sacrifice in quality.

When the plants are "related" to each other through common markets, common product lines, etc., the usual organization form is to divide the work according to the following well-known formula:

Activity	Plant	Headquarters Quality Control
Prepare the quality plan	X	X
Execute the plan	X	. . .
Audit the execution vs. plan . . .	. . .	X

Under this concept:

1. A quality plan is drafted for the approval of both the plant and Headquarters Quality Control.

2. The laboratories which are to execute the plan are made responsible to the respective plant managers.

3. The Headquarters Quality Control is required to audit this execution.

In such an arrangement, it becomes important to define with precision what is included in the term "audit." It is quite usual for the audit to include:

1. Review of the data on product quality as found by the plant laboratory. To this end, summaries of the plant data are sent regularly to headquarters. (The data plan is organized to provide ready summaries from the basic data.)

2. Test of duplicate samples to provide "audit of decisions."[14] For this purpose, the plant laboratory sends samples to headquarters under an agreed plan.

3. Surveillance of plant and laboratory quality activities and conditions. This is done by periodic visits of headquarters personnel to the plant.

4. Quarantine of nonconforming lots. Under this concept, conforming lots (the great majority) remain under the jurisdiction of the plant laboratory. However, once a lot is discovered to be nonconforming, the jurisdiction for determining whether the lot is fit for use is transferred to Headquarters Quality Control. The transfer is formalized by executing a "Hold" document. Thereafter, Headquarters Quality Control arranges for disposition of the lot under a procedure similar to that used by a Material Review Board (see Section 12).

---

[14] See Section 10, under Audit of Decisions. See also Section 11, under Product Acceptance by Operators.

Multiple-Division Organization[15] Any divisional profit-center is autonomous on matters of quality control. However, if the divisions have sufficient community of interest, there is a need for interdivisional coordination.[16] The community of interest may arise from the fact that the divisions:

Sell their products in the same or overlapping markets
Sell under the same company name or brand
Make components which will enter the same final product
Employ common technology

Organizing a useful form of coordination among divisions requires a good deal of tact because the division general managers resist any invasion of their autonomous status. The more usual forms of interdivisional coordination include:
1. Simple "crisis coordination" through direct contact between divisional general

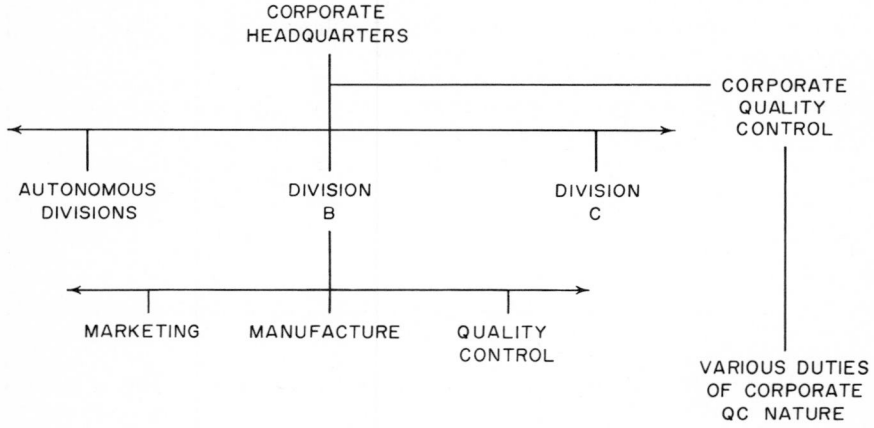

Fig. 7-7 Organization in multidivision companies featuring corporate quality staff.

managers or divisional quality managers as problems arise.
2. A broader informal coordination through the "senior" quality manager.[17] This informal coordinator acts as a sounding board for other quality managers, and he usually has access to top management.
3. A formal council of quality managers. An example is seen in the Quality Assurance Council of IBM Corporation.[18] This council identifies critical common problems and stimulates steps to be taken for their solution.
4. A corporate quality control staff. See Figure 7-7, and discussion below.
Intercompany Organization The most usual need for such organization is in large complex systems requiring extensive subcontracting. In such cases the prime con-

[15] See, in this connection, Section 6, under Multidivision and Intercompany Planning.
[16] In some divisionalized companies — the so-called "conglomerates" — there is no community of interest among the divisions except that of finance. In such cases there is no real need for interdivisional coordination on quality matters; the divisions retail full autonomy.
[17] The "seniority" may be based on one of several grounds: He is quality manager at the oldest division or at the largest division. He is the ranking quality manager in age, or in service, or in service as a quality manager.
[18] Charles W. Law, Standardization of Quality Assurance Practices in a Decentralized Corporation, *Industrial Quality Control*, December 1964, pp. 294–297.

tractor engages various subcontractors to design and build the subsystems which are to enter the total system.

For such undertakings the job for coordination is so extensive that conventional collaboration among the companies does not do the job. Instead, there is need to create a new organization whose main job is coordination. This organization, often called "Program Management," is discussed in Section 44, Complex Systems.

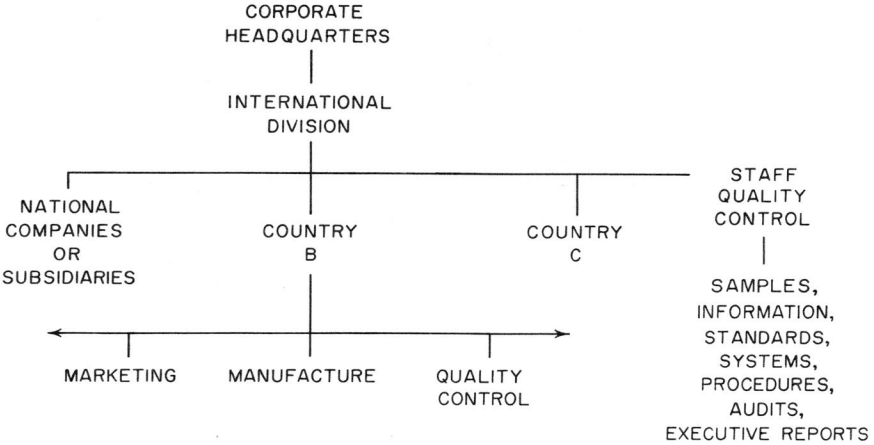

Fig. 7-8 Multinational organization for quality.

Multinational Organization   Some companies conduct their international operations through local subsidiaries. For reasons of local legislation on ownership, employee relations, taxation, etc., these subsidiaries are given a high degree of autonomy in conducting their operations. However, there are important linkages to the parent company in quality matters:

Much of the technology originates with the parent company.

The products are sold in overlapping markets, requiring a policy of international quality standards.

The subsidiaries develop know-how which needs to be shared by all.

To disseminate quality specifications and know-how and to provide a form of quality assurance, the usual practice is to create an international quality staff at company headquarters. (Figure 7-8). This staff has responsibility for:

Developing quality specifications and standards needed for international operation

Disseminating information to and among the subsidiaries

Auditing performance of the subsidiaries by appropriate means: analysis of quality reports, check of product samples, surveillance visits, etc.

Preparing and publishing executive reports on quality performance and problems

COORDINATION OF THE QUALITY FUNCTION

Coordination is the orchestration of the various quality activities around the Spiral (Section 2, Figure 2-2) into a harmonious, optimum result. In tiny companies it is simple to achieve this orchestration. In large companies it is increasingly complex, since:

Many of the activities needed to achieve fitness for use take place outside of the manufacturing company.

Other activities take place within the company but are scattered among numerous separate departments, each of which is engaged in meeting multiple goals.

The various men involved have departmental and personal goals which may take priority over fitness for use and even become antagonistic to fitness for use.

There is a range of alternatives for coordination. While there is a good deal of flexibility in the choice, the most important need is to provide a positive mechanism for coordination rather than leaving it to chance.

The principal forms used for coordination are discussed below.

The Common Boss. In small companies this is a natural and effective method. Through his knowledge of the general needs of the business, the boss can identify the quality needs (objectives), and determine how these needs should be met (plans). Through direct access to all employees, the boss can issue orders to perform those deeds which carry out his plans. Then, through this same access, he can observe to see whether the orders have been executed and whether the results have been obtained.

As the company grows, its size and complexity reach a stage such that the common boss can no longer maintain this intimate personal contact with all the people and deeds. If the boss is to continue to coordinate, he must create the tools which are a substitute for face-to-face contact: (1) the Annual Quality Program (Section 6) or other impersonal form of coordination and (2) the executive reports on quality (Section 21) or other reports of progress against plan.

If such supplementary tools are not created, then the boss loses his ability to coordinate, and coordination must be done in other ways.

Self-Coordination. Where there is no organized provision for coordination, there may well be no orchestration either, since no legitimate leadership has been established. By default, it is left on a basis of every department for itself. Despite such default, leadership may arise in the middle and lower management levels on the basis "If orchestration isn't provided by upper management, let's provide it right here."

Sometimes this leadership is successful, and through this success achieves legitimacy as well. More usually, self-coordination is successful only in dealing with "fires." Some sporadic trouble flares up, and the managers converge on the scene to solve the resulting acute problem. However, the chronic problems go on and on because there are no alarm signals to urge the managers to converge on the scene.

Committees. Industry makes extensive use of committees for orchestrating the quality function. Usually these committees deal with specific programs or projects, as for example:

Need for coordination is on the subject of:	*Coordinating committee is usually called:*
Disposing of nonconforming products	Material Review Board (see Section 12)
Reviewing new product designs	Design Review Committee (see Section 8)
Quality improvement	Quality Improvement Committee (see Section 16)
Improving motivation for quality	Quality Motivation Committee (see Section 18)

There may also be other committees on a companywide basis, depending on special needs such as product standardization, engineering changes, etc. In addition, the launching of a new activity—e.g., Quality Cost Analysis, Annual Quality Program — is commonly aided by creating committees to help guide it through its formative period.

The membership of these committees usually consists of managers whose full-time job is something else. Their committee assignments normally demand little time, because the staff specialists (who are also the committee secretaries) do the detailed fact collecting and analysis.

Precedent. Both in and out of the company, precedent plays a vital role in coordination. From numerous prior meetings, from pronouncements and actions of executives, and from successes and failures in solving problems, there arises a set of habit patterns. These habit patterns take root and create numerous vested interests in the form of status, authority, rights, seniority, etc. In turn, these vested interests act to formalize the habit patterns so that the various "rights" are officially recognized.

The great strength of precedent as a means for coordination lies in its predictability. The great weakness lies in the fact that precedent has evolved from old premises which may no longer be valid, from the personalities of people who are no longer on the job, from lack of knowledge which may since have been acquired. For reasons such as these, it is a risky thing to continue old patterns indefinitely. The swifter the pace of change in the company, the more rapidly do these patterns become obsolete.

Written Procedure. The use of written procedure presupposes that means have been created for preparing written procedure. These means are in themselves a coordination device.

Written procedure serves some vital purposes:

1. Before something is written out, it must first be thought through. Often the first time a procedure is written out is also the first time it has been thought through.

2. Before a written procedure is approved, there must be a meeting of the minds of the departments involved. Such a meeting of the minds is better assured from review of a written procedure than from oral understandings.

3. A written procedure guards against drifts of memory, provides for easier training of new people, and serves as a source of reference.

It is seen that a written procedure becomes a perpetual coordination device. It gives impersonal supervision by offering the optimum solution of the repetitive company problem. It has predictability and tends to engender a sense of law and order.

However, written procedure has its disadvantages:

1. It tends to become static, since many companies fail to provide adequate machinery for review and maintenance of procedure.

2. It provides for the usual situations. When unusual situations arise, they may well be handled in the usual way, with resulting blunders.

3. It can result in an attitude which stresses attention to the procedure rather than to the problems the procedure was designed to solve. In large organizations, whether private or public, this unimaginative devotion to procedure is known as "bureaucracy."

Staff Specialists. They can be very useful in coordination because they possess the time and skills needed to collect information from all parts of the Spiral (Section 2, Figure 2-2), analyze this information, draft proposals, and present these proposals to the line managers as an aid to decision making. A common example is use of a Quality Control Engineer for conducting quality planning or for Material Review Board studies.

An extension of the concept is the use of the project manager for new-product introduction. A project manager, usually from Engineering, is designated to guide the project not only through development and design but often on into manufacture and sometimes on into marketing and use. During the development phases the project manager may have jurisdiction of the assigned engineers as well as the budget for the project. For smaller projects the coordinator may be a small team or even one man, the project engineer.[19]

Use of staff quality specialists creates its own problems of coordination because the staff specialist usually possesses special training and is strongly oriented to his specialty. Yet his work must be coordinated with that of line managers who lack this special training and who are oriented to different functions and goals. The greater the difference in training and in orientation, the more difficult is this coordination.

The Staff Department. In some companies the delegation to the Quality Manager authorizes him to play a major role in coordination of the quality function.[20] This role is similar to the role played by the Finance Manager in the finance function. However, this delegation to the Quality Manager is of very recent origin, and is still in a state of evolution. (See Roles of the Quality Control Staff, below.)

Coordination through a staff department is achieved by the well-known approach of separating planning, execution, and audit. The staff drafts the plan, which must be approved by the line departments. Following joint approval, the execution is delegated to the line departments. (This delegation eliminates the bulk of the jurisdictional problems.) However, the staff department follows up by reviewing results to see whether the execution is in accordance with plan.

Tools for Coordination. Aside from the use of positive coordination machinery, there are many forms of coordination associated with the development of various tools of quality management: quality policies, the annual quality program, objectives and plans to meet them, executive reports, quality surveys and audits. These tools are the result of coordinated effort, and, once in use, they provide further coordination by the fact of use.

STAFF QUALITY CONTROL DEPARTMENTS

In this Handbook, the "line" (or "operating") departments are those without which the enterprise cannot exist, e.g., Marketing, Manufacture.[21] The remainder are "staff" departments which, while not vital to the existence of the enterprise, can be important to its efficient operation.

The work carried out by staff departments includes some well-known activities. Examples of these, and their counterparts in the quality functions, are set out in Table 7-3.

In practice, staff quality control departments engage in all the types of activities defined in Table 7-3. However, while the department may live on and on, the individual services or specialties keep changing much as does the "product line" of the company. The constant need to modernize its "product line" is one of the most difficult problems faced by staff departments.

Birth of a New Specialty A new staff specialty originates in one of two major ways:

1. New concepts are evolved to assist study and solution of long-standing problems, e.g., breakthrough concept, quality cost analysis.

---

[19] See, for elaboration, Section 6, under Major Project Planning; also under New-Product Planning.

[20] See also Section 17, under Quality Managers: Roles of the Quality Manager.

[21] It soon becomes evident, on reflection, that staff and line are loose, overlapping concepts which do not admit of precise, simple definition. Those who engage in debate on what is line or staff will commonly do better to devote their time to understanding clearly the deeds and activities under discussion. Once these are clear, the labels do not matter.

2. New tools are developed to do scientifically what has previously been done empirically, e.g., quantification of reliability.

These concepts and tools are tested by venturesome men who then publicize their results. The publicity stimulates other companies to try out the new ways and to

TABLE 7-3 Examples of Staff Quality Activities

Staff department activities	Examples generally	Examples in quality control
Utility service for the line departments	Materials handling; plant maintenance; employee recruitment	Laboratory test services; instrument calibration
Coordination of departmental line activities which contribute to a common plan	Budget preparation; production scheduling	Quality planning; reliability planning
Advisory services to line departments	Legal services; technological expertise	Consulting in statistical methodology, metrology, reliability analysis
Control to see that operations conform to plans	Cost and expense reporting; internal audit	Product inspection; quality audits

create new specialists to do the associated staff work.[22] In turn, the advocates for the new ways sense an opportunity to contribute to the company (and to their own aspirations) at a pace greater than normal The company may respond to their advocacy by establishing a new staff department to provide legitimacy, funds, manpower and other essentials needed to make extended use of the specialty.

Growth Phase If the specialty is successful in its pilot installations, it gains strength and extends itself over more and more areas of application. The aura of such success is not limited to the special method or tool in question, e.g. Evolutionary Operation (EVOP); the aura extends to the entire staff department and to its personnel. As a result, the department tends to attract more assignments. It also receives the benefit of the doubt on new proposals which it makes.[23]

Growth of the department can take place for a variety of reasons:

Extension of the specialties to more and more areas of application

Need for maintenance of new levels of performance as they are attained

Need for continuing support through training of line people, consultation, preparation of procedures and manuals

Added assignments resulting from the aura of success

Maturity Phase This phase is reached when a staff department has established itself as a useful member of the industrial community. At this point its continued existence depends on whether it keeps its product line fresh. This requires that it turn solved problems over to the line department while taking on the job of dealing with unsolved problems.

[22] Sometimes the publicity becomes contagious (a lot of luck enters into this) and grows to national or international proportions through the press, conferences, etc. In such cases upper management may intervene and order a test of the new methods and tools.

[23] The reverse is true if the pilot installation is botched or if the new specialty turns out to be without substance. Not only the new specialty but also the staff department and the men associated with the failure are discredited. In consequence, the department becomes more vulnerable during an economic squeeze.

The staff specialists should take the initiative in simplifying the new tools and in designing the training courses needed to facilitate their adoption by the line people. For example:

Control charts, if widely needed, should be prepared by inspectors, testers, operators, etc., rather than by quality control engineers.

Reliability prediction and allocation, if widely needed, should be done by product designers rather than by reliability engineers.

For the staff to turn activities over to the line people sounds like economic suicide, and it might well be the case in a static society. However, new problems are ever coming over the horizon.[24] These require new tools for solution and provide a basis for the staff specialists to modernize their "product line" as they turn the old, matured tools over to the line departments. To continue "doing business at the old stand," i.e., doing a maintenance job on old tools, is the surest way to decay and death of the staff department.

Evolution of the Quality Control Staff Departments These departments were first created on wide scale during the 1940s.[25] Several stimulants contributed to a wide proliferation of "Statistical Quality Control" departments:

A need for improving quality of production of goods required during World War II
A sudden and extensive growth of interest in the use of statistical methodology to aid quality control
Formation of an American Society for Quality Control (ASQC)

Because these early departments emphasized application of statistical methodology, mathematicians were in demand to carry out this work. Then, as the need for a broader approach became evident, the demand was more for engineers, and especially for Industrial Engineers, whose basic training was at that time especially useful in factory management. As such men moved into the work of quality control, the universal urge for status caused them to press for distinctive titles and job categories. Numerous titles contested for prominence, and by the end of the 1950s the title Quality Control Engineer had emerged as dominant. This was in accord with the emergence of the dominant departmental name of Quality Control Engineering.[26]

Quality Control Engineering The Quality Control Engineers began by using their statistical knowledge to design sampling plans for inspection and control charts for process control. As their experience widened, they learned to redirect their efforts to the broader aspects of quality planning and defect prevention. These redirected efforts involved them with the entire list of quality control "work elements" (see Quality Control Work Elements and Jobs, above) except those concerned with the launching of new products.

To carry out this broad list of work elements required that the Quality Control Engineers learn a good deal about "nonquality" functions of the company. To illustrate:

---

[24] See, for example, Juran, J. M., Mobilizing for the 1970's, *Quality Progress,* August 1969. See also Juran, J. M., A Note on the Mortality of QC Departments, *Industrial Quality Control,* p. 22, February 1961.

[25] However, companies which had long faced severe quality problems had created staff quality control departments much earlier in the century. The author was a member of such a department (in Western Electric Company) in the 1920s.

[26] The overemphasis on statistical methodology resulted, in some companies, in making the name "Statistical Quality Control" a liability.

Activity	Requires some knowledge of the functions of
Field complaint analysis	Sales and Sales Service
Quality cost analysis	Accounting
Motivational programs	Industrial Relations
Vendor surveillance	Purchasing

The resulting broader array of knowledge of company operation has further aided the Quality Control Engineers to identify the main quality problems and to structure their programs in a way which optimizes company rather than departmental performance.

The one major area not invaded by the Quality Control Engineers was that of launching of new products. When the need arose for modernizing this activity to meet the needs of the computer, defense, and aerospace industries, a new specialty, that of the Reliability Engineer, was created.

Reliability Engineering   In response to the urging of these new specialists, many companies, notably in the defense and aerospace industries, created new departments for Reliability Engineering (rather than expanding the scope of the Quality Control Engineering departments). In some companies a single staff department was retained but was renamed, e.g., Quality Control and Reliability Engineering.[27]

The reliability "movement" of the 1950s and 1960s involved development and application of two formalized sets of tools:

1. New *technological* tools for quantifying reliability and for using the resulting numbers in reliability prediction and analysis for systems, subsystems, components, etc. Details of this are discussed in Section 8.

2. New *managerial* tools not only to assure that use was made of the new technology but also to formalize the whole approach to the achievement of reliability through:

Creating an awareness, through publicity and training, of the inherent nature of reliability and of the role played by all departments in achieving reliability.

Establishing a policy of quantifying reliability goals and of measuring achievement against the goals in all phases of product progression, from proposal through usage.

Formal planning of broad reliability programs, including clearly defined tasks, assignment of responsibility to all departments (see Figures 6-2 and 8-3), appropriate budgets, timetables, etc.

Introduction of organized design reviews and other reviews to permit wide participation in the planning and achievement of reliability.

Provision of systems of data collection and analysis, data banks, and other facilities essential for planning and control.

Provision of the staff support needed to draft the plans, conduct the detailed analyses, and coordinate the actions. The Reliability Engineer specialty was created to provide this staff support.

In ultrahigh reliability industries such as aerospace, formal departments for Reliability Engineering are the rule.[28] These departments operate under well-defined statements of responsibility. They make use of formal reliability objectives and

---

[27] The Reliability Engineers exhibited still other professional drives. The annual National Symposium on Reliability and Quality Control was established at a time and place other than the ASQC Annual Technical Conference. However, creation of a competitive professional Society was averted. See, in this connection, Juran, J. M., A Visit to Complex Systems, Inc., *Industrial Quality Control,* pp. 37–40, January 1962.

[28] For discussion of the organization alternatives, see Figure 7-4 and Table 7-1.

time-phased programs. They conduct reviews of customer contract requirements, product specifications, test specifications, and component drawings. They establish reliability requirements, analyze qualification and failure data in all phases of progression of the product, maintain reliability data banks, and provide feedback to the respective line departments.[29]

These activities are carried out for products to be purchased as well as those to be made in-house.

When the total amount of reliability engineering requires the full time of many men, it is common practice to create subdepartments. The groups of tasks assigned to these subdepartments varies, but it is common to see subdepartments assigned to:

Reliability prediction and allocation (or reliability analysis)
Component part engineering
Environmental testing
System evaluation
Field failure analysis and feedback

In the early days of the reliability movement the proposals for reliability "programs" were quite elaborate in their scope. They involved not only the revolutionary concept of quantifying reliability, with all of its technological connotations, but also the creation of a new staff department and realignment of numerous responsibilities, including breakup of previous monopolies of decision making. They demanded extensive documentation, data banks, feedback loops, and other formalities on a scale beyond any prior practice. All this took manpower and money, the budgets being on a scale never even imagined before. Much skepticism and outright resistance had to be overcome to make the new concepts effective.

As experience was acquired in use of the programs, ways were found to moderate the extremes of elaboration. The line departments were able to take over some of the new activities from the staff specialists. Increasingly, means were found to plan for reliability as part of the overall product planning rather than to regard reliability planning as virtually an independent world.

In moderate- and low-reliability industries, the deeds needed to achieve reliability are quite similar to those needed for high-reliability industries. However, the difference in reliability levels (one or more orders of magnitude) permits doing these deeds with a degree of informality which is unacceptable in aerospace or defense projects. (Civilian managers are usually aghast at the costs of reliability programs in aerospace industries.) The reliability engineers are usually in the same department with the quality control engineers. There is less detailed planning and especially less documentation. In addition, the more moderate requirements permit an earlier and easier transfer of activities from the reliability engineers to line department personnel.

Competition between Quality Control Engineers and Reliability Engineers The first proposals to create the new category of Reliability Engineer were contested by the Quality Control Engineers, who felt that the activities in question should be carried out by widening the scope of the Quality Control Engineers. The managers nevertheless proceeded to create a new specialty and gave it responsibilities relative to the launching of new designs and the evaluation of fitness for use in all stages of the product life cycle.[30] The responsibilities of the Quality Control Engineer generally were related to the remaining quality control work elements.

---

[29] For a detailed list of 23 tasks performed, see Johnson, Melbourne D., Reliability Management, *Annual Technical Conference Transactions,* 1965, ASQC, pp. 292–299.

[30] For the results of a survey on various aspects of the work of Reliability departments, see Freedberg, Marvin, Reliability Management, a Survey, *Industrial Quality Control,* pp. 224–226, November 1966.

While the work assigned to these two major categories has differed considerably,[31] the tools and skills used by each have much in common. Both need a background education in basic science and in applied science (usually engineering). Both need to understand the concept of fitness for use and the broad progression of events through which this concept is executed. Both must understand the basic tools of the function: quality specifications, measurement, data feedback. Both must have a grounding in basic statistical tools: data collection, distributions, probability, control charts, sampling. In addition, both need basic training in the sequence of events through which problems are diagnosed and solved:

How to define the problem
How to hypothesize or theorize on causes of the problem
How to design studies and experiments to test the validity of the theories
How to collect data, analyze them, and present the findings
How to harness the modern computer to extensive problems in data collection and analysis
How to deal with cultural resistance to technological change

While the area of commonality is wide, there are differences as well. The Reliability Engineer must have mastery over some fields of knowledge not needed by most Quality Control Engineers, e.g., reliability formulas and their application to product design.[32] Correspondingly, there is an array of know-how required by Quality Control Engineers but not required by most Reliability Engineers, e.g., process capability analysis. The quantitative extent of these areas of commonality and of difference does not seem to have been analyzed.

Other Quality Staff Specialist Categories Beyond the foregoing two major categories of quality staff specialist, there are others which are trying to become "established." The proliferation of categories has included such titles as Maintainability Engineer, Material Review Engineer, Salvage Engineer, Configuration Control Engineer, Systems Analyst, Systems Engineer, Human Factors Engineer, and still others.[33] It is seldom clear, during the first few years of the emergence of a new category, whether it will become established on a broadly accepted basis.

Related Nonquality Specialties In addition to the two major staff quality specialties, there are a number of other staff specialties which, though not oriented full-time to quality function, are nevertheless engaged in activities which impinge on the quality function. The specialist categories associated with these specialties include the following:

Industrial Engineers. Their mission is one of studying systems and methods generally with a view to improving effectiveness. Their roots are in the Taylor System (see Section 2), but during the 1960s they shifted their emphasis to systems analysis and use of the computer.[34]

---

[31] For some analysis of differences, see Movshin, Joseph, Reliability Motives and Methods, *Quality Assurance*, pp. 18–22, January 1964.

[32] A background in the product design function is highly desirable. Many successful reliability engineers are former designers.

[33] Some of this proliferation has come from the companies rather than from initiative by the specialists. During 1967, one large electrical manufacturing company published multiple advertisements looking for specialists under the following titles: Quality Control In-Process Engineers, Advance Quality Control Engineers, Quality Control Project Engineers, Test Equipment Engineers, Quality Control Test Engineers, Quality Control Purchased Material Engineers.

[34] In the early days of the evolving staff quality departments, the Industrial Engineers established themselves as excellent recruits for the new specialty. They had good knowledge of factory operation, understood the means of securing costs and other economic data, were trained in a wide array of analytical tools, and had undergone a good deal of experience in

Operations Research Analysts.   Their interest is in an interdisciplinary approach for studying how to optimize the economics of the company.   Many or even most of their applications have been in the field of production and inventory control.

Value Analysts.   They are concerned mainly with analyzing the functions performed by products and with stimulating discovery of lower-cost ways of accomplishing these same functions.   See Section 16, under Value Analysis.

Statisticians.   They are no longer equated with quality control analysts.[35]   (All quality staff specialists are trained in basic statistical tools and in some advanced tools.)   The statisticians serve the quality function as consultants in complex problems and as instructors.

Project Engineers.   Their role is one of coordinating the work of all functions with respect to an assigned project, including the work needed to achieve fitness for use.   Some of the project engineers have personal competence in the staff quality specialties and may, for this reason, be given the added responsibility of directing the work of this specialty for the project.

Standardization Engineers.   This category, while limited in numbers, has a history antedating that of the quality control engineers.   Their mission is one of aiding the company to meet industry and national standards for interchangeability in products, materials, tests, etc.   They also try to moderate the urge for special designs or other nonstandard activities which increase costs and reduce interchangeability.

As in the case of the two major quality staff specialties, these nonquality staff specialties differ significantly in work assignments but have much in common as to skills and tools needed to carry out their duties.   This commonality has given rise to a school of thought which contends that with respect to skills and tools, the area of commonality is much greater than the extent of the differences; that the proliferation in staff specialties has gone too far; that the need is to create a category of "staff generalist" who would be able to perform a broad array of staff services.   This same school of thought contends that a "good man" should be able to be knowledgeable in most of the skills which now serve to separate the specialties.   Such a category of staff generalist would, under this contention, minimize the problems of recruitment and training of staff specialists, i.e., under a system of many staff specialties there are fewer men immediately qualified to step into the specialty.   As a corollary, the specialists themselves would benefit—each would have a wider range of choice of placement and a wider opportunity for promotion if he is not identified with too narrow a specialty.   The economic recession of the late 1960s and the early 1970s may have provided some stimulus to check the trend toward overspecialization.

Running through all these staff-staff conflicts is the risk of "rediscovery of scientific management."   Once a new, narrow specialty succeeds in getting results, it is tempting for the men involved to use these results as the basis for securing a broad charter plus associated budget.   This is sometimes done by phrasing the specialty in such broad language as to encompass the entire concept of "scientific management."   Some of the definitions put forward for operations research, value analysis, systems engineering, etc., have been precisely of this nature.

Managers should be on the alert for this tendency to draft broad staff charters since they are a breeding ground for staff-staff conflicts.   Preparing the charter

---

introducing technological change.   Their limitations were traceable to preoccupation with the diminishing problem of direct labor productivity and to failure to grasp major new opportunities in indirect labor and other growing problems.

[35] See, in this connection, "Careers in Statistics," The American Statistical Association, Washington, D.C.

for a new department is launching a new design—in this case, for organization structure. This design should be subjected to close "design review" by all who will be asked to live with it, both line and staff.

ADMINISTRATION OF THE QUALITY STAFF SPECIALTY

The roles of the quality control staff (see below) are mainly of a long-range character. Such a work load suggests that the department affairs be conducted under a concept of annual planning, with shorter updating if needed. The annual plan is in turn based on the projects and other activities which make up the multiple roles of this staff. Preparation of such a plan is an essential discipline for the staff department as proof that it has thought out its mission. In addition, the proposed plan permits the line departments and the upper management to judge whether the staff department is working on important problems or on trivia, on yesterday's problems or tomorrow's.

Roles of the Quality Control Staff   These include:

Analysis for Improvement Projects.[36]   In this role the staff specialists provide data collection, data analysis, and other aids to those who guide the projects. (See Section 16, Figure 16-1.) More specifically, the specialists:

Summarize past data and conduct Pareto analyses to identify vital few symptoms
Test theories of causation through the study of process capabilities, defect concentration patterns, etc.
Design and conduct studies to test theories during current production, e.g., stream analysis
Design and carry out experiments involving changes in process, instrumentation, etc.
Establish proof of cause
Test remedies to verify effectiveness[37]

Quality Planning.   In this role the staff specialists:

Identify the quality goals for the project under study
Identify the tasks which need to be performed to reach these quality goals
Study existing capabilities for carrying out such tasks
Prepare proposals for getting the needed tasks performed, including assignment of responsibility, timetable, cost estimates, methods, etc.
Convene the cognizant managers to discuss, modify and finalize these proposals[38]

Coordination.   The foregoing activities of "quality planning" imply a delegation of execution to the various departments participating in the plan. Where there is also a continuing activity of reviewing performance, revising the plan, providing improved communication, reporting progress, etc., the term "coordination" is also used. Staff specialists are often given responsibility for such continuing coordination.

Control Systems: Assurance.   Here "control" may apply broadly, e.g., quality costs, or narrowly, e.g., a process control station. The role of the quality control specialists is principally to:

[36] For an extensive discussion, see Juran, J. M. "Managerial Breakthrough," McGraw-Hill Book Company, New York, 1964, Chapters 7, 8, and 9.

[37] For elaboration of the foregoing, see Section 16.

[38] For a case discussion. see Shaw, R. A., Early Entry of Quality Assurance in the Design Stages of Product Development, *Transactions, 17th Conference on Quality Control, Metropolitan Section,* ASQC, Rutgers University, Sept. 11, 1965, pp. 138–142.

Prepare the flow diagrams and identify the necessary control subjects and control stations

Define the work to be performed at each control station and the associated criteria to be met

Provide for data feedback, both to the control station and to the supervisory structure

Establish the audit procedure to assure that execution follows the control plan

Consulting.   As the company's principal experts in the use of their specialized concepts and tools, the quality staff specialists are called in as internal consultants when these concepts or tools are needed.   In this relationship the authority of the consultant is of no consequence, since he is an invited guest.   What is decisive is his expertise, and especially the personal relations he establishes to make himself and his knowledge palatable to his clients.[39]

Troubleshooting.   In many companies the job of investigating out-of-control situations is done by the quality control staff.   These situations may involve nonconforming purchased materials, sporadic process troubles, nonconforming lots of finished product, adverse trends on executive quality reports, etc.   The staff is used here as a convenient device for conducting the investigation without preempting much of the time of line supervisors.   While this practice is widespread, there is a good deal of doubt that it should be retained over the long run.   (See Section 11, under Troubleshooting.)

Budgeting and Reporting   Budgets for quality control staff departments are set up to correspond to the roles performed, somewhat as follows:

Role	Form of budget
Quality improvement	Project by project. See, for example, Section 16, Table 16-6.
Planning	Based on anticipated extent of new products, processes, etc., requiring planning.
Consulting, control systems, assurance	Based on past history, adjusted for expected growth.

To appeal to upper management, the budget should be dominated by improvement projects.   Most of these lend themselves to justification based on return on investment, which appeals strongly to upper management.

Because the bulk of staff work is of a long-range character, the frequency of reporting should be infrequent—normally quarterly.   Each quarterly report shows the progress made during the last quarter and lists plans for the quarter ahead.   The annual report (every fourth quarter) contains the next annual plan as well.

Completed projects are reported on at the time of completion.

In reporting financial results the staff is well advised to enlist the aid of the company's Accounting Department.   Upper management gives more credibility to financial figures if they have been "certified" by the Accounting Department.

Reporting progress involves the touchy matter of "who gets the credit."   Staff people are well advised to lean over backwards to give maximum credit to line supervisors.   Some staff specialists draft reports on finished projects in the form of joint reports (with the line departments involved).

[39] For elaboration, see Purcell, Warren R., The Internal Quality Control Consultant, *Industrial Quality Control,* pp. 38–40, October 1962.   See also Juran, J. M., So You Want To Be a Quality Control Consultant, *Industrial Quality Control,* pp. 265–270, December 1966.

Introducing Change   In its creative and project work the staff department is trying to change the existing order. On the face of it, the proposed changes are technological in character. However, any technological change is accompanied by an "uninvited guest"—a "social" consequence of the change. The social consequence consists of some impact on the habits, beliefs, attitudes, practices, traditions, status, etc., of the people affected. It is the social aspect of the change which poses the real problems of introducing change.

Behaviorial scientists have given the name "cultural pattern" to this collection of habits, beliefs, etc.[40]   They point out that every continuing "society" (a group of people associating with each other) develops a pattern of behavior. This pattern is then taught to new members who enter the society, thus perpetuating the cultural pattern.

The cultural pattern is of such great importance to the society that attempts to change it are resisted. (By definition, these attempts threaten the habits, beliefs, etc., of the people involved.)   This resistance to change can easily result in rejection of a "beneficial" technological change, since the price to be paid in habits, beliefs, etc., may be too great in the minds of the people.   Because cultural patterns are found in all societies without exception, the introduction of change in industry is subject to the same forms of resistance.   There has been no lack of this resistance in factories with respect to new techniques for quality control.[41]

Dealing effectively with cultural resistance requires an awareness of the very existence of a cultural pattern and an understanding that it has evolved to provide the members of the culture with precedent, tradition, and predictability as well as status, explanations, and still other social needs.

Through such awareness and understanding, the advocate of change is better able to judge the likely effect of his proposals on the culture and to predict the nature of the resistance to which the proposal must adapt.

As the cultural pattern is understood, it becomes possible to make use of some "rules of the road" for introducing change.   These include the following:

1. Secure the active participation of those who will be affected during both the planning and the execution of the change.

2. Strip off all technical cultural baggage not strictly needed for introducing the change. (Many quality control engineers have been in violation of this.)

3. Reduce the impact of the changes by weaving them into an existing broader pattern of behavior or by letting them ride in on the back of some acceptable change.

4. Put yourself in the other fellow's place.

5. Make use of the wide variety of methods available for dealing with resistance to change.   These include:

   a. Persuasion.

   b. Change of environment in a way which makes it easy for the individual to change his point of view.

   c. Remedying the cause of the resistance.

   d. Creation of a social climate which favors the new habits.

   e. Provision of sufficient *time* for mental changes to take place. (Many changes have failed of acceptance on this ground alone.)

   f. Starting small and keeping it fluid.

   g. Avoiding surprises.

[40] For a fascinating book, see Benedict, Ruth, "Patterns of Culture," Houghton Mifflin Company, Boston, 1934.

[41] See Juran, J. M., "Cultural Patterns and Quality Control," *Industrial Quality Control,* pp. 8–13, October 1957.

6. Treat the people with dignity.[42]

Despite all careful preparation, the staff specialist will still encounter cases where his recommendations are not accepted. He has alternatives here as well:

1. Forget it. Realize that even an 80% average is excellent as an adoption rate for staff recommendations.

2. Discriminate between the vital and the trivial. Reserve the intense arguments, the appeals, the showdowns for the important cases.

3. Bring the matter up again in a few months. Sometimes it is found that the recommendation is now acceptable (or may already have been adopted) because enough time has passed for the line man to adapt himself.

4. "Surround" the line man by selling the idea to his subordinates and to his associates. As this is done and he finds himself alone, he questions his position.

5. Review the proposal to discover its social weaknesses as well as its technical weaknesses. While the outward reasons for rejection are almost always stated in technological terms, the real reasons may well have been related to the cultural pattern.

6. Review the proposal in the light of the personal aspirations of the man who disagrees. If he is security-minded, does it threaten his security? etc.

7. Agree to disagree, and agree to put the matter to higher authority.[43]

Other Staff-Line Relationships   It is almost universal that responsibility for results of operations rest on the line managers, not the staff managers. For this reason the line manager is given the right either to accept or reject the advice of staff specialists. (He does either at his own peril.) This is a good rule. If a manager is to be held responsible for results, he should have authority over the means for getting those results. To require him to accept staff advice is equivalent to transferring part of that authority to the staff (a form of authority without responsibility).

This very real responsibility of line managers makes the authority of the staff specialist an illusory thing. To be sure, the staff department has status on the organization chart. It has a budget, a table of duties, and other outward symbols of authority. These symbols certainly do confer legitimacy in some important ways — the right to secure information, to attend meetings, to present proposals. However, the real authority, i.e., the ability to secure action, is not derived from the rank of the staff manager. It is derived from his knowledge, from his proved competence in assisting line managers in improving their results, and from his personality. The matter of personality is surprisingly important. Although personality by itself solves no problems, it avoids some severe problems by converting the conflicts inherent in the staff-line relationships into innocent rivalries or even good natured collaboration.

Aside from the conflicts inherent in introducing change, there are others inherent in planning and controlling. Of these, the problem of "two bosses" is probably the most common. The problem arises when staff specialists prepare plans to be executed by line departments. For example, a plant laboratory "reports" to the plant manager. However, the Division Quality Control (staff) Department is a major force in preparing the quality plans to be used and in auditing to see that the execution follows the plans. The organization chart itself reflects a dualism. A solid line runs from the laboratory to the plant manager. However, a dotted line runs from the laboratory to the Division Quality Control Manager.

The solution lies in the fact that the plant laboratory has only one personal boss (the plant manager) but numerous impersonal bosses, of which the quality plan is

---

[42] Margaret Mead, "Cultural Patterns and Technical Change," UNESCO, 1953. Also reprinted as a Mentor Book, New American Library, Inc., New York, 1955.

[43] For a more exhaustive discussion of "resistance to change," see Juran, J. M., "Managerial Breakthrough," McGraw-Hill Book Company, New York, 1964, pp. 141–157.

but one. (Others include the personnel manual, the budget, the safety regulations, etc.) As long as there is only one personal boss, the plant laboratory head has a place for appeal to secure the final word.[44]

Careers, Training, and Professionalism for Quality Staff Specialists These topics, while pertinent to administration of the quality staff specialty, are also pertinent to manpower management. They are discussed in Section 17, under the respective headings.

THE CORPORATE QUALITY MANAGER

The term "Corporate Quality Manager" is used here in the sense of a staff corporate post in a *multidivisional* company. In such companies each autonomous Division has a full-fledged quality control organization responsible to the Division General Manager. The post of Corporate Quality Manager, when created, is located on the organization chart in the manner depicted on Figure 7-7.

The Corporate Staff Duties Although the duties of the Corporate Quality Manager vary considerably from one company to another, they usually consist of some combination of the duties in the following list:

Assistance to Corporate Management. This may include:

Development of corporate quality policy
Coordination of the work of preparing the annual quality program (major objectives, projects, plans)
Preparation and publication of executive reports on results attained
Audit of divisional quality performances
Assistance in interdivisional quality problems

Assistance to Divisional Management. This includes the following:

Appraisal of divisional quality managers. (In some companies the Corporate Quality Manager exercises a veto power over appointments to posts of divisional quality manager.)
Assistance in start up of new divisions.
Consulting service to aid divisions to attain self-sufficiency.

Coordination of Corporate Quality Matters. These include such matters as:

Relations with government agencies on quality matters[45]
Relations with Industry Associations on quality matters
Relations with Standardization bodies
Relations with Professional Societies on quality matters

Professional Development. In this capacity the Corporate Quality Manager assists in raising the professional competence of the divisional quality control people and of "nonquality" people as well. To do this, he is obliged to:

Keep informed on new developments and practices which are emerging in the specialty
Disseminate this information to the divisions
Collaborate with the divisions in trying out promising developments for company use

---

[44] For added discussion, see Juran, J. M., "Managerial Breakthrough," McGraw-Hill Book Company, New York, 1964, pp. 69–70.

[45] This excludes matters in which the government agency is a customer of the company. Such matters are handled by the company Division which is the government contractor in the case.

Develop new concepts for tryout in the company

Conduct internal company conferences on quality control

Prepare training programs, manuals, courses, and means for exchanging experiences

Publish internal newsletters, case histories of programs tried out, etc.

Command. In some cases the Corporate Quality Manager is given direct command over some corporate quality facility because such an assignment is as logical or convenient as any alternative. Examples include:

Central laboratories

Central standards laboratory

Data banks for reliability, vendor rating, etc.

Documentation, e.g., standard practice manuals

Some Negatives   Study of the foregoing lists makes it evident that there are some very real needs to be served by a corporate quality staff post.[46]   However, there are also some good reasons for *not* creating the post:

1. The authority is vague.   In practice the authority depends much more on the knowledge and personality of the corporate quality manager than on his organization status.

2. There is no agreed measure of effectiveness.   The measureable results appear in divisional performance.

3. The post is difficult to fill, since it requires a high level of professional skills along with unusual competence in "selling" programs to a wide assortment of managers.

4. The post is a dead-end job.   In most companies there is no logical progression out of the job, so that the men who fill it thus step out of the line of promotion.

With such an array of obstacles, it is not surprising that these posts have in fact undergone a high mortality rate.   They are set up with the best intentions.   Yet, a few years later, during some economic slowdown, they are abolished when someone asks, "What useful results are we getting from this department?"

ORGANIZATION FOR QUALITY IMPROVEMENT

Improvement projects require special organization design if the project is interdepartmental.   In such cases, means must be provided for interdepartmental guidance or "steering" of each project.   In addition, means must be provided for performing the detailed diagnostic work, again on some interdepartmental basis.

The general approach to such organization (for "breakthrough") is extensively discussed in J. M. Juran, "Managerial Breakthrough," Chapters 6 and 7.   The application to quality improvement is discussed in Section 16, under Organizing for Improvement.

---

[46] For a good case history, see Toeppner, Thomas G., Implementing a Corporate Quality Assurance Activity in a Multi-Product, Divisionalized Corporation, *24th Annual Technical Conference Transactions,* ASQC, pp. 1–12, 1970.

8

New-Product Quality [1]

H. D. VOEGTLEN

Assistant to Vice President, Product Effectiveness
Hughes Aircraft Company, Culver City, Calif.

INTRODUCTION

Launching a new product is a complex undertaking involving several levels of analysis and judgment.

1. The "business" analysis, which considers such questions as

---

[1] In the Second Edition, the material on Reliability programs was prepared by E. F. Dertinger.

   a. Is there a social need (e.g., a market) for this product?

   b. If the product is feasible technologically, will the cost be compatible with what the buyer is willing to pay?

  2. The "managerial" analysis, which considers how to mobilize the company's manpower and other resources in order to develop, design, produce, test, market, service, etc., the new product.

  3. The "technological" analysis, which considers such questions as

   a. Is this product technologically feasible?

   b. Precisely what should be the technological nature of the new product to strike an optimum balance among the competing parameters?

In this Handbook, the business aspects of new-product launching are discussed mainly in Sections 4 and 14. The broad planning approach is discussed in Section 6. Many of the managerial and technological problems are discussed in the present Section 8. There are also related discussions in other Sections, and these will be referenced in Section 8 where pertinent.

TABLE 8-1 Traditional versus Modern Products

Aspects of products	Traditional	Modern
Simplicity	Simple, static	Complex, dynamic
Precision	Low	High
Need for interchangeability	Limited	Extensive
Consumables or durables	Mainly consumables	Mainly durables
Environment in which used	Natural	Unnatural
User understanding of product	High	Low
Importance to human health, safety and continuity of life	Seldom important	Often important
Life cycle cost to user	Similar to purchase price	Much greater than purchase price
Life of a new design	Long; decades and even centuries	Short; less than a decade
Scientific basis of design	Largely empirical	Largely scientific
Basis of reliability, maintainability, etc.	Vague: "best effort"	Quantified
Volume of production	Usually low	Often high
Usual cause of field failures	Manufacturing errors	Design weaknesses

Traditional and Modern Products The timeless drive of human creativity has yielded a procession of new products throughout all recorded history. Within recent centuries, and especially during the twentieth century, there has emerged a category of products which we will call "modern" to distinguish it from the "traditional." Table 8-1 compares these two categories of products with respect to some important aspects as seen by producer and user.

It is evident from Table 8-1 that modern products[2] exhibit some marked differences from traditional products. Collectively, these differences add up to a revolution in the nature of products, and thereby they demand a revolution in the process for launching these modern new products. Such a revolution has grown out of

---

[2] The word "product" is used here in its generic sense. Modern products are often called "systems," "equipments," etc. There is a hierarchy of functional levels of products going from a complex system down to the elemental part. One published terminology for such a hierarchy consists of "system, subsystem, equipment, group, unit, assembly, subassembly, stage, part." (Military standard MIL-E-16400.)

actual experience. The proliferation of modern products was dramatized by the emergence of complex military systems, aerospace systems, and computers (an early example was the telephone system). Efforts to launch such products by traditional methods resulted in extensive failures and a growing awareness that a revolution was needed.

This revolution in launching new products actually consists of two revolutions. One of these relates to the *managerial* methods for launching new designs. It involves such managerial tools as the phase system for product development, early warning systems (e.g., design review) for detecting trouble ahead, etc. The second revolution relates to the new *technological* tools, e.g., quantifying reliability. Together, these two revolutions have greatly improved the launching of modern products.

Because modern products are in addition to, not instead of, traditional products, we need two processes for launching new products: (1) the traditional process for traditional products and (2) the revolutionary process for modern products. Traditional methods are not adequate to launch modern products. They were tried and they failed. As a corollary, the fact that revolutionary ways are available does not mean that they should be used for traditional products as well. For many traditional products, the traditional ways are adequate and the use of modern ways is uneconomic.

Both traditional and modern products must be fit for use and hence must meet the basic parameters of fitness for use: quality of design, quality of conformance, availability, and customer service.[3] However, closer analysis (e.g., Table 8-1) soon makes clear that modern designs are more exacting in their needs for reliability, maintainability, safety, cost effectiveness, etc. The new managerial and technological methods are a response to these more exacting needs.

The discussion which follows will consider all major tools used in launching new products, whether managerial or technological, and whether these are suitable for traditional products, modern, or both.

MANAGERIAL METHODS FOR LAUNCHING NEW PRODUCTS

These managerial methods all relate to the mobilizing of the human and other resources of the company to the task of launching new products.

Cost Effectiveness Concept   For modern products, attainment of fitness for use involves a balance among many competing parameters and costs. To help achieve this balance, there has been evolved a formalized listing of these parameters and costs, from the inception of the design to the end of its operational life.[4] This concept will be referred to as the "cost effectiveness" concept. The many other names include system effectiveness, system worth, and operational effectiveness.

Figure 8-1 shows the cost effectiveness concept broken down into its major parameters, each of which is broken down further into subparameters. The terms used in Figure 8-1 are widely accepted.)[5]   Obviously, some of the parameters are not

---

[3] For elaboration, see Section 2, under Parameters of Fitness for Use.

[4] Voegtlen, H. D., and J. A. Cafaro, The Measurement and Specification of Product Abilities, *Industrial Quality Control,* March 1962, pp. 20–25. See also Meagley, Nelson G., The System Effectiveness Concept at Continental Aviation and Engineering, *ASQC Annual Technical Conference Transactions,* 1967, pp. 53–62.

[5] "Chairman's Final Report," Weapon System Effectiveness Industry Advisory Committee (WSEIAC), U.S. Air Force Systems Command, January 1965. (Available from Superintendent of Documents, Washington, D.C.) The findings of this report are summarized in Voegtlen, H. D., A Review of the Major Findings of the Weapon System Effectiveness Industry Advisory Committee, *Proceedings, 1966 Annual Symposium on Reliability,* IEEE, pp. 22–31.

applicable to all products, but within the broad range of modern products the parameters apply widely and validly.[6,7]

Of the parameters shown in Figure 8-1,

Availability is a measure of the condition of the product at some (random) time when required for use.   For example, a product undergoing routine maintenance may at the time be unavailable for use.   (The topic of availability is elaborated below, under Maintainability.)[8]

Dependability is a measure of the product condition, given its availability when required for use.   This topic is elaborated below, under Reliability.

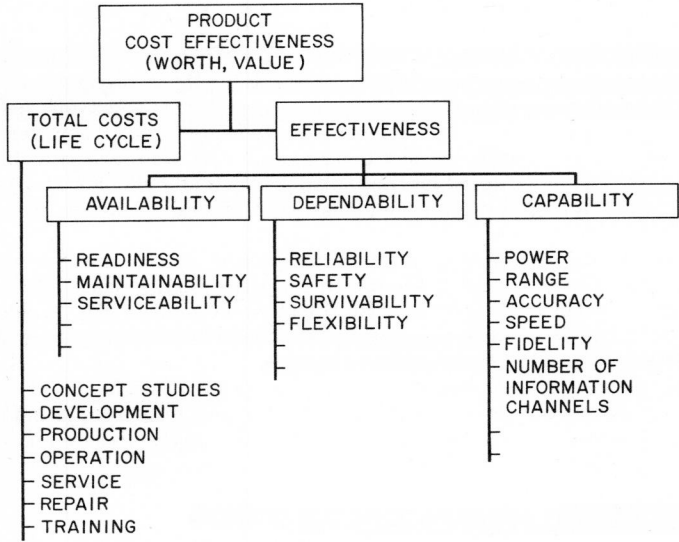

Fig. 8-1   Elements of cost effectiveness.

Capability is a measure of the extent to which the product meets its specified operational requirements during use, given its dependability during the period of use.   For example, a motor operating at its specified 3,600 revolutions per minute is exhibiting capability.

(Product) Effectiveness is the resultant of availability, dependability, and capability.

Cost is the life cycle cost of the product.[9]

Cost Effectiveness is the value received for the resources expended and is the ratio of cost to effectiveness.

The concept of cost effectiveness is ancient.   What is new is the formalized action taken to:

Identify the parameters and factors that enter the cost ratio

[6] ARINC Research Corporation, System Cost Effectiveness: Basic Concepts and Framework for Analysis, Publication 398-99-1-722, January 1967.

[7] A good deal of the literature on Systems Engineering relates to the concept of cost-effectiveness.   See Allen, T. H., Systems Engineering Bibliography, *Industrial Quality Control*, December 1967, pp. 317–321.   Includes annotations for the 46 references cited.

[8] See also, Section 2, under the "Abilities."

[9] See Section 4, under Life Cycle Costing.

Quantify these factors to permit more precise evaluation and decision making

Specify the factors in quantitative terms so that all concerned know the goals to be met

Control the factors throughout the product life cycle, again based on the goals to be met

Improve performance through feedback of results and quantified evaluation of priorities

The Phase Concept of Product Development Although the life cycle of a product is a continuum from "cradle to grave," managers have found it useful to subdivide this

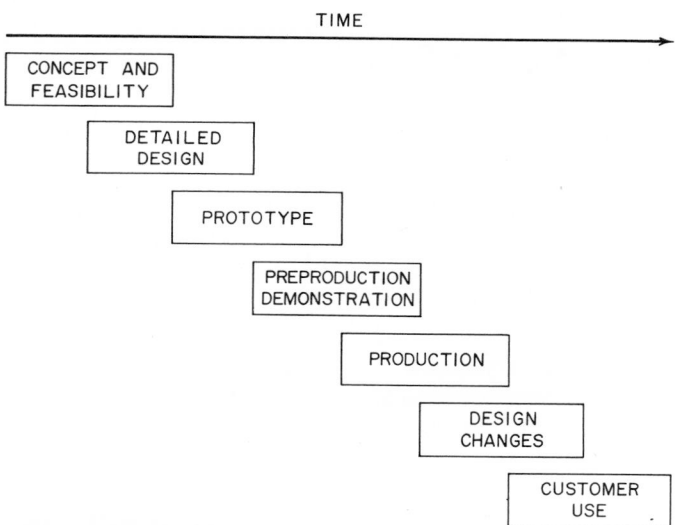

Fig. 8-2 Phases in product development.

cycle into clearly defined phases. This phase system makes it easier to define the tasks to be done, to assign responsibility, to measure results, and to make decisions on whether to continue with projects or not.

The broad concept of cradle-to-grave quality planning is discussed in Section 6, under New Product Planning. The reader is urged to study this broad planning in conjunction with the present topic—especially Figures 6-2 and 6-3 and Tables 6-2 and 6-3.

A major segment of the cradle-to-grave quality planning is "product development." This segment logically breaks down into a number of recognized phases as depicted in Figure 8-2, which also shows the time sequences of these phases. The significance of these phases can be summarized as follows:

1. *Concept and Feasibility Phase.* In this phase the known or anticipated need for a product is studied in enough detail to determine if it is feasible to design and manufacture a product responsive to the need. An important element of this feasibility is the expected cost to the company and to the customer. This phase culminates in a conclusion that it is feasible (or not feasible) to continue with the project. This conclusion recommends one or more design concepts that appear to be promising to explore in the future.

2. *Detailed Design Phase.* In this phase, the alternative design concepts are

evaluated, the most promising one is selected, and the product is designed in sufficient detail to prepare purchasing specifications for parts and materials, and to plan the manufacture of products for prototype testing. For complex products, the detailed design phase may consist of two major subphases: (1) a more detailed exploration of several design concepts uncovered in the feasibility stage (these explorations may be conducted simultaneously or sequentially), and (2) selection of a final design concept followed by a full, detailed design.

There is always the possibility that, during or after the detailed design phase, the design concept selected may prove to be poor and may have to be discarded. The cycle then starts all over. (The detailed design phase may also include major work in new-component development and may go beyond and include fabrication of hardware to evaluate the design proposed on paper.)

3. *Prototype Phase.* In this phase, the first essentially complete units of the product are built and tested. The tests may evaluate such factors as basic design capability, effects of extreme environments, and reliability for extended periods of operation. The units built may not be complete but are complete enough to test the adequacy of the basic design approach. The prototype tests should indicate that the initial design approach can be adopted and completed in detail. If not, "back to the drawing board."

Ideally, prototype units are built using the manufacturing procedures and equipment planned for full-scale production, but this is sometimes not possible. In such case, the test results may not be completely representative of what the production units will do. However, the prototype phase is a valuable means for the designer to evaluate the adequacy of his design approach ("technical feasibility") and to revise the design prior to setting up manufacturing procedures.

4. *Preproduction Demonstration.* In this phase a "production design" is prepared and is evaluated for producibility and performability.

The production design differs from the prototype design, due to design changes made for a variety of reasons: to simplify manufacturing processes, cut the cost of materials, standardize for greater interchangeability with existing products, utilize present production facilities, etc.

Next, a preproduction lot of product is made to the production design, using the production equipment.[10] This "pilot run" is then tested, sometimes under simulated use environments (proving grounds) and sometimes by selected customers under conditions of actual use.[11]

Based on the results of the tests and the experience of manufacture, the design is either released for full-scale production or sent back to be reworked.

5. *Full-Scale Production.* This is the regular production for sale and delivery to customers.

6. *Design Changes.* Based on experience gained in production, marketing, and use of the product, design changes are made to improve product performance and to eliminate field failures which showed up under the conditions of use. These design changes go through one or more of the previous phases of the life cycle.

7. *Customer Use.* This is the entire period of product useful life, including the warranty interval (if provided) and all service and repair until the product is discarded, traded in, or replaced.[12]

There are other methods of dividing the cradle-to-grave progression into logical phases. For example, some practitioners divide the prototype phase up into

---

[10] See, in this connection, Section 9, under Design of the Manufacturing Process.

[11] For some examples, see Section 14, under Competitive Evaluations.

[12] Derived from Juran, J. M., and F. M. Gryna, "Quality Planning and Analysis," McGraw-Hill Book Company, New York, 1970, pp. 114–116.

three subphases, i.e., prototype design, prototype construction, and prototype testing. There is no single method which fits all companies or even all projects within a single company.[13]

The Early Warning Concept   A long-standing aid to launching new products has been the early warning concept. Under this concept certain reviews, tests, analyses, etc., are introduced into the product development as a means of securing early warning of trouble ahead. Making and testing of prototypes provides early warning of failures during field usage. Trial production runs provide early warning of manufacturing problems during mass production.

For modern products, the early warning concept has been considerably expanded and formalized. Table 8-2 shows, for various phases of the product life cycle, the methods used for securing early warning of trouble ahead.

TABLE 8-2   Forms of Early Warning of New-Product Problems

Phases of new-product progression	Forms of early warning of new-product troubles
Concept and feasibility study	Concept review
Prototype design	Design review, reliability prediction, failure mode and effects analysis
Prototype construction	Prototype test, environmental test, overstressing
Preproduction	Pilot production lots
Early full-scale production	In-house testing (e.g., kitchen, road), consumer use panels, limited marketing area
Full-scale production, marketing, and use	Employees as test panels, special provisions for prompt feedback
All phases	Failure analysis, data collection and analysis

A major element of this expansion of early warnings has been the design review (see below). In modern products the greatest single source of field failures is weaknesses inherent in the design. Since product development and design precede usage by several years, it is most important to discover design weaknesses during the design phase itself. Failing this, the damage done by these weaknesses is multiplied enormously. It is this great multiplying effect which has stimulated the growth of formal design reviews.

Design Review   The purpose of this review is early detection and remedy of design deficiencies which could jeopardize: successful performance during use; low-cost manufacture; and low-cost, prompt field maintenance.

The design review concept is of old standing and has been carried out, for traditional products, in several ways:

1. By the head of the enterprise. In very small companies this can still be effective due to the chief executive's personal exposure to all phases of the product life cycle.

2. By the head of the Technical Department. This likewise can be effective for

---

[13] For an example as applied to consumer products, see Kato, Tetsujiro, Quality Assurance of Watches at Development Stages, *Proceedings, 14th EOQC Conference,* Lausanne, Switzerland, 1970, pp. 103–106.

very small companies. It can also be effective when the new product contains only minor departures from the old. For modern products this review is effective only for those matters in which the designer is the best expert, e.g., stress analysis. In other matters this form of review is not adequate, for reasons which will be discussed shortly.

3. By a New-Products Committee. Over the years many such committees were set up, and their duties included giving early warning of trouble ahead. For the most part, these committees were ineffective as to new product quality because:

a. They lacked the specialized staff and the modern tools of analysis needed to conduct meaningful reviews in the design phase.

b. They were not brought into the picture until it was too late, i.e., the time-table for production and marketing had seemingly been frozen up to an extent such that proposals for change became unacceptable on the grounds of disruption of the timetable.

c. They faced what seemed to be an entrenched monopolistic resistance by designers, so that proposals requiring design changes seemed futile.

4. By Manufacturing Planning. This department has traditionally looked for ways to improve manufacturing economics, including design revisions. See Section 9, under Design Review.

For modern products, the design review has been dramatically restructured through several "new" concepts:

1. Design reviews are made mandatory, either through customer demand[14] or through upper management policy declaration.[15,16]

2. The design review is conducted by a team consisting mainly of specialists who are *not directly associated with the development of the design.* Table 8-3 shows the potential membership and their respective contributions to the design review meeting. In practice the team consists of a core membership such as project manager or project engineer as chairman, product designer, reliability engineer (often the secretary), manufacturing engineer, sales engineer, service engineer. Other specialists are called in as needed.[17]

3. The design review is formal. It is planned and scheduled like any other legitimized activity. The meetings are built around prepared agendas and documentation sent out in advance. Minutes of meetings are prepared and circulated. Follow-ups for action are likewise formalized.

---

[14] Design reviews are mandatory for NASA contracts. See NHB 5300.4 (1A), *Reliability Program Provisions for Aeronautical and Space System Contractors,* 1970, paragraph 305. (Available from Superintendent of Documents, Washington, D.C.) This standard not only makes design reviews mandatory but also prescribes some minimal standards for the methods of conducting the reviews.

An elaboration of the NASA concept of design reviews has been published. ("Elements of Design Review for Space Systems," NASA SP 6502, Office of Technology Utilization, National Aeronautics and Space Administration, 1967. For sale by Clearinghouse for Federal Scientific and Technical Information, Springfield, Va. 22151.) This 57-page manual does not give mandatory requirements—it is issued for information purposes. It discusses purpose of design reviews, elements of a program, categories to be reviewed, application, and costs.

Some military contracts also make design reviews mandatory, in which case they reference the military standard MIL-R-27542.

[15] See, for example, Jacobs, Richard M., Implementing Formal Design Review, *Industrial Quality Control,* February 1967, pp. 398–404.

[16] See also Hunt, J. V., Reliability Management under Automation, *Proceedings, 1968 Annual Symposium on Reliability,* IEEE, pp. 15–20.

[17] For elaboration, see Jacobs, Richard M., *op. cit.,* from which Table 8-3 is derived.

4. The design review covers all quality-related parameters and others as well (see Table 8-3).[18]

5. The design review is conducted at several phases of the progression of the design and at several levels of the product hierarchy (system, subsystem, etc., down to specific parts).

The foregoing new approaches to design review were first applied to military and aerospace systems. The tools developed and the experience gained have since been applied increasingly to civilian products as well.[19] In both categories of products, the obvious costs of conducting the design reviews have at the outset been obstacles to gaining acceptance. With experience, the companies have developed a clearer understanding of the cost versus value aspects of the design review programs and thereby have reduced the costs while retaining the essential benefits.

A universal obstacle to design review has been the cultural resistance of the Design Department. It has been common practice for this department to hold a virtual monopoly on design decisions; i.e., these decisions have historically been immune from challenge unless actual product trouble was being encountered. With such a background, it was not surprising that the designers resisted the use of design reviews to challenge their designs. The designers contended that such challenges were based purely on grounds of theory and analysis (at which they regarded themselves as the top experts) rather than on the traditional grounds of "failed hardware." This resistance then was further aggravated in those companies which permitted the reliability engineers to propose competing designs. The designers resisted the idea of having competitors even more than they resisted the idea of design review.[20]

The emerging purpose of the design review is one of bringing to the designer inputs from the best experts available (on various essential specialties) so that the designer can optimize "his" design. In the design review meetings, the designer must listen to these inputs and respond constructively. He retains the benefit of the doubt and the last word on matters of structural integrity.[21]

Beyond the managerial and organizational aspects of design review as discussed above, there are other aspects involving use of new technological tools. These are discussed later in this Section.

RELIABILITY IN NEW PRODUCT DESIGN

The ancients faced *all* the parameters faced by modern industry. They recognized that a product should have certain performance characteristics, e.g., the dimensions of the structure, the weight of the armor, the speed of the ship. In addition, they recognized that a product should have a long total service life; that during this life it

---

[18] Of course, the emphasis on parameters is not uniform. For results of surveys on subject matter of design reviews (and other useful aspects) see McClure, J. Y., and Winlund E. S. Design Review, a Philosophy, Survey and Policy, *Proceedings 1963 Symposium on Reliability and Quality Control*, IEEE, pp. 287–300.

[19] For a good discussion, see Jacobs, Richard M., *op. cit.*, and Hunt, J. V., *op. cit.* For some useful case histories, see Jacobs, Richard M., and H. Donnell Hulme, Commercial Design Review and Data Analysis Program, *ASQC Annual Technical Conference Transactions*, 1965, pp. 229–241.

[20] For elaboration, see Jurisdiction in Product Specifications, under Management of New Product Quality, below.

[21] For elaboration, see Juran, J. M., Mobilizing for the 1970's, *Quality Progress*, August 1969, pp. 8–17.

TABLE 8-3   Design Review Team Membership and Responsibility

Group member	Responsibilities	Type of design review*		
		PDR	IDR	FDR
Chairman	Calls, conducts meetings of Group, and issues interim and final reports	X	X	X
Design Engineer(s) (of product)	Prepares and presents design and substantiates decisions with data from tests or calculations	X	X	X
Reliability Manager or Engineer	Evaluates design for optimum reliability consistent with goals	X	X	X
Quality Control Manager or Engineer	Ensures that the functions of inspection, control, and test can be efficiently carried out		X	X
Manufacturing Engineer	Ensures that the design is producible at minimum cost and schedule		X	X
Field Engineer	Ensures that installation, maintenance, and user considerations were included in the design		X	X
Procurement Representative	Assures that acceptable parts and materials are available to meet cost and delivery schedules		X	
Materials Engineer	Ensures that materials selected will perform as required		X	
Tooling Engineer	Evaluates design in terms of the tooling costs required to satisfy tolerance and functional requirements		X	
Packaging and Shipping Engineer	Assures that the product is capable of being handled without damage, etc.		X	X
Marketing Representative	Assures that requirements of customers are realistic and fully understood by all parties	X		
Design Engineers (Not associated with unit under review)	Constructively reviews adequacy of design to meet all requirements of customer	X	X	X
Consultants, Specialists on components, value, human factors, etc., (as required)	Evaluates design for compliance with goals of performance, cost, and schedule	X	X	X
Customer Representative (optional)	Generally voices opinion as to acceptability of design and may request further investigation on specific items			X

*P = Preliminary
 I = Intermediate
 F = Final

should give service with few failures; that if it did fail, it should be easy to restore service.

Quite early in recorded history the ancients succeeded in quantifying some of the performance parameters, notably length, weight, and time. They did not succeed in quantifying parameters such as reliability or maintainability. Nevertheless, they took these latter parameters seriously, as the museums, the archaeological sites, and the historical improvements in products will attest.

The Need to Quantify   The movement to quantify reliability, etc., is a twentieth century phenomenon.   The reason for the movement is the proliferation of modern products, with their impact on manufacturer and user, as is evident from Table 8-1. A major aspect of this impact is the new situation of "life behind the quality dikes"; i.e., for the first time in history, human safety, health, and convenience depend absolutely on the reliability or uninterrupted service of our power supply, communications, vehicles, drugs, computers, weapons, etc.[22]

The most acute need for quantification was that exhibited by the parameter of reliability.   This need was a logical result of the nature of the more sophisticated modern products, which involved:

Increased Complexity.   More complex systems demanded simultaneous performance from larger numbers of components, thereby demanding increased reliability of each.

More Severe Environments.   Missiles and manned aircraft moved into new environments of space.   Military strategy dictated worldwide operability, involving a wider range of atmospheric and other environment conditions.   The associated attainment of reliability required that the range and combinations of these more severe environments be quantified, along with the ability of the systems and components to perform and survive under such environments.

Compressed Product Development Cycle.   Military agencies consciously let contracts with severely compressed product development time cycles.[23]   These compressed time cycles could not be met without curtailing or omitting normal phases of product development, e.g., environmental testing, prototype construction and test, field testing.   Omission of these phases created serious risks of program failures. To reduce these risks, new methods were evolved to permit evaluating reliability (and related parameters) in the design stages.

Definition of Reliability   The starting point in quantification is the definition of terminology.   The meaning of "reliability" was standardized as follows:

Reliability is the probability of a product performing without failure a specified function under given conditions for a given period of time.[24]

The foregoing definition of reliability is basic, but it is only one of the ways of specifying reliability or of communicating the concept.[25]   Table 8-4 lists the reliability "figures of merit" in common use.   It is evident that reliability can be specified in terms of (1) probability of success for a given mission or use;[26] (2) mean time between failures; (3) mean cycles of use between failures; (4) availability, which generally includes the term "maintainability" and is discussed below.

Failure Patterns   For individual components, the failure patterns follow a stress-strain relationship superimposed on some measure of usage, e.g., hours of use, cycles of use, kilometers of travel, etc.   The general approach is discussed below under Parts Selection and Control.

[22] For an elaboration of this theme, see Juran, J. M., Mobilizing for the 1970's, *Quality Progress,* August 1969, pp. 8–17.

[23] Early makers of complex systems, e.g., the Bell Telephone System, had reached high levels of reliability through *elongated* product development cycles, involving comprehensive environmental, prototype, and field testing, supplemented by well-organized programs of field failure analysis and data feedback.

[24] "Reliability of Military Electronic Equipment," report by Advisory Group on Reliability of Electronic Equipment, Office of the Assistant Secretary of Defense (R&D), June 1957.   (This was the historic AGREE report.)

[25] See, for elaboration, Section 2, under Reliability.

[26] For single-use ("one-shot") products, e.g., the explosive bolts on a spacecraft, the reliability definition becomes merely the probability of success or the percent effective.

TABLE 8-4   Reliability Figures of Merit

Figure of merit	Meaning
Mean time between failures (MTBF)	Mean time between successive failures of a repairable product
Failure rate	Number of failures per unit time
Mean time to failure (MTTF)	Mean time to failure of a nonrepairable product or mean time to first failure of a repairable product
Mean life	Mean value of life ("life" may be related to major overhaul, wearout, etc.)
Mean time to first failure (MTFF)	Mean time to first failure of a repairable product
Mean time between maintenance (MTBM)	Mean time between a specified type of maintenance action
Longevity	Wearout time for a product
Availability	Operating time expressed as a percentage of operating and repair time
System effectiveness	The extent to which a product achieves the requirements of the user
Probability of success	Same as reliability (but often used for "one shot" or non-time-oriented products.)
b_{10} life	The life during which 10% of the population would have failed
b_{50} life	The median life, or life during which 50% of the population would have failed

As numerous parts are brought together in various configurations, the failure rates of the resulting assemblies, units, systems, etc., follow some predictable patterns which are derived from field failure data and probability considerations. Section 22, under the heading Failure Patterns for Complex Products, discusses the distribution of "time between failures," the resulting formulas relating failures to time, the relationship of component reliability to system reliability, and related matters. The reader is urged to study this discussion in Section 22, as it is fundamental to the discussion of reliability evaluation, prediction, allocation, etc.

The Reliability Quantification Process   Because quantification is fundamental to all reliability activities, it is essential for the designers, planners, etc., involved to understand the essentials of this process. Table 8-5 shows how the process operates.

The top section of Table 8-5 shows how a missile system is composed of six subsystems. At the outset, based on prior experience plus the broad needs of the Defense forces, an overall reliability objective of 0.95 is set for the missile system. This objective is then "apportioned" to the subsystems, again on the basis of experience plus engineering judgment. As a result, a reliability objective of 0.995 is set for the explosive subsystem.

The middle section of Table 8-5 shows a further apportionment within the explosive subsystem. In this apportionment, a reliability objective of 0.998 is set for the fusing circuitry. For the stated mission time of 1.45 hours, this objective of 0.998 translates into a mean time between failures (MTBF) of 725 hours as an equivalent objective.

Up to now, the quantification process has been based mostly on qualitative judgments. The lowest section of the Table is different—it is based mostly on "hard" data. The fusing circuitry is broken down into basic components, e.g., transistors, diodes. From the numbers of each of these components utilized in the circuitry and from data of failure rates of such components when used in actual service,

TABLE 8-5   Quantification of Reliability

System breakdown

Subsystem	Type of operation	Reli-ability†	Unreli-ability	Failure rate per hour	Reliability objective‡
Air frame	Continuous	0.997	0.003	0.0021	483 hours
Rocket motor . . .	One-shot	0.995	0.005		1/200 operations
Transmitter.	Continuous	0.982	0.018	0.0126	80.5 hours
Receiver.	Continuous	0.988	0.012	0.0084	121 hours
Control system . .	Continuous	0.993	0.007	0.0049	207 hours
Explosive system .	One-shot	0.995	0.005		1/200 operations
System		0.95	0.05		

Explosive subsystem breakdown

Unit	Operating mode	Reli-ability	Unreli-ability	Reliability objective
Fusing circuitry.	Continuous	0.998	0.002	725 hours
Safety and arming mechanism	One-shot	0.999	0.001	1/1,000 operations
Warhead.	One-shot	0.998	0.002	2/1,000 operations
Explosive subsystem . . .		0.995	0.005	

Unit breakdown

Fusing circuitry component part classification	Number used, n	Failure rate per part (λ) (%/1,000 hr)	Total part failure rate ($n\lambda$) (%/1,000 hr)
Transistors	93	0.30	27.90
Diodes	87	0.15	13.05
Film resistors	112	0.04	4.48
Wire-wound resistors	29	0.20	5.80
Paper capacitors	63	0.04	2.52
Tantalum capacitors	17	0.50	8.50
Transformers	13	0.20	2.60
Inductors	11	0.14	1.54
Solder joints and wires.	512	0.01	5.12
			71.51

$$\text{MTBF} = \frac{1}{\text{failure rate}} = \frac{1}{\Sigma n\lambda} = \frac{1}{0.0007151} = 1{,}398 \text{ hours}$$

* Adapted by F. M. Gryna, Jr., from G. N. Beaton, "Putting the R&D Reliability Dollar to Work," *Proceedings of the Fifth National Symposium on Reliability and Quality Control,* 1959, Institute of Electrical and Electronics Engineers, Inc., p. 65.

† In terms of probability of success for a given time period

‡ For a mission time of 1.45 hours

a *prediction* is made of the total failure rate for the fusing circuitry, using the method of adding failure rates. (Note that the adding of failure rates is analogous to adding costs or elemental standard times to predict the cost or time for an overall manufacturing operation.)   When this predicted failure is converted into a prediction of MTBF, the result is 1,398 hours, which is comfortably better than the objective[27] of 725 hours.

[27] Sometimes the reliability objective is called the "reliability budget," because the allocation process parallels the process used in financial budgeting.

Table 8-5 exemplifies several of the processes associated with the ability to quantify reliability:

Apportionment (or budgeting), i.e., the process of allocating reliability objectives among various elements which collectively make up a higher-level product.

Prediction, i.e., use of prior performance data plus probability theory to calculate the expected failure rates for various circuits, configurations, etc.

Analysis, i.e., identification of the strong and weak portions of the design to serve as a basis for improvements, trade-offs, and similar actions. For example, the lowest third of Table 8-5 makes clear that the main contributors to failure rates are (1) transistors, (2) diodes, and (3) tantalum capacitors. These three categories of parts account for about 70% of all the unreliability. Hence any real improvement must include some action with respect to these parts.

THE RELIABILITY PROGRAM

The attainment of reliability requires participation and action from all major company departments. For example, the training brochure of an automobile manufacturer[28] listed the following departmental responsibilities:

1. Engineering: for the use of reliability-proved designs, for an adequate program of tests and a good data analysis system, for maintaining a keen awareness of failure rates, for efficient communication and liaison with all departments

2. Production: for selecting the most effective processes of fabrication and assembly, for keeping informed on specific factors contributing to service failures, for maintaining the highest employee morale possible, for a constant educational effort to promote product reliability

3. Quality Control: for applying consistently the finest available inspection techniques; for the maintenance of close communication with engineering, purchasing and service; for recording all information from sampling plans, test processes, and performance history; for constant evaluation and readjustment to promote product quality

4. Reliability: for assisting in the establishment of reliability goals, for predicting the reliability of the future product, for promoting corrective action and design changes to improve the product, for an effective program of education and communication

5. Purchasing: for coordinating with quality control, production, and engineering on vendor problems; for up-to-date knowledge of quality levels and failure data

6. Material handling: for knowing and classifying all priority items and items requiring special handling

7. Service: for fast and accurate evaluation of field service problems; for providing a sound feedback system, organized to point out trends; for supplying dealers promptly all information on corrective action

The fact that reliability is a resultant of the work of many departments has led to wide adoption of a concept of a reliability "program" for the purpose of:

Defining the tasks to be performed
Assigning responsibility for the performances
Establishing a timetable for completion
Coordinating the resulting actions

The condensed version of such a reliability program typically shows the tasks to be

---

[28] Courtesy of Buick Motor Division, General Motors Corporation.

performed (i.e., the program elements) in a time-phased relationship. Figure 8-3 is a well-known example of such a time-phased program.

The task is the basic building block of the reliability program. For any given program the tasks needed will depend on many factors, such as the nature of the product (whether simple or complex), the customer and his requirements, the phases inherent in the contract (e.g., development, production, end-use evaluation), and state-of-the-art considerations (e.g., need for new materials or components). What follows below is a discussion of the major tasks which are common to most reliability programs. For further detail, the practitioner is urged to consult the cited references. In addition, there is an extensive literature on reliability, covering the full spectrum of products, customers, and program phases. The best single source is Annals of Assurance Sciences, a series entitled *Proceedings, Annual Symposium on*

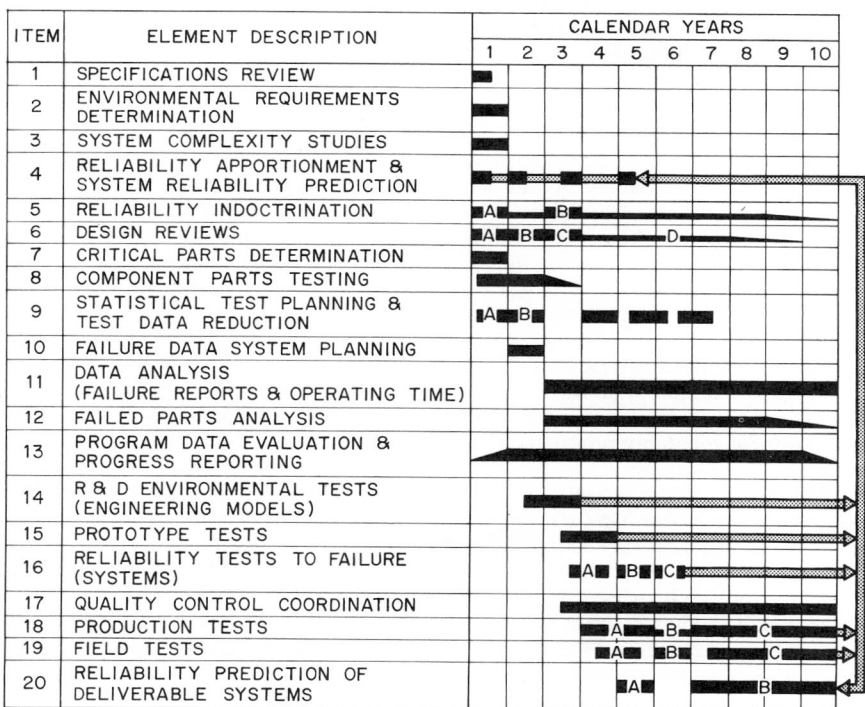

Fig. 8-3 Time-phased reliability program.

5A. Engineering personnel	16C. System 3
5B. Manufacturing personnel	18A. Early production
6A. Preliminary design review	18B. Service-evaluation test phase
6B. Interim design review	18C. Full-scale production
6C. Final design review	19A. Contractor-evaluation tests
6D. Reliability improvement committee reviews	19B. Service-evaluation tests
	19C. Service-use tests
9A. Parts tests	20A. Early production systems
9B. Systems tests	20B. Full-scale production systems
16A. System 1	→ Reliability calculations and improvement of original prediction
16B. System 2	

Reliability dating from 1954.   The 1970 volume[29] contains a cumulative index of papers, listed both by title and by author, since 1954.

The Program Plan   Some customers, especially the Military Services and the National Aeronautics and Space Administration (NASA), require submittal of a formal reliability program plan.   The plan describes the reliability tasks to be performed, the schedules and funding controls for task performance, and an identifiable reliability function in the program office organization.   The plan format is a paragraph-by-paragraph response to those items in the program "spec" that are required in the proposal request.

After approval by the customer, the reliability program plan is incorporated into the contract and becomes a basis for contractual compliance.   The customer program specifications are written broadly enough so that their requirements are subject to interpretation.   Differences in interpretation occasionally lead to changed scope of work.   It is important to submit a definitive plan with the proposal and to clarify any differences during contract negotiation.   Then the final program plan requires only minor refinement in order to receive approval.

The government specifications are rarely applied to a program across the board, so the cost of a reliability program can vary widely.   The principal variations result from the degree of parts and materials effort, and a requirement for reliability testing at any level of assembly.   Other factors—such as special analyses, training, documentation, and subcontract controls—can also create pricing variations.

In general, a program built around NASA specification NHB 5300.4 (1A), "Reliability Program Provisions for Aeronautical and Space System Contractors" (formerly NPC 250-1), is the most expensive to administer, due mainly to NASA emphasis on parts and material control and on failure analysis and documentation.[30] The greatest contract risk item is a requirement for MIL-STD-781, reliability qualification or acceptance testing at the end item level.

Nongovernmental organizations have increasingly been adopting the concept of formalized reliability program planning.[31]   Some large companies have published standards for reliability programs to be used in negotiating vendor contracts as well as for in-house guidance.

Establishing the Requirements   In line with the AGREE definition, reliability is not fully thought out until the following have been clearly defined:

1. What constitutes successful product performance? The need here is to define just what is the mission of the product and what are the conditions which prevail when the mission is successful.   As the mission is defined in detail, it becomes more clear which product failures impair the success of the mission and which do not.

2. What are the loads, stresses and other environments to which the product will be subjected during its life? Numerous product failures are traceable to a lack of meeting of the minds on what the real environments are to be; e.g., the designer designed the product to operate at $180\,^{\circ}\text{C}$, but in some applications the temperatures rise to $200\,^{\circ}\text{C}$.   Such failures have sparked some lively arguments about who is to blame.   While there have been some glaring cases of "blame," these failures are mostly traceable to insufficient service knowledge by the designer (or by the user

---

[29] *Proceedings, 1970 Annual Symposium on Reliability,* sponsored by IEEE, ASQC, ASNT, and IES, Institute of Electrical and Electronic Engineers (IEEE), 1970.   (Available from IEEE headquarters, 345 East 47th St., New York, N.Y. 10017.)

[30] For a discussion of the provisions of this specification, see Ball, Leslie W., NHB 5300.4 (1A), Reliability Program Provisions for Aeronautical and Space System Contractors, *Journal of Quality Technology,* October 1971, pp. 179–183.

[31] For a case discussion, see Stiles, Edward M., Reliability in Mass Produced Consumer Products, *Proceedings, 10th Annual Symposium on Reliability,* IEEE, 1964, pp. 85–96.

himself). One of the contributions of the reliability "movement" has been to force all parties to dig deeper in order to discover what the real environment will be.

3. What are the needed reliability goals? Here the reliability programs make a clean break with the qualitative approach of the past.[32] The programs require that the goals be quantified into some unit of measure:

a. In terms of reliability, e.g., the missile shall have 95% reliability during a mission time of 1.45 hours.

b. In terms of failure rate, e.g., during the one-year guarantee period, the failure rate of the batteries shall not exceed 1%.

c. In terms of usage, e.g., the mean time between failures shall be at least 300 hours. (Units of measure for usage include cycles of operation, kilometers of travel, etc.)

It is seen that establishing requirements involves reaching a meeting of the minds on — and hence quantifying — the definition of product performance, the environmental conditions, the reliability goal. In some cases the customer may take the initiative in establishing these requirements. Failing this, good practice now requires that the manufacturer set goals and communicate these to all concerned.

Reliability Analysis and Prediction Inherent in the establishment of reliability requirements is the need to estimate or *predict* reliability in advance of manufacturing the product. This prediction is a continuing process which takes place at several stages of the progression from design through usage. (See Table 8-6.) At the outset the predictions are "on paper," being based on design information plus past failure rate experience. In the final stages, the predictions become *measurement* based on data from consumer use of the product.

While the visible result of the prediction procedure is to quantify the reliability numbers, the process of prediction is usually as important as the resulting numbers. This is so because the prediction cannot be made without obtaining rather detailed information on product missions, environments, critical component histories, etc. Acquiring this information often gives the designer new knowledge previously not available to him. Even if the designer is unable to secure the needed information, this inability nevertheless identifies for him the areas of ignorance in which he is forced to work.

The following steps make up a reliability prediction method which analyzes the design as well as arriving at the reliability numbers:[33]

1. *Define the Product.* The system, subsystems, and units must be precisely defined in terms of their functional configurations and boundaries. This·precise definition is aided by preparation of a functional block diagram (Figure 8-4) which shows the subsystems and lower-level products, their interrelation, and the interfaces with other systems. For large systems it may be necessary to prepare block diagrams for several levels of the product hierarchy.

Given a functional block diagram and a well-defined statement of the functional requirements of the product, the conditions which constitute failure or unsatisfactory performance can be defined. The functional block diagram also makes it easier to define the boundaries of each unit and to assure that important items are neither neglected nor considered more than once. For example, a switch used to connect two units must be classified as belonging to one or the other (or as a separate unit).

---

[32] A good many states of ignorance were concealed by the qualitative approach. At meetings in which designers were asked to write down their numerical target for "high reliability," their numbers could be several orders of magnitude apart as well as being stated in different units of measure.

[33] "Reliability Theory and Practice," training program developed by ARINC Research Corporation, Washington, D.C., 1962.

TABLE 8-6   Stages of Reliability Analysis and Prediction*

	1 Start of design	2 During detailed design	3 At final design	4 From system tests	5 From customer usage
Basis	Prediction based on approximate part counts and part failure rates from previous product usage; little knowledge of stress levels, redundancy, etc.	Prediction based on quantities and types of parts, redundancies, stress levels, etc.	Prediction based on types and quantities of parts failure rates for expected stress levels, redundancies, external environments, special maintenance practices, special effects of system complexity, cycling effects, etc.	Measurement based on the results of tests of the complete system. Approximate reliability indexes are calculated from the number of failures and operating time	Same as (4) except calculations are based on customer usage data
Primary uses	1 Evaluate feasibility of meeting a proposed numerical requirement 2 Help in establishing a reliability goal for design	1 Evaluate overall reliability 2 Define problem areas	1 Evaluate overall reliability 2 Define problem areas	1 Evaluate overall reliability 2 Define problem areas	1 Measure achieved reliability 2 Define problems areas 3 Obtain data for future designs

*NOTE: System tests in (4) and/or (5) may reveal problems that result in a revision of the "final" design. Such changes can be evaluated by repeating steps 3, 4, 5.

From Juran, J. M., and F. M. Gryna, Jr., "Quality Planning and Analysis," McGraw-Hill Book Company, New York, 1970, p. 140.

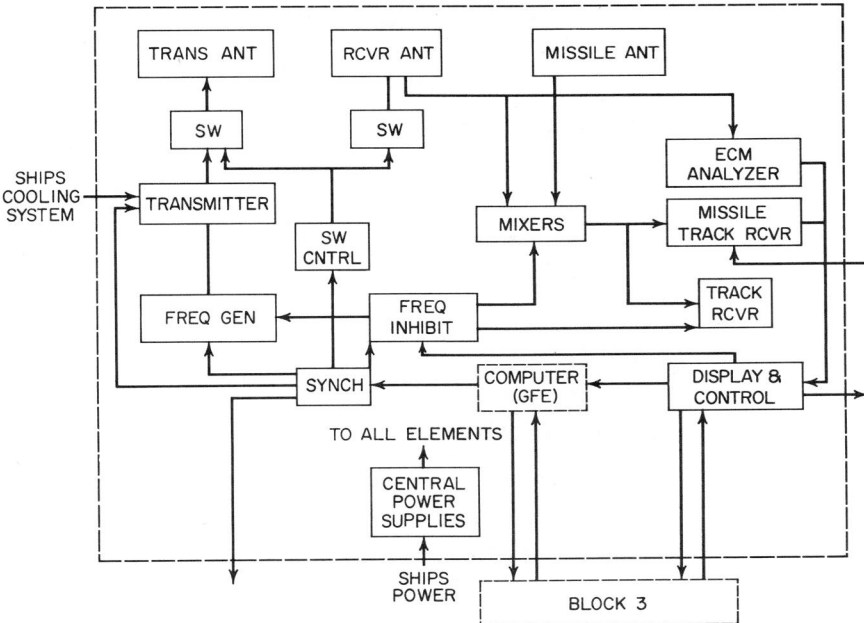

Fig. 8-4 Functional block diagram. (From "Handbook of Reliability Engineering," NAVAIR 00-65-502, courtesy the Commander, Naval Air Systems Command.)

2. *Draw a Reliability Block Diagram.* The reliability block diagram (Figure 8-5) is similar to the functional block diagram, but it is modified to emphasize those aspects which influence reliability. The diagram shows, in sequence, those elements which *must* function for successful operation of each unit. Redundant paths and alternative modes should be clearly shown. Elements which are not essential to successful operation need not be included, e.g., decorative escutcheons. Also, because of the many thousands of individual parts that constitute a complex product, it is necessary to exclude from the calculation those classes of parts which are used in mild applications. The contribution of such parts to product unreliability is relatively small. Examples of items that can generally be disregarded are tube sockets, terminal strips, knobs, chassis, and panels.

3. *List Factors Relevant to Reliability.* For each critical part, it is necessary to list all factors which are relevant to reliability. These factors include part function, part ratings, internal environments and stresses, expected external environments and stresses, and duty ("on" time) cycle. This detailed information makes it possible to perform a stress analysis which will not only provide information on the appropriate adjustments to standard input data but also serve to uncover weak or questionable areas in the design. Parts with dependent failure probabilities should be grouped together into modules so that the assumptions upon which the prediction is based are satisfied.

4. *Select Part Reliability Data.* The required part data consist of information on catastrophic failures and on tolerance variations with respect to time under known operating and environmental conditions. Acquiring these data is a major problem for the designer, since there is no single reliability data bank comparable to handbooks such as those that are available for physicial properties of materials. Instead,

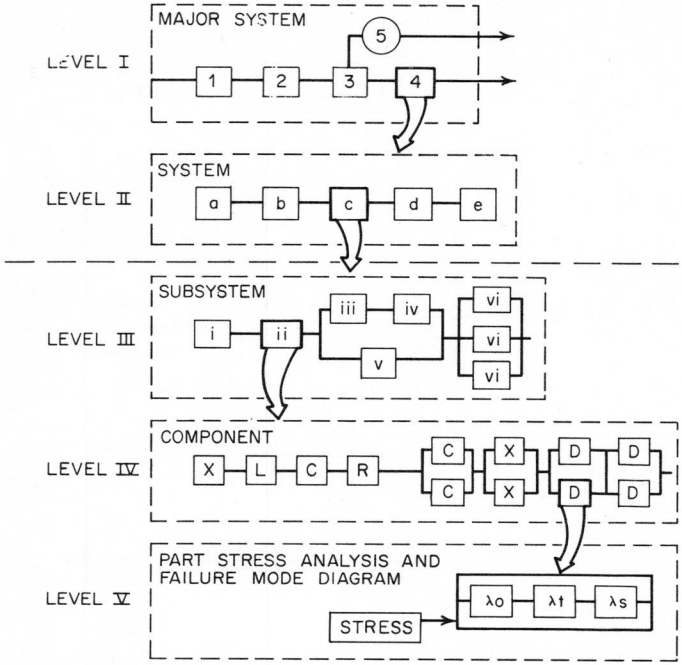

Fig. 8-5 Reliability block diagram. (From "Handbook of Reliability Engineering," NAVAIR 00-65-502, courtesy the Commander, Naval Air Systems Command.)

the designer must build up his own data bank by securing reliability data from a variety of sources:

Field performance studies conducted under controlled conditions.
Specification life tests.
Data from parts manufacturers or industry associations.
Customers' part-qualification and inspection tests.
Government agency data banks such as MIL-HDBK-217A, which contains a large amount of failure rate data together with stress analysis procedures essential to its use. [34, 35]

5. *Determine Appropriate Reliability Relationships for Each Part, Part Class, or Module in the Product.* Basic reliability data such as are acquired in Step 4 are in the form of curves (e.g., Figure 8-6) which show the relationship of reliability to various stress levels, e.g., failure rates versus ambient temperature under various ratios of operating voltage to rated voltage. Applying these curves to the specific units, applications, and environments provides the reliability numbers which become the basis of summing up failure rates in Step 6, below.

In the absence of basic reliability data, it may be feasible to make reasonably ac-

[34] MIL-HDBK-217A, "Reliability Stress and Failure Data for Electronic Equipment," December 1965.

[35] An example of an inter-agency program is the Failure Rate Data (FARADA) Program administered by the Naval Fleet Missile Systems Analysis and Evaluation Group, Corona, California.

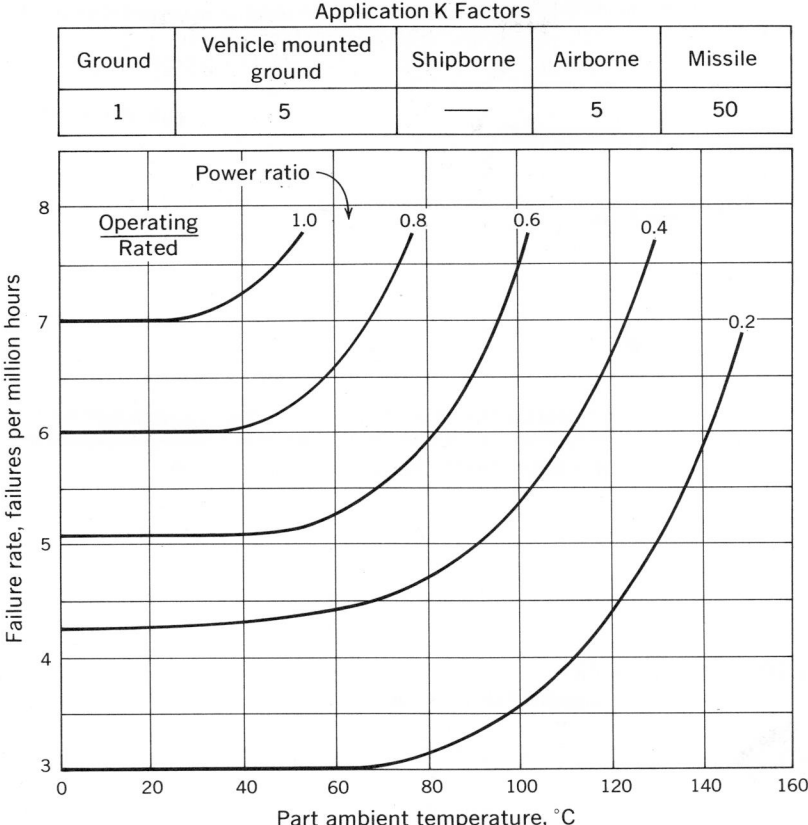

Application K Factors				
Ground	Vehicle mounted ground	Shipborne	Airborne	Missile
1	5	——	5	50

Fig. 8-6 Failure rates related to stress and ambient temperatures.

curate estimates based on past experience with similar part types. Lacking such experience, it becomes necessary to perform part evaluation tests to secure the data.

6. *Determine Block and Unit Failure Rates.* The failure data of Step 5 are added up to obtain failure rates for higher-level product units. (See Table 8-5 and associated discussion.) Pertinent subsystem or assembly correction factors, such as those taking into account the effects of maintenance, can be applied at this point. Block and unit rates are in turn combined to give subsystem and system failure rates.

7. *Determine Appropriate Reliability Unit of Measure.* This is the choice of reliability index or "figure of merit" as listed in Table 8-4, i.e., MTBF, failure rate, etc.

8. *Apply the Resulting Predictions.* The predictions not only indicate the expected reliability of the product but also point up the weak areas, the extent of improvement needed, and likely opportunities for securing improvement.

Failure Mode and Failure Effect Analysis This early warning or preventive technique provides the designer with a methodical way of studying the causes and effects of failures before the design is finalized. In essence, a product (at the system and/or lower levels) is examined for all the ways in which a failure can occur. For each potential failure, an estimate is made of its effect on the total system and of its seriousness. In addition, a review is made of the action being taken (or planned) to minimize the probability of failure or to minimize the effect of failure.

Figure 8-7 is an example of the analysis. Each hardware item is listed on a separate line, and entries are made in the appropriate columns. The analysis is elaborated to include such matters as:

Safety. This is the most serious of all failure effects and often is handled through special programs. (See below, under Safety in New-Product Design.)

Effect on downtime, i.e., must the system stop until repairs are made, or can repairs be made during an off-duty time?

Access, i.e., what hardware items must be removed to get at the failed component?

Repair planning, i.e., repair time, special repair tools, etc.

Recommendations for changes in designs or specifications, for added tests, for instructions to be included in manuals of inspection, operation or maintenance.

For most products, it is not economic to conduct the analysis of failure mode and failure effect for each component. Instead, engineering judgment is used to single out those items which are critical to the operation of the product. As the analysis proceeds, the designer will discover that he lacks ready answers for some of the failure modes and is therefore forced to dig deeper until he finds the answers.

Generally, a failure mode and effect analysis on one item is also helpful to the designers of other items in the system. In addition, the analyses are useful to the studies of maintainability and safety, and should be planned in cooperation with the specialists who work on these subjects (see below, under Maintainability, and also under Safety).

Parts Selection and Control   Table 8-5 demonstrates how system reliability rests on a base of reliability of the component parts. A dramatic example is the improvement in reliability of electronic circuitry through development of high reliability parts. During the 1960s the failure rates of these parts averaged as follows:[36]

Types of circuit elements	*Failure rate per million hours*
Pre-1960 electron tubes	48.0
1965 solid state	4.4
High-reliability solid state	0.23
Integrated circuits	0.085

The vital role played by part reliability has resulted in programs for thorough selection, evaluation, and control of parts. These programs include mainly:

1. *Parts application study.* The specification and design information supplied by parts manufacturers generally provides guidelines for application. If previous history is available from parts used in similar products, this history becomes an essential input. New applications must be subjected to qualification tests, including overstress, to determine safety factors.

2. *Approved parts list.* Preliminary component-parts lists are reviewed as early in the design phase as possible to:

Verify that proved parts (i.e., proved in previous usage) are being utilized wherever possible

---

[36] Lennon, John R., A Reliability/Cost of Ownership Approach to Microavionics, *Proceedings, Eleventh National Symposium on Reliability,* IEEE, 1965, p 38. (The data are averages for seven types of circuits.)

PERSON MAKING ANALYSIS D. R. Longabach

DATE ___10/1/69___

PROJECT NO. ___X101___

SYSTEM ___Planetary group___

P = probability of occurrence

D = likelihood of damage to surrounding components

S = seriousness of failure to the system

1 = very low or none (<1 in 10)	2 = low or minor (3 in 10)	3 = medium or (50-50)	significant			4 = high (7 in 10)	5 = very high or catastrophic (>9 in 10)

COMPONENT (PART NO.)	POSSIBLE FAILURE	CAUSE OF FAILURE (FAILURE MECHANISM)	P	D	S	EFFECT OF FAILURE ON SYSTEM	HOW CAN FAILURE BE ELIMINATED OR REDUCED
Gear, Hub Part No.	Grooved external spline teeth	Wear, case crushing	2	3	5	Will not transmit power	Heat treat splines
Plate, Reaction Part No.	Warped	Not made flat	3	2	4	Clutch slippage	Provide straightening
		Excessive heat, slippage	1	2	4	Clutch slippage	Increase engaging force
	Worn or smeared	Lack of lube	1	2	4	Clutch slippage	Increase lube oil
Disc Assembly Part No.	Warped	Excessive heat, slippage				Clutch slippage	Increase lube oil
	Loss of friction material	Bond failure	1	3	5	Clutch slippage	Develop better bonding
Spring Part No.	Broken	Fatigue	2	2	3	Lack of plate separation	Design for lower stress
		Improper assembly	1	2	3	Lack of plate separation	Provide assembly instruction

Fig. 8-7 Failure mode and failure effect analysis. *(Courtesy, Caterpillar Tractor Co.)*

Verify that unproved or questionable parts are actually capable of meeting reliability or environmental ratings[37]

Compare ratings or qualification test data with anticipated environmental (life) stresses

3. *Critical components list.* A component part is considered "critical" if any of the following conditions apply:

It has a high population in the equipment

It has a single source of supply

It must function to special, tight limits

It has not been proved to the reliability standard, i.e., no test data, insufficient usage data

The critical components list should be prepared early in the design effort, certainly well within the first six months of the program and extending at most to the end of the first year. It is common practice to formalize these lists, showing, for each critical component, the nature of the critical features, the plan to quantify reliability, the plan for improving reliability, etc. The list becomes the basic planning document for (1) test programs to qualify parts; (2) design guidance in application studies and techniques; and (3) design guidance for application of redundant parts, circuits or subsystems.

4. *Derating practice.* Derating is the assignment of a product to operate at stress levels below its normal rating, e.g., a capacitor rated at 300 volts is used in a 200-volt application. For many components, data are available showing failure rate as a function of stress levels. For example, Figure 8-6 shows how failure rate of a line of electronic components varies with ambient temperature and applied stress. The conservative designer will use such curves to achieve reliability by using the parts at low power ratios and low ambient temperatures.

Some companies have established internal policies with respect to derating. Derating is a form of quantifying the factor of safety and hence lends itself to setting guidelines as to the margins to be used.[38]

Derating may be considered as a method of determining more scientifically the factor of safety which engineers have long provided on an empirical basis. For example, if the calculated load was 20 tons, the engineers might design the structure to withstand 100 tons as a protection against unanticipated loads, misuse, hidden flaws, deterioration, etc.

A related technique[39] is that of calculating the variation of stresses to establish a "reliability boundary" at a given number of standard deviations beyond the average stress. The average strength is then specified to exceed the reliability boundary, again by a given number of standard deviations. See, in this connection, Section 22, Figure 22-19 and related discussion.

Demonstration Test Programs Demonstration tests are those conducted to verify that a product will work under operating conditions for a given length of time.

From the users' viewpoint, the most important reliability tests are those applied to the system or to the end product. However, much testing is conducted at the part, subassembly, and assembly levels prior to receipt of hardware for system tests. It is not feasible, due to cost and schedule constraints, to conduct statistically significant tests at all equipment levels. The usual emphasis is on (1) the component and

[37] This requirement may force deferment of use of new components which have attractive properties until the evidence of reliability has been established.

[38] See generally MIL-HDBK-217A, "Reliability Stress and Failure Data for Electronic Equipment," December 1965. Fig. 8-6 is derived from this.

[39] Lusser, Robert, "Reliability through Safety Margins," U.S. Army Ordnance Missile Command, Redstone Arsenal, Alabama, October 1959.

parts level and (2) the complete system level. While certain critical assemblies may be subjected to reliability qualification tests, this is held to a minimum.

Demonstration tests follow the AGREE definition of reliability and hence focus on the three elements of: performance requirements, environmental conditions during usage, and time requirements.

Performance requirements are defined uniquely for each product, e.g., the kilowatt output of a generator. During the performance, the product is subjected to stresses, and these stresses vary (e.g., a tractor works in sandy soil on one day and in rocky soil the next day). Hence stress must be viewed as a distribution rather than as a single value. Similarly, strength varies from one unit of product to the next and hence must also be viewed as a distribution. Obtaining the data needed to construct these distributions can be so costly that shortcuts have to be taken, e.g., sampling actual usage of the product by typical customers. An alternative is to simulate customer usage, e.g., in the company "proving ground." The resulting data disclose the stress levels being encountered. Tests must then be conducted to verify that the product can withstand the expected stress levels for the required time period.

Environmental conditions (e.g., temperature, humidity, vibration) are critical to many products. Here again, the problem is twofold: (1) discovering the expected environmental levels and (2) testing to verify that the product can meet them. By skillful design of test programs, it may be feasible to meet both of these needs simultaneously. For example, Figure 8-8 summarizes the testing done on six guidance systems. All six systems are first subjected to an acceptance inspection. They are then divided into two groups of three each. One group is subjected to the transportation and handling environments indicated, in order to discover the effect of transportation and handling on later operations. (The other group does not undergo these tests.) All six systems are then run through the countdown and flight test environments listed. Two systems are run at the expected flight test environment; two are run at a level 10% higher than the expected; the remaining two are run at a level 20% higher than the expected. (When feasible, raising the levels until failure occurs will provide information on the margin of safety inherent in the design.)

Time requirements are the third element of reliability testing. Testing one item of product to failure, then repairing it and testing again to failure, through several cycles, may provide good information on that particular item. It may also provide useful data on product wear-out,[40] but it will not necessarily reveal the variability that occurs among many items of the same product due to part and production variability. However, testing many items of product for a shorter period of time will produce test data and failure data which do show many effects of part and production variability. Bringing these test data to a state of statistical significance can run into cost problems both as to test facilities and as to "appraisal" costs. Nor are these tests complete—they may still fail to disclose critical early wear-out characteristics of the product.

Interpretation of time-oriented test data is aided greatly by use of the Weibull form of data plotting.[41] These plots usually approximate a straight line and simplify the extrapolation process. They are also useful for comparing the results of

---

[40] In test of an aircraft engine component, analysis showed that a single test of 800 hours duration would have been six times more likely to reveal a certain failure than tests of 200 hours each on four separate engines. See Markham, B. G., Reliability Assurance and the Concord Engines, SAE paper no. 670316.

[41] See Section 22, under Predicting Reliability during Design Based on the Weibull Probability Distribution. See especially Figs. 22-9 and 22-10, plus related discussion.

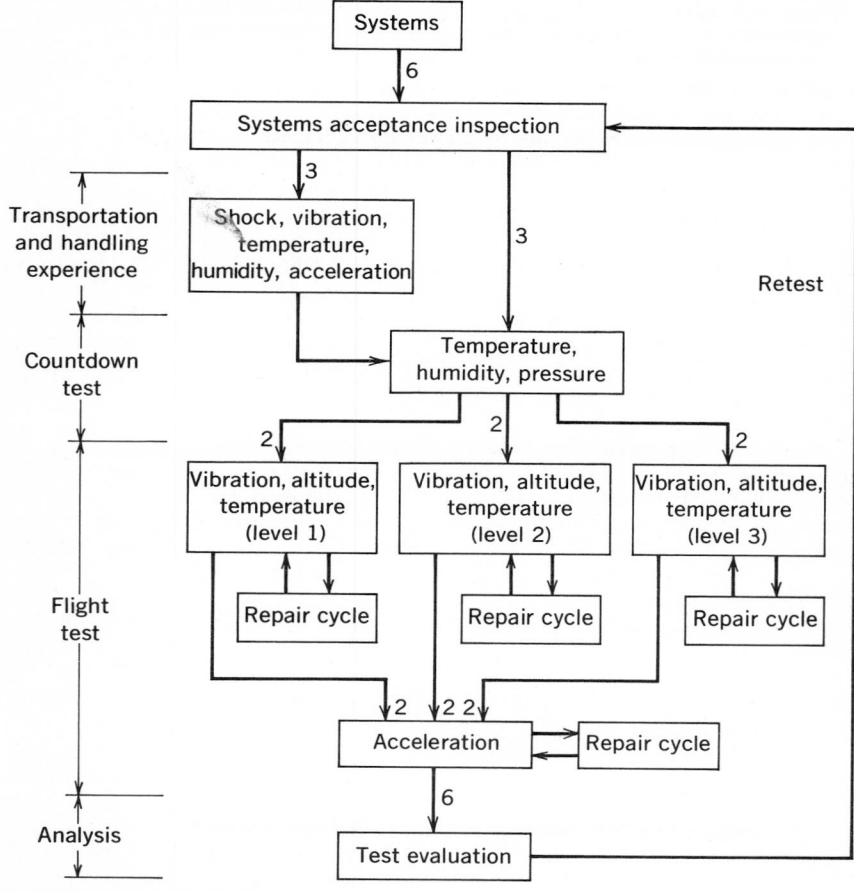

Fig. 8-8 Reliability qualification test.

accelerated testing (see below) with results of testing under normal operating conditions. This tool is a "must" for the designer.

Accelerated testing is a common form of securing reliability test data at reduced testing cost. In this form of testing, the products are made to perform at abnormally high levels of stress and/or environments in order to make them fail sooner. (Earlier failures mean less test equipment, lower testing costs, and earlier answers.) Extrapolation is then used to convert the short life under severe conditions into expected life under normal conditions. Great care is needed to assure that the accelerated test time is properly correlated to normal usage time to avoid overstating the expected life. A further problem is that accelerated testing can introduce new failure modes which do not occur during normal product usage. Taking such failure modes seriously has sometimes led to major redesigns which provided no benefit from the standpoint of the original product requirements. While the benefits from accelerated testing can be substantial, there are serious risks of being misled. It is obviously essential to apply engineering judgment in planning reliability demonstration tests so as to balance the factors of duration of test, severity of test, and size of sample.

All test results and descriptions of failures should be recorded in detail. These data serve multiple purposes:

Understanding of the nature of the product at the time of test

Comparison with subsequent part and system performance data to facilitate reliability control at later stages of the program

Inputs to the data banks

A number of Sections of this Handbook deal with the collection and analysis of test data, notably Section 12 (Inspection and Test), Section 13 (Measurement), Section 19 (Documentation), Section 20 (Computers), and Sections 22 to 28 (Statistical Methods). In addition, the "industry" Sections (29 to 47) include numerous examples of the use of performance test programs.

Both governmental and nongovernmental programs increasingly contain requirements for reliability testing. In some cases these requirements are a part of the invitation to bid. In such cases it is most important to make a "good and immediate" reliability prediction on the proposed hardware. If the prediction shows that the actual hardware reliability will be close to or less than the customer requirement, this can severely affect cost and schedule. Further, whatever the prediction shows, the penalties imposed (if the test is failed) should be carefully reviewed.

While there are many ways to demonstrate reliability, the government specifications are built around the test in the so-called AGREE report. One of these specifications[42] (MIL-R-22793) determines what the reliability is. The other specification[43] (MIL-STD-781B) determines if the actual reliability meets the requirement. Both specifications involve operation under temperature cycling and under vibration conditions.

MIL-STD-781B (the more commonly applied) is used for production items as a condition of acceptance. Usually, a sample from the first production lot is put through a reliability "qual" (qualification) test, and subsequent lot samples are tested as a condition of lot acceptance. If a sample fails the test, the entire lot is rejected, and subsequent action requires customer concurrence.

Nongovernment programs have not been extensively standardized, so that there is a good deal of individual negotiation of the contract provisions. For example, when the New York Metropolitan Transit Authority purchased new subway cars in 1971, the contract stipulated that the first eight-car train must complete 30 consecutive days in revenue passenger service without equipment failure. (Any breakdown starts the 30 days all over again.)[44]

Consumer products also have need for demonstration test programs. In these cases it is the manufacturer himself who needs the demonstration to assure himself that he will not create a marketing or warranty disaster. If the product is critical to safety and health, he may have need to assure the government regulators as well.

Specifiers should be alert to the precise wording of the reliability requirements portion of the product specification. Some critical problems have arisen because of failure to grasp the distinction between two seemingly similar wordings: (1) The MTBF shall be no less than x hours and (2) The MTBF shall be x hours.

Of these wordings, (1) states the minimum acceptable while (2) states the average

[42] MIL-R-22973, "General Specification for Reliability Index Determination for Avionic Equipment Models," October 1961.

[43] MIL-STD-781B, "Reliability Tests, Exponential Distribution," November, 1967.

[44] *Business Week*, Jan. 8, 1972, p. 72. The severity of this contract may have been the result of an earlier contract by the Long Island Railroad (a subsidiary of the same Authority) which bypassed the test of prototype models in order to gain prompt delivery. The result was a severe service problem.

value. Experience has shown that wordings such as (1) require two or three times the average MTBF of (2) to meet the minimum acceptable value!

There are further needs for caution is specifying reliability requirements:

1. For a time-oriented performance, a statement of product reliability purely in percentage is meaningless. For example, a reliability is specified as 95%. However, the buyer has in mind mission times of 1.5 hours whereas the vendor has in mind mission times of 1.1 hours.

2. When MTBF is specified as an average, the word "average" should be included in the specification, e.g., not "The MTBF shall be x hours" but "The MTBF shall average x hours." In addition, the specification should define the "units" from which the average is to be calculated.

3. In some cases, specifications have included a confidence level; e.g., "The MTBF shall be at least 100 hours at the 95% confidence level." In such cases, the MTBF needed to meet the demonstration requirement may be many times the MTBF number specified! For further discussion, see Section 22, under Statistical Estimation: Confidence Limits.

A further critical wording is the definition of what constitutes a failure. This definition can readily be decisive on whether the product meets the test.[45] It is important to determine and specify any exceptions to the failure definition early, particularly with respect to periodic maintenance, e.g.; replacement prior to wear-out. In consumer products, the definition of failure is critical to the provisions of the warranty; e.g., was the product serviced in accordance with the provisions of the service manual?

Reliability Data Systems   Reliability data serve several important purposes:

1. To detect current reliability problems and assist in their solution. An example is the use of the data feedback loop shown in Figure 8-9. This loop operates in the conventional way: failures are detected and reported, analyses are made for causes, remedies are devised and applied.

2. To provide managers with quantitative information on product performance and on the status of problems. This feedback should not be limited to information on current problems; it should include also summaries in the form of executive reports, as discussed in Section 21.

3. To assist in reliability improvement programs. (See below, under Reliability Improvement.)

4. To provide failure history and other reference data for use in product changes and in future products.[46] This is the "data bank" concept and serves the needs of reliability in a manner analogous to that served by handbooks of properties of materials (when choosing materials for specific applications).

Reliability Data Banks.   The term "data bank" implies an organized approach to data collection, classification, analysis, summary, and retrieval. Despite the seeming advantages of such an organized approach, it is very difficult and costly to

---

[45] Note the applicable paragraphs of MIL-STD-781, which cites the environmental profile ("Test Level. . . ."), the acceptance criteria ("Test Plan. . . .") and may contain a definition of what constitutes a failure.

[46] Unless data are available on failure rate history of basic components and parts, all reliability predictions are purely theoretical. Calculations of MTBF for the same design (by different reliability engineers) can readily differ by an order of magnitude or more if no experience data are available. In one survey the second most popular reason for not attaining reliability goals was "lack of field usage data." (This survey was taken in the electronics industry, which is probably the furthest advanced in creating reliability data banks.) See Freedberg, Marv, Reliability Management, A Survey, *Industrial Quality Control,* November 1966, pp. 224–226.

execute. In practice, companies make only limited use of the available data. These data originate from:

1. Engineering, preproduction, production or special tests (e.g., test track, test kitchen) under the manufacturer's control. These tests are usually conducted on the premises but may include "captive" usage tests, e.g., employee homes, consumer panels, captive sales outlets.

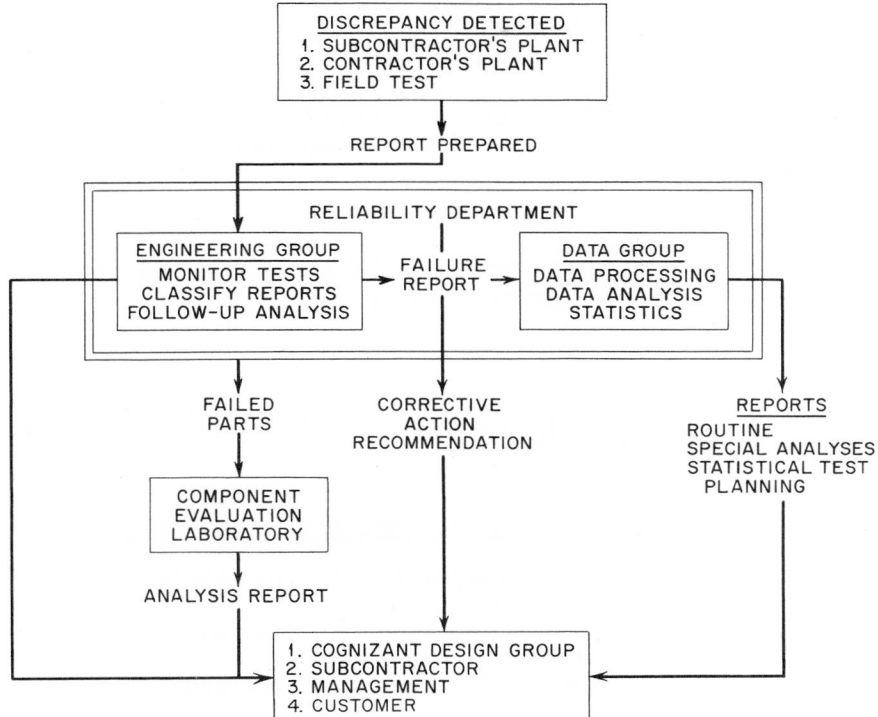

Fig. 8-9 Failure reporting, analysis and feedback.

2. Vendors and major subcontractors. Increasingly these companies are organizing their test data in forms which can be readily used by their customers for product design purposes.

3. Field performance data, including customer returns. While these data have an obvious dramatic effect on practical men, they are suspect in many ways: the sources of the data are notoriously difficult to control; the data are frequently incomplete and of dubious validity; coverage (e.g., the spectrum of environments) is incomplete. For a more extensive discussion, see Section 15, under Field Performance Measures.

4. Independent data banks. These are springing up in recognition of the fact that basic failure data can be used by many companies. For such multiple use, it may be more economic to maintain a central data bank instead of numerous duplicating company data banks. The more prominent of these banks are discussed in Section 10, under Vendor Qualification Process. In addition, there are laboratories

devoted mainly to testing products for safety, and these laboratories develop test data which have wide application.   See Section 4, under Consumer Test Services.

Acquisition of data is only the first step in creating a working data bank.   The data must be analyzed to assist specialists in finding causes and remedies.   There must be summaries to permit evaluation of trends and identification of the more important problems.   Provision must be made for ready access so that potential users will not be discouraged in their efforts to find what they are looking for.   All this involves considerable work plus special skills, as discussed in other Sections of this Handbook, mainly 19 (Documentation), 20 (Computers), and 21 (Upper Management).   Normally, a trained specialist must be given responsibility for organizing and performing this work.   It cannot be left on a basis of each man for himself.

The operational reliability of most products is determined by the four factors of design, quality of parts and materials, workmanship, use and maintenance.   Failure reporting, data banks, etc., are of value only as they contribute to improvement in one or more of these factors.   In turn, virtually all departments of the manufacturing company, as well as the vendors, subcontractors, users and repair shops, are influential either in attaining or failing to attain reliability.   It is this wide involvement which makes the failure data problem so large and complex.

The most important of the data acquisitions is the reports of failures and malfunctions which pertain to end-product reliability.   Provision should be made for securing these reports from vendors and subcontractors, from field test and usage sites, and from the manufacturers' own departments.   The latter include not only the development and test laboratories but also the activities involved with "workmanship", i.e., methods, fabrication, assembly, test, troubleshooting.

Many reliability programs are built with emphasis on field performance data and with inadequate use of in-plant test data.   It is a mistake to structure programs in this way.   Not only do they lose much of the advantage of early warning but the field data are often unreliable and incomplete for reasons noted above.   The most "cost effective" data system is that which has a positive influence on end-product quality through actions taken *early* in the development or production phases.

Reliability Improvement   The general approach to quality improvement (Section 16) is widely applicable to reliability improvement as far as the economic analysis and the managerial tools are concerned.   The differences are in the technological tools used for diagnosis and remedy.

Projects for Improvement.   These are identified mainly through use of the Pareto principle (see Section 2).   For example, a summary of flight test data on an aircraft fleet showed that 10% of the aircraft components accounted for 82% of the removals, with 2% accounting for 53% of the removals.   In consequence, assignment of reliability engineers was concentrated on 150 out of a possible 2,300 items.[47][48]

Relative contribution to failure rates is evident from quantification studies.   The lower third of Table 8-5 makes clear which components must be improved if end reliability is to be improved. Relative contribution to downtime is still another source of project ideas.   See, for example, Figure 8-11*b*, below.

Solutions for Projects.   In those cases where the predicted or actual reliability falls short of meeting the reliability goals, the designer has a variety of methods for closing the gap.   Some of these methods (e.g., derating and added factors of safety)

[47] Adkins, L. A., Jr., C-141 Reliability Flight Test Program, *Industrial Quality Control,* February 1967, pp. 370–373.

[48] For a case example of improvement, see Wagner, R. H., Designing Electronic Reliability into Commercial Automatic Pilots, *Proceedings, Ninth Annual Symposium on Reliability,* IEEE, 1963, pp. 502–512.

have been described under Parts Selection and Control, above.   Beyond these methods, the designer may:

1. *Review the users' needs* to see if the *function* of the unreliable parts is really necessary to the user.   If not, eliminate that part of the design entirely.   Alternatively, look to see if the reliability index (figure of merit) correctly reflects the real interests of the user.   For example, availability is sometimes more meaningful than reliability.   If so, a good maintenance program might improve availability and hence ease the reliability problem.

2. *Consider trade-offs* of reliability for other parameters, e.g., functional performance, weight.   Here again it may be found that the customers' real needs may be better served by such a trade-off.

3. *Use Redundancy.*   When a designer provides redundancy, he provides more than one means for accomplishing a given task in such a way that all the means must fail before the system fails.

There are several types of redundancy, a common form being parallel redundancy. A familiar example is the multiengined aircraft, which is so designed that even if one engine fails, the aircraft will still be able to continue on to a safe landing.

Under conditions of independent failures, the overall reliability for parallel redundancy is expressed by the formula

$$P_s = 1 - (1 - P_i)^n$$

where P_s = reliability of the system
   P_i = reliability of the individual elements in the redundancy
   n = number of identical redundant elements

Figure 8-10 shows some simple examples of series-parallel and parallel-series redundancies and calculates the system reliability versus that prevailing for the case of no redundancy.[49]

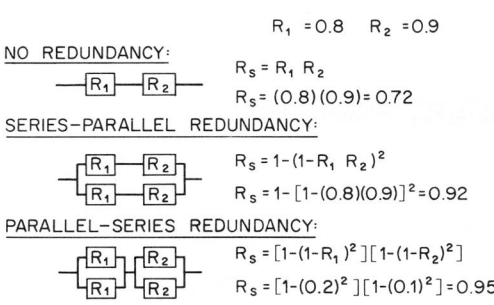

Fig. 8-10   Redundancy.

4. *Control the operating environment* to provide conditions which yield lower failure rates.   Common examples are *(a)* potting electronic components to protect them against climate and shock and *(b)* use of cooling systems to keep down ambient temperatures.

5. *Specify replacement schedules* to remove and replace low-reliability parts before they reach wear-out stage.   In many cases the replacement is made contingent on the results of checkouts or tests which determine whether degradation has reached a prescribed limit.

[49] For a more extended discussion, plus performance curves, see ARINC Research Corporation, "Reliability Engineering," Prentice-Hall, Inc., Englewood Cliffs, N.J., 1964, pp. 211–213.

6. *Prescribe Screening Tests.* These tests are intended to detect infant mortality failures and to eliminate substandard components. The tests take various forms: bench tests, "burn in," accelerated life tests.

7. *Conduct Research and Development.* This may be done to attain an improvement in the basic reliability of those components which contribute most of the unreliability. While such improvements avoid the need for subsequent trade-offs, they may require advancing the state of the art and hence an investment of unpredictable size.

Although none of the foregoing provides a perfect solution, the range of choice is broad. In some instances the designer can arrive at a solution single-handedly. More usually he must collaborate with other company specialists. In still other cases the customer and/or the company management must concur because of the broader considerations involved.

Reliability Growth   The continuing efforts to reduce failure rates result in continuing increases in reliability—a phenomenon known as "reliability growth." Some of this takes place during the design phases, through the response to design reviews and to the test data. Additional improvement takes place when field performance data stimulate further action.

Reliability growth can be measured,[50] and many programs provide for this as a check against goals. In turn, reliability goals are commonly set with an awareness that growth will take place.

There have been a number of efforts to predict reliability growth as an aid to setting goals. While prediction models are numerous, the published results based on actual data are few. One study on five different products (relatively complex aircraft accessories) reached the conclusion that failure rates decline at a rate which is inverse to the square root of product usage time.[51] For example, the products in product line X have been in operational use for a cumulative total of 20,000 hours and have attained a failure rate of 0.02. As the products continue to be used and accumulate a total of 80,000 hours, the failure rate will meanwhile have been cut to 0.01.

MAINTAINABILITY IN NEW-PRODUCT DESIGN

While product maintenance is an ancient problem (buildings, clothing, ships, etc.), the extent and importance of maintenance has grown remarkably during the twentieth century. Some of the major areas of growth have been in:

1. Central services such as electric power and telephone communication, without which the industrial societies cannot function.[52]

2. Mechanized and automated factories in which maintenance is a major force in achieving productivity.

3. New consumer products, e.g., automobiles, household appliances, and electronic entertainment products. For these products, the costs of maintenance over the service life of the products exceed the original price.[53]

---

[50] This growth is measured in units of measure which vary with the type of product and usage. For the C-141 aircraft (a large cargo carrier), the measures included departure reliability, abort reliability, maintenance man-hours per flight hour, maintenance actions per flight hour, and unscheduled removals per flight hour. See Hamilton, D. O., and W. G. Ness, Aircraft Reliability Growth Characteristics, *Proceedings, 15th Annual Symposium on Reliability,* IEEE, 1969, pp. 465–471.

[51] Private communication to J. M. Juran.

[52] See the concept of "life behind the quality dikes," in Juran, J. M., Mobilizing for the 1970s, *Quality Progress,* August 1969, pp. 8–17.

[53] See Section 4, under Life Cycle Costing, especially Table 4-6; see also Section 15, under Field Service.

4. New military equipment and systems for which costs of maintenance soared to prohibitive figures. In a comprehensive study by the author (under sponsorship of the U.S. Air Force's Rome Air Development Center), it was found that for ground electronic equipment, the *annual* maintenance costs were from 60% to five times the original cost of the equipment.[54] More recent figures, from British sources,[55] suggest that the annual cost of maintenance runs to about the following percentages of the British military budgets:

Navy. 40%
Army 20%
Air Force 40%

In response to these growing needs, a good deal of constructive activity took place. Companies organized maintenance departments to improve the effectiveness of maintenance work and to provide feedback to component manufacturers. Numerous service shops sprang up to meet the needs of consumers. Researchers and designers came up with maintenance-free materials and components, e.g., aluminum siding, self-lubricating bearings.

A more elaborate, organized approach toward maintainability was that evolved by the U.S. military services starting in the 1950s. The initial step was establishment of definitions and preparation of program specifications. Next, requirements for maintainability were introduced through special contractual provisions or amendments. By 1959, formalized program specifications became available, one of the first being the Air Force MIL-M-26512 (June 1959). Since then numerous documents and specifications have been issued applicable to many products and systems (pneumatic, hydraulic, electronic, mechanical, etc.) designed to satisfy operational requirements applicable to shipboard, aircraft, missile, and ground environments.

While the primary impetus for maintainability as a new "discipline" is attributable to the Department of Defense, general industry was also taking measures which embodied the same principles. Despite varying applications (and resulting differences in terminology), the subsequent exchanges of experience have been stimulating an emerging set of universal concepts and definitions, as discussed below. The trends in volume and complexity of long-life products and systems all point to a growing need for maintainability for the foreseeable future.[56]

Maintainability Concepts and Terms Maintainability is one of the parameters which contributes to product availability (see Section 2, Figure 2-1 and related discussion). It is broadly defined as the ease of restoration of service after failure and is expressed in any of several "figures of merit," the most usual being mean time to repair (MTTR).

Figure 8-11a shows, in greater detail, the elements which make up total available time. It is seen that repair time is but one element of downtime. In addition, there is waiting time, both for spare parts and for documentation.

Figure 8-11b shows a management type of report on availability of two types

[54] McLaughlin, R. L., and H. D. Voegtlen, Ground Electronic Equipment Support Cost vs. Reliability and Maintainability, *Proceedings, Fifth Annual Symposium on Reliability*, IEEE, January 1959, pp. 36–42.

[55] "The Reliability of Service Equipment," The Institution of Mechanical Engineers, 1969, 1 Birdcage Walk, Westminster, London SW1. This volume contains 14 papers plus discussion from an Armed Services/Industry Conference. The data quoted are from pages 4, 10, and 15 respectively.

[56] Blanchard, B. S., and E. E. Lowery, "Maintainability Principles and Practices," McGraw-Hill Book Company, New York, 1969, pp. 1–6.

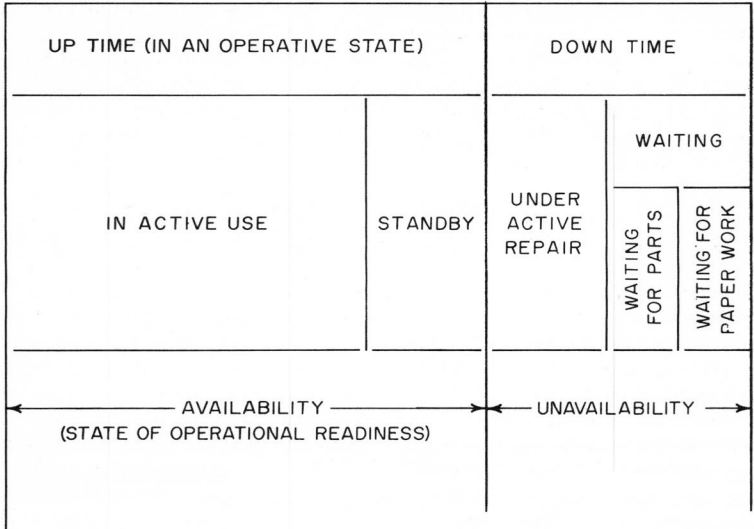

Fig. 8-11a   Ingredients of availability.

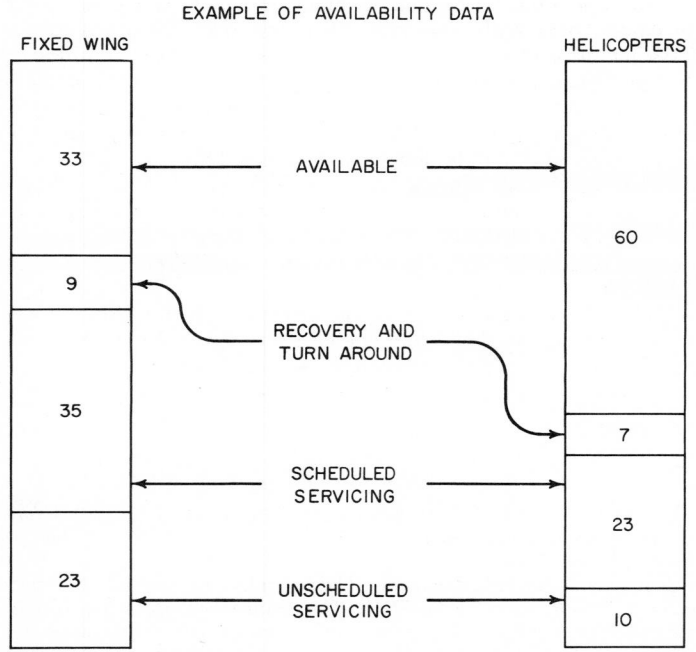

Fig. 8-11b   Example of availability data. *(Journal of the Royal Aeronautical Society.)*

of aircraft.[57] Some of the detail of Figure 8-11*b* is not included, but the presentation dramatizes the extent of the problems and opportunities.

The terminology associated with maintenance as well as the problems of carrying out field maintenance are discussed in Section 15, under Field Service: Maintenance. The reader is referred to that Section for details of definitions as well as for discussion of the problems of managing the service shops. In the present Section 8, the emphasis is on maintainability program elements and on design for maintainability.

The discipline of maintainability engineering is considered to include all the *effects* of product failures and ways of minimizing these effects. In contrast, the discipline of reliability engineering is considered to be concerned with the *causes* of product failure and their elimination.[58]

Those organizations which have adopted the concept of maintainability as a separate discipline have created a category of Maintainability Engineer. This engineer has then been assigned a role in the product design teams and has become the team specialist with respect to the topics elaborated below.

Maintainability Program Elements Formal maintainability programs start with the premise that maintainability can be programmed in the same way as the parameters of product capability or reliability. This program consists of four discrete work stages:

1. Planning, during which maintainability requirements are defined and translated into design criteria
2. Design application to establish the inherent functional and physical characteristics of the product
3. Measurement to verify quantitative and qualitative goals
4. Evaluation of the design and the results to assess areas for improvement.

These work stages are carried out through a series of tasks which consist mainly of the topics discussed below.

The Program Plan. The maintainability plan describes what is to be done, who is to do it, and when it is to be done. It includes provision for the following elements:

Allocation of quantitative maintainability design requirements and predicting achievement of these requirements.

Maintainability analysis to develop the overall maintenance concept and the general maintainability design requirements. This analysis produces and allocates *quantitative* maintenance requirements to the lower functional product levels.

A detailed maintenance concept and plan that establishes requirements for maintenance facilities, support equipment, and technical skills.

Maintainability design criteria that give specific guidance to design engineers.

Design trade-offs involving maintainability versus other parameters. (These are documented in status reports.)

Maintainability parameters (of the planned design) which must be predicted quantitatively.

Subcontractor maintainability requirements that must be included in specifications to vendors.

Design reviews that must include review of the maintainability of the design.

Maintenance data that must be collected and analyzed for repairs made during

---

[57] Beadon, J. A., The State of Affairs in the Royal Navy, *Journal of the Royal Aeronautical Society,* March 1966, pp. 394–396.

[58] This is the conceptual separation made by those who advocate a separate discipline of maintainability engineering. This view is contested by other advocates, and it is not clear whether, over the long run, the separation will endure. Of course, the activities will endure in any event.

tests.   The system must include a way of initiating corrective design action for maintenance problem areas.

Maintainability demonstrations that verify achievement of design goals.

It is seen that the program plan is all-pervasive, extending from the product design concept through the use and maintenance of the product over its entire service life.

Establishing the Requirements.   An overall maintainability goal is set for the product. This is apportioned to the various components of the product. Maintainability can be predicted on paper during the design phase, and it can finally be measured by timing the period required for certain maintenance actions on hardware. (This is analogous to goal setting, apportionment, prediction, and measurement for reliability.)

Measurement.   Figures of merit used for establishing the requirement may be any of the following:

Average maintenance time per product operating period (1,000 hours, 1 year, etc.)

Mean time to repair (MTTR)

Downtime per operating period (scheduled and unscheduled maintenance)

Availability per unit of time

Maintenance cost per unit of time

Total support cost per unit of time

An allowable task time is specified when a limit must be placed on downtime for maintenance. The customer may specify a maximum task time or he may establish a mean for all tasks. Terminology commonly used is (1) maximum time for unscheduled or scheduled maintenance, (2) mean time for unscheduled or scheduled maintenance, or (3) mean time to repair (MTTR).

A maximum task time limit, once it is clearly defined, can be imposed easily and directly at the product or component design level.

A mean task time limit is a difficult design requirement. It is usually specified at the system level and, because it is an average value, is of little or no significance to unit design engineers until it is allocated among the units of the product.

Evaluation.   Mean time, even when allocated, is a troublesome requirement for the design engineer. To determine mean task time, the engineer must weigh the time required for each individual task in accordance with the predicted frequency of that task. (For unscheduled maintenance, the frequency is essentially the predicted failure rate.) To meet this requirement, unit design parameters must be established at levels which assure that the product requirement will be met. These internal parameters may be almost arbitrary in value, but they should at least take into account the reliability predictions for the equipment. Several iterations of the maintenance task analysis are then made to assess design progress against requirements.

The customer may specify the percentage of total time that the equipment must be operable and ready. Common terms are (1) inherent availability—based on the characteristics of the design only, and (2) operational availability—based on the characteristics of the design modified by the capability of the logistic support system.

Availability is a *system* parameter and is seldom allocated to the unit level. Instead, factors which affect availability, (e.g., maintenance task time, frequency of maintenance) are estimated. These estimates are made during preliminary maintenance task and availability analyses. They are then allocated to the unit level to become internal unit design requirements. Design progress is monitored through iterations of the maintenance task and availability analyses. Unit allocations may be adjusted to make a more equitable distribution of the burden among the design areas and thus minimize product design cost.

Reliability analysis and prediction of failure rate is an essential ingredient in setting realistic requirements. In addition, routine servicing needs must be considered. Ground rules must be established and agreed upon between customer and manufacturer as to how these requirements are to be measured.

Maintainability Analysis and Prediction   Methods for analysis and prediction are still in the process of evolution, and there are several avenues of approach.[59]

1. Secure data of past experience on similar equipment, and extrapolate to make predictions on a new design.

2. Break down the maintenance task into elemental tasks needed to carry out maintenance at the various product levels. Then acquire data representing "standard" times to accomplish these tasks. These standards can then be used to build up a predicted total maintainability time in much the same way as reliability is built up from elemental failure rates or as time for manufacturing operations is built up from standard elemental times.

While this concept is basically sound, the work needed to compile the data bank of standard times is enormous.

3. Employ a widely used method developed under sponsorship of the Rome Air Development Center. A number of *dissimilar* equipments were studied in typical field use situations, in the laboratory, and through analysis of design features as shown in schematics, drawings, and early design criteria.[60,61] These studies identified nine universal tasks which occur in the vast majority of maintenance actions. Figure 8-12 shows these universal tasks and the sequence in which they are conducted to constitute a typical maintenance cycle.

The method continues on the premise that maintenance time depends on three main independent variables:

A — product design features
B — design dictates for maintenance personnel
C — design dictates for support facilities

An equation was then established to relate maintenance time, T, to these variables:

$$T = f(A, B, C)$$

Through regression analysis of actual maintenance data, constants were established for this equation as follows:

$$T = \text{antilog } (3.54651 - 0.02512A - 0.03055B - 0.01093C)$$

Once the constants for the regression equation have been computed, it remains to evaluate, for each part, the effect of the independent variables A, B, and C. This is done by the use of checklists developed for each variable. Table 8-7 shows a portion of such a checklist developed for rating variable A (product design features). Rat-

[59] Harring, Michael C., and Lyle R. Greenman, "Maintainability Engineering," Martin-Marietta Corporation, Orlando, Florida, 1965, pp. 31–71.

[60] Retterer, B. L., and H. D. Voegtlen, Advanced Maintainability Techniques for Aircraft Systems, *Proceedings, Aerospace Reliability and Maintainability Conference*, Spartan Books, Inc., Washington D.C., 1963, vol. 2, pp. 429–433.

[61] "Maintainability Prediction Technique," Phase IV Report, Contract AF30 (602) 2057, Rome Air Development Center Technical Report TDR-62-156, March 1962.

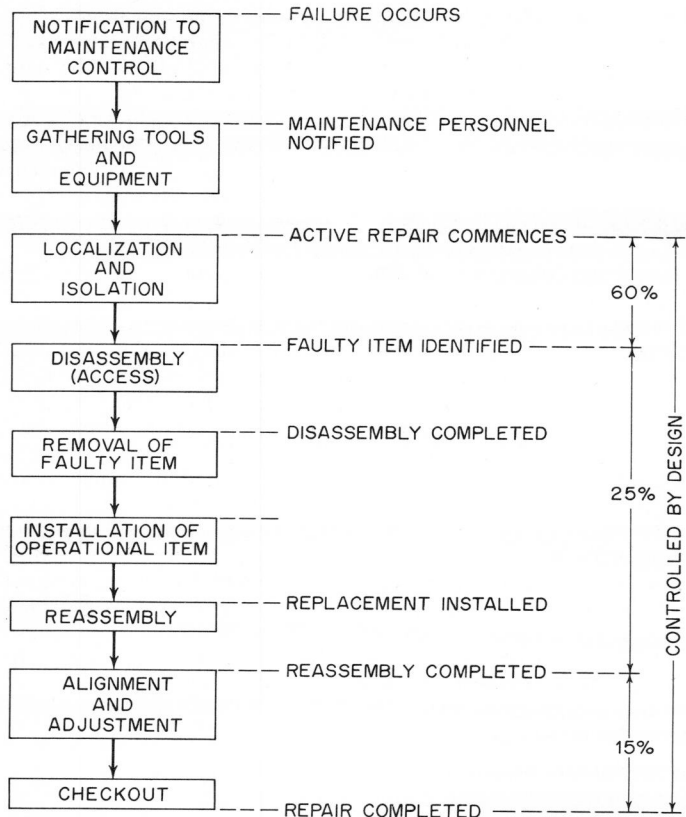

Fig. 8-12 Typical Maintenance Cycle.

ings range from 4 (minimal need for maintenance time) down to 0 (maximal need for maintenance time). Similar checklists are prepared for variables B and C.[62]

Using the design information (drawings and related technical data), the analyst applies the three checklists by rating the component under study for all the features of each checklist. The sums of the ratings become the values of the three variables A, B, and C for that component. These values are then converted into maintenance time through calculation from the regression equation or through use of an equivalent nomograph.[63]

This procedure must be repeated for each component in the system. Table 8-8 shows the results of rating numerous components for each of the variables A, B, and C. The calculated maintenance time for each component appears in the right-hand column. These time values can then be used directly with the component failure

[62] See Retterer, B. L., RADC Maintainability Prediction Technique Application, *ASQC Work Book for Second Product Maintainability Seminar*, Oct. 15 and 16, 1962.

[63] Retterer, B. L., and R. L. McLaughlin, Maintainability Prediction and Measurement. *Industrial Quality Control*, December 1963, pp. 16–20.

TABLE 8-7   Checklist for Rating Physical Design Factors

1. *Access* (External)
   a. Access adequate both for visual and manipulative tasks (electrical and mechanical). . 4
   b. Access adequate for visual but not for manipulative tasks 2
   c. Access adequate for manipulative but not for visual tasks 2
   d. Access not adequate for visual or manipulative tasks. 0
2. *Latches and Fasteners (External)*
   a. External latches and/or fasteners are captive, require no special tools, and need only
      a fraction of a turn for release. 4
   b. External latches and/or fasteners meet two of the above three criteria 2
   c. External latches and/or fasteners meet one of the above three criteria 0
3. *Latches and Fasteners (Internal)*
   a. Internal latches and/or fasteners are captive, need no special tools, and require only
      a fraction of a turn for release. 4
   b. Internal latches and/or fasteners meet two of the above three criteria 2
   c. Internal latches and/or fasteners meet one of the above three criteria. 0
4. *Access* (Internal)
   a. Access adequate for both visual and manipulative tasks (electrical and mechanical). . 4
   b. Access adequate for visual but not for manipulative tasks 2

. . . .

13. *Testing* (In Circuit)
    a. Defective part or component can be determined without removal from the circuit. . . 4
    b. Testing requires removal. 0
14. *Protective Devices*
    a. Equipment was automatically kept from operating after malfunction occurred to pre-
       vent further damage. (This refers to malfunction of such areas as bias supplies,
       keep-alive voltages, etc.). 4
    b. Indicators warned that malfunction has occurred. 2
    c. No provision has been made 0
15. *Safety* (Personnel)
    a. Task did not require work to be performed in close proximity to hazardous condi-
       tions (high voltage, radiation, moving parts, and/or high-temperature parts) 4
    b. Some delay encountered because of precautions taken 2
    c. Considerable time consumed because of hazardous conditions 0

TABLE 8-8   Maintainability Task Analysis and Time Prediction

Task	Part	Score A	B	C	Time, min
1	C618	18	22	17	172.4
2	K101	44	26	20	26.8
3	T102	24	22	16	124.9
4	V101	40	22	20	44.8
5	V102	40	22	20	44.8
. . .	. . .	. . .	. . .	. . .	. . .
47	V503	53	26	26	13.7
48	V504	35	21	17	69.2
49	V505	36	21	18	63.7
				Total	2508.2
				Mean	51.2

rates to predict total maintenance times for comparison with the design goals. In the event that there are deficiencies, the same figures are helpful in pointing out where the main contributions to high maintenance times are. These become the targets for improvement.

Table 8-9 is an example of the format in which calculated maintenance times can be made readily available to the designer.[64]

In another approach, a checklist for electronic equipment provides for rating a total of 208 product features for their relative effect on downtime, maintenance time, logistics requirements, equipment damage, and personnel injury. Maintainability is then quantified as a percentage of the favorable ratings for the applicable features. See MIL-M-55214 (EL), February 8, 1963.

TABLE 8-9   Maintenance Task Time "Standards"

	Tubes Average time (hours) to perform corrective maintenance tasks for eliminating equipment or system malfunction caused by tube failure					
	Corrective maintenance tasks					
	Diagnosis		Replacement		Test	
	Localization	Isolation	Disassembly	Reassembly	Alignment	Checkout
Part	0.021	0.265	0.313	0.438	0.156	0.175
Stage	0.029	0.315	0.231	0.362	0.077	0.167
Subassembly	0.037	0.394	0.165	0.262	0.045	0.158
Assembly	0.045	0.506	0.122	0.191	0.030	0.149
Unit	0.053	0.636	0.094	0.134	0.021	0.138
Group	0.063	0.776	0.071	0.090	0.015	0.124
Equipment	0.075	0.907	0.049	0.061	0.010	0.108
Subsystem	0.090	1.090	0.032	0.037	0.007	0.091
System	0.107	1.305	0.016	0.017	0.003	0.062
None	0.125	1.546	0.000	0.000	0.000	0.000

	Parts Average time (hours) to perform corrective maintenance tasks for eliminating equipment or system malfunction caused by part failure					
	Corrective maintenance tasks					
	Diagnosis		Replacement		Test	
	Localization	Isolation	Disassembly	Reassembly	Alignment	Checkout
Part	0.021	0.772	1.281	1.334	0.156	0.175
Stage	0.039	1.179	0.328	0.561	0.077	0.167
Subassembly	0.056	1.417	0.165	0.262	0.045	0.158
Assembly	0.073	1.569	0.122	0.191	0.030	0.149
Unit	0.089	1.700	0.094	0.134	0.021	0.138
Group	0.106	1.821	0.071	0.090	0.015	0.124
Equipment	0.121	1.924	0.049	0.061	0.010	0.108
Subsystem	0.136	2.022	0.032	0.037	0.007	0.091
System	0.150	2.100	0.016	0.017	0.003	0.062
None	0.165	2.172	0.000	0.000	0.000	0.000

[64] Derived from Margulies, G., and J. Sacks, Bureau of Ships Maintainability Specification, *Proceedings, Ninth Annual Symposium on Reliability,* IEEE, 1963, pp. 84–92.

Design Aids to Maintainability   The new attention devoted to maintainability has made clear that maintainability is an inherent part of product design planning, i.e., if the design fails to give consideration to maintainability, the result will be either a high cost of maintenance during the service life or costly design changes later in the product development cycle.[65]

To attain a proper balance between maintainability and other parameters requires that the product designer give consideration to various alternatives and trade-offs, such as the following:

Reliability versus Maintainability.   For example, given an availability requirement, should the response be an improvement in reliability or in maintainability?

Modular versus Nonmodular Construction.   Modular design requires added design effort but reduces the time required for diagnosis and remedy in the field.   The fault need only be localized to the module level, after which the defective module is unplugged and replaced.   This concept is being rapidly extended to consumer products such as television sets.

Repair versus Throwaway.   For some products or modules, the cost of field repair exceeds the cost of making new units in the factory.   In such cases design for throwaway is an economic improvement in maintainability.

Built-in versus External Test Equipment.   Built-in test features reduce diagnostic time but usually at an added investment.

Man versus Machine.   For example, should the operation/maintenance function be highly engineered with special instrumentation and repair facilities, or should it be left to skilled technicians with general-use equipment?

Beyond such widely prevailing questions, there are numerous design features which have been identified as contributing to good maintainability.   Table 8-10 is an example of a checklist used as a guide to good design for maintainability.[66]   It is also a convenient after-the-fact guide for checking the degree of maintainability actually achieved or for comparison among similar products.

Demonstration Test Programs   The demonstration consists of measuring the time needed to locate and repair malfunctions or to perform selected maintenance tasks. For products not yet in service, these malfunctions and tasks must be simulated.   An important aspect of the demonstration is the selection of which malfunctions and tasks to simulate.   The usual practice is to follow the reliability analysis of the product, e.g., if capacitor failures make up 10% of the predicted failure rate of the product, then 10% of the simulated failures will be failed capacitors.

Technicians who demonstrate the repair of the simulated malfunctions are chosen for their similarity in ability and training to the technicians who will eventually maintain the product in the field.   Conditions surrounding the demonstration must be carefully controlled so as not to influence the outcome of the tests.[67]   Time lost in obtaining parts or setting up test equipment is normally excluded, as is time lost because of random equipment failures occurring during the test.

To illustrate this procedure, Table 8-11 presents a typical calculation.   Here, the part types used in the equipment have been identified and the quantity used noted. Reliability data provides the average part failure rates.   The product of the quantity used and the failure rate yields the expected number of failures per thousand hours. In this example, it was found by totaling the part failures that 6.391 equipment

---

[65] For elaboration, and discussion of some of the principles involved, see Blanchard and Lowery, *op. cit.*, pp. 7–12.

[66] Blanchard and Lowery, *op. cit.*, Chapter 7, p. 116 *et seq.*

[67] For some data on dubious simulation practice, see Daveau, John E., Suggested Improvements for Maintainability Demonstrations, *Proceedings, Fifteenth Annual Symposium on Reliability*, IEEE, 1969, pp. 572–579.

TABLE 8-10   Maintainability Design Checklist

General
1. Standardization maximized
2. Components functionally grouped
3. Console layout optimized
4. Complexity minimized
5. Self-test incorporated
6. Max. time to repair minimized
7. Tools & test equipment. minimized
8. Labeling maximized
9. Weight minimized
10. Calibration requirements known
11. Repair/replace philosophy known
12. Maint. procedures known
13. Personnel requirements minimized
14. Trade-offs documented

Handling
1. Equipment lifting means employed
2. Equipment base reinforced (fork-lift app.)
3. Drawer/panel handles employed
4. Assembly handles employed
5. Console casters employed (as applicable)
6. Damages susceptibility minimized
7. Weight label on console

Panel displays/controls
1. Controls standardized
2. Controls sequentially positioned
3. Controls properly spaced
4. Controls adequately labeled
5. Controls adjacent to applicable display
6. Ruggedized meters employed
7. Meters externally removable
8. Panel lighting employed
9. Indicator lights "press-to-test"
10. Fuse requirements satisfied
11. Spare fuses provided
12. Warning lights employed-critical functions
13. Color of indicator lights adequate
14. Controls placed by frequency of use

Equipment racks-general
1. Drawers on roll-out slides
2. Panels hinged
3. In-position maintenance possible
4. Cables connected with drawers extended
5. Permanent cable inlets on front avoided
6. Heaviest items on bottom
7. Operator/panels optimum position
8. Air intake/exhaust provisions adequate

Connectors
1. Quick disconnect variety
2. Connector spacing adequate
3. Labeling adequate
4. Connectors keyed
5. Connectors standardized
6. Spare pins provided
7. Male connectors capped
8. Receptacles "hot" & plugs "cold"
9. Moisture prevention considered

Reliability
1. Allocated MTBF known
2. Fail-safe provisions incorporated
3. Critical/service life considered
4. Wear-in/wear-out cycles considered
5. Failures traceable by test

Servicing/lubrication
1. Servicing requirements considered
2. Servicing points accessible
3. Servicing frequencies known

Safety
1. Electrical outlets/junction boxes labeled
2. Interlocks employed
3. Fuse/circuit breaker protection adequate
4. Warning decals adequate
5. Guards/safety covers-high potentials
6. Protruding devices eliminated
7. External metal parts adequately grounded
8. Drawer/panel/structure edges rounded
9. Tool use considered

TABLE 8-11 Task Selection for Maintainability Demonstration

Part class	Quantity	Average part failures, %/1,000 hr.	Number of expected failures/1,000 hr operation	Contributions to total expected failures, %	Number of failures for sample of 50	Actual failures
Blowers/motors.	44	0.189	0.083	1.30	0.65	1
Capacitors	505	0.010	0.051	0.80	0.40	0
N-type diodes	19	2.983	0.567	8.87	4.44	4
Connectors	261	0.032	0.084	1.31	0.66	1
Relays	74	0.359	0.266	4.16	2.08	2
Coils	71	0.033	0.023	0.35	0.18	0
Resistors.	1,517	0.015	0.228	3.57	1.79	2
Switch.	176	0.045	0.079	1.24	0.62	1
Transformers	85	0.133	0.113	1.77	0.89	1
Tubes.	301	1.567	4.717	73.81	36.91	37
Miscellaneous	101	0.178	0.180	2.82	1.41	1
Total.	3,154		6.391	100.00		50

failures per thousand hours could be expected. This figure, used as a base, permits the percentage contribution for each part classification to be determined. These percentages in turn permit the apportionment of the desired sample—in this case, 50. With knowledge of the part types to be tested, a random selection process may be employed to identify the specific parts to be used.[68]

Demonstrating the maintainability of a design has important implications for a manufacturer. The demonstration can be costly, but the possibility that the product will be unacceptable due to downtime and maintenance can be far more costly. Redesign and modification of an inadequate product to improve a quantitative maintainability parameter can also be a major undertaking, since it may require advancing the state of the art. In consequence, despite the cost of maintainability demonstrations, the outlook is for a continuing acceptance of the concept in launching new designs.

Maintainability Data Systems The ultimate source of prediction of maintainability is the record of actual maintenance performance. This record is needed not only as an input to the prediction process but also as a control of field maintenance, so that the established goals (if sound) will be met in practice.

Section 15, under Field Performance Measures, discusses the basic data sources inherent in field maintenance data systems: service reports, complaint analyses, operations logs, etc. That discussion is mainly from the viewpoint of maintenance of consumer products. Use and maintenance of such products is mainly by persons who are not part of a broad organization which includes dominance over product design and manufacture. This separation complicates the problems of unified systems of documentation.

In contrast, in a broad system like that for military defense, the use and maintenance of products is done by employees of the system. This arrangement does permit the use of an all embracing system of interrelated specifications and documentation, and such has been the trend. An example is the Bureau of Naval Weapons' WR-30, "Integrated Maintenance Management for Aeronautical Systems, Weapon Systems, Related Weapons," dated May 1, 1963. This system features about a dozen basic documents, notably the Maintenance Engineering Analysis Record (MEAR), which have been prepared to meet all the needs for designing and achieving maintainability.[69]

SAFETY IN NEW-PRODUCT DESIGN

Section 14 (under Product Liability) discusses the general problem of product safety and the ways in which companies can take steps to minimize their risks. In the present Section 8, the emphasis is on the product design aspects of product[70] safety.

Quantification of Safety There is no known way of attaining absolute safety. The space exploration programs were funded virtually without restraint, and yet there were fatal and near fatal accidents. With present knowledge, some level of risk is inherent. The design problem is to reduce this to an "acceptable" level, which, to be predictable, should be quantified.

[68] For elaboration, see Retterer, B. L., and R. A. Miles, A Procedure for System Maintainability Testing, *Proceedings, Ninth Annual Symposium on Reliability*, IEEE, 1963, pp. 448–454.

[69] For an example of application, see Murphy, C. T., and R. R. Gardner, Implementation of a Maintainability Program Using MEARs, *Proceedings, Sixth Annual New York Conference on Electronic Reliability*, IEEE, New York Chapter, May 21, 1965, pp. 17–1 to 17–15.

[70] There are interactions between products and the systems in which they operate. If an automobile is considered as a product, the complex of highway transportation, including drivers, roads, signals, etc., would be considered a system. See generally Section 44.

Generally, quantification of safety has been time-related. Industrial injury rates are quantified on the basis of lost-time accidents per million man-hours of exposure.[71] Motor vehicle injury rates are on a basis of injuries per 100 million miles. School injury rates are on the basis of injuries per 100,000 student days. (It would be very useful if all measures were on the common basis of million man-hours of exposure.)

Product designers have tended to quantify safety in two ways:

1. Hazard[72] frequency. This takes the form of frequency of occurrence of an unsafe event and/or injuries per unit of time, e.g., per million hours of exposure.

2. Hazard severity. Four categories of severity are recognized:

Class I. *Negligible.* Will not result in personnel injury or product damage.

Class II. *Marginal.* Can be counteracted or controlled without injury to personnel or major product damage.

Class III. *Critical.* Will cause personnel injury or major product damage, or will require immediate corrective action for personnel or product survival.

Class IV. *Catastrophic.* Will cause death, severe injury to personnel, or product loss.

Acceptable Level of Risk   The safety equivalent of the reliability goal is the acceptable hazard rate. In the absence of agreed quantitative goals, there is great difficulty in agreeing on such goals, even more than in matters of product reliability, since human safety is at stake. There is an acute need for a rationale which will permit agreement on acceptable levels of risk.

One proposal is to use the national safety average as a demarcation line between acceptable and nonacceptable risks. The guiding principle would be that "any hour of human life should be as safe as any other hour."

For example, the national injury rate for home accidents for 1970 was about 4.8 per million man-hours of exposure. If the injury rate from glass bottles for carbonated beverages is below this level (as it seems to be), then the need for continuing improvement could logically be put on an evolutionary basis. In contrast, for products which have an injury rate above the national average, the highest priority should be assigned to making safety improvements.[73,74]

While the concept of equality of risk is one possible form of safety policy, there are other views which contest this concept:

1. A view that safety goals should be consistent with the product mission requirements. This concept is expressed in the objectives of MIL-STD-882.

2. A view that some products or jobs are inherently hazardous, and that the human beings involved should be specially compensated for the added risks.

3. A view that human life is priceless and hence nothing short of perfection is acceptable. The advocates of this view tend to be both vocal and emotional. One section of the *Final Report of the National Commission on Product Safety*[75] was concerned with glass bottles and disclosed a divergence of views among government agencies. On the one hand, the Interstate Commerce Commission and the Federal

---

[71] This is the frequency rate. There is a severity rate as well.

[72] A hazard in Safety literature is generally defined as "any real or potential condition that can cause injury or death to personnel, or damage or loss of product or property." In Reliability literature, the word "hazard" may have a different meaning, akin to a failure rate index.

[73] The foregoing is based largely on the discussion in Juran, J. M., Product Safety, *Quality Progress,* July 1972, pp. 30–32.

[74] This does *not* mean that half the products are above the average. Under the Pareto principle of vital few and trivial many, most products are under the average.

[75] Obtainable from the Superintendent of Documents, U.S. Government Printing Office, Washington, D.C.

Trade Commission felt that no further regulatory action was warranted. On the other hand, the National Commission on Product Safety felt that there was a need for new product standards. The emotional nature of the argument is evidenced by the opening paragraph in the Commission report on glass bottles, which included the statement: "'I will be blind in one eye for the rest of my life because of a defective glass bottle.' The testimony of 14-year-old Sharon Jackson of Chicago tells the tragic potential of exploding glass bottles."

4. A view that safety is a matter of balancing the economics of cost of safety against the value of safety. Under this view, an effort is made to quantify the costs of various levels of safety in an effort to find the optimum. (It is easy to demonstrate that there is an optimum.) This approach is quite meritorious when only product damage is involved. It is open to attack if human safety is involved.

At present we are only in the early stages of resolving the differences among these and other contesting views on what should be the policy on acceptable level of risk. Only after extensive quantification of hazard rates for many products will it be possible to arrive at a consensus.

Safety Analysis   The general approach is well known.

1. Review available historical data on safety of similar and predecessor products. These data obviously should include complaints, claims, and lawsuits. In addition, data are available from regulators, independent laboratories, and still other sources.

2. Study the ways in which the product has actually been used and misused. This study is especially important for products which are used by a wide spectrum of the population, e.g., consumer products or those military products which are used directly by the foot soldier. Such a wide spectrum of humanity inevitably misuses products[76] or finds uses for which the products were never designed.

Products for children (or to which children have access) are a special case because of the inexperience of youngsters and because "logic" becomes academic when injured children are displayed before a jury. A child's building block has a very high reliability. Yet the child may fall and injure himself on a corner of the block; he may throw the block and injure another child. Manufacturers may turn to the use of plastic foam for making the blocks, but now new questions arise: Could a child bite off a piece and choke on it? Would the material be toxic? Obviously, a child is misusing a block when he bites off a piece. Yet the standards on electric lamp cord have been revised to minimize ·the danger to a child who may bite through the insulation.

3. Assess the likelihood that damage will actually occur. This likelihood is the resultant of several probabilities:

     a. That the product will fail in a way which creates a hazard (this probability may be available through failure-rate analysis)

     b. That the existence of the hazard will result in damage

     c. That despite no failures in the product, it will be misused so as to result in damage

4. Quantify the exposure (time, cycles, etc.) of the product and the users to hazardous conditions.

5. Determine the severity of the effect of hazards on product or user.

While safety analyses are of long standing, the empirical, qualitative approaches of the past are giving way to more formalized, quantitative studies, as discussed below.

---

[76] The ordinary household ladder includes a small platform for holding tools, a can of paint, etc. The platform is "obviously" too flimsy to support the weight of a man. Yet enough men do stand on it and are injured by the resulting fall to suggest that the platform may need to be designed to hold a man's weight.

The Organized Program   Organized, companywide approaches to product safety have taken one of two main roads:

1. A company Product Safety Committee to coordinate activities of all company departments.   This approach is discussed in Section 14, under Product Liability.

2. A concept of Product Safety Engineering and Management which is based in the Product Design Department.   This approach has been fostered by the military agencies (and others) and is discussed below.

Safety Program Objectives.   An example of the military approach is seen in MIL-STD-882, which is frequently specified on government contracts.[77]   This standard identifies the following as objectives for safety programs:

Safety should be designed into the product to a degree consistent with mission requirements.

Hazards associated with each product (and its components and units) are to be identified, eliminated, or controlled to an acceptable level.

Control is to be established over hazards that cannot be eliminated, so as to protect personnel, equipment, and property.

Risks involved in the use of new materials, production techniques, or testing techniques are to be minimized.

Safety Tasks.   The organized program identifies specific tasks to be performed during the various phases of new-product development.   These tasks are principally as follows:

During concept formulation phase: conduct concept safety studies; perform preliminary hazard analysis (see, for example, the modernized analysis by Daedalus,[78] Figure 8-13); define product safety performance "envelope"; select product safety effectiveness measures, i.e., figures of merit.

During contract definition phase (A): prepare a proposed safety plan; update the preliminary hazard analysis; identify which are the safety requirements in the specification;[79] include safety considerations in trade-off studies.

During contract definition phase (B): implement approved contract definition safety plan; complete preliminary hazards analysis; identify safety decisions to be made before the development phase; establish a firm safety plan for the development phase, including a breakdown of safety tasks.

During development phase: implement program approved in definition phase; provide design criteria and evaluate product design through hazard analysis and safety studies; establish test requirements; participate in program reviews and in trade-off studies.

[77] MIL-STD-882, "Requirements for System Safety Programs for Systems and Associated Subsystems and Equipment," July 1969, Defense Document Distribution Center, Washington, D.C.

[78] An example of such an analysis ("the first safety analysis") has been prepared for the design project of the philosopher Daedalus who, with his son Icarus, was held captive by King Minos of Crete. Daedalus made wings of feathers, thread, and beeswax to enable them to escape. He warned his son:
> "My boy, take care
To wing your course along the middle air.
If low, the surges wet your flagging plumes;
If high, the sun the melting wax consumes."

In today's dialect, the analysis of Daedalus would be called a "Preliminary Hazard Analysis" and would take a form such as is shown in Figure 8-13. The analysis of Figure 8-13 suggests that Daedalus had additional options he might have employed beyond mere warnings to the user (a member of a species which is notorious for ignoring warnings).

[79] It is becoming common practice for safety-sensitive specification requirements to be marked with a special symbol. This symbol then carries through to vendors, manufacturing processes, test specifications, etc.

IDENTIFICATION: Mark I Flight System

SUBSYSTEM: Wings

DESIGNER: Daedalus

Hazard	Cause	Effect	Corrective or preventive measures
Thermal radiation	Flying too close to sun	Heat may melt beeswax which holds feathers together. Separation and loss of feathers will cause loss of aerodynamic lift. Aeronaut may then plunge to his death in the sea.	Provide warning against flying too high and too close to sun. Maintain close supervision over aeronauts. Use buddy system. Provide leash of flax between aeronauts to prevent one from flying too high. Restrict area of aerodynamic surfaces to prevent flying too high.
Moisture	Flying close to water surface	Feathers may absorb moisture, causing them to increase in weight and to flag. Limited propulsive power may not be adequate to compensate for increased weight and drag so that aeronaut will gradually sink into sea. Result: loss of function and mission failure. Possible drowning of aeronaut if survival gear is not provided.	Caution aeronaut to fly through middle air where sun will keep wings dry or where accumulation rate of moisture is acceptable for time of mission. Provide aeronauts with flotation gear.

Fig. 8-13 Preliminary hazard analysis.

During subsequent phases: help maintain safety precautions throughout, including audit of engineering changes.

Tools of Safety Analysis. Figure 8-14 lists some of the numerous techniques of safety analysis and shows the product situations in which they are commonly used.[80] Obviously, only the most complex products, involving detailed man-product interrelationships, will require so wide an array of techniques. More usually, a few widely used techniques will supply the bulk of the analysis needed.

The most fundamental technique is the hazard analysis exemplified in Figure 8-13. It is quite similar to the failure mode and failure effect analysis (Figure 8-7) and other tabular arrangements. In applying the techniques, columns are set up listing hazard, condition, part, event or procedural step to be studied, causes, effects, and finally preventive and corrective measures.[81]

A second technique is the fault tree analysis. This "top-down" approach starts by supposing that an accident takes place. It then considers the possible direct causes which could lead to this accident. Next, it looks for the origins of these causes. Finally, it looks for ways to avoid these origins and causes. The branching out of origins and causes is what gives the technique the name of "fault tree" analysis.[82] The approach is the reverse of the failure mode and failure effect analysis, which starts with origins and causes and looks for any resulting bad effects. (For complex products, the failure mode and failure effect analysis becomes a huge undertaking.)

These and several other techniques are exemplified in the cases of the hot water heater and the compressor tank, which follow.

Detailed Analysis of a Domestic Hot Water Heater. A safety analysis of the common domestic hot water heater will serve to illustrate the use of some of the tools of safety analysis.[83] Figure 8-15 is a diagram of the product and its principal components. The Gas Supply Subsystem is blocked out for more detailed analysis.

Figure 8-16 is a block diagram showing the sequence and interaction of the gas supply subsystem components. Sometimes called a "functional flow diagram," it is an essential step in all engineering analyses for whatever subsequent purpose.

Figure 8-17 illustrates a hazard analysis. The possible modes of failure and their probable effect from a safety viewpoint are enumerated. The relative seriousness of the hazard is indicated in the last column of the figure.

Figure 8-18, a fault tree analysis, groups related failure events by class or relative seriousness. A safety numerical analysis may now be performed for each of the hazard classes, using the following expressions:

$$p = Kft$$

where p = probability of occurrence of an unsafe event
K = severity effect of the occurrence, for example, class I (safe) = 0; class II (marginal) = 0.1; class III (critical) = 0.5; class IV (catastrophic) = 1.0
f = frequency of occurrence, i.e., event occurrence rate (probability), failure rate, and/or personnel injuries per time exposure (occurrences per hour)
t = time of operation or exposure (hours)

[80] Derived from the work of an Electronic Industry Association committee, membership unknown.

[81] Hammer, Willie, Designing a Safe System, *Machine Design,* September 3, 1970, pp. 92–97.

[82] For a good discussion with a case example, see Eisner, R. L., "Fault Tree Analysis to Anticipate Potential Failure," ASME paper 72 DE 22, 1972.

[83] Recht, J. L., System Safety Analysis: Failure Mode and Failure Effect, *National Safety News,* vol. 93, no. 2, 1965, pp. 24–26.

•—*Point* Single units, specific events, hazards, or conditions	▬—*Linear* Interrelationships between components	▭—*Area* Groups of components	⬛—*Spatial* Spatial relationships and conditions	t —*Time* Durations or sequences of events
Preliminary (gross) hazard analysis	Interface analysis	Hazard area and location identification	Environment analysis	Profiles
Catastrophe analysis	Fluid-flow analysis	Emergency route and safety zone maps	Man-equipment-space relationships	Time sequencing
Failure mode and effects analysis	Energy-flow analysis	Panel layouts	Crashworthiness, escape and rescue analysis	Normal programmed procedures analysis
Critical component analysis	Fault tree analysis	Range maps and limits	Mockups	Contingency analysis
Specific hazard analysis	Electronic circuit logic analysis		Simulators	Rescue procedures analysis
Critical incident technique	Link analysis		Prototypes	

Fig. 8-14 Types of hazard analysis and where to use them.

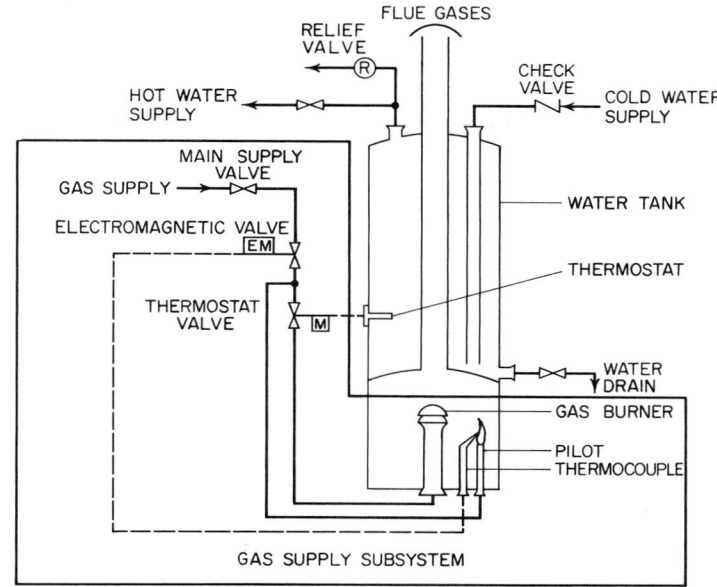

Fig. 8-15 Domestic hot water heater—product diagram.

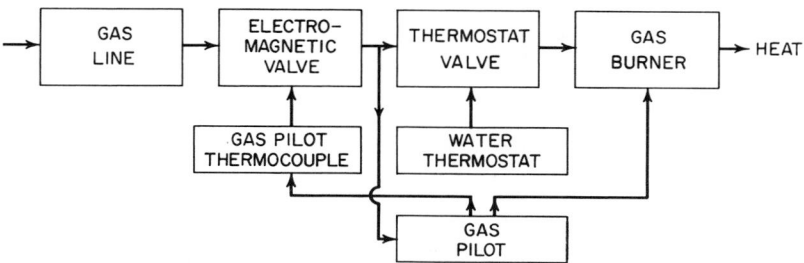

Fig. 8-16 Gas supply subsystem—block diagram.

For a gas explosion, $k = 1$. Let us assume that the summation of failure rates, including cycle time adjustments, for those events that could cause gas explosion (obtained from a reliability analysis) is 0.06×10^{-6}. This is the f term of the above equation. Let us further assume that a 10-year warranty period is the design requirement. During this period the exposure time, t, is 87,000 hours. Therefore,

$$p = (1) \ \frac{0.06}{1,000,000} \ (87,000) = 0.005$$

Since S, the safety of the system, is merely $1 - p$, it follows that

$$S = 1 - 0.005 = 0.995$$

In a similar manner, the probability of less serious events may be derived and an overall safety index calculated.

Item	Function	Hazard involved	Hazard effect on system	Hazard class
I Gas supply subsystem				
1.1 Gas line	To supply gas	1. Line leakage	Gas explosion	IV
1.2 Electromagnetic valve (normally closed)	Controls gas supply	1. External leakage	Gas explosion	IV
		2. Internal leakage or failure to close	Gas explosion	IV
		3. Failure to open	System inoperative	II
1.3 Gas pilot thermocouple	Actuates electro-magnetic valve	1. Fails to actuate	System inoperative	II
		2. Premature actuation	None	I
1.4 Thermostat valve (normally open)	Controls gas supply	1. External leakage	Gas explosion	IV
		2. Internal leakage or failure to close	System continues to heat up until relief valve opens	III
		3. Failure to open	System inoperative	II
1.5 Water thermostat	Actuates thermostat valve	1. Fails to actuate	System continues to heat up until relief valve opens	III
		2. Premature actuation	None	I
1.6 Gas pilot	Ignites gas	1. Pilot lit	None	I
		2. Pilot extinguished	System inoperative	II
1.7 Gas burner	Heats water	1. Clogged	System inoperative	II
		2. Open	None	I

Fig. 8-17 Gas supply subsystem—hazard analysis.

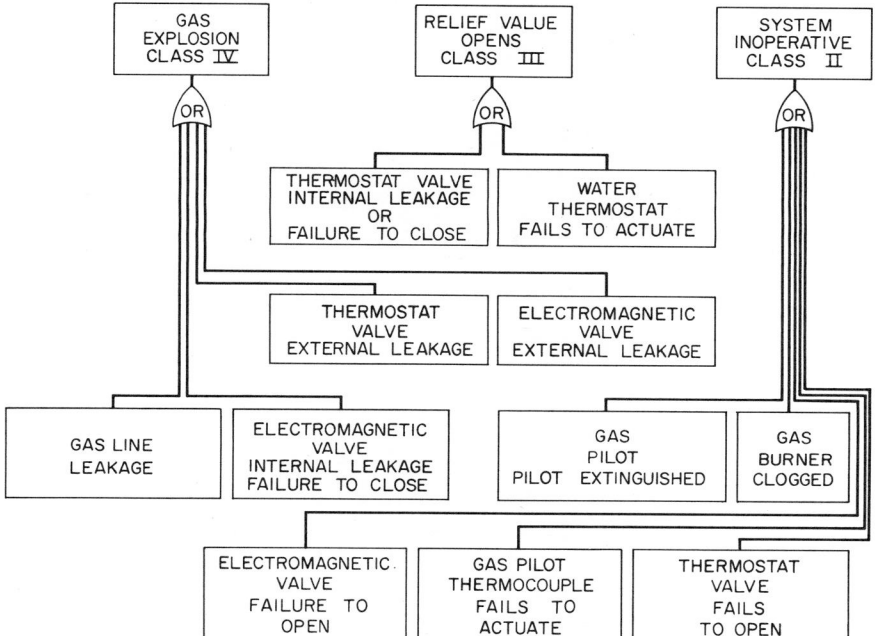

Fig. 8-18 Gas supply subsystem—fault tree analysis.

Hazard Analysis on a Compressor Tank.   Accidents generally occur because of a sequence or combination of factors rather than because of one factor alone. An example of this is shown in Figure 8-19, illustrating rupture of a compressed-air tank under pressure.[84] The event could injure personnel or cause damage to other equipment or property.   The sequence is shown in Figure 8-19, along with some measures which could be taken to prevent the event from occurring.   In practice the sequences are developed in reverse order, starting with a selected catastrophe (which may have been determined in a preliminary hazard analysis), working back through the intermediate cause and effect relationships, and terminating at the initiating cause.

Improving Safety through Design Quantified safety analysis is a useful aid for comparative evaluation of alternatives.   However, the basic task of the designer remains what it always was—to use his technological training and experience to create new and changed designs which will eliminate or minimize serious hazards. A part of this experience is to know what the potential hazards are.   Table 8-12 is a representative list.[85]   A further need is to understand the kinds of injuries which result from hazards, e.g., the list shown in Table 8-13.[86]   (No attempt has been made to show cause and effect relationship.)

The following are some examples of means used by designers to reduce the hazard levels of products:[87]

1. *Elimination of Hazard:* For example, a pneumatic or hydraulic system might

[84] Hammer, Willie, *op. cit.*
[85–87] Hammer, Willie, *op. cit.*

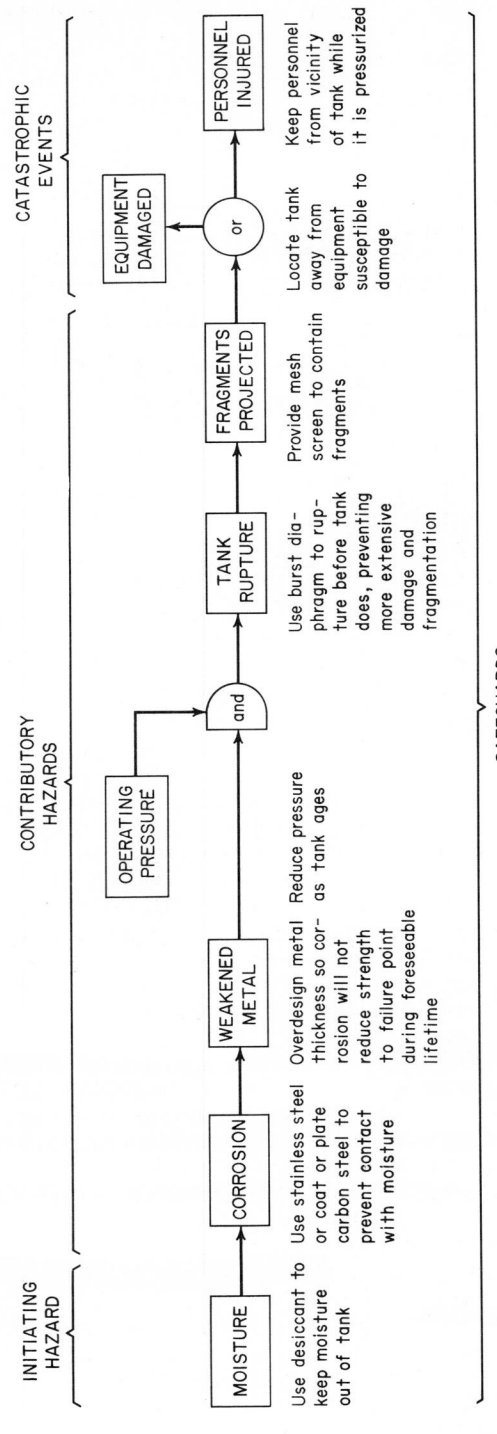

Fig. 8-19 Hazard analysis on compressor tank.

TABLE 8-12   Potential Hazards

Acceleration and motion
Chemical reactions
    Dissociation
    Oxidation
    Replacement
Contamination
Corrosion
Electrical
    System failure
    Inadvertent activation
    Shock
    Thermal effects
Explosion
Fire
Heat and temperature
    High temperature
    Low temperature
    Temperature changes
Impact and shock

Leakage
Moisture
    High humidity
    Low humidity
Power source failure
Pressure
    High pressure
    Low pressure
    Pressure changes
Radiation
    Thermal
    Electromagnetic
    Ionizing
    Ultraviolet
Structural damage failure
    Stress concentrations
Toxicity
Vibration and noise
Weather and environment

TABLE 8-13   Types of Injuries

Mechanical
    Cuts
    Punctures
    Bruises
    Broken bones
    Particles in eyes
Burns
    Electrical
    Thermal, heat
    Thermal, cold
    Radiation
    Chemical
Pressure
    Acceleration
    Crushing, fluid
    Crushing, solid mass
    Pinching
    Noise and vibration
    Dysbarism

Shock
    Electrical
    Pressure wave
    Physical contact
    Physiological
    Trauma
    Cold immersion
Toxicity
    Asphyxiation
    Organic damage
    Respiratory, system damage
    Circulatory, system damage
    Dermatosis
Others
    Heat exhaustion
    Wind chill

be used instead of an electrical system, where there is a possibility of fire, explosion, shock, or undesirable heating. Fluidic control systems are being applied more and more for these reasons.

2. *Hazard-Level Limitation:* The product can be made intrinsically safe by limiting the energy level of the potential hazard. Electricity may be essential for a system and cannot be eliminated, but use of solid-state devices—operating at low power levels—can eliminate possibilities of fire, shock, or excessive heating.

3. *Lockouts, Lockins, and Interlocks:* Isolating transformers in a vault minimizes the possibility of electrocuting personnel. Explosion-proof equipment keeps flame in electrical lines, fittings, and machinery from igniting a flammable environment which surrounds it. Pushbutton switches that must be operated in a specific sequence (if a mishap is to be avoided) can be interlocked.

4. *Fail-safe Designs:* These may be fail-passive, fail-operational, or fail-active. A fuse or circuit breaker is a fail-passive device that opens when a dangerous situation occurs, deenergizing and "safing" an electrical system.   Passing water under the disk of a boiler inlet valve, instead of over, is a fail-operational arrangement; if the disk separates from the valve stem, it is raised by the flowing water so the boiler will continue to operate safely.   A destruct system on an air-to-air missile is a fail-active device; if the missile misses its target and does not detonate within a set time, the destruct system blows the missile apart to halt its flight and limit the damage that an armed warhead or entire missile could cause by hitting the ground.

While most accidents are caused by failures[88] (of material or personnel), others are the result of hazards inherent in the product; e.g., a color television set may produce an excellent picture and sound but still generate harmful radiation.   Minimizing these inherent hazards involves a further list of methods available to the designer:

5. *Monitors:* These are devices which detect dangerous conditions or potential failures so that corrective action can be taken before an accident or failure occurs. Typical examples are temperature and pressure gages, radiation counters, infrared indicators to detect hot spots or flames, and even personnel paired in a buddy-system arrangement to guard each other's well-being in a dangerous situation.

6. *Warnings:* Generally warnings are made to personnel, but the signals generated by the monitoring systems used for warnings can also be directed to take corrective actions automatically.

7. *Minor Loss Acceptance:* A restricted amount of product damage may be accepted to assure that major damage is avoided.   For example, blowout panels in oil and gas furnaces give way in the event of an explosion and overpressurization from delayed ignition of accumulated fuel vapors.   This prevents damage to furnace walls, boiler tubes, and other equipment and structures.

8. *Escape and Survival:* Procedures must be established and equipment and means provided for leaving the scene of an accident to avoid injury and surviving in the new location.   An ejection seat permits escape of a pilot from a disabled aircraft; the parachute is necessary for survival after he has left the aircraft.

9. *Rescue:* Personnel may be incapacitated or trapped in a vehicle or structure where they may be subjected to further injury.   It is therefore necessary to provide devices, equipment, and procedures that others can use for their rescue.

10. *Isolation:* Not all hazards can be eliminated.   Frequently, control of those hazards that remain is lost and an accident occurs.   It is therefore necessary to provide safeguards to minimize injury or damage that could result.   Isolation is not only a means of avoiding accidents but can also be used to avoid or minimize damaging effects.

MANAGEMENT OF NEW-PRODUCT QUALITY

New-product programs properly extend from cradle to grave, and the management of such programs must be coextensive with this scope.   The discussion which follows deals with the special managerial problems associated with new-product programs.

Product Planning   A new design is a "project," and the planning for such projects follows the pattern shown in Section 6 (Table 6-1 and related discussion).   Small design changes are handled as routine projects, using a standard procedure.   This

---

[88] In such cases, failure rate improvement is also a means for improving product safety.   For details, see Reliability Improvement (in this Section).

procedure then serves as an impersonal means of coordinating the work of the line departments, each of which is left to plan its departmental work in its own way. As the projects grow in size, the coordination is personalized through the use of such devices as committees, project engineers, or project managers.

Reliability Planning   It is evident from an earlier major topic (The Reliability Program) that the technological activities needed to attain high reliability in modern products can consume sizable funds and can preempt much management attention. Efforts to secure such funds and attention have encountered much resistance from managers.   Some of this resistance arises from lack of awareness that new deeds, never previously performed, are an essential part of attaining the levels of reliability essential to modern products.[89, 90]   Additional resistance stems from the excesses of those reliability specialists who have urged on producers of civilian products the very elaborate programs and documentation required by the military and aerospace customers.[91]   (The published literature, which has been authored mostly by men associated with these government purchased systems, is positively frightening to producers of civilian products.) Finally, there is much cultural resistance due to myths[92] about past practice.

Collectively it adds up to a good deal of resistance to reliability planning.   As a result, several methods have been developed for justifying to inexperienced or skeptical managements the need for funding and the extent of funds required.[93] These methods include:

Quantifying failure cost data to show that improved reliability can be paid for out of reduced failure rates

Estimating life cycle costs[94] under various levels of reliability

Proposing incentive type contracts through which the added income from high reliability will pay for the reliability program (see below, under reliability incentive contracts)

Actually, since the reliability planning should start in the very earliest stages, the funding should likewise be provided in the early stages.   This concept is especially difficult for traditionalists to grasp, since the instinctive reaction is that a double price is being paid for achieving reliability.   (Again, lack of awareness that new deeds are required.)   The answer to these instinctive reactions is not logical reasoning but data on the price of unreliability.

Reliability Incentive Contracts   An alternative to imposing a detailed reliability pro-

---

[89] A related problem in reliability planning is that of reliability of manufacturing processes. For a series of articles dealing with this problem, see Plant/Equipment Reliability—1, *Chemical Engineering Progress*, vol. 66, no. 12, December 1970; also Plant/Equipment Reliability —2, *Chemical Engineering Progress*, vol. 67, no. 1, January 1971.

[90] A frequent question from managers is "Why do I have to pay extra for reliability?   Hasn't reliability always been implied in any design?"   The answer is that if there is to be *quantification* of reliability, there will be added costs.   The significant added costs are not the paper predictions but the quantification through formal test demonstration.

[91] In these complex systems the reliability problem is major; sometimes it is the limiting factor in the solution.   Hence, while the planning process has much in common with reliability planning for less sophisticated products, the organization forms and the formality of work assignment differ significantly.   See Section 44 for an elaboration.

[92] For a useful discussion of some myths about reliability practices as well as some positive thinking about reliability costs, see Ryerson, C. M., Myths and Realities in Reliability, *Technical Conference Transactions*, 1961, American Society for Quality Control, pp. 283–300.

[93] See, for a good discussion, Dertinger, E. F., Funding Reliability Programs, *Ninth National Symposium on Reliability and Quality Control*, IEEE, 1963, pp. 16–33.

[94] See Section 4, under Life Cycle Costing.

gram plan on a contractor is to establish a contract incentive based on achieved reliability.   Under this alternative, the parties negotiate a clause in their contract making the contractor's fee or profit vary depending on the extent to which reliability goals are attained or exceeded.

Generally such incentive contracts include incentive clauses for cost and delivery as well as for reliability.   There is a good deal of detail involved in spelling out the terms of the agreement and of the method of administration.

The reader is referred to the bibliography cited for details.[95]

Staff Specialist Organization   A prickly problem in organizing for new-product design is that of using the "new" disciplines such as Reliability Engineering, Maintainability Engineering, and Safety Engineering.   While the discussion which follows will concentrate on reliability, the principles involved apply generally to all these specialties.

The time required to introduce a new discipline is usually shortened if a new specialty department is created for it and if the head of the specialty understands his role.   This role is ideally one of analyzing the projects, using the tools of the new specialty, and making the results of the analysis available to the "regular line" departments — always taking care to minimize any encroachment on their traditional decision-making responsibilities.   These ideals are difficult to meet in practice, and as a result there have been many instances of false starts and many needs to revise assignment of responsibilities.

The variety of organization forms tested out is seen in Section 7, which traces the evolution of the reliability engineers.   The alternatives for organization are shown in Figure 7-4 and are discussed in Table 7-1.

Beyond these questions of "command,"[96] there are the further questions of how to allocate specific duties and activities among the line departments and staff specialties.   This is best done by (1) listing the deeds or tasks which need to be done, (2) reaching agreement on precisely what is meant by each of the terms used, and (3) deciding to whom to make the delegation.   Despite earnest contentions about "logical" ways to organize, the decisions are mainly unique to each company, e.g., the level of training of the designers is an essential factor in deciding what can be delegated to them.

The foregoing discussion has used the reliability "discipline" as a case in point. However, the needs for the parameters of safety and maintainability are quite similar, i.e., identification of tasks and clear assignment of responsibility.   These things need to be done irrespective of whether the company recognizes the parameters as the base for a new staff specialty.[97]

Product Specifications   Primitive societies require no specifications, since buyer

---

[95] See Hedger, E. F., Incentive Contracting, paper no. 13, pp. 83–88; also Mangeot, F. J. A., Contractual Aspects of Reliability, paper no. 14, pp. 89–94.   Published 1969 in "Reliability of Service Equipment."   Available from The Institution of Mechanical Engineers, 1 Birdcage Walk, Westminster, London S.W. 1.

See also Frederick, W. C., System Worth and Incentive Contracts, *Proceedings, 9th Annual Symposium on Reliability,* IEEE, 1963, pp. 6–15, and Van Dine, Howard A., Quality Performance Incentive, *Proceedings, 10th Annual Symposium on Reliability,* IEEE, 1964, pp. 591–599.

See also Section 14, under Contract Incentives for Quality.

[96] These are mainly (1) "Should there be a separate Reliability Engineering Department?" and (2) "To whom should this Department report?"

[97] In the case of safety, the extensive new legislation plus the stimulus of the insurance companies make the Safety Engineer a likely new category of specialist.   While his early role is most evident in product design, the ultimate role is probably one of coordinating the work of all company departments with respect to product safety.   See, in this connection. Section 14, under Product Liability.

and seller meet face-to-face in the market place. As commerce expands, the specification evolves, first by sample and then as a written specification. For the industrial societies of today, with material sources, factories, and markets located in multiple countries and with products and systems operating interchangeably on an international scale, the written specification has become an indispensable document for ready communication of product descriptions.

Contents of material and product specifications have become highly standardized[98, 99] and include the following:

Title	Physical characteristics
List of contents	Reliability and maintainability charac-
Historical background	teristics
Scope	Method of test and criteria for ac-
Role of the product	ceptance
Definitions	Packaging and protection
Relevant authorities	Special information and cautions
References	Field service information
Pertinent conditions of manufacture, installation, storage, and use	

The heart of the specification is the list of essential characteristics and their tolerances. Increasingly these lists include new types of characteristics such as reliability (e.g., MTBF — 1,000 hours), availability, maintainability, safety, etc. In addition, the form of the tolerances is increasingly more statistical in nature. For example, bulk or coalesced products are being defined by specifying (1) tolerances on the average values and (2) maxima for the standard deviation.

Functional and Nonfunctional Characteristics. The distinction between functional and nonfunctional is set out in Section 12, under Seriousness Classification. The distinctions are clear enough, but industrial practice can intervene to make things complicated. When both kinds of characteristics are published in the same document (as often happens), there is confusion unless it is clearly designated which is which. A major reason for clear designation is the difference in jurisdiction over waivers of nonconformance cases. Generally, the Design Department *must* be a party to any waiver of functional requirements, but not as to nonfunctional requirements. (Design also has the major voice in deciding what is functional and what is not.)

The trend is toward making clear which characteristics are functional. This is done in any of several ways:

1. Use of separate documents to carry the functional requirements
2. Designation of functional requirements by special code letters
3. Seriousness classifications of characteristics (see Section 12, under Seriousness Classification)

Standardization in Specifications. The work of specification has been greatly simplified by the growth of standards for materials, components, processes, tests, products, etc.[100] (These standards are available from numerous sources: professional societies, industry associations, standardization organizations, government

[98] See MacNiece, E. H., "Industrial Specifications," John Wiley & Sons, Inc., New York, 1953.

[99] See also "General Guide to the Preparation of Specifications," 1970, European Organization for Quality Control, P.O. Box 1976, Rotterdam 3, Netherlands.

[100] Recommendations of the International Organization for Standardization (ISO) relate to methods of test — 45%; dimensional specifications — 25%; quality — 15%; descriptive practice — 15%. See Trowbridge, Roy P., *Quality Management and Engineering,* June 1972, pp. 32 and 33.

regulators, large customers—e.g., military services—and still others.) In addition, there are standards available to assist the designer in such matters as dimensioning and tolerancing (see below, under Tolerancing). Use of preferred sizes[101] has greatly reduced problems of inventory and obsolescence while retaining flexibility in choice.

Tolerancing   The selection of tolerances has a dual effect on economics of quality. The tolerance affects:

1. Fitness for use and hence the salability of the product
2. Costs of manufacture (facilities, tooling, productivity) and quality costs (equipment, inspection, scrap, rework, material review, etc.)

In theory, the designer should, by scientific study,[102] establish the proper balance between the value of precision and the cost of precision. In practice, the designer

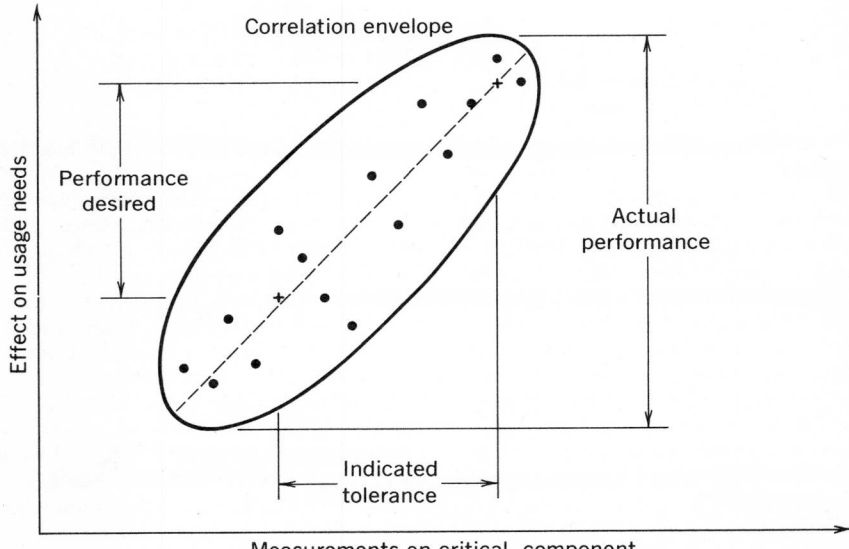

Fig. 8-20   Scatter diagram for setting tolerances.

is unable to do this for each tolerance—there are too many quality characteristics. As a result, only a minority of tolerances are set scientifically. Scientific tools for tolerancing include:

1. *Regression studies.* For example, a thermostat may be required to turn on and shut off a power source at specified low and high temperature values respectively. A number of thermostat elements are built and tested. The prime recorded data are (1) turn on temperature, (2) shut off temperature, and (3) physical characteristics of the thermostat elements. These data permit scatter diagrams to be prepared (Figure 8-20) and regression equations[103] to be computed to aid in establishing critical component tolerances on a basis which is scientific within the confidence limits for the numbers involved.

---

[101] These are mainly based on the famous Renard series. See ANSI Standard Z17.1-1936.
[102] See Section 9, under Cost of Tolerances.
[103] See generally Section 26.

2. *Tolerances for Interacting Dimensions.* Numerous designs involve "interacting dimensions." An electronic circuit may consist of 11 elements in series; a mechanical assembly may consist of a buildup of 8 elements; a single complex piece part may include a chain of 10 dimensions, starting from a base line. What these designs have in common is the existence of interaction among these elements or dimensions. Each element or dimension has its own tolerances. However, the variation of the composite (the circuit, the assembly, or the chain) will be related to the variations of the elements according to the laws of probability, i.e., it is very unlikely that all the extremes will come together simultaneously.

This unlikelihood makes it possible to establish wider tolerances on elements of such designs without significantly increasing the extent of nonconformance. The scientific approach to this is discussed in Section 22, under Tolerance Limits for Interacting Dimensions.

Most tolerances are established by methods which, in varying degrees, are less than scientific. The principal methods include:

1. By Precedent. There is much merit to use of past practice (which has stood the test of time) provided the practice is sound. As will be seen, past practice includes a serious bias toward tight tolerances.

2. By Bargaining. When proposed tolerances are challenged on the ground of high costs, it is often easier to reach an agreement by bargaining than to undergo the costs of a thorough investigation.

3. From Tolerance Systems. There has been a great deal of standardization of methods of dimensioning and tolerancing, at company,[104] industry, national, and international levels.[105] The published standards[106] become the basis of design and shop practice except for those tolerances which require special consideration.

Unrealistic Tolerances Loosely Enforced   In most companies the accumulated specifications contain an extensive array of unduly tight tolerances, i.e., tolerances not really needed to achieve fitness for use. This accumulation is a natural result of the historical forces to which the design department has been subjected:

1. The designers had clear responsibility for assuring that the product was fit for use and had only vague responsibility for assuring that the product could be made economically.

2. The designer had facilities for testing whether the design would be fit for use but lacked facilities for testing whether the design could be produced economically.

3. When the resulting tight tolerances created shop troubles, the shop often responded by exceeding the tolerances in order to meet delivery dates. Then, when many of the products performed satisfactorily, the shop drew the conclusion that the designers were needlessly tight. However, there were also cases in which exceeding the tolerances resulted in field failures. From these cases the designers drew the conclusion that the shop could not be trusted fully. One reaction of designers was to set still closer limits in order to neutralize the expected overruns.

---

[104] Many companies use preprinted notes on all drawings stating (for example) "Unless otherwise specified, all dimensions shown are to be held to ± 0.015 inches."

[105] National standardization bodies include American National Standards Institute (ANSI), British Standards Institution, Deutscher Normenausschuss, Association Française de Normalisation, Japan Standards Association, and the United States military services (MIL Standards). The international body is the International Organization for Standardization (ISO).

[106] An example of a national standard is that for dimensioning and tolerancing USASI Y14.5 (now ANSI Y14.5) published (1966) by American Society of Mechanical Engineers, 345 E. 47th St., New York, N.Y. For a discussion, see Edward S. Roth, USASI Y14.5, Dimensioning and Tolerancing for Engineering Drawings, *Journal of Quality Technology*, October 1969, pp. 277–284.

This game was detected or suspected by the shop, so that the mistrust became mutual.

Recent trends have been in the direction of reducing the biases of both the designers and the shops. However, there remains an accumulation of "unrealistic tolerances loosely enforced" which all concerned would like to convert into a situation of "realistic tolerances rigidly enforced." This conversion cannot be accomplished by the "legitimate" process of making engineering investigations and issuing engineering change orders. There are too many investigations, and the issuance of engineering change orders is too elaborate a process.

To date, no one has found a way to accomplish this conversion in an economical way. Methods in use all require restricting the conversion to selected tolerances which are creating the bulk of the cost problem. The selection may be made from: the "high dollar loss list" of the quality cost studies; the list of products for which 100% inspection is being conducted; the list of nonconforming products which has come before the Material Review Board; the list of changes requested by vendors.

Once the list of suspect tolerances has been identified, there are a number of ways in use for minimizing the conversion effort:

1. Establish an order of priority for the "vital few" and deal with them through the regular engineering change procedure.

2. For tolerances of less than vital importance, create a "short loop" for changes, i.e., designate a team (e.g., designer and quality control engineer) to make changes without going through full documentation, e.g., marking up local drawings. Later, when some other reason arises for making an engineering change, the incompletely documented cases will be included.

3. Alternatively, if the tolerance is discovered to be too tight, leave the specification unchanged, but revise the sampling plans to accept a wider dispersion of product. In most companies, changes in sampling plans are accomplished with minimal documentation.

4. Adopt the rule that three Material Review Board waivers of the same defect constitutes a permanent waiver.

Beyond these shortcuts, there is a broad solution which has not yet been fully tested in practice. It consists of devising a new system of tolerancing and enforcement of all new product lines so that they will be launched on a basis of "realistic tolerances rigidly enforced." (This will mean that there will be two systems of tolerancing and enforcement in the company simultaneously.) Then as the older designs phase out, only the new system will remain in force.

Providing Aids to Designers. Any evolutionary solution to unrealistic tolerances must include ways to minimize the bias of the designers. An essential need is to provide the designer with tools which can assist him in understanding the cost consequences of proposed tolerances. Several of these tools are available.

1. *Process capability data.* As data on process capability are worked up and made available for ready reference (see Section 9, under Process Capability: Usage), it becomes feasible to train designers in the significance and use of these data.

2. *Data on cost of precision.* A further step is to quantify the actual cost of achieving various levels of precision, e.g., how the cost in dollars increases as the tolerance in millimeters decreases. Surprisingly, the data for preparing tables or charts of these relationships are often already available in the labor standards used to measure production and inspection productivity. What has not been done is to convert these data into tables of cost versus precision. See, for example Section 9, Figure 9-4 and associated discussion.

3. *Seriousness classification.* Generally, the most important characteristics also call for the greatest precision. In consequence, use of seriousness classification of

characteristics is also a broad guide to tolerancing. [107]   See Section 12, under Serious-ness Classification, for the methodology employed, especially Table 12-6 and asso-ciated discussion.

4. *Value analysis.* This is an organized approach for improving the cost-value relationships, mainly in new designs. See Section 16, under Organizing for Im-provement: Value Analysis, for the techniques used.

5. *Sensory qualities.* There is a good deal of technique available to assist de-signers in tolerancing for sensory qualities. See Section 12, under Sensory Qual-ities.

Jurisdiction in Product Specifications Traditionally, the product designers have been granted (or have acquired) a monopoly on decision making concerning product specifications. This monopoly must now be reexamined in the light of the nature of modern products.

Quantification of Parameters. The designer is the best trained and most expe-rienced specialist as to quantification of some parameters: stress analysis, properties of materials, structural integrity. However, the designer is usually *not* the best qualified man as to quantification of other parameters: reliability, manufacturing cost, maintainability, users' life cycle costs, safety, etc. As a result, provision must be made to enable the company's most qualified specialists to contribute to the prod-uct designs. This they do through the design review.

The designer usually considers the design review as an invasion of his former monopoly on quantifying the parameters. This is precisely the intention, and for the reason that the designer is no longer the most qualified specialist as to some parameters.

Creative Design. Once the nature of the competing parameters has been clari-fied, there remains the problem of creating a design which is an optimum way of meeting all parameters. By his training and experience, the designer is the most qualified man to do this, and he should have a clear, unchallenged responsibility to do so.

Publication. Once the design is finished, there should be a monopoly on publica-tion, i.e., one and only one "legitimate" source of information on what has been specified. (Any other arrangement breeds confusion.) The Design Department has traditionally held this monopoly as to functional requirements. In addition, where the same documents carry the nonfunctional requirements as well, such dual-purpose documents have also been published by the Design Department as a monopoly. These arrangements have worked well, and there is no reason for chang-ing them.

In some companies, separate documents are used for nonfunctional require-ments. [108]   In such cases there is no need for publication to be done by the Design Department. Instead, the publication is by the department which plays the lead-ing role in deciding the requirements, e.g., Manufacturing Planning.

The privilege of publication includes the duty of keeping publications up to date in the event of design changes. For modern products, the network of documenta-tion associated with specifications has become quite complex and this has greatly

---

[107] There is some trend to industry and national standardization of seriousness classification. See, for example, MEKANRESULTAT 72006 (1972), the Swedish standard for classification of characteristics in product specifications. Available from Sveriges Mekanforbund, Box 5506, S-114 85 Stockholm, Sweden.

[108] For a discussion of functional versus nonfunctional requirements, see Product Specifica-tions, above.

complicated the process of issuing changes. The name "configuration control" has been coined to describe the activity of assuring that design changes are properly processed, both as to documentation and as to the effect on the hardware. See generally Section 19.

Cultural Resistance of Designers. Like any other "society," the Design Department evolves a "cultural pattern," i.e., a collection of beliefs, habits, attitudes, practices. This cultural pattern then acts as a stabilizer of practice, including an outward resistance to changes in practice. Applied to design review, the cultural pattern of the designers has included two main forms of outward resistance:

1. The concept of a monopoly on all aspects of specifying. The design review breaks this monopoly by designating other men as the company's best specialists for quantifying certain parameters.[109]

2. The concept of quantifying reliability from tests on hardware and in no other way. When it is proposed to quantify reliability by mathematical prediction, before any hardware has been built, the reaction of many designers is one of disbelief. Only by exposure to actual cases does this disbelief disappear.

Those who face this outward resistance from designers can deal better with it if they realize that there is nothing personal about it; i.e., "Review the design, not the designer." Cultural patterns are a very logical response to the forces with which a society must deal, and the cultural resistance of the designers is no exception. The advocates of design review should try to understand the origin and nature of the resistance before trying to deal with it.

Improving Effectiveness of Designers   For the short range, the traditional skills of the designer can be supplemented by the skills of reliability engineers and other specialists in order to meet the needs of modern product design. For the long range, the trend will certainly include bringing the designers to a greater state of self-sufficiency, so that there will be less need to rely on the continued participation of other specialists. Bringing the designers to a state of self-sufficiency is done in two main ways (1) design experience retention and (2) training.

Design Experience Retention. All design managers agree that experience is an essential requirement of a good designer. To supplement the designer's own experience, it is common to summarize the experience of other designers as well. This "experience retention" is achieved through several widely used tools:

1. *Design Standards Manual.* This book accumulates the departmental standards derived from experience along with referencing the outside standards which have been adopted. The manual is supplemented by notes, memoranda, and other "standards in the making." In large companies there is an Engineering Standards Department which prepares and maintains these standards manuals.

2. *Checklists.* These lists are a form of "countdown" to be checked out by the designer as he proceeds with his project. For example, the checklist on fire hazard would typically include the following:

What could cause a break in the fuel line or oil line?
What could cause a fuel or oil leak?
Could there be a source of ignition?
What is combustible?
How can a fire be detected?
How can the fuel be turned off?
What is the escape route for personnel?

3. *Usage and Failure Data Banks.* The performance of the product under conditions of actual use constitutes the most important single source of experience

---

[109] See Quantification of Parameters, above.

data. A data bank to collect and summarize such information becomes one of the most useful sources of design experience.[110,111]

4. *Tools for Economic Analysis.* These include charts and tables showing the relationship of cost to precision (see, for example, Section 9, Figures 9-4 and 9-27); tables of process capability, comparative costs of alternative designs, etc.

Training for Designers.[112] To attain self-sufficiency, the designers also need training. In part this training is in how to use the design experience retention and in part it is training to become proficient in the use of tools which have had their origin in other disciplines. These tools include:

1. *Quantification of Reliability.* The basic formulas and procedures are well known and have been organized into standardized training courses. It is comparatively easy to train designers in the use of these basic formulas and procedures (which have wide application). For more complex situations, access must be had to the reliability specialists.

2. *Other Quantification.* To a lesser degree, training courses have been worked up in maintainability and safety. However, enough is available to offer a useful indoctrination to designers.

3. *Design of Experiments.* The increased complexity of products and the tightening demands for statistical significance in test results has required that test programs be designed in a way which holds costs of testing to a minimum while yielding maximum information. Courses in design of experiments and the associated analysis of the resulting data have been standardized at several levels of sophistication and are widely available.

---

[110] For elaboration, see Reliability Data Systems, above; see also the discussion of data banks under Reliability Analysis and Prediction.

[111] An example of product improvement through access to failure data is seen in the field of cryptanalysis. At one time the military code clerks who compiled code books for use in transmitting messages (in shortened and secret form) lacked adequate knowledge of the weaknesses of their systems since they had no feedback from the cryptanalysts (the men who tried to "break" secret enemy messages). When one officer was given charge of both sections, he saw to it that the security of the coding systems was improved. See Kahn, David, "The Code Breakers", The Macmillan Company, New York 1967, P. 160 *et seq.*

[112] See also Section 17, Table 17-6, and associated discussion.

Section **9**

Manufacturing Planning

DONALD N. EKVALL

Manufacturing Manager, Leeds & Northrup Co.
North Wales, Pa.

J. M. JURAN

INTRODUCTION

The word "manufacture," as used in this Handbook, means:

1. Manufacturing planning, i.e., the collection of activities through which the factory is put into a state of readiness to produce to quality and other standards.

2. Production, which is the execution of the plan; i.e., usage of the machines, methods, etc., to make finished products out of purchased materials and components. (This topic is treated in Section 11.)

Manufacturing planning begins with review of a new (or changed) product design to judge producibility. It ends when all is in readiness for the factory personnel to take over and produce.

Putting the factory into this state of readiness requires that the planners carry out a series of planning activities[1] shown on Table 9-1. On this same table are shown the outward results of the planning and the identity of the department mainly responsible.

RESPONSIBILITY FOR MANUFACTURING PLANNING

A major decision in manufacturing planning for quality is the division of the planning work among:

Staff planners who operate interdepartmentally
Departmental planners
Production supervisors
Production nonsupervisors

The main factors influencing this decision are the complexities of the projects, the anatomy of the manufacturing process, the technological literacy of the work force, and the managerial philosophy of reliance on systems versus reliance on men.

Complexity of the Project   Manufacturing planning is done in response to designs for new products or processes, changed products and processes, field and shop troubles which have their origin in prior planning, and analyses for quality improvement. These and other sources provide the "projects" which become the work load for the planners.

Some of these projects are truly "major," e.g., launching a new product line, automation of a large production shop. For such major projects, the approach usually follows the concept of "project planning" as discussed in Section 6, under Major Project Planning. This approach features the creation of special organization structures, with important responsibilities for planning and coordinating activities not only for manufacture but also for other functions as well.

At the other extreme is the stream of small projects discussed in Section 6 under Routine Projects for Change. Here the interdepartmental planning consists of preparing a master (standard) procedure to coordinate the work of the departments. Once the master procedure has been made effective, departmental planning takes over, using the procedure as a repetitive coordinator.[2]

Anatomy of the Process   The vast majority of industrial processes take one of three basic forms. These forms importantly affect the extent of formal planning done as well as the choice of who does the planning.

---

[1] The manufacturing planner must accommodate the plan to meet objectives for cost, timetable, etc., in addition to quality. In this Section, the discussion concentrates on the quality problems.

[2] For projects which are a mixture of large and small, see Section 6, under Spectrum of Projects.

TABLE 9-1   Manufacturing Planning: Activities, Responsibilities, and Results

Planning activity	Planning principally performed by	End result of planning
Review design for clarity of specifications and for producibility; recommendations for change	Manufacturing Engineering*	Producible design; revised product specification
Choose process for manufacture: operations, sequences	Manufacturing Engineering	Economic, feasible process; process specification
Provide machines and tools capable of meeting tolerances	Manufacturing Engineering and Quality Control Engineering	Capable machines and tools
Provide instruments of accuracy adequate to control the process	Manufacturing Engineering	Capable instrumentation
Provide manufacturing information: methods, procedures, cautions	Manufacturing Engineering	Operation sheets
Provide system of quality controls: data collection, feedback, adjustment	Quality Control Engineering and Production (see also Section 12, under Inspection Planning)	Control stations equipped to provide feedback
Define responsibilities for quality	Line Supervision (see Section 11)	Agreed pattern of responsibilities
Select and train Production personnel	Production Supervision (see Sections 11 and 17)	Qualified production operators
Prove adequacy of planning; tryouts; trial lots	Manufacturing Engineering	Proof of adequacy

* In the process industries, the name is more usually Process Development. In the mechanical industries, alternative names are: Manufacturing Planning, Methods Engineering, etc.

The Autonomous Department. This process form receives basic materials and fabricates them into finished products, all within a single self-contained department. The schematic diagram is shown in Figure 9-1. A well-known example is the tool room.

For such autonomous departments there may well be formal planning, but in that event the planner is often a member of the autonomous department rather than a member of a staff planning department. In very small autonomous departments, the planning is done by the departmental supervision and even by the workmen.[3]

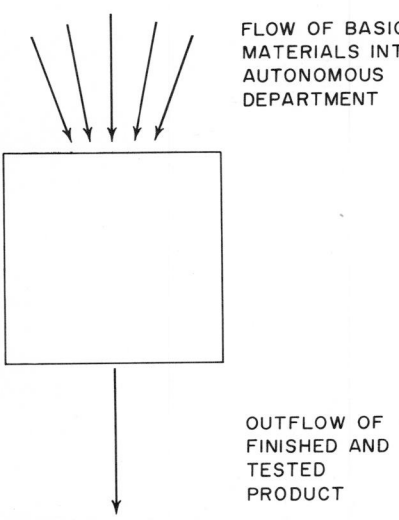

FLOW OF BASIC MATERIALS INTO AUTONOMOUS DEPARTMENT

OUTFLOW OF FINISHED AND TESTED PRODUCT

Fig. 9-1. Schematic of process for a small autonomous department.

The Assembly "Tree." This familiar process is widely used by the great mechanical and electronic industries which build automotive vehicles, household appliances, electronic apparatus, etc. The roots of the tree are numerous vendors or in-house departments making parts and components. These elements are assembled, by still other departments. Figure 9-2 shows this process schematically.

The assembly tree requires planning of two very different kinds: interdepartmental and departmental. In large operations, it becomes mandatory to use staff planners for the interdepartmental planning. However, it is not mandatory to use staff planners for departmental planning as well, though this is sometimes done.

The Procession. In this form, there are again numerous in-house departments (with occasional vendor departments). However, all the product progresses sequentially through all departments, each performing some operation which contributes to the final result. This form is exhibited by the bulk of the "process" industries.[4] It is also exhibited by mechanical industries when making complex components in large numbers, e.g., engine blocks, crankshafts, etc. Figure 9-3 shows the schematic.

As in the tree form, the procession form requires both interdepartmental and departmental planning. For the former, it is usually mandatory to make use of staff planners. For departmental planning, there are options, as discussed below.

Technological Literacy Before departmental planning can be assigned to departmental supervision and the workmen, it is necessary that they possess the technological literacy needed for the task. This literacy includes the ability to read and interpret the specifications, customers' orders, interdepartmental plans, and other informational inputs. It also includes an understanding of the machines, tools, instruments and other facilities (plus some related cost data) sufficient to make the planning judgments needed to meet standards of quality, cost, and delivery.

Where technological literacy has not yet been attained (e.g., in some "developing" countries), the departmental manufacturing planning cannot be delegated to super-

[3] For some further discussion of forms in job shop operation, see Section 45, under What Is a Job Shop?

[4] For a more detailed discussion as applied to a specific industry (metals), see Section 33, Table 33-1 and associated discussion.

visors or workmen who lack such literacy.   However, where this literacy has been attained, it is feasible to delegate the departmental planning.   The failure to do so is

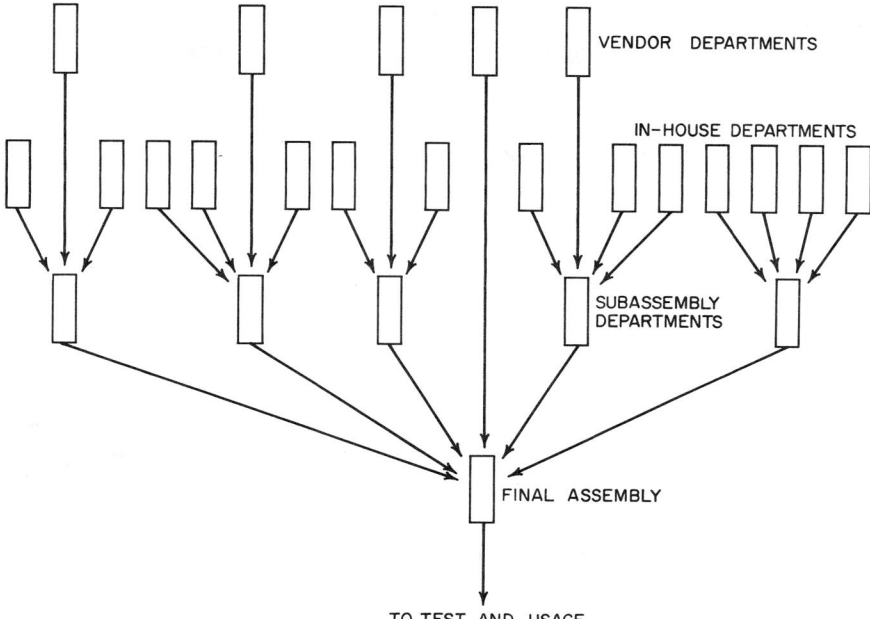

Fig. 9-2.   Schematic of the assembly "tree" form of process.

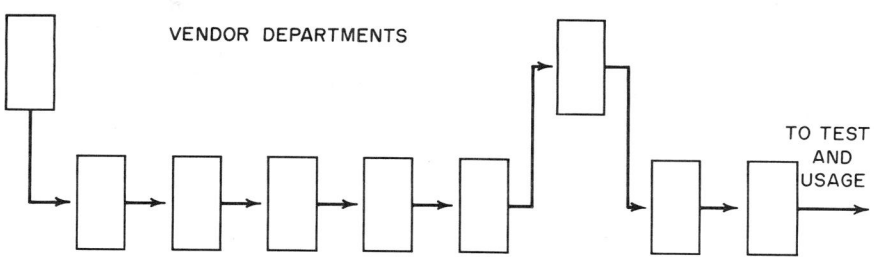

Fig. 9-3.   Schematic of the "procession" form of process.

usually due to cultural resistance by a managerial philosophy which is reluctant to make such a delegation.

Managerial Philosophy   A number of industrialized countries delegate very little of the job of manufacturing planning to the departmental supervision or to the work force.   In the United States, this situation is largely a residue of the Taylor System[5] of separating manufacturing planning from execution, i.e., from production. (See Section 18, under Role of Motivation: The Taylor System.)

[5] For a collection of Taylor's principal writings, see Taylor, F. W., "Scientific Management," Harper & Brothers, New York, 1947.

The Taylor System was proposed early in the twentieth century, at a time when education levels of foremen and workmen were very low while, at the same time, the factories were acquiring more and more complexity in technology. The system was so successful in improving productivity that it was widely adopted in the United States. It took firm root and remains as the dominant approach to manufacturing planning, not only interdepartmentally but departmentally as well.

Meanwhile, a major premise of the Taylor System, i.e., technological illiteracy of the foremen and workmen, has been made obsolete by the dramatic increase in education levels of foremen and workmen. In some countries, industrial companies have recognized the planning capacities inherent in the men who now possess such education and have delegated the manufacturing planning accordingly.[6] In the United States, the cultural pattern created by the widespread adoption of the Taylor System includes important vested interests and axiomatic beliefs among industrial managers, staff planners, union leaders, college professors, and still others. Collectively, these beliefs constitute a serious limitation on effective use of the education of the many to participate in the planning.[7]

DESIGN REVIEW[8]

The purposes of design review include improvement of manufacturing economics through the early warning concept, i.e., anticipating quality difficulties. These quality difficulties are mainly related to the product tolerances, e.g., low yields, undue precision. Other anticipated problems are related to vagueness of specifications, difficulty of access for measurement, etc.[9]

The Manufacturing Engineer and the Quality Control Engineer (as members of the design review team) have a joint responsibility to identify these potential troubles and to contribute constructive ideas for possible solutions. They also have available to them some useful tools for quantifying their proposals, as discussed below.

Classification of Characteristics   It is helpful to know, during the design review meetings, which characteristics are functional and which are nonfunctional.[10]   The former, once agreed on, must be met. However, the nonfunctional characteristics, being of a means-to-an-end nature, have an inherent flexibility which permits various modifications to be made. For example:

Control limits different from product limits to provide alarm signals in the process
Manufacturing limits on average and standard deviation rather than on individual product units to improve economics of manufacture and control
Tolerance on mating parts shifted about to optimize the economics of holding the tolerances, e.g., external and internal diameters
Tolerances on assembly components based on statistical rather than arithmetic addition (See Section 22 under Tolerance Limits for Interacting Dimensions).

It is also of value for the planners to understand which characteristics of the de-

---

[6] See generally Sections 48 and 48A.

[7] In contrast, see Section 18, under The Japanese QC Circle.

[8] The general approach to design review is discussed in Sec. 8, under Design Review. Improvement of manufacturing economics is achieved also by substitution of materials, standardization of components, redesign to simplify tooling, etc. Such improvements are only obliquely related to quality and are not discussed here.

[9] Many of the Industry Sections of this Handbook (Sections 29 through 47) discuss problems of design review as applied to specific products.

[10] See Section 12, under Seriousness Classification.

sign are critical, major, and minor. The design review discussions bring out some of this. The more complete the classification, the better able is the planner to employ the available time and money where they will do the most good.[11]

Cost of Tolerances   Discussion of tolerances is an extensive activity during design review. To aid these discussions, it is useful to provide quantitative data on the cost of holding various levels of precision. There are two available forms of these data.

Process Capability Tables. Some companies have prepared tables showing the process capability of their principal processes. During design reviews, such tables provide convenient prediction of the yields of processes and thereby a prediction of excess costs. Such quantitative data carry considerable weight in the design review meetings. Table 9-2 is an example of such a compilation for various machine tools cutting various dimensions on a variety of materials.[12]

Charts of Cost of Precision. Even though the tolerances can be met with available processes, the cost of meeting tolerances varies widely with the precision demanded.[13] The design review meetings can therefore be aided by data which show the cost of meeting various levels of precision. Figure 9-4 shows an example of relationship between cost and precision for a grinding operation.[14] The significant thing about Figure 9-4 is that no new studies were created to prepare the figure; *the data were already in the house.* The data were contained in the industrial engineering studies which had been conducted to set standards of a day's work.

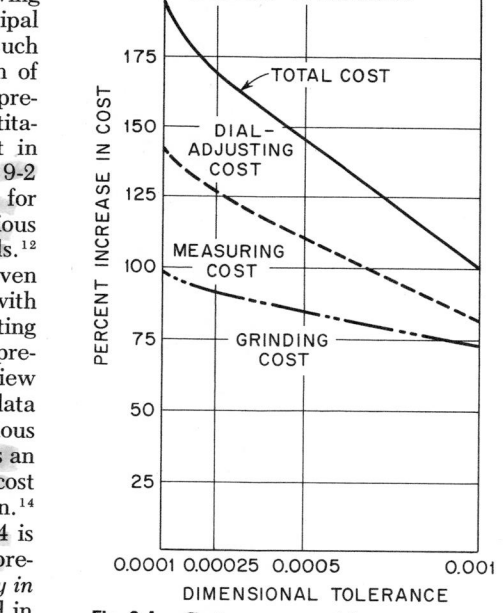

Fig. 9-4.   Cost versus precision.

Such standards data abound in most companies. Since the same studies also identify the product worked on and hence the tolerances, it is feasible to prepare summaries such as are exemplified in Figure 9-4. The relative scarcity of such summaries is due mainly to the fact that there is no clear responsibility assigned for preparing them.

---

[11] Some of the Industry Sections of this Handbook discuss seriousness classification as applied to specific products.

[12] From broader research conducted by L. A. Seder and P. D. Krensky and first published in the Second Edition of this Handbook.

[13] For an interesting, early set of cases, see discussion of paper by Hall, J. A., *Transactions ASME*, vol. 51, no. 4, pp. 16–17, January–April, 1929.

[14] Bayer, Lad J., *Tooling and Production*, August 1956, pp. 73–76.

TABLE 9-2 Process Capability (in thousandths of an inch)

Machine and operation	Material							
	Soft brass	F. M. and alloy	Stainless steel	Phosphor bronze	Aluminum	Cupronickel	Copper	Plastic
No. 00G – Brown & Sharpe:								
D–Turn.	0.4–0.7	0.5–1.5	1.0*	1.0*				
D–Form.	0.5–1.0	0.7–1.7	0.8–1.5	0.6–1.5*	1.4*			
D–Burnish.			0.3*					
D–Thread roll	0.6–2.0	3.0*			1.0*			
L–Form.	0.5–1.5*	2.0*						
L–Cut off	0.5–1.5	1.0–2.0	1.0–2.5	2.0*				
No. 0G – Brown & Sharpe:								
D–Turn.	1.0	1.0*	1.0*	1.2*				
D–Form.	0.8–1.5	0.8–1.5	1.0–1.5*	1.3–2.0				
L–Form.	0.5*		0.7*					
L–Cut off	0.8–1.0		1.5*					
L–Counterbore	1.0–2.0							
No. 2G – Brown & Sharpe:								
D–Turn.	1.0–1.2*	0.4–1.5	1.5–2.0*	1.8*		0.8*	0.6–1.0*	
D–Form.	0.8–1.5	0.5–2.2	2.5*	2.5*			2.5*	
L–Form.	0.5*		0.7*					
L–Cut off	0.5–1.0		1.5*					
$\frac{7}{16}$-inch Gridley:								
D–Turn.	1.0–1.5*							
$\frac{9}{16}$-inch Gridley:								
D–Turn.	1.0*	1.0–4.0*						
D–Form.		1.0–4.0*						
OD–Thread size.	1.0–1.5*							
L–Cut off	1.8–4.8*							

D = Diameter
L = Length
OD = Outside diameter
*Based on data from a single source. May not be representative.

DESIGN OF THE MANUFACTURING PROCESS

The manufacturing process involves two very different kinds of design:

1. The systems design, which envisions how the product is to be made from basic materials. This is an interdepartmental design and can be on a grand scale, as exemplified by the steelmaking process, Figure 33-1.

2. The work station design, which enables each "unit process" to play its role in the grand design.

For both these kinds of design the planner can make effective use of some fundamental concepts in planning for quality: concept of dominance, process capability, foolproofing, etc. These concepts are discussed in detail in this Section.

The technological approach to systems design is largely outside the scope of this Handbook. Except for instrumentation[15] and automated processes,[16] this design is not discussed in detail in this Section. The reader is referred to some of the Industry Sections of this Handbook for some examples of systems design, notably Sections 33, 34, 35, 42, and 43. See also Section 6, which deals with the broad company approach to quality planning.

Work station design requires a great deal of attention to man-machine relationships and to the details of tool design.[17] The extent of these details and relationships can be seen from an example.

An electronics company undertook a process redesign to reduce the incidence of welding defects. Metallurgical examination of numerous defective welds showed that both technological and human variables contributed to these defects. The improved technology was provided in several ways:

Standardization and specification of electrode designs, i.e., alloy and geometry for every type of weld

Standardization of tools for dressing electrodes

Standardization of process variables (current, time pressure, etc.) for each type of weld and product

Redesign of some tools to permit prompt, sure changeover

Removal of unauthorized maintenance tools

A preventive maintenance program for the tools and equipment

Improved performance by the personnel also required several new inputs:

Steps were taken to improve the industrial relations climate by facing up to some prevailing sources of resentment.

Training programs were conducted for supervisors, maintenance men, setup men and operators. These programs, using demonstrations and visual aids, explained the advantages and purposes behind the new technology, the terms used, the significance of various defect types, the likely causes of various defects, the likely remedies, etc.

New procedures were introduced to put shop personnel on a self-control basis, including data sheets for feedback purposes.

It is evident from this example that manufacturing planning involves not only the "hardware" of machines, tools, and instruments but also the "software" of method and procedures which will enable the work force to extract from the hardware the performance of which it is capable.

[15] See Quality Information Equipment, below.

[16] See Automatic Process Regulation, below.

[17] Many work stations are also control stations. See below, under Planning Process Controls: Work Stations.

Additional examples will be found throughout the Industry Sections. They make abundantly clear the vital role played by the tools, fixtures, transfer mechanisms, handling equipment, etc. Undramatic details such as locating surfaces, clamping positions, cleaning devices, etc., nevertheless require dedicated attention by competent engineers, tool makers, and technicians of all sorts.

Preproduction Trials Because the manufacturing plan starts as a mental concept, it will be "scaled up" many orders of magnitude if it goes into large-scale production. There is great risk in going directly into production from the conceptual plan primarily because of the risk of quality failures. To reduce this risk, companies make use of trial production lots (called pilot plant production, preproduction, etc.) to discover deficiencies in the planning and to remedy them before going into full-scale production. In some industries this concept is formalized into regular phases of scaling up. See, for example, Section 42.

The scaling up of production is actually a continuation of the scaling up which takes place from product design concept to prototype or model construction and test. The adequacy of the full-scale manufacturing plan cannot be judged from the record of models made in the model shop. In the model shop the basic purpose is to prove engineering feasibility; in the production shop the purpose is to meet standards of quality, cost, and delivery. The model-shop machinery, tools, personnel, supervision, motivation, etc., are all different from the corresponding situations in the production shop.

Tool Tryout. At the work station level, as new tools are completed, they are subjected to a tryout procedure which, in most companies, is highly formalized. The tryout consists of producing enough product from the new tool to demonstrate that it can meet quality standards under shop conditions. (Because multiple standards are involved, there are multiple parties to the tryout.) The proof of adequacy for quality involves participation of a quality planner or an inspection supervisor.

These formalized tryouts conclude with the execution of a formal document backed up by supporting data, which always include the quality data. The release of the tool for full-scale production is contingent on the approval of this tryout document.

Limited Trial Lots. Beyond the tryouts at individual work stations, there is need for collective tryouts. These require trial production lots, which must be scheduled for the prime purpose of proving in the manufacturing process. The trial lot is usually made in the regular production shop and provides an extensive preview of the problems which will be encountered in large-scale production. In the process industries the equivalent intermediate scaling up is the "pilot plant." It is widely used to provide the essential information (on quality, costs, productivity, etc.) needed to determine whether and how to go into full-scale production.

Some critical quality questions can be answered by limited trial lots. In the electronics industry there are cases in which the adequacy of critical materials can be proved only by actually fabricating the material into products to a degree which permits test of fitness for use. (See Section 38, under Materials Planning.) In planning the manufacture of electron tubes, it is common practice to compare the results achieved by the various teams which assemble mounts. A typical set of data at the beginning of a large production run was as follows:

Team	Number assembled	Shorted X to Y	Shorted Y to Z	Shorted W to Z
A	500	8	0	0
B	500	1	1	6
C	500	0	2	9

The data suggest that team A has some weakness which creates X-Y shorts. However, the other teams are using methods which avoid these shorts. In contrast, Team A has solved the problem of W-Z shorts, while Teams B and C have not.

Experimental Lots. The trial lot concept provides opportunities for planners to test out alternatives, and they often combine the concept of experimentation with that of proving in the nonexperimental portion of the trial. See, for example, Section 34, Figure 34-5.

Attainment of good process yields is one of the most important purposes of experimental lots. These experiments can make use of all the techniques discussed in Section 16 and in the various statistical Sections (22 through 28).

Preproduction Runs Ideally, product lots should be put through the entire system, with the deficiencies found and corrected before going into full-scale production. In practice, companies usually make some compromises with this ideal approach. The "preproduction" may be merely the first of the regular production, but with special provision for prompt feedback and correction of errors as found. Alternatively, the preproduction may be limited to those features of product and process design which are so new that prior experience cannot reliably provide a basis for good risk taking. While some companies do adhere to a strict rule of proving in the product and process through preproduction lots, the more usual approach is one of flexibility, in which the use of preproduction lots depends on:

1. The extent to which the product embodies new or untested quality features
2. The extent to which the design of the manufacturing process embodies new or untried machines, tools, etc.
3. The amount and value of product which will be out in the field before there is conclusive evidence of the extent of process, product, and usage difficulties

Release to Manufacture Companies which use formal tool tryouts and similar phased manufacturing planning also provide for a formal "Release to Manufacture." This is a documented transfer of responsibility from Manufacturing Planning to Production. It follows the trials, the needed revisions, and other actions which lead to an agreement to make the transfer of responsibility.

CONCEPT OF DOMINANCE[18]

All manufacturing processes involve numerous variables which affect the resulting quality. These variables are not equally important; they follow the Pareto principle of the vital few and the trivial many. Often one variable is so completely decisive that it "dominates," i.e., it is more important than all the rest of the variables combined. This dominance of one variable (or very few) is widespread, and many planners have instinctively made use of it. For example, in presswork, it has long been known that the die is dominant. In consequence, the systems of control have been built around this fact.[19] However, in other cases the dominance is there but is not acted on because there is no formal way to assure that it receives the attention it deserves.

The most usual forms of dominance in manufacturing processes are:

Setup-dominant[20] Here the process has been engineered to so high a degree of reproducibility that it provides an essentially uniform product during the entire

[18] The earliest published elaboration of this concept was by L. A. Seder and appeared in the Second Edition of Quality Control Handbook, Section 26, Quality Control in the Job Shop, under System-centered Approach.
[19] See Section 35, under Presswork.
[20] See also Section 24, under Lot Formation.

length of the lot. In such cases, if the original setup is correct, the entire lot will conform to standard. The planning should therefore concentrate on:

1. Creating a highly reproducible process, with little time-to-time variation. The measure of attainment of such a process is discussed below, under Process Capability.

2. Providing the setup men with the means for self-control. This discussion follows.

3. Providing adequate controls to assure that the setup is correct in the first place. This is discussed in Section 11, under Inspection Feedback to Production.

The broad concept of self-control is discussed in Section 11, under Concept of Operator Self-Control, *et seq.* To apply this concept to setups requires that the set-up man be provided with the means for:

1. Knowing where to center the setup. Sometimes this is evident from the product or process specification. In cases where this is not evident, special knowledge must be provided to the setup man. For example, a company making metal containers ("tin cans") found that while the process was highly reproducible, it was essential that certain dimensions of the setup be precisely centered. For this purpose the planners prepared a narrow limit scheme and provided the setup men with suitable narrow limits to meet. These became a mandatory requirement of the setup.[21]

2. Knowing whether the setup is actually centered. The necessary instruments, standards, etc., should be provided to the setup men for this purpose. Alternatively, patrol inspectors who are so provided should do the measuring and feed this data back to the setup men. In some cases it is feasible to make use of product data to show clearly the nature of the setup, as in the example in Section 11, Figures 11-3, 4, and 5, plus related discussion.

3. Adjusting the setup with precision. (This is often a neglected aspect of process design.) In conventional metal cutting, calibrated feed wheels accomplish this purpose. However, for many other processes, the setup men are left on a cut-and-try basis. Since they are also responsible for meeting cost and delivery standards, the cut-and-try adjustments become a temptation to "settle for a close one," since a new try may be no better.

Machine-dominant   Here the process, though reproducible, undergoes a continuing time-to-time change (e.g., depletion of reagents, wear of tools, heat buildup, etc.) of such magnitude that product nonconformance is inevitable during the production of the lot. To deal with this change, provision must be made for periodic check and adjustment.

The "periodic check" consists mainly of conventional process control techniques as discussed in Section 11, under Knowledge of "Supposed to Do."[22] The adjustment needs are quite similar to those discussed above, under Setup-dominant. However, the planners have historically done a more complete job of engineering the running of the process than of setting up the process.

Operator-dominant   In this category is a vast array of operations which are not yet fully engineered and for which the unengineered residue is the major source of defects. For such operations, the attention and skill of the operators is decisive. Hence the operations are classed as operator-dominant.

Defects from operator-dominant processes are commonly "operator-controllable." The nature of these defects is discussed in detail in Section 18. Of the remedies

---

[21] See, in this connection, Section 23, under Statistical Control Using Limits Derived from Product Specifications.

[22] See Section 23 for the statistical techniques involved.

noted there, the planner can mainly make use of (1) Foolproofing the process and (2) Discovering the knack during trial lots.

These are discussed below, under Foolproofing the Process and under Trial Lots.

Component-dominant In this category the purchased input materials, parts, etc., possess qualities which are collectively so vital that they are the main factor in deciding the quality of the final product.

The manufacturing planner has an important voice in the make or buy decision and thereby in the extent to which component dominance is allowed to grow. However, there are economic considerations which may require enduring a component-dominant process. In that event, the methods set out in Section 10 become pertinent. Since the planner also participates in these vendor relations, he can make his influence felt in the structuring of the vendor quality control programs.

There are, of course, other categories of dominance[23] and some combination forms as well. However, the categories listed above are widely prevalent and can be used to illustrate the concept.

Table 9-3 summarizes, for these four categories of dominance, some examples of

TABLE 9-3 Dominance

Setup-dominant	Machine-dominant	Operator-dominant	Component-dominant
	Typical operations		
Punching	Packaging	Arc welding	Watch assembly
Drilling	Staking	Hand soldering	Auto assembly
Cutting to length	Screw machining	Blanchard grinding	Other mechanical
Broaching	Automatic cutting	Steel rolling	assembly
Die cutting	Volume filling	Turret-lathe running	Plastics assembly
Die drawing	Weight filling	Spray painting	Electronics assembly
Molding	Papermaking	Electronic	Tube making
Coil winding	Wire enameling	"trimming"	Food formulation
Labeling	Wool carding	Hand packing	Vegetable packing
Sheet-metal bending	Resistance welding	Repairing	
Flame cutting		Adjusting	
Heat sealing		Inspecting	
Printing		Card punching	
Mimeographing		Filing	
		Order filling	
		Shoe lasting	
	Typical control systems during manufacture		
First-piece	Periodic inspection	Acceptance	Vendor rating
inspection	X chart	inspection	Incoming inspection
Lot plot	Median chart	p chart	Prior operation
Precontrol	$\bar{X}$ and R chart	c chart	control
Narrow-limit gaging	Precontrol	Operator scoring	Acceptance
Attribute visual	Narrow-limit gaging		inspection
inspection	p chart		
	Process variables check		
	Automatic recording		

[23] In job shop manufacture, what is often dominant is the "job numerics"—i.e., the totality of differences in product, tooling, control plan, end use, etc.—which distinguish one job shop order from another. The proper recognition and communication of these job numerics is a major factor in the effectiveness of job shop quality control. See Section 45, especially under The Job Numerics.

each, the typical approach to planning the process, and the typical control systems used.

PREDICTING PROCESS ADEQUACY

The planner should know in advance whether the process will be able to turn out products which are fit for use. There are several ways of making this prediction: from direct measurement of the process, from product usage data, from product conformance to specification, from process capability studies. Each of these methods has advantages and limitations, and these are summarized in Table 9-4.

TABLE 9-4   Methods of Predicting Process Adequacy

Method of prediction	Advantages	Disadvantages
By direct measurement on the process itself	Can be done without waiting for product to be available for processing. Detects errors in process facilities, and points to some causes.	Process is not under load, not being operated under shop conditions.
From successful usage of the product	Ultimate proof in the minds of practical men. Carries weight with non-technical managers.	Fails to provide a quantitative measure of capability. Knowledge is not transferable to new products not yet manufactured.
From product conformance to specification	Traditional method, long accepted by machine builders and machine users.	Fails to quantify capability relative to the variables involved. Limited as to predictability.
Measure of process capability	Provides quantitative data which can be used to predict adequacy for future designs.	Requires added effort to collect and analyze data.

Prediction from Direct Measurement of the Process. It is common practice in manufacture of machine tools to test the machines by placing dial gages, test mandrels, spirit levels, and other instruments in appropriate mountings and measuring the trueness of the machine.[24] These measurements (which are recorded by the machine builder and become part of the permanent file for that machine) have value in detecting construction errors, but they are quite limited as predictors of machine performance since the machine is not under load and is not being run under shop conditions.

In purchasing new machine tools, the practice is increasingly to specify process capability based on the uniformity of the resulting product. However, at the time the machine is shipped, there may be no material or castings available for tryout. In such cases measurement on the machine is for the moment the only basis of qualification.

In cases where the product made by the machine fails to conform to tolerances, measurement of the machine may point to causes. Figure 9-5a shows the results of testing some bore, turn, and cutoff machines for reproducibility of the front slide motion.

[24] An authoritative work is Schlesinger, Georg, "Testing Machine Tools," The Machinery Publishing Co. Ltd., London. Also The Industrial Press, New York, 1945.

Of the 26 machines tested, 5 were badly in need of maintenance, as exemplified by Figure 9-5b. Figure 9-5c depicts data from a machine which was in good order.

Prediction from Successful Usage.   In some industries (e.g., complex chemicals, drugs), the final large-scale manufacturing process evolves out of a pilot plant. This

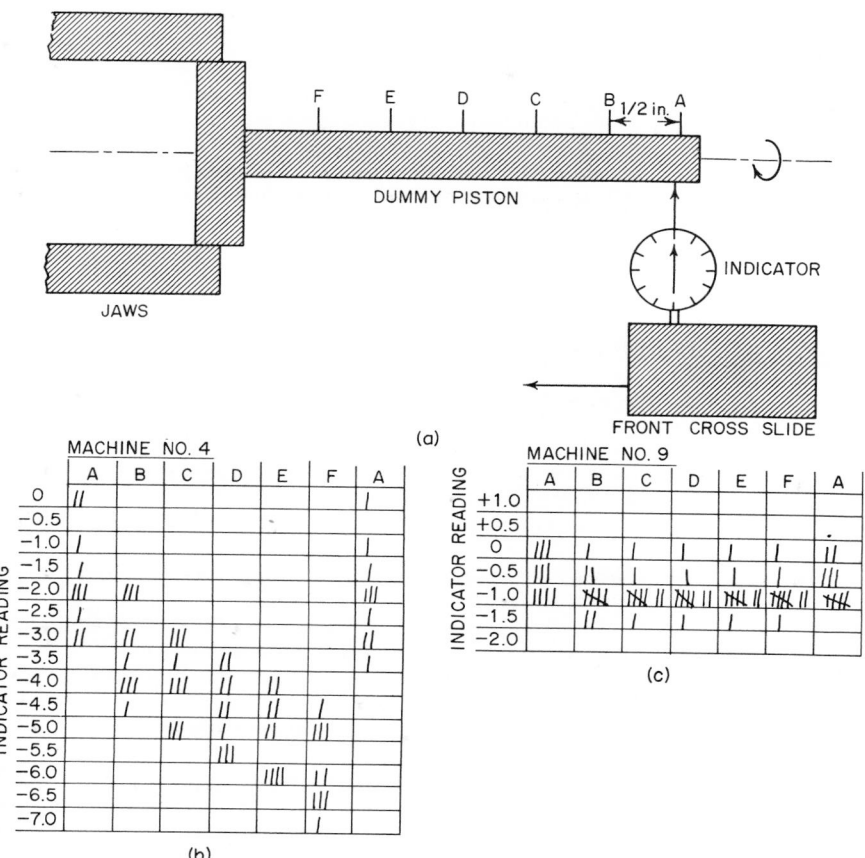

Fig. 9-5a, b, c.   Measurement made directly on machine tool.

pilot plant is under the close supervision of the product and process research personnel and is used to develop the large-scale process. The researchers tend to feel that since the pilot plant operated under close control of dedicated personnel, the pilot plant parameters are to be regarded as the ultimate criteria for judging the adequacy of a process.

This reasoning is entirely logical when the pilot plant is the only production facility and even in the early stages of operating the large-scale plant. However, as production, sale, and usage become increasingly successful, a new data input becomes available. The record of successful usage proves not only the fitness of the product for use, but *also the validity of the large-scale manufacturing process.* [25]

[25] It does not prove the validity of the pilot plant process.

Usage data provide no scientific measure of process capability. However, they are the ultimate proof of validity and carry great weight with upper management and marketing management.

Prediction from Product Conformance. This has been the classical method of judging process adequacy. The machine tool builder's job was regarded as done only when the first parts made by the machine were found to meet tolerances.

The method appeals to practical men, and it is good as far as it goes. However, it fails to quantify capability in relation to the variables encountered and thereby limits the ability to transfer the available process knowledge to product designs which have not yet been made. This limitation is fatal to good planning, which requires quantified predictability.

Prediction through Measure of Process Capability. This is a twentieth century development which has been spreading rapidly. It is discussed under the next few headings.

PROCESS CAPABILITY: THE CONCEPT

Process capability is the measured, inherent reproducibility of the product turned out by a process.

Basic Definitions   Each key word in this definition must itself be clearly defined, since the concept of capability has an enormous extent of application and since non-scientific terms are inadequate for communication within the industrial community.

Process. This refers to some unique combination of machines, tools, methods, materials, and men engaged in production. It is often feasible to separate and quantify the effect of the variables entering this combination, and such separation can be illuminating.

Capability. This word is used in the sense of a capacity, based on tested performance, to achieve measureable results.

Measured. This refers to the fact that process capability is quantified from data which, in turn, are the result of measurement of work performed by the process.

Inherent Reproducibility. This refers to the product uniformity resulting from a process which is in a state of statistical control, i.e., in the absence of time-to-time "drift" or other assignable causes of variation. "Instantaneous reproducibility" is a synonym.

Figures 9-6 and 9-7 show the concept of instantaneous reproducibility. In Figure 9-6, the measurements follow a persistent horizontal pattern without any time-to-time drift. In Figure 9-7, the process exhibits a noticeable drift. However, the instantaneous reproducibility is identical for the two diagrams, though the frequency distribution is not.

Product. The measurement is made on the product because it is product variation which is the end result.

Process capability as defined above is a measureable property of the process (much as volume in liters is a measureable property of a container). The resulting measure is expressed in terms of 6σ of variation (see below) and is *unrelated to the product tolerance;* i.e., "the process doesn't know what the tolerance is." Whether a process will actually hold any given tolerance depends on a variety of factors, but mainly on the width of the tolerance.

Process Patterns   The concept of process capability can be better understood by a brief review of some of the usual process patterns encountered. Figure 9-6 is the ideal case of a process in a state of statistical control. Figure 9-7 is the same process when subjected to a time-to-time drift, e.g., wear of tools, depletion of active solution.

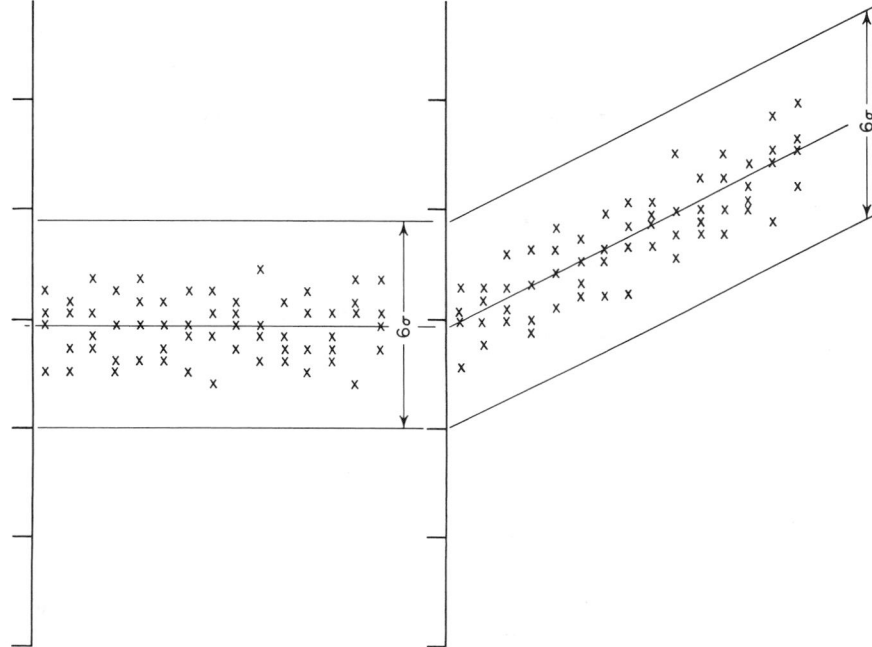

Fig. 9-6. Instantaneous reproducibility, sequence of subgroups showing no drift.

Fig. 9-7. Instantaneous reproducibility, sequence of subgroups showing drift.

Figures 9-8a through 9-8e show some of the process patterns[26] resulting from common interruptions and adjustments, as follows:

Figure no.	Result of
9-8a	Sudden size change due to tool adjustment
9-8b	Interruption, during which machine cools off and then gradually heats up again until original size is restored
9-8c	Start up of a machine on Monday morning, with associated tool adjustment
9-8d	Frequent adjustment or overcorrection
9-8e	Change in dispersion and size due to change in raw material

Standardized Formula The most widely adopted formula for process capability is:

$$\text{Process capability} = 6\sigma$$

where σ = the standard deviation of the process under a state of statistical control, i.e., under no drift and no sudden changes.

Many industrial processes, notably in the chemical process industries, do operate under a state of statistical control. For such processes, the computed process capability of 6σ can be compared directly to specification tolerances, and judgments of

[26] These figures are derived from van Gelder, K. W., Frequentiever-delingen en Proceskarten (Frequency Distributions and Control Charts), *Sigma*, vol. 7, no. 2, 1961, pp. 30–33; also no. 3, pp. 49–52.

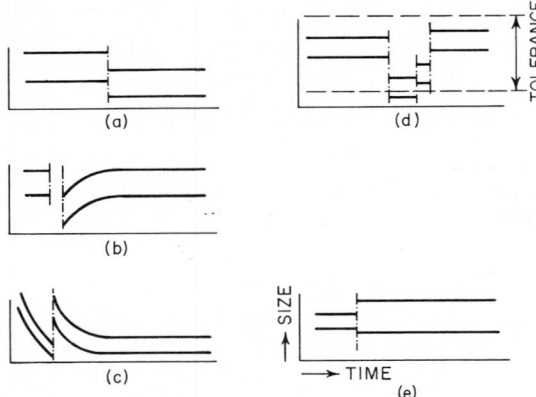

(a) Sudden size changes due to tool adjustment. *(b)* After an interruption there is a delay (heat effect) before the return to original size. *(c)* Startup of a machine on Monday morning, combined with an adjustment of the tools. *(d)* Unnecessary adjustment and incorrect adjustment. *(e)* Change in dispersion and size by using another raw material.

Figs. 9-8a through 9-8e.   Process patterns.

adequacy can be made.   However, the majority of industrial processes do exhibit drift and do exhibit sudden changes.   These departures from the ideal are a fact of life, and the practitioner must deal with them, as is discussed below under Process Capability: Relation to Tolerance.

Nevertheless, there is great value in standardizing on a formula for process capability based on a state of statistical control.   Under this state, the product variations are the resultant of numerous small variables (rather than being the effect of a single large variable) and hence have the character of random variation.   The practitioner cannot reduce this "natural" or inherent instantaneous reproducibility, which thereby becomes "unavoidable" so long as this process is used; i.e., the variability of the process can be reduced to the size of the process capability, but no further.   It is most helpful for planners to have such limits in quantified form.[27]

PROCESS CAPABILITY MEASUREMENT

A number of methods have been evolved for measuring process capability.   One of these, the control chart method, is rigorously correct; the rest are approximations.

Control Chart Method.   Typically, five consecutive pieces become one subgroup, and (typically) ten such subgroups are selected.   These subgroups need not be consecutive, since what is decisive in determining capability is variation within subgroups.   The 50 pieces are measured on a variables basis, and the resulting data are tested for lack of statistical control by means of an $\bar{X}$ and R chart (see Section 23).   If the data show no evidence of lack of control, the process capability is computed

---

[27] Some practitioners advocate a standard formula which does take into account the "extraneous" variables such as drift and sudden changes.   However, use of such a formula would remove the commonality possessed by all processes, i.e., inherent instantaneous variability. Instead, the standard formula would include the "extraneous" variables, which differ widely from one process to another.

as 6σ, which includes 99.73% of the data. The 6σ are computed by the formula:

$$6\sigma = 6s = 6\,\frac{\bar{R}}{d_2}$$

where $s =$ the calculated standard deviation of the sample

$\bar{R} =$ the average range of the 10 subgroups

$d_2 =$ the constant for converting ranges into standard deviations, for the particular subgroup size, 5 in this case

Appendix II, Table A shows the values of d_2 for various sizes of subgroups.

If the process gives evidence of lack of control, the planner may either:

1. Discard the data, try to eliminate the cause of the out-of-control condition, and repeat the process capability study.

2. Accept the computation as a good approximation of process capability. This is the usual practice when the out-of-control condition is minor.

Frequency Distribution Method. Here a sample of (typically) 50 consecutive pieces is taken, during which time no adjustments are made on the machines or tools. The pieces are all measured, the data are tallied in frequency distribution form, and the standard deviation is calculated. (See Section 22, under Measures of Dispersion.) The process capability is then regarded as equal to 6σ.

The method is an approximation, since the frequency distribution may fail to disclose process drift or process changes. For example, Figures 9-9a and 9-9b show

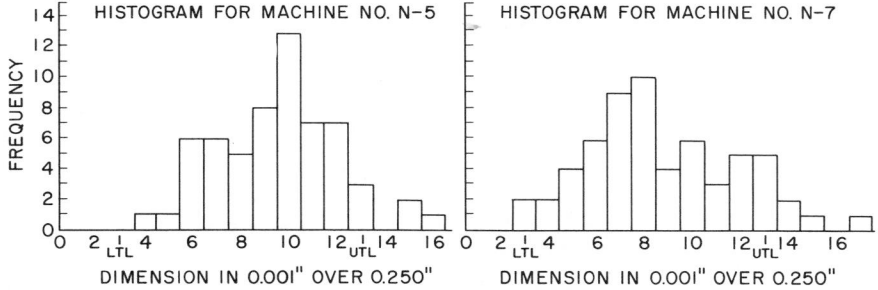

Fig. 9-9.   Two machines with similar frequency distributions.

the frequency distributions of data from two machines. The histograms show approximately the same average and dispersion. However, when the same data are tallied in a manner which shows the individual measurements within each subgroup sample in the chronological order of production (Figures 9-10a and 9-10b), the story is different. Figure 9-10a suggests an absence of drift; Figure 9-10b suggests the presence of a sizable drift. The conventional $\bar{X}$ and R charts (Figures 9-11a and 9-11b) confirm these suggestions. Computation of process capability from the frequency distributions would give a valid result for the left-hand machine but a distorted result for the right-hand machine.

Despite the risk of inflating the value of process capability, the frequency distribution method is widely used. For many processes the risk is small, since little drift takes place during a run of only 50 pieces. The method is simple to use, and the contour of the frequency distribution provides added knowledge to the experienced practitioner. The value of sigma is tedious to compute by manual

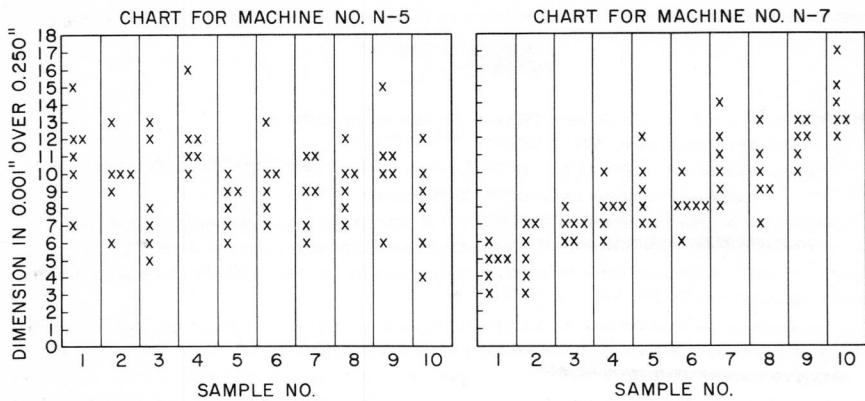

Fig. 9-10.   Important differences revealed by X charts.

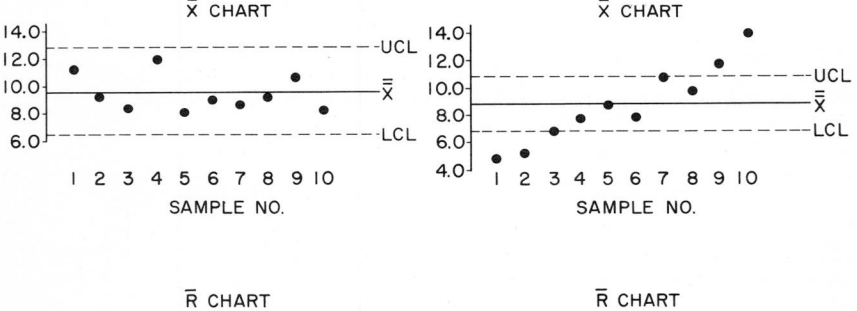

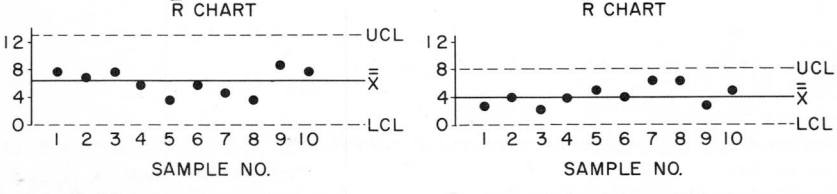

X̄ CHART FOR MACHINE N-5
SHOWS NO TIME–TO–TIME EFFECT

X̄ CHART FOR MACHINE N-7 SHOWS
A DEFINITE TIME–TO–TIME EFFECT

Fig. 9-11.   X̄ and R charts confirm suspected machine differences.

methods.[28] However, the new generations of desk-top electronic calculators include programs which eliminate the need for making these calculations manually.

Lot Plot Method. This method was originated in 1947 by Mr. Dorian Shainin[29] as a structured approach to product acceptance sampling by variables. The sample is 50 pieces, but taken *at random.* A special data recording sheet provides for ready calculation of the ranges of ten subgroups of five pieces each. (Use of subgroups and ranges is only to avoid the burden of calculating the standard deviation.) The average range is then converted to standard deviation by a constant.[30]

The well-designed data sheet and the attention devoted to making calculations easy contributed to wide adoption of the Lot Plot method for sampling by variables.[31] This adoption then extended to some use of the method for process capability calculation.

Use of Lot Plot introduces an added error due to the fact that sampling is random rather than being based on consecutive pieces. Where the lot is small and is the result of a single process setting, this added error is minimal. Where the lot is large or is the result of multiple process setups, the error can be considerable. For such cases the Lot Plot method should be avoided.

Shop Study Considerations   Measurement of process capability involves also a number of "practical" considerations which influence the validity of the results.

Who Makes the Study? It can be anyone who has the training and experience. At the outset, this is restricted to the specialists such as the Quality Control Engineer. However, most studies are quite simple, and it is feasible to train manufacturing planners, shop supervisors, and even nonsupervisors to conduct these simple studies.

Setting Up the Study. The investigator should establish a good rapport with the operator, whose collaboration can aid or hinder the study. Provision should be made beforehand to separate the product by streams, preserve the order of manufacture and otherwise separate the variables it has been concluded to study. Provision should also be made to record the status of process variables regarded as decisive (e.g., hydraulic pressure, handwheel settings, speeds, feeds, etc.). Input materials, tools, and other facilities should be checked at least for identity.

Conducting the Study. A log should be kept of all that transpires at the process during the progress of the study. The samples or specimens taken for measurement should be identified as to stream, order of production, etc. The process should be operating under its normal operating conditions unless the study is also investigating specific abnormalities, e.g., warmup during startup.

Measurement. Measurement should be by variables if at all possible. The instrument should be able to divide the product variability or the tolerance, whichever is smaller, into at least five parts. If the shop instrument cannot do this, the measurement should be done by a laboratory instrument. If the shop instrument is used, it should first be checked for calibration.[32]

---

[28] Some techniques are available for shortcuts in calculation. These are usually based on graphic methods employing probability paper in some form. See Section 22, under Methods of Summarizing Data; see also Streamline Your Appraisals of Process Capabilities, *Quality Assurance*, June 1966, pp. 29–30.

[29] See Shainin, Dorian, The Hamilton Standard Lot Plot Method of Acceptance Sampling by Variables, *Industrial Quality Control,* July 1950.

[30] See, for details, Section 25, under Lot Plot.

[31] See Shainin, Dorian, Recent Lot Plot Experience Around the Country, *Industrial Quality Control,* March 1952.

[32] For added discussion and procedures, see De Grote, Irwin A., Machine Quality Capability Studies, *Transactions, 16th Midwest Quality Control Conference,* ASQC, St. Louis, Mo., October 1961, pp. 155–169.

PROCESS CAPABILITY: RELATION TO PRODUCT TOLERANCE

A major reason for quantifying process capability is to be able to compute the ability of the process to hold product tolerances. For processes which are in a state of statistical control, a comparison of the variation of 6σ to the tolerance limits permits ready calculation of percent defective by conventional statistical theory. (See Section 22, under Probability Distributions.)

In most processes, not only are there departures from a state of statistical control but the process is not necessarily being operated to secure optimum yields, e.g., the average of the process is not centered between the upper and lower tolerance limits. To allow for these realities, planners commonly provide factors of safety. Automotive engineers use a rule-of-thumb relationship that for metal cutting, process capability must be no greater than 75% of the tolerance. For example, if a process tolerance is ±2, the total tolerance range becomes 4 and the maximum process capability allowed is 75% of 4, or 3.0. For unilateral tolerances, the rule of thumb is that process capability should be no greater than seven-eighths of the product tolerance.

A Japanese company[33] (also in the automotive industry) defines two kinds of capability, consisting of:

1. Six standard deviations as computed from frequency distribution
2. Eight standard deviations as computed from average ranges

The relation of these two values is used to judge whether time-to-time variation is excessive.

In addition, a process capability index is defined as:

$$\text{Index} = \text{tolerance width} \div \text{process capability}$$

This index is then used for making planning decisions by creating four grades of processes and establishing a pattern of decision making for each, as follows:

Value of process capability index	Resulting class of process	Decision
Above 1.33	1	More than adequate. Machine could even be speeded up.
Under 1.33, but greater than 1	2	Adequate for the job but requires close control as index approaches 1.
Under 1 but above 0.67	3	Not adequate for the job.
Under 0.67	4	Not adequate for the job.

Quite often, the failure of a process to meet tolerances is not lack of inherent process reproducibility; it is rather a failure to take full advantage of the inherent capability of the process. In such cases it is necessary to analyze the process more completely, as discussed in Process Capability Analysis, below.

PROCESS CAPABILITY ANALYSIS

Process capability *measurement* is the quantifying and predictive aspect of using the process capability concept. This measurement is conducted without any need to know what is the tolerance on the product. The 6σ value which expresses inherent capability makes no reference to the tolerance.

[33] Osuga, Yutaka, Process Capability Studies in Cutting Processes, *Reports of Statistical Applications Research,* Japanese Union of Scientists and Engineers, vol. 11, no. 1, 1964, pp. 23–35.

In contrast, use of the measured capability is largely for two main purposes, both of which do involve the tolerances:

1. As an aid to prediction—to answer the question: "Will this process be able to hold the specified product tolerance?"

2. As an aid to analysis: "Why does this process not hold the specified product tolerance?"

The term "process capability *analysis*"[34] refers to the activity of studying the process in an effort to answer both these questions.

Inherent Reproducibility versus Tolerance   The most elementary form of process capability analysis is a comparison of inherent process reproducibility with the product tolerance.   Figure 9-12 shows such a relationship graphically and makes

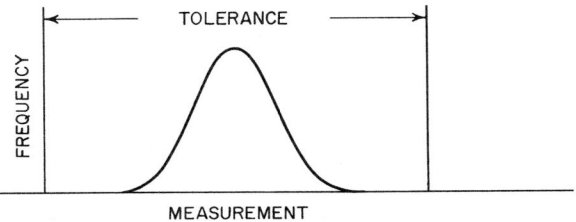

Fig. 9-12.   Inherent reproducibility adequate to hold tolerance.

it obvious that the process can meet the tolerances.   (In contrast, Figure 9-13 shows the same process as Figure 9-12, but operating to so narrow a tolerance that defects are inevitable.   Here it is obvious that the process cannot meet the tolerance.)

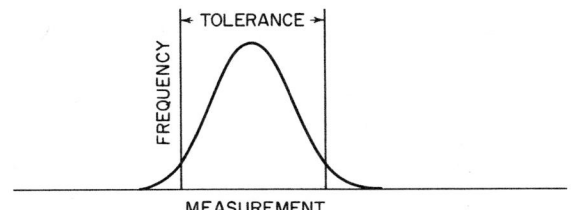

Fig. 9-13.   Identical inherent reproducibility inadequate to hold narrower tolerance.

Why Adequate Processes Fail to Hold Tolerances   In practice there are many situations in which tolerances are not met despite the fact that the inherent reproducibility of the process is adequate to meet the tolerances.   A few major reasons account for most of these failures.

Process Misdirected.   Figure 9-14 shows the same process as is shown in Figure 9-12.   However, the "centering" of the process in Figure 9-14 is marginal, and the

---

[34] The terminology is not yet standardized, and some practitioners use different terms to describe these two very different activities of process capability measurement and process capability analysis.   For this reason it is important, in studying the literature, to pay little heed to the terminology but to pay close attention to the deeds.   For an example of prevailing discussions, see Eichelberger, L. S., Process Capability, Or Is It? *Quality Progress,* January 1972, pp. 2, 3.

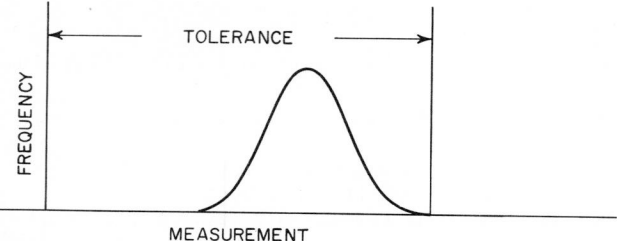

Fig. 9-14.   Process marginally centered.

process is in danger of producing defects.   In Figure 9-15, the identical process is now so poorly centered that defects are being produced.

Where the problem is one of correctly centering the process in relation to the tolerances, the planner must so structure the work station as to put the operator in a state of self-control.   (See Section 11, under Concept of Operator Self-Control.)

Instrumentation Inadequate.   A second major reason for failing to hold tolerances despite an "adequate" process is that the instruments are inadequate to enable

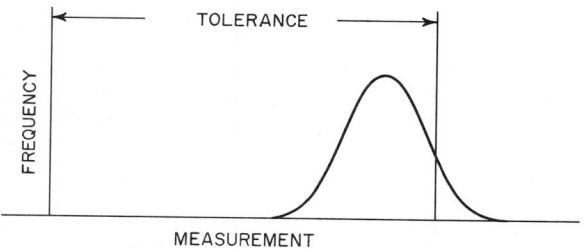

Fig. 9-15.   Poor centering creates defects.

Production to guide the process.   A common planning failure has been to assume that instruments which are adequate to judge product conformance are also adequate to guide the process.   The former practice of providing fixed-limit gages was a widespread example.   These fixed-limit gages were well suited for swift decisions on product acceptance (go or no-go).   However, they were a serious handicap to good process regulation.

Where variable instruments are provided, they must still be of adequate precision. Preferably they should be able to divide the tolerance range into ten divisions, and certainly *not less than five.*

A classic example of inadequate instrumentation was found in a study[35] (Figure 9-16) of the operation of turning the tiny shafts used in large numbers in the watch-making industry.   There had long been a controversy on whether the machines could hold the tolerances.   An engineer was stationed at one machine to collect the pieces produced, in the exact order of production, and to keep a log of the pre-

---

[35] Courtesy of G. P. Luckey, then vice president, and A. B. Sinkler, then quality manager and later president, of Hamilton Watch Company, Lancaster, Pa.   (Consulting experience of J. M. Juran.)

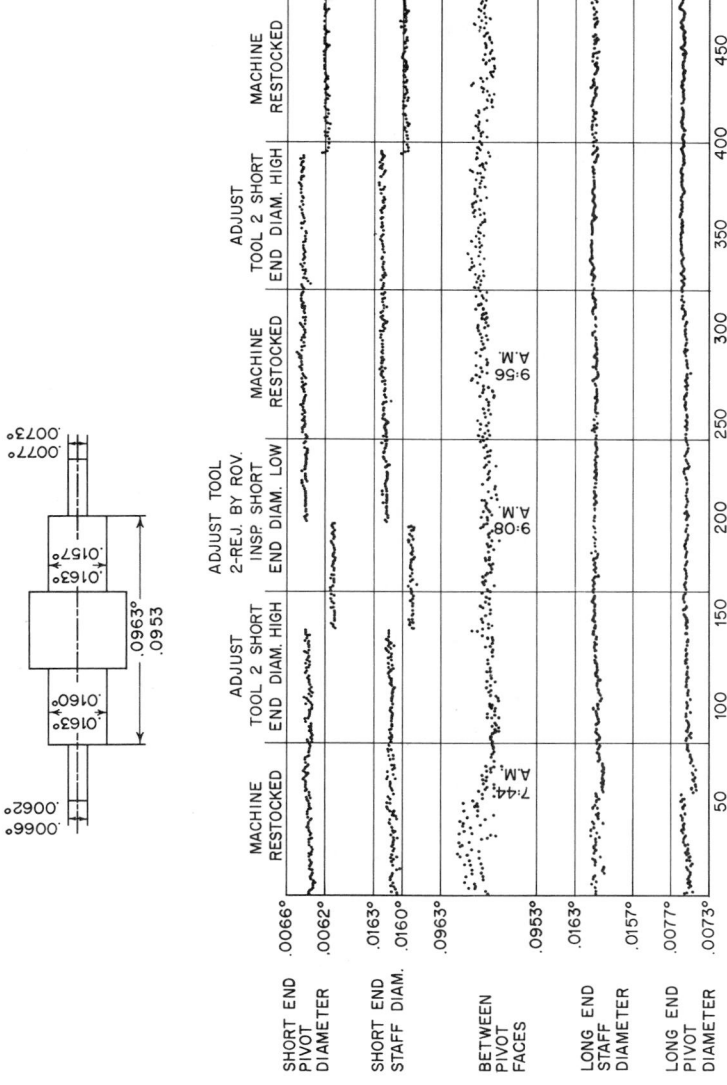

Fig. 9-16. Study of capability of machine for turning watch parts.

vailing shop practices. The pieces were then measured in the measurement laboratory for each of the five critical dimensions on each of the 500 pieces (about a day's production). Figure 9-16 shows the resulting 2,500 measurements plus pertinent notes from the log. The data made obvious some very important conclusions:

1. Progressive changes in diameter were very slight. During the run of 500 pieces, average diameter changed about 0.0001 inch, this being about a third of the narrowest tolerance range. This uniformity exceeded the expectations of most of the supervisors.

2. Changes caused by restocking the machine were less than expected and of short duration. Note the effect at pieces no. 55 and no. 493. The effect at piece no. 271 is negligible.

3. The operators' gages were inadequate to "steer" the machines. Note at piece no. 140 how both short end diameters dropped suddenly (these diameters are controlled by a single tool holder). The explanation was that the operator, *from his gage,* had concluded that the parts were becoming oversize, and he had therefore adjusted the machine downward. At piece no. 197 he restored the adjustment following a check by the patrol inspector. At piece no. 392 the operator was again misled by his gage.

4. The machine capability for the pivot-shoulder distance was easily adequate. (The greater variability of the first 50 parts was due to the investigator's unfamiliarity with the precise gage.)

The study settled once and for all the question of the adequacy of the process, and the planners were able to proceed with confidence as it was applied to new designs. At the same time the study established that the shop gages were *not* adequate for "steering" the machines, and it became necessary to provide new, more precise gages.[36]

Process Drift. The two processes, Figures 9-6 and 9-7, possess identical "instantaneous" reproducibility. A single subgroup of four consecutive pieces, whether taken from Figure 9-6 or Figure 9-7, will show the same variability, i.e., the same range of measurements on the vertical scale. When these two processes are compared with a product tolerance, as in Figures 9-17 and 9-18, it is evident that for small lots the drift is unimportant. Both the drifting and the nondrifting processes can successfully produce the small lot at a single, well-directed setting.

It is also evident that during large-lot production the effect of drift becomes very important. In the example of Figure 9-18, the drift will in time make the product 100% defective. Various steps can be taken to neutralize this drift, and these steps can all be the more effective if we first *quantify the amount of drift.*

Quantifying the drift is an exercise in data collection more than data analysis. The final measure is the rate of change per hour, per 1,000 pieces, or per some other convenient unit of process activity. Knowing this rate of change makes it easier to apply any of the following usual methods of neutralizing the drift:

1. Repeated resettings of the process based on systematic process control techniques (see Section 23). Knowledge of the rate of drift is of great value in establishing the checking schedule. In the watch shaft example (Figure 9-16) it was found that the existing checking schedule was too frequent, resulting in loss of productivity.

2. Automatic compensation for the drift, e.g., metered rate of replenishment of the solution, stepped rate of change of the mechanical setting. These rates of change are chosen based on knowledge of the rate of drift.

3. Automatic measurement of the product as it is being made and stopping of the

---

[36] The study made possible a striking reduction in dimensional defects, an increase in productivity, and a sharp reduction in the detail gaging being done. Note that the data analysis was quite simple. The real contribution was the decision to take data in a way never done before.

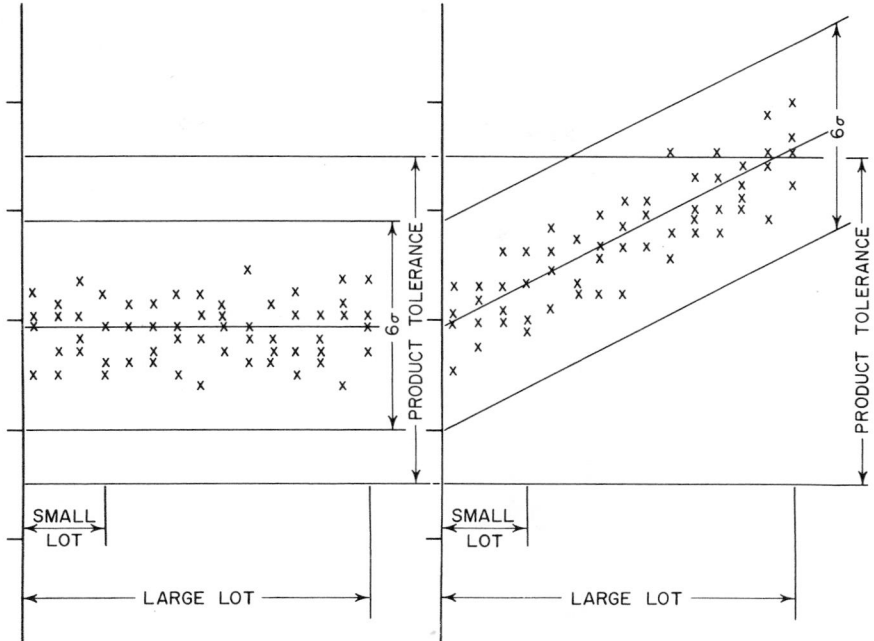

Fig. 9-17 Nondrifting process versus tolerance.

Fig. 9-18. Drifting process versus tolerance.

process when the danger line is reached.   The design of such mechanisms is aided by knowledge of the rate of drift.

4. Sequential operations.   The economics of productivity may dictate enduring the drift in a first "roughing" operation and then applying a finishing operation to remove the effect of drift of the roughing operation.   For these and other sequential operations, the quantified capabilities of the processes are an aid to manufacturing planning.   See, in this connection, Interrelation of Sequential Processes, under Process Capability: Usage, below.

Process Erratic.   The diagrams of Figure 9-8a through 9-8e give some examples of sudden changes which take place in industrial processes.   The examples given are all of familiar, recurring phenomena.   As the capability studies quantify the size of these changes and help to discover the reasons for them, appropriate planning action can be taken:

Temporary phenomena (e.g., a cold machine coming up to operating temperature) can be dealt with by scheduling warming periods plus checks at the predicted time of stability.

More enduring phenomena (e.g., change due to new material supply) can be dealt with by specifying setup reverification at the time of introducing such change.

Phenomena which, though statistically significant, are unimportant in relation to the tolerances can usually be ignored.

Product Mixture.   A common obstacle to utilizing the inherent capability of a process is that, for reasons of productivity, products from several processes are commingled at the time of manufacture.   Examples of this are widespread: multicavity plastic molding, multiple unit film deposition for electronic components, multiple spindle metal cutting, multiple mold latex dipping, multiple head filling of containers, etc. What these processes have in common is a multiplicity of "machines" mounted on a single frame. The multiple character of these producing sources superimposes a stream-to-stream variation on top of the variations inherent in any one stream. This stream-to-stream variation materially affects the ability of the process to meet the specifications.[37]

In such cases, any conventional sampling of product ends up with data which are a composite of two very different sources of variation:

1. The stream-to-stream variation, traceable to differences in the mold cavities, spindles, heads, etc.

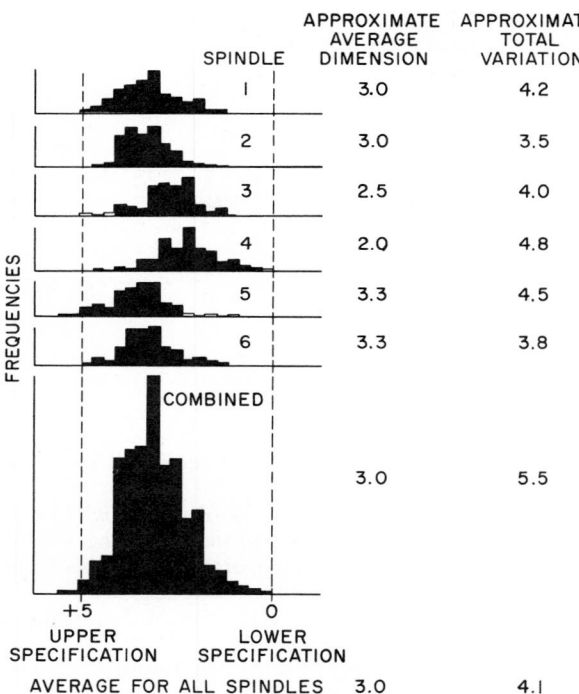

SPINDLE	APPROXIMATE AVERAGE DIMENSION	APPROXIMATE TOTAL VARIATION
1	3.0	4.2
2	3.0	3.5
3	2.5	4.0
4	2.0	4.8
5	3.3	4.5
6	3.3	3.8
COMBINED	3.0	5.5
AVERAGE FOR ALL SPINDLES	3.0	4.1

+5   0
UPPER   LOWER
SPECIFICATION   SPECIFICATION

Fig. 9-19.   Separating multiple streams, multiple spindle machine.

2. The within-stream variation, which characterizes a single "pure" process.

To quantify the stream-to-stream variation requires that the product from different streams (cavities, spindles, molds, heads) be segregated.[38] Once segregated, the data for each stream can be treated in the conventional manner. Figure 9-19 is

---

[37] A related situation is the dial feed machine in which a train of fixtures passes a common station (or series of stations) which performs the identical operation on each unit of product in the passing train. In such cases each fixture of the train represents a separate stream for process capability purposes.

[38] An incidental effect of such segregation is the identification of individual streams which are chronic sources of defects. See Section 16, under Dissection: Process and Product.

an example of such segregation and quantification for a multiple spindle screw machine.[39]

The combined effect of stream-to-stream and within-stream variation is expressed by the formula:

$$\sigma_c{}^2 = \sigma_w{}^2 + \sigma_b{}^2$$

where σ_c = composite variation
  σ_w = within-stream variation
  σ_b = stream-to-stream variation

(This formula is valid only if there is no interaction between the two variables.)

The example of Figure 9-19 typifies a great many conventional process designs of multiple-stream character. In addition, there are unconventional designs which likewise result in product mixtures. For example, the rotating arbor method of winding grids for electron tubes provides for winding a "strip" of about a dozen grids on one arbor. Analysis shows that there are substantial within-strip variations in the critical minor diameters due to the effect of starting and stopping the machine. Figure 9-20 shows how this diameter varies from grid to grid within a typical strip.

All too often, manufacturing planners have provided ingenious methods for improving productivity (through use of the multiple-stream concept) without having quantified the effect of the stream-to-stream variations on product quality. Such omissions constitute deficient manufacturing planning, since the value of the added productivity may be lost due to the resulting product quality deficiencies.

Tools for Analysis   As the process becomes complex, the analysis to measure process capability also becomes complex. As noted, the product lots are in reality composed of multiple streams, each of which can exhibit time-to-time drift and other changes. In addition, even at instantaneous time, there are piece-to-piece and within-piece variations.[40]

Several methods of analysis are available to assist the planner in quantifying these components of total variation.

Graphic Analysis.   An example is the Multi-Vari graph discussed in Section 16, under Interrelation of Variables.

SPAN Plan.   This is a structured approach to analysis and is likewise discussed in Section 16, under Interrelation of Variables.

Design of Experiment and Analysis of Variance.   This is a generalized approach, with flexibility to fit any combination of variables. For each such combination, there is prepared a tailor-made "design of experiment" for collecting the data which will permit resolution of the composite variation into its components. The resulting data are analyzed by the technique of "analysis of variance," which provides, in standardized format, the determination of significance of the variables under experiment as well as their interaction.[41]

Response Surface Methodology.   This sophisticated planning device has been increasingly used in the chemical process industries and some others to study the effects of multiple variables on yields or other desired characteristics and to find the combination which optimizes the final result.[42]

Evolutionary Operation (EVOP).   This analytical approach is aimed at securing data from manufacturing operations (as distinguished from laboratory or pilot plant

---

[39] Bayer, Harmon S., How to Determine the Quality Capability of Machines and Tools, *Tooling and Production*, May and October, 1954.

[40] Some of these are discussed in Section 16, under Dissection: Process and Product. Figure 16-4 shows this interrelation diagramatically.

[41] See generally Section 27.

[42] See generally Section 28.

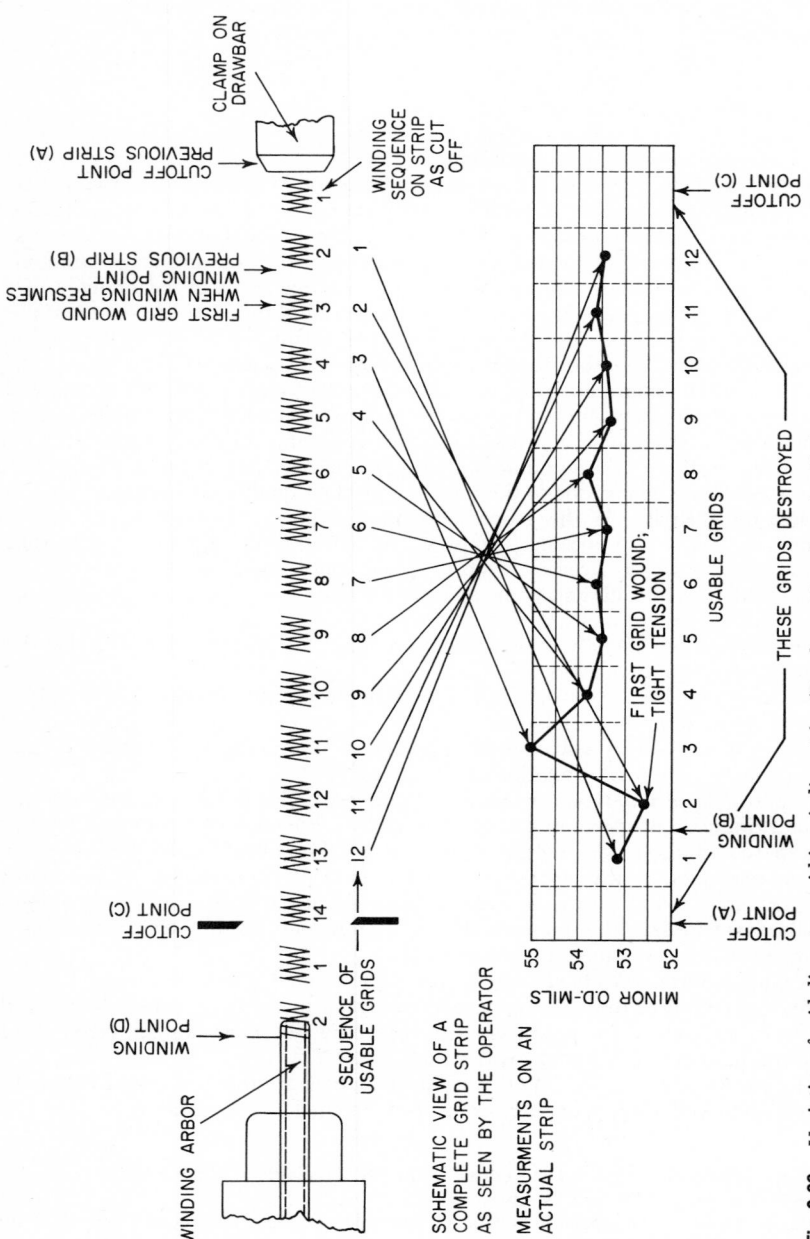

Fig. 9-20. Variation of grid diameters within winding strip. (*Raytheon Manufacturing Co.*)

experiment). Successive lots are made under process conditions which vary from one lot to another. The EVOP method goes a step further by deliberately creating some variation which will provide needed data without jeopardizing the product. Special analysis techniques then derive the relationships which form the basis of product improvement.[43]

Nonconventional Analyses Some processes, notably in the "process industries," do not readily submit to conventional forms of analysis and therefore require specially designed studies. For example, the processing of a certain type of fertilizer results in a product which is actually three fractions: (1) large lumps, called "clinker"; (2) a slurry; and (3) the fines. Chemical analysis shows that these fractions differ in their chemical composition. However, the differences are predictable within limits. Similarly, the flow of dry mixtures through hoppers results in some product segregation, but the extent of this is measureable and, within limits, predictable.

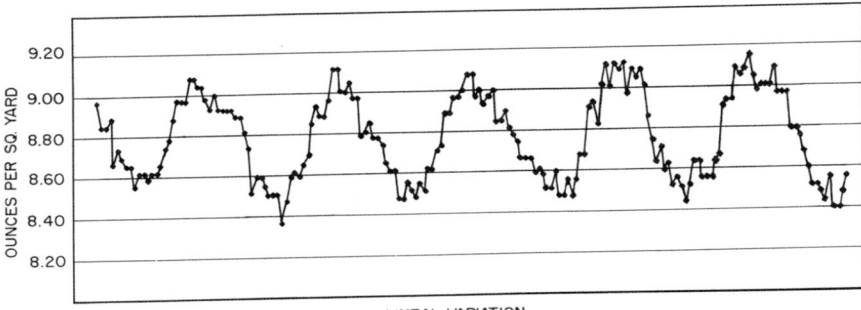

LINEAL VARIATION

Fig. 9-21. Original study—capability of calendering process.

While these complex processes demand great ingenuity from the pioneering investigator, his method of study becomes applicable to all processes of the same process family. In a study of a calendering operation used to make adhesive tape, a pioneering investigator[44] found that the process could not be measured directly; it was necessary to measure the product instead. By taking samples across the sheet and along the length, he was able to identify and measure (indirectly) such calendar factors as crown, eccentricity, etc. He was able to remedy excess cross-sheet variation with comparative ease. His problem was the lineal variation or "heartbeat" resulting from eccentricity of the rolls. Figure 9-21 shows his original process capability study.

The critical product tolerance was a minimum number of ounces per square yard. This could easily be met by raising the average amount of adhesive applied. However, the adhesive was of surgical quality and quite costly. One solution was to reduce the amplitude of the "heartbeat," which would permit lowering the average while still meeting the minimum.

The investigator next studied the capability of his *competitors' machines* by buying samples of their products and measuring the lineal variation! (Figure 9-22). In addition, he studied the capability of calenders used for other products, e.g., rubber (Figure 9-23) and plastic (Figure 9-24). Finally he found the calender of greatest capability (Figure 9-25).

---

[43] See generally Section 27A.
[44] Oladko, Anthony, Developing a Calendergraph, *Rubber Age*, September 1949.

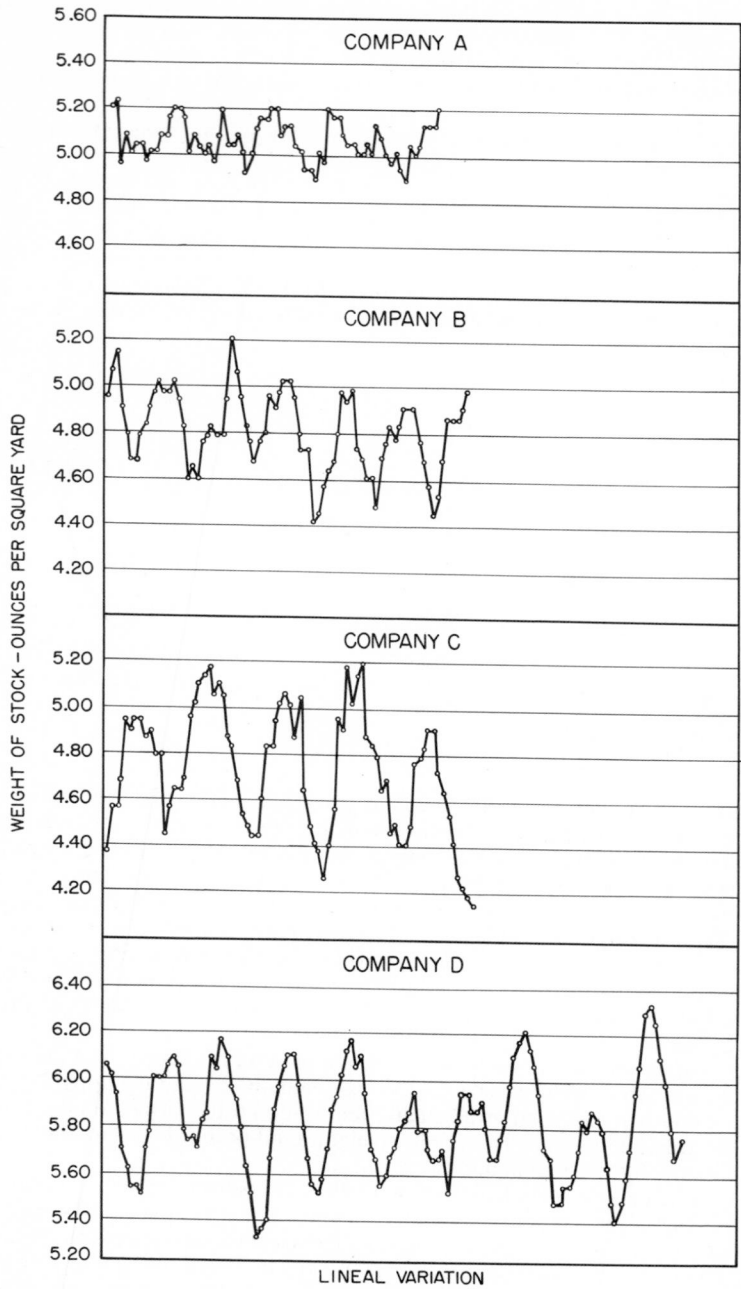

Fig. 9-22. Study of capability of competitors' machines.

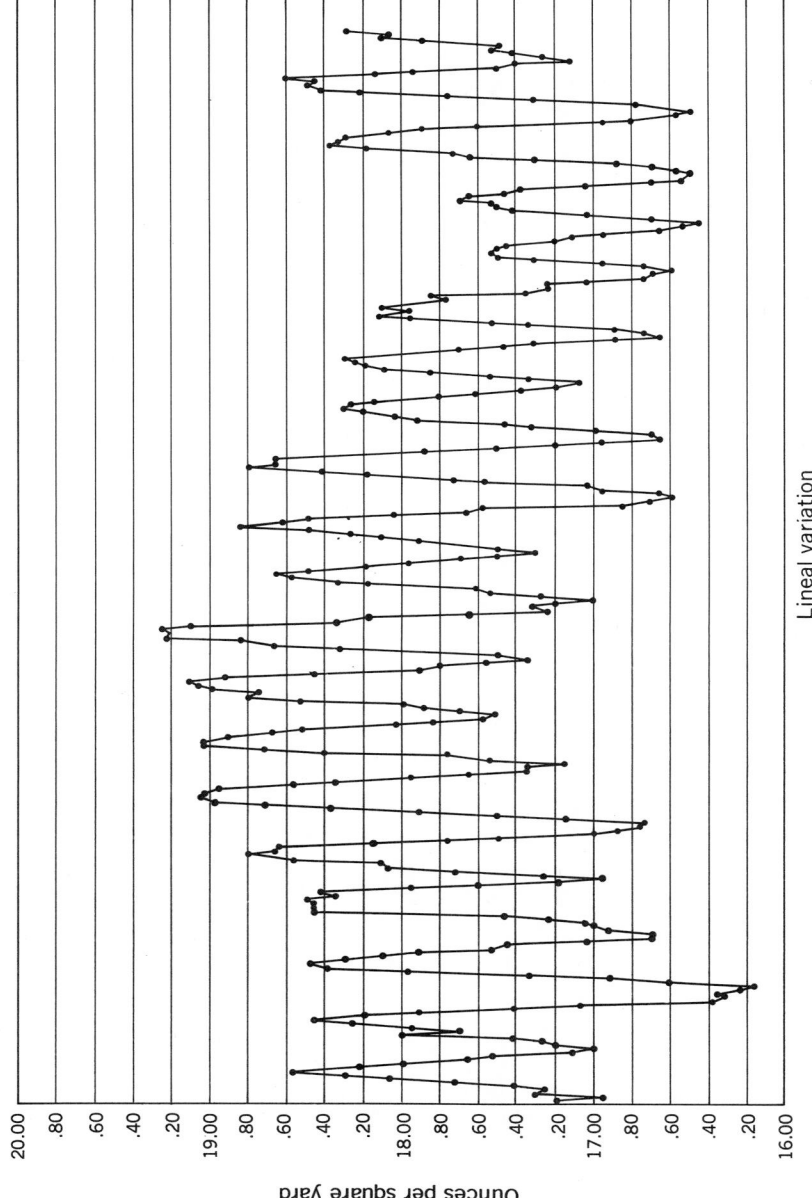

Fig. 9-23. Capability study—calendering rubber sheets.

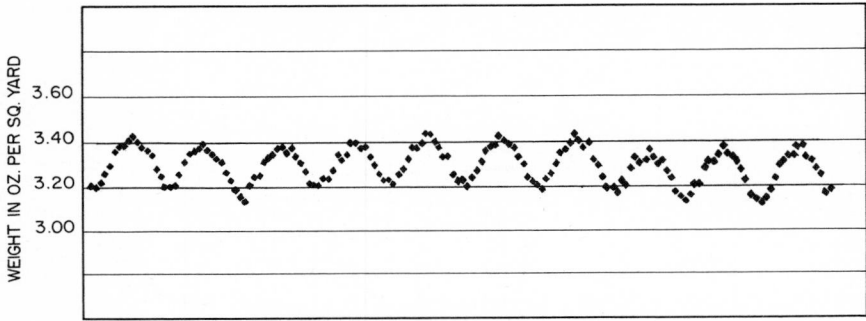

Fig. 9-24. Capability study—calendering plastic sheets.

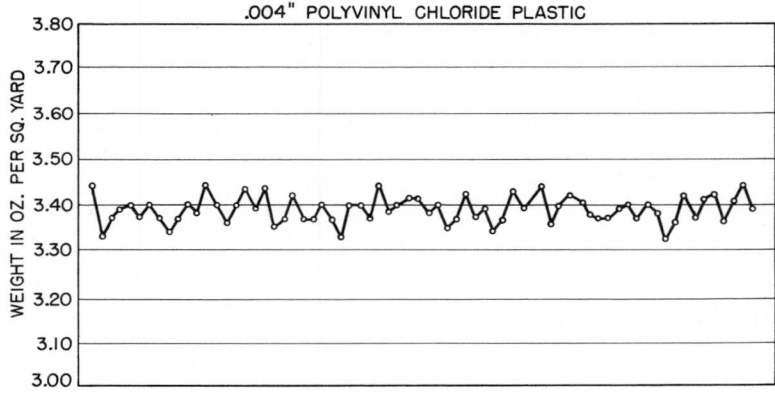

Fig. 9-25. Capability study—new roller-bearing calender.

In like manner, a pioneering capability study of woolen carding required precise measurement of small samples taken both lineally and across the width of the card, i.e., from each of the 88 yarns created by the card. Once devised, this method of study became the standard approach for the carding machine.[45] (See Section 16, Figure 16-15 and associated discussion, for some added detail.)

PROCESS CAPABILITY: USAGE

The most obvious use of process capability data during manufacturing planning is to predict whether the design tolerances can be met with the available processes. In addition, there are other uses which can simplify the job of planning.

Choice among Alternative Processes   For example, an optical company faced a

---

[45] Klock, A. G., and C. W. Carter, Woolen Carding Meets Quality Control, *Industrial Quality Control,* May 1952, pp. 35–38.

choice between mechanical chucks and vacuum-operated chucks for milling lenses. Comparative studies showed

Process	Process capability	Chipped lenses
Mechanical chuck	0.076 mm	5.3%
Vacuum chuck	0.046 mm	0.4%

These data, along with the comparative economics of the processes, simplified the decision.

The adhesive tape example (Figures 9-21 through 9-25) featured a search for an alternative process which could save material usage through superior process capability. In this instance, the concept of alternative processes extended to the *study of competitors' processes.*

Purchase of Machinery Adoption of 6σ as a standardized measure of process capability makes it possible to specify process capability in purchase orders for machinery. Such forms of specification are in actual use, though adoption has been slow. Generally, the machine tool and other machinery makers have been wary of making firm commitments. They point out that attainment of the contracted capability depends not only on the construction of the machine, but also on factors which are under the control of the buyer, i.e., design of the tools and maintenance of both machines and tools.

While it will be some years before 6σ becomes widely used in these purchase contracts, the machinery buyer is in most cases protected by the industry practice. Under this practice, the machine tool builder provides the technical service needed to prove in the machine for the purpose for which it was bought. This is really a form of guaranteed but unquantified process capability.

Interrelation of Sequential Processes There are numerous situations in which several operation stages are interrelated. In such cases the planner must prepare a virtual product design for each stage of the operation (since the functional design defines only the end product). To prepare these intermediate designs means specifying how much material to provide for subsequent removal, uniformity of locating surfaces, etc. In such cases, knowledge of the capability of the respective operations greatly facilitates the planning.

Figure 9-26 shows an example of studies of related rough and finishing operations. The data make clear how much material is removed in finishing and what the final uniformity of the product is. With this knowledge and with knowledge of the final product specification, the prior operation can be planned with confidence. (In Figure 9-26, the rough process is more uniform than the finishing process for the charted characteristic. However, the finishing process is performed to achieve high precision on a different characteristic. To do so, it must remove material.)

A further frequent need for planning sequential processes arises when the precision of an earlier operation is destroyed by a later operation. The distortion of gear teeth during the subsequent hardening operation is an example. (See Section 37, Figures 37-8 and 37-9).

Precise operations should always follow coarse operations, not the other way around. For example, in one company, an expensive, precise "hand correcting" operation was followed by a comparatively coarse polishing operation. Under statistical theory, the composite result of such a sequence should virtually destroy the usefulness of the precise operation. The shop supervisors (and the planners) were not convinced by theory. A series of split-lot experiments confirmed the theory.

A further need in planning sequential operations is to anticipate quality problems which early operations may create for later operations. For example, a plant mak-

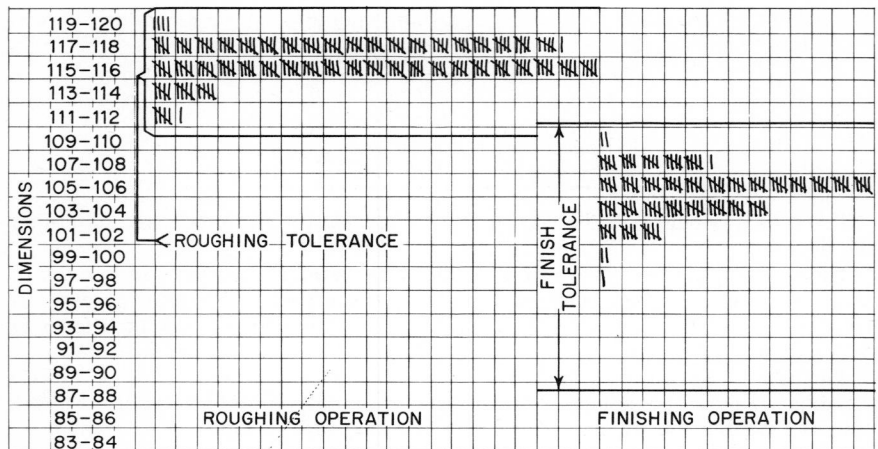

Fig. 9-26. Relation of sequential operations.

ing electric and gas ranges encountered much breakage of enamel in assembly and in the field. The trouble was traced to panels which were misshapen or bent in such a way that the assembly operation put the ceramic coating into a state of tension. (The ceramic coating, while strong under compression, breaks easily under tension.) In turn, the panels were losing their original shape during the enameling process. This process had been planned so as to achieve productivity and convenience for Production without due consideration to distortion which might create quality problems further downstream.

Data Storage and Retrieval During the early stages of use of the process capability concept, the data on process capability exist as isolated studies made by individual planners or investigators to solve specific problems. As these studies become numerous, there arises an opportunity to assemble these scattered studies and to put them into a form which can make the results readily available for use by all concerned. The most elementary form for such data summary, storage, and retrieval is a table or matrix of process capabilities corresponding to various process conditions. Table 9-2 shows such a matrix for automatic screw machines.

Some companies have enlisted the computer to provide such data storage and retrieval. In one company, the data from the studies were placed on punch cards and fed into a computer to secure process capabilities for specific machines or processes independent of the part produced. (Some standardization of procedure is needed to simplify programming.) The computer was used also to test the data for homogeneity.[46]

An extension of use of the computer is to take the process capability study data in a form which permits establishing relations between process capability and certain process variables, e.g., material hardness, depth of cut. Where this is done, the computer can be used to determine process capability expected for any new combination of process variables.[47]

[46] Fielden, Sidney, Capability Studies, *Transactions, 10th January Conference, Hamilton-Middletown Section and Cincinnati Section,* ASQC, Jan. 28, 1961, pp. 16–22.

[47] McCubbin, Robert E., Machine Tool Information System, *Technical Conference Transactions,* ASQC, 1971, pp. 235–243.

It is also feasible to show, in a broad-scale presentation, the capabilities of a wide range of processes for accomplishing related tasks. Figure 9-27 shows such a presentation as applied to 16 categories of precision.[48]

Planners should be alert to the potential value of process capability studies made in other companies and even in other industries. Such data have reference value despite the fact that they have been collected under conditions different from those which prevail in one's own company. Often such data provide a "market" measure against which to judge whether the local capabilities are competitive or not. The methods used for study likewise have value as a basis for comparison.

PROCESS CAPABILITY IMCOMPATIBLE WITH PRODUCT TOLERANCES

The planner has several alternatives in the event that process reproducibility is inadequate to hold tolerances. (What follows is premised on the assumption that inherent process reproducibility has actually been quantified. If this premise is not well founded, the planner may need to look for "Why Adequate Processes Fail to Hold Tolerances," as discussed under Process Capability Analysis, above.)[49]

"Change" the Process Such change may consist of numerous revisions short of substitution of a different, more precise process. The basic process may remain unchanged while the tools are revised. The sequence of operations may be revised. It may be possible to add an attachment to the process to improve the uniformity of a critical variable. Feeding cycles may be revised to reduce the effect of introducing new input materials. Operations may be added to reduce the variability of one or more product characteristics.

Still another form of process change is shift of work to other machines in the same process class. To do this with confidence requires that data be available as to the inherent capability of the various machines in the class. Where this is available, the planner's method instruction sheet can require the use of the precise machines for the precise tolerances.

The foregoing and other available opportunities for change present the planner with a wide variety of choice short of making a major investment in a new process.[50] In most cases, the process capability studies (made to discover the feasibility of modest changes) will incidentally shed light on the inherent limitations of the basic process and will thereby lead to the development of improved processes as well.

Revise the Tolerances To a considerable degree, the approach to securing revision of tolerances parallels the activities of design review. However, as process capability studies are made, the ability to hold the tolerance moves out of the realm of speculation and into that of reality. The very act of quantification *depersonalizes the problem.* It is no longer the planner saying that the tolerance should be widened; it is the impersonal process capability study saying that the tolerance cannot be met.

Revising tolerances likewise has alternatives. If the problem is interchangeability, revision of the tolerance for the mating component may be more economic. Experiments may establish that usage is adequate even with wider tolerances. The tolerance in question may be part of the broader problem of "Unrealistic Tolerances Loosely Enforced," discussed in Section 8.

"Suffer and Sort" Sorting the product is at best a temporary solution, since the

---

[48] Conway, H. G., The Use of Tolerance Systems, *Product Engineering,* February 1956, pp. 164–167.

[49] See also Section 16, under Remedy of Management-controllable Defects.

[50] As a rule of thumb, a process yielding 80% or more of good product can be refined to yield in the "high 90s" without major investment. (Consulting experience of J. M. Juran.)

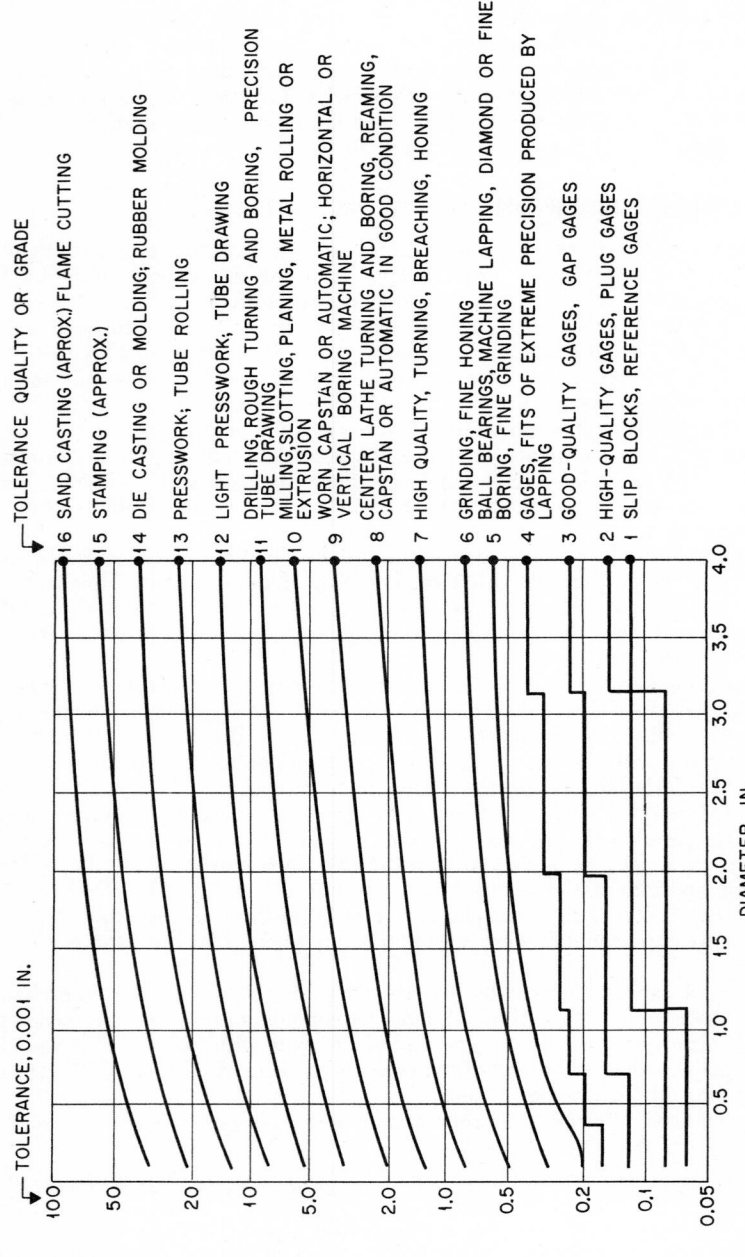

Fig. 9-27. Accuracy of various machine processes.

basic problem, i.e., the incompatibility of process capability with tolerance, has not been solved. The cost of the sorting and the (usually) greater cost of remedy for the defects goes on and on until a more fundamental solution is found.

Excess Precision   When inherent process variability is less than 50% of the tolerance band, there are also several alternative courses of action to be considered.

Sell the Excess Precision. It may be possible to secure better prices, or at least a greater share of market, by advertising the fact that the product is more precise than called for by the tolerances.

Sell the Method. Where the method of securing the superior precision has been developed within the company, it may be feasible to sell it (through licensing, etc.) to machinery manufacturers, competitors, etc.

Reassign to Less Precise Machines. Where the available machines are materially different in capability, the precise process can be reserved for close-tolerance work.

Reduce the Cost of Control. If the excess precision cannot be sold and is being attained at a cost in control work, it may be feasible to reduce the cost of controls. This achieves a cost reduction without reducing value.

One alternative which should *not* be used is to tighten the tolerances. This is a nonsolution which increases the number of borderline lots of product, adds to the process control needed, precludes any future adoption of a more economic (though less precise) process, etc. Product tolerances should be based on fitness for use, not on process capability.

FOOLPROOFING THE PROCESS

The manufacturing planners' biggest contribution to product quality has very likely been the concept of designing the process to be error free through "foolproofing." Where this type of design is economic, it provides an alternative solution to some very difficult problems:

It can eliminate[51] defects which fallible human beings would otherwise make through inadvertence.

It can make effective a "knack" which would otherwise require retraining many workers.

It can make impossible[52] the defects resulting from inattention, indifference, and other forms of worker willfulness.

It can bypass a complex analysis for causes by finding a solution even though the cause of defects remains a mystery.

Economics of Foolproofing   Figuring the cost of engineering and applying foolproofing to a process is usually a conventional exercise in cost estimating. Figuring the value is also feasible for in-house defects which would otherwise be caught at a later but more costly stage. For defects which would otherwise go to the customer, the intangibles in the estimates begin to grow larger than the known costs, so "managerial judgment" becomes increasingly the basis for decision. In the extreme cases involving safety and health hazards or potential crippling blows to the company reputation, there is no known way to secure reliable data on value. Hence managerial judgment is used, preferably broadly based over a "jury of managers" so that extreme views are balanced out.

Methods of Foolproofing   Some of the more usual forms are summarized below.

Fail-Safe Devices. These consist of:

1. Interlocking sequences. For example, to ensure that operation A is performed,

---

[51,52] Experienced practitioners are wary of words like "eliminate" or "impossible." A foolproof process or system requires maintenance from fallible human beings.

the subsequent operation B locates from a hole which only operation A creates.

2. Alarms and cutoffs. These are used to signal depletion of material supply, broken threads, or other abnormalities. The alarms are also fail safe, i.e., they are silent only if all is well. If there is doubt, they sound anyhow.

3. All-clear signals. These are designed to signal only if all remedial steps have been taken.

4. Foolproof fixtures. These serve not only as fixtures but also as instruments to check the quality of work from preceding operations.

Magnification of Senses. Examples are:

1. Locating indexes and fixtures to outperform human muscle in precision of position

2. Optical magnification to improve visibility

3. Remote-control viewing (closed circuit television) to permit viewing of the process despite distance, heat, fumes, etc.

4. Multiple signals to improve likelihood of recognition and response, e.g., simultaneous ringing of bells and flashing of lights; audiovisual systems (See Section 17, under Training Methods).

Redundancy. This consists of extra work performed purely as a quality safeguard. Examples are:

1. Multiple-identity codings to prevent product mixups, e.g., color codes or other recognition schemes on drug labels, tool steel, aluminum sheet, etc.

2. Multiple approvals. For example, the drug industry requires that formulation of recipes be checked and approved by two pharmacists working independently.

3. Audit review and checking procedures. These are widely used to assure that the plans are being followed.

4. Design for verification. The product may include specially designed provision for verification (holes for viewing, coupons for test, etc.) It also includes the rapidly growing use of nuclear tracers.

5. Multiple test stations. For example, a can-filling line may provide checks for empty cans through height gages, weighing scales, and air jets (for blowing empties off the conveyer).

Countdowns. These are arranged by structuring sensing and information procedures to parallel the operation procedures so that the operational steps are checked against the sensing and informational needs. A dramatic example is the elaborate countdown for the launching of a space vehicle. Surgical operations require countdowns, including accounting for all materials and tools used (sponges, surgical instruments, etc.). The procedure manual is a widely used form of countdown. So are job memory cards, as in the example of the abrasive cloth discussed under Planning Process Controls, below.

Error-Prone Systems Beyond the foolproofing of individual operations, there may be need to foolproof entire systems which are error-prone. For example, the presence of multiple languages for the same communication is a breeding ground for errors. See, for example, hospital drug errors (Section 47) and engineering design errors (Section 16, under Theories—Formulation and Arrangement). The planner who identifies and deals with such error-prone systems is getting a great deal of return on his effort.

In one classic example, a naval vessel was almost lost due to conflict in standards for hydraulic versus electrical systems. A hydraulic valve increases energy when turned counterclockwise; an electrical valve does the opposite. A technician who had been upgraded from the hydraulics section of the ship to the electronics section became confused during an emergency and reverted back to the hydraulic standard, causing a near disaster.

Identifying such defect-prone systems is seldom done from ordinary analysis. More usually it requires a feedback from actual problems encountered, so that some analyst can find a common cause. At the least, the planner should keep himself informed on the failures which are occurring and on the causes and remedies. To an important degree, the new ideas for planning have their origin in remedies found during troubleshooting and especially during breakthroughs.[53,54]

TRACEABILITY

The process design must provide for "traceability," i.e., the ability to identify the product and its origins. Traceability is needed principally to:

Assure that only materials and components of adequate quality enter the final product, e.g., sterility in drug materials, adequate metallurgical composition and heat treatment in structural components.

Provide obvious identification to avoid mixup of products which otherwise look alike (these cases abound).

Permit recall of suspected product on a precise basis. Many of the huge recalls of automobiles in the 1960s were the result of inadequate traceability. The defective cars were only a small fraction of the total recalled.

Localize causes of failure and take remedial action at minimal maintenance cost.

There are still other uses of traceability—in inventory control, scheduling, etc. Some of these uses also affect quality. For example, use of materials on a first-in-first-out basis reduces the risk of quality deterioration due to perishable materials.

Batch Control. The materials entering a batch are measured out in accordance with the recipe or formula. A lot number is assigned and a set of batch documents bearing that lot number is created. The "genealogy" of the input materials is recorded in the batch documents, as are the processing data (e.g., temperatures, pressures) and the product test data.[55] For complex, critical products (e.g., aerospace vehicles, drugs) the batch documents may become a formidable collection.[56] When the finished product is packaged, the lot number is imprinted on the individual

[53] In 1965, the U.S. Post Office Department printed its first tricolor stamp (The Florida Quadricentennial Commemorative). The design required multiple passes of the sheets, and the Post Office was aware of the risk of making some defectives, such as the few Dag Hammarskjöld panes which had fields upside down. A good deal of redundant foolproofing was adopted:

A lower corner on each sheet was trimmed off to make obvious any sheet which was upside down.

An electronic finger sensed the trimmed corners during sheet feeding.

A yellow block, to be photo-sensed if the sheet was improperly inserted, was printed on one side of each sheet.

A press attachment let only one sheet at a time be fed (to avoid the lower part of a double sheet missing its color).

The sheets were 100% inspected.

A "last stamp" inspection was conducted before packaging.

(*Quality Assurance,* August 1965, editor's memo.)

[54] In the original design stages it may cost no more to avoid an error-prone system than to create one, e.g., arrangement of switches in a control panel. See, for examples, Swain, Alan D., Human Factors in Design of Reliable Systems, *Proceedings of the Tenth National Symposium on Reliability and Quality Control,* IEEE, January 1964, pp. 250–259.

[55] Documents may include "travel cards" to accumulate data for the lot or batch. See Lee, George, Traceability, *Quality Assurance,* January 1970, pp. 56–58. Accountability for dispersed batches may be aided by dispersal cards. See Hafer, R. A., Critical Component Lot Identification and Control, *Automatic Control,* December 1961, pp. 58–60. Aerospace documentation is exceedingly extensive. See Dyer, Morris K., Product "Traceability" for NASA Space Systems, *Annual Technical Conference Transactions,* ASQC, 1966, pp. 202–208.

[56] See, for example, Maass, Richard A., Handling the Growing Demand for More Traceability, *Quality Assurance,* December 1967, pp. 20–23.

containers and on the mass containers, i.e., cartons, drums, skids, etc. Subsequently, when the product is sold, it may be necessary to maintain a record of customers' names through the entire distribution chain.

Continuous Production, Low Unit Value. In this form there is no natural lot, since materials of various genealogical origins keep entering the process at irregular intervals. In consequence, the designation for traceability becomes a *date code* and is based on the calendar dates of the occurrence of some cardinal event, e.g., packaging, final test, final assembly. The choice of time span is arbitrary, i.e., a week's production. (This arbitrary amount of production may still be called a "lot." However, it does not meet the strict criterion of "uniformity" required for use of the word "lot.") See Section 12, under The Nature of Lots of Product.

The documentation system for this arbitrary lot is quite similar to that used for the batch. Provision is made to record the history of the input materials, the process conditions prevailing during fabrication, and the test results. Due to the inherent nature of continuous production, traceability is now incomplete, since cutoff dates for introduction of new material batches or for process changes cannot be identified with precision. In consequence, any subsequent recalls or investigations must provide for this margin of error.

For some products having low unit value, it may be feasible to show the date code (lot number) directly on the product. More usually, for reasons of cost (and available space), the date code appears only on the containers.

Continuous Production, High Unit Value. In this form, the distinguishing feature is the unique designation of each unit of product by serial number. The documentation is then keyed to individual serial number or blocks of numbers.

The serial number is widely used in the manufacture of consumer goods as well as industrial equipment. Household appliances and home entertainment electronics use serial numbers, and the system of guarantees is keyed to these. Larger units (e.g., motor vehicles) may employ serial numbers for major subsystems (e.g., engines) as well as for the vehicle itself.

Recent safety legislation and related forces in the marketplace have greatly increased the need for traceability. In the case of passenger tires, the regulators have required that the tire makers set up to trace the sale of tires through the entire marketing chain (whether for original equipment or for replacement) to the ultimate consumer!

Achievement of traceability has much in common with configuration management. In this connection, see Section 19, under Configuration Management.

PLANNING PROCESS CONTROLS

Process controls are the "software" of manufacturing planning. Their purpose is to enable the human forces to run and regulate the processes so that the standards will be met.

Process control is based on the feedback loop as discussed in Section 6, under Planning for Control: the Universals. The steps for planning manufacturing process controls follow quite closely the universal approach for use of the feedback loop. (To an important degree, the generalized concept of the feedback loop grew out of experience in process controls.)

Process control planning has much in common with Inspection Planning (as discussed in Section 12). The latter emphasizes the planning work needed to put inspectors or operators in a position to acquire the product and process data which are essential inputs to the feedback loop. In the present Section, the emphasis is on aiding the Production work force to close the loop when the input data become available.

Process control planning also has much in common with the work of executing this control plan, as discussed in Section 11. Because it is the Production force that must make the plan work, there should be the closest collaboration between the planner and the Production supervision at the time of preparing the plan.

Flow Diagrams These are useful planning tools for showing the overall manufacturing system and the role played by the unit processes within the system. These diagrams are made in various forms to suit specific needs. Figure 39-1 shows the schematic flow of product in the textile industry. Figure 33-1 is a pictorial representation of the steelmaking process. Figure 6-5 shows, in detail, the operations and inspections involved in the manufacture of electron tubes. Figure 9-28 shows, in schematic form, the conventional flow of material in electromechanical manufacture.

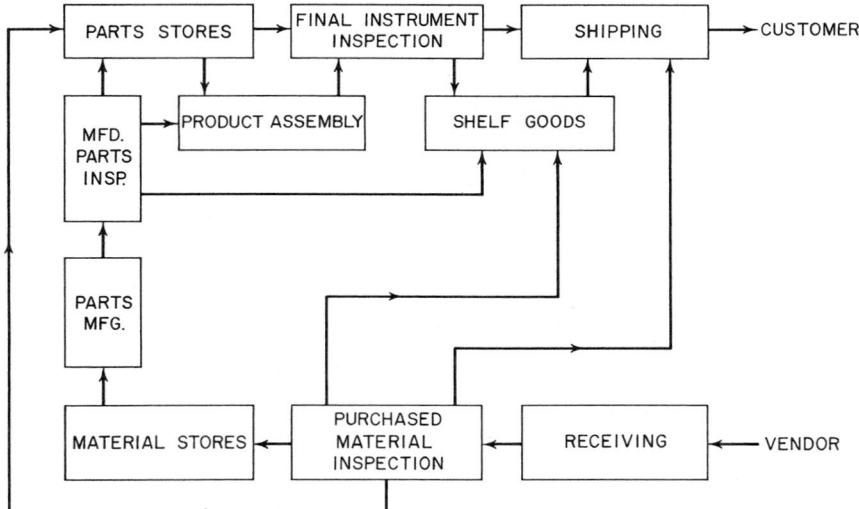

Fig. 9-28.   Schematic flow of materials and product, electromechanical industries.

Work Stations The building blocks of the manufacturing process are "operations," i.e., the elemental processes which bring about some intended change in the characteristics of the product. These operations are grouped into "work stations," which are presided over by a human operator or by automated control. Generally, but not always, the work stations are coextensive with process control stations, as discussed in Section 11 generally and in Section 12, under Inspection Planning.

For each work station the manufacturing planner prepares a work plan which is then published in a widely used document known as an Operation Sheet.[57] The Operation Sheet contains minimally:

The list of operations, in their proper sequence, to be performed at that work station

The machines, tools and instruments to be used

The materials to be used in the operations

[57] The name also varies widely: Methods Sheet, Master Route Sheet, Process Specification, etc.

Supplemental detail varies widely, the extent of detail being based on the considerations discussed under Responsibility for Manufacturing Planning, above.

Control Criteria   Historically, the Operation Sheet was devised by the forerunners of the modern Industrial Engineer. The emphasis was on productivity, not on criteria for control of quality. As the concept of quality control has evolved, it has deemphasized product inspection and has looked to process design and control as the prime source of quality of conformance. This evolution has required a corresponding evolution of process control criteria and, in turn, a structured approach to defining, recording, and meeting these criteria. The resulting process control plans are recorded in several media, including the Operation Sheet.

On close examination, it becomes clear that there are several kinds of process control criteria, each with its own cultural history.

Product Criteria. Table 12-10 (in Section 12), Criteria for Judging Conformance of Product in Units and Lots, elaborates on product control criteria, and notes that the organizations of Product Design, Quality Control, and Inspection prepare and publish these criteria. Lot control criteria are published in the Inspection Methods Sheet and in standard sampling tables. In those cases where Production is given product acceptance responsibilities, the criteria used are still prepared by the Quality Control or Inspection planners.

Process Operation Criteria. These are increasingly being published by the manufacturing planners in process specifications, Operation Sheets, etc. Where they are not, Production must do its own planning and evolve its own criteria.

For example, in one company, manufacture of some types of coated abrasives is still an art as much as a science. Because the anatomy of the process is that of a self-contained department, many process operation criteria are left to Production to work out. As an aid in quality planning, the foreman keeps an array of card files—one set for each type of product and one card for each lot made. The lot card is used to record the process conditions, i.e., temperature, speed, etc., for that lot. In addition, the subsequent laboratory test results are posted to the card, making the history of the lot complete. When a new order comes into the department, the foreman consults the card file for that product. He identifies the lots which gave the best laboratory results and then tries to re-create the process conditions which correspond to those prevailing when the best lots were made.

Process Control Criteria. Increasingly, the process operating conditions are being defined by the manufacturing planners. As this is done, the planners prepare and publish criteria (checking schedule, sample sizes,[58] allowable deviations, etc.) in accordance with the following general approach:

If process control checks are to be made by	Planning is done by	Publication is in
Inspectors responsible to Inspection Department	Inspection planners	Inspection Methods Sheet or Inspection Manual
Employees of Production Department	Inspection planners or by manufacturing planners	Operation Sheet

In those cases where the Operation sheet carries the process control procedures, the Manufacturing Engineer consults with the Inspection planner, and their joint conclusions go on the Operation Sheet.

Machine and Tool Maintenance Criteria. The trend to automated processes has emphasized a long-standing need to provide a planned approach to the maintenance of tools and machines. Traditionally this has been in the hands of Production, and

[58] See Section 23 for the statistical considerations involved.

more often than not, it has been unplanned. The trend is now to establishment of checking schedules and other maintenance criteria, including maintenance methods. See Section 35 for examples. Responsibility for establishing these criteria, whether by Manufacturing Planning, Production, or Quality Control, is still in a state of evolution.

Instrument Maintenance Criteria. The approach to instrument maintenance is well established and is set out in detail in Section 13. Responsibility for ensuring that instruments remain in calibration is usually assigned to the instrument laboratory rather than being left to the various departments which use the instruments.

Responsibilities on the Factory Floor. These are discussed in Section 11, under Quality Responsibilities on the Factory Floor.

STANDARDIZATION IN MANUFACTURING PLANNING

Throughout the foregoing discussion of manufacturing planning there has been repeated reference to standards, control, criteria, plans, etc. Collectively, these terms can be generalized into phrases such as "standard practice" or "standardization."

Several different organizations have each arrived at the concept of achieving control of quality through standard practice, though starting from different basic orientations.

Manufacturing planners are oriented to achieving goals for manufacturing cost, productivity, etc., including quality. They make wide use of the concept of standard practice to assist Production in reaching these goals.

Quality planners are oriented to product fitness for use. To this end they employ numerous technological and managerial tools, including the concept of standard practice for product and process control.

Standardization organizations are oriented to the concept of standard practice as a general-use tool for the benefit of man, including application of this general-use tool to improve the effectiveness of manufacture and of product quality.[59]

When diverse organizations and approaches all converge on the same final subject matter, there are opportunities for conflict due to jurisdictional disputes. There are also opportunities for improved effectiveness by good collaboration among diverse organizations, since each is able to contribute experience not possessed by the others. Manufacturing planners and quality planners are well advised to take the initiative in enlisting the collaboration of the pertinent Standards organizations in structuring standard practice.

QUALITY INFORMATION EQUIPMENT

The term "quality information equipment" (QIE), as used here, designates the physical apparatus which makes measurements of products and processes and feeds the resulting data back for decision making. The feedback may be to human regulators or direct to the process itself (see Automatic Process Regulation, below).

For years, the dominant use of gages and instruments[60] was to make decisions on

---

[59] For a good discussion of this point of view, see Evseenko, E., Manufacturing Process Quality Optimization, *Quality,* 1968, no. 4, pp. 111–115.

[60] "Gage" usually refers to a device for mechanical measurements. "Instrument" usually connotes electrical measurement. "Meter" usually refers to a calibrated instrument for measuring by variables. "Assay equipment" usually designates equipment for chemical or metallurgical testing. "Test equipment" commonly refers to equipment that measures finished-product characteristics.

product conformance to specification. This dominant use tended to obscure the real purpose of instrumentation, which is to provide information. While much of this information still serves to enable Inspection to make decisions on product conformance, there has been growing emphasis on other uses: process control, quality improvement, management reports. etc. These added uses have greatly influenced the evolution of instruments in two main directions:

1. The go no-go gages used for sorting product have evolved into automated mechanical gaging machines, with counterparts in automated electronic testing machines and in autoanalyzers for chemical analyses.

2. The measuring instruments have evolved into systems which also indicate, record, regulate, compute, summarize, and report. For such instruments their role in providing information is readily evident, and this role has led to a movement to change the terminology so that instruments, gages, and test sets become "Quality Information Equipment." There is merit to this movement.[61]

The complex demands placed on the new equipments have required new approaches in equipment planning, design, evaluation, and maintenance.[62] The planning cannot be limited to an examination of the needs for judging conformance to specification; it must embrace the remaining needs as well, and it is these needs which now pose the real problems (i.e., the heads of the QIE are becoming bigger than the bodies).

Two sets of planners are involved in planning for QIE. The Manufacturing Planning Engineers usually plan that QIE which is to be used by Production. However, the Quality Control Engineers usually plan that QIE which is to be used by Inspection and by the test laboratories.[63] Since the QIE provides information needed by a wide variety of departments, the two sets of planners must collaborate fully with each other as well as with the departments who are to use the equipment and with those who are to act on the resulting information.[64]

The planning for QIE starts with identifying (1) the quality decisions which need to be made, (2) who is to make these decisions, and (3) the data feedback needed to make these decisions. These needs start at the control stations, progress to laboratory testing, and continue on to supervisory and executive review. It is useful to prepare a flow diagram depicting the interrelation of these data sources and usages.

Each process control station requires an individual analysis as to the QIE needed for decision making. As processes have become more complex, this analysis has been extended to give added assistance to Production in several ways:

Provide a running trace of how the product compares with tolerance. The comparison may be projected on a television screen.

Identify cause of out-of-control condition.

Compute the amount of change needed for process correction.

[61] For some added discussion see Sussman, Bernard, Quality Information Equipment, *Industrial Quality Control*, July 1964, pp. 10–16.

[62] See, for example, Paddison, L. J., The Design of Test Equipment for High Reliability Product, *Transactions, 11th National Conference, Aircraft and Missile Division*, ASQC, Los Angeles, November 1961.

[63] In this Section, the emphasis is on use of QIE for making decisions on the process. In Section 12, under Automated Inspection, the emphasis is on making decisions on the product.

[64] For an example of allocation of responsibility in a large electrical manufacturing company, see Feigenbaum, A. V., "Total Quality Control," McGraw-Hill Book Company, New York, 1961, p. 176, Fig. 9.5. Note also the development schedule, *ibid*, p. 175, Fig. 9.4; also the checklists, p. 173, Fig. 9.3, on equipment cost, and pp. 193–196, Fig. 9.19, on equipment design. Absent from these checklists is the Occupation Safety and Health Standards, *Federal Register*, May 17, 1971, pp. 10466 through 10714.

For final test, the QIE may be required to go well beyond bare test of conformance to specification. There may be added needs to:

Prepare test programs to prove that the product will not fail under various misapplications it may meet in the field.

Provide "burn-in" and other extended simulation of use in order to remove "infant mortality." (The resulting test racks sometimes run to sizable investment.)

Provide overstress and environmental tests to estimate life and reliability through time acceleration.[65]

Beyond the collective needs of the individual control stations are the added needs for feedback into various additional summaries (e.g., executive reports, quality cost studies, quality improvement studies, etc.). The information flow diagram helps to identify these added usages and supplies added criteria for the QIE planners.

The elementary metrological criteria for QIE are well known.[66] The equipment must possess the necessary precision and accuracy. It must be rugged enough to withstand normal usage. It must reproduce its own readings and must be compatible with other equipment in use (e.g., Production and Inspection instruments must give compatible results).

Adapting the QIE for use involves added planning. The "fixturing" of mechanical test equipment should simulate usage, as should the electronic circuitry. Tests should simulate actual usage so as not to reduce the life of the product. In precise work, provision must also be made to provide environments which simulate usage. The interfaces with the product should be designed for swift, sure connect and disconnect and for convenience in operation. The esthetic design should not be overlooked—if well done it commands respect and helps to promote an aura of precision.

An increasing requirement in QIE is to simplify checking and maintenance. In part, this is done by providing master units to check the accuracy of the equipment. In addition, modular designs are used to permit easy removal and replacement, thereby shortening the mean time to repair.

An important adaptation is to provide instructions to the personnel. The trend has been to restore self-control to the control stations, whether through operator self-control or through automation. Either way, the feedback loop grows more complex and is more exacting in its demands on operators, inspectors, maintenance technicians, and supervision. The instructions and training manuals become essential tools for meeting these demands.

A further need for adaptation is to tie the QIE into the overall data processing system. The quality information flow diagram is of great value in visualizing the overall needs for data processing. Here the planners must collaborate extensively with the systems analysts and programmers who administer the control computers.[67]

---

[65] In one example involving a receiving test of electronic components, a testing system employs a transport and conditioning unit which houses the mechanical transport system and the temperature chambers. A pluggable test pack makes connections to the pulse generators, power supplies, and wave-form measuring devices. All this is coupled to a control system consisting of:

A processing unit which controls the movement of the components at the test stations

A multiplexer unit to receive analog test data from the testing unit

A data converter (analog to digital)

A card read punch

A console typewriter for printing results

From "Application Brief K20-1725, Industrial Testing System," IBM Components Division, Poughkeepsie, N.Y.

[66] See generally Section 13.

[67] See generally Section 20.

Computers are being used not only to process the data and to regulate the processes[68] but also to prepare instruction sheets. This is accomplished by storing the procedures on tape and calling them out when the associated equipment is called out.

The extensive interdepartmental effect of QIE makes it evident that the planner must follow his QIE project through to the very end. The design must now meet some exacting, complex criteria. The construction must be responsive to that design. Most important, the design must then be proved out in trials conducted under actual usage conditions.

The evolution of the automated process and the numerically controlled machine has required corresponding evolution in QIE. This is discussed below under Automatic Process Regulation.

AUTOMATIC PROCESS REGULATION[69]

In a manually regulated process, the operator receives inputs on process performance from personal observation or from measurement. Based on these inputs, the operator manually turns the valves and wheels to close the feedback loop and thus regulate the process.

In the automated process, the loop is closed without the intervention of the operator. The sensing instruments measure the process or product and signal to an effector mechanism, which may be designed in one of two basic ways:

1. The analog design. Here the sensor creates action, not information. The sensing directly energizes the effector mechanism to close the loop. (The flyball governor is an analog design which converts the sensed speed of rotation into valve motion.) A machine shop example is the continuous gaging of work done on a centerless grinder, with action to shut off the grinding when the desired dimension has been reached.

While the analog device is inherently limited to one task, many multitask analog systems are designed and built (like modular building blocks) from several analog control loops. Increasingly, these analog control systems are required to provide outputs which can be fed into broader systems through analog-to-digital conversion. In addition, analog equipment is designed for modular interchangeability to permit changes in configuration of control or to provide easy conversion of the tasks that an analog system may be required to perform.

2. The digital design. Here the sensor creates information, not action. The sensed information is processed in a computer which determines the course of action and then closes the loop.[70] The digital design can play a multiple role. It can:

Make decisions on acceptance or nonacceptance of the measured product
Identify and point to the cause of defects when trouble is encountered
Regulate the process to avoid further production of defects
Stop the process if regulation fails
Provide data summaries for managerial control

Applied to a single machine process, the digital design may be programmed to sample the product and to follow virtually any type of control scheme, e.g., narrow limit, control charts, etc. For multiple characteristics, e.g., contoured profiles, the

[68] See Automatic Process Regulation, below. Also, see generally Section 20.
[69] See generally LeJoy, Millard H., "Industrial Automatic Controls," Prentice-Hall, Inc., Englewood Cliffs, N.J., 1955.
[70] For elaboration, see Juran, J. M., "Managerial Breakthrough," McGraw-Hill Book Company, New York, 1964, pp. 192–195, 371–373.

multiple measurements must be correlated with masters to judge conformance and to signal corrective action.

Advanced control systems include means for process setup. The human operator spells out the final product requirements desired, either by setting the dials or by inserting a specification card (or tape) which bears the information. The computer then orders the creation of the necessary process conditions to make this product. The sensors keep feeding data to the computer as to actual product and process conditions prevailing. The computer then closes the loop to change the process in response to these data.[71]

Numerical Control (NC) This is the name applied to systems of control (usually for machine tools) which are based on a digital design. In this design the product specification is converted into computer language and the resulting program is stored in punched cards, punched tape, magnetic tape, etc. When a product is to be manufactured, the corresponding stored program is fed into the NC machine tool. A reader decodes the program and sends the signals through amplifiers into the motors which move the machine elements through their coordinate directions. Provision is made for sensing the actual position of the machine elements and comparing these with the programmed position for closing the loop.[72]

NC systems in their simplest forms regulate only the end points of the tool travel. More advanced is the system of tool control along the entire travel path for any coordinate. Still more advanced are the contour designs which permit generating any designed path.

Direct Digital Control (DDC) In this design a central computer takes over the decision making from local stations. This permits the computer to orchestrate the performance of these control stations rather than leaving each one to carry out a prompt "bang bang" control which is responsive to local signals but may have side effects on other product and process characteristics.

Direct digital control systems may provide for dealing with upward of 100 control loops. Since DDC is discontinuous, extensive memories must be provided along with a scheduling program which connects the computer to the control loops one at a time.

The principle of DDC also is applied to NC machines, thus becoming direct numerical control (DNC). Here a single computer handles an entire battery of NC machines. The computer memory substitutes for the punched tape (which serves as the memory for the self-controlled NC machine). In addition, "adaptive control" is in evolution, permitting compensation for time-to-time variations.[73]

Responsibility for Planning of Automated Systems Before the advent of automation, there was a comparatively clear separation of manufacturing planning work:

1. Design and manufacture of machinery (e.g., machine tools) was done by companies specializing in machine building.

2. Design and manufacture of instruments was done by different companies specializing in such work.

The growth of automation has changed this pattern of responsibilities. The design of the automated system is now a single responsibility of some systems engineer. In addition, there has been an erosion of the former boundary lines separating construction of machines from construction of instruments.

---

[71] For an advanced application, see Serafin, Eugene E., Multiple Computer System Controls Manufacturing Line, *Control Engineering*, December 1964. (Manufacture of solid logic technology cards.)

[72] For discussion of the related problem of inspection at NC machines, see Section 12, under Automated Inspection.

[73] See Metalworking: A Profile for the Future, *Mechanical Engineering*, February 1969, p. 39.

The responsibility for quality planning has undergone a parallel change.   The production machine, the sensor, and the computer are now so closely coupled that a system design is needed.   This system design still requires the support of the specialist engineers, but the coordination is cardinal.

The effect on the line departments is equally profound.   Both Production and Inspection are relieved of such repetitive jobs as making measurements, adjusting

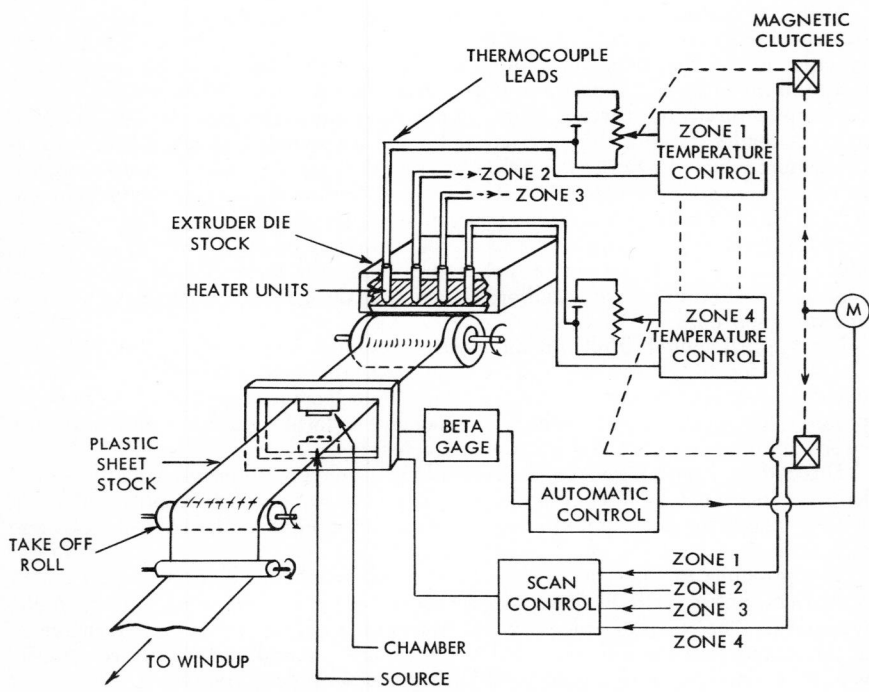

Fig. 9-29.   Control system using beta-ray gaging. *(Tracerlab Division, LFE Corp.)*

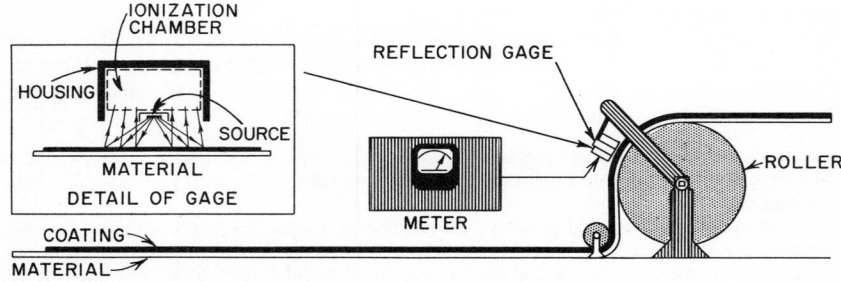

Fig. 9-30.   Back scattering thickness gage. *(Tracerlab Division, LFE Corp.)*

the process, and recording the data. Instead, the emphasis shifts to maintaining the precision of the system, correcting troubles as they arise, and studying the summarized data for trends and needs for action. All this requires less manpower. However, the remaining manpower must be better educated, better trained, and must carry greater responsibility.

Application Problems Undertaking to provide automatic regulation is not a simple matter of turning over to a servomechanism what used to be done by human beings; a whole replanning is necessary. For example, in mechanical processes, the gaging now may need to be done when the product is so hot that thermal expansion becomes significant; the gage may need to be designed to be as rugged as the production fixtures; special provision is needed to clean the measured and measuring surfaces; the need for reliability of gages is now more exacting, as is the need for observing calibration schedules.[74]

By far the most automatic process regulation is based on sampling data. Good planning and especially complete knowledge of process capability are essential to confident use of such sampling approaches. The planning is decisive not only as to sound regulation of the process; it affects product acceptance as well. The systems of automatic regulation contemplate reliance not on product inspection after the fact but on sampling and feedback control, backed up by rigid maintenance of the precision of the equipment.[75]

Figures 9-29 and 9-30 show the schematic for conventional automatic regulation of a process for making sheet material.

[74] These needs have stimulated studies of reliability of alternatives for instrumentation. One investigator found that for two similar processes, one controlled electronically and the other hydraulically, the former had a maintenance cost of $6.30 per instrument versus $9.80 for the latter. For additional data plus the results of an opinion poll, see De Lancey, M. M., A Chemical Company's Survey Gives Edge to Electronic Instruments, *Control Engineering*, October 1961, pp. 82–84.

[75] For some related problems and solutions, see Section 12, under Automated Inspection. See also Section 42, under Manufacture and under Inspection.

Vendor Relations[1]

ROBERT G. FITZGIBBONS

Rath & Strong, Inc.

J. M. JURAN

INTRODUCTION

The quality of materials and components supplied by vendors[2] obviously influences the quality of product made from those components. In many industries, e.g.,

---

[1] In the Second Edition, this Section was prepared by Dorian Shainin and L. A. Seder.

[2] The term "vendor" or "supplier" refers here to those processors or manufacturers of materials and components who sell not to consumers but mainly to (1) other manufacturers for further processing, or (2) customers who embody the vendor's products into a broad service system. Sales made by vendors to merchants in the chain of distribution sometimes have the characteristics of (1) and sometimes of (2), with plenty of gray area in between.

electronic apparatus, this influence dominates final product quality. In other industries the effect is still considerable, e.g., purchased materials account for over 25% of the costs of automotive manufacturers and over 50% of the costs of some appliance manufacturers.[3]

However, vendor relations goes beyond questions of the quality performance of the vendor. The vendor's financial stability, his prices, his ability to meet delivery promises, and still other parameters affect the overall relationship. The quality parameter must compete with all the others in arriving at a balance which optimizes the overall relationship.

Traditional and Modern Purchases The most important factor determining the pattern of vendor relations is the nature of what is being bought. It is important

TABLE 10-1   Contrast in Purchases

Traditional	Modern
Natural or semiprocessed materials	Purchase of designs, plans, and technical service in addition to materials
Tolerances wide, quality variable	High precision, high reliability
Specifications rudimentary	Sophisticated designs, quantified design parameters
Independent usage, low interchangeability	High interdependence, high interchangeability
Incoming inspection practical	Incoming inspection impractical
Limited subcontracting, geographic proximity, short feedback loop	Multiple tiers of subcontracting, wide geographic dispersion, long feedback loop
Secrecy concept by both parties	Mutual disclosures essential
Single line of communication	Multiple lines of communication
Vendor supplies goods only	Vendor supplies goods plus proof of compliance

SOURCE: J. M. Juran: Vendor Relations—An Overview, *Quality Progress,* July 1968, pp. 10–16.

to grasp this fact since modern purchases differ so remarkably from the traditional. Table 10-1 compares the nature of traditional to modern purchases.

The modern purchases are *in addition to*, not instead of, the traditional purchases. In consequence, most companies are engaged in both kinds of purchases. Such companies must be careful to use, for each kind of material purchased, the type of vendor relations which fits the case at hand.

The classification into traditional and modern is often too broad to provide clear directions for vendor relations practices. Some practitioners have suggested more detailed categories of purchases in order to establish correspondingly clear patterns of vendor relations.[4] These categories include:

[3] Alex Morrison quoted the following estimates of industry material cost percentages in the United Kingdom: electric cables, 70%; chemicals, 60%; motor vehicles, 65%; mechanical engineering, 50%; iron and steel, 70%. (Paper presented at the 1968 Conference of European Organization for Quality Control, Madrid.)

[4] Swaton, L., and W. Weaver, Five Steps to Supplier Quality Control, *Industrial-Quality Control,* May 1966, pp. 611–616. See also Holmes, Jack, Monitoring the Quality and Reliability of Supplies, *The Quality Engineer,* vol. 31, no. 2, pp. 49–52.

Standard Materials. These are common use materials made, by multiple vendors, to industry specifications. Usually the test specifications are also standardized. For such materials the buyer[5] can often limit himself to incoming inspection without becoming involved with the more complex aspects of vendor relations.

Standard "Hardware." These include many fasteners, fittings, and similar items mass produced to industry specifications. Again, the buyer can often limit himself to incoming inspection.

Minor Components. These are functional in their usage and consist of mechanical parts such as gears and bearings or electronic parts such as diodes and relays. Usually they are made to the vendors' specifications, but in many cases these are derived from industry specifications. While incoming inspection of these components can largely determine fitness for use, there is a residue which requires some use of modern vendor relations techniques.

Major Components. These perform major functions in the system and may be either proprietary (to vendors' specifications) or to the buyer's specification. They require the vendor's total capability, and the scheme of vendor relations should be structured accordingly.

Vendor Relations Objectives and Activities The objective in vendor relations is to enable the buyer to proceed with confidence in his use of the goods. For traditional products this objective becomes one of being able to use the product without the need for incoming inspection or for corrective procedures. For modern products the objective becomes one of relying on the vendor just as though he were an in-house department, i.e., that either "make" or "buy" should yield the same quality.

Attaining these objectives requires that the parties carry out a series of well-known activities:

1. Establish a vendor relations quality policy
2. Use multiple vendors for major procurements
3. Establish a formal vendor and product qualification process
4. Conduct joint quality planning; agree on responsibilities
5. Establish two-way communication
6. Set up to detect and remedy deviations
7. Conduct vendor surveillance
8. Exchange inspection data; provide certification
9. Undertake improvement programs; set up mutual assistance
10. Create and utilize vendor quality ratings

(handwritten annotations: "Modern" bracketing the list, "Traditional" bracketing items 2 and 8)

Of these ten activities, numbers 3, 5, 6, and 10 are required in most purchase situations. The need for the remaining activities depends on what is being bought. Modern products bought in large volume require the entire list of these activities. Traditional products, materials, and standard components employ 2 and 8. Proprietary products, produced to vendor specifications, are often bought by customers who lack test facilities and who therefore rely on the vendors plus a feedback from their own usage. Where the pattern of products and purchases is a mixture, the buyers face the added problem of assuring that purchase of modern products is done with modern methods while purchase of traditional products continues to be done mainly with traditional methods. (Modern methods can be a waste if applied to traditional products.)[6]

The detailed conduct of these activities is discussed under the major topics which follow.

---

[5] The terms "buyer," "vendee," and "customer" are used here in the sense of any organization which buys from a vendor.

[6] For elaboration, see Juran, J. M., Vendor Relations—An Overview, *Quality Progress,* July 1968, pp. 10–16.

A Note on "Nonproduct" Quality   Companies make extensive purchases of goods and services which neither enter the company's products nor are used in direct fabrication of the product.   The important categories include:

Equipment used for plant services: motors, pumps, valves, pallets, containers, fork-lift trucks
Supplies of all sorts, both office and plant
Office equipment of all sorts

For these categories it is common to find that the established vendor relations procedures bypass the buyer's Quality Control Department.   In consequence, there is no organized incoming inspection, vendor survey, or other positive action for quality evaluation or control.   Instead, the action is based primarily on failures in usage.

The reason usually given for bypassing the buyer's Quality Control Department is that the buyer's customers will not be affected by poor quality of these goods. This reason is by no means universally valid.   For example, poor-quality wooden pallets for product transportation result in product damage.[7]   Quality of maintenance supplies affects the stability of the manufacturing processes.   Quality of printing affects the integrity of the support operations, etc.

Quality failures in these purchases show up in numerous scattered departments. Not only is there no organized body of analysts to deal with them but there is often no awareness that they all originate from a basic problem of "nonproduct" quality. The quality cost studies (see Section 5) do not pick them up, since these studies are likewise concerned only with those qualities which go into products sold by the company.

Normally, such a state of affairs goes on and on because there is no evidence of the size of the problem.   In those companies where there is need for a basic change, the first step is for some middle manager to take the initiative and to make an estimate of the size of the problem, i.e., a quality cost study applied to nonquality products.   If the quality cost study bears out the suspicions, the way is open to justify a program for improvement.

VENDOR RELATIONS QUALITY POLICY

The general nature of quality policies is set out in Section 3.   Applied to vendor relations, the following major questions emerge and require policy decisions:

Interdependence or Not   This questions whether the vendor is to be treated mainly as an in-house department ("on the team") or left on his own as an outsider. Generally, in purchasing modern products, interdependence must prevail, whereas in traditional products the situation of two independent worlds can be retained.[8] The decision on this basic quality policy question affects virtually all other aspects of vendor relations.

Interdependence takes three major forms:

Technological.   For traditional and proprietary products, the vendor is usually self-sufficient; for modern products, he often is not.   The more complex the product, the greater is the need to give the vendor the type of technological assistance he would receive if he were an in-house department.

Technological assistance is a two-way street.   In *all* cases the buyer can learn from

---

[7] For elaboration, see Sec. 46, under Support Tasks and Their Quality Problems: Transportation.

[8] For elaboration, see Juran, J. M., Vendor Relations—An Overview, *Quality Progress,* July 1968, pp. 10–16.

the vendor. (In some cases it is the vendor who is the technological giant, selling to buyers who lack engineers and laboratories.)

Technological assistance usually requires "exchange visiting," i.e., mutual visits to see each other's operations. These visits create the risk that the visitors will make unauthorized use of the knowledge obtained during the visit. For modern products, the need to take these risks is far greater than for traditional products.

Economic. In modern products, the life cycle cost concept requires that the vendor understand the buyer's costs over the entire useful life of the product.[9] This is a revolutionary change from the relationship prevailing in traditional products and creates a new level of economic interdependence.

Managerial. Because modern products involve purchase of a wide range of vendor capabilities, the planning for use of these capabilities must be coordinated with the capabilities of the buyer. A major effect of this form of interdependence is that the assurance of good quality can no longer be derived from incoming inspection. Instead, the assurance must come from placing responsibility on the vendor to (1) make the product right and (2) furnish the proof that it is right.

Details of making effective these three forms of interdependence are discussed below, under Joint Quality Planning.

Multiple Vendors For important purchases it is well to use multiple sources of supply. A single source can more easily neglect to sharpen its competitive edge in quality, cost, and service. (It is also risky for continuity, e.g., strikes, fire.)

Despite the evident advantages of multiple sources, there is an enormous extent of use of single sources. The most dramatic cases are the huge multidivisional companies in which some divisions are vendors to others, e.g., large, integrated steel, oil, chemical, automotive, and electronic companies.[10] These operations are quite successful in using monopolistic sources of supply because they solve their quality problems through a combination of managerial tools:

1. Joint quality planning (see below)
2. Prompt feedback of deviations (see below)
3. Upper management insistence on corrective action
4. Threat of breaking the monopoly if the vendor division will not act

At the other extreme, the expense of qualifying additional sources results in use of single sources for small-volume purchases. Single sources may actually offer price advantages if the volume is not split among multiple vendors.

Published Quality Policy A good deal of unwritten vendor quality policy exists in the form of long-standing industry practices, sanctioned by the laws governing sales. There exist also some elements of written policy contained here and there in company vendor relations manuals.[11] As interdependence grows, the need for published policy grows with it. Commonly the resulting published policy is embodied in a Vendor Relations Manual, along with other information of importance and use to vendors.

On a more comprehensive scale, the U.S. Department of Defense makes wide use of MIL-Q-9858A[12] as a document to govern quality relations with contractors, including some quality policy matters.

Still another form is seen in the "Ten Principles for Vendor-Vendee Relation-

[9] See Section 4, under Life Cycle Costing.

[10] A further example is the government monopolies which prevail in many countries, notably those of Eastern Europe. See, in this connection, Juran, J. M., Quality Control under Monopoly, *Industrial Quality Control*, March 1965, p. 462.

[11] For some examples of published vendor quality policy, see Section 3, under Subject Matter of Quality Policies.

[12] The Naval Publications and Forms Center, 5801 Tabor Ave., Philadelphia, Pa. 19120.

ships" evolved by a research committee of the Japanese Union of Scientists and Engineers. In paraphrased form, these principles include:

Mutual respect and cooperation
Prior contractual understanding
Agreed methods of evaluation
Agreed plans for settling disputes
Exchange of essential information
Adequate performance on related functions, e.g., inventory control
Vendor responsible to deliver good product and supporting data
Consumers' interests preeminent

VENDOR QUALIFICATION PROCESS

A vendor of modern products qualifies himself in two very different ways:

1. As to his adequacy in business matters generally—integrity, financial capability, prompt payment, etc.

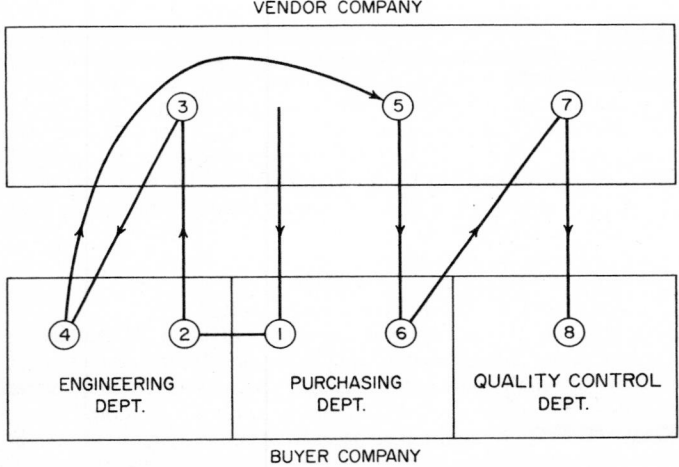

VENDOR COMPANY

BUYER COMPANY

1. LOOKING FOR BUSINESS

2. SECURE ENGINEERING REQUIREMENTS

3. PREPARE SAMPLES

4. QUALIFY SAMPLES

5. PREPARE PROPOSAL

6. ACCEPT PROPOSAL

7. PRODUCE

8. INSPECT, APPROVE

Fig. 10-1. Product qualification process. This may be supplemented by surveys and surveillance.

2. As to his adequacy in matters of product quality

To attain these qualifications requires that the vendor pass three departmental gates before he receives any income:

1. Engineering, to qualify the product
2. Purchasing, to secure a contract
3. Quality Control, for approval of regular product shipments

Figure 10-1 shows this sequence graphically.

The vendor's general business qualification is largely outside the scope of this Handbook. The qualification to meet quality requirements is discussed below.

Methods of Prediction   Buyers have evolved a variety of methods for predicting a prospective vendor's likelihood of meeting quality requirements. These include:

1. Demonstration by test on actual product. This is usually known as qualification testing.

2. Data showing the vendor's performance on similar quality requirements for other customers. These data are secured through a data bank.

3. Estimate of the vendor's capability. This is done through a Vendor Quality Survey (see below)

Qualification Testing.   The procedure here is for the vendor to make up samples of the product and submit these to the buyer's engineers for testing. These tests are not merely for instantaneous conformance to specification; they extend to life, failure rate, maintainability, and other aspects of use.

Much lead time is needed for this qualification testing, and this in turn requires good advance planning. The procedure is costly enough to limit its use to mass-production or high-reliability projects. The validity of the results is heavily influenced by the integrity of the samples. They should be made by the same production process which will be used in regular production. They should not be made by hand in the laboratory. (Nevertheless, sometimes they are.)

Data Bank on Vendor Performance.   This data bank concept is similar to that used in commercial transactions to predict the likelihood that a company will pay its debts. (In the United States, the leading national credit data bank is Dun & Bradstreet, Inc., a company which collects data pertinent to credit performance and summarizes these to arrive at credit ratings.)

At the start of the 1970s there had not yet been organized, in the United States, a national vendor quality data bank.[13] The possibilities for creating such a national bank are limited due to long-standing reluctance of companies to give out product performance information which discloses the name of the manufacturer, especially if the information is derogatory.

In other cultures, there is less reluctance to put vendor performance data into a public data bank. In 1958 the Swedish electronics industry agreed that all reliability data on electronic components should be regarded as public property unless restricted for national security reasons. A national data bank was created and the Military Electronics Laboratory was designated as the custodian.[14]

For the most part, national data banks remained to be organized.[15] However, a number of more limited banks had been organized in the United States and elsewhere. These are:

1. Data banks set up to serve a specific industry. An example is Coordinated Aerospace Supplier Evaluation (CASE). This started as an informal association of aerospace prime contractors with the objective of reducing redundant surveys of suppliers in the industry. The originator of the idea, Aerojet-General Corporation, also became custodian of the bank. Survey data were received by the bank, summarized, and issued, on request, to members of the Association, including backup data.

---

[13] See, in this connection, Juran, J. M., Management's Corner, *Industrial Quality Control,* May 1964, pp. 65 and 66.

[14] For elaboration, see "FTL—The Swedish Military Electronics Laboratory," pp. 45–50. The pamphlet, including sample data sheets, is available in English from Försvarets Forskningsanstalt, Stockholm 80, Sweden.

[15] Eastern European companies tend to be less restrictive in pooling data into data banks. (Personal observation of J. M. Juran.)

The plan included a bias, since no provision was made for reporting data on disapproval of vendors.[16]

2. Data banks set up within a single large company. A published example is General Motors Source Performance Evaluation and Reporting (SPEAR). This data bank was set up as a corporate program to pool survey reports, performance reports, and defective material reports from all divisions. The first product category tackled was fasteners.[17]

3. Data banks within the federal government. These have tended to be product-oriented rather than vendor-oriented, i.e., the main purpose is to make available test data and failure data on parts and components. Participants (contractors and government departments) "deposit" test and failure reports with the data bank. The latter processes the data and makes them available, without charge, to participants for use in design, etc. Because the data are identified by manufacturer, some aspects of vendor performance can be determined. The principal programs are *(a)* the Interagency Data Exchange Program (IDEP), which is oriented to test data, and *(b)* the Failure Rate Data Program (FARADA), oriented to failure data.

The IDEP program is operated at three centers:

Army/NASA: Army Missile Command, Redstone Arsenal, Huntsville, Alabama

Navy: Navy Fleet Missile Systems Analysis and Evaluation Group, Corona, California

Air Force: Air Force Space and Missile Systems Organization, El Segundo, California

The FARADA program is joint for all agencies and is operated by the same Navy group as operates the Navy IDEP program.

Qualified Vendors List   Vendors who successfully meet the criteria of the qualification process are added to the Qualified Vendors List. This formalized list provides a delegation of authority to various company departments to distinguish between vendors who are qualified and those who are not. Purchasing agents receive wide latitude for dealing with qualified vendors, both in inviting bids and in placing orders. Quality control procedures permit, for qualified vendors, a lower level of inspection, test, surveillance, etc., than for vendors not on the list. Still other departments make similar distinctions.

In addition, tangible evidence of the distinction may be given to the vendor in the form of a Certificate of Qualification. This has proved to be a useful public relations and motivational tool. Often the vendor takes advertising space to publicize the fact of his qualification.

Merchant companies face a special problem of vendor qualification since most of them lack the necessary technology, i.e., they have no test laboratories, inspectors, Quality Control Department, etc. The methods actually used are a combination of the following:

1. The buyer's knowledge of conditions in the product line and his discussions with the vendor

2. Inspection performed incidental to unpacking for display, sale, etc.

3. Feedback from customer usage

[16] For elaboration, see Aerospace Firms Pool Records and Reports on Suppliers, *Quality Assurance,* December 1966, pp. 22–24. See also, the Case for CASE, *Quality Management and Engineering,* May 1972, pp. 26 and 27.

[17] See, for details, Autobuilder Starts New Vendor Evaluation Program, *Quality Assurance,* November 1967, pp. 20 and 21; also Maass, Richard A., SPEAR—Blunted Weapon or Sharp Tool? *Quality Assurance,* April 1968, pp. 34–37.

Some large merchants do have Quality Control departments, laboratories, and other organized means for product qualification. The procedures used by such companies have much in common with those used by manufacturing companies.

In international purchases, there are special problems in qualifying vendors. For large or critical purchases, it is quite important to send a specialist to visit the vendor to aid in clarifying specifications and to evolve the necessary basis for joint quality planning.[18] For other purchases, the qualification may be through (1) trial orders placed to test the vendor's capability or (2) discussion with present customers of the vendor to learn about their experience with the vendor's quality.

Qualified Parts Catalog In some companies the two forms of vendor qualification (business and quality) are sharply delineated by preparing two different lists.

1. A list of qualified *vendors,* meaning vendors who have been "cleared" for integrity, credit, etc.

2. A list of qualified *products,* known variously as "qualified parts catalog," "preferred parts catalog," etc.

The product catalog is used to list those products[19] for which there is objective evidence of vendor adequacy. The evidence may come from:

1. Qualification testing
2. Appearance on a government agency Approved Parts List
3. Test results supplied by the vendor
4. A record of successful usage

The formality of two separate lists tends to make clear the fact that qualification of vendors is based largely on business considerations, whereas qualification of product is primarily technological in nature. There is an overlap, but the main significance is that qualification of a vendor does *not* automatically qualify all of his products.

VENDOR QUALITY SURVEYS

Lacking proof that the vendor has already been successful in meeting the needed quality requirements, buyers try to make a prediction in other ways.[20] An extensive form of such prediction is the vendor quality survey. Under this concept, a team of qualified observers[21] visits the vendor. The observers see the facilities, study the procedures, talk to the men, collect the pertinent data. From all this they "should be" able to make a useful prediction of the likelihood that the vendor will deliver good quality.

The Questionnaire and Checklist In practice, the survey is expanded to review the entire capability of the vendor—financial, managerial, technological. A questionnaire is sent out in advance to be executed and returned by the vendor, along with copies of his pertinent data and manuals. The survey team studies this information, becomes informed as to some matters, and becomes better prepared to make the visit—what to see and what questions to ask.

[18] See, in this connection, Section 6, under Intercompany Quality Planning. See also Section 48 generally to grasp the influence of national cultural differences in the approach to planning for quality.

[19] Sometimes what is listed is the vendor's *process,* e.g., plating.

[20] These "other ways" include general reputation of the vendor and his performance on other kinds of products. Neither of these is widely regarded as a useful predictor of vendor performance.

[21] Membership on the team varies, both in number and in the departments represented. A typical team consists of specialists from Purchasing, Project Engineering, and Quality Control.

Study of numerous company questionnaires and checklists shows a commonality[22] of check points, as follows:

Management: philosophy, quality policies, organization structure, indoctrination, commitment to quality

Design: organization, systems in use, caliber of specifications, orientation to modern technique, attention to reliability, engineering change control, development laboratories

Manufacture: physical facilities, maintenance, special processes, process capability, production capacity, caliber of planning, lot identification and traceability

Purchasing: specifications, vendor relations, procedures

Quality Control: organization structure, availability of quality control and reliability engineers, quality planning (materials, in-process, finished goods, packing, storage, shipping, usage, field service), audit of adherence to plan

Inspection and Test: laboratories, special tests, instruments, measurement control

Quality coordination: organization for coordination, order analysis, control over subcontractors, quality cost analysis, corrective action loop, disposition of nonconforming product

Data systems: facilities, procedures, effective use, reports

Personnel: indoctrination, training, motivation

Quality results: performance attained, self-use of product, prestigious customers, prestigious subcontractors

The Survey Report Following the survey, the team reports its findings. These consist of (1) some very objective findings as to facilities possessed or lacked by the vendor, (2) some subjective judgments on the effectiveness of the vendor's operations, (3) a further judgment on the extent of assistance needed by the vendor, and (4) a highly subjective prediction as to whether the vendor will deliver good product if he is awarded a contract.

Very little has been published on the correlation between surveyor's predictions and subsequent quality of actual deliveries. The Brainard study[23] concluded there was no useful correlation. In the opinion of both of the authors, proof of positive correlation remains to be established. It is quite desirable for companies to study the extent to which this correlation has been achieved by their own surveyors.

Extent of Use of Surveys The use of vendor surveys has been very extensive in military and aerospace programs but less so in commercial programs. A study by an ASQC committee reported that surveys of new vendors were being conducted by 82% of military and aerospace contractors versus 34% of commercial contractors.[24] In many cases individual vendors were surveyed and resurveyed over and

---

[22] See, in this connection, Vendor Evaluation Checklists, Hitchcock Publishing Company, Wheaton, Ill. 60187. This compilation contains several pages of questions dealing with vendors' facilities, organization, and control systems. In addition, it includes specialized lists dealing with some common products (e.g., bearings, fasteners), processes (e.g., plating, welding), test laboratories (e.g., nondestructive, environmental).

Compilations in the professional society journals include Shanazarian, Thomas E., Vendor Certification, *Industrial Quality Control*, April 1967, pp. 480–484; also Wyllie, W. W., Quality Capability Survey of Vendors, *Western Quality Control Conference*, ASQC, March 16–17, 1961.

[23] Brainard, Edgar H., Just How Good Are Vendor Surveys? *Quality Assurance*, August 1966, pp. 22–25. Brainard found that, following 151 ratings made during surveys to predict vendor quality performance, the actual deliveries correspond to the ratings for 77 vendors but failed to correspond for 74 vendors.

[24] Vendor-Vendee Technical Committee, ASQC, Publication VV-1. Imperial Reproductions, Cherry Hill, N.J. 08034.

over again by teams from numerous contractors. The resulting protests and criticisms led to some proposals for minimizing these duplications and excess costs:

1. Pooling of survey results into data banks so that multiple companies can make use of the same data. Examples are data banks such as CASE and SPEAR (see under Vendor Qualification Process, above).

2. Designating approved survey agencies whose conclusions (that a vendor is qualified) would be honored by all contractors.[25] This would require some standardization of the survey, at least for small vendors—an idea that has also received support.[26] It would also require some changes in government regulations.

A move in this direction was the 1972 proposal by the ASQC Vendor-Vendee Technical Committee to create an official, accepted source of vendor quality surveys through:

    a. A standard for the conduct of vendor surveys. (An existing standard is ASQC Standard C-1-1968.)

    b. Use of ASQC-Certified Quality Engineers to conduct the surveys

    c. Award of an ASQC Quality Accreditation Certificate to successful vendors

    d. Publication of a National Accreditation Register of accredited vendors[27]

3. Exempting certain categories of vendors from surveys. Finley[28] has suggested the following categories:

Suppliers of maintenance and repairs and of operating supplies for plant consumption

Suppliers of proprietary products which can be tested for acceptance

Low-value procurements for isolated or short-term use

Suppliers of labor or technical assistance on the buyer's premises

4. Abolishing resurveys for vendors whose delivery record is one of good quality.[29]

5. Recognizing that small vendors can operate quite effectively with minimal formalized procedures, and taking account of this fact both in scheduling and conducting surveys.

JOINT QUALITY PLANNING

In the purchase of both traditional and modern products, the end result is a delivery of the goods to the buyer. However, in the case of modern products, the purchase also includes something else—the purchase of *the vendor's capability* in product design, manufacturing planning, quality control, technical assistance, etc.[30] For modern products, this vendor capability is applied to preparing designs and plans to fit the buyer's special needs. When a buyer avails himself of these capabilities

---

[25] Logan, John K., Facilities Survey—Boon or Boondoggle? *Industrial Quality Control,* November, 1967, pp. 259–261.

[26] Cooper, David R., Don't Survey Small Suppliers out of Your Business, *Quality Assurance,* September 1966, pp. 38 and 39.

[27] Field, D. L., R. A. Maass, and T. M. Vining, ASQC Quality System Accreditation, *Annual Technical Conference Transactions 1972,* ASQC, pp. 469 and 470.

[28] Finley, Arnold B., Purchased Quality: By Objective or Objection? *Industrial Quality Control,* November, 1967, pp. 255–259.

[29] Foster, Jack B., A Unified Approach to Vendor Surveys, *Industrial Quality Control,* October 1966, pp. 176–178.

[30] In traditional products the vendor likewise supplies a capability, since he performs some processing operations. However, this capability is employed in performing standardized operations to make standard products for the use of buyers generally.

of the vendor, he is said to be buying "engineered products" as distinguished from standard products or "commodities."[31]

Some vendor planning is required in the buyer's precontract documents. Two well-known models for vendor planning are MIL-Q-9858A of the Department of Defense and NHB 5300.4 (1B) of the National Aeronautics and Space Administration. Some civilian buyers also provide such models for vendor planning.[32] However, a study of provisions for quality planning in government versus civilian contracting shows that:

1. The provisions are quite similar on matters of providing assistance to vendors.

2. The provisions are quite different as to restraints on vendors. The government contracts are the more exacting, and the differences relate largely to the needs for documented proof that the product is adequate.

Figure 10-2 shows these contrasts graphically.[33]

Effective purchase of the vendor's capabilities requires that these be coordinated with the corresponding capabilities of the buyer's organization. The chief means

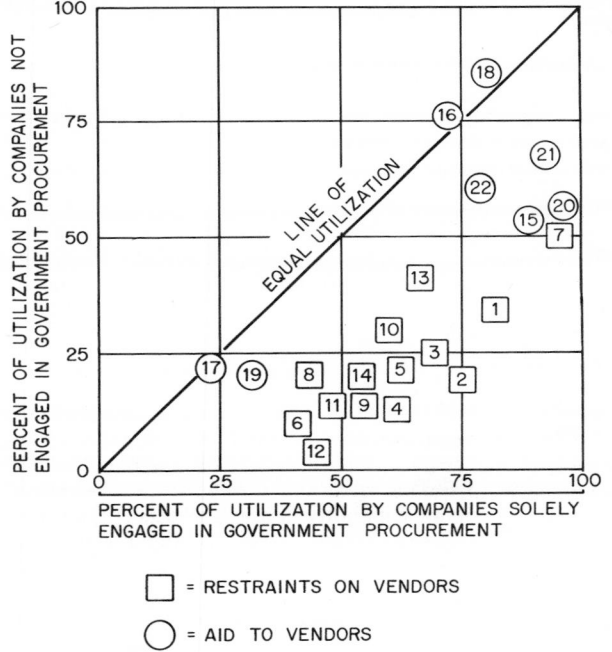

Fig. 10-2. Comparison of utilization of designated restraints on and aids to vendors. See key to numbers.

[31] Often the term "contractor" is used to describe the vendor who provides these special services along with the goods.

[32] See, in this connection, ASQC Standard C1, *Quality Progress*, May 1968, pp. 25 and 26.

[33] Derived from Vendor Vendee Technical Committee, ASQC, Publication VV-1, available from Imperial Reproductions, Cherry Hill, N.J. 08034.

Code no.	Precontract restraints on vendors	Percent of utilization by companies engaged solely in:	
		Government procurement	Civilian procurement
1	Survey of new vendors	82	34
2	Approval of vendor's quality system	75	20
3	Vendor must redelegate quality requirements	69	26
	Vendor must have written:		
4	Manufacturing instruction sheets	60	14
5	In-process inspection and test instructions. . . .	62	21
6	Workmanship standards	42	11
7	Written corrective actions	95	51
8	Approval of vendor's final inspection and test instructions	45	18
9	Vendor must be approved by buyer's QC organization to be eligible for contracts	53	15
	Restraints during execution of the contract		
10	Periodic audit of vendor's quality program	66	31
11	Conduct of source inspection.	46	14
12	Use of source representatives	44	6
13	Buyer may not accept certified test results in lieu of testing	66	42
14	Vendor may not perform Material Review Board (MRB) activities on his own product . .	51	17
	Communication and assistance to vendors		
15	Quality requirements in the contract	92	51
16	Discussion of quality requirements with vendors	73	76
17	Duplicate gages or test equipment supplied to vendor	23	22
18	Vendors notified of defects	81	85
19	Vendors provided with summaries of quality performance	31	21
20	Vendor rating system in effect.	96	55
21	Vendor ratings used to improve vendor performance.	92	67
22	Vendor rating used to disqualify vendors	77	59

Fig. 10-2 (Continued)   Key to numbers on chart.

for securing this coordination is joint quality planning. Some of this planning takes place in the precontract stage. The bulk of the planning is done after the award but before production. The remaining planning takes place following the start of production.

Precontract Planning Precontract planning is largely devoted to securing a mutual understanding sufficient to reach a decision on whether to contract or not. In this exchange the vendor needs to understand the usage requirements and specifications of what he is to meet: how will the system make use of his component; what are the interface requirements; what are the main requirements for performance, reliability, maintainability, safety, etc., what is the meaning of key words and phrases. The buyer, in turn, needs to understand just what capabilities the vendor is able to muster to meet all these requirements. (The quality survey results are an element in the buyer's quality planning.)

A simple case example is given by a vendor (manufacturer) of metal tubing. His customers buy the tubing (usually through distributors) for a wide variety of applications. Some of these applications require further processing on the tubing, e.g., redrawing, thread rolling. These different applications require different input materials. However, the vendor, not the distributor, is the expert in choice of tubing to be used for a given application. The vendor therefore takes positive steps to discover what the end use of the product will be. The vendor also has established a Material/Specification Review Board (MSRB) to review dubious inquiries and orders. The resulting classifications include the following:

(1) easy to make
(2) think we could make but need a trial order
(3) would be surprised if we could make to the specifications as written.[34]

Sometimes there is widespread vendor interest in specific contracts, i.e., the contract is very large, or the contract has a high potential for follow-on contracts. In such cases the buyer may organize bidders' conferences to reduce the effort required for individual indoctrination. During such conferences, informed officials are on hand to explain the buyer's concepts and to answer questions. One of the hopes in such conferences is that the list of bidders will be reduced to a manageable number of seriously interested vendors.

It should be noted that the buyer's basic requirements are represented by two kinds of "specifications":

1. Performance specifications defining what the product is to do, i.e., fitness for use.

2. Detailed specifications to provide details which are necessary (though sometimes not sufficient) to inform the vendor on what to do to make the product fit for use

With the award of the contract, detailed planning proceeds across all the lines of interdependence: economic, technological, managerial, procedural. This planning may cover part or all of the spectrum of activities from "cradle to grave," the specific elements being chosen to fit the special needs of each contract.

Joint Economic Planning The economic aspects of joint quality planning concentrate on two major approaches:

1. Buying value rather than conformance to specification. The technique used is to analyze the value of what is being bought and to try to effect an improvement. The organized approach is known as Value Analysis and is discussed generally in

---

[34] Harry W. Poole, Customer/Supplier or Supplier/Customer—It Works Both Ways, *Quality Assurance,* October 1970, pp. 32 and 33.

Section 16. Applied to vendor quality relations, value analysis looks for opportunities such as:

Overspecification for the use to which the product will be put, e.g., special products ordered when standard would do
Emphasis on original price rather than on cost of usage over the life of the product
Emphasis on conformance to specification, not fitness for use

2. Optimizing quality costs. To the purchase price the buyer must add a whole array of quality-related costs: incoming inspection, material review, production delays, downtime, extra inventories, etc. However, the vendor also has a set of costs which he is trying to optimize. In some respects these two sets of costs can be harmonized. However, in some respects they are squarely antagonistic, as in the "profitable spare parts business."[35] The buyer can do much to help himself by putting together the data needed to understand the life cycle costs or the cost of usage and then pressing for a result which will optimize these. The trend is to work out these arrangements in the original contract negotiations.[36]

Joint Technological Planning This involves numerous aspects of product design, process design, test procedure, etc., and is done both to optimize results and to make the systems and procedures compatible. The more usual elements of such joint planning include:

1. Agreement on the meaning of the details of the specifications.
2. Quantification of reliability requirements. (This may include imposing reliability tasks on vendors.)
3. Seriousness classification of defects to help the vendor understand where to concentrate his efforts. The approach used is set out in Section 12, under Seriousness Classification.
4. Establishment of sensory standards for those qualities which require use of the human being as an instrument (see Section 12, under Sensory Standards).
5. Standardization of test methods and checkout of measurement systems to establish their compatibility.[37] During the joint planning of the instrumentation, an effort is made to avoid duplication of expensive test equipment.
6. Establishment of sampling plans, AQL levels, and other criteria relative to inspection and test activity. Because these sampling plans affect the fate of future lots, both parties are well advised to understand what they are doing.[38] From the vendor's viewpoint, the design of the sampling plans should be such that product of usual process average will be easily accepted by the plan. From the buyer's viewpoint, the critical factor is the amount of damage which will be done by one defect getting through the sampling screen. Once this is evaluated, the balance of costs (sorting versus sampling) can be estimated as a useful input to selection of the AQL. (See, in this connection, Section 24, under Selection of an AQL on the Basis of Cost.)

---

[35] For elaboration, see Juran, J. M., Mobilizing for the 1970's, *Quality Progress*, August 1969, p. 10.

[36] For example, a manufactrer purchases castings under a contract in which the vendor is paid an increment for quality but must, in turn, pay for machining costs lost due to hidden defects in castings. See Section 34, under Customer Relations.

[37] Many contract troubles have their origin in the fact that the contract was signed despite the lack of an agreement on standardization of test method.

[38] Occasionally buyers make pronouncements that "no defects are tolerable" yet conduct sampling inspections to assure this. Purely on statistical grounds this is obvious nonsense. The buyer's protection in the case of such critical qualities comes not from the buyer's sampling plan but from the vendor's process.

The sampling plans, symbolized by the AQL,[39] can become a serious restriction on the vendor if lots of process average quality will not be readily accepted. To avoid trouble from this source, the parties are well advised first to determine the actual process average, i.e., total defectives found, divided by total sampled units inspected. This should be done for each seriousness class of defects. (This calculation excludes lots which are significantly worse than the regular production from the process.) Such prior knowledge of the process average makes it possible to calculate, for any sampling plan to be used, how many lots of process average quality will fail to be accepted. Once this information is available, there is a range of options:

a. Adopt Industry AQLs and LTPDs. Some industries, notably electronic components, have developed industry standards[40] for AQLs and LTPDs.

b. Bargain out the AQLs between the parties.

c. Make a trial run on tentative AQLs and adopt the final AQLs after the results of the trial become evident.

Beyond these participative approaches are the unilateral determinations made by an economically powerful buyer or vendor. Even if burdensome, these determinations may be endured by the weaker party when there is no ready alternative. However, the agreement is not real, and the resulting abrasion can become a continuing obstacle to good vendor relations.

Formalizing the sampling plans so they have legitimacy (become part of the contract) is done in any of several ways:

The buyer publishes an incoming inspection procedure which is referenced in the purchase contract.

The buyer publishes a Vendor Relations Manual which includes the sampling plans to be used and which is referenced in the contract.

The purchase contract contains a special provision dealing with sampling.

The product specification contains the sampling plan.

7. Establishment of a system of lot identification and traceability. This concept has always been present in some degree, e.g., heat numbers of steel; lot numbers of pharmaceutial products. More recently, with intensified attention to product safety and liability, the need for this identification to simplify localization of trouble, to reduce the volume of product recall, and to fix responsibility, etc., has become more acute. These systems, while demanding some extra effort to preserve the order of manufacture and to identify the product, can be decidedly helpful in quality control, since preserving the order makes possible greater precision in sampling.

Where the order of manufacture is not preserved, the buyer has no choice but to sample at random. This requires larger samples while yielding lower precision of results. In contrast, if the buyer knows the order of manufacture, he can utilize this knowledge along with stratified sampling to secure greater protection at lower cost. (If he has data on the vendor's process capability, he can improve his sampling effectiveness still further.) Some buyers make use of this principle by asking the vendors to select samples identified by order of manufacture and to submit these samples for test by the buyer. This procedure avoids the burdensome problem of opening containers to secure samples. The principle of "audit of decisions"

---

[39] Some vendor relations manuals no longer make reference to AQLs at all. Instead, they merely show the sampling plan the buyer intends to use for various types of characteristics. There is merit in this, since the AQL concept is quite confusing to those who have not received basic training in statistical sampling.

[40] See, in this connection, Section 38, under Incoming Inspection.

is used to establish the vendor's integrity in selecting samples (see below).

8. Establishment of a system of timely response to alarm signals resulting from defects. In many contracts, the buyer and vendor are yoked to a common timetable for completion of the final product. Usually a separate department called Production Control (or Materials Management, etc.) presides over major aspects of scheduling. However, the upper management properly looks to the people associated with the quality function to set up alarm signals to detect quality failures and to act positively on these signals to avoid deterioration, whether in quality, cost or delivery.

Pilot Lots. A major technological undertaking is that of conducting a pilot lot, including purchased components, through manufacture as the forerunner to quantity production. The activities involved are completely analogous to those set out in

TABLE 10-2   Responsibility Matrix—Vendor Relations

Activity	Participating departments		
	Product Design	Purchasing	Quality Control
New-product qualification testing.	XX	X	X
Vendor quality survey.		X	XX
New vendor qualification	X	XX	X
Communication to vendors on:			
Contracting	X	XX	X
Product design	XX	X	
Inspection and test planning	X	X	XX
Nonconformance of products		XX	X
Decision on fitness of non-			
conforming products	XX	X	X
Quality surveillance		X	XX
Planning of quality data system		X	XX
Vendor quality rating		X	XX
Quality improvement		X	XX

XX = Principal responsibility
X = Collateral responsibility

Section 9, Manufacturing Planning for Quality (and in other sections). The fact that buyer and vendor are different companies does not change the list of activities, but it does increase the difficulties of coordination. Commonly it is necessary to resort to face-to-face conferences to reach the objectives.

Joint Managerial Planning Achieving the economic and technological goals requires use of the conventional management tools of planning. These should be applied on a joint basis, as though buyer and vendor were all part of the same management team. The more usual elements of this planning include:

Definition of Responsibility: Buyer versus Vendor. When multiple departments of both companies are involved in a joint effort, it becomes important to clear up the assignment of duties as between buyer and vendor. The assignments are spelled out partly in the contracts, partly in the vendor relations manual, and partly in the conferences and other communications between the parties.

In modern products some innocent looking tasks turn out to be quite demanding, e.g., those associated with achieving reliability. These tasks should be clearly defined, and should be clearly assigned as to responsibility, before the contract is signed.

Definition of Responsibility: Within Buyer.[41]   Responsibilities within the buying organization are often more difficult to straighten out than those between buyer and vendor.   Table 10-2 shows a typical assignment of some common responsibilities.   In practice, this needs to be expanded to cover greater detail.

Documentation and Reporting.   In many contracts the vendor is required to provide documented proof that the product conforms to specification and is fit for use. (The buyer uses these proofs in lieu of incoming inspection of the product.)

Achieving this compatibility requires that a whole array of details be made compatible, details such as designs of forms, code numbers for defects, seriousness classification, data processing systems, key aspects of terminology, target dates for reports, computer programs, and still other aspects of systems and procedures.

All this compatibility is used for other essential purposes as well, e.g., data feedback, quality certifications, audits.

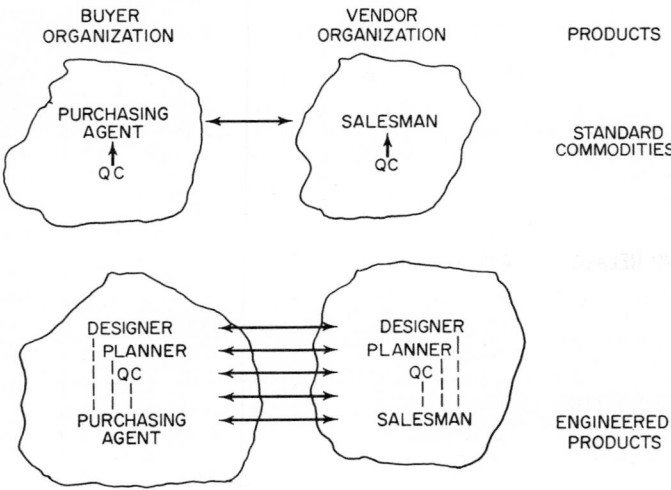

Fig. 10-3.   Vendor communication channels.

Multiple Communication Channels   The need for multiple forms of joint planning can be met only by setting up multiple channels of communication: designers must communicate directly with designers, quality specialists with quality specialists, etc.   These multiple channels are a drastic departure from the single channel, which is the method in common use for purchase of traditional products.   (See Figure 10-3.)   The multiple channels also create a risk of confusion unless coordination is provided.   One form of such coordination is to provide Purchasing and Sales with copies of all letters, minutes, etc.   However, in many cases this is not enough and needs to be supplemented with conferences at which men from the key departments of both companies are present.   It is easier to arrive at necessary understandings and trade-offs through such conferences than through detached channels alone.

---

[41] Obviously, the vendor also has internal organization problems.   These are discussed in Sections 14 and 15.

Experience in such conferences has shown that even the coordination within the individual companies is improved as well.[42]

In complex contracts the systems of procedures become correspondingly complex, requiring flow diagrams and special provisions to assure good lines of communication.[43]

A further need may be to create special coordination forms to supplement the work of the regular departments. An example is the creation of a Procurement Review Team (PRT) to coordinate requests for quotations and selection of sources. Such a team consists of members from Purchasing, Design, and Quality Control.[44]

A useful by-product of formalizing these organization structures is legitimacy. The change from a single channel to multiple channels is especially troublesome, and it is essential that the new arrangement have top management backing.

Media for Written Plans   When the parties reduce their planning to written contracts, there are several ways of putting the quality planning into the official documents:

1. Write the provisions into the purchase order
2. Incorporate some provisions, e.g., seriousness classification of characteristics, into the product specifications
3. Prepare a separate quality/reliability specification, and reference this into the purchase orders
4. Include some quality provisions (e.g., incoming inspection procedures) in a Vendor Relations Manual, and reference this manual in the purchase order

Of the foregoing methods, numbers 1 and 2 are applicable for specific products, whereas 3 and 4 are more convenient for application to many products.

THE VENDOR RELATIONS MANUAL

The manual follows the general principles applicable to any quality manual (see Section 6, under The Quality Control Manual), but these are specially tailored to the needs of vendor relations.

Typically, the contents include:

1. A statement or preamble dealing with the company's quality policies and with vendor relations generally.
2. A description of the company's operations and the role played by product quality.
3. The general plan of organization with respect to quality and especially the role of the key vendor relations departments, usually Purchasing and Quality Control. The duties of specific categories of employees are sometimes set out in detail to help the vendor understand what he can expect from whom.
4. An explanation of the nature of the company's quality specifications, standards, and other means of expressing the product requirements, including seriousness classification.
5. Copies of the sampling plans, AQLs, and other criteria used by the buyer.
6. Copies of the quality data and report forms used by the buyer.

---

[42] See, in this connection, Cook, Lawrence E., The Quality Assurance Pre-Production Conference, *Industrial Quality Control,* February 1966, pp. 408–411. Aside from listing the topics to be discussed in such conferences, Cook also discusses the method of conducting such conferences.

[43] See Langille, Noble A., Quality Assurance Procedures for Purchasing, *Quality Assurance,* June 1968, pp. 24–28.

[44] See von Osinski, Ralph, A Team Approach to Buying, *Quality Assurance,* June 1967, pp. 40–42.

7. Explanation of the buyer's plan of vendor surveys.
8. Actions expected of the vendor (these may be listed as instructions or as recommendations):

Submission of samples
Preparation of quality plans
Specific inspection and test programs needed
Specific reliability programs needed
Procedure to be used for disposition of nonconforming material
Records and reports to be kept
Procedure for making engineering changes effective

9. A glossary of the terms used by the buyer.
Publication of the manual (or a revision) is commonly an occasion for holding seminars for vendors to explain the manual and to provide other indoctrination.

TWO-WAY COMMUNICATION

With the end of the planning stage there arises a need for providing continual two-way communication during the execution of the contract. The purpose of this communication is to supply essential information, provide performance data, identify troubles which arise, stimulate corrective action, and improve the ability of the parties to work together.

Design Information and Changes   The vendor needs the design information referenced in the contract as well as the related standards, seriousness classifications, and other matters which contribute to understanding the meaning and significance of the designs. Industry has made great strides in learning how to communicate design information at the beginning of the contract. However, the record in communicating subsequent design changes is less impressive.

Design changes may take place either at the initiative of the buyer or the vendor. Either way, there is need to treat the vendor like an in-house department in the procedures for processing design changes and in configuration control (see Section 19). This need is especially acute for modern products, where design changes can affect products, processes, tools, instruments, stored materials, procedures, etc. Some of these effects are obvious, but others are subtle, requiring the opportunity for complete analysis to identify the effects. Failure to provide adequate design change information to vendors has been a distinct obstacle to good vendor relations.

Deviations   During the performance of the contract, the parties observe deviations from product, process, or procedural standards. It is essential that both parties be made aware of these deviations promptly so that they can bring their joint efforts to bear for solving the resulting problems.

Product Nonconformance.   These cases may be discovered at the vendor's plant by the vendor's inspectors or by resident buyer's inspectors. Alternatively, they may be discovered at the buyer's plant during incoming inspection.[45] Either way they tend to be well communicated since the effects are dramatic: delays in shipment, congestion of space, added costs to be absorbed, etc.

Process Nonconformance.   These cases are less dramatic than cases of product nonconformance because of confusion of process with product tolerances and confusion in the process tolerances themselves; i.e., are they advisory or are they mandatory? (For a detailed discussion, see Section 11, under Knowledge of "Supposed to Do": Process Specifications.) The fact that these confusions exist makes it neces-

---

[45] See Section 12, under Inspection at Inspection Stations: Incoming Inspection.

sary that the buyer and vendor establish clear rules as to which cases of process nonconformance are to be "written up" and communicated. Failing this, some instances of process nonconformance will not be communicated because they do not result in product nonconformance or in unfitness for use.

Procedural Nonconformance. Where the vendor is held responsible for providing proof that the product conforms to specification, this proof includes evidence of adherence to procedure. Since the buyer relies on these proofs, any departures from procedure should also be communicated to the buyer. In practice, the buyer must audit the adherence to procedure, as there are many departures which do not result in product nonconformance.

Product Unfitness for Use. These cases may be discovered through product testing, Material Review Board decisions, field complaints, service calls, returns, etc. The impact on the manufacturer is direct and severe, since the very ability to sell the product is jeopardized. Despite the importance of these feedbacks, the manufacturer may have difficulty in relaying the necessary alarm signals to the vendor. Some of this difficulty is technological; i.e., there are problems in securing adequate field data and in working out the data processing needed to separate out the information required by the various vendors. However, some of the inadequacies in communication have been due to lack of buyer awareness of the usefulness of good feedback to the vendors.

Corrective Action   The feedback loop to secure vendor corrective action requires some special emphasis due to the independent status of the vendor. Since any notification of nonconformance becomes a "complaint" to the vendor, the validity of the nonconformance should be verified. In addition, communication to the vendor must include precise description of the defects. The best description is in the form of samples given to the vendor. If samples cannot conveniently be sent, the vendor should have the opportunity to visit the site of the trouble.

The vendor should be notified promptly of all nonconformance cases, whether accepted as fit for use or not. Industrial practice is to do this in writing, using serially numbered deviation reports. (Phone calls may be added to gain time.) The notification includes the buyer's test data, the extent to which the deviation exists on the product, the theories of causes, the likely remedy, etc. The written notification is also logged on a running report, providing follow up to assure that corrective action will be taken.

Beyond the problems of corrective action, there are numerous related questions: What disposition is to be made of the defectives? Who will sort or repair? Who will pay the costs? What were the causes? What steps are needed to avoid a recurrence? These questions are outside the scope of pure defect detection; they require joint discussion among departments within each company and further joint discussions between buyer and vendor. On modern products it is no longer feasible to settle these matters through the single communication link of purchasing agent and salesman. Instead, resort is had to conferences attended by those who can make the main contribution to the problem at hand.

In important contracts it is good practice to schedule monthly (or so) meetings, attended by the key departments (Purchasing, Engineering, Quality Control) in both companies, to review progress and deficiencies. Such meetings develop a good deal of skill in securing corrective action. For other contracts, these meetings are held under the exception principle.[46]

---

[46] See, for example, Maass, Richard A., The Point of Control Is the Supplier's Plant, *Quality Assurance*, February 1967, pp. 18–21.

Records and Reports   Design of records and reports needed to provide adequate communication is largely governed by the principles and techniques set out in Section 19.   Several matters of special emphasis for vendor relations include the following:

1. For each part number, a file or "dossier" is created to hold the specifications, engineering change information, inspection instructions, and other information pertinent to that part number.   In addition, for each vendor supplying that part number, a file is set up to accumulate the correspondence and the performance data.   This includes results of qualification testing; field performance complaints; cases of nonconformance; decisions of material review boards; results of source or incoming inspection; summaries of data, e.g., process averages, control charts, etc.; and surveillance report items.

2. The data processing system is set up to provide summaries in various forms:

Trends of quality of individual components which involve high costs or critical quality characteristics

Listing of highest loss components to help establish priority of projects for corrective action and improvement

Summary of vendor performance by percent of lots rejected, loss due to defects, and other forms needed for the periodic vendor quality rating

Data processing follows the general procedures set out in Section 20, and executive-type reports are designed in accordance with the principles discussed in Section 21.

"Positive" Communication   It is a widespread practice for buyers to communicate to vendors the data evidencing nonconformance, unfitness for use, and other troubles encountered.   In contrast, it is a rather limited practice to communicate product data when the situation is trouble-free.   However, when communication from buyer to vendor is limited to reports of a negative nature, the atmosphere for constructive improvement can also become negative.   There is awareness of this problem, and there are ways of dealing with it:

1. Broaden the communication to include the positive; i.e., when performance is good, say so.   Letters of praise are rare enough to be conversation pieces.[47]

2. Create face-to-face meetings.   Such meetings (conferences, clinics, etc.) need not be limited to instances of failure.   They can be broadened to discuss positive results, to show the vendor the conditions of use, and otherwise to improve the climate of relationship.

3. Create systematic awards, e.g., Vendor of the Month.   Such awards receive considerable attention from vendors, who display them prominently and publicize them in the trade journals as well as in the house organs.

4. Create joint programs for improvement of chronic troubles.   (See below, under Vendor Quality Improvement: Mutual Assistance.

As the communications are broadened, there is greater likelihood that the vendor will move from a purely defensive posture to one of making constructive proposals. In those cases where the vendor is the giant and the buyer is small, the vendor's capability can be most helpful to the buyer.

The limited use of positive communication is partly due to unawareness of the opportunities presented (see, for example, Audit of Decisions, below).   In other cases the opportunities are known but there are serious technological limitations due to differences in "dialect."   The buyer creates his own defect code numbers,

---

[47] See, for example, Simons, R. W., Letters to the Editor, *Industrial Quality Control,* August 1965, p. 50.

chart of accounts, etc., and locks all this into his forms, procedures, and computer. The vendor, who deals with numerous buyers, has his own language yet faces the job of communicating with numerous buyers using polyglot dialects.   Industry standardization can help a lot to reduce these language problems.[48]   However, until the day when such industry solutions are complete, the standardization must come from the initiative of individual companies.[49]

PROOF OF CONFORMANCE

Buyers secure their assurance of product conformance and of fitness for use in a variety of ways:

Reliance Solely on the Vendor.   This form is in wide use for very small purchases, for purchase of standard materials, for purchase of goods not used in the product, e.g., office furniture.   The assurance is secured during the subsequent processing or use of the product.

Incoming Inspection.   This inspection is conducted, at the buyer's premises, upon receipt of the product from the vendor.   The approach is described in detail in Section 12, under Inspection at Inspection Stations.

Duplicate Samples.   Under this method the vendor selects the samples for the buyer in accordance with a prearranged selection plan.   These samples are identified as to the lots from which they are drawn, the order of manufacture being preserved, e.g., samples from a heat of steel.   The samples may be sent to the buyer to arrive in advance of the main shipment.

Under this method, the buyer first goes through a phase of convincing himself that tests of these duplicate samples correlate with tests of samples taken independently from the same lot.   Once this confidence is established, the buyer avoids sampling the lots at incoming inspection and may in due course adopt an "Audit of Decisions" (see below).

Source Inspection.   In some contracts the "incoming inspection" is conducted by the buyer *at the vendor's plant.*   This form is known as "source inspection."

Source inspection requires inspection planning and related techniques as discussed at length in Section 12, under Inspection Planning.   However, the fact that two independent companies are involved puts added requirements on formality of documentation and on communication.[50]   Some techniques originally evolved for use in vendor relations, e.g., lot plot sampling,[51] have found their way into general use for any type of inspection.

Vendor Surveillance.   (See below.)

Audit of Decisions.   (See below.)

Unless provision is made for the use of information derived from the vendor's operations (e.g., process capability, preserving the order, duplicate samples, vendor test results), the buyer has no proof of conformance beyond that derived from incoming inspection.   In that event, the extent of sampling needed at incoming inspection is determined by the laws of probability governing random sampling and by the limiting AQLs or other statistical limits established.   The resulting sample sizes can be formidable.

[48] See Section 30, under Quality Performance Feedback, for an example of an industry-generated feedback device (roll card).

[49] See, for example, von Osinski, Ralph, Get the Message to the Supplier, *Quality Assurance,* June 1967, pp. 33–35.

[50] See, for example, Swaton, L., and W. Weaver, Five Steps to Supplier Quality Control, *Industrial Quality Control,* May 1966, pp. 611–616.

[51] See Section 25.

VENDOR SURVEILLANCE

Contracts which place full quality responsibility on the vendor also require the vendor to present (1) a suitable plan for controlling quality and (2) proof that the plan has been followed.

These same contracts also permit the buyer to exercise a "surveillance"[52] over all the activities carried out by the vendor to achieve conformance to specification and fitness for use. In consequence, the surveillance includes procedural, process, and product audits as well as any inspection conducted by the buyer.

For many contracts, the buyer exercises this surveillance through periodic visits to the vendor's plant. In large contracts, it is usual for the buyer to maintain a resident auditor at the vendor's plant to provide for a continuing surveillance. This same auditor may also conduct any necessary source inspection, though this is not universal.

When well carried out, vendor surveillance can provide the buyer (and the vendor) with early warning of problems prior to product nonconformance or unfitness for use. However, attaining this goal has been difficult in practice because surveillance is difficult to administer to the satisfaction of both parties. These difficulties do not arise when critical or major defects are present, since neither party will tolerate unfitness for use. Instead, the difficulties arise due to:

1. Minor defects which have little or no effect on fitness for use
2. Vague delegation of responsibility to the buyer's resident auditor
3. Documentation requirements which do not affect fitness for use but do affect the state of proof needed by the buyer (in lieu of incoming inspection)

In the case of (1) and (2), it helps a good deal to classify the defects as to seriousness.[53] Once the classification is made, there are ways of providing different degrees of tolerance for different classes; e.g., the AQLs and acceptance numbers can be graduated to the severity of the defects. In addition, the delegation given to the resident inspectors can be made fairly broad on noncritical matters, permitting local granting of deviations without the need of a formal appeal process to higher levels. Finally, the entire surveillance process is aided by providing clear and prompt channels for appeal on those matters which the resident inspector has no authority to waive.

The documentation problem (3) is more subtle. There is not only an obvious need to provide the buyer with proof of product adequacy but also a hidden need to provide *personal* protection to the resident inspectors and others in the buyer's organization in the event of future troubles and investigations. An example of such need for personal protection is seen in the problem of certificates of compliance. (See below, under Certification.)

A good deal has been done by the government buyers to define the role of the resident inspector and to give him detailed instructions. "Quality and Reliability Assurance Handbook H 50"[54] spells out how to evaluate the contractor's quality program to see if it conforms to the provisions of MIL-Q-9858A. A related "Quality and Reliability Assurance Handbook H 57"[55] spells out how to perform reviews, evalua-

---

[52] Surveillance parallels closely the Audit of Execution versus Plans, as described in Section 21. However, in vendor relations there may be added features, e.g., a sampling validation of the reports prepared by vendors; a retest of product to establish the integrity of testing. Collectively, these and related efforts are sometimes called "source control." See, for example, Braun, S., Verify Before You Buy, *Quality Assurance,* September 1968, pp. 22–25.

[53] See Section 12, under Seriousness Classification.

[54,55] Available from Superintendents of Documents, U.S. Government Printing Office, Washington, D.C. 20402.

tions, verifications, etc., during the progress of the contract. This is done in considerable detail, including forms to be executed, records to be kept, etc.

The documentation problem can be aggravated or simplified depending on the method followed in reporting on deficiencies in documentation. In those cases where each deficiency is treated as a "federal case," even when fitness for use is not involved, the reporting will become a source of abrasion between the companies. (Surveyors who are attached to operating divisions tend to stress fitness for use. However, surveyors who are not attached to operating divisions tend to stress everything.) What must be realized is that documentation in surveillance systems is a form of proof to the buyer. A deficiency in documentation is an incompleteness in the proof but not necessarily a deficiency in the product.

A related problem in documentation arises when the vendor is organized to rely on "men rather than system." In many cultures the tradition is one of lifelong employment with the same company. Companies following such tradition tend to structure their quality assurance programs around the experience, integrity, and memory of trusted long-service employees, since these same employees will continue to be available, year after year, to carry out the programs. As a corollary, these companies have minimal need for establishing the systems of records and documentation essential to organizations which operate with high employee turnover, or which prefer to rely on "systems rather than men." When these same companies attempt to negotiate for contracts under the rules established by the American aerospace or defense industries, their reaction is that the demands for documentation are fantastic, and are largely unnecessary for achieving fitness for use. In such situations, negotiations are greatly simplified if the parties can be made aware that their differences arise from a clash between two cultures rather than from any differences in dedication toward product fitness for use.

It is useful to design the surveillance reports in a way which separates the vital few matters (affecting fitness for use) from the residue, which represents a form of nonconformance to some specification. Top management attention should be directed primarily to matters of fitness for use and to the adequacy of the *systems* (of documentation, etc.).

Some vendors minimize the problem by setting up to conduct their own surveillance. Through this means they reduce the incidence of deviations. One result is that surveillance by the buyer tends to be tapered off, since buyers concentrate their surveillance effort on the most troublesome areas.

CERTIFICATION

There are a number of forms of "certificate" and "certification" used in vendor relations.[56] These words have multiple meanings, and some of these meanings differ widely from others, resulting in extensive confusion.

Certificates   There are several forms of these:

Certificate of Test.   This term is used in the sense of *evidence that testing was done.* The evidence is embodied in a formal document called a "certificate of test." This document, issued by a test laboratory, states that certain product was tested for certain qualities. The product is identified by description, amount, lot number, etc. The test data are given, along with the conclusion on conformance or nonconformance to specification. The document is signed by a designated official.[57]

The laboratory may be an independent test laboratory or a captive laboratory,

[56] For discussion on forms of certification used in marketing, see Section 14, under Labeling.
[57] For details of the document design, see Poulos, Thomas T., Producing Certifications, *Industrial Quality Control,* February 1965, pp. 393–395.

i.e., the vendor's laboratory. (There are many situations in which recourse is had to an independent test laboratory.)

The distinguishing characteristic of the certificate of test is the objective evidence it presents—data which are the result of positive, reproducible tests[58] taken to determine the quality of the product.

Certificate of Compliance. This is an assertion that product complies to specification. The assertion is contained in a document called a "certificate of compliance." A typical wording is: "To whom it may concern: This certifies that to the best of our knowledge the material delivered under this contract is in accord with the terms of the contract." The document makes no clear identification of the product, makes no statement that tests were conducted, provides no test data. The certificates are often preprinted, including signatures, to serve as an inexpensive way of complying with the wishes of a customer who insists on having them.

One vendor conducted a study of prevailing practice with respect to certificates of compliance and concluded that they were unnecessary and redundant, though requiring a good deal of effort. He then demonstrated to the customer's inspector that the regular shipping documents said the same thing, and he succeeded in getting the certificates discontinued.[59] The certificate of compliance gives no added protection to the *organization* receiving it, though it may make the *person* requesting it feel he is better protected.

Implied Certificate. The very act of shipping product in response to a contract is an implied form of certification that the goods comply to specification. So the courts have held for centuries, and they are still holding that way.[60]

Vendor Certification This term also has multiple uses, chiefly:

1. As a synonym for vendor qualification, i.e., putting the vendor on the list of approved vendors. In some companies the formalizing of this act includes sending the vendor a document, i.e., a certificate, to attest to the fact that the vendor has reached the state of qualification described in the document.[61]

2. To designate the process used in formalizing a vendor contract which embodies seriousness classifications of defects, sampling plans, provision for disposition of defects, etc. The process is also known as "Quality Level Certification," from the title of the Ford Motor Company booklet on the subject (1951).[62]

Personnel Certification. This refers to the common practice of requiring that vendor (or other) personnel performing critical operations, e.g., welding critical to human safety, should first undergo a course of training and pass a qualifying examination. A certificate of qualification is issued as part of the formal procedure. (See Section 17, under Production Operators.)

[58] It is fundamental that buyer and vendor must agree fully on what is to be the test method.

[59] Wylie, P. A., and D. E. Lewis, That Eternal Certificate of Compliance, *Quality Assurance,* November 1968, pp. 44 and 45. As part of the same study, provision was made to give necessary test data and better material identification to the customer.

[60] Juran, J. M., Vendor Relations—An Overview, *Quality Progress,* July 1968, p. 16. See also Sherman, W. A., Certification—A Tower of Babel? *Industrial Quality Control,* August 1966, pp. 72–75. Sherman distinguishes between (1) implicit certification through product delivery and (2) explicit certification through documentation. He further divides (2) as between *(a)* lack of objective quality evidence, i.e., "Whatever it was you asked for, we gave it to you," and *(b)* presence of objective quality evidence.

[61] See, for example, Pianin, A., Hamilton Standard Guides Purchased Goods Quality in Vendor Plants, *Quality Assurance,* October 1965, pp. 34 and 35.

[62] See, for example, Wintermute, D. V., Certified Suppliers Key IBM Long Term Cost Reduction, *Quality Assurance,* October 1965, pp. 32 and 33.

Note by the Editor (Juran): Ford Motor Company was evidently the first major industrial company to put such agreements into the formal contract. See Smith, W. H., Problems of Receiving Inspection and the Assembly Line, *Industrial Quality Control,* March 1951, pp. 8–14.

Lot Certification.   This refers to the process of associating homogeneous lots with certificates of test so that multiple buyers are spared the expense of testing.   An old application of this is the use of heat numbers in the metals industry.   A more recent application is in centralized testing of electronic parts.   In some European countries this is done on a national scale.[63]

AUDIT OF DECISIONS

A buyer who receives vendor's test data has an opportunity to eliminate his own incoming inspection through use of the concept of the "audit of decisions." Under the concept, the following sequence of events takes place:

1. Along with his product shipments, the vendor arranges to transmit his test data.

2. The buyer performs a lot-by-lot incoming inspection on the product and compares his test data with the vendor's test data to determine if the vendor's laboratory can be relied on to make good product conformance decisions.

3. As the buyer develops confidence in the vendor's laboratory, the buyer stops making lot-by-lot incoming inspections.   Instead, he accepts the test results of the vendor as valid.   However, the buyer initiates a periodic check (every tenth lot or so) to verify that the vendor's laboratory continues to make good product acceptance decisions.   It is this periodic check which constitutes the audit of decisions.

Figure 10-4 shows in simplified graphic form how the concept operates.   Comparative data for the first six lots has established the following:

1. The vendor has a process which is capable of holding the tolerances.

2. The lot-to-lot variability of the vendor's process is low enough to avoid jeopardizing product conformance through inherent variation.

3. The vendor's laboratory gives results which are a sound basis for decision making.

4. There is an unexplained, consistent difference in test procedures, the vendor's test being the more severe.

Under these circumstances, the buyer begins to rely on the vendor's laboratory at lot number 7.   He then progressively increases this reliance by reducing his own testing further and further until he has converted to full audit of decisions.   This constitutes a drastic change in philosophy of testing.   At the outset, the purpose of testing was to determine "Is the product good or bad?"   Any information about the vendor's laboratory was incidental.   At the final stage, the purpose of the buyer's testing is to determine "Does the vendor's laboratory continue to make good decisions?"   Any information about the product is incidental.

Companies that contemplate use of the concept of audit of decisions always are concerned about what to do when the audit check shows a failure by the vendor's laboratory.   Usually these companies insist that means be set up for tracing the identity of all lots not tested by the buyer since the previous audit check.   This is quite a sensible requirement, and calls for joint planning that will establish clear lot identification and traceability.[64]

---

[63] Clavier, M., A Centralized System of Acceptance Control of Electronic Parts on a National Scale, *Bulletin de l'AFCIQ,* October 1960, pp. 63-78 (in French).   See also Section 38, under Testing and Inspection: Acceptance by Certification, and especially the reference to British Standard 9000.

[64] Plans which compare test data from two laboratories also encounter the statistical problems of significance.   See Section 13, under Error of Measurement, Interlaboratory Test Program.   See also Goldman, George E., Verification and Food Processing, *Food Quality Control,* September 1965, Food and Allied Industries Division, ASQC.

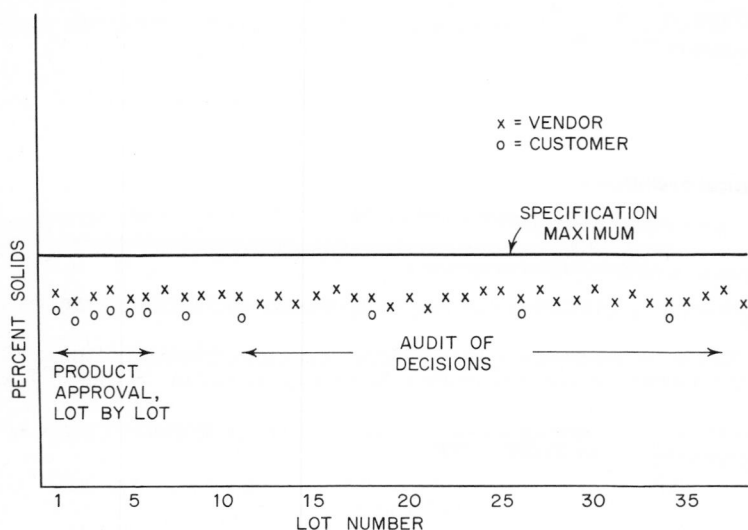

Fig. 10-4.   Concept of audit of decisions.

A variation of the concept of audit of decisions is the provision, in many sampling schemes, that the prior record of the vendor should influence the size of the sample. This prior record may be the process average, the percent of lots accepted, the vendor rating, or some other form of categorization.[65]

Use of the concept of audit of decisions requires that the vendor supply his test data to the buyer on a continuing basis. In very simple cases such as shown in Figure 10-4, the vendor commonly does this upon request by the buyer. However, many cases are not so simple, involving frequency distributions, control charts, computer printouts, etc. As a result, some vendors make a charge for the copies of the data, especially if the buyer wants these data specially processed to serve his needs. In other cases, e.g., a large vendor selling a small order to a buyer, the vendor may resist the request altogether. In still other cases, the vendor takes the initiative and supplies the data automatically as a selling device, i.e., he hopes to enlist the support of the buyer's technical and quality control people. An early example was that of Hunter Spring Company, which initiated the practice of supplying the frequency distributions of tests on lots of springs to their customers in the early 1940s. This practice may be on the increase.[66]

VENDOR QUALITY IMPROVEMENT: MUTUAL ASSISTANCE

The general approach to quality improvement (Section 16) applies fully to improvement of vendor quality. However, there are several tools or concepts which have special significance:

[65] See, for an example, Klontz, Walter C., How the Inspector/Tester Can Maximize the Use of Vendor Piece Part History or Vendor-Furnished Data, *Eighth Annual Western Regional Conference,* ASQC, March 1961.

[66] See, for example, Quality Certification System —At No Charge, *Quality Management & Engineering,* April 1971, pp. 26–27.

Identifying Chronic Troubles Beyond the problems posed by individual lots, there is the added important problem of dealing with "repeaters." These are cases in which the same problem comes up over and over again, suggesting that the cause is not a repeated error or blunder but rather a basic deficiency in the design, process, system, etc.

Some notorious chronic troubles are well known to the parties because of their frequency and severity. Others are not well known or are not agreed on. For these, the need is to establish their presence through the data system. A simple data system is the matrix which lists successive lots horizontally and defect types vertically. See Section 19, Figure 19-10c for an example.

Once identified and placed on the priority list for solution, the approach needed is that of "quality improvement" using the methods discussed below and in Section 16.

Pareto Analysis Numerous vendor improvement programs have failed because the vital few problems were not identified. Instead, the programs consisted of broad attempts to tighten up all procedures. However, there are also some difficulties in just how to conduct the Pareto analysis[67] in order to search out the vital few projects. Instances of notorious specific components are easy. So are cases of individual vendors with shocking records. Beyond these (usually) self-evident cases, the Pareto analysis may take any of a number of forms:

1. Analysis of losses (or defects, lot rejections, etc.) by material number or *part number*. Such analysis serves a useful purpose as applied to catalog numbers involving substantial or frequent purchases. See, for example, Section 38, Figure 38-7 and associated explanation.

2. Analysis of losses by *product family*. This identifies the vital few product families present in small but numerous purchases of common product families, e.g., bearings, resistors, paints.

3. Analysis of losses by *process*, i.e., classifying the defects or lot rejections in terms of the process to which they relate, e.g., plating, swaging, winding, etc.

4. Analysis by *vendor* across the entire spectrum of purchases. This can help to identify weaknesses in the vendor's managerial approach as contrasted to the technological, which more usually is correlated with products and processes.[68]

5. Analysis by *cost* of the parts. In one company, 37% of the part numbers purchased accounted for only 5% of the total dollar volume of purchases, but for a much higher percent of the total incoming inspection cost. The conclusion was that these "trivial many" parts should be purchased from the very best vendors, even at top prices. The alternative of relying on incoming inspection would be even more costly.[69]

6. Analysis by *failure family*. This sophisticated technique is used to discover major defects in the management *system*. For example, Material Review Board studies disclose multiple instances of working to the wrong issue of the specification. In such cases, the *system* used for configuration control should be reexamined. If value analysis discovers multiple instances of overspecification, the design *procedures* for choosing components should be reexamined, etc. These analyses by

---

[67] For a detailed discussion, see Section 2, under the Pareto Principle.

[68] In one company there were 222 vendors on the active list. Of these, 38 (or 17%) accounted for 53% of the lot rejections and 45% of the bad parts.

In a large aerospace company employing about 4,000 vendors, the worst 16 vendors contributed 50% of the defective lots.

(Private communication to J. M. Juran.)

[69] Private communication to J. M. Juran.

failure family are a vital means of discovering how the buyer is contributing to his own problems.[70]

Organization for Improvement   The need is for a joint approach.   Some companies make use of the monthly conference attended by the key departments (usually Purchasing, Design, and Quality Control) of both buyer and vendor.   In other cases teams are formed to conduct the analyses for specific projects.   In still other cases the buyer assigns an engineer to make periodic visits to the vendor's facility.[71] The tools used include:

Value Analysis.   This technique (see Section 16) originated in the purchasing area and has very likely reached its highest development there.   However, it is doubtful that enough use is being made of the technical know-how of vendors.[72]

Life Cycle Costing.   For long-life products, this technique may well contain the greatest single potential for reducing cost of usage.   See Section 4, under Life Cycle Costing.

Audit of Decisions.   This concept, along with preserving the order, has great potentiality for reducing the cost of vendor inspection and testing.   See above.

Mutual Assistance   The main vendor quality problems are intercompany in nature and can therefore best be solved by joint analysis and action rather than separately. Each of the parties has experience and know-how, both in management and technology, which can be of aid in the problem at hand.   These aids may consist of such matters as:

Access to experts in the technological specialty which underlies the problem
Equipment and instrumentation of a special character
Experience in solving similar problems with other buyers or vendors
Expertise in problem solving generally

The fact that the parties are independent companies requires that care be used in the conduct of mutual assistance.   The activity should be problem-oriented and should, as far as possible, be depersonalized; i.e., one *person* should not give advice to another *person*.   Instead, both should pool their knowledge for problem solving. Any consulting relationship should be by invitation and not by imposition.   In like manner, if a buyer has embarked on an improvement program in his own factories and wishes to extend this into vendor factories, this extension should be voluntary on the part of the vendor.   (See, in this connection, Section 18, under The Formal Motivation Program; Extension to Include Vendors.)

VENDOR QUALITY RATING

"Rating" of quality of work done by the vendor involves a number of very different concepts.   These include component rating, lot rating, and vendor rating.   Table

---

[70] Even more difficult is the identification of axiomatic beliefs which are nevertheless invalid.   One successful program of vendor quality improvement used the following major tools: Pareto analysis, improved feedback to vendors, technical assistance.   Included also was the denial of an axiomatic belief among vendors that their prime problem was operator-controllable defects.   See Maass, Richard A., Remember 200K?   Would You Believe 529K?   *Quality Assurance,* October 1970, pp. 24–27.

[71] See, for example, Ozasa, M., Technical Guidance to a Material Supplier, *Reports of Statistical Application Research,* Japanese Union of Scientists and Engineers, vol. 6, no. 3, 1959, pp. 30–43.

[72] A survey of vendors of electronic components yielded 18 suggestions.   Of these, 5 were to the effect that buyers were overspecifying; 4 were to the effect that buyers were not making full use of vendors' product knowledge.   See Mistakes to Avoid When Evaluating and Selecting Capacitor Vendors, *Evaluation Engineering,* May/June 1967, p. 47.

10-3 shows the purposes served by these various ratings along with the methods in use for arriving at the ratings. It is seen from Table 10-3 that "vendor quality rating" is a broad assessment of vendor quality performance and is used to assist in making decisions of the broadest nature, e.g., whether or not to continue to do business with this vendor.

Measures in Use Vendor quality rating plans are based on one or more of the following measures:

1. *Product Percent Defective.* In this plan the lot-by-lot data on pieces received and on pieces defective are summarized to give the monthly or quarterly percent defective. A variation of this is to use a six-month moving average, adding the newest month's data while dropping off the oldest month.[73]

An alternative plan is to create an adjective rating which is a composite of *(a)* the quantitative percent defective and *(b)* the estimated complexity of the product class.

2. *Percent Defective versus AQL.* In this plan the basic calculation is made by the formula:

$$LC = \text{lot calculation} = \frac{p - p'}{p'(100 - p') \div n} \tag{1}$$

where p = actual percent defective of the product
p' = AQL percent
n = sample size

Since the formula gives awkward numbers to work with, a modification such as this is made:

$$LR = \text{lot rating} = K_1 - K_2(LC) \tag{2}$$

where K_1 and K_2 are constants chosen to yield more comfortable numbers to work with. In the original Bendix[74] plan, K_1 was 70 and K_2 was 10. (In consequence, a lot with percent defective equal to AQL received a score of 70.)

The lot ratings can then be combined into a composite vendor rating (VR) by a formula such as:

$$VR = K_1 + \left(\frac{\sum LR}{N} - K_1 \right) \sqrt{N} \tag{3}$$

where N = number of lots in the composite

Another form used for relating percent defective to AQL is to use a direct ratio and then to add an empirical scale such that 0% defective yields a rating of 100, while a percent defective equal to AQL has a rating of (say) 70.

3. *Effect on Inspection Costs.* Here the vendor quality rating (VQR) consists of:

$$VQR = \frac{\text{desired cost of inspection}}{\text{actual cost of inspection}} \, 100 \tag{4}$$

The desired cost is the cost based on normal sampling and approval of acceptable product. The plan was developed for use at one of the IBM divisions.[75] A variation

[73] Gilmore, Harold L., and Laurent Paquin, Vendor Rating for Missile Reliability, *Industrial Quality Control,* September 1963, pp. 13–16.

[74] Fitzgibbons, Robert G., The Bendix Radio Vendor Quality Rating System, *Industrial Quality Control,* May 1955, pp. 38–42. See also, for some elaboration on this scheme, Duncan, Acheson J., and Robert G. Fitzgibbons, Further Comments on the Bendix Vendor Quality Rating System, *Industrial Quality Control,* July 1965, pp. 21 and 22.

[75] Nickel, Kenneth W., Quality Costs as a Method for Rating Vendors, *ASQC Convention Transactions,* 1962, pp. 95–103.

TABLE 10-3   Various Types of Rating of Vendor Quality

Rating	Purpose	Units of measure	Typical inputs and usual source	Principally used by	Examples of decisions
Vendor	To assist in making decisions on broad relations with vendors	Summaries and indexes: percent of lots accepted, percent of deliveries late, total of excess costs due to defects.	Data summaries from data processing center	Managers of Purchasing, Quality Control	Increase vendor's share of business, hold conference to discuss status, remove from approved list
Lot	To assist in disposition of lots of product	Various: % defective, degree of conformance, cost to sort, fitness for use	Inspection data from Incoming Inspection	Quality Control supervisors; Material Review Board	Accept, sort, reject
Component	To aid designers and other technical specialists in product design, test, etc.	Technological: tensile strength, MTBF, etc.	Test data from qualification laboratories	Designers, reliability engineers, quality control engineers	Specify (or do not specify) the component

is to use inspection hours,[76] i.e.:

$$VQR = \frac{\text{inspection hours for accepted lots}}{\text{total inspection hours}} 100 \tag{5}$$

4. *Weighted Disposition of Material.* A number of plans are based on the fact that the material submitted may have undergone any of a number of dispositions: completely conforming and accepted, nonconforming but with prior waiver, nonconforming but accepted by Material Review Board, nonconforming but reworked, nonusable and returned to vendor, etc. Each of these categories is assigned an arbitrary number of demerits which then becomes the lot rating for each lot in that category. The vendor rating becomes the composite of the ratings of his lots.[77]

Composite Rating Plans   Vendor performance is, of course, not limited to quality. It includes delivery against schedule, price (or effective price), and still other performance categories. These multiple needs suggest that vendor rating should include overall vendor performance rather than just vendor quality performance. The Purchasing Department is a strong advocate of this principle and has valid grounds for this advocacy.

The purchasing people have themselves been active in creating vendor rating plans which embody these multiple performances of the vendor. The National Association of Purchasing Agents has published[78] three alternative plans:

1. *Categorical Plan.* This is a nonquantitative evaluation. The buyers meet monthly and rate the vendors as plus, neutral, or minus.

2. *Weighted Point Plan.* The three principal vendor performances are rated in accordance with following plan:

Factor	Unit of measure	Weight
Quality	Percent of lots accepted	40
Cost	Low price ÷ actual price	35
Service	Percent of promises kept	25

3. *Cost-Ratio Plan.* This plan compares vendors on the total dollar cost for a specific purchase. Total costs includes quoted price plus quality costs, delivery costs, and service costs. The final rating[79] is in terms of "net value cost."

The extensive literature on vendor quality rating schemes makes clear that differences in products and in purchasing patterns require differences in rating plans. For products whose qualities are clearly identified at incoming inspection, a plan based on summarizing results of incoming inspection is adequate. For purchased components which create substantial excess processing costs, the plan should reflect the existence of these costs. For purchased components which affect the buyer's warranty and service costs, the vendor rating plan should (ideally) reflect these field troubles as well.

Because the plans must be tailor-made, it is important to clarify the purposes intended to be served by the ratings. These may include the following:

To provide objective, quantified measures of vendor performance

[76] Hafer, R. A., Supplier Delivery—Quality Conformance Rating System, *ASQC Convention Transactions,* 1963, pp. 305–308.

[77] See, for example, Siegel, Joseph, A Practical Approach to Vendor Ratings, *Industrial Quality Control,* July 1966, pp. 17–19.

[78] "Evaluation of Supplier Performance," National Association of Purchasing Agents, New York, 1964.

[79] For an example, see "Evaluation of Supplier Performance," *op. cit.* See also Juran, J. M., and Frank M. Gryna, Jr., "Quality Planning and Analysis," McGraw-Hill Book Company, New York, 1970, pp. 430–432.

To aid in arriving at a balanced judgment of vendor performance for all categories of buyer needs

To provide both buyer and vendor with common factual information on overall performance

To minimize the risk of being stampeded by isolated instances of failure

To identify troublesome areas so that corrective attention can be concentrated

The design of reports on vendor ratings is in line with these purposes. Typically, these reports summarize information by vendor, with subtotals by commodity or product class. For material under frequent delivery, these reports may be monthly; otherwise, the reports are quarterly. Summaries going to vendors are usually accompanied by details on failed lots. (The vendor had previously known these, of course, through the regular feedback of deviations.)

In addition to the above, the buyer may prepare semiannual or annual summaries. These are used in review of the list of qualified buyers and in planning next year's allocation of purchases.

Action on the Ratings   The vendor quality ratings can become an important input to decisions on future purchases. These decisions must take account of the other parameters of vendor performances as well. (The best vendor is the one who has no weakness.)

In some cases, the quality needs become so acute that the quality rating becomes dominant, and the vendor's ability to remain on the approved list is determined by his quality rating. Such ratings become both a threat and an opportunity; i.e., some vendors will not survive, but the survivors will increase their sales. In one case, a division of a large company carried out a three-year program during which vendor rejections were reduced from 22 to 6%. During this same time, the list of vendors was reduced from 1,700 to 800, so that the survivors increased their share of the division's business. In addition, the division officials gave publicity to the best vendors, including introducing them to purchasing managers of other divisions. One result was an increase of "best vendor" sales to these other divisions of nearly $30 million.[80]

LEGAL ASPECTS OF VENDOR RELATIONS

The legal basis of vendor relations is the general law governing sales. Where the sale is not specially documented by purchase orders, specifications, etc., the law of sales nevertheless implies certain warranties based solely on the actions of the parties:

1. The warranty of "merchantability," i.e., a warranty that the product is suitable for the general purposes for which products of the same description are used, and that the product is thereby suitable for moving in the channels of trade.

2. A warranty of fitness for intended use, in those cases where the vendor knows the specific use the buyer will make of the product

These implied warranties can be changed by an "exclusion" agreement between the parties. Generally, such exclusion will be enforced when the parties are both engaged in commerce. However, when one of the parties is a consumer, the courts are reluctant to enforce exclusion of warranties, and tend to find such exclusions as contrary to public policy.

Beyond the effect of the general law of sales, vendor relations may be governed by practices prevailing in the industry with respect to such matters as lot formation, bulk sampling, delivery conditions, etc. Where such recognized practices

[80] Product Evaluation and Supplier Control: $29½ Million Supplier Bonus, *Quality Management & Engineering*, March 1972, pp. 20–22.

prevail, the buyer impliedly accepts them unless he specifically states otherwise.

Generally, the warranty is not waived by the buyer's act of paying the invoice before inspection (to secure the benefit of the discount for prompt payment). In many cases the warranty also survives inspection by the buyer, e.g., hidden defects, sealed packages, etc. Here again, consumers receive added protection, extending even to cases where they sign documents to the effect that the goods were received in satisfactory condition.

A greal deal of commerce is conducted under conditions in which the documentation is extensive. Formal purchase contracts are signed, and these include many clauses in "fine print." Product specifications are referenced, as are standards of other sorts. Procedures are set out for documentation, surveillance, and other aspects of vendor relations. Such contract provisions are normally fully enforceable unless one of the parties is a consumer.

For additional discussion, see Section 14, under Warranty of Quality.

Production of Quality

J. M. JURAN

NATURE OF PRODUCTION

"Production," as the term is used here, designates the activity of running the processes, machines, and tools, and of performing the associated mental and manual operations, to make products from basic materials and components. Production is a part of the broader activity of Manufacture, which includes also manufacturing planning (see Section 9). What distinguishes production from nonproduction (i.e., manufacturing planning, machine maintenance, etc.) is that the production operations directly change the character of the product, e.g., composition, shape, etc.

Scope of Activity Production as an activity must be distinguished from the capitalized word "Production," meaning a department of that name. The Production Department is often given duties beyond those of performing direct production activities.   These added duties vary widely from one company to another, depending on several main factors:

Complexity of Product and Process.   The greater the complexity, the more the decision making is done by the technologists.[1]

Volume of Production.   Mass production requires complex machinery, tools, instruments, and controls to achieve low cost, high productivity, and high quality. Companies tend to make wide use of engineers rather than production supervisors to make the analyses and decisions associated with such complex technology.

Management Philosophy.   In many companies, the Taylor concept of separating planning from execution has been the rule for some decades.   In such companies the practice is one of giving Production a narrow assignment with respect to quality control decisions and actions.[2]

Training of Foremen.   The extent to which the production supervisors are trained in management and technology is a further factor in the willingness of the company to enlarge their scope of responsibility.

National Tradition.   In some countries there are special traditions which greatly affect the assignment given to Production supervision.[3]

Company response to these factors has resulted in a wide divergence of organization forms.   At one extreme, the department called Production has wide responsibilities for manufacturing planning, machine maintenance, and product inspection. At the other extreme, the department has a very narrow scope of activity—that of executing the plans which others have prepared.   Between these extremes are numerous intermediate forms, and life is being lived successfully (and unsuccessfully) along the entire spectrum.

QUALITY RESPONSIBILITIES ON THE FACTORY FLOOR

The factory floor is the scene of myriad decisions which affect quality.   Several categories of these decisions are so highly repetitive that companies should make crystal clear who is to make which decisions.

Principal Decision and Action Categories   The most frequent categories are the following:

Setup Approval.   The "setup" consists of assembling the proper machines, tools, instruments, and material and adjusting them so that the resulting product will conform to specification.   This setup is prepared either by the production operator or by a setup specialist.   Once the setup has been prepared, a decision must be made: "Should this process be allowed to commence production?"   This decision is known as "setup approval."[4]

Running Approval.   Once the process is running, there is need for periodic check to see if the process is still producing product which conforms to specification.   The decision to be made is: "Should the process continue to run or should it stop?"   This decision is known as "running approval"[5]

Product Approval.   As product is completed, there is periodic need to decide whether the product conforms to specification.   This decision is called product ap-

---

[1] See Section 9, under Responsibility for Manufacturing Planning.

[2] See Section 18, under Role of Motivation: The Taylor System.

[3] For an extensive discussion, see Juran, J. M., QC for Foreman and Workers, An International Summary, *Reports of Statistical Application Research, Japanese Union of Scientists & Engineers,* vol. 16, no. 4, 1969.   See also Sections 48 and 48A generally.

[4] Also "startup approval," "setup acceptance," etc.

[5] Also "running acceptance."

proval[6] as contrasted with the preceding two decisions, which together constitute process approval.

Pattern of Departmental Responsibilities In the United States, the *departmental* assignment for making these decisions is usually as follows:

Decision	Usually Assigned to
Setup approval	Production, but sometimes jointly with Inspection
Running approval	Production
Product approval	Inspection

Such is the usual *departmental* assignment. There is also the further question of how these departmental responsibilities are to be assigned to the categories of job classes on the factory floor. To answer this question it is convenient to make use of a responsibility matrix to reach agreement on who should make which decisions (see below).

DECISIONS, ACTIONS	PRODUCTION			INSPECTION		OTHER
	SETUP MAN	OPERATOR	FOREMAN	BENCH	PATROL	
PROCESS DECISIONS						
SETUP						
SETUP ACCEPTANCE						
RUN						
RUNNING ACCEPTANCE						
PRODUCT DECISIONS						
CONFORMANCE						
SORT						
FITNESS FOR USE						

Fig. 11-1 Matrix for agreeing on responsibilities for decisions and actions on quality.

Pattern of Individual Responsibilities Unless the managers decide who may make what decisions, the people on the work floor must work out among themselves who is to decide what. Some of these local agreements are an unpleasant surprise to managers once they are discovered.

Managers can quite readily work out an agreed pattern of decision making by using a responsibility matrix such as Figure 11-1. A meeting of the cognizant supervisors is convened to discuss the problem. At this meeting the blank matrix is first

---

[6] The term "product acceptance" has also been used in the past but should probably be avoided. There are really two levels of decision on the product: "Does the product conform to specification?" and (if nonconforming) "Is the product fit for use?" See, in this connection, Section 12, under Judgment of Fitness for Use.

drawn on the blackboard. The members then agree on what decisions and actions they will talk about.[7] These are listed in the left-hand column to become the headings for the horizontal rows of the matrix. Next, the members agree on who is available on the factory floor to make these decisions. These potential decisions makers become the headings for the vertical columns of the matrix.

Next, the matrix is reproduced and a copy is given to each conferee, who is asked to fill in his idea of who should make which decision and take which action. These filled-in copies (sometimes executed anonymously) are collected and all the marks

DECISIONS, ACTIONS	PRODUCTION			INSPECTION		
	SETUP MAN	OPERATOR	FOREMAN	BENCH	PATROL	OTHER
PROCESS DECISIONS						
SETUP	16	7				
SETUP ACCEPTANCE	8	3	10	1	4	1
RUN		23				
RUNNING ACCEPTANCE		19	3		5	1
PRODUCT DECISIONS						
CONFORMANCE	1		5	1	18	2
SORT		6		17		
FITNESS FOR USE			6		6	13

Fig. 11-2 Divergence of views on responsibility.

are transferred to the blackboard to show the composite belief of the membership. Figure 11-2 shows an example of such a tally.

The summary enables the members to identify their collective agreements and the extent of their differences. These differences can then be talked out until agreement is complete. This agreement can then be reduced to a written procedure, formally approved and published.

The foregoing is a proved technique for reaching agreement on any problem in responsibility. However, in such discussions, managers often ask: "Is there a right way to organize?" The answer is no. The pattern of responsibility must be designed to fit the local conditions. In one department it is convenient to assign to the same man the jobs of set up and operate; in another department setup is best done by a special setup man. In one department the process is so stable that the original setup will endure for the length of the lot; in another department the setup requires check and readjust during the life of the lot. There are differences in the

---

[7] "Responsibility" is never clear unless it is stated in terms of decisions or actions. It is futile to ask "Who is responsible for quality?" since the question does not identify a decision or action. However, a question in the form "Who is responsible for approving setups?" admits of an unequivocal answer.

extent of training, in the level of morale, etc., of the work force. The permutations of these and other differences make each department unique and require a made-to-measure design of responsibility for decision making.

CONCEPT OF OPERATOR SELF-CONTROL

Whatever the pattern of responsibilities given to an operator (or setup man) is, he can properly be held *accountable* for achieving good quality only if he has been put into a state of "self-control."[8]   An operator (or anyone else) is said to be in a state of self control only if all three of the criteria for self-control have been met. These criteria require that the operator be provided with:

1. Means for knowing what he is *supposed to do*
2. Means for knowing what he *is doing*
3. *Means for regulating* what he is doing

If all of the foregoing criteria have been met, the operator is in a state of self-control and can properly be held accountable for results. (He still may not attain 100% results for reasons which are discussed below.)

Controllability   This word is used to help identify where the ability to achieve conformance to standard lies. When all the criteria for operator self-control have been met, the resulting defects are said to be operator-controllable. If any of the criteria have not been met, the defects are said to be management-controllable.[9]

Determination of where the controllability lies requires consideration of a good deal of detail. Table 11-1 lists some typical questions which are pertinent to this determination. Once the answers to such questions are largely known, where the controllability lies becomes obvious.[10]

Effect of Lack of Self-Control   Lack of operator self-control means that responsibility for defects produced is shared or lies elsewhere. For example, the needs for self-control might be met as follows:

Needs for self-control	Supplied (by management) to
Knowledge of "supposed to do"	Inspection
Knowledge of "is doing"	Production, via Inspection
Means for regulation	Production

To the extent that the criteria for self-control are not met, the operator cannot be held responsible for the results. In the extreme case where the operator merely feeds stock into the machines, there should be no pretense that somehow he is engaged in control of quality.

This does not stop some managers from "pretending." What traps these managers is the fact that *any* operator is in a position to contribute to poor quality, e.g., by poor materials handling. However, the fact that operators can contribute to poor quality does not prove that they can also contribute to good quality. For example, an operator can damage a well-designed product through poor handling, but he cannot remedy a poorly designed product by good handling. (See, in this connection, Section 18, under Operator-controllable Errors, *et. seq.*)

---

[8] See Section 2, under Self-Control.

[9] Management-controllable defects are subclassified based on departmental responsibility, e.g., Design-controllable.

[10] It is also feasible to quantify controllability. See Section 16, under Controllability Quantification, for a case example (Table 16-8) and related discussion.

See also Section 18, under Operator-controllable Errors.

TABLE 11-1   Are Defects Operator-controllable?

I. Does the operator know what he is *supposed to be doing?*
   A. Are there specifications or instructions which apply to this operation?
      1. Are they written down? If written in more than one place, do all agree?
      2. If visual defects, are there standard samples?
   B. Does operator have access to them?
   C. Does he actually refer to them in practice?
   D. Does he really understand them?
   E. Are these specific specifications the sole criterion of acceptability (i.e., no longstanding verbal instructions which countermand them)?
   F. Does operator know whom to consult to give official interpretation of the specifications in doubtful cases?
   G. Does operator know how the product is used? Has he seen it used?
   H. Does operator know the full consequences of his failure to meet the specifications?
   I. Does Inspection usually inspect to the specifications?
      1. Are deviations rare?
      2. Do they require O.K. by higher authority?
   J. Does foreman review specifications with operator from time to time?
   K. Does operator receive specification changes automatically and promptly?
   L. Does operator know what to do with defective raw material?
   M. Does operator know what to do with defective finished product?
II. Does operator know what he *is doing?*
   A. Are gages or measuring equipments provided?
      1. Do they show how the process is doing rather than sort good from bad?
      2. Are they available to the operator?
      3. Are they adequately checked and maintained?
      4. Are they precise enough to give repeatable readings on the same unit of product?
   B. Is operator told how often to sample his work?
      1. Is time allowed on the job rate for this sampling?
      2. Is allowed time sufficient?
   C. Is operator told how many pieces (or readings) to sample?
   D. Is operator told the criteria on which he should decide to correct the process?
   E. Is there any independent check as to whether the operator actually follows the specified sample size, frequency, and adjustment criteria?
   F. Is operator required to record the results of his checks?
   G. Does anyone verify the accuracy of these records?
   H. Is operator always notified of Inspection rejections?
   I. Are inspection data fed back to the operator for his use?
   J. Does foreman have a record of operator quality performance?
   K. Is this record shown to and discussed with operator?
III. Can operator regulate the process?
   A. Is there a swift, sure adjustment operator can make to eliminate defects when they occur?
   B. Has the quality capability of this process been measured?
   C. Is the quality capability within the tolerances allowed by the specification?
   D. Does operator make his own decisions as to when the process requires correction (as opposed to having them made by foreman or patrol inspector)?
   E. Does operator know what to do if criteria for action are exceeded?
      1. Under what conditions he takes correction action?
      2. What action?
      3. Under what conditions he shuts down and seeks help?
      4. Whose help?
   F. Have the operator actions which cause the defect been written down and given to him?
   G. Have the operator actions which can prevent the defect been written down and given to him?

KNOWLEDGE OF "SUPPOSED TO DO"

The operator derives his knowledge of what he is supposed to do from a variety of sources.

Fitness for Use   This is the ideal source and is at its best in cases where unfitness for use is brought home to the operator by direct contact with the user, e.g., the village shoemaker. The recognized "trades," e.g., plumber, are added examples in which fitness for use is extensively fed back to the operator. In the industrial company, the toolmaker is an example, through his participation in the tool try-outs. The maintenance mechanic is a further example. In some types of jobbing production, the operator observes and even participates in the simulated use test on the production floor.

In cases such as these, knowledge of "supposed to do" is derived from a mixture of (1) feedback of fitness for use and (2) a structured training and qualification course which is itself likewise keyed to fitness for use. The more extensive the knowledge of fitness for use, the less is the need for specifications.

Product Specifications   These are widely used as a substitute for knowledge of fitness for use. When product specifications are chosen to provide knowledge of "supposed to do," some essential precautions must be observed:

Provide Unequivocal Information.   Sometimes the specification is clear enough, but there are conflicting provisions in other sources: the manuals; the customer's order; memoranda in the file; shop standards; inspection practices; verbal orders from the foreman; and that mysterious, durable document, the foreman's black book. The operator is usually less able to reconcile these conflicts than anyone else. To the extent that the information conflicts, to that extent there is a failure to meet the criterion of knowledge of "supposed to do."

Provide Information on Seriousness.   All specifications contain multiple characteristics, and these are not equally important. The more the operator is informed as to which are the vital few characteristics, the better can he place his emphasis.[11]

Explain the "Why."   Explanation of the purposes served by the product and by the specification enlarges the knowledge of "supposed to do" and provides motivation through the resulting feeling of participation. The understanding of the "why" adds interest and life to the inanimate specifications as well as making more obvious the seriousness classification of the characteristics.

Some of the explanations of the "why" comes from investigations associated with field complaints or with disposition of nonconforming product. The decisions and actions taken in such cases are grounded in studies of fitness for use. The reasons behind the decisions can therefore be illuminating to operators who have only product specifications as a guide.

Provide Standards.   In those cases where the specification is silent, standards should be provided. There is an extensive array of needs here, especially on widely prevailing characteristics such as product appearance. (For years, enormous numbers of electrical connections were soldered in the absence of clear standards for an acceptable soldered connection.) If these standards are not provided by the managers and engineers, then, by default, the standards will be set by the inspectors and operators.

Train the Operators.   The general aspects of operator training for quality are discussed in Section 17. Beyond this general training are the special training needs of specific jobs. For example, some welding operations affect human safety. It is common practice to require that operators undergo a training program, including welding of specimen pieces, to qualify for the job. A qualification examina-

[11] See Section 12, under Seriousness Classification.

tion is then held, including test of the specimen pieces. Operators who pass the examination are given a license to perform the operation for a stated interval of time.[12]

Process Specifications   For many operations it is not practical to provide product specifications to operators: the product characteristics will not appear until a later operation; there are no provisions for measuring the product until later stages. For such operations, the operators are provided with process criteria, e.g., ammeter reading, pressure valve reading, etc.

Much confusion surrounds the use of process specifications as the basis of operator "supposed to do." The principal forms of this confusion concern:

Confusion of Process Control Tolerances with Product Acceptance Tolerances. Table 11-2 shows in detail the distinction between these two kinds of tolerances.

TABLE 11-2   Distinction between Tolerances

	Process control	Product acceptance
Purpose of the tolerances:	To provide a basis for making decisions on the process	To provide a basis for making decisions on the product
Tolerances published in:	Process Specification	Product Specification
Specification usually issued by:	Process Engineering Dept.	Product Design Dept.
Tolerances concern:	Process conditions	Product qualities
Instrumentation is usually:	An integral part of the process	Not an integral part of the process
Usual measurement to discover compliance is by:	Production Dept. for advisory tolerances; Inspection Dept. for mandatory tolerances°	Inspection Dept.
Decisions on whether there is compliance made usually by:	Production Dept. for advisory tolerances, Inspection Dept. for mandatory tolerances	Inspection Dept.
Deviation from specification usually authorized by:	Production Dept. for advisory tolerances, Process Engineering Dept. for mandatory tolerances	Inspection Dept. for nonfunctional tolerances, Product Design Dept. for functional tolerances

° Advisory tolerances are supplied to operators for manufacturing convenience. Mandatory process tolerances must be met as a means of supplying essential product qualities, i.e., long life, safety, etc., when there is no immediate, economic test for the product quality.

In some operations the units of measure for the process are dramatically different from those used on the product. For example, in hardening of steel, the process variables are bath temperature, cycle time, etc. In contrast, the product is measured in terms of grain size, degrees of hardness, etc. In such a case the responsibility of the hardening furnace operator is clearly one of meeting the process tolerances, not the product tolerances.

In other operations, the units of measure for process and product are identical. A common example is the millimeter or inch used as a unit of measure in metal cutting. The product specification may show 1.000 ± 0.002 inches. The process specification may consist of some narrow-limit scheme.[13] In such cases it should be

---

[12] In some cases the license remains in effect until there is evidence of poor work or until the operator becomes inactive for several months. In such cases, requalification is required. See, for example, the ASME Code of Welding Qualifications.

[13] See, for example, Section 23, under PRE-Control.

made clear whether the responsibility of the operator is to meet the product tolerance or the process tolerance.

For example, in a large company making metal containers, one important operation is setup of the machines making the bodies for tin cans. Because can-making
is still regarded as involving a great deal of art, the machine setter is given wide
latitude in how to set up the machine. However, as to certain essential dimensions,
it is mandatory for him to meet prescribed process control tolerances, since previous study has disclosed that this dimensional control is needed to assure tight
seals. His instructions require that he measure samples for these dimensions, record
the data, calculate the median and range, and see that these fall within the established process tolerances. All this must be done before the machine may be allowed
to proceed with production.

Confusion When Control Charts Are Introduced into a Process. To the quality

TABLE 11-3 Operator Action Table

Type of information or decision needed	Sources of operator's information or decision		After introduction of control charts
	Before introduction of control charts; operator responsible for meeting:		
	Process specification	Product specification	
1. Information on what the process should be doing	Direct from proc-ess specification	Direct from prod-uct specification	From the control chart
2. Information on what the process actually is doing	From process in-struments or in-spectors	From measure-ments on the product	From the control chart
3. Decision on whether "is doing" differs from "should be doing" by an amount great enough to warrant process adjustment	From operator ex-perience	From operator ex-perience	From the control chart
4. Decision on extent of process adjust-ment needed	From operator ex-perience	From operator ex-perience	From operator ex-perience

specialists, the purpose of the control charts is simple and obvious—to serve as a
sensitive device for detecting process changes. To the Production force the charts
are complex and confusing. Table 11-3 shows the impact on the production operator if the control is made effective.

When these charts were first introduced in huge numbers during the 1950s, some
very pertinent questions were raised about the legitimacy or status of the control
chart:

1. What is the official status of the control chart? Is it merely an informal suggestion by the quality control engineer or is it a "legitimate" impersonal boss, like
the specification, the collective bargaining agreement, etc.?

2. Is the control to be used in addition to or instead of the specification?

3. If "in addition to," what of the cases where there is conflict; i.e., control chart
requires more frequent adjustment, process is not capable, etc.?

4. If the control chart is to be used instead of the specification, why is this not

legitimized; i.e., why is there no formal order relieving the operator of the responsibility for meeting specifications?

Little has been done by industrial companies to provide answers to these questions, despite their importance to the entire Production department.[14]

Confusion between Mandatory and Advisory Process Tolerances. Many process specifications contain two very different kinds of tolerances:

1. Mandatory tolerances. These are specified to assure fitness for use, make the product more marketable, achieve high reliability, etc.

2. Advisory tolerances. These are specified for the convenience of production, e.g., to help reduce the amount of cut and try in running the process. For example:

The process for cooking fish sticks (for frozen food marketing) includes requirements that *(a)* the cooking cycle shall be at *x* degrees for *y* minutes and also that *(b)* the cooked product shall have a golden brown color. The latter is regarded as mandatory for marketing the product; the former is advisory. For most materials, the specified temperature and time will also produce the proper color. However, the materials vary, and Production is authorized to vary the cooking cycle to suit.

Another example involves the specification for winding electrical coils, which may call for winding *n* turns to attain an inductance of *x*. The latter is mandatory; the former is advisory.

Some process specifications contain many tolerances without designating which are mandatory and which are advisory. Lacking this knowledge, Production tends to regard them all as advisory, whereas Inspection tends to regard them all as mandatory. The answer "of course" is to designate which is which. The problem is to induce busy technical departments to take the time to do the designating. Where they are unable to take the time, the Quality Manager may be driven to make his own determination.

KNOWLEDGE OF "IS DOING"

The operator needs knowledge of what he is doing. Only from such knowledge ("feedback") can he judge if he is conforming to what he is supposed to do. He secures knowledge of "is doing" from multiple sources.

Personal Observation. Many qualities can be judged by the human senses, without the need for instruments, e.g., the lock washer is present or absent. As to such qualities, the operator is naturally equipped with the means to provide his own feedback.

Measurement Inherent in the Process. Many processes are engineered to include much instrumentation. The resulting information provides a feedback to the operator to enable him to close the loop. Even where the feedback is into an automated system, the data are usually available to human operators acting as monitors.

Measurement by the Operator. In many processes, it is feasible for the operator to do the measuring so as to secure knowledge of "is doing." This is widely prevalent in the production of mechanical and electronic components. It is less prevalent in chemical processes, but even here it is sometimes feasible to design simple, reliable tests and to provide the operator with the reagents he needs to make these tests locally.

In some processes, a single measurement may provide enough information to constitute an adequate feedback for operator action. Quite often, however, there must be multiple measurement. In such cases, provision must be made to provide

---

[14] For an extended discussion, see Juran, J. M., *Cultural Patterns and Quality Control, Industrial Quality Control,* October 1957, pp. 8–13.

the operator with the needed criteria: how many measurements, how to record the data, how to interpret the results, etc. The statistical aspects of providing these criteria are discussed in Section 23.

Aside from the statistical aspects, there are added considerations in the plan for providing the operator with feedback based on his measurements. Some of these are discussed in Section 12, under Inspection Planning. Others are discussed, also in Section 12, under Product Acceptance Inspection.

Measurement by the Inspector. Inspectors who are responsible to the Inspection Department perform a great deal of measurement on the process to provide feedback data to Production.[15] In addition, the measurements made on the product (to judge product conformance) also provide feedback data. The approach to making this feedback to Production is discussed next.

INSPECTION FEEDBACK TO PRODUCTION

When Inspection makes measurements which are to serve as a basis for action by Production, the division of work is as follows:

Activity	Usually performed by
Measure the product or process	Inspection
Record and publish the data	Inspection
Analyze the data for significance	Both
Decide on a course of action	Production
Take the action	Production

Methods of Closing the Feedback Loop   There are various ways of closing the loop. The choice of these ways is influenced partly by the technology but mainly by the prevailing pattern of human relations.

Loop Closed by Inspector. At one extreme, the inspector is under orders to stop the process when there is evidence of failure to conform. This form is used in cases where the management has become unwilling to entrust the production operators with the responsibility for closing the loop. The result is usually an atmosphere of hostility, since the management mistrust is reciprocated by the workers. The workers also resent "outsiders" (inspectors) having the right to throw the switches on the machines; i.e., it is regarded as an intrusion on the "property rights" of the operators. Hence there is usually an abrasive relationship between Inspection and Production as well.

Where this form persists for any length of time, it is common for the responsibility for achievement of quality to pass from Production to Inspection. Once this has happened, it is a long road back.

Personal Feedback to Operators. In this form the inspector keeps his hands off the machine. Instead, he tells the operator of the results of measurement and advises him of the change needed. In some companies it is virtually mandatory for the operators to act on this advice. More usually, the operator decides whether to take the advice or not.

Personal Feedback to Foreman In some companies the rule is that the inspector may not communicate directly with the operator and that, instead, he should take his feedback to the foreman. This practice is sometimes the result of operator griev-

---

[15] In some processes, work done by one operation is made invisible by succeeding operations. One form of process inspection provides for each operator to inspect the work done by the preceding operation. This method was widely adopted in the European shoe factories founded by the Czech Bata.

ances to the effect that they are getting orders from someone other than the foreman. In such grievances it is common to find the labor Union and the foreman in agreement.

Where the operator is in a state of self-control, feedback through the foreman slows up the signal and may distort it as well. Usually it is better to feed back direct to the operators provided the feedback avoids the implication of being an order.

Impersonal Feedback. One way of making the feedback direct to the operator without the implication of giving orders is through depersonalizing the feedback. A special reporting format is needed for this purpose (e.g., charts, signal lights) as discussed under Timeliness of Feedback.

In some cases it is feasible to provide feedback of deeds rather than data. Numerous applications of closed-circuit television are used to permit observation of processes which are distant or which are conducted in an environment hostile to human comfort, e.g., heat, fumes, noise.

In one example, the welding of railroad tank cars is checked by x-rays. The x-ray image is converted into a visual image for display in a control-room TV monitor. A split-image scheme permits the added display of data corresponding to weld location. The technician is thereby able, by remote control, to observe the quality and to paint-spray the defects. Instant replay of the tape is also possible.[16]

The opportunity to view the deeds has the added advantage of being a "real time" feedback, i.e., the deeds and the signals are simultaneous. The response of operators to such realities tends to be more wholehearted than response to after-the-fact data.

Timeliness of Feedback Once defects are discovered, prompt feedback is needed to avoid continuing production of defects. Depending on the process, various ways have been devised for providing this prompt feedback.

Multiple Machines Where the process consists of numerous machines all producing independently (e.g., textile looms, lathes), signals are designed to identify those machines which are in need of attention. For example, signal lamps may be mounted to each machine. Green lights show that the product from those machines is under control. A red light signals that the machine is in trouble. These signals are turned on and off by Inspection.[17] There are numerous other forms of such signals at machines: colored tags, swiveling red hands, etc.

Large Assembly Lines. One form of feedback has been the large chart mounted in the assembly area so as to be widely visible. The chart is a matrix with vertical columns representing hours of the shift and horizontal rows representing various assembly defects. The results of inspection are posted hourly, so that any one square of the matrix shows how many instances of that type of defect were found in that hour. The writing is done with crayon on a sheet of plastic, the chart paper being under the plastic sheet. At the end of the shift, the whole is wiped clean.

With evolution of the new electronics, these feedbacks can be converted to instantaneous electronic readout.

Control Chart Feedback At the individual operator level these charts depict percent defective, number defective, average, range, median, cumulative sum, and still other measures. See Section 23 for the detailed approach.

When there is good rapport between Inspection and Production, it is feasible to arrange the data recording so that inspectors and operators put their data on the same sheet. This enables each to make use of all available data and improves the decision making all around. This practice is quite common in setup approval.

---

[16] See R.R. Tank Cars Are a Quality Project, *Quality Assurance,* September 1970, pp. 28–29.

[17] See, for example, Process Controls Enhance Product Quality, *Quality Assurance,* February 1967, pp. 24 and 25.

In using charts as feedback, care should be taken to choose a chart form which is consistent with the responsibility assigned to the production operator. To achieve such consistency:

If the operator's responsibility is to	The chart should present data showing
Make individual units of product so that they measure to a product specification	The measurement of individual units of product compared with product specification limits
Keep process conditions in accordance with a process specification	The measurement of process conditions compared with the process specification limits
Make averages and ranges meet statistical control limits	The averages and ranges compared with statistical control limits
Keep percent defective below some level	Actual percent defective compared with that level

When charts are used, it is well to agree on who is to do what with respect to chart design, etc. Table 11-4 shows a typical arrangement. However, the assignment of responsibilities varies widely among companies.

TABLE 11-4   Responsibility for Charting

Activity	Operator	Inspector	Foreman	Quality control engineer
Design of chart			X	XX
Measurements		XX		
Plotting of chart		XX		
Review of results	XX	X	X	
Action on results	XX	X	X	

XX = prime responsibility.
X = collateral responsibility.

Feedback Related to Operator Action   Inspection data are commonly the result of measuring the *product,* whereas operator action is commonly to make changes in the *process.* In consequence, the operator needs to know what kind of process change he should make to respond to a product deviation. He secures this knowledge in one of several ways:

1. From the planners, who have provided him with information relating process variables to product characteristics

2. From his own experience in cut and try

3. From the fact that the units of measure for product and process are identical

Lacking all these, the operator can only cut and try further or stop the process and sound the alarm.

Sometimes it is feasible for the data feedback to be converted into a form which makes easier the operator's decision of what action to take on the process.

For example, Figure 11-3 shows the tool setup used to cold-press a copper cap on which there were six critical dimensions. It was easy to measure the dimensions and to discover the nature of product deviations. However, it was difficult for the setup men to translate the product data into process changes. To simplify this translation, use was made of a "position-dimension" (P-D) diagram. The six measurements were first "corrected" (i.e., coded) by subtracting the thinnest from all the others. These corrected data were then plotted on a P-D diagram as shown in Figure 11-4. The resulting diagrams were then depicted in their relationship to the

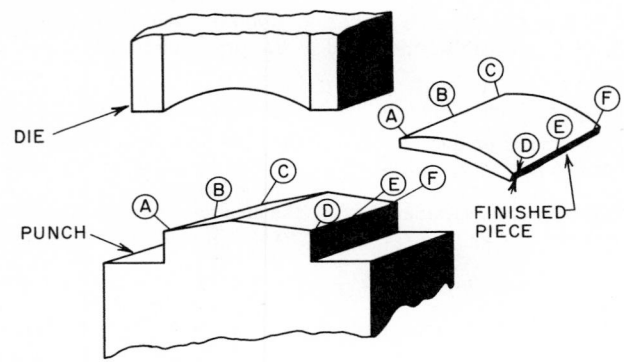

Fig. 11-3   Process for pressing copper cap.

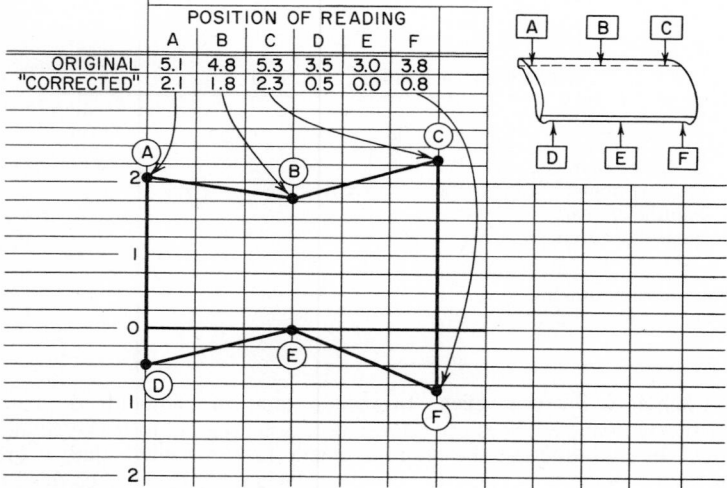

Fig. 11-4   Method of drawing P-D diagram.

	POSITION OF READING					
	A	B	C	D	E	F
ORIGINAL	5.1	4.8	5.3	3.5	3.0	3.8
"CORRECTED"	2.1	1.8	2.3	0.5	0.0	0.8

tool setup (Figure 11-5).   The setup men and operators learned how to interpret the P-D diagrams and to use them in modifying the process.[18]

Criteria for Good Feedback to Operators   It is evident from the foregoing that feedback to operators should:

Read at a Glance.   The pace of events on the factory floor is swift.   Operators should be able to review the feedback in stride.

Deal with the Vital Few.   If the trivial many defects are included, attention is diverted from the vital few defects.

Deal with Operator-controllable Defects.   Any other course provides a basis for unfruitful argument.

[18] From Seder, L. A., Diagnosis with Diagrams, *Industrial Quality Control,* January and March 1950.

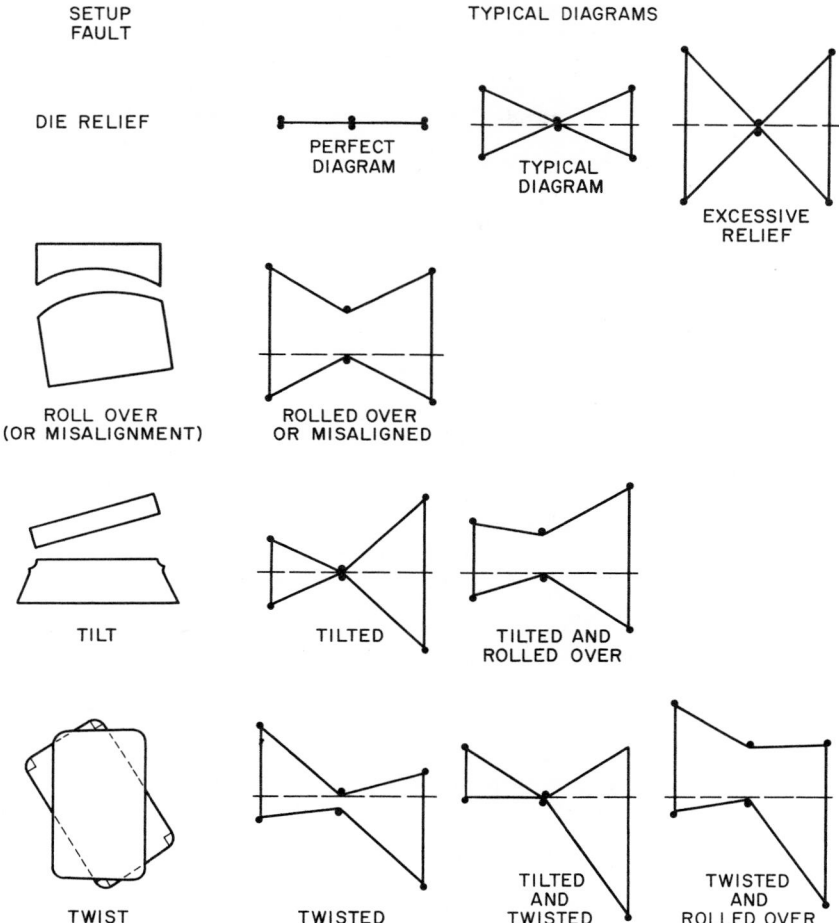

Fig. 11-5 Relation of P-D diagram to tool setup.

Provide Prompt Signals.   Timeliness is a basic test of good feedback; the closer the system is to "real time" signaling, the better.

Guide Corrective Action.   The signals should be in terms which make it easy to decide on remedial action.

A welcome added feature is a level of *interest.*   Dull, humorless presentations arouse less response then those which are periodically seasoned with showmanship and humor.

In practice, many reporting systems fall short of meeting these criteria.   Some have aimed for completeness, thereby taking attention from the vital few defects and transferring it to the trivial many.   Other systems have been designed to exercise the statistical skills of the engineer rather than to provide swift, simple, and sure understanding to the operator.   Intricate charts, complex language, fine print, numerous notes, etc., are all detrimental to good feedback.

Summaries to Foremen   Beyond the need for feedback at the work stations, there is need to provide foremen with short-term summaries.   These take several forms:

Scrap Accumulation.   In some shops it is convenient to "summarize" the defective product itself.   In Section 34 (Foundry Quality Control), an example is given of use of a daily scrap conference in which the scrap itself, along with the data, is part of the feedback.

Matrix Summary.   To assist the foreman in analysis of his problem, it is helpful to provide him with a matrix summary.   A common form of matrix is operators versus defects, i.e., the vertical columns are headed up by operator names and the horizontal rows by the names of defect types.[19]   The matrix makes very clear which defect types predominate, which operators have the most defects, and what the interaction is.   Other matrixes might be of machine number versus defect type.   A third is defect type versus calendar week, etc.[20, 21]

When the summary is published, it is usual to circle the matrix cells to highlight the vital few situations which call for attention.

An elaboration of the matrix is to split the cell diagonally, permitting the entry of two numbers, e.g., number defective and number produced.

Pareto Analysis.   Some companies prefer to minimize the detail given to the foreman.   Instead, they merely give him information on the total defects for the day plus a list of the top three (or so) defects encountered, and how many of each.   The logic is that the foreman cannot in any case deal with more than a few defects.   A lengthy list dilutes the attention given to any one defect type, including the important ones.

Computer Data Analysis and Reporting.   An extensive example is that used in an automobile assembly operation employing 1,200 people and involving numerous quality characteristics checked over an assembly line 4 or 5 miles long.   At each inspection station, provision is made to enter the data on defects into a computer via an electronic data card.   A three-digit code is used to convert the names of defects into the computer language.   The computer performs the programmed calculations and prints out the needed summaries and status data at typewriters located in the offices of the supervisors directly involved.   These are short-term reports, concerned with identifying sporadic outbreaks of defects, accumulations of unrepaired product, etc.[22]

The foreman also needs summaries of a longer-range nature to enable him to identify chronic quality troubles and to provide perspective beyond that of day-to-day firefighting.   These longer-range summaries are discussed in Section 21.

Corrective Action   Usually, Production takes corrective action on the alarm signals contained in the Inspection feedback.   When Production fails to take this corrective action, Inspection supervisors usually consider it their responsibility to apply pressure of some sort.   When the alarm signal is based on products not conforming to specification, this pressure is rather obvious through refusal to approve the product.   The inability to ship the product then comes to the attention of the upper supervision.

---

[19] See, for example, Holguin, R., Today's News—Today: a Must in Shop Corrective Action, *Industrial Quality Control,* June 1965, pp. 616–618.

[20] See, for example, Daw, H. Robert, Systematic Procedure of Trouble Spotting, *Industrial Quality Control,* March 1965, pp. 443–449.

[21] See Stawski, E., J. Birecki, and J. Weidig, Operationalism in QC, *Industrial Quality Control,* April 1961, pp. 20–22.

[22] Di Cicco, John J., Dynamic Quality Control, *Industrial Quality Control,* November 1965, pp. 235–239.   One of Di Cicco's figures appears in Sec. 42 (Fig. 42-12).

See also Smith, J. Kevin, Chrysler Instantaneous Quality Reporting, *Industrial Quality Control,* January 1967, pp. 325–328.

When the alarm signals are the result of process failure to conform to process specifications, it is more difficult for Inspection to use the ultimate threat of refusal to approve the product.   However, Inspection has a number of alternatives for stimulating correction of the process.   It can look to see whether the process non-conformance is on mandatory or advisory tolerances.   As to the former, it is feasible to enlist the support of other departments (e.g., Technical, Marketing).   It is also useful to see whether the nonconformance is sporadic or chronic in nature.   Usually the latter are beyond the capacity of Production to remedy without staff assistance.

Taking corrective action on sporadic troubles goes under the name of trouble-shooting and is discussed below.

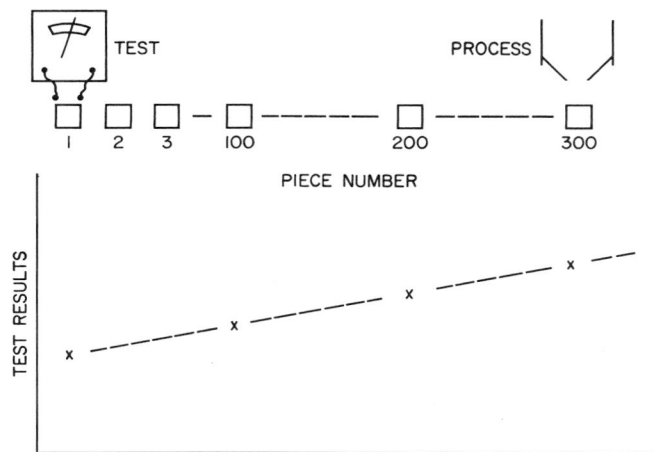

Fig. 11-6   Product and process relationship.

PRODUCT AND PROCESS RELATIONSHIP

A unit of product is the resultant of the interplay among the numerous variables of the process.   In consequence, measurement of a unit of product provides two types of knowledge:

1. The condition of that unit of *product.*
2. The condition of the *process* at the time it produced that unit of product; i.e., the product "tells" on the process.

If units of product are measured in the sequence in which they are made, the measurements will similarly provide knowledge about two trends:

1. The trend of the quality of those units of product
2. The trend of the process during the time it was producing those units of product

Figure 11-6 shows schematically the interrelation of these two trends.

It is evident that a plot of the test results on the units of product in the order of manufacture becomes also a plot of the changes in the process.   The conventional control chart (Section 23) uses exactly this principle to detect and disclose evidence of process changes.   If, in addition, data are taken on the condition of the process variables related to the same order of manufacture, it becomes feasible to quantify relationships between process variables and product characteristics.

In Section 12, under Inspection at Inspection Stations, an example (Figure 12-1) is given of preserving the order of manufacture for the purpose of product approval during process inspection.   In process control, preserving the order is also an important element in securing precise knowledge at minimal sampling.

Securing process control data based on preserving the order of production requires collaboration between the work station and the patrol inspection.   The approach used in Figure 12-1 is an example of preserving the order during mass production.   During jobbing production, the "egg crate" concept is used.   Symbolic of this concept is the compartmentalized container (Figure 11-7).   Under such a concept, Production and Inspection agree on a standard procedure for placing prod-

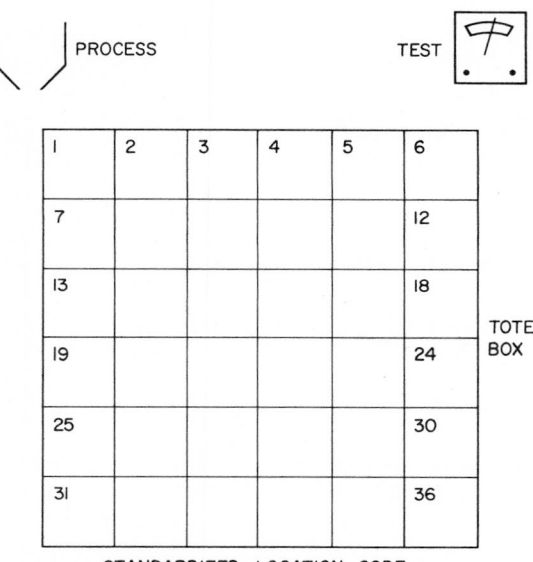

Fig. 11-7   Preserving the order; egg-crate concept.

uct in the transport containers, e.g., in horizontal rows starting with the upper left-hand corner. Such standardization has a wide variety of uses.   It facilitates the work of the operator in recalling his compliance with the checking schedule, e.g., every tenth piece.   It permits the operator to mark clearly just where he made any process changes.   It enables patrol inspectors to stratify their samples with precision and to discover more readily at which point in time any defective conditions originated.   It also permits engineers to reconstruct the conditions of the process by measuring the product.

ABILITY TO REGULATE

The third criterion of operator self-control is ability to regulate.   Whenever the product or process fails to conform to standard, the operator should be able to change the process in a way which will predictably eliminate the nonconformance.   This change may consist either of

1. Varying the technological conditions of the process, e.g., increasing the air pressure, adding more concentrate, turning the feedwheel

2. Varying the "human component," e.g., using lighter blows of the mallet

Regulation by varying the process conditions presupposes that there is some known, predictable relationship between process variables and product performance. The most basic question is, "Can the process hold the tolerances?" Where the answer is in the realm of debate, it is common for Production to believe that the process is not capable and that it is futile to "regulate"; i.e., the answer is to change the specifications. The real need in such cases is to measure process capability so as to settle the question once and for all. (See Section 9, under Process Capability.)

An important added aspect of capability is the ease of changing the adjustment in response to the signals given by product and process measurement. When the adjustment is of a cut-and-try nature, the production people can become discouraged.

For example, some of the rotating arbor machines used for winding electron tube grids are designed in a way which makes the centering of the arbors a cut-and-try operation. Experience has shown that after several tries have failed to meet specifications, the setup mechanics get fed up and settle for something close.

Along with process capability are other needs:

Measuring instruments precise enough to enable the operator to guide the process.
Adequate maintenance of the machines and tools.
Working conditions which are compatible with regulation by operators. For example, when the adjustment valves are located in areas which are repulsive (hot, odorous, humid), human beings tend to stay away. Modern technology can find ways around this through remote observation (closed-circuit television) and remote controls.

When the regulation consists of varying the human component of the operation, the question of process capability arises in a new form; i.e., does the operator have the capability to regulate? This important question is discussed in Section 18, which includes some examples of discovering operator "knack."

There is, increasingly, a trend toward designing the process with an eye to providing for both machine and man capabilities. See Section 9, especially under Foolproofing the Process.

In the chemical process industries, the concept of "adaptive quality control" is directed at quantifying the amount of process adjustment needed in response to observed process fluctuations. See Section 29, under Quality Improvement Programs: Adaptive Control.

PRODUCT ACCEPTANCE BY OPERATORS

Production operators[23] can and do make product approval decisions, i.e., decisions on whether the *product* conforms to specification. In the United States, this practice is often found in jobbing work and in small shops. In the mass production industries it exists, but as a minority practice, in those departments which make components.[24] However, it is rarely found in the final fabrication departments.

In theory, it is highly desirable that production operators should make these decisions on conformance. They are already in the mainstream of the product flow, are trained in the nature of the product characteristics, perform measurements, etc. To require a second person (to make measurements and judge conformance)

[23] "Operators" here means persons engaged in performing fabrication operations. It does not mean inspectors who are paid on the Production department payroll.

[24] The practice is more extensive outside the United States. See Secs 48 and 48A.

adds costs and delays and reduces the sense of responsibility of the operators. All this is theory.

In practice, most managers have the conviction that they dare not delegate the decision of product conformance to the operators. The belief is that some or many of the operators will solve their production quota problems by accepting poor product. This belief is based on long-standing tradition,[25] buttressed by some bitter experience, plus the contentions of the inspection and quality control specialists. Furthermore, when someone raises the question: "Why not delegate the decision only to those operators who will use it well?" the instinctive response is, "We can't make the delegation to some and not to others."

Criteria for Delegation The successful instances of delegation of product acceptance decisions to operators generally deny this instinctive response. Instead, these instances start with the principle, "We will delegate, but only to those operators who demonstrate that they will do a good job with the delegation." Even to make this selective delegation requires that the managers meet some basic criteria:

An Atmosphere of Mutual Confidence. The act of delegating the decision on product acceptance is itself a vote of confidence. This simply will not be done when the basic atmosphere is one of mutual blame and recrimination.[26]

A Capable Process. To the operator, a major proof of management's dedication to quality is the fact that the process can hold the tolerances.

A Low Level of Management-controllable Defects. This criterion needs to be met for the same reasons as the capable process.

A State of Operator Self-Control. (See Concept of Operator Self-Control, above.)

Sequence for Delegation Once the criteria have been met, the plan of delegation proceeds along the following general line:

1. Train the operators in how to make product acceptance decisions.

2. Set up the necessary system of product identification and preserving the order to assure that product decisions can be traced readily back to the operator who made them.

3. Institute a trial period of operator acceptance but retain the regular inspector acceptance during this trial period. The purpose of this dual acceptance is to discover, through data, which operators consistently make good product approval decisions.

4. Issue "licenses" (for making product acceptance decisions) to those operators who demonstrate their competence.[27]

5. For the licensed operators, institute an audit of decisions (see below). For the operators who do not qualify, retain the regular inspection acceptance.

6. Based on the results of the audits, continue or suspend the licenses.[28]

7. Periodically conduct new trials in an effort to qualify the unlicensed operators.

---

[25] For some of the contesting views see Juran, J. M., Inspectors—Headed for Extinction? *Industrial Quality Control,* October 1965, pp. 198–199; Paterson, E. G. D., Stop, Look, Inspect, *Industrial Quality Control,* August 1967, pp. 86–89. See also Juran, J. M., A Challenge to the Extinction of "Homo Inspectiens," *Industrial Quality Control,* December 1967, pp. 298–299. See also Letters to the Editor, *Quality Progress,* March 1968, pp. 33, 43, and 44.

[26] See generally Section 18, Motivation.

[27] The "license" authorizing the operator to make product acceptance decisions is to be distinguished from the more common certificate which shows that the operator has qualified to perform the production operation. See Section 17, under Production Operators.

[28] There is a difference of opinion on the merits of conferring a formal license certificate. The "con" school of thought prevails in companies which adhere to the principle of "praise in public, criticize in private." They point out that in those cases where it becomes necessary to revoke a license, this would be public criticism if the license had been formalized.

Operator response to the delegation appears to be generally favorable, the concept of job enlargement being a significant factor. However, operators who do qualify for the license commonly demand some form of compensation for this achievement, e.g., higher grade, more pay, etc. The companies meet these demands, since the economics of making the delegation are very favorable. In addition, the resulting differential tends to act as a stimulus to the nonlicensed operators to qualify themselves.

Audit of Decisions Figure 11-8 shows graphically the concept of audit of decisions. During the trial period (left-hand portion of chart) the inspection is conducted for two purposes:

1. Product approval, lot by lot
2. Comparison of inspector results with operator results

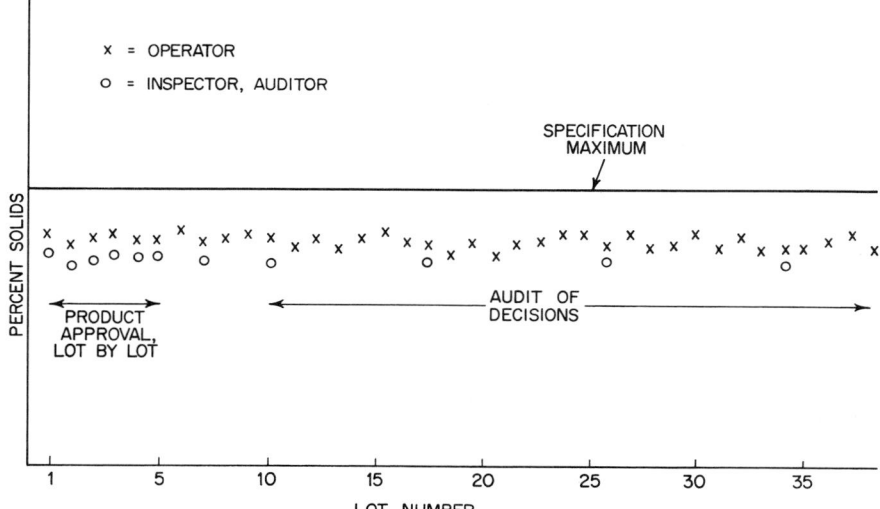

Fig. 11-8 Audit of decisions.

As the comparison establishes validity of the operator's decisions, the inspector acceptances are reduced in frequency until their prime purpose is to audit decisions. At this stage (right-hand side of Figure 11-8), any knowledge of the product is incidental.[29]

Results Achieved[30] Published reports of results of delegating product acceptance decisions to Production claim quality improvements as well as sharp reductions in inspection costs.

For example, in Northern Electric Company, Ltd.,[31] inspectors were reduced in

[29] See Section 10, under Audit of Decisions. Note also how Fig. 10-4 resembles Fig. 11-8.

[30] It must be kept in mind that good results tend to be publicized while poor results or lack of results seldom is publicized.

[31] Tucker, R. J. W., Quality Improvement by Elimination of the Traditional Inspection Department, *Annual Technical Conference Transactions,* ASQC, 1970, pp. 237–242. (Here the improvement involved also a reorganization of Production from "horizontal" lines to "vertical" lines.)

number from 350 to 250, while the demerits index was reduced from 1.5 to about 0.9.

In Quonset Point Naval Air Rework Facility, defects per 1,000 man-hours were reduced from 26.9 to 15.8; quarterly rework costs were reduced from $19,800 to $10,200; average defects per aircraft discrepancy report were reduced from 10.0 to 4.0. (See Figure 11-9.) Note that it took years for the Production force to attain a high level of percent licensed.[32]

In several cases cited in a Fortune magazine article, reductions in inspectors ranged from 30 to 75%. There were also reductions in supervision and in maintenance personnel as well as in reject rates.[33]

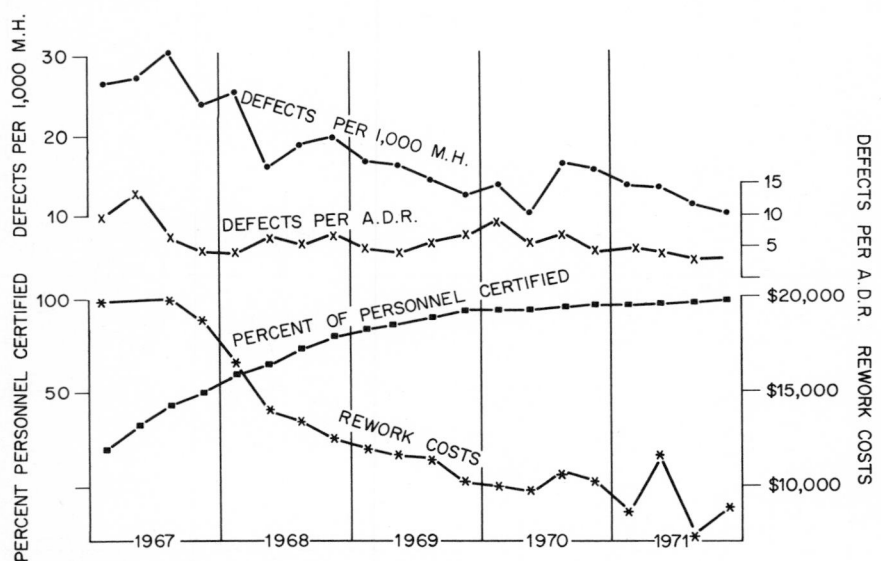

Fig. 11-9   Results of delegating product acceptance decisions to Production.

MACHINE AND TOOL MAINTENANCE

The original quality capability of processes, machines, and tools is established by process capability studies and trial lots (Section 9). Thereafter there remains a problem of maintaining these capabilities. In small companies this machine and tool maintenance is done by a single tool room which services the entire plant. As the

Machine maintenance becomes a separate service department (often combined with new machine construction).

[32] See Folloni, John R., Jr., Production Certifies Quality of Its Work. *Industrial Engineering,* November 1971, pp. 11–16. See also, for subsequent data, Folloni, John R., Jr., Employee Certification and Motivation, *1972 Technical Conference Transactions,* ASQC, pp. 397–401, from which Fig. 11-9 is taken.

[33] It Pays to Wake Up the Blue Collar Worker, *Fortune,* September 1970, p. 168.

A main tool room is retained for new tool construction and for major repairs to tools.

Branch tool rooms are created in the various production shops to store and issue tools, to sharpen them, and to perform other minor maintenance.

It is good practice to create special trays or containers which can hold all the tools and instruments needed to perform a specific operation. Such an assembly improves the housekeeping and is convenient for prompt startups. The tool crib has the responsibility for sharpening the tools and for putting the assembly into storage in readiness for doing the job on reorder.

Responsibility for Maintenance There are several solutions to this thorny question, depending on many local conditions:

The Tool Crib. Here the control is limited to what can be seen on the tool itself, since the tool crib does not measure the product. What they can see is dull tools, damaged surfaces, faulty mechanisms, etc. Repair of these obvious defects in the tools avoids very obvious defects in the product.

The Production Force. The assignment for tool control may be to the lead man, the setup man, or the operator. This control can be an improvement over tool-room control since the production people have been running the job and have gotten a feedback on product quality.

The Inspection Force. Here the approach is usually different. The quality control people tend to set up a record of tool usage plus a record of tool condition on inspection. As this record builds up there is an effort to schedule tool inspection much as is done for scheduled instrument checking. Such systems can be overdone, and many have fallen of their own weight because the elaborate record was applied to all tools rather than only to the vital few.

Setup Approval. Much tool control is done by checking the product at the start of the next job. This has the disadvantage of finding tool defects at the worst possible time. It is far better to detect and remedy these defects at a time when the pressure of schedules is not forcing compromises with quality.

Systematic Controls The control systems are all built around checking schedules which are based on some measure of tool or machine usage, i.e., volume of production made, number of jobs run, time in use, etc. (For some examples of application of these controls, see Sections 34, 35, and 42, under the appropriate headings.)

For a complex process, the checking schedule also becomes complex, so that some aspects are checked monthly, others weekly or daily, etc.[34]

Maintenance of accuracy of instruments is also of great importance to production of quality. This is discussed in Section 13.

AUDIT OF PRODUCTION QUALITY

When actions and decisions affecting quality are delegated to Production, it is quite usual to institute an audit[35] to determine how this delegation is being carried out. This audit always examines to see whether the execution conforms to the quality planning. In addition, the audit may extend to judging the adequacy of the plan itself.

---

[34] See, for example, Kawabuchi, Toshio, Preventive Maintenance of Welding Machine, *Reports of Statistical Applications Research,* Japanese Union of Scientists and Engineers, vol. 15, no. 1, 1968, pp. 45–55.

[35] The general approach to quality auditing is discussed in Section 21, under Quality Assurance. See especially Audit of Execution versus Plan in the same Section.

Audit of Execution versus Plan   There are several categories of personnel to whom this audit may be delegated:

Production Management.[36]   In this situation, the middle or upper Production managers undertake the audit of execution versus plan.   Because most production activities are highly visible, skilled observers can learn much from shop tours.   Generally, Production managers possess these skills and, in addition, put a high value on direct observation.

The strength of these audits is that the managers believe and respond to their own senses more vigorously than to an auditor's report.   The weaknesses are that the men lack the time and skills to be thorough auditors.   They seldom get thoroughly into the data and documentation or into other matters not evident from shop observation.   The fact that they are busy men limits the completeness of the audit and even the adherence to the audit schedule.   There is a risk that they will overreact to the shop observations.   Finally, they do not document their findings adequately, so that for long-range solutions the follow-up can be poor.

Inspectors.   Some inspections are conducted not to measure the product but to observe the process (see for example, the patrol beat, Section 12, Table 12-3).   Such observations are themselves a review of execution versus plan.   It is often feasible to extend these patrol inspections to review other aspects of execution.

The advantages of using inspectors are the economy (of avoiding a separate auditor) and the regularity inherent in use of patrol inspectors.   The disadvantages arise from the fact that the patrol inspector is not sufficiently detached and not sufficiently "independent." His findings are less likely to come to the attention of the middle or upper supervision than those of the independent auditor who is on the scene only occasionally.

Auditors.   For critical work the auditing should preferably be done by men who are not a part of the Inspection Department.   Usually such auditors review the practices of inspectors as well as production operators.

The independent audit tends to be more completely planned than an audit by Production management or by inspectors.[37]   In addition, the entire concept of the independent audit has the support of upper management, which receives the audit reports for review.

The audit of decisions discussed under Product Acceptance by Operators, above, requires a regular examination of product conformance along with the associated documentation.   This cannot readily be done by the independent auditors who are on the scene so infrequently.   Instead, it is assigned to a special category of auditor created at the time of making the delegation of product acceptance decisions to Production.

Audit of Adequacy of Plan   In those cases where Production performs some of the quality planning, the adequacy of the resulting plan should itself be the subject of audit.   The general approach is discussed in Section 21, under Audit of Quality Plans.

---

[36] This audit is "independent" in the sense that it is conducted by people other than the shop supervision directly involved.   However, some companies formalize audits by production foremen.   See Walden, Clyde H., The Foreman's Role in Quality Control, *1972 Technical Conference Transactions,* ASQC, pp. 513–519.

[37] For some discussion of the potentialities and limitations of independent audits, see Section 21, under Quality Audit, *et seq.*   See also Marash, Stanley A., Performing Quality Audits, *Industrial Quality Control,* January 1966, pp. 342–347; also Lubelsky, B. L., Manufacturing Reliability, *Ninth National Symposium on Reliability and Quality Control, 1963,* ASQC, pp. 240–243.

TROUBLESHOOTING

The term "troubleshooting" [38] is used here in the sense of restoring the status quo to a well-behaved process which has gone out of control. Implicit in troubleshooting is the assumption that the process had previously been "well behaved" and that some adverse change had invaded the process to throw it out of control. Under this assumption, the need is to identify this invading cause and to remove it so as to restore the process to its normal good behavior. [39]

The Troubleshooting Process   A review of numerous instances of successful troubleshooting discloses that they follow a universal sequence of events.

1. Symptoms of trouble are detected in any of various ways:

From personal observation by operators, foremen, inspectors

From data provided by the process instrumentation

From outside feedback, e.g., inspection rejections, trouble encountered by a "customer" department further down in the progression of the product, field complaints

2. These symptoms are studied and described with precision so that those who advance theories about the causes of the trouble are well informed as to the outward evidences of the trouble.

3. Theories are advanced as to the causes of the symptoms.

4. The theories are analyzed and evaluated based on logical reasoning, closer observation, experimentation, and still other means (most of these are discussed in Section 16).

5. The true cause (or causes) of the adverse change is established from the analysis.

6. Action is taken to restore the status quo by removing the cause or otherwise neutralizing it.

Responsibility for Troubleshooting   In the foregoing sequence, the road is from symptom to cause to remedy. Once the cause is known, the responsibility for remedy is clear. What is usually not clear is the responsibility for going from symptom to cause.

In broad terms, it is left to the Production personnel to see that the status quo is restored. They can either do this by themselves, or they can call in staff specialists for assistance. [40]   The extent of reliance on such "outsiders" depends largely on how well the Production foremen, lead men, investigators, and operators have been trained in conducting the activities which collectively constitute troubleshooting.

On the face of it, Production personnel should "logically" do the bulk of the analysis and remedy required for troubleshooting. Because of their constant presence on the factory floor, they are personally aware of some likely causes; i.e., they can provide good theories about causation and can also go a good distance in evaluating these theories as to their likely validity. However, if the problem does not yield easily to such analysis, it becomes necessary to dig deeper, to analyze data,

---

[38] Also known as firefighting, clearing trouble, etc.

[39] The validity of this assumption is critical to the approach used. If the trouble is chronic (i.e., the process was *never* well behaved) then the remedy is not through troubleshooting. Instead, the remedy is a "breakthrough," for which the approach is totally different. See Section 2, under Sporadic Troubles: Troubleshooting, and under Chronic Troubles; Breakthrough.

[40] In many situations, the trouble is caused in one Production department but has its effect elsewhere. Such situations usually require a staff specialist to assist in conducting the interdepartmental relations. This is not to be confused with the problems of discovering and remedying the cause of the symptoms within the Production department involved.

and even to do some experimenting. At this stage the Production personnel run into limitations because:

They are not sufficiently trained in how to conduct scientific analysis.
They lack the time needed to conduct the analysis.

These limitations give rise to proposals that troubleshooting should be conducted by those who do have training in how to analyze for causes and whose time schedule permits them to do the job; i.e., that troubleshooting should be conducted by quality control personnel,[41] or by other staff specialists.

TABLE 11-5   Contrast in Troubleshooting: Process Symptoms versus Product Symptoms

Aspects of discovering causes from symptoms	Process out of control	Product non-conforming to specification
Number of potential causes	Few	Many
Relative extent of instrumentation to causation theories.	High	Low
Length of feedback loop from symptom to cause.	Short	Long
Extent of personal observation of potential causes	High	Low
Experience in syndrome* identification . . .	Much	Little
Tendency to cover up.	Low	High

* A syndrome is a unique combination of symptoms which points to a single cause.

For the short range, the use of "outside analysts" can seem entirely logical. However, this alternative has its own deficiencies. The outsider is not in touch with the day-to-day goings on. It takes him time to tune in and still more time to secure essential information at second hand from those who already know it at first hand. Moreover, this approach fails to upgrade the Production personnel and tends to perpetuate their reliance on outside specialists.

In the judgment of the author, the long-range solution is to train the Production personnel in how to conduct the analysis which is at the heart of troubleshooting. The training needed is largely common to that needed by Production personnel generally for dealing with quality problems.[42]

Where Production personnel are trained in effective troubleshooting, they are more likely to act on process control symptoms than to wait for product noncon-formance symptoms. Table 11-5 makes clear that troubleshooting from process symptoms is easier and more effective than troubleshooting from product symptoms.

QUALITY IMPROVEMENT BY PRODUCTION

This topic has much in common with the subject of Motivation. In consequence, it is treated in Section 18 (Motivation) under the heading The Formal Motivational Program: The Prevention Package. See also, in Section 18, the discussion under International Motivation Methods.

[41] See, for example, Rodgers, F. J., Troubleshooting—A Quality Control Task, *Annual Technical Conference Transactions,* ASQC, 1965, pp. 282–285.
[42] See Section 17, especially under Production Foremen.

TRAINING OF PRODUCTION PERSONNEL

The general subject of training for quality is treated in Section 17, including those aspects of training which relate to production.   In the present Section this topic of training will be dismissed after noting the relation of this training to Production responsibilities.

The minimal training is that needed to meet present responsibilities.   However, there is a gathering belief that, given adequate training, the Production forces could accept wider responsibilities, as has been demonstrated in Japan by the example of the QC Circles.[43]   In consequence, it is well, in designing training programs for Production, to consider the future as well as the present responsibilities.   Failing this, a vicious circle develops: the proposed responsibilities cannot be assigned because Production is not trained, and the training is not given for nonexistent responsibilities.

[43] See Section 18, under The Japanese QC Circle.

Section **12**

Inspection and Test[1]

J. M. JURAN

HARDY M. COOK, JR.,
Western Electric Company

[1] For the Second Edition, portions of this Section were prepared by Edward A. Reynolds and John G. Rutherford.

INTRODUCTION

The word "inspection" has so many meanings that precise definition must precede any critical discussion. As used in this Handbook, the word "inspection" always involves evaluating the quality of some characteristic in relation to a standard. This evaluation may be described as the "inspection act" and consists of the following actions (as applied to each quality characteristic):

1. Interpretation of the specification
2. Measurement of the quality of the characteristic
3. Comparing (1) with (2)
4. Judging conformance
5. Disposing of conforming cases
6. Disposing of nonconforming cases
7. Recording the data obtained[2]

Every one of the key words in the foregoing is itself subject to much variation. The word "specification" is used in the generic sense as the *standard* for the characteristic. It may consist of a written description, a drawing, a photograph, a physical sample, an oral instruction, a hazy memory.

The term "measurement" is used in the generic sense of *evaluation,* and it has its own dialect:

When the measurement is done:	*The word commonly used to describe it is:*
By the unaided human being	Inspection (this is a second meaning for the word used in the title of this Section)
With the aid of mechanical measuring instruments	Gaging or calipering
With the aid of electronic measuring instruments	Testing
With the aid of chemical or metallurgical measuring instruments	Testing or assaying

The main purpose of inspection is to determine whether products conform to specification. This purpose is often called "acceptance inspection," or "product acceptance." However, there are other purposes as well, the more important being listed in Table 12-1. The present Section is concerned primarily with acceptance inspection, but it deals also with those purposes of inspection which are closely allied to acceptance inspection, e.g., rating of accuracy of inspectors.

---

[2] From Juran, J. M., "Management of Inspection and Quality Control," Harper & Brothers, New York, 1945, p. 23.

TABLE 12-1   The Purposes of Inspection

Inspection includes, in all instances (1) interpretation of the specification, (2) measurement of the product, and (3) comparison of (1) with (2). Inspection also includes additional elements depending on the purpose (see below).

Purpose	Usually called	Distinguishing features
a. To distinguish good lots from bad lots.	Acceptance Sampling or Sampling Inspection; also called: Vendor (or incoming) inspection......... Process inspection................. Final inspection................	Prime purpose is to classify lots of product as to whether they are acceptable or nonacceptable. Results of the sampling are used to make this classification. Data from sampling usually made available to producing department. If done by purchaser on material bought from another company If done between departments of the same company If done by seller prior to shipment of finished goods to the customer
b. To distinguish good pieces from bad pieces.	Detail Inspection, 100% Inspection, or Sorting; also called: Classification	Prime purpose is to sort the product between good pieces and bad. Any data are incidental but are usually made available to producer If process is inadequate to meet tolerances If process is adequate, but shop difficulties have created defects "needlessly"
c. To determine if the process is changing. See Sec. 23.	Control Sampling	Prime purpose is to see if the process is changing. Usually done through Shewhart control charts which compare averages of samples to statistical limit lines. Detects the entrance of significant causes of variation. Any classification of product is incidental
d. To determine if the process is approaching the specification limits. See Sec. 23	Narrow-limit control	Prime purpose is to see if the trend of change within the process is such that there is danger of producing defective product. Usually done through charts which compare measurements on individual units of product to narrowed specification limits
e. To rate the quality of product. See Sec. 21, under Product Auditing.	Product Auditing or Quality Rating	Prime purpose is to "photograph" the quality of product. Usually the seriousness of defects is recognized by assigning demerits or weights depending on the severity of defects. Results are usually charted as demerits per unit of product
f. To rate the accuracy of inspectors. See in this Section, under Measure of Inspector Accuracy.	Accuracy Inspection, or Overinspection, or Accuracy Rating, or Check Inspection	Prime purpose is to measure the effectiveness of inspectors in finding defects. Comparison is made between (1) defects found by the inspector and, (2) defects which should have been found by the inspector. The ratio of (1) to (2) is the accuracy of the inspector
g. To measure the precision of the measuring instrument. See Sec. 13.		Prime purpose is to measure the ability of the instrument to reproduce its own readings under like conditions. Usually involves repeat checks by the same instrument on the same unit of product. May involve checks by more than one instrument on the same unit of product
h. To secure product-design information.	Qualification testing	Prime purpose is to judge the service capability of the product. Sometimes involves tests of increased severity
i. To measure process capability. See Sec. 9, under Process Capability Measurement	Process-capability measurement	Quantifies inherent variation of process

The persons who are engaged full-time in inspection work commonly carry the title Inspector.[3] Other titles include Tester, Gager, Chemist, Metallurgist, Technician. Persons engaged only part-time in inspection commonly carry a job title which reflects their major activities, e.g., Lathe Operator, Adjuster, etc.

Modern acceptance inspection is a phase in a series of evolutions. It is useful to trace this evolution to gain perspective and to make more clear the distinction between the unchanging function of product acceptance and the changing manner of carrying out that function.

Prior to the advent of the modern factory, the town or village workshops were very small. The proprietor was either the only workman or he employed only a few workmen. The compactness of village life gave each workman a panoramic view of the design, manufacture, and (usually) marketing of the product. The consumer often came personally to the shop, sometimes to state his needs, sometimes to accept delivery of the product, and sometimes to return the product as being defective.

Such a panoramic view was of great aid to the workman. It made clear to him at first hand what the quality needs of the consumer were, i.e., fitness for use. In addition, the face-to-face meeting with consumers supplied a psychological stimulus to quality workmanship. In those early days, the shop proprietor would, of course, examine the product made by the workman, partly to assure that the workman was learning his trade well and partly to protect the consumer. But there were no "inspectors" as we use that term today.

As the shops grew larger and larger, several new conditions evolved:

1. The workman's contact with the consumer grew less and less. The product was no longer sold directly to the ultimate consumer in the shop itself; it was sold to one or more intermediate merchants, sometimes being shipped far away.

2. The growth of the shops also brought about a division of work so that the workman no longer made the complete product. Instead, he made only part of it, sometimes a very minute part.

3. The workman's knowledge of the design, manufacture, and marketing of the product were thus largely eliminated, being replaced by a very limited knowledge, that of the specification for the immediate operation the workman performed. Moreover, this new, narrow knowledge was impersonal, derived from cold papers instead of through warm face-to-face meeting with the consumer.

4. Furthermore, in the interest of production efficiency, the workman was often paid under a piecework arrangement, with a strong stimulus to high-quantity production.

5. This removal from full view of the industrial cycle acted not only on the workman but on the supervision as well. More and more, the direction of the workmen was by intermediate supervisors rather than by the proprietor.

6. The examination of the product devolved on these intermediate supervisors. Partly because of the great quantity of product to be examined and partly because of a conflict of interests, a new job was created—that of inspector.

This changeover from small to large shops is not complete. Many small shops of today, especially in the service industries, have no "inspectors," nor do they need them.

During the 1960s there emerged a worldwide trend toward returning to Production operators some of the responsibility for product acceptance. Details of this are discussed in Section 11, under Product Acceptance by Operators.

---

[3] The title "Inspector" is sometimes used to describe persons not concerned with industrial products or processes, e.g., Safety Inspector, Health Inspector, etc. These categories are outside the scope of this Section.

INSPECTION PLANNING

As products have grown complex and as the job of making them has been divided among many departments, the job of inspection has also become complex and divided. Most inspection is now done by inspectors who lack full understanding of fitness for use. For this more complex work it has been found necessary to engage in formal inspection planning, i.e., preparing a written plan of what to inspect for and how.

The approach to inspection planning follows closely the principles of quality planning as set out in Section 6. Application of these principles to the inspection job has been extensively studied, and good tools are available to facilitate inspection planning.

Who Plans? It depends on the work situation. Table 12-2 lists some usual inspection and test activities and the identity of the usual planner. The unifying concept

TABLE 12-2   Who does the Inspection Planning?

Products requiring inspection planning	Usual planner		
	Inspector	Inspection supervisor	QC staff planner
Components completed within single department, small series production	X		
Components completed within single department, large series production.		X	
Simple components and services, purchased or in-house (castings, plating).		X	
Complex units, small series production (machine tools)		X	
Components produced by progression through multiple departments			X
Subsystem test, interdependent units			X

within Table 12-2 is that inspection planning can be done by anyone who understands the fitness for use of the product being inspected.

Where planning is done by a staff planner, it is usual to require that his proposal be accepted by the inspection supervision before the plan becomes effective. The staff planner also is assigned a scope of responsibility within which he works. This scope determines which aspects of inspection planning he is to cover: inspection instructions, instrumentation, cost estimates, space and workplace design, documentation, etc. In large organizations the planning is sometimes divided among specialists rather than being assigned by project.

The Flow Diagram The more complex the product, the greater is the need to prepare a flow diagram showing the various materials, components, and processes which collectively or sequentially turn out the final product. Figure 6-5 (in Section 6) is an example of a flow diagram prepared to aid inspection planning.

To prepare the flow diagram, the planner visits the various locations, interviews the key people, observes the activities, and records his findings. As he prepares the complete flow diagram, the planner simplifies the picture by good use of symbols.[4]

[4] The most usual symbols are:

○   OPERATION   D   DELAY
⇒   TRANSPORTATION   ▽   STORAGE
☐   INSPECTION   ◗   COMBINED ACTIVITY

In addition, he prepares proposals for improvement based on the analysis he has made. He sends copies of the diagram to all concerned and then is ready to convene them for discussion of the diagram and the proposals.

Inspection Stations   Selection of inspection stations follows closely the criteria for selection of control stations set out in Section 6. Applied to inspection, the stations are usually placed:

At movement of goods between companies, usually called "vendor inspection"
Before starting a costly or irreversible operation, usually called "setup inspection"
At movement of goods between departments, usually called "process inspection"
Upon completion of the product, usually called "finished goods inspection"[5]

These general rules do not decide all questions of inspection stations. Complex vendor relations may require an inspection station at the vendor's plant. Some process operations may require a "station" in which the inspector patrols a large area. Other process operations may be sufficiently well in hand so that no inspection stations are used between departments (instead, there is a station after completion of all operations).[6] In still other situations, there may be an added station after packing or at the customer's premises.

For each inspection station there is need to supply the inspector with any knowledge he lacks on what to inspect for and how to do it, i.e.,

Just what the mission of that inspection station is, i.e., which qualities to check
How to determine whether a unit of product conforms to standard or not
How to determine whether a lot of product is acceptable or not ("lot criteria")
What to do with conforming and with nonconforming products
What records to make

While these categories of instruction are quite similar from one job to another, the degree of detail varies enormously.

In allocating the inspection work among the various inspection stations, the planner should be alert to the presence of "self-policing" operations. Some oversize parts will not enter tools or fixtures for further processing, or cannot be assembled. Some parts are subjected to greater stresses during manufacture than during usage. Some electrical circuit tests identify deficient components. Oil-pressure tests identify some undersize parts.[7]

List of Characteristics   For each inspection station, the planner lists the quality characteristics to be checked. To determine these, the planner considers the various sources of pertinent product information:

The needs of fitness for use
The product and process specifications as published by the engineers
The customer's order, which references the product specification but may call for modifications
The pertinent industry standards, shop standards, and other general use sources

The presence of such multiple sources of information poses a question which should be faced squarely: Should the job of finding, interpreting, and reconciling

---

[5] For complex products, such as Missile Systems, acceptance may require tests of mechanical compatibility, electrical mating, vehicle performance under specified environmental conditions, and final configuration. These are usually called "Systems Tests."

[6] In assembly lines, inspection stations may be located on the line as well as at the end of the line. See Section 41, under In-line Assembly Inspection.

[7] See, in this connection, Meagley, Nelson G., Engineering the Inspection of Industrial Processes, *ASQC National Convention Transactions,* 1952, pp. 397–407.

these sources be left to the inspector, or should the planner do it? The answer will be different depending on the situation, but it should be clear.

Interpretation of the Specification   The information in the specification is seldom complete as to the knowledge needed by the inspector to meet the realities he faces. The inspection planner can help to bridge this gap in several ways:

1. *Clear up the meaning of the words used.* Terminology for describing sensory qualities is often confusing. In one company, the term "beauty defects" was used generally to describe blemishes on the product. Some of these blemishes (scratches in the focal plane of an optical instrument) made the product unfit for service. Other blemishes, though nonfunctional, could be seen by the customers and were objectionable for esthetic reasons. Still other nonfunctional blemishes could be seen only by the company inspectors but not by consumers. However, because the multiple meanings of the term "beauty defect" had not been clarified, the inspectors rejected all blemishes. Data analysis showed that most of the blemishes were both nonfunctional and nonoffensive to customers. Hence, new terminology was created to make the distinctions needed to describe the effect of blemishes. The clarification of terminology improved yields and opened the way to improvement in manufacturing processes as well.[8]

2. *Provide supplemental information* on matters for which the specification is vague or silent, e.g., workmanship. Usually this can be done for entire commodity or component classes, with minimum individual analysis.[9] The greatest needs for supplemental standards arise in new and rapidly changing technology. In such cases it is common to find that vague standards are provided to the inspectors despite the fact that the general state of ignorance is high. (Vague standards create confusion among departments as well as among companies.)

3. *Classify the characteristics for seriousness* to help place the emphasis on the most important features of the product. (See Seriousness Classification, below.) In the case of process characteristics, make use of the Concept of Dominance, as discussed in Section 9.

4. *Provide samples,* photographs, or other reference aids to help explain the meaning of the specification. The greatest single need is for visual standards (see below).

5. *Review clarity of specifications in general.* Periodically, the inspection planners should take time out from product-by-product planning to review with the specification writers the recurring, chronic problems of interpretation. Such reviews have historically been the means for making major strides in clarifying specifications, e.g., serious classification of characteristics; quantifying widely used characteristics such as torque required to turn knobs; standardization of surface finishes; sample reference file, etc.

Written Inspection Instructions   The final results of inspection planning are reduced to writing in one of several ways:

Inspection and Test Procedure.   This is a tailor-made plan for a specific component or product type. It always lists the characteristics to be checked, the method of check (e.g., visual, gage, etc.), and the instruments to be used. It may, in addition, include the seriousness classification of characteristics; tolerances and other piece criteria; list of applicable standards; sequence of inspection operations; fre-

[8] Consulting experience of J. M. Juran. For some added examples, see Juran, J. M., Is Your Product Too Fussy? *Factory Management and Maintenance,* vol. 110, no. 8, August 1952, pp. 125–128.

[9] An example of such an approach, utilizing commodity coding for grouping families of products, resulted in cancellation of hundreds of individual instructions previously used. See Ford, Jarvis W., A Simplified Plan for Inspection Instructions, *Quality Assurance,* May 1967, pp. 30–31.

quency of inspection; sample size, allowable number of defects, and other lot criteria; inspection stamps to be applied.

Inspection and test procedures are very widely used in industry. In companies making complex systems or undergoing frequent design changes, these procedures become very numerous and consume extensive staff manpower to prepare them.

For some simple examples of Inspection and Test Procedure, see Figure 19-11, Table 37-1, and Figure 43-4 in Sections 19, 37, and 43 respectively.

Patrol Beat.   For many types of process inspection, the inspection stations require less than the full time of an inspector — often much less. A usual practice is to collect such stations into a "patrol beat" so designed that it will occupy the full time of a man. Table 12-3 is an example of such a patrol beat.[10]

Patrol beats usually involve multiple Production and Inspection departmental areas. In addition, the inspection findings are reported to several departments for information and action, i.e., Production, Inspection, Quality Control. In consequence, the planner should assure that these and other departments affected participate in the design of the patrol beat.

"Work sampling" is a useful concept in patrol inspection. Under this concept, the inspectors make *random* visits to the inspection stations. The resulting data are analyzed and become the basis for supervisory action.[11]

Finished Goods Acceptance Procedure.   There are actually a number of levels of "finished goods": materials, parts, components, subassemblies, assembled units, subsystems, systems. Each of these can be a completed product to some company or department, and thereby "finished goods" acceptance is performed at all these levels. System tests are most elaborate, not merely because of the problems of mating subsystems but because of the many complex environmental tests needed for modern apparatus.

The acceptance procedure should certainly provide inspection for new defects created by the progression of the product into higher levels of assembly and finishing operations. In addition, acceptance testing may be designed to provide redundancy against failure to detect defects missed at earlier stages of progression.

The planner should be especially alert to discover duplications between what is done at final inspection and elsewhere. When field troubles show up as a result of ineffective controls prior to final inspection, the salesmen, field engineers, and higher management all may be indifferent to the niceties of inspection stations and may urge multiple checks as a temporary measure. These bits of work can take firm root, accumulate, and endure beyond the reasons which gave them birth. The planner is in a good position to discover such out-of-date duplications and to root them out.

In conveyor assembly and test lines, the planning is usually for an entire inspection and test *team*. Sometimes the team is housed in a separate test area, the product being conveyed in and out. In other cases, the team is largely stationed on the main assembly line, the inspection stations being located amid Production stations.

Planning of such team activities requires close collaboration among the industrial neighbors involved in the common work flow. It also requires a balancing of the work load among the team members through ingenious design of test equipment, handling equipment, and work assignments.

Nonproduction Operations   The planner should be alert to the need for locating inspection stations at such operations as material handling, storage, packing, and

---

[10] From Carter, C. W., Audit Testing, *Industrial Quality Control*, March 1958, pp. 8–11.

[11] See Hecht, Bernard, The "SWAP" System of Quality Improvement, *Industrial Quality Control*, May 1962, pp. 15–21.

TABLE 12-3   Patrol Beat

No.	Test	Sampling		Testing	How results are used
		Where	Frequency	Where	
	Acid Manufacturing Process				
1	% SO_2 gas test TAPPI 603 M-45	From gas line off coolers	Once every two hours	Acid plant	This test is used for checking the automatic Leeds & Northrup SO_2 recorders
2	Temperature of gas, strong tower and weak tower M & O method		Once per hour	Acid plant	The Acid Maker controls the temperature of the gas, the strong tower, and the weak tower to regulate the speed of the gas absorption in the acid-making process
3	Acid test, total, free, and combined SO_2 TAPPI 640 M-45	From strong and weak towers	Once per hour	Acid plant	This test tells the Acid Maker how much lime rock to use. He adjusts the amount of water and gas going to the towers with this information
4	Baumé on acid in strong tower and acid in weak tower M & O method	From strong tower and weak tower	Once per hour	Acid plant	The Acid Maker controls the strength of his acid in the towers with these test results. It tells him the concentration of his acid
	Digester Cooking Process				
5	Chip moisture M & O method	Sample taken in chip bin	Once per cook	Chip room	The cook adjusts the volume of the chips he puts in the digesters with this information

shipping.   The fact that the departments doing these operations are not a part of Production is of no consequence if product quality is affected.

Aspects which may require inspection planning include:

Internal handling: use of correct containers and other handling facilities; product protection against corrosion, contamination, etc.

Internal storage: adequate identity and traceability.

Packing: product identification, lot numbers, traceability; protection against adverse environments; protection against damage due to handling, shipping and unpacking; presence of incidental small parts and information circulars.

Shipping: care in loading; special markings required by customers.

Once the planner has prepared the procedure, the interested departmental supervisors can be convened to reach agreement on who is to carry out that part of the inspection plan.

Inspection Data Planning.   The planner also determines the data recording needs for each inspection station.   In many cases, the standard inspection report forms will meet the recording needs.[12]   For finished products a special test document is usually provided.   In addition, the planner makes provision for any special recording needed for frequency distribution, control charts, certification, traceability, etc.[13]

Extent of Planning   The concept of separating inspection planning from execution has great value if properly applied.   If planning is underapplied, there is increased risk of catastrophic product failure.   If overapplied, the result is excess cost and much internal friction.   Striking a sound balance requires periodic reappraisal of the major forces in contention as well as analysis of the conventional alarm signals, e.g.,

[12] See generally Section 19.
[13] See also Inspection Data Feedback, below.

rising staff costs, abrasion between departments.   In addition, the changing job situations influence the extent of formal planning needed, notably (1) the education, experience, and training of the work force; (2) the stability of the processes; and (3) the severity of the product requirements.

Recognition of Profound Changes.   Planners should be on the alert to identify revolutionary changes in quality criteria and to provide correspondingly revolutionary procedures dealing with these changes.   To cite several examples:

1. Assembly of nuclear reactors and space vehicles requires a level of care far beyond that exercised in conventional assembly.   The Enrico Fermi reactor at Lagoona Beach, Michigan, was badly damaged in October 1966, evidently due to a foreign object blocking the flow of sodium coolant.   Pumps in nuclear reactors have been badly damaged by a loose nut being pumped through the system.[14]   Complex missiles have failed in their mission due to comparatively simple defects on mechanical components.[15]   In such situations the penalties for undetected defects rise so high that elaborate countdowns and checkouts must be instituted.

2. When the U.S. Navy undertook procurement of materials and components to build nuclear submarines, it encountered a widespread failure to adhere to specifications and sharply criticized the contractors for the nonconformances.   Actually, the contractors were doing what they had always done—shipping nonconforming products which experience had shown to be fit for use.   The big change was that the new species of submarines required rigid compliance with specifications which had been unrealistic in respect to previous applications.   In addition, there was a clash between two cultures: (1) the contractors, who took too long to discover that loose enforcement had no place in the nuclear submarine program, and (2) a new breed of Navy engineers, who were unaware that loose enforcement had long been used to neutralize the effect of unrealistic specifications.[16]

3. Soon after the Motor Vehicle Safety Act of 1966 became law, the government regulators found that a significant number of vehicle components failed to comply to standards which "industry itself" (i.e., committees of industry engineers) had set before there was legislation on the subject.   Here the two cultures involved (industry regulation and government regulation) represented different levels of enforcement, the one based on fitness for use and the other based on the concept that each instance of nonconformance now constituted a "federal case."

These cases of "massive change" can be multiplied widely.[17]   Failure to recognize their existence sets the stage for a shocking, expensive confrontation which damages many innocent people as well as the guilty.

Foolproofing.   The planner faces two responsibilities relative to inspection error: (1) avoiding built in sources of error and (2) providing positive means of foolproofing the inspection against error.   See, for a detailed discussion, Inadvertent Errors, under Inspector Errors, below.

Overplanning.   In some companies, the writing of inspection plans is extensively done.   New customer orders, new product designs, new process changes, new regulations, etc., are all occasions for scrutiny by the quality control engineers, who issue inspection plans accordingly.   As this goes to extremes, the cost of planning rises,

[14] Miller, Charles M., "Specific Quality Problems in the Manufacture of Components for Nuclear Power Plants," *ASQC National Convention Transactions,* 1959, pp. 575–583.

[15] Smiley, R. W., Government and the Inspector, *Industrial Quality Control,* April 1964, pp. 4–7.

[16] For a description of this situation as viewed by an indignant naval officer, see Rickover, H. G., The Never Ending Challenge, *Industrial Quality Control,* August 1963, pp. 12–17.

[17] Juran, J. M., Mobilizing for the 1970's, *Quality Progress,* August 1969.

and the excess formality increases the training time for inspectors, the attention to trivia, the documentation, and the control effort generally. Error rates tend to increase, with adverse effects on inspection costs and inspector morale.

Dealing with excess planning costs takes several forms. One is to do the planning by computer[18] or by other means of mechanizing much of what the engineers otherwise do manually.

A second approach is to minimize the amount of tailor-made planning by extending the use of inspection and test manuals which have broad application. See The Inspection Manual, below.

A third form is to delegate some of the planning itself to the inspection supervisors and the inspectors. To do this usually requires preparation of a manual on inspection planning plus training the inspection force to do the planning for all except the vital few characteristics, which are reserved for the staff planners.

Still another device is to agree, case by case, on the amount of detailed planning needed.[19]

Man, Machine, and System. A major decision in all planning is the extent to which tasks will be assigned to men versus machines, and the related question of delegation to men versus systems. Machines are superior for doing deeds which can be clearly defined and which require exacting attention to repetitive detail. (Contrary to popular belief, machines cannot think for men; rather, men must do the thinking for the machines. Thereafter, the machines follow the prescribed programs.)

Table 12-4 is a list contrasting intellectual activities, and proposes a division between man and machine as applied to inspection and test.[20]

The study of the interrelationship of men, machines, and system masquerades under a variety of names: Human Factors; Biomechanics; Human Engineering; Ergonomics; Industrial Psychology. Industrial managers, including Quality Managers, are commonly amateurs in the understanding of human capacities and especially human behavior. The behavioral scientists are the "professionals," but the subject is as yet hardly a science. In addition, communication between the practicing managers and the behavioral scientists is severely limited by differences in dialect and, especially, cultural background.

THE INSPECTION MANUAL

This manual elaborates the work of the Inspection Department and in addition includes much information of general interest to all company departments with respect to inspection practice.[21] It consists of:

1. A manual of inspection procedures common to all products and processes
2. Supplemental manuals for specific products and processes

---

[18] Patrick, J. F., and F. G. Brune, Quality Instructions for Missile Production, *Industrial Quality Control*, September 1962, pp. 19–22. See also Ford, op. cit.

[19] An example of the swinging pendulum is seen in setting visual inspection standards for molecular electronic circuits. In one company, the first standard consisted of several vague criteria—less than a page. Successive revisions expanded the standard to 54 (later 39) pages of closely worded criteria. A team approach was then set up to strike a middle ground, along with structuring other improvements. See Ludwig, H. D., Micro-electronics Visual Inspection —Fact or Fiction, *ASQC Annual Technical Conference Transactions*, 1967, pp. 629–635.

[20] Thompson, H. A., and E. A. Reynolds, Inspection and Testing as a Problem in Man-Machine Systems Control Engineering, *Industrial Quality Control*, July 1964, pp. 21–23.

[21] The Inspection Manual is a part of the broader Quality Control Manual (See Section 6).

TABLE 12-4   Assignment to Machines versus Men

Lower Intellectual Activities	Higher Intellectual Activities
1. Things that can be expressed exactly.	Things that cannot be expressed exactly.
2. Decisions that can be made in advance.	Decisions that cannot be made in advance.
3. Arithmetic, algebraic and chesslike symbolic logic.	Pattern recognition, judgment, creativity, foresight, leadership, and such thinking.
4. Highly repetitive and, therefore, menial.	Random, having many degrees of freedom, never exactly the same.
5. Can be reduced to logic and, therefore, programmed exactly into a machine.	Cannot be programmed exactly but can use heuristic approximations as an aid.
6. Those a small machine can handle completely, faster, and more positively.	A machine cannot handle completely and it becomes excessively large and uneconomical in attempting to do so.
7. Design and programming require a high level of intelligence but, once done, the mental activity need not be repeated.	This problem is never exactly the same and it must be reconsidered, that is, rethought out for each new decision.
8. Involves decisions as to what is right or wrong. The man guesses and the machine monitors to prevent him from making a mistake. It does this positively enough for use in safety systems.	Man uses the display which is driven by the machine and possibly a separate computer to assist him in making the choice type of decisions as to what is best, using the most advanced mathematical techniques.
9. Requires a high degree of orderliness.	Takes care of matters which cannot be arranged into any sort of orderly procedures.
10. Includes the decisions which must be made rapidly by the machine in periods of congestions and in emergencies.	Involves situations that develop more slowly, that will, sooner or later, require a considered decision.

Inspection Procedures Manual.   The contents of this manual are quite similar from one company to another and consist typically of:

The statement of legitimacy and purpose, approved by the responsible manager.

The table of contents of the manual.

The organization section, including inspection organization charts, job descriptions, and statements of responsibilities.

The general concept of inspection as used in the company.

The plan for seriousness classification of defects. (The actual classifications of defects are in the supplemental product manuals.)

The standard plans for sampling inspection: bulk sampling, tables for random sampling, continuous sampling, narrow-limit sampling.

The standard plans for use of control charts.

Vendor inspection procedures.

In-process inspection procedures.

Finished goods inspection procedures.

Measurement control procedures, including the schedule of checking intervals for general-use equipment.

Copies of all the inspection forms used and instructions for data recording and documentation. [22]

Product identification procedure.

Procedure for issuance and control of inspection stamps.

Feedback of data to Production; procedure for corrective action.

Procedure for dealing with nonconforming material.

Index and glossary.

[22] See also Section 19 for discussion of the related problems of forms design, printing, etc.

Product and Process Inspection Manuals. These specialized supplemental manuals, though dealing with a variety of products, are all organized under similar outlines, typically:

The materials section, which includes material specifications
The process section which includes:

Process specifications
Formulation control criteria
Patrol beats and associated criteria

The product section, which includes:

Product specifications and associated technical data
Product samples where feasible, e.g., textile swatches, color samples
Lists of defects, classified for seriousness
Sample sizes, frequencies, AQLs, and acceptance criteria

The test section, which includes test specifications—both internal and industry standards

PHYSICAL FACILITIES FOR INSPECTION

Inspection requires facilities in the form of work space, instruments, and supplies. The adequacy of these facilities is vital to the validity and cost of the inspection. Responsibility for providing these facilities is shared among inspection supervisors, quality control engineers, and manufacturing planning engineers, so that good coordination is essential.

The planning sequence starts with determining "activities," i.e., the inspections and tests required by the materials, process, and product. Next, the methods for conducting these inspections are determined. Finally, plans are worked out for the details of space, layout, equipment, and personnel. The determination of activities and methods is fundamental to all that follows in this sequence.

Inspection Areas A wide range of choices is available in design of the inspection area. The physical flow of work is a major influence in this choice, i.e., whether the inspector should come to the work or vice versa.

In receiving inspection, the problems of transport and unloading of the incoming product usually dictate a common area for receiving all incoming shipments. It becomes logical to locate the receiving inspection in this same common area, often with specially designed systems of transport to facilitate sampling and disposition by Inspection. [23]

In process inspection, the wide dispersion of the production areas and the sheer mass of material involved suggest that the inspector should come to the work. It is common to find patrol inspectors spending most of their time at the machines and doing their paper work at benches which are located physically in the production areas. The spectacle of all those tons of material moving into and out of numerous process inspection areas is now largely obsolete.

In final inspection, the inspectors are commonly provided with a fixed location due to the permanent installation of test facilities, power sources, etc. The problem of moving the product into and out of these locations is greatly simplified by use of conveyor transport and by sampling where feasible.

Laboratory Areas Laboratories may deal with any of numerous technological

[23] Sometimes this inspection is conducted by a resident inspector at the vendor's plant, See Section 10.

specialties: chemical, bacteriological, physical, electronic, metallurgical and metallographic, radiation, radiographic, ultrasonic, eddy current, etc. Each of these specialties requires a unique installation of instruments and supporting services, usually housed in a special environment. With some exceptions, the result is a fixed installation to which the test samples must be transported. While the test samples seldom involve tonnages of material, they do involve a problem of transporting the test samples from the points of origin, e.g., the receiving dock, the production processes. There is a time factor as well, since good process control requires prompt feedback.

These problems of transport of samples and prompt feedback are sometimes solved by special designs.

1. Use of pneumatic tubes to transport samples (even of hot metal) from the production floor to the laboratory.[24]

2. Use of modern electronic communication to feed back the data, e.g., closed circuit television.

3. Use of branch laboratories for standardized simple tests. The branch laboratory is designed to deal with a very few highly repetitive tests. The instruments, or the standard reagents, are designed so that the test will be easy to learn and largely foolproof in operation. The local inspection or production personnel are then trained in how to conduct the test and are audited periodically to verify their results.

The gage laboratory and precision measurement laboratory are special cases, since their job is primarily to measure instruments, not product. Even here, the concept of branch laboratories is widespread in large plants. An interesting form of this branch laboratory is the traveling cart or truck which can come to the instruments rather than vice versa.[25]

Storage Areas   These likewise serve a variety of purposes: to hold standard samples for reference; to file product samples for stability tests and for analysis in the event of field troubles; to store reports, correspondence, and data; to store supplies, especially perishables, e.g., photographic or radiographic film.

Much new technology has evolved which reduces the need for storage space but which introduces new problems of environment control. Microfilm, magnetic tape, punched cards, and still other devices permit drastic reductions in storage space while simplifying the ease of access. However, the special nature of these devices has favored centralizing their storage under some corporate service department. The quality planner must nevertheless inform himself of the potentialities inherent in the new technologies and the limitations on their use. Based on this knowledge, he should observe several standard precautions:

1. Safeguard against damage. Sources of damage include pilferage, flood, fire. Master samples and film records need appropriate protection against deterioration from dust, heat, etc. For important records and master copies of specifications, there may be need to send duplicates to a safe vault storage.

2. Ease of access. This involves a sound system of identification as well as a system of storage correlated to frequency of use.

3. Future requirements. Provision should be made for growth as needed. This growth should be kept in check by an adequate plan for disposition of obsolete records. See, in this connection, Section 19, under Quality Records Files.

Workplace Design   A most useful beginning is to visit some recently designed facili-

---

[24] See, for example, Proper Work Environment, *Quality Assurance*, December, 1968, pp. 134–135. See also Section 30, Table 30-3.

[25] See also, Laboratory Management, under Inspection Department Management, below.

ties of other companies in the industry, government laboratories, etc. Such recent installations reflect recent thinking and also provide a feedback of the benefits and disadvantages of the new ideas tried out. Quite often, the manufacturers of laboratory equipment have ideas to offer based on experience with customer installations.

Tailoring the design to the unique problems of each company requires consideration of some usual as well as unusual needs. Among the usual are the requirements for:

1. Safety for the personnel, and compliance with present and anticipated safety regulations.

2. Optimizing the overall cost of inspection, giving due consideration to cost of space, materials movement, etc.

3. Providing a comfortable, attractive workplace for the personnel to improve efficiency[26] as well as to reduce turnover. This includes space for personal effects as well as work space. For clerical work, an average area of 75 square feet per employee is desirable, with a minimum of 60. (This provides for usual desk and filing requirements.) Single-occupancy offices or unusual filing needs will require more space.

4. Material flow. Great care should be taken to provide for a smooth, unimpeded flow of work in and out and to keep the bottlenecks away from the inspection space.

5. Contingencies. Periodically there is need to train recruits, to hold nonconforming product awaiting disposition, or otherwise to provide for some temporary space occupancy. Lack of such provisions can seriously impede the entire operation.

6. Flexibility. It is inevitable that new products, methods, and other advances in technology will require that the workplaces be revised from time to time. Enough standardization must be provided to permit practical adaptation to these expected changes.

Examples of unusual needs include:

"Clean rooms" which maintain precise control of environments during inspection. The use of such clean rooms is expanding rapidly due to increasing precision of products.[27] miniaturization, use of ultrapure materials, etc.

Air conditioning (this is increasingly becoming usual).

Freedom from vibration, noise, odors, and other extraneous disturbances, especially when sensory qualities are involved.

Communication with other areas through electronic devices, pneumatic tubes, conveyors, etc.

Lighting Lighting is a major influence in the effectiveness of visual inspection, though lighting is needed in all other inspection activities as well—precision measurement, laboratory testing, clerical work.

The quality planner or Industrial Engineer is in the best position to study the special needs of illumination for the various inspection tasks. However, in most companies the Plant Engineering Department has the basic responsibility for decisions on lighting fixtures and on levels of illumination. Hence close collaboration is needed to assure that the inspection job needs are not ignored by overemphasis on standardization of fixtures, plant maintenance, and power consumption.

---

[26] A study at the British Royal Mint produced changes in workplace design, illumination, and work cycle, resulting in increasing efficiency of detection from 54.5 to 74% and an increase in output from 815 to 972 coins per minute. See Cox, J. G., "The Ergonomics of Coin Inspection." *Quality Engineer,* vol. 28, no. 6, November–December 1964, pp. 165–169.

[27] See, for example, the environmental needs for inspection of bearings in Starkey, Paul H., For Bearings, the Less Inspection the Better, *Industrial Quality Control,* October 1967, pp. 204–206.

The major aspects of illumination are:

Light Intensity. This is a measure of the amount of light falling on the object to be inspected and is expressed in footcandles. (A footcandle is the amount of light intensity one foot away from a standard candle. A 100 watt incandescent bulb, without reflection, gives a level of about 5 footcandles at a distance of 5 feet.)

Recommended intensity of illumination for inspection work in various industries ranges usually from 100 to 500 footcandles. For "most difficult" inspection, 1,000 footcandles is recommended.[28] The long-range trend has been to increase recommended levels of illumination. Table 12-5 presents one set of recommendations for several varieties of work. It is seen that high levels are needed for fine detail or for continuous and rapid inspection.[29]

Light Color. Product color is a special category in visual inspection because of its importance for esthetic and functional reasons. Much progress has been made in designs of systems of measurement and in instrumentation to measure product color. However, product color is still mainly judged by visual inspection, and the color of lighting used influences the results of this inspection in several ways:

1. Color of light[30] can enhance or downgrade the appearance of products. (All who shop in modern supermarkets are familiar with the green-tinted light in the vegetable sections and the slightly red-tinted light at the meat counters to improve the appearance of these commodities.)

2. In color matching, the color of light greatly influences the results. It is normal to check precise matches under two different specified lights. If the materials match under both of these, they will normally match under any light. For less critical color matching, north daylight is generally used.

Background color is highly important in detecting color variations. Normally, a neutral light gray is used for close color matching. For detecting certain color defects, a contrasting background shade of about the same luminosity is often helpful.

3. Some quality characteristics, e.g., tarnish or stains, show up much better under one color of light than another.

4. Certain colors appear to have psychological and physiological effects on the

TABLE 12-5   Recommended Levels of Illumination

Type of inspection work	Footcandles
Ordinary	50
Difficult	100
Highly difficult	200
Very difficult	500
Most difficult	1,000
By industry	
Aircraft	100
Automotive	200
Canning	200
Clothing	500
Electrical testing	100
Foundry	100–500
Glove	500
Iron and steel	100–200
Machining	Like Inspection
Paper	100
Proofreading	150
Rubber tires	200
Textile	100–500

---

[28] The human ability to distinguish details cannot be used as an indication of adequate lighting, since the human eye is remarkably adaptable. It can see at very low levels of lighting, but only at the price of eyestrain and longer comprehension time. (Bright sunshine may reach 10,000 footcandles, but people can read newspapers at 1 footcandle.)

[29] "IES Lighting Handbook," 5th ed., Illumination Engineering Society, New York, 1972. Some practitioners prefer even higher levels. See Harris, Douglas H., and Frederick B. Chaney, "Human Factors in Quality Assurance," John Wiley & Sons, Inc., New York, 1969, p. 96. See also Lane, Marshall H., Establishing Controllable Color Standards, 1972 *ASQC Technical Conference Transactions*, pp. 289–294.

[30] Color of light is commonly measured by the wavelength distribution of the light.

inspectors themselves. Psychologically, it is believed that green light tends to calm emotions. It is, therefore, frequently chosen as the wall color in areas used for odor, taste, or audio checking, where calm concentration is desired.

Light Diffusion. Diffusion refers to the softness or harshness of light in forming shadows. For detecting textural defects such as cracks in porcelain, pits in metal, etc., a hard light that will cast a sharp shadow will enable the defect to be observed much more easily than a diffused light. At the other extreme, tarnish spots or slight color variations in highly polished articles can be detected only under a very soft or diffused light. Frequently special boxes are built so that fluorescent fixtures are further diffused through white cloth, and light is reflected equally on the article from all sides.

Fluorescent fixtures are extensively used in factories and inspection areas today, and the tendency is toward increased softness of shadows. However, a harder light is frequently desirable for detection of many types of defects. In addition, variation of intensity through spotlighting is often desirable in concentrating inspector or operator attention, provided that this is not carried beyond desirable limits of background contrast. In those inspections where either shape or texture is important, angle highlighting is especially advantageous. In addition, there has been some opinion that the eye is rested by occasional changes from low to high intensities, monotony is reduced, and errors or accidents are thus prevented.[31]

Lighting Direction. For detection of shape and texture, lighting direction is equally important as light diffusion, and the direction should be such as to emphasize the defect or texture and thus make it easier to locate. In many instances, maximum detection of the defect will be obtained with the lighting heading almost toward the inspector, with resultant glare and strain. In such instances, a compromise must usually be effected. The quality engineer may also consider the possibility of polarization of the light and, in some cases (such as the detection of shiny spots on a normally dull surface), the quality engineer should also consider the use of automatic scanning methods for detection to replace or supplement the visual inspection.

Background Contrast. "Background contrast" is defined as the difference in both intensity and color between light on the object viewed and light on the background or surrounding areas. The modern trend is to illuminate industrial and inspection areas with a uniform, diffused light. However, a background contrast of the ratio of about 3 to 1 in intensity and occasionally a variation in color shade may not only make defects easier to detect but may also reduce fatigue and monotony on the part of the inspector. It is suggested that quality engineers with difficult lighting problems—particularly those requiring concentrated and rapid detection, such as conveyor inspection—give careful thought to the problem of background contrast as an aid to their inspectors.

For detection of defects, a background light which will emphasize the contrast between the defect and the good is selected. Normally, such a background light is at the opposite end of the spectrum from the defect color if the defect tends to be darker than the surrounding area. (For example, a blue light will emphasize pink stains on a white or yellow background, a red light will emphasize pink stains on a gray background.)

---

[31] One study compared the performance of manipulative and inspection tasks under the same levels of tungsten and fluorescent lighting. In some cases, the results under fluorescent lighting were superior. See Lion, J. S., The Performance of Manipulative and Inspection Tasks under Tungsten and Fluorescent Lighting, *Quality Engineer,* vol. 29, no. 3, May-June 1965, pp. 85–89.

Beyond the foregoing usual lighting aspects, there may be special situations such as (1) flickering, which may be present to an objectionable degree even though not consciously noted (particularly with single-tube fluorescent fixtures); (2) lighting cost (although, in general, the long-range economic advantages of the best possible lighting will far outweigh increased initial or operating expenses); and (3) heat generated (particularly in air-conditioned or small, confined spaces).

Many years ago C. P. Steinmetz[32] observed, "The art of illuminating engineering embraces the field of two different sciences—physics and physiology." The quality planner should bear this in mind and seek out the advice of the company Personnel and Medical departments when studying problems of lighting.

The basic reference work on lighting is the "IES Lighting Handbook," published by the Illumination Engineering Society. The field continues to be very active, and the Society's journal, *Illuminating Engineering,* is an important source for observing the progress.

Instruments   Planning for instrumentation is discussed in Section 9, under Quality Information Equipment. See also, in general, Section 13 (Measurement).

AUTOMATED INSPECTION

Automated inspection and testing[33] are used to reduce costs, improve precision, shorten time intervals, alleviate manpower shortages, avoid inspection monotony, and for still other advantages.[34]   In some industries the manpower problems now seem insoluble in the absence of automated inspection.   Already in widespread use, automated inspection is still expanding, with no end in sight.

The economics of automation involve a substantial investment in special equipment to secure a reduction in operating costs.   The crux of justifying the investment lies in the amount of repetitive work the equipment will be called on to perform.   This estimate of the anticipated volume of testing should therefore be checked out with great care.[35]

A common starting point in discovering opportunities for automated inspection is to make a Pareto analysis of the kinds of inspections and tests being conducted. The vital few types are identified.   Estimates are then made of the manpower, costs, and other current problems associated with these tests.   The economics of automation are then estimated, and the comparable figures are an aid to decision as to the feasibility of successful conversion.

For complex equipments involving depot storage and field maintenance, the question of use of automated testing is itself highly complex and requires a tailor-made study of some magnitude.[36]

Technologically, the "machine" poses many problems.   It is less adaptable than

---

[32] "Radiation, Light, and Illumination," McGraw-Hill Book Company, New York, 1918.

[33] The first large-scale applications of automated testing were very likely in Western Electric Company during the 1920s.

[34] Reductions of 90% in testing time are not unusual. See, for example, Automatic Testing— A Natural at Automatic Electric, *Quality Assurance,* September 1966, pp. 34–36.

[35] There are also cautions to be observed due to engineering bias favoring automated testing. For a useful analysis with numerous references, see Swain, Alan D., Reliable Systems vs. Automatic Testing, *Proceedings, 9th National Symposium on Reliability and Quality Control,* IEEE, 1963, pp. 380–390.

[36] For an example of such a study involving the receiver-transmitter unit of an airborne communication set, see Oyerly, Philip R., and Dewey King, A Controlled Study of Automated Testing Techniques, *Proceedings, 9th Annual Symposium on Reliability and Quality Control,* IEEE, 1963, pp. 401–414.

the human being it replaces, so some changes may need to be made in the product to offset this rigidity. For example, the machine may hold the units to be tested by grasping certain surfaces whose dimensions were previously unimportant. Now these surfaces may need to be held to close dimensions because the machine is not as adaptable as the human inspector. Alternatively, the product design may need to be changed to provide for adequate location.[37]

Beyond the work of original design, construction and prove in, the machine must be set up specially for each job.[38, 39] However, modular construction, master test pieces, and taped programs have considerably reduced setup time while improving reproducibility. Reliability has generally been high, and use of printed circuit cards and other modular components has so reduced the "mean time to repair" that downtime is generally below 5% for well-designed machines.

Automated gaging and testing is extensively used in the mechanical industries.[40] It is also widely used in the electronic industries, especially for electronic components,[41] where the problem of making connections to the automated test equipment is so severe that the original product design must provide specially for this.

In the chemical industries, the corresponding development has been the "autoanalyzer." This has already made possible some extensive cost reductions and solutions of otherwise forbidding problems of recruitment of laboratory technicians.[42, 43] The autoanalyzer makes use of some equipment common to all tests—sensors, transducers, recorders, computers. However, each type of analysis has its unique procedure for converting the material under test into a form suitable for sensing.

The advent of numerically controlled (NC) machines has required development of new inspection techniques which likewise use the NC principle. Since the machine is controlled by a tape, the validity of that tape is critical. One form of inspection control is through certifying the tapes. Once certified, the tapes become an important stabilizer in the process capability of the NC machine.[44]

Inspection of NC product can make use of the properties of the machines by substituting a stylus for the cutter.[45] The measurements made by the stylus can be checked against the master tape. A further approach is to use coordinate measuring machines, also tape-controlled, to check the NC produced components.[46] Still another approach is to make and measure a full-scale picture.[47]

[37] For some elaboration, see Smith, J. B., Automated Inspection, *The Quality Engineer,* vol. 31, no. 2, pp. 33–37, 1967.

[38] For an extensive discussion of the desired features in automated testing, see Robb, D. T., Automatic Testing in Telephone Manufacture, *Bell System Technical Journal,* September 1956, pp. 1129–1154.

[39] See generally Section 9, under Quality Information Equipment.

[40] See for example, Section 42, under Inspection.

[41] See Section 38, under Automated Tests and Data Processing.

[42] See Section 32, under Control Laboratories.

[43] See also, Anderson, Norman G., Computer Interfaced Fast Analyzers, *Science,* October 17, 1969, vol. 166, no. 3903, pp. 317–324.

[44] Tape Controlled Machines at Sundstrand Aviation, *Quality Assurance,* June 1970, pp. 30–34.

[45] Elton, H. J., Automatic Inspection, *Aircraft Production,* vol. 20, October 1958, pp. 406–409.

[46] Hunt, William F., The Economy of Numerical Control Inspection, *ASQC Technical Conference Transactions,* 1965, pp. 31–35.

[47] See Kirwan, M. S., Guaranteed Accurate Numerical Tapes, *Mechanical Engineering,* August 1972, pp. 13–17.

SERIOUSNESS CLASSIFICATION

Some quality characteristics and defects are very important to fitness for use; others are not. The village craftsman and the small shop proprietor, with their first-hand knowledge of fitness for use, are able to concentrate their efforts on the most important qualities. In modern, large, complex organizations, the workmen, inspectors, and many of the supervisors lack complete knowledge of fitness for use and thereby are not fully clear on where to place their emphasis and how to make their decisions.

TABLE 12-6   Results of Seriousness Classification of Characteristics

Characteristic classification	Effect of classification on design tolerance	Effect of classification on amount of inspection	Number of dimensions checked	
			Before classification	After classification
Critical	None	None.	154	154
Major	None	None.	110	110
Minor A.	Tolerance was increased by a specified amount (doubled, etc.) provided the part assembled satisfactorily.	Inspection was made normally, but to wider tolerances.	66	15
Minor B.	Tolerance was ignored provided the part assembled satisfactorily.	Inspection was eliminated.	352	0
Total			682	279

For example, one company studying the fabrication and inspection of machine parts classified the quality characteristics into four classes. Table 12-6 shows the effect of this classification on product tolerances and on the number of dimensions checked. The inspection time was reduced from 215 to 120 minutes. In addition, there were greater savings through lower rework costs, lower tooling costs, and lower engineering costs for disposition of nonconforming product.[48]

To provide such missing knowledge on a broad scale, there has evolved a concept of formal seriousness classification, both for quality characteristics and for defects. The quality characteristics list comes from the specifications; the list of defects comes from evidences of failures during use (e.g., service reports) and from evidence of nonconformance during manufacture (e.g., inspection reports). When these two lists are classified for seriousness, the former is used mainly for quality planning while the latter is used mainly for inspection planning and for product auditing (see Section 21).

These two lists differ in their content, though the overlap is often great. A single quality characteristic, e.g., shaft diameter 1.000 ± 001, gives rise to two defects, i.e., oversize and undersize. These defects may be assigned different degrees of seriousness depending on the extent of nonconformance. Some extensive defect lists, e.g., the list for glass bottles, have little resemblance to the list of characteristics set out in the specifications.

Some companies use the same system of classification both for characteristics and defects. However, there is enough uniqueness about each of the two lists to suggest that adoption of a single system should be preceded by a positive examination

[48] Allen, Paul E., Evaluating Inspection Costs, *ASQC National Convention Transactions,* 1959, pp. 585–596.

of the nature of the two lists. For example, the effect of seriousness classification on design decisions can be quite different from the effect on inspection decisions, as is evident from Table 12-6.

Formal systems of seriousness classification were originally evolved to serve specialized purposes.[49] However, as the systems came into being, they were found to have application in the entire progression of product from design through usage: in quality specification, manufacturing planning, vendor relations, tooling, production, salvage, product auditing, and executing reporting. Vital qualities could now be identified with greater confidence, and it also became feasible to delegate class decisions and actions on a broad scale. For example, all class C defects could be assigned a common sampling plan, thereby avoiding the need for publishing numerous individual plans.

The multiple uses of seriousness classification systems make it desirable that the job of developing such a system be guided by an interdepartmental committee which has the responsibility for drafting a plan, modifying it, and recommending it for adoption. Such a committee has a series of tasks:

1. Determining the number of strata or classes of seriousness to use
2. Defining each class
3. Classifying each defect into one of the classes

Number of Levels or Strata. In theory, the number may be large, e.g., a defect may have any weight from 1,000 down to 1. In practice, such a large number of weights is too complex to administer. The actual plans in use consist of only several classes. While choice of the actual number of classes is arbitrary, extensive experience has shown that three or four classes suffice for a wide variety of situations.

Definitions for the Classes. These will differ with the nature of the product, process, etc. However, plans in existence tend to show striking similarity in definition, due in part to the influence of the Bell System classification plan.[50] Not only was this pioneering plan uncommonly well reasoned out; the men who devised it were later consultants to some of the U.S. Armed Services during World War II, and their thinking influenced the classification plans adopted by these Services. These plans, in turn, influenced the plans adopted by the contractors to the Armed Services.

The standard definitions adopted by the Bell System[51] are shown in Table 12-7. Study of these definitions discloses that there is an inner pattern common to the basic definitions (Table 12-8).

A composite of definitions used in food industry companies is shown in Table 12-9. It is evident that there are industry-to-industry differences in products, markets, etc., which require a tailor-made wording for each industry.[52] In addition, the lists are not static. The growth of government regulation has further influenced the definitions, as has the problem of repairs and guarantees for long-life products.

---

[49] The Bell System pioneered by developing a system to permit rating of quality of finished product. The U.S. Armed Services developed systems to simplify the administration of acceptance of goods purchased from contractors.

[50] Dodge, H. F., "A Method of Rating Manufactured Product," Bell Telephone Laboratories, Reprint B-315, May 1928. For a description of a more modern version, see Dodge, H. F., and M. N. Torrey, "A Check Inspection and Demerit Rating Plan," *Industrial Quality Control,* vol. 13, no. 1, July 1956, pp. 5–12.

[51] Dodge and Torrey, *ibid.*

[52] A number of the Sections of this Handbook include some illustrations of seriousness classification as applied to specific industries, e.g., 30, Pulp and Paper; 31, Food and Allied Industries; 38, Electronic Components; 40, Graphic Arts; 42, Automotive; 43, Household Appliances.

TABLE 12-7   Seriousness Classification of Defects (Bell System)

Class A—Very Serious (Demerit Value, 100)
a. Will surely cause an operating failure of the unit in service which cannot be readily corrected in the field, e.g., open relay winding; or
b. Will surely cause intermittent operating trouble, difficult to locate in the field, e.g., loose connection; or
c. Will render unit totally unfit for service, e.g., dial finger wheel does not return to normal after operation; or
d. Liable to cause personal injury or property damage under normal conditions of use, e.g., exposed part has sharp edges.
Class B—Serious (Demerit Value, 50)
a. Will probably cause an operating failure of the unit in service which cannot be readily corrected in the field, e.g., protective finish missing from coaxial plug; or
b. Will surely cause an operating failure of the unit in service which can be readily corrected in the field, e.g., relay contact does not make; or
c. Will surely cause trouble of a nature less serious than an operating failure, such as sub-standard performance, e.g., protector block does not operate at specified voltage; or
d. Will surely involve increased maintenance or decreased life, e.g., single contact disk missing.
e. Will cause a major increase in installation effort by the customer, e.g., mounting holes in wrong location; or
f. Defects of appearance or finish that are extreme in intensity, e.g., finish does not match finish on other parts—requires refinishing.
Class C—Moderately Serious (Demerit Value, 10)
a. May possibly cause an operating failure of the unit in service, e.g., contact follow less than minimum; or
b. Likely to cause trouble of a nature less serious than an operating failure, such as substandard performance, e.g., ringer does not operate within specified limits; or
c. Likely to involve increased maintenance or decreased life, e.g., dirty contact; or
d. Will cause a minor increase in installation effort by the customer, e.g., mounting bracket distorted; or
e. Major defects of appearance, finish, or workmanship, e.g., finish conspicuously scratched, designation omitted or illegible.
Class D—Not Serious (Demerit Value, 1)
a. Will not affect operation, maintenance, or life of the unit in service (including minor deviations from engineering requirements), e.g., sleeving too short; or
b. Minor defects of appearance, finish, or workmanship, e.g., slightly scratched finish.

It is also evident that the classifications must simultaneously take into account multiple considerations such as functional performance, user awareness, and financial loss. For example, a radio receiver may have defects as follows:

Defect	Effect on functional performance	Consumer awareness
Open circuit in power supply	Set is inoperative	Fully aware
Short circuit in resistor	Excess power consumption	Seldom aware
Poor exterior finish	No effect	Usually aware
Poor dress of internal wiring	No effect	Seldom aware

Classifying the Defects. This essential task is time-consuming, since there are always many defects to be classified. If the class definitions have been well drawn, the task becomes much easier.

During classifying, much confusion is cleared up. It is found that the seriousness of important visual defects depends not so much on whether the inspector can see it as on whether the consumer can see it. It is found that some words describing de-

TABLE 12-8 Inner Pattern — Seriousness Classification System

Defect class	Demerit weight	Cause personal injury	Cause operating failure	Cause intermittent operating trouble difficult to locate in field	Cause substandard performance	Involve increased maintenance or decreased life	Cause increase in installation effort by customer	Appearance, finish, or workmanship defects
A	100	Liable to	Will surely*	Will surely				
B	50		Will surely†		Will surely	Will surely	Major increase	
C	10		Will probably		Likely to	Likely to	Minor increase	Major
D	1		May possibly Will not		Will not	Will not		Minor

* Not readily corrected in the field.
† Readily corrected in the field.

TABLE 12-9   Composite Definitions for Seriousness Classification in Food Industry

Defect	Effect on consumer safety	Effect on usage	Consumer relations	Loss to company	Effect on conformance to government relations
Critical	Will surely cause personal injury or illness	Will render the product totally unfit for use	Will offend consumer's sensibilities due to odor, appearance, etc.	Will lose customers and will result in losses greater than value of product	Fails to conform to regulations for purity, toxicity, identification
Major A	Very unlikely to cause personal injury or illness	May render the product unfit for use and may cause rejection by the user	Will likely be noticed by consumer, and will likely reduce product salability	May lose customers and may result in losses greater than the value of the product. Will substantially reduce production yields	Fails to conform to regulations on weight, volume, or batch control
Major B	Will not cause injury or illness	Will make the product more difficult to use, e.g., removal from package, or will require improvisation by the user. Affects appearance, neatness	May be noticed by some consumers, and may be an annoyance if noticed	Unlikely to lose customers. May require product replacement. May result in loss equal to product value	Minor nonconformance to regulations on weight, volume, or batch control, e.g., completeness of documentation
Minor	Will not cause injury or illness	Will not affect useability of the product. May affect appearance, neatness	Unlikely to be noticed by consumers, and of little concern if noticed	Unlikely to result in loss	Conforms fully to regulations

fects must be subdivided; i.e., a "stain" may be placed in two or three classes depending on severity and location. In many ways, the work of classifying defects is rewarding through clearing away misconceptions and through giving a fresh view to all who participate.

Classification of Characteristics. In some companies the formal "seriousness" classification is not of defects but of characteristics in the specifications. The classification may be in any of several alternatives:

1. Functional[53] or nonfunctional. Where a single set of drawings carries both functional ("end use") requirements and nonfunctional ("means to an end") requirements, it is important to make clear which is which. The purposes served by these two classes are generally alike throughout industry:

Functional requirements are intended to	*Nonfunctional requirements are intended to*
Ensure performance for intended use	Inform the shop as to method of manufacture
Ensure long useful life	Reduce cost of manufacture
Minimize accident hazards	Facilitate manufacture
Protect life or property	Provide interchangeability in the shop
Provide interchangeability in the field	Provide information to toolmakers
Provide competitive sales advantage	

"Which is which" becomes important because it directs the priorities of process design, and many aspects of economics of manufacture, as well as the jurisdiction over waivers.

When the engineers make this classification, they commonly add a designation such as E (for Engineering) to the functional characteristics. All others are then assumed to be nonfunctional.

A comparable situation prevails in process specifications, where the need is to distinguish mandatory from advisory requirements,[54] which correspond roughly to functional and nonfunctional requirements as applied to the product. However, the process specifications seldom make this distinction.

2. Seriousness classification. When this method is used, it parallels closely the classification into Critical, Major, and Minor as used for classification of defects.[55] The resulting classifications then become a supplement to the specification or are shown on the drawings themselves by some code designation, for example,

Critical — ⊕
Major A — ⊖
Major B — ○
Minor — not marked

[53] This is not to be confused with mechanical, chemical, or electrical functioning. In products such as jewelry or textiles, the most important functional requirement is *appearance*.

[54] For further discussion, see Section 11, in Process Specifications, under Knowledge of "Supposed to Do."

[55] The contention is often raised that the tolerances on the specifications are an automatic form of seriousness classification, i.e., anything with assigned tolerances must be met and is "therefore" critical. An alternative contention is that the closeness of the tolerances is a key to seriousness classification, i.e., the narrowest tolerances are assigned to the most critical characteristics. When these contentions are examined more closely, they are found to contain too many exceptions to serve as firm rules for classifications.

3. Segregation of functional requirements into a separate document, such as an "Engineering Specification" or a "Test Specification."

4. Shop practice tolerances versus special tolerances. This method is based on preparation of a Shop Practice Manual which sets out general use tolerances derived from the process capability of general use machines and tools. Once published, these shop practice tolerances govern all characteristics not specially toleranced.

Who Classifies? For defect classification, an interdepartmental committee is the ideal choice. This provides each department with the benefits derived from the process of active review, and it also produces a better final result.[56] However, some companies assign a staff specialist to prepare a proposed classification, which is then reviewed by all interested departments. The specialist is usually a quality control engineer.

When the classification is limited to specified characteristics, e.g., functional versus nonfunctional, the designer usually prepares the draft.

PRODUCT ACCEPTANCE INSPECTION

The principal decision-making assigned to inspectors is to determine whether product conforms to standard.[57] When the words "product" and "standard" are examined closely, it becomes evident that some careful distinctions must be made.

The Nature of Product   "Product" takes multiple forms. When submitted to Inspection for decision on conformance to standard, product may consist either of (1) single elements of product or (2) lots of product. Single elements exhibit one of two main forms:

Discrete Units of Product. These are separate entities such as bolts, teacups, refrigerators. The term "discrete" refers to the fact that the product is made, tested and used, as a separate unit. The approach to these activities is simplified through prior knowledge of how the product will be used.

Specimens from a Coalesced Mass.[58] These are samples from batches, e.g., a melt of steel or from continuous processes such as petroleum refining. These situations lack the common base of knowledge of the discrete units, since the product is made as a coalesced mass, tested as a specimen, and used in numerous forms not fully predictable at the time of test.

The Nature of Lots of Product   Usually, the product submitted (for decision on conformance to standard) consists of a "lot." The true lot is an aggregation of product made under a common system of causes. When this ideal is met, the lot possesses an *inherent uniformity derived from the common system of causes.* The extent to which the lot conforms to this ideal greatly influences the approach to product acceptance and especially the kind and extent of sampling.

In its simplest form, the true lot emerges from one machine run by one operator and processing one material batch, all under a state of statistical control, e.g., a single formulation of a drug product or a run of screw machine parts turned from one piece of rod on one machine. A great deal of industrial production consists of true lots.

However, a great deal of production consists of product mixtures which, in varying degrees, fall short of the ideal lot definition. Product made from several material batches, or on several machines, or by several operators, may be dumped into a com-

---

[56] Sometimes the committee goes further and establishes a plan for product rating, including demerit weights for each class. See Section 21, under Product Auditing.

[57] Another important body of decision making is whether the process conforms to standard. This is discussed in Section 11, under Inspection Feedback to Production.

[58] See also Section 25A.

mon container. In shop language this mixture is a "lot," but in precise language it is only a mixture. In continuous processes or in conveyor production, the process may well be common and constant, but the input materials may not be.

For precise and economic product acceptance decisions, it is most helpful to "preserve the order." This means that product is kept segregated in true lots or at least identified as to common cause. In addition, for those processes which exhibit a time-to-time variation or "drift" (e.g., the solution gradually becomes dilute, the tool gradually wears), preserving the order includes preserving the time sequence during which various portions of the lot were made. Any loss of order of manufacture becomes also a loss of some prior knowledge as to inherent uniformity.[59]

Some products are naturally fluid and develop a homogeneity through this fluidity. Homogeneity from this new cause can also qualify the product as a true lot, with important implications for the sampling process.

When several true lots are combined for the purposes of acceptance, the combination is known as a "grand lot."[60] Such mixtures are very common, e.g., product from multiple cavities of molding operations or from multiple spindles of screw machine operations.

The two categories of single elements of product (discrete units and specimens) have their counterparts in two categories of lots:

The Lot as Collection of Discrete Units. Here the lot consists of numerous bolts, teacups, or refrigerators each one of which is governed by the product specification. In batch production, the lot is usually determined by the obvious boundaries of the batch. In continuous production, the lot is usually defined as an arbitrary amount of production, or as the amount produced during an arbitrary time span, e.g., a shift, a week.

The Lot as a Coalesced Mass. Here the lot may also consist of a batch, e.g., the melt of steel. In continuous production, the lot is again based on some arbitrary selection, e.g., one ton, a day's production.

Product Acceptance Criteria Table 12-10 shows the criteria used for judging product conformance to standard, both for product elements and for lots, whether of discrete units or coalesced. It is evident that there are profound differences which affect decisions on how to inspect and which even affect the way of thinking about inspection.

Criteria for Discrete Units. Table 12-10 shows that criteria for judging conformance of discrete units to standard are contained in the product specifications and in the supplemental interpretations provided by the inspection planning (see Interpretation of the Specification, above). Inspection planners are greatly aided in setting these criteria because of the consistency inherent in the discrete unit concept—it is made, tested, and used as a unit. Knowledge of product usage is obtainable and can be put to work in developing added criteria for judging conformance.

Criteria for Specimens. Coalesced products usually lack the consistency among manufacture, test, and usage which characterizes discrete units of product. Quite often it is not known, at the time of testing the specimen, what the future use of the product will be. As a result, criteria for judging conformance of specimen to specification must include much discussion and common consent among the parties in interest. This is precisely what has happened, and a great deal has been done to evolve industry standards which define the specimen and prescribe how to test it.

Criteria for Lots (Collections of Discrete Units). For these lots, the lot criteria consist of rules for lot formation, sample sizes, allowable number of defects. These

---

[59] Preserving the order is also an important aid to process regulation. See Section 11, under Product and Process Relationship.

[60] This term is believed to have been first used by L. E. Simon

TABLE 12-10   Criteria for Judging Conformance of Product in Units and Lots

Aspects of conformance	Product consists of discrete units		Product consists of a coalesced mass	
	Individual unit of product	Lot = collection of discrete units	Specimen from mass	Lot = coalesced mass
Usual name of subject matter of inspection:	Part, unit, component, assembly, product, etc.	Lot	Specimen	Lot, mass
Standard usually consists of:	Product specification, plus supplemental criteria in inspection plan	Sampling plan	Material specification	Sampling plan
Standard usually published by:	Product Design Department and Inspection Planning	QC Department	Product Design Department	Product Design or QC Department
Standard usually expressed in terms of:	Natural units of measure	Percent defective	Natural units of measure	Percent conforming
Tolerance usually expressed as:	Maximum and minimum measurements	Allowable defects in sample	Maximum and minimum measurements	Maximum and minimum on averages; maximum on dispersion
Information on conformance usually derived from:	Measuring instruments	Sampling data plus prior knowledge of process (capability, order of manufacture, etc.)	Measuring instruments	Sampling data; inherent fluidity; prior knowledge of process
Criteria for judging conformance are:	Measurement versus tolerance	Actual defects versus allowable; evidence of process behavior	Measurement versus tolerance	Averages and dispersion versus tolerances; prior data

criteria are not provided in the design specifications. In consequence, they are provided as part of the inspection planning process.

Criteria for Lots (Coalesced). For some of these products the lot criteria are set up in a manner similar to that used for lots of discrete units, treating each specimen as though it were a discrete unit of product.[61] Increasingly, the lot criteria are being established by setting limits on the product mass in the form of (1) plus and minus tolerances on the average and (2) a maximum on the standard deviation. When the lot limits are in this form, the data on the various specimens are pooled together on a variables basis to permit judgment of conformance.

Sampling Criteria for Lots. Two major considerations guide the sampling plans to be established for lot acceptance:

1. The extent of knowledge available from sources other than sampling the lot. This is discussed below, under How Much Inspection?

2. The statistical principles governing sampling. These are discussed in Section 24 for attribute sampling and in Sections 25 and 25A for variables sampling.

How Much Inspection? Effect of Prior Knowledge The starting point is an awareness that product acceptance decisions must be based on product knowledge and that this product knowledge is available from multiple sources:

Prior Acceptance Decisions on the Same Lot. In some cases, the concept of "audit of decisions" has been put to work so that vendors, independent laboratories, operators, etc., have been qualified as able to give reliable product acceptance decisions and in addition have accepted this very lot. In such cases, no further product inspection is necessary (beyond that inherent in "audit of decisions"). See, in this connection, Section 10, under Audit of Decisions; also Section 11, under Product Acceptance by Operators.

Prior Knowledge of the Process. To illustrate, a press operation stamps out 10,000 pieces. If the first and last pieces contain certain specified holes of correct size and location, it follows that the intervening 9,998 pieces also carry holes of correct size and in correct locations. Such is the inherent nature of the press dies. In statistical language, the sample size is two pieces and the number of allowable defects is zero. Yet despite the tiny sample size, this is a sound way to do the inspection for these characteristics in the example given.

The press example is rather simple. In more complex cases there is need to measure process capability and to arrange specially to take the samples with knowledge of the order of production. One organized form of this is the conventional control chart method used for process control. (See Section 23.) For product acceptance, the approach is less well organized,[62] and a good deal of empirical structuring is done. For elaboration, see Section 11, under Product and Process Relationship.

Prior knowledge of the "process" as used here includes knowledge of the qualifications of the vendors, operators, etc., who run the process. Operators who have qualified for licenses require less rigorous inspection of their work than operators who have not qualified. Vendors who have established a record of good deliveries need not be checked as severely as vendors who lack such a record.

Product Fluidity. When the product is a fluid, this fluidity contributes to homogeneity. The extent of this homogeneity can be established by taking multiple specimens and computing the dispersion (another form of study of process capability). The presence of uniformity through fluidity greatly reduces the need for random sampling and thereby greatly reduces the sample sizes.

---

[61] Coalesced products exhibit defects but not defective units (defectives). Discrete units of products can exhibit either defects or defectives.

[62] See, however, Section 25, under Variables Plans for Process Parameter: Acceptance Control Charts.

Even when the product is a solid, the inspection planner should be alert to the possibility that it possesses homogeneity through former fluidity. For example, a centrifugal casting process was used to cast metal cylinders which were then cut up to make rings. Several rings from each cylinder were then destroyed during testing for strength. However, it was then found that the dispersion of several strength tests all made on one ring was not different from the ring to ring dispersion. This discovery made it possible to reduce the amount of product destroyed during test.

Prior Successful Usage. Where product, though nonconforming, has nevertheless been successfully used, this fact is a proper consideration in the question of how much inspection. (The greatest use of this knowledge is in "disposition of nonconforming product." See below, under this heading.)

Product Inspection. To the extent that the foregoing sources of knowledge are not adequate to make product acceptance decisions, the gap must be filled by inspection and test of the product.

Securing the Prior Knowledge. The "prior knowledge" does not automatically come to the inspection planner or the inspector. Some of this knowledge is already in existence as a by-product of other activities and hence can be had for the procedural cost of retrieval. Other knowledge is not in existence, and must be created by additional effort. However, this added effort is usually a one-time study, whereas the benefits then go on and on.

How Much Inspection? The Alternatives It is evident that a determination of "How much inspection?" should be made only after there has been an evaluation of the other inputs to product knowledge. This evaluation can then dictate any of several levels of inspection:

No Inspection. There is already adequate evidence that the product conforms and hence no further inspection is needed.

Small Samples. There is a high degree of prior knowledge, requiring only small *stratified* samples[63] so chosen as to verify the continuing validity of this prior knowledge, e.g., control charts, audit of decisions, preserving the order.[64,65]

Large Samples. Where there is little or no prior knowledge and no product fluidity, the main source of product knowledge becomes product inspection through *random* sampling. The amount of this inspection can be determined "scientifically" once the tolerable level of defects in accepted product has been clearly defined. However, choice of these levels (using the sampling parameters AQL, AOQL, etc.) is largely arbitrary and is usually determined by negotiation.[66]

100% Inspection. This alternative is used for final test of critical or complex products.[67] It may also be used when process capability is inherently too poor to

[63] In the absence of prior knowledge, such small sample sizes would be absurd, i.e., lots 20 or 30% defective could easily escape detection.

[64] For an application to destructive testing on a variables basis (involving a State Railway corporation) see Pistorius, Günther, *Das Problem der Aussagesicherheit auf Grund zerstörender Prüfungen aus der Sicht der Abnahme, Qualitätskontrolle,* vol. 12, no. 5, 1967, pp. 53–58.

[65] See also Section 24, under Sampling Plans Based on Prior Information, for the statistical approaches.

[66] In theory, the sampling parameters can be determined from economic considerations, i.e., the cost of detecting unsatisfactory lots verses the cost of failing to detect them. In practice, the "cost of detecting" is fairly easy to determine, but the cost of "failing to detect" is difficult to determine. For intangibles such as customer goodwill, there is no way known to make the determination with any useful precision.

For a detailed discussion, with formulas, see Section 24, under Selection of AQL.

[67] In very critical cases, to provide redundancy against the unreliability of 100% inspection, the amount may be 200% or over.

meet product specifications. Sampling is of no avail in such cases, since the accepted lots are usually no better than the rejected lots, i.e., the difference is merely the result of statistical variations in the respective samples.[68]

Planning Pitfalls in "How Much Inspection?" There are many situations in which inspection planners fail to provide for use of the information available from prior inspections, from fluidity, and especially from prior knowledge of process capability. In effect, the planners assume that all knowledge for decisions on product conformance must come from product inspection based on random sampling. This is a costly assumption, since for critical and major defects the resulting sample sizes are distressingly large. The alternative, of reducing sample sizes, results in high sampling tolerances for defect levels and is equally distressing. Neither of these alternatives is satisfactory to managers who must meet strict standards for both quality and cost.

The reasons for this widespread failure of planners to provide for use of available information are likely rooted in the history of the Statistical Quality Control (SQC) "movement." The early published sampling tables were all based on the assumption that the sole source of product knowledge was the sampling data. Such was essentially the basis of the published military sampling plans (MIL-STD-105, etc.). These plans were publicized at a time when industrial applications of "scientific" sampling were in their infancy. The enthusiasm of the SQC movement resulted in widespread use of the military sampling plans despite their *un*suitability for factory operation. There remains a large residue of this uneconomic sampling to be rooted out.[69]

JUDGMENT OF FITNESS FOR USE

Product acceptance involves two very different determinations:
1. Does the product conform to specification?
2. Is the product fit for use?

These two determinations serve different purposes. Knowledge of conformance to specification is needed to:

Provide protection to the user when usage experience is not yet available
Provide working criteria to those who lack knowledge of fitness for use
Create an atmosphere of law and order
Protect innocents from unwarranted blame

In contrast, knowledge of fitness for use is needed to:

Protect the user
Preserve marketability of the product
Avoid perfectionism

Judgment of Conformance A trained inspector, if provided with the specification, the product, and the instruments, can readily judge conformance to the specification. However, possession of these facilities is not enough to enable him to judge fitness for use. This second judgment requires added knowledge, as discussed below.

When inspection determines that the product conforms to specification, the prod-

[68] This does not apply in cases where the process is highly erratic so that some lots are truly conforming and others are not, i.e., the differences are not merely the result of statistical accidents. For such processes, sampling can be a useful way to separate the conforming lots from the nonconforming.

[69] Some random sampling plans do provide for recognition of prior performance. The Dodge-Romig tables include process average as a parameter to influence sample sizes. The MIL tables have evolved different "levels" to recognize past performance.

uct is routinely assumed to be fit for use; i.e., if the answer to question (1) is yes, question (2) is not even raised.[70]   The routines are structured to ship the product accordingly.   It is only when product fails to conform to specification that there arises the second question "Is the (nonconforming) product fit for use?"

Methods of Decision Making on Fitness for Use   There have been several methods for providing answers to this

1. Assume that all nonconforming product is unfit for use. Under this assumption, all nonconforming lots are scrapped, repaired, sorted, etc., but not shipped as is.   A great deal of waste has resulted from this assumption, since many designs are unrealistically strict and many nonconforming products are in fact fit for use.

2. Create a new agency for decision making, e.g., a Material Review Board, and give this agency the responsibility to determine fitness for use of all nonconforming product.   This arrangement is fairly practical if there is very little nonconforming material, but tends to require an elaborate apparatus for disposing of numerous small matters (as well as for the vital few cases where the elaborate apparatus is clearly warranted).

3. Create a system of multiple delegation for making decisions on fitness for use. Under such a system, the "vital few" decisions are reserved to a formal Material Review Board.   The remaining decisions are delegated to other people.   This is the emerging solution.

Methods for Multiple Delegation   When multiple delegation is used, there is also need for a clear means of designating who may decide what.   Several such means are available, all of them based on some system of defect or characteristic classification as discussed in Seriousness Classification, above.

1. Classification of characteristics as to functional and nonfunctional.[71]   Where this is done, a Material Review Board limits its jurisdiction to functional characteristics.

2. Seriousness classification of defects.   In these classifications, the lower classes (usually called "minor") do not affect fitness for use.   Hence the Material Review Board limits its jurisdiction to the critical and major classes.   Lower classes are delegated to the supervision, to engineers, and even to inspectors where they possess the knowledge needed to make good decisions.

3. Sampling criteria.   This is an impersonal form of delegation through use of larger acceptance numbers for minor defects.   Such sampling tables automatically provide easier acceptance of defects which do not affect fitness for use.

Organized Material Reviews   In the absence of any organized plan for dealing with nonconforming product, there arises a "delegation by default."   In one company[72] there existed five sources of waivers in actual use by inspection:

1. Written authority from Engineering
2. Written authority from Sales
3. Long-standing practice for which there existed no written authority
4. Measurement variations added to product tolerances
5. Inspector judgment on sensory qualities not clearly defined in the specifications

What is significant is that much nonconforming product is actually fit for use and that this fact is known to many people in middle and lower management.   Unless the authorized routines provide for legitimate ways for dealing with this practical problem, the unauthorized ways will take over, with unpredictable results.   Where Quality Control is weak or is poorly supported, there will be unauthorized shipment

---

[70] There are occasional exceptions to this.   Field reports of unfitness for use are enough to hold up deliveries even if the product under test conforms to specification.

[71] The term "nonfunctional" is not to be confused with appearance or other esthetic qualities.   For some products, esthetic qualities are quite essential to fitness for use.

[72] Consulting experience of J. M. Juran.

of nonconforming product, including some which is unfit for use. Where Quality Control is strong and zealous, there will be unnecessary waste due to failure to accept nonconforming product which is fit for use.

The hazards of delegation by default[73] have led many companies to establish an organized approach for review of nonconforming products. Some elements of this approach are virtually alike for all companies:

1. The inspector prepares a nonconformance report identifying the product involved, the nature of the defects, and related factual data. These reports are serially numbered.[74]

2. The inspector "red tags" the product, thereby creating an automatic "hold for disposition." Often the product is moved to a special "hold area" to get it out of the regular stream of production.

3. An investigator (often a Quality Control Engineer) is assigned to collect information pertinent to disposition of the impounded material. This information includes:

Value of the product
Cost to scrap, repair, or sort
Possibility of use in various ways: "as is"; with modifications; through concessions to customer; etc.

4. Based on his analysis and on the prevailing pattern of delegation of authority, the investigator takes or recommends action. One of these recommendations may be to accept the material as fit for use.

5. To recommend acceptance "as is" despite nonconformance, the investigator prepares a formal waiver request to a reviewing agency. In some companies this agency is Engineering Design. In other companies it is Marketing. In the most broad-based instances it is a Material Review Board.

Control of all tags—scrap, rework, etc.—is in the hands of the Quality Control Department, as is the hold area.

Material Review Board   This is a broad-based reviewing agency whose membership consists minimally of representatives from:

Engineering.   The cognizant designer is often the representative.

Quality Assurance.   The representative is often from Quality Control Engineering.

Customers.   The representative may be from the customer's organization (e.g., the government inspector) or from Marketing.

The Material Review Board works to a formal agenda and keeps minutes of its deliberations and actions. A universal rule is that acceptance of nonconforming material requires *unanimous concurrence* of all members of the Material Review Board.

In some companies, the role of the Material Review Board is solely one of judging fitness for use of nonconforming products. Such was the scope of these Boards when they were first set up (by the military procurement services). However, other companies broaden the scope of the Material Review Board so that it includes:

Decision on disposition of unfit lots internally—by scrap, repair, sorting, etc.
Fixing responsibility for the losses incurred

---

[73] A common example of nonconforming material is that of borderline product, i.e., measurably outside of tolerances but fit for use. Repetitive acceptance of such product acts to replace the official tolerance with a wider unofficial tolerance which, in its turn, may also be exceeded. In such cases the formal review process will, as a by-product, tend to bring the reasons for the deviation into the open and discourage repetition. In contrast, the unaided inspector is seldom able to discourage repetition, so that the condition goes on and on.

[74] For some examples of the documentation, see Section 19.

Periodic analysis of the accumulated waiver investigations to identify quality improvement projects

As Material Review Boards conduct their affairs, they tend to work out some delegations of the more routine cases to individual members to act without taking up the time of the full Board. The main form of this delegation is in fact finding, which is usually delegated to the Quality Control Engineer. However, there may be added delegations, i.e., the Product Designer for memorandum or marked print waivers in certain cases; to the Quality Control Engineer for guiding internal disposition of product, etc.

Effect of Multiple Product Usage   Fitness for use is often complicated by the multiple usage for the products under investigation. For the coalesced products, multiple forms of usage is widespread. In consequence, the study of fitness for use involves an inquiry as to how this impounded lot will be used. The resulting waiver may very well be restricted, e.g., for this customer or application only.

Product in discrete units likewise involves multiple usages, and the same principles hold. Sometimes the technological usage may be identical, but the circumstances of usage create the difference. An example is seen in many kinds of interchangeable components. These serve a multiplicity of uses:

1. To be shipped to Original Equipment Manufacturers (OEM) to be assembled into apparatus

2. To be shipped to OEM to be sold or used by them as spare parts

3. To be assembled into apparatus by the component maker himself

4. To be shipped, through intermediate merchants, to repair shops who use the components as spare parts for repair of products in the hands of the general public

At the time these components are made, it is seldom known to which of these destinations they will be shipped. However, when the OEM customer orders (1) and (2) are filled, the practice is to follow strict product acceptance procedures, since the OEM customer has great economic importance, backed up by competent engineers and inspectors who in turn operate out of well-equipped laboratories.

In contrast, components used for purposes (3) and (4) may include those which failed to make the OEM grade. In the company's own assembly department, the operators often have tools which permit them to adjust for poor components. Failing this, they put the poor parts aside and use others. In the case of spare parts to be sold to the general public (through merchants and repair shops), there are opportunities for abuses due to the technological ignorance of everyone involved, and some of these abuses take place.[75] In contrast, some companies flatly require that nonconforming components may be used only in their own assembly areas and may never be shipped out as spare parts.

DISPOSITION OF UNFIT PRODUCT

Product which is unfit for use is disposed of in a number of ways: scrap, sort, rework, return to vendor, sell at a discount, etc. Mainly these alternatives involve internal economics within the manufacturing company, and hence they can be quantified sufficiently to arrive at a logical economic balance. However, no matter what the disposition is, money is lost, schedules are disrupted and people are blamed. In such an atmosphere it is important to establish rules of conduct which minimize the costs, disruptions, and human abrasion.

When purchased products are involved, the rule should be to find that disposition

[75] See generally Juran, J. M., Consumerism and Product Quality, *Quality Progress*, July 1970.

which creates the minimum total loss to the parties.   Adherence to this rule reduces the amount at stake so that there is less to argue about.   In turn, this makes it easier to bargain out how to share this loss.   It is also well to write the purchase contract in a way which makes clear how to handle the various elements of cost which arise due to unfit product.

For self-made products, the rule should still be the same—to find that disposition which results in the minimum total loss.   On the face of it this should be obvious, e.g., any sorting of product should be done by that department which can do it at the lowest total cost to the company.   However, this logic can be frustrated by other considerations, e.g., manpower shortages or cultural resistance.

A major obstacle to "logical" solutions is the presence of an atmosphere of "blame" in the company, i.e., an official requirement that responsibility for errors should be discovered and allocated (often with associated "charging" of the departments responsible).   In such an atmosphere the disposition of unfit products is hampered at every turn by the reluctance of supervisors to agree to actions which might be construed as admissions of guilt.

A policy of charging back all cases of error pays a high price for dubious results. The price is not only the cost of analysis but also—and even greater—the effect on supervisory time and morale.   The other extreme of regarding everything as indeterminate is no better.   The middle ground is to concentrate the analysis on the chronic, vital few defects which go on and on, since these account for the bulk of the losses.   For the sporadic "trivial many" errors, analysis to fix blame is seldom warranted.   The local supervision is in the best position to study these and to find ways to minimize their recurrence.

For the vital few errors there remains a question of transfer of charges to the department responsible once responsibility is clear.   As a matter of good accounting practice, the department responsible should be charged.   However, much depends on how the budgets were prepared in the first place.   If charging is to be inaugurated, the setting up of future budgets should take this into account.   In addition, a look should be taken to assure that the costs of analysis and accounting are low in relation to the amounts at stake.

An undue atmosphere of blame can infect the nonsupervisory levels as well. Here the effect is often to conceal the evidence of defects by hiding the scrap, scrapping products which may be repairable, forgetting to execute the scrap or repair tickets, etc.   See, in this connection, Section 18, under Willful Errors: Operator-initiated Errors.

Disposition of unfit product by sorting may involve external as well as internal economics.   Several sorting situations are common:

1. The product in question is processed further within the same company, e.g., resistors wired into circuits.   In such cases it is usually feasible to evaluate:

   a. The cost of finding a defect through inspection.   This is approximately equal to the inspection cost per unit divided by the fraction defective.

   b. The cost of not finding a defect, i.e., the added costs incurred by further processing until the defect is found in later testing.   This can be estimated.

Under these circumstances (and assuming 100% accuracy of sorting) it is economic to sort the product when the fraction defective is more than the ratio of (a) to (b).[76,77]

---

[76] See, for elaboration and formulas, Shanazarian, Thomas E., Selection of Economical Quality Levels for Multicomponent Assemblies, *Industrial Quality Control,* October 1965, pp. 178–184.

[77] See also Taguchi, Gen-ichi, Quality Assurance and Design of Inspection During Production—2, *Reports of Statistical Application Research,* JUSE, vol. 17, no. 1, 1970, pp. 34–44.

2. The product in question goes to the user. Here it is still feasible to evaluate the cost of finding a defect. However, it is now more difficult to estimate the cost of not finding a defect and virtually impossible to estimate the intangible damage done to goodwill. Nevertheless, when the cost of finding a defect is *compared to the value of the product,* managers seem to be able to make a practical judgment. Commonly, managers will conclude that they are not willing to spend as much to find a defect as the sales value of the product.

For example, a line of consumer products sells for $5 each. A major defect has an incidence of one per thousand. The cost of testing to find the defect is $10 per thousand, so it costs $10 to find one defect. Most managers would not be willing to spend $10 to find a defective $5 product.

3. The product in question contains defects which are known to be a safety or health hazard. The cost of finding the defect can still be figured, but the managers make their decision almost exclusively on the fact that the hazard is present. Somehow the hazard will be eliminated or neutralized.

PHYSICAL CONTROL OF THE PRODUCT

The majority of companies apply rigid controls to movement of finished goods. Inspection approval is required before goods enter the (locked) finished goods storeroom (or are shipped to a customer). Packers, counters, and storekeepers are under strict orders to assure that inspection approval is present before finished goods move on to their destination. To a lesser degree, similar controls apply to finished components entering the assembly storeroom.

Control of nonconforming product is likewise rigid. The containers are red-tagged and usually are moved out of the stream of production to avoid mixups.

For parts, components, and intermediate products moving between production departments, the practice varies widely. At one extreme, physical control is entirely in the hands of Production people until the final product is presented to Inspection for acceptance as finished goods. At the other extreme, movement from any production department is always to an Inspection area (before dispatch to the next production department) and then only after an Inspection-approved "move ticket" has been executed.

A further form of inspection control is through approval stamps applied directly to the product during various stages of operation and especially at final test. Some stamps are coded to show the condition of the product. Stamps commonly identify the inspector to establish traceability as well as to fix responsibility.

For complex apparatus a dossier is invariably prepared to collect the history of the product, the inspection log books, calibration curves, and other matters of significance. Copies of pertinent results go to the customer as well. Seals or locks may be used to minimize unauthorized tampering with the product.

The need for elaborate control systems is obvious when a mixup could be catastrophic (pharmaceuticals). However, some companies use these elaborate systems largely because the managers do not trust the work force. Such mistrust is always mutual, and the long-range solution lies in resolving this mistrust, not in retaining elaborate systems.

Another source of elaboration of system is the human drive for self-sufficiency in floor space, equipment, etc. This drive can be accentuated by departmental loyalties and interdepartmental conflicts. Managers should be alert to distinguish cases requiring elaborate systems due to the nature of the product from those created by human beings for reasons of status, departmental loyalty, etc. For example, creation of separate Inspection areas can greatly increase the total time interval for manufacture, the process inventory, and the amount of paper work. As far as possible, the inspector should be brought to the product rather than the other way around. This principle is illustrated by patrol inspectors, assembly line inspectors, resident inspectors at vendor plants, etc. It has been applied to conveyorized production by establishing inspection stations at the conveyor. It has even been applied where, for reasons of identity and certification, a physical fence separates the production and inspection departments; i.e., a conveyor moves the product into and out of the inspection cage through windows cut for the purpose.

A similar principle is used where strict certification of inspected parts is essential. The only entrance to the fenced-in storeroom is through a fenced-in inspection area.

INSPECTION AT INSPECTION STATIONS

Inspection stations are usually manned by full-time inspectors responsible to the Inspection Department. This is by no means universal. Some final inspection stations are manned by full-time inspectors responsible to Production. Many process inspection stations are manned by Production operators whose principal job is production.

Incoming Inspection   The extent of inspection of products received from vendors depends largely on the extent of prior planning for vendor quality control.[78]   In the extreme case of using surveillance and audit of decisions,[79] there is virtually no incoming inspection except for identity. At the other extreme, many "conventional" products are bought under an arrangement which relies primarily on incoming inspection for control of vendor quality.

The inspectors and their facilities are housed in the receiving area to provide ready collaboration with other vendor-related activities, i.e., materials receiving, weighing, counting, storage. Depending on the physical bulk and tonnage of product, entire shipments or just samples are brought to the inspection floor. The documentation routines provide the inspectors with copies of the purchase orders and specifications, which are filed by vendor name.

Inspection planning is conventional, as discussed under Inspection Planning, above. However, there is usually a lack of prior knowledge of process capability, order of manufacture, etc. In consequence, the sampling plans involve random and (often) large samples, employing standard random inspection tables.[80]   Randomness becomes a severe problem in the case of large shipments, whether bulk[81] or not. However, special arrangements can be made with the vendor. (See Section 10, under Joint Quality Planning: Joint Technological Planning.)

Setting AQLs has been a troublesome problem, to such an extent that some industry standards have been worked up.[82]   In the absence of such standards, the AQLs are established based on precedent, past performance, or just arbitrarily. Then, as instances of rejection arise, the negotiations with vendors result in adjustment of the AQLs.

Data feedback to vendors follows conventional feedback practice.[83]

Process Inspection   This commonly serves two purposes simultaneously:

1. To provide data for making decisions on the *product;* i.e., does the product conform to specification?

2. To provide data for making decisions on the *process;* i.e., should the process run or stop?

---

[78] See Section 10, Vendor Quality Control, under Joint Quality Planning.

[79] See Section 10, Vendor Quality Control, under Audit of Decisions.

[80] See generally Section 24, Attribute Sampling, and Section 25, Variables Sampling.

[81] See Section 25A, Bulk Sampling.

[82] See, for example, Section 38, Electronic Components, under Testing and Inspection.

[83] In this connection, see also Section 10, Vendor Quality Control, under Two Way Communication; Deviations.

Because of the interrelation between process and product variables, process inspection involves observation of process variables as well as inspection of the product. These observations and inspections are made by both Production and Inspection personnel. The resulting interplay is discussed in Section 11, Production of Quality, under Product and Process Relationship.

Product acceptance of work in process may be done in any of several stages or by a combination of them. These stages include:

Setup Inspection. Some processes are inherently so stable that if the setup is correct, the entire lot will be correct, within certain limits of lot size. For such

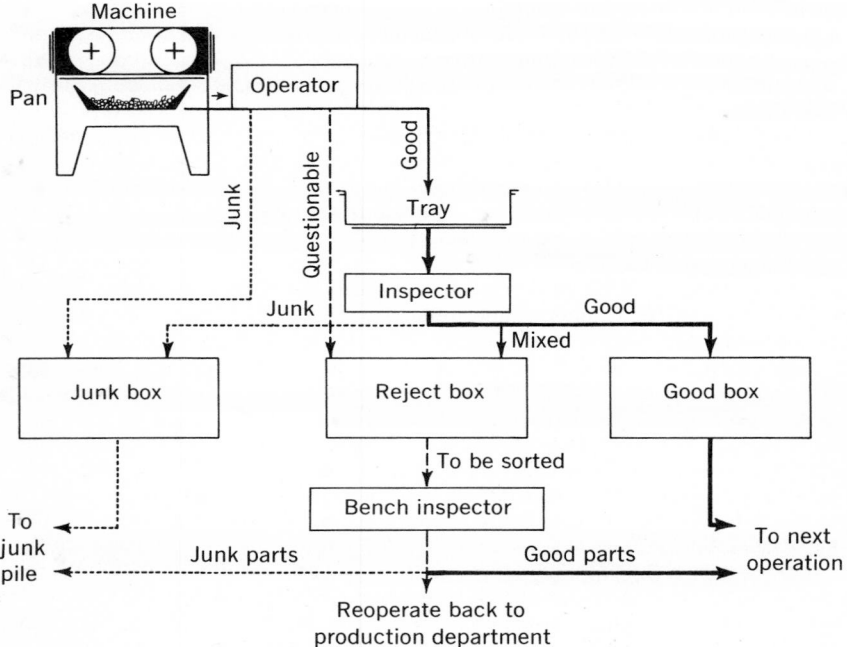

Fig. 12-1 Patrol inspection plan based on preserving the order.

processes the setup approval can also be used as the lot approval. Where a good deal is at stake, it is usual to formalize the setup inspection and to require that the process may not run until the inspector has formally approved the setup, e.g., by signing off, by stamping the first pieces, etc.[84] Some of the setup criteria make use of narrow limit or PRE-Control techniques as discussed in Section 23.

Patrol Inspection. For processes which will not remain stable for the duration of the lot, it is usual to provide for periodic sampling to be conducted during the progression of the lot, making use of various techniques described in Section 23. The numerous plans in use consist mainly of variations of the following four types:

1. Preserve the order of manufacture under an arrangement such as is depicted in Figure 12-1. In this example, the machine discharges its production into a

---

[84] See, for example, Kozich, S. S., First Article Inspection, *Transactions 8th Annual Western Quality Control Conference*, ASQC, March 1961.

small container called a "pan." The production operator periodically empties the pan into one of three larger containers:

    a. Into the junk box if the parts are junk

    b. Into the reject box if the parts are questionable or are mixed good and bad

    c. Into the "tray" if the parts are presumably good

When the patrol inspector comes to the machine, he checks the last few pieces being made. (He may also sample the tray.) Based on his check, he disposes of the tray in one of three ways:

    a. Into the junk box if the parts are junk

    b. Into the reject box if the parts are questionable or are mixed good or bad

    c. Into the "good box" if the parts are O.K. The good box goes on to the next operation

Only the inspector may dispose of the tray, and only the inspector may place any product in the good box.

The reject box is gone over by a sorter, who makes three dispositions:

    a. Junk to junk department

    b. Reoperates back to production department

    c. Good parts on to next operation

2. This method is similar to (1), but the inspection data from the last few pieces are posted to a control chart. If the process remains in control, all product made since the last check is accepted.

3. The accumulated product (e.g., in the tray of Figure 12-1) is sampled at random using some standard sampling plan, and acceptance is based on the sampling criteria.

4. The process variables are checked against a process specification, and the product is accepted provided the process conforms to specification. This method is usually restricted to cases in which there is to be a direct check on the product at later stages.

Tollgate Inspection This is a lot-by-lot product acceptance procedure. Commonly it is done after a production department has concluded its operations. Sometimes the product is moved physically to an inspection area, where it waits its turn to be inspected. Sampling is at random, using standard sampling tables.

Tollgate inspection reduces congestion at the machines and clarifies departmental responsibility. The price paid is in added material handling, added floor space, loss of order of production, and greater difficulty in fixing individual responsibility.

Finished Goods Inspection Most finished products are tested 100% for minimal simulation of use. Tests are often automated, as are the data recordings. Testing may be done either at inspection stations on the production line or in separate inspection areas. For some details, see the "Industry" Sections of this Handbook, e.g., 32, Drug and Allied Industries; 42, Automotive Industry; and 43, Household Appliances.

SENSORY QUALITIES

"Sensory qualities" are those for which we lack technological measuring instruments and for which the senses of human beings (or other animals)[85] must be used as measuring instruments. Sensory qualities may involve

Technological performance of the product, e.g., adhesion of a protective coating, friction of a sliding fit

---

[85] For some special purposes, e.g., tests of toxicity, the test panel may consist of "other animals."

Esthetic characteristics of consumer products, e.g., taste of food, odor of perfume, appearance of carpets, noise of room air conditioners

Esthetic characteristics of commercial products, e.g., appearance of buildings, noise of office machines

In common with other qualities, sensory qualities require:

1. Discovery of which characteristics, and in what degree, are required to meet the needs of fitness for use

2. Design of products which will possess these characteristics

3. Establishment of product and process standards, and of tests which will simulate fitness for use

4. Judgment of conformance to the product and process standards

This multiplicity of tasks requires a corresponding multiplicity in type of sensory test panel used, choice of test design, etc. It is easy to become confused, since the conventional terminology does not reflect the great differences needed in the approaches. Table 12-11 lists some of the main problems requiring use of sensory testing and shows the resulting differences in subject matter of test, choice of test panel, environment, statistical design, etc.

Discovery of Sensory Characteristics Required for Fitness for Use For technological sensory qualities, this determination is made using mainly the conventional methods of product development, laboratory testing, field tryouts, etc., as discussed in Section 8, New-Product Quality. Commonly it is feasible to set up, in the laboratory, test criteria which simulate field usage. Such simulation greatly simplifies discovery of the needed characteristics of the product.

Esthetic sensory qualities present a more difficult problem and pose several questions as to fitness for use:

Do consumers[86] like or dislike the esthetic quality in question, and to what degree?

Of two or more competing products (exhibiting the same sensory quality), which do consumers prefer?

At what threshold level of an esthetic quality do consumers notice its presence?

On the face of it, manufacturing company employees (managers, salesmen, engineers, inspectors) are qualified to answer these questions, since they are also members of the consuming public. However, in practice, these employees exhibit strong biases due to close association with the product, vested departmental interests, and undue sensitivity arising from intimate knowledge. Some costly instances of marketing failure and of perfectionism have been directly traceable to biased judgments of consumer preference made by company employees. The safe course is to secure answers to these questions not from company employees but from consumers (or potential consumers) in the marketplace. The cost of the market research may restrict this approach to the important qualities. (The very question of which are the important qualities is likewise best answered by consumers in the marketplace.)

The upper half of Table 12-11 deals with these same three questions and notes that to get objective answers requires that we:

Employ panel members who are representative of consumers in the marketplace. The resulting data are more likely to predict actual market response to the product.

---

[86] The term "consumer" commonly applies to the user of products made for sale and use by individuals as distinguished from enterprises. More broadly, most commercial products are also "used" by individuals, e.g., the operator running a lathe, the programmer running a computer, the employee using the cafeteria. The collective views of these industrial users become an important input to decisions on esthetic qualities for commercial products.

TABLE 12-11   Uses of Sensory Tests

Problem	Products under test—what is being measured	Panel selected from	Criteria for selection of panel members	Prior training of panel members	Test environment desired	Type of test	Results of test
To discover consumer likes and dislikes	Experimental products containing new or changed qualities	Potential consumers	Should be representative of consumers in the market	None	Conditions of regular use of the product	Quality evaluation	Rating of product on a "hedonic scale" of how well liked
To discover consumer preferences	Two (or more) different products, for the same quality	Consumers	Should be representative of consumers in the market	None	Conditions of regular use of the product	Preference test	Percent and degree of preference of product A versus product B
To discover consumer sensitivity	A controlled selection of products varying across the range under study	Consumers	Should be representative of consumers in the market	None	Conditions of regular use of the product	Special	Basis for decision on product tolerances
To discover effect, on a sensory quality, of material and process changes (for design of products and processes)	A controlled selection of products varying across the range under study	Laboratory or other company personnel	Proved ability to discriminate with respect to the quality under study	Experience with testing and with qualities under test	Controlled laboratory conditions	Various	Relationship of material and process variables to effect on quality characteristic under study
Process regulation	Samples of intermediate or finished product	Quality control laboratory or other company personnel	Proved ability to discriminate	Experience with testing and with qualities under test	Controlled laboratory conditions	Duo-trio, triangle, etc.	Basis for decision on whether to change process
Product (batch or lot) acceptance	Finished products	Quality control laboratory	Proved ability to discriminate	Experience with testing and with qualities under test	Controlled laboratory conditions	Duo-trio, triangle, etc.	Basis for decision on acceptance of product

Avoid training of the panelists. The potential and actual consumers represent a mixture of people in varying degrees of product knowledge.

Conduct the study under conditions of regular use, not in a laboratory environment. Only in this way can the data reflect the future results of actual usage.

Consumer Likes and Dislikes. One approach to prediction of consumer acceptance of a new product is to secure data on consumer likes or dislikes. For example, a food company may be interested in securing market reaction to a new ingredient (e.g., passion fruit). A new food formulation containing the ingredient under test is submitted to numerous users. Their responses are secured on a "hedonic" scale: e.g., 1. Like very much; 2. Like; 3. Neither like nor dislike; 4. Dislike; 5. Dislike very much.

The consumer panel may consist of a "standing panel" of several hundred families[87] to whom samples are sent "free." The "payment" is in data on the extent to which the family (adults, children, pets) liked or disliked the product. Alternatively, the panel may consist of other groups, e.g., passersby at a booth rented in a department store.

The data on the hedonic scale are summarized in conventional ways. As experience is gained in the response patterns to such tests, the decisions on whether to proceed further with the new product can be made with greater and greater confidence.

Consumer Preference Testing. The aim of this test is to discover consumer preferences, e.g., our product versus competitors' products, new designs versus current designs, etc. In competitive markets, such preference tests can give useful guides to decisions on product marketability, pricing, etc.

For preference testing, the submission to the consumer panel always consists of two or more samples. The responses may be "forced choice," i.e., prefer A or prefer B. Another form involves degrees of preference, e.g., strongly prefer A, prefer A, no preference, prefer B, strongly prefer B.

Figure 4-2 (from Section 4, Quality and Income) is an example showing the results of consumer preference testing of 41 products plotted against share of market. The great concentration of data along the horizontal axis suggests strongly that products with consumer preference test results of less than 30% are unable to survive in a competitive market, all other things being equal.

Consumer Sensitivity Testing. In this form of test, the purpose is to discover the "threshold" level at which consumers can detect the presence of sensory qualities. The qualities under test may be "desirable." For example, if an expensive ingredient is used in a product blend, it is very useful to know the threshold concentration level which ensures consumer recognition of the ingredient. The qualities under test may also be "undesirable." For example, a product exhibits varying degrees of visual blemish. It is very useful to know the threshold degree of defectiveness which makes the consumer respond negatively to the product.

In consumer sensitivity testing, a graduated set of samples is prepared, each exhibiting a progressively greater extent of the quality or deficiency under investigation. These samples are submitted to a consumer panel as part of an organized study.

For example, in two companies—one making sterling silverware, and the other making costume jewelry—studies were conducted to discover consumer sensitivity to visual defects. In both companies, a committee of key people (from Marketing,

---

[87] Such panels are usually contacted not by the food company but by an intermediate research company, so as to avoid any reflexes due to the name of the food company.

Design, Manufacture, Quality Control) structured a plan of study as follows:

1. An assortment of product was chosen to reflect the principal visual defects, the principal products in the product line, and the principal price levels.

2. These samples were inspected in the factory by the regular inspectors to determine the severity of the defects as judged by the frequency with which the inspectors rejected the various units of product.

3. The assortment of products was then shown to a number of consumer panels chosen from those segments of the buying public which constituted important customer classes, e.g., suburban women, college students, etc. These panels reviewed the products under conditions which simulated use of the product, e.g., silverware in place settings on a dining room table. The consumers were instructed (by a printed card) somewhat as follows: "Assume you have previously bought these products and they have been delivered to you. Naturally, you will want to look them over to see that the merchandise is satisfactory. Will you be good enough to look it over, and if you see anything which is objectionable to you, will you please point it out to us?"

The resulting data showed that the consumer panels were highly sensitive to some defects. For such defects the strict visual standards were retained. For certain other defects the consumer sensitivity was far less than factory inspector sensitivity. For such defects the standards were relaxed. In still other instances, some operations had deliberately been omitted, but the consumers proved to be insensitive to the effect of the omission. As a result, the operations were abolished.

Consumer sensitivity testing is an extension of the principle that "the consumer is right." This principle may be subdivided as follows:

1. The consumer is right as to qualities he can sense. As to such qualities, the manufacturer is justified in taking action to make such qualities acceptable to the consumer.

2. The consumer is also right as to qualities he *cannot* sense. The manufacturer is not justified in adding costs to create an esthetic effect not sensed by the consumer.

3. Where, for a given quality, the customer is sensitive to a limited level but not beyond, the manufacturer should take action to make the quality to that level but not beyond.

The intermediate marketing chain sometimes interferes with these principles. Sales clerks are proficient in emphasizing product differences, whether important or not. In turn, dealers are alert to seize on such differences to wring concessions out of competing manufacturers. A frequent result is that all manufacturers are driven to adopt wasteful standards, resulting in a needlessly high cost, e.g., finishes on nonworking or nonvisible surfaces. Elimination of such perfectionism commonly requires that the manufacturer secure data direct from consumers and then use the data to convince the distribution chain. These same data may be needed to convince other nonconsumers who exhibit perfectionist tendencies: upper management, designers, salesmen, inspectors, etc.

Visual Quality Characteristics These are a special category of sensory qualities. (Visual inspection remains the largest single form of inspection activity.) For these characteristics, the written specifications seldom describe completely what is wanted, and often the inspector is left to make his own interpretation. In such cases, the inspector is really making two judgments simultaneously:

1. What is the meaning of this visual characteristic of the specification, i.e., what is the standard?

2. Does this unit of product conform to the standard?

Where the inspector understands fitness for use, he is qualified to make both these judgments. If he lacks this knowledge, he is qualified only to make judgment

(2), no matter how long he has been on the job. Extensive experience has shown that inspectors who lack this knowledge differ widely when setting standards[88] and, in addition, do not remain consistent.

Several methods are available to planners to clarify the standard for visual characteristics:

Visual Inspection Standards. The most elementary form of visual standard is the limit sample—a unit of product showing the worst condition acceptable. In using this standard the inspector is aided in two ways:

1. the sample conveys more precise meaning to him than does the written specification.

2. the inspection is now made by comparison, which is well known to give more consistent results than judgment in the absence of comparison.

A more elaborate form of visual standards involves preparation of an exhibit of samples of varying degrees of defects, ranging from clearly defective to clearly acceptable.[89] This exhibit is used to secure the collective judgments of all who have a stake in the standard—consumers, supervisors, engineers, inspectors. Based on these judgments, standards are agreed on and limit samples are chosen.[90]

In products sold for esthetic appeal, appearance becomes a major element of fitness for use and commonly a major element of cost as well. In such cases, an exhibit of samples of various degrees of defects intermingled with perfect units of product becomes a means of measuring consumer sensitivity (or insensitivity) to various defects. Use of consumer panels to judge such mixtures of product invariably confirms some previous concepts but also denies some long-standing beliefs held by the managers as well as by the inspectors.

In the sterling silverware case, above, consumers were quite sensitive to several types of defect—they held out 22% of the defects present. However, for the bulk of defects, the consumers were quite insensitive and found only 3% of such defects. The salespeople generally found twice as many defects as consumers but still considerably less than factory inspectors.

A further use of samples of various defects is to establish *grades* of defects. The concept of different grades is vital when a plant makes products which, while outwardly similar, are used in widely different applications, e.g., ball bearings used for precision instruments and those used for roller skates, lenses for precision apparatus and lenses for simple magnifiers, sterling silverware and plated silverware. Unless the grades are well defined and spelled out in authoritative form, the risk is that the inspectors will apply one standard to all grades.

Once limit samples have been agreed on, there remains a problem of providing working standards to the inspection force. Sometimes it is feasible to select duplicates for inspection use while retaining the official standard samples in the laboratory. An alternative is to prepare photographs (sometimes stereoscopic) of the approved standards and to distribute these photographs instead.[91]

Standardize the Conditions of Inspection. Visual inspection results are greatly influenced by the type, color, and intensity of illumination, by the angle of viewing,

[88] As an example, in an optical company, study of the methods used by 18 different inspectors, engineers, etc., disclosed the existence of six methods of counting the number of "fringes of irregularity." (Consulting experience of J. M. Juran.)

[89] See, for an example involving solder connections, Hetzel, Donald E., Visual Inspection Standards Solve Subjective Squabbles, *Quality Assurance,* March 1965, pp. 29–31. The company (Boeing) uses the term "continuum" to designate the series of gradations.

[90] It is also feasible to estimate (by sampling) what the yield of the process (and thereby the cost of defects) would be for any one of the various degrees of defectiveness.

[91] See also Harris, Douglas H., and Frederic B. Chaney, "Human Factors in Quality Assurance," John Wiley & Sons, Inc., New York, 1969, pp. 157–165.

by the viewing distance, etc. Standardizing these conditions is a long step in the direction of securing uniform inspection results.

In the case of esthetic visual qualities, the guiding rule for conditions of inspection is to simulate the conditions of use, but with a factor of safety.

Establish a "Fading Distance." In some products the variety of visual defects is so great and the range of severity so wide that the creation of visual standards becomes prohibitively complex. An alternative approach is to standardize the conditions of inspection and then to establish a *fading distance* for each broad defect class. The definition for a defect becomes "anything which can be seen at the fading distance."[92]

Design of Products to Achieve Sensory Effects The approach to this product design parallels closely the general approach set out in Section 8, New-Product Quality. What is special is the absence of agreed units of measure and of instruments which can measure in terms of those units. Lacking these tools, the methods of sensory testing must be applied to the new designs, using both laboratory panels and consumer panels. Experiments involving substitution of materials, changes in process, reformulation, etc., all require sensory evaluations if cause and effect relationships are to be established. The laboratory panels provide the judgment on which these relationships can be based. The consumer panels are used to confirm the acceptability of the design in the marketplace.

The fourth row of Table 12-11 traces the use of sensory testing to discover the effect of material and process changes on sensory qualities. It is seen that the testing is done by a laboratory panel, specially selected and trained and working under controlled laboratory conditions.

Providing Standards for Sensory Qualities Once the laboratory and consumer panels have provided the technological and marketing data respectively, there remains a problem of setting standards to serve as a future basis for judging conformance. Setting these standards can be done by an organized approach which also considers factory yields and economics. This organized approach includes the following:

1. Definition of various levels of sensory quality along a "scale of measurement," i.e., a hedonic scale or a degree of defect severity as judged by panels.

2. Estimate of cost of meeting these various levels based on studies of process yields, need for added refinements in the process, etc.

3. Consideration of the effect of the various levels on product marketability based on consumer sensitivity data, competitive product analysis, etc. (See Figure 12-2.)

4. Decision on the level to be adopted as the standard. This decision should be made with full participation of all departments in interest.

5. Executive approval of the standards. This approval should be formalized. The signature of the responsible executive(s) should appear on the approved samples (or on the document evidencing the approval). This formality serves to clear the air on the fact of decision making as well as to identify the samples unmistakably. These standards take any of numerous forms: physical samples of product for visual comparison, feel, texture, etc.; photographs; sound recordings; formulation of taste and smell; and still others.

6. Duplication of the standard for shop use. For *stable* products, the sensory standard can be filed like any other master reference standard. Duplicates can be prepared for everyday use, and these duplicates can be checked against the master under a scheduled maintenance plan. For *unstable* products, new masters must regularly be prepared, at intervals shorter than the rate of deterioration. Sometimes special storage or preservatives can help to stabilize the master.

---

[92] This technique appears to have been evolved in 1951 by N. O. Langenborg of St. Regis Paper Company.

Judgment of Conformance to Sensory Standards   The lowest two rows in Table 12-11 elaborate this problem. It is evident that there are conformance problems both as to process regulation and as to product acceptance. Laboratory panels are used throughout, under controlled laboratory conditions, employing various types of sensory tests and making use of the approved standards for reference purposes.

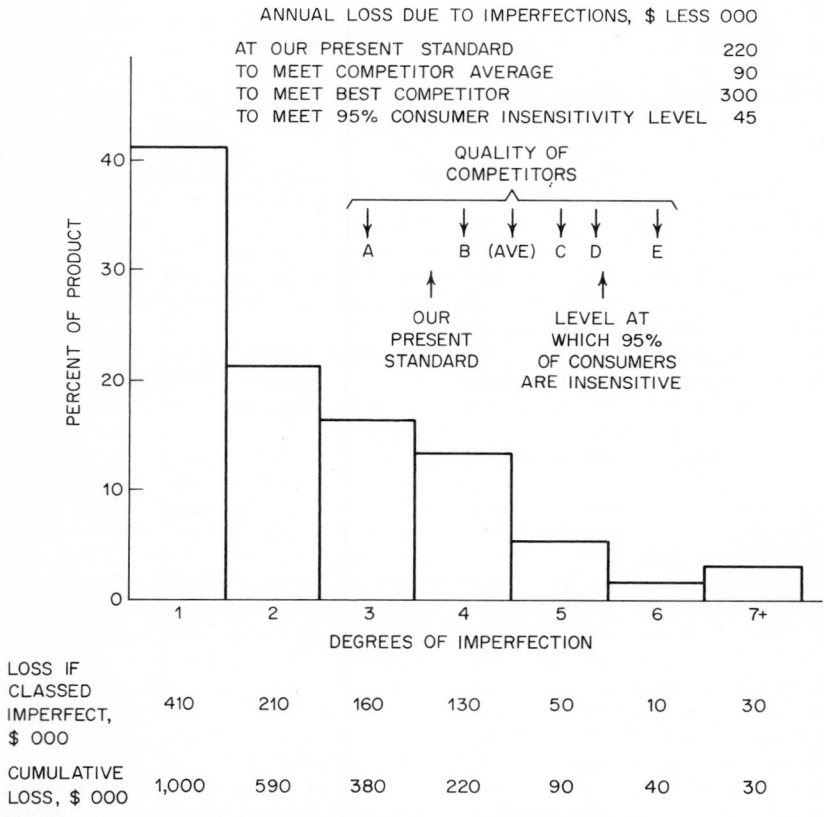

ANNUAL LOSS DUE TO IMPERFECTIONS, $ LESS OOO

AT OUR PRESENT STANDARD	220
TO MEET COMPETITOR AVERAGE	90
TO MEET BEST COMPETITOR	300
TO MEET 95% CONSUMER INSENSITIVITY LEVEL	45

	1	2	3	4	5	6	7+
LOSS IF CLASSED IMPERFECT, $ OOO	410	210	160	130	50	10	30
CUMULATIVE LOSS, $ OOO	1,000	590	380	220	90	40	30

Fig. 12-2   Summary for executive decision on sensory standards.

Panels for Sensory Testing   Panels are composed of two very different populations, and these must not be confused.

Consumer Panels.   These serve to provide information on fitness for use in its various aspects (consumer likes and dislikes, preferences, sensitivity). The prime qualification for such a panel is to be representative of the consumers in the market. Since this precludes prior selection for ability to discriminate, it follows that a proportion of the panel members will lack the ability to make discriminations (e.g., color-blindness). Training is also precluded because it introduces bias. Controlled test environments are also precluded; the conditions must be those of normal usage. These restrictions combine to make consumer panels numerically large. Often they run to hundreds of people. As a corollary, the time to conduct a test is lengthy—it can readily run to weeks and even months.

Laboratory Panels. These serve to judge conformance to standards and to provide product and process research data. Here the need is to make prompt, low-cost judgments. Selection of panel members for this purpose is based on tested ability to discriminate, and this ability is then sharpened by training. The work of these panels is carried out under controlled laboratory conditions, hence the name "laboratory panels." These features make it possible for small panels to provide prompt, low-cost data of measurable precision.

Selection of Laboratory Panels. In this selection it is first necessary to distinguish the candidate's (1) inherent ability to sense from (2) his ability to translate what he senses into a judgment. For example, in color classification, the distinguishing terms are color blindness and color ignorance. Ability to sense differs in humans, and this difference is discoverable by selection tests; i.e., tests for visual acuity, taste perception, etc. If the candidate lacks the ability to sense, it is normally not feasible nor economic to awaken this ability. If, however, the candidate has the sensory ability, then he can be trained to use this ability to render judgments.

The overwhelming source of laboratory panelists is company employees. The company makes clear its needs for panelists and invites employees to volunteer to be tested for qualification. Responses are generally good, so that there is little difficulty in selecting and training enough panelists to provide for attrition in existing panels. The job of panelist is almost always a part-time job and constitutes a welcome change from the regular job (bottling line or whatever).

Tests used for screening prospective panelists are designed to discover (1) *sensitivity*, i.e., ability to detect the stimulus under study, and (2) *consistency*, i.e., ability to reproduce results on repeated testing.[93] These tests make use of various statistical designs as discussed in Sensory Tests: Design and Analysis, below. To execute these designs, test samples are prepared to possess known concentrations or degrees of the characteristics under study.[94] The ability of the prospective panelist to judge the samples correctly is the decisive element in the panel selection process.[95]

Environment for Laboratory Panels. The laboratory panels conduct their work under controlled laboratory conditions to minimize the effect of extraneous variables, reduce the sample sizes needed, and increase the precision of results. See, for example, Figure 12-3, which shows the environment of a taste test panel. (Courtesy Schenley Distillers, Inc., Cincinnati, Ohio.) In such an environment, unwanted variables can be stratified or randomized, design of experiments can be scientific, and cost of experimentation can be held to a minimum for a given precision.

Of course, laboratory testing is not conclusive as to consumer acceptability, which is properly determined by actual use by consumers under usual usage conditions. Anything short of this fails to create the environment and the unpredictable conditions encountered in the field. Use testing by people other than consumers (hence "kitchen tested," "road tested," etc.) is still only an approximation. Simulated service testing is an approximation further removed. Materials test data (to predict *potential* service results) are an approximation still further removed.

[93] For an early, pioneering study, see Helm, E., and B. Trolle, Selection of a Taste Panel, *Wallerstein Laboratories Communications,* vol. 9, no. 28, pp. 181–194, 1946. The paper reports extensive studies made at Carlsberg Breweries, Copenhagen, Denmark, and shows results for various categories of personnel.

[94] For products made as discrete units, the examination may be based on a preselected lot of graded samples. For coalesced products, special samples, in varying degrees of concentration, are commonly prepared.

[95] For many years, industries such as brewing, food, and candy had put their confidence in a taste "expert." When, in due course, these experts were tested under statistical designs, some of the companies underwent a good deal of shock.

Sensory Tests: Design and Analysis   There are numerous designs of sensory tests, some of them quite complex.[96]   Some of the basic forms are described below.

Tests for Differences or Similarities.   These include:

1. The paired-comparison test.   Product is submitted to the panelist in pairs of samples.   One sample is identified to him as the standard or "control"; the other is

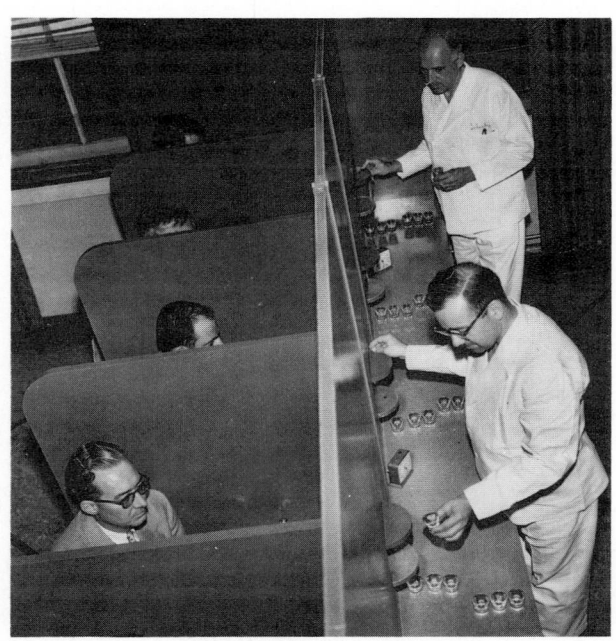

Fig. 12-3   Sensory test panel.

the test sample.   The panelist is asked to judge and record the difference on a scale of differences (such as no difference, slight difference, pronounced difference). Some of the pairs have no difference; i.e., both are "controls."

2. The triangle test.   The panelist is asked to identify the odd sample in a group of three, two of which are alike.   He may also be asked to estimate the degree of difference and to describe the difference between the odd sample and the two like samples.

3. The duo-trio test.   The panelist is asked to identify which of two samples is like the "control" to which he has previously been subjected.[97]   For example, in liquor manufacture, the aim is to make each batch indistinguishable in taste from past batches.   The duo-trio test is used as a product acceptance test.   Each pan-

[96] For a survey of taste testing evaluation procedures, see Zlobik, E. T., Subjective Product Evaluation Methods, *ASQC National Convention Transactions,* 1961, pp. 515–520.

[97] For an example of the duo-trio test in use, see Brandt, D. A., "When the Swallows Come Home," *Transactions of the Fifth Annual All-Day Conference,* Akron-Canton Section of ASQC, 1963.

elist tastes the "control," which he is told comes from previous product. Then each panelist tastes the two remaining samples, one of which is "control" and the other the batch under test. However, he is not told which is which. If the data make clear that the panel cannot distinguish the new batch from the control, the batch is accepted. Otherwise, it is reblended.

4. Ranking test. Coded samples are submitted to the panelist, who is asked to rank them in the order of concentration.

Tests for Quality Description. The panelist is asked to judge the absence, presence, or intensity of various suspected quality characteristics in the sample. A usual form is "profile" testing, in which the characteristics to be judged are listed in advance and the panelist is used as an instrument for qualitative and quantitative analysis, i.e., to "prepare a profile."

Descriptive tests are also used to identify the seeming nature of unknown qualities ("it smells like lilac").

Tests for Quality Preference or Acceptance. These are aimed at judging marketability and therefore make use of consumer panels. The most usual forms are:

1. Hedonic scale tests, which rank the product anywhere between limits, e.g., from "like very much" down to "dislike very much."

2. "Home use" testing done by a "standing" panel of consumers to whom products and instructions are delivered. The panel sends its data in return. Emphasis is on *use* testing at the point of *use.*

3. "Store testing" done by a sample of the stream of people flowing through a store. Data are recorded by a trained observer. Emphasis is on *preference* testing at the point of *sale.*

Analysis of sensory test data is mainly by conventional statistical significance tests. (See generally Section 22 under Tests of Hypotheses, and especially, Table 22-13, test number 8.) However, a specialized literature has also evolved. Methods for dealing with paired comparisons were prepared by Scheffe.[98] An early use of the duo-trio test was by Peryam,[99] who used 2.2 σ as the boundary for significance, in accordance with the formula:

$$\sigma_p = \left(\frac{pq}{n} \right)^{1/2}$$

where p = fraction correct identification of the unknown with standard
q = fraction incorrect = $(1 - p)$
n = number of samples in the series

At this level of significance, the probability is 0.014 that the lot is actually at standard despite the ratings of the panelists to the contrary. Peryam's table for sample sizes of 20 and 30 is reproduced as Table 12-12.

A comparison of operating characteristic curves for the pair, duo-trio, and triangle tests is provided by Fortuin and Van Beek.[100, 101]

[98] Scheffe, H., An Analysis of Variance for Paired Comparisons, *Journal of the American Statistical Association,* vol. 47, pp. 381–400, 1952. See also, Bradley, R. A., and M. E. Terry, Rank Analysis of Incomplete Block Designs: The Method of Paired Comparisons, *Biometrika,* vol. 39, p. 324, 1952.

[99] Peryam, David R., Quality Control in the Production of Blended Whiskey, *Industrial Quality Control,* vol. 7, no. 3, November 1950, pp. 17–21.

[100] Fortuin, G. J., and A. Van Beek, A Flavor Trial. *Statistica Nederlandica,* vol. 14, No. 2, 1960, pp. 175–185. (In Dutch).

For some added compilations of test designs, methods of analysis, and references, see Dawson, Elsie H., Sensory Testing of Foods and Beverages, *Food Quality Control,* no. 15, pp. 3–6, January 1967; also Pangborn, Rose Marie, Use and Misuse of Sensory Technology, *Food Quality Control,* no. 15, pp. 7–12, January 1967.

[101] There has also been some standardization of terminology and of procedure in specific industries. See, for example, ASTM E 253-67T, Tentative definition of terms relating to

TABLE 12-12   Rating Table for Sensory Testing

Total judgments	Number correct	Percent correct	SE distance from 50% (σ_p rating)	Percent area between 50% and this point	Percent area beyond this point
20	10	50.0	0.0	0.00	50.0
20	11	55.0	0.4	15.6	34.4
20	12	60.0	0.9	31.6	18.4
20	13	65.0	1.3	40.3	9.7
20	14	70.0	1.8	46.4	3.6
20	15	75.0	2.2	48.6	1.4
20	16	80.0	2.7	49.7	0.3
20	17	85.0	3.1	49.9	0.1
20	18	90.0	3.6	50.0 —	Very small
20	19	95.0	4.0	50.0 —	Very small
20	20	100.0	4.5	50.0 —	Very small
30	18	60.0	1.1	36.4	13.6
30	19	63.3	1.5	43.3	6.7
30	20	66.7	1.8	46.4	3.6
30	21	70.0	2.2	48.6	1.4
30	22	73.3	2.6	49.6	0.4
30	23	76.7	2.9	49.8	0.2
30	24	80.0	3.3	50.0 —	Very small

Creating New Instruments to Measure Sensory Qualities   Many sensory qualities formerly judged by human perception are now measured by instruments.   This development of new instrumentation goes on apace, using essentially the following approach (based on a procedure set out by Dr. Amihud Kramer):[102]

1. Define precisely what is meant by the quality characteristic under discussion. This must be done with participation of all interested parties.

2. Discover, through analytical study, the subcharacteristics, and define them in a way which permits, in theory, measurement by some inanimate instrument.

3. Search the literature to become informed on methods already in existence or under development for measuring these subcharacteristics.   This search will disclose a number of such possible measurement methods.

4. Choose or create product samples which vary widely for the subcharacteristics.   Test a limited number (10 to 50) of samples with each of the various measurement methods, and correlate these tests with evaluation by panels of human testers. The human evaluation here aims not to measure personal preferences but to rate the degree to which the samples possess the variable under study.   Hence the main requirement of the panel is that it be *able to discriminate* the subcharacteristics under study.   Discard those measurement methods which lack precision or which fail to reflect human evaluation.

5. For the remaining, more promising measurement methods, conduct tests on a larger number of samples (100 to 1,000) also chosen to reflect the entire range of quality variation.   In addition, conduct tests of duplicate samples using evaluation by human test panels.

6. Correlate the results of measurement against the human test panel evaluation; select that method which gives a high, outstanding correlation.   (Multiple correlation methods may be necessary.)

---

sensory evaluation of materials and products; also ASTM E 339-67, Standard method of test for discrimination of differences in the production of alcoholic beverages.

[102] Kramer, A., The Problem of Developing Grades and Standards of Quality, *Food Drug Cosmetic Law Journal*, January 1952, pp. 23–30 (Commerce Clearing House).

7. Improve and simplify the selected measurement method through further test and correlation.

8. Establish a scale of grades through use of a human sensory test panel. At this stage, the prime purpose of the human test panel is *to state preferences* along the scale of measure. Hence the main requirement of this panel is that it be representative of the producers and users of the product.

9. Weight the various subcharacteristics in accordance with their rated performance.

10. Develop the sampling procedures needed to apply the resulting method of measurement.

INSPECTOR ERRORS

The inspector, as the human element[103] in the inspection process, contributes importantly to inspection errors.[104] These inspector errors are of several categories:

Errors due to lack of capacity, skill or know-how. These will be referred to as "technique errors."

Inadvertent errors.

Willful errors.

Each of these categories has its own unique causes and remedies. Collectively, these inspector errors result in a performance of about 80% accuracy in finding defects, i.e., inspectors find about 80% of the defects actually present in the product[105] and miss the remaining 20%.

Technique Errors Into this category are grouped several subcategories: lack of capacity for the job, e.g., color blind; lack of knowledge due to insufficient education or job training; lack of "skill," whether due to lack of natural aptitude or to ignorance of the knack for doing the job. Technique errors can be identified in any of several ways:

Check Inspection. A check inspector reexamines work performed by the inspector, both the accepted and rejected product. Figure 12-4 shows an example of the results of such check inspection of the work of several inspectors. It is evident that inspectors C and F operate to loose standards while inspector B operates to tight standards. Inspector E shows poor discrimination in both directions.

Round Robin Inspections. In this analysis, the same product is independently inspected by multiple inspectors. The resulting data, when arrayed in a matrix (usually with defect type along one axis and the inspectors along the other axis), shows the defects found by each inspector in relation to the inspectors as a group.

Repeat Inspections. In this method, the inspector repeats his own inspection on the product without knowledge of his prior results. The analysis of the resulting data discloses the extent of the consistency or lack of consistency of the inspector's judgments.

Standard Sample Array. In this method the inspector takes an "examination" by inspecting a prefabricated mixture of product consisting of good units plus various

---

[103] The problem of human error is common to operators, inspectors, and anyone else. For an extensive discussion of problems of operator error, see Section 18, under Operator-controllable Errors, *et seq.*

[104] Those inspection errors which are due to the inspector are called "inspector errors" and are discussed here. Other sources of inspection errors, e.g., vague specifications, lack of standards, inaccurate instruments, etc., are discussed elsewhere in this Handbook.

[105] Note by the Editor (Juran). Numerous studies in various countries have yielded the 80-20 ratio as a broad measure of quantified inspector accuracy. However, little is known about the relative importance of each category of inspector error (lack of technique, inadvertence, and willfulness).

kinds of defectives.[106]   All units were previously carefully graded by a team of experts and numbered for ready analysis of results.   The inspector's score and his pattern of errors all point to the need, if any, for further training or other remedial steps.   (In effect, the check inspection is conducted before the inspection.)

For example, in a company making glass bottles, an attempt was made to correlate process variables with the frequency and type of defect found by inspectors stationed at the cold end of the annealing lehr.   The experiment failed because inspector variability from shift to shift exceeded product variability.   This also threw suspicion

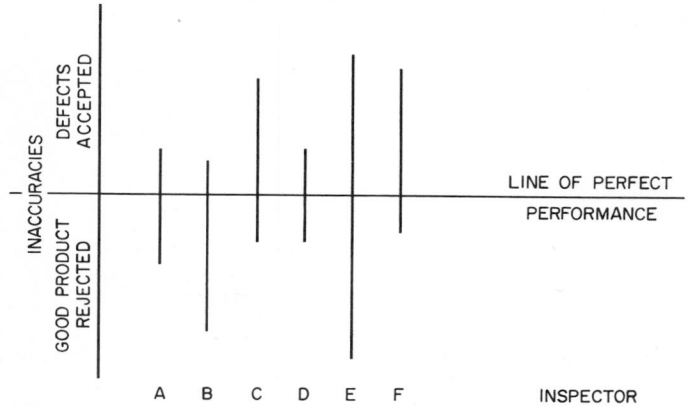

Fig. 12-4   Analysis of inspection errors.

on the accuracy of the inspection performed by the final product sorters at the end of the line.   A standard sample array of 500 bottles was created and was used to examine the inspectors.   (The examinations were conducted in the Training Department, on a miniature lehr.)   The suspicions turned out to be well founded.[107]

Remedy for Technique Errors   The need is to provide the missing skill or know-how and to answer the inspector's proper question "What should I do different than I am doing now?"   Unless the inspector is in a position to discover the answer for himself, the answer must be provided by management.   If no answer is provided, there will be no change in performance.

The various methods of analysis discussed above all can provide some clues which suggest the type of remedial action needed.   In particular, use can be made of the concept of finding the "knack," as discussed in Section 18, under Technique Errors. Under this concept, the data on inspector performance are analyzed to discover which inspectors give consistently superior performances and which inferior.   Next, a study is made of the work methods used by both types of inspectors to identify the differences in methods.   Analysis of these differences often discovers what is the secret know-how (knack) being used to get the superior performance (or what

[106] The standard sample array is known by various names, including "job sample."   For added discussion, see Harris, Douglas H., and Frederick B. Chaney, "Human Factors in Quality Assurance," John Wiley & Sons, Inc., New York, 1969, under The Inspection Job Sample, pp. 107–113.

[107] Consulting experience of J. M. Juran.

is the secret ignorance which results in poor performance). Finally, the knack can be transferred to all inspectors through retraining[108] or through being embodied in the technology.

Where the technique errors are the result of lack of job capacity, the foregoing may be of no avail, and the need may be to foolproof the operation (see below) or to reassign the inspector to a job for which he does have adequate job capacity.

Certification of Inspectors.   In critical inspections involving inspector judgment (e.g., interpreting x-rays of critical welds), it is increasingly the practice to require that the inspector be formally certified as qualified to do this job. The qualification process follows a well-standardized series of steps:

A formal training program on how to do the job
A formal examination, including a demonstration of successful performance of the job
A formal certificate attesting to the success in the examination
A license to do the job for some designated period of time
A program of audit to review performance and to serve as a basis for renewing the license

In some companies, this concept of certification has been based on the "escape rate," i.e., the extent to which defects escape detection, as determined by subsequent check inspection. (See Measure of Inspector Accuracy, below.) When this concept is used, a limited "license" (e.g., two months) is given to the inspector, subject to renewal if check inspection results continue to be favorable.

Inadvertent Inspector Errors[109]   These errors are characterized by the fact that at the time the error is made the inspector is not even aware he is making an error. Also, the best intentions are present—the inspector wants not to make any errors. The term "inadvertent" or "unavoidable" is used to connote the fact that the human being is simply unable to achieve perfection, no matter how good his intentions.

The theory of inadvertence has wavered up and down. For years it was the sincere belief of many inspection supervisors that when product was inspected 100%, the inspectors would find all the defects. Numerous unpublished and published studies have since demonstrated that human inspectors do not find all defects present. By and large, the human inspector finds about 80% of the defects present and misses the remaining 20%.[110, 111]

Inspection fallibility[112] can easily be demonstrated in the industrial classroom.

[108] See, for example, Eidukonis, Edward R., and John L. Kidwell, The Inspection Training Program. *Industrial Quality Control,* June 1967, pp. 622–628.

[109] This topic is closely related to inadvertent operator errors. See, for added discussion, Section 18, under Inadvertent Errors.

[110] While the figures of 80-20 are widely accepted, there are numerous aspects which are not fully researched, i.e., how this ratio changes with percent defective in the product, with types of inspection (visual, mechanical gaging, electrical testing), with product complexity, with amount of time allotted for inspection, etc. For a discussion from the viewpoint of "human factors" plus some supporting data (e.g., that increased product complexity results in increased inspector error), see Harris and Chaney, *op.cit.,* pp. 77–85.

[111] There is evidence that some animals can outperform human inspectors; e.g., pigeons were found to be over 98% accurate in finding defects in diodes and in empty drug capsules. See Herrnstein, Richard J., In Defense of Bird Brains, *The Atlantic Monthly,* September 1965, pp. 101–104.

[112] While there is no debate on the existence of these errors, there is some contention that human beings need not be fallible if they are adequately motivated. See, in this connection, Section 18, under Inadvertent Errors.

The following sentence has been used thousands of times:

FEDERAL FUSES ARE THE RESULTS OF YEARS
OF SCIENTIFIC STUDY COMBINED WITH
THE EXPERIENCE OF YEARS

The sentence is flashed before the audience for 30 seconds or for a full minute. Each member is asked to count and record the number of times the letter F appears. When the record slips are collected and tallied, the result is invariable. Of the F's present, only about 80% have actually been found.[113]

The existence of so extensive an error rate has stimulated action on several fronts:

1. To discover why inspectors make these errors. To date the researches have not been adequate to provide conclusive answers, so that the industrial psychologists are not agreed on what the main causes are.

2. To measure the extent of the errors. Techniques for this are now available. See Measure of Inspector Accuracy, below.

3. To reduce the extent of these errors. There is a wide assortment of remedies, as discussed below.

Remedy for Inadvertent Inspector Errors   In the absence of convincing knowledge of the causes of these errors, managers have resorted to a variety of remedies, all involving job changes in some form. These remedies include:

Foolproofing.   There are several forms of this which are widely applicable to inspection work: redundancy, countdowns, fail-safe methods. These are discussed in detail in Section 9, under Foolproofing the Process. See also Inspection Planning, above.

Automation.   This is really a replacement of the repetitive inspection by an automaton which makes no inadvertent (or other) errors once the setup is correct and stable. The economics of automation and the state of technology impose severe limits on the application of this remedy. See Automated Inspection, above.

Sense Multipliers.   Use can be made of optical magnifiers, sound amplifiers and other devices to magnify the ability of the unaided human being to sense the defects. Development of a new instrument to do the sensing is the ultimate form of this multiplication. Evidently there is an optimum to the level of magnification, and this optimum can be discovered by experimentation.[114,115]

Conversion to Comparison.   In many types of inspection, the inspector must judge the product against his memory of the standard. When such an inspector is provided with a physical standard against which he can make direct comparison, his accuracy improves noticeably. For example, in the optical industry, scratches are graded by width, and tolerances for scratches vary depending on the function of the product element (lens, prism, etc.). To aid the inspectors, plates are prepared exhibiting several scratches of different, measured width, so that the inspectors can compare the product to a physical standard.

Standards for comparison are in wide use: colored plastic chips, textile swatches, forging specimens, units of product exemplifying pits and other visual blemishes. Sometimes photographs are used in lieu of product. There are also special optical

[113] Experience of ·J. M. Juran in training courses conducted in many countries, on all continents.

[114] A U.S. Navy Department study concluded that for airborne detection of a submarine snorkel wake, the unaided eye is more effective than use of binoculars. Smith, R. P., Use of Binoculars in Search for Submarines, *National Academy of Sciences, National Research Council, Publication 712*, pp. 32–40, 1960.

[115] For some industrial studies, see Harris and Chaney, *op. cit.*, pp. 124–126 and 137–142.

instruments which permit dividing the field of view to permit comparison of product with standard. In some cases it is feasible to line up units of product in a way which makes any irregularities become highly conspicuous, e.g., lining up the holes in a row. (The childhood row of tin soldiers makes it obvious which one has the broken arm.) Some practitioners advocate inspecting units of product in pairs, to utilize the comparison principle.[116]

Templates. These are a combination gage, magnifier, and mask. An example is the cardboard template placed over terminal boards. Holes in the template mate with the projecting terminals and serve as a gage for size. Any extra or misplaced terminal will prevent the template from seating properly. Missing terminals become evident because the associated hole is empty.[117]

Masks. These are used to blot out the inspector's view of characteristics for which he is not responsible so he can concentrate on his real responsibility. Some psychologists contend that when the number of characteristics to be inspected rises to large numbers, the inspector error rate also rises.

Overlay. These are visual aids in the form of transparent sheets on which guidelines or tolerance lines are drawn. The inspector's task of judging the size or location of product elements is greatly simplified by such guidelines, since they present the inspector with an easy comparison for judging sizes and locations.

Reorganization of Work. One of the theories of cause of inadvertent inspector errors is fatigue, due to inability to maintain concentration for long periods of time. Responses to this theory have been to break up these long periods in any of several ways: rest periods; rotation to other inspection operations, several times a day; job enlargement, e.g., a wider assortment of duties, greater responsibility. Some of the behaviorial scientists urge reorganization of work on the broader ground of motivation theory, and they offer data to support this theory.[118] However, to date, there is no conclusive evidence that in Western culture, reorganization of work (to provide greater participation, etc.) will give measurably superior results in work accomplishments.[119]

Product Redesign. In some instances the product design is such that inspection access is difficult or that needless burdens are placed on inspectors. In such cases, product redesign can help to reduce inspector errors as well as operator errors. For some examples, see Section 9, under Foolproofing the Process.

Errorless Proofreading. Beyond the techniques described in Section 9, under Foolproofing the Process, there are special problems of foolproofing in inspection work. A major form of this is proofreading of text of a highly critical nature, i.e., critical to human safety and health. In such cases, the low tolerance for error has driven many companies to use of redundant checking, despite which some errors still get through.

A closer look makes it clear that proofreading is of two very different kinds:

1. Active proofreading. Here the proofreader must take an overt action, e.g., read aloud, perform a calculation, etc. Such positive actions dominate the attention of the proofreader and minimize the chance of error.

2. Passive proofreading. Here the proofreader takes no overt action. For ex-

---

[116] See Shainin, Dorian, Unusual Practices for Defect Control, *Quality Management and Engineering,* February 1972, pp. 8, 9, and 30.

[117] For added detail, see Connor, D. R., Inspection Aids for Complex Electronic Components, *Industrial Quality Control,* October 1962, pp. 21–25. Connor reports a drastic reduction in time to inspect complex boards, from over two hours to less than two minutes!

[118] See generally Harris and Chaney, *op.cit.,* pp. 201–229.

[119] See, in this connection, Section 18, under Job Enrichment.

ample, he silently reads the copy while someone else reads the master aloud. Alternatively, he silently reads both documents and compares them. In such cases it is quite possible for extraneous matters to intrude on him and dominate his attention temporarily.

For example, in blood donor centers it is usual to centrifuge the whole blood, remove the plasma, and then return the red blood cells to the donor. This return demands absolute assurance that the cells are being returned to that donor and to no one else. The system in use involves piping both the donation and the return through tubing on which there are repeats of 10-digit numbers. The tubing is cut when the donation goes to the centrifuge. Prior to return of the cells, two technicians check to compare the two 10-digit numbers on the two ends of the cut tubing. One technician actively reads the number on the tubing end attached to the donor. The other technician passively listens while comparing the number she hears with the number she sees (on that end of the tubing which is attached to the bag of blood cells).

It is feasible to make both technicians "active." For example, each is required to tap out on a keyboard the number she sees. These signals go to a computer which compares the two numbers and signals either a go-ahead or an alarm. This same principle of comparing two independent active sets of signals can be extended to any problem in proofreading.

While the foregoing are listed as remedies for inadvertent inspector errors, most of them can also be used to reduce errors due to lack of skill or errors of a willful nature.

Procedural Errors   Aside from inadvertent failures to find defects, there are inadvertent errors in shipment of uninspected product or even shipment of rejected product. These errors are usually the result of loose shipping procedures. For example, a container full of uninspected product may inadvertently be moved in with the inspected product; a container full of defectives may inadvertently be moved into the shipping area.

Such errors can be reduced by foolproofing the identification and shipping routines:

1. The inspector must *mark the product* at the time of inspection. Sometimes the inspector places the good in one box and the bad in another, or he places the good lengthwise and the bad crosswise. Lacking the markings, there is always the risk that, between shifts, during rest periods, etc., the unmarked product will go to the wrong destination.

2. The product markings should be so distinctive that the product "screams its identity" to packers and shippers.

3. The colors used for markers which identify good product should be used for no other purpose. These markers should be attached only when the inspector finds there remains nothing to be done but ship the product.

4. Issuance of markers used to identify good product should be restricted to specially chosen personnel. (These markers are a form of company seal.) For products of substantial value, serial numbers should be used as a further control.

5. The markers should provide inspector identity. In some companies the system of identification includes the operators and packers.

6. Shipping personnel should be held responsible for any shipment of goods failing to bear an inspector's approval.

Willful Inspector Errors: Management Initiated   The distinguishing features of the willful inspector error are that the inspector knows he is committing the error and that he intends to keep it up. These willful errors may be initiated by management, by the inspector, or by a combination of both.

Management-initiated errors[120] take several forms, all resulting in willful inspector errors:

Conflicting Management Priorities. Management's priorities for its multiple standards (quality, cost, delivery, etc.) vary with the state of the economic cycle. When the state of management priorities is such that conformance to quality standards is subordinated to the need for meeting other standards, the inspector's actions are inevitably affected, since he also is given multiple standards to meet.

Management Enforcement of Specifications. When management fails to act on evidence of nonconformance and on causes of defects, the inspectors properly judge management's real interest in quality from these deeds rather than from the propaganda. For example, if the supervision or the Material Review Board consistently accepts a chronic nonconformance condition as fit for use, the inspectors tend to quit reporting these defects since they will be accepted anyhow.

Management Apathy. When management makes no firm response to suggestions on quality, or to inspector complaints about vague information, inadequate instruments, etc., the inspectors again conclude that management's real interests are elsewhere. In consequence, the inspectors make do the best they can with information and facilities which they believe to be deficient.

Management Fraud.[121] Periodically a company manager attempts to deceive customers (or the regulators, etc.) through fictitious or deceitful records on quality. Seldom can a manager acting alone perpetrate such a fraud. He requires confederates who submit themselves to his orders, usually in a way which makes clear to them the real character of what is going on. Where the inspector is a willing accomplice (e.g., for a bribe) he shares in the legal responsibility. However, he may also be a most reluctant accomplice, e.g., his immediate superior gives him orders to prepare nonfactual reports or to take actions clearly contrary to regulations. In such cases the inspector cannot escape taking some kind of risk, i.e., participation in a conspiracy versus the threat of reprisal if he fails to participate.

Willful Inspector Errors: Inspector-initiated[122]   These errors likewise take multiple forms, and some take place for "good" reasons. It is important to understand the distinctions among these forms, since any misunderstandings are a breeding ground for poor industrial relations.

Inspector Fraud. The inspector is subjected to a variety of pressures. The most rudimentary forms are those by production supervisors and operators pleading for a "break." Sometimes this extends to a collusion where piecework payments are involved, both for quality and for quantity certification. At higher levels are cases in which an inspector is exposed to vendors who have a good deal at stake in the lot of product in question. Even the spectacle of an inspector dealing directly with production supervisors who outrank him substantially involves pressures to which the inspector should not be subjected.

Another form of inspector fraud consists of reporting false results solely to improve the outward evidence of his own efficiency or to make life more convenient for himself. For example, Figure 12-5 shows the results reported by an inspector after taking a sample of n pieces from each of 49 lots. There is a large predomi-

---

[120] These management-initiated errors parallel closely those associated with willful operator errors. See Section 18, under Willful Errors.

[121] With few exceptions, the major, notorious quality errors and blunders have been traceable to the decisions of managers and engineers rather than to those of the inspectors at the bottom of the hierarchy.

[122] See, for some important related matters, Section 18, under Willful Errors: Operator-initiated.

nance of three defects reported in the sample (exactly the maximum allowable number). The reason was found to be the inspector's reluctance to do the paper work involved in a lot rejection.

In the example of Figure 12-6 the inspector was to take a sample of 100 pieces from each lot, with no defects allowable. If one or more pieces were defective, an added sample of 165 pieces was to be taken, with a total of three defects allowed in the combined sample of 265. It is seen that the inspector reported defects in virtually every first sample of 100 pieces. However, he reported no defects in most of the second (larger) samples. It was found that the inspector could improve his personal efficiency by taking second samples since the time allowance for taking the second samples was liberal.[123]

Inspector fraud can be minimized by:

1. Filling inspection jobs only with persons of proved integrity.

2. Restricting the down-the-line inspector to the job of fact finding, and reserving to the inspection supervision the job of negotiating and bargaining with other supervisors or executives

3. Conducting regular check inspections and periodic independent audits to detect fraud

4. Taking prompt action when fraud is discovered.

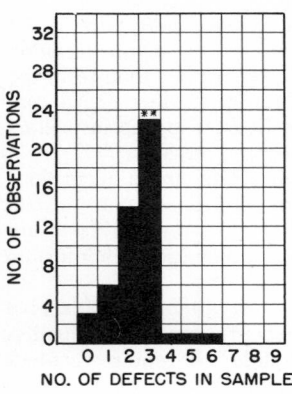

NO. OF DEFECTS IN SAMPLE

**MAX. ALLOWABLE NO

Fig. 12-5 Inspector error made for personal convenience.

Inspector Shortcuts. These may be unauthorized omissions of operations which the inspector has reason to believe are of dubious usefulness; e.g., accidental omissions had failed to give evidence of trouble. In some cases there is a shared blame, i.e., management has imposed a highly disagreeable task. For example, in a company making "tin cans," one inspection involved cutting up a can with hand-held tin shears, submerging the pieces in chloroform to remove the enamel, and measuring the thickness of the bare pieces with a micrometer. The cutting process was tedious and the chloroform was irritating to the skin, so the inspectors avoided the operation as much as possible. When better cutting tools and a different solvent were provided, the problem became minimal.

Flinching. This is the tendency of inspectors to falsify the results of inspection of borderline product. Figure 12-7 shows a frequency distribution of measurements on volume efficiency of electronic receivers. There is an "excess" of readings at the specification maximum of 30, and there are no readings at all at 31, 32, or 33. Retest showed that the inspector recorded these "slightly over" units of product as 30. By this flinching, the inspector, in effect, changed the specification maximum from 30 to 33.[124] This is a serious error.

Flinching during variables measurements is easy to detect by check inspection, which is also conducted on a variables basis. Analysis of the inspector's variables data will likewise detect flinching (as in above example).

The remedy for flinching is an atmosphere of respect for the facts as the ethical

[123] These examples are from Juran, J. M., "Inspectors' Errors in Quality Control," *Mechanical Engineering*, vol. 59, no. 10, pp. 643–644, October 1935.

[124] Juran, *op. cit.*

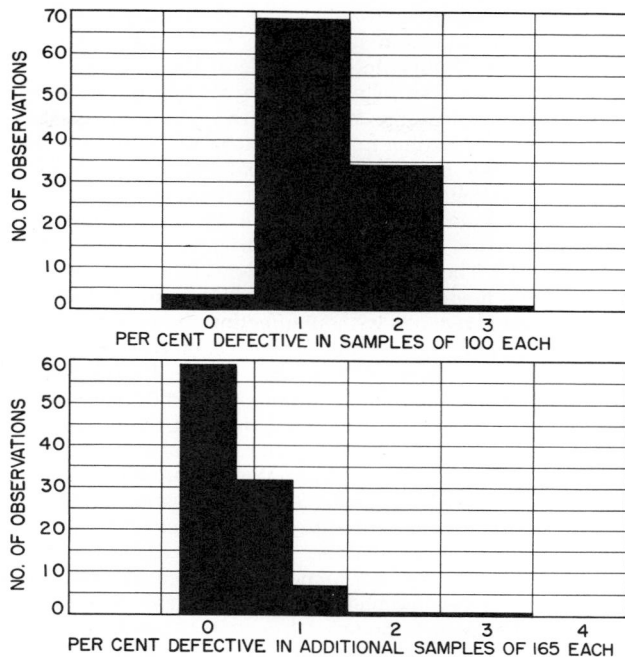

Fig. 12-6 Inspector error made to improve personal efficiency.

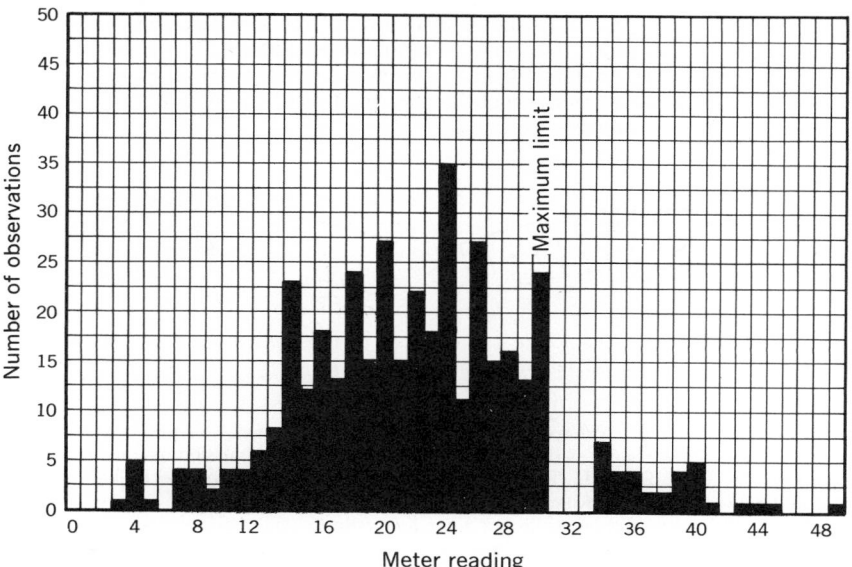

Fig. 12-7 How inspector "flinches" at design limit.

foundation of the Inspection Department. The main means for achieving this are the examples set by the Inspection supervisors.[125]

One way *not* to deal with flinching is to criticize the inspector on the basis that the pattern of readings does not follow the laws of chance. Such criticism can be interpreted as being aimed at the symptom (the unnatural pattern of readings) rather than the disease (recording fictitious instead of factual readings). The risk is that inspectors will try to meet such criticisms by trying to make the false results look more natural, hence eliminating the symptom but not the disease.

Flinching also takes place during attribute inspection. Numerous studies have shown that inspector errors in rejecting good product outnumber the errors of accepting bad product.[126] These same studies show that when check inspection is introduced and check is made *both* of product rejected and product accepted, the rejection of good product is reduced without affecting the acceptance of bad product.

Another form of flinching is to modify the inspection results to conform to the results which the inspector expects. For example, a visual inspection was being performed following a specified lapping operation. An experiment to omit the lapping operation resulted in the inspector's rejecting over half the product. A subsequent experiment, conducted without inspector awareness of omission of the operation, resulted in rejection of less than a third of unlapped product.

In some cases, flinching by inspectors is actually management-initiated through manager pressures which seem to the inspectors to leave no alternative. In one company, the inspectors making hardness tests were discovered to be flinching to an astonishing degree. It was further found that this practice had been going on for years. It developed that the manufacturing vice president had designed this hardening process himself when he was the process engineer. At the time, he had deluded himself as to its capabilities and thereby had been the author of this long-standing practice.[127]

Rounding Off. The process of dispensing with unneeded accuracy is generally referred to as "rounding off." Inspectors commonly round off their meter readings to the nearest scale division, as shown in Figure 12-8. The effect of rounding off is seen in the "picket fence" frequency distribution of Figure 12-7.

Rounding off is easy to detect from analysis of inspection data. A good analyst can, from the data alone, reconstruct the pattern of scale markings of an instrument without ever having seen the scale itself.

Fig. 12-8 Rounding off. The needle is in the same location on both charts. The charts are likely to be read as 31 and 32, left and right, respectively.

---

[125] Flinching is actually widespread among all persons who report on performance versus goals, and especially when it is their own performance. For a discussion of flinching among engineers, see Field, David L., Flinching—A Factor in Estimating Success Probabilities, *Industrial Quality Control*, February 1965, pp. 406–408.

[126] In part this arises because the good product outnumbers the bad and hence affords greater opportunity for error. But it also arises in part from the fact that acceptance of defects often comes dramatically to the attention of higher management whereas rejection of good product seldom does so.

[127] Consulting experience of J. M. Juran.

Rounding off is often a good thing, since it avoids undue attention to individual readings. But sometimes the need for precision on individual readings is great enough that rounding off should not be practiced. The planner and inspection supervisor should be on the alert to identify situations in which rounding off is not tolerable, and they should provide accordingly.[128] One practice is to require "readings to be recorded to the nearest _____."

Measure of Inspector Accuracy   The collective effort of inspector errors, from all causes, is so extensive that there is need for measuring the extent of errors and for use of the data in controlling the effectiveness of inspectors. If this measurement is made only occasionally, use can be made of standard sample arrays (see above, under Technique Errors) and cross-check among inspectors, as well as check inspection. If the measurement is to be conducted regularly so as to discover trends in performance, then check inspection is necessary.

In conventional check inspection, a second inspector, i.e., a check inspector, reviews the decisions of the inspector by reexamining the product after it has been inspected.[129] The best practice is to reexamine the rejected product as well as the accepted product. Inspector errors may consist of accepting defective units of product or rejecting good units of product. If, in addition, the check inspection reviews the procedure followed by the inspector, other errors may be found, e.g., use of wrong issue of the specification, wrong instrument, improper filling out of documents, etc.

The conventional use of check inspection data to quantify inspector accuracy is to count the errors, to assign weights, and to use the composite of errors as an index of accuracy (of inaccuracy, usually).[130] In some schemes, the errors discovered in later operations or in customer complaints are included in the data. The composite of errors may be expressed in terms of percent defective (found to exist in the inspected product) or in terms of demerits per unit. Either way, the scoring system is open to the objection that the inspector's accuracy depends, to an important degree, on the quality of the product submitted to him by the process, i.e., the more defects that come to him, the greater is his chance of missing some.

A plan for measuring inspectors' accuracy in a way which is independent of incoming quality is that evolved in 1928 by J. M. Juran and C. A. Melsheimer.[131] Under this plan the check inspector, as usual, reexamines the inspected product, both the accepted and the rejected units. In addition, the check inspector secures the inspector's own data on the original makeup of the lot, i.e., total units, total good, total defective. From these data, the following formulas emerge as applied to a single lot which has been check inspected:

$$\text{Accuracy of inspector} = \text{percent of defects correctly identified} = \frac{d - k}{d - k + b}$$

---

[128] Scale interval and pointer clearance are factors in the amount of inspector error and in the time required to read the instruments. For a quantitative study, see Churchill, A. V., The Effect of Scale Interval Length and Pointer Clearance on Speed and Accuracy of Interpolation, *Journal of Applied Psychology*, vol. 40, pp. 358–361, December 1956.

[129] For an early example (inspection of ball bearings), see Taylor, F. W., "Principles of Scientific Management," pp. 80–96. Harper & Brothers, New York, 1911.

[130] See, for example, Gilman, James R., Quality Reports to Management, *Industrial Quality Control*, May 1963, pp. 15–17. In this demerit scheme of check inspecting the work of inspectors (who are paid on piecework), the accuracy is expressed in a form which is equivalent to the number of demerits found per lot checked.

[131] The original published reference to this plan appears in Juran, J. M., Inspectors' Errors in Quality Control, *Mechanical Engineering*, vol. 59, no. 10, pp. 643–644, October 1935.

where d = defects reported by the inspector
k = number of good units rejected by the inspector, as determined by check inspection
$d - k$ = true defects found by the inspector
b = defects missed by the inspector, as determined by check inspection
$d - k + b$ = true defects originally in the product

Figure 12-9 illustrates how the percentage of accuracy is determined. The number of defects reported by the inspector, d, is 45. Of these, 5 were found by the check inspector to be good; i.e., $k = 5$. Hence $d - k$ is 40, the true defects found

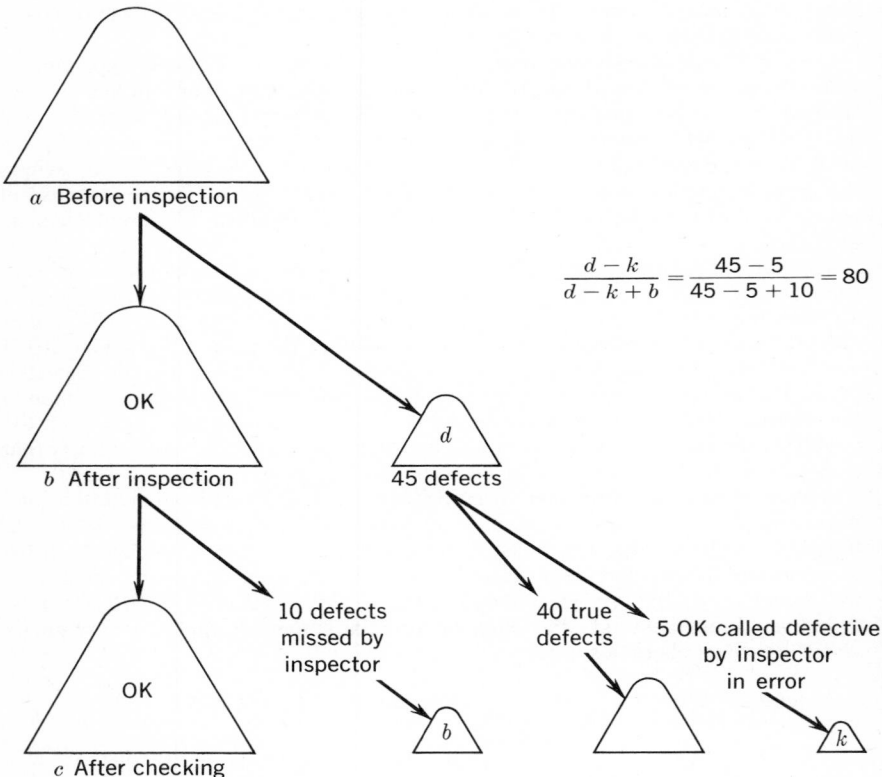

$$\frac{d - k}{d - k + b} = \frac{45 - 5}{45 - 5 + 10} = 80$$

a Before inspection

OK

b After inspection

d

45 defects

OK

c After checking

10 defects missed by inspector

b

40 true defects

5 OK called defective by inspector in error

k

Fig. 12-9 Process for determining accuracy of inspectors.

by the inspector. However, the inspector missed 10 defects; i.e., $b = 10$. Hence the original number of defects, $d - k + b$ is 50, i.e., the 40 found by the inspector plus the 10 he missed. Hence,

$$\text{Percentage of accuracy} = \frac{d - k}{d - k + b} = \frac{45 - 5}{45 - 5 + 10} = 80\%$$

In application of the plan, periodic check inspection is made of the inspector's work. Data on d, k, and b are accumulated over a period of months to summarize the inspector's accuracy, as, for example:

Job no.	Total pieces	d	b	k
3	1,000	10	0	0
19	50	3	1	0
42	150	5	1	0
48	5,000	10	4	0
Totals		200	30	0

The totals give, for percent accuracy:

$$\frac{d}{d + b} = \frac{200}{230} = 87\%$$

As is evident, the plan lends itself to simple cumulation of data. However, some compromise is made with theory to avoid undue emphasis on any one lot checked. Over a six-month period, where the cumulative checks may reach 50 or more, the need for such compromise or weighting is diminished.

The check inspector also makes errors. However, these have only a secondary effect on the inspector's accuracy. In the above example, if the check inspector were only 90 % accurate, he would have found only 27 of the 30 defects missed by the inspector. The inspector's accuracy would become:

$$\frac{200}{227} = 88.1 \text{ instead of } 87.0\%$$

In some situations, k is small and may be ignored. However, in other situations, notably for sensory qualities, the inspector may have a bias for rejecting borderline work. In such cases, it is feasible to use, as an added measure, the inspector's accuracy due to rejection of good pieces. This has been termed "waste."[132] Under the terminology used here:

$$\text{Waste} = \text{percent of good pieces rejected} = \frac{k}{n - d - b + k}$$

where n = total pieces inspected

The "percent accuracy" is also equal to the percent of material correctly inspected. This feature permits use of the plan in the pay formula of the inspector.

In the application of any plan of checking accuracy of inspectors, it is essential that the checks be at random. Neither the inspector nor the check inspector[133] should know the schedule in advance. Random dice, cards from a pack, etc., should be used. It is also essential that the responsibility be clear. The inspector who has accepted defects under orders or through inaccurate instruments, etc., cannot be held responsible for the results.

ORGANIZATION FOR INSPECTION AND TEST

Prior to the industrial revolution, manufacturing industries consisted largely of small shops, each dominated by a master. He trained the apprentices and supervised their work in various ways, including a form of quality control. This consisted of

---

[132] The term "waste" appears to have been coined by R. W. Woodward of Bausch & Lomb, Inc., to distinguish this type of loss from other losses such as scrap or rework.

[133] Where data are accumulated over a six-month period, a ratio of one check inspector to fifty inspectors appears to be sufficient to provide data of adequate statistical significance.

process surveillance and product inspection conducted until such time as the apprentice demonstrated his capability of repeatedly turning out quality products.

Emergence of the Inspector.   As the shops grew larger and larger, they outgrew the ability of the master to direct all affairs personally.   He therefore created specialized departments and appointed assistants to supervise these departments.   One of these assistants, the shop foreman, took over supervision of the workmen and continued the tradition of personally exercising the quality controls.

In due course the number of workmen grew to an extent which exceeded the capacity of the shop foreman to exercise the quality controls.   He solved this by creating the post of inspector and delegating to the inspector the job of judging fitness for use or conformance to specification.   The earliest form of this was probably in the large construction projects of antiquity.   Figure 12-10 shows an inspector using a string to measure the flatness of stone blocks while a workman is engaged in dressing the stone.   The date is 1450 B.C.

Fig. 12-10   Ancient construction inspector.   *(From C. Singer et al., "A History of Technology," Oxford University Press, 1957, Vol. 1, fig. 313.)*

The industrial revolution resulted in the growth of large manufacturing companies which included multiple production shops (foundry, lathe, etc.).   The tradition of shop inspectors reporting to the foreman was carried over, so that the organization for inspection resembled that shown in Figure 12-11.

The foremen of those shops had virtually no technical education.   Their job knowledge was derived from long association with materials, processes, and products which had remained largely static over the years.   When World War I required these shops to take on products new to them, many foremen were in deep trouble.   On the

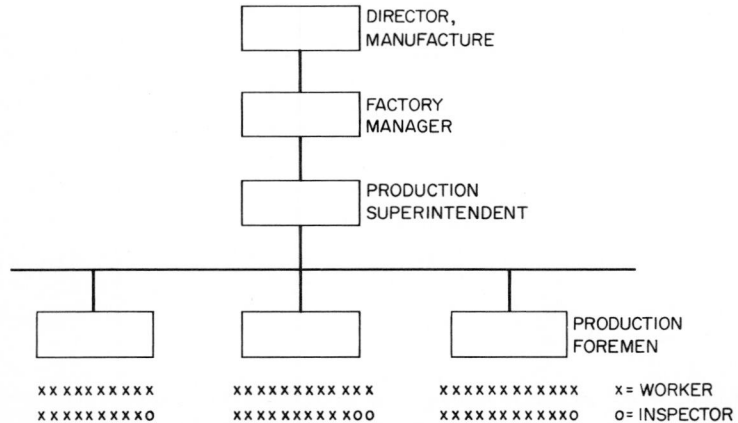

Fig. 12-11   Organization for inspection, early factories.

old products they knew from their experience how far they safely could go in overruling their inspectors.   On the new products this experience was of little help, and, in addition, they lacked the technical education which might have qualified them to make a swift transition.   In consequence, there were many serious quality failures and scandals.

Emergence of the Central Inspection Department.   Following these catastrophes and under the urging of the Taylor System[134] advocates, the companies now accepted the advice of those who had long been calling for making the inspectors independent of the Production foremen.   The companies took the inspectors away from the Production foremen and made them responsible to full-time inspection foremen instead.   Then, to provide adequate supervision for these inspection foremen, a new office, that of Chief Inspector, was created.   Figure 12-12 shows the resulting organization form in contrast to the prior form (Figure 12-11).

Inspection Department Structure   The early inspection departments generally took a form similar to that of Figure 12-13.   In due course, further developments followed, as discussed below.

Purchased Material Inspection.   All inspectors engaged in this work were brought together in a single organization section for some logical, compelling reasons.   Incoming material was received at a central receiving station, requiring also a centralized inspection station.   The purchasing routines could better be enforced by a single vendor inspection section.   The problems of dealing with vendors were special, requiring a standard vendor inspection procedure.   To a very high degree, these reasons still prevail, though new concepts of vendor relations are now needed to deal with modern subcontracting.   (See generally Section 10.)

Process Inspection.   The process inspectors were widely dispersed among the production processing departments.   The first centralizing step was to make these inspectors responsible to a Chief Process Inspector while remaining geographically

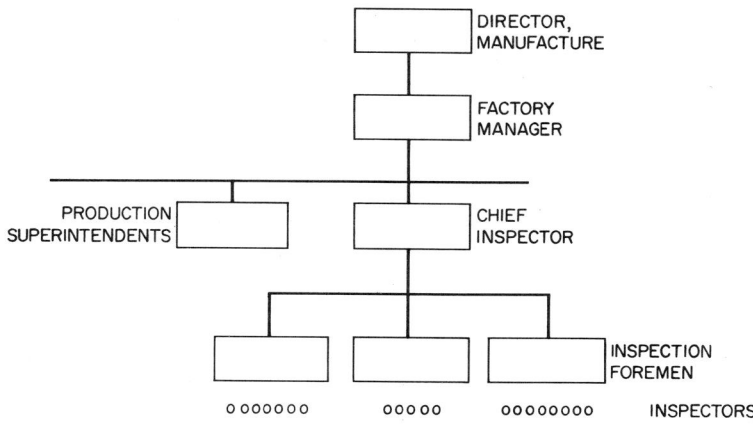

Fig. 12-12   Creation of central inspection department.

[134] Frederick W. Taylor and his school of "Scientific Management" advocated creation of specialized departments to conduct various activities (manufacturing planning, cost accounting, maintenance, inspection, etc.) previously responsible to the foreman.   See Section 18, under Role of Motivation: The Taylor System.

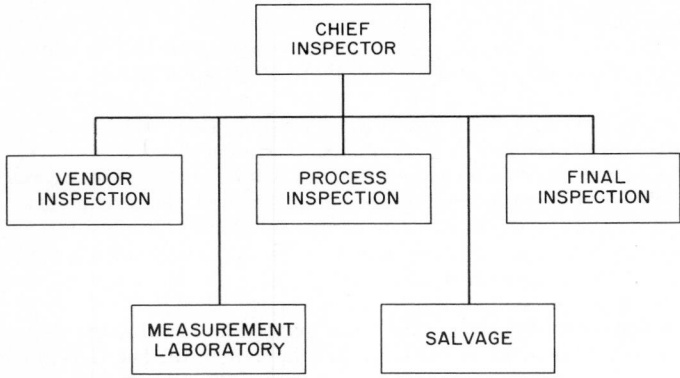

Fig. 12-13   Early central inspection department.

dispersed.   As the plants grew, multiple process inspection departments were organized to parallel the associated production departments, as shown in Figure 12-14.

Finished Goods Inspection.   This is also called "final inspection," "test," etc.
While this has long been a separate department, there have been variations in the
manner of connecting this activity into the overall organization chart.

In the mechanical and electronic industries the usual pattern has been to make
Finished Goods Inspection responsible to the Chief Inspector (Figure 12-13.)   An
alternative form has been a separation of the functional testing from the remaining
inspection (visual, gaging).   Under such an arrangement, the testing is made responsible to the Technical Department, while the remaining inspection reports to the

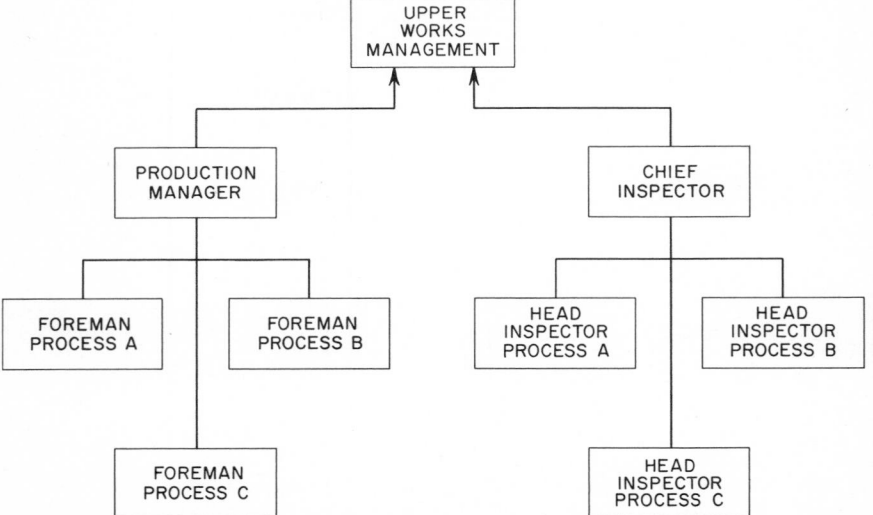

Fig. 12-14   Organization of process inspection in large plants.

Chief Inspector (Figure 12-15). Generally, the more critical the product in terms of human safety, the more likely it is that the functional testing reports to upper management, either directly or through some channel other than Manufacture.

In the process industries, there has long been a separation of critical testing (for safety, structural integrity, functional performance) from the inspection for esthetic and noncritical qualities. The critical testing was the responsibility of the laboratory, which reported to the Technical Manager. The noncritical inspection was performed by inspectors responsible to Production (Figure 12-16). To a high degree, this arrangement has persisted. In most process industries the inspectors (for noncritical properties) are brought together in a separate department which reports to a Production manager. However, in some process industries these inspectors remain dispersed organizationally and are responsible to the departmental production foremen.

In multiproduct plants there are alternatives for organizing the process and final inspection. One form is to create separate hierarchies for process and for final inspectors (Figure 12-17). Another form is to create product hierarchies, each of which includes both process and final inspectors (Figure 12-18). The choice depends largely on the extent to which the processes are unique to particular products. The plan of Figure 12-18 permits better coordination if the processes are largely unique to the associated products.

Creation of the central inspection department also created a new organizational problem: to whom should the Chief Inspector report? This problem is discussed in Section 7, under Evolution of the Quality Control Hierarchy.

Evolution of Inspection Support Activities   The formation of central inspection departments enabled the new chief inspectors to tend to some matters which had previously received scant attention. These included the following:

Metrology. Laboratories were created for calibrating, protecting, storing, is-

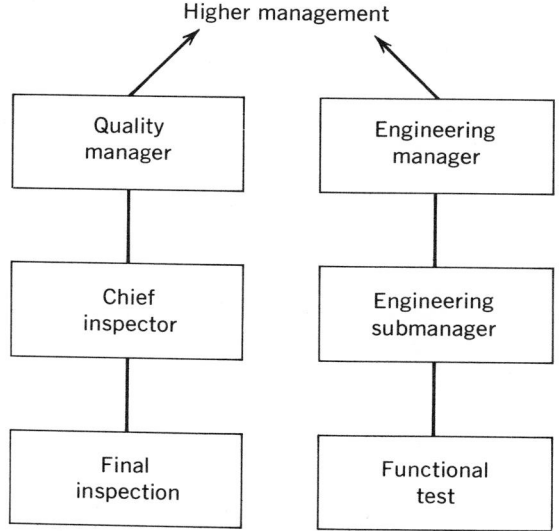

Fig. 12-15 Separation of functional test from inspection.

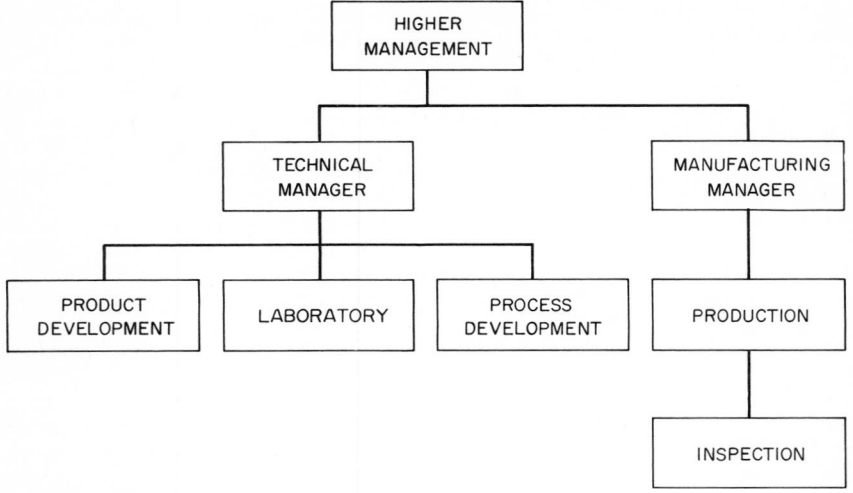

Fig. 12-16   Organization form, process industries, single plant.

suing, and otherwise regulating the precision of measuring instruments.   In addition, new skills were evolved for design of better instruments and test equipment and for planning instrumentation as part of the design of the production process and of the inspection stations.   See generally Sections 9 and 13.

Inspection Planning.   The full-time inspection supervisors evolved the concept of planning the inspection job.   Inspection methods sheets were designed to list the

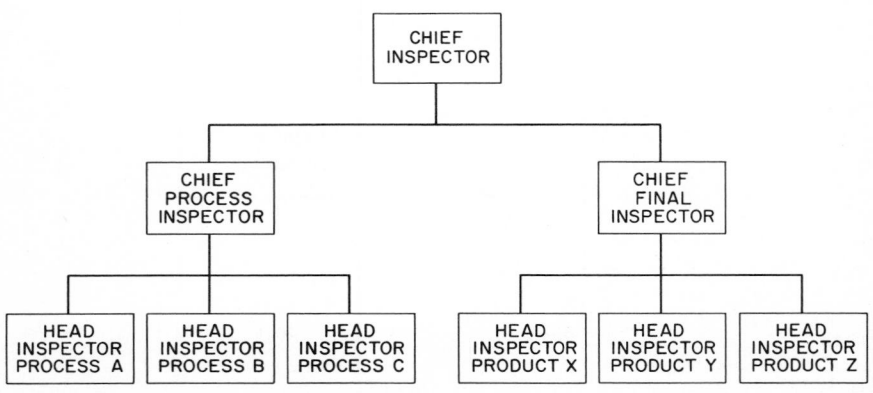

Fig. 12-17   Inspection organized by function.

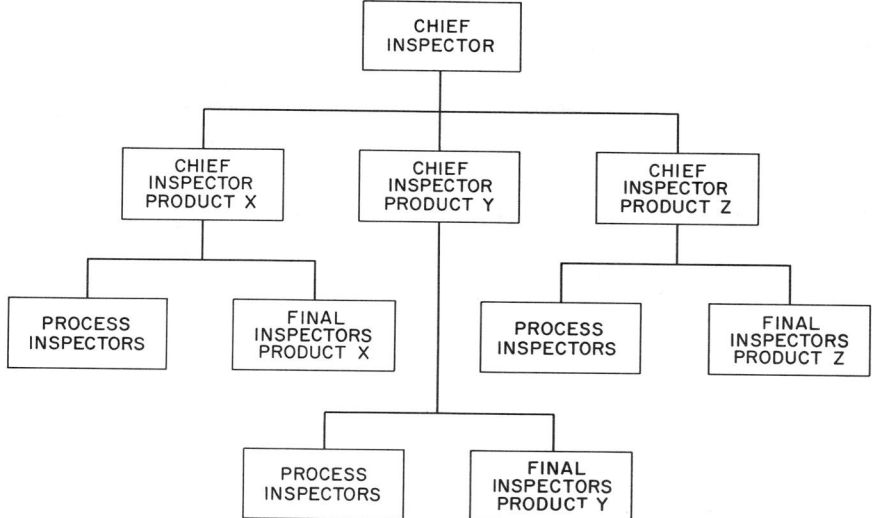

Fig. 12-18 Inspection organized by product.

inspection operations to be performed, sample sizes, allowable defects, instruments, standards, and other criteria needed by the inspectors. See Inspection Planning, above.

Inspector Selection, Training. The full-time inspection supervisors felt keenly the need for well-selected, trained inspection personnel and began to evolve the means for reaching this goal. See generally Section 17.

Salvage. The ministerial work associated with disposition of nonconforming product was gradually assigned to the Chief Inspector. It includes identification, segregation, custody, documentation and still other activities. It may involve sorting the product and planning repairs or other salvage forms.

Noninspection Operations Performed by Inspectors In many companies there are forces which try to confine work assignments to strict jurisdictional lines; i.e., inspectors should do nothing but inspection work. (A common spur to strict enforcement of jurisdictional boundaries is management pressure on departmental budgets.) However, the increasing complexity of the quality function is now tending to weaken these boundaries. The trends appear in several forms.

Counting, Weighing. Generally, the measure of amount of product has been a responsibility of the materials management departments. However, increasingly, the amount of product interfaces with quality matters. In batch processes, the ingredients must be weighed out correctly if the batch is to be correct. There must be accountability for use of some labels, seals, and other forms of certification. Spare parts and instruction booklets accompanying finished units must be counted. All this is superimposed on older forms of counting assigned to inspectors.

Some of this assignment has been on economic grounds; i.e., since the inspector handles the product anyhow, why require still another person to rehandle the product just to count it? A further reason has been the need for certifying counts for paying piecework operators. The clerk in the payroll department does not see the product on the factory floor. If he did, he would still be unable to tell whether the right operation had been performed. Yet if the piecework payments are to be made correctly, the payroll clerk must know these things. Since he cannot find them out at first hand, he must be told by someone qualified and independent. That someone is the inspector, who does so by verifying the recorded file number of the piecework operation.

Packing. The inspector usually handles all units at final inspection and sometimes in process inspection. In many cases the inspector can dispose of the product by performing the preliminary packing into the shipment boxes, thereby avoiding a duplicate handling plus the need to inspect the packing operation.[135]

It is evident that the planning of inspection work must be done with flexible concepts of jurisdiction. Failing this, the rigid enforcement of jurisdictional lines will lead to absurd duplications of work.

INSPECTION DEPARTMENT MANAGEMENT

Managing the Inspection department is accomplished through a hierarchy of supervisors whose duties have much in common. A typical list of these common duties includes the following:

Participate in inspection planning; approve all manuals and procedures to be used by the inspectors.

Approve product and process standards supplemental to engineering specifications.

Prepare the departmental budget for personnel, facilities, and supplies.

Participate in design of the inspection workplace, in choice of facilities and instruments, and in design of work methods; approve the final design.

Assign work to the inspectors; supervise and evaluate their performance; motivate inspectors to meet standards of quality and efficiency.

Collaborate with other departments in investigation and solution of quality problems and in other interdepartmental activities.

Review the condition of products found to be nonconforming; participate in the studies leading to disposition.

Review the condition of processes for which there is evidence of nonconformance to specification; collaborate in the steps needed to restore control.

Prepare and approve necessary documentation on quality.

Develop the potentialities of subordinates.

Keep informed on new industrial developments in facilities, instrumentation, inspection methods and practices; adapt for company use as appropriate.

These duties vary in detail with the specialties of the various inspection departments. The Chief Inspector carries, in addition, the broader duties of participating in discussion of numerous higher-level quality problems.

Laboratory Management   This activity involves several special problems in inspection management.

Interlaboratory Comparisons.   Despite extensive standardization of test methods, it is still necessary to conduct periodic interlaboratory comparisons among companies, between Division and Plant laboratories, between central and branch laboratories, etc.[136]

Decentralizing the Laboratory.   It is not feasible to centralize all test facilities in one laboratory. The usual forms of decentralizing are:

[135] See also, Nonproduction Operations, under Inspection Planning, above.

[136] See Section 13, under Error of Measurement: Interlaboratory Test Programs, for the methodology involved. See also Section 27 under Planning Interlaboratory Tests for methods of graphical diagnosis, especially Youden Two Sample Plots, Figure 27-10.

1. Branch Laboratories. As noted under Physical Facilities for Inspection, above, branch laboratories serve to simplify the transport of samples and to provide more prompt feedback of the resulting data. The branch laboratory may consist of:

a. A laboratory manned full-time by Inspection but located physically amid the production areas which require test service.

b. A traveling laboratory which moves from department to department on a scheduled basis. A common form of this is the gage cart or other traveling metrology laboratory used to maintain accuracy of measuring instruments.

c. A laboratory manned part-time by Production to provide prompt service without the need for requisitions and other paperwork. Such laboratories, restricted to routine testing, are located on the Production floor.

2. Independent Laboratories. These can be a useful adjunct to the company's laboratory for reasons of cost, scarce facilities, peak loads, specialized personnel, customer relations, and still other considerations. Inspection managers are well advised to keep informed on the services offered by independent laboratories and to use these as the occasion warrants.[137]

Multiple Laboratory Functions. In many companies the Inspection laboratory is the company's sole facility for making such tests. In consequence, the laboratory will be asked to make tests for a variety of purposes:

As a service to Production, which uses the data to make process control decisions
As a service to Research, which lacks a facility for making such tests
As a basis for product conformance decisions, for which the laboratory itself has the responsibility.

In such cases the laboratory is "selling" test results to multiple clients, including itself. Numerous questions of schedule priority, cost allocation, etc., arise and require that the laboratory managers make these allocations by balancing the interests of all clients rather than on the basis of departmental biases.[138]

Inspection by Production Departments There are three varieties of this, and care must be taken to identify which one is the subject under discussion:

1. Inspection conducted part-time by production operators to determine whether the process should run or stop. This is a widespread form of process control and is discussed in Section 11 under Concept of Operator Self Control *et seq.*

2. Inspection conducted part-time by production operators to make acceptance decisions on product conformance. This is discussed in Section 11, under Product Acceptance by Operators.

3. Inspection (product acceptance) conducted by full-time inspectors who report not to the Inspection Department but to the Production Department. This will now be discussed.

Most chief inspectors take a dim view of any arrangement in which full-time inspectors engaged in product acceptance report to anyone other than the Inspection Department. The usual reasons advanced emphasize the needs for professional inspection planning, special recruitment and training for inspectors, establishing a career pattern, unbiased judgment, etc. The real reason may be cultural resistance, but the asserted reasons have validity.[139]

However, use of modern staff concepts makes it possible to meet most of the ob-

---

[137] For a discussion of the pros and cons, see Maass, Richard A., The Independent Test Lab, *Quality Assurance*, April 1970, pp. 24–29 (part I); also May 1970, pp. 43–46 (part II).

[138] For some elaboration, see Woodward, Albert, Administration of a Plastic Control Laboratory, *Industrial Quality Control*, August 1966, pp. 68–71.

[139] In the judgment of the Editor (Juran), it is preferable for full-time inspectors to report to the Inspection Department rather than to the Production Department.

jections by use of a well-known formula for delegation:

| | Responsibility assigned to | |
Activity	Production	Quality Control
Prepare and approve the inspection plan	X	X
Execute the plan	X	
Audit to see that the execution follows the plan.		X

The contents of the "audit" vary depending on circumstances. For example, if the inspectors (in Production) sort or test the product 100%, a check inspection may be set up to follow this (Figure 12-19).

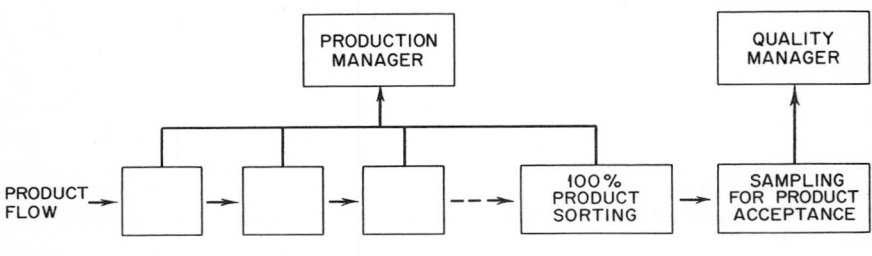

Fig. 12-19   Organization for sorting by production, with subsequent acceptance sampling.

Short-term economics are not noticeably affected by transfering full-time inspectors from Inspection to Production or vice versa. After the change, the same people perform the same duties as before. The really big effect on short-term economics is to abolish full-time inspectors by instituting "product acceptance by operators," as described in Section 11 under that heading.

The "manpower" aspects of Inspection Department Management (e.g., inspector selection, training, compensation) are discussed in Section 17. Motivational aspects are discussed in Section 18.

INSPECTION DATA FEEDBACK

Inspection generates data in profusion, and these data are widely used. Virtually all Sections of this Handbook involve some degree of reliance on inspection data, and for some Sections this reliance is extensive. Table 12-13 lists the Sections which make such extensive use of inspection data, along with the principal purpose served. In addition, Section 19 discusses some of the universal problems of data collection and documentation; Sections 22 through 28 deal with methods of data analysis; and Section 20 deals with use of computers.

Feedback to Production. This is the most extensive inspection feedback judged by volume of data and by man-hours consumed. The feedbacks serve mainly as alarm signals to identify out-of-control processes and to urge corrective action. In addition, to assist Production in problem identification, summaries are prepared by department, process, product, operator, etc., using the Pareto principle to focus on the vital few problems. The detailed methods, along with the nature of Inspection relations with Production, are discussed in Section 11, under Inspection Feedback to Production, as is the problem of corrective action.

TABLE 12-13   Uses of Inspection Data

Section number and title	Inspection data used extensively:
5 Quality Costs	As inputs to quality cost estimates
9 Manufacturing Planning	For process capability determination
10 Vendor Relations	As feedback to vendors
11 Production of Quality	As feedback to Production
12 Inspection and Test	To judge product conformance
13 Measurement	To maintain calibration of instruments
14 Marketing of Quality	To provide "feed-forward" for customer relations
15 Field Performance	To improve field service
16 Quality Improvement	To remedy chronic defects
18 Motivation for Quality	To improve human performance
19 Documentation	To identify and certify products
21 Upper Management and Quality	To prepare executive reports on quality

Data Feedback to Management.   A second extensive use of inspection data is to provide company managers with the summaries and analyses needed as part of the system of managerial control of the quality function.   See Section 21 for details, including discussion of means for auditing the system of data feedback.

Data "Feed-Forward" to the Market.   A third major use of inspection data is to identify the product, provide certificates of analysis, and otherwise to provide product information to consumers, marketers, regulators, etc.   A great deal of this is on a "To Whom It May Concern" basis through use of product markings, tags, certificates, circulars, instructions, cautions, etc.

Data System.   To provide data to meet these and other needs (Table 12-13), planners evolve a whole system of documentation such as is elaborated in Section 19.   Briefly, this system provides

Record forms and data sheets to secure the basic data.

A system of defect codes to simplify data recording and subsequent data processing

Provision for data processing, whether manually or by computer (Section 20)

BUDGETING FOR INSPECTION [140]

An invariable responsibility of the inspection supervisor is to run the department at minimal cost.   This he does through the common sequence of (1) establishing efficient methods, (2) setting standards for quality and quantity of work, (3) selecting and training inspectors to be able to meet these standards, and (4) motivating them to do so.   This responsibility for cost control is usually formalized into the company's system of budgetary control.

The inspection budget deals with the first two elements of the above sequence. These may be restated as (1) Inspection cost reduction and (2) setting standards of inspection cost performance.   Both these activities are concerned with doing deeds, though these deeds must be translated into the common language of money to meet the needs of management budgetary review.

Inspection Cost Reduction   Because a budget becomes the goal to be met, it should reflect good practice, not poor practice.   For this reason, inspection cost reduction should precede setting standards.   There are several approaches available to the Inspection supervision to achieve inspection cost reduction:

Defect Prevention.   High defect levels are the most widespread single reason for high inspection costs.   In consequence, a usual prerequisite for major reductions

[140] See also Section 5, Quality Costs.

of inspection costs is to reduce the major reasons for these costs, i.e., high defect levels. (See generally Section 16.)

Census of Inspection Costs. In this census, *all* inspection work is identified, whether done by employees of Inspection departments, of Production departments, of Laboratory departments, etc. The decisive feature for entering the census is not the titles of the people or the names of the departments to whom they report but the deeds they perform; i.e., do they examine product, compare the results to a specification, and make judgments of conformance?

Commonly the census is conducted to determine, for each department involved:

The number of equivalent full-time inspectors, and their pay

The type of work they do (sorting, sampling, etc.)., the job grade, and the approach to selection and training of inspectors

Other costs, e.g., facilities, supplies

The inspection plans used, the acceptance criteria, the procedures and other routines

The method of supervision, both in setting up the inspection plan and in seeing that the execution follows the plan

The measures of performance for accuracy and efficiency

The census is not merely a questionnaire; it includes visits to all the areas to see the manner of conducting the work. Work sampling is used to help identify the nature of the jobs being done.

The summary of the census shows the total inspection cost, which is an index of the importance of the problem in relation to other management problems. The summary also shows where these costs are concentrated, suggesting the choice of areas for more detailed study.[141]

Industrial Engineering Studies. These have wide application to inspection work. Methods study can be used to improve the design of workplaces.[142] Work standards can be applied to repetitive jobs.[143, 144] Work simplification can be used to analyze principal operations. One plan[145] is as follows:

1. Choose one of the more troublesome inspection operations for study.
2. Consider eliminating the operation entirely.
3. Failing this, break the job down as follows:
    a. List the work elements.
    b. List the equipment used.
    c. Prepare flow diagrams and workplace sketches.
    d. Discuss the job with the inspector to get his ideas.
    e. Question every detail (a checklist of 33 questions is provided).
4. Prepare a new method as the result of the study.
5. Install the new method and follow up.

Work sampling is a further industrial engineering tool available for study of the nature and content of inspection jobs.[146]

---

[141] The census may well be part of a study of Quality Costs, as discussed in Section 5.

[142, 143] For example, see Fox, J. G., The Ergonomics of Coin Inspection, *Quality Engineer,* vol. 28, no. 6, November-December 1964, pp. 165–169.

[144] Such standards can also be applied to process inspection through standard time data. See, for example, Butler, R. G. K., Work Measurement Applied to Engineering Inspection, *Time and Motion Study,* December 1963, pp. 22–26.

[145] Barry, Elmer N., Work Simplification Applied to Inspection, *Industrial Quality Control,* May 1959, pp. 56–58; also June 1959, pp. 19–20.

[146] See, for example, Backus, Fred F., Controlling Acceptable Material Flow by Work Sampling, *Proceedings ASQC Mid-Hudson Section Quality Control Conference,* September 17, 1960. (A case of improving cost of receiving inspection.)

Quality Control Engineering Studies.   These aim at a wide variety of improvements:

1. Coordinated inspection planning is used to minimize duplication of work between Inspection and Production, or between Inspection departments.

2. Automated testing is developed to replace highly repetitive manual testing.

3. Sampling is used to replace detail inspection.

4. Sampling costs are reduced by use of other available knowledge about product conformance. (See How Much Inspection?, above.) One analyst found that his inspection costs were high due mainly to wooden adherence to standard sampling plans. He thereupon designed twelve types of sampling plans to enable the quality planners to tailor the sampling to the job needs. The result was a reduction of about 30% in inspection hours per lot.[147]

5. Documentation is reduced. One manager reduced the documentation for good product (the great majority of all orders) by imprinting the Production Order with a stamp which provided space for the minimal data needed for approved lots. The conventional documentation was retained for defective material.[148]

6. Documentation is turned over to noninspectors so that the inspector can concentrate on product inspection. One form of this is to assign a separate individual to collect the papers needed by the inspector and to deliver this package to the inspector.[149]

7. Perfectionism is reduced by studying the cost of finding a defect compared to the cost of not finding it.

While means are available for reducing inspection costs by purely departmental study and action, the main opportunities are through joint study with other departments. The principal forms of this study consist of:

1. Defect prevention to reduce the need for inspection

2. Collaboration with Production to determine process capability and to preserve the order of manufacture so that the information needed for decisions on conformance is not restricted to the data derived from inspection and test[150]

3. Collaboration with Production to transfer the inspection to production operators and to regulate this through audit of decisions[151]

The Budgetary Process   The Inspection budget is only one of numerous departmental budgets. These must all be prepared under a common format, and in a common language, to permit summary and review at higher and higher levels until finally approved by top management. Because the common language is money, all the deeds must be restated in terms of money to make these summaries and reviews possible.

The common budgetary format is devised by the company's finance and accounting specialists. This format features several universals employed in the budgetary process.

Cost Centers.   These are logical subdivisions of inspection activity, chosen to fix responsibility and to provide a basis for collecting data on actual costs. The cost

---

[147] Gonet, John J., Improving the Management of Quality Cost, *1968 Technical Conference Transactions,* ASQC, pp. 261–266.

[148] See Moburg, Keith W., Defect Management by Exception. *1968 Technical Conference Transactions,* ASQC, pp. 685–690.

[149] See Kidwell, John L., and Edward R. Eidukonis, Increased Product Assurance through Inspection Upgrading and Updating, *Industrial Quality Control,* October 1965, pp. 183–188; also Kahn, Howard R., A Cost Reduction Program in the Receiving Inspection Department, *1964 Western Region Conference, ASQC,* pp. 119–122.

[150] See How Much Inspection? above; also Section 11, under Product and Process Relationship.

[151] See Section 11, under Product Acceptance by Operators.

centers usually follow organization boundaries, since responsibility becomes very clear thereby.

Activity Index. Most inspection costs vary with the amount of plant activity. Sound budgeting requires that there be discovered, for each cost center, an activity index, i.e., an expression of the relationship between plant activity and budgeted inspection costs. For different kinds of inspection, the budget will vary in different ways:

Type of inspection	Budget varies with
Receiving inspection	Number of lots
	Value of purchased goods
Process inspection	Hours of direct production labor
	Dollars of direct production labor
	Number of projects serviced
Final inspection	Units of product inspected
	Value of product inspected
	Hours of direct production labor
	Dollars of direct production labor
Test laboratory	Number of requisitions (Sometimes there is a standard time for each type of test.)
Instrument laboratory	Number of active instruments in use

There are added variables which affect budgeting in all activities and which may be of major effect in some activities. These variables include:

1. Lot Size. Inspection costs per lot do not vary greatly with lot size. However, variation in lot size can cause great variation in inspection cost per unit of product or per dollar value of product.

2. Product Mix. Budgeting is often done on the basis of a historical product mix. When this mix changes, the costs may change either way.

3. Flow of Material. The most exaggerated form of this takes place when much or even most of the product is presented for inspection in the last few days of the month.

Historical Standards. A budget for cost control is a standard for expenditures. This standard may be established in a number of ways, the most prevalent being the historical standard; i.e., we will be guided by how much we used to spend.

An example of evolution of an historical standard is seen in Figure 12-20. In this example, it had been determined that the best activity index was direct shop labor costs. Data for the last 18 months were plotted on Figure 12-20, resulting in a correlation scatter of inspection labor costs to direct shop labor costs. A line fitted to the points resulted in the relationship of a budget of $8.80 inspection labor per every $100 of direct shop labor.

Next, provision was made for the "fixed" portion of the labor budget. The supervisory and clerical force, costing $1,750 per month, were regarded as "constant" over a wide range of activity. Figure 12-21 shows how provision was made to reflect this constant into the budget.

Finally, it was determined that, at very low levels of shop activity, the "constant" force could be cut almost in two. Figure 12-21 shows how the budget line made provision for this.

On a more sophisticated level, one company identified 11 "factors" which influence the extent of inspection needed, e.g., type of product, identity of customer, degree of "black box" subcontracting, etc. For each factor, there were several degrees or levels of influence. From a study of eight prior projects, weights were

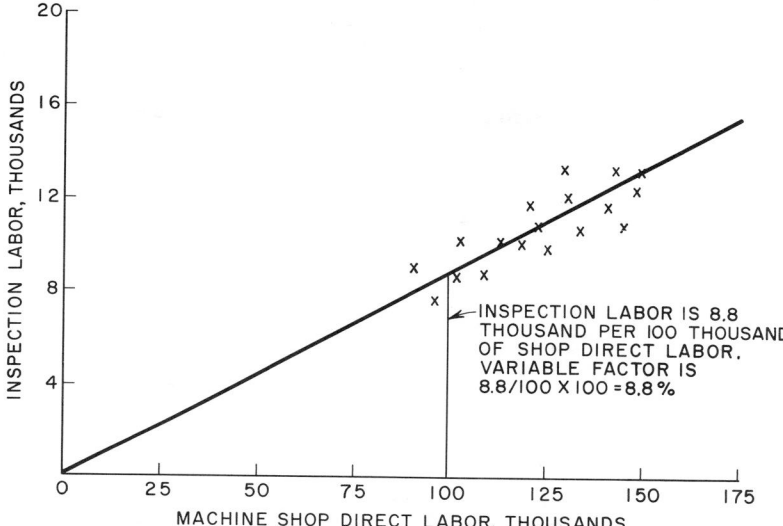

Fig. 12-20 Ratio of inspection labor costs to shop labor costs.

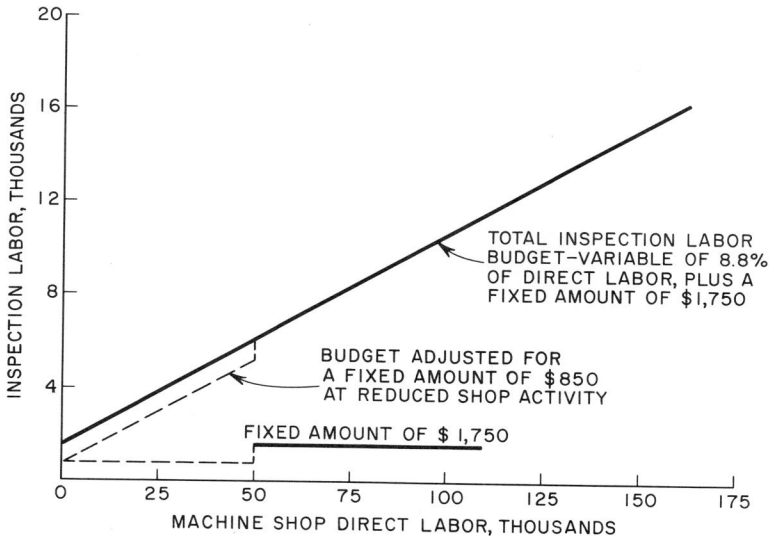

Fig. 12-21 Chart for variable inspection labor budget.

assigned to each degree of each factor. These weights were then used to analyze new contract proposals to arrive at an estimate of the inspection manpower needed.[152]

---

[152] Hutter, R. G., Inspection Manpower Planning, *Industrial Quality Control*, April 1966, pp. 521–523.

Engineered Standards.   A second basis for standards is the engineered standard; i.e., we will be guided by engineering studies in determining what ought to be spent.

Conventional industrial engineering study methods are applicable to highly repetitive inspection and have in fact been applied to such work.   Engineered standards are also common for test work of a more intricate nature, though the variability is, of course, greater.

In the case of patrol inspectors, determination of man-hours needed is based on evaluation of the patrol "beat."   Since patrol inspection is repetitive in character, it lends itself well to man-hour evaluation by conventional industrial engineering study.

Market Standards.   A third form of standard is based on the market; i.e., we will be guided by what others spend.   This form can be used only if data are obtained on costs in other plants or companies in the same industry, process, or product.   Industry surveys are one source of such data.

For example, a survey of quality control costs in the aircraft industry[153] identified over 25 different tasks performed by "Quality Control" departments.   It also studied such matters as:

Method of accounting for various activities
Principal customers
Responsibility for classifying defects
Type of quality information recorded, and recording used
Various quality control techniques used and in what activities
Ratio of inspection personnel to production personnel
Proportions of inspection personnel devoted to various tasks (clerical, receiving inspection, etc.)

In collecting these data, company activities were broken down as between airframe, engine, electronics, etc.

Data from other companies, and even from other plants within the same company, should be interpreted with caution.[154]   Costs of inspection, even for similar plants, may vary between companies or plants for a variety of reasons:

1. Organizational Assignment.   Laboratories may be under Inspection in one company and under Engineering in another, with differences in intensity of cost controls.

2. Vendor Relations.   One company may have developed sound, quality-conscious vendors and may be able to use sampling techniques on the incoming inspection of purchased materials and parts.   Another company may not be so fortunate and may have to employ a sorting function at incoming inspection in order to keep the production line operating.

3. Facilities Available.   Equipment, workplace layout, product flow, working conditions, etc., are as important to efficiency of the quality function as they are to manufacturing groups.   These factors can vary widely between plants and can produce variations in labor costs.

4. Quality-mindedness.   The general attitude toward producing a product to the necessary quality level is one of the most important indirect factors affecting the costs of the Inspection Department.   See generally Section 18.

---

[153] Allen, Paul E., How Do You Prepare Your Budget, and Where Do Quality Control Costs Go? *Transactions, Fourth Annual Quality Control Conference, Dayton Section,* ASQC, March 15, 1960.

[154] See, in this connection, Juran, J. M., What Is Par? *Industrial Quality Control,* October 1966, pp. 196–197.

Standards for Projects. A fourth form of standard is "the plan"; i.e., we will spend in accordance with a prearranged plan for a project. This device is most common when the company has secured a contract based on a bid price and now faces the problem of holding its various components of cost within the respective components of the bid.

Seldom does a company use only one form of standard for costs. The cost centers are unlike, and it is common to find different forms of cost standards used in different cost centers. Moreover, there is a measure of judgment exercised in any event. None of the methods of setting standards are precise enough to be used automatically as a basis for judging future performance.

Measure of Actual Costs The establishment of cost centers, activity indexes, and standards provides a measure of what costs should be. It remains to establish means for measuring what costs actually are. This requires added tools:

An adequate Timekeeping System. Inspectors must be provided with account numbers and forms for charging their time to proper account numbers.

A System for Computing Expenses. In like manner, there must be account numbers, requisitions, and other means for charging supplies and services to the proper accounts.

Data-processing Systems. Means must be available (manual or otherwise) for processing the basic time and expense data into prompt summaries and reports for the various cost centers.

A Budget Office. Coordination of the activities of budgeting and reporting requires that administration of the system be a separate responsibility, clearly assigned to a specific person(s).

When a company embarks for the first time on formal budgeting, it is well to go through a trial period for "debugging." During the trial period, minds are open for constructive change. Lacking a trial period, minds may close and the entire project may face defeat.

Review of Cost Performance. Reports on costs versus budgets are prepared and distributed by the budget office on a regular schedule, usually weekly or monthly. Supervisory review is concentrated on significant departure from standard. This review is often conducted as a scheduled group review of performance against budget, since there is much interrelation between causes in one department and effects in another. At these review sessions, alternative courses of action are proposed and considered.

The very act of systematically reviewing performance and questioning variances is a main factor in holding costs to standard. If variances are sure to be questioned, supervisors do their utmost to prevent variances in the first place. If there is laxity in the review, performance will soon become lax as well.

Other Cost Control Devices Whether inspection is budgeted or not, there are available various special tools for controlling inspection costs. These special tools use physical units rather than money. Some of these tools do not require use of the company's financial accounting system, though the clerks of the Accounting Department may process the special data prepared.

For example, it is usually feasible to establish a ratio indicating the number of inspection hours required as compared with the number of productive machine hours (or operator hours) spent producing the product. This ratio can then be built into the form of a variable budget. Within normal variations in volume of operation, as production hours change, inspection hours will change in the same proportion.

In some companies, data are available through history, or through industrial-engineering study, of expected inspection costs. The simplest form is associated with products made in discrete units—so many coils, condensers, tubes. Here the data are in terms of inspection hours per 100 units, or per 100 pounds, and future estimates can be based on knowledge of the future production schedule.

Slightly more complicated is the case where there is a line of product sufficiently varied so that the hours per 100 differ somewhat for the different types in the line. Inspection for the 1A gadget may require 13.2 hours per 100 as against 14.7 for the 2A gadget and 16.8 for the 3A gadget. Here, knowledge of the detailed production schedule or "mix" will permit an estimate. If details are not known, an estimate can still be made if there is no reason to believe that the "mix" has changed as compared with previous history.

This ratio of hours to hours or to units has the advantage of simplicity and ease of preparation. The main disadvantage is that only labor costs are considered, with the effect of other expenses, facility improvements, and other realities omitted.

A less precise measure is the ratio of inspectors to production workers. Beyond the deficiencies of the hours-to-hours measure, this ratio fails to consider inequalities in hours worked, absenteeism, overtime, etc.

Section **13**

Measurement

J. M. JURAN

INTRODUCTION

Conduct of the quality function depends heavily on quantification of product and process characteristics. This quantification is done through a systematic approach involving:

1. Definition of standardized units called "units of measure" which permit conversion of abstractions (e.g., length, mass) into a form capable of being quantified (e.g., meter, kilogram).

2. *Instruments* which are calibrated in terms of these standardized units of measure.

3. Use of these instruments to quantify or *measure* the extent to which the product or process possesses the characteristic under study. This process of quantification is called "measurement."

The word "measurement" has multiple meanings, these being principally:

1. the *process* of quantification; e.g., "The measurement was done in the laboratory," and

2. the resulting number; e.g., "The measurement fell within the tolerances."

Measurement rests on a highly organized, scientific base called "metrology," i.e., the science of measurement. This science underlies the entire systematic approach through which we quantify quality characteristics.

UNITS OF MEASURE

The concept of quantifying bigness and smallness is thousands of years old. At first, units of measure were in terms of parts of the human body. For example, the ancient Egyptian unit of measure for length was the royal cubit, which was defined as the length of the forearm of the reigning pharaoh.

With the expansion of commerce, and especially of international commerce, the metrologists evolved systems of international units of measure, the chief systems being the metric and the English. The metric system is entirely on a decimal basis and is largely based on units of measure which scientists have evolved in the nineteenth and twentieth centuries. The English system is only partly on a decimal basis, and includes units of measure which antedate the industrial revolution.

Metrication   The existence of multiple systems of measurement is a serious handicap to international commerce. During the twentieth century there has been extensive adoption of the metric system by countries previously using the English or other systems. At the beginning of the 1970s, all industrialized countries with the single exception of the United States had either adopted the metric system or had decided to do so. In the United States, resistance to the metric system arises from its heavy investment in the English system coupled with its low ratio of volume of international trade to total size of the economy. However, those industries which are strongly exposed to international trade have largely adopted dual systems or have converted to metric. On purely technological grounds, the metric system is widely regarded as preferable to the English.

Despite the lack of a positive national plan for converting to metric, the United States is in a slow conversion process, and this process is continuing. The gradual conversion, if continued, will likely become virtually complete in about a century, whereas a planned program would reduce the conversion time to a decade or two.[1]

Conversion costs in specific cases vary widely. Dual reading scales for instruments or dual reading dials for machines may involve less than $100 per instance. In contrast, new digital read-out systems for machine tools may run to several thousand dollars per axis.[2]

Aside from conversion of machine tools, instruments, and small tools, there are other costs[3] consisting mainly of:

Revision of specifications, standards and other documentation
Provision of dual sets of spare parts during the conversion process
Retraining of personnel

SI System   More recently there has been evolved a fully coherent international system, the Système International d'Unités (SI). This SI system consists of:

1. Six fundamental units of measure—for length, mass, time, electric current, temperature, and light intensity
2. Two supplemental units for plane and solid angles
3. A long list of units derived from (1) and (2)
4. A standardized terminology for multiples and subdivisions of all units of measure

---

[1] For further discussion, see De Simone, Daniel V., A Metric America: A Decision Whose Time Has Come, National Bureau of Standards Special Publication 345, July 1971, SD Catalog no. 13.10:345. See also the series of papers in *Mechanical Engineering*, May 1969, pp. 11–25.

[2] For some estimates for conversion of machine tools, see Blaufuss, Jo, Metric Memo, *Quality Management & Engineering*, June 1972, p. 40.

[3] For additional discussion, see De Simone, Daniel V., Moving to Metric Makes Dollars and Sense, *Harvard Business Review*, January–February 1972, pp. 100–111.

TABLE 13-1   SI System Units of Measure

Characteristic	Unit of measure	Symbol	Formula
Fundamental units			
Length	meter	m	
Mass	kilogram	kg	
Time	second	s	
Electric current	ampere	A	
Temperature	degree Kelvin	$^{\circ}$K	
Luminous intensity	candela	cd	
Supplementary units			
Plane angle	radian	rad	
Solid angle	steradian	sr	
Derived units			
Area	square meter	m^2	
Volume	cubic meter	m^3	
Frequency	hertz	Hz	(s^{-1})
Density	kilogram per cubic meter	kg/m^3	
Velocity	meter per second	m/s	
Angular velocity	radian per second	rad/s	
Acceleration	meter per second squared	m/s^2	
Angular acceleration	radian per second squared	rad/s^2	
Force	newton	N	$(kg \cdot m/s^2)$
Pressure	newton per sq meter	N/m^2	
Kinematic viscosity	sq meter per second	m^2/s	
Dynamic viscosity	newton-second per sq meter	$N \cdot s/m^2$	
Work, energy, quantity of heat . . .	joule	J	$(N \cdot m)$
Power	watt	W	(J/s)
Electric charge	coulomb	C	$(A \cdot s)$
Voltage, potential difference, electromotive force	volt	V	(W/A)
Electric field strength	volt per meter	V/m	
Electric resistance	ohm	Ω	(V/A)
Electric capacitance	farad	F	$(A \cdot s/V)$
Magnetic flux	weber	Wb	$(V \cdot s)$
Inductance	henry	H	$(V \cdot s/A)$
Magnetic flux density	tesla	T	(Wb/m^2)
Magnetic field strength	ampere per meter	A/m	
Magnetomotive force	ampere	A	
Luminous flux	lumen	lm	$(cd \cdot sr)$
Luminance	candela per sq meter	cd/m^2	
Illumination	lux	lx	(lm/m^2)

Table 13-1 lists the fundamental, supplemental, and derived units of the SI system along with the symbols used and the derivation formulas.[4]

Table 13-2 lists the terms used for multiples and subdivisions of these units of measure.[5,6,7]

[4,5] Derived from McNish, A. G., the International System of Units, *Industrial Quality Control,* March 1966, pp. 465–469.

[6] For an excellent elaboration, see Ackley, Robert A., "Physical Measurements and the International (SI) System of Units," 3d ed., Technical Publications, San Diego, California, 1970 (88 pages).

[7] See also, SI—Systeme International Rationale, *Quality Progress,* January 1972, pp. 15–18.

TABLE 13-2   SI System Multiples and Subdivisions

Multiple or subdivision	Prefix	Symbol
$1\ 000\ 000\ 000\ 000 = 10^{12}$	tera	T
$1\ 000\ 000\ 000 = 10^{9}$	giga	G
$1\ 000\ 000 = 10^{6}$	mega	M
$1\ 000 = 10^{3}$	kilo	k
$100 = 10^{2}$	hecto*	h
$10 = 10^{1}$	deca*	da
$0.1 = 10^{-1}$	deci*	d
$0.01 = 10^{-2}$	centi*	c
$0.001 = 10^{-3}$	milli	m
$0.000\ 001 = 10^{-6}$	micro	μ
$0.000\ 000\ 001 = 10^{-9}$	nano	n
$0.000\ 000\ 000\ 001 = 10^{-12}$	pico	p
$0.000\ 000\ 000\ 000\ 001 = 10^{-15}$	femto	f
$0.000\ 000\ 000\ 000\ 000\ 001 = 10^{-18}$	atto	a

* Use is discouraged.

The SI system is fully compatible with the metric system, though superseding some earlier units (e.g., liter, calorie). The SI system is not fully compatible with the English system of feet, pounds, etc., though conversion factors are, of course, available.

Nonmeasurable Characteristics   For many characteristics there are as yet no agreed units of measure. Nevertheless, useful evaluations can be made of such characteristics, by:

1. Sensory testing. Here no instrument is available for sensing, and the sensing is done by human sense organs (taste, feel, smell, etc.). For a full discussion, see Section 12, under Sensory Qualities.

2. Instrument testing. An example is the "nondestructive" testing performed to detect weaknesses in metal components (see below, under Nondestructive Testing).

Development of new units of measure and of new sensing instruments is a continuing process. All today's units of measure were evolved to replace qualitative evaluations. Presumably all today's qualitative evaluations will at some time in the future be susceptible of measurement using agreed units of measure.

MEASUREMENT STANDARDS

The six fundamental units of the International System (SI) are defined[8] as shown in Table 13-3. It is seen that except for the kilogram, all units are defined in terms of natural phenomena. (The kilogram is defined as the mass of a specific object.)

Primary Reference Standards   In all industrialized countries there exists a national Bureau of Standards whose functions include construction and maintenance of "primary reference standards." These standards consist of copies of the International Kilogram plus measuring systems which are responsive to the definitions of the fundamental units (Table 13-3) and to the derived units of Table 13-1.

In addition, professional societies, (e.g., American Society for Testing and Materials) have evolved standardized test methods for measuring many hundreds of quality characteristics not listed in Table 13-1. These standard test methods describe the test conditions, equipment, procedure, etc., to be followed. The various national Bureaus of Standards, as well as other laboratories, then develop

[8] McNish, A. G., op. cit.

TABLE 13-3   Definitions of Fundamental Units of the SI System

Meter (m).	1 650 763.73 wavelengths in vacuo of the unperturbed transition $2_{P10} - 5d_5$ in ^{86}Kr
Kilogram (kg)	Mass of the international kilogram at Sevres, France
Second (s).	1/31 556 925 974 7 of the tropical year at 12^h ET, 0 January 1900, supplementarily defined in 1964 in terms to the cesium F, 4; M, 0 to F, 3; M, 0, transition, the frequency assigned being 9 192 631 770 hertz
Degree Kelvin (°K).	Defined in the thermodynamic scale by assigning 273.16°K to the triple point of water (freezing point, 273.15°K = 0°C)
Ampere (A).	The constant current which, if maintained in two straight parallel conductors of infinite length, of negligible circular sections, and placed 1 meter apart in a vacuum, will produce between these conductors a force equal to 2×10^{-7} M.K.S. unit of force per meter of length.
Candela (cd).	$\frac{1}{60}$ of the intensity of one square centimeter of a perfect radiator at the temperature of freezing platinum.

primary reference standards which embody the units of measure corresponding to these standard test methods.

Primary reference standards have a distinct legal status, since commercial contracts usually require that "measuring and test equipment shall be calibrated . . . utilizing reference standards . . . whose calibration is certified as being traceable to the National Bureau of Standards."[9]   In practice it is not feasible for the National Bureau of Standards to calibrate and certify the accuracy of the enormous volume of test equipment in use in the shops and test laboratories.   Instead, resort is had to a hierarchy of secondary standards and laboratories, along with a system of documented certification of accuracy.

Hierarchy of Standards   The primary reference standards are the apex of an entire hierarchy of reference standards (Figure 13-1.)   At the base of the hierarchy there stands the huge array of "test equipment,"[10] i.e., instruments used by laboratory technicians, workmen and inspectors to control processes and products.   These instruments are calibrated against "working standards" which are used solely to calibrate these laboratory and shop instruments.   In turn, the working standards are related back to the primary reference standards through one or more intermediate secondary reference standards or "transfer standards."   Each of these levels in the hierarchy serves to "transfer" accuracy of measurement to the next lower level in the hierarchy.

Within the hierarchy of standards there are differences both in the physical construction of the standards and in their precision.   The primary reference standards are used by a relatively few highly skilled metrologists, and their skills are a vital contribution to the high precision attained by these standards.   As we progress down the hierarchy, the number of technicians increases with each level, until at the base there are millions of workmen, inspectors, and technicians using test equipment to control product and process.   Because of the wide variation in the training, skills, and dedication among these millions, the design and construction of test equipment must feature ruggedness, stability, and foolproofing so as to minimize errors contributed by the human beings using the equipment.

[9] This wording is from MIL-C-45662A, Military Specification-Calibration System Requirements.

[10] The terminology varies.   For a discussion, see Section 9, under Quality Information Equipment.

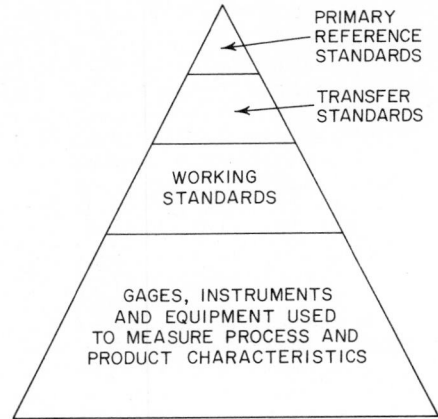

Fig. 13-1 Hierarchy of standards.

Precision of measurement differs widely among the various levels of the hierarchy of standards. At the level of primary reference standards, the precision is determined by the state of the art. For example, Figure 13-2 shows the precision attained by the U.S. National Bureau of Standards when weighing loads across the spectrum of 10^{-10} kilograms to 10^6 kilograms.[11]

At the base of the hierarchy, the precision of measurement is determined by the needs of fitness for use as reflected by the product and process tolerances. While some specialists urge that the test equipment be able to "divide the tolerance into tenths," this ideal is by no means always attained in practice.[12] However, the

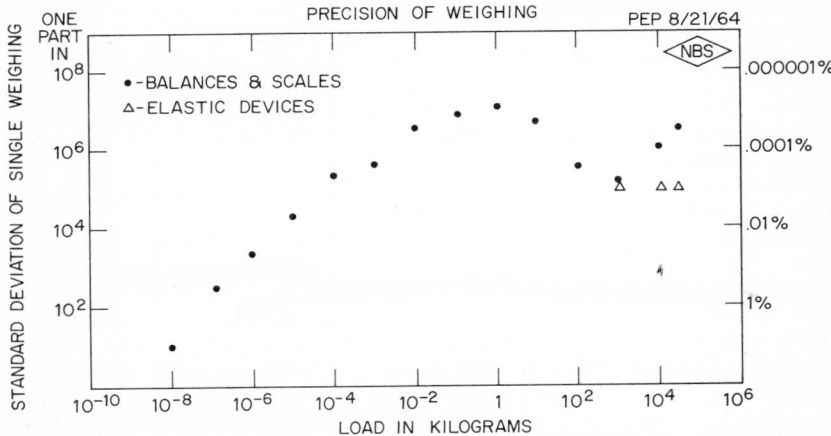

Fig. 13-2 Precision of weighing. From National Bureau of Standards Technical Note 262, Accuracy in Measurements and Calibrations, 1965, p. 4; available from U.S. Government Printing Office.

[11] National Bureau of Standards, 1961. Figure 13-2 is one of a family of such charts showing, for various parameters, the precision of measurement attained.

[12] For further discussion, see below, under Error of Measurement.

tolerances themselves have been drastically tightened over the centuries, and this tightening has generally paralleled the advances made in the state of the art.[13]

Allocation of measurement errors among the working and transfer standards has been widely discussed but has not been well standardized. The precision gap between primary reference standards and product test equipment may be anywhere from one to several orders of magnitude. This gap must then be allocated among the number of levels of standards and laboratories (transfer plus working) prevailing in any given situation.[14] When this problem of allocation was first faced, there was a tendency to conclude that each level should have a precision 10 times greater than the level it was checking. More recently, there has been growing awareness of how multiple levels of precision combine; i.e., their composite is better represented by the square root of the sum of the squares rather than by the arithmetic sum. This new awareness has caused many practitioners to accept a ratio of 5 rather than 10 for precision of working standards to product tolerances. This same ratio has also been tolerated among transfer standards as well.

ERROR OF MEASUREMENT

Product and process conformance are determined by measurements made by the test equipment at the bottom of the hierarchy of standards. Obviously, any error in these measurements has a direct bearing on the ability to judge conformance. On examination, the nature of measurement error is quite complex; even the terminology is confused. A clear understanding of the meaning of the measurements requires a minimal degree of understanding of the nature of measurement error. The starting point is to understand the nature of accuracy and precision. Figure 13-3 shows the meanings of these terms, by example and by analogy.[15]

Accuracy Suppose that we make numerous measurements on a single unit of product and that we then compute the average of those measurements. The extent to which this average agrees with the "true" value of that unit of product is called the *accuracy* of the instrument or measurement system which was employed. The difference between the average and the true value is called the *error* (also systematic error, bias or inaccuracy) and is the extent to which the instrument is out of calibration. The error can be positive or negative. The *correction* needed to put the instrument in calibration is of the same magnitude as the error but opposite in sign. The instrument is still considered *accurate* if the error is less than the *tolerance* or maximum error allowable for that grade of instrument.

Accuracy and error are quantified as a difference between (1) the average of multiple measurements and (2) the true value. As will be seen, each of these is surrounded by a fringe of doubt. In consequence, the expression of accuracy must show the extent of these doubts if the full meaning of the numbers is to be conveyed.

Precision Irrespective of accuracy of calibration, an instrument will not give identical readings even when making a series of measurements on one single unit

[13] For example, accuracy of measurement of a meter of length has progressed from an error of 1,000 per million (at the end of the fifteenth century) to an error of 0.001 per million late in the twentieth century. See Loxham, John, From Science to Technology, *Quality Engineer*, January–February 1967, pp. 16–26.

[14] Some models have been worked out to show the interrelation among: cost of developing greater precision in the primary reference standard, cost of attaining precision at each level of transfer laboratory, and number of laboratories at each level. See, for example, Crow, Edwin L., Optimum Allocation of Calibration Errors, *Industrial Quality Control*, November 1966, pp. 215–219.

[15] See, in this connection, ASTM 177-71 on use of the terms "precision" and "accuracy" as applied to measurement of the properties of materials.

Measurements on One Unit of Product by Three Instruments

Readings		Frequency Distribution of Readings	Target Analogy

Instrument A

.014	.015	.015	.017	.015
.015	.016	.014	.016	.015
.016	.016	.015	.016	.016
.017	.017	.016	.014	.016
.015	.015	.016	.014	.017

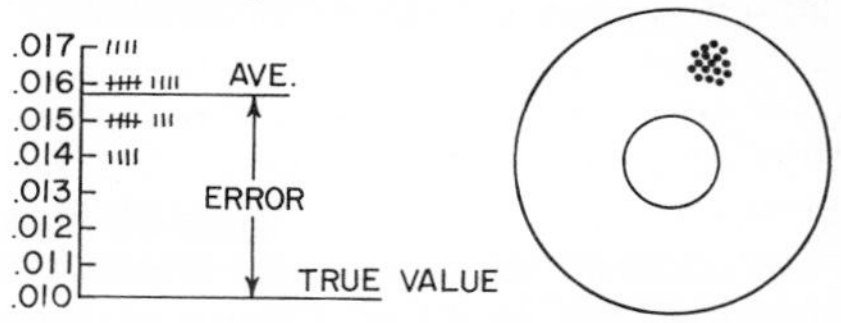

Precise, but Not Accurate

Instrument B

.009	.011	.008	:007	.011
.009	.011	.009	.016	.012
.008	.012	.014	.008	.011
.010	.013	.014	.011	.012
.010	.013	.015	.010	.013

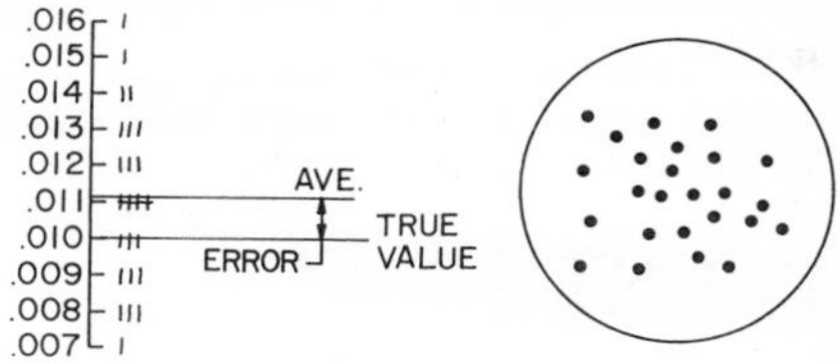

Accurate, but Not Precise

Instrument C

.009	.010	.010	.010	.009
.009	.010	.011	.011	.010
.009	.009	.011	.011	.009
.010	.011	.010	.011	.010
.010	.009	.011	.010	.010

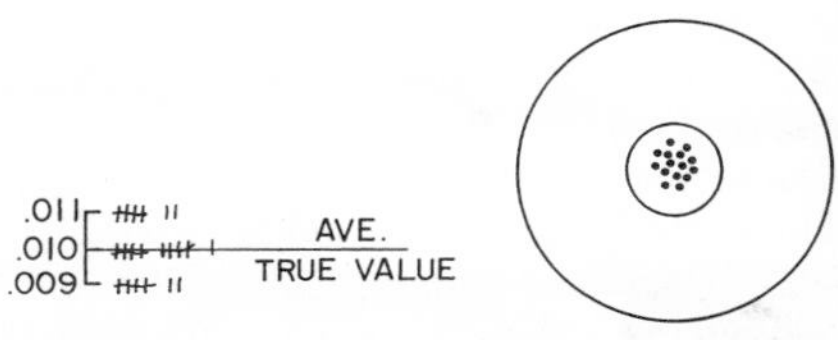

Accurate and Precise

Fig. 13-3   Accuracy and precision.

of product. Instead, the measurements scatter about the average, as exemplified in Figure 13-3. The ability of the instrument to reproduce its own measurements is called its *precision,* and this varies inversely with the dispersion of the multiple ("replicated") measurements.

Experience has shown that any measurement system has an inherent dispersion which is itself reproducible, measurable, and therefore (once known) predictable. This inherent precision of measurement parallels the inherent process capability of a machine tool.[16]

Quantification of precision is in terms of the standard deviation of replicated measurements, and is expressed by σ, the statistical symbol for standard deviation of a population.

Normally, recalibration can improve the accuracy of an instrument by reducing its error. However, recalibration normally does not improve the precision of the instrument, as this precision remains relatively constant over the working range.

Sources of Error   Systematic error and dispersion of measurements have their origin in several well-known components of measurement error.[17]

---

[16] The parallel extends to the requirement that the system be in a state of statistical control.

[17] In some industries, e.g., Chemical Process, the measurement problems are so severe that development of valid test procedures is a major step in the launching of a new product or process. See Section 29, under Manufacture of Commercial Product Quality—Organization and Responsibilities: The Analytical or Control Laboratory. See also, Section 29, under Need for Understanding Analytical Method.

Within-operator Variation. The same operator, inspector, or technician, even when using the same measuring system on the same unit of product, will nevertheless come up with a dispersion of readings. This variation is usually referred to as "within-operator" variation.

Between-operator Variation. When two operators use the same measuring system on the same product, they will usually exhibit differences traceable to differences in operator technique. These differences are called "between-operator" variation and can be exhibited both as systematic error and as differences in dispersion.

Materials Variation. In many cases it is not feasible to conduct replicated tests on the same "unit of product"; i.e., the product is changed or destroyed by testing. In other cases, the standard itself is consumable (e.g., hardness test blocks), so that material variation affects the standard as well. In these cases, where replicate testing is not feasible, the variations due to operator, equipment, and test method are composited with the materials variation. Sometimes it is feasible to resolve these composites into their components and sometimes it is not. A further complication is the case of perishable materials, which may require use of calibrations which relate time elapsed to degradation suffered.

Test Equipment Variation. Instruments are subject to numerous sources of error, both within a single instrument and between instruments: nonlinearity, hysteresis (e.g., gear backlash), drift due to temperature rise, sensitivity to extraneous "noise" (e.g., magnetic, thermal, electrical fields). Each technology is subject to its own unique array of troubles. These instrument troubles are multiplied by the "fixturing" troubles of connecting the instruments into the larger test equipment units and of connecting the test specimens for test. These fixturing troubles include such problems as making good electrical connections, fastening mechanical linkages, locating probes precisely, etc.

Test Procedure Variation. In those cases where more than one test procedure is available to conduct measurement, it is essential to determine the relative variations, since these are one of the criteria for judging the adequacy of the procedure.

Between-laboratory Variation. This is a major problem both within companies and between companies. Some major programs must await resolution of this problem before they can be concluded, e.g., industry standardization of materials, test equipment, and test procedures. In like manner, variation between vendor and buyer laboratories may be at the root of a major quality problem. So extensive is the need to reduce between-laboratory variation that standard procedures have been evolved for the purpose.[18]

Composite Errors The observed measurements are, of course, a resultant of the contributing variations. Generally this resultant or composite is related to the component variables in accordance with the formula:

$$\sigma_{obs}^2 = \sigma_w{}^2 + \sigma_b{}^2 + \sigma_m{}^2 + \sigma_e{}^2 + \sigma_p{}^2 + \text{etc}.$$

where σ_{obs} is the standard deviation of the observed measurements and where $\sigma_w, \sigma_b, \sigma_m, \sigma_e, \sigma_p$, etc. are the standard deviations reflecting the size of the variables which affect precision, i.e., within operator, between operator, material used, test equipment, test procedure, etc., respectively.[19]

[18] See below, under Interlaboratory Test Programs.

[19] This relationship is valid provided the variables are independent of each other, which they often are. Where two or more of the variables are interrelated, then the equation must be modified. If for example, variables A and B are interrelated, then:

$$\sigma_T{}^2 = \sigma_A{}^2 + \sigma_B{}^2 + \rho_{AB}\sigma_A\sigma_B$$

(footnote continues on p. 13-10)

In many cases it is feasible to quantify the effect of some component sources of variation by simple designs of experiment. When an instrument measures a series of different units of product, the resulting observations will have a scatter which is a composite of (1) the variation in the system of measurement, and (2) the variation in the product itself. This relationship can be expressed as:

$$\sigma_{\text{obs}} = \sqrt{\sigma_{\text{prod}}^2 + \sigma_{\text{meas}}^2}$$

where $\sigma_{\text{obs}} = \sigma$ of the observed data
$\sigma_{\text{prod}} = \sigma$ of the product
$\sigma_{\text{meas}} = \sigma$ of the measuring method

Now solving for σ_{prod},

$$\sigma_{\text{prod}} = \sqrt{\sigma_{\text{obs}}^2 - \sigma_{\text{meas}}^2}$$

It is readily seen that if σ_{meas} is less than one-tenth σ_{obs}, then the effect upon σ_{prod} will be less than 1%. This is the basis of the rule of thumb that the instrument should be able to divide the tolerance into about 10 parts.

To illustrate, in one shop the validity of a new type of instrument was questioned on the ground that it lacked adequate precision. The observed variation σ_{obs} was 11 (coded). An experiment was conducted by having the instrument make replicate checks on the same units of product. The σ_{meas} figured out to be 2. Then, since

$$\sigma_{\text{prod}}^2 = \sigma_{\text{obs}}^2 - \sigma_{\text{meas}}^2$$
$$\sigma_{\text{prod}} = \sqrt{121 - 4} = \sqrt{117} = 10.8$$

This was convincing proof that the instrument variation did not significantly inflate the product variation.

In another instance, involving the efficiency of an air-cooling mechanism, the observed variation σ_{obs} was 23, and the variation on retests, σ_{meas}, was 16. Thereupon

$$\sigma_{\text{prod}} = \sqrt{23^2 - 16^2} = \sqrt{529 - 256} = \sqrt{273} = 16+$$

This showed that the measurement variation was as great as the product variation. Further study disclosed that the measurement variation could be resolved into

Variable	σ of that variable	σ^2
A	14	196
B	5	25
All other	7+	52
		273

It became clear that real progress could be made only by improving variable A, and the engineers took steps accordingly.

To quantify the individual components of variation requires still more elaborate analysis, usually through a special design of experiment, as discussed below under the heading Design of Experiments.

Statement of Error   In publishing results it is necessary to make clear the extent of error in those results. Lacking clear conventions or statements, those who review

---

where $\sigma_T{}^2$ = total variance
$\sigma_A{}^2$ = variance of A
$\sigma_B{}^2$ = variance of B
ρ_{AB} = the correlation coefficient (ρ) of A and B

the results simply do not know how to evaluate the validity of the data presented. To make clear the extent of error present in the data, metrologists have adopted some guidelines which are ever more widely used.

Effect of Reference Standards. Accuracy of an instrument is expressed as the difference between T, the "true" value and $\overline{X}_m$, the average of the replicated measurements. The reference standard used is assumed to be the "true" value, but of course this is not fully valid; i.e., the standards laboratory is able to make only a close approximation.[20] If there is some need to refer to the error of the standard, the published measurements may include a reference to the standard in a form similar to "as maintained at the National Bureau of Standards."

Effect of Significant Systematic Error. When the systematic error is large enough to require explanation, the approved forms of explanation[21] consist of sentences appended to the data, stating (for example) "This value is accurate within $\pm x$ units," or "This value is accurate within $\pm y\%$."

If necessary, these statements may be further qualified by stating the conditions under which they are valid, e.g., temperature range.

It is a mistake to show a result in the form "$a \pm b$" with no further explanation. Such a form fails to make clear whether "b" is a measure of systematic error or is an expression of standard deviation of replicate measurements or an expression of probable error, etc.

Effect of Imprecision. The quantification of precision is through the standard error (standard deviation), which is the major method in use for measuring dispersion. In publishing the standard error of a set of data, care must be taken to clear up what are otherwise confusions in interpretation:

1. Does the standard error apply to individual observations or to the average of the observations? Unless otherwise stated, it should be the practice to relate the published standard error to the published average, citing the number of observations in the average.

2. If uncertainty is expressed as a multiple of the standard error, how many multiples are used?

An approved form[22] of expression is: ". . . with an overall uncertainty of ± 4.5 km/sec derived from a standard error of 1.5 km/sec."

3. Is the standard error based solely on the data presented or on a broader history of data? To clarify this requires still more intricate wording,[23] since a dispersion based solely on the current data is itself uncertain.

Effect of Combined Systematic Error and Imprecision. In these cases the expression of the published result must make clear that both types of error are present and significant. Eisenhart[24] recommends a phraseology such as ". . . with an overall uncertainty of $\pm 3\%$ based on a standard error of 0.5% and an allowance of $\pm 1.5\%$ for systematic error."

Errors Negligible. Results may also be published in such a way that the significant figures themselves reflect the extent of the uncertainty. For example in the

---

[20] In theory, the true value cannot be attained. However, the extent of error can be ascertained through the use of replication and other statistical devices. As long as the systematic error of the standard is small in relation to the error of the instrument under calibration (the usual situation), the error of the standard is ignored.

[21] Generally the "approved forms" given here are derived from "Expression of the Uncertainties of Final Results," Chapter 23 of the National Bureau of Standards Handbook 91, "Experimental Statistics" (U.S. Government Printing Office, 1963). For a brief but incisive discussion, see Eisenhart, Churchill, Expression of the Uncertainties of Final Results, *Science*, June 14, 1968, pp. 1201–1204.

[22,23] Eisenhart, Churchill, *op. cit.*

[24] Eisenhart, Churchill, *op. cit.*

statement, "The resistance is 3942.1 ohms, correct to five significant figures," the conventional meaning is that the "true" value lies between the stated value ± 0.05 ohms.

Programs to Reduce Error   As noted above in Sources of Error, there are a number of sources of variation which combine to produce the composite error.   Each major variation is in turn a composite of multiple subvariations.   Reducing the overall error usually involves two related programs:

1. Quantifying the components of error.   These components are not equally important; they follow the Pareto principle,[25] so that one or a very few are of greater influence than all the rest put together.   Through statistical design of experiment, it is feasible to quantify the main components contributing to error.   This statistical design follows the basic approach set out in Section 27, and the reader is referred to that Section for a full discussion.[26]

2. Finding ways to reduce the major variations through improved technique or new technology.   While the major variable is usually "operator technique," this finding usually concludes also that the test has not been sufficiently engineered and that new technology is needed to minimize the variations due to operator technique.

The overall approach has much in common with that discussed in detail in Section 16 for improving quality generally.

Interlaboratory Test Programs   The most complex problem of reducing error is that involving multiple laboratories.   In such cases, the approach used may be an interlaboratory test program, which is also used for some other important purposes such as:

Development of a new test method
Comparison of results of alternative test methods
Standardization of samples
Resolution of conflicts

For these and other purposes the program centers on "round robin" tests, i.e., each of the participating laboratories is to test each of an array of materials.   A good deal of exacting detail is involved in planning and executing such a program.[27] Successful programs are generally characterized by:

Appointment of a competent technical committee to plan and guide the program.
Participation, in the planning, by the laboratories who will be involved in executing the program.   (Identification of the variables to be studied must come from the technologists, not from the statisticians.)
Use of modern statistical designs of experiment.   To this end the planning team should have access to an expert statistician.   This design of experiment is not merely to reduce the cost of the test program; often enough the design is decisive as to whether the final results will meet the original objectives of the program.
An exploratory program (a "dry run") to test out the plan on a small scale before undertaking the full scale program.
A clear, detailed description of the final program agreed on, particularly a precise description of the tests to be conducted.
Multiple replications, usually about five.   (Replications are a must if principal error sources are to be quantified.)

[25] See Section 2, under The Pareto Principle.
[26] See also Section 29 under The Analytical or Control Laboratory.
[27] For a good discussion, plus numerous references, see Nelson, Benjamin A., Survey and Application of Interlaboratory Testing Techniques, *Industrial Quality Control*, May 1967, pp. 554–559.

Coded specimens and replicates, with the codes known only to the statistical planners. Preparation of these materials is "The most difficult, time-consuming and expensive task. . . ."[28]

Random assignment of specimens and replicates.

Clear instructions on how to conduct the tests with minimal bias.

Prefabricated data forms, designed to demand completeness and to foolproof the recording.

Use of analysis of variance and other advanced techniques to secure full meaning from the data.[29]

So extensive is the need for interlaboratory test programs that the approach has been subjected to some standardization. A general use standard is ASTM Special Technical Publication no. 335, "Manual for Conducting an Interlaboratory Study of a Test Method." (American Society for Testing and Materials, Philadelphia, 1963.) More specialized standards are available from the same source for specific materials, e.g., paper products, textile materials, rubber, etc. Still other standards or procedures are available.[30, 31, 32]

CALIBRATION CONTROL

Measurement standards deteriorate in accuracy (and in precision) during use, and, to a lesser degree, during storage. To maintain accuracy requires a continuing system of calibration control. The elements of this system are well known and are set out below.

(The terminology associated with "calibration control" is not yet standardized. To put an instrument into a state of accuracy requires first that it be tested to see if it is within its calibration limits. This test is often referred to as "checking" the instrument. If, upon check, the instrument is found to be out of calibration, then a rectification or adjustment must be made. This adjustment is called variously "calibration," "recalibration," or "reconditioning." In some dialects, the word "calibration" is used to designate the combination of checking the instrument and adjusting it to bring it within its tolerances for accuracy.)

While the same system can be applied to all levels of standards as well as to test equipment, there are some significant differences in detail of application. Transfer standards are exclusively under the control of standards laboratories manned by technicians whose major interest is maintaining the accuracy of calibration. In contrast, test equipment and, to some extent, working standards are in the hands of those production, inspection, and test personnel whose major interest is product and process control. This difference in outlook affects the response of these people to the demands of the control system and requires appropriate safeguards in the design and administration of the system.

New-Equipment Control The control system regularly receives new elements in the form of additional standards, new units of test equipment, and expendable materials. These elements should be of proved accuracy before they are allowed to enter the system. The approach varies depending on the nature of the new item:

---

[28] Nelson, Benjamin N., op. cit.

[29] There are also some simple yet effective techniques. See, for example, Section 27, under Planning Interlaboratory Tests: Youden Two-Sample Plots.

[30] See, for example, ASTM D990-58 (reapproved 1970), "Interlaboratory Testing of Textile Materials"; also, ASTM D2188-69, "Statistical Design in Interlaboratory Testing of Plastics."

[31] See additional references in Nelson, Benjamin N., op.cit.

[32] See also, Section 29, under Planning for Future Needs: Analytical Laboratory.

1. Purchased Precision Standards, e.g., high-accuracy gage blocks, standard cells, etc. Control is based on the vendor's calibration data and on his certifying that the calibration is traceable to the National Bureau of Standards. Where such purchased standards represent the highest level of accuracy in the buyer's company, any subsequent recalibration must be through sending the standard to an outside laboratory, i.e., the vendor himself, an independent laboratory, or the National Bureau of Standards.

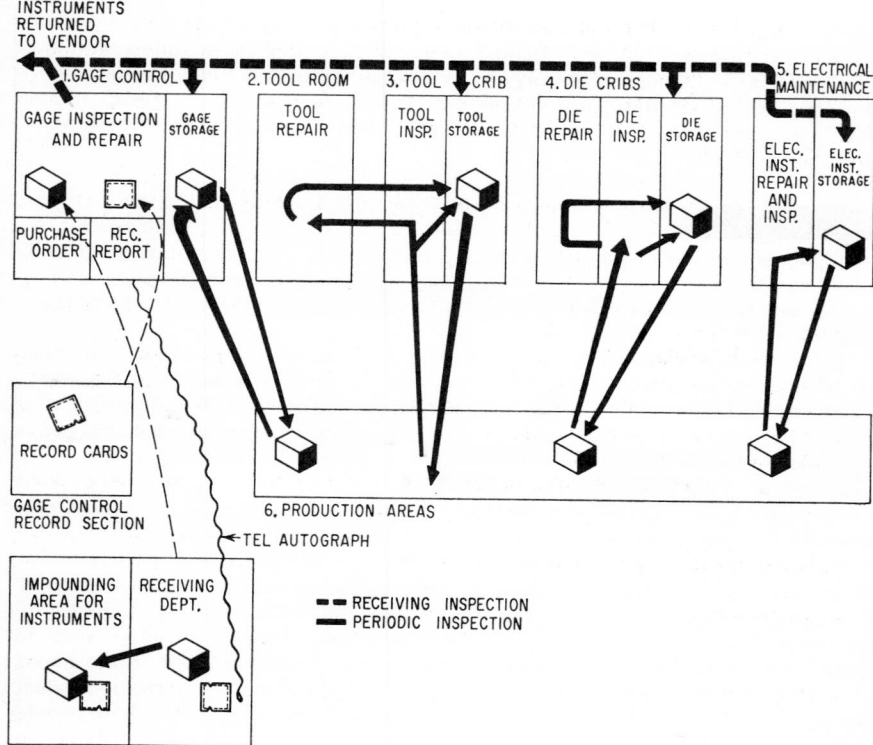

Fig. 13-4 Flow diagram for gage control. Daily—Repair orders and inspection reports sent to Gage Record Section by areas 1, 2, 3, 4, and 5. Weekly—Lists sent to gage control for periodic inspection of instruments in areas 1, 2, 3, 4, and 6. Area 5 is handled by electrical maintenance. From Meckley, D. G., III, How to Set Up a Gaging Policy and Procedure, *Am. Machinist*, vol. 99, No. 6, pp. 133–144, March 14, 1955.

2. Purchased Working Standards. These are subjected to "incoming inspection" by the buying company unless the demonstrated performance of the vendor merits use of "audit of decisions" (see Section 10).

3. New Test Equipment. This equipment is intended for use in checking products and processes. However, it usually embodies measuring instruments of various

sorts and may well include working standards as well, i.e., test pieces ("masters" for in-place check of calibration). Such new test equipment should be checked out for calibration before being put into use (Figure 13-4).[33]

4. Test Materials. These include consumable standards as well as expendable supplies such as reagents or photographic film. Variability in such materials can directly affect the associated measurements and calibrations.

For example, a manufacturer of sandpaper needed a uniform material on which to test the abrasive qualities of the sandpaper. He investigated the possibility of using plastic blocks and found that the plastics manufacturer was using this same sandpaper as a means of testing the toughness of the plastic.

For some of these materials, the vendors can provide data on variability. For the rest, it is necessary to discover the variability through analysis as discussed above, under Error of Measurement.

Inventory and Classification A systematic approach to calibration control starts with a physical inventory of all standards, instruments, and test equipment. (Where tooling is used as one of the means of product inspection, such tooling is commonly included within the list of items to be systematically controlled for accuracy.)

For each item which is to enter the system, a record card is made out. This card shows the historical origin of the item, its assigned serial number, the checking schedule, and related information. The card also provides space to record the results of check and the repairs needed.[34]

The physical test equipment is also marked with the assigned serial number for identification and traceability in the system.

Calibration Schedules These are established *by class* of equipment and are varied to reflect precision, nature, and extent of use and still other factors. At the outset, these schedules are established by judgment and bargaining. Later, as data become available on the results of checking, it becomes feasible to change the schedules in the interest of greater effectiveness and economy.

The broad intent of calibration schedules is to detect deterioration beyond tolerable levels of accuracy. This deterioration takes place mainly through usage and secondarily through the passing of time. As a result, the calibration schedules contemplate that extent of usage or of elapsed time will be evaluated in one of several ways:

1. Elapsed calendar time. This method is in widest use. It establishes a fixed calendar time, e.g., three months, as a checking interval. At the end of the three months, steps are taken to check the equipment in accordance with schedule.

2. Actual amount of usage. This is based on counting the actual usage, e.g., number of units of product checked by the equipment. The count may be made (a) manually, by the inspectors, (b) through automatic counters installed in the equipment, or (c) by programming the computers to show the amount of testing performed based on production schedules.

3. Metering of actual operating hours. For electrical equipments it is feasible to meter the actual time the equipment is drawing power. A simple device for this purpose is a direct reading coulometer (Figure 13-5). The heart of this device is a capillary tube filled with two columns of mercury separated by an electrolyte. Passage of direct current results in transfer of mercury from one column to the other.

---

[33] In addition, there are various usage criteria, as discussed in Section 9, under Quality Information Equipment. See also Section 12, under Automated Inspection.

[34] Such record cards are commercially available in various forms, including the edge-punched variety. For an example of the latter, see Schilling, Edward G., and John R. Lampus, Elements of Gage Control, *Industrial Quality Control*, September 1964, pp. 131–136.

The electrolytic gap moves as a result and serves as an indicator to measure cumulative current (and hence cumulative hours of use) on a calibrated scale.[35]

Adherence to Schedule   This vital detail makes or breaks the entire system of calibration control.

Generally, the transfer standards and most working standards pose no problem of adherence to schedule, since they are in the custody of a few standards laboratories and a relatively few associated technicians.   In contrast, the test equipment (and some working standards) are widely scattered over numerous locations and are in

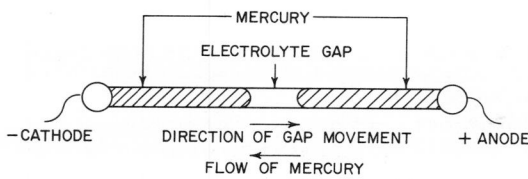

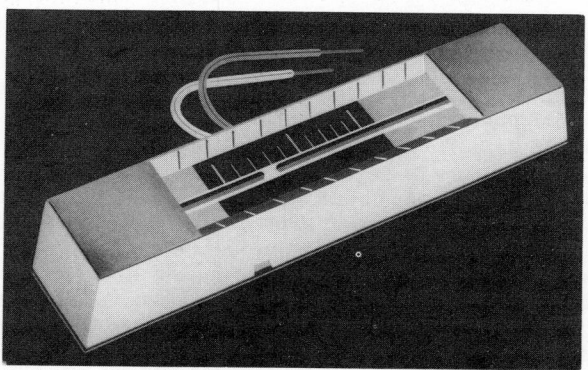

Fig. 13-5   Coulometer for recording instrument usage.

the custody of thousands of workmen, inspectors, and testers.   Some of these men can be relied on to see that the checking schedule is followed, but many cannot.

In part, the problem is one of lack of knowledge of when the recalibration is due. The shop personnel require the aid of a memory system if they are to know which piece of equipment is due to be checked that day.   They may recall what the checking intervals for each class of equipment are, but they cannot recall what the date of the last calibration was.

Some systems for adherence to schedule make use of ingenious color codes or labels which mark on each unit of equipment the date it was put back into service.[36] For large units, the expiration date is entered on a maintenance card which is attached to the unit.   Such dates are an aid to the personnel for adhering to the checking schedule.

However, an added problem is that of motivation.   The numerous users of test

[35] Available from Curtis Instruments, Inc., Mt. Kisco, N.Y.   For elaboration, see Electricalibration Intervals Set by Hours of Use, *Quality Assurance,* May, 1964, pp. 37, 38.   See also Marwell, E. M., Calibration by Use, *Instruments and Control Systems,* January 1966.

[36] These codes are often extended to identify the grades of the standards themselves, whether primary, secondary, etc.

equipment are quite concerned with recalibration when trouble is encountered but less concerned when things seem to be going smoothly. In these latter cases, interruptions for calibration can even be a nuisance.

The solution is to give responsibility (for adherence to schedule) to the standards laboratory rather than to the production, inspection, and test personnel.[37] Under this assignment, the laboratory organizes a plan of checking which will keep up with the scheduled load.[38]

In administering the checking plan, manual record cards may be used to identify the calibration dates. For example, in the time-interval system, the record card carries a calendar printed at the top. A "flag" is clipped to the card at the place representing the recalibration date. On that date, all cards so marked will have moved to the front of the pack. Alternatively, the system may be operated using the computer to provide a runoff showing which standards and equipments are due to be checked in the forthcoming week.

Calibration Practice To assure accuracy and to establish traceability, control laboratories have evolved some widely used procedures.

Individual responsibility is established by requiring that all concerned sign for their actions. The equipment record cards carry these signatures, as do the labels on the equipment.

Dates are recorded for all actions in view of the role of elapsed time in the calibration procedures.

Manuals of practice are established, including tolerances for accuracy, and methods to be used in calibration. In some types of test, these methods must be spelled out in detail, e.g., temperature or humidity controls, time cycle, human technique, etc. (Witness the detail of some of the ASTM standards on test method.)

Training programs are established for personnel, including (in some cases) formal qualification certificates to attest to proficiency.

Equipment is tamperproofed through sealing the adjusting screws. (The seals are then imprinted with the stamp of the laboratory.) In like manner, panels and drawers of test equipments are lock-wired, and the wires are lead-sealed together. (The laboratory takes no responsibility when seals are broken, and the company takes stern measures against tampering with the seals.)

As a means of assisting enforcement, quality assurance audits are conducted to review the calibration control procedures.

Record and Analysis of Results It is most useful to keep a record of the results of checking calibration and of the extent of work done to restore accuracy. Typically such a record lists:

Observed deficiencies in the equipment
Causes of out-of-calibration conditions
Repair time and recalibration time

Periodic analysis of these data then becomes the basis of:
1. Reducing the amount of checking done for equipments shown to be stable
2. Redesign of equipments to eliminate causes of repetitive failure

---

[37] When this proposal is made to practicing managers, they seldom accept it purely on grounds of theory of organization. However, when it is proposed that a sample of instruments be taken at random and checked for calibration (as a test of the existing "system" of calibration control) these same managers are quite willing to conduct such a test. The resulting disclosure of the actual state of calibration of the sample (of 25 to 100 instruments) is then decisive in convincing the managers of the need for a revision in the system of adherence to schedule.

[38] See, for example, Campbell, John P., Calibration, Heartbeat of Accuracy, *Quality Assurance,* October 1968, pp. 34–37.

Organization for Calibration Control In small companies, the control laboratory carries out the multiple functions of:

1. Establishment of a system for maintaining calibration of standards and test equipment

2. Issuance, calibration, and custody in accordance with the established system

As the company grows, the standards laboratory decentralizes, partly for reasons of geography and partly for specialization in technology.[39]

When multiple plants are located in different cities, the need for some geographical decentralization is obvious. Even in single large plants, the problems of checking test equipment may be simplified through decentralization, including the concept of mobile laboratories. For mechanical work, these take the form of the traveling gage cart equipped with surface plates, master gages, and accessories as well as an inventory of working gages.[40] In addition, the cart carries a file drawer of gage records to aid in adhering to checking schedules. An extension of the mobile gage cart is the truck or van which is equipped as a mechanical or electrical laboratory and travels from factory to factory within the same metropolitan area.

Still another form of decentralization is the "in-place" calibration. Under this concept, a working "master" is provided to simulate product or process conditions of various kinds. The test equipment must "pass an examination" by properly classifying the masters. These masters are kept physically at the test station until they are recalled for recalibration of their own accuracy.

Physical design of the laboratory workplace has been greatly complicated by the proliferation of many varieties of specialized testing: ultrasonic, x-ray, vibration, shock, acceleration, heat, humidity, etc. The details of these designs are beyond the scope of this Handbook. The practitioner must consult with the available experts: equipment manufacturers, researchers, metrologists, and still others. This must be a continuing process, since there is continuing progress in development of new tests and standards.

MEASUREMENT TECHNOLOGY

While measurement technology is beyond the scope of this Handbook, it is useful to note some of the aspects of this technology as they affect measurement generally. To this end, a brief look will be taken at trends in technology with respect to (1) measurement of length and (2) nondestructive testing. This is a small sample indeed.

Measurement of Length Except for visual inspection, measurement of length is the oldest form of measurement and occupies more laboratory and inspection time than measurement for any other quality.[41, 42] Yet this old form of measurement has undergone several revolutions during the twentieth century alone. These revolutions include:

Obsolescence of Fixed-limit Gages. Early in the century, product tolerances for metal cutting were generally of the order of 0.005 to 0.010 inches, or about 0.10 to 0.25 millimeters. With such tolerances, the fixed-limit gages, despite their error of "feel" and despite the purely "good or bad" information they provided, were an

---

[39] See generally, Section 12, under Physical Facilities for Inspection; see also Section 12, under Inspection Department Management: Laboratory Management.

[40] See, for example, Portable Gage Lab Provides Flexibility and Minimizes Downtime, *Quality Management and Engineering,* November 1971, p. 23.

[41] For a well-written basic textbook, see Busch, Ted, "Fundamentals of Dimensional Metrology," Delmar Publishers, Inc., Albany, New York, 1964.

[42] For a discussion of the "measurement" problems associated with inspection for visual and other sensory qualities, see Section 12, under Sensory Qualities.

adequate, inexpensive, and swift means for product inspection. In consequence, the preponderance of gages were of the fixed-limit type. While "variables" gages were available (i.e., dial gages, verniers, etc.), the fixed-limit gages dominated gage usage and the gage budgets. Still more precise measurement forms were also available, but these were usually carried out in the precision laboratories rather than on the shop floor.

Within several decades, the usual tolerances for metal cutting had been reduced by an order of magnitude or more, making the fixed-limit gage largely obsolete due to (1) the high error of "feel" in relation to the new level of tolerances and (2) the inadequacy of "good or bad" information for purposes of process control.

New Technological Principles. The early methods for measuring length all employed mechanical principles. To measure the numerous special configurations, e.g., inside diameters, depths, tapers, etc., many special tools were evolved: surface plates, scales, verniers, micrometers, dial mechanisms, amplification linkages, gage blocks. These were brought to higher and higher levels of mechanical precision. Finally, the economics of continuing to improve precision through extension of mechanical principles reached its limit, and it became necessary to use other principles, mainly electronic, pneumatic, and optical.

Electronic Measurement. A usual form is built around a balanced Wheatstone Bridge circuit. The gaging head or probe is used as a comparator, first resting on a known buildup of gage blocks and then on the specimen. The difference in vertical positions of this gaging head actuates a linear-variable-differential transformer which in turn unbalances the Wheatstone Bridge. The amount of unbalance can be amplified by various orders of magnitude and then read on the scale, which is calibrated in units of length. Amplifications can exceed 5,000X.

Pneumatic Measurement. The pneumatic family of instruments operates on the principle that the volume of air flowing through a gap varies with the size of the gap. In some configurations this variation is virtually linear and hence permits ready calibration. The amplification factor of these systems is surprisingly high, extending comfortably to over 10,000X; i.e., a product variation of 0.001 inches (0.0254 millimeters) would show up on the scale as 10 inches (or 254 millimeters).

Optical Measurement. There are various ways of using optical magnification for measuring length. The most precise makes use of the well-known phenomenon of "interference fringes," resulting when waves of light in the visible spectrum are alternately in phase and out of phase. A count of these fringes becomes a count of wavelengths of light. These distances are tiny—there are over a million wavelengths of visible light in each meter. The resulting precision permits magnifications of over a million in measuring with interference fringes. So precise is the method of using optical interference that the length of the meter, once defined as the length of a certain metal bar housed in the International Bureau of Weights and Measures (Paris), is now defined as 1,650,763.73 wavelengths of the orange-red line in the spectrum of krypton-86.

Still other means are available for measuring length: laser beams, holography, radiation, ultrasonics, eddy current, etc.[43] In addition, research laboratories may be in the process of working out new principles or new applications of old principles.

Nondestructive Testing (NDT) This broad term describes testing done to (1) detect flaws in materials and components and (2) measure physical properties such as dimensions, hardness, conductivity, composition, magnetic and elastic constants, etc.

This testing is done without impairing the subsequent usefulness of the product,

---

[43] For some discussion, see Abbe, Robert C., and Mike O'Brian, A Brief Report on Non-Contact Gaging, *Quality Management and Engineering*, May 1972, pp. 16–19.

hence the name "nondestructive testing." (Visual inspection is the oldest form of NDT.)

For large, critical units of product, e.g., pressure vessels, NDT is used mainly to discover flaws. Similarly, for mass produced products which are critical to safety, automated forms of NDT are used to discover defects. For example, high-pressure tubing may contain weaknesses traceable to flaws which were difficult to eliminate in the ingot and rolling stages. The resulting extent of defective tubing may be so low that nothing short of 100% testing can find the defects. Automated NDT is a practical way of conducting such 100% testing.[44] Another example is use of 100% testing to find flaws in castings and forgings.[45]

Additional uses of NDT are to check product properties. For example, thickness of coatings or dimensional variations in moving sheets may be easier to check by NDT than in any other way.[46] An increasing application is 100% automated testing of critical fasteners, e.g., bolts, nuts, to see if they have been hardened.[47]

NDT applications are not limited to metallic products (though some NDT techniques are). Some techniques are applicable and used for nonmetallic products, both for detecting flaws and for measuring properties.[48]

There are about a dozen basic technological principles which underlie the principal NDT methods. These basic methods—along with their applications, advantages, and limitations—are set out in Table 13-4. Variations in technique have multiplied the dozen basic methods several times over, and this proliferation continues. An estimate as of 1969 showed that annual sales of equipment and materials were divided about as follows[49] among the various techniques:

Equipment and materials sold	Percent of total
Radiographic equipment and film	50
Ultrasonics	18
Electromagnetic and dye penetrant	16
Eddy current	12
All other	4
	100

A 1971 survey[50] of proportion of plants (in selected industries) using NDT techniques disclosed the following:

	Percent of plants using
Penetrant dye	68
Magnetic particle	52
X-ray	45
Ultrasonic flaw detection	33
Eddy current	23
Ultrasonic thickness	22
Gamma ray	10
Infrared	7

[44] For an extensive discussion, see Debb, Arthur D., NDT Nondestructive Testing of Tubes, *Mechanical Engineering*, May 1968, pp. 32–39.

[45] See, in this connection, Section 34, under Nondestructive Testing.

[46] See, for example, Section 9, Figs. 9–29 and 9–30

[47] See Hughes, Gary M., Olds Automates Fastener Nondestructive Testing, *Quality Assurance*, July 1970, p. 48.

[48] See, for example, NDT, QA's Newest Sophisticate, *Quality Assurance*, May 1970, pp. 49–52.

[49] Turner, Ralph E., The Greening of Nondestructive Testing, *Quality Management and Engineering*, May 1972, pp. 10 and 11.

[50] Turner, Ralph E., *op. cit.*

A further survey[51] estimated an annual 11% increase in outlay for equipment and materials during the 1970s.

The versatility of NDT systems may be seen from Table 13-5, which shows the kinds of purposes or functions served by NDT systems in a great variety of test situations.

A likely moving force in the growing use of NDT is the need for greater assurance on matters of product safety, product liability, and government regulation. These forces stimulate not only testing but also formality of test programs.[52] Increasingly there are demands for certification of test equipment and of the technicians who conduct the tests, i.e., the tests are not accepted as valid unless the technicians are formally qualified to conduct the tests and interpret the results.

In addition, the technology is itself tending to become "professionalized." Here and there an engineer specialist is designated as Nondestructive Test Engineer. An American Society for Nondestructive Testing has been in existence since 1941. Under the auspices of the Society there was prepared the Nondestructive Testing Handbook.[53]

Emergence of New Functions Associated with Measurement   The early gages were designed to classify product into good or bad. The hierarchy of standards and of laboratories served to assure that these classifying gages did an accurate job of classifying. Since then, the emphasis on defect prevention and on quality planning has demanded that the shop test equipment be able to perform additional functions, mainly:

1. Indicating; i.e., the gages must show the "reading" along a scale of measurement. (The dial gage was the symbol of the indicating instrument until the advent of electronic readouts.) These readings become the feedback to operators for process control and to inspectors for product conformance decisions.

2. Regulating. In some applications it is economic to feed the measurements directly into the process so that the gage closes the loop to make the process self-regulating. See Section 9, under Automatic Process Regulation.

3. Recording. Increasingly, the burden of recording measurement data is being shifted from operators and inspectors to instruments specially designed to record data. These records are not merely a series of readings expressed in numbers. They include charts showing the data in time progression and related to tolerances or to control limits.

4. Computing, summarizing, and reporting. A further step is to feed the data into computers. Some of these computers are used to figure averages and standard deviations. Others summarize data and prepare reports for supervisory and managerial review.[54]

Collectively, these and related new functions associated with measurement have revolutionized the nature of the equipment and thereby the problems of keeping everything in calibration. It is no longer enough to assure that the mechanism which senses length remains in calibration. In addition, the entire train of attachments which indicate, control, record, compute, etc., must likewise remain in calibration. All this has greatly expanded the role of the metrologists and their supporting technicians.

---

[51] Turner, Ralph E., *op.cit.*

[52] ASTM has numerous standards on nondestructive testing, and the field is very active.

[53] Edited by Robert C. McMaster, Ronald Press Co., New York, 1959.

[54] These new and multiple functions have given rise to the name "Quality Information Equipment" to emphasize that the dominant role is to provide information. For further discussion, especially as to the planning aspects, see Section 9, under Quality Information Equipment. See generally Section 20.

TABLE 13-4 Nondestructive Testing Comparison Table (Quality Management and Engineering, May 1972, p. 20)

Type	Applications	Advantages	Limitations
Eddy current	Checks for variation in wall thickness, conductivity, metallurgical properties, coating thickness, detection of incorrect material, seams, pits, porosity, surface finish, discontinuities.	Adapts to high-speed testing without probe contact. Excellent sensitivity to such defects as pinhole leakers, stitching, and hook cracks. Operates in poor optical environment and in presence of nonconductive contaminants.	Used only in conjunction with conductive materials. Alloy and hardness dependent and affected by temperature and magnetic fields. Cannot give absolute measurement, only qualitative comparison. Sensitivity of ID defects dependent on total wall thickness and depth of defect in terms of percent of wall thickness.
X-ray.	Detects internal defects in welds, slag inclusion, penetration, lack of bond, thickness variations, cavities, metal inclusions, cracks, foreign particles.	Shows size and nature of hidden flaws or discontinuities in different thicknesses of metal. Gives permanent graphic record of defects. Radiation source can be turned off when not in use. Short time exposure. Unaffected by temperature changes or contaminants.	Has higher initial cost than gamma ray, requires power source, and has radiation hazard. Results not immediately known — requires trained technicians. Not sensitive to defects less than 2% thickness of total metal. Size and weight are generally larger than gamma. Depends on alloy uniformity.
Gamma ray	Detects interior flaws, cracks, seams, porosity, holes, inclusions, weld defects. Checks for thickness variations, integrity of assemblies.	Shows size and nature of hidden flaws or discontinuities in different thicknesses of metal. Needs no electrical power source nor oil or water cooling. Provides permanent record. Lower initial cost than x-ray.	Energy cannot be adjusted. Isotope must be chosen to meet sensitivity requirements and thickness of material. Sensitivity is not as great as x-ray. Trained technicians are needed. Results not immediately known.

Method			
Magnetic particle test	Detects surface and subsurface flaws that result from fatigue, thermal stresses, gas pockets, lack of fusion, slag inclusions, corrosion and grinding in ferromagnetic material. Locates cracks, seams, porosity, holes, inclusions.	Offers positive and simple method for finding cracklike defects at or close to the surface. Method is flexible and economical. Portable equipment is available. Immediate results.	Limited to ferromagnetic material. No indications apparent for cracks parallel to the magnetic field, so magnetism in two directions is needed to find all discontinuities. Surfaces must be clean and dry.
Penetrant dye ..	Detects all defects open to the surface. (Cracks, seams, porosity, laps, cold shuts, leaks, weld defects, fatigue cracks, processing cracks.) Used in production dip tanks or with portable units.	Detects minute cracks and leaks. Dye penetrant appears as a deep red glow on white background. Fluorescent penetrant shows under ultraviolet. Simple to apply. Accurate, fast, low initial cost and per-test cost.	Limited to surface defects. Surface must be free from oil and grease. A semidarkened area is necessary for ultraviolet inspection.
Ultrasonic: Resonance	Gages thickness of materials with relatively smooth and parallel or concentric surfaces and some moderately rough corroded surfaces.	Displays instantly size, location, orientation and degree of flaw. Accuracy not affected by temperature or pressure—2% of thickness on rough surfaces, and up to 1% on smooth surfaces. Portable units enable field testing.	Must use a couplant (oil, grease, water, glycerine) or pressure to introduce the sound into the material under test. Rough surfaces and complex geometries complicate tests. Requires trained technicians.
Pulse echo	Locates cast inclusions, internal ruptures, flaws, cracks, etc. Thickness gaging.		
Capacitive	Metallic or nonmetallic thickness and displacement gages. Dynamic vibration and high-speed inspection.	Good for both metals and nonmetals and temperature stable. Calibration relatively easy and has short response time. Readily adaptable to various configurations.	Doesn't work in liquid environments and metal parts must be grounded to system.
Fiber optical ...	Displacement, flaw detection, and overall dimensions.	High speed and not affected by type of material or magnetic fields.	Dependent on surface optical properties and affected by ambient light. Subject to contamination.

TABLE 13-5 Functional and Situational Applications of Nondestructive Testing (Courtesy, Lloyd B. Wilson)

Type of situation to be tested	Function or purpose of the nondestructive testing											
	Analysis	Detection*	Examination	Evaluation	Imaging	Identification	Inspection, checking	Location*	Maintenance (preventive)	Measurement*	Searching*	Testing*
Bonded areas							X					
Brazed areas							X					
Casting defects								X				
Cracks								X				
Defects, general		X					X	X				
Equipment				X			X	X				
Fabricating discontinuities								X				
Failure	X											
Fluid flow					X							
Foreign objects		X			X			X				
General	X	X		X	X	X	X	X	X	X	X	X
Inclusions in castings								X				
Internal parts of hardware systems			X		X			X				
Internal organs, etc., of animals			X		X			X				
Laminar defects		X						X				
Material types						X		X				
Particles	X							X		X		
Ruptures, internal								X				X
Stress—internal, residual, vibration							X	X				
Surfaces—external, internal, hidden							X	X				
Thickness, general										X		
Wall thickness: corrosion wall thinning							X					
Welds		X					X					
Weld defects							X	X				

* Functions followed with an asterisk often can be performed on an automatic or semiautomatic basis instead of manually.

Summary   The foregoing brief look at measurement technology makes clear that revolutionary changes have been extensive.   In the single parameter of length, several new technological principles have emerged to take over the bulk of precision measurement.   In nondestructive testing, the growth of new technology can properly be called explosive.   The growth of added functions associated with measurements has likewise been explosive.   For some systems "the head costs more than the body."

Developments such as these make clear that much effort is needed, on a continuing basis, to keep the laboratories, their equipment, and above all, their personnel up to date with current developments and in a state of preparation for future developments.

ACKNOWLEDGMENT

The author gratefully acknowledges the assistance of Lloyd B. Wilson, then Measurement Consultant, Sperry Gyroscope Division, Sperry Rand Corporation, in preparation of this Section.

Section **14**

Marketing of Quality

J. M. JURAN

INTRODUCTION

The quality function (Figure 2-2) includes the vital activity of marketing, which consists broadly of the steps taken by the company to secure its sales income from its customers. The quality of what the company has to sell is critical to the success of the selling effort.

This Section analyzes the business steps taken by the company to help secure sales income through quality. Closely related to these steps is the discussion in two other Sections:

1. Section 4, which discusses the forces in the economy through which quality affects income, and the approaches used to quantify these effects

2. Section 15, which discusses the company's quality activities in the market-place following sale of the product

The reader is urged to refer to these Sections, whenever noted, in order to complete his examination of the subject.

NEEDS AND SOURCES OF MARKET KNOWLEDGE ON QUALITY

To market its products, the industrial company requires a good deal of information about quality in the marketplace. Some of this information is forced on the company in the form of "alarm signals." Other information is readily available but requires positive steps in analysis and processing to put it into usable form. Still other information, though needed, is not naturally available and hence can be acquired only by special effort.

Table 14-1 summarizes the principal needs for market knowledge on quality and the principal sources for obtaining this knowledge.

Alarm Signals   The industrial company receives numerous alarm signals which tell of specific product quality failures and troubles encountered by specific customers. These signals are acted on to maintain good customer relations. When the charges involved are high or there is risk of losing an important customer, the matter receives high-level attention.[1]

The main effect of the individual alarm signal is to restore the status quo for the complaining customer. Collectively, these signals supply a rough measure of customer dissatisfaction. However, they are a very poor measure of product quality since many quality failures do not result in alarm signals.[2]

Safety and liability cases are a special category of field alarm signal. They are usually summarized on special reports which are reviewed and taken seriously by upper management.

Loss of customers due to quality failures is another form of "loud and clear" alarm signal. While summarized reports of this nature are only in the early stages of development, the Marketing people convey information of this type to upper management by informal means, and the upper managers become quite as concerned as the Marketing managers.

A formal summary in wide use is the Guarantee Account, which collects the charges resulting from failures occurring during the guarantee period. Abnormal levels of charges to this account become an alarm signal when this report is published.

Limitations Inherent in Alarm Signals   A risk in relying on alarm signals is that there exist alarming quality situations for which the conventional "quality alarms" (failures, complaints, returns) are silent.

One company reports as follows: "One of our users discovers that a competitor's product is superior for his needs. Instead of complaining to us, he merely 'switches,' and there is no quality alarm signal. The effect is there but it is hidden in share of market and sales volume, which are the resultant of many variables." (The sales force may report encountering resistance due to competition in quality, but these reports may not be given complete credibility unless the resistance borders on the massive.)

Product failures beyond the guarantee period, and nonreimbursable costs during the guarantee period, e.g., customer's downtime, do not show up in the manufac-

---

[1] See, in this connection, Section 15, under Quality Complaints.
[2] See, in this connection, Section 15, under Quality Complaints.

TABLE 14-1 Needs and Sources of Market Knowledge on Quality

Needs for market quality information	Forcibly brought to company attention by "alarm signals"	Readily available but requires analysis	Not readily available. Must be created by special studies
Individual dissatisfactions of customers	Complaints, returns, failure reports Loss of customers Salesmen's reports Safety and liability cases		
Widespread customer dissatisfactions	Loss of customers Guarantee account charges	Pareto analysis of complaints, returns Pareto analysis of salesmen's reports Analysis of decline in share of market Analysis of sale of spare parts	Study of failures beyond guarantee period Study of users' quality costs Interviews with users
Competitive quality status		Ratings from customers Ratings from consumer journals Government reports Share of market reports Salesmen's reports	Laboratory test of competing products Usage test of competing products by customers and consumers
Opportunities for improving income through quality	Pareto analyses to identify major causes of dissatisfaction Projects to eliminate these causes	Summary of above analyses; projects for improvement based on these summaries	Special field studies Projects based on these studies

turer's guarantee account and hence sound no alarm signals.[3]   However, these failures and costs can be infuriating to users.   At the least, a marketing opportunity is present, and at worst it is an alarming situation for which there are no alarm signals.

ANALYSIS OF AVAILABLE MARKET QUALITY INFORMATION

Table 14-1 shows that a good deal of market quality information can be had merely by summarizing and analyzing data already in existence.

Pareto Analysis of Field Troubles   Some of this analysis is made of the alarm signals resulting from specific field failures.   A Pareto analysis of these reported failures, complaints, returns, etc., serves to identify the vital few quality problems which cause most of these alarm signals.   This type of analysis is in wide use.

Pareto Analysis of Salesmen's Reports   Salesmen are a natural though imperfect field intelligence system.   Their reports on quality usually deal with troubles which jeopardize current customer relations.   In addition, the salesmen report on competitive products which are creating difficulties for them.   Sometimes the salesmen transmit users' ideas and their own ideas for making quality improvements.

Many companies have designed their salesmen's reports to permit ready summary. However, the summaries are made by the Marketing specialists and the emphasis is understandably on those aspects which will aid in meeting the departmental goals of sales volume, sales expense, etc. As a result, the amount of "hard" information on quality matters is limited.

Decline in Sales   Virtually all companies have good data systems to compute volume and trend of sales.   (Usually the data are summarized daily, and in some industries several times a day.)   The resulting sales analysis summaries provide the marketing and top managers with good data on sales trends.   However, only seldom are these sales analyses structured to permit evaluation of the effect of quality on sales.

The concepts for arriving at such an evaluation are clear enough.   At monthly (or other) intervals, the sales summaries are published.   These summaries show which accounts have gone up in volume and which have declined.   It is then feasible to analyze individually those accounts which have undergone a significant change.   These individual analyses require going "into the dossiers" of the individual accounts to see whether the changes were due to quality reasons or other reasons.   This review of the records must be supplemented by discussion with the cognizant marketing people.   From all this analysis it is feasible to determine:

Sales lost due to quality reasons
Sales gained due to quality reasons
Effect on profit and other financial parameters

Such is the conceptual approach.   The execution requires a good deal of new development and even invention of methods of analysis since

1. The analytical methods must be worked out jointly between the Marketing and Quality Control departments.   The former has broad jurisdiction over structuring the sales analysis, and the latter has the skills needed for determining the quality implications of the data.

2. The approach by analysis of "dossiers" can have only temporary life.   The more permanent approach would be to code the original sales documents to identify

---

[3] The sale of spare parts should be an alarm signal, but this signal is usually drowned out by the music of "profitable spare parts business."

those new sales, cancellations, etc., which are the result of product quality phenomena.

Sale of Spare Parts   These sales are often regarded as a benefit to the company because of their inherent profitability.   However, the users regard the purchase of spares as part of the overall evil of the dislocations and costs arising from product failures.   Despite the fact that many users put up with failures as a necessary evil, the manufacturers should analyze the sales of spare parts to identify major field problems.

For example, one company discovered that despite the absence of complaints, it was selling abnormal numbers of resistors to a customer as spare parts.   Investigation showed that the customer's Maintenance Department, instead of complaining, had merely set up to maintain the necessary inventory of spare parts and to keep the equipment in service.   In effect, the alarm signals had been desensitized.[4]

Data from Customers   Many large purchasers prepare data on quality performance of products purchased from vendors.   These data are then used (among other purposes) to make decisions on which vendors to favor and which to deemphasize. It is most desirable for the vendor to secure such information.

In some cases the purchaser engages in "vendor rating."   He analyzes the data and presents them in the form of comparative ratings for the competing vendors involved.[5]   These ratings are often sent to the vendors to stimulate action (competitors' names are coded).   Such published ratings are properly given great weight by the vendors.

Where the purchasers do not make the data available to the vendors, the vendors should take the initiative to secure the data anyway.   Some motor vehicle companies and appliance makers have arranged with large users (e.g., vehicle fleet operators, laundromat operators) to *buy* their data on product performance.   In such cases the manufacturers participate in design of the data plan so that the joint needs for data are given consideration.

Government Reports[6]   Governments are increasingly involved in product evaluation, mainly in their capacity as regulators but also in their capacity as purchasers. Many governments will not publish data on performance of industrial companies or products except in the aggregate, i.e., the practice is to avoid making public the performance of individual companies or of specific models of product.   Despite this limitation, the data on aggregate performance have value since they are an index to "market quality."   For example, the "Final Report of the National Commission on Product Safety"[7] summarized the number of injuries associated with use of various consumer products, including types of injuries.   Such a summary is of obvious value to companies making such products.

The increasing extent of legislation on product safety virtually assures that governments will increasingly publish safety data on a basis which discloses manufacturers' names and model numbers.   Several data collection networks are already in existence, e.g., the National Electronic Injury Surveillance System of the Bureau of Public Safety.   A related trend is publication of extent of property damage.   A group of insurance companies studied the cost to repair vehicles involved in crashes. The report, issued by the Insurance Institute for Highway Safety, named 70 models of vehicles and showed the average cost of repairs for each.[8]

---

[4] Private communication to J. M. Juran.

[5] See Section 10, under Vendor Quality Rating.

[6] See also Section 4, under Government Regulation of Quality.

[7] National Commission on Product Safety, 1970.   Available from Superintendent of Documents, U.S. Government Printing Office, Washington, D.C. 20402.

[8] *The New York Times*, Nov. 2, 1972.

An example of some years' standing is that of AB Svensk Bilprovning, the Swedish Motor Vehicle Inspection Company which carries out the national program of compulsory annual vehicle inspection. The company publishes reports summarizing the faults found for various (named) models of automobile.

Independent Laboratories   These include consumer journals, standardization organizations, and still others.[9] Some of these laboratories make comparative tests for competing lines of products. They then publish the results for the benefit of their subscribers as an aid to judicious purchasing. The overall impact of such journals is not known with precision. However, there are cases in which specific products favorably rated by such journals have shown prompt and significant increases in sales.

MARKET RESEARCH IN QUALITY

The information derived from alarm signals and from analysis of available data, while a necessary part of "market knowledge on quality," is not sufficient. It fails to disclose such things as:

Alarming situations for which there are no alarm signals

Realities which deny existing axiomatic or unsupported beliefs

Many opportunities which are present in long-standing situations but have been overlooked

Such disclosures require an organized approach to:

1. Identify what missing information is needed
2. Acquire or create this missing information

The activity of identifying and securing this missing market information is known broadly as "market research."

Organization for Market Research   When the company is small, market research is informal. Reliance is placed on the field sales force in its part-time activity as a field intelligence force. From time to time, special studies are conducted by (1) marketing supervision, (2) staff specialists, (3) outside consultants engaged on a project basis, (4) trade associations whose members feel that such an approach would be more economic or more objective.

As the company grows, the needs for market research grow to an extent which warrants the creation of a full-time Market Research Department. Usually, this activity is placed under the command of the Marketing Department. Even where Market Research is "independent," i.e., reports to top management, its main client is the Marketing Department. In consequence, most market research studies have been oriented to the selling function—sales potentials, share of market, income statistics, population growth, etc. However, the principle of studying realities and opportunities in the marketplace applies to quality as well as to sales. In some companies excellent use is made of market research *teams* to study opportunities for improving income through quality. These teams deal with individual projects. (In addition, there may be a Market Research Committee to coordinate the broader aspects of market research.)

The team concept takes on special significance when the market research study involves broad problems such as "Why is our share of market so low?" A quality specialist may look for product failures or for nonconformance to specification. However, the product may be quite in conformance with specification and not failing; the problem may rather be that the competitor's design is superior. For example, a French automobile manufacturer took advertising space to report that

[9] See Section 4, under Consumer Test Services.

he had corrected some problems which he had previously encountered in selling his product in the United States, saying:

> Our cars were not fully prepared to meet the demands of America, where sustained high speeds are normal, where a heavy foot with the clutch is normal, and where people are not used to fixing their own cars.
> More than a fair share of things went wrong with our cars. Less than a fair share of our dealers were equipped to deal with what went wrong."[10]

Market Research Objectives   As noted in Table 14-1, the main objectives are to supply the missing information needed to:

1. Discover customer dissatisfactions not evident from the alarm signals
2. Discover status of quality in relation to competitors
3. Identify opportunities for improving income through action on product quality

The details of the approaches to these objectives are discussed below, under the respective headings.

Marketing Research Planning   The most critical problem in the planning is precise definition of the objectives. Beyond this, it is necessary to distinguish clearly between two very different activities in market research.

1. Identifying the information needed to carry out the objectives. This should *always* be a team undertaking so that company needs, not departmental needs, are emphasized. It is a serious mistake to let any one department monopolize this activity.

2. Carrying out the "leg work" of acquiring or creating the needed information. This assignment cannot be made intelligently until the needed information has first been identified. Usually it will be found that the assignment must be multiple, e.g., information may be needed from laboratory tests, from dealers, from vendors, and from the complaint reports. Several specialists are then involved in collecting these different forms of information.

In some companies the annual product planning provides for market research on quality. (See the example of the "Home Company," under Competitive Evaluations, below.)

COMPETITIVE EVALUATIONS

Because users have access to competing products, it is most helpful for industrial companies to understand the state of this competition. In some cases the necessary knowledge can be estimated from laboratory testing. In other cases it is necessary to discover what the situation is *as seen by the users.*

Laboratory Evaluations   These provide useful technical data at modest expense. As to some qualities to which users may be insensitive, only laboratory testing can provide the comparisons with competitive products.

In a classic study, the uniformity of weight of adhesive on various competing tape bandages was measured. The results (see Section 9, under Process Capability Analysis, and especially Figure 9-22) were of aid not only in making judgments on market quality but also in choosing the best equipment.[11]

In some companies, competitive studies are part of the annual product planning program. For example, the "Home Company,"[12] a manufacturer of building materials, compares the performance of (say) floor tiles of competitors with its own

---

[10] From Renault advertisement (which included statements of remedial steps taken). *Time,* October 14, 1966, p. E9.

[11] Oladko, Anthony, Developing a Calendergraph, *Rubber Age,* September 1949.

[12] Actual case; name fictitious.

product. Table 14-2 is such a comparison. From this comparison, the planners can consider whether characteristics T and U, now below market, should be improved. In the case of characteristics R and S, where the Home Company now excels, they can consider whether this excellence can be sold or whether it should become the basis of a cost reduction.

TABLE 14-2   Comparison of Competitive Products

Characteristics of the product	Ranking of the companies				
	Home Co.	Competitors			
		A Co.	B Co.	C Co.	D Co.
P	3	2	1	4	5
Q	2	4	3	1	5
R	1	3	2	5	4
S	1	5	3	4	2
T	5	2	3	1	4
U	4	1	2	5	3

Securing competitive products for test is done in a variety of ways. Mass produced small items are bought in the open market, along with some of the company's own product (to include the effects of packing, shipping, storage, etc.).[13] For expensive products not involving destructive tests, it may be feasible to secure permission (to inspect and test) from some friendly dealers who market competing products. Carpets and watches are examples of products in which competitive evaluations have been made without purchase. (In the carpet example, a traveling laboratory was set up so that the examinations were performed in the storage warehouses.)

In most situations, laboratory evaluations cannot be equated with fitness for use. For example, a company making abrasive cloth found it was losing share of market despite the fact that laboratory tests showed the product to be competitive. Discussion with the (industrial) users disclosed that the user measured fitness for use based on "cost per 100 pieces polished" and that, on this basis, the competitors' cloth was superior.

Market research teams should always be alert to this distinction and should either qualify their laboratory test results or make the more extensive studies needed to discover fitness for use as seen by the users.

Field Studies   These aim to discover the users' viewpoint on fitness for use, product preference, etc. The distinguishing feature of such tests is that the user is the prime source of data. Consumer preference tests[14] are a common example.

Planning of such field studies is properly a team undertaking, involving members from Marketing, Technical, and Quality Control Departments plus others as needed. The planners must agree beforehand on what qualities they are studying and on what information they need from the users. While the information sought varies with each project, some elements of "essential information" are common to most projects. For example:

What is the relative importance of the various qualities?

What is the comparative performance of the competing products for these qualities?

What is the effect of the competing products on the users' costs, well-being, and other aspects of fitness for use?

[13] See Section 21, under Product Auditing.
[14] See Section 12, under Sensory Qualities.

A company making shaving systems was suddenly confronted with a new product feature (blade magazine and blade changing mechanism) which had been developed and was being skillfully promoted by a competitor. The company's marketing managers became concerned and demanded an equivalent feature to meet this competition.

A field study was organized to secure consumer data (through an intermediary). The planners identified the seven major qualities of a shaving system. Several hundred users were then provided with the three principal shaving systems on the market. They used all of these over a period of several months. The resulting data showed:

1. The ranking of the three systems for each of the seven qualities. For the quality in question, it was learned that the users had no preference for the new feature (no matter what the competitive advertising was then saying).

2. The ranking of the importance of the seven qualities. It turned out that the new feature concerned a quality which had the lowest importance on this ranking scale.

In consequence, the company lost interest in developing an equivalent to the new feature.

3. Quite unexpectedly, it was also learned that on another (but very important) quality, the company's product had the lowest ranking. This was considered to be a serious matter, and steps were taken to do something about it.[15]

Some companies (e.g., large manufacturers of food) conduct so many field studies that they maintain a standing consumer panel (through an intermediary). To this panel may be sent packages of new products, competitor products, changed products, etc., for securing responses.

In complex studies it is highly desirable to conduct a "dry run," i.e., to test the plan out on a few users. This is done not for the purpose of securing product data but to discover whether the plan of study itself is ready to be tried out on the broad panel of users who are to provide the data.

To minimize user bias, it is quite common to conceal the name of the company which is sponsoring the study. To this end, product identity is removed if possible. Where this is not possible, the field contacts are delegated to an outside team of market researchers so that company employees do not take part in such contacts.

In still other cases — e.g., textile fibers — the manufacturer may lack the full-scale machinery needed to test for fitness for use. In such cases a collaboration is worked out with some processors who are willing to be the guinea pigs and who participate in planning the study. The resulting data are helpful to the manufacturer in his marketing decisions and to the processor as well.

A further widespread problem is that of failure analysis for "normal" failed products, e.g., wearout. (Abnormal failures result in enough complaints to provide data on the abnormalities.) An ingenious solution is to arrange with the service shops to save failed products along with associated data. This practice is widely used in failure analysis of automotive tires, both one's own and those of competitors.

DISCOVERING MARKET OPPORTUNITIES

The market research team which sets out to discover these opportunities for quality must carry out certain essential activities:

1. *Visit the scene of action;* i.e., go out to where the product is used. This enables the team to secure first-hand information about:

  a. Conditions of use. In many ways conditions of use can differ from labora-

---

[15] Consulting experience of J. M. Juran.

tory conditions—environment, stresses, training, ignorance, misuse. Some of the conditions of use may be in violation of intended use or of instructions on how to use.[16] Yet these conditions are the realities. Arranging to discover these realities is itself realistic.

b. Problems of the user. These concern difficulties, irritations, or inconveniences as seen by the user, whether they extend to "our" product or not. For example, here is a British observer's comment on users' problems with the kitchen sink.

Because sink bottoms are back-breakingly low for most women, platforms are sold to raise the washing-up bowl to a more comfortable height. Because some draining boards slope so much that china slips into the sink, rubber mats are sold to arrest the landslide. Because the grids at the drain-hole let through bits which will later clog the pipes, little cages are sold to stop this happening. Because the flow from a tap often strikes the sink at an angle and speed which causes splashes, rubber antisplash devices are sold in every ironmonger's shop to correct the taps.

Because a flat-bottomed washing-up bowl will trap grit and grind it into the enamel of the sink, little rubber things are sold which fasten underneath the bowl by suction and raise it clear of the sink. Because detergent packs, when torn open, let out an excessive rush of detergent that is difficult to control, little plastic pourers have been devised to remedy this. Because the recess in the sink rims, intended for soap, does not drain but just collects a lot of horrid slime, ingenious minds have worked out innumerable gadgets —spiked, magnetic, ridged—to keep the soap out of its own puddle.[17]

The user sees quality in a light quite different from the view of the manufacturer of products. For example, the time required for usage is important. So is the downtime (sometimes this is the users' biggest single element of quality costs). The user may have a disagreeable chore to perform—disposal of a mess, or materials handling of a disagreeable sort. All these problems represent opportunities to an alert manufacturer.

c. Steps taken or contemplated by the user. The user sometimes comes up with solutions of his own which he has already put into effect or which he is in process of working out.[18] These ideas can be of value to the manufacturer, since they represent work done (and in process) not in the laboratory but under field conditions.

d. Needs for which the user sees no present solution. Such needs are in the nature of a list of needed inventions. For these there is opportunity to be the first to come up with a solution.

2. *Quantify the users' status.* Having secured the information from the scene of action, the research team needs to translate these findings into quantified terms which reflect the users' status. These include such matters as operating costs, downtime, maintenance costs, employee training time, employee turnover, needs for technical support. These quantified expressions of the users' status become the target to beat; the users' response to proposals will be based on whether their present status stands to be improved thereby.

3. *Understand the conditions prevailing elsewhere in the progression of events.* This understanding is needed in order to apply the "Systems Concept" (see below). The more the research teams understand what goes on in this entire progression, the

---

[16] For some examples, see Section 15, under Installation and Usage.

[17] Gundry, Elizabeth, The Trade in Afterthoughts, *Design*, November 1963. Quoted from *EOQC Newsletter*, March 1964. (To these may be added the long-standing users' irritation with metal cans of cleanser which left a ring of rust where they rested. The rust was harder to remove than the dirt. Finally, manufacturers went to plastic bottoms for these cans.)

[18] See Section 15, under Installation and Usage.

better are they able to find ways of harnessing all the available energies and skills to achieve better fitness for use.

For example, a small company making magnetic tape secured assistance from the chemical companies who made the basic film (and even from large competitors), enabling it to improve the reliability of the tape and thereby to increase its share of market.[19]

MARKET RESEARCH TOOLS

Companies make use of a variety of such tools for market research in quality. Some of these tools have already been exemplified in the foregoing discussions on market research in quality, e.g., consumer use panels, consumer preference panels, tests at customer facilities.

Normally, sizable projects require use of multiple tools. For example, one published study[20] includes the following tools applied to market research:

Telephone interviews of samples of users shortly after introducing a new model, following installation, following the first service call, and just during usage.

Surveys of prospective customers to discover what they think about products and why.

Employee panels to test out preproduction models of new products and to offer critiques and suggestions.[21]

Sampling analyses of service calls.

Other widely used research tools include:

In-House Use Testing Facilities.   Examples are the kitchens maintained by food manufacturers and the test tracks of the vehicle manufacturers. Some cosmetic makers maintain "clinics" which use members of the public as test panels. Facilities to permit employee panels to make use tests are also common, e.g., shaving laboratories maintained by makers of razor blades. One toy manufacturer invites teachers to bring young schoolchildren to play in a room full of toys while men behind one-way mirrors use stopwatches to measure how long the various toys are able to hold attention. (Later they analyze the toy breakage to identify weaknesses in design.)

Test Marketing.   Under this concept the product is marketed in a small area, e.g., a community of several hundred thousand population, before "going national." The test is structured to secure data on all aspects which contribute to income: appeal of the package, appeal of the advertising, quality of product, etc. These test markets are very costly and have drawbacks as well. They delay national marketing and thereby provide competitors with more time in which to work up and market the equivalent. However, they may be the means of avoiding catastrophic losses.

Dealer Advisory Panels.   Some companies create panels or committees of dealers, on a rotating basis, to serve as advisers in various marketing matters, including product fitness for use.

In designing all these studies there is full opportunity for use of the tools of experimental design and for analysis of the resulting data. The models for applica-

[19] *Business Week,* June 13, 1970, p. 124.

[20] Wood, Charles C., Whirlpool's Customer Assurance Program, *Industrial Quality Control,* June 1965, pp. 605–607.

[21] An example is a large manufacturer of photographic products whose Camera Club, made up of thousands of employees, is also a test panel. See Brooks, Thomas R., Quality at Kodak, *Dun's Review and Modern Industry,* June 1963, pp. 33–35, 64–67.

tion to market research are well represented in the books and journals devoted to market research, operations research, advertising research, statistics, etc.   For the general approaches, see the portion (Sections 22–28) of this Handbook devoted to statistical methods.

There is also opportunity for much creativity and invention in devising tools for market research on quality.

In launching its Pinto car (a new compact model), Ford Motor Company came up with an ingenious concept for securing market research data from business schools. The company (through an intermediate firm) provided, to professors of Business and their students, the following:

Free use of a Pinto for six weeks
Expense money of $250
A fact book on the car
Various other materials and statistics

The intent was to aid the professor in building a research project for his class, i.e., to develop market data, investigate sales promotion strategies, take opinion polls, and conduct test drives to secure reaction to product performance.

The cars were distributed to 160 campuses in 16 regions.   Prizes in the form of grants to the departments were offered for the best projects submitted.[22]

Flow diagrams can be used to identify the field "stations" from which it would be useful to have quality data.   These stations are coded to show whether the available data are adequate or not.   Such flow diagrams are useful inputs to planning the research programs.[23]

SYSTEMS CONCEPT

The needs of the user are met through the progressive efforts of various segments of the industrial society—materials men, intermediate processors, converters (manufacturers of final products), merchants, service shops, and the user himself.   To a degree, fitness for use can be improved by refinements in one or another of these segments.   However, the most spectacular historical benefits have come not from such refinements but rather from discarding the existing progression entirely in favor of some new concept of serving the user.   The term "systems approach" is here used to designate any approach which tries to improve fitness for use by restudying the entire progression rather than by accepting the present progression and refining the elements within it.[24]

There have been enough such systems revisions to enable us to identify some distinct species:

Transfer of decentralized processing to a central processing facility (e.g., centrally produced soluble coffee to replace myriads of household and restaurant coffee-makers, ready mixed concrete delivered from a central mixing plant to numerous sites, frozen food).

[22] Bazell, Robert J., in *Science,* November 27, 1969, p. 953.
A similar program, involving Mustangs, was conducted in engineering schools.
[23] For an example of such a flow diagram, though applied more broadly, see Chambers, John C., Satinder K. Mullick, and Donald D. Smith, How to Choose the Right Forecasting Technique, *Harvard Business Review,* July–August 1971, pp. 45–74.
[24] The term "systems approach" is used in several shades of meaning but all aiming to broaden the scope of the studies involved.   For a useful related discussion, see Adler, Lee, Systems Approach to Marketing, *Harvard Business Review,* May–June 1967.

Modular concepts (e.g., in construction materials; mechanical and electronic components; pallets and fork-lift trucks; roll-on–roll-off ships).

Elimination of user maintenance (e.g., self-lubricating bearings, stainless steel, aluminum building exteriors).

New central energy service (e.g., electrical energy for power and lighting to replace myriads of animals, prime movers, and oil lamps; centrally generated gas and steam for heating).

The systems concept can be the most beneficial for the user and it is the basis of the historically great business opportunities. In contrast, preoccupation with a rigid concept of "product" has resulted in some spectacular business failures[25] as well as some major government reform movements.

Applying the Systems Concept   Any user need is the focal point of multiple products and services. The user may buy a piece of equipment from one source, expendable supplies from a second source, maintenance services from a third. These purchases involve intermediate merchants, carriers, and still other industrial forms. The more completely the research team understands the user's actual needs and the way in which the existing aggregation of services converges to meet those needs, the more readily can a new system be envisioned. The benefits to the user may take the form of:

Eliminating some of the user's work entirely

Transferring work from the user to some other stage in the progression of events which can do it more easily

Improving the effectiveness of such work as still remains

Armed with the data from such studies, and—it is hoped—with quantitative information on the user's costs and problems, the market research team is able to convey to the functional company departments its recommendations on how to make life easier for the user and thereby to secure an income from him.

CONTRACTS BASED ON USAGE

One approach to optimizing the user's cost of usage is to structure the contracts so that the user pays based only on the amount of usage. Such contracts shift all the life cycle costs to the manufacturer, who then tends to redesign the system in a way which optimizes the cost of providing service.

The public utilities—e.g., telephone, power—are long-standing examples. These utilities do not sell a product nor do they often even lease a product; they sell only the service (e.g., watt-hours of electricity, message units of telephone service). In such cases the ownership of the equipment remains with the utility, which also has the responsibility of keeping the equipment maintained and repaired. The consequence is that the income of the utility is directly bound up with keeping the equipment in service. There are numerous other instances; e.g., the "U-drive" car is rented based on the actual mileage driven; laundromat machines are rented based on minutes of usage.

Sale of "products" can sometimes be converted into a sale of usage. It is common

---

[25] This was the theme of a widely read paper. Railroad managers lacked awareness that they were selling transportation; moving picture theater managers lacked awareness that they were selling entertainment, etc. In consequence, competing ways of supplying these services took the market away. See Levitt, Theodore, Marketing Myopia, *Harvard Business Review,* July–August 1960.

practice for vehicle fleets to "buy" tires based on mileage.[26]   Airlines buy engines based on hours of usage.   There is much opportunity for innovation in the use of this concept.[27]

The trend toward creating contracts based on usage is a continuing process.   A recent example is tires used by airlines.   For this usage, the mileage has no meaning; the real wear takes place during the landings.   To the airlines, the significant measure is *cost per landing.*   Such was the basis of a contract signed between Western Air Lines and Goodyear Tire & Rubber Co.[28]

For consumer products, the metering of actual usage adds many complications. Common practice is therefore to use elapsed time as an approximation of amount of usage.   For example, the guarantees on automobile batteries are based on elapsed time, often one year.   If the battery fails after nine months, it will be replaced at three-quarters the price of a new battery.

CONTRACT INCENTIVES FOR QUALITY[29]

Some contracts, notably in the aerospace and military defense industries, involve a mixture of contractor activity which includes product development, design, and manufacture.   The contract terms establish goals for cost, delivery date, and technological performance (e.g., payload, speed, reliability, maintainability).   The parties to such contracts are quite aware that the extent to which the goals will be met is not fully predictable, since no experience data are available on performance versus goals for the rather unique products (which have yet to be made for the first time).

Because of such unpredictabilities, the early contracts in these industries were structured on the basis of cost plus a percentage fee which later was changed to cost plus a fixed fee (CPFF) to eliminate the abuses of "cost plus" contracts.

During the 1960s there was evolved the concept of cost plus an incentive fee (CPIF) in order to optimize results for the users.   Under this concept, contractors would receive a bonus for exceeding the goals and a penalty for failing to reach the goals.   Successful administration of such incentive contracts required that performance be measured against goals.   This measurement posed no serious problems with respect to cost and delivery date.   However, measurement of quality performance turned out to be quite complex.

A number of concepts have been used as a basis for measuring performance with respect to quality:

1. Successful mission achievement.   For example, in the Titan III missile program, penalties and bonuses resulted from successes or failures to put the payload into orbit.[30]   The amounts at stake were as high as $810,000 per launch.

2. Failure rates and costs actually encountered during actual operation of the system.   For example, the DC-9 aircraft contract provided for evaluation of *(a)*

---

[26] The contracts become virtual leases of the tires.   The tire companies bid competitively for the awards.

[27] James Watt priced his steam engines in this manner.   Having determined that the engines offered a large fuel saving (one-third), he made a charge of 10 shillings per 10,000 strokes or £ 69 per million strokes.   He invented a stroke counter to meter the usage.

[28] Reported in *Business Week,* October 19, 1968.

[29] See also Section 8, under Management of New-Product Quality: Reliability Incentive Contracts.

[30] Move Up in Space—Win Points, *Business Week,* September 25, 1965, pp. 92–94, 96, 98, and 103.

first-year performance and *(b)* three years' performance for three parameters:

Mean time between failures (MTBF)
Time between overhauls, i.e., "airplane flight hours between scheduled removals for purposes of overhaul"
Overhaul costs in dollars per flight hour[31]

3. Performance, on sequential life test programs, for critical components. This was one of the measures used in the Skybolt missile program.[32]

4. Percent nonconformance, during the various manufacturing stages, of various processes and product components. This was another measure used in the Skybolt program.[33]

5. Performance on other matters related to quality, e.g., quality of documentation, completeness of data, number of design reviews, etc.

6. Combinations of the foregoing, sometimes under a point system which gives weights to the various categories of measured performance.

Generally, the quality parameters have been assigned about 40% of the total incentive fee, the rest of the incentive being tied to performance on cost and delivery. The quality portion may be allocated among its subparameters to an extent which becomes quite complex.[34]

When multiple mission tests are involved, it becomes feasible to use cumulative data to broaden the base of the measurement and to improve the confidence levels used to such an extent that mission success can dominate the incentive. From the user's view, this is most desirable. For programs which involve very few missions, the cost of such statistical confidence becomes exorbitant and the incentive plan must make use of other categories of measures of performance as well.[35]

The foregoing measures for use in incentive contracts go all the way from true fitness for use down to demonstrations and evidences which lack any strong correlation with fitness for use. In some instances the weaker forms have been adopted as a compromise to give the parties an incentive contract on which experience can be acquired. In other instances the weaker forms have been accepted as an alternative to an incentive contract based purely on cost and delivery.

Administration of these incentive contracts is complex because the systems and missions are complex. There must be precise definitions of what constitutes failures, and agreed rules on which failures to count and which not. Some users put great stress on remedial action and to this end provide an incentive for "quick reaction to failure mode elimination."[36]

ADVERTISING OF QUALITY

The process of disseminating commercial information is called *advertising*. The purpose of advertising is to enlarge the income of the advertiser, either through

---

[31, 32, 33] Frederickson, K. A., Incentives for Reliability, *Proceedings Tenth National Symposium on Reliability and Quality Control,* IEEE, 1964, pp. 274–285.

[34] See, for example, Van Dine, Howard A., Quality Performance Incentive, *Proceedings Tenth National Symposium on Reliability and Quality Control,* IEEE, 1964, pp. 591–599.

[35] For added discussion, see Moskowitz, Abraham I., NASA's Application of NPC 250-1 in Incentive Contracts, *Proceedings Eleventh National Symposium on Reliability and Quality Control,* IEEE, 1965, pp. 101–106.

[36] Torruella, A. R., and A. Steinberg, The Effect of Incentive Fee on Reliability Demonstration of Liquid Rocket Engines, *Second NASA Reliability & Quality Assurance Meeting,* November–December 1966, NASA Headquarters, Washington, D.C.

(1) *institutional* advertising, which aims to create a favorable image of the *company,* or (2) *product* advertising, which aims to induce people to buy the *product.*

The concept of product advertising is that human beings harbor powerful drives, needs, and wants and that through application of relatively small stimuli, these drives can be converted into decisions to buy. Under this concept, the advertiser is then faced with the dual problems of:

1. Discovering and presenting the stimuli which can best translate these human forces into action to buy. These stimuli are appeals to animal senses and to emotions.

2. Demonstrating that his product is superior to other products for meeting the human wants. This demonstration takes the form of communicating information on quality or fitness for use and is mainly an appeal to logic and reason.

In practice, many advertisements contain appeals to both emotion and reason. However, centuries of advertising have demonstrated that when human beings are buying for their own needs, appeals to the emotions generate more action than appeals to reason.

Emotional Stimuli These are widely used to advertise consumer products and, to a degree, industrial products as well. Being emotional in their nature, they are also subjective and are not susceptible to objective verification. To those who are not familiar with the underlying psychology, these stimuli are a form of diversionary shrubbery which are of little "real" value to users. [37] These stimuli take numerous forms:

Attention getters of all sorts—singing, dancing, humor, unorthodox behavior.

Product names, package colors, surrounding decor, etc., which are believed to be able to induce a favorable response from potential buyers. [38]

A vision of the well-being which, by implication, results from purchase of the product—health, comfort, social success.

An aura of company competence: the record of innovation "firsts" of the company; the prizes its products have won in competitions; the eminence of some of its scientists and engineers; etc.

An aura of inspection and test: laboratories are shown; "torture tests" are described; inspectors are counted; sophisticated instruments are pictured; precision of measurement is quoted; quality control systems are explained.

A display of "seals" from so-called "independent" laboratories (which are inherently biased since they derive their income from advertising paid for by the manufacturers to whom they award the seal).

Asserted secret ingredients, or ingredients bearing a fanciful name for which there is no standard definition.

Pseudoscientific explanations: cartoons depicting aches, pains, and their implied disappearance; staged laboratories and "scientists."

Stimuli such as the foregoing do not constitute objective evidence of fitness for use. [39] Some of the facts stated (e.g., a list of company innovations in products generally) may warrant broad inferences about the specific product being adver-

---

[37] In some countries the prevailing view is that advertising is needed only for inferior products.

[38] A great deal of study has been devoted to testing the effectiveness of advertising and promotion by using statistically structured designs of experiments and analysis of results. See, for example, Hoofnagle, William S., Experimental Designs in Measuring the Effectiveness of Promotions, *Journal of Marketing Research,* May 1965, pp. 154–162.

[39] But some make delightful reading. "Upholstery leather is chosen with extravagant care. Only one hide in every five hundred is selected. The rest are rejected because of tiny crinkles or scars. The man in charge has been at it for forty-five years. His rejects make expensive handbags" [Rolls-Royce].

tised. However, any idea that advertisers should replace emotional stimuli with objective evidence runs into some hard realities as applied to consumers:

1. The great majority of quality characteristics cannot be sensed by the consumer.
2. The great majority of factual explanations of the technological properties of products cannot be understood by the consumer.

The advertising managers have concluded, with much justification, that the emotional stimuli are an essential element of advertising of consumer products[40] and a useful adjunct to the advertising of commercial products. Many technologists and quality specialists do not welcome this emphasis, but they lack the experience of trying to sell the product without it.

Objective Evidence Advertising based on objective product and quality data is widely used for industrial products and, to a small degree, for consumer products as well. These objective presentations likewise take numerous forms:

Laboratory and inspection test results: tensile strength, frequency distribution, control chart data, Weibull plots

Usage data: mean time between failures of 10,000 hours; fuel consumption of 35 miles to the gallon; cost per unit of product, e.g., copies from a copier machine; lower schedules for adjustments, replacements, service

Listing of features possessed by the product (often to show that competitors lack these features)

Warranty provided (see below under Warranty of Quality).

Demonstrations of product usage by a series of still pictures or on television.

Evidence of user satisfaction: testimonials from named users; data on share of market, e.g., "more than all other makes combined"

Results of tests by independent test laboratories: marks or certifications from such independent laboratories

With the proliferation of complex consumer products, the traditional advertising emphasis on appeal to the emotions is running into a challenge from the consumerism movement. This challenge may well force some changes in the nature of advertising content, certainly as to "puffing" (see below) and possibly as to emotional appeal.[41] However, the potential effect on consumer buying habits is quite speculative, since the willingness to act on emotion rather than reason appears to be instinctive in the human animal.

Despite the excesses and misuse of advertising, the movement has brought extensive benefits to consumers. The urge to develop quality reputations has stimulated manufacturers to develop product quality and quality controls to levels which would back up the advertising.[42] Use of distinctive packaging has improved packaging generally and has greatly simplified distribution (but at the cost of disposal of

---

[40] For an elaboration relative to breakfast cereals, see Zalaznick, Sheldon, The Fight For a Place at the Breakfast Table, *Fortune,* December 1967.

[41] It is necessary to distinguish here between challenges to the advertising and challenges to the product. When, in the early 1970s, a consumer advocate challenged the nutritional content in breakfast cereals, some of the companies soon changed the formulation noticeably. However, there was no noticeable change in advertising, which continued to be based on subjective stimuli.

[42] An important marketing concept is "customer satisfaction," which is defined as the ratio of (1) the actual consumer experience with the product to (2) the prior consumer expectation. Since consumer expectation is in part built up by the advertising, the use of colorful advertising, while aiding short-term sales, will establish too high a level of consumer expectation and hence will reduce consumer satisfaction. (This is analogous to showing the consumer a perfect floor sample and them shipping him a shabby product from the warehouse.) A related problem exists in multiple grades of product, where the need is to match the advertising claims to the realities of the respective product grades.

the packages). Even the propaganda, being competitive, has contributed materially to the education of consumers.

Puffing   The practice of exaggerating the properties of the advertised product is known as "puffing," i.e., a self-serving exaggerated praise. Expressions like "none better," "your best buy," etc., are examples of puffing. So is the practice of creating distinctions without a difference, e.g., "fresher, smoother."

From ancient times marketers have puffed their wares, and the courts did little to stop them. The reason was that the ordinary user could do quite a bit to guard himself against deception. In those years the subjects of trade were mainly familiar materials and goods — natural foods, textiles and the like. Users had been exposed to these products from childhood, and could see, smell, and taste them in the village market place. The rule of *caveat emptor* (let the buyer beware) was a sensible rule for such products. It forced the user to grow up and thereby kept the courts out of myriads of small day-to-day transactions. Not only was there a near equality of product knowledge between buyer and seller; they lived in the same village. The resulting clear identity of the parties, in an atmosphere of village discipline, helped to keep them both honest.

Caveat emptor is still a sensible rule whenever buyer and seller meet in a small community to bargain over products with which both are familiar.

Our industrial civilization has meanwhile destroyed the premises which justified the rule of *caveat emptor,* i.e., near-equality of product knowledge, clear personal responsibility, and the pressures of village discipline. The small user is hopelessly ignorant of what the manufacturer did when he built the TV set, the tire, the automobile. In addition, the small user is caught in the confused interrelations of manufacturer, merchant and service shops, without the benefit of village discipline to keep order. The exaggerations which were once tolerable have now become misrepresentations which are no longer tolerable.

Some industrial companies are not aware that for their present products the rule of *caveat emptor* has become obsolete and that they should therefore quit this habit of centuries and start making their advertising "tell it like it is." Other companies know very well that they shouldn't exaggerate, and would prefer not to. What stops them (so they say) is that the other fellow uses misleading advertising and is taking away customers thereby. Yet this helplessness is by no means universal. Some large merchant companies do "tell it like it is," and they flourish mightily. Their practices suggest that reliability is marketable, whether in product or in advertising.[43]

We have probably reached a state where puffing and caveat emptor are obsolete as applied to technological products. The pressures of consumerism and government regulation all point in that direction.

The industrial response will likely be similar to that which created the concept of product inspection. A new category of inspector — the advertising inspector — will be created to examine the advertising and promotion, judge the conformance with the product, and approve or disapprove. It can also be predicted that the reaction of the marketing managers to such independent "advertising review" will be just as fiercely resistant as was that of the production managers to independent product inspection or that of the design engineering managers to the more recent concept of design review.

Government Regulation of Advertising   The obsolescence of caveat emptor makes necessary a considerable change in advertising practice. Some manufacturers and merchants have already taken major steps in the direction of strict objectivity. However, most of them have not, and this has led to demands for increasing government regulation. "Truth in advertising" is the slogan around which these demands are based.[44] This regulation is to be distinguished from regulation of labeling, which has long been on the statute books. (See below, under Labeling.)

---

[43] The foregoing is quoted and derived from Juran, J. M., Consumerism and Product Quality, *Quality Progress,* July 1970, pp. 18–27.

[44] Much of this "truth" relates to unit pricing, interest rates, and other financial matters which are outside the scope of this Handbook.

Extension of legislation to advertising will likely tend to regard the advertising as a form of implied warranty; i.e., since the advertiser intends the buyer to act on the representations made, he should stand behind those same representations.   The indications are that fitness for use will play a role in interpreting the validity of the advertising.

An important by-product of legislation regulating advertising is the fact that the government is empowered to act against the offender.   In the absence of regulation, the deceived buyer may, of course, proceed against the advertiser; but this is a costly, time-consuming procedure that may be frustrated by the rule of caveat emptor.[45]

WARRANTY OF QUALITY

A basic form of assurance to the customer is the quality warranty or guarantee.[46] The warranty gives the buyer certain assurances that the product is fit for use.

Implied Warranties   Warranties by the seller may be implied from his actions, under the provisions of the Uniform Commercial Code (which governs contracts of sale in virtually all states of the United States).   Under these provisions, the seller, by the mere act of sale, makes two implied warranties:

1. A general warranty of fitness for use ("merchantability" is the legal term) for the purposes for which such products are customarily used.

2. An added special warranty of fitness for the special uses to which the user will put it, provided the seller knows these special conditions.

Express Warranties   Here the seller goes beyond the mere act of sale and makes some representations about the product, i.e., properties it possesses (or lacks).   The representations may take various forms: oral promises to the buyer; display of a sample of the product; descriptions of the product in specifications, catalogs, and circulars; claims made in advertising; markings on the product itself; written statements of guarantee.

Written guarantees can be especially helpful to the parties by making clear what otherwise is usually not well understood.   When stated clearly, these written guarantees serve two basic, useful purposes:

1. They protect the buyer by spelling out the sellers' obligations to the buyer

2. They protect the seller by spelling out the limit to his obligations

The discussion which follows under the various "Warranty" headings deals with matters of money but not with human health and safety.   For the latter, see below, under Product Liability.

Warranty: Industrial Products   The parties to a sale of industrial products are knowledgeable in contract relations.   In consequence, they tend to draft the purchase contract so as to embody their known needs and to cover the contingencies which they have experienced under previous contract arrangements.   The resulting written contracts reflect a meeting of the minds on various pertinent matters including the warranty.

On those occasions when written warranty clauses are invoked, the resulting discussions are again between knowledgeable parties.   Added forces are at work urging a negotiated settlement; i.e., they usually want to continue doing business with each other.   Hence they commonly reach agreement or invoke an arbitration procedure.

---

[45] Under the British Trade Description Act (1968), the Board of Trade is empowered to proceed against offenders on consumer complaints.   In an early case, an auto dealer who had surreptitiously turned back an odometer was fined £ 1,000 ($2,800).

[46] There is a fine legal distinction between "warranty" and "guarantee."   However, industry ignores this distinction in its dialect on quality.   For additional discussion on warranties, see Section 10, under Legal Aspects of Vendor Relations.

Recent experience with warranty provisions in contracts for industrial products suggests that:

1. The "fine print" which is standard in so many contracts is no longer a reliable basis for protection. Instead, the protection must be based on prior agreement.

2. This prior agreement is best reached if there is an understanding of how the product will be used, whether that usage is protected by built-in controls, and what effects are likely to ensue if there should be defects or malfunctions. For example, defects in some materials (paper for printing, yarn for textiles) cause extensive downtime of costly machinery. The cost of the downtime has been shifting from the user to the supplier through contract revision.

3. The differences in the parties' positions on warranty should be cleared up before the price is negotiated.[47]

Some industrial purchase contracts provide for a guarantee of maintenance costs; i.e., costs beyond the guarantee are paid for by the manufacturer. Such contracts are in line with the trend to optimize the users' costs.

Warranty: Consumer Products   In contrast to the made-to-measure warranties which are written into large industrial contracts, warranties for consumer products are highly standardized. The typical consumer product warranty is printed on good-quality paper with an artwork border to make it look like a legal certificate (which it is). It includes some propaganda, i.e., a preamble stating the good intentions and care supplied by the manufacturer. Then follow the statements of the manufacturer's responsibility. These are of several varieties:

"Parts Only" Warranty.   In this warranty the manufacturer supplies replacement parts free, but the consumer pays everything else—service labor, other service costs, and transportation of the product to and from the repair site. A typical wording reads as follows:

Our obligation under this warranty shall be limited to repairing or replacing at our factory in —— any part of said appliance which our examination shall disclose to our satisfaction to be thus defective, within the time limit specified. Should any defects occur, new parts replacing such defective parts will be furnished without cost, FOB. our factory at ——.

The "parts only" warranty is an extremely narrow commitment and in the event of product failure is quite likely to create consumer dissatisfaction.

Service and Parts Warranty.   This is a broader warranty and includes a commitment by the manufacturer to restore the product to working order at no "out of pocket" cost to the user. The parts, service costs, and transportation are all paid for by the manufacturer. A typical wording is as follows:

At any time within one year from the date of delivery to the original retail purchaser, the manufacturer will repair this ——, if found by the manufacturer to be defective in material or workmanship, without cost to the owner or user. In effecting this repair, the manufacturer may, at its election, repair or replace any part which it finds to be defective.

"Delegation" Warranty.   A most controversial provision in warranties is the delegation of repair responsibilities to the retailer. A typical provision reads as follows:

The labor required to repair or replace an inoperative part is the responsibility of the dealer from whom the product was purchased.

During the first year of the warranty the —— retailer will furnish or arrange for such repair or replacements without cost to the customer, unless otherwise agreed at the time of sale.

---

[47] For elaboration, see Blackburn, Oliver M., Warranties under the Uniform Commercial Code, *The Arbitration Journal*, vol. 22, no. 3, 1967, pp. 173–182.

The root of the controversy is the contention of many retailers that they never agreed to accept this responsibility. Such "delegations" are of doubtful legal validity. However, many consumers do not know this and hence discover that neither the retailer nor the manufacturer will meet the guarantee.

Duration of Warranty. This is always spelled out and may be nonuniform as to different features of the product. For example, a one-year warranty on a product may include a five-year warranty on certain components while holding the warranty on finish to thirty days. Here is an actual wording:

> *During the first year* after purchase we provide home service (parts and labor) to repair any defect except surface finishes, which are guaranteed for thirty days. *During the second year* we provide replacement parts; labor is extra. *During the third, fourth, and fifth years* we provide replacement parts to repair the washer transmission; labor is extra.

With increasing complexity of apparatus, the problem of explaining which components are guaranteed and for how long has itself become complex. Some manufacturers name the components in a printed list. Others go further and provide an exploded diagram of the product, to identify components, along with their respective durations of guarantee.

Disclaimers. Warranties also list various conditions under which the warranty is *not* to apply, e.g., use of a home laundry machine for commercial duty, service by unauthorized personnel. There may be specific disclaimers on incidental damage, e.g., food spoiled during nonoperation of a freezer. Some disclaimers are probably of no legal effect—they are usually ruled by the courts to be contrary to public policy. Other disclaimers are probably unnecessary because they only restate the manufacturers' legal rights. However, some manufacturers use these disclaimers to discourage lawsuits or related actions.

Warranty of Reliability Conventional warranties for reliability have almost always been quantified in terms of time or in terms of measured usage of the product. More recently, these warranties have begun to include language in terms of failure rate, MTBF, and other statistical expressions for reliability.

For components produced in large numbers, guarantee of reliability is readily feasible. Reliability can be established by sampling, and the residue can then be certified as to reliability. A structured approach for doing this is now available as British Standard BS 9000 (see Section 38, under Testing and Inspection: Acceptance by Certification).

In complex systems there has already arisen a concept of including an incentive in contracts so that the price paid is related to the reliability achieved.[48] See Contract Incentives for Quality, above.

Consequential Damage Users' costs associated with product failures can go well beyond the cost of parts and service labor.

For example, a truck carrying a load of components develops a failure on the road while en route to a factory. The user's costs include:

The value of the truck during the idle time
The pay to the idle truck crew
The loss in factory production due to late arrival of the components
The cost of the emergency communication and the efforts to restore the status quo

Consumers likewise incur such added costs. For example, a food freezer fails and a load of frozen food is damaged; or the family car fails and time is lost arranging to get a service shop to repair the failure. In the second instance, substitute transportation must be paid for and an important engagement may be missed.

[48] See generally, Haddon, M. C., Guaranteed Reliability, *Industrial Quality Control,* February 1965, pp. 390–392.

Generally these consequential, pyramiding costs are not implied into the warranties and are borne by the seller only if the contract says so. Some sellers try to protect themselves further by writing a disclaimer into the warranty.

There *are* instances in which contracts will ensure payment for consequential damage. For example,

If hard castings cause tool breakage and shutdown of an automatic transfer line, the foundry pays for the broken tools and the downtime. (See Section 34, under Customer Relations.)

If breaks in paper rolls require a new setup on rotary printing presses, the paper company pays for the downtime.

If breaks in beams of yarn cause downtime on textile machinery, the yarn maker pays for the downtime.

Generally disclaimers in matters of injury to human beings are held by the courts to be contrary to public policy and hence are not enforced. However, disclaimers on consequential money damages not involving human safety are generally upheld.

Business Opportunities through Warranties   A stunning fact about consumer guarantees is the low ratio of guarantee period to average life. Only about 10% of the average life is under guarantee.

A government study[49] shows that new major household appliances purchased in 1957 had an average life expectancy running from 9 years (washing machines) to 15 years (refrigerators) and that these life spans are probably increasing. In contrast, warranty periods are usually no more than 1 or 2 years.

(Automobile guarantees have had a similar ratio, though there has been vacillation over the years.)[50]

Given such a ratio, it is evident that solution of the problem of in-guarantee service still leaves the user with a huge service problem beyond the guarantee period. It is axiomatic that any huge problem for the user is a business opportunity for the manufacturer. There are several ways in which companies are making use of this business opportunity:

Product Redesign.   Achievement of failure-free product can make the warranty an aggressive marketing device. To illustrate:

Our ——— locks are a noteworthy example. Since we've yet to hear of one of them failing, we've decided to guarantee them forever.

The great improvement in reliability of solid-state circuitry over electron tube circuitry permitted dramatic lengthening of the warranties for apparatus embodying this circuitry.

Competition in Warranties.   As experience is gained with field performance, and programs are undertaken to improve products and field service, it may be feasible to use the warranty as a competitive device. For example, in 1968 a leading maker of color television receivers extended the picture tube guarantee on new sets from one to three years and offered to make this retroactive to recent buyers.

---

[49] "Report of the Task Force on Appliance Warranties and Service," Federal Trade Commission, Washington, D.C., 1969.

[50] The cardinal events have been as follows:

1913: First warranty adopted; 90 days (no mileage limit).

1931: Changed to 90 days or 4,000 miles, whichever came first.

1960: Increased to 12 months or 12,000 miles, whichever came first.

1963: Increased to 24 months or 24,000 miles, whichever came first. Some guarantees went to 5 years but were restricted as to components.

Late 1960s: Return to 12 months or 12,000 miles, but warranty of 5 years or 50,000 miles for certain major components.

From Chesebrough, H. E., Guaranteed Reliability, Part II, *Industrial Quality Control*, March 1965, pp. 441–442.

The extension of the guarantee was attributed to product research, accelerated life testing, improved quality control and advanced production technology. A more complex example has been the changing pattern of guarantees for automobiles (see above). Competition in guarantees may take place in replacement sales as well as in original sales.

One investigator[51] compared the guarantees published for six grades of automobile tire at one retail outlet as follows:

Grade	Price	Guarantee	Price per month of guarantee
1	$13.29	18 months	$.75
2	16.79	24 months	.70
3	19.79	30 months	.66
4	24.79	36 months	.69
5	29.79	40 months	.74
6	37.04	40 months plus puncture proofing	.93

Reorientation of Marketing Emphasis. Competition in quality tends to seek out sources of user dissatisfaction and to create business opportunities by finding new ways to deal with these unsolved problems. (For the solved quality problems, the competition is not in quality but in the marketing skills.) For long-life products, a main source of user dissatisfaction has been the inability to get adequate field service when products fail. Although this problem is discussed extensively in Section 15, it bears importantly on the Marketing of Quality.

The field service problem has grown to such an extent that a major consideration in the purchase of long-life products is how to get good service if the product fails. While changes in technology are a vital element of the solution, changes in business practice are at least as important.

For example, some designs of watches permit sale based on a three-year warranty. If the watch fails during the warranty period, the user is given a new one in lieu of the failed watch. If the watch fails after the three-year warranty, it is cheaper for the user to buy a new one than to have the old one repaired.

In the watch example, the business decision involves abolition of the entire repair operation with its needs for trained specialists, inventories of spare parts, etc. For more complex products, a similar concept is worked out through use of modular designs which include instrumentation to identify the failed module. The most familiar example is a meter to signal the failure of batteries in battery-operated electronic apparatus. In such cases the user himself can remove the failed module and secure a replacement, much as he does for dead batteries.

The obstacles to the use of such concepts are similar to those discussed in Section 4, under Life Cycle Costing, i.e., data banks and cultural resistance. The manufacturer is well aware of the users' costs during the short guarantee period, since most of these are also costs to the manufacturer. However, the manufacturer lacks this information for the longer out-of-guarantee period and is thereby handicapped in his search for a better approach.

In addition, some manufacturers have a profitable spare parts business, which for the short run gives them a vested interest in product failures. Of course, for the longer run they risk losing everything—the spare parts business and the original equipment sales.[52]

---

[51] H. R. Haid in summary of Engineering Foundation Research Conference, Santa Barbara, Calif., 1968. Engineering Foundation, 345 E. 47 St., New York.

[52] For added discussion, see Section 4, under Life Cycle Costing.

Government Regulation of Warranties   In 1960, the U.S. Federal Trade Commission provided its staff with "Guides against Deceptive Advertising of Guarantees." Section I, headed Guarantees in General, is especially pertinent to quality and reads as follows:

In general, any guarantee in advertising shall *clearly and conspicuously disclose*
(a) *The nature and extent of the guarantee.*
This includes disclosure of
(1) What product or part of the product is guaranteed,
(2) What characteristics or properties of the designated product or part thereof are covered by, or excluded from, the guarantee,
(3) What is the duration of the guarantee,
(4) What, if anything, anyone claiming under the guarantee must do before the guarantor will fulfill his obligation under the guarantee, such as return of the product and payment of service or labor charges;
and
(b) *The manner in which the guarantor will perform.*
This consists primarily of a statement of exactly what the guarantor undertakes to do under the guarantee. Examples of this would be repair, replacement, refund. If the guarantor or the person receiving the guarantee has an option as to what may satisfy the guarantee this should be set out;
and
(c) *The identity of the guarantor.*
The identity of the guarantor should be clearly revealed in all advertising, as well as in any documents evidencing the guarantee. Confusion of purchasers often occurs when it is not clear whether the manufacturer or the retailer is the guarantor.[53]

Additional headings in the Guide include:

Prorata Adjustment of Guarantees
Satisfaction or Your Money Back Guarantees
Lifetime Guarantees
Savings Guarantees
Guarantees under which the Guarantor Does Not or Cannot Perform
Guarantee as a Misrepresentation

During 1967 several bills were introduced into the United States Senate to deal with warranties, as follows:

S 2726, applying to warranties of merchandise and services
S 2727, applying to automobiles (and requiring that they be warranted)
S 2728, applying to household appliances (and requiring that they be warranted)

The provisions follow the guidelines of the Federal Trade Commission but go into much more detail.[54] There are not only provisions to ensure that the warranties are clear but also some positive requirements as to what warranties may and may not include.

There has also been some Industry Association action to establish guidelines for

---

[53] The reader might find it interesting to check an ancient guarantee against these guidelines. The following record, a clay tablet, was found in the archives of the firm of Murashu Sons of Nippur. (The date is the thirty-fifth year of the reign of Artaxerxes I, which is 429 B.C. to us.)

"As concerns the gold ring set with an emerald, we guarantee that for twenty years the emerald will not fall out of the gold ring. If the emerald should fall out of the gold ring before the end of twenty years, we shall pay unto Bel-nadin-shumu an indemnity of ten mana of silver." Bursk, Edward C., *et al.,* "The World of Business," Simon and Schuster, Inc., New York, 1962, vol. 1, p. 71.

[54] For elaboration, see "Report of the Task Force on Appliance Warranties and Service," Federal Trade Commission, 1969, pp. 92–98.

advertising and other business practices, including advertising of guarantees. The American Home Laundry Manufacturers Association (which later became the Association of Home Appliance Manufacturers (AHAM) published such a set of guidelines in 1960. AHAM published recommendations in 1969 for the household refrigerator-freezer industry.

LABELING

The term "labeling" refers to actions taken by manufacturers or merchants to provide users with information about the product. As labeling has evolved, it has taken multiple but overlapping forms.

Product Labeling This refers to information about the inherent nature of the product, e.g., the net weight of the package contents, the ingredients used, instructions for operation and maintenance, warnings of danger. The information is often placed on a small tag or label, hence the term "labeling." However, the information may also be placed directly on the product, the wrapper, the container, an accompanying circular or manual, etc.

For most products, the extent of product labeling is determined by the manufacturer. In consequence, the "labels" (meaning any of the means to convey the information) are a mixture of product information and advertising. However, there are statutes on the books requiring that the product actually conform to the label. Generally, there is good adherence to these statutes as applied to the intrinsic properties of the product.

For some products, certain labeling is required by law. For example, all food packages are required by law to state the net contents and the list of ingredients. All poisonous products are required by law to be so labeled.[55]

Product Grading A second form of product information is *grade* or quality of design. For manufactured products, the grade designations are based on various contrasting intrinsic qualities which are usually measureable. When individual units of product involve substantial prices, the grade distinctions are often made in the form of *model* names or numbers to simplify user recognition. When the units of product are low in price, the grading may be done in broad classes. For example, one large merchant company uses three grade designations (good, better, best) to designate differences in quality for the same functional use.

Some grade designations are open to attack because they can readily deceive uninformed consumers. Such situations are common in consumer food products. For example, olives are graded by size into eight grades, the smallest being called "standard." Next comes "medium" and "large." Finally there are five sizes larger than "large" (extra large, giant, jumbo, colossal, and supercolossal). There are no "small" olives! In like manner, "grade no. 1" in some products (e.g., potatoes, cheese) is not the top grade, as there are hidden top grades which, though well known to the merchants, are not known to the consumers. These practices are of long standing, but they may well be doomed by the rise of consumerism.

Brand Labeling Many companies try to build a quality reputation around a distinctive name or brand for their products. They exert efforts to assure that products sold under this brand name are of a quality which will earn a good reputation. In addition, they make use of advertising to promote familiarity with and confidence in

---

[55] The Fair Packaging and Labeling Act (administered by the Federal Trade Commission) includes general provisions as to the identity of the product, identity of manufacturer (or distributor), quantity of the contents, terminology, etc. In addition, there are provisions specific to certain products. Still other provisions relate to pricing practices and promotions. (Federal Trade Commission, Washington, D.C.)

the brand name.   Application of this brand name to products is known as *brand labeling*.

The brand may be created by any of numerous organization forms (see below). Much time, expense, and dedication are required to establish user acceptance of a brand name.   However, once successfully established, the brand is of great value in marketing the branded products.   In such cases, special steps are required to guard the integrity of the brand.

Manufacturers' Brands.   Many manufacturers market their products under their own name, which then also becomes the brand name.   Other companies market the products under noncompany names (e.g., Maxwell House Coffee marketed by General Foods Corporation) or under fanciful names chosen to arrest public attention and cling to memory.   In any case, the product advertising and promotion is built around the brand name.

Manufacturers protect the integrity of their branded products through conventional systems of quality controls, as described throughout this Handbook.

In some cases, use of the manufacturer's brand is complicated because of intermediate manufacturers.   For example, the major chemical companies have created certain materials, e.g., synthetic fibers, with special properties useful to consumers. These materials are given brand names, and these brands are propagandized by advertising aimed at consumers, including guarantees which the chemical companies make *direct to these consumers*.   However, the chemical companies sell these materials not to consumers, but to the first links in the chain of yarn makers, cloth weavers, fabricators of end products (e.g., garments, blankets, carpets), retailers, consumers.   (The same applies to some industrial products, e.g., polypropylene pipe.)   Hence the chemical companies conduct these sales under a license arrangement which requires that the subsequent fabricators adhere to certain essential quality standards.   The terms of the license permit the chemical companies to establish controls which will safeguard the brand names.

Merchants' Brands.   Merchants sell products both under manufacturers' brands and under their own brands.   In the latter case, the merchant's source of supply is either a captive (owned) manufacturing source or product bought from an independent manufacturer, who agrees to apply the merchant's brand to the product.   Such products are known as "private label."   Often these products are bought under functional specifications, leaving it to the manufacturer to prepare the detailed design.

When the merchant sells manufacturers' branded products, the manufacturer is identified and the merchant's responsibilities for product quality are minimal. However, in sale of private-label products, the manufacturer is not identified and the merchant carries full responsibility.[56]

Large merchants who market extensively under their private label make use of the tools of quality control to protect their label.   Qualification testing of new designs is extensively used, as is vendor surveillance.   Regular inspection for lot acceptance is highly selective, depending on the nature of the product and the record of the vendor (who is expected to maintain an effective quality control system).   In addition, effort is exerted to use information on product failures and on user dissatisfaction to take remedial steps, both as to product and vendor.

Franchise and Chain Brands.   Some very large manufacturing and service organizations operate on a basis of a "chain" of numerous local markets, plants, restaurants, motels, etc.   Some of these local units may be owned by the chain; others may

---

[56] For elaboration, see Peach, Robert W., How Retailers Assure the Quality of Products, *Proceedings, International Conference on Quality Control,* JUSE, Tokyo, 1969, pp. 473 and 474.

be franchised under an agreement which permits them to use the brand name. The use of this brand name greatly aids the marketing efforts of the local unit.

In such chain operations the company regulations or the franchise agreements spell out the criteria under which the brand name may be used. In addition, there is provision for inspection and surveillance by a designated laboratory. This laboratory may be a corporate quality control service or even a subsidiary.[57]

For example, a large milk processing corporation consists of numerous regional operating companies. Some of these operating companies sell their milk under their own brand. However, the corporation also has a national brand which is legally owned by a subsidiary testing company. Any operating company which wishes to use the national brand must submit its plant and products to examination by the testing company.

Industry Association Brands. These are the creation of an industry association. Under the concept, a number of manufacturers collectively agree on a brand which includes minimum product quality standards. The brand is then promoted by the Association to achieve public knowledge and acceptance. Manufacturers who meet the standards may then use the brand and gain the marketing value it provides.

The product known as Harris Tweed is defined as "made from 100% pure virgin wool produced in Scotland, spun, dyed and finished in the Outer Hebrides, and handwoven by the islanders at their own homes. . . ."[58] Inspection is by the Harris Tweed Association, which authorizes use of the brand.

The integrity of the industry brand is strongly correlated with the integrity of the enforcement, which varies widely from one industry to another. Some industry associations are dominated by their members; others are powerful enough to maintain a high degree of independence.[59]

In those cases where the industry association lacks the facilities to determine whether the products comply to the terms of the brand, it may engage an independent laboratory for the purpose. Such was the action of the Boating Industry Association (BIA), which selected Underwriters' Laboratories, Inc., to determine whether manufactured boats are in compliance with BIA standards.[60]

Certification Labeling "Certification" as used here is a form of product assurance centered around a formal document or certificate. The certificate always represents the product as either conforming to specification or as fit for use. It may or may not include test data and it may be issued either by the manufacturer or by a separate testing service.[61] For a detailed discussion of these differences, see Section 10, under Certification.

---

[57] For added discussion relative to controls in service companies, see Section 47.

[58] Thomas, Veronica, The Wizard of Plockropool, *Atlantic Monthly,* July 1966, pp. 124–126.

[59] The medieval guilds made extensive use of industry quality controls. They prescribed detailed specifications for materials, processes, and products and provided independent inspections to enforce them. By the end of the thirteenth century, the cloth guild of the city of Ypres was approving 8,000 pieces of cloth per year. (See Renard, George, "Guilds in the Middle Ages," G. Bell & Sons, London, 1919.)

The famous 1662 Rembrandt painting known as *Dutch Masters* is actually a painting of a board of inspectors (sampling officials of the Drapers Guild) who had the responsibility for inspecting and awarding (or withholding) the mark for cloth produced in the city of Amsterdam. (Haak, Bob, "Rembrandt, His Life, His Work, His Time," Harry N. Abrams, New York, pp. 308–310.)

[60] News Briefs, *Quality Assurance,* October 1970, p. 82.

[61] Certification is not to be confused with conventional testing service from independent laboratories. Such laboratories provide test services to a company under a variety of conditions: the company lacks a certain instrument; the company's laboratory is momentarily overloaded; the company wants to conduct a check on its own accuracy.

In those cases where a manufacturer is "licensed" to apply an independent mark (by a government regulator or by an independent laboratory), the application of the mark is likewise a form of certification, the mark being a shorthand form of certificate; e.g., the UL mark, or the © which is the shorthand statement of "copyrighted."

It should be noted that an independent laboratory which certifies products as fit for use (or as conforming to standard) assumes some legal responsibilities. A user who relies on such certification and is damaged has the right to proceed against the independent laboratory as well as against some of the other parties directly involved.[62]

PRODUCT LIABILITY

Until the early twentieth century it was comparatively rare for users to file lawsuits based on injuries resulting from use of manufactured products. Since then, the growth in the number of these lawsuits in the United States has been remarkable. By the mid-1960s they were estimated to have reached over 60,000 annually[63] and by the 1970s had likely risen to over 100,000 per year (most are settled out of court). This growth in numbers of lawsuits has been accompanied by an equally remarkable growth in the sizes of individual claims and verdicts. From figures measured in thousands of dollars individual verdicts have grown to exceed $100,000, with some unusual cases exceeding $1 million.

Several factors have combined to bring about these growing phenomena:

1. *"Population explosion" of products.* The industrial society has placed large numbers of manufactured products in the hands of amateurs. Some of these products are inherently dangerous. Others are misused. While the injury *rate* (injuries per million hours of usage) has probably been declining sharply, the total number of injuries has been rising, thereby also creating a rise in total number of lawsuits.

2. *Erosion of manufacturers' defenses.* As these lawsuits came to trial, the courts proceeded to erode the former legal defenses available to manufacturers. Formerly, a plaintiff's right to sue a manufacturer rested on one of two main grounds:

    a. A contract for sale of product, with an actual or implied warranty of freedom from hazards. Being based on the contract relationship, the plaintiff had to establish "privity," i.e., that he was a party to the contract. The courts have in effect abolished the need for privity by taking the position that there is an implied representation that the product is safe and that this implication follows the product around, irrespective of who is the user.

    b. Negligence by the manufacturer. In such cases the burden of proof was on the plaintiff to show that the manufacturer was negligent. The courts have tended to shift the burden of proof so that the manufacturer is now required to prove that he was *not* negligent.

Manufacturers' disclaimers (published announcements of nonliability) have been held contrary to public policy.[64]

The final result of all this has been virtually liability without negligence—a theory that injuries should be paid for by those with the most assets, i.e., manufacturers.[65]

---

[62] See also, Section 4, under Consumer Test Services. See also American National Standards Institute (ANSI) Z 34.2 — 1969, relative to Certification by Producer or Supplier.

[63] "Product Liability and Reliability," Machinery and Allied Products Institute, Washington, D.C., 1967, p. 49.

[64] This probably does not apply to damages in noninjury cases. See Warranty of Quality, above.

[65] The laws are not quite as simple as the foregoing short statements. For a more detailed discussion of the legal cases through which these defenses have been eroded, see Coccia, Dondanville, and Nelson, "Product Liability: Trends and Implications," American Management Association, New York, 1970. See also Product Liability and Reliability, *op. cit.*

3. *Growing claims consciousness.* As big verdicts have been won and publicized, they have attracted the attention of injured people. In addition, the lawyers who specialize in such claims have been aggressive in stimulating claims consciousness among clients as well as in developing skills in prosecuting the cases.

Defensive Action Industrial companies do, of course, defend themselves against these risks. As a temporary measure, resort can be had to insurance, but this solves nothing fundamental. The insurance rates soon have a way of penalizing the worst record. In addition, the insurance companies tend to take steps to exclude from the insurance policies those risks which can be avoided by good management.

The basic solution is to reduce the causes of injuries at their source. Analysis soon shows that *all* company levels and functions are able to contribute to making products safer[66] and to improving the company's defenses in the event of lawsuits. The respective contributions are about as follows:[67]

Top Management. Promulgate a policy on product safety and product recalls, structure an organized approach through product safety committees[68] and formal programs, demand dating of the product and good traceability, set up an audit of the entire program, support industry programs which go beyond the capacity of the unaided company.

To this list should be added a scoreboard, i.e., a measure of the injury rate of the company's products relative to some reference level. A useful unit of measure is the number of injuries per million man-hours of usage, since some major data banks on injuries are already expressed in this form or are convertible to this form.[69]

Design. Adopt product safety as a design parameter, adopt a fail-safe philosophy of design, organize formal design reviews,[70] follow the established codes, secure listings from the established laboratories, publish the ratings, utilize modern tools of design technique.[71]

There are strong indications that product design for safety will be a target of consumerists[72] and legislators for years to come. A government report[73] estimated that 20 million Americans are injured each year in incidents involving consumer products. The same report recommended enactment of a Consumer Product Safety Act providing that a Commission "shall have authority to promulgate standards and procedures for the purpose of insuring that new consumer products are adequately designed and tested to minimize unreasonable risk of death or personal injury to the public." This recommendation was adopted. The Consumer Product Safety Act became law on October 28, 1972.

Manufacture. Establish a sound quality control program to include systems and procedures for foolproofing matters of product safety; train supervisors and operators in use of the product as part of the motivation plan; open up suggestion plans to ideas on product safety; set up the documentation needed to provide traceability and historical evidence.

The growth of product liability has sharply increased the need for documentation,

---

[66] For a case example, see Walden, Clyde H., Product Liability—Loss Prevention and Control, *1972 Technical Conference Transactions,* ASQC, pp. 339–341.

[67] Derived from Juran, J. M., Mobilizing for the 1970's. *Quality Progress,* August 1969, pp. 8–17.

[68] See, for an example, Product Liability and Reliability, *op. cit.,* pp. 88–90.

[69] For an example plus added discussion, see Juran, J. M., Product Safety, *Quality Progress,* July 1972, pp. 30–32. See also Section 8, under Safety in New Product Design: Quantification of Safety.

[70] Product Liability and Reliability, *op. cit.,* pp. 29 and 30.

[71] For an extended discussion, see Section 8, under Safety in New-Product Design.

[72] Consumerist—an advocate for consumer interests.

[73] "Final Report of the National Commission on Product Safety," U.S. Government Printing Office, 1970.

in several ways:

1. The written plan[74] which sets out the manner of designing, making, and testing products. This includes the various departmental manuals as well as the company policies and plans relating to product safety.

2. Product "traceability."[75] When hazards are discovered, there is need to identify the product suspected of causing the hazards. The more precisely this can be done, the less will be the need for massive recall. The approach has been to use individual serial numbers for large units of product and bulk designation for smaller units (lot number, heat number, date of manufacture, etc.).

3. The data collected during the processing and testing of products, from field complaints, and other sources. These are needed during investigation of troubles, for Material Review Board deliberations, and for similar situations. They are also needed in the event of government regulatory actions and lawsuits[76] arising out of injury. One large motor manufacturer requires its vendors to keep such records for five years after delivering the product. Another has told its vendors the retention period is "forever."

Sales. Provide product labeling for warnings, dangers, antidotes; train the field force in the contract provisions; supply safety information to distributors and dealers; set up exhibits on safety procedures; conduct tests after installation and train users in safety; publish the list of dos and don'ts which contribute to safety; maintain a climate of customer relations which minimizes animosity and claims.

Advertising. Set up to secure technological and legal review of copy; propagandize product safety through education and warnings. The practice of puffing (see under Advertising of Quality, above) can backfire in liability suits, e.g., a product advertised as "absolutely safe." During advertising review, one of the questions should be "How would this phrase sound in court?"

Sales Service. Observe use of the product; discover hazards inherent in this use; feed the information back to all concerned, including users, who should be warned and trained.

Consumers exhibit a wide range of intelligence, including the lowest. In consequence, actual use of the product can differ significantly from the intended use. For example, some stepladders include a light platform which is intended to carry tools or materials (e.g., paint) but is not intended to carry the weight of the user. However, some users nevertheless do stand on these platforms with resulting injury to themselves. The philosophy of the consumerists and regulators is clearly that products should be designed to stand up under actual usage and not merely intended usage.[77]

Beyond the foregoing, for which departmental responsibilities are fairly clear, there are other activities for which responsibility is often joint:

Accident investigation should be done promptly, and by qualified experts, with early notification to the insurance company. There should be a team review of claims, with provision for retaining the failed hardware as evidence. There should be defense of borderline claims to deter unjustified claims.

---

[74] See also, in this connection, Section 19, Configuration Control.

[75] See Section 9, under Traceability.

[76] During a lawsuit, the plaintiff may demand to see the records under the "discovery" (pretrial) procedure.

[77] In some instances, manufacturers merely abandon a product line rather than continue to subject themselves to claims which they feel are due solely to obvious misuse of the product. For example, a large United States electrical manufacturer abandoned the making of electric blankets due to product liability reasons. (Consumers covered the blankets during use, contrary to warnings, and caused dangerous overheating.)

Contracts should be drawn to avoid unrealistic commitments and unrealistic guarantees. Judicious disclaimers should be included, again to discourage unjustified claims.

THE MERCHANT AND QUALITY

Sale of manufactured products takes place through a chain of intermediate independent[78] merchants whose influence on quality varies widely depending on the nature of the product and the identity of the customer. Sale of technical products to industrial companies requires a high level of knowledge of the product, including some capacity to provide technical assistance. At the other extreme is self-service —the selling is done by display of the product plus prior propaganda. Between these extremes are numerous situations in which the tools and the techniques of selling play an important role in the customer's decision as to which of competing products to buy and even whether to buy at all.

Quality Activities The giant merchant companies are extensively involved in all aspects of product quality. They have Technical Departments to establish specifications and to conduct product qualification tests. Their central Purchasing Department carries out vendor selection and qualification. Their Quality Control Departments carry out vendor surveillance and incoming inspection as required by the merchandise managers.

The small merchant (retailer) lacks Technical or Quality Control Departments. However, he carries out some activities which do influence quality: unpacking, handling, display, repacking, transportation.[79] These activities afford some opportunities for finding defective product, and, even more, to create new quality problems due to product damage, confusion in identity, and misplacement of components. Storage is a further source of risk, e.g., proper stock rotation (perishable products) or proper environment (temperature of frozen foods).

Much can be done by manufacturers to minimize these risks through product design or systems redesign. As to the residue of risk, the manufacturer can provide clear information on how to care for the product, establish standards to be observed, and offer assistance in training the merchant's personnel.

In addition, manufacturers are well advised to institute audits to determine how well the merchant chain conforms to standards in matters of product quality. These audits can provide a vital input to manufacturers in their efforts to attain fitness for use.[80]

Customer Relations At the point of sale, the discussion with the customer is through the salesman, who is an employee of the merchant. This salesman is engaged in persuading the customer to buy from among the competing forms of product and from the competing brands within each form. The customer's decision to buy is influenced not only by product quality but also by delivery terms and by price, which includes (1) price of the product and (2) price of credit in the case of installment sales.

The manufacturer of branded products faces the problem of carrying the influence of his product brand through the entire merchant chain right to the point of sale. A major tool for doing this is a good reputation derived from the prior performance

---

[78] A small minority of manufacturing companies sell direct to the consumer, either through captive retail shops or through door-to-door selling by salesmen who are manufacturing company employees.

[79] At the retail store level, the large merchant also carries out these activities.

[80] See also, in this connection, the related discussions in Section 15 on merchant roles in cases of complaints and claims.

of his products to provide predictable fitness for use.   In addition, the manufacturer propagandizes his product direct to consumers through advertising and brand labeling (see under Advertising of Quality and under Labeling, respectively).   He also develops tools to aid the merchant and salesman to sell his product, e.g., product information literature, samples, demonstration kits, prepared sales training aids, etc.[81]   Some manufacturers do a superlative job of aiding merchants and customers through such means.   Particularly when the product possesses superior fitness for use, the manufacturer finds ways to sensitize the salesman to this fact so that he can in turn sensitize the prospective customer.

However, in many competitive situations, there is no clear superiority in fitness for use.   What is decisive in selling products in such cases is the marketing tools: prior reputation, attractive packaging, appealing propaganda, personable salesmanship.   In such cases, appeals to emotion prevail over appeals to precise reasoning.[82] Since the manufacturer is competing with other manufacturers for the attention and support of the merchant and salesmen, some of the manufacturer's energies must be directed to "selling" these men on himself and his product.   In part, the manufacturer does this through favorable contract terms.   In part, he sells the merchant through the same tools as the merchant uses on his customers: prior reputation, attractive packaging, appealing propaganda, personable salesmanship.

[81] For an interesting anthology, see Bursk, Edward C., Donald T. Clark, and Ralph W. Hidy, "The World of Business," Simon and Schuster, New York, 1962, vol. I.

[82] For some homespun examples, see Aspley, J. C., "How to Sell Quality," The Dartnell Corporation, Chicago, 1921.

Section **15**

Field Performance

J. M. JURAN

ROBERT W. PEACH
Manager, Quality Assurance Engineering, Sears, Roebuck and Co.

INTRODUCTION

This Section discusses those problems of product quality which are encountered after inspection and test of the product in the factory. Following the factory tests, the product undergoes an extensive series of additional steps or operations, the most usual being packaging, transportation, storage, sale, unpacking, assembly or installation, usage and service. Each of these steps can significantly affect fitness for use.

There is no standardized, concise term which describes this series of additional steps. The authors and editors have adopted the term "field performance" as a compromise term, since any deficiency in conducting these further steps becomes evident during field performance of the product rather than during factory testing.

(The term "field" is widely employed to designate the place of usage as distinguished from the factory location.)

A major difference in factory control versus field performance control lies in the quality planning. During the last few decades, the concept of formal quality planning has taken a firm hold in the Manufacturing and Quality Control Departments. However, the quality planning for the operations of packaging, transport, storage, etc., has generally lagged in effectiveness. To an important degree, this lag is traceable to the fact that these additional operations are conducted by departments such as Materials Management, Transportation, etc., whose departmental traditions have clung to informality and empiricism (as did Manufacture and Quality Control before they embarked on programs involving greater formality and science). However, it is quite obvious that the quality planning and control for these additional operations must likewise be placed on a basis of science and that, to do so, greater formality will be required. The most obvious move in this direction is to enlarge the existing quality planning concepts to include quality planning for these additional operations. Under these concepts, the staff quality specialists, in participation with Materials Management, Transportation, etc., develop a plan of control which is acceptable to all. The execution of this plan is then delegated to the regular departments (Materials Management, Transportation, etc.). In addition, an audit is instituted to check the extent to which the execution follows the plan. This audit is conducted by "independent" auditors who may be from the staff Quality Control Department or from the line department itself.

For long-life products, and to a degree for all products, the quality reputation of the manufacturer depends extensively on the quality of field performance. Fitness for use is basic to satisfaction for the user, and this cannot be complete unless all field performance activities are well conducted.

PACKAGING, TRANSPORT, AND STORAGE

All products are subject to deterioration in quality. Some of this is due to inherent instability, e.g., progressive biological activity, evaporation of solvents, crystallization of metals. The effects of such instability can be accelerated or retarded by control of the environment. In addition, quality can deteriorate due to damage during the operations which follow inspection and test. Proper quality planning and control can go far to minimize such damage, so that the product as received by the user conforms closely to that which left the factory test station.

Packaging   Several activities are carried out under this heading, and it is useful to distinguish them carefully, since the organization responsibilities differ.

Integral Environmental Packaging.   This refers to protecting the product from the environment, e.g., preserving metals from rusting, keeping moisture out of (or in) foods, shielding electronic products against electronic interference. The design of such integral environmental protection is properly a part of the original product design. As such, the protective aspects of the design should undergo the same design reviews, qualification testing, life testing, etc., as the product itself. In products such as drugs or precision electronics, the foregoing concepts are now commonplace.

In addition, the organizations engaged in conducting the designs, tests, and reviews should be the same as those engaged in these activities for the basic product itself. This organization form assures that the integral environmental packaging requirements are placed on the official product specifications and that, thereby, conformance will be enforced by the Quality Control organization.

Unitizing.   This activity is the packaging of units of product in the smallest level of container. The product may be packed only one to a container, e.g., a vacuum cleaner and its attachments. The product may also be packed many to a container, either in egg-crate fashion (e.g., a half dozen electric lamps) or in bulk (e.g., a hundred drug tablets in a bottle). During this unitizing, what is critical is to assure that:

The container marking corresponds to the product identity
The quantity shown on the container corresponds to the quantity of product actually in the container
The peripheral product (e.g., spare parts, mounting screws, maintenance supplies) are all there
The product circulars, manuals of instruction, guarantee card, and other documents are all present
The inspection stamps evidencing successful product testing are present

The packaging materials are adequate to serve as a protective cocoon to shield the products against the hazards of further packaging, transport, and storage. The design of the unit pack should be suitable and the execution of the pack on the production line must be as intended. There is often the need for specifying proper arrangement of packing materials (such as inserts) as a quality characteristic to be controlled, just as with other characteristics. If possible, the packing assembly should be foolproofed to preclude any misassembly which would reduce the effectiveness of the protection.

Final Packaging. The unit packages are usually placed into larger containers for bulk shipment and added protection during transportation. These larger packages may consist of corrugated cartons, wooden cases, etc. Once again there is need to assure that the markings on the package correspond to the contents, that the quantities are correct, that the container design is adequate for protection, that the shipping documents correspond with the goods.

Package Design The most critical aspect of quality of packaging, transport, storage, etc., is the design of the packages. For integral environmental protection, this design is increasingly a function of Product Design itself and thereby is closely coupled with the needs of the product. For unitized packaging, and especially for final packing, the practice varies widely. Often these activities are so divided among major departments that coordination is an intricate process.

For these divided responsibilities, and especially for products which undergo numerous or critical handlings, it becomes important to look at handling and packaging from a systems viewpoint rather than from the viewpoint of numerous departments. In one company, a total of 888 handlings, each a potential source of product damage, was being conducted on the materials, parts, assemblies, and packaging needed for producing and shipping a precise transmitting tube.[1] A systems review for such cases can identify opportunities to improve the overall handling by methods such as:

Modifying vendor packaging. Some electronic components are blister packaged in a way which allows testing without unpacking.
Starting unitized and other containerization at early operations or even the vendor's location. For example, the drug industry has evolved unitized packaging of dosages in which the identity of the dose (and even its own environment) are designed into the unit package and carry through to the patient.
Designing racks, trays, bins, tote boxes, etc., to provide optimal service to all companies and departments involved rather than to force added handling and repacking.

---

[1] Baker, Bronson B., Product Reliability through Integrated Packaging and Handling, *IEEE Transactions on Product Engineering and Production,* PEP-7, July 1963, pp. 1–11.

The systems concept is not limited to package design; it may need to be extended to adapt product and package to each other. In one example, office machines were being handled as much as 27 different times between the assembly line and the customer's desk, due chiefly to unboxing in sales branches for adjustment before delivery. A broad program of reliability improvement and package redesign permitted "in-box delivery" and reduced costs of makeready, delivery, and claims under warranty.[2]

Transportation   Handling and transport introduce many perils to the product. Some of these are fully predictable: climatic temperature, humidity, vibration, shock (during automated handling).   Others are the result of ignorance, carelessness, blunder, and even sabotage. For some of these perils the product is in greater danger from handling and transport than from usage.

A good deal has been done to evolve tests which can simulate shock, vibration, and other transport damage. The stresses are measured in terms of cycles per second, "G-levels" of deceleration, pulse shapes, and still other quantified measures.[3] The experience gained has found its way into specifications for packaging and vehicle loading.

Beyond the simulation tests, it is essential to secure good feedback on the actual condition of the product, including careful analysis for causation. These feedbacks are needed for planning against the "unpredictable" causes of damage as well as for improving the simulation testing.

In an early study[4] on damage to household ranges, the prevailing level of shipping damage of over 8% was regarded as an inevitable consequence of poor transportation. A study was set up to secure field data instead of just opinions. In addition, a test program was set up to measure vibration, shock, and impact. In short order (within hours), the problem areas were identified. After making six packaging changes, nine product design changes, and six processing changes, the shipping damage fell to less than 2%. See, in this connection, Figure 16-11 and associated discussion.

Storage   Immense quantities of raw materials, components, and finished products are constantly in storage, awaiting further processing, sale, or use. To minimize deterioration and degradation, various actions can be taken beyond those already discussed above.

1. Establish the "shelf life" of the product based on laboratory and field data.

2. Establish standards to place limits on time in storage.

3. Date the product conspicuously to make it easy to identify the age of the product in stock.

4. Design the package and control the environment to minimize expected and unexpected degradation.

A common weakness in these programs is the failure to "date" the product conspicuously. Sometimes this failure is just due to poor technique; e.g., iron in open storage rusts away because the color of the rust preservative is not changed annually. However, some failure to date conspicuously is the result of marketing decisions; e.g., the dates are put on the back of the product or on the front in tiny print because the advertising has priority; there is a fear of dating the product in a way which enables the consumer to know if he is getting out-of-date product. These reasons, if ever valid, now have become obsolete. Conspicuous dating on outer

[2] Reliability Drive Eliminates Pre-Delivery Field Fixes, *Quality Assurance,* January 1967, pp. 36 and 37.

[3] See, for example, Ruberton, Anthony, Transportation and Packaging Techniques to Improve Reliability, *IRE Transactions on Product Engineering and Production.* PEP 5, April 1961, pp. 45–52.

[4] Heine, R. E., How We Reduced Our Shipping Damage, *Finish,* May 1951, pp. 71–79.

cartons as well as on unit packages aids in traceability as well as in stock rotation and in establishing age of inventories.

In the special case where product is deliberately stockpiled to be used at some unknown time which may be far in the future, e.g., military supplies, some special controls are needed, notably periodic reevaluations of actual quality of the stored products.[5]

Provision for Audit   The operations of packaging, transport, and storage are widely dispersed over multiple companies and departments.   However, it is the manufacturer whose brand name is identified with the product who is inevitably regarded by the user as responsible for *any* failures, no matter how caused.   In consequence, such manufacturers are faced with the need for auditing the extent to which practice in packaging, transport, and storage conforms to specifications.

The general approach to auditing is set out in Section 21.   Application of this general approach to the operations of packaging, transport, and storage runs into some special problems, especially with such transport and storage as are conducted by independent carriers and merchants.   However, all concerned are interested in reducing claims and improving customer relations.   This common interest is usually adequate to assure that good collaboration can be worked out.

INSTALLATION AND USAGE

Before the packaged product is put into use, it undergoes additional processing during distribution, assembly, installation and checkout, etc.   These operations are quite as much a part of the progression of the product as design or manufacture, and they demand corresponding controls despite the fact that they are carried on away from the head office or factory.

Processing during Distribution   The distribution process carries out such operations as breaking bulk, readjusting, adding reagents, touching up finishes, repackaging, etc.   The planning of these operations should be a part of the overall product planning.   The results of this planning should then be embodied in specifications to be used by the distribution organizations.   Compliance to these specifications should then be audited independently.

In some cases it is found that the distribution process cannot be relied on to carry out these operations, e.g., international problems of language or culture, small retailers lacking in technological skills.   For such cases the need is for a systems redesign which eliminates the necessity for technological skills or even for the operations.   These problems can be at their worst when the operations are to be performed by the ultimate user.   (See below, under Installation by User.)

On-site Installation by Specialists   This is the assembly setup which is conducted at the user's premises to put the product in a state of readiness to operate plus installation "in place" at the site.   For some products the installation requires the services of specialists; for others the user performs his own installation.

On-site installations may require:

1. Special facilities to house the product (plus its auxiliary equipment), including means for controlling the environment.

2. Special tools and instruments.   All too often these are not as completely engineered as are the corresponding facilities in the factory due to the fact that many

---

[5] See, for example, Skolnik, S. S. J., A New Department of Defense Approach to Quality Control of Stored Material, *ASQC Convention Transactions, 1963*, pp. 219–229.   See also Mandelson, Joseph, Surveillance: Theory and Practice, *Industrial Quality Control*, June 1964, pp. 20–22, 35, and 36.   See also Cherkasky, Stanley M., Long-Term Storage and System Reliability, *Proceedings, 1970 Symposium on Reliability*, IEEE, pp. 120–127.

marketing and service departments have lagged behind the factories in use of formal quality planning and of quality specialists.

3. Special instructions.   These are increasingly needed for complex products. (There is still need for reliance on skilled installers to carry out these instructions and to meet those job problems which differ from one user location to another.)   The opportunities for errors and omissions are now so numerous that the instructions are needed for foolproofing as well as for information.

Installation by User   For the consumer (the general public) the approach must be quite different than for installation by specialists.   Now the needs are:

1. Eliminate, as far as possible, the need for installation operations to be performed by the user.

2. For the needed operations, simplify and foolproof them through designing the product that way.

3. Prepare clear, illustrated, step-by-step written instructions for the user.   A review of various failures in user installation (and operation)[6] soon discloses that the instructions had not been tested out on a panel of untrained users.   No amount of analysis or logical reasoning by company specialists can anticipate the user problems fully.   All too often the instructions are tested out only on those who are already familiar with the product.

Even with clear, well-illustrated instructions, there remain a distressing number of users who are seemingly unable to follow them.   Sometimes it is feasible to set up demonstrations to assist users generally.   Good feedback as to the types of errors made by users can become the source of further simplification of product.   However, the range of user sophistication and ignorance is so broad that it is simply not economic to provide against all degrees of user ignorance.

Usage   Once the product has been made operable, usage can begin provided the user understands how to use the product.   Here again, manufacturers have done a good deal to prepare an "Operating Manual" or other instruction for proper usage and maintenance.   These manuals are quite rudimentary for simple products and grow to elaborate handbooks for complex products.   An intermediate example is the "Owner's Manual" for owners of automobiles (see Section 42, under Field Service).

While installation and usage by specialists, (e.g., industrial equipment) tends to become rather professional, usage by consumers is characterized by much ignorance in several ways:

1. Failure to use available information.   For example, a vacuum cleaner rotary brush encounters an obstruction and stops rotating.   The Owner's Manual states clearly just what to do: remove the obstruction and reset the little red button.   The user doesn't know this because she threw the Owner's Manual away when she unpacked the cleaner, or because she kept the Owner's Manual, but has no idea where she put it, or because it doesn't occur to her to refer to the Manual, or because it is simpler to arrange to have the unit serviced.

2. Use under environments never contemplated.   For example, a householder finds his automobile door lock frozen on a subzero day.   He uses his wife's portable hair drier to thaw out the lock, and the drier fails.   (It was not designed to be operated in subzero temperatures).

3. Application of stresses never contemplated.   For example, a householder stands on his washing machine to paint the overhead ceiling.   A factory maintenance man uses a long piece of pipe to gain leverage in turning a valve and breaks the valve.

---

[6] See, for some examples, Juran, J. M., and F. M. Gryna, Jr., Quality Planning and Analysis, McGraw-Hill Book Company, New York, 1970, pp. 522 and 523.

4. Failure to maintain. Consumers are notoriously lax in following prescribed schedules for lubrication, cleaning, replacement of expendables, etc.

At the other end of the spectrum, users *improve* usage. Some men routinely tighten the screws of mechanical apparatus they buy. Some women routinely resew the critical seams of the garments they purchase. Do-it-yourself enthusiasts may perform their own maintenance even during the guarantee period.[7]

The most significant aspect of usage is the need for the manufacturer to find out *the actual usage* which takes place. As this knowledge becomes available—through field observation, through complaint analysis, etc.—the manufacturer has a wide variety of options for improving usage: consumer education, product redesign, systems redesign, etc.

QUALITY COMPLAINTS: GENERAL

As used in this Handbook, the term "complaint" is an assertion of quality deficiency. The complaint may be made by a user or a customer, e.g., a merchant. Associated with each complaint is some degree of dissatisfaction which has an impact on the manufacturer's income as well as on his costs. In consequence, the great majority of manufacturers take quality complaints quite seriously, although the methods in use for handling complaints leave much to be desired.

At the outset, it is necessary to distinguish clearly between complaints on quality and complaints on other matters. Many "complaints" arise from incorrect invoicing, late delivery, shipment of unordered goods, etc. In the discussion which follows, the term "complaints" refers to complaints about quality.

A complaint may be accompanied by a *claim* for damages resulting from the product deficiency. It may also be accompanied by *returns* of product asserted to be defective, in which case claims are made for credit and (often) for associated transportation costs. More usually, the user merely asks for service under the warranty.

Unreported Complaints Many quality failures are not reported as complaints, the principal reasons being:

1. Unimportance. Most failures on inexpensive products go unreported because the cost of complaining exceeds the value of the product. In like manner, minor defects on even costly products may go unreported; it may be easier to remedy the case at hand than to complain.

2. Assumption of "a fate, not a problem." In some situations, failures are tolerated on the assumption that nothing can be done about them. For example, a company engaged in maintaining building elevators encountered failures of resistors bought from a vendor. Instead of complaining, the maintenance crew had set up to assure that an inventory of replacement resistors would always be available. In another case, a manufacturer left a residue of welding material on a surface intended for mounting a motor. The customer's field crews sanded the defects down without complaining. (Cases such as these also are found within a single company in which one division "sells" to a sister division.)

When the users at the scene of action become shockproof, the situation can go on and on until someone else is exposed to the facts. A quality cost analysis will usually identify the chronic failures and dramatize the amounts at stake. The resulting intervention of managers looking for opportunities for cost reduction becomes the basis for challenging the premise that the problem is a fate.

3. The sheer distastefulness of it all. To most people, the whole atmosphere of

---

[7] They may also purchase supplemental components to solve problems created by inept designs. See the example of the kitchen sink, Section 14, under Discovering Marketing Opportunities.

complaint is disagreeable. The complainant questions whether he may be unduly critical in not tolerating a degree of imperfection. He hesitates to become embroiled in a potential argument with a merchant on the defensive. His prior experience with complaints may have included much futility.[8]

These unreported complaints constitute a menace to the manufacturer, since he is unaware of the real extent of failure. He may even be deluded into regarding the absence of complaints as evidence of user satisfaction.[9] To avoid this risk, companies must take other, positive steps to secure adequate knowledge of product performance.[10]

A further source of unreported failures is technological in origin, e.g., failures are not evident to the user because of circuit redundancy, undiscovered environmental causes, unit failures not causing system failures, etc.[11]

Avoidable Complaints These are extensive. On household appliances, about one-third of consumer service calls could be avoided if users followed the provisions of the Owner's Manual.[12] In some products, e.g., room air conditioners, this proportion has been over 50%.[13] When service shops return "defective" components for credit, these may be found, on retest, to include a high proportion of good product.

One appliance manufacturer conducted an experiment of providing customers with the Owner's Manual at the time of purchase and before delivery. Evidently readership and study went up, since subsequent "nuisance service calls" were only 11% against the usual 37%.[14]

The users "should" of course not make avoidable complaints. However, they do, and these complaints should be analyzed like any others to look for common patterns of causation. The remedies are not limited to educating and motivating the users, though this can help considerably. The remedies can include all the techniques used in factories for foolproofing operations against errors of negligence or inadvertence.[15]

Role of the Merchant The intermediate merchant chain strongly influences the volume and nature of quality complaints. In his warehouse and showrooms, the merchant may do a good job or a poor job in materials handling, stock rotation, and environmental control, e.g., maintaining temperature of frozen food cabinets. A policy of sale with privilege of return can result in return of products solely due to consumers changing their minds.[16] The merchant may shirk his responsibility un-

[8] It may be more accurate to say that the user complains—but to his friends rather than to the manufacturer. One study concluded that only one out of every three dissatisfied buyers of a washer or a television set complained to the manufacturer, although all may have complained to their friends. Further, it may well be that each appliance that fails soon after purchase results in adverse publicity that turns as many as ten potential customers against the brand. See Herbert E. Klein, Golden Key to Production Profits, *Dun's Review and Modern Industry,* April 1963, p. 50.

[9] For additional discussion, see Van Der Burg, Anthony R., Beware of the Non-Complaining Customer, *Quality,* 1965, no. 1, pp. 19–20.

[10] See, in this connection, Section 14, under Needs and Sources of Market Knowledge on Quality, *et seq.*

[11] Reynolds, L. G., Failure Detection in Parts, *Annual Technical Conference Transactions,* ASQC, 1965, pp. 270–276.

[12, 13] Private communication to J. M. Juran.

[14] Wood, Charles C., Whirlpool's Customer Assurance Program, *Industrial Quality Control,* June 1965, pp. 605–607.

[15] See Section 9, under Foolproofing the Process.

[16] In some cases this extends to sending multiple units to the consumer and letting her decide which to keep and which to return.

der the guarantee, forcing the user to complain direct to the manufacturer. The merchant may shut his eyes to consumer-caused damage, again inflating the manufacturer's returns and costs.[17]

It is equally likely that the merchant is following procedures that *intercept* various kinds of consumer problems, so that they do not reach the manufacturer. This can be caused by salespeople or returns clerks not following established procedures rigidly or by merchants intentionally setting a lower limit before complaints can be filed. Particularly in the case of small-value merchandise, less than half and sometimes as little as 20% of user complaints may reach the manufacturer.

Beyond the merchant's influence on consumer complaints, the merchant generates complaints of his own, e.g., shipping damage, shortages. These merchant's complaints require priority attention, since the merchant so strongly influences the manufacturer's income.

The methods of analysis for merchants' complaints have much in common with those employed for users' complaints. In addition, a look should be taken at the incidence of complaints of individual merchants when compared with merchants generally. For example, a manufacturer of ophthalmic lenses found that although claims for breakages and shortages were under 1% generally, they were consistently over 5% for some merchants. Since the products were shipped to all merchants from the same inventory, the suspicion arose that these merchants were deliberately inflating their claims. To investigate such cases (or even normal technological problems) on the customer's premises requires tact and persistence as well as technological know-how.

PROCESSING OF COMPLAINTS

In small companies involved in few field complaints, there is little need for a systematic approach to complaint analysis. As the number of complaints increases, the need for a systematic approach likewise increases. In some large companies, this lack of an organized approach has been a serious obstacle to sound customer relations.

Sources of Complaints: Registration Complaints flow in to the manufacturer from a wide variety of sources: consumers, merchants, service shops, industrial users, regulators,[18] consumer advocates, stockholders, etc. The channels of communication are also diverse: letters, telephone calls,[19] personal visits, newspaper accounts. The complaints may also be addressed to various departments in the company: Sales, Sales Service, Quality Control, any manager (especially the President), etc.

To avoid confusion amid this maze of communication, it is useful to set up a "registration desk" and to instruct all concerned to see that a copy of the complaint is routed to the desk, which will:

Register all complaints, no matter by whom received
Assign a serial number to permit tracing progress
Route the complaint to that department best qualified to conduct the analysis

---

[17] The manufacturer's own salesmen can also "marry the customer."

[18] For an example, see Section 47, under Transportation Service Quality: Airline Service Quality.

[19] A major chemicals manufacturer provides a special "hot line" telephone number for emergency calls dealing with exposure to or ingestion of hazardous products, transportation accidents, etc. The line is manned 24 hours a day, 7 days a week. The telephone number is imprinted on the bills of lading of the most hazardous products. (Private communication to R. S. Bingham, Jr.)

Assist in identifying complaint cases requiring fundamental study

Follow up to assure that adequate analyses and dispositions are made

Assist in summarized reporting

The registration desk may be located in any of several departments—Complaint Bureau, Quality Assurance, Sales Service—depending on the organization structure of the company.

Programs of Action   Each quality complaint poses several very different problems requiring several very different programs of action:

1. Satisfying the complainant. This program is oriented to the complainant and hence is needed in virtually every case of complaint.

2. Preventing a recurrence of isolated complaints. It is common practice to bring isolated complaints to the attention of those who are suspected of having caused them and to ask them what they plan to do to prevent a recurrence.

3. Identifying those "vital few" serious complaints which demand that studies be made in depth to discover the basic causes and to remedy those causes. Usually, the decisive question here is whether the complaint is isolated or widespread.

4. Analysis in depth to discover the basic causes of the complaint. This action is oriented to the product and is normally needed only in those vital few cases which are responsible for the bulk of the failures.

5. Further analysis to discover and apply remedies for the basic causes.

Satisfying the Complainant   Typically, the manufacturer must meet three needs of the complainant:

1. Restoration of service. The complainant is out of service and needs a repair or replacement. He wants this promptly, and often his need is acute.

2. Claim adjustment. Often the complainant is out of pocket due to the failure, and he wants compensation.

3. Restoration of goodwill. Even after service is restored and the claim is paid, there remains a residue of irritation due to annoyance and frustration. A proper complaint adjustment includes added effort to calm the ruffled feelings of the complainant so that he remains a customer and ally.

Execution of this program is invariably the responsibility of the Sales and Sales Service (also called "Customer Service" or just "Service") Departments. When substantial claims are involved, there is usually a review by the Financial Department or, in large companies, by a special Claims Department.

Generally, the Sales and Sales Service personnel accept the responsibilities associated with "satisfying the complainant." In contrast, it is a continuing problem to get these same men to accept responsibilities associated with the remaining programs of action. (See below.) As companies become proficient in processing complaints, they provide for a clear separation of responsibility for these various programs. A typical allocation is shown in Table 15-1.

In large companies the volume of complaints and claims may grow to an extent which requires preparation of a Sales Manual for Handling Complaints and Claims. The manual normally contains:

The company's statement of policy in handling complaints and claims.

Samples of complaint forms, properly filled out. (These forms differ greatly among companies because of differences in product, usage, etc.)

Detailed instructions for securing essential data, including explanations of *why* these data are needed.

Description of usual defects, usual causes of each, and related information for use in dealing with customers.

Statement of responsibility of salesman (or investigator) with respect to settling claims, recommending settlement, making repairs, classifying causes, etc.

Glossary of terms.
Code letters and numbers used in systematic classification.

TABLE 15-1   Responsibility for Quality Complaint Activities

Activity	Department often responsible
Satisfying the complainant	
Restore service	Service
Pay small claims	Sales
Pay large claims	Claims
Restore goodwill	Sales
Discovery and remedy of cause	
Determine whether isolated or widespread	Complaint
Determine cause	Complaint
Determine remedies	Various

Preventing the Recurrence of Isolated Complaints   Isolated complaints are usually the result of inadvertent mistakes, carelessness, errors in judgment, etc. The error has usually taken place weeks or even months before the failure takes place, so that the fundamental cause is difficult to establish, whether by a trained investigator from a central bureau or by a departmental supervisor.

Complaint registration centers often assign these isolated complaints direct to the suspect department for investigation, since the problem is similar to that of "fire-fighting" when a process sporadically goes out of control. The limitations in such assignments are that these departments usually lack training in how to conduct the necessary analyses. In addition, their objectivity is usually less than complete.[20]

Much can be done to aid these departmental investigations by training the key personnel in techniques of analysis. (See Section 17, under Production Foremen.) They can also be aided by getting them out to visit the field to see the conditions of use so as to understand better the influence of their work on product performance. An important alternative is to get the failed sample back to them to assist in the analysis as well as in motivation. It is also helpful to provide these departments with well-designed, simple forms which make clear the minimal information needed for an acceptable complaint investigation.

Identifying the "Vital Few"   This identification is based on a statistical analysis of the failures being encountered, along with managerial judgment about the seriousness, feasibility of remedy, etc.

A well-organized data system (see Basic Data Sources, below) makes it possible to identify those failures which are repetitive rather than isolated. The system can be programmed to list these "repeaters" in the order of frequency. In addition, where the system includes the costs of service, it can be programmed to list the failures in the order of costliness.

In many cases, a sampling of field failure data is quite adequate for identifying the vital few failures and for conducting the analyses.[21] Efforts to secure all failure data

[20] But they are sometimes impressively forthright. A supervisor in a container manufacturing factory came up with the following analysis: "A total of 1368 one-gallon cans got out to the customer with worm-holes in the bottoms. Foreman, Bodymaker Maintenance, Bodymaker Operator, Tester Maintenance and Quality Control were all asleep the night of October 17. No excuses." (Private communication to J. M. Juran.)

[21] See, for example, Randall, E. B., Jr., and John Mandel, A Statistical Comparison of the Wearing Characteristics of Two Types of Dollar Notes, *Materials Research & Standards*, January 1962, pp. 17–20.

may be self-defeating because too many sources are unreliable and hence reduce the quality of the data.[22]

In judging which failures to analyze in depth, managers give considerable weight to the frequency and cost of failures. In addition, consideration is given to effect on safety, environment pollution, customer goodwill, public relations, and still other factors. Once the vital few have been selected, further analysis in depth is conducted for each. This analysis is needed not to take care of today's complainant but to prevent future quality troubles and, thereby, future complaints.

Because the data processing is normally carried out in some common data center, the responsibility for identifying the most frequent and costly failures differs from that for satisfying the complainant. (See Table 15-1.)

Discovery of Causes   This analysis is undertaken for each of the vital few projects chosen by the managers for study in depth.[23] The detailed studies are usually made by full-time analysts working out of some analysis department, e.g., Complaint Bureau, Quality Control Engineering, Sales Service. The techniques employed are essentially those described in Section 16, but with some additions arising from the special conditions associated with field performance. (See, for example, Cumulative Returns Analysis, below.)

Some industries have taken the progressive step of establishing special instrumentation and data systems needed to correlate product and operating variables with field failures and even incipient field failures. Such correlations permit basic remedial action to be taken much earlier than they could be by waiting for a more extensive history of field failures.

For example, airlines increasingly use the airplane as an in-flight test bed for engines and other critical components. Special sensors are employed to measure, record, display, and analyze the conditions of these components so that failure tendencies can be detected at early stages, before they can mature into failures.[24]

Similarly, a large manufacturer of synthetic fibers has evolved a correlation of yarn breaks with causes. This he did through:

1. Equipping the process with scanners and working up a process history of each package of yarn (about 1,000 pounds).

2. Securing the history of the field performance of these packages, including capture of the broken yarns, through the field service personnel.

3. Correlation of customer results with process variables.

The resulting correlations have permitted remedial steps to be taken much earlier than they could have been by accumulating failure data in the absence of planned causation data.[25]

As data are acquired to permit correlation of observed symptoms with likely cause, it becomes feasible to prepare a syndrome[26] matrix. For example, vibration analysis of rotating machinery can be used to discover the amplitude, frequency, phase, regularity, direction, etc., of the machine vibrations. It then becomes possible to construct a matrix which simplifies the analysis for cause (Table 15-2).[27]

---

[22] See, for example, Bergere, Orland F., Organization and Operation of a Failure Analysis Laboratory, *ASQC Convention Transactions,* 1964, pp. 26–29; see also Maass, Richard A., Quality from the Top, *Quality Assurance,* May 1968, pp. 18–24.

[23] For some interesting cases plus useful associated discussion, see Flythe, T. Y., Field Complaint Investigation and Assessment, *Fifth Annual Quality Control Methods and Management Symposium, ASQC Philadelphia Section,* September 1960, pp. 71–77.

[24] For some discussion, see Cloud-9 QC, *Tooling & Production,* June 1970, pp. 65–67.

[25] Private communication to J. M. Juran.

[26] A "syndrome" is a collection of symptoms pointing to a unique cause.

[27] From Shea, Joseph M., Vibration Monitoring, *Mechanical Engineering,* October 1969, pp. 40–46.

TABLE 15-2 Syndrome Matrix

Cause	Amplitude	Frequency	Phase	Remarks
Unbalance	Proportional to unbalance Largest in radial direction	1 × rpm	Single reference mark	Most common cause of vibration.
Misalignment, couplings or bearings and bent shaft	Large in axial direction, 50% or more of radial vibration	1 × rpm usual, 2 & 3 × rpm sometimes	Single, double, or triple	Best found by appearance of large axial vibration. Use dial indicators or other method for positive diagnosis. If sleeve bearing machine and no coupling misalignment balance the rotor.
Bad bearings; anti-friction type	Unsteady — use velocity measurement if possible	Very high, several times rpm	Erratic	Bearing responsible most likely the one nearest point of largest high-frequency vibration.
Eccentric journals	Usually not large	1 × rpm	Single mark	If on gears, largest vibration in line with gear centers. If on motor or generator, vibration disappears when power is turned off. If on pump or blower, attempt to balance.
Bad gears or gear noise	Low — use velocity measure if possible	Very high, gear teeth times rpm	Erratic	
Mechanical looseness		2 × rpm	Two reference marks, Slightly erratic	Usually accompanied by unbalance and/or misalignment.
Bad drive belts	Erratic or pulsing	1, 2, 3 & 4 × rpm of belts	One or two depending on frequency Usually unsteady	Strobe light best tool to freeze faulty belt.
Electrical	Disappears when power is turned off	1 × rpm or 1 or 2 × synchronous frequency	Single or rotating double mark	If vibration amplitude drops off instantly when power is turned off, cause is electrical.
Aerodynamic hydraulic forces		1 × rpm or number of blades on fan or impeller × rpm		Rare as a cause of trouble except in cases of resonance.
Reciprocating forces		1, 2 & higher orders 1 × rpm		Inherent in reciprocating machines, can only be reduced by design changes or isolation.

Instrumentation for field failure analysis is increasingly specially designed. For example, to detect corrosion in pipelines, a recording instrument (similar in outward construction to the conventional "cleaning pig") is passed through the pipeline to collect data on corrosion and related evidences of deterioration.[28]   In like manner, noise analysis[29] and vibration analysis[30] can be used to identify incipient failures or to analyze matured failures.

In some industries the problems of failure analysis are so demanding that special failure analysis laboratories are created to do the job.   These laboratories are well equipped with special facilities and, in addition, have easy access to facilities of other laboratories.[31]   Manpower for these laboratories is specially selected and trained. Through experience, these specialists develop a high degree of sophistication in conducting failure analysis.

Discovery of Remedies   The Complaint Bureau or other investigative body can establish the cause of the product deficiency, but it cannot provide a remedy.   Instead, based on the analysis for cause, the matter is referred to that department which can remedy the known cause, e.g., Design, Manufacture.

However, good complaint investigation practice requires that the investigative bureau be a party to the tryout of the remedy to verify that the design change (or whatever) actually provides a "fix."   In addition, provision must be made for proper disposition of shop and field inventories which have been under "hold" pending the discovery of a remedy.

Trivial Many Failures   Under the Pareto principle,[32] a few types of failures account for the bulk of the field performance problems.   It is these "vital few" which deserve and usually receive the bulk of the investigative effort.   The more numerous types of failures account for a minority of the field performance problems.   These trivial many cases do not attain status on the priority list and hence receive little attention other than departmental investigations.   On purely economic grounds, this discrimination against the trivial many defects is fully warranted.   For most of them the cure costs more than the disease.   However, for some products and applications, the trivial many defects cannot be ignored.   The most obvious examples are defects which are critical to the safety of human beings.

On products like aircraft engines, the intensive efforts to eliminate recurring defects soon attains a state in which "the major contribution to unreliability is from a large number of different causes which individually occur very infrequently or after very long running lives."   For example, on one type of engine, after infant mortality causes had been dealt with, a third of the failure types occurred only after the first 500,000 hours of service experience.[33]

SIGNIFICANCE OF FIELD COMPLAINTS

Field complaints are a poor measure of product performance.   Some users complain despite the fact that the product is fit for use.   (See, for example, Avoidable Complaints, above.)   Other users do not complain, despite the fact that the product is

[28] Beaver, R. C., and Claron P. Mason, In-Place Detection of Pipeline Corrosion. *Mechanical Engineering,* June 1968, pp. 25–27.

[29] Bowen, Kenneth A., and Thomas S. Graham, Noise Analysis: A Maintenance Indicator, *Mechanical Engineering,* October 1967, pp. 31–33.

[30] Shea, Joseph M., *op. cit.*

[31] For a case description, see Pulliam, Thomas M., Analysis of Failures in Spacecraft and Aircraft Components, *Proceedings, 1969 Annual Symposium on Reliability,* IEEE, pp. 40–47.

[32] See Section 2 for a detailed discussion.

[33] Markham, B. G., "Reliability Assurance and the Concord Engines," SAE, paper no. 670316.

defective. (See Unreported Complaints, above.) In addition, there are some broad influences which affect entire classes of products and users:

1. The economic climate. Complaints fall in a seller's market and rise in a buyer's market, even for the same product.

2. The age, affluence, technological skills, etc., of users. For example, marketing of breakfast foods is done with a strong appeal to children, including offers of premiums and toys. The complaints on the premiums exceed, in number, the complaints on the food.[34] In the small world of the child, the premium occupies a large space.

3. The unit price of the product. (See Effect of Unit Price on Complaint Rate, below.)

Collectively, these influences make the complaint rate a poor index of product quality, especially on low-priced products. However, the complaint rate is an index of user dissatisfaction, and this alone is enough to require that the complaint rate be measured and watched closely.

Field Failures versus Factory Rejects   It is most illuminating to compare the list of principal field failures with the list of principal factory rejects. For example, in a company making rubber products, there was a drop in the sales of a major product type. The sales force blamed the drop on poor quality, whereupon the president ordered an improvement in quality. The factory complied by tightening up on quality standards, resulting in higher shop rejections (and higher costs) for dirt, discoloration, and other factory defects. Actually, the field problems were something else, as follows:

Principal reasons for field returns	Percent of all field returns	Principal factory defects	Percent of all factory rejections
Product has odor......	78	Dirt.........	46
Product crumbles	15	Discoloration..	22
Product tears in use....	6	Nicked......	12
All other...........	1	All other.....	20

The factory "improvement" had no significant effect on the real quality problems of the user.

In another example, in a line of ophthalmic products, the continuing check inspection of outgoing product regularly disclosed 65% to have minor appearance faults. However, there had never been a field return for these faults. Instead, 81% of the field returns were for breakage, for which the factory *had no systematic test.*

Comparison of the two lists can help to identify:
1. Lack of tests for potential field failures
2. Unjustified perfectionism in factory standards

Effect of Unit Price on the Complaint Rate   Complaint rates are strongly influenced by the unit price of the product. Table 15-3 lists some products in a wide range of unit prices along with the indicated ratio of complaints to serious defect.[35]

The data of Table 15-3 are shown graphically in Figure 15-1. It is obvious that for very low unit prices of product, the complaint rate can understate, by a couple of orders of magnitude, the extent of product inadequacy. In practice, companies find

---

[34] In one company, complaint rates on breakfast cereals run to about 1 per million packages compared to 4 per million packages for the premiums. (Consulting experience of J. M. Juran)

[35] In theory the ratio of complaints to failures can rise to over 1.0, since some users complain when there is nothing wrong with the product.

TABLE 15-3 Known Ratios of Complaints to Serious Defects for Some Products

Product	Approximate unit price	Ratio of complaints to serious defects
Razor blades	$ .05	Under 0.01
Shotgun shells	.10	About 0.02
Small articles of clothing.	5.00	About 0.10
Small electrical appliances . . .	30.00	About 0.25
Large electrical appliances . . .	200.00	About 0.50
Motor vehicles	2,500.00	About 0.75
Large engineered facilities . . .	50,000.00	1.00

it rather simple to evaluate outgoing quality of such products through check inspection.[36] The cost of this check inspection is comparatively low, since low unit prices usually are associated with a very large-volume production, permitting evaluation from a small fraction of the product.

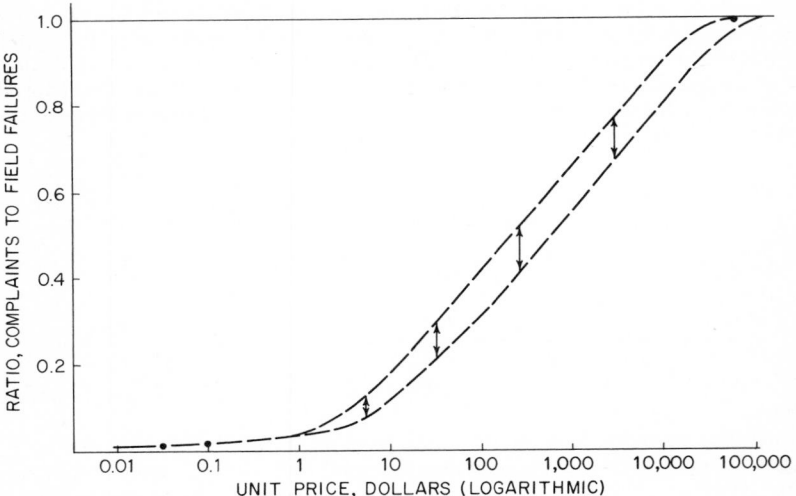

Fig. 15-1 Effect of unit price on complaint rate.

Effect of Time on the Complaint Rate For long-life products, time to first failure is a major variable determining the complaint rate. Products which "wear out," i.e., fail in "old age" after giving an acceptable service life, do not generate complaints. In contrast, "infant mortality" failures are highly complaint-prone, while the intermediate random failures attenuate in complaint rate as the extent of failure-free operation increases.[37]

The great importance of time to first failure requires that the product be "dated." The most useful date is the date when the product goes into active service. Where this cannot be secured conveniently, it may be approximated from the date of manufacture or from the date of sale. Through exercise of ingenuity, it is usually possible to secure one of these dates at nominal cost.

[36] See Section 21, under Product Auditing.

[37] For an elaboration of the concept of infant mortality, random failures, and wear-out, see Section 22, under Failure Patterns for Complex Products.

Date of manufacture is marked on the product through coded serial number, date stamps using invisible, indelible ink, decorative perforation combinations, colored thread combinations, etc. Cost of dating is minimized by doing the dating as part of some final processing operation. For many products, the day or week of manufacture is precise enough.

Date of sale is more difficult to record on 100% of the product, so the usual approach is to use sampling techniques. Where the product is serially numbered, arrangements can be worked out with selected dealers to record the date of sale on enough product to establish the interval between date of manufacture and date of sale. Alternatively, periodic inventories of dates of manufacture of goods on dealers' shelves will disclose this interval. Still another approach is to secure the data from the guarantee cards which are filled out by the dealer or user. (Sometimes the guarantee cards are serially numbered to include the coded date of manufacture.)

Date of actually going into service is normally available only for large units of product, in which case the date is secured from the attending service man or from the guarantee contract. For smaller units of product, resort must be had to sampling methods to establish the interval between date of sale and date of going into service.

Cumulative Complaint Analysis Dating the product makes possible an analysis of great value — the analysis of cumulative complaints (or cumulative returns, service charges, etc.) following the date of first usage. An example involving consumer products was an item of rubber clothing for which returns due to "tearing during usage" were a matter of concern. The prevailing design resulted in returns to an extent exemplified by the December 1951 product (Table 15-4). For the 20,000

TABLE 15-4   Data on Field Returns Since Date of Manufacture (December, 1951)

Month	Number of returns during current month	Cumulative number of returns	Cumulative percent of returns
December, 1951....	0	0	0.00
January, 1952......	8	8	0.02
February	9	17	0.08
March	4	21	0.10
April	8	29	0.14
May............	14	43	0.21
June	9	52	0.26
July............	15	67	0.33
August..........	12	79	0.39
September	14	93	0.46
October	27	120	0.60
November	17	137	0.68
December, 1952....	24	161	0.80
January, 1953......	22	183	0.91
February	24	207	1.03
March	9	216	1.08
April	33	249	1.24
May............	25	274	1.37
June	20	294	1.47
July............	21	315	1.57
August..........	16	331	1.65
September	9	340	1.70
October	21	361	1.80
November	7	367	1.83
December	23	390	1.95

units of product made and dated December 1951, the cumulative returns grew until two years later they had attained 1.95% of the original 20,000 units. When the data are charted, the resulting graph is as shown on Figure 15-2, on the curve labeled "old design."

During 1952 a new product was developed and rushed into production, the first month of full production being February 1953. The new design soon gave evidence of sharply higher rates of return, as can be seen in Figure 15-2, on the curve marked "new design."

Comparison of these two graphs is facilitated by changing the horizontal scale from calendar months to "months following manufacture." On such a scale, both graphs are moved so they begin at the origin (Figure 15-3). The graphs make dramatically clear that the new design was decidedly worse from the standpoint of tearing during usage and that this fact became evident within the first two months after full-scale manufacture.

An application of the same principle to large units of equipment is seen in Figure 15-4. These equipments, selling in the price range of $50,000 to $250,000 each, failed frequently in service and required repairs which were then paid for by the manufacturer under the guarantee he had made to the purchasers.

The engineers made design changes to eliminate the failures, but there was controversy over whether the redesigns solved the problems. The accountants summarized the repair charges monthly, but these summaries did not disclose trends with respect to individual designs.

The problem was solved through use of an analysis of cumulative repair charges. For each unit of equipment, information was available on installed price, date of in-

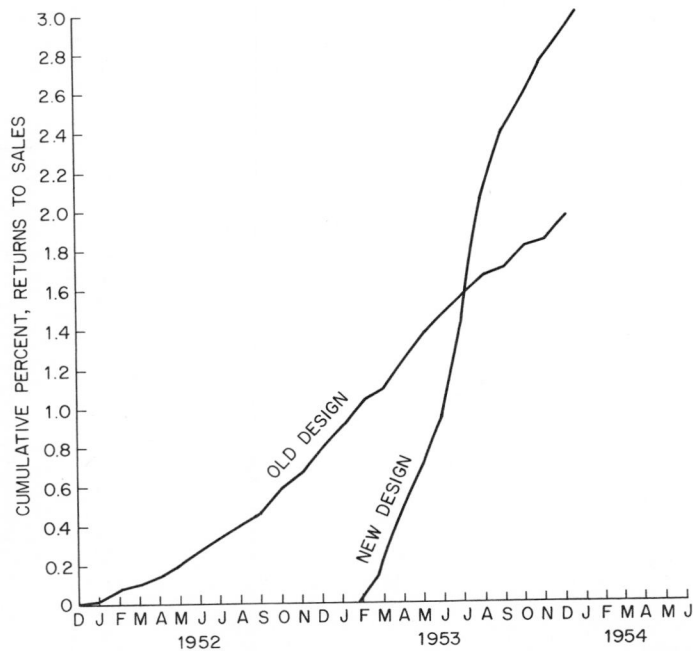

Fig. 15-2 Comparison of cumulative returns for two designs based on calendar dates of manufacture.

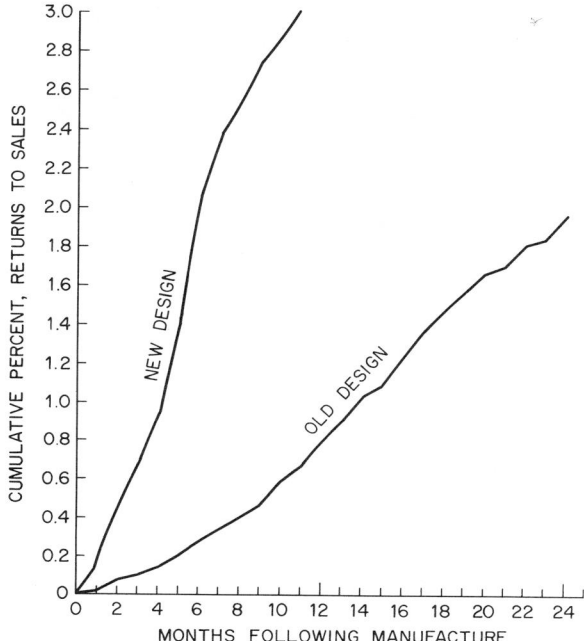

Fig. 15-3 Comparison of cumulative returns based on months following month of manufacture.

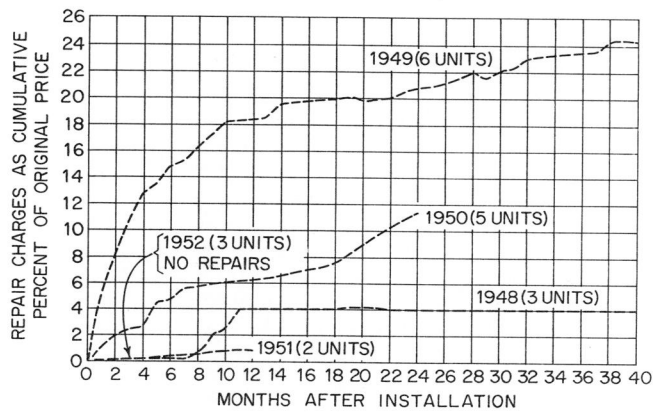

Fig. 15-4 Study of design effectiveness of large equipments through analysis of cumulative repair charges.

stallation, and repair charges month by month since date of installation. The analysis proceeded as follows:

1. For each *item* of equipment, the *cumulative* repair charges were computed, month by month, since date of installation.

2. For each *group* of equipments of identical design, the cumulative repair charges since date of installation were summed up for all members of that group, month by month, despite the fact that the equipment bore different installation dates.

3. These sums of monthly cumulative repair charges were then expressed as a percentage of the sum of the selling prices of the corresponding equipments.

4. The resulting percentages were then charted as shown in Figure 15-4.

Figure 15-4 shows that the 1948 design resulted in 4% cumulative repair charges within the first year of service, after which the equipment became stable.

The 1949 design is seen to have been a catastrophic failure problem, since cumulative repair charges soared to over 23% within three years. The subsequent effect of improving the designs is seen in the 1950 product and especially in the 1951 product, which was nearly trouble-free.

A valuable additional form of cumulative returns analysis is through use of nonarithmetic scales for charting. The Weibull chart is uncommonly flexible and useful for this purpose. It consists of a horizontal logarithmic scale of usage (time, cycles, miles, etc.), and a verticle probability scale of cumulative trouble (failures, returns, complaints). Cumulative failure data, when plotted as Weibull charts, emerge as curves which closely approximate straight lines. These curves permit ready analysis and extrapolation. (For elaboration, see Section 22, Figures 22-9 and 22-10, plus associated discussion.)

FIELD SERVICE [38]

In most companies the Marketing Department includes a specialized Customer Service Department to assist customers in various ways. Many of the activities of this special department are oriented to selling of the product and services, e.g., handling customer inquiries, conducting distribution services, providing marketing support for distributors and dealers. However, other customer service activities are closely bound up with field quality performance. It is these activities which are discussed below.

The principal quality-oriented activities carried out by the Customer Service organization include:

1. Operation of owned repair service centers and franchising of independent repair shops. (See below, under Repair Service Centers.)

2. Administration of service contracts with users. Some of these are under the original product guarantee; others are follow-on contracts.

The great increase in long-life consumer products has increased the importance of these contracts and has demanded that manufacturers understand with precision the costs involved. Most manufacturers do have adequate data as to their own costs during the guarantee period, but not as to the users' costs. In the case of the postguarantee period, few manufacturers have adequate knowledge either of product performance or of users' costs. In the future, manufacturers will find such information essential if they are to satisfy the demands of an increasingly sophisticated consumer. [39]

[38] In this Section, the work done to assist customers on field quality matters is called "field service." The department performing this work is usually called "Customer Service," "Sales Service," or just "Service."

[39] See, in this connection, Section 4, under Life Cycle Costing; see also Section 14, under Warranty of Quality.

3. Training of merchants, maintenance and repair personnel, users and others with respect to quality. Some of this training is done at the time of installation and check out. Much is done through training manuals. (See below, under Maintenance.) There are also exhibits, demonstrations, and still other forms.

4. Technical Assistance. This activity is carried on throughout all phases of customer relations. Even before sale, there is analysis of the user's application to judge product adequacy and to propose needed modification. Information is supplied on specifications, usage, and maintenance. In important cases, samples or prototypes may be prepared. Testing and laboratory services may be supplied.

As part of the sale, the Service Department may assist in installation, check out and startup. Additional assistance may include planning the supply of spare parts, the maintenance schedules, instrumentation, etc.

During usage, technical assistance is provided for analysis of performance failures. In addition, there may be monitoring, or preventive inspections. The extent of this technical assistance is determined partly by contract provisions and partly by the working relationship that has developed with the customer or user.

Repair Service Centers   These carry out repairs on failed products and serve as a base and source of supply for field representatives who carry out maintenance and repairs on the user's premises. The service centers may also sell spare parts to users for self-repair. In addition, they may sell replacements for unrepairable or obsolete products.

Repair centers for consumer products differ importantly in their ownership structure, and these differences result in wide variation in the extent and quality of repair work done. Table 15-5 lists the principal ownership forms, along with the type of work performed and the extent of support and audit by manufacturers.

During the 1960s, service shop performance in the United States came under severe criticism for several reasons: incompetent mechanics,[40] lack of prompt response, high prices, dishonesty.[41] Manufacturers and merchants have, to a degree, responded to these criticisms by:

1. Increasing the use of owned repair shops versus independents.[42]

2. Reducing the list of independent shops to whom they referred user complaints.[43]

3. Extending the use of franchise agreements and imposing standards for adequacy of repair work.

4. Extending the use of audit, in franchised shops as well as in owned shops.

5. Improving the inherent effectiveness of the service shop[44] through improved

---

[40] "Whether we like it or not, the much-discussed corporate image is often seen by consumers only in terms of the man who comes to service the products they own." Umbreit, George M., Rebuilding Customer Confidence and Satisfaction, *The Management Review*, March 1961, p. 20.

[41] See, for example, Report of the Task Force on Appliance Warranties and Service, U.S. Department of Commerce, Jan. 8, 1969. See also, Juran, J. M., Consumerism and Product Quality, *Quality Progress*, July 1970.

[42] Manufacturers who own their service shops make use of this fact in their advertising. The available evidence suggests that the question of who will provide the service is increasingly decisive in the user's decision to buy.

[43] One major manufacturer was reported to have reduced his number of service agents from 15,000 to 5,000. These survivors were franchised and subjected to audit by the manufacturer's field servicemen. A reduction of complaint letters by one-third was attributed to this revision. See Management in Practice, *American Management Association*, September 1970, p. 3.

[44] For a related commentary, see Levitt, Theodore, Production-Line Approach to Service, *Harvard Business Review*, September-October 1972, pp. 41–52. Although discussing service in the sense of the service industry rather than repairs, Levitt's point is that field operations

TABLE 15-5   Characteristics of Service Shops

Ownership	Repairs usually extend to	Repairs in or out of guarantee	Extent of support from manufacturer (training, technology, etc.)	Degree of organized audit by manufacturer
Manufacturer	A compatible line of products made by the owning manufacturer.	Mainly in guarantee	Extensive	Substantial
Dealer	Products sold by the dealer-owner.	Mainly in guarantee	Substantial	Moderate, (Receives audit from owning merchant.)
Franchised independent	A compatible line of products made by competing manufacturers, including the franchising manufacturer.	Both	Moderate	Moderate. Complaints may result in disenfranchisement.
Unfranchised independent	A compatible line of products made by competing manufacturers.	Mainly out of guarantee	Minor	None. Complaints may result in delisting from referral list.

engineering and management: design of superior facilities, diagnostic instruments, and repair tools; establishment of good systems for maintaining inventories of spare parts; training of mechanics and other personnel, etc.

6. Providing guarantees on service work. For example, a major automobile manufacturer has advertised a guarantee of his repair service for 90 days or 4,000 miles, whichever comes first.[45]

Establishment of owned repair centers cannot be justified unless minimal volumes of work are available to amortize the investment in facilities, etc. In consequence, manufacturers maintain such owned centers only in areas of extensive usage of their products. For other areas they must resort to use of dealer-owned centers or franchised independents. Beyond the economics of repair center operation is a deep-seated premise on the part of manufacturers and dealers that the repair shop is inherently unprofitable—that it exists primarily as an adjunct to marketing of the product. There is little doubt that it can assist (or hinder) marketing. However, there is much doubt about the rest of the premise. Many independent repair shops are quite profitable and could become more so through improved management.[46]

Service Center Organization. This usually consists of four main sections:

1. Customer Relations, which receives customer calls, issues work orders, maintains customer contact, issues the invoices, etc.

2. Field Operations, which consists of the crews who visit the customers' premises and perform the installations and repairs (or bring the product back to the shop for repair)

3. Shop Operations, which performs repairs on the service shop premises

4. Supply, which procures spare parts and equipment and provides these to the shop and field personnel

These departments are supported by staff specialists who also perform planning, analysis, and control activities.

Organization for Field Service Service Department activities interface extensively with other major departments involved in quality: Engineering, Sales, Quality Control, Manufacture. These interfaces, as well as the great influence of field service on company income, have resulted in the creation of agencies which can assist in meeting the needs of the user and in optimizing company performance. These agencies include:

1. *Committee on Customer Service.* The role of this committee is mainly to:

> Review field performance to identify problem areas
> Establish priorities for projects for improvement
> Coordinate improvement activity
> Review progress and stimulate action[47]

Choice of chairman and secretary varies depending on the roles of the departments in the basic organization plan of the company.

2. *Dealer Council.* In most industries the ultimate sale to the user is not by the manufacturer but by a dealer. In like manner, the repair service is carried out not

---

can become more effective if they are given the same type of technological and managerial attention as is given to the factory.

[45] *The New York Times*, Nov. 8, 1972, p. 27.

[46] An important possibility is the independent *chain* of repair centers. This may well provide the means of upgrading repair service to a level which is responsive to users' needs. For a discussion, see Juran, J. M., Consumerism and Product Quality, *Quality Progress,* July 1970. For a detailed discussion as applied to automobile dealers, see Vanderwicken, Peter. "How Sam Marshall Makes with His 'Deal,'" *Fortune,* December 1972, pp. 120–130.

[47] For a case discussion, see Cue, Dale A., Customer Complaints—Catastrophe or Cure, *Transactions 16th Midwest Quality Control Conference,* ASQC, October 1961, pp. 25–32.

by a shop owned by the manufacturer but by shops which are dealer-owned or independently owned. The fact that the dealers are so vital an extension of the manufacturer's organization has led to increasing use of a "Dealers' Council."

Under this form, dealers are chosen, on a rotating basis, to become members of the Council. Meetings are set up at which dealers and manufacturer bring up common problems for discussion. While the Council has no decision-making powers, the discussions can be influential in current lines of action and in modifying the terms of future contracts.

3. *The Ombudsman.* This Swedish term designates a public official to whom frustrated citizens can appeal for help in getting action out of a complex or unresponsive bureaucracy. In the early 1970s, manufacturers undertook to create ombudsmen to assist users in getting satisfaction from dealers, from service shops, and from the bureaucracy of the manufacturers' own departments.

Under the most usual arrangement, the manufacturer designates an official with a title such as Manager of Consumer Affairs to be the ombudsman. This appointment is announced in the press, along with the address of the ombudsman. In some cases, a toll-free telephone number is publicized so that the user may present his grievance by telephone, at no charge.[48]

Allocating Repair Labor Costs   The usual sales contract between manufacturers and dealers divides up the cost of making repairs for products still under warranty as follows:

The manufacturer pays for the cost of the failed parts (by supplying replacement parts).

The dealer pays the labor costs.[49]

Under such contracts, when high failure rates are encountered, the dealers' anticipated costs rise for reasons beyond his control. Not only does he protest these increased costs; he may discourage sale of the offending models to avoid the associated repair costs.[50]

A related and serious problem arises due to a competition between two very different marketing policies:

1. Sell a high-reliability product at a high initial price, but provide a strong warranty and a responsive service program through owned or franchised service shops.

2. Sell a low-reliability product at a low initial price but with a weak warranty which leaves it to the user to work out his service problems with the independent service shops.

In this competition, policy (1) suffers from the long-standing emphasis which consumers have given to initial price. When efforts are made to bring these prices in line with those offered by policy (2), the service costs under policy (1) can be enough to make the business unprofitable. Some very large manufacturers have abandoned entire product lines of small appliances because of inability to compete successfully with manufacturers and merchants who emphasize low initial prices and who compensate themselves by putting on the user the burden of cost of service on failed products.[51]

---

[48] The ombudsman may also be created by a trade association. See, for example, Sec. 43, under Prognosis.

[49] This is by no means universal. Many contracts provide for the dealer to charge the labor costs back to the manufacturer.

[50] For an extensive discussion, see Who Should Pay for Warranty Labor? *Domestic Engineering,* April 1964, pp. 88–95; also May 1964, pp. 75–120.

[51] For some cases, see Weeding Out the Losers, *Business Week,* March 18, 1972, pp. 22–23.

Maintenance   The term "maintenance" is generally synonymous with "keeping products in service." It includes:

Scheduled inspections, tests, and overhauls
Scheduled servicing, e.g., cleaning, lubrication, replacement of consumables
Unscheduled servicing, i.e., diagnosis of failures, and repairs to remedy the failures
Support activities such as provision of test and repair equipment, plus supply of replacement parts
Preparation of documents needed for analysis and reporting

Scheduled Inspection and Test.   These scheduled activities are planned by Service and Quality Control specialists. The planned approach is similar to that discussed in Section 12, under Inspection Planning.

The intervals between test are usually arbitrary at the outset. As data are collected, the findings can be used to schedule more scientifically. For example, in testing watt-hour meters in service, it had been the practice to test each of the 440,000 meters on an eight-year schedule. Analysis of the test data based on age of the meters and on conditions of usage showed the possibility of drastic reductions in test schedule.[52]

Scheduled Servicing.   This is also planned by specialists as to timetable and as to work to be performed. It includes replacement of components either on a planned basis or as dictated by the findings of the scheduled inspections. In addition, it includes cleaning, adjustment, lubrication, replacement of filters, etc. It may include a check-out of operation following the servicing. An extensive form of scheduled servicing is the "overhaul" which requires removing the unit from service while major scheduled servicing is performed (or scheduling the overhaul during some shutdown).

As in scheduled inspections, the data derived from scheduled servicing permit revisions of the servicing cycle. For example, commercial airlines, despite rigorous safety requirements, have been quite successful in lengthening their servicing intervals through improved instrumentation, careful recording of findings during inspection and servicing, careful observation and recording of product performance, and analysis of the resulting data.[53, 54]

Unscheduled Servicing.   This category includes diagnosis and repair of the numerous failures which put users out of service and for which they demand prompt restoration.

The nature of unscheduled servicing requires that planning be delegated largely to the technicians and supervision at the site or in the repair shops. Such delegation requires, in turn, that these men be provided with:

Test equipment and instruments which permit diagnosis[55] for locating the trouble

---

For added discussion, see Section 14, under Warranty of Quality. See also Section 4, under Life Cycle Costing.

[52] Dwon, Larry, and J. A. Morris, Statistical Approaches to Selecting Domestic Meters for Test, *AIEE Transactions,* Paper 59-167, 1959. See also, Roberts, S. W., Scheduling of Pole Line Inspections, *Bell System Technical Journal,* November 1962, pp. 1737–1758, in which the schedule is graduated to geographical areas and to type of telephone service rendered.

[53] See, for example, Ahlborg, Kurt, and Stephen Crabbe, On Condition Maintenance Programs, *Proceedings 1970 Annual Symposium on Reliability,* IEEE, pp. 300–307.

[54] In the experience of the Editor (Juran), no programs of maintenance are more effective than those of the commercial airlines.

[55] For a useful discussion of the nature of diagnosis, see de Corlieu, J., Maintainability Diagnosis Techniques, *Proceedings, 1966 Annual Symposium on Reliability,* IEEE, pp. 133–142.

Facilities and tools for conducting repairs
Training in how to do all this

Training.   The principles of training discussed in Section 17 are fully applicable to the training of maintenance personnel and are in fact applied in large manufacturing companies.   However, the numerous dealer-owned service centers, and especially the independents, are so small that they seldom make provision for formal training.   Instead, the approach is to *(a)* hire trained technicians or *(b)* perform on-the-job training.

Manufacturers have gone far to help these small service centers by establishing training courses which the technicians may attend.   Even more widespread is the preparation of special service manuals[56] for use by service centers.   These manuals provide well-designed aids for diagnosis and repair, including:

Exploded views and diagrams to show the structure of the product
Lists of parts used for various products
Color codes for wiring and components to simplify diagnosis and repair
Detailed instructions for repair, i.e., sequence of operations, tools to be used, etc.
Multinational companies prepare these manuals in various languages.

Provision of Test and Repair Equipment.   To an important degree, the test and repair facilities used in the factory have application to the service centers.   Much has been done to take advantage of this fact, though some redesign is needed to adapt the equipments to the environments of the service center.

In addition, the service centers require added equipment to take care of failure modes seldom encountered in the factory (customer misapplication, wear out, catastrophic handling damage, etc.).   Design of this supplemental equipment has been a weak element in service center management.   The problem has not been that the manufacturer lacks the technological capacity to design such equipments.   The designers are capable enough, as is evidenced by the equipment they provide for the factories.   Instead, the problem is that the service centers have not received the priorities which would enable them to draw on the time of these capable designers.   However, increasing costs of field repairs are bringing increased attention to this need.

Provision of Spare Parts.   At the root this is a conventional problem of designing and carrying out a program of inventory control.   However, the limitations inherent in the management of small shops, plus the maddening lack of standardization, have greatly complicated the problem.

This same lack of standardization creates further problems for the user.   When a manufacturer goes out of business or drops a product line, his customers are left with the products and a doubtful supply of spare parts in the distribution pipelines.   Similarly, products which have unusually long lives may be without spare parts when they do fail unless the manufacturer provides continuity of responsibility for spare parts through another organization.

Service centers can minimize these problems for themselves and their customers by careful administration of their systems of inventory control.   However, keeping adequate records of usage, and revising the order points accordingly, requires a level of dedicated management which many service centers do not attain.

Design for Maintainability.   Increasingly, the original systems and product designs are called on to meet quantified parameters for maintainability, such as mean time to repair.   (See Section 8, under Maintainability in New-Product Design.)   Some contractual requirements include development of repair techniques under

---

[56] The service manual is not to be confused with the "Owners Manual," for which the scope and treatment are different.   See Installation and Usage, above.

stated restraints.   The resulting programs set up standards for various subdivisions of mean time to repair, e.g., removal, remedy, replacement, verification test, etc.[57]

Numerous concepts are available to designers to improve maintainability:

Modular designs to permit ready plug-in repairs, e.g., printed circuit boards. Some of the modular designs permit even the users to plug in replacement assemblies.

Design for easy access to repair, e.g., swing-out or slide-out circuitry and units.

Provision of sockets which permit diagnostic equipment to make instant hookups for comprehensive checkout to locate causes of failures.

Designs which permit scheduled testing to be conducted without service interruption.

Of course, the most fundamental improvement is through failure-free designs. This will undoubtedly accelerate as the concept of life cycle costing gains headway.

Maintenance Management.   Techniques for managing the foregoing activities have much in common with those used for the Job Shop (see Section 45).   In addition, since maintenance is a "service" rather than "manufacture," the element of time is a vital ingredient of quality.[58]

It is most important that service centers acquire the habit of measuring and recording time: time of responding to users' requests for service, time to conduct repairs, time to return the user to his normal state.   These measures, when analyzed, serve multiple purposes:

Establishment of standards for service
Identification of opportunities to improve service
Establishment of standards for internal cost control[59]

Quality control of repair work (assuring that repair work is well done) is a troublesome problem for the service center.   The great majority of shops are very small, and the tradition has been self-inspection by the mechanic with only sporadic review by the service manager.   In very critical operations, e.g., aircraft maintenance, there has been much debate on whether repairs should be inspected by a separate inspector.   A likely solution to this perplexing problem is the concept of self-inspection for qualified repairmen plus an "audit of decisions" as discussed in Section 11, under Product Acceptance by Operators.

FIELD PERFORMANCE MEASURES

Measures of field performance are needed to enable managers to understand actual levels of performance, observe trends in progress, identify opportunities for improvement, and assure that improvement efforts are properly directed.   To secure such information, companies do the following:

Organize a system for collecting the basic performance data
Summarize and analyze the resulting data
Provide managers with reports suitable for study and action

Application of this conventional approach to field performance is discussed below.

[57] See, for example, Grueninger, Raymond A., An Approach to Field Repair of Avionics Computers, *Proceedings, Annual Symposium on Reliability,* IEEE, 1970, pp. 292–299.

[58] For elaboration, see Section 47, under Time as a Service Parameter.

[59] See, for example, Wilkinson, John J. How to Manage Maintenance, *Harvard Business Review,* March–April 1968, pp. 100–111.

Basic Data Sources[60]   There are several of these, and they serve multiple, overlapping purposes:

The Service Report.   This fundamental document is originated for each service call made.   It identifies the customer and his dealer.   It identifies the product by model number, serial number, date purchased, date of repair.   It records the user's asserted problem.   In addition, it provides for the service man to record:

  Description of actual trouble
  Action taken to repair the trouble
  List of parts used to make the repair
  Hours of labor required for repair

The parts used and the labor hours consumed are then priced out.   These prices are likewise recorded on the service report.

Beyond these minimal data, service reports may provide additional information: travel time and expense; measure of usage of the product[61] (e.g., odometer reading of vehicles).   In some companies, specially designed service reports are used for scheduled inspections, scheduled maintenance, overhaul, etc.   In addition, variations in the technology of the product result in variations in service report forms, especially among different industries.

Complaint Analysis Report.   This report is prepared not by service employees but by specialists working out of some Analysis Department, e.g., Reliability Engineering.   It is used to report the results of analysis of field complaints, returns, and claims.   It includes:

  Precise description of symptoms
  Results of field investigation and of laboratory retesting
  Findings on teardown and detailed study
  Conclusions as to cause and effect of failure
  Recommendations for remedial action
  Estimate of amount and value of material involved and recommendations for disposition
  Estimate of costs associated with the condition complained about

The Operations Log.   This is the diary maintained, by industrial and similar users, of the conditions of operation.   The kinds of events to be recorded in the log will vary depending on the nature of the product and should be agreed on in advance, through collaboration among the key departments involved.   Normally the log includes records of significant phenomena observed, stoppages encountered, action taken to restore operations, and proposals for improvement.   In operations critical to human safety (e.g., airline piloting), these logs are usually required by law.

In large installations there may be one or more field representatives stationed full-time at the user's facility to provide assistance and to do the failure reporting. Such representatives can be of aid in securing operating log data.

Other Data Sources.   Some companies properly feel that service reports and complaint reports do not tell the whole story, i.e., too many things go unreported. To secure this supplemental information, a variety of sources is available.

1. User return cards.   These are included with the product.   They provide checklists which the user can mark to record the state of the packaging, the appearance,

---

[60] See also Section 8, under Maintainability Data Systems.

[61] It is increasingly the practice to measure usage directly rather than by elapsed calendar time.   Where operations can be measured in cycles, counters are provided, e.g., number of copies on a copying machine.   For power-operated apparatus, a recording clock or coulometer can be wired into the power circuit.

and the initial performance of the product. Usually the card is addressed (postage prepaid) to the Quality Control department, which summarizes and analyzes the comments.

2. Telephone interviews of buyers, based on random sampling.

3. Installation of (consumer) products into employees' (and other volunteers') homes to secure operation logs and full reports of problems encountered.[62]

4. Sampling review of service calls to determine adequacy of service performed.

5. Results of tests and studies made by independent laboratories. For example, the Swedish Motor Vehicle Inspection Company (AB Svensk Bilprovning) is the authorized agency which performs the annual compulsory safety test on vehicles. Its summarized findings are published, by model number, in an annual report.[63]

Precision in Recording. The summaries, analyses, and reports cannot be accurate unless the basic records are accurate. To aid in securing accurate recording, companies may:

Prepare a glossary to standardize the terms used, so that all service men are provided with a common terminology for describing symptoms, parts, tests, causes, remedies, etc.

Establish code numbers which are keyed to standardized terms, to permit precise, easy recording of information for which the codes are descriptive. (See, for example, Section 43, Figure 43-5)

Establish aids to recording (e.g., squares to be checked) to minimize the paper work burden on the service personnel.

Provide training in the proper use of the recording system and in the appreciation of the need for precise recording.

Provide an audit of the accuracy of failure reports to identify coding and other documentation error patterns.

Use of Sampling. Data needed for analysis and reporting are of a higher quality than data needed for satisfying users or for remedying isolated troubles. This higher quality of data also means greater costs in data recording. When the amount of data is very great, this added cost of high-quality data also becomes great. Aside from having to consider these greater costs, some manufacturers have concluded that it is hopeless to try to secure high-quality data from thousands of dealers and service shops.[64]

One solution has been to use sampling. The manufacturers (1) select key dealers representing good geographical distribution and (2) use the "vital few" concept, e.g., 2% of the dealers may account for 15% of the sales, which is still a generous sample. These key dealers are visited by a team of specialists, who set up the data plan, train the personnel, arrange special compensation, and then audit for precision.[65] (For some purposes, sampling of smaller dealers may also be necessary.)

Basic Data Analyses The data derived from the various sources can be used in their raw form to aid in remedy of isolated failures and to satisfy complainants. For most other purposes, the data must undergo processing. These "other purposes" have so much in common among many companies that there has been much stan-

[62] For added discussion, see Wood, Charles C., Whirlpool's Customer Assurance Program, *Industrial Quality Control,* June 1965, pp. 605–607.

[63] AB Svensk Bilprovning, Vallingby, Sweden.

[64] In some companies, stubborn insistence on acquiring all the data has led the system to collapse under its own weight; i.e., the time required to deal with indifferent dealers, to track down errors, and to deal with the sheer volume has resulted in preoccupation with the system while the managers get no reports.

[65] For a discussion of this principle, see Gretzinger, J. R., Buick's Reliability Program, *Industrial Quality Control,* March 1965, pp. 449–453.

dardization of the end results of data processing and thereby of techniques of data processing.

Defect Matrixes. An example of this form is a table in which the horizontal lines list the principal defect types and the vertical columns list the product types. The cognizant managers and specialists are able to recognize significance in the patterns which emerge, e.g., defects which are restricted to only certain product types or which affect all product types.[66]

Listing in Order of Importance. This widely used data processing technique involves sorting and listing the basic data so that the resulting list shows the data items in their order of importance. Typically, the listing appears in such forms as:

Failure rate by defect type
Unit repair cost by product type
Total repair cost by product type
Complaint rate by customer

Often these listings include columns for cumulative totals of all elements under study.

A principal purpose of these listings is to permit focus on the "vital few" (the Pareto principle). When managers are provided with short lists of major problems, they are able, through their experience and authority, to assist in expediting solutions to these problems.

Cost Analyses. "External failures" is a standard category of "quality costs" (see Section 5). Most data systems provide for evaluating these costs, using conventional subcategories such as repair labor, parts and supplies, travel costs, etc. These cost analyses are of special interest to the Quality Control Department in its role of using the quality cost figures to justify quality improvement programs.

There are additional cost data which are of special interest to the Service Department in its role of running an effective service operation, i.e., productivity of service shops, frequency of return calls, repair costs versus budget.[67]

Spare Parts Usage. Two methods of analysis are available:

1. The record of actual usage on products, as derived from the service reports. These records reflect the real consumption of these parts, but only if the service reports are accurate and complete. Because of the problems of assuring this completeness and accuracy, the usage derived from this source includes a large potential error.

2. The sale of spare parts to the distribution chain. This is also potentially unreliable, and to a greater degree, due to (a) use of spare parts made by competitors' manufacturing sources and (b) the fact that a sale to the distribution chain is not usage — it is a transfer of inventory from one part of the chain to another.

Effect of Time Lag. Differences between usage dates, dates of sale, and dates of manufacture can create important errors in judging trends and in correlating cause (design and manufacturing variables) with effect (failure during usage).

For industrial apparatus, where dates of installation can usually be obtained, the analysis can be structured to take these dates into account. See, for example, Figure 15-4, above, and associated discussion.

For consumer products, a common measure of failure rate is failures per 1,000 units under warranty. To measure this rate accurately requires that the numerator

---

[66] See Tables 2-3, 16-2a, and 18-1 and Figure 46-1, with associated discussion. See also, Powell, Richard F., Analyzing and Interpreting Field Failure Data, *Proceedings 1970 Annual Symposium on Reliability,* IEEE, pp. 94–100.

[67] For elaboration, see Looney, James J., An Automated System for Processing Field Service Data, *Industrial Quality Control,* May 1967, pp. 543–548.

and denominator both be related to the identical product. However, the time lag between date of manufacture and date of usage is substantial. When reporting delays are added, the total time lag can be astonishingly high for some products. One evaluation[68] of the time lag between date of manufacture and receipt of failure reports showed an average interval of 6 to 32 weeks, made up as follows:

Status	Time elapsed (weeks)	
	During this state	Cumulative
In manufacturer's inventory	1–12	1–12
In transit to dealer	1–2	2–14
In dealer inventory.	1–8	3–22
In use	1–4	4–26
Undergoing service.	1–3	5–29
Being reported.	1–3	6–32

These delays distort the reported failure rate when based purely on date of manufacture or date of sale. For a new model, the reports will, at the outset, greatly understate the failure rates, since the shipments are substantial whereas the reported failures are few due to the time lag. In contrast, when the failure reports do come in, weeks or months later, the reported rate will exaggerate the actual failure rate of the units. To eliminate these exaggerations, practitioners have evolved methods for correcting failure rate data based on quantifying the time lag.[69]

A related problem is the movement of sold products into and out of the guarantee period. Where the measure of failures is based on failure rate per 1,000 units under warranty, the conventional approach is to use (for one-year warranties) the cumulative number of failures for the last 12 months divided by the cumulative number of units invoiced for the last 12 months. The resulting failure rates must be multiplied by a correction factor until the product has been on the market for an interval equal to twice the guarantee period. (See Section 43, Table 43-5 and associated discussion, for the method involved and the correction factors used.)[70]

Data Processing. Converting the basic data into usable form for managers follows conventional methods. For small amounts of data, manual processing is used (see Section 19); for great amounts, electronic data processing (see Section 20). For intermediate amounts of data, edge-punched cards provide a useful alternative.[71]

Executive Reports on Field Performance   Upper managers are quite receptive to such reports in view of the known relationship of field performance to income as well as to cost. Lacking such reports, these managers are seriously handicapped in their ability to contribute to control and improvement of field performance. In addition, in the absence of regular reports, upper managers can be stampeded by individual, isolated cases, so that they misdirect the available resources of the company.

The general concept of executive reports on quality is discussed in Section 21, under Executive Reports on Quality. The application of the concept to field performance is discussed below.

Control Subjects and Units of Measure. For field performance, the most widely used control subjects and units of measure are those shown in Table 15-6.

[68] Powell, Richard F., *op.cit.*

[69] Powell, Richard F., *op.cit.*

[70] For another approach, see Robertson, James A., Analyzing Field Failure, *Quality Progress,* January 1969, pp. 12–13.

[71] For a case example, see Miller, Robert S., Quality Control as a Service Department Responsibility, *Industrial Quality Control,* February 1962, pp. 22–24.

TABLE 15-6   Control Subjects and Units of Measure for Field Performance

Control Subject	Units of Measure in Use
Complaints	Total number of complaints
	Number of complaints per $1 million of sales
	Number of complaints per million units of product
	Value of material under complaint per $100 of sales for such products
Returns	Value of material returned per $100 of sales
Claims	Cost of claims paid
	Cost of claims per $1 million of sales
Failures	Mean time between failures (MTBF)
	Mean usage between failures, e.g., cycles, miles
	Mean time between repair calls
	Failures per 1,000 units under warranty
Maintainability	Mean time to repair (MTTR)
	Mean downtime
Service cost	Ratio of maintenance hours to operating hours
	Repair cost per unit under warranty
	Cost per service call

Beyond the control subjects listed in Table 15-6, the executive reports may include:

Breakdown of important control subjects by subcategories such as product type, department responsible, etc.

Lists of vital few problems and status of solution

Additional control subjects or added detail demanded by the special nature of the company's product[72]

A composite index which reflects the collective effect of a variety of control subjects

Status information about the Complaint Bureau (or Service Department, etc.): complaints received, closed, on hand; time required to close complaints; important unresolved cases in order of age; productivity of complaint analysis

Failures as Seen by the User.   The user's view of failures and of failure consequences differs remarkably from that of the manufacturer[73] in several respects:

1. The user is concerned with the entire service life of the product, whereas the manufacturer's data concentrate on the warranty period.[74]

2. The user faces various costs which are directly caused by failures but which are not compensated by the guarantee, e.g., downtime of machinery, idleness of machine operators.

3. The user also faces added costs which are an indirect result of failures, e.g., loss of production; failure to meet his customers' delivery dates.

Collectively these costs are known to be enormous.   Studies of life cycle costs for consumer products show that merely the costs resulting directly from failures exceed, generally, the original purchase price of the product (see Section 4, under Life Cycle Costing).

For industrial and especially for military products, the life cycle costs are even

[72] See, for example, Retterer, B. L., and R. L. McLaughlin, Maintainability Prediction and Measurement, *Industrial Quality Control,* December 1963, pp. 16–20 (numerous indexes for maintainability).

[73] For a more extensive discussion, see Section 4, under Contrast in Views: User and Manufacturer.

[74] In those cases where the user gives an annual service contract to the manufacturer beyond the guarantee period, the stage is set for collection of good data.

higher.   Air Force and Navy studies have indicated that *annual* maintenance costs may readily exceed the original equipment cost.[75, 76]

The manufacturer who lacks knowledge of these added burdens of the user incurs no immediate costs thereby.   However, he may unwittingly be losing sales.   In addition, he remains unaware of the business opportunities presented by quantified knowledge of these facts.   (See Section 4, under Contrast in Views: User and Manufacturer.)

Availability.   Although quality specialists have emphasized MTBF, failure rates, and similar measures as indexes of field performance, many users emphasize availability, i.e., the extent to which the product provides service when the user needs it. Availability as a measure is inversely related to downtime, which in processes demanding continuous operation, can be the biggest single source of user quality costs.[77]

RELATIONSHIPS: SERVICE AND QUALITY CONTROL

Once the product has gone into use, the two organizations most intensively engaged in dealing with field quality performance are Service and Quality Control.[78]   The allocation of activities varies but mainly is along the following lines:

Service is concerned primarily with providing *current* satisfaction to the user: getting his product installed and in operation, responding to his service calls, restoring service and otherwise "satisfying the complainant."

Quality Control is concerned primarily with providing *future* satisfaction to the user by analyzing quality data, identifying major quality problems, analyzing to discover the cause of these problems, taking up with the cognizant managers the means of providing remedies for these causes.

Differences in company organization structure and differences in personalities of the managers involved may result in one or the other of these departments dominating the activities of field quality performance.   However, there is no real need for dominance by either department.   As to some activities, the roles are quite different and even independent.   As to other activities, the roles are so intertwined that full collaboration is a must.

Periodically, a manager of a Service or a Quality Control Department publishes assertions to the effect that his department plays the dominant role in field quality performance in his company (or that his department *should* play the dominant role). In many cases such assertions may create misunderstandings which are detrimental to good results.   The critical need is to agree first on what the essential activities required to take care of the user are, both now and in the future.   Having agreed on what these essential activities are, the remaining need is to agree on how to perform these in a way which makes the best use of the available capabilities of both departments.

[75] Dertinger, E. F., Funding Reliability Programs, *Proceedings 9th Symposium on Reliability,* IEEE, 1963, pp. 16–32.

[76] For some case examples of dramatic effects of failures on the Navy Fleet Air Arm's safety and costs, see Stroop, Paul D., Quality Control Impact on Military Hardware, *Industrial Quality Control,* December 1964, pp. 298–304.

[77] For some case examples of use of availability, see LaVallee, R. S., A Field Study of the Maintainability and Reliability of an Interceptor Squadron, *IRE Transactions on Reliability and Quality Control,* RQC-11, No. 3, October 1962, pp. 28–34.   See also Section 8, Fig. 8-11*b*, and associated discussion.

[78] This is not universally the case.   In some companies the Complaint Bureau has much autonomy.   In others, a department known as Field Engineering may be extensively involved in installation, field repair, overhaul, customer training.   Such organization forms conduct activities which are more usually assigned to departments called Service or Quality Control.

Section **16**

Quality Improvement[1]

J. M. JURAN

IMPROVEMENT IN GENERAL

"Improvement" as used in this Section, is the attainment of a new level of performance that is superior to any previous level.[2] This superiority is attained by applying the breakthrough concept to problems of quality.

[1] For the Second Edition, this Section was prepared by L. A. Seder. Some of the techniques described in this Section were originally developed by Mr. Seder.

[2] This superiority differs from that attained by troubleshooting or by planning. See Section 2, under The Nature of Improvement.

As discussed in Section 2, under The Universal Sequence for Breakthrough, there is an invariable sequence of steps through which breakthrough is achieved.[3]   Applied to problems of improving quality,[4] this sequence may be restated as:

Proving the need for a program
Identifying the major projects; use of the Pareto principle
Securing management approval
Organizing for improvement; creation of the steering arm and diagnostic arm
Diagnosis to discover causes and remedies
Overcoming cultural resistance to technological change
Making remedies effective
Providing controls to hold the gains

The foregoing sequence becomes the outline on which the discussion of this Section is structured.[5]

TABLE 16-1   Census of Company Practices in Quality Improvement (United States)

(Do not sign your name)

In my company the effectiveness in quality improvement is about as follows:

| | Company effectiveness is: | | |
Elements of quality improvement	Strong	Adequate	Weak
Atmosphere favorable for breakthrough activity (attitude)	50	36	14
Identification of projects for improvement; proof of the need	30	48	22
Assignment of clear priorities for projects	22	41	37
Creation of steering arm	18	52	30
Creation of diagnostic arm	17	51	32
Pareto analysis	18	44	38
Use of controllability concept	13	49	38
Diagnostic competence	26	50	24
Overcoming cultural resistance to technological change	14	48	38
Determination to take action	35	51	14
Establishment of controls to hold gains at the new level	23	53	24

The effectiveness of companies in adhering to this sequence is decidedly uneven. Table 16-1 shows the results of censuses taken during the author's courses on Management of Quality Control.   The responses, from managers in hundreds of companies, are shown as percentages of all responses.

[3] For a detailed discussion of the universal sequence for breakthrough, see Juran, J. M., "Managerial Breakthrough," McGraw-Hill Book Company, New York, 1964, Chapters 2 through 11.
[4] Quality Improvement may be undertaken in any of the performance aspects associated with the quality function: reliability, shop scrap and rework, transportation damage, service effectiveness, inspection and test, storage, etc.
[5] While the foregoing activities are essential steps in launching and executing a successful *program* of quality improvement, a successful attack on specific, individual projects is often feasible by making use of a limited part of the sequence.

PROOF OF THE NEED FOR A PROGRAM

The word "program" as used here means an authorized ("legitimate"), organized mobilization of the company's resources for the purpose of improving quality. Creating such programs requires first that the upper managers become convinced that there is a real problem of sufficient size to engage their attention and to require an organized approach. Evidence of this reality and size comes from several main sources, often in combination.

Quality Costs This is a dramatic source since it is easily understandable and lends itself readily to justification on a return of investment basis. Where the cost of quality has already been estimated, these estimates are directly usable in presentations to upper management.[6] Lacking this information, the proponents of the program must usually start by putting the quality cost data together.

Putting the cost data together is discussed in Section 5, under Securing the Cost Figures. It is shown there that these figures come from a variety of sources: established financial accounts, analysis of established accounts, basic records behind the accounts, estimates, temporary special studies. The fact that estimates and other such judgments are included in the figures is entirely acceptable to managers (though not to accountants). For example, in a specific instance the quality cost for a defect type (if the facts were completely known) might be $50,000. The estimate might range from $40,000 to $60,000, or a plus or minus 20% error. Despite the wide range, the managerial decision (on whether to take on an improvement project) would be identical for all three figures, i.e., "This amount is too big to go on and on. Let's have a go at it."

Loss of Income (or threat of loss) Upper management exhibits great sensitivity to evidence of detriments to the company's income. Credible evidence consists of customer complaints and returns, failure rates, service calls, guarantee charges, lost customers, etc. Some of these elements also appear directly as quality costs, but it is widely suspected that the effect of these things on the company's income is far more significant than the measurable quality costs they create. As a result, clear evidence of adverse effects on company income carries great weight in securing upper management conviction that the problem is real and sizable.

Other Data Sources Beyond the quantified information evidencing effect on quality costs or on income, there are such sources as quality audits, study of competitive products, directions of the consumerism movement, new legislation, employee morale studies, etc.[7] No credible means exist for quantifying the effect of such things on company economics. Hence their role in providing priority to a program rests on the slippery slope of managerial judgment. There is always opportunity to be misled or even stampeded by these sources, since important intangibles such as employee morale, interdepartmental frictions, status in the industry, or public relations may be affected.

There have been many cases in which programs have been launched without knowledge of the size of the problem. Examples have been programs based on applying new techniques sponsored by some manager or staff specialist, e.g., control charts, worker motivation, etc. Such approaches have an appeal when the published papers and speeches indicate that other companies have achieved gains thereby. The approaches may be forced on the company by customer or by top management pressure. However, experience has shown that enduring results are

---

[6] See Section 5, under Presentation to Upper Management; see also Section 3, under Establishing Quality Objectives.

[7] For a broader list, see Section 3, under Establishing Quality Objectives.

far more likely to come from programs which first identify the size and nature of the problem and then select those techniques appropriate to that problem.

IDENTIFYING THE PROJECTS

The fact that large sums of money (or important intangibles) are at stake is by itself no proof of the need for a program of improvement. (In a large company, many costs are large, e.g., materials purchased, plant maintenance, etc.) A vital further need is to identify the projects—the specific few problems for which there is great potential for improvement in relation to the cost of analysis and remedy. The project list is what converts the vague program into a limited number of specific undertakings for which priorities, budgets, manpower, and other supports are legitimized.[8] A program which has not identified these projects literally doesn't know where it is going.

Pareto Analysis The guiding principle in choosing projects is to make the greatest improvement with the least effort. To find the areas of potentially greatest improvement, use is made of that indispensable tool, the Pareto analysis.[9] This tool is what enables us to identify the "vital few" projects which contain the bulk of the improvement potential.

There are several different directions in which we can look for the vital few proj-

TABLE 16-2a Pareto Analysis by Accounts—Quality Losses in a Paper Mill

Accounting category	Annual quality loss, $000	Percent of total quality loss	
		This category	Cumulative
Broke	556	61	61
Customer claim	122	14	75
Odd lot	78	9	84
High material cost. . . .	67	7	91
Downtime	37	4	95
Excess inspection	28	3	98
High testing cost.	19	2	100

TABLE 16-2b Pareto Analysis by Products—"Broke" Losses in a Paper Mill

Product type	Annual "broke" loss, $000	Percent of broke loss	Cumulative percent broke loss
A	132	24	24
B	96	17	41
C	72	13	54
D	68	12	66
E	47	8	74
F	33	6	80
47 other types	108	20	100
Total 53 types	556	100	

[8] Projects are also a form of management objective. For a general discussion, see Section 3, under Establishing Quality Objectives.

[9] See generally Section 2, under The Pareto Principle.

TABLE 16-3 Pareto Analysis by Processes — Rejections in a Job Shop

Type of process	Percent of all rejections	
	This process	Cumulative
Drill press	26	26
Layout.	11	37
Machine shop. . . .	9	46
Spot weld	8	54
Heliarc weld	8	62
Finishing	7	69
All other	31	100
Total	100	

TABLE 16-4 Pareto Analysis by Defects — Estimated Defect Costs in a Foundry

Defect name	Annual cost, $000	Percent of all defect costs		Annual cost 3 years later, $000
		This defect	Cumulative	
Pits.	315	36	36	55
Light.	78	9	45	30
Physical excess	73	8	53	40
Hard.	41	5	58	20
Wide gaps.	39	4	62	30
Thin face	32	4	66	8
Rough sides.	30	3	69	16
Broken (foundry).	30	3	72	15
Casting.	24	3	75	13
Broken (machining)	23	3	78	18
All other.	186	22	100	144
Total.	871	100	. . .	389

ects, and some experimentation may be needed to find the best of the available directions:

Accounts.   Table 16-2*a* shows the quality losses in a paper mill, subdivided by accounting category.   The "broke" loss dominates all the rest.

Products.   Table 16-2*b* shows the analysis of "broke" loss in the same paper mill. The mill makes 53 types of paper, but the worst six types account for 80% of the "broke" loss.

Processes.   Table 16-3 shows the frequency of rejections in a job shop for the various processes used.   Six of the processes contribute 69% of all rejections.

Defect Cost.   Table 16-4 shows the estimated cost of various defect types in a foundry.   The dominance pattern of the most costly defects was of direct assistance to the managers in establishing priorities for projects.

Failure Type.   A Pareto analysis in terms of money, being in the language of management, is of great aid in achieving agreement on priority of projects.   In other cases, while it may be feasible to estimate the cost for the entire category of problems (e.g., field failures), it may become too farfetched to make a second level of cost estimates as to individual types of failure.   In that event, a Pareto analysis by frequency of failure type may be adequate to enable the managers to identify the most fruitful projects.

Table 16-5 shows (in simplified form) the failure rates[10] of a certain type of auto-

[10] Failures per 100 engines over the (then) guarantee period of two years.

motive engine. It is evident that of the 200 failure types on which good data had been acquired, the top 5 categories accounted for one-third of the total failures, while the top 25 categories accounted for two-thirds of the total failures.

TABLE 16-5   Pareto Analysis by Failure Type— Field Failures in Automotive Engines

Failure type	Failure rate	Cumulative failure rate
1	40	40
2	22	62
3	16	78
4	12	90
5	10	100
. . . .		
21	4	186
22	4	190
23	4	194
24	3	197
25	3	200
. . . .		
99	0.4	280
100	0.4	280
. . . .		
199	0.1	300
200	0.1	300

Beyond the listings of problems as exemplified by the foregoing tables, use can be made of matrixes of two or more dimensions. An example is seen in Section 2, Table 2-3, where of four product classes involving three different materials, one product-material combination accounted for $24,000 out of the $37,000 total.

A second example is seen in Section 5, Table 5-3.

Return on Investment Once the cost of the vital few problems has been estimated, it becomes feasible to go a step further, and to estimate, for the more promising problems, (1) the potential improvement through analysis and remedy and (2) the cost of analysis and remedy.

These estimates permit evaluation of "return on investment."[11] In turn, this evaluation becomes an important index of priority.

Table 16-6 shows a summary of several projects presented on a return-on-investment basis. For each listed project there is shown:

The present annual costs based on accounting plus estimated information.

The estimated annual improvement. This is not only an estimate but also a projection of future results, and hence it can be wide of the mark.

The estimated investment in manpower needed to make the analysis. This is likewise an estimate of future events, but the range of error narrows as experience in conducting such projects is gained.

The time to recover the investment. This is one way of stating "return on investment." (Projects which offer recovery of the investment in less than one year commonly receive ready approval.)

The man-months of staff manpower. This is a useful addition to the presentation, since for many projects the limiting factor in analysis is the supply of staff manpower.

In Table 16-6, two of the projects are shown without any estimate of annual improvement. There is always a minority of projects in this category, and their priority is established by managerial judgment.

Priority Rating In companies actively engaged in improvement projects, the number of projects nominated commonly exceeds the digestive capacity of the managers and staff specialists. To deal with this excess, use is made of the concept of priori-

---

[11] "Return on investment" is a good deal more complex than the discussion which follows. In some companies the Industrial Engineering or the Finance department has prepared a standard procedure for computing return on investment, complete with data sheets and formulas. It is helpful for proponents of a program to enlist the aid of the Industrial Engineering or Finance specialists when estimating return on investment; the resulting presentation is likely to have greater validity and credibility.

TABLE 16-6 Return on Investment Presentation of Projects

Project description	Present annual costs	Annual improvement	Investment in manpower	Estimated Time to recover investment, months	Man-months of staff manpower
Customer claims, failures in seals....	$130,000	$100,000	$40,000	5	24
Foundry scrap for leaky castings....	88,000	44,000	30,000	8	18
Overfill in packaged chemicals......	70,000	35,000	20,000	7	12
Defects in purchased bottles	40,000	20,000	15,000	9	8
Training program for foremen	?	?	10,000	?	6
Vendor relations manual	?	?	5,000	?	3
Total..................	328,000	199,000	120,000		71

ties. By discussion and even by "voting,"[12] the managers establish a priority list. The projects to be tackled in the months ahead are then designated with the aid of the priority list. In deciding priorities, managers consider the following parameters:

The size of the potential improvement in cost or profit. One large project will take priority over several small ones.

The return on investment. Projects with prompt "payout" have little difficulty securing priorities.

The sense of urgency, e.g., customer pressure, employee pressure, consumer safety, product liability.

The extent of other problems (e.g., meeting delivery schedules) which compete for managerial and specialist time.

The ease of solution. A problem which is soluble by application of known technology will receive priority over problems which require some invention of new tools for solution.

The probable life of the product or process in question. Where this life is in jeopardy due to obsolescence, the project will be passed over.

The climate for improvement. Projects which are to be solved by management teams known to work together in harmony will receive priority over those involving managers in a state of discord.

The cultural resistance to change. Projects whose solution will likely be blocked by cultural resistance (from managers, employees, the Union, the community, etc.) will be deferred.[13]

SECURING MANAGEMENT APPROVAL

Despite its inherent merits, a program for quality improvement is in competition with other company programs and may fail to secure management support. Analysis of the fate of numerous proposals to upper management has shown that three principal criteria have great influence in upper management thinking:

1. Breakthrough or control. Upper managers strongly favor proposals for breakthrough over proposals for improving controls.

2. Business or technology. Upper management is business-oriented and favors proposals which have an obvious, if not quantified, effect on the business parameters, e.g., sales, cost, profit.

3. Language of money or things. Upper managers can best understand proposals which are presented in their language of money. See, in this connection, Section 3, Figure 3-1 ("Common languages in the company"), and associated discussion, which emphasizes the need for the middle managers and staff specialists to be *bilingual*. These middle managers and staff specialists should and do talk to the first line of supervision and to the nonsupervisors in the language of "things." They should talk to upper management in the language of money, but often do not.

Staff specialists, in particular, are prone to prepare their presentations in the dialect of the specialty. While this dialect convinces the staff specialist of the merits of the proposal, he is at first unaware that such presentation will not convince the upper managers of the merits. As this awareness dawns on him, he tries to solve the problem by offering to educate the managers in the language of the specialty. This is likewise no solution, since the upper managers really do need

---

[12] In voting on priorities, each manager ranks the entire list of project nominations in his order of priority. The rankings are then totaled, and the sums are used to structure a composite ranking list. This composite ranking becomes highly influential, though not conclusive, in the final determination of priorities.

[13] For added discussion, see Section 3, under Establishing Quality Objectives: Establishing Priorities for Objectives.

to understand the financial significance of the proposal to be able to make a sensible judgment on whether to support it or not. The specialists may actually win the battle of education yet lose the war of the proposal because their program, being presented in the wrong language, loses out in the competition against other programs which have been presented in the language of money.

A further problem in securing management approval is that of managerial attitude. Most managers (in common with people generally) do not accept proposals for breakthrough solely on the basis of data presentations and logical reasoning. Their main convictions come from seeing results successfully achieved (elsewhere) by such programs, and without undue damage to the status, beliefs, habits, and other cultural matters important to the managers involved.[14]

In some cases, ingenious dramatic presentations can assist in inducing managers to gamble on programs which are outside of their own prior experience. In other cases the presentation is doomed to failure unless the manager can be given the opportunity to see, at first hand, how a similar program has achieved results in another part of his company. Other possibilities, but progressively less convincing to the manager, are (1) to see such results in other companies, (2) to hear another manager relate his experience, at some conference, and (3) to read a paper written by a manager.

While most managers prefer to see proof of successful prior results, there are a venturesome few who are willing to take greater risks and even to be the first to try out an untested program. When the advocate of a program of quality improvement finds that the attitude of upper management as a group is lukewarm, he still has the alternative of finding one of these "venturesome few" and inducing him to try the program. If this tryout produces good results, the results will be available to convince the remaining managers.[15]

ORGANIZING FOR IMPROVEMENT

Approval of a broad improvement program sets the stage for action by providing legitimacy, budgets, and other essentials. However, improvement takes place only on a project-by-project basis. These projects do not come to fruition unless there are clear assignments of responsibility for doing the deeds required by the projects.[16] In all improvement projects, there are two critical roles for which clear assignment is a must. These are the "steering arm" and the "diagnostic arm."

The Steering Arm   This is a person or persons designated to guide the project to its conclusion.[17] The steering arm makes several essential contributions to the solution of the problem:

1. Unity of purpose. The steering arm enables the interested managers to unify their priorities and to work toward optimizing company rather than departmental performance.

2. Theories to be tested. The steering arm is the principal source of theories as to what is the cause of defects. (Breakthrough in knowledge proceeds only through affirming or denying the validity of theories.)

---

[14] For elaboration on this vital problem, see Juran, J. M., "Managerial Breakthrough," McGraw-Hill Book Company, New York, 1964, Chapter 3, Breakthrough in Attitudes.

[15] Through this method, quality improvement programs can take place even when upper managers have not been convinced of their value. However, such programs are necessarily highly localized to those areas where the middle or lower managers develop their own leadership and unity.

[16] See generally Juran, J. M., Managerial Breakthrough, McGraw-Hill Book Company, New York, 1964, Chapter 5, Mobilizing for Breakthrough in Knowledge.

[17] For an extensive discussion, see Juran, J. M., *ibid.*, Chapter 6, The Steering Arm.

3. Authority to analyze and experiment. Diagnosis requires the collaboration of various departments to secure access to data, to conduct experiments, etc. The steering arm is able to aid this collaboration, since its members usually preside over the departments in question.

4. Action on the new knowledge. Once the causes are known and remedies are designed, the likelihood that action will be taken is far greater if the departments that are to act have been represented on the steering arm.

Membership on the steering arm should be based on capacity to assist the team in making these essential contributions. The most important need is to assure that the men who will be called on to take the bulk of the ultimate remedial action are a part of the steering team from the very outset.

Typically, the steering arm for a project consists of not more than about 8 men. The chairman is preferably that line manager who will be called on to take the bulk of the ultimate action for remedy. The secretary is almost always the head of that staff department which provides the bulk of the manpower for diagnosis.

For really major projects, the members must be of high rank to stimulate ultimate action. For more specialized projects, high-ranking men are usually a detriment, since they occupy seats which could instead be occupied by those who have the real contribution to make. When both high-ranking men and subordinates are present, there is a risk of inhibiting the contributions of the subordinates.

For complex problems, the number of potential contributors is so large as to become unwieldy. In such cases the size of the steering arm should be kept down by using two categories of members: (1) the regular members who provide the bulk of the contribution and (2) the on-call members who are brought in only when they are specifically needed.

The Diagnostic Arm   This is the person or persons who conduct the detailed analysis needed to discover the causes of defects.[18] To conduct this analysis requires:

1. Time. It takes many man-hours to collect and process data, to design experiments, to carry them out, to report the results. For most projects the amount of analytical time required is beyond the capacity of the line supervision and must therefore be supplied by someone else.

2. Diagnostic skills. Diagnosis (other than for very simple projects) requires special training and experience in the study of symptoms, design of experiment, collection and analysis of data, and interpretation of results. The line supervision commonly lacks this special training and experience.

3. Objectivity. The analysis should preferably be conducted by someone who will have no involuntary (or voluntary) biases due to a vested interest in the existing order.[19]

Each of these two roles, the steering arm and the diagnostic arm, is necessary, and neither is sufficient to bring the project to its conclusion.

Anatomy of the Process   The choice of steering and diagnostic arms varies considerably, depending on the nature and size of the project and especially on the "anatomy of the process." A few examples will make this clear:

1. A division of a large automobile company launched a major program to reduce the field failure rates of the cars. A formal Reliability Committee of upper managers was created to steer the program. A large formal Reliability Engineering Department was created to do the diagnosis. (The large size of the company required that the organization structure be formalized.)

---

[18] Diagnosis is conducted at two levels: (1) to discover the causes of defects and (2) to find remedies. Generally these levels require different skills and hence are assigned to different categories of specialists. See Section 2, under The Diagnostic and Remedial Journeys.

[19] For elaboration, see Juran, J. M., *ibid.*, Chapter 7, The Diagnostic Arm.

The "anatomy" of mechanical product manufacture (such as automobiles) takes the form of an assembly "tree," as depicted in Section 9, Figure 9-2. Under this form, there is a high degree of interdependence among the various vendor and in-house departments; i.e., a defect which shows up in one department may have been caused in any of several departments on the diagram (or in some not on the diagram). In such cases, the guidance of the projects must be *inter*departmental. The diagnosis likewise must be interdepartmental, since the diagnostician must follow the trail to wherever it leads.

2. A moderate-sized plant (about 1,000 employees), making castings and then machining them into mechanical components, undertook to reduce its scrap losses. The steering arm was informal, consisting of the principal managers plus an outside consultant. The diagnostic arm consisted of a small Quality Control Engineering Department.

The anatomy of such a "process industry" factory is a "procession" and is quite different from the assembly tree. As before, there are multiple departments. However, as shown in Section 9, Figure 9-3, the product now goes sequentially through all departments and finally to test, shipment, use, etc. This anatomy likewise exhibits a high degree of interdependence among the departments and therefore requires *inter*departmental guidance and a diagnostic arm which can operate interdepartmentally.

3. A small (50-employee) plant making penicillin undertook to improve the yields of the process. Figure 9-1 (Section 9) shows the anatomy of this "autonomous" department. Basic materials enter the department, where they are completely processed into finished goods, packaged, and shipped. The process for converting the basic materials into packaged goods is virtually self-sufficient, so that the problem of improving yields is *intra*departmental. The departmental manager, if personally sufficiently versatile, can guide such a project single-handed. As it happened, the department manager was a competent pharmacologist and also trained sufficiently as a statistician to do his own diagnosis. Thereby, he was able to carry out the entire project as a "one man gang."

4. The carding department in a carpet company undertook to improve the uniformity of weight of yarn. The informal steering arm consisted of the departmental superintendent and an outside consultant. The diagnostic arm was a quality control engineer.

While the anatomy of carpet making is that of a "procession," the weight of yarn is determined in the carding department and nowhere else. In consequence, a departmental guidance of the project and a local analysis, all highly informal, were adequate to solve the problem.

5. A Japanese "QC Circle" undertook to reduce the final assembly defects present in the car radio sets assembled in its department. The QC Circle members served both as the steering arm and as the diagnostic arm.[20]

While the anatomy of the radio set factory is that of an assembly tree, the QC Circle project was restricted to final assembly defects of an intradepartmental character. Hence the QC Circle members could serve as the steering arm. In addition, the members had taken special training in the use of diagnostic tools, so they were qualified to conduct the diagnosis as well.

The approach to organization in the foregoing five cases is summarized in Table 16-7. It is seen that while the steering and diagnostic arms are always present, the form and formality vary widely. The size of the project largely determines whether the approach is to be formal or informal. The anatomy of the process is largely de-

---

[20] For details, see Juran, J. M., the QC Circle Phenomenon, *Industrial Quality Control,* January 1967, pp. 329–336.

TABLE 16-7   Forms of Organization for Improvement Projects

Case example	Steering arm	Diagnostic arm
1. Reducing field failure rates of automobiles	Formal Reliability Committee	Formal Reliability Engineering Department
2. Reducing foundry scrap losses	Informal meetings of managers plus a consultant	Formal Quality Control Engineering Department
3. Improving yields of penicillin plant	The plant manager	The plant manager
4. Improving the uniformity of weight of carpet yarns	The departmental manager plus a consultant	A quality control engineer
5. Reduction of final assembly defects in radio sets	A QC Circle of nonsupervisors	A QC Circle of nonsupervisors

cisive on whether the approach must be interdepartmental or intradepartmental.[21] The extent of training of the personnel influences greatly whether diagnosis is to be performed by "professional" diagnosticians or by trained amateurs.

Interrelation of Steering and Diagnostic Arms   The usual interplay between these two arms of organization is shown in Figure 16-1.   The activities listed are usually conducted in about the sequence shown, and the usual allocation of responsibility for decision or action is as shown.

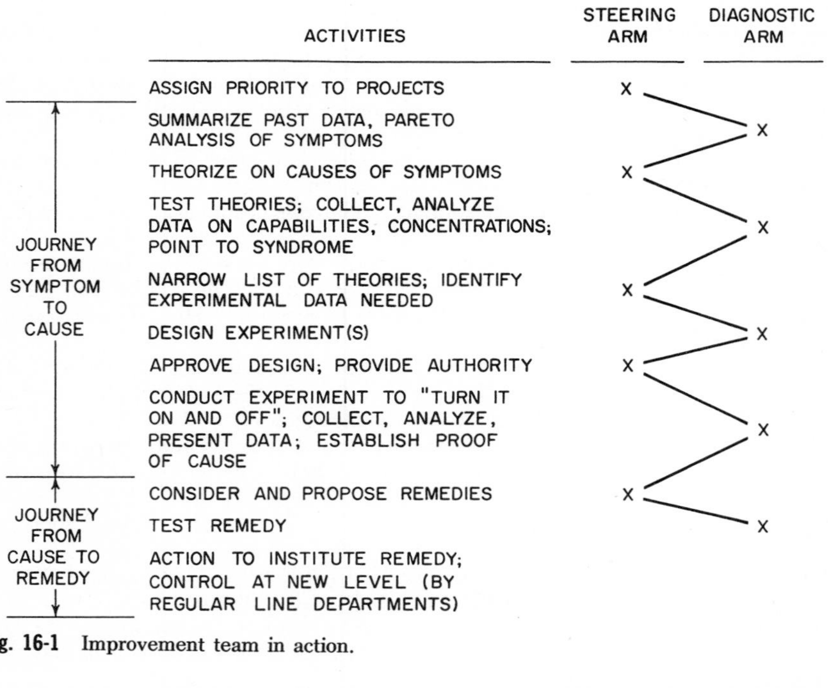

Fig. 16-1   Improvement team in action.

[21] For further discussion of anatomy of the process, (as applied to control in the metals industry), see Section 33, under The Control Plan; also Fig. 33-1, 2, and 3, Table 33-1, and associated discussion.

Section 2, under The Diagnostic and Remedial Journeys, discusses some of the universal aspects of diagnosis and remedy of chronic problems, including basic concepts and terminology. The topics which follow in the present Section 16 discuss in detail the activities listed in Figure 16-1.

Sources of Diagnosticians   Table 16-7 makes clear that there are multiple sources of manpower for doing the detailed diagnostic work—the work of the diagnostic arm. These and other sources will now be elaborated.

Staff Quality Specialists.   Quality Control Engineers are widely used for analysis of virtually any problem involving quality and especially for projects for quality improvement. Reliability Engineers also conduct such analyses, but generally for problems related to product reliability.[22]

Industrial Engineers.   These specialists are used for study of some quality costs through both the classical and modern tools of industrial engineering. The classical tools include work methods studies; setting of labor, material, and other work standards; job classifications; wage incentives; and work sampling. The modern tools include operations research, linear programming, value analysis, systems analysis, and general application of computers to assist in solution of industrial problems.

Other Staff Department Specialists.   Some companies recognize Operations Research, Value Analysis, and still other activities as separate specialties. This recognition extends to creating departments to carry out the work of the specialty and separate job categories to designate the men, e.g., Value Analyst.[23]

Consultants.   Outside consultants are used in quality improvement programs in a dual role:

1. As advisers to the steering arms in the overall conduct of the program and in the approach to specific projects
2. As trainers for the company diagnosticians

There are serious risks involved in bringing in an outsider, but these risks can be reduced by forthright discussion with managers for whom the outsider has performed similar services.[24,25,26]

Line Department Specialists.   The major line departments—such as Product Development, Process Development, Purchasing, Manufacture, and Marketing—all include specialists who have analytical skills. These skills can be enlisted to aid in diagnosis for quality improvement projects, and this is widely done. Managers of line departments, as members of steering teams, frequently accept assignments to conduct part of the diagnosis. They then delegate the detailed work to be carried out by their departmental specialists. The greatest use of these specialists is in conducting the diagnosis needed to discover remedies, but there is a significant extent of diagnosis for causes as well.

Line Department Supervisors.   These men are normally limited in their ability to conduct diagnosis owing to lack of time, lack of training in the skills of diagnosis, and involuntary bias. It helps a good deal for these men to undergo minimal training in diagnosis.[27] It enables them to do a better job of guiding projects, shortens the time needed by them for conducting diagnosis, and improves their objectivity as well.

[22] See generally, Section 7, under Staff Quality Control Departments.

[23] See Value Analysis, below.

[24] For a discussion of the role of the inside consultant see, Purcell, Warren R., The Internal Quality Control Consultant, *Industrial Quality Control,* October 1962, pp. 38–40.

[25] For an extensive discussion of problems associated with consulting in quality control, see Juran, J. M., So You Want to Be a Quality Control Consultant, *Industrial Quality Control,* December 1966, pp. 265–270.

[26] For a case example, see Ishiwara, Tatsuya, A Quality-Up Drive in the Watch Industry, *Industrial Quality Control,* September 1966, pp. 126, 134–137.

[27] See Section 17, under Non-Quality Managers and under Production Foremen.

Nonsupervisors.   The QC Circle movement of the Japanese[28] has demonstrated that nonsupervisors have the capacity to absorb training in diagnosis and to apply this training to intradepartmental projects for quality improvement.   While there are some severe obstacles to applying the QC Circle concept to other cultures, the Japanese experience leaves no doubt of the capacities of nonsupervisors to perform these deeds.

Value Analysis   During World War II (as in all wars), shortages of materials drove many companies to find substitute materials or designs for the specified materials and components.   Some of the substitutes worked out better than what was specified and were a cost reduction to boot.   These experiences led to a gathering awareness that the existing designs contained many opportunities for improvement, including improvement in quality.

Companies also found that the regular design departments exhibited little enthusiasm for restudying designs to find these opportunities for improvement.   This enthusiasm did come, however, from other engineers.   At the outset, these were usually engineers attached to purchasing departments and assigned to solve purchasing problems through substitution.   As their work came to be recognized and publicized, these engineers sought and sometimes were granted a new title and organizational recognition.   The names adopted were variously Value Analysis, Value Engineering, and still others.

While some industrial companies were willing to create a new species of engineer, others rejected the idea on the ground that the regular engineering departments already had the responsibility to conduct the "value analysis" studies.   However, the movement gained momentum when the U.S. Department of Defense supported it by recognition, publicity, and especially by offering to share savings with contractors using the value analysis concept.

The central theme of the concept is to (1) identify the necessary function to be served by a component, product, or whatever, and (2) to find the most economical way of accomplishing that function.[29]

In carrying out this theme, the value analysts have set up some terms and definitions to clarify communications.   Several categories of "value" are defined:

Use value, which is based on those properties of the product which enable it to perform work or service; i.e., the value of a nail is entirely "use."

Cost value, which is based on the minimum cost of achieving a useful function.

Esteem value, which is based on those properties of the product which contribute to pride of ownership.

Exchange value, which is based on those properties which make a product valuable for exchange purposes.[30]

The main contribution of the value analysts has probably been the concept of an *organized approach* to the improvement studies rather than continuing to rely on the idea of every engineer on his own.[31]   This organized approach has included several main elements:

1.   A more precise set of definitions of terms and elements of value to distinguish more clearly the multiple objectives to be met (see above).

---

[28] See Section 18, under The Japanese QC Circle.

[29] For elaboration, see Fallon, Carlos, Product Worth—Common Objective of Value Analysis/Quality Assurance, *Quality Assurance,* January 1971, pp. 10 and 11.

[30] Derived from Snee, Andrew J., Introduction to Value Engineering, *Quality Progress,* November 1970; see also Miles, L. D., Value Analysis and Engineering, *Fifteenth Annual Convention Transactions,* ASQC, Philadelphia, 1961, pp. 533–536.   Mr. Miles is generally regarded as the originator of the value analysis "movement."

[31] See, for example, Crouse, Robert L., Value Engineering at Honeywell, *Evaluation Engineering,* November-December 1965, pp. 10–21.

2. A Value Engineering Job Plan, which is an organized series of steps to be taken. One such series consists of:

Item selection, i.e., the product elements to be chosen for study
Determination of essential function and cost of the items selected for study
Development of alternatives to perform the essential function served
Cost analysis of alternatives
Test and verification to prove the feasibility of the alternative selected
Proposal submittal and follow-up[32]

3. Check lists to be used as countdowns in studying problems.[33]
4. Still other tools to assist engineers in making studies. These tools include:

The Pareto analysis[34] for concentrating on the high cost items
Data books of quantified costs and related pertinent accumulations
Techniques for study, e.g., brainstorming

5. Creation of training programs to sensitize men to the available techniques and to provide examples of their use.
6. Setting up teams of men from cognizant departments (often Engineering, Reliability, Quality Control) to secure a broad-based approach and to minimize jurisdictional rivalry.

A good many published papers have narrated and quoted good results achieved from value analysis. Audited savings in the U.S. Department of Defense are stated to have run to huge sums.[35] A survey prepared by the Value Engineering Division of the American Ordnance Association[36] presents data to show that along with cost improvements there are improvements in reliability, maintainability, and still other parameters. The Defense Department prepared various publications[37] on Value Engineering and generally urged its contractors to consider the technique seriously.

Organizationally, there is great variation in conducting value analysis. This variation includes:

1. The recognition of value analysis as a useful discipline or technique. As noted above, this extends from no recognition at all to setting up full-time departments.
2. The scope of the value analysts. At one extreme, the value analysts themselves conduct the studies. At the other extreme, the value analysts serve as staff catalysts by conducting training courses, providing consultation to committees, creating training materials, preparing propaganda, measuring results, publishing progress reports, etc. Between these extremes lie numerous organization setups, each responsive to the special circumstances of its own company.[38]
3. The jurisdictional lines drawn between (a) value analysts and product de-

---

[32] Adapted from Tocco, Anthony R., Value Engineering. An Economic Discipline, *Quality*, vol. 11, no. 4, Winter 1967, pp. 90–95.

[33] Some of these are formidable. Tocco, *op.cit.*, gives ten check lists and sublists totaling 101 questions.

[34] See Section 2, under The Pareto Principle.

[35] Andrew J. Snee, *op. cit.*

[36] Total Value Engineering Effectiveness, *American Ordnance Association,* Washington, D.C., August 1967.

[37] These include DOD Handbook H-111, Value Engineering. U.S. Government Printing Office, Washington, D.C., 1963; MIL-V-38352, Value Engineering Program Requirements, U.S. Air Force, 1964.

[38] See, for example, Bhote, Keki, Value Engineering—a Discipline, Not a Department, *Quality Assurance,* January 1971, pp. 12–15.

signers and *(b)* value analysts and quality specialists. These relationships likewise vary widely, and the emerging pattern, if any, is not clear.[39]

The literature on value analysis now includes books[40] as well as articles in journals.

CONTROLLABILITY QUANTIFICATION

A major fork in the road of diagnosis of a project is controllability, i.e., whether the defects are primarily operator-controllable or management-controllable. What is decisive here is whether the criteria for operator self-control have been met. As set out in Section 11, under Concept of Operator Self-Control et seq., a defect is operator-controllable if *all* the following criteria have been met:

The operator has the means of knowing what he is supposed to do

The operator has the means of knowing what he is actually doing

The operator has available to him the means for regulating his performance

TABLE 16-8   Quantification of Controllability

Defect	Percent of total	Percent controllable by		
		Operator	Uncertain	Management
Leader end off shade. . . .	17			17
Start marks.	16	8		8
Broken ends	14		14	
Creases	12	2		10
Dirt	11	7		4
Coarse filling	5			5
31 other defects	25		25	
Total.	100	17	39	44

It is feasible to quantify controllability by analyzing the major defects to see whether the foregoing criteria have all been met.[41] Such an analysis was conducted for a textile mill process. In this process, there were 37 different types of defects in the product. However, the top six defects accounted for 75% of all the defectiveness. A team consisting of the foreman and an engineer studied these six principal defects, with results as shown in Table 16-8.

As is evident from Table 16-8 the controllability was clear for two of these defects, uncertain for one of them, and divided as to the other three. (The team estimated the allocation as best they could.) With the "trivial many" defects unanalyzed, Table 16-8 indicates that the management-controllable defects dominated by about 2½ to 1.

Investigators in a number of countries have conducted studies on controllability in various industries. As reported to the author, they generally confirm his own conclusions that in industry, by and large, controllability of defects prevails as follows:

Management-controllable: over 80%

Operator-controllable: under 20%

[39] For an inconclusive discussion, see Value vs. Reliability (by Task Group M, Reliability Engineering Technical Committee, ASQC) *Industrial Quality Control*, February 1964, pp. 6-10.

[40] For example, Mudge, Arthur E., "Value Engineering," McGraw Hill Book Company, New York, 1971.

[41] For some pertinent questions, see Section 11, Table 11-1.

This ratio does not appear to vary greatly from one industry to another, but it does vary considerably from one process to another. Obviously, no one needs to accept such figures as applying to his own company. He can discover his own situation by the do-it-yourself study exemplified in Table 16-8.

In the author's experience, many managers harbor deep-seated beliefs that the bulk of defects are due to operator errors, i.e., that defects are mainly operator-controllable. The facts seldom bear this out, but the belief persists. In one printing company the managers had traditionally regarded keyboarding errors (the major component of the total error rate) as operator-controllable despite operator protests that the linotype machines made mistakes. When a program was undertaken to improve quality, the managers concluded that this issue needed to be resolved before wholehearted operator support could be enlisted. A tape operated attachment was used to test several machines by repeat casting 25 lines in succession. It was found that machine-caused errors contributed about half of the keyboarding errors and about a third of the total error rate.[42]

The controllability study is a "major fork in the road" because the approach to eliminating management-controllable errors is very different from that used to eliminate operator-controllable errors. To oversimplify, the former requires a considerable contribution from each of very few people (managers and specialists), whereas the latter requires a small contribution from each of many people.

The approach to diagnosis of operator-controllable defects is discussed in Section 18. The approach to diagnosis of management-controllable defects is discussed in the present Section, under the topics which follow.

ANALYSIS OF SYMPTOMS

The first diagnostic step is properly to understand the symptoms. If this understanding is derived solely from regular field and shop reports, the steering team can be misled through undiscovered confusion and vagueness.

Clear Concepts. The team members should develop an awareness of the distinctions among essential concepts such as defect, symptom, theory, cause, remedy, etc. Study carefully Section 2, under The Diagnostic and Remedial Journeys.

Meanings of Words Used to Describe Symptoms. It is very common for these words to have multiple meanings. Some descriptive words, e.g., "oversize," may cover several degrees of seriousness. In such cases it is quite helpful in diagnosis of symptoms to use several terms to describe these degrees, e.g., "Oversize (critical)," "Oversize (major)," "Oversize (minor)." Other descriptive words are really generic in nature, e.g., "malfunction." Such a word may be used to describe several very different symptoms (e.g., open circuit, reversed wiring, dead battery) each of which trails back to very different causes.

A widespread source of confusion is variation in departmental dialect. For example, to the accountant, "scrap" may mean anything thrown away, no matter what the reason; to the quality specialist, "scrap" is something thrown away because of nonconformance or unfitness for use.

This lack of standardization in the meanings of words can confuse managers as to the effect of defects. For example, in an optical company, the term "beauty defect" was company dialect for damaged surfaces on lenses, prisms, etc. This term failed to distinguish among several very different aspects of fitness for use:

1. Damage in the focal plane, which significantly impairs fitness for use
2. Damage which does not significantly impair fitness for use but which is visible to the user during normal use

---

[42] Grady, W. E., and L. A. Seder, Statistical Quality Control in the Composing Room, *Graphic Arts Monthly,* June 1970, pp. 66–69.

3. Damage which does not significantly impair fitness for use and which is not visible to the user during normal use

The lack of standardization can also confuse managers as to the causes of defects. In a plant making rubber products, there were several sources of torn product: the stripping operation, the machine cutting operation, and the assembly operation. The single word "tears" failed to distinguish among strip tears, click tears, and assembly tears. One of these categories was largely operator-controllable but involved only 15% of all tears. However, one important manager had assumed all the defects to be operator-controllable.

TABLE 16-9   Pareto Analysis of Defect Types in an Optical Company

Defect type	Percent of all defects	Cumulative percent
Scratches. . . .	27	27
Chips	25	52
Digs	10	62
Thickness . . .	7	69
Poor film	7	76
All other	24	100

Autopsy of Product. An essential device for cutting through the confusion in terminology is the autopsy (literally, to see with one's own eyes). The steering team (and of course the diagnosticians) should get their hands on the product and learn at first hand how the words used relate to observed conditions of the product. This seeing with one's own eyes is of added value in stimulating realistic theories of causation.

Quantification. The frequency and intensity of symptoms is of great significance in pointing to directions for analysis. The Pareto principle, applied to the records of past performance, can be of great aid in quantifying the symptom pattern.[43] For example, an optical company undertook a project to reduce quality losses in the precision components department. Table 16-9 shows the Pareto study of the defects within the department, based on three months prior data. The top five defects account for 76% of all rejections. This information is of obvious aid to the steering arm in directing the priorities of the study. The data in Tables 16-4 and 16-5 are similarly useful.

(The Pareto analysis can be dramatized by constructing a bar chart showing the size of each of the defect classes and how they accumulate to 100% of all defects. See Section 2, Figures 2-5 and 2-6.)

THEORIES: FORMULATION AND ARRANGEMENT

As symptoms of chronic defects are studied, the question is raised "What causes defect X?" The responses are mainly assertions or theories. The diagnostic process includes test of these theories, disproving some and affirming others until there is established a cause-and-effect relationship which leads to remedy. The need for a supply of theories is obvious.

Formulation of Theories. There are several sources of theories of what causes defects, including:

1. The steering arm. These men usually have had long association with the chronic problem. They have given it a lot of thought, harbor some pet theories, and have actually done some inconclusive experimenting on their own. When someone writes on the blackboard "What causes defect X?" the steering arm members have many theories to offer. In the author's experience, the causes which finally turn out to be truly dominant were for the most part on the list of theories originally propounded by the steering arm.

[43] Note that the Pareto principle applies to several levels of the quality improvement activity: finding the vital few projects, finding the vital few symptoms within a project, finding the vital few causes for a symptom, etc.

2. The diagnosticians. Once they come to grips with the data, they begin to identify possible relationships and to advance theories. Usually these serve to unify theories advanced by the steering arm, but sometimes they are brand new.

3. The work force. Through intimate association with the details of material, process, and product, the work force evolves theories of its own. Whether these theories are actually contributed depends largely on the climate of relationship between the managers and the men. This climate may inhibit the managers from asking and the men from responding.

Theories may be secured from the work force in several ways:

1. by a direct request. A factory making mechanical springs experienced field usage trouble due to some springs being too weak. The answer came from the work force. One workman had observed that during the counting of springs (by weight), the weigher would pull springs out of the entangled supply box to fill up the count. The workman's theory was that this pulling weakened some springs caught in the entanglement. He was the sole source of this theory, which turned out to identify the sole dominant cause.

2. by a standing suggestion system. The regular suggestion systems always turn up some ideas relating to quality. The Error Cause Removal aspect of some motivational programs (see Section 18) is a form of suggestion system directed specifically to quality matters.

3. from defenses set up by the work force. Workmen who are criticized for errors often defend themselves by assertions that the defects are caused in other ways. The linotype case under Controllability Quantification, above, is an example.

4. from involuntary theories. Whenever it is observed that some workmen consistently turn out work superior to that of other workmen, a shop study may disclose the cause of this difference as a form of secret knowledge. See Section 18, under Technique Errors.

Theories of Defective Systems. Theories of causation should not be limited to products and processes; they should extend to the broader systems as well. Consider several examples:

1. At a meeting of managers, one man makes the observation: "That's the third time this month we lost a lot of product due to instruments out of calibration." It is a shrewd observation, since the three lots consisted of totally different products. What is now placed under suspicion is the *system* for maintaining the instruments in calibration.

2. A manufacturer of elevators encountered a puzzling, recurring phenomenon. Various components, specified to have lengths of about 10 feet, were arriving at the field assembly site about 2 *feet* undersize. A number of these occurrences were "autopsied" by analysis of all the pertinent documents and by interviews with the men involved in the respective cases. The common cause turned out to be the existence of two languages for expressing length. For a length totaling 10 feet and 3 inches, some designers used the designations 123″, or 123 in. Other designers used the designation 10′3″. When the latter designation was used, it sometimes was read as 103″, either because the symbol for "foot" was not clearly legible or through carelessness, inadvertence, etc.

3. In the hospital study (Section 47, under Control of Hospital Medication Errors), one of the more frequent systematic contributors to medication errors was the similarity in names of different drugs. (In this study, there was also a common cause due to multiple languages—metric and apothecary.)

What these and similar cases have in common is that any one autopsy will disclose multiple causes for the error. However, over a series of autopsies made on *dissimilar* products, some systematic causes will reappear despite the dissimilarity in products.

If the list of theories advanced includes a suspected systematic error, e.g., multiple languages, it is a simple matter to test for the validity of such a theory during the individual and collective autopies. However, if the theory was not on the list of suspects, it must evolve in the mind of the diagnostician who conducted the autopsies. He deserves credit if he finds it.[44]

Orderly Arrangement. When the number of theories is small, their interrelation may be understood from seeing the written list. However, as the list grows in size it also grows in complexity to a point that the interrelations are difficult to grasp. Now it becomes desirable to create an orderly arrangement of the list of theories. There are two principal ways to create this arrangement.

TABLE 16-10   Orderly Arrangement of Theories

Raw material	Moisture content
Shortage of weight	Charging speed of wet powder
Method of discharge	Dryer, rpm
Catalyzer	Temperature
Types	Steam pressure
Quantity	Steam flow
Quality	Overweight of package
Reaction	Type of balance
Solution and concentration	Accuracy of balance
B solution temperature	Maintenance of balance
Solution and pouring speed	Method of weighing
pH	Operator
Stirrer, rpm	Transportation
Time	Road
Crystallization	Cover
Temperature	Spill
Time	Container
Concentration	
Mother crystal	
Weight	
Size	

One method is to reduce the list to writing by identifying the likely major variables. Each of these major variables has "satellites" (i.e., contributing minor variables) which are then grouped under their respective major variables. Table 16-10 shows this method used to depict the variables affecting yield of fine powder chemicals.

The second method is to use a graphic form to show the arrangement of theories. The most highly developed is the "cause-and-effect diagram."[45] Figure 16-2 shows this diagram presenting the same information as is listed in Table 16-10.

As the list or diagram of theories is studied, proposals are made for testing theories through a variety of ways: analysis of past data, study of current production, experimentation. These methods of testing theories are discussed below.

---

[44] The cultured-pearl industry, founded by Kokichi Mikimoto, was based on a series of discoveries which included an astonishing feat of autopsy and analysis. The "red current" of 1905 destroyed hundreds of thousands of oysters in his pearl farm in Ago Bay. Mikimoto opened these and found only five oysters containing spherical pearls. However, all five pearls were lodged in the identical location in each oyster.

[45] The diagram was developed in 1950 by Prof. Kaoru Ishikawa of Tokyo University and is widely used in Japan. The Japanese name is Tokusei Yoin Zu (characteristics diagram). A nickname is Sakana No Hone (fishbone). For elaboration, see Ishikawa, Kaoru, Cause and Effect Diagram, *Proceedings, International Conference on Quality Control*, JUSE, Tokyo, 1969, pp. 607–610. See also Inoue, Michael S., and James L. Riggs, Describe Your System with Cause and Effect Diagrams, *Industrial Engineering*, April 1971, pp. 26–31.

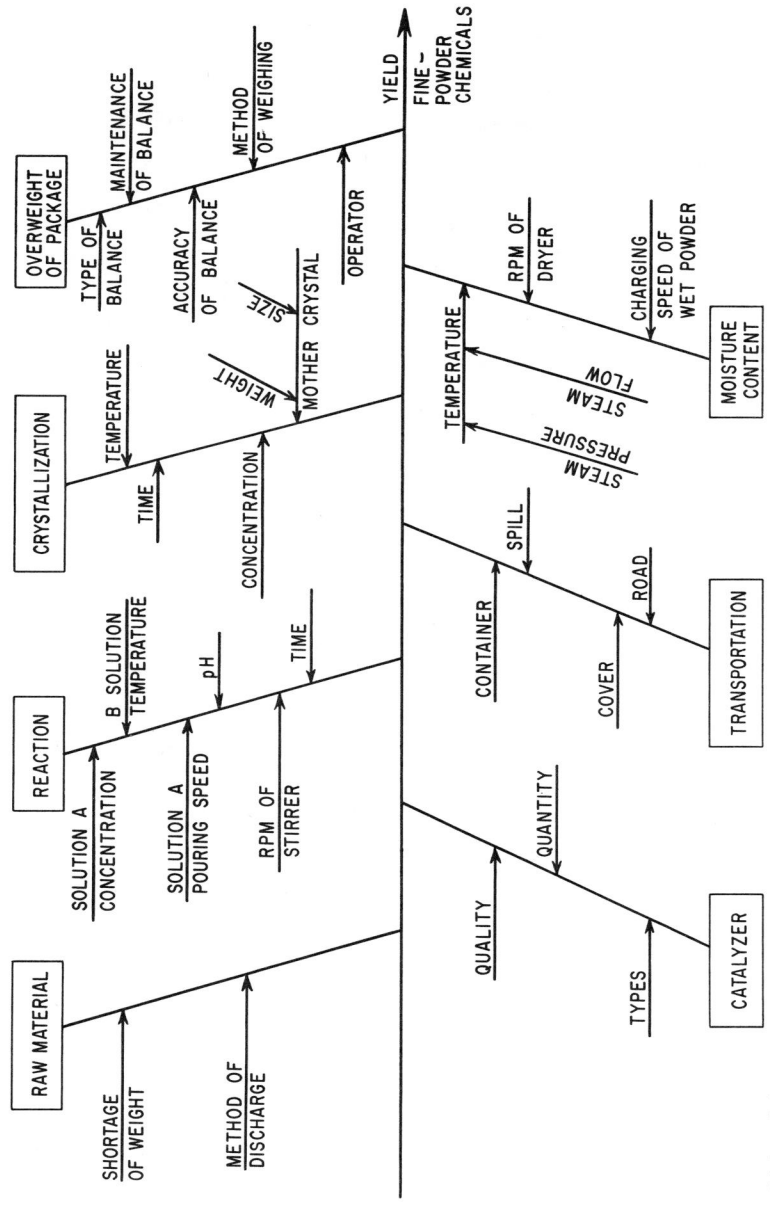

Fig. 16-2 Ishikawa cause-and-effect diagram.

TEST OF THEORIES USING PAST DATA

When theories are first propounded it is soon evident that some of them can be tested from available records without the need for experimentation or even for study of current production. This analysis from past data is an obvious early step, since it permits ground to be cleared without the need for interfering with shop operations.

The methods used in this type of analysis involve relating product percent defective to some theory of causation—process, tools, operators, etc. The relationship may be examined using various statistical devices: ranking, correlation, matrixes, etc., as exemplified below.

Ranking.   An automobile parts plant made 23 types of torque tubes. When tested for dynamic unbalance, the tubes ranged from 52.3% defective down to 12.3%, the average being 22.1%. One of the theories advanced was that a swaging operation was a dominant cause of dynamic unbalance. Since only the large-diameter tubes were swaged, it was an easy matter to prepare a ranking of tubes in order of percent defective and to identify which were swaged. Table 16–11 shows this ranking. The result was dramatic—the worst seven types were all swaged, the best seven all unswaged. The support thus given to the swaging theory resulted in a study of the swaging process. This study showed that the swaging did not control closely the coaxial relationship between the swaged and unswaged diameters, and that the specification imposed no limit on this.

Correlation.   In one foundry, it was theorized that the dominant cause of pitted castings was too large a "choke" in the pattern. (The choke is a narrow orifice designed to permit free flow of the molten metal and at the same time to obstruct the passage of lumps of sand.) Prior data were available on the percent defective of many lots of castings made from a variety of patterns. It was easy to measure the choke thickness on the physical patterns and then to correlate choke thickness against pit scrap. A positive correlation became evident (Figure 16–3.) Subsequent experimentation established 0.050 inches as the optimum choke thickness.

Matrixes.   A plant making hunting guns experienced over 10% rejections of the assembled guns due to "open hard after fire."[46] Assembly was an intricate opera-

TABLE 16-11   Test of Theories by Ranking

Type	% defective	Swaged (marked X)	Type	% defective	Swaged (marked X)
A	52.3	X	M	19.2	X
B	36.7	X	N	18.0	X
C	30.8	X	O	17.3	
D	29.9	X	P	16.9	X
E	25.3	X	Q	15.8	
F	23.3	X	R	15.3	
G	23.1	X	S	14.9	
H	22.5		T	14.7	
I	21.8	X	U	14.2	
J	21.7	X	V	13.5	
K	20.7	X	W	12.3	
L	20.3				

[46] One of the tests given to the gun is to fire it with an overweight cartridge as a safety test, i.e., to see if the chamber will burst. Following this test, some of the guns cannot be opened up to remove the spent cartridge. These guns must be disassembled and reassembled, at considerable cost.

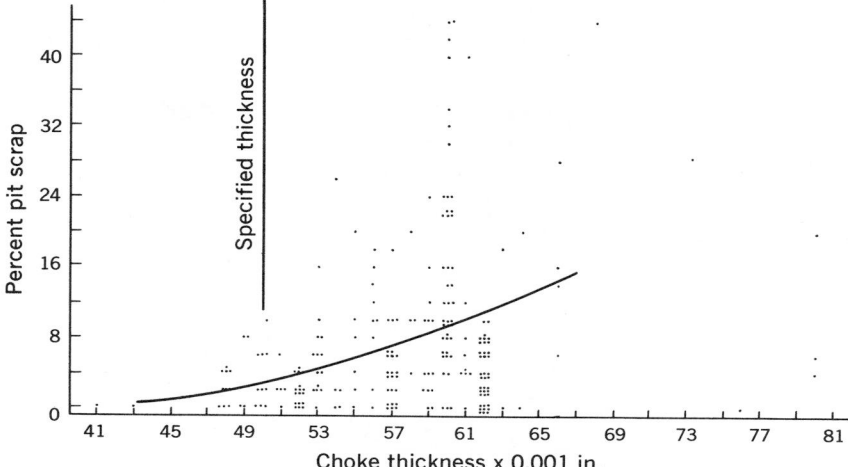

Fig. 16-3 Test of theories by correlation.

tion, requiring about an hour of the time of a skilled workman. One theory of cause of the defect was poor workmanship. This theory was vigorously opposed by the production supervision, who asserted that there were times when the defect virtually disappeared of its own accord.

Past records were available, showing, for each gun, the operator who assembled it and the results of the tests. When these data were organized into a matrix, (Table 16–12a), it became evident that there were drastic month-to-month changes in percent rejections, confirming the assertions of the production supervision. Clearly, the assemblers had not suddenly learned in January (1.8% defective) how to do this job and then suddenly forgotten it in February (22.6% defective).

Still more information was derived from this same matrix by summing up the defects for the five "best" and five "worst" assemblers (Table 16–12b). This analysis showed that during all months, good, bad, or indifferent, the five "worst" assemblers had consistently more than ten times as many defects as the five "best." This suggested that the best operators possessed some "knack" or form of secret knowledge not known to the "worst." (Alternatively, the "worst" operators possessed some form of secret ignorance.) It was found on shop study that the "best" assemblers filed away one of the critical piece part dimensions and that this constituted the knack. The managers then embodied the knack into the official technology, and the defect virtually disappeared.

In the foregoing cases, statistical techniques (ranking, correlation, matrixes) were combined with other readily available data (type of process, characteristics of tools, identity of workmen) to affirm the validity of theories. These examples do not exhaust the list of statistical techniques available nor the kind of job information available to make good use of past data. However, they do demonstrate how it is possible to make a good deal of diagnostic progress "in the office," with minimal effort and before any resort to experimentation.

TABLE 16-12*a*   Matrix Analysis

Assembly operator rank	Nov.	Dec.	Jan.	Feb.	Mar.	Apr.	Total
1	4	1	0	0	0	0	5
2	1	2	0	5	1	0	9
3	3	1	0	3	0	3	10
4	1	1	0	2	2	4	10
5	0	1	0	10	2	1	14
6	2	1	0	2	2	15	22
7	2	4	1	11	1	7	26
8	2	0	0	7	23	7	39
9	6	3	0	18	9	4	40
10	13	4	0	10	10	9	46
11	15	8	2	11	10	3	49
12	6	6	5	18	6	10	51
13	7	2	1	28	25	1	64
14	16	8	1	14	11	15	65
15	2	16	8	22	8	23	79
16	22	18	1	33	7	13	94
17	18	8	3	37	9	23	98
18	16	17	0	22	36	11	102
19	27	13	4	62	4	14	124
20	6	5	2	61	22	29	125
21	39	10	2	45	20	14	130
22	26	17	4	75	31	35	188
Total	234	146	34	496	239	241	1390
% defective. .	10.6	6.6	1.8	22.6	10.9	11.0	10.5

TABLE 16-12*b*   Matrix Analysis (*continued*)

	Nov.	Dec.	Jan.	Feb.	Mar.	Apr.	Total
5 best. . . .	9	6	0	20	5	8	48
5 worst. . .	114	62	12	265	113	103	669
Ratio	13	10	∞	13	23	13	14

TEST OF THEORIES USING CURRENT PRODUCTION

In most projects, there is need to secure information beyond that available from past data. Much of this missing information comes from the study of current production. There are multiple forms of such study and collectively they are a most valuable set of tools for diagnosis. They include process-capability studies, dissection of process and product, cutting new "windows" in the process, providing special instruments to measure with greater precision than the conventional shop instruments. All these forms of study except process-capability studies are discussed below under their respective headings.

Process-capability studies are one of the most widely used forms, since one of the theories most widely encountered is "the process can't hold the tolerances." Testing this theory requires a study of current production to determine the "process capability." Once this capability has been measured, it can be compared with the tolerances to determine whether the process can hold the tolerances.

In this Handbook, the discussion of the process-capability concept, the methods of measuring capability, and the ways of using the results are all discussed in Section 9, under Process Capability: The Concept, and subsequent headings.

Tests of theories using current production always create some interference in the affairs of the producing departments. In addition, there is the risk that the product under observation will meet some strange treatment at the hands of factory personnel who are unaware of the implications inherent in the study. In consequence, though no "experiment" may be involved, it is necessary to observe some of the cautions discussed below, under Diagnosis through Experiment.

DISSECTION: PROCESS AND PRODUCT

The collections of products known as "lots" commonly result from numerous arrays of variables, as shown in Figure 16-4. In most projects it is feasible and useful to "dissect" these multiple variables into their components so as to quantify their size and to discover which is dominant. This dissection takes various forms, as discussed below.

Stream-to-Stream Analysis   Often "lots" are the result of the confluence of several separate streams of product, as shown in Figure 16-4. These streams differ from each other due to being processed by different machines, from different material batches, by different operators, etc. When a study is made of the nature of the product coming from each stream, the results are of value in affirming or denying the validity of theories.

Common examples of stream-to-stream differences are the cases of multiple-spindle metal cutting machines, e.g., Section 9, Figure 9-19; multiple cavity molding operations (plastic, glass, metal, etc.); multiple-spindle textile machines. In all such cases the special effort required in the analysis is to segregate the product to avoid the mixtures created during normal production. Sometimes this segregation is made simple by preplanning the identification, e.g., using cavity numbers in the molding dies. In other cases, the segregation can become tedious.

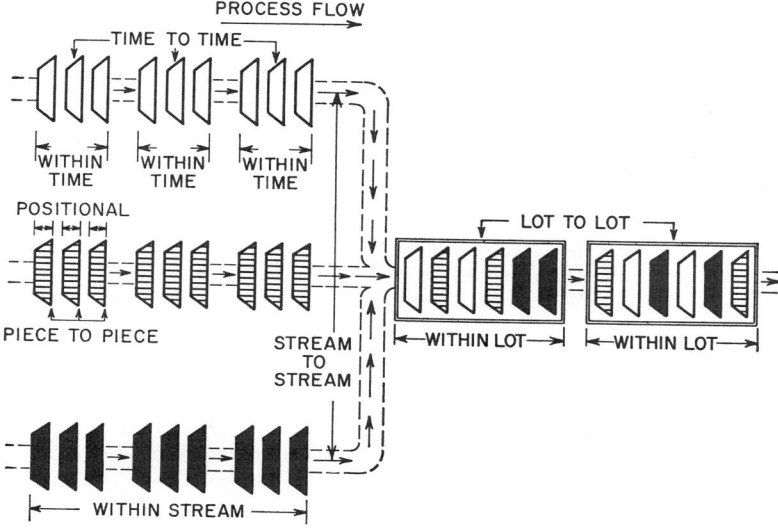

Fig. 16-4   The anatomy of lot formation.

For example, a polishing operation conveyed the parts to the polishing wheel in an endless chain of 138 holding fixtures. The polished pieces exhibited defects in the form of unpolished areas, and these defects seemed to present no orderly pattern. When a diagnostician dissected the product into 138 separate streams, each stream consisting of product held by only one of the fixtures, the "random" patterns immediately became identifiable with the respective fixtures (Figure 16–5).

Another form of such study involved leaks in the various "plumbing" joints of refrigeration circuits. By tallying the leaks based on the joints at which they occurred, a Pareto pattern was identified. Here the "streams" consisted mainly of the different designs of joints, some being much more defect-prone than others.

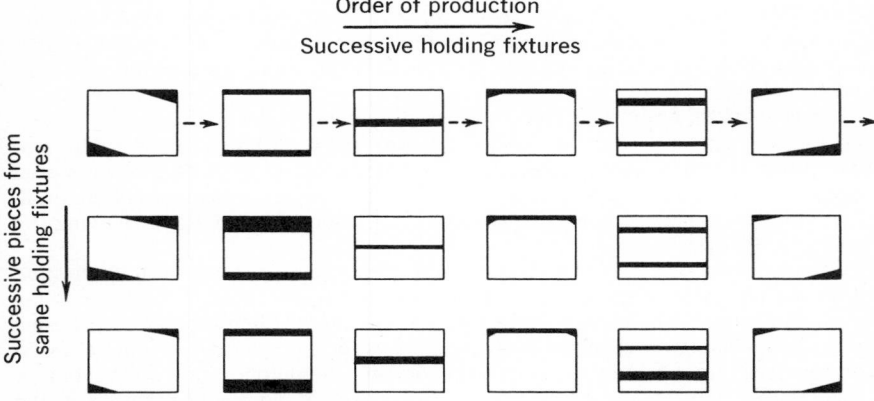

Fig. 16-5   Dissection—train of fixtures.

Time-to-Time Analysis   Within many streams, there is a time-to-time "drift"; e.g., the processing solution gradually becomes more dilute, the tools gradually wear, the operator becomes fatigued. Such drifts can often be quantified to determine the magnitude of the effect. A simple example can be seen in the process-capability study of turning the shafts for watches (Section 9, Figure 9–16). In that study there existed a slow time-to-time increase in diameter due to wear of the tools.

In an example arising out of finished product, a company making pipe joint compound found that the containers were developing internal pressures, distorting some cans out of shape and violently blowing the lids off others. Chemical analysis of the contents of distorted cans of finished product showed excess moisture. Analysis of current production showed the moisture content at the compounding operation to be near the maximum tolerance and progressively higher at subsequent operations.

Only one of the ingredients was known to be moisture-absorbing. Inquiry showed that this ingredient had, until recently, been purchased in small containers. Then someone bought a large container of the material to secure a purchasing economy. The large container, being exposed longer during usage, picked up more moisture and created the problem.

In other cases, the within-stream changes are abrupt, due to the entry of new materials, new operators, etc. For example, in a food processing operation, a recurrence of spoilage microorganisms was localized, by continuous sampling, to product turned out between midnight and 3 A.M. With this localization, the production supervisors were able to discover that the blancher operator then on duty was failing to flush and drain the blancher water during the midnight lunch hour. This failure permitted the accumulation of spoilage microorganisms.

In analyzing time-to-time variations, the length of *time between abnormalities* can be a major clue to the cause.

In a textile carding operation, there was a cyclic rise and fall of yarn weights, the cycle being about 45 minutes in length (Figure 16–6). The reaction of the production superintendent was immediate: "The only thing we do every 45 minutes or so is to stuff that feed box." In like manner, a process for making asbestos roofing shingles was found to produce abnormal weights every six minutes, on a precise

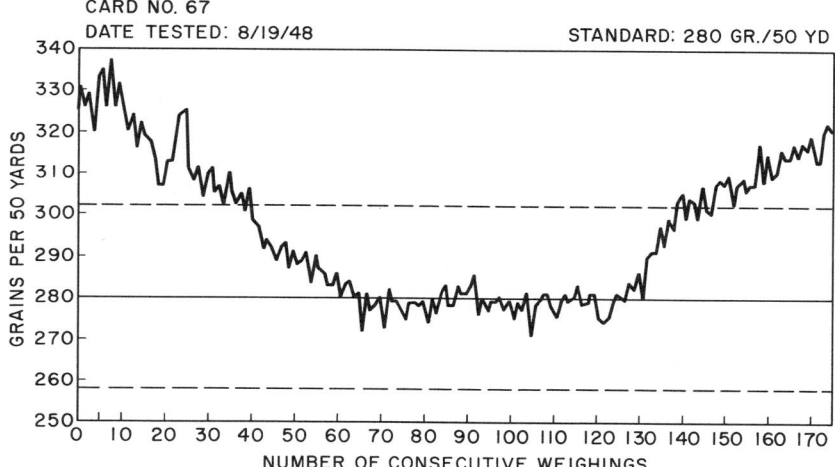

Fig. 16-6 Consecutive weighings of card yarn.

timetable. Six minutes was also the interval for dumping a new load of material into the machine.

Piece-to-Piece Analysis Products also exhibit piece-to-piece variation, which is quite independent of variations resulting from mixture of streams or from time-to-time drift.[47] Usually, measurement of this variation is done by the familiar techniques of frequency distribution. A great body of statistical methodology has been evolved to measure piece-to-piece dispersion. (See generally Section 22; also Section 9, under Process Capability Measurement.)

Beyond conventional statistical analysis, there is room for much creativity in discovering causes of piece-to-piece variation.[48] Frequently, the methods of analysis used overlap other methods, e.g., stream-to-stream, new instrumentation, etc.

For example, in a stack casting operation, one theory was that the bottom castings in the stack caused far greater scrap than the remaining castings. When the castings were processed with knowledge of their prior position in the casting stack, the theory was confirmed (Figure 16-7).

Within-Piece Analysis In some cases, what turns out to be decisive is the variation

---

[47] For very short production quantities, the drift can usually be ignored.

[48] See, for example, the case of the electron tube grid, in which some members of the strip differ consistently from others (Section 9, Figure 9-20, and associated discussion).

within individual units of product. A common example is variation in mechanical components, such as diameters out of round, unintended taper, bell-mouthed holes, eccentricity of rotating surfaces. In materials or semifinished products, some corresponding examples are segregation in mixtures or nonuniformity of sheet thickness.

The foregoing are all instances in which the variation is measureable. In consequence, the variability can be compared to other sources of variability to determine whether within-piece variability is a major or minor contributor to overall variability.

Defect-Concentration Analysis   A totally different form of piece-to-piece variation is the defect-concentration study used for attribute types of defects. The purpose

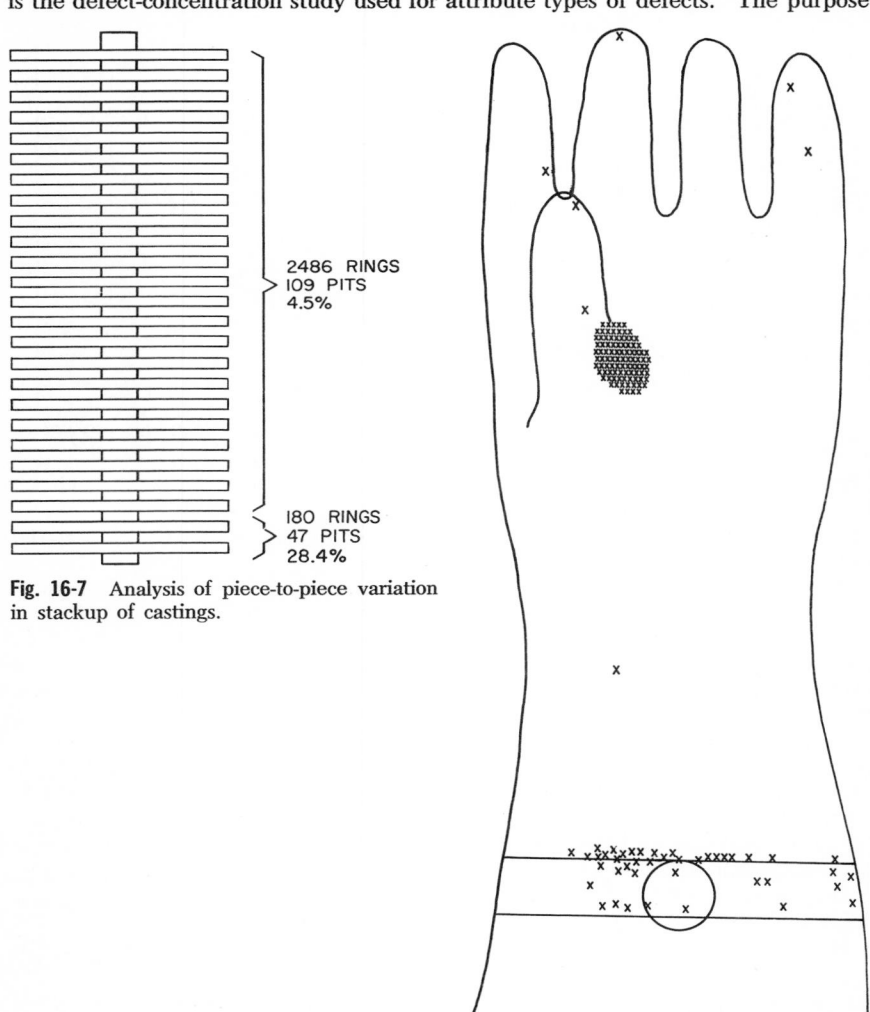

2486 RINGS
109 PITS
4.5%

180 RINGS
47 PITS
28.4%

Fig. 16-7   Analysis of piece-to-piece variation in stackup of castings.

Fig. 16-8   Concentration analysis of leaks in rubber gloves.

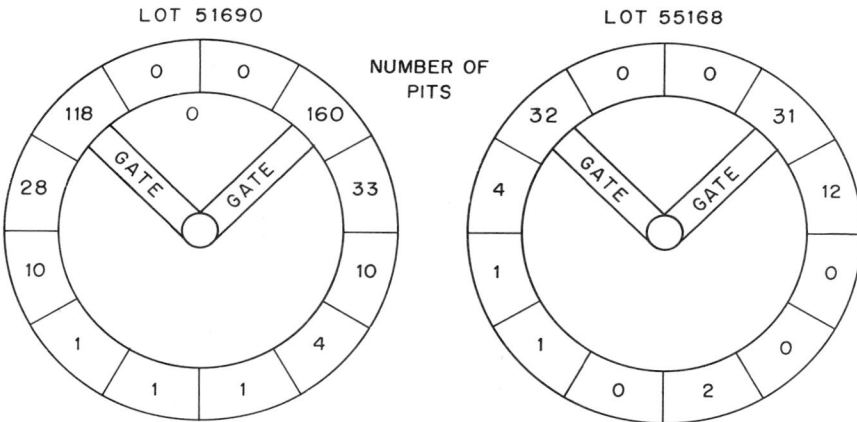

Fig. 16-9   Concentration of pits in cast rings.

is to discover whether defects are located in the same physical area.   The technique has long been used by shop personnel when they observe that *all* pieces are defective, and in precisely the same way.   However, when the defects are intermittent or become evident only in later departments, the analysis can be beyond the capacity of the shop personnel.

Figure 16-8 shows a concentration study of the location of leaks in dipped rubber gloves.   The pattern identifies the areas requiring remedy and permits comparison with future product to see if the remedy was actually achieved.

In a related example, a problem of pitted castings was analyzed by dividing the castings into 12 zones and tallying up the number of pits in each zone over many units of product.   The concentration at the gates became evident, as did areas which were remarkably free of pits (Figure 16-9).

An extension of the technique is to create a three-dimensional diagram.   In a plant making glass bottles, a cardboard model of a bottle was constructed and used to record the exact location (in three dimensions) of "checks," i.e., small incipient fractures.   The concentration was in the threads and pointed to thread mold radii as the likely opportunity for improvement.   Similarly, in a plant making hunting guns, the location of damaged wood finish on rejected guns was recorded on a three-dimensional data sheet, i.e., dots painted on a blank gunstock.   The concentration of defects was at the areas where the guns rested in the mobile storage racks and showed that on many racks the protective leather pads had rotted off.

For irregularly shaped products, an alternative approach is to use special data sheets to mark the location of the defects.   Figure 16-10 is an example of a grid used by a Spanish company for collecting data on casting defects.[49]

The defect-concentration analysis can also be applied to field failure problems. A company making household appliances was encountering chipped enamel on delivery to dealers and users.   To collect information on just where the damage was located, exploded diagrams were sent to the field service personnel.   The data, when summarized as shown on Figure 16-11, showed clearly the concentration at the corners and greatly simplified the subsequent discovery of cause and remedy.

[49] Courtesy of the Pegaso truck factory, Barrajas, Spain.

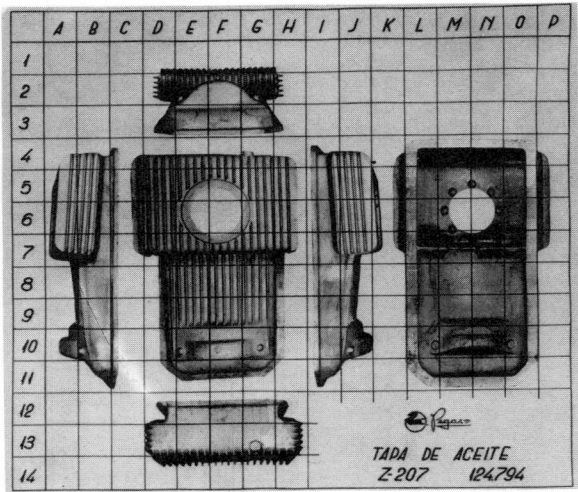

Fig. 16-10   Grid diagram used to accumulate defect-concentration data.

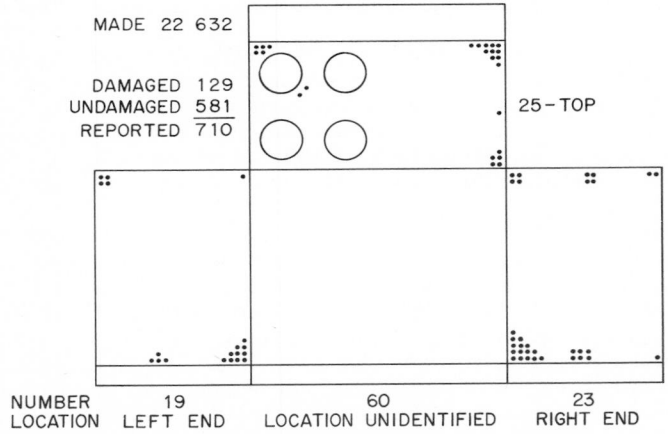

Fig. 16-11   Concentration of chipped enamel on household appliances.

INTERRELATION OF VARIABLES

The variables under study in the foregoing are always multiple in nature and are present in combination form.   While they can be studied singly, there are many instances in which the need is to study them in combination.   The aim of such studies is to quantify the size of the components of variation and to discover the extent to which they interact with each other.   The generalized methods for such combination studies are discussed in Section 27, Design and Analysis of Experiments. However, simplified forms of analysis are available for problems which do not demand the use of sophisticated tools.

Multi-Vari Chart For some purposes it is helpful to chart the variables to make more clear or to dramatize their interrelationship. A useful basic building block in such charts is a vertical line to show the range of variation of one unit of product. For example, Figure 16-12 shows the measurements on a "circular" piece which is actually slightly elliptical. The largest diameter is A, and the smallest diameter is B. The resulting values are plotted against the tolerance limits and dramatize the extent to which the elliptical condition of the piece "eats into" the tolerance.

An extension of this basic concept is seen in Figure 16-13, which depicts three different examples of the relationship of product variation to tolerance limits. The left-hand case is one in which the within-piece variation alone is too great in relation to the tolerance. Hence there is no solution unless within-piece variation is reduced. The middle example is a case in which within-piece variation is comfortable, occupy-

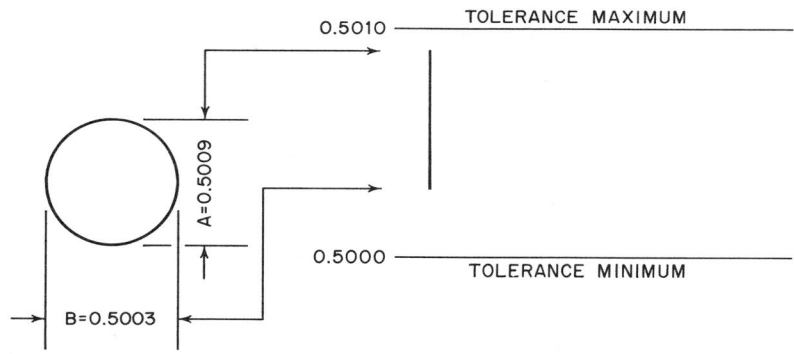

Fig. 16-12 Basic graphic representation of product variation versus tolerance limits.

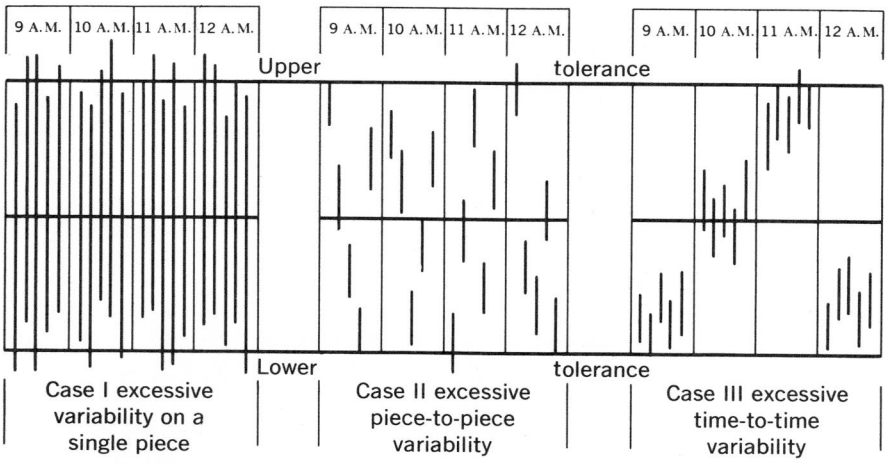

Fig. 16-13 Multi-Vari Chart.

ing only about 20% of the tolerance. The problem is piece-to-piece variation. In the right-hand example, the problem is excess time-to-time variability.[50]

P-D Diagram Another form of graphic representation is the position-dimension (P-D) diagram.[51] To use L. A. Seder's example, a copper cap was formed in a cold pressing operation. Measurement was made of six critical dimensions, as shown in Section 11, Figure 11-3. These measurements were then coded or "corrected" by subtracting the thinnest reading from all readings. This permitted a form of charting which shows the interrelationship of all dimensions on a single P-D diagram, Figure 11-4. The shape of this diagram effectively disclosed the nature of the press tool setup, as shown in Figure 11-5. The supervision, engineers, and machine setters learned to interpret the diagrams and to use them, first for quality improvement and then for holding gains. For added discussion, see Section 11, under Inspection Feedback to Production.

SPAN Plan[52] This is a structured approach to analysis of composite variations, and employs standardized data collection and analysis sheets to permit successive separation of observed total product variability into five recognized stages: lot to lot, stream to stream, time to time, within piece (or positional), error of measurement.

The plan is set out in "cookbook" fashion, so that a practitioner can collect the prescribed data, fill in the forms, and get the answers. Being a standardized procedure, the method can be used by the untrained practitioner. However, the trained analyst finds the procedure to be too elaborate for many applications and soon uses shortcuts which bypass the need for such elaboration.

Simple Vectorial Resolution Whenever the interaction among variables is negligible, the composite of multiple variations can be expressed by the relationship

$$\sigma^2_{comp} = \sigma_a{}^2 + \sigma_b{}^2 + \sigma_c{}^2 \dots,$$

where σ_{comp} = the standard deviation of the composite,
    σ_a = the standard deviation of variable a, etc.

It is evident from the formula that what is decisive about the size of variables in their contribution to the composite is not the standard deviation but the square of the standard deviation! This relationship is of great practical value in affirming or denying theories and especially in establishing priorities for mounting an attack on the critical variables.

For example, three of the operations contributing to the thickness variation of optical lenses are blocking, milling, and grinding. On one set of processes the following data were secured:

Operation	σ	σ^2
Block	1.7	2.9
Mill	1.9	3.6
Grind	2.8	7.8
Sum of squares		14.3

---

[50] The name Multi-Vari was given to this form of analysis by L. A. Seder in his paper Diagnosis with Diagrams, *Industrial Quality Control*, January 1950 and March 1950. The concept of the basic vertical line (Fig. 16-12) had previously been employed by J. M. Juran (and possibly others), who derived it from the method long used by financial editors for showing stock market prices.

[51] This term was coined by Seder, L. A., *op. cit.*, from which the example is derived.

[52] Seder, L. A., and D. Cowan, The SPAN Plan Method of Process Capability Analysis, ASQC General Publication 3, September 1956.

It is evident that the grinding, while seemingly a minor part of the variation when judged by the values of σ, accounts for more than half the sum of the squares.

Even more dramatic is the following synthetic example, which has numerous counterparts in the world of reality.

Six variables exhibit the following values of σ:

Variable	Original		Improved	
	σ	σ^2	σ	σ^2
A	9	81	6	36
B	5	25	5	25
C	3	9	3	9
D	2	4	2	4
E	1	1	1	1
F	1	1	1	1
Total squares		121		76

Under a state of complete independence, the σ of composite becomes $\sqrt{121} = 11$.

If the variability of A is now reduced from 9 to 6, the total of the squares will reduce to 76 (right-hand column), and the composite σ will reduce from 11 to 8.7.

If, however, the variability of A remains constant and the variability of all the others is reduced to *zero*, the composite σ will become 9 (the value of A).

In other words, a modest improvement in the variability of the dominant variable does more good than achievement of perfection in *all* other variables.

TEST OF THEORIES BY CUTTING NEW WINDOWS

In some cases the discovery of causes requires making measurements over and above those needed for process control and product acceptance. This is in the nature of "cutting new windows" so that we can look into more stages of the process to see what is happening where. The cutting of new windows can take several forms:

1. *Measurement at intermediate stages of a single operation.* An example is the welding of large joints in critical pressure vessels. The weld is made by running a welding "bead" helically around the joint until the welding rod is consumed. A second bead follows the first, then a third, creating layer after layer of weld material until the joint is completely built up. When the finished joint is x-rayed, any voids are identified. Those voids must be ground out and rewelded, after which the finished joint is again x-rayed. This process is repeated until the x-ray shows no voids remaining.

The steering team considered variations from a number of sources: operator, time to time, joint to joint, layer to layer, within layer, and within bead. Prior test data were available to permit analysis of the first three of these theories. The remaining three could not be analyzed, since the x-ray test was performed only when a joint was completely finished. It was necessary to "dissect the process" on some joints by making an x-ray *after each bead*. This established that the main variable was within bead variation and that the problem was concentrated at the very start of the bead.

2. *Measurement following noncontrolled operations.* A simple example was a process for machining the inside of gun barrels, consisting of a sequence of operations of drill, redrill, and ream. There was no measurement after the first two

operations.   However, after reaming, the inside diameters were measured with an air gage.   Regularly, some of the barrels were found to have inside diameters with severe gouges in one or more locations.

Did the gouging take place in the drill, the redrill, or the ream operation?   There was no way of knowing, since the air gage head could measure only the ream diameter.   When additional gaging heads were made to fit the drill and redrill diameters, the way was open to solving the problem.

3. *Measurement of additional or related properties.*   An example is the paper mill which undertook to improve the uniformity of strength of paper.   Analysis of past data established that the variation from one material batch to another dominated all other variables.   In turn, a material batch or "furnish" consisted of a load of wood chips cooked under pressure in a large sealed vessel called a digester.   Some chemical tests (if made on the cooking pulp) were known to be reasonable predictors of subsequent strength of paper.   However, these tests were not being conducted because there was no way to remove a sample from the sealed digester.   When a valve was placed in the digester, it became possible to remove samples during the cooking process and to establish correlations between (1) test results on the samples and (2) the amount of additional cooking needed.   The resulting improvement was then retained by creating a new control station based on sampling during cooking.

In other cases, measurement cannot be made of the process variable but can be made by some related property of the product.   In a problem of chipped optical lenses, one theory was that the lenses were not being squarely seated in the milling chuck and therefore were being chipped in the chucking process.   There was no practical way to measure directly whether the lens had been seated squarely or not. However, an improperly seated lens would necessarily end up with a misalignment of the optical center with the mechanical center, and this "runout" could be measured.   A comparison of the frequency distribution of runout for unchipped and chipped lenses was conclusive.   (Table 16-13.)

TABLE 16-13   Runout of Unchipped Lenses versus Chipped Lenses

Amount of runout	Frequency	
	Unchipped lenses	Chipped lenses
3	1	
4	4	1
5	6	
6	5	
7	1	
8		
9		
10		1
11		1
12		1
13		2
14		2
15		4
16		4
17		
18		
19		
20		1

4. *Study of workers' methods.* In some situations involving management-controllable defects (and many more involving operator-controllable defects), there are *consistent* differences in the defect levels coming from various production operators. Month after month, some operators are "good" and others are "poor."[53] In such situations, there must be a cause for this consistent difference in observed performance. The managers know only that the difference is there and that improvement — by bringing all workers up to the level of the best — is possible.

There are two main approaches to discovering of the cause of worker-to-worker differences:

1. Ask the workers. In a centrifugal casting operation, one team of melters was found to have significantly and consistently less pitted castings than all other melters. On inquiry, the "best" melter volunteered that each morning, before pouring any castings, he cleaned out the accumulated metal adhering to the inside surfaces of the spout used to transfer molten metal from the ladle to the casting machines. None of the other melters did this. This difference in practice provided a vital clue to bringing all melters up to the level of the best.

Asking the workers does not assure that the managers will discover the cause of the differences in worker performance. In many cases the workers do not know what it is they are doing that produces the superior product nor even that they are producing a superior product.[54] In other cases the workers do know but regard the information as a trade secret which they are unwilling to share with the management or even with workers outside their own clique. In still other cases, the problem is not secret knowledge but secret ignorance, i.e., a "bad" worker is doing something detrimental to the product but does not know it (or knows it but is not telling).

2. Study the work methods. Where the secret knowledge is not available from personal disclosure by the worker, it may be discovered anyway by studying the methods used by the "good" and "poor" workers. These studies will always disclose differences in method, and often one or two of these differences are found to be decisive. They constitute the "knack" — a small difference in method which accounts for a large difference in results.

For example, in the gun assembly case (under Test of Theories Using Past Data, Tables 16-12a and 16-12b, plus associated discussion, above), a study of differences in the work methods of the "best" and "worst" assemblers disclosed that the "best" assemblers filed away one of the critical dimensions and that this was the knack. However, the assemblers were not aware that this filing improved the product, since the test data had never been available to them. The filing very likely had its origin in an assembly operator's experiment to simplify his job of assembly and adjustment. In this case the unauthorized practice was a benefit to quality, but it could just as well have been a detriment.[55]

---

[53] What is really good and poor is the product. Whether the corresponding operators are good and poor is a theory which the facts (to be discovered) will affirm or deny.

[54] In the case of the melter above, he had not even known he was producing a superior product. Neither had anyone else known this. The superiority came to light as the result of a special study in which, for the first time in the history of the process, the identification of melter with casting was preserved through the subsequent machining operations.

[55] Studying the work methods takes some ingenuity when the failures are comparatively infrequent. In one paper mill, a study was made to improve the effectiveness of the crews in fixing breaks on the paper machine. A videotape recorder was attached to the machine, the recording being automatically started by a paper break. Replay of the tape enabled the crew to study its own performance. (Private communication to J. M. Juran.)

DIAGNOSIS THROUGH EXPERIMENT

"Experiment" as used here means mainly the creation and processing of trial lots to test the validity of theories about causes of quality deficiencies. The experiment may be conducted either in a laboratory or in the outside world—the factory, warehouse, user's premises, etc.

Criteria for Experimentation   No matter where conducted, the experiment should meet some minimal criteria. It should:

Test the theories under study and not be confused by unsuspected variables, e.g., measurement error too large in relation to the things being measured

Disclose the presence of any important cause of variation even though it has not been advanced as a theory

Keep the cost of experimentation to a level which is reasonable in relation to the quality costs under study

Provide answers with a high level of confidence

If the experiment is conducted in a laboratory, an additional criterion is that, for the variables under study, the laboratory should be a good predictor of the subsequent shop or field tryouts.

If the experiment is conducted using the shop or the field as a laboratory, there arise still other criteria. Such experiments should:

Minimize the extent of interference with day-to-day operation

Provide against unauthorized or inadvertent interference by field or shop personnel

Input Skills   To meet these criteria in practice requires a merger of several separate skills or bodies of knowledge.

1. The *managerial* knowledge about markets, costs, priorities, etc., which determines the broad goals and direction of the studies. For example, in one company there was a project to reduce the scrap due to dimensional variability of a certain machining operation. One theory advanced was that the use of wider, sturdier cutting tools would reduce the variability and thereby the scrap. When an experiment was suggested to try this out, the managers insisted on broadening the experiment in a way which would permit comparison of total cost per unit resulting from the proposed type of tool versus the regular tools in use. To make this comparison required that the experiment compare not only scrap results, but also:

Product yield per casting machined: i.e., the wider tools wasted more material since they cut more of it into useless chips.

Production per hour: i.e., the wider tools required less tool changes and hence resulted in more gross castings processed

Tool breakage: i.e., the wider tools had longer life

Tool repairs: i.e., the wider tools required less maintenance[56]

2. The *technological* knowledge of materials, process, product, instruments, etc. Here the experts are the line department personnel at all levels. The department representatives on the steering arm provide the main contributions, but the work force also has contributions to make.

3. The *statistical* skills required to design the statistical aspects of the experiment, to collect the data without bias, and to read the meanings, hidden in the data, through statistical analysis. The diagnostician provides the bulk of these skills.

---

[56] The real objective is to minimize overall costs, not project costs. The steering team should always be alert to the effect of the project under study on costs outside the study. See, for further discussion, Section 5, under Discovering the Optimum.

(He is even more effective if he has the salesmanship skills needed to convince the steering arm members in sticky cases.)

Some of these statistical skills are centered around diagnostic tools which have a wide range of application to many industry situations. These diagnostic tools (e.g., Pareto analysis, stream-to-stream analysis, defect-concentration analysis) are discussed throughout this Section under various subject headings. In addition, as the diagnostician acquires experience, he is able to identify additional universals which make some very different technological situations look very much alike.

For example, a number of "different" industrial processes (calendering, wool carding, Fourdrinier, rolling mill) turn out product in the form of a continuous sheet. These processes are fed with "different" materials (adhesives, wool fibers, wood pulp, steel blooms) to produce "different" products (adhesive tape, carpet yarns, paper, steel sheet). Yet the diagnostic approach to all is quite similar — to study variation across the sheet, along the length, from material batch to material batch, etc.[57]

4. In addition, since many trial lots must be processed "using the shop as a laboratory," there is a set of unnamed skills required to carry out the experiments with a minimum of disturbance and friction while at the same time preserving the integrity of the data. Both the steering and diagnostic arms collaborate in this task.

Unifying the foregoing skills demands a meeting of the minds on what the plan of experiment is. In simple or familiar cases this can be agreed on orally, e.g., to make a process-capability study. As the experiments grow in complexity, it becomes mandatory that the plan of experiment be reduced to writing so that there can be a formal review by all concerned to assure that the essential criteria for experimentation will be met and that full advantage is taken of the available skills and knowledge.

The Rifleshot Experiment In many projects, the analysis of available data may point strongly to only one or two suspect variables. In such cases it is common to avoid elaborate exploratory experiments and instead to conduct narrow experiments to test only the effect of the one or two suspects. Such studies are known as rifleshot experiments.

In its simplest form, the rifleshot experiment identifies, by use of the split-lot technique, which of two suspected variables is the cause. For example, of a batch of homogeneous material, half is sent through process A and the other half through process B. If the material is also a main suspect, two lots of material will be split, and each will be processed through both processes A and B, creating a two-by-two design of experiment. If three variables are involved, more combinations are needed; but now the technique of design of experiments enters to simplify the procedure. The example given by Shainin[58] illustrates the concept.

An extension cord set includes a switch, socket, and lamp. A percentage of the cord sets fail to light up at final test. In case of a defective set, is the fault in the switch, the socket, or the lamp? The answer can be found by a simple experimental design involving interchange of components from the good cord set G and the defective cord set NG, as shown in Figure 16-14. The pattern of lamps on and off conclusively demonstrates which component is defective.

A simple example of a rifleshot experiment is seen in the foundry case shown in Section 34, Figure 34-5. The purpose was to test the theory that the gating design was a major cause of excess eccentricity in the castings and of poor tension of the final product (rings).

[57] For an extended discussion, see Juran, J. M., Different to You but Alike to Me, *Industrial Quality Control,* April 1963, pp. 32 and 33.

[58] Shainin, D., When Is a Tolerance Just Right? *SAE Journal,* February 1950, vol. 11, pp. 80–83.

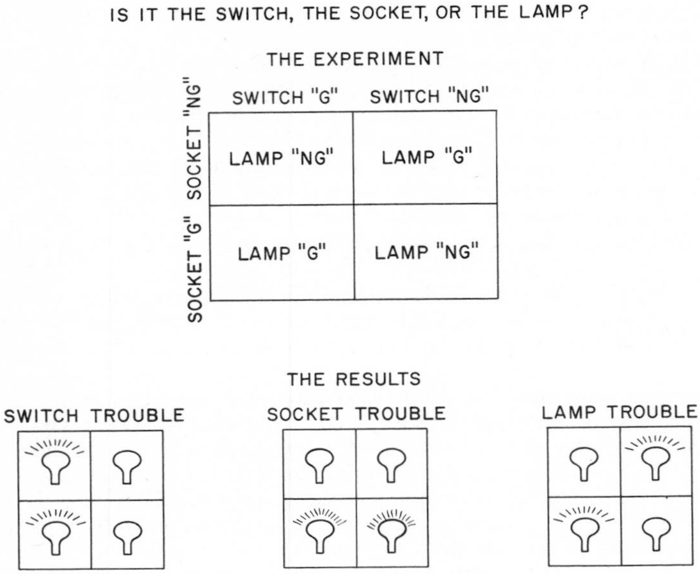
IS IT THE SWITCH, THE SOCKET, OR THE LAMP?
THE EXPERIMENT
SWITCH "G"
SWITCH "NG"
SOCKET "NG"
SOCKET "G"
LAMP "NG"
LAMP "G"
LAMP "G"
LAMP "NG"
THE RESULTS
SWITCH TROUBLE
SOCKET TROUBLE
LAMP TROUBLE

Fig. 16-14 Rifleshot experiment—defective cord sets.

An example of application of a three-variable experiment is seen in Section 34, Figure 34-8 and associated discussion. There the variables suspected of contributing to casting porosity were mold temperature, melt temperature, and operator. The experiment denied the operator theory and affirmed a combination of temperatures as dominating the causes.

The rifleshot experiment appeals strongly to practical men. It is short and to the point. It is a logical follow-up of their own thinking and will more readily win their support than will the research type of experiment which is unpredictable as to what it will prove and as to the time required to prove it. Moreover, there are times when an investigator finds an answer, fully substantiated by data, only to be unable to put this valid answer into effect *until he has disproved certain theories* which contradict the proved answer. To the investigator who thus knows the answer to his own satisfaction, it is irritating to be required to do further work just to explode some long-standing shop lore. However, this is part of the job of selling and must be done in that spirit.

The rifleshot type of experiment has the added advantage of narrowing the field of investigation and the field of opinion. As soon as any hypothesis is conclusively eliminated, those who have advocated that hypothesis gradually become reconciled to its denial and turn their thinking to other possibilities. By being dislodged from a long-standing theory, they are also forced to open their minds, and the result can be wholesome.

The rifleshot experiment has the disadvantage of limiting itself, in purpose at least, to existing theories when the solution may go beyond any of them. Seldom does an experiment made to affirm or deny an existing theory point to a variable not previously suspected.

The rifleshot experiment can be either a useful shortcut to answers or a repetitive waste of time. It depends on the experience and judgment of the diagnostician and of the steering team in choosing the right situations for use of rifleshot experiments.

The statistical designs of experiment, even for the rifleshot variety, can attain complexities which are beyond the reach of the amateur. See Section 27 for the structure of some of the more complex designs.

The Unbridled Experiment   In the absence of strong suspicions as to one or several variables being dominant, the trial-lot approach may take the form of the "unbridled" experiment. In this form, a lot (or lots) of product is followed through the successive processes under a plan which provides for making measurements of many of the suspected variables of the materials and processes. The resulting product characteristics are also measured. The hope is that the subsequent analysis will disclose all significant correlations between causes and effects.

The unbridled experiment is so much in the nature of a fishing expedition that it should be based on a written plan to assure that it is understood and that it represents a meeting of the minds. With careful planning, a well-organized unbridled experiment has a high probability of identifying the dominant causes of variability. The disadvantage is the associated high cost and long time interval to get answers.

The unbridled experiment requires both technological and statistical designs. An example of the technological design is seen in Table 16-14, involving a study by an optical manufacturer. The design shows which characteristics are to be measured and how. In addition, it shows whether the characteristics are to be:

Allowed to vary as they come naturally (M)
Held to a standardized value (S)
Deliberately randomized (R)
Deliberately varied in several classes or treatments (V)

Beyond the technological aspects of the design are the statistical aspects. These are discussed in Section 27.

A serious risk of using the unbridled experiment is that in the hands of amateurs the design becomes burdened with so many theories that it falls of its own weight. This risk can be reduced by:

1. Securing the advice of an expert statistician during the preparation of the statistical design.

2. Conducting a small-scale "dry run" of the experiment prior to running the full-scale experiment. The dry run is not for the purpose of collecting data on cause and effect; it is for the purpose of testing to see whether it is practical to carry out the experiment. (Sometimes the dry run discloses that it is not even possible, because of overcomplexity, to record the data as planned.) When the results of the dry run are reviewed by the steering arm, it is usually possible to convince the overenthusiasts that the plan must be simplified.

Processing Experimental Lots   When the experiments are conducted in laboratories, the environment, the priorities, and the responsibilities are all favorable to experimentation. In contrast, when the experiments are conducted in the shop (or in field operations), there can be handicaps at every turn:

The environment (facilities, work conditions, etc.) is designed for conducting operations, not experiments.

The established priorities are to meet the operating goals, not the needs of this experiment

The personnel regard the meeting of operating goals as their prime responsibility. The experiment may interfere with this.

Because of the obvious risks to the integrity of the experiment, provision should be made, both during the planning of the experiment and in the subsequent process-

TABLE 16-14   Detailed Plan of Experiment

Characteristic	How Measured	M, S, R or V
The Input Lenses		
1. Curvature	W gage	V
2. Visual condition	Visual	M
3. Lens type and power		S
4. Grinding cycle	Timer	M
5. Blocking conditions		M
6. Surface texture	Profilometer	M
The Tools		
1. Curve of presser	W gage	S
2. Curve of polisher body	W gage	S
3. Curve of polisher lap	Contour projector	M
4. Thickness of felt before and after	Micrometer	M
5. Diameter of polisher body	Scale	S
6. Ooze on polisher	Visual	M
7. Source of felt		S
The Process		
1. Condition of upper pin	Visual	M
2. Condition of bushing	Visual	M
3. Polishing time	Timer	S
4. Machine setting	Protractor	S
5. Machine No., spindle No.		S
6. Operator		S
7. Date, time		M
8. Process performance	Visual	M
The Finished Product		
1. Presence and location of unpolish	Microscope, visual, arc lamp	
2. Visual condition	Visual	
3. Targets	Arc lamp	
4. Curve	W gage	

ing, to guard against damage to the intent of the experiment.   The more usual needs are to assure that:

1. The data recording reflects what actually happened to the experimental lot. The most desirable approach is for the assigned diagnostician to "attach himself" to the lot and to follow it through its planned journey.   This enables him to see to it that the data collection plan is actually being carried out.   In addition, he is able to keep a log on the extraneous conditions present, since there are times when such conditions provide critical insights.   Where it is not feasible for the diagnostician to follow personally the progress of the experimental lot, the data plan should be sent, in writing, to all personnel along the line of march, with clear responsibility established for the tasks to be performed.

2. The lot must be identified throughout so that it will not be commingled with other product.   It is exasperating when an experimental lot vanishes, but it is not as inexcusable as it seems.   Changes of shifts, needs of expediters, or confusion among materials handlers can readily bring about such a result.   Obviously, the lot, if not constantly in the possession of the diagnostician, must be marked in a way that leaves no doubt of its identity, including a designation of whom to call in the event of question.

Where the experimental lot is being shipped between companies, the precautions must be even more strict. Here the collaboration should assure that a diagnostician is present both when the lot is loaded at one company and when it is unloaded at the other.

3. The lot should receive only the treatment intended by the experimental design. The fact that the lot is known to be special carries the risk that it will receive special treatment. In some cases, special identification must be *omitted* to eliminate this risk. In other cases, the observations and log of the accompanying diagnostician can provide the needed assurance.

DIAGNOSIS FOR NONDISSECTIBLE CHARACTERISTICS

A characteristic is "dissectible" if it is measurable during the process of manufacture, e.g., a shaft diameter as it progresses through a series of mechanical operations, or the viscosity of a resinous material as it is processed into a varnish.

A characteristic is "nondissectible" if it cannot be measured during such progression. Examples are the taste of a whiskey blend, the sharpness of a razor blade, the tensile strength of a casting, the electrical output of an electron tube. These examples are all alike in that the characteristics do not even exist until a whole series of manufacturing operations has been performed. Many nondissectible characteristics are in the nature of final, functional properties of the product, yet they first came into existence at the virtual conclusion of all manufacturing processes.[59]

Most of the examples cited in this Section have consisted of dissectible characteristics. For such cases, the diagnostician is greatly aided by the opportunity to make measurements at successive process stages or even to cut new windows for this purpose. The nondissectible characteristic lacks this feature, so the diagnostician must use other approaches. There are several of these:

1. Convert the nondissectible characteristics to dissectible through:

   a. Measure of related but dissectible properties, e.g., hardness used as a measure of tensile strength or viscosity used as a measure of polymerization.

   b. Creation of a new instrument, e.g., the airflow instrument for measuring uniformity of textile sliver.

   c. Use of parallel pilot plant: i.e., samples are processed in a laboratory-controlled pilot plant, thereby providing an early control against the results of production in the regular departments.

2. Correlate process variables with product results. A common approach is to take data on current production for those process variables believed to influence the product characteristics under study. The resulting product is also measured, following which use is made of statistical analysis to test for cause-and-effect relationships.

For example, a metal casting operation was diagnosed by a correlation study. Engineers were stationed in the foundry to record data on the 21 process variables proposed as theories by the steering team and to record also the practices of the foundrymen. The resulting castings were then followed into the machining operations until the quality of the (nondissectible) characteristics under study became evident. Simple regression analysis[60] was able to identify the dominant variable, which was then neutralized by process changes. Now it became possible to identify the secondary variables and to remedy them as well.

The work of staging such a study is called an "experiment," since it meets the

[59] The foregoing is paraphrased from Seder, L. A., A New Science of Trouble Shooting, *Industrial and Engineering Chemistry*, September 1951, pp. 2053–2059. The terms "dissectible" and "nondissectible" were first used in this classic paper.

[60] The statistical techniques used to make such regression analyses are discussed in Section 26.

dictionary definition of an activity conducted to test a hypothesis. While the study involves no change in the process itself, the design of the study should embody all the care which goes into the planning of trial lots, as discussed under Diagnosis through Experiment, above.

3. Experiment using trial lots. This differs from 2 because the trial lot is deliberately designed to be processed specially. This special design reduces the work of experimentation and permits drawing conclusions which have a wider range of application than would result from letting nature take its course. Details of this approach are discussed in Diagnosis through Experiment, above.

MEASUREMENT FOR DIAGNOSIS

It is surprising how often the roadblock to diagnosis is the use of shop instruments to make the measurements. These instruments were never intended for diagnosis! They were provided for entirely different purposes—i.e., process regulation and product test—and in most cases they serve these purposes well. Having long used these shop instruments for these purposes, the shop personnel can easily drift into the axiomatic belief that the same instruments can also do the necessary diagnosis for quality improvement projects. In specific situations where new instruments are provided for proper diagnosis, and produce dramatic results, the line supervisors are stunned, saying "That should have been obvious."

There are several principal categories of cases in which measurement for diagnosis must be different from measurement for control:

1. Measurement by variables instead of attributes. For example, the need may be to study process capability of machines. The available shop fixed-limit gages, though suitable for product acceptance, are not adequate to study process capability.

2. Measurement with a precision superior to that of the shop instruments. In some cases this need arises because the shop instruments themselves are a dominant cause; i.e., they are not adequate even for their intended job of process control and product acceptance. In the watch shaft case (Section 9, Figure 9-16), the shop dial gages were not precise enough to enable the operators to regulate the machines. The process capability study was made by a laboratory instrument which was more precise by an order of magnitude.[61]

Greater precision is also necessary in cases where there is need to measure fine subdivisions of the product. One of the variables in a textile carding machine is the variation "across the web"; i.e., a wide web of fibers is broken up into 88 ribbons which are later spun into yarn.[62] To study the yarn-to-yarn variation (in weight), it was necessary to cut the yarns into small lengths and weigh them with a precise gram scale (Figure 16-15). (The shop acceptance procedure of weighing large spools of finished yarn introduced variables which could not be countenanced in the diagnosis.)

3. Measurement at new "windows" cut into the process. This is exemplified by the gun barrel case and the welding case discussed under Test of Theories by Cutting New Windows, above.

4. Measurement of properties not in the specification. The paper strength problem and the chipped lenses problem are examples of this. These are also discussed under Test of Theories by Cutting New Windows, above.

[61] The standardized evaluation of precision is the σ of measurement, which should not exceed a specified ratio to the σ of product variability. See Section 13, under Measurement Standards and under Error of Measurement.

[62] The study of variation *along the length* of the yarn is depicted in Figure 16-6 and involved some related needs for precise measurement. See generally Klock, A. G., and C. W. Carter, Woolen Carding Meets Quality Control, *Industrial Quality Control*, May 1952, pp. 35–38.

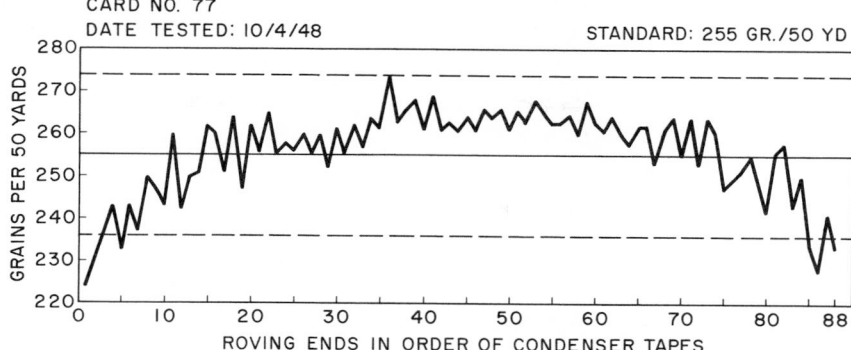

CARD NO. 77
DATE TESTED: 10/4/48   STANDARD: 255 GR./50 YD

ROVING ENDS IN ORDER OF CONDENSER TAPES

Fig. 16-15   Variation in yarn weight across the web.

5. Developing means to summarize sensory test results.   For example, in the optical industry, the extent of scratches on precise components is a major problem affecting process yields and product quality.   It is comparatively easy to judge one component for product acceptance purposes.   However, for judging process capability, or for comparing competing processes, something else is needed.   Use of percent of components scratched is a step forward, but the scratches are unequal in size and thereby in seriousness.   One optical company developed the concept of a "scratch index" which was expressed roughly as the ratio of the scratched area to the total area.   (The length of a scratch could be measured, and the width could be estimated by comparison to a standard scratch plate.)   The resulting index could be computed for entire lots of product.   It turned out to be much more sensitive than percent defective as an index for studying the effect of suspected causes of scratches, for judging process capability, and for choosing among competing processes.   A similar "chip index" was equally helpful in the problem of chipped optical components.

Sensory measurement.   Where the qualities under study are of a sensory nature, the "measurement" is done using human beings as instruments.[63]   Here again, the precision needed for diagnosis is different from that which is adequate for product acceptance.   For example, an attempt to improve the yield of glass bottle manufacture failed because inspector variability (from shift to shift) exceeded product variability.   It became necessary to go to use of a standard sample array to "calibrate" the inspectors.[64]

IMPROVEMENT IN FIELD PERFORMANCE

The "principles" of quality improvement apply to field performance[65] as well as to other parameters of fitness for use.   However, experienced practitioners know very well that application of these principles to problems of field performance is sufficiently different to require added techniques as well as special adaptation of standard techniques.

The main points of special emphasis in the improvement of field performance include the following:

[63] See generally Section 12, under Sensory Qualities.
[64] See Section 12, under Inspector Errors: Technique Errors.
[65] "Field performance" as used here refers to all problems of quality which follow manufacture, as discussed in Section 15, under Introduction.

1. The choice of projects is directed mainly at creating or retaining company income rather than at cost reduction. For example, a company making earth-moving machinery gave the highest priority to:

Total operating hours before initial service overhaul
Vehicle service life (measured in units of time)
Availability (ratio of operating hours to operating hours plus maintenance and downtime hours attributable to failure)[66]

2. A considerable extent of field failure has its origin in product design, requiring extensive collaboration of the project team with the entire span of product development and design activities.[67]

3. Even for field troubles which have their origin in manufacture, the separation of time and distance between cause and effect complicates the problems of diagnosis. Some aspects of this are discussed in Section 15, under Processing of Complaints: Discovery of Causes.

4. The difficulties of terminology are multiplied by the fact that numerous dealers, users, and repair shops are involved in the communications, each with a potentially different dialect.

5. The environments under which failures actually took place can be difficult to discover, due to user ignorance and misuse plus some lack of forthrightness.

Some companies have responded to these special problems by creating a category of Service Analyst to conduct the diagnosis in the field for multiple categories of product. Men in this category acquire wide experience as to the realities of field performance and are able to contribute this experience to the project teams. Other companies specialize their analysts by product line, so that the same analyst may be involved with studies of both shop and field problems for that product line.

STATISTICAL ANALYSIS

Analysis of quality improvement information includes statistical analysis in all of its conventional forms: frequency distributions, control charts, regression analysis, analysis of variance, etc. The techniques for these analyses are described in Sections 22 through 28. Use of computers is discussed in Section 20, while use of manual methods is discussed in Section 19.

REMEDY OF MANAGEMENT-CONTROLLABLE DEFECTS[68]

Once the diagnosis has established the needed cause and effect relationships, the project enters the remedy sequence. This involves several related activities: choice of remedy, overcoming cultural resistance to change, providing controls to hold the gains.

Finding remedies is generally easier than discovering causes. There are usually many theories about causes but few alternatives for remedy. In addition, the analysis for causes usually points out the department which should provide the remedy, so that responsibility is clear.

[66] Baba, Motomu, Quality Improvement of Bulldozers in Komatsu Mfg. Co., *Reports of Statistical Applications Research*. vol. 14, no. 3, 1967, pp. 22–27.

[67] See, for example, Kullman, L. W., and G. W. Phillips, Reliability Engineering Principles Applied to Commercial Weapons Systems—Guns and Ammunition, *Tenth National Symposium on Reliability and Quality Control* IEEE, 1964, pp. 122–136.

[68] Remedy of operator-controllable defects is discussed in Section 18.
See also, in general, Juran, J. M., Managerial Breakthrough, McGraw-Hill Book Company, New York, 1964, Chapter 10, Breakthrough in Performance—Action.

This same department nominates a remedy from the available alternatives.[69] This nomination should be reviewed by the team steering the project, since the need is to optimize company economics and since the range of choice involves interdepartmental considerations. However, there is a shift in the source of diagnostic manpower. During the diagnosis for causes, this manpower comes primarily from engineers attached to Quality Control. During the search for remedies, the diagnostic support comes mainly from the line departments that will take the final remedial action.

Remedy through Change in Technology   Many remedies involve changes in processes, instruments, methods, etc. The diagnosis for causes often points to these and clarifies the economics as well. In the watch shaft example (Section 9, Figure 9-16) the need for change of gages became obvious from the diagnosis, and the cost of new gages was obviously very small in relation to the cost of the defects.

Cases of conflicting terminology, incomplete information, vague orders or lack of standards are all forms of failure to provide the work force with knowledge of what they are supposed to do. They are usually economical to remedy.

As the cost of remedy rises (new tools, processes), the need for return on investment calculations becomes acute. Here it is useful to secure the aid of Industrial Engineering and Finance, who are skilled in preparing such studies and whose "certifications" tend to carry weight with upper management.

The greatest risk involves the cases where the process variability exceeds the necessary tolerable range yet the *process is the best known*. To improve the process would involve a form of research, with all the uncertainties associated with such a journey into the unknown. However, a solution in such cases constitutes a breakthrough (often patentable) and thereby a competitive advantage.

Remedy through Change in Standards   One of the possible remedies for chronic defects is to change the standards. In consequence, one of the directions for diagnosis should be to look at the validity of the standards. The very idea of challenging the standards is repugnant to some men on the grounds that any widening of standards represents a degradation of quality. Sometimes this resistance may be valid, but often it is not.[70]

The alarm signals which point to a review of standards include:

1. A lack of correlation between *(a)* the principal defects which stimulate field complaints and returns and *(b)* the principal defects found by the factory inspectors. See for example, Section 15, Field Failures versus Factory Rejects (under Significance of Field Complaints).

2. A situation in which the personnel who set the standards have no clear knowledge of the needs of fitness for use. These situations abound in the case of sensory qualities and require field studies on panels of users to establish realistic standards. See Section 12, under Sensory Qualities: Discovery of Sensory Characteristics Required for Fitness for Use.

3. Cases in which nonconforming components discovered in-house are regularly repaired or discarded but have never been subjected to trial of fitness for use. The need here may be to set up an experiment in collaboration with the users. Through such experiments it may be found that the nonconforming product is in fact fit for use or that the economics of use are more favorable than the economics of nonuse.[71]

Figure 16-16 shows the trend of percent scrap on a mechanical component over a

[69] For remedies during manufacturing planning, see Section 9, under Process Capability Incompatible with Product Tolerances.

[70] Aside from resistance due to cultural reasons (see below, under Cultural Resistance), the resistance to change in standards may be due to perfectionism. See Section 4, under Perfectionism.

[71] Still other solutions may be found, e.g., establishment of multiple grades.

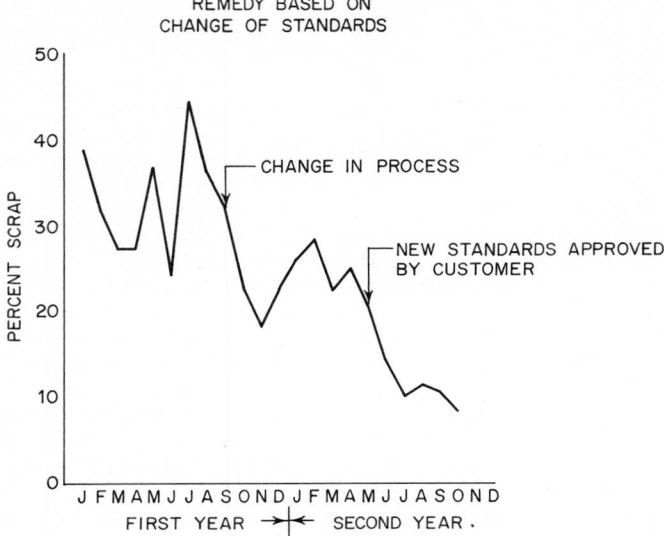

Fig. 16-16   Remedy based on change in standards.

two-year period. In September of the first year, a process change was made, and during the following eight months the scrap levels fell from 32% to 24%. Meanwhile, through collaboration with the users, a change in standards was made, resulting in a drop from 24% to 10%. The gain from change in standards (14%) exceeded the gain from change in process (8%).

4. Cases in which the user is overspecifying, to his detriment. For example, a company bidding on specifications for an instrumentation system noted that there were requirements for interchangeability not only on the subsystems but also on the components entering the subsystems. The former was obviously an essential requirement for field use; the latter was not, since the components were of a nature such that any repairs involving replacement of components could be made only at the factory site and not in the field. The situation presented an opportunity to save the buyer money if he could be convinced that the requirement for interchangeability of the components was a form of perfectionism.

The response to the foregoing alarm signals is to set up experiments which can validly establish the needs of fitness for use. A common road block to such experiments is the assumption that the designers had established their tolerances by experiment. For most tolerances this assumption is not valid.

A more valid objection arises under the following state of facts:

The prevailing product acceptance standards do not reflect the needs of fitness for use and can be relaxed. However, there is objection to this relaxation on the grounds that the process controls will then also be relaxed, thereby making the product worse and "crowding" the new (relaxed) product acceptance standards. This objection is well founded in plants where this "crowding" has been a way of life, and it is a plausible reaction in any case, even if the real resistance has its origins in the cultural pattern. A sensible response to such objection is to establish and publish a scoreboard on process performance. Such publication provides assurance to the objectors that the process is in fact being kept in control. Alternatively, it sounds a public alarm in cases of lack of control.

Remedy by Enduring the Defects   This solution is not merely a matter of "suffer and sort," though such is sometimes the economical solution.   The economics of cost of avoiding defects versus cost of enduring are largely controlling in the case of internal defects which are endured at one stage to be caught at another.[72]

Even when the defects make the product clearly unfit for use, they may be endured if they occur rarely.   In such cases, the cost of finding a defect through sorting soars as the percent defective declines.   The cost of finding a defect compared to the sales value of the unit of product is another useful comparison.[73]

Cultural Resistance to Improvement   The changes needed to effect a quality improvement are actually of two very different sorts:

1. An intended change in technology, standards, etc., to create the intended improvement.

2. An unintended effect on the status, belief, habits, and other elements of the "cultural pattern" of the people involved.   This effect on the culture is usually unwelcome and hence is resisted, thereby creating what is loosely known as "resistance to change."

The importance of this cultural resistance cannot be overstated.   The practitioners must understand its existence, the reasons behind it, and how to deal with it.   For a discussion in this Handbook, see Section 7, under Administration of the Quality Staff Specialty: Introducing Change.[74]

Holding the Gains   As action takes place to institute the remedies, there arises the problem of holding the gains.[75]   Obviously, solution of this problem is simplified if the predecessor steps have been well thought out: diagnosis, remedy, accommodation to the cultural resistance.   Nevertheless, there are enough cases in which the gains do not endure to require that the improvement plan include positive provision for holding the gains.

Mainly, the need is to institute controls, i.e., process controls and other forms as discussed variously in this Handbook.   However, the design of these controls should be specially tailored to the nature of the changes which have been introduced.   An important control special to quality improvement programs is the scoreboard on quality costs.   See Section 5, under The Control Scoreboard.   In this design, it helps to keep in mind that these changes are of two very different species:

Irreversible changes.   These are self-controlling because there is no way to undo them; e.g., the old tool has been thrown away, so there is no choice but to use the new tool.

Reversible changes.   These are not self-controlling, and they can be undone. For example, the work force has been provided with scales so that the recipe can be weighed out more precisely.   However, the workers quietly go back to estimating by eye, and the scales are not used.   Part of the improvement has evaporated, and with it, part of the results gained.

Where reversible changes are a problem, the solution is the process audit.[76]   A process auditor is designated to patrol the process, to see and record whether the changes introduced remain in effect.   This process audit is in addition to the data on process performance which are the central sources of information for process control.   The audit is needed in any case at the time of transition.   Thereafter, the results of audit will themselves disclose whether the changes have taken such firm root that the audit and other controls can be tapered off.

---

[72] In this connection, see also Section 24 under Selection of an AQL.

[73] See in this connection, Section 5, under Discovering the Optimum.

[74] For an extensive discussion, see Juran, J. M., "Managerial Breakthrough," McGraw-Hill Book Company, New York, 1964, Chapter 9, Resistance to Change: Cultural Patterns.

[75] See generally, Juran, J. M., *ibid.*, Chapter 11, Transition to the New Level.

[76] See generally Section 21, under Audit of Execution versus Plans.

THE END OF IMPROVEMENT

There is an economic limit to improvement due to the fact that the cost of improvement rises spectacularly as we approach perfection.   The economic model for this principle is shown in Section 5, Figure 5-2, and the practical application of the model is shown in Figure 5-3.

Section 17

Manpower[1]

J. M. JURAN

INTRODUCTION

Achievement of quality involves the harnessing of two very different kinds of forces:

1. The materials and energies of *nature.* For centuries, craftsmen and engineers have employed these forces on the basis of empirical knowledge. More recently, the "natural" scientists (mathematicians, physicists, chemists, etc.) have increasingly discovered laws governing these natural forces. These discoveries have been employed by engineers to harness the natural forces through development of the tools and methods of technology, e.g., thermodynamics, machine design.

[1] In the Second Edition this Section was prepared by Edward A. Reynolds.

2. The creativity and skills of *human beings*. For centuries, managers employed these forces on the basis of empirical knowledge. Late in the nineteenth century there arose the Taylor[2] movement to put this knowledge on a more scientific basis. The forerunners of today's Industrial Engineer developed tools such as methods study, work measurement, job training, and piecework incentives to improve the effectiveness of manpower.

More recently the behavioral scientists[3] have undertaken additional as well as more precise studies of the forces of human beings. Today's managers employ a mixture of empiricism, Industrial Engineering, and the work of the behavioral scientists in managing the work of the human resources of the enterprise.

This Section and the Section which follows (18, Motivation) discuss the ways in which the forces of human beings are harnessed to achieve quality. The "human beings" referred to are not merely those in the Quality Control department or even merely those in the company. They include, in addition, those people outside the company who contribute importantly to fitness for use: vendors, merchants, repair shops, government regulators, and the user himself.

TASKS, JOBS, AND CAREERS

A "task" is an identifiable segment of work and is largely synonymous with the "work element" discussed in Section 7, under Quality Control Work Elements and Jobs.

In that same discussion, a "job" is defined as a "bundle of work" assigned to one person. The job may consist of a single work element or it may include multiple work elements, of which all or only some are quality-related.

A "career" is a sequence of jobs designed to provide a logical progression for development and promotion.[4] The career concept can help in several ways:

In recruiting new employees, by showing them the long-range opportunities of the career in addition to the short-range opportunities of the starting job

In retaining qualified employees, whose identification with the company is improved through identification with a career pattern

In clearing up vagueness in the minds of the managers by creating a logical, coherent approach to manpower development instead of a crisis-by-crisis approach

Career Patterns   There are several lines of career development in the quality function.

Inspection Management.   In this line, the starting job is that of simple inspection, requiring no experience. From there the progress is to higher-grade inspection jobs, then into inspection supervision, and finally to the post of Chief Inspector. As higher levels of supervision are attained, the prime need becomes the skills of management, since the job has become one of getting results through directing other people.

Laboratory Technician.   This line of development is based on technological proficiency in metrology and testing. Recruitment requires an extent of training in technology usually beyond the high school level. The starting job is usually routine testing. Progression is into more complex testing, design of tests, instru-

---

[2] See Section 18, under Role of Motivation: The Taylor System.

[3] See Section 18, under Role of Motivation: Role of the Behavioral Scientists.

[4] For case examples, see Skolnik, Samuel S. J., Quality Control Training and Professional Development in the Department of Defense, *1962 ASQC Convention Transactions*, pp. 571–575; also Watkins, C., In-Plant Company Courses, *Proceedings, 13th EOQC Conference*, Prague, 1967, pp. 134–141.

ment design, and other forms of technological progression. The final job in the line is that of the company's chief expert in some test specialty, e.g., Nondestructive Testing, or as chief of the test laboratory.

Engineering.   This line requires, for recruitment, an engineering degree or its equivalent.   The assignments may begin with any of a variety of starting jobs: data collection and analysis, preparation of detailed quality planning sheets, etc. Progression is into the categories of Quality Control Engineer, Reliability Engineer, etc., and finally to the post of chief of the staff quality specialist department.

Other Functional Departments.   There is a degree of transfer and promotion from the Quality Control function to other functions (and vice versa).   Typical

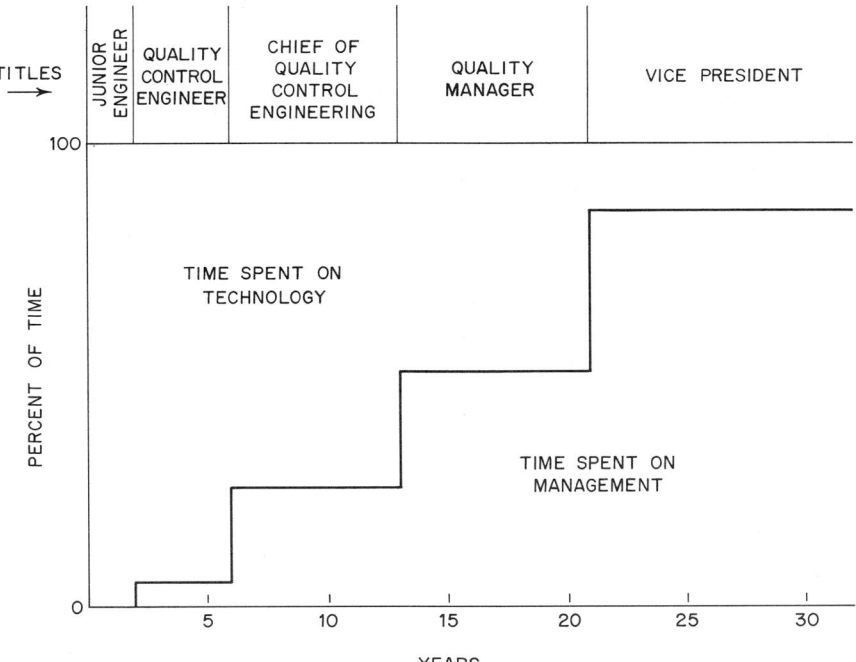

Fig. 17-1   Job progression—management and technology.

instances involve inspectors becoming shop foremen; engineers and laboratory chiefs moving into product design, process development, project engineering, etc.

General Management.   The three lines of inspection, testing, and engineering all converge into the post of Quality Manager.   This post is a halfway house between the quality specialty and general management, and is a major fork in the road. To be transferred out of this post into another function, e.g., to become Manufacturing Manager, is to leave the quality specialty and to enter the profession of management.

Actually, any job is a mixture of management and technology, the proportions changing over the years (Figure 17-1).   During the early years, the time spent on technology is so preponderant that the correct descriptive word is "engineer."   If a state is reached where the time spent on management is clearly preponderant, the correct title is clearly "manager." When both types of activity are significantly present, the titles lose their meaning.

TRAINING: THE CONCEPT

Training is a shortcut alternative to learning from experience or from accumulated mistakes. In a static society, products and processes go on without change for a man's lifetime, as do the trades and professions. For such societies, training is done once, and it lasts a lifetime. In the modern dynamic society, products and processes do not last a lifetime; many become obsolete in less than a decade. In like manner, the trade or the profession no longer lasts a lifetime. Many tradesmen or professionals, if not updated, become obsolete in less than a decade.[5]

The twentieth century forces of change have greatly affected the quality function[6] and have thereby demanded extensive programs of training. However, the response to these demands has been seriously out of balance in the United States. Generally, programs for inspectors, for quality specialists, and for the supervision in the Quality Control departments have been adequate to the needs. In contrast, programs (of training in the quality function) for other departments, for upper management, and for people outside the company have been deficient. To correct these imbalances requires development of special programs for upper management, middle management, product and process developers, manufacturing planners, purchasing specialists, field service specialists, accountants, and still others in the company. It also requires programs for people outside the company, e.g., the unions, vendors, merchants, repair shops, users, government regulators.[7]

The Training Program   The basic purpose of training is to create or update skills. Collateral with this is the transmission of information, e.g., the "briefing session." In addition, the training process so inevitably affects the attitudes of trainees that the changing of attitudes becomes one of the purposes of training.

Training cannot be done in the abstract. It must be specially designed and built into "programs" which give consideration to:

1. The quality problems and challenges faced by the company. These differ from one company to another, so the program must be tailor-made. In addition, these things keep changing from year to year, so the programs must keep pace with these changes.

2. The knowledge and skills needed to solve these problems and meet these challenges. These skills must be identified on a job-by-job basis; i.e., for each job, it is necessary to determine what skills are required to perform the quality-oriented tasks contained within that job. Table 17-1 is an example of such an analysis.

3. The knowledge and skills actually possessed by the jobholders. To understand this requires that an inventory be taken to discover the prevailing levels of knowledge and state of skill.

4. The training facilities and processes already in existence. These may include apprentice schools, on-the-job training by supervisors, self-training through manuals,

---

[5] The rate of obsolescence of knowledge is such that the "half life" of the knowledge of the manager, engineer, supervisor, or tradesman is probably about ten years; i.e., unless there has been regular updating of what becomes obsolete year by year, the man will be only 50% effective a decade later.

[6] For a detailed discussion of the massive changes in the quality function, see Juran, J. M., Mobilizing for the 1970's, *Quality Progress*, August 1969, pp. 8-17.

[7] In some programs conducted by the author, the companies have invited the attendance of some of their labor leaders, government inspectors, vendors, and customers.

company Training Department courses, collaboration with local University Extension services, etc. These existing forms are supported by vested interests, and any new program is well advised to secure the aid of these interests.

5. The prevailing climate for training, based on the record of past programs. When programs fail, it is usually for reasons such as that (a) they are not responsive to the needs of the company; (b) they have been launched without adequate prior participation of the line managers; (c) they are presented not in the language of the trainees but in the jargon of the specialist; (d) they have bypassed the established organization and methods for training. If the past record in training is negative, the new program should include proposals to remedy the failures of the past.

Role of the Supervisor   Training is a major responsibility of the supervisor, since it is basic to his managerial role of getting results through the efforts of other people. To an important degree, the supervisor personally is the trainer in:

1. Job induction, when the employee first starts on a new task
2. Job rotation, when the employee is assigned to a variety of tasks
3. Self-teaching, when the employee must study the manuals, procedures and other documentation as part of the preparation for doing his job.

Even where the supervisor is not personally the trainer, he is a major factor in any training undertaking, since he governs the essential priorities and the prevailing climate. As a consequence, *all* training programs, formal and informal, must be developed with the participation of the supervisor and must provide him with the means for carrying out his own key role.

A good deal has been done to help the supervisor in his role of training and of program development. Much can be done to assist him by preparing well-designed training materials and tools for his use.[8]

Case studies. These permit trainees to discuss a "staged" situation in which they have no prior reflexes. Well-prepared cases permit group discussion and role playing and are regarded by the majority of the trainees as well worth the time.[9]

Projects and Exercises. Many of the techniques in quality control training lend themselves to ready assignment of projects. Virtually any supervisor or nonsupervisor has access to actual job conditions which permit data collection and analysis for preparing frequency distributions, calculating mean and dispersion, measuring process capability, preparing a Pareto analysis, preparing a cause-and-effect diagram, etc. It is good practice to make such assignments, since the solution of problems from the world of reality has maximum impact on the trainee.

Examinations. When training is undertaken as a means of qualifying a person for assignment to a job, there should be a qualifying examination. In license cases, the examination is, of course, mandatory. The examination is also necessary if the training is a modular element in a broader curriculum leading to some certificate of completion.

Even when no qualification is at stake, it is usually useful to conduct examinations. The resulting feedback to the trainee serves to inform him of the extent to which he has been successful in acquiring the new knowledge. Equally important is the collective feedback to the instructors on how well they are getting their material across.

---

[8] See also Training Methods, below.

[9] For examples of cases which have been widely used, see Juran, J. M., and F. M. Gryna, Jr., "Quality Planning and Analysis," McGraw-Hill Book Company, New York, 1970 (the Metal Containers, Inc., case, pp. 643–646, and the RPM case, pp. 646–648). A number of the problems in this textbook are keyed to these case statements, e.g., a problem in vendor relations, pp. 419 and 420.

TABLE 17-1   Guide to Knowledge or Training Required for Various Quality Control Jobs

Subject	Quality director	Quality manager	Quality engineer	Inspection supervisor	Laboratory supervisor	Statistician	Statistical analyst	Inspector	Methods of training*
General Management:									
1. Personnel administration	X	X	O	X	X	O			TBU
2. Industrial organization	X	X	X	X	X	O			UBC
3. QC organization and functions	X	X	X	X	X	X	O	O	QBU
4. Basic production methods	X	O	X	O	O	O			UBC
5. Basic marketing	X	X	O	O		O			UBC
6. Cost systems and budgets	X	X	O			O			UBT
Company Operations:									
7. Policy and general plans	X	O							T
8. Organization and operations	X	X	X	X	X	O			T
9. Regulations and procedures	X	X	X	X	X	X	X	X	TB
10. Products and processes	X	X	X	X	X	X	O	X	QB
11. Eng. and prod. problems	X	X	X	O	X	O			B
12. Current industry techniques	X	X	X	O	O				
Engineering:									
13. Basic physics	O	X	X	O	X	O		O	UB
14. Basic chemistry	O	X	X	O	X	O			UB
15. Advanced chemistry—org. and phys.		O	O		X				U
16. Basic metallurgy	O	O	X	X	X	O			UBC
17. Precision measurements—elem.		X	X	X	X			X	QB
18. Precision measurements—advan.		O	X	X	O	O			BM
19. Nondestructive testing		O	X	O	X				BM
20. Lab. practices and equipment		O	X	O	X	O			QB
21. Technical report writing	X	X	X	X	X	X	X	O	TB

TABLE 17-1 Guide to Knowledge or Training Required for Various Quality Control Jobs (Continued)

Subject	Quality director	Quality manager	Quality engineer	Inspection supervisor	Laboratory supervisor	Statistician	Statistical analyst	Inspector	Methods of training*
Mathematics and Statistics:									
22. Shop math		X	X	X	X	X	X	X	TB
23. Calculus		O	X		O	X	O		UC
24. Basic SQC	X	X	X	X	X	X	X	O	QUB
25. Advanced sampling		O	X	O	O	X	O		UQ
26. Exper. design and analysis	O	O	O		O	X	O		UQ
27. Basic record and data systems	O	X	X	O		X			B
28. Data processing		O	O			X	O		BM
General:									
29. Public speaking	X	X	O	O	O	X			TU
30. Safety	O	X	X	X	X	O	O	X	T

X = Necessary.
O = Highly desirable.

*NOTE:
T — Central Training Department can provide course on request, if sufficient demand.
Q — Headquarters Quality Control Department will arrange courses as desirable.
U — University courses are available in many areas.
C — Correspondence course is available from state universities.
B — Books and technical articles are considered practical means for home study. (Books are, of course, also available for other subjects but self-study is not considered as practical.)
M — Manufacturers of equipment provide short full-time courses in various cities.

TRAINING METHODS

A wide variety of methods is available, and these can be adapted to the wide variety of trainees and of subject matter.

Classroom Training   This widely used training form has broad application to training programs in quality control.   Effective use of the classroom requires care in dealing with several elements of the learning process:

A training content which at the very outset establishes connecting links between the quality mission of the company, the unsolved quality problems, and the role of the trainee in solving those problems

A clear course outline plus prepared text material, so that the trainee can see what will be coming up and can do some advance preparation

Competent instructors, both as to the subject matter and as to ability to communicate

Well-designed teaching aids

In addition, it is well to do some judicious screening so that trainees do not get into courses for which they are seriously overqualified or underqualified.

The Quality Control Manual   These manuals are widely used for reference when procedural questions arise and for the induction of new people into jobs.   Well-prepared manuals permit a new appointee to learn a good deal about his new job through study on his own, before the problems arise.   In special situations, the manual itself becomes the main text for training seminars.[10]

Training Films[11]   These are increasingly available in a variety of quality-related subjects, such as the following:

Metrology: mechanical, optical, nondestructive testing, etc.

Statistical methods: sampling theory, control charts, design of experiments, etc.

Quality systems: product design, process control, campaigns, motivation

Reliability, maintainability

Product and process technology, mostly electronic but some others as well

New films are constantly being produced, and it is useful to maintain contact with the sources.   A prime contact is the Education and Training Institute of the American Society for Quality Control,[12] which maintains a rental service and is a source of information on training aids generally.

Audiovisual Systems   These systems consist typically of:

1. An audio tape which carries voice instructions.   These instructions are heard through earphones or a speaker.

2. A series of color slides depicting the successive stages of process and product to be attained and the methods, knack, etc., for doing the job.   These slides are displayed on a viewing screen.

3. The necessary electronic gear to play the tapes, synchronously project the slides, and provide operator control over the system—start, advance, playback, stop.

Use of these systems requires preparation of the instruction programs themselves. These are commonly tailor-made for specific operations (e.g., assembling, wiring,

---

[10] Examples are seminars organized by a company for its vendors at the time of publishing a new vendor relations manual.   In like manner, publication of a new or revised government manual is the occasion for organizing seminars to discuss the interpretation.

[11] For some detailed listings, see *Industrial Quality Control,* October 1966, pp. 192 and 193; also *Evaluation Engineering,* November/December 1966, p. 40.

[12] Located at 161 West Wisconsin Ave., Milwaukee, Wis. 53203.

inspecting) on specific products.[13] There are also available some standard programs for operations in wide general use, e.g., electronic component assembly, wiring, soldering, mechanical assembly, tool maintenance, etc.[14]

The use of audiovisual systems is evidently of great aid in complex assemblies, where it shortens the learning time and reduces the error rate.[15]

In one instance, an audiovisual script for test of automatic transmission apparatus was drafted by an engineer and reviewed by three key groups: the manufacturing engineers and product engineers, the test foremen, and six testers. The resulting critiques contributed to the adequacy and clarity of the script and to the acceptance by those who could make the program work or fail.[16]

Programmed Instruction This is another form of self-instruction based on the preparation of prefabricated training materials. These materials are designed to present successive "frames" or small segments of information for independent study. The design further permits immediate feedback to the student as to his absorption of the knowledge.

Preparation of these programs is costly, requiring considerable time by a skilled programmer plus associated consultation with the key supervision. However, once prepared, the programs permit a good deal of flexibility in training, since the instruction need not be done on the job or even in conventional classrooms at scheduled hours.

Training by Simulation There have been a number of proposals for using simulation and games as training tools. Some of these include:

1. An attribute sampling game with the objective of attaining the lowest combined cost of inspection plus loss due to defects missed.[17]

2. An extension of the foregoing involving two components which assemble to make a third. Again, the game is to minimize the total costs.[18]

3. A machine assignment game in which the player can assign work to any of several machines of different process capability and different cost per unit of product, the costs per unit being higher for the more precise machines.[19]

4. A process yield game. The players are given prior production data for the yields of 26 batches of a process along with data on certain ingredients and process variables. The game is to specify the conditions under which new lots should be made to achieve minimal costs.[20]

---

[13] Manufacturers of the audiovisual hardware usually conduct workshops to show clients how to prepare programs. In addition, there are commercial firms who offer services in preparing programs.

[14] In a broader sense these systems, in the form of training films, have been in long and extensive use. The innovations here are to tailor-make the program to specific tasks and then to put the program under the step-by-step control of the operator or inspector.

[15] See Color-Sound Slides Speed Assembly, *American Machinist/Metalworking Manufacturing*, April 30, 1962, pp. 108–110. See also Jacobsen, T. L., and R. A. Williams, Audiovisual Systems; Key to Quality Control. *Mechanical Engineering*, August 1963, pp. 46–49. Also Hill, David A., and John J. Tamsen, Videosonic System Instructions Raise Quality Standards, *Industrial Quality Control*, July 1961, pp. 15–20.

[16] Maass, Richard A., Train Inspectors with a Show, *Quality Assurance*, October 1968, pp. 40 and 41.

[17] Torgersen, P. E., and G. B. Thomas, Simulating an Acceptance Sampling Plan, *Industrial Quality Control*, December 1963, pp. 27–29.

[18] Torgersen, Paul E., and Rodney L. Cleavelin, Simulating Acceptance Sampling in a Component Assembly System, *Industrial Quality Control*, October 1966, pp. 172–176.

[19] Masing, Walter E., Kwaliteitsbeheersings-spelen (Quality Control Games), *Sigma*, vol. 9, no. 3, 1963, pp. 61–64.

[20] Daly, C., Statistical Games, *Applied Statistics*, vol. 13, no. 2, 1964, pp. 74–83.

In-Company Programs   In large companies, the central training organization (or the Quality Control Department) may create a broad program for training in quality control, offering a battery of related courses.   Some courses are conducted in-house, using company managers and engineers as instructors.   Some courses make use of invited lecturers.   Still others are offered by local universities.[21]

In Sweden, the Association of Metalworking Industries has evolved a training concept which permits companies to conduct in-house training courses for engineers. Under this concept, an industry committee:

Designs the course material and reduces it to a textbook, complete with exercises and case studies

Prepares teaching aids, video and audio

Prepares a detailed instructor's guide keyed to the textbook and teaching aids[22]

Presents the course to prospective course leaders at seminars, which include briefings to assist and motivate these men to attain effectiveness in their own teaching[23, 24]

Some Rules of the Road   Managers are strongly biased in favor of learning from the experiences of other managers.   Training programs for managers should make use of this bias by building the training around such experiences.   In the classroom, this is done by first presenting actual examples of experiences and then generalizing from these examples.   (If the generalities are presented first, the managers stop listening.)

Outside of the classroom there are also ways to present actual experiences:

Visits to Other Companies.   Managers are always stimulated by such visits. Their critiques are quite objective, since it is someone else's problems which are the target.

Management Night at the Society Meeting.   Some professional societies reserve one of their evening meetings to provide programs specially designed for managers. Such meetings may become a part of the curriculum.

Published Articles.   The industrial literature makes wide use of "success stories" showing how some companies solved problems.   Some of these stories are timely for the training program at hand and can be used as a form of learning from the experience of other managers.[25]

---

[21] See generally *Industrial Quality Control,* June 1967 (special issue on education and training), and especially the following papers: Harvey C. Charbonneau, Quality Control Training at General Motors Institute, pp. 629–631; A. J. Hitzelberger, Benefits of a Continuing Quality Training Program, pp. 631–633; Warren R. Purcell, Satisfying Industrial Quality Control Training Needs, pp. 634–636; Eugene E. Newman, Quality Training in Government, pp. 636–639.   For a case example, see Asay, K. C., and J. W. Morris, Professionalism in Quality Control, *ASQC Technical Conference Transactions, 1965,* pp. 50–56.

[22] The weakness of the concept is in the reliance on in-house instructors, many of whom, though competent technologists, lack experience in teaching and educational methods.

[23] Forseth, B., In-House Company Courses, *Proceedings 13th EOQC Conference,* Prague, 1969, pp. 130–133.

[24] For a comprehensive study of education and training for quality in European countries, see Egermayer, F., *(a)* "Report on the First EOQC Seminar on Education and Training for Quality" and *(b)* "National Systems of Education and Training for Quality," European Organization for Quality Control, P.O. Box 1976, Weena 734, Rotterdam 3003, Netherlands.

[25] These success stories tend to be colored due to company censorship.   Actually, it would be very useful if the journals were also to publish failure stories, since these are most instructive.

COURSES IN STATISTICAL METHODS

Courses in statistical methods as an aid to quality control were first conducted on a large, organized scale during World War II under the sponsorship of the War Production Board. Since then, many universities have regularly offered such courses through their extension divisions. These courses are conducted in a series of evening classes, in full-time summer seminars, and even in-house by arrangement with industrial companies. Many large companies conduct such courses in an organized in-house evening school.[26] In addition, some professional societies, consulting companies, and industry associations sponsor such courses.

The Basic Course   The content of the basic statistical course is well standardized. Typically it extends over ten full days (or equivalent) and is built around the following topics:

Variation, measures of central tendency, measures of dispersion
Frequency distributions
Control charts
Probability and sampling
Attribute sampling plans
Application to industrial quality problems, e.g., process capability, Lot Plot, narrow limit controls, statistical tolerancing.[27]

Teaching Aids[28]   Presentation of these topics to shop audiences is considerably aided by some ingenious teaching aids which simplify the presentations and enliven the meetings. They include:

1. *Attribute Sampling Demonstrators.* These consist of groups of wooden beads, some of which are colored to represent defects. Pitted paddles are thrust into the bead pile to collect a sample in the pits (Figure 17-2).[29] This sampling can be done by each member of the class, and the results can be tabulated and analyzed.

A typical proportion of colors is as follows:

Color A	1%	Color D	8%
Color B	2%	Color E	16%
Color C	4%	Natural	69%

By adding various combinations, a percent defective anywhere from 1 to 31% can be simulated.

2. *Galton's Quincunx.* This creates frequency distributions by letting beads tumble over multiple rows of pins. At each row the bead can fall to the right or the left of the pin. After a random journey over numerous rows of pins, the bead drops into a vertical slot. When many beads are dropped, the result is a frequency distribution (Figure 17-3).[30]

The device makes it easy to simulate a manufacturing process in the classroom. Each bead becomes a unit of product which can be "manufactured" and measured before the eyes of the audience. As a series of units is measured, the frequency

---

[26] In 1928, the Western Electric Company's Hawthorne Works added to its evening school offerings a course in statistical methods designed and conducted by the author.

[27] For details on these subjects, see Secs. 22 through 28, under the respective headings.

[28] For an extensive discussion, including sources of supply and a well-researched bibliography, see Schwerin, R. L., Teaching Aids for Statistics and Quality Control, *Industrial Quality Control,* June 1967, pp. 654–660.

[29] Available from Lightning Calculator Co., St. Petersburg Beach, Fla., 33736.

[30] Available from Lightning Calculator Co., St. Petersburg Beach, Fla., 33736.

Fig. 17-2 Attribute Sampling Demonstrator.

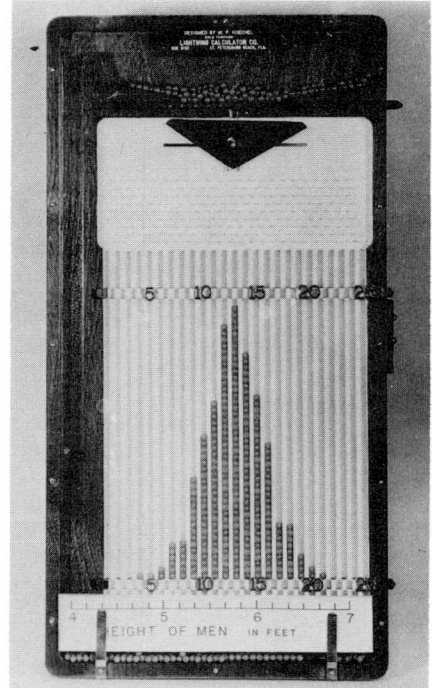

Fig. 17-3 Galton's quincunx.

distribution takes shape. The central tendency and dispersion can then be calculated, the latter representing process capability.[31]

In addition, the device can be used to demonstrate the nature of the control chart for averages and ranges. Limit lines for the "process" are calculated and drawn on the blackboard. Subsequent samples from the device represent process subgroups. The averages and ranges for these subgroups can be plotted to test for out-of-control, both when the process is undisturbed and when it is deliberately changed. (Some devices are designed to permit ready change of average; the others can only be tilted.)

3. *Statistical Tolerancing Simulator.* This device consists of several sets of blocks, each simulating a set of components waiting to be assembled. The purpose is to demonstrate that as random assembly takes place, the extremes will seldom come together. A typical set of blocks is described in Table 17-2. The class partic-

TABLE 17-2   Simulator for Statistical Tolerancing

Size, inches	Silver	Black	Red	Blue	Orange	Total
0.500						
0.600					1	1
0.700		1	1	1	1	4
0.800	1	3	2	1	2	9
0.900	5	6	4	3	4	22
1.000	8	6	6	5	4	29
1.100	5	3	4	5	4	21
1.200	1	1	2	3	2	9
1.300			1	1	1	3
1.400				1	1	2
1.500						
Totals	20	20	20	20	20	100
$s =$	0.095	0.116	0.145	0.163	0.192	

The maximum assembly is 6.5 inches and the minimum is 3.5 inches. However, since s of the composite of all five distributions figures out to be 0.327, further calculation shows that only about 2 of 100 assemblies will actually be outside of ± 0.750 around the average of 5.0.

ipates in assembling the "parts" at random and demonstrates the difficulty of reaching the worst case dimensions.[32]

Lacking the more sophisticated teaching aids, the instructor can resort to use of ordinary six-faced dice, coin tossing, the Shewhart bowl, and still other simple devices.[33]

Advanced Courses   These have likewise attained a degree of standardization as to content. The advanced course generally deals with the following subjects:

Statistical inference, confidence limits
Significance tests

[31] An earlier device, the "Shewhart bowl," contained numbered chips corresponding to a normal frequency distribution. This could be sampled to demonstrate control chart theory. It lacks the drama of Galton's quincunx.

[32] Van der Weiden, H., Statistisch Speelgoed (Statistical Toys), *Sigma*, vol. 5, no.2, 1959, pp. 28–32.

[33] See Berry, Edmund D., High School Introduction to Quality Control, *Industrial Quality Control*, June 1967, pp. 611 and 612.

Sampling by variables
Reliability quantification
Design and analysis of experiments

Here again, some teaching aids are available. One is a "process variance demonstrator," which is an electronic device for simulating industrial experimentation.[34]

The basic courses, with good teaching aids, can be taught to almost anyone with a high school education (or even less). However, the advanced courses are usually beyond the grasp of those who have not gone beyond high school. In addition, some advanced courses go so deeply into statistical theory that they are out of the reach of those who are not well grounded in college mathematics.

In large companies, in-house programs are entirely feasible due to available competent practitioners and good teaching aids.[35, 36]

OTHER COURSES

Beyond the foregoing, there are numerous specialized courses mainly for managers, engineers, and other staff specialists. Some of these are discussed in detail below under the headings of the various categories of personnel for whom they are intended. Information on availability of courses can be secured from the American Society for Quality Control[37] (which also sponsors some of these courses), from ASQC Divisions and Sections, and from other sponsors, e.g., the American Management Association.[38] Available courses include:

Management of quality costs
Vendor quality relations
Product quality auditing
Government-industry relationships, MIL specifications, Material Review Board.

Design and analysis of experiments (for engineers, scientists, and other professional specialists). These designs can become exceedingly complex, so there are several levels of advanced courses as well.

Evolutionary operation (EVOP), which has been widely conducted in the chemical process industries

Response surface methodology, also conducted mainly in the chemical process industries.

Use of computers to control processes. Again mainly for chemical processes.
Reliability and maintainability engineering
Nondestructive testing[39]

---

[34] Moder, J., Jr., A Teaching Aid for Regression, Correlation, Analysis of Variance, and other Statistical Techniques, *Industrial Quality Control*, October 1956, pp. 16–21.

[35] For an example of an in-company program, see Smith, H., Statistical Training within an Industrial Firm, *American Statistician*, April 1964, pp. 22–24.

[36] Steps have also been taken to create programmed instruction in statistics. For a discussion, see Hromi, John D., Programmed Instruction in Statistics for Industry, *Industrial Quality Control*, June 1967, pp. 640–643.

[37] Located at 161 West Wisconsin Ave., Milwaukee, Wis. 53203.

[38] Located at 135 West 50 St., New York, N.Y. 10020.

[39] For a summary of educational programs available, see Serabian, Steven, An Assessment of Education in Nondestructive Testing—Present Status and the Future Needs, *Fifteenth Annual Symposium on Reliability*, 1969, IEEE, pp. 429–443. This comprehensive presentation was based on a survey conducted by the Educational Council of the American Society for Nondestructive Testing.

Some of the ASQC Divisions sponsor courses which are oriented to the special problems of the Division, e.g., Chemical, Textile, Needle Trades. In still other cases, the Divisions sponsor "standard" courses, but with problems and cases drawn from their respective industries, e.g., Design of Experiments for the Chemical and Allied Industries.[40]

INSPECTION MANPOWER MANAGEMENT

Inspection manpower management makes use of conventional concepts of manpower management but employs various techniques appropriate to the inspection jobs.

Career Design   A short-range example is the apprenticeship program. For instance, a four-year program, covering a mixture of training and job assignments over a progression of many types of tasks, converts inexperienced high school graduates into qualified tool and gage inspectors.[41]

Job Descriptions   The job description (Figure 17-4)[42] is a basic building block in the management of manpower. It usually contains the following types of information:

Job duties and responsibilities
Qualifications needed by the jobholder (education, experience, etc.) to perform this job adequately
Qualification tests suggested as aids to judge fitness
Logical sources for recruitment
Logical directions for future advancement and criteria for qualification

The job description is used in organization planning to assist in logical assignment of responsibility. It is used in recruitment and upgrading to assist in matching employee qualifications with job needs. It is used in job grading or evaluation (see below) to help provide a logical interrelation among jobs. It has still other uses in wage and salary surveys, employee rating, etc.

Job Evaluation   Some companies use a formal plan of grading jobs as a basis for establishing pay differentials and promotion patterns. These plans operate by:

1. Defining the factors which are considered to be decisive in the value of the job, e.g., education, experience, etc.

2. Defining several degrees for each factor. For example, education and experience are defined in terms of years of exposure.

3. Assigning numerical "point" values for each degree of each factor.

4. Defining grades on the basis of total points. Each grade is assigned a zone along the scale of total points.

5. Analyzing each job and judging the degree to which it possesses each of the factors.

6. Summing up the point values and establishing the resulting grade.[43, 44]

---

[40] For a quantitative analysis of the titles of courses given by ASQC Sections and by the Chemical Division, see Raymo, C. T., Educational Activities of Sections and Divisions, *Industrial Quality Control*, June 1967, pp. 617, 618. Courses in statistical methodology were overwhelmingly in the majority.

[41] Timken "Rolls Its Own," *Quality Assurance*, April 1966, pp. 28–30.

[42] While this description is for a Junior Quality Control Engineer, the format and type of information are typical.

[43] For details, see Maynard, H. B. "Industrial Engineering Handbook," 3d ed., McGraw-Hill Book Company, New York, 1971, under Job Evaluation.

[44] The subject of inspector compensation is discussed in Compensation for Inspectors, below.

JOB DESCRIPTION

Classification Code ST-108

Date Prepared:	12-6-57	Job Title:	Junior Quality Engineer
Prepared By:	E. R.	Department:	Quality Control
Approved By:	DD, MR	Location:	All
Replaces Issue Of:	2-23-57	Salary Code:	D

Duties: Assists Senior Quality Engineer in development, installation, and operation of QC system for economic control of raw material, in-process and finished products, including:
   Preparation and audit of procedures, records, personnel requirements, etc., for inspection, testing, complaint handling, vendor contacts on quality problems.
   Making of technical and statistical investigations on quality problems, methods, and equipment; preparation of engineering reports of recommendations.
   Contacting other departments, suppliers, and customers on quality problems.
   Training of inspectors and technicians in job methods and technical studies.

Logical Sources: (1) Upgrade from Engineering Trainee or Inspector (with technical training)
   (2) Hire as engineer with min. 1 to 3 yrs. experience in quality control, inspection supervisor, testing, or related activity, or with product experience.
   (3) Hire as graduate engineer with training in statistics.

Logical Advancement To: Senior Quality Engineer (possibly to Statistician, or to Inspection Foreman)

Requirements For Advancement: Technical knowledge in statistics, inspection, testing, specifications, report writing, etc. Ability to investigate and aid in solution of quality problems. Ability to work effectively with subordinates and superiors. Experience in processes and products.

Age and Sex Requirements: None—normally male 21 to 35 yrs.

Formal Education Required: B.S. (prefer Ch. E., I.E., M.E., Math or Physics) or equivalent.

Craft Training Required: None—inspection and lab experience or related factory work helpful.

Special Training Desirable: Statistics, technical report writing, rubber and plastics technology

Experience Required: None—Quality Engineering, Inspection, or lab supervision desirable.

Manual Skills Required: None—technical hobbies and aptitudes desirable.

Physical Requirements: Normal; frequently in factory and doing close inspection, including color.

Special Personality Requirements: Will work extensively with people at all levels and contact customers and vendors on disputes. Firm but likable personality required.

Testing Suggested As Aid To Final Interview:

Test	Min. Score For Preliminary Screening
Otis or similar IQ if college marks below top third.	> 105 for college graduates
Minn. Clerical — for carefulness with data.	
Special Engineering Knowledge Test (QC-34) if not technical col. grad.	Average clerical worker 50% (about equiv. to 2 yrs. col.)

Fig. 17-4 Job description.

Inspector Selection   Inspectors differ widely in their ability to find defects, interpret specifications, etc. Unless the inferior performers are detected through test batteries or by the employment interview, their lack of ability will be disclosed only after they are on the job.

In many companies, the application for employment may contain (or be supplemented by) a questionnaire. This questionnaire elicits information which experience has shown to be a useful input to the employment decision.[45]

Most large companies and many smaller ones employ test batteries. The tests of applicants are conducted either by the central Employment Department or by an outside testing service. Table 17-3 lists some of the more usual tests conducted.[46] Collateral with these tests is the physical examination which, for inspectors, tests specially for such characteristics as color blindness.[47, 48]

Test results should be regarded as an input to the employment decision, but not as the decision itself. Correlations of test results with subsequent performance are not adequate to permit reliance solely on test results.[49] The real decision must be left to the interviewers who, in turn, should consider the test results along with other inputs. The skilled interviewer can do much to reduce the risk of misplacement through judicious questioning and follow-up of promising lines of discussion.[50]

In the United States, the 1960s brought a wave of legislation against discrimination in employment, with a resulting decline in use of aptitude and other selection tests. Since then, the use of these tests has resumed an upward trend. However, the laws against discrimination remain, and require, in effect, that application of selection tests shall not result in employment discrimination on the basis of color, race, creed, sex, etc.

Inspector Training   Much of this is done by the supervisor at the time of induction on the job. The common assumptions are that this training is responsive to the task and job requirements and that thereafter the situation improves with experience. In practice these assumptions may be invalid, so that a poor training can take root and be perpetuated.

In one electronics plant, the quality of the grids (a critical component) was a source of concern. The grid winding process was believed to be setup-dominated, and thereby the competence of the patrol inspectors became suspect. The inspectors were given an examination which tested their job knowledge, e.g., interpreting a specific grid specification, and which also required them to measure a sample of product of known quality.[51] The examination results confirmed the worst suspicions which had been raised (Figure 17-5). A training program to improve job knowledge and performance attained a measure of success (Figure 17-5) but fell

[45] The questionnaire may be extended to be a miniature examination to test qualifications. A British study concluded that this concept had demonstrated merit. See Holmes, J., B. Clayton, and H. Squire, The Selection of Inspectors, *Quality Engineer,* September–October 1964, pp. 131–136.

[46] For some useful case discussions, see Jacobson, Henry J., Management Methods of Inspection Control, *Industrial Quality Control,* July 1964, pp. 24–28. See also, Wachniak, Ray, Inspector Shortage? *Quality Management & Engineering,* May 1971, pp. 10–12.

[47] Note, however, that it is entirely feasible, through special planning, to use blind people as inspectors. See Riggs, William L., Use of the Blind and Visually Handicapped in Inspection, *Industrial Quality Control,* July 1967, pp. 7 and 8.

[48] See also the use of the "standard sample array," Section 12, under Inspector Errors: Technique Errors.

[49] For some discussion on validation of test batteries, see Harris, Douglas H., and Fred B. Chaney, Human Factors in Quality Assurance, John Wiley & Sons, Inc., New York, 1969, Chapter 11, Inspector Selection.

[50] The interview is the main means for judging the essential attribute of personal integrity.

[51] See Section 12, under Inspector Errors.

TABLE 17-3   Some Tests Used for Quality Control Personnel

Test of	Name	Available from	Comments
Vocational interests	Kuder Preference Test	SRA	Measures interest in 10 job fields—clerical, scientific, mechanical, persuasive, etc.
Emotional adjustment . . .	Adams Personal Audit	SRA	Rates seriousness, tranquillity, tolerance, persistence, etc.
Temperament	Thurstone Temperament Schedule	SRA	Evaluates impulsiveness, dominance, sociability, etc.
Inspection aptitude	Flanagan Aptitude Classification	SRA	Estimates aptitude for repetitive inspection.
Mechanical aptitude (knowledge)	SRA Mechanical Aptitude Test (Richardson, etc.)	SRA	Measures knowledge in mechanical deletions, space relations, and arithmetic problems.
Defect detection	Flanagan Industrial Test-Inspection	SRA	Checks ability to detect flaws
Clerical speed and accuracy	Minnesota Clerical Test	PC	Checks speedy perception and handling of numbers, letters, and symbols.
Understanding mechanical relations	Mechanical Comprehension (Bennett) Test	PC	Availability in several levels of complexity.
Spatial perception	Minnesota Paper Form Board	PC	Checks ability to visualize assembly of mechanical parts.
Supervisory knowledge. . .	How Supervise?	PC	Used to determine opinions on supervisory problems.
Mental ability	Modified Army Alpha Test (Wells)	PC	Measures numerical and verbal mental ability.
Mental ability	Otis Mental Ability Tests	PC	Available in several forms and levels.
Mental ability	Wonderlic Personnel Test	PC	Rapid overall intelligence test.
Color discrimination.	Farnsworth-Munsell Tests	PC	Classification of color aptitude & color discrimination.

For tests of eyesight, the Ortho-Rater (Bausch & Lomb Optical Co.) or the Keystone Telebinocular (Keystone View Co.) equipment may be of interest.

NOTE: "SRA" is Science Research Associates, Chicago, Ill.

"PC" is Psychological Corporation, New York City.

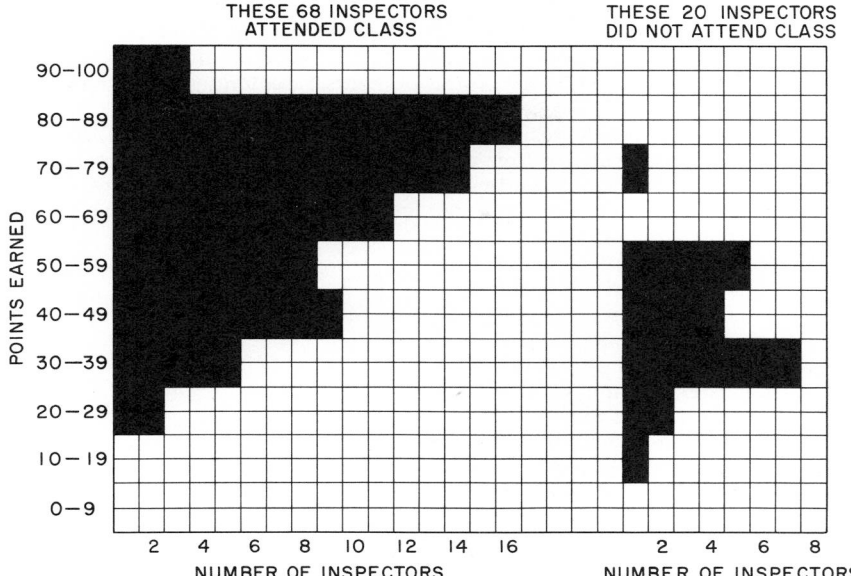

THESE 68 INSPECTORS
ATTENDED CLASS

THESE 20 INSPECTORS
DID NOT ATTEND CLASS

Fig. 17-5   Examination results of trained and untrained inspectors.

sufficiently short of the desired levels to raise some new questions about the validity of the original recruitment.

When supervisory on-the-job training is shown to be insufficient for the job needs, there are several remedial steps:

1. Improve the ability of the supervision to do training. In part this is done by training supervisors in how to train. Modern versions of the famous Job Instruction Training programs of World War II are widely available for this purpose.[52]

2. Provide the supervisor with training aids to make it easy for him to be a good trainer. See Training Methods, above.

3. Create training courses to be given directly to nonsupervisors in those cases where on-the-job training is not feasible.

One company in the aerospace industry established 58 formal courses available to inspection personnel (32 courses were also available to other personnel). Beyond the recognition provided for completing the courses, 12 of the courses involved formal certification of qualification to perform the respective tasks, and "Space Ratings" were created as symbols of achievement based on a number of factors: completion of training courses, job performance, etc.[53]

"Standard" courses for inspectors must necessarily be concerned with subjects of broad appeal, e.g., mechanical measurement, interpretation of specifications, documentation, control chart procedure. Beyond these subjects of broad appeal, the courses must be tailor-made. This requires analysis of the training needs and the

[52] For some detailed discussion about the learning process as applied to inspectors, see Harris, Douglas H., and Fred B. Chaney, *op. cit.*, Chapter 12, The Development of Knowledge and Skills.

[53] Schneider, J. G., What Are the Chief Inspectors Doing to Keep the Inspector Currently Informed? *Industrial Quality Control*, November 1965, pp. 232–235.

structuring of a program which is responsive to those needs.[54]   All this is time-consuming and therefore usually beyond the capacity of the supervisor.   In consequence, some other organization form must be used to create these courses.   In addition, the administration of all off-the-job courses requires special organization machinery.

A common form of such organization is through creation of a job of Training Coordinator (the job may be part-time rather than full-time).   The coordinator may be within the Quality Control Department or he may be a part of the Central Training Department.   In one company[55] the coordinator's duties were as follows:

1. Determine training needs
2. Assign personnel to instruct
3. Conduct classes when necessary
4. Develop and/or coordinate course material
5. Prepare course material and visual aids
6. Schedule classes
7. Administer all out-of-plant training
8. Maintain training records
9. Follow up for effectiveness

Training of inspectors also includes a miscellany of practical matters which the standard literature may not cover:

Inspectors should have maximum opportunity to learn of fitness for use, i.e., to see the usage of the product, to see the process, to read typical complaints, etc.

The training should include essential procedural matters such as documentation, data feedback, and relations with industrial neighbors.[56]

Certificates of completion should be awarded.   Beyond the status and recognition involved, these certificates are becoming increasingly important as evidence of qualification.   In some cases, e.g., nondestructive testing for certain applications, only certified employees may legally conduct the tests.

In small companies there is no in-house training department able to provide a full service to the various managers.   In consequence, the approach is one of informality and improvisation, as, for example, use of outsiders (e.g., professors, consultants) to supply prepared training material and instruction.[57]

Compensation for Inspectors   In the United States, compensation plans for inspectors are mainly linked to the job grade as determined by job evaluation.   The job grades which result from this evaluation are translated into money equivalents through wage surveys which determine what the "market" pays for similar work in the same industry, locality, etc.   The resulting money values become the basis for setting up wage or salary ranges for each grade.   The actual pay of the inspector within the salary range is determined by his length of service, his job performance, and still other factors.

While the foregoing is a systematic approach to determining compensation, the

[54] For an example of a 13-week training curriculum for advanced mechanical inspection, see McDermott, Richard J., Quality Control's Most Valuable Resource, *ASQC Technical Conference Transactions, 1970,* pp. 229–235.

[55] Eidukonis, Edward R., and John L. Kidwell, The Inspection Training Program, *Industrial Quality Control,* June 1967, pp. 622–628.   (This rewarding paper includes added useful information on facilities for training, reduction of inspection errors, etc.)

[56] For elaboration, see Hill, Paul W., Developing a Training and Rating System for Inspectors in Basic Quality Control, *Transactions, Fourth Annual Conference, Dayton Section ASQC,* March 6, 1960.

[57] See, for example, Cooley, R. L., Training Inspectors in a Small Shop, *ASQC Technical Conference Transactions, 1970,* pp. 253–262.

results are not fully satisfying to inspectors and inspection supervisors.   One of the most usual sources of dissatisfaction is the difference in pay between inspectors and production operators (for the same grade of work) arising from the fact that the production operator often has an opportunity to earn incentive pay, whereas the inspector seldom has this opportunity.   In some situations, a low-grade production job may thereby earn higher take-home pay than a high-grade inspection job.   As a corollary, production operators who are offered a promotion to inspection work may be forced to take a cut in their take-home pay as part of the bargain.

There are several ways of dealing with this long-standing[58] problem:

1. Make the inspection job a steppingstone toward promotion.   A good deal can be done to make this a reality, since the inspection job usually provides breadth of experience and a judicial sense which can be applied in many jobs.   In this connection, it is helpful if the Inspection management establishes a clear concept of a career pattern[59] as a means of showing the inspectors an image of their future.   In addition, as more and more men follow this pattern successfully, the image can be shown to be a reality.

2. Provide nonfinancial incentives for the inspection jobs.   Some of these are inherent in the jobs: a wider range of contacts, more opportunity for use of judgment, more opportunity for job planning, higher status in the social structure of the factory.

3. Provide opportunity for inspectors to earn incentive pay.

Inspection work can be measured both as to quantity and quality and hence can, in theory, be placed on an incentive payment basis once standards are established. In practice, the problems of measuring the accuracy of inspection work have tended to limit the use of incentive wage plans for inspectors.

For highly repetitive inspection, standards of a day's work can be established by conventional Industrial Engineering methods (time study, standard data, etc.).[60] For less repetitive work, use can be made of the Pareto principle by setting standards for the vital few operations.[61]   Special precautions must be taken to provide separate allowances for dealing with defective lots in order to minimize biasing the inspectors' judgment for or against finding lots defective.

While quantity of work done can be measured week after week with reasonable precision, the accuracy of inspection work cannot be measured economically over so short a period of time, owing to sampling inaccuracies.   Instead, it is necessary to collect data on accuracy over a long period of time, six months or so.   There are also special provisions needed to make the inspectors' accuracy independent of the process capability.   See, in this connection, Measure of Inspector Accuracy, in Section 12, under Inspector Errors.

If provision has been made to measure both quantity and accuracy of inspection work, it is quite feasible to make use of incentive pay plans.   The long time required to accumulate good data on inspector accuracy suggests that the pay changes be infrequent (e.g., every six months) rather than weekly as is done for production piecework operators.[62]

[58] Although the problem is of long standing, it is generally declining in importance because the use of piecework plans for production operators has been steadily declining.

[59] See Tasks, Jobs, and Careers, above.

[60] The early industrial engineers established standards for inspection work as well as for production work.   See, for example, Taylor, F. W., Principles of Scientific Management, Harper & Bros., New York, 1911, pp. 86 et seq.

[61] Lambrou, Fred H., Wage Incentives for Inspectors, *Journal of Industrial Engineering*, September–October 1956, pp. 236 and 237.

[62] For a more extended discussion involving application to a very large inspection department, see Juran, J. M., Management of Inspection and Quality Control, Harper & Bros., New York, 1945, pp. 48–57; also pp. 170–178.   See also, Butler, R. G. K., Work Measurement

(footnote continued on p. 17–22)

Probably the most complex incentive problem is that posed by patrol inspection. Here the approach has generally been to:

1. Establish a historical ratio of patrol inspection hours to production hours.

2. Based on this history plus judgment, establish a standard ratio of inspection hours to production hours.

3. This standard ratio multiplied into the actual production hours for any future period becomes the standard for patrol inspection hours for that period.

INSPECTION SUPERVISORS

Inspection supervisors have all the usual responsibilities of supervisors as to industrial relations: plan the work of the department, assign work to the inspectors, train and coach, review performance.[63]   In addition, the special nature of inspection work requires:

Decision making on conformance to standards
Disposition of nonconforming products
Investigation of quality complaints and troubles
Data collection and analysis, plus documentation

These responsibilities have guided the training courses for inspection supervisors, which typically cover the following topics:

Principles of supervision: getting results from others through planning, organizing, directing, controlling, appraising
Responsibilities of the supervisor; job scope
Statistical methodology: variation, frequency distributions, sampling, control charts, process capability
Job technology: the specifications, materials, product, process, tests[64]
Organization: company, Quality Control, and Inspection
Work planning and assignment
Measurement: metrology, instrumentation, maintenance of accuracy
Nonconformance: Material Review Board, deviation procedure
Quality analysis: troubleshooting; prevention of chronic defects
Quality motivation
Inspection budgets and cost control

QUALITY ENGINEERS AND OTHER QUALITY SPECIALISTS

In all countries these specialists have emerged and are, in varying degrees, a stimulus toward improving the effectiveness of the quality function.   In the United States, these specialists have become so numerous that they have a direction of their own.[65]

Careers for Quality Specialists   A career is a logical progression of job assignments over one's lifetime.[66]   The career which begins in some trade or profession usually also remains the career for life.   However, some people who are employed by insti-

---

Applied to Engineering Inspection, *Time and Motion Study,* December, 1963, pp. 22–26; also Brewer, E., and Pamela Kacser, A Comparative Analysis of Incentive Plans, *Time and Motion Study,* February 1964, pp. 12–23.

[63] For a list of duties common to inspection supervisors, see Section 12, under Inspection Department Management.

[64] This topic is valid only for intracompany courses.

[65] See, in this connection, Section 7, under Staff Quality Control Departments; also under Administration of the Quality Staff Specialty.

[66] For further discussion, see Tasks, Jobs, and Careers, above.

tutions gradually move out of professional work and more and more into managerial work. For example, the career depicted in Figure 17-1 is that of an engineer who starts with assignments which are 100% professional in nature. In a short time he is given an assistant. Now, to the extent that he supervises the work of this assistant, he is managing, i.e., getting results from the work of other people.

The next stage (in Figure 17-1) is the appointment to the post of head of Quality Control Engineering. Now perhaps a fourth of the time of the engineer is spent in managing. The rest of the time he is still using the tools of the engineering profession. Most people (including himself) regard him as an engineer, not a manager.

A further phase (Figure 17-1) is that of Quality Manager. Now the engineer is spending about half his time in managing. (Some people call him a manager; others still call him an engineer.) He has also reached a major fork in the road, the choice of whether he will spend the remainder of his career in the profession (quality control) or whether he will leave this profession to succeed in a hierarchical career as manager.

These two careers differ considerably in the qualifications needed to carry them out. The profession requires not only analytical competence but also intellectual honesty and a dedication to the search for basic truths. The hierarchical career[67] emphasizes leadership of men, the understanding of human nature, and the skill required for dealing with that complex variable.[68] Since few men are so gifted as to be highly qualified for both of these careers, the choice is quite important.

In all societies, both these careers are regarded as necessary and honorable callings. However, in most societies, the hierarchical career receives greater tangible rewards than does the professional, i.e., a higher salary, a larger office, more amenities, more publicity, and more of other "good things of life." These differences are visible not only to the professional but also to his family, his neighbors, his community. As a result, the professional is under pressure to attain the same tangible benefits as are received by the manager. In the large organization, he can normally achieve this result only by leaving the profession and becoming a manager. In doing so he may move into a career for which he is not well qualified, with all the risks of mediocrity or failure. In addition, on retirement, when men must look back, the tangible rewards seem less important than whether one's time has been well spent. Men who conclude they have spent many years on the wrong road can become quite embittered about it.

The man who remains in the profession has opportunities for progress other than hierarchical. Some of this can be done without leaving the organization, i.e., service on professional society committees, contributions to the literature, teaching at the local university. Other opportunities may require moving to a different organization—larger, more diverse, more challenging. Still other forms of progress involve a new environment: the university, writing and lecturing, consulting.[69]

Of course there are limits imposed on the range of choice, especially by the organization, which puts institutional needs high on the list of priorities. The needs of the staff specialists are well known and have been documented.[70] However, companies differ in their response to these needs, while individual staff specialists

[67] Managing is itself a form of profession, having already met most of the criteria which define a profession.

[68] See, in this connection, Bingham, R. S., Jr., Evolution of a Quality Control Manager, *Industrial Quality Control*, September 1962, p. 36 (Management's Corner).

[69] In this connection, see Juran, J. M., So You Want to Be a Quality Control Consultant, *Industrial Quality Control*, December 1966, pp. 265-270.

[70] See Juran, J. M., Managerial Breakthrough, McGraw-Hill Book Company, New York, 1964, pp. 104-106, The Care and Feeding of Diagnosticians. See also, Juran, J. M., Progress for QC Engineers—Horizontal or Vertical, *Industrial Quality Control*, May 1956, pp. 108 and 109.

differ in their demands. The resulting interplay leads to highly individualized situations requiring tailor-made decisions.

Professionalism for Quality Specialists   In the United States, as quality specialists proliferated in numbers, they also created means for exchanging their experiences. Their principal organization, the American Society for Quality Control (ASQC), holds numerous conferences, publishes journals, and conducts training courses. From these exchanges there has emerged a concept of "professionalism" of Quality Control.[71]

Prior to the 1960s there were efforts to create for the quality control specialty the status of a separate engineering curriculum in the universities, and a licensed "Professional Engineer" category in the states. When these efforts bore no fruit, ASQC created, during the 1960s, a category of Certified Quality Engineer, based on ability to perform "the basic work elements of Quality Control Engineering."[72] The certification program became operational in 1966. The examinations consist of three parts: Statistical, Engineering, Management.[73] Administration is by the Education and Training Institute of ASQC.[74] As of June 1971, a total of 2,744 individuals had been certified as "Quality Engineer." (Some qualified under a "grandfather clause.")

The certification programs were extended in the 1970s to create a category of Quality Technician[75] (1970) and of Reliability Engineer (1972).

Aside from the question of professionalism, there is much evidence that quality control is in fact recognized as a specialty. The industrial companies have created job titles such as Quality Control Engineer and Reliability Engineer by the thousands. They authorize these men to support the quality control conferences, seminars, etc. They place advertisements to recruit men for these job categories. These advertisements seldom demand any experience in the industry or technology of the company; they *demand only qualification in the quality control specialty.*

Training for Staff Quality Specialists   This training has undergone a considerable evolution since the concept of full-time staff quality specialists received its real impetus in the 1940s. At the outset the enthusiasm (and overenthusiasm) for the statistical tools tended to equate the newly emerging category of staff quality spe-

---

[71] The criteria for the recognized professions include an essential public service, a special codified body of knowledge; special selection of those who are to enter the profession, broad education plus training in the specialty, examination as proof of qualification to practice, a public license and monopoly for those who qualify for practice, a code of ethics, a means of livelihood.

[72] For a list of these elements see The Basic Work Elements of Quality Control Engineering, *Industrial Quality Control,* May 1961.

[73] For an extensive list of examination questions, see David C. Leaman, ASQC Quality Engineer Certification Examination, *Quality Progress,* October 1972, pp. 19–27.

[74] For a review of the program, see Astrachan, Max, ASQC Education and Your Future, The ETI Programs and Progress, *Industrial Quality Control,* June 1967, pp. 613–616. Astrachan distinguishes three different forms designating qualification:

Certification, which is done by a professional society and attests to professional qualifications.

. *Registration,* which is done by a governmental body and carries some connotations of qualification (some registration is done mainly for revenue) and to permit effective regulation if needed.

Licensing, which confers a monopoly on those practicing the recognized professions.

See also Bress, L. N., Professionalism in Quality Control, *Annual Technical Conference Transactions, American Society for Quality Control,* 1965, pp. 116–119; also Kozich, Steve, Professionalism, *ibid.,* pp. 120–135.

[75] David C. Leaman in a review of Education and Training in ASQC, *Quality Progress,* May–June 1971, p. 66.

cialists with application of statistical methods. The training programs reflected this view.

During the 1950s, this emphasis on statistical methods was contested by a school of thought which envisioned a broader role for the emerging Quality Control Engineers. The result was the creation of two main roads for training:

1. Statistical methodology as a general-use discipline in which quality control is one of the areas for application of the methods. (The resulting practitioner is called a Statistician).

2. Quality Control Engineering, in which statistical methodology is one of the tools of the "profession."

The emerging drive for professionalism had the added effect of urging structured courses which could:

Serve as a recognized body of knowledge on which the profession is based
Prepare men to meet their job requirements
Enable men to pass the (optional) certificate examinations

Courses for Quality Control Engineers   These typically cover the following topics:

Elements of Quality Control Engineering	Process control methods
Statistical methodology	Measuring equipment and metrology
Product and process quality planning	Quality cost analysis
Preproduction planning	Data systems and reports[76]
Process capability	Organizing for quality
Inspection and test planning	Training for quality
Vendor control methods	Motivation for quality

Courses for Reliability Engineers   These emerged soon after the creation of this new staff specialty. A typical course content is that contained in the 1969–1970 announcement of the Education and Training Institute of ASQC, under the title "Fundamentals of Reliability":

Introduction. Historical background. Basic concepts and definitions. Reliability functions involved. How reliability improvement enhances profit and image.

Establishing a Reliability Program. Scope of programs: commercial, defense, and space. Organizing for reliability: commercial, defense, and space. Costs of reliability vs. return on investment.

Designing for Reliability. Objectives and customer requirements. Estimation and apportionment. Failure distributions and failure rates. Data collection, analysis, and utilization. Use of computers. Trade-offs. Maintainability and availability. Failure mode and effect analysis technique. Effective design review procedure. Performance report analysis and feedback. Corrective action procedure. Reliability test planning: development, verification, and life tests.

Producing Reliable Products. Drawing and specification review and change control. Supplier selection and surveillance. Process specification review and process control. Quality Control: inspection, test, instrument and gage control.

Assuring Reliability in Use. Operation and maintenance manuals. Installation. Maintenance and field service; training. Field performance report feedback. Product warranties; product liability.

Courses for Quality Control Technicians   The "technician" is a job category employing knowledge and skills of a technological nature but not to the extent which requires an engineering degree. Typically, the quality control technician conducts sophisticated laboratory tests, assists scientists and engineers in conduct of experiments, etc.

---

[76] Increasingly, this topic involves training in the use of computers. See Section 20, under Manpower and Training.

The need for such technicians has been so extensive that new ways have been sought to provide the necessary training programs on a large scale. One approach has been to develop special curricula in the numerous technical colleges which train technicians of all sorts. This approach commonly involves creation of a Community Advisory Committee to work with the colleges in developing a curriculum which will meet the needs of the industries while utilizing the capabilities of the college.[77]

An analysis prepared in 1971 listed 150 educational institutions offering courses and degrees in quality control.[78] Many of these were technical colleges, but a significant minority consisted of leading universities in the United States. Of the 150 institutions offering such programs, 26 offered an "associate" degree, e.g., Associate in Science. These institutions were all community colleges and technical institutes.[79]

A typical curriculum for an Associate in Science degree consists of 60 units, of about 16 hours each, as follows:

Title	Units
English and Speech	9
Mathematics	6
Psychology, Political Science	6
Other general education	3
Quality Control Concepts and Techniques	6
Statistical Concepts and Techniques	3
Quality Control Engineering Principles and Techniques	6
Reliability Objectives	3
Quality Control Application (Procurement, Electronics)	6
Metrology and Nondestructive Testing	9
Supervision	3
	60

The late 1960s also witnessed the beginnings of experiments to conduct quality control education at the high school level. Collaboration between a large industrial company and local schools resulted in establishing some pilot programs which emphasized metrology and testing (mechanical and nondestructive), basic statistics, quality control engineering, general orientation.[80]

QUALITY MANAGERS

The term "quality manager" is used here in the sense of the highest ranking manager associated full-time with the quality function. His title[81] varies from one company to another: Vice President for Quality, Director of Quality and Reliability, Quality Manager, Quality Control Manager, etc.

[77] For an early case history, see Quality Control—Reliability Goes to College in San Diego, *Industrial Quality Control*, May 1965, p. 592; see also Curry, Arthur D., Inspectors Unlimited, *ASQC Technical Conference Transactions, 1967*, pp. 601–605.

[78] Guidelines for Establishing Educational Programs in Quality Control and Reliability. Published by San Diego Section, ASQC, March 1971. Available from Education and Training Institute, ASQC. This well-documented analysis sets out the approach used to establish a curriculum and gives a listing of courses, degree requirements, and text materials as well as naming the institutions involved.

[79] Beyond the "associate" degree, nine of the institutions offered degrees either as Bachelor of Science or as Master of Science.

[80] See Gelles, Paul E., Quality Control Education in the High School, *ASQC Technical Conference Transactions, 1970*, pp. 249–252.

[81] A title may contain words which designate rank only (e.g., Vice President) or role only (e.g., Reliability Engineer) or both (e.g., Vice President for Engineering).

Roles of the Quality Manager   These vary widely and consist of combinations of the following:

1. The inspection role.   He usually commands the forces which measure the products and judge conformance to specification.

2. The "customer's representative" role.   He participates in and may dominate the judgment of fitness for use.

3. The planning and coordination role.   He has participation and even leadership in establishing company quality policies, objectives, and plans.   Where he combines business knowledge with technological skills, he may become the "right-hand man" of the Chief Executive Officer on quality matters.

4. The analysis role.   He usually commands the staff specialists whose analytical studies form the basis for scientific approaches in attainment of quality and for achievement of breakthroughs.

5. The consulting role.   He is the management team specialist in the quality function and, in addition, he and his organization possess special skills which have application to other functions.

6. The assurance role.   He is the company's scorekeeper and reporter on the actual state of quality performance.   (See Section 21.)

7. The outside liaison role.   He is the company's contact with quality specialists in government, the industry, the professional societies, etc.[82]

Effectiveness of the Quality Manager   The quality manager's effectiveness in these roles is judged in various ways.

His role as chief inspector and as customer's representative is judged by the extent of internal and external quality difficulties traceable to malfunction in the role.

His role as planner and coordinator is judged by the business effectiveness of the resulting policies, objectives, and plans and by his success in securing collaboration with the line departments.[83]

His role as analyst and consultant is judged by the extent to which the analyses result in action, by the breakthroughs achieved, and by the extent to which the line departments are trained to carry on the matured specialties.

His assurance role is judged by the objectivity of the reports, by his concentration on the vital few matters, and by the constructive responses secured.

His role as a departmental manager is judged by the business orientation of his budget, by the extent of breakthrough projects, by the extent to which old services are transferred to the line departments, and by his competence in identifying needed new services.

Beyond the foregoing, the quality manager is most helpful to the company if he can:

Identify alarming quality situations not detectable by the conventional alarm signals

Structure breakthrough programs around outdated basic premises and axiomatic beliefs

Head off the cultist movements by sensing them early in the game, examining their content, and taking the initiative in proposing what to do about them

Why Quality Managers Fail   Many quality managers have lost their jobs, yet seldom is this the result of poor technological competence.   The usual reasons for

---

[82] For added detail, see Section 7, under Activities Assigned to Quality Control Departments, Table 7-2; also Section 7, under The Corporate Quality Manager; also Section 7, under Coordination of the Quality Function.

[83] See in this connection, Stiles, Edward M., Financial Aspects of Quality Management, *Seventh Annual Conference Transactions, Akron Canton Section,* ASQC, April 1965, pp. D-15 to D-24.

failure are inadequate personality or errors of business judgment such as:

Emphasizing conformance to specifications instead of fitness for use

Emphasizing problems for which the company already has adequate solutions, instead of problems which have not yet been solved (or which are not even being worked on)

Operating as loners in departmental management rather than securing inputs and ideas from all key people

Advocating their special skills as a panacea for all problems rather than diagnosing the problems first

Failing to communicate with the other key people in setting up programs and in reporting progress

Getting drawn into premature support of some passing slogan-cult movement

The quality manager can do much to guard against these causes of failure by broadening his understanding of the mission of the company and of the role played by the quality function in the achievement of this mission. Conventional programs of management development can be most helpful in securing such understanding. In addition, the quality manager is well advised to expose himself to the conduct of the quality function in a variety of materials, processes, products, companies, industries, locations, cultures. The wider this exposure, the better becomes the grasp of the universal principles which fit all situations. Opportunities for such exposure are presented in numerous ways:

Exchange visits with vendor companies, customers, industrial neighbors

Attendance at industry shows, conventions, professional society sectional meetings

Reading the literature

Work in the professional societies —local meetings, committees, etc.

Training in Management of Quality Control   Despite important differences among companies, industries, and national cultures, training needs in management of the quality function appear to have a high degree of commonality. The author's course in Management of Quality Control conducted in about 30 different countries on-all continents, for managers from widely different industries, has nevertheless met with good responses.[84]   The course content is described by the following major topical headings (Third edition, 1974):

The quality function	Quality policies and objectives
Product development	Quality planning
Vendor relations	Organizing for quality
Manufacture of quality	The Quality Manager and his job
Inspection and test	Manpower for quality
Marketing of quality	Data systems
Field performance	Quality and income
Optimizing quality costs	Upper management and quality
Improving quality	Industry applications
Motivation for quality	

Beyond this commonality, there need to be supplements or differences in emphasis for different industries. Companies making long-life products require stress on reliability planning, life cycle costing, etc. Courses for government contractors must

---

[84] For a detailed discussion, see Juran, J. M., Quality and Reliability Training for Management, *Proceedings 13th EOQC Conference,* Prague, pp. 19–22. For some early history of courses and seminars for management, see Juran, J. M., Seminars for QC Management—At Last, *Industrial Quality Control,* July 1964, p. 52.

include material on the multitudinous quality-related government specifications. Companies making products critical to health and safety face special problems, including government regulation.

For large companies, a useful training device is the companywide Quality Control Conference. Typically, the Corporate Quality Manager convenes this conference following consultation with Divisional quality managers. (If there is no Corporate Quality Manager, one of the Divisional managers may supply the leadership.)

An example of such a conference was one conducted by a large multidivision company largely in the health industry. The three-day meeting was held at a resort hotel with a program consisting of:

Presentations by some corporate and divisional officers on quality needs as seen by them

Workshops on several topics, e.g., quality costs

A seminar by an outside consultant on several quality management topics

The varieties of opportunity for development of managers can be seen in the idealized program summarized in Table 17-4. It is evident that there are numerous

TABLE 17-4   Plan of Professional Development for Managers

Sources of development	Equivalent days per year
Formal course.	5
Conventions (Industry, Professional Society)	3
Section meetings	2
Evening courses (1 hour per week).	5
Reading (2 hours per week); Books, journals, trade literature, etc.	12
Total	27

sources of training material, but that the time needed to remain informed is substantial.

PRODUCTION OPERATORS[85]

Recruitment and selection of the Production work force has been intensively studied in industrial companies, since this is usually the largest single category of employees. The selection is done with the aid of standard test batteries, in which quality is only one of the considerations.

There is more to be done to develop good correlation between operator aptitudes and achievement of quality. For example, in one electronics company a study was conducted to reduce certain wiring errors from the prevailing level of 6.0 reverses per 10,000 connections. The conductors were identified by multicolored striped insulation. The study took several directions, one involving test of the operators for color perception.

This test, using the Farnsworth-Munsell 100 Hue Test, showed a positive correlation between test score and percent of errors (Figure 17-6). It was concluded that the data justified giving a color perception test to new employees and using the results as one of the criteria for assignment to such work.[86]

Traditional training for Production operators has covered all aspects of the job, one of which is meeting quality standards. In the recognized "trades," this train-

---

[85] The word "operators" is used here in the sense of nonsupervisory Production personnel and includes setup men, process checkers, etc.

[86] Private communication to J. M. Juran.

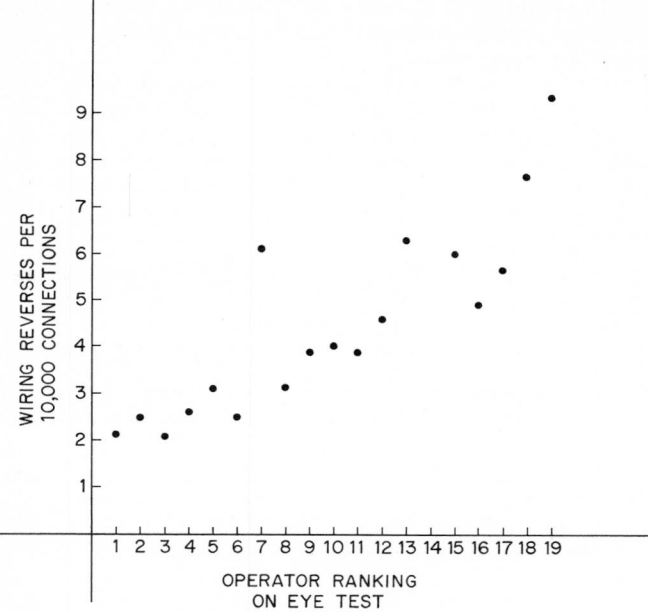

Fig. 17-6   Correlation, eye test versus wiring error rate.

ing has been substantial, sometimes running to a span of several years.   For some of these trades, the workman emerges with qualifications to plan his own work and to execute the plan.

In mass production enterprises, the broad quality planning is done by the managers and engineers.   In some countries, notably the United States, much or most of the detailed quality planning is also done by the engineers, leaving only the execution to the operators.   Such a separation of planning from execution is a negative form of training, since the training process inherent in the planning activity is denied to the operators.

During the 1960s there evolved a discernible worldwide movement to give production operators special training in quality control matters and to provide them with a broader role in quality planning and decision making.   This movement has taken several forms:

Licenses Based on Examination for Quality.   In operations critical to human health and safety (e.g. certain welding), there has been a trend to require licensing. To qualify for the license, operators must take a course in how to do the job and then pass an examination in which the quality of work done is an essential element. This trend has been accelerating under the increasing government regulation of products and processes which are critical to human safety and health.

In addition, there has been a trend to creating licenses for operations which are critical to the company's economics or which have a high technology content, e.g., machines which are numerically controlled.   There has always been an informal concept of "licensing" through restricting assignments to operators believed to be qualified.   What is new is the *formalized* training, objective testing, and formal licenses.

Product Acceptance by Operators. This is an extension of the licensing procedure. Operators whose work proves they make good acceptance decisions (and who meet some other criteria) are permitted to do their own inspection.[87] In the Polish "DO RO" plan, an actual license is issued.[88]

Operator Participation in Problem Discussion. To a degree, this is always present, i.e., when the operator is confronted with defective work and tries to defend himself. However, there has been a trend to go beyond these crisis situations. In the United States, some of the motivational programs of the 1960s included the Error Cause Removal procedure, which urged operators to come forward with ideas for quality improvement.[89] In the Soviet Union, the "Saratov System" includes provision for operator participation in quality problem discussion.[90]

Job Enlargement. In the United States, where the Taylor system[91] of separating planning from execution has been an international extreme, there has been some trend to widening the span of work performed by operators. For example, an electronics company redesigned a manufacturing process to permit an operator to assemble and test an entire radio receiver. The change required more operators and more operator training, but it reduced inspection and repair costs.[92]

Problem Solving. In this form the operators receive training in how to analyze and solve quality problems. Having been trained, they are given the opportunity to tackle actual problems and solve them. Both the training and project work are placed on a voluntary basis. During the 1960s, only the Japanese made significant use of this idea, but their use, under the name QC Circles, was massive (see Section 18, under International Motivational Methods).

In one complex case involving an overseas refinery under construction, a computer was programmed to simulate a critical subsystem of the refinery. The training of operators in how to run the refinery included creation of disturbances in the model to enable the operators to become familiar with these phenomena and to learn how to respond to them.[93]

PRODUCTION FOREMEN

A Production foreman (or other Production supervisor) is responsible for meeting multiple standards: productivity, cost, schedule, personnel relations, etc., including quality.[94] In consequence, training for foremen tends to be designed to deal with all these standards, though some modular elements of the training are strongly quality-oriented.

For example, a West German company program for training foremen (who must first pass a qualifying examination) follows a sequence consisting of:

A four-week training course in various aspects of the foreman's job, including quality problems

An eight-week course in tool setting

[87] For elaboration, see Section 11, under Product Acceptance by Operators.

[88] See generally Section 18, under International Motivational Methods.

[89] See Section 18 under The Formal Motivation Program.

[90] See Section 18, under International Motivational Methods.

[91] See Section 18, under Role of Motivation: The Taylor System.

[92] Motorola Creates a More Demanding Job, *Business Week*, Sept. 4, 1971, p. 32. See also Section 18, under Job Enrichment.

[93] Lieber, Roy E., Operators Run Simulated Refinery for Pre-Startup Experience, *Control Engineering*, September 1964, pp. 105–107.

[94] The priority of these standards keeps changing, and this complicates the job of attaining quality. See Section 18, under Willful Errors: Management-Initiated Operator Errors.

Attendance at lectures (during working hours) on general subjects of interest
Reading of periodicals relating to the foreman's work
Visits to other plants to exchange experiences with other foremen
Special three-day courses on miscellaneous subjects of interest
Reference to the Foreman's Manual, which is distributed to all foremen[95]

The widest use of foreman training courses in quality control has taken place in Japan. The first major step was the national radio course given during July–September 1956 for 15 minutes per day, six days per week. Additional radio (and TV) courses followed, as well as courses offered by the Japanese Union of Scientists and Engineers. The text used in the radio courses sold over 100,000 copies.

During the 1960s regular quality control courses for foremen were created by the Japanese Standards Association and the Japanese Union of Scientists and Engineers (JUSE). These courses have trained many thousands of foremen. Even more extensive have been the in-house courses created by many industrial companies. The cumulative number of foremen who had been trained in formal quality courses had by the beginning of the 1970s gone well into six figures.[96]

The subject matter of the (usually 40-hour) Japanese courses may be judged from the topic titles[97] of the textbook:

What is quality control?
How to take and treat data. Includes distributions, average, dispersion, histogram, Pareto diagram, Cause and Effect Diagram.
Statistical concept (of sampling).
Control charts.
Control in the workshop (how to set up controls in the shop environment).
Improvement in workshop (project identification, analysis, and action to improve).
What is a foreman?
QC Circle activities.
Human relations.
Quality Assurance and Inspection.

A vital need for foremen is knowledge of how to solve quality problems. In most companies it has been generally assumed that once an out-of-control process or other quality problem is brought to the foreman's attention, he knows how to solve it. For the most part, this assumption is not well founded; the foreman needs training in how to solve quality problems.[98]

Courses of the sort conducted in Japan include training in how to solve problems using several forms of analysis: Pareto, Cause and Effect Diagram, experiment design, data collection and analysis. In the United States and elsewhere, some special

---

[95] Müller, K., Quality-Consciousness and Responsibility in Production. *Proceedings, 13th EOQC Conference,* Prague, 1969, pp. 79–84.

[96] An index of the cumulative number of foremen trained is the cumulative sale of the "QC Handbook for Foremen." As of January 1970, the A Section (Concepts) had sold over 240,000 copies; the B Section (Methods) had sold over 110,000 copies.

[97] Ishikawa, Kaoru, Education and Training of Quality Control in Japanese Industry, *Reports of Statistical Applications Research,* JUSE, vol. 16, no. 3, 1969, pp. 21–40. See also Imaizumi, M., Foremen's Role in Quality Control—Recent Aspects of Foremen in Japan, *ibid.,* vol. 12, no. 2, 1969, pp. 10–15. Also Tosaka, S., An Example of Quality Control Education for Foremen and Workers, *ibid.,* pp. 23–27. See also generally Section 48, under Quality Control in Japan.

[98] The statistical quality control courses of the 1950s were of little help on this score. These courses stressed control charts, which are devices for identifying problems and doing so with greater precision than is possible by empirical methods. Actually, the foremen of those days knew very well, from their empirical signals, that certain quality problems needed solving. What the foremen lacked were the skills to solve these problems and the time in which to do it.

training programs have been evolved on the subject of problem solving. Some of these programs stress data collection and analysis; others stress clear communication and terminology, etc.[99]

Another foreman training need which is all too often taken for granted is product knowledge. The assumption that long years of association automatically provide this knowledge is often invalid.[100] In a company manufacturing sewing machines, an attempt was made to improve the quality of the complex shafts by instituting foreman training courses in statistical methods. Some improvement was realized, but the bulk of the problem remained. Then it was discovered that the Shaft Department foremen did not understand the usage of the product. Several approaches were used to give the foremen adequate product knowledge. Arrangements were made for the foremen to:

Visit the assembly area to observe the quality problems arising during shaft assembly

Study the product in the classroom using exploded diagrams and three-dimensional models

Assemble sewing machines

Perform sewing operations on the machines

Spend time on the assembly line

The product knowledge training program gave the foremen information which they could use in running their department. In addition, it greatly improved the atmosphere of collaboration with the Assembly Department. There was a subsequent dramatic improvement in quality, and it was believed that the training program was an important element in securing this improvement.[101]

"NON-QUALITY" MANAGERS

Outside of the Quality Control Department, the managers carry a mixture of responsibilities in which quality of product is only one of the goals to meet. The job descriptions for these people are written not by the Quality Manager but by others. The evaluations of their overall performance and their qualifications for advancement are likewise made by others. The Quality Manager sometimes has a voice in defining their quality-oriented goals, but theirs is the final word.[102]

Traditionally, the training programs for these managers have been built around their main functional responsibility. Any subsidiary goals have been given incidental treatment. However, the increasing importance of the quality function has begun to change this traditional setup.

The most extensive development of training programs (in quality control) for non-quality mangers has been in Japan. Table 17-5 shows an example of the approach as used by one Japanese company.[103] The table covers the entire hierarchy from President through engineers and foremen. (However, it omits reference to the com-

[99] A structured approach for solution of sporadic problems is contained in Kepner, Charles H., and Benjamin B. Tregoe, "The Rational Manager," McGraw-Hill Book Company, New York, 1965. The approach emphasizes clear definition of terminology, good communication, and related qualitative approaches. However, the book is under a serious misapprehension that all problems are sporadic.

[100] See Section 11, under Troubleshooting.

[101] Calahan, Richard C., Basic Product Knowledge—A Vital Link in Quality and Reliability Training, *Proceedings, 13th EOQC Conference,* Prague, 1969, pp. 54–57.

[102] There is need to rethink this very point. The overall quality planning mechanism should set out the quality-oriented goals for all departments.

[103] Ishikawa, K., Education of Quality Control in Japanese Industry, *Reports of Statistical Application Research,* Union of Japanese Scientists and Engineers, vol. 16, no. 3, pp. 21–40.

TABLE 17-5   Training Program in Matsushita Electric Industries Co.

Title of course	Held for	No. of Persons	Hours	Contents
Management Course	President and Directors	8	21	Introduction to QC, statistical way of thinking, quality assurance, development of new products, organization and administration of QC
Course for Chiefs of Departments	1. Factory Manager, Chiefs of Dept. at Head Office	22	18	Same as above top management course
	2. Sales Managers	15	6	Introduction to QC, market survey
Middle Management Course	Chiefs of Departments at factories, Chiefs of Sections (Out of 200 persons, 60 persons attended QC:MC course held by JUSE)	200	6	How to introduce and promote QC
Engineer's Course	QC engineers OR workers			Attended the courses held outside the company
Intermediate	People in charge of design and research	60	144	QC application method, statistical method, control chart method, sampling inspection method, sampling, etc.
Introductory Course	Engineers in general (Out of 260 persons, 20 persons attended the courses held outside the company) (This course has been held 5 times)	260	36	Received the training under the course corresponding to introductory course held by JUSE
Foreman Course (Primary)	Foremen	200	12	Foremen's QC text (A) used
Foreman Course (Secondary)	Foremen picked up from those getting the primary course	80	30	Foremen's QC text (B) used

pany's very extensive program of QC Circles, which includes training for many thousands of nonsupervisors.)

On a smaller scale is the use of multiple training programs by an American company with factories in 30 countries. The more common programs included:

Two or three day briefings for new marketing executives.

One or two week training for new corporate staff engineers, new Quality Control Managers and similar technical personnel.

One month in-depth training for quality audit engineers, assembly foremen, etc.

Twenty hour training for assemblers.

Five to ten hour briefing for manufacturing foremen and setup men.[104]

Detailed training programs for non-quality managers are still in the process of evolution. Experience to date[105] suggests training topics as shown in the matrix of Table 17-6. (See, in this connection, Section 8, under Improving Effectiveness of Designers: Training of Designers.)

Getting the non-quality managers to accept such training has been a long-standing problem, the most difficult being that of top management. The Quality Manager is obviously at a disadvantage in bringing this about.[106] More usually, top managers become interested in seminars for themselves when:

1. They receive clear alarm signals that they are being outperformed, e.g.,

Sales are going down due to poor quality

Although sales are rising, share of market is going down due to poor quality

Competitors who are outperforming the company have made use of such training programs

2. A team of inside managers (rather than one manager) makes the recommendation for training seminars for top management.

3. The internal Management Development Department supports the recommendation.

4. A respected outsider presents a persuasive case.

5. There is an opportunity to attend a seminar not with subordinates but with other top managers.

6. They read success stories written by top managers in other companies.[107]

In training managers, it is important to make clear to them that they are present in the course in two capacities and for two purposes:

1. As head of a specialized department (Quality Control or similar title). In this capacity their purpose is to broaden their understanding of how their *specialized duties* are carried out in industry generally. They hope, on returning to their jobs, to increase their *departmental* effectiveness, and thereby company effectiveness.

2. As a member of the company team, with an interest in the quality function generally. In this capacity their purpose is to broaden their understanding of how

---

[104] Calahan, Richard C., Basic Product Knowledge—A Vital Link in Quality and Reliability Training, *Proceedings, 13th EOQC Conference,* Prague, 1969, pp. 54–57.

[105] The author has conducted numerous seminars for top management. In addition, attendees at his courses on Management of Quality Control have included a minority of managers from Research and Development, Design, Purchasing, Production, Marketing, Customer Service, Finance, Personnel. The feedbacks from these managers are reflected in the present comments.

[106] In too many cases, in-house seminars organized for top management have been used to "sell" top management on some technique or program favored by the Quality Manager. The real need in such seminars is to clarify for top management its own role in establishing and reaching quality goals.

[107] As a corollary, the journals of professional societies should regularly devote space to success stories written by top managers.

TABLE 17-6   Matrix for Training "Non-QC" Personnel in Quality Matters

Subject matter of training	Upper Management	Middle Management	Product Design	Purchasing	Manufacturing Planning	Production	Marketing	Customer Service	Finance	Personnel
Annual quality program	X	X	X	X	X	X	X	X	X	X
Quality policies	X	X								
Quality objectives	X	X								
Planning for quality	X	X								
Organizing for quality	X	X	··	··	··	··	··	··	··	X
Quality and income	X	X	X	··	··	··	X	··	X	
Quality costs	X	X	··	··	X	X	··	··	X	
Quality improvement	X	X	X	X	X	X	X	X	X	X
Motivation for quality	X	X	··	··	X	X	··	X	··	X
Executive reports	X	X	··	X	X	X	X	X	X	X
Quality audit	X	X	X	X	X	X	X	X	X	X
Consumerism	X	X	X	X	X	X	X	X	X	X
Product liability	X	X	X	X	X	X	X	X	X	X
Government regulation	X	X	X	X	X	X	X	X	X	X
Launching new products	X	X								
Cost effectiveness	··	··	X	··	X	··	X			
Life-cycle costing	··	··	X	··	··	··	X	X	X	
Reliability program	··	··	X	X	X	··	X	X		
Maintainability program	··	··	X	X	X	··	X	X		
Product safety	X	X	X	X	X	X	X	X	X	X
Tolerancing	··	··	X	X	X					
Design of experiment	··	··	X	··	X	··	··	X		
Design review	··	··	X	X	X	··	··	X		
Vendor relations	X	X	··	X	··					
Vendor qualification	··	··	X	X	X					
Vendor survey	··	··	X	X	X					
Joint vendor planning	··	··	··	X	X					
Vendor certification	··	··	X	X	X					
Audit of decisions	··	··	··	X	··	X				
Vendor rating	··	··	··	X						
Process capability	··	··	X	··	X	X				
Traceability	··	··	X	X	X	X	··	X		
Automated process control	··	··	··	··	X	X				
Quality information equipment	··	··	··	··	X	X	··	X		
Factory quality decisions	··	··	··	··	X	X	··	··	··	X
Concept of self-control	··	··	··	··	X	X	··	X	··	X
Inspection by operators	··	··	··	··	··	X	··	X	··	X
Operator errors	··	··	··	··	··	X	··	X	··	X
Machine/tool maintenance	··	··	··	··	··	X	··	X		
Trouble shooting	··	··	··	··	··	X	X	X		

TABLE 17-6   Matrix for Training "Non-QC" Personnel in Quality Matters *(Continued)*

Subject matter of training	Upper Management	Middle Management	Product Design	Purchasing	Manufacturing Planning	Production	Marketing	Customer Service	Finance	Personnel
Operator training................	..	..	..	..	..	X	..	X	..	X
Shop process control............	..	..	..	..	X	X				
Market research in quality.......	..	..	..	..	..	..	X	X		
Sales contracts based on usage	..	..	..	..	..	..	X	X	X	
Advertising of quality............	..	..	X	..	..	..	X	X		
Quality labeling.................	..	..	X	..	..	..	X			
Quality warranties...............	..	..	X	..	..	..	X	X	X	
Service contracts...............	..	..	..	..	..	..	X	X	X	
Control of service quality........	..	..	..	..	..	..	X	X		
Quality complaint analysis.......	..	..	X	..	..	..	X	X		
Field data feedback.............	..	..	X	..	..	..	X	X		

the *overall quality function* is carried out in industry generally. On returning to their jobs, this broader understanding can aid them in developing proposals aimed at improving the *company's* effectiveness in conducting the entire quality function.

In the first of these capacities, the trainee's prime concern is with his assigned special duties. In the second, his prime concern is with the entire quality mission of the company; how to define this mission, how to appraise the company's present effectiveness in carrying out this mission, what steps the company should take to go from the present level of effectiveness to the target level of effectiveness for carrying out its quality mission.[108]

OUTSIDERS

In this category are nonemployees who nevertheless exert important influences on fitness for use. The major categories and the programs available are as follows:

Vendors. Vendor selection methods are based on vendor surveys and on vendor rating schemes as discussed in Section 10. In addition, the regular relations with vendors develop a good deal of knowledge about vendor performance and add significantly to decisions on vendor selection.

These same vendor relations are also a form of training, since this is a common meeting ground for two different cultures. In addition, the improvement programs undertaken by the manufacturer can be extended to the vendor.[109]

Conferences for vendors, sometimes used for launching new vendor relations policies, can be extended on a voluntary basis to become training seminars. Many manufacturers have assisted vendors in setting up improvement and training pro-

[108] From Juran, J. M., "Management of Quality Control" (a textbook used for manager training), 3d ed., 1974, privately published.

[109] See Section 18, under The Formal Motivational Campaign: Extension To Include Vendors; see also Section 10, under Vendor Quality Improvement.

grams through providing literature, text material, instructors, and technical assistance.

Dealers.   Manufacturers have excellent measures of dealers' sales performance. The measures of dealers' quality performance is less well done and could be improved in many cases through reviews and audits, as discussed in Section 15.   Use of these audits for dealer selection must be circumspect since, to a degree, the dealer owns the market.

Dealer training in quality is usually well done through the medium of product literature and actual training of salesmen.   In launching new products, it is common to include quality of product as an essential element of the training.

Repair Shops.   The competence of repair shops has been the weakest link in the chain which provides fitness for use for consumers.   In broad terms, the best shops have been the captive shops maintained by manufacturers and dealers.   These shops serve the user mostly during the warranty period.   Thereafter, the independent repair shops provide most of the product maintenance.

Under the prevailing organization forms, the initiative for adequate selection and training of the personnel in the independent repair shops must come from the proprietors.   On the record, this has been a highly variable performance.   The percent of incompetents is not precisely known, but obviously it is too high.

The manufacturers can be of assistance in providing good product literature and in offering training classes.   The concept of "approved shop" has merit if well audited. However, in the opinion of the author, the independent repair shop is inherently too handicapped to conduct efficient repair and must give way to more efficient organization forms, e.g., chains of repair shops, manufacturers' shops, etc.[110]

Users.   Training for users depends largely on whether the user is *(a)* an industrial company or *(b)* the consumer.   In the former case there is opportunity to supply technical assistance and knowledge during sale, installation, check out, and service. The users' personnel have the capacity to absorb this training and, in addition, to provide useful ideas for improvement.

The situation with consumers is very different due to widespread product ignorance, and (what can be worse) to indifference to training.   Many manufacturers do prepare good product literature on proper use and care of the product and on cautions to be observed.   However, experience has shown that many users pay little heed to these things.[111]

Until new concepts are evolved, manufacturers have little choice but to pursue, with best efforts, the methods available to:

Provide high reliability in the original design
Foolproof the product against hazards and misuse
Adopt modular designs to simplify user maintenance
Provide clear product use and care instructions, preferably on the product itself and certainly in the literature
Train salesmen and servicemen in how to train users

Labor Unions.   Participation of labor union leaders in quality programs and training is remarkably different under various national cultures.   In Japan and in Eastern Europe, the Unions regard their role as entirely compatible with furthering the progress of the company.   At the other extreme, as exemplified in too many United States companies, there exists a state of mutual hostility between these union leaders and the managers, so that the quality problems of the company do not engage the sympathy of the union leaders.

---

[110] For elaboration, see Juran, J. M., *Consumerism and Product Quality, Quality Progress,* July, 1970.   See also Section 15, under Field Service.

[111] See, for example, Section 43, under Customer Relations.

Sometimes, as in launching motivational campaigns, the active participation of the Unions has been enlisted, even when the overall atmosphere of collaboration is poor. However, the fundamental need is to improve this basic atmosphere. Individual instances of collaboration can help to bring this about, but the broader need is to rethink the basic relationship so as to eliminate the atmosphere of hostility.

The tradition in the established trade unions differs from that of most industrial unions. These trade unions have their roots going back to the guilds and similar forms of organization involving years of apprenticeship to qualify as a master of the trade. An important element of this training was emphasis on quality. The piece of work done by the apprentice to prove qualification for the rank of master was known as a "masterpiece," and the word retains this connotation. The official attitude of the trade unions remains one of placing high stress on quality. To this day the union publications devote space to pride in the craft, and urge employment of unionized workers on the grounds of high quality.

Government Regulators. The growth of legislation dealing with product quality has greatly increased the extent of regulation of quality. A consequence has been that more industries are now "regulated" and that many "unregulated" industries nevertheless find themselves extensively involved with regulations. It is common to find that both (the new regulatory agencies and the companies newly exposed to regulation) are awkward and mutually suspicious in their relationship to each other.

A useful training device has been to create a seminar in which the regulators are provided with information about company organization and practices as well as exposure to the company managers who appear to make presentations.

INTRODUCTION

This Section deals with the problems of stimulating people (operators, supervisors, managers, specialists) to take action to reduce those errors which lead to poor quality. As will be seen, these errors have multiple causes and hence multiple remedies, including "motivation."

The Section also deals with the means of stimulating people to participate in programs designed to improve quality.

Based on actual polls of managers, the effectiveness of diagnosis and remedy of human errors is one of the weakest areas in the conduct of the entire quality function.[1] In part, this weakness is inherent in the subject matter—we are still in the early stages of discovering the universals which underlie human error and human motivation. In particular, there has been some tendency, by managers, to equate human error with lack of motivation. This erroneous belief has been responsible for some serious misdirections of effort, so that pseudosolutions have been applied while the problems go on and on. In this Section, the author has undertaken to go back to fundamentals—to identify the prevailing premises, to evaluate their validity, and to examine the practices in use in relation to these premises.

Because most people are nonsupervisors, much of this Section is devoted to operator error, the word "operator" being used in the sense of any nonsupervisor. Where the narrower meaning of production nonsupervisor is intended, the term used is "production operator."

This Section examines the spectrum of human errors and categorizes these into their subspecies. It then deals with the causes and remedies for these subspecies of error. Finally, it examines the broad forces which are in contention and which must be confronted as part of the solution of problems of human error.

OPERATOR-CONTROLLABLE ERRORS

Operator-controllable errors are those which occur when the operator is in a state of self-control as set out in Section 2, under Self-Control.[2] To summarize, a person is in a state of self-control if he possesses the means of:

Knowing what he is supposed to be doing
Knowing what he is actually doing
Changing his performance in the event that what he is doing does not conform to what he is supposed to be doing

It is normally the responsibility of management to provide the operator with the means for meeting these criteria.[3] A failure of management to meet any of these criteria renders the resulting defects management-controllable. However, if all the criteria have been met, any resulting defects are regarded as operator-controllable.

The distinction between operator-controllable and management-controllable[4] is important because there are other, parallel distinctions between management and operators in matters such as organization structure, division of work and responsibility, social groupings, political groupings, etc. These widely used distinctions have a profound effect on the achievement of quality. Failure to grasp this distinction as applied to controllability of errors is a widespread source of confusion in the quality function.

[1] For data from these polls, see below, under Census of Company Effectiveness on Operator-controllable Errors.

[2] See also, Section 11, under Concept of Operator Self-Control.

[3] In the recognized professions and trades, the "operator" acquires most of the means for meeting these criteria through special education, apprenticeship, and experience.

[4] Management-controllable is made up of subspecies both as to function, e.g., design-controllable, and as to level of supervision, e.g., foreman-controllable.

Controllability can be quantified by analysis of the process. See, for an example, Section 16, Table 16-8 and associated discussion under Controllability Quantification. Such studies dramatize the extent of operator-controllability and help the managers to view the problems objectively. Many managers believe that the company's quality problems could be solved by the operators. Yet the overwhelming evidence is that operator-controllable defects generally are less than 20% of the total.[5]

Subspecies of Operator Error   Once the criteria for operator self-control have been met, it seems logical to conclude that management has finished its job and that now it is up to the operator to deliver good work. An extension of this logic is to conclude that since the operator is actually in a state of self-control, any errors, i.e., failure to do good work, must be the result of lack of operator motivation. Many managers observe repeated instances of defects due to operator carelessness, inattention, or blunder for which the conventional management explanation is "lack of motivation." An extension of this logic is to conclude that since operators' lack of motivation can and does result in defects, it should be possible to eliminate defects through motivation programs.

This train of logic is fatally defective on three grounds:

1. The fact that operator carelessness, etc., can create defects (in good designs) does not mean that the absence of operator carelessness will eliminate defects (in bad designs); i.e., eliminating operator-controllable defects will not eliminate management-controllable defects.

2. Because operator-controllable defects are commonly less than 20% of the overall defect problem, elimination of operator-controllable defects will at best eliminate only a minor part of the problem.

3. Many and probably most operator-controllable errors are *not* the result of lack of motivation.

This last point requires elaboration, since it runs contrary to the opinion of most managers. What convinces such managers is an example drawn from a nonindustrial source—*the golfer.*

The golfer is obviously in a state of self-control. He knows very well what he is supposed to do. He can observe with his own senses what his actual performance is. He has tools identical to those used by experts. Why then are there so many golf balls in the lakes? Under conventional logic, the reason is that the golfer is not well motivated. Such a conclusion would be laughed at by anyone who plays golf or who has observed golfers at play, since few people are as intensely motivated as golfers. Equally hilarious would be an assertion that if the proper motivation were applied to the golfer, he would make no errors.

The way out of this dilemma is the concept of *subspecies of operator error.* Once one breaks away from an axiomatic belief in motivation as a cure-all for operator-controllable defects, it becomes evident that there are several subspecies of these defects:

1. Errors due to *inadvertence* (i.e., inadvertent errors)
2. Errors due to *lack of technique* (i.e., technique errors)
3. *Willful* errors

It is this classification[6] which will be examined in greater detail in this Section.

---

[5] Based on numerous studies made by the author and on studies made by other investigators (in the United States, Czechoslovakia, Holland, Japan, and Sweden) and exhibited to the author. Curiously, there has been little material published on this point.

[6] This classification was first proposed in the author's paper Operator Errors—Time for a New Look, *Quality Progress*, February 1968, pp. 9–11. An earlier classification, for inspector errors, consisted of involuntary errors, avoidable errors, blunders, errors of ignorance, de-

(footnote continued on p. 18-4)

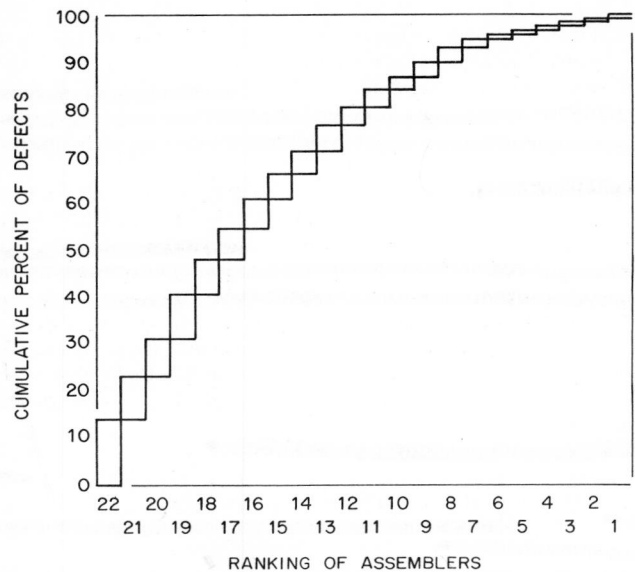

Fig. 18-1   Pareto diagram for gun assemblers.

Diagnosis of Operator Errors   There are two levels of diagnosis for operator errors:

1. Analysis of past performance data to discover the existence of *patterns of concentration* of error, e.g., by operator, by defect type. (Absence of concentration also has a significance.) These patterns identify the likely subspecies of operator error involved and point to directions for further study. These data of past performance are studied "in the office."

2. Analysis to discover the *causes* of the concentration patterns. This analysis is conducted "in the field," e.g., on the factory floor.

The principal tools used to study data on past performance are:

1. *The Pareto[7] analysis* of operator performance. For example, Figure 18-1 is a charting in the Pareto form of the gun assembler data of Sec. 16, Table 16-12a. It is evident that the five "worst"[8] assemblers contribute about half the defects, while the five "best" assemblers contribute only 4% of the defects. The implication is that the superior performances are the result of a secret knowledge or knack possessed by these "best" assemblers. Alternatively, the implication is that the worst performances are the result of lack of skill or technique by the "worst" assemblers.

2. *Trend analysis* of best and worst performances to see if they exhibit consistency. For example, the summaries of gun assembler data (Table 16-12b) show

---

liberate falsifications. See Juran, J. M., "Management of Inspection and Quality Control," Harper & Bros., 1945, pp. 39–48.

See also the classification of operator errors in Stok, Th. L., Quality Motivation in U.S. Industry, *Quality,* Summer 1964, pp. 37–41. Dr. Stok uses the categories: consciously caused, unconsciously caused, unintentional omissions.

[7] See generally Section 2, under The Pareto Principle.

[8] At this stage, "best" and "worst" are properly applied only to performances, not to operators.

the following month-to-month relationship of the five worst and five best performances:

	Nov.	Dec.	Jan.	Feb.	March	April
5 best......	9	6	0	20	5	8
5 worst.....	114	62	12	265	113	103
Ratio	13	10	∞	13	23	14

This analysis established that there was a consistency as to which operators gave the best performances and which the worst. This consistency raised the presumption that the best performances were the result of secret knowledge. This secret knowledge was then discovered by shop study of the methods used by the men.

3. *The matrix.* In its most usual form the matrix is a table showing, for each defect type, how many were produced and by which operator. Table 18-1 is an example involving an office "operation" of preparing insurance policies. The "operator" is a policy writer who starts with the order written by a salesman following the sale of a policy to a prospect. Using pertinent data in the procedures manual, the policy writer types up a printed blank policy form which later becomes the official insurance contract. When the form is completed, it is examined 100% by an inspector. Table 18-1 shows a (simplified) summary of the results of this 100% inspection over a period of three months. The summary is most revealing.

The right-hand column of Table 18-1 shows the total of errors for each error type, the grand total being 80. Of these, 19 consisted of error type three. This is a "lump" of about a quarter of all the errors. Looking horizontally across the line for error type three, it is evident that one policy writer (B) accounted for 16 of these 19 errors. Looking vertically down the column for policy writer B, it is seen that she had a total of 20 errors over the three-month period and hence only four errors other than error type three.

An experienced manager knows that there is a ready solution for these 16 type three errors committed by policy writer B. It is a case of "secret ignorance" i.e., policy writer B, *and no one else,* is widely misinterpreting some aspect of the procedures. This can be discovered by interview of policy writer B, by study of her work methods, etc., with a virtual certainty of solution.

TABLE 18-1   Matrix of Errors by Insurance Policy Writers

Error type	\multicolumn{6}{c}{Policy writer}	Total

Error type	A	B	C	D	E	F	Total
1	0	0	1	0	2	1	4
2	1	0	0	0	1	0	2
3	0	16	1	0	2	0	19
4	0	0	0	0	1	0	1
5	2	1	3	1	4	2	13
6	0	0	0	0	3	0	3
27							
28							
29							
Totals	6	20	8	3	36	7	80

TABLE 18-2 Interrelation among Error Pattern, Likely Subspecies of Operator Error, and Likely Solution

Pattern disclosed by analysis of operator error	Likely subspecies of error causing this pattern	Likely solution
On certain defects, no one is error-prone; defect pattern is random.	Errors are due to inadvertence.	Foolproof the process.
On certain defects, some operators are consistently error-prone while others are consistently "good."	Errors are due to lack of technique (ability, know how, etc.). Lack of technique may take the form of secret ignorance. Technique may consist of known knack or of secret knowledge.	Discovery and propagation of knack. Discovery and elimination of secret ignorance.
Some operators are consistently error-prone over a wide range of defects.	There are several potential causes: Willful failure to comply to standards Inherent incapacity to perform this task Lack of training	Solution follows the cause: Motivation Transfer to work for which operator is qualified. Supply training.
On certain defects, all operators are error-prone.	Errors are management-controllable.	Meet the criteria for self-control.

A second "lump" in errors by defect type is the 13 errors of type five. This time, as one looks horizontally at the pattern of error type five, it is seen that all policy writers are involved. Under the truism that "if everyone makes the same mistake, it isn't a mistake," the implication is that there is a difference in interpretation of procedures between (a) the policy writers as a group and (b) the inspector. This theory can be tested by detailed analysis of the work being performed.

The matrix is also revealing through the totals by policy writer. The total for writer B has already been discussed. However, the total for policy writer E is even larger—36 errors. As the pattern of this total is studied, it is seen that policy writer E makes errors in all categories and is the only one to do so. The past performance data alone do not make clear *why* policy writer E is so widely defect-prone. It might be any of a variety of reasons. She may not be properly trained, lack the capacity to do such exacting work, be indifferent to the needs of doing good work, be performing sabotage, have become too old for the job, etc. To obtain a clear understanding of the reason would require a study in depth.[9]

There is also a meaning to be read out of those error types which show no concentration. For example, in Table 18-1, error type two was committed only twice over the study period in what seems to be a random pattern. The implication of the random pattern is errors due to inadvertence.

Unique Patterns of Operator Error When one conducts many studies of operator errors using the foregoing tools of analysis, it soon emerges that the great majority of the analyses point to a very few unique identifiable patterns. Each of these unique patterns suggests the likely subspecies of operator error which produces such a pattern. In turn, each of these subspecies of error has its own unique program for solution. Table 18-2 shows the interrelations among: the defect patterns, the likely subspecies of error causing these patterns, the likely solutions.

[9] Some managers would have only limited interest in the reason and would solve the problem by removing this policy writer from the job.

The topics which follow will examine, in detail, those subspecies of error most frequently encountered.

INADVERTENT ERRORS

These errors are characterized by the fact that at the time of making the error the operator is even unaware that he has made an error; e.g., he adds up a column of figures and gets the wrong answer.

On the matrix of defect type by operator, inadvertent errors show a random pattern, both by defect type and by operator. The random pattern by operators precludes any assumption of lack of skill, since this would mean that none of the operators were skilled. The random pattern by defect type precludes any assumption of concentration for reasons of secret ignorance.

The errors themselves present the outward evidence of oversights, lapses in memory, inattention, etc. When one of these errors, by bad luck, results in a serious accident or a large loss, it is called a blunder or worse. The operator committing the error is seldom able to explain how it happened.

There are two main schools of thought as to the cause of inadvertent defects, each with its own remedy. One of these may be called the "fallibility" school and the other the "inattention" school.

The "Fallibility" School This assumes that human employees are fallible, that there is a limit to human capacities, and that this limit extends to the powers of memory, concentration, and other faculties needed to keep going on a continuing job. The layman's expression of this attitude is "To err is human." Under this assumption, managers have endured inadvertent errors if they were not dangerous or too burdensome economically. Where the managers were unable to endure the defects, they resorted to foolproofing[10] the operations.

Where the stakes were truly enormous, managers went to extremes to neutralize human fallibility. Inattention was a serious problem in ancient early warning systems—the watchtower, the sentry post, the ship's crow's nest. A major question for commanders was the proper length of watch. Evidently some fleets changed the lookout men every half hour.

The twentieth-century makers of complex systems faced some new orders of magnitude in dealing with errors. The unprecedented product complexity meant that even a low incidence of human failure would result in so high an incidence of product failure as to be totally unacceptable. Hence, in addition to ordinary approaches to error reduction, these manufacturers had to go to extraordinary approaches—redundant designs, foolproofing, countdowns, etc. It is quite understandable that such manufacturers would consider seriously any plausible proposal for error reduction. It was precisely such manufacturers who were drawn into the wave of motivational programs of the 1960s, some on their own initiative, some at the urging of their government customers. In contrast, makers of commercial products for sale in the competitive market place tend to resist a goal of perfection on the grounds that it is uneconomical.[11]

---

[10] The approaches to foolproofing are detailed elsewhere in this Handbook. Foolproofing against Production errors is discussed in Section 9, under Foolproofing the Process. Foolproofing against Inspection errors is discussed in Section 12, under Inspector Errors: Inadvertent Inspector Errors.

[11] See, for example, Haas, A. R. The Superior Craftsmanship Program, *Industrial Quality Control,* June 1966, pp. 665–669; also Sheffres, E. H., Zero Defects—A Quality Control Paradox, *Quality Assurance,* November 1969, pp. 49 and 50.

The "Inattention" School The "inattention" school came into prominence during the 1960s through the publicity given to the Zero Defects (ZD) programs. The advocates of such programs contended that human beings will not make errors if they are adequately motivated. Starting with this premise, they built programs on the following line of reasoning:

1. The prime cause of human error is inattention.
2. The long-standing adage "to err is human" is invalid.[12]
3. Because human beings have long accepted this invalid adage, there exists a climate of mediocrity which tolerates unnecessary errors.
4. Human beings can be convinced that errors are unnecessary and that as individuals they can avoid errors by devoting constant attention to the job.
5. This conviction can be secured by appealing to the sense of pride that human beings derive from superior performance and through other motivational devices.[13]

In the opinion of the author, the "inattention" school is inherently unsound and will not endure. As elaborated in the Historical Supplement at the end of this Section, it was an unusual combination of circumstances which resulted in many government contractors, plus some others, embarking on formal motivational programs based on the inattention theory.

Nevertheless, the concept of motivation has a great deal of attraction for managers, even as applied to inadvertent errors. The instances of gross carelessness, inattention, or blunder which regularly come to their attention cause them to question, in all sincerity, how motivated operators could possibly do such things. The very term "foolproofing" suggests what must once have been a prevailing school of thought as to the cause of inadvertent defects.

In addition, the outward evidences of extent of inadvertent error can be deceiving as to the effect of applying motivation. To illustrate:

1. A manager urges his secretary to participate in the company's motivational program by reducing typographical errors. To do so, she starts proofreading everything she writes for him. (Previously she did not proofread since she made few errors.) The proofreading finds most of these errors, which she then corrects. As seen by her boss, her quality has improved due to motivation. Someone else might conclude that she makes as many errors as before, but that she has introduced an added redundancy cost to prevent these errors from going on to the next operation.

2. An operator responds to a motivational program by setting up a check sheet to help him assure that he has carried out all the steps required and in their proper sequence. As a result he makes less inadvertent errors. The managers of the program attribute this to motivation. Someone else might conclude that what has happened is the unauthorized introduction of the countdown method of foolproofing.

The interrelation of inadvertence to process design is likewise an area which has been the subject of debate. Some processes demand more concentration than others and are thereby more susceptible to inadvertent errors. The motorist driving in the central city has much more to watch and to keep in mind than when he is driving on a country lane. When operators are assigned to processes which demand

[12] This view was urged seriously and unequivocally. For example, one of the early advocates of this school of thought stated (after relating three instances of operator-controllable error): "The common denominator in all three of these parables is human error—and contrary to most opinion, it is *not* inevitable" [emphasis in original paper]. See Crosby, Philip M., Z is for Zero Defects, *Industrial Quality Control*, October 1964, p. 182.

[13] There were numerous expressions of this philosophy. See, for example, Halpin, James F., Zero Defects, McGraw-Hill Book Company, New York, 1966, pp. 3–9. See also, Todt, Howard C., Employee Motivation, Fact or Fiction? American Management Association Bulletin 71, New York, 1965, pp. 3–10.

a high degree of concentration, they are likewise more susceptible to inadvertent errors. The growing complexity of industrial processes requires increasing recognition that there is a man-machine relationship which cannot be solved by advocacy of this or that technique. All available tools must be used, each directed at the specific problem it is able to solve. None are panaceas.

TECHNIQUE ERRORS[14]

There are many situations in which, for specific defects, there are consistent differences in error levels among operators despite the fact that the specifications, materials, processes, etc., are outwardly the same for all. The implication is that these consistent differences are the result of some special knowledge possessed by the superior performer or some secret ignorance "possessed" by the inferior performer.[15] In this Handbook such errors are referred to as technique errors, since they are the result of lack of knowledge, skill, technique, etc., of how to avoid the error.

The special knowledge possessed by the superior performer is not known to the management nor to the inferior performers, as to them it is "secret." In the author's experience, the knowledge is often a secret even to those who possess it. For example, in the gun assembly case[16] the superior performers knew they filed one of the components, but they did not know that this was decisive in eliminating the defect of "open hard after fire." In the centrifugal casting case, the "best" melter was unaware that his housekeeping was a significant factor in reducing the incidence of pitted castings.[17]

For the inferior performers, all is secret. They do not know what the superior performers do to make them superior. Neither do they know what ignorance of their own is making them inferior. Their very logical, sensible question is: "*What should I do different than I am doing now?*"

Discovery of just what this secret knowledge or secret ignorance is becomes the second level of analysis of technique errors. This discovery cannot be made from records of performance. It requires study and comparison of techniques used by operators, and this can be done only at the scene of action. The purpose of studying these techniques is to discover the "knack," i.e., that small difference in method which produces a large difference in results.

To discover the knack it is helpful first to interview the most successful operators to secure from them their beliefs as to what it is they do which makes them superior.[18] Operators always have ideas on this point, and are usually quite willing to talk about it.

The interviews should be supplemented by actual observation of the process to test out the theories advanced by the operators and to discover other differences of which they are not aware. It is common to find that these two sources of information strengthen each other. For example, in the centrifugal casting case, an engi-

[14] For a discussion of technique errors as applied to the special problems of inspectors, see Section 12, under Inspector Errors.

[15] This assumption is challenged by a school of thought which contends that consistent performance differences are due primarily to the range of human capacities rather than to acquired skill or knowledge. There is much merit in this contention when the matrix analysis shows consistent superiority (or inferiority) across a wide range of defects. However, the contention is seldom valid when applied to specific defects.

[16] See Section 16, under Test of Theories by Cutting New Windows: Study of Workers' Methods.

[17] See Section 16, *ibid.*

[18] See Section 16, *ibid.*

neering study had disclosed that the time taken to empty the supply ladle gave a positive correlation with percent defective. The subsequent interview with the "best" melter disclosed that each morning, before pouring any castings, he cleaned out the delivery funnel.[19] Since this technique likewise influenced the time required for the metal to flow (on its journey from ladle to casting machine), the managers became convinced that time of flow was the main variable and structured an improved technology around this confirmed theory.

Because the interviews and shop studies will disclose multiple differences in operator technique, some experimentation may be needed to discover which of these differences constitutes the knack. Once discovered, the secret knowledge has been transferred to the management, who is then in a position to provide an answer to that question "What should I do different than I am doing now?" The solution may be to (1) teach the knack to all operators through retraining or (2) revise the technology so that the knack becomes locked into the process.

The need for data analysis, interviews, and job study is sometimes questioned by those motivational advocates who contend that well-motivated operators will also be motivated to develop skills. The author's experience has been that in most cases it takes a trained analyst, a determined effort, and appreciable time to discover and confirm the knack or the secret ignorance. Such things are beyond the operators other than in cases like the QC Circle,[20] where the operators themselves have been trained in analysis and are willing to devote the time and effort to make such studies.

Finally, some practitioners feel that technique errors should not be classified as operator-controllable. Their reasoning is that if the operator cannot by himself discover the knack, then management has not finished its job. The contention is obviously valid if *none* of the operators has the knack. In contrast, if the great majority of operators have the knack, most managers would regard the errors as operator-controllable. In between is a gray area which can be argued either way.

ERROR-PRONE OPERATORS

One of the categories in the matrix of defect types by operator is the defect-prone operator, as exemplified in Table 18-1 by policy writer E. The remedy for this defect-prone operator is not in teaching her some knack, since her failing is not concentrated in one or several specific defects. Neither is the solution to foolproof the process; that solution is not economical, since all the other operators can do the job without the need for foolproofing. The solution is something else and depends on whether this individual's defect-proneness is the result of:

1. Lack of capacity—physical, mental, moral, etc. For individual cases, the solution is reassignment. If lack of capacity is widespread, then the *system* for recruitment and placement becomes suspect.[21]

2. Lack of preparation—education, training, etc. Remedy is again on a case-by-case basis unless lack of preparation is widespread. In that event, the system of training becomes suspect.[22]

3. Willfulness. This category of defect-proneness is discussed below under the heading Willful Errors.

---

[19] This technique had not been discovered by observation of the process. The melters commenced work at 7:30 A.M., but the diagnosticians, who were employed on the office payroll, commenced at 8:30 A.M. and missed the cleaning which took place during the first hour of the shop workday.

[20] See below, under The Japanese QC Circle.

[21,22] See generally Section 17, under the pertinent headings.

WILLFUL ERRORS

Willful errors are distinguished by the facts that (1) the operator knows how to avoid making the error, and (2) despite this knowledge, he deliberately makes the error, i.e., fails to meet the quality requirement.

On the face of it, such a combination is reprehensible. However, closer examination of numerous cases soon makes clear that willful operator errors arise from a welter of reasons, some "good" as well as "bad." In particular, willful operator errors can arise from management initiative as well as from operator initiative.[23]

Management-initiated Operator Errors   These take several well-known forms:

Conflicting Priorities.[24]   Managers are faced with meeting multiple standards of performance, e.g., quality, schedule, cost, safety. Obviously, life is always easier if the manager is able to meet all these goals. However, the changing economic climate and various added unforeseen events force the manager to give some goals a higher priority than others. In addition, because the forces pushing against the manager keep changing, he must keep shifting his priorities. In major cases, this shifting is accomplished by "drives" or "campaigns" which single out one standard to receive high priority during the drive and which, if necessary, violate other standards. For example, when deliveries to customers are behind schedule, the managers may order the factory to work overtime and to depart from strict adherence to quality standards. (In this part of the economic cycle, it is usual for the delivery standard to prevail over the quality and cost standards.) This urge to give one of the standards priority over the others does not stop with the managers; they transmit the pressure to their subordinates, who pass it on further until it includes the operators as well.

Conflicting Quality Specifications.   The durable foreman's "black book" is the classic example of a square conflict between unofficial and official specifications, with the workman often in the middle. Management actions in regularly failing to enforce specifications is also a conflict, since the repetitive action (e.g., repeated Material Review Board waivers) becomes the unofficial specification. The managers seldom give the operators reasons for the waivers, so the operators draw their own conclusions and evolve action patterns which follow observed management deeds rather than the official specifications.

Management Apathy.   In some cases, managers fail to face up to quality problems encountered by operators, forcing the latter to find their own solutions and resulting in willful violation of one standard in order to meet others. For example, in one steel company, the electrical repair shop was replacing annually over 1,500 spindles of portable hand grinders—a loss due to willful damage by the workmen. The damage consisted of hammering the lock nuts to loosen them. Investigation showed that the wrenches did not fit the locknuts and that the workmen had complained about this for years, but nothing had been done about it. When proper wrenches were supplied, the replacement of spindles dropped to under 300 per year.

Operator-initiated Errors   These likewise take several forms, some of them a matter of serious concern to the company well-being.

Inattention,[25] *Indifference.*   Some operators exhibit no interest in quality or even

---

[23] This holds for willful inspector errors as well. See Section 12, under Inspector Errors.

[24] For a broader discussion of conflict in standards (departmental versus company), see Juran, J. M., "Managerial Breakthrough," McGraw-Hill Book Company, New York, 1964, pp. 330–333.

[25] Errors due to deliberate inattention are not "inadvertent;" the real error is the inattention, which is willful.

in work. This is evidenced not only by their high error rate across many defect types but also by lack of response to the needs for corrective action, by absenteeism, etc.

Foot Dragging, Disobedience. Some operators go beyond the passive status of indifference; they take positive steps to frustrate the managers through deliberate minor sabotage (some not so minor). Defects are concealed by unauthorized repair. Scrap is not reported, and the physical evidence is concealed. Records are falsified. Orders are violated, not carried out, or deliberately misinterpreted. Delays are introduced. Programs are openly ridiculed and morale is undermined.

Shortcuts. Some operators devise unauthorized ways to increase their production at the expense of quality. Others find ways to reduce their workload so as to give themselves more leisure time on the job. Still others avoid performing disagreeable parts of their jobs.

Conflict in Loyalties. In some situations a proper operator response to job requirements will create problems for fellow workers, for the Union, or for some other institution to which the operator has a loyalty. He may choose to subordinate his loyalty to the company.

Defenses for Operator Errors The foregoing operator-initiatied errors nevertheless have defenders among Union leaders, behavioral scientists, journalists, etc. These defenders offer plausible explanations for the entire array of operator-initiated errors. Inattention and indifference are asserted to be caused by monotonous, boring jobs; deliberate failures are caused by the pressure of multiple competing standards; other errors are caused by vague standards and inadequate job information; failure to follow orders is a human response to management arbitrariness and management failure to resolve personal grievances.

To illustrate, in a classic case, the spinners in a textile plant were failing to tie the correct knots (weaver's knots) because of dislike for the foreman and because of slow action on grievances. Pleas and threats by the foreman were of no avail. Only when the Personnel Director took the (informal) leader of the spinners to the weaving department and showed her the trouble being encountered by the weavers did the problem end. Now the spinners had a good reason for tying the weaver's knots—to help the weavers.

Failure of Communications Operators are faced with numerous opportunities to compare management's words concerning quality with management's deeds concerning quality. When there is a seeming conflict between the words and deeds, the operators may conclude that management does not give high priority to quality and that hence there is no need for operators to do so either.

Management's words are always "for" quality. Collectively, the managers say so on the bulletin boards, on the wall posters, in the company newspaper, etc. The message is well stated, even eloquent.

However, management actions are often something else, *as seen by the operators.* Table 18-3 lists some actions taken by managers, shows how these actions look to operators, and indicates the probable operator interpretation. It is evident that even when management has good reasons for its actions, the operators may not be aware of this and hence may conclude otherwise.

Managers likewise face serious difficulties in discovering what the actualities on the factory floor are with respect to operator error. Such information as comes to the managers is mainly through (1) the supervisory hierarchy or (2) the Union. Transmission through either of these media distorts the message by censorship, coloration, etc. The risk is that management accepts the distorted message and acts on it. Because of these distortions, managers do not really know how many willful errors are the result of good reasons versus bad reasons or the result of management initiative versus operator initiative. However, managers have some practical alternatives to permit them to discover what the realities are.

TABLE 18-3   Operator's Views of Actions Taken by Managers

Conditions as seen by the managers	Conditions as they look to the shop operators	Probable shop interpretation
Nonconforming material judged to be fit for use after discussion with customer.	Material outside of specification was rejected by inspectors but was accepted by managers.	Management does not regard the specification as important.
Machine needs repair, but in view of a new machine being on order, it would be a waste to repair the old machine with only a few months to go.	Defects are being produced by a machine in need of repair, but management will not repair the machine.	Management is not willing to spend money to get quality.
Operator suggestion for improving quality was investigated and found to be uneconomic.	Operator suggestion for improving quality has not been answered.	Management is not interested in improving quality.
We are badly behind in delivery to customers and must act to catch up on schedules.	Scoreboards on quantity receive much more attention than scoreboards on quality.	Management is more interested in quantity than quality.
A process cannot hold the tolerances, but there is no better process known. Hence the process must be closely watched to minimize defects.	The process cannot hold the tolerances but the operators are urged to reduce the defects.	Management does not know what it is doing.

1. They can, by sample, study enough cases in depth to judge the relative proportions involved.

2. They can periodically take soundings of employee beliefs and attitudes to discover the operators' views on management's deeds versus words.[26] If, for the most part, the deeds match the words, the words will be believed and explanations of exceptions will be accepted. If the deeds generally do not match the words, a deep skepticism develops and can be eliminated only by establishing a new and continuing record of actions which do match the words.

Remedy for Willful Errors For operator-initiated errors, the major remedy is through motivation. In many companies, the basic plan of industrial relations provides for such motivation on a continuing basis. See below, under Continuing Programs of Motivation. In other companies, there is periodic need for a drive or campaign to reorient priorities with respect to quality. Such an approach is discussed below, under The Formal Motivational Campaign.

For management-initiated operator errors, the remedies must include motivation of managers, as discussed below under Quality Motivation for Managers.

Beyond the motivational solutions, there are added remedies, some requiring prior analysis of causes and others not:

Studying the operations in detail to detect systematic errors. For example, in the case of willful inspection errors, practices such as flinching, rounding off, and falsification of data can usually be detected by analysis of the data themselves.

[26] These soundings are taken by conventional methods of employee surveys, polls, etc., using the behavioral scientists as media, to minimize distortion in transmission.

Foolproofing the operation so that the options are out of the hands of the operator.[27]

Turning the more critical aspects of the job over to people whose motivation is believed to be more reliable. An example is quality planning by staff specialists.

Instituting systems of check and audit to discover cases of willful departure from standards.

Providing clear traceability to operators through identity stamps, signoffs, etc.

Removing offending operators from the jobs.

ROLE OF MOTIVATION

Motivation is the process of stimulating people to act in ways which serve the needs of the organization providing the stimulus. To oversimplify, motivation consists of discovering and applying the stimuli needed to induce the employee to carry out designated activities in specified ways.

Subject Matter of Motivation   Applied to matters of product quality, motivation is not limited to problems of reducing willful errors; it extends to the entire spectrum of activities through which we achieve fitness for use. In the case of operators, this means, at the least, that they:

Follow the established control plan and meet the criteria provided
Accept training and retraining in methods for doing the job
Adopt new technology as it is evolved

In addition, there are activities for which participation by operators is highly desirable and which may therefore be the subject of motivation:

Provide feedback to management on problems encountered
Assist in troubleshooting to restore status quo
Participate in plans for quality improvement

Motivation for quality is regarded as essentially synonymous with "quality mindedness." However, a clear distinction is made between *attitude,* which is a state of mind, and *behavior,* which is a state of action. The ultimate purpose of all the programs is to change behavior. Whether change of attitude is an essential prerequisite to change in behavior is by no means clear.

Role of the Behavioral Scientists   Discovering the stimuli to which human beings respond is an intricate process in which the managers are largely amateurs. The professionals are the "behavioral scientists," whose role may be best understood by analogy. The role of the natural scientist is to discover laws governing the forces of nature, but it remains for the engineer to apply these laws. Similarly, the role of the behavioral scientist is to discover the laws governing the forces of people, but it remains for the manager to apply these laws.[28]

Behavioral science comprises several categories of specialists active in the following major overlapping fields, all of which are concerned with human beings:

Psychology, the study of individual behavior, e.g., perception, learning, motivation
Physiology, the study of functional performance of the body, e.g., vision, hearing, muscular fatigue
Sociology, the study of the nature of human societies and institutions

[27] See Sections 9 and 12 for discussions of foolproofing for Production and Inspection, respectively.

[28] For elaboration, see Juran, J. M., "Managerial Breakthrough," McGraw-Hill Book Company, New York, 1964; pp. 367–370. See also "Behavioral Science," Studies in Personnel Policy No. 216, National Industrial Conference Board, New York, 1969.

Cultural anthropology, the study of the collected beliefs, habits, attitudes, language and other forms of group behavior evolved by human societies and transmitted to new members of the society by learning.

Specialists in these and related fields have increasingly been called on by industry to assist in diagnosis of the problems of industrial relations. The contributions of the specialists result mainly from an objective approach, free of any outdated managerial prejudices, and from use of experimental and analytical methods.[29] The failures of the specialists stem mainly from inability to translate the knowledge of the specialty into the language of the manager and from overelaborateness of approach, including a disposition to rediscover "Scientific Management" under new names, e.g., Human Factors, Human Engineering, etc.

A milestone in the relationship between the behavioral scientist and the manager was the "Hawthorne Experiments."[30]   In that project, behavioral scientists were invited to a large plant to help explain some employee behavior phenomena which were baffling to the managers. The success in this collaboration was achieved in a setting which included the following elements:

1. The study was a *joint undertaking* between behavioral scientists and practicing managers.

2. The locale of study was *the factory*, not the psychological laboratory.

3. The problem studied was not staged; it consisted of *real life.*

4. The tools used for study were the *analytical tools* of the behavioral scientists, not the empiricism of the managers.

Theories of Motivation All behavioral scientists agree that human beings act in response to stimuli which appeal to their internal needs and drives. Obviously, it is important to understand just what kinds of stimuli are effective. While the behavioral scientists agree that the needs are multiple and that they are unequal in importance, they do not agree on the order of priorities nor on the relative importance of potential stimuli. The resulting schools of thought are numerous, so that the discussion which follows is restricted to some of the more prominent among these schools.

Human Needs McGregor,[31] in an elaboration of the work of Maslow,[32] lists a "hierarchy of human needs" which the author has restated in Table 18-4, along with the form that quality motivation programs usually take in appealing to these needs.

A different classification[33] of human needs is based on the premise that job satisfactions and dissatisfactions *are not opposites.* Under this premise, stimuli which reduce job dissatisfaction are called "hygienic factors." They include wages, job security, working conditions. Inadequacy in these factors is a source of dissatisfaction. However, once adequate, they become accepted as normal and provide no stimulus to superior performance.

In contrast, stimuli which provide job satisfaction are called "motivators." They are assumed (under this premise) to relate to what the employee *does.* The employee's satisfaction is assumed to be derived from the doing. Motivators, under this premise, consist of such things as job challenges, opportunities for creativity,

---

[29] For elaboration, see Harris, Douglas H., and Frederick B. Chaney, "Human Factors in Quality Assurance," John Wiley & Sons, Inc., New York, 1969, Chapter 3.

[30] Roethlisberger, F. J., and W. J. Dickson, "Management and the Worker," Harvard University Press, Cambridge, Mass., 1939.

[31] McGregor, Douglas, "The Human Side of Enterprise," McGraw-Hill Book Company, New York, 1960.

[32] Maslow, A. H., "Motivation and Personality," Harper & Bros., New York, 1954.

[33] Herzberg, Frederick, Bernard Mausman, and B. Snyderman, "The Motivation to Work," 2d ed., John Wiley & Sons, New York, 1959.

TABLE 18-4   Hierarchy of Human Needs, and Forms of Quality Motivation

McGregor's list of human needs	Usual forms of quality motivation
Physiological needs, i.e., need for food, shelter, basic survival. In an industrial economy this translates into minimum subsistence earnings.	Opportunity to increase earnings by bonus for good work.
Safety needs, i.e., once a subsistence level is achieved, the need to remain employed at that level.	Job security, e.g., Quality makes sales; sales make jobs.
Social needs, i.e., the need to belong to a group and be accepted.	Appeal to the employee as a member of the team—he must not let the team down.
Ego needs, i.e., the need for self-respect and for the respect of others.	Appeal to pride of workmanship, to achieving a good score. Recognition through awards, publicity, etc.
Self-fulfillment, needs, i.e., the urge for creativity, for self-expression.	Opportunity to propose creative ideas, to participate in creative planning.

identification and participation with groups, responsibility for planning, "job enrichment."[34, 35]

Theory X and Theory Y   While the behavioral scientists search for a unified theory, the managers must manage, and they must do so empirically. The empirical approaches consist of managerial responses to observed phenomena. Applied to quality, the managers see various evidences of quality failures, and they evolve a coherent set of beliefs to explain these observed failures. Despite the fact that the managers observe the same outward evidences, their resulting sets of beliefs differ remarkably. These beliefs have been classified by McGregor[36] into two main categories, Theory X and Theory Y. This classification is very helpful to managers concerned with motivation for quality.

While McGregor's classification applies to industrial work generally, it can readily be paraphrased into quality control terms. Under the managers' Theory X, industrial workers have no interest in quality (or in work, for that matter). Industrial man, unlike his ancestors, is lazy, spoiled, uncooperative, and soft because he no longer is forced to meet the challenge of nature for survival. Hence the job of the managers is to combat this negative attitude with incentives for meeting standards and with penalties for failure. Implicit in Theory X is the premise that industrial workers are interested only in more money. Hence, only through increments of money (or threat of loss of money) can workers be spurred to conform to standards of quality.

Under Theory Y, industrial workers, like their ancestors, retain an internal drive for accomplishing things and derive satisfaction from producing workmanlike results. However, these workers are prevented from using this drive and getting these satisfactions because of the organization of modern industry. This organization gives men meaningless, monotonous jobs which stifle their natural drive; i.e., it is nonsense to talk of craftsmanship when the job is a monumental bore. In consequence, men are frustrated because they cannot attain the satisfactions they naturally want and thus seem to exhibit the symptoms of indifference, etc. Hence the job of the manager is to create new job conditions which will remove these frustrations and which will permit the normal human drives for accomplishment and the normal instincts of workmanship to assert themselves.

[34] For some interesting commentary, see An Interview with Frederick Herzberg, *The Management Review,* July 1971, pp. 2–15.

[35] See Job Enrichment, below.

[36] McGregor, Douglas, *op. cit.*

The managers do not merely hold these beliefs as philosophical concepts; they put their beliefs into action. Hence, while some aspects of shop operation are alike under both theories (e.g., specifications, processes, instruments), there are great differences in the design of jobs, delegation of responsibility, reliance on man versus system, etc. Table 18-5 lists some of the more usual differences in approaches to the control of quality when operating under these two theories of the managers. To oversimplify, Theory X management does not trust the men and hence relies on the system. Theory Y management does trust the men, and exhibits this trust through a wider delegation of responsibility.

TABLE 18-5   Shop Operation under Theory X versus Theory Y

Operation under Theory X	Operation under Theory Y
Extensive use of piecework rates as an incentive to meet the standard	Less emphasis on piecework rates; greater use of supervisory leadership
Emphasis on wage-penalty clauses or disciplinary measures to punish poor quality performance	Emphasis on the "why" and "how" to improve poor quality performance
Reliance mainly on inspection personnel for tool control	Reliance mainly on production personnel for tool control
Reliance placed mainly on patrol inspectors to see that setups are correct	Reliance mainly on operators and setup men for correctness of setup
Reliance on patrol inspectors to stop machines which are found by inspectors to be producing defects	Reliance on operators to stop machines which are found by inspectors to be producing defects
Extensive use of formal inspection approval for piecework payment, movement of material, etc.	Limited use of formal inspection approval
Debates on the factory floor center on authority to shut down machines, and on motives	Debates on the factory floor center on the interpretation of specifications and measurements
Relationships between operators and inspectors tense, often hostile and acrimonious	Relationships between operators and inspectors businesslike, often good-natured
Upper-management criticism for high scrap losses directed at Inspection as much as Production	Upper-management criticism for high scrap losses directed at Production
Operators exhibit no outward desire to do a quality job	Operators do exhibit the outward desire to do a quality job
Operators largely ignored as a source of ideas for improvement	Operators frequently consulted for ideas for improvement

The Taylor System[37]   To a very important extent, Theory X has its roots in the Taylor System of management. Frederick W. Taylor was a mechanical engineer who joined a factory as a lathe hand, became head of the lathe gang, and then became manager of the machine shop. It was in the late nineteenth century, when factories were beginning their conversion from "many laborers and few machines" to "many machines and few laborers." Taylor concluded that the foremen and workmen of those days lacked the educational qualifications[38] to decide how work should be done, what constituted a day's work, or how to select and train workmen. Taylor undertook to remedy all this by changing the shop organization. He created industrial engineers to plan the work methods and to establish standards of a

---

[37] For a discussion of the Taylor System as applied to manufacturing planning, see Section 9, under Responsibility for Manufacturing Planning.

[38] In those days education levels were very low by twentieth-century standards. Virtually all shop employees were technologically illiterate and some were fully illiterate.

day's work. In other ways he turned the work planning over to various specialists, leaving to the foremen and workmen only the job of executing plans prepared by someone else. One essential part of Taylor's approach was the use of piecework schemes to motivate the workmen to meet the standards of a day's work.

Taylor's approach resulted in substantial increases in productivity. These results were publicized by Taylor in his writings,[39] and they attracted wide attention. In due course, this concept of separation of planning from execution became and remains the norm for the practice of management in the United States.[40] In the decades after World War II, when the industrial companies greatly expanded their work of quality planning, they continued to follow the Taylor concept of separating planning from execution. They did so by creating new specialist positions (Quality Control Engineers, Reliability Engineers) to do the planning and analysis, leaving it to the line supervision, operators, and inspectors to execute the plans.

Meanwhile, over the decades, important changes have taken place which have made some of Taylor's premises obsolete:

The level of education has risen remarkably, so that foremen and workmen now possess a high degree of technological literacy.

The standard of living has likewise risen remarkably, thereby minimizing the effect of piecework as a stimulus to worker effort

Industrial Unionism has emerged as a major force and has required managers to bargain collectively on many matters which were previously solved by unilateral (and often arbitrary) action.

These changes, along with the studies of the behavioral scientists, have combined to raise serious questions about the current validity of the Taylor System and of Theory X operation. A good deal of ferment is taking place and there are some signs that massive changes may be in the making. Managers are paying increased attention to the findings of the behavioral scientists.[41] Experiments are under way to turn product acceptance over to production workers.[42] Incentives based on piece work have been on the decline for several decades. Case studies of use of motivators (in the Herzberg meaning) are increasingly being published and studied.[43] The reasons behind the success of the Japanese QC Circles are under active international study.

The massive change, if it takes place, will proceed slowly. American managers have a considerable investment in the Taylor System, and they cannot dismantle it easily since it is deeply rooted and has shaped much of the existing cultural pattern of managers and technical specialists. The behavioral scientists (psychologists, sociologists, cultural anthropologists) tend to arrive at solutions which emphasize their respective disciplines, thereby slowing up any trend to unified direction. Many of the specialized planners (e.g., Industrial Engineers, Quality Control Engineers) exhibit a vested interest in the status quo. It will take years of appraisal of published cases of experiments and of evaluation of various motivational programs to establish a clear direction for change.

Human Factors Schools "Human factors" is the name given by some behavioral scientists to a "new discipline" of analysis of work situations for compatibility with the psychological and physiological attributes of the human beings involved. The analysis extends to:

[39] For a collection of Taylor's principal writings, see Taylor, F. W., "Scientific Management," Harper & Bros., New York, 1947.

[40] See, in this connection, Section 9, under Responsibility for Manufacturing Planning.

[41] See, for example, Willemze, F. G., Involvement of People, *Eleventh EOQC Conference,* London, June 1967, pp. 25–27.

[42] See Section 11, under Product Acceptance by Operators.

[43] See "Behavioral Science", *op. cit.*

1. Human factors which are unique for specific individuals, e.g., "skill, knowledge, attitude, temperament and interests"

2. Physical job factors, e.g., "work layout, tools, equipment and aids"

3. Organizational factors, including "work methods, policies, type of work group, supervisory practices, and the social aspects of the organization"[44]

Applied to problems of product quality, the human factors school (schools, actually) is involved with such problems as operator error, inspector accuracy, workplace design, role of the supervisor, etc.

Commonality and Competition among Behavioral Scientists   All of these schools of behavioral scientists distinguish clearly between subspecies of error.[45] (Their classifications though unlike, contain much commonality.) All devote much attention to the patterns of human relations among employees, between employees and supervisors, etc. All devote study to the details of human behavior and to the forces believed to affect this behavior. All regard the problems of human error as resulting from a very complex interrelation of human and technological elements, i.e., the "sociotechnical system." All reject the simplistic solutions which are based on some sweeping assumption such as the "inattention theory."

Despite this commonality, the effectiveness of the behavioral scientists is reduced by the diversity of their theories,[46] by their special dialects, and by their emphasis on abstractions (attitudes, motives, conflicts, etc.). To reduce these abstractions to practical conclusions, the behavioral scientists propose what seems to the manager to be costly programs: analysis of jobs in much detail to provide inputs to understanding the sociotechnical system, interviews to discover operator attitudes toward jobs and bosses, studies of group identifications and relationships, studies of communication channels and patterns, surveys of operator and manager morale. The managers who question the need for these studies may themselves be part of the problem, since the cultural resistance of the managers is deeply rooted, thereby putting a severe burden of proof on the behavioral scientists.

The behavioral scientists also compete with each other for reasons traceable to the disciplines of their origin, e.g., psychology, sociology, cultural anthropology. In addition, these scientists as a species compete with established industrial staff categories for jurisdictional rights over the staff work needed to plan and execute not only motivational programs but even the more basic matters of original quality planning, planning of inspection and test, quality improvement, etc.[47] The quality control specialists point to their broad staff responsibility in quality matters generally.[48] The Industrial Engineer points to his long association with motivation in

---

[44] The foregoing derived from Harris and Chaney, op. cit., Chapter 2.

[45] See, for example, Rook, Luther W., ZD: Momentary or Momentous, Quality Assurance, October 1965, pp. 24–28. Dr. Rook's basic classification is (1) Situation Caused Errors and (2) Human Caused Errors.

[46] For a brief discussion, see Vaill, Peter B., Management and Human Performance. This paper is part of the U.S. Government publication "Zero Defects — The Quest for Quality," Quality and Reliability Assurance Technical Report TR 9, U.S. Government Printing Office, Washington, D.C., 1968, pp. 1–20. For a more exhaustive treatment, see Gellerman, Saul W., "Motivation and Productivity," American Management Association, New York, 1963.

[47] For some examples involving inspector error reduction, see Section 12, under Inspector Errors.

[48] In addition, reliability specialists have begun to quantify human errors in reliability terms, e.g., Mean Time Between Human Errors (MTBHE), as a means of relating human unreliability to product unreliability. See Weiser, Bernard, Human Factors Effects on Reliability, Industrial Quality Control, December 1965, pp. 297–300.

productivity problems as well as his general knowledge of improvement programs.[49]

Despite the obstacles, the behavioral scientists have compiled an impressive array of studies which have shed much light on problems of human motivation. However, good compilations and digests of these studies are rare,[50, 51] and the practicing manager has difficulty in acquainting himself with the experimental evidence. Not only is it published (and unpublished) in diverse sources; it is usually surrounded by a good deal of dense shrubbery regarded by the behavioral scientist as essential to the presentation.

CONTINUING PROGRAMS OF MOTIVATION

The prime source of motivation for quality is *not* the spectacular, publicized campaign or drive. The main source of motivation is rather the quiet, unpublicized activities which go on and on and which, if well done, make it unnecessary to resort to campaigns. These continuing motivational activities are conducted at all stages of the employment cycle, and apply to all elements of the Subject Matter of Motivation discussed above, in Role of Motivation.

The discussion which follows lists practices which are used, in various employee situations, by companies who have succeeded in attaining a high degree of motivation for quality as an inseparable part of the behavior pattern of the work force. Obviously, these practices are not universal, even among companies which have been successful in reaching a high level of quality motivation. The practices are rather listed as examples of what are among the proved methods used for attaining these high levels.

Job Design and Planning   The extent of employee motivation is strongly affected by the way in which jobs are designed and planned. As a minimum, the job plan should be such that the employee is in a state of self-control.[52] If the criteria for self-control have not been met, then in the view of the operator, management has not completed its own job. Under such a state of affairs, he may well regard a management appeal for reduction of operator errors as lacking in good faith.

In those cases where it is not feasible to meet fully the criteria for self-control (e.g., process not capable, yet the best known), the job planning should recognize this fact. For such cases, the criteria may be structured around meeting process parameters (to minimize the defect levels) rather than around product parameters.

In addition to job planning which meets the minimal requirements for self-control, there are added aspects of good job planning which are aids to operator motivation:

Identifying the knack which distinguishes good from poor performance
Identifying the cautions to be observed (sources of secret ignorance)
Providing foolproofing for sources of inadvertent error

The foregoing relates mainly to the effect of good job planning on motivation, irrespective of job design. A further influence on motivation is the job design itself, i.e., whether the job is varied and interesting, or highly repetitive and monotonous. An increasing list of companies is tending away from the traditional design of jobs

---

[49] See Snyder, D. A., Motivation Programs, Their Development and Function, *Journal of Industrial Engineering*, June 1968, pp. 274–278.

[50] A good collection of cases is contained in Managing Change, *National Industrial Conference Board*, 1967. For additional cases, see "Behavioral Science," *op. cit.*

[51] Numerous end-of-chapter references are available in Harris and Chaney, *op. cit.*

[52] See Section 2, under Self-Control; see also Section 11, under Concept of Operator Self-Control *et seq.*

through minute subdivision and from introducing job interests to provide motivators in the Herzberg sense.[53]   This form of job design, along with participation and other motivators, is discussed below under Job Enrichment.

Recruitment   Companies are well advised to project an image of attention to quality before employees are recruited and during the recruitment process itself. Some companies include an image of attention to quality as part of their product advertising and public relations propaganda. They exhibit their products in public places in the community. They sponsor activities which bear a relation to quality of product. The brochures they use to describe the company include text material and photographs stressing the emphasis on quality.

This emphasis can be carried into the process of recruiting new employees. Recruiters sent to visit local schools and colleges carry the message orally as well as through the brochures. The booklets "Welcome to the X Company" include a section dealing with the product quality image and its importance to all employees.

The new employee induction procedure can be made consistent with the public relations propaganda by emphasizing quality during the first days on the job, when the new employee is most impressionable. The employee can be shown exhibits of how the quality of the operations he performs affects subsequent operations and the ultimate user. Plant tours can be used to show the interrelation of what he does with all else.[54] Some companies use moving pictures as a more convenient form of showing this interrelationship to new recruits.

Training and Supervision on the Job   The supervisor has many opportunities to influence motivation for quality in the training he provides and in the day-to-day supervisory activities.

Training.[55]   Much of the training is concerned with meeting the criteria for operator self-control. Employees need information on the "what," i.e., what are their responsibilities for making decisions and taking actions, what is the meaning of the specifications, what distinguishes good work from defects, what is the nature of the machines and tools.

Employees also need training in the "how"—how to use the processes, the instruments, the controls.

Probably the weakest point in training is explanation of the "why." Supervisors do participate in discussions on specifications, rejections, waivers, tool changes, etc. Operators do not. The why of the decisions is usually known to the supervisor, and he can convey this knowledge to the employees.

Training does not end with inducting new employees or showing older employees just once. (A long service record is no proof that the employee is properly trained for the job.) There must be continued observation and retraining so that adverse practices do not emerge and take root.

Setting a Good Example.   The supervisor has his own responsibilities for decisions and actions with respect to quality. His performance is watched by the operators and influences their performance. The supervisor who fails to provide for keeping the equipment, instruments and supplies in good shape not only handicaps the operators in their efforts to do a good job but causes them to question management's sincerity as well.

In like manner, the supervisor's attention to quality versus his attention to productivity, cost, and other goals is watched by the operators. By praise for good work and criticism for poor work, the supervisor demonstrates his interest in quality

[53] See Human Needs (under Role of Motivation, above).

[54] See, for example, the problem of the textile spinning department and tying of weaver's knots, under Willful Errors, above.

[55] For an extended discussion on training and training methods, see Section 17.

as well as helping the operator to understand his own performance. The supervisor who gives a fair hearing to operator complaints about deficiencies in the system of self-control is also demonstrating management's interest in quality.

Meeting Employee Needs. To a degree, the supervisor can, by his own conduct, contribute to meeting the human needs shown in Table 18-4. Recognition and praise for good work contribute to self-respect and respect of others. Assigning responsibility and providing for team competitions contribute to social needs. Listening to operators' ideas and providing opportunity for participation on quality not only contributes to one's sense of fulfillment but it helps convince operators that quality has a high status in management's priorities. In contrast, a negative supervisory attitude — "You're not supposed to think" — always ends up with some fiasco in which the gleeful explanation is "I'm not supposed to think."

Communication to Employees   The company employs many media for this purpose, and most of them can be structured to include communication on quality matters.

Shop Procedures and Manuals. These contain the methods for doing work and include special information on employee safety, machine maintenance, material usage, and similar peripheral matters. Under good programs of motivation, these same procedures and manuals are used to convey special information on quality — cautions to be observed, knacks to be used, etc.

Company Journals. Many companies publish newspapers, magazines, and other journals for employee readership. These present an excellent opportunity to convey information of general interest on quality. Articles, pictures, news, interviews, etc., can be obtained from users, customers, salesmen, technical specialists, and still others. These articles describe the product designs, the sources of exotic materials, the processes, the test laboratories, the usage. When well illustrated, including pictures of the people involved, these articles are of great help in giving meaning to the work performed.

Some companies prepare periodic newsletters which are sent to the employee homes. The belief is that in the relaxed home atmosphere, these letters will become conversation pieces in the family and in the neighborhood.

Bulletins. These appear on the factory bulletin boards and are used to provide prompt official information, uncolored by transmission through the supervisory hierarchy, to the entire employee body. The bulletin boards are also used to show employees some of the activities engaged in by the company, e.g., to display copies of current advertisements which emphasize the attention to quality.

Propaganda Posters. These are time-honored, temporary attention getters and are effective for getting some messages across. For example, the concept "Quality Makes Sales; Sales Make Jobs" has been effectively projected by posters. However, posters are only a useful supplement to the broader motivational program which must deal with deeds (behavior) as well as with attitudes. Posters can never be the program itself, since they do not answer the question "What should I do different than I am doing now?"

Defective Product. This is a most effective form of communication, and there are various methods of bringing defects to the attention of employees. Some shop supervisors hold daily or weekly scrap conferences with operators. Displays may be prepared to contrast good and bad work. Complaint letters from salesmen or customers may be posted along with the defect display. (This may include periodic personal visits from salesmen or customers.) Sometimes, accumulations of defects are piled up in conspicuous displays, with placards telling the cost.

In displaying defects or in other forms of implied criticism, some companies are careful to avoid making the atmosphere tense. They soften the criticism by using cartoons or other forms of humor so that the message gets across effectively while a relaxed state of human relations is maintained. Cartoons can further be used for ingenious presentation of technological explanations.

Competitors' Product. Companies that compete in foreign markets or that face competition from abroad sometimes display competitors' products alongside their own to make clear that the competition is very real.

Quality "Cues." A very practical element of communication to operators is the identification of (1) the vital few controllable defects in the department and (2) the proved ways (the knack) of avoiding these defects.

In contrast to the propaganda posters, which aim at employee motivation generally, the quality cues are very specific as to operation. They *do* provide answers to the question, "What should I do different than I am doing now?"

A usual method of preparing quality cues is through collaboration between the supervisor and the quality control specialist. From the inspection reports, they identify the vital few operator-controllable defects. For each of these, they go further and identify the knack used by superior operators for avoiding the defect. The resulting information is assembled in a booklet which applies to this department and no other. These booklets are given to all operators in the department and may be supplemented by special wall posters which are again unique to the operations of this department. The same quality cues then become the subject of special attention by the supervisor, the training programs, etc.

Awards for Good Work. Some companies apply the concept "Praise in public, criticize in private" to quality performance. Departmental competitions are staged, with banners being awarded to the winning departments.[56]

Open House. This program is designed to permit employees, their families, and the community to see how the company operates. Usually the employees secure a prior tour and a briefing which deepens their own understanding of their contribution to the whole. In addition, when they are called on to explain their jobs to others or merely to do their jobs while family and neighbors are watching, their awareness of their own contribution rises sharply.

Annual Interviews. When used, these are significant occasions and permit two-way communication about quality as well as other matters.

Specific Provisions for Quality Motivation The company's approach to employee motivation extends over a wide area of employee conduct: absenteeism, tardiness, safety, productivity, etc., as well as quality. For example, the suggestion system accepts ideas of any kind, including those for quality improvement. In addition, there are some specific provisions aimed primarily at motivation for quality.

Certification. For some operations, only formally qualified operators may be assigned. The qualification is based on a formal training program followed by a formal examination, which includes testing the product for quality.[57]

Incentives for Quality. While direct penalties or bonuses linked to quality are very much in the minority,[58] the actual quality achieved is one of the elements in most formal performance appraisal plans. These appraisals are influential in choice of candidates for promotion, in considerations for pay increases, and in other matters important to employees.

A related incentive is that of qualification for self-inspection. The quality performance of the operator is decisive in determining whether he is given authority to approve his own product.[59] Commonly, this delegation carries with it a pay increase or other benefit.

---

[56] This can be extended to include awards for *poor* work, provided it is done good naturedly. A gaily painted barrel of junk awarded weekly to the department with the worst scrap record has been known to arouse spirited competition to *avoid* receiving the award.

[57] See generally Section 17, under Production Operators.

[58] See below, under Incentives for Defect Reduction by Operators.

[59] See generally Section 11, under Product Acceptance by Operators.

Employee Participation.   There are several levels of participation, and it is useful to distinguish these from each other.

1. Defense against unwarranted blame.   Operators defend themselves against such blame by pointing out deficiencies in the system of self-control; i.e., management has not met the criteria.   This feedback is forthcoming even if management displays no interest in operator feedback generally.

2. Collaboration on operator-controllable defects.   The operators' responsibility with respect to these defects is so clear that there is seldom a problem of securing feedback from operators.   While some of this is defensive, operators generally welcome being consulted as to their observations, experience, theories, etc.

3. Collaboration on management-controllable defects.   This level of collaboration requires special provision such as suggestion systems, Labor-Management Committees, QC Circles, etc., to legitimize the activity.   The detailed approaches are discussed below, under Incentives for Defect Reduction by Operators; Role of the Operator in Defect Reduction.

Quality Scoreboards.   The scoreboard is a most useful tool for motivation as well as for control generally.   It minimizes the controversies about just how good or bad quality is and whether quality is getting better or worse.   It is an aid to both the supervisor and employee and is taken seriously if the technical problems of scorekeeping have been solved adequately.

Quality Audits.   These likewise affect quality motivation by demonstrating that quality performance is high enough on management's priority list to be the subject of formal, independent review and report.

THE FORMAL MOTIVATIONAL CAMPAIGN[60]

For the long run, the motivation for quality should be built into the overall fabric of employee and public relations as discussed in the previous major topic, Continuing Programs of Motivation.   However, many companies encounter situations which appear to demand "action now" instead of going through the long process of restructuring the basic fabric.   The pressures for "action now" may come from a rash of troubles which appear to have their origin in lack of adequate motivation, reports of results achieved by other companies through motivational campaigns, pressures from important customers, new analyses of internal costs or external failures which point to inadequate motivation, etc.   Whatever the reason, the result is a "drive" on motivation which will be referred to here as a "campaign."

On the face of it, a motivational campaign is limited to stimulating employees, who then take all remaining action.   However, analysis of numerous campaigns, published and unpublished, makes it clear that the campaign must consist of two distinct packages:

1. A *motivation* package aimed at stimulating the employee to reduce his own (operator-controllable) errors

2. A *prevention* package aimed at stimulating the employee to assist in reducing management-controllable errors

Purposes of a Motivational Campaign   The central purposes are common to all campaigns:

[60] Motivational campaigns and programs for quality improvement go back into the recesses of history.   The texts of ancient laws include provision for punishment of sellers of poor quality products.   The published regulations of the medieval guilds included penalty provisions for failure to follow the astonishingly detailed material, process, and product specifications.

While motivation for quality is ancient, published accounts of campaigns are comparatively recent.   For a brief history of twentieth-century publications, see the Historical Supplement at the end of this Section.

To make each employee aware that the company's quality performance is important to his well-being; e.g., quality makes sales, sales make jobs

To convince each that there is something he can do, in his daily work, to contribute to this quality performance

To show each one just what it is he can do to make this contribution on his regular job

To establish and record the best way of doing each job, as a reference for future training and audit

To provide means for receiving and acting on employee ideas and suggestions for improving quality

To provide a scoreboard for measuring performance and progress[61]

Normally, the purpose of the campaign is to improve quality performance. However, in special cases, there may be added special purposes. For example, during the 1960s the urgings of military customers influenced many contractors to undertake motivational campaigns as a matter of good customer relations. In designing campaigns, care should be taken to look to the purposes to be achieved and then to design the campaign to meet those purposes. One thing to avoid is to copy the approaches of other companies whose campaigns were structured to meet special purposes unique to them or to their industry but which have little application to other companies or industries.

Prerequisites for Launching a Campaign   Many campaigns are failures when measured by the discernible effects on quality. Analysis of these failures has led to identification of the prerequisite background conditions which favor success in the campaign. They are mainly as follows:

1. The company has already done a respectable job of reducing management-controllable defects and hence is coming to the employee body with clean hands.

2. The employee-controllable defects are substantial enough, for economic or usage reasons, to warrant a serious motivational effort.

3. The extent of mutual confidence between management and employees is such that employee participation in a campaign is likely to be genuine.

4. The top managers are willing to show personal interest and especially to set an example by changing their priority of emphasis on quality in relation to other company goals.

5. The intermediate supervision is sufficiently open-minded to be willing to listen seriously to the ideas and suggestions of the employees.

6. The management is willing to provide the staff manpower needed to conduct the numerous detailed studies (discovering the knack of superior operators, investigating employee proposals, etc.).[62]

Securing Management Approval   This follows the general approach discussed in Section 16, under the same heading. In practice, motivational campaigns are often the result of initiative taken by top management.

Organization and Planning   This is done simultaneously for both the motivation package and the prevention packages. However, each has its own detailed techniques, as discussed below within this Section.

The organization structure for the campaign always requires creating (1) means for steering the campaign and (2) means for performing the detailed analyses or diagnosis.

[61] For elaboration, see Juran, J. M., Nine Steps to Better Quality, *Factory Management and Maintenance*, March 1954.

[62] For elaboration, see Juran, J. M., Quality Problems, Remedies and Nostrums, *Industrial Quality Control*, June 1966, pp. 647–652.

Steering Committee. This consists of a committee or council of managers to provide broad guidance to the program. In a large company, it is usual to appoint subcommittees, e.g., for divisions, plants, functional departments.

Committee membership is drawn from multiple departments of the company. The line departments (Production, Marketing, Design, etc.) must be represented, since the bulk of the action to be taken is by their personnel. In addition, staff departments are represented, because (1) staff people, like any others, have an opportunity to improve their own performances, and (2) the staff plays some special roles in carrying out the campaign. Examples of these special roles include:

Advertising, which has skills in selling to outsiders and helps in designing the publicity, exhibits, etc., needed to sell to insiders.

Personnel, which has special skills in communication with employees, has command over the communication media (bulletin boards, company newspapers, etc.) and helps to design new means of communication.

Accounting, which keeps score on many kinds of performance and helps in design of additional scoreboards needed for the campaign.

Quality Control Engineering, which has skills in diagnosis of quality problems, is usually a part of the Steering Committee and often plays the main role in diagnosis as well.

Diagnostic Support. The second need in organization planning is manpower to carry out the detailed coordination and to conduct the detailed studies of ideas for improvement, to establish goals, to discover the knack of superior operators, etc. This work is time-consuming and cannot normally be done by the line managers. Hence it is assigned to various staff specialists. Studies of a quality improvement nature are normally assigned to quality control specialists. Coordination of the timetable, preparation of agendas for committees, publication of minutes, and similar tasks are assigned to a coordinator. In large campaigns, the coordination grows to be a full-time job. In the Zero Defects (ZD) types of programs, the administrator is called ZD Administrator. (Usually, he reports to the Quality Manager.) In addition, the various departments may appoint representatives to be the departmental contact men to make it easier for the Administrator to do his job.

Time Phased Plan. The campaign commonly involves three groupings or phases of activity: (1) prelaunching preparation, (2) launching, and (3) carrying out the plan. Because many people must participate and many tasks need to be performed, the planning should be formalized to list the tasks, the schedules, and responsibilities for performing these tasks in the time allotted.[63]

Prior Publicity. There is a wide range of choice of media for announcing the coming program. The local press[64] as well as the company's house organ are enlisted. Use is made of wall posters, banners (on buildings and entrance gates), flags, table "tents," stickers on correspondence, inserts in payroll envelopes. Information booklets may be prepared for distribution. Some companies use the device of "teasers" in which provocative publicity is used for some weeks without disclosing the precise nature of what is coming.

The popularity of the formal campaigns has led the independent suppliers of

---

[63] For elaboration, see McClure, J. Y., Detailed Guide for Program Planning. This paper is part of the U.S. Government publication "Zero Defects—The Quest for Quality," Quality and Reliability Technical Report TR 9, U.S. Government Printing Office, Washington, D.C., 1968, pp. 156–190.

[64] Utilization of close community relations is exemplified by the "Quality Week" organized in several neighboring communities by a section (Parkersburg, W. Va.) of the American Society for Quality Control. Extensive collaboration was secured with local industries, merchants, media, etc. See The Incentive of Quality Week, *Quality Progress*, May 1968, pp. 13–18.

management services to prepare prefabricated materials for sale to companies embarking on formal campaigns. These materials include:

Information bulletins which explain motivational programs to managers and which are intended to help secure top management support

Handbooks and manuals to be used as training guides for managers and supervisors

Propaganda materials: posters, banners, badges, pins, plaques, stickers

Forms for Error Cause Removal, pledges, reports, etc.

"Giveaways": matches, pens, key chains, etc., carrying the slogans

Setting Goals. It is universal for the campaigns to set goals for accomplishment. These are set for the various departments after discussion with the supervisors involved. Commonly the goals set involve an error reduction of 25 to 50% from the levels prevailing before the program.

For Production departments, these goals are defined in the usual units of measure: percent defective, defects per unit of product, etc. However, since the programs are companywide, the need to measure goes beyond the "hardware" departments involved in production; it extends to the "software" departments performing support activities—Engineering, Accounting, Data Processing, Finance, Marketing, Materials Management, etc.[65] While all these departments have quality problems, not all of them have quantified the measure of quality, and it may be necessary to develop new units of measure for this purpose. In some cases it may be necessary to resort to a universal measure such as errors per 100 man-hours.[66]

Budgeting. The published figures[67] of $1.50 to $2.50 per employee (for the first year) represent only the out-of-pocket costs of purchasing printing, badges, etc. Not included are the larger costs of the Administrator's salary, the supervisory time, the diagnostic time, the added records, etc. Neither do they include the money awards or other substantial prizes which are an inherent part of some programs. The budget should reflect these costs so that they may be considered in relating the cost of the program to the estimated improvement in performance.

Indoctrination. It is not feasible to "sell" a program to the employee body unless the supervision is sold first. "Indoctrination" is intended to convince the supervision of the merits of the program and to help them to play their role in carrying it out. This requires prior preparation of training material, i.e., supervisors' manuals, films, etc. These materials are then used in the training sessions. Indoctrination properly starts from the top down. Meetings are held for top management, middle managers, departmental representatives, first-line supervision, union stewards, and, in due course, the work force.

Another form of indoctrination consists of the briefings for nonemployees. These include the local press (newspaper, radio, television), the Union officials, community leaders, industrial neighbors, and others who need to be informed.

Extension to Include Vendors   Some companies believe that the vendors should be included in the program in view of the impact of vendor quality on the final product. The question of whether it is "right" for a company to "shove the program down the vendor's throat" is resolved by applying the same rule as is applied to employees—it must be voluntary on the part of the vendor.

The conventional approach to vendors parallels that used for employees, but scaled up to size. The activities usually include:

[65] See generally Section 46.

[66] See "Zero Defects—The Quest for Quality," *op. cit.,* Appendix, pp. 220–232; also Halpin, James F., "Zero Defects," McGraw-Hill Book Company, New York, 1966, pp. 130–138.

[67] See, for example, Halpin, James F., *op. cit.,* pp. 24–25.

Informing the vendors of the company's action in launching a motivational program

Sending each vendor copies of the materials used to indoctrinate the company's supervisors

Structuring means for measuring vendor performance

Organizing seminars for vendors to discuss vendor relations problems and solutions

Creating a principal award, e.g., Quality Vendor of the Month

Creating subsidiary awards, e.g., Outstanding Vendor

Making ceremonial awards and publicizing these to all vendors

Preparing and distributing periodic summaries on the company's progress in vendor relations[68]

Choice of a Name for the Program   Choice of a name is a decision quite different from choice of program content.   The latter should be designed to be responsive to the company's quality problems.   The name can be chosen in a way which merely describes the program contents.   However, because these programs require selling to many people and have customer relations implications, it is usual for companies to derive added benefits by choosing a name which

Takes advantage of currently favorable publicity

Responds to the wishes of important customers

Provides a catchy slogan to improve the salability to employees

During the 1960s, these considerations led many companies to use the name ZD for their programs, since it fulfilled all the foregoing criteria.[69]   However, this was not done 100%.   For various reasons numerous other names were used: PRIDE, VIP, Superior Craftsmanship, STEP, Q-BEE, CARE, PQ, AWARE, etc.[70]

In the absence of some currently favorable publicity, it is usual for companies to build a name around their usual sales slogans or public relations image.   Alternatively, a theme is invented specially for the program, and the name relates to this theme.   Sometimes a theme character is invented, either a good character, e.g., Herr Kvaliten (Electrolux AB), or a bad character, e.g., Herm the Germ (Merck, Sharp & Dohme).

The Launching   The dramatic launching has for centuries been used by leaders to convey to followers the nature and importance of a new campaign.   In several ways, the dramatic launching can be of aid to the program.

It constitutes a spectacle—a memorable occasion—and thereby gives the program special significance and importance.

It convenes a host of people, proposes a meritorious cause, and provides opportunity for membership in this meritorious cause.

It assembles the recognized leadership and shows them to be actively behind the program.

It introduces and legitimizes the individuals designated to guide the program, i.e., the committees and the Administrator.

It pledges the managers to a new level of conduct on some matters which have in the past been obstacles to motivation, e.g., action on ideas for improvement.

Collectively these are forceful reasons for conducting the dramatic launching—so forceful that any excesses of advertising can detract from the value of the meeting.

---

[68] For a good case example, see Gerow, Arthur H., "Extending Zero Defects to Vendors," *American Management Association Bulletin* 71, New York, 1965, pp. 26–31.

[69] See, for added discussion, Juran, J. M., Nostrums—Revisited, *Industrial Quality Control,* May 1967, pp. 586–587.

[70] When such criteria are used in choosing names, it follows that the contents of the program cannot be understood from knowing the name, but only from knowing the list of deeds.

The meeting may be convened in any large hall, or outdoors, or even via closed-circuit television if several locations are involved. The dignitaries include the senior executive of the company, national and local political leaders, the Union head, an important customer, a guest of honor who is a well publicized figure. Speeches are made explaining and supporting the program. The committee and the Administrator are introduced. Films are shown. The first pledge cards are signed (by the senior executive and the Union head).

The Motivational Package This "package" consists of those activities aimed to provide employees with the added information and tools needed to reduce their own (operator-controllable) errors.[71] Design of this package is necessarily influenced by the company's premises of what causes these errors, but many of the concepts are common:

A concept of "do it right the first time."

The need to involve employees of *all* departments, not only Production.[72] (In this respect, the ZD programs of the 1960s marked a useful departure from the past.)

The awareness that many employees are engaged in repetitive, monotonous work.

The need for an organized approach which has top management support and which uses company resources to help design the package.

Beyond common concepts, there are also common ingredients of activities and ideas for influencing human behavior.

Product Awareness. The purpose is to help employees understand how the product is used, what will happen if the product fails, and how his work relates to all this. In some cases, simple exhibits can be set up to demonstrate product use. In other cases, special effort is needed. For example, in an automobile parts plant, the managers were faced with showing the metal finishers in the "white" stage the effect of any process defects on the final finish. The approach used was to display a white component (an automobile hood) adjacent to the corresponding finished component. The left side of each hood had various defects; the right side had none. The display made it very easy to see the real damage done by the process defects.[73]

Where exhibits are not feasible, they may be approximated through visual aids: posters, pictures, filmstrips, moving pictures, etc.

Usage Information. The impact of quality on customers and users can be shown in various ways: arranging visits to customer locations; inviting customers to come to the plant; display of letters from customers, either resulting from good work (repeat orders) or from bad work (complaints). Well-known users may be invited for memorable occasions, e.g., sports champions, military heroes, astronauts.

Provision for Participation in Propaganda. This is universal, and it takes many forms. Slogan or essay contests are conducted for prizes. The winning entries are then publicized, since their contents are useful propaganda. The prizes are ceremonially awarded, and this yields further publicity as well as stimulating further participation. Stamps, labels, and other forms of employee identification are provided to personalize employee contributions to product progression.

Pledge Cards. These were widely used in the ZD type of program to symbolize the individual's voluntary commitment to the program. Where used, the practice is

---

[71] A minority of companies broaden this purpose to include non-quality matters as well, e.g., cost, productivity, etc.

[72] The programs tend to be vague on the need to motivate the managerial group. The stress on employee motivation is always clear and sometimes is clearly exclusive. For example, "Design the program for the individual worker—*this is a worker program, not a managerial program*" [emphasis in original text]. See Newnham, Donald E., Zero Defects—Do It Right The First Time, *The Journal of Industrial Engineering,* January 1966, pp. 3–6.

[73] Personal observation by the author, at AB Volvo, Olofström Works, Sweden, 1972.

to give a blank form to the employee, leaving it to him to decide whether to sign it, but making clear that management hopes for a high response. Signers are given lapel badges to wear, and these may be linked to tangible rewards. For example, prizes, e.g., transistor radios, may be awarded, by lot, but only to pledge card signers. Periodic bargain lunches may be offered in the cafeteria, but only to those wearing their badges. Figure 18-2 shows a typical form of pledge card.

ZERO DEFECTS

As a concerned citizen and affected employee, I fully support the Zero Defects Program objectives. I will constantly strive for zero defects in my work.

Signed_____

Date_____

It's Up to Me!

How to Achieve ZERO DEFECTS

Remember these four "I's":

I. IDENTIFY the causes of errors
1. Investigate why errors are made
2. Grade defects in order of importance
3. Solicit suggestions

II. INSTRUCT in error-free performance
1. Explain Zero Defects limits
2. Show how to "Do it right the first time"
3. Check that skills are correctly used
4. Give recognition to Z.D. performers

III. INSPECT work as it's being done
1. Set the "It's Up to Me" example
2. Explain inspection techniques
3. Establish goals for quality effectiveness

IV. INSPIRE and motivate
1. Use a "Build-Up" campaign
2. Show employees importance of work
3. Report on progress
4. Sell "Zero Defects"

DO IT RIGHT THE FIRST TIME

ELLIOTT SERVICE COMPANY, INC.
MOUNT VERNON, N.Y.

Fig. 18-2 Example of pledge card.

Participation in the Control Process. This is also universal and takes several principal forms:

1. Attendance at indoctrination meetings at which the plan for the program is unfolded, and ideas for implementation are solicited. Attendance at such meetings may include foremen, union representatives and non-supervisors.

2. Employee councils may be formed to participate in discussion of various elements of the program.[74]

[74] See Zimmer, Merle V., Sustaining the ZD Program, "Zero Defects, The Quest for Quality," *op. cit.,* pp. 192–202.

3. Weekly (or even daily) discussions may be held to review exhibits of the previous week's (day's) principal defects and to propose remedial action.

4. The regular suggestion system may be modified to provide special awards for suggestions on quality.

5. Error Cause Removal participation may be provided (see below).

The Prevention Package   Employee response to the motivation package takes a number of forms:

Reduction of willful errors

Acceptance of retraining to acquire skills or to adopt the knack known to be used by superior performers

Acceptance of technological changes designed to minimize inadvertent errors through foolproofing, redundancy, etc.

Submission of ideas for reducing operator-controllable errors

In the usual situations, where the quality problems are dominated by management-controllable errors, the foregoing are necessarily limited in scope since they are aimed at operator-controllable errors, which are in the minority. However, in these same situations it is also feasible to enlist operator support in reduction of management-controllable defects as well. The tool used for this purpose is the suggestion system or some derivative thereof. One of these derivatives is widely referred to as "Error Cause Removal" (ECR), from the term coined during the motivational campaigns of the 1960s. The employee participation is built around an ECR form (Figure 18-3). The intent is that as employees see conditions which they believe are causing defects but which they are unable to remedy, they execute the form so that management can act to provide the remedy.[75] The same form may also be used for suggestions to improve other job aspects which might be helpful to quality, e.g., lighting.

ECR forms are turned over to the departmental supervisor, but the procedure also makes a copy available to the Administrator, who has the job of assuring that the proposal is acknowledged, analyzed, and finally concluded one way or another. Many of the ECR proposals can be acted on by the department supervisor. Failing this, he makes use of the Administrator to help secure assistance from other resources in the company. In turn, the Administrator is aided by the Committee and by the pledge made by top management that ECRs will receive prompt, serious attention.

The ECR procedure places no limitations on subject matter. Hence ECRs are submitted on management-controllable as well as operator-controllable defects. As a result, the scope of potential employee participation is widened greatly.

Some of the improvements resulting from ECR proposals make lively reading, whether because of the amount at stake or the ingenuity exercised. In consequence, companies make wide use of such cases to publicize the results and the employees involved.

Measurement of Performance   All formal programs provide for measurements of results against goals and for use of the attained results to serve as a basis for further action, i.e., recognition for achievements, stimulus for lack of results, etc.

Measurement of Group Performance.   The concept of departmental or group performance is widely used in these programs. Psychologists favor the creation of

---

[75] The original ZD program does not appear to have included this feature. The Error Cause Removal element of the programs was evidently developed by General Electric Co. (Halpin, *op. cit.,* pp. 59–61). Most companies make use of the ECR and clearly regard it as a vital element of the program. The Department of Defense Handbook is to the same effect. Such is also the judgment of the author.

QAN. 07159

ZERO DEFECTS

ERROR CAUSE IDENTIFICATION

NAME		LOCATION	MAIL POINT
OCCUPATION TITLE	DEPT.	CLOCK NO.	☐ HOURLY ☐ SALARY

IN ORDER THAT A BETTER JOB BE PERFORMED TOWARD THE GOAL OF ERROR-FREE PERFORMANCE, I AM IDENTIFYING THE FOLLOWING CAUSE OR POTENTIAL CAUSE OF ERROR:

IMPORTANT INFORMATION

IF, IN ADDITION TO IDENTIFYING ERROR CAUSE, YOU FEEL THAT YOU HAVE A WAY TO SOLVE IT, PLACE THIS SOLUTION IN THE ABOVE AREA. IF ADDITIONAL SPACE IS REQUESTED, USE A SEPARATE SHEET, ATTACH IT TO THIS FORM AND PLACE A CHECK IN THE FOLLOWING BLOCK. ☐

THE ERROR CAUSE IDENTIFICATION PORTION OF THE ZERO DEFECTS PROGRAM IS NOT A SUBSTITUTE FOR THE SUGGESTIONS AWARDS PROGRAM.

IF YOUR SOLUTION IS ADOPTED, AS A COST REDUCTION TECHNIQUE, YOU MAY ALSO BE ELIGIBLE FOR A SUGGESTION AWARD. REMEMBER, YOU MUST FILL OUT AN ADDITIONAL FORM TO BE ELIGIBLE FOR THE SUGGESTION AWARDS PROGRAM.

ERROR CAUSE IDENTIFICATION IS NOT NECESSARILY RESTRICTED TO YOUR OWN WORK AREA – THE SITUATION MAY EXIST ANYWHERE IN THE PLANT.

IN ALL CASES, THE DECISION OF THE COMPANY WILL BE FINAL. ALL IDEAS SUBMITTED BECOME THE PROPERTY OF THE COMPANY.

Fig. 18-3 Error Cause Removal form.

such groupings of employees to achieve cohesiveness and to aid the individual in identifying with a group. An extension of this concept is to use the group performances for the purpose of stimulating competition among groups.

Performance measurement always includes some aspect of product or process achievement, e.g., percent defective, error rate, demerits per unit. In addition, some programs provide for other "measures" e.g., housekeeping, materials handling. For such factors, the measurement plan is on some demerit basis, and the evaluation is based on audits.

Provision is also made for publishing departmental or group performance. This is done on charts which show performance against goals. These charts are prominently displayed in the respective departments to provide a feedback to employees, both as to progress and lack of progress.

Recognition for Groups. This concept is also widely used. In addition, there is wide use of competition among groups. Since the products, processes, etc., differ among groups, the basis of competition is in terms of universal measures, e.g., greatest percent improvement for the month.

Awards to groups are plaques or trophies which stay in the possession of the winning group for a month and then travel to the next winning group. Certificates or badges may be awarded to individual members to be retained permanently.

Individual Performance. Programs also provide for using measures of individual performance as a feedback to supervisors. These consist of the long-standing measures used for process control, plus some which may be added to measure and control operator error rate. Such measures are used between the supervisor and the individual as a source of feedback and to identify problems. The same data are used as a basis for choosing individuals for special recognition.

Companies generally avoid publication of the performance of individuals other than in the exceptional cases when an award is to be given. This is based on the concept that as to individuals, praise may be in public, but criticism must be in private.

Awards to individuals are by an Awards Committee on recommendation of the supervisor. In some companies, individual recognition may be financial: cash prizes, paid holiday trips, merchandise prizes. Other companies provide nonfinancial recognition: designation of Craftsman of the Day, badges or plaques, special parking privileges.

Whether financial or nonfinancial, the awards are made at a ceremonial presentation. Pictures and narratives appear in the house organ, in the public press, on the local television, on the "wall of fame." Commendation letters, sometimes sent to the employee's home, are used.

Results Attained Published information on results is sparse but impressive.[76] Large gains have been reported in quality costs, in reduction of workmanship errors, in defects of other classes. Some of the reports stress defect-free production of workers over long periods of time or over many units of product. Some of the reported improvements deal with the support activities, e.g., purchase requests, accuracy in teletypes, punch-card accuracy, etc.[77]

In most cases the campaigns contain both a motivation package and a prevention package. Such a combination makes it difficult to separate the relative contributions of the respective portions. When programs have the support of top management and are structured to involve all departments, it becomes very difficult to trace the source of contributions. (Major problems are always interdepartmental.)[78]

Evidently, the response of loosely structured company departments is less positive than that of highly structured departments. In one aerospace company, an anonymous questionnaire survey was conducted in various departments to secure reactions of employees to a companywide motivational program.[79] One of the questions asked for a rating of "overall opinion" of the program on a ten-point scale ranging from "no value" (zero) to "great value" (ten). The ratings given by employees in various departments were as follows: Production, 6.4; Administration, 5.6; Sales, 4.8; Engineering, 4.6; Research and Development, 2.6.

Ending the Campaign There is a difference of opinion as to whether motivational campaigns can go on and on permanently or must be limited in time. In the author's opinion, a "permanent campaign" is inherently contradictory. Instead, the permanence must be attained by restructuring the basic approaches to quality achievement as discussed under Continuing Programs of Motivation, above.

[76] For a compilation of results reported by several companies, see Berkwitt, George, Does "Zero Defects" Really Work? *Dun's Review,* August 1966, pp. 24–26, 49, 50.

[77] Newnham, Donald E., *op. cit.*

[78] See, in this connection, Haas, A. R., The Superior Craftsmanship Program. *Industrial Quality Control,* June 1966, pp. 665–669.

[79] Barrett, Gerald V., and Patrick A. Case, Zero Defects Programs: Their Effects at Different Job Levels, *Personnel,* November–December 1967, pp. 40–46.

Because of the contradictions inherent in a permanent campaign, some companies prefer to set a time limit to the campaign and to terminate it dramatically. This they do by award of the grand prizes amid a final round of publicity.

Quite aside from the merit of permanent versus temporary, there is need for assuring that the gains achieved are retained. There are a number of ways in which this is done:

Make the Changes Irreversible. When new fixtures, tools, or other physical facilities are provided, the old ones can be discarded so there can be no return to the old method.

Publish the New Methods. As new knowledge is acquired, it is incorporated into the manuals, instructions, etc., to serve as a basis for future training, retraining, reference, and audit.

Continue the Scoreboard. By continuing to measure performance, it can be determined whether the new level of results is being held or whether there is a slipping back.

Audit the Practices The audit programs should provide for periodic review of the changed processes and methods to assure that the changes remain in force.

INTERNATIONAL MOTIVATIONAL METHODS

The preceding discussions on motivation for quality have dealt mainly with the methods used in the United States. In other national cultures, the broad economic political and social forces combine to create motivational programs which differ extensively from those used in the United States. In the discussion which now follows, some of these national approaches will be examined.

(The broader forces which create these national differences are discussed in Sections 48 and 48A).

The Japanese QC Circle[80]   The QC Circle is a group of workers and work leaders within a single company department. The group, usually numbering ten or so members, is formed for the purpose of conducting studies to improve the effectiveness of work in their departments. Originally oriented to study of quality problems, the Circles have increasingly undertaken studies of other problems as well, e.g., productivity, cost, safety, etc.

The first step in the formation of QC Circles is an offer by a company to provide, to the work force, training in analysis of quality problems and in participation in QC Circles. Employee participation is voluntary,[81] and about half of the work force does volunteer. Once formed, the Circle embarks on study of projects. These projects may be nominated by the management or by the Circle itself.

Training of the Circle and study of the first project proceeds simultaneously. The training takes several forms:

1. Training "by the book." Using manuals, the QC Textbook For Foremen, etc., the Circle is instructed in a number of all purpose techniques:

Pareto analysis to identify the "vital few"
Cause-and-effect diagram (the Ishikawa diagram) to map out the variables
Statistical tools: histograms, graphs, control charts, process capability study, scatter diagram, binomial probability paper

2. Training through study of projects worked out by other QC Circles. The journal *Gemba to QC* (Quality Control for the Foreman) is a source of many such projects and is studied at Circle meetings.

---

[80] See the special bibliography at the end of this Section for references on QC Circles.

[81] This was certainly the case at the outset. Subsequent surveys have suggested that supervisory urge to join the Circles has become substantial.

3. Training during the working out of the project itself through assistance from supervisors, engineers, and others; case report presentation meetings; submission of case reports for action and for publication.

The Circles meet once or more each month, usually for one to two hours. Meetings may be held on company time or after hours (it varies with companies and circumstances). When held after hours, there is usually some form of compensation or amenity.

The movement has grown fantastically from its beginning in 1962. A decade later, the *registered* Circles numbered over 40,000, with a membership of over 400,000. The *unregistered* circles outnumber the registered circles by an order of magnitude. By mid-1972, the Japanese estimated that the total QC Circles had reached ½ million, with a membership of about 5 million.[82]

The number of projects worked out is even more fantastic, since a Circle, once it is under way, appears to average three project completions per year. (The targets established are four projects per year.) The cumulative total of completed projects during the first decade of the movement (1962–1972) is of the order of magnitude of *5 million projects!*

The money saved per project varies remarkably. However, the averages reported to the QC Circle conventions are about $5,000 per project. It must be concluded that the impact of the QC Circle movement on Japanese quality and on the economy has been simply immense.

These Circles operate in every conceivable industry. In consequence, a book of published projects exhibits great variety in the subject matter of projects and in the method of solution. To cite a few examples:

Reduction of defects in seamless stockings. After efforts to achieve improvement through operator skill were unsuccessful, the Circle developed a new "three-way needle" which was more productive and easier to handle. Productivity was increased 70% and rejects were cut in two.[83]

Improvement of yield in a crystallization process by changing the cooling rate, based on experimentation over a number of variables.[84]

Reduction of errors of counting and marking product through methods improvement and foolproofing.[85]

Improvement in uniformity of torque of bolts through experiments on variables.[86]

Reduction of welding defects and repair by foolproofing the welding gun.[87]

Improvement of ship unloading at a steel mill.[88]

A very usual QC Circle solution is to foolproof the process.[89] For example, in an operation of multiple welding of cable clamps into automobile trunks, the incidence of missing clamps was about one per thousand. A QC Circle tried several remedies, the final one being a foolproofing of the fixture so that unless all clamps were in

[82] Ishikawa, Kaoru, Quality Control Starts and Ends with Education, *Quality Progress,* August 1972, p. 18.

[83] See, at the end of this Section, reference 1, pp. 63–66.

[84] See, at the end of this Section, reference 2, 1970, pp. 91–94.

[85] See, at the end of this Section, reference 2, 1970, pp. 95–98.

[86] See, at the end of this Section, reference 2, 1970, pp. 107–110.

[87] See, at the end of this Section, reference 2, 1969, pp. 47–56.

[88] See, at the end of this Section, reference 2, 1969, pp. 97–102.

[89] In such cases, the diagnosis for cause may be incomplete or bypassed altogether. Once there is a solution by foolproofing, practical men seem content to leave the cause for the psychologists to find.

place, no welding could be done.   This brought the incidence of defects down to zero, literally.[90]

In a second case, a QC Circle undertook to reduce inadvertent missing solder as part of a broader project of defect reduction in a soldering assembly line.   It was noted that breaks in continuity of work (e.g., model changes, operator relief changes) were sources of solder omission.   As a remedy, redundance and countdown procedures were instituted to ensure continuity.   Even as to a single worker, it was found that leaving a partly finished equipment and then returning to it increased the risk of omissions, so such breaks were abolished.   Further redundancy consisted of requiring the use of audible cadence counting.[91]

An outgrowth of the QC Circle movements is the Jishu Kanri (JK) activity of the Japanese steel industry.   The literal meaning of JK is "workers' voluntary group activities."   JK was created to bring together into one unified sponsorship a number of worker group activities which had previously sprung up:

The QC Circle movement, promoted by the Japanese Union of Scientists and Engineers

The Zero Defects movement, promoted by the Japan Management Association

Other movements such as Improvement Circle, No Error, etc.

In execution of the JK activity, the target of the work groups is improvement of all sorts: productivity, quality, cost, safety, processes, machines, tools, working conditions, human relations, and even the very concept of looking for improvement.

A report describes the JK concept and its growth and direction during the first years of its existence.   The report includes case histories of projects and results in 21 plants of 15 Japanese companies.[92]

The motivations which energize the QC Circle movement in Japan are very different from those which prevail in the Western countries.[93]   As seen by a Westerner studying the QC Circle movement, the priority of motivations was about as follows:

1. Improving the company's performance.   This ranks first because of special reasons inherent in the Japanese history and culture.[94]

2. Self-improvement.   This again is responsive to a cultural imperative.

3. Recognition.   The QC Circle offers opportunity for indentification with a group, and for recognition of creative work done, in a whole hierarchy of awards: presentation of a project before company managers, publication of the report in the company journal or in the national journal, attendance at conferences, visits to other companies, national prizes,[95] membership on the team which goes abroad to study QC in other countries.

4. Creativity amid boredom.

5. Money incentives.

(The fact that money incentives is lowest in the list may come as a surprise to a Westerner, but it is not surprising in the Japanese culture.)

[90] Takasu, Hiroshi, Measures for the Omission of Wire Harness Clamps in the Body Assembly Process, International Conference on Quality Control, JUSE, Tokyo, 1929, Paper 08-28.

[91] Miyake, Ryohei, Control of Soldering in Tuner Assembly Process, *Reports of Statistical Applications Research*, vol. 15, no. 4, 1968.

[92] See, at the end of this Section, reference 3.

[93] For an illuminating discussion which goes back into the history of industrial relations in Japan, see Godo, Teruo, Characteristics of Labor Management in Japan, *Management Japan*, May 15, 1967, pp. 24–32.

[94] Reference 6.

[95] An example is the Nihon Keizai Shimbun QC Literature Prize.   (Nihon Keizai Shimbun is the Japanese counterpart of the United States' Wall Street Journal.)

Finally, it is abundantly clear to the Japanese worker that top management and the national leadership give a very high priority to achievements in quality. See Section 48 for a discussion of this phenomenon in relation to that prevailing in other cultures.

The USSR Saratov System   Saratov System[96] is the label for a movement in the Soviet Union[97] to improve quality and to shift the responsibility for achieving quality from inspectors to production workers. (Inspectors had previously sorted the product to keep the defects from going out to the user.) The concept of the Saratov System is to make achievement of quality dependent on workmanship.

To achieve this shift requires first that the criteria for operator self-control be met successfully. This is undertaken by the conventional steps of:

1. Establishing clear, valid product specifications and standards
2. Providing processes and tools capable of meeting the standards
3. Providing adequate information, instrumentation and job instructions
4. Providing training in proper use of the facilities, instruments, instructions,

As the criteria for self-control are met, there is introduced a motivation scheme which includes the following elements:

1. A concept of "Do it right the first time." This is underlined by the basic measure of operator performance which is percent of work done right the first time.

2. Provision for analysis and solution of quality problems. This is achieved in several ways:

Analysis by teams of workers. These organized teams (each known as a Community of Communist Labor) pool their job experience and knowledge with a view of solving quality problems.[98] A large factory may have many of these teams.

Open discussion of quality problems among workers, foremen, and engineers. One day of the week is designated as Quality Day, and discussions are scheduled for this day.

Use of a flying squadron of foremen and engineers to analyze more complex problems.

3. Provision is made for measuring performance, not only of workers but of operations generally. There are six indexes, as follows:

Percent of product which is right the first time (the prime measure of worker performance)

Consumer reaction: percent of claims and complaints

Percent of violations of product and process standards as determined by audit

Percent of changes in product and process specifications due to errors of product designers and process planners

Percent of continuity of plant operations

Cost of scrap, rework, etc.

These indexes are used to judge performance both before and after introduction of the Saratov System.

4. Incentives for good performance. These are both financial and nonfinancial.

Financial incentives consist of a graduated scale of bonuses based on attainment of high results as measured in percent of work done right the first time:

---

[96] The name Saratov is derived from the region of the Soviet Union in which the system was evolved.

[97] For a broad discussion of quality in Socialist countries, see Section 48A.

[98] The system does not appear to include the concept of training operators in the tools of analysis as is done in the Japanese QC Circles.

For meeting goals, 25%
For exceeding goals, 40%
For exceeding goals long enough to earn the right to self-inspection, 50%

Nonfinancial incentives are built around the attainment of the right to self-inspection. Workers whose percent "right first time" is persistently high are given the authority to inspect their own work.[99] This can extend to a literal "license," i.e., the worker receives a personal inspection stamp. Attainment of this license not only qualifies the worker for the top bonus; it also makes him eligible for designation of *Udarneek* (advanced worker) or the higher designation of *Udarneek Lenin Five-Year Plan*. Such designations carry nonfinancial distinctions and amenities of importance. In addition, if the workers in an entire shop attain licenses for self-inspection, the shop foreman also gets a form of license.

5. A concept of responsibility for results. Workers who have not yet attained the license for self-inspection have their work inspected by inspectors in conventional fashion. The finding of even one defect is reason for returning the lot to the worker for correction. For workers who do have the license, audits provide the feedback on which to base judgments for continuing the license.

Reports of improvements attained are quite similar to those in the United States journals regarding results of motivational programs. Substantial improvements take place in factory rejects, productivity, cost, service calls, etc.[100] As with other national programs, it is difficult to identify the specific origin of these improvements, since introduction of the Saratov System takes place simultaneously with other management efforts for improvement.

The Polish DO RO System   This is one of a family of systems used in Eastern Europe.[101] DO RO is an acronym for *Dobra Robota,* which in Polish means "good work." In other countries, other terminology is used, e.g., *Ohne Fehler,* the German term meaning "without defects."

The DO RO system, like Saratov, aims to put responsibility for quality on the worker. The management creates a favorable environment for workers to enroll in the DO RO system. This is done on a voluntary basis, by signing a pledge card. (As in the United States, the senior manager signs the first card.) Evidently about half the workers respond to the invitation, which involves taking training and an examination (see below).

Next, there is action to shift responsibility from inspectors to workmen. This follows an approach paralleling the Saratov System, a basic prerequisite being to meet the criteria for self-control. Inspection emphasis is shifted from final product inspection to establishment of control stations earlier in the process, using instrumentation, data feedback, chart control, etc., as appropriate. Problems turned up become the basis for analysis to provide adequate machines, processes, information, and other essentials of worker self-control.

There follows a program of training of workers, using textbooks and specially prepared training materials. Training is done in seminars and is followed up by examinations, with certificates awarded to successful trainees.

As in the Saratov System, there is a provision for awarding a self-inspection license to workers whose results justify such a step. In DO RO, a license certificate is issued

---

[99] See Section 11, under Product Acceptance by Operators.

[100] First-hand observations by the author (during multiple trips to the Soviet Union, Poland, Romania, Czechoslovakia, Hungary and Yugoslavia) from visits to plants and exhibitions, discussions with plant managers and staff specialists, discussions with officials of central bureaus, and feedback from attendees at lectures and courses conducted.

[101] See generally Section 48A.

to the employee as proof of this attainment.   This certificate, signed by the plant Director and the Chairman of the Trade Union council, is hung at the worker's machine and authorizes the inspector to accept the work on the worker's decision.   A free translation of the Polish text is as follows:

LICENSE

Taking into account a very good and zealous performance of your professional duties and high discipline in observing the principles and requirements of the technological process at your post, and especially in regard to your personal responsibility and care in the maximum elimination of the possibility of errors and defects creation, the management and trade union council, on suggestion of your direct manager, gives you the right to carry out self-control (the control of your production).

This right is a proof that you are appreciated very highly and that you are enlisted among the best workers of our enterprise.

The management of the plant, on giving you this authorization, expresses at the same time its thanks for good results of your work and wishes you a good performance in the future.

(Signed)

CHAIRMAN OF THE TRADE UNION COUNCIL

(Signed)
DIRECTOR

The license is honored not only by the factory inspectors but also by customers who accept the DO RO mark on the product as adequate proof of quality.

INCENTIVES FOR DEFECT REDUCTION BY OPERATORS

The term "incentives" as used here refers to systematic forms of motivation for quality through influencing the pay of operators and inspectors.

Traditional Quality Incentives.   Prior to the rise of modern collective bargaining, it was a widespread practice to pay production workers on a piecework basis.   These plans were almost universally based on *quantity* of work done.   However, they often included indirect incentives for quality.   For example:

The operator was paid for good pieces only and not for bad pieces.

The operator was paid for good pieces at piecework rates and for bad pieces at base rates.

The operator was required to sort good from bad, and to repair the bad, all on his own time.

These penalty provisions included many injustices, mainly that operators were often penalized for defects beyond their control.   However, the prevailing structure of industrial relations made it difficult to remedy these abuses.

Effect of Collective Bargaining.   The rise of industrial unionism in the mid-1930s resulted in widespread grievances because of unjust penalties for defective work. Discussion of these grievances disclosed that there was in fact a wide practice of penalizing operators for defects beyond their control.   In consequence, the managers abolished virtually all the penalties for defects, even those for which operators were clearly responsible.

It is unlikely that such penalty plans will ever be reinstated on any significant scale.   Aside from the resistance of the Unions, there has also arisen a degree of state legislation which imposes severe restrictions on use of such penalty provisions. For example, Section 103.455 of the Wisconsin Statute provides:

Deductions for faulty workmanship, loss, theft or damage.   No employer shall make any deduction from the wages due or earned by any employee, who is not an independent contractor, for defective or faulty workmanship, lost or stolen property or damage to property, unless the employee authorizes the employer in writing to make such deduction or unless the employer and a representative designated by the employee shall determine that such defective or faulty work, loss or theft, or damage is due to worker's negligence, carelessness, or wilful and intentional conduct on the part of such employee, or unless the employee is found guilty or held liable in a court of competent jurisdiction by reason thereof. If any such deduction is made or credit taken by any employer, that is not in accordance with this section, the employer shall be liable for twice the amount of the deduction or credit taken in a civil action brought by said employee. Any agreement entered into between employer and employee contrary to this section shall be void and of no force and effect. In case of a disagreement between the two parties, the industrial commission shall be the third determining party subject to any appeal to the court.

There does remain a residue of incentives for quality, but these are primarily of the premium type. For example, operators loading the cupola in a foundry have an incentive based on precision of charging the cupola, whereas the men who pour the castings are on a conventional quantity incentive.[102]

Effect of Affluence.   As earnings of operators have risen sufficiently to carry them well above the subsistence level, the stimulus of piecework rates has declined. In the United States there has been a gradual decline in use of piecework until it has become a minority form of motivation. The use of machine-paced production lines has been a further contributing factor. The gradual abolition of piecework has carried with it the abolition of other forms of direct money incentive for operators.

Alternatives to Money Incentives.   In lieu of money penalties for defective work, companies in the United States use mainly the following alternatives:

1. Motivation programs and campaigns as discussed in this Section, above.

2. Rating of quality of work done by operators and use of these ratings to identify superior and inferior performers, leading to discovery of knack, retraining, self-inspection, etc.

3. Job redesign and enlargement (see below, under Job Enrichment).

Role of the Operator in Defect Reduction.   Under the Taylor System of separating planning from execution, the role of the operator is one of executing plans prepared by others. This system of management imposes severe limits on the ability of the operator to contribute to defect reduction. Table 18-6 summarizes the potential contribution of the operator under this traditional management system,[103] where no training or time is provided to enable the operator to become involved in problem solving.

It is seen from Table 18-6 that the potential operator contribution is strongly influenced by the type of defect, as follows:

1. Management-controllable defects. The operator can identify failure to meet the criteria of self-control and bring these to management attention. The Error Cause Removal procedure is specially designed for the purpose. Operators accused of committing errors often point such things out in self-defense.

The operator can also theorize on the causes of the defects, and on how they might be remedied, but he lacks the time, the facilities, and the training to conduct an adequate diagnosis.

2. Operator-controllable defects (willful). Here the potential contribution of the operator is at its best, since he can respond to the motivational program and shut the defects off.

3. Operator-controllable defects (technique errors). The operator can adopt the

---

[102] Burton, James R., An Incentive for Operators Whose Production Is Machine Controlled, *Journal of Industrial Engineering,* January–February 1965, pp. 56–58. See also Sidebottom, A. W., and E. Brewer, Management's Responsibility for Quality, Output and Profitability, *Work Study,* March 1965, pp. 11–22.

[103] Derived from Juran, J. M., Operator Errors—Time for a New Look, *Quality Progress,* February 1968, pp. 9–11.

TABLE 18-6   Role of the Operator in Defect Reduction

Activity	Role of the operator as applied to			
	Management-controllable errors	Operator-controllable errors		
		Inadvertent errors	Technique errors	Willful errors
Identify the presence of errors	X	—	X	XX
Theorize as to causes	X	—	X	XX
Analyze for causes	X	—	X	XX
Theorize as to remedies	X	X	X	XX
Choose optimal remedy	—	—	—	X
Apply remedy	—	X	X	XX

XX = Large potential contribution
X = Small potential contribution
— = Negligible potential contribution

knack of better operators once this is explained to him. He can adopt new technology which embodies the knack. However, he is unlikely to discover the knack for himself unless time and training are provided to permit him to make the analysis.

4. Operator-controllable defects (inadvertent). It is doubtful that the operator can diagnose the cause of these, since even the specialists have found the problem to be very complex. The operator may have some ideas on how to foolproof the operation, but again, unless he has the time and training, he cannot prove his contentions.

The frustration of operators under the Taylor System of management has become notorious and has posed a serious problem to managers. In addition, the results reported by behavioral scientists from experiments in "job enrichment" (see below) have been of increasing interest to American managers. Finally, the astounding growth of the QC Circles has posed a clear competitive threat for which an answer must be provided. The answer may well lie in some form of job enrichment, as discussed in the next major topic.

JOB ENRICHMENT

Under Herzberg's concept of motivators and also under McGregor's Theory Y, there is need to redesign work to provide employees with something more than meaningless, repetitive, monotonous operations. The broad term applied to such redesign of work is "job enrichment," "job enlargement," etc. There are several ways of going about it.

Explanation of Why and How   Under this approach, the operations performed do not change, but the employee is provided with information on why and how. The techniques used for communicating this information are discussed in Continuing Programs of Motivation, above.

Participation   This approach likewise involves no management-initiated change in the operations performed. However, special provision is made to secure employee participation in job-related matters. There are several degrees of such participation:

1. The conventional suggestion system. While this is originally structured by management, it is left to the employee to take the initiative in volunteering ideas.

2. Personal solicitation of worker ideas on job-related matters. This differs from the usual suggestion system, since the initiative is taken by the management to open up direct discussions with employees. For example, in a metals manufacturing company, there was a problem of controlling the performance of a ball milling operation. One of the variables was the number of balls remaining in the mill (the mill grinds up the balls as well as the materials undergoing processing). Discussion with the operators disclosed that they could judge from the sound of the operation what the condition of the contents of the ball mill was. This method of control had never occurred to the managers. In another case involving a process for making synthetic yarns, there had for years existed a problem of discolored yarns, the problem being localized to only part of the process. When employee ideas were solicited as to the likely cause of the discoloration, the answer was found. The contamination came from a wooden plank which had for years been unnoticed at the bottom of one of the storage tanks.

3. Joint planning, in which the workers are asked to participate in discussions with supervisors on how best to do the job. An early form of this was the Scanlon Plan, which involved joint management-worker committees and a plan for sharing the gains.[104] A less formal approach is exemplified by the case cited by Myers.[105] The company in question was low bidder on a contract and found itself losing money. It was taking 138 hours to assemble a unit of equipment, and this had to be reduced to 100 hours to break even. The foreman took the ten assemblers off the line and into a conference room to solicit ideas for improvement. (Eight of the assemblers had prior training in problem solving.) Over a series of meetings and tryouts of ideas, the end result was to reduce the assembly time far below the 100 hours needed to break even. The success achieved on this operation led other foremen to structure similar participation meetings.

4. Creation of teams of workers so as to increase employee involvement in discussion and solution of departmental problems. The precise method of organizing these teams and of working with them varies widely—the technique is comparatively new. However, the reported results have been generally favorable and the concept may be in a growth cycle.[106]

(Note that the team concept is also inherent in the Soviet Union's Saratov System and in the Polish DO RO system.)

5. Special training of worker teams in how to solve quality problems, followed by working on projects. This is the approach of the Japanese QC Circles.

What distinguishes the participative approach from the traditional is that the work force is given a role to play in the hitherto managerial process of setting goals, planning to meet goals, analyzing problems, etc. This participation extends to involvement in projects for improvement as well as projects for control.

In the participative approach, the role of the supervisor changes as drastically as does the role of the employee. Traditionally the supervisor establishes the goals, standards, and methods. He then applies motivation to the work force to use these methods and to meet the goals and standards. Under participation, the supervisor

[104] See Gellerman, Saul W., "Motivation and Productivity," American Management Association, New York, 1963, pp. 66–69.

[105] Myers, M. Scott, Increasing Employee Motivation, in "Managing Change," National Industrial Conference Board, New York, January 1967, pp. 41–46.

[106] Huse, Edgar F. and Michael Beer, Eclectic Approach to Organization Development, *Harvard Business Review,* September-October 1971, pp. 103–112. See also Fort Lauderdale Experiment, *Quality Management and Engineering,* June 1972, pp. 12–14.

is faced with motivating employees to participate in the very managerial processes which have been supervisory monopolies.[107]

Job Change: Horizontal This is a form of job "enlargement" by increasing the span of variety of work done by the employee. For example, the assembly line of 40 workers is redesigned to consist of five lines of eight workers each. The result is a more cohesive work group, less monotony, greater opportunity to understand the complete flow, and thereby greater opportunity for creativity.[108] In the extreme case, the assembly line is abolished and each worker assembles the unit of product complete. For example, a company which abolished the assembly line for hot plates reported several improvements, including quality, in which operator-controllable defects dropped from 23% to 1%. Abolition of the assembly line for a type of electronic instruments also resulted in a quality improvement.[109]

A variation of horizontal job enlargement is to train each member of a work team to be able to do any of the jobs done by the entire team. (There may be a higher pay rate awarded to the worker who qualifies himself.) Responsibility for assigning work is turned over to the team itself, which thereby may take on a number of responsibilities previously restricted to the supervision: interviewing and hiring job applicants, filling in for absentees, scheduling work breaks, establishing work rules.[110]

Job Change: Vertical Here the job enlargement consists of adding new *functions*, e.g., the production operator may be given the added duties of product inspection, tool control, inventory control, record keeping, etc. The individual becomes a "minimanager" for that work station.

In one case, the job of process inspectors was enlarged by adding unconventional duties such as troubleshooting, disposition of nonconforming product, conducting process capability studies, planning Production station quality control criteria, establishing prevention programs, and assisting in design reviews.[111]

It is evident that there is a wide range of choice for conducting experiments to discover the method that fits the special situations of each company. The limiting factors are not so much the technology as the cultural resistance of all concerned — managers, union leaders, employees. This resistance is minimal when it is made clear that an experiment is in progress and that the long-range decisions will have to await the results of the experiment.[112]

QUALITY MOTIVATION FOR MANAGERS

No manager wants poor quality, high costs, or late deliveries. Yet many managers make decisions which do result in poor quality. In part, the reasons behind these decisions are the same as those which characterize operator-controllable errors: inadvertent, technique, and willful errors.[113] However, managerial decision making

[107] For elaboration, see Roche, William J., and Neil L. MacKinnon, Motivating People with Meaningful Work, *Harvard Business Review*, May-June 1970, pp. 97–110.

[108] For several examples, see Tuggle, Greylan, Job Enlargement, *Industrial Engineering*, February 1969, pp. 26–31.

[109] See Huse and Beer, *op. cit.*

[110] See, for example, The Plant That Runs on Individual Initiative, *Management Review*, July 1972, pp. 20–25. See also Management Itself Holds the Key, *Business Week*, Sept. 9, 1972, pp. 142–150.

[111] Maher, John, Wayne Overbagh, Gerald Palmer, and Darrell Piersol, Enriched Jobs Mean Better Inspection Performance, *Quality Assurance*, November 1969, pp. 23–26.

[112] See, in this connection, Myers, M. Scott, Overcoming Union Opposition to Job Enrichment, *Harvard Business Review*, May-June 1971, pp. 37–49.

[113] See above, under Inadvertent Errors, Technique Errors and Willful Errors, respectively.

with respect to quality goes beyond the problems of conventional errors and extends into the complexities of business management to such a degree that error classification often has little meaning.

Willful Errors   The most common source of willful managerial errors on quality is multiple standards, i.e., the fact that the line manager must meet not only quality standards but also standards for cost, delivery, safety, etc.   These multiple standards are always present, whether the problem is one of control or one of creating change.

An example of multiple standards to be met during creation of change is the launching of a new product.   The urgency of getting to market ahead of competitors may cause the managers to launch the new product before the reliability testing and other early warning tests have been concluded.   The action is called a "calculated risk" if the managers are as well informed on the quality implications as they are on the marketing implications.   However, in many companies there is an inherent inequality about these two categories of knowledge, since the top managers lack the tools needed to exercise command over the quality function whereas they do possess these tools as applied to the marketing function.

Problems of managerial control also abound in multiple standards.   In one plant making electron tubes, a consultant found that although the inspection instructions called for 100% inspection of all assembled mounts, no such inspection was in fact being conducted.   The Mount Department manager had an interesting explanation.   The 100% inspection had been in effect for several years, but with occasional exceptions.   These exceptions were the result of crises which arose in the subsequent department (Seal and Exhaust).   When this department faced a shortage of mounts, its manager would persuade the Mount Department manager to deliver uninspected mounts to keep the machines going.   This persuasion was achieved by a willingness of the Seal and Exhaust manager to accept the responsibility for any added scrap due to use of uninspected mounts.   To the surprise of the Mount Department manager, there seemed to be no discernible difference in scrap from uninspected mounts versus inspected mounts.   Nevertheless, he always reverted to the 100% inspection when each crisis was over.

Then came a time when there was a big "drive" on costs.   The proposed departmental cost reductions did not add up to enough to meet the top management goals, whereupon top management superimposed an arbitrary 10% reduction "across the board."   The Mount Department manager met this quota by quietly eliminating the 100% inspection.[114]

While multiple standards are a continuing problem for all managers, the priority assigned to each standard keeps changing.   During one year, the top priority may be on prompt delivery to customers.   During the second year, the emphasis may shift to quality; during the third year, to cost, etc.   An organized major change in these priorities is called a "drive" or a "campaign."   Obviously, it would be desirable if industrial companies could be managed without the need for "drives."   However, the managers can readily point to the fact that the forces and conditions in the marketplace continually undergo profound changes and that prompt response to these changes is the major reason for the drives.   There is much merit in these contentions.

The fact that the line manager can give uneven priority to the multiple goals is one reason for the existence of specialty departments, each oriented to some major company goal.   (Quality Control is one of these specialty departments and is oriented to the quality goals.)   The training and motivation of these specialty departments is necessarily different from that of the line departments.   The resulting differences in emphasis are an aid to assuring that the line managers maintain a

---

[114] Consulting experience of the author.

reasonable balance among all goals. However, the differences in emphasis are also the source of some potentially severe frictions between the specialty and the line departments.

For example, the line manager is asked not only to be quality-minded but also to be cost-minded, safety-minded, etc. For the line manager, life is much simpler if *all* goals can be met. When the forces inherent in the economic cycle force this manager to fall short of meeting some major goal, he is normally quite concerned about the deficiency; but he regards it as the least undesirable of the available alternatives.

In contrast, the specialty department affected by the deficiency tends to regard a violation of its goals as a high offence and the violator as a high' offender. The specialists exert considerable effort to eliminate the violation. In their zeal they may become personal about it, accusing the line managers of lacking quality-mindedness. (What the specialist usually means is that the line manager has, at the time, an order of priorities different from that of the specialist.) Such accusations breed counteraccusations and can result in a rapid deterioration of relationships between zealous specialists and conservative line managers.

Motivation for Control A major responsibility for all managers is to design and administer the plans of control, including control of quality, through which performance is measured against goals so that action can be taken on the difference.[115] Because the number of quality characteristics to be controlled is very great, the control plans are designed in a way which permits the nonsupervisors and the automated processes to do the bulk of the control work. There remains a residue of higher-level control which should not be delegated but should be exercised by the managers themselves.

In carrying out his personal control duties, the manager, through the example he sets, greatly influences motivation for quality throughout the organization. If the manager fails to act on the alarm signals, his subordinates will follow his example. If the manager takes action without explaining his reasons, his subordinates will deduce his reasons from the action (or lack of action) they observe, but these deductions can be wildly erroneous.

The pyramiding effect of the manager's actions extends also to his premises or beliefs. If an important manager is convinced that the prime quality problem is operator errors, this belief will tend to become entrenched throughout that part of the hierarchy supervised by him, with the result that the main causes of quality problems are not analyzed.

Motivation for Improvement The manager who fails to structure improvement programs never becomes liberated from the endless job of "firefighting." Only the manager who is equally at home with both control and breakthrough can reach a state in which he has time for planning the future along with conducting current operations.

The approach to quality improvement programs is discussed mainly in Section 16. Study of that Section will disclose that these programs enable the managers to guide the technologists and specialists in projects which are individually justified as sound returns on investment. In addition, these projects collectively are the means for providing the know-how needed for planning new products and processes in a way which avoids creation of troubles for the future.

Even more than for control, the example set by the manager in tackling projects for improvement is vital to the whole organization. Control sets its own priorities — when a "fire" breaks out, all concerned are forced to deal with it, then and there. In contrast, projects for improvement do not give automatic alarm signals. Neither do they force action to be taken immediately. Identifying and acting on improve-

[115] See generally Section 6, under Planning for Control *et seq.*

ment projects requires managerial initiative, and the example must be set again and again.

Fortunately, participation in successful project work is highly stimulating to most people. As they gain successes and experience, they also learn that improvement projects are a most agreeable form of relief from the monotony of repetitive operations and from the abrasive crises incidental to preoccupation with control.

Managerial Involvement   The key to managerial motivation is involvement. This is especially true for the "non-quality" managers (e.g., Production, Purchasing, Marketing). To these managers, quality is only one of a number of goals they must meet; the quality function is secondary to their departmental function.

The ultimate model for involving the non-quality managers in quality goals is the Annual Quality Program as discussed in Section 6. Through such programs, each department, whether "quality" or "non-quality," participates in the setting of quality goals for the year ahead and accepts a share of the tasks which need to be performed before the goals are reached.

Where the company does not operate under the concept of the annual quality program, the non-quality managers can still be brought into involvement. They may be asked to:

Nominate quality improvement projects or quality problems requiring solution
Serve on the steering teams which guide specific projects to a conclusion
Serve as instructors in training programs
Receive reports on the company's performance with respect to various quality goals
Serve on quality audit teams

These and other forms of active participation in dealing with quality problems are useful in broadening the understanding of the quality function and in paving the way to the setting up of the annual quality program.

Upper Management and Motivation   Upper management has a multiple role to play in motivation for quality: motivation of nonsupervisors, of the supervisory and managerial body and of upper management itself. The main emphasis to date has been on upper management's role in campaigns motivating the workers. As elaborated in The Formal Motivational Campaign, above, this role is one of approving the program and its budget in the first place, participating in the ceremonial launching, in award ceremonies, and in other propaganda essentials.

However, *most quality problems are management-controllable.* Hence the job of motivating the managers is more significant than that of motivating workers. In motivating managers, the ceremonial and propaganda aspects are of small significance. What becomes significant is the decisions and actions of upper management. The most important of these decisions and actions include:

1. Whether upper management leads, delegates, or abdicates the quality function in the first instance. The extent of upper management participation is rightly judged by other managers as the real index of the importance of the quality function, no matter what the propaganda says.[116]

2. Whether the policies are to achieve quality leadership in the industry, competitiveness, or adequacy. These policies affect the priorities given to other standards, and constitute clear signals to the managers and supervisors.

3. Whether budgetary requests for improving and maintaining quality receive an objective hearing (e.g., for machine maintenance, housekeeping, training programs, floor space, even such humble matters as paint for inspection areas or printing for data sheets).

[116] See also Section 21, under Upper Management Participation in the Quality Function.

4. Whether upper management itself has taken the time to understand enough fundamentals of the quality function to avoid being stampeded by sporadic troubles.

Upper management's propaganda is invariably good. When the decisions and actions confirm the propaganda, the words are believed and become effective in their own right. When the decisions and actions deny the propaganda, the credibility of all management pronouncement becomes suspect.

ROLE OF THE LABOR UNION

The official pronouncements of labor unions invariably support high quality of product. The medieval guilds regulated quality of materials, process, and product in great detail. Some of their restrictive and monopolistic practices were defended on the ground of protecting the public against inferior products. The modern trade unions follow this same concept and defend some of their practices (e.g., long apprenticeships, restrictions on productivity) on the ground of protecting quality of product. The trade union press often devotes space to the importance of craftsmanship as an essential ingredient in the trade.

The traditions of the industrial unions are quite different from those of the trade unions. The trade unionist undergoes a broad apprenticeship which normally enables him to plan his own work to meet the needs of fitness for use or of the "specification," which in many cases is determined by past practice as interpreted by subjective judgment. In contrast, the industrial unionist does not normally undergo a broad apprenticeship and is not normally allowed to plan his own work. Instead, the work is planned by a planning specialist who prescribes the machines, tools, methods, and instruments to be used. The same specialist (or another) sets standards of what constitutes a day's work. Another specialist establishes detailed quality criteria. The resulting multiple standards are cited by the industrial unions as a prime cause of poor quality, e.g., it is not possible to do a good job due to the speed of the assembly line.

The active role of industrial unions with respect to product quality has taken two principal directions:

1. Elimination of penalties for defective work. As discussed above in Incentives for Defect Reduction by Operators, industrial unions have been quite successful in abolishing these penalty plans and in securing legislation to restrict reinstatement of similar plans.

2. Bringing inspectors into the collective bargaining units. This effort has generally succeeded as to routine inspection work, whether it is performed by people called inspectors, sorters, operators, etc. In contrast, salaried quality auditors and other such quality specialists are generally not in the collective bargaining units.

Beyond such specific areas of activity, problems of product quality are seldom prominent in union-management relationships. Instead, the relationships are dominated by other considerations (e.g., wages, mutual confidence). The broad atmosphere created by these dominant considerations strongly influences the reception given to proposals concerning product quality.

Generally, the industrial unions of the United States were born in the 1930s during a time of severe economic distress and social upheaval. The rise of these unions was bitterly resisted by the generation of managers then in power. One consequence of the resulting antagonism was that the unions adopted some narrow, rigid views of their responsibilities for the health of the companies. The unions' main positions were:

1. The union is responsible to its members for assuring that they secure a maximum share of the companies' income. Hence the unions must contest with the managers on how to divide up this income.

2. The union has no responsibility for assisting the companies to increase their income.   Hence the unions need not collaborate with managers on how to improve the quality, productivity, profitability, etc., of the companies.

There have been some notable exceptions to the foregoing, an organized form being the Scanlon Plan.   This plan involved formal Labor-Management committees to study ways to improve company performance plus a formal agreement for sharing the resulting gains.[117]   However, these exceptions have constituted only a small minority of the union-management relationships.

Meanwhile, a growing international competition has resulted in some remarkable shifts of jobs across international boundaries.   Whole industries (e.g., shipbuilding, electronics, steel, textiles) have undergone massive losses of jobs to foreign competitors.   These losses are of profound concern to the unions and are causing a reexamination of the traditional view that the union has no responsibility for improving the health of the companies.[118,119]

TABLE 18-7   Census of United States Company Effectiveness on Operator-controllable Errors

CENSUS OF COMPANY PRACTICES ON MOTIVATION

(Do not sign your name)

In my company, the effectiveness in motivation for quality is about as follows:

	Company effectiveness is:		
Elements of motivation for quality	*Strong*	*Adequate*	*Weak*
Understanding of criteria for self-control	9	51	40
Measure of controllability	8	50	42
Separation of operator error causes	9	43	48
Errors due to lack of skill			
Identify consistently good operators	13	43	44
Discover the knack	5	34	61
Retrain	7	35	58
Motivation to remedy willful errors	10	53	37
Foolproofing, redundancy, etc. to remedy inadvertent errors	18	52	30
Motivation of operators to			
Identify gaps in self-control	4	41	55
Analyze causes of operator errors	4	35	61
Adopt knack of good operators	10	47	43
Remedy willful errors	7	56	37
Accept foolproofing, redundancy, and similar changes in technology	18	59	23

[117] For added discussion, see Gellerman, Saul W., "Motivation and Productivity," American Management Association, New York, 1963, pp. 66–69.

[118] See, for example, The Steelworkers Set Out to Rescue Steel, *Business Week,* December 11, 1971, pp. 58 and 59.

[119] It is not merely the views of the unions.   There are many managers who are unwilling to

In this reexamination of responsibilities, it is inevitable that the unions will study the forms of collaboration prevailing in those countries which have been successful in improving their own economies by outperforming their international competitors. In such countries (e.g., Japan), it is common to find that the unions, while also contesting with management on how to divide the income of the company, consider that they do have a responsibility to help improve the health of the company. The amazing growth of the QC Circles is a demonstration of this view of the unions and of the support given to this view by the employee body.

CENSUS OF COMPANY EFFECTIVENESS ON OPERATOR-CONTROLLABLE ERRORS

Table 18-7 shows the results of censuses conducted among United States managers who have participated in the author's courses on Management of Quality Control. The form used for the census was Table 18-7 in blank. Men attending the courses were usually the Quality Managers in their companies, though about a third of them were managers from Production, Engineering, Service, etc. About 200 companies are represented in these United States data.

A similar set of data representing about 200 European companies is shown in Table 18-8. (These data are the result of censuses taken during courses given by the author in Great Britain, Holland, Scandinavia, and Spain.)

It is evident that most of the men are not satisfied with the situation in their respective companies. Some of the concentrations make clear why. For example, most companies are adequately informed as to who the consistently good operators are. However, most companies do not follow through to discover the knack used by these operators or to retrain the inferior operators.

It is also evident that such a census can be conducted within a single company to discover the pattern of beliefs.

HISTORICAL SUPPLEMENT

Individual company programs of motivation for quality have been legion, but few were published prior to the twentieth century.[120] An example of a published account is that of the Bigelow Sanford Carpet Company's program, launched in 1949.[121] A generalized approach[122] to a quality motivation "campaign," published in 1954, described the following elements:

Remove reject causes controlled by Management.
Set up a plant Quality Committee to guide the program.
Convince operators of importance of quality.
Show operators how to improve quality.
Solicit operators' ideas for improving quality.
Establish quality scoreboards and goals.
Follow the scoreboard with the foremen.
Set a start and an end to the campaign.
Follow through to make improvement permanent.

---

let the unions become involved in assisting the companies on the grounds of interference with management prerogatives.

[120] The author recalls his role in structuring a large-scale program undertaken in the late 1920s in the Hawthorne Plant of Western Electric Company (which at that time employed over 40,000 people).

[121] See Hurst, R. F., Building a Quality Minded Organization, Production Series No. 183, American Management Association, New York.

[122] Juran, J. M., Nine Steps to Better Quality, *Factory Management and Maintenance,* March 1954.

TABLE 18-8   Census of European Company Effectiveness on Operator-controllable Errors

CENSUS OF COMPANY PRACTICES ON MOTIVATION

(Do not sign your name)

In my company, the effectiveness in motivation for quality is about as follows:

	Company effectiveness is:		
Elements of motivation for quality	*Strong*	*Adequate*	*Weak*
Understanding of criteria for self-control	13	55	32
Measure of controllability	9	49	42
Separation of operator error causes	12	38	50
Errors due to lack of skill			
Identify consistently good operators	20	51	29
Discover the knack	9	38	53
Retrain	8	40	52
Motivation to remedy willful errors	10	52	38
Foolproofing, redundancy, etc. to remedy inadvertent errors	14	52	34
Motivation of operators to			
Identify gaps in self-control	5	39	56
Analyze causes of operator errors	7	45	48
Adopt knack of good operators	12	48	40
Remedy willful errors	9	60	31
Accept foolproofing, redundancy, and similar changes in technology	16	62	22

The Martin Company Experience.   In the early 1960s the Orlando Division of Martin Company was producing missiles for a military customer.   On two occasions, in late 1961 and early 1962, the company exhorted its inspectors to find all discrepancies so that perfect missiles could be delivered.   When this succeeded, the company concluded to carry such an approach to the entire work force.   The slogan ZD (zero defects) was coined to publicize the ultimate goal.

Martin Company publicized their approach, results, and slogan among their military customers and vendors.   However, no significant adoption (of programs called ZD) seems to have taken place elsewhere until after June 1964, when the U.S. Army Missile Command began a series of seminars and workshops on the subject.   This was supplemented in November and December 1964 by seminars conducted by the Department of Defense.[123]   At the same time, one of the national journals published a story[124] on the Martin experience, and the resulting publicity further stimulated interest.

Military Advocacy.   Department of Defense advocacy for motivational programs

[123] For details, including estimates of numbers of companies who adopted programs, see More ZD Reports, *Quality Assurance*, August 1965, pp. 21–23.
[124] Let's See ZD, *Time*, November 6, 1964, pp. 93–94.

became substantial.   Information kits were prepared and distributed.   A handbook[125] was published in 1965.   Awards were given to contractors merely for creating programs, (at a time when it would be months before it could be known whether there would be useful results).   While most published information (e.g., the "Guide to Zero Defects") tended to be restrained, some government and military officials became zealous advocates, to a point that some and perhaps many contractors undertook programs as a matter of good customer relations.[126]

The National Aeronautics and Space Administration and the Atomic Energy Commission also tended to favor contractor adoption of motivational programs. However, these agencies were less exuberant in their advocacy than their military counterparts.

Generally, the motivational programs were confined to the government contractors.   The much larger civilian economy certainly was aware of the publicity and certainly looked to see what was going on.   The tendency was to conclude that such stress on perfection was not in keeping with the economics of the civilian industries. In consequence, such programs as were undertaken in civilian industries concentrated on the vital few defects which were usually management-controllable.

ADDED BIBLIOGRAPHY ON MOTIVATIONAL CAMPAIGNS

"A Guide to Zero Defects," Department of Defense Quality and Reliability Assurance Handbook 4155.12-H, Nov. 1, 1965.   This is a brief (16-page), well-prepared summary of the ingredients of a motivational program.   Available from Superintendent of Documents, Washington, D.C. 20402.

"Zero Defects, The Quest for Quality," Department of Defense Quality and Reliability Assurance Technical Report TR 9, Aug. 15, 1968.   This is a 232-page collection of papers on various aspects of motivational programs.   The topics are well chosen, and the papers are mainly responsive to the topics.   A good collection.   Available from the Superintendent of Documents, Washington, D.C. 20402.

James F. Halpin, "Zero Defects: A New Dimension in Quality Assurance," McGraw-Hill Book Company, New York, 1966.   This is a 228-page book setting out the views of the Director of Quality of the Martin Company's Orlando Division, the original locale of the so-called ZD programs.   Includes much useful detail on many matters of administration.   Severely biased by its one-track advocacy of the "inattention" school of why operators make errors.

Industrial Quality Control, June 1966 issue.   This issue is devoted to quality motivation and features six well-chosen papers dealing with various aspects of motivational programs: industry case histories, government views, and a consultant's critique.

BIBLIOGRAPHY ON QC CIRCLES

1. K. Ishikawa (ed.), "QC Circle Activities," QC in Japan Series, no. 1, JUSE, Tokyo, 1968 (in English).   A comprehensive history and description of the QC Circle movement, with eight case examples of how it works in action.   (This reference is the source of some of the quantitative data in the description of QC Circles given in this Section, above.)   Includes reprints of reference 6 and 7 below.

2. Reports of QC Circle Activities," JUSE (in English):
   No. 1, 1968 (21 cases)   No. 4, 1971 (12 cases)
   No. 2, 1969 (32 cases)   No. 5, 1972 (19 cases)
   No. 3, 1970 (24 cases)
   These books are part of the preparation for foreign trips made annually by a specially

---

[125] "A Guide To Zero Defects," Quality and Reliability Assurance Handbook 4155.12-H U.S. Government Printing Office, Washington, D.C.

[126] See Juran, J. M., Quality Problems, Remedies and Nostrums, *Industrial Quality Control,* June 1966, pp. 647–653.

selected QC Circle team. The selection is competitive, based on outstanding QC Circle projects. The books contain descriptions of these projects as well as information of the general approach to QC Circle activity used by the companies who are sponsoring the respective team members. The projects make rewarding study.

3. "Jishu Kanri Activities in the Japanese Steel Industry," Japan Iron and Steel Institute, Toyko, April 1971 (in English). This is similar to reference 2, but oriented entirely to the Japanese steel industry.

4. *Gemba to QC* (Quality Control for the Foreman), JUSE (in Japanese). This monthly journal, which as of 1971 had a circulation of over 90,000 copies, consists largely of lively descriptions of projects worked out by QC Circles. The competition for publication in this journal is keen, and the projects again make rewarding reading.

5. *Reports of Statistical Applications Research*, JUSE (in English). This monthly journal sometimes includes descriptions of projects of QC Circles. In addition, there is a periodic updating of the status of the QC Circle movement, e.g., by K. Ishikawa, vol. 16, no. 3, 1969.

6. J. M. Juran, The QC Circle Phenomenon, *Industrial Quality Control*, January 1967, pp. 329–336. The first full-scale report by a Westerner on the QC Circle movement. Widely reproduced and translated into numerous languages.

7. J. M. Juran (ed.), The Japanese QC Circle: Questions and Answers, *Quality*, Summer 1967, pp. 37 and 38. The discussion about QC Circles at the 1966 Stockholm Conference of the European Organizations for Quality Control.

8. Color slide series (88 slides, 35 mm) with a narration tape (in English; 28 minutes) available from Japanese Union of Scientists and Engineers. Concept and birth of a QC Circle, plus case example. See also J. M. Juran, QC For Foremen and Workers, An International Summary, *Reports of Statistical Applications Research*, Japanese Union of Scientists and Engineers, vol. 16, no. 4, 1969, pp. 15–22. This paper was the opening lecture of the 8th Conference on QC for Foremen before an audience of 3,200 foremen.

Documentation: Configuration Management

ROBERT K. RUZICKA, SR.

Brookfield Stationers*
Brookfield, Wisconsin

INTRODUCTION

Attainment of product quality requires an extensive activity of creating and using many kinds of information. Each Section of this Handbook includes discussions of those aspects of information creation and usage which are pertinent to the subject matter of that Section. Collectively, these needs for information add up to a large, complex network or system consisting of numerous interrelated subsystems.

The present Section is concerned with two major components of this information system:

1. *Documentation.* This concerns the overall system used for collection, analysis, and use of quality information. Documentation which is done mainly by manual "paper work" systems is discussed in this Section. Documentation which is done mainly by computer is discussed in Section 20, which follows.

2. *Configuration Management.* This is a special information system used to maintain product identity, especially during a time of engineering change. This special system is discussed in detail in this Section.

Several recent major trends have required that manufacturers expand their infor-

---

* At the time this manuscript was in preparation, the author was Chief Quality Engineer, Allis-Chalmers Corporation, Milwaukee, Wisconsin.

mation systems with respect to documentation and configuration management:

1. Government and commercial customers have shifted from emphasis on incoming inspection to emphasis on surveillance as a basis for vendor relations. These surveillance schemes require that the manufacturer provide extensive objective proof that all requirements have been met.

2. Government regulators are insisting on extensive documentation by manufacturers as part of the plan for protecting safety and health of users. For example, a 1971 regulation requires that manufacturers of automotive tires maintain records which will identify the ultimate purchaser of every tire.

3. Consumer advocates are urging more documentation as a means of providing information to consumers.

4. Product liability cases and threats are forcing manufacturers to establish defensive schemes of documentation.

These and other demands have worked their way into the contracts, specifications, codes, and other overriding standards of practice. Manufacturers are required to create, maintain, and retain records at all stages of product progression from design to usage, including records for such specific reasons as:

Failure or defect analysis	Corrective action
Process control	Product improvement
Product redesign	Quality cost analysis
Warranty analysis	Liability claims
Evidence of the actual state of the product	Product and component "traceability"[1]

It would be theoretically possible to create separate document networks to respond to each one of the foregoing needs. Experience has shown that where this is done, each individual involved tends to design his network around his personal experience and concepts (which may not fit the next incumbent). Often his design is built to satisfy a specific crisis rather than to handle the main stream of traffic in the most economical way. Moreover, this every-one-for-himself approach creates waste and confusion, since the networks have a great deal in common. In consequence, the trend is to provide for a comprehensive design of documentation which can meet all needs. This comprehensive response is known as the *systems approach*.

Under the systems approach, a skilled staff specialist is assigned to examine all needs for documentation and to design a system which will economically satisfy them all. His design is subject to review by the various line managers who have needs to be met, and these reviews are a check on the adequacy of the design. In turn, the staff specialist becomes a check on those managers who are overly concerned with the short range or with specific crises (provision is made for these crises under the "management by exception" principle). Such an approach also goes far to depersonalize the system, so that turnover in personnel will not render it inoperative.

The systems approach also has some disadvantages. It is a much longer process than the alternative of problem-by-problem solution. It requires an investment in salaries to specialist insiders or fees to outsiders. It is oriented more to fundamental prevention of chronic problems than to solving of sporadic problems. None of these features (lengthy analyses, investment for the long view, and emphasis on prevention) is immediately helpful to managers under the pressure of today's crises.[2]

---

[1] See Section 9, under Traceability.

[2] See, in this connection, Milroy, Neil, The Disintegration of an Information System, in R. N. Anthony (ed.), "Management Control Systems, Cases and Readings," Richard D. Irwin, Inc., Homewood, Ill., 1965, pp. 17–29.

CONFIGURATION MANAGEMENT

As a rough definition, configuration management is the means by which product and documentation are kept mutually identified. However, both the words in this term are given different meanings in different companies, so that one must understand the deeds behind the words if he is to understand the meanings given to the term in any company.

Configuration   The configuration of a product is the inherent nature of that product. The completeness of the description of this "nature" varies. In some companies, "configuration" is used in the narrow sense of size, shape, and other physical and chemical characteristics. However, in other companies, "configuration" includes facts such as the following:

1. The physical item conforms to issue 04 of the engineering drawing.
2. The steel was purchased from Feric Steel Furnace on Purchase Order Number 230656, dated 3/27/71, was made on Heat Number WX 37791, and conforms to ASTM 176-61T.
3. The welding was done by operator number 29991 using TIG process 10-721 during April 1971, at which time his license to weld was still in force.
4. The bracket on the item was rejected on April 28, 1971, because the 2.176-diameter hole was off location (2.719 instead of 2.705 ± .010), after which acceptance "as is" was authorized by Engineer Joe Jensen on May 6, 1971.

This broader definition of configuration obviously includes also the identification of the pertinent materials, processes, personnel, etc., which have collectively created the product, plus the data which proves that the resulting product conforms to specifications. Some identification may be marked on the product,[3] but mainly the identification and proof of adequacy are achieved through chains of documentation. The documents consist of engineering drawings, specifications, in-process inspection reports, acceptance inspection and test results, special test results, etc. These inputs are symbolized in Figure 19-1, along with some of the resulting outputs.

Management   In most companies, "management" of configuration is synonymous with the processing of engineering changes. However, this "processing" is given various meanings. At one extreme, the real decisions all rest with the designers, and the "processing" of engineering changes consists solely of assuring that the documentation and products are changed to conform to the intent of the engineers' designs. At the other extreme, processing the engineering change becomes a highly formalized, closely coordinated activity in which the coordinating agency carries a good deal of weight in the decisions which are made.

The trend has been toward the more formalized, coordinated approach. The reason is that as products have become more complex, the effect of an engineering change has multiplied in complexity and in cost.[4] Since more is at stake and the chance for error is multiplied, the companies have made their review structure more elaborate in order to guard against unneeded or unwise changes and against errors in introducing needed changes.

Taken together, the words "configuration management" are in many companies regarded as synonymous with a formalized approach for assuring that engineering changes are correctly carried out. Providing this assurance involves several elements which collectively constitute configuration management in these companies.

---

[3] For further discussion on physical product identification and traceability, see Section 9, under Traceability.

[4] In one important type of aircraft, a total of 195 engineering changes were processed in one year at an average cost of about $127,000 per change. Haddenhorst, R. G., Paper 69-DE-54, Design Engineering Conference, American Society of Mechanical Engineers, May 1969.

Organization   Special organization machinery is set up to coordinate the engineering changes.   This machinery consists of some combination of the following.

1. A published procedure which defines the role of each department.   Action is by the line departments and coordination is by the procedure.   This approach is sometimes the sole engineering change machinery, e.g., in small companies for noncritical changes or in any company for situations in which there is a continuing procession of many small changes.

Inputs	Documentation system	Outputs and uses
Configuration data		Corrective action loops
Contracts		Discrepancy identification
Product development data	Forms	Failure analysis
Design specifications		Corrective action
Process, other specifications	Procedures	
Engineering changes		Configuration management
	Data recording	Engineering change control
		Traceability
Inspection and test data from:	Data processing	
Receiving inspection	Manual	Improvement programs
Vendor surveillance	Electronic	Quality cost analysis
Process control	Other	Quality improvement
Final inspection, test		
Field performance results	Distribution	Executive reports by time
		Product, responsibility, etc.
	Filing	Vendor performance
Discrepancy data	Retention	In-house performance
Vendor failures	Retrieval	Field performance
Process out of control		Cost results
Scrap rework		Improvement projects
Field complaints, claims		
Warranty charges		Quality assurance to:
Product safety claims		Management
		Customers
		Regulators
		Etc.

Fig. 19-1   Model of documentation system.

2. A project engineer plus "sign off" by the line departments, usually Design, Manufacture, and Quality Control.   Here the project engineer provides coordination.

3. An Engineering Change Committee which provides not only coordination but also a degree of decision making as to the merits of the proposed change.

4. A Project Change Administrator who prepares plans, secures approvals, publishes reports, expedites, etc.   Use of such Administrators tends to be limited to cases where engineering changes are very complex and costly.

Classes of Change   A convenient aid for configuration management is to classify the changes as to priority.   Companies which use only two classes[5] define them somewhat as follows:

Class A Changes.   These are changes ordered by the customer or changes in-

---

[5] Some companies use three or more classes, with appropriate definitions for each.

tended to provide remedies for product safety hazards, deficiencies in field usage, high costs, late deliveries, inadequate field interchangeability, retrofits in the field.

Class B Changes.   These are any changes not classed in Class A, e.g., minor improvements, phasing out of obsolete products.

In companies using such systems of classifying changes, the class of change is decisive as to:

1. The choice of organization to be used in coordinating the change; e.g., for Class A changes, the combination of Committee and Administrator may be used, but not for Class B changes.

2. The extent to which the change will be made effective in various categories of product: in field service, in the finished-goods pipeline, in process of manufacture, etc.

Formalized Review Procedure   As the formalized coordination concept takes hold, there evolves a structured review procedure. A sequence of essential tasks is established,[6] and forms are designed to require that all changes go through this sequence.[7]

In the formalized reviews, close attention is paid to clear definition of the "baseline," i.e., the intended design. (During the various phases of product development, there are several design stages.) Unless this base line is clear, the reviews and actions will become confused and will work at cross purposes.[8]

Once the baseline and the intended changes are clear, the effect of the change is determined. This requires "tracking" the changes through assembly "trees," parts lists, processes, tools, instruments, etc. This tracking must be done through the entire hierarchy of product: system, subsystems, units, components, etc. Increasingly, computers are used to perform most of the tracking in the case of complex products.[9]

As it becomes clear just what aspects of the product are affected, it becomes possible to evaluate the cost and the benefit of the change. For this purpose it is also necessary to secure an inventory of the physical product which will be affected by the change; i.e., how many are in field use, how many in the pipeline, how many in a semifinished state. There may also be an effect on maintenance support, i.e., spare parts, repair parts, diagnostic instruments, and repair tools.

Control over this array of information and action is maintained by assigning a project number to each change and establishing for that project the same array of controls as goes with any complex project: list of activities, schedules, cost estimates, cost accounting, status reports, and documentation. This is done over the entire life cycle of the change, from design concept through being made fully effective.

In situations involving sizable, complex inventories, the "effectivity" of the change likewise becomes complex. If the units of product are serially numbered, then these serial numbers are used to define effectivity, e.g., serial numbers under 450 will undergo no change; serial numbers 451-620 will undergo change J only; serial numbers 621 and over will undergo changes J and K. Where serial numbers are not used, an alternative is to base the effectivity on status of the product in the pipeline,

[6] For a good deal of elaboration, see "Configuration Management Training Course," ASQC, 1968. Available from American Society for Quality Control, 161 W. Wisconsin Ave., Milwaukee, Wis. 53203.

[7] See, for example, Veith, Walter, Configuration Management, *Mechanical Engineering,* February 1967, pp. 20–25.

[8] For some elaboration on the definition of baselines, see Christiansen, E. G., What Is Configuration Management? *ASQC Technical Conference Transactions,* 1972, pp. 245-251.

[9] See, for example, Crossfield, A. Scott, and Torben O. Thams, Traceability and Configuration Data System, *Annual Technical Conference Transactions,* ASQC, 1965, pp. 36–40.

e.g., product already sold will undergo no change; product in finished goods or spare parts inventories will undergo change J; product in process will undergo changes J and K.

Provision is made for countdown, i.e., checking with all affected departments and verifying all critical elements affected.[10]

It is evident that what is called configuration management is several rather different though related functional activities. One classification of these activities consists of:

Configuration "Control." This is the basic decision making of what changes are to be made, the time schedules, the budgets, the extent of effectivity, etc.

Configuration Identification. This is the establishment of the necessary documentation, etc., for maintaining the integrity of identification and proof of conformance.

Configuration Accounting. This activity is concerned with following the progress of the change, verifying adherence to plan and procedure, and reporting progress.[11]

THE DOCUMENTATION SYSTEM

A documentation system is an information conversion process, as depicted in Figure 19-1. Numerous kinds of data enter as inputs from the left. The system converts these into outputs of various kinds, as listed on the right.

A study of Figure 19-1 soon makes clear that serving these multiple needs from such a wide array of inputs is best optimized by a "systems approach." The potentialities inherent in such a systems approach are so attractive that many companies have taken this road. They have evolved a coordinated system for originating and processing all documentation relating to the quality and reliability of the product.[12] These documents originate in, and are used by, numerous company departments. Hence the responsible departmental managers review the design of the system and concur both in the original content and in subsequent changes.

Scope and Purpose At the very outset, those who are to design the system should prepare a statement of scope and purpose. This statement should set out what the system is intended to provide, such as:

1. Identification of the information needed by company managers, customers, regulators, etc., for meeting specific customer requirements, taking corrective action, improving quality, reducing quality costs, analyzing field performance, etc.

2. Systematic means for collection, reduction, retention, and retrieval of the objective quality data needed to supply this information

3. Traceability of the data to the physical product at the various levels of completion and use

4. Design and provision of the data forms, report forms, etc., needed to collect, process, and report information to all concerned

5. Creation of a record file for information retrieval and retention

Unless scope and purpose are well defined at the outset, the managers who are being asked to approve creation of a "system" do not really understand what they are being asked to approve.

[10] See, for example, Kintigh, L. A., Management and Control of Product Engineering Changes—For Automobiles, Paper 69-DE-61, Design Engineering Conference, May 1969, American Society of Mechanical Engineers.

[11] For elaboration, see Schnipper, Joseph, Configuration Management and Quality Management, *ASQC 1971 Technical Conference Transactions,* pp. 53–60.

[12] See, for example, Smurthwaite, R. S., Meeting R & D Requirements for Reliability and Quality Control Data, *Journal of the Electronics Division,* ASQC, October 1966, pp. 3–12.

Policy   Proposals should be made to upper management to accept some broad policies governing the systems of documentation. Mainly these policies concern such matters as:

Organization.   Allocation of responsibility for creating and implementing the system should be made clear. This allocation varies from one company to another (due to size, complexity, history, etc.), but the tasks to be carried out are quite similar and consist of the following:

1. Design of the System. In very large companies this is usually done by the Quality Control Department in collaboration with the central Systems and Procedures Department (which often carries also a basic responsibility for Forms Management). In moderate-sized companies, the design may be by a systems analyst or by an outside consultant. In very small companies, the design will be by the owner-manager or by one of his assistants.

2. Review of the Design. The departments affected are asked to review and approve the design (or take exception to some of its features). These managers provide essential inputs to the design, since they carry responsibility for various essential decisions. For example, the Legal Department may require a ten-year retention period for certain types of test data. Marketing may require a provision, outside the regular system, for flexibility in dealing with special customer requirements for records and traceability. Other departments may require a high degree of autonomy as to certain subsystems, e.g., Production Engineering and their drawing control system.

3. Managing the System. The practice varies. In some companies the Quality Control Department has the responsibility. In others the Systems and Procedures Department is made responsible. In still others there are split responsibilities between Corporate Headquarters and Divisions, etc. All are workable so long as the responsibility is clear. Of course, the budget allocations should follow the assigned responsibilities.

4. Publication. This is commonly done by one of the staff departments, e.g., Systems and Procedures.

5. Design of Forms. This is often done by the department chiefly involved, but with review and veto power by the staff department. (See Forms Control, below.)

The presence of a staff Systems Department simplifies a good many tasks which are otherwise awkward to handle. These include preparing a budget for facilities, developing expertise in identifying the most appropriate office equipment and supplies, choosing good vendors (for forms, printing, etc.), maintaining the central file, observing retention periods, distributing changes, preparing training programs, and conducting audits. Of course, some of these tasks may be taken over by other departments; e.g., Purchasing may handle selection of vendors for office equipment and supplies.

Forms Control.   It has been a universal experience that when the various departments are given unchecked authority to create forms to meet departmental needs, the long-range result is a widespread duplication and accumulation of unnecessary paper. (The duplicate paper is often only the visible tip of the waste—the main waste is in the resulting duplication of data recording and processing.) To defend against this wasteful proliferation, many companies have instituted the concept of "Forms Control." Under this concept, someone with an interdepartmental outlook on the system (e.g., a forms analyst) must review the need for the form along with the related procedure, the form design, cost, etc., before the form is released for purchase and implementation.

The forms-control reviewer should have knowledge of the needs served by the present system, the way in which the present forms contribute to these needs, and the costs involved. In reviewing a proposed new or changed form, he should determine whether the need is already being met or can be met by a modification in some existing form. He should also determine if the use of standard business forms commercially available can do away with the need for a special form.   The published catalogs of standard business forms make it easy to conduct such a search. (Such catalogs are usually on file in the Purchasing Department.)

The forms-management group should conduct its own affairs in a way that makes forms easily traceable.   Each proposed form, intermediate draft, and approved draft should bear a unique distinguishing number in accordance with a mnemonic code.   The number assigned to each approved form then becomes its catalog number, and becomes the "specification" number for purchase or printing orders (without risk of confusion with other forms of similar title or description).   The forms analyst commonly aids in selecting the printer and becomes directly involved in the planning and execution of the printing order.

Investigation and Analysis of Needs   The most critical question in any documentation system is, "What outputs do we need?"   Some of the answers are obvious, e.g., the contract or the customer specifies certain documentation; the government regulators require certain documentation; the legal department requires certain documentation practices for product liability reasons.

In contrast, there are other "needed" outputs about which there is doubt.   These doubts can be resolved only by a clear understanding of just what *use* will be made of the output, and by whom.   It takes good analysis and persistence on the part of the analyst to determine just what the use will be.   Unless he persists, the risk is that some outputs will be merely a carryover of past practice to serve needs which are no longer valid.

An example of a positive approach to identifying needs is discussed in Section 21, under Executive Reports on Quality.   The reader is urged to review that discussion along with Table 21-3, as these exemplify a determined approach toward identification of needs.

The skilled analyst soon learns to identify the main sources which can contribute to a good system design.   In some line departments, the most useful source is not the manager (who may require a courtesy call in any event) but some key individual who can think incisively about systems.   The analyst should also be on the alert for instances in which the company's staff departments have a contribution to make. A problem of traceability may involve securing inputs from such departments as Legal (regulation, liability), Public Relations (consumerism), Personnel (employee identification).[13]

Tools and Methods   Design of the documentation system is aided by use of several well-known tools and study methods:

Flow Diagrams.   These are widely used in system design.   For example, Figure 21-3 (of Sec. 21) shows a flow diagram of the quality report system in a company making household appliances.   This diagram shows the essential information network of the system: what the input documents are, where they are introduced and what data they contain, how these data are processed and converted, who receives the processed information, which departments get what reports.   The flow diagram is always helpful to the analyst; without it he cannot explain the problem to some of

[13] The analyst should also look to the sources in the literature.   A major source is the publications of the American Society for Quality Control: The annual Proceedings of its conferences, the publications of its Divisions, the journals *Quality Progress* and *Journal of Quality Technology*.   Other sources include *Quality Management and Engineering,* Hitchcock Publishing Co., Wheaton, Ill.; and *Administrative Management,* Geyer-McAllister Publications, New York.

the other people. In complex cases he cannot explain the problem even to himself unless he creates the flow diagram.

Traffic Density. The analyst should also study the "traffic pattern" to be sure that what he designs is responsive to the usual situation, not the unusual. A "system" is essentially a multiple-use plan—a device for impersonally coordinating repetitive deeds over and over again without having to repeat the planning over and over again. The repetitiveness may involve requests for proposals, customer contracts, engineering changes, disposition of nonconforming materials, processing of customer complaints, etc. The analyst should carefully avoid designing the system around one or several exceptional cases which are brought to his attention by defensive managers. He should listen to these, but he should also examine a representative sample of the repetitive events around which his system is to be built. Such a sample will be more likely to disclose the nature of the great majority of cases, and it is around these that the main stream of the system should be designed. If the system is designed to meet the few unusual cases, it will force all the usual cases to carry the extra costs which are warranted only for the unusual cases.

Manual or Electronic Data Processing? While electronic data processing is in wide use, manual methods remain, and most companies make use of some of each. Hence the analyst must consider these alternatives, since the detailed design of the system is greatly influenced by this choice. This choice is usually dictated by the volume of data, the extent of multiple use, and the general progress the company has made in going to electronic systems.

One trap to avoid is to assume that the system for dealing with discrepant material must be the same as that for nondiscrepant material. In many situations, the best system for discrepant material may remain manual even if a different system is used for nondiscrepant material. For example, in one company, as part of a major revision of the quality reporting system, it was decided to use an electronic data system for recording and processing data on conforming lots of product but to use a manual system of the edge-punched-card variety (see below) for nonconforming lots of product.[14]

Even more serious is the trap of assuming that all product lines must use the same system. Some product lines demand elaborate documentation systems which are a waste for other product lines. In such cases the preferred practice is to establish alternative systems, each able to meet the needs of its product line. The analysis then includes a determination of which of the alternatives to apply.[15]

Edge-punched Cards. An ingenious method of simplifying analysis of data without use of electronic machinery is the edge-punched card (Figure 19-2). The card may be used both as an original data recording form and as a method of analysis. The coding consists of notching the cards so as to leave some holes intact and obliterate others. Sorting is then done by inserting several long needles into the pack of cards to pick up those which have been unnotched for the variables under study (Figure 19-3).

The method is economically applicable to intermediate arrays of data which require multiple sorting during analysis.

Procedures Once the system has been agreed on, it is reduced to written procedures which set out the details of how the agreed on system is to be operated. Procedure writing may be done either by the Systems and Procedures Department or

---

[14] Private communication to J. M. Juran. See, in this connection Cohen, G. B., EDP or Pencil and Paper, *Industrial Quality Control,* May 1964, pp. 8–10.

[15] A parallel is seen in the problems of quality planning. See Section 6, under Spectrum of Projects.

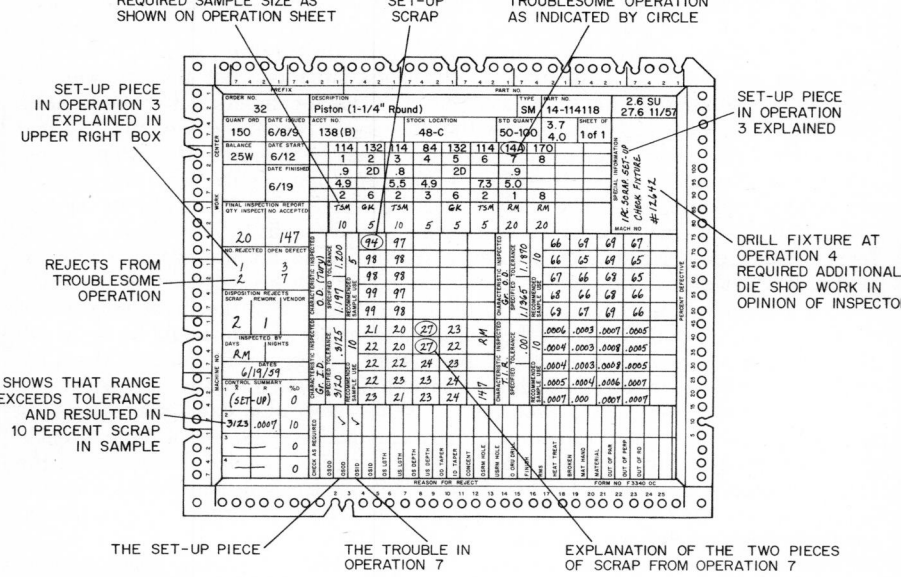

Fig. 19-2   Edge-punched card.

by the Quality Control Department.   Either way, the procedure follows the format of the Quality Control Manual[16] and becomes a part of it.   A typical format would be:

1. Scope and purpose
2. Applicable documents
3. Responsibilities
4. Procedures

The writeup should be in enough detail to make clear who is to do what and how, along with why, when, and where.   It is good practice to include flow diagrams as an aid to quick, sure understanding.

Approval routines for procedures commonly provide for "signing off"; i.e., the departments other than the issuing department sign the final document to show their review and concurrence.   It is a useful practice, since managers can be changed and memories can be fallible.

Audit   The general approach to audits in the quality function is set out in Section 21, under several headings commencing with Audit of Quality Plans.   This general approach applies fully to audit of systems to see if the execution follows the plan.

Where the use of systems is extensive, audits can make use of the concept of random sampling; i.e., if there are 60 forms in a system, 5 may be audited each month on a random number basis.   Other features of the system can likewise be audited at random, e.g., retention dates, security of classified papers, etc.   It is useful, when auditing, to maintain a record of the degree of compliance to system.

Training   Well-written procedures plus the associated flow diagrams are in themselves good training devices.   However, it is useful, especially at the time of introducing new procedures, to set up training seminars, so that those who are to make

---

[16] See generally Section 6, under The Quality Control Manual.

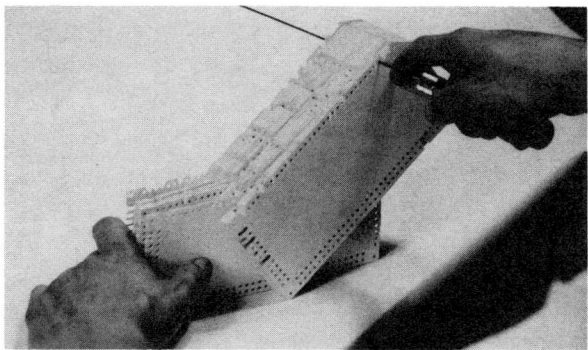

Fig. 19-3   Edge-punched-card sorting.

the system work understand what is expected of them.   See, in this connection, the general approach to training in Section 17.

FORMS DESIGN

A *form* is a preplanned document which accommodates the entry of specified information.   By its nature, it contains hints or clues on the type and amount of information to be entered by the originator.   This is accomplished by accurate box descriptions. By the numbering or color of the copies made at one writing (by the originator) it may also indicate who will get copies of the information being recorded.

The form is a preplanned activity; i.e., before the form can be designed and used, someone must determine what information is needed on the form, what information is available to be entered on the form, what information must be extracted from the form, and the information which must be added.   As related to a data system, a form is a key item used as input and output.   It may consist physically of a tag, card, sheet of paper, or a rubber stamp.

As an input document, the title of the block or brief descriptions on the form gives greater assurance that all the required data will be entered instead of leaving it to the memory and judgment of the originator to write it on a blank piece of paper. Continuity and consistency of information are improved.   Within the paper-work process, forms are used to summarize, classify, and rearrange source data for transmission to another analyst, work station, or decision maker.

The Forms Designer   Many persons with systems experience can design adequate single-sheet forms for departmental use or for conveying information to one other department.   Examples of such simple forms are Inspection Reports, Test Reports, Minutes of Meetings, Data Sheets, Reports.   However, it is useful to establish a standard such as is shown in Table 19-1.   Such a standard can help the amateurs turn out work of a more professional nature.

For more complex purposes, the forms also become more complex (e.g., multiple copies, spot carbon, die cuts), and the need arises for an experienced specialist to do the forms design and forms management.   (It is no place for a newly hired college graduate to receive his company orientation or for make-work projects.)   The specialist may be a person in the Quality Control Department, in which case part of his time must be budgeted for this purpose.   Alternatively, the specialist may be someone of recognized talents from another department, e.g., Marketing or Advertising.   Specialist service is also available from the vendors of printed forms and office equipment.   These vendor companies also offer a wide array of standard busi-

TABLE 19-1   Forms Design Standards*

The following standards should be applied by the initiating unit when drawing a rough sketch of the form to be submitted with the forms requisition. The forms management staff in reviewing the request will make any necessary adjustment of specifications before forwarding the requisition for duplicating or printing.

1. Cut Form Sizes

Any size that can be cut from 32 x 42 inches without waste, particularly sizes $3\frac{1}{2}$ x 8, 4 x $5\frac{1}{4}$, 8 x $10\frac{1}{2}$ and 16 x $10\frac{1}{2}$.

Normal file card sizes: 3 x 5, 4 x 6, 5 x 8.

Post card sizes: $3\frac{1}{4}$ x $5\frac{1}{2}$.

Considerations:
   (a) Avoid crowding content;
   (b) Conform to dimensions of storage and filing facilities (i.e., legal size, letter size, etc.);
   (c) Fit to standard office machines for fill-in (i.e., typewriter, bookkeeping machine, etc.);
   (d) Fit to standard-size envelopes.

2. Paper Weight and Grade

Operating unit ordinarily should specify one of the following four:

Mimeograph. . . . . 36 lb. (basis 17 x 22)
Card . . . . 180 lb. (basis $25\frac{1}{2}$ x $30\frac{1}{2}$)
Sulphite. . . . . 32 lb. (basis 17 x 22)
Bond (25% rag). . . . . 32 lb. (basis 17 x 22)

Selection should be based upon:
   a. Handling requirements;
   b. Writing method;
   c. Number of copies to be made at one writing;
   d. Length of time the form will be retained;
   e. Printing requirements (i.e., printing on two sides, by a given process, etc.);
   f. Filing and storage space requirements (affected by thickness of paper).

3. Color of Paper

Specify color only when needed for emphasis or for more efficient filing, routing or sorting. Reduce the need for colored paper by use of sorting symbols, bold headings, heavy ruled lines or other devices when possible. Exceptions permissible for specific organization or operating requirements.

4. Color of Ink

Specify other than black ink only when fully justified by volume and increased efficiency in use of the form and when the more economical possibilities of colored paper are inadequate. Two colors should be avoided except under extreme justification.

5. Identification and Heading

Heading may be centered across entire top of form or centered in space to the left of any entry boxes placed in upper right. (Upper right should be designed for file or other ready reference entries if needed.) Within space decided upon, arrange generally as follows:

Form number and issuance or revision date—upper left corner.

Agency name and location (if needed)—upper left (under form number) or top center (depending on its importance in use of form).

Form title—center of top (under agency name and location, if that item is centered). Use conspicuous type.

*Reproduced from "Forms Management," "Records Management Handbook," FPMR 101-11.2, U.S. Government Printing Office, Washington, D.C., 1969.

TABLE 19-1 Forms Design Standards *(Continued)*

Bureau of the Budget number and expiration date, for Federal report forms—upper right corner.
Exception: Run identification across bottom of vertical-file-card forms unless needed for file-reference purposes.

6. Instructions

Well designed forms require few instructions other than captions and item headings. When required, instructions usually should—
a. Be set in two or more narrow columns rather than full-width lines.
b. Be listed as numbered items rather than in paragraph style.
c. Be placed as near items to which they apply as possible (unless length would detract from effective layout).
When instructions are segregated on form, they should be placed—
a. At top right or top center, if concise and applicable to the whole form.
b. At bottom, if that will make possible more economical use of space.
c. On reverse, if no space available on face.

7. Address

If name and address are inserted on form by agency prior to mailing, position of name and address should be suitable for window-envelope use. Forms requiring return to an agency should be properly identified as provided under Standard No. 5.
Forms intended for use in window envelopes must conform to postal regulations, which in general provide that nothing other than name and address, and possibly mailing symbol, shall appear in the window. The form must fit the envelope to avoid shifting of the address. Standard-size envelopes only should be used. *Post Office Department Schedule of Award of Contracts for Envelopes* is the guide to standard envelope sizes.

8. Pre-printed Names or Facsimile Signatures

If form is to be stocked for continuing use, personal names or signature of official may be preprinted only on special justification or by legal requirement (to avoid having large numbers of forms made obsolete by change of officials). Preprinting of titles only or the use of rubber stamps or automatic signature inscribers are alternatives to be considered.

9. Form Arrangement

a. Align beginning of each writing space on form vertically for minimum number of tabular stops.
b. If box design is used:
 (1) Serially number each box in its upper left-hand corner;
 (2) Start caption in upper left-hand corner, to right of number, leaving fill-in space below caption;
 (3) Draw box size to provide sufficient space for fill-in.
c. Place essential information where it will not be obscured by stamps, punches, or staples, or be torn off with detachable stubs.
d. Group related items.
e. Include "to" and "from" spaces for any necessary routing.
f. Provide for use of window envelopes, when appropriate, to save additional addressing.
g. To the extent practicable, provide same sequence of items as on other forms from which or to which information is to be transferred.
h. Arrange information for ease in tabulating or transferring to machine punch cards, if those are involved.

TABLE 19-1   Forms Design Standards *(Continued)*

10. **Check Boxes**

Use check boxes when practicable.
   a. Place check boxes either before or after items, but all in the corresponding positions within any line series.
   b. Avoid columnar grouping of check boxes if possible, because of poor registration when carbon copies are required. Place check boxes before first column and after the second column when there are two adjacent columns of questions.

11. **Margins**

Printing Margin. Printed all-around borders usually should not be used since they tend to increase production problems and costs. In any event an extra margin of 3/8 inch or not less than 3/10 inch from edge of paper should be allowed on all 4 sides for gripping requirements in printing and as a safety margin for cutting. No printing—neither border nor text—should be permitted in that space.
Binding Margin. For press-type fastener, side or top, 1 inch; for ring binder, 1 inch (printing permitted but no fill-in within these margins).
Fill-in Margin. Top typewriting line, at least 1 1/8 inch from top of paper if possible. Bottom typewriting line, not less than 3/4 inch from bottom. Hand fill-in permissible above or below these lines.

12. **Space Requirements for Fill-in**

Typewritten— 10 characters to the horizontal inch to accommodate both elite and pica typewriters;
   3 fill-in spaces to the vertical inch, each space being double typewriter space.
Handwritten— 1/3 more space horizontally than for typewritten fill-in;
   3 spaces to the vertical inch, each space double that of typewriter space.

13. **Rulings**

   a. Use heavy 1 1/2-point or parallel 1/2-point rulings as first and last horizontal lines, between major divisions, and across column headings.
   b. Use 3/4-point rulings across bottom of column headings, and above a total or balance at the foot of a column.
   c. Use hairline rulings for regular lines and box lines when no emphasis required.
   d. Use 3/4-point rulings for vertical subdivision of major sections or columns.
   e. Use leaders as needed to guide eye in tabular or semi-tabular items.

14. **Signature and Approval Date**

Single handwritten signatures usually go at bottom right of last page. Allow 1/2 inch (three single typewriter spaces) vertically and three inches horizontally.
Two handwritten signatures, normally left and right at bottom of last page.
Space below the 3/4-inch bottom typewriter margin generally reserved for handwritten signatures and dates.

15. **Two-Sided Forms**

   a. Two-sided forms ordinarily should be printed head to foot (top of front to bottom of back), especially if top-punched for binder use.
   b. If punched in left margin for binder use, 2 sided forms should be head to head.
   c. Three- or 4-page forms (one sheet folded once) should be head to head throughout if open-side style, and head to foot if open-end (so that, when opened for use, head of third page follows foot of second page).

TABLE 19-1   Forms Design Standards *(Continued)*

d. Head-to-foot open-end forms are preferable for machine fill-in.

e. For multi-page forms, separate sheets of proper page size should be used instead of larger sheets folded to page size, unless the larger sheets can be cut economically from standard paper sizes and run on standard printing or duplicating equipment.

16. Prenumbering

Use prenumbered forms only if accounting or control is required for each form or document. Place number in extreme upper right corner.

17. Punching

For standard press-type and 3-hold ring binders:
Distance from edge of paper to center of hole should measure $\frac{3}{8}$ inch;
If 2 holes are punched, for press-type fastener, the distance between centers should be $2\frac{3}{4}$ inches;
If 3 holes are punched, distance from center to center of adjacent holes should be $4\frac{1}{4}$ inches.

---

ness forms which can be purchased in small quantities with the customer's name and address imprinted thereon. Alternatively, rubber stamps can be used to overprint the standard form (see Figure 19-4). Finally, design service can be bought from companies which specialize in this.

In large corporations there are always staff departments which include specialists who are available as in-house consultants. Such specialists commonly take on the broad responsibility for systems analysis, forms design and construction, forms layout, vendor selection, etc.

The Work Elements   These involve a great deal of detail, most of which is beyond the scope of this Handbook.[17] The high points may be summarized as follows:

Establish the Need.   Some of this has already been noted in the discussion of The Documentation System, above, under the heading Investigation and Analysis of Needs. In addition, the analyst should study the information network to understand the impact of the new form, i.e., Are there added uses beyond those known to the proponent? Is the information already available from other sources? (Often enough, two or three unrelated documents already include the information.) In addition, there are some questions which must be answered to provide essential detail for the remaining list of activities. For example: How often will the new form be executed? In how many copies? Where, how long, and under what criteria will the form be filed? Which copy will be designated as the official file copy? Which copies will be designated as working copies? Will other departments want to enter data of their own on the form?

The prime method for securing first answers to the foregoing is the interview. This should not be limited to the requester; it should extend to key people among users and among the supporting services, e.g., duplicating, filing. A flow chart such as that in Figure 19-5 is of great aid in identifying who the key people are and what the likely problems will be, e.g., storage, retention.

Estimate of Costs.   This includes the one-time initial costs of labor and material for drafting, plate making, and first printing. It also includes the subsequent, repetitive costs. From these estimates and from estimates of savings, decisions on

---

[17] For additional detail, see Osteen, Carl E., Forms Analysis, Office Publications, Inc., Stamford, Conn., 1969. See especially Chaps. 4 through 9. See also Kaiser, Julius B., Forms Design and Control, American Management Association, 1968.

RECEIVING RECORD

No. 0056	DATE March 27 to 71	Purchase Order No. or Returned Goods 160560

RECEIVED FROM	LM Woodworking		PREPAID

ADDRESS	9106 N Green St		COLLECT

VIA	their truck	FREIGHT BILL NO.	

	QUANTITY	ITEM NO.	DESCRIPTION
1	500	1	$\frac{1}{4}$"x 1" dowels
2			
3			
4			
5			ACCEPT/REJECT INSPECTION
6			
7			Lot 500 Insp 20 Def 5 Acc 15
8			Sort No 480
9			
10			Date 3/29/71 By RJR
11			Defects Qty Disp Resp By
12			$\frac{1}{16}$ 1 Crack 3 use as is LMW cnt

REMARKS: CONDITIONS, ETC. $\frac{1}{4}$" is $\frac{9}{32}$ 3 use as is LMW cnt

No. Packages 2	Weight 10 lbs.	Received By L.M.R.	Checked By J.K.J.	Delivered To Stock
Rediform 2H 260		BE SURE TO MAKE THIS RECORD ACCURATE AND COMPLETE		

Fig. 19-4 Use of rubber stamp to overprint standard form. *(Courtesy Rediform Office Products.)*

optimum reorder quantities and on still other economic questions can be made, e.g., combining forms.

Layout of Forms. The first step is to define precisely what data are to be entered on the form. Next, a rough layout is prepared on quadrille paper or on layout sheets provided by vendors. The data boxes are mapped out for convenience in either data entry or data usage. (See Table 19-1, paragraph 12, for recommended spacing to avoid crowding.)

Some data blocks are of the forced-choice type, e.g., Figure 19-6. Others permit the originator to make a narrative entry. Experience shows that forced-choice entries are more objective and accurate and that they permit easier data processing.

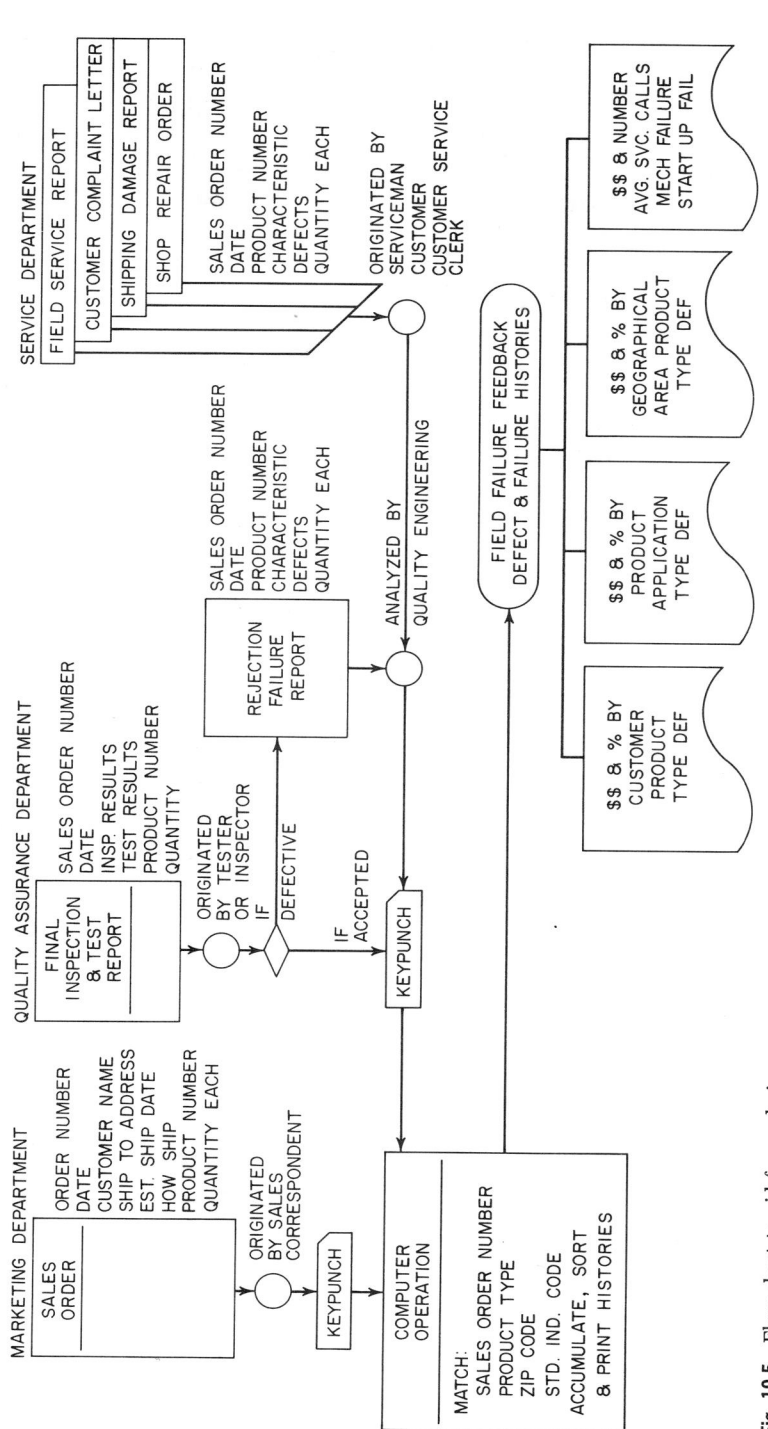

Fig. 19-5 Flow chart to aid forms design.

An additional method of improving the accuracy of data entries is through establishing a standard system of code designation for product names, defect names, etc.[18] Such standardization clears up misunderstandings among departments. In addition, the use of code numbers simplifies data entry and especially data processing.

Form size represents a constant struggle among three competing needs: (1) making the blocks large enough, (2) getting all needed information on the form, and (3) keeping the overall size of the form within a given standard.

---

3. DISCOVERED DURING

1 ☐ Receiving Inspection/Test	5 ☐ In-Plant Inspection
2 ☐ Process Capability Study	6 ☐ Final Acceptance Inspection
3 ☐ First Piece Inspection	7 ☒ Final Acceptance Test
4 ☐ Initial Sample Approval	8 ☐ Product Quality Audit
0 ☐ Other:	

---

4. DESCRIPTION OF DEFECT

CHARACTERISTIC

1 ☐ Cleanliness	4 ☐ Finish	7 ☒ Length	10 ☐ Straightness
2 ☐ Diameter	5 ☐ Flatness	8 ☐ Location	11 ☐ Squareness
3 ☐ Depth	6 ☐ Height	9 ☐ Radius	12 ☐ Thickness
0 ☐ Other:			13 ☐ Width

OBSERVED VALUE: *1.365   1.392   1.372*

DEFECT TYPE

1 ☐ Under Low Limit	4 ☐ Corrosion	7 ☐ Burrs
2 ☒ Over High Limit	5 ☐ Foreign Material	8 ☐ Cracks
3 ☐ Out of Specification	6 ☐ Damaged/Broken	9 ☐ Voids
0 ☐ Other:		

CAUSE

1 ☐ Not Determined	4 ☐ Careless Handling	7 ☐ Storage
2 ☐ Unknown	5 ☐ Improper Cleaning	8 ☐ Wrong Item
3 ☐ Transportation	6 ☐ Stock Rotation	9 ☐ Workmanship
0 ☒ Other: *Jig in error*		

Fig. 19-6   Format for forced-choice entries.

Standardization of sizes permits economic use of paper, i.e., less waste from use of standard sheet sizes, and economic use of file space. Standardization of contents permits other economies: multiple factories may use the same basic form (imprinting is added), larger runs may be printed, similar form designs may be "gang printed," etc.

When first developing a form, it is good practice to prepare a low-cost model and test this out in actual usage. The feedback from such usage and especially the

---

[18] See for example, Ziegler, Manfred, A Manual Defect Data Collection System, *Industrial Quality Control,* September 1965, pp. 113–115. In this example, the code letters are reproduced on the record blank as a convenience for the originator of the form. For examples in this Handbook, see Section 35, Table 35-2; also Section 43, Fig. 43-5.

errors made (i.e., error type and error frequency) will provide good information from which to revise the form for final layout and production.

Preparation of Procedure. The procedure is the widely used instruction in how to fill in and process the forms. What is helpful here is not to elaborate on the obvious, e.g., entering a part number. Instead, emphasis should be on the main sources of confusion and error as discovered from trial usage or from experience with similar forms. Normally the procedure is checked out with all departments involved in the flow diagram. Their sign-off approves the procedure and the associated form.

Forms Construction This concerns the physical attributes of the form other than layout and format. It includes such matters as number of copies, how these copies reproduce, how they are held together. It includes weight and color of paper, color of ink, etc.

Form construction interfaces with all other aspects of the documentation system: clerical labor or shop labor in originating the form; cost of providing copies for regular or occasional needs; adaptability to use in office machines; ease of subsequent use of the form for data additions, data removals, data processing, filing, storage.

Selection of paper is a major element of form construction. Paper must be chosen not only for its merits in current usage (e.g., opacity, erasability) but also for its suitability for storage (e.g., durability, permanence). Many storage requirements now extend beyond ten years due to new demands for record retention on matters of safety, liability, traceability, etc. Table 19-2 shows types and uses of paper and provides a basic knowledge of terms.

Specification of Forms Once form construction has been established, a specification embodying all technical information—i.e., type of paper, type of ink, method of fastening, etc.—is prepared for the form. This specification becomes the basis for future purchase. However, experience has shown that it is worthwhile to discuss the specification personally with the printer, especially if he is new to your company. Such personal discussion assures uniform interpretation and also secures the printer's suggestions for quality improvement or cost reduction.

Selection of Printer The general approach used for Vendor Qualification (see Section 10) applies to qualifying printers as vendors. Other than for very large printers, this industry does not use formal quality "systems" for controlling product quality.[19] In consequence, reliance must be placed on the adequacy of the printer's equipment, the evident competence of the supervision, and the submission of printed "proofs" prior to production runs.

Implementation This activity again follows the conventional practice used in introducing change. Target dates and lead times should be realistic. Training should be provided to the individuals involved, along with orientation for the supervision, the extent obviously depending on the complexity of the change. In some cases there is no substitute for workshop sessions in which the new forms are actually filled out, processed, etc., by those who will be required to do so thereafter. The training should also include persons outside the company (vendors, dealers, etc.) where they are critically involved.

QUALITY RECORDS FILE

There is extensive use of such files for current reference and as repositories. In small companies there may be only one such file, under the jurisdiction of the owner-manager or the chief inspector. As the company grows, there arise multiple files under multiple jurisdictions. Quality Control may maintain inspection records; Purchasing may maintain vendor quality records; Marketing may maintain product

---

[19] See Section 40, Graphic Arts Industry.

TABLE 19-2   Selection Guide for Types of Paper

Suggested use	Type of paper	Remarks
Permanent records or those having retention cycle, frequent handling, erasing, and posting	Rag or cotton	Usually available in the range of 25 through 100% cotton fiber content and substances of 9 through 20 lb. in a cockle or smooth finish. High erasability, handling, permanency. These characteristics increase in direct proportion with the percentage rag or cotton content.
Permanent and semipermanent	Sulphite bond	General-use for forms. Characteristics are good for usual applications.
For use with spirit duplicators	Duplicator bond	One type available for masters and another type for making copies. Usually available in substance of 16 or 20 lb.
Detect tampering	Safety bond	Used to detect tampering with entries on paper.
For uses in which handling, posting of figures, and erasing are great	Ledger bond	Has greater strength, opacity, erasability, and durability than other bond papers. Usually available in a substance of 28 lb.
Blueprints or blue or black line prints	Translucent	Has least opacity, so that information can be reproduced on diazo equipment which transmits light through the paper.
Light weight and for second copy	Onionskin	Also thin, which conserves file space. Usually available in 9-lb substance. This is also a bond type of paper.
File folders, cards, tags	Bristol	Stiff and heavy. Suitable for a great deal of handling.
File folders, index tags, and tags	Tag board	Strong and tough, but not as much as index bristol.
Tissue type used for second, third, etc. copy in multipart forms	Manifold	Similar in characteristics to bond. Available in an 8-lb substance.

warranty records, etc.   No matter what the jurisdiction, the underlying principles for keeping good record files are alike.

Files need not be physically centralized—more usually their location is based on easy access for the major user.   Nor is there need to establish a central file which contains copies of everything; relatively few records warrant the extra expense (space, file cabinets, labor, etc.) of such duplication.   What is important is to establish clear responsibility for custody plus good procedures for keeping the records complete, orderly, and secure.

Record File Content.   Mass filing requires that those who understand the subject matter should instruct the file clerks or the filing machinery on where to put what. This is done by creating numerical or word codes or indexes which then become the basis of document classification, filing, and retrieval.

Classification indexes are a detail of the utmost importance, since ease of filing and especially of retrieval is heavily influenced by the design of the indexing system. Extensive study has been devoted to this problem, and some good references are available.[20]   In addition, competent advice can be secured from professional librarians and from office equipment suppliers.   The latter have good literature describing indexing systems as well as ingenious equipment for making these systems effective.

Indexes can be set up on one or a combination of several bases, e.g., alphabetical-subject, numerical, document type.   For example, rejection reports might all be in the same file, subdivided by part number and in order of date.   However, with growth it becomes necessary to create a numerical index analogous to the Dewey Decimal System used in libraries.   For example, a major category may be 100 — Administration.   The subcategory Correspondence might have the number 110, and the sub-subcategory Announcements the number 111.   Below this, there might be Safety Announcements—111.1; Personnel Announcements—111.2; etc.

While choice of index categories is tailor-made, the following will satisfy the needs of most quality or inspection organizations:

100 — Administration
200 — Objective evidence
300 — Engineering Drawing and Specification
400 — Supplier
500 — Technical information

An example of subcategories structured around this list is shown in Table 19-3.

For each of the subcategories, filing criteria must be established on how to file, e.g., chronological, alphabetical, etc.   In addition, retention periods must be set up. Figure 19-7 is an example of a procedure setting up such criteria.

Information Retrieval.   The sole purpose of all the foregoing effort is to enable information to be "retrieved" accurately and economically within a reasonable time. If the record file has been badly designed or is poorly maintained, the effects will show up in high document retrieval costs, in long waiting times, and in a percentage of inability to retrieve at all.

A special problem in information retrieval is *data retrieval.*   The usual problem here is the compilation of information which may be scattered among numerous documents.   To make data retrieval possible requires that the data be entered in the documents in a way which permits ready retrieval, e.g., key punching on data processing cards.   Here again, indexes or codes are needed.   Some consist of the serial numbers of documents, e.g., sales orders, repair reports, invoices.   For other purposes, a number of familiar codes may be used:

Purpose of sorting is by:	*Familiar code numbers available*
Geographical locations	Post office zip code (the first three digits are usually adequate), telephone area code
Industry	Bureau of Labor Statistics Standard Industrial Classification Code (SIC)
Person	Social Security Number
Quality control subject matter	ASQC Literature Classification System code (LCS)

Filing Procedures.   It is good practice to reduce to writing the procedures for operation of the quality records file.   One section of this procedure references all applicable documents, e.g., the Quality Control Manual or the company's general manual on Records Management.   Another section makes clear the responsibilities involved; e.g., which department has custody of which records.

Filing Equipment.   Office equipment manufacturers offer a wide assortment of

[20] For example, Guidelines for the Development of Information Retrieval Thesauri, U.S. Government Printing Office, Washington, D.C., 1967.

TABLE 19-3   Quality Records File Index*

100 ADMINISTRATION	400 SUPPLIER
101 Department Budget	401 Supplier Surveys
102 Business Plans	402 Active Suppliers
103 Employee Personnel Records	403 Inactive Suppliers
104 Personnel Certification	404 Quality Ratings
105 Quality Systems	405 Supplier Corrective Action Requests
106 Customer Usage	406 Qualified Supplier Lists
107 Professional Societies	407 Special Studies and Investigations
108 Training Courses	408 Test Records
109 Textbooks, Journals, etc.	409 Process Capability Studies
110 Definitions	410 First Piece Inspection Records
111 Quality Reports	411 General Correspondence
112 Correspondence	
113 Request for Quotation Review	500 TECHNICAL INFORMATION
114 Customer Contracts	501 Quality and Reliability Specifications
	502 Quality Standards
200 OBJECTIVE EVIDENCE	503 Calibration System
201 Inspection Reports	504 Statistical Calculations
202 Rejection Reports	505 Computer Programs
203 Process Capability Studies	506 Quality Audits
204 Part, Component Data History	507 Process and Manufacturing Techniques
205 Quality Engineering Reports	508 Quality Manual Masters
206 Corrective Action Requests	509 Test Specifications
207 Field Failures, Defects, Complaints	510 Measurement Equipment
208 Customer Order File	511 Tooling
209 Part, Component, Assembly Product	512 Product Quality Plans
Reliability Data	513 Test and Inspection Equipment
210 Special Studies and Investigations	514 Catalogs and Sales Literature
	515 Company Product Literature
300 ENGINEERING DRAWINGS AND	516 Tooling Literature
SPECIFICATIONS	517 Parts and Component Literature
301 Materials	518 Competitor Product Literature
302 Detailed Parts	
303 Standard Components	
304 Subassemblies	
305 Assemblies	
306 Functional Systems	
307 Final Product	

* Courtesy Allis Chalmers Corporation.

filing cabinets, both as to size and as to methods of operation. The alternatives are well described in their catalogs, which they make readily available. These catalogs should be acquired and studied as a first step in selecting filing equipment. Design of filing equipment has been so aggressively pursued by the manufacturers that they have standard equipment which adequately solves virtually any problem in filing.

Retention Cycles. Documents are retained in one of two states:

1. Active. Such documents are held in readily accessible locations.

2. Inactive. These documents are also held, but not necessarily in readily accessible locations.

The state of activity is determined for various categories of documents through standardized retention periods and starting dates, as exemplified in Figure 19-7. At the end of the active period, the files may be transferred to an inactive file. At

INDEX NUMBER	CATEGORY	FILE CRITERIA	ACTIVE	FROM	INACTIVE
100	ADMINISTRATION-GENERAL				
100.1	Quality Records Index, Q.A.I. No. 301-1	Title	Current	N/A	N/A
101	Correspondence	Subject	2 yrs.	Dated	1 yr.
102	Quality Costs	Title	2 yrs.	Dated	5 yrs.
103	Personnel Certifications	Name/Type	Current	Termination	7 yrs.
104	Quality Systems	Subject	Permanent	N/A	N/A
105	QE Report (Masters)	Report No.	3 yrs.	Yr. Date	12 yrs.
106	Status Reports	Title	2 yrs.	Dated	5 yrs.
*110	Quality Manual (Masters)	Procedure No.	Superseded	Eff. Date	See 110.1
*110.1	Quality Manual (Record Copy)	Procedure No.	7 yrs.	Superseded Date	Permanent
*111	QA Instructions (Masters)	Q.A.I. No.	Superseded	Eff. Date	See 111.1
*111.1	QA Instructions (Record Copy)	Q.A.I. No.	7 yrs.	Superseded Date	Permanent
112	Training	Subject	1 yr.	Dated	3 yrs.
*120	Request for Quotation Review	Name & Bid No.	Awarded or 1 yr.	Dated	N/A
*121	Contracts	Name & SO No.	Until Ship Date	Awarded	N/A
130	Projects/Products (Overall Plans)	Name	Current	Date	7 yrs.
	*See 4.6 and 4.7 of Procedure for special instructions.				
200	OBJECTIVE EVIDENCE				
210	Nonconformance Reports	Yr. & Part No.	3 yrs.	Date	6 yrs.
215	Deviation from Specification	Yr/Qrtr/Product	2 yrs.	Date	5 yrs.
217	Part, Component, Product Data	Part No.	3 yrs.	Date	6 yrs.
220	Circuit Breaker Insp., & Test Data	Type & Serial No.	3 yrs.	Ship Date	6 yrs.
223	Insp. Record, Swgr.-Swbd. (6302)	Product & SO No.	3 yrs.	Ship Date	6 yrs.
225	Assembly, Product Data (Misc.)	Product & SO No.	3 yrs.	Ship Date	6 yrs.

Fig. 19.7 File categories and retention cycles. (*Courtesy Allis Chalmers Corporation.*)

the end of the inactive period, the files should be destroyed. The mechanism for administering these actions varies, one method being to mark the file folders themselves (Figure 19-8).

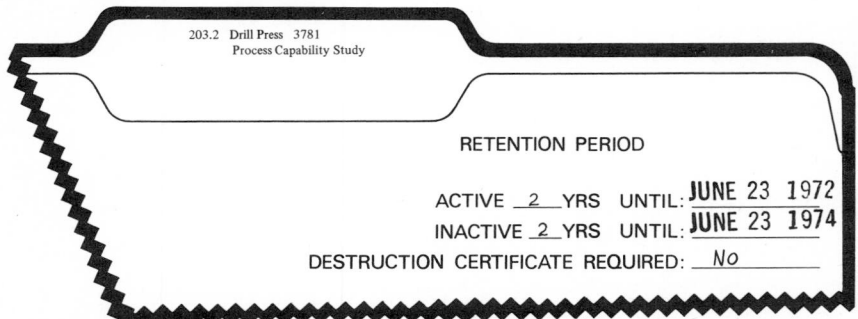

Fig. 19-8   Retention cycles printed on standard file folder.

Retention periods are chosen based on the following considerations:[21]

1. The frequency and extent of reference to the record by personnel of the organization

2. The existence of the same type of information elsewhere

3. The extent to which the record is transcribed or summarized in another record to be retained for a longer period of time

4. The necessity of the record as a support or explanation of another record to be retained for a long period of time

5. The importance of the record as an integral segment of the historic documents of the organization

6. The usefulness of the record for studies of procedures, company operations, and production

7. The value of the record in legal or other investigations

8. The effect that a change of law, regulation, or procedure may have on the value of the record

Record Security.   Record security is of two kinds:

1. Protection against unauthorized use, e.g., theft, espionage. The usual practice is to place restricted files in a restricted area presided over by a custodian. Such files are released only to persons who can establish adequate identification and who sign out the records. In such arrangements, the custodian is a key figure and should be chosen on the basis of a known record of integrity.

2. Protection against damage from natural causes, e.g., heat, water, dust, etc. This protection is provided by adequate design of the storage area itself. In addition, use may be made of redundancy, i.e., duplicate copies of important documents may be retained in a separate and even remote storage facility.

Microphotography.   Recent scientific developments have made it possible to miniaturize records through microphotography to a point that they occupy as little as 2% of the space occupied by the originals. The miniaturization has several forms, e.g., *microfilm,* which puts numerous document copies on a continuous film strip, and *microfiche,* which puts the copies on a card. Appropriate machines are available for reading these miniatures and for making full-sized copies from them.

---

[21] "Guide to Record Retention Requirements," U.S. Government Printing Office, Washington, D.C., 1970.

Assembly Name Mechanical Drive			Assembly No. 963234-03		Order No. 23-161-50		Date Jan.10'71	Serial No.
Part Name Linkage			Part No. 963234-651-03		Machine 41-031		Originated by P.L.B.G	
Lot Size 10	Qty Insp. 3	Qty Def. 2	Total Def. Pcs. 9	Vendor Name, Code	Purchase Order No.		Customer Name, Order No.	
CHARACTERISTIC	Acceptance Criteria		Description of Defects	Qty of Defects	DISPOSITION	Sorting Results		
						UseAsIs	Repair	Scrap
Length	1.931±.005		1.938,1.939	2	Repair		5	
Diameter	.625±.010		.637	1	Scrap			1
					Accepted	1		

ESTIMATED HRS	Dept. & Acct. Charged		Total	3	Total Pieces 1 7 2		Order No.	Qty.	Disp.
Scrap	Material	Labor	% or Amt.		Authorized Disposition Signature				
Repair 14.0	149	176	100%		Quality Assurance ✓ J.Hunt	Date 1/15/71			
Lost Labor 3.0					Engineering R.E.July	Date 1/15/71			
Total 17.0					Purchasing	Date			
By M.R.G									

Fig. 19-9 Inspection form—single lot.

This process has a definite place in record retention, but it must be employed with caution because of the costs involved and because of technical limitations. Generally, the use of microphotography is advantageous when:

1. A large volume of records is to be retained permanently.
2. It is desired to destroy the original copy of the record.
3. The condition of the record is such that microphotography is required to preserve the record during its retention period.
4. A large volume of computer output can bypass the computer printer and enter directly on microfilm. This temporarily retains large masses of information for subsequent selective reproduction.

SELECTED FORMS

The most basic form in the quality function is the Inspection Report (Figure 19-9). It is usually the first form created. In a small operation it may be the only form in use. The report may be designed in various ways, the most usual being:

1. To show the results of inspection of a single lot of product (Figure 19-9).
2. As a diary showing results of inspection of successive lots of product from different vendors (Figure 19-10a).
3. As a diary showing the daily results of inspection by one individual, covering multiple lots, which may involve multiple kinds of product (Figure 19-10b).
4. As a "ledger" form which accumulates the results of inspection for a single product over multiple days and by multiple inspectors (Figure 19-10c).

RECEIVING INSPECTION REPORT		Part Name			Surface Top				Part Number	23161-003	
Vendor Code	Purchase Order Nr.	Lot/Batch	Quantity	Def.	Insp. by	Date	Description of Defects				Rejection Report #
3125	0065 W	250	32	5	JAW	12/16/71	Surface Scratches ⅛" Long				5431
3125	0192 W	300	32	0	FXS	12/19/71	——				——
6971	0229 W	300	32	0	FXS	12/19/71	——				——

(a)

IN-PROCESS INSPECTION REPORT				Inspected by: Frank Kasper Date 12/17/71 Dept Machine Shop				
Part Number, Name Lot, Batch Serial Nr.	Quantity Lot/Batch	Insp.	Rejected % Def've	Nature of Observation & Type of Deficiency Found	Qty	Action Taken Disposition	Resp.
6036 Yoke Bracket	600	80	5 6%	1.163±.005 Length 151.171-1.175 .625±.005 DIA. 15.635¢.638	5 2 7	Repair Scrap Sort Lot	MFG MFG
51257 Stringer	50	8	0	Checked Per Inspection Instr.	0	Accepted	

(b)

PART NUMBER 2300-013		PART NAME Drawer Channel Support									AQL 2.5%	AOQL 3.5%		QUALITY CONTROL INSPECTION REPORT	
Refer to proper Inspection Instruction. Record all inspection results in this form Refer to defect codes below.											LTPD .05	LQ .05	25%		
Order/Lot Batch No.	Lot Size	Sample Size	Def't've Pieces	DEFECT CODES*									Total Defects	Insp. By	Rejection Report No.
				A	B	C	D	E	F	G	H	J			
5882	98	20	8		3		7		8		I		19	FXS	7757
7691	125	20	0										0	GLC	——
8239	210	32	I		I		I						3	PMR	——
8491	623	80	4	2	3		4						9	RAD	——
8641	550	80	10		6		10		3				19	GLC	7963
9314	2	2	0										—	GLC	——

(c)

Fig. 19-10a,b,c   Three types of general inspection reports.

INSPECTION INSTRUCTION	PART NAME Channel Support		PART NO. 2300-013	
ORIGINATED Paul Michaels	DATE 9/17/70	SAMPLING PLAN AQL 1.0% LTPD_____ β _____		
APPROVED John Francis	DATE	AOQL 1.5% LQ 10% .05		
Drill Press 6391		NO Mil Std 105D Level II		
DESCRIPTION	SPECIFICATIONS	TOOL	REMARKS	
Diameter	0.625-.030	Plug Gage	Record all results	
Length	1¼ ± 1/32	Scale	on Inspection Report	
Width	3½± 1/32	Scale		
Hole Location	2⅜x 5¼± 1/32	Scale		
Burrs	1/32 max	Magnifying Glass	20X	

Fig. 19-11   Inspection Instruction.

A second major form is that used for nonconformance material. This may be identical with the form used for reporting conforming material. (See, for example, Section 45, Figure 45-4.) Alternatively, it may be a special design, with space to describe in detail the nature of the nonconformance as well as the subsequent disposition, e.g., Use as Is, Rework, Scrap, Return to Supplier. The multiple copies become source documents for various departments, e.g., Accounting for costing, Production Control for reorder, Material Review Board for disposition, Quality Control for analysis. Sometimes, one copy is designed to be the material identification tag.

Design of the inspection and nonconformance reports for subsequent data processing is decisively affected by the volume of forms to be processed. Where this volume is small, the processing will be done manually, and conventional types of forms may be used, taking care to have like data recorded in like locations on the form to reduce error.

For large masses of data, the forms are designed to simplify the subsequent key punching or other steps in the data processing sequence. It is common practice to record the original data on data processing cards (see Section 20, Figure 20-6).

There is also an awkward level of data—too large for manual processing and too

TABLE 19-4   Examples of Use of Forms

Type of form	Use is exemplified in figure or table number:
Coding plan	Figures 35-2, 39-3, 43-5
Control chart	Figures 23-1, 23-6, 23-7, 23-8, 23-9, 25-10, 29-7, 29-16, 29-18
Control chart data sheet	Figure 23-2
Corrective Action Request	Figures 19-12, 45-4
Data flow plan	Figures 19-5, 21-3, 37-6, 39-6, 42-12
Defect description	Figure 19-6
Defect travel card	Figure 43-5
Edge punched card	Figures 19-2, 19-3
Error Cause Removal form	Figure 18-3
EVOP work sheet	Figures 27A-3, 27A-5
Failure reporting plan	Figures 8-9, 42-18
Field return card	Figures 30-7, 41-2
Flow diagrams, product and process	Figures 6-3, 6-5, 9-1, 9-2, 9-3, 9-28, 29-6, 29-7, 29-8, 29-12, 29-14, 29-15, 29-17, 30-1, 30-2, 32-3, 33-1, 33-3, 34-1, 35-1, 35-4, 36A-1, 36A-3, 37-1, 39-1, 40-1, 41-5, 41-6, 42-8, 42-9, 43-2, 43-3
Inspection instruction	Figure 19-11, Table 37-1, Figure 41-7, Figure 43-4
Inspection plan	Figures 37-15, 39-3, 41-8, 43-3
Inspection record	Figures 19-4, 19-9, 19-10, 30-5, 31-5, 41-9, 41-10
Ishikawa diagram	Figures 16-2, 35-5, 37-11
Lot Plot	Figure 25-9
Probability paper	Figures 22-6, 22-7
Product description tag	Figure 4-4
Report system	Figure 21-3, Tables 21-3, 41-1, 41-2, Figure 43-8
Responsibility matrix	Figures 6-1, 6-2, Tables 6-2, 10-2, 11-4, 35-4, 39-5, 43-1, 43-4
Sampling plans, attributes	Tables 24-4 through 24-11
Sampling plans, variable	Tables 25-3, 25-5, 25-6, 25-8, 25-14, 25-18, 25-19, 25-21, 25-22
Specifications, product and process	Figure 31-1, Tables 31-2, 31-3, Figures 39-2, 40-2, 41-4, Table 43-2
Weibull diagram	Figures 22-9, 22-10, 22-11, 42-19

small to warrant programming the data processing machinery. For this level, the edge-punched card is a convenient solution (see Figures 19-2 and 19-3).

A third major form is the Inspection Instruction. See Figure 19-11, also Figures 37-15 and 43-4. It standardizes the work to be performed at the control stations no matter who is doing the job. Sometimes the same form provides the inspection instructions plus space to record the data.

Numerous other forms and formats are in use. They are not reproduced here since they can be found in other Sections of this Handbook. See Table 19-4.

Smaller companies should make use of the numerous standard business forms which are available from business stationers. Among the most usual are the aids to correspondence. In one variety, the originator completes the top half of a triplicate form and the addressee replies on the lower half. These are quite convenient for such uses as Corrective Action request (Figure 19-12). Still other forms available are engineering log books or notebooks, chart paper of all sorts, calculation forms, etc.

speedimemo

TRIP

TO
F. X. Francis, Chief Engineer

DEPT.-LOCATION
6209 Product Engineering

FROM
A. M. Jeans, Quality Engineer

DEPT.-LOCATION
6106 Quality Engineering

SUBJECT
CORRECTIVE ACTION REQUEST, End Table Top 768952-02

DATE
1 / 24 / 72

MESSAGE

REPLY REQUESTED BY: Feb. 8, 1972

PROBLEM:

1. Pin holes present in surface of finish

2. Filler material tends to squeeze put of wood pores.

35 complaints received during last two weeks from six distributors.

ORIGINATOR-DO NOT WRITE BELOW THIS LINE

SIGNED A M Jeans

REPLY

CAUSE: 1. Filler improperly applied. Pin holes are due to air being trapped in pores.
2. Flowout of filler is due to improper wash coat applied between stain & filler.

CORRECTIVE ACTION: Process to be revised.
1. Require slower brushing motion & thinner but more coats of filler.
2. Change wash coat mix from ¼ turpentine & 3/4 filler to 1/3 turpentine & 2/3 filler.

EFFECTIVE: Lot # 715-002 on Order 19768

DEPT.-LOCATION
6209 Product Engineering–Process Section

SIGNED F X Francis

DATE
2 / 3 / 72

SEND PARTS 1 AND 3 WITH CARBON INTACT. - PART 3 WILL BE RETURNED WITH REPLY.

Rediform® 4S 470

Fig. 19-12 Standard business form used as Corrective Action Request *(Courtesy Rediform Office Products.)*

ACKNOWLEDGMENTS

My appreciation is extended to the companies who furnished information and copies of their forms. Because of space limitations, many of these forms could not be published; but they nevertheless provided much data for my research on the subject.   In particular, Armstrong Cork Co., American Machine and Foundry Co., Western Electric, Eli Lilly and Co., The L. S. Starrett Co., Automation Industries, Inc., Bowser-Morner Testing Laboratories, Inc., Stanley Tools, Sylvania Electric Products, Inc., Associated Testing Laboratories, Inc., American Paper Institute, The Drawing Board, United Fruit Co., Celanese Fibers Co., The Institute of Paper Chemistry, and Mattel, Inc. were generous in the material provided.   For typing, proofreading, arranging, and most of all for encouragement and patience, thanks to my wife, Jean.   My appreciation to Mrs. Menzel for the final typing of the manuscript, twice!

Section **20**

Computers in Quality Control[1]

J. E. BLUM
Assistant Manager, Operations Research,
Consolidated Papers, Inc.

R. S. BINGHAM, JR.

[1] In the Second Edition, this Section was prepared by International Business Machines Corporation.

INTRODUCTION

This Section identifies those needs of the quality control function which are best satisfied by high-speed computers.[2] It identifies the criteria which determine whether manual or automatic computation should be done. It discusses the capabilities of available computer systems pertinent to quality control needs. It analyzes the impact of modern data processing on quality control effectiveness. It also provides detailed checklists for deriving computer systems specifications, for implementation of plans, and for revision of existing systems.

TABLE 20-1   Computer Use Described in Other Sections

Handbook Section no.	Computer use
5	Provide quality cost data
8	New-product design, reliability quantification, data banks, etc.
9	Process regulation, process control feedbacks, automated testing, etc.
10	Vendor relations programs
12	Automated inspection and test, and data feedback
13	Control of calibration
14	Market research and sales analysis
15	Field performance feedback
16	Quality improvement analysis
17	Training in use of computers
19	Configuration control and documentation, e.g., inspection reports, corrective action requests, indexes or codes; see also for Systems Approach
21	Management reporting
22–28	Statistical analysis (e.g., see Section 26, Regression, for detailed explanation of computer use to evaluate predictor equations, sample problems, and computer printouts.)
29–47	Case histories in various industries, products, and processes (See Table 20-3 for added detail.)

Numerous Sections of this Handbook are concerned with various aspects of computers and their application to quality control. Table 20-1 provides a cross reference.

Since the 1950s, amazing changes in computer capabilities have occurred, and with them outstanding opportunities for quality control have arisen. Because computers currently available to Quality Control Departments range all the way from desk-top computers to huge multiprocessing computing centers, it is useful to trace briefly the development of modern high-speed computer operation and its programming.

In the "calculator," a *punched card* is read;[3] the information is cycled through a sequence of *instructions;* sums, differences, quotients, and products are accumulated in a limited number of *registers;* and, finally, results are printed on an "accounting machine." The characteristics of that age of calculators included:

"Hard wired" computing steps (if the calculations were to be changed, the "plugboard" was rewired)

---

[2] In this Section, "computer" refers to the class of stored programmable electronic machines having a supervisory system controlling the functions of *input, output,* job scheduling, and calculating on a *real-time multiprogramming* basis. Comments on smaller desk computers are found under Minicomputers. Also see Glossary for definitions of other terms which are shown in italics the first time used.

[3] See Figures 20-8 and 20-9 for examples of punched cards.

A limited number of items stored in fixed format
A limited number of *program* steps accomplished with one wiring panel

Internal storage using *stored programs* eliminated the plugboard. The initial step in using such a computer was to read in the program[4] instructions. These were followed by the data in format as described above.

This computer usage was characterized by stepwise, small programs, the output of one being input to the next. The limited internal storage required considerable skill in balancing the number of program steps internally stored with the amount of data read in, and with intermediate results temporarily stored. (The trick was to subdivide the program to have the right instructions present when specific accumulations in data had been accomplished.) Also characteristic of both these computers were instructions written in *machine language.*

The next improvement in programming came with *compilers.* They used pseudo-English statements[5] to describe the computations needed. These statements were punched into cards. The deck was then fed into the computer and acted upon by a previously loaded program. The output was a set of machine-readable instructions similar to those which would have been prepared by a programmer. Divorcing the program writer from the original machine language is perhaps *the* most significant step forward in using computers. Scientists, engineers, and practitioners not knowledgeable in how the computer operates can now prepare instructions for calculations using compilers known as FORTRAN, BASIC, COBOL, PL/I, etc.

Interactive programs appeared about 1965. These permit the program writer to prepare compiler language programs one line at a time, each rapidly tested for validity. If errors are found, the diagnostic code tells the writer the kind of error he has made. Upon correction, the next program step is entered until all are completed. This interactive capability for scientific and technical work usually shortens both program writing and *debugging.* The interactive approach normally operates on a *time-shared* basis[6] (by this we mean that several users are simultaneously addressing the computer with demands, yet each acts as though he were the sole user.)

At this stage in computer development, several significant events have taken place. Some of the capabilities originally "hard wired" into the computer have been separated from the electronics and instead included in the "software," e.g., floating-point arithmetic. (*Software* is a list of program instructions prepared by the computer vendor and available to the user. It aims to optimize computer hardware usage, e.g., operating systems, compilers, utility routines.) In addition, "canned programs," i.e., sets of instructions specifically written to accomplish limited goals but incorporable in other programming efforts, have been issued. (These include statistical analysis, plotting, etc.). These pretested programs have both faults and virtues (see below, Translating Design Specifications into Computer Requirements —Software). A substantial improvement in software allows the preparation of pretested *subroutines* "callable" from an on-line library into any number of programs as needed without requiring additional computer storage.

---

[4] In this Section, "program" refers to a sequence of computer instructions (sometimes called computer coding) which direct input, output, arithmetic operations; i.e. in general, what is to be done and its sequence, including tests for invalid conditions as well as corrective measures to overcome them. See Glossary; also Bingham, R. S. Jr., Automatic Programming Answers a Need, *Univac Review,* vol. 2, no. 2, pp. 6–11, Summer 1959.

[5] Such as READ, WRITE, IF, GO TO, EXECUTE and using symbols *,/,+,−,**, and SQRT for multiply, divide, add, subtract, exponentiate, and square root, respectively.

[6] Kemeny, J. G., "Man and the Computer," Charles Scribner's Sons, New York, 1972, describes time-sharing and Dartmouth's interactive compiler, BASIC, in a very readable primer which forecasts future computer uses.

The net effect of these improvements has been to reduce the cost of computing and to make computers easier to use. At the same time, there remains an aura of mystery about computers and their use that quality control practitioners seem to have difficulty penetrating.

BASIC CONCEPTS OF DATA AND DATA PROCESSING

Most newcomers to the field of data processing have difficulty because they do not know where to start. Some of this has to do with jargon in the business, lack of familiarity with the capabilities of computers in general, and assumptions about manual computing that have been overlooked.

For example, all computations must necessarily deal with four steps:

Data input
Storage and retrieval
Processing
Output

In *manual* systems, this is accomplished with the following approaches:

1. A language (using a set of explicit instructions to describe generally what is to be done).

2. Data descriptors,[7] telling the *kind* of data to be manipulated, and providing sufficient identification so that they may be uniquely obtained or separated from available reports.

3. Arithmetic operators—a series of mathematical procedures encompassing addition, subtraction, multiplication, and division.

4. A number system (including a definition of zero, plus and minus, and infinity, but utilizing the axioms of closure, commutativity, associativity, identity, inverse, and transposition).

5. Control—where to start, when to stop, and what to do if errors or incomplete instructions are met.

In addition, a trained statistical clerk is expected to have operational capability using a particular mechanical calculator; manual dexterity in handling and manipulating data records (normally data recorded on paper, cards, forms); ability to follow in sequence a given set of instructions; ability to identify at a glance "obvious" errors in the data record; and the capacity to follow through by obtaining clarification of the doubtful data and correcting them on the record. Training also aids the clerk in separating different jobs as they are received, identifying which statistical operations should be carried out on each job, and determining the form in which the results are to be reported.

Computer systems have the same five elements described above but differ in their capacity to exercise intelligence. While at first glance the computer appears to be more inflexible, its language offers distinct advantages by minimizing the number of decisions its user has to make:

Its conventions are defined and unambiguous.

It is intolerant of dialects, forcing correction of vague instructions.

It is unforgiving about invalid arithmetic operations (such as dividing by zero) but calls for immediate correction.

It has diagnostic capability providing gentle admonitions and suggested corrections for improperly used instructions.

[7] Descriptors: "Division, Plant, Production Line, Machine Type, Process Type, Operator, Production Run Number, Customer, Raw Material Lot, Production Shift (7-3, 3-11, 11-7), Measured Property, Part Number, etc."

It is modular, encouraging use at successively more sophisticated levels as learning occurs.

It temporarily stores every data element fed into it (each can be copied, subdivided, and erased).

With suitable definition, it distinguishes one data element from another—knowing where each starts and ends—while linking to it an appropriate descriptor.

It combines information handling and mathematical calculations equally well.

Properly instructed, it follows the instructions indefinitely in sequence without failure (thus complex mathematical subroutines may be designed once and used repetitively without involving engineers in the reviewing of basic mathematical theory).

Table 20-2 summarizes computational system differences of manual and computer systems. Figure 20-1 shows the flow sheet for calculating average, variance, standard deviation, and confidence limits for the average of any number of data items all from the same data file. Figure 20-2 provides the corresponding computer programming steps. These two figures illustrate input-output, decisions (branching), arithmetic processing, looping, control (starting and stopping), and use of callable subroutines.

QUALITY CONTROL NEEDS SERVED BY COMPUTER SYSTEMS

Computer systems are particularly appropriate in seven key areas of quality control:

Data accumulation
Data reduction, analysis, and reporting
Real-time process control
Automatic testing and inspection
Statistical analysis
Information retrieval
Quality management-related techniques

Table 20-3 gives examples pertinent to each of these areas and principal benefits to be expected. Each is discussed below.

Data Accumulation   One of the principal problems of every quality control operation is that of identifying and collecting data pertinent to the department's objectives. More data may be collected than necessary for control decisions. Ancillary data may be taken in anticipation of future demands. The data may be descriptive in nature —identifying time, place, occasion, production line, run number, operators, or supervisors, etc. The data may represent process or product properties. They may represent different costs associated with alternative inspection schemes. The traceability of data is frequently required in industries that demand high precision or high quality. This poses a special problem of being able to link data from one organizational function to another within a corporation. In manual systems, the cost of additional *descriptors* on laboratory reports, inspection forms, etc., to identify, classify, and provide traceability is generally overlooked. In computer systems, this identification may occupy more storage than the actual data. Ideally, identification *redundancy* is held to a minimum. As indicated in Section 19, Documentation, structures can be established to connect these various data elements.[8] Modern computer systems use data-base management techniques[9] to minimize the cost of

---

[8] See, in this Section, Concepts of Data and Data Processing, above, for use of descriptors.

[9] Data-base management is related to the design and creation of the data base, the operation of the administration system, and the use of data manipulation languages. See Schubert, R. F., Basic Concepts in Data Base Management Systems, *Datamation,* July 1972, pp. 42–47;

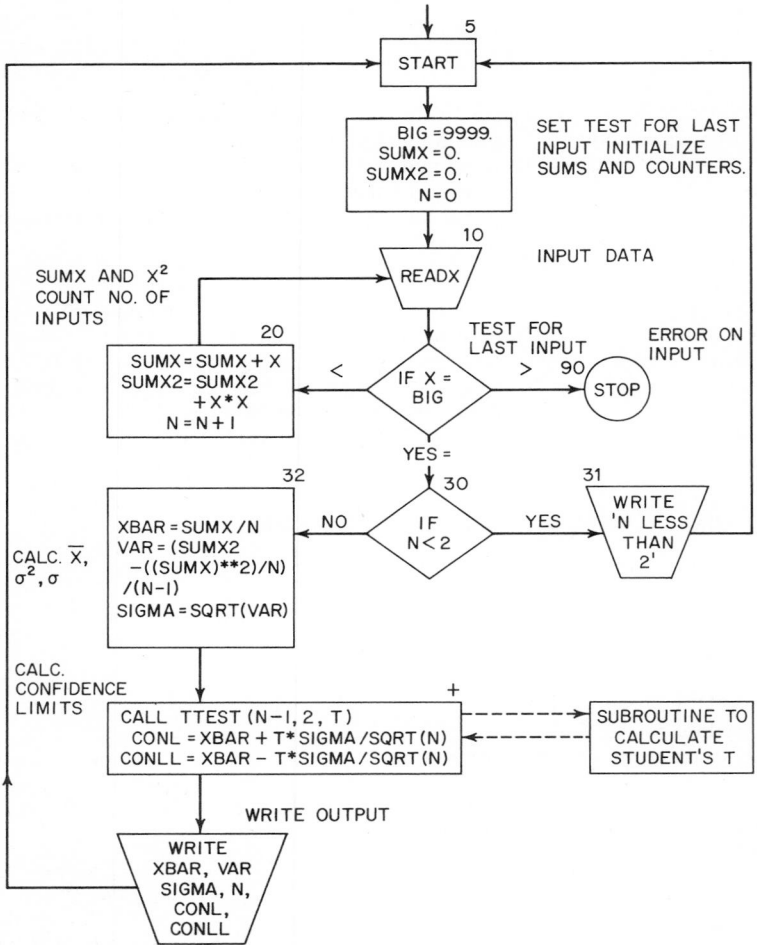

+"TTEST" IS THE NAME OF SUBROUTINE CALCULATING THE CRITICAL (T)
VALUE OF STUDENT'S T-DISTRIBUTION FOR F DEGREES OF FREEDOM,
L LEVEL OF SIGNIFICANCE ONE-TAILED.

Fig. 20-1. Flow chart for calculating average, variance, standard deviation.

manipulating such data and maintaining the relationships of the various elements, purging files, etc. without losing the ability to classify the data for multiple analyses.

Data Reduction, Analysis, and Reporting   Once data have been accumulated in computer-retrievable form, a variety of techniques can be applied to expedite quality activities and minimize department costs.   For example, routine data can be automatically plotted and inspection records tabulated—reporting percent defects by

Patterson, A. C., Data Base Hazards, *Datamation,* July 1972, pp. 48–50; McLaughlin, R. A., Building a Data Base, *Automation,* July 1972, pp. 51–55; and Coupe, R. J., Applying Data Base Management to Production Scheduling and Control, *Automation,* August 1972, pp. 32–37.

```
   5 BIG = 9999.
     SUMX = 0.
     SUMX2 = 0.
     N =  0
  10 READ(7,1) X
   1 FORMAT(F10.3)
     IF(X - BIG)  20,30,90
  20 SUMX = SUMX + X
     SUMX2 = SUMX2 + X * X
     N = N + 1
     GO TO 10
  30 IF(N - 2) 31,32,32
  31 WRITE(9,2)
   2 FORMAT(' N LESS THAN 2')
     GO TO 5
  32 XBAR = SUMX/N
     VAR = (SUMX2 -((SUMX)**2) /N)/(N-1)
     SIGMA = SQRT(VAR)
     F = N -1
     L = 2
     Z = N
     CALL TTEST(F,L,T)
     CONL = XBAR +(T * SIGMA/SQRT(Z))
     CONLL = XBAR - (T * SIGMA/SQRT(Z))
     WRITE(9,3) XBAR,VAR,SIGMA,N,CONL,CONLL
   3 FORMAT(' ',3F10.3,I10,2F10.3)
     GO TO 5
  90 CALL EXIT
     SUBROUTINE TTEST(F,L,T)
   C PROGRAM STUDENTS  T - SUBROUTINE          F = DEG. FREEDOM
   C CHOOSE  (1)   .95   (2)   .975   (3)  .995  L = LEVEL ONE TAIL
     DIMENSION C(5)
     IF(L -2) 10,20,30
  10 C(1)  = 1.6449
     C(2)  = 3.5283
     C(3)  = 0.8560
     C(4)  = 1.2209
     C(5)  = -1.5162
     GO TO 40
  20 C(1)  = 1.9600
     C(2) =   .60033
     C(3) =   .95910
     C(4) = -.90259
     C(5) =   .11588
     GO TO 40
  30 C(1)  = 2.5758
     C(2) = -.82847
     C(3) = 1.87450
     C(4) = -2.23110
     C(5) =  1.5631
  40 T =.(F * C(1) + C(2) + C(3)/F) /(F + C(4) + C(5) /F)
     RETURN
     END
```

Fig. 20-2.   Computer programming steps.

machine, department, shift, attributes, etc.   Unusual situations can be reported on an exception basis using built-in decision rules.[10]

For production operations where it is common to find many characteristics on each product important to quality decisions, status reporting can be done economically to meet operating quality review requirements.   In the process industries, quality levels and uniformity can be reported "run-by-run."   In the area of complaint analysis, sorting of data by quality attributes, customer, product line, production area, dollar value of complaint, and nature of complaint can be added to normal recordkeeping (formal or informal; even forecasts of additional complaints to be anticipated are possible).   For bulk materials, the validity of complaints can be

[10] Hagie, L. T., in The Computer as a Quality Control Tool, *Transactions, 25th Annual Technical Conference*, ASQC, 1971, Chicago, Ill.   This paper describes machine-drawn control charts and product quality data summaries.   It shows input formats, statistics calculated, sample reports, and charts.

TABLE 20-2 Computational System Differences

System element	Manual	Automatic
Systems analysis	Minimal; specific to current job	Extensive; relates current job to others, to future needs.
Data input	Inspection record, lab report, process log	Same; usually via keypunch or input terminal; wherever possible replacing a source document.
Data screening	Visual, casual; done after trouble is encountered or when unusual analysis appears	Editing built-in based on expected results. Automatic alarming for doubtful values. Gives directions for correction.
Data reduction	Specific to need, usually limited to one method	Selected by programs after preliminary analysis adaptive to changing needs.
Data analysis	"Quick and dirty," simple, restricted to fast methods (control charts, distributions, etc.) on few properties	As extensive as needs and systems analysis justify. Statistical methods selectable sequentially during analysis.
Programming	Limited to forms design, preparing computational aids, nomographs, tables	Amount depends on complexity of screening, reduction, analysis, and report generation; ability to use data already in core or previously programmed subroutines.
Training	Limited for each person doing work but usually frequently repeated due to personnel turnover. Variable	Once programs are tested and accepted, only operators need be trained. (Users are easy to train due to documentation.)
Documentation	Minimal, reference to Q.C. manuals, textbooks, or notes	Extensive for systems maintenance and revision, and for interrelating with other computer systems (so subroutines can be shared; any malfunctions can be detected.)
Reliability	"Excellent to poor" depending on: design training personnel motivation	"Excellent to poor" depending on: design data validity computer operator performance
Interpretation of results	"Variable to uniform" due to uncertainties in: input choice of screening statistical methods used	Uniform due to standardized system.
Report generation	Handwritten, typed. Delayed	Standardized by design. Complete. (Volume depends on design.) On exception basis, if planned.

judged by comparing products shipped to different customers but made at the same time on the same production equipment. The ability to automatically process complaint information, once properly classified, avoids overlooking trend situations which should serve as early warnings of potential major claims.

To quality managers covering a vast number of production areas, automatic data reduction and analysis with exception reporting permits scanning all of the process areas rather than simply covering only those most recently in trouble.[11] Consistent

---

[11] Portable data logging with computer-compatible output for process studies is described in Bicking, C. A., R. S. Bingham, and R. L. Weiss in Automatic Data Logging for Experimentation and Quality Control, *Industrial Quality Control*, vol. 20, no. 6, pp. 12–16, December 1963.

TABLE 20-3 Quality Control Computer Applications and Benefits

Area of use	Examples	Principal benefits from computer use	No.	Examples in Handbook Section Title
1. Data accumulation	1. Transmission of data as generated from raw material receiving areas, production process inspection stations, testing labs, and outgoing quality audit.	1. Faster transmission, fewer errors, reduced delay time from inspection or test to communication of results, lower collection costs.	39 42 41	Textiles Automotive—about data input via scanner, teletypes, and data banks. Assembly—under Data Collection and Feedback, the use of Touch Tone telephones.
2. Data reduction analysis, and reporting	2. Screening of data for obvious errors, conversion to common units (errors/1,000 units, defects/ton, etc.); scaling or transformation to achieve normality (use of arcsine, logs, square root, reciprocal, other); time phasing data collected from different steps in the same process; arithmetic adjustment prior to analysis. (See 5 below.) Standardized reporting to several different shop and management levels from the same data over different time periods.	2. Consistent, uniform application of selected rules and procedures derived from previous process analysis: Low cost use of advanced techniques not manually possible in time allowed or with limited personnel Automatic reduction and analysis triggered by data as accumulated Exception reporting to preplanned list according to situation severity	39 38 40 42	Textiles Electronic Components—computer-aided design. Graphic Arts—photo-composition computer-assisted Automotive—computer graphics for designing, rough drawings, and preparing NC computer tapes
3. Real-time process control	3. Control of stock flow rate, headbox air pressure, etc., to paper machine, continuously sensing basis weight and moisture, comparing to standards, calling for automatic valve adjustment of variables according to control equations when action limits exceeded.	3. More uniform process control and product quality with continuous process inspection—combines 1 and 2 above with knowledge of process dynamics to make correct size process changes for upset or shift sensed. Safer operation with hazardous processes.	29 30 33	Chemicals Pulp and Paper Metals Industry

TABLE 20-3 Quality Control Computer Applications and Benefits (Continued)

Area of use	Examples	Principal benefits from computer use	No.	Examples in Handbook Section Title
4. Automatic testing and inspection	4. Sample taken automatically from process line (line first purged, sample weighed, passed through sensing heads of colorimeters, hazemeters, particulate counters, spectrophotometers, etc.). Comparison of test results may call for additional testing. In electronics, circuit check at different voltages, after temperature cycles; use of diagnostics to advise repair service if action is to be taken (identified by terminal strip junction, part, etc.).	Can build in fail-safe mechanism, greater frequency of inspection and automatic gauge calibration. 4. Few personnel needed for menial or, alternatively, for highly complex but repetitive tasks. Minimize sampling handling. Corrective steps can be automatically looked up in a table stored in the computer; frequency of failure logged by defect, related to various measurements, etc.	32 32 38 38	Drugs, Product Surveillance Drugs Electronic Components Electronic Components
5. Statistical analysis	5. Use of any and all methods (as needed) described in Sections 22, 23, and 26. Once data are in retrievable form, analysis can be made via control charts, frequency distribution, correlation with other data, comparison with standards or previous averages, ranges, standard deviations, ratios, etc. Tabulations by defect type, production area, process type, etc., can be checked for unusual occurrence with statistical significance tests.	5. Complete flexibility in processing data through a wide variety of analytical techniques, at low cost, using methods prechosen for specific situations or in specific sequences. Can use best numerical methods (recommended by mathematicians, programmed for computers by software specialists, and purchasable).	29	Chemicals

TABLE 20-3 Quality Control Computer Applications and Benefits *(Continued)*

Area of use	Examples	Principal benefits from computer use	No.	Examples in Handbook Section — Title
6. Information retrieval	6. Look up specifications, complaint records, production problems by product line for quality planning; search out previous cost experience historically; examine process change record to avoid repetition of previous failures; compile standardized inspection instruction.	6. Assurance that specifications file contains latest changes (i.e., easy maintenance of specifications). Uncover allied (product or customer) complaint histories economically. Programs available for defining files, data bases and for specifying keywords for search.	19 29 45 8	Documentation Chemicals—data banks Job Shop—memory systems and "Job Setup Cards" New Product Quality
7. Quality Management-related techniques	7. Planning for inspection, manpower, new production facilities, process control via discrete and continuous process simulation (CSMP). Project planning via PERT or CPM.	7. Time saving. Simulation allows studies of various options prior to installation of inspection schemes, test stations, publication of test frequencies. With CSMP, finding optimum parameter values minimizes process delays and sluggish feedback. Find and eliminate bottlenecks.	29	Chemicals, *see* Adaptive Control

checkpoints and action limits can be built into the automatic analysis, generating highlight reports and also automatically calling for more detailed analysis in the troubled areas. (Based on the decision rules built into the programs, sequences of data can be listed along with the analysis to that point.)

Real-Time Process Control   As indicated in Section 9, for some production circumstances, adequate sensors are now available to measure the important process variables rapidly enough to maintain the process on target. Computers are pertinent to process control situations where (1) more than one control variable is measured, (2) the variables are interrelated or correlated, (3) time delays make feedback slow, or (4) variables must be time-related to be properly interpreted. (In some instances, uniformity depends upon process level, and control limits must be adjusted as the process is shifted to make different grades of product.)

Real-time process control requires:

Proper selection of process controller set points
Assurance that feedback loops are as tight as necessary
Proper identification of interrelations and limiting of their number so control actions can be defined, referenced, and executed for each out-of-control situation or trend alert
Current knowledge of "process dynamics," including delay times, gains, and corrective actions specific to each control loop

With "adaptive control" (see Section 29) it is necessary to update the control parameters. This can be built into the process control loop and periodically reported to the quality manager.

The computer provides the opportunity for monitoring several industrial processes concurrently, including shifting priorities to handle extreme out-of-control conditions.[12]   (See under Process Control Applications, in this Section.)

Automatic Testing and Inspection   As indicated in Section 12, under Automated Inspection, two needs must be satisfied when inspection or testing are automated: the inspection itself, and the calibration of the inspection equipment. Automatic testing may be used on high-volume production lines to provide go no-go answers. When multiple properties are measured or product under test must be sequenced through a variety of environmental conditions or monitored over time, computer systems can continually follow the product under test. Thus, data collection and production analysis as well as exception reporting can be combined with automatic testing.[13]

In automatic inspection of electronic assemblies, the inspection is normally sequenced through the various circuits. If substandard voltages or responses are obtained, a diagnostic routine is called automatically by the computer to determine whether repair is possible and, if so, to identify to a repair operator what should be done. (See Section 38, under Automated Tests and Data Processing.)

When automatic testing is applied to products made from numerically controlled machines, computers can be used to generate automatic test instructions simultane-

---

[12] Ralston, E. L., The Process Control Computer—A New Tool for Quality Control, *Transactions of the 21st Annual Technical Conference,* ASQC, pp. 343–348, 1967, Chicago, Ill. This paper describes the fundamentals of process-control computers, including use of punch cards, magnetic tape, paper tape, typewriters, etc., along with contact sensing, analog conversion, contact operating interrupts, etc., and leads from closed loop control to direct digital control.

[13] See Bingham, R. S., Jr., Density Control by Weight And Dimensional Measurement Control, *Industrial Quality Control,* vol. 16, no. 2, pp. 22–25, August 1959, for a unique combination of measuring and inspection decision rules to determine if acceptability had to be judged by computing product density for each unit of product.

ously with the numerical control tape preparation itself. (This relates to defining the location of the reference point on the product as well as on the inspection table.[14]) Thus the computer ties together the entire automatic testing, data reduction, and reporting cycle.

Statistical Analysis   Once programmed, the statistical techniques described in Sections 22 through 28 can be used to diagnose unusual process conditions. Either routinely or on an exception basis, the computer determines, for a given process:

Capability to perform at a specified level
If current specifications are appropriate
Whether the process is in control

To carry out this analysis, the quality engineer, from his knowledge of the process, specifies a particular sequence of statistical tests to be used under each set of conditions. The results of these tests suggest any additional statistical calculations needed. If a critical condition is discovered, an alarm is sounded for taking appropriate process action.

Once the analysis is programmed to occur automatically, the same or other data can be examined by an almost endless variety of statistical methods individually or in sequence. The cost saving and minimization of staff are incidental to the power built in for problem diagnosis in short periods of time.

Information Retrieval   Quality Departments frequently have great need for retrieval of historical information in the areas of specifications, performance reporting, complaint analysis, or run records. The specific requirement may be to search out conditions under which certain unusual process anomalies were reported or to determine whether a process change had adversely affected quality levels. In product development and process improvement, a review of customer history identifying previous run difficulties can alert production departments to avoid similar problems. Search of inspection records by defect types can identify need for quality engineering studies. It is typical of most information retrieval problems that Quality Control must identify process relationships or defect dependencies.

Quality Management-Related Techniques   Just as modern planning and scheduling techniques[15] are available for other department managers, the quality manager can utilize Critical Path Methods (CPM), Program Evaluation and Review Technique (PERT), Line of Balance (LOB), and simulation. The techniques are applicable in inspection planning, in quality control planning for new production facilities, or in evaluating effectiveness of testing and inspection.

Via computer simulation, it is possible to obtain measures of process dynamics necessary for real-time process control (CSMP—a Continuous System Modeling Program, is commonly used). Using discrete simulation, the number of testers necessary to man a production testing station can be determined (GPSS—General Purpose System Simulator, finds wide use[16, 17]).

As indicated in Section 17, Manpower, an important function of quality manage-

---

[14] See Section 9 under Automatic Process Regulation, for numerical control; Section 12, under Automated Inspection, for inspection devices.

[15] In this Section, see Advanced Techniques for details and applicable software references.

[16] See White, J. R., Computer Simulation in Quality Control, *Transactions of the 23rd Annual Technical Conference,* ASQC, pp. 139–147, 1969, Los Angeles. This paper tells how to select a strategy to minimize the percent of batches exceeding specifications and maximize the production capacity of a batch chemical system. Eleven figures illustrate problem formulation, simulation model building, the computer program, and how to evaluate the experiment.

[17] Brennan, R. D., in Continuous System Simulation for Quality Control Studies, *Transactions of the 24th Annual Technical Conference,* ASQC, pp. 441–448, 1970, Pittsburgh. This paper uses a fabrication facility model to show the effect of management pressures on worker performance and the effect on scrap losses of sampling control during fabrication.

ment is to assure that the best techniques are used for process control. Several computer-aided games have been developed to assist in training operators and engineers.[18]

The computer is particularly valuable in quality management when using these techniques, because of the time-saving possible. Using computer-retrievable data directly from the production stream or inspection records and via previously programmed "software packages" specifically designed to solve PERT, CPM, LOB, GPSS, and CSMP problems, the quality manager can add considerable power to his planning.

ELEMENTS OF A COMPUTER APPLICATION

The purpose of this discussion is to describe preliminary planning and other considerations to be met for effective use of computers in quality control. These include:

Criteria for electronic data processing
Discipline in planning
Standardization of analysis and presentation
Economics
Sequential implementation
Equipment sharing

Criteria for Electronic Data Processing   Computers are beneficially applied to situations where:

1. A large volume of data must be handled
2. Each product unit has many measured quality properties
3. The calculations are lengthy or complex
4. Error-free results are necessary
5. The data are used for several purposes
6. The same analysis is likely to be performed many times on different data sets of different sizes

If several of these characteristics are present, it is reasonable to expect that computerization will substantially reduce quality costs.[19]

To illustrate, if a statistical clerk calculates the average and standard deviation for hundreds of tests each day, if complex or lengthy calculations on an unwieldy number of properties are made, if a number of quality attributes per item must be accurately calculated because the report is to be given to a customer, then the computer can do the calculations much faster and much more accurately than is possible manually. Once the data have been stored in computer files and are available for immediate access, they can be manipulated in many ways.

To achieve the benefits described in Table 20-3, extensive planning is required. While computers can be thought of as high-powered slide rules, they are not as easy to use as most computer salesmen would have us believe. A systematic approach is necessary.

Discipline in Planning   The time and money to be invested in any computer application are significant enough to necessitate complete planning. A computer application must be so thoroughly examined that a flow sheet can be drawn relating data input, analysis methods, and expected output.

[18] Reynolds, J. H., SIMCEL—3: A Quality Control Game, *Technical Conference Transactions,* ASQC, pp. 691–696, 1969.

[19] See Economics, below, concerning cost reduction. Many nonrepetitive, small sample problems contain computer payoffs though not necessarily satisfying these criteria. In this Section, see Computer System Design Specifications.

Detailed planning requires the programming of all alternatives.   Each time a choice exists, the decisions to be made and their bases must be spelled out.   For example, where a Quality Control Analyst is able to use good judgment or rules of thumb in a manual system, the computer must have clear-cut decision rules to follow. (These are conveniently summarized in decision tables using statements of this type: "If event A occurs, do D and F. If events A, B, *and* C occur, then do D, E, F, and G."[20])   Since programs must be flexible enough to allow for every possible situation, this causes quality management to define (preferably in writing) the applicable rule for each possibility.   The extent of this detail may seem excessive, yet in practice it is common to discover inconsistent use and even misuse.

Assume, for example, the computer is to collect and analyze all quality data.   The planning must determine:

What data—are the data timely, accurate, unbiased?
How will the data be described or accessed?
How fast are answers needed and how often?

The data must be screened for obvious errors (this assumes a knowledge of feasible results).   Data reduction techniques must be chosen and applied.   Before the computer can decide, it must be told what decisions to make, what actions to take and when to take them, how much to change control variables (which interrelated variables must be decoupled), who must be notified, what reports must be generated and when.

Standardization of Analysis and Presentation   Statistical analysis can be standardized without loss of output flexibility.   It is not unusual for several corporate divisions to prefer reporting similar data in different forms, each selected because of special emphasis or ease in interpretation.   However, these differences make it difficult for general management to compare performance.

For adequately described data, alternative report formats (e.g., one for corporate, one for division Quality Control) can be generated without paying the price of data collection again.   Using selected descriptors, the data file can be accessed and the corresponding data sorted, collated, summarized, or ranked.   Thus, one customer may want run averages reported; another, ranges and medians; a third, individual test values beyond specifications.   Generally, for data handling, anything that can be done manually, a computer can be programmed to do faster and cheaper.

A word of warning—standardized formats have their place.   Reports of a division dominated by long production runs are not likely to serve another division with very short runs and frequently changing product lines.   By dictating standardization of report layout and content, the computer report may not serve as intended but instead lead to the duplication of manual effort.   In the most serious cases, the computer report is likely to be ignored.

Economics   The economies of using computers are associated with their high-speed data handling and calculating abilities.   A Quality Department with no previous experience using computers may achieve cost reduction or cost avoidance by replacing statistical clerks with the computer.   However, as indicated by Diebold,[21] "Cost displacement is not enough—operational gain must result."   In quality control, primary benefits can be expected from special statistical studies using "canned

---

[20] For example, if one point exceeds the 3σ control limit (Event A), then call the foreman (Action D) and double the sampling rate (Action F).

[21] Diebold, J., Bad Decisions on Computer Use, *Harvard Business Review,* January–February 1969, pp. 14–16, 27, 28, and 176.   More experienced users find that computers do not reduce quality staffs but rather increase their effectiveness.

programs" and from operational quality reports for plant use.[22] Executive reports are more likely to contribute to overhead expense.

Computer costs generally fall into three categories: program development, computer operations, and conversion. Program development includes systems analysis, programming, test, and debug.[23] Computer operation costs for routine reports normally include, in addition to computer charges, data collection, key punching, and verification of output documents. Conversion costs relate to (1) modifying existing programs or hardware to satisfy new needs or (2) changing all existing systems from one computer vendor to another.

The payback on computerizing a manual job can be estimated by dividing the approximate development cost by the difference between the manual and computer costs per run. For example, for the program in Figure 20-2, flowcharting took 0.2 hours, programming 0.5 hours, keypunching 20 minutes, and two computer runs at 2.0 minutes per run to compile, test, and debug the 52 statements. Estimated development cost was $22. Using hourly rates shown in Table 20-4 each time after 22 uses, the computer program would save approximately $1.50 per run over normal calculation.[24]

Table 20-4 shows the run time and costs for the analysis of 20 observations by four different statistical programs, along with the approximate number of computer statements in each program. The time to prepare the punched cards for these programs ranged from three to nine minutes.

In the case of a new report using parts of existing data files, only systems analysis and programming costs will be incurred. The additional calculations, as contrasted with manual calculation, may be programmed at minor additional charge for manipulating the same data again. (The steps for computer report design are discussed below, under Planning.)

While computing costs depend on the specific computer used, type of data input, and labor costs, an approximate quality control computing budget can be constructed. For example, the Diebold Group, Inc., has reported that a typical large manufacturing corporation allocates on the average 0.90% of corporate sales to data processing.[25] Typically, manufacturing uses 24% of the total budget, applying it generally: 30% for new systems development, 60% for ongoing applications, and 10% for conversion. Carr[26] reports a breakdown of hardware, 39%; personnel, 57%; and supplies, 4%. Of these, personnel costs were subdivided as follows: programmers and systems analysts, 49%; operators, 11%; keypunchers and verifiers, 14%; and administration, 26%. For supplies, costs were typified as printer paper, 63%; punch cards, 19%; magnetic tape, 11%; printer ribbon, 5%; and disc packs, 2%.

Typical data covering purchase, monthly maintenance, and short-term lease prices are available from vendors or in comparisons published by Datapro Research Corporation (in their "EDP Buyers Bible") or by Auerbach Info, Inc. (in Auerbach Computer Characteristics Digest, Desk Reference Series, or Data Handling Reports).

[22] In this Section, see Tables 20-10 and 20-11 for lists of programs specific to quality control and statistical analysis.

[23] See Systems Analysis, under Organizing for Computer Services; also Software, under Planning.

[24] This assumes 20 minutes per manual calculation, including table lookup, etc., and 30 seconds computer time.

[25] Few Yardsticks Available for Gaging EDP Expenditure, *Automation,* vol. 19, no. 2, p. 4, February 1972.

[26] Carr, F. J., Computers Fundamentals, in H. B. Maynard (ed.), "Industrial Engineering Handbook," 3d ed., McGraw Hill Book Company, 1971, New York, sec. 9, chap. 1.

TABLE 20-4 Program Development, Time, Costs, and Payback

Program name	No. of computer statements	Approximate programming* Time (man-days)	Approximate programming* Cost, dollars	Time (min.) to Prepare data	Time (min.) to Keypunch data	Time (min.) to Run computer	Total variable computer cost/run, dollars	Estimated manual cost, dollars	Payback–‡ no. of uses to pay off programming costs
Process capability...........	114	1	88	3	2	1.03	2.51	4.20	52
Linear regression............	193	2	176	4	2	1.22	2.96	12.60	19
Multiple regression..........	323	3	264	3	1.4	0.47	1.38		
ANOVA....................	1,000	5	440	9	4.3	1.01	3.44		
Hourly rates used, dollars†			11.00	6.25	9.40	110.00		7.20	

* Programmed in FORTRAN, run on IBM 360/40 computer.
† Times are typical, rates and overhead representative.
‡ Programming cost/(estimated manual cost per run − total variable computer cost per run)

Sequential Implementation   This concept helps to meet timetables and provide interim service.   Once thorough analysis of a quality control system is completed, it may be possible to implement the system in phases; e.g., after data files are developed to accept information, the system can be implemented one division at a time.   This accomplishes two objectives:

It provides the capability for debugging computer programs and correcting systems problems at one division.

It reduces the time for total implementation at all divisions, since basic program errors discovered at the first division are eliminated prior to extension.

Since computer programs can be *segmented* (or broken into subroutines), it is possible to write a master program whose principal job is to cycle data through various combinations of subroutines.

Each subroutine is planned and programmed separately to overall master program specifications, e.g., in the statistical area, individual subroutines can be programmed to plot control charts, to make t-tests, F-tests, tests of nonrandomness, etc.   (See Tables 20-10 and 20-11, below, for lists of programs specific to quality control and statistical analysis.)   The master program has the principal function of transferring data in a general manner to all subroutines so that new quality control routines or reports can be added easily.

Equipment Sharing   Modern third-generation computers provide high-speed input and output required for commercial applications as well as calculation speed essential for scientific computing.   This offers the potential for sharing a computer among departments.

Further flexibility derives from the ability to partition the main memory into separate areas to facilitate multiprogramming, in which more than one program or program task can be executed at the same time.   It is quite possible for *real-time* programs for inventory control, order entry, or shipping status to be executed in one partition while a second area handles the routine or batch jobs.   These could include invoicing, payroll, quality control, accounts receivable, or scientific analysis.[27]

Because third generation computer investments are large, and conversions time-consuming, it is essential that someone knowledgeable in quality control participate in the specification and design of new computer systems.   This means the quality control staff must have communicated its long-range plans to the corporate data processing department.   (See below, Planning.)   Failure to plan jointly may make it so difficult or costly to include quality control application programs in any new computer system that the quality projects would not be attempted.

Sharing computer systems may also have its disadvantages because of corporate organization or attitude; i.e., typically the computer department is controlled by the financial staff.   This came about because historically, in most companies, the first computer was a bookkeeping machine assigned to the Finance Department.   As computers were extended to scientific users, priorities and scheduling problems arose.   Although the equipment can be shared and costs separated and charged, the control of the computer is typically not shared.   (See Organizing for Computer Services, in this Section.)

PLANNING

Planning is essential to assure efficient design of computer systems.   There are two

---

[27] See Leavey, R. A., Software for Start-Up Computer Systems, *Automation,* vol. 19, no. 10, pp. 50–54, October 1972, for the elements of a production information and control system.

aspects to the planning: devising the computer system design specifications and translating these specifications into a computer design proposal.[28]

It is most important to clarify the key elements in proper planning for a data processing system; e.g., what questions are to be answered by the collected data and its subsequent analysis? Although the computer can analyze retrievable data at high rates and relatively low cost, the right information must be stored and, subsequently, planning must anticipate broad use rather than individual problems. Line quality control supervisors and production managers play a major role in the system specification by describing the results they need.

Dynamic Quality Control Departments require flexibility, so that initially captured data and analysis methods can be changed to give new insight into production inefficiencies, product design inadequacies, or substandard field performance.

Computer System Design Specifications   To derive computer systems specifications requires a systems approach or a systems analysis, meaning a look at the total picture instead of just a specific part of it. (Typically, the quality function interrelates with all other business systems in the company.) To take these interrelations into account, systems analysis determines the needs for decision making based on information; the availability of information; the hardware and related devices necessary to acquire, store, process, retrieve, and display this information; and the methods required to utilize the information for decision making. Through such an approach, the final proposed specifications will include analysis and recommendations pertinent to all related functions.

For example, a computerized reporting system has been designed to report the daily average outgoing quality for all routine tests. The programs were written to generate the necessary reports. Three months later, the Quality Control Manager decided that because the information generated was so valuable, he should use the computer to calculate process capabilities. However, this required that individual test results be retained, a feature not included in the original design and one which would now require additional disk or tape devices be purchased. Each program that processed the input data had to be changed to generate the detail files for storage of the individual readings. This doubled the programming and systems analysis cost.

It is wise to include the examination of all possible uses for the data of the quality function under consideration to assure that future requirements have been anticipated. Although the optimum system may be too expensive or require more of the Data Processing Department's time than can be spared, the longer-range view frequently uncovers unannounced latent needs.

Figure 20-3 outlines the planning steps necessary for computerization.[29] The analysis begins with the initial inquiry, problem definition, problem analysis, and the subsequent preliminary design. Verification of the problem definition along with preliminary justification, benefits, alternatives, and importance must be considered. Once this has been completed, agreement must be reached on the quality information design specifications. The inevitable expansion of the design usually warrants further search for additional benefits. Systems analysis is then made to determine the human and computer factors relevant to the quality function under consideration (and to the interrelated functions). This analysis must be coordinated into the com-

[28] Computing Policies are discussed separately under Organizing for Computing Services (below), since they are usually established once and changed rarely. They set the framework within which planning is done.

[29] User - D.P. involvement ratio suggested by Dr. W. Harden, of John Nuveen & Co., during AMR International, Inc., Conference on Managing D.P. For Top D.P. Management, November 1972.

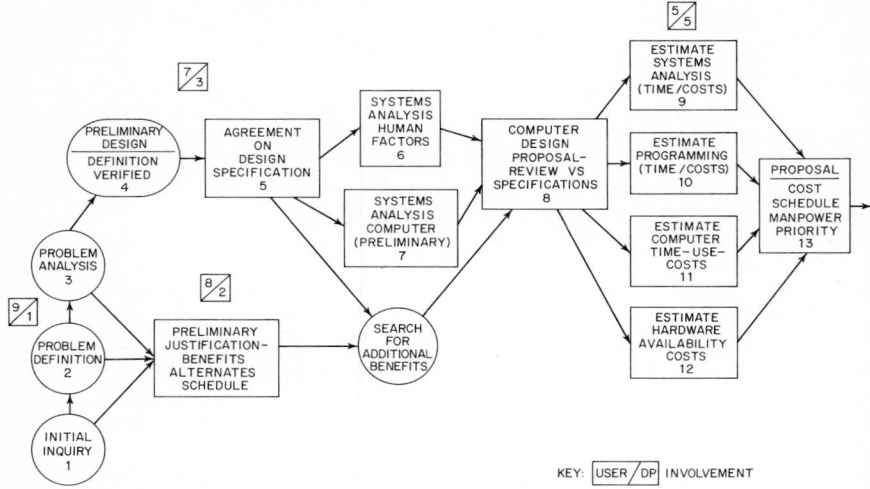

Fig. 20-3. Computer planning.

puter design proposal, which is then reviewed for conformance to the specifications. This design proposal includes in it the identification of all facets of the quality tasks being considered and a recommendation for satisfying the requirements.

Once this has been accomplished, an estimate is made of the computer analysis, programming, computer usage, and hardware costs to generate a proposal management can evaluate on the basis of cost versus benefits. This proposal should also include the schedule for completion of the project, the number of man-hours required, and the relative priority of the project.

At this point, the computer proposal is screened.[30]   This review may highlight areas of weakness and require more systems analysis or justification; or the review may accept the proposal but lower its priority.   Once the project has been accepted, the Data Processing Department schedules it and allocates manpower to do the systems analysis, programming, debugging, documentation, and implementation of the system.   It is also their responsibility to review the system periodically to assure that the original objectives have not changed and have been met.

Justification   The justification of a computerized application in a quality area can take many different forms.   Actual dollar savings may not necessarily be the only means for justifying the computer application, but it is still the easiest.   Computerization can also be justified by an increase in information to management that allows them to make decisions on a basis more objective and more timely than was previously possible.

Justification may also be based on more efficient use of technical capability.   In periods of economic slowdown when companies are forced to reduce their work forces, it becomes a problem of fewer people doing more things.   Computerization of a quality function gives the Quality Manager and his staff greater capability and flexibility, although their numbers may be limited.

Justification of a quality computer application becomes a problem when the existing computer facility or capability is already fully taxed.   As noted above, typically

[30] See Computing Policies, under Organizing for Computing Services, concerning responsibility for computer project selection consistent with top management corporate goals.

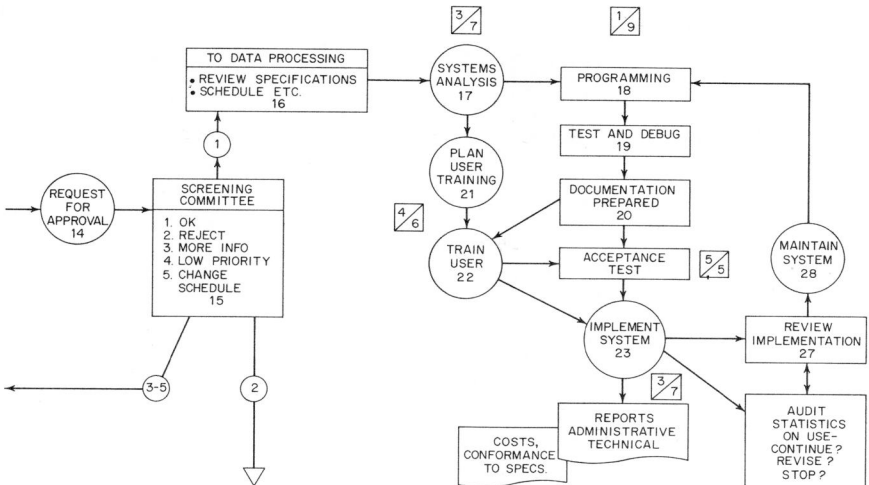

Fig. 20-3. Computer planning. *(Continued)*

the financial people control the computer. Once a computer becomes loaded to capacity, the priority of scientific or quality applications sometimes is downgraded to a point of inadequacy. This makes it essential that a good systems analysis has been made of the proposed application and that sound arguments can be made for establishing a realistic priority. For additional justification discussion, see Organizing for Computing Services, below.

Translating Design Specifications into Computer Requirements The flow diagram, Figure 20-3, shows the overall computer planning network. The text which now follows expands on Figure 20-3 and sets out in detail the essential steps in computer planning. Each step suggests how to deal with specific needs or requirements as determined by the systems analysis phase of the computer systems design. Collectively these steps can be looked on as a checklist which can stimulate thought as to the many types of computer peripheral equipment available today.[31]

1. *Data Collection.* There are many methods of converting data into computer-retrievable form. Table 20-5 describes the more common methods of collection, their characteristics, major disadvantages and advantages, and examples of use. This evaluation must examine both input and subsequent data processing. As indicated in Table 20-6, speeds of various computer units range several thousand fold, card input being the slowest. This emphasizes the need to plan multiple uses of the same data, either sequentially at one time after input, or delayed analysis on data stored on a high-speed memory device, tape, disc, or drum. It is not enough to keypunch data and request statistical analyses one at a time through a battery of programs.

Each alternative means for data collection should be evaluated as to economy,

---

[31] For example, "Auerbach Computer Characteristics Digest," Desk Reference Series, Auerbach Publishers, Inc., Philadelphia, Pa., tells of new developments, specifics on computer characteristics, performance, pricing, overall performance of competitive computer systems, range of choices in computer equipment selection, and techniques for preparing requests and evaluating proposals from computer manufacturers. See also "Datapro 70, EDP Buyers Bible," Datapro Research Corp., 1 Corporate Center, Moorestown, N.J.

TABLE 20-5   Data Collection Methods

Type	Examples	Transmission rate*	Characteristics	Advantages/ disadvantages	Typical use
Manual	Keypunch	Keypunch rate 100 – 2,100 cards per hour, depending on number of columns punched. Typical card readers – 600 cards per minute.	80-column card.	Can be implemented without "communications gear" (i.e., telephone lines, modems, software); relies on flow of source documents to the data processing center.	Quality data, inventory, payroll, manually operated or can be tied to automatic instruments.
	Port-A-Punch		Can be used in field without power.		
Semiautomatic	IBM 1030 data collection system	60 characters per second.	Communication between remote location and the central processing area.	Data entered at a remote location via several types of input; card, badge, slides; reasonably inexpensive, can be off-line.	Quality test data collection; time reporting; job cost accounting.
	IBM 1259 magnetic character reader	600 six-inch-long documents per minute.	Reads magnetic-ink-printed data from cards or paper documents.	Usually for preprinted checks so have a "constant" number; eliminates need for "stiff" checks; quality demands for magnetic printing higher than typing.	Check cancelling and tabulating.
	IBM 1231 optical mark page reader	Maximum 1,600 pages, 8½ x 11, per hour.	1,000 mark positions per side; connects directly to computer.	Eliminates keypunching; care must be taken to avoid extra pencil marks; slow; costly.	Answer sheets for tests; record data at source.

*NOTE: The physical recording rate is a function of the type of collection devices used and the application. An Industrial Engineer can provide assistance in simulating true recording rates for a given application.

TABLE 20-5   Data Collection Methods   *(Continued)*

Type	Examples	Transmission rate	Characteristics	Advantages/ disadvantages	Typical use
	IBM 2260 Display Station	2,600 characters per second.	Rapid man-machine communication by direct cable to computer displays; up to 960 characters in 12 lines on a 3 x 9 inch area of a cathode ray tube.	Visual verification of input; program controllable, can be preformatted; because it needs program control, the time to implement and the cost are greater.	Order entry, on-line work-in-process reporting.
Automatic	Analog to digital	Highly dependent on devices selected.	Automatic gathering and transferral of data from a source to the central processing unit.	Eliminates manual effort and possible errors, can easily handle large volumes of data; may require complex programming to provide for analysis capabilities desired.	In-process automatic testing and data collection and analysis.

TABLE 20-6   Relative Transfer Speeds — UNIVAC 1106

Form of storage	Characters per second
Card reader	800
Tape.	91,000
Disk	416,000
Internal CPU.	2,666,666

speed, convenience, suitability for work environment, etc. as a possible means for fulfilling the computer design specification.   Auerbach, DataPro, and others[32] list the cost of these input devices for all vendors.

2. *Data Analysis.*   For each type of analysis, the appropriate assumptions and the consequences of needs not being met must be considered.   For example, considera-

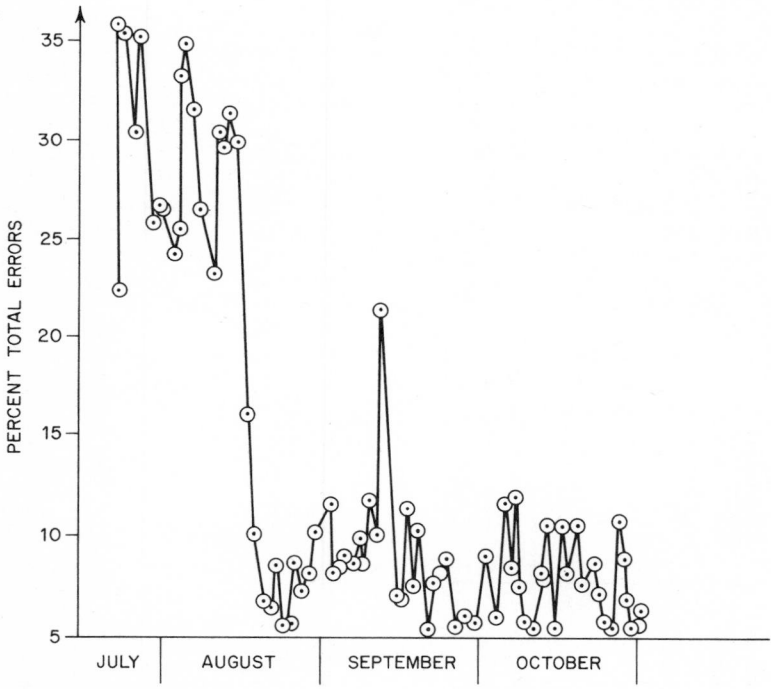

Fig. 20-4.   Input error control.

tion must be given to the need for data transformation, screening for obvious errors, replacement of missing or inaccurate data, multiple analyses of the same data, varying volumes of input data, and retention periods.

Nonnormal distributions or changes in underlying distribution assumptions must be anticipated.   If calculated results are to be compared to operating specifications,

[32] See Auerbach, *op. cit.* (in footnote 31), under Translating Design Specifications into Computer Requirements.

the frequency of specification change should be determined to optimize later computer operations.   Since available statistical and mathematical algorithms vary in efficiency, numerical analysis[33] may be worthwhile prior to specifying the necessary computation.

3. *Reports.* If the computer proposal is to provide useful information, the output or reports to be developed must take into account:

a. The types of reports required—detail, exception, summary.

b. Who will use the reports (reports differ for various levels in the company).

c. Frequency required—daily, monthly, on demand.

d. Timing required—must the reports be prepared for a certain morning meeting or by a certain day of the month?

e. Purpose to be accomplished by the reports—are they to serve as monthly run histories, or are the reports used to correct daily process upsets?

f. Report volume—if too thick, it may lose its appeal.

g. Reproducibility by conventional duplicating methods; also must information on the report be available for further analysis?

4. *Systems Security.* Systems security includes correction of input errors, data verification, and selective capability of file access.   If erroneous data enter the computer system and are not corrected, credibility will be lost as the errors show up in the reports.   A common means of avoiding the problem is to use an edit program that screens the input data for obvious errors.   Each entered value is checked against an operating range, and if it is outside the range, it is not allowed into the computer file but flagged by a special error report sent back to the Quality Control Department.   These "obvious" operating ranges can be automatically calculated from the data stored in the computer files.   An average of the last three to four months' (or whatever provides a representative sample) operating values $\pm$ 4 times the standard deviation of these values is useful as the obvious operating range.   Figure 20-4 shows the change resulting from the introduction of automatic calculation of obvious operating ranges in an input edit program.   Total errors include changes in product specifications, name, and identification codes as well as data errors; e.g., omission of one "run number" may flag each subsequent data entry as an "error." Insertion of the missing run number would thereby correct from 10 to 100 "errors." The error rate as shown in Figure 20-4 depends on how errors are defined.

In this way, the Quality Control Department has full control of the system and has the option of correcting or reentering data if it is in error.   "Garbage" is eliminated from the computer files.[34, 35]

Certain product specifications in computer files may be proprietary or confidential and represent a competitive edge for a company.   To prevent outsiders from accessing these files, most computers have the capability of requiring user-identifying codes at the file level.   This means that unless the program accessing a file can provide the correct identification, it will not be permitted to enter the file.

Unauthorized program modification is usually prevented by computer operations

---

[33] See Numerical Analysis, under Standards (in this Section).

[34] Error prevention by 100% inspection of punched cards is commonly practiced by data processing centers and is called "verification." Its efficiency is not 100%, nor does it obviate the need for input editing.

[35] See Minton, G., Inspection and Correction Error in Data Processing, *Journal of the American Statistical Association,* vol. 64, no. 328, pp. 1256–1275, December 1969; and Minton, G., Verification Error in Single Sampling Inspection Plans for Processing Survey Data, *Journal of the American Statistical Association,* vol. 67, no. 337, pp. 46–54, March, 1972. Also Fasteau, H. H., J. J. Ingram, and G. Minton, Control of Quality of Coding in the 1960 Censuses, *Journal of the American Statistical Association,* vol. 59, no. 305, pp. 120–132, March 1964.

control, more to avoid incomplete system changes (e.g., changing three files loaded by a program but overlooking a fourth later used) than to prevent theft, fraud, or misleading output.   Appropriate documentation (described below, under Software) assists.[36,37,38,39]

5. *Software.*   The programs identified in the systems analysis phase either have to be coded or obtained from another source, i.e., the vendor or a third party. "Canned" programs have the (supposed) advantage of having been previously tested and debugged.   Evaluation and modification take time, which should be included in the planning schedule.

One means for evaluating vendor-canned programs is through the use of programmer reference manuals.   A FORTRAN description typically contains the following elements: FORTRAN V Reference, Assembler Language Reference, Argument and Function Range, Functions Referenced, Error Conditions, Mathematical Method, Accuracy (ranges used in the test, number of argument values per argument range in the test, maximum relative error, root mean square of the relative error, maximum number of erroneous bits, percent of test function values with full length accuracy), Timing, Main Storage Requirements.[40,41]   The data processing department must be included in the investigation since not all programming languages can be used on all computers.

Software evaluation can be costly and time-consuming if the specifications are not clear to the potential user or if the documentation,[42,43] as is often the case, is incomplete.

Documentation is a *very* important part of every computer system, and the system is no better than its description.   Good documentation is best done as the programming proceeds.   This assumes that later revisions can be made without generating more errors than are being corrected.   Clarity and standardized presentation assist in minimizing delay and inconvenience during training and program revision.

To assure that all corrections to a system have been made accurately, test data or special inputs are planned and in some cases designed into the original system so that subsequent revisions will be carefully scrutinized.

6. *Hardware.*   In addition to the input equipment described in (1) above, the limitations of the existing computer hardware must be reviewed regularly.   The

---

[36] See also Wasserman, J. J., Plugging the Leaks in Computer Security, *Harvard Business Review*, pp. 119–128, September–October 1969; and Computers—Happiness Is Security, *Quality Progress*, vol. 3, no. 6, p. 31, June 1970.

[37] Halting the Electronic Hijacker, *Management Review*, November 1968, pp. 45–49, condensed from *Modern Office Procedures*, September 1968, gives a 16-point control checklist.

[38] Sauter, J. L., Reliability in Computer Programs, *Mechanical Engineering*, February 1969, pp. 24–27, offers seven recommendations to minimize malfunctions due to poor system design, oversight, or poor judgment in trade-offs between hardware and software.

[39] "Management Control of EDP," IBM, F20-0006-0, 1965, prepared by Price Waterhouse and Company, describes, via two case studies, responsibilities and control techniques for system design, source data, programming, data processing, output validity.   Interests of controller, auditor, and outsiders are considered.   Checklist included.

[40] See also Numerical Analysis, under Standards.

[41] Univac 1100 Series, Fortran V Library, Programmer Reference, UP-7876, Section 2. Mathematical Functions, Articles 2.1 through 2.2.

[42] "Documentation" means an explanation of program logic; reason for its choice; definition of input, output, and file formats; error message listings; and the scope of the diagnostics. For programs with little input/output but extensive computing, checkpoints, restart locations, and interrupt points are commonly specified.

[43] See also McCracken, D. D., and G. M. Weinberg, How to Write a Readable FORTRAN Program, *Datamation*, vol. 18, no. 10, pp. 73–77, October 1972.

data processing industry is so dynamic that the hardware and the books soon go out of date. To keep up to date requires periodic study of reliable publications[44] whose sole purpose is to describe capabilities of up-to-date hardware. A further must is "see your data processing manager."

7. *Systems Audit.* Each third-generation computer has the ability to log usage information for each of its components. Analysis of this information is essential for systems optimization and verification that each program is still needed. Both operating bottlenecks and obsolete systems can be spotted from statistics on file access, tape usage, subroutine calls, etc., augmented with program logic reviews highlighted by emergency restarts or operating reruns.[45]

QUALITY INFORMATION SYSTEM EXAMPLES

The following examples are designed to illustrate the general principles described above.

Process Review   The flow sheet shown in Figure 20-5, part A, illustrates the information flow for one of several testing laboratories. Information associated with process type 1 was of substantial volume as compared to that for other process types. In the laboratory, a tester, after completing the tests, marked an optical page reader sheet (see Figure 20-6). At the end of the day, these sheets were trucked from the various outlying divisions to the data processing center where the sheets were "read" directly into the computer and daily detail and summary cards were punched.

The information for other processes (small volume) was sent directly to the data processing center, where it was individually keypunched. The cards were sorted and collated. Following this, a computer analysis was performed to produce reports which were sent to the quality control engineers and management on an exception basis. (Table 20-7 is an example of the exception report produced.)

This system had several disadvantages, including inaccuracies associated with extreme sensitivity of the optical page reader, poorly marked sheets, excessive time spent by testers filling out the page reader sheets, slow input of the page reader to the computer, and occasional delays in the trucking of the data to the data processing center. To overcome these weaknesses, the system was redesigned to transmit the information after each test was completed through a badge and manual entry station via telephone lines to an off-line card punch located in the data processing center (see Figure 20-5, part B). This eliminated the trucking and the manual entry on the optical page reader sheet and allowed the operator to verify the accuracy of his own data as entered. An edit program was built into the computer operations to test for "obvious errors" (as described above under Planning: Systems Security). One of the controls on the input was an error listing sent to each Quality Control Department daily. From this, necessary corrections were marked and returned to data processing. (Figure 20-4 illustrates the level of errors when the system was first introduced without the obvious error check and the level achieved after its addition.)

With both systems, the data were obtained for process *review* purposes rather than for instantaneous process *control.* A third phase in the evolution of this quality

[44] See Federal Information Processing Standards (FIPS) Notes, *NBS Technical News Bulletin,* vol. 55, no. 5, pp. 126 and 127, May 1971, for a list of ADP software information resources including Business Software Information Service, Computer Program Abstracts, Computer Programs for Chemistry, etc.

[45] See Bell, T. E., "Choose Your Tools to Check Your Computer," *Computer Decisions,* vol. 4, no. 11, pp. 12–15, November 1972, for recommendations on operational control, equipment selection, and system tuning.

PART A – FIRST SYSTEM

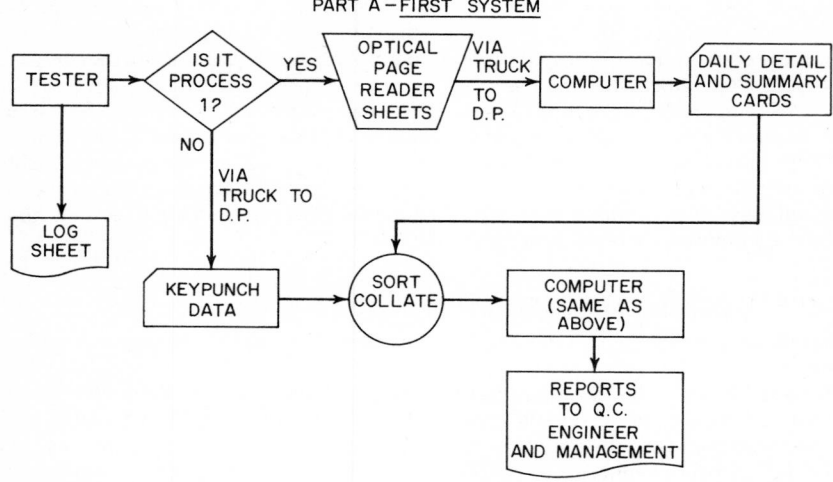

PART B – REVISED SYSTEM

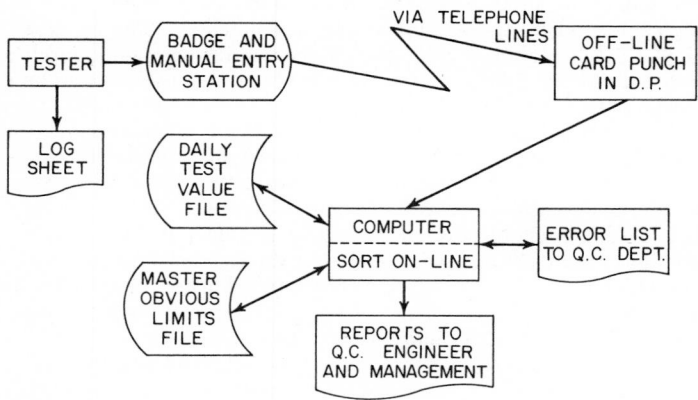

Fig. 20-5. Information flow—process review.

information system is to provide direct entry to the computer system on-line (replacing the off-line card punch) with feedback to the test station and output either via cathode ray tube or on-line printer calling for corrective action when points are out of control, trends are seen, or some unusual behavior, such as nonrandomness in the data, is detected.

This type of quality information system is particularly useful where the number of quality attributes measured is large, and individual control charts on each would be too time-consuming and interfere with the testing function. Furthermore, the purpose of quality review was to determine whether or not product and in-process specifications should be changed as well as to provide calibration data for testing instrument maintenance.

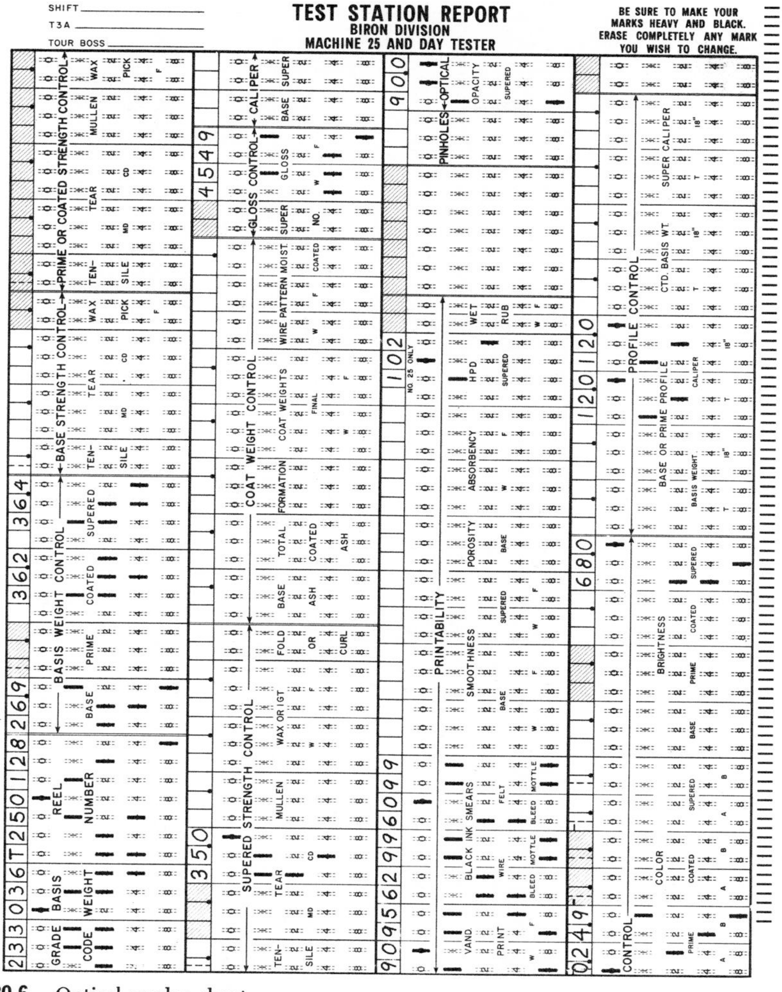

Fig. 20-6. Optical reader sheet.

Field Quality Evaluation The information flow shown in Figure 20-7 reflects reports filled out on a service call by the service man. (Figure 20-8 is an example of the service call report written on a punch card, which later becomes the source document.) The call report is forwarded through the branch office to the main office for review prior to keypunching and verifying.

Periodically, the computer sorts the input, compares the name and code file against the master file, and prepares two reports, an aging report and a 90-day trouble analysis designed to identify manufacturing and quality control problems. (Table 20-8 is an example of the 90-day trouble summary.) The aging report aims to identify basic product design deficiencies. Both of these are sent to the quality control engineer for evaluation as well as to management.

TABLE 20-7 Exception Report*

DAILY AVERAGE SUPERED PAPER TEST QUALITY EXCEPTION REPORT

OCT. 7, 1966   WX/IGT/SB   PAGE 1

MACH, GRADE, & WT.	NO OF REELS	PRINT W	PRINT F	GLOSS W	GLOSS F	COLOR A	COLOR B	BR.	OP.	MOIST.	W	F	MULL.	TEAR CD	TEN. MD	CAL.	HPD/ POR.
11 CC DB2 60	32					3.6 .4—				5.1	113 23	113 23					1737
11 PL DB2 60	10							80.7 1.3—		5.1							
12 PG DB2 70	4	61	60							5.3	8 1		30.9 3.9	67 8			521
12 FG RC 50	7							72.2 1.2	90.0 2.0—	5.7			18.3 2.7—				
14 CWM RC 50	8	31	32			4.8 .5			92.2 1.8—	4.5		148	20.7 2.7	41 3			179
14 CWM RC 60	31	33	33							4.4		138	27.9 3.9	55 7			185

*For any values paired vertically, the lower represents the difference from standard, if a standard exists.

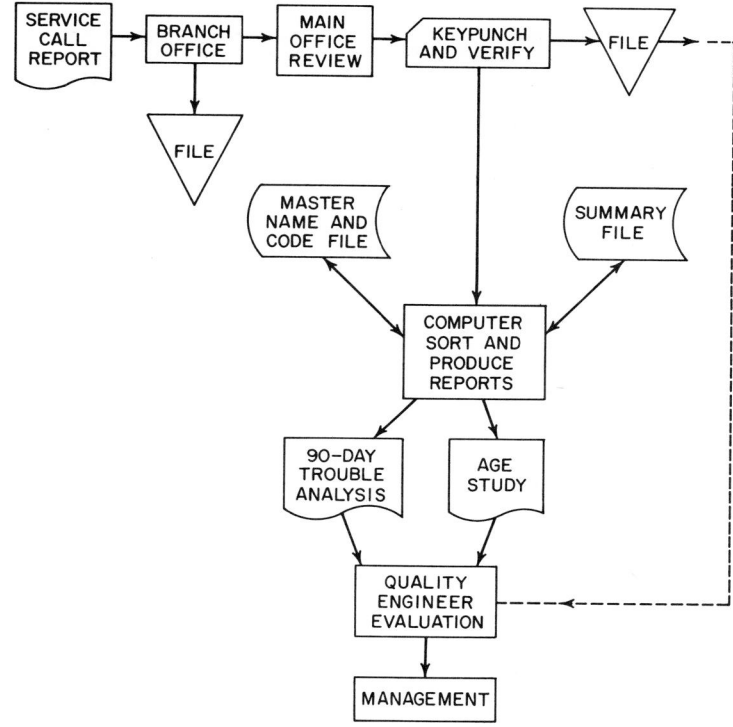

Fig. 20-7.   Information flow for field quality evaluation.

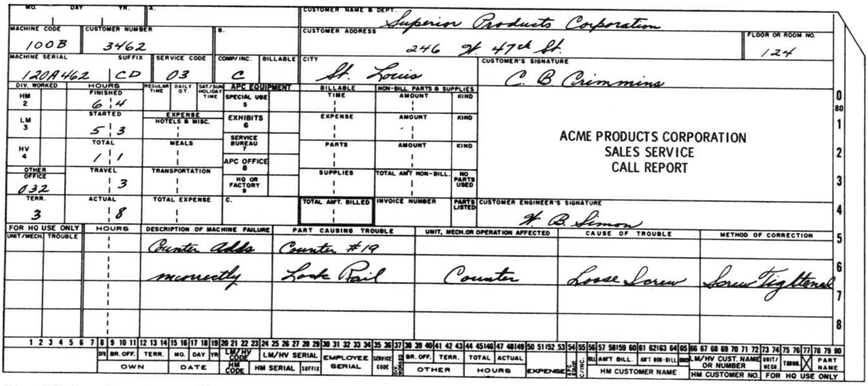

Fig. 20-8.   Service call report.

TABLE 20-8 Ninety-day Trouble Summary

90-DAY TROUBLE SUMMARY
Sales Service Department

Period						Products analyzed	Total for Period		Average per product per month		% of unit of part hours to type hours	Aver. per prod. per month all yrs. of mfg.
Mo or Yr of MFG	Product type	Unit code	Part code	Unit or part name	Trouble code	Quantity by type	Calls	Hours	Calls	Hours		Hours
	199	12		CONTACT UNIT		50	125	507.3	.83	3.36	25.5	
	199	08		FEED UNIT		50	104	311.4	.69	2.08	15.7	
	199	42		RELAY UNIT		50	135	181.7	.90	1.21	9.1	
	199	30		CIRCUIT BREAKER UNIT		50	64	167.2	.43	1.11	8.4	
	199	14		MAGNET UNIT		50	46	145.2	.31	.97	7.3	
	199	20		VARIABLE SPEED DRIVE UNIT		50	22	105.5	.15	.70	5.3	
	199	18		AUTO VALUE UNIT		50	33	67.4	.22	.45	3.4	
	199	35		SEN RECT UNIT POWER SUPPLY		50	25	51.3	.17	.34	2.6	
	199	03		CLUTCH UNIT		50	18	49.2	.12	.33	2.5	
	199	42		BASE UNIT		50	13	41.6	.09	.28	2.1	
	199	48		EXHAUST UNIT		50	15	27.7	.10	.18	1.4	
	199	60		CAM UNIT		50	20	24.9	.13	.17	1.3	
	199	25		IMPELLER UNIT		50	16	12.3	.11	.08	.6	
	199	15		TUBE CONTROL UNIT		50	5	9.2	.03	.06	.5	
	199	45		PUNCH UNIT		50	4	3.6	.03	.02	.2	
	199	05		MOTOR AND DRIVE UNIT		50	1	2.8	.01	.02	.2	
	199			NO UNIT MENTIONED		50	46	116.3	.31	.78	5.9	

Period   4th quarter

TABLE 20-8 Ninety-day Trouble Summary (*Continued*)

90-DAY TROUBLE SUMMARY

Sales Service Department

Period	4th quarter											
Mo or Yr of MFG	Product type	Unit code	Part code	Unit or part name	Trouble code	Products analyzed			Average per product per month		% of unit of part hours to type hours	Aver. per prod. per month all yrs. of mfg.
						Quantity by type	Total for Period					
							Calls	Hours	Calls	Hours	Hours	Hours
	199			NO TROUBLE FOUND		50	18	103.4	.12	.69	5.2	
	199			CUSTOMER ERROR		50	26	45.6	.17	.30	2.3	
	199			CUSTOMER POWER SUPPLY		50	3	9.4	.02	.06	.5	
	199			UNASSIGNABLE UNIT NTF		50	2	2.3	.01	.02	.2	
	199			CUSTOMER ATTACHMENTS		50	1	3.2	.01	.02	.2	
				TYPE 199 PRODUCT		50	742	1988.5	4.96	13.25		
	199			ASSIST TIME		50		272.6		1.82	13.7	

PERIOD SAMPLED 13 WEEKS

Trouble codes

01 Adjustment	18 Burred-nicked	22 Dirty-corroded	41 Off punch	61 Stripped	70 Worn
04 Alignment	16 Burned	25 Dry	42 Open	64 Tension	97 Other
07 Bent-warped	10 Jam	27 Leaking	46 Shorted	65 Timing	98 No trouble found
09 Blown	20 Damaged	34 Loose	52 Slipping	66 Tripped-unlatched	
13 Broken	21 Defective	36 Missing	56 Sticking-binding	67 Weak	

DETAIL CARD – CLUSTER INFORMATION

COLOR	GRADE	FINGER LENGTH	B BB BC BM BN BP BR	C CE CH CI CM CR CS CT CW	DEFECTS D DC DS DT	F FF FR	G GR	L LS	M MF ML MS	O OC	RETAIL STORE	NO. OF FNG.	CARD NO.
0	0	0	T T T T T T	T T T T T T T	T T T	T T	T	T T T	T	0 0 0	0 0	0 0
1	1 1	1 1	L L L L L L	L L L L L L L	L L L	L L	L	L L L	L	1 1 1	1 1	1 1
2	2 2	2-2	M M M M M M	M M M M M M M	M M M	M M	M	M M M	M	2 2 2	2 2	2 2
3	3	3	S S S S S S	S S S S S S S	S S S	S S	S	S S S	S	3 3 3	3 3	3 3
4	4	4-4	N P R S	SB SC SD SK SL SM SP SR	T W TB TC TH WP	1 2 3 4 5 6 7 8					4 4 4	4 4	4 4
5	5	5	NI NR PD RB RE RR								5 5 5	5 5	5 5
6	6	6-6	T T T T T T	T T T T T T T	T T T	T	T T T T T T T			6 6 6	6 6	6 6
7	7	7	L L L L L L	L L L L L L L	L L L	L	L L L L L L L			7 7 7	7 7	7 7
8	8	8-8	M M M M M M	M M M M M M M	M M M	M	M M M M M M M			8 8 8	8 8	8 8
9	9	9	S S S S S S	S S S S S S S	S S S	S	S S S S S S S			9 9 9	9 9	9 9

HEADER CARD – GENERAL INFORMATION

TYPE INSP.	SHIP	DATE DISCH.	DATE INSP.	AREA	PORT	BRAND NAME	PROD. DIV.	VARIETY	PACKING	UNIT	INSPR. NO.	BOX CODE STA. NO. TURBO	BOX COMB.	PROJECT NO.	GREEN GROSS	RIPE GROSS	TARE	LOOSE FINGERS	CARD NO.
AR	0 0 0	M 0	M 0	0 0 0	0 0	VA	PS	CL	0 0	0 0 0	0 0	0-0	0-0	-0	0 0	0 0
RE	1 1 1	A 1 1	A 1 1	EU 1 1	1 1	GM	BA	FG	1 1	1 1 1	1 1	1 1-1	1 1-1 1-1	1 1	1 1
	2 2 2	M 2 2	M 2 2	JA 2 2	2 2	CA	NK	HD	2 2	2 2 2	2 2	2 2-2	2 2-2 2-2	2 2	2 2
	3 3 3	J 3 3	J 3 3	SO 3 3	3 3	LA	PP	3 3	3 3 3	3 3	3 3-3	3 3-3 3-3 3	3
	4 4 4	J 4	J 4	EA 4 4	4 4	PO	SF	4 4	4 4 4	4 4	4 4-4	4 4-4 4-4 4	-4
	5 5 5	A 5	A 5	WE 5 5	5 5	NA	PB	5 5	5 5 5	5 5	5 5-5	5 5-5 5-5 5	55
	6 6 6	S 6	S 6	CE 6 6	6 6	TP	6 6	6 6 6	6 6	6 6-6	6 6-6 6-6 6 6	66
	7 7 7	O 7	O 7	7 7 7	7 7	7 7	7 7 7	7 7	7-7	7-7 -7 7 7	77
	8 8 8	N 8	N 8	8 8 8	8 8	8 8	8 8 8	8 8	8-8	8-8 -8 8	88
	9 9 9	9	D 9	9 9 9	9 9 9	9 9	9 9 9	9 9	9-9	9-9 -9 9 9	99

Fig. 20-9. Port-A-Punch cards.

Applications of this technique are used in a number of industries in which it is desirable to classify complaints or field service experience by category. In many instances, comparison of specific defects in different geographical locations or under different environmental conditions helps to identify either product improvement required or customer misuse.

Perishable Foods Inspection Figure 20-9 shows a Port-A-Punch card used by inspectors for recording perishable food quality in the field. The card is unique in that the elements of the card in which information is to be coded have been die-cut so that, in place of conventional keypunching, the punches can be produced with a stylus. The cards are carried in the field by the inspector and the information is recorded by punching out the holes with a stylus. The cards are collected and airmailed from various spots around the world on a once-per-week basis to the main office data processing center. Competitive information is collected on a similar sampling basis. Executive reports illustrating available quality about perishable product are produced on a weekly basis and, after evaluation and highlighting by the quality director, forwarded to management for information.

The key to this quality information system is the unique design of the card, which permits recording information in 66 columns instead of the conventional 40 in each card. The system relies strongly on a well-known classification of defects used universally and worldwide within this company.[46]

For additional examples in other Sections of this Handbook, see Table 20-1. See also Process Control Applications, Automatic Measurement Systems, and Minicomputer, under Special-purpose Computer Applications.

[46] Private communication.

ORGANIZING FOR COMPUTING SERVICES

Ideally, priorities for computing services should be established on the basis of team decisions. In practice, these priorities are strongly influenced by the organization structure (i.e., to which Department does Data Processing report). This influence diminishes as real-time interactive computing becomes available or when computing capacity is comfortable. In that event the obstacle to good service is not access to the computer but systems analysis and programming.

Responsibility for Computing When the priorities for computer access, systems analysis, and programming are favorable, the Quality Control Department is content to receive computing services from some service department. Such an arrangement enables Quality Control to give attention to its primary mission without becoming deeply involved with a support specialty. However, when total computing needs exceed capacity, the departments that have difficulty in getting priorities from the central service source will turn to other sources, either purchased services or in-house departmental services.

Purchased Services These can be obtained through service bureaus, through time sharing[47,48,49,50] with an adjacent bank or other corporation, through consultants, or through a "turnkey" purchase. In the latter, specifications are given to a vendor who provides all services including systems analysis, programming, purchase or rental of computing hardware, documentation, and training to use the new system. This is a suitable approach when computing skills within the corporation are nil and the needs are high. Table 20-9 describes pros and cons of purchased services.

Purchased services should be considered when the main memory of the in-house computer is too small for occasional very large jobs (which would preempt the entire computing schedule for long stretches at a time) or when a computing operating system is required which is foreign to the in-house computer.[51,52]

Internal Services The alternative, in-house computing, goes all the way from Quality Control having its own computer to sharing one with another department; it includes considerations of "open and closed shop." In "open shop" any computer user has complete access to all aspects of the computer system or actually takes over its operation during his assigned time. In "closed shop" operation, all computing is done by the department assigned the responsibility; input is presented according to prescribed standards, specifications must be met in all ways relative to design of programs, justification, operating times, etc., and direct access is normally not available.

Because engineers tend to look on computers as oversized slide rules to be used

---

[47] See Stewart, M., "Will Time-Sharing Help You?" *Management Review*, June 1970, pp. 37–41, for classes of use best solved by time sharing.

[48] See Kemeny, J. G., "Man and the Computer," Charles Scribner's Sons, New York, 1972, for details of BASIC programming.

[49] Time Sharing: One More Q.C. Tool, *Quality Progress*, vol. 3, no. 6, pp. 26–28, June 1970, describes TIME/WARE, a series of 25 quality control programs, costs and a sample problem.

[50] A similar service is available through other computer "service bureaus." Software is also available, e.g., Quality Control Operating System (QCOS)^{TM}, from John A. Keane and Associates, Princeton, N.J.

[51] For example, APL, a powerful interactive mathematical language, is reported to require a minimum of 256 K bytes memory on IBM 360/370 operating under OS—thereby putting it beyond the reach of most quality departments.

[52] Guides are available for selecting leased equipment to meet speed and cost requirements. See Auerbach, *op.cit.*, for evaluation of benchmark problems, including matrix inversion and generalized mathematical problems (which include a combination of arithmetic operations, input, output, and manipulation of fifth-order polynomial subroutines). Speed improvements of better than 2,500/1 are possible.

TABLE 20-9   Advantages and Disadvantages of Purchased Services—Closed Shop and Open Shop

Choices	Advantages	Disadvantages
Purchased Services	1. Provide quick, cost-controlled computing specifically designed for chosen problems. 2. Uses available or proprietary software. 3. Pay only for computer time and services used. 4. Immediate access according to negotiated schedule. 5. Avoid supervisory and personnel expense. 6. Gain quick expertise.	1. No residual systems analysis, programming, or overall computing skill developed. 2. Purchased software difficult to evaluate—may be inefficient, costly, but defects are difficult to detect. 3. Cost per computer hour greater. 4. Highly vulnerable during systems analysis and programming to vendor personnel turnover. 5. Hookup, telephone line charges, travel expense add to cost. 6. Potential security problem.
In-house computing closed shop	1. Single responsibility assignment to another department for effective use of the computing function, for keeping abreast of changes in the computing field, for making all changes in computer operating systems, and in disseminating impact of these to all users. 2. Bears the brunt if oversights or errors in running happen. 3. Responsible for correct translation of input data into machine-readable form. 4. Sets standards for documentation, input/output, and decides if operating diagnostics are adequate. 5. Responsible for new hardware and contracted software purchase decisions.	1. Same as any tightly controlled organization with high fences—may not adequately disseminate information about the computing center configuration, its principal use, or its degree of use. 2. May not encourage innovation or examination of its operating methods and computing capabilities (thus, it may perpetuate inefficient and expensive operating programs).
In-house computing open shop	1. Direct access to the computer. 2. Faster turnaround time for "one-time" programs. 3. Reduction in documentation cost. (With well-disciplined users, debugging time can be shortened.) 4. New programs implemented more rapidly.	1. Possible abuse of the computer center (due to poor debugging or an excessive number of undocumented programs—which cannot be run by anyone other than the designer). 2. Lack of understanding of actual computer center use. (This can be overcome by job records of main-frame time used and an audit of excessive debugging.) 3. Inefficient programming if skills of computer center personnel not used.

when needed rather than as machines to be kept busy, some Quality Control Departments have justified having their own computers. This justification is more clearly seen in closed shop operations in which the Computing Department lacks mathematical and statistical skills and where the Quality Control Department would have to describe in excessive detail the statistical or mathematical calculations required. In many cases, the explanation time exceeds the programming time. In each case, the solution to these potential problems is found in clear-cut computing policies.

Computing Policies   As Diebold[53] has pointed out, executive management has the primary responsibility for deciding what computing is to be done within a corporation and how it is to be organized. The following must be examined:

1. Priorities—who comes first when there has been an operational upset—lost time (does quality control take a back seat to payroll, accounts receivable, etc.)

2. Turnaround time—does the computing environment include "job stream" queuing, or is lengthy advance notice required (this can also come about with too little time assigned for quality control computing).

3. Corporate strategy—is there dedication to a high-quality product line, to high level of customer service, and to traceability through such things as run records including raw material, processing, inspection records, etc.?

4. Budget—does quality control have a budget sufficiently large to accommodate its required computing, and does it have a voice in determining relative priorities of new programming effort?

5. Computer use justification—does top management have an adequate understanding of the importance of computing to quality control; is justification measured both in cost replacement *and* value of information in terms of what it can do for quality management, in terms of the consequences of omission or error, and in the desire to multiply the effectiveness of technical people?[54]

Systems Analysis   The decision as to whether some systems analysis capability should be resident within the quality control function is dependent on the size of the systems analysis activity within the company and its availability to the Quality Control Department. With good assurance that all quality control needs can be met, systems analysis can be assigned elsewhere. On the other hand, if extensive effort is required to translate quality control needs into data processing language, then it is likely to be more economical for at least a residual systems capability to be present within quality control. In some cases, this can be a part of inspection planning or preproduction analysis activities. As indicated in Section 19, these skills may already be at hand in companies having high engineering change or traceability requirements. Basically, the user must be assured that his computing output will be in a form directly usable and intelligible to him.

Manpower and Training   With an increasing trend toward providing systems analysis and programming capability within the Quality Control Departments, personnel must be carefully selected and training[55] provided for them and for other users within the quality control function. Generally the training would cover:

1. How the company responds to computing needs in general

2. Existing quality control computing programs—what they do—why—who uses them—cost—payback

3. How to identify quality control needs best served by computing

4. Procedures for obtaining computing services

---

[53] Diebold, J., "Bad Decisions on Computer Use," *Harvard Business Review*, January–February 1969, pp. 14–16, 27, 28, and 176, urges top management to take a direct hand in deciding its corporation's computer master plan.

[54] Diebold, *op. cit.*

[55] See Section 17.

5. Limitations and constraints on computing relative to the specific Quality Control Department

In addition, for the systems analyst and programmers,[56] a specific training program should be developed in concert with the vendor and department principally responsible for computing if it is external to the Quality Control Department.

STANDARDS

Effective use of the computer relies on suitable standards in four areas:

Systems analysis and programming
Numerical analysis
Data validity
Operational performance

The data processing industry has been active in generating its own standards. However, because the profession itself is young, the Quality Control Department will do well to see that operating procedures are well documented with suitable controls.[57,58]

Systems Analysis and Programming   Standards in these areas emphasize thoroughness in coverage of the function being studied (use of checklists) and systemizing the approach to the programming task itself.

Considerable progress can be expected in the 1970s in converting the estimating phase of programming from an art to something that is closer to a science.[59]   With various degrees of complexity, currently used methods commonly include the following:

Complexity of existing system
Number of input and output documents
Number of clerical functions now performed
Number of new steps to be introduced
Is the system totally new?

Computer vendors can be of assistance in establishing analysis and programming standards.   For example, allocation of time to *programming activities* has been reported as:

Program logic	35%
Coding and developing test data	25%
Testing and debugging	35%
Final documentation	5%
Total	100%[60]

[56] The authors are disbelievers in the notion of training all quality control engineers in FORTRAN or other computer languages.   Instead, we recommend that they acquire an understanding of what can be accomplished with the computer.   Engineers can be encouraged to collect data and analyze their problems in terms of available computer programs if computer input and use are simplified.

[57] See generally Section 19, Documentation.

[58] See in this Section, Systems Security under Translating Design Specifications into Computer Requirements.

[59] "Planning for an IBM Data Processing System," GF20-6088-3, IBM, White Plains, N.Y., discusses preinstallation planning, systems design, program preparation, standardization, program testing, etc., for both commercial and scientific installations.

[60] "Management Planning Guide for a Manual of Data Processing Standards," C20-1670-0, IBM, White Plains, N.Y., covers need for EDP standards, sources of standards, policies, programming and estimating standards, systems analysis (flow charting, file formats, definitions), testing rules, etc.

Automating flow charting[61] and updating programming changes conveniently will help minimize operating manual preparation.[62]   (The computer program listing is a ready reference.)

In each situation, it is to the Quality Manager's advantage to inquire exactly what estimating procedure is used. If none is apparent, the comparison between forecast and accomplishment using control charts may be helpful. (In this Handbook, see Section 46, Support Operations.)   Currently, few data processing centers use quality assurance techniques, although the trend is in this direction[63, 64, 65, 66]

Numerical Analysis   This topic is associated with choices in programming to assure accurate and valid results. Because most digital computers use a binary mathematical base, exact decimal representation is not possible. Inherent in every computer is a limitation on accuracy associated with "word length" (in a desk calculator, number of digits stored).   Furthermore, many subroutines in compilers use infinite series or approximations to calculate square root or to exponentiate.

Several approaches are available to minimize errors accumulating from lengthy calculations or due to poor choices of approximations:

Become familiar with the field of numerical analysis.[67, 68, 69]

Investigate limitation of single and double precision related to your computer software.

Note accuracy statements associated with your compiler (FORTRAN, COBOL, etc., see Programmer Reference Manual).

Choose statistical algorithms or programs evaluated by more knowledgeable statisticians (see below, Computer Programs for Quality Control Use).

Choose approximations having adequate error control.[70, 71, 72]   A few examples will illustrate the advantages of considering the numerical analysis aspects of computing.

---

[61] Chapin, N., Flow Chart Packages and the ANSI Standard, *Datamation,* vol. 18, no. 9, pp. 48–53, September 1972, as related to COBOL programming, compares costs, output in terms of flow chart, cross referencing, source, and diagnostics. In the references, it comments upon programs documentation for six software packages.

[62] See generally Section 19, Documentation.

[63] Coutinho, J. DeS., Quality Assurance of Automated Data Processing Systems (ADPS), *Journal of Quality Technology,* vol. 4, no. 3, pp. 145–155, July 1972; also see vol. 4, no. 2, pp. 93–101, April 1972, describes attitudes and techniques for ADP process controls.

[64] See Damon, H. H., "Controlling the Quality Computer System," *Quality Progress,* vol. 3, no. 2, p. 35, February 1970, for a description of the organization and program within the General Electric Medium Systems Department to cope with quality computer systems.

[65] See Reorganization of ANSI Standards Committee X3, and Approved ANSI Standards on Computers and Information Processing, *NBS Technical News Bulletin,* May 1970, pp. 100–102, for a list of standards and active standards committees.

[66] Harris, W. P., Quality and Aerospace Software, *Quality Progress,* vol. 3, no. 2, p. 43, February 1970.

[67] Householder, A. S., "Principles of Numerical Analysis," McGraw-Hill Book Company, New York, 1953.

[68] Milne, W. E., "Numerical Calculus," Princeton University Press, Princeton, N.J., 1949.

[69] Faddeeva, V., "Computational Methods of Linear Algebra," Dover Publications, Inc., New York, 1959, English translation from Russian.

[70] Hastings, C., Jr., "Approximations for Digital Computers," Princeton University Press, Princeton, N.J., 1955.

[71] Abramowitz, M., and I. A. Stegun, "Handbook of Mathematical Functions," AMS55, U.S. Government Printing Office, Washington, D.C., June 1964.

[72] Wilde, D. J., "Optimum Seeking Methods," Prentice-Hall, Inc., Englewood Cliffs, N.J., 1964.

Calculation of Variance.   Of the several formulas available, (1) is more accurate than (2).

$$s^2 = \frac{\sum (x_i - \bar{x})^2}{n - 1} \tag{1}$$

$$s^2 = \frac{\sum x^2 - (\sum x)^2 / n}{n - 1} \tag{2}$$

This is because it multiplies differences $(x_i - x)$, which tend to be smaller than the individual values (x_i). Its accuracy is paid for by one less squaring operation and by $n - 1$ more differences; in general by a "second pass of the data"—the first pass calculates the average. Other approaches possible include "scaling the data" by subtracting a constant from each value and adjusting the calculated average.

$$s^2 = \frac{n \sum x^2 - (\sum x)^2}{n(n - 1)} \tag{3}$$

While (3) is more convenient on a desk calculator, its chances for "overflow" and thereby inaccuracy are even greater than (2).

Choice of Algorithm to Satisfy Accuracy.   Polynomial equations, continued fraction expansions, power series, etc., are all candidates for approximating statistical test values such as student's t, F, χ^2.[73,74,75] The choice depends on error rates tolerable. For example, an approximation to the mean square successive difference critical values[76] can be made using the following equation:

$$CL = b_o + n\left[b_1 + n(b_2 + nb_3)\right]$$

If a maximum deviation from the published values no greater than -0.018 is acceptable, b_3 can be set equal to zero[77] (saving one multiplication and one addition step). Otherwise, the accuracy is at least $-.012$.

Computing Programs for Quality Control Use.   Table 20-10 lists tested programs for many quality control uses. Table 20-11 lists statistical algorithms meeting a specific set of requirements[78] (including accuracy and failure indications) which may be imbedded in other more general master programs.[79,80,81]

Programming Choices.   Building unnecessary sophistication into a computer program can be expensive. For example, Table 20-12 compares two different methods for calculating the square root of a number, the $X^{**}Y$ being more general and more

---

[73] Abramowitz, M., and I. A. Stegun, *op. cit.*

[74] Algorithms for computing critical values of key statistics can be found as follows: *F*-Distribution, *Communications of Association for Computing Machinery*, vol. 7, no. 12, p. 725, December 1964; Student's *t*-Distribution, *Technometrics*, vol. 7, no. 1, pp. 71 and 72, February 1965.

[75] Dudewicz, E. J., and S. R. Dalal, "On Approximations to the t-Distribution," *Journal of Quality Technology*, vol. 4, no. 4, pp. 196–198, October 1972. These authors highlight the difficulties in selecting rigorous computing algorithms. They point out that the formula was given in 1964 and restated in 1970, but the proof was not demonstrated earlier and is not generally known, although widely applicable.

[76] Bingham, R. S., Approximations for Mean Square Successive Difference Critical Values, *Technometrics*, vol. 10, no. 2, pp. 397–400, May 1968.

[77] Values for b_0, b_1, and b_2 change also.

[78] Nelder, J. A., et al., "The Construction and Description of Algorithms," *Applied Statistics*, vol. 17, no. 2, pp. 175–179, 1968, describes the procedure and details for publication of computing algorithms relevent to statistical problems. The two-part items cover the description and the algorithm itself. (Contains a good checklist for judging completeness of "canned" programs.)

[79] Nelder, J. A., et al., Statistical Computing 1970, *Applied Statistics*, vol. 20, no. 1, pp.

TABLE 20-10   Computer Programs for Quality Control Use*

Volume	Number	Pages	Issue	Contents
1	1	68–71	January 1969	Seven statistics (median, mean, range, variance, standard deviation, coefficient of variation, skewness) and frequency histogram plots.
1	2	149–152	April 1969	Plots $\bar{X}$ and $\bar{R}$ charts (constant subgroup size $2 \le n \le 10$; automatic scaling); computes $\bar{R}$, $\bar{\bar{X}}$, 3σ limits.
1	3	217–220	July 1969	Plotting p and np charts (3σ for constant and varying sample size).
1	4	285–288	October 1969	Plotting c and u charts (constant sample size c chart; variable sample size u chart) and average sample size u chart; 3σ limits.
2	1	54–57	January 1970	Plotting cusum charts (both individual and grouped data).
2	2	109–111	April 1970	Algorithm for scale selection in computer plots (modified from AS 21).†
2	3	174–176	July 1970	Two- to five-point Lagrangian Interpolation. Up to eight pairs of observations; data sets read sequentially.
2	4	243–245	October 1970	Student's t-test (one- and two-sample, equal and unequal sample sizes).
3	1	38–41	January 1971	Scatter plots (up to 500 pairs).
3	2	95–97	April 1971	Coefficient of correlation (r). (Calculates r, upper and lower 95% limits using $Z = 0.5\,ln\,(1 + r)/(1 - r)$ and $\sigma_r = 1/\sqrt{n - 3}$ for sample size $n > 3$.)
3	3	138–143	July 1971	Simple linear regression (omits F test for replicates).
3	4	184–189	October 1971	Multiple linear regression.
4	2	113–117	April 1972	Fitting two widely useful nonlinear models: $(Y = B_0 + B_1 B_2{}^x)$ $(Y = B_0 + B_1 X_{B_2})$
4	2	117–118	April 1972	Scaled midpoints for a histogram. (References vol. 2, no. 2 and vol. 3, no. 1.)
4	3	168–171	July 1972	Single sampling plans given an AQL, LTPD, producer and consumer risks (uses Poisson distribution).
4	4	205–209	October 1972	Double sampling plans (uses Poisson distribution).
5	1	39–42	January 1973	Multiple sampling plans.

* References to *Journal of Quality Technology* (programs in FORTRAN IV).
† *Applied Statistics* computing algorithm 21. (See Table 20-11.)

25–79, 1971, covers a series of papers on statistical computing and computer languages including coverage of internal data structures, operating system considerations for statistical computing, input/output in statistical programming, and a report on the work of the Dutch Working Party on statistical computing.

[80] Muller, M. E., Computers as an Instrument for Data Analysis, *Technometrics*, vol. 12, no. 2, pp. 259–293, May 1970. An excellent paper describing the state of the art. Presents the specifications for a statistical computing language and then provides description of STAT JOB. [Note comment on paper by Leone (54), Abstracts of Statistical Computer Routines, which reports the limitations in programs, their writeups, and the quality of the computational techniques.]

[81] See Milton, R. C., and J. A. Nelder, "Statistical Computation," Academic Press, New York, 1969, for a recent compendium on topics of specific interest to computing statisticians.

TABLE 20-11   Computing Algorithms for Statistical Analysis*

	General				
	Volume	Number	Pages	Year	Title
	17	2	175–179	1968	The Construction and Description of Algorithms
	19	1	110	1970	Preparation of Typescript for Algorithm Descriptions
	19	1	82–92	1970	A Conversational Statistical System for Medical Records

	Remarks				
AR Number	Volume	Number	Pages	Year	Remark on algorithm
1	18	1	116–117	1969	AS 1—Subroutine Package
2	18	3	299–300	1969	AS 2—The Normal Integral (as to speed and accuracy)
3	20	1	117	1971	AS 10—(for equally spaced points; speed, storage saving)
4	20	2	216	1971	AS 10—The Use of Orthogonal Polynomials (corrects two possible failure modes)

		Algorithms				
	AS Number	Volume	Number	Pages	Year	Title
	1	17	2	180–185	1968	Simulating Multidimensional Arrays in One Dimension
	2	17	2	186–188	1968	The Normal Integral (computes ordinates lower and upper tail area from a given standardized x)
C†	3	17	2	189–190	1968	The Integral of Student's t-Distribution (area from $-\infty$ to t_v)
C2	4	17	2	190–192	1968	An Auxiliary Function for Distribution Integrals
C	5	17	2	193–194	1968	The Integral of the Noncentral t-Distribution
C	6	17	2	195–197	1968	Triangular Decomposition of a Symmetric Matrix
C	7	17	2	198–199	1968	Inversion of a Positive Semidefinite Symmetric Matrix
	8	17	3	277–279	1968	Main Effects from a Multiway Table
	9	17	3	279–283	1968	Construction of Additive Table
	10	17	3	283–287	1968	The Use of Orthogonal Polynomials
	11	17	3	287–288	1968	Normalizing a Symmetric Matrix
	12	17	3	289–292	1968	Sums of Squares and Products Matrix
	13	18	1	103–104	1969	Minimum Spanning Tree
	14	18	1	105–106	1969	Printing the Minimum Spanning Tree

*References to *Applied Statistics*.
† C or C2 indicates correction (see below).   "Ref" refers to AS Number indicated.

TABLE 20-11   Computing Algorithms for Statistical Analysis *(Continued)*

					Algorithms
AR Number	Volume	Number	Pages	Year	Title
15	18	1	106–110	1969	Single Linkage Cluster Analysis
16	18	1	110–114	1969	Maximum Likelihood Estimation from Grouped and Censored Normal Data
17	18	1	115–116	1969	The Reciprocal of Mill's Ratio
18	18	2	197–199	1969	Evaluation of Marginal Means
19	18	2	199–202	1969	Analysis of Variance for a Factorial Table
20	18	2	203–206	1969	The Efficient Formation of a Triangular Array with Restricted Storage for Data
C 21	18	2	206–208	1969	Scale Selection for Computer Plots
22	18	3	283–287	1969	The Interaction Algorithm
23	18	3	287–290	1969	Calculation of Effects
24	18	3	290–293	1969	From Normal Integral to Deviate
25	18	3	294–298	1969	Classification of Means from Analysis of Variance
26	19	1	111–113	1970	Ranking an Array of Numbers
27	19	1	113–114	1970	The Integral of Student's t-Distribution (from t to $+\infty$)
28	19	1	115–118	1970	Transposing Multiway Structures
29	19	2	190–192	1970	The Runs Up and Down Test
C 30	19	2	192–196	1970	Half Normal Plotting
31	19	2	197–203	1970	Operating Characteristics and Average Sample Size for Binomial Sequential Sampling
32	19	3	285–287	1970	The Incomplete Gamma Integral
33	19	3	287–289	1970	Calculation of Hypergeometric Sample Sizes
34	19	3	290–292	1970	Sequential Inversion of Band Matrices
C 35	20	1	99–104	1971	Probabilities Derived from Finite Populations
36	20	1	105–110	1971	Exact Confidence Limits for the Odds Ratio in a 2 x 2 Table
37	20	1	111–112	1971	Inversion of a Symmetric Matrix
38	20	1	112–115	1971	Best Subset Search
39	20	1	115–117	1971	Arrays with a Variable Number of Dimensions
Ref. 40	20	2	192–194	1971	The Cumulative Construction of Minimum Spanning Trees
40	20	2	204–206	1971	Updating a Minimum Spanning Tree

TABLE 20-11   Computing Algorithms for Statistical Analysis *(Continued)*

<table>
<tr><td colspan="7" align="center">Algorithms</td></tr>
<tr><th colspan="2">AS
Number</th><th>Volume</th><th>Number</th><th>Pages</th><th>Year</th><th>Title</th></tr>
<tr><td></td><td>41</td><td>20</td><td>2</td><td>206–
209</td><td>1971</td><td>Updating the Sample Mean and Dispersion Matrix</td></tr>
<tr><td></td><td>42</td><td>20</td><td>2</td><td>209–
213</td><td>1971</td><td>The Use of Orthogonal Polynomials with Equal x-Values</td></tr>
<tr><td>C</td><td>43</td><td>20</td><td>2</td><td>213–
216</td><td>1971</td><td>Variable Format in Fortran</td></tr>
<tr><td></td><td>44</td><td>20</td><td>3</td><td>327–
331</td><td>1971</td><td>Scatter Diagram Plotting</td></tr>
<tr><td></td><td>45</td><td>20</td><td>3</td><td>332–
335</td><td>1971</td><td>Histogram Plotting</td></tr>
<tr><td></td><td>46</td><td>20</td><td>3</td><td>335–
337</td><td>1971</td><td>Gram-Schmidt Orthogonalization</td></tr>
<tr><td></td><td>47</td><td>20</td><td>3</td><td>338–
345</td><td>1971</td><td>Function Minimization Using a Simplex Procedure</td></tr>
<tr><td></td><td>48</td><td>21</td><td>1</td><td>97–
99</td><td>1972</td><td>Uncertainty Function for a Binary Sequence</td></tr>
<tr><td></td><td>49</td><td>21</td><td>1</td><td>100–
103</td><td>1972</td><td>Autocorrelation Function for a Binary Sequence</td></tr>
<tr><td></td><td>50</td><td>21</td><td>1</td><td>103–
112</td><td>1972</td><td>Tests of Fit for a One-Hit vs. Two-Hit Curve</td></tr>
<tr><td></td><td>51</td><td>21</td><td>2</td><td>218–
225</td><td>1972</td><td>Log-Linear Fit for Contingency Tables</td></tr>
<tr><td></td><td>52</td><td>21</td><td>2</td><td>226–
227</td><td>1972</td><td>Calculation of Power Sums of Deviation about the Mean</td></tr>
<tr><td colspan="7" align="center">Corrections</td></tr>
<tr><th colspan="2">AS
Number</th><th>Volume</th><th>Number</th><th>Pages</th><th>Year</th><th>Correction</th></tr>
<tr><td colspan="2">3-7</td><td>18</td><td>1</td><td>118</td><td>1969</td><td>Omission, sequence</td></tr>
<tr><td colspan="2">4</td><td>19</td><td>2</td><td>204</td><td>1970</td><td>$- h, - a$</td></tr>
<tr><td colspan="2">30</td><td>20</td><td>1</td><td>118</td><td>1971</td><td>a_5</td></tr>
<tr><td colspan="2">21</td><td>20</td><td>1</td><td>118</td><td>1971</td><td>Negative Minimum</td></tr>
<tr><td colspan="2">35</td><td>20</td><td>3</td><td>346</td><td>1971</td><td>Three Errors</td></tr>
<tr><td colspan="2">43</td><td>20</td><td>3</td><td>346</td><td>1971</td><td>Three Errors</td></tr>
</table>

expensive. Not only is the less general coding (SQRT) almost three times faster, but it requires approximately one-fourth as much main storage and is more accurate. These programming choices can be checked during programming planning or in a preinstallation audit. (See UNIVAC FORTRAN V Programmer Reference Manual, op. cit.)

Multiple Regression and Matrix Inversion. The problems involved in binary numbering systems most normally evidence themselves in the algorithms used for computing parameters of a multiple regression analysis or similar statistical techniques in which matrix inversion is involved. Wampler[82, 83] has shown that the inversion techniques used in several well-known regression programs are not satis-

[82] Wampler, R. H., A Report on the Accuracy of Some Widely Used Least Squares Computer Programs, *Journal of the American Statistical Association,* vol. 65, no. 330, pp. 549–565, June 1970.

[83] Wampler, R. H., The Evaluation of Linear Least Square Computer Programs, *Journal of Research,* National Bureau of Standards, Series B, 73B, no. 2, pp. 59–90, April-June, 1969. Wampler ranks available programs as to effectiveness and usability.

TABLE 20-12   Comparison of Two Methods for Computing Square Root*

Performance factor	SQRT	$X**Y$
Timing	9.3 or 40.1 μs	106 to 117 μs
Number of instructions.	33	125
Data area size	10	42
Total main storage requirement . . .	43	167
Maximum error (10^{-8})	-0.74 to 0.73	-0.85 to -1.17
Full-length accuracy %	100	75 to 95

*Data abstracted from UNIVAC 1100 Series FORTRAN V Library Programmer Reference (UP-7876), pages 2–55 through 2–56 and 2–69 through 2–71, op. cit.

factory for some ill-conditioned matrixes. This failure is basically caused by the round-off methods selected.[84]

Data Validity   Success in this venture is measured by the proportion of sufficiently accurate data transmitted to the right location at the right time.   Accuracy is relative and data checking and editing should be limited wherever possible.   Extraneously recorded or printed digits clutter up reports and can slow down access to computer files.

Methods for assuring validity for computer use include:

Verification or 100% inspection of punched cards
Use of buffered input devices which permit sensed errors to be corrected prior to transmission or punching
Visual displays of keyed input for visual verification
Comparison against "obvious" error limits[85]
Statistical tests for outliers ("wild values")
Automatic retransmission and comparison when "parity" or "check bits" are lost, etc.
Quality motivation programs to locate errors and prevent recurrence via training[86]

Published results are sketchy and range from 10 to 98% *defective* in an unusual combined classification and keypunching operation.[87,88,89]   Verification has been reported as 96 to 97% effective.

Vendors publish expected error rates and indicate how often per day a telecommunication terminal should have to retransmit prior to maintenance.

[84] See also Mayer, R. P., and R. A. Stowe, Would You Believe 99.9969% Explained?, *Industrial and Engineering Chemistry*, vol. 61, no. 5, pp. 42–46, May 1969, on regression interpretation.

[85] Freund, R. J., and H. O. Hartley, A Procedure for Automatic Data Editing, *Journal of the American Statistical Association*, vol. 62, no. 318, pp. 341–352, June 1967.   These authors have proposed using a gross check, an internal consistency check, and a least squares correcting procedure.

[86] Mandel, J., Quality Control Basic Data, *Quality Progress*, vol. 3, no. 6, pp. 16–19, June 1970, describes reasons for errors.   Methods for detecting, controlling, and correcting them are described along with training and selection of personnel.

[87] Minton, G., *op. cit.*, under Planning, Data Analysis.

[88] O'Reagan, R. T., Relative Costs of Computerized Error Inspection Plans, *Journal of the American Statistical Association*, vol. 64, no. 328, pp. 1245–1255, December 1969, describes how to calculate breakeven as a function of input error rates for computer editing versus post-computer edit choices.

[89] "In one unpublished study, keypunching error rates for 63 jobs performed within one month ranged from zero to 4.21 errors per 1,000 key strokes, averaging 0.291 errors per 1,000 key strokes.   The jobs had from 4 to 17,454 cards per job, with from 6 to 73 columns punched per card.   Seven operators on the *same* job ranged from zero to 0.443 errors per 1,000 key

Operational Performance Standards for computer operational efficiency can be obtained in the same manner as on any production unit but with the added complication that, under time sharing and executive system control, the central computer and its peripheral equipment may be used simultaneously by all, some, or none of the programs. Typically, operating "uptime" is logged on all units individually.

Performance can be enhanced by good feedback from the operator of run difficulties, including errors causing restarts or reruns along with the time lost. Scheduling is usually data processing's responsibility, but clear input labeling and program identification (both physically and printed out on the operator console unit) help assure error-free runs. The Quality Control Department shares, with its system analyst and programmer, responsibility for suitable documentation leading to good operating instructions. (In this Section, see Software, under Planning, for additional comments.) This is to include learning run times for each program, advising operators in recovery procedures and describing backup data and program locations.

Periodic review with the Data Processing Department of program usage, errors detected, reruns, etc. will help sustain performance.

Process Control. Performance on continuously operating computers has been reported by Hubbe.[90] Based on 1969 information, 12 paper mills responding, covering 5 large systems averaging 214 loops and 7 small systems averaging 56 loops, mean time between failure (MTBF), mean downtime (MDT) and availability [defined as 100 MTBF (MTBF + MDT)], the conclusions were as follows:

1. MTBF ranged from 109 to 1,633 hours (for the latter about 5 failures a year on all hardware for all causes).

2. MDT averaged 5.2 hours with a median of 3.7.

3. Availability averaged 99.1% with a median of 99.34.

(The above figures include outside factors, e.g., air conditioning failures, power failures, and human errors.) Excluding these, the median MTBF rose to 954, median MDT 3.4, median availability 99.46%.

4. The comparison of software failures on user and supplier programs showed that all software failures occur less than half as often as all hardware failures.

5. Average availability due to all software problems was 99.8% (as compared with 99.1% due to all hardware problems).

6. On supplier only programs, MTBF has more than doubled (from 1,448 to 3,622 median) and availability has increased accordingly.

Every mill reported that no paper production was lost due to computer failures (presumably based on sufficient analog control backup).

SPECIAL-PURPOSE COMPUTER APPLICATIONS

The computers described above, whether operating in a commercial or scientific environment, are primarily general-purpose in nature and thereby have greater capabilities and higher costs than may be justified in industrial situations. Availability of low-cost, special-purpose computers for use in laboratories, offices, and manufacturing plants has accelerated a trend toward automatic process control, data gathering, and analysis.[91, 92] These applications are described below.[93]

---

strokes. Two of the operators exceeded the upper control limit and two the lower control limit in this study."

[90] Hubbe, P. D., Control Computer Dependability Study, *TAPPI,* vol. 53, no. 9, p. 1,777, September 1970.

[91] See Williams, T. J., "The Present Status of Automatic Production and Control Devices and Expected Featured Developments," *Technometrics,* vol. 8, no. 1, pp. 73–89 February 1966, for a list of vital factors in process industry mathematical modeling, use of process dynamics, and gains expected from use of theoretical models.

Process-control Applications   Section 9, Manufacturing Planning, under Planning Process Controls, Quality Information Equipment, and Automatic Process Regulation sets the scene for more detailed discussion of how to match computer to process[94] for optimum control.   Benefits to be expected include:

Closer control of process level to target
Reduction in process variation
More uniform application of control procedures during startup, operations, and shutdown
Tending of many process elements by fewer people
Less lost time in meeting new quality targets during grade change
Consistent sequencing of control actions during process upsets or in emergencies
Reduction in instrument costs under DDC

The payoff is greatest when rapid response to process upsets or changes avoids significant loss in production or product quality and when process control variable interrelationships are complex.

The planning requirements contain all the steps described in this Section under Planning as well as additional ones related to setting priorities on corrective control actions, importance of maintenance if calibration is lost, and measuring process dynamics.   The following are necessary steps in process control applications:

1. Define the principal results wanted, i.e., what is to be controlled, why, benefits expected.

2. Describe the operating process, controlling mechanisms, sensing elements and factors to be adjusted, etc.

3. Determine time relationships and dependencies among control variables which will have to be decoupled; i.e., lags, response times, and relative gain factors of correlated variables.

4. Evaluate sensing—sensitivity, linearity over the control range, calibration procedures, robustness in operating environment, output level and type, whether pneumatic, electrical, or mechanical.[95]

5. Determine the interface necessary to relate the sensing signal to the computer (includes signal level, impedance, stability, etc.) and the nature of input: analog, digital, switch closure, or time passage.

6. Select computing and control algorithms *(a)* to scale input and output signals, *(b)* to analyze material and heat balances, *(c)* to calculate process adjustments necessary for control.

7. Select control variables to be manipulated; relate timewise (see 3 above);

[92] See Williams, T. J., annual reviews, Computers in Process Control, *Industrial and Engineering Chemistry,* vol. 61, no. 1, pp. 76–89, January 1969, vol. 62, no. 2, pp. 28–40, February 1970.   Williams notes the rapid acceptance of the minicomputer and the beginnings of standardization of process control software.   Also vol. 62, no. 10, pp. 94–107, December 1970 (emphasizes the rapid price decrease of the minicomputer).

[93] See Dyck, A. W. J., New Developments and Trends in Process Control, *American Paper Industry,* vol. 53, no. 12, pp. 26–32, December 1971, for a state-of-the-art report on process-control computers for the paper industry.   Reports typical costs for a process control system over a five-year period are $950,000 for computer, software development, instrumentation, facilities and cables, and $516,000 for manpower.

[94] Aron, J. S., Real-Time Systems in Perspective, *IBM Systems Journal,* vol. 6, no. 1, pp. 49–67, 1967, describes special characteristics of real-time systems including input (rate, message length, types, device response), priorities, response time, operating characteristics, output characteristics, software, reliability.

[95] See Mardon J., et al., How to Select Hardware for Process Control Systems, and How to Select Process Control Computers, *Pulp and Paper Magazine of Canada,* vol. 71, nos. 23–24, pp. 115–124, December 4-18, 1970.

choose method for transmitting signal, verifying its receipt, that action starts and is completed.

8. Compare measuring and control action time with available computer cycle time.

9. Design failure detection and fail-safe operating mode. Decide strategy for process restart if computer or instrumentation fails.

10. Select hardware;[96] order, install, program, test, debug and document.

11. System test (include all elements of control loop including failure mode).

12. Recheck control parameters for algorithm.

Automatic Measurement Systems As rapidly as interfaces could be developed between instruments (manual and automatic) and data recording units (keypunches, paper and magnetic tape, etc.), the intermediate step has been eliminated where volume and economic feasibility warranted. Primary benefits are lower cost of data input, error-free data collection, and minimum supervisory needs.[97]

A natural extension of the concept is to hook the instrument directly to a central computer or a dedicated one. (See below, Minicomputers.) Special devices have been built into many systems to indicate end of record for each sample or measurement.[98] The published examples range from hospital laboratories[99] to process areas.[100, 101, 102, 103] Pribor and Kirkhan[104] describe a typical application in which a CLAS 300 Spear Computer with a 4,000-word core memory and 12 analog input channels costing about $50,000 is part of a hospital data system directly linked to a Technicon SMA 12 Autoanalyzer, a SMA 4, and a Beckman Analytrol Scanning Densitometer. They report cutting time (from test request to report) from 24 to 4 hours in most cases, clerical errors minimized, and costs lowered to about 7 cents per patient day versus 40 cents per patient day for a moderately large computer. Physically located in the laboratory and run by regular laboratory technicians, the

[96] See Lehigh, W. R., and R. H. Mosher, Correct Computer Control Design Can Improve Mill Operations, *Paper Trade Journal*, vol. 155, no. 46, pp. 82-83, Nov. 15, 1971.

[97] Edwards, R. A., Laboratory Automation Based Systems, Presented at COMMON Meeting, Cincinnati, Ohio Sept. 8, 1967.

[98] Bicking, C. A., R. S. Bingham, and R. L. Weiss, Automatic Data Logging for Experimentation and Quality Control, *Industrial Quality Control*, vol. 20, no. 6, pp. 12–16, December 1963.

[99] Biochemical Hospital Records, *Quality Progress*, vol. 3, no. 6, pp. 5–6, June 1970.

[100] Young, W. R., Quality Control of an Automated Chemical Assay Utilizing the IBM 1130, *Transactions of the 23d Annual Technical Conference*, ASQC, pp. 173–180, 1969, Los Angeles, Calif., describes a systems analysis to maximize the reliability, accuracy, and the amount of useful information obtainable from an automated assay while concurrently minimizing the cost of these innovations through the improvement of existing computer software — a detailed discussion from transmittance readings through monitoring performance.

[101] Downing, J. C., How to Process Quality Control Data Electronically, *Transactions of the 21st Annual Technical Conference*, ASQC, pp. 43–50, 1967, Chicago, describes an IBM 1460 computer system at Johnson & Johnson used to prepare daily exception variable and attribute sampling reports, highlighting troublesome machines and operators for Production Management's corrective action.

[102] Schwartz, M. C., An Automated Record Keeping and Data Retrieval System for a Quality Control Laboratory, *Transactions of the 25th Annual Technical Conference*, ASQC, pp. 137–143, 1971, Chicago, describes the design and installation of a semiautomatic record keeping and data retrieval system at Mead Johnson in Evansville, Indiana and its subsequent evolution providing on-line data entry and retrieval.

[103] Kemner, W., and R. Gordon, Putting the Computer to Work in Steel Analysis, *Transactions of the 22d Annual Technical Conference*, ASQC, pp. 223–229, 1968, Phila. Pa., describes spectrographic and statistical analysis of iron and steel samples with direct information feedback to the B.O.F. floor. (IBM 360 computer plus telecommunications experience reported.)

[104] Pribor, E. C., and W. R. Kirkhan, In-Lab Computer Links Directly to Instruments, *Laboratory Management*, June 1968, pp. 14–49.

system handles virtually the entire laboratory load, producing analysis of specimens, storing of results, updating patient's report with every new test, and, in some cases, providing diagnosis. It eliminates transcription of data and typing of separate reports.

Minicomputers   While the decade of the 1960s was one of rapidly growing computer capacity, the 1970s will be typified by the growth of computer accessibility. This greater access will more than likely be provided by minicomputers. The small, inexpensive ($10,000 to $30,000) general-purpose digital computers can do almost anything that large computers can. They perform the same type of logical and arithmetic operations, use the same data storage and input/output devices that the larger computers do. The difference is that minicomputers are a lot smaller and a lot less expensive and have less core capacity than big computers.[105]

Rather than use the central computer for quality control reporting, it is possible to use a minicomputer to collect the data from a test laboratory on a daily basis and provide interim reports.[106] These data can then be transferred to the central computer for retention. Minicomputers have been interfaced with practically every type of instrument found in industrial research and quality laboratories.[107, 108]

Minicomputers usually require programming at the most basic programming level rather than by compilers.[109] This and their limited core requires specialized training and leads to slower programming. This is important only during initial implementation and for (one hopes) rare program changes. Although capable of application to a wide *variety* of problems, these small computers are usually used for a *limited* special purpose at any one time.

Desk Calculators. In addition to minicomputers, desk calculators have become increasingly useful in the analysis of quality data. Models exist ranging from programmable (up to hundreds of steps) to simple adding machines. A new Hewlett-Packard interface allows its programmable calculators to be used for applications traditionally performed by minicomputers. The interface connects the HP9800 series programmable calculators to coupler/controllers to control instrument systems for data acquisition, process control, and automatic testing.[110] Wang, Monroe, and Hewlett-Packard (to name a few) have numerous desk calculators which can provide many statistical functions by pressing a single key. The functions include but are not limited to standard deviation, variance, correlation coefficient, linear regression, F and t tests, random number generator, trigonometric and logarithmic functions, permutations and combinations, etc. It is even possible to attach a plotter to several calculators including the Hewlett-Packard Model 9100 A.[111]

ADVANCED TECHNIQUES

The computer puts in the hands of the quality manager the capability of utilizing more advanced techniques than he can with pencil and paper. Since the methods of operations research are outside the scope of this Handbook, the following discus-

[105] Decastro, Edson D., What Can You Do With A Minicomputer? *Industrial Research,* November 1969, pp. 45–51.

[106] Cashman, M., Small Business Computer, *Datamation,* June 1972, pp. 51–57, indicates the results of a survey of vendors catering to the small business user and includes characteristics of their computers.

[107] For use in calibration work see Kreyer, L. S., Minicomputer-Driven System Offers Savings In Electronic Calibration, *Quality Management and Engineering,* April 1972, pp. 17–19.

[108] See Young, N. F., Minicomputer Tests Minicomputers in Q.A. Program, *Quality Management and Engineering,* April 1972, pp. 12–13.

[109] Compilers are available for use on larger computers to produce code for minicomputers, e.g. IBM 1800 FORTRAN for System 7.

[110] *Computer World,* March 1, 1972.

[111] Outfit-Your-Own-Calculator, *Quality Progress,* vol. 4, no. 11, pp. 5–6, November 1971.

sion is limited to indicating applications important to quality management that the computer makes possible.

Simulation Techniques   These methods are aimed at determining "What would happen if." Essentially, they are substitutions of a model of an existing business system with a computer system. As indicated in Thierauf, they may be deterministic or probabilistic.[112] For example, production management is frequently reluctant to substitute sampling acceptance for 100% inspection, particularly when customer requirements are stringent. With extensive 100% inspection information in computer files, any number of pertinent inspection plans can be tested against the same data by random sampling. The computer results demonstrate the proportion of the defects present in the submitted lots or process flow which would be detected (or overlooked). In one application, such a test, comparing Dodge's CSP-3 continuous sampling plan with 100% inspection for two different sampling inspection levels (25% and 10%) led to savings of $100,000 in the first year.[113]

One of the authors[114, 115] has used simulation to demonstrate the power of EVOP and selected experiment designs in meeting possible changes in furnacing parameters. In one instance, four different models of changing furnacing conditions were simulated to show the power of a particular statistical design in studying the effect of intentional changes in resistor composition and processing.[116]

In a number of companies, Quality and Industrial Engineers jointly study process flows for increased productivity and cost reduction. Computer simulation of process flows using GPSS[117] or SIMSCRIPT permits evaluation of the effect of changing such things as the number of inspection stations,[118] inspectors, roving quality technicians, or the frequency of quality audit on in-process quality levels under various degrees of quality variation. Using FORTRAN, it is possible to study the effect of inventorying work in process whose quality is known only as a result of in-process sampling. Knowing the effect of quality level on inventory size, and subsequent production upset due to off-quality goods, can be instrumental in improving customer service.

In the field of automated process control, where engineering must take into account process perturbations, CSMP[119] permits modeling and studying computer-

---

[112] Thierauf, R. J., and R. A. Grosse, "Decision Making through Operations Research," John Wiley & Sons, Inc., New York, 1970, Chap. 15, especially pp. 480–482.

[113] Bingham, R. S., An Application of Continuous Sampling Plans for Chemical Acceptance and Control, *Transactions,* Statistical Methods in the Chemical Industry, Chemical Division, ASQC, Hoboken, N.J., January 12, 1957, pp. 67–85.

[114] Bingham, R. S., Try EVOP for Process Improvement, *Industrial Quality Control,* vol. 20, no. 3, pp. 17–23, September 1963.

[115] Bingham, R. S., Getting Around Environmental Trends—Angular Randomized vs. Augmented Factorial Designs, *1960 Metropolitan ASQC Conference,* New York.

[116] Choksi, S. C., Computer Can Optimize Manufacturing Tolerances for an Economical Design, *Transactions of the 25th Annual Technical Conference,* ASQC, 1971, pp. 323–330, Chicago, describes the rationale, flow diagram, and results in a computer simulation of tolerance stackup. Principal benefit claimed is the ability to determine whether a given tolerance can be increased or not at minimum cost.

[117] Simulation software is available (free) as part of computer rental, or at additional charge, or as a proprietary item from independent software companies, depending on the computer vendor.

[118] Staab, T. C., Can Computer Simulation Help Improve Quality? *25th Annual Technical Conference Transactions,* ASQC, 1971, pp. 481–489, Chicago, illustrates simulation techniques via the determination of the number of inspectors required and the correct sample size for a particular problem. (Flow sheets and sample data are given.)

[119] See Continuous Simulation and Process Design, *IBM Computing Report,* Winter 1972, pp. 6–9, for a discussion of applications of CSMP and a description of optional graphic output on the IBM 2250 unit interactively in conjunction with FORTRAN IV.

collected data to determine the appropriate response function to avoid under- or overcontrol.

Model Building and Planning The first step in simulation, after deciding the technique is germane, is to list the questions to be answered by the study. From this, a model is constructed to reflect adequately the industrial environment present. This is of limited scope yet capable of responding to the questions. After verifying that the model is pertinent and valid, it is converted into computer language and made ready for test.[120]

Role of the Computer The computer provides the capability of testing the model repeatedly with a variety of different conditions suitable to the questions to be answered. Normally, the computer programs either generate or call for random elements providing, in a very short period of time, a test of the model equivalent to years of actual use. Furthermore, the compiler software normally permits the model builder to generate reports, frequency distributions, tracings of specific transactions to identify which routes they took, and, if pertinent, identification of specific defects which would have been ignored by the particular model. (Note it is possible to include statistical tests of randomness to verify validity of the data examined during the study.)

To illustrate the power of the simulation software, GPSS/360 (IBM), for example, has the following building-block capabilities:

Equipment-oriented: Seize, Release, Preempt, Return, Storage, Enter, Leave, Logic, Gate

Transaction-oriented (time delays): Advance, Generate, Terminate, Split, Assemble, Match, Gather, Assign, Index

Flow Modification: Transfer, Loop

In addition, random generators, distribution functions, Boolean algebra, statistical tests and queuing tables are available.

Scheduling, PERT-CPM, and Personnel Allocation For some quality control functions, the juggling of manpower as a supervisory function in the face of varying union rules and restrictions consumes considerable time. This can be saved by using carefully constructed computer programs, taking into account skills and weaknesses of quality control inspectors, technicians, and engineers. These are particularly useful when a wide variety of quality control projects are under way or critical products are being introduced. Particularly, with high rates of absenteeism, the ability to use on-line linear programming[121] for personnel allocation can simplify a quality supervisor's job.

With the problems of project management, it is important to meet inspection planning and quality control schedules. The use of PERT[122] and CPM[123] techniques for identifying bottlenecks in both overall project planning and within the quality control portion of the project itself can avoid oversights and missed schedules. These techniques are particularly useful for corporate coordination of quality efforts in a multiplant environment.

---

[120] Sundstom, J. F., Simulation—Tool for Solving Materials Handling Problems, *Automation*, vol. 16, no. 12, pp. 90–93, December 1969, reports the subdivision of time spent on each step of a simulation analysis: problem definition, 10%; data collection, 30%; model definition, 20%; computer programming, 10%; debugging and validation, 10%; actual computer runs, 5%; and analysis of output, 15%. (In the example described, the model was tested some 30 times during the course of the study, which took approximately a six-month period.)

[121] Vajda, S., "Readings in Linear Programming," John Wiley & Sons, Inc., 1958, Chapter 11.

[122] Thierauf, *ibid.,* Chapter 5.

[123] Shostack, K., and C. Eddy, Management by Computer Graphics, *Harvard Business Review*, vol. 49, no. 6, pp. 52–63, November–December 1971.

FUTURE APPLICATIONS OF COMPUTERS TO QUALITY CONTROL

The biggest stumbling blocks in greater application of computers to quality control problems lie in the area of awareness and training. With greater awareness of the contributions computing can make to quality management and subsequent analysis of quality information needs, we can expect greater demands for computing. Information management is not yet acknowledged as a significant discipline in many corporations.[124] As it becomes better accepted, training in computer techniques will become more widespread. Training not only in computer capabilities but in quantitative methods will add to the demand for computer availability.

The net effect of greater computer applications will be to shorten the time required for product development. One indication is that we are already seeing computers as an element in a closed loop "experiment-analysis-decision" procedure.[125, 126] This technique of analyzing the data directly from the experiment and in turn changing the parameters *during* experimentation will again shorten the product design evaluation time.

As quality management information systems become more commonplace, greater information retrieval will shorten time for preparation and distribution of specifications, for editing and publication of quality procedures, and for interrelating quality costs with production planning. In general, we can expect more analysis, and a greater proportion of that will be more sophisticated and include a greater number of defect classifications as well as mathematical and statistical techniques.

The accelerated demand for computing will be assisted by the improvements in hardware, including availability of minicomputers,[127] programmable deskside computers with plug-in programs, and with greater application of interactive graphic techniques.[128, 129] Access via time-sharing computers to large main memories will permit remote terminal users to use graphic techniques in more routine problem solving. Principal developments needed are in the software area.

Software Developments   Until recently, there was no compiler specifically designed to write statistical programs utilizing full computer capability.[130] Teams of numerical analysts and statisticians will undoubtedly offset this in the near future. Greater attention is being placed on numerical efficiency not only to reduce computing costs but also to assure that misleading results are not being produced.[131] New software will undoubtedly include the ability to dictate programs orally to the computer, using voice recognition and thereby bypassing the input problem.

Programs are already available for flow-charting of computer programs, and the

[124] Prince, T. R., "Information Systems for Management Planning and Control," rev. ed., Richard D. Irwin, Inc., Homewood, Ill., 1970.

[125] Time-Shared Computer Runs Experiments, *NBS Technical News Bulletin,* vol. 54, no. 1, pp. 4–5, January 1970.

[126] Secrest, D., Time-Sharing Experimental Control on a Small Computer, *Industrial and Engineering Chemistry,* vol. 60, no. 6, pp. 74–80, June 1968.

[127] Prince, *op. cit.*

[128] Shostack and Eddy, *ibid.*

[129] Medlin, C. H., and R. E. Bingham, The Use of Graphical Display Unit (Light Pen and Scope) For Regression Analysis, *25th Annual Technical Conference Transactions,* ASQC, 1971, pp. 157–162, Chicago, cite and illustrate the time-saving and model-selection advantages of interactive statistical analysis using light pen and CRT input-output. See also Peikert, E. W., Interactive Graphics - A New Dimension, *IBM Computing Report,* vol. 5, no. 5, pp. 4–7, November–December 1969, for a discussion of GATD (Graphic Analysis of Three-Dimensional Data) and photos of CRT output.

[130] See Muller, M. E., *op. cit.,* under Numerical Analysis in this Section.

[131] See Wampler, *op. cit.,* under Numerical Analysis in this Section.

same technique can be applied to constructing process flow charts. These will be useful in inspection planning.

In the field of numerical control, the programs for tape control computers are commonly prepared in the engineering department. To our knowledge, none of this has yet taken advantage of network flow analysis, which would assure optimum production processing and automatic inspection efficiency.

Adaptive quality control[132] is expected to make strong inroads where control charting is used extensively. It requires periodic updating of the control parameters. Just as these can be done automatically by computer, so can AOQLs, AQLs, and other sampling plan parameters be adjusted in light of automatically analyzed results. (For example, the decision to change control limits as additional data are accumulated can be tested and carried out automatically according to program decision rules.)

Chronic Problems   There is no reason why the Pareto rule cannot be applied by computer to identify the "ten most chronic quality problems." By doing this periodically and using automatic information retrieval from the quality management information system, progress in overcoming these problems should be highlighted, becoming both faster and more economical. The interrelation between production losses, difficulties in manufacturing, preshipment inspection, and customer experience should produce a more responsive quality system. Under management information systems (depending on the discipline used within the company) it will be possible for any executive to interrogate the data bank to examine quality performance historically in comparison with program forecasts. A log of the number of times the quality data bank was interrogated and the types of questions asked of it could provide additional insight as to management's concern.[133]

COMPUTER GLOSSARY

The following, taken from "A Brief Computer Glossary," *Quality Progress*, vol. 3, no. 2, p. 37, February 1970, with permission of the American Society for Quality Control, has been supplemented with terms from a variety of other sources.[134] The serious worker interested in a definitive work will refer to the "American National Standard Vocabulary for Information Processing" (latest edition), ANSI X3.12-1970, available from the American National Standards Institute, 1430 Broadway, New York 10018.

Absolute Address   (1) An *address* that is permanently assigned by the machine designer to a storage location.

(2) A pattern of *characters* that identifies a unique storage location without further modification.

Access time   The time it takes a computer to locate data or an instruction word in storage and transfer it to an arithmetic unit for use.

---

[132] See Section 29, Adaptive Control under Quality Improvement Programs.

[133] See also MacMillan, M. A., and D. M. McNamara, in The Impact of Computers on Quality: Past, Present and Future, *Transactions of the 23d Technical Conference*, ASQC, 1969, pp. 741–747, Los Angeles, who speculate on how computers are likely to affect quality systems of the future.

[134] Other published glossaries include Grant, R., *Paper Trade Journal*, vol. 154, no. 37, pp. 57–58, 1970; Digest of Computer Terms, *Automation*, July 1970, pp. 73–75 (abstracted from "A Glossary of Commonly Used Computer Terms," General Automation, Inc., Orange, Calif.); Wegner, C. S., Computer Graphic Terms, *Automation*, vol. 19, no. 7, pp. 51–53, July 1972, a general glossary of terms (written for the layman) for graphic terminals designed for interactive use; and Friend, G., Data Communications Glossary, *Automation*, vol. 19, no. 11, pp. 47–48, November 1972 (selected terms to help the newcomer to the computer data communications field).

Algorithm A prescribed set of well-defined rules or processes for the solution of a problem in a finite number of steps, e.g., a full statement of an arithmetic procedure for evaluating sin x to a stated precision.

Analog computer A computer that represents variables by physical analogies; a computer that solves problems by translating physical conditions into related mechanical or electrical quantities and uses mechanical or electrical equivalent circuits as an analog for the physical phenomenon being investigated.

Binary A characteristic, property, or condition in which there are only two possible alternatives.

Binary coded decimal A decimal notation in which the individual decimal digits are represented by a pattern of ones and zeros.

Bit A single character in a binary number or a single pulse in a group of pulses; a unit of information.

Branch Selection of possible paths in the flow of control based on some criterion.

Byte A measurable portion of consecutive binary digits, such as a combination of bits.

Card 80-column A punch card with 80 vertical columns representing 80 characters. Each column is divided into two sections, one with character positions labeled 0 through 9; the other is labeled 11 and 12. The latter also are referred to as the X and Y zone punches.

Channel A path along which information may flow.

Character One symbol of a set of elementary symbols such as those corresponding to typewriter keys. Symbols usually include digits 0 through 9, letters A through Z, punctuation marks, operation symbols and any other single symbols that a computer may read. A character may be represented by a group of other elementary marks such as bits or pulses.

COBOL COmmon Business Oriented Language

Compare To examine the representation of a quantity to discover its relationship to zero; to examine two quantities usually to discover identity or relative magnitude.

Compile To prepare a *machine language* program from a computer program written in another programming language by making use of the overall logic structure of the program, or to generate more than one machine instruction for each symbolic statement, or both. Includes assigning *absolute addresses* and codes for symbolic ones.

Compiler A program that *compiles.*

Computer A device capable of solving problems by accepting data, performing prescribed operations on the data, and supplying the results of these operations. Various types of computers are calculators, *digital computers,* and *analog computers.*

Control field A constant location, e.g., on a punch card, at which instructions are placed that will control one or more operations.

Data Basic elements of information which can be processed or produced by a computer.

Deck A collection of cards punched for a specific purpose.

Digital computer A computer that processes information represented by combinations of discrete or discontinuous data as compared with an analog computer for continuous data. A device that performs sequences of arithmetic and logical operations not only on data but its own program.

Disk A storage device (generally magnetic) on which information is recorded.

Double precision Pertaining to the use of two *computer words* to represent a number, thereby increasing the number of significant digits retained.

Edit To modify the form or format of data, e.g., to insert or delete characters such as page numbers or decimal points or to check data validity.

Flow chart A graphical representation for the definition, analysis, or solution of a problem in which symbols are used to represent operations, data, flow, and equipment.

FORTRAN (FORmula TRANslating system) Any of several mathematical procedure-oriented languages.

Hardware Physical equipment, e.g., mechanical, magnetic, electrical, or electronic devices. Contrast with *Software.*

Immediate access The ability to use a storage device or register directly without delay due to other units of data.

Input Information transferred from an external source to the internal storage of the computer.

Input equipment Equipment used for transferring data and instructions into an automatic data processing system; equipment by which an operator transcribes original data and instructions to a medium that may be used in an automatic data processing system.

Instruction   A set of characters that defines an operation together with one or more addresses (or no address) and which, as a unit, causes the computer to perform the operation on the indicated quantities.

Keypunch   A keyboard-actuated device that punches holes in a card to represent data.

Loop   A self-contained series of instructions in which the last instruction can modify and repeat itself until a terminal condition is reached.   A communications circuit between two private subscribers or between a subscriber and a local switching center.

Machine-oriented language   A language designed for interpretation and use by a machine without translation.   The language may include instructions that define and direct machine operations and information to be recorded by or acted upon by these machine operations.

MODEM (MOdulator and DEModulator)   A device used to translate analog signals to digital signals for transmission over telephone lines, with provision at the receiving end for reconversion to analog signals.

Multiprocessing   Pertaining to the simultaneous or *interleaved* execution of two or more programs or sequences of instructions by a computer or computer network.   Multiprocessing may be accomplished by *multiprogramming, parallel processing,* or both.

Off-line equipment   Peripheral equipment or devices not in direct communication with the central processing unit of a computer.

On-line equipment   Peripheral equipment or devices in a system under control of the central processing unit in which information reflecting current activity is introduced into the data processing system as it occurs, directly in line with the main flow of transaction processing.

Output equipment   Equipment used to transfer information out of a computer.

Parity bit   A check bit that indicates whether the total binary "1" digits in a character or word (excluding the parity bit) is odd or even.   (If a "1" parity bit indicates an odd number of "1" digits, a "0" bit indicates an even number.   If the total number of "1"—including the parity bit—is always even, the result is an even parity system.   The parity bit of a word is tested against the "1" digits in that word to assure data validity before or after arithmetic operations, data transmission, etc.

Peripheral equipment   Auxiliary machines that may be placed under the control of the central computer, e.g., card readers, card punches, magnetic tape feeds, high-speed printers. Peripheral equipment may be used on-line or off-line depending upon computer design, job requirements, and economics.

Processor   A general term that includes assembly, compiling, and generation; a shorter term for an automatic data processor or arithmetic unit.

Program   To devise and write a *computer* routine.

Random access   The process of obtaining information from or placing information into storage where the time required is independent of the location of information most recently obtained or placed in storage, without effective time penalties.

Real time   (1) Pertaining to the actual time during which a physical process transpires.   (2) Pertaining to the performance of a computation during the actual time that the related physical process transpires so results of the computation can guide the physical process.

Register   Hardware used to store bits or characters, usually containing transistors or tubes.

Routine   Coded instructions sequentially arranged to direct the computer to perform a specific operation or sequence of operations.

Segment   That portion of a routine too long to fit into internal storage but short enough to be stored entirely in the external storage, such as a segment containing the coding necessary to call in other segments automatically; as a verb, to divide a routine into parts each of which consists of an integral number of subroutines and each of which is capable of being stored entirely in the internal storage.

Set (character)   A set of characters from which selections are made to denote and distinguish data, e.g., 0 to 9 or A to Z.

Software   (1) The collection of *programs* and *routines* associated with a computer, e.g., *compilers, library routines.*   (2) All the documents associated with a computer, e.g., manuals, circuit diagrams.   (Contrast with *Hardware.*)

Storage   Synonymous with but preferred to *memory.*   A device in which data may be stored and later obtained as desired.

Stored program computer   A digital computer that, under control of internally stored instructions, can synthesize, alter, and store instructions as though they were data and can subsequently execute these new instructions.

Systems analysis Examination of an activity, procedure, method, technique, or business to determine what operations are necessary and how they may best be accomplished.

Tape Material strip that may be punched, coated, or impregnated with magnetic or optically sensitive substances for use with data input, storage, or output.

Time sharing Pertaining to the *interleaved* use of the time of a device.

BIBLIOGRAPHY

Data Collection

"New Dimensions in Code Reading High-Speed Optical Scanners," *Modern Materials Handling,* vol. 27, no. 10, p. 50, October 1972.

Ford, R. F., Production Monitoring with Computers, *Automation,* vol. 19, no. 11, pp. 38–42, November 1972.

Sharan, S., An Economical System for Rapid Retrieval of Quality Data, *Quality Progress,* vol. 3, no. 6, pp. 20–21, June 1970.

Data Reduction, Analysis, and Reporting

Quality Control Programs for Inspection Analysis, *Computer Decisions,* vol. 4, no. 10, p. 61, October 1972.

Continuous Process Evaluation by EDP, *Quality Assurance,* vol. 9, no. 8, pp. 16–19, August 1970.

Miles, R. A., Capability by Computer, *Quality Assurance,* November 1969, pp. 54–55.

Milton, R. C., and J. A. Nelder, "Statistical Computation," Academic Press, New York (1969).

Real-Time Process Control

Andrews, D. L., Computer Successfully Controls Glatfelter's No. 8 Paper Machine, *Paper Trade Journal,* vol. 156, no. 25, pp. 40–41, June 12, 1972.

Angelo, N. B., Process Computers—Which One for the Job?, *Industrial Quality Control,* October 1965, pp. 167–170.

Computer Controls Moisture and Basis Weight at Garden State, *Paper Trade Journal,* vol. 154, no. 42, pp. 58–61, Oct. 19, 1970.

Lehtikoski, O., Integrated Computer Control System Proves Successful in Finland, *Paper Trade Journal,* vol. 154, no. 8, pp. 36–37, Feb. 23, 1970.

Grant, R., What is a Computer Really? How Does it Work? What Can it Do for Us?, *Paper Trade Journal,* vol. 154, no. 37, p. 48, September 1970.

Wickstrom, W. A., Evaluation of an On-Line Colorimeter, *TAPPI,* vol. 52, no. 2, pp. 222–228, February 1969.

McMahon, T. K., Control Model Formulation for the Pulp and Paper Industry, *TAPPI,* vol. 47, no. 2, pp. 84–88, February 1964.

Moore, J. F., and N. F. Gardner, Process Control in the 1970's, *Chemical Engineering,* June 2, 1969 (reprint); hierarchy of control objectives.

Bernard, J. W., and G. M. Howard, Organizing Multilevel Process Control Systems, *Automation,* March 1970, pp. 78–83.

Burkhardt, R. C., and M. Asgari, Kraft Pulp Bleaching Under Computer Control—When Vendor and User Collaborate, *Paper Trade Journal,* vol. 154, no. 35, pp. 74–77, Sept. 21, 1970.

Boozer, R. F., and E. C. Fox, Automatic Control of a Kraft Continuous Digester, *Paper Trade Journal,* June 11, 1962, pp. 42–46.

DeRidder, F. P., Batch Digester Scheduling Meets Reasonable Demands, *Pulp & Paper,* vol. 41, no. 21, pp. 19–20, 32, July 1967.

Ewing, R. W., et al., "Generalized Process Control Programming System," Humble Oil & Refining Company, Baytown, Texas (GPCP) PROSPRO/1800.

Savas, E. S., Computer Control in the Paper Mill, *TAPPI,* vol. 47, nos. 2–5, pp. 164A–168A; 149A–152A; 181A–188A; 127A–133A respectively, February–May 1964.

Fellows, F. H., Multi-Loop Anticipator Computer Control Systems, *Paper Industry,* vol. 45, no. 2, pp. 92–94, May 1963.

Dreisbach, D. A., Practical Considerations of Computer Color Control, *TAPPI,* vol. 54, no. 8, pp. 1298–1301, August 1971.

Automatic Test and Inspection

Computer + TV Keeps You Tuned In, *Quality Assurance,* vol. 9, no. 11, pp. 22–23, November 1970.
The Products of a Psychedelic Age, *Business Week,* no. 2135, p. 82, Aug. 1, 1970.

Information Retrieval

All the News That Fits on Fiche, *Datamation,* vol. 18, no. 11, pp. 169–172, November 1972.
Terminal Provides Electronic Copy Editing, *Automation,* vol. 17, no. 7, p. 10, July 1970.

Top Management

Hanold, T., An Executive View of MIS, *Datamation,* vol. 18, no. 11, pp. 65–71, November 1972.
Brandon, D. H., Does Your Contract Really Protect You?, *Computer Decisions,* vol. 3, no. 12, pp. 22–25, December 1971.
Wight, O., "The Executive's NEW Computer, 6 Keys to Systems Success," Reston Publishing Company, Inc., Reston, Va., 1972.
Harnessing the Computer, *Automation,* vol. 17, no. 8, p. 6, August 1970.
Patterson, A. C., "Data Base Hazards," *Datamation,* July 1972, pp. 48–50.
Rau, P., Evaluating the EDP Function, *Datamation,* vol. 18, no. 9, pp. 72–73, September 1972.
When EDP Goes Back to the Experts, *Business Week,* Oct. 18, 1969, pp. 114–116.

Numerical Control

CDC 6600 Carves Parts for Giant Jets, *Application Report,* Control Data Corporation, 1969.
Report on APT, EXAPT 2 Use, Development, *CDC Physical Science News,* February 1970, vol. 21, p. 2.

Engineering Design Assists

GM's Mini: the Very Model of Automation, *Business Week,* Aug. 8, 1970, vol. 2136, p. 26.

Production Control

Successes Turn Detractors to Computer-Methods Converts, *Computer Decisions,* vol. 4, no. 1, pp. 36–40, January 1972.
Perry, D. C., Are You Ready for Computerized Materials Control? *Automation,* vol. 19, no. 2, pp. 38–42, February 1972.

Upper Management and Quality

J. M. JURAN

INTRODUCTION

This Section is concerned mainly with the role of upper management in the quality function. Because upper management makes wide use of certain special tools in order to carry out its role, these tools (quality audits, surveys, and executive reports) are also subjects for discussion in this Section.

"Upper management" as used here consists of the chief executive officer and his immediate assistants. In a United States single-division[1] company, these men

---

[1] The word "division" as used here is an organization unit conducting an essentially autonomous business and responsible for the profitable operation of that business. The head of the division has the responsibility of general manager, and his subordinate managers carry responsibility for such vital functions as product design, manufacture, marketing, quality, etc.

usually carry the titles of President and Vice Presidents respectively. In a multi-division company, the division leadership (general manager and his immediate subordinates) is regarded as "upper management" for that division.[2]

UPPER MANAGEMENT PARTICIPATION IN THE QUALITY FUNCTION

This participation can vary all the way from formal leadership to abdication. This spectrum may conveniently be divided up into three principal zones: positive leadership, delegation, default.

Positive Leadership   In this form of participation, upper management takes command of the quality function in much the same way as it (usually) commands the finance function.

The leadership of our quality function seldom comes from our top managements. More often it comes from our quality control specialists, from inspired middle managers, from determined customers or from no one. In contrast are other functions, notably finance and marketing, where top management leadership is the rule. What makes the difference?

In part the difference is historical. Only recently has the quality function risen to top management importance. Hence the tradition of top management leadership is too new to make this leadership widespread in the quality function. However, in part the difference lies in the maturity of the tools and skills through which top management can make its leadership effective. We would all make a big contribution to our companies if, during the 1970's, we were to make effective the concept of the annual quality program—the equivalent, in the quality function, of the budget of the financial function.[3, 4]

To exercise leadership of the quality function requires that upper management first create the tools which make this type of participation possible. The indispensable tools consist of:

1. The Annual Quality Program as discussed in Section 6, under that heading. This program requires that upper management actively participate in establishment of quality policies,[5] quality objectives,[6] and plans for meeting objectives.[7] In turn, this same participation requires that upper management become actively involved in:

Creating an organization structure which provides for orchestration of the quality function (see Section 7).

Training of the management team in understanding of the nature of the quality function and in their respective roles for achieving departmental and company objectives. United States companies have generally concentrated such training in staff quality specialists and managers, while leaving the rest of the management team to rely largely on experience plus these trained specialists. In consequence, most United States companies have a large backlog of development and training waiting to be done with respect to the quality function (see Section 17).

Motivation of all levels to give to the quality function the priority required by

[2] For additional discussion, see Section 7, under The Quality Control Hierarchy in Practice.

[3] Quoted from Juran, J. M., Mobilizing for the 1970's *Quality Progress,* August 1969, pp. 8–17.

[4] For a discussion of how upper management commands the finance function, see Financial Analogy, in Section 6, under The Annual Quality Program. For elaboration on the finance function parallel, see Juran, J. M., The Two Worlds of Quality Control, *Industrial Quality Control,* November 1964, pp. 238–244; see also J. M. Juran, Mobilizing for the 1970's, *Quality Progress,* August 1969, pp. 8–17.

[5] See Section 3, under Subject Matter of Quality Policies, *et seq.*

[6] See Section 3, under Quality Objectives, *et seq.*

[7] See generally Section 6.

the new economic forces: consumerism, liability, life behind the quality dikes, etc. (see Section 18).

2. Executive reports on quality performance, as discussed in the present Section 21. These reports enable upper management to see whether the policies, objectives, and plans are actually being carried out.

In a case example of a company's shift in upper management participation, the approach consisted of:

1. Creation of a top management task force on quality and reliability consisting of the nine group executives and chaired by the vice president for management services.

2. Creation of broad "Total Quality Assurance" programs for quality improvement, based on policy formation, objectives, plans, manuals, etc.

3. Measure of performance against plan. This includes monthly review of progress by the top management task force.

4. A scheme of annual certification of plants based on the degree of success in implementing the program.[8] (Evidently the scoreboard on quality costs receives great weight, as does an audit conducted by the corporate quality control staff.)

Delegation   Instead of providing positive leadership of the quality function, upper management may choose to delegate this leadership in one of several ways:

1. Creation of broad committees with special responsibilities for coordinating activities in the entire quality function[9]

2. Creation of a broad-based Quality Control Department whose duties include coordination of the activities in the entire quality function[10]

3. Adopting special programs which in themselves contribute to coordination, e.g., quality cost programs, formal design reviews, formal vendor qualification procedures, etc.

4. Setting up the surveys, audits, and executive reports needed to provide upper management with information on how the quality function is being conducted

The prime difference between this "delegation" and "positive leadership" is the prior responsibility for decision making. Under the concept of "positive leadership," it is upper management which makes the decisions on quality policies, objectives, and plans. The formal annual quality programs are structured in a way which demands this type of decision making.

Default   In this form, there is no provision for coordination of the activities of the quality function. The reason in specific companies may be that the quality function is of low importance compared to other functions, the upper managers are unaware of the importance, long experience with informal coordination has given satisfactory results, etc.

It is important to distinguish between default and absence of formality. In many situations good quality can be attained without formal programs due to the small size of the company, the lack of complexity in the product, etc. (In such cases formal programs may be a detriment to cost with no useful gain in quality.) The significant thing about default is that upper management has not faced up to the question: "How shall we coordinate the activities of the quality function?" Deciding to make no special provision for orchestration is not necessarily a mistake; the decision may be right or wrong. The mistake is in failing to face up to the question.

Under the "default" form of leadership (or rather lack of leadership), upper management becomes involved mainly in response to crises. On evidence of a crisis, upper management may well move in and participate in putting out the fire.

[8] See the Quality World of Allis Chalmers, *Quality Assurance*, December 1970, pp. 10–24.
[9] See Section 7, under Coordination of the Quality Function.
[10] See Section 7, under Evolution of the Quality Control Hierarchy.

In addition, even under the default concept, upper management does receive some modicum of information on quality performance through complaints, returns, service performance reports, quality cost reports, etc. These are acted on under the exception principle, and these actions do constitute a form of upper management participation.

QUALITY ASSURANCE: GENERAL

In this Handbook, "quality assurance" is the activity of providing, to all concerned, the evidence needed to establish confidence that the quality function is being adequately performed.[11]   The confidence is derived from objective evidence, but the type of evidence differs widely, depending on the persons requiring the assurance and on the nature of the product.   Table 21-1 shows some of the more usual forms of objective evidence through which various people secure assurance that the quality function is being well conducted.

It is seen in Table 21-1 that for natural products, quality assurance comes from direct sensory examination of the product, e.g., freshness of vegetables in the village marketplace.   For manufactured products of a simple, short-lived nature, the sensory evidence must usually be supplemented by laboratory testing.   Those who lack test facilities must rely on the word of the manufacturer or on feedback from use testing.   (For short-lived products this feedback is prompt.)

For longer-life products, none of the foregoing evidence (sensory examination, laboratory testing, or use testing) is adequate to provide assurance of proper conduct of the quality function.   More elaborate testing (environmental, life) can provide added assurance, but most merchants and users lack such test facilities.   Hence they must secure their added assurance from such forms as the manufacturer's quality reputation, or test by some independent laboratory, or warranties.

As products grow more and more complex, the evidences from testing, even if they include the more sophisticated environmental and life tests, are no longer adequate to provide full quality assurance, since:

They fail to guard against inadequate product designs, process designs, and quality planning which are present at the very outset of a project and can thereby lose years of time and effort before they are discovered during product usage

They fail to deal with those aspects of quality performance which show up after final test, e.g., packing, transport, storage, usage, maintenance.

To meet these added needs for quality assurance, there has been evolved a concept that the manufacturer must not only produce the product but also prepare and make available to the customer the *proof* that the product is fit for use.

In complex products this proof usually consists of:

1. A formal plan which spells out, for all phases of product progression "from cradle to grave," how fitness for use will be achieved

2. A system of reviews to verify that the plan, if followed, will result in fitness for use

3. A system of audits to verify that the plans are actually being followed

The foregoing concept has some similarity to the concept of the financial audit, which provides assurance of financial integrity by establishing, through "independent" audit, that:

1. The plan of accounting is such that, if followed, it will correctly reflect the financial condition of the company.

2. The plan is actually being followed.

[11] The term "quality assurance" also has other meanings, and it is necessary to understand clearly the distinctions involved.   See Section 2, under Quality Assurance.

TABLE 21-1 Forms of Objective Evidence Used for Quality Assurance

Persons requiring quality assurance	Natural products	Simple manufactured products		Complex products
		Short-lived	Long-lived	
Consumers	Direct sensory examination	Usage	Prior reputation of manufacturer; warranty	Prior reputation of manufacturer; warranty
Customers lacking technological capability	Direct sensory examination	Usage	Prior reputation of manufacturer; warranty	Prior reputation of manufacturer; warranty
Customers with technological capability	Direct sensory examination; test	Test; usage	Life test; usage data banks	Surveys; audits; test and usage data banks
Regulators	Direct sensory examination; test	Test	Life test; usage data	Surveys; audits; test and usage data
Managers of the manufacturing companies	Direct sensory examination; reports of complaints and returns	Executive reports of test results; usage, complaint, and returns data	Executive reports of life tests; usage, complaints, returns; surveys, audits	Executive reports; surveys; audits

The concept of quality assurance through plan, review, and audit requires extensive documentation, both as to the planning and execution. The reviews and audits are sufficiently time-consuming to call for the creation of special departments to carry out the concept. These special departments are often called Quality Assurance departments.[12, 13]

The deeds used to provide the evidence for quality assurance masquerade under a variety of names: audit, survey, surveillance, rating, review, etc. In the topics which follow, these deeds and their definitions are discussed in detail.

QUALITY AUDIT: GENERAL

A quality audit is an independent review conducted to compare some aspect of quality performance with a standard for that performance. The term "independent" is critical to the concept of audit and is used in the sense that the reviewer (called the auditor) is neither the person responsible for the performance under review nor is he the immediate supervisor of that person.

There are sound reasons for emphasizing the independence of the auditor. Many failures to meet quality standards are management-initiated, due largely to the problem of meeting multiple standards. (See Section 18, under Willful Errors.) Self-audit is known to carry a high risk of repeating the original errors. Audit by one's subordinates carries the risk of suppressing the findings due to dominance by rank.

Quality audits are used mainly:

1. by a company[14] to evaluate its own quality activities
2. by a company to evaluate the quality activities of its vendors, licensees, agents, etc.
3. by a regulatory agency to judge the quality activities of the organizations it is assigned to regulate.

The subject matter of quality audits extends across the entire spectrum of the quality function, but the bulk of the auditing is done under several well-established categories

Audit of Policies and Objectives   This review is conducted at the highest level of company operations and hence is normally done by the upper management, using the concept of the Annual Quality Program (as discussed in Section 6, under that heading). The standard used to judge adequacy of quality policies and objectives is a mixture of past performance, performance of competitors, and subjective judgment.

In Japan there emerged, during the 1960s, a concept of a "companywide quality audit" which may be coupled with the preparation of the Annual Quality Program. Either way, the scope of the audit extends to the business aspects of the company's quality activities as well as the technological aspects. The subjects of such audits

---

[12] For a discussion of where to put these Quality Assurance departments on the organization chart, see Organization for Assurance, in Section 7, under Evolution of the Quality Control Hierarchy. (The terminology has not been standardized. See Section 2, under Quality Assurance.)

[13] Some quality assurance is departmental in nature, e.g., process controls, vendor qualification. Such forms of departmental assurance are discussed in the respective functional Sections of the Handbook. Those aspects of quality assurance which are required by upper management are discussed in the present Section.

[14] The term "company" here includes any organization engaged in manufacture of products and services.

include quality policies, objectives, performance against objectives, programs for quality improvement, needs for investment, etc.[15]

In these companywide quality audits, the audit team is headed by the company President[16] and includes the members of upper management. A consequence of this arrangement is that preliminary or subsidiary audits are first conducted at departmental levels, under the leadership of the departmental heads. The results of these lower-level audits are summarized to become, progressively, the major inputs to the higher-level audits.

The concept of a companywide quality audit is also used extensively in the United States, but the scope is more limited and generally excludes the business implications of the quality function. A well-standardized example is the guide provided for evaluating Department of Defense contractors' quality programs.[17] The guide is intended to be used in conjunction with MIL-Q-9858A *(Quality Program Requirements).*[18]

Audit of Performance against Company Objectives   Because company objectives are quite broad, this review is based largely on the data presented by the executive reports on quality. (See below, under Executive Reports.)   The reviews are conducted by upper management, the usual frequencies being quarterly or monthly, with some subjects being reviewed annually.

Other Audit Forms   These include:

Audit of Plans, Systems, and Procedures, to judge their adequacy for enabling the company to meet its quality policies and goals
Audit of Execution, to see if execution follows the plans, systems, and procedures
Product Audit, to see if the product meets the specifications and the needs of fitness for use

These audit forms are used extensively and are all discussed below, under the respective headings.

Common Features of Audits   Despite wide variation in subject matter, all audits exhibit commonality in various ways:

1. They are legitimate. If internal, they are clearly authorized by the responsible managers. If conducted externally (e.g., a vendor's facility), they are authorized by agreement.

2. They consist of a study of actual practice against some concept of good practice, i.e., they avoid a "fishing expedition."[19]

3. They are carried out by trained or experienced persons who are "independent"; i.e., they have no direct responsibility for the conduct of the activity undergoing audit.

4. They are scheduled in advance rather than being conducted as a response to a crisis.

[15] For elaboration, see Mizuno, Shigeru, Company-Wide Quality Activities in Japan, *Reports of Statistical Applications Research,* vol. 16, no. 3, 1969, pp. 2–13; Mizuno, Shigeru, Quality Systems in Japan, *Reports of Statistical Applications Research,* vol. 13, no. 1, 1968, pp. 32–44; Kondo, Y., Internal QC Audit in Japanese Companies, *Proceedings 13th EOQC Conference,* Prague, August 1969, pp. 112–117; Asaka, Tetsuichi, Quality Control Audit, *Reports of Statistical Applications Research,* vol. 16, no. 3, 1969, pp. 14–20.

[16] Hence it is sometimes called "the President's audit."

[17] Quality and Reliability Assurance Handbook H 50, "Evaluation of a Contractor's Quality Program."   Available from Superintendent of Documents, U.S. Government Printing Office, Washington, D.C.

[18] Available from The Naval Publications and Forms Center, 5801 Tabor Ave., Philadelphia, Pa. 19120.

[19] This is not realized 100%, since "good practice" is not 100% standardized and since auditors periodically come up with important findings which had previously been overlooked.

5. They are scheduled and conducted with the knowledge and participation of those whose work is being audited (no secrets or surprises).[20]

6. The facts turned up in the audit are agreed on before the report issues to higher levels.

7. The findings and recommendations are reviewed at higher levels and are then followed to secure action.

The various reviews, controls, and reports carried out by the line people and their supervision lack the feature of "independence" and hence are not usually regarded as part of the plan of "quality assurance." However, care should be taken to avoid being confused by the terminology. In many companies the internal controls, even though not "independent," are nevertheless highly dependable. As this fact is discovered from independent audits and surveys, the extent of independent auditing can be reduced to take advantage of this dependability.

AUDIT OF QUALITY PLANS

Table 21-1 makes clear that the more complex the product, the greater is the need to review the quality plans, systems, procedures, etc., to judge their adequacy.[21] In this Section, the term "audit of quality plans" refers to review of the entire family of elements of quality planning to judge their adequacy for meeting the quality mission of the company, the needs of fitness for use, etc.

Reference Standards Audit of quality plans requires reference standards against which to judge the adequacy of the plans. (Failing this, the audit becomes heavily subjective.) The reference standards normally available include:

The written policies of the company as they apply to quality
The stated objectives in the budgets, programs, contracts, etc.
The customer and company quality specifications
The pertinent government specifications and handbooks[22]
The company, industry, and other pertinent quality standards
The published guides for conduct of quality audits
The pertinent Quality Control departmental instructions
The general literature on auditing

Because standards for audits are still in a state of evolution, the written material is not complete and there remain important unresolved questions.

Scheduling Audits of quality plans are usually conducted on a programmed, scheduled basis, since they consume much time not only of the auditors but of busy line managers as well.[23] The usual schedule provisions include the following:

[20] While such is the majority practice, there is a school of thought which feels that the scheduled audit results in biased results, since those who are the subject of audit have an opportunity to "dress up" the activity prior to the audit. There is merit in this contention. However, the unscheduled audit is known from experience to create a different set of undesirable results, one of which is a serious abrasion between the auditor and the line departments.

[21] For a useful elaboration, see Law, C. W., Expanding the Scope of Quality Assurance Audits, *Quality Progress*, October 1970, pp. 31 and 32. See also Alaimo, A. P., Quality Systems Audit in a Multi-Plant Manufacturing Division, *ASQC 1972 Technical Conference Transactions*, pp. 211–218.

[22] These may be issued by regulatory bodies or by contracting bodies. Examples are the Department of Defense MIL-Q-9858A *(Quality Program Requirements)* and Handbook H50 *(Evaluation of a Contractor's Quality Program)*; also NASA's NHB 5300.4 (1B), *Quality Program Provisions for Aeronautical and Space System Contractors.*

[23] There is also a minority practice of unannounced audits. See, for example, Reis, P. S., and S. I. Fahrenbruch, Quality Audit—An Effective Management Tool, *Industrial Quality Control*, February 1966, pp. 402–407.

For new product or projects: audit during original planning or soon after launching of the project

For stable product lines: audits on a regular cycle, every one to three years

For specific quality problems: specially scheduled by agreement

In addition, consideration is given to such factors as:

Performance of the product

Feedback from customers and other sources

Findings of previous audits

A proposed schedule of audits is drafted by the audit group, discussed with the line managers, and finally approved. Thereafter this schedule is followed except as special conditions require additions or deletions.

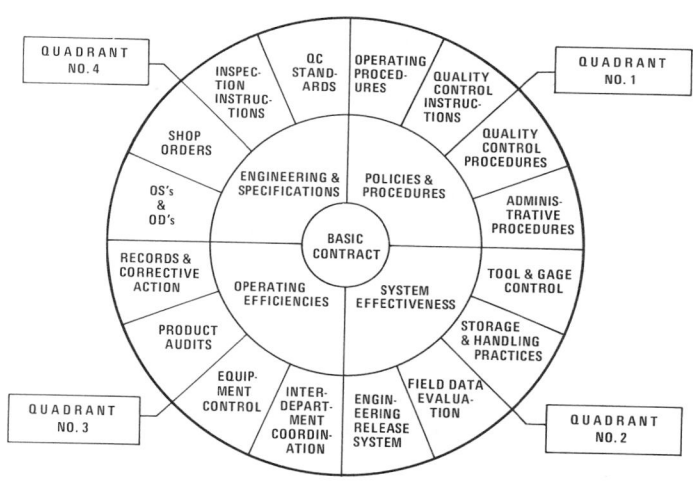

Fig. 21-1 Subject matter for audit of quality plans.

Subject Matter Because audit of quality plans can extend into virtually all activities of the company, steps are taken to define clearly just what should be the subject matter of specific audits. Usually this is done by:

1. Identifying the broad areas of quality activity. For example, Figure 21-1 shows, for one major program, the subjects chosen for audit.[24]

2. Establishing, for each chosen subject, a detailed checklist of the features to be studied and the questions to be raised. Many checklists have been published and are available in the literature.[25] However, each company must prepare its own checklist to meet its own unique situation.

Life Cycle of an Audit A typical sequence of events is shown in Figure 21-2, derived from Ozeki.[26] In this sequence, a statement of audit policy, objectives, and proce-

[24] Reis and Fahrenbruch, op. cit.

[25] See, for example, Bogumil, W. A., Evolution of Quality Control Systems, *Production,* September 1967, pp. 130–133. See also, Matthews, C. N., Auditing Quality Systems, *Quality Assurance,* October 1970, pp. 28–31; see also, Marash, Stanley A., Performing Quality Audits, *Industrial Quality Control,* January 1966, pp. 342–347.

[26] Ozeki, Kazuo, An Actual Example of Quality Audit in Machine Parts Industry, *Reports of Statistical Application Research,* JUSE, vol. 12, no. 1, 1965, pp. 66–71. See also, Marguglio, Benjamin W., Quality Systems Audit, *Industrial Quality Control,* July 1963, pp. 12–15.

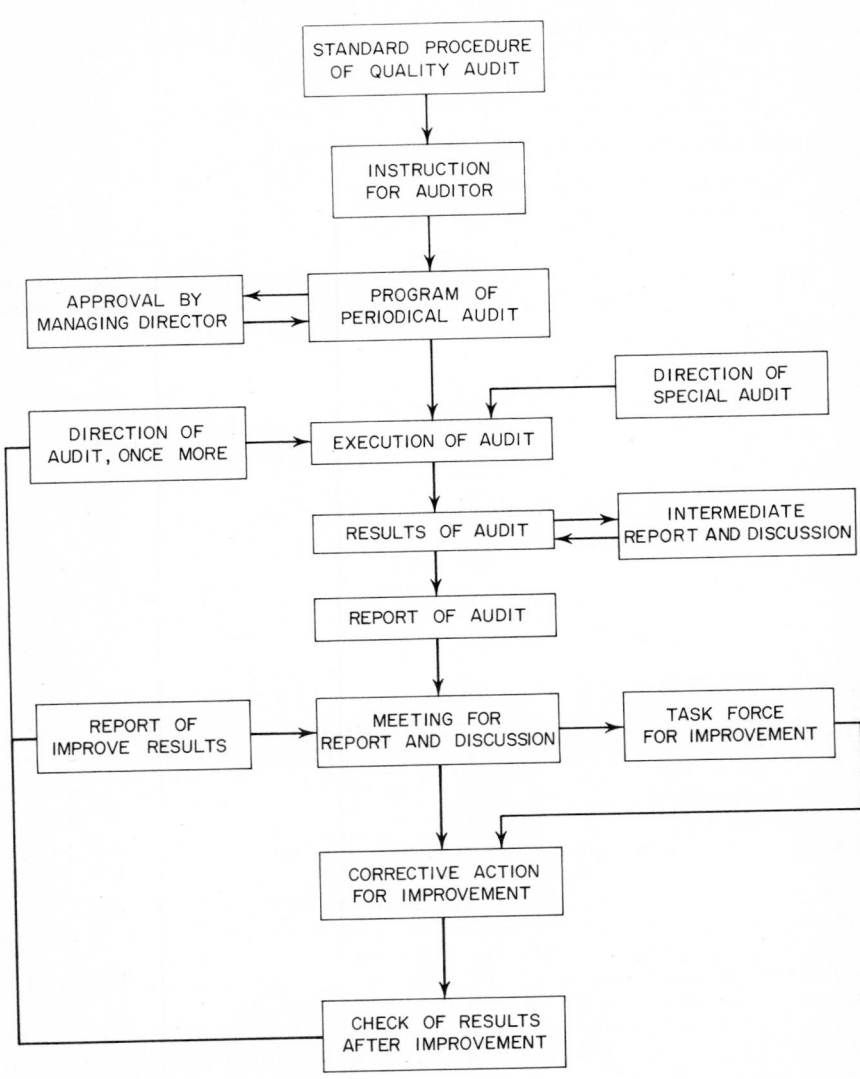

Fig. 21-2 Life cycle of an audit.

dures is drafted, reviewed, and finally approved by upper management. This statement becomes a continuing charter for the auditors and is brought up to date periodically, based on experience gained.

The auditor(s) then conducts the audit, covering the various audit elements as set out in the procedure plus those matters which, though not covered by procedure, appear to warrant attention. He examines, without exception, each of the "vital few" audit elements. These consist usually of:

1. Elements which are critical to safety or which are known to involve large economic risks

2. Chronic problem cases

3. Troubles turned up in prior audits

4. Elements specifically singled out for review by either the staff or line departments involved

The remaining audit elements are of the "trivial many" variety. These the auditor samples, in view of their huge volume. The sampling discloses the incidence of errors and also reveals whether the structure of plans and systems is inherently sound.

A well-conducted audit is not limited to study of documents, important though these are. The real need is to *understand the deeds* which have been performed. (The documents are the main evidence of the deeds.) In consequence, the auditor should also examine at first hand those matters which cannot be reflected solely by documents, e.g.: the state of knowledge, motivation, and morale of the personnel; the atmosphere of creativity and improvement; the level of mutual confidence and collaboration.

Having done his fact collecting, the auditor discusses the findings with the interested line managers to clear up any differences as to the facts. Once the facts are agreed on, the auditor prepares the report—listing his findings, the action already taken, and offering any needed recommendations. This report goes to the interested managers. Finally, there is a follow-up procedure requiring the managers to respond to the recommendations so that there is a final disposition; i.e., the recommendation is acted on, modified, or not acted on.

The individual audits are each important in their own right and serve to secure corrective action for the subject matter of that audit. In addition, the audits are collectively important for identifying the systematic weaknesses in the entire company's approach to quality planning and systems. For example, the headquarters quality control office of a large electrical manufacturer found, upon auditing divisional programs, that the following were the main weaknesses (in order of frequency):[27]

Inadequate control of issuance and recovery of drawings so that factory people lack the latest issue

Inadequate analysis of available quality data

Emphasis on firefighting and underemphasis on prevention

Inadequate control of instrument calibration

Poor material handling and storage with resultant product damage

Weaknesses in vendor quality control programs

Inadequate instructions on the factory floor

Weaknesses in product identification and segregation of defects

Incomplete reporting of quality costs

Inadequate local internal quality audits

In some companies, provision is made to quantify the results of audit by:

Counting the discrepancies found

Assigning weights or degrees of seriousness to various types of discrepancies

Working up a weighted measure of discrepancies per opportunity for discrepancy

AUDIT OF EXECUTION VERSUS PLANS

This form of audit is for the purpose of seeing whether the conduct of operations is in accordance with the plans, procedures, specifications, etc.

---

[27] Jones, L. F., Corporate Quality Control Audit Program, Address to Akron Canton Section Conference, ASQC, March 21, 1970. See also Matthews, C. N., Auditing Quality Systems, *Quality Assurance,* October 1970, pp. 28–31, for use of the Pareto principle in analysis of audit findings.

On the factory floor, the review of execution versus plans may be done by:
1. Impersonal means, e.g., automated instruments.
2. The operators engaged in checking their own activities.
3. The production supervisors during their review of what goes on in their departments.
4. Patrol inspectors engaged in carrying out an independent review of operations. While these men are not called auditors, the work they do meets the criteria for what constitutes an independent audit.
5. Auditors who check the state of factory operations as part of a broader audit of execution.

The amount of execution of plans is simply enormous. In consequence, the audit of execution must be based on sampling; even the choice of sampling methods turns out to be an intricate problem.[28]

In one large electronics company the audit of divisional practice (conducted by corporate staff auditors) uses a plan of sampling based on selected combinations of:

The product lines made by the company
The functional activities engaged in, e.g., design, production
The subject matter within these products and activities, e.g., instrument accuracy, record keeping, etc.

This sampling approach replaced the former approach of auditing a specific product line within a specific division and reporting the results with recommendations for action.[29]

Another form of audit sampling is by product control centers. In this approach a group of related product control stations is regarded as a center for sampling purposes. Each month (or so) a sample of 100 (or so) *decisions* is chosen at random and checked for adequacy. Based on the findings, the center is allowed to proceed, the sample is extended, or a product audit is instituted.

In theory, the audit of operations should be coextensive with the plans, which may extend from "cradle to grave." In practice, the main emphasis is usually on review of the product and process to see if they conform to specification. Product auditing (see below) is an example of such emphasis.

In addition to product auditing, there is a review of many other aspects of execution.[30] The activities reviewed may include:

Response to quality alarm signals—effectiveness of analysis, action
Control and improvement of quality costs
Control of essential documentation, especially engineering change documents
Material identification and traceability
Maintenance of machines, tools, measuring instruments
Vendor evaluation and rating
Extent of use of statistical and other scientific tools where appropriate
Record keeping—completeness, timeliness

When the overall approach to auditing is by product line, it is usual for the same auditor to audit the adequacy of the plans as well as the adequacy of the execution. All findings are then embodied in a single report to the managers.

In those cases where vendor relations are conducted under a plan of assurance

[28] In contrast, the "sampling" for audit of plans is fairly simple. Plans change slowly, so that periodic audits, even every two or three years, are adequate.
[29] See Purcell, Warren R., Sampling Techniques in Quality Systems Audits, *Quality Progress,* October 1968, pp. 13–16.
[30] For a useful discussion, see Handbook H 50, "Evaluation of a Contractor's Quality Program," U.S. Government Printing Office, Washington, D.C.

rather than incoming inspection, the review of execution versus plan is used widely, often being called "surveillance."[31]   The customer's representative (he is not called auditor) is extensively engaged in assuring that the vendor is following the agreed plan.   (See Section 10, under Vendor Surveillance.)

An importance stimulus to audit of execution vs. plan has been the growing extent of government regulation of products. As the regulatory agencies gain experience, they turn to the audit concept as a means of covering maximum ground with the available personnel.[32]   When these audits turn up discrepancies which create unwelcome attention and publicity for the companies, the companies respond, in part, by creating or strengthening their own audits (self-audits).

Quality auditing is also needed in the service industries, where the close relationship to consumers requires special techniques for auditing. See Section 47, under Conformance to Design: Audit for Assurance.

QUALITY SURVEY

The quality survey can be regarded as a quality audit in which the limitations are removed.[33]   The audit is concerned almost exclusively with conformance of various sorts: conformance of plans to standards of good planning, conformance of execution to plan, conformance of product to specification and usage needs.   Such audits provide answers to some vital questions and must be regarded as an essential element of quality assurance.   However, they are not sufficient to provide full assurance to upper management that all is well with respect to quality, since they commonly are not concerned with such matters as:

Discovery of alarming situations for which there exist no present alarm signals

Analysis of users' situations with respect to cost, convenience, etc., over the life of the product

Challenge to Development, Design, and other "monopolistic" departments on quality adequacy, perfectionism, cost, etc.

Challenge to top management itself with respect to policies, goals, premises, and axiomatic beliefs

To provide such missing elements of quality assurance requires a broader review than the structured audit.   This broader review is often called a "survey."   (The terminology has yet to be standardized.)

An early form of quality survey was that used by the Bell System in reviewing the adequacy of its approach to quality.   These surveys were conducted by committees engaged full-time in quality matters.   The Bell System survey brought together information from six related investigations, as follows:

1. An examination of the product design specifications from the standpoint of product fitness for use, completeness, and freedom from ambiguity

2. An examination of the manufacturing specifications and procedures, for similar reasons

---

[31] The term "surveillance" is also used in the sense of the process of conducting quality surveys (see below).   It is necessary to understand the deeds to understand what is meant by the words.

[32] See, for example, the discussion in Section 32 on government regulation as applied to the drug industry's "good manufacturing practice."

[33] Some authorities use the words "audit" and "survey" interchangeably.   In this Section, the word "audit" implies the existence of agreed criteria against which the plans and execution can be checked.   In contrast, the word "survey" implies the inclusion of matters not covered by agreed criteria.   In a sense, the audit discovers discrepancies and alarm signals; the survey goes further and also discovers opportunities and unexpected threats.

3. A review of customer quality complaints and of the action taken in diagnosis and remedy

4. A review of product audit data and shop performance data to appraise the state of product quality and of process controls

5. A study of inspection performance, inspector accuracy, test equipment accuracy, and other aspects of inspection integrity

6. An examination into the quality performance and understanding of the shop personnel

The detailed investigations were conducted by full-time staff specialists, and their findings were reviewed by the managers who were members of the survey committee. The resulting reports and follow-ups received the attention of upper management as well as local management.[34]

Another example of quality survey is that conducted by the Japanese Deming Prize Committee in its examination of companies nominated for this prize. The principal elements examined are as follows: Company's quality control; organization and management; training in and dissemination of quality control ideas and practices; collection, feedback, and utilization of information; analysis of information data; active utilization of statistical methods; standardization; process control; quality assurance; results attained; future planning.[35]

When a really fundamental examination is to be made, the managers guiding the survey should keep in mind that they are part of the problem. To provide assurance against their own biases, they should have recourse to outsiders[36] who have the independence and competence to identify those problems and causes which have their origin in upper management itself. A further need is to take note of new forces and phenomena to which traditional programs have not given weight.

For example, during the early 1960s, product safety, pollution, consumerism, product liability, government regulation, and still other quality-related problems were not regarded as major factors to be considered in quality policies, objectives, and plans. A decade later every single one of these things had become recognized as a major problem. Those companies who had foreseen some of this through their long-range planning thereby gained important head starts over their competitors.

PRODUCT AUDITING

Product auditing[37] is an independent evaluation of product quality to determine its fitness for use and conformance to specification. The evaluation is carried out by a separate group of product auditors (checkers, etc.) responsible (usually) to a Quality Assurance Department. Some product auditing is done on a continuing

---

[34] Derived from Juran, J. M., Management of Inspection and Quality Control, Harper & Brothers, New York, 1945, pp. 186 and 187. To a considerable degree, these same concepts continue to prevail in the Bell System. See, for example, Gause, C. R., The Quality Survey, *Industrial Quality Control*, January 1964, pp. 17–20. See also Bradley, G. H., Jr., and E. M. Hodges, The Quality Survey in Quality Assurance Operations, *Industrial Quality Control*, April 1965, pp. 489–494.

[35] Mizuno, Shigeru, Quality Systems in Japan, *Reports of Statistical Application Research*, JUSE, vol. 15, no. 1, pp. 32–44, 1968. The Deming Prize is the most prestigious quality status attainable by a Japanese company. See QC in Japan Series no. 3, "Deming Prize," JUSE, Tokyo.

[36] Outsiders may be consultants, educators, selected dealers, "public members" of committees, etc.

[37] Also called "rating of product quality," "product rating," "finished product quality audit," "check inspection."

TABLE 21-2 Potential Stages for Product Auditing

Stage at which product auditing is conducted	Pros and cons of using this stage
After acceptance by inspectors	Most economical, but does not reflect effect of packing, shipping, storage or usage.
After packing but before shipment to field	Requires unpacking and repacking, but evaluates effect of original packing.
Upon receipt by dealers	Difficult to administer at such multiple locations, but reflects effect of shipping, storage.
Upon receipt by users	Even more difficult to administer, but evaluates the added effects of dealer handling and storage plus effects of shipment to user and unpacking.
Performance in service	The ideal, but also the most difficult to administer due to the number and variety of usages. Can be simplified through sampling.

basis and therefore requires product auditors assigned full-time to specific product lines. In other cases the product auditing is done periodically, e.g., annually. In that event the product audit is usually coupled with the audit of plans and systems and is carried out by the same men who audit the plans.

Stage of Evaluation Ideally, the product audit should compare actual service performance with users' service needs. This ideal is so difficult and costly to administer that most product auditing consists of an approximation, i.e., comparison of laboratory test results with specifications. Even this approximation can be carried out in any of several stages of product progression, as shown in Table 21-2.

For many simple, stable products, the approximation of test results versus specification is a useful and economic way of conducting the product audit. Even for products not so simple, the majority of quality characteristics identifiable by the user are also completely identifiable while the product is still at the factory. In consequence, the design of product audit should be done based on assuring that those product characteristics which are essential to usage are properly evaluated at some appropriate stage, whether in the factory or in some more advanced stage of progression.

As products become increasingly complex, the product auditing is increasingly conducted at several of the stages shown in Table 21-2. The bulk of the characteristics may be evaluated at the most economical stage, i.e., shortly after factory inspection. However, the remaining (and usually more sophisticated) characteristics may be evaluated at other stages.

In conducting product auditing after shipment to the field, there are further alternatives. If the product consists of small, stable units, it may be feasible to send samples back to a central laboratory for evaluation.[38] If the product consists of large units, it may be more economical to send an audit team out to the field. For example, in the Graphic Arts industry, a supplier of coated paper may send a team out to the field to observe (1) product warehoused by customers and (2) actual running of the paper on the customer's presses, e.g., printing of magazines.[39]

In addition to test of fitness for use, the product audit may include a subsequent "tear down" of some units to evaluate workmanship and other adherence

[38] For example, grinding wheels. See Schilling, Edward G., and Harold J. Davies, Quality assessment—A Missing Link, *ASQC Convention Transactions*, 1964, pp. 279–287.

[39] Private communication to J. M. Juran.

to standards.[40]   The resulting findings are included in the overall quality evaluation.

Sampling for Product Audit   When the purpose of the audit remains one of assurance rather than control,[41] the sample size is arbitrary and is a balance between the cost of large samples and the unreliability of small samples.   One pioneering company chose the formula:

$$\text{Monthly sample size} = a\sqrt{2N}$$

where N is the monthly production and a is a constant depending on the nature of the product.[42]

A large appliance manufacturer uses minimum daily samples from specific product groups in accordance with the formula

$$\text{Sample size} = 0.008\ N + 2$$

where $N =$ daily production.

This sample size is doubled for more complex products and during the introduction of new products.[43]   Of course, no matter what the sample size, it is feasible to compute the confidence limits and to judge whether this is adequate for assurance purposes.

In order that the samples shall be representative of the production "mix," it is necessary to plan the sampling with a knowledge of the production schedules. The usual rules of random sampling are then observed.

For products made in mass production, sample sizes needed for high levels of confidence are still a very small fraction of the product.   In contrast, for products made as large units and in small series, the conventional concepts of sampling confidence limits are prohibitively costly.   In such cases, sample sizes are arbitrary and may seem ridiculously small viewed from conventional probability considerations.   However, these large units involve large numbers of quality characteristics.   Hence the sample sizes in terms of characteristics also extend to large numbers.   The resulting evaluations of product quality usually satisfy the needs of practical managers even if they cannot be demonstrated to be sound statistically.[44]

Quality Standards   Introduction of product auditing invariably has a beneficial effect on clarifying quality standards.   This effect is the result of:

1. The inevitable discussions between the auditors and the line organizations who contest some of the findings of the auditors.

2. The differences in viewpoint due to differences in emphasis.   The product audit is specifically set up to reflect the user's viewpoint,[45] whereas the line

---

[40] See, for example, Wilson, Myron F., The Quality Your Customer Sees, *ASQC Journal of the Electronics Division,* July 1967, pp. 3–16.   See also Modine's "Centralized" System Gets Results, *Quality Assurance,* August 1965, pp. 24 and 25.

[41] Sometimes it does not.   Some redundant inspections are aimed at discovering and remedying errors but are called "product audit" despite the fact that the data are incidental.   In other cases the purpose of the inspections is short-range control rather than long-range assurance.   The purpose to be served markedly influences the sample sizes and the method of sampling (whether at random or stratified).

[42] Dodge, H. F., and M. N. Torrey, A Check Inspection and Demerit Rating Plan, *Industrial Quality Control,* July 1956, pp. 5–12.

[43] Sandholm, L., Program to Reduce the Need for Servicing Domestic Appliances, *First Scandinavian Conference on Quality and Reliability,* Göteborg, May 1968.

[44] See Wilson, Myron F., *op. cit.* Wilson reports using a standard sample of five units, but with flexibility to meet various practical considerations.

[45] For example, the definition of quality responsibilities in a large motor manufacturing company makes the product audit ". . . responsible for reporting from a customer standpoint the quality level of vehicles based on new car audits, warranty parts inspection, and war-

organizations have a strong tradition of emphasizing conformance to specification.

3. The use of product audit results to provide a running scoreboard of product performance. Such a continuing scoreboard requires that the quality standards be consistent from month to month.

A consequence of the need for clear, uniform standards is that the quality auditors play a role, sometimes the dominant role, in defining quality standards from the viewpoint of the user.

Action on Discrepancies   When the quality auditor finds defects or discrepancies in his samples, he brings these to the attention of the line supervisors concerned for two reasons:

1. To secure their verification of the factual situation so that the subsequent quality rating is based on agreed facts

2. To alert them to the alarm signals inherent in the presence of defects amid product which has already been approved for shipment to customers

When the product audit sampling turns up critical or major defects, the audit procedures normally provide for documenting these cases fully, just as is done for any other discovery of a serious internal or field failure. A discrepancy form is executed to put corrective action machinery into motion.[46] The case is then followed to a conclusion by the organizations regularly assigned to such problems.

Quality Rating   Most product auditing is done under a broader concept of preparing a continuing score or "rating" of quality. This running score is then used as one of the inputs for the executive reports on quality.

Seriousness Classification.   The results of product audit appear in the form of presence or absence of defects, failures, etc. Because these discrepancies are unequal in importance, a simple summary such as percent defective is not acceptable to the managers involved. In consequence, most of the approaches to executive reporting include development of a system for classifying the defects into several levels of seriousness, e.g., critical, major, minor, incidental. The details of establishing a system of "seriousness classification for defects" are discussed in Section 12, under Seriousness Classification.

Weighting.   Once seriousness classification has been accomplished, it is comparatively easy to assign weights to each class to quantify the seriousness. Usually a weight of 100 "demerits" is arbitrarily assigned to the most serious defect class. Then the committee which is guiding the design of the rating plan "votes" on the following question:

Assuming that the most serious class of defects is to be given 100 demerits, what is your opinion on what should be the demerits for the remaining three classes?

The votes are then tallied in frequency distributions. The resulting concentrations are discussed (and usually rounded off) to arrive at the final agreed values.

Study of numerous choices of weightings shows a consensus somewhat as follows:

Seriousness classification	Weight or demerit value
A (critical)	100
B (major)	35 to 75
C (minor)	10 to 25
D (incidental)	1 to 10

---

ranty reports." Quoted in Maass, Richard A., Find the Problems; Fix Them, *Quality Assurance*, March 1970, pp. 34–42.

[46] See for example, Wilson, Myron F., *op. cit.*

Summary. Once the demerit values have been agreed on, it is easy to convert the defects found in the product audit to a common basis of demerits and to arrive at a composite demerits per unit. For example, during a given month, the following were the results of product audit on one product line:

Defect class	Weight	No. of defects found	Total demerits
A (critical)............	100	2	200
B (major)	50	7	350
C (minor)	10	28	280
D (incidental).........	1	26	26
Total			856

Since there were 2,500 units of product audited during the month, the demerits per unit came to $856 \div 2{,}500 = 0.34$.

For mass production products, the unit of product may be a simple concept, e.g., lamps, gallons, tons. When the product line is miscellaneous in nature, it is necessary to find some common index which expresses the extent of opportunities for defects, e.g., number of electrical connections, weight of airframe, number of quality characteristics, "possible error count." Use of such a common index opens the way to making comparisons with past history, with competitors, across product lines, etc.

The scoreboard in terms of demerits per unit is by no means universally accepted. Some managers prefer a scale of numbers which equates 100 with perfection and a score such as 70 as a "passing grade." In consequence, some companies convert their demerits per unit score into an equivalent quality rating. For example, if 3 demerits per unit is regarded as a passing grade of 70, the conversion might take the following form:

Demerits per unit	Equivalent quality rating
0	100
1	90
2	80
3	70
4	60
5	50

There is nothing scientific about such conversions. If they make it easier for the managers to interpret the results, they are good conversions.

A further reluctance to use demerits per unit arises from the fact that this index combines the findings of critical and major defects with minor and incidental defects. In most lines of product, the problems of fitness for use and customer relations are almost entirely associated with the incidence of the important defects. Managers in such industries properly want ready access to the figures on critical and major defects, feeling that these are the real problems no matter what the figure of demerits per unit is.

Standard for Comparison. To be meaningful, the score on demerits per unit (or the conversion thereof) must be compared with some "standard." The usual standard is past practice; i.e., the managers want to see whether quality is getting better or worse.

To quantify past practice, the auditors conduct the product audit over enough months to acquire stable data. This period is known as the base period. In calculating the base period, it is usual to exclude known abnormalities such as new-product troubles, effect of temporary crises, etc. The resulting "refined" base period then becomes a basis for comparison, much as previous years' costs or expenses.

Alternatively, the standard for comparison may be "market quality." In such cases, the product audit plan is applied to competitive products in the same way it is applied to the company's own products. The methods of securing competitive products follow the practices discussed in Section 14, under Competitive Evaluations.

When competitive products are to be audited in the field, special inspection and test provisions may be needed. For example, a carpet company undertook to apply its product audits to competitors' products as well as its own. To avoid purchasing the competitors' products, arrangements were made to do the auditing in the warehouses of friendly merchants. This required that the company design a portable inspection facility with standard lighting, which could be taken by the auditors from city to city, to minimize the variation due to conditions of inspection.

Reporting. Conventional practice is to give the line managers two types of feedback:

1. The reports of discrepancies found made at the time of discovery.

2. Monthly (or so) summaries of demerits per unit and product rating. These reports are charted in the manner typical of executive reports (see below). If desired, statistical control limits can be calculated and added to the charts.[47]

Designing the Audit Plan Because the plan of product auditing has a wide impact on executive decision making, it is essential that the plan be designed with full participation of the departments affected. The usual approach is to designate an interdepartmental committee to guide the preparation of the plan, leaving it to the Quality Assurance Department to do the detailed work in the interim between meetings. Lacking such broad-based participation, there is a risk that the audit will reflect the departmental outlook of the auditors rather than the needs of fitness for use.

In one company, a continuing product audit placed great emphasis on the appearance of the product. The findings of the audit during one four-month period were as follows:

Rank	Nature of defect	Percent of all defects found in the audit
1	Poor finish	65
2	Assembly wrong	10
3	Defective parts	6
4	Wrong parts	6

During the same period, defects returned from the field showed the following pattern:

Rank	Nature of defect	Percent of all defects found in the adult
1	Material breakage	73
2	Solder joint failures	16

The same analysis turned up the fact that the product audit included no test for the two serious defects that dominated field returns. In contrast, the emphasis on finish was the result of perfectionism.[48]

---

[47] See Dodge, H. F., A Method of Rating Manufactured Product, *Bell System Technical Journal,* vol. 7, pp. 350–368, 1928.

[48] Consulting experience of J. M. Juran.

Product Audit Manual   As product auditing becomes accepted as a regular use tool for quality assurance, there evolves a manual of procedure to guide the auditors in their work.   Typically, the manual contains:

Purpose of the product audit plan
Organization and responsibilities
Selection of samples: sample sizes; frequency of sampling; method of selection
Selection of samples of competitors' products
Specifications and test procedures
Visual inspection procedures
Verification of defects by line departments
Definition of seriousness classes
List of all defects and their seriousness classification
Procedure for data recording, data processing, and summary
Procedure for reporting.
Copies of forms used, illustrating the recording, processing, and reporting of data

EXECUTIVE[49] REPORTS ON QUALITY

To participate in the quality function, managers must have information on what is going on.   It is not enough to wait for crises.   There should be a regular report structure which provides the managers with:

1. Control reports, showing progress toward goals and giving alarm signals in the event of adverse developments.   Such reports help the manager participate in the control process.[50]

2. "Opportunity signals" which identify opportunities for improvement.   Such signals help the manager participate in the breakthrough process.[51]

A well-designed battery of executive reports can serve all these purposes simultaneously.

Matrix of Executive Reports   Table 21-3 is a matrix showing, for the more usual "control subjects" of executive reports on quality, the typical

Units of measure
Standards used for comparison
Report formats
Frequency of reporting
Departments providing the basic data

Table 21-3 is a broad generalization of the approach to executive reports on quality as practiced in a wide variety of industries.   The reader is urged to look also at the plans of executive reports as used in specific industries.   Most of the industry Sections in this Handbook (Sections 29-47) include material on executive reports for control of quality.[52]

Control Subjects   Effective executive control is built around a selection of control subjects.   While these control subjects vary a good deal in detail among industries and companies, they exhibit much commonality as to categories of subject matter. Most of the control subjects listed in Table 21-3 are widely used, no matter what the industry.

[49] The word "executive" is used here in the sense of a member of middle or upper management.

[50] For an extensive discussion of the entire control process, see Juran, J. M., Managerial Breakthrough, McGraw-Hill Book Company, 1964, pp. 181–344.

[51] See Juran, op. cit., pp. 15–179.

[52] See also the similarities in the control process as used on the factory floor, as discussed in Section 11, under Inspection Feedback to Production, especially Criteria for Good Feedback to Operators.

Since all control is built around specific control subjects, the choice of these subjects is the most critical element in the entire control system. If a vital control subject is omitted, the managers will lack a vital instrument on their instrument panel. If an unimportant control subject is included, it will receive undue attention while diluting the attention given to more important matters.

The choice of control subjects is so important that it should not be left to the decision of some one department manager. Neither should the choice be left to the accumulated evolution of response to crises. Periodically there should be a positive review of the control subjects to discard those which have outlived their usefulness and to add new subjects which have meanwhile grown in importance. Such a positive review can usually be made on the initiative of the quality manager. Armed with a matrix similar to Table 21-3, this manager "makes the rounds," calling on all other key managers and securing their nominations for control subjects to be added or deleted along with their views on the other elements in the table (unit of measure, etc.).[53]

Once the nominations have been collected, it is feasible to design a plan of executive reports which responds to the consensus of the managerial views. A draft report is then prepared and distributed to the managers for their study. Finally, a meeting is convened to discuss the draft, a "final" design is adopted, and this design is used until the next such review several years later.[54]

In the absence of such periodic reviews, it is common to find that the executive reports remain narrow in scope. In some companies the "executive report" is virtually a departmental report by the Quality Manager and devotes much space to his departmental problems of budgets, manpower, equipment, etc.

Hierarchy of Controls   When the number of quality characteristics in specifications, processes, tools, etc., is multiplied into the units of product, the result is a fantastically large number of things to be controlled. To achieve this control with minimal human attention, managers and engineers make extensive use of stable processes, foolproof operations, automated regulation, and similar devices. Superimposed on this inanimate control are several layers of control by people: nonsupervisors, first-line supervisors, middle managers, upper managers. The lower layers rely largely on personal observation of the operations but supplement this with control through information. In contrast, the upper layers exercise control mainly from reports, supplemented by personal observation.[55]

Paralleling the hierarchy of controls is a hierarchy of information. At the base is an enormous number of bits of information, each used for hour-by-hour or piece-by-piece control. This same information, when progressively summarized to serve higher and higher levels of managers, becomes a major input to the executive report system. In large companies there are several such levels of summarization, e.g., foreman, superintendent, middle manager, and upper manager.

To oversimplify, quality controls may be separated as between operational controls and executive controls. Table 21-4 presents such a separation and shows how very different the extremes of the hierarchy are. Although they originate from a common base, they end up as virtually two separate worlds. The manager who receives an executive report on the twenty-fifth day after the end of the month and

---

[53] The managers should keep an eye on the control subjects which are increasingly under emphasis by the press, the reformers, the regulators, the legislators, etc. For example, the Federal Trade Commission's key statistical measures for identifying industrial sources of consumer problems include consumer complaints and accidents caused by products. Quoted in The FTC Builds a Model Informer, *Business Week*, March 11, 1972, p. 94.

[54] For further discussion, see Juran, *op: cit.*, Chapter 13, Choosing the Control Subject, pp. 197–217.

[55] For elaboration, see Juran, *op. cit.*, pp. 181–189.

TABLE 21-3   Matrix of Executive Reports on Quality*

Control subject	Typical unit of measure	Usual departmental source of data	Typical standard	Typical format	Typical frequency
Negative customer reactions					
Complaints	Number of complaints per 1,000 units; per $000 of sales	Field Service	Historical	Narrative	M
Returns	Value of returns per $000 of sales	Accounting	Historical, market	Narrative	M
Service calls	Number of service calls per 1,000 units under warranty; cost of service calls per 1,000 units under warranty	Field Service	Historical, market	Tabulation	Q
Guarantee charges	Dollars per 1,000 units under warranty	Accounting	Historical, market	Tabulation	Q
Field performance					
Product reliability	Failure rate; mean time between failures	Field Service	Engineered, historical, market	Charts	M
Spare parts sales	Dollars of sales	Accounting	Historical	Tabulation	A
Product conformance on inspection, test	Defects per unit; process average for specific qualities	Inspection, Test	Historical, engineered	Charts	M
Outgoing quality based on product audit	Demerits per unit	Quality Assurance	Historical market	Charts	M
Vendor quality performance	Dollars of cost per dollars of purchases	Accounting, Quality Control	Historical	Tabulation	Q
Quality costs: appraisal, failure, prevention	Dollars per hour of direct labor; per dollar of direct labor, shop cost, processing costs, sales; per unit of product, equivalent product	Accounting, Quality Control	Historical, budget	Tabulation, charts	Q

TABLE 21-3 Matrix of Executive Reports on Quality* *(Continued)*

Control subject	Typical unit of measure	Usual departmental source of data	Typical standard	Typical format	Typical frequency
Surveys; audits other than product audit	Various	Quality Assurance	Plan	Narrative	S
Opportunities	Return on investment, other	Quality Control	—	Narrative, tabulation, charts	Q
Customer relations on quality (other than alarm signals)	Various	Marketing, Field Service, Quality Control	—	Narrative	Q
Sales income gained or lost due to quality	Dollars	Marketing, Accounting, Quality Control	—	Tabulation Narrative	Q
Results of quality improvement programs	Dollars, return on investment	Quality Control	Plan	Tabulation, narrative charts	Q

*Frequency code: M = monthly
                Q = quarterly
                A = annual
                S = special

TABLE 21-4   Operational Quality Controls versus Executive Quality Controls

Aspect	Application to operational quality controls	Application to executive quality controls
Control subjects	Physical, chemical, specification requirements	Summarized performance for product lines, departments, etc.
Units of measure	Natural physical, chemical (ohms, kilograms, etc.)	Various. Often in money. See Table 21-3
Sensing devices	Physical instruments, human senses	Summaries of data
Who collects the sensed information	Operators, inspectors, clerks automated instruments	Various statistical departments
When is the sensing done	During current operations	Days, weeks, or months after current operations
Standards used for comparison	Specification limits for materials process, product	History, competitors, plan
Who acts on the information	Servo mechanisms, nonsupervisors, first-line supervisors	Managers
Action taken	Process regulation, repair, sorting	Motivation, change of plan, disciplinary action

complains about "ancient history" is confusing these two worlds, as is evident from Table 21-4.

Leading and Lagging Indicators   A further distinction in controls is whether they provide information before, during, or after operations.   Operational controls are obviously designed to assist in the conduct of day-to-day operations (Table 21-4).

Executive control reports are regarded as lagging indicators because the reports come out weeks or even months after the operations have been performed.   Such reports are nevertheless of great value in showing trends, identifying substantial failures to meet goals, measuring performance of managers, etc.

The degree of lag varies considerably.   The summarized scrap or rework reports may lag only one month behind the day-by-day events.   However, warranty charges may lag several months behind the date of manufacture and years behind the date of product development

In contrast, some executive reports are leading indicators.   Market research on quality may lead product development by months.   Design review is a leading indicator of failure rates.   Product audit lags behind date of manufacture but is a leading indicator of quality as received by the user.

The well-balanced system of executive reports makes use of leading indicators ("early warning signals") as well as summaries which lag behind operations.[56,57]

Feedback Loop   The idealized control structure is the feedback loop which is built around each control subject.   The conceptual approach is discussed in Section 6, under Planning for Control.   A graphic representation of the feedback loop for control of quality is shown there in Figure 6-4.

The elements of the feedback loop are well known: unit of measure, sensor, standard, collator, effector.   In the model loop, every control subject must be equipped with every one of these elements.   The application of this model to executive controls on quality is discussed under the topics which follow.

Units of Measure   In operational control, the choice of unit of measure is simplified by the fact that the things being measured are largely homogeneous.   As a result,

[56] For further discussion, see Juran, op. cit., Sensing before, during, and after the fact, pp. 258–263.

[57] For an example, see Knevels, Robert H., Quality Information for Management Action, *Automotive Industries,* June 1, 1969, pp. 55–62, 84.

most of the units of measure in use are "natural" units, e.g., ohms, hours, tons, meters.

The executive report, being a summary, usually deals with things which are not homogeneous. In consequence, it is necessary to create new units of measure which permit summary of unlike things. There are several ways of doing this:

1. Arbitrary weighting. For example, defects are classified as to seriousness and each class is assigned a weight (demerits). This makes it possible to use demerits per unit of product as new unit of measure. (See Product Auditing above.)

2. Conversion into a common natural unit. A well-known example is the use of money as a common measure of scrap, rework, service work, etc., despite wide differences in products and processes. Another example is the concept of "opportunities for failure" used as the denominator of indexes of performance, e.g., number of electrical connections.

3. Conversion into statistical equivalents. In this approach, the historical performance in natural units is equated to 100% (for example). A 10% departure from this level becomes a score of 90%, no matter what the natural unit is. This method also permits preparing composite scores for several performances by weighting.[58]

Sensing   This is the technical term for measuring performance in terms of the unit of measure. At the bottom of the company this measuring is done by the personnel of several departments: Inspection, Test, Quality Control, Quality Assurance, Field Service, Accounting, and still others. Logically, these same departments carry out the work of summarizing their data. In consequence, as is evident from Table 21-3, preparation of the executive reports on quality involves a good deal of precise coordination among these departments in order to:

Standardize terminology such as names of defects, parts, and other names which enter the data system

Standardize the code numbers which are used to translate this terminology into the language of the computer[59]

Standardize the calendar dates for defining time intervals (weeks, months) and for meeting report deadlines

Agree on the form of delivery of information to minimize the problems of preparation of the final executive reports[60]

Define the respective responsibilities of all departments associated in this cooperative venture[61]

It is also important to keep an eye on the distinction between the deeds and the data (which are only the evidence of the deeds). The realities are the deeds, and the surest control is through personal observation of the deeds: "I don't care what the report says—the bins are empty."

The successive layers of summary and the creation of unnatural units of measure all carry the risk that the data will fail to reflect the deeds due to coloration, statistical quirks, and just plain mistakes.[62] Careful checking and auditing are needed to maintain the full connection between deeds and data.

Data Processing   Information on quality originates as myriads of small bits of data, each unimportant to the manager. The need is to convert this mass of bits into a

---

[58] For a more extensive discussion, see Juran, *op. cit.*, Chapter 14, The Unit of Measure.

[59] Many of these code number systems are designed to be mnemonic in order to simplify electronic data processing. See, for example, Section 43, Fig. 43-5.

[60] See also, Juran, *op. cit.*, The Sensor, pp. 257–274.

[61] For added discussion, see Juran, *op. cit.*, pp. 295–297; also pp. 312–314.

[62] For example, an index may give a false signal because the cutoff date for the data in the numerator differs from that used in the denominator.

few summarized facts, each of vital importance to the manager.   The mechanism for making this conversion is the system of data processing.

Processing of the data is sometimes done by manual means (see Section 19) but more usually with the aid of computers (see Section 20).   The applications include chemical products,[63] electrical products,[64] automotive assembly,[65] defense products.[66]

The computer becomes indispensable when large amounts of basic data must be multiple-sorted to produce a variety of executive reports on different subjects for different recipients.   For example, Figure 21-3 shows a network of executive reports designed to serve the needs of Electrolux, a Scandinavian manufacturer of household appliances.   The reports deal with quality by classes of parts, by process, by product class, by plant, and for the corporation.   The input information comes from several sources located in the factories as well as from field sources.   The output consists of seven species of executive reports, with distribution to the appropriate managers and specialists.[67]

Standards   The system of executive controls should provide standards against which to compare performance.   In the absence of standards, it is easy for managers to overreact to individual complaints or to other alarm signals.   (The "sensationalist" type of reformer uses precisely this technique of dramatizing individual failures then generalizing as though these cases were widespread.)

At the technological level the standards are *engineered* and are embodied into the material, process, and product specifications.   Other engineered standards include material usage and labor usage.   Next are the *historical* standards in which current performance is compared with the past.   A further standard is the *market,* i.e., what other people do when faced with similar problems.   Competitive performance is the most usual market standard for quality.   A fourth standard is the *plan,* e.g., the budget, quota, schedule.   The plan is established by human judgment after the other inputs—technology, history and market—are considered.[68]

Upper management is strongly attracted to use of market comparisons as a check on what a good performance is.   In quality matters there are several sources of market data:

1. Customers who purchase from competing sources.   Often they are willing to prepare comparative data, though without identifying competitors.

2. Trade associations who become a data bank, again preserving anonymity.

3. Independent laboratories who publish comparative test results, often naming the competitors.

[63] Wilson, James R., Computerized Quality Control for Multibranch Production Lines, *Chemical Engineering,* vol. 69, no. 11, May 28, 1962, pp. 140–146.

[64] Daw, H. Robert, Records and Reports of Quality, *Industrial Quality Control,* March 1965, pp. 443–449, also Shapiro, Samuel S., Computerized Reliability Reporting System, *Industrial Quality Control,* April 1961, pp. 13–15.

[65] DiCicco, John J., Reporting Quality Information, *Industrial Quality Control,* November 1965, pp. 235–239; also Smith, J. Kevin, Records and Reports of Quality, *Industrial Quality Control,* January 1967, pp. 325–328.

[66] Ziegler, Manfred, Quality Level Information System, *Industrial Quality Control,* September 1967, pp. 163–167.

[67] Sandholm, Lennart, Improving Quality Assurance, *European Organization for Quality Control, 9th Conference,* Rotterdam, 1965.   See also, Demos, N. P., The Master Control System in General Electric, *Industrial Quality Control,* October 1955, pp. 17–21.   For an extension of this concept to reliability reporting, see Shapiro, *op. cit.*

[68] For an extensive discussion, see Juran, *op. cit.,* Chapter 15, The Standard.   For a discussion of standards for quality costs, see Section 5 (of this Handbook), under Discovering the Optimum.

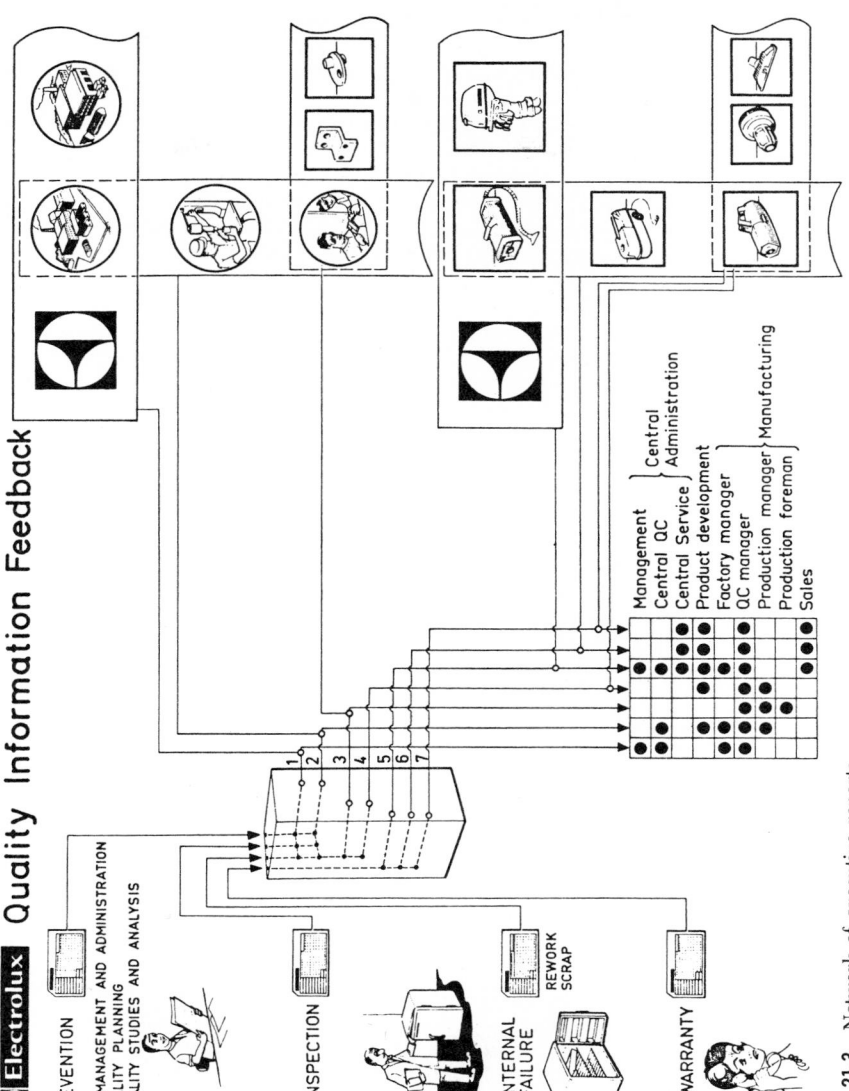

Fig. 21-3   Network of executive reports.

4. Government regulatory bodies who publish test results, sometimes naming names.[69]

5. Professional society research studies. This method has potential, but to date has been used only to a limited degree.[70]

To go beyond these sources requires special studies. See, for added discussion, Section 14, under Competitive Evaluations. See also Section 4, generally.

Indexes In making comparisons, managers are not content merely to compare the respective summaries, e.g., this month's scrap loss versus last year's monthly average. Often the managers want to take notice of the changing bases behind the figures, e.g., the scrap levels may be higher because the level of production is higher. To take account of these changes in bases, managers have evolved the concept of an index. Applied to executive reports on quality, this index is a fraction in which the numerator expresses the intensity of the phenomenon under observation (e.g., cost of scrap, number of failures) and the denominator expresses the size of the opportunity for existence of the phenomenon under observation (e.g., volume of production, number of units in active service).

The typical units of measure shown in Table 21-3 include further examples of indexes.[71]

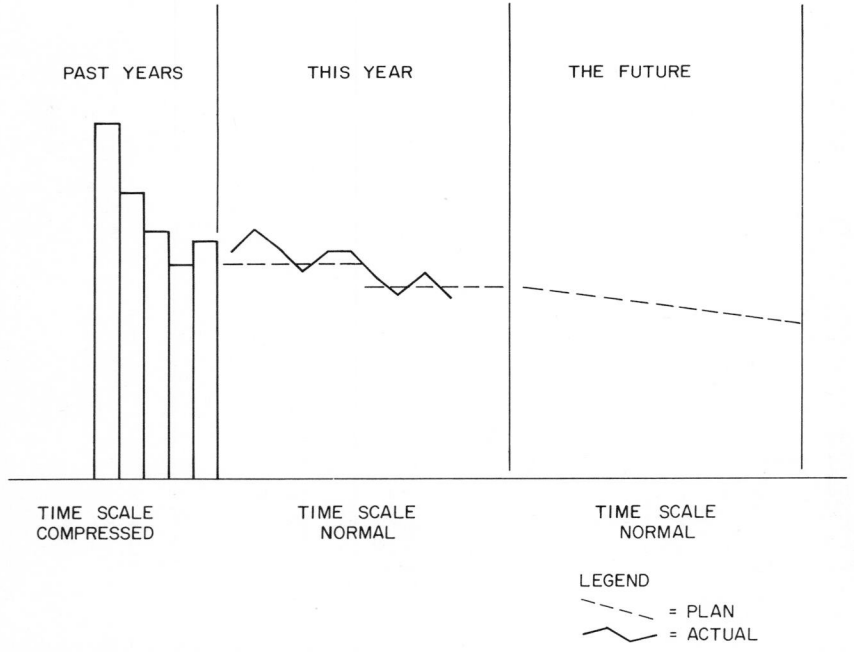

Fig. 21-4   Basic graphic presentation for executive reports.

[69] For example, AB Svensk Bilprovning, the Swedish Motor Vehicle Inspection Company which conducts the compulsory annual vehicle inspection, publishes summarized results of its findings. For each model tested, the summary shows the percentage of faulty headlights, exhaust systems, brakes, etc., encountered during the year's testing.

[70] See Juran, J. M., What is Par? *Industrial Quality Control,* October 1966, pp. 196 and 197.

[71] See also Section 5, Bases for Comparison (under The Control Scoreboard) for some examples of indexes used in reporting quality costs.

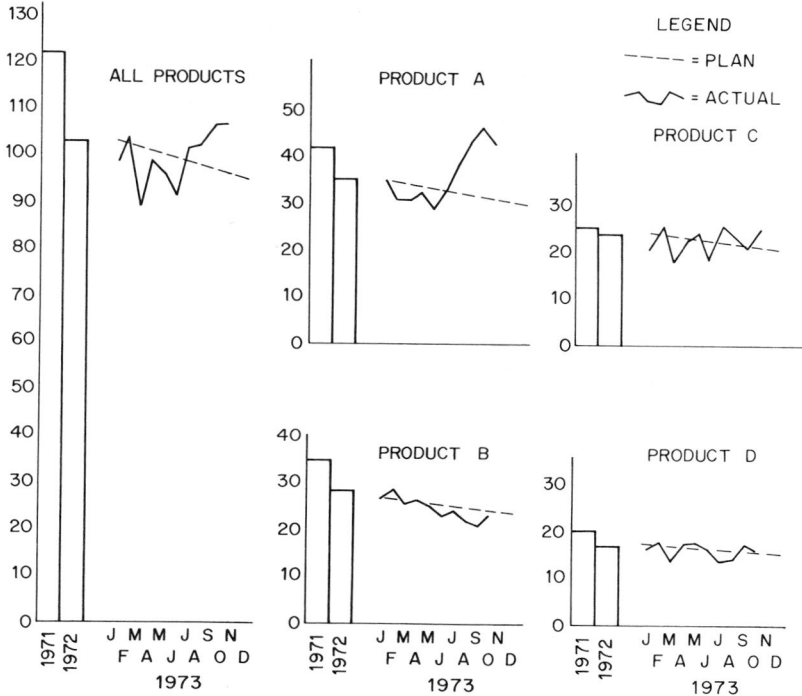

Fig. 21-5 Graphic presentation for multiple levels of summary.

Format Executive reports should be designed to read at a glance and to permit easy concentration on the exceptional matters requiring executive attention.

Tabulations of data are the most primitive format. Some of these consist of forbidding stacks of pages from a computer print-out or from a statistical department. These masses of data are an imposition on busy executives, who are in effect being asked to do the summarizing which someone else should have done.

Summarized tabulations are a long step in the right direction. They do not give a perspective in time, but they do tabulate the three essential current figures: standard, actual, and variance. In some companies the significant deficiencies or improvements are marked in a distinctive way to simplify the job of reading the tabulation.[72]

Graphic presentation requires added work by the reporting departments but greatly simplifies interpretation by the executive. The basic form of graphic presentation is shown in Figure 21-4. The graph shows full perspective: the past (history), the present (current performance), the future (objective or budget). The physical size of the fluctuations is an aid to judging significance of variances even in the absence of statistical control limits.

Figure 21-5 shows how graphic presentation can present multiple levels of summary. The breakdowns may be by product line, by department responsible, by defect type, etc.[73]

[72] See, for example, Daw, *op. cit.*
[73] Even by product components. In one ingenious example, a schematic of a circuit is pre-

Charting technique has been studied exhaustively and is readily available in the literature.[74] Figure 21-6 shows some examples extracted from the reports used in a company making electronic entertainment products.[75]

When numerous charts are needed, it is feasible to make use of a standardized format to create a coordinated "executive instrument panel." In the absence of such standardization, the managers are faced with a problem of frequent "tuning in and out" due to the variety of format. As a result, their reviews are slowed down and the opportunities for error are increased.

Publication   It is useful to assemble the principal executive reports on quality into a comprehensive package which is published regularly and which can in due course earn a status as the authoritative source of essential information on quality, i.e., an official executive instrument panel. To reach such a status requires years of dedicated reporting using unquestioned objectivity, good format, and careful attention to the needs of the executives who are the users.

Whether as a comprehensive package or on a piece-by-piece basis, the reports are distributed to the men on the distribution list. From there, the action pattern differs. In some companies there is a monthly or quarterly meeting of upper managers specially devoted to review of quality problems.

Some companies maintain a "control room" which houses enlarged versions of the charts.[76] Provision is made to keep these charts current for ready reference and available for easy access to all concerned. In such companies, the monthly managerial review briefing and discussion may take place in the control room.

Interpretation[77]   The editor of the executive reports can provide useful illumination of the facts through the inclusion of supplemental information which does the following:

Identifies the vital few quality problems, whether in field usage, vendor relations, factory operations, etc. Preferably this list does not exceed ten items. Managers are quite willing to lend their experience, knowledge, and authority to help solve this "vital few." However, if they are given a list of hundreds or even just dozens of problems, they will become involved in none, not even the vital few.

Reports on the status of major quality programs under way; results achieved, work in progress; what the next move is and who is to take it; need, if any, for action by upper management.

Summarizes the findings of audits and surveys, whether in-house or of vendors.

Discusses major developments which are taking place with respect to quality due to industry programs, government action, competitor action, consumer organizations, and other outside forces.

Previews proposals which will be coming up for upper management consideration.

The editor of the reports must also take pains to avoid the common errors which lead to erosion of confidence in the reports. These include:

---

sented with hollow circles to designate failures and red painted circles to designate failures remaining after corrective action. This is called a "measles chart." See Mills, J. E., A Reliability Audit in Military and Space Electronics, *Industrial Quality Control,* September 1966, pp. 123–126.

[74] An excellent compilation is *Engineering and Scientific Graphs for Publications,* American Standard Z 15.3-1947; also *Time Series Charts—A Manual of Design and Construction,* American Standard Z 15.2-1938. Both are available from ANSI or ASME.

[75] For a good case example, see the charts in Powell, Richard F., Assuring Reliability in Your Hi-Fi Set, *1968 Annual Symposium on Reliability,* IEEE, pp. 6–14.

[76] See, for example, Massaker, W. E., Guidelines for Problem Analysis and Resolution, *ASQC Annual Technical Conference Transactions,* 1968, pp. 119–130.

[77] See also, Juran, *op. cit.,* Chapter 18, Interpretation, pp. 301–322.

Failure to distinguish between what is important and unimportant. A common example is the assumption that because some deviation is statistically significant, it must also be economically significant.

Too many false alarms, resulting from failure to check the alarm signals.

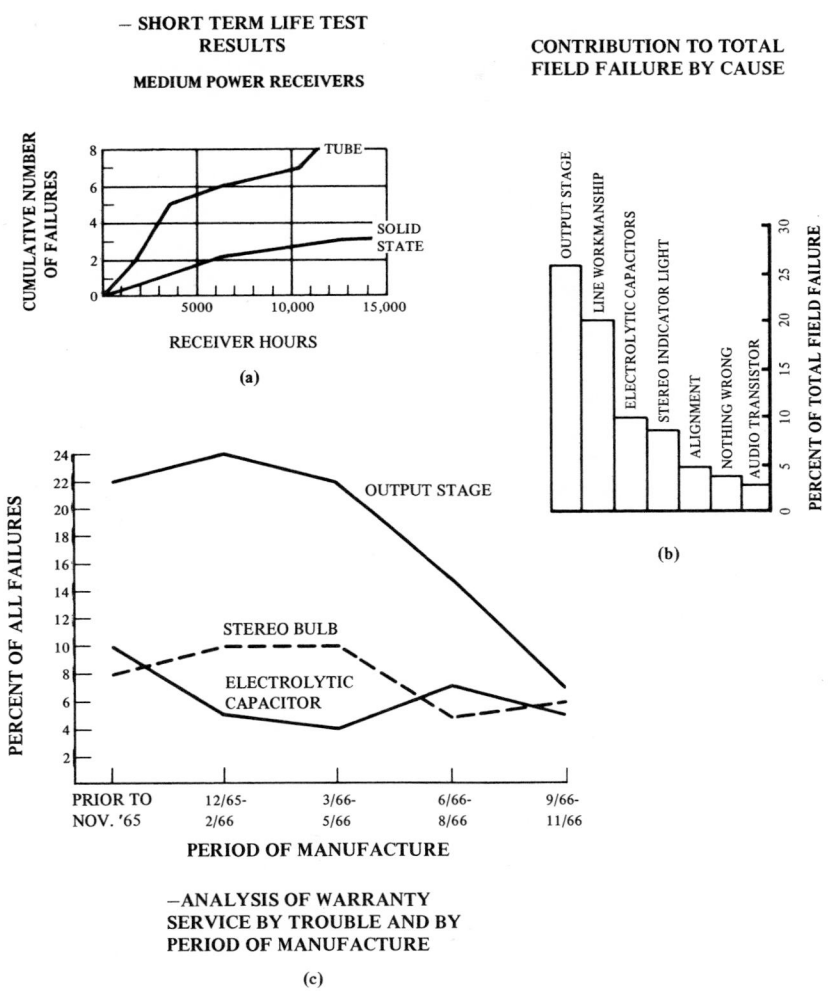

Fig. 21-6 Examples of charts used in executive reports.

An atmosphere of "blame" in the reports, rather than one of constructive search for remedy and improvement.

"Overkill" in its various forms. A common example is emphasis on nonconformance when fitness for use is adequately protected.[78, 79]

[78] This is always easier to understand when someone else does it, e.g., government regulators.
[79] See also Why Quality Managers Fail, in Section 17, under Quality Managers.

Reports on Opportunities While control reports have been largely standardized as to content and format, reports on opportunities are still in the early stages of evolution. An example of a well-standardized report on opportunities is the quality cost analysis. In its early phases, this analysis:

Estimates the total quality costs and the main contributing categories.

Identifies the vital few improvement projects and presents these in the language of management to "sell" programs for improvement.[80]

A second major form of report on opportunities is the Pareto analysis when applied to any major problem which is susceptible of improvement.[81]

An underdeveloped form of report on opportunities is that of improving sales income or share of market. As elaborated elsewhere,[82] there are ways to identify these opportunities through such methods as:

Sales analysis to identify decreases and increases in sales to major customers.

Further analysis, case by case, to discover which of these changes are for quality reasons

Estimate of the sales improvement potential, the likely cost of realizing this potential, and the resulting return on investment

Customer contact, laboratory testing, and market research to discover the programs needed to secure sales increases through action on quality

Finally, there are opportunities for which conventional presentations (e.g., chart trends, return on investment) are of no avail, yet which are of great significance to the company. They include such matters as:

Identifying out-of-date basic premises and axiomatic beliefs which are a roadblock to motivation for quality. (See Section 18, expecially Tables 18-7 and 18-8.)

Identifying the various management "movements" which are ever emerging in industry, examining them, and conducting enough tryout to judge whether they are cults or whether they have useful application in the company.

Identifying the forces in the economy which are serious threats for the future and which therefore are a form of alarming situation for which the company has no alarm signals.

To make matters worse, these categories of opportunity are not special to the quality function — they are so fundamental in their nature that they strongly influence other major functions as well. In consequence, a functional manager, e.g., the quality manager, must enlist a broad-based array of support from other functions before he is able to carry conviction.

QUALIMETRY

"Qualimetry" is a word coined within the U.S.S.R. Committee on Standards, Measurement, and Measuring Instruments to designate a new "science" of measuring quality. The stated intention is to find a system of evaluation of quality in the broadest sense, i.e., fitness for use and its components: quality of design, quality of conformance, availability for continuing use (reliability, maintainability, etc.), adequacy of field service. The U.S.S.R. All-Union Research Institute for Standard-

---

[80] For an extensive discussion, including the detailed methodology, see Section 5 (Quality Costs).

[81] See Section 16, under Identifying the Projects.

[82] See Section 4, under Quality and Share of Market *et seq.*; also, Section 14, under Analysis of Available Market Quality Information, *et seq.*

ization has created a project to develop a science of qualimetry, plus subsidiary sciences (e.g., in related fields such as metrology or standardization) as may be needed. It recognizes that there are national differences which may affect the evolution of qualimetry as a science. However, it feels that there are universal principles as well. [83]

The concept of a broad measure for quality has long intrigued quality specialists. Early attempts at preparing such measures centered around the development of product rating, as discussed in Product Audit, above. Under this concept, quality is measured in terms of the presence of defects as determined by product audit. The various defects are classified for seriousness, and a weight (in demerits) is assigned for each class. The composite of demerits per unit becomes the measure of quality. As a measure of quality of conformance to specification, this product rating has much practical value despite the fact that neither the seriousness classification nor the choice of weights is established by scientific methods.

More recently, progress has also been made in measuring quality in its other forms. For long-life products, several interrelated measures have been set up for continuity of service (e.g., mean time between failures; mean time to repair). There is promise of quantifying users' economics for long-life products through the concept of life cycle costing. [84]

Some proposals have also been advanced for preparing a composite measure of quality in its broadest sense. None of these proposals has met with sufficient acceptance to be regarded as a serious contender for an agreed rationale.

Obviously, the quality specialists in the Capitalistic economies would welcome a broad measure of quality if one were developed. However, many of them doubt the value of devoting the effort needed to develop such a measure, since the forces of the marketplace operate to evaluate the contesting qualities and thereby to make extinct those products which are unable to compete successfully.

The Socialistic economies face a greater need for solving this problem. These economies include a good deal of central planning, and the planners are handicapped in their work if they are unable to quantify so important a factor in the economy as quality. Lacking this quantification, they have greater difficulty in establishing pricing structures for the products, in allocating investments for quality, in judging what broad programs to undertake, etc.

A comparable problem in Capitalistic economies is the quantification of such factors as cost of living, extent of unemployment, extent of crime. These factors are so important to the citizenry that means have been evolved for quantifying them. Once they are quantified, it become possible to see what the trends and the regional differences are and whether there are needs for specific programs to help the economy to reach a better balance among the contesting forces.

During the early 1970s the project of developing Qualimetry as a science had just been launched. [85] If it can be brought to a successful conclusion, it will be of aid to all economies.

[83] Conversation between A. V. Derbisher (Director, U.S.S.R. All-Union Research Institute for Standardization) and the author, Lausanne, June 1970.

[84] See Section 4, under Life Cycle Costing.

[85] See Azgaldov, G. G., et al., Qualimetry, *Quality*, EOQC, vol. 12, no. 3, 1968, pp. 92 and 93; see also Glichev, A., et al., Qualimetry—Its Contents, Objectives and Methods, *EOQC Newsletter*, no. 75, pp. 2–8 April 1971 (Special Feature); also, Glichev, A., Qualimetry and Man, *16th Annual Conference*, EOQC, Oslo, June 1972.

MANPOWER[86] FOR QUALITY ASSURANCE

There are multiple sources of this manpower, and these sources bear a logical relationship to the subject matter of the audit.

Upper Management   These men participate actively in the companywide quality audit or the preparation of the Annual Quality Program.   In such cases, the audit team is headed by the chief executive and includes a number of the other upper managers.   In Japan, this team makes use of outside consultants and internal specialists to assist with the staff work and to provide added objectivity.[87]

A further use of upper managers for audit is the "plant tour" type of audit conducted by upper managers when they visit a company location.   The structure is quite loose, since the makeup of the audit team is not by design but by the fortuitous visiting schedules of the executives.   The audits are quite informal: there is no firm checklist, the review usually includes not only quality but other matters as well, the review is anything but systematic.

The positive value of such an upper management audit is the evidence conveyed to the lower levels of an interest and participation by upper management.   On the negative side is the unprofessional nature of the audit and the risk that the top managers will overreact to their observations.

Middle Managers   A significant number of companies make use of teams of middle managers to conduct quality audits on a part-time basis.[88]   These teams include not only quality managers but managers from other functions as well, e.g., Production, Personnel, Marketing, Purchasing.

This device is useful for conducting the pilot audits which serve as a precedent for subsequent scheduled audits carried out by "professional" auditors.   In addition, the managers derive useful personal feedback and development from participating in these audits.   However, it is seldom possible to carry out this team concept as a continuing program due to manager turnover, low priority given to something so easily deferred, etc.

Outside Consultants   This source of manpower is used in special situations when:

The company has some major unsolved quality problems which have prevailed for years and for which there is no end in sight.

The upper managers are not agreed among themselves and may even question their own objectivity; i.e., are they part of the problem?

The upper managers lack full confidence in their own professionals and wish to check their judgment.

If the outsider is well qualified (this can be checked with his prior clients on similar assignments), he may well be able to shorten the time required by the company to identify its quality weaknesses.   (To the company, the review may be an "audit," but the consultants usually call it a "survey.")

Full-time Auditors   Increasingly, the source of manpower for independent audits has been the creation of a new category of specialist who is assigned full-time to auditing.   These auditors are located in a special Quality Assurance Department (or similar title) which normally reports to the Quality Manager.

The use of full-time auditors greatly improves the competence of the auditing. The auditing job exposes the men to a wide variety of company activities so that

---

[86] For a discussion of the broader aspects of manpower in the quality function, see Section 17 generally.

[87] Mizuno, Shigeru, Quality Systems in Japan, *Reports of Statistical Applications Research,* vol. 13, no. 1, pp. 32–44, 1968.

[88] See, for example, *Quality Assurance,* September 1968, pp. 16–20.

they undergo intensive training and development, especially during the first two years or so of their assignment. As a result, the auditors soon become well-trained professionals. As a direct consequence of their audits, they participate in discussions of quality specifications, standards, and procedures. Their study of discrepancies gives them an understanding of peripheral "non-quality" matters which nevertheless have a bearing on quality. Their resulting broad exposure also increases their capacity to take on added responsibilities. They are aware of this to such an extent that they become restive after several years.

One approach for dealing with this personnel problem is to make a bargain with the man at the time he is assigned to an auditing job, e.g., that he will be reassigned at the end of three (or so) years to a new job which takes advantage of the development he has undergone on the auditing job. In such cases the auditors tend to stick it out. In contrast, if the assignment is for an indefinite period and if there is no clear evidence of new opportunity, the auditor tends to look for new opportunities outside the company.

A further problem with auditors is the case in which the auditing is *not* full time; e.g., a quality control engineer is assigned to a mixture of quality planning, analysis, and auditing. The overwhelming experience in such cases is that the auditing receives the lowest priority of all the assignments and soon is not being done at all. As far as possible, the rule should be to make auditing a full-time job. Where the amount of auditing is less than one man's full time, it may be feasible to do the auditing seasonally, so that during the months the man is assigned to auditing he has no other assignments.

In finance function, the great public need for integrity of the financial reports of publicly owned companies has given rise to a licensed professional auditor, the Certified Public Accountant. It is quite conceivable that there will evolve a category of Certified Public Quality Auditor to provide a corresponding certificate to companies based on compliance to accepted standards for quality planning and execution.[89]

Product Auditors Product Auditing is usually a full-time job; often the product auditor remains full-time on the same product line year after year.

The general practice is to fill these posts from the ranks of inspectors who have long experience and who have demonstrated a high level of objectivity and integrity. These auditors select the samples as prescribed, inspect and test them to the specifications, and do the associated paper work. Sometimes, but not usually, they participate in the associated discussions of the findings and implications.

Because of the managerial importance of the product audit, the product auditor job is graded above that of the inspector working on the same product. The auditor is usually on the salaried rather than the hourly payroll, and the job is usually exempt, i.e., not in the labor union of the hourly rated employees. However, the job of product auditor is not rated in the "professional" category.

---

[89] At the 1972 ASQC Technical Conference there was proposed a National Quality System Accreditation plan (for vendor qualification) which would involve:

A National Accreditation Register.

Use of ASQC Standard C-1-1968 *(General Requirements for a Quality Program)* as a standard for accreditation. (This has since been issued as an American Standard, ANSI Z 1.8, approved November 18, 1971.)

Use of ASQC-certified Quality Engineers to evaluate quality systems and award accreditation.

See Field, D. L., R. A. Maass, and T. M. Vining, ASQC Quality System Accreditation, *ASQC 1972 Technical Conference Transactions,* pp. 469 and 470.

Basic Statistical Methods

FRANK M. GRYNA, Jr.

THE STATISTICAL TOOL KIT

Most of the decision making in the quality function rests on a base of statistics — the collection, analysis, and interpretation of data. For the practitioner, "statistics" can be thought of as a kit of tools which helps to solve problems. The statistical tool kit shown in Table 22-1 lists the problem to be solved, the applicable statistical tool, and where in this Handbook the tool is to be found.

TABLE 22-1   The Statistical Tool Kit

Problem	Statistical tool	Reference pages
Planning a statistical investigation	Planning and analyzing data for solving specific problems	22-66, 68
Summarizing data	Frequency distributions, histograms, and indices	22-3 to 8
Predicting future results from a sample	Probability distributions	22-8 to 20
Determining a probability involving several events	Basic theorems of probability	22-20 to 21
Predicting performance without failure (reliability)	Reliability prediction and analysis	22-21 to 33
Determining the significance of difference between two sets of data or between a set of data and a standard value	Tests of hypothesis	22-33 to 48
Determining the sample size required for testing a hypothesis	Sample size determination for hypothesis testing	22-48
Determining the ability of a sample result to estimate a true value	Confidence limits	22-48 to 51
Determining the sample size required to estimate a true value	Sample size determination for estimation	22-51 to 52
Determining tolerance limits on single characteristics	Statistical tolerance limits	22-53 to 56
Determining tolerance limits for interacting dimensions	Tolerance limits for interacting dimensions	22-56 to 61
Incorporating past information in predicting future events	Bayes' theorem	22-61 to 63
Incorporating economic consequences in defining decision rules	Statistical decision theory	22-63 to 65
Converting data to meet statistical assumptions	Transformations of data	22-65 to 67

Controlling process quality by early detection of process changes:
  1. Using measurements data
  2. Using go no-go measurements data
	
	Variables control charts
	Attributes control charts
		
		23-1 to 17
		23-17 to 24

TABLE 22-1   The Statistical Tool Kit (Continued)

Problem	Statistical tool	Reference pages
Evaluating quality of lots to a previously defined quality level:		
1. Quality measured on a go no-go basis	Attributes sampling plans	24-1 to 44
2. Quality measured on a variables basis	Variables sampling plans	Sec. 25
3. Sampling to determine reliability	Reliability sampling plans	Sec. 25
4. Bulk product	Bulk sampling plans	Sec. 25A
Evaluating the relationship between two or more variables by determining an equation to estimate one variable from knowledge of another variable	Regression analysis	Sec. 26
Planning and analyzing experiments:		
1. Investigating the effect of varying one factor	One-factor experiment	Sec. 27
2. Investigating the effect of varying two or more factors	Designs for two or more factors	Sec. 27
3. Investigating the variability of laboratory measurements	Interlaboratory tests	Sec. 27
4. Experimenting under process conditions to determine optimum settings of variables	Evolutionary operations	Sec. 27A
5. Determining the optimum set of values of a group of variables that affect a response variable	Response surface methodology	Sec. 28

METHODS OF SUMMARIZING DATA

Practical methods of summarizing data stress simplicity. Sometimes, one method provides a useful and complete summarization. In other cases, two or even three methods are needed for complete clarity. Three key methods are the frequency distribution, the histogram, and measures of central tendency and dispersion.

The Frequency Distribution The frequency distribution is a statistical tool for presenting numerous facts in a form which makes more clear the central tendency and the dispersion along the scale of measurement.

Table 22-2 shows "raw data" representing the measurement of electrical resistance of 100 coils. A practitioner scanning these 100 facts has difficulty in grasping their meaning.

Table 22-3 shows the same data after tabulation. Note how the analyst's tallies in the column "Tabulation" make more evident where is the central tendency and what

TABLE 22-2   Resistance (Ohms) of 100 coils

3.37	3.34	3.38	3.32	3.33	3.28	3.34	3.31	3.33	3.34
3.29	3.36	3.30	3.31	3.33	3.34	3.34	3.36	3.39	3.34
3.35	3.36	3.30	3.32	3.33	3.35	3.35	3.34	3.32	3.38
3.32	3.37	3.34	3.38	3.36	3.37	3.36	3.31	3.33	3.30
3.35	3.33	3.38	3.37	3.44	3.32	3.36	3.32	3.29	3.35
3.38	3.39	3.34	3.32	3.30	3.39	3.36	3.40	3.32	3.33
3.29	3.41	3.27	3.36	3.41	3.37	3.36	3.37	3.33	3.36
3.31	3.33	3.35	3.34	3.35	3.34	3.31	3.36	3.37	3.35
3.40	3.35	3.37	3.32	3.35	3.36	3.38	3.35	3.31	3.34
3.35	3.36	3.39	3.31	3.31	3.30	3.35	3.33	3.35	3.31

TABLE 22-3   Tally of Resistance Values of 100 Coils

Resistance, ohms	Tabulation	Frequency	Cumulative frequency
3.45			
3.44	I	1	1
3.43			
3.42			
3.41	II	2	3
3.40	II	2	5
3.39	IIII	4	9
3.38	JHT I	6	15
3.37	JHT III	8	23
3.36	JHT JHT III	13	36
3.35	JHT JHT IIII	14	50
3.34	JHT JHT II	12	62
3.33	JHT JHT	10	72
3.32	JHT IIII	9	81
3.31	JHT IIII	9	90
3.30	JHT	5	95
3.29	III	3	98
3.28	I	1	99
3.27	I	1	100
3.26			
Total		100	

is the dispersion. The column "Frequency" is merely a recorded count of these same tallies. The column "Cumulative Frequency" shows the number of coils with resistance equal to or greater than the associated resistance value.

Table 22-3 exhibits a range of values from 3.44 to 3.27, or 17 intervals of 0.01 ohm each. When it is desired to reduce the number of such intervals, the data are grouped into "cells." Table 22-4 shows the same data grouped into a frequency distribution of only six cells, each 0.03 ohm wide. Grouping the data into cells simplifies presentation and study of the distribution but loses some of the detail. (However, one can always go back to the original data if necessary.)

TABLE 22-4   Frequency Distribution of Resistance Values

Resistance		Frequency	Cumulative frequency
Boundaries	Midpoints		
3.415–3.445	3.43	1	1
3.385–3.415	3.40	8	9
3.355–3.385	3.37	27	36
3.325–3.355	3.34	36	72
3.295–3.325	3.31	23	95
3.265–3.295	3.28	5	100
		100	

The following are the steps taken to construct a frequency distribution:
1. Decide on the number of cells. Table 22-5 provides guidelines[1] which are

---

[1] These guidelines aim not only to provide a clear summary of data but also to reveal any underlying pattern of variation.

TABLE 22-5 Number of Cells in Frequency Distribution

Number of observations	Recommended Number of cells
20–50	6
51–100	7
101–200	8
201–500	9
501–1,000	10
Over 1,000	11–20

adequate for most cases encountered. These guidelines are not rigid and should be adjusted when necessary.

2. Calculate the approximate cell interval i. The cell interval equals the largest observation minus the smallest observation divided by the number of cells. Round this result to some convenient number.

3. Construct the cells by listing cell boundaries. As an aid to later calculation:

a. The cell boundaries should be to one more decimal place than the actual data and should end in a 5.

b. The cell interval should be constant throughout the entire frequency distribution.

4. Tally each observation into the appropriate cell and then list the total frequency f for each cell.

The Histogram There are several ways of showing a frequency distribution in graphic form. The most popular is the frequency histogram. Figure 22-1 shows the electrical resistance data of Table 22-4 depicted in histogram form. The diagram is

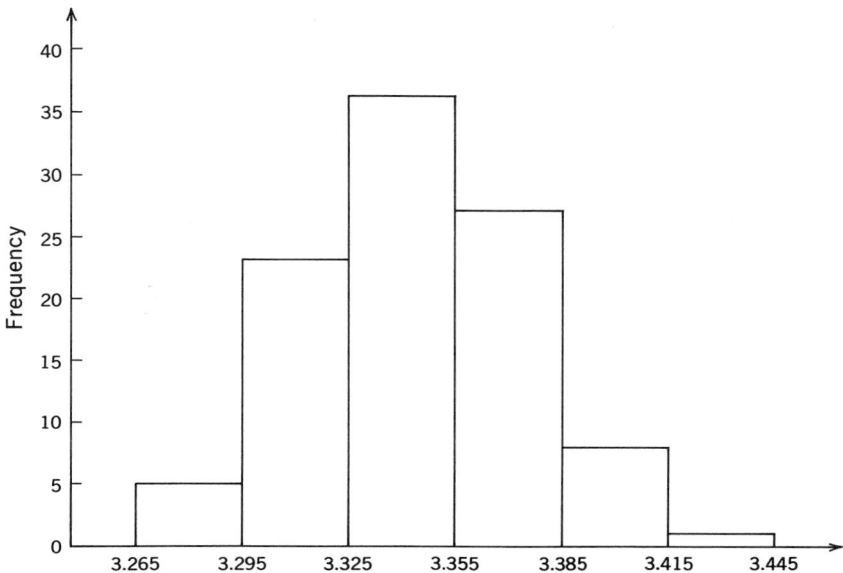

Fig. 22-1 Histogram of resistance.

so easy to construct and interpret that it is widely used in elementary analysis of data.

One example of wide, effective use of frequency histograms is comparison of process capabilities with tolerance limits. The histogram of Figure 22-2 shows a process which is inherently capable of holding the tolerances drawn on the same figure. The high degree of defectives being produced is the result of running this process at a setting which does not locate its central tendency near the midpoint of the tolerance range.[2]

Analyses of histograms to draw conclusions beyond the sample data should be based on at least 50 measurements.

Measures of Central Tendency Most frequency distributions exhibit a "central tendency," i.e., a shape such that the bulk of the observations pile up in the area between the two extremes. The measure of this central tendency is one of the two most fundamental measures in all statistical analysis.

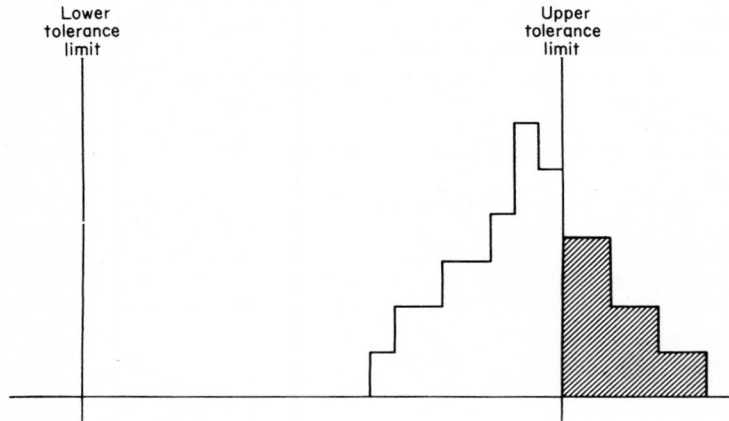

Fig. 22-2   Histogram of a process.

There are three principal measures of central tendency.

1. *Arithmetic mean* (the ordinary "average"), used for symmetrical or near symmetrical distributions, or for distributions which lack a clearly dominant single peak.

The arithmetic mean $\bar{X}$ is the most generally used measure in quality work. It is employed so often to report average size, average yield, average percent of defective, etc., that control charts have been devised to analyze and keep track of it. Such control charts can give the earliest obtainable warning of significant changes in the central value (see Section 23).

The mean is calculated by adding the observations and dividing by the number of observations. A short method for calculating the mean is given in a subsequent example under Measures of Dispersion.

2. *Median* (the middle value when the figures are arranged according to size), used for reducing the effects of extreme values, or for data which can be ranked but are not economically measurable (shades of color, visual appearance, odors) or for special testing situations. If, for example, the average of five parts tested is used to decide whether a life test requirement has been met, then the lifetime of the third

[2] See Section 9, under Process Capability Analysis, for other examples.

part to fail can sometimes serve to predict the average of all five, and thereby the decision of the test can be made much sooner.

3. *Mode* (value which occurs most often in data), used for severely skewed distributions, describing an irregular situation where two peaks are found, or for eliminating the effects of extreme values.

The statistical "efficiency" of these measures varies. See Dixon and Massey (Ref. 1, chap. 9) for elaboration.

Measures of Dispersion   Data are always scattered around the zone of central tendency, and the extent of this scatter is called dispersion or variation. Measure of dispersion is the second of the two most fundamental measures in all statistical analysis.

There are several measures of dispersion. The simplest is the range, which is the difference between the maximum and minimum values in the data. As the range is based on only two values, it is most useful when the number of observations is small (about 10 or less).

The most important measure of variation is the *standard deviation*. The definition of the standard deviation is a formula:

$$s = \sqrt{\frac{\sum (X - \bar{X})^2}{n - 1}}$$

where s = sample standard deviation
Σ = "sum of"
X = observed values
$\bar{X}$ = arithmetic mean
n = number of observations

For calculation purposes, an equivalent formula is

$$s = \sqrt{\frac{n \sum (X^2) - (\sum X)^2}{n(n - 1)}}$$

The square of the standard deviation is called the *variance*.[3]

With data in frequency distribution form, shortcut calculations can simplify find-

TABLE 22-6   Calculation of Average and Standard Deviation

Midpoint (1)	Frequency f (2)	d' (3)	fd' (4)	$f(d')^2$ (5)
3.43	1	+2	2	4
3.40	8	+1	8	8
3.37	27	0	0	0
3.34	36	−1	−36	36
3.31	23	−2	−46	92
3.28	5	−3	−15	45
	$\Sigma = 100$		$\Sigma = -87$	$\Sigma = 185$

[3] There is also an index called covariance which gives information on the relationship between pairs of observations on characteristics X and Y. This is defined as

$$s_{XY} = \frac{\sum [(X - \bar{X})^2 (Y - \bar{Y})^2]}{n - 1}$$

For an application, see Section 26, under Example—Computer Output.

ing the average and the standard deviation. This is illustrated in Table 22-6. To start, an arbitrary origin A is assumed as 3.37.

A zero is arbitrarily placed on this line in the d' column. The other figures in this column indicate how many cells the entry is above or below the arbitrary zero. Minus signs are attached when the entry is smaller than the assumed value, 3.37. The fd' values in column (4) are found by multiplying together the entries in columns (2) and (3). Similarly $f(d')^2$ is found by multiplying the figures in columns (3) and (4). Note that the totals in the last two columns are identified in the formulas as $\Sigma fd'$ and $\Sigma f(d')^2$, respectively, and i is the cell interval. As the multiplications are small enough to be carried out mentally, the complete table can be made quickly.

$$\bar{X} = A + \left(\frac{\Sigma fd'}{n}\right)i = 3.37 + \left(\frac{-87}{100}\right)0.03 = 3.344$$

$$s = i \sqrt{\frac{n\Sigma f(d')^2 - (\Sigma fd')^2}{n(n-1)}}$$

$$s = 0.03 \sqrt{\frac{100(185) - (-87)^2}{100(99)}} = 0.031$$

For sample sizes of about 10 or fewer observations, the standard deviation can be approximated from the range by calculating R/d_2, where d_2 is a factor in Appendix II, Table A. For example, suppose the first column of values in Table 22-2 represents a sample of 10. The range is $3.40 - 3.29$, or 0.11. From Table A in Appendix II, $d_2 = 3.078$. The estimate of the standard deviation is therefore $0.11/3.078 = 0.036$. This is much simpler than calculating the standard deviation directly. Subsequent topics in this Section further illustrate this feature of the range. Dixon and Massey (Ref. 1, pp. 136–140) furnish procedures and tables for a variety of applications of the range.

A final measure of variation is the coefficient of variation. This is defined as the standard deviation divided by the mean and is thus a relative measure of variation. It can be helpful in comparing several sets of similar data that differ in mean value but may have some commonality in *relative* variation.

The methods of summarizing data covered in the previous paragraphs can be placed on a computer (see Larson, Ref. 2). Also see Sec. 20, Tables 20-10 and 20-11, for additional information on computer programs for quality control.

PROBABILITY DISTRIBUTIONS

A distinction is made between a sample and a population (or "universe"). A sample is a limited number of measurements taken from a larger source. A population is a large source of measurements from which the sample is taken.

A probability distribution function is a mathematical formula which relates the values of the characteristic with their probability of occurrence in the *population*. Figure 22-3 summarizes some distributions and their functions. When the characteristic being measured can take on any value (subject to the fineness of the measuring process), its probability distribution is called a continuous probability distribution. For example, the probability distribution for the resistance data of Table 22-3 is an example of a continuous probability distribution because the resistance could have any value, limited only by the fineness of the measuring instrument. Experience has shown that most continuous characteristics follow one of several common probability distributions, i.e., the "normal" distribution, the "exponential" distribution, and the "Weibull" distribution. These distributions find the probabilities

DISTRIBUTION	FORM	PROBABILITY FUNCTION	COMMENTS ON APPLICATION
NORMAL		$y = \dfrac{1}{\sigma\sqrt{2\pi}}e^{-\frac{(x-\mu)^2}{2\sigma^2}}$ μ = Mean σ = Standard deviation	Applicable when there is a concentration of observations about the average and it is equally likely that observations will occur above and below the average. Variation in observations is usually the result of many small causes.
EXPONENTIAL		$y = \dfrac{1}{\mu}e^{-\frac{x}{\mu}}$	Applicable when it is likely that more observations will occur below the average than above.
WEIBULL		$y = \alpha\beta(x-\gamma)^{\beta-1}e^{-\alpha(x-\gamma)^\beta}$ α = Scale parameter β = Shape parameter γ = Location parameter	Applicable in describing a wide variety of patterns of variation, including departures from the normal and exponential.
POISSON*		$y = \dfrac{(np)^r e^{-np}}{r!}$ n = Number of trials r = Number of occurrences p = Probability of occurrence	Same as binomial but particularly applicable when there are many opportunities for occurrence of an event, but a low probability (less than 0.10) on each trial.
BINOMIAL*		$y = \dfrac{n!}{r!(n-r)!}p^r q^{n-r}$ n Number of trials r = Number of occurrences p = Probability of occurrence q = 1-p	Applicable in defining the probability of r occurrences in n trials of an event which has a probability of occurrence of p on each trial.
NEGATIVE BINOMIAL*		$y = \dfrac{(r+s-1)!}{(r-1)!(s!)}p^r q^s$ r = Number of occurrences s = Difference between number of trials and number of occurrences p = probability of occurrence q = 1-p	Applicable in defining the probability that r occurrences will require a total of r + s trials of an event which has a probability of occurrence of p on each trial. (Note that the total number of trials n is r + s.)
HYPERGEOMETRIC*		$y = \dfrac{\dbinom{d}{r}\dbinom{N-d}{n-r}}{\dbinom{N}{n}}$	Applicable in defining the probability of r occurrences in n trials of an event when there are a total of d occurrences in a population of N.

Fig. 22-3 Summary of common probability distributions. Asterisks indicate that these are discrete distributions, but the curves are shown as continuous for ease of comparison with the continuous distributions.

associated with occurrences of the *actual values* of the characteristic. Other continuous distributions (e.g., t, F, and chi square) are important in data analysis but are not helpful in predicting the probability of occurrence of actual values.

When the characteristic being measured can take on only certain specific values (e.g., integers 0, 1, 2, 3, etc.), its probability distribution is called a discrete probability distribution. For example, the distribution for the number of defectives r in a sample of 5 items is a discrete probability distribution because r can only be 0, 1, 2, 3, 4, or 5. The common discrete distributions are the Poisson, binomial, negative binomial, and hypergeometric (see Figure 22-3).

The following paragraphs explain how probability distributions can be used with a sample of observations to make predictions about the larger population.

CONTINUOUS PROBABILITY DISTRIBUTIONS

The "Normal" Probability Distribution   Many engineering characteristics can be approximated by the normal distribution

$$y = \frac{1}{\sigma \sqrt{2\pi}} \, e^{-(X - \mu)^2 / 2\sigma^2}$$

where $e = 2.718$
$\pi = 3.141$
$\mu =$ population average
$\sigma =$ population standard deviation

Problems are solved with a table, but note that the distribution requires estimates of only the average μ and standard deviation σ of the population[4] in order to make predictions about the population. The curve for the normal probability distribution is related to a frequency distribution and its histogram. As the sample becomes larger and larger, and the width of each cell becomes smaller and smaller, the histogram approaches a smooth curve. If the entire population[5] were measured, and if it were normally distributed, the result would be as shown in Figure 22-3. Thus, the *shape* of a histogram of sample data provides some indication of the probability distribution for the population. If the histogram resembles[6] the "bell" shape shown in Figure 22-3, then this is a basis for assuming that the population follows a normal probability distribution. Hahn (Ref. 3) gives a practical discussion of assuming normality.

Making Predictions Using the Normal Probability Distribution   Predictions require just two estimates and a table. The estimates are:

$$\text{Estimate of } \mu = \bar{X} \qquad \text{Estimate of } \sigma = s$$

The calculations of the sample $\bar{X}$ and s are made by one of the methods previously discussed.

For example, from past experience, a manufacturer concludes that the burnout time of a particular light bulb he manufactures is normally distributed. A sample of 50 bulbs has been tested and the average life found to be 60 days, with a standard deviation of 20 days. How many bulbs in the entire population of light bulbs can be expected to be still working after 100 days of life?

[4] Unless otherwise indicated, Greek symbols will be used for population values and Roman symbols for sample values.

[5] In practice, the population is usually considered infinite, e.g., the potential production from a process.

[6] It is *not* necessary that the sample histogram be perfectly normal. The assumption of normality is applied only to the population. Small deviations from normality are expected in random samples.

The problem is to find the area under the curve beyond 100 days (see Figure 22-4). The area under a distribution curve between two stated limits represents the probability of occurrence. Therefore, the area beyond 100 days is the probability that a bulb will last more than 100 days. To find the area, calculate the difference K between a particular value and the average of the curve in units of standard deviation:

$$K = \frac{X - \mu}{\sigma}$$

In this problem, $K = (100 - 60) \div 20 = +2.0$. Table B in Appendix shows, for $K = 2$, a probability of 0.9773. Applied to this problem, the probability that

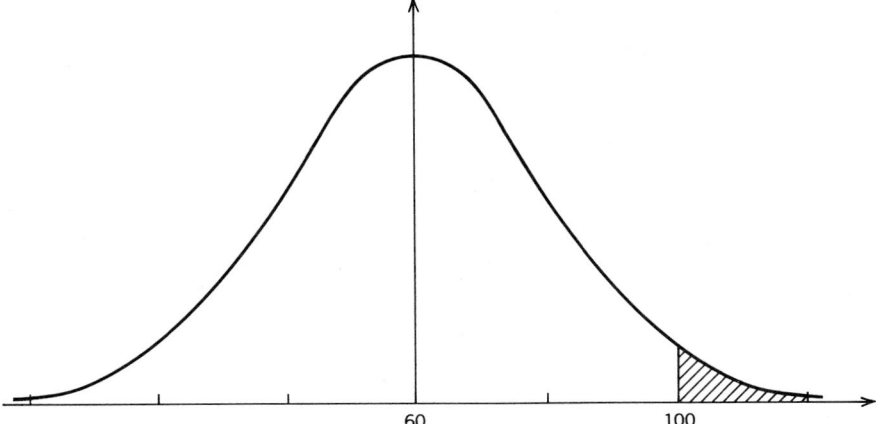

Fig. 22-4 Distribution of light bulb life.

a bulb will last 100 days or less is 0.9773. The normal curve is symmetrical about the average and the total area is 1.000. The probability of a bulb's lasting more than 100 days then is $1.0000 - 0.9773$, or 0.0227, or 2.27% of the bulbs in the population will still be working after 100 days.

Similarly, if a characteristic is normally distributed and if estimates of the average and standard deviation of the population are obtained, this method can estimate the total percent of production that will fall within engineering specification limits.

Figure 22-5 shows representative areas under the normal distribution curve.[7] Thus 68.26% of the *population* will fall between the average of the population plus or minus 1 standard deviation of the population, 95.46% of the population will fall between the average $\pm 2\sigma$, and finally, $\pm 3\sigma$ will include 99.73% of the population. The percentage of a *sample* within a set of limits can be quite different from the percentage within the same limits in the population. This important fact is an underlying principle of testing hypotheses (covered later in this Section).

Another way of making predictions based on a normal distribution employs probability paper. Probability paper is so constructed that data from a particular kind of distribution plot as a straight line; i.e., a sample of data from a normally distributed population plots approximately as a straight line on normal probability paper. (Small deviations from a straight line are expected because the data represent a

[7] These can be derived from Table B in Appendix II.

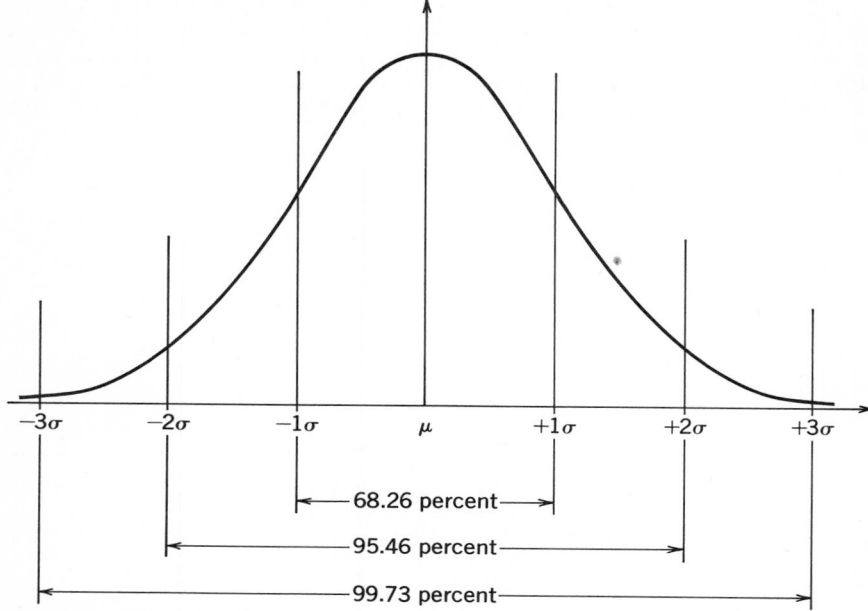

Fig. 22-5   Areas of a normal curve.

sample of the population.)   The following are the steps taken to plot data on probability paper:
1. Arrange the observations in ascending values.   The smallest value is given a
rank *i* of 1 and the largest value a rank of *n*.
2. For each value, calculate the cumulative frequency.
3. For each value, calculate

$$\frac{\text{Cumulative frequency}}{n+1} \times 100$$

This provides the mean rank probability estimate, in percent, for plotting the data.
4. Plot the observed values against their mean rank probability estimate.
If the observations are in frequency distribution form, the procedure is the same
except that instead of using the observed values the probability estimates are plotted
against the cell boundaries.   This is illustrated for the resistance data (see Table
22-7).

TABLE 22-7   Resistance Data

Cell boundaries	Frequency	Cumulative frequency	$\dfrac{\text{Cumulative frequency}}{100+1}(100)$
3.415–3.445	1	1	0.99%
3.385–3.415	8	9	8.9
3.355–3.385	27	36	35.6
3.325–3.355	36	72	71.3
3.295–3.325	23	95	94.1
3.265–3.295	5	100	99.0
	100		

The plot is shown in Figure 22-6. Lower cell boundaries are plotted against the last column of Table 22-7 using the upper (Percent Over) scale. The line has been drawn in by eye, and the fit appears reasonable. This line represents an estimate of the population, and predictions like those obtained from the normal probability table can be read directly from the graph. For example, 5% of the population of coils will have resistance values greater than about 3.39. Also, 95% will have values greater than about 3.29. (Therefore, 95 − 5, or 90%, will have values between 3.29 and 3.39.)

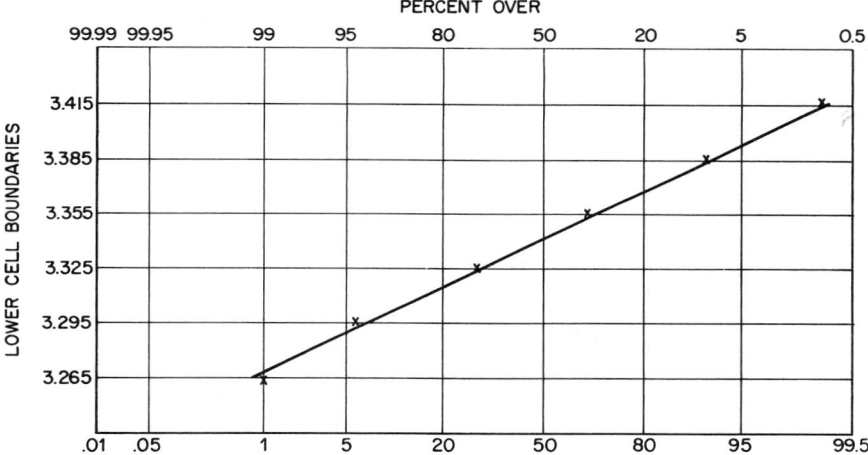

Fig. 22-6 Cumulative probability plot of Table 22-7.

Figure 22-7 shows a form[8] which incorporates probability paper plotting with further analysis such as confidence limits and control limits.

King (Ref. 4) gives a practical description of probability paper procedures for the normal and other important distributions.

The Exponential Probability Distribution The exponential probability function is

$$y = \frac{1}{\mu} \ e^{- X / \mu}$$

Figure 22-3 shows the shape of an exponential distribution curve. Note that the normal and exponential distributions have distinctly different shapes. An examination of the tables of areas shows that 50% of a normally distributed population occurs above the average value and 50% below. In an exponential population, 36.8% are above the average and 63.2% below the average. This refutes the intuitive idea that the average is always the 50% point! The property of a higher percentage below the average sometimes helps to indicate applications of the exponential. For example, the exponential describes the loading pattern for some structural members because smaller loads are more numerous than larger loads. The exponential is also useful in describing the distribution of failure times of complex equipments.

Making Predictions Using the Exponential Probability Distribution Predictions based on an exponentially distributed population require only an estimate of the popula-

---

[8] This type of form was originally developed by E. F. Taylor. Further information may be obtained from the General Electric Co., Medical Systems Business Division, Milwaukee, Wisconsin, 53201.

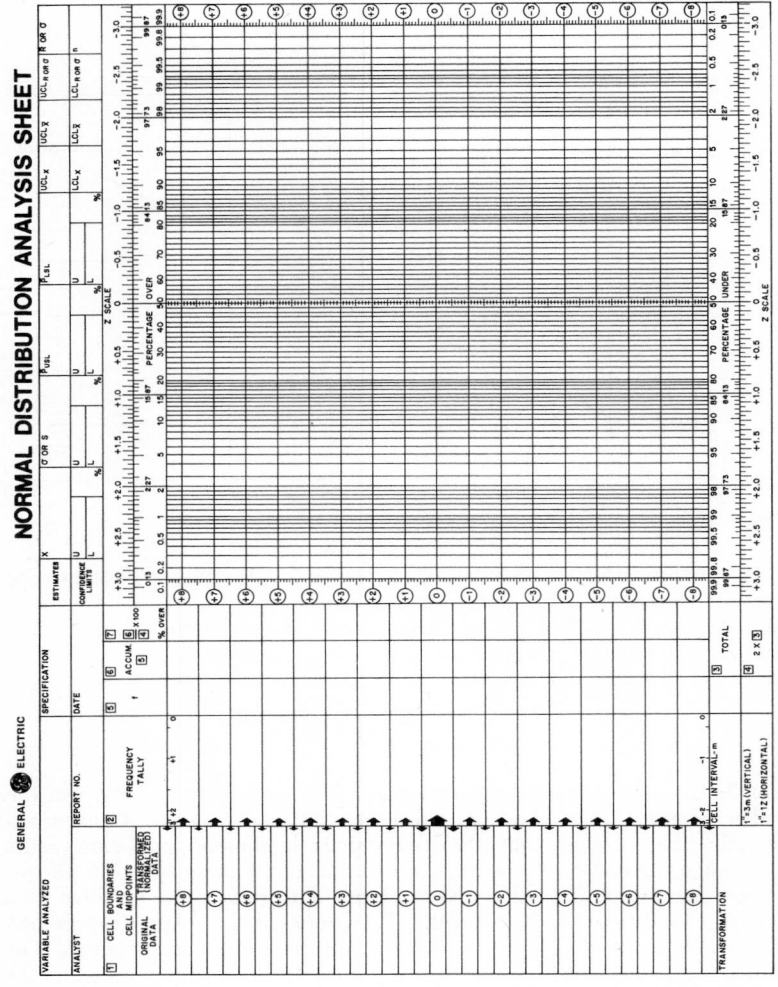

Fig. 22-7 Normal distribution analysis sheet.

tion average.   For example, the time between successive failures of a complex piece
of equipment is measured and the resulting histogram is found to resemble the exponential probability curve.   The results of a sample of measurements indicate that the
average time between failures (commonly called MTBF or mean time between failures) is 100 hours.   What is the probability that the time between two successive
failures of this equipment will be at least 20 hours?

The problem is one of finding the area under the curve beyond 20 hours (Figure
22-8).   Table C in Appendix II gives the area under the curve beyond any particular
value X that is substituted in the ratio X/μ.   In this problem,

$$\frac{X}{\mu} = \frac{20}{100} = 0.20$$

From Table C in Appendix II the area under the curve beyond 20 hours is 0.8187.
The probability that the time between two successive failures is greater than 20

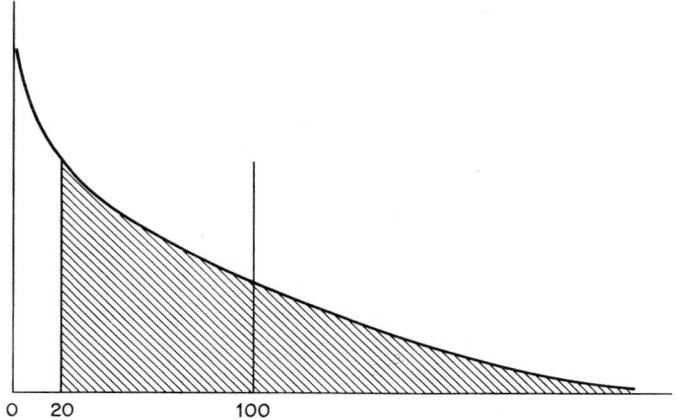

Fig. 22-8   Distribution of time between failures.

hours is 0.8187; i.e., there is about an 82% chance that the equipment will operate
without failure continuously for 20 or more hours.   Similar calculations would give
a probability of 0.9048 for 10 or more hours.   Later in this Section, this probability
is calculated for the specified "mission time" of a product, and the result is called
"reliability."   These analyses could also be made using exponential probability
paper.

The Weibull Probability Distribution   The Weibull distribution is a family of distributions having the general function

$$y = \alpha\beta \, (X - \gamma)^{\beta - 1} \, e^{\, - \, \alpha \, (X - \gamma)^{\, \beta}}$$

where α = scale parameter
β = shape parameter
γ = location parameter

The curve of the function (Figure 22-3) varies greatly depending on the numerical
values of the parameters.   Most important is the shape parameter β, which reflects
the pattern of the curve.   Note that when β is 1.0, the Weibull function reduces to
the exponential and that when β is about 3.5 (and $\alpha = 1$ and $\gamma = 0$), the Weibull
closely approximates the normal distribution.   In practice, β varies from about $\frac{1}{3}$ to

5. The scale parameter α is related to the peakedness of the curve; i.e., as α changes, the curve becomes flatter or more peaked.

The location parameter γ is the smallest possible value of X. This is often assumed to be 0, thereby simplifying the equation. It is often unnecessary to determine the values of these parameters because predictions are made directly from Weibull probability paper. King (Ref. 4, pp. 136–140) gives procedures for graphically finding α, β, and γ.

The Weibull covers many shapes of distributions. This makes it popular in practice because it reduces the problem of examining a set of data and deciding which of the common distributions (e.g., normal or exponential) fits best.

Making Predictions Using the Weibull Probability Distribution An analytical approach for the Weibull distribution (even with tables) is cumbersome, and the predictions are usually made with Weibull probability paper. For example, five heat-treated shafts were stress-tested until each of them failed. The fatigue life (in terms of number of cycles to failure) is shown below:

10,263
12,187
16,908
18,042
23,271

The problem is to predict the percentage failure of the population for various values of fatigue life. The solution is to plot the data on Weibull paper, observe if the points fall approximately in a straight line, and if so, read the probability predictions (percentage failure) from the graph.

Although Weibull plotting can follow the mean rank procedure of normal probability paper, much of the literature on Weibull applications uses "median ranks." Table D in Appendix II gives, for various sample sizes, the values of the median rank.[9] The median ranks necessary for this particular example are based on a sample size of five failures and are as shown in Table 22-8. (The mean rank estimates are shown for comparison.) The cycles to failure are now plotted on the Weibull

TABLE 22-8   Table of Median and Mean Ranks

Failure number i	Median rank	Mean rank $= \dfrac{i}{5+1}$
1	0.1294	0.1667
2	0.3147	0.3333
3	0.5000	0.5000
4	0.6853	0.6667
5	0.8706	0.8333

graph paper against the corresponding values of the median rank (see Figure 22-9). These points fall approximately in a straight line;[10] so it is assumed that the Weibull distribution applies. The vertical axis gives the cumulative percent of failures in the population corresponding to the fatigue life shown on the horizontal axis. For example, about 50% of the population of shafts will fail in less than 17,000 cycles. About 90% of the population will fail in less than 24,000 cycles. By appropriate subtractions, predictions can be made of the percent of failures between any two fatigue life limits.

It is tempting to extrapolate on probability paper, particularly to predict life. For

[9] Note that the mean rank procedure does not require a table.
[10] King (Ref. 4, pp. 126–128) describes how to modify a plot to help obtain a straight line.

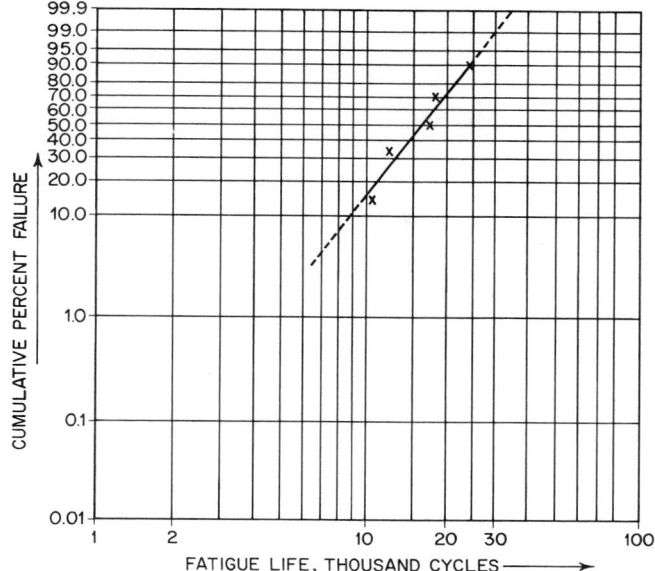

Fig. 22-9 Distribution of fatigue life.

example, suppose the minimum fatigue life were specified as 8,000 cycles and the 5 measurements above were from tests conducted to evaluate the ability of the design to meet 8,000 cycles. As all 5 tests exceeded 8,000 cycles, the design seems adequate and therefore should be released for production. However, extrapolation on the Weibull paper predicts that about 8% of the *population* of shafts would fail in less than 8,000 cycles. This suggests a review of the design before release to production. Thus, the small *sample* (all *within* specifications) gave a deceiving result.

Extrapolation can go in the other direction. Note that a probability plot of life test data does *not* require that all tests be completed before the plotting starts. As each unit fails, the failure time can be plotted against the median rank. If the early points appear to be following a straight line, then it is tempting to draw in the line *before* all tests are finished. The line can then be extrapolated beyond the actual test data and life predictions can be made without accumulating a large amount of test time. The approach has been applied to predicting, *early in a warranty period,* the "vital few" components of a complex product which will be most troublesome. However, extrapolation has dangers. It requires the judicious melding of statistical theory and engineering experience and judgment.

Moult (Ref. 5) describes the use of a Weibull plot in comparing the suitability of two types of steel for use in bearings. The plot is shown in Figure 22-10.

Nelson and Thompson (Ref. 6) discuss several types of Weibull paper. Probability graph paper is available for the normal, exponential, Weibull, and other probability distributions.[11] Although the mathematical functions and tables provide the same information, the graph paper reveals *relationships* between probabilities and values of X that are not readily apparent from the calculations. For example, the reduction in percent defective in a population as a function of wider and wider tolerance limits can be easily portrayed by the graph paper.

[11] A source is Technical and Engineering Aids for Management, Lowell, Mass. 01852.

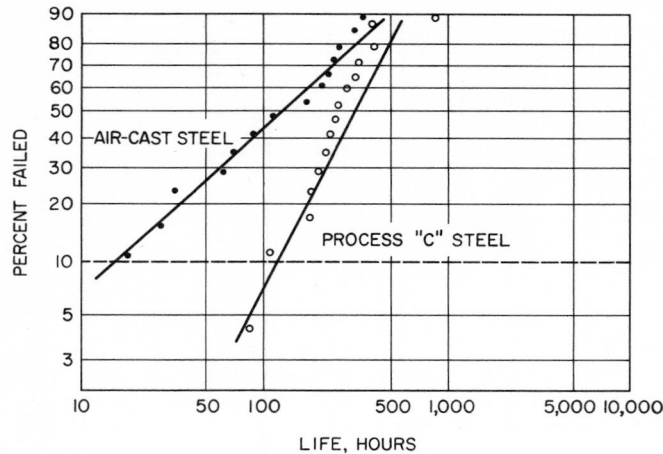

Fig. 22-10   Composite fatigue endurance—process "C" vacuum degassing vs. air cast AISI 8620.

DISCRETE PROBABILITY DISTRIBUTIONS

The Poisson Probability Distribution   In practice, the most important discrete distribution is the Poisson.   It is an approximation to more exact distributions and applies when the sample size is at least 16, the population size is at least ten times the sample size, and the probability of occurrence p on each trial is less than 0.1.   (These conditions are often met.)

Figure 22-3 states the Poisson probability function, but the real work is done by cumulative probability tables.

Making Predictions Using the Poisson Probability Distribution   A lot of 300 units of product is submitted by a vendor whose past quality has been about 2% defective. A random sample of 40 units is selected from the lot.   Table E in Appendix II provides the probability of r or less defectives in a sample of n units.[12]   Entering the table[13] with a value of np equal to 40 (0.02), or 0.8, gives Table 22-9.   Individual probabilities can be found by subtracting cumulative probabilities.   Thus, the probability of exactly 2 defectives is $0.953 - 0.809$, or 0.144.

TABLE 22-9   Table of Poisson Probabilities

r	Probability of r or less in sample
0	0.449
1	0.809
2	0.953
3	0.991
4	0.999
5	1.000

[12] The application of these probabilities is explained in Section 24, under Operating Characteristic (OC) Curve.

[13] A graphical equivalent is explained in Section 24, under Constructing the OC Curve.

The Binomial Probability Distribution   If the probability of occurrence p of an event is constant on each of n independent trials of the event, then the probability of r occurrences in n trials is

$$\frac{n!}{r!(n-r)!} p^r q^{n-r}$$

where $q = 1 - p$.

In practice, the assumption of a constant probability of occurrence is considered reasonable when the population size is at least ten times the sample size.[14]   (Note that the binomial has fewer assumptions than the Poisson.)

Table F in Appendix II provides partial tables for the binomial and gives references for more complete tables. King (Ref. 4, chaps. 20–22) discusses binomial probability paper. Muench (Ref. 7) explains a binomial computer.

Making Predictions Using the Binomial Probability Distribution   A lot of 100 units of product is submitted by a vendor whose past quality has been about 5% defective. A random sample of six units is selected from the lot. The probabilities of various sample results are given in Table 22-10.

TABLE 22-10   Table of Binomial Probabilities

r	P (exactly r defectives in 6) $= [6!/r!(6-r)!](0.05)^r (0.95)^{6-r}$
0	0.7351
1	0.2321
2	0.0306
3	0.0021
4	0.0001
5	0.0000
6	0.0000

In using the formula, note that $0! = 1$. Table F in Appendix II lists binomial probabilities in cumulative form, i.e., the probability of r or fewer occurrences in n trials. For the above example, the probability of 1 or less defectives in a sample of 6 can be read from the table as 0.9672. Note that this is the sum of the probabilities for $r = 0$ and $r = 1$, i.e., $0.7351 + 0.2321 = 0.9672$.

Negative Binomial Distribution   The negative binomial distribution is related to special cases of the Poisson distribution. Johnson and Leone (Ref. 8, pp. 88–91) give an example.

The Hypergeometric Distribution   Occasionally, the assumptions of the Poisson or binomial cannot be met. Subject only to the assumption of a random sample, the hypergeometric gives the probability of exactly r occurrences in n trials from a lot of N items having d defectives as

$$\frac{\binom{d}{r}\binom{N-d}{n-r}}{\binom{N}{n}}$$

where $\binom{N}{n}$ is the combination of N items taken n at a time and is equal to $N!/[n!$ $(N-n)!]$, where $N! = [N(N-1)(N-2)\ldots 1]$ and $0! = 1$. The calculations can be avoided by using tables such as those prepared by Lieberman and Owen (Ref. 9).

---

[14] Under this circumstance, the change in probability from one trial to the next is negligible.

Duncan (Ref. 10, pp. 88–89) compares the results of Poisson, binomial, and hypergeometric distributions.

Making Predictions Using the Hypergeometric Probability Distribution   A lot of 100 units is submitted by a vendor whose past quality has been about 5% defective. A random sample of 20 units is selected from the lot. To calculate the probability of 0 defectives in 20, note that the lot has 5 defectives and 95 nondefectives. Then:

$$P(0 \text{ in } 20) = \frac{\binom{5}{0}\binom{95}{20}}{\binom{100}{20}} = \frac{\left[\dfrac{5!}{0!(5-0)!}\right]\left[\dfrac{95!}{20!(95-20)!}\right]}{\dfrac{100!}{20!(100-20)!}} = 0.319$$

Repeat substitutions into the formula are made to find P (r in 20), where r in this example is 0, 1, 2, 3, 4, and 5.

Testing a Distribution Assumption   In practice, a distribution is assumed by evaluating a sample of data. Often, it is sufficient to evaluate the shape of the histogram or the degree to which a plot on probability paper follows a straight line. These convenient methods do require judgment (e.g., how "straight" must the line be?) because the sample is never a perfect fit. Be suspicious of the data if the fit is "perfect." "Goodness of fit" tests (see Tests of Hypothesis later in this Section) evaluate any distribution assumption using quantitative criteria.

BASIC THEOREMS OF PROBABILITY

Probability theory underlies all decisions which are based on sampling. Probability is expressed as a number which lies between 1.0 (certainty that an event will occur) and 0.0 (impossibility of occurrence).

A convenient definition of probability is one based on a frequency interpretation:

If an event A can occur in s cases out of a total of n possible and equally probable cases, then the probability that the event will occur is

$$P(A) = \frac{s}{n} = \frac{\text{number of successful cases}}{\text{total number of possible cases}}$$

Example   A lot consists of 100 parts. A single part is selected at random, and thus, each of the 100 parts has an equal chance of being selected. Suppose a lot contains a total of 8 defectives. Then the probability of drawing a single part that is defective is 8/100, or 0.08.

The following theorems are useful in solving problems:

Theorem 1.   If $P(A)$ is the probability that an event A will occur, then the probability that A will not occur is $1 - P(A)$.

Theorem 2.   If A and B are two events, then the probability that either A or B occurs is

$$P(A \text{ or } B) = P(A) + P(B) - P(A \text{ and } B)$$

A special case of this theorem occurs when A and B cannot occur simultaneously (i.e., A and B are "mutually exclusive"). Then the probability that either A or B occurs is

$$P(A \text{ or } B) = P(A) + P(B)$$

Example   The probabilities of r defectives in a sample of 6 units from a 5% defective lot were found previously by the binomial. The probability of 0 defectives was 0.7351; the probability of 1 defective was 0.2321. The probability of 0 or 1 defective is then 0.7351 + 0.2321, or 0.9672.

Theorem 3.   If A and B are two events, then the probability of the joint occurrence of both A and B is

$$P(A \text{ and } B) = P(A) \times P(B/A)$$

where $P(B/A)$ = probability that B will occur assuming A has already occurred.

A special case of this theorem occurs when the two events are independent, i.e., when the occurrence of one event has no influence on the probability of the other event. If A and B are independent, then the probability of both A and B occurring is

$$P(A \text{ and } B) = P(A) \times P(B)$$

Example A complex system consists of two major subsystems. The probability of successful performance of the first subsystem is 0.95; the corresponding probability for the second subsystem is 0.90. Both subsystems must operate successfully in order to achieve total system success. The probability of the successful operation of the total system is therefore $0.95 \times 0.90 = 0.855$.

The theorems above have been stated in terms of two events but can be expanded for any number of events.

FAILURE PATTERNS FOR COMPLEX PRODUCTS

Complex products often follow a familiar pattern of failure. Consider the data in Table 22-11. Assume that one unit was started on test and the time when it failed

TABLE 22-11 Failure History for a Unit of Electronic Ground Support Equipment

Time of failure, infant mortality period		Time of failure, constant failure rate period		Time of failure, wear-out period	
1	7.2	28.1	60.2	100.8	125.8
1.2	7.9	28.2	63.7	102.6	126.6
1.3	8.3	29.0	64.6	103.2	127.7
2.0	8.7	29.9	65.3	104.0	128.4
2.4	9.2	30.6	66.2	104.3	129.2
2.9	9.8	32.4	70.1	105.0	
3.0	10.2	33.0	71.0	105.8	
3.1	10.4	35.3	75.1	106.5	
3.3	11.9	36.1	75.6	110.7	
3.5	13.8	40.1	78.4	112.6	
3.8	14.4	42.8	79.2	113.5	
4.3	15.6	43.7	84.1	114.8	
4.6	16.2	44.5	86.0	115.1	
4.7	17.0	50.4	87.9	117.4	
4.8	17.5	51.2	88.4	118.3	
5.2	19.2	52.0	89.9	119.7	
5.4		53.3	90.8	120.6	
5.9		54.2	91.1	121.0	
6.4		55.6	91.5	122.9	
6.8		56.4	92.1	123.3	
6.9		58.3	97.9	124.5	

was recorded. The unit was repaired, again placed on test, and the time of the next failure recorded. The "failure rate" for the unit can be calculated for equal time intervals as the number of failures per unit time.[15] When the failure rate is plotted against a continuous time scale, the resulting chart (Figure 22-11), known as the "bathtub curve," exhibits three distinct periods or zones. These zones differ from

---

[15] Some applications require the use of a "hazard rate" instead of "failure rate." For the distinction, see Section 25, under Variables Plans for Process or Lot Parameter—Life Testing and Reliability.

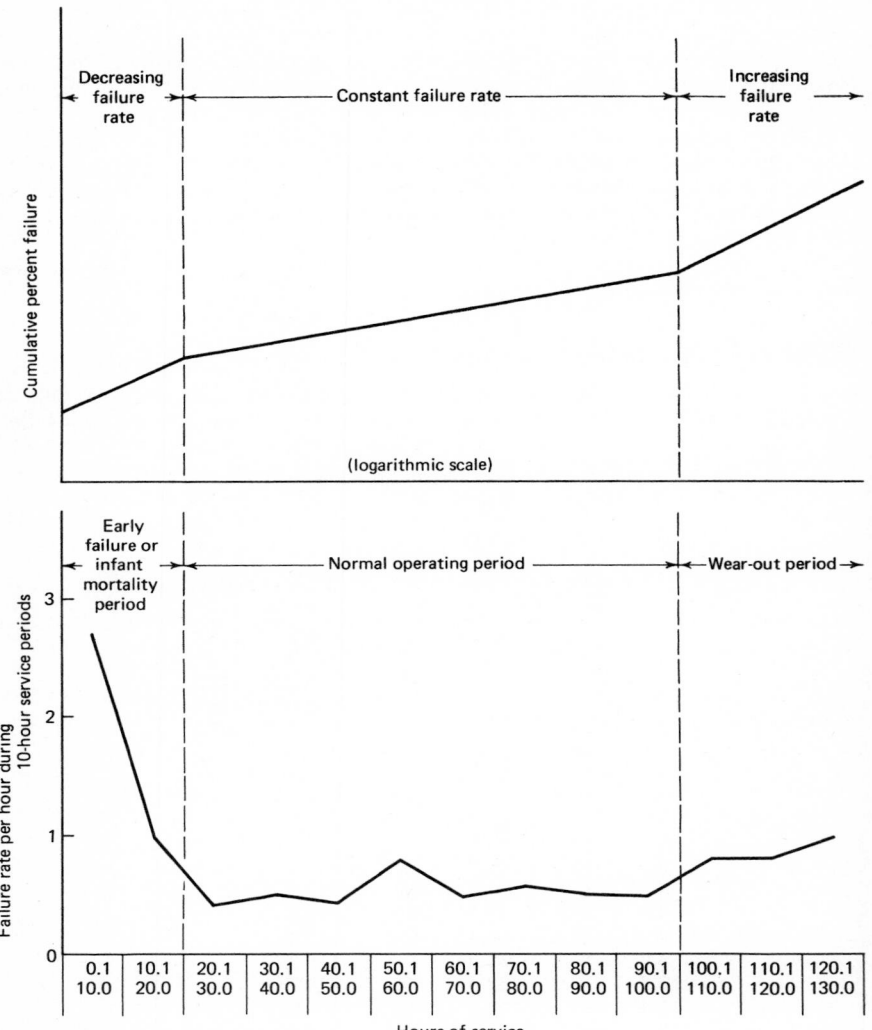

Fig. 22-11   Failure rate vs. time.

each other in frequency of failure and in the failure causation pattern as follows:

1. The infant mortality period.   This is characterized by high failure rates which show up early in usage.   Commonly these failures are the result of blunders in design, manufacture, or usage or of misapplication and other identifiable causes. Sometimes it is possible to "debug" the product by simulated use test or by overstressing (in electronics this is known as burn-in).   The weak units still fail, but the failure takes place in the test rig rather than in service.

2. The constant failure rate period.   Here the failures result from the limitations inherent in the design plus accidents caused by usage or poor maintenance.   The latter can be held down by good control on operating and maintenance procedures. However, a reduction in the basic failure rate requires a basic redesign.

3. The wear-out period. These are failures due to old age; e.g., the metal becomes embrittled or the insulation dries out. A reduction in failure rates requires preventive replacement of these dying components before they result in catastrophic failure.

The top portion of Figure 22-11 shows the corresponding Weibull plot when a $\gamma = 2.6$ was applied to the original data. The values of the shape parameter β were approximately 0.5, 1.0, and 6.0, respectively. A shape parameter of less than 1.0 indicates a decreasing failure rate, a value of 1.0 a constant failure rate, and a value greater than 1.0 an increasing failure rate (see Figure 22-11.)

The Distribution of Time between Failures (TBF)   Users are concerned with the length of time that a product will run without failure. For repairable products, this means that the "time between failures" is a critical characteristic. The corresponding characteristic for nonrepairable products is usually called the "time to failure." The variation in time between failures can be studied statistically (Figure 22-12a).

When the failure rate is constant, the distribution of time between failures is distributed exponentially. Consider the 42 failure times in the constant failure rate portion of Table 22-11. The time between failures for successive failures can be tallied, and the 41 resulting TBF's can then be formed into the frequency distribution shown in Figure 22-12a. The distribution is roughly exponential in shape, indicating that when the failure rate is constant the distribution of time between failures (not *mean* time between failures) is exponential. This is the basis of the exponential formula for reliability.

The Exponential Formula for Reliability   The distribution of time between failures indicates the chance of failure-free operation for the specified time period. The chance of obtaining failure-free operation for a specified time period *or longer* can be shown by changing the TBF distribution to a distribution showing the number of intervals equal to or greater than a specified time length (Figure 22-12b). If the frequencies are expressed as relative frequencies, they become estimates of the probability of survival. When the failure rate is constant, the probability of survival (or reliability) is

$$P_s = R = e^{-t/\mu} = e^{-t\lambda}$$

where $P_s = R =$ probability of failure-free operation for a time period equal to or greater than t

$e = 2.718$

$t =$ a specified period of failure-free operation

$\mu =$ mean time between failures, or MTBF (the mean of the TBF distribution)

$\lambda =$ failure rate (the reciprocal of μ)

Note that this formula is simply the exponential probability distribution rewritten in terms of reliability.

Example   Previous experience shows that the mean time between failures of a radar set is 240 hours. Assuming a constant failure rate, what is the chance of running the set for 24 hours without failure?

$$R = e^{-t/\mu}$$

$$R = e^{-24/240} = 0.90$$

There is a 90% chance of obtaining 24 hours or more of failure-free operation.

The assumption of a constant failure is rightly questioned. However, experience suggests that the assumption is often a fair one to make. (More fundamental than arguing the validity of the assumption is the need to take design actions to yield a constant failure rate. For example, the careful determination of burn-in periods

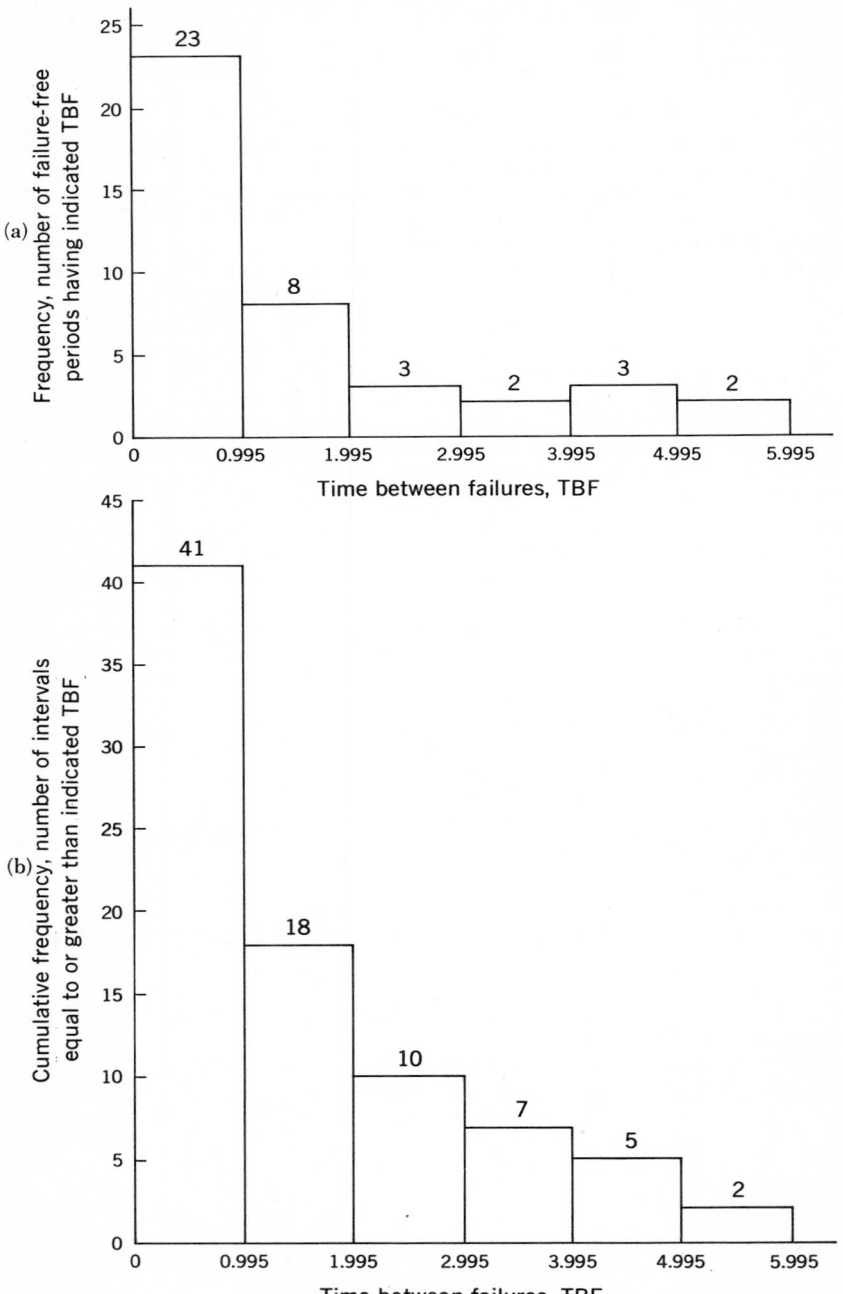

Fig. 22-12   *(a)* Histogram of time between failures.   *(b)* Cumulative histogram of time between failures.

and replacement periods for both parts and systems is good design practice that will help achieve a constant failure rate.)

The Meaning of "Mean Time between Failures"   Confusion surrounds the meaning of mean time between failures (MTBF). Further explanation is warranted.

1. The MTBF is the mean (or average) time between successive failures of a product. This definition assumes that the product in question can be repaired and placed back in operation after each failure. These conditions are not always met. Furthermore, the MTBF is not always the most appropriate index for a product. For example, some other index such as percent uptime[16] is more pertinent when a product operates continuously as compared with the product needed for specific mission times (e.g., petroleum refinery equipment vs. a guidance system for a missile).

2. If the failure rate is constant, the probability that a product will operate without failure for a time equal to or greater than its MTBF is only 37%. (R is equal to 0.37 when t is equal to the MTBF.) This is contrary to the intuitive feeling that there is a 50-50 chance of exceeding an MTBF.

3. MTBF is not the same as "operating life," "service life," or other indices which generally connote overhaul or replacement time. In Figure 22-11, "life" is the *length* of the constant failure rate period while MTBF is the reciprocal of the failure rate (*height* of the bathtub curve.)

4. An increase in an MTBF does not result in a proportional increase in reliability (the probability of survival). If $t = 1$ hour, the following table shows the mean time between failures required in order to obtain various reliabilities:

MTBF	R
5	0.82
10	0.90
20	0.95
100	0.99

A fivefold increase in MTBF from 20 to 100 hours is necessary to increase the reliability by 4 percentage points as compared with a doubling of the MTBF from 5 to 10 hours to get 8 percentage points increase in reliability. This is important because MTBF is often used as the criterion for making important decisions affecting reliability, whereas the probability of survival for a specified time t may be the more important index to the user.

Alternative methods[17] of denoting reliability are sometimes used to avoid the serious consequences of misinterpreting the meaning of MTBF. One alternative is the reciprocal of MTBF, i.e., the failure rate. This eliminates the confusion with "service life" or "operating life." Another recognizes that MTBF is really just a substitute for the reliability percent R and its associated time t. Reliability is then stated as (1) the percent reliability required and (2) the mission time, instead of condensing these two numbers into one number (MTBF).

The Relationship between Part and System Reliability   It is often assumed that system reliability (i.e., probability of survival P_s) is the product of the individual reliabilities of the n parts within the system: $P_s = P_1 P_2 \ldots P_n$. This is known as the product rule. The formula assumes (1) that the failures of any part will cause failure of the system and (2) that the reliabilities of the parts are independent of each other, i.e., that the reliability of one part is not dependent on the reliability of another part. (Evans, Ref. 11, gives a good discussion of this and other assumptions in reliability calculations.) A set of lights in series on a Christmas tree demonstrates the product rule. These assumptions are usually not 100% correct. However, the formula is a

---

[16] Uptime is equivalent to percent operative (as contrasted with downtime).

[17] See also Section 8, Table 8-4.

convenient approximation that should be refined as information becomes available on the interrelationships of parts and their relationship to the system. (The redundancy formula[18] is an example of this.) The following illustrates the product rule:

Example   The following reliability requirements have been set on the subsystems of a communications system:

Subsystem	Reliability (for a 4-hour Period)
Receiver	0.970
Control system	0.989
Power supply	0.995
Antenna	0.996

What is the expected reliability of the overall system if the above requirements are met?

$$P_s = (0.970)\,(0.989)\,(0.995)\,(0.996) = 0.951$$

The chance that the overall system will perform its function without failure for a 4-hour period is 95%.

If it can be assumed that each part follows the exponential distribution, then

$$P_s = e^{-t_1\lambda_1}\,e^{-t_2\lambda_2} \cdots e^{-t_n\lambda_n}$$

Further, if t is the same for each part,

$$P_s = e^{-t\Sigma\lambda}$$

Thus, when the failure rate is constant (and therefore the exponential distribution applies), a "reliability prediction" of a system can be made based on the addition of the part failure rates. This is illustrated in the next section.

Predicting Reliability Based on the Exponential Distribution   Section 8, under Reliability Analysis and Prediction, presents a procedure for reliability prediction based on the exponential distribution. The extensive use of the exponential reliability function warrants further discussion.

The mechanism underlying the exponential is that of random or chance failures which are independent of accumulated life and consequently are individually unpredictable. The justification of this type of "failure law" involves several conditions.

1. Many forces can act upon the product and produce failure. For example, various deterioration mechanisms, part failure rates, and environmental conditions often result in stress-strength combinations that produce failures randomly in time.

2. A constant failure rate often occurs for the total product regardless of the failure pattern of individual parts. This is a result of the mixing of ages of parts by replacement or repair of parts. (This concept is called the "approach to a stable state.")

3. Many parts have multiple failure modes. For example, a resistor may open or a lead may break off; a transistor may go outside tolerance limits or it may abort. For some parts, the failure modes representing random catastrophic failures are likely to occur before wear-out characteristics become evident. For other parts, catastrophic failures are not likely. However, tolerance failures—which are usually associated with wear-out—can be induced both by time and by environmental conditions. The question then is whether a tolerance failure is more likely to result from wear-out or from environmental peaks. The latter case often leads to a constant failure rate.

Because of the simplicity of the exponential function, it has been used extensively

[18] See Section 8, under Reliability Improvement.

in reliability work.   However, the assumption is valid only if supported[19] by the failure data collected.   For noncomplex products when the principal failure mechanism is wear-out, the exponential assumption is not valid.   Blanton and Jacobs (Ref. 12) discuss various reliability prediction techniques including data sources and recommended uses.

Predicting Reliability during Design Based on the Weibull Distribution   Prediction of overall reliability based on the simple addition of component failure rates is valid only if the failure rate is constant.   When this assumption cannot be made, an alternative approach, based on the Weibull distribution, can be used.

1. Graphically or analytically use the Weibull distribution to predict the reliability R for the time period specified.   Do this for each component.

2. Combine the component reliabilities using the product rule and/or redundancy formulas to obtain the prediction of system reliability.

Rich, Smith, and Korte (Ref. 13) give an example of predicting the reliability of a tractor pump for a 500-hour period and a 1,500-hour period (see Table 22-12).   The first analysis was on a proposed design.   Note how the prediction highlights the "vital few" parts such as the oil seal and control valve.   The analysis after some design changes on these parts shows a significant increase in reliability and decrease in failure cost per tractor.   (Table 22-12 lists data for important items only and then summarizes reliability and cost for the complete assembly of 68 parts.)

Reliability as a Function of Applied Stress and Strength   An individual component is satisfactory if its strength is greater than the stress applied to it.   For the same design, strength will vary from component to component.   The applied stress will also vary.   The variation in each of the two parameters is depicted in Figure 22-13.   Consider the *difference* between strength and applied stress in a given instance.   The probability of successful performance ("reliability") is the probability that this

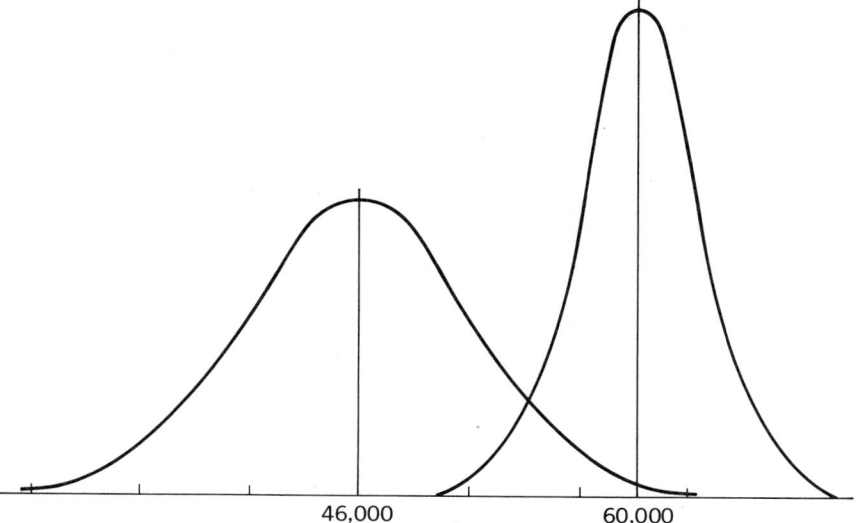

Fig. 22-13   Stress and strength distributions.

46,000   60,000

[19] For testing the assumption with data, see Test 12b (Table 22-13) under the subsequent discussion of Tests of Hypothesis.

TABLE 22-12   Reliability Prediction for a 1.38 Cubic Inch per Revolution Variable Displacement Pump

Part name (only parts with significant percent failure are listed)	First analysis Percent failure at 500 hours	First analysis Percent failure at 1,500 hours	First analysis $/tractor at 500 hours	Analysis after changes Percent failure at 500 hours	Analysis after changes Percent failure at 1,500 hours	Analysis after changes $/tractor at 500 hours
Pump drive coupling special screws	0.6	3.0	0.21	0.2	1.0	0.07
Pump drive coupling	0.07	0.8	0.01	0.07	0.8	0.01
Hydraulic pump shaft	0.02	0.06	0.01	0.02	0.06	0.01
Pump shaft oil seal	3.7	20.0	0.41	1.0	5.0	0.10
Pump shaft bushing	0.75	2.25	0.30	0.25	0.75	0.10
O-ring packings (11) (evaluated separately)	0.63	2.10	0.08	0.63	2.10	0.08
Stroke control valve	13.0	38.0	0.77	0.05	0.15	0.02
Assembly reliability (68 parts):						
At 500 hours		80%			97.3%	
At 1,500 hours		49%			92.0%	
Cost at 500 hours			2.18		$0.77	0.77

difference is greater than 0. Figure 22-14 shows a distribution of the *difference* between strength and stress. Assuming independence of strength and stress:

$$\mu_{\text{difference}} = \mu_{\text{strength}} - \mu_{\text{stress}}$$

$$\sigma_{\text{difference}} = \sqrt{\sigma_{\text{strength}}^2 + \sigma_{\text{stress}}^2}$$

If normality is assumed, the probability of a difference greater than 0 can be estimated by finding the area under the curve.

Example   Suppose the following estimates apply to a part:

	Strength, psi	Applied stress, psi
Average	60,000	46,000
Standard deviation	3,000	5,500

Then   average   difference $= 60,000 - 46,000 = 14,000$

$$\sigma_{\text{difference}} = \sqrt{(3,000)^2 + (5,500)^2} = 6,260$$

$$K = \frac{0 - 14,000}{6,260} = -2.24$$

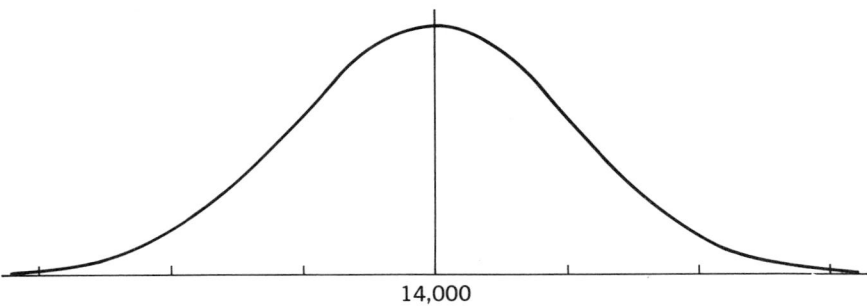

14,000

Fig. 22-14   Distribution of (strength — stress).

From Table B in Appendix II, the area greater than 0 is 0.9875; i.e., the reliability is 98.75%.

This discussion has been simplified in order to stress a basic concept. The key point is that *variation* in addition to average value must be considered in design. Designers have always recognized the existence of variation by using a "safety factor" in design. However, safety factor is often defined as the ratio of average strength to the worst stress expected. (Kececioglu and Cormier, Ref. 14, discuss various definitions.)

Note that in Figure 22-15, all the designs have the *same* safety factor. Also note that the reliability (probability of a part having a strength greater than stress) varies considerably. Thus the uncertainty often associated with this definition of safety factor is in part due to its failure to reflect the *variation* in strength and variation in stress. Such variation is partially reflected in a "safety margin" (see below).

The implications of recognizing variation are far-reaching. For example, consider the following basic formula in strength of materials:

$$s = \frac{Tr}{J}$$

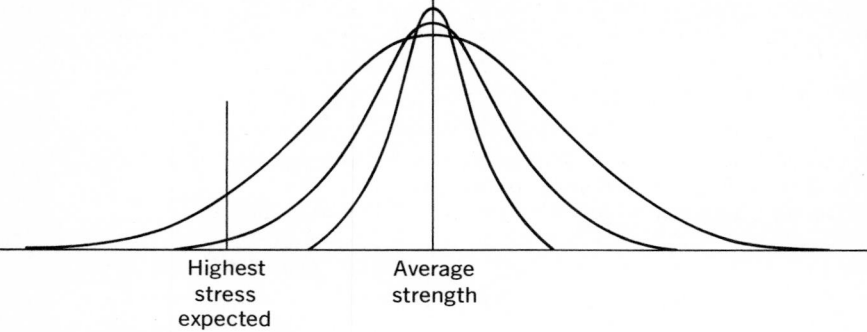

Highest
stress
expected

Average
strength

Fig. 22-15   Variation and safety factor.

The torque T, radius r, and polar moment of inertia J each have variabilities which contribute to the variability in shearing stress s. This variability is generally recognized in total by using a safety factor in design. The uncertainty in a safety factor can be narrowed by estimating standard deviations for T, r, and J and using statistical methods to estimate the variation in shearing stress in a manner similar to that used in calculating the standard deviation of the difference between strength and stress. The approach would also apply to many other design formulas.

Quantifying Conditions of Use and Design Capability—"Safety Margin"   The conditions of use and design capability can be reflected in specifications in the form of a minimum value of the *safety margin* defined as

$$\frac{\text{Worst stress — average capability}}{\text{Standard deviation of capability}}$$

This recognizes the variation in capability but is conservative because it does not recognize a variation in stress.

Quantifying the conditions of use and capability requires data. The data are often difficult to obtain, but the resulting payoff (as will be shown) justifies the effort. For example (Ref. 15), operating temperature is a critical parameter and the maximum expected temperature is 145° F. Further, the capability is indicated by a distribution having a mean of 165° F and a standard deviation of 13° F (see Figure 22-16). With knowledge of only the maximum temperatures, the safety margin is

$$\frac{145 - 165}{13} = -1.54$$

The safety margin says that the average capability is 1.54 standard deviations above the maximum expected temperature of 145°. Table B in Appendix II can be used to calculate a reliability of 0.938 (the area greater than 145°).

The reliability estimate of 0.938 assumes that the device will always be subjected to 145° F. Now suppose that data were available indicating that temperature was normally distributed with a mean of 85° F and a standard deviation of 20° F. The picture of stress and capability is then shown in Figure 22-17. The reliability would then be evaluated in terms of a distribution of the *difference* between capability and stress.

$$\mu_{\text{difference}} = 165 - 85 = 80$$
$$\sigma_{\text{difference}} = \sqrt{(20)^2 + (13)^2} = 24$$

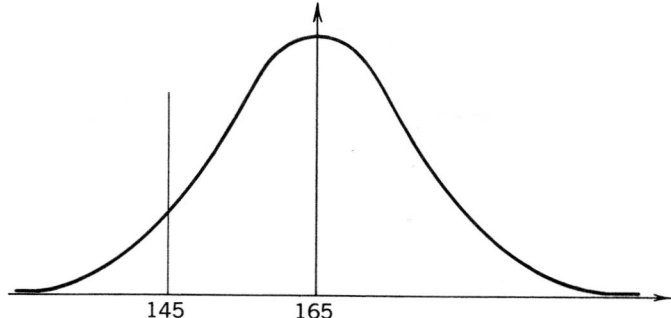

Fig. 22-16 Distribution of strength.

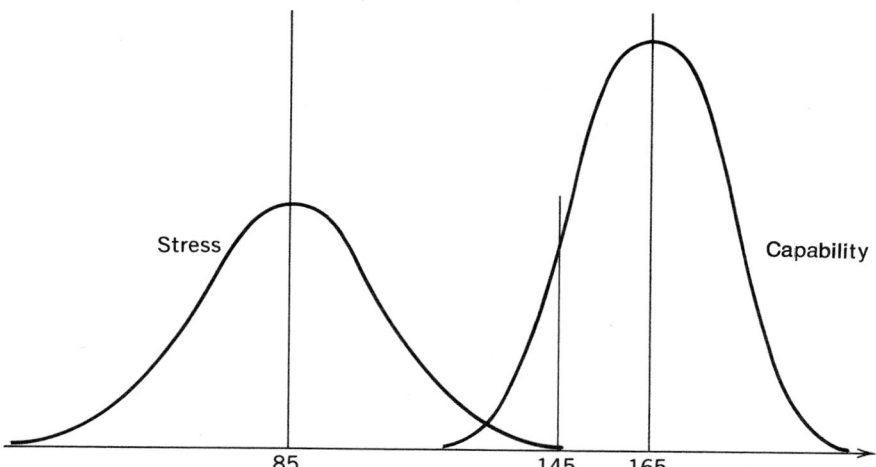

Fig. 22-17 Distributions of stress and strength.

The distribution of the difference is shown in Figure 22-18. The safety margin is

$$\frac{0 - 80}{24} = -3.33$$

Table B in Appendix II would predict a reliability of 0.9996. This compares with with 0.938 estimated without knowledge of the variation in stress.

In many instances, distribution information is not readily available on expected stress, and so the reliability boundary would have to be based on engineering judgment instead of specifying the boundary in terms of a safety margin. However, the specification could require a capability safety margin of (say) 5.0. This would mean that tests would be required to show that the average capability is at least five standard deviations above the reliability boundary.

Lusser (Ref. 16) proposed the use of safety margins in specifications for critical products such as guided missiles (Figure 22-19). He suggested safety margins for

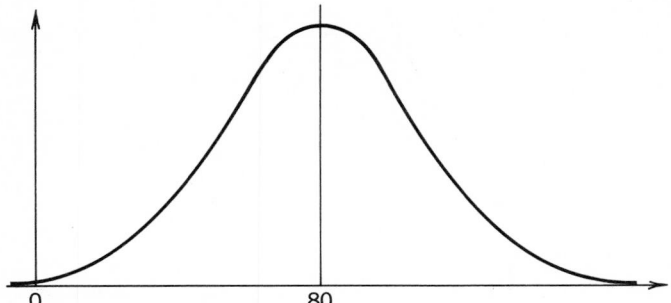

Fig. 22-18 Distribution of difference between strength and stress.

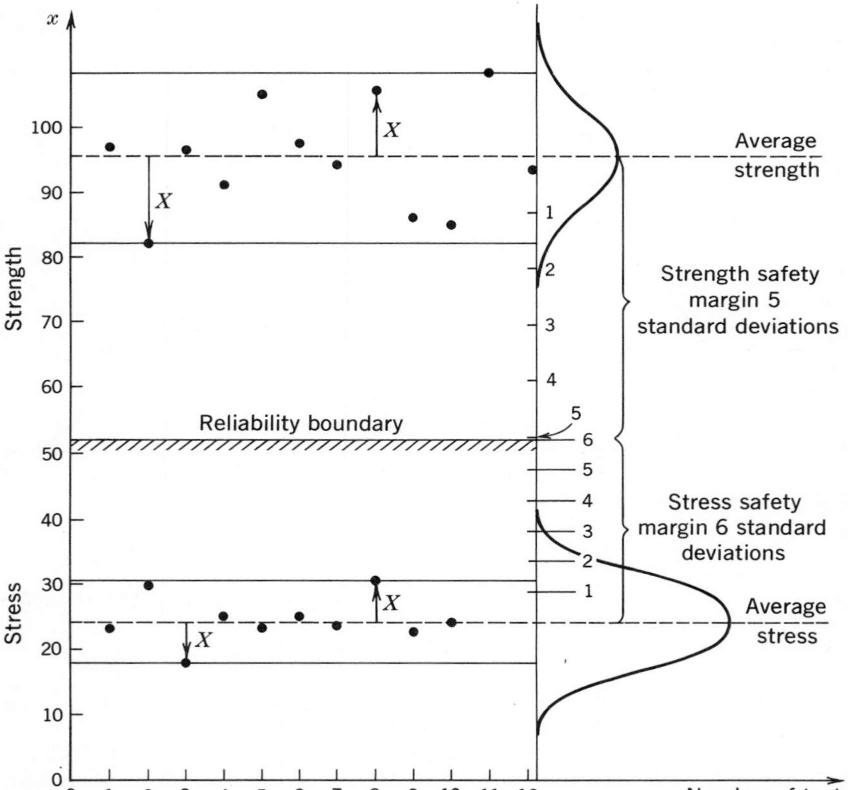

Fig. 22-19 Illustrating how scatterbands of stresses and strengths shall be separated by a reliability boundary.

strength and stress. Specifically, the reliability boundary (maximum stress) was to be defined as six standard deviations (of stress) above the average stress. The average strength would have to be at least five standard deviations (of strength) above the reliability boundary. These minimum values of safety margin were suggested for products requiring extremely high reliability.

TESTS OF HYPOTHESIS[20]

Basic Concepts "Hypothesis" as used here is an assertion made about a population. Usually the assertion concerns the numerical value of some parameter of the population. For example, a hypothesis might state that the mean life of a population of batteries equals 30.0, written as $H:\mu_0 = 30.0$. This assertion may or may not be correct. A "test of hypothesis" is a test of the validity of the assertion, and is carried out by analysis of a sample of data.

There are two reasons why sample results must be carefully evaluated. First, there are many other samples which, by chance alone, could be drawn from the population. Second, the numerical results in the sample actually selected can easily be compatible with several different hypotheses. These points are handled by recognizing the two types of sampling error.

The Two Types of Sampling Error In evaluating a hypothesis, two errors can be made:

1. *Reject* the hypothesis when it is *true*. This is called the "type I error" or the "level of significance" and is denoted by α.

2. *Accept* the hypothesis when it is *false*. This is called the "type II error" and is denoted by β.

These errors are defined in terms of probability numbers and can be controlled to desired values.

The type I error is shown graphically in Figure 22-20 for the hypothesis $H:\mu_0 = 30.0$. The area between the vertical lines represents the "acceptance region" for the test of hypothesis. If the sample result falls within the acceptance region, the hypothesis is accepted. Otherwise, it is rejected. Notice that there is a small por-

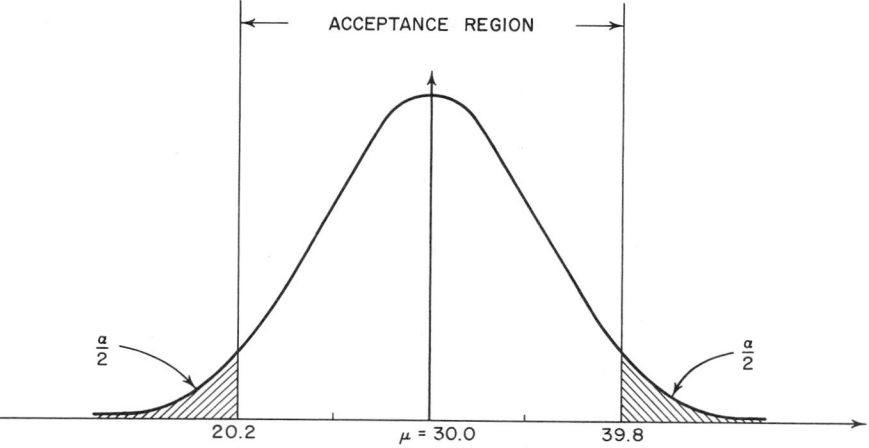

Fig. 22-20 Acceptance region for $H:\ \mu_0 = 30.0$.

[20] Also called "tests of significance."

tion of the curve which falls outside the acceptance region. This portion (α) represents the probability of obtaining a sample result outside the acceptance region, even though the hypothesis is correct.

Suppose it has been decided that the type I error must not exceed 5%. This is the probability of rejecting the hypothesis when, in truth, the true average life is 30.0. The acceptance region can be obtained by locating values of average life which have only a 5% chance of being exceeded when the true average life is 30.0. Further, suppose a sample n of four measurements is taken and $\sigma = 10.0$.

Remember that the curve represents a population of sample *averages* because the decision will be made on the basis of a sample average. Sample averages vary less than individual measurements according to the relationship[21] $\sigma_{\bar{x}} = \sigma/\sqrt{n}$. Further, the distribution of sample averages is approximately normal even if the distribution of the individual measurements (going into the averages) is not normal.[22] The approximation holds best for large values of n but is adequate for n as low as 4.

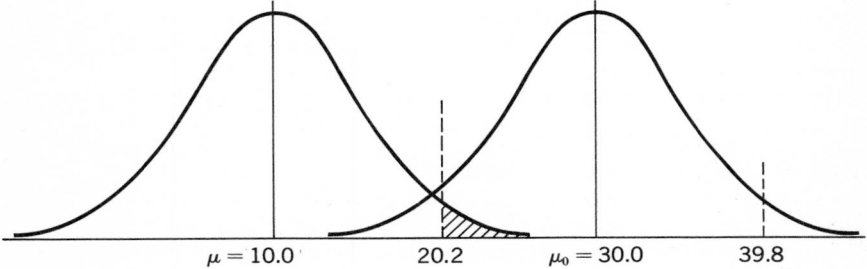

$\mu = 10.0 \qquad 20.2 \qquad \mu_0 = 30.0 \qquad 39.8$

Fig. 22-21   Type II or β error.

Table B in Appendix II shows that a 2.5% area in each tail is at a limit which is 1.96 standard deviations from 30.0. Then under the hypothesis that $\mu_0 = 30.0$, 95% of sample averages will fall within $\pm 1.96\,\sigma_{\bar{x}}$ of 30.0, or

$$\text{Upper limit} = 30.0 + 1.96\,\frac{10}{\sqrt{4}} = 39.8$$

$$\text{Lower limit} = 30.0 - 1.96\,\frac{10}{\sqrt{4}} = 20.2$$

The acceptance region is thereby defined as 20.2 to 39.8. If the average of a random sample of four batteries is within this acceptance region, the hypothesis is accepted. If the average falls outside the acceptance region, the hypothesis is rejected. This decision rule provides a type I error of 0.05.

The type II or β error, the probability of accepting a hypothesis when it is false, is shown in Figure 22-21 as the shaded area. Notice it is possible to obtain a sample result within the acceptance region, even though the population has a true average which is *not* equal to the average stated in the hypothesis. The numerical value of β depends on the true value of the population average (and also on n, σ, and α). This is depicted by an "operating characteristic" (OC) curve.

The problem now is to construct an operating characteristic curve to define the magnitude of the type II (β) error. As β is the probability of *accepting* the original

[21] See Section 23, under Concept of the Control Chart.
[22] See Grant and Leavenworth (Ref. 17, pp. 69–71).

hypothesis ($\mu_0 = 30.0$) when it is *false*, the probability that a sample average will fall between 20.2 and 39.8 must be found when the true average of the population is something other than 30.0. This has been done for many values of the true average, and the result is shown in Figure 22-22.[23] (Juran and Gryna, Ref. 18, pp. 195-199, gives the detailed calculations.) Thus, the OC curve is a plot of the probability of accepting the original hypothesis as a function of the true value of the population parameter (and the given values of n, σ, and α).

The Use of the Operating Characteristic Curve in Selecting an Acceptance Region The acceptance region was determined by dividing the 5% allowable α error into equal parts (see Figure 22-20). This is called a two-tail test. The entire 5% error could

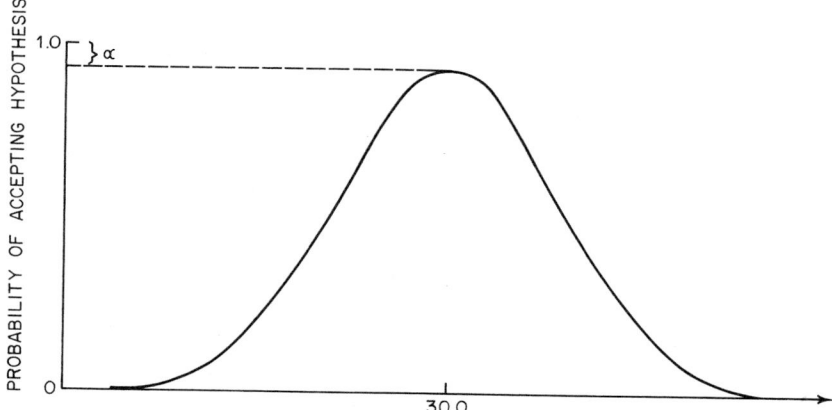

Fig. 22-22 Operating characteristic curve.

also be placed at either the left or the right tail of the distribution curve (Figure 22-23). These are one-tail tests.

Operating characteristic curves for tests having these one-tail acceptance regions can be developed following the approach used for the two-tail region. Although the α error is the same, the β error varies for the three tests.

In some problems, knowledge is available to indicate that if the true average of the population is *not* equal to the hypothesis value, then it is on one side of the hypothesis value. For example, a new material of supposedly higher average strength will have an average equal to or *greater than* that of the present material. Such information will help select a one-tail or two-tail test to make the β error as small as possible. The following guidelines are based on the analysis of OC curves:

Use a one-tail test with the entire α risk on the right tail if (1) it is suspected that (if μ_0 is not true) the true mean is $>\mu_0$ or (2) values of the population mean $<\mu_0$ are acceptable and we are interested only in detecting a population mean $>\mu_0$.

Use a one-tail test with the entire α risk on the left tail if (1) it is suspected that (if μ_0 is not true) the true mean is $<\mu_0$ or (2) values of the population mean $>\mu_0$ are acceptable and we are interested only in detecting a population mean $<\mu_0$.

Use a two-tail test if (1) there is no prior knowledge on the location of the true

---

[23] This curve should not be confused with that of a normal distribution of measurements. In some cases, the shape is similar, but the meanings of an OC curve and a distribution curve are entirely different.

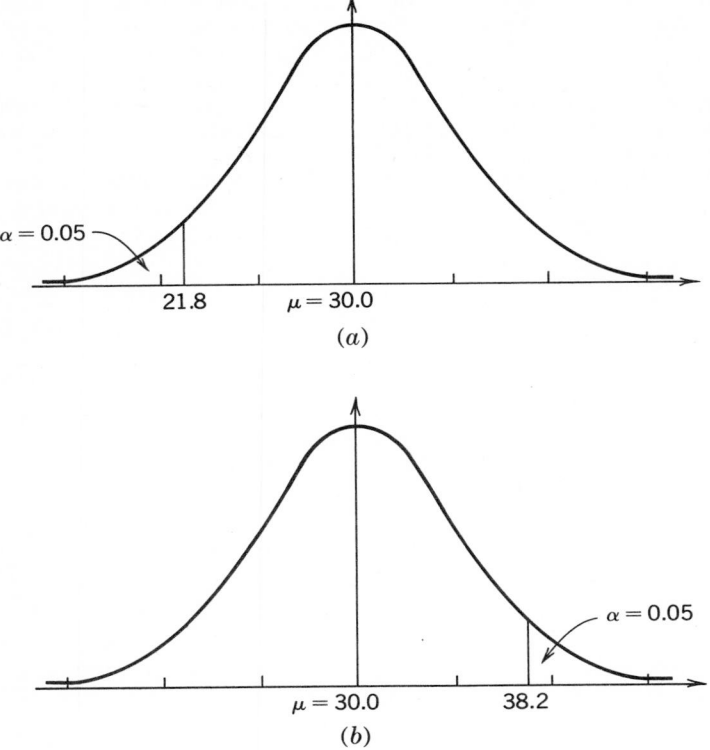

Fig. 22-23   *(a)* Entire 5% error on left tail.   *(b)* Entire 5% error on right tail.

population mean or (2) we are interested in detecting a true population mean $<$ or $>$ the μ_0 stated in the original hypothesis.[24]

Every test of hypothesis has an OC curve. Duncan (Ref. 10) and Natrella (Ref. 19) are good sources of OC curves. (Some references present "power" curves, but power is simply 1 — the probability of acceptance.)

With this background, the discussion now proceeds to the steps for testing a hypothesis.

TESTING A HYPOTHESIS WHEN THE SAMPLE SIZE IS FIXED IN ADVANCE

Ideally, desired values for the type I and type II errors are defined in advance and the required sample size determined (see later discussion on Determining the Sample Size Required for Testing a Hypothesis). If the sample size is fixed in advance

---

[24] With a two-tail test, the hypothesis is sometimes stated as the original hypothesis H_0: $\mu_0 = 30.0$ against the alternative hypothesis $H_1:\mu_0 \neq 30.0$. With a one-tail test, $H_0:\mu_0 = 30.0$ against the alternative $H_1:\mu_1 < 30.0$ if α is placed in the left tail or $H_1:\mu_1 > 30.0$ if α is placed in the right tail.

because of cost or time limitations, then usually the desired type I error is defined and the following procedure is followed:

1. State the hypothesis.
2. Choose the type I error. Common values are 0.01, 0.05, or 0.10.
3. Choose the test statistic for testing the hypothesis.
4. Determine the acceptance region for the test, i.e., the range of values of the test statistic which result in a decision to accept the hypothesis.
5. Obtain the sample of observations, compute the test statistic, and compare the value to the acceptance region to make a decision to accept or reject the hypothesis.
6. Draw an engineering conclusion. Table 22-13 summarizes some common[25] tests of hypotheses. The procedure is illustrated through the following examples. Further examples and elaboration of the procedure are provided in Dixon and Massey (Ref. 1), Johnson and Leone (Ref. 8), Duncan (Ref. 10), and Natrella (Ref. 19). Table 22-13 lists a few unique or additional references for certain tests.

Example   Tests on eight units of an experimental engine showed that they operated, respectively, for 28, 26, 31, 29, 25, 27, 28, and 27 minutes with 1 gallon of a certain kind of fuel. A proposed specification states that the engine must operate for an average of at least 30 minutes. Does the engine meet the requirement? Assume a 5% significance level.

Solution.   Using Test 1b of Table 22-13,

$$H:\mu_0 = 30$$

Test statistic: $$t = \frac{\bar{X} - \mu_0}{s / \sqrt{n}}$$

Acceptance region: Degrees of freedom[26] DF $= 8 - 1 = 7$

$$t \geq -1.895$$

Analysis: $$\bar{X} = 27.6 \qquad s = 1.86$$

$$t = \frac{27.6 - 30.0}{1.86 / \sqrt{8}} = -3.68$$

Conclusion.   Reject the hypothesis. There is sufficient evidence to conclude that the engine does not meet the requirement.

Example   Solve the previous example using the range instead of the standard deviation.

Solution.   Using Test 1c of Table 22-13,

$$H:\mu_0 = 30.0$$

Test statistic: $$\tau_1 = \frac{\bar{X} - \mu_0}{R}$$

(Text continues on p. 22-45)

[25] These are tests commonly mentioned in the literature and used in practice. A number of them assume a normal distribution. Harter and Dubey (Ref. 20) defines tests for the mean and variance but assuming a Weibull distribution (which really covers a family of distributions).

[26] A mathematical derivation of "degrees of freedom" is beyond the scope of this handbook, but the underlying concept can be stated. "Degrees of freedom" is a measure of the assurance involved when a sample standard deviation is used to estimate the true standard deviation of a universe. When the true standard deviation is known, DF $= \infty$. More generally, DF equals the number of measurements used to determine the sample standard deviation minus the number of constants established from the data in order to compute the standard deviation. In this example, it was necessary to establish only one constant (the sample average) in order to compute the standard deviation. Therefore, DF $= 8 - 1$.

TABLE 22-13 Summary Table of Tests of Hypothesis

Test statistic and its distribution	Assumptions	Remarks
Test 1. The mean of a population is equal to μ_0 ($H: \mu = \mu_0$)		
(a) $U = \dfrac{\bar{X} - \mu_0}{\sigma / \sqrt{n}}$ Normal distribution (Appendix II, Table B)	X is distribution-free but should be continuous and have only one mode	Standard deviation of population is known
(b) $t = \dfrac{\bar{X} - \mu_0}{s / \sqrt{n}}$ t distribution with DF $= n - 1$ (Appendix II, Table G)*	X is normally distributed	Standard deviation of population is estimated by sample s
(c) $\tau_1 = \dfrac{\bar{X} - \mu_0}{R}$ T_1 distribution (Appendix II, Table H)	X is normally distributed	Dispersion of the population is estimated from sample range
(d) $r =$ number of occurrences of less frequent sign for a two-tail test (or number of positive or negative signs for a one-tail test) Distribution of r (Appendix II, Table I)	Distribution-free but population should be continuous and symmetrical	Data are analyzed by evaluating signs of $(X_i - \mu_0)$. (This is a "sign" test.)
Test 2. The means of two populations are equal ($H: \mu_1 = \mu_2$)		
(a) $U = \dfrac{\bar{X}_1 - \bar{X}_2}{\sqrt{\sigma_1^2 / n_1 + \sigma_2^2 / n_2}}$ Normal distribution (Appendix II, Table B)	X_1 and X_2 are distribution-free but should be continuous and have only one mode. If the populations are not normally distributed, sample sizes n_1 and n_2 should be large so that sampling distribution of U is approximately normal	Standard deviations of populations are known

*For explanation of DF, see footnote 26.

TABLE 22-13 Summary Table of Tests of Hypothesis (*Continued*)

Test statistic and its distribution	Assumptions	Remarks
(b) $t = \dfrac{\bar{X}_1 - \bar{X}_2}{\sqrt{\dfrac{1}{n_1} + \dfrac{1}{n_2}} \, \sqrt{\dfrac{(n_1 - 1)s_1{}^2 + (n_2 - 1)s_2{}^2}{n_1 + n_2 - 2}}}$ t distribution with DF $= n_1 + n_2 - 2$ (Appendix II, Table G)	$\sigma_1 = \sigma_2$ X_1 and X_2 are normally distributed	Standard deviations of populations are estimated by sample s_1 and s_2
(c) $\tau_d = \dfrac{\bar{X}_1 - \bar{X}_2}{1/2\,(R_1 + R_2)}$ Distribution of τ_d (Appendix II, Table J)	X_1 and X_2 are normally distributed	Dispersions of populations are estimated by sample ranges
(d) $t' = \dfrac{\bar{X}_1 - \bar{X}_2}{\sqrt{s_1{}^2 / n_1 + s_2{}^2 / n_2}}$ t distribution with $\text{DF} = \dfrac{(s_1{}^2 / n_1 + s_2{}^2 / n_2)^2}{\dfrac{(s_1{}^2 / n_1)^2}{n_1 - 1} + \dfrac{(s_2{}^2 / n_2)^2}{n_2 - 1}}$ (Appendix II, Table G)	X_1 and X_2 are normally distributed	Standard deviations of populations are estimated by sample s_1 and s_2 (no assumption that $\sigma_1 = \sigma_2$)
(e) $t = \dfrac{\bar{d}}{s_d / \sqrt{n}}$ t distribution with DF $=$ number of pairs $- 1$, (Appendix II, Table G)	Populations are normally distributed	Data are taken in n pairs and difference d within each pair is calculated
(f) $r =$ number of occurrences of less frequent sign for a two-tail test (or number of positive or negative signs for a one-tail test) Distribution of r (Appendix II, Table I)	n_1 and n_2 each ≥ 6 Populations must be continuous and symmetrical; each of the two observations on a pair has been obtained under similar conditions	Data are analyzed by evaluating signs of $(X_1 - X_2)$. (This is a "sign" test.)

TABLE 22-13   Summary Table of Tests of Hypothesis   *(Continued)*

Test statistic and its distribution	Assumptions	Remarks

Test 3.   Two characteristics on one product have specified population means ($H: \mu_X = \mu_{X_0}$ and $\mu_Y = \mu_{Y_0}$) [Johnson and Leone (Ref. 8)]

$$T^2 = \frac{s_Y^{\,2}}{s_X^{\,2} s_Y^{\,2} - s_{XY}}(X - \mu_{X_0})^2$$

$$- \frac{2 s_{XY}}{s_X^{\,2} s_Y^{\,2} - s_{XY}}(X - \mu_{X_0})(Y - \mu_{Y_0})$$

$$+ \frac{s_X^{\,2}}{s_X^{\,2} s_Y^{\,2} - s_{XY}}(Y - \mu_{Y_0})^2$$

where $s_{XY} = \dfrac{n \sum(XY) - \sum X \sum Y}{n(n-1)}$

critical value for $T^2 = \dfrac{2(n-1)F}{n-2}$

where the F distribution has $DF_1 = 2$; $DF_2 = n = 2$ (Appendix II, Table K)

Assumptions	Remarks
Bivariate normal distribution	Population standard deviations are estimated by s_X and s_Y (T^2 is called Hotelling's T^2)

Test 4.   The standard deviation of a population is equal to σ_0 ($H: \sigma = \sigma_0$)

$$\chi^2 = \frac{(n-1)s^2}{\sigma_0^{\,2}}$$

Chi square distribution with $DF = n - 1$ (Appendix II, Table L)

Assumptions	Remarks
Population is normally distributed	Standard deviation of population is estimated by sample s

TABLE 22-13 Summary Table of Tests of Hypothesis *(Continued)*

Test statistic and its distribution	Assumptions	Remarks

Test 5. The standard deviations of two populations are equal ($H: \sigma_1^2 = \sigma_2^2$)

Test statistic and its distribution	Assumptions	Remarks
(a) $F = \dfrac{s_1^2}{s_2^2}$ F distribution with $DF_1 = n_1 - 1$ $DF_2 = n_2 - 1$ (Appendix II, Table K)	Populations are normally distributed	Standard deviation of populations are estimated by sample s_1 and s_2
(b) $F' = \dfrac{R_1}{R_2}$ Distribution of F', (Appendix II, Table M)	Distribution-free but X_1 and X_2 should be continuous	Dispersions of populations are estimated by sample ranges

Test 6. The proportion of a population exhibiting a certain characteristic is p_0 ($H: p = p_0$)

Test statistic and its distribution	Assumptions	Remarks
(a) $U = \dfrac{X - np_0}{\sqrt{np_0\,(1 - p_0)}}$ Normal distribution (Appendix II, Table B)	$n \geq 100$ Only for large sample sizes	Proportion of population is estimated by sample proportion
(b) Determine confidence limits (Appendix II, Table N) and observe if p_0 falls within the limits		Proportion of population is estimated by sample proportion (useful when $n < 100$)

Test 7. The proportions in two populations are equal ($H: p_1 = p_2$)

Test statistic and its distribution	Assumptions	Remarks
$U = \dfrac{X_1/n_1 - X_2/n_2}{\sqrt{\hat{p}(1 - \hat{p})\,(1/n_1 + 1/n_2)}}$ where $\hat{p} = \dfrac{X_1 + X_2}{n_1 + n_2}$ Normal distribution (Appendix II, Table B)	$np > 5$ for each population. Sample sizes n_1 and n_2 must be large so that sampling distribution of U is approximately normal	Proportions in populations are estimated by sample proportions

TABLE 22-13 Summary Table of Tests of Hypothesis (*Continued*)

Test statistic and its distribution	Assumptions	Remarks

Test 8.   Proportion of correct decisions on a sensory evaluation is p_0 ($H: p = p_0$)

Test statistic and its distribution	Assumptions	Remarks
(a) $U = \dfrac{X/n - 0.50}{\sqrt{0.25/n}}$ Normal distribution (Appendix II, Table B)	$p = 0.5$, n should be > 30	Judge is asked to identify which of two specimens is the same as a control specimen originally given to him. (This is a "duo-trio" test.)
(b) $U = \dfrac{X/n - 0.33}{\sqrt{0.22/n}}$ Normal distribution (Appendix II, Table B)	$p = 0.33$, n should be > 30	Judge is asked to identify which of three specimens is different from the other two. (This is a "triangle" test.)

Test 9.   Samples are from identically distributed populations $[H: F(X_1) = F(X_2)$ where $F(X) =$ distribution function]
[Johnson and Leone (Ref. 8)]

Test statistic and its distribution	Assumptions	Remarks
(a) For evaluation of means $T' =$ sum of ranks in smaller sample Distribution of T' (Appendix II, Table O)	Distribution-free; If $n_1 > 8$ and $n_2 > 8$, the distribution of statistic T' can be closely approximated to normal	Data are evaluated by ranking the combined observations from the two samples (1 for the smallest, 2 for next smallest, etc.) Then calculate the sum of the ranks in the smaller sample. A rejected hypothesis leads to the conclusion that the means are different. (This is a "rank sum" test.)
(b) For evaluation of standard deviations $T' =$ sum of ranks in smaller sample Distribution of T' (Appendix II, Table O)	Distribution-free; If $n_1 > 8$, and $n_2 > 8$, the distribution of statistic T' can be closely approximated to normal	Data are evaluated by ranking the combined observations but ranking assigns 1 to smallest observation, 2 to largest observation, 3 to next smallest, etc. The sum of the ranks for the smaller sample is calculated. A rejected hypothesis means that the standard deviations are different. (This is a "rank sum" test.)

TABLE 22-13 Summary Table of Tests of Hypothesis *(Continued)*

Test statistic and its distribution	Assumptions	Remarks
Test 10. The observations in a sample have been randomly drawn from a single population [Bennett and Franklin (Ref. 21) and Dixon and Massey (Ref. 1)]		
(a) u = number of runs Distribution of runs (Appendix II, Table P)	$n_1 \geq 10,\ n_2 \geq 10$	Data are evaluated in terms of number of sequences or "runs" above and below the median. (This is a "run" test.)
(b) $\displaystyle M = \frac{\sum_{i=1}^{n-1}(X_{i+1}-\overline{X_i})^2}{\sum(X_i-\overline{X})^2}$ $\displaystyle U = \frac{1 - M/2}{\sqrt{(n-2)/[(n-1)(n+1)]}}$ Normal distribution (Appendix II, Table B)	1. $n \geq 4$ 2. Normal population	Data are evaluated in terms of differences between successive observations in a sequence $(X_{i+1}-X_i)$. (This is the "mean square successive difference, M, test.")
Test 11. An observation does belong to the same population as the other observations in a sample (Ref. 1), Grubbs (Ref. 22)]		
Both X_1 and X_n are to be evaluated if extreme observations in either direction are undesirable.	X is normally distributed. Population mean and standard deviation are unknown	Data are evaluated by arranging data in order of magnitude and comparing the distance of one extreme observation from other observations with a measure of variability

n	r
$3 \leq n \leq 7$	$r_{10} = \dfrac{X_2 - X_1}{X_n - X_1}$
$8 \leq n \leq 10$	$r_{11} = \dfrac{X_2 - X_1}{X_{n-1} - X_1}$
$11 \leq n \leq 13$	$r_{21} = \dfrac{X_3 - X_1}{X_{n-1} - X_1}$
$14 \leq n \leq 25$	$r_{22} = \dfrac{X_3 - X_1}{X_{n-2} - X_1}$

Distribution of r (Appendix II, Table Q)

TABLE 22-13 Summary Table of Tests of Hypothesis *(Continued)*

Test statistic and its distribution	Assumptions	Remarks

Test 12.   A sample of data comes from a population with the specified probability function

Test statistic and its distribution	Assumptions	Remarks
(a) D = largest deviation of actual % cumulative frequency from theoretical % cumulative frequency Distribution of D (Miller and Freund, Ref. 23, p. 409)	Distribution should be continuous	Data are evaluated by first plotting on probability paper. The largest deviation of a plotted point from a straight line is then evaluated. This test applies particularly where $n < 30$. (This is the "Kolmogorov-Smirnov test.")
(b) $\chi^2 = \sum \dfrac{(f_a - f_e)^2}{f_e}$ *Distribution* *DF* Normal. . . . . Number of cells minus 3 Exponential. . . . . Number of cells minus 2 Weibull. . . . . Number of cells minus 4 Poisson. . . . . Number of cells minus 2 Binomial. . . . . . . Number of cells minus 2 Test statistics for all distributions follow the chi square distribution (Appendix II, Table L)	$n > 30$ and preferably > 100	Data are evaluated by first constructing a frequency distribution. Theoretical frequencies (based on the distribution assumption) are calculated for each cell. The actual (f_a) and theoretical (f_e) frequencies are then compared. This test can be used for continuous and discrete distributions. If any theoretical frequency is less than 5, the cell involved should be combined with one or more adjacent cells

Acceptance region: $\qquad\qquad\tau_1 \geq -0.388$

Analysis: $\qquad\qquad \tau_1 = \dfrac{27.6 - 30.0}{6} = -0.40$

Conclusion. Reject the hypothesis. There is sufficient evidence to conclude that the engine does not meet the requirement.

Example Solve the previous example using the sign test.

Solution. Using Test 1d of Table 22-13,

$$H:\mu_0 = 30.0$$

Test statistic: Number of positive signs r
Acceptance region: $r = 1$ (one tail test)
Analysis: $X \qquad X - \mu_0$

28	$-$
26	$-$
31	$+$
29	$-$ $r = 1$
25	$-$
27	$-$
28	$-$
27	$-$

Conclusion. Reject the hypothesis. There is sufficient evidence to conclude that the engine does not meet the requirement.

Example Five batches of rubber were made by each of two recipes and tested for tensile strength with the following results:

Recipe 1	Recipe 2
3,067	3,200
2,730	2,777
2,840	2,623
2,913	3,044
2,789	2,834

Test the hypothesis that average strength is the same for the two recipes. Assume a 5% significance level.

Solution. First, Test 5a of Table 22-13 tests the assumption of equal variances. The outcome of this is used to decide whether to use Test 2b or 2d to evaluate the question about average strength

$$H:\sigma_1{}^2 = \sigma_2{}^2$$

Test statistic: $\mathrm{DF}_1 = 5 - 1 = 4 \qquad \mathrm{DF}_2 = 5 - 1 = 4$

$$F = \frac{(s_1)^2}{(s_2)^2}$$

Acceptance region: $\dfrac{1}{9.60} \leq F \leq 9.60$

Analysis: $s_1{}^2 = 16{,}923.7$

$\qquad\qquad\qquad s_2{}^2 = 51{,}713.3$

$$F = \frac{16{,}923.7}{51{,}713.3} = 0.33$$

Conclusion. Accept the hypothesis. This is used to satisfy the assumption of equal variances in the following test of hypothesis. Now, using Test 2b,

$$H : \mu_1 = \mu_2$$

Test statistic: $t = \dfrac{\bar{X}_1 - \bar{X}_2}{\sqrt{\dfrac{1}{n_1} + \dfrac{1}{n_2}} \sqrt{\dfrac{\left[(n_1 - 1)s_1{}^2 + (n_2 - 1)s_2{}^2 \right]}{n_1 + n_2 - 2}}}$

Acceptance region: $DF = 5 + 5 - 2 = 8$

$$-2.306 \leq t \leq +2.306$$

Analysis: $t = \dfrac{2{,}867.8 - 2{,}895.6}{\sqrt{\dfrac{1}{5} + \dfrac{1}{5}} \sqrt{\dfrac{(5 - 1)16{,}923.7 + (5 - 1)51{,}713.3}{5 + 5 - 2}}}$

Conclusion.   Accept the hypothesis. There is insufficient evidence to conclude that the recipes differ in average strength.

Example   Solve the previous example using ranges instead of standard deviations.

Solution.   First, Test 5*b* of Table 22-13 tests the assumption of equal variances.

$$H : \sigma_1{}^2 = \sigma_2{}^2$$

Test statistic: $F' = \dfrac{R_1}{R_2}$

Acceptance region: $0.32 < F' < 3.2$

Analysis: $R_1 = 3{,}067 - 2{,}730 = 337$

$$R_2 = 3{,}200 - 2{,}623 = 577$$

$$F' = \frac{337}{577} = 0.58$$

Conclusion.   Accept the hypothesis. This is used to satisfy the assumption of equal variances in the following test of hypothesis. Now, using Test 2*c*,

$$H : \mu_1 = \mu_2$$

Test statistic: $\tau_d = \dfrac{\bar{X}_1 - \bar{X}_2}{\frac{1}{2}(R_1 + R_2)}$

Acceptance region: $-0.493 \leq T_d \leq +0.493$

$$R_1 = 3{,}067 - 2{,}730 = 337$$

$$R_2 = 3{,}200 - 2{,}623 = 577$$

Analysis: $\tau_d = \dfrac{2{,}867.8 - 2{,}895.6}{\frac{1}{2}(337 + 577)} = -0.061$

Conclusion.   Accept the hypothesis. There is insufficient evidence to conclude that the recipes differ in average strength.

Drawing Conclusions from Tests of Hypotheses   The payoff for these tests of hypotheses comes from reaching useful conclusions. The meaning of "Reject the hypothesis" or "Accept the hypothesis" is shown in Table 22-14 along with some analogies to explain the subtleties of the meanings.

When a hypothesis is rejected, the practical conclusion is "the parameter value specified in the hypothesis is wrong." This conclusion is made with strong conviction — roughly speaking at a confidence level of $(1 - \alpha)$ percent. The key question

TABLE 22-14   The Meaning of a Conclusion from Tests of Hypotheses

	If hypothesis is rejected	If hypothesis is accepted
Adequacy of evidence in the sample of observations	Sufficient to conclude that hypothesis is false	Not sufficient to conclude that hypothesis is false. Hypothesis is a reasonable one but has not been proved to be true
Difference between sample result (e.g., $\bar{X}$) and hypothesis value (e.g., μ_0)	Unlikely that difference was due to chance (sampling) variation	Difference could easily have been due to chance (sampling) variation
Analogy of guilt or innocence in a court of law	Guilt has been established beyond a reasonable doubt	Have not established guilt beyond a reasonable doubt
Analogy of a batting average in baseball	If player got 300 base hits out of 1,000 times at bat, this is sufficient to conclude that his overall batting average is about 0.300	If player got 3 hits in 10 times, this is not sufficient to conclude that his overall average is about 0.300

then is "just what is a good estimate of the value of the parameter for the population"? Help can be provided on this question by calculating the "confidence limits" for the parameter. This is discussed later under Statistical Estimation: Confidence Limits.

When a hypothesis is accepted, the numerical value of the parameter stated in the hypothesis has not been proved, but it has not been disproved. It is not correct to say that the hypothesis has been proved as correct at the $(1 - \alpha)$ percent confidence level. Many other hypotheses could be accepted for the given sample of observations and yet only one hypothesis can be true. Therefore, an acceptance does not mean a high probability of proof that a specific hypothesis is correct. (All other factors equal, the smaller the sample size, the more likely it is that the hypothesis will be accepted. Less evidence certainly does not imply proof.)

With an acceptance of a hypothesis, a key question then is "what conclusion, if any, can be drawn about the parameter value in the hypothesis"? Two approaches are suggested:

1. Construct and review the operating characteristic curve for the test of hypothesis. This defines the probability that other possible values of the population parameter could have been accepted by the test. Knowing these probabilities for values relatively close to the original hypothesis can help draw further conclusions about the acceptance of the original hypothesis. For example, Figure 22-22 shows the OC curve for a hypothesis which specified that the population mean is 30.0. Note that the probability of accepting the hypothesis when the population mean μ is 30.0 is 0.95 (or $1 - \alpha$). But also note that if μ really is 35.0, then the probability of accepting $\mu = 30.0$ is still high (about 0.83). If μ really is 42.0, the probability of accepting $\mu = 30.0$ is only about 0.33.

2. Calculate confidence limits on the sample result (see subsequent topic of Statistical Estimation). These confidence limits define an interval within which the true population parameter lies. If this interval is small, then an acceptance decision on the test of hypothesis means that the true population value is either equal to or close to the value stated in the hypothesis. Then, it is reasonable to act as if the parameter value specified in the hypothesis is in fact correct. If the confidence interval is relatively wide, then this is a stern warning that the value stated in the hypothesis has not been proved and that the true value of the population might be far different from that specified in the hypothesis.

Care must always be taken in drawing engineering conclusions from the statistical conclusions, particularly when a hypothesis is accepted.[27]

DETERMINING THE SAMPLE SIZE REQUIRED FOR TESTING A HYPOTHESIS

The previous sections assumed that the sample size was fixed by nonstatistical reasons and that the type I error only was predefined for the test. The ideal procedure is to predefine the desired type I and type II errors and calculate the sample size required to cover both types of errors.

The sample size required will depend on (1) the sampling risks desired (α and β), (2) the size of the smallest true difference that is to be detected, and (3) the variation in the characteristic being measured. The sample size can be determined by using the "operating characteristic" curve for the test. Table 22-15 summarizes methods useful in determining the sample size required for two-sided tests of certain hypotheses.[28]

TABLE 22-15   Summary of Sample Sizes Graphs and Tables

Hypothesis	Graph or table
1. Mean of a population $= \mu_0$ (σ known)	Appendix Chart R
2. Mean of a population $= \mu_0$ (σ estimated by s)	Duncan (Ref. 10, p. 483)
3. Mean of two populations are equal (σ_1 and σ_2 known)	Natrella (Ref. 19, pp. T-16, T-17)
4. Mean of two populations are equal ($\sigma_1 = \sigma_2$ but estimated by s_1 and s_2)	Natrella (Ref. 19, pp. T-16, T-17)
5. Standard deviation of a population $= \sigma_0$	Duncan (Ref. 10, p. 288)
6. Standard deviations of two populations are equal	Duncan (Ref. 10, p. 515)

Suppose it were important to detect the fact that the average life of the batteries cited previously was 35.0. Specifically, be 80% sure of detecting this change ($\beta = 0.2$). Further, if the true average was 30.0 (as stated in the hypothesis), there should be only a 5% risk of rejecting the hypothesis ($\alpha = 0.05$). In using Appendix II, Chart R, d is defined as

$$d = \frac{\mu - \mu_0}{\sigma} = \frac{35.0 - 30.0}{10} = 0.5$$

Entering with $d = 0.5$ and $P_a = 0.2$ (the beta risk), the curves indicate that a sample size of about 30 is required.

Duncan (Ref. 10) discusses the calculation of the sample size required to meet the type I and II errors. In practice, however, one is often not sure of desired values of these errors. Reviewing the operating characteristic curves for various sample sizes can help to arrive at a decision on the sample size required to reflect the relative importance of both risks.

STATISTICAL ESTIMATION: CONFIDENCE LIMITS

Estimation is the process of analyzing a sample result in order to predict the corresponding value of the population parameter. For example, a sample of 12 insula-

---

[27] Rutherford (Ref. 24) discusses a procedure for drawing conclusions which requires that a choice be made between two policies for drawing conclusions, i.e., conservative and liberal.

[28] Further sources of OC curves are Duncan (Ref. 10) and Natrella (Ref. 19).

tors has an average impact strength of 4.952 foot-pounds. If this is a representative sample from the process, what estimate can be made of the true average impact strength of the entire population of insulators?

1. The "point estimate" is a single value used to estimate the population parameter. For example, 4.952 foot-pounds is the point estimate of the average strength of the population.

2. The "confidence interval" is a range of values which includes (with a preassigned probability called "confidence level") the true value of a population parameter. "Confidence limits" are the upper and lower boundaries of the confidence interval. Confidence level is the probability that an assertion about the value of a population parameter is correct.

Duncan (Ref. 10, p. 456) provides a thorough discussion of confidence limits. The explanation here indicates the concept behind the calculations.

If the population mean is μ, then the probability that the sample mean will lie between

$$\mu \pm 1.96 \frac{\sigma}{\sqrt{n}}$$

is equal to 0.95. Or,

$$P\left(\mu - 1.96 \frac{\sigma}{\sqrt{n}} \le \bar{X} \le \mu + 1.96 \frac{\sigma}{\sqrt{n}}\right) = 0.95$$

This is equivalent to saying that the probability that the sample mean plus 1.96 standard deviations of means lies above μ and the sample mean minus 1.96 standard deviations of means lies below μ equals 0.95. Or,

$$P\left(\mu \le \bar{X} + 1.96 \frac{\sigma}{\sqrt{n}} \quad \text{and} \quad \bar{X} - 1.96 \frac{\sigma}{\sqrt{n}} \le \mu\right) = 0.95$$

Combining:

$$P\left(\bar{X} - 1.96 \frac{\sigma}{\sqrt{n}} \le \mu \le \bar{X} + 1.96 \frac{\sigma}{\sqrt{n}}\right) = 0.95$$

Or the 95% confidence interval on μ is $\bar{X} \pm 1.96 \, (\sigma/\sqrt{n})$. This interval has a 0.95 probability of including the population value. Strictly speaking, 95% of the sets of such intervals would include the population value. In practice, this is interpreted to mean that there is a 95% probability that the confidence limits based on one sample will include the true value.

For the sample of 12 insulators suppose $\sigma = 0.25$. Then, the 95% confidence limits are

$$\bar{X} \pm 1.96 \frac{\sigma}{\sqrt{n}} = 4.952 \pm 1.96 \frac{(0.25)}{\sqrt{12}} = 4.811 \text{ and } 5.093$$

This is interpreted to mean that there is 95% confidence that μ is between 4.811 and 5.093. The 95% is the confidence level[29] and 4.811 and 5.093 are the limits of the confidence interval. A confidence level is associated with an assertion based on actual measurements and measures the probability that the assertion is true. Confidence limits are limits which include the true value with a preassigned degree of confidence (the confidence level).

Table 22-16 summarizes confidence limit formulas for common parameters. The following examples illustrate some of these formulas.

---

[29] Confidence levels of 90, 95, or 99% are usually assumed in practice.

TABLE 22-16   Summary of Confidence Limit Formulas and Graphs

Parameters	Formulas
1. Mean of a normal population (standard deviation known)	$\bar{X} \pm K_{\alpha/2} \dfrac{\sigma}{\sqrt{n}}$ where $\bar{X}$ = sample average K = normal distribution coefficient σ = standard deviation of population n = sample size
2. Mean of a normal population (standard deviation unknown)	$\bar{X} \pm t_{\alpha/2} \dfrac{s}{\sqrt{n}}$ where t = distribution coefficient (with $n - 1$ degrees of freedom) s = estimated σ
3. Standard deviation of a normal population a. Using sample standard deviation	Upper confidence limit = $B_U s$ Lower confidence limit = $B_L s$ where B_U and B_L are numerical factors given in Natrella (Ref. 19, p. T-34)
b. Using sample range	Dixon and Massey, Ref. 1, p. 140
4. Population fraction defective based on attribute data (fraction defective in sample)	See Chart N in Appendix II.
5. Population fraction defective based on variables data ($\bar{X}$ and s in sample)	Kirkpatrick (Ref. 25)
6. Difference between the means of two normal populations (standard deviations σ_1 and σ_2 known)	$(\bar{X}_1 - \bar{X}_2) \pm K_{\alpha/2} \sqrt{\dfrac{\sigma_1{}^2}{n_1} + \dfrac{\sigma_2{}^2}{n_2}}$
7. Difference between the means of two normal populations ($\sigma_1 = \sigma_2$ but unknown)	$(\bar{X}_1 - \bar{X}_2) \pm t_{\alpha/2} \sqrt{\dfrac{1}{n_1} + \dfrac{1}{n_2}}$ $\times \sqrt{\dfrac{\sum (X - \bar{X}_1)^2 + \sum (X - \bar{X}_2)^2}{n_1 + n_2 - 2}}$
8. Mean time between failures (based on an exponential population of time between failures)	Upper confidence limit = $2T/\chi_{\alpha/2}^2$ Lower confidence limit = $2T/\chi_{1-\alpha/2}^2$ where T = total test time on all units and DF = $2r$, where r is a preassigned number of failures
9. Reliability (based on a Weibull population)	Thoman, Bain, and Antle (Ref. 26)
10. Availability (based on an exponential population of time between failures and log normal population of repair time)	Gray and Lewis (Ref. 27)

Example   Sixty-one specimens of brass have a mean hardness of 54.62 and an estimated standard deviation of 5.34.   Determine the 95% confidence limits on the mean.

Solution

$$\text{Confidence limits} = \bar{X} \pm t \frac{s}{\sqrt{n}}$$
$$= 54.62 \pm 2.00 \frac{5.34}{\sqrt{61}}$$
$$= 53.25 \text{ and } 55.99$$

There is 95% confidence that the true mean hardness of the brass is between 53.25 and 55.99.

Example   A radar system has been operated for 1,200 hours, during which time eight failures occurred. What are the 90% confidence limits on the mean time between failures for the system?

Solution

$$\text{Estimated } m = \frac{1,200}{8} = 150 \text{ hours}$$

Upper confidence limit $= 2(1,200)/7.962 = 301.4$
Lower confidence limit $= 2(1,200)/26.296 = 91.3$

There is 90% confidence that the true mean time between failures is between 91.3 and 301.4 hours. (Epstein, Ref. 28, discusses several cases of making estimates from life test data).

Confusion has arisen on the application of the term "confidence level" to a reliability index such as mean time between failures. Using a different example, suppose the numerical portion of a reliability requirement reads as follows:

"The MTBF shall be at least 100 hours at the 90% confidence level." This means:

1. The minimum MTBF must be 100 hours.

2. Actual tests shall be conducted on the product to demonstrate with 90% confidence that the 100 hour MTBF has been met.

3. The test data shall be analyzed by calculating the observed MTBF and the lower one-sided 90% confidence limit on MTBF.

4. The lower one-sided confidence limit must be $\geq$ 100 hours.

The term "confidence level," from a statistical viewpoint, has great implications on a test program. Note that the observed MTBF must be *greater* than 100 if the lower confidence limit is to be $\geq$ 100. Confidence level means that sufficient tests must be conducted to demonstrate, with statistical validity, that a requirement has been met. Confidence level does *not* refer to the qualitative opinion about meeting a requirement. Also, confidence level does *not* lower a requirement; i.e., a 100-hour MTBF at a 90% confidence level does *not* mean that 100 hours is desired but that 0.90×100, or 90 hours, is acceptable. Such serious misunderstandings have occurred. When the term is used, a clear understanding should be verified and not assumed.

Determination of the Sample Size Required to Achieve a Specified Precision in an Estimate
Additional tests will increase the precision of the estimates obtained from a test program. The increase in precision usually does not vary linearly with the number of tests—doubling the number of tests usually does *not* double the precision (even approximately)! Further, if the sample is selected randomly and if the sample size is less than 10% of the population size, then precision depends primarily on the absolute size of the sample rather than the sample size expressed as a percent of the population size. Thus a sample size which is 1% of the population of 100,000 may be more precise than a 10% sample from a population of 1,000 (see Hahn, Ref. 29).

The cost of additional tests must be evaluated against the value of the additional precision. Confidence limits can help to determine the size of test program required to estimate a product characteristic within a specified precision. Suppose it is desired to estimate the true mean life of the battery previously cited. The estimate must be within 2.0 hours of the true mean if the estimate is to be of any value. The variability is known as $\sigma = 10.0$. A 95% confidence level is desired on the confidence statement. The 2.0 hours is the desired confidence interval or

$$2.0 = \frac{(1.96)(10)}{\sqrt{n}} \qquad n = 96$$

TABLE 22-17   Summary of Sample Size Formulas and Graphs

Parameters	Formulas
1. Mean of a normal population (σ known)	$n = \dfrac{K_{\alpha/2}^2 \, \sigma^2}{E^2}$ where K = normal distribution coefficient E = maximum allowable error in estimate (desired precision)
2. Mean of a normal population (σ estimated)	Appendix II, Chart S
3. Standard deviation of a normal population	Appendix II, Chart T
4. Fraction defective of a population	$n = p(1 - p)\left(\dfrac{K_{\alpha/2}}{E}\right)^2$ where p = estimate of the population fraction defective. If no estimate of p is available, assume "worst case" of p $= 0.5$

A sample of 96 batteries will provide a mean which is within 2.0 hours of the true mean (with 95% confidence). Notice the type of information required: (1) desired width of the confidence interval (the precision desired in the estimate), (2) confidence level desired, (3) variability of the characteristic under investigation. The number of tests required cannot be determined until the engineer furnishes these items of information.

Table 22-17 summarizes formulas and graphs useful in determining the sample size required to estimate a population parameter with a specified precision. The following examples illustrate some of the formulas.

Example A sample must be selected to estimate the population mean length of a part. It appears reasonable to assume that length is normally distributed. An estimate of the standard deviation is not available, but process knowledge suggests that "almost all" production falls between 2.009 and 2.027 inches. As a first approximation, the standard deviation is estimated as $(2.027 - 2.009)$ divided by 6, or 0.003 inch. It is desired that the estimate of μ be within 0.001 inch of the true μ and that the estimation statement be made at the 95% confidence level. Referring to Appendix II, Chart S, $E/s = 0.001/0.003 = 0.33$, and the required sample size is about 37. It is instructive to calculate n for other values of E and s (see Table 22-18).

Such a "sensitivity analysis" is helpful in evaluating the cost of extra tests against the value of extra precision.

TABLE 22-18   Effect of E and s on n

Maximum error E	Standard deviations s		
	0.002	0.003	0.004
0.0008	27	56	98
0.001	18	37	64
0.002	7	12	18

Example It is desired to estimate the standard deviation of a population σ within 20% of the true value at the 95% confidence level. Referring to Appendix II, Chart T, the required degrees of freedom is about 46 and, therefore, the sample size is $46 + 1$, or 47.

Relationship of Confidence Limits and Tests of Hypotheses Confidence limits provide a set of limits within which a population parameter lies (with specified probability). Tests of hypotheses evaluate a specific statement about a population parameter.

These procedures are related, and most tests of hypotheses can also be made using confidence limit calculations.

Example A sample of 12 insulators has an average strength of 4.95 foot-pounds. The standard deviation of the population is known to be 0.25. It is desired to test the hypothesis that the population mean is 5.15.

Solution Using Tests of Hypotheses. Table 22-13 defines the test statistic 1a as $U = (\bar{X} - \mu_0)/(\sigma/\sqrt{n})$, and U is normally distributed. If $\alpha = 0.05$, the acceptance region is a U between ± 1.96. Then

$$H : \mu = \mu_0 = 5.15$$

$$U = \frac{4.95 - 5.15}{0.25 / \sqrt{12}} = -2.75$$

As the sample index is outside the acceptance region, the hypothesis is rejected. The procedure using confidence limits is:

1. State the hypothesis concerning the value of a population parameter.
2. Obtain a sample of data and calculate confidence limits for the population parameter.
3. If the hypothesis value falls within the confidence limits, accept the hypothesis. If the hypothesis value falls outside the confidence limits, reject the hypothesis.

Solution Using Confidence Limits

$$H : \mu = \mu_0 = 5.15$$

From Table 22-14, parameter 1, the confidence limits are

$$\bar{X} \pm K_{\alpha/2} \frac{\sigma}{\sqrt{n}}$$

The 95% confidence limits are $4.95 \pm 1.96 \ (0.25/\sqrt{12}) = 4.81$ and 5.09. As the hypothesis value falls outside the confidence limits, the hypothesis is rejected. This is the same conclusion reached by using the hypothesis testing procedure.

Confidence limit concepts and tests of hypotheses are therefore alternative approaches[30] to evaluating a hypothesis. As discussed under Drawing Conclusions from Tests of Hypotheses, confidence limits can often be a valuable supplement to the test of hypothesis procedure.

STATISTICAL TOLERANCE LIMITS

"Statistical tolerance limits" are similar to "process capability," i.e., they show the practical boundaries of process variability,[31] and therefore can be a valuable input in the determination of engineering tolerance limits (which specify the allowable limits for product acceptance). Methods for calculating statistical tolerance limits are of two types—those which assume a normal distribution and those which do not require any distribution assumption. Table 22-19 summarizes these methods.

Table 22-20 shows data for illustrating these methods. Five samples of four each were taken and an outside dimension of a cathode pole recorded.

A confidence level of 95% and a population percentage of 99% have been chosen. Using method 1 and the standard deviation s, the statistical tolerance limits are

$$\bar{X} \pm Ks = 1.00287 \pm 3.615(0.00034) = 1.00164 \text{ and } 1.00410$$

---

[30] For certain hypotheses, these two approaches will result in slightly different type I errors (see Barr, Ref. 30).

[31] See Section 9, under Process Capability.

TABLE 22-19   Methods for Calculating Statistical Tolerance Limits

Method	Distribution assumption	Formula for limits	Source of factor
1. Measure a sample of n items and calculate the average $\bar{X}$ and standard deviations s	Normal	Two-sided limits: $\bar{X} \pm Ks$ One-sided limit: $\bar{X} + Ks$ or $\bar{X} - Ks$	Appendix II, Table V Appendix II, Table V
2. Measure a sample of n items and calculate the average $\bar{X}$ and range R	Normal	Two-sided limits: $\bar{X} \pm K_1 R$	Appendix II, Table U
3. Measure N samples of n items each and calculate the grand average $\bar{\bar{X}}$ and average range $\bar{R}$	Normal	Two-sided limits: $\bar{\bar{X}} \pm K_2 \bar{R}$	Bingham, (Ref. 31, p. 37)
4. Define the population percentage P which must be included between the tolerance limits. Measure a sample of n and observe the largest and smallest values	None	Two-sided limits: The probability is γ that at least $P\%$ of the population will be between the sample extremes One-sided limit: The probability is γ that at least $P\%$ of the population will be less than the sample (or greater than the smallest value)	Appendix II, Table W Natrella (Ref. 19 p. T-76)

TABLE 22-20   Data on Cathode Pole Dimension

	Sample 1	Sample 2	Sample 3	Sample 4	Sample 5	
	1.00263	1.00306	1.00293	1.00291	1.00310	$\bar{X} = 1.00287$
	1.00298	1.00328	1.00343	1.00247	1.00281	$s = 0.00034$ (standard deviation of the
	1.00293	1.00274	1.00239	1.00268	1.00256	20 observations about $\bar{X}$)
	1.00285	1.00303	1.00274	1.00365	1.00231	
$\bar{X}$	1.00285	1.00303	1.00287	1.00293	1.00269	$\bar{R} = 0.00078$
R	0.00035	0.00054	0.00104	0.00118	0.00079	$R = 0.00134$

Using method 2 and the overall range R of the combined data, the limits are

$$\bar{X} \pm K_1 R = 1.00287 \pm 1.005\,(0.00134) = 1.00152 \text{ and } 1.00422$$

Using method 3 and the average of the ranges R, the limits are

$$\bar{X} \pm K_2 R = 1.00287 \pm 1.783\,(0.00078) = 1.00148 \text{ and } 1.00426$$

These methods assume that the characteristic is normally distributed. Method 4 is "distribution-free" and assumes only that the distribution is continuous and the sample is a random one (these assumptions apply to all methods). The statistical tolerance limits by this method are simply the extreme observations in the combined sample, i.e., 1.00231 and 1.00365. Appendix II, Table W indicates that at least 78.4% of the population will be included within these limits. (Note that Appendix II, Table X provides the sample size required to include 99% of the population; i.e., a sample of 473 is needed to be 95% confident that the sample extremes would include 99% of the population.)

When it is feasible to assume a normal distribution, method 1 is preferred because it usually provides the narrowest set of limits while recognizing the variation in the sample. Methods 2 and 3 are good approximations. If normality cannot be assumed, then method 4 is appropriate but at the cost of a larger sample size. In practice, a partial sample can first be obtained to evaluate the assumption of normality. If normality can be assumed, the partial sample is then used to determine statistical tolerance limits. Otherwise, the full sample should be taken and the distribution-free approach (method 4) applied to determine the limits.

All the above methods involve two probabilities, i.e., a confidence level γ and the probability P of falling within limits. This is confusing, but these two probabilities are needed to obtain a mathematically correct statement concerning the limits. An approximation uses the sample average $\bar{X}$ and standard deviation s and regards these as highly reliable estimates of μ and σ. If normality is assumed, then 99% statistical tolerance limits are calculated as

$$\bar{X} \pm 2.56s$$

where the value of 2.56 is obtained from the normal distribution table (Appendix II, Table B).

$$\bar{X} \pm 2.56s = 1.00287 \pm 2.56\,(0.000274)$$
$$= 1.00217 \text{ and } 1.00357$$

These limits are then interpreted to mean that 99% of the population is within 1.00217 and 1.00357. Another approach sets the limits at simply $\bar{X} \pm 3s$. At best, these are only approximate because $\bar{X}$ and s are not exactly equal to μ and σ. Bingham (Ref. 31) discusses the $X \pm 3s$ approximation. (Confidence limit calculations could indicate the size of the possible error.)

Another approach to simplify the probability statement uses the Tchebycheff inequality theorem which holds for any continuous distribution. The theorem states that the probability of obtaining a value which deviates from μ by more than k standard deviations is less than $1/k^2$. For the limits to include 99%.

$$0.01 = \frac{1}{k^2}$$

$$k = 10$$

The 99% limits would be calculated as $\bar{X} \pm 10s$. These limits are distribution-free and the prediction statement is simple; i.e., at least 99% of the population is within

$\bar{X} \pm 10s$. However, the multiple of 10 is highly conservative and results in limits much wider than any of the other methods.

For the methods listed in Table 22-19, no provision is made for the division of the remaining $(1 - P)$ percent between the upper and lower tails of the distribution. Owen and Frawley (Ref. 32) give a procedure and tables for setting limits which do provide for controlling the percentage outside each of the two limits.

Statistical tolerance limits are sometimes confused with other limits used in engineering and statistics. Table 22-21 summarizes the distinction among five types of limits. Hahn (Ref. 33) gives an excellent discussion with examples and tables to illustrate the differences among several types of limits.

TABLE 22-21   Distinction among Limits

Name of limits	Meaning
Tolerance limits	Set by the engineering design function to define the minimum and maximum values allowable for the product to work properly
Statistical tolerance limits	Calculated from process data to define the amount of variation that the process exhibits. These limits will contain a specified proportion of the total population
Prediction limits	Calculated from process data to define the limits which will contain all of k future observations
Confidence limits	Calculated from data to define an interval within which a population parameter lies
Control limits	Calculated from process data to define the limits of chance (random) variation around some central value

TOLERANCE LIMITS FOR INTERACTING DIMENSIONS

Interacting dimensions are those which mate or merge with other dimensions to create a final result. Setting tolerance limits on such dimensions is discussed in the following paragraphs. Setting tolerance limits on noninteracting dimensions makes use of the methods presented under Statistical Tolerance Limits in this Section and in Section 8 (see especially Fig. 8-20 and associated discussion).

Conventional Method Relating Tolerances on Interacting Dimensions   Consider the simple mechanical assembly shown in Figure 22-24. The lengths of components A, B, and C are interacting dimensions because they determine the overall assembly length.

The conventional method of relating interacting dimensions is simple addition:

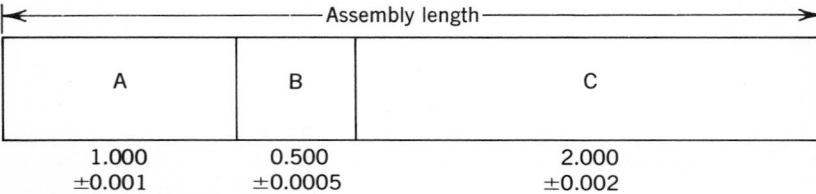

Fig. 22-24   Mechanical assembly.

For the example of Figure 22-24,

Nominal value of the result = nominal value$_A$ + nominal value$_B$ + nominal value$_C$

Tolerance T of the result = $T_A + T_B + T_C$

Nominal value of assembly length = $1.000 + 0.500 + 2.000 = 3.500$

Tolerance of assembly length = $0.001 + 0.0005 + 0.002 = \pm 0.0035$

This method assumes 100% interchangeability of components making up the assembly. If the component tolerances are met, then all assemblies will meet the assembly tolerance determined by the simple arithmetic addition.

The approach of adding component tolerances is mathematically correct but is often too conservative. Suppose that about 1% of the pieces of component A are expected to be below the lower tolerance limit for component A and suppose the same for components B and C. If a component A is selected at random, there is on the average 1 chance in 100 that it will be on the low side, and similarly for components B and C. The key point is this: If assemblies are made at random and if the components are manufactured independently, then the chance that an assembly will have all *three* components simultaneously below the lower tolerance limit is

$$\frac{1}{100} \times \frac{1}{100} \times \frac{1}{100} = \frac{1}{1,000,000}$$

There is only about one chance in a million that all three components will be too small, resulting in a small assembly. Thus, setting component and assembly tolerances based on the simple addition formula is conservative in that it fails to recognize the extremely low probability of an assembly containing all low (or all high) components.

Statistical Method of Relating Tolerances on Interacting Dimensions This method states for the example of Fig. 22-24:

Nominal value of the result = nominal value$_A$ + nominal value$_B$ + nominal value$_C$

Tolerance of the result = $\sqrt{T_A{}^2 + T_B{}^2 + T_C{}^2}$

Then:

Nominal value of the assembly = $1.000 + 0.500 + 2.000 = 3.500$

T of the assembly = $\sqrt{(0.001)^2 + (0.0005)^2 + (0.002)^2}$

= ± 0.0023

Practically all (but not 100%) of the assemblies will fall within 3.500 ± 0.0023. This is narrower than 3.500 ± 0.0035 (the result by the arithmetic method).

In practice, the problem often is to start with a defined end result (e.g., assembly length specification) and set tolerances on the parts. Suppose the assembly tolerance was desired to be ± 0.0035. Listed in Table 22-22 are two possible sets of component tolerances which when used with the quadratic formula will yield an assembly tolerance equal to ± 0.0035. The tolerance set using the conventional formula is also shown.

TABLE 22-22 Comparison of Statistical and Conventional Methods

Component	Statistical		Conventional
	Alternative 1	Alternative 2	
A	± 0.002	± 0.001	± 0.001
B	± 0.002	± 0.001	± 0.0005
C	± 0.002	± 0.003	± 0.002

The advantage of the statistical formula is larger component tolerances. With alternative 1, the tolerance for component A has been doubled, the tolerance for component B has been quadrupled, and the tolerance for component C has been kept the same as the original component based on the simple addition approach. If alternative 2 is chosen, similar significant increases in the component tolerances may be achieved. This formula, then, may result in a larger component tolerance with *no* change in the manufacturing processes and *no* change in the assembly tolerance. Note that the *largest single* tolerance has the greatest effect on the overall result.

The disadvantage of the quadratic formula is that it involves several assumptions which, even if met, will still result in a small percent (theoretically 0.27%) of results not conforming to the limits set by the formula. The assumptions are:

1. The component dimensions are independent and the components are assembled randomly. This assumption is usually met in practice.

2. Each component dimension should be normally distributed. Some departure from this assumption is permissible. See Burr, Ref. 34.

3. The actual average for each component is equal to the nominal value stated in the specification. For the original assembly example, the *actual* averages for components A, B, and C must be 1.000, 0.500, and 2.000, respectively. Otherwise, the nominal value of 3.500 will not be achieved for the assembly, and tolerance limits set about 3.500 will not be realistic. Thus, it is important to control the *average* value for interacting dimensions. This means that process control techniques are needed using variables measurement rather than go no-go measurement. Burr (Ref. 34) presents a method of specifying and controlling the *distribution.*

A summary of the two methods of tolerance is given in Table 22-23.

TABLE 22-23   Comparison of Conventional and Statistical Tolerancing

Factor	Conventional	Statistical
Risk of items not interacting properly	No risk; 100% interchangeability of items	Small percent of final results will fall outside limits (but these can sometimes be corrected with selective assembly)
Utilization of full tolerance range	Method is conservative; tolerances on interacting dimensions are smaller than necessary	Permits larger tolerances on interacting dimensions
Special process control techniques	None	Average of each interacting dimension must be controlled using variables measurement
Statistical assumptions	None	Interacting dimensions must be independent and each must be normally distributed
Lot size for components	Any size	Lot size should be moderately large (to assure balancing effect on extreme interacting dimensions)

The statistical tolerancing formula applies both to assemblies made up of physically separate components and to a chain of several interacting dimensions within one physical item. Further, the result of the interacting dimensions can be an outside dimension (assembly length) or an internal result (clearance between a shaft and hole).

Example Illustrating Format for Analysis   Figure 22-25 shows an example illustrating both conventional and statistical tolerancing.

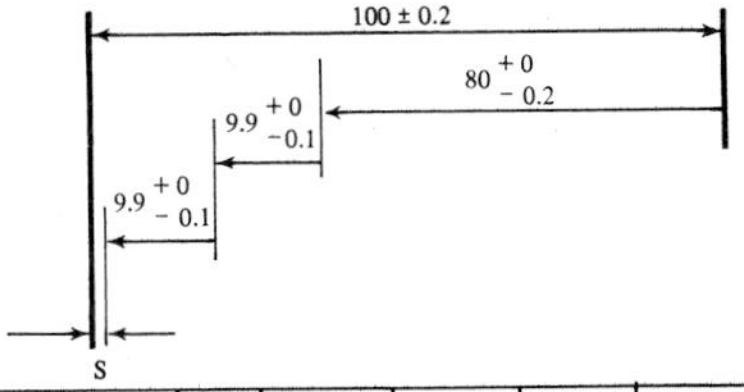

Nominal	Tolerance (without direction)		Tolerance (with direction)		Total Toler-ance	Revised Nominal		100T	present (100T)²	revised (100T)²	Total Toler-ance	Nominal	Tolerance
	Lower	Upper	Lower	Upper									
1	2	3	4	5	6	7	8	9	10	11	12	13	14
+100	−0.2	+0.2	−0.2	+0.2	0.4	+100	$T_s = 0.8$	40	1600	3600	60	100	±0.3
−80	−0.2	0	0	+0.2	0.2	−79.9	modified $T_s = 0.8$	20	400	1600	40	79.8	±0.2
−9.9	−0.1	0	0	+0.1	0.1	−9.85	$(100T_s)^2 = (80)^2$	10	100	400	20	9.85	±0.1
−9.9	−0.1	0	0	+0.1	0.1	−9.85	= 6400	10	100	400	20	9.85	±0.1
+100						+100							
−99.8						−99.6							
+0.2			−0.2	+0.6	0.8	+0.4			2200	6000			
										6400			

Fig. 22-25 Format for conventional and statistical tolerancing. (*Adapted from "Tolerances and Fittings, Calculations of Tolerances for Linear Measuring Chains, Description of Worksheet for Tolerance Establishment." AEG–Telefunken Co., Germany.*)

The top of the form shows a schematic of the specifications on a component which contained three rollers in a housing. The solid line at the left is a reference point for the first measurement. The base of the arrows shows the reference point for subsequent measurements. There are four component dimensions which interact to yield the resulting dimension S.

The first seven columns in Figure 22-25 use conventional tolerancing but convert all the tolerances to bilateral (plus and minus) rather than unilateral as some of them are. The first three columns enter the nominal and tolerance limits directly from the schematic. Columns 4 and 5 are identical to 2 and 3 for dimensions in the positive direction; otherwise columns 4 and 5 just reverse the signs of columns 2 and 3. Column 6 is the total tolerance range. Column 7 is, in effect, a revised nominal value with the two-sided tolerance shown in column 6. Note that the total tolerance in column 6 is 0.8.

Column 8 enters this 0.8. No rounding off was deemed necessary, and finally the value was multiplied by 100 and squared for convenience in using the statistical approach. Therefore 6,400 is the maximum allowable sum of squared tolerances.

Columns 9 and 10 list the present bilateral tolerances and their squares. As column 10 is much less than 6,400, the tolerances on the interacting dimensions may be increased. This is done in column 11 (there would be many sets of new tolerances). As the sum in column 11 is within 6,400, this is acceptable, and the square roots can be taken to yield the new tolerances (in terms of total tolerance range). These tolerances are shown in column 12. The nominal and bilateral tolerances are listed in columns 13 and 14. (The effect of statistical tolerancing can be seen by comparing columns 6 and 12.)

Further Applications of Statistical Tolerancing. It is easy to be deceived into concluding that the statistical method of tolerancing is merely a change from an expression of tolerances in the form of limits on each component to a form of:

1. Upper and lower limits on the average $\bar{X}$ of the mass of components.

2. An upper limit to the scatter σ of the components.

The change is much more profound than mere form of the specification. It affects the entire cycle of manufacturing planning, production, inspection, quality control, service, etc. It is, in effect, *a new philosophy of manufacture.*

The first published example of a *large-scale application* of statistical tolerancing appears to be that of the L-3 coaxial system (a broad-band transmission system for multiple telephone or television channels). Dodge, Kinsburg, and Kruger (Ref. 35) discuss the application.

The general plan was:

1. Discovery of the key quality characteristics of each component element of the system.

2. Determination of the precision of measurement, to separate measurement variability from process and product variability.

3. Collection of data on process capability for the key qualities, to aid in establishing realistic tolerances.

The foregoing were preliminary to:

4. Establishment of tolerances for the key quality characteristics in the dual form of a maximum on the standard deviation σ and limits on the average $\bar{X}$. The limits on X were established as $\pm \frac{1}{3}\sigma$ around the nominal.

5. Establishment of control procedures.

It was recognized that the limits on σ and $\bar{X}$ required further interpretation if the intent of the designers was to be carried out by the manufacturers. To this end, three forms of product acceptance were established:

1. Control charts. Shewhart control charts for $\bar{X}$ and σ could be used for product acceptance, provided "eligibility" was established (seven consecutive subgroups,

of five pieces each, all met the control limits for X and σ) and provided subsequent statistical control was maintained (based on chart results plus absence of major changes in process).

2. Batch control. This was based on examination of a sample of (normally) 50 pieces by variables measurements, with limits on $\overline{X}$ and σ appropriate to the sample size of 50. Each batch stood or fell on its own measurements.

3. Detailed classification. Product which did not qualify under 1 or 2 was measured in detail. The resulting conforming units were classified into one of three variable classes. The packaging was then done by selecting classified units in such a way that each package contained an assortment of product which conformed to the intent of the design as to $\overline{X}$ and σ.

Grant and Leavenworth (Ref. 17, chap. 10) discusses statistical tolerancing including an application to shafts and holes. The Western Electric Handbook (Ref. 36, pp. 122–127) presents examples and discusses the assumptions. Gelling and Schaafsma (Ref. 37) provides further development of the concept, including a special method of specifying the average value. Peters (Ref. 38) discusses statistical tolerancing, including a method for recognizing cost differences among components. Choksi (Ref. 39) discusses the use of computer simulation to determine optimum tolerances.

The concept may be applied to several interacting variables in an engineering relationship. The nature of the relationship need *not* be additive (assembly example) or subtractive (shaft and hole example). The formula can be adapted to predict the variation of results that are the product and/or the division of several variables. Mouradian (Ref. 40) discusses these applications.

A textbook is available giving numerous problems, worksheets, and solutions for a variety of situations involving interacting dimensions. See Wade (Ref. 43).

BAYES' THEOREM AND STATISTICAL DECISION THEORY

The techniques presented under Tests of Hypothesis consist of analyzing a sample of observations and reaching a conclusion (with defined sampling risks) to accept or reject the hypothesis. The experimenter considers the consequences of the type I and type II errors and, to a lesser degree, the likelihood that extreme values of the population parameter will occur. However, this is usually done on a qualitative basis and involves judgment. In practice, a sample size is limited by economics and the experimenter defines the type I error (usually 0.05 or 0.01) in numerical terms and then must accept the type II error that results with the sample size fixed by economics. There is a methodical way of defining the consequences of the type I and type II errors and the likelihood of extreme values. The approach involves "Bayes' theorem" and "statistical decision theory."

Bayes' Theorem This theorem uses past ("prior") information to supplement actual test data. The approach is based on a theorem originally proposed by Rev. Thomas Bayes in 1763. The theorem is:

If $\mu_1, \mu_2, \ldots, \mu_n$ are mutually exclusive events (i.e., they cannot happen simultaneously) of which one must occur, and if these events can be associated with another event A, then

$$P\left(\frac{\mu_i}{A}\right) = \frac{P(\mu_i)P(A \mid \mu_i)}{\sum\limits_{\text{all } i} [\,P(\mu_i)P(A \mid \mu_i)\,]}$$

For example, suppose it is desired to evaluate the mean life of an engine. The requirement is 5,000 hours. Experience in the development department on similar engines is summarized as follows:

"We are fairly certain (80%) that the new engine will have a mean life of 5,000 hours.

"There is small chance (15%) that the new engine will have a mean life of only 2,500 hours.

"There is a smaller chance (5%) that the new engine will be poor and achieve a mean life of only 1,000 hours."

The three values of mean life are the events μ_1, μ_2, and μ_3. The percentages are the values of $P(\mu_i)$, that is, the probability that the mean life of the population will be μ_i.

The following test program has been proposed: run 11 engines each for 1,000 hours; if four or fewer failures occur, conclude that the design meets the 5,000-hour requirement. Here, the event A is the passing of the above program (i.e., running 11 engines and having four or fewer failures). Assuming an exponential distribution, calculations[32] can be made to find the probability of passing the test given that the true mean is μ_i.

These probabilities are $P(A/\mu_i)$ in Bayes' theorem. Summarizing:

μ_i	$P(\mu_i)$	$P(A/\mu_i)$
5,000	0.80	0.95
2,500	0.15	0.71
1,000	0.05	0.10

Suppose the test program is conducted and passed. The probability[33] that the 5,000-hour mean life requirement has been met is

$$P(\mu = 5,000 \,/\, \text{test passed}) = \frac{0.8\,(0.95)}{0.8\,(0.95) + 0.15\,(0.71) + 0.05\,(0.1)} = 0.87$$

Thus, the test program would give reasonably high assurance (87%) that the design meets the requirement (if the test is passed). Simultaneously, if the design is extremely poor ($\mu = 1,000$), there is only a small chance (10%) that it will pass the test. (A 71% chance of passing a design with a mean of only 2,500 hours may not be tolerable.)

The controversial question is the determination of the values of $P(\mu_i)$; for example, what is the basis of saying that there is an 80% chance that the engine will achieve the 5,000-hour mean life? It may often be possible to synthesize such probabilities from past experience on similar products or parts of products. This experience may be test data or proved scientific principles. For example, suppose it is desired to predict the probability that an object will drop a specified height. Six such objects are released and do drop the height. Calculations (based on the binomial distribution, not on Bayes' theorem) predict, with 90% confidence, that the probability of success on a seventh trial is at least 0.68. However, a scientific principle (i.e., the law of gravity) states with certainty (1.0) that the object will drop, and therefore the statistical prediction (0.68) is conservative.

It is often impractical to perform statistically sufficient tests using only current products, and engineering managers have used and will continue to use past experience in drawing conclusions on current products. They often do this in an informal

---

[32] See this Section, under Making Predictions Using the Exponential Probability Distribution.

[33] This probability of 0.87 is called the posterior probability as compared with the prior probabilities $P(\mu_i)$.

and qualitative manner. Bayes' theorem, when applicable, provides an opportunity to evaluate this extremely valuable past experience in a more methodical manner.

There is controversy on the Bayes' vs. the conventional approach to analysis of data. The viewpoints as applied to evaluating a new design are summarized in Table 22-24.

Statistical Decision Theory This concept requires two items of information not formally used in classical analysis:

1. The economic consequences of making type I or type II errors.
2. The probabilities that different values of the population parameter will occur. (The classical approach has no assumption concerning different values of the population parameter, and therefore really assumes equal probability for all values of the parameter.)

TABLE 22-24 Bayes' vs. Conventional Statistical Approach in Evaluating a New Design

Factor	Bayes'	Conventional
Role of past experience	Past experience is valuable in helping to predict performance of a new design	Not applicable because the new design is different. Evaluation of new design must be based solely on test results of new design
Purpose of development test program on new design	Confirm or deny expected performance of new design as predicted from past experience	Supply the data for evaluating the new design
Validity of conclusions about the new design	Depends on ability to quantitatively relate past experience to new design	More conservative than Bayes' because evaluation is based solely on test results of new design
Number of tests required on new design	Bayes' approach requires less than conventional approach because it makes use of applicable past data	

This discussion shows how each of these items of information can change the decision rule as compared with the classical approach to testing hypotheses. Consider the problem of defining an acceptance sampling plan which will have a high probability of accepting lots 1% defective and a low probability of accepting lots which are 10% defective. Suppose a proposed sampling plan consists of taking a random sample of 40 observations from a lot and accepting the lot if one or fewer defectives are found in a sample of 40. (Perhaps this plan was found from a set of sampling tables or perhaps it was decided on the basis of convenience.) The effectiveness of this proposed plan can be evaluated by determining the type I and the type II errors. The type I error is the probability of rejecting a 1% defective lot. This is the probability of obtaining a sample of 40 which contains one or fewer defectives from a lot which is 1% defective. From Appendix II, Table E, with $np = 40 \times 0.01 = 0.4$, the probability of one or fewer defectives is 0.938. This means that the probability of rejecting a 1% lot is $1 - 0.938$, or 0.062. The type II error is the probability of accepting a lot which is 10% defective. This is the probability of obtaining a sample of 40 with one or fewer defectives from a lot which is 10% defective. Again, from Appendix II, Table E, with $np = 40 \times 0.10 = 4.0$, the probability of acceptance is 0.092.

If the risks of 0.062 of rejecting good quality and 0.092 of accepting bad quality are deemed reasonable, then the proposed sampling plan would be instituted. All this illustrates the classical statistical approach to testing the hypothesis that the percent defective in the lot is equal to 1%. Now consider the decision theory approach—in two steps. First, suppose that economic information is available on the consequences of each type of error (see Table 22-25).

TABLE 22-25   Loss Table

	$p = 0.01$	$p = 0.10$
Accept lot	0	$200
Reject lot.	$20	0

A $20 expense is incurred if a good lot is rejected and a $200 expense is incurred if a bad lot is accepted. An evaluation of decision rules can be made by calculating the expected loss if a decision rule is used over and over again. The expected value is the average value in the long run and is obtained as the summation of the products of a particular value and the probability of occurrence. The expected loss for the decision rule proposed above is calculated as follows:

Expected loss $= 0(0.938) + 20(0.062) + 200(0.092) + 0(0.908) = 19.64$

This is the expected loss based on a decision rule which permits one or fewer defectives in a sample. However, perhaps the decision rule should permit zero defectives in the sample or two defectives in the sample. As the decision rule changes, the probabilities of acceptance for either 1% defective lot or 10% defective lot will change, but these can easily be calculated using Appendix II, Table E. The expected loss for each of some other decision rules is shown in Table 22-26.

The decision rule with the lowest expected loss is the decision rule for the acceptance number of zero. Thus, when the economic consequences are taken into account, the correct decision rule requires zero defectives in the sample. This is more stringent than the original sampling procedure (which allowed one defective), but it makes intuitive sense when it is realized that the serious error in the procedure is to accept a bad lot (an economic consequence of $200 vs. only a $20 loss if a good lot is rejected). In this case the economic consequences say that the type I error is

TABLE 22-26   Expected Loss Considering Economic Consequences

n	c	Expected loss
40	0	$ 10.20
40	1	19.64
40	2	47.76
40	3	86.62
40	4	125.80

small compared with the type II error, and the statistical decision theory approach generates an appropriate rule.[34]

Now suppose information was also available on the relative likelihood that a lot submitted would be 1% defective or 10% defective. Specifically, suppose on the basis of lots previously submitted by the supplier, it is estimated that the "prior" probability of a 1% defective lot is 0.8 and the "prior" probability of a 10% defective lot is 0.2.[35] This information can be incorporated into the expected loss. For the original decision rule of one or fewer defectives in the sample, the expected loss is now

Expected loss $= 0.8[0(0.938) + 20(0.062)] + 0.2[200(0.092) + 0(0.908)] = 4.67$

The results for the other decision rules are shown in Table 22-27. Table 22-27 indicates that the optimum decision rule in this case allows one or fewer defectives in the sample.

[34] It is instructive to calculate the type I and type II errors for this new decision rule of zero defectives in the sample. The type I error is about 0.33 and the type II error is about 0.018. A type I error of 0.33 for an acceptance sampling plan would often be considered high. However, such a conclusion is based on a conventional way of selecting sampling plans which does not take into account the economic consequences of a wrong decision.

[35] If test information from the present lot was available, Bayes' theorem could convert these prior probabilities to posterior probabilities which could then be used in the subsequent analysis.

Now suppose the prior probabilities had been 0.99 and 0.01 for the 1% defective and 10% defective lots, respectively. The expected loss for each of the decision rules is shown in Table 22-27. With this new set of prior probabilities, the optimum

TABLE 22-27   Expected Loss Considering Economic Consequences and Probability of Occurrences

		Expected loss	
n	c	$P_1 = 0.8; P_{10} = 0.2$	$P_1 = 0.99; P_{10} = 0.01$
40	0	$ 7.00	6.57
40	1	4.67	1.41
40	2	9.65	0.63
40	3	17.34	0.89
40	4	25.16	1.26

decision rule allows two or fewer defectives in a sample. In this case, even though the economic consequences of accepting a 10% lot are large ($200), the low likelihood of such a lot being submitted (a probability of only 0.01) results in a final conclusion to use a sampling plan which allows two or fewer defectives.[36]

Statistical tables and sampling plans based on Bayes' theorem or statistical decision concepts are not common, but the concepts can have a significant effect, and therefore development work seems imminent and worthwhile. Oliver and Springer (Ref. 41) give an example of Bayesian acceptance sampling tables. Hadley (Ref. 42) provides background material including examples on tests of hypotheses, confidence limits, and acceptance sampling plans.

TRANSFORMATIONS OF DATA

Most of the statistical methodology presented in this section assumes that the quality characteristic follows a defined probability distribution. The analysis and conclusions that result are, of course, valid only to the extent that the distribution assumption is correct. Under Tests of Hypothesis a "goodness of fit" test was presented for quantitatively evaluating a set of data to judge the validity of a distribution assumption. Moderate deviations of a sample of observations from a theoretical population assumption are to be expected because of sampling variations. The goodness of fit test determines whether the deviation of the sample from a theoretical assumption is likely to have been due to sampling variation. If it turns out as unlikely, then it is concluded that the assumption is wrong.

Sometimes, a set of data does not fit one of the standard distributions such as the normal distribution. One approach uses "distribution-free" statistical methods for further analysis. Some of these were listed under Tests of Hypothesis, and Natrella (Ref. 19) presents further material. However, these methods often require larger sample sizes than conventional methods for equivalent statistical risks. Some other approaches to analysis are:

1. Examine the data to see if there is a nonstatistical explanation for the unusual distribution pattern. For example, the output of *each* of several supposedly identical machines may be normally distributed. If the machines have different means or standard deviations, then the combined output probably has an unusual distribution pattern. In this case, separate analyses could be made for each machine.

2. Analyze the data in terms of averages instead of individual values. As stated

---

[36] For a sampling plan with a sample size of 40 and two or less defectives allowed, the type I error is about 0.008 and the type II error is about 0.238.

under the Two Types of Sampling Error, sample averages closely follow a normal probability distribution even if the population of individual values from which the sample averages came is not normally distributed. If it is sufficient to draw a final conclusion on a characteristic in terms of the average value, then the normal distribution assumption can be applied. However, the conclusions apply only to the average value and not to the individual values in the population. (Predicting the percent of a population falling within engineering tolerance limits illustrates the situation where analysis in terms of the average would not be sufficient because engineering tolerance limits refer to individual values rather than averages.)

3. Use the Weibull probability distribution. The Weibull distribution is really a group of many continuous distributions with each distribution uniquely defined by numerical values of the parameters of the Weibull probability function (e.g., a beta value of 1.0 indicates an exponential distribution). If a set of data yields an approximate straight-line plot on Weibull paper, the straight line then directly provides estimates of the probabilities for the population. Whether the exact form of the probability distribution is normal, or exponential, or another distribution becomes somewhat secondary because the straight-line plot provides the needed probability estimates.

4. Make a transformation of the original characteristic to a new characteristic that is normally distributed. Figure 22-26 summarizes several of these mathematical transformations. These transformations are useful for (a) achieving normality of measured results, (b) satisfying the assumption of equal sample variances required in certain tests, and (c) satisfying the assumption of additivity of effects required in certain tests. Natrella (Ref. 19) discusses transformations for all these uses.

PLANNING AND ANALYZING DATA FOR SOLVING SPECIFIC PROBLEMS

The previous material in this Section presented many statistical techniques. In practice, these techniques must be used in an effective manner that yields a return for the cost of using them. To achieve this return, it is not sufficient to plug numbers into formulas. The full process is careful planning of data collection, analysis of the data to draw statistical conclusions, and making the transition to answer the original technical problem. A checklist of steps to achieve this is:

1. Collect sufficient background information to translate the engineering problem statement into a specific statement that can be evaluated by statistical methods.

2. Plan the collection of data.

   a. Determine the type of data needed. Variables data (readings on a scale of measurement) may be more expensive than attributes data (go or no-go data), but the information is much more useful.

   b. Determine if any past data are available that are applicable to the present problem.

   c. If the problem requires an evaluation of several alternative decisions, obtain information on the economic consequences of a wrong decision.

   d. If the problem requires the estimation of a parameter, define the precision needed for the estimate.

   e. Determine if the error of measurement is large enough to influence the sample size or the method of data analysis.

   f. Define the assumptions needed to calculate the required sample size.

   g. Calculate the required sample size considering the desired precision of the result, statistical risk, variability of the data, measurement error, and other factors.

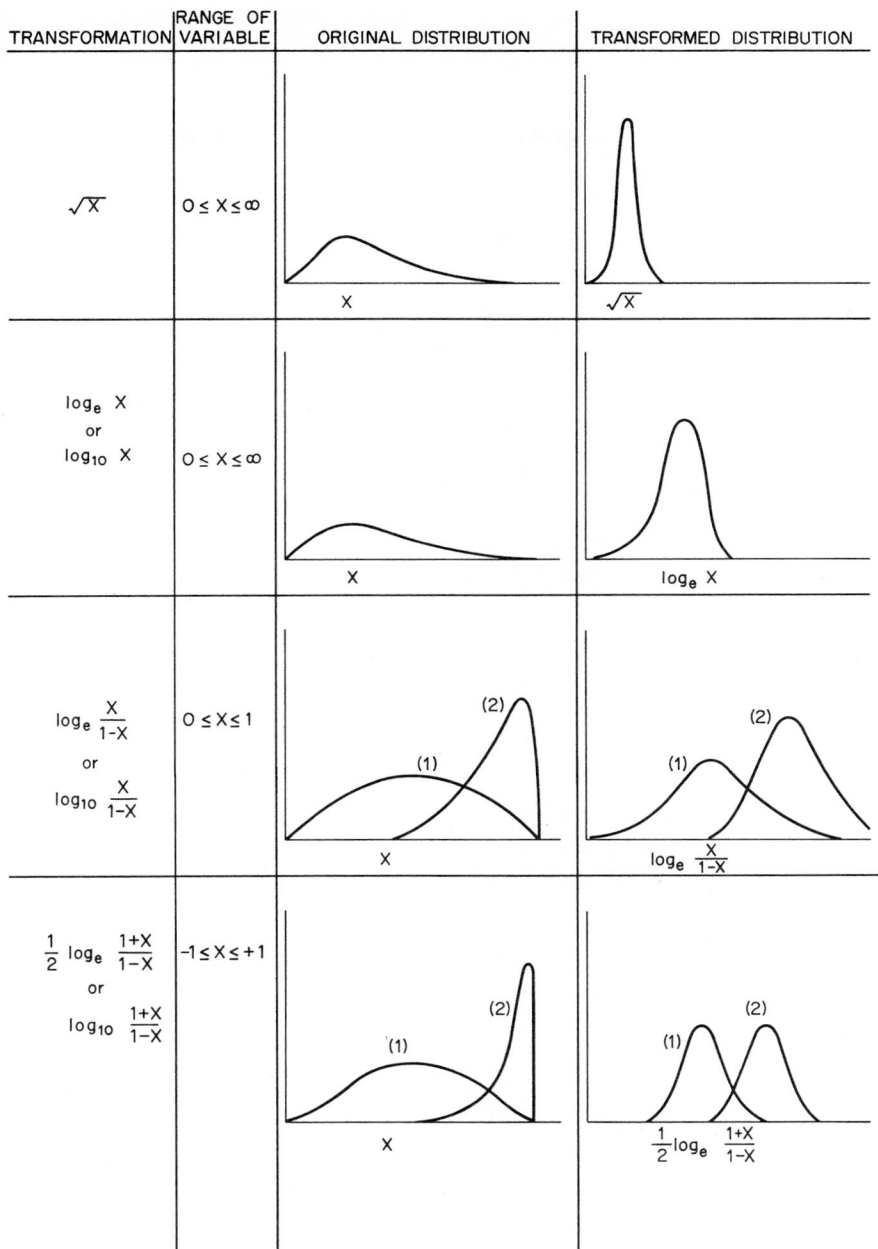

Fig. 22-26 Summary of some transformations.

  h. Define any requirements for preserving the order of measurements when time is a key parameter.
  i. Determine any requirements for collecting data in groups so defined to reflect different conditions which are to be evaluated.
  j. Define the method of data analysis and any assumptions required.
  k. Define requirements for any computer programs which will be needed.
3. Collect the data.
  a. Use methods to assure that the sample is selected in a random manner.
  b. Record the data and also all conditions present at the time of each observation.
  c. Examine the sample data to assure that the process shows sufficient stability to make predictions valid for the future.
4. Analyze the data.
  a. Evaluate the assumptions stated for determining the sample size and for analyzing the data. Take steps (including additional observations) if required.
  b. Apply statistical techniques to evaluate the original problem.
  c. Determine if further data and analysis are needed.
  d. Conduct "sensitivity analyses" by varying key sample estimates and other factors in the analysis and noting the effect on final conclusions.
5. Review the conclusions of the data analysis to determine if the original technical problem has been evaluated or if it has been changed to fit the statistical methods.
6. Present the results.
  a. State the conclusions in meaningful form by emphasizing results in terms of the original problem rather than the statistical indices used in the analysis.
  b. Present the results in graphical form where appropriate. Use simple statistical methods in the body of a report and place complicated analyses in an appendix.
7. Determine if the conclusions of the specific problem apply to other problems or if the data and calculations could be a useful input to other problems.

REFERENCES

 1. Dixon, Wilfrid J., and Frank J. Massey, Jr., "Introduction to Statistical Analysis," 3d ed., McGraw-Hill Book Company, New York, 1969.
 2. Larson, Kenneth E. (ed.), The Summarization of Data, *Journal of Quality Technology,* vol. 1, No. 1, pp. 68–71, January 1969.
 3. Hahn, Gerald J., How Abnormal Is Normality? *Journal of Quality Technology,* vol. 3, No. 1, pp. 18–22, January 1971.
 4. King, James R., "Probability Charts for Decision Making," The Industrial Press, New York, 1971.
 5. Moult, John F., Critical Agents in Bearing Fatigue Testing, *Lubrication Engineering,* December 1963, pp. 503–511.
 6. Nelson, Wayne, and Vernon C. Thompson, Weibull Probability Papers, *Journal of Quality Technology,* vol. 3, No. 2, pp. 45–50, April 1971.
 7. Muench, J. O., "The Cumulative Binomial Distribution Computer," Sandia Corporation Monograph, SC-R-64-1348, October 1964; available from Clearinghouse for Federal Scientific and Technical Information, National Bureau of Standards, U.S. Department of Commerce, Springfield, Va.
 8. Johnson, Norman L., and Fred C. Leone, "Statistics and Experimental Design," vol. I, John Wiley & Sons, Inc., New York, 1964.
 9. Lieberman, G. J., and D. B. Owen, "Tables of the Hypergeometric Probability Distribution," Stanford University Press, Stanford, Calif., 1961.
10. Duncan, Acheson J., "Quality Control and Industrial Statistics," 3d ed., Richard D. Irwin, Inc., Homewood, Ill., 1965.
11. Evans, Ralph A., Problems in Probability, pp. 347–353, *Proceedings of the Annual Symposium on Reliability,* Institute of Electrical and Electronics Engineers, Inc., 1966.

12. Blanton, H. Elmore, and Richard M. Jacobs, A Survey of Techniques for Analysis and Prediction of Equipment Reliability, *Industrial Quality Control*, vol. XIX, No. 6, pp. 18–25, December 1962; vol. XIX, No. 7, pp. 13–18, January 1963.
13. Rich, Barrett G., O. A. Smith, and Lee Korte, "Experience with a Formal Reliability Program," SAE Paper 670731, Farm, Construction and Industrial Machinery Meeting, Society of Automotive Engineers, 1967.
14. Kececioglu, D., and D. Cormier, Designing a Specified Reliability into a Component, *Proceedings of the Third Annual Aerospace Reliability and Maintainability Conference*, p. 546, Society of Automotive Engineers, Washington, D.C., 1964.
15. "Reliability for the Engineer," Book 5, "Testing for Reliability," pp. 29–31, Martin Marietta Corp., Orlando, Fla., 1966.
16. Lusser, R., "Reliability through Safety Margins," United States Army Ordnance Missile Command, Redstone Arsenal, Alabama, October 1958.
17. Grant, E. L., and R. S. Leavenworth, "Statistical Quality Control," 4th ed., McGraw-Hill Book Company, New York, 1972.
18. Juran, J. M., and Frank M. Gryna, Jr., "Quality Planning and Analysis," McGraw-Hill Book Company, New York, 1970.
19. Natrella, Mary G., "Experimental Statistics," National Bureau of Standards Handbook 91, Government Printing Office, Washington, D.C., 1963.
20. Harter, H. Leon, and Satya D. Dubey, "Theory and Tables for Tests of Hypotheses Concerning the Mean and the Variance of a Weibull Population," AD 653593, Clearinghouse for Federal Scientific and Technical Information, U.S. Department of Commerce, Washington, D.C., 1967.
21. Bennett, Carl A., and Norman L. Franklin, "Statistical Analysis in Chemistry and the Chemical Industry," chap. 11, John Wiley & Sons, Inc., New York, 1954.
22. Grubbs, Frank E., Procedures for Detecting Outlying Observations in Samples, *Technometrics*, vol. 11, No. 1, pp. 1–21, February 1969.
23. Miller, Irwin, and John E. Freund, "Probability and Statistics for Engineers," chaps. 10, 11, Prentice-Hall, Inc., Englewood Cliffs, N.J., 1965.
24. Rutherford, John R., A Logic Structure for Experimental Development Programs, *Chemical Technology*, March 1971, pp. 159–164.
25. Kirkpatrick, R. L., Confidence Limits on a Percent Defective Characterized by Two Specification Limits, *Journal of Quality Technology*, vol. 2, No. 3, pp. 150–155, July 1970.
26. Thoman, D. R., L. J. Bain, and C. E. Antle, Maximum Likelihood Estimation, Exact Confidence Intervals for Reliability and Tolerance Limits in the Weibull Distribution, *Technometrics*, vol. 12, No. 2, pp. 363–371, May 1970.
27. Gray, H. L., and Truman Lewis, A Confidence Interval for the Availability Ratio, *Technometrics*, vol. 9, No. 3, pp. 465–471, August 1967.
28. Epstein, Benjamin, Estimation from Life Test Data, *Technometrics*, vol. 2, No. 4, pp. 447–454, November 1960.
29. Hahn, Gerald J., The Absolute Sample Size Is What Counts, *Quality Progress*, vol. V. No. 5, pp. 18–19, May 1972.
30. Barr, Donald R., Using Confidence Intervals to Test Hypotheses, *Journal of Quality Technology*, vol. 1, No. 4, pp. 256–258, October 1969.
31. Bingham, R. S., Jr., Tolerance Limits and Process Capability Studies, *Industrial Quality Control*, vol. XIX, No. 1, pp. 36–40, July 1962.
32. Owen, D. B., and W. H. Frawley, Factors for Tolerance Limits Which Control Both Tails of the Normal Distribution, *Journal of Quality Technology*, vol. 3, No. 2, pp. 69–79, April 1971. See also Frawley, W. H., C. H. Kapadia, J. N. K. Rao, and D. B. Owen, Tolerance Limits Based on Range and Mean Range, *Technometrics*, vol. 13, No. 3, pp. 651–656, August 1971.
33. Hahn, G. J., Statistical Intervals for a Normal Population, Part I, Tables, Examples and Applications; Part II, Formulas, Assumptions, Some Derivations, *Journal of Quality Technology*, vol. 2, No. 3, July 1970; vol. 2, No. 4, October 1970.
34. Burr, Irving W., Specifying the Desired Distribution Rather than Maximum and Minimum Limits. *Industrial Quality Control*, vol. 24, No. 2, pp. 94–101, August 1967.
35. Dodge, H. F., B. J. Kinsburg, and M. K. Kruger, The L3 Coaxial System—Quality Control Requirements, *Bell System Technical Journal*, vol. 32, pp. 943–1005, July 1953.

36. "Statistical Quality Control Handbook," Western Electric Company, Inc., Mack Printing Co., Easton, Pa., 1956.
37. Gelling, H., and A. H. Schaafsma, Process Accuracy and Tolerances, *Quality,* vol. VII, No. 4, pp. 85–96, winter 1963.
38. Peters, J., Tolerancing the Components of an Assembly for Minimum Cost, ASME Paper 70-Prod.-9, *Transactions of the ASME Journal of Engineering for Industry,* American Society of Mechanical Engineers, New York, 1970.
39. Choksi, Suresh, Computer Can Optimize Manufacturing Tolerances for an Economical Design, *Annual Technical Conference Transactions,* pp. 323–330, American Society for Quality Control, 1971.
40. Mouradian, G., Tolerance Limits for Assemblies and Engineering Relationships. *Annual Technical Conference Transactions,* pp. 598–606, American Society for Quality Control, 1966.
41. Oliver, Larry R., and Melvin D. Springer, A General Set of Bayesian Attribute Acceptance Sampling Plans, *Technical Papers of the 1972 Conference, American Institute of Industrial Engineers,* pp. 443–455.
42. Hadley, G., "Introduction to Probability and Statistical Decision Theory," Holden-Day, Inc., Publisher, San Francisco, 1967.
43. Wade, Oliver R., "Tolerance Control in Design and Manufacturing," Industrial Press, Inc., New York, 1967.

Process Control by Statistical Methods

C. A. BICKING
Expert, United Nations Industrial Development Organization

FRANK M. GRYNA, Jr.

PROCESS CONTROL DEFINED

"Process" as used in this Section is any combination of machines, tools, methods, materials, and men employed to attain the qualities desired for products or services. Most of the processes discussed in this Handbook are manufacturing processes, but some are service processes. Still others are support operations common to both manufacturing and service industries.

"Control" as used in this Section is the managerial process of establishing and

23-1

meeting standards.[1]   The basic control device is the feedback loop, which is widely used in biological organisms, engineering mechanisms, and management systems. Throughout, the feedback loop serves the common purposes of detecting adverse changes, identifying the causes of these changes, and taking steps to eliminate these causes.[2]

This Section of the Handbook is concerned with those statistical tools which have been evolved to quantify the elements of the feedback loop and to put process control on a quantified basis.   Other aspects of process control are discussed elsewhere in the Handbook, and include:

Topic	Discussed in
Management universals of the feedback loop	Section 6, under Planning for Control—the Universals
Ability of the process to meet standards	Section 9, under Process Capability
Control systems for dominant process variables	Section 9, under Concept of Dominance, especially, Table 9-3
Product acceptance problems	Section 25, under Variables Plans for Process Parameter
Attainment of optimum process conditions	Section 27A and Section 28
Role of the process control personnel in closing the loop	Section 11, under Concept of Operator Self-Control
Measuring process dynamics, lags, disturbances	Section 29, under Adaptive Control

CONCEPT OF THE CONTROL CHART

The ultimate objective of processes is to make products which conform to specifications.   Once the manufacturing planning has provided capable processes,[3] it is the role of process control to get the most out of these processes by running them at well-aimed and uniform levels of performance.   A major tool for doing this is the control chart.

A control chart[4] is a graphic comparison of process performance data to computed "control limits" drawn as limit lines on the chart.   The process performance data usually consist of groups of measurements ("rational subgroups") selected in regular sequence of production while preserving the order.

The prime use of the control chart is to detect "assignable causes" of variation in the process.[5,6]   The term "assignable causes" has a special meaning, and it is essential to understand this meaning in order to understand the control chart concept.

Process variations are traceable to two kinds of causes, (1) random, i.e., due solely to chance, and (2) assignable, i.e., due to specific "findable" causes.   See Table 23-1.

[1] See generally, Section 2, under Control and under Quality Control.

[2] See Section 6, under Planning for Control—The Universals.

[3] See Section 9, under Process Capability.

[4] The control chart was invented in 1924 by Dr. Walter A. Shewhart, and was first expounded in his book, "The Economic Control of Quality of Manufactured Product," D. Van Nostrand Company, Inc., New York, 1931.   At first it was known as the Shewhart control chart, but extensive usage has led to the shorter term "control chart."

[5] Some control charts are used to detect production of nonconforming product.   See Section 25, under Acceptance Control Charts.

[6] For still other uses of control charts, and a comparison of the types of charts depending on the intended use, see Ref. 1.

TABLE 23-1   Distinction between Random and Assignable Causes of Variation

Random (chance) causes	Assignable causes
Description	
Consists of many individual causes	Consists of one or just a few individual causes
Any one random cause results in a minute amount of variation (but many random causes act together to yield a substantial total)	Any one assignable cause can result in a large amount of variation
Examples are human variation in setting control dials, slight vibration in machines; slight variation in raw material	Examples are operator blunder, a faulty set-up, or a batch of defective raw material
Interpretation	
Random variation cannot economically be eliminated from a process	Assignable variation can be detected; action to eliminate the causes is usually economically justified
When only random variation is present, the process is operating at its best; if defectives are still being produced, a basic process change must be made or the specifications revised in order to reduce the defectives	If assignable variation is present, the process is not operating at its best
An observation within the control limits of random variation means the process should not be adjusted	An observation beyond control limits usually means the process should be investigated and corrected
With only random variation, the process is sufficiently stable to use sampling procedures to predict the quality of total production or make process optimization studies (e.g., EVOP)	With assignable variation present, the process is not sufficiently stable to use sampling procedures for prediction

Ideally, only random causes should be present in a process, because this represents the minimum possible amount of variation. A process which is operating without assignable causes of variation is said to be "in a state of statistical control," which is usually abbreviated to "in control." A process which is in control is not only doing the best possible production job; the state of control also permits realization of important fringe benefits of the type listed in Table 23-1. Attainment of these basic and fringe benefits is what makes it so useful to identify and eliminate assignable causes of variation, and that is a key purpose of a control chart.

The control chart distinguishes between random and assignable causes of variation through its choice of the control limits. These are calculated from the laws of probability in such a way that highly improbable random variations are presumed to be due not to random causes, but to assignable causes. When the actual variation exceeds the control limits, it is a signal that assignable causes entered the process and the process should be investigated. Variation within the control limits means that only random causes are present and the process should be left alone.[7]

Use of the control chart to detect assignable causes of variation in the process takes two forms:

1. To determine whether an "unknown" process is in a state of control. (This is called "control with no standard given.")

[7] An important exception involves nonrandomness usually indicated by "runs" on a control chart. See the discussion under Interpretation of Control Charts.

2. To determine whether a "known" process remains in a state of control. (This is called "control with standard given.")

The steps needed to set up these two types of control chart are quite similar. However, there are differences in the formulas for calculating the control limits, in the symbols used for the statistics, and in some of the concepts of significance.

For most control charts, the control limits are calculated on a basis of the average $\pm\, 3$ times the standard deviation of the statistic used. (This will be developed further as the various kinds of charts are discussed in detail.) Use of $\pm\, 3$ times the standard deviation means that if random causes alone are present, 99.7% of the charted values will fall within the control limits. The remaining 0.3% become false alarms, but this frequency is so low that the $\pm 3\sigma$ limits are often used to distinguish between random and assignable causes of variation.

While $\pm 3\sigma$ limits are the most widely used, some situations call for different limits and result in different degrees of false alarm. Use of $\pm 2\sigma$ limits results in 4.5% of

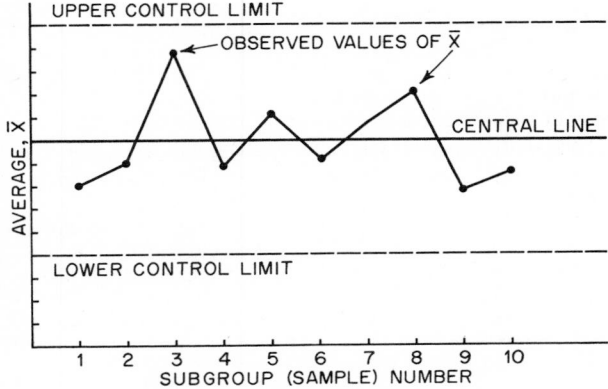

Fig. 23-1   Generalized control chart for averages.

false alarms if only random causes are present. Use of $\pm 1\sigma$ limits similarly results in 31.7% false alarms.

Figure 23-1 shows the essential features of a control chart as applied to sample averages. The sample averages are plotted chronologically, and if they fall within the control limits, the process is said to be in a state of statistical control.[8] A final note of caution! A state of "statistical control" merely means that only random causes are present. It does *not* necessarily mean that the product meets specifications. (This important point is elaborated later in Table 23-15 and associated discussion.) Conversely, a process which is not in statistical control may still be producing product which conforms to specification. Action on such a process usually has a much lower priority than action on processes which are producing nonconforming product.

As the reader gets into the details of how to construct and use control charts, he should keep in mind what is the purpose behind doing it at all. The ultimate pur-

---

[8] The control chart is a perpetual test of hypothesis. For example, on an $\overline{X}$ chart each point tests the hypothesis that the mean is equal to the center line of the chart. If the point falls within control limits, the hypothesis is accepted; otherwise it is rejected. With 3σ limits, the type I error is 0.0027. See Section 22, under Tests of Hypothesis.

pose of the processes is product fitness for use. Sometimes it is economic to keep a process "in control" as a better means of meeting the product specifications. In turn, it is sometimes economic to plot control charts as an aid to keeping processes in control. However, use of these means (charts, controlled processes) should be restricted to those situations where the means can economically aid the basic purpose of meeting product specifications. Considering the vast number of quality characteristics which are present in a modern plant, *control charts are justified for only a small minority of the quality characteristics.* Furthermore, once they have served their purpose (for problem analysis for breakthrough or control), most should be taken down and the effort shifted to other characteristics needing improvement.

STEPS IN SETTING UP CONTROL CHARTS

A. Choose the characteristic to be charted. This is a matter of judgment, but use the following guides:

1. Give high priority to characteristics that are currently running defective. These may be on basic or intermediate items such as parts and subassemblies or the final end product. A Pareto analysis[9] can establish priorities.

2. Identify the process variables and conditions contributing to the end product characteristics to define potential charting applications from raw material through processing steps to final characteristics. For example, pH, salt concentration, and temperature of plating solution are process variables contributing to plated smoothness.

3. Choose characteristics which will provide the kind of data needed for diagnosis of problems. Attribute data (e.g., percent defective) provide summary information but may need to be supplemented by variables data (e.g., numerical diameter of individual pieces) to diagnose causes and determine action.

4. Determine the earliest point in the production process at which testing can be done to get information on assignable causes so that the chart can serve as an effective early warning device to prevent defectives.

B. Choose the type of control chart. Table 23-2 compares several basic control charts.

C. Decide the center line to be used and the basis of calculating the control limits. The center line may be the average of past data, or may be a desired average (i.e., a standard value). The limits are usually set at ± 3 standard deviations, but other multiples may be chosen for different statistical risks. For example, $\pm 3\sigma$ limits involve a very small risk (usually less than 3 in 1,000) of looking for trouble that does not exist. However, these 3σ limits may have a large risk of failing to detect trouble when it does exist.[10] Limits set at $\pm 2\sigma$ would have a larger risk of the first type of error but a smaller risk of the second type. These risks depend on the sample size and other factors (see below). A study by Duncan (Ref. 2, p. 398) found that "charts using 2σ or even 1.5σ limits are more economical than charts using the conventional 3σ limits. This is true if it is possible to decide very quickly and inexpensively that nothing is wrong with the process when a point (just by chance) happens to fall outside the control limits; i.e., when the cost of looking for trouble when none exists is low. Contrariwise, it will be more economical to use charts with 3.5σ to 4σ limits if the cost of looking for trouble is very high."

D. Choose the rational subgroup.[11] The data chronologically plotted on a control

[9] See Section 2, under The Pareto Principle.

[10] These are called the type I and type II errors (see Section 22, under Tests of Hypothesis).

[11] The term sample is often used for subgroup. The latter will be used here to emphasize the group of n values as distinct from a sample which can be interpreted as only one value.

TABLE 23-2   Comparison of Some Control Charts

Statistical measure plotted	Average X and range R Average X and standard deviation σ Individual X Cumulative sum $\Sigma(X - R_0)$	% defective p Number of defectives np	Defects per unit u Number of defects c
Type of data required	Variables data (measured values of a characteristic)	Attribute data (number of defective units of product)	Attribute data (number of defects per unit of product)
General field of application	Control of individual characteristics	Control of overall fraction defective of a process	Control of overall number of defects per unit
Significant advantages	1. Provides maximum utilization of information available from data 2. Provides detailed information on process average and variation for control of individual dimensions	1. Data required are often already available from inspection records 2. Easily understood by all personnel 3. Provides an overall picture of quality	Same advantages as p chart but also provides a measure of degree of defectiveness
Significant disadvantages	1. Not understood unless training is provided. Can cause confusion between control limits and tolerance limits 2. Cannot be used with go no-go type of data	1. Does not provide detailed information for control of individual characteristics 2. Does not recognize different degrees of defectiveness in units of product	Does not provide detailed information for control of individual characteristics

chart consist of groups of units of product, and the groups are called rational subgroups. Grant and Leavenworth (Ref. 3, p. 157) state: "subgroups should be chosen in a way that appears likely to give the maximum chance for the measurements in each subgroup to be alike and the maximum chance for the subgroups to differ one from the other." The main points in choosing the rational subgroups are:

1. Lots from which the subgroups are chosen. Order of choice of the lot is a vital factor in determining whether a particular kind of variable is concealed or revealed. Any one lot should, so far as possible, have been made under like conditions, so that the pieces in that lot are as alike as possible. The order of choice of the lots can be in one of several ways:

   a. By suspected cause of variation. In this case, each lot is composed of product originating through a single "system of causes." For example, a six-spindle machine may be delivering product into a common delivery chute. To test whether any one of the spindles is a significant cause of variation, the product delivered by the six spindles should be kept segregated and would thereby constitute separate lots. In like manner, the product of different operators, different machines, different shifts, material, process conditions, etc., form a natural basis for dividing the product into lots and for subsequently choosing the subgroups from the segregated portions.[12]

   b. From equal quantities of product produced. This is especially useful for detecting continuing changes such as dilution of chemical solutions or wear of

[12] See Section 12, under The Nature of Lots of Product.

tools. If the "equal quantities" are chosen so as to synchronize with other suspected variables (change of materials, etc.), this method will automatically test for such suspected variables.

c. Over equal time intervals. This is especially useful for disclosing causes which vary with time. Choice of lots over equal time intervals is easy to organize and administer. Most control charts used for *retaining control* are on either an equal-time or an equal-quantity basis.

d. Avoid identification of lots at all and simply choose subgroups directly from the process at regular time intervals or at regular quantity intervals. This method, while the simplest of all to administer, is also the least informative if there is evidence of lack of control. In addition, the failure to identify lots loses the order and complicates the problem of corrective action. Obviously, knowledge of the technical process can aid greatly the separation of the product into rational groups or lots from which the rational subgroups are to be drawn. The main effort is to assure that *the specimens in any one subgroup have been produced under essentially the same conditions.*

2. Composition and frequency of the subgroup. When the chart is used for process control purposes, the pieces within each subgroup should be consecutive pieces in the order of production. This is desirable in order to obtain an estimate of chance variation which will yield control limits sensitive enough to detect process changes. If the pieces are taken at random from a lot, the changes that take place as the lot progresses will serve to increase the dispersion in the subgroup, resulting in wider control limits, thereby reducing the sensitivity of the chart.[13]

The decision on frequency of subgroups must balance the cost of taking subgroups against the value of the data obtained. Duncan (Ref. 2, p. 398) reached the following conclusions with respect to the frequency of sampling for $\bar{X}$ and R and the need to detect process change in order to minimize overall cost:

a. If a shift in the process average causes a high rate of loss, i.e., high relative to the cost of inspection, it is better to take small subgroups quite frequently than large subgroups less frequently. For example, when the rate of loss is high, subgroups of 4 or 5 taken every ½ hour are better than subgroups of 8 or 10 taken every hour.

b. If the unit cost of inspection is relatively high, the most economical design is one that takes small subgroups (say subgroups of 2) at relatively long intervals (say every 4 to 8 hours) with narrow control limits, say at $\pm 1.5\sigma$.

Experience data are helpful in judging proper frequency of sampling. The known rate of tool wear or the known rate of deterioration of a chemical solution will help to decide how much time or product may go by before there is danger of failure to meet specification. At the outset it is well to sample frequently until the data indicate that the frequency can be reduced.

3. Subgroup size. The subgroup size decides the width of the limit lines and thereby decides the maximum extent of change which will go undetected. The sensitivity of a chart for detecting process changes of varying degrees with different subgroup sizes can be defined by an operating characteristic curve.[14] Suggestions for size are given in the subsequent discussion of the various charts.

E. Provide the system for collecting the data. If the control chart is to serve as a day-to-day shop tool, it must be made simple and convenient for use. Measurement must be simplified and kept free of error. Indicating instruments must be designed

---

[13] A subgroup which is to be used for acceptance purposes rather than for detecting process changes should be formed by taking the specimens in random order from the entire lot on which a decision is to be made. But also see Section 12 under Product Acceptance Inspection.

[14] An example is given later in this Section. For an application to several types of control charts see Ref. 2, chaps. 19–22.

to give prompt and reliable readings. Better yet, instruments should be designed which can record as well as indicate. Recording of data can be simplified by skillful design of data or tally sheets. The working conditions are a factor. A machine department which abounds in cutting oil cannot keep respectable records with ordinary pencil and paper. Protective covers can be made, special paper and crayons provided. Copies of day-to-day data should be avoided.

F. Calculate the control limits and provide specific instructions on the interpretation of the results and the actions which are to be taken by various production personnel (see subsequent paragraphs).

CONSTRUCTING A CONTROL CHART FOR ATTAINING A STATE OF CONTROL ("CONTROL WITH NO STANDARD GIVEN")

The chart problem here is one of testing whether an "unknown" process is in a state of control. The general procedure is to:

1. Take a series of samples ("subgroups") from the process, as a source of data.
2. During the collection of these data, keep a log of any process changes which take place, e.g., changes in material, operator, tools, etc.
3. Compute trial control limits from these data.
4. Chart the data against the trial control limits to determine if any samples are "out of control."

If no samples are out of control, the process is said to be in control, and the way is open to prepare a control chart to aid in *maintaining* control. See Constructing a Control Chart for Maintaining Control in the Future (Control with Standard Given), below.

If the process is shown to be "out of control," the way is open to investigate the "out-of-control" points, find and eliminate the assignable causes, and retest the process for the existence of a state of control.

X̄ and R Chart   This chart is particularly helpful for machine-dominant processes. From the viewpoint of efficient utilization of all information contained in a series of measurements, a pair of charts—one showing average $(\bar{X})$ values and one showing range (R) values—is best.[15] $(R = \text{maximum} - \text{minimum values.})$ The chart of $\bar{X}$ values tells when a change has occurred in central tendency. This might be due to such factors as tool wear, a gradual increase in temperature, a new batch of material of greater toughness, or a different method used by a night-shift workman. The chart of R values indicates when a significant gain or loss of uniformity has taken place. A loss in uniformity might be due to such causes as worn bearings, a loose tool post, an erratic supply of coolant, careless chucking of stock, variability of pieces as received from a previous roughing operation, or lack of concentration of the operator.

Control limits[16] for subgroup averages[17] are

$$\bar{X} \pm 3\sigma_{\bar{X}} = \bar{X} \pm \frac{3\sigma'}{\sqrt{n}}$$

where $\sigma_{\bar{X}} = $ standard deviation of the population of *averages* of subgroups

---

[15] Standard deviation is sometimes used in place of the range.

[16] Careful on the meaning of symbols. In the Third Edition of this Handbook and in most statistical literature, the symbols σ and s, respectively, are used to designate the standard deviation of the population of individual values and the standard deviation calculated from a sample. This contrasts with σ' and σ used in some control chart literature. In this Section, the prime notation will be used when needed to tie in easily with other control chart literature.

[17] Averages vary less than individual values according to the relationship $\sigma_{\bar{X}} = \sigma' / \sqrt{n}$. See Section 22, under The Two Types of Sampling Error.

σ' = standard deviation of the population of *individual* values

n = number of values in each subgroup

In practice, the use of sample ranges simplifies the calculations by eliminating the need to calculate standard deviations.

A series of small subgroups are measured and the average $(\overline{X})$ and range (R) calculated. The subgroup size is constant,[18] say 4, and preferably[19] 25 such subgroups should be collected. The grand average $(\overline{\overline{X}})$ and the average range $(\overline{R})$ are calculated.

The three standard deviation control limits are given by the following formulas:

Statistic	Upper limit	Lower limit
Averages	$\overline{\overline{X}} + A_2\overline{R}$	$\overline{\overline{X}} - A_2\overline{R}$
Ranges.	$D_4\overline{R}$	$D_3\overline{R}$

The values of the factors[20] are given in Table 23-3.

TABLE 23-3   Control Limit Factors*

n	A_1	A_2	B_3	B_4	D_3	D_4	E_1	E_2
2	3.759	1.880	0	3.267	0	3.268	5.318	2.660
3	2.394	1.023	0	2.568	0	2.574	4.146	1.772
4	1.880	0.729	0	2.266	0	2.282	3.760	1.457
5	1.596	0.577	0	2.089	0	2.114	3.568	1.290
6	1.410	0.483	0.030	1.970	0	2.004	3.454	1.184
7	1.277	0.419	0.118	1.882	0.076	1.924	3.378	1.109
8	1.175	0.373	0.185	1.815	0.136	1.864	3.323	1.054
9	1.094	0.337	0.239	1.761	0.184	1.816	3.283	1.010
10	1.028	0.308	0.284	1.716	0.223	1.777	3.251	0.975

* Values of A_1, A_2, B_3, B_4, D_3, D_4, E_1, E_2 and graphs of $3\sigma_p$ and $c \pm 3\sqrt{c}$ are given in Appendix Table Y. A partial tabulation of the first eight factors is reproduced here for the convenience of the reader in the following text.

An example is shown in Figures 23-2 and 23-3.

Table 23-4 summarizes the formulas and other matters for this type of chart.[21]

The literature has a wealth of examples on average and range charts. The Western Electric Company Handbook (Ref. 5) is especially strong on illustrative examples and detailed instructions for application. Grant and Leavenworth (Ref. 3) is a fine blend of examples, procedures, and conceptual background. Erdman, Bailey, and Knowler (Ref. 6), and Bicking (Ref. 7) give examples of published case histories that include technical process details.[22] Reference 6 is also an example of a blow-by-blow story of a problem from start to finish.

INTERPRETATION OF CONTROL CHARTS

First, examine the chart for unusual points or patterns, i.e., nonrandomness. It is customary to place the charts for $\overline{X}$ and R one above the other so that average and

---

[18] If this is not possible, see Grant and Leavenworth (Ref. 3, pp. 173–174) for procedures to follow.

[19] Hillier (Ref. 4) discusses the risks with various numbers of subgroups and gives procedures for calculating limits with as few as two subgroups.

[20] A formula for each of these factors is given in the Glossary of Symbols.

[21] Section 20 gives computer program references for plotting many of the control charts discussed in this Section.

[22] See also Section 29, under Semicontinuous Processes.

CONTROL CHART DATA SHEET

PART NUMBER: 102J	DESCRIPTION: SHAFT		
LOT NO.: 195	ORDER NO.: 7-18	MACHINE NO.: SBL-20	DEPT.: M
OPERATION: FACING TO LENGTH	OPERATOR: BROWN	SHIFT: 1 DATE 12-17-48	INSPECTOR: SMITH

SAMPLE #	1	2	3	4	5	6	7	8	9	10	11	12	13
	.9382	.9382	.9385	.9379	.9384	.9385	.9385	.9387	.9388	.9381	.9386	.9386	.9386
	.9378	.9380	.9382	.9380	.9385	.9385	.9385	.9386	.9382	.9385	.9387	.9384	.9386
	.9385	.9380	.9383	.9384	.9387	.9385	.9385	.9385	.9386	.9383	.9387	.9385	.9386
	.9375	.9382	.9379	.9384	.9386	.9385	.9387	.9382	.9386	.9386	.9385	.9384	.9381
													.9539
TOTAL	3.7520	3.7524	3.7529	3.7527	3.7542	3.7540	3.7544	3.7540	3.7542	3.7535	3.7545	3.7538	3.7539
X̄	.93800	.93810	.93822	.93818	.93850	.93850	.93860	.93850	.93855	.93838	.93862	.93845	.93848
R	.0010	.0002	.0006	.0005	.0003	.0000	.0002	.0005	.0006	.0005	.0002	.0001	.0005

SAMPLE #	14	15	16	17	18	19	20	21	22	23	24	25
	.9382	.9386	.9388	.9385	.9387	.9388	.9385	.9386	.9384	.9387	.9387	.9390
	.9387	.9387	.9387	.9387	.9387	.9385	.9387	.9390	.9386	.9388	.9387	.9389
	.9388	.9387	.9387	.9385	.9383	.9386	.9386	.9390	.9386	.9388	.9389	.9389
	.9388	.9386	.9386	.9384	.9389	.9386	.9386	.9389	.9388	.9386	.9390	.9390
TOTAL	3.7545	3.7546	3.7549	3.7541	3.7538	3.7545	3.7539	3.7553	3.7544	3.7549	3.7553	3.7558
X̄	.93862	.93865	.93872	.93852	.93865	.93862	.93865	.93888	.93860	.93872	.93882	.93895
R	.0006	.0001	.0002	.0003	.0006	.0003	.0003	.0004	.0004	.0002	.0003	.0001

NO.	X̄	R
1	.93800	.0010
2	.93810	.0002
3	.93822	.0006
4	.93818	.0005
5	.93855	.0003
6	.93850	.0000
7	.93860	.0002
8	.93850	.0005
9	.93855	.0006
10	.93838	.0005
11	.93862	.0002
12	.93845	.0001
13	.93848	.0005
14	.93862	.0006
15	.93865	.0001
16	.93872	.0002
17	.93852	.0003
18	.93865	.0006
19	.93862	.0003
20	.93865	.0003
21	.93888	.0004
22	.93860	.0004
23	.93872	.0002
24	.93882	.0003
25	.93895	.0001
TOTAL	23.46353	0.0090

$$\bar{\bar{X}} = \frac{23.46353}{25} \qquad \bar{R} = \frac{0.0090}{25}$$

$$\bar{\bar{X}} = .938541 \qquad \bar{R} = .00036$$

LIMITS FOR AVERAGES CHART

UPPER CONTROL LIMIT = $\bar{\bar{X}} + A_2\bar{R}$
LOWER CONTROL LIMIT = $\bar{\bar{X}} - A_2\bar{R}$

$\bar{\bar{X}} = .938541$ COMPUTED FROM INSPECTION DATA. SEE
$\bar{R} = .00036$ } LAST TWO COLUMNS ON THIS SHEET.

CONSTANT A_2 IS OBTAINED FROM TABLES (SEE FIGURE 22). FOR A SAMPLE SIZE = 4, A_2 = .729

$A_2\bar{R}$ = .729 x .00036 = .000262
U.C.L. = .938541 + .000262 = .938803
L.C.L. = .938541 - .000262 = .938279

LIMITS FOR RANGES CHART

UPPER CONTROL LIMIT = $D_4\bar{R}$
LOWER CONTROL LIMIT = $D_3\bar{R}$

$\bar{R}$ = .00036 (SEE LAST COLUMN ON THIS SHEET)

CONSTANTS D_3, D_4 ARE OBTAINED FROM TABLES (SEE FIGURE 22). FOR A SAMPLE SIZE = 4, D_3 = 0.000, D_4 = 2.282

U.C.L. = 2.282 x .00036 = .00082
L.C.L. = 0 x .00036 = 0

Fig. 23-2 Data sheet for determining if a process is in control.

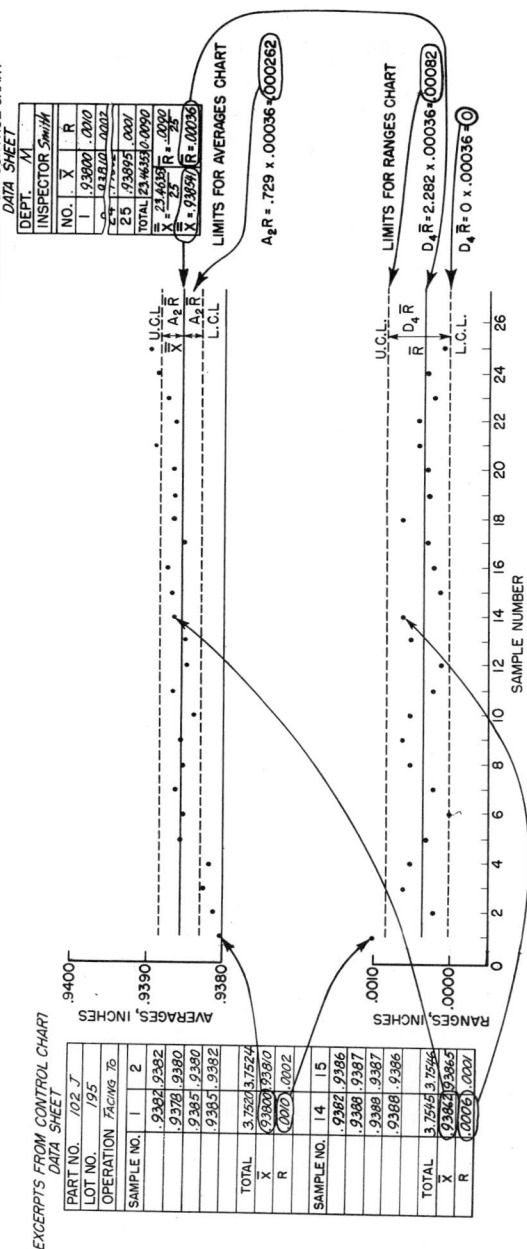

Fig. 23-3 How to construct the Shewhart control chart.

TABLE 23-4   Summary of Control Chart for Average and Dispersion

Typical problems for application:
  Meeting specifications on a numerical characteristic
  Underadjustment or overadjustment of a process
  Mating components causing assembly problems
  Data expensive or difficult to obtain
Characteristics plotted:
  Average $\bar{X}$ and range R or standard deviation σ
Formulas for control limits:
  Averages: $\bar{\bar{X}} \pm A_2\bar{R}$ or $\bar{\bar{X}} \pm A_1\bar{\sigma}$
  Ranges: $D_4\bar{R}$ and $D_3\bar{R}$
  Standard deviations: $B_4\bar{\sigma}$ and $B_3\bar{\sigma}$
Subgroup size:
  With subgroup ranges, n is usually 4 or 5. If n exceeds 10, standard deviation
  should replace the range

Some common patterns of plots	Examples of meaning (see Ref. 5)
Cyclic up and down movements	$\bar{X}$ chart: seasonal environmental effects, rotation of operators
	R chart: maintenance schedules, operator fatigue
Trends in single direction	$\bar{X}$ chart: tool wear, deterioration of plating solution
	R chart: homogeneity of raw material (better or worse)
Concentration of consecutive points at several different values	$\bar{X}$: change in machine, operator, material, or setup
	$R:$ same
Correlation between $\bar{X}$ and R charts	If the averages tend to move in the *same* direction as the ranges, the population is positively skewed (long tail on high side). Movement in the opposite direction means negative skewness

Some cautions:
1. Investigate out-of-control points on the range chart *before* interpreting the chart for averages
2. Determine the form of the distribution of individual measurements before comparing process variability with specifications (normality should not be assumed)
Statistical distribution assumptions:
1. Subgroup *averages* from a population in control are distributed normally
2. The control chart factors (A_2, D_4, D_3, etc.) assume a normal population of individuals, but moderate deviations are acceptable

range for any one sample are in the same vertical line.   Observe whether one, both, or neither indicates lack of control for any given sample.   If a point falls outside these provisional control limits, it is strong evidence that the out-of-control sample did not come from the same cause system as the others.

If a sample *average* falls outside the limit lines, it is evidence that a general change affecting all pieces has occurred between samples.   Study the log kept during the collection of data to see if, for the associated subgroup, there was a change in materials, process, or other factor which might account for the point out of control.

If a sample *range* falls outside limits, it is evidence that the uniformity of the process has changed.   Where time has been used as the basis for subgrouping, this may mean a change in either man, machine, or material factors affecting variability.   It may also reflect a sudden shift in process (such as the start of a new tray of parts or another bar of steel) which happened to occur within the lot from which the sub-group was being taken. In the latter case both average and range might well be outside limits.

In addition to points outside control limits, look for "runs," i.e., a succession of points on one side of the center line.[23]

1. Length of run (a long run indicates nonrandomness). Reference 5 (p. 26) recommends the following as indicators of nonrandomness:

2 out of 3 successive points at 2 standard deviations or beyond
4 out of 5 successive points at 1 standard deviation or beyond
8 successive points on one side of the center line.[24]

2. Number of runs about the center line (too *few* runs indicates nonrandomness). Section 22, under Tests of Hypothesis, defines such a run test.

Special cases of runs are cycles and trends. Tests of runs to supplement the 3σ limits are important in detecting nonrandomness.[25, 26]

Table 23-4 lists some common patterns[27] of plots and examples of their meaning. At this point, technical knowledge of the process is crucial to tracking down the assignable causes and taking steps to eliminate them.

The next step in interpretation compares the process data with specification limits. This is discussed in a subsequent paragraph, under Constructing a Control Chart for Maintaining Control in the Future (Control with Standard Given).

WHY USE AVERAGES IN CONTROL CHARTS?

The question is often asked, "Why are averages used in control charts rather than individual pieces?" The answer lies in the fact that *averages are more sensitive to change* than are individuals (see Figure 23-4). Consider a process in which σ for individual pieces is 50 and the average of the process is 1,000. The 3σ range of individuals is 150, and therefore the limit lines will be from 1,150 to 850. A change in process from the old level of 1,000 to a new level of 1,100 will change the 3σ range of individuals to new values of 1,250 to 950. However, the chance of an indi-vidual specimen's falling outside the *old* limit lines will be about 16 in 100. If it is desired to detect such a change in the process with a certainty of 99 in 100, it would take on the average *twenty-seven* subgroups of one specimen each.

On the other hand, if a control chart for averages of 4 is used, the limit lines will be

$$\frac{3\sigma}{\sqrt{n}} = \frac{3 \times 50}{2} = 75$$

on either side of the average of 1,000, or an upper limit of 1,075 and a lower limit of 925. Assume the same change in average from 1,000 to 1,100. Then the chance that the average of a group of four will fall outside the *old* limit lines will be about

[23] Duncan (Ref. 2, pp. 132–137) discusses and gives tables for several run tests.
[24] See Section 39, under Tests for Detecting Instability in the Process. Also, see Ref. 2, p. 930, for the number of successive points as a function of the total number of points.
[25] However, some risks are involved. Hilliard and Lasater (Ref. 8) have investigated the use of three tests singly or in combination on an $\overline{X}$ and R chart. The tests were a point beyond control limits, length of run, and number of runs. One finding showed that if all three tests are used on each chart, the chance of getting a *false* indication of nonrandomness is about 0.25. The reference provides guidance on the use of the three tests.
[26] Barish, Hauser, and Ehrenfeld (Ref. 9) evaluate six rules on whether and how much to adjust a process.
[27] Reference 5 is an excellent reference for control chart patterns.

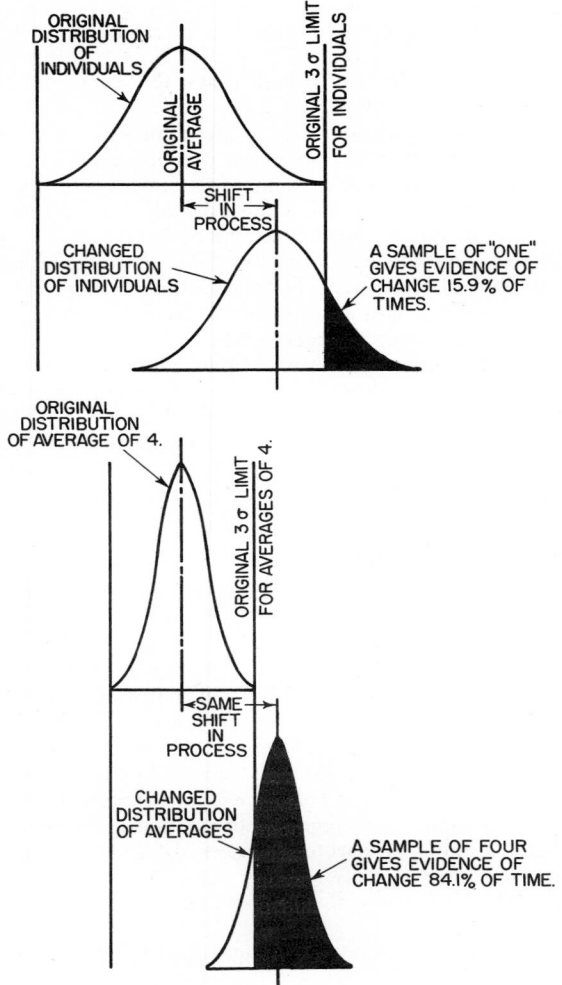

Fig. 23-4   How averages are more sensitive in detecting change than individuals.

84 in 100.   If it is again desired to detect such a change with a certainty of 99 in 100, it would take on the average only *two* or *three* subgroups of four specimens each.

THE OPERATING CHARACTERISTIC (OC) CURVE FOR A CONTROL CHART

This curve tells how sensitive the chart is for detecting process changes of varying degrees.   More specifically, the chart is a plot of the true value of a process param-eter (e.g., the average) against the probability that a single sample will fall within the control limits. Figure 23-5 shows an OC curve[28] for an $\bar{X}$ control chart based on an average of 45.8, a standard deviation of individual pieces of 2.9, and a sample size $n = 4$. For example, if the process average shifts from its previous average of 45.8 to 40.0, the probability that the average of a single sample of 4 will fall within control limits is about 0.16. That is, there is only a 16% chance that a change of this magnitude will go undetected. If the process average shifted only to 43.0, the probability that a sample average will fall within control limits would be about 0.84, or an 84% probability that the shift would be undetected on the basis of 1 sample of 4. In a given problem it is unlikely that the shift would go undetected very long. For example, the probability of this shift's going undetected in 5 samples of 4 units each is $(0.84)^5$, or 0.418.

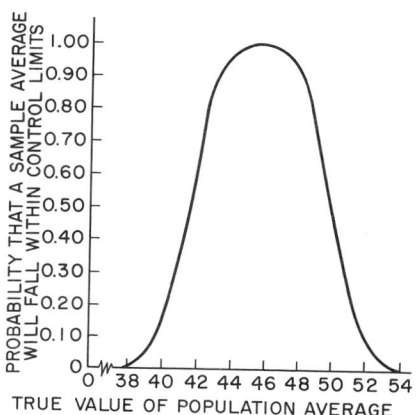

Fig. 23-5 Operating characteristic curve for a control chart.

The previous discussion, under Steps in Setting Up Control Charts, stated some rules often followed in practice on subgroup size and control limits. These rules try to strike a balance between the cost of looking for trouble that does not exist and the cost of failing to look for trouble that does exist. In a given problem, a control chart system can be designed based on the uniqueness of the problem. The OC curve can be the basis of the design. The OC curve is a function of the subgroup size n, width of control limits $t\sigma$ (e.g., 1.5σ, 2σ, 3σ), and the value of the standard deviation. By evaluating the OC curve for various subgroup sizes and control limits, a chart can be designed with realistic values of n and t. Duncan (Ref. 2) has excellent discussions on the methods of constructing OC curves for $\bar{X}$ and R, p, and c control charts, and on conclusions to be drawn from these OC curves.

OTHER CONTROL CHARTS

Control Charts for Individuals X This chart is a plot of individual observations, one by one, and is useful when only one observation can be conveniently obtained per lot or batch of material. The chart of individuals is not as sensitive[29] as the $\bar{X}$ chart (see Why Use Averages in Control Charts?). However, it does avoid possible misunderstandings concerning subgroup averages and specification limits—control limits for individuals may be directly compared with specification limits.[30]

The control chart for X is an extension of the control chart for $\bar{X}$ and R, using the same central line as the $\bar{X}$ chart and appropriate control limits based on the variation within rational subgroups. The measure of variation may be the range or standard deviation of subgroups.

[28] This curve should not be confused with that of a normal distribution of measurements. In some cases, the shape is similar, but the meanings of an OC curve and a distribution curve are entirely different.

[29] For this reason, 2σ control limits are sometimes used.

[30] See Section 29 for several examples.

The procedures are analogous to those described for the $\bar{X}$ chart. Control limits should be based on at least 15 individual measurements. The 3σ control limit formulas based on subgroup ranges are:

	Upper limit	Lower limit
Individuals	$\bar{\bar{X}} + E_2\bar{R}$	$\bar{\bar{X}} - E_2\bar{R}$
Ranges.	$D_4\bar{R}$	$D_3\bar{R}$

Values of the numerical factors are given in Table 23-3.

Examples of Control Chart for X A batch-type resin manufacturing process is controlled by measurement of the flow point. Two batches are made per day, so that a daily subgroup of two is a rational one. However, it is desirable to examine the results for possible corrective action batch by batch. Accordingly a control chart for individual batches is indicated. Data are given in Table 23-5.

TABLE 23-5   Flow Point of Resin

Subgroup	Measurements		Range R
	X_1	X_2	
1	133.5	117.5	16.0
2	124.0	126.5	2.5
3	132.5	130.5	2.0
4	118.0	126.5	8.5
5	127.5	133.5	6.0
6	131.5	128.5	3.0
7	124.0	124.0	0
8	137.0	143.5	6.5
9	132.5	133.5	1.0
10	133.0	126.5	6.5
11	126.0	135.5	9.5
12	121.5	131.0	9.5
13	135.5	131.5	4.0
14	136.0	128.0	8.0
15	127.5	126.0	1.5
16	125.0	123.5	1.5
17	130.0	130.0	0
Totals		4,391.0	86.0
Averages		129.15	5.06

For the X chart,
Center line $= \bar{\bar{X}} = 129.15$
Control limits $= \bar{\bar{X}} \pm E_2\bar{R}$
$= 129.15 \pm (2.660)\,(5.06)$
$= 142.61$ and 115.69

For the range chart,
Center line $= \bar{R} = 5.06$
Control limits $= D_4\bar{R}$ and $D_3\bar{R}$
$= 3.27\,(5.06)$ and $0(5.06)$
$= 16.6$ and 0

Individual batch results and ranges[31] are plotted on charts with these limits.

[31] In practice, the range chart is often omitted when experience shows it to stay in control.

The chart is not shown, but by observation, it can be seen that the second batch on the eighth day is out of control on the high side. (All the ranges are in control.) The reasons for this would be investigated.

An alternative way of subgrouping in a situation like this is to use moving ranges (i.e., ranges of consecutive measurements). A new subgroup is formed by including the latest measurement and deleting the oldest one. If a single measurement spans much time (e.g., a day or longer), moving ranges make it possible to calculate a range after each individual measurement rather than wait for a complete new subgroup of measurements. For the resin flow point example, the moving ranges are obtained as in Table 23-6.

TABLE 23-6   Partial Listings of Moving Ranges, Flow Point of Resin

Subgroup	Consecutive pairs		Moving range
1	133.5	117.5	16.0
2	117.5	124.0	6.5
3	124.0	126.5	2.5
4	126.5	132.5	6.0
5	132.5	130.5	2.0
•	•	•	•
•	•	•	•
•	•	•	•
33	130.0	130. 0	0
Total			169.5
Average			5.14

For the X chart,
Center line $= \bar{\bar{X}} = 129.15$
Control limits $= \bar{\bar{X}} \pm 2.660 \bar{R}$
$= 129.15 \pm (2.660)(5.14)$
$= 142.82$ and 115.48

For the range chart,
Center line $= \bar{R} = 5.14$
Control limits $= 3.27 (5.14)$ and $0(5.14)$
$= 16.8$ and 0

As before, the one batch with flow point of 143.5 is out of control. In this example, either of the methods of subgrouping is equally effective.

The examples given in Tables 23-5 and 23-6 illustrate two approaches to calculating and using the range in a chart for individual measurements. When there is a definite rational basis for grouping the observations into rational subgroups (e.g., four successive batches in a single shift), the conventional calculations of the range (Table 23-5) may be followed. When there is no definite basis for grouping the data, control limits can be based on variation between batches as obtained from moving ranges (Table 23-6). The same data were used in the examples to illustrate the two methods.[32]

Table 23-7 summarizes the control chart for X.

Control Charts for Attributes Data   Control charts for $\bar{X}$, R, or X require that actual numerical *measurements* be made, e.g., a length. Control charts for attributes data require only a *count* of observations on a characteristic. Table 23-8 summarizes the attributes charts to be discussed in the following paragraphs. Control charts for

---

[32] Grant and Leavenworth (Ref. 3, pp. 157–182, 302–304) further explains the importance of subgroupings.

fraction defective p and for number of defectives np are the first types of attribute charts to be described, followed by control charts for defects per unit u and for number of defects c.

TABLE 23-7 Summary of Control Chart for Individual Measurements

Typical problems for application:
  Each batch or lot is evaluated by a single measurement
  A long time span occurs between measurements
  Short cycles or trends are present in the process and must be detected quickly
  A direct comparison of plotted measurements to specification limits is needed
  Chart is needed that avoids statistical explanations to operators of $\bar{X}$ and R limits
Characteristics plotted:
  Individual measurements (ranges or moving ranges of subgroup are sometimes plotted)
Formulas for control limits:
  Individuals: $\qquad \bar{\bar{X}} \pm E_2 \bar{R}$ or $\bar{\bar{X}} \pm E_1 \bar{\sigma}$
  Ranges: $\qquad\quad D_4 \bar{R}$ and $D_3 \bar{R}$
  Standard deviations; $\ B_4 \bar{\sigma}$ and $B_3 \bar{\sigma}$
Subgroup size:
  Depends on difficulty of obtaining individual measurements, but often $n = 2$
Some common patterns of plots:
  Similar to those for $\bar{X}$ and R charts (see Table 23-4)
Some cautions:
  1. Decide process action knowing that the chart is less sensitive than an $\bar{X}$ chart
  2. Determine the form of the distribution before comparing process variability with specifications
  3. Have sufficient data before drawing conclusions on apparent trends or cycles. If possible, check with an $\bar{X}$ chart which will dampen extreme individual measurements and highlight long-term trends and cycles
  4. Interpret moving ranges carefully—two successive moving ranges are not fully independent* since they share one measurement in common
Statistical distribution assumption:
  Individual measurements are distributed normally

* For a discussion of the analysis of correlated measurements see Section 29, under Evaporation and Crystallization.

Control Charts for Fraction Defective p An example of attributes data consists of the ratio of the number of items or occurrences having some given attribute to the total number of items in a subgroup. Usually this is designated as the fraction defective p.

The fraction defective p is most useful when tests are of a "go no-go" nature but may also be used when measurements made on a scale are recorded. In the latter case, p is the fraction of the measured values falling outside a limit or limits. A control chart for p (or other attributes data) works well for both machine-dominant and operator-dominant processes.

The p chart is less sensitive than charts for variables (for example, $\bar{X}$ and R charts) and is not so helpful in diagnosing causes. In spite of this it is commonly found that the introduction of this simple chart is accompanied by reductions in the average fraction defective. Its value lies in giving information to supervisors as to *when* to apply pressure for improved quality. But let the engineer beware of assuming that "the chart did it." The fact is that, when top management presses for improved quality, it applies this pressure to *both* the line and the staff organization. If there had been no chart, the improvement might have come anyway, because of the simultaneous pressure on the line supervisors.

TABLE 23-8   Summary of Control Chart for Attributes

Typical problems for application:
   Informing all levels of management on overall quality levels
   Problems where it is difficult to make a numerical measurement
   Problems where several types of defects must be grouped together
Characteristics plotted:
   Fraction defective p
   Number of defectives np
   Defects per unit u
   Number of defects c
Formulas for control limits:

Fraction defective:
$$\bar{p} \pm 3 \sqrt{\frac{\bar{p}(1 - \bar{p})}{n}}$$

Number of defectives:
$$n\bar{p} \pm 3 \sqrt{n\bar{p}(1 - \bar{p})}$$

Defects per unit:
$$\bar{u} \pm 3 \sqrt{\frac{\bar{u}}{n}}$$

Number of defects
$$\bar{c} \pm 3 \sqrt{\bar{c}}$$

Subgroup size:
   p chart: $n > 50$ or $n\bar{p} \geq 4$
   np chart: $n > 50$ or $n\bar{p} \geq 4$
   u chart: 1 or more (but subgroup size constant)
   c chart: 1 or more (but subgroup size constant)
   (The *better* the quality, the *larger* the subgroup size needed to detect lack of control)

Some common patterns of plots   Examples of meaning
   Cyclic up and down movements Regular changes in suppliers
   Trends in single direction   Poor trend due to tool wear; tightening of requirements.
                                      Good trend due to increased skill; relaxation of require-
                                      ments
Some cautions:
   1. Beware of small subgroup size on a p chart— control limits tend to be wide and show a
      process in control
   2. Interpret carefully when each point reflects several characteristics—a process in control
      may be due to a balancing of good and bad characteristics. Plot separate charts if possible
Statistical distribution assumptions:
   p chart: binomial
   np chart: binomial
   u chart: Poisson
   c chart: Poisson

The fraction defective may be used with respect to a single quality characteristic or with respect to two or more characteristics considered collectively. A distinction is made between a "defect" and a "defective." A "defect" is a single instance of nonconformance to some requirement, whereas a "defective" is a unit containing one or more "defects."

The control chart lines for samples of size n are

	Central line	Control limits
Control chart for p	$\bar{p}$	$\bar{p} \pm 3 \sqrt{\dfrac{\bar{p}(1 - \bar{p})}{n}}$

where $\bar{p}$ is the total defectives in all samples divided by the total units in all samples and n is the number of units in any subgroup. If the samples are equal or nearly equal in size, the average sample size $\bar{n}$ may be used.[33]

If feasible, the samples should be large enough so that the presence of no defects in the subgroup indicates a significant improvement over the standard. This requires a sample size (n) greater than $(9 - 9\bar{p})\bar{p}$ articles, where n = number of articles in subgroup and $\bar{p}$ = average fraction defective. The dotted line on the graph for p-chart limits (Appendix II, Chart Z) shows, for each $\bar{p}$ value, the smallest sample that will have this property. For example, suppose that $\bar{p} = 0.05$. Find the intersection of the diagonal line marked 0.05 with the dotted line. Move downward on the page to find $n = 171$ on the lower scale.

TABLE 23-9 p Chart Data

Subgroup: Production during week			Inspected at: Final assembly and test	
Week No.	Week ending	No. magnets inspected	No. defective magnets	Fraction defective p
1	12/3	724	48	0.067
2	12/10	763	83	0.109
3	12/17	748	70	0.094
4	12/31	748	85	0.114
5	1/7	724	45	0.062
6	1/14	727	56	0.077
7	1/21	726	48	0.066
8	1/28	719	67	0.093
9	2/4	759	37	0.049
10	2/11	745	52	0.070
11	2/18	736	47	0.064
12	2/25	739	50	0.068
13	3/4	723	47	0.065
14	3/11	748	57	0.076
15	3/18	770	51	0.066
16	3/25	756	71	0.094
17	4/1	719	53	0.074
18	4/8	757	34	0.045
19	4/15	760	29	0.038
Totals.		14,091	1,030	
Averages		741.6	54.2	0.073

The control chart for p is most effective when samples are large, that is, greater than 50, or when the expected number of defective units per sample is four or more. When $\bar{p}$ is small, for example, less than 0.10, the control limit formula may be simplified to $\bar{p} \pm 3 \sqrt{\bar{p}/n}$. For samples of unequal size, control limits are usually based on the average n.

Example of Control Chart for p   Table 23-9 shows the results of final testing and inspection, during a period of 5 months, of certain permanent magnets used in elec-

---

[33] Theoretically, control limits should be calculated separately for each sample size (a pooled estimate of $\bar{p}$ having been calculated from the number of defectives np divided by the total number of observations). However, such varying control limits are deadly to explain to management or operators. Another approach is a "stabilized p chart." This plots fraction defective expressed in standard deviation units. See Pollitzer (Ref. 10) for a discussion and nomograph.

trical relays. The total number of magnets tested was 14,091. The total number found to be defective was 1,030. The average sample size was

$$\bar{n} = \frac{14,091}{19} = 741.6$$

The average fraction defective was

$$\bar{p} = \frac{1,030}{14,091} = 0.073$$

Control limits for the chart were placed at

$$\bar{p} \pm 3\sigma_p = \bar{p} \pm 3\sqrt{\frac{\bar{p}(1-\bar{p})}{\bar{n}}} = 0.073 \pm 3\sqrt{\frac{0.073(1-0.073)}{741.6}}$$

$$= 0.073 \pm 0.0287 = 0.102 \text{ and } 0.044$$

The value 0.0287 is found either by direct calculation or by referring to Chart Z (in Appendix II). To use the graph, find the sample size on the lower scale, move

CHART FOR FRACTION DEFECTIVE

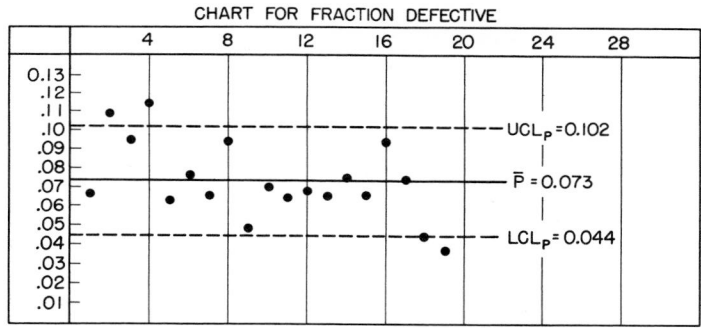

Fig 23-6 p chart for permanent magnets.

upward to the intersection with the solid diagonal line at $\bar{p}$ (interpolate to find 0.073). Then move to the left-hand scale to obtain the value of $3\sigma_p$, which is given there as 0.029. The upper limit for p is thus $\text{UCL}_p = 0.073 + 0.029 = 0.102$, and the lower limit is $\text{LCL}_p = 0.073 - 0.029 = 0.044$. The resulting control chart is shown in Figure 23-6. Note that the last sample is below the lower control limit, indicating a significantly low fraction defective. Although this might mean that there is some assignable cause resulting in better quality, such points can also be due to an inspector's accepting some defective units in error. Grant and Leavenworth (Ref. 3) gives additional examples.

Control Chart for Number of Defectives np A control chart for the number of defectives is equivalent to the control chart for p. It is a practical alternative when all samples have the same size n. It makes direct use of the count of number of defectives. See the column headed "No. defective magnets" in Table 23-9.

Formulas for control chart lines are

	Center line	Control limits
Control chart for np . . .	$n\bar{p}$	$n\bar{p} \pm 3\sqrt{n\bar{p}(1-\bar{p})}$

For small $\bar{p}$ the control chart limit formula is simplified to $n\bar{p} \pm 3\sqrt{n\bar{p}}$.

Example of Control Chart for np For the example in Table 23-9,

Center line $= n\bar{p} = 54.2$

Control limits $= n\bar{p} \pm 3\sqrt{n\bar{p}} = 54.2 \pm 3\sqrt{54.2}$

$$= 54.2 \pm 22.1 = 76.3 \text{ and } 32.1$$

The simplified formula is used because $\bar{p}$ is less than 0.10. The same subgroups are out of control on this basis as in the control chart for p (Figure 23-6). The charts are identical except for the vertical scale; so the np chart has not been reproduced. The sample sizes in this example vary slightly but are sufficiently similar to be treated as equal.

Control Chart for Defects per Unit u The control chart for u is most useful when several independent defects (they must be independent) may occur in one unit of product. This is likely to happen in complex assemblies.

The control chart lines for sample size n are

	Central line	Control limits
Control chart for u	$\bar{u}$	$\bar{u} \pm \sqrt{\dfrac{\bar{u}}{n}}$

where $\bar{u}$ is the total number of defects in all samples divided by the total number of units in all samples, that is, the defects per unit in the complete set of test results. For samples of unequal size, control limits are computed for each size separately, using a pooled value of $\bar{u}$.

Example[34] of Control Chart for u Table 23-10 gives inspection results for 25 consecutive lots of a product. The lot size was essentially constant; so a constant sample size ($n = 10$) was used. All defects were counted because two or more defects of the same or different kinds could occur on each item. The defects per unit are found by dividing the number of defects found by the sample size.

Then, for the control chart for u,

$$\text{Central line} = \bar{u} = \frac{37.5}{25} = 1.5$$

$$\text{Control limits} = \bar{u} \pm 3\sqrt{\frac{\bar{u}}{n}} = 1.50 \pm 3\sqrt{\frac{1.50}{10}}$$

$$= 1.50 \pm 1.16 = 2.66 \text{ and } 0.34$$

The control chart is given in Figure 23-7. The ninth sample is out of control. At the time this occurred, an investigation was worthwhile to turn up the reason for an excessive defect rate.

Control Chart for Number of Defects c A control chart for number of defects in a sample is the equivalent of the control chart for u. It is a practical alternative when all samples are of the same size n. It is particularly effective when the number of defects *possible* on a unit is large but the percentage for any single defect is small. Examples are physical defects such as surface irregularities, flaws, or pinholes on continuous or extensive products such as yarn, wire, paper, textiles, or other sheeted materials. The chance of a defect's occurring at any one spot may be small, but the overall opportunity for defects may be great.

The chart for c makes direct use of the count of defects. See the column headed "Total Defects in Sample c" in Table 23-10.

---

[34] Also see Section 39, under Shewhart Control Chart for Attributes. Grant and Leavenworth (Ref. 3) provides additional examples.

TABLE 23-10   Number of Defects

Sample No.	Total Defects in Sample c	Defects per Unit u
1	17	1.7
2	14	1.4
3	6	0.6
4	23	2.3
5	5	0.5
6	7	0.7
7	10	1.0
8	19	1.9
9	29	2.9
10	18	1.8
11	25	2.5
12	5	0.5
13	8	0.8
14	11	1.1
15	18	1.8
16	13	1.3
17	22	2.2
18	6	0.6
19	23	2.3
20	22	2.2
21	9	0.9
22	15	1.5
23	20	2.0
24	6	0.6
25	24	2.4
Total...	375	37.5

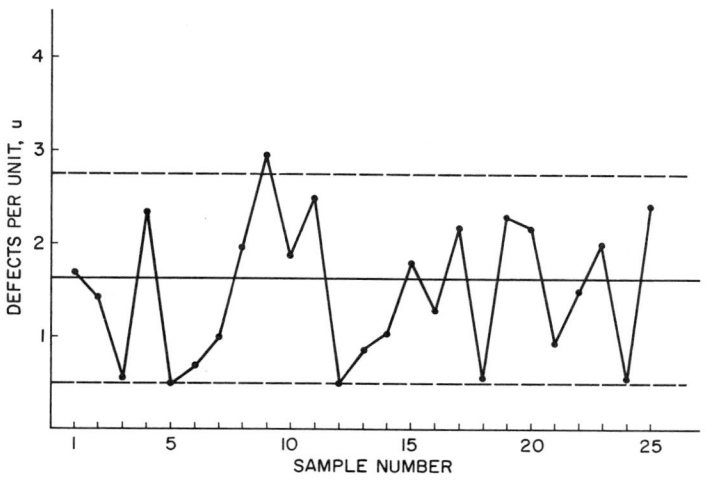

Fig. 23-7   Control chart for u.

Formulas for control chart lines are

	Central line	Control limits
Control chart for c ...	$\bar{c}$	$\bar{c} \pm 3\sqrt{\bar{c}}$

where $\bar{c}$ is the total number of defects in all samples divided by the number of samples, that is, the average number of defects per sample.

Examples of Control Charts for c For the example in Table 23-10,

$$\text{Central line} = \bar{c} = \frac{375}{25} = 15.0$$

$$\text{Control limits} = \bar{c} \pm 3\sqrt{\bar{c}} = 15.0 \pm 3\sqrt{15.0}$$

$$= 15.0 \pm 11.6 = 26.6 \text{ and } 3.4$$

The same sample, No. 9, is out of control on this chart as in the control chart for u. The charts are identical except for the vertical scale; so the c chart has not been reproduced.

TABLE 23-11. c Chart Data

Sheet number	Number of pinholes	Sheet number	Number of pinholes
1	8	14	6
2	9	15	14
3	5	16	6
4	8	17	4
5	5	18	11
6	9	19	7
7	9	20	8
8	11	21	18
9	8	22	6
10	7	23	9
11	6	24	10
12	4	25	5
13	7	Total	200

An example of the control chart for c to control defects of a sheeted material follows. Table 23-11 shows the results of a series of pinhole tests of paper intended to be impervious to oils. Specimen sheets 11 by 17 inches in size were taken from production at intervals, and colored ink was applied to one side of the sheet. Each individual inkblot which appeared on the other side of the sheet within 5 minutes was counted as a defect.

The center line of the chart is located at $\bar{c} = 200/25 = 8.0$ defects per sheet. Control limits, which are at $8.0 \pm 3 \sqrt{8.0}$, may be computed directly or found from Chart AA (in Appendix II). The average value, 8.0, is located at either the upper or lower edge of this chart. The points at which the vertical line through 8.0 crosses the solid curves are noted. The corresponding limits are found at the side of the chart. In this case, the upper 3σ limit is found at 16.5 and the lower 3σ limit at zero. The resulting c chart is pictured in Figure 23-8. Grant and Leavenworth (Ref. 3) provides additional examples.

CUMULATIVE SUM CONTROL CHARTS

Another type of control chart is the cumulative sum control chart (CSCC). A CSCC for subgroup averages is particularly well adapted to detecting abrupt changes in

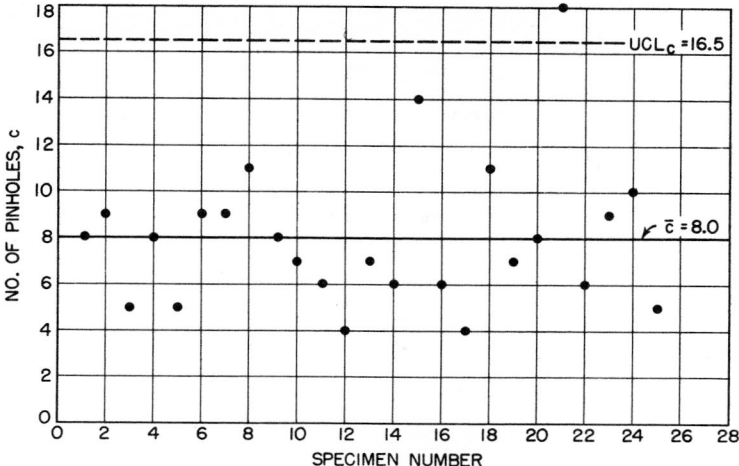

Fig. 23-8 *c* chart for pinholes in paper.

process level (shifts of about $0.5\sigma_{\bar{x}}$ to $2.0\sigma_{\bar{x}}$) that remain with the process (say for at least five sampling periods).

The distinguishing feature of CSCC is that the plotted points contain information from all the observations up to and including it. Usually, each point equals the preceding point *plus* the value of a statistic computed from the last subgroup, thus the name "Cumulative Sum." (In standard control charts, each point represents the data of one subgroup only.)

The interpretation of these charts depends on comparing plotted points with critical limits. Unlike the limits of a Shewhart control chart, which are fixed and parallel, in CSCC applications, the limits vary in position and can be applied by laying a suitably shaped mask over the chart with a fixed origin coinciding with the last plotted point.

A summary for this chart is given in Table 23-12.

As an example, the data in Table 23-13 summarize measurements from 20 subgroups of 4 each on the percent of water absorption in common building brick. The reference value R_0 was 10.0. To illustrate the CSCC, the original data were modified to introduce a decrease in the overall average of 2.0% starting with subgroup 11.

Following the procedure in Table 23-12, $\sigma_{\bar{x}}$ was estimated as

$$\frac{\bar{R}}{(d_2)\sqrt{n}} = \frac{8.08}{2.059(\sqrt{4})} = 1.96$$

It was desired to detect a process shift D of $1\sigma_{\bar{x}}$, and therefore $\delta = 1.96/1.96 = 1.0$. The conventional a for a standard $\bar{X}$ chart was selected, i.e., $a = 0.00135$. The scale factor k was defined as $2\sigma_{\bar{x}} = 2(1.96) = 3.92$, and this was rounded to 4.

From Appendix BB, read the lead distance d for the mask as 13.2. With D/k of $1.96/4$ or about 0.5, read θ (from Appendix BB) as 14°.

Figure 23-9 shows the CSCC with the mask located at subgroup 13. The mask was moved from left to right with the 0 point on the mask placed over each plotted point. For the first 12 points, the mask did not cover any of the plotted points. This meant no shift in process level. At point 13, the mask detected the shift and indicated that the shift started at about the time subgroup 10 was taken (it really started at subgroup 11).

TABLE 23-12   Summary of Control Chart for Cumulative Sum for the Average

Typical problems for application:

Controlling a process tightly by detecting moderate shifts in the average (i.e., shifts of about $0.5\sigma_{\bar{X}}$ to $2.0\sigma_{\bar{X}}$) with a minimum number of tests because of high costs of a shift or high test costs

Characteristic plotted:

Cumulative sum of deviation of subgroup averages from a reference value

Formulas for control limits:

1. Obtain an estimate of $\sigma_{\bar{X}}$.   (From $\bar{X}$ and R data, the estimate is $(\bar{R}/d_2)/\sqrt{n}$)
2. Determine the least amount of change D in the average that it is desired to detect, and calculate $\delta = D/\sigma_{\bar{X}}$.
3. Determine the probability level at which decisions are to be made.   For limits equivalent to standard control limits, $\alpha = 0.00135$
4. Define the scale factor k as the vertical scale distance per unit of the horizontal scale. Ewan (Ref. 11) recommends this be between $1\sigma_{\bar{X}}$ and $2\sigma_{\bar{X}}$ and preferably closer to $2\sigma_{\bar{X}}$.   (The horizontal scale represents subgroup number)
5. Read the lead distance d from Appendix BB.   This requires knowledge of δ
6. Calculate D/k and read the angle θ of the mask from Appendix BB.   Enter at row with $\delta = D/k$
7. Using d and θ construct the mask to define the control limits

Subgroup number:

The guidelines for $\bar{X}$ and R charts apply, but for best results Ewan (Ref. 11) suggests:

$$n = \frac{2.25s^2}{D}$$

(where s is an estimate of the population standard deviation) and an interval between subgroups of $T/6$ where T is the permissible average time before the shift of D is detected

Some common patterns of plots:

The mask is placed over the last point plotted.   If any of the previous points are covered by the mask, a process shift has occurred (the process is "out of control").   Points covered by the top of the mask means a decrease in the average; the bottom of the mask detects an increase.   The first point covered by the mask indicates the time at which the shift in average started.   If all the points are exposed by the mask, the process is considered in control

Some cautions:

1. Periodically check with an R chart to see if the standard deviation is constant before drawing conclusions on the average
2. Watch for *gradual* changes in the process average or changes that enter and leave the process (say in less than 5 sampling intervals).   These conditions are not as apparent on a cumulative sum chart as on an $\bar{X}$ chart

Statistical distribution assumption:

The population of individual measurements is distributed normally

---

Figure 23-9 also shows the standard $\bar{X}$ chart.   It would not have detected the shift on the basis of an $\bar{X}$ beyond $\pm 3\sigma_{\bar{X}}$ control limits.   However, note that by subgroup 15 the shift would be detected by 4 out of 5 successive points beyond $1\sigma_{\bar{X}}$.

A comparison of the cumulative sum chart and the standard $\bar{X}$ chart involves the concept of average run length (ARL).[35]   The ARL is the average number of sample points plotted at a specified quality level before the chart detects a shift from a previous level.   Ewan (Ref. 11) compares the ARL for the two charts for various amounts of shift in a process average.   For shifts between about $0.5\sigma_{\bar{X}}$ and $2\sigma_{\bar{X}}$, the cumulative sum chart detects the shift with roughly half the number of subgroups as

[35] The procedure for determining d and θ can reflect desired values of the average run length.   See Ewan (Ref. 11) and Bowker and Lieberman (Ref. 12, pp. 495–498).

TABLE 23-13   Data on Percent Water Absorption

Subgroup number	$\bar{X}$	$\bar{X} - 10.0$	$\Sigma(\bar{X} - 10.0)$
1	15.1	5.1	5.1
2	12.3	2.3	7.4
3	7.4	−2.6	4.8
4	8.7	−1.3	3.5
5	8.8	−1.2	2.3
6	11.7	1.7	4.0
7	10.2	0.2	4.2
8	11.5	1.5	5.7
9	11.2	1.2	6.9
10	10.2	0.2	7.1
11	7.6	−2.4	4.7
12	6.2	−3.8	0.9
13	8.2	−1.8	−0.9
14	7.8	−2.2	−3.1
15	6.8	−3.2	−6.3
16	6.1	−3.9	−10.2
17	4.3	−5.7	−15.9
18	8.5	−1.5	−17.4
19	7.7	−2.3	−19.7
20	9.7	−0.3	−20.0

Note: $\bar{R} = 8.08$

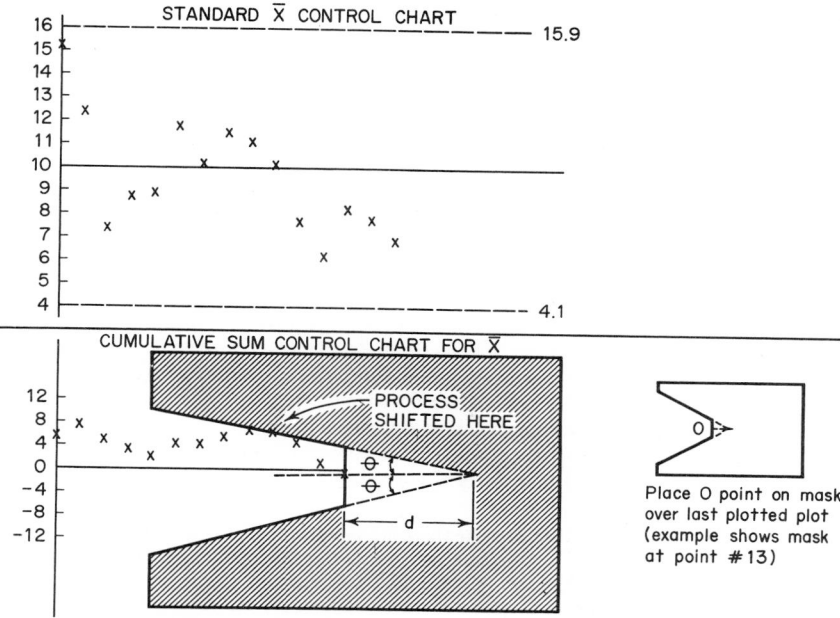

Fig. 23-9   Comparison of cumulative sum and standard control chart.

the standard $\bar{X}$ chart.[36] The standard Shewhart $\bar{X}$ seems best for large shifts (say greater than $2\sigma_{\bar{X}}$) or short-term shifts. The difficulty production people have in understanding the cumulative sum chart must also be recognized.

The discussion here has been restricted to a CSCC for the average value. Johnson and Leone (Ref. 13, pp. 320–340) provides a thorough discussion and procedures (including scale value, lead distance, and mask angle) for applying the concept to sample ranges, variances, number of defectives, fraction defective, and number of defects.

CONSTRUCTING A CONTROL CHART FOR MAINTAINING
CONTROL IN THE FUTURE (CONTROL WITH STANDARD GIVEN)

Continuing to Use the Control Charts   Most industrial processes are not in control when first analyzed by control chart methods. Therefore, it is common to find at first many points outside the control limits. It is also possible to track down the reason for some of these instances of lack of control and to take remedial action. (It is useful to mark right on the chart the explanations found for any points out of control.)

As remedies are made to a process, a new set of data should be collected, statistical control limits recalculated, and the new data plotted against these revised limits. (Even if no process changes have been knowingly made, it is a good idea to calculate the overall average value for a chart periodically, say every 25 subgroups, and compare[37] it with the previous data.)

If the originally appearing causes of variation are corrected but it is inconvenient to collect a new set of data for future limits, it is acceptable to remove the out of control subgroups from the original set of data and recalculate limits against which the next data to be acquired are plotted. The cycle of removing assignable causes and recalculating limits may be repeated[38] until the process finally shows a state of control (control is often attained by degrees). If the control band is sufficiently narrow and is positioned satisfactorily with respect to specification limits, the process is ready for the next stage, control with respect to a given standard.

Control: Standard Given   As a process is brought into control, data become available as to what is the expected level of the process and what is the expected dispersion. From these data it is possible to establish the expected range of variation for the process. This expected range of variation then becomes the standard against which subsequent samples are compared to detect the entry of significant causes of variation.

Use of the expected range of variation as a standard will detect significant changes in the process. Whether these changes would cause defects or not is quite another matter and depends on the relation of the product specification limits to the control limits.

The data from the process are the actual average values and are so designated, as

$$\text{Grand average} = \bar{\bar{X}}$$
$$\text{Average fraction defective} = \bar{p}$$
$$\text{Average number of defects} = \bar{c}, \text{ etc.}$$

If these factors are used to specify the expected future values from the process,

---

[36] The comparison gets involved because there are modifications to the standard $\bar{X}$ chart that are pertinent (see Ref. 11). Also, the cumulative sum chart is superior only for certain significance levels (see Johnson and Leone, Ref. 13, pp. 340–342).

[37] In practice, these averages are often compared without the use of any formal test, but the procedures in Section 22, under Tests of Hypothesis, could also be used.

[38] For examples of an X chart see Section 29, under Gas Absorption and Polymerization. For an $\bar{X}$ and R chart, see Juran and Gryna (Ref. 16, pp. 299–304).

then the same quantities are simply redesignated, as "standard" values, by substituting the "prime" symbol for the bar, so that

$$\text{Expected or "standard" average} = \bar{X}'$$
$$\text{Expected or standard fraction defective} = p'$$
$$\text{Expected or standard number of defectives} = c'$$

If the past data are not precisely the same as the desired standard, control limits based on the desired standard can still be set up but only if there is evidence or real reason to believe the standard value can be achieved.

These standard values are for the entire volume of material to be manufactured; i.e., they are desired population values. Since the range theoretically expected in a normal population is infinitely wide, it is necessary to adopt some other measure as the standard for dispersion. The measure σ', which is equal to $\bar{R}/d_2$ or to $\bar{\sigma}/c_2$, is customarily used.

See Table 23-14 for a full table of values and control limits.

TABLE 23-14   Chart Factors for Control with Respect to a Given Standard*

If, for the controlled process	Then, in a chart for maintaining control to a given standard		
	The central line is at	The lower-limit line is at	The upper-limit line is at
The average is $\bar{\bar{X}}$	$\bar{\bar{X}}$ (now called $\bar{X}'$)	$\bar{X}' - A\sigma'$	$\bar{X}' + A\sigma'$
The fraction defective is $\bar{p}$	$\bar{p}$ (now called p')	$p' - 3\sqrt{\dfrac{p'(1-p')}{n}}$	$p' + 3\sqrt{\dfrac{p'(1-p')}{n}}$
The number of defects is $\bar{c}$	$\bar{c}$ (now called c')	$c' - 3\sqrt{c'}$	$c' + 3\sqrt{c'}$
The number of defectives is $n\bar{p}$	$n\bar{p}$ (now called np')	$np' - 3\sqrt{np'(1-p')}$	$np' + 3\sqrt{np'(1-p')}$
The standard deviation is $\bar{\sigma}$	$\bar{\sigma}$ (now called $c_2\sigma'$)	$B_1\sigma'$	$B_2\sigma'$
The range is $\bar{R}$	$\bar{R}$ (now called $d_2\sigma'$)	$D_1\sigma'$	$D_2\sigma'$

n	A	c_2	B_1	B_2	d_2	D_1	D_2	n
2	2.121	0.5642	0	1.843	1.128	0	3.686	2
3	1.732	0.7236	0	1.858	1.693	0	4.358	3
4	1.500	0.7979	0	1.808	2.059	0	4.698	4
5	1.342	0.8407	0	1.756	2.326	0	4.918	5
6	1.225	0.8686	0.026	1.711	2.534	0	5.078	6
7	1.134	0.8882	0.105	1.672	2.704	0.205	5.203	7
8	1.061	0.9027	0.167	1.638	2.847	0.387	5.307	8
9	1.000	0.9139	0.219	1.609	2.970	0.546	5.394	9
10	0.949	0.9227	0.262	1.584	3.078	0.687	5.469	10

* More complete tables of A, B_1, B_2, D_1, and D_2, as well as charts showing values for the factors for p and c charts, are given in Appendix CC.

STATISTICAL CONTROL USING LIMITS DERIVED FROM PRODUCT SPECIFICATIONS

Comparing the Process Data with Specification Limits   An analysis of the process vs. the specification can start with one of the several methods described in Section 9, under Process Capability Measurement. For example, one method uses control chart data and estimates the standard deviation of individual measurements as simply $\bar{R}/d_2$ (where d_2 is a numerical factor) and then process capability is calculated as six standard deviations.[39] (Strictly speaking, a process should be in a state of statistical control before evaluating the capability. Two reasons: statistical control assures that the process is doing its best and is stable enough for prediction purposes.)

Once the process variation has been measured in terms of process capability, a comparison with the tolerances follows. This comparison must reflect both the variation in the process (the width of the distribution curve) and the aim of the process (the center of the curve). This is discussed in Section 9, under Process Capability Analysis.[40] Further, there are numerous situations in which a process is not in control but requires no action, since the product tolerances are being met easily; there are also numerous situations in which a process is in control but the product tolerances are not being met. Table 23-15 shows the more usual permutations encountered.

The control chart for $\bar{X}$ does not show specification limits. When the chart is used for purposes of process control (as contrasted to purposes of product acceptance[41]) it is wise *not* to include specification limits on the same chart with statistical control limits. A comparison of the two would be wrong because specification limits usually refer to *individual* measurements and control limits refer to *averages* of subgroups. As averages vary less than individual measurements comprising the averages,[42] control limits cannot be compared with specification limits.

The literature presents material on further statistical analyses to aid in deciding action based on a control chart. Taylor (Ref. 14) presents an example of deriving a rule on when to adjust a machine based on optimizing economics. Ott (Ref. 15) shows the application of the Shewhart control chart to production experimentation and particularly to the situation of examining the last k points on a chart. Evolutionary Operation[43] provides a structured approach to making process changes and evaluating results.

Conventional control charts provide control limits based solely on the observed variation of the process and therefore provide the means of detecting any change.[44]

In other instances, it is important to detect the presence of only those changes which might cause defectives. For such cases, control limits are derived from a combination of (1) the observed variation and (2) product specifications. The process is then permitted to change gradually or even abruptly (assignable causes present) as long as defectives do not become imminent. The chart gives alarm signals only when defectives threaten. One model for this approach[45] assumes that the average of the process must be kept far enough away from the specification limit to avoid defects being made.

PRE-Control

An example of the approach is the PRE-Control technique.[46] PRE-Control starts a process centered between specification limits and detects shifts that might result in

---

[39] The use of $6(\bar{R}/d_2)$ is an approximation. For other methods see Section 22, under Statistical Tolerance Limits.

[40] See particularly Figs. 9-12 through 9-15.

[41] See Section 25, under Acceptance Control Charts.

[42] See Section 22, under The Two Types of Sampling Error.

[43] See Section 27A.

[44] The control limits are supplemented by tests of randomness such as runs as described previously, under Interpretation of Control Charts.

[45] The literature often refers to "modified control limits," "reject limits," or "narrow limits" (see Grant and Leavenworth, Ref. 3, pp. 298–301). For a discussion of charts that reflect both consumer and producer risks, see Section 25, under Acceptance Control Charts.

[46] The discussion here is based on that by Arnold O. Putnam in the Second Edition of this Handbook.

TABLE 23-15   Action to Be Taken

	Product meets tolerances		Product does not meet tolerances	
	Process variation small* relative to tolerances	Process variation large* relative to tolerances	Process variation small relative to tolerances	Process variation large relative to tolerances
Process is in control	Consider cost reduction through less precise process; consider value to designer of tighter tolerances	Generally no action	Process is "misdirected" to wrong average. Generally easy to correct permanently	Process may be misdirected and also too scattered. Correct misdirection. Consider economics of more precise process vs. wider tolerances vs. sorting the product
Process is out of control	Generally no action	Investigate cause for lack of control. Decision to correct based on economics of corrective action	Process is misdirected or erratic or both. Correct misdirection. Discover cause for lack of control. Consider economics of more precise process vs. wider tolerances vs. sorting the product	

* As a rule of thumb, a process variation (sometimes called natural tolerance $= 6\sigma$) less than a third of tolerance is small; more than two-thirds of tolerance is large.

making some of the parts outside a print limit. PRE-Control requires no plotting and no computations from sample parts, and it needs only three pieces to give control information. The technique utilizes the normal distribution for the determination of significant changes in the aim or the spread of a production process — changes that could result in the increased production of defective work.

The principle of PRE-Control is demonstrated by assuming the worst condition that can be accepted from a process capable of quality production, i.e., when the natural tolerance is the same as the print allows, and when the process is precisely centered and any shift would result in some defective work.

If two PRE-Control (PC) lines are each set one-fourth of the way in from each print-tolerance limit (Figure 23-10a), then 86% of the parts will be inside the PC lines, with 7% in each of the outer sections. In other words, 7%, or 1 part in 14, will occur outside a PC line under normal circumstances.

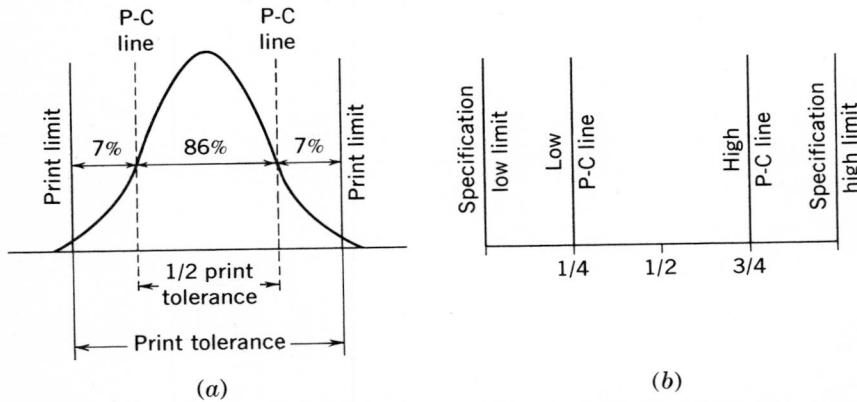

Fig. 23-10   (a) Assumptions underlying PRE-Control. (b) Location of PRE-Control lines.

The chance that two parts in a row will fall outside a PC line is $\frac{1}{14}$ times $\frac{1}{14}$, or $\frac{1}{196}$. This means that only once in about every 200 pieces will two parts in a row occur in a given outer band. When two in a row do occur, there is a much greater chance ($\frac{195}{196}$) that the process has shifted. It is advisable, therefore, to reset the process to the center. It is equally unlikely to get a piece beyond one given PC line and the next piece outside the other PC line. In this case, the indication is not that the process has shifted but that some factor has been introduced which has widened the dispersion to an extent that defective pieces are inevitable. An immediate remedy of the cause of the trouble must be made before the process can safely continue.

These principles lead to the following set of rules[47] that summarize the technique of PRE-Control:

1. Divide the specification tolerance band with PC lines at one-fourth and three-fourths of the tolerance, as in Figure 23-10b.

---

[47] This set of PRE-Control rules is the one most widely used. It applies when 1 to 3% defective is permissible and the 6σ process dispersion is a maximum of 88% of the tolerance range. For other rules covering other quality levels and process dispersion, see D. Shainin, Techniques for Maintaining a Zero Defects Program, *American Management Association Bulletin* 71, 1965; also, N. Raymond Brown, Zero Defects the Easy Way with Target Area Control, *Modern Machine Shop,* July 1966, pp. 96–100.

2. Start job.

3. If first piece is outside specification limits, reset.

4. If first piece is inside specification limit but outside a PC line, check next piece.

5. If second piece is also outside same PC line, reset.

6. If second piece is inside PC line, continue process, and reset only when two pieces in a row are outside a given PC line.

7. If two successive pieces show one to be outside the high PC line and one below the low PC line, action must be taken immediately to reduce variation.

8. When five successive pieces fall between the PC lines, "frequency gaging" may start and continue as long as the average number of checks to a reset is 25. While waiting for five, if one piece goes over a PC line, start count over again.

9. During frequency gaging, make no process adjustments until a piece exceeds a PC line. Check the very next piece and proceed as in 6 above.

10. When machine is reset, five successive pieces inside the PC lines must again be made before returning to frequency gaging.

11. If the operator checks more than 25 times without having to reset his process, his gaging frequency may be reduced so that more pieces are made between checks. If, on the other hand, he must reset before 25 checks are made, increase the gaging frequency.[48] An average of 25 checks to a reset is indication that the gaging frequency is correct.

The PRE-Control technique indicates changes in process aim and process variation. It is simple to use, can use go no-go gages, and can guarantee a specified percent defective if corrections are made when required.

Process control techniques that use narrow limits should be introduced to the shop with great care. Unless fully explained, these limits appear to be tightening up the tolerances. Such a misunderstanding is difficult to correct, and it is best to record to the narrow limits in the quality control office until shop personnel are trained in the meaning and usefulness of the limits on the shop floor.

SPECIAL CHARTING TECHNIQUES

Table 23-16 lists some of the many variations of the control charts discussed in this Section.

Some of the standard control charts assume normality. When measurements are distributed nonnormally, they can sometimes be "transformed" mathematically[49] and the transformed measurements then treated by standard control limit formulas. Cowden (Ref. 20, chap. 21) discusses this and other means of handling nonnormal measurements. Be particularly careful of special types of data such as ranks or ratios of two characteristics. Rank data are usually nonnormal. Ratios are sometimes normal but must be carefully analyzed from the viewpoint of statistical control because of possible interacting conditions between the two characteristics comprising the ratio.

STATISTICAL CONTROL OF AUTOMATED PROCESSES

Section 9, under Automatic Process Regulation, defines some of the basic approaches used in automating manufacturing processes. Section 20, Computers in Quality Control, discusses the role of computers in both automated and nonautomated processes.

---

[48] Practice has shown that it is proper to consider any single run between 21 and 29 not to differ from an *average* of 25.

[49] See Section 22, under Transformations of Data.

TABLE 23-16   Special Control Charts

Name of chart	Feature	Reference
Median	No arithmetic computations when subgroup size is odd	Grant and Leavenworth (Ref. 3, pp. 304–305)
Moving average and moving range	Has smoothing effect to emphasize trends; new average plotted with each individual measurement	Grant and Leavenworth (Ref. 3, pp. 177–182)
Geometric moving average; exponentially smoothed average	Combines successive measurements; effective in detecting small process shifts	Freund (Ref. 17), Wortham and Heinrich (Ref. 18)
Demerits	Permits weighting of defects by degree of seriousness	Grant and Leavenworth (Ref. 3, pp. 284–286); see also Section 21, under Product Auditing
Adaptive	Evaluates process data against predicted value and quantifies adjustment needed	Section 29, under Adaptive Control
T^2	One chart evaluates two or more related variables that have a joint effect on a quality characteristic	Montgomery and Wadsworth (Ref. 19)

From the viewpoint of data analysis in process control, the march toward automation has sparked these innovations:

1. Continuous reading instrumentation which yields large amounts of data on process variables and quality characteristics. Arnold (Ref. 21) and Lindstrom (Ref. 22) present examples.

2. Automation of statistical analysis (e.g., calculation of means, standard deviations, control limits). This is discussed in Section 20 and also by Toole and Klein (Ref. 23).

3. Comparison of process results with preset numerical standards. This comparison may result in *(a)* the generation of a document giving pertinent information on a nonstandard condition or *(b)* the generation of an error signal that automatically makes a process adjustment. An intriguing example is the Adaptive Control approach with its own control chart technique (see Section 29). References 21 and 23 discuss other examples. Bishop (Ref. 24) presents some principles and examples of automatic feedback control to quality problems.

These techniques are often used on the production floor ("on line") and simultaneous with production ("real time").

REFERENCES

1. Page, E. S., Comparison of Process Inspection Schemes, *Industrial Quality Control,* vol. 21, No. 5, pp. 245–249, November 1964.
2. Duncan, Acheson J., "Quality Control and Industrial Statistics," 3d ed., Richard D. Irwin, Inc., Homewood, Ill., 1965.
3. Grant, E. L., and R. S. Leavenworth, "Statistical Quality Control," 4th ed., McGraw-Hill Book Company, New York, 1972.
4. Hillier, Frederick S., $\bar{X}$- and R-Chart Control Limits Based on a Small Number of Subgroups, *Journal of Quality Technology,* vol. 1, No. 1, pp. 17–26, January 1969.
5. "Statistical Quality Control Handbook," Western Electric Company, Mack Printing Co., Easton, Pa., 1956.

6. Erdman, Eric J., Larry E. Bailey, and William C. Knowler, The Production Line SQC Helped, *Quality Progress,* vol. 2, No. 8, pp. 20–22, August 1969.
7. Bicking, Charles A., New Angles on Old Problems of Measurement and Data Analysis, *Industrial Quality Control,* vol. 22, No. 10, pp. 510–551, April 1966.
8. Hilliard, Jim E., and H. Alan Lasater, Type I Risks When Several Tests Are Used Together on Control Charts for Means and Ranges, No Standard Given, *Industrial Quality Control,* vol. 23, No. 2, pp. 56–61, August 1966.
9. Barish, Norman N., Norbert Hauser, and Sylvan Ehrenfeld, Choosing Economic Control Designs, *1969 Annual Technical Conference Transactions,* pp. 633–644, American Society for Quality Control.
10. Pollitzer, E. A., A Stabilized *p*-Chart Nomograph, *Quality Progress,* vol. 1, No. 6, pp. 9–10, June 1968.
11. Ewan, W. D., When and How to Use Cu-Sum Charts, *Technometrics,* vol. 5, No. 1, pp. 1–22, February 1963.
12. Bowker, Albert H., and Gerald J. Lieberman, "Engineering Statistics," 2d ed., Prentice-Hall, Inc., Englewood Cliffs, N.J., 1972.
13. Johnson, Norman L., and Fred C. Leone, "Statistics and Experimental Design," vol. I, John Wiley & Sons, Inc., New York, 1964.
14. Taylor, Howard M., Statistical Control of a Gaussian Process, *Technometrics,* vol. 9, No. 1, pp. 29–41, February 1967.
15. Ott, E. R., Analysis of Means—A Graphical Procedure, *Industrial Quality Control,* vol. 24, No. 2, pp. 101–109, August 1967.
16. Juran, J. M., and Frank M. Gryna, Jr., "Quality Planning and Analysis," McGraw-Hill Book Company, New York, 1970.
17. Freund, Richard A., Graphical Process Control, *Industrial Quality Control,* vol. XVIII, No. 7, pp. 15–22, January 1962.
18. Wortham, A. W., and G. F. Heinrich, Control Charts Using Exponential Smoothing Techniques, *1972 Annual Technical Conference Transactions,* pp. 451–458, American Society for Quality Control.
19. Montgomery, Douglas C., and Harrison M. Wadsworth, Jr., Some Techniques for Multivariate Quality Control Applications, *1972 Annual Technical Conference Transactions,* pp. 427–435, American Society for Quality Control.
20. Cowden, Dudley J., "Statistical Methods in Quality Control," Prentice-Hall, Inc., Englewood Cliffs, N.J., 1957.
21. Arnold, W. E., Quality Control and Digital Control Computers, *1965 Annual Technical Conference Transactions,* pp. 329–340, American Society for Quality Control.
22. Lindstrom, William M., Computer Control of a Blast Furnace Operation, *1963 Annual Technical Conference Transactions,* pp. 55–60, American Society for Quality Control.
23. Toole, Patrick A., and Robert F. Klein, On Time Quality Control, *1966 Annual Technical Conference Transactions,* pp. 835–840, American Society for Quality Control.
24. Bishop, Albert B., Automation of the Quality Function, *Industrial Quality Control,* vol. 21, No. 10, pp. 509–514, April 1965.

Section **24**

Sampling by Attributes

J. M. WIESEN

Systems Planning Staff Chairman, Sandia Laboratories

SAMPLING—COMMON CONCEPTS

Sampling inspection is conducted to learn about the quality of a lot of product, in many cases quite large, from careful examination of a small number of units of product (the sample) drawn from that lot. Most sampling is done for the purposes of lot approval or process control. However, there are other purposes, and these can be seen in Table 12-1 (of Section 12).

Attributes and Variables   The approach to sampling is quite different depending on whether the characteristics under study are:

1. Attributes, e.g., the product is in a state of good or bad; the gaging is on a basis of go or no-go.

2. Variables, i.e., the product can be evaluated along a scale of measurement.

In this Handbook, inspection by attributes is the subject of the present Section 24. Inspection by variables, including the special case of bulk sampling, is discussed in Sections 25 and 25A. However, to avoid duplication, some concepts which are common to both attributes and variables sampling will be discussed only in Section 24.

Advantages and Disadvantages of Sampling   Compared with 100% inspection, sampling has some attractive advantages:

1. Economy due to inspecting only part of the product.

2. Less handling damage during inspection.

3. Fewer inspectors, thereby simplifying the recruiting and training problem.

4. Upgrading the inspection job from monotonous piece-by-piece decisions to lot-by-lot decisions.

5. Applicability to destructive testing, with a quantified level of assurance of lot quality.

6. Rejections on vendors or shop departments of entire lots rather than mere return of the defectives, thereby providing stronger motivation for improvement.

Sampling also has some inherent disadvantages:

1. There are risks of accepting "bad" lots and of rejecting "good" lots.

2. There is added planning and documentation.

3. The sample usually provides less information about the product than does 100% inspection.

Assumptions Made in Sampling Plans   These plans commonly assume:

1. The inspectors follow the prescribed sampling plan.

2. The inspection is made without error; i.e., no human or equipment mistakes are made in measurement or in judging conformance.

In practice, these assumptions are not fully valid. See Section 12, under Inspector Errors.

Units of Product   These may consist of (1) discrete pieces or (2) specimens from bulk material, The criteria used for judging the conformance of a single unit of product to standard are somewhat different for these two categories. The criteria used for judging lot conformance differ even more widely. See, for elaboration, Section 12, under Product Acceptance Inspection, and especially Table 12-10.

Seriousness Classification of Defects   Many sampling plans set up their criteria for judging lot conformance in terms of an allowable number of defects in the sample. Since defects differ greatly in seriousness, the sampling plans must somehow take these differences into account.

Where there exists a formal plan for seriousness classification of defects (see Section 12, under Seriousness Classification), the sampling plans may be structured so that

1. A separate sampling plan is used for each seriousness class, e.g., large sample sizes for critical defects, small sample sizes for minor defects.

2. A common sampling plan is used, but the allowable number of defects varies for each class, e.g., no critical defects are allowed, but some minor defects are allowed.

3. The criteria may be established in terms of defects per hundred units, the allowable number being different for each class.

4. The criteria may be based on demerits per unit; i.e., all defects found are converted to a scale of demerits based on the classification system.

In the absence of a formal system of seriousness classification, all defects are considered equally important during the sampling inspection. However, where nonconforming lots are subsequently reviewed to judge fitness for use, the review board gives consideration to the seriousness of the defects.

Lot Formation   The general approach to lot formation is discussed in Section 12, under The Nature of Lots of Product. While most acceptance sampling plans can be validly applied regardless of how lots are formed (skip-lot plans are an exception), the economics of inspection and the quality of the accepted product are greatly influenced by the manner of lot formation.

The interrelation of lot formation to economics of inspection is discussed in Section 12, under How Much Inspection? and will not be elaborated here. The interrelation of lot formation to quality of accepted product can be seen from a single example.

Ten machines are producing the same product. Nine of these produce perfect product. The tenth machine produces 100% defectives. If lots consist of product from single machines, the defective product from the tenth machine will always be detected by sampling. If, however, the lots are formed by mixing up the work from all machines, then it is inevitable that some defects will get through the sampling plan.

The fact that lot formation so strongly influences outgoing quality and inspection economics has led to some guidelines for lot formation.

1. Do not mix product from different sources (processes, production shifts, input materials, etc.), unless there is evidence that the lot-to-lot variation is small enough to be ignored.

2. Do not accumulate product over extensive periods of time (for lot formation).

3. Do make use of extraneous information (process capability, prior inspections, etc.) in lot formation. (See in this connection, Section 12, under How Much Inspection?) Such extraneous information is especially useful when product is submitted in isolated lots, or in very small lots. In such cases the extraneous information may provide better knowledge on which to base an acceptance decision than the sampling data.

4. Do make lots as large as possible consistent with the above to take advantage of low proportionate sampling costs. (Sample sizes do not increase greatly despite large increases in lot sizes.)

When production is continuous (e.g., the assembly line) so that the "lot" is necessarily arbitrary, the sampling plans used are themselves designed to be of a "continuous" nature. These Continuous Sampling Plans are discussed later in these Sections.

Lot-by-Lot Inspection   When product is submitted in a series of lots (termed lot-by-lot) the acceptance sampling plans are defined in terms of

N = lot size

n = sample size

c = acceptance number, i.e., the allowable number of defects in the sample

r = rejection number

When more than one sample per lot is specified, the successive sample sizes are designated as n_1, n_2, n_3, etc. The successive acceptance numbers are c_1, c_2, c_3, etc. The successive rejection numbers are r_1, r_2, r_3, etc.

Single Sampling, Double Sampling, and Multiple Sampling   In single-sampling plans, the decision to accept or reject a lot is based on the results of inspection of a single group of units drawn from the lot. In double-sampling plans, a smaller initial sample is usually drawn, and a decision to accept or reject is reached on the basis of this

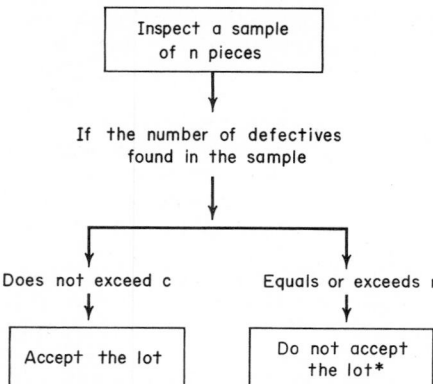

Fig. 24-1 Schematic operation of single sampling. Asterisk means that in practice the lot may be repaired, junked, etc. Sampling tables usually assume that the lot is detail-inspected and that the defective pieces are all repaired or replaced by good pieces.

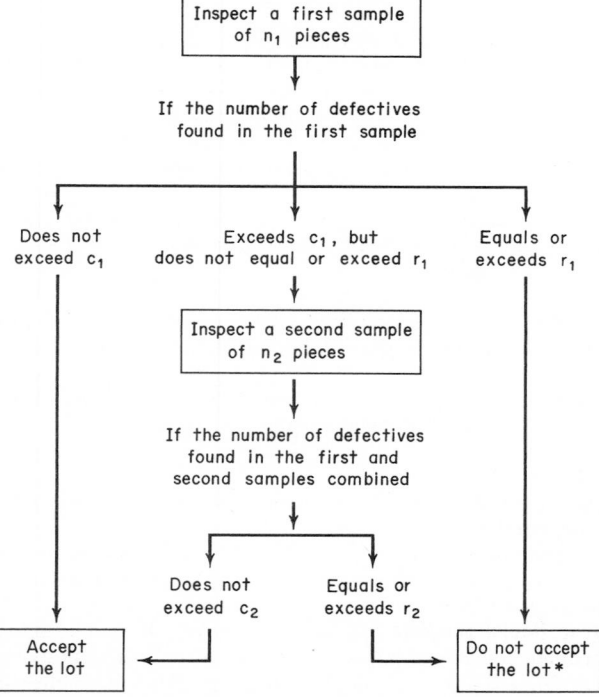

Fig. 24-2 Schematic operation of double sampling. Asterisk means inspect the remainder of the pieces, replacing or repairing defective pieces.

smaller first sample if the number of defectives is either quite large or quite small. A second sample is taken if the results of the first are not decisive. Since it is necessary to draw and inspect the second sample only in borderline cases, the average number of pieces inspected per lot is generally smaller with double sampling. In multiple-sampling plans, one, or two, or several still smaller samples of n individual items are taken (usually truncated after some number of samples) until a decision to accept or reject is obtained. (The term "sequential-sampling plan" is generally used when a decision is possible after each individual unit has been inspected.) The operating instructions for the three types of plans are shown schematically in Figures 24-1, 24-2, and 24-3.

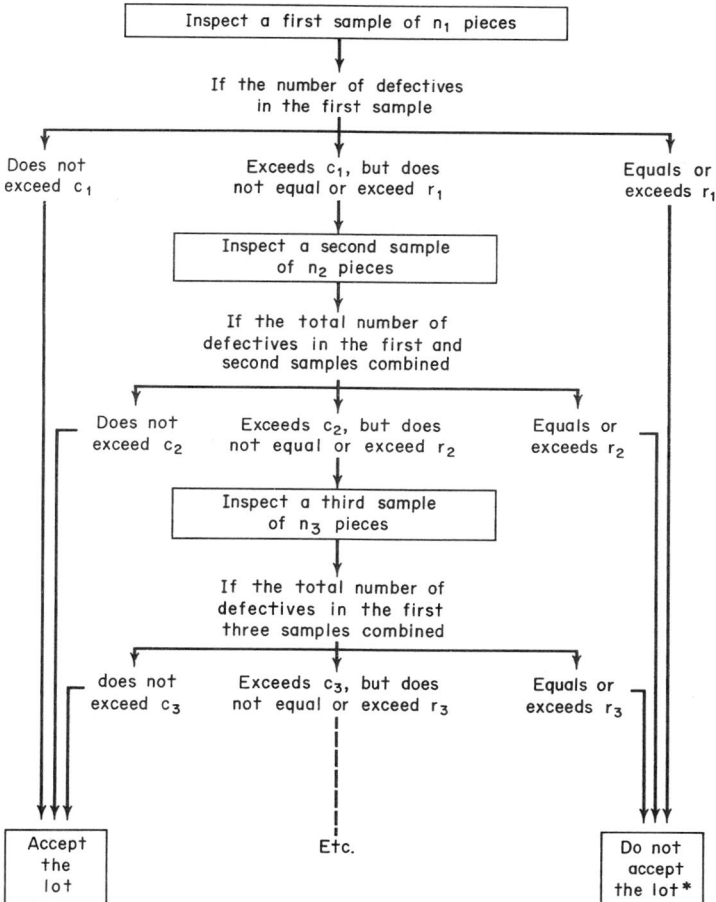

Inspect a first sample of n_1 pieces

If the number of defectives in the first sample

Does not exceed c_1 | Exceeds c_1, but does not equal or exceed r_1 | Equals or exceeds r_1

Inspect a second sample of n_2 pieces

If the total number of defectives in the first and second samples combined

Does not exceed c_2 | Exceeds c_2, but does not equal or exceed r_2 | Equals or exceeds r_2

Inspect a third sample of n_3 pieces

If the total number of defectives in the first three samples combined

does not exceed c_3 | Exceeds c_3, but does not equal or exceed r_3 | Equals or exceeds r_3

Accept the lot | Etc. | Do not accept the lot*

Fig. 24-3 Schematic operation of multiple sampling. Asterisk means some of these plans continue to the "bitter end," i.e., the taking of samples continues if necessary until the lot is fully inspected, unless the plan has meanwhile "made up its mind." Other plans, described as "truncated," are designed to force a decision after a certain number of inconclusive samples have been examined.

In general, all three sampling schemes can be planned to give lots of specified qualities nearly the same chance of being accepted; i.e., the operating characteristic curves, to be described later, can be made quite similar if desired. However, the best type of plan for one producer or product is not necessarily best for another. The suitability of a plan can be judged by considering the following factors:

1. Average number of parts inspected
2. Cost of administration
3. Information obtained as to lot quality
4. Acceptability of plan to producers

The advantages and disadvantages of the three forms of sampling plans are tabulated in Table 24-1. All these features should be taken into account in selection of a plan. For example, in cases where the cost of inspection of each piece is substantial,

TABLE 24-1   Comparative Advantages and Disadvantages of Single, Double, and Multiple Sampling

Feature	Single sampling	Double sampling	Multiple sampling
Acceptability to producer	Psychologically poor to give only one chance of passing the lot	Psychologically adequate	Psychologically open to criticism as being indecisive
Number of pieces inspected per lot	Generally greatest	Usually (but not always) 10 to 50% less than single sampling	Generally (but not always) less than doubling sampling by amounts of the order of 30%
Administration cost* in training, personnel, records, drawing and identifying samples, etc.	Lowest	Greater than single sample	Greatest
Information about prevailing level of quality in each lot	Most	Less than single sample	Least

*This is not to be confused with total cost of inspection, which includes administration cost of the plan.

the reduction in number of pieces inspected may justify use of multiple sampling despite its greater complexity and higher administrative costs. On the other hand, single sampling may be preferable if the cost of training personnel or the selecting, unpacking, and handling of parts is appreciable. Still further, double-sampling plans have been demonstrated to be simple to use in a wide variety of conditions, economical in total cost, and acceptable psychologically to both producer and consumer.

The practicability of using multiple-sampling schemes can be increased where circumstances permit the same plan to be used repeatedly. Practical aids such as special parts trays or special data sheets can be used to simplify the inspector's work.

SELECTING THE SAMPLE

The results of sampling are greatly influenced by the method of selecting the sample. In acceptance sampling, the sample "should be representative of the lot." In those cases where the inspector has knowledge of how the lot was formed, he can use this knowledge in selecting the sample by stratification (see below). Lacking this knowledge, the correct approach is to use random sampling.

Random Sampling   All published sampling tables are prepared on the assumption that samples are drawn at random; i.e., at any one time each of the remaining uninspected units of product has an equal chance of being the next unit selected for the sample. To conduct random sampling requires that (1) random numbers be generated and (2) these random numbers be applied to the product at hand.

Random numbers are available in prefabricated form in tables of random numbers (Appendix II, Table DD). One uses such a table by entering it at random (without "looking") and then proceeding in some chosen direction (up, down, right, left, etc.) to obtain random numbers for use. Numbers which cannot be applied to the product arrangement are discarded.

Random numbers may also be generated by various mechanical devices. These include:

1. A bowl of numbered chips or marbles. After mixing, one is withdrawn and its number recorded. It is then replaced and the bowl is again mixed before the next number is withdrawn.

2. Random number dice. One form is the icosahedron (20-sided) dice. There are three of these, each of a different color, one for units, one for tens, and one for hundred. (Each die has the numbers from 0 to 9 appearing twice.) Hence one throw of the three dice displays a random number within 000 to 999. (Available from Japanese Standards Association and distributed by R. Wachniak, Milwaukee, Wis. 53222.)

3. Still other techniques, for example, the random sampling bulb (Ref. 1).

Once the random numbers are available, they must still be adapted to the form in which the product is submitted. For systematically packed material, the container system can be numbered to correspond to the system of random numbers. For example, a lot might be submitted in 8 trays, each of which has 10 rows and 7 columns. In such a case, the trays might be numbered from 0 to 7, the rows from 0 to 9, and the columns from 0 to 6. Then, using three-digit random numbers, the digits are assigned to trays, rows, and columns, respectively.

For bulk packed materials, other practical procedures may be used. In the case of small parts, they may be strewn onto a flat surface which is marked with grid lines in a 10×10 arrangement. Based on two-digit random numbers, the cell at the intersection of these digits is identified. Within the cell, further positional identity can be correlated with a third digit.

For fluid or well-mixed bulk products, the fluidity obviates the need for random numbers, and the sample may be taken from "here and there."

Stratification of Samples   When the "lots" are known to come from different machines, production shifts, operators, etc., the product is actually multiple lots which have been arbitrarily combined. In such cases, the sampling is deliberately stratified; i.e., an attempt is made to draw the sample proportionately from each true lot. However, within each lot, randomness is still the appropriate basis for sampling.

A further departure from randomness may be due to the economics of opening containers, i.e., whether to open few containers and examine many pieces from each, or to open many containers and examine few pieces from each. See, for elaboration, Section 25A.

Sampling Bias   Unless rigorous procedures are set up for sampling at random and/or by stratification, the sampling can deteriorate into a variety of biases which are detrimental to good decision making. The more usual biases consist of:

1. Sampling from the same location in all containers, racks, or bins.

2. Previewing the product and selecting only those units which appear to be defective (or nondefective).

3. Ignoring those portions of the lot which are inconvenient to sample.

4. Deciding on a pattern of stratification in the absence of knowledge of how the lot was made up.

The classical example is the legendary inspector who always took his samples from the four corners and center of each tray and the legendary production operator who very carefully filled these same spots with perfect product.

Because the structured sampling plans do assume randomness, and because some forms of sampling bias can significantly distort the product acceptance decisions, all concerned should be alert to plan the sampling to minimize these biases. Thereafter, the supervision and auditing should be alert to assure that the actual sampling conforms to these plans.

SAMPLING RISKS AND PARAMETERS

When acceptance sampling is conducted, the real parties of interest are the producer (vendor or Production Department) and the consumer,[1] i.e., the company which buys from the vendor or the department which is to use the product. Since sampling carries the risk of rejecting "good" lots and of accepting "bad" lots, with associated serious consequences, producers and consumers have gone far to standardize the concepts of what constitutes good and bad lots, and to standardize also the risks associated with sampling. These risks are stated in conjunction with one or more parameters, i.e., quality indices for the plan.

Producer's Risk   The Producer's Risk α is the probability that a "good" lot will be rejected by the sampling plan. In some plans, this risk is fixed at 0.05; in other plans, it varies from about 0.01 to 0.10. The risk is stated in conjunction with a numerical definition of "good" quality such as an Acceptable Quality Level.

Acceptable Quality Level (AQL)   The AQL is the maximum percent defective (or maximum number of defects per hundred units) that, for the purpose of sampling inspection, can be considered satisfactory as a process average (Ref. 2). A sampling plan should have a low Producer's Risk for quality which is equal to or better than the AQL.

Consumer's Risk   The Consumer's Risk β is the probability that a "bad" lot will be accepted by the sampling plan. The risk is stated in conjunction with a numerical definition of "bad" quality such as a Lot Tolerance Percent Defective.

Lot Tolerance Percent Defective (LTPD)   The LTPD is the level of defectiveness that is unsatisfactory and therefore should be rejected by the sampling plan. A Consumer's Risk of 0.10 is common and LTPD has been defined as the lot quality for which the probability of acceptance is 0.10; i.e., 10% of such lots will be accepted. [LTPD is a special case of the concept of Limiting Quality (LQ) or Rejectable Quality Level (RQL). The latter terms are used in tables that provide plans for several values of the Consumer's Risk as contrasted to a value of 0.10 for the LTPD.]

A third type of quality index, Average Outgoing Quality Limit, incorporates another assumption and will be discussed later in this Section.

The Producer's and Consumer's Risks and associated AQL and LTPD are summarized graphically by an operating characteristic curve.

OPERATING CHARACTERISTIC (OC) CURVE

For attributes sampling plans, the OC curve is a graph of lot fraction defective vs. the probability that the sampling plan will accept the lot.

Figure 24-4a shows an ideal OC curve for a case where it is desired to accept all lots 3% defective or less and reject all lots having a quality level greater than 3%

---

[1] The word "consumer" as used here and in "Consumer's Risk" (see below) refers to the buying company and *not* to "small users." There are historical reasons for this terminology, which remains in use.

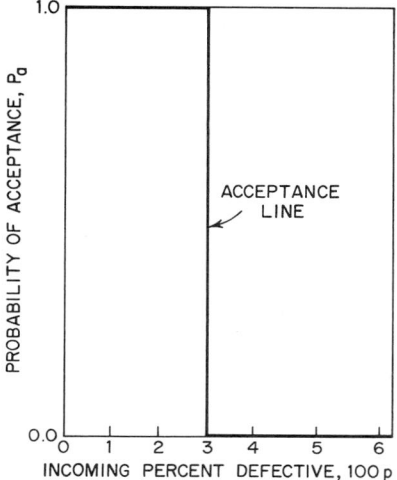

Fig. 24-4a   An ideal sampling plan performance.

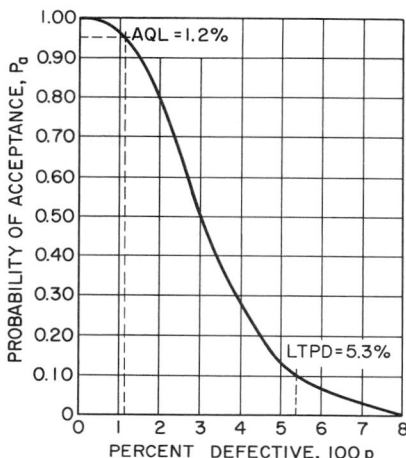

Fig. 24-4b   An actual sampling plan performance.

defective. Note that all lots less than 3% defective have a probability of acceptance of 1.0 (certainty); all lots greater than 3% defective have a probability of acceptance of 0. Actually, however, no sampling plan exists that can discriminate perfectly; there always remains some risk that a "good" lot will be rejected or that a "bad" lot will be accepted. The best that can be achieved in practice is to control these risks.

Figure 24-4b shows the curve of behavior that would be obtained if an inspector were instructed to take a sample of 150 pieces from a large lot and to accept the lot if he found no more than 4 defective pieces.

It is seen from this curve that a lot 3% defective has one chance in two of being accepted. However, a lot 3.5% defective, though technically a "bad" lot, has 39 chances in 100 of being accepted. (The probability of 0.39 applies only when and if a quality level of 3.5% is submitted. As this is "bad" quality, relatively few such lots should be submitted by the producer. Therefore, only 39% of the few bad lots submitted will be accepted.) In like manner, a lot 2.5% defective, though technically a good lot, has 34 chances in 100 of *not* being accepted.

Actually the lack of a sharp distinction may not be too serious. Economically, it may be a matter of indifference whether a lot 3% defective is accepted or sorted. In the case of lots 2.5 or 3.5% defective it makes a difference, but the difference may not be great in relation to the cost of trying for greater precision, and in view of the imponderables which are still present in computing break-even points.

The effect of parameters of the sampling plan on the shape of the OC curve is demonstrated in Figure 24-5, where the curve for perfect discrimination is given along with the curves for three particular acceptance sampling plans. The following statements summarize the effects:

1. When the sample size approaches the lot size or, in fact, approaches a large percentage of the lot size, and the acceptance number is chosen appropriately, the OC curve approaches the perfect OC curve (the rectangle at p_1).

2. When the acceptance number is zero, the OC curve is exponential in shape, concave upward (see curves 2 and 3).

3. As the acceptance number increases, the OC curve is pushed up, so to speak,

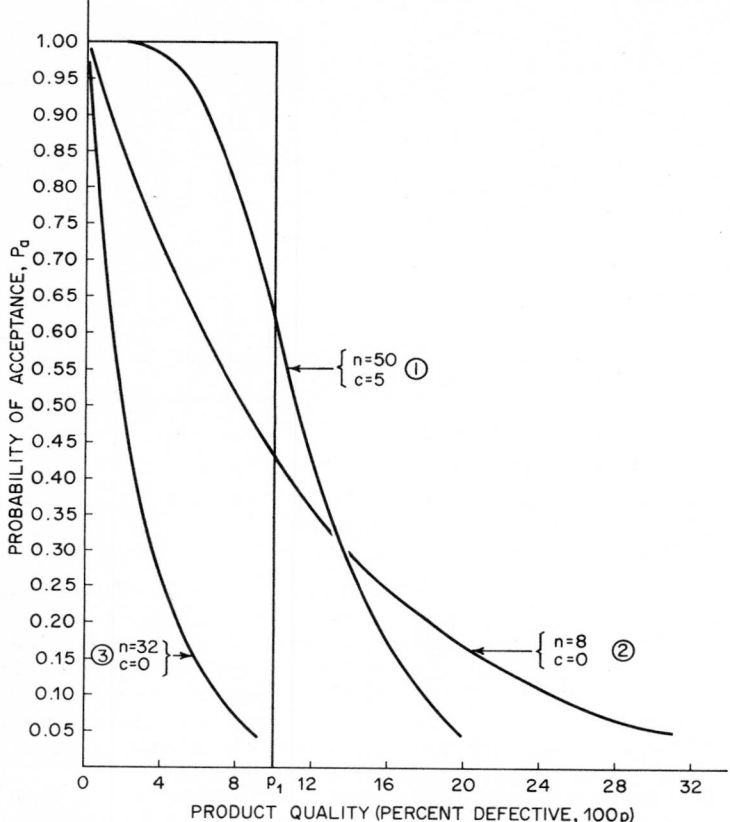

Fig. 24-5 Shape of the OC curve.

for low values of p, and the probability of acceptance for these quality levels is increased, with a point of inflection at some larger value of p (see curve 1).

4. Increasing the sample size and the acceptance number together gives the closest approach to the perfect discrimination OC curve (see curve 1).

It is sometimes useful to distinguish between type A and type B OC curves (Ref. 3, pp. 56–59). Type A curves give the probability of acceptance for an individual lot that comes from finite production conditions that cannot be assumed to continue in the future. Type B curves assume that each lot is one of an infinite number of lots produced under essentially the same production conditions. In practice, most OC curves are viewed as type B. With the few exceptions noted, this Section assumes type B OC curves.

CONSTRUCTING THE OC CURVE

The OC curve can usually be constructed based on the graphical summary of the Poisson distribution (Appendix II, Chart E). The procedure is illustrated in Figure 24-6. A value of fraction defective p is assumed and multiplied by the sample size n

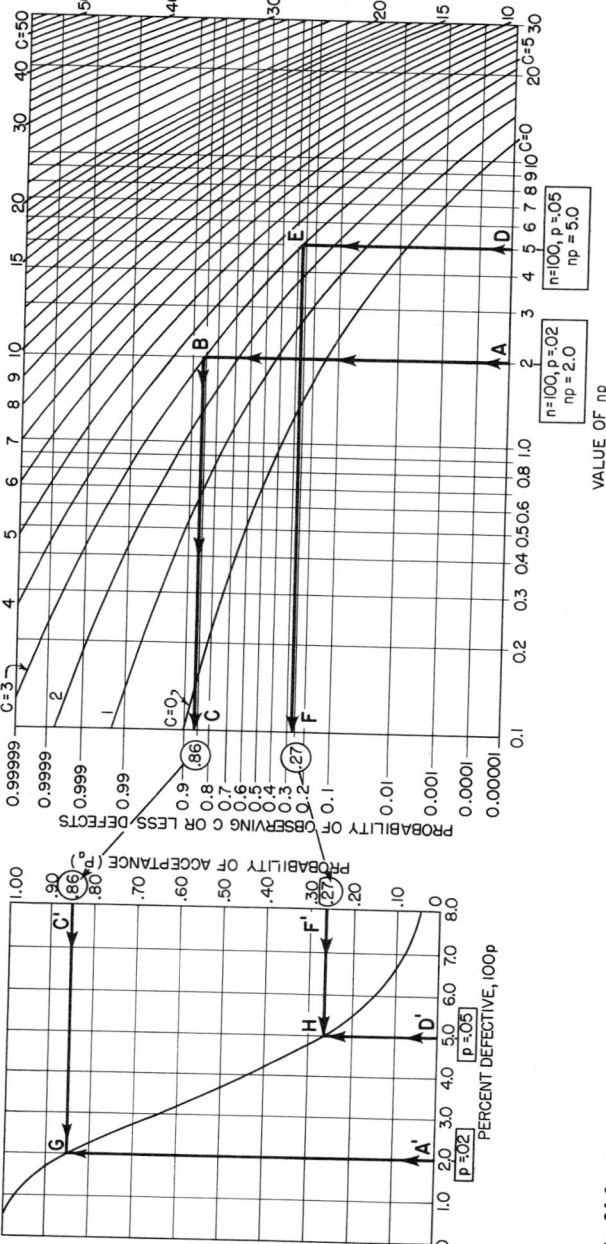

Fig. 24-6 Procedure for obtaining the operating characteristic curve. Sample $(n) = 100$; allowable number of defects in the sample $(c) = 3$.

and the product np located on the horizontal scale of the chart. The curve for the allowable number of defectives in the sample is then intersected and the probability value read on the vertical axis. This gives the probability of c or fewer defectives in a sample of n from a lot with a fraction defective p. This is the probability of acceptance. The procedure is repeated for several values of p until the complete OC curve is obtained.

The Poisson distribution is used here as an approximation to the binomial and hypergeometric distributions. These distributions are defined and illustrative OC curve calculations given in Section 22. For reasonable accuracy in using the Poisson and binomial, the lot size should be at least ten times the sample size. Furthermore, use of the Poisson requires that p be small, say less than 0.10. Use of the hypergeometric is free of both these assumptions. Type A OC curves should be constructed using the hypergeometric, although the binomial may be a good approximation.

Selection of a Sampling Plan to Pass through Two Points   In practice, existing sampling tables can usually provide plans which meet a required Producer's Risk (and corresponding AQL) and a required Consumer's Risk (and corresponding LTPD). When this is not possible, a sampling plan can easily be devised to pass through the two points on an OC curve. This is discussed by Burr (Ref. 4, pp. 319–320). Cameron (Ref. 5) also gives tables for constructing such plans. The method, based on the Poisson distribution, provides a good first cut for an exact derivation of a single sampling plan.

Selection of an AQL   The AQL cannot be set scientifically and hence must be set by bargaining or arbitrarily. (An exception, discussed below, is the determination on the basis of internal costs.) In concept, the AQL represents a balance point between (1) the cost of achieving a better quality level (increased vendor's inspection, additional controls, more precise manufacturing equipment) and (2) the cost of permitting a worse level (assembly rejections, wasted product, increased downtime). In practice, the AQL is a compromise between vendor capability and buyer requirements.

Although these costs are not easy to determine, it is possible to find an approximate break-even point for the cost of accepting a defective vs. the cost of inspection. This can then be compared with a vendor's capability and a final value reached by bargaining to reflect past vendor performance and industry standards. In some cases, an AQL may be set arbitrarily on a trial basis until performance data are available to establish a permanent value.

Selection of an AQL on the Basis of Cost.   A break-even point can be determined which balances the cost of finding and correcting a defective against the loss incurred if a defective slips through an inspection procedure (see also Section 12, under Product Acceptance Criteria). Enell (Ref. 6) has shown that the break-even equation is

$$A = R = \frac{I}{p} + C$$

where A = unit cost of acceptance (damage done by a defective piece which slips through inspection)
I = cost of inspecting one piece
C = cost of repairing or replacing a defective once found
p = (unknown) fraction defective in the lot
R = unit cost of rejection (cost of finding a defective in a rejected lot, plus expense of correcting it)

If the cost C to replace the piece is small compared with A, the damage done by a defective, then the break-even fraction defective p_b is approximately

$$p_b = \frac{I}{A} = \frac{\text{cost to inspect one piece}}{\text{damage done by one defective}}$$

Theoretically, lots having a quality level less than p_b should be accepted without sorting; lots having a level greater than p_b should be sorted and the defectives corrected. The variability in quality from lot to lot is an important factor in deciding the amount of inspection. If past history shows that the quality level is much better than the break-even point and is stable from lot to lot, little if any inspection may be needed. If the level is much worse than the break-even point, and consistently so, it will usually be cheaper to use 100% inspection rather than sample. If the quality is at neither of these extremes, then sampling will pay for itself. Thus, the AQL should generally be less than the break-even point.

For example, suppose the unit inspection cost for pieces of mica film is 0.1 cent and the damage done by a defective slipping through is 10 cents. Then $p_b = 0.1/10 = 0.01 = 1\%$.

As a 1% defective quality level is the break-even point between sorting and sampling, the appropriate sampling plan should provide for a lot to have a 50% probability of being sorted or sampled; i.e., the probability of acceptance for the plan should be 0.50 at a 1% defective quality level. Suppose the mica is submitted in lots of 15,000 pieces. The operating characteristic curves in a set of sampling tables such as MIL-STD-105D (Ref. 7), Inspection Level 2, Code Letter M, can now be examined to determine an AQL. Examination of these operating characteristic curves shows the plan closest to having a P_a of 0.50 for a 1% level is about midway between the plans with AQL of 0.40 and 0.25. Either of these, but preferably the one with the lower AQL, is the plan to adopt.[2]

Average Outgoing Quality Limit (AOQL)   The Acceptable Quality Level (AQL) and Lot Tolerance Percent Defective (LTPD) have been cited as two common quality indices for sampling plans. A third commonly used index is the Average Outgoing Quality Limit (AOQL). The AOQL is the worst, or "limit" of average quality of outgoing product including accepted lots and rejected lots which have been screened.

The AOQL concept stems from the relationship between the fraction defective before inspection (incoming quality) and the fraction defective after inspection (outgoing quality) when inspection is nondestructive and rejected lots are screened. When incoming quality is perfect, outgoing quality must likewise be perfect. However, when incoming quality is very bad, outgoing quality will also be perfect, because the sampling plan will cause all lots to be rejected and detail inspected. Thus at either extreme—incoming quality very good or very bad—the outgoing quality will tend to be very good. It follows that between these extremes is the point at which the percent of defectives in the outgoing material will reach its maximum. This point is known as the AOQL.

If p is incoming quality, P_r is the probability of lot rejection, and all rejected lots are screened and made free of defects (i.e., 0%), then

$$\text{AOQ} = (p)P_a + (0)P_r = (p)P_a$$

This calculation assumes that all defective units identified in the samples from accepted lots are retained in the lots while all defective units in rejected lots are identi-

---

[2] For a discussion of other approaches to setting an AQL on the basis of cost see Cecil Peterson, Selecting a Product Quality Level, *Industrial Engineering*, August 1970, pp. 23–26.

TABLE 24-2 Computations for Average Outgoing Quality Limit (AOQL)
For this example, $n = 78$, $c = 1$

Incoming quality fraction defective $= p$	np	Probability of acceptance $= P_a$	Average outgoing quality (AOQ) $= p \times P_a$
0.005	0.39	0.940	0.00470
0.010	0.78	0.820	0.00820
0.015	1.17	0.680	0.01020
0.020	1.56	0.550	0.01100*
0.025	1.95	0.430	0.01075
0.030	2.34	0.330	0.00990
0.035	2.73	0.250	0.00875
0.040	3.12	0.190	0.00760
0.045	3.51	0.140	0.00630
0.050	3.90	0.100	0.00500
0.055	4.29	0.075	0.00402
0.060	4.68	0.050	0.00300

* AOQL $\cong$ maximum AOQ $\cong 0.01100 = 1.1\%$.

fied[3] and either repaired or replaced by nondefective units. No account is taken of the change in outgoing quality if, e.g., the defective units are simply discarded. Other actions can require other modifications to the formula. Burr (Ref. 4, pp. 307–311) discusses this in some detail. In most cases, especially when the ratio of sample size to lot size is small, the above formula is adequate.

Table 24-2 shows a calculation for a specific sampling plan to demonstrate this principle (Figure 24-7 was used to find the value of P_a).

Figure 24-8 shows graphically the manner in which the curve of the average out-going quality begins at zero, rises as incoming quality gets worse, and then falls again as the incoming quality gets still worse.

From the viewpoint of the consumer, a plan affords its least protection if the average incoming quality $\overline{p}$ happens to be the one beneath the crest of the curve. Generally, the AOQL is about one-half the incoming quality level which yields the AOQL. For sampling to be economical, the average quality should be no worse than the AOQL.

Average Sample Number (ASN) and Average Total Inspection (ATI) The ASN is the average number of units inspected per lot in sampling inspection ignoring

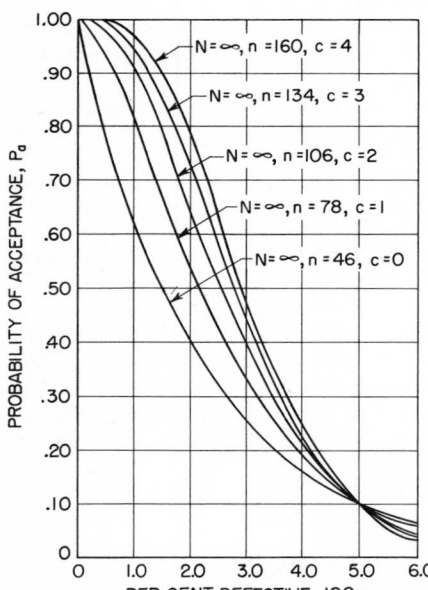

Fig. 24-7 Family of sampling plans each having LTPD = 0.05.

[3] For a discussion of the effect of inspection errors on AOQL see A. H. Jaehn and R. S. Bingham, Jr., Decision Rules for Inefficient Sorting, *Annual Technical Conference Transactions*, pp. 311–318, American Society for Quality Control, 1972.

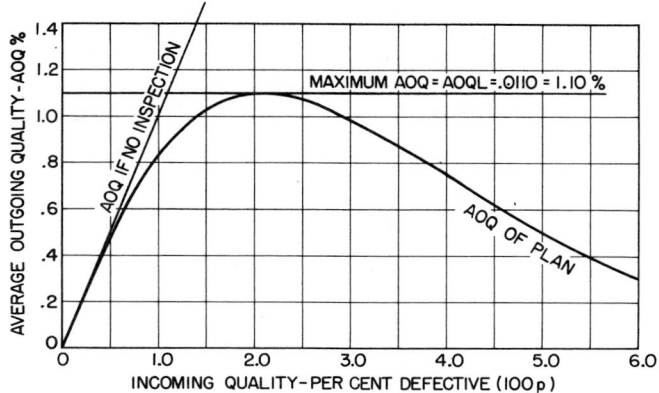

Fig. 24-8   AOQ curve and AOQL for a typical sampling plan.

the 100% inspection of rejected lots. In single-sampling inspection the ASN is equal to n, the lot sample size.   However, in double- and multiple-sampling plans the probability of not reaching a decision on the initial sample and consequently being forced to inspect a second, third, etc., sample must be considered.   Suppose a double sampling plan has sample sizes n_1 and n_2.   Let P_{a1} be the probability of accepting the submitted lot on the first sample and P_{r1} the probability of rejecting the submitted lot on the first sample.   Then $(1 - P_{a1} - P_{r1})$ is the probability of requiring a second sample, and the average sample number then is $\text{ASN} = n_1 + (1 - P_{a1} - P_{r1})n_2$, since a decision will always be reached at the end of the second sample.   This assumes complete inspection of all samples drawn regardless of when a decision to accept or reject can be made.[4]   Likewise, if n_1, n_2, n_3, . . . , n_k are the k sample sizes for a multiple-sampling plan and P_{ai} and P_{ri}, $i = 1, 2, . . . , k$, are the probability of acceptance and rejection, respectively, on the k samples conditioned by the probability of no decision on a prior sample, the ASN can be computed by a simple extension of the technique used for the double-sampling plan.   The formula will not be derived here.

The comparison for some specific plans is shown in Figure 24-9.   (The calculations assume that all samples selected are completely inspected.)   As indicated, double and multiple sampling generally lead to economies over single sampling when quality is either very good or very poor.   In this illustration, when p is equal to 0.03 to 0.04 double sampling offers little advantage while the multiple-sampling plan ASN peaks but still offers considerable advantage.   There are instances where the ASN curves for double- and multiple-sampling plans peak above the single-sample plan line defining a region of incoming quality where single sampling is most economical.

The Average Total Inspection (ATI) takes into account the likelihood of 100% inspection of rejected lots when this is possible; i.e., inspection is nondestructive.   The lot size N must now be taken into account.   Again with single-sampling plans

---

[4] In order to obtain adequate information on the process average quality, the custom is always to inspect the first sample completely in double and multiple plans but to curtail inspection as soon as a decision can be made on later samples.   This means the actual ASN will generally be lower than that given by the formulas here.   For the extent of this reduction see Burr (Ref. 4, pp. 311–313).

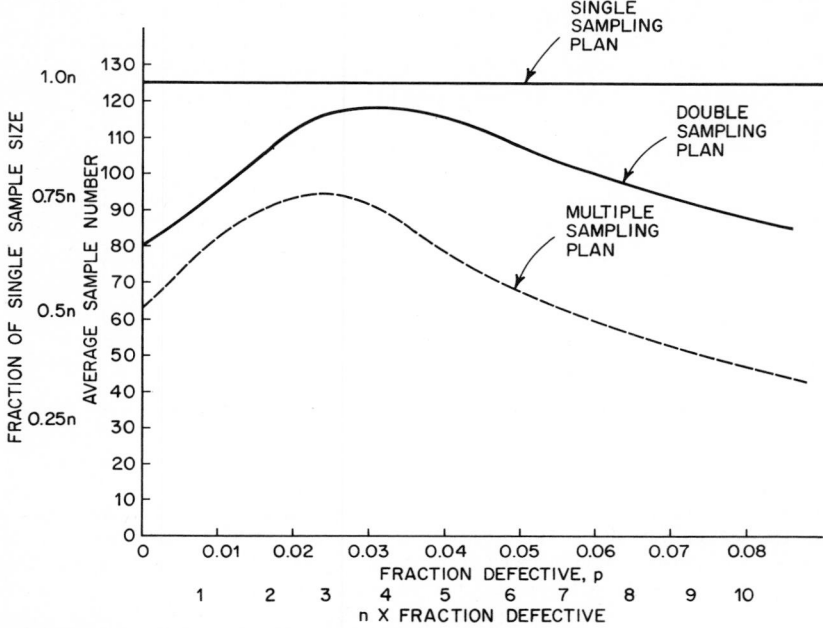

Fig. 24-9 Average sample number vs. fraction defective.

with sample size n, lot size N, probability of acceptance P_a, and probability of rejection P_r,

$$\text{ATI} = P_a n + P_r N$$

An extension to double sampling is simply

$$\text{ATI} = P_{a1} n_1 + P_{r1} N + (1 - P_{a1} - P_{r1})\big[P_{a2}(n_1 + n_2) + P_{r2}(N)\big]$$

where the symbols are defined as before. Extension to multiple-sampling plans of k levels is straightforward and will not be derived here.

Minimum Inspection per Lot I_m Minimum inspection per lot, for a given type of protection, can be illustrated by the following example.

Assume that a consumer establishes acceptance criteria as an LTPD of 0.05. A great many sampling plans meet this criterion. Some of these plans are:

Take from each lot a sample n of	Accept the lot if the number of defectives does not exceed the maximum acceptance number c
46	0
78	1
106	2
134	3
160	4

Figure 24-7 shows the corresponding operating characteristic curves. Each plan has an LTPD of 0.05; i.e., the probability of acceptance of a submitted inspection lot with fraction defective of 0.05 is 0.10. Which plan should be used? One logical

TABLE 24-3   Computation of Minimum Inspection per Lot for 5 Alternative n-c Combinations Appropriate to Lots of $N = 1,000$ Articles

All plans have the same lot tolerance percent defective.   Incoming material has a process average percent defective, $\overline{p} = 0.5\%$.

Sample size n	Allowable number of defects c	Probability of acceptance by sampling P_a	Probability of inspecting residue of lot $1 - P_a$	Average no. pieces inspected		
				In sample* n	In rest of lot† $(N - n) \times (1 - P_a)$	Total inspected per lot
46	0	0.795	0.205	46	196	242
78	1	0.940	0.060	78	55	133
106	2	0.983	0.017	106	15	121‡
134	3	0.995	0.005	134	4	138
160	4	0.998	0.002	160	2	162

* The sample size indicates the number inspected from each lot.

† The size of the uninspected residue of the lot, multiplied by the probability that it will have to be inspected because of rejection of the sample.

‡ This is the minimum sought.

basis for choosing among these plans is to use that one which gives the least inspection per lot.

The total number of units inspected consists of (1) the sample which is inspected for each lot and (2) the remaining units which must be inspected in those lots which are rejected by the sampling inspection.   The number of lots rejected in turn depends on the normal level[5] of defectives in the product so that minimum inspection is a function of incoming quality.

A sample computation of minimum inspection per lot is shown in Table 24-3.   It is assumed that rejected lots are detail inspected.   For small acceptance numbers the total inspection is high because many lots need to be detailed.   For large acceptance numbers the total is again high, this time because of the large size of samples.   The minimum sum occurs at a point between these extremes.

From the foregoing it is seen that for any conditions of

> Lot tolerance percent defective
> Consumer's Risk
> Lot size
> Process average

it becomes possible to derive the values of

> n = sample size
> c = allowable number of defectives in the sample, to obtain
> I_m = minimum inspection per lot

Similar reasoning may be applied in making a selection from a group of sampling plans designed to give the same average outgoing quality limit (AOQL).

Complete tables for sampling have been derived for minimum inspection per lot for a variety of $\overline{p}$, LTPD, and AOQL values.   These will be described later.

PUBLISHED SAMPLING SCHEMES AND TABLES

Table 24-4 summarizes the principal published sampling tables[6] showing, for each, their area of application, main features, and quality index.

[5] See discussion of process average $\overline{p}$ under Dodge-Romig Sampling Tables.

[6] For a comparison of the features of these plans and those developed in several European

The published plans cover three quality indices: AQL, LTPD, and AOQL.

AQL Plans Sampling schemes indexed by AQL are designed to give high assurance for type B[7] situations and give high assurance of lot acceptance when process quality is equal to or better than the specified AQL; i.e., the process fraction defective is less than or equal to that AQL. These plans are devised for producer's protection or to keep the Producer's Risk small. Lesser consideration is given to what might be called the other end of the plan, the Consumer's Risk. If there is interest in controlling both Producer's Risk and Consumer's Risk with the use of schemes indexed by AQL values, the best approach is to study the OC curves and choose the plan which provides adequate protection against both types of risks.

MIL-STD-105D is the best-known sampling scheme indexed by AQL. The AQL's presented in this standard form a sequence which is evident in the standard. The sequence chosen, while arbitrary, does provide a sensible grouping and indexing of plans for use.

LTPD Plans Sampling schemes indexed by LTPD or other values of Limiting Quality (LQ) are designed for type A situations and are essentially the mirror image of plans indexed by AQL. That is, the plans are chosen such that the Consumer's Risk of accepting a submitted lot of product with quality equal to or worse than the LQ is equal to or less than some specified value. Specifically, LTPD plans provide a 10% probability of accepting lots of the listed LTPD quality. The Dodge-Romig sampling scheme is the best-known set of plans indexed by LTPD. MIL-STD-105D also provides some LQ plans.

AOQL Plans Sampling schemes indexed by AOQL are derived to provide assurance that the long-run average of accepted quality, given screening of rejected lots, will be no worse than the indexed AOQL value. The Dodge-Romig plans provide the best available tables of sampling plans indexed by AOQL.

The steps to be applied in any lot-by-lot sampling acceptance procedure are summarized as:

Establishment of standards (by inspection executive):
Decide what shall be a unit of product.
Classify the quality characteristics for seriousness (see Section 12).
Fix an acceptable quality level for each class.
Fix an inspection level for the product.
Installation of procedure (by inspection supervisor):
Arrange for formation of inspection lots.
Decide what type of sampling shall be used (single, double, multiple).
Choose sampling plan from tables.
Operation of procedure (by line inspector):
Draw sample units from each inspection lot.
Inspect each sample unit.
Determine whether to accept or reject the inspection lot (if sampling for acceptance) or whether to urge action on the process (if sampling for control).
Review of past results (by inspection supervisor):
Maintain a record of lot acceptance experience and cumulative defects by successive lots.
Determine whether to tighten or reduce inspection on future lots.

The specific plans are now discussed.

---

countries see Ernst P. Rossow and E. D. vanRest (eds.), "Introduction to the Principles and Application of Sampling Plans by Attributes," The European Organization for Quality Control, Rotterdam 3, Netherlands, March 1969.

[7] As mentioned earlier, when the sample size is much smaller than the lot size, the type B OC curve closely approximates the corresponding type A OC curve.

TABLE 24-4   Summary of Published Attributes Sampling Plans for Lot-by-Lot Inspection

Name of plan	Type of sampling	Type of application	Key features
MIL-STD-105D	Single, double and multiple	General application whether or not rejected lots can be 100% inspected	Maintains average quality at a specified level or better. Aims to minimize rejection of good lots. Also provides single-sampling plans for fixed consumer risks and average quality levels in the long run. Tables and mechanics of operation are simplified to minimize training required to use plan
Dodge-Romig	Single and double	General application where rejected lots can be 100% inspected	One type of plan has a Consumer's Risk of 0.10 of accepting bad quality. A second type of plan limits the average quality level in the long run. Protection is provided with minimum inspection per lot
Chain sampling	Single- and two-stage	Particularly useful when inspection involves destructive or costly tests	Aims to minimize sample sizes without a large risk of rejection of good lots. Occurrence of a single defective does not necessarily cause rejection of lot
Bayesian plans (discovery sampling)	Generally single	General application where probability of occurrence of defective lots can be estimated a priori	Smaller sample size required as compared with standard attribute schemes
Skip-lot sampling plans	Single	Particularly useful when indicated quality level is high and inspection involves costly or destructive tests	Aims to minimize inspection with adequate protection against major degradation in quality
H107	Continuous single-level	General application when production is truly continuous and inspection is nondestructive	Although plans are indexed by AQL, plans actually limit the average quality in the long run
H106	Continuous multilevel	Same as above	Plans limit the average quality in the long run
Cumulative sum	Continuous single-level	General application when production is truly continuous and no restriction on the nature of inspection	Plans limit the average quality in the long run but in sense different from above

MIL-STD-105D SAMPLING TABLES

MIL-STD-105 was first issued in 1950 as MIL-STD-105A with the current issue, MIL-STD-105D (Ref. 7), published Apr. 29, 1963. The current issue includes many important improvements over previous issues and will be the only one discussed here. Pabst (Ref. 8) describes the theoretical aspects and characteristics of issue D. The reader interested in these matters, as well as comparison of issue D with important aspects of previous issues, should study that reference.

The quality index in MIL-STD-105D is the Acceptable Quality Level (AQL):

A choice of 26 AQL values is available ranging from 0.010 to 1,000.0. (Values of 10.0 or less may be interpreted as percent defective or defects per hundred units. Values above 10.0 must be interpreted as defects per hundred units.)

The probability of accepting AQL quality varies from 89 to 99.5%.

Defects are classified as critical, major, or minor.

The purchaser may, at its option, specify separate AQL's for each class or specify an AQL for each kind of defect which a product may show.

The purchaser also specifies the relative amount of inspection or inspection level to be used. For general applications there are three levels, and level II is regarded as normal. The three levels involve inspection in amounts roughly in the ratio 1 to 2.5 to 4. Level II is generally used unless factors such as the simplicity and cost of the item, inspection cost, destructiveness of inspection, quality consistency between lots, or other factors make it appropriate to use another level. The Standard also contains special procedures for "small-sample inspection" where small sample sizes are either desirable or necessitated by some aspects of inspection. Four additional inspection levels (S1 through S4) are provided in these special procedures.

The procedure for choice of plan from the tables is outlined below.

1. The following information must be known:
   - *a.* Acceptable Quality Level (AQL).
   - *b.* Lot size.
   - *c.* Type of sampling (single, double, or multiple).
   - *d.* Inspection level (usually level II).
2. Knowing the lot size and inspection level, obtain a code letter from Table 24-5.
3. Knowing the code letter, AQL, and type of sampling, read the sampling plan from one of the nine Master Tables (Table 24-6 is for single-sampling normal inspection; the Standard also provides tables for double and multiple sampling).

For example, suppose that a purchasing agency has contracted for a 1% AQL for a certain characteristic. Suppose also that the parts are bought in lots of 1,500 pieces. From the table of sample size code letters (Table 24-5) it is found that letter K plans are required for inspection level II, the one normally used. Then the plan to be used would be found in Table 24-6 in row K. The sample size is 125. For AQL = 1.0, the acceptance number is given as 3 and the rejection number as 4. This means that the entire lot of 1,500 units may be accepted if 3 or fewer defective units are found in the sample of 125 but must be rejected if 4 or more are found. Where an AQL is expressed in terms of "defects per hundred units," this term may be substituted for "defective articles" throughout.

The system for choosing the initial sampling plan takes account of the quality of product actually submitted only in the limited sense that the AQL is thought to be attainable. When the material later submitted is of generally high quality, the functions of inspection emphasized are somewhat different from those when submitted material is of generally poor quality. If the average quality is high, sampling gives information on the prevailing quality level and provides some assurance that any sudden deterioration in quality will be detected and the resulting low-quality lots rejected. The functions of sorting good lots from bad and of applying pressure

TABLE 24-5 Sample Size Code Letters*

Lot or batch size			General inspection levels		
			I	II	III
2	to	8	A	A	B
9	to	15	A	B	C
16	to	25	B	C	D
26	to	50	C	D	E
51	to	90	C	E	F
91	to	150	D	F	G
151	to	280	E	G	H
281	to	500	F	H	J
501	to	1,200	G	J	K
1,201	to	3,200	H	K	L
3,201	to	10,000	J	L	M
10,001	to	35,000	K	M	N
35,001	to	150,000	L	N	P
150,001	to	500,000	M	P	Q
500,001	and	over	N	Q	R

* Sample size code letters given in body of table are applicable when the indicated inspection levels are to be used. The Standard includes an added table of code letters for small-sample inspection.

to cause the supplier to improve quality are less important. Moreover, poor or borderline material is seldom submitted for inspection (because it is usually detected by the producer in his inspection); so a relatively small amount of inspection is all that is economically justified.

If the quality of product submitted is consistently low, most lots will be rejected. Also, it is unfortunate but true that the few inspection lots accepted in these circumstances will not be appreciably better than those rejected. If the AQL were properly chosen and is one that can or has been met by this or other suppliers, it becomes necessary to apply greater pressure to bring this supplier's quality into line. In addition, the sampling inspection has greater need for sharp discrimination between good and bad material in order to reduce the consumer's risk. Accordingly, MIL-STD-105D provides two variations in sampling severity from that chosen as normal, the choice of Reduced or Tightened inspection as mentioned earlier.

INSPECTION SEVERITY—DEFINITIONS AND GENERAL RULES FOR CHANGING LEVELS

The commonly used attributes acceptance sampling plans make provision for shifting the amount of inspection and/or the acceptance number as experience indicates. If many consecutive lots of submitted product are accepted by an existing sampling plan, the quality of submitted product must exceed that specified as necessary for acceptance. This makes it desirable to reduce the amount and cost of inspection (with a subsequent higher risk of accepting an occasional lot of lesser quality) simply because the quality level is good. On the other hand, if more than an occasional lot is rejected by the existing sampling plan, the quality level is either consistently lower than desired or the quality level fluctuates excessively among submitted lots. In either case it is desirable to increase the sampling rate and/or reduce the acceptance number to provide greater discrimination between lots of adequate and inadequate quality.

Three severities of inspection are usually provided: Normal, Tightened, and Re-

TABLE 24-6 MIL-STD-105D Master Table for Normal Inspection (Single Sampling)

Acceptable Quality Levels (normal inspection)

Sample size code letter	Sample size	0.010		0.015		0.025		0.040		0.065		0.10		0.15		0.25		0.40		0.65		1.0		1.5		2.5		4.0		6.5		10		15		25		40		65		100		150		250		400		650		1000	
		Ac	Re	Ac	Re	Ac	Re	Ac	Re	Ac	Re	Ac	Re	Ac	Re	Ac	Re	Ac	Re	Ac	Re	Ac	Re	Ac	Re	Ac	Re	Ac	Re	Ac	Re	Ac	Re	Ac	Re	Ac	Re	Ac	Re	Ac	Re	Ac	Re	Ac	Re	Ac	Re	Ac	Re	Ac	Re	Ac	Re
A	2	↓		↓		↓		↓		↓		↓		↓		↓		↓		↓		↓		↓		↓		↓		↓		↓		0	1	1	2	2	3	3	4	5	6	7	8	10	11	14	15	21	22	30	31
B	3	↓		↓		↓		↓		↓		↓		↓		↓		↓		↓		↓		↓		↓		↓		↓		0	1	1	2	2	3	3	4	5	6	7	8	10	11	14	15	21	22	30	31	44	45
C	5	↓		↓		↓		↓		↓		↓		↓		↓		↓		↓		↓		↓		↓		↓		0	1	1	2	2	3	3	4	5	6	7	8	10	11	14	15	21	22	30	31	44	45	↑	
D	8	↓		↓		↓		↓		↓		↓		↓		↓		↓		↓		↓		↓		↓		0	1	1	2	2	3	3	4	5	6	7	8	10	11	14	15	21	22	30	31	44	45	↑		↑	
E	13	↓		↓		↓		↓		↓		↓		↓		↓		↓		↓		↓		↓		0	1	1	2	2	3	3	4	5	6	7	8	10	11	14	15	21	22	30	31	44	45	↑		↑		↑	
F	20	↓		↓		↓		↓		↓		↓		↓		↓		↓		↓		↓		0	1	1	2	2	3	3	4	5	6	7	8	10	11	14	15	21	22	30	31	44	45	↑		↑		↑		↑	
G	32	↓		↓		↓		↓		↓		↓		↓		↓		↓		↓		0	1	1	2	2	3	3	4	5	6	7	8	10	11	14	15	21	22	30	31	44	45	↑		↑		↑		↑		↑	
H	50	↓		↓		↓		↓		↓		↓		↓		↓		↓		0	1	1	2	2	3	3	4	5	6	7	8	10	11	14	15	21	22	30	31	44	45	↑		↑		↑		↑		↑		↑	
J	80	↓		↓		↓		↓		↓		↓		↓		↓		0	1	1	2	2	3	3	4	5	6	7	8	10	11	14	15	21	22	30	31	44	45	↑		↑		↑		↑		↑		↑		↑	
K	125	↓		↓		↓		↓		↓		↓		↓		0	1	1	2	2	3	3	4	5	6	7	8	10	11	14	15	21	22	30	31	44	45	↑		↑		↑		↑		↑		↑		↑		↑	
L	200	↓		↓		↓		↓		↓		↓		0	1	1	2	2	3	3	4	5	6	7	8	10	11	14	15	21	22	30	31	44	45	↑		↑		↑		↑		↑		↑		↑		↑		↑	
M	315	↓		↓		↓		↓		↓		0	1	1	2	2	3	3	4	5	6	7	8	10	11	14	15	21	22	30	31	44	45	↑		↑		↑		↑		↑		↑		↑		↑		↑		↑	
N	500	↓		↓		↓		↓		0	1	1	2	2	3	3	4	5	6	7	8	10	11	14	15	21	22	30	31	44	45	↑		↑		↑		↑		↑		↑		↑		↑		↑		↑		↑	
P	800	↓		↓		↓		0	1	1	2	2	3	3	4	5	6	7	8	10	11	14	15	21	22	30	31	44	45	↑		↑		↑		↑		↑		↑		↑		↑		↑		↑		↑		↑	
Q	1250	↓		↓		0	1	1	2	2	3	3	4	5	6	7	8	10	11	14	15	21	22	30	31	44	45	↑		↑		↑		↑		↑		↑		↑		↑		↑		↑		↑		↑		↑	
R	2000	↓		0	1	1	2	2	3	3	4	5	6	7	8	10	11	14	15	21	22	30	31	44	45	↑		↑		↑		↑		↑		↑		↑		↑		↑		↑		↑		↑		↑		↑	

⇩ = Use first sampling plan below arrow. If sample size equals, or exceeds, lot or batch size, do 100 percent inspection.
⇧ = Use first sampling plan above arrow.
Ac = Acceptance number.
Re = Rejection number.

duced.   All changes between severities are governed by rules associated with the sampling scheme.   Normal inspection is generally adopted at the beginning of a sampling procedure and continued until evidence of either lower or higher quality than that specified exists.   Schematically, the rules for switching severities specified in MIL-STD-105D are given in Figure 24-10.

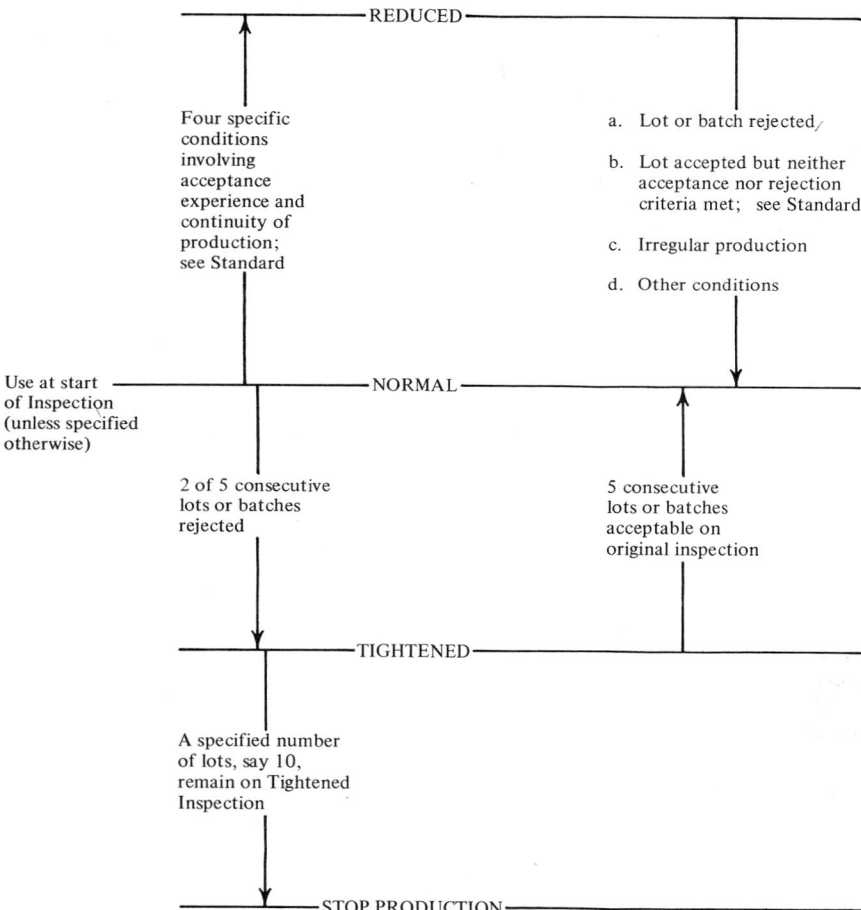

Fig. 24-10   Rules for switching inspection severity, MIL-STD-105D.

From the schematic it can be seen that the criteria for change from Normal to Tightened and back to Normal are simple and straightforward.   (This is a vast improvement over past issues of MIL-STD-105.)   Again, the change from Reduced to Normal is straightforward and occurs with the first indication that quality has slipped.   Considerably more evidence is required to change from Normal to Reduced.

In using schemes like MIL-STD-105D, the customer assumes that the changes from Normal to Tightened and Reduced to Normal are a necessary part of the scheme.   (Recall that such AQL plans provide primarily producer's assurance that quality at the AQL level will be accepted.) The change from Normal to Tightened or Reduced to Normal occurs when evidence exists that quality level has deteriorated. In this way the consumer's protection is increased.

On the other hand, the supplier is interested in keeping inspection costs as low as possible consistent with the demands placed upon him. He certainly would want to change from Tightened to Normal inspection when conditions warrant. He generally would want to change from Normal to Reduced except in those cases where record-keeping costs or bother exceed the saving in reduced sampling effort. The initiative for these types of changes generally rests with the supplier; only in those instances where an economic advantage exists would a customer insist on reduced inspection. This might occur, e.g., when the customer himself is using these sampling plans, or where inspection is destructive or degrading.

The case could arise where a complex item is being inspected for many characteristics, some of which are classified as critical, some major and some minor. A different sampling plan could be in effect for each class. It is also possible on this same product to have reached the situation where, e.g., Reduced inspection could be in effect for critical defects, Tightened inspection for major defects, and Normal inspection for minor defects. The bookkeeping involved with complete flexibility of sampling plan choice by classification of characteristic and inspection severity can be enormous. On the other hand, the savings involved with lower inspection rates, especially with destructive inspection, could be sizable. Inspection cost and convenience, along with the consequences of the error of applying an improper sampling plan, are the main determinants in any decision to use anything but the highest sampling rate associated with all defect classifications and whether to take advantage of Reduced inspection for one or more defect classes when allowed. Of course, when Tightened inspection is dictated by sampling experience, there is no recourse but to adopt it for at least that classification or characteristic, other than to discontinue acceptance inspection of submitted product.

MIL-STD-105D also provides four sampling levels, S1 through S4, which may be used where relatively small sample sizes are necessary and larger sampling risks can or must be tolerated. Adoption of these levels is not based on any routine statistical evaluation of sampling experience but is negotiated on the basis of desire or necessity.

MIL-STD-105D also provides Limiting Quality (LQ) single-sampling plans with a Consumer's Risk of 10% (LTPD) and 5% for use in isolated lot acceptance inspection. If other levels of LQ are desired, the individual OC curves can be examined to adopt an appropriate plan.

Finally, MIL-STD-105D provides a table of AOQL values for each of the single-sampling plans for Normal and Tightened inspection. These may also be used as rough guides for corresponding double- and multiple-sampling plans.

The sampling plans in MIL-STD-105D are sufficiently varied in type (single, double, multiple), amount of inspection, etc., to be useful in a great number of situations. The inclusion of operating characteristic curves and average sample size curves for most of the plans is a noteworthy advantage of the Standard. The reader is also referred to the excellent supplementary publication, H-53 (Ref. 9), which discusses and provides recommendations on many of the practical problems that arise during the day-to-day application of the standard.

DODGE-ROMIG SAMPLING TABLES

Dodge and Romig (Ref. 3) provide four different sets of tables:
1. Single-sampling lot tolerance tables (SL)
2. Double-sampling lot tolerance tables (DL)

3. Single-sampling AOQL tables (SA)

4. Double-sampling AOQL tables (DA)

All four types of plans were constructed to give minimum total inspection for product of a given process average. All lots rejected are assumed to be screened, and both the sampling and the expected amount of 100% inspection were considered in deriving the plan which would give minimum inspection per lot. This is a particularly appropriate approach for a manufacturer's inspection of his own product, as when the product of one department is examined prior to use in another. Practically, it may be reasonable to use the same theory even when the sampling is done by the purchasing company and the detailing of rejected material is done by the supplying company, since in the long run all the supplier's costs to provide material of a specified quality are reflected in his price.

The first and second sets of tables are classified according to lot tolerance percent defective at a constant Consumer's Risk of 0.10. Available lot tolerance plans range from 0.5 to 10.0% defective. In contrast, the third and fourth sets of tables are classified according to the average outgoing quality limit (AOQL) which they assure. Available AOQL values range from 0.1 to 10.0%. Lot tolerance plans emphasize a constant low Consumer's Risk (with varying AOQL's). In other words, they are intended to give considerable assurance that individual lots of poor material will seldom be accepted. The AOQL plans emphasize the limit on poor quality in the long run but do not attempt to offer uniform assurance that individual lots of low quality will not get through. The relative importance of these two objectives will guide the choice of types.

Table 24-7 shows a representative Dodge-Romig table for single sampling on the lot tolerance basis. All the plans listed in this table have the same risk (0.10) of accepting submitted lots that contain exactly 5% of defective units. The table has six columns. Each of these lists a set of plans appropriate to a specified average value of incoming quality. For example, if the estimated process average percent defective is between 2.01 and 2.50%, the last column at the right gives the plans that will provide the minimum inspection per lot. However, the assurance that a lot of quality 5% defective will be rejected is the same for all columns; so an initial incorrect estimate of the process average would have little effect except to increase somewhat the total number of pieces inspected per lot. The selection of a plan from this table thus requires only two items of information: the size of the lot to be sampled and the prevailing average quality of the supplier for the product in question.

Process average is determined from past records, modified by any supplemental knowledge useful for predicting the expected level of defects. The following are suggested as useful rules for determining process average:

1. Compute from the first samples[8] taken on about 25 lots, the total inspected, the total defects found, and the resultant average fraction defective $\bar{p}$.

2. Eliminate any samples from "abnormal" lots. This is done by finding any instances in which the fraction defective for one sample exceeds the average fraction defective $\bar{p}$ by an amount greater than $3\sqrt{\bar{p}(1-\bar{p})/n}$, where n is the size of the sample for the lot under suspicion.[9]

3. Recompute $\bar{p}$ with the abnormal cases eliminated (or corrected by the Dodge-Romig method). The new value of $\bar{p}$ is to be used as process average $\bar{p}$.

[8] If this computation is made from all samples, the results will be biased, since second samples are taken only from lots of borderline quality.

[9] Dodge and Romig (Ref. 3) recommend that these abnormal samples be not eliminated but rather corrected through equating them to $\bar{p} \pm 2\sqrt{\bar{p}(1-\bar{p})/n}$ depending on the direction of the abnormality.

TABLE 24-7   Dodge-Romig Table* for Lot Tolerance Single Sampling

Lot Tolerance Percent Defective = 5.0%

Process average % Lot size	0–0.05			0.06–0.50			0.51–1.00			1.01–1.50			1.51–2.00			2.01–2.50		
	n	c	AOQL %	n	c	AOQL %	n	c	AOQL %	n	c	AOQL %	n	c	AOQL %	n	c	AOQL %
1–30	All	0	0	All	0	0	All	0	0	All	0	0	All	0	0	All	0	0
31–50	30	0	0.49	30	0	0.49	30	0	0.49	30	0	0.49	30	0	0.49	30	0	0.49
51–100	37	0	0.63	37	0	0.63	37	0	0.63	37	0	0.63	37	0	0.63	37	0	0.63
101–200	40	0	0.74	40	0	0.74	40	0	0.74	40	0	0.74	40	0	0.74	40	0	0.74
201–300	43	0	0.74	43	0	0.74	70	1	0.92	70	1	0.92	95	2	0.99	95	2	0.99
301–400	44	0	0.74	44	0	0.74	70	1	0.99	100	2	1.0	120	3	1.1	145	4	1.1
401–500	45	0	0.75	75	1	0.95	100	2	1.1	100	2	1.1	125	3	1.2	150	4	1.2
501–600	45	0	0.76	75	1	0.98	100	2	1.1	125	3	1.2	150	4	1.3	175	5	1.3
601–800	45	0	0.77	75	1	1.0	100	2	1.2	130	3	1.2	175	5	1.4	200	6	1.4
801–1,000	45	0	0.78	75	1	1.0	105	2	1.2	155	4	1.4	180	5	1.4	225	7	1.5
1,001–2,000	45	0	0.80	75	1	1.0	130	3	1.4	180	5	1.6	230	7	1.7	280	9	1.8
2,001–3,000	75	1	1.1	105	2	1.3	135	3	1.4	210	6	1.7	280	9	1.9	370	13	2.1
3,001–4,000	75	1	1.1	105	2	1.3	160	4	1.5	210	6	1.7	305	10	2.0	420	15	2.2
4,001–5,000	75	1	1.1	105	2	1.3	160	4	1.5	235	7	1.8	330	11	2.0	440	16	2.2
5,001–7,000	75	1	1.1	105	2	1.3	185	5	1.7	260	8	1.9	350	12	2.2	490	18	2.4
7,001–10,000	75	1	1.1	105	2	1.3	185	5	1.7	260	8	1.9	380	13	2.2	535	20	2.5
10,001–20,000	75	1	1.1	135	3	1.4	210	6	1.8	285	9	2.0	425	15	2.3	610	23	2.6
20,001–50,000	75	1	1.1	135	3	1.4	235	7	1.9	305	10	2.1	470	17	2.4	700	27	2.7
50,001–100,000	75	1	1.1	160	4	1.6	235	7	1.9	355	12	2.2	515	19	2.5	770	30	2.8

n = size of sample; entry of "All" indicates that each piece in lot is to be inspected.

c = allowable defect number for sample.

AOQL = average outgoing quality limit.

* Tables 24-7 and 24-8 are reproduced from Dodge and Romig, "Sampling Inspection Tables," 2d ed., John Wiley & Sons, Inc., New York, 1959, by permission of the publisher and of Bell Telephone Laboratories, Inc.

Instead of using single sampling, one can select a double-sampling plan for the same lot tolerance from the table provided. A comparison of the sample sizes under the single- and double-sampling plans will show that for comparable situations, fewer units will be inspected under double sampling, provided that a decision can generally be reached on the basis of the first sample.

If a borderline quality necessitates drawing a second sample with high frequency, the total number of pieces inspected may be greater for double sampling than for single sampling (see discussion of ASN and ATI).

Table 24-8 is a typical table from the Dodge-Romig AOQL plans using double sampling. In distinction to the lot tolerance tables, this table gives plans which differ considerably as to lot tolerance but have the same AOQL of 1%. (The corresponding lot tolerances are, however, given.)

AOQL plans are appropriate only when all rejected lots are 100% inspected. It is this averaging of the perfect quality of the screened lots with the poor quality of the unsatisfactory lots occasionally accepted (owing to the unavoidable Consumer's Risk) that determines the average outgoing quality and makes a limit possible. AOQL schemes are open to question where rejected lots are returned to an outside supplier since there is no directly controlled assurance that they will be 100% inspected and returned.[10]

Sampling becomes uneconomical if the average quality submitted is not considerably better than the AOQL specified. For this reason the Dodge-Romig AOQL tables do not give plans for process averages which exceed the AOQL. Similarly, lot tolerance plans are not given for process averages greater than one-half of the specified lot tolerance. Actually, 100% inspection is often less expensive than sampling if the average incoming quality is poor enough to cause 40% or more of submitted lots to be rejected, since the expenses of administration of the sampling plan and of double handling of rejected lots are eliminated.

In comparison with MIL-STD-105D, the Dodge-Romig plans make no distinction for type of defects, but a lower value of AOQL or LTPD could be adopted for major defects than for minor or incidental defects. Also, Dodge-Romig gives no direct provision for Tightened or Reduced inspection, although the sample size is adjusted as $\bar{p}$ varies. Also, tightening can always be effected by adopting a lower AOQL or LTPD.

The MIL-STD-105D Sampling Tables will undoubtedly be more commonly used in sampling inspection, especially where final acceptance of military product is concerned. Although the Dodge-Romig tables have general utility, the most usual application may be to within-plant inspection situations.

CHAIN-SAMPLING PLANS

Chain-sampling plans utilize information over a series of lots. The original plans (Ref. 10), called ChSP-1, utilize single sampling on an attributes basis with n small and $c = 0$. The distinguishing feature is that the current lot under inspection can also be accepted if one defective unit is observed in the sample provided that no other defective units were found in the samples from the immediately preceding i lots, i.e., the chain. Clark (Ref. 11) presented additional OC curves for ChSP-1, and Dodge and Stephens (Refs. 12, 13) derived some new chain-sampling plans which make use of cumulative inspection results from several samples and are generalizations and extensions of ChSP-1. Conversely, ChSP-1 is a subset of the new plans, and the discussion here will be in terms of the new two-stage plans.

[10] This is one of the prime reasons for the preference for AQL schemes by the procurement agencies of the armed forces.

TABLE 24-8 Dodge-Romig Table for AOQL Double Sampling Average Outgoing Quality Limit = 1.0%

Process average %	0-0.02						0.03-0.20						0.21-0.40					
	Trial 1		Trial 2			p_t %	Trial 1		Trial 2			p_t %	Trial 1		Trial 2			p_t %
Lot size	n_1	c_1	n_2	n_1+n_2	c_2		n_1	c_1	n_2	n_1+n_2	c_2		n_1	c_1	n_2	n_1+n_2	c_2	
1-25	All	0	—	—	—	—	All	0	—	—	—	—	All	0	—	—	—	—
26-50	22	0	—	—	—	7.7	22	0	—	—	—	7.7	22	0	—	—	—	7.7
51-100	33	0	17	50	1	6.9	33	0	17	50	1	6.9	33	0	17	50	1	6.9
101-200	43	0	22	65	1	5.8	43	0	22	65	1	5.8	43	0	22	65	1	5.8
201-300	47	0	28	75	1	5.5	47	0	28	75	1	5.5	47	0	28	75	1	5.5
301-400	49	0	31	80	1	5.4	49	0	31	80	1	5.4	55	0	60	115	2	4.8
401-500	50	0	30	80	1	5.4	50	0	30	80	1	5.4	55	0	65	120	2	4.7
501-600	50	0	30	80	1	5.4	50	0	30	80	1	5.4	60	0	65	125	2	4.6
601-800	50	0	35	85	1	5.3	60	0	70	130	2	4.5	60	0	70	130	2	4.5
801-1,000	55	0	30	85	1	5.2	60	0	75	135	2	4.4	60	0	75	135	2	4.4
1,001-2,000	55	0	35	90	1	5.1	65	0	75	140	2	4.3	75	0	120	195	3	3.8
2,001-3,000	65	0	80	145	2	4.2	65	0	80	145	2	4.2	75	0	125	200	3	3.7
3,001-4,000	70	0	80	150	2	4.1	70	0	80	150	2	4.1	80	0	175	255	4	3.5
4,001-5,000	70	0	80	150	2	4.1	70	0	80	150	2	4.1	80	0	180	260	4	3.4
5,001-7,000	70	0	80	150	2	4.1	75	0	125	200	3	3.7	80	0	180	260	4	3.4
7,001-10,000	70	0	80	150	2	4.1	80	0	125	205	3	3.6	85	0	180	265	4	3.4
10,001-20,000	70	0	80	150	2	4.1	80	0	130	210	3	3.6	90	0	230	320	5	3.3
20,001-50,000	75	0	80	155	2	4.0	80	0	135	215	3	3.6	95	0	300	395	6	2.9
50,001-100,000	75	0	80	155	2	4.0	85	0	180	265	4	3.3	170	1	380	550	8	2.6

TABLE 24-8   Dodge-Romig Table for AOQL Double Sampling Average Outgoing Quality Limit = 1.0%

Lot size	0.41–0.60 Trial 1 n_1	c_1	Trial 2 n_2	n_1+n_2	c_2	p_t %	0.61–0.80 Trial 1 n_1	c_1	Trial 2 n_2	n_1+n_2	c_2	p_t %	0.81–1.00 Trial 1 n_1	c_1	Trial 2 n_2	n_1+n_2	c_2	p_t %
1–25	All	0	—	—	—	—	All	0	—	—	—	—	All	0	—	—	—	—
26–50	22	0	—	—	—	7.7	22	0	—	—	—	7.7	22	0	—	—	—	7.7
51–100	33	0	17	50	1	6.9	33	0	17	50	1	6.9	33	0	17	50	1	6.9
101–200	43	0	22	65	1	5.8	43	0	22	65	1	5.8	47	0	43	90	2	5.4
201–300	55	0	50	105	2	4.9	55	0	50	105	2	4.9	55	0	50	105	2	4.9
301–400	55	0	60	115	2	4.8	55	0	60	115	2	4.8	60	0	80	140	3	4.5
401–500	55	0	65	120	2	4.7	60	0	95	155	3	4.3	60	0	95	155	3	4.3
501–600	60	0	65	125	3	4.6	65	0	100	165	3	4.2	65	0	100	165	3	4.2
601–800	65	0	105	170	3	4.1	65	0	105	170	3	4.1	70	0	140	210	4	3.9
801–1,000	65	0	110	175	4	4.0	70	0	150	220	4	3.8	125	1	180	305	6	3.5
1,001–2,000	80	0	165	245	4	3.7	135	1	200	335	6	3.3	140	1	245	385	7	3.2
2,001–3,000	80	0	170	250	5	3.6	150	1	265	415	7	3.0	215	2	355	570	10	2.8
3,001–4,000	85	0	220	305	6	3.3	160	1	330	490	8	2.8	225	2	455	680	12	2.7
4,001–5,000	145	1	225	370	7	3.1	225	2	375	600	10	2.7	240	2	595	835	14	2.5
5,001–7,000	155	1	285	440	8	2.9	235	2	440	675	11	2.6	310	3	665	975	16	2.4
7,001–10,000	165	1	355	520	9	2.7	250	2	585	835	13	2.4	385	4	785	1,170	19	2.3
10,001–20,000	175	1	415	590	11	2.6	325	3	655	980	15	2.3	520	6	980	1,500	24	2.2
20,001–50,000	250	2	490	740	14	2.4	340	3	910	1,250	19	2.2	610	7	1,410	2,020	32	2.1
50,001–100,000	275	2	700	975	18	2.2	420	4	1,050	1,470	22	2.1	770	9	1,850	2,620	41	2.0

n_1 = size of first sample; n_2 = size of second sample; entry of "all" indicates that each piece in lot is to be inspected.
c_1 = allowable defect number for first sample; c_2 = allowable defect number for first and second samples combined.
p_t = lot tolerance per cent defect corresponding to a consumer's risk (P_c) = 0.10.

Before discussing the details of the plans, the general characteristics of chain sampling are described. Chain-sampling plans, in comparison with single-sampling plans, have the characteristic of "bowing up" the OC curve for small fractions defective while having little effect on the end of the curve associated with higher fractions defective. The effectiveness of chain-sampling plans strongly depends upon the assumptions on which the plans are based, namely:

1. Production is steady, as a continuing process.
2. Lot submittal is in the order of production.
3. Attributes sampling is done where the fraction defective p is binomially distributed.
4. A fixed sample size from each lot is assumed.
5. There is confidence in the supplier to the extent that lots are expected to be of essentially the same quality.

Chain-sampling plans are particularly useful where inspection is costly and sample sizes are relatively small. However, they may also be found useful with large sample sizes. The advantage over double-sampling plans is the fixed sample size. The disadvantage is that moderate changes in quality are not easily detected. However, major changes in quality are detected as easily with chain-sampling plans having much smaller sample sizes than single-sampling plans with the same AQL.

The new chain-sampling plans are two-stage plans with acceptance based on cumulation of defectives in each stage separately and defined by the parameters and designators:

n = sample size, constant over all samples

k_1 = maximum number of samples for cumulation of defectives in the first stage

k_2 = maximum number of samples for cumulation of defectives in the second stage and in the "normal" period following the second stage

C_1 = allowable number of defectives in the cumulative results of k_1 or fewer samples in the first stage

C_2 = allowable number of defectives in the cumulative results of $k_1 + 1$ to k_2 or fewer samples, or the last k_2 samples

d = number of defectives in a sample

d_i = number of defective units in the ith sample

D = cumulative number of defectives in a series of samples

D_i = cumulative number of defective units at the ith sample with cumulation performed according to the plan

The acceptance criterion is a cumulative results criterion (CRC). At the start (initial application of the plan) and at a restart, the CRC for k_1 must be satisfied. To establish the normal acceptance period, the CRC for k_2 must be satisfied and the normal period continues as long as the CRC is satisfied for the last k_2 lots. Restart occurs whenever the CRC is not satisfied. The flow chart for the plan, reproduced from Dodge and Stephens (Ref. 13), is given in Figure 24-11. The letters in the blocks have been added to facilitate the example given later.

Dodge and Stephens adopt the designation ChSP-0, 2, e.g., to designate a two-stage sampling plan with $C_1 = 0$, $C_2 = 2$ and n, k_1, k_2 as unspecified or open parameters. A plan with $n = 10$, $k_1 = 1$, $k_2 = 3$, $C_1 = 0$, $C_2 = 2$ would be a particular plan in ChSP-0, 2. Additional sets of plans would then be designated by ChSP-0, 1; ChSP-1, 2; etc.

The ChSP-1 plans defined in Ref. 10 had $k_1 = k_2 - 1$ and k_1 was designated as i. The scheme there is to inspect a sample of n units from a lot, accept the lot if zero defectives were found in the n units, or accept the lot if one defective was found in the sample and no defectives were found in the samples from the immediately preceding i lots. Thus for ChSP-1 comparison with ChSP-0, 1; $n = n$, $k_1 = k_2 - 1 = i$, $k_2 = i + 1$, $C_1 = 0$, $C_2 = 1$, and ChSP-1 is a subset of the new two-stage plans.

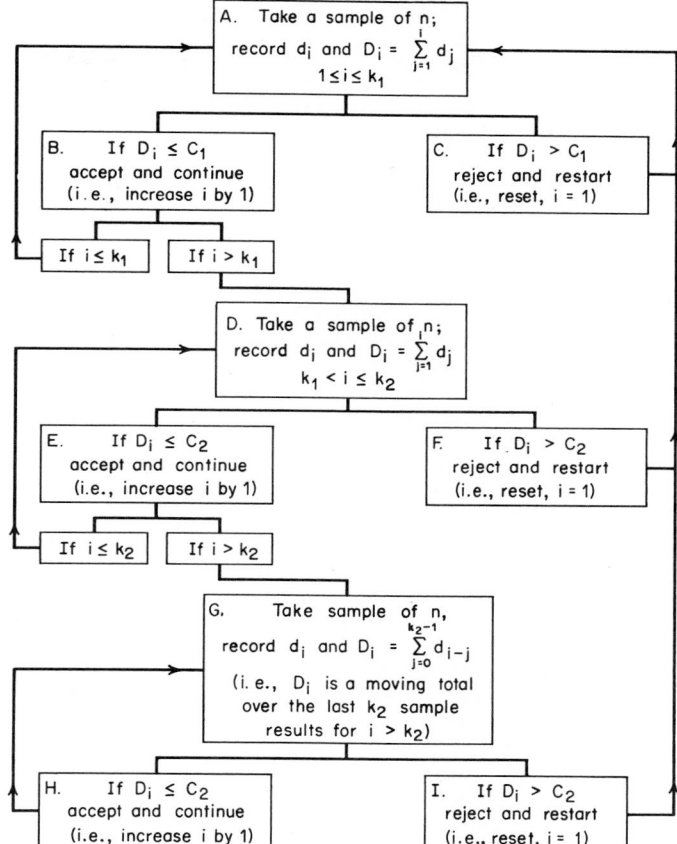

Fig. 24-11 Flow chart of operations, two-stage chain-sampling scheme.

An example based on the ChSP-0, 2 with $n = 10$, $k_1 = 1$, $k_2 = 3$, $C_1 = 0$, $C_2 = 2$ may be helpful. The example can best be followed through use of Figure 24-11.

1. Set $i = 1$ and draw a sample of 10 units from lot 1. If d_1 and $D_1 = 0$, accept the lot and set $i = 2$ (blocks A and B) and proceed to block D; otherwise reject the lot and reset $i = 1$ (block C).

2. If $i = 2$, draw a second sample of 10 units from lot 2. If $d_2 = 0, 1$, or 2, then $D_2 = d_1 + d_2 = 0, 1$, or 2; accept the lot (block E), set $i = 3$, and return to block D; otherwise reject the lot and reset $i = 1$ (block F).

3. If $i = 3$, draw a third sample of 10 units from lot 3. If $D_3 = d_1 + d_2 + d_3 = 0$, 1, or 2, accept the lot (block E), set $i = 4$, and proceed to block G, the normal period; otherwise reject the lot and reset $i = 1$. (In the above d_1 must be zero to proceed to block D. If $d_2 = 1$, then $d_3 = 1$ would allow acceptance of both lot 2 and lot 3. If, however, $d_2 = 2$ and lot 2 is accepted, then d_3 must equal zero for acceptance of lot 3.)

4. If $i = 4$, draw a fourth sample of 10 units from lot 4. If $D = d_2 + d_3 + d_4 = 0$,

1, or 2, accept the lot (block *H*), reset $i = 5$, and continue in block *G;* otherwise reject the lot and reset $i = 1$.

5. Continue to select samples from lots and cumulate the number of defective units over the last three samples. As long as this moving cumulation of number of defective units over the last three samples remains less than or equal to 2, the individual lots are accepted. Whenever the cumulation exceeds 2, the current lot is rejected and the plan is restarted.

Formulas for the OC curves for ChSP-0, 1; ChSP-0, 2 and several OC curves for various values of n, k_1, and k_2 are given in Refs. 12 and 13. All are based on the type B sampling situation.

The published OC curves of Refs. 10, 11, 12, and 13 may be used directly for chain-sampling plans. The user may find it necessary to compute his own OC curves, using the published ones as a guide, if additional plans in either the single- or two-stage scheme are desired. Additional plans should not be adopted without first examining the OC curve, since only in this way can the real advantages of chain-sampling plans to single, double, or multiple plans be compared when the use of the chain-sampling scheme is valid. This last point of validity must be carefully considered in any instance.

SPECIAL PROCEDURES FOR SMALL-SAMPLE INSPECTION

In situations where small samples are necessary because inspection is destructive or extremely costly, where items are submitted in small lots, or where "check" samples are desired, the following procedures may be applicable (Refs. 14, 15). In the case of attributes sampling acceptance, a Reference Quality Level (called RL here for Reference Level and to avoid confusion with the more common use of RQL for Rejectable Quality Level) in terms of fraction defective p is established prior to initiating the plan. The RL is an engineering estimate of what the quality at delivery should be. In the situations cited above, no sampling plan can economically assure compliance with the RL, but cumulation of results once nonconformance is indicated can be utilized to detect quality levels (in terms of fraction defective) that are larger than the RL and to initiate corrective action. The procedures assume conditions similar to those assumed for chain-sampling plans and are given in Ref. 15.

In implementing the procedure a regular sampling plan, usually a single-sampling plan, with small n and c is chosen. Each submitted lot is accepted or rejected according to this plan. When a lot is rejected, the submitting agency is informed that the cumulative results criterion will apply to succeeding lots. Each lot under the cumulative results criterion is accepted or rejected according to the original n and $c;$ but, in addition, the fraction defective is cumulated over a number m of succeeding sample units, like $m = 100$. If the observed fraction defective exceeds the allowance prior to satisfying $m = 100$, or if a lot is rejected under the individual plan, that lot on which the cumulative criterion was violated or the nonconforming lot is rejected. The process is then declared nonconforming, and no further lots may be submitted until the submitting agency provides evidence that corrective action has been taken. After such evidence has been provided, submittal and inspection are started again on a new sequence of cumulative results. If the cumulative results are satisfactory over the next m units, the cumulative results criterion is removed. If the results are not satisfactory, submittal is once more halted, higher authority is informed, stronger evidence of corrective action is required, and cumulative results criterion is again imposed.

No extensive tables exist for this type of plan on a fraction defective basis, and implementation might require some experimentation. For example, given an RL of 2.5% and $N = 100$, the appropriate single-sampling plan from MIL-STD-105D with an AQL of 2.5% would have $n = 20, c = 1, r = 2$. The testing of 20% of the items might be impossible for various reasons, and consequently a sampling plan with $n = 5$, $c = 1$, $r = 2$, and AQL = 10% might be chosen. Following a lot rejection under the adopted plan a cumulative results criterion might be established such that no more than one additional failure will be permitted in the next 50 sample units inspected. Even though individual lots might be conforming under the $n = 5$, $c = 1$ plan, submittal may be halted due to failure to conform to the cumulative results criterion. Once again, experimentation with approaches such as the above along with calculation of what long-run quality can be consistently accepted and how many false alarms can be created is necessary.

DEMERIT SAMPLING PLANS

Demerit sampling schemes are based on a classification of defects, a weighting for each class, and comparison of the cumulated demerits observed with a standard, thus providing an index used for acceptance decisions. For example, if there are four classes of defects with demerit weights of 100, 50, 10, and 1, depending on seriousness of the defect, the cumulative number of demerits is the sum of the number observed in each class multiplied by the weight for that class. When the statistical distribution for this index can be established, it is possible to set acceptance criteria for lot inspection. Section 12 discusses the approach used to establish the seriousness classification. A cumulative results plan on a demerits sampling basis is also discussed in Ref. 15.

SAMPLING PLANS BASED ON PRIOR INFORMATION

General Concept   The concept that experience or analytical studies can yield prior frequency distributions of the quality of submitted lots and that these "prior" distributions can in turn be used to derive lot-by-lot sampling plans has gained some popularity in recent years. This is generally termed the Bayesian approach. Bayes' theorem and decision theory (Bayesian) concept are discussed in Section 22. The manner in which prior information may be used to modify a conventional acceptance sampling plan is also demonstrated there. The general concept of the use of prior information is discussed in Section 12, under How Much Inspection?

Bayesian Sampling Plans   Considerable literature exists on Bayesian sampling. However, very limited sampling tables based on particular prior distributions of lot quality are available. It is generally true that a Bayesian plan requires a smaller sample size than does a conventional sampling plan with the same Consumer's and Producer's Risk. Among others, Schafer (Ref. 16) discusses single sampling plans by attributes using three prior distributions of lot quality. Given specified risks α and β, sampling plans which satisfied these risks and which minimized sample size were determined. For example, with a particular prior distribution, $n = 6$ and $c = 0$ gave protection equivalent to a conventional sampling plan with $n = 34$, $c = 0$.

Advantages similar to those quoted above are usually cited. However, one prime factor is frequently ignored; i.e., how good is the assumption on the prior distribution. Hald (Ref. 17) gives an extensive account of sampling plans based on discrete prior distributions of product quality. In addition, on pages 305 and 306 he states:

For the further development of the theory of sampling inspection, it is an important problem on the basis of experience from process control and sampling inspection to specify properties of the sequence of prior distribution $f_N(X)$ i.e., the probability that a lot of N items contains X defective items. Unfortunately, published data on prior distributions are very scarce. It is important to notice that consideration regarding $f_N(X)$ should also be based on models of the production process itself so that the theories of process control and lot-by-lot sampling inspection in this way may be linked closer together than at present.

The mixed binomial distribution may be generated by a process where each lot of size N is produced in a state of statistical (binomial) control but where the process average varies from lot to lot in accordance with the distribution function $\Phi(p)$. Until better models have been developed the mixed binomial distribution may well serve as an approximation, and probably a rather good one for the purpose of developing sampling plans. . . .

Hald also employs a simple economic model along with the discrete prior distributions and the hypergeometric sampling distribution to answer a number of basic questions on costs, relationship between sample size and lot size, etc. Schafer (Ref. 18) also considers the Bayesian operating characteristic curve.

A Bayesian plan can sometimes be installed in parallel with a conventional plan until sufficient history is obtained to evaluate and adjust the prior distribution. When this can be done, conversion to the Bayesian plan can be made with good justification.

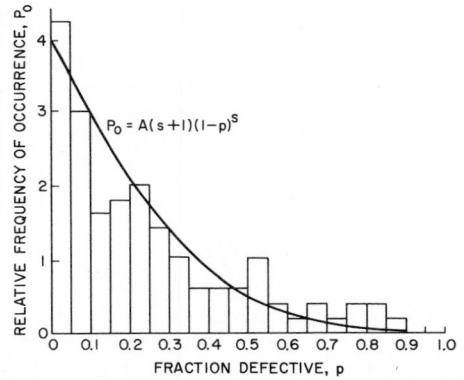

Fig. 24-12 Probability-of-occurrence distribution.

Discovery Sampling Discovery Sampling (Ref. 19) is a scheme akin to the Bayesian approach. It can be installed and compared with practically any inspection plan (including 100% inspection) without disturbing the existing plan, and at the cost only of collecting and analyzing small additional amounts of data.

Reference 19 reports that wide inspection experience shows the probability of occurrence of lots of product with fraction defective p is adequately described by the curve in Figure 24-12 with $s = 3$ and where A is the ratio of the number of partially defective lots to stock to the total number of lots to stock. Given this prior distribution—a process average expressed in terms of lots of product rather than units of product, the ratio of lots sampled to the total number of lots inspected, and a desired AOQL—then the existing sample size can be adjusted for the next sampling period. A formula and nomograph are provided for determining sample size along with a flow chart describing installation of the plan.

Evaluations of Discovery Sampling have been made (Ref. 20). In comparisons with conventional sampling plans, it is reported that smaller sample sizes with at least equivalent protection have occurred.

SAMPLING PLANS FOR CONTINUOUS PRODUCTION

General Concepts Some production processes deliver product in a continuous stream rather than on a lot-by-lot basis. Separate plans have been developed for such continuous production. These plans generally start with 100% inspection until

TABLE 24-9   Continuous Sampling Plan Code Letters

Number of units of product produced in a production interval*	Inspection levels			
	I	II	III	
	CSP-1 and CSP-2	CSP-1 and CSP-2	CSP-A	CSP-1 and CSP-2
2–8	C	B	$\underline{A'}$	A
9–25	D	C	$\underline{B'}$	A
26–65	E	D	$\underline{C'}$	B
66–110	F	E	$\underline{D'}$	B
111–180.	F	E	$\underline{E'}$	C
181–300.	G	E	$\underline{F'}$	C
301–500.	G	F	$\underline{G'}$	D
501–800.	G	F	$\underline{H'}$	E
801–1,300	H	F	$\underline{I'}$	E
1,301–3,200	H	G	$\underline{J'}$	F
3,201–8,000	I	H	$\underline{K'}$	G
8,001–22,000	J	I	$\underline{L'}$	H
22,001–110,000	K	J	$\underline{M'}$	I
110,001 up.	K	K	$\underline{N'}$	J

* The production interval is the period of time, usually a shift or a day, during which a number of units of product or a homogeneous batch of product is produced. The choice of the number of units of product or of the duration of the production interval must be estimated from prior information.

some consecutive number of units free of defects are found and then provide for inspection on a sampling basis until a specified number of defective units is found. One hundred percent inspection is then instituted again until a specified number of consecutive good pieces is found, at which time sampling is reinstituted. Continuous sampling plans have been proposed by Harold F. Dodge and modifications developed by Dodge and Miss M. N. Torrey (Ref. 21). Reference 22 recounts these and other developments in the evolution of continuous sampling plans. The following paragraphs describe these plans as adapted by the U.S. Department of Defense.

H107 (Ref. 23) lists the following prerequisites for application of the single-level continuous sampling plans:

1. The inspection must involve "moving product," i.e., product which is flowing past the inspection station, e.g., on a conveyor belt.

2. Rapid 100% inspection must be feasible.

3. The inspection must be relatively easy.

4. The product must be homogeneous.

The handbook contains three types of continuous sampling plans: CSP-1, CSP-2, and CSP-A plans.

CSP-1 Plans CSP-1 plans use 100% inspection at the start. When i successive units are found to be acceptable and when there is assurance that the process is producing homogeneous product, 100% inspection is discontinued and sampling is instituted to the extent of a fraction f of the units. The sampling is continued until a defective unit is found. One hundred percent inspection is then reinstated and the procedure is repeated.

To choose the proper plan it is necessary to know only the quantity produced in a production interval, and the AQL (or AOQL). For example, suppose 400 units are produced each day on a continuous production line. A continuous sampling plan is desired for an AQL of 2.5%. Referring to Table 24-9 and using inspection level II for 400 units, the sampling frequency code letter is read as F. The sampling plan is then read from Table 24-10. (Both Tables 24-9 and 24-10 are representative tables from H107.) One hundred percent inspection is used until 35 successive units are found nondefective. Sampling, at the rate of 1 unit in 10, is then instituted. If a defective is found, 100% inspection is reinstituted and continued until 35 successive units are found nondefective, at which time sampling is reinstituted. The table also shows that the procedures of the plan will result in an AOQL of 3.09%.

CSP-2 Plans CSP-2 plans were developed to permit sampling to continue even if a single defective is found. Again, 100% inspection is used at the start until i successive units are found free of defects. When sampling is in effect and a defective is found, 100% inspection is instituted only if a second defective occurs in the next i or fewer sample units inspected. Separate tables are provided for the CSP-2 plans. The tables for CSP-1 and CSP-2 have the same sampling rates, AQL, and AOQL values. However, the number of successive acceptable units i required for sampling is higher under the CSP-2 plans—ranging from about 50% higher for the low code letters to about 25% higher for the high code letters.

Stopping Rules for CSP-1 and CSP-2 Both CSP-1 and CSP-2 plans contain provisions for stopping inspection if 100% inspection persists too long. For each of the plans, a table of L, or limiting values, is given in terms of the duration of 100% inspection. If this value is exceeded, 100% inspection can be stopped until the supplier identifies the causes of the defective product and corrects his process. Murphy (Ref. 24) has investigated four different "stopping rules" for use with CSP-1 plans. He concludes that a useful rule is to stop when a specified number of defectives is found during any one sequence of 100% inspection.

CSP-A Plans The CSP-A plans incorporate the principle of a total of $(a + 1)$ defective units in an inspection period which is usually one day. The total includes defective units found in both 100% inspection and sampling inspection. At the start, 100% inspection is instituted and transfer to sampling is permitted if i successive units are found free of defects before a total of $(a + 1)$ defective units are found. If during sampling inspection, a single defective unit is found, and it is not the $(a + 1)$st for the inspection period, 100% inspection is reinstituted as at the start but all previously detected defective units are counted in $(a + 1)$. Inspection is discontinued whenever $(a + 1)$ defective units are found during the inspection period, whether this defective unit was found on 100% or sampling inspection. Inspection will be restarted, with a new inspection period, only after assurance from the supplier that corrective action has been taken. The values of i are generally smaller for CSP-A than for CSP-1; the stopping rule incorporated into the plan might be considered an advantage, but the complexity of administration might be considered a disadvantage.

Multilevel Continuous Sampling.

The Department of Defense has developed a set of continuous sampling plans, H106 (Ref. 25), which reduce the sampling rate beyond that of other plans when the quality level is better than a defined AOQL. In addition, sudden changes in the amount of inspection are avoided by providing for several "levels" of inspection. Figure 24-13 outlines the procedure for using the plan. The procedure provides for reducing the sampling rate each time i consecutive units are found to be free of defects. The first sampling rate after leaving 100% inspection is f, and each succeeding sampling rate is f raised to one larger power. The number of sampling levels is k. Thus, if $f = \frac{1}{2}$ and $k = 3$, the successive sampling rates are $\frac{1}{2}$, $\frac{1}{4}$, and $\frac{1}{8}$.

The plans are indexed in terms of AOQL and procedures provided for values of AOQL from 0.10 to 15.0%; $f = \frac{1}{2}$ and $f = \frac{1}{3}$; and 1 to 5 sampling levels k. The following example will illustrate the plan:

The example deals with a contract for 750 generators. The AOQL was estab-

TABLE 24-10 Continuous Sampling Plan Table

Values of i for CSP-1 Plans

Sampling frequency code letter	f	AQL, %													
		0.015	0.035	0.065	0.10	0.15	0.25	0.40	0.65	1.0	1.5	2.5	4.0	6.5	10.0
A	1/2	240	180	120	100	75	50	33	25	20	12	9	5	4	2
B	1/3	390	290	200	170	130	80	55	43	34	20	15	9	6	4
C	1/4	500	380	260	220	170	100	75	55	45	27	19	12	8	5
D	1/5	600	450	320	270	200	130	90	70	55	33	23	14	9	6
E	1/7	750	560	390	330	250	150	110	85	65	40	29	17	12	8
F	1/10	920	690	480	410	310	190	140	100	80	50	35	22	15	10
G	1/15	1,110	840	590	500	380	230	170	130	100	65	43	27	18	12
H	1/25	1,380	1,040	730	620	470	290	210	160	130	75	55	34	22	15
I	1/50	1,780	1,340	940	800	600	370	260	200	160	100	70	42	29	19
J	1/100	2,210	1,660	1,150	980	740	450	320	250	200	120	85	55	36	24
K	1/200	2,630	1,970	1,370	1,170	880	530	380	300	240	150	100	65	43	28
		0.12	0.16	0.23	0.27	0.36	0.59	0.83	1.08	1.35	2.20	3.09	4.96	7.24	10.70
		AOQL, %													

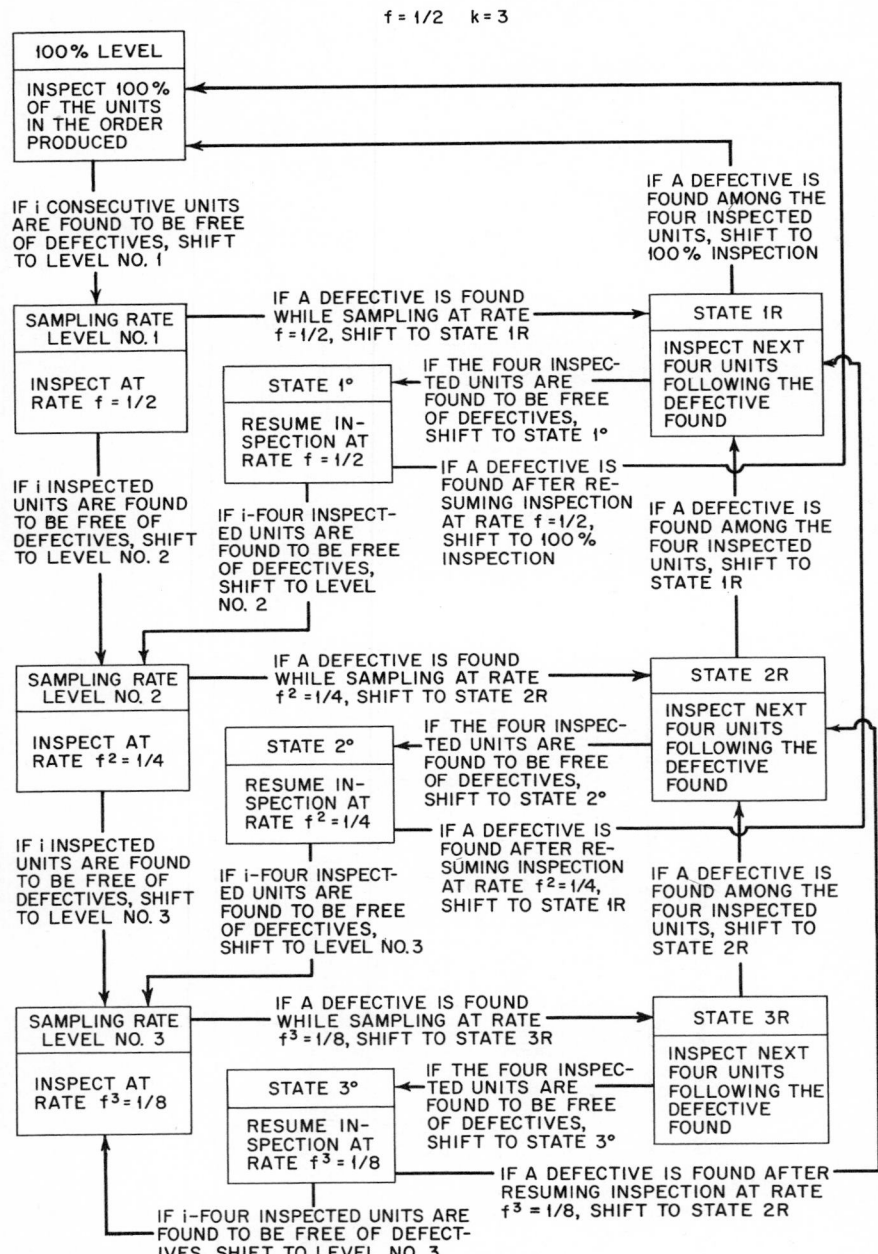

Fig. 24-13 Procedure for multilevel continuous sampling.

lished at 5.0% for major defects, and a sampling rate $f = \frac{1}{2}$ was desired. From Table 24-11 the inspector selected the appropriate plan, $f = \frac{1}{2}$, $k = 3$, and $i = 15$. As the generators, serially numbered, are released for inspection, the inspector started 100% inspection and recorded the serial numbers on the first line of his work sheet which had been ruled into blocks (any convenient type of work sheet may be used). A notation indicating the unit's acceptability is made as each unit is inspected. The fifth generator was defective, and the inspector recorded that fact in the fifth block. He initiated corrective action and then started recording on the second line of the work sheet so that there would be no mistake about knowing both when the last defective was observed and how many nondefective units had been inspected since then. A total of 15 nondefective units were inspected, so the inspector began sampling at the rate of $\frac{1}{2}$. He tossed a coin each time to decide whether to or not to inspect each unit as it was presented. While sampling at the rate of $\frac{1}{2}$, 15 nondefective units were inspected and recorded on the third line of the work sheet. He then shifted to the rate of $\frac{1}{4}$ (again by tossing a coin twice and inspecting a given generator if two heads were obtained) and started recording the results on line 4. The ninth unit inspected proved to be defective, so he shifted to the 2R state and started recording the results on line 5. The next 4 units were good, so he shifted to the 2° state and proceeded to sample at the rate of $\frac{1}{4}$ until a total of 15 good units had been inspected since the defective, i.e., 11 nondefective after leaving state 2R. These results were recorded in line 6. He then shifted to level 3 and inspected at the rate of $\frac{1}{8}$, again by some random selection. No defectives were found in the first 15 inspected. Since the plan called for 3 levels, the inspector started a new line and continued to inspect at the rate of $\frac{1}{8}$. This was recorded on line 8. The tenth unit inspected on line 8 was defective; so he shifted to the 3R state and inspected the next four items. The inspector continued in accordance with the sampling plan, and each time a defective was found, he initiated corrective action. The inspector kept a record of the causes and the corrective action taken.

H106 contains curves for average outgoing quality and expected average fraction inspected for all the plans. H107 also provides characteristic curves for the single-level continuous sampling plans. Note that these are not Operating Characteristics (OC) curves in the sense previously used. The characteristic curves of H107 for CSP-1 and CSP-2 give "Percent of Product Accepted on a Sampling Basis" as an ordinate vs. "Percent Defective of Submitted Product." For CSP-A plans the ordinate is "Percent of Time Inspection Will *Not* Be Stopped" vs. "Percent Defective of Submitted Product." Since these plans are actually designed on an AOQL basis, the AOQ curves and the Expected Average Fraction Inspected Curves of H106 would be more useful.

Notice that all the continuous plans discussed so far are based on the AOQL concept, i.e., requiring periods of 100% inspection during which only nondefective product is accepted. This action controls the average defectiveness of accepted product at some predetermined level. In all these cases, inspection must be non-destructive to employ the AOQL principle.

SKIP-LOT PLANS

Skip-lot sampling plans are used when there is a strong desire to reduce the total amount of inspection. The approach is to satisfy some initial criteria, such as 10 or so consecutively accepted lots, and then determine what fraction of lots will be inspected. Given this fraction, the lots to be inspected are chosen using some random selection procedure. The assumptions on which the use of skip-lot plans are based are much like those for chain-sampling plans. OC curves for the entire skip-

TABLE 24-11 Multilevel Continuous Sampling Plans for $f = 1/2$

N Contract size or Production rate		0.10	0.15	0.25	0.35	0.50	0.75	1.0	1.5	2.0	3.0	5.0	7.5	10.0	15.0
4–65	i									↓	↓	5		4	
	k											1		2	
66–135	i								↓	18	11		↓		
	k									1	1				
136–200	i							↓	25			↓	6		
	k								1				2		
201–300	i							39				↓	11		
	k							1					2		
301–400	i						↓			↓	20			↓	
	k										2				
401–500	i						54		↓	31			↓	6	
	k						1			2				3	
501–700	i					82		↓	43			↓	9		4
	k					1			2				3		4
701–1,100	i				119		65				↓	15		↓	
	k				1		2					3			
1,101–1,500	i		↓	167			↓			↓	26	↓	↓	8	
	k			1							3			4	
1,501–2,700	i	↓	218		↓	↓	88		↓	40	↓	18	11		
	k		1				2			3		4	4		
2,701–4,000	i	421		↓	197	132			55	↓	31				
	k	1			2	2			3		4				
4,001–5,500	i		↓	269				↓	↓	47					
	k			2						4					
5,501–8,500	i		446			↓	↓	83	63						
	k		2					3	4						
8,501–10,500	i	↓			↓	168	112	↓							
	k					3	3								
10,501–15,000	i	675		↓	241	↓	↓	95							
	k	2			3			4							
15,001–21,000	i		↓	337	↓	193	128								
	k			3		4	4								
21,001–32,000	i	↓	564	↓	275										
	k		3		4										
32,001–50,000	i	847	↓	386											
	k	3		4											
50,001–80,000	i	↓	636												
	k		4												
80,001–150,000	i	969	↓												
	k	4		↓	↓	↓	↓	↓	↓	↓	↓	↓	↓	↓	↓
150,001 and over	i	1,059	706	422	302	210	140	104	69	51	34	20	13	9	5
	k	5	5	5	5	5	5	5	5	5	5	5	5	5	5

Use the sampling below, or at the point of, the arrow. When the value of i equals or exceeds N, every unit must be inspected. (In such cases, sampling in accordance with MIL-STD-105D may be preferable.)

lot sampling scheme are generally not derived, but an AOQL concept does apply. Strong dependence is made on the constancy of production and consistency of process quality as well as faith in the producer and inspector.

The skip-lot sampling scheme was devised by Dodge (Ref. 26) and is, in essence, an extension of Continuous Sampling Acceptance Plans. He designated the scheme as SkSP-1.

The application of skip-lot sampling should be confined to those instances where a continuous supply of product is obtained from a reasonably stable and continuous process. The parameters of the plan (in terms of Continuous Sampling) are:

i = number of successive lots to be found conforming to qualify for skipping lots either at the start or after detecting a nonconforming lot

f = fraction of lots to be inspected after the initial criteria have been satisfied

n = sample size per inspected lot

c = acceptance number for each inspected lot

For example, if $i = 15, f = \frac{1}{3}$, n $= 10, c = 0$, the plan is to inspect 10 units from each lot submitted until 15 consecutive lots are found conforming, i.e., have no defectives in the sample. Then one-third of the submitted lots are chosen at random (by drawing beads from a bowl, cards from a deck, etc.) for inspection and inspected to the same n and c. As long as all lots are found to be conforming, the f-rate applies. When a nonconforming lot is identified, reversion to inspecting all lots occurs until again 15 consecutive lots are found to be conforming, and then skipping is permissible again.

Many values of f and i are possible, and these may be obtained from the Basic Curves for Plan CSP-1 (Ref. 26). For instance, for an AOQL of 2%, f values ranging from 0.50 to about 0.10 are reasonable with corresponding i values of 13 to 54.

The AOQL mentioned above requires some explanation. If, when a lot is found to be nonconforming it is 100% inspected and all defective units removed and the reconstituted lot accepted; or if nonconforming lots are replaced by lots known to be conforming, then the AOQL of $X\%$ means: on the average, not more than $X\%$ of the accepted lots will be nonconforming for the characteristic(s) under consideration. Note the similarity of this definition to that given previously; here the AOQL means $X\%$ of *lots* accepted; previously, it meant $X\%$ of *units* accepted.

One further consideration is whether to apply the skip-lot procedure to only one characteristic of a product, to all characteristics simultaneously, or just to some. The plan is obvious and straightforward when applied only to one product characteristic, perhaps a particularly expensive one in time or dollars. If applied to several characteristics, it might be best to inspect the f fraction for these characteristics on each lot. For example, if 6 characteristics are candidates for skip-lot sampling and $f = \frac{1}{3}$, perhaps 2 of these would be examined on one lot, two on another, and two on the third, again in some random fashion, so that all lots receive some inspection. Of course, if the most expensive part of the sampling scheme was forming the lot, sampling from it, and keeping records, the choice might be to inspect all characteristics on the same sample units. This argument may be extended to the case where all inspection characteristics are on a skip-lot basis; but if inspection is very complex, this is difficult to visualize.

CUMULATIVE SUM SAMPLING PLANS

A scheme has been devised (Ref. 27) whereby the continuous inspection approach may be employed when inspection is destructive. Acceptance or rejection of the continuously produced product is based on the cumulation of the observed number of defectives. In addition, it is possible to discriminate between two levels of quality, an Acceptable Quality Level (AQL) and a Rejectable Quality Level (RQL).

Prior to the development of Cumulative Sum Plans the following situation frequently occurred when inspection was destructive. Since production was continuous, usually there was no technically rational procedure for defining lots. A common procedure was to accumulate product until a lot was formed and then sample and make the acceptance or rejection decision. Two objections to this were: the time delay in making a decision on the product was too long, and a few short periods of bad production could cause a large quantity of good product to be rejected. Various approaches to lessening this jeopardy were used, all with some logical or practical drawback.

The procedure of Ref. 27 establishes two zones, an accept zone and a reject zone, and product is accepted or rejected according to the cumulative sum of defectives observed. Figure 24-14 illustrates the scheme. To implement the plan, a sample

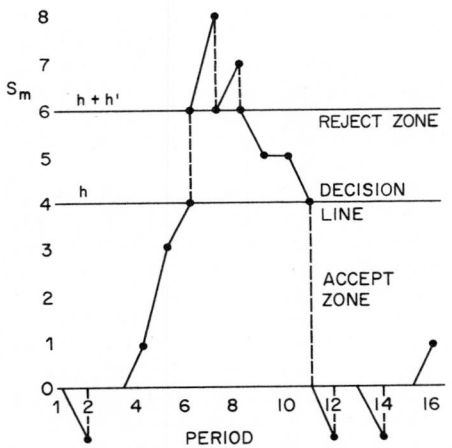

Fig. 24-14   Form of chart for acceptance under cumulative sum sampling plans.

of size n is chosen at regular intervals from production. The units are inspected and the number of defective units d_i in the ith sample recorded. Then,

$$S_m = \sum_{i=1}^{m} (d_i - k)$$

is accumulated, where k is a parameter of the scheme and S_m is computed and plotted according to the following rules:

1. Start the cumulation, S_m, at zero.
2. Accept product as long as $S_m < h$, where h is a second parameter of the scheme. When $S_m < 0$, return the cumulation to zero.
3. When h is crossed or reached from below, reject product and restart the cumulation at $h + h'$ (h' is a third parameter of the plan).
4. Continue rejecting product as long as $S_m \geq h$. When $S_m > h + h'$, return calculation to $h + h'$ and continue rejecting product until $S_m < h$.
5. When h is crossed or reached from above, accept product and restart cumulation at zero.

The discriminatory capability of the plans is controlled through the choice of k, h, and h' and their combinations. In familiar terms, k is akin to an acceptance number and h defines how far one is willing to deviate from this number over a long run and still accept product. The quantity h' is essentially how much evidence is required to be assured the process has been corrected.

The protection offered by this type of plan, which is similar to a type B acceptance situation, is defined by an OC curve which is determined by the ratio of the average run length (ARL) in the accept zone to the sum of the ARL in the accept and reject zones. An example, taken from Ref. 28, follows.

A production situation exists where thermal batteries are produced at the rate of 50 per day. Testing is destructive, and a suitable number for testing is five per day. Based upon the reliability requirements of the system for which the battery is a component, a sampling plan with $P_a \approx 0.95$ at $p = 0.025$ (AQL = 0.025) and $P_a \approx 0.10$ at $p = 0.15$ (RQL = 0.15) was appropriate.

On the basis of the desired AQL and RQL, two comparable plans were suggested: (1) a conventional single-sampling plan with $n = 35$, $c = 2$, and (2) a cumulative sum plan with $n = 10$, $h = 1$, $h' = 2$, $k = 1$. The OC curves of these two plans coincide.

The two plans are compared during a period of 70 days' production of 50 batteries per day. For Plan 1, a sample was generated by taking five batteries per day for 7 days, and from this sample the total number of defective batteries was recorded. If there were two or fewer observed defective batteries, the 7 days' production was accepted; otherwise it was rejected.

For Plan 2, a sample was formed by taking five batteries per day for 2 days, and from this sample the total number of defective batteries was recorded. The cumulative sums $\Sigma(d - 1)$, since $k = 1$, was then ploted for each 2-day period, and the decision to reject or accept these periods of production was based on the value of $\Sigma(d - 1)$.

The results of the comparison showed that 21 days' production with three observed defectives was accepted by the single-sampling plan and 30 days' production with four observed defectives was accepted by the cumulative sum plan. Thus, the cumulative sum plan provided a 42% greater yield of batteries with the same protection and approximately the same (0.027 vs. 0.028) estimated quality of accepted product.

The above example points up the weakness of using a conventional single-sampling plan when the quality is spotty where just a few isolated days of bad product can cause several days' production to be rejected. Conversely, the cumulative sum procedure was able to adapt to the sporadic quality and appears to be well suited for such a process.

The reader should be cautioned that the Cumulative Sum Scheme has not had widespread use to date. The reason seems to be the unfamiliarity rather than any theoretical or practical shortcoming of the scheme.

REFERENCES

1. Hamaker, H. C., and H. J. Prins, The Random Sampling Bulb, *EOQC Bulletin*, pp. 327–329, Philips Research Laboratories, Eindhoven, Netherlands, December 1960.
2. "Definitions and Symbols for Acceptance Sampling by Attributes," ASQC Standard A2-1971/ANSI Std. Z1.6-1971, American Society for Quality Control, Milwaukee.
3. Dodge, H. F., and H. G. Romig, "Sampling Inspection Tables," 2d ed., John Wiley & Sons, Inc., New York, 1959.
4. Burr, I. W., "Engineering Statistics and Quality Control," McGraw-Hill Book Company, New York, 1953.
5. Cameron, J. M., Tables for Constructing and for Computing the Operating Characteristics of Single Sampling Plans, *Industrial Quality Control*, July 1952, pp. 37–39.
6. Enell, J. W., What Sampling Plan Should I Choose? *Industrial Quality Control*, vol. X, No. 6, pp. 96–100, May 1954.

7. "Sampling Procedures and Tables for Inspection by Attributes," MIL-STD-105D, Government Printing Office, Washington, D.C., 1963.
8. Pabst, W. R., Jr., MIL-STD-105D, *Industrial Quality Control*, vol. XX, No. 5, pp. 4–9, November 1963.
9. "H53, Guide for Sampling Inspection," Government Printing Office, Washington, D.C., June 30, 1965.
10. Dodge, H. F., Chain Sampling Inspection Plan, *Industrial Quality Control*, vol. XI, No. 4, pp. 10–13, January 1955.
11. Clark, C. R., OC Curves for ChSP-1 Chain Sampling Plans, *Industrial Quality Control*, vol. XVII, No. 4, pp. 10–12, October 1960.
12. Dodge, H. F., and K. S. Stephens, Some New Chain Sampling Inspection Plans, *Transactions of the Nineteenth Annual Technical Conference, American Society for Quality Control*, May 3–5, 1965, p. 8–17.
13. Dodge, H. F., and K. S. Stephens, Some New Chain Sampling Inspection Plans, *Industrial Quality Control*, vol. 23, No. 2, pp. 61–67, August 1966.
14. Dodge, H. F., A Cumulative-results Sampling Plan for Small Sample Inspection, *Technical Report* 11, Statistics Center, Rutgers, The State University, New Brunswick, N.J., Apr. 27, 1962.
15. Cone, A. F., and H. F. Dodge, A Cumulative Results Plan for Small Sample Inspection, *Industrial Quality Control*, vol. 21, No. 1, pp. 4–9, July 1964.
16. Schafer, R. E., Bayes Single Sampling Plans by Attributes Based on the Posterior Risk, *Naval Research Logistics Quarterly*, vol. 14, No. 1, pp. 81–88, March 1967.
17. Hald, A., The Compound Hypergeometric Distribution and a System of Single Sampling Inspection Plans Based on Prior Distributions and Costs, *Technometrics*, vol. 2, No. 3, pp. 275–340, August 1960.
18. Schafer, R. E., Bayesian Operating Characteristic Curves for Reliability and Quality Sampling Plans, *Industrial Quality Control*, vol. 21, No. 3, pp. 118–122, September 1964.
19. Taylor, E. F., Discovery Sampling, *Proceedings of the Ninth Annual ASQC Convention*, American Society for Quality Control, Inc., Milwaukee, 1955.
20. Taylor, E. F., "The Reliability of Sampling Plans," The Martin Company, Baltimore, Md., 1960.
21. Dodge, H. F., and M. N. Torrey, Additional Continuous Sampling Inspection Plans, *Industrial Quality Control*, vol. 7, No. 5, pp. 7–12, March 1951.
22. Dodge, H. F., Notes on the Evolution of Acceptance Sampling Plans, Part IV, *Journal of Quality Technology*, vol. 2, No. 1, pp. 1–8, January 1970.
23. "H107, Single-level Continuous Sampling Procedures and Tables for Inspection by Attributes," Government Printing Office, Washington, D.C.
24. Murphy, R. B., Stopping Rules with CSP-1 Sampling Inspection Plans in Continuous Production, *Industrial Quality Control*, vol. 16, No. 5, pp. 10–16, November 1959.
25. "H106, Multi-level Continuous Sampling Procedures and Tables for Inspection by Attributes," Government Printing Office, Washington, D.C.
26. Dodge, H. F., Skip-lot Sampling Plans, *Industrial Quality Control*, vol. XI, No. 5, pp. 3–5, February 1955.
27. Beattie, D. W., A Continuous Acceptance Sampling Procedure Based upon a Cumulative Sum Chart for the Number of Defectives, *Applied Statistics*, vol. 11, No. 3, pp. 137–147, November 1962.
28. Prairie, R. R., and W. J. Zimmer, Graphs, Tables and Discussion to Aid in the Design and Evaluation of an Acceptance Sampling Procedure Based on Cumulative Sums, *Journal of Quality Technology*, vol. 5, No. 2, pp. 58–66, April 1973.

Sampling by Variables

EDWARD G. SCHILLING, Ph.D.

Consulting Statistician,
General Electric Company,
Lamp Business Division

INTRODUCTION

Specifications are often written in terms of a simple *classification* of product into categories of defective and nondefective (e.g., broken pieces in a shipment). Attributes sampling plans are appropriate for the discrete data resulting from inspection to this type of specification. Such plans involve comparison of the number of defectives counted in the sample to an acceptance number to determine the acceptability of the lot.

When specifications are stated in terms of *continuous measurements* on individual units of product (e.g., weight of each of the pieces in a shipment), attributes plans may still be used on a go no-go basis by gaging or by classifying sample measurements simply as defective or nondefective. However, considerable savings in sample size may be achieved by applying a variables sampling plan directly to the measurements themselves. Variables plans may also be used when primary interest is in process level rather than percent defective.   Both types of variables plans involve comparison of a statistic (such as the mean) computed from a sample of the product, with a limiting value or acceptance limit, to determine the disposition of the lot.[1]

Types of Variables Plans   Attributes plans are generally applied on a percent defective basis.   That is, the plan is instituted to control the proportion of product which is defective or out of specification.   *Variables plans for percent defective* are also used in this way.   Such plans provide a sensitivity greater than attributes but require that *the shape of the distribution of individual measurements must be known and stable.*   The shape of the distribution is used to translate the proportion defective into specific values of process parameters (mean, standard deviation) which are then controlled.

Variables plans can also be used to control process parameters to given levels when specifications are directed toward the process average or process variability and not specifically to percent defective.   These *variables plans for process parameter* do not necessarily require detailed knowledge of the shape of the underlying distribution of individual measurements.

Sampling plans used in reliability and in the sampling of bulk product are generally of this type.   Published plans in the reliability area, however, usually require detailed knowledge of the shape of the distribution of lifetimes.

COMPARISON OF ATTRIBUTES AND VARIABLES PLANS

Some of the important features of attributes and variables plans for percent defective are compared in Table 25-1.

The principal advantage of variables plans for percent defective over corresponding attributes plans is a reduction in the sample size needed to obtain a given degree of protection.   Table 25-2 shows a comparison of variables sample sizes necessary to achieve the same protection as the attributes plan: $n = 125$, $c = 3$ (MIL-STD-105D, Code K, Inspection Level II, 1% AQL used for comparative purposes in Section 24).

Probably the most important consideration in the application of variables sampling plans is the requirement that the shape of the underlying distribution of measurements to which the plan is to be applied must be known.   For example, if the diameters of individual units of product are to be inspected, those diameters must be distributed in a known pattern.   This means that statistical tests on past data must show that the distribution of the measurements involved is actually that assumed by the plan.   Control chart evidence is also desirable to indicate process stability.   This point cannot be overemphasized, since a principal use of the distributional assumption in variables acceptance sampling for percent defective is with regard to individual units and not sample means, which can usually be assumed to be normally distributed.   While it has been argued[2] that variables plans may be roughly correct when applied to distributions other than the distribution assumed, judicious application requires confirmation that the underlying distribution of the process to which the plan is applied is actually that assumed by the plan.

---

[1] The basic concepts of acceptance sampling include much that is common to both sampling by attributes and sampling by variables.   Because of this commonality and to avoid duplication, these common concepts are presented in Section 24, under Sampling—Common Concepts.   Readers are urged to consider that material as part of this introduction to Sampling by Variables.

[2] Jennett, W. J., and B. L. Welch, The Control of Proportion Defective as Judged by a Single Quality Characteristic Varying on a Continuous Scale, *Journal of the Royal Statistical Society,* Series B, vol. VI, pp. 80–88, 1939.

TABLE 25-1   Comparison of Attributes and Variables Sampling Plans for Percent Defective

Feature	Attributes	Variables
Inspection	Each item classified as defective or nondefective. Go no-go gages may be employed	Each item measured. Inspection more sophisticated. Higher inspection and clerical cost
Distribution of individual measurements	Need not be known	*Must* be known (normal usually assumed)
Type of defect	Any number of defect types can be assessed by one plan	Separate plan required for each type of defect
Sample size	Depends on protection required	Smaller sample size for same protection as attributes (at least 30% smaller*)
Process information	Percent defective	Percent defective plus valuable information on process average and variability for corrective action
Severity	Weights all defectives of a given kind equally	Weights each unit inspected by its proximity to specifications
Evidence to supplier	Defectives available as evidence	Possible for lot to be rejected on sample containing no defectives
Measurement errors	Measurements not recorded	Measurements available for review
Screened lots	No effect on performance of plan	Screened lots may be rejected in error even though they contain no defectives

*Bowker, A. H., and H. P. Goode, "Sampling Inspection by Variables," pp. 32–33, McGraw-Hill Book Company, New York, 1952. Assumes single sample of one characteristic.

TABLE 25-2   Comparison of Variables and Attributes Sample Sizes*

$$p_1 = 0.0109 \qquad \alpha = 0.05$$
$$p_2 = 0.0535 \qquad \beta = 0.10$$

Plan	Sample size
Single-sampling attributes.	125
Variables:	
σ known	19
σ unknown (s).	52
σ unknown ($\bar{R}$ of groups of 5)	75
Sequential sampling, σ known (ASN at p_1)	10.3

Based on MIL-STD-105D, Code K, 1% AQL.
*Specifications assumed to be $> 6\sigma$ apart if two-sided. ASN (Average Sample Number), p_1, and p_2 as defined in Section 24.

In applying variables plans, it is advantageous to use a "known standard deviation" plan whenever possible. This usually requires a control chart, in control, with about 20 or more samples plotted to assure a stable level of standard deviation. The chart is maintained as long as the known standard deviation plan is being used. In the absence of such a chart, unknown standard deviation plans may be used, although knowledge of the shape of the distribution is still required for variables plans for percent defective. The construction and use of control charts are discussed in Section 23. The discussion, in Section 24, of lot formation and sample selection is also of critical importance.

AREAS OF APPLICATION

Since some fundamental knowledge of the process producing the product is required for proper application of variables sampling plans for percent defective, a natural area of application of such plans is to in-house inspections, e.g., process control or final inspection. Use of these plans in incoming inspection should be restricted to product from known and trusted suppliers with a confirmed history of a reasonably stable process steadily producing product with a known shape of distribution. Process history should be initially developed under an attributes sampling plan. A switch to variables may be considered after a plot on probability paper or a goodness of fit test (see Section 22) indicates that the distribution of product is as assumed. A control chart for at least 20 lots is useful to confirm process stability. There are times when the inspection situation demands the use of fewer lots. In such situations, appropriate limits for a 10-lot control chart have been developed by Hillier.[3] Variables plans are inappropriate for inspection of single lots unless the sample size is large enough to allow for meaningful goodness of fit tests to confirm that the shape of the underlying distribution of measurements is as assumed.

Variables plans for process parameter may be used whenever specifications are stated in terms of process mean or standard deviation. While control charts assess the consistency of process levels, acceptance sampling plans should be used to determine conformance to specifications. This is important, since both consumer and producer risks should be considered in acceptance sampling, while conventional Shewhart control charts consider only the producer's risk at one specified level ($\alpha = 0.003$).

JUSTIFICATION OF VARIABLES PLANS

Some of the background justification for variables sampling plans for percent defective is illustrated in Fig. 25-1, which assumes the underlying distribution of measurements to be normal with standard deviation σ known.

Suppose the following sampling plan is used to test against an upper specification limit U:

1. Sample n items from the lot and determine the sample mean $\overline{X}$.
2. Test against an acceptance limit $(U - k\sigma)$, k standard deviation units inside the specification.
3. If $\overline{X} \leq (U - k\sigma)$, accept the product; otherwise reject the product.

If the distribution of individual measurements is normal, as shown, a proportion p of the product above the specification limit U implies the mean of the distribution must be fixed at the position indicated by μ. Means of samples of size n are, then, distributed about μ, as shown; so the probability of obtaining an $\overline{X}$ not greater than $(U - k\sigma)$ is indicated by the shaded area of the distribution of sample means. This shaded area is the probability of acceptance when the fraction defective in the process is p. Note that the normal shape supplies the necessary connection between the distribution of the sample means and the proportion of product defective. While, for reasonable sample sizes, the distribution of *sample means* will be normal, regardless of the shape of the underlying distribution of individual measurements, it is the underlying distribution of measurements itself that determines the relationship of μ and p. Hence, the plan will be quite sensitive to departures from normality.

[3] Hillier, F. S., $\overline{X}$- and R-chart Control Limits Based on a Small Number of Subgroups, *Journal of Quality Technology*, vol. 1, No. 1, pp. 17–26, January 1969.

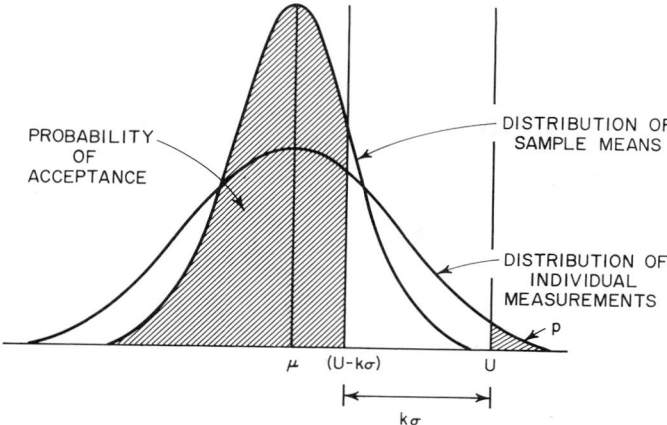

Fig. 25-1 $(U - k\sigma)$ method.

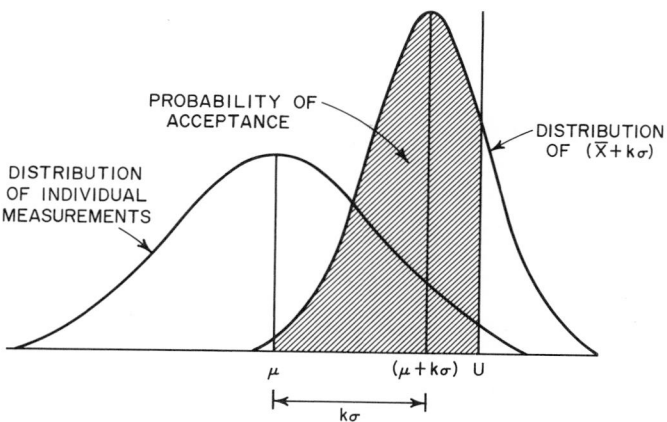

Fig. 25-2 $(\overline{X} + k\sigma)$ method.

Since $\overline{X} \leq U - k\sigma$ is equivalent to $\overline{X} + k\sigma \leq U$, the above sampling plan may be expressed as follows:

1. Sample n items from the lot and determine the sample mean $\overline{X}$.

2. If $\overline{X} + k\sigma \leq U$, accept the product; otherwise reject the product.

This is the method used to specify variables sampling plans in MIL-STD-414.[4]   Diagrammatically, this second method of specifying a sampling plan is indicated in Figure 25-2.   Adding $k\sigma$ to each $\overline{X}$ moves the distribution of the sample means to the right a distance $k\sigma$, so that the upper specification limit U plays the role of the acceptance limit.   This can be seen by comparing Figure 25-1 with Figure 25-2.

Using Figure 25-1 or Figure 25-2 and normal probability theory, it is possible to

[4] "Sampling Procedures and Tables for Inspection by Variables for Percent Defective," MIL-STD-414, U.S. Department of Defense, Military Standard, Government Printing Office, Washington, D.C., 1957.

calculate the probability of acceptance P_a for various possible values of p, the proportion defective. A graph of P_a vs. p traces the operating characteristic curve of the acceptance sampling plan. Figure 25-3 shows the operating characteristic curve of the variables plan $n = 19$, $k = 1.908$, testing against a single-sided specification limit with known standard deviation. For comparative purposes, the OC curve of the attributes plan $n = 125$, $c = 3$ is also given. Note that the OC curves intersect at about $p = 0.01$ and $p = 0.05$, indicating roughly equivalent protection at these fractions defective.

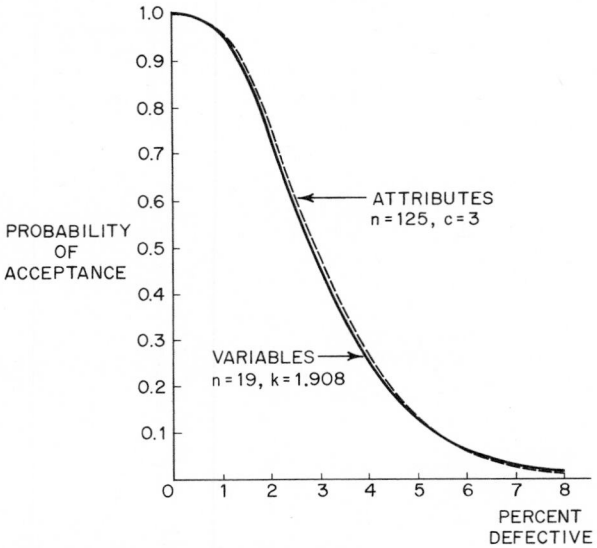

Fig. 25-3   Operating characteristic curve.

Probability theory appropriate to other methods of specifying variables plans (e.g., standard deviation unknown, double specification limits) can be used to give the OC curves and other properties of these procedures. Formulas for determining plans to meet specific prescribed conditions can also be derived. Note that the OC curves of variables plans are generally considered to be type B as discussed in Section 24. That is, they are regarded as sampling from the process producing the items inspected, rather than the immediate lot of material involved.

When process parameters are specified, sampling plans can be developed from analogous tests of significance with corresponding OC curves. These plans do not require percent defective to be related to the process mean, since the specifications to which they are applied are not in terms of percent defective.[5] This means that assumptions of process distribution may not need to be as rigorously held as in variables plans for percent defective.

There is often much more involved in acceptance sampling than simple tests of hypotheses. *Sampling plans* applied individually to guard against an occasional discrepant lot can be reduced to hypothesis tests. Sampling plans, however, may be combined into *sampling schemes,* intended to achieve a predetermined objective.

[5] However, such a relationship may have been in the original specification of process level.

Sampling schemes, as overall strategies using one or more sampling plans, have their own measures such as AOQ (Average Outgoing Quality) or ATI (Average Total Inspection), not to be found in hypothesis testing. Thus, MIL-STD-105D and its variables counterpart MIL-STD-414, are sampling schemes which specify the use of various sampling plans under well-defined rules.

BASIC ELEMENTS OF SAMPLING PLANS

Application of any acceptance sampling plan to a specific lot or unit of product requires knowledge of three elements:

1. Sample size—the number of items to be sampled from a specific lot or process
2. Statistic—a value determined from the sample to serve as an index of lot or process quality
3. Decision criteria—specification of values of the statistic leading to lot or process acceptance or rejection:
    a. Acceptance criterion—values leading to acceptance
    b. Rejection criterion—values leading to rejection

The sampling plan is implemented as follows: a sample of the stated size is taken, and the statistic is computed from the sample results[6] and then compared with the decision criteria for acceptance or rejection.

Table 25-3 provides a summary of variables plans in common use. Most of the plans in this Section are explained in tables which define the step-by-step procedure for employing the three elements involved and present an example.

Each of the procedures shown for variables plans for process parameter and for percent defective is illustrated using a set of data adapted from MIL-STD-414.[7] The data follow below, and will be used repeatedly to exemplify the use of the plans.

DATA TO BE USED IN EXAMPLES

"The specification for electrical resistance of a certain electrical component is $650.0^\pm 30$ ohms. A lot of 100 items is submitted for inspection. Inspection Level IV, normal inspection, with AQL = 2.5%. . . . Suppose the values of the sample resistances in the order reading from left to right are as follows:"[8]

$$643, 651, 619, 627, 658, 670, 673, 641, 638, 650$$

Should the lot be accepted?
For these data,

$$\bar{X} = 647$$

$$s = \sqrt{\frac{\sum(X - \bar{X})^2}{n-1}} = 17.22$$

In examples where known standard deviation is required, it will be assumed that $\sigma = 13$.

VARIABLES PLANS FOR PERCENT DEFECTIVE

When interest is centered on the proportion of product outside measurement specifications, and when the underlying distribution of individual measurements is known, variables plans for percent defective may be used. These plans relate the

---

[6] It is assumed that the precision of the measuring process, Section 13, is adequate.
[7] *Op. cit.*
[8] MIL-STD-414, *op. cit.*

TABLE 25-3 Summary of Variables Sampling Plans

Type of plan	Plan	Assumed distribution	Criteria specified	Features	Reference
Percent defective	MIL-STD-414	Normal	Acceptable quality level (percent defective)	Tables and procedures for lot evaluation to a specified AQL. Includes tightened and reduced inspection. OC curves given	Table 25-4, Table 25-7
	Mixed variables –attributes (MIL-STD-414)	Normal	Acceptable quality level (percent defective)	For use with MIL-STD-414 when lots have been screened before submission to sampling inspection	Table 25-11
	Lot plot	None	Allowable percent defective	Requires 50 measurements. Simple calculations and graphical procedure used to evaluate lot	Table 25-12
	Single-sampling variables plan	Normal	Acceptable and rejectable percent defective	Formulas for determining sample size and acceptance criteria to meet defined risks	See reference on page 25-17
Lot or process parameter—general	Test of hypothesis	Appropriate for test	Mean or standard deviation	Formulas for determining sample size and acceptance criteria to meet defined risks	Section 22
	Acceptance control chart	Appropriate for determining acceptable and rejectable values of mean	Mean	Graphical procedure to determine if mean falls within defined limits	Table 25-13

TABLE 25-3 Summary of Variables Sampling Plans (*Continued*)

Type of plan	Plan	Assumed distribution	Criteria specified	Features	Reference
	Sequential sampling	Normal	Mean or standard deviation	Procedures for evaluating one measurement at a time to determine if mean falls within defined limits. Complex but total sample size lower than with other plans	Pages 25-28 to 25-29
Lot or process parameter— reliability and life testing	H108	Exponential	Mean life	Tables for lot evaluation for testing with and without replacement of failed items and for tests terminated based on preassigned time or failures. Also sequential testing	Table 25-17
	MIL-STD-690B	Exponential	Failure rate	Tables for process rather than lot evaluation. Designed for application to electronic parts	Pages 25-33 to 25-35
	MIL-STD-781B	Exponential	Mean life	Tables for process and lot evaluation. Designed for application to electronic parts	Page 25-35
	TR-3 TR-4 TR-6	Weibull Weibull Weibull	Mean life Hazard rate Reliable life	Tables for evaluating reliability with Producer's Risk of 0.05 and Consumer's Risk of 0.10. Tables cover Weibull parameter from 1/3 to 5 and thus include most common shapes	Table 25-20 and pages 25-35 to 25-39

TABLE 25-3   Summary of Variables Sampling Plans *(Continued)*

Type of plan	Plan	Assumed distribution	Criteria specified	Features	Reference
	TR-7	Weibull	Same as TR-3, TR-4, TR-6	Relates mean life, hazard rate, and reliable life plans to attribute plans in MIL-STD-105D	Page 25-39
Lot or process parameter – bulk sampling	Specific bulk sampling models	Appropriate for test	Mean	Formulas for determining sample size to estimate mean with specified confidence interval. Applicable for gaseous, liquid, or solid products which occur in nondiscrete units	Sec. 25A

proportion of individual units outside specification limits to the population mean through appropriate probability theory. The sample mean, usually suitably transformed, is then used to test for the position of the population mean in the manner of the variables plans for process parameter.

Assume the distribution of individual measurements is known to be normal and a plan is desired such that the OC curve will pass through the two points $(p_1, 1 - a)$ and (p_2, β) where

$p_1 =$ acceptable proportion defective
$1 - a =$ probability of acceptance at p_1
$p_2 =$ rejectable proportion defective
$\beta =$ probability of acceptance at p_2

The OC curve should appear as indicated in Figure 25-4. Some important plans of this type are described below.

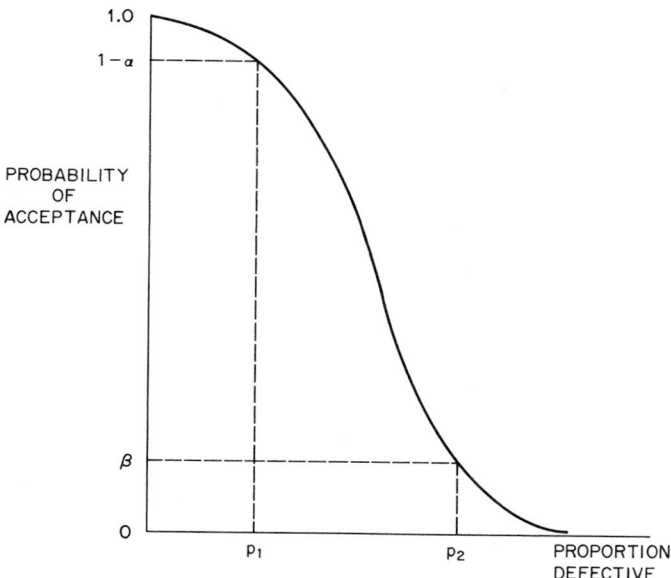

Fig. 25-4   Operating characteristic curve.

Military Standard 414   Military Standard 414[9] is an AQL[10] type of sampling scheme which assumes the individual measurements to which it is applied to be normally distributed.

The standard allows for the use of three alternative measures of variability: known standard deviation σ, estimated standard deviation s, or average range($\bar{R}$). If the variability of the process producing the product is known and stable as verified by a control chart, it is profitable to use σ. The choice between s and $\bar{R}$, when σ is unknown, is an economic one.[11]   The range requires larger sample

[9] *Op. cit.*
[10] See Section 24, under Sampling Risks and Parameters.
[11] A general procedure for using the range in variables sampling plans is described in A. J. Duncan, "Quality Control and Industrial Statistics," 3d ed., pp. 250–252, Richard D. Irwin, Inc., Homewood, Ill., 1965.

sizes but is easier to compute. The operating characteristic curves given in the standard are based on the use of s, the σ and $\bar{R}$ plans having been matched, as closely as possible, to those using s.

MIL-STD-414 offers two alternative procedures. In addition to the method using an acceptance constant k, the standard also presents a procedure for estimating the proportion defective in the lot from the variables evidence. The former method is called Form 1; the latter is called Form 2. Form 2 is the preferred procedure, since the switching rules for reduced and tightened inspection cannot be applied unless the fraction defective of each lot is estimated from the sample.

These two procedures can be compared with equivalent forms of attributes sampling. One possibility is to compare the number of defectives found in the sample d with an acceptance number c. Alternatively, the proportion defective in the population could be estimated from the proportion defective in the sample, and that estimate then compared with some acceptance limit (M). These possibilities are compared with their variables counterparts in Figure 25-5.

	Attributes	Variables
Form 1	$d \leq c$	$z = \dfrac{U - \bar{X}}{s} \geq k$
Form 2	$p = \dfrac{d}{n} \leq \dfrac{c}{n} = M$	$Q = \dfrac{U - \bar{X}}{s}$ is used to estimate p
		$p \leq M$

Fig. 25-5   Criteria for acceptance (sample of n).

The standard is composed of sections indexed by measure of variability, type of specification (single or double), and Form of the acceptance procedure. Only Form 2 is officially available for the case of double specification limits; however, factors are provided for application of Form 1 if desired. The structure of the standard is shown in Figure 25-6.

Application of MIL-STD-414 follows the pattern of MIL-STD-105D, which is also an AQL sampling scheme. Sample sizes are determined from lot size, and after choosing the measure of variability to be used and the Form of the acceptance procedure, appropriate acceptance limits are obtained from the standard. As in MIL-STD-105D, operating characteristic curves are included in MIL-STD-414 and should be consulted before a specific plan is instituted. Note that the plans contained in these two standards do *not* match.

Since it is an AQL scheme, MIL-STD-414 is based on an overall strategy which incorporates *switching* rules to move from normal to tightened or reduced inspection and return depending on the quality observed in the previous 10 lots. These switching rules are indicated in Figure 25-7 and should be used if the standard is to be properly applied.

A check sequence for application of MIL-STD-414 is given in Figure 25-8. Tables 25-4 and 25-7 show the specific steps involved in application of the two Forms using the sample standard deviation as a measure of variability. Procedures for upper, lower, and double specification limits are indicated in these Tables together with appropriate references to the standard and an illustrative example. Modifications to the procedure, necessary when variability is measured by average range or a known standard deviation, are described. Table 25-10 shows the relationship of the statistics and procedures used under the various measures of variability allowed, for each of the Forms.

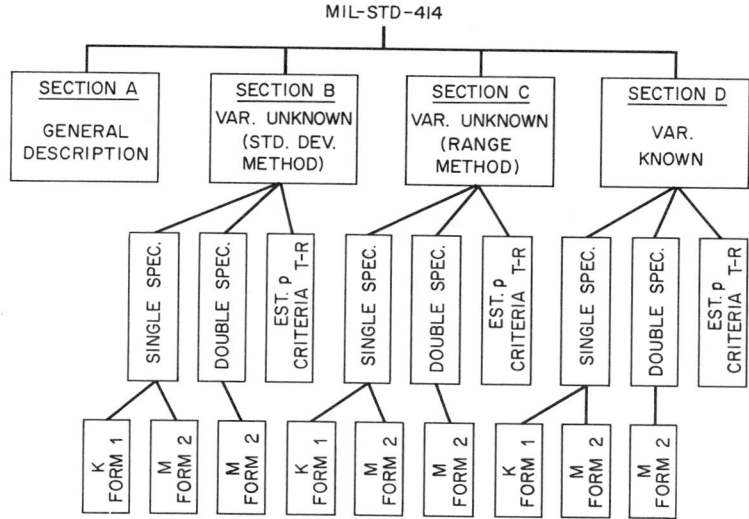

MIL-STD-414

| SECTION A | SECTION B | SECTION C | SECTION D |
| GENERAL DESCRIPTION | VAR. UNKNOWN (STD. DEV. METHOD) | VAR. UNKNOWN (RANGE METHOD) | VAR. KNOWN |

Fig. 25-6   Structure of MIL-STD-414. (*E. G. Schilling, Variables Sampling and MIL-STD-414, Transactions of Twenty-sixth Quality Control Conference of the Rochester Society for Quality Control, Mar. 30, 1970, pp. 175–188.*)

MIL-STD-414 has a liberal supply of excellent examples. The reader is referred to the standard for more detailed examples of its applications.

Mixed Variables—Attributes Plans   Attributes plans reject on the basis of the number of defects found in a sample. Variables plans, however, use statistics (such as $\bar{X}$ and s) to indicate the quality of the lot. When all defectives are removed in a screening process, the resulting screened lot cannot be rejected by an attributes plan, since there are no defectives contained therein (assuming 100% accuracy in screening).

One disadvantage of variables plans is the fact that screened lots may at times be rejected by a sample $\bar{X}$ or s indicating percent defective to be high when, actually, the discrepant material has been eliminated. To prevent rejection of screened lots, double-sampling plans have been developed which use a variables criterion on the first sample and attributes on the second sample. Lots are accepted if they pass variables inspection; however, if they do not pass, a second sample is taken and the results are judged by an attributes criterion. In this way screened lots will not be rejected, since rejections are made only under the attributes part of the plan. This type of plan was proposed as early as 1932.[12] The procedure has been discussed in some detail by Bowker and Goode,[13] Gregory and Resnikoff,[14] and Schilling and Dodge.[15] MIL-STD-414 allows for the use of such procedures. The steps involved are shown in Table 25-11.

[12] Dodge, H. F., Statistical Control on Sampling Inspection, *American Machinist,* October 1932, pp. 1085–1088.

[13] Bowker, A. H., and H. P. Goode, "Sampling Inspection by Variables," McGraw-Hill Book Company, New York, 1952.

[14] Gregory, G., and G. J. Resnikoff, Some Notes on Mixed Variables and Attributes Sampling Plans, *Technical Report* 10, Applied Mathematics and Statistics Laboratory, Stanford University, Mar. 15, 1955.

[15] Schilling, E. G., and H. F. Dodge, Procedures and Tables for Evaluating Dependent Mixed Acceptance Sampling Plans, *Technometrics,* vol. XI, No. 2, pp. 341–372, May 1969.

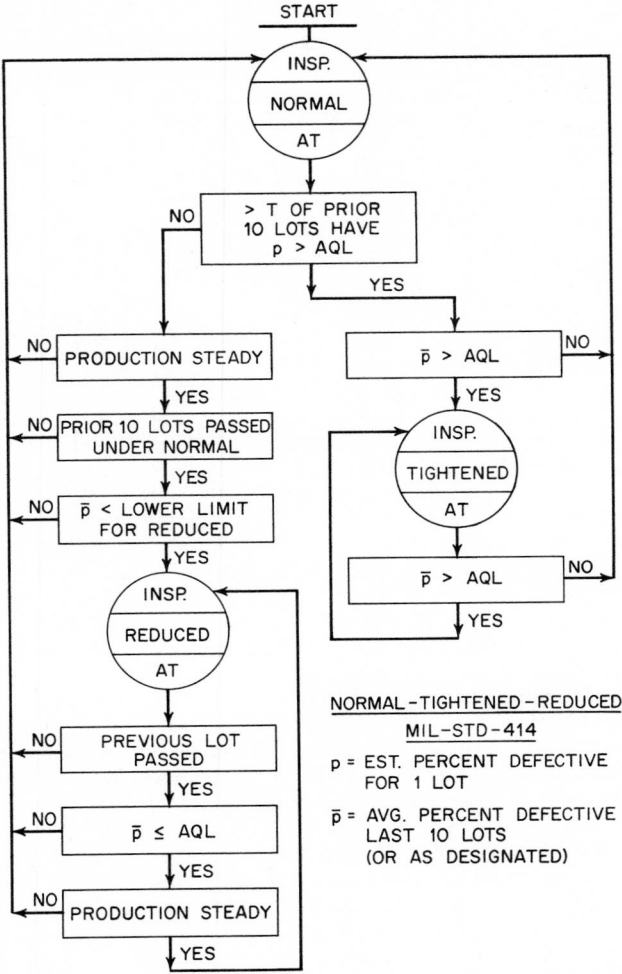

Fig. 25-7   Switching rules. *(E. G. Schilling, Variables Sampling and MIL-STD-414, Transactions of Twenty-sixth Quality Control Conference of the Rochester Society for Quality Control, Mar. 30, 1970, pp. 175–188.)*

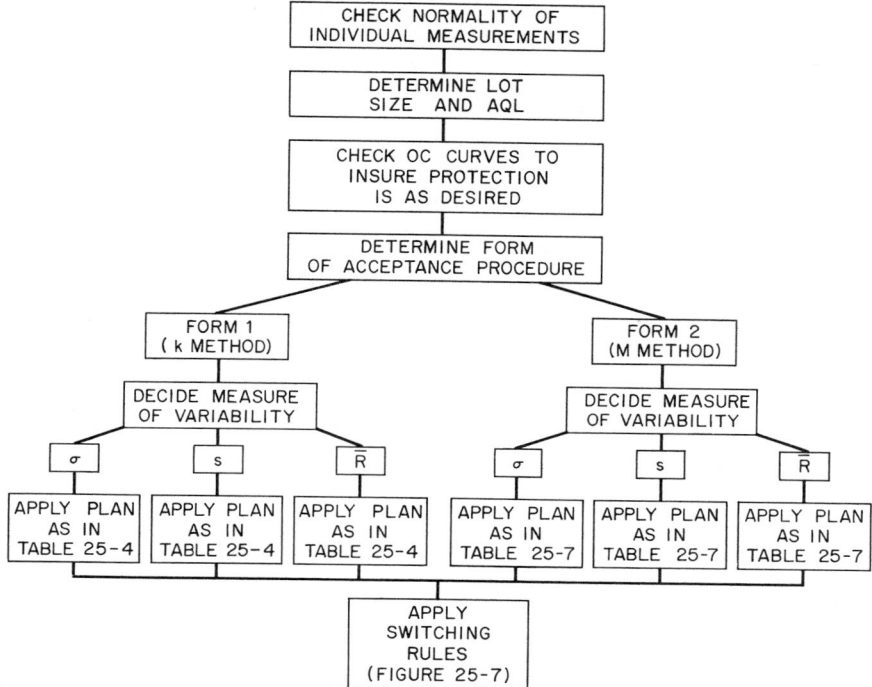

Fig. 25-8   Check sequence for MIL-STD-414.

Lot Plot   Probably no variables acceptance sampling plan matches the natural inclination of the inspector better than the Lot Plot method.[16]   Developed by Dorian Shainin at the Hamilton Standard Division of United Aircraft Co., the procedure employs a histogram (see Section 22) and rough estimates of the extremes of the distribution of product to determine lot acceptance or rejection.   A standard sample size of 50 observations is maintained.

While the method has been questioned on statistical grounds,[17] particularly for nonnormal distributions, it is useful as a tool for acceptance sampling in situations where more sophisticated methods may be inappropriate or not well received by the parties involved.   The Lot Plot plan is especially useful in introducing statistical methods.   The subjective aspects of the plan (classification of frequency distributions, their construction, etc.) and its fixed sample size suggest the use of more objective procedures in critical applications.   Its wide initial acceptance[18] attests to its appeal to inspection personnel.   The Lot Plot method is outlined in Table 25-12.   See Grant and Leavenworth[19] for details.

[16] Shainin, D., The Hamilton Standard Lot Plot Method of Acceptance Sampling by Variables, *Industrial Quality Control,* July 1950, pp. 15–34.

[17] Moses, L. E., Some Theoretical Aspects of the Lot Plot Sampling Inspection Plan, *Journal of the American Statistical Association,* vol. LI, pp. 84–107, 1956.

[18] Shainin, D., Recent Lot Plot Experiences around the Country, *Industrial Quality Control,* March 1952, pp. 20–29.

[19] Grant, E. L., and R. S. Leavenworth, "Statistical Quality Control," 4th ed., McGraw-Hill Book Company, New York, 1972.

TABLE 25-4   MIL-STD-414, Variability Unknown, Standard Deviation Method, Form 1

Example: Use the data given under Data to Be Used in Examples, above. Should the lot be accepted?

Summary of plan	Calculations
I. Restrictions: Individual measurements normally distributed	
II. Necessary information	II
A. Lot size	A. Lot size $= 100$
B. AQL	B. AQL $= 2.5\%$
C. Severity of inspection: Normal, Tightened, Reduced	C. Normal inspection
III. Selection of plan	III
A. Determine Code Letter (Table 25-5) from Lot Size and Inspection Level (Normally, Inspection Level IV is used)	A. Code F
B. From Code Letter and AQL, determine (Table 25-6)	B
1. Sample size $= n$	$n = 10$
2. Acceptance constant $= k$	$k = 1.41$
C. Double specification limits: obtain MSD $= F(U - L)$, where F is obtained from appropriate Table in the Standard	C. MSD $= 0.298(680 - 620)$ $= 17.88$
IV. Elements	IV
A. Sample size: See above	A. $n = 10$
B. Statistic	B. $T_U = (680 - 647)/17.22$
1. Upper specification: $T_U = (U - \bar{X})/s$	$= 1.92$
2. Lower specification: $T_L = (\bar{X} - L)/s$	$T_L = (647 - 620)/17.22$
3. Double specification: T_U and T_L	$= 1.57$
C. Decision Criteria	C
1. Acceptance criterion	
a. Upper specification: $T_U \geq k$	$1.92 > 1.41$
b. Lower specification: $T_L \geq k$	$1.57 > 1.41$
c. Double specification: $T_U \geq k$, $T_L \geq k$, and $s \leq$ MSD	$17.22 < 17.88$
2. Rejection criterion: Reject otherwise	
V. Action: Dispose of lot as indicated and refer to switching rules for next lot	V. Accept the lot
VI. Characteristics: OC curves given	
VII. References: "Sampling Procedures and Tables for Inspection by Variables for Percent Defective," MIL-STD-414, U.S. Department of Defense, Military Standard, Government Printing Office, Washington, D.C., 1957	
VIII. Remarks (use appropriate tables from Standard)	
A. Range method	
1. Use $\bar{R}$ of subsamples of 5 if $n \geq 10$; use $\bar{R}$ if $n < 10$	
2. Substitute $\bar{R}$ for s in statistics	
3. Double specifications—use values of f (for MAR) in place of F (for MSD), where MAR is the Maximum Allowable Range (see MIL-STD-414)	
B. Variability known: Substitute σ for s in statistics	

TABLE 25-5 Sample Size Code Letters*

Lot size	Inspection levels				
	I	II	III	IV	V
3–8	B	B	B	B	C
9–15	B	B	B	B	D
16–25	B	B	B	C	E
26–40	B	B	B	D	F
41–65	B	B	C	E	G
66–110	B	B	D	F	H
111–180	B	C	E	G	I
181–300	B	D	F	H	J
301–500	C	E	G	I	K
501–800	D	F	H	J	L
801–1,300	E	G	I	K	L
1,301–3,200	F	H	J	L	M
3,201–8,000	G	I	L	M	N
8,001–22,000	H	J	M	N	O
22,001–110,000	I	K	N	O	P
110,001–550,000	I	K	O	P	Q
550,001 and over	I	K	P	Q	Q

* Sample size code letters given in body of table are applicable when the indicated inspection levels are to be used.

Tables 25-5, 25-6, 25-8, and 25-9 are reproduced from "Sampling Procedures and Tables for Inspection by Variables for Percent Defective," MIL-STD-414, Government Printing Office, Washington, D.C., 1957.

A special Lot Plot card is helpful in simplifying some of the calculations. Figure 25-9 shows the form filled out for the example given in Table 25-12.

General Method for Deriving Single-sampling Plans by Variables MIL-STD-414 and Lot Plot are examples of variables plans that define sample size, acceptance criteria, and step-by-step procedures based on specified sampling risks.

If the sampling risks in these plans are not satisfactory, a single-sampling plan can be derived to meet two previously specified points on an OC curve. The procedure is given in Duncan.[20]

VARIABLES PLANS FOR PROCESS PARAMETER

When specifications are stated in terms of process location or variability, as measured by specific values of the mean μ or the process standard deviation σ, interest is centered not on fraction defective but rather on controlling the parameters of the distribution of product to specified levels. From specifications of this type, it is usually possible to distinguish two process levels which may be used as bench marks:[21]

1. APL = Acceptable Process Level—a process level which is acceptable and should be accepted most of the time by the plan

2. RPL = Rejectable Process Level—a process level which is rejectable and should be rejected most of the time by the plan

[20] op. cit., pp. 219–252.

[21] Freund, R. A., Acceptance Control Charts, *Industrial Quality Control*, October 1957, pp. 13–23.

TABLE 25-6   Master Table for Normal and Tightened Inspection for Plans Based on Variability Unknown, Standard Deviation Method
(Single Specification Limit, Form 1)

Sample size code letter	Sample size	Acceptable quality levels (normal inspection)													
		0.04	0.065	0.10	0.15	0.25	0.40	0.65	1.00	1.50	2.50	4.00	6.50	10.00	15.00
		k	k	k	k	k	k	k	k	k	k	k	k	k	k
B	3	→	→	→	→	→	→	→	↓	↓	1.12	0.958	0.765	0.566	0.341
C	4	→	→	→	→	→	→	→	1.45	1.34	1.17	1.01	0.814	0.617	0.393
D	5	→	→	→	→	→	→	1.65	1.53	1.40	1.24	1.07	0.874	0.675	0.455
E	7	→	→	→	→	→	1.88	1.75	1.62	1.50	1.33	1.15	0.955	0.755	0.536
F	10	→	→	→	2.24	2.11	1.98	1.84	1.72	1.58	1.41	1.23	1.03	0.828	0.611
G	15	2.64	2.53	2.42	2.32	2.20	2.06	1.91	1.79	1.65	1.47	1.30	1.09	0.886	0.664
H	20	2.69	2.58	2.47	2.36	2.24	2.11	1.96	1.82	1.69	1.51	1.33	1.12	0.917	0.695
I	25	2.72	2.61	2.50	2.40	2.26	2.14	1.98	1.85	1.72	1.53	1.35	1.14	0.936	0.712
J	30	2.73	2.61	2.51	2.41	2.28	2.15	2.00	1.86	1.73	1.55	1.36	1.15	0.946	0.723
K	35	2.77	2.65	2.54	2.45	2.31	2.18	2.03	1.89	1.76	1.57	1.39	1.18	0.969	0.745
L	40	2.77	2.66	2.55	2.44	2.31	2.18	2.03	1.89	1.76	1.58	1.39	1.18	0.971	0.746
M	50	2.83	2.71	2.60	2.50	2.35	2.22	2.08	1.93	1.80	1.61	1.42	1.21	1.00	0.774
N	75	2.90	2.77	2.66	2.55	2.41	2.27	2.12	1.98	1.84	1.65	1.46	1.24	1.03	0.804
O	100	2.92	2.80	2.69	2.58	2.43	2.29	2.14	2.00	1.86	1.67	1.48	1.26	1.05	0.819
P	150	2.96	2.84	2.73	2.61	2.47	2.33	2.18	2.03	1.89	1.70	1.51	1.29	1.07	0.841
Q	200	2.97	2.85	2.73	2.62	2.47	2.33	2.18	2.04	1.89	1.70	1.51	1.29	1.07	0.845
		0.065	0.10	0.15	0.25	0.40	0.65	1.00	1.50	2.50	4.00	6.50	10.00	15.00	
		Acceptable quality levels (tightened inspection)													

All AQL values are in percent defective.

↓ Use first sampling plan below arrow, that is, both sample size as well as k value. When sample size equals or exceeds lot size, every item in the lot must be inspected.

TABLE 25-7   MIL-STD-414, Variability Unknown, Standard Deviation Method, Form 2

Example: Use the data given under Data to Be Used in Examples, above. Should the lot be accepted?

Summary of plan	Calculations
I. Restrictions: Individual measurements normally distributed	
II. Necessary information	II
A. Lot size	A. Lot size $= 100$
B. AQL	B. AQL $= 2.5\%$
C. Severity of inspection: Normal, Tightened, Reduced	C. Normal inspection
III. Selection of plan	III
A. Determine (Table 25-5) Code Letter from Lot Size and Inspection Level (normally, inspection Level IV is used)	A. Code F
B. From Code Letter and AQL, determine (Table 25-8)	B
1. Sample size $= n$	$n = 10$
2. Value of M	$M = 7.29$
IV. Elements	IV
A. Sample size: See above	A. $n = 10$
B. Statistic	B. $Q_U = (680 - 647)/17.22$
1. Upper specification: $Q_U = (U - \bar{X})/s$	$= 1.92$
2. Lower specification: $Q_L = (\bar{X} - L)/s$	$Q_L = (647 - 620)/17.22$
3. Double specification: Q_U and Q_L	$= 1.57$
C. Estimate Percent Defective from Table 25-9	C
1. Upper specification: estimate $p_U(\%)$ from Q_U and n	$p_U(\%) = 1.68$
2. Lower specification: estimate $p_L(\%)$ from Q_L and n	$p_L(\%) = 4.92$
3. Double specification: estimate $p(\%) = p_U(\%) + p_L(\%)$	$p(\%) = 6.60$
D. Decision criteria	
1. Acceptance criterion	
a. Upper specification: $p_U(\%) < M$	
b. Lower specification: $p_L(\%) < M$	
c. Double specification: $p(\%) < M$	D. $6.60 < 7.29$
Note: if AQL's not equal on upper and lower specifications, obtain M for each and apply a, b, c, above, using larger of two M values in c	
2. Rejection criterion: Reject otherwise	
V. Action: Dispose of lot as indicated and refer to switching rules for next lot	V. Accept the lot
VI. Characteristics: OC curves given	

VII. Reference: "Sampling Procedures and Tables for Inspection by Variables for Percent Defective," MIL-STD-414, U.S. Department of Defense, Military Standard, Government Printing Office, Washington, D.C., 1957

VIII. Remarks (use appropriate tables from Standard)
    A. Range method — similar except:
        1. Use $\bar{R}$ of subsamples of 5 if $n \geq 10$; use R if $n < 10$
        2. Substitute $\bar{R}/c$ for s in statistics, where c is a scale factor given with n and M in the Standard
    B. Variability known — similar except:
        1. Substitute σ/v for s in statistics, where v factor is given with n and M in the Standard

TABLE 25-8 Master Table for Normal and Tightened Inspection for Plans Based on Variability Unknown, Standard Deviation Method
(Double Specification Limit and Form 2, Single Specification Limit)

Sample size code letter	Sample size	Acceptable quality levels (normal inspection)													
		0.04	0.065	0.10	0.15	0.25	0.40	0.65	1.00	1.50	2.50	4.00	6.50	10.00	15.00
		M	M	M	M	M	M	M	M	M	M	M	M	M	M
B	3	→	→	→	→	→	→	→	→	→	7.59	18.86	26.94	33.69	40.47
C	4	→	→	→	→	→	→	→	1.53	5.50	10.92	16.45	22.86	29.45	36.90
D	5	→	→	→	→	→	→	1.33	3.32	5.83	9.80	14.39	20.19	26.56	33.99
E	7	→	→	→	→	0.422	1.06	2.14	3.55	5.35	8.40	12.20	17.35	23.29	30.50
F	10	→	→	→	0.349	0.716	1.30	2.17	3.26	4.77	7.29	10.54	15.17	20.74	27.57
G	15	0.099	0.186	0.312	0.503	0.818	1.31	2.11	3.05	4.31	6.56	9.46	13.71	18.94	25.61
H	20	0.135	0.228	0.365	0.544	0.846	1.29	2.05	2.95	4.09	6.17	8.92	12.99	18.03	24.53
I	25	0.155	0.250	0.380	0.551	0.877	1.29	2.00	2.86	3.97	5.97	8.63	12.57	17.51	23.97
J	30	0.179	0.280	0.413	0.581	0.879	1.29	1.98	2.83	3.91	5.86	8.47	12.36	17.24	23.58
K	35	0.170	0.264	0.388	0.535	0.847	1.23	1.87	2.68	3.70	5.57	8.10	11.87	16.65	22.91
L	40	0.179	0.275	0.401	0.566	0.873	1.26	1.88	2.71	3.72	5.58	8.09	11.85	16.61	22.86
M	50	0.163	0.250	0.363	0.503	0.789	1.17	1.71	2.49	3.45	5.20	7.61	11.23	15.87	22.00
N	75	0.147	0.228	0.330	0.467	0.720	1.07	1.60	2.29	3.20	4.87	7.15	10.63	15.13	21.11
O	100	0.145	0.220	0.317	0.447	0.689	1.02	1.53	2.20	3.07	4.69	6.91	10.32	14.75	20.66
P	150	0.134	0.203	0.293	0.413	0.638	0.949	1.43	2.05	2.89	4.43	6.57	9.88	14.20	20.02
Q	200	0.135	0.204	0.294	0.414	0.637	0.945	1.42	2.04	2.87	4.40	6.53	9.81	14.12	19.92
		0.065	0.10	0.15	0.25	0.40	0.65	1.00	1.50	2.50	4.00	6.50	10.00	15.00	
		Acceptable quality levels (tightened inspection)													

All AQL and table values are in percent defective.

↓ Use first sampling plan below arrow, that is, both sample size as well as M value. When sample size equals or exceeds lot size, every item in the lot must be inspected.

TABLE 25-9 Table for Estimating the Lot Percent Defective Using Standard Deviation Method

Q_U or Q_L	3	4	5	7	10	15	20	25	30	35	40	50	75	100	150	200
0.1	47.2	46.7	46.4	46.3	46.2	46.1	46.1	46.1	46.0	46.0	46.0	46.0	46.0	46.0	46.0	46.0
0.2	44.5	43.3	42.9	42.5	42.4	42.2	42.2	42.2	42.2	42.1	42.1	42.1	42.1	42.1	42.1	42.1
0.3	41.6	40.0	39.4	38.9	38.6	38.4	38.4	38.3	38.3	38.3	38.3	38.3	38.2	38.2	38.2	38.2
0.4	38.7	36.7	35.9	35.3	34.9	34.7	34.6	34.6	34.6	34.6	34.5	34.5	34.5	34.5	34.5	34.5
0.5	38.8	33.3	32.4	31.7	31.4	31.2	31.1	31.0	31.0	31.0	31.0	30.9	30.9	30.9	30.9	30.9
0.6	32.6	30.0	29.0	28.3	27.9	27.7	27.6	27.6	27.6	27.5	27.5	27.5	27.5	27.5	27.4	27.4
0.7	29.3	26.7	25.7	25.0	24.7	24.5	24.4	24.3	24.3	24.3	24.3	24.3	24.2	24.2	24.2	24.2
0.8	25.6	23.3	22.5	21.9	21.6	21.4	21.3	21.3	21.3	21.3	21.2	21.2	21.2	21.2	21.2	21.2
0.9	21.6	20.0	19.4	18.9	18.7	18.5	18.5	18.5	18.5	18.4	18.4	18.4	18.4	18.4	18.4	18.4
1.0	16.7	16.7	16.4	16.1	16.0	15.9	15.9	15.9	15.9	15.9	15.9	15.9	15.9	15.9	15.9	15.9
1.1	9.8	13.3	13.5	13.5	13.5	13.5	13.5	13.5	13.5	13.5	13.5	13.5	13.6	13.6	13.6	13.6
1.2	0	10.0	10.8	11.1	11.2	11.3	11.4	11.4	11.4	11.4	11.4	11.5	11.5	11.5	11.5	11.5
1.3	0	6.7	8.2	8.9	9.2	9.4	9.5	9.5	9.6	9.6	9.6	9.6	9.6	9.6	9.6	9.7
1.4	0	3.3	5.9	7.0	7.4	7.7	7.8	7.9	7.9	7.9	7.9	8.0	8.0	8.0	8.0	8.0
1.5	0	0	3.8	5.3	5.9	6.2	6.3	6.4	6.5	6.5	6.5	6.6	6.6	6.6	6.6	6.6
1.6	0	0	2.0	3.8	4.5	4.9	5.1	5.2	5.2	5.3	5.3	5.3	5.4	5.4	5.4	5.4
1.7	0	0	0.7	2.6	3.4	3.8	4.0	4.1	4.2	4.2	4.2	4.3	4.4	4.4	4.4	4.4
1.8	0	0	0	1.6	2.5	2.9	3.1	3.2	3.3	3.4	3.4	3.4	3.5	3.5	3.5	3.6
1.9	0	0	0	0.9	1.8	2.2	2.4	2.5	2.6	2.6	2.6	2.7	2.8	2.8	2.8	2.8
2.0	0	0	0	0.4	1.2	1.6	1.8	1.9	2.0	2.0	2.1	2.1	2.2	2.2	2.2	2.2
2.1	0	0	0	0.1	0.7	1.2	1.3	1.4	1.5	1.5	1.6	1.6	1.7	1.7	1.7	1.8
2.2	0	0	0	0	0.4	0.8	1.0	1.1	1.1	1.2	1.2	1.2	1.3	1.3	1.3	1.4
2.4	0	0	0	0	0.1	0.3	0.5	0.5	0.6	0.6	0.7	0.7	0.7	0.8	0.8	0.7
2.6	0	0	0	0	0	0.1	0.2	0.3	0.3	0.3	0.3	0.4	0.4	0.4	0.4	0.4
2.8	0	0	0	0	0	0	0.1	0.1	0.1	0.1	0.2	0.2	0.2	0.2	0.2	0.2
3.0	0	0	0	0	0	0	0	0	0.1	0.2	0.1	0.1	0.1	0.1	0.1	0.1

Sample sizes

TABLE 25-10   Application of MIL-STD-414*

Step	Section	Form 1	Form 2
Preparatory		Obtain k and n from appropriate tables	Obtain M and n from appropriate tables
Determine criteria	Section B *(s)*	$T_U = \dfrac{U - \bar{X}}{s}$ $T_L = \dfrac{\bar{X} - L}{s}$	$Q_U = \dfrac{U - \bar{X}}{s}$ $Q_L = \dfrac{\bar{X} - L}{s}$
	Section C *(\bar{R})*	$T_U = \dfrac{U - \bar{X}}{\bar{R}}$ $T_L = \dfrac{\bar{X} - L}{\bar{R}}$	$Q_U = \dfrac{(U - \bar{X})c}{\bar{R}}$ $Q_L = \dfrac{(\bar{X} - L)c}{\bar{R}}$
	Section D *(\sigma)*	$T_U = \dfrac{U - \bar{X}}{\sigma}$ $T_L = \dfrac{\bar{X} - L}{\sigma}$	$Q_U = \dfrac{(U - \bar{X})v}{\sigma}$ $Q_L = \dfrac{(\bar{X} - L)v}{\sigma}$
Estimation			Enter table with n and Q_U or Q_L to get p_U or p_L
Action	Single specification	Accept if $T_U \geq k$ or $T_L \geq k$	Accept if $p_U \leq M$ or $p_L \leq M$
	Double specification	Accept if† $T_U \geq k, T_L \geq k$ and $s <$ MSD or $\bar{R} <$ MAR	Accept if $p_U + p_L \leq M$

$c =$ scale factor.

$$v = \sqrt{\frac{n}{n - 1}}$$

*E. G. Schilling, Variables Sampling and MIL-STD-414, *Transactions of Twenty-sixth Quality Control Conference of the Rochester Society for Quality Control,* Mar. 30, 1970, pp. 175–188.

†Not official procedure.

TABLE 25-11   Variables Plans for Percent Defective—Mixed Variables-Attributes Plans, MIL-STD-414

Example: Use the data given under Data to Be Used in Examples, above. Should the lot be accepted?

Summary of plan	Calculations
I. Restrictions: Measurements normally distributed	
II. Necessary information	II
A. Lot size	A. Lot size $= 100$
B. AQL	B. AQL $= 2.5\%$
III. Selection of plan	III

A. Using AQL and Lot Size, select appropriate variables plan from MIL-STD-414, Normal Inspection	A. Same as Table 25-7
	     $n = 10$
	     $M = 7.29$

B. Using AQL and Lot Size, select single-sampling attributes plan from MIL-STD-105 using Tightened Inspection	B. MIL-STD-105D gives Code F
	     $n = 32$
	     $c = 1$

IV. Elements	IV

A. Sample size
     See above. Use items drawn in first sample as a part of second sample
	A. First sample: $n = 10$
	     Second sample:
	     $n = (32 - 10)$

B. Statistic: Use appropriate statistics from MIL-STD-414 and MIL-STD-105 as indicated in each standard	$n = 22$
C. Decision criteria	C. Table 25-7 indicates
1. Apply MIL-STD-414 plan	MIL-STD-414 plan
a. Accept lot if MIL-STD-414 plan accepts	accepts. If MIL-STD-414 rejected the lot, an
b. Otherwise, apply MIL-STD-105 plan, taking additional samples to satisfy MIL-STD-105 sample size requirements	additional 22 samples would be drawn and the MIL-STD-105D plan applied
2. Apply MIL-STD-105 plan if necessary	to the number of defectives in the
a. Accept lot if MIL-STD-105 plan accepts	combined sample of 32
b. Otherwise reject lot	
V. Action	V. Accept the lot
A. Dispose of lot as indicated	
B. Switching rules not applicable to Mixed Variables-Attributes inspection	
VI. Characteristics	
A. Since the procedure outlined in MIL-STD-414 is a "dependent" mixed plan, see the following references:	

     1. σ known: Schilling, E. G., and H. F. Dodge, Procedures and Tables for Evaluating Dependent Mixed Acceptance Sampling Plans, *Technometrics,* vol. XI, No. 2, pp. 341–372, May 1969

     2. σ unknown: Gregory, G., and G. J. Resnikoff, Some Notes on Mixed Variables and Attributes Sampling Plans, *Technical Report* 10, Applied Mathematics and Statistics Laboratory, Stanford University, Mar. 15, 1955

     3. Approximation for σ unknown: Bowker, A. H., and H. P. Goode, "Sampling Inspection by Variables," McGraw-Hill Book Company, New York, 1952.

VII. Reference: "Sampling Procedures and Tables for Inspection by Variables for Percent Defective," MIL-STD-414, U.S. Department of Defense, Military Standard, Government Printing Office, Washington, D.C., 1957.

TABLE 25-12   Variables Plans for Percent Defective Lot Plot

Example: A Lot Plot is to be used in inspecting the width of caps. A sample of 50 is taken in 10 subgroups of 5 with the following results:

1	2	3	4	5	6	7	8	9	10
0.2538	0.2581	0.2556	0.2531	0.2501	0.2521	0.2541	0.2555	0.2489	0.2529
0.2519	0.2571	0.2542	0.2566	0.2506	0.2557	0.2499	0.2569	0.2557	0.2579
0.2508	0.2521	0.2521	0.2534	0.2534	0.2569	0.2514	0.2553	0.2542	0.2565
0.2537	0.2545	0.2521	0.2557	0.2516	0.2541	0.2536	0.2496	0.2529	0.2577
0.2529	0.2563	0.2518	0.2519	0.2559	0.2524	0.2492	0.2512	0.2546	0.2541

These data are shown analyzed in Fig. 25-9. Should the lot be accepted?

Summary of plan	Calculations

I. Restrictions: None

II. Necessary information: Specification limits

III. Selection of plan

    A. Plan is constant lot to lot

    B. A special form (Fig. 25-9) is used to apply plan

IV. Elements

    A. Sample size: A random sample of 50 pieces is taken from the lot in 10 subsamples of 5 each. Subsample identification is maintained

    B. Statistic (for symmetric distribution)

        1. Statistic is $\bar{X} \pm 3\hat{\sigma}$ calculated as follows:

            a. Construct cells for frequency distribution on chart

                (1) Determine mean $\bar{X}_1$ and range R_1 for the first subgroup

                (2) Position $\bar{X}_1$ at line number 0 on Lot Plot form

                (3) Set cell width w so that $w \simeq R_1/4$

                (4) Fill in Lot Plot form with cell midpoints

            b. Tally measurements for frequency distribution using subsample number as tally mark. Tally marks form a histogram

            c. Record range of each subsample on form in terms of number of cells between lowest and highest tally mark for each subgroup

            d. Calculate grand mean $\bar{\bar{X}}$ from frequency distribution in terms of line numbers above $(+)$ and below $(-)$ arbitrary origin taken as the zero cell

            e. Draw $\bar{\bar{X}}$ on chart in terms of line numbers

Calculations:

B

1*a.* $\bar{X}_1 = 0.2526, R_1 = 0.003$

$\bar{X}_1 \sim 0.253$ at 0

$$w \simeq \frac{0.003}{4} = 0.00075$$

take $w = 0.001$

1*b.* See Fig. 25-9

1*c.* See Fig. 25-9 under "range" on right side

1*d.* Zero cell shown as arrow in Fig. 25-9

$\bar{\bar{X}} = +0.14$

1*e.* $\bar{\bar{X}}$ drawn 0.14 cell widths above middle of zero cell

Summary of plan	Calculations

f. Estimate 3σ of line numbers from average of subsample ranges

$$3\hat\sigma = 3\bar{R}\,/\,d_2 = 1.29\,\bar{R}$$

1*f.* $3\hat\sigma = 1.29\left(\dfrac{51}{10}\right) = 6.6$

g. Label $\bar{\bar{X}} \pm 3\sigma$ in terms of line numbers as
  (1) ULL = Upper Lot Limit $(\bar{\bar{X}} + 3\hat\sigma)$
  (2) LLL = Lower Lot Limit $(\bar{\bar{X}} - 3\hat\sigma)$

1*g.* See Fig. 25-9 marked ULL and LLL

h. Draw specification limits on chart

1*h.* See Fig. 25-9 marked SPEC

C. Decision criteria
  1. Acceptance criterion
    a. Symmetric distribution well within specification limits—accept automatically
    b. Symmetric distribution other than above
      (1) Lot Limits within specification—accept
      (2) Lot Limits outside specification—estimate proportion of product outside specification with special technique using code strip. If less than allowable value—accept. See reference below
    c. Nonsymmetric, bimodal distributions, etc. Special technique provided for estimating proportion out of specification using code strip. See reference below. If less than allowable value—accept
  2. Rejection criterion: Reject otherwise
V. Action: Dispose of lot as indicated. The Lot Plot form provides a useful communication device with vendor

V. Reject the lot

VI. Characteristics: See reference below and Moses paper*

VII. Reference: Shainin, D., The Hamilton Standard Lot Plot Method of Acceptance Sampling by Variables, *Industrial Quality Control,* July 1950, pp. 15–34

---

*Moses, L. E., Some Theoretical Aspects of the Lot Plot Sampling Inspection Plan, *Journal of the American Statistical Association,* vol. LI, pp. 84–107, 1956.

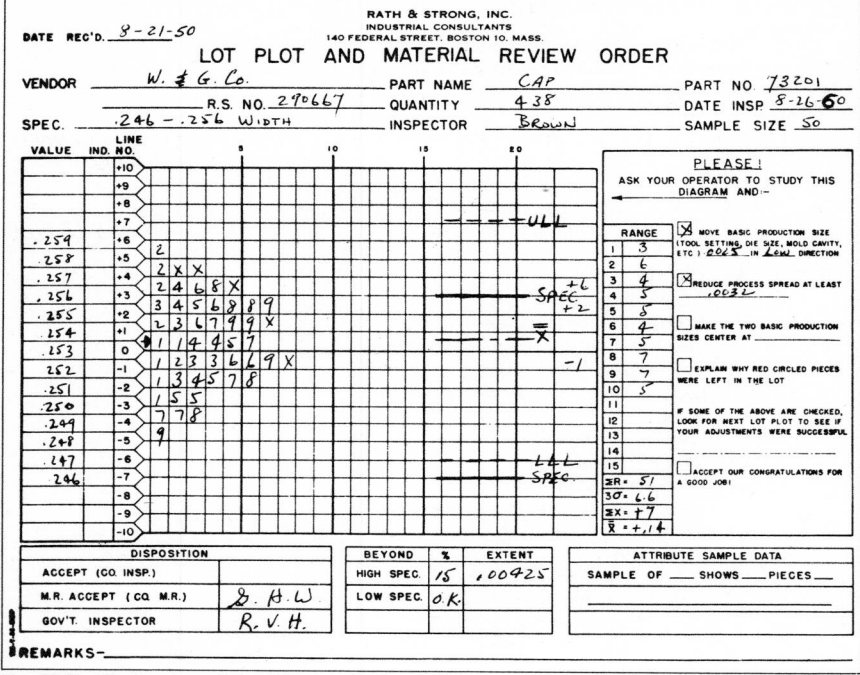

Fig. 25-9 *Illustration of Lot Plot method.*

The probability of acceptance for each of these process levels is usually specified as:

1. $1 - \alpha$ = probability of acceptance at the APL
2. β = probability of acceptance at the RPL

where α = Producer's Risk, β = Consumer's Risk

Single-sampling Plans for Process Parameter   Variables plans appropriate for this type of specification can be derived from the operating characteristic curves of appropriate tests of hypotheses. This is the case for single-sampling plans for process parameter which are, simply, appropriately constructed tests of hypotheses, e.g., testing the hypothesis that μ equals a specific value, against a one- or two-sided alternative. Thus, the statistical tests presented in Section 22 can be used for this type of acceptance sampling plan.

Acceptance Control Charts   Acceptance control charts offer a unique answer to the problem of sampling for process parameter when an Acceptable Process Level (APL) and Rejectable Process Level (RPL) are defined in terms of the mean value. They satisfy the natural desire of inspection personnel to observe quality trends and to look upon sampling as a continuing process.

These charts incorporate predetermined values of consumer and producer risk in the limits and so provide the balanced protection for the interested parties that is often lacking in the use of a conventional control chart for product acceptance.

It is not necessary that the population of individual measurements be normally distributed. The distribution must be known so that acceptable and rejectable values of the mean can be calculated. The procedure then uses the normal distribution in the analysis of the sample *mean* because the distribution of sample means of samples of reasonable size may be regarded as normal for any distribution of individual measurements.

The procedure for implementing this technique is shown in Table 25-13.

TABLE 25-13   Variables Plans for Process Parameter—Acceptance Control Charts

Example: Use the data given under Data to Be Used in Examples, above. The specification limits are 620 and 680, the AQL 2.5%, and the standard deviation 13. Assuming a normal distribution of individual measurements, the mean may be as low as 620 + 1.96 (13), or 646, or as high as 680 − 1.96 (13), or 654. This pair of values represents the range of the Acceptable Process Level (APL). It was decided that the Rejectable Process Level would occur when 14% was beyond a specification limit. Thus, the range of RPL was 620 + 1.08 (13) and 680 − 1.08 (13), or 634 and 666. Should the lot be accepted?

Summary of plan	Calculations
I. Restrictions: None	
II. Necessary information (single-sided specification)	II
$\quad$ A. σ = known standard deviation	$\quad$ A. $\sigma = 13$
$\quad$ B. μ_1 = APL (Acceptable Process Level) with $P_a = 1 - a$	$\quad$ B. $\mu_1 = 654, P_a = 0.95$
$\quad$ C. μ_2 = RPL (Rejectable Process Level) with $P_a = \beta$	$\quad$ C. $\mu_2 = 666, P_a = 0.10$
III. Selection of plan: See below	
IV. Elements	IV
$\quad$ A. Sample size $$n = \left[\frac{(z_\alpha + z_\beta)\sigma}{\mu_2 - \mu_1}\right]^2$$	$\quad$ A. $n = \left[\dfrac{(1.645 + 1.282)(13)}{12}\right]^2$ $\quad n = 10.06 \sim 10$
$\quad\quad$ where z_p cuts off upper tail area of p in standard normal curve	
$\quad$ B. Statistic: $\overline{X}$ = mean of sample of n	$\quad$ B. $\overline{X} = 647$
$\quad$ C. Decision criteria $\quad\quad$ 1. Compute: $$d = \frac{z_\alpha}{z_\alpha + z_\beta}|\mu_2 - \mu_1|$$	$\quad$ C. $d = \left(\dfrac{1.645}{1.645 + 1.282}\right)(12)$ $\quad\quad = 6.74$
$\quad\quad$ and set the Acceptance Control Limit, ACL, a distance d from APL in the direction of the RPL. Sign of $|\mu_2 - \mu_1|$ ignored.	$\quad\quad$ Upper ACL = 654 + 6.74 $\quad\quad\quad = 660.74$ By symmetry Lower ACL = 646 − 6.74 $\quad\quad\quad = 639.26$
$\quad\quad$ 2. Construct an acceptance control chart (Fig. 25-10) and accept if $\overline{X}$ falls within acceptance control limits; reject otherwise. Double-sided specification chart shown (see remarks below). Use appropriate half of chart for single-sided specification	$\quad\quad$ Plot as in Fig. 25-11
V. Action: Single lot disposed of as indicated by chart	V. Accept the lot
VI. Characteristics: Two points originally specified give indication of OC curve	
VII. Reference: Freund, R. A., Acceptance Control Charts, *Industrial Quality Control,* October 1957, pp. 13–23	

Summary of plan   Calculations

VIII. Remarks   VIII
    A. Above formulas are for single upper or single   A. Can use both upper and
       lower process limits, or for both if (Upper   lower limits since

$$\text{ACL} - \text{Lower ACL}) \geq k\sigma / \sqrt{n}\ \text{where:}$$ $$(660.74 - 639.26) >$$

α	k
0.05	5
0.01	6
0.001	7

$$\frac{(5)(13)}{\sqrt{10}}$$

$$21.48 > 20.56$$

    If (Upper ACL — Lower ACL)$< k\sigma / \sqrt{n}$,

    see above reference for appropriate factors
    B. If standard deviation is estimated from control
       chart, see reference above for appropriate
       limits
    C. Advisable to run range chart with Acceptance
       Control Chart to ensure stability of variation

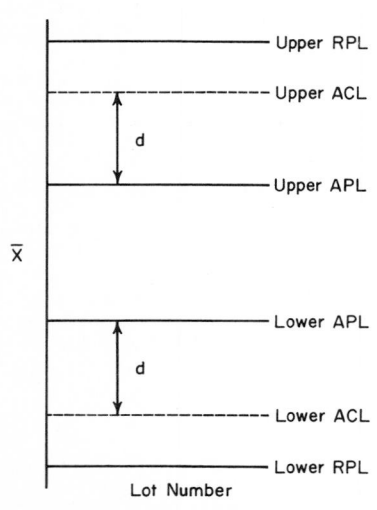

Fig. 25-10 Acceptance Control Chart concept.

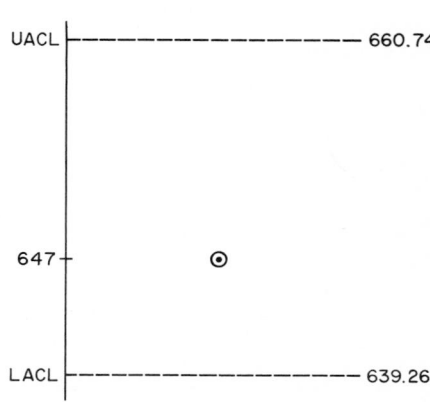

Fig. 25-11 Acceptance Control Chart example.

Sequential Sampling Plans for Process Parameter Sequential sampling procedures have been developed which are particularly useful when levels of process parameters are specified. They usually offer a substantial decrease in sample size over competing procedures, although they may be difficult to administer. Sequential sampling involves:

1. Take a sample of one measurement at a time.
2. Plot the cumulative sum T of an appropriate statistic against the sample number n.
3. Draw two lines
$$T = h_2 + sn$$
$$T = -h_1 + sn$$

where the intercepts h_1 and h_2 are values associated with the plan used and the symbol s is not a standard deviation but is a constant computed from the values of the Acceptable Process Level (APL) and the Rejectable Process Level (RPL). The use of s here corresponds to its use in the literature of sequential sampling plans.

4. Continue to sample if the cumulative sum lies between these lines, and take the appropriate action indicated if the plot moves outside the lines.

Procedures for constructing such plans and determining appropriate values of h_1, h_2, and s are given in detail in the literature.[22]

VARIABLES PLANS FOR PROCESS PARAMETER—
LIFE TESTING AND RELIABILITY

Variables sampling plans for life and reliability testing are similar in concept and operation to the plans previously described. They differ to the extent that, when units are not all run to failure, the length of the test becomes an important parameter determining the characteristics of the procedure. Further, time to failure tends to conform naturally to skewed distributions such as the exponential or as approximated by the Weibull. Accordingly many life test plans are based on these distributions. When time to failure is normally distributed and all units tested are run to failure, the variables plans assuming normality, discussed above, apply; attributes plans such as MIL-STD-105D may also be used.

Life tests, terminated before all units have failed, may be:

1. *Failure terminated*—a given sample size n is tested until the rth failure occurs. The test is then terminated.

2. *Time terminated*—a given sample size n is tested until a preassigned termination time T is reached. The test is then terminated.

Furthermore, these tests may be based upon specifications written in terms of one of the following characteristics:

1. *Mean Life*—the mean life of the product
2. *Hazard Rate*—instantaneous failure rate at some specified time t
3. *Reliable Life*—the life beyond which some specified proportion of items in the lot or population will survive
4. *Failure Rate (FR or λ)*—the percentage of failures per unit time (say 1,000 hours of test)

Several sets of plans are available for the testing of life and reliability. Table 25-14 summarizes some of these plans.

Conversion of Life Characteristics   Tables 25-15 and 25-16 will be found useful in converting life test characteristics. Formulas for various characteristics are shown in terms of mean life μ. Thus, using the tables, it will be found that a specification of mean life $\mu = 1,000$ hours for a Weibull distribution with $\beta = 2$ is equivalent to a hazard rate of 0.000157 at 100 hours or to a reliable life of 99.22% surviving at 100 hours.

Data to Be Used in Examples for Life Testing and Reliability   Each of the procedures shown for life testing and reliability is illustrated in terms of the following example adapted from H108.[23]

"Find a . . . procedure which will accept a lot with acceptable mean life . . . 1,500 hours, 95 percent of the time and will reject a lot with unacceptable mean life . . . 300 hours, 90 percent of the time."

[22] Duncan, *op. cit.*, pp. 272–286.

[23] "H108, Sampling Procedures and Tables for Life and Reliability Testing (Based on Exponential Distribution)," U.S. Department of Defense, Quality Control and Reliability Handbook, Government Printing Office, Washington, D.C., 1960.

TABLE 25-14   Summary of Some Life Testing and Reliability Plans

Document	Plans in terms of					Type of test		
	Basic distribution and type of plan	Mean life	Hazard rate	Reliable life	Failure rate (FR)	Failure terminated	Time terminated	Sequential
H 108[a]	Exponential, Lot by Lot	X			X	X	X	X
MIL-STD 690B[b]	Exponential, Lot by Lot				X		X	
MIL-STD-781B[c]	Exponential, Sampling Scheme	X					X	X
TR-3[d]	Weibull, Lot by Lot	X					X	
TR-4[e]	Weibull, Lot by Lot		X				X	
TR-6[f]	Weibull, Lot by Lot			X			X	
TR-7[g]	Weibull, (Lot by Lot, converts MIL-STD-105D)	X	X	X			X	

[a]"H108, Sampling Procedures and Tables for Life and Reliability Testing (Based on Exponential Distribution)," U.S. Department of Defense, Quality Control and Reliability Handbook, Government Printing Office, Washington, D.C., 1960.

[b]"MIL-STD-690B, Failure Rate Sampling Plans and Procedures," U.S. Department of Defense, Military Standard, Government Printing Office, Washington, D.C., 1968.

[c]"MIL-STD-781B, Reliability Tests: Exponential Distribution," U.S. Department of Defense, Military Standard, Government Printing Office, Washington, D.C., 1967.

[d]"TR-3, Sampling Procedures and Tables for Life and Reliability Testing Based on the Weibull Distribution (Mean Life Criterion)", U.S. Department of Defense, Quality Control and Reliability Technical Report, Government Printing Office, Washington, D.C., 1961.

[e]"TR-4, Sampling Procedures and Tables for Life and Reliability Testing Based on the Weibull Distribution (Hazard Rate Criterion)", U.S. Department of Defense, Quality Control and Reliability Technical Report, Government Printing Office, Washington, D.C., 1962.

[f]"TR-6, Sampling Procedures and Tables for Life and Reliability Testing Based on the Weibull Distribution (Reliable Life Criterion)", U.S. Department of Defense, Quality Control and Reliability Technical Report, Government Printing Office, Washington, D.C., 1963.

[g]"TR-7, Factors and Procedures for Applying MIL-STD-105D Sampling Plans to Life and Reliability Testing", U.S. Department of Defense, Quality Control and Reliability Technical Report, Government Printing Office, Washington, D.C., 1965.

TABLE 25-15   Life Characteristics for Two Failure Distributions

$$\text{Exponential } f(t) = \frac{1}{\mu} e^{-t/\mu}$$

$$\text{Weibull* } f(t) = \frac{\beta t^{\beta - 1}}{\eta^{\beta}} e^{-(t/\eta)^{\beta}} \text{ where } \mu = \eta\,\Gamma\left(1 + \frac{1}{\beta}\right)$$

Life characteristic	Exponential	Weibull
Proportion $F(t)$ failing before time t	$F(t) = 1 - e^{-t/\mu}$	$F(t) = 1 - e^{-g(t/\mu)^{\beta}}$
Proportion $R(t)$ of population surviving to time t	$R(t) = e^{-t/\mu}$	$R(t) = e^{-g(t/\mu)^{\beta}}$
Mean life, ML or mean time between failures	μ	μ
Hazard rate, $Z(t)$, instantaneous failure rate at time t	$Z(t) = \dfrac{1}{\mu}$	$Z(t) = \dfrac{\beta g t^{\beta - 1}}{\mu^{\beta}}$
Cumulative hazard rate $M(t)$ for period 0 to t	$M(t) = \dfrac{t}{\mu}$	$M(t) = \dfrac{g t^{\beta}}{\mu^{\beta}}$
Failure rate λ or average hazard rate period 0 to t, $m(t)$	$\lambda = \dfrac{1}{\mu}$	$m(t) = \dfrac{g t^{\beta - 1}}{\mu^{\beta}}$

* Weibull parameters explained in discussion of TR-3 (p. 100) and in Section 22.   The formulas given here are those of H108 (exponential) and TR-3 (Weibull).   They correspond to Section 22, where the parameters a and γ are taken to be $a = 1/\eta^{\beta}$ and $\gamma = 0$ here.   See Table 25-16 for values of g.

Table 25-16   Values of $g = [\Gamma(1 + 1/\beta)]^{\beta}$ for Weibull Distribution*

β	0.0	0.1	0.2	0.3	0.4	0.5	0.6	0.7	0.8	0.9
0.0	—	4.5287	2.6052	1.9498	1.6167	1.4142	1.2778	1.1794	1.1051	1.0468
1.0	1.0000	0.9615	0.9292	0.9018	0.8782	0.8577	0.8397	0.8238	0.8096	0.7969
2.0	0.7854	0.7750	0.7655	0.7568	0.7489	0.7415	0.7348	0.7285	0.7226	0.7172
3.0	0.7121	0.7073	0.7028	0.6986	0.6947	0.6909	0.6874	0.6840	0.6809	0.6778

β	0.33	0.67	1.33	1.67	3.33	4.00	5.00
g	1.8171	1.2090	0.8936	0.8289	0.6973	0.6750	0.6525

* The columns of this table are subdivisions of the rows.   Thus when $\beta = 1.2$, the value of g is 0.9292.

Assume the first 12 failures occur at 25, 55, 70, 100, 160, 190, 200, 225, 235, 290, 320, and 335 hours.

Exponential Distribution: H108   Quality Control and Reliability Handbook H108[24] presents a set of life test and reliability plans based on the exponential model for time to failure. The plans contained therein are intended for use when mean time to failure θ is specified[25] in terms of Acceptable Mean Life θ_0 and Unacceptable Mean Life θ_1. Testing may be conducted:

With replacement—units replaced when failure occurs. Test time continues to be accumulated on replacement unit.

Without replacement—units not replaced upon failure.

The handbook contains three types of plans:

1. Life tests terminated upon *occurrence of a preassigned number of failures.* Here, n units are tested until r failures occur. The average life is calculated and compared with an acceptable value defined by the plan, and a decision is made.

2. Life tests *terminated at a preassigned time.* Here, n units are tested for a specified length of time T. If T is reached before r failures occur, the test is stopped and the lot accepted. If r failures occur before T is reached, the test is stopped and the lot rejected. This type of plan is explained in Table 25-17.

3. *Sequential life testing plans.* Here, n units are placed on test and time and failures are recorded until sufficient data are accumulated to reach a decision at specified risk levels. Periodically throughout the test, the time accumulated on all units is calculated and compared with the acceptable amount of time for the total number of failures accumulated up to the time of observation. If the total time exceeds the limit for acceptance, the lot is accepted; if the total time exceeds the limit

TABLE 25-17   H108, Exponential Life and Reliability Plans, Time Terminated

Example: Use the data under Data to Be Used in Examples for Life Testing and Reliability, above, and assume that a test of about 100 hours is economically feasible, testing with replacement. Suppose first four failures occur at 25, 55, 70, 100 hours. Should the lot be accepted?

Summary of plan	Calculations
I. Restrictions: Exponential distribution of lifetimes	
II. Necessary information	II
A. θ_0 = Acceptable Mean Life with $P_a = 1 - a$	A. $\theta_0 = 1{,}500$, $P_a = 0.95$
B. a = Producer's Risk	B. $a = 0.05$
C. θ_1 = Unacceptable Mean Life with $P_a = \beta$	C. $\theta_1 = 300$, $P_a = 0.10$
D. β = Consumer's Risk	D. $\beta = 0.10$
	so, $\theta_1/\theta_0 = \frac{1}{5} = 0.20$
III. Selection of plan	III
A. Obtain Code Designation from a, β, and θ_1/θ_0. Table 25-18 provides Code Designation for most plans indexed by a, β, and θ_1/θ_0.	A. Table 25-18 indicates Code B-4
B. Using Code Designation, find appropriate value of T/θ_0. Values of T/θ_0 designated by Code and indexed by r and n as a multiple of r are provided in the standard:	B. If test is terminated at about 100 hours, then
1. Table 2C-1 (without replacement)	$T/\theta_0 = 100/1{,}500 =$
2. Table 2C-2 (with replacement)	0.067 and Table 25-19
where T = termination time	for Code B-4 shows
r = termination number	$T/\theta_0 = 0.068$ and
n = sample size	$r = 4$ for sample size $5r = 5(4) = 20$

[24] *Ibid.*
[25] Note that elsewhere in this Handbook the mean value is described by the symbol μ.

Summary of plan	Calculations

C. Multiply value of T/θ_0 given, by θ_0 to obtain termination time T

C. $T = \theta_0(T/\theta_0$
$= 1500(0.068)$
$T = 102$

Test Plan Summary:
1. Place 20 units on test
2. Terminate test at 102 hours
3. If < 4 units fail accept; otherwise reject

D. Note, additional values of n and r indexed by α, β, θ_1/θ_0, and T/θ_0, not designated by Code, are provided in the standard
  1. Table 2C-3 (without replacement)
  2. Table 2C-4 (with replacement)
E. A table with suitable instructions for use with plans based on proportion of lot failing or failure rate is also provided

IV. Elements
  A. Sample size: See above
  B. Statistic
    $T_r =$ time of rth failure in sample of n
  C. Decision criteria
    1. Accept if fewer than r failures occur by time T
    2. Reject on rth failure if time $< T$ and terminate test if desired
V. Action: Dispose of lot as indicated

IV
A. 20 units on test
B. First 4 fail at 25, 55, 70, 100 hours
  $T_r = 100$

V. Reject the lot since 4 failures occurred in 102 or fewer hours of test (test actually terminated at 100 hours)

VI. Characteristics: OC curves are provided for plans designated by Code and are indexed by α, β, and θ_1/θ_0 in Table 2A-1 in H108.
VII. Reference: "H108, Sampling Procedures and Tables for Life and Reliability Testing (Based on Exponential Distribution)," U.S. Department of Defense, Quality Control and Reliability Handbook, Government Printing Office, Washington, D.C., 1960.

---

for rejection, the lot is rejected. If the total time falls between the two limits, the test is continued.

Plans are given for various values of the consumer and producer risks, and operating characteristic curves are provided for life tests terminated at a preassigned number of failures or preassigned time. Special tables are also included showing the expected saving in test time by increasing the sample size or by testing with replacement of failed units.

Exponential Distribution: Other Plans (MIL-STD-690B, MIL-STD-781B) MIL-STD-690B[26] is a military standard concerned primarily with "process qualification," i.e., an *explicit* decision on the process rather than the lot. The Standard provides plans that evaluate the ability of the process to produce electronic parts that meet a specified failure rate requirement. It presents three sets of plans (Tables I, II, and IV of the Standard), based on Failure Rate (FR) Levels expressed in percent failures

[26] "MIL-STD-690B, Failure Rate Sampling Plans and Procedures," U.S. Department of Defense, Military Standard, Government Printing Office, Washington, D.C., 1960.

TABLE 25-18   Life Test Sampling Plan Code Designation*

$a = 0.01$ $\beta = 0.10$		$a = 0.05$ $\beta = 0.10$		$a = 0.10$ $\beta = 0.10$		$a = 0.25$ $\beta = 0.10$		$a = 0.50$ $\beta = 0.10$	
Code	θ_1/θ_0	Code	θ_1/θ_0	Code	θ_1/θ_0	Code	θ_1/θ_0	Code	θ_1/θ_0
A-1	0.004	B-1	0.022	C-1	0.046	D-1	0.125	E-1	0.301
A-2	0.038	B-2	0.091	C-2	0.137	D-2	0.247	E-2	0.432
A-3	0.082	B-3	0.154	C-3	0.207	D-3	0.325	E-3	0.502
A-4	0.123	B-4	0.205	C-4	0.261	D-4	0.379	E-4	0.550
A-5	0.160	B-5	0.246	C-5	0.304	D-5	0.421	E-5	0.584
A-6	0.193	B-6	0.282	C-6	0.340	D-6	0.455	E-6	0.611
A-7	0.221	B-7	0.312	C-7	0.370	D-7	0.483	E-7	0.633
A-8	0.247	B-8	0.338	C-8	0.396	D-8	0.506	E-8	0.652
A-9	0.270	B-9	0.361	C-9	0.418	D-9	0.526	E-9	0.667
A-10	0.291	B-10	0.382	C-10	0.438	D-10	0.544	E-10	0.681
A-11	0.371	B-11	0.459	C-11	0.512	D-11	0.608	E-11	0.729
A-12	0.428	B-12	0.512	C-12	0.561	D-12	0.650	E-12	0.759
A-13	0.470	B-13	0.550	C-13	0.597	D-13	0.680	E-13	0.781
A-14	0.504	B-14	0.581	C-14	0.624	D-14	0.703	E-14	0.798
A-15	0.554	B-15	0.625	C-15	0.666	D-15	0.737	E-15	0.821
A-16	0.591	B-16	0.658	C-16	0.695	D-16	0.761	E-16	0.838
A-17	0.653	B-17	0.711	C-17	0.743	D-17	0.800	E-17	0.865
A-18	0.692	B-18	0.745	C-18	0.774	D-18	0.824	E-18	0.882

Producer's Risk a is the probability of rejecting lots with mean life θ_0.

Consumer's Risk β is the probability of accepting lots with mean life θ_1.

* Tables 25-18 and 25-19 are reproduced from "H108, Sampling Procedures and Tables for Life and Reliability Testing (Based on Exponential Distribution)", U.S. Department of Defense, Quality Control and Reliability Handbook, Government Printing Office, Washington, D.C., 1960.

TABLE 25-19   Master Table for Life Tests Terminated at Preassigned Time — Testing with Replacement
Values of T/θ_0 for $a = 0.05$

Code	r	Sample size									
		$2r$	$3r$	$4r$	$5r$	$6r$	$7r$	$8r$	$9r$	$10r$	$20r$
B-1	1	0.026	0.017	0.013	0.010	0.009	0.007	0.006	0.006	0.005	0.003
B-2	2	0.089	0.059	0.044	0.036	0.030	0.025	0.022	0.020	0.018	0.009
B-3	3	0.136	0.091	0.068	0.055	0.045	0.039	0.034	0.030	0.027	0.014
B-4	4	0.171	0.114	0.085	0.068	0.057	0.049	0.043	0.038	0.034	0.017
B-5	5	0.197	0.131	0.099	0.079	0.066	0.056	0.049	0.044	0.039	0.020
B-6	6	0.218	0.145	0.109	0.087	0.073	0.062	0.054	0.048	0.044	0.022
B-7	7	0.235	0.156	0.117	0.094	0.078	0.067	0.059	0.052	0.047	0.023
B-8	8	0.249	0.166	0.124	0.100	0.083	0.071	0.062	0.055	0.050	0.025
B-9	9	0.261	0.174	0.130	0.104	0.087	0.075	0.065	0.058	0.052	0.026
B-10	10	0.271	0.181	0.136	0.109	0.090	0.078	0.068	0.060	0.054	0.027
B-11	15	0.308	0.205	0.154	0.123	0.103	0.088	0.077	0.068	0.062	0.031
B-12	20	0.331	0.221	0.166	0.133	0.110	0.095	0.083	0.074	0.066	0.033
B-13	25	0.348	0.232	0.174	0.139	0.116	0.099	0.087	0.077	0.070	0.035
B-14	30	0.360	0.240	0.180	0.144	0.120	0.103	0.090	0.080	0.072	0.036
B-15	40	0.377	0.252	0.189	0.151	0.126	0.108	0.094	0.084	0.075	0.038
B-16	50	0.390	0.260	0.195	0.156	0.130	0.111	0.097	0.087	0.078	0.039
B-17	75	0.409	0.273	0.204	0.164	0.136	0.117	0.102	0.091	0.082	0.041
B-18	100	0.421	0.280	0.210	0.168	0.140	0.120	0.105	0.093	0.084	0.042

For explanation of the Code, see par. 2A3.2 and Table 2A-1 in H108.

per 1,000 hours of operation (%/1,000 hours). The standard is intended as a tool for the assessment of:

1. Qualification of the process at the initial FR level
2. Extension of qualification to lower FR levels
3. Maintenance of FR level qualification
4. Lot conformance FR inspection

Operating characteristic curves for the qualifying plans are provided, and confidence levels are also specified. The plans involved are similar in operation to the time terminated sampling plans of H108, which are presented in that handbook in terms of Mean Life (ML). Note that

$$ML = \frac{100,000}{\%/1,000 \text{ hours}} = \frac{100,000}{FR}$$

An excellent discussion of MIL-STD-690B is given by Grubman, Martin, and Pabst.[27]

MIL-STD-781B[28] provides a standard set of acceptance testing plans for both process qualification and lot acceptance testing in production. This Standard was developed for electronic *equipment* as contrasted to MIL-STD-690B developed for electronic *parts*. Much of the standard is devoted to test conditions and procedural considerations. The sampling plans given are expressed in terms of mean time between failures (MTBF) and are used with switching rules in a manner similar to MIL-STD-414 or MIL-STD-105D. The standard presents the following plans:

1. Standard Probability Ratio Sequential Tests (Table 2 of Standard)
2. Short-run High Risk Probability Ratio Sequential Tests (Table 3 of Standard)
3. Fixed Length (Time Terminated) Tests (Table 4 of Standard)
4. Other: Longevity and All-equipment Tests (Table 4 of Standard)

The sequential tests operate in a manner analogous to those presented in H108. The Fixed Length Tests are also similar to the time terminated tests of H108; however, no specific sample size is set, much in the manner of the failure terminated plans of H108. Note that MTBF in MIL-STD-781B is analogous to ML in H108. The plans given in MIL-STD-781B are indexed by producer's risk α, consumer's risk β, and discrimination ratio θ_0/θ_1. OC curves are given for the sequential tests and the all-equipment screening test. An outstanding review of the standard has been given by Neathammer, Pabst, and Wigginton.[29]

Weibull Distribution: TR-3, TR-4, TR-6 Defense Department Quality Control and Reliability Technical Reports TR-3,[30] TR-4,[31] and TR-6[32] present sampling plans

[27] Grubman, S., C. A. Martin, and W. R. Pabst, Jr., MIL-STD-690B Failure Rate Sampling Plans and Procedures, *Journal of Quality Technology,* vol. 1, No. 3, pp. 205–216, July 1969.

[28] "MIL-STD-781B, Reliability Tests: Exponential Distribution," U.S. Department of Defense, Military Standard, Government Printing Office, Washington, D.C., 1967.

[29] Neathammer, R. D., W. R. Pabst, Jr., and C. G. Wigginton, MIL-STD-781B Reliability Tests: Exponential Distribution, *Journal of Quality Technology,* vol. 1, No. 1, pp. 58–67, January 1969.

[30] "TR-3, Sampling Procedures and Tables for Life and Reliability Testing Based on the Weibull Distribution (Mean Life Criterion)," U.S. Department of Defense, Quality Control and Reliability Technical Report, Government Printing Office, Washington, D.C., 1961.

[31] "TR-4, Sampling Procedures and Tables for Life and Reliability Testing Based on the Weibull Distribution (Hazard Rate Criterion)," U.S. Department of Defense, Quality Control and Reliability Technical Report, Government Printing Office, Washington, D.C., 1962.

[32] "TR-6, Sampling Procedures and Tables for Life and Reliability Testing Based on the Weibull Distribution (Reliable Life Criterion)," U.S. Department of Defense, Quality Control and Reliability Technical Report, Government Printing Office, Washington, D.C., 1963.

based on an underlying Weibull distribution of individual measurements t.   The cumulative probability distribution function at time t_0 is

$$F(t_0) = p' = P(t \le t_0) = 1 - \exp\left[-\left(\frac{t_0 - \gamma}{\eta}\right)^{\beta}\right]$$

with density function

$$f(t) = \frac{\beta(t - \gamma)^{\beta - 1}}{\eta^{\beta}} \exp\left[-\left(\frac{t - \gamma}{\eta}\right)^{\beta}\right] \qquad t \ge \gamma$$

The symbol p' is used for cumulative probability in the Technical Reports. The three reports provide plans for reliability criteria developed from the following relationships:

$$\mu = \gamma + \eta\,\Gamma\left(1 + \frac{1}{\beta}\right)$$

where Γ is the gamma function[33]

$$Z(t) = \frac{\beta}{\eta}\left(\frac{t - \gamma}{\eta}\right)^{\beta - 1}$$

$$\rho_r = \gamma + \eta\,(-\ln r)^{1/\beta}$$

where γ = location (or threshold) parameter
$\quad\ \beta$ = shape parameter
$\quad\ \eta$ = scale parameter (characteristic life)
$\quad\ \mu$ = mean life
$\ Z(t)$ = hazard rate—instantaneous failure rate
$\quad\ \rho_r$ = reliable life—life beyond which some specified proportion r of the items
$\qquad\quad$ will survive

In general the location parameter γ is taken to be zero.   If it is not zero, say $\gamma = \gamma_0$, then the observations t are adjusted to $t' = t - \gamma_0$; so accordingly $\mu' = \mu - \gamma_0$, and the analysis proceeds in terms of t' and μ'.   Then, the final results are reported in terms of t and μ by reversing the process, so that

$$t = t' + \gamma_0$$

$$\mu = \mu' + \gamma_0$$

for final results t' and μ'.

Plots on probability paper or goodness of fit tests must be used to assure that individual measurements are distributed according to the Weibull model.   When this distribution is found to be an appropriate approximation to the failure distribution, methods are available to characterize a product or a process in terms of the three parameters (γ, β, and η) of the Weibull distribution (see Section 22).   These include probability plots and also point and interval estimates.   Sampling plans are available for use with the Weibull approximation, which assumes β and γ to be known.   The plans are given in the technical reports mentioned above and are based on the following criteria:
1. Mean Life Criterion (TR-3)
2. Hazard Rate Criterion (TR-4)
3. Reliable Life Criterion (TR-6)
The tables cover a wide range of the family of Weibull distributions by providing

---

[33] A table giving the values of gamma is given in Richard S. Burington and Donald C. May, "Handbook of Probability and Statistics with Tables," 2d ed., McGraw-Hill Book Company, New York, 1970.

plans for shape parameter β from $\frac{1}{3}$ to 5. The technical reports abound in excellent examples and detailed descriptions of the methods involved.

Mean Life Criterion   Technical Report TR-3 provides plans and procedures for developing and applying Weibull plans using mean life μ as the criterion for acceptance. The dimensionless ratio t/μ is related to the cumulative probability p'. Values of t or μ can easily be determined for either of the constituents of the ratio t/μ once the other is specified. Since p' is the proportion of product failing before time t, it can be used in the role of "percent defective" in any attributes plan. The relationship of p' to t/μ, then, ties the "percent defective" to specified values of test time t and mean life μ. Seven tables, using this relationship, present factors and classifications useful in designing life test plans when the underlying distribution is Weibull. Each is indexed by various values of the shape parameter β. The tables included in TR-3 are:

Table 1—Values of $(t/\mu) \times 100$ indexed by p' (%)
Table 2—Values of p' (%) indexed by $(t/\mu) \times 100$
Table 3—Values of sample size n and $(t/\mu) \times 100$ for which $P_a \geq 0.95$ (shown in parentheses) indexed by acceptance number c and $(t/\mu) \times 100$ for which $P_a \leq 0.10$
Table 4—Values of the discrimination ratio $\mu_{0.95}/\mu_{0.10}$ indexed by acceptance number c
Table 5—Conversion of MIL-STD-105B to Weibull life test; values of $(t/\mu) \times 100$ for which $P_a \leq 0.10$ indexed by AQL and related $(t/\mu) \times 100$ and also by Sample Size Code Letter
Table 6—Values of $(t/\mu) \times 100$ indexed by related AQL values
Table 7—Single-sampling acceptance criteria for MIL-STD-105B

Tables 1 and 2 allow the direct conversion of any attributes plan to a Weibull life test. Tables 5 and 7 give factors to convert MIL-STD-105B. Tables 3 and 4 provide for the construction of Weibull life tests on the basis of the discrimination ratio $\mu_{0.95}/\mu_{0.10}$. The use of Tables 3 and 4 in TR-3 is shown in Table 25-20.

TABLE 25-20   TR-3, Reliability Plans—Weibull Mean Life Criterion

Example: Use the data under Data to Be Used in Examples for Life Testing and Reliability above, and assume that a test of approximately 150 hours is economically feasible, testing without replacement. Suppose the first four failures occur at 25, 55, 70, 100 hours. Should the lot be accepted?

Summary of plan	Calculations
I. Restrictions: Failure times Weibull with β known and $\gamma = 0$	
II. Necessary information	II
A. μ_0 = Acceptable Mean Life with $P_a = 0.95$	A. $\mu_0 = 1,500$, $P_a > 0.95$
B. μ_1 = Unacceptable Mean Life with $P_a = 0.10$	B. $\mu_1 = 300$, $P_a = 0.10$
C. β = shape parameter of Weibull distribution	C. $\beta = 1$
III. Selection of plan	III
A. Form discrimination ratio μ_0/μ_1	A. $\mu_0/\mu_1 = 5$
B. Table 25-21 indicates approximate appropriate Acceptance Number c for given shape parameter β	B. $c = 3$
C. Table 25-22 for specific values of β and c gives:	
1. Sample size (body of table)	
2. Dimensionless ratios	
a. $(t/\mu_1) \times 100$ at $P_a = 0.10$ (top of table)	
b. $(t/\mu_0) \times 100$ at $P_a = 0.95$ (in parentheses in body of table)	

Summary of plan	Calculations

D. To find sample size
1. Determine approximate time of test t desired and calculate $(t/\mu_1) \times 100$. Enter Table 25-22 with this value and c to determine sample size. If exact value of dimensionless ratio is not listed, use closest value and calculate test time to be used as

$$t = \left[\left(\frac{t}{\mu_1}\right) \times 100 \right] \frac{\mu_1}{100}$$

2. Alternatively, $(t/\mu_0) \times 100$ may be calculated. Enter the table with this value, shown in parentheses, and c to determine sample size. If exact value of this dimensionless ratio is not listed, use closest value and calculate test time to be used as:

$$t = \left[\left(\frac{t}{\mu_0}\right) \times 100 \right] \frac{\mu_0}{100}$$

D. Wish to test for about 150 hours; therefore, $(t/\mu_1) \times 100 = (150/300) \times 100 = 50$. Table 25-22 gives $n = 15$ at intersection of $(t/\mu_1) \times 100 = 50$ with $c = 3$. Test Plan Summary:
1. Place 15 units on test for 150 hours
2. If ≤ 3 units fail, accept; otherwise reject the lot

IV. Elements
  A. Sample size: See above
  B. Statistic: $Y =$ number of failures prior to time t
  C. Decision criteria: Accept the lot if $Y \leq c$ at time t; reject otherwise
V. Action: Dispose of lot as indicated

IV
  A. Test 15 units
  B. Fourth unit fails at 100 hours

V. Reject the lot and terminate test

VI. Characteristics: Given β, n, t, and c, Table 3 in TR-3 may be entered to find ratios $(t/\mu_0) \times 100$ and $(t/\mu_1) \times 100$. Dividing $(100 \times t)$ by these ratios will give μ_0 and μ_1, respectively, to roughly approximate the OC curve

VII. Reference: "TR-3, Sampling Procedures and Tables for Life and Reliability Testing Based on the Weibull Distribution (Mean Life Criterion)", U.S. Department of Defense, Quality Control and Reliability Technical Reports, Government Printing Office, Washington, D.C., 1961

Hazard Rate Criterion   Technical Report TR-4 is patterned after TR-3, using the product $tZ(t) \times 100$ in place of the dimensionless ratio $(t/\mu) \times 100$. Note that the value of t given is the termination time of the test. If hazard rates are specified for other times, tables are provided which convert the hazard rate specified into a corresponding hazard rate at the termination time of the test. The cumulative probability p' is related to $tZ(t) \times 100$. Resulting values and classifications useful in converting any attributes plan to a Weibull life test, where hazard rate is specified, are presented in seven tables, each indexed by various values of the shape parameter β. These tables are analogous to those found in TR-3. The use of Tables 3 and 4 in TR-4 corresponds to Tables 3 and 4 in TR-3; hence, the procedure of Table 25-20, above, remains the same for plans based on a Hazard Rate Criterion, with $(t/\mu) \times 100$ replaced by $tZ(t) \times 100$. Since $tZ(t) \times 100$ is a product, not a ratio, the formulas given in Table 25-20 must be converted by substituting $1/Z(t)$ for μ.

Reliable Life Criterion   *Technical Report* TR-6 is also patterned somewhat after its predecessors, TR-3 and TR-4, but uses the Reliable Life (ρ) Criterion. It uses the dimensionless quantity $(t/\rho) \times 100$ in the manner of $(t/\mu) \times 100$ and $tZ(t) \times 100$

in the previous reports. The cumulative probability p' is related to $(t/\rho) \times 100$, and resulting values and classifications useful in converting any attributes plan to a Weibull life test where reliable life is specified are presented in six tables, each indexed by various values of the shape parameter β. Plans are provided for values of reliable life of 0.50, 0.90, and 0.99. These tables are similar to those given in the previous two technical reports. Tables 3 and 4 are analogous to Tables 3 and 4 of TR-3; hence the procedure of Table 25-20 above remains the same for plans based on a Reliable Life Criterion, with $(t/\mu) \times 100$ replaced by $(t/\rho) \times 100$ and μ replaced by ρ in the formulas.

Conversion of MIL-STD-105D Plans: TR-7 Technical Report TR-7[34] provides factors and procedures for adapting MIL-STD-105D plans to life and reliability testing when a Weibull distribution of failure times can be assumed. Tables of the appropriate conversion factors are provided for the following criteria:

Table	Criterion	Conversion factor
1	Mean life	$(t/\mu) \times 100$
2	Hazard rate	$tZ(t) \times 100$
3	Reliable life $(r = 0.90)$	$(t/\rho) \times 100$
4	Reliable life $(r = 0.99)$	$(t/\rho) \times 100$

Each table is presented in three parts, each of which is indexed by 10 values of β ($\beta = \frac{1}{3}, \frac{1}{2}, \frac{2}{3}, 1, 1\frac{1}{3}, 1\frac{2}{3}, 2, 2\frac{1}{2}, 3\frac{1}{3}, 4$). TR-7 is used in a manner analogous to the three technical reports.

TABLE 25-21 Table* of Mean Life Multipliers

Approximate values for $\mu_{0.95}/\mu_{0.10}$

					β				
c	$\frac{1}{3}$	$\frac{1}{2}$	1	$1\frac{2}{3}$	2	$2\frac{1}{2}$	$3\frac{1}{3}$	4	5
0	. . .	. . .	45	10	6.7	4.6	3.1	2.6	2.2
1	2,000	150	11	4.3	3.3	2.6	2.1	1.8	1.6
2	325	45	6.7	3.1	2.6	2.1	1.8	1.6	1.5
3	140	25	5.0	2.6	2.2	1.9	1.6	1.5	1.4
4	75	17	4.1	2.3	2.0	1.8	1.5	1.4	1.3
5	50	13	3.6	2.2	1.9	1.7	1.5	1.4	1.3
6	35	11	3.2	2.0	1.8	1.6	1.4	1.3	1.3
7	27	9.1	3.0	1.9	1.7	1.6	1.4	1.3	1.3
8	23	8.0	2.8	1.9	1.7	1.5	1.4	1.3	1.2
9	20	7.0	2.7	1.8	1.6	1.5	1.3	1.3	1.2
10	18	6.4	2.5	1.8	1.6	1.5	1.3	1.3	1.2
11	16	6.0	2.4	1.7	1.6	1.4	1.3	1.3	1.2
12	14	5.6	2.3	1.7	1.5	1.4	1.3	1.2	1.2
13	13	5.2	2.2	1.6	1.5	1.4	1.3	1.2	1.2
14	12	5.0	2.2	1.6	1.5	1.4	1.3	1.2	1.2
15	11	4.8	2.1	1.6	1.5	1.4	1.3	1.2	1.2

* Tables 25-21 and 25-22 are reproduced from "TR-3, Sampling Procedures and Tables for Life and Reliability Testing Based on the Weibull Distribution (Mean Life Criterion)," U.S. Department of Defense, Quality Control and Reliability Technical Report, Government Printing Office, Washington, D.C., 1961.

[34] "TR-7, Factors and Procedures for Applying MIL-STD-105D Sampling Plans to Life and Reliability Testing," U.S. Department of Defense, Quality Control and Reliability Technical Report, Government Printing Office, Washington, D.C., 1965.

TABLE 25-22   Table of Sampling Plans for $\beta = 1$

n

c	\multicolumn{13}{c}{$(t/\mu) \times 100$ ratio for which $P(A) = 0.10$ (or less)}
	100	50	25	10	5	2.5	1	0.5	0.25	0.1	0.05	0.025	0.01
0	3 (1.7)	5 (1.0)	10 (0.51)	24 (0.20)	46 (0.11)	92 (0.06)	231 (0.02)	461 (0.01)	922	2,303	4,606	9,212	230-2
1	5 (8.0)	9 (4.2)	17 (2.1)	40 (0.90)	79 (0.45)	158 (0.22)	389 (0.09)	778 (0.05)	1,556 (0.02)	3,890 (0.01)	7,780	156-2	389-2
2	7 (14)	12 (7.4)	23 (3.7)	55 (1.5)	108 (0.76)	216 (0.38)	533 (0.15)	1,065 (0.08)	2,129 (0.04)	5,322 (0.02)	106-2 (0.01)	213-2	532-2
3	9 (19)	15 (10)	29 (5.0)	69 (2.0)	135 (1.0)	271 (0.50)	669 (0.20)	1,337 (0.10)	2,673 (0.05)	6,681 (0.02)	134-2 (0.01)	267-2	668-2
4	11 (22)	19 (12)	34 (6.2)	82 (2.4)	164 (1.2)	324 (0.61)	800 (0.24)	1,600 (0.12)	3,200 (0.06)	8,000 (0.02)	160-2 (0.01)	320-2	800-2
5	13 (25)	22 (13)	40 (7.0)	96 (2.8)	191 (1.4)	376 (0.69)	928 (0.28)	1,855 (0.14)	3,710 (0.07)	9,275 (0.03)	186-2 (0.01)	371-2 (0.01)	928-2
6	14 (30)	25 (15)	46 (7.5)	109 (3.0)	216 (1.5)	427 (0.77)	1,054 (0.31)	2,107 (0.16)	4,213 (0.08)	105-2 (0.03)	211-2 (0.02)	421-2 (0.01)	105-3
7	16 (33)	28 (16)	51 (8.2)	122 (3.3)	242 (1.7)	477 (0.83)	1,178 (0.34)	2,355 (0.17)	4,709 (0.08)	118-2 (0.03)	235-2 (0.02)	471-2 (0.01)	118-3
8	18 (35)	31 (17)	57 (9.0)	135 (3.5)	267 (1.8)	527 (0.89)	1,300 (0.36)	2,600 (0.18)	5,200 (0.09)	130-2 (0.04)	260-2 (0.02)	520-2 (0.01)	130-3
9	20 (36)	34 (18)	62 (9.3)	147 (3.7)	292 (1.9)	576 (0.94)	1,421 (0.38)	2,842 (0.19)	5,683 (0.10)	142-2 (0.04)	284-2 (0.02)	568-2 (0.01)	142-3
10	22 (38)	37 (19)	70 (9.5)	162 (3.9)	316 (2.0)	624 (1.0)	1,541 (0.40)	3,082 (0.20)	6,163 (0.10)	154-2 (0.04)	308-2 (0.02)	616-2 (0.01)	154-3
11	23 (40)	40 (20)	76 (9.8)	175 (4.0)	341 (2.1)	672 (1.1)	1,660 (0.42)	3,320 (0.21)	6,640 (0.10)	166-2 (0.04)	332-2 (0.02)	664-2 (0.01)	166-3
12	25 (42)	43 (20)	81 (10)	187 (4.2)	365 (2.2)	720 (1.1)	1,780 (0.43)	3,557 (0.22)	7,113 (0.11)	178-2 (0.04)	336-2 (0.02)	711-2 (0.01)	178-3
13	27 (42)	45 (21)	86 (10)	200 (4.3)	389 (2.2)	768 (1.1)	1,896 (0.45)	3,792 (0.22)	7,584 (0.11)	190-2 (0.05)	379-2 (0.02)	758-2 (0.01)	190-3
14	29 (44)	48 (22)	91 (11)	212 (4.4)	413 (2.3)	815 (1.1)	2,013 (0.46)	4,026 (0.23)	8,052 (0.12)	201-2 (0.05)	403-2 (0.02)	805-2 (0.01)	201-3
15	31 (44)	51 (22)	97 (11)	224 (4.6)	437 (2.4)	863 (1.2)	2,130 (0.47)	4,260 (0.24)	8,517 (0.12)	213-2 (0.05)	426-2 (0.02)	852-2 (0.01)	213-3

$(t/\mu) \times 100$ ratios in parentheses are for $P(A) = 0.95$ (or more).   The figure following the dash in sample size numbers shows the number of zeros

CONCLUSION

As Lord Kelvin has indicated, ". . . when you can measure what you are speaking about and express it in numbers you know something about it; but when you cannot express it in numbers, your knowledge is of a meagre and unsatisfactory kind."[35]   The subtleties of measurement, however, often becloud this simple proposition.   Numbers used must adequately reflect the characteristic considered, they must be carefully obtained, and they must justify the assumptions inherent in computational procedures applied to them.   Only then can they supplement our knowledge.   Too often numbers are used which do not sufficiently represent the characteristic they are ultimately supposed to measure, gages and instruments are employed without the benefit of gage control, and assumptions (frequently of normality) are made without analysis—assumptions which may not even be justified by existing data. It was not without foresight that the authors of MIL-STD-414 wrote:

It is important to note that variables sampling plans are not to be used indiscriminately, simply because it is possible to obtain variables measurement data.   In considering applications where the normality or independence assumptions may be questioned, the user is advised to . . . determine the feasibility of application.[36]

ACKNOWLEDGMENTS

The author wishes to express his appreciation to all those who contributed to the preparation of the manuscript and especially to my associate, Helen J. Mikulski, Statistician, General Electric Company, Lamp Business Division, for her valuable comments, criticisms, and suggestions.

[35] Kelvin, W. T., "Popular Lectures and Addresses," vol. I, p. 80, Macmillan & Co., Ltd., London, 1891.
[36] MIL-STD-414, *op. cit.*, p. vii.

Section **25A**

Bulk Sampling*

ACHESON J. DUNCAN, Ph.D.

Professor Emeritus of Statistics,
The Johns Hopkins University,
Baltimore, Maryland

NEED FOR SPECIAL DISCUSSION

Bulk material may be of gaseous, liquid, or solid form. Usually it is sampled by taking increments of the material, blending these increments into a single composite sample, and then, if necessary, reducing this gross sample to a size suitable for laboratory testing.

If bulk material is packaged or comes in clearly demarked segments, if it is for all practical purposes uniform within the packages, but varying between packages, and if the quality of each package in the sample is measured, then the sampling theory developed for discrete units may be employed.[1]

A special theoretical discussion is necessary for the sampling of bulk material:

1. If the packages are uniform but the increments from individual packages are not tested separately; instead they are physically composited, in part at least, to form one or more composite samples that are tested separately.

2. If the contents of the packages are not uniform so that the question of sampling error arises with respect to the increments taken from the packages.

3. If the bulk material is not packaged and sample increments have to be taken from a pile, a truck, a railroad car, or a conveyor belt.

*Copyright, Acheson J. Duncan, 1974.
[1] See Section 25.

In the above circumstances, the special aspects that make bulk sampling different from the sampling of discrete indivisible units are:

1. The possibility of physical compositing and the subsequent physical reduction (or subsampling) that is generally necessary.

2. The need in many cases to use a mechanical sampling device to attain the increments that are taken into the sample. In this case the increments are likely to be "created" by the use of the sampling device and cannot be viewed as preexisting.

OBJECTIVES OF BULK SAMPLING

In most cases the objective of sampling bulk material is to determine its mean quality. This may be for the purpose of pricing the material or for levying custom duties or other taxes, or for controlling a manufacturing process in which the bulk material may be used. It is conceivable that interest in bulk material may also at times center on the variability of the material or if it is packaged, on the percent defective, or on the extreme value attained by a segment or package.[2] In view of the limited space that is available the discussion will be restricted to estimation of the mean quality of a material.

SPECIAL TERMS AND CONCEPTS

A number of special terms and concepts are used in the sampling of bulk material. These are:

1. *Lot* — the mass of bulk material the quality of which is under study — not to be confused with a statistical population.

2. *Segment* — any specifically demarked portion of the lot, actual or hypothetical.

3. *Strata* — segments of the lot that are likely to be differentiated with respect to the quality characteristic under study.

4. *Increment* — any portion of the lot, generally smaller than a segment.

5. *Sample increments* — those portions of the lot initially taken into the sample.

6. *Gross sample* — the totality of sample increments taken from the lot.

7. *Composite sample* — a mixture of two or more sample increments.

8. *Laboratory sample* — that part of a larger sample which is sent to the laboratory for test.

9. *Reduction* — the process by which the laboratory sample is obtained from a composite sample. It is a method of sampling the composite sample. It may take the form of hand-quartering or riffling or the like.

10. *Test-unit* — that quantity of the material which is of just sufficient size to make a measurement of the given quality characteristic.

11. *Quality of a test-unit* — the expected value of the hypothetically infinite number of given measurements that might be made on the test-unit. Any single measurement is a random sample of one from this infinite set. The analytical variance is the variance of such measurements on the infinite set.

12. *Mean of a lot* — If a lot is exhaustively divided into a set of M test-units, the mean of the qualities of these M test-units is designated the mean of the lot. It is postulated that this mean will be the same no matter how the M test-units are obtained. This assumes that there is no physical interaction between the quality of test-units and the method of division. See item 16 below.

13. *Mean of a segment* (stratum, increment, composite sample, or laboratory sample) — defined in a manner similar to that used to define the mean of a lot. It is assumed that the segment is so large relative to the size of a test-unit that any excess over the integral number of test-units contained in the segment can be theoretically

[2] See Ref. 1.

ignored. If this is not true, then the quality of the fraction of a test-unit remaining is arbitrarily taken to be the quality of the mean of the segment minus this fraction.

14. *Uniformity*—a segment of bulk material will be said to be uniform if there is no variation in the segment. If, for example, every cubic centimeter of a material contains exactly the same number of "foreign particles," the density of these particles would be said to be uniform throughout the segment. See the note under item 15, however.

15. *Homogeneous*—a segment of bulk material will be said to be homogeneous with respect to a given quality characteristic if that characteristic is randomly distributed throughout the segment.

Note: The character of being uniform or homogeneous is not independent of the size of the units considered. The number of foreign particles may be the same for every cubic meter of a material, and with respect to this size unit the material will be said to be uniform. For units of size 1 cubic centimeter, however, there may be considerable variation in the number of foreign particles, and for this size of unit the material would not be judged to be uniform. The same considerations are involved in the definition of homogeneity. The number of foreign particles per cubic meter could vary randomly from one cubic meter to the next, but within each cubic meter there might be considerable (intraclass) correlation between the number of foreign particles in the cubic centimeters that make up the cubic meter.

16. *Systematic physical bias*—if the property of the material is physically affected by the sampling device or method of sampling employed, the results will have a systematic bias. A boring or cutting device, for example, might generate sufficient heat to cause loss of moisture.

17. *Physical selection bias*—if a bulk material is a mixture of particles of different size, the sampling device may tend to select more of one size particle than another. This means that if a segment was exhaustively sampled by such a device, early samples would tend to have relatively more of certain size particles than later samples.

18. *Statistical bias*—a function of the observations that is used to estimate a characteristic of a lot, e.g., its mean, is termed a *statistic*. A statistic is statistically biased if in many samples its mean value is not equal to the lot characteristic it is used to estimate.

MODELS AND THEIR USE

Sampling plans for discrete product have been cataloged in a number of tables (see Sections 24 and 25). This has not yet been possible for bulk sampling, and instead, a "sampling model" must be created for each type of bulk material and the model used to determine the sample size and acceptance criteria for specific applications.

A bulk sampling model consists of a set of assumptions regarding the statistical properties of the material to be sampled plus a prescribed procedure for carrying out the sampling. A very simple model, for example, would be one in which it is assumed that the quality characteristics of the test-units in a lot are normally distributed and simple random sampling is used.

With the establishment of a model a formula can generally be derived for the sampling variance of an estimate of the mean of a given lot. This must be uniquely derived based on the type of product, lot formation, and other factors. The specific formula (for the variance of an estimate of the mean) is given in this Section for certain important cases. The reader is urged to consult the references for other cases. From an estimate of this sampling variance, confidence limits can be established for the lot mean and/or a decision with given risk can be made about the acceptability of the lot.

Let the variance of a sample mean be denoted as $\sigma_{\bar{X}}^2$ and its estimate as $s_{\bar{X}}^2$.

Then "0.95 confidence limits" for the mean of the lot[3] will be given by

$$0.95 \text{ confidence limits for } \mu = \bar{X} \pm t_{0.025} s_{\bar{X}} \tag{25A-1}$$

where μ is the mean of the lot, $\bar{X}$ is the sample mean, and $t_{0.025}$ is the 0.025 point of a t-distribution for the degrees of freedom involved in the determination of $s_{\bar{X}}^2$.

If a decision is to be made on the acceptability of a lot,[4] a criterion for acceptability will take some such form as

Accept if $\dfrac{\bar{X} - L}{s_{\bar{X}}}$ is positive or if it has a negative value numerically less than $t_{0.05}$ $\qquad(25A-2)$

where L is the lower specification limit on the product and $t_{0.05}$ is the 0.05 point of a t-distribution for the degrees of freedom involved in the determination of $s_{\bar{X}}^2$.

STRATEGY FOR ESTIMATION OF SAMPLING VARIANCE

When an isolated lot is involved, there is no choice but to estimate the sampling variance directly from measurements on the lot itself. When a given lot, however, is one in a stream of lots from a production process, and when information on the prior output of the process is available, say from an initial pilot study, then the estimate of sampling variance may be based on this prior knowledge. When prior information is so used, some test should be made of the continued validity of the prior estimates.

The advantage of the use of prior data is that it will allow a considerable reduction in the cost of sampling and measurement required for reliable estimation of the mean quality of a current lot. A pilot study will probably be very expensive, but if this initial cost can be spread over many subsequent lots, the long-run average cost per lot may be considerably less than if the sampling variance has to be obtained separately for each lot. This, of course, assumes a prescribed standard for reliability of estimation.

DETERMINATION OF THE AMOUNT OF SAMPLING

Since the variance of a sample mean $\sigma_{\bar{X}}^2$ is a function of the amount of sampling, say the number of increments taken, then once a model has been adopted and a formula obtained for $\sigma_{\bar{X}}^2$, it becomes possible to determine the amount of sampling required to attain a confidence interval of a given width or to attain a specified probability of making a correct decision.

For an isolated lot some preliminary measurements can be made on the lot to give a preliminary estimate of $\sigma_{\bar{X}}^2$ for an arbitrary amount of sampling. Where the results of a pilot study are available, a similar estimate of $\sigma_{\bar{X}}^2$ can be obtained from this. Then if the desired width of a 0.95 confidence interval is 2δ, a target value for $\sigma_{\bar{X}}^2$ (call it $_T\sigma_{\bar{X}}^2$) can be established from the relationship

$$_T\sigma_{\bar{X}}^2 = \left(\frac{\delta}{t_{0.025}^s} \right)^2 \tag{25A-3}$$

where $t_{0.025}^s = 1.96$ in the case of an isolated lot or is the $t_{0.025}$ factor for a t-distribution for the degrees of freedom involved in the pilot estimate of $\sigma_{\bar{X}}^2$. If n is an index of the amount of sampling that is needed, say the number of increments, n can be so chosen that

$$s_{\bar{X}}^2 = {}_T\sigma_{\bar{X}}^2 \tag{25A-4}$$

---

[3] See Section 22 under Statistical Estimation: Confidence Limits.
[4] See Reference 18.

In the case of an isolated lot, if the amount of sampling so obtained yields an ultimate t-factor [for use in equation (25A-1)] with degrees of freedom less than 30, then $t^*_{0.025}$ should also be treated as an ordinary t-factor and hence a function of n, and equation (25A-4) should be solved by trial and error.

Similar calculations are involved in determining the amount of sampling to get a desired set of risks for lot acceptance and rejection.

Let L = lower specification limit for the mean of a lot (no upper limit)
Producer's Risk = 0.05 (i.e., a 95% chance of acceptance if the lot mean equals L)
Consumer's Risk = 0.10 (i.e., a 10% maximum chance of acceptance if the lot mean is $\leq L - \Delta$, where $L - \Delta$ represents the mean of a lot that is deemed barely tolerable)
DF = degrees of freedom for the estimate of $\sigma_{\bar{X}}^2$
Then choose the amount of sampling (say the number of increments) such that

$$T^{\sigma}\bar{X} = \frac{\Delta}{\lambda \sqrt{DF + 1}} \tag{25A-5}$$

where λ is given in Table 25A-1 for the designated value of DF. For an isolated lot for which preliminary results yield a preliminary estimate of variance, and for which

TABLE 25A-1 Table for Determining Sample Size*

Degrees of freedom DF	λ
2	2.76
3	2.16
4	1.61
6	1.26
9	1.00
14	0.79
19	0.68
29	0.54
49	0.42
74	0.33
99	0.29

For λ less than 0.29, $n = 8.57/\lambda^2$, where $n = DF + 1$.
* Values of λ were read from Fig. 13.31 of A. H. Bowker and Gerald J. Lieberman, "Handbook of Industrial Statistics," Prentice-Hall, Inc., Englewood Cliffs, N.J., 1955. DF is one less than Bowker and Lieberman's N.

the amount of sampling will determine not only $s_{\bar{X}}^2$ but also the degrees of freedom, Table 25A-1 can be used to determine the amount of sampling by trial and error as shown in the first example.

In the discussion that follows attention is given to the determination of the estimated variance $s_{\bar{X}}^2$ for several important models.

MODELS FOR DISTINCTLY SEGMENTED BULK MATERIAL ("WITHIN AND BETWEEN" MODELS)

Much bulk material comes in distinctly segmented form. It may be packaged in bags, bales, or cans, for example, or may come in carloads or truckloads.

For distinctly segmented material it can be established that the overall variance of individual test-units is, for a large number of segments each with a large number of test-units, approximately equal to the sum of the variance between segments and the average variance within segments. In what follows the variance within segments is assumed the same for all segments.

Model 1A. Isolated Lots, Nonstratified Segments[5] For an isolated lot of distinctly segmented material, the sampling procedure will be to take an increment of m test-units from each of n segments, reduce *each* increment to a laboratory sample, and measure its quality X. The mean of the n test-units is taken as an estimate of the mean of the lot.

On the assumption that both the number of segments in the lot and the number of test-units in a segment are large relative to n and m and on the further assumption that selection of an increment from a segment is the practical equivalent of drawing a random sample of m test-units from that segment, the sampling variance of $\overline{X}$ will be

$$\sigma_{\overline{X}}^2 = \frac{\sigma_b^2 + \sigma_w^2/m + \sigma_{r(m)}^2 + \sigma_t^2}{n} \tag{25A-6}$$

where σ_b^2 = variance between means of segments in the lot

σ_w^2 = variance of test-units within segments, assumed the same for all segments

$\sigma_{r(m)}^2$ = reduction variance involved in getting a laboratory sample from an increment of m test-units

σ_t^2 = test variance (= variance associated with the sampling of the laboratory sample plus the analytical variance)

If the n test results are $X_1, X_2, \ldots X_n$, an estimate of $\sigma_{\overline{X}}^2$ will be given by

$$s_{\overline{X}}^2 = \frac{1}{n}\frac{\sum_i (X_i - \overline{X})^2}{n-1} \tag{25A-7}$$

To determine the amount of sampling needed to attain a confidence interval of $2\,\delta$ (see above), one increment each can be taken from a preliminary sample of $n_1 \ (= 10$, say) segments, and $s_1^2 = \sum_i (X_i - \overline{X}_1)^2/(n_1 - 1)$ can be computed.

The final n can be found by setting $n = s_1^2/{}_T\sigma_{\overline{X}}^2$, where ${}_T\sigma_{\overline{X}}^2 = (\delta/1.96)^2$. If the n so obtained is less than 30, then an n can be found by trial-and-error methods such that $s_1^2/n = [\delta/t_{0.025(n-1)}]^2$ where the t-factor is the 0.025 point for a t-distribution with $n-1$ degrees of freedom.

To obtain an acceptance sampling plan with prescribed risks (see above), a preliminary sample of n_1 increments can be taken as described in the previous paragraph. Then Table 25A-1 is entered with $\lambda = \Delta/s_1$ and the final sample size n is taken equal to $DF + 1$.

Example 1 An inspector has the task of determining the mean density of a lot of 300 bags of chalk. He selects a preliminary sample of 10 bags at random and takes a small increment from each bag. Each increment is reduced to a laboratory sample and its density is measured. Let the mean density of the 10 results be 0.134 gram per cubic centimeter and the sample variance be $s_1^2 = 0.000049$.

It is required that the width of the confidence interval be 0.007 gram per cubic centimeter, which leads to setting ${}_T\sigma_{\overline{X}}^2 = (0.0035/1.96)^2 = 0.00000319$. A 0.95 confidence interval of width 0.007 gram per cubic centimeter (2δ) thus requires a total of $n = 0.000049/0.00000319 \cong 15$ bags. Since this is less than 30, the inspector checks the width of the confidence interval with a sample of 15. For $n = 15$, $t_{0.025}$ for $15 - 1 = 14$ degrees of freedom is 2.145. With an s^2 of 0.000049, the width of the confidence interval may be expected to be $2\,(2.145)\,(0.000049/15)^{1/2}$

---

[5] *Cf.* Ref. 1.

$= 0.00775$, which is a little larger than desired. The inspector therefore tries $n = 18$. This yields

$$2t_{0.025}(n-1)s/\sqrt{18} = 2(2.111)(0.000049/18)^{1/2} = 0.00696$$

which is almost on target. Hence the inspector decides to sample a total of 18 bags.

A sampling plan for a lower specification limit of 0.135 and a $\Delta = 0.004$ would require that $\lambda = 0.004/0.007 = 0.57$, and Table 25A-1 would show the required sample size of 28.

Model 1B. One of a Series of Lots   Suppose the current lot is one of a series of lots of distinctly segmented material and that estimates of $\sigma_b{}^2$ and $\sigma_w{}^2$ have been made in a pilot study, together with estimates of the reduction variance and test variance (Ref. 1). It will be assumed that the reduction variance yielded by the pilot study is valid for larger amounts than that used in the study.

With the given prior information, an estimate of the sampling variance for the current sample estimate of mean lot quality can be based on the pilot study, and there is need only for a current check on the continued validity of this study. Consequently composite samples can be used requiring only a few measurements, and the cost of inspection of the current lot may be considerably curtailed. Let the sampling plan consist of selecting n segments at random from the lot and drawing an increment of m test units from each segment. Let h subgroups of n/h increments each be selected at random from the n increments,[6] let a composite sample be formed of each of these subgroups, let each composite sample be reduced to a laboratory sample, and let the quality of each be measured.

The measurement of the h composite samples may first be used to test the validity of the prior estimates of variance. This may be done by constructing an R-chart with

$$\text{Central line} = d_2 \left(\frac{s_b{}^2 + s_w{}^2/m}{n/h} + s_r{}^2 + s_t{}^2 \right)^{1/2} \tag{25A-8}$$

$$\text{Upper control limit} = D_2 \left(\frac{s_b{}^2 + s_w{}^2/m}{n/h} + s_r{}^2 + s_t{}^2 \right)^{1/2} \tag{25A-9}$$

where d_2 and D_2 are in Appendices A and CC (for a sample size of h). The continuing validity of the prior estimates of variance is accepted if the range of h measurements falls below the upper limit on this R-chart. If the range of the h measurements falls above this limit, a shift should be made to a model for an isolated lot and further sampling undertaken.

If the validity of the prior estimates is accepted, the mean of the h composite measurements $\bar{X}_{c(h)}$ is taken as an estimate of the lot mean with a sampling variance equal to

$$s^2_{\bar{X}_{c(h)}} = \frac{s_b{}^2 + s_w{}^2/m}{n} + \frac{s_r{}^2 + s_t{}^2}{h} \tag{25A-10}$$

From this result 0.95 confidence limits for the mean of the lot will be given by

$$\bar{X}_{c(h)} \pm t_{0.025}\, s_{\bar{X}_{c(h)}} \tag{25A-11}$$

where $t_{0.025}$ is the 0.025 point of a t-distribution with degrees of freedom given by[7]

---

[6] It is assumed, of course, that n is divisible by h.

[7] This is Satterthwaite's procedure for approximating the distribution of a linear function of independent mean squares. See Ref. 8, p. 605.

$$DF = \frac{(s_{\bar{X}_{c(h)}}^2)^2}{\frac{1}{f_b}\left(\frac{s_b^2}{n}\right)^2 + \frac{1}{f_w}\left(\frac{s_w^2}{mn}\right)^2 + \frac{1}{f_r}\left(\frac{s_r^2}{h}\right)^2 + \frac{1}{f_t}\left(\frac{s_t^2}{h}\right)^2} \tag{25A-12}$$

the f's being the degrees of freedom with which the respective prior estimates of variance were determined. For the most likely f-values, $t_{0.025}$ will fall within the range 1.99 to 2.09.

Example 2 A pilot study has shown that the basic variances related to the manufacture and sampling of a 10-10-10 granulated fertilizer in bags are as follows (data relate to the percent of potash in the fertilizer):

Variance between bags $s_b^2 = 0.2516$, based on 24 degrees of freedom.

Variance between increments from the same bag using a sampling device of the kind to be employed $s_w^2/m = 0.0144$, based on 25 degrees of freedom.

Variance of reduction, assumed reasonably constant for composite samples of the size expected $s_r^2 = 0.0256$, based on 19 degrees of freedom.

Variance of testing and analysis $s_t^2 = 0.0100$, based on 20 degrees of freedom.

An inspector wishes to set up 0.95 confidence limits for the mean percent potash content of 200 bags of the given fertilizer and wants a confidence interval of width 1.0% or a $\delta = 0.5\%$ using two composite samples. Solving equation (25A-10) for n and putting $s_{\bar{X}_{c(h)}}^2 = (\delta/2.09)^2$,

$$n = \frac{s_b^2 + s_w^2/m}{s_{\bar{X}_{c(h)}}^2 - [(s_r^2 + s_t^2)/h]}$$

Then the number of bags required is

$$n = \frac{0.2516 + 0.0144}{(0.5/2.09)^2 - [(0.0256 + 0.0100)/2]} = 6.77$$

This is rounded up to the next *even* number yielding $n = 8$. ($n = 6$ could be used but this gives rise to greater risks than desired.)

The inspector then selects 8 bags at random from the lot and takes an increment from each bag. Four of these increments are chosen at random, composited, and reduced to a laboratory sample. The remaining four increments are also composited and reduced to a laboratory sample. A determination of the percent potash is made for each sample. Suppose the results are 9.7 and 9.2%. From equations (25A-8) and (25A-9) an R-chart for a sample of 2 has

$$\text{Central line} = 1.128\left(\frac{0.2516 + 0.0144}{4} + 0.0256 + 0.0100\right)^{1/2}$$

$$= 1.128(0.3195) = 0.3605$$

Upper control limit $= 3.686(0.3195) = 1.18$.

Since the difference $9.7 - 9.2 = 0.5$ is less than 1.18, the inspector accepts the validity of the pilot study variances and proceeds with estimation of the lot mean.

The mean of the two sample results, 9.45%, is taken as the best single estimate of the lot mean. The reliability of this estimate is given by 0.95 confidence limits. On using equations (25A-10) and (25A-12),

$$s_{\bar{X}_{c(h)}}^2 = \frac{0.2516}{8} + \frac{0.0144}{8} + \frac{0.0256}{2} + \frac{0.0100}{2} = 0.0510$$

and $$DF = \frac{(0.0510)^2}{\frac{(0.03145)^2}{24} + \frac{(0.0018)^2}{25} + \frac{(0.0128)^2}{19} + \frac{(0.0050)^2}{20}} \cong 50$$

From equation (25A-11), the 0.95 confidence limits for the mean of the lot are

$$9.45 \pm 2.009\sqrt{0.0510} = 9.00 \text{ and } 9.90$$

Since the inspector was conservative in the determination of n, the confidence interval is somewhat narrower than the target value of 1%.

The "Within and Between" Models: Stratified Segments   In some situations the quality characteristic of the bulk material may be stratified in that in each segment it may vary from layer to layer and is not randomly distributed throughout the segment. Difficulties in formulating a model for stratified segments of this kind can be overcome if the strata are reasonably parallel and if the increments taken from the sample segments are taken perpendicular to the strata and penetrate all strata. In taking a sample from a bale of wool, for example, a thief could cut a sample running vertically from top to bottom of the bale.[8]

An increment derived by directional sampling of this kind from a stratified segment can no longer be viewed as a random sample of m test-units from the M test-units that make up the segment. The proper approach in this case is to view the sampling of a segment as the random selection of one directed increment from the totality of directed increments that make up the segment. If we assume further that the variability between directed increments within segments is basically the same for all segments, then the variance formula will be the same as formula (25A-10) except that s_w^2/m will be replaced by s_{DI}^2 where s_{DI}^2 is an estimate of the variance of the directed increments within segments, assumed the same for all segments.

MODELS FOR BULK MATERIAL MOVING IN A STREAM

In many instances the bulk material to be sampled is moving in a stream, say on a conveyer belt. In such instances it is the common practice to take increments systematically from the stream, the increment being taken across the full width of the stream.

Isolated Lots   If increments are taken at random from the stream, we would have a simple random sample from the lot and we could proceed much as indicated for isolated lots of distinctly segmented material.

If increments are taken systematically, as is usually the case, and are composited into a single composite sample, no estimate of variance can be obtained. A compromise would be to take h interpenetrating[9] systematic samples each with a separate random start, but there would have to be h independent samplers or sampling devices, operating simultaneously to acquire increments at the same intervals but with different starts. The increments of each set could be composited, reduced, and measured, and the h results could be treated as a simple random sample of h measurements. Since each measurement would be based on a composite of a number of increments, the sampling variance of the mean of the h measurements would not be as great as the sampling variance of the mean of h randomly selected individual increments. It is unlikely, however, that the variability due to reduction and testing would be any different in the two cases; so there would be a limit to the gain that could be obtained by the compositing procedure.

Model 2A. A Stream of Lots: A Segregation Model   When a stream of bulk material persists for some time, with possible interruptions, determinations of quality and/or action decisions may have to be made for a number of lots. Here, a pilot study might be profitable.

---

[8] If the bottom layers cannot be reached, some adjustment might be made for this. See Ref. 5.

[9] One systematic sample might be taken, for example, every hour at 12 minutes after the hour, a second every hour at 28 minutes after the hour, and a third every hour at 41 minutes after the hour, the 12, 28, and 41 being random selections from a 60-minute period.

The kind of pilot study needed will depend on the assumptions about the statistical properties of the material in the stream. If the quality of the material varies randomly in the stream, then a pilot study based on a number of randomly or systematically taken increments would be sufficient to determine the variance of the material, and this could be used to set up confidence limits for the means of subsequent lots or make decisions as to their acceptability, even though in each of these lots a single composite sample was taken.

Frequently bulk material in a stream shows local segregation. A model that allows for this has been applied to the sampling of coal (see Ref. 2) and might be useful for other bulk material. We will call this the "segregation model."

The segregation model views the stream of material as composed of a series of increments (e.g., scoopsful) across the stream made up of, say, M test-units each. Over the whole stream, which is assumed to be very large, the variance between increments σ_I^2 can be expressed approximately as

$$\sigma_I^2 = \frac{\sigma^2}{M} + \left(1 - \frac{1}{M}\right)\rho\sigma^2 \qquad (25A\text{-}13)$$

where σ^2 is the variance between individual test-units in the stream of material and ρ is the intraclass correlation coefficient between test-units in the same increment. A further assumption is that over the range of likely values of M, the parameter ρ is independent of M; hence formula (25A-13) will give the variance between increments whatever the size of the increments. The possible approximate validity of such an assumption has been suggested by the work of J. Visman.[10]

Given the above model for the statistical properties of the stream of bulk material, the task of the pilot study is to estimate the basic parameters[11] σ^2 and ρ. The pilot study recommended by ASTM "Standard Methods for Sampling Coal" (Ref. 2) consists of taking a set of 30 large increments and a contiguous set of 30 small increments (in size about 0.25% of the large increments). The variance of the 30 small increments is computed and designated as s_A^2. Similarly the variance of the 30 large increments is computed and designated as s_B^2. In equation (25A-13) the term σ^2/M is replaced by σ_u^2/W, where W is the weight of the bulk material that makes up an increment and σ_u^2 is the variance of an increment of unit weight. It is assumed that $1/M$ (or $1/W$) is small enough to be neglected, and the variance formula that is employed in the pilot study is

$$\sigma_I^2 = \frac{\sigma_u^2}{W} + \sigma_{seg}^2 \qquad (25A\text{-}14)$$

where σ_u^2 is called the "random variance" and σ_{seg}^2 ($= \rho\sigma_u^2$) is called the "segregation variance."

On the assumption that ρ remains constant with variations in W and with the symbols s_{ran}^2 and s_{seg}^2 used as estimates of σ_u^2 and σ_{seg}^2, the random and segregation variances are estimated from the equations

$$s_A^2 = \frac{s_{ran}^2}{W_1} + s_{seg}^2 \qquad (25A\text{-}15)$$

$$s_B^2 = \frac{s_{ran}^2}{W_2} + s_{seg}^2 \qquad (25A\text{-}16)$$

where W_1 and W_2 are the weights of the small and large increments, respectively. These yield

---

[10] Also see Ref. 7.
[11] Actually, estimates are made of σ^2 and $\rho\sigma^2$.

$$s^2_{\text{ran}} = \frac{W_1 W_2 (s_A{}^2 - s_B{}^2)}{W_2 - W_1} \qquad (25A\text{-}17)$$

and
$$s^2_{\text{seg}} = s_B{}^2 - \frac{s_{\text{ran}}{}^2}{W_2} = \frac{W_2 s_B{}^2 - W_1 s_A{}^2}{W_2 - W_1} \qquad (25A\text{-}18)$$

The above results assume that the reduction and testing variances are negligible.

Although in ASTM D2234 the pilot study is used only to estimate s^2_{ran} and s^2_{seg}, it is probably wise in addition to test the assumption of a constant segregation variance by taking an additional set of 30 middle-sized increments. If the assumption is valid, the variance computed for the middle-sized increments should compare reasonably well[12] with that predicted for that size increment by formula (25A-13), using the values of s^2_{ran} and s^2_{seg} computed from the variances of the large and small increments.

With estimates available of σ^2 and $\rho\sigma^2$, given by s^2_{ran} and s^2_{seg} from the pilot study, an estimate can be made of the sampling variance of a mean of n increments, each of size M test-units or weight W, from a current lot. Suppose n increments are selected at random from the current stream of material or are selected systematically and the additional assumption made that the variation between increments in the stream is random. Further, suppose the n increments are grouped at random into h-subgroups, each subgroup being composited, reduced to a laboratory sample, and tested. Then the mean of the h results will have the estimated sampling variance

$$s^2_{\bar{X}_{c(h)}} = \frac{s^2_{\text{ran}}}{nW} + \left(1 - \frac{1}{W}\right) \frac{s^2_{\text{seg}}}{n} + \frac{s^2_r (nW/h) + s_t{}^2}{h} \qquad (25A\text{-}19)$$

where $s^2_{r(nW/h)}$ is the reduction variance for composite samples of size nW/h and s^2_t is the test variance, both estimated in supplementary pilot studies. As with other models, this formula for the sampling variance can be employed to determine the number of increments n to use for a given size increment W in order to get a confidence interval of prescribed width or to be assured of certain minimum risks in acceptance or rejection of the lot. Before the confidence limits are actually computed, however, or the decision made to accept or reject, the continued validity of the pilot study estimates s^2_{ran} and s^2_{seg} should be tested. This can be done by plotting the range of the h composite results on an R-chart with

$$\begin{array}{l}\text{Central} \\ \text{line}\end{array} = d_2 \left[\frac{s^2_{\text{ran}}}{nW/h} + \left(1 - \frac{1}{W}\right) \frac{s^2_{\text{seg}}}{n/h} + \sigma^2_{r(nW/h)} + \sigma_t{}^2 \right]^{1/2} \qquad (25A\text{-}20)$$

$$\begin{array}{l}\text{Upper} \\ \text{control} \\ \text{limit}\end{array} = D_2 \left[\frac{s^2_{\text{ran}}}{nW/h} + \left(1 - \frac{1}{W}\right) \frac{s^2_{\text{seg}}}{n/h} + \sigma^2_{r(nW/h)} + \sigma_t{}^2 \right]^{1/2} \qquad (25A\text{-}21)$$

The primary difficulty in this model is that in practice sample increments are generally taken systematically and not at random. The question thus becomes that of the randomness of the variation between increments in the stream of material taken at the given interval. If practicable, the pilot study should cover at least as much material as is likely to be included in a subsequent lot and to have the increments taken at the same interval. It might also be well to make the 30 large increments of the pilot study consist of 5 interpenetrating[13] systematic samples of 6

[12] An F-statistic can be set up for comparing the variance of the middle-sized increments with that predicted for it from the estimated values of σ^2_{ran} and σ^2_{seg}. The degrees of freedom for the predicted value may be determined by Satterthwaite's formula. See Ref. 8, Sec. 2.2.2, chap. XXX.

[13] See footnote 8.

increments each, the 5 systematic samples having independent random starts. If the variation between the mean of the 5 systematic samples is significantly greater than is to be expected on the basis of the intrasample variation, it would be wise to abandon the use of the model or at least not to use systematic sampling.

Example 3   In a pilot study ASTM D2234 gives the variance of 30 small increments of coal, each weighing 0.27 pound, as $s_A^2 = 29.2$ and also the variance of 30 large increments, each weighing about 106 pounds, as $s_B^2 = 1.3$. The large and small increments are taken contiguously from the stream of coal at more or less regular intervals. (The small samples are actually a subsample obtained by riffling from a larger sample of 4 to 20 pounds. The 106-pound samples are reduced by normal methods that seek to make the test samples representative of the whole.) In another pilot study the variance of reduction and analysis is determined to be 0.0465.

From the values of s_A^2 and s_B^2, the random variance and segregation variance are computed to be $s_{ran}^2 = 7.6$ and $s_{seg}^2 = 1.3$ [see formulas (25A-17) and (25A-18)]. If in evaluating a subsequent lot, increments of weight W and four composites are to be used, the total number of increments n needed can be found from equation (25A-19). For a confidence interval of approximate width 2δ use the n that comes close to satisfying the relationship

$$\frac{7.6}{nW} + \left(1 - \frac{1}{W} \right) \frac{1.2}{n} + \frac{0.0465}{4} = \left(\frac{\delta}{1.96} \right)^2$$

Thus if $\delta = 1$ and $W = 100$ pounds, n should be such that

$$\frac{0.076}{n} + 0.99 \frac{1.2}{n} + 0.0116 \cong 0.26$$

Since the n adopted will have to be a multiple of 4, $n = 8$ comes the closest to the desired result.

Obtaining the Test-units   Three factors are important in obtaining the test-units:

1. The models discussed above assume random sampling. Either the increments are picked at random (using preferably random numbers if the units can be identified) or the increments are selected systematically from material that is itself random. Random sampling may have to be undertaken while the material is in motion or being moved. If random sampling cannot be used, special efforts should be made to get a representative picture of a lot, noting strata and the like. Some element of randomness must be present in a sampling procedure to yield a formula for sampling variance.

2. Grinding and mixing. In the processing of bulk material and in the formation of composite samples, grinding and/or mixing may be employed in an attempt to attain homogeneity or at least to reduce the variability of the material.[14]

If a material can be made homogeneous for the size increment that is to be used in subsequent sampling, then an increment of that size can be viewed as a random sample of the material. The attainment of homogeneity of bulk material in bags, cartons, barrels, etc., is thus a worthy objective when the contents of these containers are to be sampled by a thief or other sampling instruments. However, random sampling does not guarantee minimum sampling variation, and grinding and mixing may lead to a reduction in overall sampling variation without attaining homogeneity.[15]

Although grinding and mixing are aimed at reducing variability, these operations may in some circumstances cause segregation and thus increase variability.

---

[14] Some interesting theoretical work on grinding and mixing has been done by H. Sakamoto. See Ref. 14 for an abstract.

[15] *Cf.* Ref. 7.

3. Reduction of a sample to test-units. Measurements often may be made directly on the sample itself. However, sometimes a portion of the sample must be carefully reduced in either particle size or physical quantity to facilitate laboratory testing. The unreduced portion of the sample may be retained for subsequent reference for legal purposes or verification of results. An example of a technique is coning and quartering. The material is first crushed and placed in a conical pile, which is then flattened. The material is then separated into quarters and opposite quarters selected for further quartering or as the final test-units.

References 3 and 4 provide unique details on obtaining test-units for a large variety of specific bulk products.

TESTS OF HOMOGENEITY

The homogeneity of bulk material may be tested by $\bar{X}$-charts and c-charts (see Section 23). For mixtures of particles that can be identified, local homogeneity may be tested by running a χ^2 shortest-distance test. See Ref. 15.

REFERENCES

1. "Recommended Practice for Sampling Industrial Chemicals" (E300-70), American Society for Testing and Materials.
2. "Standard Methods of Test for Sampling Coal" (D2234-68), American Society for Testing and Materials.
3. Bicking, C. A., The Sampling of Bulk Materials, *Materials Research and Standards,* March 1967.
4. Bicking, C. A., T. A. Donovan, T. S. Sosnowski, and C. M. Bicking, "Bibliography on Precision, Bulk Sampling and Related Applications of Statistics—Supplement," CA Report 10, *TAPPI,* 1967.
5. "Methods of Sampling Chemical Products," Parts I–IV (P.S. Drafts 69/6168–6171), British Standards Institution.
6. Cochran, W. G., Relative Accuracy of Systematic and Stratified Random Samples from a Certain Class of Populations, *The Annals of Mathematical Statistics,* vol. XVII, pp. 164–77, 1946.
7. Cochran, W. G., "Sampling Techniques," 2d ed., John Wiley & Sons, Inc., New York, 1963.
8. Duncan, A. J., "Quality Control and Industrial Statistics," 3d ed., Richard D. Irwin, Inc., Homewood, Ill., 1965.
9. Duncan, A. J., Bulk Sampling: Problems and Lines of Attack, *Technometrics,* vol. 4, pp. 319–344, 1962.
10. Duncan, A. J., An Experiment in the Sampling and Analysis of Bagged Fertilizer, *Journal of the Association of Official Agricultural Chemists,* vol. 43, pp. 831–904, 1960.
11. Hebden, J., and G. H. Jowett, The Accuracy of Coal Sampling, *Applied Statistics,* vol. I, pp. 179–191, 1952.
12. Jowett, G. H., The Accuracy of Systematic Sampling from Conveyor Belts, *Applied Statistics,* vol. I, pp. 50–59, 1952.
13. Jowett, G. H., The Comparison of Means of Industrial Time Series, *Applied Statistics,* vol. IV, pp. 32–46, 1955.
14. Sakamoto, H., Statistical Theory of Systematic Sampling and Mixing Methods of Bulk Materials, *Proceedings of 35th Session,* International Statistical Institute, pp. 883–884, Beograd, 1965. Abstract.
15. Shinner, R., and P. Naor, A Test of Randomness for Solid-Solid Mixtures, *Chemical Engineering Science,* vol. 15, Nos. 3/4, pp. 220–229, 1961.
16. Visman, J., Tests on the Binomial Sampling Theory for Heterogeneous Coals, *Symposium on Coal Sampling,* pp. 141–152, ASTM S.T.P. 162, 1955.
17. Visman, J., A General Sampling Theory, *Materials Research and Standards,* vol. 9, pp. 9ff., 1969. See Comments by A. J. Duncan, *Materials Research and Standards,* vol. II, p. 25, and further discussion by J. Visman, A. J. Duncan, and M. Lerner, *Materials Research and Standards,* vol. II, pp. 32ff and discussion by J. Visman and A. J. Duncan, *Journal of Materials,* vol. 7, pp. 345–350, 1972.

18. Grubbs, Frank E., and Helen J. Coon, on Setting Test Limits Relative to Specification Limits, *Industrial Quality Control*, March 1954, pp. 15–20.

Section **26**

Regression Analysis[1]

JOHN S. RAMBERG, Ph.D.

Departments of Industrial and Management Engineering
and Statistics, The University of Iowa

USES OF REGRESSION ANALYSIS

Numerous problems encountered in quality control require the estimation of relationships between two or more variables. Often interest centers on finding an equation relating one particular variable to another set of one or more variables. For example, how does the life of a tool vary with cutting speed? Or, how does the octane number of a gasoline vary with its percentage purity?

Least squares is a statistical technique for estimating the parameters of an equation relating a particular variable to a set of variables. Some authors refer to this as least squares or curve fitting, whereas many practitioners call it regression analysis and call the resulting equation a regression equation. The latter convention will be used here, although the precise definition of the term regression analysis is more restrictive.

Some experimental data for the tool life example are given in Table 26-1[2] and plotted in Figure 26-1. Tool life is the response variable (also called the dependent variable or the predictand) and cutting speed is the independent variable (also called the predictor variable). In this case, the independent variable is controllable; i.e., it is fixed by the experimenter or the operator of the machine. In the second exam-

---

[1] In the Second Edition, this Section was prepared by Besse Day Mauss.
[2] Ref. 10, p. 380.

TABLE 26-1 Tool Life (Y in minutes) vs. Cutting Speed (X in feet per minute)

Y	X	Y	X
41	90	21	105
43	90	13	105
35	90	18	105
32	90	20	105
22	100	15	110
35	100	11	110
29	100	6	110
18	100	10	110

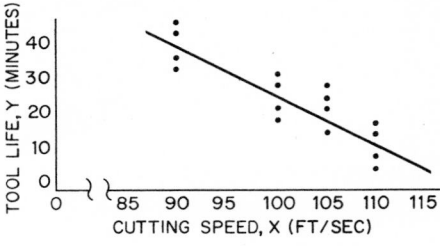

Fig. 26-1 Tool life Y vs. cutting speed X.

ple, both the octane number and the percentage purity are random. The data for this example are given in Table 26-2 and plotted in Figure 26-2. Since the goal is to predict the octane number, it is regarded as the dependent variable, and the percentage purity is considered as the independent variable. Of course, in many problems there are a number of independent variables, and in some cases this set of independent variables includes both random and controllable variables.

The computations for two-variable regression problems can be done quite easily on a desk calculator, but when there are many variables, the number of computations becomes overwhelming. However, with the advent of the modern digital computer and multiple regression computer programs, the number of variables is no longer a severe restriction. To understand and interpret the results of multidimensional problems, a thorough knowledge of the two and three variable cases is necessary.

There are many reasons for constructing regression equations, and although the motives do not affect the calculations, they do affect the interpretation of the results. In some cases, regression analysis is used to describe the nature of a relationship in a quantitative manner. Often, however, the goals are more specific. In the first example where the cutting speed is controllable, the objective might be to find the particular value of cutting speed which minimizes the tool wear or some cost function based on tool wear. Least squares regression can also be used to determine the important independent variables in a process, e.g., whether process variables such as moisture, pressure, or temperature affect a quality characteristic of the product such as strength.

In other problems, where the independent variable is not controllable, the goal may be to predict the value of the dependent or response variable. This might be done because the independent variable is easier to measure than the dependent variable. Or the independent variable may be available before the dependent

TABLE 26-2 Octane Number Y vs. Percentage Purity X*

Y	X	Y	X
88.6	99.8	86.1	99.2
86.4	99.7	87.3	99.1
87.2	99.6	86.4	99.0
88.4	99.5	86.6	98.9
87.2	99.4	87.1	98.8
86.8	99.3		

* Excerpted by special permission from *Chemical Engineering*, March 1956.

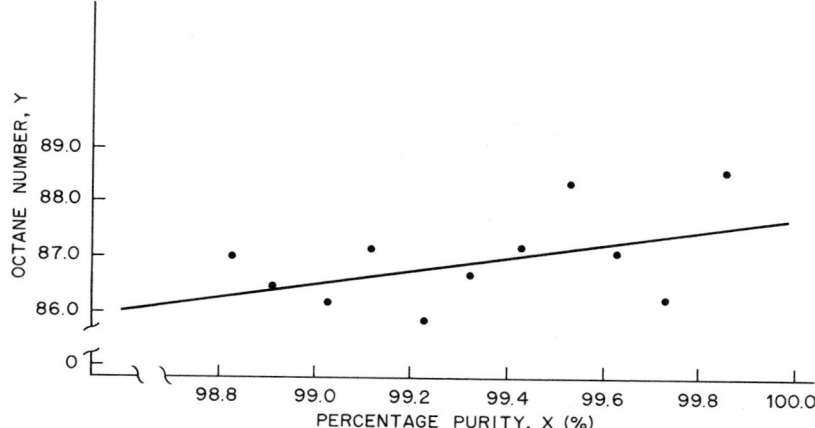

Fig. 26-2 Octane number vs. percentage impurity.

variable, and hence it would be desirable to forecast the value of the dependent variable before it occurs. In still other cases it might allow a destructive test to be replaced by a nondestructive test.

The following list includes a number of uses of regression equations, some of which are interrelated:

1. Forecasting and prediction
2. Quantitatively describing the relationship between a particular variable and another set of variables
3. Interpolating between values of a function
4. Determining the important independent variables
5. Locating the optimum operating conditions
6. Discriminating between alternative models
7. Estimating particular regression coefficients

SUMMARY OF STEPS IN A REGRESSION STUDY

For any of the goals stated above, the basic steps in a regression study are:

1. Obtain a clear statement of the objectives of the study. Determine which variable is to be the response variable and which variables can be included as independent variables. In addition, obtain some measure of the precision of the results required—not necessarily in statistical terminology. It is important to have a thorough understanding of what use will be made of the regression equation, since this may preclude the use of certain variables in the equation and will also help to give an understanding as to how much effort and money should be devoted to the project.

2. Collect or specify collection procedures for the data. The end results can only be as good as the data upon which they are based. Careful planning at this stage is of considerable importance and can also simplify the analysis of the data.

3. Prepare scatter diagrams (plots of one variable vs. another) of the data to obtain information about the relationships between the variables. If there are many variables or many observations, it may be worthwhile to have the data punched on cards, so that the scatter plots can be done on a computer.

4. Calculate the regression equation.

5. Study the equation to see how well it fits the data. This includes looking at

transformations of variables for a better fit, or the removal of variables from an equation if they do not improve the prediction equation.

6. In addition to providing the equation, give measures of the precision of the equation and any procedure for using the equation. Also specify procedures for updating the equation and checks to determine whether it is still applicable, including control charts for the residuals (observed value—predicted value).

A number of texts have been written on regression, including Acton (Ref. 1), Daniel and Wood (Ref. 3), Draper and Smith (Ref. 4), and Johnston (Ref. 11). References 3 and 4, which are the most recent, include computer programs and output. They complement each other nicely and are highly recommended. Many applied statistics texts have at least one chapter devoted to regression, e.g., Brownlee (Ref. 2), Hald (Ref. 7), and Johnson and Leone (Ref. 10). In addition to regression, several other techniques have been devised for the analysis of multivariate data. An excellent series of articles on this subject by Kramer and Jensen (Ref. 12) appeared in the *Journal of Quality Technology*.

Our discussion of regression begins with a single predictor problem, proceeds to problems with more than one predictor variable using matrix expressions where needed, and concludes with a discussion of computer programs.

SIMPLE REGRESSION

Many problems involve only a single predictor variable X. The dependent variable Y is often related to other predictor variables, but these have either been held constant during the experiment or their effects have been judged to be much smaller than that of X. These problems are often referred to as simple linear regressions.

Graphing the Data   The first step in any study of relationships between variables is to plot a graph of the data, often called a scatter diagram. The usual convention is to plot the response variable on the vertical axis and the independent variable on the horizontal axis. A graph can provide a great deal of information concerning the relationship between variables and often suggests possible models for the data. The data plotted in Fig. 26-1 suggest that Y is linearly related to X over the range of this experiment. If this were not the case, various transformations of the data as well as curvilinear relationships could also be considered. Often the relationship can be "linearized" by taking the logarithm of one or both of the variables.

A graph can also indicate whether any of the observations are outliers, i.e., observations which deviate substantially from the rest of the data. These outliers may be due to measurement errors or recording errors, in which case they should be corrected or deleted. Or they may be due to process changes or other causes, and the investigation of these changes or causes may provide more information than the analysis of the rest of the data. No outliers are apparent in Fig. 26-1.

A closer inspection of the graph can give an indication of the variability of Y for fixed X. In addition, it may show that this variability remains constant over all X or that it changes with X. In the latter case the method of weighted least squares (see Section 2.11 of Ref. 4) may be preferred to the standard least squares technique discussed here.

The Model   After graphing the data, we may want to obtain an equation relating Y to X. To do this, a model for the data must be postulated or entertained. The term entertain is used to emphasize that the proposed model may be modified during the course of the study and is just a starting point.

A possible model for the data in Figure 26-1 is

$$Y = \beta_0 + \beta_1 X + \varepsilon \tag{26-1}$$

where β_0 and β_1 are the unknown intercept and slope, respectively, of the regression line. The model assumes that Y is a linear function of X plus a random error term, denoted by ε. This random error may be due to errors in the measurement of Y and/or to the effects of variables not included in the model, which is called equation error. The X's are assumed to be measured with negligible error. For the data in Figure 26-1 the X's are fixed; however, the same model can be used when the X's are random as in Figure 26-2.

Estimating the Prediction Equation   The objective in this section is to find estimates (b_0, b_1) of the unknown parameters (β_0, β_1) and thus obtain a prediction equation

$$\hat{Y} = b_0 + b_1 X \qquad (26\text{-}2)$$

where $\hat{Y}$ is the predicted value of Y for a given value of X.

Least squares provides a method for finding estimates of these parameters from a set of N observations $(Y_1, X_1), \ldots, (Y_N, X_N)$. The estimates are called least

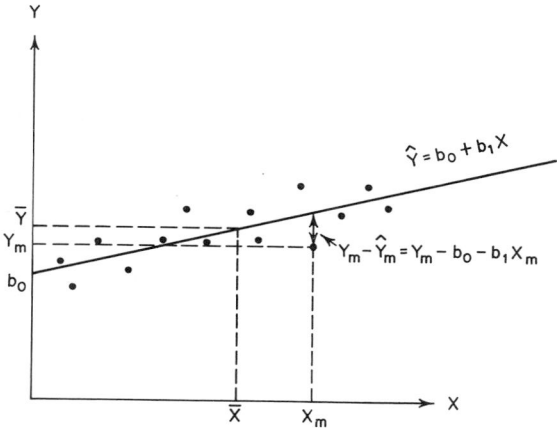

Fig. 26-3   Least squares.

squares estimates because they minimize the sum of the squared deviations between the observed and predicted values of the response variable $\Sigma(Y_m - \hat{Y}_m)^2 = \Sigma(Y_m - b_0 - b_1 X_m)^2$. These ideas are illustrated in Figure 26-3. For a derivation of the estimates, see any of the texts mentioned in the introduction.

If (1) the observations are independent, (2) the variance of the errors is constant over these observations, and (3) the linear model postulated is correct, then the least squares estimates are the "best linear unbiased estimates." That is, in the class of linear unbiased estimates of the parameters, the least squares estimates have the smallest variance. Even if these conditions are not satisfied, the least squares technique can be used, although modifications or other methods may provide better estimates. Note that no assumption has been made concerning the distribution of the random error, and in particular a normal distribution is not necessarily assumed. No assumption on this error term will be required until confidence intervals and tests of hypothesis are constructed.

The least squares estimates for the parameters of the linear model (1) are

$$b_1 = \frac{\Sigma(X_m - \bar{X})(Y_m - \bar{Y})}{\Sigma(X_m - \bar{X})^2}$$

$$b_0 = \bar{Y} - b_1 \bar{X} \qquad (26\text{-}3)$$

where $\bar{X} = \Sigma X_m/N$ and $\bar{Y} = \Sigma Y_m/N$ are sample averages. All these summations range from $m = 1$ to $m = N$. Except where needed, the additional notation will be omitted for typographical simplicity.

As can be seen from (26-3), b_1 is related to the sample correlation coefficient

$$r = \frac{\Sigma(X_m - \bar{X})(Y_m - \bar{Y})}{\sqrt{\Sigma(X_m - \bar{X})^2 \Sigma(Y_m - \bar{Y})^2}} \qquad (26\text{-}4)$$

by

$$b_1 = r\sqrt{\frac{\Sigma(Y_m - \bar{Y})^2}{\Sigma(X_m - \bar{X})^2}}$$

However, the concept of correlation is meaningful only when both the variables are random, whereas b_1, the least squares estimate of the rate of change of Y per unit change in X has meaning for both the case of random X and controllable or fixed X.

The sums, sums of squares, and sum of cross products for the data ($N = 16$) given in Table 26-1 are

$$\Sigma X_m = 90 + 90 + \ldots + 110 = 1,620$$
$$\Sigma Y_m = 41 + 43 + \ldots + 10 = 369$$
$$\Sigma X_m^2 = 8,100 + 8,100 + \ldots + 12,000 = 164,900$$
$$\Sigma Y_m^2 = 1,681 + 1,849 + \ldots + 100 = 10,469$$
$$\Sigma X_m Y_m = 3,690 + 3,870 + \ldots + 1,100 = 36,170$$

which can be computed in one pass on many desk calculators. It is worthwhile to note here that whenever doing calculations of this type it is advisable to repeat the calculations as a check.

The summary statistics are computed from the raw statistics using the following computational forms:

$$\bar{X} = \frac{\Sigma X_m}{N} = 101.25 \qquad \bar{Y} = \frac{\Sigma Y_m}{N} = 23.06$$

$$\Sigma(X_m - \bar{X})^2 = \Sigma X_m^2 - \frac{(\Sigma X_m)^2}{N} = 164,900 - \frac{(1,620)^2}{16} = 875.00$$

$$\Sigma(Y_m - \bar{Y})^2 = \Sigma Y_m^2 - \frac{(\Sigma Y_m)^2}{N} = 10,469 - \frac{(369)^2}{16} = 1,958.94$$

$$\Sigma(X_m - \bar{X})(Y_m - \bar{Y}) = \Sigma X_m Y_m - \frac{\Sigma X_m \Sigma Y_m}{N}$$

$$= 36,170 - \frac{(1,620)(369)}{16}$$

$$= -1,191.25$$

From these results the least squares estimates can be calculated as

$$b_1 = \frac{-1,191.25}{875} = -1.3614$$

$$b_0 = 23.06 - (-1.3614)(101.25) = 160.9018$$

and hence the prediction equation is

$$\hat{Y} = 160.90 - 1.3614X$$

The prediction equation (26-2) is sometimes written in terms of deviations from averages; i.e., $\hat{Y} = \bar{Y} + b_1(X - \bar{X})$, which for this example becomes

$$\hat{Y} = 23.06 - 1.3614(X - 101.25)$$

Examining the Prediction Equation After estimating the coefficients of the prediction equation, the equation should be plotted over the data to check for gross calculation errors. Roughly half the data points should be above the line and half below it. In addition, the equation should pass exactly through the point $(\bar{X}, \bar{Y})$.

A number of criteria exist for judging the adequacy of the prediction equation. One common measure of the adequacy of the prediction equation is the proportion of variation R^2 explained by the prediction equation. To compute R^2, the sum of the squared deviations of the Y_m about $\bar{Y}$ is partitioned into two parts, the sum of squares due to regression and the residual sum of squares; i.e.,

$$\sum(Y_m - \bar{Y})^2 = SS(REG) + SS(RES)$$
$$= \sum(\hat{Y}_m - \bar{Y})^2 + \sum(Y_m - \hat{Y}_m)^2 \qquad (26\text{-}5)$$
$$= b_1 \sum(X_m - \bar{X})(Y_m - \bar{Y}) + \sum(Y_m - \hat{Y}_m)^2$$

From this, the proportion of the variation $\sum(Y_m - \bar{Y})^2$

explained by the regression is computed as

$$R^2 = SS(REG)/\sum(Y_m - \bar{Y})^2$$
$$= \frac{b_1 \sum(X_m - \bar{X})(Y_m - \bar{Y})}{\sum(Y_m - \bar{Y})^2}$$
$$= \frac{(-1.3614)(-1,191.25)}{1,958.94} = 0.828$$

Thus, for this example, the prediction equation explains 82.8% of the variation of the tool life.

Another interpretation of R^2 (when both the independent and the dependent variables are random) is as the square of the sample multiple correlation coefficient. When there is only one independent variable, this reduces to the square of the sample correlation coefficient r^2 defined in (26-4).

Although R^2 is a useful measure of the adequacy of the prediction equation, an estimate of the variability of the Y's about the regression equation is usually more important. Either the sample variance s^2 or its square root s, called the standard error of the estimate, can be used. The latter is often preferred, because it is measured in the same units as Y. Both of these, as well as other results, can be obtained from the analysis of variance (ANOVA) given in Table 26-3.

TABLE 26-3 ANOVA Table (Linear Model)

Source	Sum of squares	Degrees of freedom	Mean square
(1) Due to regression (b_1) . . .	$b_1 \sum(X_m - \bar{X})(Y_m - \bar{Y})$	1	MS (REG) = SS (REG)/1
(2) Residual	$\sum(Y_m - \hat{Y}_m)^2$*	$N - 2$	MS (RES) = SS (RES)/$(N - 2)$
(3) Total corrected for the mean	$\sum(Y_m - \bar{Y})^2$	$N - 1$	

* Obtained by subtracting (1) from (3).

The corrected total sum of squares[3] and the regression sum of squares are calculated from the summary statistics and the estimate of the regression coefficient. Although the residual sum of squares can be calculated directly, it is more easily obtained as the difference between the corrected total sum of squares and the sum of squares due to regression. Each of these sums of squares has an associated degrees of freedom.[4] The corrected total sum of squares has $N - 1$ degrees of freedom, since one degree of freedom is used in estimating the mean. For this *one* variable model, there is *one* degree of freedom associated with the regression sum of squares, leaving $(N - 1) - 1 = N - 2$ degrees of freedom associated with the residual sum of squares. The mean squares (MS) are calculated by dividing the sum of squares by their associated degrees of freedom. The estimate of the variance of Y about the regression line is $s^2 = $ MS (RES), and hence the standard error of the estimate is $s = \sqrt{\text{MS(RES)}}$.

From the mean squares an F statistic can be calculated as

$$F_{\text{CALC}} = \frac{\text{MS(REG)}}{\text{MS(RES)}}$$

If (1) the ϵ's in the original model are normally distributed with a common variance, (2) the observations are independent, and (3) the postulated linear model is correct, the regression can be tested for significance, i.e., the statistical hypothesis

$$H_0 : \beta_1 = 0$$

can be tested against the alternative hypothesis

$$H_1 : \beta_1 \neq 0$$

by comparing F_{CALC} with the tabulated F at an appropriate level of significance α. If $F_{\text{CALC}} > F_{\text{TAB}}$ we conclude that the regression is significant and that the prediction equation is a better predictor of Y than $\bar{Y}$. Although it is difficult to check the assumptions stated above, it is of some comfort to know that the test is not extremely sensitive to departures in the distribution of ϵ from normality if the number of observations is relatively large. If the X's are random, this test must be interpreted in a conditional sense, i.e., given the values of the X's.

For the example, the analysis of variance (ANOVA) table[5] is given in Table 26-4. The regression is significant at an $\alpha = 0.01$ level ($F_{\text{TAB}} = 8.86$) and $s = \sqrt{24.08} = 4.91$.

It is important to note that even when the regression is significant, the unex-

---

[3] Some authors include the total sum of squares (uncorrected) in the ANOVA table, partitioning it into two parts—the corrected sum of squares and the sum of squares due to $\bar{Y}$ (or b_0). See Draper and Smith (Ref. 4, p. 15).

[4] See Section 22, under Testing a Hypothesis When the Sample Size is Fixed in Advance.

[5] See Section 27, under Completely Randomized Design—A Simple One Factor Experiment.

TABLE 26-4   ANOVA Example

Source	Sum of squares	Degrees of freedom	Mean square	F_{CALC}
(1) Due to regression	1,621.80	1	1,621.80	67.35
(2) Residual.	337.14	14	24.08	
(3) Total corrected for the mean	1,958.94	15		

plained variability can still be large, and the prediction equation may not be of any value.

Lack of Fit—Replicated Observations   If it is feasible to replicate, i.e., take more than one observation on Y at one or more values of X, the adequacy of the model can also be tested.[6]   In this case the SS (RES) can be partitioned into two parts—that due to pure error, SS (PE), and that due to lack of fit, SS (LF).

Suppose that there are N_m readings $Y_{m1}, Y_{m2}, \ldots, Y_{mN_m}$ at X_m, where $m = 1, 2, \ldots, k$.   The contribution to the sum of squares due to pure error for X_m is

$$\sum_{j=1}^{N_m} (Y_{mj} - \bar{Y}_m)^2 = \sum_{j=1}^{N_m} Y_{mj}^2 - \frac{(\sum_{j=1}^{N_m} Y_{mj})^2}{N_m}$$

and the associated degrees of freedom is $N_m - 1$.   The SS (PE) is just the sum of these k contributions and the associated degrees of freedom (DF) is

$$\sum_{m=1}^{k} (N_m - 1) = \sum_{m=1}^{k} N_m - k$$

For the example given in Table 26-1:

X_m		SS (PE)	DF
90	$41^2 + 43^2 + 35^2 + 32^2 - (151)^2/4 =$	78.75	3
100	$22^2 + 35^2 + 29^2 + 18^2 - (104)^2/4 =$	170.00	3
105	$21^2 + 13^2 + 18^2 + 20^2 - (72)^2/4 =$	38.00	3
110	$15^2 + 16^2 + 6^2 + 10^2 - (42)^2/4 =$	41.00	3
	Total	327.75	12

The SS (LF) is found by subtraction as

$$\text{SS (LF)} = \text{SS (RES)} - \text{SS (PE)} = 337.14 - 327.75 = 9.39$$

and the lack of fit degrees of freedom is obtained in a similar manner as $14 - 12 = 2$.   The mean squares are then found by dividing the sum of squares by the appropriate degrees of freedom and

$$F_{\text{CALC}} = \frac{\text{MS(LF)}}{\text{MS(PE)}}$$

If the F_{CALC} is greater than the tabled F, the lack of fit is "significant" and a better or more complete model is needed (e.g., $Y = \beta_0 + \beta_1 X + \beta_2 X^2$).   Plots of the residuals $(Y_m - \hat{Y}_m)$ vs. X_m are particularly helpful in suggesting alternative models. Some examples are given in Fig. 26-4.[7]   In each case the model $Y = \beta_0 + \beta_1 X$ was postulated and the plots are of the resulting residuals.

If F_{CALC} is less than the tabled F, then the model is accepted.   This does not mean that other variables should not be considered in the model, but only that the form of X in the model is adequate.

The calculations for our example are summarized in Table 26-5.   The lack of fit is judged not significant at an a level of 0.05 ($F_{\text{TAB}} = 3.89$).   Hence, the postulated model is accepted and the residual mean square is used as the estimate of the variance.

---

[6] An estimate of the pure error may sometimes be available from sources outside the immediate experiment.

[7] Daniel and Wood (Ref. 3, pp. 19–24) present graphs of a number of nonlinear functions and give transformations which "linearize" them.

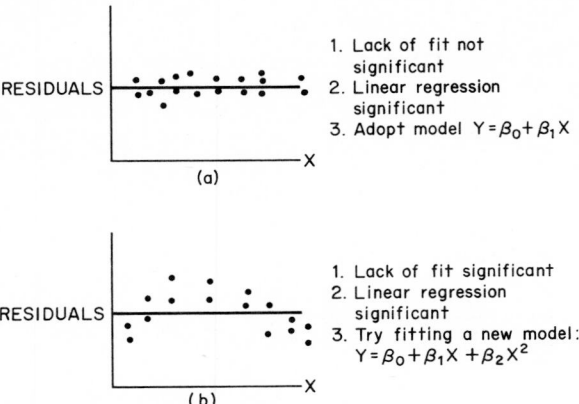

Fig. 26-4   Residuals and lack of fit.

TABLE 26-5   ANOVA Lack of Fit Example

Source	Sum of squares	Degrees of freedom	Mean square	F_{CALC}
Lack of fit	9.39*	2	4.695	0.172
Pure error	327.75	12	27.3125	

*Obtained by subtracting SS (PE) and SS (RES)

If replication is not possible, e.g., X is random rather than controllable, the Y values corresponding to X values which are close together can be used to obtain an estimate of the variability and hence judge the lack of fit.[8]

Confidence Intervals   Both R^2 and s^2 provide measures of the reliability or adequacy of a prediction equation.   Confidence intervals provide another measure of the reliability of the various estimates.   All these confidence intervals are based on the square root of the residual mean square.   A $(1 - a)$ two-sided confidence interval for the slope β_1 is given by

$$b_1 \pm \frac{ts}{\sqrt{\sum (X_m - \bar{X})^2}} \qquad (26\text{-}6)$$

where the value t is obtained from Appendix II, Table G, with $N - 2$ degrees of freedom.   (See Section 22 for a discussion of confidence intervals and the t-distribution.)   The term in the denominator plays the role that $n^{1/2}$ plays in confidence intervals on population means.   For the example, the 0.95 confidence interval on β_1 is

$$-1.36 \pm \frac{(2.145)(4.91)}{\sqrt{875}} = -1.36 \pm 0.356$$

The term $s/\sqrt{\Sigma(X_m - \bar{X})^2}$ is often called the standard error of the regression coefficient.

[8] See pp. 123–125 of Daniel and Wood (Ref. 3).

In addition to the confidence interval on β_1, confidence intervals can also be constructed for the mean of Y at a given value of X. The $(1 - \alpha)$ confidence interval on the *mean* of Y at X (or equivalently on $\beta_0 + \beta_1 X$) is

$$b_0 + b_1 X \pm ts \sqrt{\frac{1}{N} + \frac{(X - \bar{X})^2}{\sum (X_m - \bar{X})^2}} \qquad (26\text{-}7)$$

where X is the value at which the confidence interval is being constructed and t again has $N - 2$ degrees of freedom. By letting $X = 0$, a confidence interval for β_0 is obtained.

In addition to the assumptions previously stated, these confidence intervals also require (1) that the independent variable is fixed rather than random and (2) that the errors are normally distributed. However, if the X's are random, confidence intervals can still be calculated, but they must be interpreted in a conditional sense. Confidence intervals are not sensitive to departures from normality if the sample size is reasonably large. This is not the case for the following interval, which is very sensitive to the normality assumption.

In addition to a confidence interval on the expected value of Y at a given X, there may be a need for an interval estimate for a future individual observation on Y at X.[9] In this case the interval must also take into account the variability of Y about $\beta_0 + \beta_1 X$, and the result is

$$b_0 + b_1 X \pm ts \sqrt{1 + \frac{1}{N} + \frac{(X - \bar{X})^2}{\sum (X_m - \bar{X})^2}} \qquad (26\text{-}8)$$

where t has $N - 2$ degrees of freedom. Computations of these intervals for various values of X are given in Table 26-6.

MULTIPLE REGRESSION

Although there are many problems involving single predictor variables, more often there are many predictor variables. A generalization of the least squares technique, previously discussed, can be used to estimate the coefficients of the multivariable prediction equation. This problem is called multiple regression.

The General Model For a problem with k predictor variables, the model can be written as

$$Y = \beta_0 + \beta_1 X_1 + \ldots + \beta_k X_k + \varepsilon \qquad (26\text{-}9)$$

where the β's are unknown parameters and ϵ is the random error. These variables may be transformations of the original data. For example, in predicting gasoline yields from data on the specific gravity and vapor pressure of crude oil, Y may be the log of the gasoline yield, X_1 the crude oil specific gravity, X_2 the crude oil vapor pressure, and X_3 the product of the crude oil specific gravity with its vapor pressure.

The general model includes polynomial models in one or more variables, such as

$$Y = \beta_0 + \beta_1 X_1 + \beta_2 X_2 + \beta_3 X_1{}^2 + \beta_4 X_2{}^2 + \beta_5 X_1 X_2 + \varepsilon$$

This is still considered a linear model, since the term linear model means that the model is linear in the β's.[10]

---

[9] A more complete discussion of confidence intervals is given in Draper and Smith (Ref. 4). See Daniel and Wood (Ref. 3) for a confidence interval which simultaneously includes the whole line.

[10] See chap. 10 of Draper and Smith (Ref. 4) for a discussion of models which are nonlinear.

TABLE 26-6 Computation of Confidence Limits

X (1)	$b_0 + b_1 X$ (2)	$\dfrac{(X - \bar{X})^2}{\Sigma(X_m - \bar{X})^2}$ (3)	$\sqrt{\dfrac{1}{N} + (3)}$ (4)	$t\,s \times (4)$ (5)	90% confidence limits on the mean of Y at X		$\sqrt{1 + \dfrac{1}{N} + (3)}$ (8)	$t\,s \times (8)$ (9)	90% prediction limits on Y at X	
					Lower (2) − (5) (6)	Upper (2) + (5) (7)			Lower (2) − (9) (10)	Upper (2) + (9) (11)
90	38.37	0.14464	0.4551	3.94	34.43	42.31	1.0987	9.50	28.87	47.87
100	24.76	0.00179	0.2535	2.20	22.56	26.96	1.0316	8.92	15.84	33.68
($\bar{X}$) 101.5	($\bar{Y}$) 23.06	0.0	0.2500	2.17	20.89	25.23	1.0308	8.91	14.15	31.97
110	11.15	0.08750	0.3870	3.36	7.79	14.51	1.0724	9.27	1.88	20.42

Numbers in parentheses are column numbers.

$t_{14,0.95} = 1.761$.

Estimating the Prediction Equation   The objective now is to find the least squares estimates $(b_0, b_1, \ldots, b_k)$ of the unknown parameters $(\beta_0, \beta_1, \ldots, \beta_k)$ and obtain a prediction equation

$$\hat{Y} = b_0 + b_1 X_1 + \ldots + b_k X_k \tag{26-10}$$

where $\hat{Y}$ is the predicted value of Y for the given values of $X_1, \ldots, X_k$. Letting $x_i = X_i - \bar{X}_i$ and using the fact that

$$b_0 = \bar{Y} - b_1 \bar{X}_1 - \ldots - b_k \bar{X}_k$$

this prediction equation can be expressed in the following alternative form:

$$\hat{Y} = \bar{Y} + b_1 X_1 + \ldots + b_{k} \hat{y}_k \tag{26-11}$$

This form will be used in the remainder of this Section.

To simplify the formulas, the observations can also be expressed as deviations from their sample averages; i.e., for the mth observation $x_{im} = X_{im} - \bar{X}_i$ and $y_m = Y_m - \bar{Y}$. Then the least squares estimates of the $k + 1$ parameters of the multivariable linear model (26-9) can be obtained from the following set of $k + 1$ linear equations:

$$b_1 \sum x_{1m}{}^2 + b_2 \sum x_{1m} x_{2m} + \ldots + b_k \sum x_{1m} x_{km} = \sum x_{1m} y_m$$
$$b_1 \sum x_{1m} x_{2m} + b_2 \sum x_{2m}{}^2 + \ldots + b_k \sum x_{2m} x_{km} = \sum x_{2m} y_m$$

$$\tag{26-12}$$

$$b_1 \sum x_{1m} x_{km} + b_2 \sum x_{2m} x_{km} + \ldots + b_k \sum x_{km}{}^2 = \sum x_{km} y_m$$
$$b_0 = \bar{Y} - b_1 \bar{X}_1 - b_2 \bar{X}_2 - \ldots - b_k \bar{X}_k$$

All the above summations are on m and range from 1 to N. This convention will be followed throughout the remainder of the Section.

Solving these "reduced normal" equations simultaneously can be tedious. To simplify the task, a matrix algebra approach will be used. A knowledge of matrix algebra is essential to understand certain of the remaining portions of this Section. However, the required knowledge can be easily learned from Appendix A at the end of the Section.

Equation 26-12 can be written in matrix notation as

$$\begin{bmatrix} \sum x_{1m}{}^2 & \sum x_{1m} x_{2m} \cdots \sum x_{1m} x_{km} \\ \sum x_{2m} x_{1m} & \sum x_{2m}{}^2 \quad \cdots \sum x_{2m} x_{km} \\ \vdots & \vdots \qquad \vdots \\ \sum x_{km} x_{1m} & \sum x_{km} x_{2m} \cdots \sum x_{km}{}^2 \end{bmatrix} \begin{bmatrix} b_1 \\ b_2 \\ \vdots \\ b_k \end{bmatrix} = \begin{bmatrix} \sum x_{1m} y_m \\ \sum x_{2m} y_m \\ \vdots \\ \sum x_{km} y_m \end{bmatrix} \tag{26-13}$$

Denoting the $k \times k$ matrix by S and the $k \times 1$ vector on the right-hand side of the equation by a, (26-13) can be written as

$$\mathbf{S} \, \mathbf{b} = \mathbf{a} \tag{26-14}$$

All these quantities can be computed on a desk calculator. The computational forms for the s_{ij} and a_i are

$$s_{ij} = \sum x_{im}x_{jm}$$

$$= \sum X_{im}X_{jm} - \frac{(\sum X_{im})(\sum X_{jm})}{N}$$

$$a_i = \sum x_{im}y_m \qquad \qquad (26\text{-}15)$$

$$= \sum X_{im}Y_m - \frac{(\sum X_{im})(\sum Y_m)}{N}$$

It is important to note that the b's are the unknowns in this set of linear equations and all other quantities are calculated from the data. To solve these equations for the b's requires the inverse of the matrix $\mathbf{S}$. Premultiplying both sides of (26-14) by the inverse of $\mathbf{S}$ (denoted by C), the following equation results:

$$\mathbf{b} = \mathbf{Ca} \qquad \qquad (26\text{-}16)$$

At this point the utility of a computer and a regression program should be apparent. There are a number of "programmable" desk calculators which are also capable of this task when k is not too large. These calculators are not costly and should be considered as an alternative to using a general-purpose computer. If neither of these is available, the results can be calculated on a desk calculator. One such method for finding the inverse matrix and the b's is given in Appendix B of this Section.

Examining the Prediction Equation   After obtaining C and $\mathbf{b}$, an ANOVA table can be constructed and the adequacy of the prediction equation evaluated by a number of criteria. The ANOVA table, which is a generalization of that derived for the single predictor variate, is given in Table 26-7. The third row in Table 26-7 is the same as in Table 26-3. Note that the expressions in the first row reduce to those in the first row of Table 26-3 when $k = 1$.

Since there are k variables in the model, the sum of squares due to regression has k degrees of freedom associated with it. In addition since k coefficients and one intercept have been estimated, the residual sum of squares has $N - (k + 1) = N - k - 1$ degrees of freedom associated with it. The F statistic is calculated as before [i.e., $F = $ MS (REG)/MS (RES)] and $s = \sqrt{\text{SS (RES)}/(N - k - 1)}$. In this case the F statistic can be used to test the statistical hypothesis

$$H_0 : \beta_i = 0 \qquad (i = 1, 2, \ldots, k)$$

TABLE 26-7   ANOVA Table (Linear Model)

Source	Sum of squares	Degrees of freedom	Mean square
(1) Due to regression	$\mathbf{b}'\mathbf{a}^{*}$	k	MS (REG) $=$ SS (REG)/k
(2) Residual	$\Sigma(Y_m - \hat{Y}_m)^2$†	$N - k - 1$	MS (RES) $=$ SS (RES) / $(N - k - 1)$
(3) Total corrected for the mean......	$\Sigma(Y_m - \overline{Y})^2$	$N - 1$	

* The sum of squares due to regression can be written as $\mathbf{b}'\mathbf{a} = b_1 \Sigma x_1{}_m y_m + b_2 \Sigma x_2{}_m y_m + \ldots + b_k \Sigma x_{km} y_m$. (Note that $\mathbf{b}'$ is the transpose of the $\mathbf{b}$ vector.)
† Obtained by subtracting (1) from (3).

against the alternative statistical hypothesis

$$H_1 : \text{Some } \beta_i \neq 0 \quad (i = 1, 2, \ldots, k)$$

The only change is in the degrees of freedom used to look up the F_{TAB} ($k, n - k - 1$ vs. $1, n - 2$).

The proportion of variation explained by the equation (R^2) can be obtained from the ANOVA table. Note that R^2 does not depend on the number of variables in the equation, but s^2 does. In fact, if a new variable is added to the model (and the least squares estimates and ANOVA table are recomputed), the value of R^2 cannot decrease. However, s^2 can either increase or decrease, since it depends on the residual degrees of freedom in addition to the residual sum of squares, which decreases by one when a new variable is added.

Confidence Intervals   Confidence intervals for individual β's can be developed using the fact that the variance of b_i is $c_{ii}\sigma^2$, where c_{ii} is i^{th} diagonal element of the C matrix. A confidence interval with confidence coefficient a for β_i is given by

$$b_i \pm ts\sqrt{c_{ii}} \tag{26-17}$$

where t has $(N - k - 1)$ degrees of freedom.

Since the $b_i (i = 1, \ldots, k)$ have a joint distribution and are in general not uncorrelated, care must be taken in the interpretation of sets of these confidence intervals.[11]

In addition, a confidence interval on the regression equation at a point $\mathbf{x} = (x_1, \ldots, x_k)$ where $x_i = X_i - \bar{X}_i$ is given by

$$\bar{Y} + b_1 x_1 + \ldots + b_k x_k \pm ts\left(\frac{1}{N} + \mathbf{x}'C\mathbf{x}\right)^{1/2} \tag{26-18}$$

where t has $N - k - 1$ degrees of freedom and $\mathbf{x}'C\mathbf{x}$ is a quadratic form which takes into account the covariances and variances of the b's.

In a similar manner an interval for a future Y at $\mathbf{X}$ is given by

$$\bar{Y} + b_1 x_1 + \ldots + b_k x_k$$
$$\pm ts\left(1 + \frac{1}{N} + \mathbf{x}'C\mathbf{x}\right)^{1/2} \tag{26-19}$$

where t has $N - k - 1$ degrees of freedom.

An Example   The methods discussed in the previous section will be illustrated by an example furnished by Mason E. Wescott[12] with $k = 2$ predictor variables. The problem is to relate the green strength (flexural strength before baking) of electric circuit breaker arc chutes to the hydraulic pressure used in forming them and the acid concentration. The data are given in Table 26-8, with hydraulic pressure and green strength given in units of 10 pounds per square inch (psi) and the acid concentration given as a percent of the nominal rate for 20 observations. Two-variable plots of the data are given in Figures 26-5, 26-6, and 26-7. Summary statistics including sums, sums of squares, and cross products, both raw and corrected, as well as the sample means are given in Table 26-9.

The Doolittle computations (see Appendix B) proceed as follows:

$$s_{31} = s_{11} = 3,436.8$$

---

[11] See, for example, Draper and Smith (Ref. 4, pp. 55, 64–67).
[12] Example 5 from Mimeo Notes, Mason E. Wescott, Rochester Institute of Technology, Rochester, N.Y.

TABLE 26-8   Arc Chute Data

Green strength Y in units of *10 psi*	Hydraulic pressure X_1 in units of *10 psi*	Acid concentration X_2, as % of *nominal rate*
665	110	116
618	119	104
620	138	94
578	130	86
682	143	110
594	133	87
722	147	114
700	142	106
681	125	107
695	135	106
664	152	98
548	118	86
620	155	87
595	128	96
740	146	120
670	132	108
640	130	104
590	112	91
570	113	92
640	120	100

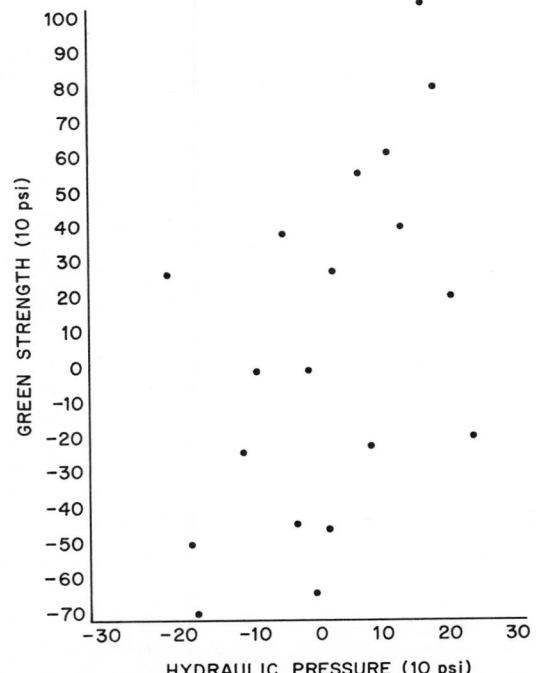

Fig. 26-5   Green strength vs. hydraulic pressure (deviations from averages).

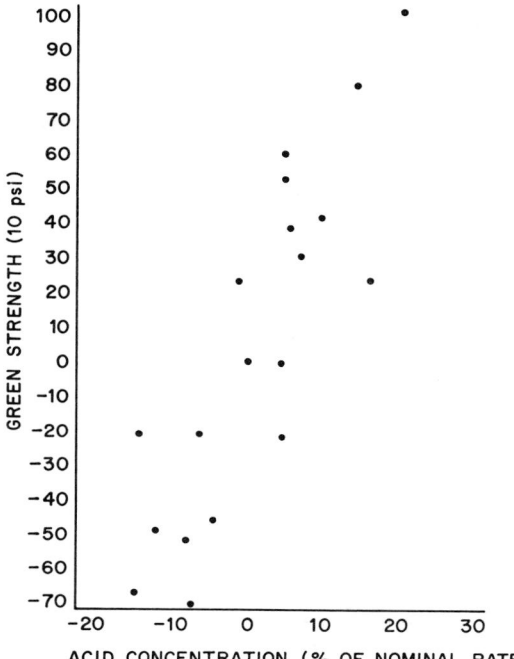

Fig. 26-6   Green strength vs. acid concentration (deviations from averages).

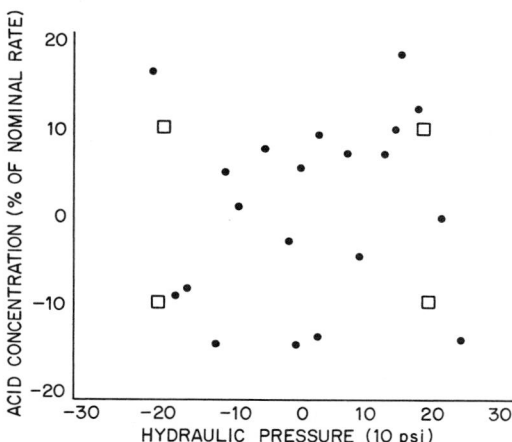

Fig. 26-7   Acid concentration vs. hydraulic pressure (deviations from averages).   Rectangles indicate points at which confidence intervals have been calculated.

TABLE 26-9   Summary Statistics

$N = 20$		
$\Sigma Y_m = 12{,}832$	$\Sigma X_{1m} = 2{,}628$	$\Sigma X_{2m} = 2{,}012$
$\Sigma Y_m^2 = 8{,}286{,}988$	$\Sigma X_{1m}^2 = 348{,}756$	$\Sigma X_{2m}^2 = 204{,}500$
$\Sigma X_{1m} Y_m = 1{,}693{,}226$	$\Sigma X_{2m} Y_m = 1{,}300{,}253$	$\Sigma X_{1m} X_{2m} = 264{,}785$
$\bar{Y} = 641.6$	$\bar{X}_1 = 131.4$	$\bar{X}_2 = 100.6$

S		a
$s_{11} = 3{,}436.8$	$s_{12} = \quad 408.2^*$	$a_1 = 7{,}101.2\dagger$
$s_{21} = \quad 408.2$	$s_{22} = 2{,}092.8$	$a_2 = 9{,}353.8$

$$
\begin{aligned}
{}^* s_{12} &= \Sigma x_{1m} x_{2m} = \Sigma X_{1m} X_{2m} - (\Sigma X_{1m} \Sigma X_{2m}/N) \\
&= 264{,}785 - [(2{,}628)\,(2{,}012)/20] \\
&= 408.2
\end{aligned}
$$

$$
\begin{aligned}
\dagger a_1 &= \Sigma x_{1m} y_m = \Sigma X_{1m} Y_m - (\Sigma X_{1m} \Sigma Y_m/N) \\
&= 1{,}693{,}226 - [(2{,}628)\,(12{,}832)/20] \\
&= 7{,}101.2
\end{aligned}
$$

$$s_{32} = s_{12} = 408.2$$

$$a_3 = a_1 = 7{,}101.2$$

$$s_{41} = \frac{s_{31}}{s_{31}} = 1$$

$$s_{42} = \frac{s_{32}}{s_{31}} = \frac{408.2}{3{,}436.8} = 0.118773$$

$$a_4 = \frac{a_3}{s_{31}} = \frac{7{,}101.2}{3{,}436.8} = 2.06622$$

$$s_{52} = s_{22} - s_{42}s_{32} = 2{,}092.8 - (0.118773)\,(408.2) = 2{,}044.316861$$

$$a_5 = a_2 - s_{42}a_3 = 9{,}353.8 - (0.118773)\,(7{,}101.2) = 8{,}510.369172$$

$$s_{62} = \frac{s_{52}}{s_{52}} = 1$$

$$a_6 = \frac{a_5}{s_{52}} = \frac{8{,}510.36917}{2{,}044.31686} = 4.16294.$$

These computations are summarized in Table 26-10.   Six decimal places were carried in the computations to protect against the accumulation of roundoff error.

TABLE 26-10   Forward Doolittle Example

Row:			
1	3,436.8	408.2	7,101.2
2	408.2	2,092.8	9,353.8
3	3,436.8	408.2	7,101.2
4	1.0	0.118773	2.066224
5	0	2,044.316861	8,510.369172
6	0	1	4.162940

The computations of the estimates are:

$b_2 = a_6 = 4.162940$

$b_1 = a_4 - s_{42}b_2 = 2.066224 - (0.118773)(4.162940) = 1.571779$

$b_0 = \bar{Y} - b_1\bar{X}_1 - b_2\bar{X}_2 \doteq 16.27475$

The computation of the C matrix follows:

$c_{22} = \dfrac{1}{s_{52}} = \dfrac{1}{2,044.31686} = 0.00048916$

$c_{12}(= c_{21}) = -c_{22}s_{42} = -(0.000489160)(0.118773) = -0.000058099$

$c_{11} = \dfrac{1}{s_{31}} - c_{12}s_{42} = \dfrac{1}{3,436.8} - (-0.000058099)(0.118773)$

$$= 0.00029787$$

Hence

$$C = \begin{vmatrix} 297.869 & -58.099 \\ -58.099 & 489.160 \end{vmatrix} \times 10^{-6}$$

To verify these results, the matrix product of C and S is computed:

$$C \cdot S = \begin{vmatrix} 1.0000002 & 0.0000005 \\ 0.0000005 & 0.9999980 \end{vmatrix}$$

It should equal (within rounding error) the 2×2 identity matrix (I).

The prediction equations corresponding to (26-10) and (26-11) can be calculated from the Doolittle results as

$$\hat{Y} = 16.277 + 1.572\,X_1 + 4.163\,X_2$$

$$\hat{Y} = 641.600 + 1.572\,(X_1 - 131.400) + 4.163\,(X_2 - 100.600)$$

The latter form will be used in the remaining computations.

The ANOVA table (Table 26-11) for the example follows directly from the summary statistics of Table 26-9 and from Table 26-7. The residual mean square error is 228.0, and hence the standard deviation s is 15.100.

The 95% confidence intervals on β_1 and β_2 are obtained as

$$1.572 \pm 2.110 \times 15.100 \times \sqrt{297.869} \times 10^{-3}$$

$$1.572 \pm 0.550 = 1.02 \text{ and } 2.12$$

TABLE 26-11   ANOVA Example

Source	Sum of squares	Degrees of freedom	Mean square
(1) Due to regression	50,100.8*	2	25,050.40
(2) Residual.	3,876.0†	17	228.0
(3) Total corrected for the mean	53,976.8	19	

* $(1.571779)(7,101.2) + (4.16294)(9,353.8) = 50,100.825$.
† By subtraction.

and

$$4.163 \pm 2.110 \times 15.0997 \times \sqrt{489.16} \times 10^{-3} = 4.163 \pm 0.705 = 3.46 \text{ and } 4.87$$

Confidence intervals for $\beta_0 \times \beta_1 X_1 \times \beta_2 X_2$ and for a future observation of Y at five combinations of X_1 and X_2 are given in Table 26-12. (The five points at which the confidence intervals are computed are also indicated in Figure 26-7.)

COMPUTER PROGRAMS

Because of the widespread popularity of regression, almost every computer facility has at least one and most have many regression programs. These programs may have been locally written, or they may have been obtained from other sources. In the latter case, the program usually has been modified in some manner, so that it can be run on the local computer system and satisfy the needs of the local users.

Recent studies by Longley (Ref. 13) and Wampler (Ref. 15) indicate that the user should carefully check his regression program. In particular, he should not presume that the program has been checked, just because a sample data problem is given in the program manual. Unfortunately a number of the algorithms used in these programs are often taken directly from desk calculator instructions. While these algorithms may be efficient for desk calculators, they are often not good enough for digital computers. The reason is that digital computers carry about eight significant digits and these routines do not take into account round-off or truncation errors and hence can produce numerically inaccurate results, even in double precision. For example, Longley found that many of the programs computed the squared deviations of a variable about its mean by the computational formula $\Sigma X_m{}^2 - (\Sigma X_m)^2/N$, rather than by $\Sigma (X_m - \bar{X})^2$. Since these quantities are the base for most of the regression calculations, numerical errors may be present in all the results.

Since the user may not be able (or simply does not want to invest the time) to check completely the coding of his program, a few simple checks for this purpose, taken from Ref. 13, are given below. These can be used to gain some idea of the limitations of a program.

1. Add the residuals about the regression line. They should sum to zero, within rounding error.

2. If the residuals sum to zero, make additional runs of the problem after adding 10, 100, 1,000, 10,000, etc., to each variable. The coefficients will begin to change at a point where round-off error occurs.

3. As a check on the accuracy of the inversion routine, run a problem with two variables X_1 and X_2. Then make another run with the same response variable but two new independent variables $X_1^* = X_1 + X_2$ and $X_2^* = X_1 - X_2$. The following results should hold: $b_1 = b_1^* + b_2^*$ and $b_2 = b_1^* - b_2^*$.

Longley (Ref. 13) gives some additional checks, and Wampler (Ref. 15) lists results on many of the commonly used regression programs.

A write-up is usually available with regression programs. It should include a complete discussion of the input required and an explanation of the output and options available, as well as a complete statement of the calculation formulas and a sample problem. Although documenting a program is a difficult task, a poorly written documentation is often a warning of a poorly or improperly written computer program.

While the input formats of regression programs vary, most programs have an option which allows the user to specify a variety of transformations of the data, such as logs, powers, and cross products. Typical regression outputs include ANOVA tables, residuals plots, and other statistics in addition to the estimates of the regression coefficients. Although often omitted, an "echo-check," i.e., a printout of the

TABLE 26-12 Computation of Confidence Intervals

X_1 (1)	X_2 (2)	$\hat{Y}$ (3)	$(x'Cx)$ (4)	$\sqrt{\frac{1}{N}+(4)}$ (5)	$ts \times (5)$† (6)	95% confidence limits on the mean of Y at X_1, X_2 Lower (3)−(6) (7)	Upper (3)+(6) (8)	$\sqrt{1+\frac{1}{N}+(4)}$ (9)	$ts \times (9)$ (10)	95% prediction limits on Y at X_1, X_2 Lower (3)−(10) (11)	Upper (3)+(10) (12)
111.4	90.6	568.53	0.1457*	0.4424	14.10	554.43	582.63	1.0935	34.84	533.69	603.37
111.4	110.6	651.79	0.1922	0.4921	15.68	636.11	667.47	1.1145	35.51	616.28	687.30
131.4	100.6	641.60	0.0	0.2236	7.12	634.48	648.72	1.0247	32.65	608.95	674.25
151.4	90.6	631.41	0.1922	0.4921	15.68	615.73	647.09	1.1145	35.51	595.90	666.92
151.4	110.6	714.67	0.1457	0.4424	14.10	700.57	728.77	1.0935	34.85	679.82	749.52

Numbers in parentheses are column numbers.

*Since $x' = (111.4 - 131.4, 90.6 - 100.6) = (-20, -10)$.

$$x'Cx = (-20, -10) \begin{bmatrix} 297.869 & -58.099 \\ -58.099 & 498.160 \end{bmatrix} \times 10^{-6} \begin{bmatrix} -20 \\ -10 \end{bmatrix} = (-5,376.39, -3,819.62) \times 10^{-6} \begin{bmatrix} -20 \\ -10 \end{bmatrix} = 0.1457$$

† t_{TAB} with 17 degrees of freedom is 2.110, $s = 15.100$.

original and transformed data, is essential. More often than not "strange" regression results can be traced to a misplaced decimal point in an observation, the wrong variables being read in, or the incorrect use of the transformation option. If this is not available in a program, ask the computer center to modify the program so that it is automatically printed out unless the user deletes it.

Stepwise Procedures   In many situations there are a large number of possible variables for a model and the problem is to select the "vital few" from these "trivial many," instead of obtaining the complete regression equation. There are many reasons for not using all the variables. For example, it has been shown that a subset of variables can provide a better prediction equation than the full set, even though the full set has a higher R.[13] More important, equations with fewer variables are easier to understand and hence more likely to gain acceptance and be used.

Unless the data come from a properly designed experiment, there is no simple test for significant variables. Since there are $2^k - 1$ possible prediction equations to evaluate, for large k, it is obvious that even with a digital computer, a brute force approach is not feasible; i.e., for $k = 10$, $2^k - 1 = 1,027$.

Stepwise regression is a heuristic technique for avoiding this computation problem. It begins by selecting the single independent variable which is the "best" predictor in the sense that it maximizes R^2. Then it adds variables to the equation in a sequential manner, in order of importance. At each step the variable added is the one which increases the sum of squares (and hence R^2) or equivalently reduces the residual sum of squares by the largest amount. This procedure not only selects variables, but deletes variables previously selected, if at some point they no longer appear important.

This procedure does not guarantee that the "best" set of variables will be included in the final equation. However, it does provide an efficient method for finding "good" regression equations and at present seems to have found many successful applications. Stepwise regression programs are widely available. For a complete discussion of the methodology of stepwise regression and references to stepwise computer programs, see Draper and Smith (Ref. 4).

In addition to stepwise regression, numerous other techniques have been developed. One which seems to have great potential was developed by Hocking and Leslie (Ref. 8) and improved by LaMotte and Hocking (Ref. 9). Their algorithm finds the "best" subset of variables of size $1, 2, \ldots, k$, where k is the total number of variables submitted. Although the computations require more time than the stepwise procedure, this procedure guarantees the best subset in the R^2 sense and in addition gives a number of the "contending" subsets. Of course, if the number of variables is small, we could compute all regressions. These "best" regression algorithms have not yet found widespread usage, but as they become more readily available they should prove increasingly popular.

The set of possible variables should be selected on the basis of preliminary investigations of the factors which influence the response variables. The indiscriminate use of regression analysis to "find" relationships, where no physical facts suggest the existence of a relationship, often leads to nonsensical results.[14] Unfortunately, this is usually discovered after the prediction equation fails miserably in predicting future observations.

If a large amount of data is available, one portion of it can be used for selecting

[13] See Narula, S. C., and J. S. Ramberg, The Mean Square Error Criterion and Subset Regression, Letter to the Editor, *The American Statistician*, vol. 26, No. 5, p. 42.

[14] See Box, G. E. P., Use and Abuse of Regression, *Technometrics*, vol. 8, pp. 625–629; Nov. 1966 for a more complete discussion of the limitations of regression analysis.

BEST SUBSET REGRESSIONS
USING LAMOTTE-HOCKING METHOD
DEVELOPED BY KENNETH DEMAY
UNDER THE DIRECTION OF J. S. RAMBERG
INDUSTRIAL AND MANAGEMENT ENGINEERING DEPARTMENT
UNIVERSITY OF IOWA

VARIABLE		MEAN	STANDARD DEVIATION
STRNGH	1	641.60000	53.29995
PRESS	2	131.40000	13.44932
ACID	3	100.60000	10.49511

COVARIANCE MATRIX

VARIABLE NUMBER	1	2	3
1	2840.884	373.747	492.305
2		180.884	21.484
3			110.147

CORRELATION MATRIX

VARIABLE NUMBER	1	2	3
1	1.000	0.521	0.880
2		1.000	0.152
3			1.000

Fig. 26-8 Sample regression program output. *(Continued on following pages.)*

```
FULL REGRESSION EQUATION

ALL PREDICTOR VARIABLES IN THE EQUATION


R SQUARE-FULL EQUATION        0.928



STD. ERROR OF EST.       15.09963
```

ANALYSIS OF VARIANCE

	DF	SUM OF SQUARES	MEAN SQUARE	F RATIO
REGRESSION	2	50100.818	25050.409	109.871
RESIDUAL	17	3875.982	227.999	
TOTAL	19	53976.800		

VARIABLES IN EQUATION

VARIABLE		COEFFICIENT
CONSTANT		16.27659
PRESS	2	1.57178
ACID	3	4.16294

LIST OF RESIDUALS

OBSERVATION NUMBER	Y X(i)	Y COMPUTED	RESIDUAL
1	665.0000	672.0732	-7.0732
2	618.0000	636.2639	-18.2639
3	620.0000	624.4983	-4.4983
4	578.0000	578.6206	-0.6206
5	682.0000	698.9643	-16.9643
6	594.0000	587.4989	6.5011
7	722.0000	721.9031	0.0969
8	700.0000	680.7407	19.2593
9	681.0000	658.1834	22.8166
10	695.0000	669.7383	25.2617
11	664.0000	663.1550	0.8450
12	548.0000	559.7593	-11.7593
13	620.0000	622.0780	-2.0780
14	595.0000	617.1064	-22.1064
15	740.0000	745.3090	-5.3090
16	670.0000	673.3488	-3.3488
17	640.0000	653.5535	-13.5535
18	590.0000	571.1433	18.8567
19	570.0000	576.8780	-6.8780
20	640.0000	621.1840	18.8160

Fig. 26-8 *(Continued)*

variables and estimating coefficients, saving the remainder of the data for testing the derived equations. In any case, the equation should be periodically reviewed as new data become available.

Example—Computer Output A printout of a typical regression program for the example problem is given in Figure 26-8, with some comparisons of results.

The means, standard deviations, and covariances can be calculated from the summary statistics in Table 26-9. The off-diagonal correlation coefficients are calculated from the covariance matrix by dividing the corresponding entry by the square root of the product of the two appropriate diagonal elements, which are variances.

THIS PROBLEM WAS RUN ON SELECT,
A PROGRAM IMPLEMENTING THE LAMOTTE-HOCKING METHOD
FOR THE SELECTION OF SUBSET REGRESSIONS
BY L.R.LAMOTTE, INST. OF STAT., TEXAS A&M UNIVERSITY

CALCULATION SUMMARY FOR FINDING BEST 1-SUBSET OF 2 VARIABLES

TOTAL NUMBER OF REGRESSIONS COMPUTED   2
FRACTION OF TOTAL POSSIBLE   1.000

SUMMARY OUTPUT FOR THE   1-TH REGRESSION

        R SQUARE-FULL EQUATION   0.928
        R SQUARE-THIS EQUATION   0.775

        STD. ERROR OF EST.   26.00198

    ANALYSIS OF VARIANCE

	DF	SUM OF SQUARES	MEAN SQUARE	F RATIO
REGRESSION	1	41806.945	41806.945	61.835
RESIDUAL	18	12169.855	676.103	
TOTAL	19	53976.800		

    VARIABLES IN EQUATION

VARIABLE	COEFFICIENT
CONSTANT	191.96684
ACID 3	4.46951

SUMMARY OUTPUT FOR THE   2-TH REGRESSION

        R SQUARE-FULL EQUATION   0.928
        R SQUARE-THIS EQUATION   0.272

    VARIABLES IN EQUATION

VARIABLE	COEFFICIENT
CONSTANT	370.09811
PRESS 2	2.06622

Fig. 26-8 *(Continued)*

The diagonal elements are, of course, one. For fixed X's the computational formulas remain the same. However, these expressions are not really sample covariances or sample correlations, since covariance and correlation are measures which refer to random variables.

The ANOVA table and the b coefficients agree (within rounding error) with those calculated using the Doolittle technique. (Although it is not printed out here, the C matrix is available on many programs.) Residual plots are also available in addition to the table of residuals. (These plots as well as the "echo-check" were deleted to save space.)

REFERENCES

1. Acton, F. S., "Analysis of Straight-line Data," John Wiley & Sons, Inc., New York, 1959.
2. Brownlee, K. A., "Statistical Theory and Methodology in Science and Engineering," John Wiley & Sons, Inc., New York, 1965.
3. Daniel, Cuthbert, and Fred S. Wood, "Fitting Equations to Data," John Wiley & Sons, Inc., New York, 1971.
4. Draper, N. R., and H. Smith, "Applied Regression Analysis," John Wiley & Sons, Inc., New York, 1966.
5. Gorman, J. W., and R. J. Toman, Selection of Variables for Fitting Equations to Data, Technometrics, vol. 8, No. 1, pp. 27–51, February 1966.
6. Graybill, F. A., "Introduction to Matrices with Applications in Statistics," Wadsworth Publishing Company, Inc., Belmont, Calif., 1969.
7. Hald, A., "Statistical Theory with Engineering Applications," chap. 18, John Wiley & Sons, Inc., New York, 1952.
8. Hocking, R. R., and R. N. Leslie, Selection of the Best Subset in Regression Analysis, Technometrics, vol. 9, pp. 531–540, November 1967.
9. LaMotte, L. R., and R. R. Hocking, Computational Efficiency in the Selection of Regression Variables, Technometrics, vol. 12, No. 1, pp. 83–93, February 1970.
10. Johnson, N. L., and F. C. Leone, "Statistics and Experimental Design in Engineering and the Physical Sciences," vol. 1, John Wiley & Sons, Inc., New York, 1964.
11. Johnston, J., "Econometric Methods," McGraw-Hill Book Company, New York, 1963.
12. Kramer, C. Y., and D. R. Jensen, Fundamentals of Multivariate Analysis, Journal of Quality Technology, vol. 1, Nos. 2, 3, 4, 1969; vol. 2, No. 1, 1970.
13. Longley, J. W., An Appraisal of Least Squares Programs for the Electronic Computer from the Point of View of the User, Journal of the American Statistical Association, vol. 62, pp. 819–841, September 1967.
14. Volk, William, Industrial Statistics, Chemical Engineering, pp. 165–190, March 1956.
15. Wampler, R. H., On the Accuracy of Least Squares Computer Programs, Journal of the American Statistical Association, vol. 65, pp. 549–565, June 1970.
16. Williams, E. J., "Regression Analysis," John Wiley & Sons, Inc., New York, 1959.

APPENDIX A: MATRIX OPERATIONS

Some elementary matrix operations, which are useful in regression analysis, are given in this appendix. Further results and more details can be found in any book on matrices.

A matrix X is a rectangular array of elements with n rows and k columns and will be denoted by a boldfaced uppercase letter. For example, a set of $n = 3$ observations on $k = 2$ variables can be recorded as

$$X = \begin{bmatrix} x_{11} & x_{12} \\ x_{21} & x_{22} \\ x_{31} & x_{32} \end{bmatrix} = \begin{bmatrix} 5 & 6 \\ 1 & 2 \\ 3 & 1 \end{bmatrix}$$

where the first subscript denotes the row number and the second subscript denotes the column number. A column vector is a special case of a matrix, consisting of one column, e.g., $n \times 1$. Vectors will be denoted by boldfaced lowercase letters. For example, a column vector of three observations on a single variable can be written as

$$x = \begin{bmatrix} x_1 \\ x_2 \\ x_3 \end{bmatrix} = \begin{bmatrix} 2 \\ 4 \\ 1 \end{bmatrix}$$

The transpose of matrix or a vector is denoted by a prime; i.e., for the previously defined matrix X, and column vector x,

$$X' = \begin{bmatrix} 5 & 1 & 3 \\ 6 & 2 & 1 \end{bmatrix} \qquad x' = (2, 4, 1)$$

where x' is a row vector. Addition or subtraction of matrices is defined only if they have exactly the same number of rows and the same number of columns. The sums or differences of two matrices are then the sums or differences of the corresponding elements of these matrices; i.e., if X is as defined before and

$$Z = \begin{bmatrix} z_{11} & z_{12} \\ z_{21} & z_{22} \\ z_{31} & z_{32} \end{bmatrix} = \begin{bmatrix} 3 & 3 \\ 2 & 4 \\ 3 & 2 \end{bmatrix}$$

Then

$$X + Z = \begin{bmatrix} x_{11} + z_{11} & x_{12} + z_{12} \\ x_{21} + z_{21} & x_{22} + z_{22} \\ x_{31} + z_{31} & x_{32} + z_{32} \end{bmatrix} = \begin{bmatrix} 8 & 9 \\ 3 & 6 \\ 6 & 3 \end{bmatrix}$$

and

$$X - Z = \begin{bmatrix} x_{11} - z_{11} & x_{12} - z_{12} \\ x_{21} - z_{21} & x_{22} - z_{22} \\ x_{31} - z_{31} & x_{32} - z_{32} \end{bmatrix} = \begin{bmatrix} 2 & 3 \\ -1 & -2 \\ 0 & -1 \end{bmatrix}$$

Multiplication of two matrices is defined only if the number of columns of the first matrix A is equal to the number of rows of the second matrix B. Then an element c_{ij} of the resulting element C is given by

$$c_{ij} = \sum_{m=1}^{n} a_{im} b_{mj} \qquad \begin{aligned} i &= 1, \ldots, p \\ j &= 1, \ldots, k \end{aligned}$$

where p is the number of rows in A, n is the number of columns in A (rows in B), and k is the number of columns in B such that C is a $p \times k$ matrix.

Thus, if,

$$W = \begin{bmatrix} 1 & 2 \\ 3 & 4 \end{bmatrix}$$

then

$$XW = \begin{bmatrix} 5 & 6 \\ 1 & 2 \\ 3 & 1 \end{bmatrix} \begin{bmatrix} 1 & 2 \\ 3 & 4 \end{bmatrix} = \begin{bmatrix} 23 & 34 \\ 7 & 10 \\ 6 & 10 \end{bmatrix}$$

Since W has 2 columns and X has 3 rows, the product WX is not defined, and thus we see that in general WX is not equal to XW.

A special matrix which occurs frequently is the square identity matrix denoted by I. For $n = k = 4$,

$$I = \begin{bmatrix} 1 & 0 & 0 & 0 \\ 0 & 1 & 0 & 0 \\ 0 & 0 & 1 & 0 \\ 0 & 0 & 0 & 1 \end{bmatrix}$$

The identity matrix belongs to the class of symmetric matrices. A symmetric matrix is one in which $x_{ij} = x_{ji}$ for all (i,j); a matrix X is symmetric if $X = X'$.

Although division is not defined for matrices, the inverse of a matrix A (denoted by A^{-1}) which is a generalization of the inverse (or reciprocal) of a scalar is defined. Inverses are defined only for square matrices and have the following properties:

$$AA^{-1} = A^{-1}A = I$$

Inverses exist only if the matrix is nonsingular, i.e., if the determinant is nonzero. The forward Doolittle method (Appendix B) is one method of finding the inverse of a symmetric matrix.

APPENDIX B: THE FORWARD DOOLITTLE TECHNIQUE

The forward Doolittle technique is a convenient method for solving regression problems on a desk calculator, provided there are not more than four variables. For a larger number of variables the work becomes excessive and a digital computer with a multiple regression program should be used. Even for smaller problems this method is recommended, because of the many side benefits available in most regression programs such as transformations of variables and residual plots. For purposes of illustration, we will assume that there are three predictor variables, so that S is 3 by 3 and $\mathbf{a}$ is 3 by 1.

In Table 26-13, after writing down the symmetrical matrix S, we insert the $\mathbf{a}$ vector as an additional column.

TABLE 26-13   Sum of Squares and Cross Products Matrix*

s_{11}	s_{12}	s_{13}	a_1
s_{21}	s_{22}	s_{23}	a_2
s_{31}	s_{32}	s_{33}	a_3

* An additional column $\left(W_i = \sum_j S_{ij} + a_i \right)$ is often appended to this matrix as a check.

These W's are then operated upon in the same manner as the s's and a's. At every stage the W_i entry should be equal to $\sum_j s_{ij} + a_i$.

The rows of the forward Doolittle technique are obtained as follows: Row 1 is repeated directly after row 3 as row 4, i.e.,

$$s_{41} = s_{11}, s_{42} = s_{12}, s_{43} = s_{13}, a_4 = a_1$$

Next row 5 is constructed from row 4 as

$$s_{51} = \frac{s_{41}}{s_{41}} = 1, s_{52} = \frac{s_{42}}{s_{41}}, s_{53} = \frac{s_{43}}{s_{41}}, a_5 = \frac{a_4}{s_{41}}$$

Row 6 is obtained from rows 2, 4, and 5 by

$$s_{61} = s_{21} - s_{52}s_{41} = 0$$
$$s_{62} = s_{22} - s_{52}s_{42}$$
$$s_{63} = s_{23} - s_{52}s_{43}$$
$$a_6 = a_2 - s_{52}a_5$$

Row 7 is obtained by

$$s_{7j} = \frac{s_{6j}}{s_{62}} \text{ and } a_7 = \frac{a_6}{s_{62}}$$

Row 8 is obtained from rows 3, 5, 6, 7, and 8 as

$$s_{81} = s_{31} - s_{53}s_{41} - s_{73}s_{61} = 0$$
$$s_{82} = s_{32} - s_{53}s_{42} - s_{73}s_{62} = 0$$
$$s_{83} = s_{33} - s_{53}s_{43} - s_{73}s_{63}$$
$$a_8 = a_3 - s_{53}a_4 - s_{73}a_6$$

Row 9 is obtained by

$$s_{9j} = \frac{s_{8j}}{s_{83}} \text{ and } a_9 = \frac{a_8}{s_{83}}$$

Table 26-14 summarizes these calculations.

From these equations the b's can be computed directly as

$$b_3 = a_9$$
$$b_2 = a_7 - s_{73}b_3$$
$$b_1 = a_5 - s_{52}b_2 - s_{53}b_3$$

The procedure can be extended to more variables in an obvious manner, treating the steps given previously in a pairwise manner.

TABLE 26-14   Forward Doolittle Technique

Row:				
1	s_{11}	s_{12}	s_{13}	a_1
2	s_{21}	s_{22}	s_{23}	a_2
3	s_{31}	s_{32}	s_{33}	a_3
4	s_{41}	s_{42}	s_{43}	a_4
5	1	s_{52}	s_{53}	a_5
6		s_{62}	s_{63}	a_6
7		1	s_{73}	a_7
8			s_{83}	a_8
9			1	a_9

In addition the inverse of the S matrix (which we denote by $C = S^{-1}$), is also symmetric and follows from these results. This matrix, which is useful in interpreting the regression results, is calculated as follows:

$$c_{33} = \frac{1}{s_{83}}$$

$$c_{23} = -c_{33}s_{73}$$

$$c_{13} = -c_{33}s_{53} - c_{23}s_{52}$$

$$c_{32} = c_{23}$$

$$c_{22} = \frac{1}{s_{62}} - c_{23}s_{73}$$

$$c_{12} = -c_{23}s_{53} - c_{22}s_{52}$$

$$c_{31} = c_{13}$$

$$c_{21} = c_{12}$$

$$c_{11} = \frac{1}{s_{41}} - c_{13}s_{43} - c_{12}a_{42}$$

A more detailed explanation of the forward Doolittle technique is given in Johnson and Leone (Ref. 10).

Section 27

Design and Analysis of Experiments[1]

MARY G. NATRELLA

Statistical Engineering Laboratory,
Institute for Basic Standards,
National Bureau of Standards

[1] Contribution of the National Bureau of Standards, not subject to copyright.

INTRODUCTION

An experiment has been defined, in the most general sense, as a "considered course of action aimed at answering one or more carefully framed questions." This Section discusses a more restricted kind of experiment in which the experimenter chooses certain factors for study, deliberately varies those factors in a controlled fashion, and then observes the effect of such action.   The Section discusses how to design such experiments and how to interpret the resulting data.

The Section is organized into the following subdivisions:

1. An Introduction, which provides those basic definitions which are essential to the understanding of any problem in experimental design and analysis.   (Other definitions are provided later, as needed.)

2. A series of typical problems in design and analysis of experiments, starting with the simplest, and increasing in complexity.   For each of these problems there is presented the method of structuring the experiment and analyzing the resulting data.   General comments on each design are also presented.

3. A discussion of the size of the experiment, assumptions, and other matters pertinent to all designs, plus reference to other works.

Basic Definitions   Several fundamental terms are widely used throughout this Section:

Factor.   A factor is one of the things being studied in the experiment.   A factor may be quantitative, e.g., temperature in degrees, time in seconds.   A factor may also be qualitative, e.g., different machines, different operators, switch on or off.

Level.   The levels of a factor are the values of the factor being examined in the experiment.   For quantitative factors, each chosen value becomes a level; e.g., if the experiment is to be conducted at four different temperatures, then the factor "temperature" has four levels.   In the case of a qualitative factor, "switch on or off" becomes two levels for the switch factor.   If there are six machines run by three operators, the factor "machine" has six levels while the factor "operator" has three levels.

Treatment.   This is a single level assigned to a single factor during an experimental run, e.g., temperature at 800°.   A *treatment combination* is one set of levels for all factors in a given experimental run.   For example, an experimental run, using 800° temperature, machine 3, operator A, and switch off would constitute one treatment combination.

Experimental Materials. These consist of the objects to which treatments are being applied.   They may be biological entities, natural materials, fabricated products, etc.

Experimental Environment. This comprises the surrounding conditions which may influence the results of the experiment in known or unknown ways.

Block. This is a portion of the experimental material or of the experimental environment which is likely to be more homogeneous within itself than are different portions.   For example, specimens from a single material batch are likely to be more uniform than specimens from different batches.   A group of specimens from such a single batch would be regarded as a block.

Experiment Design (also called experimental pattern).   This is the formal plan for conducting the experiment. It includes the choice of the factors, levels, and treatments, and use of certain tools called planned grouping, randomization, and replication.

Some Tools for Sound Experimentation *Planned Grouping or Blocking.* Beyond the factors selected for study, there are other "background" variables which may affect the outcome of the experiment. Where the experimenter is aware of these variables, it is often possible to plan the experiment so that:

1. Possible effects due to background variables do not affect information obtained about the factors of primary interest.

2. Some information about the effects of the background variables can be obtained.

In designing experiments, wide use is made of the uniformity within blocks to minimize the effect of unwanted variables and to accentuate the effect of the variables under study. Designs which make use of this uniformity within blocks are called "block designs," and the process is called "planned grouping."

Randomization. The assignment of specimens (to treatments) in a purely chance manner is called randomization in the design of experiments. Such assignment increases the likelihood that the effect of uncontrolled variables will balance out. It also improves the validity of estimates of experimental error and makes possible the application of statistical tests of significance and the construction of confidence intervals.

There are many famous examples of experiments where failure to randomize at a crucial stage led to completely misleading results. However, the beneficial effects of randomization are obtained in the long run, and not in a single isolated experiment. Randomization may be thought of as insurance and, like insurance, may sometimes be too expensive. If a variable is thought unlikely to have an effect, and if it is difficult to randomize with respect to the variable, we may choose not to randomize.

Replication. This is the repetition of an observation or measurement. It is done to increase precision and to provide the means for measuring precision. (In some kinds of experiments there is no outside source for measuring precision, so that the measure must come from the experiment itself.) In addition, replication provides an opportunity for the effects of uncontrolled factors to balance out, and thus aids randomization as a bias-decreasing tool. (In successive replications, the randomization features must be independent.) Replication also helps to detect gross errors in the measurements.

Table 27-1 lists some requisites for sound experimentation, and shows the way in which these tools contribute to meeting the requisites. For discussion of the general principles of experimentation, the book by Wilson (Ref. 1) is especially recommended. A checklist which should be helpful in all phases of an experiment is given by Bicking (Fig. 27-1).

CLASSIFICATION OF EXPERIMENT DESIGNS

Statisticians, by themselves, do not design experiments, but they have developed a number of structured schedules of taking measurements which they call experiment designs. These designs have certain rational relationships to the purposes, needs, and physical limitations of experiments. They also have certain advantages in economy of experimentation and yield straightforward and unbiased estimates of experimental effects and valid estimates of precision.

There are a number of ways by which experiment designs might be classified, e.g.,

1. By the number of experimental factors to be investigated (e.g., single-factor vs. multifactor designs)

TABLE 27-1   Some Requisites and Tools for Sound Experimentation

Requisites	Tools
1. The experiment should have carefully defined objectives. See Fig. 27-1	1. The definition of objectives requires all the specialized subject-matter knowledge of the experimenter, and results in such things as: *a.* Choice of factors, including their range *b.* Choice of experimental materials, procedure, and equipment *c.* Knowledge of what the results are applicable to. See Fig. 27-1
2. As far as possible, effects of factors should not be obscured by other variables	2. The use of an appropriate *experimental pattern* helps to free the comparisons of interest from the effects of uncontrolled variables, and simplifies the analysis of results
3. As far as possible, the experiment should be free from bias (conscious or unconscious)	3. Some variables may be taken into account by *planned grouping*. For variables not so taken care of, use *randomization*. The use of *replication* aids *randomization* to do a better job
4. Experiment should provide a measure of precision (experimental error)*	4. *Replication* provides the measure of precision; *randomization* assures validity of the measure of precision
5. Precision of experiment should be sufficient to meet objectives set forth in requisite 1	5. Greater precision may be achieved by: refinements of technique, *experimental pattern* (including *planned grouping*), *replication*

* Except where there is well-known history of the measurement process.

2. By the structure of the experiment design (e.g., blocked designs vs. randomized designs)

3. By the kind of information the experiment is primarily intended to provide (e.g., estimates of effects or estimates of variability).

Some of the common statistical experiment designs are listed in Table 27-2. Basic features of the designs are summarized in terms of these criteria of classification. The details of design and analysis are given under the topics which follow. [The analysis is based on a statistical model unique for the specific design. Johnson and Leone (Ref. 2) explain the models for many designs.]

COMPLETELY RANDOMIZED DESIGN—A SIMPLE ONE-FACTOR EXPERIMENT

General   The design is appropriate to the situation where only one experimental factor is being investigated. A total of N experimental units are available for the experiment. There are k treatments (or levels of the factor) to be investigated. Of the total number $N = n\,k$ units, n units are assigned at random to each of the k treatments.

Example   An investigation was made of the effect of three different conditioning

A. *Obtain a Clear Statement of the Problem*
  1. Identify the new and important problem area
  2. Outline the specific problem within current limitations
  3. Define exact scope of the test program
  4. Determine relationship of particular problem to whole research or development program
B. *Collect Available Background Information*
  1. Investigate all available sources of information
  2. Tabulate data pertinent to planning new program
C. *Design the Test Program*
  1. Hold a conference of all parties concerned
    a. State the propositions to be proved
    b. Agree on magnitude of differences considered worthwhile
    c. Outline the possible alternative outcomes
    d. Choose the factors to be studied
    e. Determine practical range of factors and specific levels at which tests will be made
    f. Choose the end measurements which are to be made
    g. Consider the effect of sampling variability and of precision of test methods
    h. Consider possible interrelationships (or "interactions") of the factors
    j. Determine limitations of time, cost, materials, manpower, instrumentation, and other facilities and of extraneous conditions, such as weather
    k. Consider human-relations angles of the program
  2. Design the program in preliminary form
    a. Prepare a systematic and inclusive schedule
    b. Provide for stepwise performance or adaptation of schedule if necessary
    c. Eliminate effect of variables not under study by controlling, balancing, or randomizing them
    d. Minimize the number of experimental runs
    e. Choose the method of statistical analysis
    f. Arrange for orderly accumulation of data
  3. Review the design with all concerned
    a. Adjust the program in line with comments
    b. Spell out the steps to be followed in unmistakable terms
D. *Plan and Carry Out the Experimental Work*
  1. Develop methods, materials, and equipment
  2. Apply the method or techniques
  3. Attend to and check details; modify methods if necessary
  4. Record any modifications of program design
  5. Take precautions in collection of data
  6. Record progress of the program
E. *Analyze the Data*
  1. Reduce recorded data, if necessary, to numerical form
  2. Apply proper mathematical statistical techniques
F. *Interpret the Results*
  1. Consider all the observed data
  2. Confine conclusions to strict deductions from the evidence at hand
  3. Test questions suggested by the data by independent experiments
  4. Arrive at conclusions as to the technical meaning of results as well as their statistical significance
  5. Point out implications of the findings for application and for further work
  6. Account for any limitations imposed by the methods used
  7. State results in terms of verifiable probabilities
G. *Prepare the Report*
  1. Describe work clearly, giving background, pertinence of problems, meaning of results
  2. Use tabular and graphic methods of presenting data in good form for future use
  3. Supply sufficient information to permit reader to verify results and draw his own conclusions
  4. Limit conclusions to objective summary of evidence so that the work recommends itself for prompt consideration and decisive action

Fig. 27-1 Checklist for planning test programs. *(From Charles A. Bicking, Some Uses of Statistics in the Planning of Experiments, Industrial Quality Control, vol. 10, No. 4, p. 23, January 1954.)*

TABLE 27-2 Classification of Designs

Design	Type of application	Structure	Information sought
Completely randomized	Appropriate when only one experimental factor is being investigated and when material is homogeneous and background conditions can be controlled	*Basic:* One factor is investigated by allocating experimental units at random to treatments (levels of the factor) *Blocking:* None	1. Estimate and compare treatment effects 2. Estimate precision
Factorial	Appropriate when several factors are to be investigated at two or more levels and interaction of factors may be important	*Basic:* Several factors are each investigated at several levels by running all combinations of factors and levels *Blocking:* None	1. Estimate and compare effects of several factors 2. Estimate possible interaction effects 3. Estimate precision
Blocked factorial	Appropriate when number of runs required for factorial is too large to be carried out under uniform conditions	*Basic:* Full set of combinations of factors and levels is divided into subsets so that some high-order interactions are equated to blocks. Each subset constitutes a block. All subsets are run *Blocking:* Blocks are usually units in space or time. Estimates of certain interactions are sacrificed to provide blocking	1. Same as factorial except certain high-order interactions cannot be estimated
Fractional factorial	Appropriate when there are many factors and levels and it is impractical to run all combinations	*Basic:* Several factors are investigated at several levels but only a subset of the full factorial is run *Blocking:* Sometimes possible but not necessary	1. Estimate and compare effects of several factors 2. Estimate certain interaction effects (some cannot be estimated) 3. Small fractional factorial designs will not estimate precision
Randomized block	Appropriate when one factor is being investigated and experimental material or environment can be divided into blocks or homogeneous groups	*Basic:* Each treatment or level of factor is run in each block *Blocking:* With respect to one other experimental variable	1. Estimate and compare effects of treatments free of block effects 2. Estimate block effects 3. Estimate precision

TABLE 27-2   Classification of Designs   *(Continued)*

Design	Type of application	Structure	Information sought
Balanced incomplete block	Appropriate when there is one primary factor but all the treatments cannot be accommodated in a block	*Basic:* Prescribed assignments of treatments to blocks are made. Every treatment will appear at least once in the same block with every other treatment *Blocking:* With respect to one other experimental variable	1. Same as randomized block design. All treatment effects are estimated with equal precision
Partially balanced incomplete block	Appropriate if a balanced incomplete block design requires a larger number of blocks than is practical	*Basic:* One primary experimental factor. Prescribed assignments of treatments to blocks are made *Blocking:* With respect to one other experimental variable	1. Same as randomized block design but all treatments are not estimated with equal precision
Latin square	Appropriate when one primary factor is under investigation and results may be affected by two other experimental variables, or by two sources· of nonhomogeneity. It is assumed that no interactions exist	*Basic:* Two cross groupings of the experimental units are made corresponding to the columns and rows of a square. Each treatment occurs once in every row and once in every column. Number of treatments must equal number of rows and number of columns *Blocking:* With respect to two other variables in a two-way layout	1. Estimate and compare treatment effects, free of effects of the two blocked variables 2. Estimate and compare effects of the two blocked variables 3. Estimate precision
Youden square	Same as Latin square but number of rows, columns, and treatments need not be the same	*Basic:* Each treatment occurs once in every row. Number of treatments must equal number of columns *Blocking:* With respect to two other variables in a two-way layout	Same as Latin square
Nested	Appropriate when objective is to study relative variability instead of mean effect of sources of variation (e.g., variability of tests on the same sample and variability of different samples)	*Basic:* Factors are strata in some hierarchical structure; units are tested from each stratum	1. Relative variation in various strata

TABLE 27-3   Breaking Strength of Cement Briquettes — Results

	Method 1	Method 2	Method 3
	553	553	492
	550	599	530
	568	579	528
	541	545	510
	537	540	571
Total T_i	2,749	2,816	2,631
n_i	5	5	5
Mean $\bar{X}_i$	549.8	563.2	526.2

methods on the breaking strength (pounds per square inch) of cement briquettes. Fifteen briquettes were available from one batch and were assigned at random to the three methods. The results are summarized in Table 27-3.

The purpose of the experiment is to investigate the effect of conditioning methods on breaking strength, and the analysis is designed to answer the question "Does the mean breaking strength differ for these methods?"

This is an example of a one-factor experiment, since only one experimental factor (method of conditioning) is under study. There are three of these methods; so the number of treatments k is 3. The number of units n assigned at random to each treatment is 5. The total number of experimental units N is 15.

Analysis   The analysis is made by testing the hypothesis[2] that the *mean* response for all treatments is the same. The analysis of variance (ANOVA) technique is basic, and is illustrated for the data in Table 27-3. A technique using the range, which requires somewhat less computation, is shown for the same data.[3] A ranks test, which is useful when the assumptions of ANOVA cannot be met (see Assumptions for Analysis of Data below), is illustrated for a different set of data.

Analysis of Variance (ANOVA).   Referring to Table 27-3, the total T is:

$$T = \sum T_i = 8,196 \qquad N = \sum n_1 = 15$$

Calculate the following:

$$C = \text{a special constant} = \frac{T^2}{N} = 4,478,294.4$$

$$SS_B = \text{between sum of squares} = \frac{\sum T_i{}^2}{n} - C$$

$$\frac{22,409,018}{5} - C = 4,481,803.6 - 4,478,294.4$$

$$= 3,509.2$$

$$SS_T = \text{total sum of squares}^4 \quad \sum_{i=1}^{k} \sum_{j=1}^{n} X_{ij}{}^2 - C$$

$$= 4,488,348 - 4,478,294.4 \qquad 10,053.6$$

$$SS_W = \text{within sum of squares} = SS_T - SS_B$$

$$= 10,053.6 - 3,509.2 = 6,544.4$$

(SS_W is here obtained by subtraction. It may be calculated directly by calculating $\sum X^2 - [(\sum X)^2/n]$ for each treatment and summing for all treatments.)

---

[2] For a discussion of tests of hypotheses, see Section 22.

[3] For an analysis based on regression techniques, see Ref. 3.

[4] In some literature, this is called the "Total Sum of Squares Corrected for the Mean."

TABLE 27-4   Analysis of Variance for a One-factor Experiment

Source of variation	Sum of squares	Degrees of freedom	Mean square
Between treatments	$SS_B = 3,509.2$	$k - 1 = 3 - 1 = 2$	$MS_B = SS_B/(k - 1)$ $MS_B = 3,509.2/2 = 1,754.6$
Within treatments	$SS_W = 6,544.4$	$k(n - 1) = N - k = 3(4) = 12$	$MS_W = SS_W/k(n - 1)$ $MS_W = 6,544.4/12 = 545.4$
Total	$SS_T = 10,053.6$	$N - 1 = 15 - 1 = 14$	

These calculated quantities are inserted in a table such as Table 27-4.

$$\text{Calculate } F = \frac{MS_B}{MS_W}$$

$$= \frac{1,754.6}{545.5} = 3.22$$

Choose α, the significance level of the test. If the calculated F exceeds $F_{1 - \alpha}$, from Appendix II, Table K for $k - 1$, $k(n - 1)$ degrees of freedom[5] conclude that there are differences among treatment means. For example, $\alpha = 0.05$ level, $F_{0.95}$ for $(2,12)$ degrees of freedom $= 3.89$. The calculated F does not exceed this value, and we conclude that the mean breaking strength is not different for the different conditioning methods.

Note: In this example the n_i are all equal. When the n_i are not all equal, use the following formula for the between sum of squares:

$$SS_B = \frac{T_1{}^2}{n_1} + \frac{T_2{}^2}{n_2} + \ldots + \frac{T_k{}^2}{n_k} - C$$

MS_W will be obtained by subtraction, or by calculating the variance within each treatment and pooling these estimates. The pooled estimate has $N - k$ degrees of freedom.

Range Test. This is a shortcut test that uses the range instead of variance (see Ref. 4). However, the test assumes normality and that all n_i are equal.

Procedure

1. Choose α, the significance level of the test.
2. Look up L_a in Appendix Table GG, corresponding to k and n. $n = n_1 = n_2 = \ldots = n_k$, the number of observations on each treatment.
3. Compute $w_1, w_2, \ldots, w_k$ the ranges of the n observations on each treatment.
4. Compute $\bar{X}_1, \bar{X}_2, \ldots, \bar{X}_k$, the means of the observations on each treatment.
5. Compute $w' = w_1 + w_2 + \ldots + w_k$.

Compute w'', the difference between the largest and the smallest of the means $\bar{X}_i$.

6. Compute $L = nw''/w'$.
7. If $L > L_a$, conclude that the averages of the k products differ; otherwise, there is no reason to believe that the averages differ.

Example

1. Let $\alpha = 0.05$.
2. $k = 3$ $n = 5$ $L_a = 1.19$
3. $w_1 = 31$ $w_2 = 59$ $w_3 = 79$
4. $\bar{X}_1 = 549.8$ $\bar{X}_2 = 563.2$ $\bar{X}_3 = 526.2$
5. $w' = 169$ $w'' = 563.2 - 526.2 = 37.0$

[5] See Section 22, under Testing a Hypothesis When the Sample Size Is Fixed in Advance.

TABLE 27-5   Life Tests of Stopwatches

	Condition 1	Condition 2	Condition 3
	1.7 (1)*	13.6 (6)	13.4 (5)
	1.9 (2)	19.8 (8)	20.9 (9)
	6.1 (3)	25.2 (12)	25.1 (10.5)
	12.5 (4)	46.2 (16.5)	29.7 (13)
	16.5 (7)	46.2 (16.5)	46.9 (18)
	25.1 (10.5)	61.1 (19)	
	30.5 (14)		
	42.1 (15)		
	82.5 (20)		
Sum of ranks $= R_i$	$R_1 = 76.5$	$R_2 = 78.0$	$R_3 = 55.5$
n_i	9	6	5
$R_1{}^2/n_i$	650.25	1,014.00	616.05

* The numbers shown in parentheses are the ranks, from lowest to highest, for all observations combined, as required in Step 3 of the Procedure and Example.

6. $L = \dfrac{185}{169} = 1.09$

7. Since L is less than L_a, there is no reason to believe that the group averages differ.

Ranks Test.   This is the Kruskal-Wallis one-way analysis of variance using ranks. It does not require the assumption of normality.

A number of stopwatches were stored in three different environments and then tested until some part of the mechanism failed.   The data in Table 27-5 are thousands of cycles (on-off-restart).   The question to be answered is "Does the average length of life differ for the three storage conditions?"

Procedure

1. Choose α, the significance level of the test.

2. Look up $\chi^2{}_{1-a}$, for $k-1$ degrees of freedom in Appendix II, Table L, where k is the number of treatments to be compared.

3. We have $n_1, n_2, \ldots, n_k$ observations on each of the treatments $1, 2, \ldots, k$ and $N = n_1 + n_2 + \ldots + n_k$.

Assign a rank to each observation according to its size in relation to all N observations.   That is, assign rank 1 to the smallest, 2 to the next larger, etc., and N to the largest.   In case of ties, assign to each of the tied observations the average of the ranks which would have been assigned had the observations differed slightly.   (If more than 20% of the observations are involved in ties, this procedure should not be used.)

4. Compute R_i, the sum of the ranks of the observations on the ith treatment, for each of the treatments.

5. Compute

$$H = \frac{12}{N(N+1)} \sum_{i=1}^{k} \frac{R_i{}^2}{n_i} - 3(N+1)$$

6. If $H > \chi^2{}_{1-a}$, conclude that the averages of the k treatments differ; otherwise, there is no reason to believe that the averages differ.

Note: When using this Procedure, each of the n_i should be at least 5.   If any n_i is less than 5, the level of significance α may be considerably different from the intended value.

Example
1. Let $\alpha = 0.10$.
2. $k = 3 \qquad \chi^2_{0.90}$ for 2 DF $= 4.61$
3. In Table 27-5, $N = 9 + 6 + 5 = 20$. The assigned ranks are shown in Table 27-5.
4. $R_1 = 76.5 \qquad R_2 = 78.0 \qquad R_3 = 55.5$
5. $H = \dfrac{12}{420}(2{,}280.30) - 63 = 2.15$

6. Since H is not larger than $\chi^2_{0.90}$, there is no reason to believe that the averages or the three storage conditions differ.

GENERAL COMMENTS ON A COMPLETELY RANDOMIZED DESIGN

The plan is simple and may be the best choice when the experimental material is homogeneous and when background conditions can be well controlled during the experiment:
The advantages of the design are:
1. Complete flexibility in terms of number of treatments and number of units assigned to a treatment
2. Simple analysis
3. No difficulty with lost or missing data
In planning the experiment, n units are assigned at random to each of the k treatments. When the data have been taken, the results are set out in a table which looks like Table 27-6.
Set out this way, the results of experiments are indistinguishable from a situation where there has been no design and no allocation at all, but where several different samples have been tested from each of several different sources of material, or several observations made at each of several different conditions. Whether the observations come from units randomly allocated to several different treatments or from units obtained from several different sources, the data table looks the same, and in fact the analysis will be essentially the same.
This simple one-factor design is called "completely randomized" to distinguish it from other experiment designs where the principle of "blocking" or planned grouping has been made part of the structure.

TABLE 27-6 Completely Randomized Design (One-factor)

Observation	Treatments				
	1	2	3	. . .	k
1					
2					
3					
⋮					
n					

One-Way Analysis of Variance—Models The results of an experiment run according to a completely randomized design are summarized in a one-way table such as Table 27-3. The analysis of a completely randomized design is called a one-way analysis of variance. The analysis shown may also be used for any one-way classification of data, whether or not the data came from a designed experiment. The data might consist of a number of samples from different manufacturers, or of different types of stopwatches, as in the example used for the one-way analysis using ranks. To discuss the general analysis of variance for a one-way classification of data, statisticians speak of the "models" in analysis of variance. Which model is appropriate is determined by answering the question "Do the several groups (by which the data are tabulated) represent all such groups that the experimenter is interested in?" If they do, the model is Model I, the Fixed Effects Model. If, on the other hand, the groups are considered to be a random sample from some population made up of such groups, the model is Model II, the Random Effects Model. For example, suppose that the data in Table 27-3 were not from a completely randomized design where 15 briquettes were allocated at random to 3 conditioning treatments. Suppose instead the column headings were "Batch 1, 2, 3," and that there were 5 briquettes tested per batch. The 3 conditioning treatments of the designed experiment presumably were the only 3 treatments of interest to the experimenter at that time and therefore represent a Fixed Effects Model, whereas 3 batches presumably are a random sample of batches made by some standard procedure and represent a Random Effects Model.

For both Model I and Model II, the experimenter is trying to determine whether the 3 groups are different in mean value. For Model II, he is also interested in knowing what is the relative variation—between samples from the same batch, and between batches. Knowledge of the relative variability of different samples within a batch or of different batches will help in planning how many samples to test.

Data obtained from a designed experiment, as described for this completely randomized design, will usually be Model I, since presumably the experimenter included all the treatments of interest. Data obtained in other ways can be Model I or Model II depending upon how the experimenter answers the question posed. If such data are of the Model I kind, any of the foregoing analyses may be used as given. If the data correspond to Model II, use the analysis of variance F test and add one extra step. Add an extra column to Table 27-4 and label it Expected Mean Square.

	Expected mean square
Between groups	$\sigma_w^2 + n\sigma_b^2$
Within groups.	σ_w^2

For the data in Table 27-3, we have:

	Mean square	Expected mean square
Between groups	$MS_B = 1{,}754.6$	$\sigma_w^2 + 5\sigma_b^2$
Within groups	$MS_W = 545.4$	σ_w^2

σ_b^2 is called the between component of variance, and σ_w^2 is called the within component of variance. MS_B is an estimate of the Expected between Groups Mean Square. MS_W is an estimate of the Within Groups Expected Mean Square. Therefore, estimates s_w^2, s_b^2 of σ_w^2, σ_b^2 are obtained as follows:

MS_B is set equal to $s_w^2 + ns_b^2$
MS_W is set equal to s_w^2

$$s_w^2 = 545.4$$

$$s_b^2 = \frac{1{,}754.6 - 545.4}{5} = \frac{1{,}209.2}{5} = 241.8$$

The total variance s_t^2 is estimated as $s_t^2 = s_b^2 + s_w^2$.

There is a simple user-oriented computing system called OMNITAB (Ref. 5), which in response to the one-word command ONEWAY, gives back automatic printout of almost everything that could be calculated for a one-way classification of data —e.g., the complete analysis of variance table, the results of the ranks analysis of variance, the group means and standard deviations and their confidence intervals, the components of variance (to be used if appropriate), the results of multiple comparisons of group means, and the results of three tests of homogeneity of variance.

FACTORIAL EXPERIMENTS—GENERAL

Terminology   In a factorial experiment we control several factors and investigate their effects at each of two or more levels. The experimental plan consists of taking an observation at each one of all possible combinations that can be formed for the different levels of the factors. Each such different combination is called a treatment combination.

Suppose that we are interested in investigating the effect of current level and force on the measured resistivity of silicon wafers. In the past, one common experimental approach has been the so-called "one at a time" approach. This kind of experiment would study the effect of varying current at some constant force, and then study the effect of varying force at some constant current. Factors would be varied "one at a time." The results of such an experiment are fragmentary in the sense that we have learned about the effect of different current levels at one force level only (and the effect of different force levels at one current level only). The measured resistivity of the wafer at different current levels may depend on the force level used; if we had chosen a different force level, our observed relation of resistivity to current might have been quite different. In statistical language, there may be an interaction effect between the two factors within the range of interest, and the "one at a time" procedure does not enable us to detect it.

In a factorial experiment, the levels of each factor we wish to investigate are chosen, and a measurement is made for all possible combinations of levels of the factors. Suppose that we had chosen 5 levels of current and 4 levels of force. There would be 20 possible combinations of current and force, and the factorial experiment would consist of 20 trials. In our example, the term *level* is used in connection with quantitative factors, but the same term is also used when the factors are qualitative.

In the analysis of factorial experiments, we speak of main effects and interaction effects (or simply interactions). Main effects of a given factor are always functions of the average response or yield at the various levels of the factor. In the case where a factor has two levels, the main effect is the difference between the responses at the two levels averaged over all levels of the other factors. In the case where the factor has more than two levels, there are several independent components of the main effect, the number of components being one less than the number of levels. If the difference in the response between two levels of factor A is the same regardless of the level of factor B (except for experimental error), we say that there is no interaction between A and B, or that the AB interaction is zero. Figure 27-2 shows two examples of response or yield curves; one example shows the presence of an interaction, and the other shows no interaction. If we have two levels of each of the factors A and B, then the AB interaction (neglecting experimental error) is the difference in the yields of A at the second level of B minus the difference in the yields of A at the first level of B. If we have more than two levels of either or of both A and B, then the AB interaction is composed of more than one component. If we have a levels of the factor A and b levels of the factor B, then the AB interaction has $(a - 1)$ $(b - 1)$ independent components. A two-factor interaction (e.g., AB) is called a second-order interaction.

For factorial experiments with three or more factors, interactions can be defined similarly. For example, the ABC interaction is the interaction between the factor C and the AB interaction (or equivalently between the factor B and the AC inter-

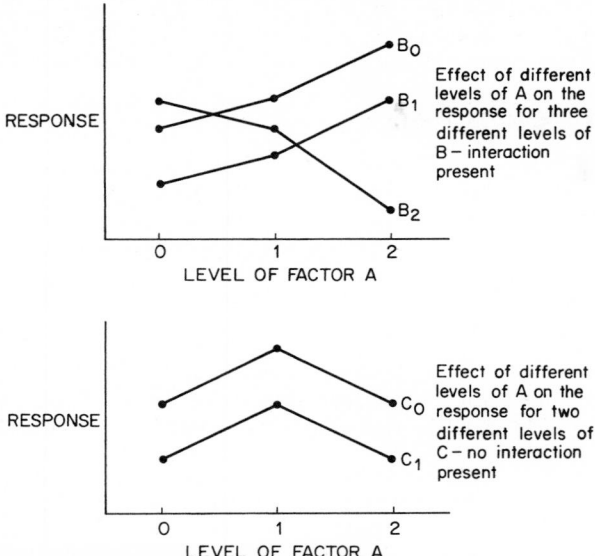

Fig. 27-2   Response curves showing presence or absence of interaction.

action, or A and the BC interaction). A three-factor interaction (e.g., ABC) is called a third-order interaction.

Example of a Factorial Experiment with Two Factors   A two-factor experiment is the simplest kind of multifactor experiment, and the recommended design is a two-factor factorial design; i.e., all possible combinations of the levels of the two factors are run.

For example, measurements of resistivity of a silicon wafer are usually made at one current level I_0 and using 150 g force. An investigation is in progress to see what happens when the method is extended to other values of force and current. Four values of force are used (25, 50, 100, 150 g) and five levels of current (levels 1, 2, 3, 4, 5 where level 3 is the standard level). An experimental trial is made at each of the $4 \times 5 = 20$ possible combinations. The data are summarized in a two-way table as in Table 27-7. This is a two-factor factorial experiment, and some books will describe it as having two "crossed" factors, and label the analysis as the analysis of two crossed classifications.

The problem here is to decide whether there are significant effects due to varying levels of force and to varying levels of current. Judgments about possible interacting effects of force and current may be made if the experiment is replicated, or if the experimenter has a valid estimate of experimental error from similar work. The data as shown in Table 27-7 will be used as an example of an unreplicated experiment.

(In the real experiment replicate measurements were, of course, made since the investigator was interested in finding out about interactions, and since it was not known whether the precision of the method would be the same at the extreme values of the factors.)

ANOVA can be used to test two hypotheses: (1) the mean resistivity for all levels of force is the same, and (2) the mean resistivity for all levels of current is the same.

The analysis would proceed as follows:

r = number of rows = 4

c = number of columns = 5

T = grand total = $\Sigma C_i = \Sigma R_i = 236.77$

n = total number of observations = $r \times c = 20$

$$C = \frac{T^2}{n} = 2{,}803.00164$$

Row sum of squares = $SS_R = \dfrac{\Sigma R_i{}^2}{c} - C = 0.014855$

Column sum of squares = $SS_C = \dfrac{\Sigma C_i{}^2}{r} - C = 0.021430$

Total sum of squares = $SS_T = \Sigma(\text{all observations squared}) - C = 0.041855$

Error (or residual) sum of squares = $SS_E = SS_T - SS_R - SS_C = 0.005570$

The analysis of variance table for a two-factor factorial (unreplicated) is shown in Table 27-8.

For rows: Conclude a significant effect of rows if the F value is greater than $F_{1-\alpha}$ for $r-1$, and $(r-1)(c-1)$ degrees of freedom (from Appendix II, Table K).

For columns: Conclude a significant effect of columns if the F value is greater than $F_{1-\alpha}$ for $c-1$ and $(r-1)(c-1)$ degrees of freedom (from Appendix II, Table K).

The analysis of variance table is only one part of an analysis of data. Plots are always useful and in this case would point up what an eye-scan of the data may have shown—the noticeably higher values at current level 5, and the apparent decrease in resistivity with increasing force, particularly at the outer values of current. When the factors are quantitative and the levels equally spaced, there are simple methods to check on various types of trend (linear, quadratic, etc.) in the measurements as a function of varying levels of a factor (see Hicks, Ref. 6).

The model postulated for the data assumed that the factor effects were additive. One way to check on this assumption is by computing Tukey's test for nonadditivity (see Ref. 7), which would check against the possibility that the effects of a factor were, for example, multiplicative rather than additive. The test for nonadditivity on these data is not significant; so presumably the effects may be considered additive.

It is useful to make a table of row effects and column effects (Table 27-9). (Row effect = row mean minus grand mean.)

It is useful to make a two-way table of residuals, where the residual for the cell in the ith row, jth column is equal to the observation in that cell minus (grand mean + ith row effect + jth column effect). Examine the table of residuals for individual large values (indicating a possibly erroneous observation) and for patterns in sign and size. Plot the residuals against the order in which treatment combinations were actually run. The treatment combinations were supposed to have been run in random order, but sometimes these directions are not followed.

Shortcut techniques (using ranges) for comparisons of means in a two-way classification have been given by Kurtz et al. (Ref. 4).

The discussion thus far has assumed that only one determination per cell was made. If we want to have an estimate of error from this experiment, we must replicate the experiment. It will be useful to have a table like Table 27-7, where the entry in each cell is now the average of k determinations. In addition, make a

TABLE 27-7   Resistivity Measurements

Force	Current					Total
	Level 1	Level 2	Level 3	Level 4	Level 5	
25 g	11.84	11.83	11.84	11.81	11.96	$R_1 = 59.28$
50 g	11.84	11.88	11.88	11.87	11.90	$R_2 = 59.37$
100 g	11.77	11.80	11.80	11.81	11.88	$R_3 = 59.06$
150 g	11.79	11.80	11.80	11.80	11.87	$R_4 = 59.06$
Total........	$C_1 = 47.24$	$C_2 = 47.31$	$C_3 = 47.32$	$C_4 = 47.29$	$C_5 = 47.61$	$T = 236.77$

TABLE 27-8   Analysis of Variance of Resistivity Measurements of Table 27-7

Source of variation	Sum of squares (SS)	Degrees of freedom (DF)	Mean square $= \dfrac{SS}{DF}$	$F = \dfrac{\text{mean square (source)}}{\text{mean square (error)}}$
Rows (force)........	0.014855	$r - 1 = 3$	0.00495	10.67*
Columns (current)........	0.021430	$c - 1 = 4$	0.00536	11.54*
Error........	0.005570	$(r - 1)(c - 1) = 12$	0.000464	
Total........	0.041855	$rc - 1 = 19$		

* Significant at the 1% level.

TABLE 27-9   Table of Effects

	Row mean	Row effect
1	11.8560	0.0175
2	11.8740	0.0355
3	11.8120	−0.0265
4	11.8120	−0.0265
	Column mean	Column effect
1	11.8100	−0.0285
2	11.8275	−0.0110
3	11.8300	−0.0085
4	11.8225	−0.0160
5	11.9025	0.0640

The means were calculated from the totals in Table 27-7. The row effects (and the column effects) will sum to zero. Look at their relative size—for example, there is one big column effect (corresponding to level 5 of current).

table where the entry in each cell is the variance of the k measurements about this average. The latter table may be scanned to see whether the variances are pretty much alike, or homogeneity of variance tests (Refs. 7, 8) may be made. Since the analysis of variance procedure will assume that these variance estimates are homogeneous and pool them, they should be examined before pooling.

A plot of each cell mean vs. cell variance (or standard deviation) may be revealing. Look for individual outlying points, or for a pattern of dependence of variability on mean value (in the latter case, consider the need for a transformation of the data).

The analysis of variance of the replicated experiment is easily modified from that of the unreplicated one.

Proceed as follows: Calculate the following quantities and insert in Table 27-10:

r = number of rows
c = number of columns
k = number of determinations per cell
n = total number of observations = krc
T = grand total

$$C = \frac{T^2}{n}$$

$$\text{Row sum of squares} = SS_R = \frac{\sum R_i^2}{kc} - C$$

$$\text{Column sum of squares} = SS_C = \frac{\sum C_i^2}{kr} - C$$

TABLE 27-10   Analysis of Variance Table for Two-factor Factorial (k Replicates per cell)

Source of variation	Sum of squares	Degrees of freedom DF	Mean square	F
Rows.	SS_R	$r-1$	$SS_R/DF = MS_R$	MS_R/MS_E
Columns	SS_C	$c-1$	$SS_C/DF = MS_C$	MS_C/MS_E
Interaction.	SS_I	$(r-1)(c-1)$	$SS_I/DF = MS_I$	MS_I/MS_E
Error.	SS_E	$rc(k-1)$	$SS_E/DF = MS_E$	
Total.	SS_T	$krc-1$		

$$\text{Interaction sum of squares} = SS_I = \frac{\Sigma(\text{cell mean})^2}{k} - SS_R - SS_C - C$$

Total sum of squares $= SS_T = \Sigma$ (all observations squared) $- C$

Error sum of squares $= SS_T - SS_R - SS_C - SS_I$

The foregoing instructions will fill in all the cells in the "Sum of Squares" column of the analysis of variance table (Table 27-10), but the similarities to Tabel 27-7 should be noted.

The value of MS_E in Table 27-10 can be obtained by pooling the $(r \times c)$ estimates of within cell variance.

A real experiment like the one described would surely have been replicated, and this one was. The investigator is trying to extend the range of the test method, and wants to check that the precision is the same at the extended levels of the variables, and to check on interacting effects of the factors. The full set is not shown here.

FACTORIAL EXPERIMENTS WITH n FACTORS (EACH FACTOR AT TWO LEVELS)

Symbols   A factorial experiment in which we have n factors, each at two levels, is known as a 2^n factorial experiment. The experiment consists of 2^n trials, one at each combination of levels of the factors. To identify each of the trials, we adopt a conventional notation. A factor is identified by a capital letter, and the two levels of a factor by the subscripts zero and one. If we have three factors A, B, and C, then the corresponding levels of the factors are A_0, A_1, B_0, B_1; and C_0, C_1; respectively. By convention, the zero subscript refers to the lower level, to the normal condition, or to the absence of a condition, as appropriate. A trial is represented by a combination of small letters denoting the levels of the factors in the trial. The presence of a small letter means that the factor is at the level denoted by the subscript 1 (the higher level for quantitative factors); the absence of a letter means that the factor is at the level denoted by the subscript zero (the lower level for quantitative factors). Thus, the symbol a represents the treatment combination where A is at the level A_1, B is at B_0, and C is at C_0. The symbol bc represents the treatment combination where A is at the level A_0, B is at B_1, and C is at C_1. Conventionally, the symbol 1 represents the treatment combination with each factor at its zero level. In an experiment with three factors, each at two levels, the $2^3 = 8$ combinations, and thus the eight trials, are represented by (1), a, b, ab, c, ac, bc, abc, This system is illustrated in the following example.

Example   The data in Table 27-11 are taken from a larger experiment on fire-retardant treatments for fabrics. The excerpted data are intended only to provide an example for demonstrating the technique of analysis. The experiment has four factors, each at two levels, i.e., is a 2^4 factorial. Note that all factors are qualitative in this experiment. The experimental factors and levels are:

Factors	*Levels*
A—Fabric	A_0—Sateen
	A_1—Monk's cloth
B—Treatment	B_0—Treatment x
	B_1—Treatment y
C—Laundering condition	C_0—Before laundering
	C_1—After one laundering
D—Direction of test	D_0—Warp
	D_1—Fill

TABLE 27-11   Results of Flame Tests of Fire-retardant Treatments (a 2^4 Factorial Experiment)

		A_0				A_1			
		B_0		B_1		B_0		B_1	
C_0	D_0	4.2	(1)	4.5	b	3.1	a	2.9	ab
	D_1	4.0	d	5.0	bd	3.0	ad	2.5	abd
C_1	D_0	3.9	c	4.6	bc	2.8	ac	3.2	abc
	D_1	4.0	cd	5.0	bcd	2.5	acd	2.3	$abcd$

The observations reported in Table 27-11 are inches burned, measured on a standard-sized sample after a flame test.   For reference, the conventional symbol representing the treatment combination appears beside the resulting observation.

Analysis: Estimation of Main Effects and Interactions   Yates' method is a systematic method for obtaining estimates of main effects and interactions for two-level factorials.   The method may be found in various textbooks (Cochran and Cox, Ref. 9, and Davies, Ref. 10).   The method as given here applies to factorials, blocked factorials, and fractional factorials, for which we have 2^n observations.[6]   The first step in Yates' procedure is to make a table with $n + 2$ columns, where n is the number of factors in the factorial experiment.   For example, see Table 27-12, where $n + 2 = 6$.   In Table 27-12 the treatment combinations are listed in a standardized order in the first column, and after following the prescribed procedure, estimated main effects and interactions result in the last column (column $n + 2$).   The order in which the treatment combinations are listed in column 1 determines the order of estimated effects in column $n + 2$.   The generation of the values in the table is explained below.

[6] In a $1/2^b$ fraction of a 2^n factorial, there are $2n'$ observations, where $n' = n - b$.

TABLE 27-12   Yates' Method of Analysis Using Data of Table 27-11

Treatment combination (1)	Response (yield) (2)	(3)	(4)	(5)	g (6)	
(1)	4.2	7.3	14.7	29.2	$57.5 = g_T$	
a	3.1	7.4	14.5	28.3	$-12.9 = g_A$	, an estimate of $8A$
b	4.5	6.7	14.5	-5.2	$2.5 = g_B$	, an estimate of $8B$
ab	2.9	7.8	13.8	-7.7	$-3.5 = g_{AB}$	, an estimate of $8AB$
c	3.9	7.0	-2.7	1.2	$-0.9 = g_C$	, an estimate of $8C$
ac	2.8	7.5	-2.5	1.3	$-0.5 = g_{AC}$	, an estimate of $8AC$
bc	4.6	6.5	-3.5	-0.8	$1.3 = g_{BC}$	, an estimate of $8BC$
abc	3.2	7.3	-4.2	-2.7	$0.5 = g_{ABC}$	, an estimate of $8ABC$
d	4.0	-1.1	0.1	-0.2	$-0.9 = g_D$	, an estimate of $8D$
ad	3.0	-1.6	1.1	-0.7	$-2.5 = g_{AD}$	, an estimate of $8AD$
bd	5.0	-1.1	0.5	0.2	$0.1 = g_{BD}$	, an estimate of $8BD$
abd	2.5	-1.4	0.8	-0.7	$-1.9 = g_{ABD}$	, an estimate of $8ABD$
cd	4.0	-1.0	-0.5	1.0	$-0.5 = g_{CD}$	, an estimate of $8CD$
acd	2.5	-2.5	-0.3	0.3	$-0.9 = g_{ACD}$	, an estimate of $8ACD$
bcd	5.0	-1.5	-1.5	0.2	$-0.7 = g_{BCD}$	, an estimate of $8BCD$
$abcd$	2.3	-2.7	-1.2	0.3	$0.1 = g_{ABCD}$	, an estimate of $8ABCD$
Total	57.5					
Sum of squares	219.15				3,506.40	

For factorials or blocked factorials, the treatment combinations should be listed in "standard order" in the first column, i.e.,

For two factors: (1), a, b, ab

For three factors: (1), a, b, ab, c, ac, bc, abc

For four factors: (1), a, b, ab, c, ac, bc, abc, d, ad, bd, abd, cd, acd, bcd, abcd

.

.

.

etc.

"Standard order" for five factors is obtained by listing all the treatment combinations given for four factors, followed by e, ae, be, abe, . . . , abcde (i.e., the new element multiplied by all previous treatment combinations). Standard order for a higher number of factors is obtained in similar fashion, beginning with the series for the next smaller number of factors, and continuing by multiplying that series by the new element introduced.

The estimated main effects and interactions also appear in a standard order:

For two factors: T, A, B, AB

For three factors: T, A, B, AB, C, AC, BC, ABC

.

.

.

etc.

where T corresponds to the overall average effect, A to the main effect of factor A, AB to the interaction of factors A and B, etc.

The systematic procedure for Yates' method is as follows:

Procedure

1. Make a table with $n + 2$ columns. In the first column, list the treatment combinations in standard order.

2. In column 2, enter the observed yield or response corresponding to each treatment combination listed in column 1.

3. In the top half of column 3, enter, in order, the sums of consecutive pairs of entries in column 2. In the bottom half of the column, enter, in order, the differences between the same consecutive pairs of entries, i.e., second entry minus first entry, fourth entry minus third entry, etc.

4. Obtain columns 4, 5, . . . , $n + 2$, in the same manner as column 3, i.e., by obtaining in each case the sums and differences of the pairs in the preceding column in the manner described in Step 3.

5. The entries in the last column (column $n + 2$) are called g_T, g_A, g_B, g_{AB}, etc., corresponding to the ordered effects T, A, B, AB, etc. Estimates of main effects and interactions are obtained by dividing the appropriate g by 2^{n-1}. g_T divided by 2^n is the overall mean.

Note: The remaining steps of this procedure are checks on the computation.

6. The sum of all the 2^n individual responses (column 2) should equal the total given in the first entry of the last column (column $n + 2$).

7. The sum of the squares of the individual responses (column 2) should equal the sum of the squares of the entries in the last column (column $n + 2$) divided by 2^n.

8. For any main effect, the entry in the last column (column $n + 2$) equals the sum of the responses in which that factor is at its higher level minus the sum of the responses in which that factor is at its lower level.

Example

1. The example shown in Table 27-11 is a 2^4 factorial ($n = 4$). Therefore, our table will have six columns, as shown in Table 27-12.

2. See Table 27-12.

3. See Table 27-12.

4. See Table 27-12.
5. In Table 27.12,

$$g_A = -12.9$$

The estimated main effect of

$$A = \frac{-12.9}{8} = -1.6$$

$$g_{AD} = -2.5$$

The estimated effect of AD interaction $= \dfrac{-2.5}{8} = -0.3$, etc.

Note: The following steps are checks on the computations in Table 27-12.
6. The sum of column 2 should equal g_T,

$$57.5 = 57.5$$

7. The sum of squares of entries in column 2 should equal the sum of squares of the entries in the last column divided by 2^4 ($=16$),

$$219.15 = \frac{3,506.40}{16}$$

$$= 219.15$$

8. $g_A = (a + ab + ac + abc + ad + abd + acd + abcd)$
$\qquad - [(1) + b + c + bc + d + bd + cd + bcd]$
$\qquad = (22.3) - (35.2) = -12.9$

Procedure for Testing for Significance of Main Effects and Interactions

1. Choose α, the level of significance.
2. If there is no available estimate of the variation due to experimental error,[7] find the sum of squares of g's corresponding to interactions of three or more factors in Table 27-12.
3. To obtain s^2, divide the sum of squares obtained in Step 2 by $2^n \nu$, where ν is the number of interactions included. In a 2^n factorial, the number of third and higher interactions will be $2^n - (n^2 + n + 2)/2$. If an independent estimate of the variation due to experimental error is available, use this s^2.
4. Look up $t_{1 - \alpha/2}$ for ν degrees of freedom in Appendix Table G. If higher-order interactions are used to obtain s^2, ν is the number of interactions included. If an independent estimate of s^2 is used, ν is the degrees of freedom associated with this estimate.
5. Compute

$$w = (2^n)^{1/2}(t_{1 - \alpha/2})s$$

6. For any main effect or interaction X, if the absolute value of g_X is greater than w, conclude that X is different from zero; e.g., if $|g_A| > w$, conclude that the A effect is different from zero. Otherwise, there is no reason to believe that X is different from zero.

Example

1. Let $\alpha = 0.05$.
2. Using Table 27-12,

$$g^2_{ABC} + g^2_{ABD} + g^2_{ACD} + g^2_{BCD} + g^2_{ABCD} = 5.17$$

3. $n = 4 \qquad [\nu] = 5$

[7] See General Comments on Factorial Designs.

$$2^n[v] = 16(5) = 80$$

$$s^2 = \frac{5.17}{80} = 0.0646 \qquad s = 0.254$$

4. $t_{0.975}$ for 5 DF $= 2.571$

5. $w = 4(2.571)(0.254) = 2.61$

6. $|g_A| = 12.9$ and $|g_{AB}| = 3.5$ are greater than w; therefore, the main effect of A and the interaction AB are believed to be significant.

Half-Normal Plots.   Daniel (Ref. 11) proposed a simple and effective technique for use in the interpretation of data from factorial experiments where all factors are at two levels.   This technique, called "half-normal plots" helps to study the magnitude of the effects, identify which interactions can reasonably be assumed to be zero, and detect wild observations, and it may give evidence that the conditions of the actual experiment have inadvertently departed from the assumptions usually made in the analysis.   Half-normal plots are easily made on special probability paper by extending the calculations from Yates' method.

Detection of "Wild Values."   Half-normal plots can be used to detect an aberrant value.

Hunter (Ref. 12) has proposed a method in which the procedure of Yates' algorithm is reversed, using significant coefficients only, to obtain predicted values for each treatment combination.   Residuals (difference between observed values and predicted values) are then obtained and examined.   Large residuals may indicate aberrant observations and should be investigated.

BLOCKED FACTORIAL EXPERIMENTS (EACH FACTOR AT TWO LEVELS)

When the number of factors to be investigated is more than just a few, it may be that the required number of trials 2^n is too large to be carried out under reasonably uniform conditions—e.g., on one batch of raw material, or on one piece of equipment. In such cases, the design can be arranged in groups or blocks so that conditions affecting each block can be made as uniform as possible.   The use of planned grouping within a factorial design (i.e., a blocked factorial) will improve the precision of estimation of experimental error, and will enable us to estimate the main effects free of block differences; but the structure of the designs is such that certain interaction effects will be inextricable from block effects.   See Refs. 10 and 13 for examples of these designs.

FRACTIONAL FACTORIAL EXPERIMENTS (EACH FACTOR AT TWO LEVELS)

The Fractional Factorial Designs   If there are many factors, a complete factorial experiment, requiring all possible combinations of levels of the factors, involves a large number of tests—even when only two levels of each factor are being investigated.   The complete factorial experiment may overtax the available facilities, or it may not be practical to plan the entire experimental program in advance, and we may wish to conduct a few smaller experiments to serve as a guide to future work.

In these cases, it is useful to have a plan that requires fewer tests than the complete factorial experiment.   Recent developments in statistics have considered the problem of planning multifactor experiments that require measuring only a fraction of the total number of possible combinations.   The fraction is a carefully prescribed subset of all possible combinations, its analysis is relatively straightforward, and the use of a fractional factorial does not preclude the possibility of later completion of the full factorial experiment.

In Figures 27-3, 27-4, and 27-5, let the letters A, B, C, D, E, F, and G stand for seven factors to be investigated, and let the subscripts zero and one denote two alternative levels of each factor. The 128 $(= 2^7)$ possible experimental conditions

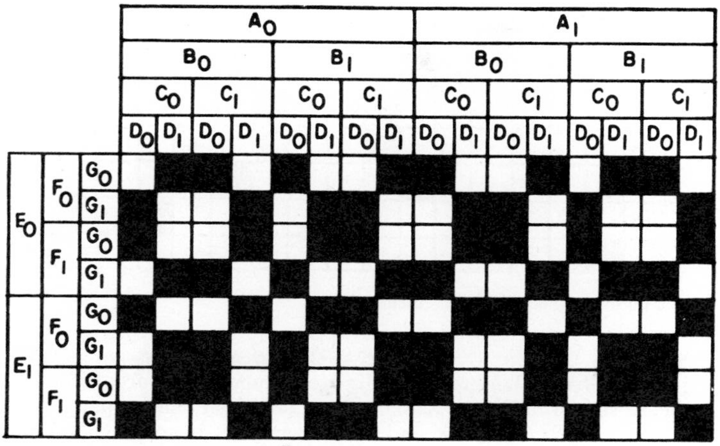

			A_0						A_1			
			B_0		B_1			B_0		B_1		
			C_0	C_1	C_0	C_1		C_0	C_1	C_0	C_1	
			D_0 D_1	D_0 D_1	D_0 D_1	D_0 D_1	D_0 D_1	D_0 D_1	D_0 D_1	D_0 D_1		
E_0	F_0	G_0 / G_1										
	F_1	G_0 / G_1										
E_1	F_0	G_0 / G_1										
	F_1	G_0 / G_1										

Fig. 27-3   A one-half replicate of a 2^7 factorial.

			A_0						A_1			
			B_0		B_1			B_0		B_1		
			C_0	C_1	C_0	C_1		C_0	C_1	C_0	C_1	
			D_0 D_1	D_0 D_1	D_0 D_1	D_0 D_1	D_0 D_1	D_0 D_1	D_0 D_1	D_0 D_1		
E_0	F_0	G_0 / G_1										
	F_1	G_0 / G_1										
E_1	F_0	G_0 / G_1										
	F_1	G_0 / G_1										

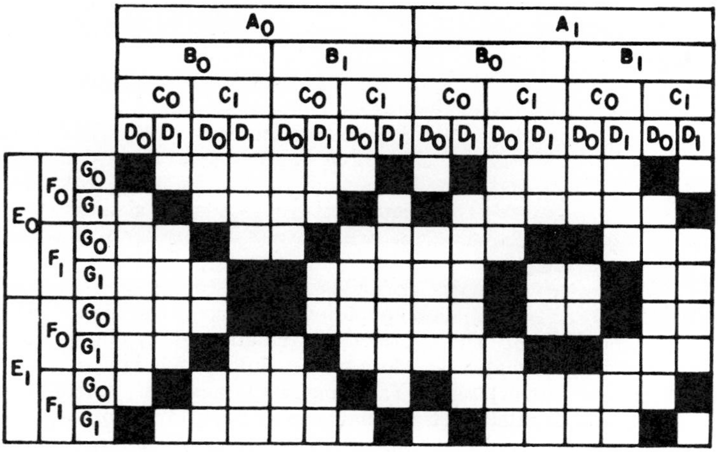

Fig. 27-4   A one-quarter replicate of a 2^7 factorial.

are represented by the 128 cells of Figure 27-3. The shaded squares represent those experimental combinations to be investigated if the experimenter wishes to measure only half the 128 possible combinations. In the same way, the shaded cells in Figures 27-4 and 27-5 illustrate plans requiring only 32 and 16 measurements, respectively, instead of the full set of 128.

Fractional factorial experiments obviously cannot produce as much information

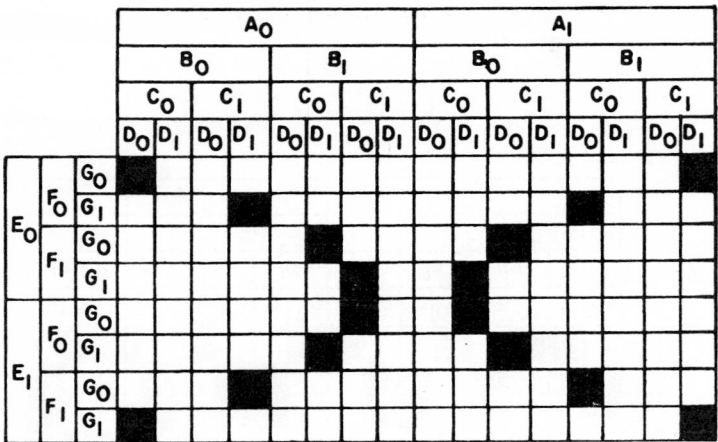

Fig. 27-5   A one-eighth replicate of a 2^7 factorial.

as the full factorial. Economy is achieved at the expense of assuming that certain of the interactions between factors are negligible. Some of the larger fractions (e.g., the half-replicate shown in Figure 27-3) require only that third-order (and higher) interactions be assumed negligible, and this assumption is not uncommon. However, the plan calling for one-eighth of the possible combinations, as shown in Figure 27-5, can only be used for evaluating the main effects of each of the seven factors, and will not allow the evaluation of any two-factor interactions.

In a complete factorial experiment we have 2^n tests. In the analysis of a complete factorial, we have n main effects, $2^n - n - 1$ interaction effects, and an overall average effect. The 2^n tests can be used to give independent estimates of the 2^n effects. In a fractional factorial (say the fraction $1/2^b$) there will be only 2^{n-b} tests and therefore 2^{n-b} independent estimates. In designing the fractional plans (i.e., in selecting an optimum subset of the 2^n total combinations), the goal is to keep each of the 2^{n-b} estimates as "clean" as possible—i.e., to keep the estimates of main effects and if possible second-order interactions free of confusion with each other.

If we plan to test whether or not certain of the effects are significant, we must have an estimate of the variation due to experimental error which is independent of our estimates of the effects.

Table 27-13 gives two examples of two-level fractional factorial plans, together with the effects that can be estimated (assuming three-factor and higher-order interaction terms are negligible). The treatment combinations should be randomly allocated to the experimental material. More two-level plans may be found in Refs. 10 and 13, with detailed instructions for Yates' method of analysis. A large catalog of two-level plans is found in Ref. 14, fractional factorial plans for factors at three levels may be found in Ref. 15, and plans for mixed two-level and three-level factors in Ref. 16.

During the past decade, there have been many developments and publications in the area of fractional factorial designs. This has been one of the most active areas in the statistical design of experiments. For estimating missing values in unreplicated two-level factorial and fractional factorial designs, see Draper and Stoneman (Ref. 17). For methods of construction of fractional replicate plans, see Addelman (Refs. 18, 19, and 20). For methods of partial duplication, augmentation, and sequencing of fractional factorial designs, see Patel (Ref. 21), Daniel (Refs. 22 and 23), John

TABLE 27-13   Examples of Fractional Factorial Plans

Plans	Treatment combinations*	Estimated effects
Plan 1:	(1)	T
Four factors ($n = 4$)	ad	A
½ replication ($b = 1$)	bd	B
8 observations	ab	$AB + CD$
	cd	C
	ac	$AC + BD$
	bc	$BC + AD$
	$abcd$	D
Plan 2:	(1)	T
Five factors ($n = 5$)	ae	A
½ replication ($b = 1$)	be	B
16 observations	ab	AB
	ce	C
	ac	AC
	bc	BC
	$abce$	$-DE$
	de	D
	ad	AD
	bd	BD
	$abde$	$-CE$
	cd	CD
	$acde$	$-BE$
	$bcde$	$-AE$
	$abcd$	$-E$

* The order given is the proper order for Yates' method of analysis; see Estimation of Main Effects and Interactions under Factorial Experiments with n Factors (Each Factor at Two Levels).

(Ref. 24), and Addelman (Ref. 25).   For an example of Yates' method and inverse Yates' method in a metallurgical context, see Duckworth (Ref. 26).

GENERAL COMMENTS ON FACTORIAL EXPERIMENTS

Verification of a Factorial Design   The analyses presented previously apply only to a true factorial design where every level of one factor can be combined with every level of the other factors.   In a full factorial, observations are required at all combinations.   Sometimes, a data table appears to represent a factorial design but information on the experimental conditions reveals that the design was not a factorial.

Consider the following experiment which could be summarized in a two-way table (Table 27-14).

This is not a factorial experiment.   Three batches of *each* of 3 types of cement have been made, and some property measured.   Batch 1, from cement type 1, is unique and has nothing in common with Batch 1 from type 2 or type 3; so there is no overall batch effect, and no interaction between types and batches.   The two factors, types and batches, are said to be "nested," i.e., the levels of one factor exist only within the levels of another factor.   In fact it is probably a mistake to call them factors at all.   This is a hierarchical experiment to investigate differences between types and between batches within types (possibly between samples within batches), etc. (see Nested Designs).

The example of cement types and batches might not cause trouble, since this is so clearly a nested design, but consider the two-way table (Table 27-15).

TABLE 27-14   A Plan Which Is Not a Factorial

Batch	Cement type		
	1	2	3
1			
2			
3			

TABLE 27-15   A Plan Which May Be a Factorial

Head	Machine		
	1	2	3
1			
2			
3			

It would never be obvious from the two-way table whether these data form a factorial experiment or not. One must know how the experiment was run. If in fact, Head 1 was the same head and was used on each machine, it was a factorial design. If on the other hand, three different heads were used on each machine, it was not a factorial.

Estimates of Experimental Error for Factorial-Type Designs

Internal Estimates of Error. As in any experiment, we must have a measure of experimental error to use in judging the significance of the observed differences in treatments. In the larger factorial designs, estimates of higher-order interactions will be available. The usual assumption is that high-order interactions are actually estimates of experimental error. As a working rule we often use third- and higher-order interactions for error. This does not imply that third-order interactions are always nonexistent. The judgment of the experimenter will determine which interactions may reasonably be assumed to be meaningful, and which may be assumed to be nothing more than error. The latter interactions may be combined to provide an internal estimate of error for a factorial experiment of reasonable size. For very small factorials, e.g., 2^3 or smaller, there are no estimates of high-order interactions, and the experiment must be replicated (repeated) in order to obtain an estimate of error from the experiment itself.

In blocked factorial designs, some of the higher-order interactions are confounded with blocks and are not available as estimates of error. When a 2^3 factorial is arranged in two blocks of four observations, the single third-order interaction provides the blocking (the means of subdividing the experiment into homogeneous groups), and therefore estimates block effects, not error. Here again it may be necessary to replicate the experiment or at least part of it in order to have an estimate of experimental error.

In the case of fractional factorials, there may be no point in replication of the experiment; further experimentation would probably be aimed at completing the full factorial or a larger fraction of the full factorial. The smaller fractional factorial designs do not contain high-order interactions that can suitably be assumed to be error. Accordingly then, an independent estimate of error will be required when using a small fractional factorial. Occasionally and cautiously we might use second-order interaction effects to test main effects, if the purpose of the experiment were to look for very large main effects (much larger than second-order effects). In using interactions as estimates of error, we may tentatively decide before conducting the experiment (or at least before having a knowledge of the responses or yields) which of the effects may be assumed to be zero, so that they may be used in the estimate of the variation due to experimental error. Half-normal plots may be used to check on these assumptions.

Estimates of Error from Past Experience. In the cases discussed that do not provide adequate estimates of error from the experiment itself, we must depend on an estimate based upon past experience with the measurement process. In laboratory and industrial situations, this information is often at hand or can be found by simple analysis of previously recorded data.

Analysis of Factorial Experiments A discussion of the analysis of two-factor experiments was given in this section, followed by discussions of multifactor factorial experiments where all factors are at two levels. For examples of analyses of more generalized factorials—multifactor with various numbers of levels per factor—see any of the recommended texts (Refs. 1, 6, 9, 10, 27, 28, 29, 30).

Yates' method of analysis, given for the two-level factorials, has been generalized (Ref. 31). This method is particularly useful as part of a computer program for the analysis of factorial experiments.

BLOCK DESIGNS

General It is easier to first think of blocked designs as one-factor designs in the sense that there is one experimental factor of primary importance. The several levels of the one factor are called "treatments."
In the simplest blocked designs (those with one-way blocking), the data, when taken, will be summarized in a two-way table which looks like Table 27-16.

In spite of the two-way summary table, it can be thought of as a one-factor design because the factor or variable which provides the blocks is usually of secondary interest. The experimenter's aim is to measure the effects of the primary factor, free of any effects caused by the variable-called-blocks, with perhaps a secondary aim of estimating the effects of the variable-called-blocks. For example, if the blocks in the experiment are time periods, the first aim of the experiment is to evaluate the effects of the primary variable free of the effects of time-caused differences. A secondary aim might actually be to measure the effects of the time periods to help in planning future experiments.

TABLE 27-16   A Simple Block Design

	Treatments			
	1	2	...	k
Block 1	—	—	...	—
Block 2	—	—	...	—
.	.	.	...	.
.	.	.	...	.
.	.	.	...	.
	—	—	...	—
	$\bar{X}_1$	$\bar{X}_2$	...	$\bar{X}_k$

This secondary interest in the variable-called-blocks may exist in several different degrees, e.g..

1. The aim of the experimenter is to estimate effects of treatments free of block effects—he does not particularly want to have numerical estimates of block effects. If blocks are days, day-to-day differences should be eliminated but are of no particular interest in themselves.

2. Primary aim is to estimate effects of treatments, but he would also like to have numerical estimates of block effects.

3. Sometimes the variable-called-treatments and the variable-called-blocks are of almost equal interest. In this case a "block design" is almost a "two-factor experiment"—but the experimenter must be sure that the two factors do not interact before he uses a block design. If interaction between factors exists or is suspected, he must use the design and analysis for a factorial experiment with two factors.

In other words a block design (with one-way blocking) can be considered as a one-factor design or a two-factor-no-interaction design. The simplest design with one-way blocking is the "Randomized Block Design." This and others will be discussed.

RANDOMIZED BLOCK DESIGNS

Planning In comparing a number of treatments, it is clearly desirable that all other conditions be kept as nearly constant as possible. Often the required number

TABLE 27-17   Conversion Gain of Resistors

Resistor (blocks)	Test set (treatments)						Total	Mean
	1,463	1,506	1,938	1,946	1,948	2,140		
3	138.0	141.6	137.5	141.8	138.6	139.6	$B_1 = 837.1$	$b_1 = 139.52$
4	152.2	152.2	152.1	152.2	152.0	152.8	$B_2 = 913.5$	$b_2 = 152.25$
5	153.6	154.0	153.8	153.6	153.2	153.6	$B_3 = 921.8$	$b_3 = 153.63$
6	141.4	141.5	142.6	142.2	141.1	141.9	$B_4 = 850.7$	$b_4 = 141.78$
Total.....	$T_1 =$ 585.2	$T_2 =$ 589.3	$T_3 =$ 586.0	$T_4 =$ 589.8	$T_5 =$ 584.9	$T_6 =$ 587.9	$G =$ 3,523.1	
Mean.....	$t_1 =$ 146.30	$t_2 =$ 147.32	$t_3 =$ 146.50	$t_4 =$ 147.45	$t_5 =$ 146.22	$t_6 =$ 146.98		

of tests is too large to be carried out under similar conditions. In such cases, we may be able to divide the experiment into blocks, or planned homogeneous groups. When each such group in the experiment contains exactly one observation on every treatment, the experimental plan is called a randomized block plan.

There are many situations where a randomized block plan can be profitably utilized. For example, a testing scheme may take several days to complete. If we expect some systematic differences between days, we might plan to observe each item on each day, or to conduct one test per day on each item. A day would then represent a block. In another situation, several persons may be conducting the tests or making the observations, and differences between operators are expected. The tests or observations made by a given operator can be considered to represent a block. The size of a block may be restricted by physical considerations.

In general, a randomized block plan is one in which each of the treatments appears exactly once in every block. The treatments are allocated to experimental units at random within a given block. The results of a randomized block experiment can be exhibited in a two-way table such as Table 27-17, assuming we have b blocks and t treatments.

Since each treatment occurs exactly once in every block, the treatment totals or means are directly comparable without adjustment.

Example The data in Table 27-17 represent conversion gain of four resistors measured in six test sets. Conversion gain is defined as the ratio of available current-noise power to applied direct-current power expressed in decibel units, and is a measure of the efficiency with which a resistor converts direct-current power to available current-noise power. We are interested in possible differences among treatments (test sets) and blocks (resistors).

Analysis The analysis of a randomized block experiment depends on a number of assumptions. We assume that each of the observations is the sum of three components. If we let Y_{ij} be the observation on the ith treatment in the jth block, then[8]

$$Y_{ij} = \phi_i + \beta_j + e_{ij}$$

where β_j is a term peculiar to a given block. It is the amount by which the response of a given treatment in the jth block differs from the response of the same treatment averaged over all blocks, assuming no experimental error.

ϕ_i is a term peculiar to the ith treatment, and is constant for all blocks regardless of the block in which the treatment occurs. It may be regarded as the average value of the ith treatment averaged over all blocks in the experiment, assuming no experimental error.

e_{ij} is the experimental error associated with the measurement Y_{ij}.

[8] In some literature the first term in the model is the grand mean and the terms for blocks and treatments represent the effects of individual blocks and treatments from the grand mean.

In order to make interval estimates for, or to make tests on, the ϕ_i's or the β_j's, we generally assume that the experimental errors e_{ij}'s are independently and normally distributed. However, if the experiment was randomized properly, failure of this assumption will, in general, not cause serious difficulty.

Estimation of the Treatment Effects   A treatment effect ϕ_i is estimated by the mean of the observations on the ith treatment. That is, the estimate of ϕ_i is $t_i = T_i/b$.

For example, see Table 27-17. The estimate of the effect of Test Set 1,463 is $t_1 = T_1/4 = 585.2/4 = 146.30$. Similarly, $t_2 = 147.32$, $t_3 = 146.50$, $t_4 = 147.45$, $t_5 = 146.22$, $t_6 = 146.98$.

The q test, described below, tests two hypotheses:
1. The mean gain for all test sets is the same and
2. The mean gain for all resistors is the same. The test compares two means at a time.

Testing and Estimating Differences in Treatment Effects. Procedure
1. Choose α, the significance level of the test.
2. Look up $q_{1-\alpha}(t, \nu)$ in Appendix Table EE, where

$$\nu = (b-1)(t-1)$$

3. Compute the sum of squares of the treatments

$$SS_t = \frac{T_1{}^2 + T_2{}^2 + \ldots + T_t{}^2}{b} - \frac{G^2}{tb}$$

4. Compute the sum of squares of the blocks

$$SS_b = \frac{B_1{}^2 + B_2{}^2 + \ldots + B_b{}^2}{t} - \frac{G^2}{tb}$$

5. Compute

$$SS = \sum_{i=1}^{t} \sum_{j=1}^{b} Y_{ij}{}^2 - \frac{G^2}{tb}$$

i.e., compute the sum of the squares of all the observations, and subtract G^2/tb.
6. Compute

$$s^2 = \frac{SS - SS_b - SS_t}{(b-1)(t-1)}$$

and s.
7. Compute

$$w = \frac{q_{1-\alpha}s}{\sqrt{b}}$$

If the absolute difference between any two estimated treatment effects exceeds w, decide that the treatment effects differ; otherwise, the experiment gives no reason to believe the treatment effects differ.

Note: It should be noted that for all possible pairs of treatments i and j, we can make the statements

$$t_i - t_j - w \leq \phi_i - \phi_j \leq t_i - t_j + w$$

with $1 - \alpha$ confidence that all the statements are simultaneously true.

Example
1. Let $\alpha = 0.05$
2. $q_{0.95}(6,15) = 4.59$

3. $S_t = 517,181.998 - 517,176.400 = 5.598$
4. $S_b = 518,104.065 - 517,176.400 = 927.665$
5. $S = 518,123.13 - 517,176.40 = 946.73$

6.
$$s^2 = \frac{13.467}{15} = 0.8978 \qquad s = 0.9475$$

7.
$$w = \frac{(4.59)(0.9475)}{\sqrt{4}} = 2.175$$

8. Since there is no pair of treatment means whose difference exceeds 2.175, we have no reason to conclude that test sets differ.

Estimation of Block Effects   The block effect β_j is estimated by the mean of the observations in the jth block minus the grand mean. That is, the estimate of β_j, the jth block effect, is $b_j = B_j/t - G/bt$.

For example, in Table 27-17, the grand average equals $G/bt = 3,523.1/24 = 146.80$.

$$
\begin{aligned}
b_1 &= 139.52 - 146.80 & b_3 &= 153.63 - 146.80 \\
&= -7.28 & &= 6.83 \\
b_2 &= 152.25 - 146.80 & b_4 &= 141.78 - 146.80 \\
&= 5.45 & &= -5.02
\end{aligned}
$$

Testing and Estimating Differences in Block Effects.   Procedure
1. Choose α, the significance level of the test.
2. Look up $q_{1-\alpha}(b,v)$ in Appendix Table EE, where
$$v = (b - 1)(t - 1)$$

3.⎫
4.⎪ Same as Steps 3, 4, 5, and 6, for "Testing
5.⎬ and Estimating Differences in Treatment Effects."
6.⎭
7. Compute
$$w' = \frac{q_{1-\alpha}\, s}{\sqrt{t}}$$

8. If the absolute difference between any two block effects exceeds w', conclude that the block effects differ; otherwise, the experiment gives no reason to believe that block effects differ.

Note: As in the case of treatment effects, we can make simultaneous statements about the difference between pairs of blocks i and j, with confidence $1 - \alpha$ that all the statements are simultaneously true. The statements are, for all i and j,

$$b_i - b_j - w' \le \beta_i - \beta_j \le b_i - b_j + w'$$

Example

1. Let $\alpha = 0.05$.
2. $v = (4 - 1)(6 - 1)$
     $= 15$
     $q_{0.95}(4,15) = 4.08$
3 $S_t = 5.598$
4. $S_b = 927.665$
5. $S = 946.73$
6. $s^2 = 0.8978 \qquad s = 0.9475$

7. $w' = \dfrac{(4.08)\,(0.9475)}{\sqrt{6}} = 1.578$

8. The absolute difference between two block effects does exceed 1.578, and we conclude that resistors do differ.

BALANCED INCOMPLETE BLOCK DESIGNS

Planning   In this design there is one primary experimental factor, but all the treatments cannot be accommodated in a block.

We define r, b, t, k, λ, E, and N as follows:

r = number of replications (number of times each treatment appears in the plan)

b = number of blocks in the plan

t = number of treatments

k = number of treatments which appear in every block

λ = number of blocks in which a given treatment-pair appears,

$$\lambda = \frac{r(k-1)}{t-1}$$

E = a constant used in the analysis, $E = t\lambda/rk$

N = total number of observations, $N = tr = bk$

Using this nomenclature, it is possible to enumerate the situations in which it is combinatorially possible to construct a balanced incomplete block design.   Plans are indexed in Table 27-18 for $4 < t \leq 10$, $r \leq 10$ and two examples given.   For some other balanced incomplete block plans, see Refs. 9 and 13.

If we wish to estimate and to make tests of block effects as well as treatment effects, we should consider the plans where $b = t$; i.e., the number of blocks equals the number of treatments.   In such plans, called symmetrical balanced incomplete block designs, differences between block effects are estimated with equal precision for all pairs of blocks.

To use a given plan from Table 27-18, proceed as follows:

1. Rearrange the blocks at random.   (In a number of plans in Table 27-18, the blocks are arranged in groups.   In these plans, rearrange the blocks at random within their respective groups.)

2. Randomize the positions of the treatment numbers within each block.

3. Assign the treatments at random to the treatment numbers in the plan.

The analysis of this design is discussed in Refs. 9 and 13.

GENERAL COMMENTS ON BLOCK DESIGNS

Table 27-2 outlines the characteristics of Randomized Blocks, Balanced Incomplete Blocks, Partially Balanced Incomplete Blocks.   In the simplest type of block design, Randomized Blocks, the blocking is with respect to one experimental variable (or source of inhomogeneity), and the block is large enough to accommodate all the treatments we wish to test.

In "Incomplete Block Designs," the blocking also is one-way, but the block size is not large enough for all treatments to be tested in every block.   One class of incomplete block designs, called "Balanced Incomplete Block Designs," has certain restrictions on the assignment of treatments to blocks which lead to equal precision in the estimation of differences between treatments.

If Randomized Block and Balanced Incomplete Block Designs do not meet the needs of the experimenter with regard to number of blocks, size of blocks, number of treatments, etc., other kinds of plans are available.   An important recent develop-

TABLE 27-18   Balanced Incomplete Block Plans (4 $\leq t \leq 10$, $r \leq 10$)

				Index		
t	k	r	b	λ	E^*	Plan number†
4	2	3	6	1	2/3	1
	3	3	4	2	8/9	†
5	·2	4	10	1	5/8	2
	3	6	10	3	5/6	†
	4	4	5	3	15/16	†
6	2	5	15	1	3/5	3
	3	5	10	2	4/5	4
	3	10	20	4	4/5	5
	4	10	15	6	9/10	6
	5	5	6	4	24/25	†
7	2	6	21	1	7/12	†
	3	3	7	1	7/9	7
	4	4	7	2	7/8	8
	6	6	7	5	35/36	†
8	2	7	28	1	4/7	9
	4	7	14	3	6/7	10
	7	7	8	6	48/49	†
9	2	8	36	1	9/16	†
	3	4	12	1	3/4	11
	4	8	18	3	27/32	12
	5	10	18	5	9/10	13
	6	8	12	5	15/16	14
	8	8	9	7	63/64	†
10	2	9	45	1	5/9	15
	3	9	30	2	20/27	16
	4	6	15	2	5/6	17
	5	9	18	4	8/9	18
	6	9	15	5	25/27	19
	9	9	10	8	80/81	†

* The constant $E = t\lambda/rk$ is used in the analysis.

†Indicates plans that may be constructed by forming all possible combinations of the t treatments in blocks of size k.   The number of blocks b serves as a check that no block has been missed.

Plan 1: $t = 4$, $k = 2$, $r = 3$, $b = 6$, $\lambda = 1$, $E = 2/3$

Group I	Group II	Group III
(1) 1, 2	(3) 1, 3	(5) 1, 4
(2) 3, 4	(4) 2, 4	(6) 2, 3

Plan 2: $t = 5$, $k = 2$, r $= 4$, $b = 10$, $\lambda = 1$, $E = 5/8$

Group I	Group II
(1) 1, 2	(6) 1, 3
(2) 2, 5	(7) 2, 4
(3) 3, 4	(8) 3, 2
(4) 4, 1	(9) 4, 5
(5) 5, 3	(10) 5, 1

ment has been the classification and enumeration of partially balanced incomplete block designs (Ref. 32). These designs may be useful if a balanced design requires a larger number of blocks than is practical.

Another kind of plan, called the "Chain Block Plan" is useful when observations are expensive and the experimental error is small; it can handle a large number of treatments relative to the total number of observations. See Ref. 13 for the structure and details of analysis.

Two-way Blocking Designs are available which provide for two blocked variables (in Table 27-2, see Latin squares and Youden squares). Descriptions for Latin square designs and for Youden squares are given in this section.

Mandel (Ref. 33) has discussed generalized chain block plans which have two-way blocking—the only restrictions for the generalized designs being that the number of blocks be even and the number of treatments be a multiple of the number of blocks.

LATIN SQUARE DESIGNS

Planning A Latin square plan (or the Youden square plans described later) is useful when it is necessary or desirable to allow for two specific sources of nonhomogeneity in the conditions affecting test results. Such designs were originally applied in agricultural experimentation when the two directional sources of nonhomogeneity were simply the two directions on the field, and the "square" was literally a square plot of ground. Its usage has been extended to many other applications where there are two sources of nonhomogeneity that may affect experimental results—for example, machines, positions, operators, runs, days. A third variable, the experimental treatment, is then associated with the two source variables in a prescribed fashion. The use of Latin squares is restricted by two conditions:

1. The number of rows, columns, and treatments must all be the same.
2. There must be no interactions between row and column factors (see Factorial Experiments—General, for discussion of interaction).

Youden square plans are less restrictive than Latin squares; the number of rows, columns, and treatments need not be the same, but only certain number combinations are possible.

As an example of a Latin square, suppose we wish to compare four materials with regard to their wearing qualities. Suppose further that we have a wear-testing machine which can handle four samples simultaneously. Two sources of inhomogeneity might be the variations from run to run, and the variation among the four positions on the wear machine. A 4×4 Latin square will allow for both sources of inhomogeneity if we can make four runs. The Latin square plan is as shown in Table 27-19 (the four materials are labeled A, B, C, D).

TABLE 27-19 A 4 X 4 Latin Square

Run	Position number			
	(1)	(2)	(3)	(4)
1	A	B	C	D
2	B	C	D	A
3	C	D	A	B
4	D	A	B	C

Examples of Latin squares from size 3×3 to 7×7 are given in Table 27-20. In the case of the 4×4 Latin square, four are given; when a 4×4 Latin square is needed, one of the four should be selected at random. The procedure to be followed in using a given Latin square is as follows:

1. Permute the columns at random.
2. Permute the rows at random.
3. Assign letters randomly to the treatments.

(If squares of 5×5 and higher are used very frequently, then, strictly speaking, each time we use one we should choose a square at random from the set of all

TABLE 27-20   Selected Latin Squares

3 X 3	4 X 4			
A B C	1	2	3	4
B C A	*A B C D*	*A B C D*	*A B C D*	*A B C D*
C A B	*B A D C*	*B C D A*	*B D A C*	*B A D C*
	C D B A	*C D A B*	*C A D B*	*C D A B*
	D C A B	*D A B C*	*D C B A*	*D C B A*

5 X 5	6 X 6	7 X 7
A B C D E	*A B C D E F*	*A B C D E F G*
B A E C D	*B F D C A E*	*B C D E F G A*
C D A E B	*C D E F B A*	*C D E F G A B*
D E B A C	*D A F E C B*	*D E F G A B C*
E C D B A	*E C A B F D*	*E F G A B C D*
	F E B A D C	*F G A B C D E*
		G A B C D E F

possible squares.   Fisher and Yates (Ref. 34) give complete representation of the squares from 4 × 4 to 6 × 6, and sample squares up to the 12 × 12.

The results of a Latin square experiment are recorded in a two-way table similar to the plan itself.   The treatment totals and the row and column totals of the Latin square plan are each directly comparable without adjustment.

The analysis of the Latin square design is discussed in Refs. 10 and 13.

YOUDEN SQUARE DESIGNS

Planning   The Youden square, like the Latin square, allows for two experimental sources of inhomogeneity.   The conditions for the use of a Youden square, however, are less restrictive than for the Latin square.   The use of Latin square plans is restricted by the fact that the number of rows, columns, and treatments must all be the same.   Youden squares have the same number of columns and treatments, but a fairly wide choice in the number of rows is possible.   We use the following notation:

t = number of treatments to be compared
b = number of levels of one source of inhomogeneity (columns)
k = number of levels of the other source of inhomogeneity (rows)
r = number of replications of each treatment
λ = number of times that two treatments occur in the same block

In a Youden square, $t = b$ and $k = r$.

In the example of a Latin square, we wished to test four materials with regard to their wearing qualities.   There were two sources of inhomogeneity; these were the variation among the four positions on the machine, and the variations from run·to run.   In order to use the Latin square plan, we had to make four runs.   A Youden square arrangement for this case would require only three runs.   Some Youden square plans are indexed and an example given in Table 27-21.

The results of an experiment using a Youden square plan are recorded in a two-way table which looks like the plan itself.

For methods of analysis, see Refs. 9 and 10.   For an experimental example of Plan 5, see Ref. 30.

TABLE 27-21   Youden Square Arrangements ($r \le 10$)

Plan number	$t = b$	$r = k$	λ	$E = t\lambda/rk$	Remarks
				Index	
1	3	2	1	3/4	✿
2	4	3	2	8/9	✿
3	5	4	3	15/16	✿
4	6	5	4	24/25	✿
5	7	3	1	7/9	
6	7	4	2	7/8	Complement of Plan 5†
7	7	6	5	35/36	✿
8	8	7	6	48/49	✿
9	9	8	7	63/64	✿
10	10	9	8	80/81	✿
11	11	5	2	22/25	
12	11	6	3	11/12	Complement of Plan 11
13	11	10	9	99/100	✿
14	13	4	1	13/16	
15	13	9	6	26/27	Complement of Plan 14
16	15	7	3	45/49	
17	15	8	4	15/16	Complement of Plan 16
18	16	6	2	8/9	
19	16	10	6	24/25	
20	19	9	4	76/81	
21	19	10	5	19/20	Complement of Plan 20
22	21	5	1	21/25	
23	25	9	3	25/27	See Ref. 9, pp. 529–535
24	31	6	1	31/36	See Ref. 9, pp. 529–535
25	31	10	3	93/100	See Ref. 9, pp. 529–535
26	37	9	2	74/81	See Ref. 9, pp. 529–535
27	57	8	1	57/64	See Ref. 9, pp. 529–535
28	73	9	1	73/81	See Ref. 9, pp. 529–535
29	91	10	1	91/100	See Ref. 9, pp. 529–535

✿ Blocks in these plans are columns of Latin squares with one row deleted.

† The "complement" of a plan is developed as follows: Construct the first block (column) by writing all treatments that did not appear in the first block of the original plan. With these letters as starting points, complete each row by writing in alphabetical order all remaining treatment letters followed by A, B, C, . . . until every treatment letter appears once in each row. For example, Plan 6 is developed from Plan 5 as follows: The first block of Plan 5 is ABD; its complement and therefore the first block of Plan 6 is CEFG. The complete layout for Plan 6 is:

Row	1	2	3	4	5	6	7
				Block			
1	C	D	E	F	G	A	B
2	E	F	G	A	B	C	D
3	F	G	A	B	C	D	E
4	G	A	B	C	D	E	F

Plan 5: $t = b = 7$, $r = k = 3$

Row	1	2	3	4	5	6	7
				Block			
1	A	B	C	D	E	F	G
2	B	C	D	E	F	G	A
3	D	E	F	G	A	B	C

NESTED DESIGNS

Most experiment designs are primarily intended to provide estimates of the effects of experimental treatments or factors. In sampling studies and in investigations of test methods, however, the "factors" may be hierarchical sources of variation and the primary information sought is knowledge of the relative variability of the sources. Designs intended to provide this information, i.e., estimates of variance at various stages, are called "nested designs" and can be very simple in structure. A simple

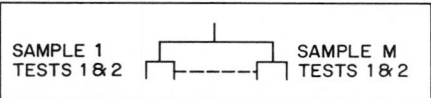

Fig. 27-6   A two-stage balanced nested design. *(Reprinted with permission from T. R. Bainbridge, Staggered Nested Designs for Estimating Variance Components, Industrial Quality Control, vol. 22, No. 1, pp. 12–20, July 1965.)*

example is the design shown in Figure 27-6, where two samples are taken and duplicate tests made on each sample. The primary information sought is the variability of tests on the same sample and the variability of different samples. This is a two-stage "balanced" nested design. (If the same number of subunits is taken from each unit at any stage, the design is called "balanced.")

In experiments which are not sampling studies or investigations of hierarchical structures, but where some experimental factors are "nested" rather than "crossed" (see Two-factor Experiments), similar information is sought for some factors—e.g., the variability among levels of one factor which is nested within another factor.

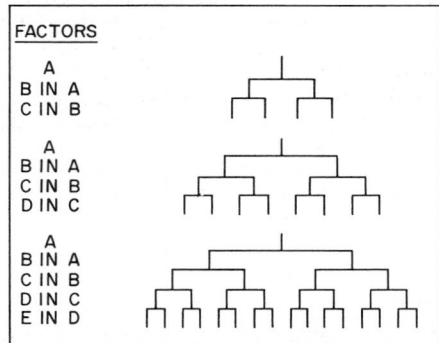

Fig. 27-7   Balanced nested designs for three, four, and five factors *(Reprinted with permission from T. R. Bainbridge, Staggered Nested Designs for Estimating Variance Components, Industrial Quality Control, vol. 22, No. 1, pp. 12–20, July 1965.)*

In Figure 27-6, the first stage (samples) could be called Factor A and the second stage (tests) could be called Factor B. Figure 27-7 shows one A unit for a balanced three-, four-, or five-stage nested design.

The analysis of balanced completely nested designs may be found in standard textbooks—see Appendix 6B of Davies (Ref. 35). For the analysis of a two-stage nested design, see the analysis of variance for "Completely Randomized Designs" in this section and calculate the components of variance as described for the Random Effects Model under One-way Analysis of Variance—Models. For the more complicated "nested factorials," where some factors are "crossed" and some are "nested," see Hicks (Ref. 6); some useful rules for determining the expected mean squares in the analysis of variance of such designs are given by Lenter (Ref. 36).

Note Figure 27-7. At each stage only two subunits of each unit are taken, but the total number of tests multiplies rapidly as the number of stages (or factors) increases. Because of the rapidly increasing total number of tests, only a few units are usually used at the top levels. In other words, balanced nested designs tend to provide too little information on the upper levels (the initial stages, or Factors A and B) and often provide more than enough information at the bottom levels (Factor E, for example). Bainbridge (Ref. 37) has considered alternative "unbalanced" nested designs with a fixed total number of tests. He prefers a design which he calls a staggered nested design which is easy to administer and which provides about the same number of degrees of freedom for each factor. He shows staggered nested designs for three, four, five, and six factors (see Figure 27-8 for the designs and their analysis).

MIXTURE DESIGNS

In some experiments with mixtures, the property of interest depends on the proportions of the components of the mixture, not on the amount of the mixture. For example, stainless steel is a mixture of different metals, and its tensile strength depends on the proportions of the metallic elements present; gasoline is ordinarily a blend of various stocks, and the octane rating of the final blend depends on the proportions going into the blend. The proportions of the components of a mixture must of course add up to one, and in the most general case the proportion of any component may range from zero to one. The factor space available for experimentation is thus constrained. It has been shown that, if the number of components in the mixture is q, the factor space is a regular $(q-1)$-dimensional simplex (e.g., a triangle for $q = 3$, a tetrahedron for $q = 4$).

A natural approach would be to take a uniformly spaced distribution of experimental points over the whole available factor space. This results in the so-called simplex lattice design proposed by Scheffé (Ref. 38). A (q,m) lattice, for example, is a lattice for q components, where the proportions for each component have $m + 1$ equally spaced values from 0 to 1, i.e., the values $0, 1/m, 2/m$, etc. For three components, the proportions of each component would be $0, \frac{1}{2}, 1$ when $m = 2$; $0, \frac{1}{3}, \frac{2}{3}, 1$ when $m = 3$. The lattice resulting when $m = 2$ is called the quadratic lattice, the lattice resulting when $m = 3$, the cubic lattice, etc. (see Figure 27-9).

In addition, modified lattices can be made by adding center points to the two-dimensional face or faces of the quadratic lattice. This provides a design called the special cubic lattice, which has proved to be very useful in experimentation.

The number of points k required for any lattice except the special cubic is found using the formula

$$k = \frac{(m + q - 1)!}{m!(q - 1)!}$$

The number of points required for the special cubic is

$$k = \frac{q(q + 1)}{2} + \frac{q(q - 1)(q - 2)}{6}$$

Sources of Variance	Sums of Squares	Degrees of Freedom	Expectations of Mean Squares	Format of A–Units
A	(5) – CF	m–1	$\sigma_c^2 + 1\frac{2}{3}\sigma_b^2 + 3\sigma_a^2$	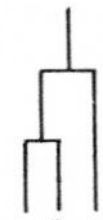
B in A	(3)+(4)–(5)	m	$\sigma_c^2 + 1\frac{1}{3}\sigma_b^2$	
C in B	(1)+(2)–(3)	m	σ_c^2	
Total	(1)+(2)+(4)–CF	3m–1	4A Three Factors	a b c
A	(7) – CF	m–1	$\sigma_d^2 + 1\frac{1}{2}\sigma_c^2 + 2\frac{1}{2}\sigma_b^2 + 4\sigma_a^2$	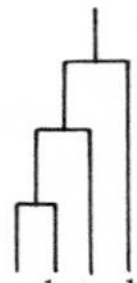
B in A	(5)+(6)–(7)	m	$\sigma_d^2 + 1\frac{1}{6}\sigma_c^2 + 1\frac{1}{2}\sigma_b^2$	
C in B	(3)+(4)–(5)	m	$\sigma_d^2 + 1\frac{1}{3}\sigma_c^2$	
D in C	(1)+(2)–(3)	m	σ_d^2	
Total	(1)+(2)+(4)+(6)–CF	4m–1	4B Four Factors	a b c d
A	(9) – CF	m–1	$\sigma_e^2 + 1\frac{2}{5}\sigma_d^2 + 2\frac{1}{5}\sigma_c^2 + 3\frac{2}{5}\sigma_b^2 + 5\sigma_a^2$	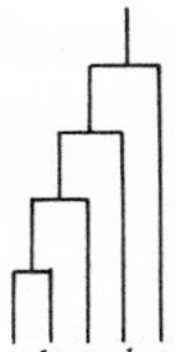
B in A	(7)+(8)–(9)	m	$\sigma_e^2 + 1\frac{1}{10}\sigma_d^2 + 1\frac{3}{10}\sigma_c^2 + 1\frac{3}{5}\sigma_b^2$	
C in B	(5)+(6)–(7)	m	$\sigma_e^2 + 1\frac{1}{6}\sigma_d^2 + 1\frac{1}{2}\sigma_c^2$	
D in C	(3)+(4)–(5)	m	$\sigma_e^2 + 1\frac{1}{3}\sigma_d^2$	
E in D	(1)+(2)–(3)	m	σ_e^2	
Total	(1)+(2)+(4)+(6)+(8)–CF	5m–1	4C Five Factors	a b c d e
A	(11) – CF	m–1	$\sigma_f^2 + 1\frac{1}{3}\sigma_e^2 + 2\sigma_d^2 + 3\sigma_c^2 + 4\frac{1}{3}\sigma_b^2 + 6\sigma_a^2$	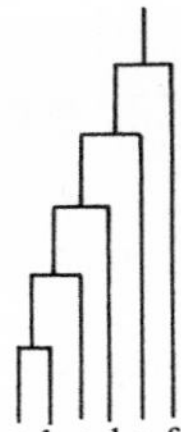
B in A	(9)+(10)–(11)	m	$\sigma_f^2 + 1\frac{1}{15}\sigma_e^2 + 1\frac{1}{5}\sigma_d^2 + 1\frac{2}{5}\sigma_c^2 + 1\frac{2}{3}\sigma_b^2$	
C in B	(7)+(8)–(9)	m	$\sigma_f^2 + 1\frac{1}{10}\sigma_e^2 + 1\frac{3}{10}\sigma_d^2 + 1\frac{3}{5}\sigma_c^2$	
D in C	(5)+(6)–(7)	m	$\sigma_f^2 + 1\frac{1}{6}\sigma_e^2 + 1\frac{1}{2}\sigma_d^2$	
E in D	(3)+(4)–(5)	m	$\sigma_f^2 + 1\frac{1}{3}\sigma_e^2$	
F in E	(1)+(2) – (3)	m	σ_f^2	
Total	(1)+(2)+(4)+(6)+(8)+(10)–CF	6m–1	4D Six Factors	a b c d e f

TOTALS NEEDED TO GET SUMS OF SQUARES

(1) $= \Sigma a^2$

(2) $= \Sigma b^2$

(3) $= \dfrac{\Sigma (a+b)^2}{2}$

(4) $= \Sigma c^2$

(5) $= \dfrac{\Sigma (a+b+c)^2}{3}$

(6) $= \Sigma d^2$

(7) $= \dfrac{\Sigma (a+b+c+d)^2}{4}$

(8) $= \Sigma e^2$

(9) $= \dfrac{\Sigma (a+b+c+d+e)^2}{5}$

(10) $= \Sigma f^2$

(11) $= \dfrac{\Sigma (a+b+c+d+e+f)^2}{6}$

$CF = \dfrac{(\text{Grand Total})^2}{\text{Total No. of Tests}}$

Fig. 27-8 Staggered nested designs for three, four, five, and six factors (*Reprinted with permission from T. R. Bainbridge, Staggered Nested Designs for Estimating Variance Components, Industrial Quality Control, vol. 22, No. 1, pp. 12–20, July 1965.*)

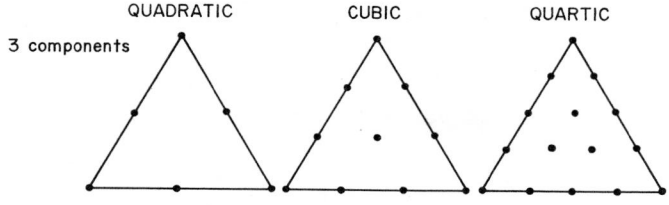

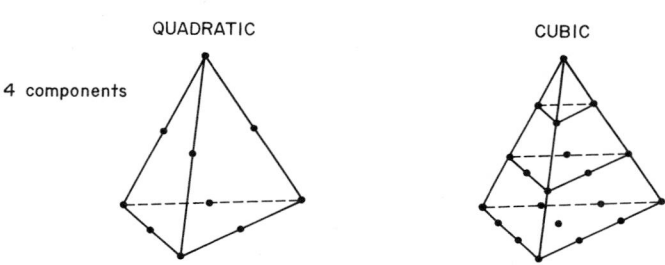

Fig. 27-9 Lattice designs for three- and four-component mixtures. *(Reprinted with permission from J. W. Gorman and J. E. Hinman, Simplex Lattice Designs for Multicomponent Systems, Technometrics, vol. 4, No. 4, p. 464, November 1962.)*

The number of points required for several values of m and q is given in Table 27-22.

The property of interest is measured at each of the design points (corresponding to mixtures of different proportions). Simplified polynomials are used to relate the response variable Y to the various mixture proportions used.

A very useful design called the "special cubic" by Scheffé requires seven points for three-component mixtures—the six points of a $(q = 3, m = 2)$ lattice plus a seventh point at $X_1 = \frac{1}{3}, X_2 = \frac{1}{3}, X_3 = \frac{1}{3}$.

The seven mixtures are the three pure components, the three binary mixtures, and the ternary mixture, as shown in Table 27-23.

The "special cubic" corresponds to the equation

$$Y = \beta_1 X_1 + \beta_2 X_2 + \beta_3 X_3 + \beta_{12}X_1X_2 + \beta_{13}X_1X_3 + \beta_{23}X_2X_3 + \beta_{123}X_1X_2X_3$$

The computed coefficients are

$$b_1 = Y_1 \qquad b_2 = Y_2 \qquad b_3 = Y_3$$
$$b_{12} = 4Y_4 - 2(Y_1 + Y_2)$$

TABLE 27-22   Number of Points Required for Lattice Designs

Number of components q	Type of lattice			
	Quadratic $m = 2$	Special cubic $m = 2$	Cubic $m = 3$	Quartic $m = 4$
3	6	7	10	15
4	10	14	20	35
5	15	25	35	70
6	21	41	56	126
8	36	92	120	330

$$b_{13} = 4Y_5 - 2(Y_1 + Y_3)$$
$$b_{23} = 4Y_6 - 2(Y_2 + Y_3)$$
$$b_{123} = 27Y_7 - 12(Y_4 + Y_5 + Y_6) + 3(Y_1 + Y_2 + Y_3)$$

An excellent discussion of such designs is found in an article by Gorman and Hinman (Ref. 39). They give the polynomials and their solutions for quadratic, special cubic, cubic, and quartic lattices — specifically for three-component mixtures, and the general formulas for q-component mixtures. These authors also give methods for testing the fit of the polynomials and estimating the variances of predicted values, graphical methods to explore suitability of models, an example of a study of the octane-blending characteristics of a three-component system, plus the general caution that there are risks involved in attempting to define an unknown part of a system from empirical study of a part of the system.

TABLE 27-23 Design Points for Special Cubic (Three-component Mixture)

Point number	X_1	X_2	X_3	Response
1	1	0	0	Y_1
2	0	1	0	Y_2
3	0	0	1	Y_3
4	1/2	1/2	0	Y_4
5	1/2	0	1/2	Y_5
6	0	1/2	1/2	Y_6
7	1/3	1/3	1/3	Y_7

Since the original designs proposed by Scheffé, modifications and extensions have been made by various people for various special cases and situations.

Kurotori (Ref. 40) considers a three-component mixture where each component has a lower bound and gives an example of a propellant involving a mixture of binder oxidizer, and fuel.

Kenworthy (Ref. 41) used ratios to design factorial experiments for situations where the percentage of each component was greater than zero with upper and lower bounds.

McLean and Anderson (Ref. 42) discussed designs for factors with two-sided constraints other than zero and one.

Scheffé (Ref. 43) proposed a new design to consist of the 2^{q-1} points which represent mixtures of all possible subsets of the q-components present in equal proportions.

The original mixture designs were such that some of the experiments do not contain any of one or more ingredients of the mixture. In some applications this may be unsatisfactory, and Draper and Lawrence (Refs. 44 and 45) proposed alternative designs for three- and four-component mixtures.

Thompson and Myers (Ref. 46) considered proportions in a well-defined area of interest (possibly near current operating levels) rather than an exploration of the whole factor space.

Lambrakis (Ref. 47) proposed an alternative to the simplex-lattice design in which all the features of the design are maintained except that the pure mixtures are replaced by the $(q-1)$nary mixtures.

GROUP SCREENING DESIGNS

Experimental designs for finding the few effective factors out of a large number of possible factors have been called "screening designs." The design described here has the following structure: form groups, each containing several factors; test the groups; and then test individual factors of the groups that prove to contain significant factors. Such designs were proposed by Connor (Ref. 48) and further studied by Watson (Ref. 49), and are intended to minimize the amount of experimentation required.

The experimental variables are divided into groups, and each group is treated as a single variable until an effect on the response variable is shown.

The following assumptions are made:

1. All factors are assumed initially to have the same probability of being effective.
2. The factors do not interact.
3. The directions of effects, if they exist, are known.

The number of factors is $f = gk$, where g = number of groups and k = number of factors per group. For example, consider an experiment with nine factors. The nine factors are divided into $g = 3$ groups of $k = 3$ factors each. The upper and lower levels of the groups are defined as follows:

Group Factor X consists of Factors A, B, C.

Level 1 — all three factors at lower level (0,0,0)

Level x — all three factors at upper level (1,1,1)

Group Factor Y consists of Factors D, E, F.

Level 1 — all three factors at lower level (0,0,0)

Level y — all three factors at upper level (1,1,1)

Group Factor Z consists of Factors G, H, I.

Level 1 — all factors at lower level (0,0,0)

Level z — all factors at upper level (1,1,1)

The first-stage design studies the group factors. It may be done using a half-replicate of a 2^3 factorial, requiring the four group treatment combinations x, y, z, and xyz which correspond to treatment combinations for the nine factors as follows:

$x(1,1,1,0,0,0,0,0,0)$

$y(0,0,0,1,1,1,0,0,0)$

$z(0,0,0,0,0,0,1,1,1)$

$xyz(1,1,1,1,1,1,1,1,1)$

The results of the first-stage experiment will indicate which group factors contain at least one effective factor. A second-stage experiment, which may consist of a half-replicate of a 2^3, will then be run on each effective group factor to determine which of the individual factors are effective. For further details, see Ref. 49. Patel (Ref. 50) gives detailed procedures for two-, three-, and four-stage screening tests.

Daniel (Ref. 51) and Carr and McCracken (Ref. 52) have also discussed procedures for identifying important effects in a large group of factors using group-screening designs and fractional factorial designs.

The application of group-screening designs discussed here has been to the identification of effective experimental factors, but there is also extensive literature relating to the screening of effective compounds and drugs and to the group testing of individuals.

PLANNING INTERLABORATORY TESTS

This topic presents a few simple techniques that are useful in planning and analyzing the results of interlaboratory (or round-robin) tests. The article by Wernimont (Ref. 53) is a good introduction to the general problem. More specific techniques of analysis, some of which are given here, may be found in Youden (Ref. 54), Mandel (Ref. 29), and an ASTM publication (Ref. 55). Reference 56, which is a compilation of previously published papers on statistical concepts and procedures, includes eight articles on Interlaboratory Tests.

A Rank Sum Test for Laboratories   In almost any set of interlaboratory test data, some reported results are so far out from the main body of results that there is a real question whether those data should be omitted in order to avoid distortion of the true picture. It is always a difficult problem to decide whether or not outlying results should be screened. One does not wish to discard a laboratory's results

TABLE 27-24   Approximate 5% Limits for Ranking Scores*

Number of laboratories participating	Number of materials												
	3	4	5	6	7	8	9	10	11	12	13	14	15
3	...	4	5	7	8	10	12	13	15	17	19	20	22
	...	12	15	17	20	22	24	27	29	31	33	36	38
4	...	4	6	8	10	12	14	16	18	20	22	24	26
	...	16	19	22	25	28	31	34	37	40	43	46	49
5	...	5	7	9	11	13	16	18	21	23	26	28	31
	...	19	23	27	31	35	38	42	45	49	52	56	59
6	3	5	7	10	12	15	18	21	23	26	29	32	35
	18	23	28	32	37	41	45	49	54	58	62	66	70
7	3	5	8	11	14	17	20	23	26	29	32	36	39
	21	27	32	37	42	47	52	57	62	67	72	76	81
8	3	6	9	12	15	18	22	25	29	32	36	39	43
	24	30	36	42	48	54	59	65	70	76	81	87	92
9	3	6	9	13	16	20	24	27	31	35	39	43	47
	27	34	41	47	54	60	66	73	79	85	91	97	103
10	4	7	10	14	17	21	26	30	34	38	43	47	51
	29	37	45	52	60	67	73	80	87	94	100	107	114
11	4	7	11	15	19	23	27	32	36	41	46	51	55
	32	41	49	57	65	73	81	88	96	103	110	117	125
12	4	7	11	15	20	24	29	34	39	44	49	54	59
	35	45	54	63	71	80	88	96	104	112	120	128	136
13	4	8	12	16	21	26	31	36	42	47	52	58	63
	38	48	58	68	77	86	95	104	112	121	130	138	147
14	4	8	12	17	22	27	33	38	44	50	56	61	67
	41	52	63	73	83	93	102	112	121	130	139	149	158
15	4	8	13	18	23	29	35	41	47	53	59	65	71
	44	56	67	78	89	99	109	119	129	139	149	159	169

Note: Let L laboratories test each of M materials. Assign ranks 1 to L for each material. Sum the ranks to get the score for each laboratory. The mean score is $M(L + 1)/2$. The entries are lower and upper limits that are included in the approximate 5% critical region.

*Reprinted with permission from W. J. Youden, Ranking Laboratories by Round Robin Tests, *Materials Research and Standards,* vol. 3, No. 1, pp. 9–13, January 1963.

without good reason; on the other hand, if a laboratory is careless or not competent, one does not wish to "punish" the test method. A ranking test for laboratories due to Youden (Ref. 57), reprinted in Ref. 56, is described here. See also the paragraph below on Youden Two-sample Plots.

An interlaboratory test usually involves sending several materials to several laboratories. The ranking test for laboratories uses the materials to rank the laboratories. The data from the interlaboratory test are usually summarized in a two-way table with materials as rows and laboratories as columns (or vice versa).

For each material, the laboratory having the largest result is given rank one, the next largest rank two, etc. (Tied values are treated as is usual in ranking procedures, each tied value being given the average of those ranks which would have been assigned if the values had differed a little.)

For each laboratory, the assigned ranks are summed over all materials. A laboratory which is consistently high will show a lower rank sum and a laboratory which is consistently low will show a higher rank sum than the average or expected rank sum. The question is whether such rank sums are excessively high or excessively low. To decide this, tables have been provided (see Table 27-24).

A Ruggedness Test for Use by the Initiating Laboratory   Very often a test method is judged to have acceptable precision by the original laboratory, but when the test is performed by several laboratories the results are disappointing. The reason is usually that the original laboratory has carefully controlled conditions and equipment and that the operating conditions in other laboratories are slightly different. (There are always slight deviations which are permissible within the instructions contained in the standard procedure for the test method.) Youden (Ref. 54) proposed that the initiating laboratory investigate the effects of such deviations by deliberately introducing small variations in the method so that they may be prepared for the variations resulting when the test is used by other laboratories. In order to minimize the extra work required for the original laboratory, he proposed that some very efficient designs (Plackett-Burman designs, available for 7, 11, 15 factors) be used to detect such effects. One of these, described in Ref. 54, permits the examination of seven factors in eight runs, provided the factors do not interact.

If significant effects result from such variations of conditions in a single laboratory, the method needs further refinement before interlaboratory tests are run.

Youden Two-sample Plots   A simple plan to investigate the performance of laboratories and of the test procedure itself was suggested by Youden (Ref. 58), reprinted in Ref. 56. Samples of two materials (A and B) are sent to each laboratory in the program. The two materials should be similar in kind and in the value of the property to be measured. The laboratories should have the same internal precision. The pairs of results are used to plot a graph where the X and Y scales are equal, and where each laboratory is represented by one point. A laboratory's result on Sample A is the X-coordinate and its result on Sample B is the Y-coordinate of that point. There will be as many points as there are laboratories. For graphical diagnosis, a vertical line is drawn through the median of all points in the X-direction, and a horizontal line through the median of all points in the Y-direction. The lines could be drawn through the X and Y averages just as well, but the medians are convenient for quick graphical analysis.

Individual points which are very far removed from the main body of the results indicate laboratories that should probably be screened from the analysis. The two intersecting median lines divide the space into four quadrants, and the first (and often revealing) step in the analysis is to look at the distribution of points among the quadrants. If only random errors of measurement were operating, there would be a circular scatter of points with roughly equal numbers in each quadrant. The plots of most real-life interlaboratory data, however, show concentrations in the upper-right and lower-left quadrants (see Figure 27-10). If a laboratory is high on both samples, its point will lie in the upper right, if a laboratory is low on both samples, its point

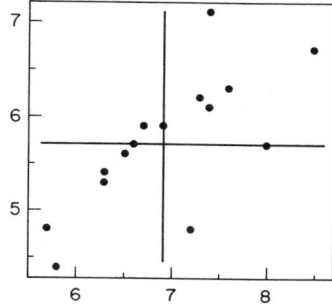

Fig. 27-10 Percent phthalic anhydride in two paint samples—Youden plot showing systematic differences.

TABLE 27-25 Multiples of the Standard Deviation

Percent of points within circle	Multiple of the standard deviation
90	2.146
95	2.448
99	3.035

will lie in the lower left. Being high (or low) on both samples is an indication that a laboratory has somehow put its own stamp on the procedure—i.e., that there are systematic differences among laboratories. Where these systematic differences exist, the points will tend to lie in a long narrow ellipse. Assuming that the two materials are similar in kind and value of the property measured, as prescribed, and that the scatter in results for A does turn out to be approximately the same as the scatter for Sample B, we can calculate an estimate of the standard deviation of a single result as follows:

1. Calculate the "signed differences" $d = A - B$ for each laboratory. (For the ith laboratory $d_i = A_i - B_i$.)
2. Calculate $\bar{d}$, the algebraic average of the d's.
3. Calculate $d_i' = d_i - \bar{d}$.
4. Take the absolute values of the d' and calculate their average. Multiply this value by 0.886 to get an estimate s of the standard deviation of a single result. (The value 0.886 is $1/d_2$, Appendix II, Table A, for $n = 2$.) A circle can be drawn which is expected to contain any stated percentage of the points. The circle is centered at the median point and its radius (for stated percentage to be contained within it) is obtained by multiplying s (from Step 4) by the factor given in Table 27-25.

Points lying outside the circle usually indicate laboratories with systematic differences. Further deductions are possible from such plots (see Ref. 54 or 56); they have been used in a wide variety of applications including chemical and engineering tests and standards comparisons.

PLANNING THE SIZE OF THE EXPERIMENT

Methods for determining the number of observations required for estimating the mean and variability with certain precision, or for comparing two sets of data with regard to mean and variability with certain risks of error, are given in Section 22, under Basic Statistical Concepts. A method for determining the number of observations required when comparing the means of several groups is given here.

For example, the analysis of variance F-test (see Completely Randomized Designs) is designed to test the hypothesis that all group means are the same, i.e., $\mu_1 = \mu_2 = \ldots \mu_k = \mu$. The outcome of the test depends on the significance level α at which the test is done, the true variability of individual observations, the number of observations per group, and the size of the true difference (if any) between group means. When planning experiments, if there are no restrictions on the number of observations which can be made, one should specify the size of differences in means that are considered important from a practical standpoint. The significance level at which the test is to be made is also specified; the sample size (number of observations per group) can be determined using existing tables or charts to achieve a stated probability $(1 - \beta)$ of detecting differences of that size. To use such tables, we compute a quantity ϕ^2:

$$\phi^2 = \frac{\sum(\mu_i - \mu)^2 / k}{\sigma^2 / n} = \frac{n \sum(\mu_i - \mu)^2}{k\sigma^2}$$

where n = number of observations per group (to be determined)
k = number of groups
σ^2 = true value of within-group variability (assumed same for all groups; can be estimated from previous similar work)

μ_i = true mean for ith group

μ = average of all μ_i

Let $(\mu_i - \mu) = d_i$. $\sum\limits_{i=1}^{k} (\mu_i - \mu)$ must equal zero.

Appendix Table FF gives values ϕ^2 for $\alpha = 0.01$ and $\beta = 0.2$ $(1 - \beta = 0.80)$, and DF_1 and DF_2 degrees of freedom. In the simple case used in the example, $DF_1 = k - 1$ and $DF_2 = k(n - 1)$. Other charts and tables are available in slightly different form and for additional values of α and β. See, for example, Refs. 59 and 60.

Example Consider an experiment like the one shown in Table 27-3. Suppose that another experiment is to be run, and that we wish to determine beforehand how many briquettes to test using each method, in order to achieve certain discrimination in comparing the means for the three methods. If the statistical test is to be done at the $\alpha = 0.01$ level, and if we want the probability of detecting the postulated differences to be at least 0.8, we can use Appendix Table FF. Assume $\sigma^2 = 545$, an estimate from the previous experiment. Suppose the following sizes of differences are considered practically important:

$$d_1 = \mu_1 - \mu = -30$$
$$d_2 = \mu_2 - \mu = +20$$
$$d_3 = \mu_3 - \mu = +10$$

(Obviously, many different values for the d's will yield the same value for Σd^2 and therefore the same ϕ^2. The d's chosen are what are thought to be meaningful for a particular experimental situation. Here we have postulated only certain sizes of differences—in some situations, the pattern of the differences might be meaningful. For example, if the groups were increasing levels of a quantitative variable such as temperature, a meaningful pattern for the d's might be a constant change in mean from one level to the next higher one. Remember that the d_i must sum to zero.)

In the example $\Sigma d_i = 1,400$.

Calculate

$$\phi^2 = \frac{n \sum\limits_{i=1}^{k} d_i^{\,2}}{k\sigma^2}$$

$$\phi^2 = \frac{n(1,400)}{3(545)} = \frac{1,400\,n}{1,635} = 0.86\,n$$

$$DF_1 = k - 1 = 3 - 1 = 2$$

$$DF_2 = k(n - 1) = 3n - 3$$

Using Appendix II, Table FF, we must find two values of n, one which gives ϕ^2 larger than required and one smaller.

n	$DF_2 = 3n - 3$	Tabled ϕ^2	Desired $\phi^2 = 0.86n$
7	18	6.05	6.02
8	21	5.83	6.88

The "tabled ϕ^2" for $n = 8$ was obtained using linear interpolation. The solution lies between $n = 7$ and $n = 8$, and we take the larger n. Eight observations per group will give us an 80% chance of detecting the postulated differences when we do an F-test at the $\alpha = 0.01$ level.

This method may be used for multifactor experiments provided the proper values for DF_1 and DF_2 are used.   It is used when the purpose of the experiment is to compare group averages, and it works for any number of groups, provided the number of observations per group is large enough.   In this case and in the case described below, equal numbers of observations should be taken in each group.

For another kind of experiment where the purpose is to compare the between-group variability with the within-group variability (see discussion of Model II, Random Effects Model, under One-way Analysis of Variance—Models), there is a *minimum* number of groups required to achieve desired discrimination in terms of the relative variability.   For example, see Table 27-26, where α and β are the risks of the two kinds of error (see Section 22). δ_0 is an "acceptably small" value of the ratio σ_b/σ_w (i.e., a ratio of between-group variability to within-group variability not large enough to be practically important). δ_1 is an "unacceptably large" value for the ratio σ_b/σ_w (large enough that we want to achieve a significant result).

Useful discussions on determining the number of observations are also given in Refs. 9 and 28.

TABLE 27-26   Minimum Number of Groups—Random Effects Model*

$\alpha = \beta = 0.05$		$\alpha = \beta = 0.01$	
δ_1/δ_0	Minimum number of groups	δ_1/δ_0	Minimum number of groups
1.5	35	1.5	68
2	14	2	25
2.5	9	2.5	16
3	7	3	12

* Reprinted with permission from Ref. 2.

GENERAL REMARKS ON ANALYSIS OF DATA

Assumptions for Analysis of Data   The usual analysis assumes that the observations are normally distributed, and that the variability of results within a treatment is the same for every treatment.   Where there is serious doubt about normality, consider the use of a transformation (see Section 22).   For the simple design called "Completely Randomized," a special analysis using ranks and not requiring the assumption of normality has been given.

The assumption of equal variability should be investigated.   If there are more than a few treatments, plot each treatment mean vs. a measure of the variability within a treatment (i.e., range or standard deviation).   If the plot shows that the variability increases as the mean increases, for example, consider using a transformation on the data (see Section 22, under Transformation of Data) and performing an analysis on the transformed data.   In addition to a rough graphical check of this sort, there are tests of homogeneity of a set of variance estimates.   See Refs. 7 and 8.   These tests are, unfortunately, more sensitive to departures from normality than are the tests which will be used to compare the means of treatments.   The experimenter's own feelings about whether the variability should be the same in different groups should not be ignored.

Remarks on Computing   The methods of analysis given here, and those found in most textbooks, are methods which are intended for hand or desk calculators, but there has been much activity in the development of packaged computer programs to do various kinds of analysis of variance computations.   For information on packaged programs, see Section 20.   Two general cautions are in order: (1) the computing methods given in this section should not be literally translated into a computer program—they would be very inefficient, and (2) the user of packaged statistical programs should be as critical a consumer of programs as he is of everything else.

Missing Values   If there are missing values in the data from a designed experiment (observations lost, not completed, etc.) consult Ref. 9 or 10 for the particular kind of design. Rules are given for supplying one or a few missing values so that the analysis can be done in the regular way.

REVIEWS OF RECENT DEVELOPMENTS IN DESIGN OF EXPERIMENTS

An article by Herzberg and Cox (Ref. 61) reviews developments since 1957 and includes a bibliography of about 800 items covering this period.

Ostle (Ref. 62) gives a review of articles on the statistical design of experiments which have appeared in *Industrial Quality Control* and *Technometrics*. This review is more concerned with actual applications. For applications in chemistry, the periodic reviews on "Statistics in Chemistry" in *Analytical Chemistry* will be useful.

REFERENCES

1. Wilson, E. Bright, Jr., "An Introduction to Scientific Research," McGraw-Hill Book Company, New York, 1952.
2. Johnson, Norman L., and Fred C. Leone, "Statistics and Experimental Design in Engineering and the Physical Sciences," vol. II, John Wiley & Sons, Inc., New York, 1964.
3. Mendenhall, William, "Introduction to Linear Models and the Design and Analysis of Experiments," Wadsworth Publishing Company, Inc., Belmont, Calif., 1968.
4. Kurtz, T. E., B. F. Link, J. W. Tukey, and D. L. Wallace, Short-cut Multiple Comparisons for Balanced Single and Double Classifications, *Technometrics*, vol. 7, No. 2, pp. 95–165, 1965.
5. Hogben, David, Sally T. Peavy, and Ruth N. Varner, "OMNITAB II User's Reference Manual," National Bureau of Standards *Technical Note* 552, Government Printing Office, Washington, D.C. 20402, 1971.
6. Hicks, Charles R., "Fundamental Concepts in the Design of Experiments," Holt, Rinehart and Winston, Inc., New York, 1964.
7. Snedecor, George W., and William G. Cochran, "Statistical Methods," 6th ed., The Iowa State University Press, Ames, Iowa, 1967.
8. Duncan, Acheson J., "Quality Control and Industrial Statistics," 3d ed., Richard D. Irwin, Inc., Homewood, Ill., 1965.
9. Cochran, William G., and Gertrude M. Cox, "Experimental Designs," 2d ed., John Wiley & Sons, Inc., New York, 1957.
10. Davies, Owen L. (ed.), "The Design and Analysis of Industrial Experiments," Hafner Publishing Company, Inc., New York, 1954.
11. Daniel, Cuthbert, Use of Half-normal Plots in Interpreting Factorial Experiments, *Technometrics*, vol. 1, No. 4, pp. 311–341, 1959.
12. Hunter, J. S., The Inverse Yates Algorithm, *Technometrics*, vol. 8, No. 1, pp. 177–183, 1966.
13. Natrella, Mary G., "Experimental Statistics," National Bureau of Standards Handbook 91, Government Printing Office, Washington, D.C. 20402, 1966.
14. Statistical Engineering Laboratory, "Fractional Factorial Experiment Designs for Factors at Two Levels," National Bureau of Standards Applied Mathematics Series No. 48, PB176119, National Technical Information Service (NTIS), Department of Commerce, Springfield, Va. 22151, 1957.
15. Connor, W. S., and Marvin Zelen, "Fractional Factorial Experiment Designs for Factors at Three Levels," National Bureau of Standards Applied Mathematics Series 54, Government Printing Office, Washington, D.C. 20402, 1959.
16. Connor, W. S., and Shirley Young, "Fractional Factorial Experiment Designs for Experiments with Factors at Two and Three Levels," National Bureau of Standards Applied Mathematics Series 58, Government Printing Office, Washington, D.C. 20402, 1961.

17. Draper, Norman R., and David N. Stoneman, Estimating Missing Values in Unreplicated Two-level Factorial and Fractional Factorial Designs, *Biometrics,* vol. 20, No. 3, pp. 443–458, 1964.
18. Addelman, Sidney, Irregular Fractions of the 2^n Factorial Experiments, *Technometrics,* vol. 3, No. 4, pp. 479–496, 1961.
19. Addelman, Sidney, Techniques for Constructing Fractional Replicate Plans, *Journal of the American Statistical Association,* vol. 58, No. 301, pp. 45–71, 1963.
20. Addelman, Sidney, Symmetrical and Asymmetrical Fractional Factorial Plans, *Technometrics,* vol. 4, No. 1, pp. 47–58, 1962.
21. Patel, M. S., Partially Duplicated Fractional Factorial Designs, *Technometrics,* vol. 5, No. 1, pp. 71–83, 1963.
22. Daniel, Cuthbert, Sequences of Fractional Replicates in the 2^{p-q} Series, *Journal of the American Statistical Association,* vol. 57, No. 298, pp. 403–429, 1962.
23. Daniel, Cuthbert, Parallel Fractional Replicates, *Technometrics,* vol. 2, No. 2, pp. 263–268, 1960.
24. John, Peter W. M., Augmenting 2^{n-1} Designs, *Technometrics,* vol. 8, No. 3, pp. 469–480, 1966.
25. Addelman, Sidney, Sequences of Two-level Fractional Factorial Plans, *Technometrics,* vol. 11, No. 3, pp. 477–509, 1969.
26. Duckworth, W. E., Statistical Method in Metallurgical Development, *The Statistician,* vol. 15, pp. 7–30, 1965.
27. Chew, Victor (ed.), "Experimental Designs in Industry," John Wiley & Sons, Inc., New York, 1958.
28. Cox, D. R., "Planning of Experiments," John Wiley & Sons, Inc., New York, 1958.
29. Mandel, John, "Statistical Analysis of Experimental Data," John Wiley & Sons, Inc., New York, 1964.
30. Youden, W. J., "Statistics for Chemists," John Wiley & Sons, Inc., New York, 1951.
31. Cooper, B. E., The Extension of Yates 2^n Algorithm to Any Complete Factorial Experiment, *Technometrics,* vol. 10, No. 3, pp. 575–577, 1968.
32. Clatworthy, W. H., "Tables of Two-Associate-Class Partially Balanced Designs," National Bureau of Standards Applied Mathematics Series 63, Government Printing Office, Washington, D.C. 20402, 1973.
33. Mandel, John, Chain Block Designs with Two-way Elimination of Heterogeneity, *Biometrics,* vol. 10, No. 2, pp. 251–272, 1954.
34. Fisher, R. A., and F. Yates, "Statistical Tables for Biological, Agricultural and Medical Research Workers," 6th ed., Stechert-Hafner, Inc., New York, 1964.
35. Davies, O. L., "Statistical Methods in Research and Production," 3d ed., Hafner Publishing Company, Inc., New York, 1967.
36. Lenter, M. M., Listing Expected Mean Square Components, *Biometrics,* vol. 21, No. 2, pp. 459–466, 1965.
37. Bainbridge, T. R., Staggered, Nested Designs for Estimating Variance Components, *Industrial Quality Control,* vol. 22, No. 1, pp. 12–20, 1965.
38. Scheffé, Henry, Experiments with Mixtures, *Journal of the Royal Statistical Society,* Series B, vol. 20, pp. 344–360, 1958; Corr. vol. 21, p. 238, 1959.
39. Gorman, J. W., and J. E. Hinman, Simplex Lattice Designs for Multicomponent Systems, *Technometrics,* vol. 4, No. 4, pp. 463–487, 1962.
40. Kurotori, I. S., Experiments with Mixtures Having Lower Bounds, *Industrial Quality Control,* vol. 22, No. 11, pp. 592–596, 1966.
41. Kenworthy, O. O., Factorial Experiments with Mixtures Using Ratios, *Industrial Quality Control,* vol. 19, No. 12, pp. 24–26, 1963.
42. McLean, R. A., and V. L. Anderson, Extreme Vertices Design of Mixture Experiments. *Technometrics,* vol. 8, No. 3, pp. 447–456, 1966.
43. Scheffé, Henry, The Simplex Centroid Design for Experiments with Mixtures, *Journal of the Royal Statistical Society,* Series B, vol. 25, No. 2, pp. 235–251 (discussion pp. 251–263), 1963.
44. Draper, Norman R., and Willard Lawrence, Mixture Designs for Three Factors, *Journal of the Royal Statistical Society,* Series B, vol. 27, No. 3, pp. 450–465, 1965.

45. Draper, N. R., and W. E. Lawrence, Mixture Designs for Four Factors, *Journal of the Royal Statistical Society*, Series B, vol. 27, No. 3, pp. 473–478, 1965.
46. Thompson, William O., and Raymond H. Myers, Response Surface Designs for Mixture Problems, *Technometrics*, vol. 10, No. 4, pp. 739–756, 1968.
47. Lambrakis, D. P., An Alternative to the Simplex-lattice Design for Experiments with Mixtures, *Journal of the Royal Statistical Society*, Series B, vol. 31, No. 2, pp. 234–245, 1969.
48. Connor, W. S., Group Screening Designs, *Industrial and Engineering Chemistry*, vol. 53, pp. 69A–70A, 1961.
49. Watson, G. S., A Study of the Group Screening Method, *Technometrics*, vol. 3, No. 3, pp. 371–388, 1961.
50. Patel, M. S., Group Screening with More than Two Stages, *Technometrics*, vol. 4, No. 2, pp. 209–217, 1962.
51. Daniel, Cuthbert, Factor Screening in Process Development, *Industrial and Engineering Chemistry*, vol. 55, pp. 45–48, 1963.
52. Carr, Jesse M., and E. A. McCracken, Statistical Program Planning for Process Development, *Chemical Engineering Progress*, vol. 56, No. 11, pp. 56–61, 1960.
53. Wernimont, Grant, Design and Interpretation of Interlaboratory Studies of Test Methods, *Analytical Chemistry*, vol. 23, p. 1572, 1951.
54. Youden, W. J., "Statistical Techniques for Collaborative Tests," Association of Official Analytical Chemists, Inc., Washington, D.C., 1967.
55. "ASTM Manual for Conducting an Interlaboratory Study of a Test Method," ASTM Special Publication 335, American Society for Testing and Materials, Philadelphia, Pa., 1963.
56. Ku, Harry H. (ed.), "Precision Measurement and Calibration—Statistical Concepts and Procedures," National Bureau of Standards Special Publication 300, volume 1, Government Printing Office, Washington, D.C., 20402, 1969.
57. Youden, W. J., Ranking Laboratories by Round-robin Tests, *Materials Research and Standards*, vol. 3, No. 1, pp. 9–13, 1963.
58. Youden, W. J., Graphical Diagnosis of Interlaboratory Tests, *Industrial Quality Control*, vol. 15, No. 11, pp. 1–5, 1959.
59. Dixon, Wilfred J., and Frank J. Massey, Jr., "Introduction to Statistical Analysis," 3d ed., McGraw-Hill Book Company, New York, 1969.
60. Owen, D. B., "Handbook of Statistical Tables," Addison-Wesley Publishing Company, Inc., Reading, Mass., 1962.
61. Herzberg, Agnes M., and D. R. Cox, Recent Work on the Design of Experiments: A Bibliography and a Review, *Journal of the Royal Statistical Society*, Series A, vol. 132, Pt. 1, pp. 29–67, 1969.
62. Ostle, Bernard, Industry Use of Statistical Test Design, *Industrial Quality Control*, vol. 24, No. 1, pp. 24–33, 1967.

Evolutionary Operation

E. HARVEY BARNETT

Corning Glass Works, Corning, New York

EVOLUTIONARY OPERATION

A plant should produce, in addition to its product, information for its own improvement. This is the heart of the Box system for increased profit called Evolutionary Operation (EVOP), Ref. 1.

EVOP involves the introduction of small, planned, changes in operating conditions. Results are analyzed, and when a direction for improvement has been established, new process conditions are adopted. Since small changes continue to be used in routine operation, further improvements can be detected. When the rate of finding improvements slows down, the small changes may be applied to a different selection of operating variables to obtain more improvement in results.

This Section establishes the philosophy of EVOP in greater detail and shows how to start and run it.

INTRODUCTION

The "process industries" are so-named because their production is dependent on a "process"—a procedure for effecting a change in (usually) the chemical composition of raw material. Besides the chemical industry itself, such industries as paper, paint, plastics, glass, and steel are included. Many of their processes are based on complex technology, and the optimum adjustment of operating conditions is not obvious or even readily determined. It is common to find that their variables interact. For example, if the flow is increased, the temperature must be raised to prevent loss of yield.

Laboratory and pilot plant information on optima is helpful in optimizing a plant but is not likely to give the exact plant optimum. This is called "scale-up uncertainty" and occurs because certain factors have not been quantified as they change with equipment size. These include effect of agitation on mass transfer, film coefficients, degree of mixing, efficiency of distillation stages, and so on.

In short, a full-scale plant must be optimized by work on the same plant.

There are two effective ways to do this: designed experiments and Evolutionary Operation (EVOP), Ref. 2. To say "designed experiments" implies a limited number of runs and changes in operating conditions large enough to be recognized. This often requires special precautions, a test task-force, and some risk of off-specification product. EVOP uses small changes that can hardly be noticed, but these changes are repeated several times. Progress is not as fast, *but no additional manpower* is used and changes in product quality and quantity are minute.

The cost of running EVOP is so low that most plants should continue to run it indefinitely. This is done to obtain data on the location of the optimum as gradual changes in raw material, catalyst activity, residue buildup, and so on, occur over a period of time.

While EVOP was originated by G. E. P. Box with reference to process industries, it has spread widely and can be found in any industry that has an operation for which the best adjustments are not immediately obvious. Even assembly plants may have a pickling, anodizing, or electroplating department, for example, which can be improved by EVOP. For an example in the electronic components industry, see Section 38, under Quality Improvement, particularly Figure 38-4.

The savings obtained through EVOP are large but generally considered proprietary in the highly competitive chemical industry. The author was informed[1] that one EVOP increased a plant capacity by 67% and increased profit in one year by $1 million. He has reason to believe that such records are not rare.

As "the mills of God grind slowly, yet they grind exceeding small," so too is EVOP slow but capable of finding small improvements. It therefore makes slow progress and is not appropriate when a quick improvement is required. At the same time, the steps needed for fast action are usually risky, and the relative merits of these alternative approaches must be weighed.

If the consequences of bad settings of variables, moves in the wrong direction, and so on, are not very harmful, then large changes should be made by a selected experimental design such as a factorial. These cases are not common in plants.

BACKGROUND

The original paper by Box (Ref. 1) included all the essential features of EVOP; the many papers on the subject in recent literature contain only minor modifications and case histories. A thorough review was published in 1965 (Ref. 3)—see particularly Refs. 4, 5, 6, and 7 at the end of this Section. Since 1965, the literature has been concerned mostly with more complex methods (e.g., Ref. 8). A theoretical text which covers many methods is given in Ref. 9. Neophyte and expert alike will benefit from reading the Box and Draper (Ref. 10) text on the subject. It contains all the statistical background on which EVOP is founded, many variations of the basic designs which may be used with worked examples, and extensive discussions of strategy and philosophy.

A typical definition of "optimum" is:

Optimum conditions are those which make specification product at maximum long-term profit.

Data are usually obtained on production rate and yield or efficiency. The optimum is determined by calculation for various rates of sales. The plant cannot be at

---

[1] Private communication.

optimum if it outproduces the sales department for very long, for inventory costs will overwhelm any production savings.   There may also be the capability of making different grades of product, or the proportions of by-products may vary.

With increased and critical emphasis on pollution, data on by-product production have become very important. A by-product may have a large negative value in treating or disposal cost, or in community relations. For chemical reactions an increase in yield of the main product is accompanied by a decrease in a by-product, or there is less unreacted raw material. It is therefore doubly important to quantify these relations. These dual benefits can be put in the optimization calculation.

Another benefit sometimes obtained from EVOP is to increase the capacity rating of the plant, thus delaying or eliminating the necessity for capital expansion.

RESPONSE SURFACE[2]

A response surface is the mathematical or graphical representation of the connection between important independent variables and a dependent variable.[3] Most pro-

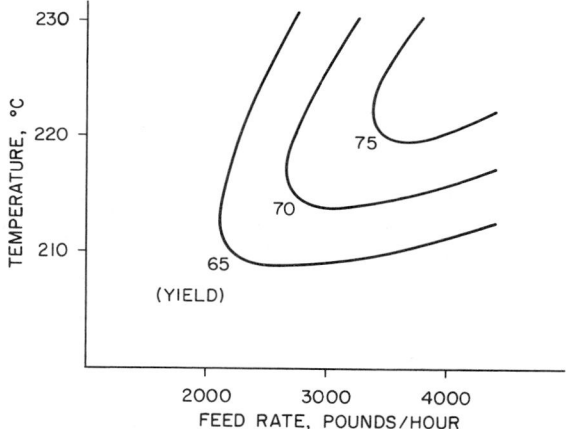

Fig. 27A-1 Typical response surface: yield as a function of feed rate and temperature for a catalytic reactor.

cesses have several dependent variables such as yield, assay of the product, and pounds per hour of a by-product. These responses are usually smooth and may be graduated approximately by a simple figure such as a family of circles or of parabolas. We are ordinarily working on processes that have unknown response surfaces —if they were known, the work would not be necessary.

A response surface for a process might look like the one in Figure 27A-1, which shows the yield of a catalytic oxidation as a function of temperature and feed rate of hydrocarbon.[4] If this information were known, the pounds per hour of product could be calculated and an optimum could be selected for any desired production

---

[2] See Section 28, Response Surface Methodology.
[3] An independent variable is a factor that is, or conceivably could be, controlled. Examples are flow rate and temperature. The value of a dependent variable is the result of the settings of one or more independent variables.
[4] See also Section 28, Fig. 28-1, for another lucid example.

rate.   The response surface is initially unknown, but improvement can be made if we only find out which way is up.   After several moves have been made (see below), multiple regression can be used to approximate the response contours (see Section 26, under Multiple Regression).

EVOP TECHNIQUE

The problem, then, is to increase profit in an operating plant with minimum work and risk and without upsetting the plant.   These are the steps:

1. Survey company reports and open literature on the process.   Study cost, yield, and production records.

2. Study this section on EVOP and preferably the definitive text (Ref. 10).

3. Obtain agreement and support from production management.   Hold training sessions.

4. Select two or three independent variables which are likely to influence profit (see definition of optimum).

5. Change these variables in small steps according to a plan.

6. After the second repetition of the plan (Cycle 2) and each succeeding cycle, calculate the effects.

7. When one or more of the effects is significant, change the midpoints of the variables and perhaps their ranges.

8. After eight cycles, if no variable has been shown to be effective, change the ranges or select new variables (Ref. 11).

9. Continue moving the midpoint of the EVOP plan and adjust the ranges as necessary.

10. When a maximum has been obtained, or the rate of gain is too slow, drop the current variables from the plan and run a new plan with different variables.

The following topics explain these steps in detail.

Literature Search   EVOP can be done without any reference to the physics, chemistry, or kinetics of the system.   It is done essentially this way for training purposes. See Training for EVOP, below.

When the problem is real, it is much better to learn all the facts that are already available.   Then there will be no need to search for variables that are already known to be important.   Sources include the process instructions, company reports, manufacturers' literature, patents, textbooks, and encyclopedias of technology.   Do not neglect people.   Company personnel, consultants, and operators can all contribute. Search for information on

1. Important independent variables

2. Test methods for intermediate and final results

3. Recommended procedures

4. Records of good and bad results and their causes

5. Long-term history of results; plant production rate and yield by week or month, and similar data; effect of past changes in equipment and conditions

When information is contradictory, this is a candidate idea for an EVOP; the conflict can be resolved by data.

Always consider the physical and chemical principles that apply.   When two chemicals react, important independent variables are likely to be concentration of reactants, temperature, catalyst concentration, pressure (if a gas is present), and space velocity or time.

The EVOP Design   EVOP uses planned runs that are repeated over and over (replicated).   A sound plan in wide use is the two-level complete factorial, discussed in detail in Section 27.   There are real and psychological reasons to maintain observations on the result of known conditions, called a "reference point."   For simplicity in the present discussion, let this point be the center of the square.

Example   This example shows coded data from an actual EVOP in the author's experience (Ref. 12).   This was a batch organic reaction, and after the steps above were followed, the two variables and their ranges were selected as shown in Figure 27A-2. Y is a coded yield in pounds per batch and should be maximized.   By this diagram we mean that the reference run (batch) was made at 130 ° C for 3½ hours.   The next batch was made at 120 ° C for 3 hours, and so on.   The first *cycle* contains five runs, one at each of the conditions.   Samples were taken from each batch and analyses were obtained.

If the process were continuous, it would be allowed to stabilize after each change of conditions, perhaps by waiting for three residence times[5] or preferably by determining the actual time to equilibrium by a test.

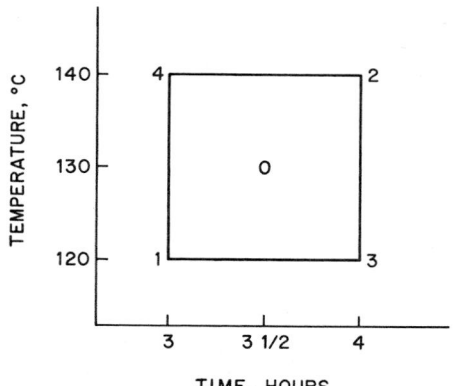

TIME, HOURS

Fig. 27A-2   An EVOP plan.   Numbers are in run order.   0 is the reference run.

Warning: It is not unusual to have difficulty in obtaining a representative sample. Procedures and tests are discussed in Sections 22, 24, and 25A.

Effects could be calculated at the end of Cycle 1, but since the estimate of error depends solely on the before-EVOP estimate, it is better to proceed with Cycle 2. After the latter is completed, calculate the effects and their confidence intervals on a form (Ref. 12) such as Figure 27A-3, which shows this example.   A form like this helps reduce the work and minimizes mistakes.   Instructions should be printed on the reverse side (see Figure 27A-4).

This calculation is different from the one that does the same job in Section 27. Here, the error term that puts the magnitude of effects into perspective is obtained from the range by use of factor K first derived by Box and Hunter (Ref. 13).   The uncertainty in estimating the effects is stated as a confidence interval and the Change-in-mean effect (CIM) is calculated by comparing the results at the outer four corners with the result in the center.   The use of this last information is discussed below.

A *phase* is defined as all the cycles that use the same settings of the same variables.   The phase mean shows the general level of results and can be used to compare different phases.

The left part of the form is used to record data and calculate effects.   It also has the scaled diagram of the phase.   The right third calculates the error limits of effects and corner averages.   Following Box and Draper, the error limits are called "2 S.E."

---

[5] Residence time is volume of the vessel divided by the flow rate in appropriate units.

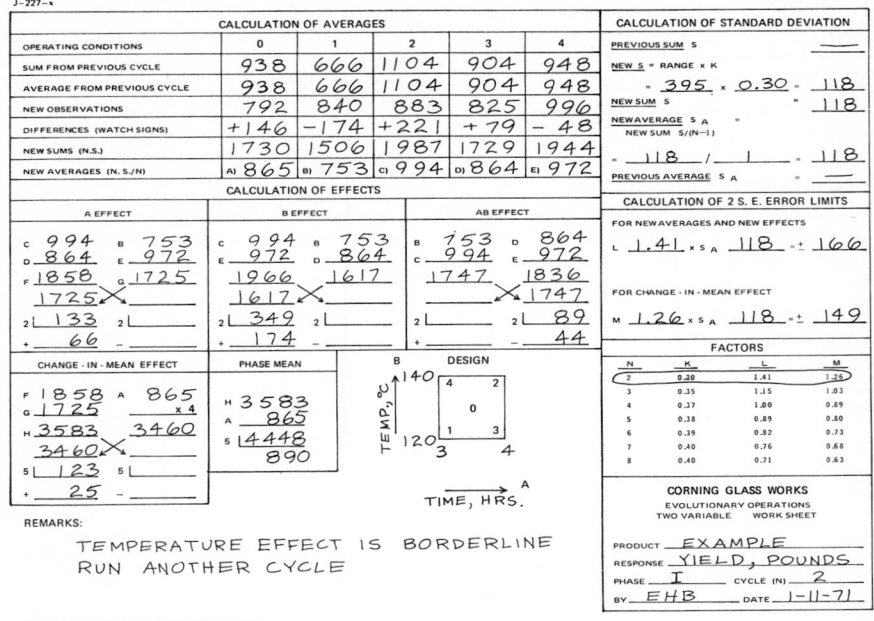

Fig. 27A-3   Calculation form at the end of Cycle 2 (modified from Ref. 12).

Note: The numerical illustrations apply to the data of Fig. 27A-3.

Differences   —Subtract new observations from old averages.   Note the algebraic sign of the difference. $(938 - 792 = 146)$

New Sums   —Add the new observations to the old sums. $(938 + 792 = 1,730)$

New Averages—Divide the new sums by N, the number of the cycle. $(1,730/2 = 865)$

Calculation of Effects   —(For example, the A effect)
Write the new averages for operating conditions 2 and 3 opposite (C) and (D). Add these two to get the number in space (F). Carry out corresponding operations to get the number for space (G).
The next operation is subtraction. If (F) is larger than (G), recopy (G) under (F) and subtract (G) from (F). If (G) is larger than (F), recopy (F) under (G) and subtract (F) from (G). In either case divide by 2 and the sign of quotient is shown on the form. (The A effect is +66.)

Change-in-mean effect —Copy (F) and (G) as shown and add these two. (A) is multiplied by 4. The next operation is subtraction as above. Divide by 5. (The Change-in-mean effect is +25.)

Phase Mean   —Copy (H) and (A) from Change-in-mean box, add them, and divide by 5. (The phase mean is 890.)

Calculation of Standard Deviation   —Range. The range is the algebraic difference between the most positive and most negative differences. The range is always positive. (The range of +146, −174, +221, +79, and −48 is 395.) The standard deviation is then equal to the range times K.

Constants   —Read K, L, and M factors from the table.

Fig. 27A-4   Instructions for EVOP form.

for "two standard errors." This indicates that they cover approximately the usual 95% confidence region. The confidence for a few cycles is less than 95%. Caution should be exercised in claiming significance after two or three cycles unless a previous estimate of *s*, the standard deviation of a run, is sound and has been averaged with current data.[6] Barnett's paper increased factors *L* and *M* by the ratio (Student's *t*)/2 as partial correction for this uncertainty, and the previously estimated *s* was not used. There is some basis for not putting too much faith in the previously estimated *s* because the "halo effect" is not uncommon. This occurs when the process variability during EVOP is less because of increased attention by operators and supervisors, and perhaps because of improved sampling and analysis instituted during the preparatory work.

For the present example at the end of Cycle 2, the *A* effect (time) is estimated as 66 ± 166; it lies somewhere between -100 and $+232$. The true value of this effect could be negative, positive, or nil. The *B* (temperature) effect, however, is estimated to be 174 ± 166, or in the range $+8$ to 340. Technically, it is likely to be a positive real effect. The interaction *AB* is small, and so is the change in mean. Since the confidence region for *B* is so close to zero and following the advice above to be cautious at Cycle 2, another cycle is run. Its results are shown in Figure 27A-5.

After Cycle 3, the *B* effect (temperature) was declared significant, since its likely values fall in the range of 169 ± 92, or $+77$ to $+261$. Thus it does not appear that data from more cycles would change the conclusion that temperature should be increased to increase *Y*.

When significance is found for one independent variable but not for the other, *move* the plan in the desirable direction for the first variable and increase the range

J-227-X

CALCULATION OF AVERAGES

OPERATING CONDITIONS	0	1	2	3	4
SUM FROM PREVIOUS CYCLE	1730	1506	1987	1729	1944
AVERAGE FROM PREVIOUS CYCLE	865	753	994	864	972
NEW OBSERVATIONS	934	853	1066	852	953
DIFFERENCES (WATCH SIGNS)	− 69	− 100	− 72	+ 12	+ 19
NEW SUMS (N.S.)	2664	2359	3053	2581	2897
NEW AVERAGES (N. S./N)	A) 888	B) 786	C) 1018	D) 860	E) 966

CALCULATION OF STANDARD DEVIATION

PREVIOUS SUM S 118
NEW S = RANGE x K = 119 x 0.35 = 42
NEW SUM S = 160
NEW AVERAGE S A = NEW SUM S/(N−1) = 160 / 2 = 80
PREVIOUS AVERAGE S A = 118

CALCULATION OF EFFECTS

A EFFECT: C 1018, D 860, F 1878; B 786, E 966, G 1752; 1878 − 1752; 2 | 126; + 63

B EFFECT: C 1018, E 966, 1984; B 786, D 860, 1646; 1984 − 1646; 2 | 338; + 169

AB EFFECT: B 786, C 1018, 1804; D 860, E 966, 1826; 1826 − 1804; 2 | 22; − 11

CALCULATION OF 2 S. E. ERROR LIMITS

FOR NEW AVERAGES AND NEW EFFECTS: L 1.15 x S A 80 = ± 92

FOR CHANGE - IN - MEAN EFFECT: M 1.03 x S A 80 = ± 82

CHANGE - IN - MEAN EFFECT: F 1878, G 1752, H 3630; A 888 x 4 = 3552; 3630 − 3552; 5 | 78; + 16

PHASE MEAN: H 3630, A 888, 5 | 4518, 904

DESIGN: B (TEMP, °C) 140: 4, 2; 0; 120: 1, 3; A (TIME, HRS.) 3, 4

FACTORS

N	K	L	M
2	0.30	1.41	1.26
3	0.35	1.15	1.03
4	0.37	1.00	0.89
5	0.38	0.89	0.80
6	0.39	0.82	0.73
7	0.40	0.76	0.68
8	0.40	0.71	0.63

CORNING GLASS WORKS
EVOLUTIONARY OPERATIONS
TWO VARIABLE WORK SHEET

PRODUCT EXAMPLE
RESPONSE YIELD, POUNDS
PHASE I CYCLE (N) 3
BY EHB DATE 1-12-71

REMARKS:
TEMPERATURE EFFECT IS + 77 → + 261
INCREASE TEMPERATURE & START PHASE II

MANUFACTURING AND ENGINEERING DIVISION

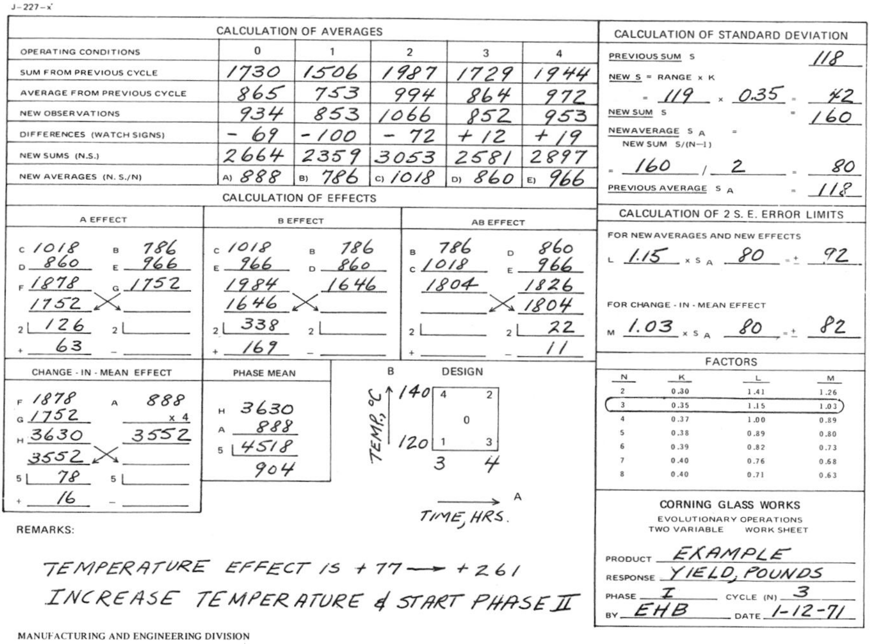

Fig. 27A-5 Calculation form after Cycle 3.

[6] Put it in the slot for "Previous sum *s*" on the form for Cycle $N = 2$ and use 2 as the divisor.

for the second (nonsignificant) one, as shown in the lower right-hand drawing of Figure 27A-6. When significance is found for both variables, move the center of the plan in two directions, and do so in proportion to the size of the effects. This is the direction of steepest ascent (see Section 28, under Determine Direction of Steepest Ascent). Whenever the plan is changed, a new *phase* is started. During the second and later phases, considerable confidence can be attached to the previous estimate of standard deviation, since this was obtained under the current operating method.

Moves   To be conservative, as EVOP should be, moves are contiguous; i.e., one or more of the points in the old phase and new phase coincide. This limits the moves to those types shown in Figure 27A-6.

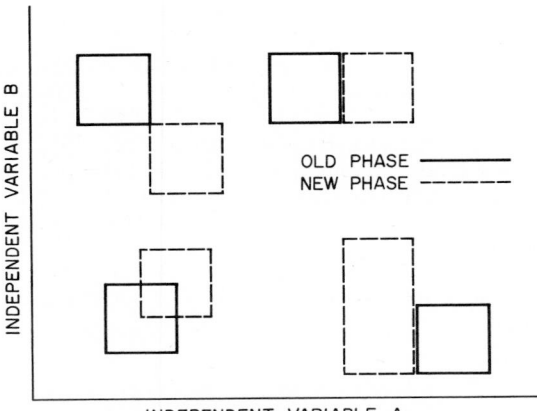

Fig. 27A-6   Possible relations of old phase and new phase.

There is nothing "magic" about drawing these plans as squares. One hour does not equal 20° C anyway.

A particularly strong signal may justify a move to a plan that does not adjoin the previous one. Remember, however, that many processes have a maximum and you may jump "over the hill."

Change-in-Mean   The Change-in-mean effect is the difference between the results at the center point and the average of the other four points. It is therefore a signal of curvature as shown in Figure 27A-7, and it shows the relation between the range of the independent variables and the curvature of the response. It is used in conjunction with the effects to indicate when a maximum (or a minimum) has been reached, and the sensitivity of the response to changes in the independent variable. In rare cases it may happen that the first phase is located symmetrically about the maximum with respect to the two independent variables chosen. In this case the variables should be nonsignificant but the Change-in-mean may be significant, or it will be after the ranges are increased sufficiently. This is expected to occur in any case after several phases have been run.

In addition, the CIM for the profit variable at each phase measures the cost of EVOP if the reference conditions are in the center of the design. If not, similar calculations must be made to compare the reference conditions with the average of the four experimental points.

Blocking   The results of a process ordinarily change slightly with time. This does not mean that the process can read a clock or a calendar, but reflects changes in sources of raw material, changes in air temperature from day to night, and so on. These may appear as cycles, and identification of their period helps to locate their causes.

Runs made close together in time are expected to be more nearly alike than those over a longer interval. Blocking is used to minimize the trouble caused by changes of this type. For the EVOP calculations shown here, a block is one cycle. Changes in average level that occur between cycles are completely canceled from the estimated effects, as can be seen by adding a constant to the five runs of Cycle 3 and recalculating the effects. (The phase mean is changed, of course.)

Multiple Dependent Variables   So far the explanation has been in terms of a single dependent variable. This is rather unrealistic except for the profit variable. Most

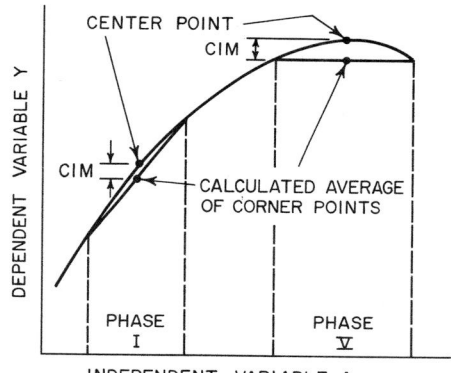

Fig. 27A-7 Cross section through a response surface. CIM indicates curvature.

processes have several dependent variables that must be measured and calculated, such as yield, production rate, percent impurity, or pounds of by-product. A calculation sheet is made for each dependent variable, and significance may be noted on one dependent sheet but not on others. In this case, it may be well to run another cycle or two to get more information on the other dependent variables before a move is made.

The most troublesome case occurs when the indicated directions for improvement of two variables (say production rate and percent impurity) do not coincide. Of course, percent impurity can be increased to the limit of the specification, but be sure to leave sufficient leeway to allow for normal plant and laboratory variation. At this point, introduce one or more new variables in the EVOP plan that may influence one of the dependent variables but not the other. Except for this, no general advice can be given. However, a great advance will have been made by quantifying the situation, even if no further improvement is possible with existing equipment. Data may give evidence of the profit available from new equipment, such as a larger purification column.

REPORTING RESULTS

Ordinarily, several managers have an interest in the current status of an EVOP. These may be the department supervisor, production superintendent, plant manager, and technical superintendent. As each cycle is calculated, it is convenient and

advisable to prepare a summary of the results for them.   This same information is
likely to be posted in the plant and is called the "Information Board."   It is shown in
Figure 27A-8 after Cycle 3 of the example.

Plant operators should participate in suggesting variables and ranges, and hence
this feedback to them is psychologically essential.

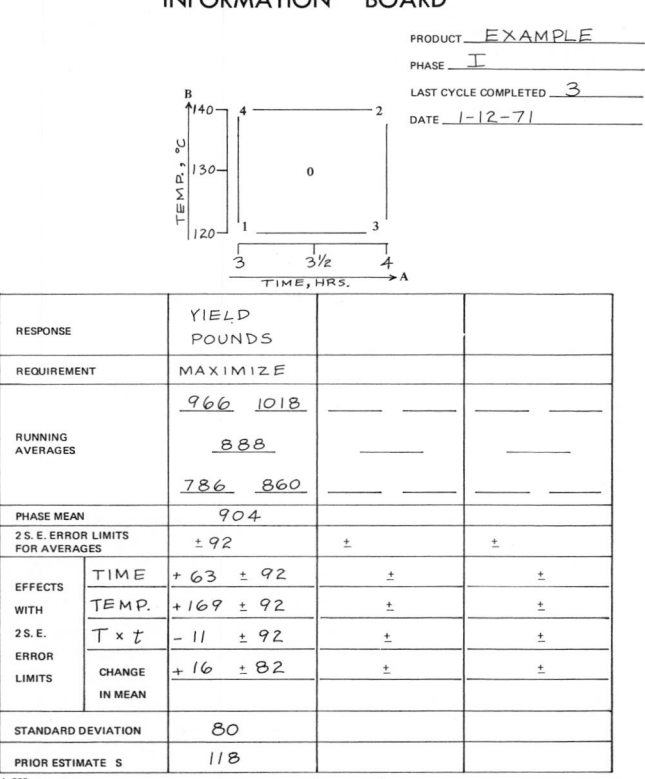

EVOLUTIONARY   OPERATION
INFORMATION   BOARD

PRODUCT EXAMPLE

PHASE I

LAST CYCLE COMPLETED 3

DATE 1-12-71

RESPONSE	YIELD POUNDS		
REQUIREMENT	MAXIMIZE		
RUNNING AVERAGES	966 1018	— —	— —
	888	—	—
	786 860	— —	— —
PHASE MEAN	904		
2 S. E. ERROR LIMITS FOR AVERAGES	± 92	±	±
EFFECTS WITH 2 S. E. ERROR LIMITS	TIME	+ 63 ± 92	±	±
	TEMP.	+169 ± 92	±	±
	T × t	− 11 ± 92	±	±
	CHANGE IN MEAN	+ 16 ± 82	±	±
STANDARD DEVIATION	80		
PRIOR ESTIMATE S	118		

J—226—x

Fig. 27A-8   Information Board after Cycle 3.   In this example, space has been provided for
three dependent variables.

THE EVOP ADVISERS

While one man can design and run an EVOP, it is still true that the greatest success
comes from the best ideas.   A small group with varied backgrounds should be
formed to generate and discuss ideas, to study the data, and to decide when and how
to move.   This group may consist of the department supervisor, technical representative, and research chemist, for example.   They meet before the EVOP starts and
on call to turn empirical feedback (use of the bare data) into scientific feedback (use
of data after comparison with scientific principles, knowledge of operating habits,
etc.) (Ref. 14).

CHOICE OF PROCESSES

Since EVOP is on trial in a plant when it is first used, and because it is better to get larger benefits soonest, a selection of the best candidate must be made if the plant has more than one process. Factors to be considered in selecting processes for study are:

1. Possible profit gain
2. Likelihood of success
3. Safety and process considerations
4. Personal and organizational factors

For the last, see Section 16, under Identifying the Projects—Priority Rating.

In the case of safety and process, remember that no process ever runs at perfectly constant conditions. Normal variations probably give enough room to do EVOP. If a pressure or temperature limit cannot be exceeded, it is usually possible to run at slightly milder conditions.

For processes that have not been subjected to designed experiments, the probability of profit gain is surely better than 0.75; some authorities say better than 0.95. Use your best estimate.

Again, for processes that have not been subjected to designed experiments and in the absence of a better figure, the estimated increase in profit can be taken as one-fifth of the difference between perfection and the current figure. If the process is a chemical reaction with less than 100% yield (not limited by equilibrium), then 100% yield is "perfection." Other cases will be more difficult, but a reasonable estimate can usually be made.

For those processes amenable to EVOP (check safety and personal factors), multiply the profit to be gained by the probability of success, and rank these numbers. Choose one from the top two or three processes.

TRAINING FOR EVOP

Plant personnel who have not dealt with designed experiments and statistical decisions tend to resist EVOP. They have what seem to them perfectly valid reasons, some of which are cataloged here to improve understanding.

1. EVOP will upset the process.
2. Off-specification material will result.
3. Plans are too complicated for operators to perform.
4. It is impossible to attribute effects to a single variable when more than one was changed at the same time.
5. Calculations are too complicated and time-consuming.
6. The process will be in better shape for EVOP when new equipment is installed next year.

These usually reduce to a common factor: fear of the unknown. The remedy for this is training, so that these people understand as much about the method as they need for their part in it. This training should include the operators, extend at least as high as the local manager, and perhaps include his superior. Time spent and course content should be tailored to the particular groups involved. Plant personnel may attend a commercial short course[7] of two or three days. These usually have topflight instructors and computer simulation.

The main effort, however, should be in the plant with some version of a simulated

---

[7] The journal *Quality Progress* frequently carries course announcements, or you may write to Executive Secretary, American Society for Quality Control, Milwaukee, Wis. 53203.

EVOP as a final examination. The simulated response surface can be contours sketched on a sheet of graph paper, it can be the internal wiring (Ref. 15) of a "black box" (process analog), or it may be an equation in a computer. In any case, random error is added to the readings for realism, and the students decide when a variable is important and make their moves as they will later on a real process (Ref. 16). Students work in groups of three or four as an EVOP committee. The instructor should answer questions on techniques and strategy fully, but he must preserve the secrecy of the true response surface. In this way, the groups demonstrate to themselves that they can find the direction of improvement on an unknown surface. Plants with inadequate staff may engage a consultant for this training and to guide them through a phase or two of the first EVOP. His fee will be well repaid in fewer cycles run in each phase, for EVOP as described in this Section is more conservative than necessary.

OTHER PLANS

Most plans are based on the two-level factorial design. It is common to choose either two or three independent variables and to add the reference condition in the center.

TABLE 27A-1   A Table of Values of $f_{k,n}$[*]

Number of cycles, n	Number of runs in the block k								
	2	3	4	5	6	7	8	9	10
2	0.63	0.42	0.34	0.30	0.28	0.26	0.25	0.24	0.23
3	0.72	0.48	0.40	0.35	0.32	0.30	0.29	0.27	0.26
4	0.77	0.51	0.42	0.37	0.34	0.32	0.30	0.29	0.28
5	0.79	0.53	0.43	0.38	0.35	0.33	0.31	0.30	0.29
6	0.81	0.54	0.44	0.39	0.36	0.34	0.32	0.31	0.30
7	0.82	0.55	0.45	0.40	0.37	0.34	0.33	0.31	0.30
8	0.83	0.55	0.45	0.40	0.37	0.35	0.33	0.31	0.30
9	0.84	0.56	0.46	0.40	0.37	0.35	0.33	0.32	0.31
10	0.84	0.56	0.46	0.41	0.37	0.35	0.33	0.32	0.31
15	0.86	0.57	0.47	0.42	0.38	0.36	0.34	0.33	0.31
20	0.86	0.58	0.47	0.42	0.38	0.36	0.34	0.33	0.32

[*]From Ref. 13, p. 94.

Designs other than the example can be handled without much difficulty, but the calculation form must be altered, and the factors K, L, and M are usually different.

The factor K, which converts range into estimated standard deviation, depends on the number of runs in a cycle and the cycle number. It is tabulated in Table 27A-1 as $f_{k,n}$.

The factors L and M are related to $t/\sqrt{n}$ of the familiar expression for the confidence interval, $E \pm tS\sqrt{n}$. Following Box and Draper, 2.0 is always used for t, n is the cycle number, E is the effect being estimated (difference between averages), and S is the standard error of *that same effect*.

The standard error of the effect is derived from the formula for calculating the effect, using a procedure for the variance of a linear combination.

In the example above,

$$\text{CIM} = \frac{1}{5}[Y_1 + Y_2 + Y_3 + Y_4 - 4(Y_0)]$$

where Y_1, Y_2, etc., are observations on a dependent variable at the design locations

1, 2, etc. The variance of CIM after one cycle is obtained by squaring all the coefficients and adding:

$$\sigma^2_{CIM} = (1/25)(\sigma^2 + \sigma^2 + \sigma^2 + \sigma^2 + 16\sigma^2) = (20/25)\sigma^2$$

where σ^2 is the variance of a single run, assumed equal for all conditions. After the third cycle, the calculation is the same but each value is the average of three observations and each σ^2 is replaced by the variance of the average of three observations, $\sigma_3{}^2 \doteq \sigma^2/3$. The formula at this stage is

$$\sigma^2_{3,CIM} = (20/25)\sigma_3{}^2$$

and in terms of the variance of an individual run it is

$$\sigma^2_{3,CIM} = (20/25)\frac{\sigma^2}{3} = 0.267\sigma^2$$

The standard deviation *of the effect* is

$$\sigma_3 = \sqrt{0.267s^2} = 0.517s$$

where s is the standard deviation of an individual run and is an estimate of $\sqrt{\sigma^2}$. Putting in 2 for t, the half-range of the confidence interval is 1.03, as shown on the form.

Similar calculations must be made to obtain the multiplying factors L and M for any scheme which differs from the example.

STATISTICAL ASSUMPTIONS

Certain theoretical assumptions were made in the derivation of this method. They mostly involve the central limit theorem, the normal distribution, and independent random errors.

Randomization has been sacrificed for simplicity. It is advisable to check other operations for their relation to the experimental runs. For example, suppose each cycle has 5 runs. If a tank car of raw material lasts for 10 runs, get in step with tank cars and they will be blocked out. On the other hand, if a filter coat is renewed every 5 runs and is likely to influence results, every cycle should be arranged with the runs in a different order.

Normality is required only approximately, and this will be achieved by averages after four or five cycles.

Lack of independence of errors can be illustrated by yield of a batch chemical process. Suppose a batch is not completely transferred to the measuring tank. The apparent yield is low: a negative error. This amount is added to the following batch, and its yield is high: a positive error. These errors are correlated (not independent). Try to arrange that every run has a fair chance to demonstrate its correct average value.

These assumptions are not generally troublesome; common sense and detailed knowledge of how the plant operations are carried out will usually suffice to make EVOP work as it was designed to do.

REFERENCES

1. Box, G. E. P., Evolutionary Operations; A Method for Increasing Industrial Productivity, *Applied Statistics*, vol. 6, No. 2, pp. 81–101, 1957.
2. Koehler, T. L., How Statistics Apply to Chemical Processes, *Chemical Engineering*, vol. 67, No. 25, pp. 142–152, Dec. 12, 1960.

3. Hunter, W. G., and J. R. Kittrell, Evolutionary Operation: A Review, *University of Wisconsin Department of Statistics Technical Report* 55, December 1965. The same paper is in *Technometrics*, vol. 8, No. 3, pp. 389–397, August 1966.
4. DeBusk, R. E., Evolutionary Operation at Tennessee Eastman Company, *Industrial Quality Control*, vol. 19, No. 4, pp. 15–21, 1962.
5. Koehler, T. L., Evolutionary Operation, *Chemical Engineering Progress*, vol. 55, No. 10, pp. 76–79, 1959.
6. Spendley, W., G. R. Hext, and F. R. Himsworth, Sequential Application of Simplex Designs in Optimization and Evolutionary Operation, *Technometrics*, vol. 4, pp. 441–461, 1962.
7. Bingham, R. S., EVOP for Systematic Process Improvement, *Industrial Quality Control*, vol. 20, No. 3, pp. 17–23, 1963.
8. Barneson, R. A., *et al.*, Picking Optimization Methods, *Chemical Engineering*, vol. 77, No. 16, pp. 132–142, July 27, 1970.
9. Himmelblau, David M., "Process Analysis by Statistical Methods," John Wiley & Sons, Inc., New York, 1970.
10. Box, G. E. P., and N. R. Draper, "Evolutionary Operations," John Wiley & Sons, Inc., New York, 1969.
11. Box, G. E. P., and N. R. Draper, Isn't My Process Too Variable for EVOP? *University of Wisconsin Technical Report* 106, March 1967. The same paper is in *Technometrics*, vol. 10, No. 3, pp. 439–444, August 1968. The answer to the question is "No!"
12. Barnett, E. H., Introduction to Evolutionary Operation, *Industrial and Engineering Chemistry*, vol. 52, pp. 500–503, June 1960.
13. Box, G. E. P., and J. S. Hunter, Condensed Calculations for Evolutionary Operation Programs, *Technometrics*, vol. 1, No. 1, pp. 77–95, February 1959.
14. Box, G. E. P., A Simple System of Evolutionary Operation Subject to Empirical Feedback, *Technometrics*, vol. 8, No. 1, pp. 19–26, February 1966.
15. Moder, J. J., A Teaching Aid for Regression, Correlation, Analysis of Variance, and Other Statistical Techniques, *Industrial Quality Control*, vol. 13, No. 4, pp. 16–21, October 1956.
16. Russell, E. R., and K. S. Stephens, An EVOP Teaching Game Using a Simulated Process, *Journal of Quality Technology*, vol. 2, No. 2, pp. 61–66, April 1970.

Section **28**

Response Surface Methodology

WILLIAM G. HUNTER

University of Wisconsin

TRUMAN L. KOEHLER

American Cyanamid

THE EXPERIMENTAL SITUATION

Different Objectives of Experimental Programs Experiments are performed for a wide variety of reasons. The best strategy to adopt depends on the objectives of the study. Sometimes investigations are undertaken to determine which are the most important variables on an industrial process. This problem is one of *screening* variables, and techniques that have proved of considerable value for this purpose are factorial and fractional factorial designs.[1] If the most important variables are known, the problem facing the experimenter is often the following: How do these variables affect the process? For example, how do the concentration and the time affect the yield of the chemical reaction? More specifically, the problem may be one of *optimizing* the process with respect to the important variables. For example, what are the best settings for concentration and time?

[1] See Section 27 of this Handbook.

Response Surface Methodology Response Surface Methodology (RSM) has been successfully used to optimize many different kinds of industrial units, processes, and systems. It is an experimental approach. It has been applied in research and development laboratories and sometimes on actual plant equipment itself. In the latter situation, however, Evolutionary Operation[2] is often more appropriate. Evolutionary Operation is a gentle form of RSM that is useful for both objectives of screening and optimizing.

With RSM, selected important variables of the process are varied in a carefully chosen way, measurements are made on the operating capabilities of the process, and these data are analyzed to indicate in what ways the variables should be adjusted to improve performance. These steps may be repeated as often as is required. It is not necessary to be a statistician or mathematician to use these ideas. Quality control engineers can easily learn the fundamental principles and put them to use.

In implementing RSM, a number of statistical procedures discussed in other sections of this Handbook are used.[3] The concept of RSM was first developed and described by Box and Wilson (Ref. 3) in 1951. At first RSM was used primarily as an experimental optimization technique in the chemical industry. Since then, however, it has found application in many other fields (see Hill and Hunter, Ref. 9). RSM can be usefully regarded as consisting of two stages:

1. First-order stage, in which a first-order mathematical model is contemplated, a factorial or other first-order design performed, the data fitted, the contours of the response surface drawn, and the direction of steepest ascent determined and pursued.

2. Second-order stage, in which a second-order mathematical model is contemplated, a central-composite or other second-order design performed, the data fitted, the contours drawn, a canonical analysis performed, and an optimum located.

Response surface methodology is actually more flexible than these brief definitions indicate. A skeletal outline, which shows some of the possible paths through an RSM study, is given in flow-diagram form in Figure 28-1.

Weakness of One-Variable-at-a-Time Approach A popular method of experimentation is the one-variable-at-a-time approach (see Section 27). Each variable, in turn, is varied while all the rest of the variables are held at some fixed, constant levels. One trouble with this approach is that a false optimum can be reached. Consider the following hypothetical illustration.

Example Under study is a chemical reaction in which there are two variables of interest, the concentration of one of the reactants and the time reaction. What settings for these two variables will maximize the yield? The best known settings, at the outset of the investigation, are a concentration of 25% and a time of 1 hour.

Following a one-variable-at-a-time approach, the engineer first runs a series of experiments by varying the time, while holding the concentration at 25%. The results show that a maximum yield of about 65% is obtained when the time is 1.9 hours. Holding the time fixed at this value and varying concentration, and obtaining a maximum at 25%, he reaches the conclusion that the maximum yield (65%) is achieved when the concentration is 25% and the time is 1.9 hours. This conclusion, however, is incorrect.

Response Surface The actual situation, unknown to the experimenter, is shown in Figure 28-2. Here the yield is shown as a function of both concentration and time. The solid curved lines in the figure are contour lines of constant yield. For example, there is an entire set of conditions of concentration and time that give an 80% yield.

[2] See Section 27A of this Handbook.
[3] See Section 27 for factorial designs and Section 26 for regression analysis and analysis of variance.

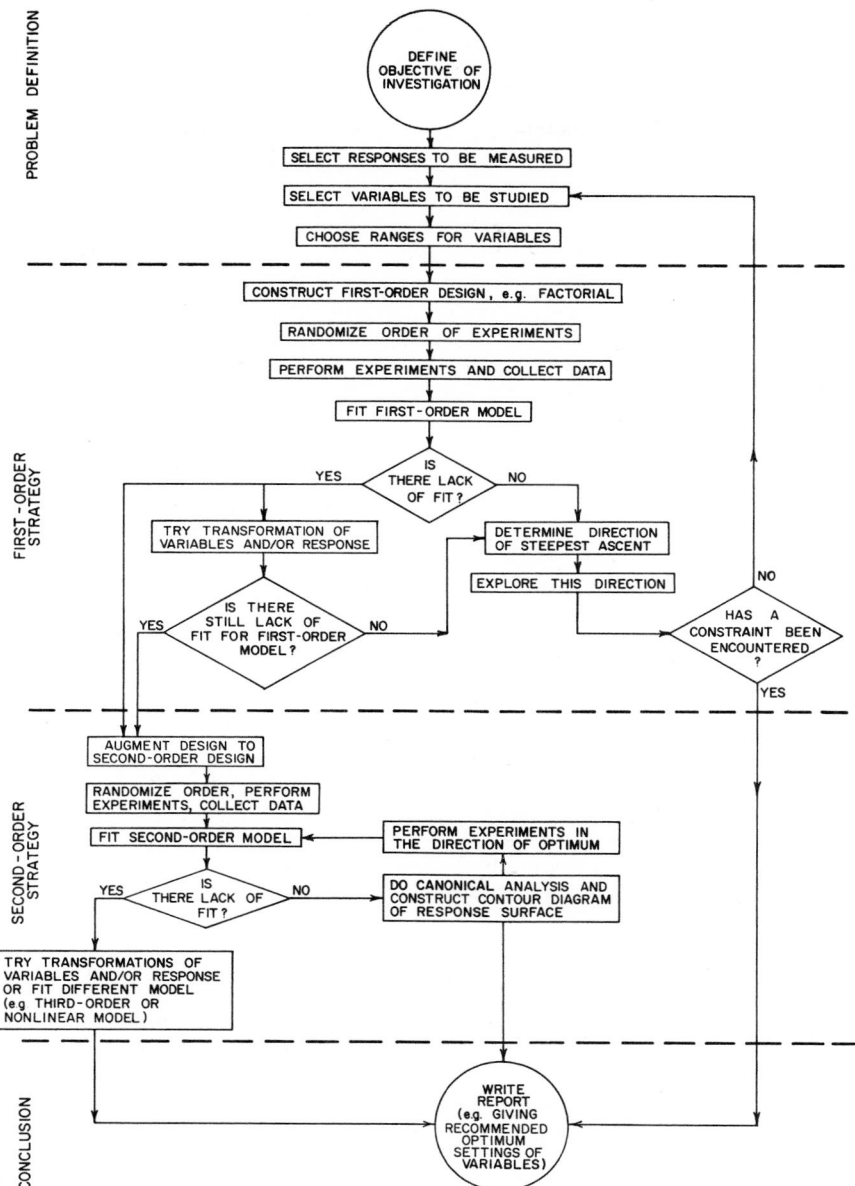

Fig. 28-1. Outline of main ideas of response methodology.

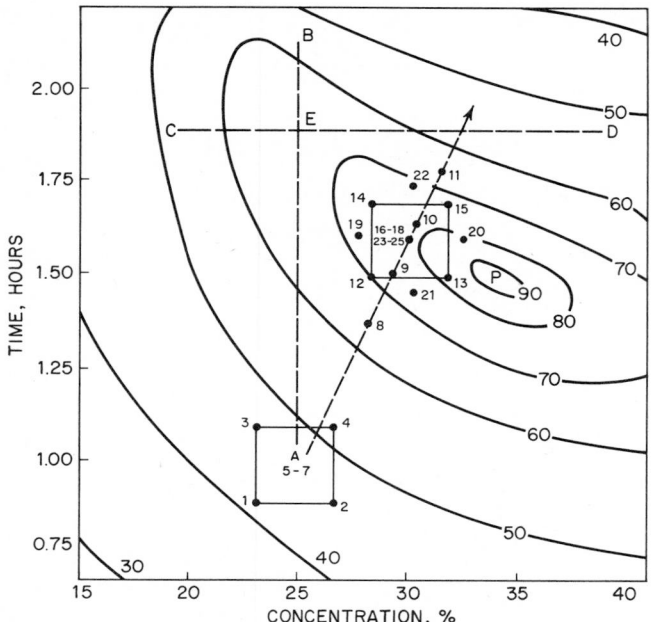

Fig. 28-2.   Response surface showing yield of a chemical reaction as a function of concentration and time.

The contour surface can be viewed as a mountain; the peak of the mountain is the point P.   The contours of 90, 80, and so forth, can be viewed as altitudes.   These numbers represent the percentage yields.

The engineer's objective was to find those settings for the concentration and time which would give the maximum yield.   Viewed geometrically, what he was trying to do was climb to the highest point on the mountain.   He has failed for a fairly simple reason.

Figuratively speaking, by varying time, he first traversed the hill going along a path from point A to point B (see Figure 28-2).   Between A and E he was walking up the mountain, but then at point E he started to go down the other side.   From point E to point B he was walking down the other side of the hill.   The traverse for varying concentration (C to E to D) is shown.

The experimenter has achieved a yield of only 65% (at E), whereas a yield in excess of 90% (at P) is possible.   This higher yield can be achieved by *simultaneously* increasing concentration and decreasing time from the experimenter's reported "optimum" values.

If the contours of the hill were circular and there were no experimental error, this one-at-a-time-procedure would have taken the engineer to the highest point on the hill.   In general, the contours of real response surfaces are not circular or spherical, and thus what is needed is a more sophisticated experimental strategy such as RSM.

BEGINNING OF PROGRAM

The RSM approach (see Figure 28-1) will now be applied to the example of maximizing the yield.

Define Objective of Investigation[4] It is of the utmost importance to define clearly the objective of the study to be undertaken. It is surprising how often in practice this step is either ignored or not given the careful attention it deserves. This often leads to difficulties later on. In the present example the objective is to maximize the yield. The objective, in general, may involve multiple criteria.

Select Variables and Ranges The next step is to select the variables to be studied together with the ranges over which they are to be studied. It is necessary to understand the technical aspects of the experimental situation for this to be done intelligently. The specific *scale* in which each variable is to be studied must also be chosen. For example, instead of varying time linearly in units of hours, the experimenter might choose the basic scale to be the logarithm of the number of hours. In the present example, the variables concentration and time are selected. Initially, it is decided to vary concentration from 23 to 27% and time from 0.9 to 1.1 hours.

FIRST-ORDER STRATEGY

Construct Design and Collect Data The 2^2 factorial design with three center points,[5] shown in Table 28-1, is constructed. The order of the seven runs is randomized, the experiments are performed, and the results shown in Table 28-1 are obtained. (Assume that, unknown to the engineer, the true relationship between X_1 and X_2 and the yield of product is given by the response surface shown in Figure 28-2.) The results are also shown in Figure 28-3.

Fit First-Order Model and Check for Lack of Fit The analysis of these results can be carried out in either one of two equivalent ways. The effects and interaction[6] of the factorial design can be calculated with their associated 95% confidence intervals, as is shown below:

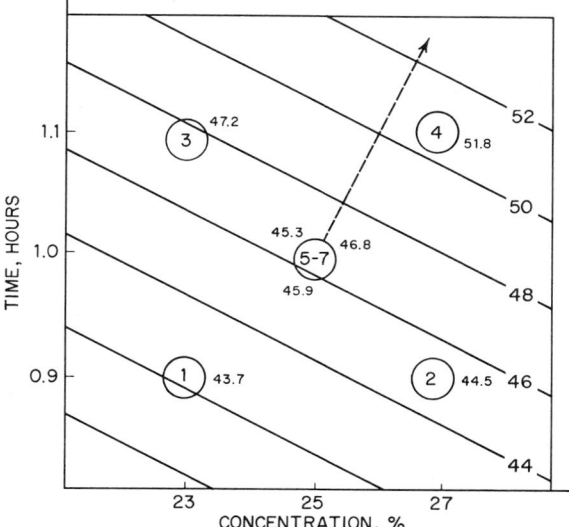

Fig. 28-3. Results of first-order design with fitted first-order (planar) response surface.

[4] See Section 27 of this Handbook.

[5] Further discussion of the number of center points and other matters on setting up the design is given in Refs. 4 and 10.

[6] See Section 27 of this Handbook.

TABLE 28-1   Results of First-order Design

Run number	$X_1 =$ concentration		$X_2 =$ time		$Y =$ yield
	%	Coded units	Hours	Coded units	%
1	23	-1	0.9	-1	43.7
2	27	$+1$	0.9	-1	44.5
3	23	-1	1.1	$+1$	47.2
4	27	$+1$	1.1	$+1$	51.8
5	25	0	1.0	0	46.8
6	25	0	1.0	0	45.9
7	25	0	1.0	0	45.3

Calculation of main effects:

Concentration: $(-Y_1 + Y_2 - Y_3 + Y_4)/2 = (-43.7 + 44.5 - 47.2 + 51.8)/2 = 2.7$

Time: $\qquad\quad(-Y_1 - Y_2 + Y_3 + Y_4)/2 = (-43.7 - 44.5 + 47.2 + 51.8)/2 = 5.4$

Interaction: $\quad(+Y_1 - Y_2 - Y_3 + Y_4)/2 = (43.7 - 44.5 - 47.2 + 51.8)/2 = 1.9$

Curvature: $\quad(+Y_1 + Y_2 + Y_3 + Y_4)/4 - (Y_5 + Y_6 + Y_7)/3 = 46.8 - 46.0 = 0.8$

Calculation of confidence intervals:[7]

Concentration: $\pm 2ts/\sqrt{n} = \pm 2(4.30)(0.755)/\sqrt{4} = \pm 3.25$

Time: $\qquad\quad \pm 2ts/\sqrt{n} = \pm 2(4.30)(0.755)/\sqrt{4} = \pm 3.25$

Interaction: $\quad \pm 2ts/\sqrt{n} = \pm 2(4.30)(0.755)/\sqrt{4} = \pm 3.25$

Curvature: $\quad \pm ts\sqrt{(1/n) + (1/n_0)} = \pm(4.30)(0.755)\sqrt{(1/4) + (1/3)}$

$\qquad\qquad\qquad\qquad\qquad\qquad\qquad\qquad\quad = \pm 2.48$

Effects	Calculated 95% confidence interval (in units of percent yield)
Concentration ...	2.7 ± 3.25
Time..........	5.4 ± 3.25
Interaction......	1.9 ± 3.25
Curvature	0.8 ± 2.48

Table 28-1 shows how these confidence intervals were calculated. Note that Y_i is the yield for run number i, n is the number of runs in the factorial design (in this case four), n_0 is the number of center points (in this case three), and t is the appropriate t-value for a 95% confidence interval. The quantity s is the square root of

$$s^2 = \frac{\sum_{i=5}^{7}(Y_i - \overline{Y}_0)^2}{n_0 - 1}$$

where $\overline{Y}_0$ is the average of the center points Y_5, Y_6, and Y_7. Of course, confidence intervals at levels different from 95% may be calculated. A curvature effect has been calculated, which is the difference between the average of the factorial design points (runs 1 to 4) and $\overline{Y}_0$ the average of the center points (runs 5 to 7).

As the center-point conditions have been repeated three times, an estimate of the variance can be readily obtained. (If repeat runs have not been performed, it might be possible to obtain an appropriate estimate in some other way, for example, from

---

[7] The concept of confidence intervals is discussed in Section 22, under Statistical Estimation: Confidence Limits.

some external source, past experience, or from a technique like half-normal plots; see Daniel, Ref. 5.) With the three values 46.8, 45.9, and 45.3, $s^2 = 0.57$ is calculated as an estimate of the variance of an individual observation with two degrees of freedom.

These intervals suggest first that, since the statistics measuring second-order effects (interaction and curvature) are small, the relationship between time, concentration, and yield may be described geometrically as a plane. That is, there is no apparent lack of fit of the first-order model. Second, it appears that time is clearly important. The data suggest that longer time and perhaps higher concentration produce increased yield. A more precise analysis can be made using the equation

$$Y = \beta_0 + \beta_1 X_1 + \beta_2 X_2 + \varepsilon \qquad (28\text{-}1)$$

where the β's are constants whose values we can estimate from the data, Y is the measured value of the response (the yield), ε the random error, and

$$X_1 = \frac{\text{concentration}(\%) - 25}{5} \qquad (28\text{-}2)$$

$$X_2 = \frac{\text{time}(\text{hours}) - 1.0}{0.1} \qquad (28\text{-}3)$$

The formulas for X_1 and X_2 code the original values of the settings, i.e., $+1$ for the high level, 0 for the middle level, and -1 for the low level (see Table 28-1).

From our data, the fitted first-order model becomes

$$\hat{Y} = 46.46 + 1.35 X_1 + 2.70 X_2 \qquad (28\text{-}4)$$

which is a regression equation the coefficients of which can be obtained by standard regression techniques.[8] Alternatively, in this case since a factorial design has been employed, the constant term can be obtained by calculating the average, that is, $\bar{Y} = 46.46$, and the other two values can be obtained by calculating $\frac{1}{2}$ concentration effect$=\frac{1}{2}(2.7) = 1.35$ and $\frac{1}{2}$ time effect $= \frac{1}{2}(5.4)=2.70$.

A second method for evaluating the fit is to use the analysis of variance. The resulting ANOVA table (Table 28-2) indicates that the first-order model [equation (28-4)] adequately fits the data.[9] The ratio of the lack of fit mean square divided by the pure error mean square is 4.13, and since this value is less than $F_{2,2}(0.95)=19.0$, there is no evidence of lack of fit of the first-order model. Since there is no evident

TABLE 28-2 ANOVA Table: First-order Model, First Design,*

Source	Sum of squares	Degrees of freedom	Mean square
Mean b_0	15,107.86	1	
b_1	7.29	1	7.29
b_2	29.16	1	29.16
Lack of fit	4.71	2	2.36
Pure error	1.14	2	0.57
Total.	15,150.16	7	

* In the literature of response surface methodology, it is customary that the ANOVA table include a term for the sum of squares for the mean. In other uses of ANOVA, some authors exclude the sum of squares for the mean (e.g., see Sections 26 and 27).

[8] See Section 26 of this Handbook.
[9] See Section 26 of this Handbook. For further details, see Draper and Smith, Ref. 8.

TABLE 28-3   Results of Second-order Design

Run number	Concentration (coded units) X_1	Time (coded units) X_2	Yield, % Y
First-order design:			
12	-1	-1	69.3
13	$+1$	-1	85.1
14	-1	$+1$	72.8
15	$+1$	$+1$	73.6
16	0	0	80.9
17	0	0	78.4
18	0	0	80.4
Augmenting runs:			
19	$-\sqrt{2}$	0	71.4
20	$+\sqrt{2}$	0	78.9
21	0	$-\sqrt{2}$	73.9
22	0	$+\sqrt{2}$	69.1
23	0	0	76.4
24	0	0	78.5
25	0	0	76.3

lack of fit, it is reasonable to study the implications of the fitted first-order model [equation (28-4)]. The plane which is described by this equation is represented in Figure 28-3 by the straight contour lines.

Determine Direction of Steepest Ascent   The direction of steepest ascent[10] is indicated in Figure 28-3. It is perpendicular to the contour lines. Four experiments (numbers 8 to 11) in this direction indicate that the center of a second design should be approximately at a concentration of 31% and a time of 1.6 hours. The design employed and the data obtained after performing the runs in random order are shown in Table 28-3 as runs 12 to 18. An analysis of the data shows apparent lack of fit (Table 28-4). The ratio of the lack of fit mean square divided by the pure error mean square is 26.8, and since this value is greater than $F_{2,2}(0.95)=19.0$, there is evidence of lack of fit of the first-order model.

SECOND-ORDER STRATEGY

Construct Design and Collect Data   Since lack of fit is detected, the design is augmented by adding runs 19 to 25 to form the second-order (central composite) design shown in Table 28-3. (In general, if a model does not fit, it may be advantageous, instead of immediately considering a higher-order model, to consider transforma-

TABLE 28-4   ANOVA Table: First-order Model, Second Design

Source	Sum of squares	Degrees of freedom	Mean square
Mean b_0	41,734.32	1	
b_1	68.89	1	68.89
b_2	16.00	1	16.00
Lack of fit	94.12	2	47.06
Pure error	3.50	2	1.75
Total.	41,916.83	7	

[10] For further details, see Cochran and Cox, Ref. 4, p. 357, or Davies, Ref. 6, chap. 11.

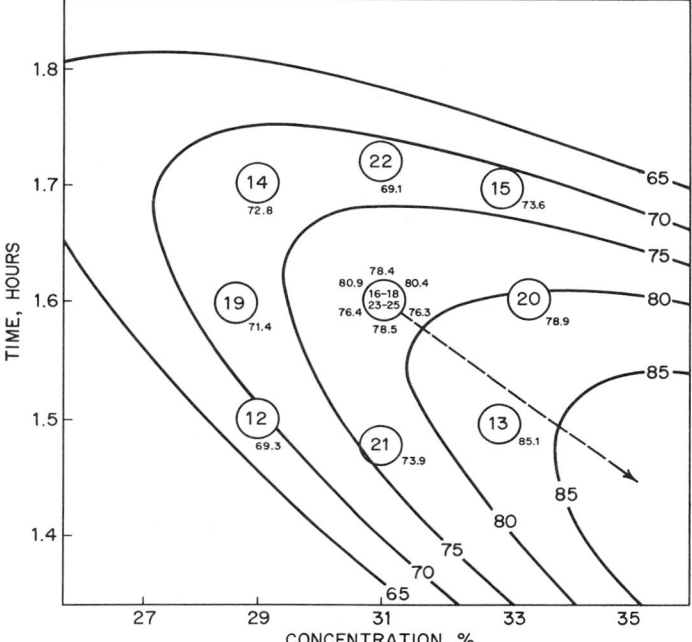

Fig. 28-4. Results of second-order design with fitted second-order (nonplanar) response surface.

tions of the variables and/or the responses. See Box and Cox, Ref. 1, Box and Tidwell, Ref. 2, and Draper and Hunter, Ref. 7.)

Fit Second-Order Model and Check for Lack of Fit   The fitted second-order equation is

$$\hat{Y} = 78.50 + 3.40X_1 - 1.85X_2 - 3.75X_1X_2 - 1.21X_1^2 - 3.03X_2^2 \quad (28\text{-}5)$$

The contours of this equation are shown in Figure 28-4 with the second-order design results. No lack of fit is evident from either visual inspection or statistical calculation (see Table 28-5). The form of equation (28-5) can be simplified so the shape of the response surface can be better appreciated. It is difficult to visualize the surface from equation (28-5) because it contains six constants. A canonical analysis,[11] which involves a translation and rotation of the coordinates from the original (X_1, X_2) axes to the new (Z_1, Z_2) axes, gives an equation which contains only three constants:

$$Y - 173.83 = -0.0332Z_1^2 - 8.4075Z_2^2 \quad (28\text{-}6)$$

This equation indicates, because of the negative coefficients for Z_1^2 and Z_2^2, that the fitted response surface has a maximum point. A direction in which to proceed at the next stage to search for the maximum is indicated by the arrow in Figure 28-4. The arrow points toward the "top of the mountain." The investigation might terminate after experimenting in this direction, perhaps with a few added points in the vicinity of the maximum. In some situations it may be useful to perform a full second-order design near the final optimum.

---

[11] For further details on canonical analysis and RSM in general, see Davies, Ref. 6.

TABLE 28-5   ANOVA Table: Second-order Model

Source	Sum of squares	Degrees of freedom	Mean square
Mean b_0	81,016.07	1	
First order b_i . .	119.87	2	59.94
Pure second order b_{ii}	80.73	2	40.37
Mixed second order b_{ij}	56.25	1	56.25
Lack of fit	2.23	3	0.74
Pure error	21.77	5	4.35
Total.	81,296.92	14	

The ratio of the lack of fit mean square divided by the pure error mean square is 0.17, and since this value is less than $F_{0.95}$ for 3, 5 degrees of freedom (5.41), there is no evidence of lack of fit of the second order model.

APPLICATION OF RSM IN PRACTICE

The example has illustrated a typical RSM approach, but many variations are possible, some of which are shown in Figure 28-1. A summary of some specific designs is given in Figure 28-5. Details are provided in the references cited.

Characteristics   Among RSM's desirable characteristics are: (1) It is a sequential procedure, the results at each stage guiding the direction to be taken at the next. (2) It represents the experimental problem in readily understood geometrical terms (for example, the problem of climbing a mountain). Contour plots are highly effective. (3) It approximates the response in terms of a first-order model up to the point where it is found inadequate, at which stage a second-order model is used. (4) It is applicable for any number of variables.

RSM has been used since about 1950 on a wide variety of real problems and has been demonstrated to work. RSM is useful not only for optimization but also for specification problems. Here, several responses are studied simultaneously for a given system and the question is whether it is possible to manufacture a product that will satisfy all specifications and, if so, what settings of the variables should be used.

Constraints   In exploring the direction of steepest ascent in the first-order stage of RSM, the investigator may encounter a constraint. For instance, in the example considered above suppose that when experiments number 8, 9, 10, and 11 were run (the points along the direction of steepest ascent), it was discovered that a certain impurity in the product exceeded the upper specification limit for conditions 9, 10, and 11. Careful analysis (and perhaps further runs) may show that the optimum conditions were near those for experiment number 8. Higher yields could not be realized because the impurity level would be too high for the product to be marketable.

Many Variables   RSM can be used for more than two variables, and in fact, as the number of variables increases, the relative efficiency of RSM increases when compared with strategies such as a one-variable-at-a-time approach.

Importance of Understandable Presentation of Results   The end of an RSM study is not a set of mathematical equations, and this is a point frequently overlooked in practice. The statistical results must be translated into terms that are meaningful to those who must act on the results. Graphical summaries such as contour plots have proved highly effective for this purpose. Technical and economic data on several alterna-

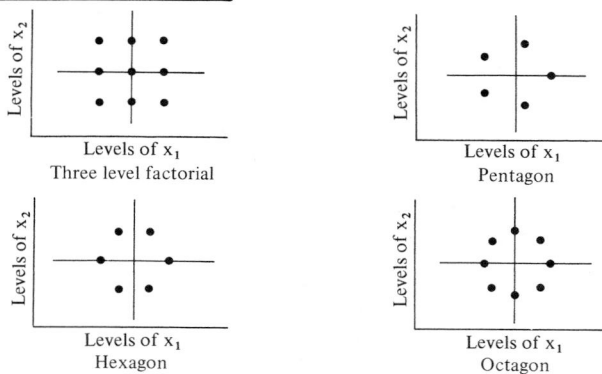

Fig. 28-5. Summary of some designs useful in response surface exploration.

First-Order Designs

Two variables x_1 and x_2 — Ref. 10

Two-level factorial

Two-level factorial with center points

Triangular

More than 2 variables (some 2^{k-p} fractional factorial designs) —Ref. 4.

No. of variables	Number of runs	p
3	8	0
4	8	1
4	16	0
5	8	2
5	16	1
5	32	0
6	8	3
6	16	2
6	32	1
6	64	0

Second Order Designs

Two variables x_1 and x_2 — Ref. 10

Three level factorial

Pentagon

Hexagon

Octagon

More than 2 variables (some rotatable* designs) — Ref. 4

No. of variables (k)	Number of Points for 2^{k-p} fractional factorial	Augmenting Points	Center	Total Points
3	8 (p = 0)	6	6	20
4	16 (p = 0)	8	7	31
5	16 (p = 1)	10	6	32
6	32 (p = 1)	12	9	53

*A rotatable design is one that has equal predictability for responses at equal distances from the center of the design in all directions.

tive conditions including, say, the maximum yield value can be presented.   The ultimate problem is not one of mathematics but of communication.

ACKNOWLEDGMENT

We wish to thank Mr. P. Kartha for assistance with the worked example.

REFERENCES

1. Box, G. E. P., and D. R. Cox, An Analysis of Transformations, *Journal of the Royal Statistical Society*, Series B, vol. 26, p. 211, 1964.
2. Box, G. E. P., and P. W. Tidwell, Transformation of the Independent Variables, *Technometrics*, vol. 4, p. 531, 1962.
3. Box, G. E. P., and K. B. Wilson, On the Experimental Attainment of Optimum Conditions, *Journal of the Royal Statistical Society*, Series B, vol. 13, p. 1, 1951.
4. Cochran, William G., and Gertrude M. Cox, "Experimental Designs," 2d ed., chap. 8A, John Wiley & Sons, Inc., New York, 1957.
5. Daniel, C., Use of Half-normal Plots in Interpreting Factorial Two Level Experiments, *Technometrics*, vol. 1, p. 311, 1959.
6. Davies, O. L. (ed.), "Design and Analysis of Industrial Experiments," chap. 11, Hafner Publishing Company, Inc., New York, 1954.
7. Draper, N. R., and W. G. Hunter, Transformations: Some Examples Revisited, *Technometrics*, vol. 11, p. 23, 1967.
8. Draper, N. R., and H. Smith, Jr., "Applied Regression Analysis," John Wiley & Sons, Inc., New York, 1966.
9. Hill, W. J., and W. G. Hunter, A Review of Response Surface Methodology: A Literature Survey, *Technometrics*, vol. 8, p. 571, 1966.
10. Hunter, J. Stuart, Determination of Optimum Operating Conditions by Experimental Methods, Part II, 1, 2, 3, *Industrial Quality Control*, December 1958, January and February, 1959.

Section **29**

Chemical Process Industries

C. A. BICKING

Expert, United Nations Industrial Development Organization

JOHN D. HINCHEN

Senior Research Specialist—Statistics, Monsanto Industrial
Chemicals Company, St. Louis, Missouri

R. S. BINGHAM, JR.

INTRODUCTION

General Background   Chemical and process industries generally are engaged in performing physical and chemical changes on materials. The starting materials may be "raw," e.g., ore, sand, clay, rosin, wood chips, air, water. They may also be products of other chemical operations such as coke manufacture or oil cracking. The broad area of chemical manufacturing includes rubber, food, beverages, heavy chemicals, pharmaceuticals, petroleum, and plastic materials.[1]

To build the desired properties and performance characteristics into the finished product, the processes must be controlled. Important to this control are the properties of the raw materials, the characteristics of the unit processes and operations required, residence time under specified temperatures, pressures, and concentrations, and the methods of measurement employed.

In addition to conventional quality control problems, the chemical industry faces other problems which differ from the conventional:

1. The measurement methods may in themselves be miniature chemical processes requiring control.[2]

2. Reaction kinetics continue with time, making it necessary to protect samples from delay in delivery, contamination with air, freezing, container contamination, etc.

3. In-process samples may differ markedly in composition from the finished product.

4. Control of isomers of the desired product may be difficult.

5. Testing time may be relatively long compared with the batch reaction time, requiring control decisions to be anticipated.

6. Product specifications may not fully define performance under widely varying customer conditions.

In this industry the same materials may be applied to multiple customer uses. In consequence, the quality controls must achieve the dual purposes of:

1. Assuring that the materials produced possess the correct physical and chemical properties.

2. Assuring that the materials will perform satisfactorily in the customer's process and product. For example, a polyvinyl chloride resin must be readily processable in a floor tile plant, and must also impart good wear characteristics and soil resistance in the finished floor tile.

The chemicals industry shares with all industries the problems of rapid product obsolescence and the need for prompt conversion of research effort into profitable production. In particular, the quality needs of the marketplace can change rapidly and, often, unpredictably. To illustrate, concern with ecology and consumer safety may require: development of different fuels and lubricants for automobile engines; flame-retardant paints and textiles; biodegradable detergents, fertilizers, weed killers, and insecticides.

While the ultimate purpose of all this change is superior fitness for the user, the industry must learn, with precision, just what are the effects of raw material quality and process conditions on product properties and performance. To learn all this, the industry must also continually develop new tests which simulate usage but can be conducted in the laboratory. In addition, as specifications for chemical purity become more stringent, more sensitive and precise methods of determining trace impurities are needed. Developing such new tests and precisions requires extensive

---

[1]See also Sections 30 and 31.

[2]See Wernimont, Grant, The Basis for Interpreting Results from a Testing Process, *Experientia Supplementum*, vol. 5, 1957.

collaboration among suppliers and users, new technology in testing procedures, correlation of chemical and physical tests with use-type tests, and finally, correlation of all these with field performance.

Organization for Quality The industry tradition has been to concentrate responsibility for achieving quality controls in three broad areas as discussed below.

The Research and Development Laboratory. This unit has basic responsibility for:

Inventing the product
Defining the technology for making it
Identifying competing reactions causing reduced yield or substandard quality
Providing sufficient data to design the plant
Pinpointing from theoretical considerations when, where, and how process control should be exercised

The most economic quality control is achieved by building the right conditions into processes before they commence full-scale manufacture. Changing a going process is enormously costly compared with *controlling research* on how to design the process originally. The key is not necessarily to spend more time in the process development and pilot plant stages, but to structure the best possible *design of experiment* during those stages. The special methods of experiment design and statistical analysis now available are of paramount importance in learning the most from a minimum amount of information.[3] The research and development laboratory is expected to use all techniques available to it.[4]

The Analytical or Control Laboratory. Laboratory measurements are the bases for acceptance of raw materials, manufacturing process decisions, and release of outgoing product. Also, they are the means for product uniformity improvement through assessment of how process variables affect equipment behavior and operating procedures. Quantitative knowledge of the extent of variation due to sampling and to the accuracy and precision of the analytical test is essential to the most effective use of laboratory measurements. Activities and methods for obtaining such knowledge are normally the responsibility of the analytical or control laboratory.

The Manufacturing Plant. Prime responsibility for delivering on time according to specifications lies here. Manufacturing decides whether to ship, reblend, rework, or scrap. When it cannot meet its specifications (whether they be yield, cost, quality, or safety), it calls for Research and Development or Engineering assistance and advises the Sales Department of possible impact on customers.

The plant also enhances major process improvements by close attention to process behavior.[5] Opportunities abound in the chemical industry to obtain higher conversions, larger yields, less scrap or waste, and fewer recycles for reworking through improved manufacturing control. Success in achieving these goals lies in being able to discover the specific influence of the important process variables on the product characteristics and to devise the routine control procedures for steadily maintaining

[3]See Section 27.
[4]Throughout this Section the authors have recommended, wherever possible, the most appropriate statistical procedures which have been practically used. As many of the examples show, the $\bar{X}$ or range control chart is frequently suitable for the task. However, many problems are more rapidly solved by what may *appear* to be unnecessarily complex methods. See G. Wernimont (Evaluation of Laboratory Performance of Spectrophotometers, *Analytical Chemistry,* May 1967, p. 554) for a problem requiring characteristic vector analysis for its solution; anything less skirts the real problem.
See Polymerization, in this Section — a typical case history using control charts and regression analysis for problem definition. Control charts provide operator control.
[5]See Coutie, G. A., Use Statistics for Optimization, *Chemical Engineering,* Nov. 16, 1959, pp. 190–191.

these variables at the desired levels.   The chemical industries look to the manufacturing plants to take the initiative in making these improvements.

The functions of these three major centers are elaborated here and there in the remainder of this Section.

THE CONTROL PLAN

The New Product Cycle   The chemical industry follows conventional practice in discovering market needs and in mobilizing its technological and managerial resources to respond to those needs.   The general industrial approach (Section 6, under New Product Planning) is largely applicable to the chemical industry.   In like manner, field trials and customer feedback largely follow conventional practice.[6] However, in the initial project formulation stages, the chemical industry faces an "experimental space" which is uncommonly broad and multidimensional. Extensive literature searching of patents, technical journals, and company reports via computer indexing and information retrieval methods serves to limit the "space" to be explored.   This essential first step is rarely omitted.

Formulation and Methodology   Many variables need to be considered in the laboratory, and the experiment designs will usually be of a screening type.   The fractional factorial, primarily the 2^n series,[7] is of considerable value to screen out the less important variables and to retain those which appear to have the greatest effects on the desired properties.   The screening designs may be followed by Simplex or Central Composite designs[8] to optimize.   Analysis of variance and multiple regression are the statistical techniques principally employed.[8]

If the product is to be a blend of several ingredients, and the properties will blend linearly (in direct proportion to the amounts of each component present), then linear programming techniques can be used.   These procedures permit the researcher to obtain a minimum cost formulation consistent with the product specifications.   If the properties do *not* blend linearly, a combination of linear and nonlinear multiple regression techniques can be employed to obtain a best fit via computer to a set of desired properties (one of which may be cost).   Harrington's Desirability Function is such an approach.[9]

Laboratory Scale Evaluation   The candidate product is evaluated in the Research Laboratory on the basis of chemical and physical properties as well as prototype performance tests.   In addition, the product will be checked against industry standard tests, and for conformance to government and other specifications, e.g., Underwriters' Laboratories, FDA, SAE, specific customer requirements.   During this phase of product design, it is advisable to seek out, whenever possible, theoretical relationships among various measurable characteristics, each generally giving insight into its successor:

Molecular structure→chemical properties→physical properties→performance tests

Based on this work, a product is eventually selected for field trial.   Quantities of the product may be synthesized on a laboratory scale, and shipped to potential customers' plants for field evaluation.   These tests may result in tentative acceptance by the customer, or feedback of information for product modification.

[6]See Section 14, under appropriate headings.
[7]See Sections 27 and 26.
[8]See Sections 27 and 26.
[9]Harrington, E. C., Jr., The Desirability Function, *Industrial Quality Control*, vol. 21, p. 10, April 1965.

Field Trials and Customer Feedback   In addition to following conventional practice as described in Section 14, the chemical industry must face several additional problems:

At the research stage only small quantities are available for customer evaluation.

Most customers are industrial users who further process the new product prior to consumer testing (performance both in-plant and at consumer level is important).

Many products require lengthy field evaluation (shelf life, weathering, aging, degradation under environmental exposure) under different climatic conditions (relative humidity, temperature, ozone, salt spray, etc.).

Technical data describing typical properties, toxicity, safe handling practices, preferred storage, etc., take time to develop, especially when the new product is an ingredient (and frequently only a minor one) in many other products.

The customer may also be a competitor and may deny observation of the new product in his plant, making informed comparison of old and new product sketchy.

Wherever possible, time and effort can be saved by suitable choice of statistical designs.[10]   These can be used to develop technical data to introduce the product and to assist the customer in his evaluation.[11]   In any event, field trials and customer acceptance are key steps in establishing quality controls.

DESIGN OF PROCESS—RESEARCH AND DEVELOPMENT PHASE

Initial Experimentation   Process design presents separate problems from product design (although sometimes handled concurrently).   With an understanding of product requirements, the research effort is directed toward finding the best way to make it.[12]   To be considered are raw material quality, the process type (continuous vs. batch), equipment to be used, variables to be studied, unit processes and unit operations required, number of process stages, variables at each stage and their effects on subsequent stages, etc.   All these things and more ideally should be tied down before the process is turned over to the manufacturing department.

Once the process type and equipment decision has been made, prototype equipment (glassware, small-scale reactors, etc.) is set up and the task of quantifying process variables begins.   After a few feasibility experiments, the experimenter may use screening designs such as the Plackett and Burman series,[13] or other fractional factorial designs.[14]   These experiments are to pick out the *important* process variables and decide which will be held constant, which deliberately varied, which will be allowed to vary but will be recorded, etc.   One of the more popular designs looks

---

[10] See Section 27.   Latin square, incomplete block, and factorial designs can usually be constructed to meet the need.

[11] See Bingham, R. S., Ten Minutes with Top Management, *Industrial Quality Control,* vol. 18, no. 4, pp. 5–8, October 1961, on the impact of testing and manufacturing variation relative to the amount of testing necessary in a customer's plant.

[12] See Bobis, A. H., and L. E. Andersen, An Approach for Economic Discrimination between Alternative Chemical Syntheses, *Technometrics,* vol. 12, no. 3, pp. 439–456, August 1970.

[13] See Plackett, R. L., and J. P. Burman, The Design of Optimum Multifactorial Experiments, *Biometrika,* vol. 33, pp. 305–325, 1946.

[14] See also Daniel, C., Factor Screening in Process Development, *Industrial and Engineering Chemistry,* vol. 55, p. 5, May 1963.

at the main effects of seven variables in eight experimental runs:

Run No.	Variable						
	A	B	C	D	E	F	G
1	0	0	0	1	1	1	0
2	0	0	1	1	0	0	1
3	0	1	0	0	1	0	1
4	0	1	1	0	0	1	0
5	1	0	0	0	0	1	1
6	1	0	1	0	1	0	0
7	1	1	0	1	0	0	0
8	1	1	1	1	1	1	1

0 = low level of variable
1 = high level of variable

Other experiment designs like Latin squares and fractional factorials may be used as screening designs. (See Section 27 for a more complete discussion.)

Optimization of Process Conditions   Once important variables have been selected, optimizing processing conditions is next. The experimenter using reaction kinetics, if they are known, will use experiment designs to calculate rate constants. Physical and chemical characteristics of the process may enter into this phase.[15]

If the reactions are numerous and complex, or if the kinetic models are not known, an empirical approach to optimization via a central composite or 3^n factorial design is often used. Data analysis frequently calls for multiple regression allowing the desired equation to be examined analytically for optima, areas of constant results, etc. A quadratic equation in n variables is frequently used:

$$Y = C_0 + C_1 X_1 + C_2 X_2 + C_3 X_3 + \ldots + C_n X_n + \ldots + C_{11} X_1{}^2 + C_{22} X_2{}^2$$
$$+ C_{33} X_3{}^2 + \ldots + C_{nn} X_n{}^2 + C_{12} X_1 X_2 + C_{13} X_1 X_3 + \ldots + C_{n-1,n} X_{n-1} X_n$$

The Y-term can be yield, conversion, or any of several desired quality characteristics. The X's may include time, temperature, catalyst concentration, reactant ratios, etc.[16] Most computer systems are equipped with programs for obtaining the least squares solutions[17] and should also provide:

1. A means for calculating the value of Y corresponding to values of X_i which may not actually have been run.

2. Predicted values of Y for comparison with those actually obtained at the design values of X_i.

3. Determination of optimum conditions by differentiating the equation with respect to each X in turn.

4. Contour plotting of the values of Y against any pair of X's (contours of equal Y make it easy to pick out ranges of operating conditions within which the desired results may be obtained). (See Figures 29-1 and 29-2.) (For process analysis purposes as described below, cumulative sum plots may also be used.)[18]

Definition of Raw Material Quality Required   One of the elements to be considered in the optimization step is the quality of the raw material (or materials) used. These

[15] See Atkinson, A. C., and W. G. Hunter, Design of Experiments for Parameter Estimation, *Technometrics,* vol. 10, no, 2, pp. 271–290, May 1968 (may be useful for nonlinear-type experiment design).

[16] See Caul, L. D., and R. S. Bingham, Jr., A Statistically Designed Study of a Phenol-formaldehyde Resole, *Preprint Series,* American Chemical Society Division of Organic Coatings and Plastic Chemistry, vol. 21, no. 1, pp. 12–18, March 1961, demonstrates the procedure for a well-known thermosetting polymer intermediate.

[17] See Sections 26 and 20.

[18] See Section 23.

may be materials purchased from another company, and in such situations, a quality specification may already exist.   On the other hand, the starting raw material may be an in-house product or intermediate, or even a by-product of another process. In such cases, variability from lot to lot may be large, and it is the function of Research to define the limits within which the raw material must be maintained to produce a satisfactory process.[19, 20, 21]   This information can then be included in a formal Raw Material Specification and used for vendor negotiations on price and quality.

Tentative Process or Tentative Operating Procedure   From the Process definition, a Tentative Process is written prior to turning it over to manufacturing or pilot plant personnel.   This document contains pertinent information on how the process is to be operated, subject to demonstration of its feasibility.   It commonly includes Introduction, Synopsis of Process, Flow Sheet, Equipment Required, Bill of Materials, Process Detail, Discussion of Important Variables, Raw Material Specifications, Finished Material Specifications, Analytical Methods, and Toxicity and Hazards. This document is read and approved by the departments concerned prior to the next stage, scale-up to larger equipment.

DESIGN OF PROCESS—PILOT PLANT OR INTERIM PRODUCTION PHASE

Need for Partial Scale-up   In scaling up a process from the laboratory to the manufacturing plant, there is often an intermediate or Pilot Plant stage.   Usually, this is a manufacturing unit, larger than laboratory-scale equipment, but smaller than the ultimate commercial manufacturing unit.   Manufacturing the new product on this intermediate scale provides a better look at problems which may occur in the final plant, especially in cases where a new plant is being built.   The Pilot Plant stage provides:

Solution of scale-up problems
Sufficient material for long-term testing or large-scale trial run at customers' plants
Development of Standard Operating Procedures

Process Simulation and Reaction Kinetics   Ideally, scaling up a process to larger equipment, whether pilot plant or full-scale manufacturing plant, uses all available technology.   This includes reaction kinetics and the mechanisms for agitation, heat transfer, and other physical phenomena.   This information can be scaled up theoretically to the dimensions of the larger equipment. Simulating the process on a computer is becoming more prevalent.   If this is done, by varying the computer conditions one may predict (subject to verification) what can be expected in plant-scale equipment.

Validating Empirical Equations   When the process information consists primarily of empirical equations developed on the laboratory scale, the scale-up operation can be aided by selected sequential experimentation in the pilot plant.   Using this technique, a single experiment is substituted for one of those made in the laboratory scale equipment, the regression is run again, and any changes in fit or in coefficients

---

[19] See Bingham, R. S., A Program for Controlling Incoming Chemical Quality, *Chemical Purchasing*, vol. 1, No. 1, pp. 14–16, January-February 1965.
[20] See Mitchell, J. A., Quality Control in Raw Materials Acceptance and Chemical Specifications, *Industrial Quality Control*, vol. 4, No. 3, November 1947.
[21] Bingham, R. S., J. L. Gioele, and V. B. Shelburne, Studies in Ore Car and Abrasive Grain Sampling Variation, ASTM Symposium on Bulk Sampling, Special Technical Publication 242, pp. 45–56, May 1959, Philadelphia, Pa. describe sampling and testing as they relate to vendor comparisons and specifications.

are noted. This procedure is iterated until the coefficients stabilize, or until sufficient evidence is uncovered that the operations are essentially the same.[22, 23]

Material for Field Trials   The pilot plant also aids in the development of a quality product by providing sufficient material to permit definitive field trials by a large number of customers. Information fed back can be used to revise the process and product if required. If the full-scale manufacturing plant is not ready, interim production to obtain and hold new markets can be carried out in the pilot plant.

MANUFACTURE OF COMMERCIAL PRODUCT—QUALITY ORGANIZATION AND RESPONSIBILITIES

Research and Development   This group is responsible for three tasks related to manufacturing:

Process demonstration
Major process modifications
Approval of procedures, specifications, and process changes

Each is discussed below.

The Research Department is commonly called upon to demonstrate the new process prior to its being accepted by Manufacturing. A series of plant runs in full-scale production equipment is made, supervised by the Research team responsible for the process and product development. During this period, operating and quality difficulties are ironed out. If these are not readily surmountable, the responsibility for further work remains with Research. Normally, once a predetermined amount of product or number of runs are made without mishap, the process is accepted for regular production by the Manufacturing Department.

If for any reason, after a long period of successful operation, the process changes or ceases to produce the desired quality and yield, Research may be called in to ascertain the reasons and to assist Manufacturing in correcting the situation. This can occur if unforeseen variables enter the picture, such as changes in raw materials source, customer requirements, or competitive action. Transfer of process responsibility back to Research is negotiated between Manufacturing and Research.

Sometimes continuous experience with a process will identify operating improvements to increase profitability or obtain better quality. Amendments to Tentative Processes, Standard Procedures, or Finished Material Specifications when required are usually subject to the approval of the Research Department.

The Analytical or Control Laboratory   A major key to successful manufacture of a quality chemical is to have valid, pertinent analytical methods to monitor product quality. In many situations, standard test methods already exist in the literature. Adaptation of these methods to the particular product or process is the responsibility of the Analytical or Control Laboratory. It may also be asked to develop new tests relating to customer performance requirements. In filling these various needs it is responsible for selecting testing methods whose accuracy, precision, reliability, and pertinence match the particular need.[24, 25, 26]   Whether the new tests are passed

[22] Harrington, E. C., Jr., J. Novak, R. O. Lynn, Process Scale-up by Sequential Experimentation and Mathematical Optimization, *Chemical Engineering Progress*, vol. 58, No. 2, February 1962.

[23] See also Mandel, J., A Method for Fitting Empirical Surfaces to Physical or Chemical Data, *Technometrics*, vol. 11, No. 3, p. 411, 1969.

[24] See McFarren *et al.*, Criteria for Judging Acceptability of Analytical Methods, *Analytical Chemistry*, March 1970, p. 358.

[25] See also Mandel, J., Statistical Methods in Analytical Chemistry, in I. M. Kolthoff and P. J. Elving (eds.), "Treatise on Analytical Chemistry," Part III, vol. I, Interscience Publishers, a division of John Wiley & Sons, Inc., New York (in press).

[26] See also Linnig, F. J., and J. Mandel, Which Measure of Precision? *Analytical Chemistry*, vol. 36, pp. 25a–29a, 32a, December 1964.

on to the Analytical Laboratory from Research, or the new development takes place completely in the Analytical Laboratory, control charts, experiment design, and regression analysis are very helpful. [27, 28]

Intelligent interpretation of process data—whether from the manufacturing or pilot plant—requires an exact knowledge of the degree to which the sample represents the product, and the accuracy and precision of the test methods. [29] Quantitative determination of these variabilities rests primarily on obtaining valid data, statistically analyzing the data, and expressing the results in a meaningful form. [30] Almost inevitably, such quantitative determination leads to reduction in *overall* variation, once the major sources of excessive variability have been disclosed. Thus, time is usually well spent in studying laboratory test methods.

Test Method Development—Satisfying Multiple Criteria. In developing a new test method, the analytical chemist will search for equipment, techniques, and conditions to determine the desired property as accurately and precisely as needed. He will also be concerned with costs, difficulty of operation, time required to obtain a result, etc. Just like the process chemist or engineer, he may have many criteria for deciding which of many possible methods is the best. [31]

Suppose an analyst is interested in measuring the amount of by-product A in a sample of finished product from a manufacturing process. The nature of A is such that to measure its concentration, it must be converted to compound B which can be titrated directly. Conversion requires heating A in the presence of a catalyst for a period of time. Some B may be lost at extreme conditions. The analyst is searching for the combination of time, temperature, and catalyst concentration to produce the *maximum* amount of B, and the combination which produces the *most consistent amounts* of B. He hopes these conditions will be the same.

In light of the optimization objectives, a three-factor central composite experiment design is chosen. [32] Temperature is varied over the range of 105 to 125° C, reaction time from 15 to 75 minutes, and catalyst concentration from 0.1 to 0.5%. Using a large uniform sample of Material A, the reaction to produce B is run at 15 different experimental conditions, each repeated 3 times. The order of the 45 runs is a random sequence. The experimental conditions and the amount of B determined are shown in Table 29-1.

To obtain an estimate of the conditions producing the highest *yield* of B and the

---

[27] See Hill, H. M., and R. H. Brown, Statistical Methods in Chemistry, *Analytical Chemistry,* vol. 40, No. 5, pp. 376R–380R, April 1968; vol. 38, No. 5, pp. 440R–442R, April 1966, two review articles covering significant papers in the areas of Statistical and Quality Control Methods, Models and Design of Experiments, Precision, Inter-laboratory Studies, Analytical Methods, Chemical Processes, Optimization, Kinetics, and Regression.

[28] See also Bingham, R. S., Development and Utilization of a Quality Control Program, in I. M. Kolthoff and P. J. Elving (eds.), "Treatise on Analytical Chemistry," Part III, vol. 1, Sec. B, chap. 13, Interscience Publishers, a division of John Wiley & Sons, Inc., New York (in press), for 245 references pertinent to Quality Control in Analytical Chemistry.

[29] See Bicking, C. A., A Statistical Approach to the Study of Test Precision, I, Defining Precision Standards, *TAPPI,* vol. 40, No. 3, pp. 191–192, March 1957; Bicking, C. A., The Use of Statistics for Analysis of Testing Results, *TAPPI,* vol. 38, No. 9, pp. 573–576, September 1955; and McArthur, D. S., *et al.,* Evaluation of Test Procedures, *Analytical Chemistry,* vol. 26, No. 6, pp. 1012–1018, June 1954.

[30] See Hinchen, J. D., and W. E. Koerner, Propagation of Analytical Error in Normalized Data, *Analytical Chemistry,* February 1965, p. 283.

[31] See Lawton, W. H., and E. A. Sylvestre, Self Modeling Curve Resolution, *Technometrics,* vol. 13, No. 3, pp. 617–634, August 1971; and Mandel, J., and F. L. McCrackin, Analysis of Families of Curves, *Journal of Research of the National Bureau of Standards,* vol. 67A, No. 3, p. 259, 1963, for aids when the response is a curve.

[32] See Section 28 for details of this design.

TABLE 29-1   Test Method Development—Experimental Conditions

Condition No.	Time, minutes	Temp., °	Catalyst, %	Yield of B (3 runs)	
				Avg.	Range
1	30	110	0.2	15.4	0.48
2	30	110	0.4	17.4	0.45
3	30	120	0.2	17.7	0.49
4	30	120	0.4	20.7	0.46
5	60	110	0.2	19.7	0.39
6	60	110	0.4	21.7	0.36
7	60	120	0.2	20.9	0.40
8	60	120	0.4	23.9	0.37
9	15	115	0.3	14.6	0.51
10	75	115	0.3	22.1	0.33
11	45	105	0.3	15.6	0.41
12	45	125	0.3	20.1	0.43
13	45	115	0.1	15.3	0.46
14	45	115	0.5	20.3	0.39
15	45	115	0.3	24.7	0.42

smallest variability, the data are fitted to the following empirical equation as a first approximation:[33]

$$\text{Yield} = C_0 + C_1 X_1 + C_2 X_2 + C_3 X_3 + C_{11} X_1{}^2 + C_{22} X_2{}^2 + C_{33} X_3{}^2 + C_{12} X_1 X_2 + C_{13} X_1 X_3 + C_{23} X_2 X_3$$

where $X_1 = $ time $- 45$ minutes
$X_2 = $ temperature $- 115°$
$X_3 = $ catalyst $- 0.3\%$

The same model is also used to determine the equation for the *range*, and also for the *ratio* of the *range* to the *average yield*. The equations obtained by computer using the backward regression method are:

$$\text{Yield} = 24.67 + 0.125 X_1 + 0.225 X_2 + 12.50 X_3 - 0.007 X_1{}^2 - 0.0683 X_2{}^2 - 170.833 X_3{}^2 - 0.00333 X_1 X_2 + 0.50 X_2 X_3$$

$$\text{Range} = 0.422 - 0.003 X_1 + 0.001 X_2 - 0.1625 X_3 + 0.1163 X_3{}^2$$

$$\text{Range/yield} = 0.0171 - 0.00032 X_1 - 0.00023 X_2 - 0.0242 X_3 + 0.000008 X_1{}^2 + 0.000066 X_2{}^2 + 0.1795 X_3{}^2 + 0.000008 X_1 X_2 + 0.000387 X_1 X_3$$

These equations can be solved for maxima or minima by differentiation, and the optimum conditions for each obtained. However, it may be more useful to place certain restrictions on the results, such as "the test method is to have minimum error and still report 25% recovery of compound B."

Figure 29-1 shows the contour plot[34] of range/yield vs. time and temperature, at a catalyst concentration of 0.3%. The ratio appears to have a minimum value near

[33] See Section 26, Regression Analysis, for details on empirical curve fitting and Section 28 for optimizing-type models.

[34] Contour plots (plots of equal response Y) may be obtained, once the coefficients have been estimated, by setting the response Y and all but one of the X's to selected values, and solving the equation for the unspecified X. A new level of one X is taken and the process repeated until the values of X of interest have been evaluated. The Y value is changed and the process repeated. Most computer programs restrict evaluation to the levels of the experiment design but permit selecting many levels for the response. Figure 29-1 has 11 levels for the range/yield response.

65 minutes and 116°. (The area surrounded by the contour line symbolized by "O" will give ratios of less than 0.0150.) Figure 29-2 shows that the area of maximum yield is found near 55 minutes and 116°. The yield will be 25% or more within the area symbolized by the "A" contour line. Optimum conditions for both error and yield occur where these two areas (minimum ratio and maximum yield) overlap.

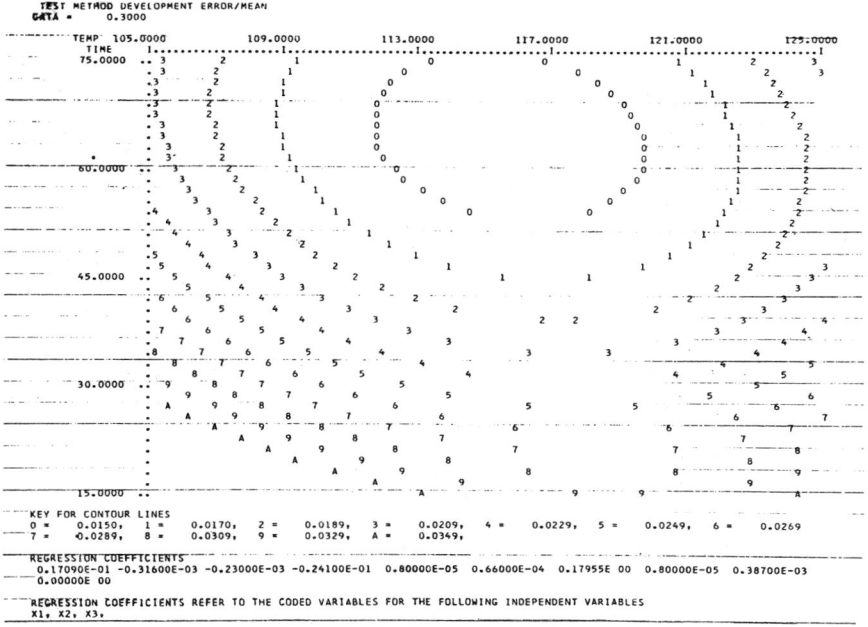

Fig. 29-1   Contour plot—test method development (range/yields).

Test Method Development—Comparison of Equipment and Techniques.   In developing test methods, the interest may not be in optimizing a reaction as part of the experimental procedure. The problem may be one of deciding which piece of equipment, sample size, or operating technique might optimize the recovery and error in measuring a particular component in a sample. In gas-liquid chromatography (GLC) studies, for example, the variables might be column-detector combinations, methods of integration, and sample size for analysis of several different classes of material. One experiment design useful in a study of this type is shown in Table 29-2. Three observations were taken on each combination of these factors. By analysis of variance, it was possible to select a column-detector combination, sample size and integration technique to minimize error and bias on each of the sample types tested.[35] As shown in Table 29-3, more precise results

[35] More details are given in Emery, E. M., The Role of Quantitation in Gas Chromatography, *Journal of Gas Chromatography*, December 1967.

were generally obtainable at higher component concentrations, the digital integrator gave better results than the disk integrator or peak height (see Table 29-4), and only the thermistor detector was poorer in precision than the other techniques studied (see Table 29-5).

Once the pertinent method has been selected, its long-term reliability may be determined.[36]

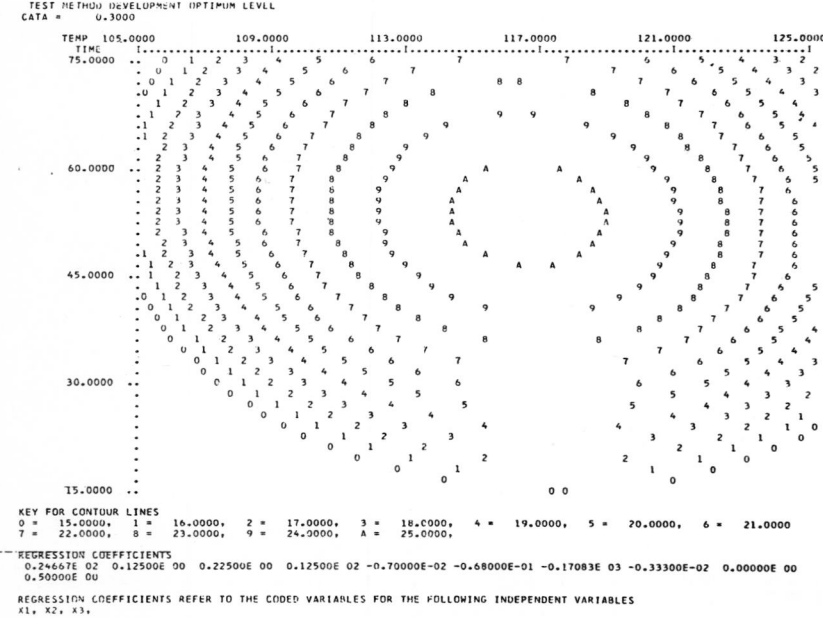

Fig. 29-2   Contour plot—test method development (yield).

Determining Test Method Reliability.   In examining the reliability of a chemical method, "nested" classifications provide measures of variation between duplicates run on the same sample, between replicates analyzed on the same shift or day, or between samples from various parts of a boxcar.   Knowledge of these variations permits optimum construction of a sampling schedule to meet a given precision requirement.   A sampling and analysis plan similar to that shown in Figure 29-3 allows comparison of two laboratory methods, each on several days while assessing the size of sample-to-sample fluctuations and duplicate repeatability.   The plan can be enlarged to include comparisons of analysts or equipment, but in new-methods

[36] See also Tingey, F. H., Experimental Designs in Analytical Chemistry, Part I, vol. 10, and Mandel, J., Statistical Methods in Analytical Chemistry, in I. M. Kolthoff and P. J. Elving (eds.), "Treatise on Analytical Chemistry," Part III, vol. 1, Interscience Publishers, a division of John Wiley & Sons, Inc., New York (in press), for other examples of test method development.

development it is frequently advantageous to limit the work to one analyst until the method is pretty well defined; then its reliability can be tested by other chemists or technicians.[37,38]

In this example, prior to the analysis, a carboy of solution was prepared and well agitated. Pint samples were withdrawn and labeled. One-half the bottles were chosen at random for analysis by each of the methods, and the order of analysis as well as method (weight or volumetric) was decided by lot also. Only the last stage

TABLE 29-2   Experiment Design for Chromatography Study

Column type		I		II		III		IV	
Sample size		Small	Large	Small	Large	Small	Large	Small	Large
Material	Integration								
A	1								
	2								
	3								
B	1								
	2								
	3								
C	1								
	2								
	3								
D	1								
	2								
	3								

Column types:
  I—packed column, hot wire
  II—packed column, thermistor
  III—packed column, flame ionization
  IV—capillary column, flame ionization
Materials:
  A—gas mixture
  B—low-boiling liquid
  C—medium-boiling liquid
  D—high-boiling liquid

Integrators:
  1—digital
  2—disk
  3—peak height

of analysis, titration, was duplicated on an aliquot of the sample. Statistical analysis of the data in Table 29-6 is shown in Table 29-7. Comparing differences between samples with differences between duplicates, it is evident that the latter severely

[37] See Marcuse, S., Optimum Allocation and Variance Components in Nested Sampling with an Application to Chemical Analysis, *Biometrics,* September 1949, pp. 189–206; Mitchell, J. A., Control of the Accuracy and Precision of Industrial Tests and Analyses, *Analytical Chemistry,* vol. 19, No. 12, pp. 961–967, December 1947; Wernimont, G., A Symposium on Design of Experiments for Developing New Analytical Methods; Introduction Remarks, *Analytical Chemistry,* vol. 20, p. 12, December 1948, and Newchurch, E. J., *et al.,* Quality Control in Petroleum Research Laboratory, *Analytical Chemistry,* vol. 28, pp. 154–157, February 1956.

[38] Nested and staggered nested designs are further explained in Section 27, or see Bainbridge, T. R., Staggered Nested Designs for Estimating Variance Components, *Industrial Quality Control,* vol. 22, pp. 12–20, July 1965, and Goldsmith, C. H., and D. W. Gaylor. Three Stage Nested Designs for Estimating Variance Components, *Technometrics,* vol. 12, No. 3, pp. 487–498, August 1970.

TABLE 29-3   Precision Study Results, Sample Type and Component Concentration Comparison

Sample mixture	Digital integrator areas relative 2s in parts per hundred
Gas	1.11
Low-boiling liquid	0.67
Medium-boiling liquid	1.14
High-boiling liquid	1.15
Component concentration:	
10%	1.34
30%	0.95
60%	0.60

TABLE 29-4   Precision Study Results, Integrator and Sample Size Comparisons

Normalized peak values	Relative $2s$* in parts per hundred	
	Small sample	Large sample
Digital integrator	1.17	0.73
Disk integrator.	2.00	1.69
Peak height	1.54	1.77

* Relative $2s$ = two standard deviations as percent of mean value.

TABLE 29-5   Precision Study Results, Column-Detector Comparison

Combination	Digital integrator areas relative 2s in parts per hundred
Packed column, hot wire	0.93
Packed column, thermistor.	1.23
Packed column, flame ionization	0.80
Capillary column, flame ionization	0.89

underestimate the variability of both the methods. Failure of the day-method interaction to reach significance signifies that, whatever the day-to-day effects are, they are uniform in their action on all samples. Since the methods do not differ, the volumetric, being quicker, was chosen.

Confidence Limits for Single Determinations. From the components of variance, confidence limits can be estimated for the analytical differences on samples. The methods for making these estimates are discussed in detail, with examples, in Section 22, under Statistical Estimation: Confidence Limits.

$$\sigma^2_{\text{duplicates}} + 2\sigma^2_{\text{samples}} = 194.50$$

$$\sigma^2_{\text{dup}} = 5.72 \qquad \text{(from data)}$$

$$\sigma^2_{\text{sam}} = 94.39 \qquad \text{(by solving above equation)}$$

$$\sigma^2_{\text{total}} = 100.11$$

$$\sigma_{\text{total}} = 10.0$$

$$\sigma_{T(\text{decoded})} = 0.10$$

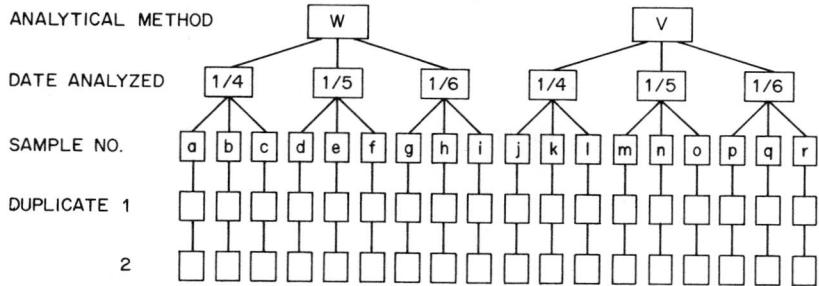

Fig. 29-3   Test layout in analytical method development.

For the 12 degrees of freedom available,[39, 40] $t = 2.18$.   Hence, 95% confidence limits for a *single* sample analyzed *once* on a given day are $\pm L = t\sigma_T = 2.18 \times 0.10 = 0.218$.   Inasmuch as the existing specification range was only 0.50%, neither method was adequate.   Solution temperature control eliminated the day effect and additional analysts were trained in the volumetric method before the

TABLE 29-6   Development of a Test Method to a Given Precision

Method	Weight								
Days	¼			⅕			⅙		
Sample	*a*	*b*	*c*	*d*	*e*	*f*	*g*	*h*	*i*
Duplicates:									
1	62	44	45	48	54	48	81	52	60
2	64	44	42	42	50	44	78	52	61
Average	63.0	44.0	43.5	45.0	52.0	46.0	79.5	52.0	60.5
Day average	. . .	. . .	50.2	. . .	. . .	47.7	. . .	. . .	64.0

Method	Volumetric								
Days	¼			⅕			⅙		
Sample	*j*	*k*	*l*	*m*	*n*	*o*	*p*	*q*	*r*
Duplicates:									
1	35	42	44	52	58	48	79	50	58
2	37	42	40	45	54	43	77	50	59
Average	36.0	42.0	42.0	48.5	56.0	45.5	78.0	50.0	58.5
Day average	. . .	. . .	40.0	. . .	. . .	50.0	. . .	. . .	62.2

Data shown are coded ($-$ 15.00, $\times$ 100).

tests shown in Table 29-8 were made.   The statistical analysis (Table 29-9) verified that differences among analysts compared with the replicate sample variance were no larger than could be expected by chance alone.   Hence, the precision of the laboratory method was calculated from the total sum of squares, resulting in a stan-

[39] A rule of thumb to use here is:
"When the mean squares are significantly different (or do not estimate the same variance) use the degrees of freedom of the biggest variance."
A more exact procedure is that of F. E. Satterthwaite (An Approximate Distribution of Estimates of Variance Components, *Biometrics Bulletin*, vol. 2, pp. 110–114, 1946).
[40] See also Davies, O. L. (ed.), "Statistical Methods in Research and Production," 3d ed. rev., pp. 144–149, Oliver & Boyd Ltd., Edinburgh, 1957, for procedures for confidence limits *for individual components of variance*; 95% limits for σ of samples are 0.0558 and 0.130.

TABLE 29-7   Analysis of Variance

Source	Degrees of freedom	Sums of squares	Mean squares	F ratio	Expected mean squares** (EMS)
Methods.	1	93.44	93.44	< 1	$\sigma_d{}^2 + l\sigma_S{}^2 + jkl\sigma_M{}^2$
Days	2	2,164.50	1,082.25	5.6*	$\sigma_d{}^2 + l\sigma_S{}^2 + ikl\sigma_D{}^2$
Days × methods.	2	243.06	121.53	< 1	$\sigma_d{}^2 + l\sigma_S{}^2 + kl\sigma_{DM}{}^2$
Sample (within days). . .	12	2,334.00	194.50	34.0***	$\sigma_d{}^2 + l\sigma_S{}^2$
Duplicates (within samples).	18	103.00	5.72	. . .	$\sigma_d{}^2$
Total.	35	4,938.00			

Significant at 0.05 (*) and 0.001 (***) levels.
** Mathematical model:

$$y_{ijkl} = \mu + M_i{}^F + D_j{}^F + (DM)_{ij}{}^F + S_{k(ij)}{}^R + d_{l(ijk)}{}^R$$

where M = methods ($i = 1, 2$; 1 = weight; 2 = volumetric)
$\quad\quad\quad D$ = days ($j = 1, 2, 3$)
$\quad\quad\quad DM$ = method × day interaction
$\quad\quad\quad S$ = samples within days and methods ($k = 1, 2, 3$)
$\quad\quad\quad d$ = duplicates within samples, days, and methods ($l = 1, 2$)
$\quad\quad\quad F$ = fixed factor, R = random factor

Set EMS = mean squares and solve; i.e., $\sigma_d{}^2 = 5.72$; $\sigma_d{}^2 + 2\sigma_S{}^2 = 194.50$; $\sigma_S{}^2 = 94.39$.

TABLE 29-8   Test of Modified Method by Several Analysts

Replicate Sample No.	Analyst identification*				
	A	B	C	D	E
1.	9	8	6	8	6
2.	3	4	6	8	2
Average. . . .	6	6	6	8	4

* Data coded (-15.00, × 100)(one test per sample).

TABLE 29-9   Analysis of Variance

Source	Degrees of freedom	Sums of squares	Mean squares	F ratio
Analysts.	4	16	4.0	< 1
Sample replicates	5	34	6.8	
Total	9	50		

dard deviation of 0.0235, only one-fourth as large as earlier obtained, and significantly smaller at the 0.02 level as judged by an F test:[41]

$$F = \left(\frac{0.100}{0.0235}\right)^2 = 18.1; F(0.02; 12, 9) = 5.1$$

Number of Samples to Analyze.   In deciding whether several samples[42,43] should

[41] A double-tailed test was used since it was unknown *a priori* which variance would be least.
[42] *Samples* are to be replicated here since $\sigma = 0.0235$ represents variation due to *both* sample-to-sample difference and analytical-test-method variation.   A preferred way is to use

be analyzed and the results averaged to improve precision of the estimate, the following approach can be taken. If precision is wanted such that only 10% of the specification range is consumed by the measuring method, the number of samples needed can be calculated directly from the specifications. Given a specification of 16.00 $\pm 0.25\%$, the uncertainty of any reported analysis should not exceed $\pm 0.025\%$. The number of samples n to be analyzed and averaged is

$$n = \left(\frac{t\sigma}{\pm L} \right)^2 = \left(\frac{2.26 \times 0.0235}{\pm 0.025} \right)^2 = 4.52 \text{ or } 5$$

using $t = 2.26$ based on 9 degrees of freedom and 95% confidence limits.

Control samples (five randomly taken at a time) submitted for analysis would be judged acceptable or not as the average of the five determinations fell within control limits for an averages chart;[44]

$$\bar{\bar{X}} \pm \frac{2\sigma'}{\sqrt{n}} = 16.00 \pm \frac{2 \times 0.0235}{\sqrt{5}} = 16.00 \pm 0.021$$

$$UCL = 16.021 \ \%$$
$$\bar{\bar{X}}' = 16.000 \ \%$$
$$LCL = 15.979 \ \%$$

Cumulative Average Chart. An alternative technique, sequential in nature, compares successive cumulative averages based on one, two, three, etc., tests until it truncates at a given number, with appropriate limits, as shown in Figure 29-4. Note that additional analysis is called for in certain cases when even though the average lies within specifications it falls within the no-decision zone. The cumulative average limits represent the test error divided by the square root of cumulative sample size.

Relation of Test Limits and Specification Limits. A third method is to establish a predetermined relationship between test limits and specification limits.[45]

Control Chart to Check Test Method. Range control charts are commonly used to monitor the analytical process. See Section 23, under Concept of the Control Chart, et seq.

Need for Understanding Analytical Method An important consideration in establishing test limits or charts for controlling accuracy or precision of laboratory methods is proper identification of the testing scheme.[46] Since precision of an average is im-

---

a nested design, as in Fig. 29-3, but with *analyses* replicated (in the sense of Fig. 29-5). See Section 25A, Bulk Sampling, for more details. Also see Bicking, C. A., The Sampling of Bulk Material, *Materials Research & Standards*, vol. 7, pp. 95–116, March 1967.

[43] See also Youden, W. J., and J. M. Cameron, Use of Statistics to Determine Precision of Test Methods, ASTM Symposium on Statistical Analysis, *Special Technical Publication #103*, pp. 27–34, October 1949.

[44] See Section 23, under Control Charts for Average and Range; note that the average of five analyses will show as an out-of-control point about 6 times in 10 if the process average has shifted more than 0.025% from the nominal, or about 99 times in 100 if it has shifted more than 0.050% from the nominal. See also Ferris, C. D., F. E. Grubbs, and C. L. Weaver, Operating Characteristics for the Common Statistical Tests of Significance, *Annals of Mathematical Statistics*, vol. XVII, pp. 178–192, 1946.

[45] Grubbs, F., and H. Coon, On Setting Test Limits Relative to Specification Limits, *Industrial Quality Control*, vol. 10, No. 5, pp. 15–20, March 1954. See also, same issue, pp. 10–15, Eagle, Alan R., A Method for Handling Errors in Testing and Measuring.

[46] See Wernimont, Grant, The Basis for Interpreting Results from a Testing Process, *Experientia Supplementum*, vol. V, 1957.

proved only if the average represents two or more *independent* results, it is usually rewarding to draw the flow sheet of the testing process. Method A of Figure 29-5 represents the typical "duplicate" analysis, where only the titration repeatability is checked; no measure of precision of steps 1 through 3 is available in the differences between the titrated results. Method B represents the true independent "replicate," in which each stage is performed independently of any previous weighing. Note that weighing in step 1 is *not* carried out first for replicate 1 then 2; but preferably all of replicate 1 is completed prior to starting replicate 2. This is not always feasible, and different-sized samples, clearing the balance pan of weights, and other complete "startover" methods can be used.[47]

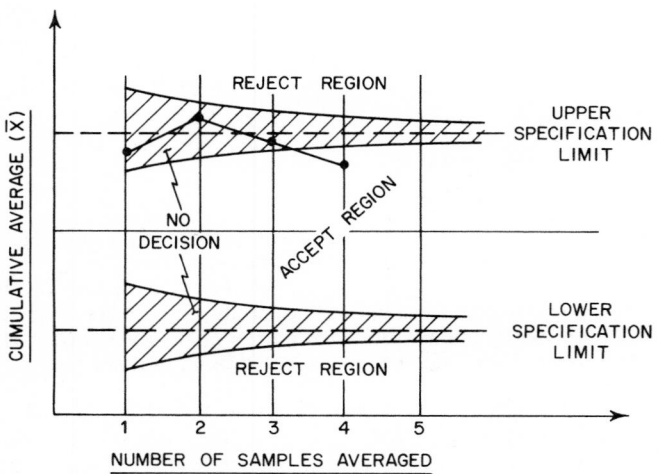

Fig. 29-4 Test on cumulative average.

Control of Product Quality This requires sampling and testing of raw materials, analysis of samples during manufacture, and analysis of finished products. Each is discussed below.

Most raw materials for chemical processes are purchased on the basis of chemical analysis, with standard specifications typical.[48] The methods and philosophy of sampling and testing depend upon the nature of the material (bulk solids, bulk liquids, type of packaging, etc.). (See Section 25A on Bulk Sampling.) Once a vendor's quality has been established as acceptable and uniform, the raw material may be accepted on the basis of the vendor's analysis. Control charts or certification of statistical control of the vendor's process may accompany the invoice.[49]

Process control of product quality on the basis of tests *after* the product is made may be too little and too late. Instead, samples are taken during the operation,

[47] See also Calder, A. B., Statistical Approach in Analytical Chemistry: Why It Is Important, *Analytical Chemistry,* vol. 36, pp. 25A–34A, August 1964; Higgins, J., Subtracting the Blank Value, *Analyst,* vol. 89, pp. 211–215, 1964; and Hsi, B. P., Optimization of Quality Control in the Chemical Laboratory, *Technometrics,* vol. 8, pp. 519–534, August 1966.

[48] See Patek, J. M., Specifications, in I. M. Kolthoff and P. J. Elving (eds.), "Treatise on Analytical Chemistry," Part III, vol. 1, Interscience Publishers, a division of John Wiley & Sons, Inc., New York, 1968, for detailed discussion pertinent to this industry.

[49] See also Section 10, under Vendor Quality.

and based on the results, process adjustments made.   The tentative process as received from Research usually specifies the control points and action to be taken, but the initiative of the control chemist is required when problems arise.   Regression studies are useful in determining the relationship between control test results and finished product properties.[50]   Many companies beneficially use continuous sampling devices to provide continuous control and avoid blending composite grab samples.   Connected to gas-liquid chromatographs and other instruments, they provide continuous monitoring of the process stream.   These automatic instruments may in turn be connected to a digital computer so sample composition can be calculated immediately.   Open-loop control, subject to operator action, predominates

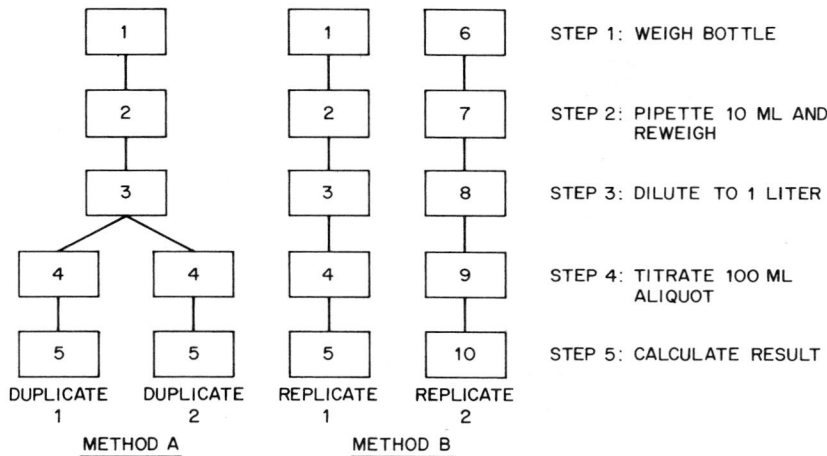

Fig. 29-5   Relation of duplicates and replicates.

currently, but closed-loop computer control is rapidly replacing obsoleted instruments.

When chemical control tests are run by operators at plant test stations, commonly the analytical laboratory maintains the equipment, standardizes test solutions, and occasionally checks operator results.[51]

Finished product testing is done by the Analytical Laboratory to determine specification conformance and the state of process control.   Normally, the sample is delivered to the laboratory by the manufacturing personnel responsible for the process.   Occasionally the laboratory will actually obtain a sample of the finished material.   Responsibility for maintaining the accuracy and precision of the tests belongs to the laboratory, and based on the results, material is accepted or rejected.   *Disposition* of rejected finished product is not a laboratory function.[52]

[50] See Hinchen, J. D., Correlation Analysis in Batch Process Control, *Industrial Quality Control,* March 1955.

[51] See Wernimont, G., Use of Control Charts in the Analytical Laboratory, *Analytical Edition, Industrial and Engineering Chemistry,* vol. 18, p. 587, 1946; and Mitchell, J. A., Control of the Accuracy and Precision of Industrial Tests and Analyses, *Industrial and Engineering Chemistry,* vol. 19, pp. 961–967, December 1947.

[52] Manufacturing usually decides how the rejected product is to be modified (blended, treated, recycled, scrapped, etc.).   The Sales Department is notified if customer specifications cannot be met.

The finished product results are reported to manufacturing as each batch or lot is tested.[53] Results are also recorded in a permanent ledger and are available for statistical analysis.[54]

Control Charting and Reporting of Results.   In many laboratories it is the practice to maintain control charts, either in the laboratory or preferably adjacent to process units in the plant.   Laboratory personnel monitor these charts on a day-to-day basis, and call production personnel's attention to trends, shifts in level, out of control points, etc., as they occur whether the individual lots remain in specification or not.   The charts also can be reviewed periodically with Production Supervision, Marketing Technical Service personnel, and Quality engineers.   In this way they form a basis, together with field performance information, for periodic Quality Audits for each product.

Modifications of the standard Shewhart Control Chart are quite common in chemical process quality control.   These include cumulative sum charts which are very sensitive to shifts in level, narrower control chart limits (2σ vs. 3σ), individual charts and moving-range charts.[55]   For process use, careful weighing of the risks involved has often resulted in the use of 2σ limits and even in some unusual instances of 1.5 or 1σ limits.   For average charts, the narrowed limits are directly proportional to the reduced number of standard deviations.[56]

Individual measurement and moving-range charts are particularly suited for study of batch-type processes.   The individual measurement chart may be used with average and range charts or alone.   Since, characteristically, data accumulate slowly in batch operations, it is often advantageous to use the moving-range method of calculating control chart limits for the individual measurements.   This consists of averaging the differences between consecutive pairs of measurements[57] (viz., between 1 and 2, 2 and 3, etc.) and substituting constants in the following formula for 2σ limits:

$$\bar{\bar{X}} \pm 2/3\,(1.88\bar{R}\sqrt{2})$$

which reduces to $\bar{\bar{X}} \pm 1.77\bar{R}$

THE MANUFACTURING DEPARTMENT

Raw Material Acceptance   In many companies, the responsibility for acceptance of raw material lies with the Manufacturing Department.   If all specifications are met, or if the vendor has certified that the material is of standard quality, there is no problem.   However, if one or more properties deviate from standard, and it is judged that by process modification, satisfactory product can be made from the raw material, manufacturing management may exercise the prerogative of accepting the material.   In such cases, the material will be used under a limited procedure, which

[53] Hinchen, J. D., Control Charts in Batch Processes, *New England Quality Control Conference Papers,* Aug. 22, 1952, pp. 113–120.

[54] See Bingham, R. S., Jr., An Application of Continuous Sampling Plans for Chemical Acceptance and Control, *Transactions, Statistical Methods in the Chemical Industry,* Jan. 12, 1957, pp. 67–85, American Society for Quality Control, Chemical Division, Hoboken, N.J., for a description of an application of Dodge's CSP-3 plan to multiple attributes of an organic product.

[55] See Section 23 for details.

[56] See Section 23 for the increase in "power" afforded.

[57] See Section 23, Process Control by Statistical Methods, on the number of observations to establish "state of control."

is subject to the review and approval of the Research Department, as well as several responsible individuals in manufacturing. The vendor, of course, is notified of the discrepancy in raw material quality.[58]

Process Control   Quality control during manufacturing rests with the Manufacturing Department. This includes preparation of Standard Operating Procedures, Operating Instructions for chemical operators, and taking specific action based on control test results. Production Supervision is responsible for recognizing and correcting unusual situations, and has the sole responsibility for shutting down a line that is producing off-quality product.

In many instances exceptionally fine control of quality is unnecessary because of the ease of blending, reworking, or making alternate classification of materials of variable qualities. However, the prevalence of these practices often affords an opportunity for substantial cost reduction by careful process control. Every such instance should be examined on its merits.

In batch-type operations, in particular, the control of processing time is often the most important source of saving in processing costs as well as a means of improving quality level and uniformity. A great deal about effect on quality of formulations, operating conditions, and personnel performance can be learned by intelligent use of a combination of charts on processing time and quality measurements.[59]

Much of the effectiveness of quality control and especially of the use of control charts is their psychological effect. In many instances, major improvements in quality level and uniformity have come about almost immediately upon installation of charts in operating areas. Removal of the charts has resulted in poorer quality performance. The same kind of thing is probably present, to some degree, in all parts of the effort to improve quality.[60] The human aspects of application of the scientific method are always as important as its technical phases. The supervisor or chemist using the techniques must learn to accept a way of thinking which is often contrary to parts of his academic training.[61] A new generation of scientific and engineering personnel may well come into industry better equipped originally for the job of quality control.

In any application of industrial statistics, no matter what the industry, the general form of the statistical method applying to a particular kind of problem is essentially the same. The general forms of the most widely applicable techniques have been set forth in Sections 22 through 28 of this Handbook. For the chemical industries at least, greatest interest is likely to center on the manner of approaching the solution of a series of typical problems rather than a rigorous development of the statistical methods used. The general outline of what follows is to state the problem as clearly as possible; provide a background of general information to orient the reader; describe in some detail the preparation made for the work, and the psychological and technical approach followed; indicate with tables or charts the principal steps in the statistical analysis of the data; and finally, point out the results of the work done.[62]

[58] See Mitchell, James A., Quality Control in Raw Materials Acceptance and Chemical Specifications, *Industrial Quality Control,* vol. 4, No. 3, November 1947.

[59] See Traylor, W. S., Use of Statistical Methods for Time Study of Batch Processes, *Industrial Quality Control.* vol. 4, No. 4, January 1948, for a noteworthy paper.

[60] See Section 18, under Role of the Behavioral Scientists.

[61] See Hampton, D. R., C. E. Summer, and R. A. Webber, "Organizational Behavior and the Practise of Management," Scott, Foresman and Company, Glenview, Ill. 1968, especially pp. 413–425, Innovation and Conflict in Industrial Engineering, and pp. 273–355, The Impact of Informal Organization: Social Factors in Organizational Behavior.

[62] See Bennett, C. A., and N. L. Franklin, "Statistical Analysis in Chemistry and the Chemical

UNIT OPERATIONS (OR PHYSICAL CHANGES)—BATCH OPERATIONS

Mixing   The unit operation of mixing involves the blending of two or more materials into a homogeneous lot.   The materials mixed may be either dry, liquid, or a combination of dry and liquid ingredients resulting in a solution, a paste, or any agglomerate of varying degrees of dryness.   Mixing may be continuous; but in the

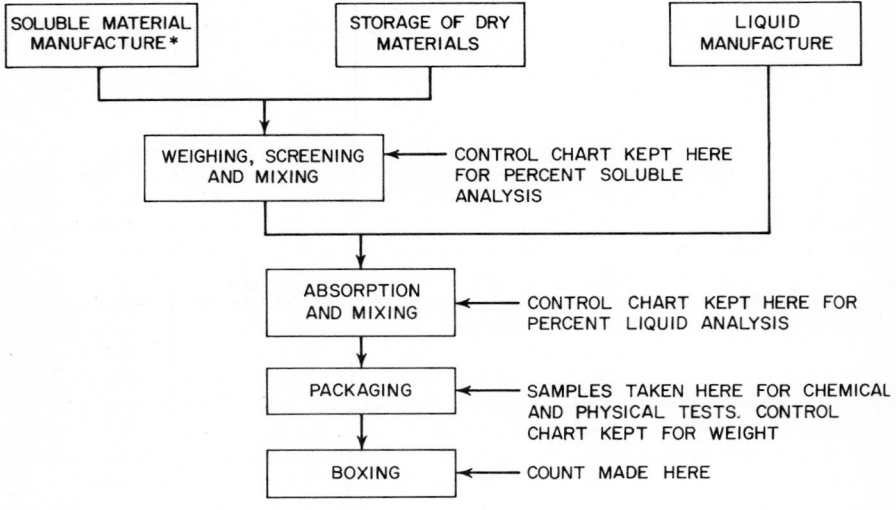

* SEE SECTION ON CRYSTALLIZATION

Fig. 29-6   Simplified flow sheet for mixing operation.

manufacture of typical products such as fertilizer, dynamite, paints, lacquers, or dyes, a batch operation is most common.

The example considered is improvement during manufacture of the uniformity of proportions of various chemical constituents of a damp mix for the purpose of controlling closely an important performance characteristic.   In addition to providing a simple, workable system for process control of chemical constituents, the full solution calls for measuring the reproducibility of the analytical methods used and discovering how well product performance is correlated with chemical content.   Typically, the problem finally involves study of another production operation which supplies one of the principal ingredients.

The manufacturing procedure consists of the absorption of a liquid in a mixture of nonsoluble materials with some soluble ingredients which add to the efficiency of product performance (see Figure 29-6).

Since the formulations in which the product are made are determined in advance,

Industry," John Wiley & Sons, Inc., New York, 1954; Davies, O. L. (ed.), "Design and Analysis of Industrial Experiments," 3d ed. rev., Oliver & Boyd Ltd., Edinburgh, 1957; and Daniel, C., Application of Statistical Methods in Chemical Engineering, *Industrial and Engineering Chemistry,* vol. 48, No. 9, pp. 1392–1402, September 1956, for additional examples amplifying these points.

control of the quality of the product depends principally on the quality and uniformity of ingredients and on operator attention to weighing, mixing, and packaging. Normally, all the critical ingredients are prepared at the site of the mixing, so that variations are known and taken into account. For example, control data from manufacture of the principal soluble material permit classification and blending of that material when necessary. Furthermore, manufacture of the liquid component proceeds as needed under unvarying, closely watched conditions.

One of the deterrents to easy systematic control of the process is its batch nature and the fact that rarely is one formulation made for a great number of consecutive batches on the same equipment. Control charting of all formulations made would

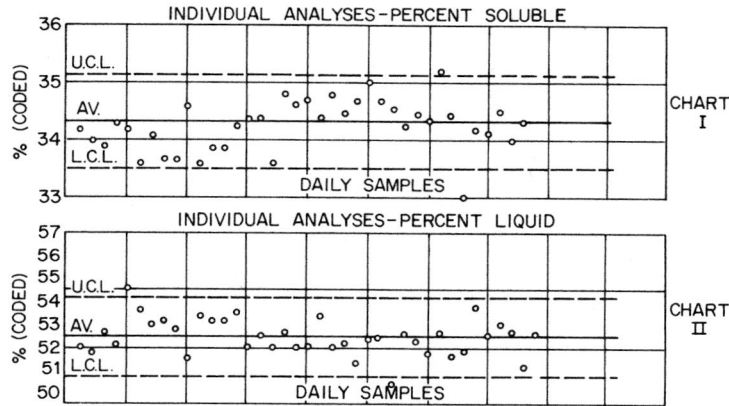

Fig. 29-7 Mixing-operation control.

involve an excessive amount of paperwork, and produce information on the less common formulations at such a slow rate as to be of limited value. Consideration is given, therefore, to the regular charting of results only from the most frequently made formulations.

Three very important determinations are made on daily samples from each formulation manufactured in quantity: (1) percent of soluble, (2) percent of liquid content, and (3) a performance rating. Each of these series of measurements is suitable for control charting by operators at points where they exercise definite control over quality. The most useful form of chart shows test results by the control laboratory on samples from the individual batches. Figure 29-6 indicates the points at which each of these factors, in turn, is susceptible to control. The locations for the charts for the first two properties are obvious, but the direct application of a chart for performance in the operating area is not so readily justified.

The percent of soluble chart may be kept at the preliminary mixing stage where care following the formulation instructions and in weighing will influence the amount of soluble material included. The percent of liquid chart may be kept at the final mixing stage where the care in addition and mixing of the liquid will influence the dampness of the sample. Typical are Charts I and II for percent of soluble and percent of liquid, respectively, given in Figure 29-7. Perhaps the most troublesome part of the control of percent of liquid is the tendency toward the formation of lumps of large size compared with the size of sample used for chemical analysis. Presence of lumps may give inordinate values for percent of liquid. The magnitude of the effect of the poor test reproducibility due to this sampling difficulty may be appreciated by inspection and analysis of a set of typical duplicate analytical results.[63]

To make meaningful decisions in interpreting analytical data, the precision of the test method must be determined. Table 29-10 gives a set of 16 duplicate results and the computation of the test precision.

TABLE 29-10   Calculation of Precision of Analysis for Percent of Liquid Content

Original Data (Coded)

Sample No.	Duplicate tests on same samples		Ranges
1	1.2	2.4	1.2
2	1.4	0.6	0.8
3	1.8	0.5	1.3
4	0.8	1.2	0.4
5	0.8	0.2	0.6
6	0	0.7	0.7
7	0.9	0.1	0.8
8	0.9	0.9	0
9	1.8	0.6	1.2
10	0.8	0.8	0
11	3.1	0.7	2.4
12	2.5	0.4	2.1
13	0.5	0.3	0.2
14	0.5	0.7	0.2
15	1.1	0.9	0.2
16	1.1	0.8	0.3

Total 12.4
Average 0.775

$$s = \frac{\bar{R}}{d_2} = \frac{0.775}{1.128} = 0.687$$

95% confidence limits of individual tests (test precision) $= \pm L = \pm ts$.
For 16 degrees of freedom, $t = 2.12$, $\pm L = \pm 2.12 \times 0.687 = \pm 1.46$.

The test variation is more than 14% of the specified liquid content. Moreover, more complete information which became available showed that the test variation accounted for more than 78% of the total variation in results. This situation pointed out the necessity for improvement of the test method. Several methods were tried to bring about this improvement, with some resultant satisfaction.[64]

The product performance chart can be kept either in the packaging area or at the boxing operation (preferably the former) for convenience in correcting the process

[63] In this Section, see under Analytical Laboratory relative to the importance of suitable accuracy and precision. See also Section 25A on Bulk Sampling.

[64] Test methods sometimes have unnecessary variation built in as a result of efforts to "improve" the method. For example, in chemical standards preparation, substantial reduction in analytical effort and test variance may be possible. J. A. Speckman, *Journal of Research of the National Bureau of Standards*, vol. 68B, pp. 49–53, April–June 1964, has shown that the practice of taking measurements until two *identical* readings are obtained cannot be justified since the average of the first two readings almost always gives a better estimate of the measured quantity.

where the weight per package could be closely watched. However, a more direct subject for control is weight per package, which is critical. The real matter of interest at this stage is the density of packing of the damp mix because of its influence on performance. Weight is directly correlated with density because the greater the density of packing, the greater the weight.

The effect of chemical content on performance was one of the first things studied. Multiple regression measured the effect of percent of soluble (as two different in-

TABLE 29-11   Multiple Regression of Percent of Liquid (Other Than Water), Percent of Water, Percent of No. 1 Soluble, Percent of No. 2 Soluble, with Product Performance Rating

Original Data (Coded)

Rating y	Liquid (other than water) x_1	Water x_2	Soluble No. 1 x_3	Soluble No. 2 x_4
− 35	0.75	0.01	0.55	0.10
− 75	0.35	0.06	0.90	0.45
− 105	0.45	0.01	− 0.25	0.40
− 55	0.25	0.04	0.80	0.25
− 25	0.15	0.06	− 0.05	− 0.30
5	0	0.01	0.25	− 0.35
− 95	0.30	− 0.01	− 0.80	− 0.10
− 55	0.25	0.01	− 0.20	0.05
5	− 0.15	0.06	1.00	1.30
− 20	0.15	0.01	0.90	0.90
− 35	0	0.01	1.00	1.05
− 45	− 0.15	0.01	− 0.30	1.65
90	0.35	0.14	1.30	− 0.75
35	0.90	0.09	0.15	0.70
145	0.85	0.11	1.10	− 0.50
95	0.35	0.11	1.00	− 0.30
− 170	4.80	0.73	7.35	4.55

gredients separately); percent of liquid; and moisture, as water, on the performance characteristic. A predicting equation of the form

$$Y = b_0 + b_1 X_1 + b_2 X_2 + b_3 X_3 + b_4 X_4$$

was sought, where coded values were

Y = performance rating
X_1 = liquid other than water, percent
X_2 = water, percent
X_3 = soluble No. 1, percent
X_4 = soluble No. 2, percent

The data are shown in Table 29-11.

A backward stepwise regression program produced the following equation:[65]

$$Y = -68.11 + 1,259.88 X_2$$

Water Content X_2 was significant at 99% + and explained 67.42% of the total variance of the performance rating Y. No other factor was significant.

[65] See Draper, N. R., and H. Smith, "Applied Regression Analysis," John Wiley & Sons, Inc., New York, 1966; also Section 26.

Another factor affecting performance—the fineness of crystals in the principal soluble material—was next examined. Correlation studies showed an important connection between these factors, explained by the better performance associated with fine crystals, presumably because of their greater surface area. Since more uniform crystals of optimum size were wanted, this led to the crystallization study described next.

Evaporation and Crystallization These two unit operations often follow in sequence.[66] They involve heat application to remove moisture and, when formation of crystals is important, require careful application of motion for crystal size control. The operation is usually batch rather than continuous. Typical products are organic and inorganic salts, caustic soda, phosphoric acid, glycerin, and sugar.

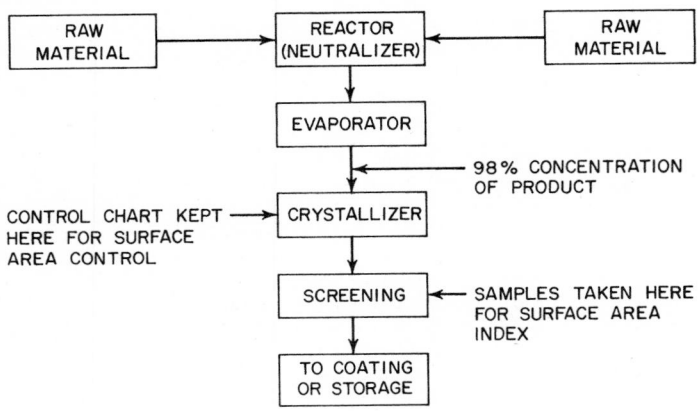

Fig. 29-8 Simplified flow sheet for evaporation and crystallization.

In this example, after the chemical reaction is completed, the product is in a dilute aqueous solution. The resulting solution is evaporated to 98% solids in open vats, crystallized, and grained under rolling motion in agitated, steam-heated kettles. The crystals are screened to return fines to the crystallizer and acceptable grains either to a coating operation to increase water resistance or to storage. Figure 29-8 gives the simplified flow sheet.

The desirable property for this material is large surface area, i.e., small particles. Crystal size control is the most critical item in its manufacture. Periodic crystal size measurements must be made prior to adjusting crystallizer temperature or agitation speed. This may be done by selective screening. A physical method for determining an index number representing average crystal size of a lot was devised for rapid charting to assist in production control. This particle-size index was plotted on a control chart kept alongside the crystallizer kettle. As long as control was exhibited, no change in crystallizer operation was made. If lack of control occurred, appropriate action was to be taken at once by the operator.

"Two-sigma" limits for individual surface-area determinations were chosen because of previous successful use of this kind of chart in production processes where surface area was important. It is significant that this development came only after

---

[66] See Box, G. E. P., and J. Chanmugam, Adaptive Optimization of Continuous Processes, *Industrial and Engineering Chemistry,* vol. 54, p. 2, February, 1962, as to the inflation of process variance if "heels" or residues are left in tanks or reactors, i.e., because of correlated errors.

a new method of obtaining a surface-area index made it possible to correlate variables expected from technical knowledge to affect the problem.

UNIT OPERATIONS—SEMICONTINUOUS

Solvent Extraction Solvent extraction consists of the physical separation of two or more materials which have been in close association. It may separate a soluble from an insoluble material by a solvent under heat and pressure, or separate two liquids by means of a solvent in which the liquids are unequally soluble, as in countercurrent extraction. Typical products of processes in which solvent extraction is in-

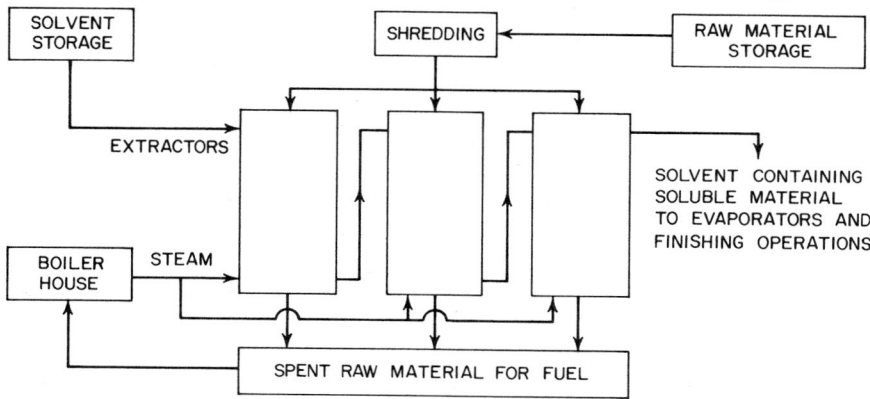

Fig. 29-9 Simplified flow sheet for solvent-extraction operation.

volved are coal gas, insecticides, perfumes, oils, acetic acid, rosin, and lubricating oils.

The example describes a process in which a shredded raw material is subjected to alternate periods of solvent pumping and steam heating under pressure. The extractors are arranged in a battery so that, as a new charge is placed in the cycle, an exhausted charge is removed. At this stage, the process continues intermittently, although preparation of the raw material, evaporation, and subsequent finishing operations are continuous. Figure 29-9 gives a simplified diagram of the extraction operation.

The raw material contains approximately 20% of extractable materials. All but a fraction of 1% of these extractable substances are readily removed. However, the tonnage handled is so great that extraction of an additional 0.05% would increase the value of product by about $400 per day. Very close control and lowest possible level of extractable material remaining in the spent charge is desirable. As a means of analyzing existing efficiency and of readily following the effect of changes, a control chart like the one in Figure 29-10 is effective. Weekly average values are plotted on this chart because of the greater precision of averages of a test which is not highly reproducible. The control limits are based on the average range of weekly subgroups made up of seven daily test values.[67]

A number of long-term factors affect extraction efficiency. Their influence is so gradual that, though they may be control charted, the charts are not effective as a

[67] See also Vance, F. P., An Economic Basis for Setting Confidence Limits, *Industrial Engineering Chemistry*, vol. 58, p. 2, February 1966, for an alternative approach to setting limits.

direct means of process control. Two of these basic factors are the amount of raw material processed and seasonal factors (the latter is concerned with methods of handling and storing the raw material; each can modify its moisture content). Also, over a period of years, a change in the quality of the raw material may become apparent. The relative importance of these factors may be tested by correlation studies of monthly or quarterly averages. The correction of their effects usually involves major equipment changes, such as the addition of more extractors to the battery, decreasing rate of production by lengthening the extraction cycle, location of a higher grade of raw material, or bulk drying of the raw material before extracting it.

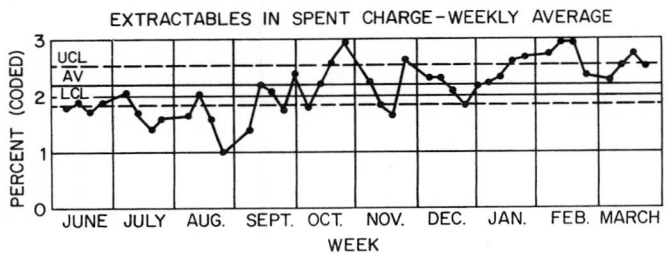

EXTRACTABLES IN SPENT CHARGE – WEEKLY AVERAGE

Fig. 29-10   Solvent-extraction efficiency.

After the long-term factors have been taken into account, something can be done by the operators in the extraction area to reduce the extractables in the spent material. Their efforts may be guided by control charts to follow variations in the critical operating conditions.

Fourteen processing measurements are regularly made and recorded in the processing log. With this many variables affecting efficiency, it is difficult for the operator to know what to do when in trouble. Even if all 14 factors were control charted, it would be difficult because little is known of the *combination* of factors or interactions which may affect the result. What is required before the operator can change the controls with beneficial effect is to pinpoint his attention on the few most critical points of control.

All 14 factors were studied by multiple regression, and 11 were eliminated successively until only three factors remained. The outcome was to ask the operators to keep three control charts and take action when control limits were exceeded on:

1. Quality of the solvent
2. Concentration of the extractable in the solvent at the end of the cycle
3. Size of shreds

The quality of the solvent can be controlled by greater attention in the solvent-recovery procedure, the concentration by varying the rate of pumping of solvent, and the size of shreds by screening and reshredding when necessary. Figure 29-11 shows diagrammatically the direct relationships among the principal processing factors. The high residual extractables at A are explained by a peak in the curve of solvent quality and in the concentration curve. Similarly, peak B is explained by large-sized shreds and high concentration. Finally, the low residual at C is based on unusually good solvent quality and low concentrations.

These charts are scaleless, but the extent of departure from control limits is in proper proportion in each instance. The correspondence of shaded areas in the three lower charts with shaded areas in the upper chart leads to the conclusion that often lack of control in one or another of the three critical processing factors will reflect in lack of control in efficiency. It follows that action to correct for lack

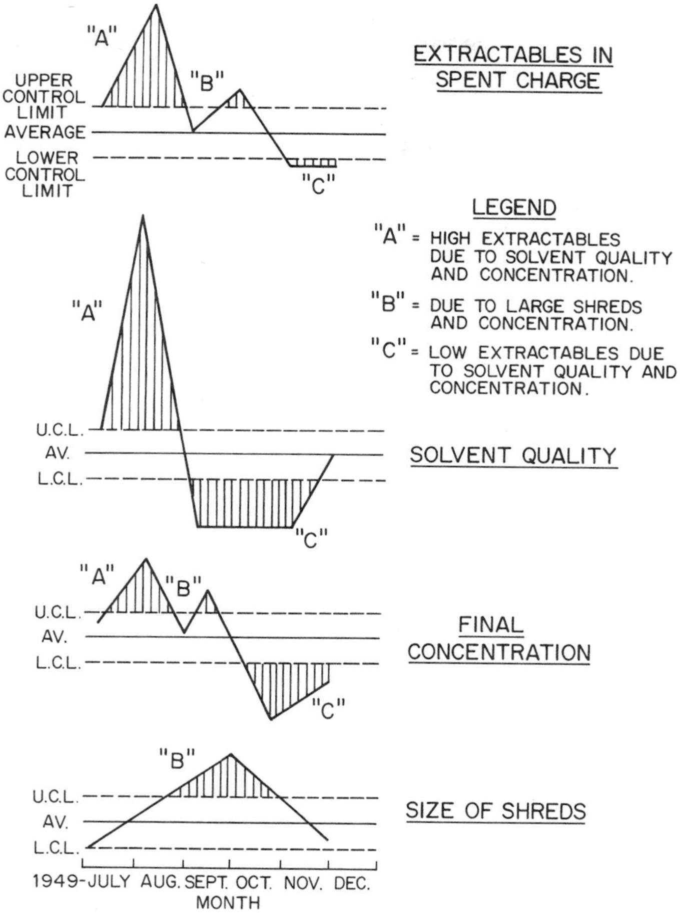

Fig. 29-11   Solvent-extraction efficiency compared with process variables.

of control in the process control charts (or to reproduce exceptional conditions in the more favorable direction) will improve control of efficiency.

The action charts to be used for control of solvent quality, concentration of solvent, and size of shreds will be similar to Figure 29-10, except that the limits should be changed to limits for daily measurements and daily results plotted as they are obtained.[68]   The charts should be kept in the operating area where the area superintendent, shift supervisors, and operators may follow them continually.   Charting may be done by control-laboratory personnel, a records clerk, or the operator, depending on plant preference.

Sedimentation and Decantation   The unit operations of sedimentation and decanta-

---

[68] Alternatives for closer process control include moving average charts, cumulative sum charts (see Section 23) or Adaptive Control (see below).   The choice in part is determined by individual preference.   However, for the results to be meaningful, they must reflect process response time (to adjustments) and test variability.

tion involve the action of gravity in settling or separation of sediment or sludge from a solution and subsequent drawing off of one portion. The removal of froth or skim is a similar operation. These procedures are required in the manufacture of products like potassium salts and caustic soda. The separation of slag in metal purification and withdrawal of sludge in certain types of chemical reactions are also typical.

The example describes the removal of sludge in a polymerization process. (A further description of the complete study of the polymerization process is given under Semicontinuous Processes. See Figure 29-15 for the simplified flow sheet.) The level of the sludge in the separator kettles was indicated by bobs which hung down in front of a blackboard and were connected by a chain-and-pulley system with floats inside the kettles. A rough scale was marked off in inches on the board. When the bobs hung low, sludge levels were high in the kettles, and vice versa. When the bobs seemed low enough to the operator, as judged by eye, a pump was turned on which began pumping the sludge from the kettle. When the operator thought the bob had risen high enough, the pump was turned off. Since the amount of sludge was known to affect product quality, this proved to be a rather loose way of controlling a critical stage of the process.

Sludge levels were read and recorded hourly in the operating log. Accordingly, it was easy to tabulate a portion of these data on control chart data sheets and calculate control limits. Subgroups of three hourly readings each were chosen arbitrarily. Limits for individual hourly readings were calculated by conventional methods, for $\overline{X}$ and R.[69] The calculated limits were chalked on the blackboard in the operating area, and the operators were instructed in their use. Pumps were to be turned on when the bobs reached the lower limit and turned off when they reached the upper limit.

The original limits for kettle No. 2 were 23.1 inches $\pm$ 13.1 inches. A few weeks after use of the chalked limits was begun, limits for this kettle were, as calculated in the sample, 23.1 $\pm$ 9.1. In the meantime, as the result of other statistical analyses, automatic level controllers were installed on some of the other kettles. A typical set of limits calculated from a kettle having automatic controls was 23.2 inches $\pm$ 2.3 inches. Subsequently all kettles were supplied with automatic controls with significant improvement in product quality.

Filtration   A serious matter for statistical analysis in filtration is the loss of fines in the filtrate. Particularly in the manufacture of expensive chemicals, a significant increase in the amount of fines can mean a huge monetary loss. Correlation of amount of fines with type of filter material used is an analysis that pays dividends. It is also likely that many other factors, such as pumping pressure, time of filtration, temperature of filtrate, and scheduling of filter changes, may be important. A control chart kept on amount of fines may enable the operator to identify these or other causes of unusual losses and make the necessary corrections.

UNIT OPERATIONS—CONTINUOUS

Fluid Flow and Absorption   Although these two unit operations do not necessarily go together, water-conditioning and effluent treatment, extremely important to the process industries, involve both.[70]

[69] See Section 23, under Examples of Control Chart for $\overline{X}$.

[70] Space does not permit adequate discussion of the details, but the quality engineer faced with problems in these areas should understand bulk sampling (including automatic samplers, pros and cons of sample compositing; etc.) (see Section 25A); stratification of sludge in river-beds, biological methods for judging river quality, as well as state and federal regulations governing sampling, testing, and reporting of results when under "orders." At this writing, standards are in a great state of flux. See also Razzeel, W.E., Pitfalls and Procedures in BOD Tests, *Pulp and Paper Magazine of Canada*, vol. 73, No. 7, pp. 86–89, July 1972.

Typically, control charts are used to follow incoming and outgoing quality. Equipment volume sets residence time and dictates sampling frequency.

Gas Absorption. This unit operation may have as its purpose the removal of impurities in a gas or the absorption of the gas itself in water. The process is carried out by passing the gas through absorption towers filled with the absorbing material,

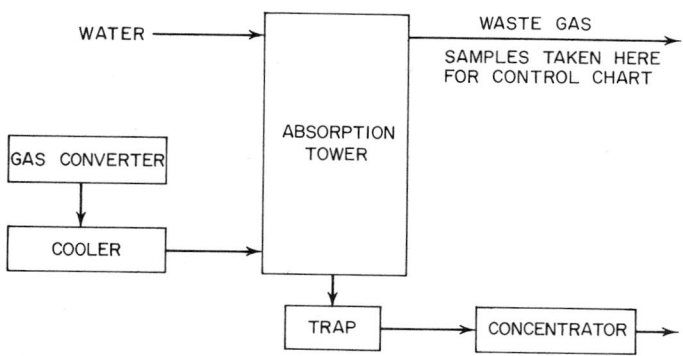

Fig. 29-12   Simplified flow sheet for gas-absorption operation.

baffles, plates, or various types of inactive packing. Typical products in which impurities are removed are distilled coal products, fuel gases, and industrial gases such as carbon dioxide. Examples of products in which the gas itself is absorbed in water are bleach, nitric acid, and hydrochloric acid.

In the example, a gas is passed up through bubble plates in an absorption tower countercurrent to the flow of water through the tower. The finished acid is drawn off through a trap and later concentrated. Figure 29-12 gives the simplified flow sheet.

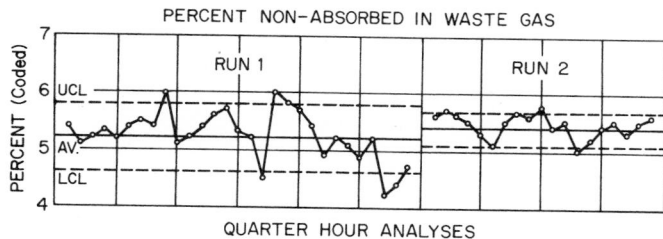

Fig. 29-13   Gas-absorption operation.

Control of absorption is only a part of the problem, but samples of the waste gases are taken for this as well as for other control purposes. Two runs of the percent unabsorbed gas are plotted on a control chart similar to Figure 29-13. From ranges of four analyses made every quarter hour, control limits for individual analyses were calculated. Lack of control indicates need for adjustment in such controllable factors as rate of gas flow or amount of cooling water. During the second run, the limits were much narrower, indicating much closer attention to control. If these limits are used on subsequent charts and adjustment is made immediately on the basis of lack of control (and only on that basis), the recurrence of wide and uncontrolled variation is unlikely.

UNIT PROCESSES (OR CHEMICAL CHANGES)—BATCH PROCESSES

Causticization   In modern large-scale plants, causticization proceeds continuously as in the continuous digestion of wood pulp. Caustic soda is used in large quantities in the manufacture of rayon, explosives, soap, paper, and many other products.

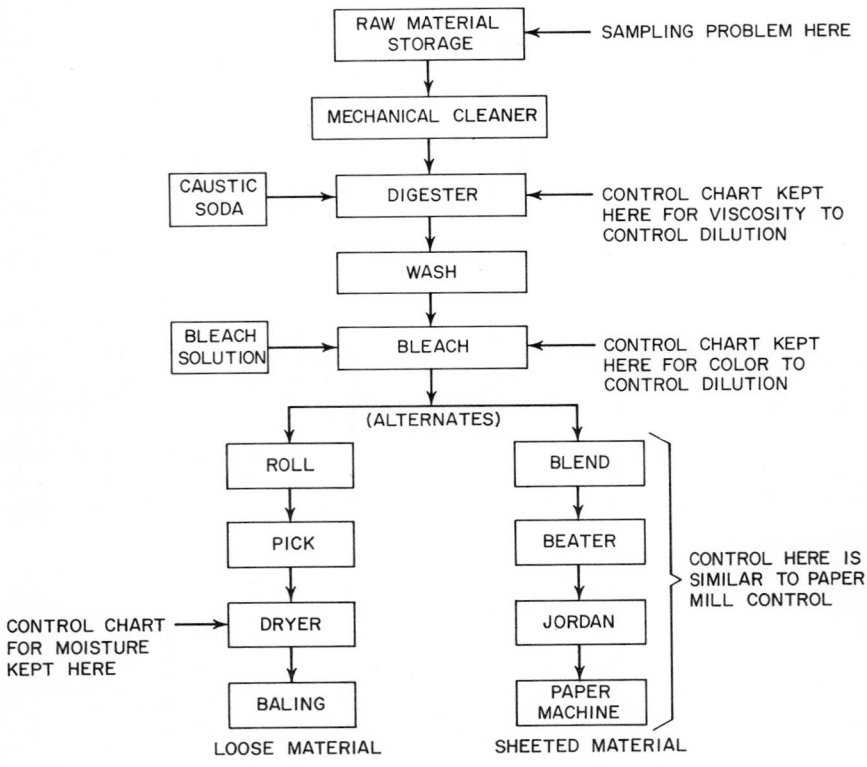

Fig. 29-14   Simplified flow sheet for a causticization process.

The causticized material is usually nitrated, acetylated, ethylated, or otherwise reacted, then spun, extruded, or cast to make final products such as celluloid, lacquers, film, and fibers. The process consists essentially of boiling with a dilute caustic solution to purify or modify the original raw materials.

The batch causticization described in the example is as straightforward an operation as can be found in the chemical industry. However, some nice statistical problems are associated with manufacturing. Uncontrolled variations at several points in the operation have far-reaching effects on properties of materials made in subsequent processes for which the causticized product is the principal raw material.

Figure 29-14 indicates some facets of the process control problem. Raw materials are received in bulk or in bales. Variations in physical properties, residual contaminants, dirt, and other properties are tremendous. The bulk sampling principles are directly applicable to the problem of selecting bales or lots for processing. Causticization control in the digester reflects directly in the viscosity of many end products, and bleaching success directly influences final product colors. Simple control charts for individual batches apply at both these stages in processing, as indicated on the flow sheet.

A mill survey of the purification stages uncovered the following information. Process variables enter all along the line during purification and are partially listed as follows:

Degree of wetting of raw material
Proportions of digester charge
Amount and properties of black liquor (partially spent caustic solution)
Fresh caustic concentration
Digester temperature, pressure, and cycle
Nature, concentration, agitation, and time of bleach
Number, agitation, and time of washes
Differences between individual pieces of equipment
Differences between shifts

Important properties such as color, filterability, dirt, HCl insoluble, and viscosity are determined largely before the end of this stage of the process. Within the limits imposed by equipment and operating instructions, the care exercised by the operators is an important factor in the variability of the product. The ability of the operators to control temperatures, pressures, feed rates, and concentrations is a profitable subject of study by area supervisors. However, the control of variables at the purification stage is primarily a concern of the laboratories.

The principal quality problem illustrated in this application concerns color variation *between lots* of causticized intermediate material and color variation *between batches* of a plastics material made from the same lots by a later reaction.

Analysis of variance offers so much in the study of this process that an example of its use is given.[71] Tables 29-12 and 29-13 show that color of causticized material has a greater effect on plastics color than variables in the plastic-manufacturing process. The proper place for further work to improve plastics color is in the causticization process, very possibly through closer control of the bleaching of the raw materials.

Esterification   As a batch-type process, esterification is typical of many operations in which attention to control of both final quality and the processing *time* is important. Products employing this process are represented by xanthate or viscose rayon, acetate rayon, and ethyl and vinyl acetate.

Final quality charts are useful in following trends from batch to batch, particularly in locating relatively slow acting causes of lack of control such as an instrument drift or the gradual degradation of a raw material. Chart choice and setup details are similar to batch-type unit operations. Individual batch charts with limits calculated from small subgroups, often moving ranges of two measurements, are common.

Final quality charts are much more useful if used in conjunction with time-cycle control charts. The time of each element in the production cycle is recorded separately, and for each component, the results for a small number of batches are sub-

---

[71] See Section 27 for details on Analysis of Variance generally. See also Mandel, J., The Partitioning of Interaction in Analysis of Variance, *Journal of Research of the National Bureau of Standards,* vol. 73B, no. 4, p. 309, 1969, for added analytical sensitivity.

TABLE 29-12 Comparison of Color Variation in Lots of Causticized Product with Color Variation between Plastics-material Batches

Original Data

Causticized material lot No.	Color of individual plastics batches processed	Total	Average
1	4.2, 3.9	8.1	4.05
2	4.9	4.9	4.90
3	5.2, 4.2	9.4	4.70
4	4.5, 3.0, 3.8	11.3	3.77
5	3.5, 3.5, 3.3, 3.4	13.7	3.43
6	5.0, 5.5, 4.4, 5.7, 5.9	26.5	5.30
Total	....	73.9	

Calculations:

(1) $\quad 4.2^2 + 3.9^2 + \ldots + 5.9^2 = 334.09 = \sum x^2$

(2) $\quad \dfrac{8.1^2}{2} + 4.9^2 + \dfrac{9.4^2}{2} + \dfrac{11.3^2}{3} + \dfrac{13.7^2}{4} + \dfrac{26.5^2}{5} = 330.93 = \sum \left(\dfrac{\text{total}^2}{n} \right)$

(3) $\quad \dfrac{73.9^2}{17} = 321.25 = \dfrac{\text{grand total}^2}{\sum n}$

TABLE 29-13 Analysis of Variance

Source	Sums of squares	Degrees of freedom	Mean squares	F ratio	Significance
Causticized lots.....	(2) — (3) = 9.68	$r - 1 = 5$	1.936	6.7	High 0.01
Plastics process.....	(1) — (2) = 3.16	$n - r = 11$	0.287		
Total..........	12.84	$n - 1 = 16$			

grouped to obtain limits for charts for individual batches.[72] A separate chart is kept for each element of the cycle and also usually for the total time involved in manufacture of the batches. The effect of the human factor is soon evident; and based on lack of control, action can be taken to minimize its importance. The effect of pump, raw material conveyor, or boiler-plant capacity, unequal temperature and pressure, and of operating condition unevenness will all show up on the chart for the part of the cycle where they are important. Experimentation with operating conditions may be carried out, watching effect on both time of operations and final product quality.

Although dual charting is somewhat different from practices in mechanical industries, only the simplest control charting procedures are needed.[73]

SEMICONTINUOUS PROCESSES

Polymerization Polymerization is used in the petroleum industry and in manufacture of synthetic rubber and of many organic materials. In polymerization, a

[72] An alternative is to plot the mean square successive difference (MSSD). See Section 22 and Bennett, C. A., and N. L. Franklin, "Statistical Analysis in Chemistry and the Chemical Industry," pp. 677–684, John Wiley & Sons, Inc., New York, 1954.

[73] See Section 23.

reaction occurs in which two or more molecules of the same substance combine to form a compound from which the original substance may or may not be regenerated.

An example from a polymerization process illustrates the condition common to the more involved reactions.[74] Rather complete statistical analysis of all the measurable variables in the process precedes the use of any simple method to assist control. The step-by-step approach described provides a pattern for handling many other processes of similar complexity.

The first step by the quality control engineer was to assemble as much information as possible about the process, including process control and final quality measurements over a period long enough to permit analysis. The type of generalized information needed is shown in the simplified flow sheet in Figure 29-15.

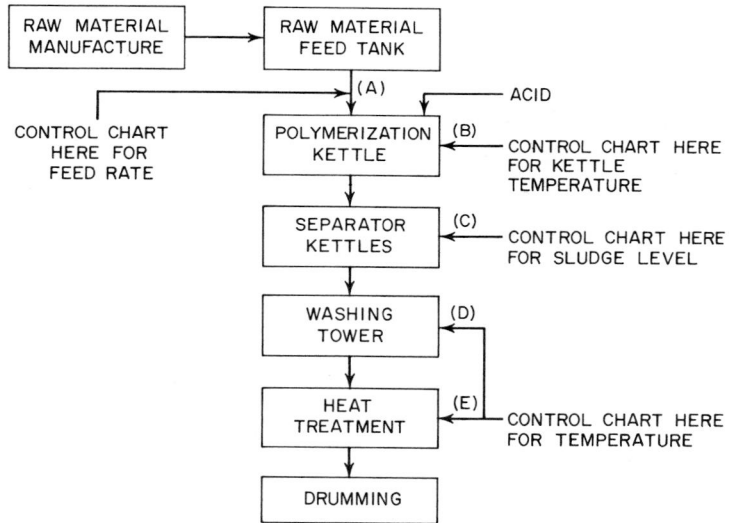

Fig. 29-15 Simplified flow sheet for polymerization process.

The first control chart was based on previous final quality measurements from the process. About 25 subgroups of 4 hourly measurements each were taken from a past period of acceptable operation to be used as a standard against which to compare future results. The original limits for the three principal quality measurements are given in the left half of the charts in Figure 29-16. A typical series of hourly readings from the normal period before starting the statistical study is plotted between the limits. These provide what is known as a master control chart, or an overall picture of quality results. It is suitable for keeping in the operating area so that the operators and quality control engineer may see the results of their joint efforts to improve quality.

Lack of control occurs frequently on the original charts. If possible, action should be taken to adjust the process on the basis of lack of control. An operator closely following a process may be able to identify on the charts results of some of his adjust-

[74] See also Bingham, R. S., Jr., Control Charts in Multi-stage Batch Processes, *Industrial Quality Control*, vol. XIII, no. 12, pp. 21–26, June 1957, and Bingham, R. S., Jr., Practical Chemical Process Control, *Industrial Quality Control*, vol. XIII, no. 11, pp. 46–56, May 1957, for examples of countercurrent, multistage operations.

ments and thus receive direct assistance in future handling of the process. It is more likely, however, that this master control chart will portray results based on more detailed process studies. These studies may use special statistical analyses or action-control charts spaced at strategic spots in the process.

When the process was initially surveyed, it was realized that before charts could be placed, an analysis of several variables had to be made. Variables affecting

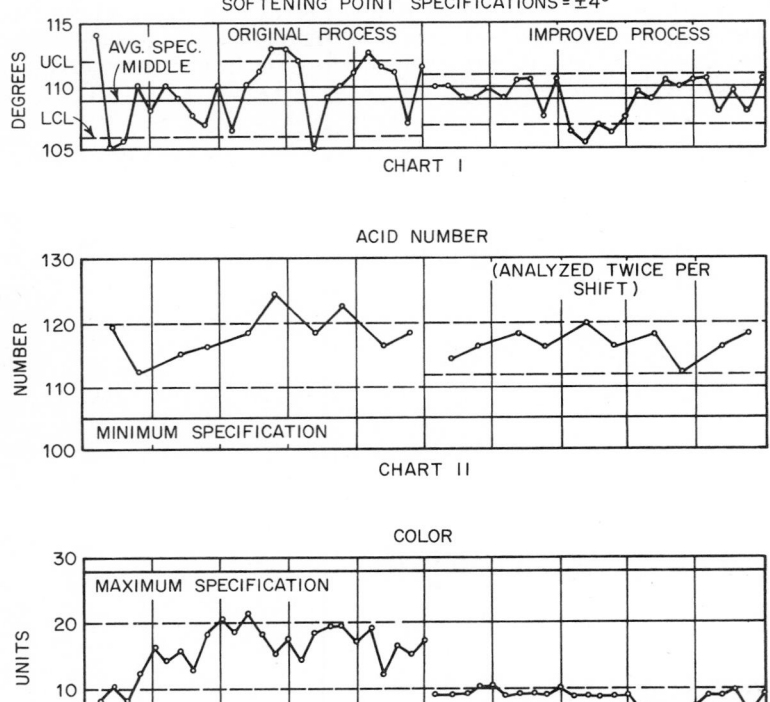

Fig. 29-16 Master control chart—polymerization.

softening point of the product were studied first by multiple regression: feed rate, polymerizer temperature, and sludge levels in the separator kettles. The regression showed all three factors significantly affected softening point. Together they accounted for 78% of the total product variation. Past performance for these three variables was then plotted on action-control charts. Corrective action for each is different and is described in turn.

Fluctuations in the *feed rate,* which sent its action chart out of control so often, were beyond the power of the polymerization-area operators to regulate. The production area supplying the raw material for polymerization frequently reduced production rate or diverted the supply to other finishing areas. Naturally, lack of control occurred on those occasions on the action chart, and the effect could even be traced to fluctuations in the product quality as portrayed in the master control chart. Once identified, remedial action was justified. A large storage tank was installed so raw material could be accumulated during periods of high availability. This evened out the flow rate to such an extent that good control was obtained and maintained on the first action chart. Charting of feed rate was then discontinued.

A new multiple regression was then made of the three variables mentioned earlier: feed rate, temperature, and sludge level against softening point. This time

TABLE 29-14 Regression Analysis—Softening Point of Polymerization Product

Source	Sums of squares	Degrees of freedom	Mean squares	F ratio	Probability of significance
Temperature.	19.48	1	19.48	32.5	99.9%
Sludge level	13.77	1	13.77	23.0	99.9%
Feed rate	0.37	1	0.37	. . .	None
Residual	12.63	21	0.60		
Totals	46.25	24			

the *flow rate* turned out to be *nonsignificant* while the other two significant factors continued to account for about the same proportion of the total variation in softening point as they originally did (see Table 29-14).

While the feed rate work was going on, sludge levels were studied by a second action chart chalked on a blackboard in the operating area. (See Sedimentation and Decantation above.) This was a real action chart because the start and end of pumping periods were determined by float bob position with respect to the control limits. As long as the operators maintained close watch over the positions of the

TABLE 29-15 Regression Analysis—Softening Point of Polymerized Product, Partial Sludge-level Control

Source	Sums of squares	Degrees of freedom	Mean squares	F ratio	Probability of significance
Temperatures.	19.48	1	19.48	16.1	99.9%
Sludge level	0.12	1	0.12	. . .	None
Residual	26.65	22	1.21		
Totals.	46.25	24			

bobs, good control was maintained. However, though reduced slightly from the start, the limits were still wide. Also, as shown in Table 29-14, the variance due to sludge levels was still significant.

Once again it was time for action. This time only part of the engineering action decided on was taken initially on a trial basis. Automatic sludge-level controllers were installed on part of the kettles. Regression of the data from the controlled kettles showed the effect of sludge levels had disappeared[75] (see Table 29-15).

Subsequently, all kettles were equipped with automatic controls, and temperature was left as the sole significant source of variation measured. The cost of automatic feed and acid rate control was then investigated to determine the feasibility of further reducing quality variation by a third process adaptation. (This step had not been taken at the time represented by the right half of the control charts in

[75] See Hinchen, J. D., Multiple Regression with Unbalanced Data, *Technometrics*, vol. 2, no. 1, pp. 22–29, January 1970. He outlines the errors in interpretation possibly resulting when specific degrees of correlation among the independent variables exist.

Figure 29-16. It will be seen from the chart that the softening point had become better controlled within a more uniform range.)

So far, the charts spotted at points *A, B,* and *C* in Figure 29-15 have been discussed. Much the same procedure was carried out in setting up charts at *B, D,* and *E* for color improvement.

A regression of feed color, bleaching property of the feed, and heat-treatment temperature showed that the first and last significantly accounted for 46.5% of the product color variation. Nothing could be done immediately about the feed color. However, other variables could be studied to identify causes of a larger proportion than 46.5% of the total variation. Accordingly, kettle temperatures, wash-tower temperature, sludge levels, solution concentration, contamination of feed, and acidity of wash water were added to the regression. The first two were found to be additional significant factors which brought the accounted-for variation to a satisfactory total.

Control on polymerizer kettle temperature had already been arranged because of its effect on softening point. Action charts were prepared for installation at the washing tower and at the heat-treater as shown on the flow sheet. The resulting improvement in product color is shown vividly in the right-hand portion of the master control chart (Figure 29-16).[76]

CONTINUOUS PROCESSES

Hydrogenation and Hydrogenolysis Typical products of these processes are ammonia from nitrogen, hydrochloric acid from chlorine, hydrogenated oils and fats, detergents (hymolal class), petroleum products, and methane from carbon monoxide.

The hydrogenation process provides an excellent illustration of process control chart use at the very outset of a program. This was possible because the process is relatively simple, and because two or three factors, all under the operator's control, are decisive in normal control of quality.

The simplicity of the process may be seen from the flow sheet in Figure 29-17. The important processing factors are feed rate, temperature, and pressure. However, these factors were not charted, but rather the final performance quality measurements.

The first two curves of Figure 29-18 show the original charts used for process analysis before the control program was started. From their very first use, important new knowledge was obtained about quality control.

First, the extremes of high and low refractive index showing up as lack of control could be tied in with process interruptions due to renewing the catalyst charge in a part of the reaction sequence or equipment maintenance. Sometimes the interruptions were unscheduled and unintentional (for example, when a pipeline clogged or equipment failed). It was clear at once that *interruptions* should be avoided whenever possible. This made a study of the schedule for changing catalyst and for maintenance work desirable. It also showed the need for new equipment when unscheduled shutdowns occurred oftener than they should have.

The refractive-index chart, in particular, showed an unrealistic relationship between the control limits (or natural specifications) of the process and the manufacturing specifications. The upper control limit exceeded the specification limit. This meant in the normal course of events a certain proportion of off-grade material could be expected. Furthermore, adjustments were being made to the process when the specifications were exceeded regardless of whether control still existed.

---

[76] See also Pasteelnick, L. A., and W. B. Leder, Statistical Analysis in a Polymerization Process, *Chemical Engineering Progress,* vol. 53, no. 8, pp. 392–395, August 1957, for further information on polymerizer control.

Another peculiarity shown by this chart was the tendency for plateaus to occur near or at the upper specification level. Actually, the data distribution appeared skewed because of this phenomenon. It may have its explanation in a custom of resampling when borderline results are obtained, or it may be due to an unconscious bias for obtaining results within specification.[77]

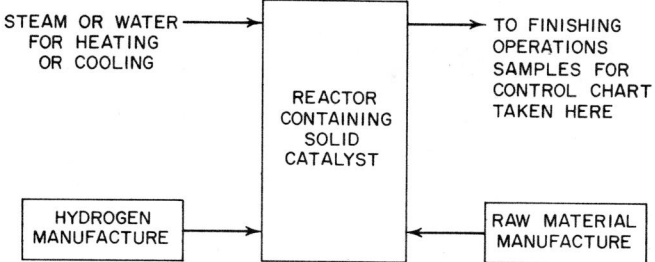

Fig. 29-17   Flow sheet for hydrogenation process.

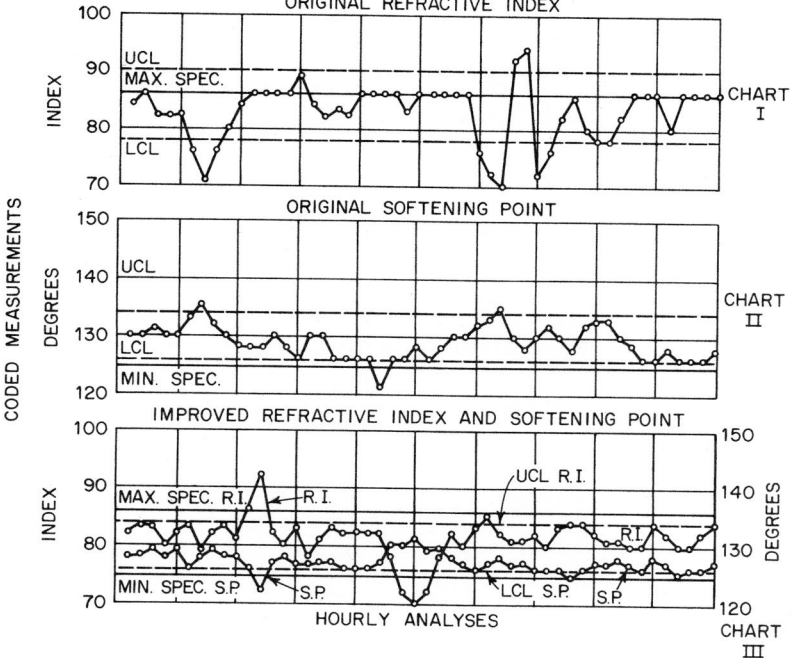

Fig. 29-18   Hydrogenation process control.

To overcome this, the operating goal for refractive index was set lower so that the tendency to favor results just within the specification would be lessened. Operators were directed to make process adjustments only on the basis of lack of control. These revised practices led immediately to a slightly lower average result, an upper limit below the maximum specification, and a better degree of control. Better

[77] See Flinching, Section 12, under Willful Inspector Errors—Inspector Initiated.

uniformity in the quality measurement reflected in higher throughput—in contrast to the former effort to get high throughput by pressing the refractive index as close to the maximum specification as possible.

In normal periods of operation, small changes in feed rate, temperature, or pressure reflected immediately in the quality results on the chart. Therefore, the operator could watch the chart and see the effects of adjustments readily. The chart became a real instrument of control. After a few months of use, the operators stated that they would rather run the process with the chart than without it.

The unique features of the chart eventually put in use are illustrated in the lower part of Figure 29-18. Only the *upper* control limit for refractive index and the *lower* control limit for softening point were used. The two sets of measurements were plotted in different colors. When the curve for refractive index approached or exceeded the upper limit, the operator observed the location of the corresponding points for softening point. If they, too, were approaching or had exceeded their lower limit, no simple process adjustment to regain control quickly could be made. However, if there was some leeway for reducing the softening point without going out of control, proper adjustment such as reducing the rate of feed could be made. This often brought the refractive index back into control without dangerously lowering the softening point. Thereafter, the process was controlled by careful adjustments of the few control valves to obtain a steady relationship between the two variables and to keep both inside the control limits.[78,79,80] When this normal control pattern was supplemented by a revised maintenance schedule and fewer catalyst changes, optimum results from the process were assured. The control chart shows graphically uniformity improvement. This was done at very little cost with increased efficiency in plant operation, which made a higher total throughput possible at this better quality level.

ANALYSIS OF FINISHED PRODUCT QUALITY

Classification of Product   One of the incentives for producing a product "right the first time" is the classification of substandard product at a lower valuation than first quality product. Correction of this situation then becomes economically desirable to the manufacturing supervisor. Charts on "Percent Right First Time" maintained in the operating area, and competition between various crews often results in improved quality. Since the process capability vs. specification range may vary from product to product, quality *percentage* standards are set up for individual products, with the goal being to exceed the standard.

Substandard product may be reworked, blended off, scrapped, or sold at reduced price or occasionally at full price with customer and Marketing Department approval.

Determination of Causes of Off-Grade Production.   The chemical industry has its share of instances in which off-grade materials are produced. The reasons are numerous: lapses in control, changes in raw material lots, catalyst degradation, equipment wear, etc.

---

[78] An alternative procedure when two or more attributes are correlated uses multivariate control charts (Hotelling's T^2). See Johnson, N., and Leone, F. C., "Statistics and Experimental Design," vol. I, pp. 347–348, John Wiley & Sons, Inc., New York, 1964.

[79] See also Hicks, C. R., Some Applications of Hotelling's T, *Industrial Quality Control,* vol. XI, no. 9, pp. 23–26, June 1955.

[80] See Jackson, J. E., Quality Control Methods for Two Related Variables, *Industrial Quality Control,* vol. XII, no. 7, pp. 4–8, January 1956; and DeBaun, R. M., and A. M. Schneider, Some Examples of Multivariate Analyses, *Mid-Atlantic Conference Transactions,* February 1957, pp. 19–26, American Society for Quality Control.

However, the industry also has some good means for dealing with these instances. The data system is usually well developed and includes records of operating conditions, material batch numbers, and logs of difficult or unusual occurrences. In addition, the companies are usually self-sufficient in the availability of engineers to analyze and solve problems. The methods of analysis follow conventional practice for the most part (see Section 16). However, there are many pitfalls, since operating variables are interrelated and time lags exist between a variable change and the resultant product property change.[81]

Investigation of Customer Complaints and Returned Goods Reports. This follows conventional practice as described in Section 15, under Complaint Analysis.

QUALITY IMPROVEMENT PROGRAMS

Much of the conventional approach to quality improvement (see Section 16) is directly applicable to the Chemical Industry. However, the tools of analysis often must be quite sensitive, since many chemical industry products are high-volume, low-profit (commodity) materials. In such cases, large sums of money rest on small differences in yield. The tools of analysis needed to deal with such small differences must be flexible enough to accommodate numerous variables, many of which are nonlinear, and which may interact with other variables. Such tools do exist, and the chemical industry has made much progress in applying them to improve yields and controls.[82]

Evolutionary Operation   This technique, developed by G.E.P. Box, was pioneered in the chemical industry and applied profitably in hundreds of chemical operations.[83]

Adaptive Control   Control charts as described in Section 23 are designed to detect shifts in process level, increases or decreases in process variability, or nonrandomness (as typified by trends, cycles, etc.). As such, control charts "call for action." The kind or amount of action is not always clear.

Adaptive control, a technique developed by Box and Jenkins,[84] aims to improve process control and thereby outgoing product by "anticipating" where the process will wander if left unadjusted. Furthermore, it describes *when* action is called for and the *amount* of correction. The aim is to eliminate all but random variation in the quality or composition of products. The procedure is appropriate when:

There is a "dead time" or delay before the adjustment takes effect.

The adjustment begins to take effect immediately, but the full effect of the change is not felt for some period of time.

Improper choice of either the *amount* of correction or the *timing* of the correction

---

[81] See Hinchen, J. D., Multiple Regression in Process Development, *Technometrics*, vol. 10, pp. 257–270, May 1968; Draper, N., and H. Smith, "Applied Regression Analysis," John Wiley & Sons, Inc., New York, 1966; and Section 26, Regression Analysis.

[82] Some additional examples are given in Bingham, R. S., Jr., Quality Control Applications in the Coated Abrasive Industry, *Industrial Quality Control*, vol. XIX, no. 5, pp. 5–12, November 1962; Coutie, G. A., Use Statistics for Optimization, *Chemical Engineering*, Nov. 16, 1959, pp. 190–191; Bingham, R. S., and J. L. Gioele, Statistical Methods for Ceramic Process Control and Experiment Planning, *Journal of the Canadian Ceramic Society*, vol. 28, pp. 46–49, 1959; Addendum, *Journal of the Canadian Ceramic Society*, vol. 30, p. 135, 1961; and Bingham, R. S., Jr., and J. L. Gioele, Ceramic Pressing—Optimization of Equipment Effectiveness through Experimental Design, *Transactions, 14th Annual All Day Conference on Quality Control*, Sept. 8, 1962, pp. 61–77, New Brunswick, N.J.

[83] See Section 27A for full discussion, examples, and extensive references, most relating to process industry application.

[84] Box, G. E. P., and G. M. Jenkins, "Time Series Analysis, Forecasting and Control," Holden-Day, Inc., Publisher, San Francisco, 1970.

may cause the process to oscillate, overshoot the desired target, or undershoot the target.

It is not possible to control one or more inputs to the process, but the effect of variation in these inputs can be measured and correction taken to offset them (i.e., the process adjustments minimize the effect of the input upsets on the output quality).

Changes in the process level are selected from time to time (e.g., to make different "grades" of a product) and it is desired to get from one process level to another in the shortest time or with minimum "off grade" product made.

The benefits likely to be achieved from using adaptive control include:

Faster response to unexpected disturbances
Closer match of process level to process set point
Elimination of overcontrol
Faster startup

The technique is ideally suited to the chemical and process industries because it permits optimal process control as well as process optimization. As indicated earlier, in the process design stage the plant process equipment, piping, storage tanks, mixers, towers, etc., are sized to match plant capacity specifications. At this time, valves are selected, tower packing chosen, etc., to acknowledge reaction kinetics and transport phenomena. In these engineering calculations, commonly analog or digital computer models of the proposed process are utilized. By doing so, expected process upsets and dynamics can be superimposed on the plant design to determine the appropriate method for process control.[85]

When the process is unusually complex, or the chemical reaction kinetics unknown, empirical approaches as described earlier and in Section 27 can be used to approximate reaction kinetics. Furthermore, the plant typically finds after startup that the process is not "tuned" for optimum operating conditions. In actual plant practice, competing reactions may have modified the kinetics, the piping may have been rerouted, valve action rendered sluggish, mixing effectiveness reduced, catalyst activity degraded, tower packing fouled, or flow turbulence reduced. Under such conditions, the appropriate control action may be quite different from that taken to meet "theory" or from that taken immediately after startup or a "piping boilout."

Essentially, Box and Jenkins have built on the practices of control engineers who typically have designed into the mechanical or electronic linkages of automatic controllers *derivative, proportional,* and *integral* action. Their procedure uses mathematical equations or charts whose parameters can be changed instead of changing the controller mechanism.

The following steps are common to the procedure:

1. *Process identification*—determine the nature of disturbances commonly seen by the process, including estimates of process variance.

2. *Process prediction*—derive an equation for predicting where the process level would be if unadjusted, when disturbed as in step 1 above. (The equation may include the latest measurement, the differences between successive measurements, and the cumulative algebraic sum of the deviations of a series of measurements from their predicted value.)

3. *Process correction*—derive an adjustment equation including measures of "process gain"—the change in the "output" (response) variable to adjustment of an "input" or control variable. (This equation takes into account process dynamics

---

[85] See Section 20, under Simulation Techniques, for details on Continuous System Modelling Program (CSMP).

including lags between the time an adjustment is made and the time the effect is observed *at the sampling point.*)

4. *Chart control*—construct charts to be used by the operator to simplify the prediction and calculation of adjustments. (In computer control, automatic adjustment would replace operator correction.)

Viscosity Control by Adaptive Control—An Example. The following example[86] illustrates the elements of the technique but is not meant to be all-inclusive. It concerns viscosity control of a process in which gas is injected into a liquid in a continuous reactor. Twenty-five of some 200 observations available are shown in Table 29-16.

1. *Process identification.*

Process objective: Resultant mixture viscosity is to be between 86 and 98 centipoise with 92 the target.

Process disturbance: The incoming gas composition varied within commercially acceptable limits but with substantial impact on the mixture viscosity.

Process adjustment: Reaction control was achieved by feeding in more or less gas.

Process gain: Experimentally, it was observed that a change in gas rate of 50 pounds per minute eventually produced a viscosity change of 10 centipoise, i.e., $g = 10/50 = 0.2$.

TABLE 29-16 Adaptive Control—Viscosity of Product of Gas Reactor

Hour	Viscosity	Hour	Viscosity
1	90	14	92
2	94	15	93
3	94	16	96
4	95	17	90
5	98	18	88
6	90	19	93
7	92	20	87
8	89	21	90
9	93	22	91
10	94	23	95
11	91	24	91
12	95	25	97
13	91		

Process dynamics: The viscosity change was observed to be exponential[87] with time; half of the expected change occurred in 1 hour. Over a period in which *no* adjustments were made, changes in viscosity level appeared to occur stepwise. (The inference is that gas composition varied stepwise and shifted the viscosity to higher or lower levels rather than trending upward or downward.)

2. *Process prediction.* To predict[88] the next viscosity result $(\hat{z}_{p+1})$, the optimal predictor would be the previous result (z_p), i.e., $\hat{z}_{p+1} = z_p$.

3. *Process correction.* In light of the step function disturbance, and the exponential process dynamics,[89] the appropriate corrective adjustment uses the change

[86] Example modified from Box and Jenkins, "Time Series Analysis, Forecasting and Control," Holden-Day, Inc., Publisher, San Francisco, 1970.

[87] Fraction changed $(y/x) = 1 - \exp(-x)$. $x = T/TC$, where $T =$ time in hours, $TC =$ time constant in hours. See Harrison, H. L., and J. G. Bollinger, "Introduction to Automatic Controls," 3d printing, pp. 66–67, International Textbook Company, Scranton, Pa., August 1966.

[88] Box and Jenkins describe several methods for theoretically and empirically determining the appropriate predictor and correction equations, e.g., when the disturbance is not approximated by a step function or the process dynamics by an exponential function. One trial-and-error method evaluates, over limited ranges within a so-called "stability region," choices of three parameters having similar effect as the "derivative, proportional, and integral" control action used by control engineers. See Table 29-17 and discussion related to it. See also Box, G.E.P., and G. M. Jenkins, Some Statistical Aspects of Adaptive Optimization and Control, *Technical Report* 8, NSF-G14768, University of Wisconsin, May 1962; Some Statistical Aspects of Adaptive Optimization and Control, *Journal of the Royal Statistical Society,* No. 2, pp. 297–333, 1962.

[89] $\triangle e_p = e_p - e_{p-1}$, where $e_p =$ deviation of latest reading from the process target or set point.

in error $\triangle e_p$ plus the latest error e_p. Algebraically, this becomes twice the current difference from set point minus the previous difference from set point.

$$\text{Correction } (X_{p+1}) = \frac{-1}{g(\triangle e_p + e_p)} = \frac{-1}{g(2e_p - e_{p-1})}$$

This should be intuitively satisfying, since only one half of the corrective effect is felt by the time the next sample is taken.

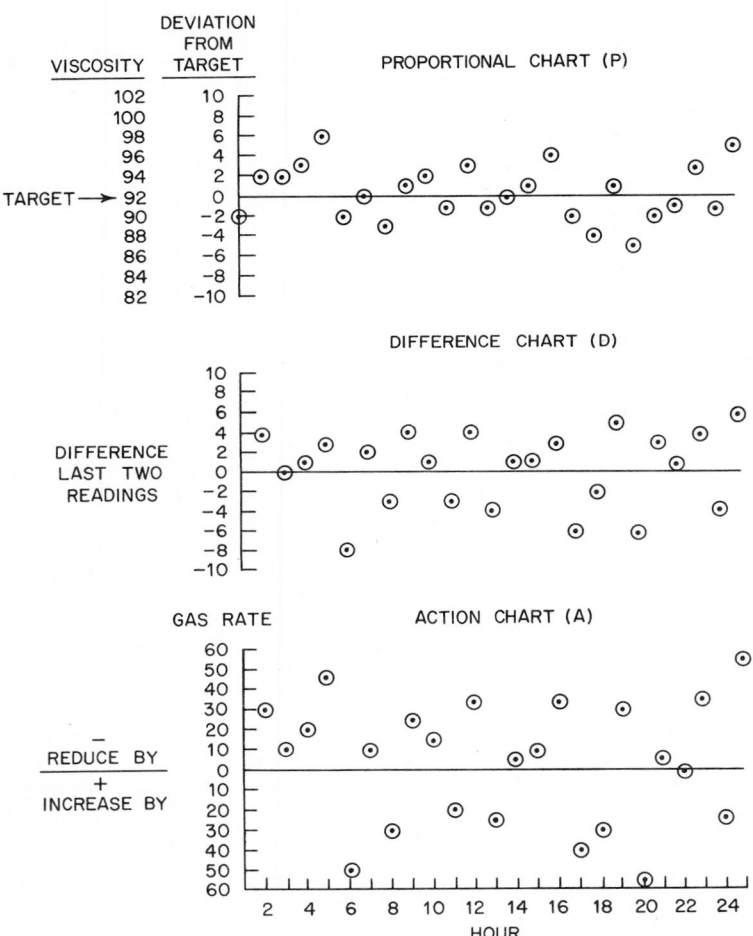

Fig. 29-19 Adaptive quality control charts.

4. *Chart control.* The charts to control the process are shown in Figure 29-19. The proportional (P) chart is a plot of the hourly readings from Table 29-16. The horizontal line is drawn at the target value, 92. The second scale shows the deviations from target value and represents e_p in the correction equation.

On the difference chart (D), the difference between successive readings is plotted. (For example, the first point is the difference between hour 2 and hour 1, 94−90 =

+4. The second point, $94 - 94 = 0$, etc.) These differences are plotted about a horizontal line at zero. They represent $\triangle e_p$ in the correction equation.

The third chart is the action *(A)* chart. On this chart the sums of the deviations on charts P and D are plotted. (For hour 2, $2 + 4 = 6$; for hour 3, $2 + 0 = 2$, etc.) Hence chart A represents $\triangle e_p + e_p$. The action chart is plotted on a scale ($-1/g$ times the sum of the deviations) which shows directly the adjustment required.

Each hour, the operator enters the viscosity result on the P chart, calculates and plots D, then adds the deviations on P and D to get A. He reads the appropriate correction from the A scale and makes the required adjustment to the gas rate.

Extensions of Adaptive Control: The adaptive control charts can be modified to take care of lags through a process, i.e., elapse of time before an adjustment takes effect. Also, there can be large changes in the prediction and correction equation weighting factors (G0, G1, GM1)[90] without much effect on the efficiency of the technique. In other words, the dynamics do not need to be exactly represented. Box and Jenkins[91] have shown "the choice of the coefficients is not very critical; a sum of squares slightly greater than the smallest value can be obtained over a fairly wide area of the (G0, G1, GM1) parameter space." Table 29-17 illustrates this. Part A summarizes the combinations of G0, G1, and GM1, giving minimum sums of squares of prediction error (SSE) for the data of Table 29-16.[92, 93, 94]

The minimum SSE (shown on the last line of Part A) was obtained for $G0 = 0.20$, $G1 = 0.0$, and $GM1 = 0.0$ for these 25 observations. (Box and Jenkins differed only with $G0 = 1.0$.) Note that the approximate 95% confidence region (Approx. CL.) for this subset of their data (0 to 0.592 D03) includes *all* SSE in Part A.

Further demonstration of the insensitiveness of the SSE region to G0, G1, GM1 choice is given in Part B of Table 29-17. For $GM1 = 0.0$, note that the confidence region includes $G0 = 0.0$, $G1 = 0.0$, implying randomness and that no better control is possible.[95]

Box and Jenkins have also described:

"Zone adjustment" in which the Action Chart (A of Figure 29-19) is marked off into bands with one corrective adjustment made for all points falling within a band.

"Constrained" correction procedures which limit the variance of the controlled variable (gas flow in this example). They give methods for calculating the increase in output variance (viscosity in the example) due to less than full correction.

Forecasts and their variances more than one observation ahead.

[90] Box and Jenkins use γ_0, γ_1, and γ_{-1} where G0, G1, and GM1 are used here.

[91] Box, G. E. P., and G. M. Jenkins, Some Statistical Aspects of Adaptive Optimization and Control, *Technical Report* 8, NSF-G14768, University of Wisconsin, May 1962; Some Statistical Aspects of Adaptive Optimization and Control, *Journal of the Royal Statistical Society*, No. 2, pp. 297–333, 1962.

[92] Here e is defined as "predicted value $-$ observed value" or $e_p = \hat{z}_p - z_p$. The computing procedure for a chosen set of G0, G1, GM1 starts by setting $\hat{z}_1 = z_1$ so that $e_1 = 0$, $\triangle e_1 = 0$, $Se_1 = 0$. Then $\hat{z}_2$ is predicted by substituting z_1, e_1, $\triangle e_1$, Se_1 in the equation

$$\hat{z}_{p+1} = z_p + G0e_p + G1Se_p + GM1\triangle e_p$$

From the new $\hat{z}$, e, $\triangle e$, and Se are calculated and the process repeated. The "sum of squares" (SSE) being minimized is

$$e_1{}^2 + e_2{}^2 + e_3{}^2 + \ldots + e_n{}^2$$

$(Se_p = e_1 + e_2 + e_3 \ldots + e_p. \quad \triangle e_p = e_p - e_{p-1}.)$

[93] Within the stability region described by Box and Jenkins, the combination explored covered the range of GM1 from -0.80 to 0.80 in steps of 0.20 [i.e., $-0.80\ (0.20)\ 0.80$]. Likewise G0 and G1 ranged $0.0\ (0.2)\ 4.0$ as appropriate.

[94] Sums of squares of errors are in "floating point notation" with the exponent following. Hence, 0.234168D 03 equals 234.168.

[95] Box and Jenkins suggest procedures for testing adequacy of the prediction and correction models. They recommend 200 to 400 points rather than the 25 used for illustration here.

TABLE 29-17   Adaptive Control—Sums of Squares of Error

Part A—Minimum SSE over All G0, G1, GM1 Combinations

Minimum SS	G0	G1	GM1	Approx. CL.[1]
0.319383D 03	1.40	0.0	—0.80	
0.288391D 03	1.20	0.0	—0.60	
0.263378D 03	0.80	0.0	—0.40	
0.246631D 03	0.60	0.0	—0.20	
0.234168D 03*	0.20	0.0	0.0	
0.243435D 03	0.20	0.0	0.20	
0.286536D 03	0.20	0.0	0.40	
0.347497D 03	0.10	0.0	0.60	
0.453580D 03	0.0	0.0	0.80	
0.234168D 03*	0.20	0.0	0.0	0.592201D 03

1. Approx. CL. = SE (1+CHISQ/DF); N IS   25
* = minimum   SSE.

Part B—Sums of Squares of Errors, Observed—Predicted, GM1 = 0.0

G0 IS = G1	0.0	0.2	0.4	0.6	0.8	1.0
0.0	0.325D 03	0.234D 03*	0.242D 03	0.260D 03	0.294D 03	0.351D 03
0.2	0.692D 03	0.393D 03	0.314D 03	0.313D 03	0.349D 03	0.421D 03
0.4	0.128D 04	0.451D 03	0.363D 03	0.365D 03	0.413D 03	0.509D 03
0.6	0.121D 04	0.540D 03	0.431D 03	0.429D 03	0.496D 03	0.628D 03
0.8	0.216D 04	0.740D 03	0.499D 03	0.505D 03	0.606D 03	0.792D 03
1.0	0.247D 04	0.749D 03	0.546D 03	0.606D 03	0.758D 03	0.102D 04
1.2	0.188D 04	0.658D 03	0.620D 03	0.759D 03	0.967D 03	0.137D 04
1.4	0.103D 04	0.649D 03	0.781D 03	0.986D 03	0.126D 04	0.193D 04
1.6	0.738D 03	0.801D 03	0.108D 04	0.128D 04	0.168D 04	0.287D 04
1.8	0.751D 03	0.123D 04	0.152D 04	0.164D 04	0.240D 04	0.420D 04
2.0	0.136D 04	0.214D 04	0.197D 04	0.212D 04	0.379D 04	0.725D 04
2.2	0.370D 04	0.325D 04	0.227D 04	0.305D 04	0.604D 04	
2.4	0.808D 04	0.337D 04	0.277D 04	0.524D 04	0.103D 05	
2.6	0.897D 04	0.311D 04	0.409D 04	0.960D 04		
2.8	0.420D 04	0.422D 04	0.780D 04	0.158D 05		
3.0	0.472D 04	0.650D 04	0.181D 05			
3.2	0.132D 05	0.136D 05	0.267D 05			
3.4	0.193D 05	0.469D 05				
3.6	0.463D 05	0.573D 05				
3.8	0.206D 06					
4.0	0.321D 06					

1.2	1.4	1.6	1.8	2.0	Min SSE
0.442D 03	0.593D 03	0.853D 03	0.124D 04	0.216D 04	0.234D 03*
0.542D 03	0.753D 03	0.112D 04	0.160D 04		0.234D 03
0.677D 03	0.983D 03	0.148D 04	0.262D 04		0.234D 03
0.867D 03	0.132D 04	0.194D 04			0.234D 03
0.115D 04	0.180D 04	0.323D 04			0.234D 03
0.158D 04	0.242D 04				0.234D 03
0.225D 04	0.410D 04				0.234D 03
0.312D 04					0.234D 03
0.535D 04					0.234D 03
					0.234D 03
					0.234D 03
					0.234D 03
					0.234D 03
					0.234D 03
					0.234D 03
					0.234D 03
					0.234D 03
					0.234D 03
					0.234D 03

Using *iterative* steps in process identification, prediction, and correction modeling, the technique provides control adaptive to a wide range of process industry disturbances and dynamics.

Plant Experimentation   Ideally, experimentation in the factory aimed at improving quality, yield, and throughput will make full use of Experiment Designs. Because of the large number of variables commonly present in chemical plants, more use is apt to be made of the screening designs described by Plackett and Burman,[96] or fractional factorials listed by Daniel, Hunter, and others.[97] To make optimum use of data as obtained, sequential experimentation may be used.[98,99]

Process optimization is frequently the goal of plant experimentation. The central composite designs of Box,[100,101] and Hunter[102] are very useful, combined with multiple regression and response surface plotting. These designs may be used sequentially to seek an optimum under various strategies.[103,104,105]

One of the dangers in plant experimentation is that the pressures for output and quality may not permit running all the planned experiments. In one such example, a 2^6 factorial design was set up to study the factors affecting product quality. Gathering information took several weeks, during which all shifts were involved. After 96 runs had been made, only 33 were found to be a part of the original design. The other 63 runs were repeats of some of the design; others were points not originally planned. It was possible to analyze the data using multiple regression. However, many of the interactions of interest were not measurable, with considerable information lost.

Multiple regression is valuable in plant experimentation and in analyzing data which may be produced as a by-product of normal operation.[106]

Process Automation   One of the keys to building better quality into chemical products is adequate control of the operating variables. The old days when an operator could stick his thumb into the product and "adjust" the quality level are fast disappearing. Instead, continuous viscometers, continuous samplers, on-line gas-liquid chromatographic analyzers, etc., are being installed by many companies. These techniques give instantaneous pictures of how the process is doing. In ad-

[96] Plackett, R. L., and J. P. Burman, The Design of Optimum Multifactorial Experiments, *Biometrika*, vol. 33, pp. 303–325, 1946.

[97] Daniel, C., Fractional Replication in Industrial Experimentation, *Transactions, National Convention*, pp. 229–233, American Society for Quality Control, 1957.

[98] Harrington, E. C., Jr., J. Novak, and R. O. Lynn, Process Scale-up by Sequential Experimentation and Mathematical Optimization, *Chemical Engineering Progress*, vol. 58, no. 2, February 1962.

[99] Daniel, C., Use of Half-normal Plots in Interpreting Factorial Two Level Experiments, *Technometrics*, vol. 1, no. 4, November 1959.

[100] Box, G. E. P., Exploration and Exploitation of Response Surfaces, *Biometrics*, vol. 10, no. 1, March 1954.

[101] Box, G. E. P., and P. V. Youle, The Exploration and Exploitation of Response Surfaces, II, An Example of the Link between the Fitted Surface and the Basic Mechanism of the System, *Biometrics*, vol. 11, pp. 287–323, 1955.

[102] See Section 28 and Box, G. E. P., and J. S. Hunter, The 2^{k-p} Fractional Factorial Designs—Part I, *Technometrics*, vol. 3, no. 3, August 1961; Part II, *Technometrics*, vol. 3, no. 4, November 1961.

[103] Marquardt, D. W., Generalized Inverses, Ridge Regression, Biased Linear Estimation and Nonlinear Estimation, *Technometrics*, vol. 12, no. 3, pp. 591–612, August 1970.

[104] Hoerl, A. E., and R. W. Kennard, Ridge Regression—Biased Estimation for Nonorthogonal Problems, Technometrics, vol. 12, no. 1, pp. 55–68, February 1970.

[105] Hoerl, A. E., and R. W. Kennard, Ridge Regression—Application to Non-orthogonal Problems, *Technometrics*, vol, 12, No. 1, pp. 69–82, February 1970.

[106] See Draper, N., and H. Smith, "Applied Regression Analysis," John Wiley & Sons, Inc., New York, 1966, on advantages and pitfalls of this approach. See also Section 26.

dition, automatic controls on temperature, pressure, product feed rate, etc., permit restraint of these variables within very narrow limits. Control engineers have developed computer-monitored open- and closed-loop systems. In some of these, all sampling, analysis, calculation of results, and corrective signal to the controlling device are coordinated by the computer.[107]

Data Banks A relatively new computer-aided approach to quality improvement is the data bank concept. Operating information from a process is taken continuously on punched paper or magnetic tape. Periodically, the information is plotted out on a computer in the form of cumulative sum charts, together with the quality information stored. Comparisons can then be made over a period of time and action taken on those conditions which appear difficult to control. As described in Section 20, via multiple regression the same information may give clues as to why some conditions vary.

Quality Motivation Programs In the chemical industries, the managers are quite aware that control over product quality is primarily in the hands of the technical specialists rather than the work force. In consequence, the industry has generally avoided undue enthusiasm for structured motivation programs.[108] However, the industry makes wide use of some elements of quality motivation:

Employee training[109] includes information on what happens to the product when standard procedures are not followed. (This is extended to explain how and why processes work, how instruments, controllers, and computers control, etc.)

Examples are used to show how customer problems are related to the measured chemical and physical properties of the product. These examples underscore the importance of the job of controlling those properties.

Display racks may be set up to contrast good with poor product, and to publicize the relation of control testing to product quality.

The "employees" who can affect quality adversely include auxiliary personnel as well as operators. Products can be contaminated when lines and tanks are used for more than one product if the auxiliary personnel fail to clean the containers properly. In such cases, foolproofing and redundancy can be of help to all: special fittings, color coding, tags, etc.

PLANNING FOR FUTURE NEEDS

The industry uses conventional means to discover the changing needs of the market: competitive analysis, customer contact, and still others as discussed in Section 14. The evaluations require conventional collaboration between Marketing, Research, and Analytical Laboratories. Membership and active participation in Technical Society and industry committees provides added opportunities for keeping ahead of changing quality needs and even for guiding their direction. The ideal feedback is quantified data on future market demands, but soundly based opinions can be helpful in providing Research with directions for product improvement work and new product developments.

Research The bulk of research is directed to product and process improvement.[110] It focuses on existing products and processes, investigating new raw material sources, improving yields, comparing batch- and continuous-type processes,

---

[107] See Section 20.

[108] See generally Section 18.

[109] See Bingham, R. S., Chalk Dust and Chemicals—S.Q.C. Training for the Chemical Industry, *Industrial Quality Control*, vol. XVIII, No. 10, pp. 15–18, April 1962.

[110] Ideally, a small but consistent portion of resources should be expended in fundamental research to answer basic questions of "why and how," and in the hope of being rewarded by an occasional fundamental discovery.

seeking better methods of control, etc.   These defensive strategies aim to offset
future quality problems.

When a new product is developed to fit an existing or new need, the prudent
research manager may often continue the research effort, and come up with the
so-called "second generation" or "third generation" product.   These anticipate
the projected requirements two or three years hence.   The ability to pull a new product off the shelf as required often permits a company to get the jump on competition, or at least have an answer ready if competition moves first.   For example, the
aim of a project might be to replace carbon tetrachloride as a cleaning fluid.   The
table below shows the properties desired, and the degree to which the candidate
fluids fulfill the requirements.   The numbers are subjective ratings, with 1 indicating fully satisfactory.   Generation I is a product which has a cost base making
it competitive now.   Generation II is a better product with a slightly lower profit
margin and some properties which are not currently required.   It could be our "new,
improved Clean-O" next year.

Property	CCl_4	Generation I	Generation II
Nontoxicity	0.0	1.0	1.0
Nonflammability	1.0	1.0	1.0
Low viscosity	1.0	0.9	1.0
Cleaning ability:			
Dust, lint	0.8	0.9	1.0
Grease	0.9	1.0	1.0
Water-soluble dirt	0.1	0.8	1.0
Nonpolarized organics	0.1	0.5	0.7

Analytical Laboratory   The analytical laboratory can prepare for future quality
problems by being alert to new testing needs and by improving existing methods
and equipment.   Continual monitoring of test accuracy and precision directed
toward definite improvement goals will permit acceptance of tighter test precision
standards when such needs arrive.[111]   If existing equipment and methodology fail
to provide desired and foreseen test reliability, it is the responsibility of the analytical laboratory to investigate, purchase, and check out newly developed testing
equipment.

One of the foreseen problems resulting from changing quality requirements may
be the need for increasing test load from time to time.   Automation of testing equipment and computerizing test calculations may alleviate the situation.   Some companies already have interfaced gas-liquid chromatography and Instron testing equipment to provide input to computers for computation.   Any equipment where large
numbers of repetitive tests are run is fair game for this approach.[112]

[111] Within-company laboratory comparisons are commonly made.   Further, cooperative,
"round robin" or interlaboratory "programs" are effective in deriving standardized test meth-
ods of known accuracy and precision traceable to the National Bureau of Standards.   See
Lashof, T. W., Ranking Laboratories and Evaluating Methods of Measurement in Round Robin
Tests, *Materials Research & Standards,* vol. 4, pp. 397–407, August 1964; Wernimont, G.,
Precision and Accuracy of Test Methods, *ASTM Symposium on Applications of Statistics,*
Special Technical Publication 103, pp. 13–26, 1950; Youden, W. J., Ranking Laboratories
by Round Robin Tests, *Materials Research & Standards,* January 1963, pp. 9–13; Youden,
W. J., "Statistical Techniques for Collaborative Tests," AOAC, Washington, D.C., 1967,
and Wernimont, G., Evaluation of Laboratory Performance of Spectrophotometers, *Analytical
Chemistry,* May 1967, p. 554; for classical descriptions of test techniques.   See also Section
27, under Interlaboratory Tests.

[112] See Secrest, D., Time Sharing Experimental Control on a Small Computer, *Industrial
and Engineering Chemistry,* vol. 60, p. 9, September 1968, for papers on automation of analytical testing methods and uses of computers in the analytical laboratory.   See also Sections
20 and 32.

Manufacturing Department The Manufacturing Department investigates, purchases, and installs new equipment to increase yield, productivity, and quality. Better instrumentation can help in process studies aimed at determining the effects of operating conditions on product quality and in developing controls which keep the process on target. New equipment and instrumentation can lead to automatically controlled plants in which a computer becomes part of the control loop, providing information for operator control, or even sending impulses to the operating equipment to regulate the process.

Interfacing of process instrumentation, automatic sample analyzers, and the computer has been successfully accomplished and data logging used for process improvement and control.[113] In highly interacting processes where corrective adjustment to one portion of the process results in a disturbance elsewhere, it is necessary to look at everything at once, which the operator is unable to do. But this is just what a computer does well, and a description of such a plant is given by Shah and Stillman.[114,115]

It is also important to improve packaging and storage techniques in anticipation of changing market needs. For example, if a customer formerly purchased material in drums and now wants truck or tank-car shipments, the quality of the material must be protected in storage and in transit. The Manufacturing Department may often maintain a staff of packaging and shipping experts whose function is to solve these problems. In addition, packaging changes may be needed to stay abreast of or anticipate competitive action.

BIBLIOGRAPHY

Bennett, C. A., and N. L. Franklin, "Statistical Analysis in Chemistry and the Chemical Industry, John Wiley & Sons, Inc., New York, 1954.

Davies, O. L., ed., "Statistical Methods in Research and Production with Special Reference to the Chemical Industry," 3d ed. rev., Hafner Publishing Company, Inc., New York, 1957.

Davies, O. L., ed., "Design and Analysis of Industrial Experiments," 2d ed., Oliver & Boyd Ltd., Edinburgh, 1956.

Hinchen, J. D., "Practical Statistics for Chemical Research," Methuen & Co., Ltd., London, 1966.

Johnson, N. L., and Leone, F. C., "Statistics and Experimental Design in Engineering and the Physical Sciences," 2 vols., John Wiley & Sons, Inc., New York, 1964.

Youden, W. J., "Statistical Methods for Chemists," John Wiley & Sons, Inc., New York, 1951.

---

[113] See Bicking, C. A., R. S. Bingham, and R. L. Weiss, Automatic Data Logging for Experimentation and Quality Control, *Industrial Quality Control,* vol. XX, No. 6, pp. 12–16, December 1963; see also Williams, T. J., Computers and Process Control, *Industrial and Engineering Chemistry,* vol. 59, No. 12, pp. 53–68, December 1967, a review article on current practice.

[114] Shah, M. J., and R. E. Stillman, Computer Control and Optimization of a Large Methanol Plant, *Industrial and Engineering Chemistry,* vol. 62, p. 12, December 1970.

[115] See also Sections 20 and 30.

Pulp and Paper Industries[1]

A. H. JAEHN

Manager, Quality Systems, Consolidated Papers, Inc.,
Wisconsin Rapids, Wisconsin

R. S. BINGHAM, JR.

INTRODUCTION

Beginning in the 1970s, paper and board mills in the United States totaled 825 and pulp mills 309.[2] Facilities range from family-owned single mills to large corporate multimill operations. Mergers and diversification have changed the face of the in-

---

[1] In the Second Edition, this Section was prepared by Warren R. Purcell.

[2] See "Post's 1970 Pulp & Paper Directory," Miller Freeman Publications, San Francisco, Calif., for breakdown by states and type of mill.

dustry. What used to be called the paper industry is now a complex of paper, packaging, and wood products producers. This has led to more stringent and scientific management controls and systems by the larger mills, including wider application of quality control procedures, particularly those using computers.

Product quality requirements are being more closely specified by the end user. Many customers have organized their own quality control programs, including testing facilities, to evaluate the quality characteristics of pulp, paper, and paperboard products on receipt, and to correlate these results with their performance. High-speed printing presses demand papers that not only give desired printability but provide almost trouble-free pressroom performance. In the coated papers industry, for example, the standard for web breaks for a major pressroom on a particular grade and size has been reduced in a period of 12 years from 15 to 5 breaks per 100 rolls.[3] In the corrugating industry, the advent of high-speed automatic packing lines has led customers to demand tighter specifications, particularly in dimensional tolerances.

The paper industry is somewhat unique in comparison with other process industries in the exchange of technical know-how directly between competing companies, by suppliers serving the industry, technical organizations, and educational institutions. It is common for production and quality control personnel to visit other companies to view operations and talk over joint quality control problems. Extensive technology has been developed by educational institutions specializing in pulp and paper technology such as the Institute of Paper Chemistry, and the Universities of Maine and Western Michigan.

The trend in the industry is toward standardization of mill practices and test methods, particularly those associated with mill technical effort. Much of this work has been accomplished through industry-sponsored projects of the Paper Industry Management Association (PIMA), the Canadian Pulp & Paper Industry Association (CPPA), and the Technical Association of the Pulp and Paper Industry (TAPPI).

The major challenges facing quality control in the industry include:

1. Reduction of waste and "job lot" through control of losses caused by process variation and product defects. ("Job lot" means substandard paper sold at below standard price.)

2. Meeting the tighter performance standards required by customers spurred by the high downtime cost of high-speed automated processing equipment.

3. Successfully launching new products through early involvement of quality control in the planning and pilot stages.

4. Continually updating control procedures and practices as new technology is developed. This is particularly pertinent in the areas of on-line computer control where Quality Control must help assess the accuracy, precision, and reliability of the associated instrumentation plus auditing new control program effectiveness.

5. Sound application of statistical techniques in determining process, test, and sampling variation to evaluate and describe in-process and finished product quality performance.

The following discussion traces quality practices typical of this industry coincident with the process flow from raw materials to shipping. Special problems are examined under the headings Testing and Inspection, Establishing Specifications, and Statistical Methods. Since much of the narrative emphasizes publication and book paper production, other key control aspects are highlighted under Quality Control in Other Segments of the Industry.

---

[3] Jont, K. A., "Paper Problems—How They Affect the Publisher and Printer," 1970 Testing, Graphic Arts, and Reprography Conference, Minneapolis, Minn., Sept. 24, 1970.

RAW MATERIAL CONTROL

Purchased raw materials in this industry can be categorized generally as:

Pulpwood
Pulping and bleaching chemicals
Papermaking chemicals
Purchased fiber

As in other continuous processes, raw material uniformity is vital in maintaining product quality. Generally, little raw material testing is performed by the mills. Rather, reliance is placed on the supplier to meet quality requirements. New sources of supply are, however, introduced into the mill on a trial basis. The need exists for proper trial design in evaluating new raw materials.[4] (See Improvement through Mill Trials, under Quality Improvement, below.)

Pulpwood Wood represents 85 to 90% of the fiber used in papermaking. Measurement of amount of wood is needed for quality reasons (e.g., wood-yield ratios) as well as for supplier payment, inventory control, etc. The most widely used form of measurement is volumetric, the usual unit of measure being the cord (an $8 \times 4 \times 4 = 128$ cubic foot pile), or the cunit (100 cubic feet of solid wood, exclusive of bark). Volume measurement is not a completely accurate indication of solid wood content, as volume is affected by irregularities in size and shape of logs, degree of pile compactness, and amount of bark. Before any cordage measurement can be usefully applied, the exact method of measurement and character of the wood must be known.

Roundwood converted to chips can be measured much more accurately by weighing. However, as wood weight is affected by moisture content, representative samples are needed for ovendry moisture testing or one of the newer continuous measurement methods based on microwave, nuclear, or capacitance principles.[5]

Pulping and Bleaching Chemicals Pulping and bleaching chemicals enter the mill in carload quantities. These are supplied through major heavy chemical producers with the shipment assay generally provided to the mill by the supplier's control laboratory.

Papermaking Chemicals Chemical additives are used to improve some properties of the paper or board. The industry is the largest consumer of white clays and is second to the food industry in the consumption of starches. Major suppliers have pilot facilities for product evaluation, plus a wide background of practical experience in the application of their products under varying conditions at different mills. Because of the extensive use of nonfibrous raw materials, common industry tests have been developed to ascertain quality level.[6]

Purchased Fibers

Wood Pulp. Although the majority of the large paper and board manufacturing companies include pulping operations in their total manufacturing system, requirements for purchasing wood pulp do exist to satisfy special furnish needs or when there is an imbalance of pulp manufacturing capability with product demands.

---

[4] See Bicking, C. A., and A. C. Barefoot, Sampling and Preparing Wood for Analysis, *Proceedings TAPPI Testing Conference*, Savannah, Ga., September 1971, for a suggested revision to TAPPI Standard T-11 on Sampling of Wood which combines a formal statistical sampling approach and an "engineered" sample, i.e., "one based on experiment or engineered trial to assure as good a sample as the situation permits."

[5] Accurate Raw Material Measurement Vital to Efficient Operations, *Paper Trade Journal,* vol. 153, no. 28, pp. 61–68, July 14, 1969.

[6] Pertinent test methods are discussed in Testing and Inspection, this Section.

Integrated pulp mills afford the paper manufacturer immediate direct control advantages over pulp quality. Users of purchased pulp have the distinct advantage of being able to use pulp blends from various suppliers, thus minimizing short-term quality deficiencies from any one particular source. Pulp ratios are commonly manipulated as necessary, based on paper mill quality test data.

Wastepaper. Wastepaper is a substitute raw material for wood pulp, for ecological and economical reasons. Approximately 20% of the fiber used by paper and board mills in the United States comes from this source (40% in Japan). Wastepaper is generally supplied to the mills presorted by large-volume dealers.

Efforts of wastepaper suppliers must be closely coordinated with the paper stock consumer to provide the correct grade. Strength, cleanliness, and brightness requirements of the end product dictate the amount and grades which may be employed. Wastepaper testing for grade classification and product suitability is a key function of both the wastepaper dealer's laboratory and the consuming paper mill laboratory.[7] Wastepapers to be deinked and bleached have much more exacting specifications than those used for construction papers and boxboards.[8]

PULP MILL CONTROL

Uniform and high-quality pulp for paper products is ever more important as demands for paper quality requirements increase. These demands focus pulp producers' attention on in-process quality control programs. Pulp manufacture uses unit operations such as gas absorption, evaporation, extraction, and filtration, which are common to many chemical processes (see Section 29).

Chemical Pulping Figure 30-1 depicts a simplified flow diagram for a typical kraft chemical pulp mill highlighting key control points.

TABLE 30-1   Wood and Chip Quality Factors

Factors Affecting Quality	Suggested Control Programs
Wood species variation	Continual record of chip analysis
wood supply:	
Variation in wood moisture	1. Rapid moisture testing 2. Plot running averages
Purchased chip vs. roundwood	1. Check on proportion of each 2. Evaluate chip suppliers for moisture, density, chip size distribution, species, bark, and tramp metal
Age of logs or chips	1. Minimize storage time 2. Maintain records of wood age in each yard and pile
Site location (growth rate, age of tree, size of tree, etc.)	Limited control over these factors (influences must be recognized)
Bark content	Physically separating and weighing bark present in a known weight of representative chips (apply to each chip supplier and mill system)
Chip size	Chip classification testing

Wood and Chips. Table 30-1 outlines the significant factors affecting wood and chip quality, and the suggested control programs as described by Green.[9] A com-

[7] Wastepaper market prices in 1971 reflect the value of separated fibers; mixed paper at $2 per ton, old corrugated containers $12 per ton, hard white envelope cuts $75 per ton. Compare these with virgin fiber: groundwood $90, kraft bleached softwood $146 per ton.

[8] See Ref. 38, vol. 1, chap. 14, for further information on wastepaper processing.

[9] Green, R. P., Control of Pulp Quality in a Bleached Kraft Pulp Mill, *Tappi,* vol. 46, no. 3, pp. 14–26, March 1963.

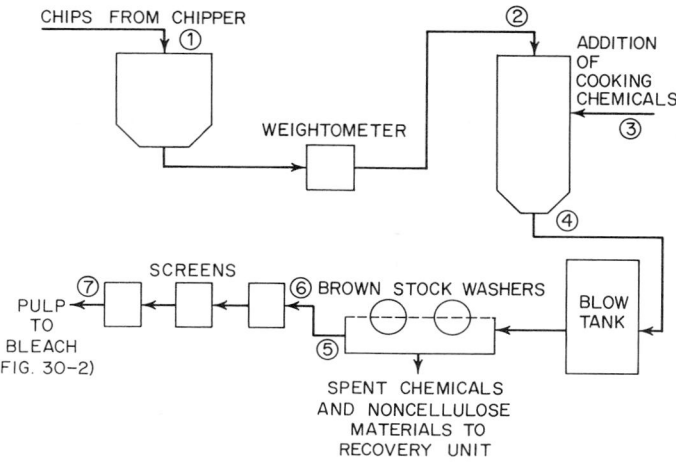

CHIPS FROM CHIPPER

WEIGHTOMETER

ADDITION OF COOKING CHEMICALS

SCREENS

PULP TO BLEACH (FIG. 30-2)

BROWN STOCK WASHERS

BLOW TANK

SPENT CHEMICALS AND NONCELLULOSE MATERIALS TO RECOVERY UNIT

Sampling Point	Material	Test
(1)	Chip from chipper	Chip classification (including chip length)
(2)	Chips to digester	Moisture
(3)	Cooking chemicals	Active alkali
(4)	Blow line pulp	Permanganate number
(5)	Brown stock	Salt cake loss
(6)	Stock-screen inlet	Consistency
(7)	Stock-screen outlet	Consistency

Fig. 30-1 Testing control program for typical chemical pulp mill.

prehensive control program may not always be justified at all pulp mills. Each operation must be examined in light of its own particular problems.

Digestion. Other than wood supply, key areas of the kraft digestion process influencing final product quality include:

1. Control of the relative amounts of wood, white liquor, and black liquor in the charge. Wood moisture variation can result in incorrectly adjusting the active alkali charge for the actual dry weight of chips. Wood moisture tests help the digester operator compensate for changes in moisture level when necessary. Liquor testing is of paramount importance, since these results determine the amount of liquor added to the digester. (White liquor is tested for active alkali and sulfidity at the control station by conventional chemical liquor analysis.)

2. Time-temperature control during pulping. Automatic control of digester heating schedules alleviates variations in pulp quality. However, individual digesters differ because of scaling of heat exchangers, variations in chip loading and packing, liquor circulation patterns, steaming, and relief practices. All these factors relate primarily to poor heat distribution or liquor circulation. Systematic pulp sampling from each digester to spot variation within and between digesters for key pulp characteristics—permanganate number and viscosity—is essential to good pulp mill control.

Brown Stock Washing and Screening. Thorough brown stock washing prevents chemical losses and improves color and bleachability. Screened pulp must be carefully observed for shives and dirt.   This avoids increased chemical costs and excessive fluctuation in strength and brightness which commonly occur when excessive bleaching is used to overcome lack of pulp cleanliness.

Pulp Bleaching   Bleaching is a continuation of the cellulose purification process started at the digester.   Process conditions are controlled to give the final desired brightness yet maintain the necessary pulp strength.   A typical bleaching sequence used for high bright pulps has five stages: chlorination, caustic extraction, chlorine dioxide, caustic extraction, and chlorine dioxide (CEDED).   (Figure 30-2 shows

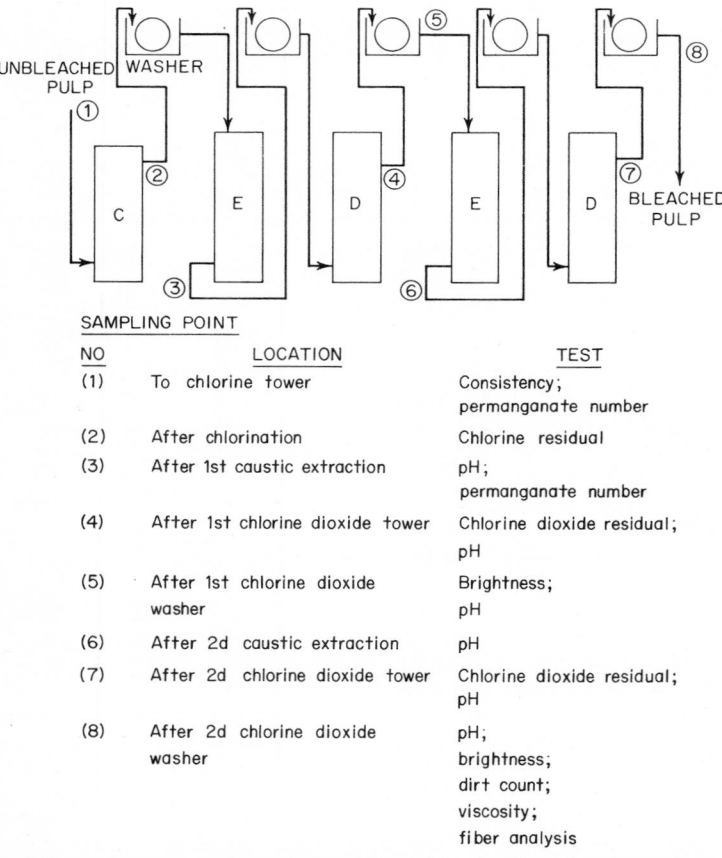

SAMPLING POINT		
NO	LOCATION	TEST
(1)	To chlorine tower	Consistency; permanganate number
(2)	After chlorination	Chlorine residual
(3)	After 1st caustic extraction	pH; permanganate number
(4)	After 1st chlorine dioxide tower	Chlorine dioxide residual; pH
(5)	After 1st chlorine dioxide washer	Brightness; pH
(6)	After 2d caustic extraction	pH
(7)	After 2d chlorine dioxide tower	Chlorine dioxide residual; pH
(8)	After 2d chlorine dioxide washer	pH; brightness; dirt count; viscosity; fiber analysis

Fig. 30-2   Pulp testing program for typical multistage bleach plant.   See also Ref. 38, vol. 1, chaps 9–11 for details on chemical pulping.

typical sampling points for process testing.)   Where strength and final brightness are not of prime concern, the number of stages may be reduced.   The following briefly describes the control aspects pertinent to the bleaching process.

Chlorination.   In this stage, aqueous or gaseous elemental chlorine is added to a suspension of pulp in water to remove lignin.   High brightness in later stages and maintenance of pulp strength depend primarily upon initial chlorination control.   Insufficient chlorination results in subsequent excessive chlorine dioxide usage, high chemical costs, and difficulty in achieving uniform and high-brightness pulp. Excessive chlorination, on the other hand, increases initial chlorine costs and reduces pulp strength. Chemical addition rates, pulp consistency, pH, temperature, and time are key variables for chlorination control.

Caustic Extraction. Removal of chlorinated lignins from the pulp is accomplished in the caustic extraction stages so that oxidative bleaching agents in subsequent stages can be efficiently utilized. In kraft pulps, the alkaline extraction stage very effectively removes many dyelike substances. Again, chemical addition (the amount of applied alkali), pulp consistency, pH, temperature, and time are important controlling factors.

Chlorine dioxide is generally used as a finishing bleach to obtain high-brightness pulps. It normally raises pulp brightness without any loss in pulp strength, as it attacks and oxidizes the lignin without attacking the cellulose. Pulp brightness measurements following the first chlorine dioxide stage determine the degree of bleaching achieved in the process to this point.

Pulp Mill Testing Successful control of pulp quality is keyed to the mill control laboratory. It makes routine control tests at prescribed frequencies to provide process control and outgoing quality information. Results posted on operations control charts direct attention to quality trends and to factors contributing to variations. When statistically significant departures from standard occur, the shift testers immediately report these to the manufacturing foreman. On major control tests, plant operators receive their reports immediately after completion of the analysis, while routine reports pertaining to various departments are issued daily.

The tests described in Figures 30-1 and 30-2, although not complete, are typical. See Testing Methods (this Section) for additional information on pulp mill testing procedures.

Mechanical Pulping Groundwood is produced by a grinding process whereby debarked logs are forced against a continuously revolving grindstone. The most important control problem is that of maintaining a uniform grade of groundwood to the paper machine. Pulp quality characteristics are determined by wood species and age, fineness of grindstone surface, burr design, type of grinder, and grinder operating conditions.

Groundwood Testing. Commonly, groundwood is a mixture of pulps from a battery of grinders—a blend of long and short fibers plus fibrous fragments. No one test can be used for quality control. Operator judgment guided with test information is necessary.

Of the quality control tests, the subjective "blue-glass" test is the oldest and one still in use in many mills. Operating personnel observe a dilute suspension of fiber and water poured onto a sheet of dark blue glass lighted from below, noting the condition of the fiber bundles. The Canadian Standard Freeness Tester measures drainage (expressed numerically for a standard consistency and stock temperature). It attempts to measure the drainage of water from the stock as it would actually take place on a paper machine. Other control laboratory tests on pulp handsheets include bursting strength and tear. Pulp fiber classifiers have been developed, such as the Bauer-McNett, to separate selectively the fibers of various length and size. The results are worthwhile in process development and characterizing existing operations. The procedure is too lengthy for process control.

Control Charts. Process control charts for consistency and freeness avoid overcontrol, i.e., excess variation resulting from unnecessary changes. Generally, action limits are set at ±2 standard deviations based on past performance about the given standard value. Table 30-2 illustrates the type of improvement reported by Breen[10] at one mill after 6 months' experience with a control chart system.

[10] Breen, J. K., Statistical Control Charts—Their Application in Groundwood Mills, *Pulp and Paper Magazine of Canada*, vol. 70, no. 14, pp. 61–63, July 18, 1969.

TABLE 30-2   Improvement in Groundwood Uniformity after 6 Months' Experience with Control Chart System

Test	Location	% improvement*
Consistency	Paper machine proportioners	41
	Washed stock chest	20
	Deckered stock chest	46
Freeness	Paper machine proportioners	35
	Washed stock chest	35
	Deckered stock chest	37
Brightness	Washed stock chest	46
	Deckered stock chest	15

$$* \% \text{ improvement} = \frac{\text{original variance} - \text{variance after 6 months}}{\text{original variance}} \times 100$$

PAPER MILL CONTROL

Control of the papermaking process involves bringing together three basic papermaking functions—stock preparation, wet end, and dry end—and coordinating them for maximum mill efficiency and product quality.   Also, many papermaking processes include coating either on or off-machine, which can further complicate the paper mill process control system.   A flow diagram of the total paper mill complex is illustrated in Figure 30-3.   See Ref. 39 for further details on papermaking equipment and technology.

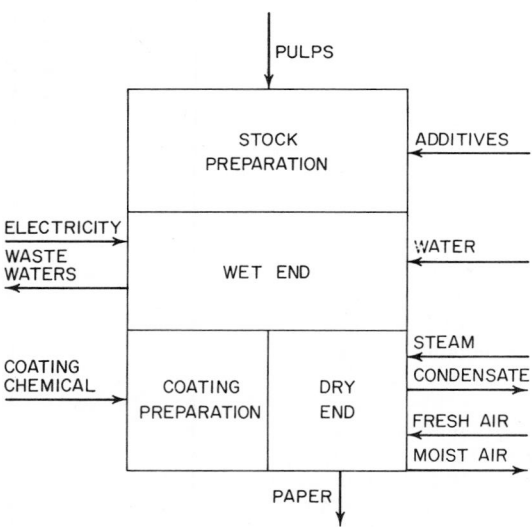

Fig. 30-3   Paper mill complex.

The complexity of papermaking control requires close operator process surveillance.   Knowledge of process variables, interrelationships, causes and effects, and the type and extent of machine adjustments required to achieve optimum quality comes about only after much training and experience.   Operators produce quality paper partly as an art and partly as a science.   Test stations perform routine tests for specific quality characteristics, on-machine instruments measure and control critical process variables, and in more recent years, computers guide operators in their control function.

Operator Control Control of quality in paper manufacturing prior to the technical evolution of the early twentieth century was entirely in the hands of the paper-maker. Years of experience have made the papermaker a good judge of paper quality as made (but not necessarily in terms of its use). He prides himself on being able to derive a great deal of information regarding paper quality as produced by observing process conditions. By watching the "wet-line," couch vacuum, crumbing, press stickiness, fiber buildup on doctors, and other observable but nontestable properties, he "tunes" the equipment to assure meeting product specifications. He informally tests for product quality by rattling the sheet, tearing it slowly in the machine and cross direction, and inspecting uniformity of texture ("formation")—viewing the sheet against a strong light. Such visual characteristics as cleanliness, opacity, brightness, and gloss can be judged well by the experienced eye. Commonly the papermaker has evaluated smoothness by feeling the surface with his fingers or tongue, and determining the degree of sizing by touching his tongue to the sheet and noting the time for the saliva to be absorbed. Being subjective, many of these "craftsman" tests are susceptible to excessive variation because of differences in senses and interpretation between operators. Further, they lack a numerical scale for judging control.

Test Station Control The above problems have been at least partially overcome by:

1. Developing mill control test methods that provide numerical values of paper quality characteristics

2. Establishing mill control stations where these tests can be made by trained personnel, independent of manufacturing operation

The most important and immediate use of test station control data is, of course, to assure that operating faults or problems are corrected with minimum delay. With proper statistical analysis of accumulated test data, routine testing programs can detect subtle quality trends relatable to process, equipment, or operational changes.

Paper mill management for the most part justifies mill test station control as a means to guide the papermaker in his work. Besides providing speed, accuracy, and precision, test stations also add a psychological value, since continuous process monitoring generally leads to greater operator care.

Test Station Forms. Test station control effectiveness can be considerably improved with properly designed quality log sheets. Their design must emphasize all the important quality characteristics and their relationship in terms of both properties and timing. It may even be advantageous to repeat an element from another form (such as freeness, furnish, or coating changes) to establish cause-and-effect relationships. Test station forms are more than just a system of recording measurements. They are tools for rapid surveillance of current and past quality performance by mill operators and supervisors. (See Section 19 for forms design.)

Sampling Problems. The major problems associated with test station control of the papermaking operations relate to testing the paper after its removal from the paper machine at the reel turnup. This presents problems in:

1. Obtaining a representative sample at the reel

2. Time delays in sample delivery and testing

3. Relaying information to the paper machine crew for corrective action

Although sampling at reel turnup is and will continue to be an established practice for most paper mills, cross direction (CD) and machine direction (MD) variation in paper test characteristics within a reel must be recognized.[11,12,13] These varia-

[11] Benya, V. R., Wet End Tuning Improves Machine Balance, Increases Output, *Pulp and Paper*, vol. 41, No. 24, pp. 40–44, June 12, 1967.

[12] Early papers on CD-MD models include: Bicking, C. A., The Fundamentals of Control

tions can be determined by a conventional two-factor analysis of variance or staggered nested designs. (See Section 27, Design and Analysis of Experiments.) Computers simplify data collection and analysis on a regular basis from a series of runs on desired properties. Normally, data consist of a fixed number of measurements across the paper web ("front, front center, center, back center, and back" positions), which are repeated at intervals in the machine direction. The length selected in the machine direction can be varied to study both short-term (within-reel) and long-term (reel-to-reel) variation. Sampling schemes for paper testing must take into account these MD and CD variations plus the test error of each particular measurement. Only this way can mill Quality Control arrive at optimum sampling schemes to detect important shifts in level. (Further details pertaining to sampling and testing and their relationship to specifications are described in this Section under Testing and Inspection and under Establishing Specifications.)

TABLE 30-3   Overcoming Communication Problems from Laboratory to Machine Floor

Problem	Solution

1. *Sample delivery* to test station
     a. Must protect sample from moisture pickup, dirt, etc.
     b. Be fast over long distances
	1. a. Use nonpermeable pouches, plastic gloves to handle samples
	     b. Pneumatic tube system for pouch delivery ($\frac{1}{2}$ mile in 80 seconds); move test station close to machine

2. Must *condition* sample to standard relative humidity and temperature for 4–72 hours before testing	2. Use accelerated conditioning for preliminary results; follow up with specified conditioning for historical results
3. Testing time	3. Automatic test equipment, digital output
4. Feed information back to machine operators	4. Use telautograph remote receiving stations; closed-circuit TV cameras scanning laboratory test logs under remote operator control; telephone; remote terminal entry to computer system

Operator-Laboratory Communication. For process control, tests must be quickly made and results returned rapidly. Table 30-3 lists some of the problems to be overcome. In general, on-machine continuous instrumentation is preferred whenever it can be justified economically. Because of the large number of interrelated processing conditions and variables, the machine foreman is usually encouraged to visit the test station. There he can spot changes in pulp brightness, freeness, refining, etc., as well as in-process tests which help predict final paper properties.

On-Machine Quality Measurements   Gages for on-machine quality measurements have been developed, and their effectiveness in automatic control applications is

Charts, *Tappi*, vol. 36, No. 12, pp. 544–549, December 1953; Bicking, C. A., and R. G. Trelfa, Some Influences of Paper Machine Design and Operation on Variability of Paperboard, *Industrial Quality Control.* vol. X, No. 2, pp. 17–19, September 1953; Burkhard, G., and P. E. Wrist, The Evaluation of Paper Machine Stock Systems by Basis Weight Analysis, *Tappi*, vol. 37, No. 12, pp. 613–630, December 1954. (Discusses CD × MD models using the "interaction" term as the random component and suggests an analysis of both random component vs. speed and studies of periodicity in terms of time series analysis using serial covariance and autocorrelation. Contains a useful discussion of stability of the cross direction profile—especially helpful for those interested in constructing mathematical models of paper machines.)

[13] Lake, L.O., Sheet Properties That Affect Machine Direction Register on Gravure Presses, *Tappi*, vol. 53, No. 10, pp. 1964–1967, October 1970, relates rate of change in MD elasticity (as influenced by MD basis weight changes) to gravure press register problems; a direct process-to-customer use cause-and-effect explanation.

being exploited by many mills.   Traversing gages for basis weight and moisture measurement have found widespread acceptance throughout the industry, while new systems for numerous other quality control measurements as listed in Table 30-4 are continually being introduced.

TABLE 30-4   On-machine Gaging Systems for Measuring Characteristics of Paper*

Property	Method
Strength:	
Basis weight	Radiation gaging
Moisture.	Infrared, dielectric, conductivity, microwave
Caliper.	Magnetic reluctance
Formation.	Optical
Density	Basis weight/caliper
Fiber weight.	Basis weight minus moisture
Optical:	
Opacity	Optical transmitted light
Gloss	Optical reflected light
Color	Optical reflected light
Flaws.	Optical transmitted and reflected light
Formation.	Optical transmitted light
Permeability	
Air permeability	Air transmission

* Smith, B. W., and J. Boersma, On-machine Measurements of Paper Uniformity, *Tappi*, vol. 49, No. 7, pp 80–82, July 1966.

Scanning gages offer the advantage of presenting an accurate average value and a cross direction *profile* display.   They are essential for caliper measurement since caliper control is entirely cross directional.   For color, fixed point measurements are satisfactory, as variation is usually MD oriented.   (The standard method of color control with pigments or dyes does not lead to cross direction variability.)

Computer Control   With on-machine quality measurements the amount of quality data generated often is so great that machine crews are confused and fail to respond properly to interrelated process variables.

Computers help solve this problem by selective data logging as an operator guide or by direct automatic control.   (See Section 20 for detailed approaches to computer applications.)   Stout's compilation[14] of computer benefits shows reduction in rejects, product variability, grade change time, plus machine speed increases of 10 to 20%.

Justification Needed.   Paper mill computer process control can be justified normally only through increased productivity.   Good[15] suggests most paper machines are not ready for computer control because the predominant process control problems have not yet received cheaper, more efficient, conventional control analysis and solution.   Specification reevaluation, good sampling and testing procedures, and control charts in the machine room are effective precursors.

FINISHING

Finishing includes all the operations involved in transforming a reel of paper into the product form required by the customer.   These include winding and rewinding, supercalendering, sheeting, trimming, and inspection.

[14] Stout, T. M., Would You Believe—Process Computers Can Be Successful in the Paper Industry? *Paper Trade Journal*, vol. 153, No. 15, pp. 54–57, Apr. 14, 1969.
[15] Good, J. L., Paper Industry Computer Control—Fact or Fiction? *Paper Trade Journal*, vol. 153, No. 13, pp. 76–81, Mar. 31, 1969 (see below, under Improvement through Process Control).

Quality control in the finishing area is primarily involved in maintaining workmanship standards and inspection procedures to provide a product that will perform satisfactorily in subsequent customer operations.

Winding and Rewinding   The process of *winding* consists of unwinding a full *reel* of paper (machine width), trimming the edges, and simultaneously slitting it into one or more *rolls*.   *Rewinding* is considered as the unwinding of a *roll* that was made on a winder and making it into one or more rewound rolls.   From the standpoint of manufacturing control, winding and rewinding are identical.

Roll Quality Requirements.   Winding requires that rolls produced be:

1. Consistently trimmed to the width ordered by the customer.   (This means maintaining accurate and reliable web guiding systems.)

2. Free from mechanical defects that affect their runnability in subsequent converting operations.   (Not all mechanical defects are winder-caused.   *Wrinkles, bags,* and *corrugations* are often in the paper before it reaches the winder.   Minimizing these defects generally requires maintaining uniform basis weight, caliper, and moisture profiles in papermaking, sizing, and coating.)

Roll runnability is often more important to the printer than printability.   No matter how excellent a printing job can be achieved, if the rolls do not run properly on the presses, they will cause low productivity and excess waste and cost, and they will be rejected and returned to the producing mill.   The needs of some web-fed converting operations may be even more critical than those required by high-speed presses.   For example, register bond and computer papers are required to have extremely uniform wound-in tension throughout the rolls to maintain register in the converting operation.

Defect Classification.   Much has been done to classify and identify roll defects that cause converting problems.[16]   However, more effort is still required in standardizing nomenclature for proper communications between paper manufacturer and customer.   (See Inspection Methods, this Section.)

Mechanical defects tend to be grade-oriented.   Defects considered serious in one grade may be insignificant in others.   See Table 30-5 for the more common defects for various grades of paper.

Roll Quality Measurement.   For many years, mill roll quality was measured by thumping with a club across the entire roll face and listening to the sound produced.   (The hand is also used to estimate the resiliency of the roll in this procedure.)   Recently, roll hardness testing devices such as the Beloit Rhometer[17] have been developed along the same basic principles.   It consists of a device to strike the roll and a circuit to measure sound transmission through the roll.   The harder the roll, the faster the sound travels.   The system is calibrated in arbitrary "rho" units on a 0 to 100 scale.   Mills employ these devices to obtain roll hardness profiles and relate them to machine conditions, supercalender crowns, and potential mechanical performance problems.[18]

Another new approach to measurement of roll quality is that of monitoring variations in roll diameter by a special roll checking device.[19]   The theory is that high caliper areas or humps in the roll cause stretched paper, which results in slack

[16] Production Operating Communication Standards for Magazine Paper Mills, Printers, and Publishers, *Tappi CA Report* 13, October 1967.

[17] Pfeiffer, J. D., Internal Pressures in a Wound Roll of Paper, *Tappi,* vol. 49, No. 8, pp. 342–347, August 1966.

[18] TAPPI Useful Method 402, Hardness of Paper Rolls (Using Schmidt Concrete Test Hammer), *Tappi,* vol. 54, No. 7, pp. 1177, July 1971.

[19] Quint, R. J., Measurement and Control of the Condition of Paper Rolls, *Paper Trade Journal,* vol. 152, No. 9, pp. 52–54, Feb. 26, 1968.

TABLE 30-5   Common Mechanical Defects for Specific Grades of Paper*

Paper Grade	Defects
Newsprint	Loose cores
	Overstretched (bags or breaks) on the outer diameter
	Out-of-round rolls
Coated grades	Tension bursts
	Shear bursts
	Bags
Business form	Bags
	Offsets
	Off-center cores
Grocery bag	Dishing
	Loose cores
	Off-center cores
Carbonizing	Dishing
	Corrugations
	Stars

* Forsberg, G., Emphasis on Better Rolls Means More Attention to Roll Structure, *Paper Trade Journal,* vol. 153, No. 17, pp. 36–40, Apr. 28, 1969.

or baggy areas as the roll unwinds (and wrinkles if the paper is later cut into sheets). This test equipment consists of an arm traversing the length of the paper roll, measuring and recording the deviation from a perfect cylinder of paper. (See Testing and Inspection in this Section, and Section 36B, Plastic Film Quality, for additional details on roll quality inspection.) Daly[20] reported shipping roll defects and explanations for their causes as related to winding.

Supercalendering   This operation is designed to improve the printing surface and appearance of the sheet as judged by gloss level and uniformity. From a quality control viewpoint the most important control variables in supercalendering are sheet moisture, calender pressure, and amount of localized steam. Gloss is measured as surface light reflectance. Various instruments are available for gloss measurement both on and off line; results are recorded directly as a percentage of reflected light. On-line gloss instrumentation has generally been stationary. Thus, gloss recorder chart readings can be misleading in maintaining the specification level if a large variation in cross direction gloss variability exists on the web. Mill laboratory gloss testing on a reel-to-reel basis across the entire web is common. (The average is used for control of *level* and the range for CD *uniformity.*) Audits of gloss on top of shipping rolls are often useful in characterizing outgoing quality because, owing to rewinding, they are made on the opposite end of the roll normally tested for process control.

Sheeting   Paper is generally cut from the winder rolls on a rotary cutter. The rolls are placed on a backstand section holding 1 to 12 rolls depending on the quality and basis weight of the paper.

Defect Prevention Measures.   In cutter backstand setup it is imperative that:

1. The number of rolls cut at one time does not exceed that which the knife will cut cleanly without causing broken edges or dust (generally monitored by the cutter operator).

[20] Daly, D. A., Study of Defects in Wound Rolls Leads to Better Winding Control, *Paper Trade Journal,* vol. 151, No. 49, pp. 46–48, Dec. 4, 1967.

2. The set of rolls to be cut is uniform in visual appearance (color, brightness, opacity, gloss).

3. Defective rolls which would cause recurring defects repetitively are not included.

Roll matching for sheeting to assure within-load uniformity can be expedited in the finishing room by having test data for optical properties of the parent reels from which the rolls were cut. In many cases the *range* of color, brightness, etc., to obtain a reasonable visual match may be tighter than the normal *long-term* process capability for the specific grade, thereby making it necessary to establish separate tolerances for the sheeting operation. Obviously, defective rolls must be detected earlier in the process at the paper machine, winders, coater, supercalenders, etc., to minimize underruns and expedite process control. (Cutter speeds are too high for inspection during cutting except for the grossest defects; furthermore, overlap of sheets conceals 50 to 90% of the area.)

Sheeting Inspection Systems. Inspection for visual defects has traditionally involved either 100% sorting or fanning of loads[21] after cutting. These inspection procedures suffer from low efficiency due to monotony and fatigue, and in the case of fanning, the inability to view the entire sheet.[22]

Statistical acceptance sampling plans have been adopted by many mills, resulting in substantial cost reductions.[23] The materials handling aspects, to avoid damaging the product, suggest the samples be taken soon after cutting and before stacking. This requires pulling sheets periodically from the layboy for examination by the operator or an assigned inspector. Alternatively, automatic sampling devices on cutters at many mills assure both nondestructive sampling and adequate random sample. An automatic actuated gate diverts the sample sheets to a secondary layboy below the existing sheeting equipment for accumulation and subsequent lot-by-lot inspection[24] or to a moving belt for continuous inspection. In this way, visual inspections of each sheet in a clip[25] at a predetermined random frequency can determine whether or not the load being cut goes directly to trimming or to sorting. These plans are especially useful on grades where 100% manual or electronic inspection is not economically justified or possible. (See Statistical Acceptance Sampling in this Section.)

Automated Inspection Systems. Fully automated inspection systems are generally feasible in finishing room applications *only* for top-grade papers which otherwise would have to be hand-sorted. The most important application of defect detection equipment has been on the cutter-sorter (in-line) and sheet sorter (off-line).

The cutter-sorter combines high-speed cutting and inspection. Guillotine trimming is often eliminated by its precision features. Sheet sorters lend themselves

---

[21] A "load" is defined as the maximum quantity of cut sheets that can be accumulated at the delivery layboy. "Skids" represent a subdivision or multiple of the load, counted, weighed, and on a skid or pallet; usually wrapped and banded for shipment. The number of sheets on a skid depends on customer order or specifications, or trade practice.

[22] Obvious difficulties with fanning inspection were reported by R. M. Soth, Hammermill's Quality Acceptance Sampling Plan, *Paper Trade Journal,* vol. 145, No. 47, pp. 39–41, Nov. 20, 1961. Only 60% of the sheet is "seeable;" an average person fanning 115 reams in 7 ½ hours looks at 230,000 edges of 57,500 sheets while standing under glaring lights in a huge room full of distractions.

[23] Mead, G. W., Sheet Finishing Process Improves Overall Papermaking Efficiency, *Paper Trade Journal,* vol. 148, No. 39, pp. 28–29, Sept. 28, 1964.

[24] Haselow, W. J., Acceptance Sampling for Visual Quality Control, *Tappi,* vol. 46, No. 2, pp. 161A–163A, February 1963, describes a system developed at Consolidated Papers, Inc., employing sample frequency adjustment feature.

[25] All the sheets cut at one time are referred to here as a "clip." It is the natural sampling unit when multiple sheeting, containing a sheet from each roll.

to inspecting random samples or rejected loads. The sheet sorter consists of a feeding mechanism, scanning inspection station, and a double delivery system (one for the "accepts" and the other for "rejects").

At present, automated inspection systems are limited to detecting defects categorized as holes, lumps, wrinkles, or spots. Other defects such as hair cuts, calender cuts, streaks, blade scratches, and pinholes are not economically detectable with equipment commercialized[26] to date.

Trimming   In this operation, the slightly oversize cut sheets are trimmed to final size, usually in a block of several reams. This aligns the edges for automatic feeding in a printing press, folder, collator, etc.

Quality problems of trimming are primarily related to workmanship. Operator carelessness causes out-of-square sheets with subsequent pressroom problems in obtaining accurate register. Excessive pressure on the clamp bar may leave an impression on the top sheets; insufficient pressure may cause slipping and result in uneven cutting. Knife dullness will cause rough and *dusty* edges. Inadequate examination of the trimmed stack may allow sheets with *turned corners* to go undetected, later causing blanket damage on offset printing presses. Periodic quality audits of the trimming operation are used to assure a specified quality level leaving the mill and to pinpoint problem areas needing immediate corrective action.

TESTING AND INSPECTION[27]

Testing Methods   Design of reliable, rapid tests has proved difficult for many of the material, process, and product properties of this industry. Test *limitations* must be understood. Many of the tests measure more than one property, making their interpretation difficult if the immediate circumstances are not known.

These difficulties are reflected in the TAPPI classification of its methods as: *Useful* (formerly "Routine"), *Suggested Methods* (usually precision, accuracy, or reliability not yet established), and *Standards*.

Substantial progress has been made in improving and understanding test methods since Bicking pointed out the incompleteness of TAPPI methods. Greater attention to the importance of testing and the benefits of statistical methods has identified need for additional research into the basis for commonly used tests. This has of necessity extended into reappraising test equipment itself, frequently disclosing unsuspected limitations or even misuse. Table 30-6 highlights some of this development.

In pulp testing, the *need* for sound test methods is even greater than in paper testing. As indicated in Table 30-6, present methods are best limited to detecting lack of uniformity within one pulp or furnish and not for cross comparisons. Reference pulps (see Table 30-6) provide a calibration for pulp test methods and equipment.[28]

Test Precision Statements.   When stating the precision of a test method, the exact conditions of the test evaluation must be described.[29] Specifically, the precision statement must report:

1. If the variation described results from multiple tests on
The same area; or

---

[26] Functional and sensitivity details of automated inspection systems available are described in Scharf, E., What Are the Justifications for Instrumented Paper Inspection? *Paper Trade Journal,* vol. 154, No. 2, pp. 50–55, Jan. 12, 1970.

[27] See generally Sections 12, Inspection and Test, and 13, Measurement.

[28] For further detail on pulp and paper testing see in this Section, Pulp Mill Testing.

[29] See "Precision Statement for Test Methods," TAPPI T1206 OS-69, but realize the measures of precision "repeatability, comparability, and reproducibility" are not universally accepted or even meaningful in some situations. Hence, the advantage in clearly defining conditions for data collection. See also Section 13, under Errors of Measurement.

TABLE 30-6   Testing Development

Precision and Accuracy

1. *Statements of Precision; Precision Data Available.* Drew attention to need for precision statements and urged committee action. Bicking, C. A., The Use of Statistics for Analysis of Testing Results, *Tappi,* vol. 38, No. 9, pp. 573–576, September 1955. Also Bicking, C. A., Precision Data Available on Commonly Used Tappi Standard Methods of Test, *Tappi,* vol. 42, No. 1, pp. 89A–91A, January 1959.

Of 36 standard methods for testing pulp, 9 had a section dealing with sampling, 27 made no statement about precision, 1 specified accuracy expected, and none indicated pertinent probability levels. Bicking, C. A., Survey of Sampling and Precision Requirements in Present Tappi Test Methods, *Tappi,* vol. 44, No. 1, pp. 42–46, January 1961.

The measures of precision "repeatability, comparability, and reproducibility" are not universally accepted or even meaningful in some situations. "Precision Statements for Test Methods," TAPPI T1206 OS-69.

2. *Related Statistical Methods and Bibliographies.* Role of Statistical Methods. Bicking, C. A., Statistical Approaches to the Study of Test Precision, *Tappi,* vol. 40, No. 3, pp. 191–192, March 1957.

Traces improvements and advances generally. Bicking, C. A., Bibliography on Precision, Analysis of Test Data, and Applied Statistics in the Pulp and Paper Industry, *Tappi,* vol. 46, No. 8, pp. 182A–196A, August 1963; *Tappi,* vol. 46, No. 9, pp. 227A–240A, September 1963.

Update through 1965. Includes Interlaboratory Testing. *Tappi CA Report* 10, September 1967.

Test Method and Equipment Evaluation

1. *Brightness.* Concept, state of the art, and depth of technical detail. Van den Akker, J. A., L. R. Dearth, and W. M. Shillcox, Is the Concept of Standard Brightness Suitable Today? *Tappi,* vol 46, No. 5, pp. 202A–207A, May 1963; also No. 11, pp. 183A–187A, November 1963; also pp. 187A–190A.

2. *Tearing Strength.* "Differences can be introduced by clamping (10% or more) by the number of plies tested (as high as 100%), with a change in the *nature* of the tear . . . the splitting of paper as it occurs in the Elmendorf is not encountered in most instances of tear failure in the usual applications of paper." Wink, W. A., and R. H. Van Eperen, Does the Elmendorf Tester Measure Tearing Strength? *Tappi,* vol. 46, No. 5, pp. 323–325, May 1963.

3. *Opacity.* Comparison of Printing Opacity Determined with Several Selected Instruments. Dearth, L. R., W. M. Shillcox, W. A. Wink, and J. A. Van den Akker, Study of Instruments for the Measurement of Opacity of Paper—V, *Tappi,* vol. 53, No. 3, pp. 436–441, March 1970.

4. *Color.* Needless basic defects in colorimetric instruments designed to measure color limit the accuracy and the usefulness of the data. Dearth, L. R., Numerical Evaluation of Color Employing Suitable Instrumentation, *Tappi,* vol. 46, No. 10, pp. 146A–151A, October 1963.

Presently available instruments must be used with full awareness of their limitations and that appropriate "hitching posts" must be employed if satisfactory correlation is to be obtained between vendor and buyer. Wurzburg, F. L., Jr., Survey of Instruments for Color Specification, *Tappi,* vol. 46, No. 7, pp. 155A–159A, July 1963.

5. *Gurley Stiffness.* "Light and Medium weight coated papers . . . cannot be compared . . . to similar basis weight *uncoated* papers." "Conversion factors supplied . . . with respect to sample length . . . for card and cover stocks, file folders, and various types of paper boards, either coated or uncoated, are not strictly valid." Verhoeff, J., and I. C. White, Some Aspects of the Gurley Stiffness Tester, *Tappi,* vol. 53, No. 7, pp. 1316–1319, July 1970.

6. *Viscosity.* During development of in-process testing, difficulties with one coating clay were associated with unusual rheological behavior. Hussain, S. M., *et al.,* An Ultra High Shear Recording Viscometer, *Tappi,* vol. 53, No. 1, pp. 96–101, January 1970.

7. *Roughness.* Misuse can result from a change in product specification. "An excellent instrument for the evaluation of newsprint . . . but *magazine* papers today are so smooth that the Bendtsen roughness tester values are in the lowest and rather inaccurate range of the instrument." Also describes improper calibration procedures. Haefeker, G., Calibration of the Bendtsen Roughness Tester, *Tappi,* vol. 53, No. 1, pp. 114–115, January 1970.

"Differences up to 40% were noted between the results . . . with 23 different Bendtsen instruments used by one Australian company." (Agreement within 10% was achieved following overhaul of the flowmeters, recalibration, addition of new measuring head pressure controls, etc. Zubryn, E., and G. L. Hook, Deficiencies in Bendtsen Roughness and Porosity Testers and Their Correction, *Appita,* vol. 23, No. 4, p. 279, 1970).

8. *Mullen.* Mullen test on corrugated board has an uncontrolled factor producing variation of up to ± 30% of test results. In use for over 50 years, method was first published in 1966 and declared inadequate in 1970. Hood, P. F., Standardization of the Burst (Mullen) Test Procedure, *Tappi,* vol. 53, No. 2, pp. 253–256, February 1970.

Proposed standardization method. Maltenfort, G. G., S. A. Morse, and J. Babakitis, Standardization and Calibration of the Mullen Burst Test by Electronic Instrumentation, *Tappi,* vol. 54, No. 7, pp. 1122–1127, July 1971.

9. *Pulp Properties.* Present routine methods could give very misleading information about the efficiency of a process, ranking of various pulp grades, or suitability of a given furnish for a certain application. Gavelin, G., How to Describe and Test Pulp Properties or Characteristics, *Paper Trade Journal,* vol. 155, No. 27, pp. 40–42, July 5, 1971.

10. *Beater Tests.* Unusually uniform testing was a clue to spurious performance. (The experiment design, data, results, analysis, and coefficients of variation for six widely different pulps are included.) Hughes, F. P., A Comparison of the Performance of the Valley and PFI Laboratory Beaters, *Pulp and Paper Magazine of Canada,* vol. 71, No. 16, pp. 75–80, Aug. 21, 1970.

Calibration Materials

1. *Pulps.* Twelve properties are reported on a *time, revolution,* and *freeness* basis with the standard deviation and number of tests required (based on the number made) to assure, with 95% confidence, that the means fall within ± 5% of the stated value. Ten Valley beater, four PFI mill, and one Kollergang evaluation covered. Frost, P. J., 1969 Tappi Reference Pulp Preliminary Results, *Tappi,* vol. 54, No. 4, pp. 598–601, April 1971.

2. *Paper.* Institute of Paper Chemistry, Appleton, Wis., circulates paper samples for industry-wide calibration.

A TAPPI-NBS collaborative reference program; over 120 laboratories participate calibrating over 12 paper properties. Additional Interlaboratory Reference Tests for Paper and Rubber, *National Bureau of Standards Technical Bulletin,* vol. 56, No. 10, p. 251, October 1972.

Similar services include correlation service of Central Laboratories of the Swedish Paper Industry.

Interlaboratory Testing (See Section 13 generally)

Consult *before* conducting interlaboratory studies. "Interlaboratory Evaluation of Test Methods Used with Paper and Paper Products" TAPPI Standard Method T1200 OS-69; also "ASTM Manual for Conducting an Interlaboratory Study of a Test Method," *Special Technical Publication* 335, ASTM, Philadelphia, Pa., 1963.

Examples of interlaboratory studies. (Components of variance are reported.) Lashof, T. W., and J. M. Patek, Interlaboratory Evaluation of a Method for Indicated Brightness of Papers Containing Fluorescent Brighteners, *Tappi,* vol. 45, No. 7, pp. 566–570, July 1962; also Lashof, T. W., Precision of Methods for Measuring Tensile Strength, Stretch, and Tensile Energy Absorption of Paper, *Tappi,* vol. 46, No. 1, pp. 52–59, January 1963.

Testing Maintenance

Procedure reports average coefficient of variation for *specimens* and *units* on eight properties. Ernst, J. O., *et al.,* Maintenance of Validity in Physical Tests of Paper, *Tappi,* vol. 54, No. 4, pp. 550–552, April 1971; also Halverson, C. O., Improvement of Mill Testing Accuracy and Inter-mill Test Conformity, *Tappi,* vol. 49, No. 4, pp. 39A–42A, April 1966.

Survey of Current Usage

Few methods are used unabridged. Lyne, L. M., The Use of Tappi Standards and Routine Control Methods by Paper Mills and Converters, *Tappi,* vol. 50, No. 1, pp. 43A–44A, January 1967.

Different areas on the same sheet; or
Different sheets from the same roll.
2. If the value determined for each test relates to
The same operator;
The same instrument;
Within the same time period; and
Within the same laboratory.

It is common practice to determine the laboratory precision of destructive paper tests by testing adjacent strips taken in the machine direction. In most cases, this minimizes the effect of within-sample variation; short-term MD variation (representing only a fraction of a second of machine time) is generally much less than that exhibited by the CD profile of a particular property.

Knowledge of between-laboratory precision is highly important to avoid manufacturer-customer disputes, and in monitoring several mill test stations by a central laboratory.[30]

Auditing Test Calibration and Uniformity.   Because many tests are subjective or reflect correlations with specific customer needs, it is especially important to maintain test uniformity and calibration.[31]   This assists a company indirectly in four ways:

Assures appropriate product disposition
Minimizes process over- or undercontrol
Prevents misdirection of research and development effort
Assesses changes in competitive products

In multimill companies, staff auditing of mill instruments and test methods is commonplace.   C.O. Halverson has reported[32] remarkable improvements in testing accuracy and uniformity among widely separated Kimberly-Clark mills.   Using a "percent testing error" system to express the deviation from the mean of audit samples as a percentage of the grade standard tolerance, improvements from 21 to 8% were obtained in 3 years.   The program necessarily includes audit of testing procedures.

Prior to starting an extensive interlaboratory calibration program it is usually productive to survey test needs.[33]

Test and Inspection Survey   Mill control tests, inspection, and reporting systems for many companies have been constructed piecemeal over many years, reflecting numerous customer problems and personnel changes.   A periodic survey of all routine testing and inspection to determine current applicability and justification frequently leads to cost reduction or capacity to accommodate the latest testing demands without increasing costs.   See Section 12, under Budgeting for Inspection, for a discussion of various approaches to improving inspection effectiveness.   The survey should point out excessive testing or inspection, plus needed process control procedures, especially in areas where quality losses are high or product performance poor.

Inspection Methods   Properly judging appearance and mechanical paper quality is one of the more complex problems in this industry.   To avoid subjective decisions,

[30] It cannot be overemphasized that extensive evaluation of any *proposed method* within a single laboratory must be undertaken to expose all potential factors and determine their influence.   Then, and only then, should a *proposed method* be included in interlaboratory evaluation.

[31] Reference pulps and papers are available.   See Table 30-6.

[32] See Table 30-6 for this and other pertinent references.

[33] Even for one-mill companies not involved in interlaboratory testing, a Test and Inspection Survey can be extremely enlightening.

quality standards are best established through joint efforts of manufacturing, quality control, and customer representatives. Paper samples or photographs illustrating the degree of defect allowable are helpful in supplementing written descriptions.[34] Photographs are imperative in defining roll quality mechanical defects.

Numerical Quality Indicators. The advantages of expressing appearance and mechanical quality in numerical terms are discussed more fully in Section 12, under Sensory Qualities. Common uses in papermaking include:

1. Specifying the number of dirt particles above a certain size in a given area.[35,36]

2. Setting reference standards of various product quality levels in terms of numerical ratings 0, 1, 2, 3, etc., e.g., uniformity of reflectance, undertone, and print quality. In use, the test is made, the print is rated numerically by comparison against standard prints, and decision is made relative to minimum specification values in accordance with customer performance feedback.

Defect Terminology and Inspection Standardization. Lack of standardized defect terminology and inspection methods is a major industry problem. The same defect may be called many names depending on the mill or operator; e.g., in roll inspection, "cracked edges" are also called "broken edges, tears, foldovers, dog-ears, snags, winder cracks, and edge cuts." A corrugation may be called a "rope mark, twist, or chain mark."

Standardization is best achieved by providing an inspection manual describing the defect, inspection procedure, and numerical quality rating.[37,38,39]

Quality Control's role in the inspection effort is dependent on the quality responsibility pattern established by management.[40] General industry practice is that Manufacturing is accountable for product quality. Quality Control commonly monitors adherence to standards. Often, roving inspectors audit products in-process.

In-Process Product Certification. Section 11, under Product Acceptance by Operators, describes creating operator quality awareness. Streit (Ref. 37) illus-

---

[34] See Bingham, R. S., Q.C. Applications in the Coated Abrasives Industry, *Industrial Quality Control,* vol. XIX, No. 5, pp. 5–12, November 1962 for an example of inspector-tightened standards. (Product Engineering accepted 67%, inspection only 54%—a statistically significant difference for this special study of over 1,000 abrasive disks.)

[35] See TAPPI Method T437, which uses an "Equivalent Black Area" *(eba)* to define defectiveness. Inspection combines location of dirt spots, matching their size with printed dots of known size.

[36] In these cases, it is wise to determine the type of statistical distribution through methods described in Section 22 and establish control limits accordingly. (The Poisson process commonly describes dirt distribution as found in paper. Too often the area examined is too small for discrimination. Increasing the area markedly increases the *power* of the test for this distribution.)

[37] For an example of defect identification, classification, description, inspection procedure, grading, and numerical coding, along with photographs of the standards, see Table 1 and Figs. 7 and 8, from Wickstrom, W. A., Operation Roll Quality Standards, *Pulp and Paper,* vol. 41, No. 51, pp. 35–40, Dec. 18, 1967.

[38] See TAPPI publication "Defect and Remedy Manual for Corrugated Box Plants" (Oct. 1, 1962) for an example of inspection nomenclature and standards.

[39] For inspection of *rolls* using statistical principles to verify defect distributions and to decide acceptability, see Fairfield, J. H., and R. S. Bingham, Statistical Evaluation of Cloth Surface Quality—Applications for Coated Abrasives, *The Quality Engineer,* vol. 28, No. 2, pp. 47–53, March–April 1964 and No. 4, pp. 120–121, July–August 1964. This procedure is appropriate primarily for very expensive products or for defect distribution studies with web-guided winders.

[40] See Quality Responsibilities, below.

trates a plan specifically designed for this industry using a traveling ticket on which succeeding operators can agree or disagree with previous quality ratings as the product passes along the process flow. Mechanical roll quality and appearance defects are marked.

Statistical Acceptance Sampling[41]   The major application of statistical acceptance sampling in the industry (and this industry has lagged others) has been in sheeting.

Implementation.   Acceptance sampling must be preceded by a definite management policy statement of outgoing quality level. Existing mill quality levels, customer complaints for specific defects, competitive information, and market conditions must be considered. Many mills selected AQLs or AOQLs to assure the same or slightly better quality than offered by previous fanning and sorting methods, the major aim being to reduce sheet inspection cost.

Impact of defects on product performance is important when establishing sampling plans.[42] A classification of defects shown developed at Consolidated Papers, Inc.,[43] relates defects to their effect on customer pressroom operation:

Major defects, i.e., those likely to cause press shutdown
Minor defects, i.e., of immediate concern but not necessarily press stoppers
Incidental defects, i.e., of concern for informational purpose, individually not a problem unless present in large numbers

Selection of sampling plans whether single, double, or sequential depends on knowledge of possible defect distribution within the load. Process studies are usually necessary to determine whether defects are *sporadic* (e.g., contamination, slime holes, holes), *stratified* (off-color, wrinkles, wet streaks), or *random* (oil drops, water drops, coating spray) in occurrence.[44] If defects are random, double and multiple sampling schemes are advantageous, particularly in reducing sampling and inspection costs. If defects are stratified, single sampling plans are advantageous in defect detection due to larger sample size requirements.

Sorting efficiency of rejected loads is a necessary consideration in evaluating the inspection system. Figure 30-4 shows a typical OC curve for major defects assuming a 70% sorting efficiency of rejected loads. Note the inability to improve the outgoing percent defective when incoming percent defective reaches a high level. Although inspection efficiency is less than perfect, no across-the-industry solution has been found. Generally, good practice is to sell as job lot or beater paper when defects as indicated by the sample exceed levels where sorting is incapable of upgrading to the desired quality.[45]

STATISTICAL METHODS

While not all segments of the industry employ statistical methods extensively, their use is growing. As indicated under Testing Methods, they are very helpful in test development, standardization, and interlaboratory testing. The discussion under Improvement through Mill Trials emphasizes how they help avoid erroneous con-

---

[41] See Section 24, Sampling by Attributes.

[42] See Section 12, under Product Acceptance Inspection, *et seq.*

[43] Haselow, W. J., Acceptance Sampling for Visual Quality Control, *Tappi*, vol. 46, No. 2, pp. 161A–163A, February 1963.

[44] This information is essential for valid sampling plan design, speeds process correction, and in cases where corrective action is not yet clear, increases effectiveness of mill trial planning (see below).

[45] Jaehn, A. H., and R. S. Bingham, Decision Rules for Inefficient Sorting, *American Society for Quality Control Conference Transactions,* May 1972, pp. 311–318, describe procedures for minimizing costs and protecting outgoing quality when *sorting* is inefficient.

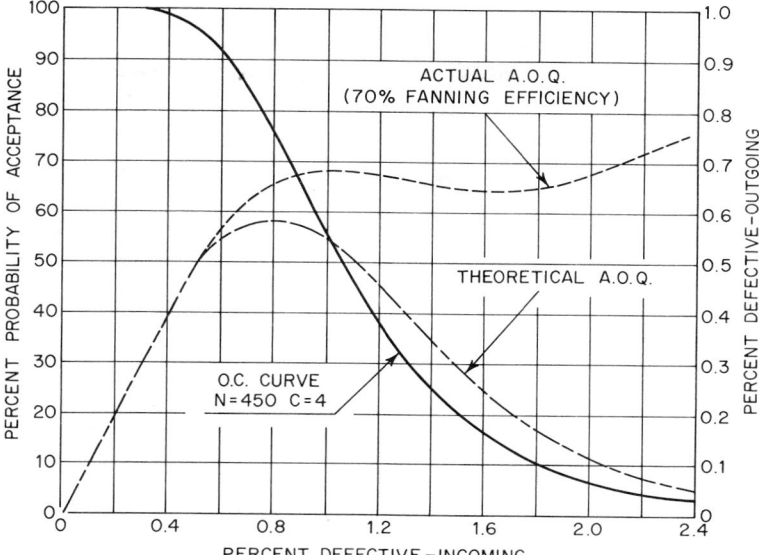

Fig. 30-4 Sampling plan for major defects. *(From Haselow, W. J., Acceptance Sampling for Visual Quality Control, Tappi, vol. 46, No. 2, pp. 161A–163A, February 1963.)*

clusions in process and product development. As variation due to methods and sampling is better understood, wider and more sophisticated use can be expected. Even so, the range of applications to date is impressive.[46] Table 30-7 classifies significant techniques annotated under references by process area. To further illustrate, areas for profitable application in pulping follow.

Control Charts One excellent use of control charts in the bleaching operation tells when process adjustments are necessary. Control limits are commonly calculated from pulp brightness data taken from selected process points during a period of satisfactory operation (see Figure 30-2). Temperatures, chemical rates, etc., are adjusted when out-of-control conditions occur.[47]

Analysis of Variance When two or more variables are to be examined at the same time, factorial designs[48] are of great value. In bleaching studies, the effects of temperature, type of bleaching chemical, pH levels, and consistency can be investigated as to their effect on pulp brightness, dirt and shive removal, or refining characteristics. In pulping studies, chip sizes, pretreatment techniques, cooking temperature-time cycles, liquor concentration, and composition may be related to yield, bleachability, refining characteristics, etc. (Besides estimating the effects of major variables, measures of interactions can be obtained. Frequently these are important for thorough process behavior understanding.)

Regression Analysis When planned experimentation is difficult because of production limitations in the mill, or when processing conditions do not permit resetting conditions of *all* control variables to selected levels, multiple regression analysis[49]

[46] See Bicking, Table 30-6, for two bibliographies covering the period to 1965.
[47] See Section 23.
[48] See Section 27, Design and Analysis of Experiments.
[49] See Section 26, Regression Analysis.

TABLE 30-7   Application of Statistical Methods to Process Areas*

Process area	Basic statistics	Control charts	Analysis of variance	Regression	Design of experiments	Optimization	Multivariate analysis	Sampling
Raw materials.......	...	...	...	...	.....	...	...	19
Timberlands........	...	...	6	...	.....	...	...	6
Pulping...........	...	2, 15	7, 9	7, 12	5, 7, 13, 17, 18	1, 13	...	2, 17
Bleaching.........					16	16		
Papermaking.......			8	11				
Converting........	14			4	4			
Inspection........		14					10	
Testing...........		14	9	12	17		10	
Test development...		3	3	3, 12	17			

* See Reference below for details. See also Table 30-6 and Table 30-8 for additional references.

1. Laboratory-scale batch studies using response surface methods to derive second-order regression equations. Three-dimensional models illustrate results. Bailey, R. N., et al., A Statistical Analysis and Optimization Procedure for the Kraft Pulping Process, Tappi, vol. 52, No. 7, pp. 1272–1275, July 1969.

2. See Mechanical Pulping, this section, for details. Breen, J. K., Statistical Control Charts—Their Application in Groundwood Mills, Pulp and Paper Magazine of Canada, vol. 70, No. 14, pp. 61–63, July 1969.

3. Excellent example of test development using statistical methods. Brown, D. S., C. J. Kremer, and A. C. Smith, Jr., An Underwater Beam Strength Test for Waxed Corrugated Board, Pulp and Paper Magazine of Canada, vol 61, No. 12, pp. T555–T558, December 1960.

4. A ½ replicate of a 2^5 fractional factorial run on a full-sized hot head pressure curtain coater studied head height, pump speed, wax temperature, belt speed, and slot opening, using two different high-viscosity wax-resin blends. Results were judged by changes in dimensions, strength, and barrier properties. Correlation coefficients were determined for film thickness, basis weight, burst strength, puncture, stiffness, flat crush, and short column crush. Useful interpretations relating to operating aids and testing methods. Brown, D. S., and W. F. Lewis, Waxing Corrugated by Pressure Curtain Coating, Tappi, vol. 46, No. 1, pp. 172A–178A, January 1963.

5. Graeco-Latin square used to study the effect of concentration, temperature, time, and pressure on 9 species during development of a suitable pulp. The assumption of independence among the variables is discussed. Cabella, S., The Cold Soda Pulping of Southern Hardwoods, Tappi, vol. 46, No. 4, pp. 196A–199A, April 1963.

6. Demonstrated sampling plan design. Clark, A. III, and A. F. Ike, Using Variance Components and Cost Analysis to Improve Sampling Efficiency in Wood Density Surveys, Tappi, vol. 53, No. 2, pp. 295–299, February 1970.

7. Urges mill pulp yields be determined from precise laboratory studies; discusses impact of pulping and measuring variables on precision and accuracy; reports via nested analysis of variance model. Regression of yield on permanganate number given. Hatton, J. V., and J. L. Keays, Relationship between Pulp Yield and Permanganate Number for Kraft Pulps: I, Pulp and Paper Magazine of Canada, vol. 71, Nos. 11-12, pp. 123–132, June 5–19, 1970.

8. A special report by the British Research Association for the Paper and Board, Printing and Packaging Industries comparing two headboxes. Details planning, data collection, statistical two-way analysis of variance, residual component of variances before and after the installation of the new

headbox, and an analysis of long-term and cyclical variation. Howarth, J., and N. Shoumatoff, Statistical Evaluation of a Paper Machine Head Box's Performance, *Paper Trade Journal*, vol. 155, No. 26, pp. 60–63, June 28, 1971.

9. Microdigester design serves as background to discuss precision problems in pulping and their impact on processing costs. Reports within and between cook variation of yield. Keays, J. L., and J. M. Bagley, Digester Assembly for Precision Pulping Studies, *Tappi*, vol. 53, No. 10, pp. 1935–1940, October 1970.

10. A tutorial paper demonstrating tests of sample means vs. hypothetical means, comparison of two-sample means, *k*-sample means; a comparison of a sample covariance matrix vs. a hypothetical covariance matrix, and two-sample covariance matrices, one against another as well as homogeneity of variance for *k* groups. These techniques will be more important in the paper industry in light of the apparent correlation among most measured properties. Control charting is expected to utilize multivariate control charts such as Hotelling's T^2 chart. Jackson, J. E., Some Multi-variate Statistical Techniques Used in Color Matching Data, *Journal of the Optical Society of America*, vol. 49, No. 6, pp. 585–592, June 1959. (Addenda and errata – same journal, vol. 52, No. 7, pp. 835–836, July 1962.)

11. Multiple regression explains the effect of contact length, shell thickness, basis weight, speed, number of pressure rolls, nip pressure, steam pressure, and percent moisture to the Yankee on paper drying rate, water drying rate, percent moisture from the drier, and Yankee surface temperature. Maahs, H. G., and L. N. Johanson, Yankee Drying Rate; Statistical Analysis of Data, *Tappi*, vol. 45, No. 10, pp. 760–765, October 1962.

12. Regression analysis helped reduce errors in estimating moisture of wood chips from 3.9 to 1.0%, evaluated differences between neutron radiation and gamma ray radiation. Note: 50% of the error was due to oven testing and instrument variability. Mann, A. A., Statistics – Important Tool in Mill Technical Work, *Tappi*, vol. 48, No. 9, pp. 122A–124A, September 1965.

13. A second-order response surface fitted to time-to-temperature, time-at-temperature, temperature, and active alkali concentration variables to explain pulp permanganate and kappa numbers, brightness, rejects, and beating time. Mill scale batch digester studies. McKibbins, S. W., *et al.*, Statistical Analysis of Kraft Pulp Mill Digester Operation, *Tappi*, vol. 53, No. 9, pp 1750–1752, September 1970.

14. Frequency distributions, data collection, $\bar{X}$, and R charts, and uses of special probability paper to demonstrate variation in corrugated box joint gaps. Nelson, H. G., Process Capability Studies in Corrugated Box Plants, *Tappi*, vol. 49, No. 47, pp. 83A–88A, July 1966.

15. Start-up of a pulp drying machine using a two-sided cumulative sum chart and the averages of a single sample from the front, center, and back to determine whether the process setting is adequate. Olree, J. G., Sequential Start-up Procedure for Pulp Drying Machine, *Tappi*, vol. 44, No. 9, pp. 678–684, September 1961.

16. A two-level factorial experiment in four variables led to a central composite design to optimize the effect of pH, temperature, and consistency during bleaching. Statistical patterns are credited with clarifying a picture confused using classical methods. O'Meara, D., and C. E. J. Mair, The Effect of Hypochlorite Bleaching Variables on Sulfite Pulp Properties, *Tappi*, vol. 45, No. 7, pp. 578–582, July 1962.

17. The importance of knowing precision and accuracy of test methods is emphasized. Describe use of a nested design with six levels of furnish, four blocks of stock samples within each furnish level, and two independent tests within each block, completely randomizing all factors over the whole experiment, including each step in the preparation of the test furnishes (sulfite and groundwood). Thaxter, R. D., and P. Hubbe, The Application of Experimental Design to the Study of a Test Method, *Tappi*, vol. 46, No. 12, pp. 189A–194A, December 1963.

18. Statistically designed experiments, computer analysis, and computer plotting of the derived equation employed to determine effects of pulp steeping and pressing variables on filterability of viscose. Wyatt, W. R., Optimum Viscose Process Studies—Steeping and Pressing, *Tappi*, vol. 49, No. 10, pp. 464–468, October 1966.

19. Over 1,000 listings covering precision, bulk sampling, and related application of statistics in the pulp and paper industry. Bicking, C. A., *et al.*, Bibliography on Precision, Bulk Sampling and Related Applications of Statistics, *Tappi CA Report 10*, 1965. Bicking, C. A., Bibliography on Sampling of Raw Materials and Products in Bulk, *Tappi*, vol. 47, No. 5, pp. 147–170A, May 1964.

is suggested. However, test data must be screened to verify that independent variables spanned a sufficient range of levels.

QUALITY RESPONSIBILITIES

The life of a product in this industry from development through full commercialization is quite similar to that described in Section 29. See also Section 6, especially Figure 6-3, Table 6-2, and associated discussion.

The responsibility for quality control is commonly vested in the Production Department with routine quality decisions made by machine tenders, rewinder operators, and when doubt exists, operating foremen. Frequently, finishing room inspectors report to a Converting Manager. The quality control function is exercised through issuance of specifications, sampling, testing, and overall surveillance of outgoing quality.

For those companies making products directly used by consumers, it is not unusual to find an organization in which a "Customer Representative" reports outside the local mill management. That representative makes final decisions about product acceptability prior to packaging. For more technical products, final acceptance may depend on laboratory tests, simulated in-use tests, and visual inspection results. Then, final acceptance is more likely to be determined by a service department such as Quality Control or, in sensitive sales situations, by a Product Manager.

Quality responsibilities are taken seriously with the full realization that product quality and service may be the determining factor in an industry known for overcapacity and demand fluctuations.[50]

ESTABLISHING SPECIFICATIONS

Specifications for paper products differ considerably depending on whether the end use is consumer products or industrial applications. Consumer products tend to have the fewest specified qualities, and most of these are sensory in nature (color, appearance, "hand," softness, crispness, crackle). Industrial products vary widely in specified qualities (because of many types of application) and include such diverse properties as surface smoothness to resist erasures, waterproofness, resistance to gas transmission, electrical conductance, ability to hold ink on the surface, and fire-retardant properties. In general, industrial paper specifications have become better defined in proportion to the user's understanding of his needs and the paper industry's ability to supply them.[51] The addition of *selected* chemical additives rather than commercially available by-products has tended to make specifications more technical.[52]

Consumer Products Users of consumer products, while able to express their likes and preferences, are unable to make technological contributions to solve the problems of specifying and testing. In consequence, the burden is on the manufacturer to develop the technology himself. Solution of individual specification problems requires use of the general approach set out in Section 12, under Sensory Qualities.

[50] Rich, S. U., Pricing Strategy Considerations for Pulp and Paper Producers, *Tappi,* vol. 53, No. 7, pp. 1282–1285, July 1970.

[51] See Baldwin, J. G., The Packaging Specification in "New Directions in Packaging," pp. 36–43, American Management Association, Inc., New York, 1970, for departments both internal and external to a company influenced by specifications.

[52] For example, early sizing agents were glues, starches, and rosin derivatives, some highly variable in nature. As their chemistry and refining practices became better understood, the effects of the various derivatives could be separated and more clearly specified. This, in turn, meant final paper attributes could be more clearly established with less variability from run to run.

The "ultimate" solution of new instruments is discussed in Section 12, under Creating New Instruments to Measure Sensory Qualities.

Industrial Products   Much progress has been made in developing specifications, test methods, and instruments for the industrial papers.   The fact that many industrial users have technological capability has contributed importantly to this progress.   For example, major publishers often specify opacity values (i.e., show-through characteristics) of lightweight paper, and audit mill conformance to specifications by testing at their printing plants.

For industrial products, assistance can be secured from progressive customers. Mill Quality Control must be ready to assist such customers in preparing meaningful tests and specifications.[53]   Customers must specify only properties which can be related to *performance* in their operations. A good example is provided by C. H. Bubb,[54] describing Xerox's quality acceptance program developed jointly with their paper suppliers.

Because of paper's relatively low cost, inevitably specifications become a compromise: strength sacrificed for opacity, opacity for basis weight, stiffness for fold, etc. They are further complicated by the effect of moisture.[55]

One approach to resolve the moisture problem has been to *condition* paper (holding it at constant temperature and humidity[56]) and then test.   Conditioning is partially defeated because of the time required to bring a sample to standard conditions.[57]   For process control, it is impossible.   To illustrate, basis weight controls by sample tearout at the dry end of the machine can only acknowledge the moisture content at that instant. Since dry paper rapidly absorbs moisture, special handling methods are required if the basis weight is to be measured away from the immediate sampling point. The basis weight as determined by a customer on a conditioned sample is not likely to match that obtained under manufacturing conditions. Quality Control must be closely involved in recommending the most suitable test to avoid having the customer specify unnecessary, irrelevant, or correlated tests.[58, 59, 60, 61]

Not only is the problem that of avoiding irrelevant tests; in-process controls demand knowledge of other properties which may or may not be closely related to end use

---

[53] Many test methods do not measure basic paper properties.   Being empirical or attempting to simulate end use performance, they may focus attention on a secondary property rather than on an important primary characteristic; e.g., paper smoothness may be examined by an air-leak device, a profile meter, or low-angle lighting.   Whether such a test is purposeful depends on the *need* for smoothness, e.g., to avoid glare, for intimate surface contact, for decorative appeal, to avoid surface roughness or harshness, or to obtain continuous printed ink films of high reflectivity.   This emphasizes the need for close manufacturer-customer rapport in describing fitness for use and how to measure it.

[54] Bubb, C. H. "The Evolution of a Quality Control Program," TAPPI Conference, Feb. 16, 1970, reports that tensile, fold, burst, and tear were initially included in the testing program but later dropped because the physical tests could not be tied into performance problems.

[55] See Ref. 38, chap. 16 by W. Gallay.   (He describes the effect of water on cellulose and emphasizes that paper fibers are chemically highly polar long-chain polymers.)

[56] See TAPPI Standard T402, "Standard Conditioning and Testing Atmospheres for Paper, Board, Pulp Handsheets, and Related Products."

[57] *Tappi*, vol. 53, No. 4, pp. 716–717, April 1970, a proposed revision to TAPPI Standard T402, OS-49 calls for *preconditioning times* of 1 to 24 hours and *conditioning times* of 4 to 72 hours, depending on product.   An appendix points out that the "hysteresis effect" is "5 to 25% of the test value for many physical properties."

[58] This is especially true since, according to W. Gallay, "All paper properties — physical, optical, or penetrability — are directly or indirectly strongly influenced by cellulose-water relationship." Ref. 38, vol. 1, p. 405.

[59] See also Crook, D. M., and W. E. Bennett, "The Effect of Humidity and Temperature on the Physical Properties of Paper," RA/T/90, February 1962 (copyright by B.P.&B.I.R.A.) for their direct effect on testing.

product tests. Furthermore, different paper companies can meet the same *end use requirement* using different furnishes and manufacturing techniques. Yet, available test methods would show substantially different test properties, but in the case of printing papers, the printed piece would look substantially the same.

An indication of the kind of customer specifications likely in the future for printing papers was given by Jont.[62] He listed 16 properties which "seriously affect the printed result and costs."

1. Smoothness
2. Porosity
3. Color
4. Brightness
5. Gloss
6. Basis weight
7. Caliper
8. Impression tolerance
9. Winding
10. Stretch
11. Moisture content
12. Ink holdout
13. Dimensional stability
14. Tensile
15. Tear
16. Tensile at the fold

He further notes "roll quality" is generally specified in terms of workmanship detail. For example, there must be an absence of baggy rolls, poorly made splices, hair cuts, fiber cuts, calender cuts, slime holes, bursts, etc.

To indicate the extent of the quality compromise which practically occurs, he states, "given two papers of equal print quality, the one that performs with the fewest delays on press will emerge as far superior printability. In fact, a most desirable printing quality can be obtained on an even slightly inferior sheet from a printability standpoint if it is superior to another in runnability."

CUSTOMER RELATIONS

Customer Service   In most large paper manufacturing companies, a customer service organization is available to assist the converter, printer, or user in resolving product quality problems. These are skilled specialists who have in-depth knowledge of customer operations, sometimes being experienced "craftsmen" in a particular end use field, e.g., union card carrying printers who have excellent rapport with pressroom supervisors and operators. Such skills pinpoint the source of trouble (paper, ink, press, or a combination of these) through a well-organized and supervised stepwise approach on a specific job on the press. When these specialists visit customer plants, they feed back product performance and competitive information. Some companies emphasize the importance of customer quality acceptance by having mill managers or other executives accompany sales and customer service personnel on pressroom visits.

Complaint Analysis   Maintaining customer complaint records focuses attention on major mill quality problem areas. Quality complaint summaries can be placed in perspective relative to grades produced, defect type, and complaint frequency, and by using total tonnage or number of orders processed during a given period. Complaints stemming from recent production usually get immediate attention and investigation to determine if a sizable quality problem is at hand.

[60] Fetsko, J. M., and A. C. Zettlemoyer, Factors Affecting Print Gloss and Uniformity, *Tappi*, vol. 45, No. 8, pp. 667–681, August 1962, make the case for agreeing to a *single* empirical test when gloss tendencies depend on various inks.

[61] In *Tappi CA Report* 8076, R. S. Hunter claims, "The chief obstacle to the successful application of gloss measurements of ink films is the absence of established procedures." He describes "what has been or can be done to place gloss measurements . . . on a scientific basis." See Methods for Evaluating the Gloss of Ink Films, *Tappi*, vol. 46, No. 7, pp. 162A–167A, July 1963.

[62] Jont, K. A., "Paper Problems—How They Affect the Publisher and Printer," 1970 Testing, Graphic Arts, and Reprography Conference, Minneapolis, Minn., Sept. 24, 1970.

The mill Technical Department typically performs laboratory investigations on submitted samples, and reviews process test data and operating conditions prevailing during the manufacture of product. Comprehensive complaint analysis helps assign the deficiency to product design, manufacturing operational problems, quality control system failure, improper communications, or misuse by the customer.

Quality Performance Feedback In publication paper manufacture, timely pressroom feedback aids the *producing* mill by expediting and strengthening corrective action to reduce defect frequency and severity. Also routinely reporting pressroom data helps the *printer* judge the performance of *his* suppliers.

Defect Evidence. Properly identified *physical* evidence of defects is vital. Pressrooms are encouraged to save paper samples contiguous to or causing a web break; or printed signatures in the case of poor printing. The samples are attached to the supplier's roll card and returned for analysis.

Roll Cards. To overcome problems of incorrect reporting, a standard roll card has been developed and endorsed by many technical associations of the paper and printing industries. The paper mill supplies the necessary information on the front of the card; the printer supplies that on the back. For computerized reporting systems, roll card information provides the input.

In use, the pressman refers to a "Glossary of Paper Defects"[63] and identifies the defect by placing its number and other relevant data in the boxes provided. The pressman helps the mill in troubleshooting by marking on the card where the web break occurred relative to its distance from the core.

Computerized Reporting Systems. These have been developed by many larger mills and publishers to evaluate continually the web break and printing performance in the pressroom. Prompt and consistent feedback is required to make these reports meaningful to the paper mill. Figure 30-5 illustrates a typical pressroom 12-month

PRESSROOM SUMMARY - WEB BREAKS/100 ROLLS BY MFG. DATE

REPORT 2-C

GRADE	WT	SIZE	MACH	PRINTER	MFG. DATE	ROLLS SHIP	ROLLS RETURN	BREAK FREQ.	LIMITS UCL	LIMITS LCL
LTI	50	34.70	91	ABC	DEC	700	594	11.10	12.60	7.40
					JAN	638	612	9.20	12.56	7.44
					FEB	914	900	8.20	12.11	7.89
					MAR	1742	1668	14.10H	11.55	8.45
					APR	931	854	4.20L	12.16	7.84
					MAY	1001	962	17.10H	12.04	7.96
					JUN	414	413	3.20L	13.11	6.89
					JUL	600	552	4.10L	12.69	7.31
					AUG	741	702	6.50L	12.39	7.61
					SEP	947	934	8.20	12.07	7.93
					OCT	401	16	22.80	25.80	0.00
					NOV	943	312	0.00	13.58	6.42
					TO DATE	9972	8519	6.82L	10.69	9.31
LT2	50	52.50	91	DEF	APR	850	800	4.50L	12.24	7.76
					JUN	1000	936	9.40	12.07	7.93
					AUG	968	900	10.70	12.11	7.89
					SEP	1250	853	12.36H	12.17	7.83
					OCT	760	550	13.10H	12.70	7.30
					NOV	925	120	18.00H	15.77	4.23
					TO DATE	5753	4159	8.60L	10.98	9.02

Fig. 30-5 Computerized pressroom summary.

[63] See *Tappi, CA Report* 13, Product Operating Communication Standards. October 1967.

summary computer report, used to judge mill web break performance in meeting the target established by the printer (in this case 10.0 web breaks per 100 rolls).[64] The tally of rolls shipped and cards returned gives evidence to the mill on the representativeness of the sample.

Control limits are placed at

$$c \pm 2\sigma_c = c \pm 2\sqrt{\frac{c}{n}}$$

where c = web break target (breaks per 100 rolls)

n = number of rolls reported per 100

To illustrate, if the web break target were 10 breaks per 100 rolls and 594 rolls were reported to have a break frequency of 11.10 per 100 rolls, control relative to target would be calculated as follows:

$$\text{Controls limits} = 10 \pm 2\sqrt{\frac{10}{5.94}} = 10 \pm 2.60$$

These limits are provided on the first line of Figure 30-5 and show that the reported break frequency of 11.10 per 100 rolls is in control. ("H" or "L" in Figure 30-5 means out of control limits, high or low.)

Other options for isolating web break causes, including breaks by defect type, breaks by roll position, by winder, by press, etc., can also be programmed if warranted. The results are used to judge whether the performance of a particular paper run is unique to one pressroom, press, paper machine, winder, etc. Shifts in most defect types can usually be traced to papermaking operational problems or furnish changes, when not identified with press problems (such as web tension, roll alignment, or drier temperatures).[65]

QUALITY IMPROVEMENT

The general approach to quality improvement is fully applicable to the pulp and paper industry.[66] It is helpful to commence with a study of quality costs (see Sec-

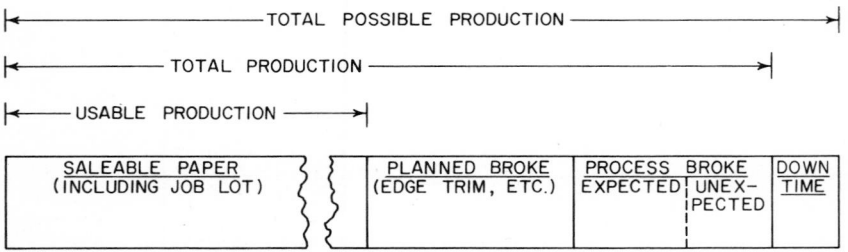

Fig. 30-6   Relationship of broke to production balance.

[64] The report is real; "defects per unit" data are hypothetical to conceal printer's information.

[65] See also Section 40, Graphic Arts Industry.

[66] See Section 16, Quality Improvement, relative to breakthrough, use of Pareto analysis, and choice of projects. See also Section 2, under the Nature of Improvement, which includes discussion of concepts for troubleshooting of sporadic problems, planning of new products and processes, and "breakthrough" of chronic problems.

tion 5) to quantify the various categories and the total. In some segments of the paper industry, quality costs approach 10% of gross annual sales (see Par, below).

Survey of Quality Losses The second phase of improvement programs is a Pareto analysis of the major categories of quality costs.[67] It is usual to find that the category of "broke" is the largest (even though it may be repulpable). Figure 30-6 shows the broad relation of broke to total possible production. It is most useful to go a step further and to classify process broke losses by Pareto analysis (see Figure 30-7). At some mills, on-line computers have significantly reduced expected broke during start-up and grade change (basis weight, color, etc.). Unexpected broke from off-standard quality is frequently best attacked by sharpening operator quality awareness at each manufacturing stage to isolate each problem source. Similar Pareto analyses are carried out for other main loss categories, e.g., customer returns, substandard paper sold at reduced prices (job lot), and rework (rewinding and sorting).

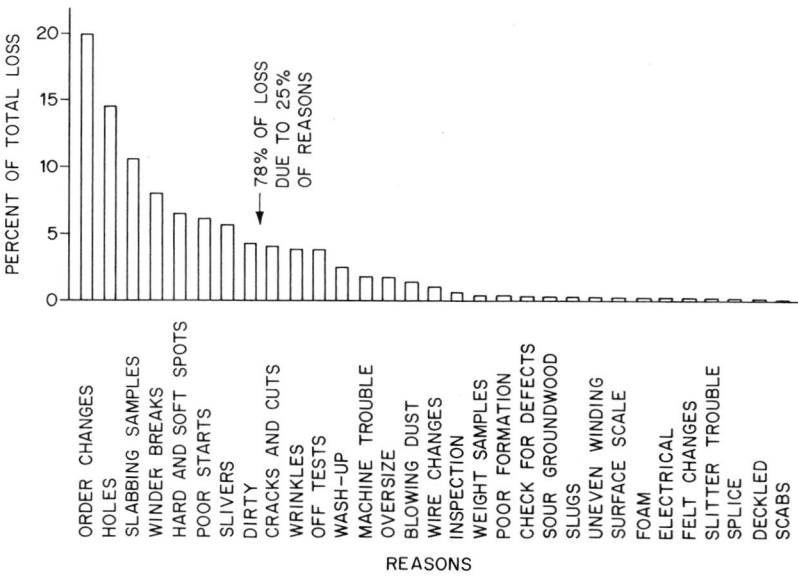

Fig. 30-7 Distribution of process broke by reasons. For example, "washup" means paper broked because of unscheduled paper machine shutdown and start-up. *(From Carter, C. W., and L. C. Paulson, A Quality Control Program, Tappi, vol. 40, No. 12, pp. 207A–209A, December 1957.)*

Improvement through Process Control A second approach to quality improvement for many paper products is through extending the use of early warning sensors and on-line instrumentation to control the process in contrast to laboratory testing of occasional samples. Fastest response to process disturbance requires an on-line

[67] See Section 16, Tables 16-2a and 16-2b for examples.

process control computer. The literature[68] shows widespread application for at least some *process* variables. The missing link has been a reliable sensing element for measuring many of the *product* attributes. In some cases, the measurement method is available but the technology for "testing the process" is not completely understood.[69] Usually, extensive piping changes are required to overcome the sluggishness of the process to effect rapid correction of paper currently being made. Failing this, data would be stored in the computer memory, and the best operating conditions would be fed back for the next run of the same grade.

As additional sensing elements become commercially available, more "self-tuning" control will be used. Some companies have computer programs which tell the machine tender when additional machine speedup is possible. The program tests if the grade is being run as fast as possible (speed may be limited by drive capacities, drying section capabilities, uniformity of profile, or other self-imposed quality restrictions). It tests for constraints being violated and, if not, prints out the tentative speed increase. The operator approves the increase, the computer makes the changes, the machine responds along a trajectory-calculated path, and the computer checks the constraints again.

Improvement through Mill Trials   The pulp and paper industry makes use of "mill trials," which are common in all process industries.[70] The difficulties inherent in such trials likewise parallel those encountered in other industries: small-scale equipment[71] vs. commercial production machinery; Technical supervision vs. Production supervision, etc. The predictability of mill trials can be aided by understanding the more usual problems encountered and the solutions which experience has shown to be possible.[72] (See Section 16, under Diagnosis through Experiment, and especially under Processing Experimental Lots.)

The trials are typically used to evaluate second sources of supply; alternative raw materials for cost reduction, process improvement, or ease of manufacture; or alternative methods of drying, pressing, or calendering to alleviate manufacturing problems.

Cost limitations on commercial trials normally constrain severely the amount of machine time which can be set aside for sampling. If short trials are run, substantial paper machine time will be used to bring the machine to the new equilibrium conditions. Once reached, "okayed" paper must be reeled immediately before the trial conditions have to be abandoned for the manufacture of the next grade. A detailed knowledge of process flows, including white water holdups, silo contents, and recycle times, can improve machine trial planning.

Statistical Designs for Machine Trials.   These designs demand high competence in use of statistical designs,[73] which must be tailored to the problem at hand. However, these designs are greatly simplified if certain conditions can be met:

---

[68] See References 13 to 21, and Section 20.

[69] The early practice of computer data logging *every* available process variable and finding regression equations relating these to product characteristics has been largely replaced by studying process dynamics. (See Section 29, under Adaptive Control, for further discussion.)

[70] See, for example, Sections 29 and 33.

[71] Laboratory-scale investigation as an alternate to mill trials has special handicaps in this industry: e.g., edge effects on fourdrinier wires, mass aspects of large rolls; momentum and temperature rate of change in mill equipment differ markedly from small-scale equipment. Hand sheets can be used in bench-scale work to study a variety of factors, but not formation or printability or, in general, any property where dynamics of the equipment play a major role.

[72] With the exception of products totally new to a company, the *product* made on mill-scale equipment is *normally* usable by the customer. Because of cost, volume, and customer considerations, mill trials reflect conservative changes.

[73] See Statistical Methods in this Section and Section 27 for preferred experiment designs.

1. The "before" and "after" processes demonstrate statistical control.[74]
2. Normal test variability has been determined for each important property.
3. Process variability has been established, both CD and MD.
4. Calculations have been made to quantify the extent of sampling and testing needed for various levels of confidence in detecting technically important changes.
5. Instructions for sampling and testing have been prepared in advance.
6. The men responsible for supervising the mill trials have been encouraged to identify clearly the key variables for which they expect to find changes:

The size of the changes considered to be of technical significance

Secondary attributes or variables they anticipate might possibly change or be correlated with the primary attributes

The significant changes in levels below which the process will be assumed to be operating *unsatisfactorily*

"No-go" situation such that if the necessary conditions are not achieved, the trial will be aborted

Assuring Valid Data.   Before mill trials are conducted, a review should be made of the equipment and process conditions which may be encountered, e.g., filled felts, worn wires, marginal pH, variable slimicide dosages, inexact furnish proportions, variable refining circumstances, and unrepresentative sampling.   The conditions necessary to a successful trial should be spelled out and discussed with the machine crews to simplify the selection of circumstances favorable for running the trials. Before the trial begins, the operating conditions should be confirmed.   This is to include laboratory reappraisal of current base sheet properties (e.g., two-sidedness, fines distribution) and crew verification of CD profile levelness because of their special influence on so many final product properties.

Failure to plan completely cannot be overcome by collecting data under "normal conditions" and attempting to separate the "high settings" from the "low settings." Attempting to associate these with changes in product properties is fraught with uncertainty primarily because machine conditions are not normally varied from one level to another over a sufficient *range* to produce the changes expected.[75]   Instead, if the same grade is made repeatedly, EVOP can be used to assess the influence of two or more variables (see Section 27A).

QUALITY CONTROL IN OTHER SEGMENTS OF THE INDUSTRY

Our purpose has been to demonstrate typical industry problems and solutions.   Obviously, Quality Control needs differ in accord with customer needs, product value, ease of manufacturing to specifications, etc.   Table 30-8 indicates a sampling of literature useful in other segments not discussed here.

---

[74] See Section 22 for appropriate statistical tests: *t*-tests of *before* and *after* vs. *trial* averages and *F*-tests of pooled *(before-after)* variance vs. *trial* variance, or control charts of appropriate averages and ranges are useful in deciding if significant changes in level of variation occurred. (Results from "after" conditions frequently do not approximate "before" conditions. Hence, combining "standard operating data" from one period to another for comparison with "trial" data is apt to be frustrating if not misleading.)

"Appropriate" implies modeling the sampling plan to reflect known sources of process variation important to this study.   See Bingham, R. S., Bulk Sampling—A Common Sense View point, *Tappi*, vol. 46, No. 5, pp. 288–296, May, 1963, also Section 25A, Bulk Sampling.

[75] Davies, O. L., "Statistical Methods in Research and Production," 3d ed. rev., pp. 236–238, Hafner Publishing Company, Inc., New York, 1957.

TABLE 30-8   Quality Control in Other Paper Industry Areas

Newsprint

General. Predicting runnability and print performance of newsprint. Furnish control. Ullman, U., Newsprint Quality Control, *Pulp and Paper Magazine of Canada*, vol. 72, No. 4, pp. 71–72, April 1971.

Roll Quality. Newsprint defect terminology. Anon., Glossary of Newsprint Terminology, *The American Pressman*, vol. 78, No. 11, pp. 12–14, November 1968.

Recommended tolerances by *The New York Times* covering manufacture of gravure printing papers for subsequent insertion into newspapers. Millen, R. W., and G. L. Larocque, Spectra Color—The Manufacture and Insertion of High Quality Preprinted Colour into the Daily Newspaper, *Pulp and Paper Magazine of Canada*, vol. 66, No. 6, pp. T303–T312, June 1965.

Quality problems common to papermaker and printer. Quality requirements, associated test and inspection methods. Steinberg, S., Press Problems with Newsprint, *Pulp and Paper Magazine of Canada*, vol. 64, No. 1, pp. T19–T26, June 1963.

Testing. Paper properties that influence print quality and ink transfer. Methods for measurement of roughness distribution of surfaces. Estimating half-tone quality from density and nonuniformity of solid prints. Parker, J. R., Letterpress Printability, *Paper Technology*, vol. 7, No. 4, pp. 359–366, August 1966.

Instrumentation and Measurement. Special instrumentation used for control of headbox, press angle takeoff, and web tension. Unique method of measurement of basis weight based on direct weighing of paper reel combined with measurement of paper length. Johansen, L., and V. Torok, Drive and Control Distinguish Europe's Largest Newsprint Machine, *Paper Trade Journal*, vol. 152, No. 14, pp. 42–47, Apr. 1, 1968.

Specialty Papers

Case History. Quality control techniques for manufacturing high-quality specialty papers. Setting up quality control system: specifying quality levels, inspection, information feedback, audits, corrective action, and control. Wadsworth, J. K., Quality Control—A Service to Management, *The Quality Engineer—Journal of the Institute of Engineering Inspection*, vol. 25, No. 1, pp. 14–20, January–February 1961.

Sheeting Quality Control. Quality control to overcome problems of sheeting sensitive grade papers. Eberth, P. J., SCM's Automatic Sheeting System Protects Fragile Copy Paper, *Paper Trade Journal*, vol. 155, No. 16, pp. 40–41, Apr. 19, 1971.

Instrumentation. On-line caliper control for manufacture of photographic papers. Anon., Kodak Focuses on Caliper Control with Non-contacting Gauge, *Pulp & Paper*, vol. 44, no. 5, p. 82, May 1970.

Vendor-Vendee Programs. Procedures to judge papers for copier-duplicator work. Bubb, C. H., "The Evolution of a Q. C. Program," TAPPI 55th Meeting, Feb. 16, 1970.

Tissue

Quality Control Programs. Scott Paper's quality control program for towels and tissue. Howell, C. M., Development of a Quality Control Program, *Tappi*, vol. 38, No. 8, pp. 150A–152A, August 1955.

Computer Aids. Consumer paper quality system. Computer aids to meaningful interpretation of quality control test data. Mottl, N. J., and P. M. Shiah, Systems Engineering Approach to Quality Control, *Transactions, American Society for Quality Control Technical Conference*, pp. 497–505, Chicago, Ill., 1971.

Instrumentation. On-line infrared measurement of basis weight and moisture in lightweight, creped tissue. Brunton, D. C., and O. C. Miller, On-line Moisture/B. W. for Creped Tissue by Infrared Techniques, *Paper Trade Journal*, vol. 155, No. 40, pp. 43–44, Oct. 4, 1971.

Packaging Paper

Test and Inspection. Quality control methods for converters (bags, wrapping paper). Grading evaluation of printed color, register, and cleanliness for bag manufacture. Grimes, W. S., Raw Material Evaluation and Quality Control Testing for Flexography, *Tappi*, vol. 46, No. 3, pp. 197A–198A, March 1963.

Test equipment and procedures used in Coating/Laminating process, evaluating quality of incoming films, foils, glassines, papers, adhesives, coatings, and solvents. *Paper, Film & Foil Converter*, vol. 45, No. 10, p. 52, October 1971; vol. 45, No. 11, pp. 44–46, November 1971; vol. 45, No. 12, p. 40, December 1971. Continues through 1972.

Paperboard

General. Nontechnical approach to quality control function in a paper converting plant. Allen, G. C., Q.C.—A Production Management Viewpoint, *Pulp and Paper Magazine of Canada*, vol. 72, No. 9, pp. 111–112, September 1971.

Quality Control Programs. Guidelines for a quality control program. Rubinstein, S. P., Process Control in the Corrugating Industry, *Tappi*, vol. 49, No. 9, pp. 107A–110A, September 1966.

Equipment selection; in-process and finished product inspection; downtime control. Scally, W., How to Set-up Quality Controls for Corrugated, *Paperboard Packaging*, vol. 48, No. 12, pp. 68–70, December 1963.

Methods for control. Includes organization and function of personnel, production methods, inspection and sampling plans; physical testing equipment. Beamish, J. R., Quality Control in the Corrugated Container Industry, *Food Quality Control*, vol. 3, No. 2, pp. 11–23, January 1963.

Specifications, Sampling, and Testing. Specifications for corrugated shipping containers; case sampling, conditioning and routine testing procedures; suppliers evaluation. Holt, R. J., Quality Control Inspection from the Customer's Viewpoint, *Tappi*, vol. 42, No. 4, pp. 24A–28A, April 1959.

Test equipment and suppliers for paperboard manufacturers, converters, packagers, and material vendors. Hecht, M., Quality Control Buyer's Guide, *Paperboard Packaging*, vol. 49, No. 9, pp. 34–42, September 1964.

Simulated use testing. Miller, C. E., Poultry Box Test Performance—Progress Report of the Research Subcommittee of the Corrugated Box and Container Board Committee, *Pulp and Paper Magazine of Canada*, vol. 72, No. 11, pp. 91–92, November 1971.

Dimensional Control. Sheet length control, automatic adjustment of count for defective sheets; computer scheduling. Rubinstein, S. P., Electronics, Automation, and Computers for the Corrugated Industry, *Tappi*, vol. 47, No. 4, pp. 170A–175A, April 1964.

Quantifying Appearance and Quality. Includes schedule of assigned demerits for physical tests and visual quality. McGrattan, W. W., and H. J. Ostrowski, A Method for Visual and Physical Quality Audit Rating of Corrugated Boxes, *Pulp and Paper Magazine of Canada*, vol. 72, No. 8, pp. 88–90, August 1971.

Coating

Process Selection—Effect on Quality. Description of various coating methods with respect to the quality of surface they produce. Booth, G. L., How the Printing Surface Depends on the Coating System Used, *Paper Trade Journal*, vol. 155, No. 38, pp. 63–67, Sept. 20, 1971.

End-use Requirements. Coated paper characteristics required by different printing processes. New trends. Smith, K. F., Quality Aspects in the Coating Process, *American Paper Industry*, vol. 50, No. 3, pp. 27–37, March 1968.

Precontrol Testing. Coating preparation control techniques and instruments. Keefer, W. L., Coating-Makedown Instrumentation—A Neglected Area of the Mill, *Paper Trade Journal*. vol. 153, No. 20, pp. 77–79, May 19, 1969.

Instrumentation. Design and use of coating weight control systems. Hoath, W. D., Automatic Coating Weight Control of an Air Knife Coater, *Tappi*, vol. 53, No. 5, pp. 491–496. March 1970.

PAR

Although there is relatively free exchange of technical information among even competing companies, only recently have significant loss and quality cost data been established. TAPPI committee surveys are a potential source of such data. (API data are restricted to member companies.)

Quality Costs Defining quality costs in this industry follows the conventional approach set out in section 5, and is subject to all the limitations noted there.

In the corrugated industry, Rubinstein[76] reports that quality costs in all phases can run to 7 to 10% of sales. Generally, the cost of quality control departments in relation to total sales is 0.5 to 1.0%. Table 30-9 presents direct quality control department costs for companies producing various grades of board, paper, and specialty products.[77]

TABLE 30-9   Cost of Quality Control Department

Grade of paper	Approx. selling price, $/ton	Quality Control Department costs	
		$/ton	%
Paperboard	200	0.98	0.5
Paper	155	1.47	0.9
Paper	250	2.00	0.8
Paper	400	3.32	0.8
Specialty	1,000	6.50	0.7

Finishing Problems A TAPPI survey[78] includes a list of major problems (or complaints) experienced by mills within each functional area in finishing. The top five problems for each finishing area were:

Supercalendering
1. Filled roll problems
2. Scale
3. Corrugations
4. Finish requirements
5. Wrinkles

Sheeting
1. Wrinkles
2. Cutter dust
3. Production efficiency
4. Jogging
5. Dimensional tolerance

Winding
1. Slitter dust
2. Offsets
3. Maintaining tension
4. Bursts
5. Baggy rolls

Trimming
1. Size and squareness control
2. Knife life
3. Equipment malfunction
4. Production efficiency
5. Dusting

FUTURE PROJECTIONS

Pricing and capacity have had major impact on this industry's profitability. Efforts for greater productivity at higher speeds with wider paper machines and continuous

[76] Rubinstein, S. P., Organized Quality Control Training, *Tappi,* vol. 46, No. 1, pp. 159A–163A, January 1963.

[77] Ware, H. O., A New Look at Product Quality and Financial Well-being, *American Paper Industry,* vol. 48, No. 12, pp. 76–79, December 1966.

[78] A Study of Paper Finishing: Equipment, Problems, and Trends, *Tappi CA Report* 22, November, 1969.

pulp digesters will obsolete much old equipment and many operating methods. Crew training on process instrumentation and machine automation will become well entrenched. Conventional quality control functions will have to be introduced and modified more rapidly than in the past. The sensitive areas include recycling, environmental protection, computers, and off-line testing.

Recycling. Increased pressure by the general public for paper reuse will result in greater dependence upon recycled fiber as a raw material source. Quality control can be expected to set standards and analyze incoming recycled pulp to safeguard mill product quality for each specific end use. Packaging grades will get special attention to avoid food contamination due to trace chemicals from recycled fibers or process waters.

Environmental Protection. Greater emphasis on air, water, and solid waste management, including in-plant water conservation, will require that Quality Control be alert to possible process upsets and product quality deterioration. Stringent state and federal government regulations on pollution control will call for Quality Control expertise in sampling and measurement procedures to assure meeting requirements. A thorough understanding of the representativeness of samples, sample-to-sample variation, and test calibration, variation, and bias will be essential to protect manufacturing facilities from legal action.

Computers can be expected to take over many of the established quality control functions. On-line instrumentation will vastly reduce dependence on periodic laboratory "top-of-reel" testing for machine control, except for limited tests lacking on-line sensors.

Quality control will turn to on-line instrumentation and computers for data storage, reduction, and process capability studies. Direct entry of real-time laboratory test data will integrate one aspect of quality control into the computerized process control system.[79] The time-sharing features of most process computers will permit reduction and analysis of quality control data beyond the normal summary or exception reports. More advanced statistical techniques (such as spectral analysis, multivariate analysis, adaptive control, and process modeling) pertinent to complex machine-fiber processing systems will give clearer insight into appropriate controls and process interrelationships.

Off-Line Testing. Empirical and subjective off-line testing techniques will be questioned as to their validity in predicting end-use performance (burst strength, tear strength, folding quality, smoothness, absorbency of various liquids, curl, etc.). Better use of fundamental tests (basis weight, moisture, tensile strength, opacity, color, brightness, etc.) for characterization of product quality is envisioned.

Confidence in off-line testing will further increase because of standardization of techniques and greater precision of instruments. Digital readout coincident with instrument improvements will aid interfacing to computers and lead to automated laboratory testing.[80] Quality Control will need to stay continually abreast of instrumentation and test improvements to gain needed precision, reliability, and time-saving.

[79] Fisher, J. M., "Opportunities for Quality Control through Computerization of Paper Machines," *American Society for Quality Control* Midwest Conference, Minneapolis, Minn., Oct. 17, 1970, emphasizes that the modern process control system could eliminate the need for the Quality Department, at least as it is now structured in the industry. He concludes that Quality Control needs to be an interface function that interprets changing requirements and provides quality information systems.

[80] Anon., Electronics Eliminates Errors and Speeds Routine Paper Testing, *Paper Trade Journal,* vol. 152, No. 38, pp. 66–67, Sept. 16, 1968, describes a system that automates reading and zeroing of instruments, recording, calculation, typing of reports, and a probability test for rejection of "outliers."

ACKNOWLEDGMENT

The authors are indebted to Consolidated Papers, Inc., for encouragement and permission to publish this Section. It reflects helpful discussions and comments from L. W. Murtfeldt, R. J. Mader, H. W. Bennett, C. A. Normington, W. J. Byers, F. F. Oehme, as well as many Technical Managers and Quality Control Supervisors within the Company. The Research and Development library deserves thanks for extensive literature searching. C. A. Bicking and M. S. Renner gave special help by criticizing early drafts of the manuscripts and providing both direction and guidance over the past 20 some years. Secretarial assistance from Mrs. L. Lecy and Mrs. E. Wittrock made all this possible.

REFERENCES

Process Analysis

1. Junt, M., The Nondestructive Testing of Paper on the Paper Machine, *Tappi,* vol, 45, No. 11, pp. 170A–172A, November 1962.
2. Howe, B.I., J.A. Hopkins, and T.W. Stokes, A Study of Basis Weight and Formation from the Multigrade Headbox, *Pulp and Paper Magazine of Canada,* vol. 71, No. 1, pp. 46–62, Jan. 2, 1970.
3. Knox, D., Moisture Determination by Machine Sampling at the Reel, *Tappi,* vol. 49, No. 3, pp. 72A–76A, March 1966.
4. Mardon, J., *et al.,* Machine Problems and Paper Uniformity, *Paper Trade Journal,* vol. 149, No. 50, pp. 50–55, Dec. 13, 1965.
5. Rhorer, C. R., Diagnosis and Correction of Moisture Profile Problems on Paper Machines, *Tappi,* vol. 54, No. 1, pp. 43–46, January 1971.
   Ljungvist, K. J., Analysis of Chip Characteristics with Use of a Slotted Screen, *Paper Trade Journal,* vol. 153, No. 47, pp. 68–70, Nov. 24, 1969.
7. Clark, J. D'A., Freeness Fallacies and Facts, *Tappi,* vol. 53, No. 1, pp. 108–113, January 1970.

See also Table 30-7

Computers

8. Anon., PTJ Survey Reveals NA Process Computer Status and Practice, *Paper Trade Journal,* vol. 154, No. 35, pp. 87–91, Aug. 24, 1970.
9. Anon., Where NA Mills Are Using Process Computers and with What Benefits, *Paper Trade Journal,* vol. 154, No. 35, pp. 25–31, Aug. 31, 1970.
10. Anon., Computer Controls Moisture and Basis Weight at Garden State, *Paper Trade Journal,* vol. 154, No. 42, pp. 58–61, Oct. 19, 1971.
11. Chao, H., and W. Wickstrom, The Development of Dynamic Color Control on a Paper Machine, *Automatica,* vol. 6, pp. 5–18, 1970.
12. Dahlin, E. B., Interactive Control of Paper Machines, *Control Engineering,* vol. 17, No. 1, pp. 76–81, January 1970.
13. Ekstrom, A., and G. Sangregorio, Automating the Control Loops on a Swedish Kraft Paper Machine, *Pulp and Paper,* vol. 41, No. 14, pp. 30–34, Apr. 3, 1967.
14. Grant, R., Computer Applications—from Stock Preparation to Shipping, *Paper Trade Journal,* vol. 155, No. 29, pp. 38–43, July 19, 1971.
15. Hambleton, A., Coordinated Control of a Workable Alternative to Computerization, *Paper Trade Journal,* vol. 155, No. 22, pp. 34–37, May 31, 1971.
16. Holm, R. A., and J. F. Perry, Review of Process Control, *Tappi,* vol. 53, No. 9, pp. 1638–1649, September 1970.
17. Mardon, J., W. H. Mehaffey, and J. E. Barrett, Centralized Control of a Paper Machine, *Pulp and Paper Magazine of Canada,* vol. 68, No. 6, pp. 81–92, June 1967.
18. Mounce, G., and S. Persik, Computer Directed Multiple Sensor Process System for a Newsprint Machine Measurement, *Pulp and Paper Magazine of Canada,* vol. 71, No. 4, pp. 60–63, Feb. 20, 1970.
19. Sanborn, I. B., Consolidated Takes a Hard Look at Process Computer Profitability, *Paper Trade Journal,* vol. 154, No. 22, pp. 46–47, June 1, 1970.

20. Sullivan, M. D., Process Control Pays at Consolidated, *Pulp and Paper*, vol. 44, No. 12, pp. 65–69, November 1970.
21. Wickstrom, W. A., and M. Horner, Closed-loop Color Control for Printing Papers, *Tappi*, vol. 53, No. 5, pp. 784–791, May 1970.

Instrumentation

22. Gartland, W. T., *et al.*, A Paper Ash Gage for On-line Measurements, *Tappi*, vol. 54, No. 3, pp. 425–427, March 1971.
23. Mercer, P., Problems in On-machine Measurement of Cross-machine Profiles, *Paper Trade Journal*, vol. 153, No. 5, pp. 46–48, Feb. 3, 1969. See also Beta Gauge Debate Continues, *Paper Trade Journal*, vol. 153, No. 21, pp. 61–62, May 26, 1969.
24. Scrivens, D. B., Application of Infrared Moisture Measurement to Paper Machines, *Paper Trade Journal*, vol. 154, No. 3, pp. 42–46, Jan. 19, 1970.
25. Ziegenhagen, P. D., New Device Measures Stock Density, *Pulp and Paper*, vol. 40, No. 9, pp. 40–41, Feb. 28, 1966.
26. Locke, I. I., Do Your Instruments Solve Problems?—Or Contribute to Them? *Paper Trade Journal*, vol. 147, No. 33, pp. 24–27, Aug. 19, 1963.
27. Cyr, L. A., Yardage Meters Applicable to Winders and Rewinders, *Pulp and Paper Magazine of Canada*, vol. 71, No. 18, pp. 78–80, Sept. 18, 1970.

See also Table 30-8.

Sampling, Inspection, and Testing

28. Sampling a Single Lot of Paper, Paperboard, Fiberboard, or Related Product (Proposed Revision of T-400 ts-64 as a Standard), *Tappi*, vol. 53, No. 2, pp. 342–343, February 1970.
29. Benzing, J. A., How Champion Electronically Inspects Lightweight Coated Papers, *Paper Trade Journal*, vol. 154, No. 32, pp. 37–38, Aug. 10, 1970.
30. Nash, P., Automation of Inspection of Uniform Fast Flowing Sheet Materials, *Tappi*, vol. 54, No. 6, pp. 923–927, June 1971.
31. Ward, E. J., Roll Quality Control in Mill Type Winders, *Pulp and Paper Magazine of Canada*, vol. 71, No. 18, pp. 85–90, Sept. 18, 1970.
32. Kohler, J. B., and G. R. Mounce, Paper Flaw Detection and Inspection Methods, *Tappi*, vol. 45, No. 11, pp. 172A–174A, November 1962.

See also Tables 30-6, 30-7, and 30-8.

Statistical Methods

See Tables 30-6, 30-7, and 30-8.

Specifications

33. Stickney, R. L., and C. E. Upham, "Paper Properties Which Cause Variations in Print Quality," TAPPI 6th Graphic Arts Conference, Kiamesha Lake, N.Y., Oct. 7–10, 1969.
34. Anon., Control of Paper and Board Quality Featured at British Conference, *Paper Trade Journal*, vol. 155, No. 18, pp. 54–57, May 3, 1971.

See also Table 30-8.

General Quality Control

35. Brewster, D.B., Economic Gains from Improved Quality Control, *Pulp and Paper Magazine of Canada*, vol. 71, No. 6, pp. 55–58, Mar. 20, 1970.
36. Mosher, R. H., and D. S. Davis, "Industrial and Specialty Papers," vol. II, pp. 194–245, Chemical Publishing Company, Inc., New York, 1970.
37. Streit, F., "Paper Quality Control," Lockwood Publishing Co., Inc., New York, 1968.

See also Table 30-8.

Texts

38. Libby, C. E., Pulp and Paper Science and Technology, vol. 1, "Pulp," vol. 2, "Paper," McGraw-Hill Book Company, New York, 1962.
39. Casey, J. P., "Pulp and Paper: Chemistry and Chemical Technology," vol. 1, "Pulp and Bleaching"; vol. 2, "Papermaking;" vol. 3, "Paper Testing and Converting," Interscience Publishers, Inc., New York, 1960–1961.
40. Joint Textbook Committee of the Paper Industry of the United States and Canada, "Pulp and Paper Manufacture," vol. 1, "The Pulping of Wood"; vol. 2, "Control of Secondary

Fiber, Structural Board, Coating"; vol. 3, "Papermaking and Paperboard Making," Mc-Graw-Hill Book Company, New York, 1970.

Bibliographies

41. Roth, L., and J. Weiner, "Quality Control—Pulp and Paper Industries," Bibliography Series 189, Institute of Paper Chemistry, Appleton, Wis., 1959. (See also Byrne, J., and J. Weiner, Supplement 1, 1968.) See also Table 30-6, above.

Section **31**

Food and Allied Industries

DR. H. L. STIER

Vice President, Quality Control,
United Brands Company, Boston, Massachusetts

INTRODUCTION

This Section describes the quality control techniques successfully used for:
1. "Perishable" food products
2. "Nonperishable" or processed foods
3. Food containers and packaging materials

The Section discusses the importance of federal and state regulations, voluntary requirements, and industry codes in deriving specifications and control plans. It illustrates sampling plans and statistical control chart techniques useful in the food industry. The Section also relates quality information systems to production, packaging, processing, and marketing of foods. No attempt has been made to include information concerning the technological aspects of equipment, product handling methods, or processing and packaging procedures. The examples illustrate different types of application rather than providing broad coverage of all food products.

The most important problems in food quality control, as listed by the industry in reponse to the 1964 survey by Brokaw and Kramer[1] were:

[1]Brokaw, C. H., and A. Kramer, Quality Control in Processing Foods, *Food Technology*, vol. 18, No. 9, pp. 73–78, September 1964.

Need for more recognition by top management
Need to upgrade personnel
Insufficient quality consciousness of production line people
Cooperation with other departments
Need for more standards based on objective methods

Progress in these areas is noted as appropriate here and there in the Section and in the Bibliography. In what follows, the general approach has been to identify the standards and then relate these to the Control Plan typically used.

LEGISLATIVE AND VOLUNTARY REQUIREMENTS

Federal and State Laws   Many federal and state laws and regulations have a direct and important impact on quality control in the food industry. They are:

The Federal Food, Drug and Cosmetic Act (FDAC)[2]
The Fair Packaging and Labeling Act (FPLA)
Regulations of the Federal Food and Drug Administration for implementing the FDAC and FPLA
U.S. Department of Agriculture Grade Standards for Fruits, Vegetables, Poultry and Meats
The U.S. Department of Interior Standards for Fishery Products
Federal Food and Drug Administration Standards of Identity, Quality, and Fill
The Perishable Agricultural Commodities Act
State and local health laws and regulations
State and local weights and measures laws and regulations

Especially important to food processors are the Good Manufacturing Practices regulations issued in 1969 and the Better Process Control regulations issued in 1973. Revisions and additions to the Regulations of the FDAC are being made constantly. Therefore, it is important that each food processor keep continually informed of all the regulations which pertain to his operations and products. This can be done through direct contact with the FDA, through trade associations or trade publications. Analytical procedures used by the FDA are published in the Official Methods of Analysis of the Association of Analytical Chemists. (The eleventh edition was published in 1970.) Whenever applicable, food processors should include these test methods in their control laboratory procedures or specify them when chemical analyses are done by outside laboratories.

Federal Food and Drug Act   The nature and extent of early quality control efforts in the food industry were determined to a large degree by federal legislation and regulations. The Pure Food and Drug Act was passed in 1906 to assure the purity, wholesomeness, and safety of the nation's food supply. To comply with its requirements, all food processors had to exercise careful controls over product quality and container fill. Leaders in the food industry early realized that public confidence in their products was essential if the food processing industry was to grow and prosper. They participated actively in drafting the Act, and their trade associations conducted research programs to determine the processing times, temperatures, and procedures necessary to assure the complete safety of processed food products. They also cooperated actively with the federal government (FDA) in the enforcement of the Act. The original Act was augmented and replaced in 1938 by the passage

[2]Copies may be obtained from Food and Drug Administration, U.S. Department of Health, Education and Welfare, Washington, D.C., 20250; or Government Printing Office, Washington, D.C.

of the Federal Food, Drug and Cosmetic Act. In 1966 the Fair Packaging and Labeling Act (Public Law 89-755) further amplified those parts of the Act dealing with packaging and labeling. Other important amendments with which every food processor should be familiar are:

Tolerances for Pesticide Chemicals incorporated in Section 408 of the Act, originally passed as the Miller Act (Public Law 518) in 1954
The Food Additives Amendment of 1958 — Section 409 of the Act
The Color Additives Amendment of 1960 — Section 706 of the Act

Tolerances (some very low) have been established for various pesticides and each food and color additive. Every food quality control program should incorporate adequate safeguards to ensure compliance of the raw product and the processed product with these parts of the Act.

Microbiological contamination of a food product is by far the most serious condition that can occur, and no tolerance for error is permitted. The wholesomeness and safety of food products has long been considered a "sacred trust," and the food industry has accepted and enforced it as such. Three parts of one section of the FDAC deal specifically with microbiological bases that are used for determining when a food is "adulterated" under the Act:

1. Section 402(a)(1) states that a food is adulterated "if it bears or contains any poisonous or deleterious substance which may render it injurious to health." The presence in food of specific infectious bacteria such as salmonellae or toxins of staphylococci and *Clostridium botulinum* is considered adulteration. No other supporting evidence is required.

2. Section 402(a)(3) states that a food is adulterated "if it consists in whole or in part of any filthy, putrid or decomposed substance or if it is otherwise unfit for food." A food is considered adulterated under this section if it contains excessive coliform bacteria or an excessive total population of various kinds of microorganisms (total plate count). To establish that such contamination by microorganisms actually constitutes *filth* requires evidence of insanitary conditions in the plant.

3. Section 402(a)(4) states that a food is adulterated "if it has been prepared, packed, or held under insanitary conditions whereby it *may* have become contaminated with filth or whereby it may have been rendered injurious to health." Thus, inspection evidence of insanitary practices may constitute a basis for legal action.

Regulations of the Food and Drug Administration The FDA, which is charged with the enforcement of the Food and Drug Act and its various amendments, has issued implementing regulations and standards. These regulations and standards are mandatory and have the force of law since they can be enforced by seizure and injunction proceedings in federal courts. Many state and local agencies also issue and enforce regulations that directly affect processors and marketers of food products. The most important are the state and local health departments, and the weights and measures agencies. The federal regulations cover four broad areas: (1) pesticide residues; (2) food additives; (3) color additives; and (4) good manufacturing practices. Following are some of the key elements in these regulations, which will have a direct bearing on food quality control programs:

Pesticide residue tolerances apply specifically to the fresh product, but processed foods must meet the following requirements:

1. The poisonous or deleterious pesticide residues must be removed during processing to the extent that the remaining concentration is less than the permissible tolerance.

2. The concentration of a pesticide in the preserved or processed food when ready to eat cannot be greater than the tolerance permitted on the raw agricultural commodity. The recommendations issued by the National Canners Association in 1960

entitled "Preventing Contamination of the Raw Product" will prove useful to every food processor who wants a high degree of assurance that there are no hazardous residues in his product.[3]

Food additives regulations are included in Part 121 of the Code of Federal Regulations. Those issued through 1971 were:

A — Definitions and Procedural and Interpretative Regulations

B — Exemption of Certain Food Additives from the Requirement of Tolerances

C — Food Additives Permitted in Feed and Drinking Water of Animals, or for the Treatment of Food Producing Animals

D — Food Additives Permitted in Food for Human Consumption

E — Substances for which Prior Sanctions have been granted

F — Food Additives Resulting from Contact with Containers or Equipment and Food Additives Otherwise Affecting Food

G — Radiation and Radiation Sources Intended for Use in the Production, Processing and Handling of Food

Those food additives exempted from tolerances have been published by the FDA in a listing of additives that are "Generally Recognized as Safe" (GRAS). This list is continually revised and updated. Additives originally included in the GRAS list are sometimes deleted and added to lists of additives with tolerances. Such lists should be constantly monitored and food quality control programs adjusted accordingly.

As methods of chemical analysis have become more sophisticated, the migration of chemical compounds from food packaging materials into the packaged food product has been discovered. To prevent or minimize chemical contamination of foods from their packages, tolerances have been established and limitations in the use of certain materials decreed by the FDA. Packaging materials for meat and poultry products must be approved by the U.S. Department of Agriculture (USDA) before use.

Color additives for food use have been listed by the FDA in two categories: (1) those subject to certification and (2) those exempt from certification. Regulations have been issued which provide for the identity, specifications, uses, restrictions, labeling requirements, and certification. The Color Additive Amendment to the FDAC was effective in July 1960. Since that date, review and certification of color additives for food use have been continual. The intended use of any color additive in a food product should be checked to ensure that it has been certified for food use by the FDA.

The Good Manufacturing Practices Regulations added legal "teeth" to the enforcement of sanitation requirements. Prosecution for failure to comply became a reality. These regulations include specific requirements concerning the sanitation of plant and grounds (Part 128.3), equipment and utensils (128.4), sanitation facilities and controls (128.5), sanitary operations (128.6), processes and controls (128.7), and personnel (128.8). The "processes and controls" section contains specific requirements concerning:

Inspection and care of raw material and ingredients
Sanitation of containers and carriers of raw ingredients
Food processing areas and equipment
Food processing controls
Chemical and microbiological testing procedures

---

[3]"Consumer Confidence in Canned Foods: Industry's Responsibility," National Canners Association, Supplement to Information Letter 1766, February 13, 1960.

Coding of processed products
Quality maintenance and sanitation during storage and transportation

Also included in this section is the requirement concerning packaging: "Packaging processes and materials shall not transmit contaminants or objectionable substances to the products, shall conform to any applicable food additive regulations, and should provide adequate protection from contamination."

Better Process Control Regulations   Late in 1971 the FDA proposed a new set of regulations to be issued in 1972 after review and comment by industry to ensure better process control in food processing plants.[4] The proposal reflected a general reorientation and shift in emphasis by the FDA from the inspection of food processing to the inspection of the management of food processing or, more specifically, quality control.[5] The proposed regulations, aimed primarily at better control over the processing of low-acid foods—those in which botulism can occur—set forth specific requirements concerning (1) the kinds of temperature measurement and recording equipment to be used, (2) the frequency of inspection of the top double seam and measurements to be recorded, and (3) the kind of information and records to be maintained to assure complete documentation of the process.

The National Canners Association, who first proposed the Better Process Control Regulations to the FDA, listed the major provisions of the regulations[6] as follows:

1. Food processors would be required to file with the FDA: (a) a list of the low-acid products packed; (b) a description of the processing procedures used specifying the retort or cooker type, the minimum initial temperature, and the time and temperatures of the process used for each product in each container size.

2. Codes on containers of low-acid foods would be changed periodically so that they would be related to shift, batch, or volume of products rather than merely to the time period.

3. Records would be retained for a period of at least 3 years.

4. All retorts would be equipped with temperature-time recording devices to provide a permanent record of the process. These records would be related to the codes so that at any time the process received by cans of a specific code could be checked.

5. The following action would be taken if the records reveal a slight inadvertent deviation in the process: (a) Set aside the lot involved for further evaluation in accordance with procedures recognized by competent processing authorities as being adequate to detect any potential hazard to health. (b) A record of the evaluation procedures used and the results would be made and retained by the processor. (c) If spoilage having a potential health significance were found in any lot which in whole or in part had any distribution, the canner would be required to report this fact to FDA (this has been industry practice in the past).

6. FDA inspectors would be authorized to inspect and copy the required low-acid processing records when they make their routine visits. They also would inspect the processing equipment to see that it is appropriate and in keeping with the requirements of the Regulations.

7. Specific requirements for processing equipment, as well as container closure, would be followed.

8. Supervisors of retort operations and can seam inspectors would be required to

[4]Food and Drug Administration, Proposed Rule Making—Manufacture and Processing of Canned Foods, *Federal Register*, vol. 35, No. 219, Nov. 12, 1971.
[5]Edwards, C. C., The Need for More Regulations, *Proceedings, 65th Annual Convention of the National Canners Association*, Jan. 31, 1972, pp. 21–22.
[6]Somers, I. I., N.C.A.—FDA Better Process Control Plan, *Proceedings, 65th Annual Convention of the National Canners Association*, Jan. 31, 1972, pp. 25-27.

attend, and be certified by, an approved school as having completed the prescribed course of instruction within 1 year after the effective date of the regulations.

Industry Code for Frozen Foods   For frozen food products the Association of Food and Drug Officials of the United States (AFDOUS) adopted a Frozen Food Code in 1961 containing specific guidelines for the handling of frozen food products.   This AFDOUS Code is more detailed than the Good Manufacturing Practices Regulations (which cover all types of foods, including frozen) and has been adopted in whole or in part by a number of states.

Federal Grades and Standards   Standards of Identity, Quality, and Fill of Container have been issued by the FDA for a wide range of products, including canned vegetables, fruits, fish, jams, jellies, preserves, frozen concentrates, and specialty products.   These standards are issued as regulations and thus have the force of law. For all the products covered by these standards their requirements become the minimum that the food processor must include in his own product specification.

Voluntary or permissive quality standards have been developed in cooperation with growers, processors, packers, handlers, wholesalers, and retailers of food products.   The USDA has issued such grade standards for processed and fresh fruits and vegetables and poultry and meat products, and the U.S. Department of Interior (USDI) for fishery products.   In addition, grade standards have been issued by individual states for certain regional products.   The USDA Quality Grade Standards are frequently used by the food processor and marketer to provide a common basis for the quality evaluation of the product.   An inspection and certification service is provided by the USDA and permits the designation of the food product in the appropriate U.S. grade.   Food products may be inspected on a lot inspection basis or on a continuous basis in plants by USDA inspectors, and an inspection certificate issued and shipping cases stamped to indicate the grade attained by the lot.

Some government agencies purchase large quantities of food products — the USDA for the school lunch program; the Department of Defense (DOD) for the various armed services installations; and the General Services Administration (GSA) for various other government agencies.   When federal grade standards exist for the food product, these are usually required and included in the specifications.   However, there are a number of food products for which such federal standards do not exist, and the federal agency will prepare its own specification or standard.   These food product specifications are usually quite comprehensive, and provide the food processor with another source for guidelines concerning quality attributes of a food product not included in existing federal quality grade standards.   Some examples of food specifications issued by federal agencies are shown in Table 31-1.

See Gunderson[7] for a comprehensive listing and sources of all federal food standards, federal specifications, and military specifications.

QUALITY SPECIFICATIONS

The preparation of written quality specifications for each product is an important first step in planning a useful quality control program.   The quality policy of the firm and the objective of top management should be reflected in the quality specifications.   They should indicate not only the level for each quality attribute, but also the permissible variations or tolerances, the methods of measuring, and the sampling procedure for determining conformance with the specifications.

The basis of the product quality specifications may be a federal specification, the

---

[7] Gunderson, F. L., H. W. Gunderson, and E. R. Ferguson, Jr., "Food Standards and Definitions in the United States.   A Guidebook," Academic Press, Inc., New York, 1963.

TABLE 31-1   Examples of Food Specifications

Item	Date	Agency	Federal Specification No.*
Apple butter, canned	1969	U.S. Dept. of the Army	Z-A-00616D (Army-GL)
Beans, dry	1969	U.S. Dept. of the Army	JJJ-B-106E
Catsup, tomato.	1969	U.S. Dept. of the Army	JJJ-C-91F
Cheese, cottage	1970	GSA	C-C-281E
Cheese, natural Swiss. . . .	1969	U.S. Dept. of the Army	C-C-00302B (Army-GL)
Cheese, pasteurized processed Swiss, and pasteurized processed Swiss and Cheddar, or American.	1969	U.S. Dept. of the Army	C-C-00305B (Army-GL)
Flour, rye	1969	U.S. Dept. of the Army	N-F-471C
Frankfurters, chilled and frozen	1970	U.S. Dept. of the Army	PP-F-660E
Ice cream; ice milk; sherbet; and ices	1970	GSA	EE-I-00116D (AGR-C&MS)
Milk, flavored (chocolate) and flavored dairy drink (chocolate)	1970	GSA	C-F-1392A
Potatoes, white, dehydrated	1969	U.S. Dept. of the Army	JJJ-P-630B

* Available from the Government Printing Office, Washington, D.C., 20250, or the issuing department.

USDA Grade Standard, or an independently prepared specification based upon the company's goals and objectives, and the results of a consumer survey. Above all they should be consumer-oriented. Consumer survey data should be combined with process capability studies made in the company's production facility to assure realism and economic feasibility. The tolerances that are included in the specification should reflect the ability of the process to make the product in question.

Reactions and preferences change as consumers are exposed to improvements in product quality, new food products, consumer education, and greater affluence. Consequently, it is important that consumer surveys be updated periodically. The rapidity of new product development in foods is such that only about 20% of the products on retail shelves at any one time were there 5 years earlier. Accordingly, if specifications are to reflect current preferences and are to result in a product that is truly competitive in the marketplace, consumer data should be updated every 3 years.

Agreement on Standards   As a prelude to the consideration and discussion of specific tolerances and grade descriptions, it is important that Production, Marketing, and Research agree on basic concepts. Experience has shown that the following ground rules are usually applicable:

1. Reflect all safety and wholesomeness requirements, as well as those characteristics which the buyers (jobber and retailer) and consumers recognize, and which influence the price they are willing to pay.

2. Provide tolerances and allowances which reflect the actualities of the product as produced, handled, and marketed.

3. Specify factors which are to be measured objectively, and provide guides for those which are to be evaluated subjectively.

4. Restrict the number of different grades (quality levels); any one grade should represent not less than 15 to 20% of the total volume of product sold.

5. Review specifications for revision whenever changes occur in consumer requirements, in competitive standing of the product, or in relevant regulations and standards of the FDA.

Figure 31-1 shows the format for a processed product.

Quality Specifications for perishable products are quite similar to those for processed products on matters of General Characteristics, Packaging, Coding of Containers, and Quality Control Inspections. The defect lists are of course different, as are the seriousness classifications and the use of variables measurements to judge

---

(Company Name and Address)

QUALITY SPECIFICATIONS—(PRODUCT NAME)

Quality Level: (Grade or Brand Name)

Date effective: _____

A. *Raw Product*
Each of the significant characteristics of the raw product should be listed on separate lines with the required value at the right of the form. For example, for processed fruits or vegetables under this section might be included stage of maturity with appropriate objective (instrumental) measures such as soluble solids, texture, and tenderness. In addition, other requirements that might be listed include tolerances for physical damage and insect and disease damage, and any other attribute deemed important.

B. *Processed Product*
The average and the permissible range for individual containers should be included here for such factors as net weight, vacuum, headspace, pH, consistency, color, and extraneous material.

C. *Food Container*
Specific dimensions and important characteristics should be listed here. For cans this section should also include the average and permissible range of measurements for the top double seam.

D. *Shipping Container*
Include under this section material (corrugated fiber board, etc.), dimensions, printing (size, color, and location), and structural strength requirements.

E. *Coding of Containers*
Specify the type of code, size of letters or digits, and location on the individual containers and the shipping container. The code should identify product, plant, and time of production by 4-hour periods but at least for each 8-hour shift.

F. *Quality Control Inspection to Determine Conformance with Specifications*
1. Sampling Plan.
2. Inspection Procedure.
3. Acceptance and Rejection Criteria.

(Signed) _____

(Quality Manager

Approved:

_____ Date: _____

Fig. 31-1 Example of a specification for a processed product.

conformance to permissible frequency. Container Fill and Net Weight is a separate characteristic for perishable products.

THE CONTROL PLAN

Because of the great number and variety of food products, it is not possible in this Section to include detailed descriptions of the quality control procedures used for individual products. Instead two broad groups of products are covered—perishable foods and nonperishable, processed foods. These two categories account for a large proportion of all foods and represent both old and new applications of quality control in the food industry.

Perishable foods are those which remain edible for relatively short periods of time. They include unprocessed foods which are consumed in the raw state such as fresh fruits and vegetables and certain sea foods as well as some processed foods such as bakery and confectionary products. In contrast, those processed foods which are packed in hermetically sealed containers in a microbiologically sterile condition are, for all practical purposes, nonperishable. They remain edible indefinitely.

Statistical Quality Control The use of statistical techniques (e.g., formal sampling plans, control charts) for perishable foods is relatively new and much less frequent than for processed foods. In contrast, application of statistical methods in food processing plants was clearly in evidence during the 1940s. By 1954, 64% of food processing plants had used, or were using, some form of statistical quality control.[8] However, many of the applications were limited and infrequent. Greatest usage at that time was shown by the beverage industry (77%) and the canning and preserving industry (75%). Stier[9,10] reported that in 1954, statistical methods were used by food canners most frequently in packaging and manufacturing operations. Usually one of the first and most successful applications was the control of container fill. By 1964, 86% of food processing plants were using statistical control charts to some degree.[11]

Quality Control of Perishable Foods Perishable foods are subject to continual change and quality deterioration over the whole life cycle of the product. For effective control, inspections, reporting, and corrective action must be provided at each step in the progression from grower to consumer. Preventive quality control[12] is especially important. These controls require close collaboration among all departments, and are especially important for branded products.

Planning the Program. Quality of perishable foods may be affected at each of the many steps in their preparation for packaging and marketing. As a corollary, there are numerous potential control points and numerous opportunities for inspections and audits. Proper choice of control points is critical to profitable operation since

1. Failure to control can multiply the costs of poor quality as the product progresses into the more costly stages, and especially to the marketplace.

---

[8] Hosking, F. J., Quality Control Techniques Used in the Food Industry, *ASQC Convention Transactions* 1955, pp. 292–297.

[9] Stier, H. L., Statistical Quality Control in the Canning and Preserving Industry, *National Canners Association Bulletin,* 1955.

[10] Stier, H. L., How Statistical Quality Control Is Used in Food Processing Industries, *Transactions ASQC Technical Conference,* 1959, pp. 663–674.

[11] Brokaw and Kramer, *op. cit.*

[12] "Preventive" quality control puts the emphasis on loss of inherent product quality as a result of disease, insect infestation, poor handling, etc. This is further expanded on in this Section, under Quality Improvement.

2. Overcontrol, i.e., too many control points or overinspection at selected control points, is an added cost from which no corresponding value is derived.

Striking an economic balance between these two risks requires that the quality program be planned with the full participation of upper management, operating management, and the Quality Control staff. Such participation assures that the cost and income considerations are fully presented and helps to minimize biases toward uneconomical levels of quality—high or low.

The purposes and end results of the participative planning are to:

1. Identify the key quality characteristics through consumer surveys and preference tests. (These should be updated at least every 3 years.) For example, appearance of perishable foods in the marketplace influences the consumer's *initial* impression of quality. However, the overall quality evaluation is largely based upon the degree of acceptability when the product is eaten.

2. Prepare quality specifications, standards, and tolerances which reflect consumer preferences, competitive superiority, and process capabilities.

3. Study the price/cost/quality relationships. These studies include (a) prices paid for products purchased from contract producers (or others) vs. resulting effect on processing costs and attainable selling price; (b) cost of inspections at various control stations vs. costs incurred through lack of inspections; and (c) costs of prevention of damage during production, handling, and transport vs. damage incurred by lack of prevention.

4. Prepare standards for maximum product waste at all stages.

5. Prepare standards and means for evaluating quality deterioration through each step of the product progression from harvest, through distribution, to the consumer.

6. Provide for processing of customer and consumer complaints to acknowledge, to provide satisfaction, and to take steps to prevent recurrence.

7. Establish a quality information system to provide (a) regular feedback of performance to operating personnel, (b) evaluation of quality in relation to competitive products, and (c) useful periodic reports to upper management and operating management with proper attention to any failure in meeting product standards.

8. Arrange for top management final approval for the quality control system established for each product and for each major operating department.

9. Assign to operating management the responsibility for (a) implementing corporate quality policies, (b) carrying out the approved quality plans, and (c) taking the corrective action required to meet established quality standards.

Selecting the Critical Control Points   Out of 25 or 30 possible points where quality inspections might be made for the control of quality of a perishable food, very effective control can usually be exercised by inspection at only five points provided they are "critical points of control." These are the points in the production and distribution process where control is critical to assure conformance with laws and regulations and to prevent quality deterioration.[13] In recent years the number of critical points has increased, and the importance of others has increased, because of the more stringent requirements with respect to pesticide residues, food additives, etc. As a starting point in the selection of the critical control points in a quality control program for a perishable food, list every step from the first production decision to sale to the consumer. Each step should be rated with respect to the magnitude of its effect on product quality or compliance with federal law or regulations. Following is such a list for a fresh fruit or vegetable. An asterisk indicates possible points for "critical control."

1. *Production and cultural practices.*

*a. Variety selection. Does it produce a high proportion of product that meets the quality specification, in addition to high yields, disease resistance, etc.?

[13] See Section 12, under Inspection Planning.

b. Planting.

c. Cultivation.

d. Fertilization.

e. Irrigation.

*f. Insect and disease control. Residues of pesticides may be a special problem on certain perishable products, such as fresh fruits and vegetables. The types of pesticides and the rates and timing of application should be carefully planned and monitored throughout the production period. Quality control checks can be very important in assuring conformance with existing regulations and laws. If there is any possibility that the amount of any residue on the product exceeds existing tolerances, then random samples should be analyzed by the recommended procedures to determine actual concentrations on the product.

*2. Preharvest inspection is a very important inspection for certain crops to assure the optimum stage of maturity at harvest and to estimate the proportion that will meet the specifications of each grade or quality level when harvested. For example, in pineapple preharvest inspection a random sample of 10 pineapples is checked for soluble solids, and the shell color (color index) is recorded beginning about 1 week before harvest. The requirement for the top quality level is an average of 12% soluble solids with no single pineapple less than 10%. When the sugar content of the pineapples approaches the required level, a sample of 20 is taken to provide greater reliability of the estimate.

3. Harvesting.

a. Instruction to supervisors and laborers.

b. Identifying correct stage of maturity.

*c. Quality sorting as harvested. If the selection and sorting into the various quality levels is done in the field as in field wrapping and packing of lettuce, then quality audits should be made of a random sample of packed cartons. This will be the only opportunity to correct errors in packing since field packed product will go directly to the rail or truck carrier.

d. Placing in field container.

4. Transporting from field to packing house. The potential for handling damage in this operation can be great. Those methods and techniques which are least damaging should be determined and used.

*5. At the packing house. The selection of packed containers at random from the line throughout the day and the inspection of the product in each container is usually desirable for perishable products. The inspection should provide the information necessary for corrective action in quality selection, net weight, packing techniques, and excessive handling damage. Typical operations performed at the packing house include:

a. Unload.

b. Wash.

c. Trim.

d. Sort according to size, quality, etc.

e. Weigh.

f. Pack.

g. Seal container.

h. Stamp code on containers.

i. Place in carrier or storage room.

6. Transport to market.

a. Load on carrier.

b. Ice or check refrigeration unit.

c. Check temperature and condition of product at intermediate points in transit.

d. Inspect upon arrival and record quality deterioration.

7. Market Quality.

*a. Obtain and inspect random samples at wholesale and at retail to determine quality deterioration and handling damage that occurred after packing. An example of a record form used for this purpose is shown in Figure 31-2.

b. Obtain competitive products at both the wholesale and retail market for comparison.

c. Determine retail "shelf life" under usual conditions of handling.

COMPARISON OF QUALITY SCORE OF THE SAME LOTS AT PACK AND IN THE MARKET

Product: Iceberg Lettuce
Quality Level: _____

Pack Code	Date Insp.	City	No. Hds. Insp.	Days From Pack To. Insp.	Maj. Defects Pts. Ded.	Quality Score	Quality Score	Diff. From Mkt. Score	Maj. Defects Pts. Ded.
		Market Quality - Wholesale(W) Retail(R)						At Pack	
KD379	2/23	Boston	24	12 days	RD-18	54(W)	92	+38	LB-2
JD379	2/24	New York	3	14 days	PR-14	51(R)	91	+40	ML-2
CKA158	2/24	New York	6	13 days	LB-12	53(R)	94	+41	LB-1
CKA158	2/24	Florida	6	13 days	LB-3 RD-8				
CKA166	2/24	Florida							

Fig. 31-2 Comparison of quality score of the same lots at pack and in the market.

d. Determine changes in packaging, methods of handling, or storage that will prolong shelf life and reduce quality deterioration during distribution.

Defects and Quality Scores   The quality control program should include a Seriousness Classification of Defects. Wherever possible, each defect classificaction is related to its effect on edible quality. Sections 12 and 24, under this title, deal extensively with the approach used. (See especially Table 12-9, Composite Definitions for Seriousness Classification in Food Industry.) Figure 31-3 shows an application of this concept to the defect of fruit spot of bananas. In this case the defect is classed as major, but the number of demerits per defect is not a constant. Instead, the demerits vary depending on the severity of the defect. Usually, the product rating is merely the number of demerits per unit of product (in the samples inspected). Alternatively, a rating of 100 is established for perfect product, and the demerits per unit are deducted from 100 to give the actual rating of the product.

Inspection   *Sampling and inspection in the field prior to harvest* call for care and planning to assure a random selection of the units to be inspected. One way to assure randomness is to select the general locations by the random choice of numbered squares from a drawing (grid) on a sheet representing the field (Figure 31-4) and then randomly locating the plant or plants to be sampled within each square.[14]

Inspection after packing calls for a random selection of cartons. From each carton selected, at least two units should be inspected to provide a measure of quality variability *within* individual cartons.[15]   When defect severities and incidence become low, both the sample size and the frequency of inspection should be reduced. Alternatively, inspection can be omitted for those defects whose incidence is very low. The inspection record should be carefully planned and so organized that the data obtained during inspection can be easily entered and summarized.[16]

[14] The grid system for ensuring random sampling has been used by the author (for cranberries) and by others for peas, corn, etc.
[15] See Section 24, Sampling by Attributes, for general information on setting up sampling procedures.
[16] See Section 19 for details on forms design and good practice.

PITTING DISEASE *(Fruit Spot)* (PD)

(Color photograph generally required
to adequately describe these defects)

Description: Small round depressions in early stages, developing up to ⅜ inch in diameter in the advanced stage. Interior of spot reddish-brown to black in color, sometimes with an orange halo. May appear anywhere on fingers or on crown. Number as well as the size of spots increase after fruit is harvested, but especially during ripening.

Cause: Fungus infection caused by *Pyricularia grisea.*

Classification: Major

Method of Rating:

Severity rating	No. of spots	
	On a hand	On a cluster
Trace	1 to 12	1 to 6
Light.	13 to 24	7 to 12
Medium	25 to 40	13 to 20
Severe.	41 or more	21 or more

Note: Include spots on crown and pedicel as well as on the peel of the finger.

Fig. 31-3 Boxed bananas: defects.

Quality inspection *after packaging* should answer the following questions:

1. Do net weights meet legal requirements and are they within company standards?

2. Is the arrangement (packing technique) in the package correct?

3. How much product damage occurred during packaging?

4. What are the nature and causes of defects and damage found?

5. Is carton condition good enough to prevent product damage during transit?

6. Are cartons properly coded for identification of product, packing plant, packer, pack date, etc.?

7. What is the overall quality packed?

8. What is the degree of quality variability between and within cartons?

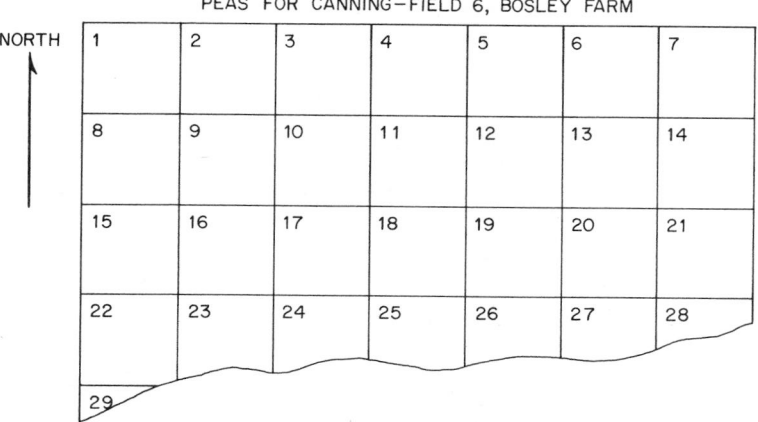

PEAS FOR CANNING—FIELD 6, BOSLEY FARM

Fig. 31-4 Field sampling diagram.

Quality inspection *at destination* should provide the following information:
1. Nature and degree of damage in transit.
2. Quality score upon arrival in the marketplace.
3. Percent of units that do not meet the quality specifications.
4. A basis for price adjustment or decision concerning disposition of the product in the event of serious damage.

The size of sample and the frequency of sampling at each of the above three points (preharvest, after packaging, at destination) should be based upon the importance of any one or all of the factors listed under each point. Sampling and inspection may not be necessary or desirable if

a. The value of the inspection is less than the cost.

b. The perishable product is not a branded product or one classified in a standard grading system such as the USDA Produce Grades.

c. Quality deterioration or damage in transit is invariably slight.

When buyer and seller have agreed on a certain grade level or quality specification for a perishable product, inspection should be made at the point of packing. It is frequently desirable to inspect the product upon arrival at the packing shed immediately before packing to correct promptly any deficiencies in the procedure or instructions for selecting or preparing the produce prior to packing. A random sample of cartons inspected after packing helps to correct any packing deficiencies and to obtain a record of the quality shipped.

Competitive Quality. To determine the relative quality of competitive products, regular sampling inspection and quality evaluations should be made. Five to ten containers of each competitive product should be purchased from wholesalers or retailers. Each unit in the cartons should be inspected carefully, and the defect scores awarded by the same scoring system as that used for company products.

Because defect severity ratings are sometimes subjective, each inspector should be carefully instructed, supervised, and occasionally tested concerning his knowledge of defect identification and severity rating. Such a procedure is absolutely necessary to ensure accuracy in the inspection record and comparability of the data between inspectors and from lot to lot.

QUALITY CONTROL OF PROCESSED FOODS

Because of the less perishable nature of processed foods the inclusion of the transportation and marketing phases in the quality control system is not nearly as important as it is for perishable foods. Usually manufacturers of processed foods consider their quality control program to end after packaging and labeling. This is especially true of those processed products which are heat sterilized and packaged in hermetically sealed containers. However, during the past decade more recognition has been given to the importance of quality maintenance in the channels of distribution. Many processed foods, such as bakery, confectionery, and frozen food products, are all susceptible to significant quality deterioration in storage and during marketing when conditions are not properly controlled. For these types of products the extension of the quality control system to the marketplace can be important in reducing losses and improving consumer acceptability and market share.

Important aspects of the quality control system for processed foods are:
1. Raw product quality

Adequate economic sampling and inspection procedures using objective methods for measuring raw product quality

Correlation of raw product quality with processed product quality

Payment to suppliers based on delivered quality

2. Control of container quality for both incoming shipments and after sealing and processing

3. Process control, including determining the critical points of control, periodic monitoring and recording procedures to assure adherence to processing requirements, container fill control, and verification of organoleptic and microbiological quality of the processed product

4. Monitoring quality changes during storage and transportation
Product stability and container damage in transit

5. Use of customer and consumer complaint information

Raw Product   There is usually high correlation between the raw product quality and processed food product quality unless processing causes excessive deterioration. The correlation is especially high for nonformulated products like canned or frozen fruits and vegetables.   In formulated products, end product quality can be altered by varying the proportions of ingredients and by the use of additives such as spices and thickening agents.   Many studies have been made to determine the correlation between certain attributes of the raw product and the quality of the processed product.   These usually involve correlation of organoleptic and physical-chemical tests. Characteristics such as color, texture, firmness, viscosity, and sweetness can be "objectively" measured.   Many of the instruments developed for the measurement of these characteristics are now in general use by food processors for measuring and controlling quality.   Descriptions of the instrument developed for measuring the kinesthetic characteristics of foods have been published by Kramer[17,18] Szczesniak,[19] and others.

For certain products, such as peas and sweet corn, the time of harvest of the raw product is critical in determining the quality of the raw product.   Thus the first sampling and measurement of raw product quality should be made from a random sample taken from the field to be harvested.   Tenderometer readings of raw peas will accurately indicate when the crop should be harvested for optimum quality and yield.   To ensure a random sample, a grid system for locating areas in the field should be used in combination with a random numbers table.   Figure 31-4 shows such a sampling grid.

When the crop is harvested and delivered to the processing plant, a sample should be taken upon arrival, and each of the significant quality factors measured.   The results determine the quality level designation for the processed product.   Sometimes different qualities of the raw product can be effectively blended with lower or higher quality of the same product to give the desired finished product quality. The raw product record form should be so designed that averages and ranges can be easily calculated for use in control charts.[20]   The use of instrumental methods for measuring quality permits the use of the more sensitive $\bar{X}$ and R charts.   Three-sigma limits for individual measurements provide a basis for accurately estimating the proportion of the finished product that will meet the specifications for a given quality level.

The record of the incidence and severity of insect or disease damage in the raw product is sometimes important in estimating the proportion of the product that may have to be discarded, as well as providing an accurate picture of the effectiveness of disease and insect control measures.

If the raw product is purchased from growers or other suppliers, then the sampling inspection and quality record provide a sound basis for payment, and for determination of the extent to which the product meets agreed-upon specifications.

---

[17] Kramer, A., Definition of Texture and Its Measurement in Vegetable Products, *Food Technology,* vol. 18, No. 3, pp. 46–49, 1964.

[18] Kramer, A., Measuring and Recording Rheological Properties of Gels, *Food Technology,* vol. 20, pp. 111–115, 1966.

[19] Szczesniak, A. S., Texture Measurements, *Food Technology,* vol. 20, pp. 52–58, 1966.

[20] See generally Section 23, Process Control by Statistical Methods.

Many food processors pay contract growers a price based upon the quality of the product delivered.

Process Control   As continuous processing replaces batch operations in the food processing industry, automatically operated machinery and automatic recording devices find greater use.   In a few plants, computers control the process.   There has been some tendency to become wholly dependent upon the automatic recording and controlling devices rather than on observation and action by trained process engineers or food technologists.   However, several serious food spoilage outbreaks have made clear that the food process control system must include provisions for frequent, periodic human monitoring and data recording for each critical control point.   The interpretation and action by a trained, responsible supervisor cannot be wholly replaced by automatic recording and controlling devices.

It is equally important that a record be made during the monitoring and inspection process.   An example suitable for a shift or day's production, which meets the requirements of the Better Process Control Regulations, issued by the FDA in 1973, is shown in Figure 31-5 for aseptic processing of a canned fruit.   Typical entries illustrate its use.   Production stoppage in Section H is an important part of this record.   On the back, recorded measurements of the top double seam assist in prompt seamer adjustments as necessary.

The critical points for control should be selected as outlined above on perishable foods.   To ensure safety of the product from a public health standpoint, the attainment of the desired temperatures for the required length of time should be the first critical control point checked in every food processing operation.   When hermetically sealed containers are used, the integrity of the seam operations and the container become critical points of control.

Container Fill   Statistical control of container fill is usually one of the earliest and most useful applications in the food processing operation.   One of the first steps should be machine and process capability studies of the filling operation.   The range in net contents of containers from each filling head of a filler is determined, and the total variation of the machine calculated.   Taking a sample of consecutively filled containers, one for each filling head, and plotting the weight data on a lot-plot[21] form, is a convenient method for determining machine capabilities and significant differences between filling heads.[22]   Calculating 3-sigma limits for individuals enables the processor to estimate the percent of containers that will be below the declared container label weight when the average weight is set at a given level.   Conversely, the processor can accurately determine the average net weight for which the machine must be set to limit the extent of containers under label weight to any predetermined proportion.   For example, if the standard deviation of individual container net weights σ_x is 0.1 ounce, and the declared weight on the label is 16 ounces, then the average fill weight required to have "none"[23] under 16 ounces is 16.3 ounces (declared weight of 16 ounces plus 3 standard deviations of individual weights).

As described in Section 23, plotting values on $\bar{X}$ and R charts provides positive evidence of the control of container fill, and pinpoints the time of significant variations, both when to look for assignable causes and when to leave the process alone. Frequently in food processing operations unnecessary changes are made in machine settings, thereby increasing variability in the operation.

A convenient and frequently used sample size is five containers.   Each of the five containers should be taken consecutively from the line to minimize variation be-

---

[21] See Section 25, under Lot Plot.

[22] See Giesecker, L., and L. V. Strausburger, A Modified Lot-Plot Sampling Procedure for Controlling Container Fill, *Transactions ASQC,* 1955, pp. 265–273.

[23] Actually, 0.13%.

tween containers. The sampling frequency depends upon the production rate as well as the degree of control attained. For example, small baby food containers, produced at the rate of 1,000 per minute, require more frequent sampling than No. 10 cans produced at the rate of 40 to 50 a minute. Once statistical control has been established, sampling every 20 to 30 minutes is sufficient. More frequent sampling

Quality Control Record
CANNED MASHED BANANAS — NO. 10 CANS OR 5 GALLON CANS

01642 (7-72)	A. PLANT LOCATION Greenfield	B. QTY. PRODUCED 1485 Cases	C. TIME & PACK DATE 0648 Sep.18'72	D. LOT CODE 2622

E. RAW PRODUCT

TIME OF DAY	WASH WATER FREE CHLORINE ppm	SOLUBLE SOLIDS %
0700	10-5-1	21.6-21.6
0900	10-0.5-0	22.6-22.6
1300	10-2.5-2.5	21.4-21.4
1500	10-2.5-1.5	22.6-22.6

F-1. OFF-ODOR; OFF-FLAVOR; OFF-COLOR

F. CANNED PRODUCT

TIME OF DAY	GROSS WEIGHT gms.	VACUUM in. Hg	PH	SOLUBLE SOLIDS %	CONSISTENCY cm./30 sec.	EXTRANEOUS MATERIAL
0700	3643	5	5.3	22.8-22.0	6.3-5.9	Neg.
0900	3647	Full	5.3	22.8-23.2	5.5-5.0	Neg.
1000	3623	3	5.3	23.4-23.0	6.5-6.0	Neg.
1300	3639	2	5.3	23.0-22.6	6.0-5.5	Neg.
1435	3650	Full	5.3	23.0-22.6	6.5-6.0	Neg.
1535	3670	Full	5.3	23.8-22.6	5.0-5.6	Neg.

DAILY AVERAGE   CONTAINER   TARE   WEIGHT   (gms.)

G. PRODUCT FLOW RATES AND PROCESS TEMPERATURES

TIME OF DAY	TIMING PUMP SETTING rpm	HEATING THERMUTATORS A	B	C	HOLDING TUBE MERC. THERM.	HOLDING TUBE OUTLET TEMP.	COOLING THERMUTATORS D	E	F	CANNING RATE cans/min.	CAN STERIL.	COVER STERIL.	FILL CHAMBER	SEAMER HOUSING
0730	78-116	226	256	272	NMT	270	200	140	92	25	460	360	280	380
0900	80-118	230	260	272	NMT	270	200	142	90	24	465	360		
1000	80-116	224	248	272	NMT	272	200							
1330	80-116	228	252											

TOP DOUBLE SEAM DIMENSIONS

K. LOT CODE	L. PACK DATE											All Measurements 0.001"

M.	Loc.	TIME SAMPLE TAKEN 730	800	830	1000	1030	1330	1400	1430	1530	1600		
COUNTER SINK	1	62	68	56	60	56	57	53	55	53	52		
	2	63	64	56	59	58	58	55	57	55	54		
	3	63	62	54	64	59	68	55	54	59	56		
SEAM THICKNESS	1	66	67	67	64	64	66	65	65	65	65		
	2	65	67	67	67	67	67	66	66	66	66		
	3	66	68	68	67	67	67	67	68	68	68		
SEAM LENGTH	1	126	130	128	126	128	128	120	127	127	126		
	2	126	131	128	126	129	128	128	128	128	128		
	3	127	128	127	127	129	129	129	129	129	128		

TIME SAMPLE

Fig. 31-5 Continuous processing quality control record. Top, front; bottom, back.

is necessary to spot and correct out-of-control situations at the beginning of an operation, or to establish statistical control of the process. Convenient control chart and record forms used by food processors are described in detail by Stier,[24] and Kramer and Twigg.[25]

[24] See Stier, H. L., Statistical Quality Control for Canners, *Proceedings, 53rd Annual Convention of the National Canners Association* (Information Letter 1764, Jan. 30, 1960).
[25] Kramer, A., and B. A. Twigg, "Quality Control for the Food Industry, 3d ed., vol. I, "Fundamentals," chap. 15, AVI Publishing Co., Inc., Westport, Conn., 1970.

Ingredients, Supplies, and Equipment   Acceptance-inspection of incoming ingredients and supplies is an important part of the overall quality control of a food processing plant.   If some of the minor ingredients in a formulated product do not meet specifications, the end product quality may be below desired quality standards, or may not meet legal or regulatory requirements even though the major raw products may be of high quality.   The first step in a useful quality control program for these items is the establishment of realistic specifications as described under Quality Specifications, above.

CONTAINER AND PACKAGING QUALITY CONTROL

Complete specifications and an acceptance-inspection procedure are required for containers used by food processors.   Defects of the incoming container, especially side seams and the bottom double seam, can result in serious spoilage from the entry of microorganisms.   Incoming sampling and inspection of containers has substantially reduced spoilage losses of canned products.   A reduction of 80% was reported by Way and Weimerskirch.[26]   Figure 31-6 shows the sampling-inspection record form they used.

An in-plant top double seam inspection and control system is an important adjunct to receiving inspection of containers.   Proper adjustment of the closing machine is necessary to ensure correct dimensions for each part of the top double seam and to prevent leakage and subsequent product spoilage.   Standards (dimensions) for the top double seam are an obvious starting point.   During processing, after control has been established, the top double seam is measured on closed containers from each line every 2 to 4 hours.   During the precontrol phase or when trouble develops, measurements are made every 30 minutes.   The checks should involve both visual inspection and recorded measurements at two or three locations around the circumference of the top double seam.   The first measurement should be taken close to the side seam of the can body, the next about 120° around the circumference, and the third one an additional 120°.   Using a special can micrometer, measurements should be made of the seam length and thickness, length of the cover hook, body hook, countersink, and overlap.   (The latter two measurements are of lesser importance and are sometimes omitted.)   The average and the range of the two or three measurements on each container are commonly plotted on a control chart.   In the beginning of canning, during initial stages of seamer adjustment, machine capabilities should be determined and compared with previously established specifications.   If the capabilities are wider than the specifications, the specifications should be reviewed.   If they are the minimum required for top double seam operations, some major change must be made in the process, such as major repair or the purchase of a new seamer.

Fiberboard cartons are commonly used as shipping containers for canned foods and perishable foods such as fresh produce.   Establishing quality specifications and making incoming quality inspections can pay for itself in large operations.   A checklist for a fiberboard box specification is given in Table 31-2.   Sampling and inspection procedures should be incorporated in the specification, e.g., use of MIL-STD-105D Sampling Plans for large shipments of containers.

Sometimes failure and collapse of a fiberboard food container may be caused by incomplete or poor adhesive application during corrugated board manufacturing.   Such deficiencies can be detected by established tests.[27]

[26] Way, C. B., and R. I. Weimerskirch, A Mutual Approach to Quality Control by Can Manufacturer and Food Processor, *Food Quality Control*, vol. 2, No. 2, pp. 10–17, 1962.

[27] See TAPPI Suggested Test Method T812 su-70, "Ply Separation of Solid and Corrugated Fiberboard (Wet)"; Table 30-6 lists other applicable TAPPI Standard, Suggested, and Useful Test Methods.

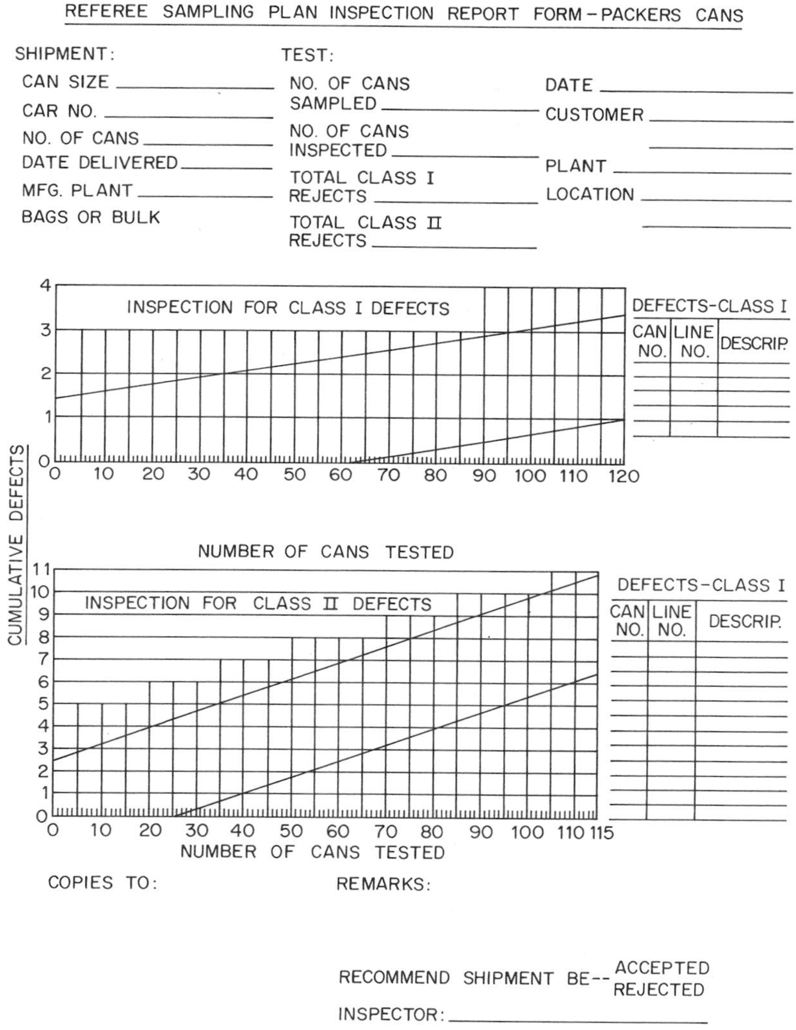

REFEREE SAMPLING PLAN INSPECTION REPORT FORM – PACKERS CANS

SHIPMENT: TEST:

CAN SIZE _____   NO. OF CANS   DATE _____

CAR NO. _____   SAMPLED _____   CUSTOMER _____

NO. OF CANS _____   NO. OF CANS

DATE DELIVERED_____ INSPECTED _____ PLANT _____

MFG. PLANT _____   TOTAL CLASS I   LOCATION _____
                              REJECTS _____

BAGS OR BULK   TOTAL CLASS II
                              REJECTS _____

Fig. 31-6   Referee sampling plan inspection report form.

Plastic containers are also important in the food industry. Specifications developed with the supplier should clearly state the characteristics and performance qualities which containers must have, so tolerances and ranges in film thickness, dimensions, etc., will be realistic, e.g., capable of being accomplished within the process capabilities of the manufacturer. Table 31-3 lists the attributes to be included in specifications for plastic bags, as an example. See Section 36B for a more complete discussion of quality control of plastic films.

TABLE 31-2   Checklist for a Fiberboard Box Specification

1. *General Characteristics* (with appropriate reference to attached drawing)
2. *Dimensions* (with appropriate reference to attached drawing)
   It is suggested that both inside and outside dimensions be listed together with the cubic area of the box (outside).   The dimensions listed should be nominal or average, but the permissible tolerance should also be included in the specification
3. *Vents* (with appropriate reference to attached drawing)
   Size, shape, and location
4. *Handholds* — dimension and location (with reference to attached drawing)
5. *Printing on Cover*
   a. Words
   b. Logotypes
   c. Location
   d. Color
6. *Composition of Fiberboard*
   a. Top
   b. Body
   c. Liner (if any)
   d. Tunnel pad (if any)
7. *Quality of Corrugated Board*
   For each of the following the average (nominal) and tolerance or permissible range to be shown:
   a. Caliper of combined board
   b. Flat crush
   c. Pin adhesion
   In addition to the above, some other tests might be specified which are considered important.   The procedure and method of measuring should be referenced or specified for each factor
8. *Manufacturing Code*
   a. General description — five digits without spaces or dashes (day, months, and year)
   b. Size of digits
   c. Location
      (1) On body
      (2) On cover
9. *Component Assembly*
   Under this heading should be a statement of method of assembly and binding of flaps — staples or glue.   If staples are used, then the heading could be simply "Stapling" with the following subheads:
      Number of staples
         Body
         Cover
      Type of staples (material and dimensions)
      Location (pattern of staples) — attached illustration
10. *Inspection to Determine Conformance with Specifications*
    a. Sampling
    b. Inspection procedures
       (1) Measurement
       (2) Tests
    c. Reporting
11. *Box Type* — code designation (upper right)
12. *Effective Date* (upper right)
13. *Revision Number and Date* (upper right)
14. *Date Prepared and Preparing Department* (lower left corner)
15. *Approval Signatures*

TABLE 31-3   Quality Specifications — Polyethylene Bags

(Company Name and Address)

Effective Date: _____

A. General Characteristics

B. Dimensions	Average	Permissible Range (Individual Measurements)
1. Film gage		
2. Bag width		
3. Bag length		
4. Vent holes		

    a. Diameter
    b. Location
    c. Die cuts *not* removed

  5. Tear strip
    a. Width
    b. Holes for wicket
    c. Location of perforation

  6. Gusset
    a. Width
    b. Length
    c. Taper

C. Pack Unit

D. Printing
  1. Legibility
  2. Layout
    a. Style and size of letters
    b. Colors of printing ink
    c. Color registration
  3. Ink splatter

E. Coding of Bags

F. Packaging
  1. Packing carton
  2. Dimensions of carton
  3. Method of packing
  4. Number of wickets per packing carton
  5. Information on outside of packing carton
    a. Bag type
    b. Total number of bags in carton
    c. Dimensions of bag (length and width)
    d. Manufacturer's name
    e. Plant location
    f. Date packed

G. Quality Inspection to Determine Conformance to Specifications
  1. Sampling plan
  2. Inspection procedure
  3. Acceptance and rejection criteria

(Signed) _____

Approved:

MICROBIOLOGICAL ASPECTS OF FOOD QUALITY CONTROL

Food products are subject to contamination by foreign matter of all kinds. Frequently the contamination does not constitute a health hazard but makes the food product undesirable because of aesthetic or palatability considerations. An important part of every food quality program is the identification and reporting of all extraneous matter and contamination. Of special importance is the detection, quantification, and control of contamination by biological sources such as bacteria, molds, yeasts, insects, and rodents. When live pathogenic microorganisms are present in a food product, it becomes potentially a public health hazard. Although nonpathogenic (spoilage) organisms may not cause food poisoning, their effect on the food may seriously affect color, texture, or flavor of the product to such a degree that it becomes inedible.

Because of the great number of potential sources of contamination, control measures must be comprehensive, especially for perishable foods. The most effective quality control procedures are those which prevent contamination. However, microbiological analyses of ingredients, raw product, and finished product should be considered a major responsibility of the quality contol staff of a food company. See Kramer and Twigg[28] for a discussion of microanalytical and microbiological techniques and the minimum equipment needs of a food microbiological laboratory.

Microbiological methods used in the quality control of a food product should provide for not only the positive identification of pathogenic organisms, but also the numbers per gram. Only in this way can sufficient information be obtained to assess the true health hazard of the product. Although many improvements have been made recently in microbiological techniques, resulting in faster and more accurate identification of organisms, one of the major deficiencies is still the long time (over one day) required to obtain a "microbiological reading" for a product. When there is trouble, the information is available too late to take corrective action on the line to prevent contamination of a substantial part of production. Therefore, the Quality Control Manager should keep up to date on all improvements which speed up microbiological analysis.

To prevent microbiological contamination, strict sanitation of plant and equipment is an absolute necessity. The Quality Control Department should make periodic (daily or for each shift) sanitation surveys and follow up to see that deficiencies are corrected. A method of quantifying sanitation surveys and using control chart analysis has been proposed by Stier.[29] To keep populations of microorganisms at a low level on perishable products, they must be handled quickly and carefully, and refrigerated after packing or processing. Microbiological checks should be made of incoming raw product ingredients and finished product. Chlorinated water should be used for washing and preparation of raw materials such as fresh fruits and vegetables. The water should contain 1 to 4 parts per million of active chlorine. A quality control inspector should check the chlorine content throughout the day to ensure the proper level. Other elements which should be included in the quality control program to ensure safety in the food product are:

1. Microbiological checks of equipment to detect bacterial buildup
2. Processing time and temperature checks to assure conformance with the prescribed process
3. Microbiological analysis of water in cooling tanks

---

[28] Kramer and Twigg, op. cit., chap. 10, Microanalytical and Microbiological Methods.
[29] Stier, H. L., Methods of Statistical Control for Sanitation Operations, *Modern Sanitation and Building Maintenance,* vol. 10, No. 6, pp. 16–18, 1958.

4. Microbiological analysis of container runways to determine possible buildups and points of contamination

5. High-temperature incubation of sample containers after processing (95 °C for 15 days)

6. Microscopic examination of the processed product

Microscopic examination should be used on the production line to determine the microbiological "load" of the product. Although this rapid control method does not distinguish between live or dead organisms, it serves to adjust the sampling frequency for less rapid culturing and detailed examination as the "load" varies.

The Howard mold counting procedure[30] is frequently used for determining the mold content of a product. If a maximum mold count has been established for a product, a cumulative graphical procedure can be used to determine conformance to the specification (see Figure 31-7).

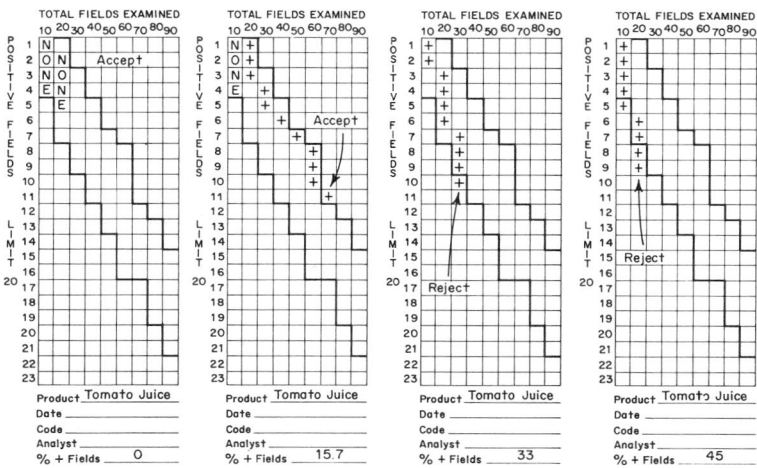

Fig. 31-7   Howard mold counts.

SENSORY EVALUATION OF FOOD QUALITY

Objective methods of measuring texture and color of food products are widely used, but because of the complex nature of food flavor it is still most effectively determined organoleptically by the use of taste panels. Taste panels are used extensively in the food industry to determine:

Product uniformity during production
Flavor changes during storage
Differences between products when formulation changes are made
Effect of process changes on flavor and other quality attributes
Consumer acceptability of products
Off-flavors caused by additives or pesticides

[30] This and many other procedures are described in the "Official Methods of Analysis of the Association of Analytical Chemists," 11th ed., 1970; see also "Laboratory Manual for Food Canners and Processors," vols. I, II, National Canners Association, AVI Publishing Company Westport, Conn., 1968.

Taste panels should be used as an integral part of a food quality control program. The Institute of Food Technologists has issued a Sensory Testing Guide[31] which contains a comprehensive description of various taste panel methods, the types of problems for which each should be used, and the methods of statistical analysis of the data. (See Section 12, under Sensory Qualities, for further discussion.)

QUALITY IMPROVEMENT

Many of the conventional techniques for quality improvement are used in this industry.[32] At State Agricultural Experiment Stations and company research farms, attention is focused on new product strains and hybrids, as well as pest and insect control for yield improvement. The latter takes the form of prevention in which the crop is afforded as much protection as possible from planting through harvest, processing, and distribution.

Preventive quality control is an important aspect of any quality control program, but it is especially important in the quality control of perishable foods. For perishable foods such as fresh fruits and vegetables, effective disease and insect control, together with care in harvesting and handling, are important in preventing quality deficiencies and product waste. A useful quality control program at this stage will minimize quality downgrading and maximize the proportion of total production that meets the top quality standards.

Measurement and reduction of product waste is an important function of quality control. In quality control programs for perishable foods, waste measurement can be done at two points, in the field and in the packinghouse. Realistic goals for maximum product waste should be established by management. Quality control periodically measures total product waste, and when it exceeds the desired level, a detailed inspection of waste is made to determine causes, thus providing the basis for corrective action. This detailed record of waste causes is made only after the gross waste exceeds 8%. Such studies can be made on a sampling basis, in this case samples of 100 pounds taken randomly throughout one day's operation.[33]

QUALITY REPORTING

Periodic reports summarizing key quality information should be prepared and distributed to operating and top management.[34] There must be an orderly system of summarizing the basic data. Some individual should be charged with the responsibility for reviewing the summarized data and for selecting those items which are worthy of analysis and reporting. The data summarization can be manual or, if the volume warrants, computerized. The computation of standard deviations and significant differences should be an integral part of a computer program. An intermediate summary form of some kind is needed if the summarization is to be done clerically. Forms that have been carefully prepared may permit much of the summarization of the basic inspection record to be done by the inspectors themselves. Figure 31-8 shows a summary report used for perishable products.

These data, when summarized on a weekly basis and after both tabular and graphic interpretations of the key data are made, will provide management with

[31] Dawson, E. H., Sensory Testing Guide for Panel Evaluation of Foods and Beverages, *Food Technology*, vol. 18, No. 8, pp. 25–31, 1964. See also Section 12, under Sensory Qualities.

[32] See Section 16, Quality Improvement; Section 27, Design and Analysis of Experiments; and Section 27A, Evolutionary Operations.

[33] See Section 19, Documentation, Configuration Management, relative to record forms design combining sampling instructions and data recording.

[34] See also Section 21, under Executive Reports on Quality.

QUALITY SUMMARY: ICEBERG LETTUCE

Type Inspection	City		Brand		Type Pack		No. Heads Inspected	
RETAIL	Arlington, Massachusetts				Soft Wrap		6	

Quality Score	Avg. Firmness (Index)			Avg. Head Dia. (In.)	Dia.Min. Max.		Week Ending
57	53			5.4	5.1" - 5.7"		9/5/70

Defect Name	Defect Code	Heads Affected at Indicated Severity									Points Deducted	
		Total		Trace		Light		Medium		Severe		Avg. Per
		No.	%	No.	%	No.	%	No.	%	No.	%	Total	Head Insp.
Bitterness	BI	2	33			2	33					4	0.7
Torn Leaf	TL	6	100	1	17	1	17	2	33	2	33	27	4.5
Excessive Wrapper Leaves	EW	1	17	1	17							1	0.2
Bruised Leaves	LB	5	83	5	83							15	2.5
Bruised Midrib	BR	5	83	3	50	2	33					21	3.5
Close Trim	CT	2	33	1	17	1	17					9	1.5
Dirt	DT	3	50	2	33			1	17			18	3.0
Pink Rib	PR	1	17	1	17							3	0.5
Too Soft	TS	2	33	1	17	1	17					9	1.5
Undersize	US	4	67	2	33	2	33					18	3.0
Decay	DY	1	17							1	17	72	12.0
Insect Damage	ID	2	33	1	17	1	17					36	6.0
Rusty Brown Discoloration	RD	1	17			1	17					24	4.0

Fig. 31-8 Quality summary: iceberg lettuce.

the facts needed for evaluating quality performance and taking corrective action. A brief summary consisting of three to five points of one or two sentences each should be included at the beginning of the report.

BIBLIOGRAPHY

Processed Foods

Bakunts, G., Quality Determination Method for Minced Meat, *Myasnaya Industriya USSR*, vol. 40, No. 12, pp. 9–10, 1969.

Duran, H. L., Quality Control during the Canning of Vegetables, *Alimentaria*, vol. 6, No. 26, 39–47, 1969.

Perishable Foods

Becker, F., Quality Control and Evaluation of Butter, *Deutsche Molkerei-Zeitung*, vol. 91, No. 26, pp. 1182–84, 1970.

Fiqueiredo, M. P., de, Quality Assurance of Liquid Eggs, *Food Technology*, vol. 25, No. 7, pp. 730–736, 1971.

Fox, M., and A. Kramer, Objective Tests for Determining Quality of Fresh Green Beans, *Food Technology*, vol. 20, No. 12, 88–92, 1966.

Container Fill

Beazley, C. C., and G. J. Boehmer, The Use of Statistical Methods in Package Net Weight Studies, *Food Quality Control*, vol. 2, No. 1, pp. 7–16, 1961.

Bonner, B., Legal and Statistical Aspects of Package Weight Control, *Food Quality Control*, vol. 1, No. 2, pp. 3–13, 1961.

Lieberman, W. L., Methods for Identifying Filled Containers with Filling Heads, *Food Quality Control*, vol. 3, No. 2, pp. 9–10, 1963.

Rounds, H. G., The Major Considerations in the Problem of Package Weight Control, *Food Quality Control*, vol. 2, No. 3, pp. 17–25, 1962.

Rowe, G. A., Statistics of Determining a Shortage, *Food Quality Control,* vol. 13, pp. 7–11, May 1966.

Stack, P. W., and P. R. Humbaugh, Improved Weight Control of Volumetric Packing Lines, *Journal of Industrial Engineering,* vol. 19, No. 6, 285–288, 1968.

Way, C. B., Fill Control in the Canning Industry, *ASQC Convention Transactions,* vol. 9, pp. 505–512, 1955.

Inspection

Francis, F. J., and F. M. Clydesdale, Colour Measurement of Foods, *Food Products Development,* vol. 3, No. 8, pp. 44–54, 1969.

Goldman, G. E., Verification and Food Processing, *Food Quality Control,* vol. 12, pp. 3–5, September 1965.

Sampling

Bartlett, R. P., Jr., and J. B. Wegener, Sampling Plans Developed by the USDA for Inspection of Processed Fruits and Vegetables, *Food Technology,* vol. 11, No. 10, pp. 526–532, 1957.

Filipello, F., Random vs. Stratified Sampling Methods for Tomato Inspection, *Food Technology,* vol. 11, pp. 434–436, August 1957.

Microbiological

Elliott, R., "Microbiological Standards for Meat and Poultry Products under Federal Inspection, Symposium on Microbiological Standards for Foods," Food Research Institute, University of Wisconsin, Madison, Wis., Apr. 9, 1969.

Mossel, D. A. A., M. A. R. Salazar, and H. L. O. Indacochea, Control of Microbiological Quality in the Food Industry, *Alimentaria,* vol. 8, No. 36, pp. 5–56, 1971.

Peeler, J. T., An Application of Mathematical Sampling Models to Microbiological Inspection, *Food Quality Control,* vol. 29, pp. 3–8, November 1969.

Smith, F. R., "Microbiological Controls in the Frozen Foods Industry," presented at The Food Research Institute, University of Wisconsin, Madison, Wis., Apr. 9, 1969.

Stearman, R.L., Statistical Concepts in Microbiology, *Bacteriological Reviews,* vol. 19, No. 3, pp. 160–215, 1955.

Cereals and Baking

Cirilli, G., Analysis Applied to Flour Milling, Macaroni and Feed Industries, III, Macaroni Analysis, *Tecnica Molitoria,* vol. 20, No. 10, pp. 272–276, 1969. (Italian Abstracts in English in *Food Science* and *Technical Abstracts.*)

Cookson, M. A., Product Control in the Bakery. Consumers Want Consistent Quality, *Baking Industry Journal,* vol. 3, No. 2, pp. 19–20, 1970.

Fiqueiredo, M. P. de, Total Quality Control in the Baking Industry, *ASQC Technical Conference Transactions,* New York, 1966, pp. 835–855.

Fornari, D., The Control of Macaroni and Oven Product Quality, *Tecnica Molitoria,* vol. 20, No. 2, pp. 8–20, 1969. (Italian Abstracts in English in *Food Science* and *Technical Abstracts.*)

Confectionery Products

Habersaat, F. C., Quality Control of Confectionery Products Containing Alcohol, *Susswaren,* vol. 14, No. 5, pp. 218–224, 1970. (German Abstracts in English in *Food Science* and *Technical Abstracts.*)

Howat, G. R., Chocolate—Maintaining Quality, *Process Biochemistry,* vol. 5, No. 5, pp. 63–64, 1970 (Cadbury Bros. Ltd., 4 Savile Row, London).

Meursing, E.H., Quality Control of Cocoa Powder: Methods for Analysing 7 Properties, *Manufacturing Confectioner* vol. 49, No. 11, pp. 43–47, 1969.

Vittadini, A., Quality Control in Confectionery Industries, *Industrie Alimentari,* vol. 8, No. 2, pp. 59–68, 1969. (Italian Abstracts in English in *Food Science* and *Technical Abstracts.*)

Packaging

Barnes, J. E., Span Plan Procedures in Polyethylene Manufacture, *Food Quality Control,* vol. 3,.No. 1, pp. 3–16, October 1962.

Beamish, J. R., Quality Control in the Corrugated Container Industry, *Food Quality Control,* vol. 3, No. 2, pp. 11–23, January 1963.

Lang, K. F., Maintaining Quality of Glass Containers through Acceptance Sampling, *Food Quality Control*, vol. 14, pp. 3–7, 1966.

Morrissey, K. C., Quality Control in Can Manufacture and Its Relation to Product Quality, *Food Quality Control*, vol. 12, pp. 7–9, September 1965.

Statistical Design and Sensory Evaluation

Bradley, R. A., Statistical Designs for Taste Test Panels, *ASQC Technical Conference Transactions*, 1955, pp. 621–626.

Carroll, M. B., The Use of Subjective Evaluation in Product Control and Development, *Food Quality Control*, vol. 3, No. 3, pp. 8–18, 1963.

Dawson, E. H., Sensory Testing of Foods and Beverages, *Food Quality Control*, No. 15, pp. 3–6, January 1967.

Kramer, A., and L. P. Ditman, A Simplified Variables Taste Panel Method for Detecting Flavor Changes in Vegetables Treated with Pesticides, *Food Technology*, vol. 10, No. 3, pp. 155–159, 1956.

Mahoney, C. H., H. L. Stier, and E. A. Crosby, Evaluating Flavor Differences in Canned Foods, I, Genesis of the Simplified Procedure for Making Flavor Difference Tests; II, Fundamentals of the Simplified Procedure, *Food Technology*, vol. 11, No. 9, pp. 29–43, 1957.

Pangborn, R. M., Use and Misuse of Sensory Methodology, *Food Quality Control*, vol. 15, pp. 7–12, January 1967.

Settergren, R. C., Statistical Evaluation of Batch-type Operation, *Food Quality Control*, vol. 1, No. 2, pp. 14–18, 1961.

Stewart, R. A., Sensory Evaluation and Quality Assurance, *Food Technology*, vol. 25, No. 4, pp. 401–404, 1971.

Von Sydow, E., Flavor—A Chemical or Psychophysical Concept? *Food Technology*, vol. 25, pp. 40–44, January 1971.

Way, C. B., Statistical Quality Control Applications in the Food Industry, *Industrial Quality Control*, vol. 17, No. 11, pp. 30–34, 1961.

General and Miscellaneous

Bowman, A. P., Quality Control as a Management Tool, *Food Quality Control*, vol. 3, No. 2, pp. 2–9, 1963.

Geary, Nathaniel L., The Self-certification Pilot Program, *Food Quality Control*, No. 27, pp. 1–5, July 1969.

Girardot, Norman F., Methods of Measuring Consumer Preferences, *Transactions ASQC Regional Conference (Hamilton-Middletown and Cincinnati Sections)*, January 27, 1962, 12 pp.

Hebden, W. H., The Role of the Quality Control Department in the Food Industry, *Food Technology in New Zealand*, vol. 5, No. 12, pp. 492–496, 1970.

Hopkins, E. W., Life and Quality of Food Products, *ASQC Technical Conference Transactions*, 1964, pp. 209–214.

Jones, J. W., Application of Quality Control Procedures in the Food Industry, *Food Quality Control*, vol. 3, No. 3, pp. 1–4, 1963.

Kramer, A., Experience with Some Novel Quality Control Applications in the U.S. Food Industry, *Maryland Processors' Report—Fruits & Vegetables*, vol. 15, p. 4, October 1969.

Mrak, Emil M., Food Control in the Seventies, Talk at Food Research Institute, University of Wisconsin, Madison, Wis., Mar. 31, 1970.

Schutz, H. G., A Food Action Rating Scale for Measuring Food Acceptance, *Journal of Food Science*, vol. 30, No. 2, pp. 365–374, 1964.

Stier, H. L., Quality Control Practices and Problems in Food Processing," *Quality Control & Consumers Conference Papers*, Rutgers, N.J., 1957, pp. 21–23.

Szilagyi, J. A., et al., Development and extension of the Official Food Quality Control System, *Elelmiszervizsgalati Kozlemenyek*, vol. 16, Nos. 4/5, pp. 173–180, 1970. (Hungarian) English summary.

Victor, R. D., "Computer-automated Quality Control in Food Processing," *20th Annual Technical Conference, ASQC Food and Allied Industries Division*, New York, June 1–3, 1966.

Willinsky, M., et al., Quality Control, *Food in Canada*, vol. 30, No. 7, pp. 14–26, 1970.

Wright, W., M. Fracchia, and H. Rosoff, The Sensory Evaluation of Beer, *Food Quality Control*, vol. 3, No. 3, pp. 4–7, 1963.

Ziemba, J. V., QC and Sanitation Key Efficient, *Food Engineering*, vol. 42, No. 6, pp. 88–90, 1970.

Section **32**

Drug and Allied Industries

H. LATHAM BREUNIG, PH.D.

Eli Lilly and Company

INTRODUCTION

The "Drug and Allied Industries" (DAI) recognize four broad categories of products:

1. *Medicines for humans,* which may be administered either internally or externally, in both the preventive and therapeutic senses. This classification embraces "such terms as drug, substance, preparation, derivative, mixture and admixture."[1] Such medicines are covered by the general designation of pharmaceuticals. In addition this classification includes medicines of a biological nature, e.g., vaccines, toxoids, and serums.

2. *Medicines for animals,* which may be used not only for preventive and therapeutic purposes in the veterinary sense but also as feed additives to modify physiological response, i.e., growth stimulants.

3. *Cosmetics* for cleansing, adornment, or disguise. These are chiefly for external application, and may include mechanical devices as well as chemical substances. Cosmetics are also used in the therapeutic sense, e.g., acne treatment, nail hardeners.

4. *Agronomical and horticultural* chemicals, which are applied to soil, crops, and grasses and include insecticides, fungicides, and herbicides. A number of crops so treated may eventually reach human usage by indirect means.

The main activity of DAI consists of converting raw materials of natural or syn-

---

[1] Davis, H., The Quality Control of Medicine, *The Pharmaceutical Journal (England),* vol. 27, February 1965.

thetic origin into forms suitable for administration to humans, animals, and crops, in accordance with some intended purpose.   For instance, medicines for humans may be administered in one or more of over 35 different pharmaceutical dosage forms ranging from aerosols and ampoules through lotions and ointments to tinctures

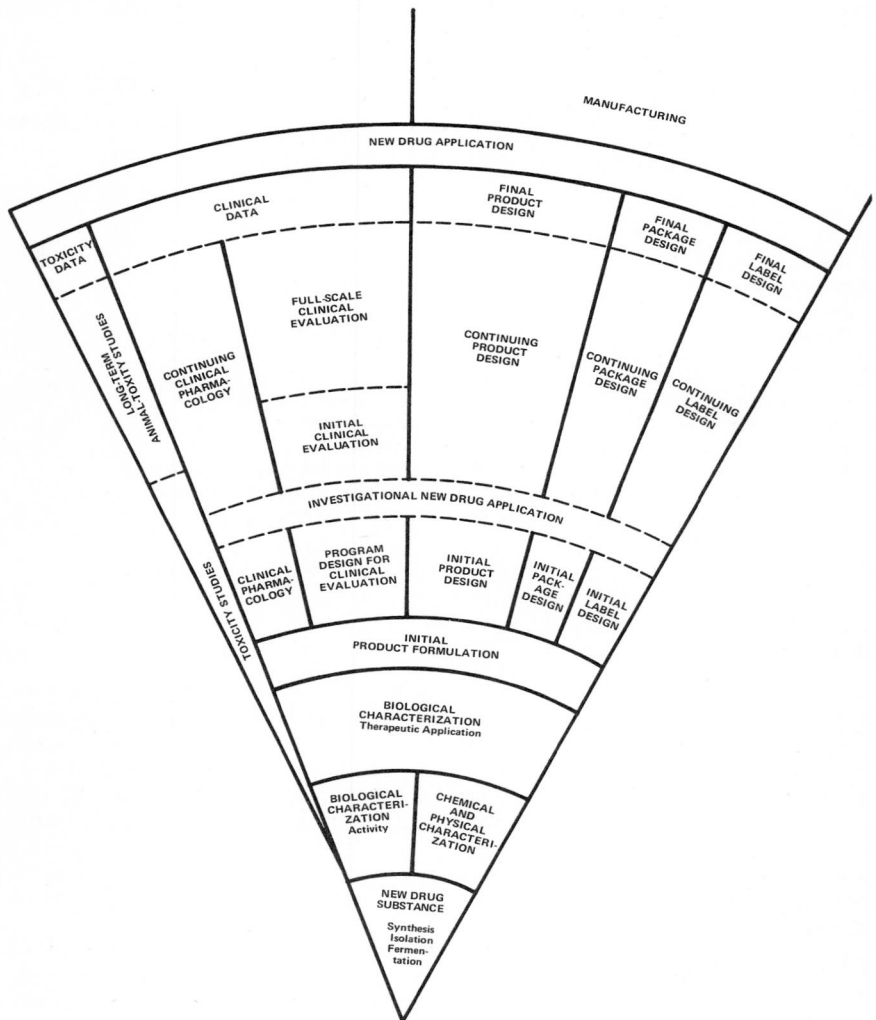

Fig. 32-1 Evolution of a pharmaceutical product. *(Courtesy Eli Lilly and Company.)*

and tablets.   More than one strength of each may be marketed.   Cosmetic items number in the tens of thousands.

The drug and allied industries possess a basic similarity to the chemical process industry.   As a result, many of the techniques discussed in Section 29 are applicable to DAI.   However, the DAI also differ from the chemical process industries in two major ways:

1. Techniques have been developed from ancient times to the present day for enhancing the bioavailability of chemical or biological ingredients of interest through incorporation into the different pharmaceutical and cosmetic dosage forms. These permit the active medicament to be assimilated at varying rates into the organism following administration by one of several routes such as by mouth or other bodily orifice, by injection, or by topical application.

2. Since DAI products are intended, either directly or indirectly, for human usage, and since the consumer is rarely in a position to evaluate quality ("the tablet you take is one which has not been assayed"), considerations of identity, efficacy, bioavailability, and safety have led to a vast system of voluntary control procedures as well as involuntary governmental controls.

This Section identifies and stresses those aspects and techniques of the quality function which are special or critical to DAI.

NEW PRODUCT EVOLUTION

The evolution of a new drug product follows rather closely the path depicted in Figure 32-1. Experience with many such new product evolutions has led to a subdivision of this path into four relatively standardized stages: New Drug Discovery, Development, Investigational New Drug (IND), and New Drug Application (NDA). These distinctions are a logical result of differences in the following stages:

1. The scientific and technological disciplines inherent in each stage

2. The makeup of the managerial teams needed to guide the projects through the stage

3. The organizational groupings of the scientists and technologists

4. The combinations of outside participation, e.g., medical doctors, hospitals, government regulators, etc.

These stages are also "time-phased," and the transitions are marked by "milestones", e.g., transfer of jurisdiction to different committees, reassignment of principal responsibility, submission to government agencies. Figure 32-2 shows schematically how this time-phasing proceeds from research to production.

New Drug Discovery   This stage is concerned with creating or identifying new drug substances which generate biological activity able to combat specific ailments for which existing medication may be inadequate or absent. Pharmaceutical companies spend a great deal of effort in investigating a tremendous store of potential agents to find those few which are active in a promising way. Extensive screening programs are carried out whereby large numbers (i.e., 3,000 per year) of compounds may be submitted to initial testing. Group screening increases the rate at which compounds may be tested, since a high proportion of compounds are "inactive" yet replication must be adequate to control the number of "false positives" passed on for further testing. In such extensive searching an incidental role is played by serendipity; i.e., a synthesized compound found to be ineffective for the original intended purpose may turn out to be useful for some other purpose.

The same compound may be submitted to several screens through multistage sequential procedures for such drug activity as:

Anticonvulsant	Antitumor
Hypotensive	Hypoglycemic
Diuretic	Antibacterial
Analgesic	Antiviral

to name a few of the possible screens.

This screening effort applies not only to new compounds but also to molecular modification of existing compounds or the formation of new salts or derivatives. These new compounds may be of natural origin from plants, animal glands, or mold

spores, or they may be strictly synthetic chemicals. Essential areas in the research effort are toxicology and pharmacology, which investigate, respectively:
1. The possible dangers inherent in the new drug to biological systems[2]
2. The physiological action of the new drug substance on specific animal species
    Research in the cosmetics field encompasses such areas as application of new polymers to hairsets and skin creams, developing new synthetic fragrances and colorings, and the effect of hormones and vitamins on the skin.

DOMESTIC PHARMACEUTICALS

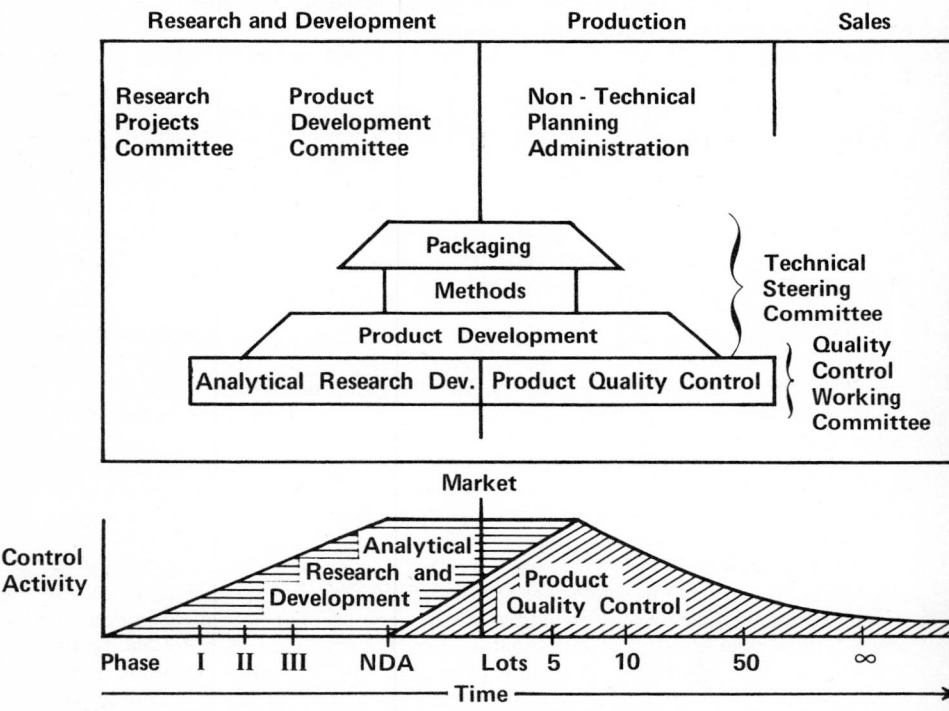

Fig. 32-2 Time-phased development of a pharmaceutical product. *(Courtesy Eli Lilly and Company.)*

Development Once it has been agreed, on the basis of biological, chemical, and toxicological considerations, and on therapeutic application (Figure 32-1) that a compound has potential for human, animal, or other appropriate use, the project enters the development stage. This transition commonly includes a change in guidance from a Research Project Committee to a Product Development Committee (Figure 32-2). The objective of the development stage is to prepare the initial product formulation and to conduct the other developmental activities prerequisite to an Investigational New Drug application (see below).
Since drug substances are seldom administered in their pure form, a critical part of the development is the incorporation of the drug into an appropriate delivery

[2] A notable example of failure of the test battery to detect teratological defects was that of the tranquilizer Thalidomide.

vehicle and dosage form for administration. Scientific development of dosage forms has emerged (from empiricism) as a complex and vital aspect of "quality of design" or formulation.

The end objective of the product development is a formulation which has an optimal selection of product components and processing steps to attain essential physical properties such as solubility, dispersibility, compressibility, particle size, and sensitivity to environments, all influential in dosage form or in therapeutic efficacy.

Development of tests to demonstrate suitability of the dosage form to the physiological environment is likewise an essential part of the development program; e.g., intravenous injections must not produce hemolysis; skin preparations should possess appropriate rheological properties; tablets need to disintegrate within definite limits under the conditions existing in the gastrointestinal tract. The resulting parameters such as tonicity, pH, specific gravity, surface tension, sedimentation rate, or friability provide guideposts for product utility and quality.

In addition, product formulations and dosage forms should be designed so that meeting the quality requirements does not depend on processes which are unstable or overly sensitive to changes in raw materials. Neither should the tolerances on materials or processes tax the limits of known technology.[3]

Following the establishment of an appropriate delivery vehicle, the analytical research and development is charged with developing assay methods for the drug substance in both the delivery vehicles and the body fluids.

Investigational New Drug (IND)   Once the new compound has met the requirements of development and animal experimentation stages, it becomes a candidate for an Investigational New Drug (IND). It is now ready for its first trials on human beings or, in the case of animal products, on an appropriate animal species. For agricultural products, field trials are in order. For cosmetics, testing is more or less subjective through consumer preference testing.

The trials for an IND are conducted in three phases (Figure 32-2) which are spelled out in the Code of Federal Regulations[4] issued by the Food and Drug Administration (FDA) of the Department of Health, Education and Welfare (HEW), which must approve an application for an IND before trials may begin. These phases begin at certain identifiable milestones:

1 When the new drug is first introduced into man. Up to this point only animal and *in vitro* data are available.

2. When initial trials begin on a limited number of patients for specific disease control or for prophylaxis purposes.

3. When clinical trials are set up to assess the drug's safety and effectiveness, and to establish optimum dosage schedules.

At certain points during the IND trials the FDA may request additional information based upon inputs from the investigators. This close regulatory supervision is based on the experience that "each new drug is unique in its therapeutic and toxic effects, and is not amenable to testing to standards applicable to previously existing drugs."[5]

Clinical trials must be conducted on a scale sufficient to establish the dangers and

---

[3] The foregoing three paragraphs have been paraphrased or quoted from Cooper, Jack, Quality Design and Quality Maintenance, *Control Procedures in Drug Production,* Proceedings of a Seminar, University of Wisconsin, Madison, Wis., July 17–22, 1966.

[4] "Code of Federal Regulations," Title 21, Part 130, Government Printing Office, Washington, D.C., 20402, 1968.

[5] Kahn, A. R., "The Role of Standards in Biomedical Instrumentation," Presented at the 25th Annual Technical Conference, American Society for Quality Control, Chicago, Ill., May 19–21, 1971.

effectiveness of the new drug before it may be marketed.   Such trials protect the patients and physicians from product claims which are not based on established testing protocols.

Biological products in the investigational stage, as well as during subsequent processing and distribution, are covered by the biologics standards of the U.S. Public Health Service Act[6] which controls vaccines, sera, and toxins.   Cosmetics are at present not covered by similar preclearance regulations, but the industry has developed its own guidelines.

In addition to the mandatory phases of the IND, it is common for companies to monitor the performance of drugs after approval of the NDA.   The approach varies, but always involves investigation of reports of adverse reaction.   In addition, there may be further studies to substantiate or rule out suspected toxicity, and to extend claims of safety and efficacy where indicated,[7] carried out by teams consisting of:

1. A principal clinical investigator who provides active leadership to the project
2. A biostatistician
3. An extensive array of support personnel: physicians, scientists, research fellows, nurses, laboratory technicians, secretarial staff, etc.[8]

Aside from reviews by the cognizant Product Development Committee, the trials are governed by guiding principles both scientific and ethical.[9,10,11,12]

Paralleling the IND studies are the in-plant studies in several areas (Figure 32-1). Short-and long-term toxicity studies continue.   Analytical development chemists are working to devise the best assay methods for eventual quality control of the drug in its various dosage forms (Figure 32-2).   Development of appropriate packaging forms is going on, as is planning of descriptive literature.   Studies are being carried on to determine product stability in appropriate containers and if expiration dating will be needed.   Development studies of chemical manufacturing capabilities, and improvement of dosage form are also part of the continuing effort.

New products in the areas of veterinary science normally go through the same IND stages as those for human medicine.[13]   Pesticide control is covered by regulations of the U.S. Department of Agriculture.[14]   Animal feeds containing drugs are also regulated.[15]

New Drug Application (NDA)   Once the new drug has successfully gone through the IND phases, an NDA is filed with the Food and Drug Administration.   The requirements are spelled out in the code of Federal Regulations.[16]   At the same time, all

[6] Biologics Standards, Public Health Service Regulations, *Federal Register,* vol. 35, No. 171, Washington, D.C., Sept. 2, 1970.

[7] DeHaan, Raymond, Clinical Studies to Evaluate Safety and Efficacy in Phase IV Investigations, *Drug Information Bulletin,* vol. 2, No. 3, p. 84, 1968.

[8] Martin, Christopher M., Controlled Evaluation of Drugs in Man, *Drug Information Bulletin,* vol. 1, p. 101, 1967.

[9] Martin, Christopher M., Controlled Evaluation of Drugs in Man, *Drug Information Bulletin,* vol. 1, p. 102, 1967.

[10] World Health Organization, Principles for the Clinical Evaluation of Drugs, *World Health Organization Technical Reports,* Series 403, 1968.

[11] World Health Organization, Principles for Pre-clinical Testing of Drug Safety, *World Health Organization Technical Report,* Series 134, 1966.

[12] Herrick, A. D., and McK. Cattel, "Clinical Testing of New Drugs," Revere Publishing Co., New York, 1965.

[13] Veterinary Biological Law, Virus, Serum and Toxin Act, 1944, Part F, Title III, Public Law 410, Code of Federal Regulations, Title 9, Department of Health, Education and Welfare.

[14] Federal Insecticide, Fungicide and Rodenticide Act (1947), Code of Federal Regulations, Title 7, Part 162, Government Printing Office.

[15] Food Additives (Animal Feeds) Law, Code of Federal Regulations, Title 21, Parts 121–146, U.S. Department of Health, Education and Welfare.

[16] *Ibid.,* Part 130.

pertinent supporting documentary evidence is submitted to the FDA. During the FDA review of the NDA, development work continues, since the FDA frequently requests additional supporting evidence or asks for changes in the proposed promotional literature.

Once the NDA is approved, the new drug goes into manufacturing, marketing, and usage. These large-scale activities create new information pertinent to the NDA but not available during the much smaller scale of manufacture and usage inherent in the clinical trials. There is provision in the FDA regulations to permit filing of amendments to the NDA in the light of experience gained during manufacture, marketing, and usage, as well as from continuing developmental studies. The CFR spells out requirements for records and reports concerning experience, such as number of dosages put out, incidence of side effects, and complaints on drugs for which an approval is in effect.

The intent of the foregoing kinds of regulations has been to broaden the base of clinical and governmental judgment weighing the benefit to risk ratio for potential patients. On the other hand it has, in many cases, lengthened the time required for development and may, in addition, discourage some developments altogether.

QUALITY OF CONFORMANCE

In common with certain other industries requiring destructive testing, e.g., automobile tires, food products, a striking feature of DAI is its virtual inability to test the individual units of product before they reach the consumer because of the destructive nature of chemical and biological tests.

Because of safety requirements in human and animal use, the DAI has developed elaborate control procedures which are all-pervasive as to plant environment, facilities, materials, processes, personnel identity, documentation, and packaging.

Sources of Specifications   Control procedures used in the industry are in response to two main sets of requirements:

1. The unique specifications for individual drug products set forth in approved NDAs, the compendia (see below), and still other sources of product definition.

2. Various regulatory requirements of multiple origin

The FDA Regulations.   In 1963, the Food and Drug Administration published regulations concerning Good Manufacturing Practice (GMP) for finished pharmaceuticals which largely recognized industry standards adopted by the Pharmaceutical Manufacturers Association in 1961. These regulations, representing a consensus, were amended in 1965 and revised in 1971.[17] The broad scope of these regulations is indicated by the topic headings:

Definitions	Production and control procedures
Finished pharmaceuticals; manufacturing practice	Product containers and their components
Buildings	Packaging and labeling
Equipment	Laboratory controls
Personnel	Distribution records
Components	Stability
Master production and control records	Expiration dating
	Complaint files

The FDA has issued a handbook containing selected reference material supple-

[17] Good Manufacturing Practices, Code of Federal Regulations, Title 21, Chapter 1, Subchapter C, Part 133, *Federal Register,* vol. 36, No. 10, January 1971.

menting and amplifying a number of the topics listed above.[18] Some aspects of DAI manufacturing practice are demanding in the extreme. An example is the environmental requirements for control of contamination, and especially, for maintaining sterility. Such requirements are all-pervasive, affecting not only the material, containers, closures, etc. The very design of manufacturing space and processes must be special, extending to the plan of airflow, control over quality of the air itself, control over employee-originated contamination, etc. For some related examples, see Sections 31, Food and Allied Industries, and Section 36B, Plastic Film Quality, under the pertinent headings.

Compendia. In addition to the GMP, the manufacture of some pharmaceutical products is governed by two major compendia: the United States Pharmacopeia (USP)[19] and the National Formulary (NF).[20] Although privately published, these compendia have achieved legal status (through being incorporated by reference in the Food, Drug and Cosmetic Act), and all manufacturers are required to follow the provisions therein. These compendia are reissued at 5-year intervals, with supplements being issued every 6 months or so.

The compendia define officially accepted methods of assay, certain minimum standards, e.g., tolerances on percent active ingredient, minimal sampling plans, and still other standards. However, it is quite common for ethical manufacturers to establish in-plant controls and tolerances more strict than the minimal standards set out in the compendia.

Most countries have agencies which are the national equivalent of the FDA, and which monitor products of their DAI, e.g., the National Institute of Pharmacology and Bromatology of Argentina. In addition, many of these countries have their own official compendia, e.g., the British Pharmacopeia.[21] Multinational companies are thereby required to conform to the regulatory requirements in force in each country in which they are operating.

Other Regulations. Regulations issued by the FDA to implement the cosmetics part of the Food, Drug and Cosmetic Act are summarized in Food, Drug and Cosmetic Law Reports.[22] The cosmetics industry is not covered by official requirements for premarketing clearance, processing, or distribution but has developed its own Quality Assurance Guidelines (QAG)[23] which have been adopted by the Cosmetics, Toiletry and Fragrance Association. These are quite similar, in form, to the Good Manufacturing Practices of the drug group. These are minimum requirements, and as with the drug group, the manufacturer of high-quality product tends to develop his own system of stricter controls.

The Pesticides Law,[24] the Veterinary Biological Law,[24] and the Animal Drug Food Additive (Animal Feeds)[24] Law cover these respective areas, not only for preclearance but also for processing and distribution.

Government Purchases. Still other standards are those established by the government not in its role as a regulator, but in its role as a purchaser. For example, the Defense Personnel Support Center (DPSC) has issued its own standards,[25]

[18] FDA Bureau of Voluntary Compliance, "FDA Drug Industry Workshop Handbook," U.S. Department of Health, Education and Welfare, Food and Drug Administration, 1968.

[19] United States Pharmacopeia XVIII, United States Pharmacopeial Convention, Bethesda, Md., 1970.

[20] National Formulary XIII, American Pharmaceutical Association, Washington, D.C., 1970.

[21] "British Pharmacopeia," The Pharmaceutical Press, London, England, 1968.

[22] "Food Drug Cosmetic Law Reports," Commerce Clearing House, Inc., New York.

[23] "Quality Assurance Guidelines," Quality Control Reports, Wallace Werble, Publisher, Washington, D.C., February 1971.

[24] See footnotes 13, 14, and 15, under Investigational New Drugs, above.

[25] DPSC Standards for the Manufacture of Drugs, Pharmaceuticals and "Biological Products," Defense Support Personnel Center, Philadelphia, Pa., September 1968.

which may be different from those of the USP, NF, or FDA. These standards are used as a basis for qualifying drug manufacturers and packagers in accordance with the requirements of the Armed Services.

Raw Material Control   The concepts of vendor quality control as discussed in Section 10 are generally applicable to DAI. The emphasis is on completeness of specifications, exacting requirements for purity, close control of material identity, and completeness of documentation. Concepts in common use include multiple vendors, vendor evaluation based upon questionnaires and site visits, and technical assistance.

Containers, closures, and similar general-use supplies may create some annoying and even serious problems. Manufacturers of such supplies sometimes have difficulty in applying to a small portion of their output the exceptional controls demanded by the DAI, and it may be necessary for a DAI company to set up added operations to meet such special needs as stability and freedom from contamination. In other cases the DAI company gives up on trying to purchase these supplies from the large vendors, and turns to specialty vendors instead.

Many vendor plants making critical raw materials for DAI are subject to FDA inspections similar to those conducted for the DAI group. There are other special situations, some of which are discussed in the literature.[26,27,28,29]   The practice of exchange of assay data between vendors and the DAI companies is to be recommended.

Process Controls   Generally, the available techniques of process control (see Section 23) are applicable, and largely adequate to the DAI. During the bulk stages of the batch processing, the control techniques have much in common with those used in chemical processes generally (see Section 29). Figure 32-3 shows a flow diagram of production of an antibiotic, and illustrates the extent of the control problem for a complex process.

As the bulk stages progress into the final stages, the resulting dosages involve very large numbers for which conventional sampling techniques, control charts, etc., are fully applicable.

Bulk sampling is conventional and is generally covered by the discussions of Section 25 A. However, sample sizes at the dosage stages have been a thorny problem. The assays are costly, and time delays are created by assaying large samples.

The GMPs refer only to "representative" samples, while the DPSC standards go somewhat further and state that raw materials "shall be sampled by an experienced, knowledgeable person who is under the supervision of a qualified person in quality control," and for finished products, "Samples of each lot shall be selected on a random basis. . . ." Because of practical considerations relative to production and storage conditions the truly random sample is virtually impossible. So compromises need to be made. Various types of sampling schemes are discussed by Slonim.[30] Sampling from bulk containers may be carried out by "stratified random sampling" whereby the shipment or lot is divided into a beginning, a middle, and an end. Con-

[26] Piersma, Henry D., "Inspection Procedures in Quality Control Operations," First National Symposium on Drugs and Medicaments Control, National Institute of Pharmacology and Bromatology, Buenos Aires, Argentina, Nov. 2–7, 1969.

[27] Elkas, Robert W., Bulk Specifications for Process and Final Ingredient Materials, "Control Procedures in Drug Production," University of Wisconsin Bookstore, Madison, Wis., 1966.

[28] Byers, T. E., Legal Requirements for Domestic and Imported Raw Materials, "Control Procedures in Drug Production," University of Wisconsin Bookstore, Madison, Wis., 1966.

[29] Hopes, Ted M., Quality Control of Raw Materials, *Drug and Cosmetic Industry*, vol. 110, No. 4, p. 46, April 1972.

[30] Slonim, M. E., Sampling in a Nutshell, *Journal of the American Statistical Association*, vol. 52, p. 143, 1957.

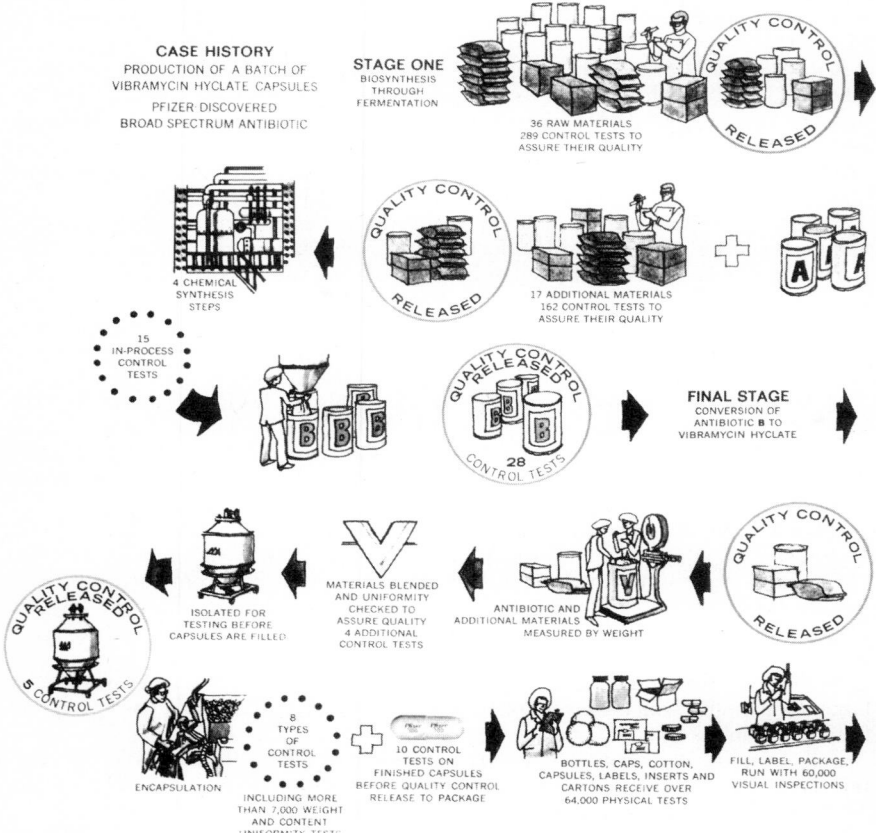

Fig. 32-3   Controls on an antibiotic production process. *(Courtesy Chas. Pfizer & Co., Inc.)*

tainers are randomly chosen from each stratum for sampling. The sample may or may not be composited, depending upon whether the material is in bulk powdered or similar form or whether the batch comprises containers or single dosage units, e.g., tablets or capsules which may need to be identified.

Sampling from production equipment such as tablet compression machines may be handled by "systematic sampling with a random start."

The question of sample size is a thorny one, and no general rules are applicable. The problem of sampling in a pharmaceutical house has been discussed by Breunig and King.[31] Military Standards 105D[32] and 414[33] relate sample size to lot size. These, however, take no account of a priori information concerning process capa-

[31] Breunig, H. L., and E. P. King, Acceptance Sampling of Finished Pharmaceutical Products, *Journal of Pharmaceutical Science,* vol. 51, p. 187, 1962.

[32] "Sampling Procedures and Tables for Inspection by Attributes," Military Standard 105D, Government Printing Office, Washington, D.C., 1963.

[33] "Sampling Procedures and Tables for Inspection by Variables for Percent Defective," Military Standard 414, Government Printing Office, Washington, D.C., 1957.

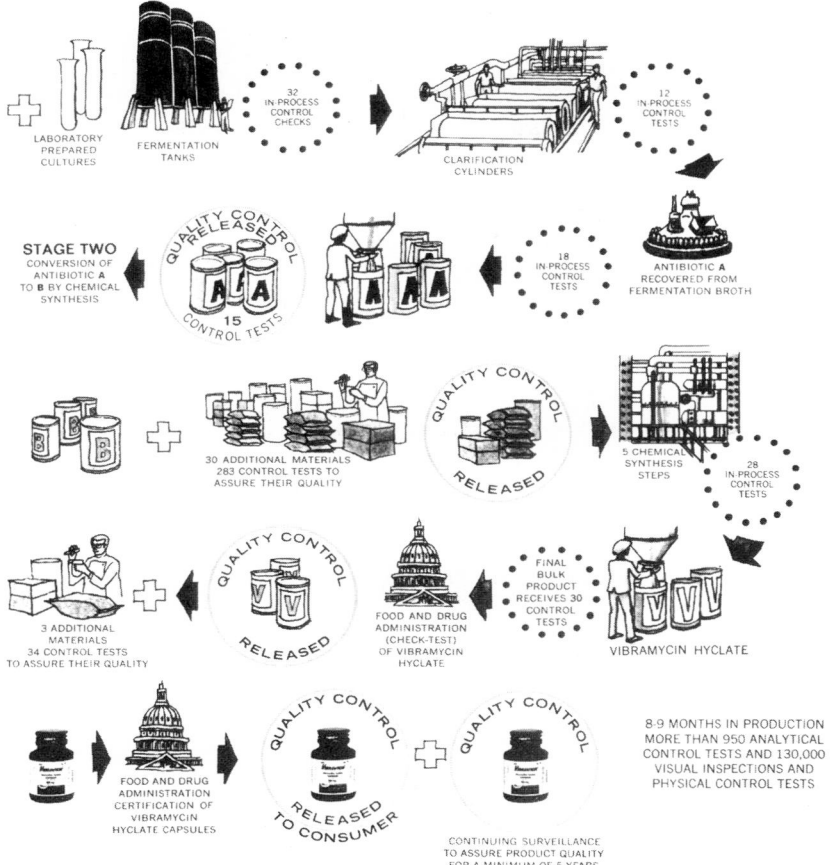

Fig. 32-3   *(Continued)*

bility or of preserving the order of manufacture and hence demand comparatively large samples, especially from the large lot sizes prevailing in the DAI.   Thus sample sizes at normal inspection levels become unreasonably large in the context of lot sizes of one million or more tablets.   So recourse must be made to "special inspection levels" with reduced sample sizes.   This increases the consumer's risk, but if the product is correctly manufactured in the first place, the AQLs (acceptable quality levels) become quite small and the risks are not unreasonable.   The dilemma of the pharmaceutical manufacturer is brought out by Olson and Lee.[34, 35]

The advent of automated testing and of computer analysis of the resulting data will in all likelihood make possible an extension of sampling of individual dosages by variables along with more effective use of the resulting data.

The introduction of high-speed packaging lines has put new demands on freedom

[34] Olson, T. N. T., and I. Lee, The Application of Statistical Methods in the Pharmaceutical Industry, *Journal of Pharmaceutical Science,* vol. 55, p. 1, 1966.

[35] For a general discussion, see Section 12, under How Much Inspection?

from bottle defects, missing bottle labels, etc. It is unlikely that these demands can be met by adjusting sample sizes. The likely road will be foolproofing the processes.

A critical aspect of DAI process controls is product identification and traceability. These controls are exercised by

1. Extensive documentation built around the lot number

2. Complete identification of the physical product as it progresses through the operations

3. Programs for accountability in the usage of materials and products, labels, containers, etc., as a redundant form of ensuring identity by matching inputs and outputs

Documentation   This is a special problem in DAI because of the overriding importance of product identity and product traceability. When a consumer suffers an adverse reaction from some DAI product, it is essential that all other products traceable to the same origin be identified and quarantined. This need and related needs are met by a highly developed system of lot numbers which are keyed to the batch system of production characteristic of DAI.

When a batch is formulated, a lot number is assigned, and a batch document is created to accumulate all data associated with that lot. These data include the input materials (which carry their own lot numbers), the process variables, the product assays, etc. The lot number is carried through into packaging so that the skid loads, cases, cartons, and bottles all carry the lot number. (All this is now part of the mandatory Good Manufacturing Practice.) The completed batch-production record bears the initials of every individual associated with the process from the weighing out of the ingredients through the release of the product by Quality Assurance. In the case of complex processes, the complete batch record can be a formidable document.

When the product is sold, the lot number is recorded so that it can be traced. In turn, the entire distribution chain records the lot number as the product progresses through wholesalers, retailers, e.g., hospital and community pharmacies, to the patient. An important step in product identification was taken when individual dosages were labeled to show (by code number) the identity of the drug in that dose. In this breakthrough, the systems concept was one of recognizing that product identity is critical all the way to the point of use by the patient, and that by applying this identification at the point of origin, the risk of errors is reduced for the entire series of subsequent opportunities for mistakes. Another development for identifying the product from manufacturer to patient has been the "unit dose package" in which each dose is packaged in a minicontainer (e.g., a sealed envelope) which identifies the contents.

In cases where a product recall must be made, the suspect lot numbers are broadcast to the distribution chain so that the product is quarantined. In extreme cases resort may be had to registered letters, telephone calls, visits, etc.

While many of the methods of documentation set out in Section 19 have application to DAI, there is much about DAI documentation that is unique to consumer products. The use of computers has considerably improved the efficiency of information assembly and retrieval. It is now entirely feasible to follow a drug and the derived product from the manufacturer through all processing and control stages on to the pharmacies and hospitals.

Control Laboratories   The Drug and Allied Industries maintain a number of laboratories to conduct assays of samples drawn from all stages of product progression: raw materials, in process, finished products. These control laboratories encompass a broad spectrum of professional disciplines, e.g., chemical, pharmacological, biological, microbiological, and are manned by trained personnel. Their assays provide essential facts on which to judge product conformance to specification. These same assays also provide a form of assurance that the manufacturing and other procedures have been followed.

The control laboratories are guided by the assay procedures of the official compendia and by the requirements set out in the approved NDA. In addition to these mandatory requirements, many control laboratories develop their own supplemental controls.

Operation of the control laboratories is to a large extent conventional, as discussed in Sections 12 and 13 and other general Sections of this Handbook. What is unique is the overwhelming importance of product identity, safety, and efficacy. All these require strict adherence to rigorous procedures.

During the 1960s, the control laboratories became involved in two movements of a revolutionary nature:

1. Automated assays, whereby manual manipulations are replaced by programmed operations, calculations, and readouts. This concept has already provided the means for making fast, economic assays on individual dosages, permitting larger samples, greater statistical validity, and shorter intervals for decision making.[36] In addition, the concept promises to contribute substantially to solving what was fast becoming a critical manpower shortage of trained laboratory technicians.

2. Computer analysis of assay data. This development has already proceeded into conventional computation of test averages, ranges, etc., for acceptance and control chart purposes.[37,38] In addition, extension is under way to provide for data storage and retrieval for a wide variety of purposes.[39]

Beyond these rather revolutionary developments, the control laboratories face a continuing need for development of new assay procedures as well as updating of existing procedures to take advantage of new scientific knowledge. This development work is usually done by a separate assay development group. Commonly this group reports to the Quality Control head (as does the control laboratory) to ensure close liaison.[40]

Stability; Expiration Dating   Drug manufacturers guarantee the stability of their products, in both the design and the conformance stages of product evolution.[41] In addition, much effort is devoted to quantifying the rates of degradation so as to be able to predict shelf life and establish expiration dates. Dramatic evidence of this effort is provided by the size of the "file" of products maintained by drug manufacturers to serve as a source of material for continuing stability testing. Further evidence is provided by the need for using computers to retrieve the data, calculate the regression equations, and schedule future assays.[42,43]

---

[36] A useful, extensive reference is *Annals of the New York Academy of Sciences,* vol. 130, Art. 2, pp. 483–868. This consists of the papers presented at the conference on Automation in Industrial Pharmaceutical Process and Quality Control. The 38 papers cover the choice of apparatus and the design of laboratory technique needed to automate a wide variety of assays.

[37] Gill, J. M., and S. P. Perone, Computer Automation of Gas Chromatography, *Journal of Chromatography Science,* vol. 7, p. 709, 1969.

[38] Tochner, M., J. A. Magneson, and L. Z. Saderman, Time Sharing—A Powerful Approach for Gas Chromatographic Data Reduction, *Journal of Chromatography Science,* vol. 7, p. 740, 1969.

[39] Schwartz, M., An Automated Record Keeping and Data Retrieval System for a Quality Control Laboratory, *Quality Progress,* vol. 5, No. 1, p. 22, 1972.

[40] Piersma, Henry D., Quality Control Looks to Research and Development, "Control Procedures in Drug Production," University of Wisconsin Bookstore, Madison, Wis., 1966.

[41] Lachman, L., H. A., Lieberman, and J. L. Kanig, "The Theory and Practice of Industrial Pharmacy," chap. 23, Lea & Feibiger, Philadelphia, 1970.

[42] Blanco, M., S. Eriksen, and M. Boghosian, Computer Control of Drug Stability, *Drug and Cosmetics Industry,* vol. 106, p. 44, December 1970.

[43] Lintner, C. J., J. I. Northam, and R. J. Cole, Use of Computer Tables and Printouts for

These efforts have borne fruit. Most drug products are highly stable, running to several years and beyond, despite the fact that "shelf life" often is equated with a degradation of only 10% loss of potency. Considerations in cosmetic shelf life include such areas as fragrance and color, stability, and prevention of rancidity. However, despite such achievements, the DAI faces extensive problems with product stability for several reasons:

1. Drugs may be stored in the distribution pipeline for years because of slow demand in some localities.

2. Drug storage, especially in the distribution chain, may take place in environments, e.g., temperature, different from those stipulated by the manufacturer.

3. Stock rotation may be inadequate in the distribution chain. Manufacturers contribute a stimulus to good stock rotation by giving credit for out-of-date products under a policy which is among the most liberal in the economy.

When stability testing is done at room temperatures, the measure of shelf life may consume years of calendar time. In consequence, considerable experimentation is devoted to testing at higher than room temperatures to accelerate aging.[44] While this approach is an aid to the development chemist during the design stage, it has obvious limitations in the usage stages because of the extent of testing required, and the questions about the assumed kinetic models. The FDA has been reluctant to accept shelf life predictions based on accelerated aging, and has generally insisted on data taken during storage at usual room temperatures.

Based on the results of test programs, expiration dates are established.[45] While the FDA Good Manufacturing Practice requires that "suitable" dates be established based on "reliable, meaningful and specific test methods," there has been no clear standardization of a procedure for this purpose, and there is therefore some variation in industry practice.

Field Feedback   The pharmaceutical component of DAI is properly sensitive to adverse reactions among users of drug products. Reports of adverse reactions may come from patients performing self-medication, from physicians, or from pharmacists. These reports may be made through the medical service representatives or direct to the company offices.

Adverse reactions are investigated promptly by teams of specialists chosen in response to the nature of the problem. In addition, most companies designate a department to accumulate the results of investigation of all adverse reactions and to publish summarized reports for review by management, the medical staff, the research group, and quality assurance. These reports are classified by cause, as for example in Figure 32-4. In some cases there may be other classifications such as dose-subject relationship[46] exemplified in Figure 32-5. A good deal of this complaint activity is susceptible to the approach used in industry generally, as discussed in Section 15, under Processing of Complaints, et seq.

The FDA requires the pharmaceutical industry to report to it all known instances of adverse reaction. The FDA has its own investigation organization, and often carries out studies independently of those conducted by the pharmaceutical companies. From these studies the FDA reaches it own conclusions, which in some

---

Interpreting and Predicting Drug Stability Data, *American Perfume and Cosmetics,* vol. 84, p. 31, 1970.

[44] Garrett, Edward E., Kinetic Approaches and Limitations, "The Dating of Pharmaceuticals," p. 45, University of Wisconsin Bookstore, Madison, Wis., 1970.

[45] Comer, J. P., Processing of Stability Data for FDA Submission, "The Dating of Pharmaceuticals," p. 93, University of Wisconsin Bookstore, Madison, Wis., 1970.

[46] Koch-Weser, Jan, Definition and Classification of Adverse Drug Reactions, *Drug Information Bulletin,* vol. 2, No. 3, p. 74, 1968.

PARTIAL BREAKDOWN BY CLASSES

Class 1—Pharmaceutical
- A. Analytical standards or tolerance difficulties
- Q. Formula and processing difficulties or quality deviation
- P. Production difficulties
- U. Unjustified
- O. Old or outdated merchandise
- T. Transit damage

Class 2—Biological
- A. Analytical standards or tolerance difficulties
- Q. Formula and processing difficulties or quality deviation
- P. Production difficulties
- U. Unjustified
- O. Old or outdated merchandise
- T. Transit damage

Class 3—Therapeutic
(Includes reports of reactions, sensitivity, ineffectiveness, etc., when treatment of a patient by a doctor is involved)

Class 4—Inspection
- F. Finishing
- B. Bulk
- S. Statistical

Class 5—Packaging
(Complaints on products where the difficulty is entirely due to a component part of the package)

Fig. 32-4 Classification of complaints.

1. Misdosage			
a. deliberate misuse	dose related	all subjects	predictable
b. medication error			
c. titration			
2. Pharmacologic			
a. undesired, expected		most subjects	
b. desired, excessive			
c. undesired, unexpected		some subjects	unpredictable
3. Nonpharmacologic	not dose related		
a. allergic			
b. idiosyncratic			

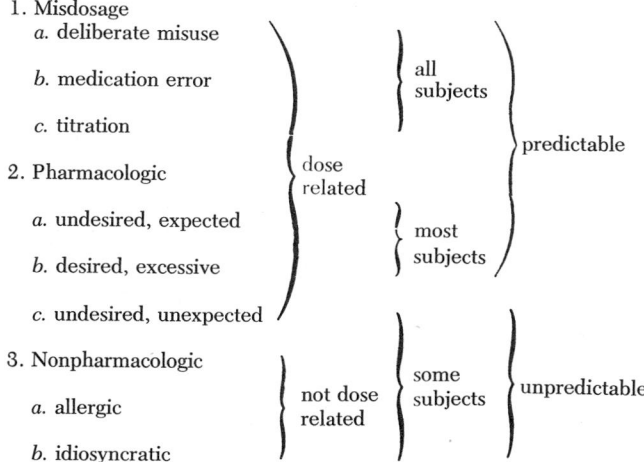

Fig. 32-5 Unfavorable drug effects and their dose-subject relationships.

cases vary from those reached by the companies.   Any differences are then resolved through discussion between the regulators and the companies.

Other agencies which have for some time been active in assembling data on adverse reactions include the American Medical Association's Council on Drugs, and the World Health Organization Group on Monitoring Adverse Drug Reactions.[47]

ORGANIZATION FOR QUALITY

The DAI problems of organization are largely conventional, and respond to the principles set out in Section 7.   However, application of these principles is strongly influenced by the presence of two related forces: (1) the risks inherent in manufacture and marketing of products critical to human health and (2) the extent of government regulation.

Organization Structure   Organization charts of DAI industries respond to these forces of risk and regulation in several ways.

1. They create committees whose major or sole reason for existence is the regulatory presence.   These committees exercise the functions described by their titles: Government Liaison Committee; Committee on Product Recalls; Committee on Good Manufacturing Practice, etc.   Of course, the forms used vary from one company to another.

2. They set up full-time departments to deal with the regulators on New Drug Applications, FDA Intensified Drug Inspection Program (IDIP), and still other critical relationships.

3. They provide a high degree of autonomy to the Quality Control Departments in their role of determining conformance to specification.   This autonomy is not necessarily hierarchical, e.g., by drawing the chart so that the head of Quality Control reports to the President.   Rather the autonomy derives from the fact that conformance to specifications is an essential part of the entire production process, from raw materials to distribution of finished product.   In such an atmosphere there can be no challenge to the findings of Quality Control that nonconforming product is unfit for marketing.

A further aspect of Quality Control autonomy lies in the wide extent of quality-oriented procedures.   Many activities which in other industries are left to the functional departments involved, e.g., Production Planning, Inventory Control, Packaging, or Printing, are brought into the formal quality control procedures, both in the planning and in the subsequent execution.   In some cases, for example, printed cartons intended to hold bottles of product are printed with an edge mark which is added solely as a redundancy to safeguard product identity.   When the folded cartons are stacked up, the edge marks form an unbroken straight line unless one of the cartons is for the wrong product.   Extreme care is taken that the right label is on the right product in the right carton.

Through such all-pervasive quality planning and inspections, the ratio of Quality Control personnel to other personnel is increased to levels well beyond those prevailing in industry generally.   In addition, the "nonquality" personnel devote much time to "quality" matters, partly because the procedures demand it and partly because of their awareness of the critical importance of the products to human health.

Definition of Responsibilities   The same forces of risk and regulation have influenced the delegations of responsibilities for relations with the regulators.   Official contacts are designated, and the regulators are advised accordingly.

Executive Reports   Top managers in the DAI receive and take seriously summary

---

[47] Sadusk, Joseph F., Jr., The Monitoring of Adverse Reactions to Drugs, *Drug Information Bulletin,* vol. 2, No. 3, p. 60, 1968.

reports such as those on adverse reactions and the results of the internal quality audits.

Executive control over quality costs is exercised through the regular budgetary reviews rather than through quality cost studies (as discussed in Section 5). In some companies cost reduction activities in the quality control area are regarded with suspicion, on the ground that the effort may be to reduce these costs at the expense of quality.

Manpower   The DAI problems of manpower for quality are largely conventional, as discussed in Section 17. Some special needs arise from regulations requiring "Qualified Professional Persons" in production and quality control management positions as defined by Defense Personnel Support Center (DPSC) Standards[48] which spell out in some detail personnel and other criteria for qualifying suppliers.

While the DAI have done much to establish foolproof and redundant systems, they have also undertaken programs of motivation for quality. These programs have stressed the importance of the products to human health, the pride that comes from doing a high-quality job, and the opportunities for eliminating errors through suggestions for improvement.[49]

The exacting technology in the DAI demands personnel trained in the sciences and technology which underlie the DAI products. The job of recruiting and training this personnel is simplified by the existence of long-standing professional specialties, school curricula, recognized degrees, and state licensing. Courses are also available to enable personnel to keep up with new developments in science and technology. In addition, there is a considerable array of literature for self-training, i.e., professional journals, books, trade literature, etc. Generally the DAI company personnel respond to these opportunities, and the result is a widespread high level of scientific and technological competence.

In contrast, the DAI research and quality control personnel exhibit wide variability in their competence to handle the statistical aspects of experimental design, data collection, data analysis, etc. Some companies have structured training programs which have brought their personnel to a high degree of self-sufficiency in meeting these daily problems.

Generally, the statistical techniques discussed in Sections 22 through 28 are applicable to Drug and Allied Industries. The special problem of consumer preference testing for cosmetics has much in common with the general problem of sensory testing as discussed in Section 12, under Sensory Qualities.

Beyond these generally used techniques practitioners in the DAI have made numerous applications of statistical methods and have published papers describing these applications. Some of these papers are included in a special bibliography at the end of this Section.

GOVERNMENT REGULATION

Government regulation of the DAI is among the most intense of those for manufacturing industries, particularly in the drug component. The pattern of regulation is all-pervasive, influencing the conduct of all company departments and personnel. In the discussion which follows, only those company functions which are most heavily influenced are discussed in any detail.

New Product Development   As discussed in New Product Evolution, above,

---

[48] See DPSC Standards, under Government Purchases, above.

[49] Sinotte, L. Paul, Ph.D., "Attitudes and Motivation," Symposium on Good Manufacturing Practices in the Pharmaceutical Industry. International Federation of Pharmaceutical Manufacturers Associations, Geneva, Switzerland, 1971.

FDA approval is required for IND's and NDA's. Thus any stage involving tests on human beings requires prior approval by the FDA. Thereby the regulators control to some extent the amount of experimentation and data needed, through their authority to grant or withhold approval of the NDA, without which the product may not be marketed.

Quality Planning   In reviewing the NDA, the FDA is also reviewing the quality plan for making and testing the product. Many of the exceptions taken by the FDA relate to the adequacy of the process control and test programs. A positive response to these exceptions is also a revision of the quality plan in order to meet the views of the regulators.

A further participation in quality planning is the promulgation of the Good Manufacturing Practice, which is itself a broad quality plan. The compendia likewise are a major element in quality planning, since they impose limits on choice of test methods, product variability, etc.

Product Acceptance   Under existing legislation, certain products, e.g., insulin, antibiotics, require FDA test and certification before being released for use. This practice seems to have originated in years when some company test laboratories were not equipped or able to make the necessary assays. However, the practice has continued even though many manufacturer laboratories are admirably equipped and competent to do the testing, as evidenced by the scarcity of noncertifications.

Quality Audit   This is accomplished by FDA visits to manufacturing plants to review company compliance with the quality plans. (These plans include Good Manufacturing Practice as well as the material, process, product, and test specifications.)

The FDA inspectors have given the name Intensified Drug Inspection Program (IDIP) to the audit conducted at the manufacturing plants. The audit is carried out in great detail. The exceptions taken and recommendations made are discussed with the responsible plant personnel, and followed by a report to the company management.

These audits may sometimes turn up instances of noncompliance with the procedures, e.g., missing signatures, incomplete records.[50] These noncompliances seldom result in product unfitness for use, because of the redundancies built into the control systems. However, the findings have likely provided added stimulus to manufacturing companies to keep these noncompliances to a minimum. In some cases, manufacturing companies have gone to more formal plans of self-audit. In addition, it is likely that some policy matters previously left vague have been brought out into the open and settled as an indirect result of questions raised by the IDIP audits.

Complaints   As noted under Field Feedback, above, companies are required to report to the FDA all known cases of adverse reaction. In investigating these and other sources of feedback from usage, the FDA exerts a powerful influence on the DAI's customer relations, since the FDA has the power to require quarantines and recalls.

Marketing   The regulators also exert controls over the manufacturers' marketing activities. An example is the wording of the package circular, which serves as a form of advertising (it makes various claims for the usefulness of the product) as well as a form of product description. The FDA often proposes that claims be reworded or that reports of product difficulties be added. The basic reasons behind government regulation of the DAI are (1) the obvious risk of dangers to human health, and (2) the fact that the consumer has no choice but to rely on the competence and integrity of the manufacturers. In recent years the regulators and DAI

---

[50] Brodsky, Philip, FDA Control Drug Inspection, "Control Procedures in Drug Production, p. 127, University of Wisconsin Bookstore, Madison, Wis., 1966.

have improved their relationships through cooperative effort. The Good Manufacturing Practice regulations, where both groups participated in the preparation, is an example of this. The atmosphere is increasingly one of rapport, rather than that of adversary roles.

LOOKING AHEAD

In the DAI extensive product research is continuing, so that the coming years will continue to see more new and improved products. Process development is likewise continuing, and will be reflected in new and improved processes which give emphasis to sterility and automated controls.

Instrumentation and analytical methods are undergoing a revolutionary development which includes automated assays as well as greater precision.[51] Another revolution—that of computerized data collection, analysis, and retrieval—will make possible a high degree of utilization of the data generated by the new instrumentation. Direct computer control of processes (already in wide use in other industries) is a further development.

These developments will reduce the extent of personnel needed for making day-to-day assays and inspections. The emphasis will shift to the proper utilization and maintenance of the integrity of the measurement equipment and the computers. This change in emphasis will call for corresponding changes in emphasis by the Quality Control departments so that they will be fully competent to:

1. Determine the form and extent of the data needed for quality control and improvement
2. Program the production equipment and instruments through computers to deliver these data
3. Interpret the data, with statisticians playing an increasingly important role
4. Maintain surveillance over the integrity of the new systems

The knowledge and skills demanded by these activities will require extensive new training in statistical methods, instrumentation, and computer programming. In addition, the organization structure of the Quality Control departments will need some changes to give leadership and emphasis to the new developments.

SUMMARY

The drug and allied industries have contributed importantly to the extensive improvements made in the human life span, in animal health, in agricultural productivity, and in many other aspects of human well-being. New product developments have been the visible, dramatic symbol of these improvements. However, the subsurface activities, i.e., the manufacturing and quality control processes, have been no less significant in accomplishing these results. The dosages of drugs and the usages of other products run to fantastic numbers, yet at very high levels of safety and efficacy. The industry and government personnel whose joint efforts have brought these results to fruition deserve much credit for these achievements.

SPECIAL BIBLIOGRAPHY ON STATISTICAL METHODS AS APPLIED TO DRUG AND ALLIED INDUSTRIES

Statistical techniques are widely used in the DAI, at every stage from new product evolution through product usage. To a large degree, these techniques are conventional, and are discussed in Sections 22 through 28 of this Handbook. However,

---

[51] A useful, extensive reference is *Annals of the New York Academy of Sciences*, vol. 130, Art. 2, pp. 483–868.

the DAI is developing a subliterature of its own, as exemplified by the following, in addition to those references previously cited:

Malone, M. H., and R. C. Robechaud, A Hippocratic Screen for Pure or Crude Drug Materials, *Lloydia,* vol. 25, p. 320, 1962.

Federer, W. T., Procedures and Designs for Screening Material in Selection and Allocation, with a Bibliography, *Biometrics,* vol. 19, p. 553, 1963.

Dunnett, C. W., Statistical Theory of Drug Screening, "Quantitative Methods in Pharmacology," pp. 212–231, North-Holland Publishing Company, Amsterdam, 1961.

King, E. P., A Statistical Design for Drug Screening, *Biometrics,* vol. 19, p. 429, 1963.

Redman, C. E., and E. P. King, Group Screening Utilizing Balanced and Partially Balanced Incomplete Block Designs, *Biometrics,* vol. 21, p. 865, 1965.

Litchfield, J. R., Sequential Analysis, Screening and Serendipity, *Journal of Medicinal and Pharmaceutical Chemistry,* vol. 2, p. 469, 1960.

Finney, J. D., Statistical Problems of Plant Selection, *Bulletin of the International Statistical Institute,* vol. 36, p. 242, 1958.

Finney, J. D., An Experimental Study of Certain Screening Processes, *Journal of the Royal Statistical Society,* Series B, vol. 28, p. 88, 1966.

"Remington's Pharmaceutical Sciences," chapter on Statistics, Mack Publishing Company, 1970.

Breunig, H. Latham, Some Uses of Statistical Control Charts in the Pharmaceutical Industry, *Industrial Quality Control,* vol. 21, No. 2, p. 79, August 1964.

Comer, J. P., H. L. Breunig, D. E. Broadlick, and C. B. Sampson, Estimation of Mean Potency and Content Uniformity of Tablets: A New Approach, *Journal of Pharmaceutical Science,* vol. 59, p. 210, 1970.

Roberts, Charles D., Fill Weight Variation Release and Control of Capsules, Tablets and Sterile Solids, *Technometrics,* vol. II, p. 161, 1969.

Sampson, C. B., H. L. Breunig, J. P. Comer, and D. E. Broadlick, Characterization of the Content Uniformity Plan, *Journal of Pharmaceutical Science,* vol. 59, p. 1653, 1970.

Sampson, C. B., H. L. Breunig, J. P. Comer, and D. E. Broadlick, Characterization of the USP XVIII Content Uniformity Plan, *Journal of Pharmaceutical Science,* vol. 60, p. 957, 1971.

Sampson, C. B., and H. L. Breunig, Some Statistical Aspects of Pharmaceutical Content Uniformity, *Journal of Quality Technology,* vol. 3, p. 170, 1971.

Colquhoun, D., "Lectures on Biostatistics," Oxford University Press, Fair Lawn, N.J., 1971.

Cooper, M. S. (ed.), "Quality Control in the Pharmaceutical Industry," Academic Press, Inc., New York, 1972.

Section **33**

Metals Industry

DR. C. H. WALDEN

Director of Process Technology, Kaiser Aluminum & Chemical Co.

INTRODUCTION

The modern metals industry produces over thirty *basic* types of metals in a wide diversity of alloys and grades. This spectrum is then processed into a wide variety of forms such as sheet, coil, wire, rod, ingot, and billet, each with its own quality problems. Despite the myriad of permutations of metals and shapes, there is much commonality in the underlying quality control principles employed to meet the needs of fitness for use and to do so economically. This commonality is well exemplified by the problems and practices of the steel and aluminum industries. It is these industries (with which the author has some degree of familiarity) which will mainly be discussed in this Section. In like manner, the Section will concentrate on those aspects of quality control and improvement which are widely prevalent in the industry and can therefore be regarded as a main road amid a bewildering array of side roads.

The metals industry has exhibited an impressive pace of improving technology and adopting new concepts of process control. There was a day, not too long ago, when most metals processes were governed by the state of the art, and were heavily dependent upon operator skill. Computer control is now becoming commonplace, the tools of the applied statistician are being put to use, and it is a safe prediction that by the end of the 1970s, the industry will be highly automated and will have assimilated the most advanced of quality control techniques.

Economic factors have a direct bearing upon the type of quality control problems as well as upon the attempts to resolve these problems. The industry is closely coupled to its source of raw material, the ore body, and this places restrictions upon its flexibility to adopt new processes. On the other hand, as the older ore bodies are depleted, the basic smelting processes must be modified to consume new ore sources. These new sources usually present new and often more difficult processing problems. The metals processes must accomodate to the raw material that is available, and there is only limited ability to select ores that are optimum for the process. This limitation on the availability of a variety of ores also pertains to the supplementary raw materials such as coal, coke, pitch, and limestone. These materials constitute very significant cost factors and are used in large quantities. Hence, the economic concerns are often more determinative in the selection of raw materials than are the quality factors. These economic realities have had an influence on the extent of the quality control effort directed to raw materials. Still another economic characteristic is that expansion of production capability requires immense outlays of capital funds. Prudence dictates that these funds be directed to proved processes, and there is necessarily a reluctance to make process changes which would obsolete existing investments. This provides an inertia working against rapid changes in processes and equipment.

In recent years the metals industry, along with many other basic industries, has been confronted with the problems associated with its influence on the environment. There is no doubt that the nation's goal of improving the environment will have very significant impacts on the design and the controls of the metals processes of the future.

The subject matter will be treated under four main topics. *The Control Plan* will treat the subjects related to controlling an existing process in order to achieve maximum product quality at minimum cost. *Quality Improvement* will be directed to those techniques which will yield breakthrough in technology, equipment, and controls that will permit operating at new, higher levels of quality that are so important for an industry to remain competitive and forge ahead. *Measures of Performance* is directed to techniques for guiding the quality improvement effort, for determining that the control plan is working and that the gains predicted from quality improvement activities are realized. Finally, the subject of *Quality Problems* gives recognition that today's quality will not suffice for tomorrow's market.

THE CONTROL PLAN

The control plan for a specific metals process depends upon a number of basic considerations. Of prime concern is the nature of the product and its quality requirements. The design of the control plan also depends upon the volume of metal being processed and the anatomy of the process. Process anatomy is the functional structure of the total process and can best be explained by referencing some representative metals processes.

1. Figure 33-1 illustrates in schematic form the flow diagram of the process of manufacturing steel mill products from the basic raw materials of iron ore, limestone, and coal. That portion of the total operation concerned with the smelting of iron ore to iron is concerned with a single process and a single product and is categorized here as a Type I process. This Type I process has its counterpart in aluminum, where bauxite ore is converted to refined aluminum oxide. The types of controls employed in this type of process, as well as the approach one takes to quality improvement, will differ from other types of processes concerned with a variety of products and/or a variety of processes.

The Type I process concerned with a single process and a single product allows for the concentration of quality control effort to be directed to a rigid control of process variables. Little, if any, effort is directed to customer contacts or to developing new products. Quality of raw materials is an important consideration for quality and cost. Since process efficiency depends heavily upon continuous operation, a concerted effort is made to provide a preventive "front-end"[1] type of control over this type of process.

2. Figure 33-2 illustrates in schematic form a process of a different anatomy calling for a different logic of control. It depicts the process for converting aluminum oxide into molten aluminum metal. It employs a multitude of individual electrolytic reduction cells each producing the same product but operating almost completely independently of each other. This type of process will be referred to as a Type II process. It has its counterpart in the chemical industry wherein chlorine and caustic are produced from sodium chloride in banks of individual electrolytic cells. The unique feature of this type of operation is the large number of units[2] which are operated in an almost independent manner.

The Type II process differs from a Type I process in that it is concerned with a multitude of small identical processes producing a single product. For economic reasons, the total process control effort is likely to be spread lightly over a host of production units with considerable reliance for quality being placed upon "operator skill." Should process upsets occur in a few of the units, it would have a relatively small impact upon the whole plant, and as a result, one is likely to drift into a posture of "back-end" control. The principal control effort is then directed to finding the process upsets and restoring control by compensative corrective action.

3. In Figure 33-1, the Basic Oxygen Furnace unit operating on a batch basis represents a third type of process that will be referred to as a Type III process. It has its counterpart in the casting of aluminum alloys by increments of individual heats.

A Type III process is generally referred to as a batch process. The logic of control here is directed to controlling on an incremental basis with provisions made for process adjustments on a batch basis. Quality problems are readily detected and defective product can be easily isolated. The exposure to major process upsets is at a minimum. Less emphasis is required on controlling the inputs when the opportunities exist for correction.

4. Figure 33-3 illustrates in schematic form the anatomy of the process for converting aluminum metal into the variety of mill products needed to satisfy the requirements of a wide range of customers and end uses. It is being designated as a Type IV process and is also illustrated by the steel fabrication operations shown in Figure 33-1. It is a multiunit, multiproduct type of process that requires increased emphasis on individual customer requirements. This type of process can be likened to a large job shop.

A Type IV process presents a formidable control problem. It requires that a major effort be directed to customer relations and it calls for frequent process modifications in order to satisfy a range of customer requirements. Operating procedures must be rather formal and complex in order to convey the exact production practices for each product. The inspection function must be extensive, since it is directed to a large number of products and customers. Reliance must be placed upon the equipment operator to control his process, and only a minimum amount of quality control surveillance over the process is economically feasible. Since the material progresses through a number of operations, there are opportunities for in-process inspection that prove useful for detecting processing problems prior to final inspection.

---

[1] The term "front-end" refers here to a type of control plan that is directed to the control of important process parameters as opposed to a "back-end" control that is geared to react in a compensative fashion when the process output is nonconforming.

[2] It is common for the number of individual units to number in the hundreds.

The raw materials of steelmaking must be brought together, often from hundreds of miles away, and smelted in a blast furnace to produce most of the iron that goes into steelmaking furnaces. Air and oxygen are among the most important raw materials in iron and steelmaking.

PELLETS

IRON ORE

BLAST FURNACE

SINTER

LIMESTONE

BASIC OXYGEN FURNACE

SCRAP OR PREREDUCED ORE

CRUSHING

MOLTEN IRON TRANSFER CAR

COAL

COKE OVENS

SLAG

OPEN HEARTH FURNACE

COKE OVEN BY-PRODUCTS

CASTING PIG IRON

MIXER

A FLOWLINE ON STEELMAKING

This is a simplified road map through the complex world of steelmaking. Each stop along the routes from raw materials to mill products contained in this chart can itself be charted. From this overall view, one major point emerges: Many operations—involving much equipment and large numbers of men—are required to produce civilization's principal and least expensive metal.

ELECTRIC FURNACE

Fig. 33-1   Flow diagram of steelmaking. *(American Iron and Steel Institute.)*

Because the process is product- and customer-oriented, the process control as well as the quality improvement activities are likely to be concentrated on individual products rather than on basic process deficiencies.

The above is intended to give the reader some appreciation of the factors that go into developing a control plan for a specific metals process.

The remaining discussion of the control plan will cover the control techniques and problems for the entire sequence of activities through which the products are designed, manufactured, marketed, used, and serviced. The treatment will start with an understanding of those customer relations aspects which influence the selection of the type of controls to be employed. It will then consider the types of controls that are exercised over new products and the special problems experienced in the metals industry. The manufacturing control plan will then treat the three basic

Molten steel must solidify before it can be made into finished products by the industry's rolling mills and forging presses. The metal is usually formed first at high temperature, after which it may be cold-formed into additional products.

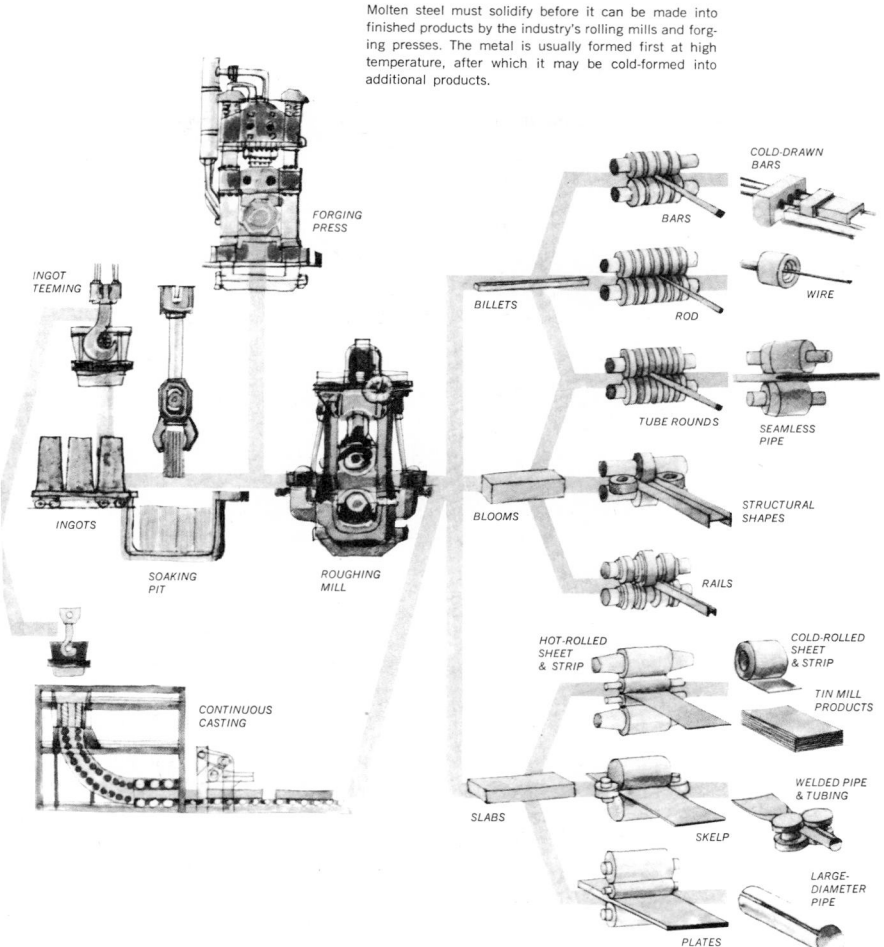

COLD-DRAWN BARS

FORGING PRESS

BARS

INGOT TEEMING

BILLETS

WIRE

ROD

TUBE ROUNDS

SEAMLESS PIPE

INGOTS

BLOOMS

STRUCTURAL SHAPES

SOAKING PIT

ROUGHING MILL

RAILS

HOT-ROLLED SHEET & STRIP

COLD-ROLLED SHEET & STRIP

CONTINUOUS CASTING

TIN MILL PRODUCTS

WELDED PIPE & TUBING

SLABS

SKELP

LARGE-DIAMETER PIPE

PLATES

Fig. 33-1 *(Continued)*

elements of control: (1) Raw Material Control, (2) Process Control, and (3) Product Control. Emphasis will be placed on those elements of control which appear to be common to the industry.

Table 33-1 summarizes the effect of the anatomy of metals processes on the control plan.

Customer Relations [3]

Identification of Customer Requirements. A large volume of metal products is sold to customers whose end-use requirements are well understood and whose basic quality requirements are stated in the standards and codes published by ASTM, various trade associations, or governmental agencies. These basic requirements, in

---

[3] For a discussion of customer relations generally, see Sections 14 and 15.

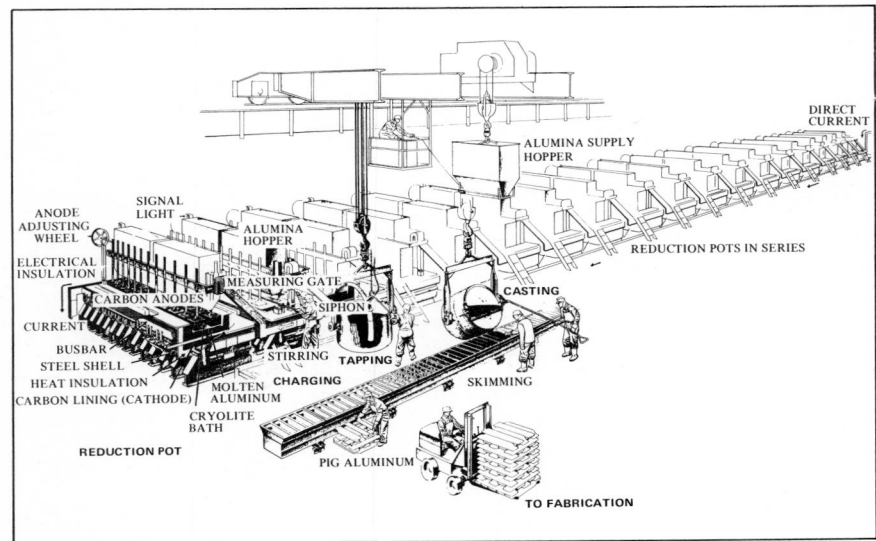

Fig. 33-2   Flow diagram of aluminum reduction.   *(Metals Engineering Institute–American Society of Metals.)*

TABLE 33-1   **Effect of Anatomy of Metals Processes on Plans of Process Control**

Anatomy of process	Type I	Type II	Type III	Type IV
Process and product characteristics	Single product Single process Continuous operation One or few large production units	Single product Single process Continuous operation Numerous small production units	Multiple products Batch process	Multiple products Multiple processes
Plan of control emphasizes	Control of input raw materials Rigid control of process variables Control of important process parameters	Signals to indicate process upsets Prompt response to nonconforming units Reliance on operator skills Product inspection after completion	Means for making incremental adjustments to variables in input materials and in process conditions	Clear understanding of customer requirements Formal procedures for filling customer orders Process modifications to meet customer needs Reliance on operator of equipment with minimal process surveillance Process inspection between operations Final product inspection

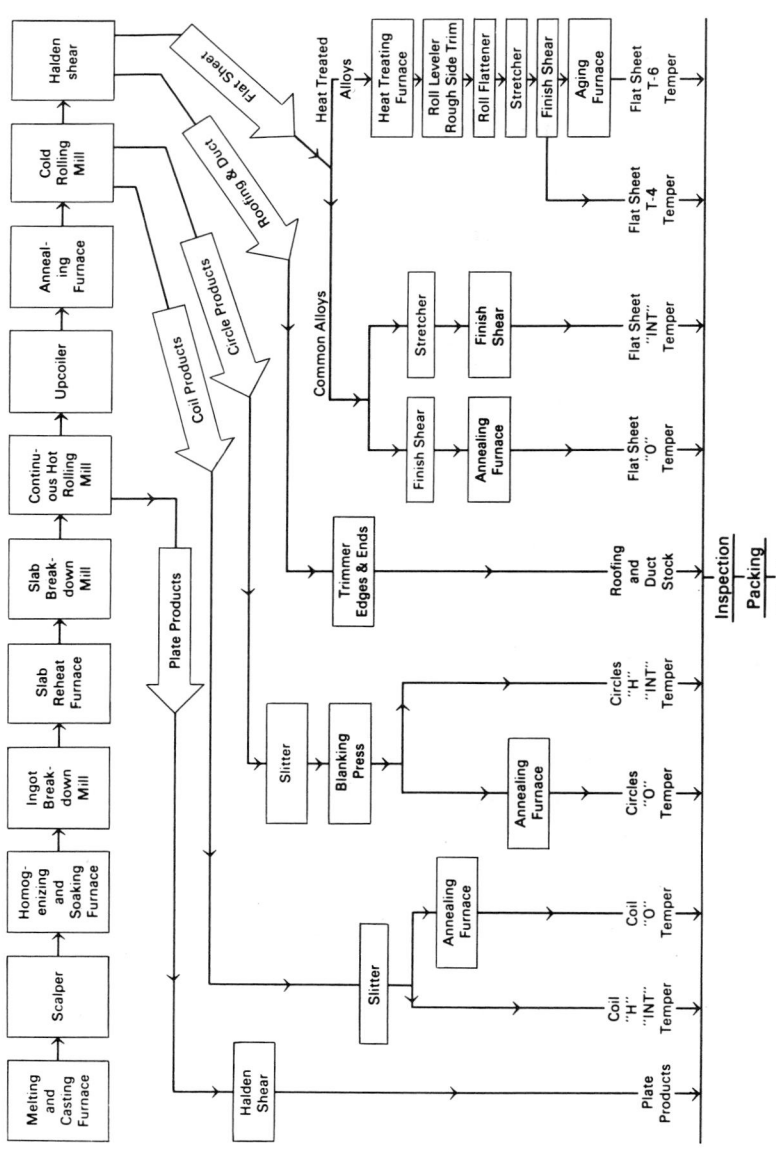

Fig. 33-3 Flow diagram for aluminum conversion. *(Metals Engineering Institute–American Society of Metals.)*

most instances, have to be augmented by individual customer requirements that make the product amenable to specific end uses. It is a common practice for the customer to reference the standard and then add to this his special requirements. A metals plant dealing with a large number of customers requires a well-organized system of order entry in order to capture all such information and program it into the manufacturing and quality control plans. Orders for new customers and new products are commonly reviewed by quality control and/or metallurgical personnel before the order is approved for manufacture. It is also a common practice to maintain a file on quality problems experienced with individual customers so that this information can be used to avoid repetitive problems.

In addition to the large quantity of standard products sold, a variety of products are sold that are not adequately described in existing and recognized standards. The customer has a specific end use but may lack sufficient knowledge to state his exact needs in terms of alloy, temper, and functional requirements. The product is being ordered on a "fitness for use" basis, and it is left up to the metal producer to gain an understanding of the customer's requirements and to produce to meet these needs. It is also not uncommon for a customer to order a standard product without full knowledge that it will work in his application. Again, the burden falls to the metal producer to determine the actual requirements for this customer. The metals industry has recognized this need to assist the customer in determining his quality requirements and has developed technical specialists who work directly with the customer in determining his unique requirements. The lack of complete product specifications can and does lead to misunderstandings with the customers and, at times, to monetary losses for both the metal producer and the customer. More and more products are coming within the provinces of standards organizations, and many customers are developing definitive purchase specifications. Concurrent with this trend, the metal suppliers are developing more specific sales specifications describing their standard mill products.

The above remarks are addressed to the broad subject of product specification and customer requirements, and do not apply to the chemical composition of metals and their alloys. The metals industry has a very keen appreciation of the importance of chemical composition in determining metal performance. Alloy designation and composition limits are very carefully defined and rigidly adhered to in the quality control of the product. This attention to the control of chemistry has served the industry well, and we find it a common practice for a customer to specify the composition of the metal as well as its performance requirements.

A third type of customer relation is the sale of metal through distributors. The distributor may handle a number of different metals and stock a variety of alloys, compositions, and physical shapes. These are products that he has found to have general use but usually in quantities which would not warrant the customer placing an order directly to a metal producer. There is the added advantage to the customer that he can generally receive prompt delivery. The customer relations responsibility at the metals plant may then take on a dual character, with the principal responsibility and contact being to and with the distributor but still maintaining a secondary responsibility to the ultimate customer.

Information Feedback from the Customer. A vital part of the producer-consumer relationship is a system for providing prompt and accurate feedback of information to the mill should the customer experience quality problems. When quality problems are detected in their early stages, corrections can be made in product design or control that will avert major customer dissatisfaction.

The Sales Department is usually the first to hear of customer quality problems, and accepts the prime responsibility for the initial inquiry and investigation. It is a common and recommended practice that the salesman immediately notify the Quality Control Department at the producing mill of any quality problem so that immediate action can be taken on any additional orders for this product which might be in the process of being manufactured. This action often calls for a holdup in production until the full facts have been determined. The salesman servicing the customer has the additional responsibility of obtaining all the facts and completing a complaint and/or claim form which will be directed to the Quality Control Department at the producing mill. He may be called upon to supply a sample of the defective product and will exercise judgment as to whether or not the seriousness and complexity of the claim require that a mill representative visit the customer in order to review the technical aspects of the problem. Should the Quality Control or Metallurgical Departments sense a serious problem, they may elect, on their initiative, to visit the customer's plant, but in most cases the problems can be resolved by telephone calls, samples, and correspondence. In some instances the customer will request technical assistance from the metal producer in order to help in fabricating the metal or in more clearly defining the product requirements.

The activities described above for obtaining information feedback from the customer are, at times, assigned to field engineers working from regional sales offices with little or no dependence upon mill personnel traveling to the customer's plant. This system provides a prompt and accurate feedback of quality information and avoids having mill personnel leave their work assignments to investigate quality problems.

New Products Controls[4]   The metals industry as treated within the scope of this Section is not called upon to produce a host of new products each year in order to maintain market position. Since the products are for the most part standard mill products that are used as raw materials for subsequent processing, they are not as subject to frequent redesign as are those which are manufactured for the consumer market. The metal forming customer may be called upon for frequent introduction of new products, but he is usually able to accomplish this by modifications within his own process, and he seldom requires major changes in the metal supplied to his process. As a result, there is a relatively high degree of stability of the basic design characteristics of standard mill products.

There are a number of new product controls which are somewhat unique to the metals industry and merit some discussion.

The Trial Order. It is usual for orders placed for mill products to run into thousands of pounds. When such an order fails to perform, financial claims of major magnitude arise. For this reason, it is common and recommended practice for a metals plant to first undertake the production of a new product (or an old product for a new use) on the basis of a small trial order, with the major production quantities to be produced only after the trial order material had been successfully utilized by the customer. This approach has merit on a number of counts:

1. The small trial order minimizes the possible economic loss should the new product fail to perform.

2. It affords the opportunity for close surveillance by Quality Control and/or Metallurgy of the actual manufacture of the trial order. This is helpful in validating the manufacturing procedures and assures that the trial order material will be representative of the normal production product.

3. By working with the customer on the basis of a trial order, it is possible to avoid many misunderstandings. The customer is aware that the product is being manufactured on a trial basis. Should the trial order fail to perform, the producer's quality image is not damaged, and avenues are left open for subsequent trial orders.

4. It is common practice for a Quality Control and/or Metallurgical representative from the mill to be present during the processing of the trial order in the customer's

---

[4] For a discussion of new products controls generally, see Section 8.

plant. This provides an excellent opportunity for the producing mill to understand more completely the manner in which its product will be used and to observe the product's shortcomings should it fail to perform.

This need for the trial-order approach points up the inadequacies of the present standards and specifications to predict sufficiently the fitness for use of many metal products. This apparent deficiency is not attributable to a lack of diligence upon the part of the metal producer to describe his product adequately or to his ignorance of the various metal forming processes. It is, in part, attributable to the diversity of uses to which these mill products are applied. The customer often has unique metal forming requirements that relate to his equipment and process.

In studying this problem, one finds that many of the common quality control assurance tests fail to measure all the product attributes which lead to its successful use. It suggests the need for more product assurance tests that simulate the customer's use of the product. There is a challenge to the technologist in the metals industry to develop more tests which will predict good processing characteristics— fitness for use.

New Product Availability. The manufacture of mill products, from a quality control viewpoint, can often be likened to a large job shop. The basic metal can be manufactured in a myriad of final mill products which vary by composition, by temper, by physical shape, or by surface condition. It is a common practice for the metal companies to publish sales data sheets describing their available standard products, but it is understood that additional products can be made available upon inquiry. Requests for new product availability go to the Quality Control Department as well as other interested departments before a determination can be made as to whether or not the mill has the capability of producing the product in a profitable manner. The role of the Quality Control and/or Metallurgical Department is to determine if the processes have the inherent capability for producing to the quality levels specified on the customer inquiry.

In actual practice, the decisions concerning process capability are frequently made without the benefit of a statistically designed capability study but are based on experience and a nonstatistical study of performance data. The metallurgist or quality control engineer assigned this responsibility would do well to become familiar with the techniques for performing capability studies as they are described in Section 9. The quantitative information from these studies can then augment the engineers' close familiarity with the problems encountered on similar products in order to render a proper decision as to the plant's ability to produce the proposed new product.

Qualification Tests for New Products. A great many of the new products generated by the metals industry concern only minor adaptations to standard products in order to meet the specific processing requirements of individual customers, but there are still others that represent very significant changes in composition, physical properties, and end-use application. The latter category requires more rigid controls.

Products that are associated with major changes in metal composition and basic manufacturing methods are generally the result of a company's Research and Development Program and are directed to specific new needs in the marketplace. The basic development work, along with the attendant product testing, is often done in a research environment and then, when feasibility has been demonstrated, it is programmed for mill production. These new products often require new equipment or complete new facilities and must be manufactured in accordance with new standard operating procedures. They also require new methods of quality assurance. The new product control system for these major innovations is more rigid and exhaustive than that described above for minor changes in standard products.

The routine product acceptance testing will seldom suffice for determining that a new product will perform as intended. The development work associated with these major changes in product design must be supported by tests that will serve to predict reliability in service, and they must be broad enough in scope to detect the unexpected modes of failure. These tests, generally referred to as qualification tests, are commonly performed on the product produced in the research and development effort but are sometimes overlooked when evaluating the first production offering. An adequate new product control system should call for a complete review by personnel competent in the fields of technology, statistics, and quality assurance and familiar with the end-use application. This intensive review of the test data supporting the adequacy of the design of new products is taking on increasing importance as we experience rapid changes in the laws governing product liability.

Raw Material Controls The metals industry has some unique problems associated with the control of raw material quality. The principal raw material is the ore, which usually comes from a predetermined source. Variations in the processing quality characteristics of the ore can have a profound influence upon the quality of the metal as well as the efficiency of the process. It is a common practice to blend ores from various mining areas in order to achieve a more uniform feed to the smelting operation. In the aluminum operation the bauxite ore undergoes a chemical processing operation that converts it to a purified aluminum oxide before it is consigned to the smelting operation for conversion to metal. In some metals industries there are often types of ore beneficiation operations which are directed to the task of concentration, removal of harmful impurities, and achieving greater uniformity. In many instances the metals process must be made to conform to the quality of the ore available.

Other basic raw materials such as coal, coke, pitch, limestone, and recycle metal are, for economic reasons, subject to much the same types of limitation in respect to assuring uniformity. There are, however, lesser quantities of raw materials such as alloying components, chemicals, rolling mill coolants, and refractories which are used in the metals industry and are amenable to formal vendor controls.[5]

It is a common practice in the metals industry for the responsibility of evaluating raw material quality to be assigned to the Metallurgical Department with little or no involvement on the part of the Quality Control Department. It is the opinion of the author that raw material control systems as we now know them in the metals industry would improve if the task of controlling to a quality level were considered a quality control function.

Many of the raw materials are purchased on the basis of commercial specification, and it is only on rare occasions that a plant is in an inventory or purchasing position to reject a shipment that fails to conform. The industry does, however, carry out a considerable amount of sampling of raw materials and performs a wide variety of analysis upon these samples in the chemical laboratories. Most of the raw materials vary widely in particle size and uniformity and present some challenges in obtaining a representative sample. See Section 25A for the general approach to the subject of sampling of bulk materials. Bertholf[6] treated this subject as it applies to the steel industry.[7]

---

[5] For a discussion of vendor controls generally, see Section 10.

[6] Bertholf, W. M., The Sampling of Bulk Materials in the Steel Industry, *American Society for Quality Control, Technical Conference Transactions,* 1955, pp. 105–116.

[7] See also, Takahashi, U., and M. Imaizumi, Sampling Experiment of Fine Iron Ore, *Reports of Statistical Applications Research,* vol. 18, No. 1, pp. 22–32, 1971. See, further Sato, T., K. Ito, S. Chujo, and U. Takahashi, Example of Experiments on Systematic Sampling of Iron Ore, *ibid.,* pp. 33–40.

There is an ever-increasing awareness of the importance of raw material quality to the metals industry, and the quality control function should, in the coming years, be expected to contribute in a very significant manner.

The problem of controlling the quality of raw material from the smelter to the casting and fabrication operation is usually one of internal quality controls. The molten metal is sampled, analyzed, and graded, and this system serves the industry well in controlling the quality of the composition of the metal. This control point will take on increased importance as the metals industry moves more and more to continuous types of process.

Process Controls   The process control plans employed in the metals industry are so many and varied that only three basic operations will be considered:

1. Ore smelting
2. Molten metal casting
3. Metal fabrication

Ore Smelting.   At the smelting stage of a metals process, the raw materials represent the major input to the process, and hence, the process control plan should be addressed to their control. The plan should contain provisions for either controlling the uniformity of raw material quality or detecting shifts in quality and altering the process to cope with these shifts. This is not a simple task. For many of the metals processes, consideration of the cost and availability of raw materials overshadow the concerns about their quality characteristics. Coal, limestone, and metal-bearing ores are naturally occurring materials, do not possess the uniformity of manufactured materials, and present problems in obtaining a representative sample. Seldom are alternative sources of supply readily available. Despite these formidable problems, process control plans can accomplish a great deal in smoothing out the variations. Most smelting processes have flexibility for operating efficiently with varying grades of raw materials if the changes can be anticipated. An adequate knowledge of raw material quality presents opportunities for the blending of materials possessing wide variations in quality into a uniform feed to the smelting process.

After due consideration of the control of raw materials, the process control plan must treat the important operating variables such as raw material feed rates, energy inputs, and reaction times. These vary from process to process depending upon the chemistry of the process as well as equipment design. Some of these variables are amenable to instrumented control, but many depend upon operator skill and attention.

The process control plan for a smelting operation must also address itself to the quality of the metal produced. It requires a regimen for collecting metal samples and submitting these to chemical testing. These tests are directed to metal purity and are usually carried out by instrumented x-ray or spectrographic methods that provide for a rapid feedback of data to the smelter.

Molten Metal Casting.   Many of the quality attributes of metal products are imparted at the time the molten metal is cast into a form suitable for subsequent fabrication. The composition of the metal or metal alloy is determined at this stage of the process. Metal received from smelting must be further refined or modified by the addition of alloying ingredients in order to achieve the desired level of chemical composition.

In order to accomplish this control, accurate calculations have to be made of the alloying ingredient requirements. The molten metal is sampled and analyzed before it is ready for casting. Provisions are made for adjusting chemical composition if required. An important element of the process control plan for metal casting is the means for monitoring the melting and casting practices. Most of these practices are not amenable to instrumented control, and considerable reliance must be placed upon the operator's skill and willingness to follow metallurgical practices. An effective process control plan calls for audits of the operator's activities by either the foreman or the Quality Control Department.

The final chemistry of the metal is determined at the time of casting. A visual inspection of the ingot is used to detect the presence of casting defects that might result in problems during fabrication.

Metal Fabrication. The process control plan for a metal fabrication process is directed to the product attributes that are of importance to the customer. We will consider four principal types of product characteristics.

1. *Metallurgical Characteristics.* The metals industry has developed sophisticated controls for both process inputs and product outputs related to strength and function. In addition to effective control of metal composition as described above, fabrication practices are designed to achieve the correct balance of properties to satisfy both the strength and the function requirements for the product.

These fabrication practices are concerned with the heat treating and rolling of the metal. Heat treating procedures are defined in detailed operating practices, and the accuracy and uniformity of the equipment used for these operations is closely monitored. The sequence of operations during fabrication is important to the control of metallurgical characteristics and this is defined in operating practices.

In order to be assured that the fabrication practices are followed, some form of auditing is employed. In many instances this is the informal auditing carried on during routine supervision. However, a more formal and documented audit plan provides greater assurance.

2. *Thickness.* Thickness control is achieved either by operator skill or, increasingly, through a closed-loop computer control system. In either case, the final result is recorded in chart form by a continuous thickness measuring device, and the operator has a continuous display of actual strip thickness available to him.

3. *Surface Appearance.* While audits of roll conditions, tensions, speeds, etc., are employed in an effort to control appearance, the fundamental approach in rolling is still to examine one end of some predetermined fraction of the coils produced, such as every fourth or fifth coil, and to take corrective action if defects are found. At slitting, sheeting, and leveling operations, operators examine the sheet as it passes at operating speeds, which presents some obvious control limitations. Frequent examination and maintenance of the rolls which come in contact with the strip are the primary controls for conditions developed at these operations.

4. *Flatness.* Use of optimum rolling speeds, lubricants, and reduction sequences is relied upon for flatness control, along with continuous observation of flatness by the rolling mill operator. For products which require a high degree of flatness, subsequent flattening operations are required. Recent developments in this area have substantially reduced the reliance on operator skills and have provided the opportunity for effective process control through the use of predetermined machine settings to compensate for a wide variety of as-rolled buckle or wave conditions. See Quality Improvement, below.

Product Controls   In the metals industry, product assurance controls can be logically grouped into the following three categories:

1. Control of metal composition
2. Control of mechanical properties
3. Control of dimensional and visual characteristics

There are, however, a number of inspection and testing problems which are unique to the metals industry.

Control of Metal Composition. The control of metal composition starts at the smelting operation, at which time a level of metal purity is established. A subsequent control at the time of casting is directed to the chemical composition of the metal alloy or grade of metal as well as to the extent of the nonmetallics such as oxides, carbides, and dissolved gases. The control of chemical composition is required if the metal is to be able to develop the desired mechanical properties during fabrication and to perform as intended in product service. The control of nonmetallics is required in order to assure product uniformity and to prevent flaws and discontinuities in the metallic structure that could lead to product failure during subsequent metal fabrication or in its ultimate end use.

The procedures for sampling molten metal and for performing the chemical analysis are well developed and are generally carried out in accordance with ASTM approved procedures.[8] The analytical work is conventionally performed by spectrographic or x-ray techniques that make use of modern instrumentation[9] and provide rapid and simultaneous determinations for a wide range of chemical elements.

The metals industry generally uses melt or heat numbers that are associated with specific casts of metals, and these numbers follow the product no matter how often the lot is divided. This practice has served the industry well in relating metal composition to problems encountered in end use. This ability to provide traceability may well become more valuable in view of the surge of product liability problems.

The control of nonmetallics is dependent upon a rigid adherence to casting practices that have been designed to scavenge these impurities from the metal. It proves difficult to sample and verify by analytical techniques that this control has been completely achieved. Process audits provide an adequate degree of product assurance for most products, but when it is critical that the level of nonmetallics be maintained at a very low level, the ultrasonic, nondestructive testing technique is employed.[10]

Control of Mechanical Properties. Mechanical properties of metals include such attributes as tensile strength, yield strength, percent elongation, electrical conductivity, resistance to stress corrosion, forming ability, and hardness.

These quality characteristics are built into the product by control of metal composition as well as by the in-process controls exercised during fabrication. These controls relate to casting conditions, ingot preheat, rolling techniques, heat treating, etc. The proper sequencing of the operation as well as the control of the operating parameters in each operation are required in order to develop the required properties. These are specified in operating practices and are incorporated into the manufacturing procedures for each product.

An assurance of these controls is obtained by sampling each lot of material after fabrication and performing on this sample the various standard tests that have been developed by ASTM,[11] the industry, or the customer. Most of these requirements are included in the product standards, but the customer may order material to his own and often more restrictive specification.

The effectiveness of the test in controlling quality depends to a large measure upon the representative nature of the sample. A test lot is usually associated with a single casting lot. For critical applications, this may be further restricted to a single ingot within the casting lot. The sample from the lot is conventionally taken from the end of the coil, and there is a definite limitation on the ability to select a

[8] See Standards and Specifications, below.

[9] Kemner, W., Putting the Computer to Work in Steel Analysis, *American Society for Quality Control, Technical Conference Transactions,* 1968, pp. 223–229.

[10] For an understanding of these techniques, the reader is referred to pp. 279–411 in the textbook "Ultrasonic Testing of Materials" by Krautkramer, J., and H. Krautkramer, Springer-Verlag New York Inc., 1961.

[11] ASTM, "Physical and Mechanical Testing of Metals," Part 31.

random sample.[12,13] In order to provide an adequate margin of safety, it is a common practice to establish internal control limits for both the chemical composition and mechanical properties. These internal control limits are more restrictive than the specification requirements. Material testing between the control limits and the specification limits is subject to resampling and additional testing before a decision is made to accept or reject the product.

For metal products used in critical end-use application, it is a common practice for the customer to require a certification[14] of test results. These are typed listings of chemical and mechanical properties and are attested to by a Quality Control or Metallurgical representative before forwarding to the customer. This quality assurance procedure is often the result of government-directed quality activities and has in the past played a useful role. (It is questionable how well it serves to add to the reliability of metal products, since the metals industry has long recognized its responsibility to supply products that conform to chemical and mechanical properties and has developed the internal controls that provide a high degree of product assurance.) There are additional requirements for metal products destined to be used in defense or aerospace activities that call for the government specification number to be marked directly upon the metal.

Control of Dimensional and Visual Characteristics. Metal products are produced in all manner of physical shapes and sizes, and with a wide range of permissible variations in dimensional tolerances and visual characteristics. The dimensions and the visual appearance are determined during the fabrication operations, and in-process controls are exercised by the operational personnel at each step of the operation. The product assurance controls for dimensional and visual characteristics are exercised either at the time of the final operation or by inspection carried out in an inspection area. The responsibility for these controls is assigned to the Inspection Department, which may report to the Metallurgical or the Quality Control Department or, in some cases, reports independently to the Plant Manager. In some instances, the responsibility for packaging the material is also assigned to the Inspection Department.

A number of specific problems associated with the inspection[15] of dimensional and visual characteristics in the metals industry merit some discussion here.

1. *Coil Inspection.* The inspection of metal products produced in a coil form presents a difficult problem.[16] For the most part, the equipment operator has to be looked upon as an inspector for coil products, since it is not feasible to recoil and inspect the product independently of the final operation. The operator is called upon to inspect a moving strip and often at speeds that make it difficult to detect all the visual flaws or problems relating to lack of flatness. Special auxiliary techniques such as the use of strobe lights or the introduction of slack loops in the moving strip are sometimes employed to increase the effectiveness of this inspection. There have been attempts[17] to develop optical types of instrumentation which would provide an opportunity for continuous visual monitoring.

---

[12] Sturtevant, J. V., Variability of Mechanical Properties of Flat Rolled Sheet Product, *American Society for Quality Control, Technical Conference Transactions,* 1957, pp. 181–189.

[13] Occasione, J. F., Acceptance Sampling of a Continuously Extended Product: Steel Wire in Coils, *American Society for Quality Control, Technical Conference Transactions,* 1956, pp. 589–599.

[14] See Section 10, under Certification.

[15] For a discussion of inspection generally, see Sections 12 and 13.

[16] Lewis, S. S., Inside the Mill—Sampling? or Crystal Ball Gazing? *American Society for Quality Control, Technical Conference Transactions,* 1969, pp. 434, 436.

[17] Reynolds, P. M., The Surface Inspection of Metal Sheet and Strip by Optical Methods, *Metallurgical Reviews,* vol. 11, pp. 89–96, 1966.

Samples, several feet in length, are removed from the ends of the coiled product, and these have been found to correlate amazingly well with the material in the center of the coil. These samples provide an opportunity to verify width of the coil as well as the thickness as it occurs at either end of the coil. When thickness uniformity throughout the coil is critical, use is made of continuous recording gages at the final operation. The material that fails to conform to thickness tolerance can then be removed or the coil rejected. The strip chart from these gages can be used to augment the inspection performed at the end of the coil.

Pearson[18] describes an invention that was directed to the problem of detecting out-of-flatness conditions on a moving strip, but the author has no familiarity with its success. It is anticipated that new measurement techniques will some day provide a breakthrough in this area of continuous inspection of coil.

2. *Problems of Visual Standards.* Aside from the problem of visual inspection on a coiled product, there is a more general problem of establishing adequate standards of visual quality. The industry often falls back upon what is referred to as a standard of commercial quality. This is not a well-defined standard and it must be defined for each type of product, giving proper consideration to the end use and the customer's stated requirements. This still leaves much to be desired. There are varying degrees of severity for each type of visual defect, and it proves difficult to express these in written form. In addition to the categories of visual discontinuities termed defects, there is another type of discontinuity which is referred to as a "condition," meaning that the visual discontinuity is an inherent result of the manufacturing process and is not a cause for rejection.

This problem of establishing definitive visual standards has never been adequately treated by the groups responsible for establishing industry standards, and it becomes a matter of negotiation with each customer. Visual display boards and photographs are often used to help define the visual standards. Some companies have issued technical publications which define and illustrate the defects and conditions associated with its products, but these do not always establish standards for acceptance.

3. *Problems of Flatness Standards.* There is an expressed or an implied requirement for adequate flatness in all metal products sold in either sheet or coil form. To achieve adequate flatness requires extremely close control of the rolling operation and often corrective measures after rolling. As a result of the customer concern and the production problems associated with flatness, a significant amount of the product inspection effort is being directed to the flatness quality characteristic. Despite this concern for flatness, the industry lacks well-defined standards for flatness. This aspect of product quality, like that of visual appearance, is scarcely treated in the industry product standards, and when it is treated, it fails to cover the subject adequately.

It is quite difficult to express the degree of flatness in a simple quantitative fashion. Conventionally, out-of-flat conditions have been expressed as height of waves on specified center-to-center of adjacent waves. For example, the tolerance might be expressed as 1/2-inch wave on 2-foot wave centers. These waves do not occur with any sort of regularity, and this type of tolerance is difficult to apply in inspections. Recently it has been suggested[19] that a fractional difference in the length of the taut and slack portion of the sheet would be a better way to specify and eval-

[18] Pearson, W. K. J., Shape Measurement and Control, *Journal of the Institute of Metals,* vol. 93, pp. 173–178, 1964–1965.

[19] Pearson, W. K. J., Shape Measurement and Control, *Journal of the Institute of Metals,* vol. 93, p. 171, 1964–1965.

uate the quality of flatness. The Aluminum Association[20] has issued flatness tolerances in the conventional wave height manner for sheet and certain types of coil product.

Supplementary Product Controls. It is a common practice to have operating personnel inspect cast ingots before they are sent to rolling. This inspection is for the purpose of sorting out ingots which are obviously defective because of cracks and other surface conditions. The main purpose of this control is to avoid further manufacturing effort on product that will prove defective at a later point in the operation.

The visual inspection of metal as it moves from step to step in the metals process is commonly a part of the operator's responsibility. This in-process inspection serves to detect manufacturing problems as well as to avoid the application of more work to an already defective product. It also serves to notify the Scheduling Department that additional metal will be required to meet the customer's requirements.

Another type of supplementary product control that is gaining some acceptance in the metals industry is that of product auditing. These audits represent a second inspection performed on a small sample of the product by a salaried representative of the Quality Control Department, conducted independently from the routine inspection. The merits of product audits are presented in Section 21 of this Handbook and are treated in detail by Woltz.[21] Product audits provide a method of measuring the effectiveness of the product control plan and also provide a reliable estimate of the average quality shipped to the customer. This approach has some special implications in the metals industry.

1. *Control of Visual Standards.* Because of the difficulty of defining visual standards of quality, a great deal of reliance has to be placed upon the experience and skill of the inspector to make correct decisions concerning visual quality. By and large, the training provided these inspectors proves effective, but many metals plants are faced with changes in job assignments which can leave the task of visual inspection in the hands of inspectors with relatively little experience. The audit proves useful in assuring that the eyes of the inspector are in constant calibration with the eyes of the product specialist in quality control who is fully versed as to the customer's requirements.

The subject of measuring inspector performance has been treated by Wallack and Adams.[22] In this treatment they discuss inspector accuracy in detecting surface defects in tinplate as well as visual and gaging defects in machine parts. The results reported by this emphasize the need for product audit activities. See also Section 12, under Accuracy of Inspectors.

2. *Control of Special Customer Requirements.* Quite often a metals plant is called upon to produce a wide variety of products to the specific requirements of a large number of customers. These specific requirements cover product quality, packaging requirements, product identification, and restrictions on the size of lots or items. While systems are established for conveying these requirements through the operation, it presents opportunities for oversights and errors. A product audit system proves effective in reducing such errors.

The product audit technique is also used at times in the metals industry by the supervision in the Inspection Department. These audits have proved to be a useful management tool for the inspection foreman who has the responsibility to see that the inspectors are trained and that they are following the inspection plan.

[20] Aluminum Standards and Data, The Aluminum Association, New York, 1970–1971.

[21] Woltz, J. R., Product Quality Audit System, *American Society for Quality Control, Technical Conference Transactions,* 1963, pp. 291–295.

[22] Wallack, P. M., and S. K. Adams, A Comparison of Inspection Performance Measures, *American Institute of Industrial Engineers, Transactions,* June 1970, pp. 97–105.

A third type of supplementary control that is gaining some acceptance in the metals industry is that of process audits.[23] These audits are directed to the critical process parameters known to influence the quality of the product. The audits serve the dual purpose of increasing the reliability of the process and of assuring greater product uniformity. The observations may be carried out by technicians operating under the control of the Metallurgical or Quality Control Department, or they may be the accepted responsibility of the Production supervision. The process audits relate to product control insofar as they provide assurance that the product has been manufactured in accordance with design and that quality has hence been "built into" the product. They provide an increased measure of assurance that the customer will receive a uniform product from shipment to shipment and from item to item. This has extreme relevance to those product characteristics for which an adequate laboratory test is lacking.

Standards and Specifications   Many of the standards and specifications associated with metal products had their origin in governmental requirements but are still basic to the industry. The ASTM has played a significant role in developing specifications, and the various trade associations of the metals industry have assumed a responsibility for developing the more universal standards which treat commercially available products.[24] ASTM has also played a very significant role in standardizing sampling and testing procedures. Technical societies[25] representing the consumers of metals products have developed standards which are germane to their field of interest. The large aerospace and defense-related contractors have seen the need to superimpose their own requirements on those of governmental and trade associations. The entire subject of standards and specifications in the metals industry is extremely complex, and most metals companies find the need for employing one or more specification engineers, assigned to the task of keeping abreast of the subject matter and providing an information service to Sales, Development, Manufacturing, and Quality Control. These specialists are called upon to interpret the complex requirements and to ferret out any conflicts which may exist between the customers' requirements and the product capabilities. These standards and specifications concern themselves with product characteristics, test methods, and even the elements of the quality control system used in the producing plant. The requirements frequently change, and one must be sure that he is referencing the most recent amendment of the specification. Many customers' orders make reference to specification documents, and a plant order entry system must be capable of reviewing the requirements of the referenced specification before the order is accepted for fabrication.

The problem of keeping apprised of all applicable codes, standards, and specifications is likely to get more complex as the government becomes more involved in product quality and as trends in product liability place more burden on the manufacturer for becoming familiar with the end-use requirements.

For a rather complete listing of the various sources of standards and specifications, the reader is referred to a book by Struglia.[26] In addition to this general information source, the following listed sources are a useful start toward becoming more familiar with standards and specifications in the metals industry.

[23] Walden, C. H., and P. L. Widener, Quality Control of an Aluminum Sheet Mill, *American Society for Quality Control, Technical Conference Transactions,* 1967, pp. 23–24.

[24] The publication *Aluminum Standards and Data Mill Products,* issued by the Aluminum Association, is an excellent source of standards for aluminum products.

[25] For example, ASME Boiler and Pressure Vessel Code, The American Society of Mechanical Engineers, New York 10017.

[26] Struglia, E. J., *Standards and Specifications Information Sources Mangement Information Guide* 6, Gale Research Company, Book Tower, Detroit, Mich. 1965.

Sources for Standards and Specifications

1. Specifications and Methods of Testing (issued annually), ASTM Publication, American Society for Testing and Materials, Race St., Philadelphia, Pa.   Part 3—Steel Sheet, Strip, Bar, Rod, Wire, Metallic, Coated Products.   Part 5—Copper and Copper Alloys.   Part 6—Die-cast Metals, Light Metals and Alloys.   Part 32—Chemical Analysis of Metals, Metal Bearing Ores.

2. Aluminum Standards and Data, 1970–1971, The Aluminum Association, 750 Third Avenue, New York 10017.

3. "Carbon Steel Sheet Product Manual," American Iron and Steel Institute, 150 East 42d Street, New York.

4. "Standards Manual for Copper and Copper Alloys, Mill Products," Copper and Brass Research Association, 420 Lexington Avenue, New York 10017.

5. "SAE Handbook," ASM Index, lists over 1,000 SAE Aerospace Material Specifications on Metals. Society of Automotive Engineers, 485 Lexington Avenue, New York 10017.

6. Kardonorsky, S. P., Guide to Material Standards and Specifications, reprint from *Materials in Design Engineering*, March, April, May, June, July, August, 1958 issues.

7. "Military Standardization Handbook—Aluminum and Aluminum Alloys," Mil-HDBK-694 A(MR).

8. "Military Handbook—Metallic Materials and Elements for Aerospace Vehicle Structures," Mil-HDBK-5A.

QUALITY IMPROVEMENT

The metals industry in its early beginnings started on the basis of art rather than science, but even in these early years it made rapid improvements in product quality that were sufficient to support the metals requirements of the industrial revolution. It offered products of unique but at the same time versatile characteristics that led to breakthroughs in man's effort to master his environment. Each succeeding decade has seen new advances that have included new metals as well as improvements in the quality of older metals. We have more recently seen the advent of the new exotic metals such as uranium and titanium that hold much promise for the future. The great wonder of these quality improvements is that they have been accompanied by parallel improvements in the efficiencies of the process. This has led to an ever broader use of metal products.

Much of the credit for these successes should be given to the profession of metallurgy, which has developed the metals process into a true science. Metals processes have been developed which are capable of fabricating metal products with a tremendous range in properties and which demonstrate a high degree of reliability. The physical metallurgist has developed the skills of alloying and fabrication while the extractive metallurgist, the chemist, and the engineer have provided continual improvements in the treatment of ore and its conversion to high-grade metal. Many of the basic metals processes that started on the basis of art have now become sciences.

The Climate for Improvement   Many factors have worked in a positive manner to hasten quality and process improvements and a few have, at times, worked in opposition to change. The metals industry is one of the largest industries in our total economy and thus has been able to attract the talent of high-caliber men in developing new processes and products. Competition has always been keen within each segment of the industry, and quality improvements that have filled new requirements have always yielded market share improvement. The various metals have had to compete with one another as well as with other products such as wood, refractories, and plastics.

Defense industries and space exploration have offered great challenges to the metals industry. The response has doubtless contributed very signficantly to improvements in technology and product quality.

The industry's high capital investments as well as very significant operating costs have spurred the search for newer and more efficient processes. High capital investment has also acted to retard rapid innovation when it called for replacing costly existing processes. It is not uncommon to see the same product made in one plant by an old process and in a new plant by the most modern of processes. The significance of this reluctance to replace the older and inefficient processes was vividly displayed after World War II when the war-torn countries of Europe and Japan rebuilt their metals industry with new processes which have produced major breakthroughs in product quality and manufacturing costs.

The climate for applying the best quality control practices toward the goals of quality improvement has not been consistently good in the metals industry. Only in most recent years do we see the acceptance of the concepts of modern quality control. Quality control has generally grown as an arm of the Metallurgical Department, and many of the tasks normally assigned to Quality Control remain within the province of the metallurgist. The net result has been a slow acceptance, by the metals industry, of the quality control methodology that can contribute to product improvement. In addition, the main thrust of the Metallurgical Department has been toward the metallurgical aspects of the operation with lesser emphasis placed on the nonmetallurgical aspects of fabrication. The knowledge of the equipment engineer and the skill of the equipment operator have been looked to for providing product improvements relating to visual appearance and dimensional control. Quality Control, working with the metallurgist, has, however, played a very significant role in achieving quality improvement through its customer contacts and indentification of the product characteristics that required improvement.

Project Identification   In the metals industry, there are a number of sources of information that are useful for identifying areas for quality improvement.[27] The most common sources relate to the following:

Yield or recovery information	Raw material cost variances
Customer claims and complaints	Information of competitors' quality
Excessive rework costs	Products that require excessive manufacturing
Promised delivery performance	operations

From such a range of source information, it is not difficult to identify potential quality improvement projects, but the question does arise as to the relative priority of projects. How do we pick the vital few and avoid the pitfall of working on projects of marginal value? The priority of many products can be determined by their obvious economic significance but, in other instances, must be based upon judgment.

Some quality improvement projects specific, if not unique, to the metals industry warrant some elaboration.

Yield Improvement Projects.   It is common practice in the metals industry to use the process yield[28] as one of the principal measures of manufacturing efficiency. Many of the causes of low yield are quality related and are therefore appropriate targets for quality improvement.[29] Quality problems can reduce process yields

---

[27] For a discussion of project identification generally, see Section 16.

[28] The term "recovery" is often used in preference to yield.

[29] Rosenzweig, G., "Less Steel in the Scrap Bucket," Yield Improvement Program in a Rolling Mill, *American Society for Quality Control, Technical Conference Transactions,* 1968, pp. 217–221.

either in the form of defective finished product or in the more usual form of in-process scrap. For this reason, the percentage of defective finished product cannot be used as the exclusive index of relative importance of quality improvement projects; i.e., the main losses may have been experienced during processing. In addition, a distinction must be made between:

1. "Quality" losses due to failures of conformance.
2. Other scrap losses considered to be inherent in the processes, e.g., the trim removed from the sides of rolled coils due to the invariable irregularities at these edges. These "inherent" losses are sometimes called "natural waste."

The metals industry can recycle much of the metal that is scrapped during fabrication, but nevertheless the recycling costs represent a major cost factor and hence an opportunity for process and quality improvement. It is a common practice to maintain records pertaining to yield, and when these are maintained in sufficient detail, they represent an excellent source for identifying areas where quality improvement could contribute to reduced manufacturing costs. Many times these sources of loss have long been accepted as an essential aspect of the process and are overlooked as opportunities for improvement.

It is useful to supplement these yield data with a system of scrap identification and nomenclature which describes the observed defects ("symptoms") in precise enough language to provide clues to the causes of the defects. Widely used terms such as "trim losses" or "mill damage" are of no help for this purpose. The Pareto principle of identifying and working on the vital few can best be applied when scrap is properly categorized in the above manner.

Customer Claims and Complaints. The metals industry has its share of dissatisfied customers. In the case of large shipments, the customer will not only complain if inadequate quality exists; he will also ask for a refund and will want to return the material. In some of these cases the customer has received product outside his stated requirements as well as outside the generally accepted commercial standards. The usual remedy to these problems is increased quality assurance measures. However, in many instances, the product in question may be found in accord with commercial standards as well as the stated customer requirements but still fails to perform in the customer's plant. In other words, it is not fit for the customer's intended use. If the claim is significant in size and the reason is not readily obvious, a product engineer or a metallurgist most familiar with the type of product in question is usually dispatched to the customer's plant in order to identify the product quality deficiency and to decide upon the validity of the claim. This customer contact activity often yields information that can focus attention on the need for some basic quality improvements if this market is to be satisfactorily serviced.

Promised Delivery Performance. For mills producing products to customer orders rather than carrying warehouse inventories of standard items, there is always a problem of producing and shipping promptly in accordance with a promised date for shipment or delivery. Since most customers desire to carry a minimum-sized inventory, the shorter lead times become a sales asset, while failure to meet promises on delivery can erode customer relations.

The manufacturing problem of failing to meet promised delivery dates may seem unrelated to the need for quality improvement, but upon close examination one finds that quality problems relate to an appreciable number of missed promises. In some instances, the quality problem may cause a delay of the entire shipment. In other instances it produces an unexpected low yield and results in the shipment of a partial order. The reasons for missed promises can be analyzed and can lead to the identification of the main needs for quality improvement.

Organizing for Quality Improvement   In most metals plants, the quality control function reports to the same department head as the process engineer and/or metallurgist. This department may be designated as the Technical Department or, at times, the Metallurgical Department.

One distinct advantage of this organizational setup is that the quality control engineer can work closely with those individuals who are responsible for technology, when he is called upon to work on quality improvement projects. A disadvantage is that the quality control effort is slow to adopt new quality control methodology and that the quality control function seldom achieves the organizational stature required.

The concepts[30, 31] of an interdepartmental approach of organizing a plant's resources for achieving a breakthrough in quality have been put to very good use in a number of metals companies. This approach offers the opportunity to bring a broader-based task force into the act of seeking quality improvement. It is helpful in overcoming many of the cultural problems associated with removing the art from a process.

The quality control engineer makes his greatest contribution to the quality improvement effort by collecting and analyzing the facts and steering the work clear of the pitfall of acting on the basis of opinion.

Special Problems   The metals industry is faced with a number of problems which work against achieving rapid and permanent quality improvements.

Plant Experimentation.   Many quality improvement projects call for some form of experimentation in the plant. At best, these experiments interfere with the production activity. They may also create inordinate amounts of scrap. Primary metals products are produced by processes which are massive in size, often continuous in nature, and hence not readily amenable to plant experimentation. An alternative course is to develop pilot plant equipment, but this, too, is expensive and often yields results that are not predictive of full-scale production operation.

Another factor that deters plant experimentation is the fact that many aspects of the metals operation are under operator cognizance without benefit of written practices and instrumental control. This makes it difficult to carry out well-controlled plant experiments.

All the above problems emphasize the necessity for well-designed experiments as discussed in Sections 27 and 28. The statistically designed approach to experimentation will yield the maximum information with the least cost.

Holding the Gain in Quality Improvement.   A quality improvement project also provides increased knowledge of the process. If this increased knowledge can be consistently applied to the process, the resulting quality improvement can also be retained. This calls for revised manufacturing practices and greater attention to one or more of the manufacturing variables. For metals operations that rely on written operating practices and formal methods of process control, this presents very few problems. However, for processes that rely principally upon the knowledge and the skill of the production operator, there are serious problems of making sure that the new knowledge is put to use. These problems can be handled only by educating the operator as to the importance of the new controls and then following up with process audits that provide assurance that the operator is conforming.

Wide Range of Product Types.   Most metals operations produce a wide range of products which are, in turn, sold to a large number of customers having a variety of requirements. When quality problems arise, they often appear as being related to a single product rather than to a basic process deficiency. In the face of marketing a host of products with a variety of quality problems, it is difficult to select the area for improvement which will yield the most results. Quality improvement

---

[30] See Section 16, under Organizing for Improvement.

[31] Juran, J. M., "Managerial Breakthrough," pp. 67–68, McGraw-Hill Book Company, New York, 1964.

effort is often dispersed over many products and fails to produce the breakthrough types of solution that contribute to improvements throughout the plant.

Cultural Problems It is to be expected that an industry as old as the metals industry will experience some cultural resistance in adopting the changes in operating practices required for achieving a breakthrough in quality improvement. In the metals industry, this cultural resistance is greatly influenced by two long-standing practices:

Technical Organization.[32] Usually the technical organization in a metals plant is headed by a Chief Metallurgist. The evolution of this metallurgical-centered type of organization is understandable, since over the years, the science of metallurgy has been the main contributor to the basic technology of the industry. The metallurgists responsible for these advances have properly gained the respect of other departments, and have been awarded high organization status for their contributions.

A subtle by-product of this organization form has been the equating of the metallurgical function to the total technical function. This has often resulted in two failures to balance priorities:

1. Nonmetallurgical technology (e.g., chemical analysis, mechanical equipment) has received less emphasis than metallurgy.

2. The concepts of a quality function, and of nonmetallurgical skills for solving quality problems, e.g., quality planning, statistical methods, motivation, and quality costs, have not been fully grasped or aggressively utilized.

Aside from the Plant Chemist, charged with directing the chemical analysis, it is not uncommon to find the entire technical staff possessing a metallurgical education. Certainly, some of these men broaden their field of technical knowledge and demonstrate capabilities for making contributions beyond the limits of metallurgical phenomena, but the strong metallurgical connotation has resulted in technical organizations having a narrow charter in respect to the entire technology of the process. As a result, other departments have been called on to supply much of the nonmetallurgical technology; e.g., Plant Engineering and Production have supplied much of the equipment technology. These arrangements have worked, but there is a good deal of question as to whether they might not have worked better had the technical function been built on a broader base, with the total process in mind.

Operator Cognizance. In its infancy, the metals industry depended almost entirely upon the skill of the equipment operator to achieve good processing results in both smelting and fabrication. It took some time to convince the melter in the steel industry that a laboratory analysis might yield a processing decision which excelled his visual skill for determining the quality of a heat. The aluminum industry still depends a great deal upon operator skill for the operation of electrolytic reduction cells. The skill required to operate a large rolling mill was long considered to be the epitome of craftsmanship. As a result of this heritage, many metallurgical processes operate based on operator skill and under operator cognizance. This condition is changing rapidly with the advent of new equipment, computer controls, and increased technology. The metals industry has witnessed the advances made in motivational programs[33] in the United States and Japan and is applying this knowledge to its operations.

---

[32] This portion of the author's original draft has been substantially revised by the Editor (Juran). In the opinion of the Editor, the proper development of the quality function in the metals industry has been retarded by making the Quality Control organization subordinate to the Metallurgy Department.

[33] For a discussion of motivational programs generally, see Section 18, and especially, the Jishu Kanri activities in the Japanese steel industry (a derivative of the Japanese QC Circles).

The Role of Statistics in Improvement   The metals industry explored the use of statistical tools for quality control long before it considered the broader concepts of quality control. Two European authors[34] appear to have been the first to use statistical methods for analyzing variables in the steel industry. However, the technique was slow in spreading. Such success as was achieved was the result of individual effort rather than a general acceptance of the discipline.

An early direction of study was the search for cause and effect relationships in the processes. Use was made of the statistical tools of correlation and regression analysis. Some of the early papers published still merit referencing.[35, 36, 37, 38, 39]

While the present author can report that use of statistical methods is on the increase, the metals industry cannot yet be regarded as one of the leaders in applying statistics.

In more recent years, computers have played a significant role in bringing about the use of statistics in the metals industry, for they present the opportunity to analyze the copious metals plant production data. The quality control literature of the 1960s contained relatively few publications concerning the use of statistics in the metals industry, but there are a number of papers which merit mention.[40, 41, 42, 43] From other indications, it is evident that the metals industry is making use of statistical methods, but apparently the results from these applications are going unreported or are being published only in journals relating to metals technology.

The opportunites afforded by experimentation using techniques of factorial designed experiments and EVOP will likely await the general acceptance of statistical methodology as an essential part of the metallurgical curriculum or until the methods gain acceptance for plant use after their worth has been demonstrated in the research and development laboratories.

Statistics has played a significant role in steering the quality improvement efforts in the metals industry. The use of capability studies has resulted in attention being focused on process deficiencies and this, in turn, has resulted in a direction of technical effort to those areas requiring improved capability. The basic statistical tech-

---

[34] The first published paper appears to have been "Metallurgy and Probability" by A. Jude, delivered in 1922 and published in the *Journal of the Birmingham Metallurgical Society,* vol. VIII, No. 8, pp. 309 *et seq.* A portion of this paper was reproduced in *Quality (Journal of European Organization for Quality Control)*, vol. XV, No. 1, pp. 19–22. More widely known is the 1923 paper by Dr. Karl H. Daeves, *Stahl und Eisen,* vol. 43, No. 14, pp. 462–466 (in German).

[35] A pioneering paper was that of H. J. Hand, The Utility of Statistical Methods in Steel Plants, *Transactions AIME,* vol. 131, pp. 231–260, 1938.

[36] Rogers, W. T., Multiple Correlation Applied to Steel Plant Problems, *ASM, National Transactions,* 1947, pp. 935–953.

[37] Woods, A. P., Jr., Statistical Methods Applied to Steel Plant Operations, *American Society for Quality Control, Technical Conference Transactions,* 1954, pp. 279–288.

[38] Leckie, D. S., Applications of Regression Analysis to Steel Plant Problems, *American Society for Quality Control, Technical Conference Transactions,* 1955, pp. 419–432.

[39] Curry, J. A., Searching for Assignable Causes in an Integrated Steel Plant, *American Society for Quality Control, Technical Conference Transactions,* 1956, pp. 89–97.

[40] Lewis, S. S., Inside the Mill—Sampling? Or Crystal Ball Gazing? *American Society for Quality Control, Technical Conference Transactions,* 1969, pp. 427–437.

[41] McCune, D. C., Variables Selection in Multiple Regression, *American Society for Quality Control, Technical Conference Transactions,* 1967, pp. 27–32.

[42] Hanajiri, A., An Application of Multiple Regression Analysis to Cupola Melting Operations, *American Society for Quality Control, Technical Conference Transactions,* 1966, pp. 156–161.

[43] McMahon, D. J., Applications in the Steel Industry of the 3-parameter Weibull Distribution, *American Society for Quality Control, Technical Conference Transactions,* 1970, pp. 275–281.

niques such as the control chart and the histogram have been used to identify the nature of process control problems.

Results   The industry has been seriously challenged by imports, by competition from plastics and other competing materials, by problems of oversupply, and by the escalating cost of new process facilities.   All these challenges plus the universal problem of rising labor costs have placed increased emphasis on the need for new technology.   The basic oxygen furnace process has revolutionized the manufacture of steel.   Modern gage instrumentation and computers have allowed an increase of rolling speeds as well as increased capability for holding a close tolerance on gage and flatness.   The industry has been successful in tailoring its products to meet a myriad of customer requirements.   Aluminum has created a host of new products that utilize its combination of strength, light weight, good electrical conductivity, and uniformity of surface appearance.

The metals industry has found ways to overcome the complex problems associated with the processing of uranium and titanium.   It has found profitable uses for its by-products.   It has responded well to the requirements of national defense and space exploration.

Specific quality problems in which the industry has been able to achieve significant improvements include the following.

Improvement in Thickness Control.   Thickness control is essential at each step of metal rolling.   The product must be thick enough to provide structural integrity for the intended use.   However, excess thickness is an economic loss.   Hence customers have continually demanded closer tolerances on thickness, and these demands have required control over both the nominal and the range of thickness throughout the product.   In addition, uniformity of thickness is vital to achieving flatness (see below).

The metals industry has responded to these needs by constantly improving its ability to roll a strip to closer thickness tolerances.   More recently this improvement has come from application of improved measuring devices such as x-ray and nuclear gages to the computer controls of rolling mills.   Not only have the thickness tolerances been tightened but this has been achieved at increased rolling speeds.

Flatness of Sheet and Coil.   A prerequisite for achieving flatness is uniform thickness of the input material.   In addition, the reduction during rolling must be uniform across the width of the strip.   Any area of the sheet which is reduced in thickness more than others becomes longer as well.   This extra length then creates either edge waves or center buckling, depending on the reduction profile.   Nonuniform rolling may be caused by such variables as deflection of mill work rolls, nonuniform heat buildup in the rolls, or use of the same roll contour for a variety of widths.

Significant improvements in thickness measurement have been realized by employing x-ray and nuclear gages.   The rolling equipment has been improved, and fine adjustments can now be made by means of computer controls, all of which result in improved flatness.   Coincidentally with these advances, there has been the development of a whole new generation of leveling equipment that is capable of reworking a strip until it is flat.   Devices have been developed[44] for measuring the state of flatness even under the operating condition when the strip is under tension.

Computer Controls.   The metals industry has also recognized the need for improving the instrumentation of its process so that it might achieve the benefits of operating with computer controls.   These controls have been successfully applied to nearly all aspects of the metals process.   Lindstrom[45] describes the computer con-

[44] Pearson, W. K. J., Shape Measurement and Control, *Journal of the Institute of Metals*, vol. 93, pp. 173–178, 1964–1965.

[45] Lindstrom, W. M., Computer Control of a Blast Furnace Operation, *American Society for Quality Control, Technical Conference Transactions*, 1963, pp. 55–60.

trols of a blast furnace. Computer controls in hot strip mills are becoming common-place.[46,47] Computers have gained widespread use for process control in Japan.[48] They are also used in simpler tasks such as controlling billet cutting.[49] The use of computers in all these different applications has allowed increased productivity without large increases in capital investment and manpower. To accomplish this task successfully, the technology of the process had to be enhanced, and new abilities in instrumentation and computer controls had to be developed for direct application to the metals industry. Shaw[50] reports on some of the serious problems encountered with on-line measurement in the steel industry.

MEASURES OF PERFORMANCE

The metals industry makes use of several measures of quality performance, as set out in Table 33-2. Despite the value of these measures, further work remains to be done to evolve a method of expressing quality performance in simple terms understandable by upper management as well as by managers in Technical, Production, and Sales.[51] Lacking an adequate measure, quality performance is commonly equated with the cost of customer claims or with percent scrap. Such indicators fall short of presenting an overall picture, and are not adequate to relate quality to income and profit. These same shortcomings make it difficult for Quality Control to provide management with adequate information about quality performance and about needs for quality improvement.

Measures in Current Use Metals plant operation generates a great deal of information needed for process regulation and for making decisions on product conformance. These data serve their intended purpose but are not easily reduced to a form which permits measuring quality performance. The type and quantity of these data vary throughout the metals industry, and this variation is attributable to the nature of the metallurgical process and to the size of the effort that a company sees fit to expend in controlling its processes. Hayter[52] and Rogers[53] reported on the type of quality performance data available in a steel mill and how they are used to improve quality and productivity. Teschner[54] reports on the use of computers for informational control.

Turning to the measure of quality performance listed in Table 33-2, cost of customer claims does provide some index of customer satisfaction and hence has gained acceptance. It has limitations since it is an after-the-fact measure, provides no early

[46] Staff Control Engineering, Hot Strip Steel Mills Computer Controls Begins to Pay Out, *Control Engineering,* vol. 10, No. 12, pp. 24–25, December 1963.

[47] Samuel, G. H., On-line Computer Boosts Steel Mill Output, *Control Engineering,* vol. 14, No. 6, pp. 80–84, June 1967.

[48] Katsura, K., M. Imaizumi, and S. Nakamura, An Application of Computer for Process Control in Steel Industry, *Reports of Statistical Application Research, Union of Japanese Scientists and Engineers,* vol. 12, No. 2, pp. 21–36, June 1965.

[49] Clyne, J. P., Simple Computer Billets Five Ways, *Control Engineering,* vol. 11, No. 1, pp. 81–84, February 1964.

[50] Shaw, D., Some Problems in On-line Measurements in the Steel Industry, *Quality Engineer,* vol. 31, No. 5, pp. 132–135, 1967.

[51] See generally Section 21, under Executive Reports on Quality.

[52] Hayter, W. T., Process and Quality Control for Management, *American Society for Quality Control, Technical Conference Transactions,* 1961, pp. 61–66.

[53] Rogers, W. T., Total Quality Control in an Integrated Steel Plant, *American Society for Quality Control, Technical Conference Transactions,* 1962, pp. 481–491.

[54] Teschner, H. G., Controlling Data Flow in a Steel Mill, *Control Engineering,* vol. 15, No. 4, pp. 76–80, April 1968.

TABLE 33-2 Measures of performance

Application	Control subject	Unit of measure
Metals industry generally	Customer claims	Percent of claims to sales
Metals industry generally	Process yield	Percent acceptable product to material input
Ore smelting	Raw material usage	Usage vs. standard
Aluminum reduction	Power consumption	Ratio of power used in reduction to total power consumption
Metals industry generally (recent)	Quality losses	Losses vs. standards

alert to unfavorable trends, and fails to reflect internal plant losses due to poor quality.

Process yield (or percent recovery) expresses the "survival rate," i.e., the percentage of material (introduced into an operation) which emerges as acceptable product. This yield does bear a relation to product quality but is usually considered as a measure of manufacturing efficiency rather than of quality performance.

In ore beneficiating and smelting, some economic indicators (of the efficiency with which the raw materials are used) also serve as measures of quality performance.

In electrolytic reduction of aluminum oxide to aluminum metal, an important process performance indicator is that percentage of total power consumption which is used in converting the oxide to the metal.

Some metals companies[55,56] have recently established procedures for expressing their quality performance in terms of the total economic loss attributable to poor quality[57] and have coupled this with the cost of quality appraisal to arrive at a measure of quality performance in terms of dollars. A new approach to this problem was developed by the author and is reported upon by Burtenshaw and Klein.[58] This method makes use of indicators which have been developed on the basis of establishing standards of quality performance and then measuring and reporting conformance to these standards. This type of quality indicator is easily understood by management and serves to complement measurements of productivity which have been developed on the basis of work standards.

Standards for Comparison Practically nothing is available in the literature that would serve as a basis for establishing "norms" of quality performance in the metals industry. There is an understandable reluctance on the part of any industry to disseminate quality performance data even though they might be proud of their performance, because of sales and technical implications.

It is generally recognized that the level of customer claims runs quite low and that the metals industry is motivated to correct customer problems more by a desire to satisfy the customer than for the purpose of reducing losses. Martin[59] reports that justified returns from customers amount to appreciably less than 1% of the weight of products shipped. Since the returned material has an appreciable salvage value, the actual loss would be somewhat lower than the amount returned.

[55] Dunn, D. S., Quality Control for Profit Improvement in the Speciality Steel Industry, *American Society for Quality Control, Technical Conference Transactions,* 1966, pp. 152–155.

[56] Hains, R. W., Economics of Quality, *American Society for Quality Control, Technical Conference Transactions,* 1969, pp. 439–443.

[57] For a discussion of quality and costs generally, see Section 5.

[58] Burtenshaw, O. L., and N. A. Klein, Let's Put Quality Control in Its Place, *American Society for Quality Control, Technical Conference Transactions,* 1969, pp. 417–418.

[59] Martin, A. R., Control of Product Quality in the Wrought Aluminium Industry, *The Production Engineer,* vol. 36, No. 4, p. 263, April 1967.

QUALITY PROBLEMS

The summary which follows discusses some principal current and future quality problems of the metals industry. Because these problems are inherent to the manufacturing processes employed, they are representative of the industry.

Current Problems

Surface Appearance. This is a major reason for product rejection and customer dissatisfaction. This deficiency may be merely a matter of a nonuniform surface texture, or it may involve measurable surface flaws imparted by the fabrication equipment. Many metal products such as those manufactured from aluminum are designed to be used with the natural mill surface finish or, at most, with a thin coating. The customer expects a product having a uniform, eye-pleasing appearance, but to achieve such a product consistently requires rigorous controls at each operation and an effective method for inspecting and sorting the product. Tinplate has a susceptibility to nonuniform appearance which is objectionable to the customer. Metal used in building products or in the transportation field must conform to rigid standards of surface quality.

Many factors in a metal operation work in opposition to achieving a uniform surface. Metallic oxides introduced in the rolling operation erode the surface, and the mechanical operations inherent to the rolling process take their toll. The product experiences handling damage in the plant and is subjected to further damage during shipping and exposure to the elements.

There are no easy solutions to the problems associated with surface appearance. The reasons for the imperfections are many and are highly dependent upon operator control. While improvements have been made in surface quality, the customer continually increases his demand for surface uniformity.

Flatness. In recent years significant progress has been made in improving the flatness of sheet and coil products, but the lack of adequate flatness remains as one of the principal problems of the industry. Further improvements are needed in the industry's ability to roll a flat sheet and to be able to inspect for this characteristic during manufacture.

Yield Improvement. The metals industry recognizes the need to increase its process yield if it is to increase its profit and minimize the need for capital expenditures. There are many factors which detract from high yields. Some of these relate to process design, but others are attributable to chronic and sporadic quality problems that require identification and resolution.

Thickness Control. Major improvements have been made in the metals industry's ability to achieve tighter tolerance for the thickness of its rolled products. These improvements have resulted from improvements in rolling mill equipment, gage instrumentation, and computer controls. These improvements have been significant, but the problem remains paramount as the customer continues to demand ever tighter tolerances. The uniformity of thickness relates to the product processing characteristics in the customers' plants, while the adherence to the optimum level for nominal gage plays a major role in the economics of utilizing the metal.

Future Problems

The metals industry will be confronted with a host of problems in the coming decade. It will be required to remain price competitive with imports while it will experience increased costs for wages and for capital expenditures required to solve environmental problems. The metals industry customers will require improved product quality with little or no increase in price. The consumerism movement, and trends in product liability are bound to affect the industry. Quality control methodology should prove helpful in coping with the emerging problems, as discussed below.

Product Liability. Many products rely on metal components for their structural integrity. The trends in product liability disputes require increased attention to quality assurance in all company departments.[60] New designs require controls which help discover any hidden hazards in new products and new applications. Quality Control will be called on to improve the planning of the manufacturing and inspection processes to minimize product hazards. Increased attention must be given to customer problems of usage and failure. Improved data collection and analysis will be needed to identify the "vital few" sources of liability risks.

Environmental Controls. In order to meet air and water pollution standards, the metals industry will be required to make major process modifications and to provide means for controlling and monitoring the quality of all air and water effluents. The quality control profession can help in providing the methodology of control for these side-streams. The procedures for sampling, testing, auditing, and taking corrective action on side-streams can well be patterned along the line of the procedures used for controlling the process. The Quality Control function might well be assigned the responsibility for exercising these controls.

Control of Maintenance. The metals industry can improve costs and productivity by increasing the effectiveness of the maintenance activity. It is becoming evident that the quality control concepts developed for the manufacture of a product apply equally well to the maintenance activities.[61] Audit techniques should prove useful in detecting the need for preventive maintenance as well as for determining the effectiveness of the maintenance work.

Yield Improvement. There remain major opportunities in the metals industry for profit improvement through improvements in yield. Metal trim and other sources of scrap, now considered standard for a process, must be made the target for yield improvement activities.

Increased Customer Requirements. The customer of the basic metals industry is going to be searching for means to improve his process and will increase his demands for improved product quality. The customer will expect more uniformity in his raw material so that it will respond to automated and high-speed equipment. He will insist on material free of any defects which might be reflected in his product, since he will be selling to a more quality-conscious market.

Changes in Process Control. The metals process of the future will likely be more continuous in nature. It will be more highly automated, and less reliance will be placed upon the skill of the operator for controlling the process. This places increased demands on technology and control methods. More cause and effect information will be required so that computers can be properly programmed to control and take compensatory corrective action. Subsidiary controls must be established that ensure the reliability of instruments. Quality information must be made available in a nearly continuous manner so that process upsets can be quickly detected.

Worker Motivation. Despite the fact that the trend is toward increased automation and computer control, we will still find the worker performing a vital function in controlling the process and determining product quality. Concepts of motivation will have to be employed to convert an operator from an individual craftsman to a qualified technician in a more sophisticated process.

---

[60] See generally Juran, J. M., Consumerism and Product Quality, *Quality Progress*, July 1970.

[61] Cornell, P. W., "Interfacing Maintenance and Quality Control during the Seventies," American Society for Quality Control, Western Regional Conference, 1970.

Foundry Quality Control [1]

K. F. PACKER

President, Packer Engineering Associates, Inc.

W. C. TRUCKENMILLER

Vice President, Packer Engineering Associates, Inc.

INTRODUCTION

The foundry is a fundamental source of structural components for our industrial civilization. Thousands of foundries produce, annually, millions of tons of ferrous and nonferrous castings. These castings undergo subsequent machining, heat treating, and finishing operations, but the quality of the castings is vital to the ultimate use of the product and to the economics of the machine shops as well.

When compared with other metal structural forms (forgings, weldments) the casting gives a good account of itself.[2] Once the patterns are available and proved, production is rapid and costs are low, especially in large quantities. Almost any shape can be made, and in sizes adequate for the great majority of applications. The metallurgical properties are influenced by the technique exercised but can reach a high level of attainment.

Castings are made from a wide assortment of base metals, often alloyed and/or thermally treated to attain the special properties needed for the end use. In addition, there are several basic casting processes, each with variants in machines, tools, etc. However, these processes all stem from a deceptively simple concept. A metal is selected, melted, and poured into a previously prepared cavity. When the re-

---

[1] In the Second Edition, this Section was prepared by D. G. Meckley III and H. F. Singer.
[2] Hall, H. T. Aspects of Quality and Reliability in the Foundry, *The British Foundryman*, vol. 61, pp. 191–201, May 1968. See especially Table III, p. 193.

sulting casting has solidified and cooled, it is removed from the mold, subjected to some mechanical and perhaps some metallurgical operations, cleaned, and shipped.

Successful execution of this basically simple concept is beset with many obstacles, chiefly process variables. To permit reuse of patterns, the molds are split, creating problems of making and matching the halves precisely. The molds are made of cohesive sand, a material which is not completely understood. The castings require holes and cavities here and there, demanding the use of cores, also made of sand. The molten metal must enter the mold from the outside, requiring sprues and runners. Loose sand must be kept out of the mold, requiring chokes and risers. The metal shrinks nonuniformly during solidification, creating voids, warpage, and stresses.

During the twentieth century, great strides have been made in foundry science and technology. The nature of metals is much better understood, thanks to much research and to new instrumentation. Foundry equipment has undergone a major revolution, permitting a high degree of mechanization, with better controls and uniformity. The concept of quality control by data and analysis has gained a foothold. Nevertheless, there remain many variables which are still handled by empirical methods. Most important, applying the available scientific knowledge still runs into formidable cultural resistance, since the industry has long been rooted in empiricism.

This Section limits itself to discussion of quality control of *ferrous* castings, which constitute the bulk of all casting tonnage. However, the concepts and the methods in use for the quality control of ferrous castings are, to a high degree, applicable to nonferrous castings as well.

QUALITY PLANNING

Some foundries are independent companies whose customers are manufacturers. Other foundries are "captive shops," i.e., departments within a manufacturing company whose "customers" are sister departments.[3] Either way, the quality planning process is a series of events requiring close collaboration between the foundry and its customers. The need for collaboration arises from the fact that there are two designs: (1) the drawing of the part or component needed by the customer, and (2) the drawing of the casting needed to make the component.

Product Specification. This is always prepared by the customer. It shows the final part dimensions after machining, and specifies the end-use requirements (e.g., tensile strength, hardness) and any special tests to be made. Sophisticated customers usually specify the metal to be used, and many prepare a casting drawing as well. In addition, the customer specifies the limits on composition, structure, and metallurgical properties, or refers to published standards for these.

It is important for the foundry to understand not only the part drawing but also *how the part will be used,* i.e., what will be the environment, the stresses, the intended life. In addition it is well to understand which characteristics are critical, major, and minor. The more the foundry understands these things the more the resulting casting will be responsive to the customer's needs.

Casting Design. The foundry engineers review the customer's specification not only to design the casting but also to propose product design changes which might reduce cost of pattern equipment, improve productivity, and provide better quality. Following this review, the engineers prepare a casting drawing showing the casting

---

[3] While the text of this Section is generally oriented to the independent foundries, the quality control problems are virtually identical for the captive shops. The differences are minor, and exist mainly in the area of customer relations.

dimensions needed to provide material for machining. Usually the customer proposes a metal capable of attaining the required end-use properties, and the tests to be made to verify this attainment. These proposals may be based on ASTM standards.

A great deal of future quality trouble can be created or avoided at this design stage. Much has been done to identify casting design features which are defect-prone, e.g., fillet radii, ribbing patterns, junctions, symmetry.[4] The standards published by the various foundry research and trade associations include much useful design knowledge. (See a partial listing in the Bibliography at the end of this Section.)

Because of uncertainties in design and foundry practice, the designers have traditionally applied substantial factors of safety in the casting designs. With improved technology, better controls, and availability of nondestructive testing, these factors of safety have now come under challenge.[5]

The casting design requires simultaneous consideration of pattern design, casting tolerances, draft, partings, gating, risering, and cores, as well as adaptability to available melting, molding, and coremaking equipment.

The foundry engineers also design and recommend the pattern equipment most appropriate to the customers' needs. For product in large volume, this equipment becomes extensive and may need to be duplicated as redundant protection for the customer.

Design Review. Once the casting drawing is approved, a considerable investment in money and calendar time elapses before the next milestone is reached for discovering any basic defect in the design. In addition, the quotations of price, production, and delivery are all built around the casting design. It is therefore most important for the foundry and customer to review the casting design. The customer will be concerned with any changes affecting his original part drawing. The foundry will be concerned with assuring that it fully understands what it is undertaking, and that it has the facilities, process capability, and skills to make the casting successfully. Neither the customer nor the foundry can proceed on a reasonable risk basis until customer requirements and the foundry's ability to meet those requirements are both known and compatible.

Once agreement has been reached, a final casting drawing can be made which will show dimensions, tolerances, draft, parting line, machining and locating points, material specifications, and possibly gating and risering. As is evident, this action leaves the phase of product design and enters that of manufacturing planning.

Samples for Qualification Testing. The concept of qualification testing commonly used in vendor relations[6] is applicable to the foundry. When used, the concept calls for samples to be made by the foundry and submitted to the customer to check out his machining setups and to test the usage characteristics of the product.

When such samples are made, they should as far as possible represent the future volume production.[7] Failing this, there is a risk of unpleasant surprises for both the foundry and the customer. Many foundries require written approval (of qualification samples) by the customer before scheduling full production.

[4] For some examples of correct and incorrect mechanical design features, see Hall, H. T., Aspects of Quality and Reliability in the Foundry, *The British Foundryman,* vol. 61, pp. 191–201, May 1968. See also Caine, John B., How to Design Reliable Castings, *Foundry,* vol. 90, pp. 70–73, March 1962; also Waindle, R. F., Specifying Reliability of Castings vs. Wrought Products, *Foundry Trade Journal,* vol. 112, pp. 427–433, Apr. 5, 1962.

[5] Hall, *op. cit.*

[6] See Section 10, under Vendor Qualification Process. See also Section 42, under Purchasing—Quality Assurance by the Vendor.

[7] In this connection, see the discussion of Trial Runs under Manufacturing Planning below.

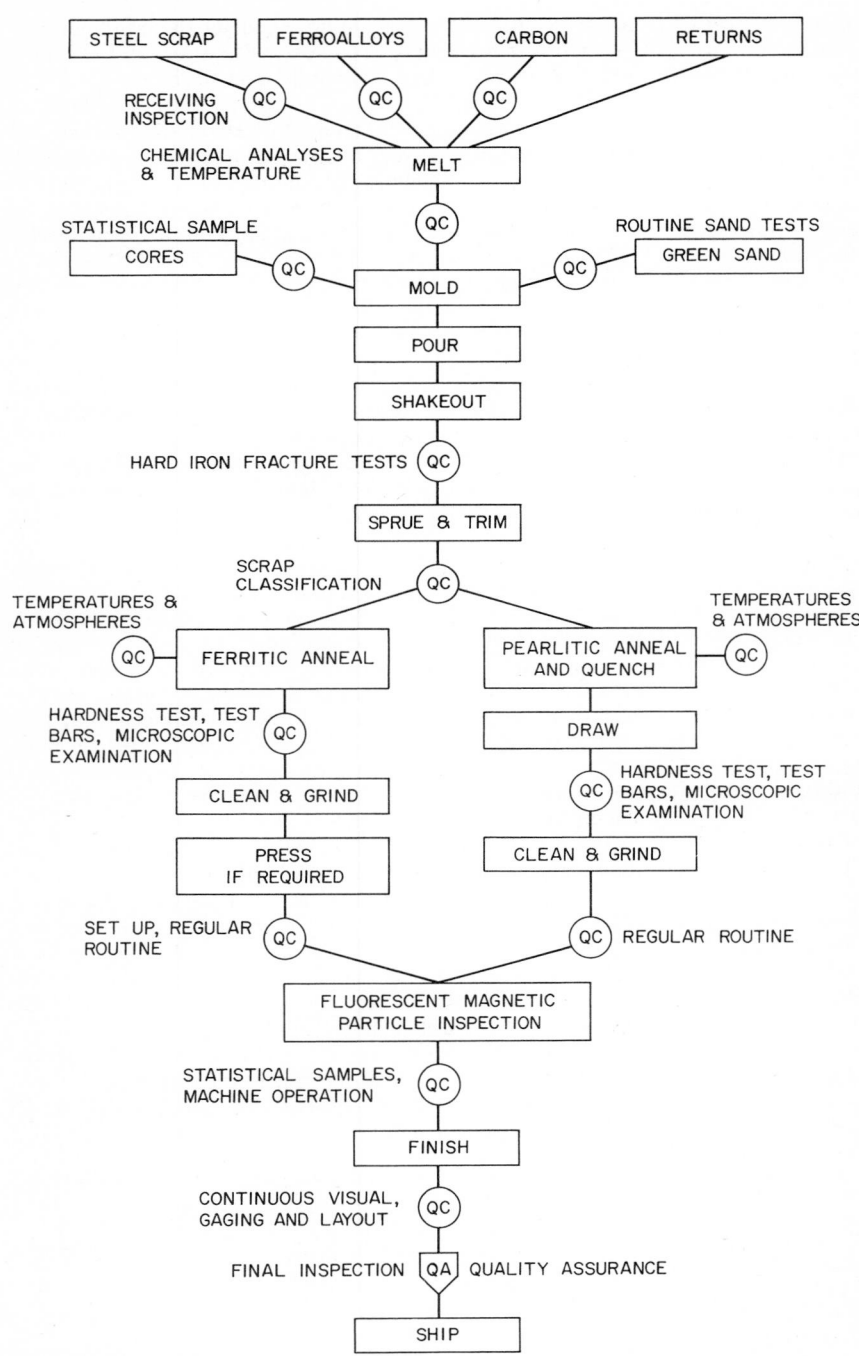

Fig. 34-1 Flow diagram of casting manufacture.

MANUFACTURING PLANNING

The agreements reached on customer's specification, on casting drawing, and on qualification samples (if any) also constitute agreement on the basic manufacturing process to be employed. As the foundry proceeds with the risks of scaling up to full production, it faces a wide array of operations, as shown on the flow diagram in Figure 34-1.

The flow diagram makes clear that several broad classes of technology and practical know-how are involved in achievement of quality: Metallurgical; "Foundry Practice," which is largely concerned with the mechanical types of operations; Inspection; Testing; Statistical Analysis. The more the foundry acquires mastery over these disciplines, the less risk it takes when embarking on manufacture of a new casting. In addition, the foundry can make use of several aids and options in its approach to planning for manufacture.

Use of Practical Experience. In contrast to the relatively high degree of science underlying the metallurgical, testing, and statistical areas, foundry practice is still largely based on experience. This is not as bad as it sounds. So long as a foundry engages in making familiar products, shapes, etc., using familiar materials and processes, the accumulated experience of its personnel is of great value in planning how to make additional, similar products.

The limitation in sole reliance on this accumulated experience is that the foundry must avoid unfamiliar products, materials, etc. Otherwise it risks getting into trouble and staying there until sufficient added experience is acquired.

Process Capability. The ability of a process or machine to reproduce its results is known as "process capability" and is expressed as 6σ of the variability of the product made by the process.[8] Process capability is measurable and, once measured, provides a valuable prediction of the ability of the process to meet the various tolerances which may be imposed on it.

Metallurgical research has done much to provide the foundry with good prediction of the effect of metallurgical properties on product qualities. Some of these predictions are sufficiently standardized to become incorporated in the industry handbooks (see Bibliography). Other relationships must be evolved from special studies.

For example, Figure 34-2 shows the relationship of pouring station to the quality of castings for cylinder heads.[9] Another example (Figure 34-3) is seen in the relationship between pouring temperature and casting defects for blowholes and porosity.[10]

Dimensional reproducibility has likewise undergone process capability studies, and these studies have led to industry standards. For example, Figure 34-4 is a guide to dimensional tolerances for malleable castings. The same publication[11] recommends other tolerances for core dimensions, core location dimensions, finishing process capabilities, coining, straightening, and sizing.

A committee (of the Institute of British Foundrymen) studying the relationship of process variables to dimensional variation in the castings came up with a regression equation (significant at the 0.1% confidence level):

$$\sigma = 0.812 \times \text{drawing dimension} + 0.02453 \times \text{projected area of core} + 2.711$$

[8] See generally Section 9, under Process Capability.

[9] Fuller, A. G., Statistical Aids for Quality Control, *The British Foundryman,* vol. 58, pp. 25–37, January 1965.

[10] Palmer, S. W., Organization of Quality Control in Iron Foundaries, *Foundry Trade Journal,* vol. 123, pp. 349–352, 357–360, Sept. 14, 1967.

[11] "Malleable Castings Dimensioning Guide," Malleable Research and Development Foundation, Cleveland, Ohio 44115.

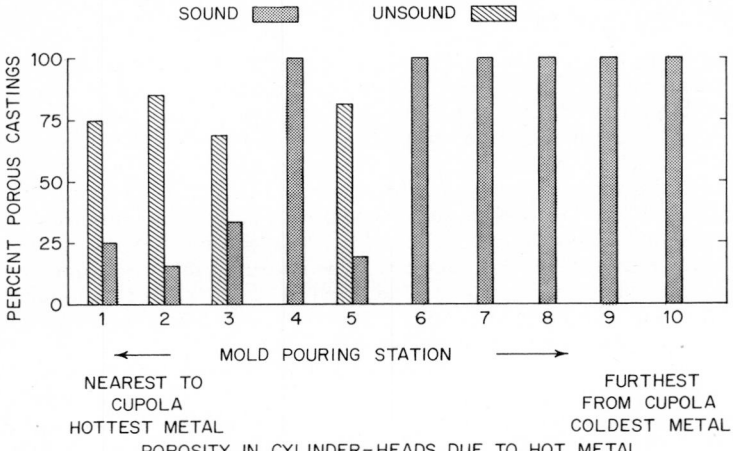

Fig. 34-2   Relationship of pouring station to cylinder head casting quality.

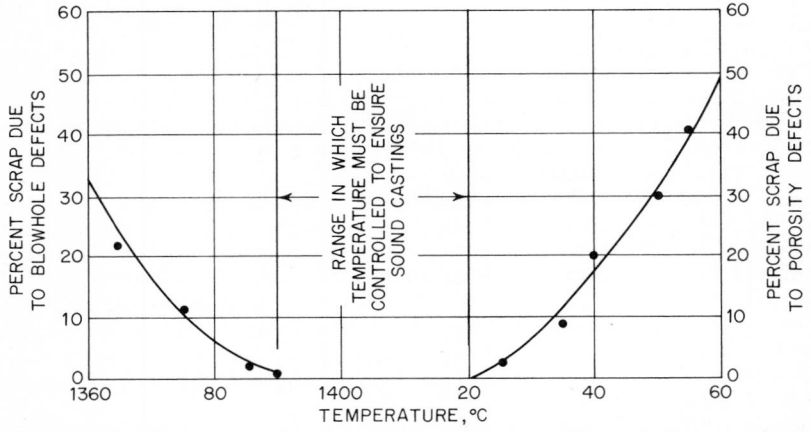

Fig. 34-3   Effect of pouring temperature on cylinder block casting quality.   *(Courtesy of British Cast Iron Research Association, Alvechurch, Birmingham, England.)*

$\times$ number of mold joints crossed $+ 6.851$, where σ is expressed in thousandths of an inch, drawing dimension is expressed in inches, projected area of the core is expressed in square inches, and number of mold joints is expressed in units.[12]

Generally, the industry research studies are addressed to broad problems of wide application, and each foundry should avail itself of this growing body of knowledge. The foundry should supplement these broad studies by conducting its own studies on unique problems such as those exemplified by Figure 34-2.

Trial Runs.   The trial run technique consists of making a limited number of cast-

[12] First Report of Technical Subcommittee TS71, Dimensional Tolerances in Castings, *The British Foundryman*, vol. 62, pp. 179–196, May 1969.

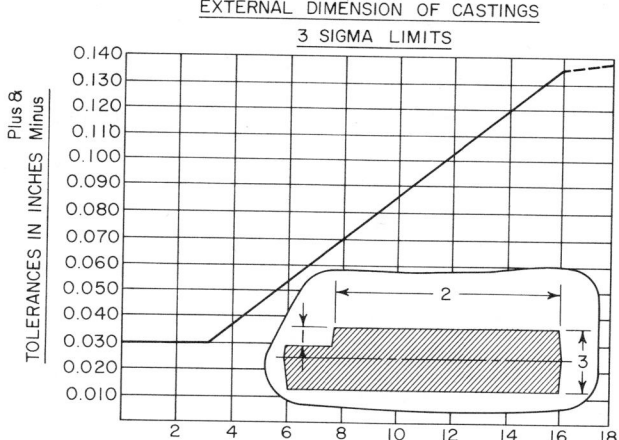

Fig. 34-4 Guide to dimensional tolerances for malleable castings. Conditions for tolerances are: 1. Solid vertical dimension not influenced by a parting line or core; green sand molding. 2. Solid horizontal dimension not influenced by a parting line or core; green sand molding. 3. Solid vertical dimension affected by parting line, not affected by core; green sand molding. *(From Malleable Castings Dimensioning Guide, 1964; courtesy of Malleable Research and Development Foundation.)*

ings (based on applying known technology) and recording carefully the results and problems encountered. Based on the experience of the trial lot, appropriate changes are made before going into full production.[13]

The trial may be limited to only those features for which existing techniques are untried. It may also be limited to determining optimum conditions (e.g., pouring temperature) for a new application. Figure 34-5 shows a trial made to discover the optimum gating for circularity of castings for piston rings and for the resulting tension of the product. The well-presented final results show that use of two gates 180 degrees apart gives excess eccentricity in the castings. The study also shows that use of three gates 120 degrees apart is unsatisfactory because of excess variability of tension in the finished product. The remaining two plans of gating are adequate for both eccentricity of castings and tension of final product. Hence the single gate, being slightly better, and cheaper as well, is chosen for use.[14]

In some situations it is feasible to combine the trial run with the qualification sample procedure, above.

Formal Manufacturing Planning. This has been the emerging approach in all but small foundries. Under this concept, standards and procedures are prepared for all the activities shown in the flow diagram (Figure 34-1). The method follows closely the general approach to manufacturing planning as discussed in Section 9. The results of all this planning are recorded in manuals, operation sheets, job cards, and other appropriate forms for reference by the work force and for audit.

The detailed application of this manufacturing planning concept to foundry operation is set out in Manufacturing Control, below.

[13] See, for example, Haney, C. E., Cost Control through Process Control, *Modern Castings,* vol. 40, pp. 110–117, October 1961.
[14] Consulting experience of J. M. Juran.

The manufacturing planning and controls needed for the foundry are quite conventional. However, the foundry tradition has long been one of manufacturing planning and control by the Production supervision and the work force. Prior to the availability of the new technologies, it was these "artists" who were the main source of foundry know-how, and there is understandable cultural resistance toward surrendering so much of the planning to an impersonal "system."

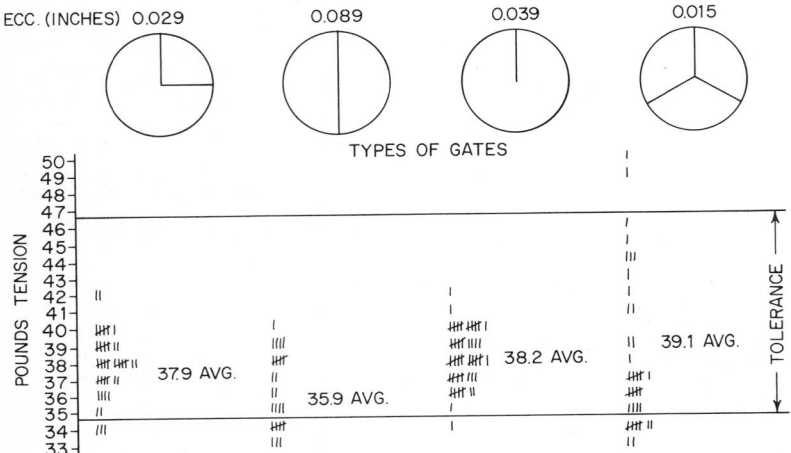

Fig. 34-5   Trial run to discover optimum gating.

MANUFACTURING CONTROL

The increasing complexity and precision demanded of the foundry have required increasing use of formal control systems to supplement the traditional reliance on the Production work force to achieve control. These supplementary systems have included establishment of:

Process specifications, both job oriented and process oriented
Controls over the quality of incoming materials and tools
Controls over all stages of the production process
Scheduled maintenance of machines, tools, and gages
Inspection and test to judge product conformance to specification (see Inspection and Test, below)
Data collection and analysis to provide aids for both quality control and improvement (see Data Collection and Analysis, below)

Job Oriented Specifications.   These consist of "job cards," one for each casting drawing, showing the tools to be used and the process conditions to be observed when making that casting. The job card is placed in a job folder which contains the drawing and other pertinent information, including "flags" or cautions to be observed when running this job.

The job folders are also used to accumulate the records of how the process was actually run, and the results achieved. For this purpose, a "job record form" (Table 34-1) is created and filled out (one for each lot run) including the defects made, test

TABLE 34-1   Data List for Job Record Card

Part number	Date molded
Part name	Core sand
Pattern number	Molding sand
Alloy number	Molder
Customer code number	Line number
Customer order number	Machine number
Pieces per mold	Air pressure, drag
Casting weight	Air pressure, cope
Flask size, type	Number of jolts
Drag height	Metal heat number
Cope height	Additions
Sprue diameter, height	Data poured
Riser height	Pouring temperature
Furnace type	Molds per ladle

results, etc.[15,16]   As these filled out forms accumulate, it becomes easier and easier to discover what process conditions tend to create good results and what other process conditions tend to create bad results.[17]   Analysis of this accumulation results in improved standards for good practice, and recommendations for change in practice.

Process Oriented Specifications.   These are the conventional process specifications so widely used in industry.   The key variables (control subjects) are identified, and standards are set for each.[18]   Then, measurements are made to assure conformance to those standards.[19,20]

In contrast to the job record card, which is the basic document for job oriented controls, the chronological data chart is the basic document for process oriented controls.[21]

The application of these job oriented and process oriented controls will now be discussed, following generally the progression of the casting through the activities shown in Figure 34-1.

Incoming Material Control   Quality control of purchased materials is quite conventional and follows the practices discussed in Section 10.   The purchases critical to casting quality include:

Materials entering the melting furnace: base metals, scrap, alloying metals, fuels, fluxes

Materials entering the molds: sand, binders

Tools: patterns, coreboxes, flasks

There has been a good deal of material standardization in the industry, especially

---

[15] Derived from Daugherty, S. P., Better Information Flow for Better Castings, *Modern Castings,* vol. 47, pp. 73–76, March 1965; and Riddell, Fred R., Practical Control Procedures, Part III, *Foundry,* vol. 94, pp. 90–93, March 1966. See also Sully, W. J., Quality Control in the Light Alloy Foundry, *Foundry Trade Journal,* vol. 119, pp. 573–579, Oct. 28, 1965.

[16] See, in this connection, Section 45, under The Repeat Job Approach.

[17] See, for example, Krueger, Lawrence S., How One Foundry Meets Reliability Standards, *Foundry,* vol. 90, pp. 86–93, March 1962.

[18] For some foundry examples of process checklists, see Haney, C. E., Cost Control through Process Control, *Modern Castings,* vol. 40, pp. 110–117, October 1961.

[19] See generally Section 6, under Planning for Control.

[20] For an example of the use of process oriented control on a broad scale, see the comment on the Japanese Book "Quality Control in the Foundry Industry" in the Bibliography below.

[21] See Chronological Charts, under Data Collection and Analysis, below.

with regard to metals. Standard specifications and test methods are widely available. The foundry should purchase its materials to these standard specifications, adding such supplemental requirements as are needed, e.g., weight and shape, special precautions.

The extent of incoming inspection varies with supplier reliability and with special material situations. Frequent checking is the rule when (1) the price is graduated to the analysis (e.g., pig iron bought on the basis of silicon content), (2) the analysis is needed in formulation, or (3) the materials bought are subject to change (e.g., moisture content in sand). In addition, unproved suppliers are checked frequently until confidence is established in the supplier's performance. Thereafter, "audit of decisions" can be established as discussed in Section 10. This concept requires that the foundry receive copies of the test results from the suppliers' laboratories.

Oil and gas fuels are highly standardized, and the supply sources are usually quite reliable. Coke is likewise purchased to standards, the tests being performed and certified by the coke producers together with experimental cupola reports. Any incoming inspection is usually for formulation or for economic reasons, e.g., moisture and ash content. The final check on coke quality is based on comparing present vs. past performance for burning (ignitibility, combustibility, and reactivity) and for usage under operating conditions.

Limestone specifications carry limits for several oxides and for sulfates and phosphates as well as screen size. Analyses should be made and checked against suppliers' certificates until the supplier is qualified. The minor fluxes (e.g., fluorspar and soda ash) are seldom checked, because of the economics.

Foundry sand should be purchased to specification for grain size, clay, fluxing constituents, and organic material, and each shipment should be checked for conformance to specifications.

Bentonites and other bonding materials and sand additives are purchased by trade name, and their acceptance is normally based only on performance in the sand system.

Refractories have little effect on product quality, but their life and performance are important to foundry economics. They are purchased to specification but are qualified solely on the basis of performance.

Purchased tooling (patterns, coreboxes, and flasks) should be checked against the tool drawings. Following recording of the results of check, these tools must be tagged to designate their status, e.g., For Layout Only; OK to Sample; Awaiting Customer Approval; OK for Trial Run; Do Not Use.

All purchased material, whether analyzed or not, should be checked for identity, after which it should be placed in clearly marked storage. Scrap should be inspected for contamination (which can create serious problems) and should be carefully segregated.

Organization for purchased material control is conventional. The technical departments set the specifications and standards, while Purchasing conducts the commercial negotiations with the suppliers. Inspections are performed by inspectors responsible to the Quality Control Department.

In-process Controls The operations of melting, molding, and pouring (Figure 34-1) are all critical to casting quality and are mainly in the hands of the Production work force. These men have numerous standards to meet aside from quality. The in-process controls are designed to assist these men in the attainment of product quality as well as to provide assurance that the quality standards have been met.

Melting. For each metal type the charge is specified. The ingredients are checked for identity and are weighed out, often on recording scales. Control of weight is by the production operators, with inspection check on the resulting recorded weights.[22] Computerized weight control has already begun.[23]

Melting is done in a variety of furnaces: cupola (Figure 34-6)[24], air furnace, arc, or induction electric. In all cases there are two principal variables: composition and temperature. Metal composition is governed by very strict specifications and must be checked before pouring, with prompt adjustment in case of failure to meet stan-

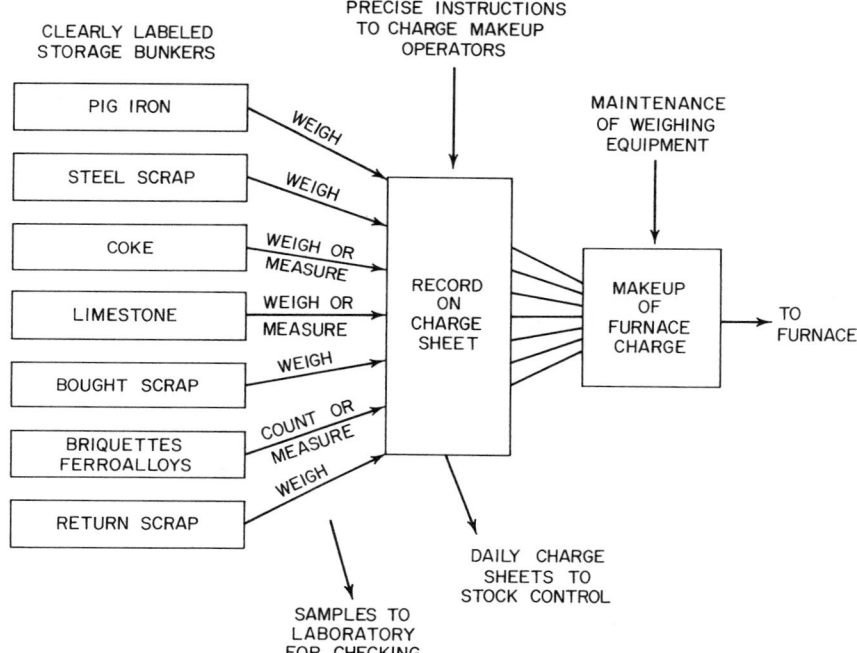

Fig. 34-6 Control of cupola charge. *(Courtesy of British Cast Iron Research Association, Alvechurch, Birmingham, England.)*

dards. The traditional analysis, using wet chemistry (supplemented by visual appraisal of fractured test bars), has steadily been giving way to direct-reading spectrometers and other sophisticated instruments. These instruments are more precise and give results more promptly.[25] Universal adoption of these instruments is limited only because they are too costly for many foundries.

Because of the great reading speed of the new instruments, the time to measure composition now depends on the speed of getting the sample to the laboratory plus getting the data back to the furnace. The former is speeded up by pneumatic tube

[22] For an example of paying a premium to the cupola crew based on adherence to weight specifications, see Burton, James R., An Incentive for Operators Whose Production Is Machine Controlled, *The Journal of Industrial Engineering*, January–February 1965, pp. 56–58.

[23] Eshelman, Ralph, Process Controls Assure Quality Castings, *Quality Assurance*, April 1967, pp. 28–30.

[24] Palmer, *op. cit.*

[25] For some comparisons, see Gupta, B. K., Modern Techniques for Iron Control, *Foundry*, vol. 95, pp. 66–71, November 1967.

delivery from furnace to laboratory.   The latter is speeded up by use of electronic transmission (e.g., closed-circuit television) from laboratory to furnace.[26]

Metal temperature at pouring (into the molds) is very critical and is held to close tolerances (see below).   The furnace temperature, being the means for attaining pouring temperature, must also be held to close tolerances based on known relation-

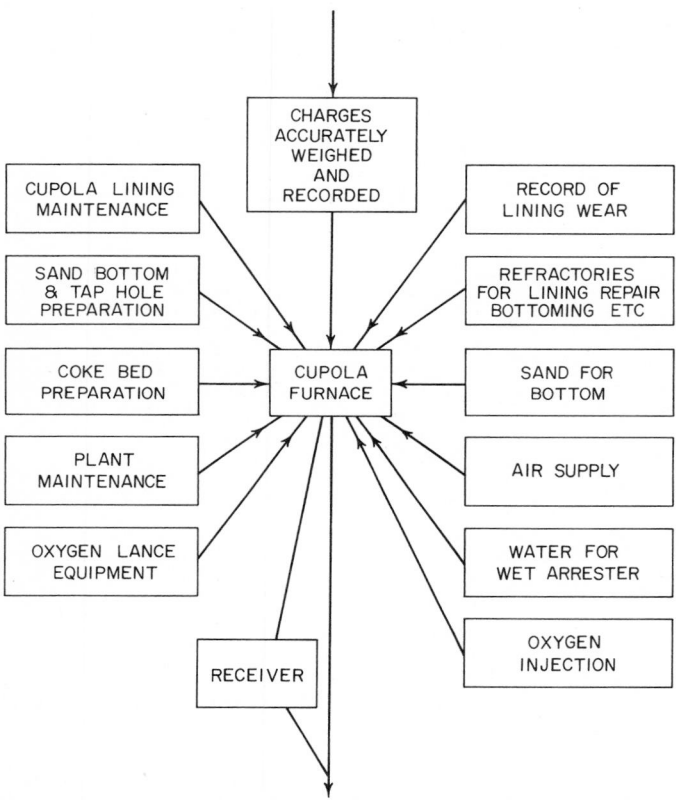

Fig. 34-7   Controls for cupola furnace operation.   *(Courtesy of British Cast Iron Research Association, Alvechurch, Birmingham, England.)*

ships between the two.   Furnace temperature is measured by conventional means, and the trend is toward automatic regulation.[27]

A great deal of setup and maintenance technique surrounds the operation of the cupola, which remains the principal form of furnace.   The variables involved in this operation (Figure 34-7) are known to affect the metal temperature and melting rate.[28]   Standard practice should be developed for these operations, and the actual practice should be audited by the quality control staff.

[26] Foundry Survival: Product Quality and Modernization, *Quality Management and Engineering*, April 1971, pp. 18–22.

[27] Eshelman, *op. cit.*

[28] Palmer, *op. cit.*

Coremaking. The quality of cores is determined by the coreboxes, the core sand, and operator practice.

Coreboxes are made to drawings and are commonly checked against those drawings by the inspectors.

Core sand is covered by specifications, and most foundries provide an inspection schedule for screen analysis. In addition, there are schedules calling for preparation of samples as test specimens to be baked and tested for cured strength, hot strength, and bakeability. Core mixes should be prescribed for each job, and these should be controlling on the coremaker and muller operator unless modified by the control personnel.

The shape of the core is determined primarily by the corebox, but only if the box remains clean and free from damage. Foundries commonly put on the coremaker the responsibility for monitoring the condition of the coreboxes while at the same time exercising care in handling and observing his product.

It is most helpful to spell out written procedures for the coremaking, setting, assembling, and curing operations. Such standard practice instructions are often seen posted on the walls of the core room along with sketches of good practice, all of which makes it more likely that uniform cores will be made. In addition, the written procedures make it possible for the inspectors to enforce the intentions of the engineers. This inspection is commonly of the patrol type. The inspector examines finished cores, including kind and location of supporting rods, venting, etc. The patrol includes the subsequent operations of baking, coating, washing, assembly, and transport to the molding department. The results of these inspections should be charted to make the trends evident.

Molding Sand. Raw sand is well covered by specifications and is checked upon receipt from suppliers. However, green sand deteriorates rapidly with use, and frequent retests as well as replenishment are necessary.[29] Testing should be done hourly (or even more frequently if deterioration is unusually rapid) for moisture, green compressive strength, green shear strength, deformation, and permeability. Moisture content is quite critical and must be accurately controlled. Other added checks are for active clay, combustibles, screen analysis, and AFS[30] clay.

The test results should not just be entered in some laboratory log book. They should be charted on control charts bearing limit lines so that the trends are clear and can be acted on promptly. It should also be made clear whose job it is to act.

It is desirable that sand be handled and stored in enclosed conveyors and silos as far as possible, to avoid contamination.

Molding. Molders should be provided with a manual of information on good molding practice for those aspects of operation which are common to all parts, e.g., condition of flask pins and holes; cleanliness of molds prior to closing. In addition, for the important parts, the molders should be provided with job cards which show the tools (e.g., flask size), special process conditions and needs (e.g., mold hardness, chaplets), and special cautions to be observed.

Mold hardness is an important variable and should be measured often enough to ensure uniformity as well as correct level.[31] Soft molds cause oversize or locally swollen castings. Once a proper level has been attained, process conditions, e.g., air pressure, must be maintained to hold this level.

The molding operation is highly vulnerable to operator error and to tool failure.

[29] One rule is that the amount of sand discard should be equal to 10% of the total weight of metal cast, and replaced with new sand. Palmer, *op. cit.*

[30] American Foundrymen's Society standard.

[31] See Fuller, *op. cit.*, for a discussion of mold hardness measurement, plus an example of a control chart on averages and ranges of mold hardness.

For these reasons there should be prompt feedback of quality information back to the molding department, at least daily, and oftener (even hourly) in special situations. See, in this connection, Error Correction, below.

Pouring. Metal temperature is known to be critical to making sound castings. However, the "right" temperature varies among different casting designs. Because of the difficulties of experimenting, it is useful to record the actual pouring temperature and to accumulate this information on job cards so that the resulting history will identify the optimum temperature. Once identified, the temperature must be held to close limits, since the defect-free range is usually quite narrow, e.g., for automobile cylinder blocks, between 1390 and 1420°C (Figure 34-3).[32]

Pouring technique also affects casting quality. Slag must be held back by an appropriate "dam" or by use of "teapot" spouts. The molds should be filled rapidly, while avoiding turbulence, with the sprue cup remaining full during pouring. Ladles should be well maintained with refractory linings and should be regularly cleaned of slag and dross. Ladles should be preheated on first usage and after breaks in production. Alloying at the ladle calls for strict controls of several sorts.[33]

Shake-out, Sprue, and Trim. Shake-out is generally not critical to quality, other than the risk of mechanical damage. However, poor technique in removal of sprues, flash, and fins can damage castings or add unnecessarily to the subsequent costs of machining.

Heat Treatment. This operation is often carried as part of the foundry activity and is for the purpose of enhancing the final properties of the product. Proper heat treatment requires both process specifications (e.g., time cycle, temperature, atmosphere) and product specifications (e.g., hardness). The procedures should provide for measurement and recording of the process and product data, plus a feedback to the shop floor in those cases where the recording is not automatic. The data are also needed for analysis of causes of improper heat treatment. In addition, considerations of product traceability and product liability require retention of heat treatment data for long periods of time.

Cleaning. This consists of operations such as sandblasting, shot blasting, grinding, and chipping. The purpose is

1. Removal of scale, sand, gates, and fins to the extent required by the customer
2. Exposure of surface defects for ready visual detection

In this operation it is important to understand clearly the usage of the product, so that the customer's needs will be met without perfectionism. For example, one foundry making automotive differential housings had for years carefully ground the casting ingates. A review with the customer disclosed that gates not in excess of ¼ inch would be entirely fit for use. (The aesthetics of a slightly projecting gate was of no consequence for a part out of sight under an automobile.) Both the foundry and the customer shared the savings resulting from the change in standard.

Machine and Tool Maintenance Foundry machines and tools are subject to rapid deterioration due to the extremes of heat, abrasion, and other severe conditions inherent in the foundry environment. Such deterioration calls for strict controls on the fitness of the equipment to avoid deterioration of the product.

The organized approach to machine and tool maintenance is well known[34] and is fully applicable to the foundry. It consists of

1. Creating a history card for each piece of equipment
2. Establishing a checking schedule for the critical features

---

[32] Palmer, *op. cit.*

[33] Palmer, *op. cit.* See also McNair, G. D., and J. Jarvis, Some Examples of Foundry Control, *The British Foundryman,* vol. 57, pp. 335–343, August 1964.

[34] See generally Section 11, under Machine and Tool Maintenance.

3. Assigning clear responsibility for adhering to the schedule

4. Recording the results of check and the revisions made

5. Auditing to see that the system is followed

On high-volume production, the flasks and patterns require frequent check. Precision of flask pins and bushings is important to casting quality and should be under a strict schedule of inspection and replacement.

As patterns undergo thousands of usages, they are gradually abraded away by the sand. The maintenance checklist should provide for regular measurement of pattern wear. In this case it is necessary to inform the customer of the trends and when replacement is needed, since the customer usually pays for the patterns.

Responsibility for adherence to the checking schedule is divided among several foundry departments. Commonly, Quality Control checks the tools for features which bear directly on product quality. For other aspects of tools and for machines, various foundry engineers, tool engineers, or maintenance personnel may have the responsibility. What is important is that the responsibility be clear.

Error Correction   This term refers to eliminating current, abnormal troubles but does not include reduction of chronic defect troubles, which are discussed under Quality Improvement, below.

A restatement of this distinction is a foundry classification of three kinds of scrap problems:

1. Gradual rise due to wear of bushings, deterioration of sand, etc.

2. Sudden adverse rise due to a new design, a breakdown, blunder, etc.

3. Chronic scrap being endured month after month [35]

Error correction deals with any current abnormality such as types 1 and 2 above. This "fire" must be put out, and commonly the factory supervision and the work force can do just that provided they are given adequate information feedback and other essentials.

Daily Scrap Conference.   The daily feedback to the shop consists typically of the daily scrap meeting. This is a stand-up conference at a special area set aside for collecting the day's scrap. The supervisor reviews the main scrap piles with the work leaders, and they agree on what action to take.

This physical feedback is often supplemented by daily summaries of the number of pieces or pounds involved, where the defects were first found, and any test information which has been compiled.

Any sudden epidemic of defects which may have turned up at any subsequent department is reported promptly without waiting for the daily scrap conference.

Weekly Summaries.   A further short-term feedback is the weekly scrap and rework summaries processed by the data system. Typically these show:

Total scrap produced relative to total weight cast

Analysis of this scrap by part number, defect, or other appropriate subdivision

The choice of "appropriate subdivision" can be important here. For a product line of castings consisting of a family of very similar designs, the most useful method of analysis is by "common cause," i.e., by defect, process, etc., which are common to all members of the family. In contrast, for very different families, or for product lines which consist of widely diverse casting designs, the analysis needs to be separated by family grouping and by important individual designs. [36]

These weekly summaries are commonly reviewed at a weekly scrap conference

---

[35] Derived from Osborn, John, Handling Multiple Variables in Analyzing Scrap, *Foundry*, vol. 93, pp. 78–80, August 1965.

[36] See in this connection, the extended discussion in Section 45, under Job Shop Control, *et seq.*

held in the foundry superintendent's office. Samples of the "vital few" defects or part numbers are on hand, and the meeting agrees on corrective action. The attendees usually also include members from Technical and Quality Control departments, who can be called on for assistance.

Machining Feedback. A further short-term feedback is from the machines which process the castings into finished parts. Machineability is regarded as an essential quality of castings, it being one of the reasons for user preference for castings vs. wrought products. In addition, some dimensional qualities of the castings affect the ability of the machine shop to fixture adequately and to cut metal economically.

For captive foundries within the same plant location as the machine shop, the feedback is relatively easy to set up. When foundry and machine shop are in different plants the feedback gets complicated, and this accentuates further for the independent foundry.

TABLE 34-2   Causation Table for Shrink in Castings

Shrink may be caused by the following:
Sand. The hot strength may be low, causing a swell in the late stages of fluidity
Pouring may be short in the mold, thereby reducing the amount of head metal left in the riser
Metal: Low carbon, low silicon, or both
Foundry practice. Soft rammed mold resulting in a swell, or cope riser connection does not properly meet drag connection
Equipment. Insufficient cope height; wrong part of the pattern in the cope; insufficient riser height
Insufficient riser diameter or riser neck causes shrink adjacent to the riser
Insufficient number of risers causes a shrink remote from the risers
Improper placement of riser

The need, in all cases, is for an open line of communication between machine shop and foundry, with as few relay stations as possible. Setting up this line must be tailor-made for each situation, since the organization patterns and availability of field representatives vary from company to company.

For further discussion on customer feedback, see Customer Relations, below.

Causation Tables. Much has been done to identify the likely causes of various types of defects. These findings have been widely published in table form.[37] In addition, many companies have prepared their own tables to fit their unique process and product situation. Table 34-2 is an extract from such a table.

To make best use of these tables requires that the men see samples of the defects. Where this is not feasible, it is most important that the defect be described with great precision.

Scrap Investigator. Error correction is often slowed up because the supervisors lack the time to make the necessary investigations. In such cases one aid to prompt action is to assign some of the analysis work to a scrap investigator. (In smaller shops this may be a part-time assignment for an inspector.)

The investigator not only has more time — he also has the mobility to visit the areas where scrap is found, study the circumstances, and bring samples back to the likely departments of origin. This visiting can be extended to the machining areas of the customer in important cases.

Training Delegation to the work force requires training in how to do the work delegated. The general approach is discussed in Section 17, under Training.

One foundry was able to organize an out of hours training program for the work

---

[37] See Hall, *op. cit.*; Haney, *op. cit.*; also Palmer, *op. cit.*; also Merz, P., Modern Methods of Improving Quality of Castings, *Foundry Trade Journal,* vol. 124, pp. 241–247, Feb. 15, 1968.

force. The instructors were various departmental specialists who explained practice in sand control, coremaking, molding, pouring, etc.[38]

INSPECTION AND TEST

Foundry inspection and test are done both as controls on the process and as checks on the product.

Inspection   The flow diagram in Figure 34-1 shows that inspection is conducted at numerous stations throughout the process. Most of these inspections have been discussed under the various operation categories listed under the heading Manufacturing Control above.

In all these inspections there is a common approach of inspection planning to list the essential characteristics of product and process, establish inspection criteria and schedules, etc. This follows conventional practice as set out in Section 12, under Inspection Planning.[39]

While each foundry is faced with identifying its own check lists of characteristics, most of these are quite common and are frequently used in a wide variety of situations. An example of such a list is seen in Table 34-1.

Final Inspection.   The foundry has traditionally conducted a final product inspection following the cleaning operation. In addition to checking the adequacy of the cleaning, this inspection also looks for visual defects of all sorts, e.g., scabs, shrinks, or breakage.

Standards for visual inspection involve the usual problems inherent in using human beings as instruments.[40] Some visual characteristics have been embodied in national standards. These are supplemented by local standards which may be written descriptions, photographs, or limiting product samples.

As during process control, inspected product must be carefully classified for fitness, whether

1. Ready to ship, all operations complete.

2. Rework, in which case, the defects and the repair operations to be performed are clearly defined.

3. Scrap. In this case, the reasons for scrapping are listed to aid in defect prevention studies. In addition, the last good operation performed is listed to aid in the cost accounting.

Scrap and rework castings should be promptly removed from the processing areas to avoid the risks of mixup with good product.

In some foundries, the detailed final inspection is performed by Production employees, who may be either part time or full time inspectors. In such cases it is usual for Quality Control to sample the accepted product as part of the audit plan. In addition, the nonconforming product set aside by the (Production) inspector is reviewed, and a decision made to accept, salvage, or scrap.

Some customers, especially in regulated industries, require special documentation for lot identity and traceability. These requirements are usually part of the purchase contracts, and require compliance.[41]

---

[38] Krueger, Lawrence S., How One Foundry Meets Reliability Standards, *Foundry*, vol. 90, pp. 86–93, March 1962.

[39] When inspection is first introduced into a foundry, some special problems of cultural resistance must be overcome. See Deaton, J. W., Inspection and Quality Control in a Foundry Producing Automobile and Tractor Castings, *The British Foundryman*, vol. 53, pp. 325–329, July 1960.

[40] See generally Section 12, under Sensory Qualities.

[41] See generally Section 19.

Salvage. Repair of some pressure castings is largely governed by ASTM specifications, which impose limits on the type of defects for which repair is permitted, and on the nature of the repair itself. More commonly, salvage methods are established by agreement with the customer.

Gage Control. This is entirely conventional and is covered in Section 13, under Maintaining Calibration Control.

Testing The traditional tests for metallurgical and mechanical properties have largely been destructive in nature. These tests have included:

1. Tensile strength on the product itself or on test specimens or coupons
2. Hardness, through indentation penetration and measurement
3. Impact test such as Charpy or Izod
4. Microstructure, determined by microscopic examination after polish and etch

These and other tests (including nondestructive testing, below) have been extensively standardized by bodies such as the American Society for Testing and Materials (ASTM)[42] and their international counterparts.

Until the 1960s almost all casting specifications were based on properties of separately cast test bars. These test results provided the users with only indirect knowledge of the properties of the castings themselves. Moreover, the users' tests were generally limited to hardness tests plus review of vendor test data. What the user really needed was tests which were aimed at assuring that the product would be fit for its end use; e.g., if the product is subjected to impacts during use, then impact testing should be a part of the test program. There was a need and a search for suitable tests which could be made directly on the product and which could be readily available to both the foundry and the user.

This search has led to standardized specifications (ASTM and SAE) for high-carbon, ferrous materials based on hardness and microstructure. These product characteristics correlate well with machinability and service performance. In addition, they can be readily integrated into the foundry process and quality control systems.

Microstructure standards (graphite shape and size) have long existed in the gray iron industry and, more recently, in the ductile iron industry. In the malleable iron industry the standards include also other variables such as surface condition.

Because these test results are so essential to customer fitness for use, the foundry must find ways to adapt these tests and test results into its process and product controls. In addition, the foundry should record these data to permit data analysis to be made, as discussed under Data Collection and Analysis, below.

Nondestructive Testing (NDT) In recent decades numerous instruments have been developed to permit nondestructive testing.[43] These instruments have greatly expanded the foundry's ability to assure quality and to improve its processes. For the foundry, the more important forms of NDT include:

Radiography. This involves use of x-ray and gamma-ray radiation to identify hidden flaws in castings. In combination with ultrasonic inspection (to give preliminary indication of defects) these methods are effective and essential, especially for important steel castings.[44] Because radiography is commonly done to meet customer's specifications, the radiographic standards should be approved by the customer.

Sonic and Ultrasonic Testing. In these tests, vibrations are induced in the castings under test. The response is then compared with that of castings known to be defect-free.

---

[42] For a good discussion, and an extensive reference to applicable standards, see Bremer, Edwin, Inspection Procedures Relating to Quality, *Foundry,* vol. 94, pp. 58–67, April 1966.

[43] See generally Section 13, under Measurement Technology, Nondestructive Testing.

[44] Merz, *op. cit.* It is even feasible, for research studies, to take x-ray moving pictures of such phenomena as gas bubble formation and path of impurities during pouring. See Rose, Harold, Using X-ray Movies to Improve Casting Quality, *Foundry,* vol. 94, pp. 92–97, June 1966.

Sonic testing can be used to detect certain types of flaws and to evaluate microstructure. It also may give good predictions of the actual tensile strength of the casting.[45] Ultrasonic testing is used for flaw detection and for such variables as thickness, elastic modulus, and graphite distribution.

These tests can be made on castings in the "as-cast" condition, and lend themselves readily to automated testing once the calibration curves have been established. Because sonic tests are very sensitive, they may reject good product if the calibration is not thorough.

Penetrant—Magnetic. This involves the use of liquids to aid in finding surface cracks. One form of this test employs fluorescent magnetic particles which adhere to defective areas under a magnetic field.

Penetrant—Nonmagnetic. This form of test employs dyes which enter cracks and pores through capillary action, and make the defects clearly visible when a developer is applied.[46]

Eddy Current Testing. This form employs electromagnetic currents to aid in detecting flaws, voids, inclusions, and other defects. It can be adapted to determine hardness, microstructure, and other metallurgical properties. It also lends itself to mechanization for high-speed testing.

Limitations. Use of NDT techniques is subject to some limitations:

1. Each application is unique, requiring its own program of evaluation of parameters and calibration of standards.

2. The test setups should include a fail-safe design, or provision for frequent check of calibration (usually by testing with masters).

3. Because equipment cost is relatively high, the economic justification must be based on *(a)* reduced testing costs per unit or *(b)* increased product reliability. Either way, the volume of production must be adequate to amortize the investment.

4. The design of some castings is such that some variables cannot be tested with NDT.

The combined forces of safety legislation, threats of liability, and consumerism will likely stimulate increasing use of 100% automated test programs. In high-volume production requiring 100% casting integrity it becomes economic to set up machines which may employ two or more NDT techniques at successive test stations. It is also feasible to use direct computer control as an aid to test. In one molding line, the computer is set up to digest data from laboratory analysis and then signal "accept" or "reject" at shake-out.[47]

DATA COLLECTION AND ANALYSIS

Quality data play a vital role in the foundry, both for current control and for quality improvement. Throughout the discussion on Manufacturing Control, and Inspection and Test, above, there have been repeated references to the need for data recording, analysis, and feedback, and various examples were given. The discussion which follows deals with some of the ways in which these quality data are collected and analyzed to be used in feedback for control.[48] A later topic will deal with the use of quality data in quality improvement.

[45] Moss, C. W., Sonic Testing in Foundry Production Control, *The British Cast Iron Research Association (BCIRA) Journal,* vol. 12, pp. 141–148, March 1964.

[46] Starr, C., Penetrant Testing Techniques, *The British Foundryman,* vol. 58, pp. 143–148, April 1965. See also Sanders, L. H., Dye Penetrant Eliminates Pressure Testing of Castings, *Metalworking Production,* vol. 109, pp. 55–58, Mar. 31, 1965.

[47] Eshelman, *op. cit.*

[48] See generally Section 19 on documentation; also Sections 22 through 28 for various forms of statistical analysis. See also Fuller, *op. cit.*

Data Recording.   Basic data sources include automatic process recorders, production operators, inspectors, laboratory technicians, and still others.   These data may be recorded on job record forms, on conventional defect list forms, or directly on chronological charts.

The recording system should provide for defect codes to simplify the work of recording as well as the subsequent data processing.[49]

Chronological Charts.   Increasing use is being made of charts which exhibit trends of important characteristics, critical defects, and summarized results.   A common form is the Shewhart-type control chart,[50] which is widely used in sand control, molding control, melting control, final product characteristics, and still others.[51]

Other chart forms include merely the daily posting of ranges of observed values, e.g., silicon or carbon content.   These provide a measure of levels and trends and lay the groundwork for later establishment of process capabilities and control limits.

It is useful to enter on the chronological charts the notations of known changes which have entered the process, e.g., corrective actions taken, new designs, and new material sources.   Such entries make it easier to discover relationships between known external causes and resulting change (or lack of change) in the process.

The "control limits" on the chronological charts are the trip wires which set off alarm signals when process or product changes are excessive.   These lines require periodic review to strike the correct balance between (1) failure to signal and (2) excessive false alarms.

Histograms.[52]   For some types of test data it is convenient to construct monthly summaries in the form of histograms as an aid in understanding the realities of product performance.   These are in use for chemical properties, metallurgical properties, and still others.[53]

Pareto Analysis.   In the foundry there are literally dozens of different quality characteristics and defect types. However, a "vital few" of these account for the bulk of the current troubles, in accordance with the universal Pareto distribution of the "vital few and trivial many."[54]

This principle should be utilized in data feedback by concentrating supervisory and managerial attention on the few items most in need of attention.[55]   When data are processed electronically, the computers can be programmed to single out the vital few items, for the same purpose.

Record Retention.   The data needed for control, identification, certification, etc., are collectively a formidable total.   Some of these, e.g., test records on structural integrity, are needed in the event of customer complaints, studies by government regulators, or potential lawsuits.   Others are needed to provide long-range data on chronic quality problems.   Still others have a short useful life, being needed only for daily or weekly control.

These different usages of the data point to the need for discrimination in record retention.   The company's Legal Counsel should be consulted on matters of statutory requirement and potential lawsuits.   Customers should be consulted as to their

---

[49] See in this connection Daugherty, *op. cit.*

[50] See Section 23 for the basic types in use, plus methods of construction.

[51] See Zobel, S. P., Some Foundry Applications of Statistical Quality Control, *Transactions, ASQC Forum on Quality Control,* Hamilton, Canada, Nov. 5, 1960, pp. 45–53; also Zaludova, A. H., Statistical Quality Control in the Foundry, *Production Engineer,* vol. 43, pp. 88–100, February 1964; also Renwick, W. Eugene, Controlling Casting Quality, *Foundry,* vol. 96, pp. 59–61, November 1968; also Fuller, *op. cit.*

[52] See generally Section 22.

[53] See, for example, Fuller, *op. cit.* (Brinell Hardness).

[54] See Section 2 under The Pareto Principle; also Section 16 under Pareto Analysis.

[55] See Daugherty, *op. cit.,* for a discussion on use of this principle in the foundry.

needs for traceability. Based on these and other inputs, appropriate retention schedules should be set up.[56]

QUALITY IMPROVEMENT

Foundry quality improvement is derived from a variety of sources:

1. New equipment and instruments, usually developed by their respective industries, based on understanding of foundry needs

2. New metallurgical knowledge, usually developed by the foundries and the casting users

3. Improved foundry practice, usually developed by the foundries based on analysis of cause and effect relationships in their own shops

The discussion which follows will be limited to improvements of type 3, though some of these must make use of the other forms as well.

Organizing for Improvement. Quality improvement is distinguished from error correction by the fact that the former is directed at long-standing, chronic quality problems. For these, the procedures used in error correction are not adequate. What is needed is a team approach structured along the lines set out in Section 16 (Quality Improvement). To use this approach, the foundry must:

1. Set up a Quality Improvement Committee to guide the improvement program, choose the improvement projects, establish priorities, and provide essential diagnostic services. This team is composed of upper managers from key departments and is commonly chaired by a line manager.

2. Appoint task groups to pursue specific projects. The members are chosen on the basis of their potential contribution to the solution.

3. Assign Quality Control, Technical, and other specialists to carry out the data collection, data analysis, experimentation, and other studies needed by the task groups to find answers to the problems.

The methods for using these three organization devices to conduct quality improvement are set out in detail in Section 16, and these methods are readily applicable to the foundry. The Pareto principle is especially applicable, since in most foundries, over 50% of the scrap results from no more than five types of defect. Commonly the most fruitful Pareto distributions are by part number and by defect type, but seldom by process.[57]

The workings of this organized approach can be seen in the example which follows. A committee undertaking a scrap reduction program secured analyses from Quality Control showing that:

1. The most frequent defect (by Pareto analysis) was cracked castings.

2. There was no trend—the month to month defects were in a steady state.

Theories of causes of cracked castings were now advanced:

1. Hot tears in the mold

2. Handling at shake-out, transfer, spruing, cleaning, or trimming

3. Stresses in heat treatment

4. Pressing operations

5. Inherent in design

A task group (Quality Control Supervisor, Foundry Engineer, Laboratory Supervisor) was appointed to dig deeper to:

1. Determine the three high-production jobs which exhibited the greatest percentage of cracked castings.

2. Discover the nature of the cracks (hot tears, hard iron, or soft iron).

---

[56] See generally Section 19, under Quality Records File—Retention Cycles.

[57] See also the discussion in Section 45, under Quality Improvement, *et seq.*; also Palmer, *op. cit.*

3. Catalog the locations of cracks on these castings together with their frequency in each location.

The ensuing report of this group at the next meeting showed:

1. Three differential carrier castings showed the highest scrap rate due to cracks.

2. These cracks were almost exclusively hard iron breaks.

3. These cracks occurred at specific locations around the large bowl faces with relative frequencies determined.

Two areas of investigation were suggested by these results: (1) rough hard iron handling and (2) design sensitivity to cracking.

Now an experiment was designed to be carried out by the Foundry Engineer and two technicians. Five lots of castings were processed each in a different way, to identify more closely which operation seemed most to be associated with the cracking. These five lots were:

1. Hand carried from shake-out to heat treat without spruing

2. Hand carried to a special careful spruing, and then placed in heat treat

3. Removed from process just ahead of spruing

4. Run through the normal process except individually carefully handled after spruing

5. Processed normally

Examination for cracks was made by fluorescent magnetic particle inspection. The results of the test showed:

1. No castings were broken in heat treatment

2. One casting was broken in a 100-piece sample of the carefully sprued casting.

3. One casting was broken in a 150-piece sample when castings were removed from the system just before spruing.

4. Four castings were broken in the sample normally processed through spruing and subsequently hand carried lot of 100.

5. Six castings were broken in the normally processed sample of 100.

6. Cracks in all except one instance were in two preferred locations.

Tentative conclusions reached by the committee at this point were:

1. Particular areas of the casting were more than normally susceptible to cracking.

2. Spruing and subsequent handling accounted for nearly all the cracking observed.

Next indicated actions were to:

1. Sharpen spruing grooves (Foundry Engineer).

2. Observe and improve production spruing operation (Foundry Engineer and Finishing Supervisor).

3. Improve handling after spruing (Foundry Engineer and Finishing Supervisor).

4. Modify design in readily cracking areas with customer approval (Tooling Engineer and Foundry Engineer).

In subsequent observation and testing, spruing operators were further instructed, handling of castings after spruing was improved, the handling system itself was modified, slight design change of the parts was accomplished, and the shapes of the spruing groove and the ingate were modified. Each change was separately checked by test.

Subsequent follow-up established a 60% reduction in the cracking of the three parts under test and a significant but lesser reduction in cracking of other castings. Further action to improve other and similar castings was still indicated.[58]

Regression Analysis.[59]   This technique is used to discover quantitative relation-

---

[58] Personal experience of the authors.
[59] See generally Section 26.

ships such as between process variables and their effect on product quality. Comparatively simple examples of foundry application include: use of sonic test results to predict tensile strength;[60] test bar tensile strength vs. casting tensile strength;[61] pouring temperature vs. porosity, elongation, yield, tensile strength.[62]

On a more sophisticated level are the studies which tackle numerous variables and, through "multiple regression," try to discover useful relationships. These are advanced techniques, requiring statistical experts to set up the equations, and computers to do the calculating. (See Section 26 for the general approach.) For example, Hanajiri[63] studied the effect of process variables on product qualities in the cupola operation using multiple regression.

Some discussion is also available on the general approach to use of computers on such foundry problems.[64]

		Mold temperature			
		Lo	Medium	Hi	Average
Melt temperature	Lo	Op_1 15-H 20-H 4-H	Op_2 11-M 13-M 5-M	Op_3 24-L+ 10-M 6-M	H—
	Medium	Op_2 25-M 14-M 18-M	Op_3 9-M 2-L 16-M	Op_1 1-L 26-L 23-L	M—
	Hi	Op_3 8-L 22-L 17-M	Op_1 7-L 19-L 3-L	Op_2 27-O 21-O 12-O	L—
Average		M	M—	L	

Average result for operators Op_1 L+
    Op_2 M—
    Op_3 L+

Fig. 34-8 Latin square experiment to discover cause of porosity.

Designed Experiments. In some cases analysis of past data will not provide adequate answers, and it becomes necessary to design experiments, as in the example of cracked castings, above, or as in Figure 34-5. A more advanced example is related by Shainin.[65] In one study of the cause of porous castings, the main suspected variables were operators, mold temperature, and melt temperature. A 3 × 3 Latin square experiment[66] was designed (Figure 34-8) to permit pouring of 27 castings by three operators at three levels of mold temperature and three levels of melt temperature. The porosity results are designated as H = heavy,

[60] Moss, *op. cit.*

[61] Fuller, *op. cit.*

[62] Riddell, Fred R., Practical Control Procedures, Part II, *Foundry,* vol. 94, pp. 74–77, February 1966.

[63] Hanajiri, A., An Application of Multiple Regression Analysis to Cupola Melting Operations, *ASQC Technical Conference Transactions,* 1966, pp. 156–166.

[64] Davidson, M. H., J. W. Sprinkle, and J. Keverian, Computer Identification of Factors Controlling Quality in Castings Production, *Modern Castings,* vol. 46, pp. 529–536, September 1964.

[65] Shainin, Dorian, Prevent Defects and You Control Quality, *Foundry,* vol. 90, pp. 77–81, March 1962.

[66] See generally Section 27.

M = moderate, L = light, O = none. The analysis makes clear that the combination of high mold temperature and high melt temperature avoids the porosity.

CUSTOMER RELATIONS

The foundry sells more than pounds of castings. It may also sell an engineering design service, a manufacturing capability, a quality capability, and still other elements which can make the customer's product an asset to his marketing efforts. Some foundries utilize this concept in their customer relations. The sales force is provided with brochures and charts explaining the quality capability of the foundry. A moving picture film is used to explain to customers the nature of the foundry process.[67]

Contracting for Quality. To the user, the foundry is a vendor whose products include defects which create quality costs. Foundries have traditionally taken responsibility for some of these costs by replacing defective castings free of charge, by paying the costs of sorting defective lots, by paying the incidental charges for transportation, etc.

There are other user costs which the foundries have commonly not paid for, e.g., machining work done on defective castings before the defect is discovered; machine down time, resulting from interruptions; investigation time; cost of field failures resulting from defective castings.

As contracts increasingly are revised to optimize the users' costs[68] it is inevitable that the foundry will become drawn into such contracts. An example is seen in a contract between a large user of castings and a foundry. The parties:

1. Determined the actual machining costs.
2. Divided this by 2 on the assumption a defective casting will, on the average, be halfway through the machining process when the defect is detected.
3. Added this half-cost to the price paid for castings (the increment came to 3%).
4. Agreed that the foundry would pay the user one-half the subsequent cost of machining defective castings (aside from replacing each with a sound casting).[69,70]

In this example, the customer also evolved a Quality Performance Index. To compute the Index, he first added up the following costs:

Value of castings returned to vendor
Labor costs incurred working on defective castings
Salvage costs incurred on defective castings

This sum was then expressed as a percentage of the value of castings originally purchased, to become the Index. The Index could be computed cumulatively for each vendor, and used as a basis for vendor selection.

Customer Feedback. The foundry's traditional "passive" approach to feedback is to wait for evidence of customer dissatisfaction. This time-honored method has the three-way *dis*advantage of (1) evidence of foundry lack of interest in customer problems, (2) feedback too late for proper corrective action, and (3) probable inaccuracy of relayed information.

[67]See Foundry Survival: Product Quality and Modernization, *Quality Management & Engineering,* April 1971, pp. 18–22. See also Barlow, T. E., You Can Sell Quality Control, *Foundry,* vol. 90, pp. 94–95, March 1962.
[68] See Section 14, under Contracts Based on Usage.
[69] Dalton, W. M., and J. J. Shellabarger, Quality Control Leads to Guaranteed Castings, *Foundry,* vol. 90, pp. 82–85, March 1962 (written by the foundry in the case).
[70]Boll, V.V., Effective Piece Price for Buying Castings, *Foundry,* vol. 92, pp. 57–61, January 1964 (written by the customer in the case).

Modern patterns of customer relations require an active approach to feedback. This approach requires that foundry representatives call on the customer regularly quite aside from the visits demanded by quality complaints. These calls minimize every one of the disadvantages of the passive approach.

The various foundry departments should collaborate with their field service representatives in designing a checklist of the kinds of reports, information, and samples needed by the foundry to remain knowledgeable about casting quality as seen by the user. (Cost of machining, per 100 castings, is one of the user's measures of casting quality.) Such calls, as well as complaint investigations, should be made by technically qualified specialists. In most companies this means the service representative rather than the salesman.[71]

The format of service reports should likewise be designed by a team so that the resulting information serves the needs of all departments. These reports should be circulated promptly and acted on promptly to give the customer and the service representative confidence that the foundry team is really behind them.

An essential element of reports of defects is the return of samples. No amount of oral or written description is as good as a sample in the hands of the men who know best what to look for, and who have the instrumentation to help do this.

Special attention must be given to prompt feedback of customer problems with machinability and fixture fits as these immediately affect his ability to produce. If need be, direct contact between the two quality control organizations should be authorized to provide such prompt feedback.

The great importance of customer feedback also requires that summaries be prepared monthly or quarterly as a report to upper management. See, in this connection, Section 21, under Executive Reports on Quality.

QUALITY ASSURANCE

Foundry management requires knowledge of how well the overall quality function is being carried out. The means for doing this follow conventional practice as set out in Section 21, under Quality Assurance.

Reports. Quality performance summaries are commonly prepared monthly for such control subjects as:

Weight of castings scrapped vs. weight cast
Cost of errors per direct labor hour, total and by department
List of principal defects, and estimated cost of each
List of most costly jobs, and estimated cost of each
Number of field complaints, with details on most serious cases
Cost of chargebacks from customers, with list of principal causes, by defect or by pattern
Histograms and other report forms on major product properties

Audit. The wide delegation given by the foundry to the lower supervision and the work force makes it desirable to audit how well this delegation is carried out. The method of audit follows usual practice, both as to product[72] and as to process.[73]

Subjects for audit should not be limited to the direct production processes. They should include such pertinent indirect matters as product handling, maintenance of equipment and tools, and adequacy of record keeping.[73]

[71] See Section 15, under Processing of Complaints.
[72] See Section 21, under Product Auditing.
[73] See Section 11, under Audit of Production Quality; also, Section 21, under Audit of Execution vs. Plan.

BIBLIOGRAPHY

Books

American Foundrymen's Society, Des Plaines, Ill. "Analysis of Casting Defects," 2d ed., 1966. An excellent discussion of nature and likely causes of foundry defects, with hundreds of photographs. "Cast Metals Handbook," 4th ed., 1957. "Design of Ferrous Castings" (by John B. Caine), 1963.

American Society of Metals, Metals Park, Ohio, "Casting Design Handbook," 1962.

American Society for Testing and Materials (ASTM), Philadelphia, Pa. Publishes numerous standards of great importance to foundry quality control.

American Zinc Institute, New York, "Die Casting with Zinc," 1965. Chapter 5 deals with dimensional tolerances.

Japan General Foundry Center, Kikaishinkokaikan, Shiba-Koen, Minato-ku, Tokyo, Japan. "Quality Control in the Foundry Industry," 1966, by Arao Kita (in Japanese). The bulk of this 263-page book is devoted to showing, for various types of metal casting (cast iron, malleable iron, cast steel, copper alloys, light alloys, and die casting) the following tables of information:

  Process flow of operations
  Location of control stations
  Specification limits at each control station
  Organization responsibility for control activities
  Instruments to be used
  Method of checking
  Control charts to be maintained
  Responsibility for action on abnormalities
  Methods for securing collective action
  Code numbers of standards
  Documentation needed

Malleable Founders Society, Union Commerce Building, Cleveland, Ohio. "Malleable Castings Dimensioning Guide," MR and DF Bulletin 28. "Malleable Iron Castings," 1960. "Metallurgy of Malleable Iron," 1971, edited by Hans J. Heine. "Microstructure Standards for Malleable Iron," MR and DF Bulletin 64.

Steel Castings Research and Trade Association (formerly British Steel Casting Research Association), East Bank Road, Sheffield S2, 3PT, England. "Quality Standards for Steel Castings," 1966.

Steel Founder's Society, Cleveland, Ohio. "Steel Castings Handbook," 4th ed., 1970.

Articles

Caspers, K. H., Kontrollkarten und Stichprobenprüfplane als Basis der Qualitätskontrolle im Giessereibetrieb, *Giesserei Praxis,* No. 15, pp. 312–322, Aug. 10, 1968.

Finch, Leroy, Quantovac Analysis in the Foundry, *Journal of Metals,* vol. 19, pp. 55–56, February 1967.

Fuller, A. G., Quality Control in the Iron Foundry, *Metal Working Production,* July 7, 1965, p. 53.

Fuller, A. G., Quality Control of Iron Casting, *Foundry Trade Journal,* vol. 119, pp. 69–78, July 15, 1965.

Hall, J. R., and D. A. Hudson, Shop Floor Control Methods in the Non Ferrous Founding Industry, *The British Foundryman,* vol. 58, pp. 289–296, August 1965.

Herrman, Robert H., Punch Card Data Help Improve Casting Quality, *Foundry,* vol. 88, pp. 120–123, June 1960.

Knight, C. F., Computer Technology in the Foundry Industry, *Modern Casting,* September 1967, p. 89. (Includes a survey of 395 foundries as to various problems. One-third of the returns asserted chronic or serious problems on quality or on data for feedback.)

Krueger, Lawrence S., Meeting the Challenge of Quality, *American Foundrymen's Transactions,* vol. 69, p. 549, 1961.

Lilliard, P. D., Providing Castings with a Full Guarantee, *Foundry Trade Journal,* vol. 129, pp. 237–239, Aug. 20, 1970. A foundry contract with a customer involving penalties for cost of machining defective castings. Scrap was cut from 22 to 7% in one year.

Mikelonis, Paul J., 75 Years Progress—in Quality Control and Inspection, *Modern Casting,* February 1972, pp. 43–49. A short history, emphasizing progress in instrumentation and in use of statistical methodology.

Palmer, S. W., The Prevention of Scrap in Iron Foundries, *The British Foundryman,* vol. 58, pp. 83–92, March 1965.

Riddell, Fred R., Practical Control Procedures, Part I, *Foundry,* vol. 94, pp. 56–59, January 1966.

Stolarczyk, J. E., The Structure and Properties of Sand Cast Gunmetals, *The British Foundryman,* vol. 53, pp. 531–548, December 1960.

Section **35**

Metal Fabricating[1]

SHIRO MATSUZAKI

President, Nippon Dia Clevite Co., Ltd.; Formerly Director and General
Manager, Nissan Motor Company, Ltd., Tokyo, Japan

INTRODUCTION

Metal fabrication comprises a considerable sector of industrial activity, in which
numerous processes (forging, turning, etc.) are performed on numerous varieties of
metals. The resulting permutations of process with material are so numerous that
only the more important processes have been selected as examples to illustrate the
sequence of activities and the techniques through which quality control is achieved
in metal fabrication generally.

The organization of this Section is both by kinds of quality control activity and by
types of metal fabrication process. Those quality control activities and techniques
(e.g., process capability, lot formation) which are universal to all metal fabrication
processes will be discussed under separate headings for the respective quality control techniques. Those quality control techniques which tend to be special to certain
metal fabrication processes will be examined under the heading of that process
which is the most demanding with respect to that technique (e.g., milling).

The author's experience has been mostly in the automotive industry, which employs virtually all types of metal fabrication. This experience has been enlarged by

---

[1] This section is concerned primarily with metal fabrication used in mass production of
(mainly) standardized metal components. Discussion of quality control for special, critical
mechanical components is amplified in Section 37, Mechanical Components.

discussion with engineers in leading manufacturing companies in Japan, with the result that the examples and views given present a generalized approach to the subject.

PRODUCT PLANNING

In metal fabricating, product planning generally proceeds as shown in the flow chart in Figure 35-1.

At the very outset there is need to reconcile the product design with the manufacturing capabilities so as to optimize quality, cost, etc. Attainment of this optimum is greatly aided by compilation and publication of data on process capability and other *quantified* information relative to ability to hold tolerances and to the effect of process variables on product quality. In the absence of such data, it is very difficult for the parties involved to agree on what is properly the optimum. Figure 35-2 gives an example of a compilation of surface roughness actually attained in the metal fabrication processes of one automobile manufacturer. It is at once evident how such factual compilations can simplify collaboration between designer and manufacturer. From such data it is easier to have a meeting of the minds as to choice of processes, need for multiple operations, need to restudy tolerances, etc.

These quantified compilations of data can be equally helpful in setting up the quality control plan. When the inherent uniformity of the process is sufficient to ensure meeting the tolerance, there is no need to provide controls. For example, a nominal 10-millimeter size drill is suitable for holding a tolerance of 10 ± 1 millimeters; it cannot, as a practical matter, make holes outside the tolerance. Hence the hole dimension need not be a control point if the drill size is checked originally. In contrast, to hold a turned diameter of 30 ± 0.03 millimeters on a lathe requires continuing measurement and control on a time-to-time basis even under the best process conditions.[2]

PROCESS CAPABILITY

Process capability is a vital consideration in all metal fabrication. The chief source of good capability varies from one process to another. In press work, it is the die which is decisive. In turning or boring, the main factor is the machine tool. In forging, the heat treatment is a major factor in process capability.

The actual capability achieved depends not only on the hardware, i.e., machine tools, cutting tools, lubrication, etc.; it depends also on the "software," i.e., the job planning, control plan, worker training, motivation, etc.

Process capability must be quantified before it can be used with confidence for planning and other decision making. The general approach to quantifying process capability is discussed in Section 9. However, this Section on Metal Fabricating presents an example of how process capability analysis succeeded in solving a difficult lathe problem. (See under Metal Cutting, Machine Tools, Process Capability below.)

MATERIAL CONTROL

Metals used for fabrication are defined by specifications, usually highly standardized, and verified by tests and inspections which likewise are highly standardized.

[2] For a general discussion of the use of process capability data plus knowledge of sequence of manufacture to improve the effectiveness of process control while reducing inspection cost, see Section 11, under Product and Process Relationship; also Section 12, under How Much Inspection?

For such materials, the general approach to vendor relations is covered in Section 10 of this Handbook, and the reader is referred to that Section for particulars.

While metal fabricating shops do not set up to duplicate the incoming inspection of vendor products, they do find themselves involved in some special problems of material control such as:

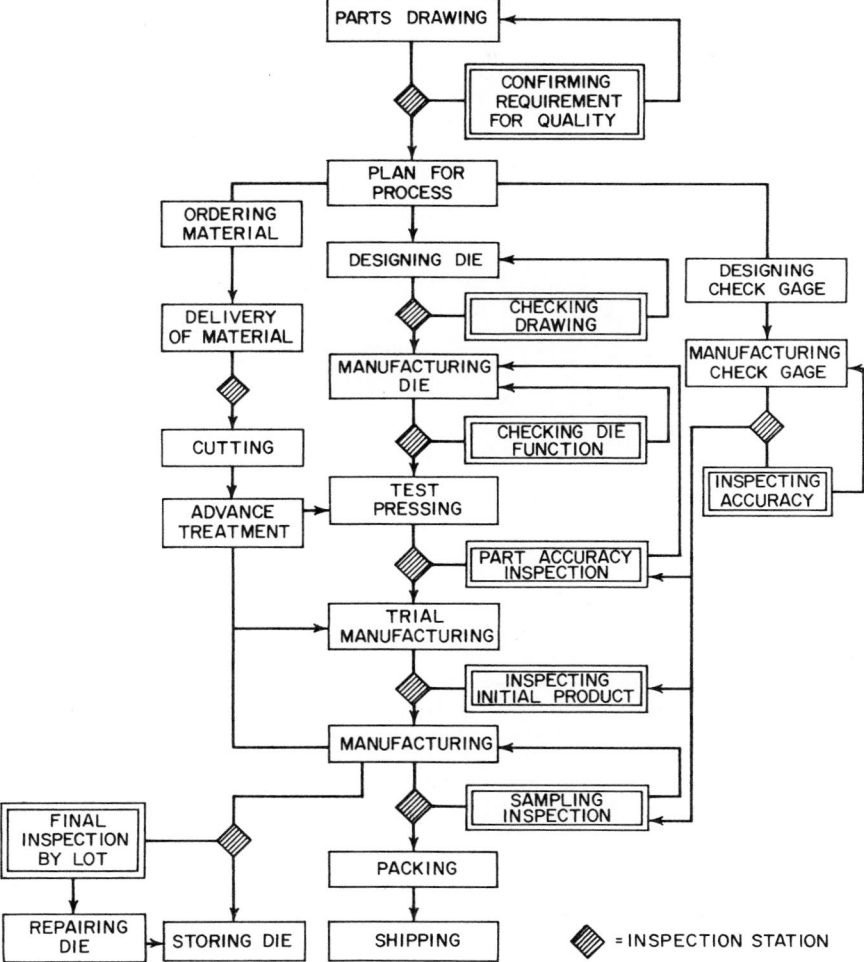

Fig. 35-1 Flow diagram, new product planning.

1. Check for correct identity of material. This is usually limited to a critical dimension such as thickness of sheets; i.e., incorrect thickness could damage a die.

2. Feedback of usage data. For some characteristics, e.g., cracking during deep draw, it is not known how to ensure, through specification alone, that the material will draw successfully. Hence the real measure of fitness for use is the successful fabrication rather than conformance to specification.

3. Traceability of metallurgical characteristics. In some cases, e.g., forgings, the critical nature of the heat treatment requires ensuring that the incoming materials possess known metallurgical properties and that the lot identity has been preserved. It is therefore usual practice for vendors to identify forging material with heat number, and to submit with each lot the data behind the heat number. These data, along with results of inspection and test by the parts maker, should be retained on file for future traceability and other reference purposes. (See also, in this connection, Section 33, Metals Industry.)

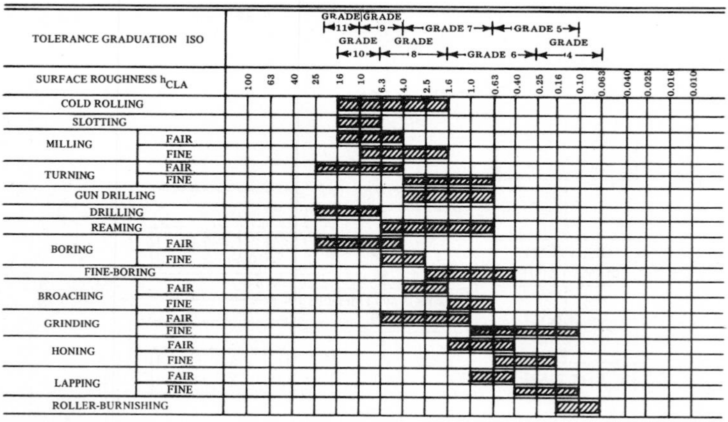

Fig. 35-2 Surface roughness resulting from various processes; h_{CLA} represents the centerline average height. This chart has been based on actual conditions at an automobile manufacturer, and there is not necessarily any theoretical relation with the surface roughness.

LOT FORMATION; TRACEABILITY

The concept of a "lot" in metal fabrication serves several useful purposes:

1. To preserve uniformity of metallurgical properties. For example, in steel forging not only must the material come from the same original "heat" of steel; the subsequent batch processes of heat treating and quenching require that strict identity control be established on the lots created by these processes. In turn, this identity control requires creation of lot numbers which will accompany the product through forging and heat treating. These lot numbers may be based on forging die number, date, or other convenient method. Once created, the lot number must remain with the product, and the lot must be processed under essentially uniform conditions.

2. To simplify process controls. For example, many press operations and metal cutting operations are so well engineered that there is very little time-to-time change in dimensions as mass production proceeds. In such cases, the process controls can be concentrated on the first few pieces made (during machine setup) and on the last few pieces made. For a process which undergoes little time-to-time change, if the first and last pieces of the lot are good, the lot is also good.

3. To simplify subsequent operations. When uniform parts are supplied to later operations, these operations also will be performed more uniformly.

4. To provide "traceability" in case of failure. When failures occur (and especially field failures), the problems of analysis, remedy, and product recall are all simplified if lot identity can be traced.

Some aspects of lot formation are natural, e.g., heat number of metals, and batch production generally. In continuous or very long series production, the lot is necessarily arbitrary, based on production over a certain time period, of a certain quantity, etc.

MEASUREMENT

The great majority of measurement activities in metal fabrication are conventional and are described in Section 13 of this Handbook.

In metal fabrication it is quite common for measurement to be used not only to judge product conformance but also to provide data for process control. In the latter case, the conditions of measurement are often severe because of presence of heat, lubricant, metal particles, dirt, etc. Both design and usage of instruments must provide for achieving accuracy despite these adverse conditions.

In addition, it is common in metal fabrication for instruments to be in the custody of many setup men, machine operators, inspectors, foremen, etc. With such wide dispersion, it is necessary that rigid procedures be in force to ensure that each instrument is actually checked, at the specified checking interval, to the tolerance for that instrument class. Standards should be established for method of checking, and adequate documentation should be provided for audit and analysis purposes.

PRESS WORK (FORMING)

Forming is a type of metal fabrication which changes the shape of metal sheets through pressing them with power-driven tools (dies). A special die is required for each operation performed on each design of part. The operation is conducted (without heating the metal) by using the inherent plasticity at normal temperatures. While there are numerous variables in the process, the most important is the die. In consequence, the long-standing tradition of concentrating on design and manufacture of good dies for press work has continued to the present day.

Formed parts vary from simple cups to complex automotive and electronic parts. Naturally, the quality characteristics vary with usage, but typical essential characteristics include dimensional and structural accuracy, limits on sheet thickness, mechanical strength, appearance, and surface finish.

Dimensional and structural accuracy pose no significant problems where the dies are well built and properly positioned. More usually, there is a problem because of elastic recovery, or springback, of the material after the part is removed from the die. This phenomenon is always present in some degree, so that even before the dies are built, consideration should be given to whether the elastic recovery can be tolerated or not.

Quality of appearance is a widespread need, since many formed parts are later finished to exhibit beauty of shape and surface. The principal visual defects are caused by dirt, foreign matter, seizures, etc., or by faulty material. These defects show up as scars, lines, pits, recesses, distortion, etc. Inspection for such defects is mainly visual, supplemented by feel or by projection. Such inspections are complicated by the difficulty of setting objective standards and by the high manufacturing speeds. A further consequence is that improvement of quality of appearance commonly requires an intricate technical study. However, setting of visual standards largely follows conventional practice as set out in Section 12, under Sensory Qualities.

Die Planning This activity cannot be overemphasized. Not only is the die decisive in product quality; it takes a long time and much expense to design, build, try out, and correct a die. Once built there is no simple, prompt way of making any fundamental change. Instead, the same lengthy, costly process must be repeated. (Often what must be done is to compromise the product design rather than to delay the project.)

To minimize the possibility of ending up with an unsatisfactory die, use can be made of various aids to good planning:

1. Reference should be made to available die design standards and handbooks.

2. Check sheets or countdown procedures should be prepared to minimize the possibility that some essential aspect of design is overlooked.

3. The progress of the work should be reviewed regularly by the departments affected.

4. Inspection should be instituted at strategic stations to guard against errors (see Figure 35-3).

5. Minor components should also be standardized to minimize design effort and to permit buying from specialized manufacturers of such components. Standards prepared by Ford Motor Company and General Motors Corporation are recommended for reference.

6. There should be a continuing updating of standards through analysis of new experience and knowledge gained from the most recent projects.

Die Design and Construction   For symmetrical parts of simple shape this has been studied extensively, and handbook standards are available showing recommended die design ratios for various materials. There are also limits for extent of deep drawing and overhang which can cause the material to crack or "neck." For complicated shapes these standard data are incomplete, and the die design must be worked out from experience with similar components, plus corrective action after tryout.

Beyond the dimensional contours and tolerances in design of dies, there is an extensive body of precise technology and practical experience in designing, building, setting, and maintaining these tools. Die designing, die making, and die setting are recognized as being among the elite of the highly skilled occupational specialties, requiring long training and experience, and properly commanding high rates of pay.[3]

It is most useful to make continuing analyses to establish relationships between die variables and product quality. Such analyses, when reduced to published standards, can be of aid in product design, die design, economic studies, and in still other ways. Table 35-1 is an example of such an analysis.

Trial Manufacture   Before a die is released to the regular production forces for use, a tool tryout is conducted. The purpose is to verify the adequacy of the die as to (1) correct functioning of the die itself, (2) quality of the parts produced, and (3) productivity. (There are numerous subsidiary details surrounding these objectives.) Once die function and product quality have been successfully achieved, a trial lot is manufactured under shop conditions to ensure that proper productivity can be achieved under normal operating conditions. At this point, the work conditions are determined, and operating standards are prepared.

Process Control   Following successful tool tryout, full-scale production can proceed. During this production, quality controls are exercised in several forms:

1. Control of setup. The first pieces made are checked to ensure their correctness and thereby the correctness of the die setting.

2. Control during production. Periodic inspection is made to ensure that the die setting has remained stable. For many qualities, this proof of stability means that

---

[3] Formal training texts and schools are available, e.g., Acme School of Die Design Engineering, South Bend, Ind.

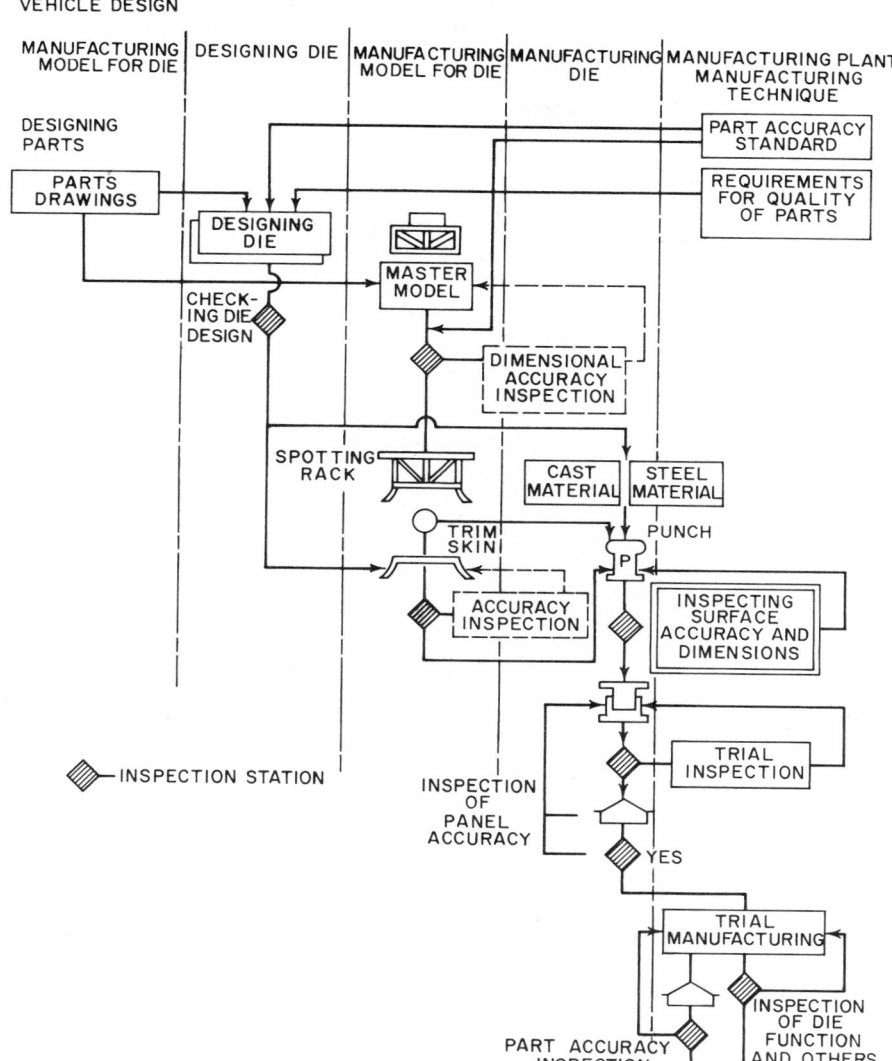

Fig. 35-3 Check points in drawing die construction.

the intervening uninspected pieces are also correct, in accordance with the principles of process capability and preserving the order.[4]

3. Control at the end of the lot. This inspection serves two purposes: *(a)* to qualify the final sublot produced, *(b)* to provide information for tool maintenance to be

[4] See generally Section 11, under Product and Process Relationship.

TABLE 35-1   Die Type and Product Accuracy (millimeters)

Die type	Accuracy of opening shape or circumferential shape			Relative accuracy between opening and circumferential shapes		
	Material thickness					
	0.1–1	1–2	2–4	0.1–1	1–2	2–4
Circumferential trimming die:						
Class A and B.........	± 0.05	± 0.08	± 0.12			
Class C and D.........	± 0.1	± 0.15	± 0.2			
Opening trimming die.....				± 0.08	± 0.12	± 0.2
Tandem type:						
Pilot feeding..........	± 0.08	± 0.12	± 0.2	± 0.15	± 0.15	± 0.20
Notch feeding.........	± 0.08	± 0.12	± 0.2	± 0.08	± 0.10	± 0.15
Full trimming die........	± 0.04	± 0.06	± 0.10	± 0.04	± 0.06	± 0.10

performed before the die is used to produce subsequent lots.   (See Tool Maintenance, below.)

Good inspection is aided by preparation of adequate inspection planning sheets showing qualities to be checked, instruments to be used, data to be recorded, etc. (See Section 12, under Inspection Planning.)   In addition, the gages should be well designed for work of this type—rugged, simple, precise, etc.   (See Section 13.) For sensory qualities, limiting samples should be prepared in consultation with the users.

Tool Maintenance   Product inspection is also an indirect form of tool inspection— the defects on the product point to the need for tool adjustment, sharpening, or repair.   In addition, it is necessary to inspect the tools themselves when the lot is completed.   From these inspections, decisions are made as to whether the tool needs repair before being stored to await further usage.

In large press shops it is useful to systematize the die repair.   For this purpose it becomes convenient to create a mnemonic code system for describing die defects (Table 35-2).   In addition, it is useful to set up the data system which can establish the relationship between number of pieces manufactured and the need for die repair.   (Virtually all presses have attachments for counting the number of pieces processed.)   Table 35-3 is an example of the type of information which can be evolved from such data.

Departmental Responsibilities   Press shop responsibilities are quite conventional. Inspection is responsible for providing and maintaining inspection procedures, inspection gages, and limit samples; selecting and training inspectors; deciding on product conformance.

Production is responsible for creating an atmosphere of good quality motivation; maintaining tools and equipment in good order; correct setup and running of the process; handling the product to minimize damage.

Tool Design and Process Engineering are responsible for planning changes in die design, process, or product to solve problems which the shops cannot solve in their daily repair and maintenance.

Quality Control is responsible for analysis of product returned by customers as unsatisfactory and for giving the results of these analyses to the departments which can provide remedies.

Naturally, there is much need for interdepartmental collaboration to accomplish the foregoing.

METAL FORGING

Metal forging is a process in which heated metal is subjected to plastic deformation by the pressure of a forging die actuated by one of various machine tools — hammer, forging press, upsetter, or rolling machine. At the same time the internal structure of the metal also undergoes improvement. So-called "free forging" (which does not use a die) is not discussed here, but involves the same basic concepts.

TABLE 35-2   Mnemonic Code for Die Defects

Code	Condition and cause	Code	Condition and cause
1.0	Economical die has been manufactured completely	11.0	Knockout trouble
1.1	Economical die has been manufactured completely (die is not ground)	11.1	Bent knocker plate, poor steel quality
1.2	Economical die has been manufactured completely (die is ground)	11.2	Bent knocker plate, too thin
2.0	Failed in manufacturing economical die (owing to cause other than die trouble)	11.3	Bent knocker plate, off center
		11.4	Bent knocker pin, poor steel quality
		11.5	Bent knocker pin, too thin
2.1	Order stop	11.6	Bent press knockout, poor steel quality
2.2	Production plan requires operation change	12.0	Worn guide pin and bushing
2.3	Material stock on hand is zero	12.1	Wear or scar, poor material
2.4	Material fails in gaging (over or short)	12.2	Wear or scar, improper lubrication
2.5	Improper material or substituting material	12.3	Wear or scar, press or die misalignment
. . . .	. . . .	13.0	Die shoe
8.0	Punch trouble	13.1	Bending or breakdown, poor material
8.1	Damage or grinding distortion	13.2	Bending or breakdown, too weak
8.2	Damage or breaking, improper heat treatment	13.3	Bending or breakdown, improper setting
8.3	Damage or breaking, clogging or blocking	14.0	Spring
8.4	Damage or breaking, miscut	14.1	Breakdown, fatigue
8.5	Scarred, improper heat treatment	14.2	Weakened, fatigue
		14.3	Weakened, defective spring
8.6	Scar, insufficient or poor quality of lubricant	15.0	Pilot
8.7	Scarred, too deep setting	15.1	Bending or breaking, miscut
8.8	Loosened, improper punch and holder fitting	15.2	Bending or breaking, improper feeding
9.0	Die section trouble	15.3	Scar, poor steel or improper heat treatment
9.1	Damage, grinding distortion	16.0	Parts cannot be drawn
. . . .	. . . .	16.1	Dimensional tolerance is questionable
9.8	Loosened, improper die holder inner fitting	16.2	Sizing die is required
10.0	Stripper	16.3	To be returned to tool shop
10.1	Bending or breaking, clogging, blocking	17.0	Die damaged during transporting or storing
10.2	Bending or breaking, broken punch	18.0	Problem exists on press. Use press trouble card and record necessary data on the recording tag
10.3	Bending or breaking, broken bolt		
10.4	Bending or breaking, damaged spring	19.0	Problem exists on feeder, rewinder, stacker, etc. Record necessary data on die recording tag
10.5	Bending or breaking, too thin		

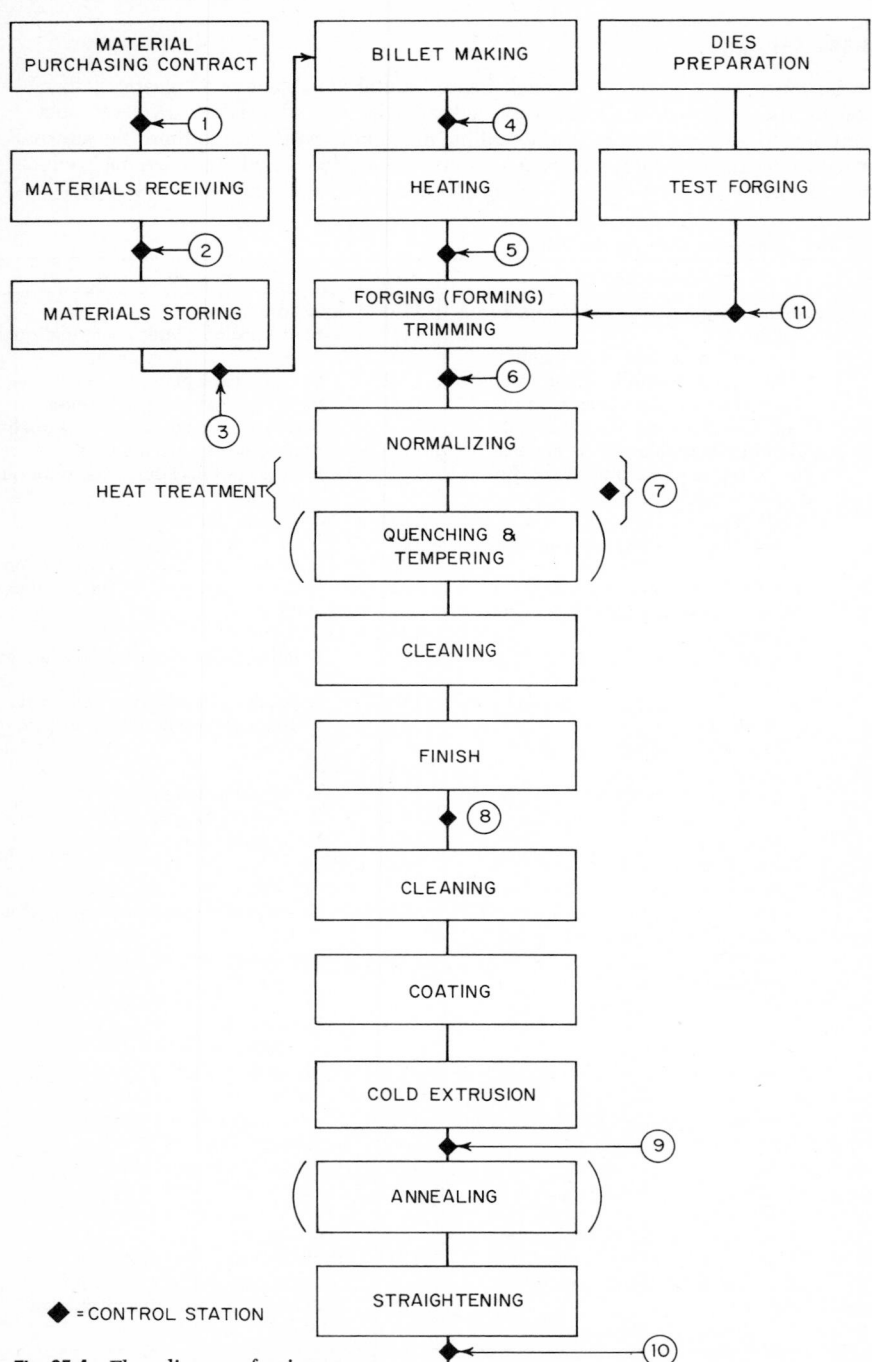

Fig. 35-4 Flow diagram, forging process.

Flow Diagram and Control Stations   New product development follows conventional practice, after which the production process follows generally the flow diagram in Figure 35-4. The control stations are numbered and involve the following activities:

1. Vendor control follows conventional practice (see Section 10).
2. Identification of heat number plus check of hardenability.
3. Heat number maintained.
4. Control of dimensions, volume, and cross section.
5. Temperature control.
6. Control of dimensions, shape, and surface in accordance with standards. Also, control of lubrication and die life (includes recording of die usage).
7. Control of process variables: processing time, furnace temperature, temperature gradients, and refrigerant temperature. Hardness is checked to estimate mechanical qualities.
8. Check for dimensions, grain structure, fiber flow, and other product characteristics.
9. Final inspections are conducted for dimensions, shape, surface.
10. Mechanical qualities are checked.
11. Results of checking dies and test forging are correlated with product results.

In forgings, the main quality consideration is the mechanical properties of the product. Hardness is an essential property since it strongly influences strength, durability, and resistance to wear. Improper hardness often makes the product unacceptable and hence is classed as a serious defect. Achievement of hardness and other mechanical properties requires material of correct metallurgical characteristics, correctly processed to avoid foreign contamination, and correctly heat treated.

Surface defects include cracks, inclusions, underfill, and excessive burr. Internal defects include metallurgical segregation, cavities, abnormal grain size, and season cracks.

Dimensional accuracy is not a major consideration in forgings unless strength of product is affected. The main factor in dimensional control is the precision of the die, which therefore becomes the subject of dimensional control.

Process Control   Table 35-4 shows a common assignment of responsibilities for process control of forging as used in a Japanese factory.

The production operator is responsible for setting up the tool so it will produce good product. Working to operation standards, the operator checks for various defects. For dimensional control he charts the data to conventional $\overline{X}$ and R control charts. He is responsible for taking action on out of control situations, and also for judging service life of dies.

In the heat treatment shop the operator carries out similar duties. He checks hardness and uses the data to adjust quenching and tempering temperatures, aided by a data recording sheet and a conventional control chart.

Operators are also responsible for checking the product for internal defects and surface defects. These inspections require special training for operators.

A checker, also in the Production Department,[5] patrols the forging and heat treating shops, checking the products in accordance with a preplanned check card, and providing the resulting information to production operators and foremen.

The Inspection Department is responsible for verifying the final product characteristics. Automated hardness testers now make it possible to test hardness of all products. Surface defects are often checked with fluorescent magnaflux testers.

---

[5] Note by the editor: In the United States, the checker would commonly be called a patrol inspector, and would be a member of the Inspection Department.

TABLE 35-3   Relation of Die Classes to Amount of Production

Class	Produced quantity	Die set	Die material	Accuracy, mm	Die					Accessories
					Type	Finishing	Thickness, mm	Lip clearance	Punch	
A	100,000–2,000,000	Cylinder guide type 2- to 4-guidepost type Subpress type	Die steel Nonshrink steel High-speed steel Cemented carbide alloy	± 0.025	Split type or single unit	Full grinding lapping finish	30–45	15'	Grinding lapping finish	Bushing is inserted into stripper punch hole. Auto-stop, finger stop, material guide, guide plate, backing plate
B	100,000–300,000	2-guidepost type	Die steel Nonshrink steel Carbon tool steel, class 3	± 0.05	Split type or single unit	Full grinding or grinding finish	22–35	30'	Grinding or polishing	Same as above
C	5,000–100,000	Punch holder Die holder Without guidepost	Die steel Carbon tool steel, class 3 or 4	± 0.075	Split type or single unit	Full grinding or grinding finish	18–30	1°	Grinding or polishing	Auto-stop or pin stop
D	500–30,000	Commonly used die set	Carbon tool steel, class 3 to 5	± 0.1	Single unit	Grinding finish	13–20	1–2°	Grinding or polishing	Auto-stop or pin stop

To aid in uniform interpretation of these tests, standards should be set for the test conditions, i.e., direction of magnetism, magnetizing current, density of magnetic liquid, etc.

Because of the high degree of production operator control, inspection feedback should be complete. In addition, performance evaluation should be prepared for production teams and departments.

Tool and Machine Maintenance As forging dies are used, they wear and deform,

TABLE 35-4 Process Control Responsibilities, Forging Operation

Object	Cutting material → trimming		Heat treat- ment, operator	Inspector
	Operator	Checker		
Dimension:				
Dies	X	X		
Die setting accuracy	X			
Machine accuracy.		X		
Product	X	X		X
Measuring instrument and gage. . .				X
Hardness:				
Anneal, normalize			X	X
Quench			X	X
Temper.			X	X
Surface defect:				
Material.				X
Product	X	X	X	X
Inner defect:				
Material.	X			X
Forging temperature.	X			
Product	X			X
Shipping inspection				X

causing the product to be out of dimensions, underfilled, etc. Because of severe usage, forging dies should be kept under close observation, and corrected promptly whenever the product begins to deviate. Such prompt maintenance not only keeps up the quality of product, it extends die life and thereby improves operating efficiency and product cost.

Die service life is affected by numerous variables, as is evident from Figure 35-5. Die inspection is done indirectly by inspecting the product, and directly by examining the die itself. In addition, the die impressions are measured by pouring babbitt metal or plaster into the die. Die manufacture should be held to tolerances which are one-tenth of the product tolerances.

Die repair and maintenance is usually done by toolroom personnel, working to preplanned standards. Repairs should be verified by inspection and by setup control of the next lot manufactured.

It may be added that forging presses operate under conditions more severe than is usual for machine tools. In consequence, machine troubles occur more frequently, and machine accuracy deteriorates more rapidly. (A common problem is worn slides, causing mismatched dies and surface defects.) Because of this special problem, maintenance of forging presses involves daily inspection schedules, checklists, accuracy standards, and adequate inventories of replacement parts.

Heat and Temperature Controls In forging steel the forging temperature is fundamental. Higher temperatures make it easier to deform the metal, but excessive heat burns the metal, causing brittle and weak product.

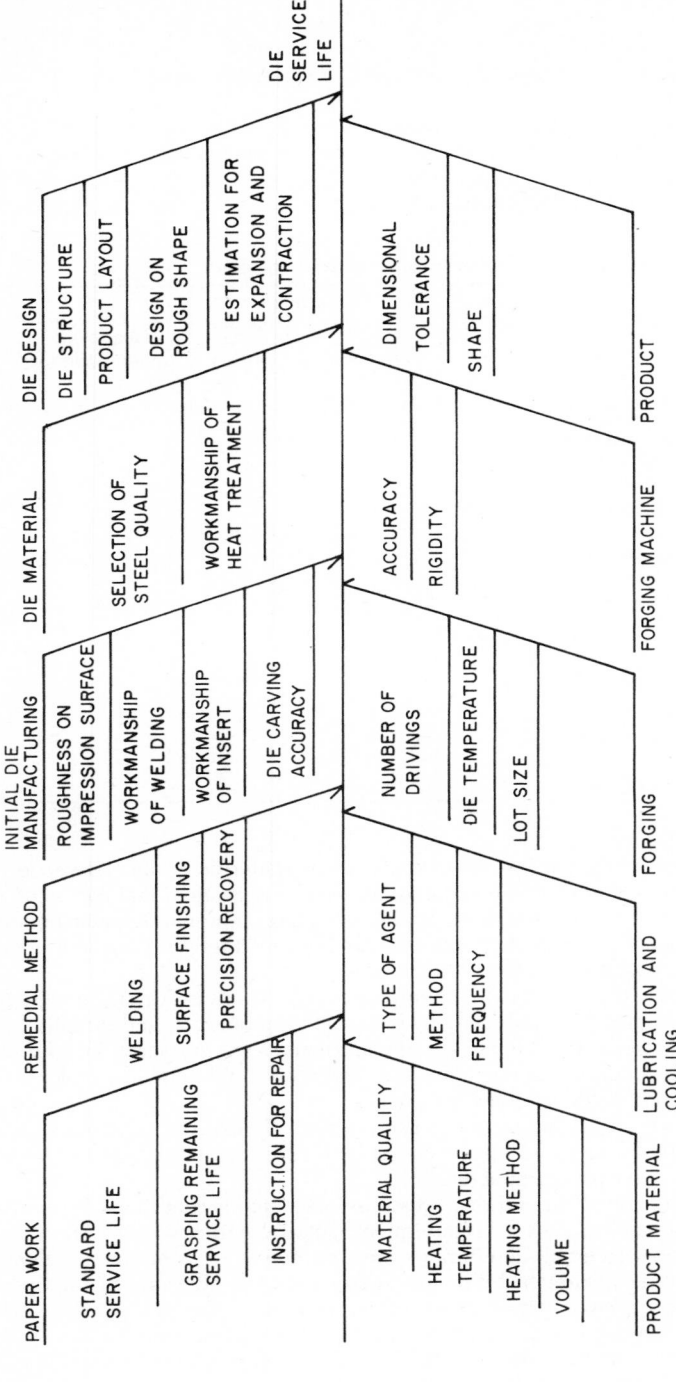

Fig. 35-5 Factors affecting life of forging dies.

Temperature may be measured either on the surface of the piece itself, or in the heating furnace. Various methods are used for measurements:

Visual, based on color of flame. This observation requires training in use of standard flame color charts, since the observation is affected by numerous environmental variables.

Optical pyrometer. This can be reliable, provided the operator is well trained in its use.

Radiation pyrometer. This largely removes operator error, and permits automatic recording of the data. However, good cleaning and maintenance are needed since the instrument is subject to error from vibration, dust, etc.

Thermocouple. This has declined in favor of other forms of measurement.

Furnace temperatures are seldom controlled automatically, it being left to the operator to adjust the controls based on the measurements. However, high-frequency induction furnaces use servocontrols which are adequate so long as the load remains constant. Such furnaces should be equipped with safety devices to guard against sudden changes in load.

Heat treatment temperatures and cooling agent temperatures must also be controlled accurately. Commonly, thermocouples are used as pyrometers for the heat treating furnace. Quenching agents are checked with thermometers, oils being usually held within the range of 60 to 80°C, and water within the range of 30 to 35°C. Long usage causes deterioration in the cooling performance of oil, requiring periodic check and replacement. Of course, all instruments should be subject to regular check and maintenance.

METAL CUTTING

Metal cutting is a method for metal removal using cutting tools to create internal stresses which create a metal break. Other forms of metal removal (electrochemical, electronic, etc.) are not considered in the examples which follow. However, the quality control methods described here are generally applicable.

The metal cutting processes use a variety of tools. Turning and boring are done with single-point tools. Drilling and reaming are done with spiral-bladed tools, tapping with threaded tools. Milling and broaching employ multiple cutter tools, while grinding is done with abrasives.

Dimensional control is a major requirement in all metal cutting. To aid this control use is made of the following:

Standard operating procedures to reduce variations in work methods.

Design of workpieces to minimize built-in machining difficulties. Figure 35-6 shows some designs to be avoided.

Automatic machines to minimize worker variability.

Statistical methods for analyzing data on machine and product fluctuations.

Seriousness classification of quality characteristics to place the main emphasis on the few really critical qualities.

While atmosphere is not usually controllable, illumination (to assist in reading instruments), and ventilation (to minimize thermal expansion[6] and contraction) can usually be kept under control. In other instances (see Figure 35-7) the effect of atmosphere can be measured, and compensating action taken.

Turning and Boring   These are processes in which cylindrical shapes are cut on

---

[6] See, in this connection, McClure, E. R., and H. Thal-Larsen, Thermal Effects in Precision Machining, *Mechanical Engineering*, July 1971, pp. 11–14.

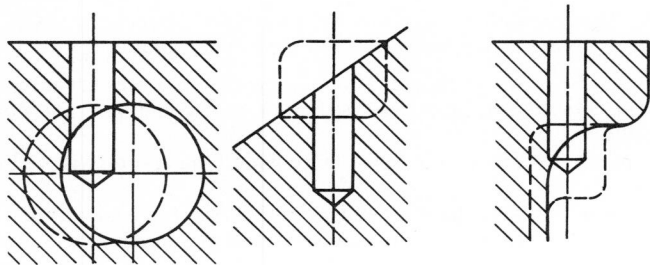

Fig. 35-6 Product designs to be avoided.

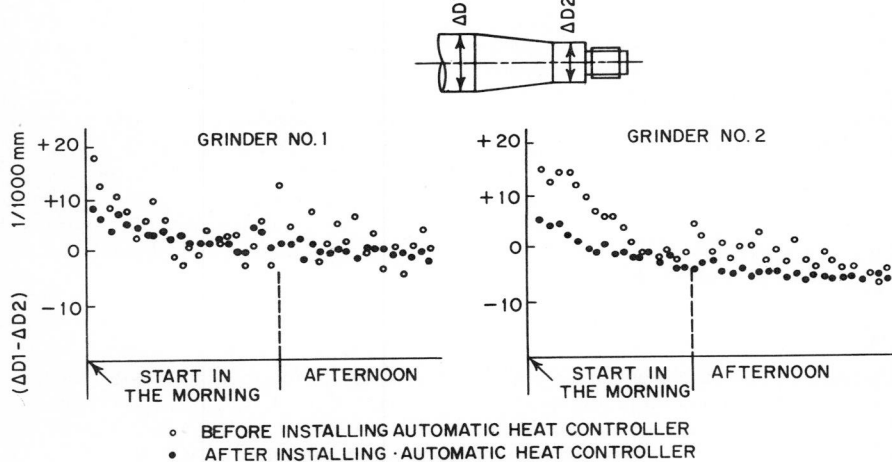

○ BEFORE INSTALLING AUTOMATIC HEAT CONTROLLER
● AFTER INSTALLING ·AUTOMATIC HEAT CONTROLLER
ΔD =DEVIATION FROM NOMINAL DIAMETER

Fig. 35-7 Effect of temperature control on precision grinding.

external or internal surfaces of rotating workpieces. (End surfaces may be cut simultaneously.) Cutting is done through chip removal by a single-point tool or "bit." Modifications include thread cutting.

Accuracy attainable by turning or boring is commonly as follows:

Tolerance of outside diameter . . . . Coarser than IT grade 6
Roundness (eccentricity) . . . . Up to 3 microns TIR
Cylindricity[7] . . . . Approximately one-half of tolerance of outside diameter

For greater precision it becomes necessary to make several cuts. Figure 35-8 is a recommended relationship between precision and number of operations.

The method of clamping the workpiece can readily affect product accuracy. Attainment of cylindrical surfaces concentric on a common axis is best done by simultaneous operation in one clamping. Clamping can also distort the workpiece

[7] Cylindricity refers to the absence of taper and is expressed by the differences in diameter per unit of length.

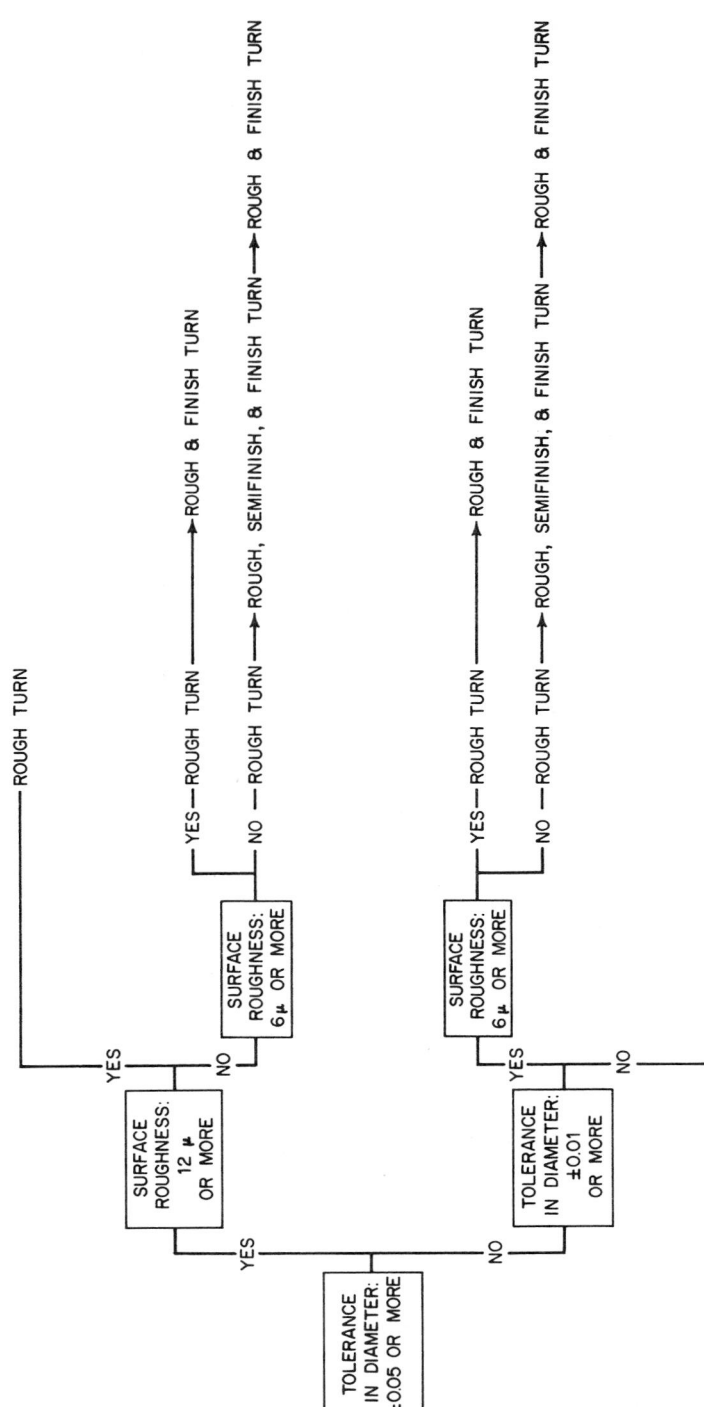

Fig. 35-8 Relation between number of operations and precision.

so that the dimension after release differs from the dimension as cut. This can be minimized by reducing the clamping force to be only slightly higher than the cutting force. Alternatively, the distortion can be measured, and compensation can be provided during the cutting to allow for the distortion.

K E S	日 立 川 崎 技 術 規 程	第 8 6 3 号
		具 1 〜 6 7
Cemented carbide cutting tool use limit judging standard		頁 4 − 2

Segment	Item to be judged	Judging standard	Measurement	Remarks
Wear of tip	Even wear of side flank	For rough cutting, when wear width reaches the value shown in Table 2, the cutting tool should be judged as it is in use limit. Table 2 	Type	Use limit	 	S	0.6	 	G	0.8		Thoroughly clean and remove metal particles from the face, and measure by the use of a magnifying glass having scale of 0.1 mm.	Even wear of side flank means a wear evenly occurred along cutting edge as shown in Figure 2, and this mainly affects cutting resistance. Fig. 2 Even wear of side flank
	Crater	In the case of type S, when depth of crater reaches 0.05 mm, the cutting tool should be judged as it is in use limit.	Thoroughly clean and remove metal particles from the rake, scratch standard crater piece with finger tip, and make judgement of depth by comparing from finger tip feeling.	Crater means a loss of metal from rake face which occurs when chip runs away through the face during cutting. In the case of type G, ordinarily, depth of crater is too minor to judge at the site.

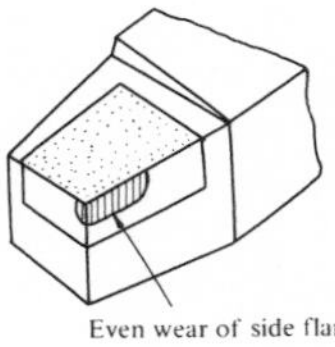

昭和　年　月　日作製		昭和　年　月　日実施
昭和　年　月　日	日立製作所川崎工場	昭和　年　月　日

Fig. 35-9 Standard for maintaining cutting tools.

Tool Control   Except for specially contoured bits, the cutting edge of turning and boring tools is formed by three intersecting planes. Traditionally, the regrinding of these bits was done by the lathe operator, and his performance was strongly influenced by this regrinding.

In modern machine shops, tool regrinding is done in a special tool crib equipped with special facilities for this purpose. In addition, standards are established for wear limits, surface, crater, chips, dimensions, etc. Figure 35-9 is a portion of such a standard as prepared by the Machining Committee of the Kawasaki Works of Hitachi, Ltd.

Adequate maintenance of tools requires periodic inspection to guard against damage beyond the possibility of repair. In lot production, it is usual to require tools to be returned to the tool crib for this purpose. In continuous production, it is necessary to provide means for positive collection of tools rather than leaving it to shop operators to adhere to the tool inspection schedules.

Machine Tools; Process Capability   Machine tools should be able to make use of cemented carbide cutting tools and should have a wide range of speeds so that surface roughness tolerances can be held. Accuracies both static and dynamic should be measured against national or international standards.

It is important to install the machine correctly. If the foundation is not precisely aligned, the machine bed becomes deformed. This reduces the inherent precision of the machine and worsens the vibration. (The importance of correct installation is often disregarded.)

The real capability of the machine can be measured only when the cutting tools have been mounted and are making the product. The usual measure of capability is 6σ. The adequacy for any tolerance is based on the relation of 6σ to T, the tolerance.

During machine tool tryouts, the number of test pieces may be limited, and an approximation must be used. For this purpose, a range of pieces of $\frac{1}{2}T$ is regarded as satisfactory. With large-scale production, 6σ can be determined with precision. (Note by the editor: In the United States automotive industry, the usual requirement is that 6σ shall be no greater than $0.7T$ to allow room for setting up and for time-to-time shift in the average.)

Process capability can be improved by careful analysis of the contributing factors. One Japanese electrical equipment manufacturer[8] faced the problem of meeting a tolerance of 10 microns when the lathe process had a σ of 5.25. (Hence 6σ was 31.5, and thus 3.15 times the tolerance.) They analyzed the variables and found the components to be

σ of operator = 5.1
σ of measurement = 0.7
σ of roundness = 0.5
σ composite = 5.25

Further analysis showed that the workplace lacked adequate illumination for reading the dials, the tool had excessive play, the machine vibrated excessively because of improper installation, and the stop position fluctuated excessively because of improper adjustment of feed screw. Improvement of these conditions reduced operator variation to $\sigma = 2.6$ and composite capability to $\sigma = 3.2$. Further analysis identified a worn machine spindle and an effect due to rise in temperature. The resulting improvements brought operator variation down to $\sigma = 1.5$ and composite capability of $\sigma = 2.4$, or $6\sigma = 14.4$. This was still too large in relation to the tolerance of 10 microns. However, functional tests on the product showed that the tolerance was unrealistic. When the tolerance was increased to 25 microns, the capability of 14.4 was entirely adequate.

Machine Tool Maintenance   Production operators should, as a regular part of their duties, inspect machine tools before starting and after ending each job.

Beyond this routine examination there should be a scheduled inspection of a more profound nature. For this purpose, it is useful to classify machine tools as to whether they are "common" or "significant." The latter are machines which exhibit one or

[8] Hitachi, Ltd., Kawasaki Works.

more of the following special characteristics: required for safety; required for legal reasons; difficult to replace; unusually costly; has unusually high precision, productivity, or efficiency. (The actual classification into common or significant is made by joint discussion between the production shop and the maintenance shop.)

One Japanese machine tool manufacturer has prepared a standard for machine

Classification	Simple static accuracy inspection	Dynamic accuracy inspection	Function inspection
Significant machine	2 to 4 times per year	Not performed periodically but on as required basis	2 to 4 times per year
Common machine	Not performed periodically but on as required basis	Once a year	Once a year

Fig. 35-10 Inspection cycle for machine tools.

tool inspection cycles based on the above classification (Figure 35-10). In this standard, the types of inspection are defined as follows:

Functional inspection: for vibration, noise, temperature rise, wear, operation, and electrical performance

Dynamic accuracy inspection: for precision of test pieces actually machined

Static accuracy inspection: based on national or international standards for those characteristics which are subject to change in level

An example of these machine tool accuracy standards is that for engine lathes, as defined in the Japanese JIS B6201, B6202, etc. Use of this standard requires static accuracy measurements to be made on the machine tools at various increments along all three axes. A formula is provided which sums up all measurements in relation to permissible values, and expresses the composite in an index value. In turn, these index values decide the grade of the machine tool in accordance with a scale set out in the standard. This accuracy index can readily be charted to provide a machine history.

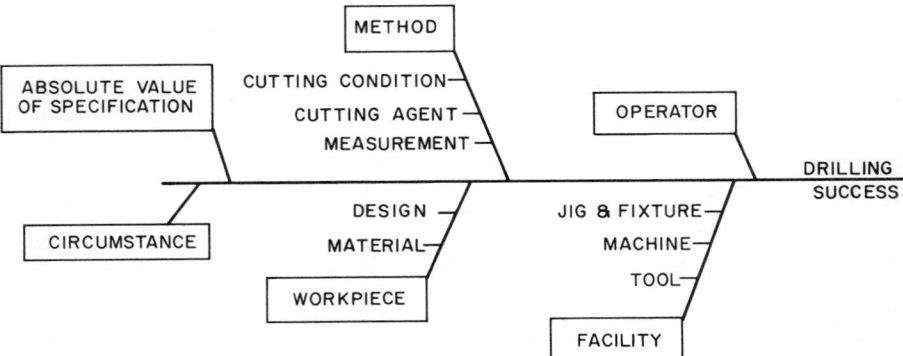

Fig. 35-11 Factors affecting drilling success.

DRILLING, REAMING, AND TAPPING

These processes, like turning and boring, involve metal cutting by chip removal. Although the workpiece is stationary and the bits do the revolving, the quality prob-

TABLE 35-5   Limits of Precision for Drilling and Reaming

	Drilling	Reaming
Fluctuation in bore	1% (large bore)– 2% (small bore)	0.2% (large bore)– 0.8% (small bore)
Fluctuation in hole position	± 0.1	± 0.05
Fluctuation in relative hole position . .	± 0.05	± 0.03
Tilting of hole.	0.2/50	0.1/50

lems are quite analogous. Whereas reaming and tapping are final process operations, drilling may be either a final operation or a step preliminary to reaming or tapping. Factors affecting drilling success are shown in Figure 35-11.

Quality control of these processes has been studied extensively, and much has been done to standardize practice. For example, Table 35-5 shows limiting stan-

TABLE 35-6   Standards for Drilling Feeds and Speeds

Work material	V, m/min	Feed rate, mm/rev
0.2–0.3% C steel	24–40	Medium
0.4–0.5% C steel	21–30	Medium
Low-alloyed steel	15–25	Medium
High-alloyed steel	15–30	Medium
Stainless steel	10–20	Medium
Cast steel	32–50	High
Chilled steel	21–30	Low
Malleable cast iron. . . .	24–40	Low
Brass	60–90	High

ϕ	Feed rate, mm/rev		
	High	Medium	Low
6.5	0.20	0.13	0.08
13	0.25	0.20	0.10
19	0.40	0.25	0.14
25	0.50	0.30	0.19

TABLE 35-7   Standards for Deep Holes

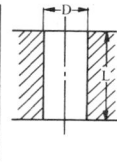

L/D Reducing percentage	V	Feed
3	10	10
4	20	10
5	30	20
6	35–40	20

dards of precision for drilling and reaming common metals. Feeds and speeds are also standardized, and Table 35-6 shows the practice for usual situations. For deep holes, modification is made as shown in Table 35-7.

Product design can also affect processing quality. Part shapes such as those shown in Figure 35-6 must be avoided, since they have a bending effect on the tools.

Precision drilling requires use of locating jigs equipped with hardened bushings to

TABLE 35-8 Maintenance Standard for Cutting Tools

General item	Detailed item	Illustration	Measuring instrument and method of measurement	Judgment standard		Sampling method
Cutting edge	Outer diameter		Passameter micrometer	Range of OD 7 to 10 mm 10 to 18 mm 18 to 30 mm 30 to 50 mm 50 to	Permissible tolerance +0 to −22μ +0 to −27μ +0 to −33μ +0 to −39μ +0 to −46μ	All pieces
	Deflection		Deflection measuring instrument	Range of OD to 30 mm 30 to 50 mm 50 to	Permissible tolerance 0.04 mm 0.06 mm 0.08 mm	All pieces
Tool angle	Tip angle		Protractor	±3°		All pieces
	Error of half angle α1 to α2		Protractor	1°		All pieces
Shape of chisel	Eccentricity of chisel point		Scale measuring	Range of OD to 10 mm 10 to 18 mm 18 to 30 mm 30 to	Permissible tolerance 0.07 mm 0.10 mm 0.15 mm 0.20 mm	All pieces

TABLE 35-9   Basis of Judging Life of Tools

Judgment factor	Drill	Reamer	Tap
Number of drilled holes. . . .	71	3	18
Finished surface	9	13	34
Wear	55	8	47
Accuracy of hole	16	9	49
Cutting sharpness	8	9	
Color of chip.	4		
Shape of chip	5	1	
Sound (noise)	4	3	
Perception	1		42
Others	2	5	5

ensure correct location of holes and to stabilize the swing of the drill. Precision reaming also requires use of a jig to prevent hole deformation due to reamer swing. Correct hole position must be controlled at drilling, since reaming cannot completely remedy poor hole location.

Tool and machine maintenance generally follow the practice used in connection with turning and boring. However, it is essential that hand grinding be avoided for drills, reamers, and taps. These are precision tools which require maintenance to be done in a separate tool crib, by skilled specialists equipped with special regrinding facilities. Here again, standards should be provided for use of the toolroom. Table 35-8 is an example of a maintenance standard.

Table 35-9 shows some interesting results from a survey conducted by a Japanese machining factory to discover how people in the industry determine the service life of tools. It is seen that drill life is determined mainly by number of holes drilled (not total length of drilling). Reamer life is determined mainly by visual judgment of surface roughness. In the case of taps, the leading basis is thread accuracy as measured with a limit gage.

MILLING

This process also involves chip removal, using multiple cutting edges whose profile is traced on the workpiece. The principles of process capability, process control, etc., are similar to those found in other metal cutting processes. However, special requirements are also present because of the inherent nature of the milling process.

1. The workpiece must have adequate strength and rigidity to withstand the powerful, fluctuating cutting forces. This strength and rigidity should be provided in the original product design, using reinforcing ribs if necessary. Alternatively, the direction of the cutting forces should be modified. Even the material is a factor here, since cast iron (for example) is high in damping capacity, whereas high-tension steel is low.

2. The fixture and toolholder must likewise be designed to stand up under the heavy fluctuating forces. To this end it is good practice to:

Make the fixture sufficiently massive to achieve damping and to minimize vibration

Establish clamping position with due consideration of direction and fluctuation of cutting forces

Clamp the workpiece as close as possible to the cutting surface

Minimize cutter overhang, use maximum arbor diameters and, preferably, avoid a cantilevered arbor entirely

Attach a flywheel to improve smoothness of cutter rotation, but only at speeds less than 80 rpm, to avoid spindle damage where starting or stopping

3. The milling cutters must be precisely ground so that all cutting edges perform equally. Otherwise the result will be lower precision, inferior surface quality, reduced tool life, and greater vibration. Usual standards for tool precision are as follows:

Unbalance of cutting edges, full back cutters or side cutters, 0.02 to 0.03 millimeter.

Run out for shank or center hole for face cutter or end-mill cutter, 0.01 to 0.02 millimeter.

Unbalance for all type of cutters, 0.01 to 0.02 millimeter.

Achievement of these levels of precision requires that cutter maintenance be carried out in a special tool crib, by specialist tool regrinders using special facilities. In addition, the cutters should be checked by special inspectors using instruments specially chosen for the purpose.

Milling cutters employing removable tips require an operation sheet setting out in detail the method of disassembly, regrinding, reassembly, and verification checking.

BROACHING

Broaching also involves tracing a cutting tool profile onto the workpiece. However, in contrast to milling, the cutting edge engages continuously with the workpiece, thereby achieving a smooth surface. Broaching is able to form shapes unattainable by any other mass production process. However, the broaching tool is quite expensive to construct. In addition, the broaching operation requires careful attention to controls if product quality is to be maintained. These controls include:

1. Material quality should be controlled for uniformity. Nonuniformity (e.g., partial chill in cast iron or work hardening in steel) runs the risk of collapsing the first blade. It is common practice to probe the material or to verify its adequacy before broaching so that only safe materials are used. Results of such checks should be fed back to the preceding process.

2. The broaching process requires special attention to cooling. (The chips, having no outlet, are wound into the narrow space between blades. Cutting blade temperatures become very high, and the generated heat has no easy escape.) While coolant is supplied generously, the coolant deteriorates, and requires a formal program of periodic analysis and replacement.

3. Broaching tools are so fragile that special precautions are needed during regrinding, storage, and setup. The toolroom usually assigns specialists to regrind and reset these tools. Similarly, the production shop assigns special personnel to set up broaching tools, except for simple round broaches or spline broaches. Even the storage of broaching tools is special. They should be suspended vertically to avoid bending or distortion.

4. Broaching fixtures also present special problems because of severity of wear and vibration. Inadequate maintenance risks a chain reaction. It is therefore necessary to adhere to a scheduled check and maintenance for these fixtures.

5. Finally, the levels of the broaching machines, both horizontal and vertical, should be checked twice a year.

GRINDING AND HONING

These processes use abrasives to remove tiny chips of metal from the workpiece. The processes operate at very high speeds and are widely used to produce highly finished surfaces on enormous numbers of metallic parts. Quality controls are important, especially in regard to the following:

1. Choice of grinding wheel. Grinding wheels vary widely in form, dimensions, grain size, bonding material, hardness, etc. Choice of the combination appropriate to the workpiece is guided by standards available in metal cutting textbooks and handbooks. Generally speaking, hard wheels are used against soft material and vice versa. Higher speeds tend to make wheels act as though they were harder. Hence worn wheels (with reduced circumference) should be speeded up to retain designed surface speed.

2. Grinding depth. Economics of the process favors minimal removal of material. However, attainment of good economics requires close control on the prior operations so that the parts entering the grinding operation are themselves uniform with respect to dimensions, toolmarks, etc. To coordinate controls among these interrelated operations, it is necessary to establish standards for uniformity of prior operations and for grinding depth.

3. Cooling methods. Cooling is essential to the process to minimize thermal expansion of the workpiece and to avoid hairline cracking. Large-capacity reservoirs, pumps, and filters must be provided. For extreme accuracy of dimension and surface, it may be necessary to use automatic temperature control rather than regular checking with a thermometer. Regular checklists and regular maintenance schedules should also be provided for cleaning the coolant of accumulated contaminants. Standards for coolant maintenance are available from manufacturers.

4. Distortion. It is common to demand accuracy measured in microns (0.001 millimeter) for grinding performance. At this level of accuracy, thermal expansion, mechanical distortion, and play of moving parts are serious contributors to inaccuracy. Temperature control of both lubricating oil and hydraulic oil (for power transfer) are essential for grinding to tolerances under 10 microns. If automatic control is not feasible, operator observation of a temperature gage is minimal for control. Figure 35-7 shows the improvement in precision of taper before and after installing an automatic heat controller.

Mechanical distortion of the workpiece can be minimized by well-designed backup to oppose the force of the grinding wheel. Design of the backup can be checked by measurements. The optimum conditions can then be recorded in the operating standards.

5. Measurement. At prevailing accuracies of grinding, special provisions are needed to ensure that precision of measurement is compatible with product tolerances. Fixed limit gages often lack the needed precision; so use must be made of precise direct measuring indicator gages or comparator gages. Normally, gage error should not exceed 10% of product tolerance.

Most grinders are equipped with comparators or limit gages to permit measurement during cutting. Such instruments are subject to wear and should be checked daily for accuracy. Since these instruments must operate in unfavorable conditions of vibration, temperature change, coolant variations, and wear, data should be accumulated on instrument performance so as to discover the instrument types and operating variables best suited for good measurement.

GEAR CUTTING

Gear cutting is a specialized form of metal cutting which, in combination with material and heat treatment characteristics, creates parts to meet exacting requirements, e.g., power transmission efficiency in automobiles, high speeds and loads in turbines, high reliability in aircraft, and high precision in instruments.

Some of the special problems of metal fabrication in gear cutting are discussed in Section 37, Mechanical Components, and the reader is referred to that section for details.

Section **36A**

Plastic Molding

JOHN C. LOUER

Artag Plastics, Chicago, Illinois (Retired)

INTRODUCTION — SCOPE

Plastics molding is a processing function which makes discrete pieces from bulk raw material. The dominant process starts with plastic materials, usually in pellet form. These are heated and then shaped in molds, usually metal, to fuse them into a new shape. Some materials act like sealing wax; i.e., on being heated they soften and can undergo physical reshaping without chemical change. On cooling they harden, and this cycle can be repeated. Such materials are called thermoplastic. Other materials undergo a chemical change during heating. For these materials, called thermosetting, the cycle cannot be repeated. The "discrete pieces" resulting from plastic molding are fantastically varied in size, shape, color, and function, e.g., refrigerator doors, golf tees, "pipe" lighted control panels, gearshift knobs.

Plastics molding is a segment of the broader plastics industry, which is already one of the leading suppliers of raw materials for all end uses. By the beginning of the 1970s, production had reached about 18 billion pounds per annum. About 10% of this poundage is products shaped by molding, which is the subject of this Section.[1] Two of the major materials used for molding are phenolics and cellulosics. At the beginning of the 1970s, the extent of major molded products from these materials was as given in Table 36A-1.[2]

[1] The next Section, 36B, deals with plastic film quality.
[2] *Modern Plastics,* January 1970.

Several aspects of plastics molding combine to put quality control emphasis on prevention. High-volume items are produced in multiple cavity molds (some over 100 cavities). Process cycles are short, and profit markups over direct costs are very small. Salvage or rework is usually uneconomical. Under these conditions, while some process monitoring is unavoidable, the major quality emphasis must be on making it right the first time.

In consequence, this Section concentrates on the molding process and the associated control activities. Final product inspection and testing follows conventional practice as discussed in Section 12, Inspection and Test.

TABLE 36A-1   Molded Products, Millions of Pounds

Products molded from phenolics		Products molded from cellulosics	
Electric switchgear	59	Blister packaging	40
		Personal items (pens,	
Automotive parts	47	pencils, brushes)	29
		Industrial sheeting	
Appliance parts	41	(signs, machine guards)	25
Electrical controls	32	Other packaging.	22
Wiring devices	31	Automotive	18
Utensils, handles.	26	Other.	62
Other.	70		
Total	306	Total	196

NEW PRODUCT CYCLE

Figure 36A-1 shows the flow diagram for putting a new product design into production. A good deal of quality control effort is carried out within this flow, as is evident from the numerous checking stations (which review matters of productivity, costs, etc., as well as quality).

Product Design   The design, as prepared by the customer, often requires revision to reduce tool costs, avoid subsequent trouble in manufacture, and improve the performance characteristics. Optimum choice of material is a major aspect of this redesign, but there are others, as for example:

1. Inserts. These are widely used to improve strength, reduce wear, provide threaded holes without higher tool cost, improve decoration, and even to add weight.

2. Wall thickness. A prime need is to ensure structural integrity. It may also be necessary to provide buttressing, e.g., around inserts and at stressed areas. In other cases the solution may be to reinforce the wall, as with glass fibers.

Material Selection   Some customer specifications are very definite about choice of materials. More usually, the customer specifies a material family (e.g., nylon, polypropylene), leaving to the molder the selection within the family. For example, nylon is available from several suppliers and in about a dozen varieties. The suppliers assist the molders in this decision by publishing tables which show material properties by grade, typically in terms of data determined by ASTM procedures. Figure 36A-2 on acrylics shows the format used. Despite the fact that the molded parts do not usually duplicate the data, these tables are a useful aid to material selection, and a useful base for comparison.

Design Review   This follows conventional practice as discussed in Section 8. The purpose is to reconcile the customer's needs with the capabilities of the molding

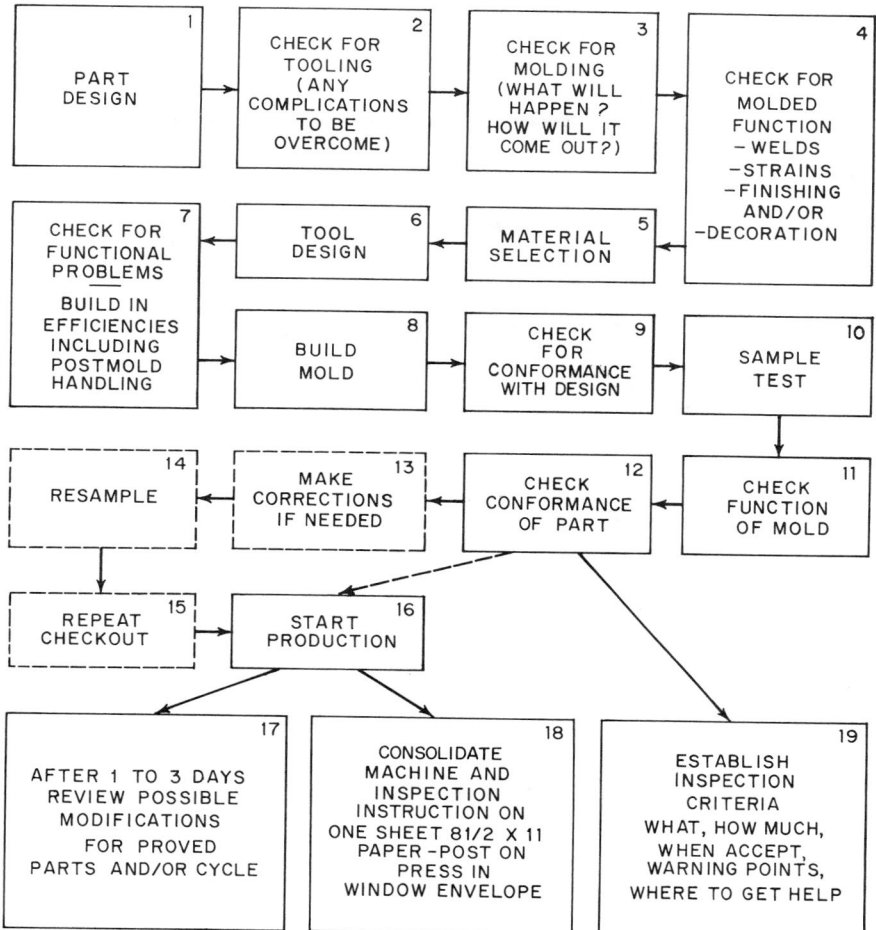

Fig. 36A-1 Flow diagram, new product cycle.

tools and process, to optimize the costs, and to head off quality failures resulting from unrealistic designs.

Tool Design The mold is a major variable in the whole panorama. It must be able to hold its precision despite many thousands of openings and closings (sometimes a quarter million cycles) under alternating high and low pressures and alternating high and low temperatures. In turn, the mold design is decisive as to mold performance. All this points to need for a rigorous check of the mold design for such features as allowance for part shrinkage so as to be in tolerance after cooling to room temperature, conformance to customer needs, location of parting lines and gating to minimize finishing, ease of control by the molding machine operator, and adequacy of foolproofing to minimize inadvertent errors.

Tool Tryout Before releasing the mold to Production, tool checks and tryouts are

Property	Test conditions	Plexiglas V (811)	Plexiglas V (044), V (045), V (052)	Plexiglas VM
Refractive index, n_D	ASTM D 542-50	1.49	1.49	1.49
Specific gravity	ASTM D 792-64T	1.19	1.19	1.18
Tensile strength	ASTM D 638-64T, ⅛ inch specimen (0.2 inch per minute), maximum, psi	10,500	11,000	9,600
Flexural strength	ASTM D 790-66, span-depth ratio 16 (0.1 inch per minute), maximum, psi	16,000	16,000	15,000
Compressive strength	ASTM D 695-68T (0.2 inch per minute), maximum, psi	17,000	17,000	14,500
Impact strength	ASTM D 256-56 (1961) Izod molded notch (per inch of notch) foot-pounds	0.4	0.4	0.4
Rockwell hardness	ASTM D 785-62	M–97	M–96	M–89
Light transmission "as received"	ASTM D 1003-61, total white, %	92	92	92
Effect of accelerated weathering on appearance of clear material	LY 406a-6024 (240 hours)			
Crazing		None	None	None
Discoloration		None	None	None
Warping		None	None	None
Unmolding		None	None	None
Deflection temperature under load, un-annealed	ASTM D 648-56 (1961), 3.6°F per minute, 264 psi	198°F	189°F	176°F
Melt flow rate by extrusion plastometer:	ASTM D 1238-63T grams per 10 minutes		V(044) V(052) / V(045)	
Condition H		1.2	0.45 0.53	4.0
Condition I		5.0	1.7 2.0	15.0
Flow temperature	ASTM D 569-59 (1961)	320°F	322°F	284°F

Property	ASTM method	230	220	190
Vicat softening point, 3.6°F per minute, 10-mil penetration, 1,000-gram load	ASTM D 1525-58T, °F	230	220	190
Shrinkage from mold dimension	ASTM D 955-51 (1961) (cold mold to cold piece) mils per inch, 48 hours	2–6	2–6	2–6
Dielectric strength	ASTM D 149-64 volts per mil	500	500	500
Dielectric constant	ASTM D 150-68, 60 cycles	3.7	3.7	3.7
Power factor	ASTM D 150-68, 60 cycles	0.05	0.05	0.04
Loss factor	ASTM D 150-68, 60 cycles	0.19	0.19	0.16
Arc resistance	ASTM D 495-61, seconds	No tracking	No tracking	No tracking
Flammability	ASTM D 635-68 burning rate, inches per minute	0.7	0.7	0.6
Water absorption	ASTM D 570-63, weight gain on 24 hours water immersion	0.3	0.3	0.3
Dimensional change on immersion, %		None	None	None

Fig. 36A-2   Average physical properties of Plexiglas molding pellets.   (*Courtesy Rohm and Haas.*)

conducted to detect and remove difficulties before large-scale production starts. This again follows conventional practice, as discussed in Section 9.

Review for Measurement   During the preproduction stage, the quality control people from both molder and customer should review the approach to be used for measurement.   A vital aspect of this is to agree on locating surfaces and gage points to avoid subsequent differences.   This review can be extended to include agreement on design of gages (if needed), on who will build them, the time schedule, etc.

THE PROCESS CONTROL PLAN

Figure 36A-3 shows the flow diagram for normal production.   During this sequence the regular Production, Inspection, and Quality Control forces take over the quality controls.

Material Control   Raw material pellets as received by the molder are usually chemically complete and ready to use, including color.   These materials are commonly bought from major chemical suppliers whose quality controls are well established.   In consequence, noncritical molders avoid the expense of laboratory confirmation, and limit themselves to identity checking.   In the event of trouble, use of the telephone, plus air mail for samples, usually secures prompt service.

Very large users tend to conduct bulk sampling of the incoming shipments. (See Section 25A.)

Identity Control   Very different materials can look very much alike.   Any resulting mixups can be costly.   In the author's experience, virtually every size of incoming container has been known to arrive with insufficient identification.   This is less common with the major suppliers.   However, the custom molding plant may be forced by its customers to deal with other suppliers as well.

To minimize the chance of mixups, material identification is a must.   This identification is needed not only in the office records or by the quality control people; it is needed by all who have occasion to contact the material: material handlers, operators, inspectors, etc.   Hence the identification must be on the material itself and must persist throughout the entire flow: storage, drying, preheating, molding.

Setup Control   A good deal of machine preparation precedes the actual molding operation.   Much of this relates to quality: setting of timers, temperature and pressure controls, etc.   There are numerous opportunities for error, including identity and preheating of the raw materials.   Of course, the Production force creates these setups, but Quality Control can provide the checks which assist in minimizing the setup errors.

Process Observations   In some molding shops the Industrial Engineer is responsible for monitoring the cyclic performance at the machine.   Lacking such monitoring, Quality Control should arrange to make this check, which properly includes not only the machine variables (especially the vital cycle time) but the operator practices as well.

For example, the time required to remove parts sticking in the mold may delay the molding cycle sufficiently to cause overheating of the material in the supply cylinder.   Mold surface integrity may be jeopardized because of risk of contact with steel pliers, screwdrivers, etc.   (Good practice limits such exposure to brass, and that in the hands of a trained worker.)

Given a well-prepared checklist, an inspector can easily check a machine out in 5 minutes or less.

A good deal of the effectiveness of these checks depends on the inspector's ability to read and interpret the available signals from the product.   Borderline product (or worse) may be signaled by the condition of the sprue, by parts sticking to the mold, light colors, carbon inclusions, etc. The process also may be giving signals, e.g., dew on a mold surface, frequent on-off signal lights on the heat circuits. Through good feedback of such findings, Quality Control can make constructive contributions to defect prevention and to raising the effectiveness of Production people in monitoring the process as well.

In addition, as Quality Control improves its effectiveness in reading the signals, it can also reduce the cost of inspection. With a properly designed tool, a hole that is present in current product, and was there at this time yesterday, has a high likeli-

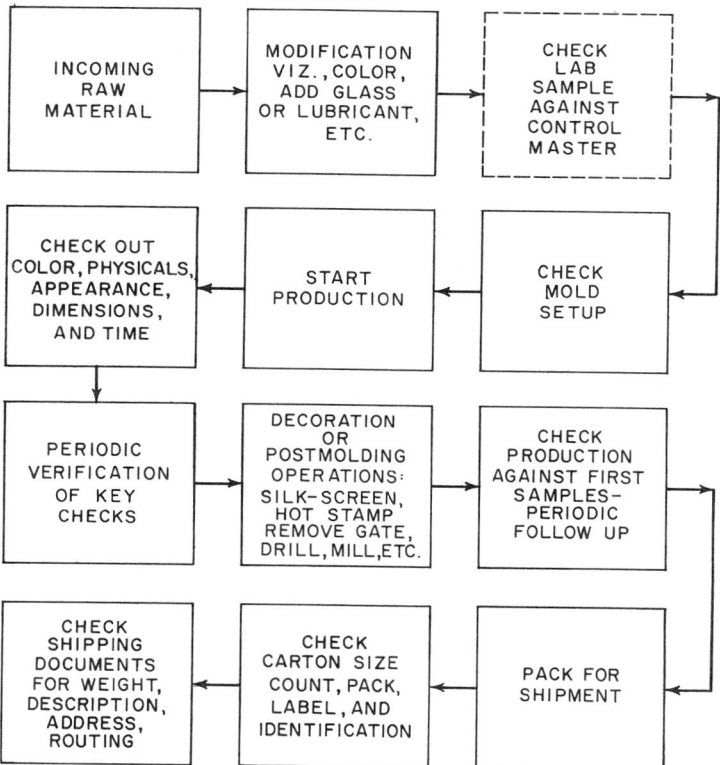

Fig. 36A-3 Flow diagram, plastic molding production.

hood of being present in every piece in between. On the other hand, a pin (plastic) in a parallel condition has no valid means of assurance; a short shot might have shortened or failed to fill it altogether.

In some shops there is no formal procedure authorizing Quality Control to make these checks. It is then necessary for the Quality Control people to do it anyway, securing their authority by persuasion and personality, plus a record of providing useful feedback to the Production force.

Corrective Action For some product quality problems it is feasible to correct or modify the mold. Alternatively, it may be possible to provide the operators with added means for control during the cycling. Other solutions may involve finding ways to use the nonconforming product, e.g., relax unrealistic tolerances or modify mating parts. Seldom does the industry start over by making a new mold. The expense and the long delay make this a matter of last resort.

MANUFACTURING PROBLEMS

Some of the principal quality problems have their origin in tooling and manufacturing practice. Notwithstanding the numerous product shapes, sizes, colors, etc., the quality problems discussed below are widely prevalent.

Parting Lines and Flash The mold is commonly created by mating two polished steel blocks each shaped to provide, between them, the cavity which will be filled by hot plastic flowing under pressure. The resulting product exhibits telltale "parting lines" wherever the blocks join; e.g., rubber balls made within two hemispherical molds exhibit an equatorial ring at the joint. If the mold halves do not close completely (e.g., a gap above 0.0003 inch in the case of nylon), the hot plastic enters the resulting crack and, on cooling, forms a characteristic "flash," i.e., a thin plastic fin attached to the product.

Most thermosetting materials generate gases during the molding processes. A common way of letting these gases out is to design the mold with an open crack at the parting line, thereby deliberately creating flash.

Molding flash creates problems of appearance or function for which the industry has evolved several solutions:

1. Hide the flash. In some cases the parting line can be placed where it is not visible during usage.

2. Incorporate the flash into the design. Sometimes the flash is planned to be a visible part of the decor—making a virtue out of necessity.

3. Remove the flash. In some cases it is feasible to do this by a mass removal process. For example, thermosetting flash is brittle and can often be removed by tumbling with smooth stones, lead shot, or waxed maple pegs, or by air blasting with peach pits. Alternatively, the removal may be by filing, etc., to be followed by a finishing operation.

For some expensive items, perfume caps, plumbing knobs, and the like, mold parting lines are actually removed, the intent being to give a hand fabricated appearance. On less sophisticated items, buffing is used to round the sharp edges, e.g., on telephone handles, small radio cabinets, some toys. In these cases, touch and appearance justify the extra costs.

4. Avoid the flash. In theory, this is feasible by use of precisely matched steel edges. However, these razor edges become factory safety hazards and are easily damaged when struck against or by metal objects. More usually, a trace radius is put on the edges, and this makes the parting line more obvious.

Hinges Under suitable molding conditions, particularly with the polyethylene, polypropylene, and polyolefin groups of materials, it is possible to mold or coin (from sheet or after molding) hinges integral with, say, a case and lid. If properly oriented, these are good for hundreds of thousands of flexes, (they have been so tested) so long as the load is at right angles with the length of the hinge in any position of opening, and generating no appreciable load lengthwise in shear. That is, it will bend almost indefinitely, but it may tear relatively easily.

Failures may arise from starving the wall (it may be less than ten-thousandths of an inch so that it does not have full thickness). Failures may also result from starting a crack or break in the thin section, as when one edge of the hinge end sticks on the wrong side of the mold, or when someone carelessly pulls on a corner instead of the middle.

Control consists of periodic verification of the actual thickness. If the mold operates without flash, once or twice a shift may be sufficient. It is also necessary to examine the hinge under magnification (3X to 10X) to watch for any damage such as corrosion (possibly brought on by trapped gases) or nicks caused by a breakdown of the tool geometry.

Weld Lines   While flowing into the mold cavity, the plastic may meet an obstruction, e.g., a mold pin used to produce a hole in the finished product. In such cases, the plastic stream divides to flow around the obstruction, and rejoins on the far side to create a "weld." Such welds may be present starting from each hole. They may also appear at some point opposite the gate. Depending on the surface temperatures of the two faces of the stream and on the amount of pressure acting to squeeze them together, the result may be:

1. A good bond. Some welds are almost as strong as the adjoining material.
2. An unbonded but tightly filled meeting surface.
3. An incompletely filled plane with a groove or open crack on the outside surface.

Tests are available to determine the weld strength, whether in tension, compression, flection, or shear. However, there are problems of interpretation of these tests, and further problems in judging what to do to improve the results. The welds can be relocated (but not eliminated) through changing the flow pattern, e.g., relocation of the gate or provision of ribs or heavy sections. To a degree, skills in molding can influence the visibility.

There are also problems in visual interpretation; e.g., is it or is it not a crack. This has not yet been put on a scientific basis.

Threads   The mold for a male (external) thread commonly starts with two flat blocks polished and lapped to each other. An oversized hole (to allow for plastic shrinkage) is then drilled and tapped, centering on the matching surface, and creating a round thread. However, after the blocks are hardened,[3] the resulting scale must be removed by grinding. This removal of about 0.002 inch from each block makes the thread about 0.004 inch out of round. This worsens because of subsequent grindings (to reduce flash).

Out of roundness is not a problem with inside threads, since the mold member which forms the thread is not split. However, the inevitable featheredge on this same member may chip off, creating a different set of quality problems.

Male threads may also be formed without the use of a split in that part of the mold. However, this requires that every thread molded thereafter be unscrewed individually, rather than being liberated by the opening of the mold halves.

The problem of plastic shrinkage greatly complicates tool construction for threads. Not only must the tool diameters be made oversize; the length must also be made oversize, and hence the number of threads per inch (of tool) must be reduced proportionately. Also the shrinkage is not uniform, being greater at the base of the thread than at the thin edge. The solid center (male) or wall (female) behind the thread may shrink enough to destroy both allowances.

Other Problems   The foregoing does not exhaust the list of manufacturing problems. Space does not permit more than brief mention of two of the many added problems:

"Craze" is surface condition of fine cracks, seemingly with no rational pattern. These are usually traceable to stresses of chemical or mechanical origin.

"Splash" and "splay" are also surface conditions, but with some order to the pattern, e.g., sunbursts or parallel lines. The usual cause is insufficiently dried material.

Troubleshooting   With experience, the shop people learn to theorize efficiently

---

[3] Unhardened steel is used to permit easier thread cutting. When long runs are not anticipated, the initial out of round can be avoided by use of prehardened steel and carbide cutters.

on the likely causes of observed defects. The more usual cause and effect relationships, based on such experience, are shown in Figure 36A-4.

INSPECTION PROBLEMS

The resilience of "solid" plastics creates a number of inspection problems, both in measurement and in judging fitness for use. Some of the most important of these problems are discussed below.

Thread Function and Gaging Specifications for threads in plastics generally follow those used for threads in metals. However, except for a limited number of sources, the bulk of the thread molding is not in the precision category. This is not

Observed defect	Likely causes
Insufficient material	Mold too cold; insufficient pressure; fill blocked by air, mold release, small gate or small runners
Excess material	Reverse of "insufficient material"
Poor appearance.	(1) Moisture in material; i.e., moisture turns to steam at mold temperatures. (2) Burned spot, i.e., hot air under molding pressures burns plastic and even corrodes metal. Vents are required. (3) Colors are heat sensitive. (4) Damaged after molding, e.g., by dents, scratches, grease
Unfilled cavities	(1) Runner system and gates not balanced (within thousandths of an inch). (2) Heat and cooling not uniform throughout the mold
Irregular product (some good, some bad)	(1) Overcontrol by operator. (2) Nonuniform material, e.g., poorly mixed regrinds, reinforcing fibers, or pigments. (3) Machine defects, e.g., relays, timers, heat controls. (4) "Rush hour" drop in water pressure (changes rate of cooling), or drop in electrical voltage (changes heater output). (5) Day to night changes due to window openings and closings, solar temperatures, air movement, or roof temperature (low ceiling, single story)
Short count	(1) Multiple cavity molds failing to deliver full quota each shot (make a cavity number count to identify which cavities are missing). (2) Gates plugged. (3) Pieces of runner stick, etc.

Fig. 36A-4   Defect cause and effect relationships.

as bad as it sounds, since threads which fail to conform to specification are usually fit for use anyway.

For example, at a magnification of 50X on the optical projector, a plastic thread may show up as out of specification in pitch diameter and contour. Yet in actual usage, the property of resilience allows the plastic thread to accommodate itself to the mating thread.

In other forms of thread measurement, even judgment of conformance becomes a problem. When checking identically dimensioned threads in metal and in plastic, the conventional go no-go gages may reject the former and accept the latter, even when the plastic is a firm, tough material such as nylon. When one recalls that the tolerances for $\frac{1}{4}$-inch threads are only about ±0.002 inch, it becomes evident that gaging plastic threads with fixed limit gages requires interpretations which are different from those used for metal parts.

There is agreement in the industry that application of the metal thread specification to plastics is inadequate. However, the author is unaware of any accepted industry standards aimed at defining sound performance or minimal strength of plastic threads, although some large companies, e.g., IBM, have developed in-house standards based on torque.

Until the specification problem is solved, the emphasis must be on fitness for use. This approach should, of course, be a part of the contract negotiations to avoid the rigid positions which are taken after rejection.

Gear Precision There are many molders of plastic gears, few of whom are equipped to do precision work. The problem is traceable to the variable shrinkage of the plastic. There is shrinkage in the basic disk, which affects the critical pitch diameter, and this shrinkage is different for various diameters, thicknesses, web geometry, etc. The shrinkage also varies within the individual gear teeth because of their nonuniform cross section.

Measurements at 50X magnification make it abundantly clear that most molded gears can be used only in noncritical applications. For precision work, the contours must be machined. The alternative is a very complex calculation of shrinkages, since precision gears require accuracies down to four decimal places (in inches). The investment in gaging equipment is considerable, and in machining equipment is even more so, to say nothing of the sophisticated molding setup.

Thin Walls — Soft Materials Molded products such as the very flexible squeeze bottles (made from soft vinyl, polyethylene, or other rubber-like materials) exhibit unique measurement difficulties. The necks of the bottles are molded with external threads which mate with the internal threads of the bottle caps. To achieve interchangeability requires dimensional control of these external threads, which are molded of about 0.015- to 0.020-inch material on a diameter of about ½ inch. However, these necks and threads distort readily when subjected to conventional gaging.

For more consistent results, a tapered pin could be placed in the neck to keep it round. However, there is no escape from the need for developing inspector skills in working with such soft materials. The author has known operators (inspectors) who developed skills to a point which permitted reproducible measurements to within 0.001 inch, even without internal support.

Hole Measurement Holes in plastic parts are sometimes elliptical because of uneven shrinkage. In addition, the hole is usually tapered, with the exposed surface exhibiting a smaller diameter than below the surface.

Measurement for such out of round or tapered conditions calls for appropriate technique. The conventional round pin checks accurately only the minimum diameter at the surface. Beyond that, checking with a pin requires interpretive skills; e.g., in an oval hole, the major diameter permits an angular pin oscillation, while the minor diameter holds the pin at right angles.

At the larger diameters, it becomes feasible to check the product with inside micrometers. Even here, the inspector should watch for an odd number of lobes evenly spaced, in which case measurement by two-point contact is in error. At small diameters (¼ inch or less) there may be no room to insert the fine measuring tools. In such cases it becomes necessary to section the piece to make the measurement.

As in thread gaging, there are problems due to resilience of the plastic. However, hole measurement is easier to standardize. One way is to standardize the pressure. For very light parts, it is feasible to let them hang vertically from the measuring jaws, noting the reading at the precise instant the part falls off.

Special Functions In some designs, small amounts of plastic serve as insulation for wires, as bearings, anchors, and braces. These applications can be critical. For example, blasting wire sets require only tiny dabs of plastic to space the ends of two wires each over a foot long. Positioning such wires so that they will not get pinched in the mold closing (especially where magnets cannot assist) is a delicate problem. Making three-conductor telephone or radio jack plugs is another variation of the same problem.   The amount of plastic is almost negligible—though critically positioned.

Control consists of meticulous training not only in proper motions and sequences, but in the basic realization of how important each of those motions is to a finished functioning assembly.   A 100% test check-out is necessary on some of these operations to prove positively that they were accomplished.   Microscopic inspection is not uncommon to verify that no wire damage occurred.

Packing Inspection   Molded parts are manually removed from the machine in most cases, though some machines are fully automatic.   If the part is complete as it comes from the press, it may be packed into a container which is not again opened until it gets to the customer's assembly line or to a retail store.   However, other parts may go through some further processing or packing which is so elaborate as to make the molding a minor part of the whole.   For example:

Milk "bags" involve a valve and outlet assembly, welding, and sterilizing.

Bedpans require a solvent cement assembly, a milling operation, and incidental buffing.

Doll furniture may require meticulous packing in sets.

Other items may require packing in individual containers, and these in turn in multiple units, all suitably labeled.

The packing work, as well as the production operations which follow the molding, are part of the product quality as seen by the user, and as such, they should be checked by Quality Control.

Inspection Records   Inspection and test records for plastic molding follow conventional practice (see Sections 12 and 19).   On the factory floor these may extend to preparing scoreboards on operator performance, control charts, and other control records.   However, the industry includes many small shops that operate with minimal paper work, relying on the know-how of the supervision and the mechanics.

The great importance of good tools requires that good maintenance be provided for the molds.   Here again, many shops rely on the know-how and memory of the foremen and setup men.   However, progressive shops have formalized their maintenance, using written work orders and keeping a "hospital record" of each mold to aid in preventive maintenance and in improving designs.

BIBLIOGRAPHY

Debing, Lawrence M. (ed.), "Quality Control for Plastics Engineers," Reinhold Publishing Corporation, New York, 1957.

Dawes, Edgar W., Improving Quality/Productivity in Plastic Molding. *Quality Progress,* vol. VI, No. 11, pp. 22–26, November 1973.

Peace, Archie, Zero In on Precision Injection Molding, *Quality Progress,* vol. I, No. 10, pp. 18–20, October 1968; reprinted, *Society of Plastics Engineers Journal,* vol. 25, No. 3, pp. 38–40, March 1969.

Roberts, L. W., Quality Control in Molding Precision Plastic Parts, *Society of Plastics Engineers Journal,* vol. 25, No. 12, pp. 69–72, December 1969.

Roberts, L. W., Quality Control of Precise Thermoplastic Injection Molding, *Quality Progress,* vol. IV, No. 2, pp. 24–26, February 1971.

Plastic Film Quality

T. R. JONES

Manager, Quality Assurance, Packaging Department,
The Dow Chemical Company

BACKGROUND

Plastics in general and plastic films in particular have experienced considerable growth in recent years. Table 36B-1 shows that this industry has approximately doubled in the decade spanning the 1960s. As indicated in the table, a number of film types are manufactured, and this variety is continually increasing, particularly in the coextrusion area. Polyethylene film occupies a dominant portion of the plastic film market, accounting for as much volume as all other film types combined. These thermoplastic materials find a variety of end uses, ranging from packaging materials for foods and soft goods to uses in agriculture, construction, and industrial applications. Frequently, they may be combined with other plastic films, foils, or papers to form flexible or rigid packaging materials, thereby offering additional physical, protective, or aesthetic qualities. The ASTM glossary includes definitions of both plastic film and plastic sheeting. However, there is little evidence of widespread industry acceptance of these terms, and often they are used interchangeably. In our discussion, film will be considered as material having a nominal thickness of less than 0.010 inch. Quality problems and practices encountered in the various types of plastic film are basically similar and therefore lend themselves to a generalized type of discussion.

Several elements of plastic film quality programs have a degree of commonality with those of other industries, and reference to the appropriate Sections in the Handbook is advised. For example, the raw materials used in plastic films and their related incoming inspection controls are similar to those used in Plastic Molding, Section 36A. Certain segments of plastic film making operations can be classified as job shop operations (see Section 45), since customized films are produced involv-

TABLE 36 B-1*   Growth of Packaging Film Market, Millions of Pounds

	1959	1965	1971
Cellophane	436	405	330
Polyethylene	250	615	1,100
Polypropylene	—	40	90
Polystyrene	2	10	15
Pliofilm.	11	15	3
Vinyl	12	30	125
Polyvinylidene chloride . . .	15	20	23
Polyester.	1	8	9
Cellulose acetate	5	5	5
Coextrusions	—	—	40
Miscellaneous	1	4	17
Total.	733	1,152	1,757

* "These estimates are based on consultation with a number of authorities in the field. The totals should be regarded only as approximations. In some instances the various sources give estimates that range considerably higher or lower than those reported here. Based on partial year reports." Miscellaneous includes fluorocarbon, ionomer, nylon, polycarbonate, polyvinyl alcohol, and others.

Data source: McGraw-Hill, "Modern Packaging Encyclopedia," 1971.

ing a number of variables such as gage, slip, color, optical properties, treatment, length, and width. Batch blending of various composition components to impart specific characteristics to a film requires rigid controls for the accurate proportioning of ingredients and to prevent cross contamination of materials. These controls are similar to those employed for batch blending in the drug industry. (See Section 32.) Plastic films are often used as food packaging material. Then they are subject to government regulations akin to those relating to foods. (See Section 31, Food and Allied Industries, and Federal Regulations, this Section, below.)

Plastic film quality programs are unique in several ways:

1. Production combines both job shop and continuous processing.

2. Raw materials constitute a major portion of the total product cost.

3. The weblike materials produced have both physical and optical properties important to film functionality.

4. The wide variety of end uses for which these films are destined frequently involves compliance with federal regulations relating to sanitation and toxicity of food packaging materials.

PRODUCTION METHODS

There are three principal methods of producing plastic film:

1. *The blown extrusion process.* In this process, molten plastic is extruded through an annular orifice or die, producing a tubular plastic form in a semimolten state. Air is induced into the tube, which is pinched nearly closed farther along the film path beyond the point of extrusion, causing expansion of the plastic into a bubble as it is continuously drawn away from the extrusion die. This trapped air bubble also serves to cool the film as it is wound up into rolls.

2. *The cast extrusion process* is an extrusion process using a long, flat slotted die opening from which molten plastic is forced or drawn and subsequently cooled on a water-cooled chilling drum or roll prior to being wound into rolls.

3. *The coextrusion process* is an adaptation to either the blown or cast process whereby similar or dissimilar types of plastic resins are simultaneously extruded from two or more extruders, thus forming a multilayer type of film.

Each has its own set of significant process variables that influences film quality. Considerable technology has been developed in these areas by the resin suppliers, and normally it is made available to their customers. Although each process has its own peculiar quality control problems, there are also many mutual or common quality problems having essentially similar solutions.

Film Properties   Plastic film properties are normally classed into two categories — optical properties and physical properties. Table 36B-2 lists the more frequently tested properties generally used to characterize a plastic film.

Specifications and Test Methods.   Numerous federal and military specifications, plus commercial standards, exist for the major film types and are available from the

TABLE 36B-2   Plastic Film Properties

Properties	Typical testing instrument	ASTM test method	Other test methods
Optical properties:			
Haze..................	Gardner hazemeter	D 1003	CS 227-59
Gloss.................	Gardner glossmeter	D 2457	TAPPI
Clarity transparency.......	Gardner clarity meter	D 1746	CS 227-59
Opacity...............	Gardner reflectometer	E 97-55	NFPA TR-18
Gels, inclusions	Polarized light, magnification, visual		
Physical properties:			
Accelerated aging.........	Circulating air oven	D 756	
Coefficient of friction (slip) ..	Egan slip tester	D 1894	CS 227-59
Conditioning for testing.....		D 618	
Heat sealability	Sentinel heat sealer		CS 227-59
Tear strength............	Elmendorf tear tester	D 689	
Folding endurance	Tinius Olsen MIT fold endurance tester	D 643	
Impact strength	Plas-Tech dart drop tester	D 1709	CS 227-59
Blocking	See Test Method	D 1893	TAPPI T-477
Water vapor transmission rate	....	E 96	
Gas transmission rate		D 1434	
Ultimate elongation	Instron	D 882	
Ultimate tensile	Instron	D 882	
Thickness (gage)..........	Beta gage, dead weight dial micrometer	D 374	CS 227-59
Thickness multilayer films. . .	Photomicroscope		
Orientation stress release . . .	Strain gage, constant temperature bath	D 1504	
Basis weight (yield)	See Test Method	D 2103	TAPPI T-410 CS 227-59
Odor..................	Panel or gas chromatograph	D 2103	TAPPI T-483 CS 227-59 NFPA TR-2
Flatness...............	See Test Method	D 1604	
Treatment.............	Pressure sensitive tape	D 2141	NFPA TR-5
% shrink	Oven, template, scale	D 1204	
Composition............	Infrared		

The specific instruments mentioned above are not the only equipment available on the market for the purpose indicated. Other manufacturers also produce suitable equipment. CS 227-59 is U.S. Department of Commerce Commercial Standard CS 227-59 for Polyethylene Film. NFPA is the National Flexible Packaging Association. Details of testing methods are given in Commercial Standards CS 227-59 and the current ASTM Annual Standards, Volumes 26 and 27. TAPPI is Technical Association of the Pulp and Paper Industry. Also, see "Modern Packaging Encyclopedia," *Modern Packaging Magazine*, 1973.

Government Printing Office. ASTM and other technical societies also have published plastic film specifications and test methods. See ASTM Volume 27 for a partial listing.

While ASTM test methods appear to predominate, methods from either government sources or technical and trade associations are also available and in common use. The availability of these tests and, in most cases, the rather moderate investment in equipment and operator training permit both the plastic film manufacturer and converter to establish ample testing facilities for product quality control. A majority of these tests are easily reproducible and therefore provide an adequate basis for film characterization between customer and supplier. For all practical pur-

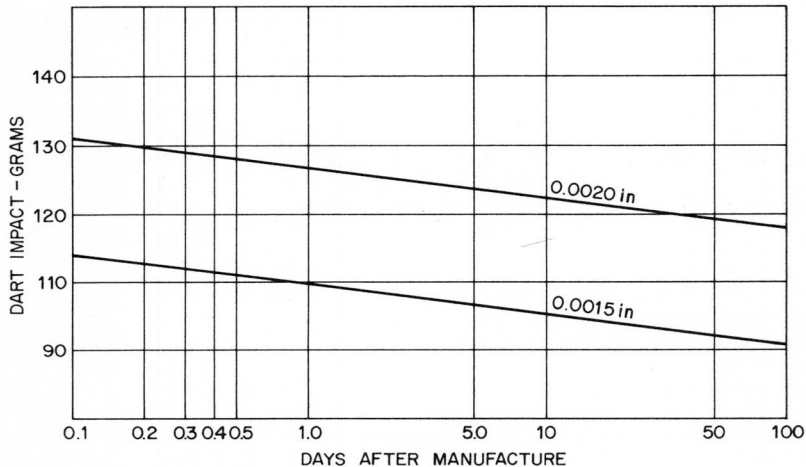

Fig. 36B-1 Plastic film—age testing.

poses, properties classified as optical will generally relate to the film's aesthetic or visual acceptability, while those classed as physical are more relatable to the film's machinability and functionality. With few exceptions, film testing is generally destructive in nature. The optical and physical properties may vary with a film's composition, age, thickness, and in some instances, whether the film is tested in the machine direction or cross-machine direction.[1]

A common practice followed in the plastic film industry marketing literature is to refer to typical or average properties of a film. This evasion of direct reference to maximum or minimum values for film characteristics undoubtedly stems from the desire to present a product in its most favorable light plus an unwillingness to reveal product information relating to process capability that conceivably would be of value to competitors. Consequently the development and use of AQLs for plastic films has been quite limited except for military and federal specifications.

Surveillance Tests. Certain physical and optical properties of some plastic film types may change with time. They must be tested not only at the time of manufacture but at subsequent intervals, since some of the additives used migrate or bloom to the film's surface, thereby causing certain properties to change with age. Accelerated age testing and aging correlation studies are often used to establish or predict the ultimate level at which the property will stabilize. Figure 36B-1 illus-

[1] Editor's note: Section 30 discusses similar problems in paper.

trates the aging effect on the impact strength of a plastic film. For quality control use specification levels at various points in time can be established from charts such as this one.

THE CONTROL PLAN

Specification Systems   Product definition or characterization is of considerable importance in the plastic film industry, and the specification method is frequently

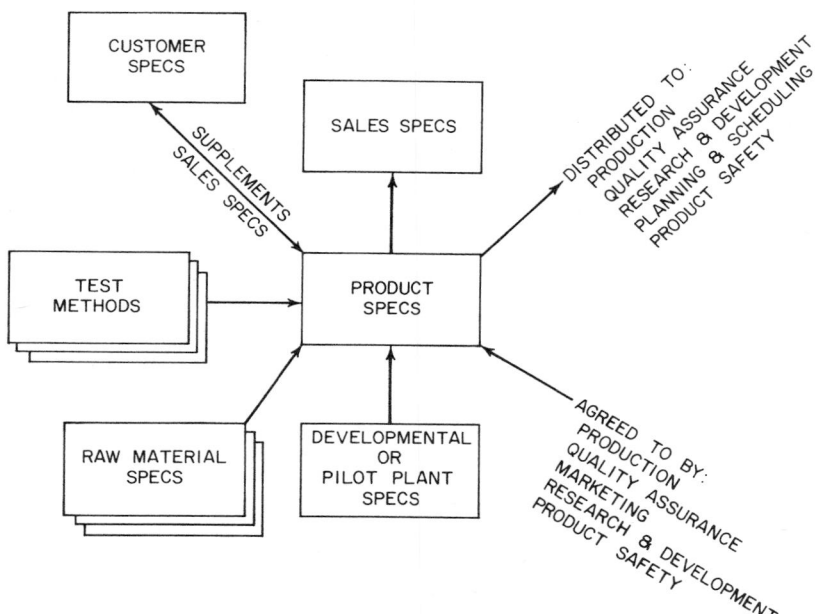

Fig. 36B-2   Specification system—plastic films.

used.   The specification system defines composition, properties, and test methods, and is a key element in the control plan. Figure 36B-2 illustrates a system which effectively communicates product information to Production, Research and Development, Quality Assurance, Planning and Scheduling, Marketing, etc. In multiplant operations where the same product is being produced at more than one location, this type of system is of primary importance to ensure consistent and correct product.   Typically, a product specification is an internal document containing composition, physical, and optical properties as well as a listing of their required testing methods.   Occasionally, it may also include frequency of sampling or test.   Values for the various specification parameters are usually statistically determined based on process capabilities, with maximum or minimum limits often being placed at a plus or minus three standard deviations.

As previously indicated, some plastic films are used in food packaging.   The definition and regimentation of composition afforded by a specification system provide a vehicle for reviewing and assuring the products' compliance with federal regulations relating to food packaging materials.   (See this Section—Federal Regulations, below.)

Raw Material   Plastic resin or polymer in the form of pellets or powder is the basic raw material. Some of these resins are relatively expensive, while others approach a commodity status. Various ingredients may be added to the base polymer to perform specific functions during fabrication or end-use application of the film. These ingredients, or additives which are usually in the parts per million range, serve as plasticizers, lubricants, antioxidants, coloring, and antistatic agents. They are either blended into the resins at their point of manufacture or added during the extrusion process. Many film making processes recycle their internally generated trim, thereby creating an additional composition component requiring control.

Receiving Inspection The quality level of the incoming raw material for plastic film manufacturing is of considerable importance to film producers, since bulk handling and storage systems for the resins are widespread. Contamination of these systems by the introduction of off-grade material can lead to serious processing and product quality problems. The resin producer is relied upon to perform various chemical and physical property tests on the resin to assure its acceptable quality level and to ensure that the resin is placed in clean, noncontaminated containers for transportation to the ultimate user. Frequently, the user will request the vendor to verify that his shipment complies with an agreed-upon raw material specification by providing certification of the lot shipped. As a precautionary measure, a film converter may quarantine an incoming resin shipment, draw representative samples, and check for contamination such as dirt, moisture, and foreign matter. This simple visual inspection consists of spreading a sample out on a clean table and looking for obvious gross defects such as pellet size, color, and foreign matter contamination.

A basic identity test is often made on the resin sample using testing techniques such as the melt flow rate.[2] A more thorough, but time-consuming test is the use of infrared spectrophotometric analysis of the resin sample. This type of testing is most useful for making an analytical dissection of the sample. "Fingerprint" analysis of this type is useful when correct additive levels in the resin are a requisite or where contamination of a chemical nature would adversely affect the processing. As a final precaution before placing the incoming resin in a bulk handling system, a sample may actually be extruded using either a laboratory extruder or production equipment. Production conditions are achieved or simulated in this performance-type testing, thereby providing an excellent means of resin evaluation.

Bulk Sampling ASTM Standard D 1898-68, "Sampling of Plastics," lists recommended practices for sampling bulk materials such as the resins used for plastic films. Several different methods are commonly employed to obtain resin samples for testing of bulk shipments at the receiving location. Although not statistically sound, these methods are practical and relatively reliable. One method has the supplier sending an "in-stream" grab sample with the shipment. A second uses a sample thief rod, a device frequently employed in checking grain and bulk chemicals to obtain material samples from multiple levels within a bin, bulk container, or hopper-type railcar. (See also Section 25A on Bulk Sampling.)

Process Control Product quality control efforts are normally directly related to process variability and process capability, with testing frequency based on an accrued knowledge of process variation and a ranking of properties in importance by their net effect on functionality. Inspection and control commonly consist of a mixture of in-process operator inspection, automatic inspection via instrumentation, patrol inspection, and final product inspection prior to shipment as described below.

1. *Operator Control.* Although instrumentation is used in varying degrees in plastic film making, the machine operator plays a major role in monitoring and

[2] ASTM D 1238-70, "Measuring Flow Rates of Thermoplastics by Extrusion Plastometer," vol. 27.

regulating process conditions influencing product quality. He is relied upon to detect any visually discernible film defects that may be present in the film web during extrusion and windup. This is true even at production speeds approaching several hundred feet per minute. Film defects included in this category are gels, discoloration, die lines, scratches, gage bands, bag or sag, poor roll windup, and surface imperfections. One relatively simple method of evaluating and recording these defects is illustrated in Figure 36B-3. In this approach, the machine operator records his ratings of various film defects on a card. By referring to standardized guidelines, he rates the quality visually as "good, slight, passable, or scrap." These guidelines may be actual samples of film, photographic standards, or written definitions. Although relatively subjective in nature, these methods make possible Pareto analyses of roll defects while providing routine quality control checks and records.

2. *Inspection Frequency.* First-piece setup inspection is typical in job shop operations where films are custom formulated for specific end uses or customers. Inspection frequency is related to the process variability of each specific characteristic, with the inspection activity best described as being routine, audit, or historical audit in nature.

3. *On-line Instrumentation.* The more commonly used on-stream instrumentation devices (where continuous or semicontinuous measurements are taken) include pinhole detectors, film thickness readings via infrared or beta gage, and film color or opacity readings. Often these instruments are coupled into process control equipment, providing automated controls. Most on-stream devices generate a charted tracing of their data, thereby providing a record of process drifts and corrections with elapsed time. This information is often useful in locating off-specification material in the production stream. Automatic on-stream instruments are complex devices. Their proper calibration at appropriate intervals must be maintained to prevent misinformation. (Instrument calibration cards are one method of showing the frequency, type, extent, etc., of calibration to be performed, and provide a documented record of when and by whom the calibration was performed. These cards are often placed in obvious locations near the instrument. Calibration cards are also advisable for test equipment not used directly on-stream but located in the inspection stations or laboratories of the patrol or final inspectors.) Some test devices, such as those for checking film optical properties, are by necessity calibrated with each use. (See also Section 13.)

TROUBLESHOOTING PROCESS PROBLEMS

Detailed process knowledge is necessary to design a sensitive in-process control system. As an example, consider roll geometry, by which we mean uniform diameter; hardness and tension across the roll; and absence of telescoping, starred ends, etc. Mill roll geometry is perhaps the most common problem plaguing the plastic film industry. Mill rolls are large rolls produced directly off the extrusion process and are either sold as is to converters or are slit into reels of narrower widths and smaller diameters prior to shipping. Poor roll geometry can be attributed to many causes, but overall, it results from a combination of inadequate process control and knowledge plus mechanical deficiencies in the film making equipment. Competently done process capability studies will aid in identifying the process variables and, consequently, in stabilization of the process. Mechanical aspects such as machine alignment, level, web tension, and guides should be considered as potential sources of roll conformation problems. Commercial mill roll scanning devices for measuring variations in the mass of material passing between a radiation source and its detector provide a full-scale, one-to-one longitudinal graphical profile analysis of the completed roll. They give valuable web profile feedback information to the

Fill out one card for each roll produced. Refer to list for details of coding.

Use O, 1, 2, or 3 to indicate General Level of Defect or Roll Quality. Use list of alphabetic abbreviations to describe details. Evaluate and record roll conditions. If no defects are apparent, rate roll as O.

Report Edge Depression as fractions of an inch to nearest 1/8 inch.

Report Telescoping as fractions of an inch to nearest 1/8 inch.

Comment on Edge Condition, Gauge Bands, or Wind when applicable.

Evaluate Film Surface Condition in manner similar to that used for Roll Condition.

Comment on Surface Condition when applicable.

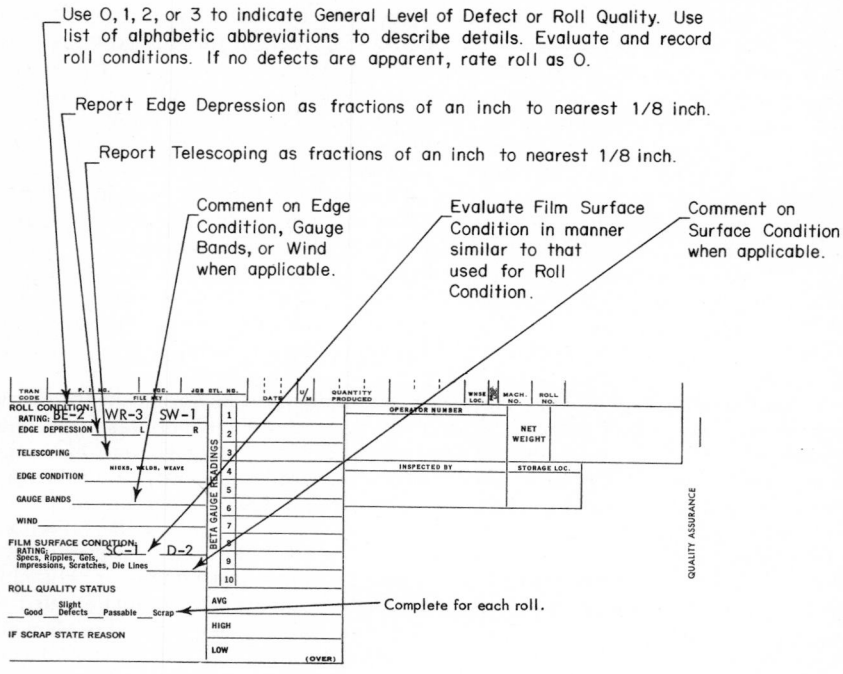

Complete for each roll.

Quality Level Rating

0   Good, no defects
1   Slight, just noticeable
2   Passable
3   Scrap

Defects

AB	Air bubbles	HZ	Haze
BA	Baggy	KC	Knife cut bad (dust, fuzz)
BE	Belled edge	PD	Polymer drippings
BL	Blocking	PI	Pimples and pock marks
BU	Burn or blush	RG	Ridges
CC	Crushed core	SC	Scratches
CI	Continuous impressions	SE	Soft edge
CL	Core length	SP	Splice
DC	Dirt or carbon	SW	Soft wind
DL	Die line	TL	Telescope
FE	Feathered edge	TN	Torn or broken edge
GB	Gage band	WB	Washboard
GL	Gels	WI	Width
HO	Holes	WR	Wrinkles
HS	Hard spot	WS	White spots

Fig. 36B-3   Roll quality rating and defect identification card.

extrusion operation.   The full-scale web profile chart also offers selective or programmed roll slitting to avoid hard and soft spots which would result in conical or tapered slit rolls.[3]

Another property to monitor to avoid processing problems is that of gage.   For most films, control of gage or thickness and its uniformity is of considerable importance as it directly relates to both the economics of raw material usage and film functionality.   Gage variations often become quite apparent in the finished roll, manifesting themselves as gage bands and poor roll conformation.   Certain film

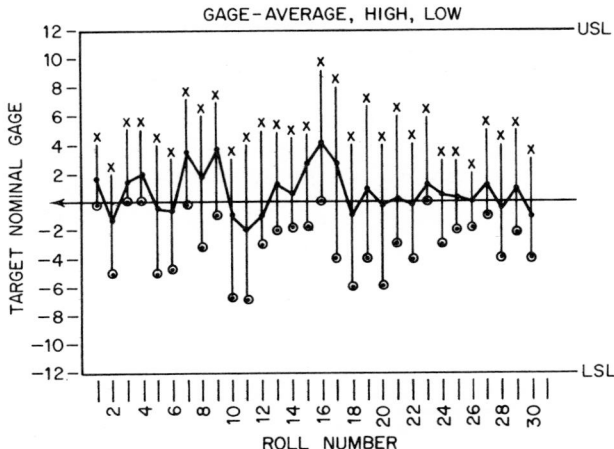

o AVERAGE GAGE OF FILM DETERMINED FROM FULL WEB
   WIDTH BETA GAGE ON 10 SAMPLES PER ROLL

x LARGEST INDIVIDUAL GAGE READING IN BETA GAGE TRACE

⊚ LOWEST INDIVIDUAL GAGE READING IN BETA GAGE TRACE

Fig. 36B-4   Plastic film rolls gage.

processes permit oscillation of the film extruding mechanism or windup equipment in the direction of the takeup reel axis to minimize the apparent effects of gage variation.   Although the standard method of measuring gage is with a deadweight dial indicator or hand micrometer, a recent trend has been toward the use of nuclear beta gages for film thickness measurement and control.   In the more sophisticated installation, these gages are installed so that on-stream gage measurements automatically record their data on continuous charts which provide visual data relatable to position in the film web.   Off-stream beta gages are also used for measuring film thickness and uniformity (in either single or multiple plies) and to provide a profile of the gage variation across the film width.[4]

A graphical technique for showing film gage on a roll-to-roll basis is illustrated in Figure 36B-4.   This simplified process capability chart provides a general picture of gage variation with time.   By relating the charted data via roll numbers to process

---

[3] Editor's note: The same problem exists in varying degrees in other weblike materials.   See Sections 30 (Pulp and Paper Industries), 33 (Metals Industry), and 39 (Textiles).

[4] See Section 9, under Automatic Process Regulation, especially Figures 9-29 and 9-30.

and machine condition logbooks, considerable insight can be obtained as to probable causes of gage variation. For product quality control this chart provides data on each roll's average gage, the range of film gage, and the high and low gage values in the web profile. It also provides a pictorial means of observing process shifts or trends. When beta gages are used, a tracing or chart of the film's gage profile is obtained, thereby locating high and low gage spots or gage bands in the film. Integrating attachments can be incorporated to provide automatically an average gage of the web profile track.

Another information source for control and troubleshooting comes from the industry practice of selling by the pound but satisfying customer specifications for fixed roll diameter or lineal footage. Since each roll's net weight is part of the production records, when rolls are wound to a specific footage, a theoretical roll weight can be calculated based on the nominal gage, footage, and roll width. Comparison of *actual* roll weight to *theoretical* weight then gives an indication if the average gage within a roll is above or below the nominal or targeted gage. Similarly, if a roll is wound to a specific *diameter*, then the variation of the actual footage from the theoretical footage yields information as to the average gage within the roll. Both techniques lend themselves to control charting.

QUALITY ASSURANCE

The overall control plan includes, in addition to the specification system, a system of documentation, data flow, and data analysis. These follow conventional practice.[5] Quality control manuals are prepared, and provide a compilation of policies, procedures, forms, etc. Audits and surveys are conducted, again in conventional manner.[6]

A form of assurance special to the industry is the use of interplant uniformity studies of products manufactured at more than one location. Although all locations may be producing to the same specification, subtle differences in process and testing techniques may result in significant differences in the same product produced at different locations. By combining a round robin testing and sample exchange program, it is possible to obtain data on both product uniformity and interlaboratory uniformity. ASTM *Technical Publication* 335 and TAPPI Standard T-1200ts provide the details and statistical methods to be used in an interlaboratory study; these can similarly be applied to interplant uniformity studies.

Comparative Data   Industry data for comparative purposes is lacking, since no major trade or technical association exists that is exclusively concerned with plastic films. Being highly competitive, the industry does not publish yardsticks for comparing productivity, scrap and waste rates, percent field rejections, quality control costs, etc. If film types were roughly divided into commodity-type films and specialty-type films, experience would probably indicate a field rejection rate of less than 1% for the commodity films, while specialty films would predictably be somewhat greater. A similar relationship on operating expenditures as a percentage of sales is likely to exist with regard to the quality control effort.

FEDERAL REGULATIONS—FOOD PACKAGING MATERIALS

A significant portion of the plastic films produced is utilized in packaging applications for food, drugs, and cosmetics. Federal regulations have been established in several areas relating to these packaging materials:

1. The Federal Food, Drug, and Cosmetic Act of 1938 and its amendments, the

[5] See generally Sections 12, 19, and 20.
[6] See generally Section 21.

1958 Food Additives Amendment, the Color Additives Amendment of 1960, and the New Drug Act Amendment of 1962 (Title 21)

2. The Meat Inspection Act (Title 9)

3. The Federal Hazardous Substances Labeling Act (Title 15)

4. Good Manufacturing Practice (GMP) (Title 21, Part 128 and 133)

Federal regulations provide a listing of acceptable food additives that can be safely ingested by man or animals. Packaging materials are composed of materials which are covered under the Food Additives lists or materials that will not migrate to the food substance as shown by food simulated migration experiments. Revisions or additions to this list are published in the *Federal Register* either when such changes are proposed or when they become effective. Periodically, the published federal regulations are revised to include these changes; however, if it is desired to keep current on a day-to-day basis, a continuing review of the *Federal Register* by trained and technically competent personnel is suggested.

Compliance   Packaging materials destined for food, drug, or cosmetic end uses must be scrutinized for compliance with the applicable federal regulations. As a part of the product specification system, this is normally accomplished by reviewing in detail the composition of the product, its intended end uses, and its end-use conditions (temperatures, contact materials, etc.). Compliance with these regulations is generally practiced on a "self-determination" basis which involves:

1. Examination of the composition of the packaging material to determine if a potential food additive is present.

2. If a potential additive is present, determination of whether or not it is covered by an appropriate existing regulation. If it is covered, what limits if any are there on its food packaging applications?

3. If a component of the packaging material is not covered by regulation, a determination must be made as to whether it can migrate to the food to be packaged. Normally, this requires a laboratory study. If migration is detected, then the material is either deemed unsuitable or preparations are made to petition FDA for acceptance. Petitioning is a lengthy and involved procedure.

4. If the composition of a vendor's raw material is unknown, a letter stating compliance of his product with FDA regulations should be obtained from an authorized representative.

Meat Packaging   Packaging of meat and poultry in federally inspected meat packaging plants is monitored by the Animal and Plant Health Inspection Service of the U.S. Department of Agriculture (commonly abbreviated to APHIS, USDA). Approvals from USDA must be obtained for materials used to package meat or poultry. An application is made to the agency for each specific type of packaging material to be used in a meat or poultry plant under USDA jurisdiction. The application requires revealing a specific packaging material's composition and therefore is treated as confidential information not to be revealed to any other agency, manufacturer, or customer.

Hazardous Substances   The Hazardous Substances Act covers items that are neither foods nor drugs, but which might be hazardous (inflammatory, explosive, toxic, radioactive, etc.) or which may be hazardous when accidentally handled by children. For plastic films this consideration is best handled when working with the customer in developing the product end use, but material hazards must also be considered when the composition of the material is being evaluated.

Safeguards   Failure to comply with any of the regulations could result in civil or criminal actions by the government. Every safeguard must be taken to avoid either. Conscientious adherence to a product specification system is a front line "control" that can effectively ensure obtaining the necessary clearances of the material components with requirements of the regulatory agencies. This, coupled with an effective quality control program for incoming raw materials, component blending, and product conformance to specification, provides an effective mechanism for continued compliance.

Good Manufacturing Practice   Federal regulations pertaining to Good Manufacturing Practice (Sanitation) have been promulgated with regard to the manufacture, processing, or holding of human foods.   These regulations, which are Part 128 of Chapter 1 of the Federal Food, Drug, and Cosmetic Act, provide guidelines directed toward the food processors and packers.   However, many of their provisions are observed by manufacturers of food packaging materials as a matter of policy.   This should be of particular concern since Part 128 states: "Packaging processes and materials shall not transmit contaminants or objectionable substances to the products. . . ."

Good manufacturing practice consists essentially of the operation and administration of methods and facilities to assure that food packaging products are properly identified, are made under acceptable conditions of cleanliness, and meet the qualities required by the appropriate specifications.

Recommended guidelines for establishing good manufacturing practices are as follows:[7]

1. Buildings should be of suitable design, size, and construction to provide for adequate manufacturing, laboratory, and storage facilities.

2. The final product must be appropriately identified as to date and place of manufacture, order, lot or batch number, and including a specific product identity name and/or number.

3. A traceability trail must provide the capability to trace the finished product back through the various steps of manufacture to its raw material component batch or lot numbers and their suppliers.

4. Letters of certification from raw material suppliers should be readily available for those items destined for food, drug, or cosmetic contact end-use applications. These letters provide added assurance that the components of the raw material comply with federal regulations.

5. Warehouse and plant housekeeping and employee hygiene practices should be such that they ensure an appropriate level of cleanliness and prevent potential contamination of products from insects, birds, rodents, or other sources.

6. The Product Quality Assurance function should have adequate facilities and should make the necessary checks and tests to maintain the identity, and conformance to specification, of each lot or order.   Representative samples of the product should be retained wherever practical.   Minimum retention time should be equated to shelf life.

Specific FDA definitions of good manufacturing practice as they relate to food additives are given in Subpart F of Regulation 121.2500.

The foregoing discussion on Federal Regulations is necessarily a general summary. Since interpretation of these regulations is still in a state of evolution, the reader is urged to consult with competent technical and legal advisers when critical questions arise.[8]

[7] See also "Self-inspection and Quality Assurance," 1969, a pamphlet available from the FDA Bureau of Compliance, Food & Drug Administration, U.S. Department of Health, Education and Welfare, Washington, D.C.

[8] For a more detailed discussion, see Statutory and Religious Regulations Affecting Food Packaging, chap. 14 of Sacharow and Griffin, "Food Packaging," AVI Publishing Company, 1970.

Section **37**

Mechanical Components

IWAO IWASAKI

President, Komatsu Machinery Works, Ltd., Tokyo, Japan

INTRODUCTION

Mechanical components vary widely in material, shape, size, end use, etc. Some are mass produced; others are made in small quantities. However, in terms of the quality control methods commonly applicable, mechanical components may be classified into three main categories:

Critical Special Components. These are mechanical parts such as cylinders, pistons, linkages, and weldments. Although they are widely used as mechanical components, they are specially designed, manufactured, and assembled to be used in specific designs of machines. This category of mechanical components will be discussed in this Section by explaining the methods of quality control which are applied to a weldment such as is designed and made for use in construction machinery or in industrial vehicles.

Critical Standard Components. These are parts such as bearings, gears, and shafts which, though critical, are highly standardized. This category of mechanical components will also be discussed in this Section, using the example of a gear to illustrate the category.

Highly Standardized Minor Components. Examples are nuts, bolts, washers, springs, fasteners, etc., made in enormous numbers on special machinery. This category is *not* discussed in this Section. However, Section 35, Metal Fabricating, deals with the quality control methods used in some of the principal processes which make this category of components. In addition, other Sections, e.g., Section 9, Manufacturing Planning, and Section 11, Production of Quality, deal with the broad approach to any process.

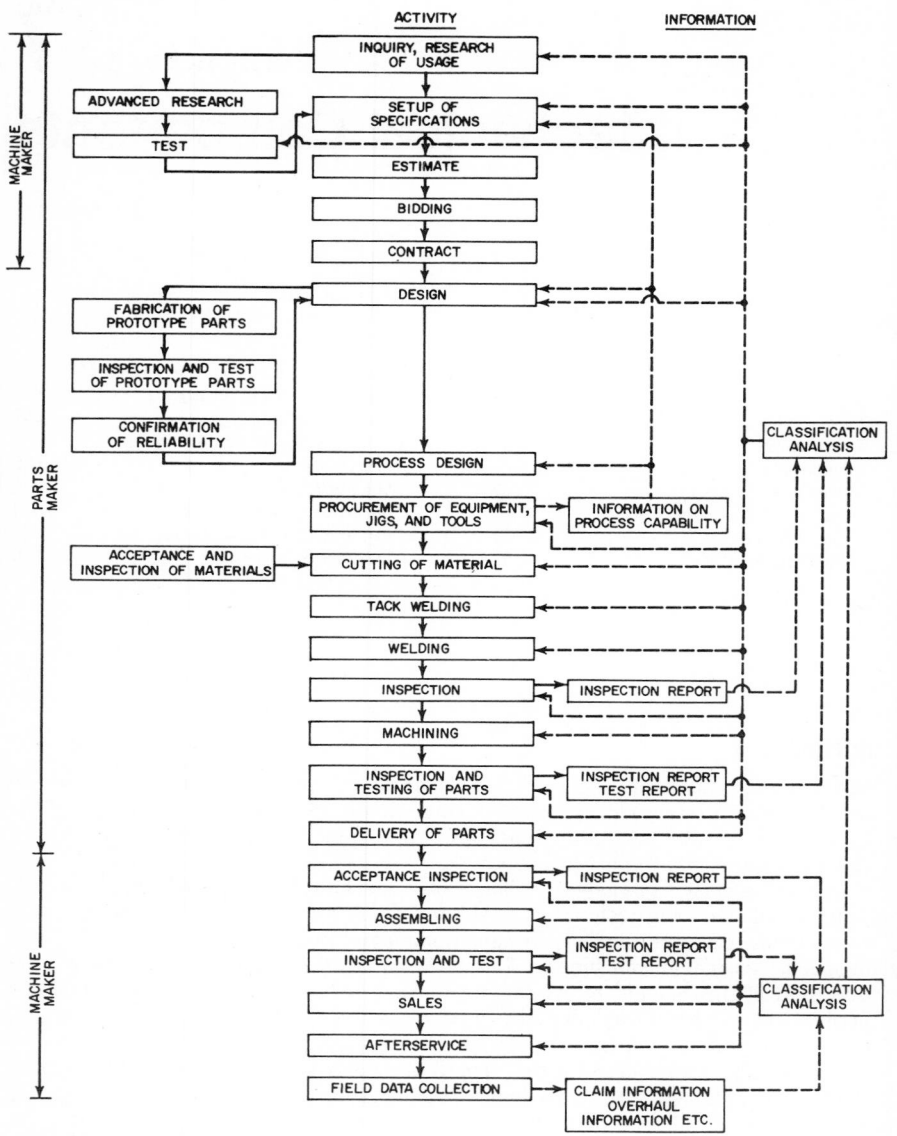

Fig. 37-1 Flow chart of welded parts.

QUALITY CONTROL OF CRITICAL SPECIAL COMPONENTS

The flow diagram (Figure 37-1) shows the stages and activities involved in the progression of a weldment ordered from a parts maker by a machine maker. The activities extend from original identification of the need for such a part through actual usage in the field, and include the associated flow of information. (While the example used is that of a purchased component, the same technological activities and most of the same managerial activities are also required for the simpler case of a self-made component.)

Specification, Estimating, and Bidding to Secure Contracts During contract negotiations between machine maker and parts maker, it is important to clarify the quality characteristics required. The following inputs are commonly needed to set up reliability objectives and to finalize specifications:

1. Information on environmental and usage conditions, e.g., tropical or frigid zone, high altitudes, desert terrain, pollution from harmful gases, vibration, and impacts. Products to be exported require knowledge of the industrial level in the country of usage and of the technical level of machine operators in that country. While the machine maker provides much of this information, the parts maker must supply some of it himself. In addition, there is need to confirm that after-sale services are available in the country of usage.

2. Study of quality of similar parts, based on quality problems encountered in usage of machines, including competitive products. This study is facilitated by setting up a system of usage data retrieval as discussed below under Feedback of Usage Data.

3. Study of assemblies or subsystems in which the parts are used, and the required functions.

4. Study of reliability of the parts and of the assemblies in which the parts are used, so as to meet the reliability goals of the completed machines.

5. Study of reliability requirements in relation to users' actual needs as a check against excessive cost to users.

Fig. 37-2 Photoelastic test of model.

Where the parts maker lacks experience data, it is necessary to conduct reliability testing. For example, a parts maker wishes to use high-tensile-strength steel to reduce weight, but lacks experience data in use of this material. In such cases, design and specification of welding conditions must be complete, and reliability must be confirmed by actual specimen testing. At the same time, photoelastic testing is conducted on models to obtain data on stress concentration. See Figure 37-2 for an example.

Estimating. Conventional cost estimating includes such costs as materials, processing, heat treating, plating, painting, packaging, transportation, and overheads.

However, special components may involve added costs due to the need for special materials, operations, equipment, etc. The cost estimating should identify these special needs and provide for them in the estimate.[1]

Contracting. The contract should embody the agreements reached on the quality control programs. These agreements may appear in quality specifications referenced by the contract, or in provisions of the written contract itself. The agreements may include such matters as:

1. Surveillance examination of vendor's manufacturing equipment, processes, and final inspection

2. Method of inspection to be used on delivery of parts

3. Methods for varying the amount of inspection (up or down) in accordance with vendor's quality performance

4. Quality data to be submitted by vendor

5. Conditions under which payment is to be made for parts delivered

6. Amount and extent of compensation to the machine maker for damage caused by inferior parts (e.g., disassembly and reassembly of machines following discovery of defective parts in completed machines)

7. Amount, extent, and duration of warranty to cover claims of users resulting from defective parts causing troubles during usage

Generally, the relationship between vendor and vendee should be governed by correct basic principles of conduct. See, in this connection, Section 10, under Vendor Relations Policy.

Engineering Design for Specific Applications Design criteria are decided after detailed negotiation with the machine maker in accordance with the specifications of the contract. Based on these design criteria, drawings are prepared and prototype parts are built. The designed quality of the parts is then confirmed. In addition, laboratory and field tests are conducted to check the estimated life of the parts.

Engineering Design. The following inputs are studied during engineering design of the parts:

1. Information on quality of similar parts, including test data, record of difficulties, claims, reliability data, etc.

2. Process capability and producibility in manufacturing, and interchangeability of spare parts

3. Application of results of advanced research for new designs

4. Application of accumulated standards, e.g., for selection of materials, welding of joints

(Items 1, 2, and 3 should also be analyzed and compiled into standards.)

Confirmation of Designed Quality. Prototype parts are made in accordance with the design. These parts are checked for dimensions, weight, etc., and are tested for performance. The results are fed back to the Design Department, along with information of any difficulty encountered in production or quality.

Confirmation of Reliability. The reliability goals for the parts must be confirmed on the prototype parts. The usual method is through simulated use testing in the laboratory. This is supplemented, if needed, by assembling parts into machines and performing field tests. If numerous quality characteristics are to be confirmed in these tests, it becomes desirable to make use of "design of experiments" (see Section 27) to conduct multiple tests on multiple parts for multiple criteria, all at an

---

[1] Cases involving extensive special tests sometimes make use of separate estimates. In the early days of the "reliability movement" there were some separate estimates for entire reliability programs.

economic level of cost of testing.   In conducting such tests it is helpful to provide some spare parts in case of inadvertent breakage during test.

The prototype parts used for testing should be measured completely and the results carefully recorded.   It is these measurements, rather than the dimensions on the drawing, which describe the parts which were tested.   Subsequent calculations should likewise bear in mind this distinction.

Laboratory testing for reliability requires careful attention to the following:

1. Design test conditions.   Tests should be programmed for severe conditions in order to shorten test hours as far as possible.   Actual test conditions must be carefully recorded to ensure correct interpretation and for future reference.   The test program and test facilities should be up to date so that field troubles which develop after sale of machines can be reproduced in the laboratory.

2. Interpretation of test results.   The life of the parts must be estimated from the test results through statistical analysis of the test data.

3. Procedure when reliability goals are not met.   The results should be reviewed by the Design Department and others concerned.   A frequent course is to make some remedial change and then to repeat the tests for confirmation of reliability. However, it is also necessary to consider more broadly the relation of the parts to the subsystem into which they are assembled, since the ultimate purpose is subsystem and system reliability.   Such consideration may suggest unit test of assemblies containing prototype parts, as a means of confirming reliability of both units and parts.   Figure 37-3 shows a portion of a reliability test in progress on welded parts.   A data recorder had previously been used to record the magnitude and varia-

Fig. 37-3   Low-cycle fatigue test of prototype part.

tions of stress exerted on machines in actual use in the field.   From analysis of these data, the test conditions and test programs are set up.

While laboratory tests are commonly adequate to confirm the reliability of individual parts, field tests are commonly needed to confirm the reliability of these parts when used as a component of complete assemblies.   It is most useful to compare the results of laboratory testing with field testing as a means of further improving laboratory testing.

Manufacturing Planning   Special parts require tailor-made manufacturing planning, including the following principal planning elements:

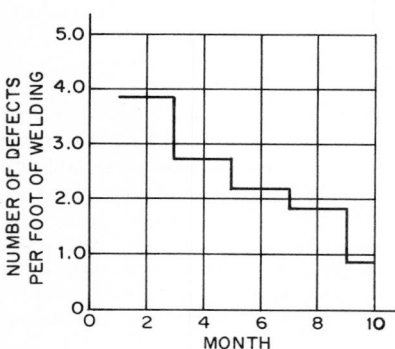

Fig. 37-4   Evaluation of skill of welder.

Process Design.   This consists of the sequence of operations to be performed; the machine tools to be used at each operation; the small tools, jigs, and fixtures; and the sheet metal cutting plan. Obviously, the process design affects quality as well as productivity.

Equipment Procurement.   It is common for standard machine tools to be purchased from machine tool makers.   However, specialized machine tools are usually self-designed, and are often self-built as well.   The advantages of self-building include early stabilization of process capability, in-house repair capability, and security of information representing advanced know-how.   This is also true of small tools and jigs.

Operation Standards.   These standards serve partly as a source of information and instruction, and partly as a supplement to quality specifications.   An example of the latter is seen in welded parts.   Because of the limitations of inspection, it is necessary to impose rigid operation standards and methods of operator control to secure required quality of welds.

Virtually all operation standards provide a breakdown of the sequence of operations; the machine tools to be used; the feeds and speeds of the machines; the small tools, jigs, and fixtures; the measuring instruments.   In addition, there are usually provided the standard machine hours and operator hours, the standard material usage, and the principal tolerances to be met.   Beyond these usual provisions there are others which are special to special parts.

Sheet metal standards also show the material thickness and other characteristics of the plate, the cutting conditions such as number of cutting tips and cutting order, and the groove dimensions.

Tack welding standards also show the tacking conditions, the type of welding and of welding rod, the root opening, dimensional limits, and measuring points.

Other welding standards also show the type of welding rod, the voltage and current to be used, the volume of gas, the welding speed, the limits for dimensions, penetration and measuring points, and the method of quality check of weld.

Measuring Instruments.   These should be considered in the original process design, along with jigs and fixtures, to provide adequate precision during both production and inspection.   Special parts may also require special design of instruments, and in some cases, automated measurement.

Training and Qualification of Workmen.   In spite of much standardization of welding technology, welding quality is known to vary significantly depending on the knowledge and skill of the workmen. In consequence, provision must be made for training workmen in how to weld, evaluating their welding skill from test pieces actually welded, and qualifying those workmen whose skill meets minimal standards. A common measure of welding skill is number of defects per unit length of weldment. Figure 37-4 shows an example of use of this unit of measure in following the progress of a workman. It is also important to keep a running record of operator performance to identify needs for further training.

Inspection and Test Planning This complements the manufacturing planning by providing adequate methods and tools to permit confirmation of manufactured quality. The planning should provide for the following principal elements:

Inspection Standards. Inspection methods, as in the example of Table 37-1, are established based on experience with similar products and from analysis of failure data. A critical need is provision for nondestructive testing (see below).

First-Piece Inspection. As manufacture starts, this inspection provides a further confirmation of the adequacy of the process, machine tools, jigs, etc. In addition, it confirms the capability of the workmen. As this information is fed back to the Design Department and to Production Engineering, the designs and processes are modified and stabilized. Thereafter, steps can be taken to reduce the extent of inspection.

Inspection Equipment. The work of inspection and test requires measuring instruments able to measure the product characteristics and to do so with proper accuracy. Some of these instruments will be standard; others will be special in their nature. Either way, time must be provided for design, procurement, installation, and prove-in. In addition, a plan must be provided for periodic check to maintain the precision of the instruments.

Nondestructive Testing. Because welding quality cannot be judged solely by exterior inspection, use is made of many forms of nondestructive testing: x-ray, supersonic testing, magnetic testing, fluorescence detection, and color check. In addi-

TABLE 37-1   Inspection Method

No.	Defect	Inspection method	Inspection standards
1	Undercut		
2	Overlap		
3	Uneven bead	Magnetic inspection	Inspection through comparison with standard samples
4	Crack	Color check	
5	Residual slag		
6	Spattering	Visual inspection	
7	Pitting		
8	Blowhole		
9	Slag inclusion	X-ray test	Inspection standards and judgment standards for x-ray test and other nondestructive tests
10	Poor penetration		

tion, stress is measured with electrical resistance strain gages, and residual stress with x-ray diffraction. Figure 37-5 illustrates detection of internal welding flaws using a supersonic flaw detector.

Feedback of Usage Data The ultimate proof of quality is in actual usage, and it is necessary to establish a feedback of usage data from product users back to the machine makers and the parts makers. This feedback should also include the failed or overhauled parts which can be so valuable in study of causes for failures. Figure

Fig. 37-5 Supersonic test of welded part.

37-6 shows an example of an information system for feedback of usage data. Two aspects of the system deserve special emphasis:

Early Usage Data. The early (e.g., the first three) months of usage are of special importance because the "infant mortality" failures commonly appear during this interval. Aside from alerting all concerned to provide prompt feedback, it is also desirable to send factory inspectors to the usage sites to study field troubles at first hand.

Reliability Data. Both the machine maker and the parts maker need usage data which confirm (or fail to confirm) the reliability estimates. These data are fed back to the design departments for remedial action. The information system of Figure 37-6 provides for this feedback as well.

QUALITY CONTROL OF CRITICAL STANDARD COMPONENTS

A good example of critical but standardized mechanical components is gears. It is this example which will be used to illustrate the approach to quality control for this category of components. The discussion which follows will emphasize reliability, precision, testing procedures, and feedback of usage data. Discussion of production processes (as described above under Critical Special Components) will be minimal.

Specifications for gears are standardized in many industrialized countries of the world. In such countries gears are produced in accordance with the respective standards (see Table 37-2).

Strict Reliability Requirements Gears are used for power transmission and for speed reduction (or increase), usually in combination with other gears. Many power train gears are subjected to very severe operating conditions, e.g., in construction equipment, off-the-highway trucks, heavy-duty trucks, lift trucks. However, being critical parts, their high reliability is indispensable. This reliability must be achieved in spite of limitations imposed on available space, speed reduction ratio, weight, price, etc. (These limitations necessarily influence the choice of size, material, and tooth profile.)

Quality Objective. Setting of quality objectives requires consideration of the required reliability of the entire gear assembly including gears, gear combinations, shafts, bearings, gear cases, lubricants, etc. In addition, the quality objective for the gears must bear a reasonable relation to the life of the machines, taking into ac-

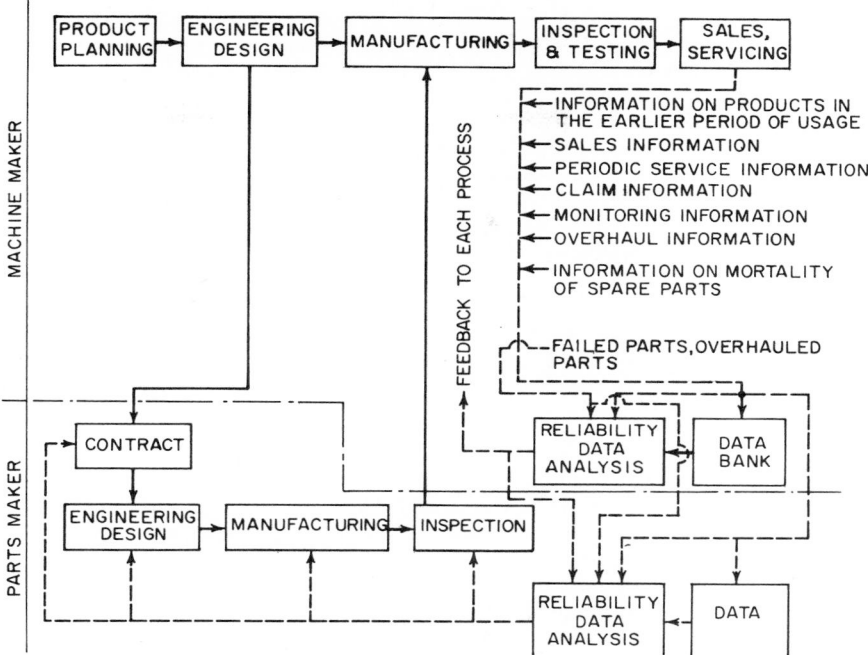

Fig. 37-6 System for feedback of usage data.

count the users' costs as affected by spare parts availability and service technique. Gear life can be too long as well as too short. Neither is advantageous to users.

Quality Specifications. These are prepared based on the quality objectives, and serve to provide against the following principal defects of gears:

1. Surface deterioration due to wear, elastic yielding, welding, fatigue, etc.

2. Tooth breakage due to overload, fatigue, cracking, quenching, etc.

3. Noise due to insufficient precision, rough surface, wear, etc.

Prevention of these defects requires careful study of the environmental and loading conditions under which the machines are operated. Based on the estimate of the probable life of the gears, design decisions are made:

1. Materials should be selected with due regard to bending strength of tooth root, contact pressure on tooth surface, core hardness, tooth surface hardness, heat treatment for required depth of hardening, and costs.

TABLE 37-2 Gear Standards

Country	Standard
United States.	AGMA (American Gear Manufacturers Association)
Great Britain.	BS (British Standard)
West Germany.	DIN (Deutsche Ingeniere Normen)
Japan	JIS (Japanese Industrial Standard); JGMA (Japanese Gear Manufacturers Association)
USSR	ГOCT (State System of Standardization)
Switzerland.	VSM (Verein Schweizerischer Machinenindustrieller)

2. Tooth surface hardness and depth of hardening are specified after study of process capability of heat treating equipment and after analysis of reliability data on matters such as tooth surface hardness and surface deterioration, hardened depth and surface deterioration, core hardness and surface deterioration, distribution of surface hardened layer and bending failure, surface hardness and life of mating gear.

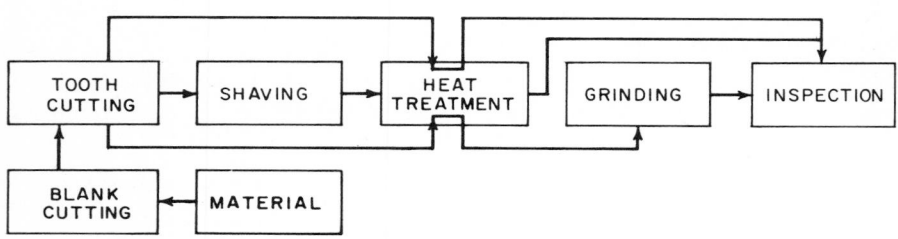

Fig. 37-7   Processes of gear manufacturing.

3. Tooth profiles are selected based on dynamic meshing characteristics, life and noise of gears in relation to factors such as basic tooth profile, amount of profile modification, amount of crowning, tooth profile error and its allowable limit.

Where shortage of reliability data precludes estimate of gear life, experimental testing is needed to confirm the life of such gears. Of course, design criteria and reliability data should constantly be updated from usage reports so that new designs reflect the best information available.

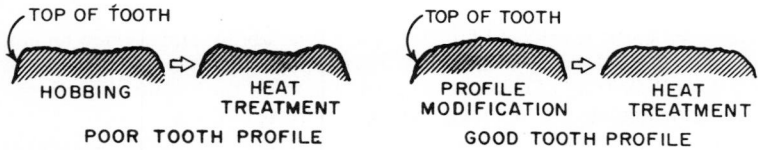

Fig. 37-8   Deformation of tooth profile in heat treatment.

Attainment of High Precision   The critical factor in making high-precision gears is the manufacturing process design. Figure 37-7 shows the stages of processing used for critical gears. Practically all gears go through heat treatment. The resulting risk of deformation requires precise controls (1) in the heat treating process and (2) in preceding stages to provide for the effects of deformation. In turn, these controls require that manufacturing processes be designed based on known capability in profiling, machining, heat treatment, etc., if the specified precision is to be met for tooth profile, hardness, depth of hardness, surface finish, etc.

Process Design.   Insufficient precision in gears is evidenced by the following defects: tooth profile error, pitch error, lead error, runout. To prevent these defects requires precision in the following categories:

1. Gear blank. Accuracy of gear blanks strongly influences the precision of the subsequent operations. Gear blank machinery should provide for adequate precision to permit the subsequent processes of tooth cutting, shaving, and grinding to be done precisely.

2. Gear tooth cutting. The precision of gear tooth cutting is influenced by several variables. The machine tools are decisive as to tooth profile error and pitch error.

Inadequate cutting tools may cause tooth profile deviation. Improperly set jigs may cause tooth profile error, lead error, runout, etc.

Even though tooth cutting machines may have sufficient process capability, deformation due to heat treatment may create dimensional defects in all defect categories. Because the type of deformation differs with the heat treating process used, the remedial measures are also different.

Where heat treatment consists of carburizing and quenching, the tooth profiles are deformed with a tendency of increasing pressure angle due to heating. (The amount of deformation varies depending on shapes of spur gears, heat treating conditions, etc.) The tooth profiles of hob cutters and shaving cutters should be chosen based on the observed extent of heat deformation.

Where induction hardening is used, the heat deformation tends to enlarge the top and root of the tooth, and to decrease the pressure angle. Knowledge of the extent of the deformation should be used as a basis for changing the tooth profiles of the cutting tools. Figure 37-8 shows an example of improvement of tooth profile achieved by such change in the cutting tools.

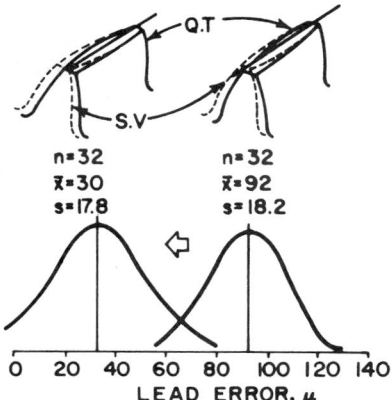

Fig. 37-9 Slight change of tooth profile, through shaving, for prevention of lead error in heat treatment; n = sample size; $\bar{x}$ = average; s = standard deviation; S.V. = after shaving; Q.T. = after quench treatment.

Lead error is also a potential defect due to heat deformation. The remedy lies in a machining process design which includes adjustments so that the final process can finish the gears exactly to the drawing dimensions.

3. Shaving. Tooth deformation caused by heat treatment subsequent to shaving affects the axial lead. To compensate for this, the gear teeth can be inclined in advance based on the observed deformation due to hardening. Figure 37-9 shows how this remedy can be provided.

In the case of profile error, there is some correlation between gear hobbing and shaving as shown in Figure 37-10. The high correlation points to the need for precise hobbing in order to attain precision during the shaving operation.

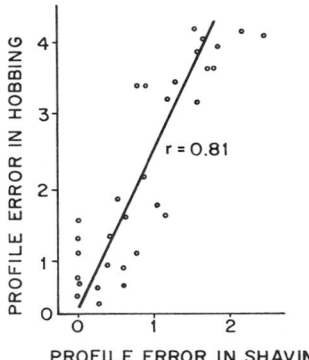

Fig. 37-10 Correlation of profile error before and after shaving.

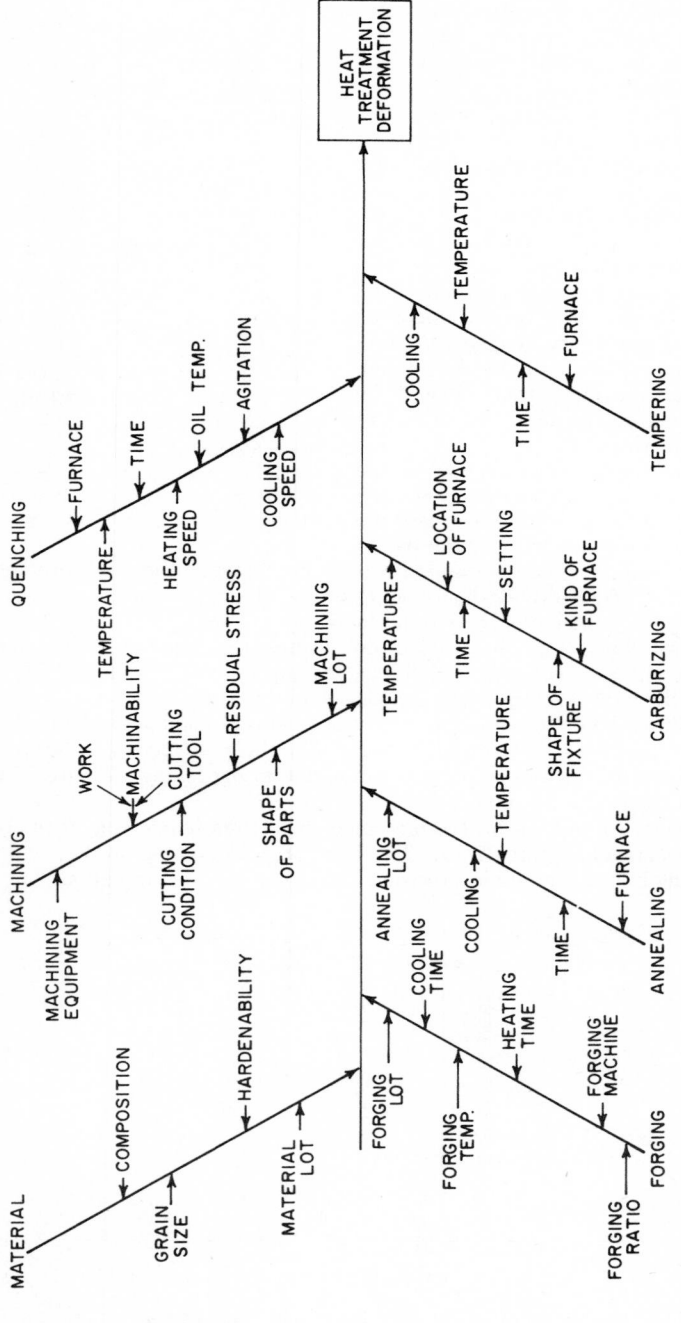

Fig. 37-11 Cause and effect diagram of deformation in heat treatment.

4. Heat treatment.   The cause and effect diagram in Figure 37-11 shows the interrelation of the variables causing heat treatment deformation. As noted above, some remedy for this deformation can be provided through compensations in preceding operations. However, these compensations all assume a uniform amount of subsequent deformation. Hence controls must be exercised in the heat treating process to hold this uniformity. A principal variable in the heat treating is the manner of charging the containers. For example, deformation during carburizing and quenching is strongly influenced by the method of piling, hanging, or placing the parts on the trays. In consequence, the process design must include clear decisions on these matters. Figure 37-12 shows an example in which lead error is high or low depending on whether the parts are placed right side up or upside down during induction hardening. Discovery of such relationships is part of the study of process capability.

In designing the details of such processes, it is useful to solicit the opinions of the workmen because they are fully acquainted with the minute details of the operation of the process. For this same reason, the activities of QC Circles are also effective.

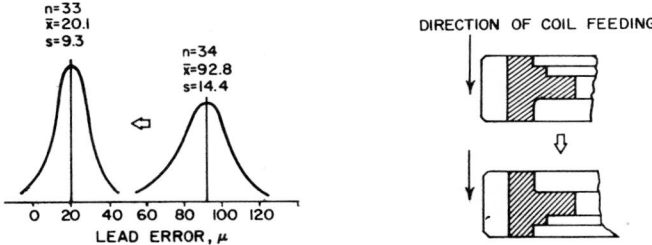

Fig. 37-12 Effect, on lead error, of gear position during hardening.

Hardness. Because hardness of gears has a major influence on reliability, it is most important to assure that hardness requirements are met. A great deal of this assurance comes from careful attention to small details during process capability studies. Figure 37-13 shows, for example, how surface carburization varies with position of the piece in the furnace. In turn, this surface carburization affects the hardness. Based on such studies, it becomes feasible to set up operating standards such as methods of placing materials in the furnace, methods of operating the furnace, cooling capacity, and time cycle. Such standards are needed for the various furnaces, quench tanks, etc.

It is also found that tooth surface hardness varies within the tooth. Figure 37-14 shows an example of this variation. Since the bending strength of gear teeth is increased through improved hardness at the root of the teeth, the heat treatment

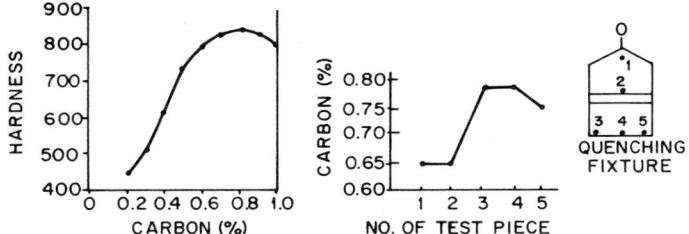

Fig. 37-13 Variation in hardness due to amount of surface carburization, and variation in amount of surface carburization depending on positions in carburization furnace.

design including the cooling method (which has extensive influence on variation in hardness) should be structured accordingly.

Process Control. The approach here is quite conventional. Check points are clearly identified, checking frequency is determined, and responsibility is assigned, to either Production or Inspection, to make the checks at the frequencies specified. Figure 37-15 gives an example of such a plan.

Close attention is paid to process changes as a further means of process control. The following process changes are the most critical: machine tools in the process, jigs and fixtures, operating conditions, heat treating furnace, heat treatment conditions, heat treatment fixtures. Upon such changes, the process capabilities are studied through first-piece inspection. The resulting data are fed back to the process design section of the shop for further improvement in manufacturing process.

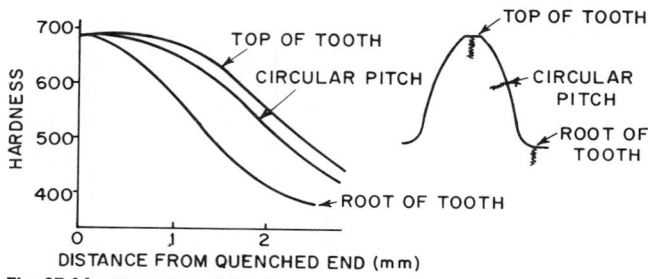

Fig. 37-14   Variation of hardness on tooth surface.

Inspection. An added form of assurance of high precision is through inspection in several forms:

1. First-piece inspection. This is carried out (see above) upon changes in machines, processes, furnaces, etc. Inspection results are analyzed to evaluate the process capabilities and to feed back essential information to process designers, inspection planners, etc. Important inspection results are filed for product history purposes.

2. Process inspection. Daily routine inspection is conducted through measurement of first piece and last piece of a lot. In those cases where Production is unable to measure precisely, a measurement service is provided by Inspection, as shown in Figure 37-15, to evaluate quality control activities in the shop.

Heat treated parts are punch marked to designate lot number and furnace and to facilitate traceability in the event of product failures. As before, important inspection data are filed for future analysis and for product history purposes.

3. Measuring instrument control. This follows the conventional approach discussed in Section 13 of this Handbook.

Rigorous Testing Procedures   Gears have comparatively simple shapes, and their theoretical analysis for strength has progressed significantly. In consequence, design procedures have become standardized, and life of gears can be estimated with some confidence. However, gears are critical components in machines, so that trouble in gears can develop into serious failures. It is therefore necessary to measure gear unit durability through reliability tests and to confirm the attainment of unit durability. Tests may be conducted in either the laboratory or the field, but if possible, accelerated tests should be given to shorten the time required to arrive at usable test results.

Laboratory Testing. The objective may be to investigate any of a number of potential failures: tooth face deterioration, bending failure, noise. While testing

Process	Production Dept. — Process Control				Production Dept. — Check of Dimensions of Parts					Inspection Dept. — Check of Process	Inspection Dept. — Check of Parts
	Item	Spec.	Frequency	Name	Check Point	Sampling Size — Start	Sampling Size — Intermediate	Sampling Size — End	Name		

Blank cutting	1. Periodic check of machines
	2. Daily check of machines
	  a. Detection of defect on table
	  b. Leakage of oil.
		(Omitted)	(Omitted)	(Omitted)	1. Outer diameter
					2. Inner diameter
					3. Breadth
					4. Degree of parallel of two ends
						(Omitted)	(Omitted)	(Omitted)	(Omitted)	1. Periodic inspection of measuring instruments
										2. Periodic inspection of machines
										3. Periodic inspection of jigs
										4. Daily check of machines, tools and jigs
										  a. Wear of tools
										  b. Damage to jigs
										  c. Defect on table
										  d. Bending of work arbor
										  e. Bending of hob arbor
										To be confirmed at shops from daily check sheet
											1. Tooth profile error
											2. Lead error
											3. Single pitch error
											4. Pitch variation
											5. Runout

Tooth cutting	1. Periodic check of machines
	2. Daily check of tools jigs
	  a. Clearance of hob head and hob arbor
	  b. Bending of hob arbor
	  c. Clearance between metal and hob arbor
	  d. Backlash between master wheel and worm
					1. Tooth profile error
					2. Lead error
					3. Runout
					4. Displacement over a given number of teeth						

Shaving	1. Periodic check of machines
	2. Daily check of jigs and tools
	  a. Deviation of roller center
	  b. Deviation of table center
	  c. Clearance of cutter shaft
	  d. Damage to jigs
					1. Tooth profile error
					2. Lead error
					3. Displacement over a given number of teeth						

Heat treatment	(Omitted)				(Omitted)						
Grinding	1. Periodic check of machines. 2. Daily check of tools and jigs a. Detection of defect on table.				1. Inner diameter 2. Breadth 3. Degree of parallel of two ends						

Fig. 37-15 Quality controls for gear precision in Production Department and Inspection Department.

can be done in a pair of gears, it is preferable to use the gear assembly which simulates the actual state of machine usage. Loading for the test should preferably be programmed to simulate field loading conditions.

While accelerated testing has important advantages, the testing load should not be excessive, as it may cause welding of gear teeth surfaces. In consequence, a maximum limit for the program load needs to be established in the original test design.

Field Testing. The ultimate proof of reliability of the machines, including component parts, is through field test. Such field testing should be done under the most severe conditions imposed by actual use. Data should be prepared to correlate laboratory test results with field test results, since such correlations multiply the value of future laboratory testing. It is also useful to provide a prompt feedback to all departments concerned as accelerated testing (e.g., on loading or revolutions) is conducted. Through such prompt feedback, the data can be available in time for the production of the parts. The data can also be utilized to standardize methods and duration of testing, to set up the system of information feedback, and in preventing recurrence of failures.

Feedback of Usage Data   The data system diagrammed in Figure 37-6 is largely applicable to critical standard parts as well. Usage data are collected by machine makers from service reports; overhaul reports; operation, repair, and overhaul information from monitoring users. When needed, these are analyzed by computer and filed for future design reference.

Parts makers must set up their data systems so as to acquire needed data from the machine maker (who has natural access to much usage data). In addition, the parts maker should maintain active direct contact with machine users to collect pertinent data. These data serve multiple purposes: a data bank for subsequent designs, a source of information for improving reliability testing through correlation of laboratory test data with field usage data, a source of information for improving manufacturing and inspection technique.

Generally, the failure data do not by themselves show the causes of the failures. Discovery of these causes requires also that failed parts be sent back for analysis. In addition, it may be necessary to send appropriate engineers to the usage site to analyze the conditions of use. When the failed parts are badly worn or broken, their precision cannot be analyzed. In such cases the original factory records may provide historical data which are helpful in the analysis. This is especially true of the history of the heat treatment of the gears, and emphasizes the need for standardizing the filing and use of the historical data on production processes, inspection processes, etc.

Section **38**

Electronic Components

EDWIN S. SHECTER

Manager, Quality Assurance,
Government & Commercial Systems, RCA, Inc.

INTRODUCTION

The term "electronic components" covers a multitude of devices which are used in electronic circuits and subsystems. Some of these components are relatively simple, e.g., resistors, capacitors, and semiconductor devices. More elaborate are components such as large-scale integration (LSI) devices, cathode-ray tubes, and lasers.

These electronic components are made in huge numbers by an industry which underwent an explosive growth during the 1960s. (This growth trend is likely to continue into the remainder of the twentieth century.) A major stimulus to this growth has been an astonishing rate of product development. In one well-known example, the vacuum tube has been largely replaced by the transistor, which is being replaced by the integrated circuit, which in turn is being replaced by Medium Scale Integration (MSI) and Large Scale Integration (LSI), which make possible thousands of circuit elements on a tiny semiconductor chip. In like manner, printed circuit assemblies are being replaced by thick and thin film hybrid devices. Resistors have gone from carbon composition and wirewound to metal film, deposited carbon, and chip resistors. Capacitors have proliferated from the traditional ceramic, mica, and paper types into tantalum, film polycarbonate, film polystyrene, and polyester film.

These product developments have enormously influenced the problems of product quality. On the positive side they have improved ruggedness and reliability, the latter sometimes having been improved by several orders of magnitude. On the negative side these product developments have made severe demands on manufacturing processes by requiring new orders of precision in process design and in measurement. Because these demands have not been fully met, the process yields have suffered. Some processes actually operate with yields of about 5%; i.e., 95% of the product is nonconforming. (In contrast, the well-developed processes operate at yields of over 95%.) Naturally, these low yields are a major factor in the prices of the associated products, e.g., LSI devices. In such products major price reductions can be made as yields are improved. In high-yield products, the cost competition is not primarily in yields, but in the more conventional approaches to cost reduction.

The presence of these unsolved problems of yields and quality costs is properly a subject of intensive study in the industry. This Section of the Handbook, while designed to provide an overview of major quality problems and solutions in the industry, will likewise emphasize the approaches used in dealing with the problems of quality yields and costs.

PRODUCT DESIGN

Design of electronic components follows generally the broad principles of product design set out in Section 8. However, application of these principles to electronic components is heavily influenced by the fact that some usual problems are present to an unusual degree; i.e., technology is not fully understood and not fully predictable; process yields can be shockingly poor; reliability requirements can be so severe that testing alone cannot provide adequate assurance. To respond to these special problems, the industry has evolved its own special emphases in the approach to product design.

An illustration of technological problems is the thick film hybrid devices. In these devices, a combination of pastes or inks provides conductive or resistive paths which are screened onto a ceramic substrate. The balance of the circuit comprises integrated circuit, transistor, or diode chips which provide active signal controls, plus subminiature chip capacitors and (occasionally) subminiature coils. The completed device may replace an entire printed circuit board using so-called "discrete devices," which are larger, self-contained versions of the same circuit elements. Figure 38-1 shows a comparison of two functionally identical circuits.

In designing such a device, the circuit function is determined and the overall physical limitations are established. Then the designer must establish the detailed characteristics such as line width of pastes, spacing between paths, power dissipation, semiconductor chip mounting, type of package, location and method of interconnecting chips, stability requirements, longevity of operation, sealing technique, testing requirements, and interface with external circuitry, all the while conforming to established design practice. In establishing these and other characteristics[1] the designer should consider the environments the device will see in service as well as the manufacturing process limitations.

Specification Review   To a growing extent, electronic components are designed to meet special customer requirements of relatively low volume. These requirements are reviewed, in the normal course of events, by the application engineers and the design engineers, whose main job is to determine what design will best suit these customer specifications. The caliber of these reviews varies widely

[1] There are over 100 known characteristics to be defined.

among companies, and all too often the approach is one of good design creativity but without taking into account the factory yield problems created by stringent design requirements. In such cases the technical agreements reached are not reflected in the quoted price, with resulting losses or subsequent painful confrontations to change the specifications.

One method of avoiding these situations is to bring into the specification review those quality engineers who can provide quantified information on the factory yield

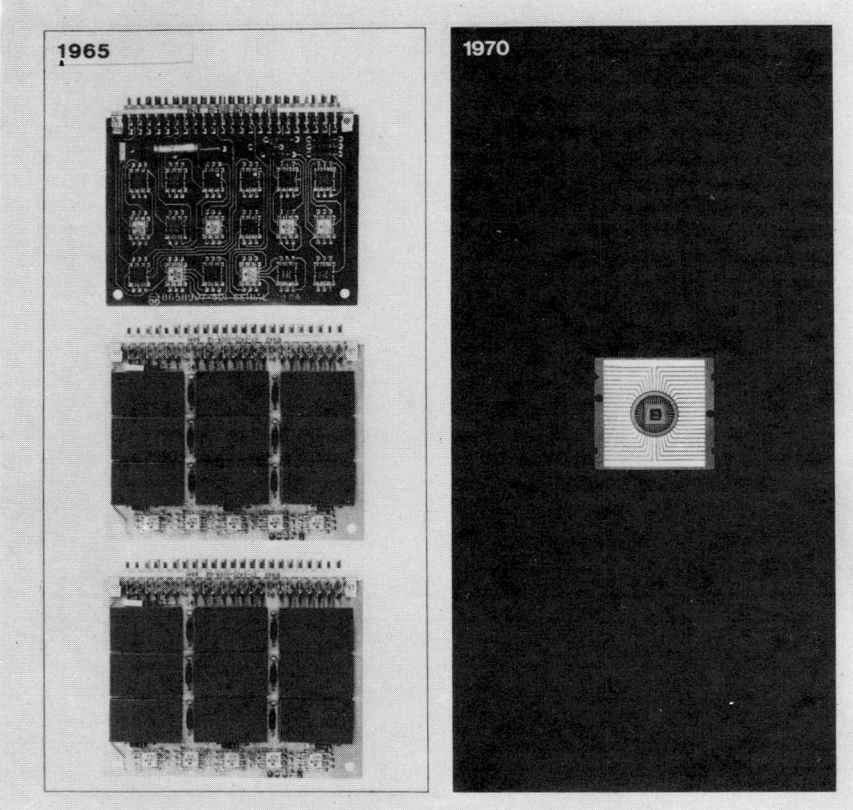

Fig. 38-1 Miniaturization in electronic parts.

problems posed by such special customer specifications; i.e., to what extent must the natural product distributions be truncated to meet the requirements? In like manner, these quality engineers are able to contribute data on the field performance to be expected, and on the extra testing costs which may need to be incurred.

Design Review The electronics industry follows closely the approach discussed in Section 8, under Design Review. These reviews are commonplace in circuit design but have not been fully exploited in electronic part design.

Design review teams put the main emphasis on functional performance, manufacturing capabilities and yields, test capabilities, material sources, handling practices, and personnel training.

It is widely recognized that specification and design reviews are of value in reducing the incidence of design-caused difficulties. However, it is also recognized that some degree of difficulty is virtually inevitable. The best that can be hoped for is that these will be kept to a minimum, and that catastrophic events will not develop.

Both design review and specification review should include provision for accumulating the knowledge gained and setting up standards and guides to be used by the designers in preparing their designs in the first place. The more that such design guides can be made available to the designer, the less is the risk that his design

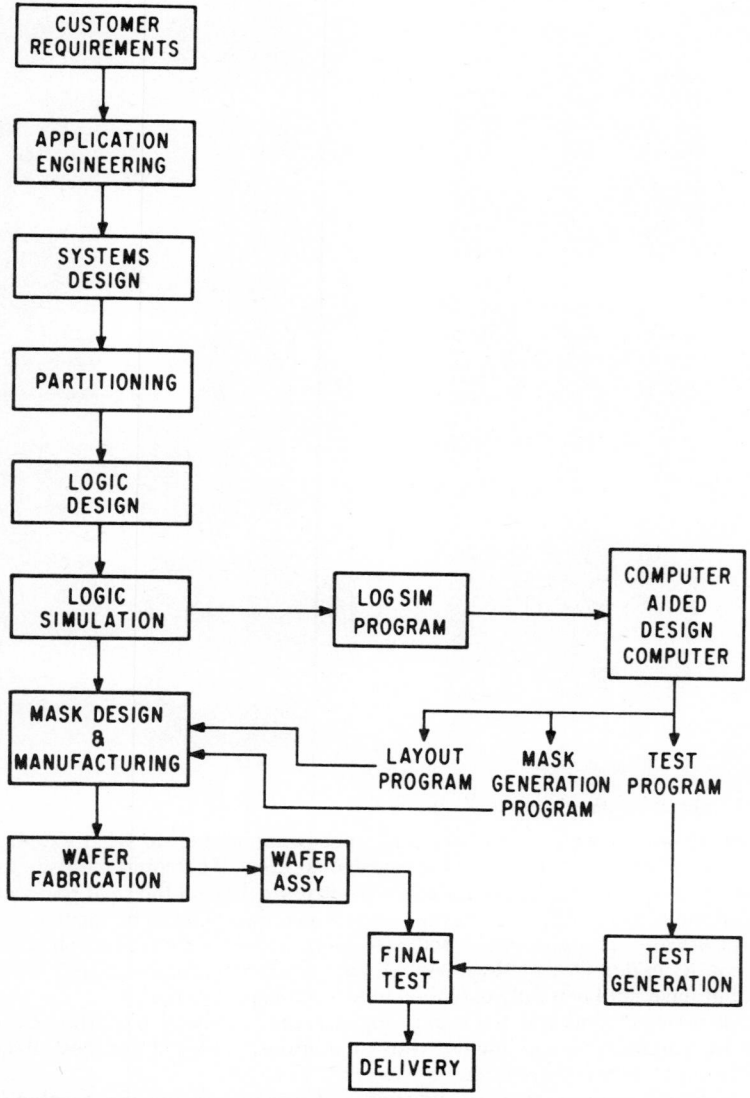

Fig. 38-2 Flow diagram, computer-aided design.

will fail to perform its intended functions, or will impose uneconomic yields on the factory.

For example, many processes use high-temperature furnaces to cure pastes, fasten chips, and seal lids to packages. Since these temperatures will damage some product qualities, the product design must consider the sequences of operations so that temperature sensitive features of the product are not exposed to the furnace operations.

In like manner, the design must consider the test and experience data on failure modes, physics of failure phenomena, process capability and test equipment limitations. (Completeness of yield and failure mode data varies widely among companies, and in some companies is very poor.) Data on field performance are of special importance both because actual usage is involved and because of disclosure of failure modes not found during in-house tests.

These test and experience data do not provide automatic answers; there is still much need for interpretation and for application to the case at hand. However, there are also many instances of underutilization of available data.

Computer-aided Design Computers are increasingly being used in design of complex electronic parts such as monolithic and hybrid integrated circuits. These computer-aided designs permit lower design cost and better delivery schedules.

In using this approach (Figure 38-2), the application engineer designs the functional system which utilizes standard cell functions and logic. The "catalog" of standard logic cells and design rules has previously been incorporated into the computer. The computer processes a logic simulation program and partitioning of circuitry information. The computer also generates:

Layouts for the circuitry

Computer input to a mask generation program (which develops the patterns to be used for subsequent processing of the semiconductor wafer)

A computerized test program (see Automated Tests and Data Processing, below).

The role of the quality engineer in this process is not yet fully defined. To play a useful role it is obviously desirable that he have knowledge of computer programming and that he be able to apply information collected from failure analyses to improve computer programs for yield maximization. Although the data gathering and feedback is important in this design cycle, it is not clear whether this can best be performed by the design or quality engineers. Traditionally, the designer will devote efforts to new creations, while the quality engineer may devote his time to design optimization.

QUALITY PLANNING

Quality planning plays an essential role in the electronics parts industry, and the main measure of success is the attained level of process yields. The factors principally affecting these yields are the process, facilities and equipment, materials, and personnel.

Process Planning This follows conventional practice in several respects (see Section 6, under Planning for Control). A *flow chart* is prepared (Section 6, Figure 6-5) showing the operations and the control stations. For each operation, a *process specification* must be prepared, defining in detail the exact operations to be performed, and their exact sequence. Ambiguity cannot be tolerated, since each vague provision becomes one more process variable. Even the environmental disturbances created by the operators (perspiration, hair spray, hand cream, cosmetics, etc.) must be controlled or neutralized by specification. The process specification must be given the stature of an engineering specification so it cannot be changed or temporarily waived without formal procedure and documentation.

The process planning also identifies the *control stations*. These are created to inspect and test the product or process characteristics and so to produce data to be used (1) for making decisions on the product; i.e., does the product conform or not; and (2) for making decisions on the process; i.e., should the process run or stop.

For each control station, complete *criteria* must be spelled out: how often to look, what to look for, what standards to use, how many to examine, how many defects to tolerate, what records to keep. (Some of the techniques and their use are described later in this Section.)

It has been the experience in the industry that for some processes it cannot be assumed that multiple machines (or multiple heads of machines) are alike. Hence, for facilities such as vacuum deposition chambers or certain types of furnaces, it may be necessary to tailor-make separate control criteria for each separate facility.

Facilities and Equipment Mass production and high precision of electronic components require precise, reliable processes to produce quality products at good yields. Precision (or repeatability) is quantified by process capability studies (see Section 9, under Process Capability). In addition, the processes must be able to maintain their repeatability over a long time span with little or no correction required. For example, in single integrated circuits it is common to have as many as 80 bonds, any one of which can cause a defective device. Such bonding processes must be carefully engineered to eliminate sources of variability. (Alternatively, it may be necessary to revise product designs, as in this instance, to use beam leads or flip chip methods for device interconnection.) In addition, control procedures must be provided for continuing appraisal of the equipment.

In many operations, environmental facilities are also critical. Some products require clean benches or a "clean room." The cleanliness requirement is normally met by utilizing a laminar flow of air in either the horizontal or vertical direction to prevent submicroscopic particulate matter from being deposited on the product or on the materials used in processing the product. Clean room technology is defined in Federal Standard 209.[2] Provision must be made for deionized or distilled water or filtered chemicals during the process cycle. When work is performed, under microscopes, benches may have to be shock mounted to minimize vibration which will increase operator fatigue. Humidity is a critical factor in the manufacture of metal oxide semi-conductor (MOS) devices.

A further problem is the susceptibility of MOS and bipolar semiconductor devices to electrostatic influence. In consequence, the presence of "static generating" parts such as plastics cannot be tolerated. Certain liquids create static as they flow through orifices. Operators must wear grounding straps. Equipment and bench tops must be grounded. Carrying trays and floors must also be non-static-generating.

The foregoing are some of the more usual quality problems in facilities and equipment. There are, of course, other factors, but they are more specialized by industry or process. However, good lighting and adequate temperature controls are always helpful.

Materials Planning Materials planning is unusually critical in the electronic components industry. In most processes, the materials are critical and in some they are absolutely decisive. Hence, while the general approach to Vendor Relations (see Section 10) has much application to electronic components, there are also some aspects of material planning which demand special consideration:

1. *Use Testing.* For some critical materials, incoming inspections and laboratory

---

[2] Federal Standard 209, Clean Room and Work Station Requirements — Controlled Equipment.

tests are unable to prove fitness for use, and it is necessary to conduct usage tests to prove the adequacy of the materials as well as to qualify the vendors.

Sintered powder is an example of such materials. Some mechanical parts, e.g., screens for battery plates or cores for capacitors, require an actual use test for proper evaluation. Cathode spray material for electron tubes is another example. Each mix must be tried out, and the resulting cathodes must be made up into tubes, and evaluated after 500 or 1,000 hours of life test. The new hybrid technology requires similar evaluation. Inks or pastes used to print resistors on ceramic substrates must be evaluated through accelerated thermal cycling to assure minimum resistance drift with time, and uniform resistivity with good adhesion.

2. *Handling and Storage.* Some materials used in the industry are sensitive to the environment, e.g., light, heat, humidity. Some materials must be stored in a dry nitrogen chamber to prevent degradation. On a less exotic scale, the containers used for transportation, storage, and transfer (into the process) must be scrupulously free from contamination. Materials planning must anticipate these special problems of handling and storage.

3. *Materials Usage.* Some of the processes are sensitive to the effects of material replenishment. For example, adding chemicals to restore plating solution concentration can affect some yields or product characteristics. In such cases, the planning must specify the technique to be used.

4. *Auxiliary Materials.* In this industry there is an uncommon extent of use of materials which do not enter the product but which do have significant effect on process performance and product quality. These materials should be brought squarely into the quality planning and control procedures. They should not be regarded as "supplies" if the routine for regulating "supplies" falls outside the rigorous quality control approach.

Personnel   The problems of employee selection, training, and motivation are mostly conventional (see Sections 17 and 18). The special problem of miniaturization requires extensive use of microscopes. Dextrous personnel and special training are needed to use these without undue fatigue. Information from reputable manufacturers can help here. Another special condition is extreme cleanliness, which has an impact on the personnel because of the need for special clothing and for controlled personal habits, e.g., cosmetics.

INCOMING INSPECTION

The management of incoming inspection is largely conventional. The usual approach is discussed in other Sections of this Handbook as follows:

Organization for incoming inspection, in Section 12, Inspection and Test
Use of incoming inspection vs. other forms of vendor control, in Section 10, Vendor Relations
Choice of sampling plans and associated criteria, in Sections 22 through 25

The electronic components industry has become increasingly based on chemical processes rather than on the earlier mechanical and electronic processes. Very little electronic evaluation is performed in incoming inspection except for complex hybrid devices which utilize semiconductor or capacitor chips.

Mechanical parts are commonly sampled, and MIL-STD-105 is often the sampling plan used. Double sampling is usually the most economical. AQLs range mostly from 0.10% for critical to 4.0% for incidental or minor items. Further achievement of economy can be realized by utilizing an "exploratory sampling plan."[3] There is

---

[3] A sampling table using zero acceptance number for an equivalent LTPD.

also a trend in the industry toward use of LTPD or LQ as the governing criteria. In addition, skip-lot sampling per MIL-HBK-106 is being put to use. Variables sampling using MIL-STD-414 has made little headway as yet, though the growth of computer applications may change this.[4]

Use of prior knowledge of process capability plus preserving the order of manufacture has wide potential application. (See generally Section 11, under Product and Process Relationship.) However, utilizing this concept requires special arrangements with vendors so they will provide treaceability of lots. For example, a plating lot is commonly smaller than a punch press lot because of equipment limitations. Only if arrangements are made with the vendor to identify the sublots can advantage be taken of the inherent uniformity within lots and sublots for control and sampling purposes.

A further opportunity for good collaboration lies in using vendor test results in lieu of retesting. This approach is described in Section 10, under Audit of Decisions.

As noted under Materials Planning, above, some materials require actual usage tests to establish fitness for use. For some critical materials, this usage testing must continue on and on, lot after lot. Such an arrangement requires close collaboration between vendor and manufacturer to ensure good product traceability. For example, inks for ceramic substrates are shipped in batches with lot numbers, and it is necessary only to take a small representative sample and to fabricate several devices in order to evaluate the overall performance level of that lot of ink. Many ink manufacturers include data and test chips (of that particular batch of ink) with each ink shipment. It is sufficient in such cases to utilize, as an incoming inspection procedure, a simple control chart for $\bar{X}$ and R.

Data feedback to vendors is conventional, use being made of data sheets which accumulate vendor data and permit identification of repeat defects. For individual lots, a more complete feedback can be made via variables data such as Lot Plot (see Section 25).

Vendor rating follows conventional practice (see Section 10).

A number of indexes are available to judge the effectiveness of Incoming Inspection:

1. The number of lots processed per inspector
2. The cost of the Incoming Inspection function per $1,000 of procured material
3. The number of lots backlogged
4. The average time required to process a lot
5. The percentage of lots creating floor problems
6. The percentage of lots accepted (this is also a measure of engineering specifications and purchasing competence)
7. Average time required for close out of corrective action requests to vendors

Because performance (as judged by these measures) varies widely within the industry, the usual standard of comparison is past history.

MANUFACTURING PROCESSES

The chemical and metallurgical processes which abound in the electronic components industry determine the electrical performance of the parts. Together with the job of making electrical connections (e.g., soldering, welding, brazing, bonding), these processes comprise about 90% of all operations involved in manufacture of electronic parts.

Chemical and Metallurgical Processes A vital need here is to establish a sensitive, sure signal from measure of product characteristic back to the controlling process

---

[4] See generally Section 20.

variable. Failure to create this signal is a source of much difficulty in the industry. An example is seen in the widespread problem of keeping chemical solutions replenished to proper levels. To illustrate, plating operations involve characteristics such as solution concentration, pH, temperature, time cycle, current, and impurities. Some characteristics are checked regularly, and the data may be recorded. Data listings are used as action devices and are then filed. More comprehensive checks are also made periodically, though less frequently. When these disclose deficiencies, adjustments are made. Simple graphs or control charts (rather than data listings) can show trends or cyclical results, or operation off nominal value. Further study may show that excessive adjustments must be avoided to keep from "shocking" the solution, or that small but more frequent adjustments improve product uniformity.

The foregoing technique involves simple graphs and simple analysis, yet achieves superior plating results. It has application not only in plating operations but in all problems of depletion of chemicals. The resulting "manual control" may seem to be less scientific than computerized control, but in the author's experience, manual methods are adequate in most instances, and are less expensive. (However, precautions must be taken to avoid overcompensation.) In addition, with experience, it becomes possible to reduce frequency of analysis and thereby the cost of control.

A related problem arises in process setup. A technique with widespread application is "Narrow Limit Gaging," which is described in Section 23. For example, in spraying cathodes for electron tubes, the natural tendency is to spray to the minimum (underspray is easily corrected, but excess spray is not). However, use of narrow limit gaging enables the operators to "center" the level of spray with confidence.

Control of Connections   The industry makes a fantastic number of interconnections among parts, and each of these is a potential source of circuit failure. Two main categories of connections are made: (1) those in which material is added to make the connection (soldering or brazing) and (2) those in which no material is added (welding and bonding, ultrasonic, and others).

Soldering and Brazing   A number of variables must be well controlled:

1. The materials being joined and those used to do the joining. While materials are subject to their own controls, a change in material batch or lot may introduce changes in results. Hence the soldering and brazing controls should provide for observation of the effect of changing to new material batches.

2. The fluxes used, which require controls similar to those applied to materials.

3. The surface treatment procedure, which is designed to cleanse parts of contaminants. Cleanliness of parts is a principal source of variation, because of the numerous sources of contamination: environment, body oils, hand or hair creams, paper and paper products, containers.

4. The soldering process, which sometimes includes prefluxing and preheating.

In establishing controls it must be kept in mind that soldered components may later undergo additional soldering upon insertion into the external circuit. Generally these later insertions take place at temperatures of 480 to 510° F. However, uncontrolled hand soldering methods may exceed the upper temperature limits. Hence the earlier part soldering should use solder of the highest practicable melting point to guard against damage from the later insertion soldering.

Control over solder temperature, exposure time, and part steadiness is essential. Because the immediate controls on the completed joints are based on visual appearance, the controls over these underlying variables should be such that well-controlled joints also present a uniform appearance.

Visual appearance of good solder joints has been well defined, the major criteria being a smooth, even flow with low dihedral angles. Many companies have published internal standards on quality of soldered joints.

5. Removal of residual flux is essential to assure that the joint will not degrade. Some fluxes contain etchants which remain active and hence must be removed promptly and completely. Since the completeness of removal is difficult to judge by visual inspection, the process must have an ample safety margin.

6. The brazing process uses no flux but otherwise presents problems similar to the soldering process. The brazing environment is usually nonoxidizing, but purity of the gas used and the flow rate are critical variables.

Welding and Bonding   These connection processes create an intermetallic joint but without adding metals (as done by soldering and brazing). Figure 38-3 shows various bonding methods in use. (See also Section 41, Figure 41-4, and associated discussion.)

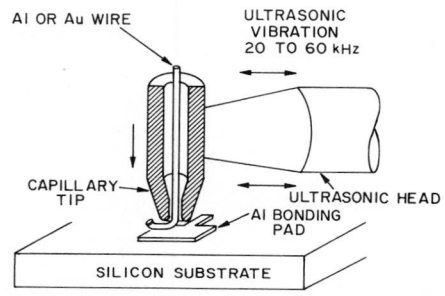

Fig. 38-3a   Bonding methods for electronic components—ultrasonic bonding.

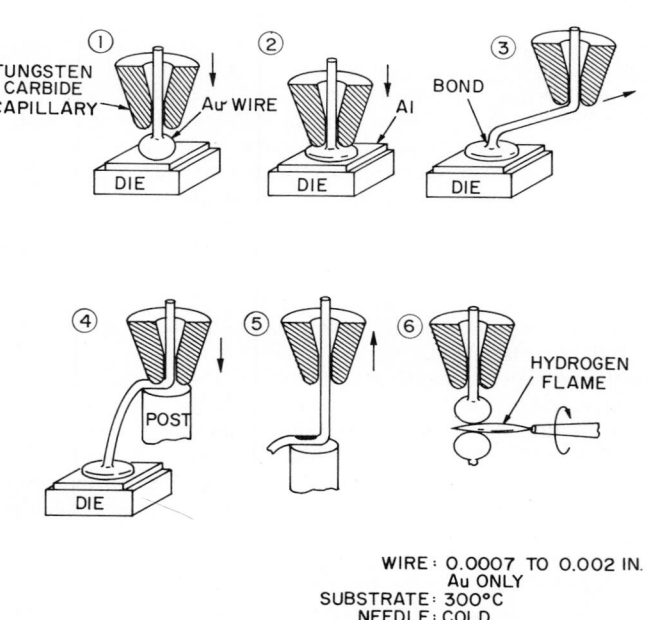

WIRE: 0.0007 TO 0.002 IN.
Au ONLY
SUBSTRATE: 300°C
NEEDLE: COLD
GAS: N_2 AT 2CFH
WEIGHT: 50 GRAMS

Fig. 38-3b   Bonding methods for electronic components—ball bonding.

Welding and bonding include some variables common to soldering and brazing, i.e., materials being joined, and cleanliness of these materials, the latter again being critical. In addition, there are some new sources of variation:

1. The electrode material and shape. These are chosen (as is the welding or bonding equipment) so that the type of weld pulse and follow-through cycle remain relatively constant. For some products this is difficult, as when the electrode material contaminates the product. It may be necessary to plate or clad the electrode to solve this problem. An alternative solution is to use, as electrode material, the same material as the metal being joined. This risks fusing the electrode to the metal being joined, and requires cooling the electrode or using special electrode shapes.

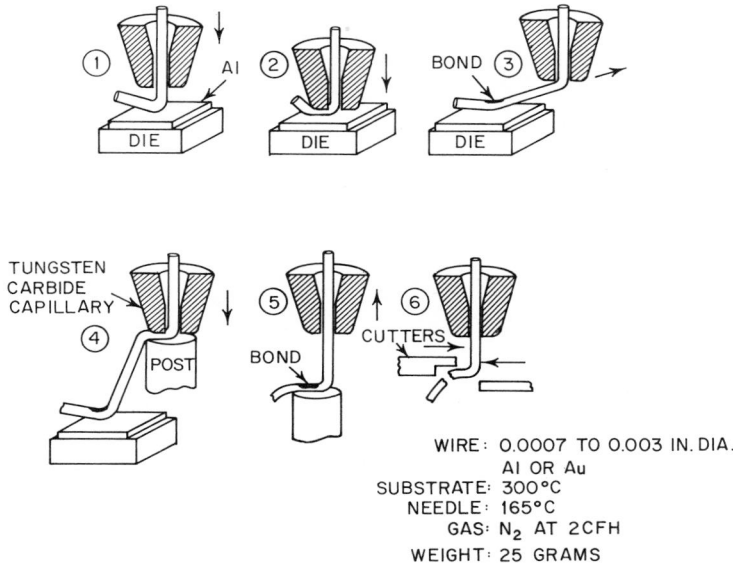

WIRE: 0.0007 TO 0.003 IN. DIA.
AI OR Au
SUBSTRATE: 300°C
NEEDLE: 165°C
GAS: N₂ AT 2CFH
WEIGHT: 25 GRAMS

Fig. 38-3c Bonding methods for electronic components—stitch bonding.

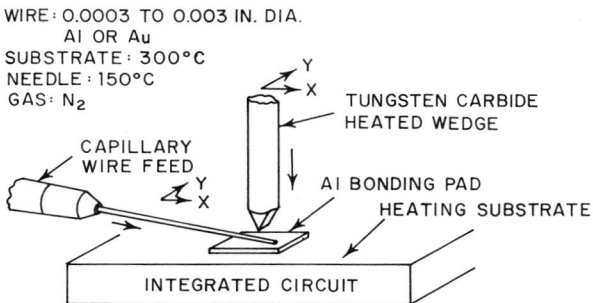

WIRE: 0.0003 TO 0.003 IN. DIA.
AI OR Au
SUBSTRATE: 300°C
NEEDLE: 150°C
GAS: N₂

Fig. 38-3d Bonding methods for electronic components—wedge bonding.

2. The weld schedule, which consists mainly of defining values for the parameters of electrode pressure and watt-seconds of energy. A useful device for preparing this schedule is the isostrength chart (Figure 38-4).

To prepare the isostrength chart, the electrode material, shape, and other fixed parameters are selected and kept constant. A sample of five welds (bonds) is made up using values of electrode force and energy at the low end of the expected range for these parameters. These welds are pull tested, and the failure strengths and modes are recorded. A second sample of five welds is made at the same low electrode pressure, but at a higher value of energy. These welds are likewise pull

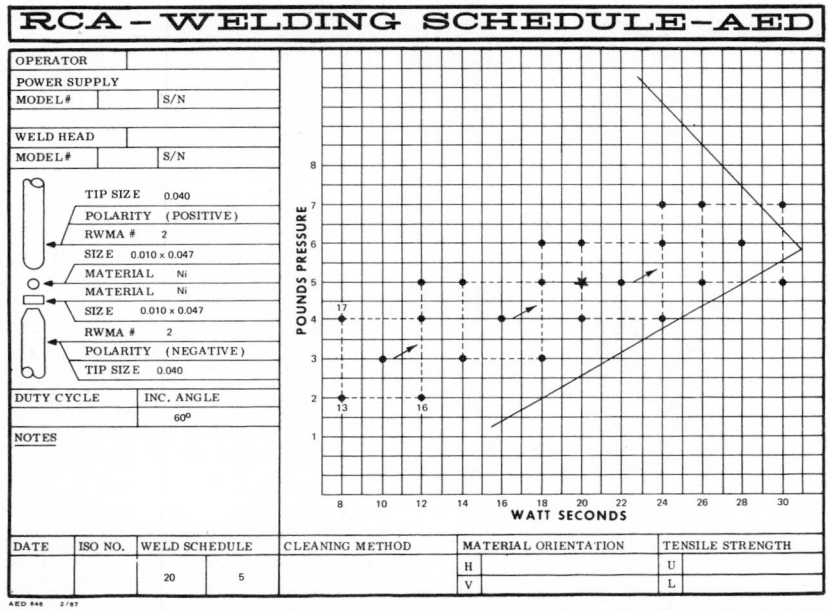

Fig. 38-4 Isostrength diagram. (From Aroian, Leo A., and James R. Gates, Welded Electronic Circuits and the Use of Response Surfaces, *Transactions, 8th Annual Western Regional Quality Control Conference,* ASQC, March 16–17, 1961.)

tested. This process is repeated for a number of levels of electrode pressure and of energy. In preparing Figure 38-4, a total of 23 sets of samples of 5 welds were tested, involving various combinations of 6 levels of electrode pressure and 12 levels of energy.

The resulting 23 averages are plotted in matrix form (Figure 38-4). The central point of the "response surface" becomes evident.[5] This is then verified by making a sample of 50 welds at the indicated pressure and energy. (The resulting average and standard deviation become the basis for future control by conventional $\overline{X}$, R control charts.) In addition, it is desirable to prepare a microsection to ascertain that a nugget or fused region has actually been created by the weld. This sectioning and etching are essential in welding for heavy-duty current capacity, e.g., batteries.

[5] For detailed discussion, see Section 27A, Evolutionary Operation, and Section 28, Response Surface Methodology.

TESTING AND INSPECTION

The testing and inspection problems posed by huge numbers of electronic components, each with multiple quality characteristics, have precluded solution by traditional methods of test, inspection, and data handling. The industry has, in consequence, made wide use of new technological and managerial tools, some specially invented to meet the special needs of the industry.

Reliability Testing The great proliferation of long-life products has enormously increased the need for reliability testing. The extent of the testing needed precludes use of manual methods, so that automated testing and data logging, aided by computer control, becomes a necessity. It is not unusual to spend over $100,000 for equipment to be used to test products which are to sell in the range of $0.50 to $50 per unit. Environmental testing is an important complicating factor, and greatly increases testing costs.

The economics of testing require use of life test racks, but this is complicated by the proliferation of product types which demand, at the least, a variety of sockets, and at the worst, an extensive investment in racks which are seldom used. In some cases, it is feasible to make a few standard types with every production lot, to be used as test samples.

Another approach to reducing the cost of life testing is to increase the effective lot size by (1) accumulation over a longer time span, or (2) combining similar types which undergo common processing. In the case of microelectronic devices, MIL-M-38510 and MIL-STD-833 set out test methods and tables of sample sizes to be used for life testing and for various categories of environmental tests.

Accelerated testing is a technique of great value for reducing sample sizes and for shortening the calendar time needed to determine the Mean Time Between Failures (MTBF). However, the test designer must be alert to avoid failures in modes which will not occur under rated conditions. It is helpful in such designs to establish the relationship between accelerated and nonaccelerated tests on the same Weibull[6] plot.

Life Testing One of the more commonly used life test models is the Weibull distribution, although the exponential distribution is widely assumed. In practice, the sampling procedures used to accept product are defined in the applicable product test specification or the sampling procedures in MIL-STD-690 or 781.[7] The trend during the 1960s was to get away from process acceptance and convert to individual lot acceptance. A typical sampling plan is that contained in MIL-M-38510. This procedure is likely to be reversed in the future for those types of electronic components which are highly complex in construction and of small volume but which are made by the same basic processes. This reversal will affect only how many types of items are sampled, but not the sampling plans. (Here again, the many parameters measured make it practical to use computers for data tabulation and analysis. Computer calculation of MTBF and failure rates has become routine.)

There has been a trend toward more severe life test requirements, both in commercial applications and in government contracts, and this trend is likely to continue. Not only does this trend require larger sample sizes; it creates greater problems for the manufacturer in case of life test failures. In addition to the lot rejected, the product in the production line (and often in the distribution pipeline) also becomes suspect. If the defect is basic to the process, there may be no recovery technique, so that losses are severe. This problem alone is a spur to rigorous con-

---

[6] See Section 22 under The Weibull Probability Distribution, *et seq.*
[7] The Naval Publications and Forms Center, Philadelphia, Pa. 19120.

trol of processes and to life testing methods which give the earliest possible signals. As a corollary, the engineering of the processes requires top-caliber people.

Environmental Tests Environmental failures can be discovered earlier than life test failures and are generally easier to remedy. However, environmental failures are serious enough to require close control and early feedback on performance. The usual approach is to use approximation tests which give early warnings of major problems, even on a daily basis. Examples of such tests are thermal cycling, shock, and vibration. Leakage testing on semiconductor devices is usually done on 100% of the product, followed by a sampling audit, using 0.65 or 1.0% AQL.

Other Tests; Measurement Technology There is a wide assortment of "other tests," some of which involve extreme precision:

1. Film thicknesses of the order of several to several hundred angstroms (1 angstrom $= 10^{-8}$ centimeter) are controlled with the aid of the spectrophotometer.

2. Surface and window areas in integrated circuit manufacture are examined with the aid of the scanning electron microscope, which permits magnifications of 400,000 times.

3. Leakages on the order of 10^{-8} cubic centimeter per second are measured with the helium mass spectrometer.

4. Chemical analyses are made (some down to trace amounts) in numbers requiring the use of automated methods.

5. Radiography is used to examine internal structures so as to identify undesired metal particles, distortions in diode springs and bond wires, or other unwanted conditions.

6. Still other measurement techniques include high-precision optics and lasers, coordinate measuring machines, flame analysis, x-ray television, eddy current, ultrasonic testing, etc.

The electronic parts industry has been a leader both in creating and in adopting new measurement technology[8] and new levels of precision. These developments, for which no end is in sight, have required substantial outlays for new equipment. However, the equipment has in turn been essential to control of quality as well as to keeping down the costs of test, which would be prohibitive under former technology. As an important by-product, new training programs have been required, and some new certifications of test technicians have been created. In addition, there has been a resurgence of the importance of the measurement function in the Quality Control organization charts.

Final Product Acceptance Beyond the testing discussed above, electronic components are subjected to more conventional inspections and tests for the remaining quality characteristics. The industry makes wide use of seriousness classification of defects, and these classes[9] are decisive in establishing the acceptance sampling criteria to be used. (Most often, the process is such that the major parameters must be 100% inspected or tested prior to the sampling acceptance checks.)

Acceptance sampling plans used by the industry are mainly designed on the "Lot Tolerance Percent Defective" (LTPD) concept rather than on the "Acceptable Quality Level" (AQL) concept.[10] The LTPD schemes are based on a common criterion of a probability of 10% of accepting lots of tolerance percent defective. Tables in effect use LTPD values in the range of 4 to 15%, depending on the seriousness

---

[8] See generally Section 13.

[9] See generally Section 12, under Seriousness Classification.

[10] There are historical reasons for the creation of these different concepts. In terms of ease of getting the product accepted, the AQL schemes favor the producer, and the LTPD schemes favor the buyer. See generally Section 24.

classification. AQL values range to 0.25% (for electron tubes and semiconductors) and have been decreasing over the years. Sampling acceptance criteria are widely spelled out in military specifications,[11] and the commercial requirements are similar in format.

Lots usually consist of one week's production, but low-volume special-purpose devices may be accumulated over longer time periods. For environmental tests, lots of different devices may be combined for sampling purposes.

It is anticipated that the trend to tighter sampling criteria will continue, and likely will reduce values of LTPD to a range of 1.0 to 1.5%, and even tighter. For the short run this will conflict with the trend to put more functions on a semiconductor chip (and thereby to create more opportunity for trouble). However, for the long run the user's requirements will prevail, with solutions provided by ingenuity, under the spur of competition.

While the basic purpose of acceptance sampling is to make decisions on the product, the data are a valuable feedback for identifying problem areas. The industry makes wide use of these feedback opportunities to investigate causes and to take remedial action.

Acceptance by Certification   An interesting formal method for "certification acceptance" of electronic parts is in use in Europe. The basic concept is similar to that long used in the metals industry[12] and embodies the following considerations:

1. Much of the supply of electronic components has its origin in large production batches which are then subdivided into small shipments for sale to original equipment manufacturers and to the distribution chain.

2. It is hopelessly uneconomic for purchasers to conduct adequate test programs on these small shipments. The way to do the testing is on the large production batch.

3. The original production batch test data can serve all the buyers of the small shipments derived from the original batch, provided that the parts manufacturer is qualified to design and carry out the necessary quality control and test activities.

4. In consequence, what the buyer of the small shipment needs is: (a) proof that the parts manufacturer is qualified to conduct valid test programs. (b) a copy of the test certificate issued by this qualified manufacturer with respect to the original production batch from which the small shipment is drawn.

To meet these needs of the buyers, the French National Federation of Electronic Industries established a scheme in which qualification of manufacturers is done under "CCTU" specifications established by a committee of the Federation, Comité de Coordinations des Telecommunications. A central laboratory acting for numerous customers audits the test operations.[13]

In Great Britain a similar scheme has been set up under the British Standards Institution (BSI), the provisions being spelled out in a published standard (BS 9000). Qualification of parts manufacturers, "stockists," and test laboratories is done by BSI under established criteria. Test specifications are likewise covered by

---

[11] For example, in MIL-R-39D (fixed wirewound resistors); also in MIL-C-39003 (tantalum capacitors).

[12] In the metals industry each original melt of metal is given a lot number ("heat number") and is tested for metallurgical and chemical properties. The test certificate then follows the product no matter how often the lot is subdivided. These test certificates are widely accepted as valid.

[13] Clavier, M., A Centralized System of Acceptance Control of Electronic Parts on a National Scale (in French), *Bulletin de l'AFCIQ,* October 1960, pp. 63–78. See also Eldin, M. J., Résultats du "Controle Centralisé" de Qualité dans le Domaine de l'Évaluation de la Fiabilité, *Bulletin de l'AFCIQ,* December 1966, pp. 35–39.

established criteria.   An independent audit is provided by the Electrical Quality Assurance Directorate of the Ministry of Technology.[14]

Beyond the national schemes exemplified above, there has been much urge to internationalize the concept of acceptance by certification.   As of the early 1970s, the 13 Western European country members of Comité Europeen de Coordination des Normes Electro-techniques (CENEL) had reached an advanced state of agreement to this end.

The foregoing concepts of certification acceptance are basically sound and have wide application in many industries.[15]

Automated Tests and Data Processing   Automated test equipment, now the dominant method of test, offers many advantages over the manual methods prevailing in the 1960s.   Many more units can be tested, and many more parameters can be evaluated.   On a complex LSI device the computer can test literally hundreds of characteristics in a matter of seconds.   Less complex product can be tested in fractions of a second.   The limiting factor in speed of test is often the setup time of placing the device to be tested in the testing environment.

These same automated test methods can generate such large amounts of test data that they can overwhelm the organization beyond its capacity to digest and use the information.   For this reason, it is necessary to identify, at the outset, the information really needed for evaluation and corrective action.   The data processing should then be set up to meet these needs, and not to process added data which do not contribute to these needs (see Section 20).

Both attribute and variables data require processing.   The former are used to identify the prevailing defect types, to determine yields, and to classify parts into categories for a variety of purposes, e.g., special rework.

Variables data can be processed into frequency distributions for analysis (central tendency, dispersion, etc.).   Control charts can be plotted by the computer, which can store the parameter values.   The computer can also perform statistical analyses of various sorts, e.g., correlation coefficient, regression lines, confidence limits.[16]

The basic use of test data is, of course, the validation of the product.   However, in many cases in this industry, it is not enough to deliver the product; the test data must also be delivered.   This practice has great value for the smaller user of complex devices.   He is unable to make the tests himself—the cost of the equipment is prohibitive.   Hence he makes use of the test data to aid him in acceptance of the delivered product and in subsequent use.   (For elaboration, see Acceptance by Certification, above.)

QUALITY ANALYSIS AND REPORTING

The industry makes wide use of quality analysis and reporting.   Most of this work can be grouped under several well-recognized specialties.

Failure Analysis   Many of the conventional tools for failure analysis (e.g., Pareto analysis, stream to stream analysis) as discussed in Section 16 are widely applicable to electronic components.   However, the growing complexity of the manufacturing processes has also complicated the *technology* of failure analysis.   As a result, failure analysis may require the services of atomic physicists, chemical engineers, and process specialists[17] as well as the use of advanced analytical equipment.

[14] An interesting feature of BS 9000 is the "Certified Test Record," which is an updated summary of test results for the last 6 months and for the last 3 years.   The manufacturer is required to supply a copy to any user on request.

[15] See also Section 10, under Audit of Decisions.

[16] See generally, Section 20.

[17] The professional disciplines involved can be implied from the names of some of the defect

For example, a problem of open circuits had developed in components made by a process which employed sequential photographic and etching operations to prepare windows for metallizing. Examination with the scanning electron microscope identified a sharp step which had developed during an etching process, causing the metal to fracture, thereby causing open metallization (see Figure 38-5). Based on this disclosure, the etching method was changed to create a shallower slope in the etched window. Thereafter, the scanning electron microscope became a regular instrument for control of processing.

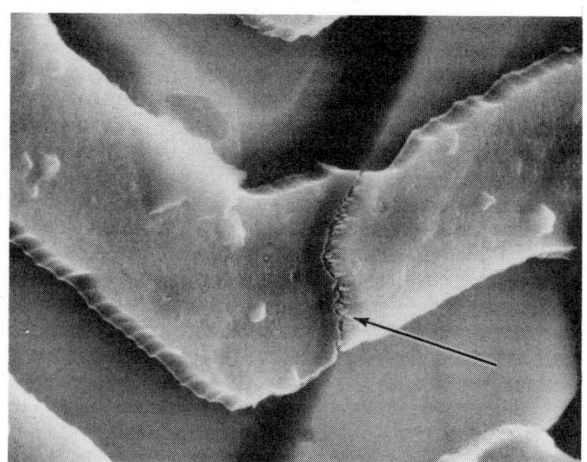

Fig. 38-5 Scanning electron microscope photograph of MOS device.

Aside from such electronic-oriented failure, the industry faces some other special failure problems. An example is the sealing of the components by a brazing or fusing operation on glass. Brazing particles may break off from the main brazed body and lodge in places where they cause short circuits or noise. Fused glass may carry strains which are a source of future failures. Special materials are used in glass-to-metal seals to get around the differentials in thermal expansion which would otherwise cause cracks during thermal cycling.

Beyond such special problems the industry has the usual quota of the more conventional failure sources such as poor soldering or welding and improper cleanliness. These are detectable by more prosaic methods and are analyzed and remedied through general use technology.

Customer and Field Liaison   The electronic components industry makes wide use of information from customers. Some of this information is sought out through field visits, usually by applications engineers. Other information is initiated by the customer in the form of returns, complaints, letters, etc. The general approach to dealing with all this feedback is set out in Section 15.

Customer returns are an important form of feedback. The returns for quality reasons should be carefully segregated from other returns. These quality returns can be summarized in the form of units returned vs. units shipped. However, there

---

symptoms and causes: oxide-metal interactions, recrystallization, eutectic formations, transverse and lateral ion migration, precipitation, etc.

is a time lag between date of manufacture and date of return. By estimating the average time lag (at say 1 month) and by using a 3-month running average, a figure of merit can be arrived at as follows:

$$\% \text{ returns (April)} = \frac{\text{total returned in February, March, and April}}{\text{total shipped in January, February, and March}}$$

It is also useful to analyze returns by defect type, customer, and product line to help identify clues to causes of exceptionally high or exceptionally low returns. These analyses are made easier when the data are arrayed in matrix form to establish whether defects are unique to certain types of product or certain customers.

Retesting of returns also provides clues to causes. Customer return of product which is good on retest may point to differences in test method, incomplete specifications, etc.

Field reports should be summarized to enter the upper management reports on quality. See Section 21, under Executive Reports on Quality, for the approach used.

Quality Cost Analysis The general approach to quality cost analysis is described in Section 5 of this Handbook, and is fully applicable to electronic components. However, the severe yield problem and the equally severe price competition make it most important that companies in the industry conduct quality cost analyses as a step preparatory to cost reduction.

Type of product	Total quality costs	% of total		
		Prevention	Appraisal	Failure*
Low cost:				
High yield	5–15	0–10	20–70	20–50
Medium yield. .	10–20	0–10	20–70	30–60
Low yield	12–25	0–25	20–80	30–70
High cost:				
High yield	5–15	5–25	20–75	10–40
Medium yield. .	10–30	5–30	20–75	30–60
Low yield	10–60	5–30	20–80	40–80

* A combination of internal failure costs and external failure costs.

Fig. 38-6 Typical quality costs as a percent of sales.

The quality cost figures in the industry reach some stunning levels, as high as 60% of sales. (This is ten to twenty times the company's profit.) Surprisingly, some companies are not aware of the size of these costs. Others are aware of the size, but have not developed effective methods of reducing these costs. Companies in both categories are often drugged by their own standard cost system, which builds in reject allowances and then sounds the alarm signals only when these allowances are exceeded.

Figure 38-6 shows typical quality costs as a percent of sales for the industry, broken down by the usual categories of Prevention, Appraisal, and Failure.

Starting with the quality cost analysis, the company should, by use of the Pareto principle, identify vital few kinds of defects which contribute to the high quality costs. These then become the subjects for quality improvement projects.

Quality Improvement The wide prevalence of poor yields makes it mandatory that projects for improving yields be identified and pursued aggressively. An example is seen in manufacture of one type of battery. For reasons peculiar to this type, variables data were plotted weekly on two of the tests conducted, i.e., capacity at high discharge rates and capacity at low discharge rates. Figure 38-7 shows these data.

The accepted product was originally of marginal quality on both tests. (There were defects as well, but the chart shows only the accepted product.) Gradually the high discharge rate capacity was improved, but the low discharge rate capacity remained marginal. (The low discharge rate performance depends mainly on plate volume, whereas the high discharge rate performance depends mainly on surface

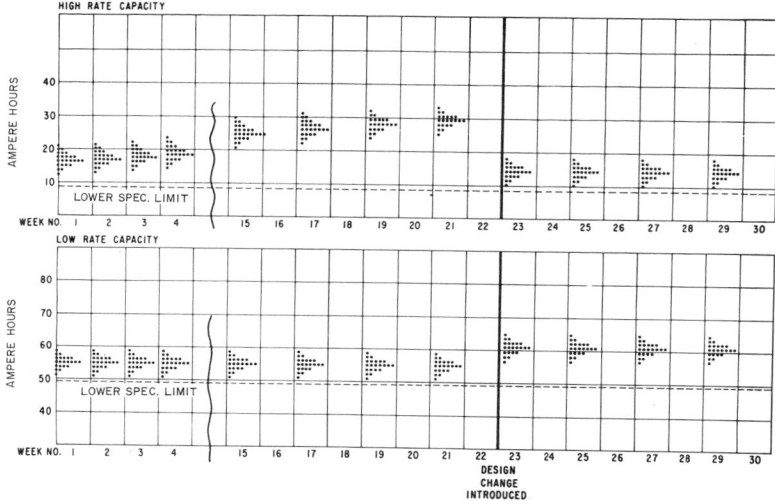

Fig. 38-7   Study of battery capacity.

area.) Guided by the chart, it was feasible to redesign the product to bring both the capacities comfortably within specification limits. A cost reduction of about 30% accompanied this product improvement.

Some of the improvement projects involve material usage, even of materials not consumed in the product. For example, manufacturing of one type of nickel cadmium battery involves an electrolysis employing sodium hydroxide (NaOH). The original process design required discard of the NaOH after use, on the theory that reuse of this caustic would degrade the product. However, this theory was challenged, and an experiment was conducted to evaluate the extent of degradation resulting from reuse. The plan of experiment involved two levels of temperature and three levels of use (Figure 38-8). An analysis using the methods described in Section 27 showed that the NaOH could be reused up to fifteen times without degradation. The material saving was about $50,000 per year.

The wide prevalence of chemical processes in the electronic components industry means also that Evolutionary Operation (EVOP) has wide application. (See generally Section 27A.) An example, also involving nickel cadmium batteries, arose out of periodic difficulty with low ampere-hour capacity. The suspected controlling variable was the nickel nitrate concentration, for which good control was available through a closed-cycle chemical solution system.

An EVOP experiment was designed by subdividing the concentration specification into five difference bands and then controlling the process at each of these five levels

(a)

Processing Temperature	NaOH reuse cycles			
	0	5	10	15
T_1	$n = 5$	$n = 5$	$n = 5$	$n = 5$
T_2	$n = 5$	$n = 5$	$n = 5$	$n = 5$

(b)

Process temperature	Number of reuses				
	0	5	10	15	
T_1	$\overline{X} = 3.2$	3.6	3.4	3.0	$\overline{\overline{X}} = 3.3$
	$R = 0.6$	0.7	0.6	1.0	
T_2	$\overline{X} = 3.4$	3.1	3.8	2.9	$\overline{\overline{X}} = 3.3$
	$R = 0.7$	0.7	0.7	0.6	
	$\overline{\overline{X}} = 3.3$	3.35	3.6	2.95	$\overline{\overline{X}} = 3.3$

(1)
$$\overline{R} = \frac{5.6}{8} = 0.7$$

$$\frac{\overline{R}}{d_2} = \frac{0.7}{2.35} = 0.298$$

For comparison of reuse cycles
Degrees of freedom (DF) $= 0.9 \ (n-1) \ k$
where $n =$ number of observations
$k =$ number of comparisons
$0.9 \ (10\text{-}1) \ (4) = 32$
For 5% one-tail test of significance
(2)
$$t = 2.04 \text{ for } 30 \text{ DF}$$
$$1.02 \ (0.298) = 0.304 \approx 0.3$$
$$3.3 \pm 0.3 = 3.6 \text{ to } 3.0$$

(c)

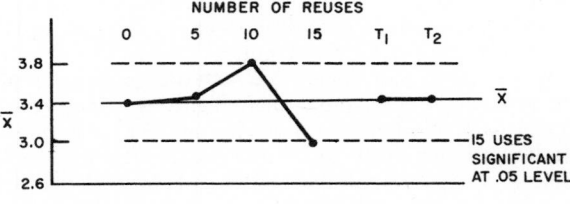

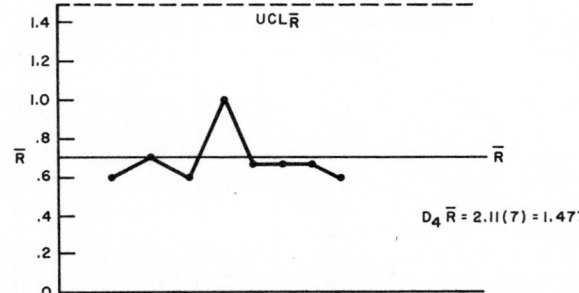

Fig. 38-8 Experimental design and analysis. *(a)* Experimental design matrix. *(b)* Analysis of means table. *(c)* Control chart analysis.

for 2 weeks.   Figure 38-9 shows the test results over the entire 10-week period. It is obvious that the level used during weeks 7 to 8 gives the best product results.

With swift-changing technology there are numerous cases in which process standards are established from limited data.   These standards should, of course, be followed until new knowledge demonstrates the need for change.   However, there should be aggressive pursuit for this new knowledge, on a project-by-project basis.

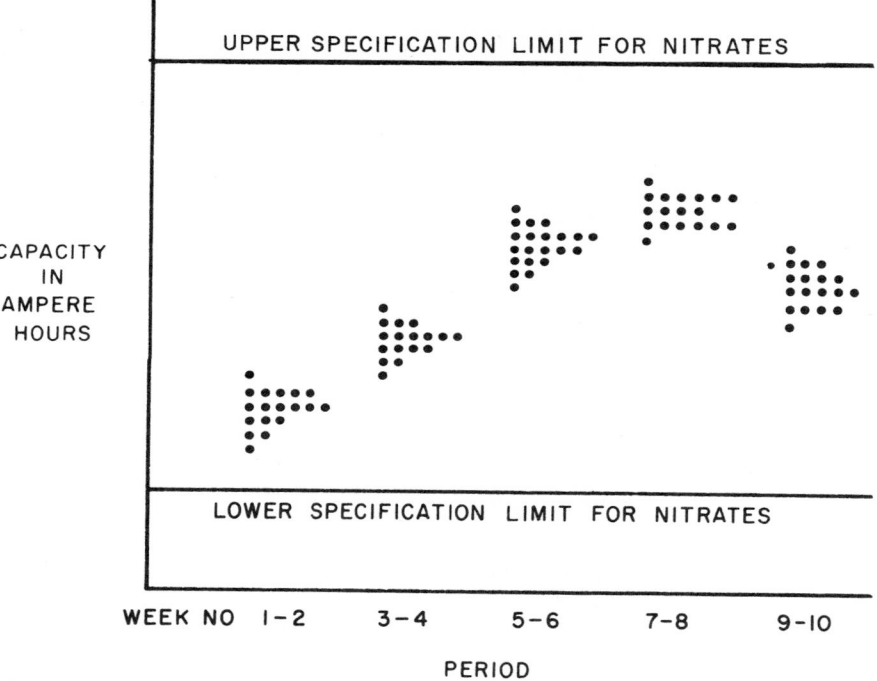

Fig. 38-9   Evolutionary operation experiment.

The EVOP[18] technique has wide application in the processes used to make semiconductor devices.   While these processes are sensitive and delicate, they are highly reproducible.   Hence such variables as gas flow, concentration, and temperature can be studied to measure their effect on the yield of the parts.

Quality Reporting   The extensive inspection and testing generate an enormous amount of quality data.   At the bottom of the company these data are used for product and process regulation.   The problem here is mainly technological —how to measure accurately and how to feed the measurements back to the control stations which can act on them promptly.   These stations need their information in terms of defect descriptions, highlighted by identifying the main contributors to the total defectiveness, and providing a primitive analysis by shifts, machines, operators, and other suspected causes.   See Section 11, under Inspection Feedback to Production, for the general approach used.

There is also a managerial problem of designing and preparing summarized re-

[18] Note that the isostrength diagram (Figure 38-4) is actually the result of an EVOP-type study.

ports for supervisory and management information and action. The governing principles set out in Section 21, under Executive Reports on Quality, are applicable.

CONCLUSIONS

The rapid changes which have characterized the electronic components industry should continue through the decades ahead, creating a vital and challenging task for the Quality profession. Overcapacity in some segments of the industry will be further complicated by expansion of facilities in other parts of the world. Quality technology in Japan is easily as advanced as that in the United States and will present no problems for the American manufacturer using Japanese facilities. On the contrary, the problem is in meeting the high quality standards of Japanese producers. Quality levels in other parts of the world fall somewhat short of United States standards but are being upgraded.

In a technological sense the semiconductor industry will see increasingly complex devices. Expanded use of computer-aided design will speed the design and manufacturing cycle, and will make small-quantity production more feasible. Since device complexity and cost will increase, means are being sought for identifying deficient portions of devices, to enable the balance of the circuits to be used. Consideration is being given to built-in test circuits to enable isolation of defective areas in semiconductor chips and to interconnect around this defective area.

In other segments of the industry, processing equipment is continually being improved to increase the number of variables that can be controlled and to do a better job in controlling those variables. This will tend to decrease variability of products being manufactured and at the same time improve reliability. The commonly used bathtub curve depicting higher failure rates due to infant mortality may change its shape by reducing or eliminating the initial high failure rate. In addition, stabilized part failure rates will continue their decreasing trend as failure studies disclose more information about the basic physics of component parts.

To keep abreast of the narrowing tolerances and reduced variability, measuring systems will become still more precise.

The trends toward smaller facilities—the so-called "hybrid shops"—will continue for awhile but may very well be reversed as companies begin to recognize that costs of high-precision measurement and supporting reliability testing become very significant. These facilities will need controls equivalent to those established at larger operations, and when this becomes evident, laboratories will be combined. Alternatively, their missions will be changed to provide a "breadboard" capability only.

The use of computer-controlled test equipment will expand to permit better collection and analysis of data, and concurrently, improved corrective action. The failure analysis function will also be increased, and will support the corrective action program.

Application of statistical methods is already extensive. However, this should be increased through cost-effective application of advanced statistical methods such as Design of Experiments and Evolutionary Operation.

Although electronic components are a part of the electronic industry, many of the manufacturing operations are chemical in nature. In consequence, the methods of quality control used in the chemical industry[19] apply to the electronic parts industry. To a large extent, profit depends upon yield, and yield depends upon control. Once the process has been engineered to achieve high yields, the holding of those yields depends on control—on the ability to detect and eliminate out-of-control conditions as they arise.

---

[19] See Section 29.

Failure rates have been coming down, and this trend is likely to continue. A survey[20] published in 1966 listed some estimates of attained and predicted failure rates for integrated circuits (percent failures at $25\,^{\circ}C$ equivalent) as follows:

        1964 (best attained levels) 0.0028
        1966 (best attained levels) 0.0012
        1968 (consensus by geometric mean). . . 0.00062
        1978 (lowest thought capable) 0.000062

The factors which have contributed to fitness for use of electronic products will remain as they have been. The scientists and engineers will provide the basic processes, materials, and facilities. The production force will provide the skills needed for operation. The Quality professions will provide the ingredients of control and statistical expertise which can help to optimize the overall quality performance.

BIBLIOGRAPHY

Bazovsky, Igor, "Reliability and Theory and Practice," Prentice-Hall, Inc., Englewood Cliffs, N.J., 1961.

Boyle, Arthur J., Ron Danklefs, and Homer Thornton, Testing MOS, *Electronic Engineer,* October 1970, pp. 42–46.

Bristol, Robert G., Design Guide to Hybrid Package Size, *Electronic Engineer,* September 1969, pp. 45–46.

Duncan, A. J., Chi Square Tests of Independence and the Comparison of Percentages, *Industrial Quality Control,* vol. XI, No. 5, pp. 9–13, February 1955.

Hamiter, Leon C., Jr., How Reliable Are MOS IC's? *Electronics,* June 23, 1969, pp. 106–110.

Holden, P. L., LSI Reliability Predictions, *Evaluation Engineering,* November–December, 1970, pp. 16–18.

Honig, R. E., Materials Characterization at RCA Laboratories, *RCA Product Engineering,* 1968.

Kochendarfer, David C., and W. R. Pabst, Jr., MIL-STD-883 and Related Documents, *Journal of Quality Technology,* July 1971, pp. 129–137.

Lloyd, David K., and Myron Lipow, "Reliability: Management, Methods and Mathematics," 2d ed., Prentice-Hall, Inc., Englewood Cliffs, N.J., 1964.

Madland, Glen R., and John Jolly, Integrated Circuits Course, *Electronic Industries,* April 1966.

Nair, K. R., The Distribution of the Extreme Deviate from the Sample Mean and Its Studentized Form, *Biometrika,* vol. XXXV, pp. 118–144, 1948.

Olmstead, P. S., How to Detect the Type of Assignable Cause, Parts I and II, *Industrial Quality Control,* vol. IX, Nos. 3 and 4, November 1952, pp. 32–38, and January 1953, pp. 22–32.

Ott, Ellis R., Analysis of Means, *Technical Report* 1, August 10, 1958. Prepared for Army, Navy, and Air Force under Contract 404 (11) Task NR. 042-921, with the Office of Naval Research.

Ott, Ellis R., and August B. Mundel, Narrow Limit Gaging, *Industrial Quality Control,* March 1954, pp. 21–28.

Weibull, W., A General Method for Estimating Distribution Parameters, *Report* AD689405, Defense Documentation Center, Cameron Station, Alexandria, Va. 22314, April 1969.

Motorola Reliability Engineering—Motorola Integrated Circuits, "MOS Reliability Test Program Plastic Encapsulated 14 Pin Dual-In-Line," February 1971.

EE's 6th Annual Semiconductor/IC Reference, *Evaluation Engineering,* November–December 1970, pp. 10–13, 24.

[20] Rodrigues de Miranda, William R., Reliability of Integrated Circuits, Analysis of a Survey, *Proceedings 1966 Annual Symposium on Reliability,* IEEE, pp. 450–463.

Section 39
Textiles

JOHN H. REYNOLDS

Consultant, formerly with Celanese Fibers Company

INTRODUCTION

Definition of Textile Materials Textile materials are "fibers, yarn intermediates, yarns, fabrics, and products made from fabrics which retain more or less completely the strength, flexibility, and other typical properties of the original fibers or filaments."[1] Fibers are manufactured from many different substances and are prepared from many different materials occurring in nature. The list of these materials includes asbestos, jute, flax, ramie, cotton, glass, nylon, graphite, polypropylene, wool, polyester, and cellulose acetate. This list, while not complete, does indicate the wide range of materials, both natural and man-made, from which textile materials are produced.

Material and Product Flow Textile yarns and fibers are made of two general types of materials, those found in nature and those produced by man. Usually the natural material occurs in fiber form which can be subsequently put into yarn form. Generally, man-made materials are first formed into continuous filaments which may subsequently be cut into staple fibers which may subsequently be spun into yarn again. Fabric is formed from the fibers or yarn and then made into various items such as shirts, skirts, panties, and slipcovers. Figure 39-1 is a very much simplified diagram which shows this flow of materials.

[1]"ASTM Standards Part 24," Standard Definitions of Terms Relating to Textile Materials, ASTM D 123-66, Philadelphia, Pa., 1966.

Quality Problems   It is not surprising that with so much variety in materials to be processed, and with added variety in the processes, the textile industry has quality problems.   However, this variety is not the major cause of these problems.   Some of the industry's major quality problems are the following:

1. The fiber from production to the final form passes through many operations and stages, usually through a number of different manufacturing plants.   As in other industries, production rates continue to be increased by using improved and automated machinery.   Each stage then puts more pressure on the preceding stages to produce a uniform and high-quality product which can be processed in one standard way and without costly machine stoppages.

2. The textile industry has a higher number of production workers per unit of product produced than any other industry.   The industry's value added per year per production worker, excluding chemical fiber production, is only $8,704, the

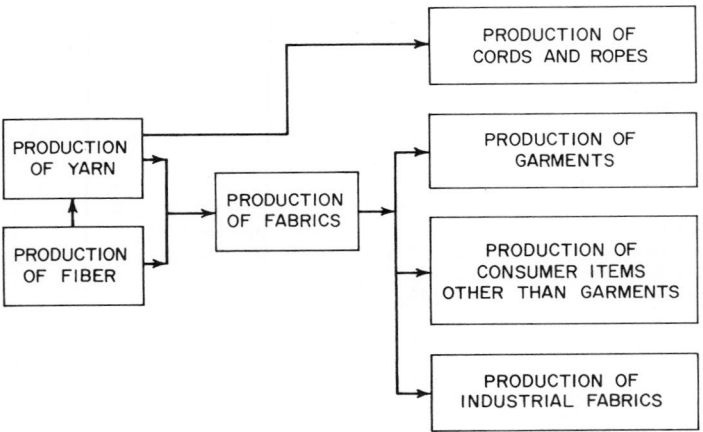

Fig. 39-1   Flow of product in the textile industry.

lowest of all industries, compared with a national average of $18,555.   The industry next above textiles is leather at $8,765.[2]   (The highest industry is petroleum and coal products, $53,560.)   This high number of workers makes it difficult to maintain the high-quality individual workmanship which is necessary to prevent errors and quality accidents.

3. The problem of increased demand for improved physical properties of textiles continues.   Industrial uses are ever more demanding.   For example, larger aircraft need fabric with higher strength and less weight for the tires; more traffic in a hotel lobby requires a better carpet.

4. There is an increased need for quality control for quick development of new products and variations of old products.   Two forces have brought this about.   New products are needed to meet new uses and desires, for example, space suits, outdoor carpets, and easy-care clothes for jet-age travel.   But probably the most pressure for quick development comes because of the increased rate of style change.   Better communication facilities, including advertising, and more widespread affluence largely account for this.

To meet these new needs and desires, new designs and new materials have been introduced into textile products. Some of these designs and materials have been unfamiliar to the consumer, who requires instruction and guidance in the most advantageous way to use the products. This, coupled with growing government regulation, has prompted textile manufacturers to put greater emphasis than ever on safety and care of their products.

In those relatively small plants of the textile industry, quality control has not kept pace with the rest of the textile industry. This, among other things, has brought them into sharp competition with imports from Japan. Since World War II, Japan has revolutionized its organization and training for quality control. Dr. Juran has described it as "the quality miracle of the century."[3] This is an extremely serious quality problem for the cotton textile producers. Japan's ability to obtain a significant part of the market in America is due to a combination of high quality of textile materials, a reputation for quality products in all fields, development of efficient textile processing machinery, and the lower wages paid to Japanese textile workers. The combination of low prices and good quality is a significant factor which contributes to the growing Japanese share of the world textile market.

THE CONTROL PLAN

The textile industry consists of many different segments. The quality control plan will differ in detail for each segment. But there are many overall similarities, and examples of selected typical techniques used to solve the quality control problems will give a general picture of the industry's quality control methods.

To facilitate discussion of the control plan, it has been divided into seven segments: customer relations, new product development and control, the control stations, criteria in decision making at control stations, the responsibility pattern, the data plan, and the audit plan.

Customer Relations   The ease of information flow between the producer and his customer in the textile industry ranges all the way from resistance to completely free interchange of quality and performance information. All the large man-made yarn and fiber producers have active customer service organizations. Their purpose is to help customers process and use the products properly, to receive and interpret complaints, and to transmit the complaints and their interpretation to the manufacturing organization. These customer service organizations, because of their close contact with the customer and his needs, participate in the design of new products and the revision of specifications for current products.

In some multistore retail organizations, customer complaints about garments and other textile consumer items are analyzed very carefully. The results of these analyses are then used to guide changes in the control systems in the manufacturing plants which supply the retail stores.

These two examples of customer relations provide for reporting on the quality of products *after* they have been produced. It is much more effective, though more difficult, to obtain an agreement between supplier and customer on how the product is to be produced and how its quality is to be controlled *before* production is begun. After production, the control and production procedures can be changed for the next production lot on the basis of observed product performance. In some areas of the cotton production industry this combination of feedforward and feedback control is just beginning to be used. A cotton mill will contract to buy a farmer's entire cotton crop on the basis of a description of how the production of the cotton is to be controlled from planting through care in the field, harvesting, and ginning.

New Product Development and Control   Proper design review of new products is important in all industries, and no less so in the design of garments, including so-

---

[3] Juran, J. M., Mobilizing for the 1970's, *Quality Progress,* vol. 2, No. 8, p. 13, August 1969.

called "high-fashion" designs. Some garment manufacturers place a technical person on the review board from the start. This is done to ensure that the design can be executed in the manufacturing plant, and to ensure that the specification of construction (for example, such things as sewing thread, closures, seams, and fabric composition) will be adequate for the intended use.

It is the practice in some companies to develop, concurrently with the development of the process, a quality control system while the new product is still in the pilot plant. This has two advantages. A system is immediately available to use in guiding the changeover from pilot plant to production plant, and the production plant is not given the frustrating task of trying to achieve unrealistic specifications, since process capability will have already been fairly well estimated.

The quality control system, when it is complete, will include both process and product specifications. Of course, these specifications may be revised as time goes on and as experience is gained in the production plant.

Complete *process* specifications will include:

1. A brief description of the process
2. A list of all vessels, machinery, and other apparatus used in the process, giving references to dimensions and characteristics such as engineering drawing numbers or manufacturer's catalog numbers
3. A list of all raw materials used, referring to their specification numbers
4. A list of all pertinent operating conditions, including tolerances and equipment replacement and servicing schedules
5. A list, in order of performance, of the steps required to execute the process
6. A list of all tests and inspections, referring to sampling and test procedures to be used, with their frequencies of performance and with the desired values and necessary tolerances

It is estimated that, outside of the man-made fiber and yarn producers and the industrial products producers, only about 1% of all textile and garment plants have written process specifications as described above.

Complete *product* specifications (both in-process and final) will include:

1. A definition of the product and a statement which describes its intended use
2. A list of all the product characteristics which are to be specified, giving the desired values and tolerances; references to sampling and analytical procedures to be used for testing each listed characteristic; a statement of the parameters which define the lot quality protection plan, if the item is usually produced in lots of individual units
3. A statement of how and to whom out-of-limits results are reported; a description of what is to be done with the material from which the out-of-limits samples were taken
4. A description of packaging requirements

All government agencies write such specifications for all items that they buy. Outside of government, producers and purchasers seldom write such detailed and specific specifications.

Figure 39-2 gives an example of a textile product specification.

The performance of textile materials is difficult to predict from laboratory tests. Therefore, it is necessary for success in development of new products to conduct field tests in the environment in which the products are to be used. Sometimes this environment can be satisfactorily simulated in the laboratory. Washing and pressing, for example, can be done in the laboratory, using the same machines and tools that a housewife uses, with the same results she obtains.[4] But it is not possible

---

[4] See also Measurement of Garment and Fabric Characteristics, under Special Problems of Analysis, below.

to reproduce in the laboratory the hazards to which a carpet will be exposed in a hospital. Similarly, the vital matter of customer acceptance of a garment can be determined only by exposure in a retail store.

Control Stations *Control Stations from Yarn to Garment.* Figure 39-3 lists and locates the principal controls for quality exercised along the sequence of activities in extruding cellulose acetate into yarn, winding it onto beams for warp knitting, warp knitting into fabric, fabric dyeing, and making a garment from the fabric. Parts of this sequence of operations illustrate typical control procedures used in processing yarns and fabrics of many different types.

Glossary of Textile Terms. Given here is a glossary of the textile manufacturing terms used in the description of the control procedures which follow:

Batch: Fabric batching is sewing two or more pieces of fabric together and winding relative short pieces into one longer piece.

Beam: (1) A cylinder of wood or metal, usually with a circular flange on each end, on which warp yarns are wound. (2) The many ends of yarn after being wound onto the cylinder.

Creel: A framework arranged to hold packages of yarn.

Denier: A measure of yarn size; grams per 9,000 meters.

Doff: To take off. For example, to take off, from their spindles, bobbins which have been filled with yarn.

End: One strand of yarn.

Lease: (1) To arrange and secure the ends of a warp in orderly fashion so that they will maintain the same relative positions with respect to one another. (2) The arrangement obtained by leasing.

Sinker: A thin, notched blade of steel which works in conjunction with the guides and needles in forming a stitch on the knitting machine.

Slub: A lump or thick place in yarn. In filament yarn usually the result of broken filaments being stripped back.

Tenter frame: A machine used to finish a fabric to a given width under tension. The machine consists essentially of a pair of continuous traveling chains fitted with clips or fine pins on horizontal tracks. The fabric is held firmly at the selvages by the two chains, which are adjusted to diverge as they advance to bring the fabric to the desired width. The fabric is carried through a heated chamber and dried to size.

Acetate Yarn Extrusion and Take-Up. The process begins with cellulose acetate flake being dissolved in a mixture of acetone and water. This solution is called dope. This dope is filtered, and then extruded to form a bundle of filaments. The dissolving and filtering processes require careful control in accordance with the general principles of quality control in chemical processing.

Dope is extruded through tiny holes in a spinneret into a cabinet containing flowing hot air, and is drawn out by a feed roll. The temperature and acetone content of the air in the cabinet are measured and recorded continuously by instruments. The velocity of the air is controlled by a standard orifice and constant-speed motor-driven fans.

Between the outlet of the cabinet and the take-up roll a lubricating assembly is installed. This device applies lubricant to the yarn. There usually are associated yarn guides outside the lubricating assembly and at the outlet of the cabinet. Before installation, these devices are inspected for freedom from defects and for conformance to specified dimensions. Yarn bearing surfaces are inspected (at intervals of about 6 months) for freedom from defects and wear which might damage the yarn as it passes over them.

After the yarn passes over the take-up roll, it is collected on a suitable package.

During extrusion and take-up, patrol inspections are made of the machine for conformance with specified operating conditions, especially for cleanliness and prop-

XYZ MILLS	SOUTH GASTONIA PLANT SPECIFICATION	
TITLE 8/3 White Sewing Thread on Cones	SPECIFICATION NO. M-1011C	
TYPE Purchased Product	DATE 10 June 70	PAGE 2 OF 2

Use ASTM Method D 2258 to determine sample sizes. This will give confidence intervals for means of about ± 3% at a probability level of 90%. Some few individual cones outside of specifications are to be expected and tolerated.

Out-of-Limits Action

If average strength requirement is not met proceed as follows:

1. Measure other specified characteristics.

2. Notify Receiving Stores Foreman to hold lot for possible return.

3. Notify Quality Control Manager.

4. Notify Purchasing Agent.

5. Return sample cones to Receiving Stores for Repacking.

If individual cone is below required minimum strength, hold it in the laboratory for disposition by the Quality Control Manager.

Packaging

Precision-wound 7-inch cone. Inside diameter of base to be 1 3/4 inches (nominal).

APPROVALS		SUPERSEDES
MANUFACTURING	QUALITY CONTROL	DATE 3 Aug. 1951 PAGE 1 OF 1

Fig. 39-2 Purchased product specification.

XYZ MILLS	SOUTH GASTONIA PLANT SPECIFICATION	
TITLE 8/3 White Sewing Thread on Cones	SPECIFICATION NO. M-1011C	
TYPE Purchased Product	DATE 10 June 70	PAGE 1 OF 2

Definition and Use

A soft, natural sewing thread, 8-count, 3-ply, usually used for sewing ends of fabric together for batching for sizing, dyeing, finishing, etc.

Requirements and Tolerances

Characteristic	Requirements and Tolerances
Color	Natural cotton
Moisture regain	7.0%, minimum for individual cones
Count (total), average	2.67, target 2.52, minimum

Single strand strength
   Average
   Individual cone
	
	6.5 lb, minimum
	5.9 lb, minimum

Turns twist per inch average	4.80 ± 0.25
Yards per cone individual	2,120, minimum

Perform only the strength tests for routine acceptance sampling.

Sampling and Testing

Characteristic	Test Method
Color	None
Moisture regain	XYZ-2895
Count	ASTM D 204
Single strand strength	ASTM D 204
Turns twist per inch	ASTM D 204
Yards per cone	ASTM D 204

APPROVALS		SUPERSEDES
MANUFACTURING	QUALITY CONTROL	DATE 3 Aug. 1951 PAGE 1 OF 1

Fig. 39-2 *(Continued)*

er threading of the yarn through the guides, lubricating assembly, and collecting devices.

At the time of doffing, a record is made of the number of less than full packages doffed. This gives a record of the number of ends which broke during the time from start-up to doff. After doffing of the take-up packages, samples of yarn are taken to the laboratory for measurement of lubricant content, denier, tenacity, elongation, filament cross-section shape, and filament cross-section size variation.

Yarn Beaming. Guide surfaces, tension devices, and end out detectors are inspected prior to installation on the creel of the beamer. The tension devices are calibrated to ensure that the proper tension is applied.

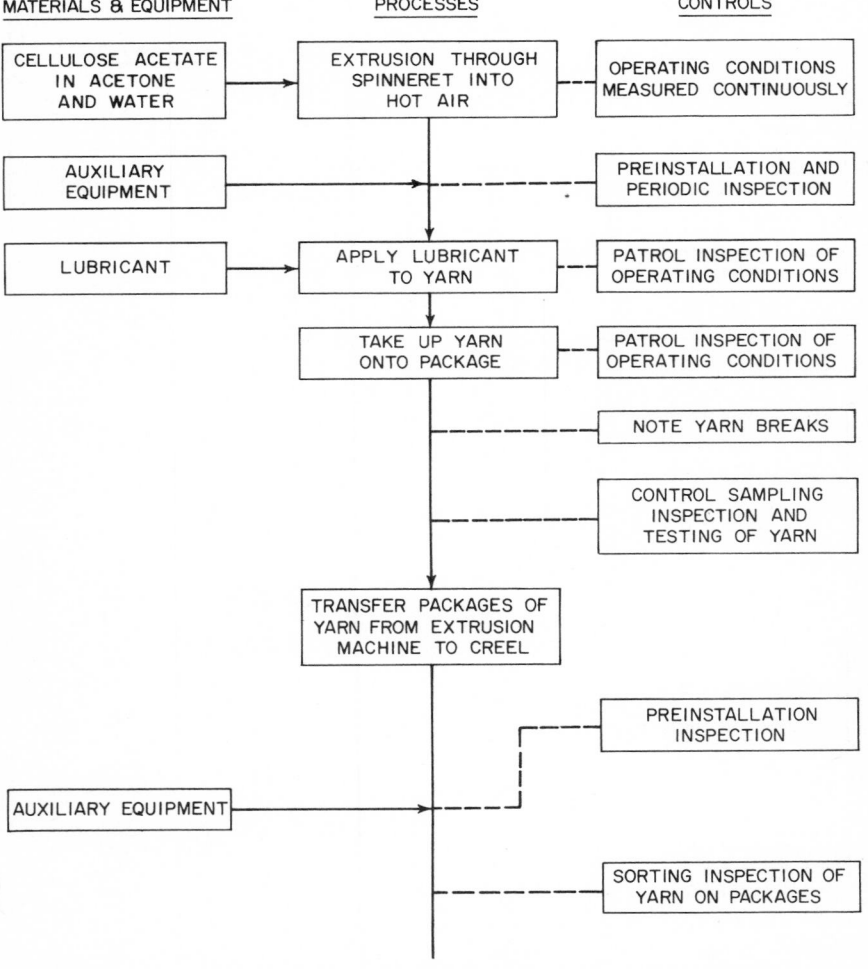

Fig. 39-3 Quality control stations in a textile process from yarn manufacture through garment manufacture.

A sorting inspection of the yarn on the packages is performed at the time the packages are tied in in the creel. Packages which appear as though they will not wind without breaking or will lower the quality of the beam are sent either to waste or to some other use.

After mounting, the insides of the flanges of the empty beams are inspected for roughness by feeling with the fingers. Any rough spots are buffed while the beam is in the warper.

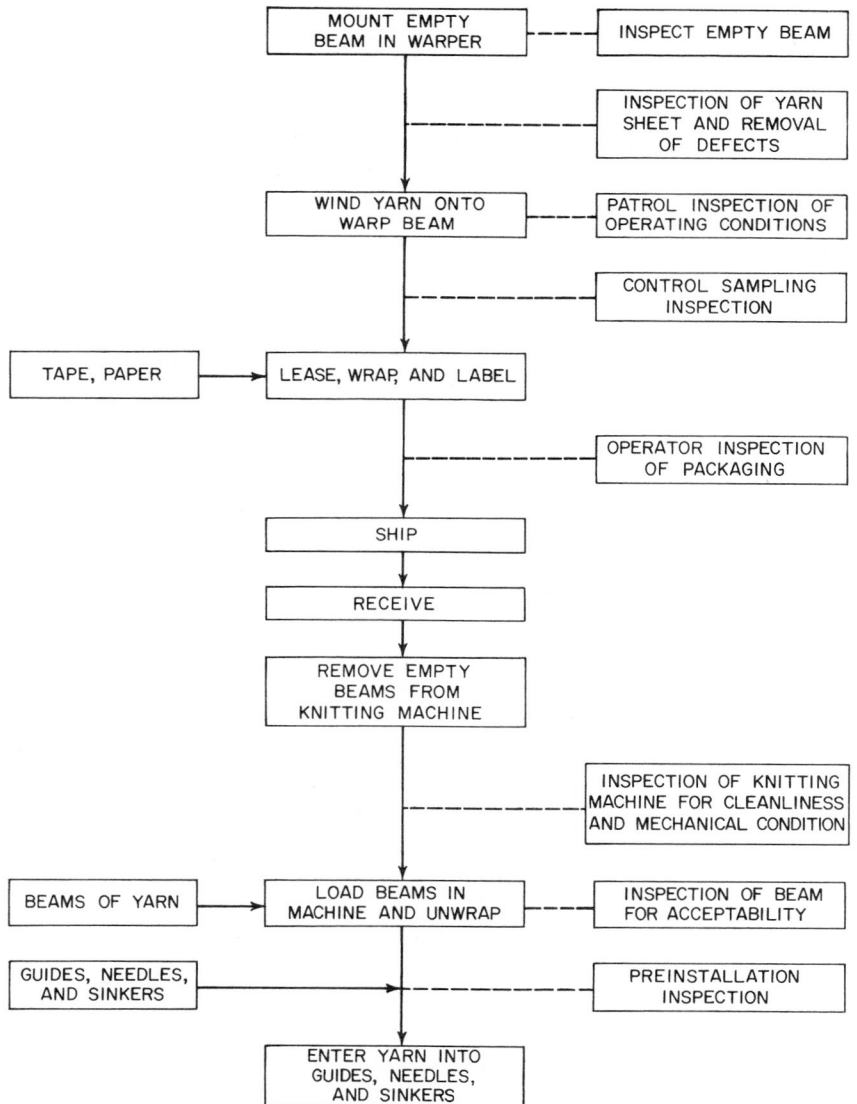

Fig. 39-3 *(Continued)*

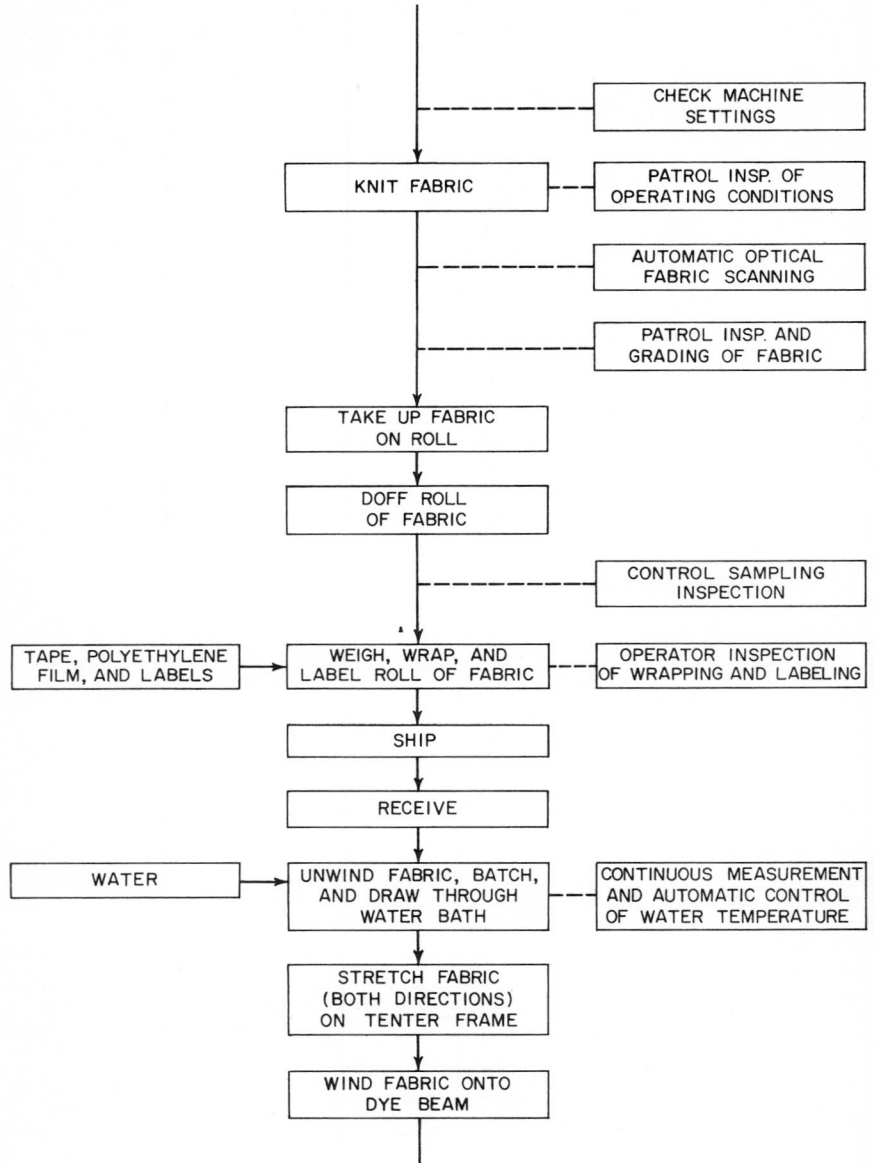

Fig. 39-3 *(Continued)*

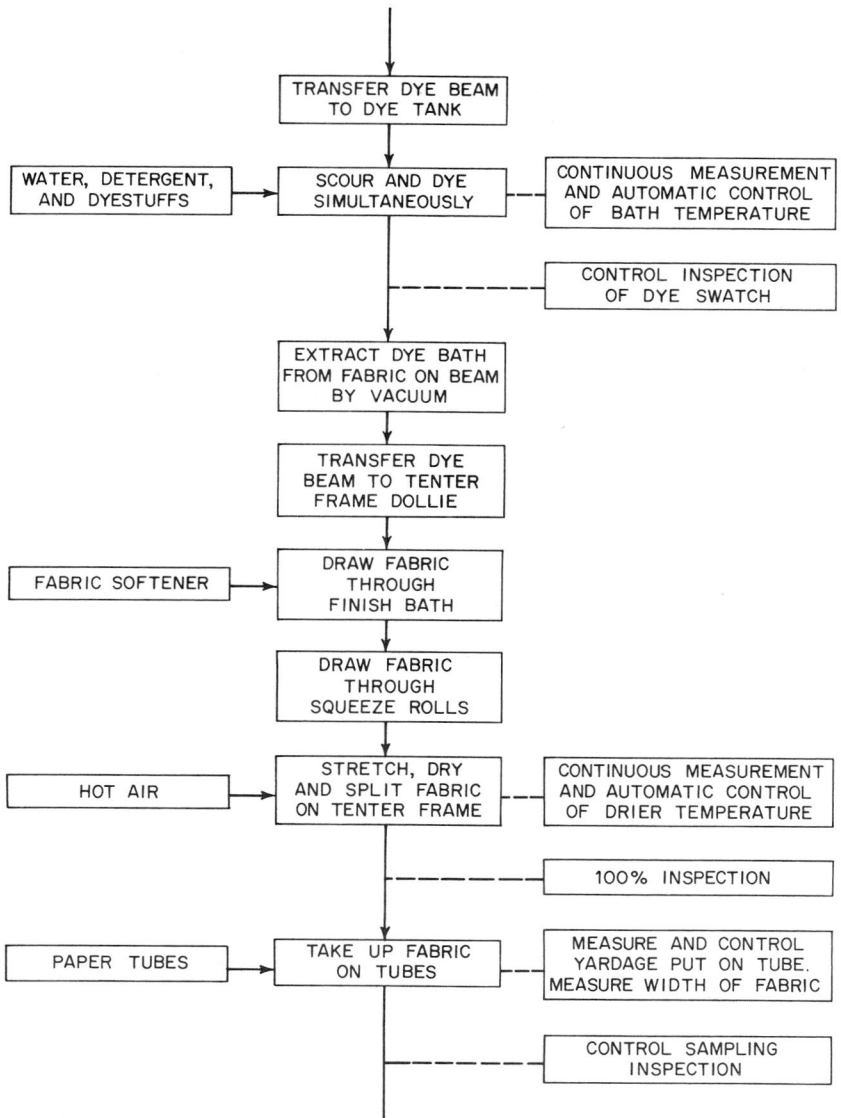

Fig. 39-3 *(Continued)*

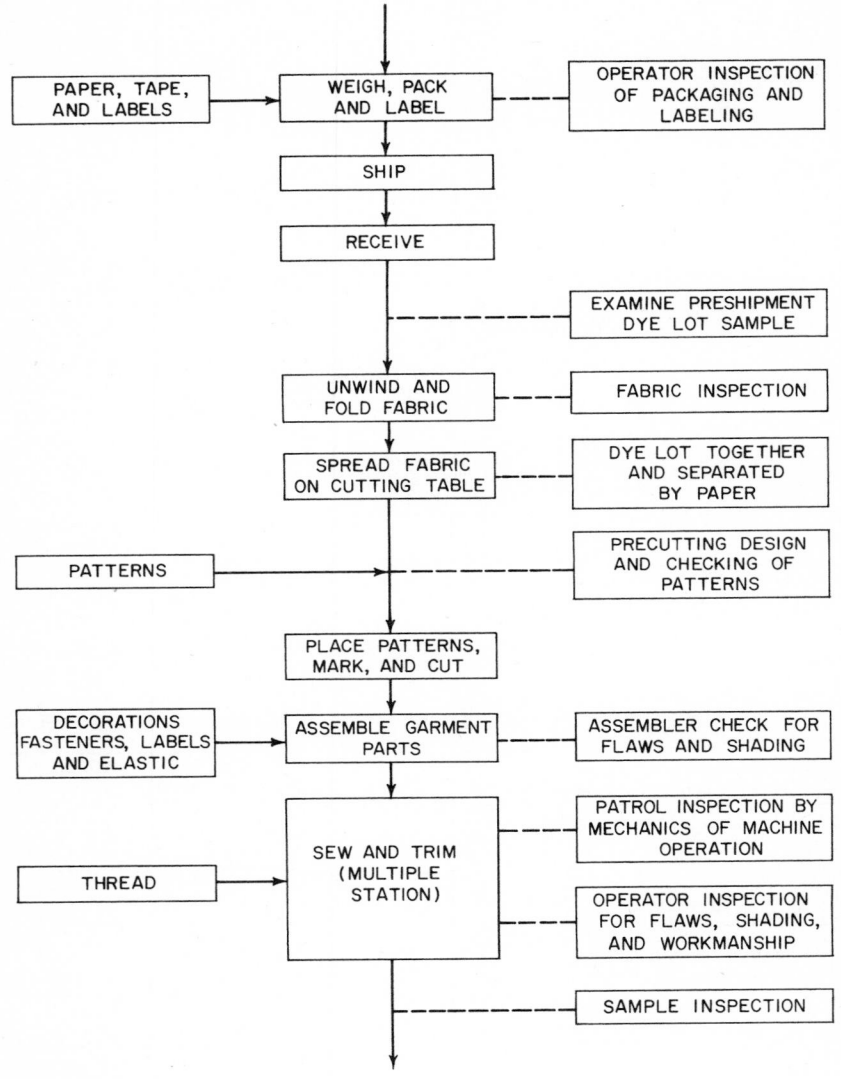

Fig. 39-3   *(Continued)*

While the yarn is being wound onto the beam, it is continuously inspected for slubs and broken filaments by an automatic photoelectric device. This device is usually set to detect a minimum change in yarn sheet thickness of somewhere between 4 and 12%. If a passing slub in the yarn increases the thickness of the yarn sheet, this will be detected, and the beam winding will automatically be stopped. When this occurs, the operator removes the slub, reties the end, and restarts the beamer.

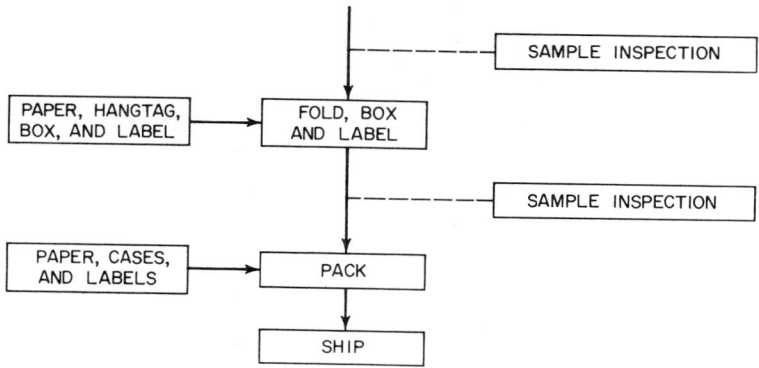

Fig. 39-3   *(Continued)*

While winding onto the beam is taking place, patrol inspections are made for conformance to specified operating conditions: tension on individual ends, winding speed, proper threading through guides, and centering and spread of yarn ends on the beam.

Also during the winding, the beam is stopped from time to time for close inspection of the outside layers of yarn for defects such as broken filaments, slubs, and soil spots. After the beam is wound, its hardness and circumference are measured and compared with a standard. Hardness is measured using an instrument which determines the resistance to penetration offered by the beam to a standardized plunger. Uniformity of hardness and circumference are necessary to accomplish uniform rates of unwinding in knitting.

Tricot Knitting. At the tricot knitting machine, after the empty beams have been removed, the machine is serviced and cleaned. Then it is inspected for cleanliness and mechanical condition.

After the full beams are loaded into the machine and unwrapped, they are inspected for acceptability. No measurements or counts are made, but what can be seen on the outside is compared with labels. The beams are also examined for possible damage in shipping.

Before replacement, yarn guides, needles, and sinkers are inspected at receiving inspection for conformance to purchase specifications. They are accepted from their manufacturer on a sampling inspection basis.

After entering the yarn ends into the machine, a short length of fabric is knit, and closely examined to be sure that the machine is functioning properly and that the machine is set up to produce the desired style of fabric.

While the knitting machine is running, an operator makes a patrol inspection for conformance to standard operating conditions.

As the knitted fabric is wound into a roll from the needles, it is held to its full width by selvage stretchers. At this time the fabric is scanned optically back and forth across its width by a photoelectric device. A hole in the fabric or a missing end reduces the amount of reflected light, and this is detected by the scanner. When this happens, the machine is automatically stopped, preventing further production of fabric containing a flaw. When the fabric is of such a construction that without flaws the reflected light would vary, a different end-out detection device is used. Between the beam and the guides there is a tension bar which extends the full width of the machine. The ends pass over the front side of this bar. A light source passes a beam of light to a photosensitive cell, just in front of the yarn sheet from the bar to the guides. Air jets behind the sheet blow any broken ends into the light beam. There they are detected, and the machine is automatically stopped.

Since the scanner does not detect all types of fabric defects, an inspector patrols a group of machines. looking for faults in the fabric, and stopping the machine when one is observed. This inspector scores the faults found, using a system similar to that described under ASQC Fabric Grading System, below. When the fabric is doffed, this inspector assigns the roll a grade in accordance with the system being used.

After doffing, but before wrapping, rolls of fabric are sampled from the stream of production and inspected. The purpose of this sampling inspection is to audit the whole quality control system.

Fabric Dyeing. In scouring and dyeing, the amount of detergent in the water is not critical, just so long as there is enough. What is critical is the amount of the different dyestuffs in the bath and the temperature of the bath. Great care is exercised in weighing the dyestuffs to be added. The quantities are in proportion to the weight of the fabric on the beam. The temperature of the bath is automatically controlled.

The dye beam has holes in it, and one end is fitted to accommodate a hose connection. The dye bath is pumped through the hose, into the inside of the dye beam, and thus out the holes and through the fabric, being received in the tank, and then recirculated through the fabric until dyeing is completed. There is a trap in the recirculating line in which is placed a swatch of the fabric being dyed. When dyeing is nearly completed, circulation is stopped, and the swatch is removed. The swatch is compared with a standard piece of the same type of fabric the shade of which has been previously passed upon by the intended purchaser. (Almost all tricot fabric dyeing is done to order and not for stock.) The dyer may accept the fabric without further ado, or he may continue recirculation, or he may add more of one or more dyestuffs to the dye bath, and then recirculate.

When dyeing is completed, the fabric is treated with a softener, stretched on a tenter frame, dried, and split. The temperature of the drying air is controlled automatically.

As the fabric is being wound onto tubes, it may or may not receive an inspection, depending upon its end use and on the confidence placed in its manufacturer and in the dyeing process. Defects such as streaks, areas not uniformly dyed, undesired moire patterns, scum spots, oil spots, fabric flaws not detected at knitting, nonuniformly stretched fabric, torn edges, and clip marks on the edges are looked for by the inspector. This inspector marks the places where there are defects in the fabric. He may grade the fabric using a system agreed upon between the vendor and vendee.

In fabric winding, the yardage put onto a tube is measured and controlled to a specified length and width. Control of the length and weight per unit length is achieved by adjustments at the two tenter frames.

Sample swatches are taken from the end of each roll of fabric. They are compared with a standard to make sure that the desired shade has been obtained. One swatch is retained for reference and another is usually sent to the purchaser of the fabric for his approval before the roll of fabric itself is shipped.

Fabric Cutting. In the sewing plant, the preshipment dye lot sample is usually examined and compared with a standard before the shipment is unpacked or even received.

At unpacking the fabric is folded in preparation for putting on the cutting table.

At the same time, the fabric is again given an inspection, and defective places are marked.

When the fabric is spread on the cutting table, fabric from each dye lot is spread together. One of the problems here is to try to minimize mismatching of shade which might occur in joining parts later on. One of the ways to do this is to separate each dye lot by laying a piece of paper between them.

After a garment design has been selected by a design review board, patterns are made to use in cutting the fabric. Before the patterns are used to cut a production lot of garments, sample garments are cut by the patterns and sewn. These test garments are then submitted to the design review board for approval on both live models and manikins.

As garment parts are assembled into bundles, the assembler checks for fabric flaws and shade matching. Defective parts are removed from the bundle and replaced by good parts.

Garment Sewing. As the garment parts are being sewn together, the operator again inspects for fabric flaws and shading, and also for workmanship on the present job and preceding sewing jobs. Common workmanship defects are such things as seam pucker, missing fasteners, failure to trim, parts not properly aligned, and improper stitch formation.

Also as the sewing is being done, mechanics patrol, looking for machines which are not performing properly. This patrolling makes mechanics readily available to operators for attention to their machines at the very first sign of trouble.

After each critical sewing operation samples are taken for inspection. See Skip Bundle Sampling, under Audit Plan, below, for a detailed description of this sampling and inspection operation.

After the last sewing operation and after boxing, some of the samples taken for control inspection are checked for proper fit by being put on manikins. The folding and boxing operation itself is also checked at the last sampling inspection.

Quality Improvement and Failure Correction. The emphasis at each control station is to make the product right so that the product will not have to be downgraded, reprocessed, or repaired, and so that there will be no process interruptions because of yarn, fabric, or assembly defects.

Quality improvement or correction of failure in this or any process is directed first at that critical or dominant "system" which largely determines the quality. Quality failures may arise in more than one system. However, quality failures are classified here by systems whose failure most frequently results in the quality failure. (See generally Section 9, under Concept of Dominance.) These cause systems are:

1. *Setup Dominant.* Failures are the direct result of the accuracy of instruments or the preciseness of adjustment of the setup.

2. *Machine Dominant.* Failures occur at random times or are dependent on adjustment of machine or process settings which are subject to change after the initial adjustment.

3. *Operator Dominant.* Each individual unit of product is exposed to a certain probability of being defective; that probability depends on the skill or decision-making ability of the operator who makes it.

4. *Material Dominant.* Quality failures are directly related to defects or fluctuations in the quality of input materials.

Table 39-1 gives a classification of quality failures in the acetate extrusion and beaming process by dominant systems.

Criteria for Decision Making at Control Stations

In a control loop the criterion for decision making is the standard. Standards are described in process and product specifications. The element in a control loop which compares the test or inspection result with the standard is called the collator. The types of specifications and collating techniques used in the textile industry are many and varied. The following types of criteria, and examples of their uses for decision making at the control stations, are described in this Section: the Shewhart control chart for variables, including control chart procedures and tests for process instability, interpretation of control chart patterns, changes in level of process variability, and changes in level of process average; the Shewhart control chart for attributes; comparison with physical standards; go no-go appearance; exponentially weighted moving average; the ASQC fabric grading system; and fabric color shade matching.

TABLE 39-1   Dominant Causes of Process or Product Quality Failure

Process or product quality	Setup dominant	Machine dominant	Operator dominant	Material dominant
Extrusion:.				
Air temperature	. . .	X	. . .	. . .
Acetone content of cabinet exhaust air	. . .	X	. . .	. . .
Velocity of air	. . .	X	. . .	. . .
Rate of less than full packages	. . .	. . .	. . .	X
Proper thread-up.	. . .	. . .	X	. . .
Machine cleanliness.	. . .	. . .	X	. . .
Lubricant content of yarn.	. . .	X	. . .	. . .
Denier of yarn	. . .	X	. . .	. . .
Tenacity of yarn	. . .	X	. . .	. . .
Elongation of yarn.	. . .	X	. . .	. . .
Filament cross-section shape.	. . .	X	. . .	. . .
Filament cross-section size variation.	. . .	. . .	. . .	X
Wind of yarn on packages	. . .	X	. . .	. . .
Beaming:				
Stops	. . .	. . .	. . .	X
Tension on end	. . .	X	. . .	. . .
Speed of beam	. . .	. . .	X	. . .
Proper thread-up.	. . .	. . .	X	. . .
Lay of yarn on beam	. . .	X	. . .	. . .
Broken filaments on beam	. . .	. . .	. . .	X
Soil on beam.	. . .	. . .	X	. . .
Beam circumference	X	. . .	. . .	. . .
Beam hardness	X	. . .	. . .	. . .

Shewhart Control Chart for Variables.[5]   It is common practice to use Shewhart statistical quality control charts of averages and ranges to guide control of variables in textile processes. These charts are used for four purposes: to detect signs of instability, to aid in troubleshooting, to detect changes in variability of the variable, and to detect changes in the average of the variable. (See Section 23.)

Tests for Detecting Instability in the Process.[6]   Instability in a process or product characteristic indicates that the cause system is changing. The four commonly used tests for instability are applied in this manner. Consider only one-half of the control chart at a time; that is, consider the area above the center line and below

[5] See generally Section 23.

[6] These tests are described and discussed in detail in "Statistical Quality Control Handbook," pp. 25–29, Western Electric Company, Incorporated, Mack Printing Company, Easton, Pa.

the center line separately, but consider both halves. Divide each of the two areas between the center line and the two control limits mentally into three equal zones. Since the control limits are at plus and minus three standard deviations from the centar line, each zone will be one standard deviation wide. See Figure 39-4. Instability in the process is indicated if any of the following combinations are formed in the various zones:

1. A single point falls outside the three-sigma limit (beyond Zone A).

2. Two out of three successive points fall in Zone A or beyond. (The odd point may be anywhere.)

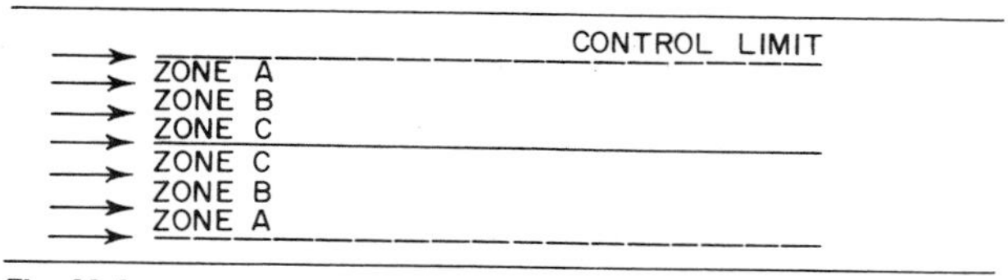

Fig. 39-4 Zones for applying tests for instability.

3. Four out of five successive points fall in Zone B or beyond. (The odd point may be anywhere.)

4. Eight successive points fall in Zone C or beyond.

Patterns on Control Charts. Competent troubleshooters know that one does not want all the facts, but only the pertinent facts. Different sets of situations produce different patterns of points with respect to the three control lines on control charts. If a particular pattern appears, it could mean that a particular set of conditions could not have occurred, and that this is one set of possible occurrences that the troubleshooter need not investigate. Putting it positively, the troubleshooter should concern himself with possible occurrences in the process which could have caused such a pattern to appear on the control chart. All together there are 15 patterns which appear on control charts.[7]

Tests for Change in Level of Variability. Changes in variability level can be detected by use of the four tests for instability described above applied to a control chart for ranges.

The Run Sum Test for Change in Average. To detect changes in the average level of a variable, a run sum test is sometimes used. A run is a sequence of observations which are all above or below a specified value. This value can be the process average X'. Wherever a point falls on the opposite side of the specified value from that of the preceding point, one run terminates, and another begins. Scores are assigned to observations, depending on the extent by which the observations depart from the specified value. The run sum is the sum of the scores in a run. Scores may be positive or negative, integral or nonintegral values. (See also Section 23, Figure 23-9 and associated discussion.)

One concludes that the process average has changed when the run sum reaches a specified value.[8]

---

[7] These control chart patterns are described and discussed in detail in "Statistical Quality Control Handbook," pp. 161–180, Western Electric Company, Incorporated, Mack Printing Company, Easton, Pa.

[8] Reynolds, John H., The Run Sum Control Chart Procedure, *Journal of Quality Technology,* vol. 3, No. 1, pp. 23–27, January 1971.

Run sum tests which are the simplest, and which are the most useful in quality control, can be denoted by

$$RS_k\left[L_0,(S_0),L_1(S_1),L_2(S_2),\ldots\right]$$

where the L's and S's denote limits and scores, and k denotes the minimum absolute value of the run sum that indicates that the process average has shifted from $\bar{X}'$. The observation X is assigned a score of S_i if

$$\bar{X}'+L_i\,\sigma'<\bar{X}\le X'+L_{i+1}\sigma'$$

where σ' is the standard deviation of the X's.

If $0 = L_0 < L_1 < L_2 < \ldots$, and $0 \le S_0 < S_1 < S_2 < \ldots$, then RS_k describes a test for increase in process average; if $0 = L_0 > L_1 > L_2 > \ldots$, and $0 \ge S_1 > S_2 > \ldots$, then RS_k describes a test for decrease in process average.

A commonly used run sum test is the symmetrical two-sided test where

$$RS_5\ [0,\,(0),\ 1,\ (1),\ 2,\ (2),\ \ldots]$$

and
$$RS_5\ [0;\ (0);\ -1;\ (-1);\ -2;\ (-2);\ \ldots]$$

are used together. Table 39-2 describes how this test operates. It gives the average number of observations required to conclude that a shift upward has occurred when indeed a shift has occurred. The distances of the shifts are given in σ' units.

TABLE 39-2 Average Number of Observations for Run Sum to Reach 5

Process average shift in σ' units	Average number of observations
0.0	685
0.5	49
1.0	11.7
1.5	5.6
2.0	3.8
2.5	2.9
3.0	2.4
3.5	2.1

TABLE 39-3 Run Sum Test of Nylon Elongation*

Day No.	Elongation, %	Score	Run sum
1	23.58	-1	-1
2	24.38	$+0$	$+0$
3	23.90	-0	-0
4	24.91	$+1$	$+1$
5	25.32	$+1$	$+2$
6	25.27	$+1$	$+3$
7	25.88	$+2$	$+5$

* $\bar{X}' = 24.20\%$; $\sigma' = 0.6\%$.

The average number of observations required to say that the process has moved up or down (two-sided test), when in truth there has been no change at all, is one-half the number shown in the table for a shift upward. As the process average departs farther and farther from the center line, the average number of observations needed to detect a change using the two-sided test becomes closer and closer to the average for the one-sided test until at a shift of one-half a standard deviation the two averages are almost the same.

Table 39-3 shows how this two-sided run sum test is applied during manufacturing to detect changes in the level of elongation to break of nylon 6 yarn which will be used in making tire cord. After take-up at the extrusion machine, nylon 6 is stretched on another machine to accomplish the desired molecular orientation. One measure of this orientation is the yarn's elongation. The greater the stretch, the higher the tenacity, and the lower the elongation. The chemical character of the yarn changes from time to time. This will change the elongation. To compensate, the amount of stretch is changed. In this way the average elongation can be kept constant.

The average elongations of one break on each of four packages of yarn from consecutive days are listed in the second column of Table 39-3. The target elongation is 24.20% and the standard deviation of these averages is 0.6%. Each average was given a score according to the two-sided run sum test RS_5 described above. Here the target elongation is 24.20%. One-sigma limits are at 24.20 ± 0.60%; two-sigma limits are at 24.20 ± 1.20%; three-sigma limits are at 24.20 ± 1.80%.

Figure 39-5 shows the scoring scheme graphically. In actual practice it is easy to estimate from the control chart the intervals in which the plotted points lie, and thus it is not necessary to draw the lines at one sigma and two sigmas. In fact it is preferable to omit these lines, and draw only those at the center line and at plus and minus three sigmas, because the additional lines tend to interfere with seeing the pattern of points relative to the center line and the three-sigma limits.

The data of Table 39-3 are also plotted in Figure 39-5, and their scores and run

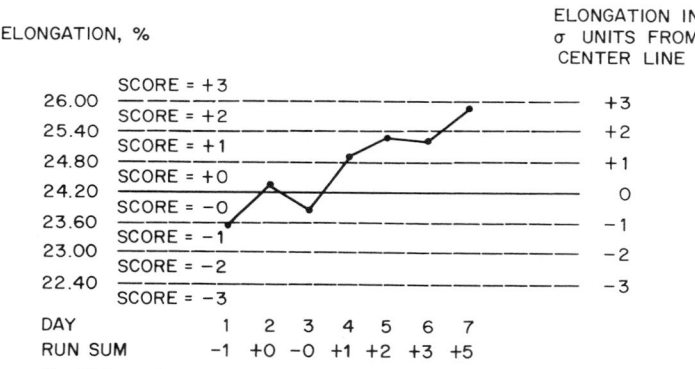

Fig. 39-5 Scheme for scoring run sum test of nylon elongation.

sums are shown. For example, the average elongation of 23.58% (for day 1) falls in the interval 23.00 to 23.60 for which the score is—1, and the run sum is −1. Although zero has no algebraic sign, signs are associated with it simply to aid in determining when one run ends and a new run starts. When a new run begins, cumulation of scores should begin anew. Between day 1 and day 2 the score changed from −1 to +0, indicating the end of one run and the beginning of a new one. The run sum for the new run as of day 2 is thus +0. After day 2 the score changed from +0 to −0, indicating again the end of one run and the beginning of another. In this way the scores were summed in each run.

On the seventh day the run sum reached 5. This was an indication that the average elongation was not now 24.20%, and that, if no other corrective action is to be taken, the amount of stretch should be changed.

Shewhart Control Chart for Attributes. One of the measures of the productivity of cotton spinning is the number of times there is a spindle not producing per 1,000 spindle hours. This number not producing is called the number of "ends down" because the end of yarn is not winding onto the bobbin. A change in the ends down rate may be caused by various changes in the process from cotton mixing to the spinning frame. But any change should be investigated. Changes can be detected by using a control chart.

A count of ends down may be made as often as once a day. It is made less frequently when things are running well. Counts are made of the number of times there is an idle spindle in a particular group of spindles during some time interval. The time interval may vary from ½ to 8 hours. The result of the count is reported as number of ends down per 1,000 spindle hours. Call this number u. Then $u = 1,000C/SH$, where C is the number of idle spindles counted, S is the total number of spindles observed, and H is the number of hours during which the count was made. A separate u is calculated for each group of spindles producing different yarns.

A control chart is established using $\bar{u}$ as the center line, where $\bar{u}$ is the average u for 15 or 20 days. The control limits for u are set at $\bar{u} \pm 3\sqrt{1{,}000\bar{u}/SH}$. For example, if $\bar{u} = 13.27$, and if $S = 240$ and $H = 1$, then the control limits for u would be $13.27 \pm 3\sqrt{1{,}000(13.27)/240}$, or 0 to 34.57.[9]

Comparison with a Physical Standard. The grade and staple length of cotton indicate to a large extent the spinning utility and hence the market value. These indicators of quality are used by farmers to appraise their methods of production, harvesting, and ginning; and to market advantageously. They are also used by cotton merchants to buy and sell cotton efficiently, and by mills to buy and blend.

Cotton grade is composed of three factors: color, leaf, and preparation. Upland cotton is normally white, but owing to various causes it may become spotted or discolored, becoming darker gray, or yellow bluish gray. Leaf and other trash refers to foreign matter remaining in the cotton after ginning. "Preparation" is the term used to describe the degree of smoothness or roughness with which the cotton has been ginned. The U.S. Department of Agriculture publishes a description of 40 different grades of American upland cotton along with specifications for how to do the grading.[10] Some of the grade names are Strict Good Ordinary, Strick Middling Light Spotted, Middling Spotted, Strict Low Middling Tinged, Good Middling Yellow Stained, Strict Low Middling Light Grey, and Good Middling Grey. For 15 of these 40 grades a set of physical standards is prepared once a year by the Cotton Division of the Agricultural Marketing Service of the U.S. Department of Agriculture. The range of each grade is represented by 12 samples put up in an official box. The original set of the physical standards in effect is sealed and deposited in a vault at the Department of Agriculture in Washington, D.C. Copies of these, known as practical forms, are prepared, sent to the cotton classing offices of the Agricultural Marketing Service, and sold to whoever wants to buy them. A grade is assigned to a bale of cotton based on matching a sample from the bale with a physical standard (a practical form), using a specified set of conditions under which the matching is performed.

Go No-Go Appearance. There are many situations in which textile materials are put into one of two quality classifications based on whether or not the item being inspected has a soiled place on it. For example, if a finished shirt has an oil or dirt spot on it, it is downgraded from first quality to second quality.

Exponentially Weighted Moving Average. For measuring cumulative results (e.g., productivity over a long time period) the Shewhart control chart for attributes has limitations, particularly during periods when there is lack of statistical control. It is just during these periods that the plant manager will be most likely to ask, "How is the spinning room running?" Today's ends down rate may be very misleading, but the manager wants one number, and he does not have time to look at the control chart. In situations like this the one number used is sometimes the exponentially weighted moving average of the daily ends down rates. This number is an excellent estimate of the current true average ends down rate. It is calculated as follows: $u'_t = au_t + (1 - a)u'_{t-1}$, where u' is the exponentially weighted mov-

[9] Since the control limits depend on S and H, it makes interpretation easier if they are kept constant.

[10] The Classification of Cotton, U.S. Department of Agriculture, *Miscellaneous Publication* 310.

ing average at day t, u is the ends down rate for day t, and a is a smoothing constant.[11]

Table 39-4 illustrates the calculation of an exponentially weighted moving average. In this example a is set equal to 0.20. The choice of a value for a involves judgment covering several factors. Depending on the particular set of circumstances, a is commonly assigned values in the range from 0.1 to 0.6.

ASQC Fabric Grading Systems. A number of different fabric grading systems exist, but probably the most commonly accepted and used is the so-called "ASQC system" (sometimes called the "four point system").[12] In this system a piece of

TABLE 39-4 Ends Down Rates Exponentially Weighted Moving Average (EWMV)*

Day	Ends down per 1,000 spindle hours u_t	Ends down EWMV u'_t
1	13.27	13.27
2	9.22	12.46
3	16.41	13.25
4	18.63	14.33
5	7.31	12.93
6	5.75	11.49
7	30.40	15.27
8	16.63	15.54
9	9.68	14.37
10	38.94	19.28

* $a = 0.20$. When $t-1 = 0$, set $u'_{t+1} = u_t$

fabric is inspected for defects of every type, including those resulting from imperfections in yarn, weaving (or knitting), dyeing, printing, or finishing. At inspection a point value is assigned to each defect depending on its length in accordance with the following schedule:

Length of Defect, Inches	Point Value
Up to 3	1
3 to 6	2
6 to 9	3
Over 9	4

But no yard of fabric (in the warp direction) is ever assigned more than four points. After assignment of points to defects, the average number of points for the piece is calculated in one of two ways. Either

$$P_1 = \frac{100D}{Y} \quad \text{or} \quad P_2 = \frac{3,600D}{YW}$$

where P_1 is the average number of points per 100 linear yards, P_2 is the average number of points per 100 square yards, D is the total number of defect points as-

[11] See, for elaboration, Wortham, A. W., and G. F. Heinrich, Control Charts Using Exponential Smoothing Techniques, *1972 Annual Technical Conference Transactions*, ASQC, pp. 451–458.

[12] Giese, David W. (ed.), Standard Procedure of Quality Evaluation for Woven Textiles with a Manual of Defects and Imperfections, The National Shirt, Pajama and Sportswear Manufacturers and the Textile Division of the American Society for Quality Control. This is the one officially recommended to its members by the American Apparel Manufacturers Association.

signed, Y is the number of linear yards in the piece, and W is the width of the piece in inches.

This system does not attempt to define a good or first-quality piece of fabric, but it does provide a grading system which buyer and seller can use to describe the quality level. They can agree among themselves what is an acceptable quality level and the sampling plan to be used.

Fabric Color Shade Matching. Although some use is made of instrumental color measurement, no completely satisfactory instrumental way has yet been devised to provide a means of matching shades of color of fabric. Therefore, shade matching is done visually by inspectors who have been tested for color and shade perception and who have been trained in what is a commercially acceptable match. It is the general practice to compare rolls of fabric visually, and to pack in the same case only those rolls which are thought to match in shade. Even this is not good enough for cutting and sewing some garments, for example, fine business and sports shirts for men. For this use, no attempt is made to match rolls of fabric in the stack. Only those garment pieces cut from the same layer in the stack of fabric on the cutting table are sewn into the same garment. This ensures that all the parts of the same garment come from portions of fabric at most about 80 yards apart in the same roll.

The Responsibility Pattern In the textile industry, as in other industries, there are in use a number of different names for departments or groups which perform the same function. There are also groups which perform one or more functions. In some sections of the industry, the quality control function is executed by Manufacturing, together with the people associated with the laboratory. In this case when one says "the Laboratory," one means "Quality Control." Sometimes a group called "Quality Control," among other duties, operates the laboratory. "Engineering" usually refers to a group which is charged with the responsibility for construction, maintenance, machine design, and similar functions, but not with product design or development. Design of new products and redesign of old is done in some instances by a group called variously Research, Development, or Design. Especially in the fabric and garment parts of the industry, and for design of the aesthetic features of a product, the function is executed by a group called the Design Department. Table 39-5 indicates the most usual pattern of responsibility for the performance of various activities related to quality control.

The Data Plan After control stations have been established, and after decision criteria have been developed, it remains necessary to get the information, in an appropriate form, from the stations to the people responsible for taking action. As might be expected, there are many different data plans in use in the textile industry. They range from the simplest to the most complex, from simple indicating instruments to closed-loop controllers employing a computer with a built-in model of the process; from notes made on the back of an envelope to automatic input to a computer which prints analyses of the data with exception notices.

Mechanized Data Processing. Figure 39-6 is a generalized flow chart for mechanized data processing for quality control being used in the industry. Raw data are introduced into the system in various ways: directly from measuring instruments or machine status sensors (in the form of analog signals) to analog or digital converters, punched paper tape (from a special typewriter); punched cards; cards marked for machine sensing; and still other ways.

First, if required, laboratory-type calculations are made. For example, to obtain the linear density, expressed in denier units, of rayon tire cord one must make the calculation $D = 9,000W/L,$ where D is the calculated denier, W is the ovendry weight, in grams, of the test specimen, and L is its length in meters.

Next the data are examined to determine whether or not they should be accepted into the system. This gives some protection from transposed digits, wandering dec-

TABLE 39-5 Typical Responsibility Pattern for Quality Control Related Activities

Activity	Design	Research	Development	General engineering	Quality control	Industrial engineering	Manufacturing	Marketing	Customer service
Design and development of:									
New product	XXA	XXF	X	...	X	...	...	X	X
Modified product	XXA	X	XXF	...	X	...	...	X	X
New process	...	XX	X	X	X	X	X		
Modified process		X	XX	X	X	X	X		
Product specifications	X	...	X	...	XX	...	X	X	
Quality engineering	...	...	...	...	XX	X	...		
Processing and fabricating:									
Raw materials inspection and acceptance	...	...	...	...	XX	...	XX		
Process inspection	...	...	...	...	...	...	X		
Product inspection	...	...	...	...	XX	...	...		
Product and process audit	...	...	...	...	XX	...	...		
Inspection results coordination	...	...	...	X	XX	...	X		
Routing of in-process material	...	...	...	...	X	...	XX		
Release of product for shipment	...	...	...	...	XX	...	X		
Customer relations:									
Customer satisfaction	...	...	...	...	X	...	...	X	XX
Customer feedback utilization	X	...	X	...	XX	...	X	X	X

XX = prime responsibility.
X = collateral responsibility.
A = responsible for aesthetic aspects.
F = responsible for functional aspects.

imal points, and incorrect identification. Of course, there are occasions when out-of-line data should be accepted; so provision is made to allow overriding of the automatic rejector.

After acceptance, the data are reduced. For example, at the end of each week, a weekly average and range might be calculated. With the introduction of each new piece of data, a series of these data are analyzed in much the same way an engineer would do in looking at a control chart.

At this point it is a fairly simple matter to predict the value of the next observation, i.e., by exponentially weighted moving average.

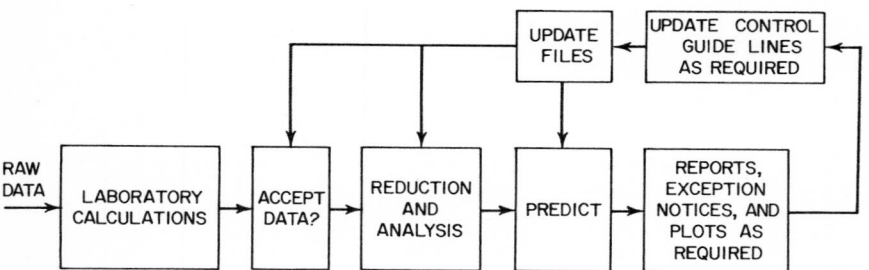

Fig. 39-6 Flow chart for data processing for quality control.

In the next step, in accordance with the results of the data analysis, reports, exception notices, and data plots are produced as required. In this step, exception notices may be produced which call attention to the need to revise control chart lines. Their revision is indicated in the succeeding block of the diagram.

Last, the files are updated, adding the newest data and discarding the oldest, substituting new control guidelines for old when these have been revised.

In some situations this system of mechanized data processing is not appropriate. Whenever it is required that an operator take action immediately, on the results of measurements or analyses made at frequent intervals, this system causes too much delay. For example, in the process of doubling and drawing staple fiber in preparation for spinning, one of the doublings and drawings of sliver[13] is done on a machine called a finisher drawing frame. The finisher drawing sliver goes next to a machine called a slubber, which produces roving.[14] At finisher drawing is the last chance to make effective machine adjustments in the linear density of the sliver, roving, and yarn without upsetting other characteristics of the yarn. Samples of finished drawing sliver are taken at frequent intervals, and linear density is determined. The results of these measurements are reported to the operator who plots a control chart for each frame, and uses these to guide himself in the adjustment of the frames.

Mechanized Data Collection. Many mechanized and automatic data collection systems are used in the industry. Two examples are loom stop recording and analysis, and yarn defects counting and analysis. In the first system, whenever a loom stops, a signal is sent automatically to a special-purpose computer. The stop and the length of time the loom remains stopped are recorded. The number of stops are accumulated in three categories, those due to a filling end break, those due to warp

---

[13] A continuous, ropelike strand approximately uniform in cross-sectional area and composed of loosely assembled fibers without twist.

[14] A loose assemblage of fibers drawn or rubbed into a single strand with very little twist; an intermediate state between sliver and yarn.

end break, and those due to all other causes. The machine efficiency is calculated for each machine and each category. Each day the data are summarized and reported by fabric style, loom fixer section, weaver section, and the three shifts. In addition, because this information gives productivity as well as quality data, the computer gives work incentive pay for the operators. In some systems the computer can be queried at any time for efficiencies from the first of the shift to the time of the query. Query and digital display stations are located so that operators and foremen alike may use them whenever they wish.

In the second system, broken filaments and slubs in continuous filament yarn are counted as the yarn is being beamed. Detection is done by sensing the interruption of a beam of light by a yarn defect. Each interruption automatically sends a signal to a special-purpose computer which accumulates the counts. When the winding of a beam has been finished, the operator, using a special-purpose keyboard, sends additional information to the same computer. This information is summarized in various ways, analyzed, and reported by the computer, including exception notices and control charts concerning the quality of the yarn being beamed.

The Audit Plan   In order to appraise the functioning of the quality control system, audits are made at various points along the production and distribution stream. Descriptions of some of these audits follow.

Patrol Inspections.   Manufacturing is of course responsible for seeing to it that the process is operated according to specifications. This means that Manufacturing inspects the process. Frequently, however, Quality Control will employ patrol inspections to audit Manufacturing's conformance to specified operating conditions such as proper thread-up and cleanliness of machines.

Inspection after Packing.   Usually textile materials of all kinds are given a cursory visual inspection just prior to packing. In the case of packages of yarn, every package is inspected; in the case of fabric, every yard of every roll is inspected; in the case of garments, every garment is inspected. A notable exception to this practice is in the plants which produce high-quality men's business and sports shirts and slacks. Here there are no final inspections at packing. As an audit of the quality control system up to this point, random samples are taken of packed materials. The packages are opened and are inspected for adherence to packaging specifications, for proper identification, and for conformance to product specifications.

Cotton Grading Control.   The Cotton Division of the Agricultural Marketing Service of the U.S. Department of Agriculture classes samples of cotton as a service to farmers. A farmer may have one sample classed from each bale he produces, free of charge. This is done in a number of different offices which service different regions. The quality of the classing is controlled very carefully. After a sample has been classed, it is retained for a period of time. From these retained samples some are selected at random and are reclassified by one member of a monitoring group. In this way checks are made on the original classers' standards, work station, and current practices.

Skip Bundle Sampling.[15]   In garment manufacturing, quality is highly dependent upon individual operators. Bundles of garment parts and partly assembled garments are passed along from one operator to another. Each person performs a limited number of operations using specialized equipment. The kinds of operations are turn and press collar, make buttonholes on fronts, attach cuffs, sew in label, and join sleeves to body. Bundle sizes range from about 35 to 100 units. Quality of

---

[15] For the original paper on this subject see Heiland, Robert E., Skip Bundle Sampling—A New Economical Method for Process Control in the Sewing Room, *Textile Quality Control Papers,* vol. 6, 1969, Textile and Needle Trades Division, American Society for Quality Control.

workmanship is largely dependent upon training, special instructions, understanding of instructions, machine setup, machine maintenance, materials, and supervision. Systems are employed to control these items.

To audit the quality control system, a technique called "skip bundle sampling" is used. This audit plan includes a feature which provides for a variable amount of auditing, more when quality is bad, and less when quality is good. The application of skip bundle sampling makes possible the elimination of final inspection mentioned earlier.

Four parameters describe a skip bundle sampling plan: n, the sample size, is the number of units to select from a bundle; c, the acceptance number, is the maximum number of defects allowed in the sample to permit a bundle to pass inspection; s is the skip interval, and $1/s$ is the average fraction of bundles sampled when the production is free of defects; m, the clearance interval, is the number of bundles to be sampled, following a bundle rejection, before random selection may be resumed.

Figure 39-7 is a diagram of the skip bundle sampling procedure. To execute the audit, one proceeds as follows: From $1/s$ of the bundles, on the average and chosen randomly, from the work of an operator on a critical operation, select at random sample of n units. Accept the bundle if there are no more than c defects in the sample. If there are some defects, but fewer than c, return the units with defects to the responsible operator for repair; then reassemble the bundle and release it to the next operation. If more than c defects are found, return the whole bundle to the responsible operator for sorting and repair. After the bundle is reassembled, take another sample of n units, inspect, and if the bundle passes this time, release it to the next operation; if not, return it to the operator, and continue this procedure until the bundle passes. Whenever a bundle is returned to an operator, begin sampling every bundle from that operator, instead of randomly sampling, until m successive bundles from the operator have been passed.

A typical plan would be $n = 30$, $c = 1$, $s = 4$, and $m = 2$. The allowable outgoing quality level (AOQL) for this plan is about 3.7% defective units for bundle sizes of 72 units.[16]

QUALITY IMPROVEMENT

Attitudes toward Improvement In the textile industry attitudes toward quality improvement cover the whole range from completely negative to highly positive; from "no improvement can be made in the quality of the product or of the control system" to "we want to be known in the industry as the producer of the highest-quality products." While there are some negative attitudes, in general, in all sections of the industry, there is a healthy climate for creative change. Such changes are actively encouraged by the industry's various technical and trade organizations.

Project Identification Since in our culture one of the primary objectives in operating a manufacturing enterprise is to make a profit, the identification of quality improvement projects can be accomplished by looking for the quality problems which cause the greatest avoidable cost. This concept is discussed in Section 5.

Organization for Improvement Sometimes when one asks, "what kinds of quality control coordination meetings do you have?" the response is, "weekly meetings take up too much time; anyhow, representatives of Quality Control and Manufacturing see each other several times every day." What is really being said is that their efforts in holding a weekly conference have been failures, and that because of this not much forward planning gets done, resulting in the necessity to meet daily

---

[16] For a discussion of how attribute sampling plans operate, see Section 24.

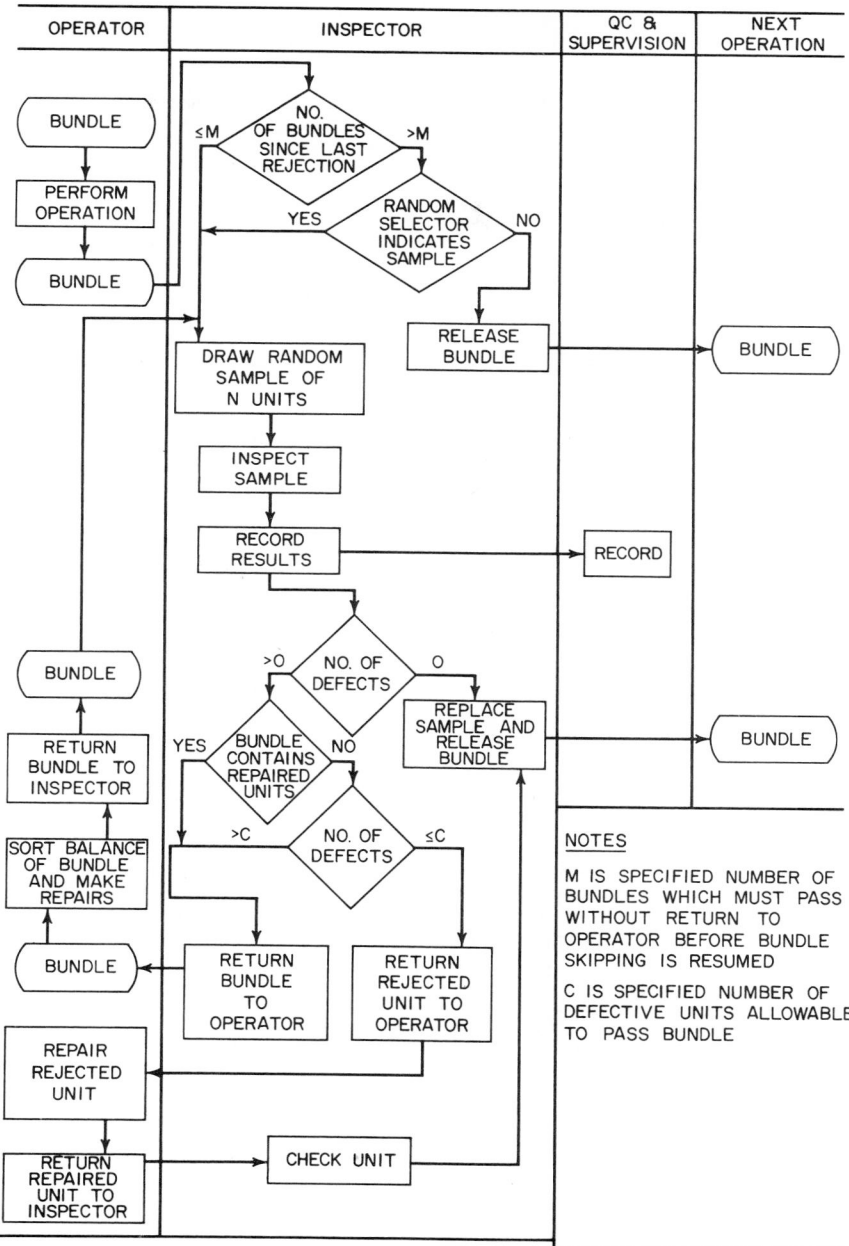

Fig. 39-7 Diagram of skip bundling sampling audit.

to take care of numerous emergencies which could be avoided with a little planning ahead. Too much time and energy is spent in fighting fires instead of preventing them.

Another answer to the question is, "representatives of Engineering, Development, Quality Control, and Manufacturing get together weekly and review the past week's performance. Action plans are formulated for study of problems or for overcoming them." This is much more useful than the no-meeting system, but it too

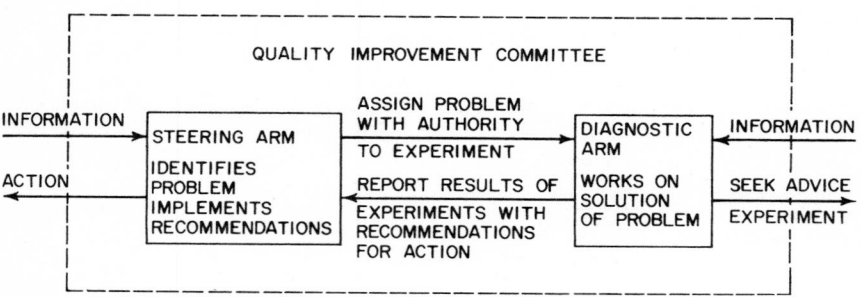

Fig. 39-8 Functions of Quality Improvement Committee.

has its pitfalls and disadvantages. Unless the conference is conducted with great skill, it will deteriorate into a session where each department tries to put the blame for the problem on another department, where no real diagnostic work is done, and where the subject is dismissed after deciding on a course of action suitable for a short-range solution of expediency, in the light of present knowledge or conditions, with no solution for the fundamental problem being found.

Juran[17] gives a complete description and discussion of the sequence of events by which breaking through into new levels of performance is achieved. Two steps in this sequence are the formation and activation of a "steering arm" and a diagnostic arm." Both arms are necessary.

An organizational technique used at the plant operational level in some textile companies to accomplish these two steps and to provide communication between these two arms is to institute the two arms with the following composition: steering arm — managers from Manufacturing, Development, Quality Control, and Engineering; diagnostic arm — a foreman from Manufacturing, a staff engineer from Development, Quality Control, and Engineering. These two arms hold a joint committee meeting once a week. Figure 39-8 gives a diagram of the committee's function. The steering arm assigns problems to its diagnostic arm for solution, suggests hypotheses to be tested, and receives and acts on the recommendations of its diagnostic arm. But the committee as a whole does not attempt to solve problems. It does not allow itself to discuss any other matters than those enumerated above. The diagnostic arm works by itself on the solutions of problems, testing hypotheses as authorized by the steering arm. The diagnosticians meet every day at a regular time for a short period for consultation and coordination of their own activities. They report their findings and recommendations to the steering arm. (For a generalized approach, see Figure 16-1 and associated explanation.)

Special Problems of Analysis Process capability studies and analysis of variance

[17] Juran, J. M., "Managerial Breakthrough," McGraw-Hill Book Company, New York, 1964.

(discussed in other sections of this Handbook) are invaluable tools to use in diagnosing troubles. These two statistical techniques usually suffice for the analysis of most textile problems.

Many Machines and Many Operators. Special diagnostic problems arise from two circumstances peculiar to this industry. It requires more operator attention than other industries, and frequently there are many machines (except in special cases, 400 to 1,800 looms in one plant) usually with many positions or with many ends of yarn. In such situations diagnosis is facilitated by plotting a control chart for each machine or operator, using the same control lines on each chart. This will make possible the identification of very good or very bad operators or machines.

Usually the correction for individual machine or position problems is to discover the differences between the good and the bad, and then make all of them like the good ones.

Usually the correction of operator problems is retraining. Training must include not only how to do the job, but also why it must be done in that precise way. Sometimes an operator may be working incorrectly, not because he does not know how to do it correctly, but because he is not convinced that what he has been told to do is necessary.

Visual Acuity. Sometimes one finds that inspectors and operators who depend on visual evaluation of their work will have very different performance records. This is often due to uncorrected defective eyesight. Because garment appearance in the retail store is the most important quality characteristic to the customer, fabric inspection and color matching in the weaving or knitting plant, in the dyeing and finishing plant, and in the garment plant are of crucial importance. Inspectors and color matchers should have their vision checked for both form and color acuity at least once a year. Charts for checking form vision are well known. Though less well known there is a simple, comprehensive, and scientifically valid test for detecting, classifying, and estimating the degree of defective color vision. It is the use of the American Optical Corporation's H-R-R Pseudoisochromatic Plates. Another very useful device is called the Glenn Colorule, obtainable from the American Association of Textile Chemists and Colorists. It consists of two rows of colored fabric swatches, each on a separate sliding bar, the swatches on the two rows being dyed with different dyestuff combinations. Use of this device provides a reliable means for the comparison and selection of light sources and color matchers.

Measurement of Garment and Fabric Characteristics. Mrs. Virginia H. Knauer, the President's adviser on consumer affairs, says,[18] "Many manufacturers of finished textiles evidently do not know the performance factors of the fabrics used in their products, and thus have a natural hesitation to suggest the proper way to care for them." With the coming of government requirements of permanent care labeling of garments, this lack of knowledge will pose quite a problem of analysis. To help in this regard, the Apparel Research Foundation, Incorporated, has published a booklet[19] which presents the details of minimum, intermediate, and advanced textile testing programs for evaluating the appearance and performance properties of materials and components used by the apparel industry. This booklet gives a list of eight pieces of equipment needed in the minimum testing program, and the information which can be obtained by using them:

1. Automatic domestic washer and tumble drier. The evaluation of the following properties after laundering serves as a check on claims made by the supplier, deter-

[18] Ray, Keith, What Nixon's Consumer Expert Expects of the Textile Industry, *Textile World,* March 1970.

[19] Blandford, J. M., and P. L. Bensing, Testing Programs for the Apparel Industry, Part I, National Bureau of Standards, Washington, D.C., 1968.

mines the compatibility of fabric and components, and provides information for laundering instructions:

   a. Appearance of fabrics and seams after laundering.
   b. Colorfastness to laundering.
   c. Delamination of bonded fabric.
   d. Durable-press properties.
   e. Shrinkage.
   f. Soil-release properties.

2. Balance, laboratory. Fabric weight of piece goods can be determined and checked for conformance to actual purchase specifications.

3. Crockmeter, standard. Evaluation of colorfastness to crocking (rubbing), both dry and wet, assesses whether coloring matter is transferred from a colored cloth to another cloth with which it comes in contact.

4. Dry-cleaning machine, coin-operated, available for use in local area (or local dry-cleaning plant). For use in determining the performance of bonded fabric in terms of delamination, shrinkage, and color permanence to dry cleaning; provides information for care label instructions.

5. Hand iron. Evaluation of colorfastness to perspiration and to pressing.

6. Spray test apparatus. Evaluates the resistance, to wetting, of fabric with or without a water-repellent finish.

7. Tape measure. Measure of the width of piece goods is always important information for any cutter.

8. Thread counter. Used to determine number of warp ends and picks per inch in woven goods, and wales and courses per inch in knit goods. Checks conformance to purchase specifications and possibility of improper finishing which could cause shrinkage problems.

Successful Quality Improvement Projects Illustrative of textile quality improvement projects are two recently reported projects successfully completed. Both of these have to do with garment manufacture.

Effect of Machine Settings on Seam Pucker. Paul R. Langston[20] reports the results of a study to determine the effect of sewing machine settings on seam pucker. By use of a fractional factorial experimental design and multiple regression analysis, he studied the relationship of five machine variables to seam pucker. The five machine variables were needle size, presser foot pressure, feed dog height, stitches per inch, and throat plate hole size. Seam pucker was rated both before and after washing.

In beginning his study, he made a literature search to learn what other work had been done on this subject. He found many tests described in the literature, but unfortunately most of them had the serious limitation that they showed only the relationships of single variables, but no interactions. In his study he found two interactions to be the most important variables affecting seam pucker.

The variables he found significant and in the order of their importance:

Stitches per inch and feed dog height interaction
Feed dog height and needle clearance in throat plate hole interaction
Stitches per inch
Needle clearance in throat plate
Feed dog height

---

[20] Langston, Paul R., Improving Garment Seam Performance, *Textile Quality Control Papers,* vol. 16, 1969, Textile and Needle Trades Division, American Society for Quality Control.

From his analysis he made the following recommendations to minimize seam pucker:

1. Use a small throat plate hole (0.042 inch) when possible.

2. Raise feed dog height, when using a small throat plate hole with a high number of stitches per inch (10 or more).

3. Lower feed dog height, when using a large throat plate hole size with a few stitches per inch.

4. Use as few stitches per inch as possible consistent with the quality demanded by the garment.

5. Use throat plate hole and needle tolerance of 0.010 to 0.020 inch for shirting weight fabrics. Use tolerance of 0.015 to 0.025 inch for heavier-weight fabrics.

Quality Control Cost Reduction. Richard D. Sikora[21] reports on the successful reorganization of the quality control system in a garment manufacturing plant, documenting not only the improved product quality but also the improved quality costs.

He lists the symptoms which demanded attention: high amount of rework and seconds; production bottlenecks in sewing room required overtime; reprocessing and rehandling caused excessive soilage; six to eight repair operators needed in addition to quality function; excessive fabric inspection in the cutting room; 10 to 12% defective outgoing packaged product.

He identified shortcomings which were thought to be causing the symptoms:

In-process inspection plan ineffective
Quality Audit inspection overstaffed
Too many bundles rehandled or reprocessed
In-process coverage inadequate
Insufficient identification of poor operators
Excessive number of cutting room inspectors
Ineffective operator training program

He also made a quality cost analysis. It was found that the total measurable quality costs for November 1966 were more than $18,000, exceeding 50% of direct labor earnings, and that not all quality costs could be documented. The distribution was much like that for the first quarter of 1967 shown in Table 39-6.

Analysis of the quality costs for the last quarter of 1966 (which were estimated to be in total $57,087), and of the list of shortcomings, led to a program for improvement. The program was outlined and implemented in December 1966. A target date for completion of this program was set at 8 months from the start. The program to be accomplished in five steps was as follows:

1. Develop an effective in-process inspection plan, and implement the plan at one station.

2. Implement the entire in-process inspection plan, and modify the quality audit inspection procedure.

3. Reduce the number of quality audit inspectors, create an additional in-process inspection station, eliminate sampling inspection conducted by main office, reduce the number of repair operators, and perform as much trimming at operations as possible.

4. Place the trim-inspection activity on a sampling plan, and increase the number of in-process inspectors from three to four.

5. Begin a formal garment fit and wear material testing, eliminate the need for cutting room inspection, and install incoming fabric inspection.

[21] Sikora, Richard D., Quality Costs! Actual Case History in the Garment Industry, *Textile Quality Control Papers*, vol. 16, 1969, Textile and Needle Trades Division, American Society for Quality Control.

TABLE 39-6 Quality Cost Distribution in Dollars (1967); Excluding Cutting Room

Source	First quarter	Second quarter	Third quarter*	Fourth quarter	Total
Failure prevention:					
Quality Control planning...	892	253	150	145	1,390
Quality Control administration...	600	600	450	550	2,250
Total...	1,492	853	600	695	3,640
Appraisal:					
In-process inspection...	2,599	2,523	2,367	3,485	10,974
Final inspection...	6,162	6,637	4,468	5,193	22,460
Quality Control audit...	780	780	780	812	3,152
Fit and wear test...			NA	147	147
Total...	9,541	9,940	7,615	9,637	36,733
Internal failure:					
Final repair...	6,855	6,221	3,404	3,389	19,869
Recut...	NA	174	422	451	1,047
Operator repair...	1,361	1,316	1,617	1,160	5,454
Finished seconds...	19,279	17,533	5,339	7,565	49,713
Finished thirds...	8,798	5,443	1,977	2,758	18,976
Garment losses...	3,004	981	141	395	4,521
Total...	39,294	31,668	12,900	15,718	99,580
External failures:					
Returned garments...	NA	174	422	451	1,047
Total...	50,327	42,635	21,115	26,050	140,127

*Contains 2 weeks vacation shutdown.
NA = not available.

Two objectives of the program were to improve the outgoing quality and at the same time to reduce quality costs.

The program was completed on schedule. Total quality costs per quarter decreased from $50,327 for the first quarter to $26,050 for the last quarter of 1967. Total quality costs as percent of direct labor dropped from a high of 45.9% in January to 18.5% in December. During the same period, direct labor personnel decreased 7.5%, individual operator earnings increased 10.8%, and the production rate increased 8.9%.

In January, 13% defective product was being delivered to trim and inspectors who were detecting 3% and passing 10%. The next December, the process was producing 3% defective product and the inspectors were detecting 1.5% and passing 1.5%.

Thus it was possible to improve quality, increase production rate, and reduce quality control costs all at the same time.

Analysis of Variables. Some of the pioneering studies in analysis of variables in the textile processes were by L. H. C. Tippett. For some of his applications, see his "Technological Applications of Statistics," John Wiley & Sons, Inc., New York, 1950.

For a classic study in process capability, leading to improved uniformity in carding of woolen yarns, see A. G. Klock and C. W. Carter, Woolen Carding Meets Quality Control, *Industrial Quality Control,* May 1952. This paper received the Brumbaugh Award (best published paper) of the American Society for Quality Control for 1952.

QUALITY PERFORMANCE NORMS

Following are some typical quality performance norms in the textile industry. These norms are estimates which were gathered during a private survey.

Quality Indicators by Process Performance Dyeing, printing, and finishing—10% of piece dyed goods must be redyed for all reasons to attain first quality status. Overall seconds in printing are 7.5%, 3.5% due to contamination, oil, dirt, mark-off, 3% due to printing defects, and 1% due to other causes.

Weaving—Efficiency of shuttleless looms weaving narrow-gage sheeting of cotton polyester blend is 95.5%; yield of first quality is 98.5%. Cotton (alone) gray mill seconds are 3%.

Tricot knitting—The defect rate is about 0.9 defect per 100 yards of fabric for 55 denier acetate in a medium-weight plain style fabric as it comes off the knitting machine. First-quality fabric yields exceed 99%.

Cotton spinning—15 ends down per 1,000 spindle hours is considered good.

Acetate yarn—95% of all cones of yarn produced are first quality.

Consumer Items Men's business shirts—2% of shirts produced are not first quality; almost all of these that fail to pass do so because of fabric faults. Two and one-half percent of the shirts produced are identified as needing repairs, and are repaired. (In the 1950s, 20% needed repair.)

Pillowcases—2% of cotton polyester blend pillowcases shipped to customers as first quality may have some form of defect.

Sheets—6% of dyed finished fitted cotton polyester sheets produced have defects which prevent their being graded as first quality; final inspection is 50% efficient; that is, 50% of the sheets which have defects are detected and removed at final inspection.

FUTURE QUALITY PROBLEMS

Future quality problems will be caused by the emergence of new fibers at an accelerated rate, competition of other new materials for uses which are now fulfilled by textiles, the fact that customers seem to be growing more demanding, and the increasing regulation of textile labeling by government. The likely ways of dealing with these problems will be through the increased use of field tests, the development of additional laboratory tests to predict field results, the development of basic quality standards for textiles voluntarily adopted by the whole industry, and the increased use of automatic machines and controls.

The industry as a whole is steadily progressing along the path of automation and computerization.[22] Now there are many dyeing and finishing operations with on-line continuous automatic controls of the various bath concentrations and conditions. In staple fiber processing there is automatic doffing, and automatic sensing and adjusting of sliver weights. There is an automatic pocket cutting and setting machine in pants sewing. With the flip of a dial a foreman or plant manager is able to get a report in seconds on the efficiency of 1,500 looms. All this makes quality control easier. Those plants without the new equipment and methods will have serious problems in keeping up with their competition.

BIBLIOGRAPHY

Fabric Grading

Blackmon, A. G., Portrayal of Fabric Quality through Point Grading, *Textile Quality Control Papers,* vol. 12, 1965, Textile and Needle Trades Division, American Society for Quality Control.

Wilson, Frank C., 100% Inspection—Fact or Fiction? *Textile Quality Control Papers,* vol. 13, 1966, Textile and Needle Trades Division, American Society for Quality Control.

Testing Textile Materials

"ASTM Standards for Textile Material," Philadelphia, 1969. Blandford, Josephine M., and Phyllis L. Bensing, *Testing Programs for the Apparel Industry,* National Bureau of Standards, 1968. In two parts. Part I gives description of testing programs for evaluating the appearance and performance properties of materials and components used by the apparel industries. Part II gives test procedures referenced in Part I.

Cotton Grading

"The Classification of Cotton," U.S. Department of Agriculture, 1965.

Garment Care and Labeling Instructions

"A Voluntary Industry Guide for Improved and Permanent Care Labeling of Consumer Textile Products," National Retail Merchants Association, 1967.

Use of Data from Customer Garment Returns

Peach, Robert W., How the Garment Manufacturer Can Make Use of Customer Returns Data, *Proceedings of the Textile Wear Test Symposium,* Raleigh, N.C., 1969.

Quality Control in Cotton Production

Ramey, H. H., Quality Control Concepts in Agricultural Production, presented at Annual Meeting of the American Society of Agronomy, 1966.

Motivation for Quality in the Textile Industry

Jones, T. Creighton, The Riegel Zero Defects Story, *Textile Quality Control Papers,* vol. 13, 1966, Textile and Needle Trades Division, American Society for Quality Control.

Process Control in Garment Manufacturing

Heiland, Robert E., Skip Bundle Sampling—A New and Economical Method for Process Control in the Sewing Room, *Textile Quality Control Papers,* vol. 6, 1959, Textile and Needle Trades Division, American Society for Quality Control.

Artim, Edward, Quality Control Manual for the Needle Trades, *Textile Quality Control*

---

[22] For a description of a new automated plant see Anon., Spring's $35 Million Katherine Plant: "A Buck Well Spent," *Textile World,* April 1970.

Papers, vol. 12, 1965, Textile and Needle Trades Division, American Society for Quality Control.

A Landmark in the Technology of Cotton Mixing

Denmark, J. B., Quality Control in Cotton Mixing, *Textile Division Supplement to Industrial Quality Control,* No. 1, 1952.

Dyeing Quality Control

Norwick, Braham, Color Quality Control in Textiles, *Color Engineering,* vol. 8, No. 1, pp. 39–46, February 1970.

Graphic Arts Industry

LAWRENCE J. SCHEWE

Senior Engineer, Printing Development, Western Electric Company, Inc.

INTRODUCTION

Graphic arts began as early as A.D. 770 when the Japanese printed from wooden engravings. Printing as an art, however, did not begin to blossom until the middle of the fifteenth century following Johannes Gutenberg's invention of movable type. This invention opened the way to coordinate the five basic factors necessary for a transition from hand-lettered manuscripts to books printed from type forms:

1. A supply of single letters cast in type
2. A method of locking the type into a solid form
3. A surface such as paper to receive the impressions
4. An ink to register the impressions on the paper
5. A method of bringing the paper and type form together under pressure[1]

From the middle of the fifteenth century until the latter part of the nineteenth century, printing by means of metallic type was the only process capable of reproducing reading matter in bulk. Other processes, such as etching, lithography, or engraving, were generally used to produce pictures and illustrations in a separate process.[2]

The next revolution began with the printing of the Nov. 29, 1814, issue of the *London Times* newspaper. It was printed on Friedrich Koenig's flatbed steam press, the first cylinder press utilizing a rotating cylinder to press the paper against a flat type bed, at a speed capability of 1,100 sheets per hour. In 1869, the *London Times* printed a newspaper on a continuous roll of paper from curved stereotype plates.

[1]"Pocket Pal," pp. 8–9, International Paper Company, New York, 1966.
[2]Strauss, Victor, "The Printing Industry," p. 8, Printing Industries of America, 1967.

Between 1870 and 1880, Richard Hoe of New York improved the printing press by developing methods for printing and delivering a completely folded newspaper from a continuous roll of paper.   During the next decade, composing and photo-engraving were improved with Ottmar Mergenthaler's Linotype in 1884, Tolbert Lanston's Monotype in 1885, and Frederic Ives' introduction of the crossline screen or halftone in 1885–1886.

The twentieth century developments have been so extensive that it may fairly be concluded that the printing and publishing industry is undergoing its greatest revolution since Gutenberg's invention.   A major direction of the recent developments has been high-speed automated processes, employing widely diversified and complex technologies.   A major example is in composition, where phototypesetting and computers are being used to set fully formatted pages at speeds of thousands of characters per second.   Telephone directories, for example, are being set at rates of two to three pages a minute.

Such developments have been a prime factor in the growth of the graphic arts industry, which has attained the status of a major United States industry, ranking tenth in industrial production and eighth in employment. [3]

While these developments have improved productivity and precision, they have been accompanied by customer demands for better quality, shorter delivery dates, and improved service.   In turn, printers are demanding increased speeds, more efficient operation, and lower costs.   Collectively, these demands, plus the revolution in technology, require a response, also revolutionary, in the approach to achievement of quality.   The prime thrust of the new approach is added control "before the fact" to ensure that large modern customers, with their complex requirements and their tight time schedules, are not placed in situations where they are driven to accept inferior quality because of the pressure of the timetable.   The nature of these supplemental controls and practices will be discussed in detail below.

"Graphic arts" as used in this Section refers to those arts in which impressions are printed from various kinds of blocks or plates by one of the four basic processes: relief (letterpress and flexography), intaglio (gravure), planographic (offset), and porous (screen process) printing. [4]

The scope of this Section includes fundamental principles and techniques of quality control generally applicable to these graphic arts.   The discussion is directed more specifically to the letterpress and offset printing processes, which account for over 90% of all the commerical printing performed by the industry.   In 1968, 50% of all commercial printing ($3.3 billion) was printed by offset, 41% ($2.7 billion) by letterpress, and 9% ($0.6 billion) by other processes including gravure and screen printing.   Use of the offset process for printing commercial work has increased so rapidly that in 1966 it surpassed use of the letterpress process. [5]

Gravure printing is largely excluded from the scope of this Section.   It involves a specialized process of etching the printing plates, and this process has featured a sophisticated form of detailed inspection by highly skilled craftsmen.   The gravure industry is in the process of developing modern methods for achieving a higher degree of scientific control for this etching. [6]

Quality of paper is vital to all printing processes, since most graphic arts images use paper as the medium.   For a discussion of paper quality, see Section 30.

While paper is the dominant medium, a great deal of printing is also done on

[3]General Business Indicators, *Survey of Current Business,* U.S. Department of Commerce, Office of Business Economics, September 1970.

[4]Strauss, *op. cit.,* pp. 2–7, 208–274.

[5]Bruno, Michael H., Printing's Progress in 1969, and Its Future for the 70's, *Inland Printer,* January 1970, pp. 54–55.

[6]Strauss, *op. cit.,* p. 251.

metal foil, plastic films, and many other materials. Each of these materials is "special" in demanding unique solutions to its printing problems. Space does not permit consideration of these special problems in this Section. However, many of the approaches described for printing on paper have a degree of application to printing on other materials.

Figure 40-1 portrays a typical flow of work in the industry.

QUALITY SPECIFICATIONS AND STANDARDS

Aesthetic value and artistic taste traditionally have been prime considerations in the historical development and growth of the industry. Such a strong tradition has had an inhibiting effect on the establishment of standards, specifications, and controls. Strong unions also have had a predominant effect on the industry's reticence to accept "radical changes." However, increasing competitiveness, demands for high productivity and efficiency, and recent scientific advancements have combined to demand that the printing industry create standards and specifications. Until such industry standards are created, subjective judgment and sensory perception must continue to be the base on which quality is judged, although variations in introspective judgments of quality are being minimized through the establishment of standards for individual jobs by many printers.[7, 8, 9] For small jobs and simple processes, these local standards can be made to work, and will likely continue to be used. However, for complex processes involving large-scale continuous production, there is no adequate assurance of trouble-free operation unless specifications and standards are established for materials, processes, and products.

Such programs of standardization must continue to be built on the sound base of experience over a long period of time. Processes and materials which are known to have given good results can be analyzed to arrive at requirements and tolerance limits. These requirements and limits are then embodied into formal specifications, which, if followed in the future, will reproduce the good results previously attained.

For example, the National Geographic Society has established quality standards based on experience over a long period of time for the following paper and ink characteristics:[10]

Ink:
  Fade-o-meter 64-hour test
  Spectrophotometer (process shades)
  Trapping
  Luster qualities
  Dilatant and thixotropic properties (tendency to thicken or thin with beating)
Paper:

Color of white	Wrinkle resistance
Finish (gloss)	Ink absorbency and holdout
Thickness (bulk)	Moisture content
Resiliency (cushion)	Tear strength (fibers)
Surface smoothness	Folding endurance
Opacity (show through)	Coating pick resistance

---

[7]Siren, Arne A., Setting Quality Control Standards, *Printing Impressions,* February 1966.

[8]Benzinger, Raymond B., Setting Standards for Quality Control in Publication Printing, *Printing Magazine/National Lithographer,* Part I, July 1964, pp. 64–66; Part II, August 1964, pp. 88–89.

[9]See also Section 12, under Sensory Qualities.

[10]Benzinger, *op. cit.*

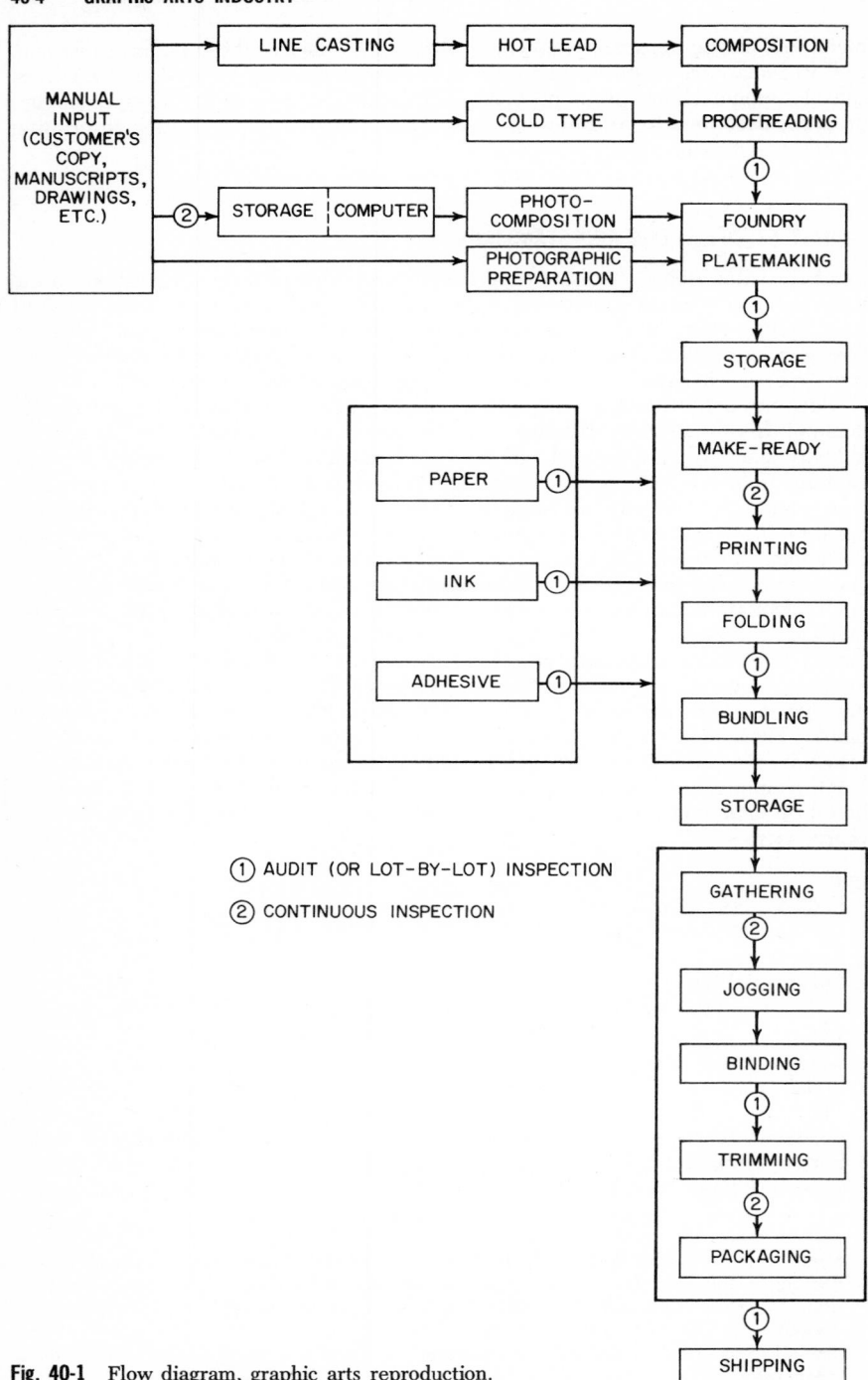

Fig. 40-1 Flow diagram, graphic arts reproduction.

Other types of operations may require additional ink specifications, e.g., for viscosity, pH, or tackiness of ink.[11] Standards for plates (such as material, physical dimensions, etching, relief, film density), presswork, and binding may also need to be established for those types of job runs where such characteristics are a major consideration in determining the quality of the final product.

Such standardization programs provide printers with a firmer grip on the three basic causes of most inefficiency and waste:

Wide variations in certain critical characteristics
Lack of accurate knowledge of permissible variations
Inability to control the output to meet consistently the stated requirements

Establishment of specifications is also necessary to remove the extremes of subjective judgment which are prevalent in the graphic arts industry. Once established, the specifications provide an accepted base for use by both production craftsmen and inspectors to judge the quality of product at any stage of production, and to predict the extent of difficulties which may be encountered in subsequent operations.

There are two basic procedures for establishing specifications in the printing industry:[12]

1. *Empirical.* This method involves experimentation, trial and error procedures over a long period of time, and requires a high degree of experience and ability from craftsmen, plus expertise in judging product quality. Such procedures have been successful in establishing specifications and standards for equipment and for raw materials such as paper and ink. In applying this method, characteristics are measured, recorded, and evaluated with respect to production problems encountered. Experience over a long period of time will permit the establishment of standards which yield the desired results for a particular press and type of product. The National Geographic Society example, above, is an application of this empirical method for establishing standards for characteristics of paper and ink.

2. *Scientific, statistical.* This method involves a control chart[13] or process capability[14] approach to measure and record specific characteristics of samples chosen over a short period of time to determine the quality capability of a process. The procedure is widely applicable to production processes, although it can also be used in conjunction with the empirical method discussed above.

For example, the tuck folding characteristics of a web letterpress were studied to evaluate the 6σ process capability in relation to customer requirements. A conventional control chart analysis based on 14 subgroups of 4 samples each showed a process capability of $6\sigma = 5.32$ (in 64ths of an inch). The study pointed the way to process improvement, and the improved result was $6\sigma = 3.06$ (in 64ths of an inch).

An example of a specification derived from such studies[15] is shown in Figure 40-2.

Aside from the benefits in greater uniformity of product and improved within-company communication, the product specifications are a constructive force for improved printer-customer relationships.

[11] Brawata, George, Color Is Major Factor in Offset Lithography, *Inland Printer/American Lithographer,* September 1967, pp. 82–83.

[12] Schewe, Lawrence J., Development of Quality Control Standards and Specifications in the Graphic Arts Printing Industry, a paper presented to the Annual Production Management Conference of the Printing Industries of America, April 22–24, 1971, Chicago, Ill. Published in PIA Management Services *PAR-lance,* No. 106, September 1971, p. 2.

[13] For discussion and examples, see Section 23.

[14] See Section 9, under Process Capability.

[15] Schewe, Lawrence J., An Application of Statistical Quality Control to Graphic Arts, *Annual Technical Conference Transactions* ASQC, pp. 209–220, 1970.

SUBSCRIBER DIRECTORY
DIMENSIONAL SPECIFICATIONS
4-COLUMN ALPHABETICAL SECTION

	Tolerance	4 column
Trim size of page[1]		
Width (inches)	$\pm \frac{1}{16}''$	9" (54¼ picas)[1]
Height (inches)	$\pm \frac{1}{16}''$	11" (66¼ picas)
Type size of page		
Width (picas)	$\pm \frac{1}{4}$	49½
Height (picas)	$\pm \frac{1}{4}$	63
Listing line displacement per page[2]	$\pm \frac{0}{1}$ per column[6]	428[7]
Type size (points)		7-solid[7]
Margins		
Top (picas)	$\pm \frac{1}{2}$	1½
Bottom (picas)	$\pm \frac{1}{2}$	1¾
Outside (picas) [1]	$\pm \frac{1}{2}$	1¾
Inside (picas) [1]	$\pm \frac{1}{2}$	3
Space between columns (picas)		Min ½
Column width (picas)	$\pm \frac{1}{4}$	12
Metal grade [3]		Hard
Type of binding [4]		Perfect[1]
Paper [5]		As Spec.

(1) The trim width and margins specified for 4 column are for 9" × 11" perfect bound directories. When side-wire stitching is specified, the trim width should be increased to 9¼", the inside margin increased by 1 pica, and the outside margin by ½ pica.

(2) Line displacement specified is based on type size of page, and includes 2 lines per column for running heads. The number of listing lines per page will be equal to (the line displacement/col. times number of columns) less (the displacement of the running heads/column times number of columns including the running head) (e.g., when 2 lines/column are used in 2 of 4 columns for running heads, listing lines per page will be 428).

(3) See QC 100.1 Para. 4.4.

(4) See QC 100.1 Para. 5.0.

(5) See QC 100.1 Para. 2.0.

(6) In cases where printer uses metal plates curved head-to-foot, the tolerance shall be $\pm \frac{0}{8}$ to allow 2 lines for curvature.

(7) When 6-solid type size is specified, number of lines/page shall be 496.

Note: When applicable, it shall be the responsibility of the Telephone Company (through its traffic printer) to furnish molds which meet the specified dimensions. (e.g., Stereotype, Electrotype, Vinylite).

Fig. 40-2   Product specification.

The prevailing state of specifications and standards is a changing mixture of the empirical and scientific. Generally, the leaders in the scientific approach have been the large suppliers (of machinery, paper, ink, etc.) and the very large printers. The remaining printers, while very numerous, have made only limited contributions.

However, it should not be assumed that a broad extension of scientific standards along with available instrumentation and other technology will convert printing into a science. Applying science in the printing shops to a degree comparable with that used in certain other industries (e.g., electronics, optics, fine chemicals) faces severe practical obstacles:

The prime test of fitness for use is still sensory (visual) and is open to subjective valuations along with the psychological problems of standardizing visual qualities.[16]

---

[16] See Section 12, under Sensory Qualities.

The user is concerned with the final product, after all colors have been applied and dried. The pressroom sees all this as an application of individual colors, and sometimes on proof stock which is not the same as the final product.

Many pressroom problems will remain on an empirical basis even if all materials were put on a fully scientific basis. The empirical know-how developed by the pressrooms is a vital input to any future standards and science for pressroom operation.

QUALITY PLANNING

The flow diagram in Figure 40-1 shows how the material inputs and operations of the main graphic arts processes combine to produce the final product. The flow diagram makes it evident that the quality levels attained at any operation are influenced, often decisively, by predecessor operations. For example, the flow diagram includes blocks for computer and photocomposition, because photocomposition is rapidly becoming a major form of typesetting. (A cathode-ray phototypesetter involves an expenditure of $300,000 or more, and can be justified only for large installations.)[17] However, when a computer and photocomposer provide a film output which is used directly to produce a printing plate, there is no opportunity for low-cost corrections. Hence the quality controls must concentrate on controlling the input to the computer.

Figure 40-1 also shows the quality control stations as they commonly prevail in the industry. The work done at these stations, and the formality of doing it, varies greatly with the size and sophistication of the printing company.[18] As a corollary, the extent of quality planning also varies greatly.

In the small shop, which performs only a few of the operations of Figure 40-1, and on a small scale, the experience of the owner and of the workmen may be sufficient to get the job done without the need for formal planning. However, in the large and even medium-sized shops, the operations shown in Figure 40-1 can each become departmental in size. In such cases, putting a job through all those departments takes on an interdepartmental flavor. The departmental foremen may be able to do much or most of their departmental planning, but they cannot do the overall planning in the absence of some coordination machinery.

Aside from the new need for coordinated quality planning (which is managerial in nature) there are new technological needs as well. The work of each department is influenced by the quality achieved in predecessor departments, so that process quality standards, process capabilities, and still other seemingly departmental matters now also have an interdepartmental character, and hence require coordinated quality planning.

Responsibility for Quality   The general industrial approach to quality planning is spelled out in Section 6, under Planning for Control. However, application of this approach to graphic arts is complicated by the lack of trained quality control engineers and by the deeply rooted tradition of reliance on craftsmanship. Because of this tradition, it is unlikely that the industry will accept a clean split of quality planning from execution (with planning to be done by the quality control engineers,

---

[17] Anderson, P. L., Phototypesetting—A Quiet Revolution, *Datamation*, Dec. 1, 1970, pp. 22–27.

[18] Historically, graphic arts quality was achieved by a combination of controls consisting of:

1. Craftsmanship and operator inspection during setup and running of the job
2. Sorting of good product from bad in case of errors
3. Reruns in case of customer dissatisfaction

These practices are still the rule in many small shops.

and execution to be done by Production and Inspection personnel). Instead, the pattern of responsibility for quality planning will need to recognize this tradition, and give an appropriate planning role to all concerned (management, supervision, operators, and inspectors) as well as to the emerging quality control engineers. In addition, the plans themselves will tend to respond to tradition by placing the basic responsibility for achieving quality on the craftsman.

Within this pattern of responsibility, the quality control engineer normally establishes the specifications, tolerance limits, and other requirements needed to make the product acceptable to the customer. In addition, he establishes the broad inspection and process control procedures needed to ensure that the specified levels are being met.

The inspectors perform the function of measuring the product at various stages of production to determine conformance to standards. They also record the data needed for analysis and evaluation.

The production operators (casting machine operator, compositor, pressman, etc.) retain the responsibility of setting up, running, and adjusting the processes.

Responsibility for Inspection   This responsibility is divided in several ways:

1. Operator inspection. The industry tradition of craftsmanship has placed on the operator the responsibility of inspection, for the purpose of making both process control decisions and product acceptance decisions. For many years this was the only inspection conducted, and this will likely continue to be the rule in the small job shops. However, the growth of the shops plus the interdepartmental nature of modern processes have required the creation of new forms of inspection. These new forms are designated on Figure 40-1 by the code numbers 1 and 2.

2. Patrol[19] inspections. These are the inspections designated by the code number 1 on Figure 40-1. The inspections are intended to assure that materials entering the processes are satisfactory. In addition, they check to see that various processes are performing at a satisfactory, economical level.

The patrol inspections are often structured so as to make use of tailor-made planning such as process capability studies and control charts. The inspections are carried out as a formal response to this planning, and the resulting data are formally recorded for subsequent analysis.

As is implied by the words "patrol" or "roving," the inspectors cover a "beat" of several stations. They travel from one station to another to take samples, judge the product, and record the data. They are fully engaged in patrol inspection work, and they report not to any Production department, but rather to the Quality Control Manager.

3. Continuous[20] inspection. (Designated by the code letter 2 on Figure 40-1.) This inspection work is done to guard against setup errors or sudden process changes which could create large quantities of defective product in a short time. In addition, it is intended to guard against certain types of process defects which the operator inspection alone is not able to control fully, e.g., machine errors which are difficult to control, or inadvertent operator errors.

The people performing these continuous inspections are physically stationed in a specific production department but do inspection as a full-time job (in contrast to production operators whose inspection work is always a part-time adjunct to the work of production). These inspectors are often employees of the Production Department involved, but they are not classed as production operators.

---

[19] "Patrol" is the term used in industry generally. In graphic arts, the terms "periodic" and "roving" are more usual.

[20] In other industries the term used might be setup inspectors, process inspectors, bench inspectors, etc.

The details of the inspections to be performed will, of course, vary with the characteristics involved, the speed of production, etc.   Moreover, the creation of these full-time inspection jobs is intended as a supplement to, and not a replacement for, the inspections which the operators and craftsmen must perform while regulating their own work.   However, as has happened in all industries, the introduction of full-time inspectors into Graphic Arts has raised some valid questions of jurisdiction.   In addition, there have been the inevitable differences of opinion, the misunderstandings, and the other consequences of introducing a new function into a going culture.   Some of these differences are inevitable because of differences in departmental goals.   Other differences are not inevitable; they have their origin in the personalities involved.   It all points to the need for choosing with care the men who are to guide the introduction of the new concept of inspection so as to minimize the frictions of the transition period.

The future of an "independent" inspection department in small and medium-sized plants is by no means certain.   In some companies, the new departments have been successful and seem destined to become a permanent feature.   In other companies, the new departments, though launched with the best intentions, have not been able to reach the objectives for which they were created and hence have been cut back or even eliminated.   Presumably, this fluid state will go on until the accumulated evidence suggests that one or the other of these methods of control offers a clear superiority.

PROCESS CONTROL

Printing plant process control procedures consist of three main categories: [21]

Setup Control [22]   This applies to stable processes which are not likely to change during the production run.   Hence, if the process is set up correctly, the entire lot can be safely run off, without the need for further inspections during the production. Examples of such processes are:

1. Placement of line slugs and engravings in galleys in the composition room

2. Imposition and placement of pages and paste-ups in offset plate preparation

3. Dimensioning of letterpress plates (i.e., squareness, beveling, curvature, thickness)

4. Imposition of plates (particularly letterpress plates) on plate cylinders of large presses

5. Adjustment of side-wire and saddle stitching mechanisms for proper spacing, length, and crimping of staples

A long-standing example of make ready or setup inspection is proofreading.   This has always been done as a separate inspection operation, and has largely been a duplication of checking which had already been done by the operators.   Yet the companies have continued to pay for the duplication, because the independent check has paid for itself in reducing the cost of subsequent rework and rejections.

There are many other areas where a similar independent check of the setup might be justified on similar grounds.   For example, side-wire and saddle stitches are often too long because the operator has neglected to readjust the mechanism when a different size of book, magazine, or pamphlet was run on the machine.   In the judgment of the author, there are many opportunities in the industry to use this

[21] Schewe, Lawrence, J., Development of Quality Control Standards and Specifications in the Graphic Arts Printing Industry, a paper presented to the Annual Production Management Conference of the Printing Industries of America, April 22–24, 1971, Chicago, Ill.   Published in PIA Management Services *PAR-lance,* No. 106, September 1971, pp. 4–5.

[22] The term "make ready" is used in the graphic arts industry to designate "preparation to run."   In this Handbook, the usual term is "setup."

concept of requiring an independent check by an inspector to verify the operator's setup as "OK to run."

Control During Production   This form of control applies to processes which *do* change during the production run.   For such processes it is not enough to exercise control over the setup; the control must provide for periodic checks during production.

Historically, the industry has done a great deal of such checking, relying on the operators to do it by informal, empirical methods.   This approach is in many situations obsolete, and "should" be replaced by more formal checks made by inspectors. This formality should include use of control charts as aids to detecting significant changes in requirements such as:

1. Raw material characteristics (i.e., ink, paper, adhesives)
2. Page pull tests (strength of adhesion in perfection binding)
3. Print contrast variations (ink density)
4. Film density of negatives
5. Paper spoilage during press make-ready
6. Web breaks per unit number of rolls
7. Collating or gathering failures per unit of time
8. Quantity of printed matter emerging from the trimmer with bleeding pages or improper trim

Printing plant craftsmen have commonly adhered to a philosophy of "do the best." However, the concept of what is best has differed widely among craftsmen.   Control charts are a step in the direction of achieving consistency among craftsmen as well as minimizing process variations resulting from subjective judgments.

Whether empirical control during production "should" be replaced by inspectors, control charts, etc., is by no means a universal conclusion in the industry.   While managers and especially engineers advocate such a change, the pressroom foremen, operators, and unions have yet to be convinced.

Quality Improvement Studies   In process control, the industry has emphasized empiricism, not science.   Faced with numerous day-to-day crises, and lacking a staff of scientists or engineers, the printer has traditionally resorted to ingenious, empirical solutions to his process difficulties.   This tradition has in turn fostered a spirit of "can do" and a pride in self-sufficiency through empiricism.

A by-product of this tradition is that numerous process problems which might be solved once and for all by a more fundamental approach have remained as recurring problems, either to be "solved" over and over again (but always temporarily) or to be endured unnecessarily.   The more usual categories of such recurring process control problems include:

1. Difficulties traceable to worn machine parts which were not detected or replaced in time.   (The real difficulty may be lack of a system of maintenance.)

2. Operator errors which started as minor inconsistencies in operating procedure and which, through continued use, became "standard operating procedure."

3. Usage of materials and supplies which were "just outside" acceptable limits but could still be used.

4. Inadequate protection against environmental effects.   An example is the handling of raw materials, particularly paper.   Many pressroom and bindery difficulties are traceable to improper packaging of paper, storage in unheated areas subject to severe changes in relative humidity, or use without proper conditioning.

Among printers there is a widely prevailing concept that such difficulties are inherent or special to the graphic arts industry.   However, numerous cases have demonstrated that the industry need not endure these problems—that it can apply the same tools for fundamental solutions which have been used successfully by other industries.

For example, thickness of printing plates has a major effect on the amount of ink transferred to the paper during high-speed web press operation. A study of variation in thickness of plates (Figure 40-3) made possible the establishment of standards which could thereafter be used as a basis for control.[23]

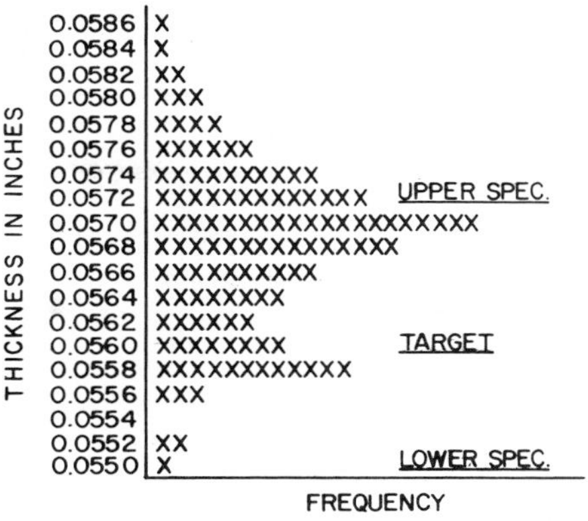

For some processes there is a pressing need to determine quantitatively the process capabilities and the time-to-time variation during the production run. Lacking this information, it is unrealistic to expect predictable performance. Examples which fall in this category are:

1. Certain raw material requirements (dependent on ordering, receiving, and plant usage procedures)

2. Film processing chemicals and mixtures

3. Error rates of line casting machines and operators

4. Error rates of composing room personnel

5. Page pull tests of perfection bound magazines and books

6. Accuracy of proofreaders

7. Signature folding capability of different types of folders and electronic cutoff controls

The resulting process capability data should be put to multiple uses:

Establishment of specifications and standards

Establishment of process control limits

Feedback to supervisors and planners to assist in quality improvement and defect prevention.

```
           0.0586 | X
           0.0584 | X
           0.0582 | XX
           0.0580 | XXX
  S        0.0578 | XXXX
  E        0.0576 | XXXXX
  H        0.0574 | XXXXXXXXX
  C        0.0572 | XXXXXXXXXXXXXX   UPPER SPEC.
  N        0.0570 | XXXXXXXXXXXXXXXXXXX
  I        0.0568 | XXXXXXXXXXXXXXX
  S        0.0566 | XXXXXXXXX
  S        0.0564 | XXXXXXXX
  E        0.0562 | XXXXXX
  N        0.0560 | XXXXXXX           TARGET
  K        0.0558 | XXXXXXXXXXX
  C        0.0556 | XXX
  I        0.0554 |
  H        0.0552 | XX
  T        0.0550 | X                 LOWER SPEC.
                    FREQUENCY
```

Fig. 40-3   Study of thickness of plastic printing plates.

ROLE OF THE QUALITY CONTROL DEPARTMENT

As a formal Quality Control Department is organized, it acquires a whole list of functions critical to attaining and improving quality. Two of these functions are the broad quality planning and the establishment of product specifications and standards, as discussed above. In addition, there are other functions.

Preparation of Inspection Plans   These consist of the conventional determination of the work to be done at each inspection station, and the criteria to be used.[24]   Application of this conventional approach to graphic arts inspection depends largely on the quality characteristics, type of work, size of plant, etc. For example, inspection of raw materials such as ink and paper may call for a variables inspection plan.[25]   Product emerging from a trimmer may be better inspected by an attributes plan.[26]   Sheets or signatures emerging from a sheet-fed or web-fed press may make use of

---

[23] Rickmers, Albert D., Statistical Quality Control; Application in the Graphic Arts, *Graphic Arts Progress,* March 1971, pp. 3–11 (published by Rochester Institute of Technology).

[24] See generally Section 12, under Inspection planning.

[25] See generally Section 25. See also Section 30 (as to paper). Although ink is measured quantitatively, the resulting evaluation is seldom used as a formal basis for acceptance or rejection.

[26] See generally Section 24.

variables inspection for some characteristics and attribute inspection for other characteristics.

In roving inspection the plan may be structured in any of several ways, as, for example:

Check of important setups, as in layout, backup, plate imposition, press make ready

Check following certain process changes, such as plate changes or check of pagination following press stoppage

Periodic sampling of continuous production, e.g., every 10,000 to 15,000 press impressions

The inspection plan also includes the inspection data recording plan. The design of this aspect of the plan requires:

1. Determination of data needed for feedback to Production and for management reporting,[27] e.g., summaries by machine, process, defect type, operator, shift number, etc.

2. Design of forms for data recording[28]

3. A planned procedure for inspectors to record their findings

Data Analysis and Evaluation   Inspection feedback to Production is commonly in simple, easily digestible form requiring little added analysis or evaluation. However, summaries for use of the upper supervision do require such analysis. In addition, the studies for quality improvement involve extensive analysis to discover trends, concentrations, etc.

Further data analysis is required for special studies such as process capability studies or designed experiments.

Quality Cost Analysis   The well-known approach to quality cost analysis[29] has application to the graphic arts industry. For example, one large printing company undertook to answer the question "How much less would it cost us to operate if we had no defects?" The analysis disclosed figures on "costs of quality"[30] as shown in Table 5-2 of Section 5.

The analysis made clear that despite all the work being done by the craftsmen, the quality costs were a major problem, and that little was being done to bring them down. The concentration of the costs was also evident, and led to the identification of specific projects for improvement.

As in most industries, the department most likely to come up with a quality cost analysis is the Quality Control Department. Of course, the analysis is but the first step in securing the improvement, since the defect prevention studies are still needed on a project-by-project basis.

Quality Improvement[31]   Usually the Quality Control Department is best situated organizationally to stimulate quality improvement programs. It can do this through identifying the chronic, "vital few" defects and conducting the analyses needed to discover the causes of these defects.

For example, a printing plant undertook to reduce the error rates in typesetting, composition, and proofreading operations. An attempt was made to stimulate the operators to reduce keyboarding errors. They responded with the assertion

[27] See generally, Section 11, under Inspection Feedback to Production, *et seq.* See also Section 21, under Executive Reports on Quality.

[28] See generally Section 19, under Forms Design.

[29] See, generally, Section 5.

[30] Private communication to J. M. Juran.

[31] See Section 16, for a complete approach to this problem. See also the discussion of quality improvement studies under Process Control, above.

that the typesetting machines made mistakes. This theory was tested by attaching tape control mechanisms to the machines under suspicion and cycling the same tape over and over again. It was found that the machines made from one-third to one-half of all the keyboarding errors! The results were a program to remedy the machine errors, and a more wholehearted collaboration from the operators.[32]

Other examples of improvement studies have involved use of data collection and analysis to determine folding capabilities of web presses producing 64, 72, and 96 page signatures at speeds up to 20,000 impressions per hour;[33] prediction of the effect of folding variations in the pressroom on the number of books with bleeding pages emerging from a trimmer in the bindery;[34] control of photographic film density to continually acceptable limits.[35]

Nominations for improvement projects may come from a variety of sources:

Disclosures from the quality cost analysis
Predominant customer complaints
Repetitive, chronic process control problems
Ideas from the inside: managers, foremen, craftsmen
Ideas from the outside: material suppliers, machine builders, competitors, customers

The Quality Control Department can play a useful role by collecting these nominations from insiders and outsiders, evaluating the likely usefulness of the ideas, and updating the quality improvement program periodically to provide adequate priority to the promising projects.

Quality cost analyses and quality improvement programs serve still another essential purpose—the justification of the very existence of a Quality Control Department. In an industry which clings to a tradition of process control by craftsmen, it is difficult to prove the value of successful process control activity and similar work done to hold levels and standards. In contrast, it is easy to show the effectiveness of successful improvement projects. The Quality Control Department that establishes a good record on reducing costs through quality improvement projects soon finds that its budgets have easier sailing. Its proposals for manpower to take on further projects are given the benefit of the doubt, and this carries over to its proposals for control efforts as well.

Customer Quality Relations A major customer relations function is that of investigation and evaluation of customer complaints. Almost all printing plants maintain procedures for such analysis, following closely the methods discussed in Section 15. The results of these analyses should, of course, be made available, on a case-by-case basis, to the interested company supervisors and to the customers involved. In addition, there should be periodic summaries, e.g., quarterly or annually, to identify complaint concentrations which are chronic in nature and require a fundamental remedy.

Some large magazine publishers make use of roving or even resident representatives in the pressroom. In addition, some paper suppliers send representatives to visit the pressroom periodically, as often as weekly,[36] to meet with representatives of *both* the pressroom and the customer. Such joint efforts are of many years stand-

---

[32] Grady, William E., and L. A. Seder, Statistical Quality Control in the Composing Room, *Graphic Arts Monthly*, June 1970, pp. 66–69.

[33] Schewe, *loc. cit.*; see also Rickmers, *op. cit.*, p. 5.

[34] Personal experience of the author.

[35] Personal experience of the author.

[36] See Section 30, under Customer Relations.

ing and have been helpful not only in solving current problems but in building a more scientific approach toward future operations.

Product Auditing[37]   The graphic arts industry is beginning to make use of the concept of rating the quality of outgoing product using generally the methods described in Section 21, under Product Auditing.   The plans in use involve classifying the product defects for seriousness, under a general set of definitions.   Figure 40-4 is an example of such definitions as used for classifying seriousness of defects in printed telephone directories.   The definitions are then used to classify each defect for

---

DEFINITION OF DEFECTS

Major Defects
   Class A: Very Serious, Critical—100 Demerits
Defects which will render any portion of a directory unusable and will surely result in adverse comment, criticism, or reaction by numerous subscribers (e.g., completely illegible or missing columns, pages, or signatures; misplaced, inverted, or completely loose pages or signatures; severely or numerous bleeding pages)
   Class B: Serious, Not Critical—50 Demerits
Defects which will render any portion of a directory (1 or 2 lines) unusable, or a larger portion difficult to read, or will (a) surely result in adverse comment, criticism, or reaction by a few subscribers or (b) probably result in adverse comment, criticism, or reaction by numerous subscribers (e.g., completely illegible, missing, or misplaced listing, line of type, or classified advertisement; partly legible or almost illegible portion of a column or classified advertisement)

Minor Defects
Class C: Moderately Serious—10 Demerits
Defects which probably will not render any portion of a directory unusable and (a) definitely will not result in adverse comment, criticism, or reaction by numerous subscribers but (b) may result in adverse reaction by few subscribers [e.g., difficult to read (distorted or fuzzy) listings or lines of type; dirty, wrinkled, torn pages or cover; duplicated lines of type; uneven ink distribution; objectionable show through; no margin]
Class D: Not Serious—1 Demerit
Defects which probably will not result in adverse reaction by subscribers (e.g., general appearance items which are not objectionable such as a very light smudge or dirty spots on a page or a slightly bent corner of a cover; staples slightly misplaced; margins which are slightly outside limits or skewed)
   Note: The degree of seriousness has been based on possible adverse subscriber reaction.

Fig. 40-4   Definitions of defects for seriousness classification.

seriousness.   Figure 40-5 shows a portion of an actual classification for telephone directories, the total list consisting of 129 defects.

   The auditing involves sampling the outgoing product, inspecting for the presence of defects, and reporting the results in demerits per unit of product.   The summaries are commonly charted for executive report purposes.

   An extensive seriousness classification of graphic arts industry defects is contained in a series of research publications of the Institut für Rationalisierung in der Druckindustrie (Institute for Scientific Management in the Printing Industry, Frankfurt am Main).   As of 1971 there were 31 such "catalogs," which collectively analyze quality characteristics of all materials used in the broader graphic arts industry (e.g., paper, carton, color, lacquer, glue, bindery materials) for all important reproduction techniques, the three principal printing processes, letterpress, offset, and intaglio, and for most of the products of the printing industry (books, pamphlets, packaging, and posters).   Each of these catalogs contains:

[37] Also called quality rating, product assurance, etc.

Subscriber Directory — Defects/Demerits List

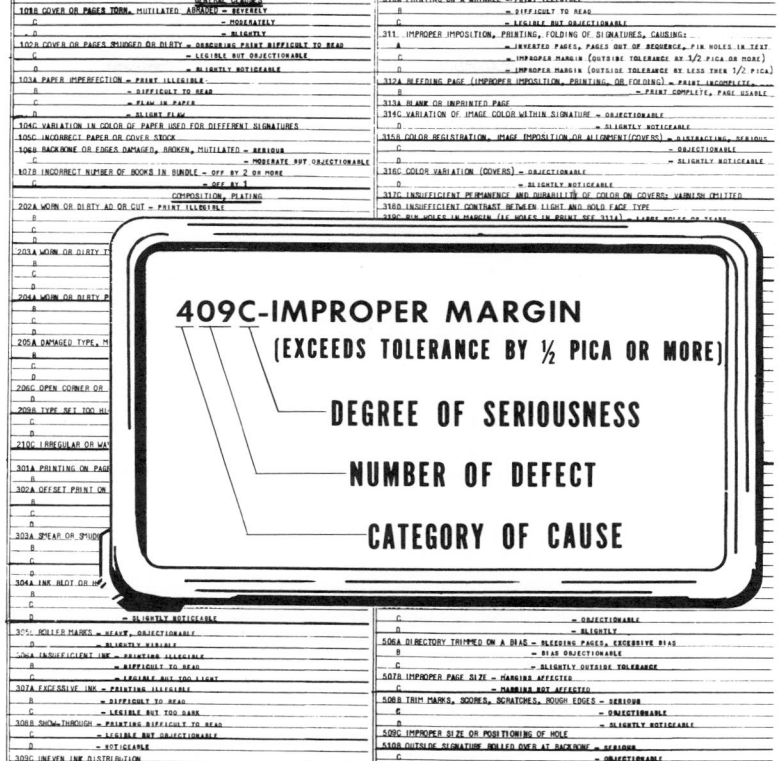

Fig. 40-5   Defect classification, telephone directories.

A listing of the respective quality characteristics. For each characteristic the possible defects are described, and are classified according to type and severity.

Reference to test methods for measurement, and discussion about possible test differences

Proposals for seriousness classification of possible defects into five classes (safety, critical, major, incidental, irrelevant)

The catalogs also show, as far as possible, the pattern of failure causes, classified by material, machine, prior planning, etc.

The extent of the research may be judged from the coverage: about 300 quality characteristics, 1,200 defect types, 140 defect patterns, and 1,100 defect causes.[38]

[38] For elaboration, see Müller-Rossow, K., Kataloge für Qualitätsmerkmale in der Druckindustrie, *15th Annual Conference, EOQC,* Moscow, June 1971, pp. 58–59. (Full paper in *Qualität und Zuverlässigkeit,* September 1971, pp. 197–201.) See also Müller-Rossow, K., and Hanns-Peter Lullich, Qualitätskontrolle in Faltschachtel-Betrieben, *Papierverarbeiter,* March 1970; also Müller-Rossow, K., Fehlerklassen und Fehlergewichtung, *Qualitätskontrolle,* December 1968, pp. 151–155. (All the above in German.)

Quality Reporting The pattern of quality reports discussed in Section 21, under Executive Reports on Quality, is appropriate for the graphic arts industry, though with some variations in application.

Summaries of results of process control inspection can be prepared in conventional manner, e.g., by department, process, defect type, etc. Trend charts and other graphic presentations are again conventional.

Progress in quality improvement is usually reported on a project-by-project basis, both for information and to stimulate participation.

Quality cost information has a high priority in an industry which has long regarded a quality control department as a nebulous overhead.

SUMMARY

The great advances made in the graphic arts industry have come mainly from the outside, i.e., from process designers, machine builders, and material suppliers. Contributions from within the industry have been less significant. This difference in scientific contribution is perhaps natural, considering the fact that the printers have consisted mainly of numerous small shops, each preoccupied with the day-to-day problems of getting out customer orders. Lacking the tradition of a scientific approach, the industry has emphasized empiricism, and has developed empirical skills to a high level of effectiveness. These skills, which still serve the industry well, are not sufficient to cope with the more modern and the future quality problems of the industry. The need is to replace empiricism with science, and some of the larger companies have already undertaken active programs to help meet this need.

In many other United States industries the conversion of empiricism to scientific quality control has made broad use of Quality Control Departments plus specialists such as quality control engineers. This method is one of the options available to the graphic arts industry, but it is unlikely that the graphic arts industry will go as fast or as far as have other industries in making use of this option; the craftsmanship concept is too deeply rooted to permit a revolutionary pace of change.

However, the movement to convert to scientific quality has already begun and is proceeding to influence company after company. For each of these companies the pace of change will necessarily be guided by its own needs, which in turn, are decided by such factors as:

The extent to which its products and processes are in the category of high technology

The level and nature of customer complaints and usage difficulties

The pattern of repeat orders, new orders, and growth

Individual companies have made some admirable improvements through use of scientific quality control. Some of these cases have been published, and collectively these demonstrate the capacity of the industry to solve its problems. The industry would be well advised to encourage its members to continue this sharing of knowledge for the benefit of all companies and, thereby, for the benefit of the industry.

A further major factor is the industry's view on training. The concept of apprenticeship and training is deeply rooted in the industry so far as original qualification and employment is concerned. In addition, some of the unions as well as the managements are quite progressive in recognizing the need for continuing programs of training to keep pace with the march of technology. However, the union orientation is strongly one of retaining the control in the crafts and not one of sharing this with a separate inspection department. This cultural resistance is a fact of life in the industry, and requires that any control plan based on independent inspection solve the human relations problems as well as the technological problems.

BIBLIOGRAPHY

A major source of reference material is the compilation "Quality Control, Application and Use in the Graphic Arts Industry," 1971.   Available from Rochester Institute of Technology, Graphic Arts Research Center, One Lomb Memorial Drive, Rochester, N.Y. 14623.   This is a compilation of abstracts of 195 papers and other publications dealing with various aspects of quality control in the graphic arts industry.   The dates are mainly in the 1960s and early 1970s.

See also:

Evanoff, Philip C., Current Trends in Papers and Printing, *Inland Printer/American Lithographer,* March 1970, pp. 33–44.

Hull, Harry H., Use and Misuse of Instruments in the Control of the Quality of the Printed Product, *Transactions 1972 Technical Conference, ASQC,* pp. 295–300.

Jaspert, W. P., Web Offset in Europe Today, *Lithoprinter,* October 1969, pp. 26–40.

Kelley, Edward J., Web-offset Pressman Must Watch Dots, *Inland Printer/American Lithographer,* March 1970.

King, Charles F., Color Proofing, Platemaking: Keys to Quality Assurance, *Inland Printer/American Lithographer,* May 1970, pp. 104–106.

Kolb, Edwin R., Computer Printing Forecast for '70's, *Datamation,* Dec. 1, 1970, pp. 28–31.

Lehrer, Leo, The Problem of Film Control Strips, *Printing Impressions,* May 1969.

Linebarger, John S., and James L. O'Brien, Quality Control Applied to Printing, *Administrative Applications Division Conference Transactions, American Society for Quality Control,* Mar. 13, 1970, pp. 3J1–3J21.

"NPIRI Test Method Index for Printing Inks, Raw Materials and Related Products", 1st edition, September 1969, National Printing Ink Research Institute, Lehigh University, Bethlehem, Pa.

Sitterley, Eugene Fletcher, Effective Quality Control Is More than Inspection, *Inland Printer/American Lithographer,* August 1968, pp. 52–53.

Thomas, D. W., Chairman, Handbook Committee; Bonnie B. Small, Chairman, Writing Committee, et al. "Statistical Quality Control Handbook," Western Electric Company, 1956, third printing, June 1967.

Whitney, James R., Printing Production and Offset Quality Control at the National Geographic Society, *Inland Printer/American Lithographer,* May 1970, pp. 91–94, 98, 101.

Winkler, J. Homer, How Research and Development Spark the Printing Industry, *Inland Printer/American Lithographer,* November 1968, pp. 37–41.

Assembly Quality Control[1]

A. J. HITZELBERGER

Motorola, Inc., Franklin Park, Illinois

INTRODUCTION

Most products are built from numerous basic materials or parts, progressing through a series of assemblies into subcomponents, components, units, equipments, subsystems, and systems. Many assembly techniques are available: mechanical, metallurgical, chemical, etc. The final products exhibit the many end-use characteristics needed by an industrial civilization: mechanical, electronic, optical, etc.

Despite the enormous numbers of combinations of input materials, assembly processes, and end-use characteristics, there are some major aspects of quality which are common to all assemblies:

1. "Cradle to grave" planning. The complexity of most assemblies, plus the needs for high reliability and long life, requires that extensive planning precede the conduct of operations. Most of this planning is discussed in other Sections of this Handbook:

Broad planning of major projects . . . . Section 6
Planning of new products, reliability, etc. . . . . Section 8
Manufacturing planning . . . . Section 9
Inspection and test planning . . . . Section 12

The special problems of assembly planning are discussed in the present Section 41.

2. Quality of materials and parts. To a considerable extent, quality of assembled products depends on the quality of the input materials. This problem is discussed generally in Section 10. The special quality problems of mechanical and electronic components are discussed in Sections 37 and 38, respectively.

---

[1] For the Second Edition, this Section was prepared by Albert E. Aubin.

3. Quality during production. Assembly operations create a great many intermediate quality characteristics, requiring detailed specifications and strict process control. The applications to assembly work are discussed below.

4. Inspection and test. This is likewise conducted at many intermediate stations as well as for end-use characteristics. The general approach is discussed in Sections 12 and 13, and some applications are discussed below.

The present Section 41 is devoted to the application of these and other recognized broad approaches to the special problems of assembly. Wherever possible, these applications are generalized to be representative of all types of assembly. Because the author's main background and experience have been in electronic products, his examples exhibit an "electronic flavoring." For added discussion relative to assembly of mechanical apparatus, see Sections 42 and 43.

THE CONTROL PLAN

The concept of cradle to grave planning is diagramed in Section 6, Figure 6-3. A flow diagram for an assembly-type industry (automotive products) is shown in Section 42, Figure 42-1. Of special significance for control of assembly quality is the proliferation of detailed standards and requirements, as projects for assembled products advance beyond the stages of market research and product development. The many parts to be bought or made require standards, tools, gages, and methods. These same needs extend to the many assembly and control stations through which the progressive stages of subassembly finally converge into final assembly. (See Section 9, Figure 9-2, for the concept of this assembly "tree.") This convergence puts special burdens on final inspection and test, which is the last opportunity, prior to consumer usage, to detect prior errors, poorly calculated risks, and compromises.

Experience has shown that it is bad economics to leave it to this final inspection and test to detect all errors. In consequence, modern methods of assembly quality control aim to:

1. Minimize errors through adequate new design control and preproduction planning.

2. Detect and correct as many errors as possible in the component, or preassembly stages.

3. Detect and correct those errors which do get through to the assembly stage.

4. Provide for detection and correction of those defects which reach the user or which become evident during usage.

The plan of responsibilities for carrying out these aims follows generally that depicted in Section 6, Table 6-2.

The emphasis in the discussion which follows is on preproduction activities to prevent defects, and on detection and correction of errors which get through to the assembly stage.

CUSTOMER-CONSUMER RELATIONS

Figure 41-1 shows the seven major channels of sale for most assembled products.

Sales in channels 1 and 2 often undergo a degree of acceptance inspection, so that feedback data are usually available and prompt. In contrast, sales through the remaining channels do not automatically yield such data, so that special provisions must be made for this purpose, over and above the program of in-house quality and reliability testing.

Sales to Distributors (Figure 41-1, channel 3) Some distributors (and dealers) purchase in large volume (though they sell to consumers one at a time). One approach for securing feedback is to select certain servicing dealers as special data sources. A joint data program is worked out, and the dealers are given an agreed extra compensation to provide the data called for by the program.

A further approach, used with selected distributors who have product test facilities, is a program of "open and test." This is done on a sampling basis related to quantities purchased, and in collaboration with the manufacturer's field representatives.

Data such as the foregoing serve two main purposes:

1. A prompt feedback of troubles encountered
2. A source of analysis, and of correlation with other data (see below)

Sales to Consumers (Figure 41-1, channels 4 through 7) These sales are made one at a time to consumers who lack test facilities and even technical knowledge of the product. However, they are able to respond in other ways.

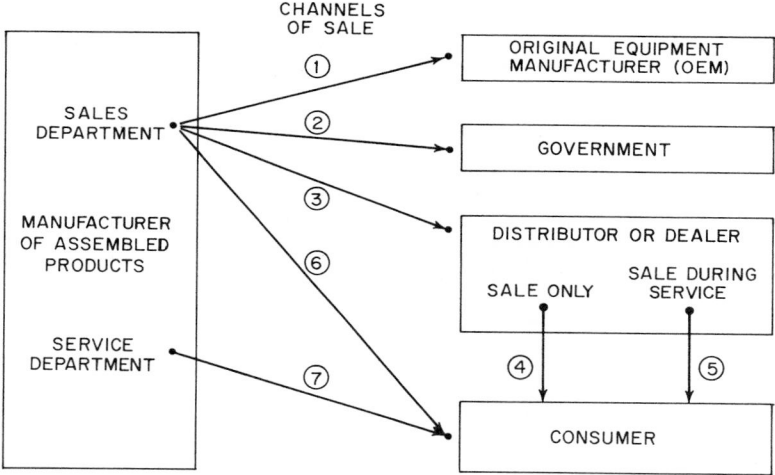

Fig. 41-1   Channels of sale.

One technique in wide use is the "arrival card." This is a prepaid business reply-card (Figure 41-2)[2] included with some or all the product shipped.[3]

Experience with arrival cards suggests that:

1. A return rate of 8 to 10% is regarded as good.[4]

2. Customers who encounter problems are more likely to reply than those who do not. A ratio of four "bad" to one "good" is normal on some types of product.

3. The cards must be date-coded by date of manufacture, since the most meaningful analysis must relate the data back to the conditions prevailing at the time of manufacture.

4. The analysis must take account of the time interval between date of manu-

---

[2] Figure 41-2 shows only the data feedback portion of the card. The reverse is the mailing address and preprinted postal permit. In addition, the card may include the manufacturer's appeal for data, some propaganda, some market research questions, etc.

[3] Where the number of units sold is very large, sampling is used to avoid being overwhelmed by data.

[4] Some manufacturers offer incentives, e.g., "trading stamps," for each card returned by the service depot.

facture and date of sale. Failing this, it is easy to be trapped into immediate and unwarranted process action. (Time lag between date of manufacture and date of sale normally averages about 6 months.)

5. Return card data can be verified and amplified by in-depth questionnaires, or by interviews.[5] (Personalized questionnaires sent to consumers who have identified themselves on the return card yield returns as high as 80%.) From the date the product first went into operation, and from industry data on average daily usage, it

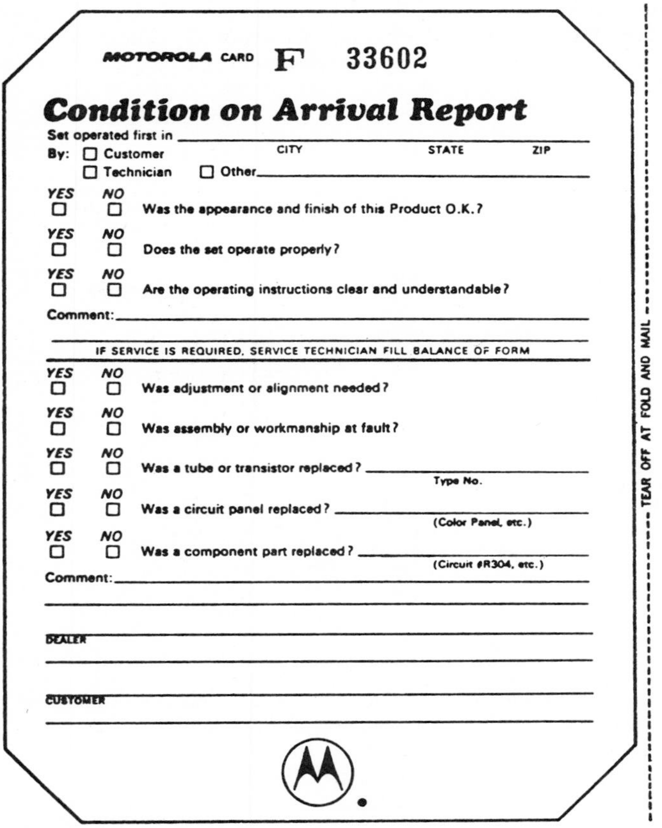

MOTOROLA CARD F 33602

Condition on Arrival Report

Set operated first in ______ CITY STATE ZIP

By: ☐ Customer ☐ Technician ☐ Other______

YES NO ☐ ☐ Was the appearance and finish of this Product O.K.?

YES NO ☐ ☐ Does the set operate properly?

YES NO ☐ ☐ Are the operating instructions clear and understandable?

Comment: ______

IF SERVICE IS REQUIRED, SERVICE TECHNICIAN FILL BALANCE OF FORM

YES NO ☐ ☐ Was adjustment or alignment needed?

YES NO ☐ ☐ Was assembly or workmanship at fault?

YES NO ☐ ☐ Was a tube or transistor replaced? ______ Type No.

YES NO ☐ ☐ Was a circuit panel replaced? ______ (Color Panel, etc.)

YES NO ☐ ☐ Was a component part replaced? ______ (Circuit #R304, etc.)

Comment: ______

DEALER ______

CUSTOMER ______

TEAR OFF AT FOLD AND MAIL

Fig. 41-2 Arrival card.

is possible to derive estimates of Mean Time Between Failures, and to compare these with in-house reliability test results.[6]

Data Analysis[7] Beyond the analysis discussed above, it is most useful to correlate data from all sources: dealers, consumers, and in-house testing.

Arrival cards are summarized by quarter (or month). (The negative comments

[5] See Section 43, under Quality Assurance—Measures of Field Performance.

[6] The questionnaire may also be designed to provide data on field service performance.

[7] In connection with analysis of data, see Section 15, under Significance of Field Complaints; also under Field Performance Measures. See also Section 21, Figure 21-6 and related discussion. See also Section 42, under Field Service. See also Section 43, under Quality Assurance.

may be subdivided by categories of defects, e.g., electrical, mechanical, cabinetry, etc.) These data can be charted.

"Open and Test" data can be summarized and charted by quarters, based on date of manufacture.

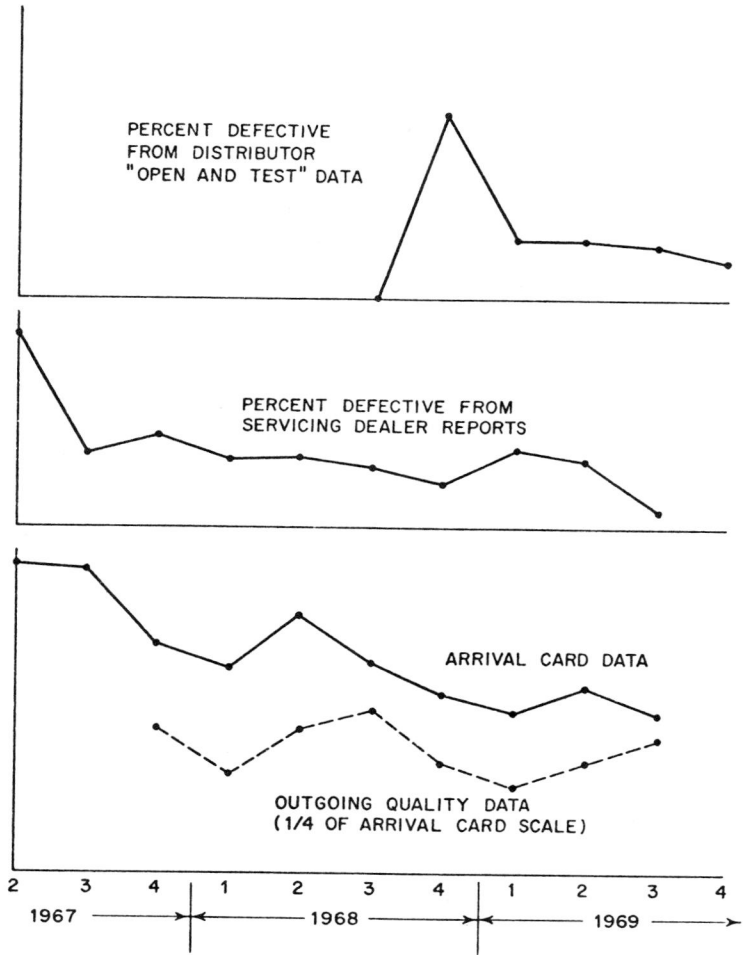

Fig. 41-3 Quarterly correlation of product quality d...a.

Reports from servicing dealers can likewise be charted by quarters, based on date of manufacture.

Because all data are related back to date of manufacture, it becomes feasible to place all charts on a single sheet for comparison.[8] See Figure 41-3, which shows

[8] In some presentations, each chart is drawn on a separate transparent sheet. These sheets can then be superimposed to see the relationships among the individual charts.

several of these graphs in the correct time relationship (based on common dates of manufacture).

NEW PRODUCT CONTROL

Launching of new assembled products involves the conventional phases of product development discussed in Section 8. As the new development progresses into manufacture, the pilot production run is widely used as a means for getting early warning of trouble ahead, and to provide time for investigation and solution of problems prior to making the scheduled full production runs.

The general approach to this pilot run is discussed in Section 9 (under Design of the Manufacturing Process). Applied to assembled products, there are some aspects of the pilot run procedure which require special attention.

Engineering Tests. Samples of initial product should be checked for conformance to engineering specification. These checks should be conducted using the planned Quality Test Instructions. In addition, each unit of product should be fully inspected for good workmanship practices. [9]

All data should be logged, and this log should include the list of specifications against which the inspections and tests were conducted. The results should be summarized and fed back to all interested departments.

Packed Product Tests. These are conducted on samples which have been completed and packaged. The prescribed tests should be performed.

In addition, attention must be paid to the qualities which are evident to the user. Finish and appearance should be checked as well as those functions which the user can sense. The information contained in the owner's manual should be reviewed carefully; *look for errors, omissions, or vague instructions.*

The analysis of these test data should include a comparison with performance of similar prior models. The reports should include comments on changes needed to improve the acceptability of products in the field.

A quantity of the accepted products should be held for shipping tests, drift tests, and life tests.

Shipping Tests. These are conducted to assure that a good product, well protected, will be able to perform its intended functions when it arrives at its final destination. Test programs include inclined impact tester, vibration, shake, drop, etc.

Drift Tests. These are used to determine the stability of the new product, i.e., changes in characteristics with the passing of time. These tests are both short-term and long-term in nature.

Life Tests. Pilot run models are also tested to determine the reliability of the product. The number of units tested varies with the nature of the product. For television receivers, a minimum of 10 units is required for significant information.

Start of Production. In large-volume production, it is advisable to submit the first 500 to 1,000 units of product to a short (4- to 16-hour) life test under mild overstress conditions, e.g., 10% overvoltage, speed, pressure, etc. [10] The resulting failures are subjected to intensive analysis for cause and remedy.

Some Universals for Pilot Run Testing. For test results to be valid predictors of product performance, the pilot run should simulate the final production conditions as closely as possible. The units should be built by the trained crew which will, in due course, become the instructors for the regular production forces. In addition,

[9] As to inspection and test generally, see Section 12.

[10] The number on test and the duration of the test must be adjusted to fit the variables of production quantities, complexity of design, nature of characteristics, and likely duration of model.

the input parts and materials should be representative of the variations which will be encountered during full-scale production; i.e., they should not be specially selected for uniformity. At the same time, these parts should have undergone prior measurement so that they are known to be conforming to their respective specifications, or at the least that they are "dynamically operative," i.e., fit for use. Failure to use parts of known prior status can reduce the value of the pilot run by burdening the analysis with problems of nonconforming parts.

There are some universals for test and analysis as well. Measurements should be made on a variables basis, and process capabilities[11] should be determined for the principal control points. All problems evident from the test and analysis should be followed up; the pilot run is only a small part of the total production-to-be, and even one deviation in the pilot run can be expected to multiply in mass production.

CONTROL DURING MANUFACTURE[12]

Typically, "new product planning" does a thorough job of planning for manpower, materials, and equipment. This same planning also provides for production methods and procedures to be worked out before full-scale production starts. In addition, the planning provides final test procedures. What has often been neglected is the planning needed for complete process control during manufacture.

Assembly Process Specifications All control is carried out through feedback loops, one for each control subject or control point. Application of this simple principle to the assembly job requires first that there be identified, with precision, just what is it that needs to be controlled during manufacture in order for the final product to serve the needs of the user. This identification is commonly done through establishment of control specifications which define the characteristics to be controlled.

These characteristics must be defined in measurable terms or in other ways which permit objective appraisal against a standard. There should also be an allowable tolerance to take care of normal processing and material variations. Establishing such standards in measurable form takes a good deal of technical skill, especially for processes which are new and complex. Setting such standards also takes a good deal of persistence, since the job must be done under considerable pressure from the planning timetable. However, such persistence pays off by eliminating vagueness which can create later delays at higher cost. Failure to persist in setting these assembly process specifications is a form of incomplete planning. In due course the planning will have to be completed anyhow, but under even more difficult circumstances.

Figure 41-4 is an example of a process specification of the type needed for assembly processes. *A similar specification is needed for each and every assembly process.*

Measurement Preparation of assembly control specifications must be paralleled by provision of adequate methods of measurement as discussed in Sections 12 and 13. Where the characteristics are of a sensory nature for which no measuring instruments are in existence, the methods available in Section 12, under Sensory Qualities, can be used.

Organization of Control Stations Once assembly process specifications, tolerances, and measurement capability have been set up, it remains to establish the feedback

---

[11] See Section 9, under Process Capability.

[12] The nature of the feedback loop for control is discussed generally in Section 6, under Planning for Control. The broad approach to control during manufacture is discussed under various headings in Sections 9 and 11, while related control activities through inspection and test are discussed in Section 12.

ACCEPTABLE SOLDER CONNECTIONS FOR VARIOUS TYPES OF COMPONENT AND HOLE LAYOUTS ON PRINTED CIRCUITS, ETCHED, SINGLE-SIDE PANELS

1. Soldering

    a. Bonding coverage should be in accordance with Table PC-1 for various components.

    b. Rosin connections. Doubtful, grainy, or flux-covered connection should be checked by exerting slight pressure on the component or lead, and noting if connection is secure.

    c. Potential shorts. Contact or potential contact between two dissimilar circuits due to solder bridging, where slight flexing of panel creates a short, is unacceptable.

    d. Dross. Evidence of "dross" (solder pot surface oxides) on panel is unacceptable. Contact Maintenance personnel when this is noted.

    e. Appearance. Refer to illustrations A, B, C, D, E, F, and W for judging acceptability of printed circuit solder connections. (Only A and B are shown below.)

2. Component Leads

    a. Excessive lead penetration. Leads should not penetrate more than ⅛ inch from underside of panel. Some areas require less penetration to prevent shorting with subsequent assemblies. Refer to illustrations or prototypes for critical lead penetration requirements.

    b. Lead-outs and tilted components. Component leads that do not penetrate bottom of panels should be inspected by exerting slight upward pressure on the lead to determine if it is securely soldered. Particular attention should be given to tilted components. Tilted transformers or other multiterminal components should be checked as follows:

. . . .

3. Printed Panel Deviations

    a. Solder Resist Flaking. . . . .

    b. Off Registry Copper on Printed Circuits . . . .

    c. Cracked Panels. . . . .

    d. Open Copper Print . . . .

    e. Lifted Copper. . . . .

    f. Mounting Holes. . . . .

    g. Interconnecting Receptacles . . . .

. . . .

TABLE PC-1*

Components	Figure	Hole layout	Terminals, min. hole closure 100%	75%	50%
Capacitor, small tubular (horiz.-flush mount)	N	F	0	2	0
Capacitor, small tubular (clinched lead).	N	W	0	0	2
Capacitor, small tubular (vertical mount).	P	F	1	1	0
Diodes (horiz. or vert. mount).	R	F	0	2	0
Diodes (clinched lead)	R	W	0	0	2

. . . .

*Numbers in last three columns indicate the number of leads for that component and minimum hole closure for the lettered figures. This specification was excerpted from a comprehensive solder treatise by James Alopondis of Motorola, Inc.

PRINTED CIRCUIT SOLDER CONNECTIONS

FIGURE "A" FLAT TERMINALS RECTANGULAR HOLES

 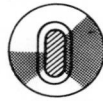

100%   75%   50%   LESS THAN 50% UNACCEPTABLE

Fig. 41-4 Assembly process specification.

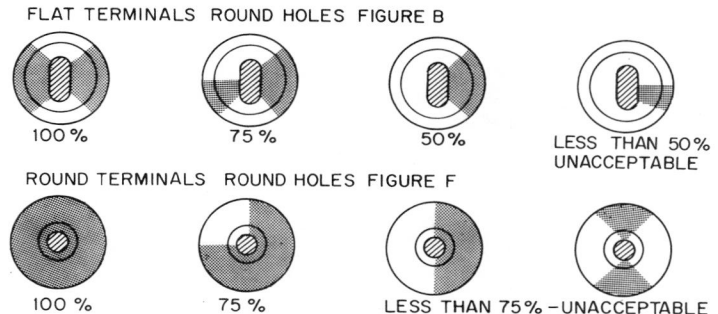

Fig. 41-4 *(Continued)* Assembly process specification.

loops through which control is attained. This is done by organizing "control stations," i.e., recognized locations at which measurement is to be done and feedback provided.

The number of assembly process characteristics is so great that both formal and informal control stations must be established. The informal stations are manned by production operators whom the process planning has placed in a state of self-control.[13] The formal stations employ Inspection personnel to do the measuring and to provide feedback.

This division of work between formal and informal control stations requires an analysis to determine which characteristics should be controlled formally. Generally, formal control is used in situations such as:

Characteristics are critical to safety or basic function.
Cost of poor yields is high in relation to cost of measurement and control.
Capability of the process is poor or marginal in relation to tolerances.

For those characteristics chosen for formal control, experience has evolved some useful principles to be observed:

1. Control should be established as close as possible to the production operation where the characteristics are generated. This minimizes the time lag between production of defectives and discovery of their presence. The lag is obviously minimal when the same person, i.e., the operator, carries out all the functions of operation, measurement, and adjustment.

2. Processes of marginal capability should be analyzed for potential solution through process improvement or through relaxing the tolerances. Where such solutions are not available, provision must be made for sorting the product at the most economical stage, and for repairing the defectives.

3. Criteria should be established as part of the control procedure, both for production operators and for inspectors. These criteria include how many measurements to make, and what action to take based on the observed results. Here again, the nature of the process (capability, drift, etc.) can aid the planners in establishing the criteria.[14]

Planning Checklist   When the product is complex, the number of things to be controlled becomes so great that it is necessary to resort to checklists or countdowns to assure that nothing is overlooked. In television receiver manufacture, a master flow chart (Figure 41-5) plus subsidiary flow charts (Figure 41-6) are used as checklists to guard against incomplete planning.

[13] See Section 11, under Concept of Operator Self-Control.
[14] See generally Section 9, under Planning Process Controls; see also Section 11, Concept of Operator Self-Control *et seq.*; also Section 12, under Inspection Planning.

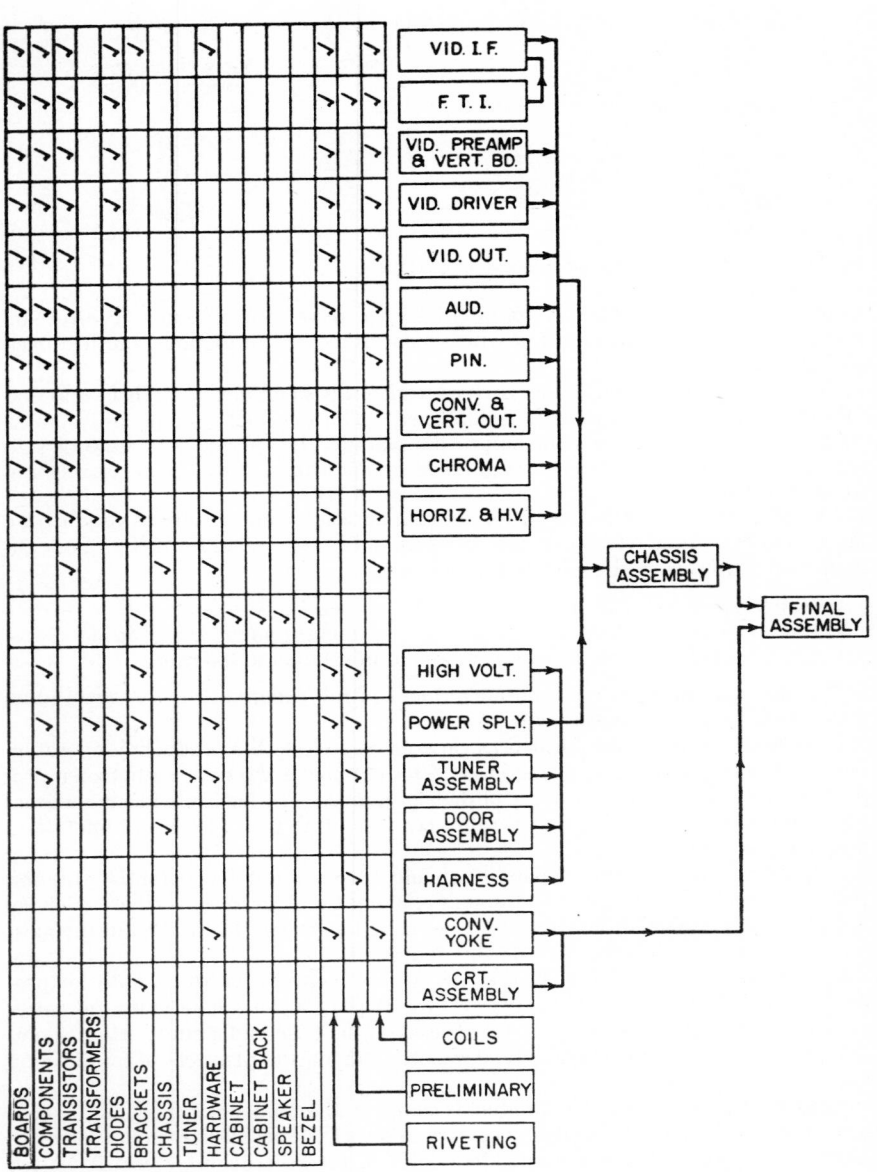

Fig. 41-5 Master flow chart.

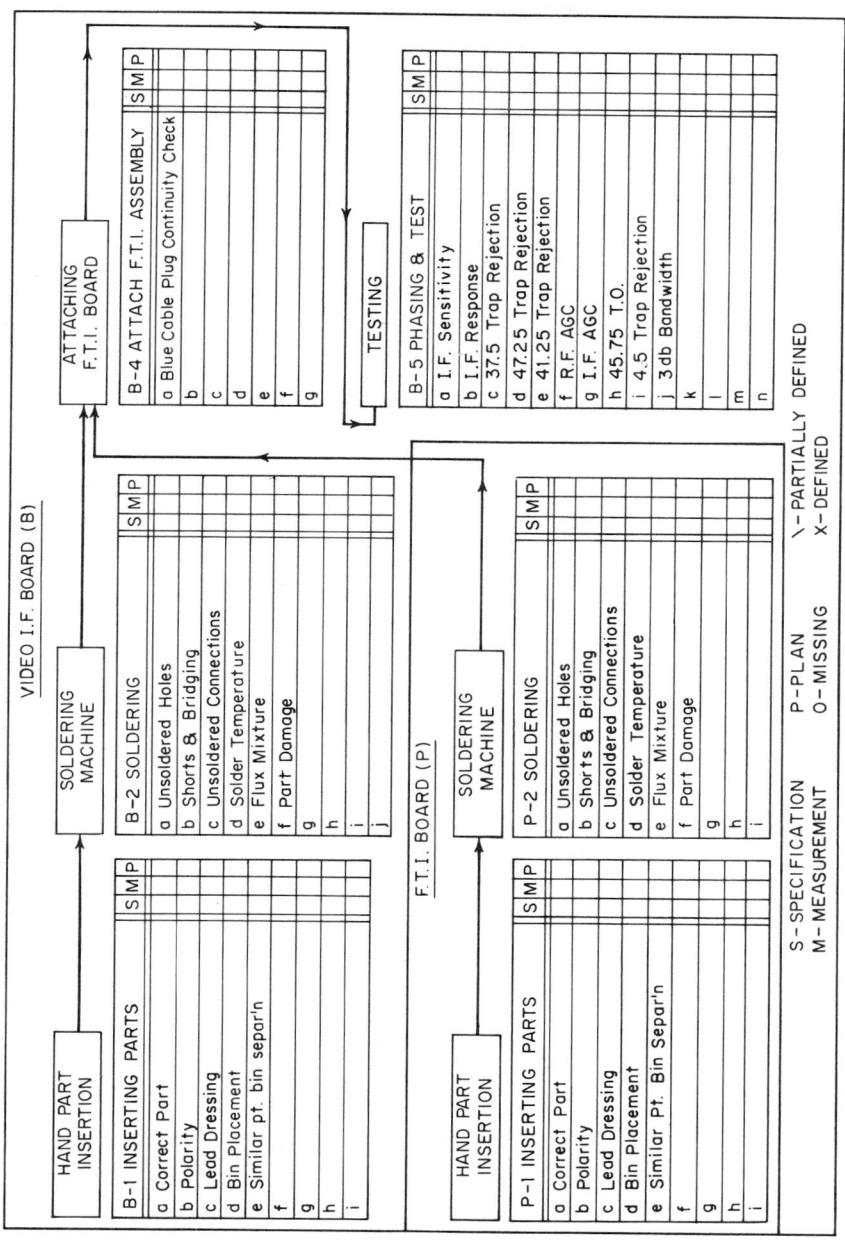

Fig. 41-6 Subsidiary flow chart.

The master flow charts show the operations in their natural sequence in order to make more evident the interrelation of the characteristics under analysis. In addition, the charts are segmented into logical subgroups, each corresponding to some component, subassembly, subsystem, etc. The subsidiary charts are broken down to individual control points, i.e., the characteristics or defects around which the individual feedback loops are built. The rectangles permit use of coded designations to show status of completion of assembly process specifications, methods of measurement, and control plans.

In-Line Assembly Inspection   Adherence to the principle of bringing controls as close to the operations as possible requires that inspectors be stationed on the assembly line itself.[15] Here again it is necessary to be selective, since it is uneconomic to apply inspection uniformly to all production stations. One way of determining how to concentrate the inspection is through analysis of the errors made at the various stations. In electronic assembly, a typical distribution of errors is as follows:

Errors per Day	% of Line Population
0 or 1	60–65
1 to 3	20–25
Over 3	10–15

Securing the data for this distribution requires a special study. Trained inspection personnel of proved accuracy are assigned to audit each work station for a period of time long enough (about a month) to establish the station-to-station variability. The operators are then classed A, B, and C, respectively. These classifications are then used, in accordance with the Pareto principle, as an aid in planning the distribution of inspection effort among the assembly line stations.

A typical arrangement for a line of 70 stations might result in assignment of inspectors (sometimes also called auditors) as follows:

	Production Station Numbers
Auditor I	1–19
Auditor II.	20–37
Auditor III	38–54
Auditor IV	55–70

Generally, inspectors near the beginning of the line are assigned more stations than those at the end of the line. To remove bias and to establish inspection sequences, each auditor is provided with a set of "coins," each numbered to match one of the production station numbers. The auditor draws the coins from a bag, at random, to establish the inspection sequence for the day.

It is also necessary to provide each inspector with the usual criteria to be applied to each production station: sampling plan, acceptance numbers, data plan, etc. The general approach is discussed in Section 12, under Inspection Planning. In addition, conventional statistical tools are available to assist the planner, notably control charts (Section 23) and special sampling plans (Section 24, under Sampling Plans for Continuous Production).

Application of these general use methods to in-line assembly inspection may require some adaptation:

---

[15] The alternative of placing all inspectors at the end of the line is a waste of inspection effort. It also increases the lag between operation and detection. In cases where prior operations are buried by later operations, no ready check is possible at the end of the line.

1. AOQLs must be established based on optimizing customer requirements and factory economics.

2. The presence of multiple defects on single units of product may require sampling plans based on defects per unit rather than on the more common basis of fraction defective.

3. Rules must be established for dealing with defects encountered beyond the allowable number. Since production is continuous, these rules usually include provision for 100% inspection while collateral steps are being taken to find and remedy the cause of the defects. In some cases these rules include provision for transfer of charges (from Inspection to Production) for 100% inspection performed.

Figure 41-7 shows in detail some of the types of rules which are evolved for conduct of in-line inspection.

1. During 100% inspection, each inspector will be examining only a small portion of the complete product; he can probably handle three or four 100% inspection requirements. A 4-hour charge to the producing departments should be made for each out of control station.

2. When a wrong part is used in many successive units because of a widespread error (stocking error, operator error, etc.), 100% inspection may be withheld if immediate corrective action takes place. The next round of the first sample should be used to verify that the necessary action has been taken.

3. Only those defects found to be the responsibility of the audited station are to be recorded on the work sheet. Any defect from another area should be separately noted and tagged. These defects are to be considered as nonchargeable.

4. The line station categories (A, B, or C) should be reviewed on a weekly basis, using the audit statistics from the previous 2-week period. The QC Department has the responsibility to make any needed reclassification.

5. Weekly forum meetings should be held with the people affected (supervisor, foreman, etc.) to review problems and assign responsibility for corrective action.

INSTRUCTIONS TO THE INSPECTORS

1. Establish the sequence of station inspections using the numbered coins provided.

2. Establish each work station's responsibilities from the applicable documents: process chart, layout plan, procedure specifications, or standards.

3. Inspect the number of units called for by the sampling plan, divided into 5 subgroups.

4. To avoid biasing an operator with your presence, do your inspection of his work at a point 3 or 4 stations later. This means that the units you inspect will all have been completed by that operator before you commence your inspection.

5. Identify all rejects both chargeable and nonchargeable.

6. If the number of defects exceeds that allowed by the first sample, proceed to the second sample if applicable. Should the number of defects again exceed that allowed, establish 100% inspection through your supervisor.

7. If the number of defects does not exceed the limits of the plan, proceed to the next station.

8. Record the number of units inspected, and identify and record all defects with the work station. Use the forms provided.

Fig. 41-7   Rules governing in-line inspections.

ESTABLISHING QUALITY LEVELS

Assembled products require extensive use of sampling plans, both during process control and in the finished product stages. Each of these plans requires the setting of a quality level, i.e., a limiting extent of defects to serve as a basic parameter for the sampling plan. The numerous sampling plans required for these products demand a correspondingly large number of these quality levels to be set. Figure 41-8 shows, in flow diagram form, some of the types of quality levels used for electronic assemblies. The same chart also shows some typical numerical levels encountered.

The general approach to establishing such quality levels is discussed in Section 24, especially under the heading Constructing the OC Curve—Selection of an AQL, *et seq.* As noted there, it is possible to establish these quality levels on a basis of optimizing total costs provided the defects are sure to be detected in the factory. For defects which can pass out to the field, the intangibles preclude a fully scientific approach, and use must be made of managerial experience and judgment.

Assembled products follow this general approach. For qualities which will affect the end use (and hence the customers) the emphasis on setting quality levels is to secure the best experience and judgment from all interested departments. For purely "internal" qualities, the emphasis is on cost studies to find that level which results in minimal total cost.

The network of quality levels extends to materials and parts received from vendors or from supporting "captive" plants. For example, in Figure 41-8 the inputs from supporting plants I and II and from departments I and II (left-hand side of chart) are set at a 1% AOQL. This is entirely practical, since these inputs consist of subassemblies which are logically treated as lots, and are sampled and accepted by conventional methods. In contrast, material received from vendors is sampled in accordance with AQLs established by contractual agreement. These vary from 0.25% for critical or hazardous items to 2.5% for complex assemblies or parts, e.g., a color picture tube involving 75 to 100 quality characteristics.

The presence of so many input process levels requires also that limits be established on the "pileup." Figure 41-8 exemplifies this by showing limits for defects per hundred (DPH) at various stages. These limits are established from past experience, pilot runs, etc. Once established, they are used to sound warning signals when the samples taken show that the levels are significantly exceeded.

DATA COLLECTION AND FEEDBACK

The general approach to inspection feedback (Section 11, under Inspection Feedback to Production) has wide application in assembly processes. There are also some special applications of these universals.

For simple situations, the simple tally sheet is as good as it always was (Figure 41-9). For more complex cases (such as the wall chart at the end of the assembly line) a more complex scoreboard is designed to permit hour-by-hour tallies to be entered (Figure 41-10).

During the 1960s there was a clear trend to use of electronic data processing, not only for summarized after-the-fact reporting but for "instantaneous" feedback as well. The latter is made possible by use of electronic encoding stations using "touch tone" telephones as a basic numerical code transmitter. These transmitters, located at strategic points in the process, deliver their data to a central computer which, in turn, transmits summaries for simultaneous electronic display or report to multiple departmental receiving stations.[16]

---

[16] See Di Cicco, John J., Dynamic Quality Control, *Industrial Quality Control,* November 1965, pp. 235–239. See also Section 42, Figure 42-12 and associated discussion. See also Section 43, under Quality Assurance—Executive Reports. See also Section 20, Computers in Quality Control.

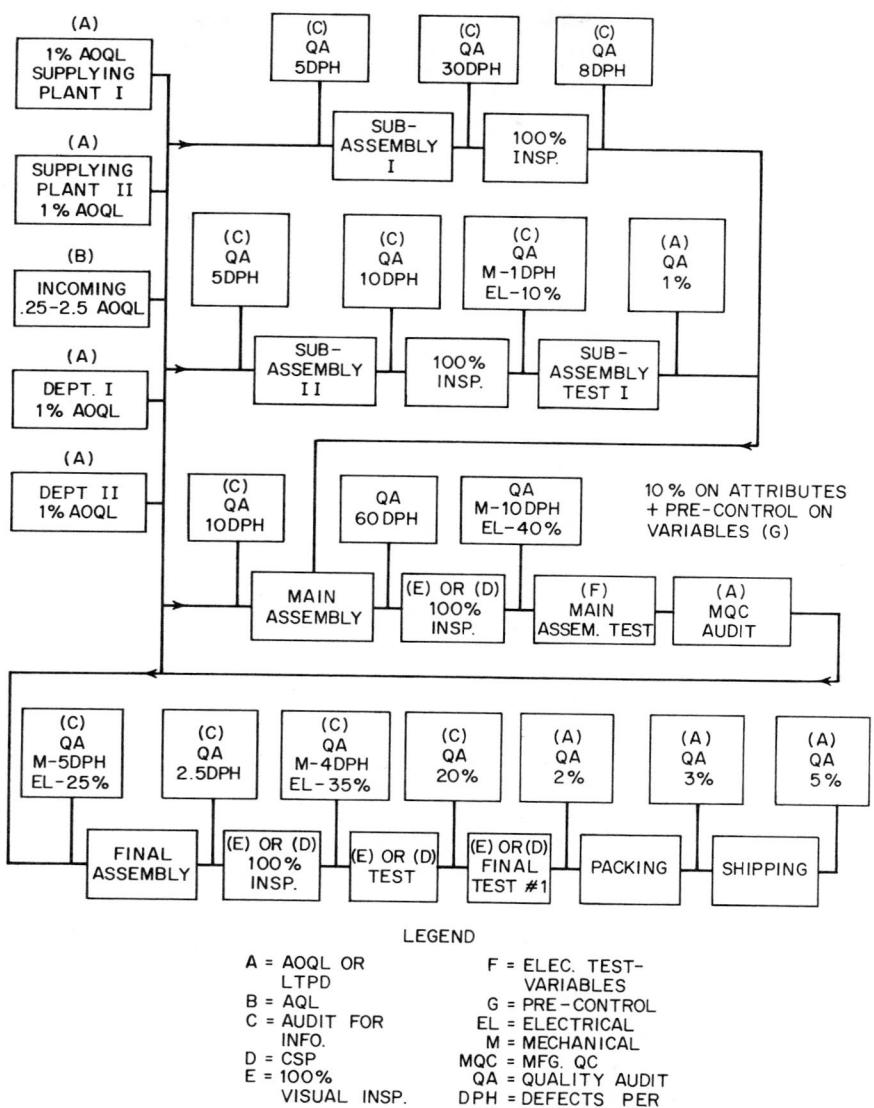

Fig. 41-8 Quality levels in use on electronic assemblies.

INSPECTION REPORT	
DATE _10-15-57_ INSP. STA. NO. _1_ DEPT. NO. _3_ INSPECTOR _Columbo_	
DEFECTIVE PLATE	~~////~~ //
DEFECTIVE PAINT	///
DEFECTIVE SCREWS	~~////~~ ~~////~~ ~~////~~ ////
DENTS	~~////~~ ~~////~~ /
WRONG PARTS	~~////~~ /
LOOSE COVER	~~////~~ ///
NAMEPLATE MARRED	///
MISSING PARTS	//
UNITS INSPECTED	~~////~~ ~~////~~ ~~////~~ ~~////~~ ~~////~~ ~~////~~
''	~~////~~ ~~////~~ ~~////~~ ~~////~~ ~~////~~ ~~////~~ ~~////~~

Fig. 41-9 Simple tally sheet for assembly defects.

A simple system using touch telephone encoders with an interface to a central computer can be installed for about $50,000 for 50 positions, or about $75,000 for 125 positions. These figures refer to the first-time equipment cost. In succeeding years, the cost is mainly the computer time.

Assembly operations can throw off enormous quantities of data, so that a limiting factor in design of the data processing system is the capacity to act on the information. Experienced managers make use of two vital concepts for balancing the information coming to them against their ability to use it:

1. The Pareto principle.[17] Under this principle, managers receive information as to the "vital few" problems, and leave the rest to be handled by someone else (or to wait their turn).

2. The "hierarchy of controls." This is the concept of the existence of multiple layers of feedback, which go to different levels of organization, for different purposes, and at different frequencies.[18] Table 41-1 shows how these factors are interrelated in a typical report system used for electronic assemblies. Table 41-2, which is keyed to Figure 41-8, shows the variegated forms of reporting associated with the control systems shown in Figure 41-8.

An added factor in design of the report system is the speed of assembly; the higher the speed, the greater the need for high-speed feedback. Failing this, a breakdown in some essential process can create a major congestion. For example, if large units are being assembled at the rate of 100 per hour and a vital defect goes unreported, one "hour's worth" of defects can overtax any repair facility. In such cases, defect trends must be identified and signaled as soon as possible.

FINAL AUDIT

It is common practice to use sampling audits of the finished product for any or all of the following purposes:

1. As a check on the effectiveness of the prior in-process control plan.

2. To provide a continuing report on the outgoing quality. (This is similar to product auditing as discussed in Section 21.)

3. To provide an added control on outgoing quality in the form of an acceptance sampling plan.

When used as an acceptance sampling plan, the final audit is usually structured on the lines of a continuous sampling plan (CSP), as discussed in Section 24, under Sampling Plans for Continuous Production. These plans are most advantageous

[17] See Section 2, under The Pareto Principle.

[18] For a more extensive discussion, see Section 21, under Executive Reports on Quality.

QUALITY CONTROL – TALLY SHEET

END OF FINAL ASSEMBLY LINE   DATE 3/6/50

HOUR	1	2	3	4	5	6	7	8
PRODUCTION COUNT	50	50/100	50/150	50/200	50/250	50/300	50/350	50/400

TOTAL OK UNITS (tally marks) ... 41 / 42 / 43 / 44 / 45

OK UNITS	40	42/82	43/125	42/167	40/207	44/251	46/297	45/342
DEFECTS								
FENDER BKT LOOSE	/			//	/	//	/	/
FENDER BOLT LOOSE		/			/			
FIT FENDER	//	///	//	///	//	/		/
FDR. TO SHIELD SCREW	///	///	////	///	///	//	///	///
FIT HOOD	/	/		/		/	/	/
FIT 1/4 MOLDING	7HL	7HL /	////	///	7HL	///	///	//
FIT DOOR			/	/	/	//		
FIT DECK LID	/	/			/			//
BUMPER BOLTS LOOSE	/ o			/	/	/	//	/
GEN. MISC.								
SPARE WHEEL LOOSE			/	/				
BRK. LINE OUT OF CLIP	/	/	/	/	///	//	//	/

Fig. 41-10 Hourly summary tally sheet for assembly defects.

TABLE 41-1   Report System for Electronic Assembly

Type	Purpose	Characteristics	Responsibility for action
Hourly	Adjust process	Word-of-mouth reporting, tallies of all rejects (or against bogies or standards), measurements showing departure from norms (e.g., carbon levels, hardness readings, surface finish readings). Short-term reports are usually kept in log without reference to cost	Production workers, lead men, technicians
Daily by shifts	Corrective action on previous day's errors, etc.	Summary of defects and defective product related to total production from previous day's operations by each work area and work shift	Shop supervision, production engineers
Weekly by shifts or work areas	Analyze trends, Paretoize by shifts, areas, operators, defects	Dollar impact of each source of quality costs. Identification of problem areas. Comparison with previous averages for variance analysis	Middle management of all types such as plant superintendent, technical directors, quality control manager, product control manager
Monthly	Assign resources for corrective action (long-term)	Dollar impact on profits by defect types and work areas. Project identification with assignment for corrective action. Three-month projection of defect levels	Top management and key middle managers
Yearly	Provide data for breakthrough programs to new and lower levels of avoidable costs	Overall evaluation of potential savings. Projections of long-term breakthrough programs	Top management and key middle managers

TABLE 41-2 Types of Reporting Associated with Various Control Systems

Code Letter	Control system	Reporting system	Usage	Charting required	Reference
A	AOQL or LTPD	Lots accepted vs. lots rejected	1. Items that can readily be accumulated in lots 2. Process in control 3. 100% reinspection practical	No	Section 24; Dodge-Romig Sampling Tables
B	AQL	Supplier history cards. Lots OK vs. lots rejected	1. Usually incoming material from vendors 2. 100% inspection not practical or too costly	No	Section 24; MIL-STD-105D Tables
C	Audit	Usually written report on adherence to quality plan	Small sample to confirm adherence to quality procedures, but can be expanded to AQL or AOQL if necessary	No	
D	CSP-1, 2, 3	Number of times 100% inspection is triggered	Continuous production flow	No	Section 24; H-107 Tables
E	100% inspection	P-charts until control is established	Process not capable of meeting specifications	Yes	Sections 9, 23
F	Variables measurements	$\bar{X}$ and R charts	Machining, electronic measurements, processes, any variables stations	Yes, until process control is established	Sections 23, 25
G	Precontrol	Number of times process readjustment is necessary	Same as above	No	Section 23

when the product is large and unwieldy, or where lot acceptance 100% reinspections might cause more damage than benefit.

Generally, the continuous sampling plans provide for going to 100% inspection when the sampling criteria are significantly exceeded. Going to 100% inspection creates a manpower problem which is met by borrowing personnel from Production and/or reducing sampling temporarily on those lines which have been exhibiting good control.

For smaller items (clocks, motors, amplifiers, servos, etc.) standard lot sampling of the Dodge-Romig type or MIL-STD-105 type are probably the most economical.[19]

Even when the final audit is not on an acceptance sampling basis, the finding of defects in the sample is taken seriously. Assignments are made to the supervision or to engineers to discover causes and find remedies. In some cases, all or a portion of the sample may be placed on short-term reliability tests or on continuous monitor to provide added information on the effect of the defects.

OVERALL PERFORMANCE STANDARDS AND MEASURES

Researches on broad performance of assembled products have been few and inconclusive. Some industry data are available on valid service calls per 1,000 household appliances. (See Section 43, Figure 43-1 and associated discussion.) Even these data, which were prepared by an industry association, show a variation of 3 to 1 among different types of appliances, as well as a general downward trend from year to year.

A second customer-oriented measure is the extent of negative comments on the "Condition on Arrival" cards. In the author's experience, once an effective arrival card system has been set up and is working, any customer returns exceeding 0.5% of total product should be a cause for deep concern.

Failures due to shipping range from 1% in prevention-oriented companies to 10% in companies relying mainly on inspection. The corresponding figures for customer complaints range from 2 to over 10%.

Another broad performance measure is that of quality costs. In the experience of the author, companies which lack a fundamental "systems" approach to control of quality have quality costs as high as 12 to 20% of sales. In contrast, companies with well-structured quality control systems are more usually in the range of 2.5 to 5.5% of sales.

A further measure of internal performance is that of product rejection rates. The following are the prevailing orders of magnitude for prevention-oriented vs. inspection-oriented companies:

	Rejection rates, %	
	Prevention-oriented	Inspection-oriented
Incoming material. . .	2–3	10–15
Electronic assembly. .	5	50–100
Electronic test	10	50

These figures are comparatively uniform for prevention-oriented companies but tend to vary widely among inspection-oriented companies.

Table 41-3 shows the author's judgment of attainable levels of defects, for various types of assembled products, at the point of leaving the manufacturer's plant. To

[19] See Section 24 for details.

TABLE 41-3   Attainable Levels of Outgoing Quality (Critical and Major Defects)*

Assembly grade	Products	Approx. AOQL, %
Simple	Irons, mixers, heaters, small radios, clocks, clock radios, auto radios, cabinets, ignition systems, batteries, alternators, motors, etc.	0.1–1
More complex	Monochrome TV sets, stereo AM-FM sets, power mowers, stoves, refrigerators, freezers, air conditioners (portable and stationary), color TV tubes, transmissions	1.0–1.75
Complex products . .	Single units of large electronic systems, transmitters, automobiles, color TV sets, numerical control units, small computers, mobile communications systems	1.75–3
Complex systems . . .	Assemblies of complex products, radar, sonar, fire control, complete communications systems	5

* Major defect—any legitimate defect requiring a service call.   Critcal defect—inoperative or unusable.

these levels must be added another 0.5 to 1.5% to allow for shipping and environmental damage prior to arrival at the consumers' premises.

QUALITY IMPROVEMENT

The assembly process makes wide use of quality improvement projects.   These follow the general approach discussed extensively in Section 16.

Because assembly process problems are highly interdepartmental in nature, the organization for improvement must likewise be interdepartmental.   It is common practice to use interdepartmental teams to guide projects and to use specialist engineers for data collection and analysis, again on an interdepartmental basis.

For example, a line of electronic products was arriving at consumer destinations with too high a defect level.   An attempt was made to solve the problem by adding yet another sorting operation, i.e., "burning-in" of each unit of product.   However, subsequent analysis showed that units which had undergone burn-in gave no better results than units without burn-in, while failure modes on the two sets of product were identical.

As a result, the attempt to solve the problem by a sorting operation was abandoned.   Instead, a fundamental improvement project was undertaken to discover root causes.   An investment was made in quality control engineering (from the money formerly used for the heat check).   The resulting interdepartmental project was singularly successful—quality costs were cut in one year from $10 to $7 per unit.

FUTURE TRENDS

A major quality problem on assembled products has been poor field service.   (See Section 15, under Customer Service.)   Manufacturers have been actively taking steps to reduce the need for this service through product designs which are inherently higher in reliability.   In a different direction, steps are being taken to design products in a way which improves maintainability in the field.[20]

A growing trend, which seems destined to reach great proportions, is that of "modularization."   Under this concept, assembled products are designed for easy disassembly of those segments or "modules" which are most likely to develop failure

[20] See generally Section 8.

or damage in service. Examples have included the color television set that usually "stays in the home" and home appliances which can be serviced by nontechnical persons.

Modularization also simplifies the quality control job in the factory, since modular subassemblies can be lot accepted on their quality characteristics before the module is buried in a maze of other parts. This simplification also extends to the operations, through creating smaller assembly teams for the modules, reducing training time, etc.

International competition has begun to be evident in product quality, in addition to the long-standing competition in price. Awareness of this new competition has given added stimulus to a prior movement to raise the quality function to a major status in hundreds of large companies.

International competition has also tended to improve industry collaboration among companies which face a common adversary. One evidence of this is an increasing willingness to exchange product quality information. Another evidence is seen in the joint efforts being undertaken to upgrade the industry quality image (under the added stimulus of the consumerism movement).[21]

Within the factory, increased automation has been a growing response to low-cost foreign competition. The resulting high-speed production reduces the time available to react to quality problems as they arise. To deal with these problems in hours and even minutes (to avoid production of large quantities of poor product meanwhile) requires computerization in various forms: computerized process control; on-stream data collection; computerized checkout; data analysis and feedback; computerized quality planning, etc.[22]

Assembled products did not fully satisfy the consumer of the 1960s. While a significant share of the dissatisfaction was the result of consumer ignorance and misuse, there were enough real problems to enable consumer groups and political groups to stimulate new legislation not only with respect to product safety but in other directions as well: advertising, labeling, repair practices, etc. Some of this legislation is of little benefit to the consumer—it raises the cost of products without adding corresponding value. However, the momentum which has been generated will likely remain in force until there has been a demonstrable improvement in product quality, as well as an evaluation of the excess of the consumerism movement.

[21] See, for example, Section 43, under Prognosis.
[22] See Section 20, Computers in Quality Control.

Section **42**

Automotive Industry

DR. SOICHIRO TOYODA

Senior Managing Director, Toyota Motor Company, Japan

INTRODUCTION

The automobile is a twentieth century concept for providing personalized transportation direct from point of origin to destination, with a high degree of safety, speed, and comfort. To avail themselves of this useful concept, the industrialized societies have built vast networks of surfaced roads and have relocated factories, dwelling communities, markets, etc. In addition, these societies have built the huge facilities needed to make and maintain automotive vehicles, as well as the equally massive facilities needed to provide fuel, parking space, roadside meals and lodging, etc. In turn, the availability of these facilities has stimulated wider use of motor vehicles to a point of no return; i.e., the automobile has become an indispensable form of transportation.

Quality Parameters Because the automotive industry has become a vital segment of each national economy and because vehicle performance now affects the daily lives of millions of citizens (and voters), the parameters of vehicle quality are of unusual importance, nationally and internationally. Mainly, these parameters involve:

Transportation Characteristics. The basic function of the vehicle is point-to-point transportation under the guidance of the driver. A great deal of effort has gone into man-machine designs which can provide such transportation in a wide variety of environments. Generally, the industry has done quite well in meeting these needs.

Economy. The automobile is a major investment for the user. (Only the dwelling house is larger.) The users' costs of transportation are a resultant of four main costs: vehicle depreciation, cost of operation (e.g., fuel, tires), cost of maintenance, and resale value. In incurring these costs, the user deals with multiple industries, including vehicle manufacturers, each trying to optimize its own costs. These suboptimizations do not optimize the users' costs; sometimes they are antagonistic to the users' costs.[1] The consumerism[2] movement will likely include an urge for optimizing the users' costs through devices such as life cycle costing.[3]

Reliability. Failure *rates* for specific components have been coming down for decades, and this trend is likely to continue. However, the *number* of failures has been rising because of increasing vehicle population and increasing complexity of vehicles. (Frequent model changes contribute to failures by introducing new designs which are a breeding ground for quality troubles.) There is evidence that consumers will tolerate a degree of vehicle failures provided that they can receive prompt restoration of service at a reasonable charge. In the United States there are serious deficiencies in this service, and it is the large manufacturers, not the numerous small service shops, who become the most visible targets for attack.[4]

Aesthetics. The vehicle not only serves as a source of transport; it is also a major source of aesthetic satisfactions, e.g., appearance or status. In consequence, styling and color are essential features of vehicles which compete for sale in a free market. In addition, the aesthetic reasons for user dissatisfaction (e.g., visible blemishes, rough surfaces, noises, discomforts) become a major source of user complaints and returns. There is also evidence that users' standards for such defects have been tightening up over the years.

Safety. Highway accident and fatality rates have declined remarkably since the early days of the automobile. One study[5] concluded that fatality rates (per million man-hours of exposure) have declined from about 1,000 in 1900 to about one in 1960, an improvement of three orders of magnitude! However, the number of fatalities rose during the same period because the man-hours of vehicle usage has increased by even more orders of magnitude. In the United States alone, highway deaths reached a level of about 50,000 per year by the late 1960s.

In matters of highway safety it is important to distinguish between two very different phenomena:

1. The "first crash," i.e., the collision of a vehicle with something external, i.e., another vehicle, a pedestrian, a road obstacle, etc. This first crash is due to deficiencies in driver, road, or vehicle. Of these, the driver, and especially the drunken driver, is the main contributor. To quote from an authoritative study, "*. . . alcohol has been found to be the largest single factor leading to fatal crashes.*"[6] (emphasis in the original, page 11).

Vehicle malfunctions contribute a minority of these crashes, and thereby the

---

[1] Juran, J. M., Mobilizing for the 1970's, *Quality Progress*, August 1969, pp. 8–17.

[2] Juran, J. M., Consumerism and Product Quality, *Quality Progress*, July 1970, pp. 18–27.

[3] See Section 4, under Life Cycle Costing.

[4] Juran, J. M., Consumerism and Product Quality, *op. cit.*

[5] Starr, Chauncey, Social Benefit versus Technological Risk, *Science*, vol. 165, pp. 1232–1238, Sept. 19, 1969.

[6] 1968 Alcohol and Highway Safety Report, a Study Transmitted by the Secretary of the Department of Transportation to the Congress, in Accordance with the Requirements of Section 204 of the Highway Safety Act of 1966, Public Law 89-564, Government Printing Office, Washington, D.C., 20402.

manufacturers have the opportunity and duty to further improve the safety features of the vehicles. However, since the major causes of the first crash are not vehicle related, the major solutions lie elsewhere.

2. The "second crash," i.e., the collision which results when the occupants of a speeding vehicle are hurled against the interior during sudden deceleration. The available evidence suggests that development of suitable restraints may result in dramatic reductions in fatalities and injuries, assuming the public is willing to accept such restraints.[7]

Air Pollution. The automobile is a major source of urban air pollution. In some areas this pollution has reached serious proportions, and poses a growing health hazard. In consequence, it is imperative that the manufacturers develop vehicles which can operate with markedly lower emission rates.

The Industry Structure   To make, sell, and maintain automotive vehicles on a large scale requires the creation of an elaborate industry structure. Economic imperatives have dictated the basic nature of this industry structure, which does not differ greatly from one country to another.[8] The industry functions are carried out as follows:

Design and Manufacture. This is carried out in a very few, very large companies owing to the need for enormous investments in research and development, and in manufacturing facilities.

Product design is an extensive activity owing to the complexity of the vehicles and the severity of the quality parameters, which require exhaustive environmental and reliability testing. The frequency of style change adds further to the design load, as does the compressed timetable.

Plants for making components are large because of the high volume of production. Assembly plants, especially for final vehicle assembly, are even larger in size because of the large-series production and the numerous components per vehicle. Extensive use is made of vendors, so that a car company may have several thousand vendors in spite of self-making most components.

The extent of concentration of these facilities may be judged from the following United States data[9] for 1967:

Vehicle manufacturing companies...	4
Vehicle assembly plants..........	46
Parts manufacturing companies.....	1,500
Parts plants.................	5,000

Marketing. The "market" for automobiles is actually a wide spectrum of user affluence and taste superimposed on basic needs for transportation. To respond to these variations in user demand, the industry has created multiple grades of automobile as well as frequent model changes, and has provided for marketing these grades through its distribution channels.

In the United States these distribution channels culminate in over 30,000 dealers (as of the early 1970s). These dealers are mainly independent companies who

[7] This point remains in doubt. During the early 1970s (5 years after lap belts and shoulder belts became mandatory original equipment) usage had attained only about 30% for lap belts, and only about 3% for shoulder belts. See Juran, J. M., Product Safety, *Quality Progress*, July 1972, pp. 30–32.

[8] See, in this connection, the European study: Survey of Quality Organisation in the Automotive Industries, 1972. Available from European Organization for Quality Control. P.O. Box 1976, Rotterdam 3005, Netherlands.

[9] Compliance Procedures Study PB 177 705, p. 12, Clearinghouse for Federal Scientific & Technical Information, U.S. Department of Commerce, Springfield, Va. 22151, October 1967.

operate under a franchise arrangement. They are extensively involved with quality through the maintenance they perform both during and after the guarantee period.[10] In addition, the dealers are a vital source of data on vehicle quality performance.

A significant amount of marketing is international in scope, creating severe problems of conformance to multiple environments, laws, and customs. The problems of data feedback also become more severe owing to difficulties with language, distance, etc.

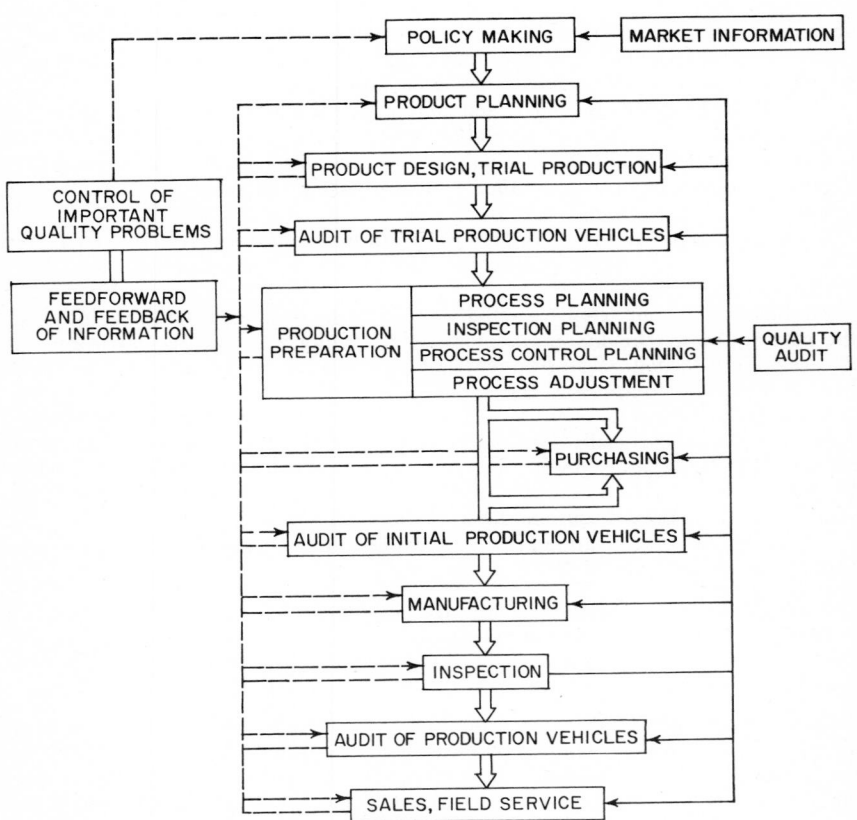

Fig. 42-1 System for quality assurance.

Vehicle Maintenance. The number of repair facilities for vehicle maintenance is very large, since it includes the independent shops and the many "filling stations" who perform repair service. See Field Service, below, for a detailed discussion.

The External Climate The great economic and social importance of the automotive industry, and the immense size of the manufacturing companies has properly been a source of concern to the public, and thereby, to legislators, journalists, re-

---

[10] The dealers also perform some manufacturing-like operations as part of the selling arrangement.

formers, etc. The collective efforts of these external forces have intensified power-ful movements which concern the industry:

Product Liability. The automobile manufacturers were among the first to feel the effect of the increase in lawsuits and the associated erosion of defenses in matters of product liability.[11] In the related field of personal injury lawsuits between motorists, the proliferation of lawsuits had reached a level which was clogging the law courts. The enactment of "no-fault" legislation has dramatically reduced these suits and the size of the associated claims. The experience gained may stimulate some legislation with respect to product liability as well.

Government Regulation.[12] In the United States the National Traffic and Motor Vehicle Safety Act of 1966 empowered a federal government agency to establish and enforce safety standards for motor vehicles and equipment. This legislation has profoundly affected the industry as to specifications, enforcement practices, documentation, traceability, recall policy, etc. It has also significantly raised the costs of the vehicles.[13] It remains to be seen what will be the effect on motor vehicle safety.

Concept of Quality Assurance[14] It is evident from the foregoing that for the auto-motive industry, the concept of quality assurance has implications which extend far beyond conventional practice. The concept does include the conventional needs of fitness for use and conformance to specifications. However, because the industry is so vital to the national economy and to the daily well-being of so many people, it must look well beyond the conventional if it is to retain its freedom of action. With this in mind, automobile manufacturers have tried their best to fulfill these broader needs of quality assurance, considering the recent consumerism[15] movement as well.

In the language of the quality control specialists, this concept of quality assurance requires that the manufacturer understand precisely all factors which affect quality, from original concept through the final scrapping of the car. Based on this under-standing, the manufacturer must enlist the participation of all concerned, vendors, marketers, service shops, related industries, etc., to establish the best overall quality assurance system.

A model for this concept is shown in Figure 42-1. While this model[16] refers specifically to Toyota Motor Co. Ltd. practice, a similar approach is followed by most car companies around the world. The remainder of this Section sets out in detail the manner in which this concept is executed.

PRODUCT PLANNING

The considerations discussed in the Introduction, above, require that the automotive industry do a thorough job of product planning before undertaking the great risks inherent in mass production and marketing of so complex a product. The auto-mobile companies do in fact carry out such planning, following the general approach discussed in Section 6 under The Planning Concept, Major Project Planning, and New Product Planning; also in Section 8 generally.

[11] See generally Section 14, under Product Liability.

[12] See generally Section 4, under Government Regulation of Quality.

[13] See Juran, J. M., Consumerism and Product Quality, *Quality Progress,* July 1970, pp. 18–27.

[14] The term "quality assurance" is used here in the sense of meeting the needs of the user and, in addition, being responsive to the broader needs of society.

[15] See generally Section 4, under Consumerism.

[16] For further discussion, see Mizuno, Takaharu, Total Quality Control Concept Applied to the Industrial Management System, *Proceedings, International Conference on Quality Control,* Japanese Union of Scientists and Engineers (JUSE), pp. 9–12, Tokyo, 1969 (in English).

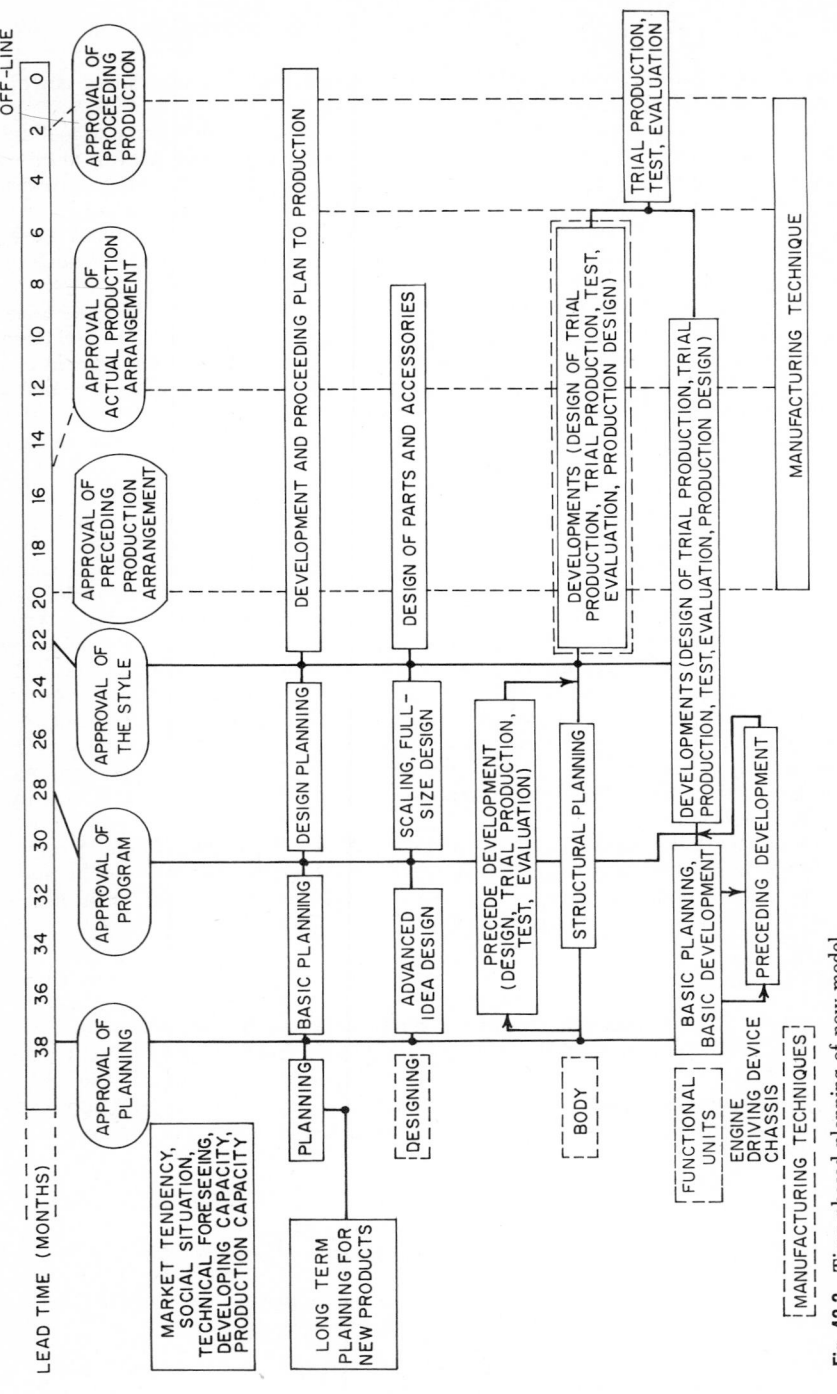

Fig. 42-2 Time phased planning of new model.

Time Phased Planning   Figure 42-2 typifies the formalized approach to new model planning[17] as carried out in the industry.   For any model this approach is preceded by long-range planning and by market research.   The lead time from embarking on a specific new model plan until the start of mass production is typically 3 to 4 years.

Long-Range Planning; Market Research.   The long-range planners study the trends in the economy, as to forces external to the industry, e.g., economic, social, political.   In addition they study the internal strengths and limitations, e.g., technology, production capacity.   The trends in consumer buying habits and especially in new car purchases, are of great importance, e.g., Figure 42-3.

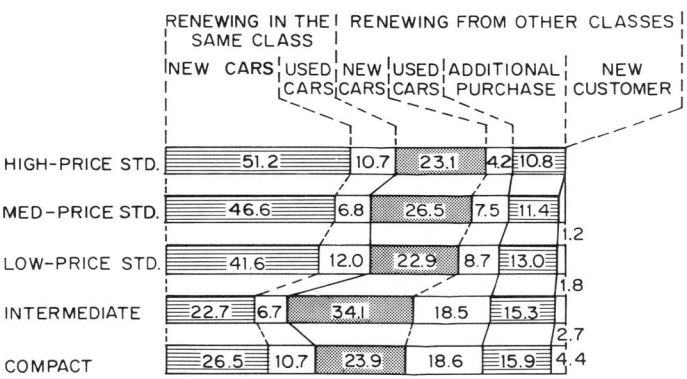

Fig. 42-3 Patterns of vehicle purchases.

The market research approach follows the practices set out in Section 4 and especially in Section 14, under Market Research on Quality, *et seq.*   Based on these studies, proposals are made for bringing new models of automobiles to market.

New Model Proposal.   This proposal sets out the parameters of the new model sufficiently to provide a basis for detailed planning.   The defined parameters include:

1. Vehicle type (sedan, hardtop, station wagon, etc.)

2. Quality policy and parameters (basic specifications for function and performance, reliability, service system, maintenance cycle, response to legislation, etc.)

3. Schedule for execution of the plan (see, for example, Figure 42-2)

4. Cost and finance parameters (vehicle weight, cost estimates, selling price, estimated profit)

Critical Quality Problems.   An essential aspect of the new model proposal is the identification of the critical quality problems.   For each of these critical problems, "idea models" are set up to evaluate progress to date and to establish goals for achievement.   The respective design specialists then supply the technology needed to reach these goals.   Figure 42-4 is an example of such an idea model as applied to body structure.[18]

Design Planning   During this phase the specialist design departments determine

---

[17] See Section 6, Figure 6-2, for an example of time phased planning which in addition defines organization responsibility.

[18] Takizawa, Kiyotake, Tadao Hashizume, and Noboru Watanabe, Durability and Reliability of Body Structure, *Journal of the Society of Automotive Engineers of Japan,* vol. 124, No. 2, p. 127, 1970 (in Japanese).

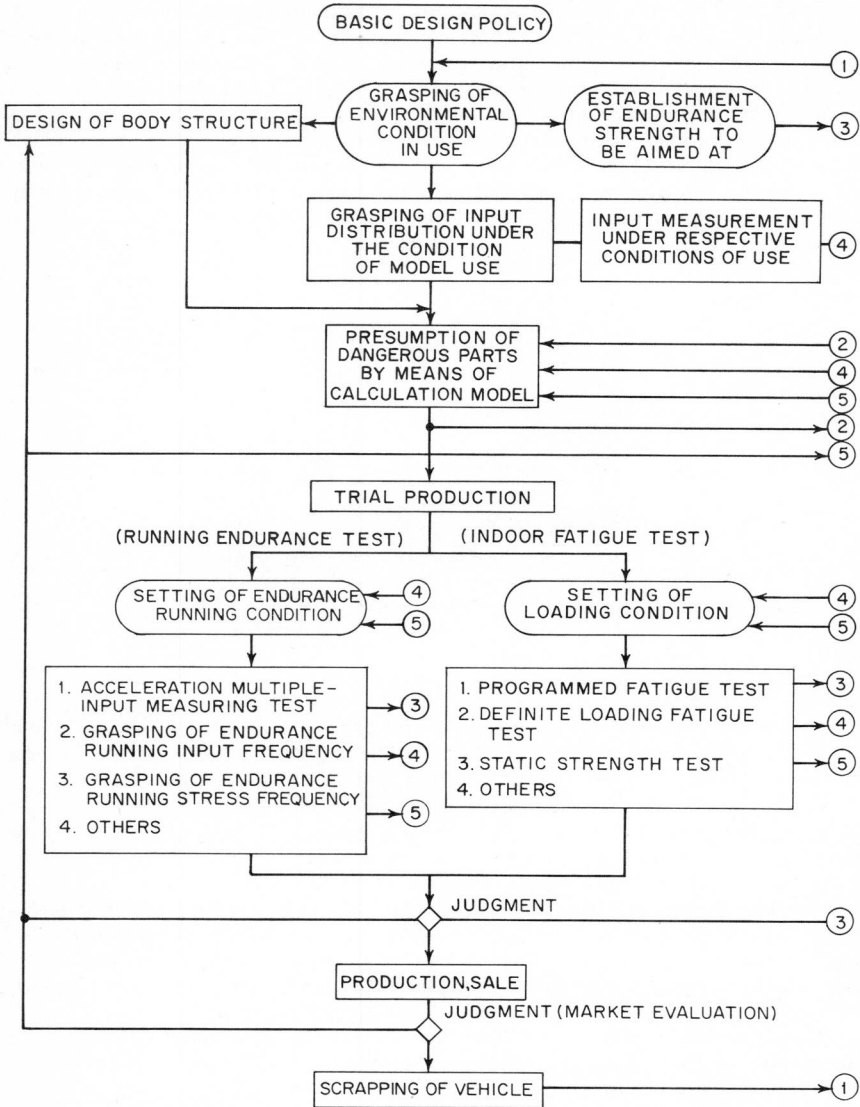

Fig. 42-4   Idea model for body strength.

major dimensions and detailed specifications for the engines and other components. They also prepare full-scale models of the finished vehicle (in clay), the actual plan of frame construction, and the layout drawings for the vehicle. In executing the design plan, consideration is given to various technical standards, quality of past and present products, productivity, and process capability.

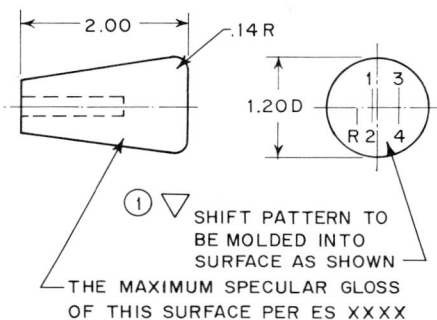

Fig. 42-5 Marking of safety characteristics (inverted delta).

Design Review. This is an essential aspect of the design planning. Formal provision is made for review by the various specialist departments,[19] for example:

Reviewing Department	Checks for
Quality evaluation	Function and performance
Manufacturing planning	Producibility
Quality control	Reliability
Field service	Maintainability
Design	Errors in design and drafting

Special provision is made to ensure that product safety features cannot be overlooked. Commonly the designers give a distinctive mark to the safety characteristics to ensure that they are fully reviewed. Figure 42-5 exemplifies this technique.[20]

Design Evaluation by Laboratory Test. A great deal of design evaluation is done by making up trial production samples of materials and components, and testing these for function, durability, and still other characteristics. These evaluations apply to vendor-designed as well as to self-designed components. (Vendors should be given the same opportunity to participate in the planning and design processes as is provided to in-house departments.) In conducting these evaluations, increasing use is being made of statistical design of experiments and of statistical analysis of test results, as by the Weibull diagram.[21]

Test facilities are extensive. They include many conventional mechanical, electronic, and chemical laboratories for testing materials and components. Specialized laboratories test the response of principal components (e.g., engines, steering, and brakes) to simulated driving conditions, using test programs coupled to electronic

[19] The approach follows generally that set out in Section 8, under Design Review. Because departmental names and functions differ from company to company, the assigned responsibilities for design review will also differ.

[20] Knowles, J., Engineering Reliability into Today's Automotive Vehicles, *Proceedings, 14th Annual Symposium on Reliability, IEEE,* pp. 67–74, 1968.

[21] See, for example, Schmudde, A. A., New Engine Designs — A Reliability Evaluation, *Mechanical Engineering,* November 1970, pp. 28–32.

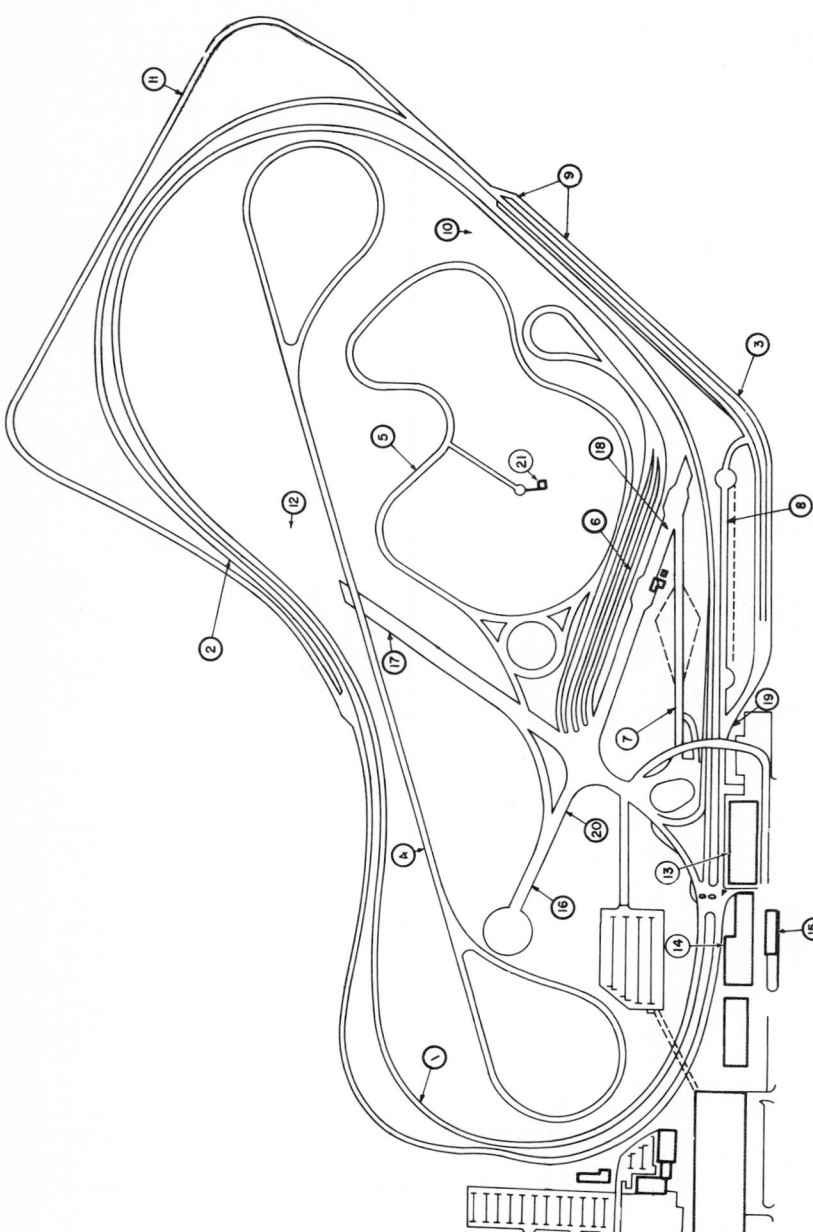

Fig. 42-6 Test track. 1, high-speed circuit (concrete); 2, circuits of varying surfaces; 3, gravel road; 4, straight road (concrete, three-lane); 5, test course for handling operation; 6, special road surface; 7, high climbing road (17 to 30%); 8, noise-generating road; 9, muddy road; 10 road covered with salt; 11, gravel road; 12, weather center; 13, car test room; 14, wind tunnel; 15, distributor; 16, north-south straight road; 17, east-west straight road; 18, safety test ground; 19, land bridge; 20, special test course with a short sloping road; 21, central communication station. (*Ford Motor Co.*)

computers. Environmental laboratories simulate storms of all sorts (rain, snow, dust, wind), winter cold, summer heat, etc. Still other facilities include a room for evaluating models for dimensional and visual characteristics (under various lighting and colors), [22] a wind tunnel for investigating response to high speeds and side winds, an acoustical chamber to test response to vibration and noise. New test facilities are constantly being developed as demands for quality continue to advance.

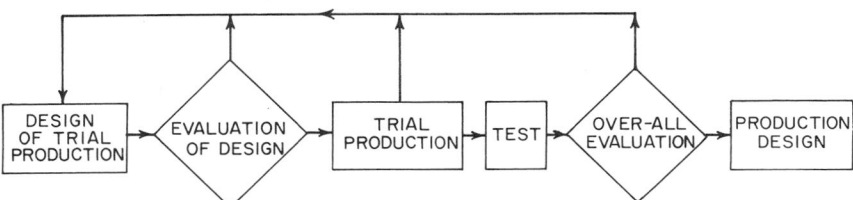

Fig. 42-7 Feedback of design evaluations.

Design Evaluation by Usage. The ultimate test of the designs is usage in the vehicle under actual driving conditions. For this purpose most car companies (as well as some tire companies) maintain a test track which simulates a wide spectrum of road surfaces (Figure 42-6). The test track is an elaborate and costly facility, since it is called on to evaluate a wide variety of vehicle and component performances.

Another form of usage evaluation is by collaboration with vehicle fleets. For example, a car manufacturer, aiming to provide a 5-year warranty on transmissions, arranged to install prototypes in New York City taxicabs to obtain usage data under severe operating conditions. [23]

Safety and Health Evaluation. Impact safety of vehicles is evaluated at an outdoor test ground equipped with test facilities for head-on collisions, barrier collisions, and vehicle rollover. Laboratory facilities include an impact simulator for reproducing collision phenomena indoors, analyzing driver and passenger behavior, and confirming the performance of safety devices. Still other impact tests evaluate the safety of parts.

Test facilities for accident prevention include a psychological laboratory and a driving simulator room for physical and psychological evaluation of driver response to disturbance, visual range, comfort and fatigue, as well as ease of manipulation of various switches and levers.

Exhaust emissions are analyzed and measured by chassis dynamometer, engine dynamometer, exhaust gas analyzer, and blow-by gas measuring devices which are combined by means of an electronic computer. A test on exhaust emission from an engine itself is conducted in a test room.

Overall Evaluation The results of design review, laboratory testing, and usage testing are constantly fed back to the product planning and product design departments as diagramed in Figure 42-7. In addition, overall evaluations are conducted to see how the model compares with competition, whether the model is responsive to users' complaints and service needs, and whether the model has remedied various quality troubles prevailing in existing models.

[22] Ishihara, Yasumasa, The Automation of Diesinking Automobile Stamping Parts, *Journal of the JSME,* vol. 73, No. 620, p. 58, September 1970 (in Japanese).

[23] Chesebrough, Harry E., Quality through Competition, *Industrial Quality Control,* May 1964, pp. 31–32.

From these evaluations, and from the evaluations of pilot production line performance (see below), the Product Planning department determines the extent to which the attainment of planned goals for quality, cost, and production capacity permits the project to proceed to mass production and marketing.

Preparation for Production   Concurrently with design planning there is planning for mass production. In some car companies this planning centers on a pilot production plant which has the capacity to assemble a few cars daily.[24] The pilot production lines, which start up about 9 months ahead of mass production, are closely observed by the Design, Methods, Quality Control, and Production departments to identify the problems inherent in scaling up production into large numbers. The pilot plant also enables the company to evaluate tooling and processing adequacy, and to train key supervisors from the assembly plants. These men then train the remaining assembly supervision in their respective plants. The pilot plant also assembles many of the engineering prototypes, which again enables Manufacturing personnel to identify potential tooling, production, and quality problems at an early date.

Organization for New Model Planning   In the large car companies, new model planning always requires elaborate, formal coordination of the work of the "regular" departments (Design, Manufacture, etc.). This coordination is provided by:

1. Full-time planners assigned to the new model project
2. Committees of various kinds to carry out special coordination tasks,[25] and to aid in interdepartmental communication
3. Formalized written plans which embody the agreements and which become a form of impersonal supervision for the project
4. Formalized procedures such as written sign-offs

The formal, organized planning process goes by various names, e.g., Quality Validation. The flow diagrams vary in detail, but not in conceptual approach.

PURCHASING

Automobile manufacturers usually purchase from 25 to 50% of the finished components assembled into the vehicle. The quality of this huge volume of purchased goods affects the car company in several important ways:

1. Internal scrap and rework traceable to defective purchased products
2. Downtime of the automated production lines due to stoppages caused by defective purchased materials and components
3. Customer claims and dissatisfaction traceable to unreliable purchased components

Vendor Relations   For many purchased components, the car companies write only the performance specification, whereas the vendor provides the product design needed to meet this specification. In this way the car company buys not merely the physical product; it buys also the design capability of the vendor, as well as his manufacturing and quality control capabilities. To purchase these collective capabilities (rather than merely purchasing standard commodities) has required a drastic revision in vendor relations programs.[26]

Prior to this revision, the scheme of vendor relations featured a high degree of

[24] For an early example, see New Quality Control Center for Ford Motor Co., *Industrial Quality Control,* January 1959, p. 18.

[25] Reliability committees have been an example. See Gretzinger, J. R., Buick's Reliability Program, *Industrial Quality Control,* March 1965, pp. 449–454.

[26] This revision is quite similar to that undergone in industry generally. See Section 10, under Joint Quality Planning.

vendor independence and isolation, with the purchaser relying largely on incoming inspection for his quality control. The new relationship has established a high degree of interdependence which features:

1. Broad-spectrum contracts which require extensive vendor qualification activities prior to product delivery, and guarantees subsequent to delivery. An example of such a contract[27] is seen in Table 42-1.

TABLE 42-1   Example of Vendor Contract

We agree to maintain and improve the quality of products purchased by you, and to conform to the terms of the regulations hereunder.

1. We will assure that the products you purchase meet your requirements for function, performance and reliability.

2. We assume full responsibility for this assurance, including the purchased products from subcontractors.

3. We will maintain and improve quality through improvement in each of the required characteristics.

4. We agree that the acceptance inspection is to be performed by the sampling plan and acceptance standard contained in your "Standard of Acceptance Inspection."

5. We will make the following disposition of defective product:

a. We will take back rejected lots or defectives at our expense.

b. In case a claim occurs in the market because of our parts, we will treat it according to the "Continued Sales Contract" we have concluded with you.

6. When defects occur in your firm or in the market, we will quarantine our defects while we analyze the cause and prevent a recurrence.

7. We will make available to you the data you need for quality assurance.

8. In case you need to survey our manufacturing process, we will furnish you with data and assistance required for such a survey.

2. Direct communication between the corresponding specialists in the two companies, e.g., product designers, manufacturing planners, quality engineers. This follows general industrial practice.[28] (See Section 10, under Multiple Communication Channels.)

3. An extensive concept of joint planning in which the vendor's plan of quality control must satisfy the car company. In return, the car company provides the vendor with technical know-how and, in some cases, with the dies, jigs, and tools needed in the operation.

A major effect of the new relationships has been a shift by the car companies away from emphasis on incoming inspection and toward the concept of surveillance. In addition, the new relationships have tended to reduce vendor turnover, and thereby to reduce start-up quality troubles.

An open question in vendor relations is the extent of vendor responsibility for guarantee charges resulting from field failure of vendor components. Generally the vendors are willing to supply replacement components at no charge but have been unwilling to pay the labor charges required to restore service.

Vendor Selection   While Purchasing is the company's prime contact with the vendor, the decision on vendor selection is a broad-based determination in which Product Design and Quality Control play important roles.

One aspect of this joint determination is the vendor survey concept which is widely used by the car companies. The survey is a study of vendor quality capability

---

[27] Shirane, L., *Statistical Quality Control*, chap. 8, Vendors, vol. 15, No. 8, p. 81, 1964 (in Japanese).

[28] However, some car companies have centralized certain aspects of the control system such as delivery schedule, delivery control, schedule changes, and disposition of quality troubles. (This constitutes a combining of the previously separate systems of production control and quality control.)

and is conducted prior to any contract award.   The car company practice follows general industrial practice as set out in some detail in Section 10, under Vendor Quality Survey.[29]

However, the car companies do not purchase from vendors based solely on the findings of the survey.   They also require the vendor to prepare production samples of the product as proof that his product design and manufacturing processes are adequate to meet the product quality requirements.   In addition, they may require the vendor to establish an adequate control system as a condition of contract award.

Vendors who succeed in qualifying their samples are formally placed on the "Approved Vendor List" for that product.   The vendors' presence on the approved list authorizes Purchasing to buy regular production quantities and has effects in other ways as well, e.g., incoming inspection practice.

When very large car companies are organized in several car divisions, these divisions have often contracted with the same vendor for the same component, with resulting multiple surveys, multiple qualification of samples, etc.   During the 1960s there was a trend in these large companies to designate one of the divisions to do such survey and qualification work for all.   In addition, a move was begun to create internal data banks to collect data on vendor performance and to make the data available for all.[30]

Quality Assurance by the Vendor   The vendor is faced with the same problems of product planning, design planning, manufacturing planning, etc., as is the car company, though on a lesser scale of complexity.   In consequence, most of the topics discussed in this Section with respect to the car company apply to the vendor as well, and hence will not be listed a second time.   However, several elements do require elaboration.

Understanding the Specifications.   Whatever the vendor makes is always part of a broader system which has been designed by the car company.   It is essential for the vendor to understand the nature of this broader system and the role of his component in it.   It is also important for him to understand the relative importance of the various quality characteristics so that his efforts are properly concentrated and so that his control standards and criteria are in harmony with the needs.[31]

Sample Approval.   The samples[32] submitted to the car company for test and validation should come from the regular production processes.   Failing this, both the car company and the vendor may be fooled; i.e., if the samples test out successfully, they may prove the validity of the product design, but they do not prove the validity of the mass production process, since they were made by other methods. Many serious delays have been caused by failure to observe this rule.

Comparison of Test Methods.   The sample approval procedure should also include a check of the compatibility of test methods.   For this purpose, the vendor should include the test data with the test certificate attached to the samples.   (This should include results such as destructive testing and accelerated life testing.)   In turn, the vendor should receive the car company's test results to help discover and correct any differences in testing technique.

[29] It is evident from the discussion in Section 10 that the validity of vendor surveys as a predictor of vendor performance is open to serious question.   In practice, many managers consider that the record of actual deliveries by the vendor is the really reliable predictor of what the vendor may do in the future.

[30] For detail, see Section 10, under Vendor Qualification Process.

[31] A vendor selling the same component to several automobile manufacturers nevertheless finds it necessary to tailor-make his approach to meet the varying practices of these manufacturers, e.g., in system design, in sampling criteria, or in documentation requirements.

[32] The number of samples is negotiated based on the needs for destructive testing, life testing, and dispersion data.

Sampling Acceptance Criteria. Sampling for process control follows conventional practice.[33] However, the sampling of the final product before it goes to the car companies is often governed by agreement, either in the purchase contract or in the referenced documents. Sometimes the guiding criteria are the car company's manual on incoming inspection plans. In such cases, the vendor commonly chooses a plan somewhat more severe than that to be used by the car companies.

The new legislation on car safety has made it necessary that all attribute sampling plans involving safety features be designed with an acceptance number of zero; i.e., they allow no defects in the sample. Any published sampling plan allowing one or more defects in the sample is subject to attack on the (fallacious) ground that it legitimizes the acceptance of unsafe products.

Controls on the Vendor The car companies maintain multiple controls on the vendor. Some of these precede production, e.g., vendor survey, sample approval, and joint quality planning. Other controls take place during production and after production.

Acceptance Inspection. For the first 1 to 3 months of mass production the automobile manufacturer may conduct random sampling (e.g., using MIL-STD-105D) of the finished purchased products to ensure that they conform to the levels represented by the approved samples. If defects are found, sampling is extended and action is taken as needed. However, if the mass production conforms to the approved samples, the sampling is phased out and is replaced by examination of the vendor's test certificates plus periodic audit. This is a very desirable goal, since it avoids duplicate inspections and makes the vendor fully responsible for delivering good product plus the proof that it is good.

Audits. Aside from controls through product sampling, the automobile companies review the vendors' adherence to the quality control plan.[34] This involves visits to the vendors' premises, to review items such as those set out in Table 42-2.

TABLE 42-2 Example of Vendor Audit Subjects

Quality control systems, policies	Materials control
Organization	Special process controls (e.g., heat treatment, welding)
Quality control procedures	Control of reference documents (specifications, drawings)
Company standards	Disposition of defectives
Inspection standards	Lot identification and traceability
Operation standards	Packaging, transport, and storage
Measuring instruments and test sets	Warranty system
Manufacturing facilities	Housekeeping

The audits also include a review of completeness of documentation, especially as to meeting legal obligations imposed by safety legislation.

In addition, it is usual to reconfirm test results by sampling checks to see if the vendors' test data are reproduced. Where the tests are destructive, the reconfirmation is by actual test at the time of audit.

Vendor Rating. A final control on vendors is achieved by summarizing data on vendor performance of various sorts: percent of deliveries which conform fully to quality standards; internal losses due to vendor defects; results of quality audits; extent of field failures traceable to vendor's product, etc. These summaries may be converted into vendor rating[35] terms for the purpose of comparing vendors or observing long-range trends and for use during contract negotiation.

[33] See generally Section 23.
[34] Shirane, *op. cit.*
[35] See Section 10, under Vendor Quality Rating.

MANUFACTURE

Figure 42-8 shows the main flow for automotive production.[36]   Starting with basic materials, the mechanical components are fabricated, sometimes in batch processes (e.g., forging, casting, stamping) and sometimes in continuous production (e.g., machining, heat treatment).   Subsequent progression (e.g., assembly, painting) is on a continuous flow basis.

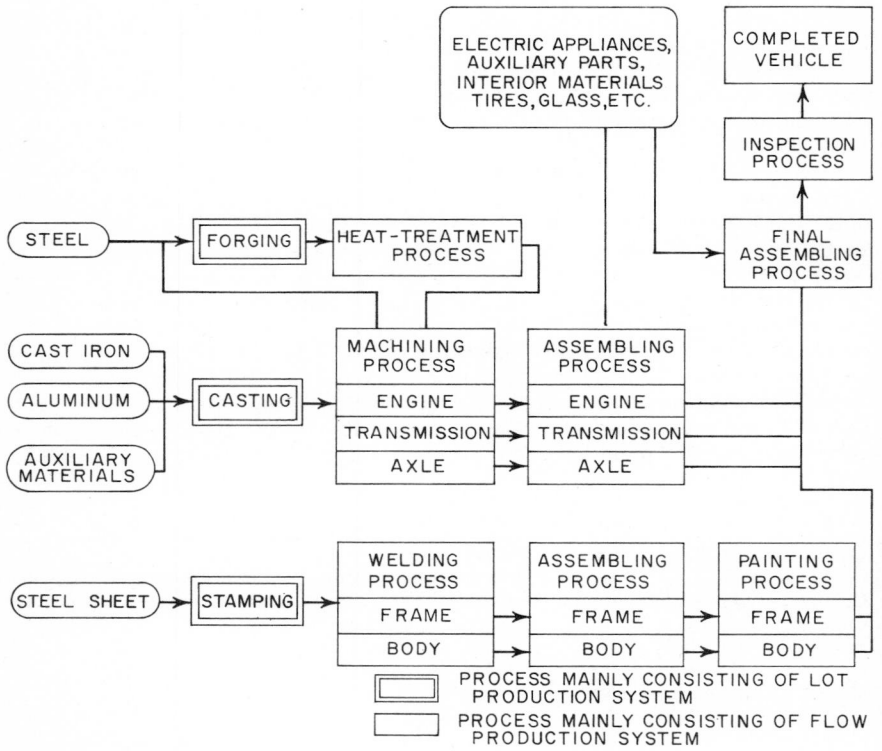

Fig. 42-8   Flow of production process.

Development of Manufacturing Methods   With growth in volume of vehicle production, the economics of automated manufacture became more favorable.   However, experience showed that automated machines and associated transfer devices demanded improved uniformity of input components if the automated processes were to maintain continuous production.   To meet these demands, the industry developed manufacturing and quality control techniques which in turn have profoundly affected the approach to quality control for the entire industry.   It turned out that under automation it was possible to improve productivity, make more economic use of manpower, and at the same time attain a higher quality of product.

[36]"Automotive Engineers Handbook," Section 13, chap. 1, pp. 13–1, 13–7, Society of Automotive Engineers of Japan (SAEJ), 1970 (in Japanese).

To maintain the quality of the automated process it has become necessary for the car manufacturers to develop:

1. Machines equipped with electronic brains for process control
2. Automated instruments capable of making 100% inspection
3. Machines capable of performing difficult operations traditionally performed by human workers

The industry has been quite successful in meeting these challenges. For example, Figure 42-9 shows the flow diagram for finishing the engine crankshaft. It is seen that the process utilizes automated sizing, automated inspection for numerous important qualities, and machining control using a minicomputer.

The earlier applications of mechanical automation concentrated on machining operations, e.g., transfer machines for cylinder blocks. More recently there has been a large-scale extension to use of industrial robots for such tasks as automatic welding of the main body[37] (Figure 42-10).

Production Preparation   All car companies maintain specialized departments which collectively carry out the preparatory steps through which the production force will be able to achieve and maintain the required quality. Several of these preparatory steps require some discussion.[38]

Facilities and Process Planning.   The process planning step specifies what operations are to be performed, the tools and machines to be used, and other aspects of production technique.[39] A critical element of this planning is whether the quality capability[40] of the process is adequate for the tolerances specified on the design drawing. In the case of critical quality characteristics (e.g., safety, basic vehicle function) it is necessary to choose processes which are extremely stable, or to fool-proof the production and inspection systems.

As the process plans are completed, they are classified by machines, tools, instruments, conveyors, etc., to provide a basis for facility planning and procurement.

Increasingly, the quality of tooling is being aided by modern computer methods. Figure 42-11 shows how a press die for a body component is manufactured in this way.[41] Computer graphics are used to prepare rough drawings from an idea sketch. A clay model is made to these rough drawings and, after modification, is measured by use of an automatic comparator to prepare an intermediate drawing. After further discussion and drawing modification, a full-scale clay model is prepared for final review. The resulting approved clay model is measured to provide the final design drawing. This in turn permits making the template, the master model, the part model, and the model for die milling. A copying machine prepares a tape from the contours of the die milling model, and this tape then drives the numerically controlled machine which makes the die.

Aside from greatly improving the efficiency of die manufacture, this method yields dies of high quality and reproducibility. The accuracy of body fits is improved, contributing to avoidance of later assembly defects.

Trial Mass Production.   Based on the planned factory layout, the facilities are installed and the tools, jigs, gages, etc., are prepared for production. At this stage a

[37] Kobayashi, Tokuo, Labor Saving by Production Engineering in Mass Production Field, *Journal of the Society of Automotive Engineers of Japan* (SAEJ), vol. 24, No. 7, p. 741, 1970 (in Japanese).

[38] Some of these specialized departments deal with such matters as cost estimation or time schedule. These matters, though obliquely related to quality, will not be discussed in any detail.

[39] For a general discussion, see Section 9.

[40] See generally Section 9, under Process Capability.

[41] Ishihara, *op. cit.*

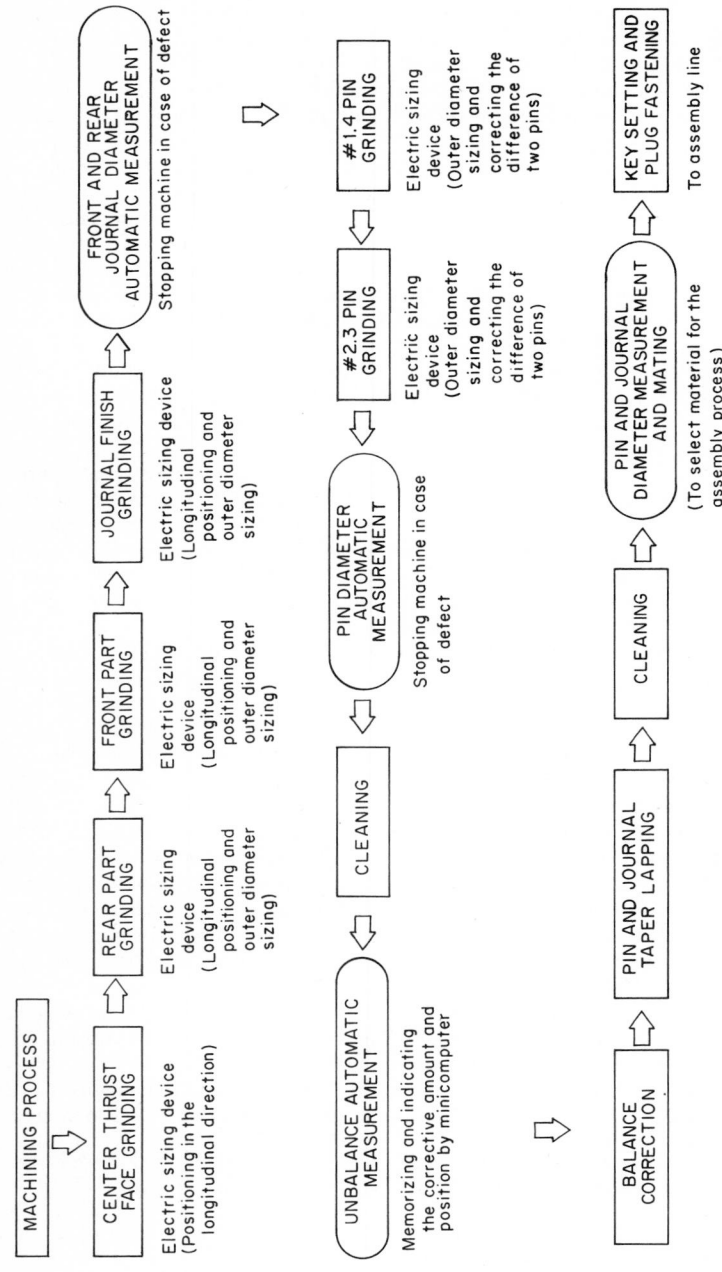

Fig. 42-9 Automated process for finishing crankshaft.

trial mass production is carried out to confirm that the quality performance (also productivity, etc.) can be attained. A vital aspect of this trial is to investigate fully the variability or dispersion of the product at all stages, from manufacture of parts through final assembly and test as automobiles. These same dispersion data

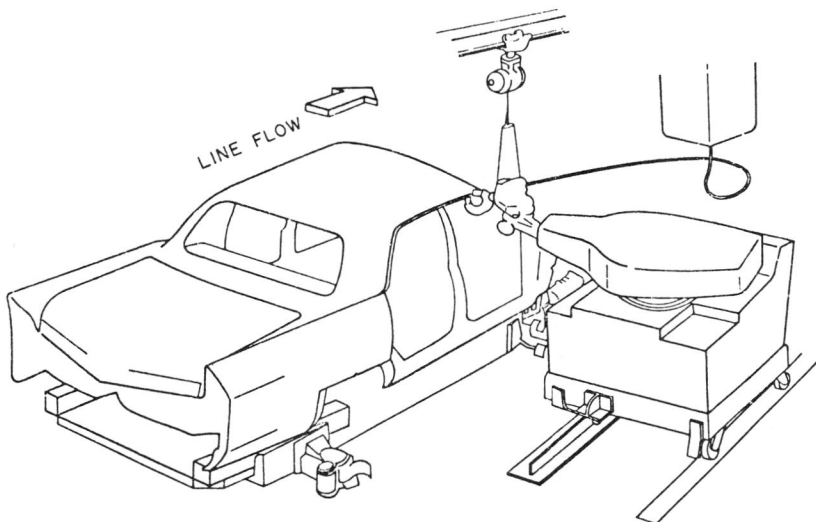

LINE FLOW

Fig. 42-10   Automatic welding of main body by industrial robot.

are needed to confirm the adequacy of the processes and to identify those requiring improved uniformity or revised standards.

The trial mass production serves also to identify needed changes in tooling so that final corrections can be made prior to regular production. In addition, the trial provides a basis for establishing responsibilities and schedules for tool control. Responsibility for tool control is assigned differently in different companies and company departments. However, the control plans can always be more wisely established if the process capability data are available.

Process Control   Two recent trends have helped to simplify the quality control of the manufacturing process:

1. Automation, which is based on superior quality planning and which eliminates much human error

2. Computer processing and feedback of quality data, which simplify data feedback for control

However, there remains a great deal of production which is still carried out by older, conventional processes. Such processes are more susceptible to worker variability. Hence there is need for thorough standardization of technique and for adequate training in use of correct technique. In addition, these processes are subject to worker errors for reasons of monotony, carelessness, etc. Prevention of such errors requires foolproofing of processes as well as worker motivation.[42]

Feedback of Inspection Data.   The industry has long recognized the need for prompt identification of quality troubles, and feedback of the necessary alarm sig-

[42] See generally Section 18.

nals to those who can act to remedy the situation.   However, the great size and complexity of the plants has made it difficult to execute this feedback by written data methods.

More recently, the companies have begun to employ the computer to process the

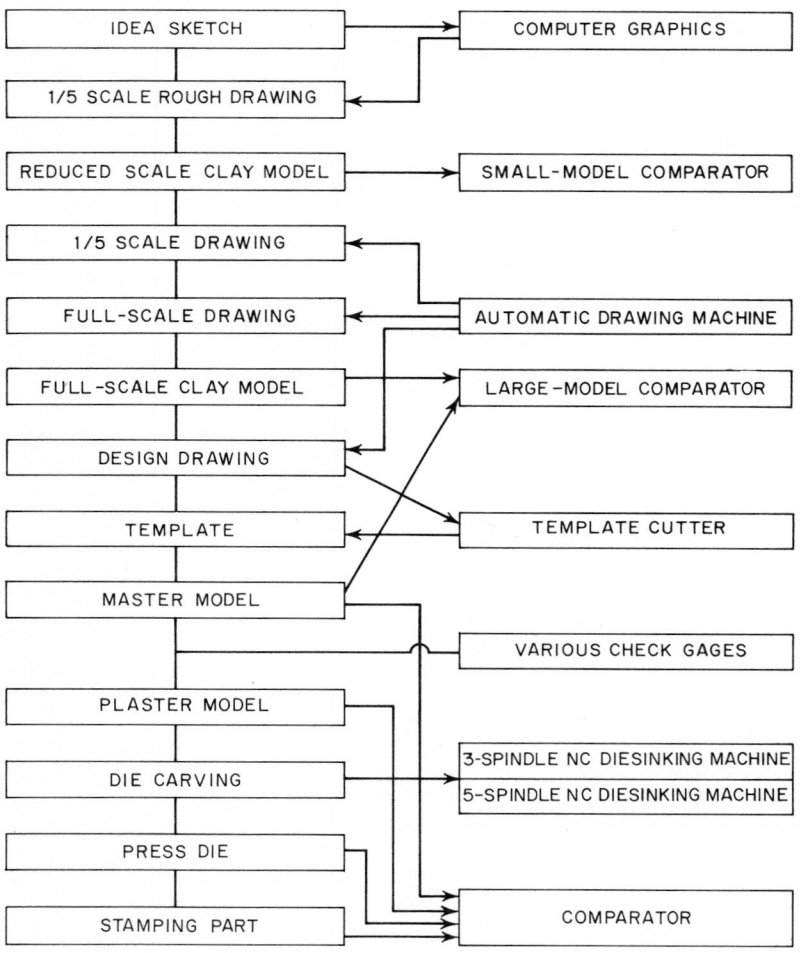

Fig. 42-11 Manufacturing process of press die.

quality data and to provide prompt feedback to the supervisor concerned.   A typical example of such a system, as applied to the final assembly shop, is seen in Figure 42-12.   Under the system, any trouble discovered in the shop is transmitted from the inspection station to the computer, which immediately relays the information to the supervisors involved.[43]

[43] Di Cicco, John J., Dynamic Quality Control, *Industrial Quality Control,* November 1965, pp. 235–239.

Conventional control charts can play a useful, continuing role in some processes, and they are extensively used in the industry.

Control of Process Capability.   The automotive industry makes wide use of the concept of process capability.   The approach is conventional, as discussed in Section 9, under Process Capability.   Usual practice in the automotive industry is to regard a process as able to hold the tolerance when 6σ of the process is no greater than 0.75 of the tolerance limits (for unilateral tolerances, no greater than about 0.87 of the limits).

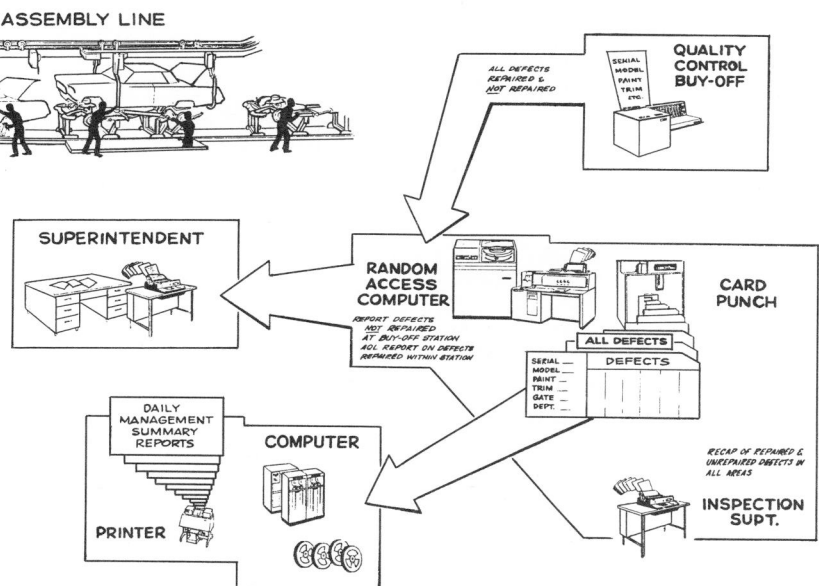

Fig. 42-12   Flow of inspection information.

Because process capability can vary with process conditions, it is useful, for some processes, to maintain a running record of process capability, and to investigate any significant deterioration.   Figure 42-13 is an example of such a record.

Operator Self-Control.   The automotive industry has been undergoing a worldwide movement to put the operators in a state of self-control.   In its earlier stages this movement has emphasized meeting the well-known criteria for self-control as set out in Section 11, under Concept of Operator Self-Control, *et seq.*   As the managers meet these criteria, the operators have increasingly been put into a state where they are able to regulate the process so that the quality specifications will be met.

More recently, this movement has been expanded to include the concept of operator self-inspection; i.e., the operator not only makes decisions on whether the process should run, stop, or be adjusted; he also makes decisions on whether the product conforms to specification or not.   The approach used follows generally the plan set out in Section 11, under Product Acceptance by Operators.

Maintenance of Automatic Controls.   As in industry generally, the automotive industry has traditionally made wide use of automatic controls in its chemical and metallurgical processes.   More recently the concept has been extended widely to the machining operations as well.   The control methods follow generally the approach discussed in Section 9, under Automatic Process Regulation, making use of

工 程 能 力 推 移 一 覧 表

機番	IG-27	機名	内 エアマイクロ	品番	$8\phi^{+0.025}_{\ -0}$	品名	A

測定要因：測定器　内面研削 経　測定単位 0.001　刃工具 DA80L　図面寸法　公差巾(T) 0.025

No.	測定年月日（推移値）	σ_p	$6\sigma_p$	$Cp=\dfrac{T}{6\sigma_p}$	等級	σ_m	$6\delta_m$	$8\delta_m$	$**Cp=\dfrac{T}{8\delta_m}$
1	46.3.20	0.0037	0.0222	1.13	2	0.0025	0.0150	0.0200	1.25
2	4.11	0.0033	0.0198	1.26	1	0.0021	0.0126	0.0168	1.49
3	5.15	0.0034	0.0204	1.23	1	0.0023	0.0138	0.0184	1.36
4	6.13	0.0035	0.0210	1.20	2	0.0024	0.0144	0.0192	1.30
5	7.18	0.0032	0.0192	1.30	1	0.0020	0.0120	0.0160	1.56
6									
7									
8									
9									
10									
11									
12									

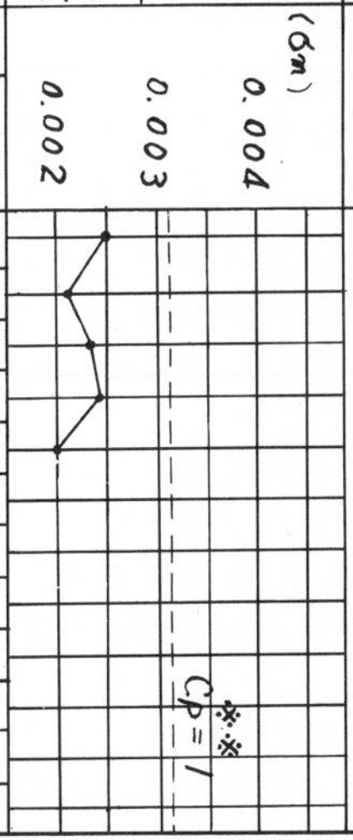

判定基準

判定	等級
$Cp > 1.33$	1
$1.33 \geqq Cp > 1$	2
$1 > Cp > 0.67$	3
$0.67 \geqq Cp$	4

グラフ：(δ_m)　0.004　0.003　0.002　公差巾(T) 0.025　$Cp = 1$ ※※※

備考欄
　σ_p : standard deviation of process
　　　　　(indicating the process capability)
　σ_m : standard deviation of quality fluctuation due to machine

Fig. 42-13 Process capability record.

automatic measurement and feedback for regulation, all without human intervention.

However, maintenance of the systems does require human intervention, and is built around the concept of maintaining the process capability. To this end, technicians are specially trained in inspection and maintenance of these automatic control systems. In response to the maintenance schedule administered by a special control center, a technician checks the process capability and conducts the necessary repair and replacement.

Process Improvement An essential aspect of automotive manufacture is constant improvement of the products and processes. The industry has long been active in such improvements through the efforts of the supervision and engineers.[44] The contribution of the workers, usually through suggestion systems, has varied greatly from company to company, and has usually been relatively minor in importance.

During the 1960s, the Japanese industries undertook extensive educational programs for foremen and workers on how to control and improve quality by modern technique. For example, in the Toyota Motor Company, such educational programs started in 1961. Manufacturing supervisors and foremen were trained in such matters as concept of quality control, Pareto diagram, characteristic factor (Ishikawa) diagram, histograms, control charts, and correlation diagrams. Following this, "QC Circles"[45] were organized to solve intradepartmental quality problems under the guidance of the work leaders. The originality and energy of these QC Circle members have contributed remarkably to process improvement.

Based on the QC Circles, a campaign was started in 1967 to eliminate defects and claims due to process deficiencies and operator error. The projects chosen for improvement are displayed on the information bulletin board in the form shown in Figure 42-14. In the example shown, the project was to reduce operator errors on the meter cable clamp. (In 4 months, the defects were eliminated completely.)

INSPECTION

The automotive industry makes extensive use of inspection to confirm the attainment of quality of materials, components, assemblies, and completed vehicles. These same inspections provide the data needed to regulate the processes, detect and eliminate troubles, make quality improvements, and prepare control reports for the managers.

While the inspections are extensive, many of them are quite conventional and follow the principles and practices set out in Section 12, Inspection and Test. Such inspections will not be discussed in any detail, and the reader is referred to Section 12 for a more extensive discussion. There are, however, some features of inspection which are unique to automotive manufacture which will be treated more extensively in the present Section.

Seriousness Classification of Defects The industry gives wide recognition to the concept that defects are not equal in importance. In most companies this concept is standardized into a formal seriousness classification scheme following the conventional procedures set out in Section 12, under Seriousness Classification. A typical example as used in the automotive industry is shown in Table 42-3. Once the classifications have been made, the sample sizes, AQLs, allowable number of defects, and other inspection criteria take account of the differences in defect seriousness.

---

[44] See generally Section 16, for the organized approach to quality improvement of management-controllable defects.

[45] See Section 18, under The Japanese QC Circle.

Organization for Inspection　The car companies follow the conventional practice of grouping their inspections by process stages, i.e., incoming, process, and final inspection.　In addition, the great size of the plants leads to specialized test laboratories which become a second basis for organizing, either by scientific discipline, e.g., chemical, metallurgical, or by product, e.g., engine test.

Inspection methods are prescribed by inspection supervisors or by specialist engineers depending on the nature of the product.　These methods are formalized in

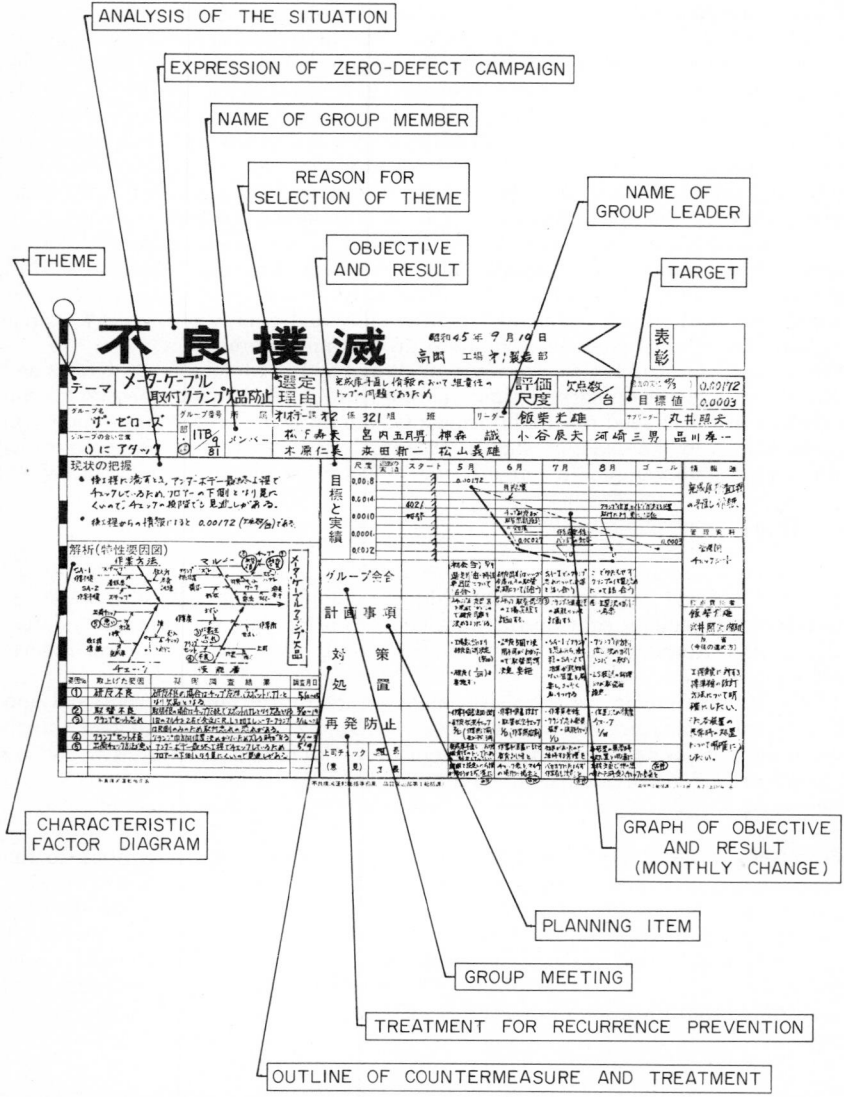

Fig. 42-14　Bulletin display of improvement.

TABLE 42-3   Seriousness Classification of Automotive Defects

Class	Nature	Description	Examples
A	Critical to safety; essential to vehicle function	Defects which can endanger human life or can render the vehicle inoperative in an essential functional degree	Heat treatment of kingpins; pressure resistance of hydraulic brake hose
B	General function of vehicle; function of essential parts; appearance essential to the user	Nonsafety defects which might affect primary vehicle function; essential appearance characteristics	Noisy brakes; trunk lock will not open; body finish discolored
C	Functions of minor parts; appearance not essential to user	Defects which do not affect vehicle function or appearance essential to user. Defects neither A nor B	Rust on chassis; crooked identification decals on components

conventional manner as discussed in Section 12, under Inspection Planning.

The actual inspection plans differ widely depending on the nature of the process. Press operations, being controlled by very stable tools, require very small samples, generally on an attribute basis. Machining operations are usually inspected on a variables basis, sometimes aided by chart control. Major components and finished vehicles receive much 100% test and detailed documentation as well.

In some companies the inspection stations ("buy stations") are established with considerable formality, including formal written signatures as evidence of inspection approval. In turn, the material handlers have no authority to move material out of any department unless the inspection signatures authorize such moves. The advent of government safety regulations has sharpened the need for formal designations of authority to approve for quality, and for formal documentation to record the day-to-day approvals.

Raw Material Inspection.[46] Mainly this is done by highly standardized tests and examinations. Metals are checked for chemical compositions and for physical and dimensional properties, using conventional test equipment. Test of machining qualities (by tool bits, grinding wheels, etc.) is necessary for future productivity. Nondestructive testing is widely used for hidden metallic defects. Nonmetallic materials similarly undergo conventional testing, though special tests apply to materials vital to safety, e.g., glass sheets, which are checked for heat resistance, shock, strain, transparency, quick cooling, and strength (for tempered glass).

Process Inspection. This again follows conventional practice,[47] but with emphasis on the special needs of the industry. Casting inspection includes analysis of a furnace specimen for chemical composition and for tensile, bending, and hardness tests. (Chemical composition of castings is very important, and is closely checked by highly sophisticated modern instruments.)[48] Forgings undergo similar chemical and metallurgical tests.[49]

Mechanical processes such as stamping and metal cutting[50] are characterized by

---

[46] See generally Sections 10 and 12. See also "Automotive Engineers Handbook," Section 13, chap. 11, Inspection, Society of Automotive Engineers of Japan (SAEJ), 1970 (in Japanese).

[47] See generally Section 12, Inspection and Test; also "Automotive Engineers Handbook," *op. cit.*

[48] See also Section 34 (Foundry Quality Control).

[49] See also Section 35 (Metal Fabricating), under Metal Forging.

[50] See also Section 35, under Press Work and under Metal Cutting.

mass production, high-speed, automated lines working to very close tolerances. Inspection for these lines has required a corresponding development of precise automated instruments,[51] some of which perform functions beyond measurement; i.e., they control the process, record the data, analyze the data, prepare reports, etc.[52] On safety-critical parts the tests may be performed 100%, e.g., automated 100% test of hardening depth of rear axle shafts.

Use of automated measuring devices requires careful attention to instrument calibration and maintenance of accuracy. See generally Section 13.

Subassemblies consisting of functioning units (e.g., engine, clutch, transmission,

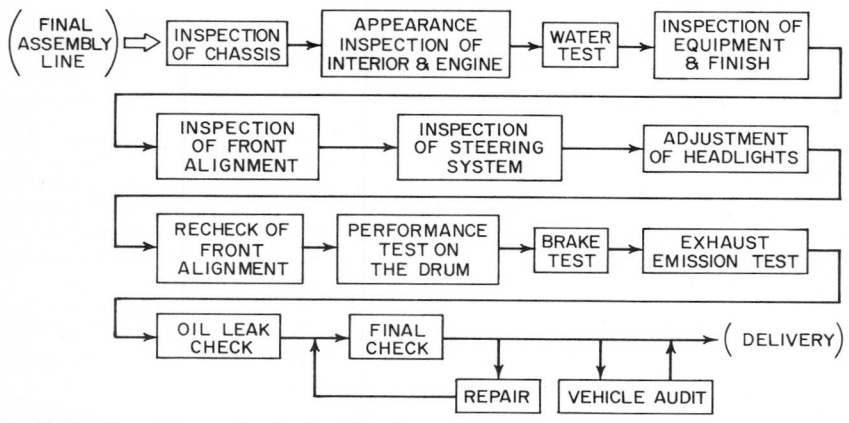

Fig. 42-15   Flow diagram for final vehicle inspection.

front and rear axles, steering assembly) are commonly checked before entering final assembly. Emphasis is on the performance and functional characteristics, for which special test equipment is necessary. Generally only sample testing is done. However, for vital characteristics the testing is 100%.

Test equipment is designed for high-speed automated operation. Examples are (1) the dynamometers used to test engines for power, torque, fuel consumption, oil consumption, exhaust emission, etc., and (2) test programs to simulate actual running of automatic transmissions.

Final Vehicle Inspection.   All finished vehicles undergo a series of inspections and tests as shown in the flow diagram in Figure 42-15. The visual inspections are conventional but the tests are mainly unique to automotive vehicles.

1. Water test. The vehicle, under simulated driving conditions, is moved through a simulated rainstorm to test for water invasion.

2. Front wheel alignment. The toe and camber of the front wheels are checked with a dynamic tester. It operates on the principle that if a wheel runs on two parallel rollers, any toe and camber will generate measurable reaction forces.

3. Headlight aim. The headlight alignment is checked by a photoelectric receptor directed squarely at the headlights.

4. Drum tester. Each vehicle is driven on a drum equipped with the same inertia

[51] See, for example, Ford Engine Plant Emphasizes Automatic Gaging, *Quality Assurance,* July 1970, pp. 56, 57.

[52] See, for example, Now, Doughnuts to Computers, *Quality Assurance,* July 1970, pp. 58, 59.

as the vehicle. Among the tests are speedometer, acceleration, transmission operation, vehicle noise, rolling resistance.

5. Brake test. The braking force of each wheel is measured by applying a specified foot pressure to the brake pedal as the wheel rotates on two parallel rollers.

6. Chassis dynamometer. This is equipped with flywheels and a power absorption unit giving inertia and road load equivalent to the vehicle. It measures engine power, fuel consumption, acceleration, and vehicle noise of each vehicle.

7. Exhaust emission analyzer. While each vehicle operates on a chassis dynamometer, the exhaust gases are connected to an analyzer to measure emissions of carbon monoxide, carbon dioxide, hydrocarbons, and nitrogen oxides. A data processing unit attached to the analyzer calculates the final results.

A traveling inspection card accompanies each vehicle. Any defects found are entered on the card and serve to inform the repairmen of what needs to be corrected. The information on defects found is also fed back to the production departments to make corrections in the processes and procedures.

The trend has been to electronic data feedback. In one system, the defect data are fed into a computer through scanners. The computer calculates the current quality levels and compares them with the target levels stored in its memory bank. The resulting deviations are sent by immediate teletype to the man in direct charge for process and procedural correction. In addition, the computer, through the vehicle serial number, watches to see whether vehicles sent back for correction have been properly corrected.[53]

Visual vehicle inspections face all the problems of using human beings as instruments.[54] To avoid a tendency to either undue looseness or perfectionism, it is necessary to sample review the decisions made by inspectors to retain a good balance.

In one interesting experiment, 600 cars (which had already gone through regular inspection and were ready for shipment) were set aside and given a further inspection by quality specialists who were playing the role of a customer checking out the operation of his new car. All defects found were noted and corrected. For the following 16 months the warranty claims on these "special" vehicles were closely watched and compared with the claims on the regular product. It was found that the "special" vehicles had lower warranty claims, resulting in savings which were close to the cost of the added inspection (of about 1 hour per vehicle). Further analysis showed that application of the Pareto principle permitted 95% of the defects to be found by only about 20 minutes of added inspection per vehicle.[55]

FIELD SERVICE

Automobile sales are seldom direct from the car company to the user; mostly they take place through intermediate distributors and dealers. Because the automobile is a long life product, the manufacturer's continuing obligations for product performance and reliability are also transmitted through this distribution chain.

Role of the Dealer[56] The dealer's contract with the car company imposes on him various obligations with respect to product quality. The dealer's role is not only to sell cars, but also to:

1. Deliver the vehicle in good condition to the user, and transmit manufacturers' information (on vehicle care, etc.) to the user

---

[53] Building the Chevrolet Vega, *Automobile Engineer,* November 1970, pp. 456–461.

[54] See Section 12, under Sensory Qualities.

[55] Buick's "Product Integrity," *Quality Assurance,* July 1970, pp. 50–51.

[56] See generally "Automotive Engineering Handbook," Section 12, chap. 8, pp. 12–47, Sales Arrangement, Society of Automotive Engineers of Japan, 1970 (in Japanese).

2. Maintain good customer relations with the user, including repair service and claim adjustment

3. Provide the manufacturer with data on user experience and vehicle performance, as a feedback for improving present products and for planning new products

4. Accept used vehicles as trade-ins on new car sales

The Vehicle Service System   The automobile operates over long distances and in many geographical areas. During this operation it requires local sources of fuel,

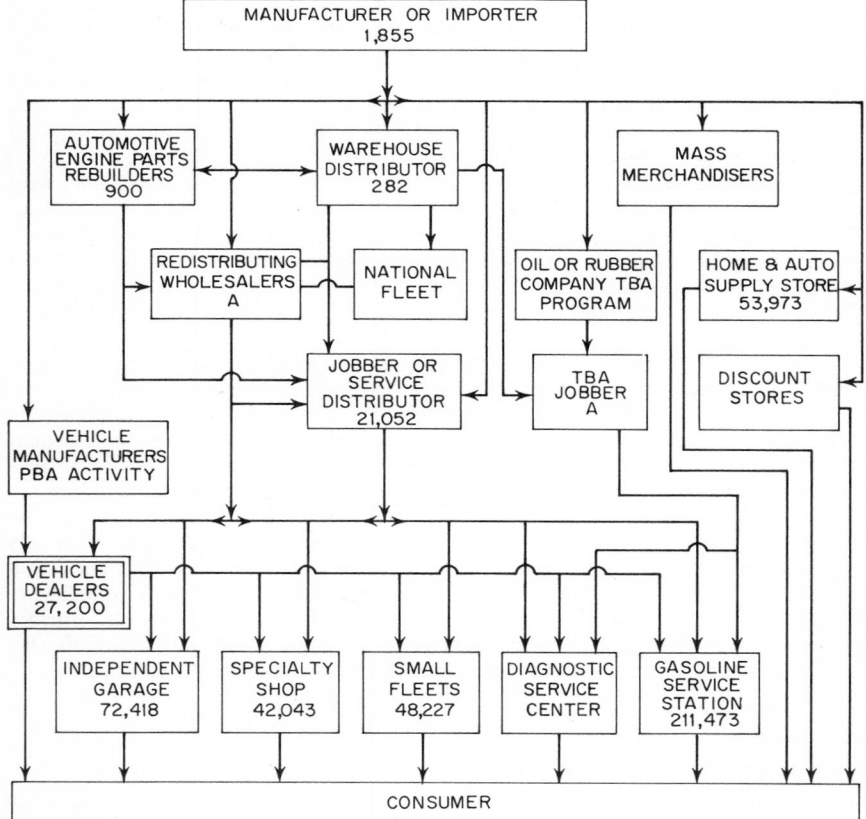

Fig. 42-16 Automotive parts aftermarket channels of distribution. (A) Redistributing and TBA jobbers are included in the jobber or service distribution total of 21,052.

other supplies, inspection service, and repair service. To meet these needs there has evolved a system of vehicle service organized (in the United States) along the lines shown in Figure 42-16.[57]

The Service Shop.   The lower blocks in Figure 42-16 show that there are in the United States several hundred thousand shops which provide inspection and repair service. During the guarantee period the vehicle dealers dominate this service.

[57] Automobile Parts Market in America and Europe, *Report of Third Inspection Team on the Distribution System for Automobile Parts,* p. 26, Junsei News Company, 1970 (in Japanese).

Thereafter the user has a range of choices, including the vehicle dealer shops. The numerous gasoline service stations are equipped to make the more frequent, minor repairs and replacements. More extensive repairs require the services of garages or specialty shops.

The Spare Parts Supply System. Repairs and replacements require spare parts, and these reach the repair shops through an "aftermarket" (i.e., after original vehicle sale) network of supply.

The spare parts may have been made by (1) the car manufacturer, (2) the vendor to the car manufacturer, or (3) independent spare parts makers. In contrast to the strict quality controls observed by car makers before assembling components into new cars, the spare parts distribution system, being composed of merchants and lacking test laboratories, exercises very little control over quality of spare parts.

Because of the essential character of automobile transport,[58] it is necessary that the repair shops maintain an adequate inventory of spare parts to permit prompt repair.

The New Car Warranty.[59] Despite the prevailing, rigorous quality control systems, it has not been feasible to eliminate automobile defects or field failures. In consequence, all manufacturers provide, as part of the original purchase arrangement, a guarantee that they will repair, free of charge, defects due to faulty design or manufacture. The terms of the guarantee have varied from time to time[60] and from manufacturer to manufacturer. Table 42-4 is an example of the wording of such a guarantee.

TABLE 42-4   Example of Wording of Car Guarantee

WHAT IS WARRANTED AND FOR HOW LONG

Buick (Buick Motor Division, General Motors Corporation) warrants to the owner of each 1971 model Buick passenger car that for a period of 12 months or 12,000 miles, whichever first occurs, it will repair, or at its option replace, any defective or malfunctioning part of the car — except tires, which are warranted separately by the tire manufacturer.

The 12 month/12,000 mile warranty period shall begin on the date the car is delivered to the first retail purchaser or, if the car is first placed in service as a demonstrator or company car prior to sale at retail, on the date the car is first placed in such service.

This warranty covers only malfunctions resulting from defects in material or workmanship.

While the car company stands behind the guarantee, the actual repair is carried out by the vehicle dealer.[61] However, sometimes service problems arise between dealers and consumers. The following are some examples of actions taken by car companies concerning the recent consumerism movement. (It is still the car companies who must solve certain problems):

---

[58] Polls published in the early 1970s indicate that workers use cars for transport to their places of work in the following degrees: United States, 81%; Europe, 20 to 45%; Japan, 26%.

[59] The terms "warranty" and "guarantee" will be used interchangeably. There are some technical differences in meaning which are not important here.

[60] The earliest warranties, dated 1913, were of 90 days duration. In 1931, this was changed to 90 days or 4,000 miles, whichever came first. In 1960, there was a major change to 12 months or 12,000 miles, whichever came first. (For elaboration, see Chesebrough, H. E., Guaranteed Reliability, Part II, *Industrial Quality Control*, March 1965, pp. 441–442.

[61] A common contention of dealers is that the flat rate allowances for warranty repairs are insufficient to cover the costs. In turn, the flat allowances, where imposed, are mainly the result of car company conclusions that prior to the flat rate allowances, the dealers' charges were too high in relation to a good standard for efficient repair.

1. Some companies have publicized the name and address of a key official, e.g., Vice President of Consumer Affairs, urging users to write to this official in case of service and other problems which are not resolved.

2. Other companies have publicized free use of substitute cars to provide the user with transportation while his car is being repaired.[62]

VEHICLE SAFETY MAINTENCE SCHEDULE (Refer to Owner's Manual for Details)	Service to be Performed at Mileage Intervals Indicated by ●								
CHECK OFF EACH ITEM UNDER MILEAGE AS SERVICE IS PERFORMED	6000	12000	18000	24000	30000	36000	42000	48000	54000
Brakes and Power Steering — Check all lines and hoses.	●	●	●	●	●	●	●	●	
—Check condition of brake linings and parking brake adjustment		●		●		●		●	
Chassis — Lube and check all fluid levels *	●	●	●	●	●	●	●	●	●
—Check condition of front and rear suspension and steering system.	●	●	●	●	●	●	●	●	●
Exhaust System — Check condition of system and underbody.	●	●	●	●	●	●	●	●	●
Tires and Wheels — Check condition. (Check tire pressure at least monthly.)	●	●	●	●	●	●	●	●	●
Engine — Change oil * Check condition of all belts.	●	●	●	●	●	●	●	●	●
— Replace oil filter (at 1st oil change and then every 2nd change)	●		●		●		●		
— Check air cleaner every 12,000 miles; replace every 24,000 miles		●		●		●		●	
— Replace PVC valve.				●				●	
— Service exhaust emission control systems (see Owner's Manual).	●	●	●	●	●	●	●	●	
— Change coolant every two years.				●				●	
Throttle Linkage — Check operation and condition.		●		●		●		●	
Headlights — Aim.		●		●		●		●	
Transmission (Automatic) — Change fluid and service filter.				●				●	

(right margin: CONTINUE SERVICES AT LIKE INTERVALS)

*SERVICE EVERY 4 MOS. OR 6,000 MILES, WHICHEVER OCCURS FIRST.   SEE OWNER'S MANUAL FOR ADDITIONAL VEHICLE MAINTENANCE REQUIREMENTS

Fig. 42-17   Vehicle safety maintenance schedule.

3. All car companies have gone forward with improved programs of training and technical assistance for dealers, as well as improved technology to reduce defect levels and to make diagnosis and repair easier and more effective.

4. All car companies have improved their audit of dealer performance (see below).

Service Shop Effectiveness. Because the guarantee contract covers only about 15% of the average useful life of the vehicle, the great majority of repairs and replacements take place outside the guarantee period. This fact, together with the enormous growth in automobile usage, has stimulated the proliferation of many independent and specialty service shops. However, some users feel that service shops should perform better service. Because the extent of field service has tended to grow and become complex, in both quantity and quality, the service stations sometimes find it difficult to satisfy all the requirements of the users. In such diffi-

[62] See, for example, New Buyer Protection Plan of American Motors, *Quality Management and Engineering,* October 1971, pp. 14–17.

cult situations, automobile manufacturers are making efforts to meet the requests of users, in both managerial and technological aspects.

The technological reasons are traceable to the trends in automobile technology, with increasing complexity, and especially with use of electronic systems and exotic materials. The conventional service shop, operating with empirical knowledge, finds it difficult to cope with complicated field troubles. The car companies are developing sophisticated diagnostic systems to permit confident detection and analysis of field troubles. In addition, the car companies are developing repair techniques which will permit easier repair by the mechanic and even by the user, e.g., modular construction. The effectiveness of these efforts by the car companies will be influenced greatly by the response of the service shops.

The managerial reasons for service shop ineffectiveness are also significant. For the vehicle dealer and the gasoline service station, the repair service is an adjunct to the main business, which is selling cars and supplies, respectively. For the garages and specialty repair shops, the main business is repairs. However, the size of these units is too small to support the development of modern technology, adequate training for personnel, and modern business systems for inventory control, cost control, data processing, etc. It is likely that a new business system, e.g., large chains of repair shops, may need to be evolved to solve this problem.[63]

Vehicle Usage. A critical element of field service is the extent of misuse of the vehicle by the owner. Conditions of usage vary widely, but there is much the user can do to minimize the need for service.

All car companies provide an "Owner's Manual" which explains in detail the proper use and care of the vehicle. For example, the Manual for one 1971 model covers over 70 pages, and deals with the following topics: Before driving your car; Starting and operating; Safety checks; In case of emergency; Air pollution control systems; Appearance care; Service and Maintenance; Maintenance schedule; Specifications, owner relations, service manual.

Although the Manual provides instructions for care and maintenance of the vehicle, the great majority of users rely on the service shop to do this. Hence the Manual also establishes a schedule for vehicle maintenance. Figure 42-17 is an example of such a schedule.

Owner adherence to the schedule is aided by the fact that the guarantee provisions are usually contingent on the owner's following the maintenance schedule. In addition, some car companies (e.g., Toyota Motor Co.) require the dealer to maintain a record of the service history of each vehicle, using a "customer control card." Through information retrieval, the dealer can stimulate the user to adhere to the schedule. (The same card is also an element of traceability in the event of recalls.)

Feedback of Field Quality Information Field performance, and especially field failures, are a source of intense attention by the automobile manufacturers because of their effect on customer satisfaction and on sales. Only product safety receives more attention.

The basic feedback flow is shown in Figure 42-18. However, securing this flow is an intricate operation because of the number of dealers (often running into thousands) and because of the geographical dispersion of dealers, owners, and vehicles.[64] To secure adequate data on field performance, the car companies make use of a number of data sources:

Warranty Data System. For each repair made under warranty, the dealer shop

---

[63] See in this connection, Juran, J. M., Consumerism and Product Quality, *Quality Progress,* July 1970.

[64] See, in this connection, Von Heising, K., Assuring Serviceability and Service, *IXth EOQC Conference,* Rotterdam, September 1965, pp. 117–119.

originates a document which serves as a repair order and also as his claim for reimbursement from the car company. This document is designed to provide the car company with essential data, i.e., dealer and customer identification, vehicle serial numbers, date, odometer reading, description of defect, description of repair, com-

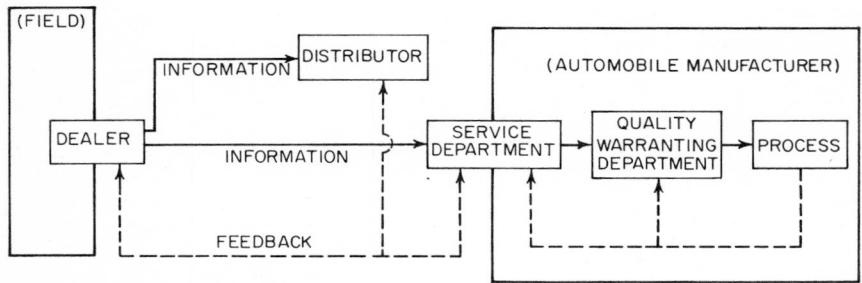

Fig. 42-18 Flow of field quality information.

ponents replaced and their cost, hours of repair labor and their cost, etc. Data coding is widely used to simplify subsequent electronic data processing. The trend has been to on-line data processing through communication circuits between dealers and distributors.[65]

TABLE 42-5 Warranty Input Information

Car line	Delivery date
Model year	Sales district
Assembly plant	Repair date
Serial number	Mileage at repair
Body style	Part number
Engine type	Defect code
Transmission type	Vendor code
Axle ratio	Cost of repair
Month of production	

Table 42-5 is an example of a warranty report input to electronic data processing.[66]

A major use of these summaries is problem identification. Whenever the summaries disclose multiple occurrence of the same defect, or other evidence of the need for corrective action, the car companies display an impressive mobilization for action. Their specialists and laboratories tear down and examine the failed components. If necessary, their investigators go to the field to study local conditions which may contribute to the trouble. The final result is a "fix" by change of design, tool, vendor practice, operator practice, etc.

A second major use of the summaries is to prepare analyses and reports of all sorts, e.g., long-range reliability, warranty costs, repair rates. All companies compare warranty costs by model, and some use warranty costs as a major measure of plant performance. The analyses are also used to make predictions of warranty expense, repair rates, and other factors needed for managerial control.

For example, Figure 42-19 is a summary showing cumulative repairs against

[65] Some manufacturers have experienced difficulty in securing good field performance data from several thousand dealers and have instead resorted to a sampling approach for prompt, reliable feedback. In such cases a limited number of dealers (e.g., 25 to 50), well dispersed geographically and accounting for about 5% of the sales, become a special data source. A factory team visits these dealers to train them and arrange the necessary documentation (and compensation) for prompt data feedback.

[66] Simpson, B. H., "Reliability Prediction from Warranty Data," SAE Paper 660060, 1966.

mileage on a Weibull plot.[67]   The broken line above 10,000 miles is a prediction based on the warranty data.

Technical Information from Service Staff of Dealer and Distributor.   This is a special feedback on safety defects, critical parts, frequent occurrences, or unusual technical phenomena as observed by dealer and distributor personnel.   Such feedback is useful not only for early warning purposes but also for elaboration of defect causes and for reporting on defects not included in the warranty information.

Conferences.   Periodically, meetings are organized to be attended by service

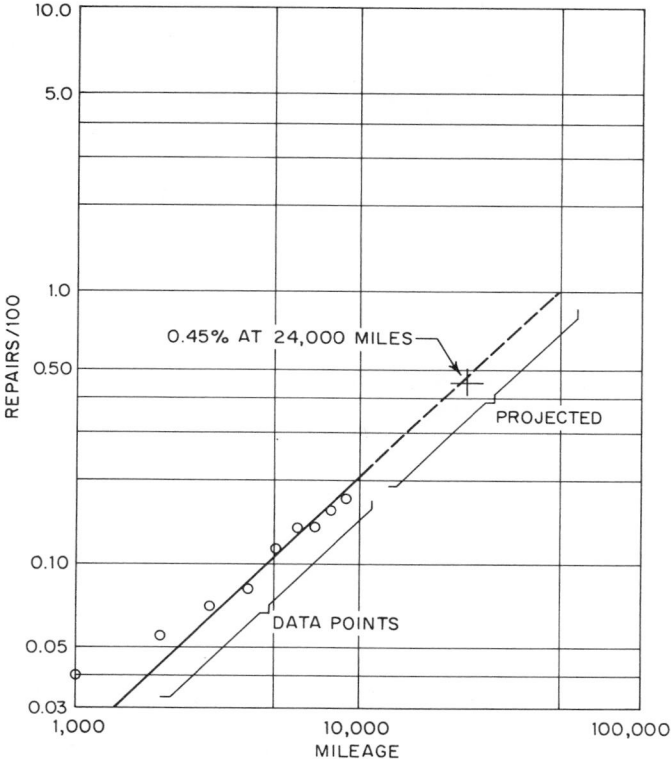

Fig. 42-19   Weibull plot of cumulative repairs.

specialists from dealers and distributors and by engineers from the car company. At such meetings specific quality and reliability problems are discussed in detail.

Market Research Studies.   These involve choosing a sample of users and conducting studies in depth through questionnaires, interviews, monitoring of vehicle results, and similar methods of market research.   Such studies disclose information which is not normally communicated through the warranty or complaint channels.

Direct Complaints from Owners.   For various reasons, owners may contact the car company directly, by letter, telephone, or even personal visit.   The car com-

[67] Simpson, *op. cit.*

panies analyze these contacts carefully to maintain good customer relations and because they sometimes include information useful for product improvement.

Field Service beyond the Warranty Period   This has been a perplexing problem. Under the existing contracts, the manufacturers' legal obligations for field service terminate with the end of the guarantee period. In practice, the manufacturer has a decided interest in seeing to it that the owners (of vehicles made by him) are able to receive good service.

Some of the steps taken to improve service during warranty (e.g., redesign of vehicles for easy maintainability; development of better diagnostic and repair equipment) can also improve service after warranty. However, such deficiencies as marketing of inferior spare parts, or incompetent repair shops would remain.

Audit of Field Service   The car companies have long been aware of the importance of good field service. However, while they have maintained a degree of surveillance over the actual service rendered by the dealers, it has been difficult to attain, for field service, as strict a level of quality assurance as has been achieved in product planning, purchasing, manufacture, and inspection.

With the increase of international competition and with the pressures of consumerism, the trend is increasingly to a more strict definition of standards for good service. In addition, the extent and formality of audit of field service by dealers and distributors are likewise on the increase.

QUALITY AUDIT

All vehicle manufacturers conduct "audits" to determine the degree to which the planning, design, purchasing, manufacture, inspection, and field service have collectively succeeded in providing vehicles which are fit for use. These audits take place at all stages, but concentrate on the finished vehicle.

The most critical need for quality data is at the time of first mass production of some major change, i.e., a new model car, a new major mechanism, a major design change in product or process. In such cases each day of delay in detecting trouble may result in hundreds or even thousands of cars being shipped with a percentage of defects and with the potential need for large recalls. The audit concept is employed as an added source of quality data at the time of such major changes.

Vehicle Audit.   This is a check of finished vehicles which have passed all tests and are ready to ship (see Figure 42-15). The audit is conducted on a small sample of the vehicles and consists of various inspections and tests in accordance with a checklist which has been designed to reflect the users' viewpoint. The contents of the checklist include:

1. Torque test of various fastenings.[68]
2. Adequacy of "customer acceptance" items such as paint, door fit, and interiors.
3. Water test. This is a more extended test of placing the vehicle in the simulated rainstorm for a long time, plus driving in water puddles on the test track.
4. Functional test. This is the most vital part of the audit. It is intended to check if the vehicle systems actually perform their intended function. Some of this check is by laboratory test, but to a large degree it is done by road test, either on the test track or in other usage.[69] Operating characteristics of engine, transmission, brake,

---

[68] Torque tests still involve human interpretation, and there even remains a residual question of whether the test should be by tightening or loosening.

[69] "Other usage" takes multiple forms. Some companies issue new cars to supervisors and engineers who use them over the weekend and then bring back the cars and the data. Other usage may consist of test driving in various difficult environments, e.g., deserts, mountains. In still other cases, usage data are bought from fleets, e.g., rental car companies.

steering, and other moving parts are measured by many meters. Safety standards and exhaust emission standards are included in the checklists.

The vehicle audit is widely regarded as an essential source of data for management reports on quality. Daily summaries are prepared for supervisory review and action, while weekly or monthly summaries are prepared for upper management review.

In addition, some companies make use of their seriousness classification of defects to arrive at a composite measure of demerits per vehicle.[70] Important defects are assigned high demerit values, while lesser defects are assigned low demerit values.

Vendor Quality Audits. These are likewise intensely conducted. See under Purchasing, above.

Process Audits. The concept of audits is also widely used for certain processes, e.g., heat treatment, welding, painting. In such processes some quality characteristics cannot be easily checked on the product. As an added safeguard, audits are conducted to ensure that the process is being carried out as prescribed in the specifications and procedures.

Component Audits. Still another audit form is on finished components after they have been accepted by Inspection. Samples of such components are taken, either following inspection, or from the finished component stores. Inspection and test are carried out under a structured plan, and the resulting data are summarized (by extent of defects) for supervisory review and action. Such component audit is quite common among vendors but is done by only a minority of car companies.

Field Service Audit. This audit is now intensifying, as has been discussed under Field Service, above.

ACKNOWLEDGMENTS

The author and editors gratefully acknowledge the assistance of the following industry experts who were kind enough to review the outline and manuscript, and to make suggestions for improvement:

E. H. Amidon, retired, formerly Director, Quality and Warranty Control, Chrysler Corporation, Detroit

Helge Castell, General Manager, AB Volvo Bus Division, Göteborg, Sweden

Dr. C. Cerruti, Director of Quality Control, FIAT, Turin, Italy

Owen W. Keeler, Manager, Product Program Planning, Chrysler Corporation, Detroit

B. R. Sweeney, Director, Product Quality Office, Ford Motor Co., Dearborn, Mich.

J. Garcia del Valle, Director of Engineering and Quality, Leyland-Authi SA, Madrid, Spain, formerly Director of Engineering and Quality, Metalurgica de Santa Ana SA, Linares, Spain

---

[70] See specifically Chrysler's Corporate Audit, *Quality Assurance,* July 1970, pp. 52, 53. For the generalized approach to product auditing by demerit systems, see Section 21, under Product Auditing.

Section **43**

Household Appliances

LENNART SANDHOLM [1]

Quality Control Consultant, Bjorklund & Sandholm, Stockholm, Sweden

INTRODUCTION

Household appliances trace their origin to the fireplaces and hearths of our fore-fathers. They used fire to cook their food and warm their bodies. They used primitive tools to wash their clothes and clean their dwellings. From these crude beginnings the household appliance industry has emerged to meet some vital human needs and to perform numerous household tasks through a wide variety of special-ized appliances. These appliances can be grouped as to the systems of which they are an integral part:

Food preservation and preparation: refrigerators and freezers, ranges, ovens, food mixers, toasters, coffee makers, frying pans, dishwashers, garbage disposal units

Fabric maintenance: washing machines, driers, irons

Floor care: vacuum cleaners, floor polishers

Climate control: air conditioners, heating units, humidifiers

Most household appliances are powered by electricity, but a significant minority use gas. They are utilized in conjunction with other products such as food, clothes, carpets, and detergents. This interrelation with other industries requires that the

[1] Formerly Corporate Quality Control Manager, AB Electrolux, Stockholm, Sweden.

household appliance industry keep up to date on developments in these related fields.

As consumer affluence rises, the use of household appliances grows extensively. A survey of usage of household appliances in the United States, as of Jan. 1, 1968, showed the following extent of saturation in a base of about 60 million households:[2]

Refrigerators	99.7	Gas ranges	63.6
Home freezers	27.2	Electric ranges (free-standing)	34.1
Clothes washers	94.3	Electric ranges (built-in)	12.9
Clothes driers	34.6	Dishwashers	18.1
Vacuum cleaners	92.0	Room air conditioners	36.7

The annual production needed to maintain and increase this saturation is equally impressive, running to an order of magnitude of 5 to 7 million units per annum for refrigerators, ranges, washing machines, air conditioners, and vacuum cleaners. The bulk of this manufacturing is done in several very large companies, and the concentration has been increasing.[3] The resulting mass production factories produce and test the finished units, which are assembled from purchased as well as fabricated components.

Purchased materials and parts often account for about half the cost of an appliance. The household appliance industry constitutes the largest market for electric motors and for fasteners, the second largest for flat rolled steel and for die castings, and the third largest for industrial coatings. Consumption of plastics of various kinds is also appreciable.

In-plant operations consist of fabrication of components, finishing, and assembly. Most of the fabrication involves sheet metal, and there has been an extensive trend to convert from lot-type manufacture to line-type manufacture. A collateral development has been automation, so that refrigerator doors, for example, are often made on fully automated lines which include stations for cutting, roll forming, punching, bending, and welding. Finishing (usually painting or enameling) is done to provide corrosion protection and appearance. Here, also, there is a trend to automation, largely through the introduction of the electrostatic spray coating method. Assembly work, which accounts for about half the man-hours, has been more difficult to automate but has nevertheless been increasingly mechanized.

New developments in the industry continue to emphasize work saving for the user: self-cleaning ovens, no-frost refrigerators, automatic dishwashers, all-fabric automatic clothes washers. These new developments include use of new technology: microwave ovens, solid state controls, urethane foam insulation, electrostatic spray coatings, thermoforming, magnetic door gaskets, electroplating of plastics. Such developments make products and processes more complicated than ever before.

Some of this new technology is the result of development work done by manufacturers of materials and components. Such innovations become simultaneously available to all appliance manufacturers. Other developments are by the manufacturers themselves: new products, new models, new styles. Competition in the industry is intense, and manufacturers feel impelled to bring new models out frequently, usually every 2 or 3 years. Often the main changes are in styling, trim, color, and other appearance appeal, giving the stylists a wide field in which to apply their talents.

---

[2] Report of the Task Force on Appliance Warranties and Service, U.S. Department of Commerce, Jan. 8, 1969, p. 166.

[3] The four largest United States manufacturers of refrigerators accounted for 65% of the units in 1958 and 73% in 1963. Task Force report, *op. cit.,* p. 162.

CUSTOMER RELATIONS

Household appliances serve to transfer tedious and disagreeable tasks from the consumer to the appliance factory, and this is the main reason that consumers buy them.[4] This transfer of work is done in conjunction with other elements of the system, e.g., frozen foods, semiprepared foods, detergents, fabrics. Once the user has shifted over to a system embodying a household appliance, he comes to depend on the continued functioning of that appliance.[5] A faulty refrigerator spoils food and may force the householder to eat his meals in a restaurant. A washing machine failure may force him to use a commercial laundry. These are wasteful, time-consuming interruptions, and consumers naturally expect long continuity of service from their appliances. In the event of failure they want prompt restoration of service. This service aspect of the industry has created so many problems for consumers that they are attaching increasing importance to the adequacy of service facilities.

Marketing of household appliances follows two main routes: (1) bulk sales to building contractors, laundromats, caravan manufacturers, etc., and (2) sales to individual consumers through intermediate appliance dealers, department stores, and discount houses.

Service facilities are provided in several different ways: factory owned service companies,[6] franchised service companies, distributor service departments, selling dealers, utility companies, independent service centers, and self-maintenance (by large users, e.g., laundromats). Most common is a combination of selling dealers and independent service centers.

Effective repair service requires good original design for maintainability, trained repairmen, and a supply of spare parts. The growing complexity of appliances has required use of training courses, service repair manuals, parts lists, "exploded" views, and other aids for improving the skills and competence of the repairman.

The supply of spare parts has likewise become complex, to a point that the original planning for a new model must include provision for having spare parts available once the model goes on sale. Neglect of such planning (and weak inventory controls) has caused long delays for some consumers. In addition, discontinuance of manufacture of a model does not abolish the need for spare parts, since the appliances in use will need spares for years to come. Reputable manufacturers usually keep a stock of spare parts for about 10 years after discontinuing production of the model. In widespread marketing areas, and especially in international distribution, these stocks are difficult to maintain.

As many as 30 to 50% of all service calls could be avoided if consumers followed the provisions of the "use and care" manuals provided by manufacturers. However, surveys have shown that these manuals are seldom read, and are often merely put aside or discarded once the appliance has been unpacked or installed. Some manufacturers attach the essential information directly to the product in some permanent manner.

Government surveys tend to show that unsatisfactory service is the biggest single source of consumer complaints on appliances.[7] Other important complaint categories are product failures and fulfillment of warranties. The Task Force study included analysis of 415 letters containing about 1,000 complaints on appliances.

---

[4] There are other reasons as well: economic (servants expensive or unavailable), status, aesthetic, etc.

[5] For elaboration, see Section 4, under Life behind the Quality Dikes.

[6] Only a few manufacturers have their own service facilities. See Task Force report, *op. cit.*, pp. 141, 142.

[7] Peterson, Esther, Do You Know Your Consumers? *Home Appliance Builder*, March 1966, pp. 14–16.

Service complaints dominated, stressing mainly (lack of) competence of repairmen and unavailability of service or parts. Most complaints dealt with manufacture and sales, especially quality and design which resulted in defects such as burned-out motors, broken plastic parts, clogging disposers, "sweating" freezers, faulty timers, and corroding ovens. Another major category concerned inadequacy of warranties; e.g., the most frequent breakdowns were the most expensive but the least covered by guarantee.[8]

Household appliances are understandably one of the prime focal points of the consumerism[9] movement. At the very outset, when the consumer is considering purchase, he is confronted with numerous choices of brands and models. Yet he lacks the objective information needed to choose that which best meets his needs, despite the fact that the appliance is for him a sizable or even a major expenditure. As noted, any failures disturb the orderly daily life he has built on the assumption the appliance will provide continuing service. The very real difficulties of securing satisfaction on the warranties, and of securing service after the warranty period, have aggravated matters further. It is therefore not surprising that appliance users have been among the most vocal in their complaints. In addition, having concluded that many manufacturers are not responsive to the complaints of individual consumers, the appliance users have been among the most energetic in turning to alternative sources of product information and alternative organization forms in an attempt to get satisfaction. These alternatives extend to all the forms available: independent laboratories, consumer unions, government agencies, standardization bodies, etc. See generally Section 4, under Consumer Test Services, *et seq.* The Task Force report[10] is an instance of a study directed specifically at appliances.

PLANNING FOR QUALITY

The general approach to planning for quality (Section 6) is fully valid for household appliances. However, there are some aspects of emphasis and detail which are specially relevant. For planning purposes, the industry operates generally under the following idealized stages:

Definition Included in this stage are the compilation and examination of product ideas, and an analysis of proposed new products. Parameters for the project are studied and established. These include the market for which the product is intended and consequently the environment in which it will be used as well as any safety requirements, etc. (e.g., Underwriters' Laboratories, American Gas Association Laboratories) which the product must satisfy. Some manufacturers include these requirements in a product specification which then forms the basis for continued work on the project.

Preliminary Design This stage includes design, preparation of drawings, and prototype construction and test.

Final Design Design work continues into the final stages. Drawings and specifications are approved and distributed. Samples are prepared for tests of various sorts. Units are supplied to independent laboratories, e.g., Underwriters' Laboratories (UL) or American Gas Association Laboratories (AGA), whose ratings may be required.

Pilot Production During this stage, three major elements of planning take place: manufacturing planning, including selection of machines and processes, plus design and ordering of tools; vendor selection and subcontracting; inspection planning.

---

[8] Task Force report, *op. cit.*, pp. 126–131.
[9] For a general discussion, see Section 4, under Consumerism.
[10] *Op. cit.*

In addition, this stage serves to verify that quality standards can be met under conditions of full-scale production. Appliance manufacturers do this by making, testing, and evaluating units produced in prepilot and pilot runs. Tests are carried out in laboratories, in test kitchens, and in private homes. Obviously it is desirable that the tools used in preparing these units be the same tools which will be used in full-scale production. However, some of the latter are not always ready, and some hand-made parts must be used. This is a calculated risk which sometimes loses, resulting in serious disturbances in manufacture and marketing. At worst there can be canceled deliveries, dealer returns, and a delayed sales launch.

Production   In this stage the plans for full-scale production and quality control are carried out. Product quality data are collected, analyzed, and acted on. Necessary product improvements are carried out, entailing changes in design, production, or inspection.

Use   This stage commences with sale of the product. Usage experience and service reports are analyzed in comprehensive quality meetings attended by key departments: Product Development and Design, Production, Quality Control, and Service. Decisions are reached and conveyed to departments responsible for action.

Table 43-1 shows a typical allocation of responsibility for the various departments.

SPECIFICATIONS

Even in the early planning stages it is necessary to set out, in a preliminary product specification, the essential requirements of use, safety, appearance, etc. Some manufacturers create a special document (usually called a "product specification") to contain these parameters. As development and design proceed, it becomes necessary to amend this product specification. By the time production starts, it has become finalized, and becomes the authoritative statement of quality requirements.[11]

This product specification should be prepared in a systematic, comprehensive manner. It should reference all essential codes, standards, test methods, etc., stipulated by the manufacturer and cognizant outside institutions, including pertinent national and international standards. An example of a format for an appliance product specification is seen in Table 43-2. This same layout is also used when specifying requirements for critical components, e.g., thermostats, timers, compressors, switches, and electric motors.

Test Standardization   It is in the interest of consumers and manufacturers alike to employ methods of test which permit objective comparison of performance of appliances made by different manufacturers or in different years. In response to this need, much work has been done (and continues in progress) by national and international standardization bodies.

In the United States, the Association of Home Appliance Manufacturers (AHAM) prepares "AHAM Recommended National Standards" for voluntary adoption. A governing policy[12] is that "AHAM standards shall be related to realistic consumer needs and foreseeable misuse." AHAM also proposes its standards for recognition by national standards bodies such as American National Standards Institute (ANSI).[13]

Standards for gas appliances are prepared in conjunction with American Gas Association (AGA) Laboratories and published by ANSI.

Other important national standards for household appliances include those issued

---

[11] Of course, the numerous drawings and parts lists define the requirements for materials, components, etc.

[12] AHAM Policy and Procedures Governing Standards, May 15, 1969.

[13] Earlier names have been American Standards Association (ASA), and United States of America Standards Institute (USASI).

TABLE 43-1   Table of Responsibility

Activity	Functions or departments available for participation								
	Market Research	Marketing	Service	Product Development and Design	Manufacturing Planning	Purchasing	Production	Inspection	Quality Control
Definition stage:									
Identification of consumer quality needs	XX	X		X					
Definition of new product in terms of product specification	X	X		XX					
Preliminary design stage:									
Judging and testing components				XX					
Making prototypes				XX					
Testing and analysis of prototypes				XX					X
Design review			X	XX	X	X			X
Final design stage:									
Testing components (continued)				XX					X
Testing and analysis of prototypes (continued)				XX					
Establishing tolerances and classification of characteristics				XX					
Establishing visual standards for appearance	X	X		XX					
Preparation of component specifications				XX					
Design review			X	XX	X	X			X
Pilot production stage:									
Planning of manufacturing setup				X	XX		X		X
Design, ordering, and tryout of tools and other equipment					XX		X		X
Design and ordering of quality information equipment				X	X		X	X	XX
Selection of vendors				X		XX			X
Evaluation of new vendors (in respect to quality)				X		X			XX
Planning of process inspection and final inspection				X	X			X	XX

TABLE 43-1   Table of Responsibility   (Continued)

Activity	Functions or departments available for participation								
	Market Research	Marketing	Service	Product Development and Design	Manufacturing Planning	Purchasing	Production	Inspection	Quality Control
Pilot production stage (continued):									
Planning of incoming inspection				X	X			X	XX
Initial sample inspection								X	XX
Evaluation of parts to be used in prepilot and pilot runs				X	X			X	XX
Prepilot and pilot runs					XX		X	X	X
Testing and evaluation of units produced in prepilot and pilot runs				X					XX
Prepilot and pilot run review				XX	X		X		X
Planning of maintenance and calibration of quality information equipment									XX
Preparation of service manuals and spare parts lists			XX	X					
Preparation of use and care manuals		XX	X	X					
Production stage:									
Operating processes as specified					X		XX		
Executing inspection as specified								XX	X
Disposition of parts and materials not meeting the specifications				X	X	X			XX
Reporting and analysis of internal failures				X			X	X	XX
Quality rating of outgoing product				X			X	X	XX
Life testing									XX
Use stage:									
Reporting and analysis of external failures		X	XX	X					X
Meetings for solving quality problems			X	X	X		X		XX
Reporting quality costs									XX

XX = prime responsibility.
X = collateral responsibility.

TABLE 43-2   Contents of Product Specification

1. Applicable documents
    a. Internal: Main drawing. Packaging drawing. Component specifications
    b. External: Rules and standards (e.g., UL, AGA)
2. Product description
    a. General features
    b. Variants
3. Product provisions
    a. Function: General data. Operating characteristics. Acceptable noise level. Reliability (mean life, guarantee service rate)
    b. Materials and workmanship
    c. Grounding and insulation (safety requirements)
    d. Dimensions
    e. Finish: Appearance. Corrosion resistance
    f. Marking (contents and location of data plate)
4. Manufacture
    a. Fabrication
    b. Painting
    c. Assembly
5. Shipping
    a. Packaging: Requirements. Tests
    b. Marking (contents and location of labels)
6. Inspection

by British Standards Institution (British Standards, BS), and by the West German Deutscher Normenausschuss (Deutsche Normen, DIN).

On the international level, the International Organization for Standardization (ISO) and the International Electrotechnical Commission (IEC) are engaged in preparing standards for household appliances.

ISO has issued two publications dealing with refrigerators.[14] These publications, which are also issued in French and Russian, define specifications of household refrigerators (of both the compression and absorption types) and lay down methods of measurement for the determination of their performance. Testing methods are described for door seal, mechanical strength of shelves and similar components, doors and fittings, no-load adjustment, no-load operation, ice making, absence of odor of materials, thermal insulation, compartment temperature. ISO intends also to issue recommendations for freezers and for refrigerator controls.

In 1965, IEC appointed a technical committee (TC 59) called "Performance of Household Electrical Appliances." This committee was formed to "state and define the characteristics to be used to determine the performance of domestic electrical appliances in order to inform the consumer; to describe the standard methods for measuring these characteristics." Consequently, the intention is not to specify performance requirements but to standardize methods of testing that will give similar results wherever they are used. The work of IEC is carried out by various subcommittees for different types of products: electric dishwashers, cooking appliances, small heating appliances, home laundry appliances, ironing and pressing appliances, floor treatment appliances, small kitchen machines. IEC has issued publications (in both English and French) on electric blankets, irons, and vacuum cleaners.[15] Next

[14] Household Refrigerators, Part I, Performance Requirements, ISO Recommendation R 824, 1968; Household Refrigerators, Part II, Special Low-temperature Compartments for the Storage of Frozen Foodstuffs, ISO Recommendation R 825, 1968.

[15] Measurement of the Performance Characteristics of Electric Blankets, IEC Publication 299, 1969; Methods of Measurement of Performance of Electric Irons for Household or Similar Use, IEC Publication 311, 1970; Methods of Measurement of Performance of Vacuum Cleaners for Household and Similar Use, IEC Publication 312, 1969.

in line for publication are testing methods for ranges, floor polishers, dishwashers, water heaters, washing machines, toasters, warming plates, steam irons, ironing machines, and food preparation machines.

Reliability   The conventional measures of reliability, i.e., failure rate, mean time to failure (MTTF), and mean time between failures (MTBF), are useful for quantifying the reliability of household appliances and their components. A supplemental measure of great value is the ratio of number of service calls to the number of units in service. Applied to the product still under guarantee, this ratio is called the guarantee service rate and is expressed as the service calls per hundred (or per thousand) units under guarantee. This ratio is widely used in management reports on quality. Some examples of the actual ratios prevailing are shown in Figure 43-1.

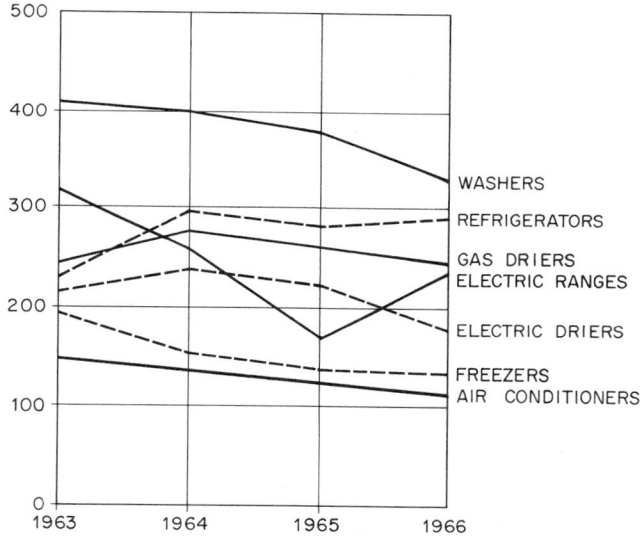

Fig. 43-1   Valid service calls per 1,000 units during first year of use.

Mean life is a useful measure of the reliability of household appliances, but the data on mean life are difficult to acquire. Manufacturers generally think in terms of mean life of 10 to 15 years, since beyond that time span most appliances are replaced by the user because of obsolescence. To "measure" mean life in the laboratory requires making many assumptions on how the appliances will actually be used by consumers. Data on mean life during actual usage are commonly based on the years of retention by the original owner before he replaces the unit with a new model. Some studies on this basis, by the U.S. Bureau of the Census, suggest an average life of about 11 years for household appliances generally.[16]

Appearance   This is more important in household appliances than in many other products. It is the result of styling, color, and finish—qualities which are notoriously difficult to specify and evaluate objectively. Yet appearance is the very characteristic about which consumers form strong personal opinions.

Because of the importance of appearance, and the cost of achieving it, manufac-

[16] Task Force report, *op. cit.*, pp. 22, 23. The report quotes a Bureau of the Census study which found that life expectancy of new units purchased in 1957 varied from 9 years for washing machines to 15 years for refrigerators. Evidently the trend of life expectancy has been on the increase.

turers distinguish between surfaces exposed to consumer view and those not exposed. The drawings reflect these distinctions, and the shop processes are regulated accordingly. For example, tools for plastic molding are designed in such a way that marks and weld lines will appear only on surfaces not exposed to consumer view.

The appearance of a surface depends on several factors such as color, luster, and texture. It is extremely difficult to specify and measure these characteristics. In practice, it is often necessary to use the human eye in conjunction with visual standards. One of the most commonly used systems for specifying color is the Munsell system, which identifies color in terms of three attributes: hue, value (lightness), and chroma (saturation). At present, color chips for approximately 1,500 Munsell notations are available, with both glossy finish and mat finish.[17] The luster of a surface is specified in the simplest manner as glossy, semiglossy, or mat. Sometimes luster requirements are indicated by a value referring to a certain type of equipment for measuring luster, such as Gardner 60°.

Defects of various kinds such as scratches and dents may occur on the surface of a part. These defects may be noticeable to a greater or lesser degree, depending on their size, quantity, and location. It is extremely difficult to stipulate requirements in this respect as well as to measure the results. As a rule, visual standards are used—one for the lowest level that is to be accepted and one for the highest level that is to be rejected.[18]

STANDARDS FOR SAFETY

Safety in household appliances usually means freedom from accidental injury due to mechanical or electrical failure. It is generally believed that the safety record of appliances is quite good.[19] This record is due not to chance but to the determination with which manufacturers, testing laboratories, and regulatory bodies have attacked and eliminated unsafe conditions.

Most countries have published codes or standards governing the safety of household appliances. In some countries compliance is mandatory by law. In other countries compliance is voluntary. However, manufacturers usually find it necessary for marketing and product liability reasons to follow existing safety standards to the letter and to permit independent testing laboratories to test whether the products incorporate the required degree of safety.

Underwriters' Laboratories (UL) develops and publishes standards for safety of electrical household appliances (and other products). Some of these standards have been approved as United States standards through American National Standards Institute (ANSI). UL also examines and tests products to determine whether they

[17] Available from Munsell Color Company, Inc., 2441 North Calvert Street, Baltimore, Md. 21218. Color tolerance sets for visually evaluating color differences from a specific reference color are also supplied.

[18] See generally Section 12, under. Sensory Qualities.

[19] Quantified safety data are not readily available. In the United States, the Final Report of National Commission on Product Safety (Government Printing Office, June 1970) estimated that injuries involving appliances numbered about 500,000 annually, out of about 15 million injuries involving consumer products generally. For a population of about 210 million, the overall injury rate is about 8 per million hours of exposure. The injury rate during actual usage of appliances is probably below the overall rate.

Wringer washing machines appear to account for a disproportionate number of injuries involving appliances.

For added discussion on "scorekeeping" of product safety, see Juran, J. M., Product Safety, Quality Progress, July 1972, pp. 30–32. See also Section 8, under Safety in New Product Design.

conform to the required standards. Approved products are "listed," i.e., they are included in UL's lists of approved products. Manufacturers of listed products are authorized to apply the UL mark to their products. There are also some provisions for checking to see whether manufacturers maintain the safety level exhibited on the original units tested by UL.

American Gas Association (AGA) Laboratories govern the safety of gas appliances in a manner quite parallel to that followed by UL for electrical appliances.

In Europe the International Commission on Rules for the Approval of Electrical Equipment (CEE) has prepared safety regulations for electrical household appliances (and other products). CEE consists of about a score of European organizations, each of which is responsible in its own country for specifying the rules for electrical equipment and for testing, where this is carried out. Member organizations are not forced to follow CEE regulations, but the relevant authorities in the various countries are advised to adopt the regulations to as large an extent as possible. CEE has issued regulations in English and French governing electric motor-operated appliances (CEE Publication 10) and electric cooking and heating appliances (CEE Publication 11). These regulations consist of Part I, general clauses, and Part II, sections dealing with specific products.

Safety regulations for electrical household appliances are also prepared by the International Electrotechnical Commission (IEC).[20] It is the intention of IEC to prepare regulations for the majority of electrical household appliances.

PREPRODUCTION ACTIVITIES[21]

The marketing of household appliances requires that dealers be provided with stocks of finished units before the sales campaign is launched. To provide these stocks

TABLE 43-3 Plan of Early Warning

Checkpoint	Design review	Laboratory testing	Field testing	Transport testing	Pilot production
Design concept	XX				
Components used.	XX	XX			
Prototypes.	XX	XX		X	
Prepilot runs		XX	XX	XX	XX
Pilot runs		XX	XX	XX	XX
Limited production runs . . .		X	X	X	XX

XX = primarily.
X = secondarily.

requires manufacture of thousands of units before consumer usage discovers any widespread defects previously overlooked. To guard against such unpleasant surprises, manufacturers make use of various forms of early warning reviews and tests. These early warnings are set up at various checkpoints in the manner shown in Table 43-3.

Some of this early warning is derived from past or current experience with similar products. Previous designs, components, or materials may have created quality problems in production, field failures, high quality costs, frequent service calls,

---

[20] Safety Requirements for the Electrical Equipment of Refrigerators and Food Freezers for Household and Similar Purposes, IEC Publication 316, 1970; Safety of Household and Similar Electrical Appliances, Part 1, General Rules, IEC Publication 335-1, 1970.

[21] See also Planning for Quality, above, and Table 43-1.

difficult repairs. Data reflecting these experiences are an essential input to the new designs and the parameters of the new products.

As the early warning reviews and tests listed in Table 43-3 are conducted, they provide information essential to attaining a high level of achievement for the various quality characteristics of the appliance. Table 43-4 shows this relationship.

TABLE 43-4   Relation of Early Warnings to Product Characteristics

Characteristic	Design review	Laboratory testing	Field testing	Transport testing	Pilot production
Performance	XX	XX	XX		
Reliability	XX	XX	XX	XX	
Safety.	XX	XX	X	X	
Maintainability	XX		XX		
Producibility	XX				XX
Controllability	XX				XX
Usability	XX	X	XX		

XX = primarily.
X = secondarily.

Design Review   The purpose of design reviews is to ensure at the earliest possible stage, i.e., in the design stage, that the new product will perform successfully and that it will be easy to manufacture, inspect, and repair. The design engineer obtains the views of various departments—chiefly production planning, production, quality control, and service departments—on the proposed design. Also of value are the views of the home economists that most manufacturers of household appliances employ in their organizations. In many cases, design reviews are not conducted in accordance with any fixed program but are carried out in an informal manner by means of discussions among the various parties concerned.

Laboratory Testing   Laboratory tests provide information concerning performance, reliability, and safety. Tests are usually carried out on complete products, but individual components are also tested separately for reliability.

Safety of household appliances is tested in accordance with existing standards. Even if tests are to be carried out by an independent testing laboratory, manufacturers carry out their own tests before sending the product to the independent laboratory for approval. This is to ensure that as far as possible, the new product will pass the tests and be awarded a seal of approval. If approval is not granted, the project may be delayed, as it will then be necessary for the independent laboratory to test the product afresh.

Most manufacturers of household appliances have a test kitchen of their own, in which practical performance tests can be carried out on their own products and those of their competitors. An important part of the work of these test kitchens is, of course, to try out prototype products and report on them. Test kitchens also help to prepare instructions, users' manuals, and sales promotion materials. As a rule, test kitchen employees have a Home Economist degree.

Field Testing   As a rule, laboratory tests can be performed only on a small number of units. In addition, it is difficult to simulate practical conditions in the laboratory. As a result, field tests are carried out in addition to laboratory tests. Units are placed in selected homes for use under normal, everyday conditions. In some cases, units are also placed in commercial laundries, restaurants, and similar places where they are likely to be exposed to exceptionally arduous duties.

In many cases, employees are allowed to use the products in their homes. A wider range of test homes is sometimes required, and units are then loaned or sold to households within a limited geographical area. However, products should be sold only in these cases when the manufacturer is fairly sure that the product is of the intended quality, such as when a modification has been introduced on an existing model.

A special problem in field testing is the gathering of information. Information received from the field may be extremely meager unless the manufacturer makes a deliberate effort to obtain it by means of personal calls and interviews at the selected test homes or by sending out questionnaires. Persons selected for testing the product should be given clear instructions as to the procedure they should adopt in the event of a fault's arising in the product. Any repairs necessary should be carried out by specially assigned personnel. The Development Department or Quality Control Department sometimes assumes the responsibility for servicing units on test in the field.

Transport Testing   On the way from the factory to the user, a household appliance is exposed to mechanical stresses in conjunction with handling, storage, and transport. These stresses can be simulated in the laboratory. The most common tests carried out on the packaged product are drop tests, compression tests, vibration tests, and shock tests. Packaged units are occasionally dispatched to various destinations in accordance with a program designed to reproduce the conditions encountered in actual practice. This program includes transportation by rail and road, transshipment, etc. Units are checked before and after transport. The stresses to which products are subjected during a trial despatch route cannot, of course, be checked in the same way as those induced in laboratory tests. However, by using impact recorders, it is possible to gain some knowledge of the stresses to which the units have been exposed.

Pilot Production   The purpose of pilot production is to show whether the manufacturing and inspection procedures that have been chosen will result in the desired level of quality when production is commenced. It is therefore important that the tools, jigs, and methods that will be used for full-scale production are also used to as great an extent as possible for pilot production runs. Pilot production may be carried out in several stages: prepilot run, pilot run, and limited production run. The number of units manufactured is increased in each stage. In the United States it is usual among major manufacturers of household appliances for a prepilot run to embrace 10 to 20 units and pilot run to embrace 50 to 200 units. These figures apply to major appliances.

Example   Before commencing full-scale production of a completely new washing machine, a manufacturer initiated six preproduction runs in varying sizes and at various intervals prior to the scheduled full production date, as follows:

Number of units	Lead time, months	Number of units	Lead time, months
50	9	375	3
300	7	1,500	2
475	5	6,000	1

All tooling was completed 5 months before the scheduled production date. A short assembly line was set up 3 months before full-scale production was due to start. Preproduction runs were carried out under the supervision of the Quality Control Department. Washing machines were placed in selected homes and commercial laundries for testing. The Development Department was responsible for all service on these machines and also kept all records.[22]

[22] The Story behind GE's 12-Pound Washer, *Appliance Manufacturer*, vol. 9, No. 12, pp. 39, 41–44, December 1961.

MANUFACTURE

Control during appliance manufacture follows closely the general approaches set out in other sections of this Handbook: Section 9, Manufacturing Planning; Section 10, Vendor Relations; Section 11, Production of Quality; Section 12, Inspection and Test. However, the job of meeting the basic aims of high quality of outgoing product and low manufacturing cost is influenced by the nature of the products and processes. Figure 43-2 shows the basic flow chart, including location of quality control stations, for manufacture of refrigerators.

Vendor Relations The appliance manufacturer makes extensive purchases of materials, e.g., sheet metal, tubing, plastic granulate, paint, and enamel. He also purchases many components, e.g., compressors, timers, thermostats, gaskets, nameplates. Not only are large sums of money involved; the quality of the purchased goods is vital to the quality of the appliance.

Vendor products are first qualified through an "initial sample" procedure. These samples are prepared by the vendor for new or changed designs or for modifications in manufacturing practice. The samples should be representative of future production.

These initial samples should be measured and tested exhaustively, and the results fully documented. Such documentation ensures complete communication as well as minimizing disputes in connection with future deliveries. Approval of the samples results in vendor qualification much as is discussed in Section 10. Discrepancies must be cleared up by revision of either the parts or the specifications, depending on technological and economical considerations.

Following vendor qualification, it is common to use incoming inspection as a further control against defectives entering the production line. The inspection is usually done through sampling by attributes, employing (in the United States) standard plans such as MIL-STD-105-D, with AQL values usually in the range of 0.65 to 6.5.

The trend in the industry is toward closer cooperation between manufacturers and vendors. Evidences of this are seen in the increasing use of multiple communication lines, joint quality planning, audit of decisions, supplier certification of inspection and test data, and vendor rating.[23] A collateral development is the trend toward tighter inventories, which further intensifies the need for control of vendor quality at the source.

Process Inspection Various inspection controls are used to regulate quality during manufacture. During fabrication, which consists largely of sheet metal work, both setup (first-piece) inspection and patrol inspection are used. In line-type manufacture, 100% inspection is sometimes used prior to costly operations. Sometimes the inspection can be combined with another operation, e.g., visual inspection and grinding of refrigerator doors prior to painting.

Setup inspection aims to detect conditions which affect adversely all units of product, e.g., misinterpretation of drawings, faulty tools, faulty instruments. Setup inspectors therefore check for correctness of drawing number, correctness of material identity, quality of material surface, and dimensions produced by the setup. The first pieces checked are marked for reference while the rest of the lot is being completed.

Patrol inspection checks work in progress at the various machines, using largely the same criteria as are used in setup inspection. Once defects are found, all production made since the previous patrol inspection becomes suspect and should be

---

[23] See generally Section 10.

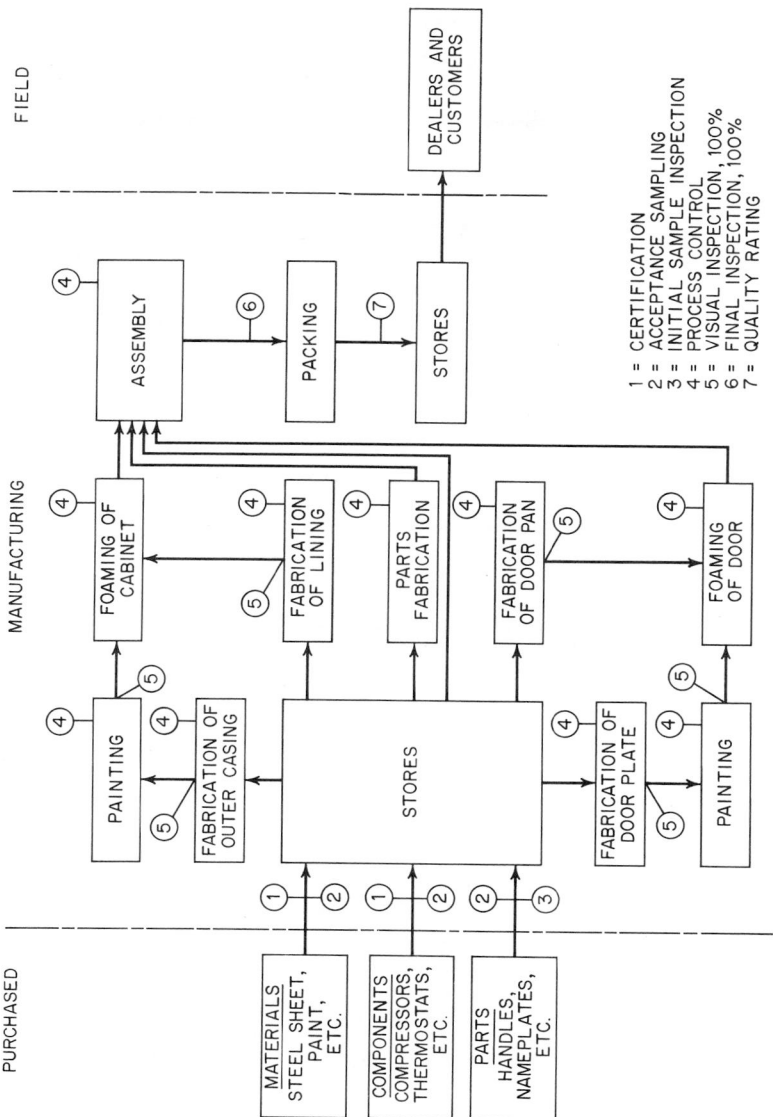

Fig. 43-2 Flow chart for refrigerator manufacture.

checked. Usually it is well to record the results of patrol inspection, sometimes on control charts. It is good practice also to check the last piece made as a form of tool control. Faulty tools then have a maximum time interval for repair before starting the next lot.

Figure 43-3 shows typical forms of inspection used in manufacture of refrigerator cabinets, and their location in the work flow. For each inspection station, instructions are prepared showing characteristics to be checked, instruments to be used, and sample sizes (Figure 43-4).

The finishing process (usually line-type) includes controls on mixtures, viscosity, and temperatures. Control charts are very helpful here. Inspection after finishing is done 100%, often in conjunction with conveyor unloading. Inspection is for the usual finishing defects, and employs visual standards as an aid to making judgments. Other characteristics are checked by conventional ASTM procedures. These include thickness, color, gloss, hardness, adhesion, flexibility, and resistance to humidity, grease, acid, alkali, and fruit stains.

Inspection of subassemblies and assemblies is also planned using flow charts and inspection instructions similar to Figures 43-3 and 43-4. The characteristics checked are those which are difficult to check in the final state, e.g., soldering, wiring thermal insulation, screw tightness. By checking closer to the operations, the feedback loop is shorter.

To check performance, the unit is connected to a source of power and is operated. For refrigerators, the temperature inside the cabinet or on the evaporator is measured. For ranges, the operations of hotplates, ovens, timers, and rotisserie motors are checked. Washing machines and dishwashers are run through at least one full cycle of their program. Noise level is checked for all units.

Performance checking requires adequate space for numerous units, since the time interval for the tests can run to over an hour. Conveyors can facilitate handling during these tests.

Safety checking is usually governed by published regulations which prescribe what is to be checked and how. Examples are products "listed" with Underwriters' Laboratories, and features which have been the subject of legislation, e.g., the door opening force on refrigerators. Electrical safety checks usually include a high potential test, earth circuit test, current leakage test, and polarity test.

Appearance is checked visually, a check also being made that the product has the correct accessories and literature. In order to reduce the possibility of the inspector's overlooking anything, he should follow a standard routine which constitutes a systematic check of the entire product. This must be taken into consideration when preparing inspection instructions.

Units which do not pass final inspection are returned to a repair area where they are examined and repaired. It is important to send the repaired units back for final inspection where they will be completely checked once again before being passed out.

Inspection is an important source of data feedback to Production and other departments concerned with keeping defects at low levels. This feedback takes two common forms:

1. Tally sheets kept by the inspector on a form similar to the inspection instruction (sometimes the two are combined).

2. Travel cards which accompany the unit on its journey through assembly and final inspection. A section of such a card is shown in Figure 43-5. A mnemonic code system is designed to number the types of defects and to simplify machine data processing. The inspector circles the appropriate code number for each defect he finds. After final inspection, the cards are collected and summarized.

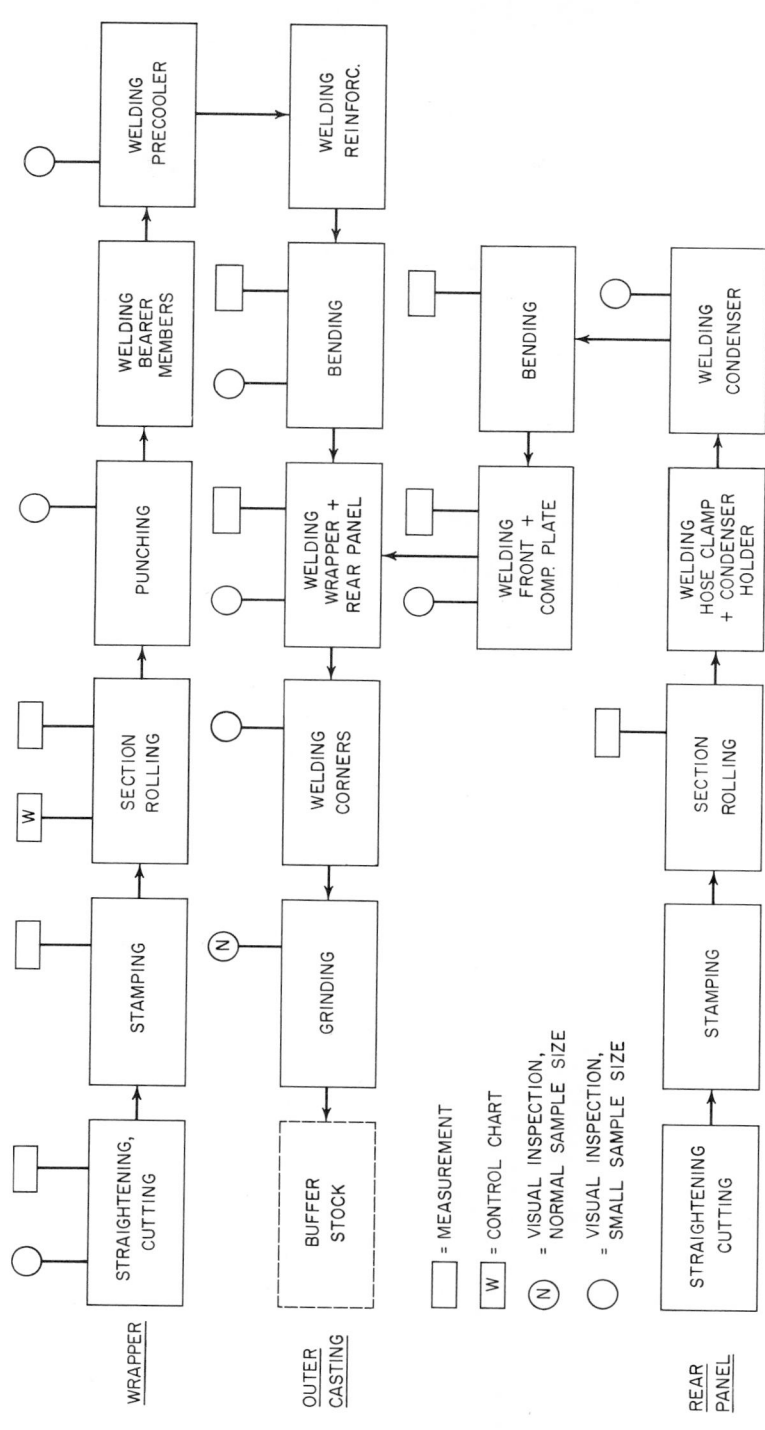

Fig. 43-3 Flow chart showing inspection controls in manufacture of refrigerator cabinets.

43-17

Part name Casing		Part no. 200 10 68	Dwg. index 1	Rev. 1
Intended for Bending of outer casing		Insp. group alt. op. KAT	Date issued 10/10/70	Issued by RZ
Item no.	Characteristic	Inspection method		Sample size
1.1	Corner cut undamaged	Visual inspection		5 per day
1.2	Corner cut slit not exceeding 0.5 mm	Visual Inspection		
1.3	Tube holders intact close to bending points	Visual inspection		
1.4	Height 1190 ± 1, 1490 ± 1, 1690 ± 1	Steel measuring tape		
1.5	Width 595 ± 0.5, 800 ± 0.5	Sliding caliper		
1.6	Lower hinge hole position 1106, 1406, 1606 ± 1	Steel measuring tape		
1.7	Intermediate bearer member position 800.5 ± 0.5 or 300.5 ± 0.5, 38.8 ± 0.5, 16.4	Fixture V-41071		
1.8	35 ± 0.5	Sliding caliper		
1.9	Tube flattening in bending minute 5.5	Sliding caliper		

Fig. 43-4 Inspection instruction.

QUALITY ASSURANCE

The managers of appliance manufacturing companies require the usual forms of summarized quality information through which they can measure results against goals and take action as needed. The usual information categories required are discussed under separate headings below.

Measures of Field Quality Performance The first of these measures is the extent of complaints on product failures and deficiencies. To secure this information, all complaints, whether by letter or telephone, and no matter from what source, should be directed to a single department in the company. Because complaints usually lead to servicing action, the service orders and job orders comprise an important source of information. This information is especially valuable during the guarantee period when the consumer turns almost exclusively to the manufacturer's service organization to have his product repaired. (Beyond the guarantee period, the data are much less reliable, since the consumer often turns to other repair sources.) Automatic data processing makes it possible to analyze service orders and job orders for the extent of failures, most frequent categories, most costly categories, etc.

Spare parts usage is a second measure of field quality performance, both during and after the guarantee period. However, this information source does not reveal failures which can be remedied without need of spare parts, or through use of parts acquired from other sources.

A third measure is through interviews and questionnaires. One company reports that it interviews 15,000 appliance users each year.[24] Users of the company's prod-

[24] Wood, Charles C., Whirlpool's Customer Assurance Program, *Industrial Quality Control,* vol. 21, No. 12, pp. 605–607, June 1965.

ucts are included in this interview program. Soon after a new model has been released on the market, persons who have purchased this model are interviewed. These customers are interviewed again one year later to see if their reaction has changed.

Additional information on consumer reaction is available from the comments and reports of salesmen and dealers. However, these reports often lack supporting data, and carry a risk of bias as well.

Results of tests made by consumer organizations are still another measure of field quality performance. These tests commonly are made on competing products, and comparative test data are usually presented in the reports. See in this connection, Customer Relations, above: also Section 4, under Consumer Test Services.

Measures of Service Performance Consumers may put up with appliance failures

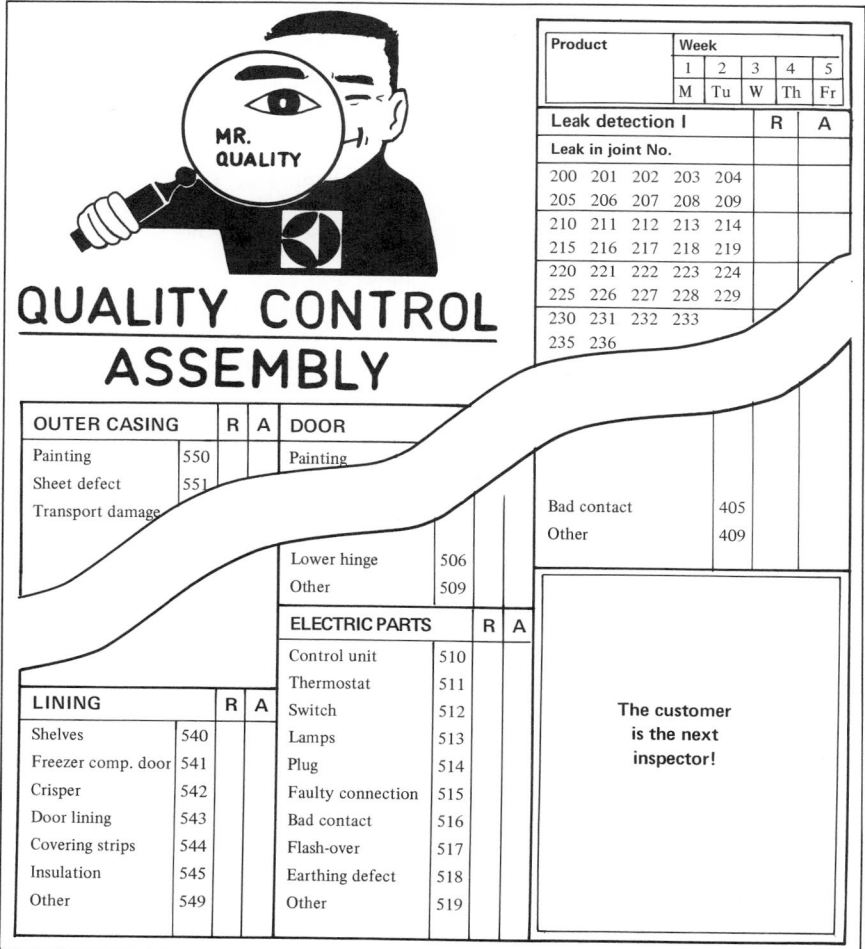

Fig. 43-5 Defect travel card.

if they can secure prompt, reliable service. In the absence of such service, consumers display sharp dissatisfaction with the product and its manufacturer. As a consequence, the emerging belief is that the behavior and efficiency of the service department are becoming a main criterion by which the consumer judges the quality of the product.

The performance of the service organization can be measured by methods paralleling those used for measuring product performance. Complaints about service, like product complaints, should be directed to a single department of the company. To facilitate this, it is useful to give information to the consumer as to where to address his complaint if he is dissatisfied with the repair. Some companies provide this information in the papers left with the consumer in conjunction with a service call. In the United States, company sensitivity to consumer dissatisfaction with service has resulted in some newspaper advertisements to provide information on whom to contact.

Data processing applied to service orders makes it possible to secure summaries of essential characteristics of good service:

Number of return calls per 100 service calls
Average waiting time (between reporting a failure and making the repair)
Time spent per service call
Costs incurred per service call

This data can be broken down by region, serviceman, etc., to discover which are the best performances and which the inferior performances. Further analysis of causes of the difference in performance can lead to discovery of the "knack" inherent in good results, and transfer of this knack to all men.

In some companies, service inspectors call on a sample of consumers to secure their reactions to the repair just made and to study the repair itself. Telephone interviews and questionnaires are also used. Through such reviews the reactions of consumers and the integrity of the repairs can be measured.

Quality Rating of Manufactured Product This is the conventional form of securing a preview of the nature of the outgoing product through reexamining completed units which have already been packed and are ready for shipment. The general principles are set out in Section 21, under Product Auditing.

Every day a small number of units are chosen at random, unpacked, and thoroughly checked according to an instruction (Figure 43-6). Because the defects are unequal in importance, a seriousness classification is used according to the principles discussed in Section 12, under Seriousness Classification. In the example of Figure 43-6, four classes are used, based on the likelihood of the defects leading to complaints (will certainly lead to complaints, will probably, will probably not, and will not).

Units selected for this check inspection are checked for performance, safety, appearance. Performance testing is done under conditions which simulate use. In addition, the units are partially dismantled for further checks on performance and safety. The packaging and marking are also checked, as is the presence of the correct accessories and literature (care and use manuals, warranty cards, etc.).

The results of the check inspection are passed on daily to the supervisors involved.[25] Weekly and monthly summaries in the form of demerit per unit reports are provided to middle and upper management under the general principles discussed in Section 21, under Executive Reports on Quality.

---

[25] While the basic purpose of check inspection is to "take a photograph of the outgoing product," the finding of a major defect becomes an alarm signal for the supervision involved. They commonly extend the sampling of packed product, review the present process, etc., to discover whether the condition is isolated or general.

Product subgroup Vacuum cleaners		Ref. FV 5120	Rev. 6	Page 1	
Model A 30, A 40	Date issued 10.6.68	Issued by B.N.	Date approved 17.6.68	Approved by CE-PK	

Item No.	Characteristic	Class			
		A	B	C	D
	PACKING, MARKING				
	Packing				
	Defects on carton, wrong fastening, lat. support missing, etc.			x	x
	Packing defects (contents squeezed, cleaner askew in carton, etc.)		x	x	x
	Label (See data plate and fan unit)				
	Missing			x	
	Wrong marking of voltage and type (e.g., Z 89 inst. of Z 90)	x			
	Other defects (indistinct, torn, etc.)			x	x
	Data plate (See label and fan unit)				
	Missing	x			
	Wrong marking of voltage or approvals marking	x			
	Poor fastening (riveting)	x	x	x	
	Wrong plate fitted (e.g., Z 89 instead of Z 90)		x		
	Accessories and printed matter				
	Missing and/or wrong: hose, extension tube, and combination nozzle	x			
	Missing and/or wrong: other accessories		x		
	Missing directions for use or other printed matter			x	x
	Too many accessories				x
	APPEARANCE				
	General appearance of the cleaner				
	Poor fitting body—rear hood—handle frame—sleighs—books		x	x	x
	Impurity in space for dust container			x	x
	Poor cleaning (dust, thumbprints, marking color, etc.)			x	x
	Surface defects (stains, scratches, etc.) on:				
	Plastic moldings (diffuser grille, handle frame, front cover, knob, rear hood, switch, and brake button, etc.)		x	x	x
	Die castings (front ring, hooks, locking bolt)		x	x	x
	Nickel-plated details (emblem holder, sleighs)			x	x
	Body complete				
	Outer cover: blisters or spot welding visible		x	x	x
	" " : other defects (damaged, wrong fitting, text, etc.)		x	x	x
	Body deformed (dents, etc.)		x	x	x
	Emblem				
	Missing	x			
	Wrong emblem fitted (text Electrolux, Luxomatic, etc.)	x			
	Poor fitting (e.g., falls out of emblem holder)	x	x	x	
	Surface defects (e.g., poor print, damaged)			x	x
	Accessories				
	Exterior defects on hose, extension tube, comb. nozzle		x	x	x
	Exterior defects on other accessories			x	x

Fig. 43-6 Quality rating instruction.

The quality rating is frequently augmented by accelerated life testing done on units selected at random. Usually this is performed on products such as washing machines and dishwashers involving moving parts which cannot be tested separately. A further supplement is the testing of products in test kitchens. Makers of ranges, especially, often take units direct from the production line to the kitchen to check roasting performance, etc.

Quality Costs   The general approach to quality costs (Section 5) is fully applicable to the appliance industry. An important departure from this general approach results from the time lag between date of manufacture and date of usage. Because of successive warehousing at the factory, distributor, and dealer, plus intervening transportation, it is not unusual for complaints to be received more than one year after date of manufacture. (The warranty period starts with date of sale to the consumer.)

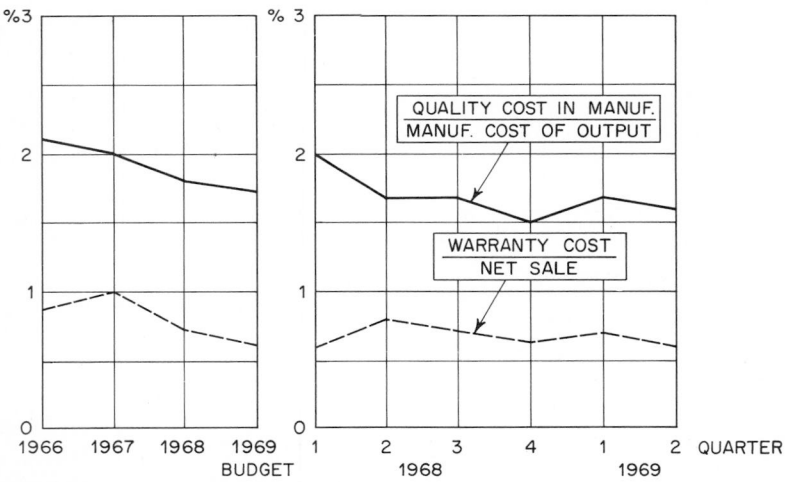

Fig. 43-7   Quality cost trends.

Because of this lag it is necessary to keep internal quality costs separate from external failure costs. The former can properly be related to direct labor manufacturing cost or contributed value expended within the same time period. However, the external failure costs must be related to a base such as "net sales billed six months earlier" if the comparison is to be valid. The seasonal variation in sales, a common phenomenon in the appliance industry, is an added reason for taking steps to secure a correct time relationship between external failure costs and the base for comparison.

Figure 21-3 (in Section 21) shows schematically the plan for collecting, summarizing, and distributing quality cost reports for a large appliance manufacturer making a variety of appliances at several factories.[26] An example of the charted summaries is shown in Figure 43-7.

Data Plan   While the data plan must be adapted to fit the product line, organization structure, and size of each company, it should in general be able to:

[26] Sandholm, L., Improving Quality Assurance, *Proceedings IXth EOQC Conference*, pp. 185–203, European Organisation for Quality Control, Rotterdam, 1965.

Provide essential details: product identification, time in service, location of defect, failure mode, corrective measure
Indicate the extent of failures encountered
Identify the most frequent or most costly failures
Provide data which can become the basis for statistical and technological failure analysis
Provide a basis for following up the measures taken to prevent failures
Provide a source of information for experience retention
Do all these things at a modest cost

Meeting these criteria of a good data plan requires attention to some essential, unspectacular details. These essential details include:

1. A data plate attached to each unit at a location easily accessible for view. The data plate should show the model number and serial number and some code for date of manufacture. The latter can be coded for simple data processing; e.g., 124 may mean week 24 in the year 1971.

2. A code to make easy the reporting of which component has failed and what is the failure mode. Ingenious design of the code makes it applicable to a variety of products and simplifies data reporting by the repairmen.[27]

3. A design of service order or job order which permits it to be filled in easily and unambiguously so that it can also be used for subsequent data processing.

The processing of data should yield at least three widely used summaries:

1. Some overall indexes of the extent of failures. One of these is the guarantee costs per unit under guarantee. This shows the field share of the "gold in the mine," and helps managers to make decisions on whether to structure improvement programs.

A second index is the guarantee service rate, i.e., the number of service calls (made during the guarantee period) per 100 units under guarantee. This is a very practical measure, but there are some technical difficulties to be solved before a valid index can be computed. The difficulties arise mainly from the fact that failure rates (and hence guarantee charges) are not uniform over the guarantee period, plus the fact that the population of units covered by the guarantee period is rarely spread evenly, month by month, over the guarantee period. When these problems are analyzed, it becomes evident that an adequate (though not precise) index can be computed by making the following assumptions: (1) the length of guarantee is one year, (2) the failure rate is constant during the guarantee period, (3) the number of units under guarantee equals the number of units sold during the 12 months immediately preceding the report month, and (4) the number of units sold per month is constant.

Under these assumptions, once 24 months have passed since the first units were sold, the guarantee service rate reaches a state of continuity and equals the ratio of of accumulated service calls (during a 12-month period) to the number of units sold during the 12 months immediately preceding. Until these 24 months have passed, it becomes necessary to multiply the above ratio by a correction factor which varies depending on the months elapsed between the report month and the date of sale of the first units.[28]   (Table 43-5)

[27] There are also some disadvantages to a universal code. See Sandholm, L., Program to Reduce the Need for Servicing Domestic Appliances, *First Scandinavian Conference on Quality and Reliability*, Gothenburg, May 27–28, 1968.

[28] Sandholm, L., Improving Quality Assurance, *Proceedings IXth EOQC Conference*, pp. 186–203, European Organisation for Quality Control, Rotterdam, 1965. See, in this connection, Powell, Richard F., Analyzing and Interpreting Field Failure Data, *Proceedings 1970 Annual Symposium on Reliability*, pp. 94–100, IEEE.

TABLE 43-5   Correction Factor for Guarantee Service Rate

n	1	2	3	4	5	6
Factor		12.00	8.00	6.00	4.80	4.00
n	7	8	9	10	11	12
Factor	3.43	3.00	2.67	2.40	2.18	2.00
n	13	14	15	16	17	18
Factor	1.85	1.62	1.45	1.33	1.24	1.17
n	19	20	21	22	23	≥ 24
Factor	1.12	1.07	1.04	1.02	1.01	1.00

NOTE: The guarantee service rate is equal to the ratio between the accumulated number of service calls during a 12-month period and the number of units sold during 12 months immediately preceding the last month n in this period multiplied by the correction factor. For the first month the product was sold, $n = 1$.

In the experience of the author, use of these correction factors permits a good prediction of the stabilized guarantee service rate for new models from only 3 or 4 months of data. Failure to use the correction factors results in an underestimate of the true guarantee service rate, creates false hopes, and loses time in taking preventive measures.

2. A second useful summary is the listing of the most frequent or the most costly failures. These follow the Pareto principle, so that they account for the bulk of the trouble due to failures, and also present the bulk of the opportunity for improvement.

3. A third summary is a listing of failures by date of manufacture (or some equivalent dating). Such summaries make it possible to see whether product made after some corrective change results in fewer failures than product made before the change.

Even with good data systems, the appliance industry is subject to long delays between date of manufacture and date of going into service. These delays create the risk that numerous finished units contain potential servicing problems unknown to the manufacturer. As a result, manufacturers are on the alert to create early warning signals which will detect these conditions. One form is that described under Quality Rating of Manufactured Product, above. Another early warning signal is created by arranging to secure data from "early warning shops," i.e., those shops which receive the units most recently manufactured. A good mutual relationship is established with these shops, and information about problems is received promptly.

In-Plant Quality Data Additional inputs for quality assurance can be secured from in-plant data. The overall level of defectives and the "top ten" most frequent defects are useful to plant management in structuring programs and in concentrating attention. The travel card (Figure 43-5) can provide the basic data for such summaries.[29]

Executive Reports The broad approach to executive reports on quality is discussed under that heading in Section 21. The principles set out there apply fully to the household appliance industry.

Of course, the detailed choices of control subjects is special to each industry. Figure 43-8 shows a list of control subjects used for the annual report on quality in one appliance manufacturing company.

[29] The bulk of in-plant data are used for day-to-day control and are so voluminous that they should not be permitted to dilute the reports used for quality assurance reporting.

QUALITY IMPROVEMENT

Quality improvement in the appliance industry follows the general approach set out in Section 16, Quality Improvement.

Improvement projects are identified by applying the Pareto principle to the data summaries of field failures, quality rating of outgoing products, quality costs, etc.

---

1. Quality cost
   a. Prevention
   b. Appraisal
   c. Internal failure
   d. External failure
2. Per product line
   a. Refrigerators and freezers
   b. Ranges
   c. Home laundry equipment
   For each product line: Quality cost. Service rate. Result of quality rating. Problems. Remarks
3. Per factory
   a. Factory A
   b. Factory B
   c. Factory C
   For each factory: Quality cost. Result of quality rating. Problems. Remarks
4. Per sale outlet
   a. Outlet X
   b. Outlet Y
   c. Outlet Z
   For each outlet: External failure cost. Problems. Remarks
5. Employees in quality control
   a. Categories (engineers, inspectors, etc.)
   b. Areas (quality engineering, incoming inspection, etc.)
6. Vendor relations
   a. Vendor rating
   b. Complaint rate
   c. Cost of incoming inspection
   d. Vendor surveys
7. Activities accomplished
   a. Changes in policy and objectives
   b. Systems introduced
   c. Training accomplished
   d. Professional society activities
8. Activities planned
   a. New systems
   b. Training

Fig. 43-8   Control subjects for annual report on quality.

Discovery of causes of chronic defect symptoms usually requires analysis in depth, both statistical and technological. The wide geographic dispersion of use and the problems of transportation add to the complexity of the problems and thereby to the need for competent analytical skills.

Appliance manufacturers often make special arrangements with a few selected service shops to secure all replaced parts involving defects under study, along with related repair information. This may be supplemented by special questionnaires or report forms to be filled out by repairmen, especially in studying damage caused in transit. Such forms provide for showing the nature and location of the damage on the appliance, and the location of the damaged appliance in the transport vehicle.

Remedies for causes of chronic defects follow conventional practice (Section 16). As a follow-up to see if the changes have produced the desired improvement, use is made of the date of manufacture to compare the performance of units made before and after the change.

Organization for appliance quality improvement almost always requires an inter-departmental approach, though the degree of formality varies. Some manufacturers make use of formal committees, with members from Design, Production, Quality Control, Sales, and Service. These committees are given wide latitude for guiding projects and stimulating action.

PROGNOSIS

Over the years, the appliance industry has been quite progressive in improving the performance and safety of its products. However, the popular movement known as consumerism[30] has focused attention on the deficiencies and has accelerated some trends which had been proceeding at a more leisurely pace:

Legislation is emerging to protect consumers from vague or deceptive guarantees.

Existing laws are being interpreted more harshly from the manufacturer's point of view.

Manufacturers' defenses in liability suits are being eroded away.

Awards in damage suits are increasing in size.

Competing sources of product information are receiving increasing support, e.g., testing institutes, standardization bodies.

New offices are being set up to receive and act on consumer complaints, e.g., government departments, newspaper columns.

Appliance manufacturers must respond to these forces, and the early 1970s saw clear evidences of new responses. Some appliance manufacturers have publicized a telephone number or a man to call in event of inability to get satisfaction. The Association of Home Appliance Manufacturers (AHAM) created an independent Major Appliance Consumer Action Panel (MACAP) to perform the duties of an ombudsman.[31] In all likelihood these and other responses from manufacturers will expand for the foreseeable future.

A further likely development will be increased attention to optimizing the users' costs as well as the manufacturers' costs. A pioneering study of appliance users' quality costs was conducted by Gryna.[32] The study divided users' costs into major categories and collected cost data for these, principally on automatic washing machines. The data showed that cost of operation and maintenance over the life of the appliance ran from 0.8 to 3.8 times the original price; i.e., it usually cost more to use the appliance than to purchase it. Users paid between 1.3 to 6.9 times as much for repairs as the manufacturer/dealer paid for guarantee repairs. Data such as these suggest that there may be new business opportunities present in offering to optimize users' costs.

Further discernible trends include:

More complex products and production processes

---

[30] See Section 4, under Consumerism.
[31] See Section 4, under Consumerism.
[32] Gryna, Frank M., Jr., User Costs of Poor Product Quality, University of Iowa, 1970 (Doctorate Thesis).

Increased international trade, with resulting problems in standardization, vendor relations, etc.

New markets, usually with special local requirements, as affluence spreads into developing countries

Such developments, along with increasing quality requirements by consumers, and the pressures of the consumerism movement all add up to more severe demands and greater stress on quality. These demands will spur the household appliance industry to greater efforts in achieving fitness for use.

Complex Systems

DR. LESLIE W. BALL

Director, Safety Office,
George C. Marshall Space Flight Center,
National Aeronautics and Space Administration,
Formerly, Director of Product Assurance,
The Boeing Company

INTRODUCTION

In an engineering context, a complex system may be defined as "a set of equipments, people, and procedures that collectively accomplishes a specified objective." Among the most familiar complex systems are those which accomplish aerospace transportation objectives. For example, the Apollo/Saturn system accomplishes the objective of transporting men to the surface of the moon and returning them to earth. The somewhat less dramatic commercial airplane systems accomplish the objective of transporting people from place to place on the earth. Other familiar complex systems include telephone communication, television entertainment, and human waste disposal systems.

Each of the cited examples is predominantly an engineering system. However, recent public concern with socioeconomic problems has extended the use of the term "complex systems" well beyond the realm of traditional engineering into areas such as crime control and environmental protection. While some of the practices that have proved to be successful in developing complex engineering systems do have potential for helping to solve socioeconomic problems, this Section will be limited to quality assurance in relation to systems where the problems are predominantly in the areas of system engineering and development program management.

Quality Assurance Objective The primary quality assurance objective for complex systems is identical with that for the simplest consumer product. In both cases, the objective is tersely and comprehensively expressed by the term "fitness for use" employed by Juran (see Section 2).

What then merits a separate Section of the "Quality Control Handbook" on the subject of quality assurance for complex systems? Part of the answer is that experience in developing complex systems has shown that it is necessary to supplement traditional simple product quality assurance disciplines with enough formal system engineering and development program management techniques to assure at least three types of integration.

These types of integration are:

1. *Integrated Requirements Definition.* The total system design requirements, including all functions from design through manufacturing, installation, maintenance, and operation, must be set forth in a sequence of phased baseline requirement definition documents.

2. *Integrated Technical[1] Program Plans.* All the technical activities which are critical to achieving a successful system must be set forth in a sequence of program plans for each phase in the system life cycle from concept through definition, development, production, and operation to obsolescence and disposal. Particular emphasis must be placed on planning the activities of specialist engineers, such as reliability, maintainability, and value engineers.

3. *Integrated Business Structure.* Items 1 and 2 are technical. Together they constitute the essence of system engineering as defined in MIL-STD-499, "System Engineering Management."[2] These technical factors must be supplemented by a business management system that provides for integration of all cost and schedule planning and control. This integration must encompass not only the customer organization and a prime contractor, but also a hierarchy of autonomous subcontractors and vendors including a multitude of organizational units within each customer agency or industrial company. This type of integration is based on a "work breakdown structure" as defined in MIL-STD-881, "Work Breakdown Structures for Defense Material Items."

This Section of the Handbook will summarize present practices for achieving the above types of integration through:

1. The Program Management Function
2. Quality Assurance Support to the Program Management Function

THE PROGRAM MANAGEMENT FUNCTION

It is inevitable in any discussion of complex system that new terms will be introduced or old terms will be given new meanings. Already the primary term "development program management," and the associated terms "phased baseline," "requirements definition document," "technical program plan," "specialist engineering," and "work breakdown structure" have been used. None of these terms include the word "quality." However, all of them represent concepts and practices that are essential to the quality assurance of complex systems.

An understanding of the relationship of the development program management[3] function to the traditional "design the product," "make the product," and "support

---

[1] In this Section the adjective "technical" is used in contrast to "cost" and "schedule." Thus technical program plans define technological objectives and how they will be achieved by technical activities, while cost plans define the budgets that will be required, and schedule plans define the dates when activities will begin and end.

[2] Copies of the Military Standards and Documents of the National Aeronautics and Space Administration cited in this Section can be obtained from the Government Printing Office, Washington, D.C. 20402.

[3] For an elaboration of this type of organization see Cleland, David I., and William R. King, "Systems Analysis and Project Management," McGraw-Hill Book Company, New York, 1968.

the product" functions is absolutely essential to understanding how fitness for use is achieved during the development of a new complex system.

Traditionally, the development program management function has been exercised by a "development project engineer." For example, in a company that produced domestic appliances, the man (or woman) who was made responsible for developing a new dishwasher would be called the "Model X Project Engineer." Within the company there might have been a dozen such project engineers all of whom accomplished their new product development responsibilities through the existing functionally oriented organization structure.

Even now, the project engineer approach to development program management is usually preferred for relatively simple products, but for complex products it has become customary to establish a "program" or "project" type of organization. In a pure project type of organization, a program manager is appointed by top management and is given the responsibility and line authority for all program objectives, i.e., cost, schedule, and technical performance,[4] for one major product and perhaps for one customer. He draws personnel for his program from the functional departments (e.g., engineering, manufacturing) in much the same way that a building contractor hires architects, carpenters, plumbers, and electricians and directs their work until a new building is designed and its construction is finished. When a development program is finished, the people who have been reporting to the program manager return to their "home" departments. Thus the program has the flexibility to draw upon a reserve of specialists as they are needed and also to achieve a transfer of knowledge and experience between programs.

Quite often a dominant customer such as a government agency or commercial airline will request that a project type of organization be established. Their reasons for doing so include the belief that centralization of responsibility and authority in a project organization will provide for rapid development of the new system and for good communication between contractor and customer people.

It is often said that the essence of program management is the effective management of change. Although a great deal of planning is done, a program manager is continuously reviewing his previous decisions on assignments of budgets, schedules, and technical requirements and he is continuously adjusting these assignments on the basis of the most recent project status data. A project type of organization greatly facilitates the required rapid and economical management of change.

Potential compromises of performance objectives resulting from program managers' decisions are subject to the check and balance provided by routine contact with the functional organizations from which program personnel were borrowed. Conflicts do arise, but when all concerned have experience with this form of organization, the conflicts are viewed as a normal mode of operation that helps to provide balance among cost, schedule, and performance.

Figure 44-1 illustrates this relationship in a way that emphasizes the integration and audit aspects of the relationship of the program management function to the traditional functions. Figure 44-2 illustrates the same relationship by means of a generalized organization chart.

Each of the basic functions of product design, product manufacture, and product support has its own "primary products." In this context, the term "primary products" is used with the meaning of the essential output that results from the work done by each of the three traditional major functions and the relatively new program management function. The primary products of the design function are design decisions as set forth in design disclosure documents, including drawings, specifica-

---

[4] The terms "technical performance" and "technical performance measurement" are defined well in paragraph 5.3.7 of MIL-STD-499.

NEW	TRADITIONAL BASIC FUNCTIONS		
PROGRAM MANAGEMENT	DESIGN SYSTEM	MAKE SYSTEM	SUPPORT SYSTEM
TOTAL QUALITY CONTROL			
PROGRAM ASSURANCE	DESIGN ASSURANCE	QUALITY ASSURANCE	SUPPORT ASSURANCE
BASED ON CRITICAL PLANNING AND CONTROL ACTIVITIES	BASED ON CRITICAL DESIGN GUIDE AND CHECK ACTIVITIES	BASED ON CRITICAL MAKE GUIDE AND CHECK ACTIVITIES	BASED ON CRITICAL SUPPORT GUIDE AND CHECK ACTIVITIES

Fig. 44-1 The program management function.

tions, and operating procedures. The primary products of the manufacture function are the parts, components, and subsystems which collectively form the total hardware system. The primary products of the support function, which includes maintenance, repair, and logistics, are ready to use systems. It should be noted that whereas a simple product, such as a bicycle, is ready to use as soon as it is shipped from a factory, complex systems, such as telephone communication systems, require the support functions of installation and check-out before they are "ready to use" the first time. Also, they require the support functions of maintenance and repair to keep them in a "ready to use" condition.

Figure 44-1 illustrates that within each of the traditional basic functions of design, manufacture, and support, there are "guide activities" and "check activities" that are performed by the appropriate line organizations. For example, design decisions are guided by performing development analysis and development test activities, and they are checked by performing design review and design verification test

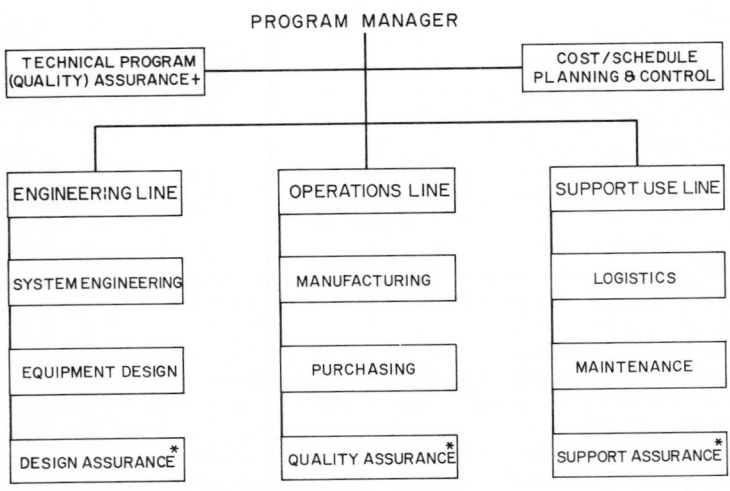

+ INDEPENDENT AUDIT OF ALL CRITICAL ACTIVITIES
* PERFORM GUIDE ACTIVITIES AND CHECK ACTIVITIES

Fig. 44-2 Line/staff project organization.

activities. In manufacturing and support, the guide activities include the training and certification of craftsmen and the inspection of incoming material, while check activities include the inspection of the product after it has been manufactured or maintained.

Figure 44-1 uses the term "design assurance" to illustrate that performing guide and check activities within the design and test organizations is the primary method of assuring the quality of design decisions. It uses the term "quality assurance" to illustrate that performing guide and check activities within the manufacturing and quality control organizations is the primary method of assuring the quality of manufacturing. It uses the term "support assurance" to illustrate that performing guide and check activities within the support organizations is the primary method of assuring the quality of installation, check-out, maintenance, and repair. What then, is contributed by the program management function? As suggested by Figure 44-1,

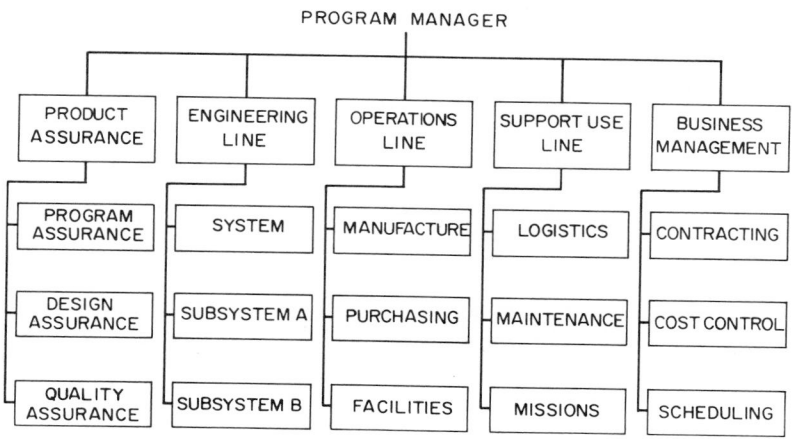

Fig. 44-3   All-line project organization.

the program management function provides an extra level of assurance that all primary products and all the critical activities performed by the line organizations will be coordinated and controlled.

Consequently, in the development of a complex system, we may regard the program management function as a "supra-quality assurance function." Another way of stating this is that the program manager and his staff do not themselves design the product, they do not themselves manufacture the product, they do not themselves support the product. What they do do, is to provide an extra level of assurance that the work of the basic design, manufacture, and support functions will be planned and controlled in the highly integrated manner that experience has shown is essential to assuring fitness for use.

This statement and the format of Figure 44-1 might lead to the conclusion that the program management function is simply a practical way of achieving the objectives of what quality engineers call "Total Quality Control." In a general way, this conclusion would be correct. However, it is extremely important for the quality engineer to recognize the implications of the types of organization illustrated by Figures 44-2 and 44-3.

First, these types of organization establish the Program Manager as the direct line boss of the whole development organization. Second, it is the Program Manager who has the overall responsibility for assuring development of a system which will meet all the requirements of the customer and thereby achieve "fitness for use." Third, although the job of quality assurance manager in an operation or product assurance line organization is very important to the successful development of complex systems, the types of organization shown in Figures 44-2 and 44-3 provide for the Total Quality Control function to be divided among the following four organizational groups:

Design Assurance
(Manufacturing) Quality Assurance
Support (Quality) Assurance
(Technical) Program Assurance

Figure 44-3 illustrates an alternative to the line/staff project organization as shown in Figure 44-2. It provides for bringing together design, manufacturing quality, support quality, and program assurance functions under a line Product Assurance boss. However, even a line product assurance manager assures only that all the necessary control data are developed. It is still the Program Manager who is responsible for assuring achievement of "fitness for use" in the new complex system.

The design assurance function, or more specifically the important segments of this function, such as reliability, maintainability, producibility, and systems effectiveness are essentially the same for a complex system as for a single product. They are discussed in Section 8 of this Handbook. The same is true for manufacturing quality assurance (Section 11) and for support quality assurance (Section 15). Consequently, in this Section we will concentrate on overall objectives and then on program assurance techniques. More specifically, we will describe the techniques by which a relatively small program assurance staff group of the type shown in Figure 44-2 is able to assist a development program manager in controlling the risks that are inherent in the development of a new complex system.

DEVELOPMENT RISK CONTROL

A narrow interpretation of the term "fitness for use" might limit the scope of assurance objectives to cover only assurance that a complex system would perform its mission or satisfy its markets, irrespective of development cost or development schedule. Obviously, this would be an unwarranted interpretation, because a product that the customer cannot afford or which is not developed when he needs it does not really provide fitness for use. Consequently, total quality control in the development of complex systems must address itself to the following three types of development risk:

1. *Cost Risk.* This is the risk that technical success will be achieved within schedule, but at a development or production cost far in excess of that which was predicted at the beginning of the development.

2. *Schedule Risk.* This type of risk covers technical success within development costs, but with serious schedule delay.

3. *Technical Risk.* This type of risk covers failure to achieve one or more vital system performance characteristics.

It is grave concern with controlling these development risks that has driven many companies to adopt the line Program Management type of organization for developing complex systems and to place upon the shoulders of the program manager the primary responsibility for controlling cost, schedule, and technical risks.

However, adoption of program management organizational forms and control techniques often has met with resistance from management people, particularly those who have achieved past successes using only the basic design, manufacture, and support functions.

Understanding of why there has been resistance to program management methods may be helped by defining and contrasting the terms "Established Product" and "New Product."

An "Established Product" is one for which cost, schedule, and technical risks can be controlled by technologies that are based on statistical analysis of production and service data.

For example, the cost, schedule, and technical risks involved in producing newsprint, food containers, or automobile tires can be and are controlled by industrial engineering, quality control, and value analysis techniques, all of which depend on statistical analysis of production and service data.

A "New Product" is one for which the development cost, schedule, and technical risks cannot be controlled simply by applying current product data.

Not all products that superficially appear to be new will meet the above criterion. For example, even an "all new" automobile is not new from the point of view of risk control unless it includes innovations for which adequate risk control data are not available.

Today, the pressures of international trade competition and the extremely large investments required to finance the development of a new system that does meet the above criterion necessitate a deliberate consideration of and decision on the type of development program that is most likely to produce a salable product without disastrous cost overruns or schedule slippage. These two options are available:

1. A minimum amount of predictive analysis and program planning and control (paper work) to be followed by multiple cycles of design, manufacture, and test

2. Enough predictive analysis and program planning and control to achieve success with only one cycle of design, manufacture and test

Many companies who have achieved past successes by using the first method now find that they can afford neither the development costs nor the development time required for repeated cycles of design, manufacturing, and test. In spite of aversion to so-called "paper work" they must choose to adopt a combination of the program management type of organization with the program management techniques of technical performance predictions, technical program planning, and cost and schedule planning and control in order to provide the best foundation for controlling new system development risks.

THE TECHNICAL PROGRAM ASSURANCE FUNCTION

It is to be expected that the title of this function will cause much debate and that many variations will occur. The title "Program Quality Assurance" has the advantage of indicating that the function is part of a total quality control system. However, in many companies, this title would cause confusing of the program management staff function with the line (manufacturing) quality assurance organization.

Whatever the title, the essential features of this function are:

1. It is a program management staff function.

2. It is responsible for the technical segment of a program manager's integrated cost-schedule-technical control system.

3. It is responsible for assuring development and application of technical risk management techniques that cover all system characteristics and all development phases.

4. Its methodology has evolved from the mathematical and program control methods set forth in reliability, quality control, and other product assurance specifications.

Again, it must be emphasized that technical program assurance is only a staff function. It is the program manager himself who has the responsibility for using his line authority to assure fitness for use by controlling development risks. In the next part of this Section of the Handbook a "Risk Management Model" will be developed and described. This model provides a practical basis for defining technical program assurance techniques and for relating them to the design, manufacturing, and support assurance functions.

DEVELOPMENT RISK MANAGEMENT MODEL

All quality assurance is based on establishment of agreed standards and on techniques for assessing actual design, manufacturing, or support achievements against

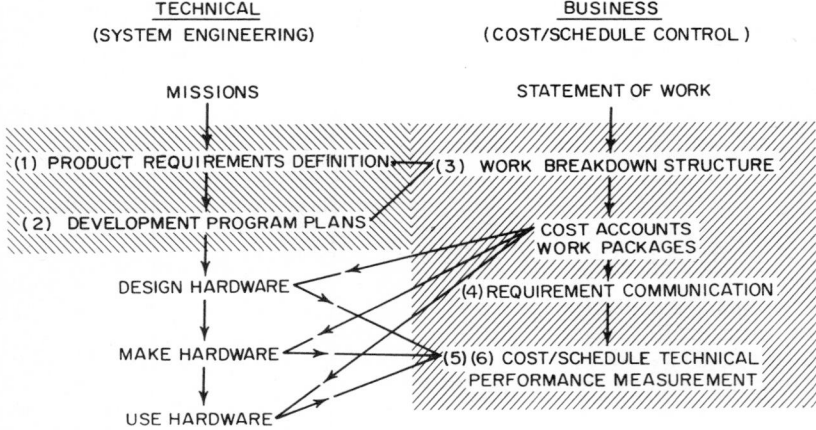

Fig. 44-4 Evolution of formal risk management.

the agreed standards. For the simplest product, quality assurance is based on inspection techniques. These techniques assess the quality achieved by the manufacturing function by comparison of product characteristics with standards established by design documentation or by an actual physical model that represents the agreed workmanship quality.

For an intermediate product, acceptance inspection is supplemented by techniques, such as incoming material inspection, process control measurement, and shipping inspection. Each of these techniques is based on comparison with an agreed standard. Even the certification of manufacturing personnel is based on comparing their training and capability with agreed standards.

What then is the nature of the agreed standard on which quality assurance of a complex system development program can be based? The answer is represented by Figures 44-4 and 44-5.

Figure 44-4 illustrates how formal disciplines for control of development risk have evolved from traditional simple product practices. The words outside the cross-hatched area represent the essential steps in the development of a simple product. In the left-hand "Technical" column, the word "missions" represents formal identification and documentation of what the Department of Defense (DOD) or National Aeronautics and Space Administration (NASA) would call a mission or what a consumer product businessman would call the market opportunities. In the right-hand "Business" column, the term "statement of work" covers either a simple contract to develop a product or, within an industrial company, an authorization by the board of directors to proceed with spending company funds on the development of a product. The words "design hardware," "make hardware," and "use hardware" represent the situation in which, once a mission or market has been defined and a statement of work has been issued, the development organization can get right on with the design, manufacture, and use of the product.

The items within the crosshatched areas represent the additional disciplines that experience has shown to be necessary to assure control of the cost, schedule, and technical risks that are inherent in the development of a complex system.

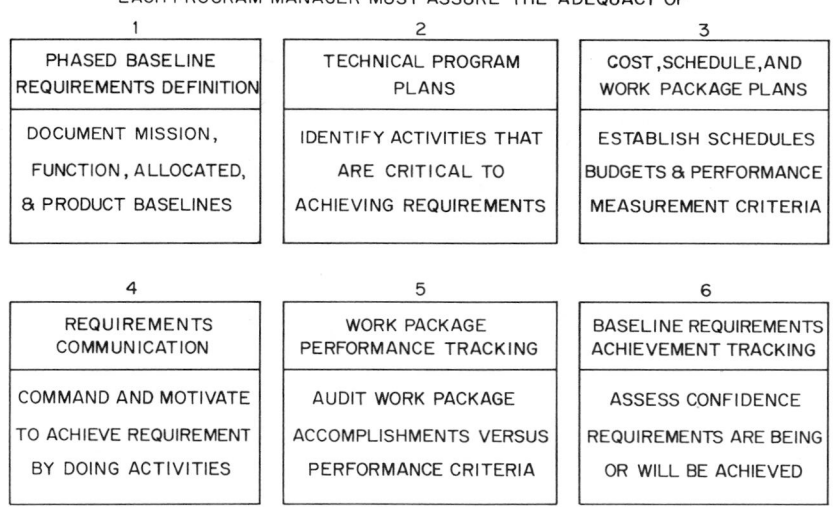

EACH PROGRAM MANAGER MUST ASSURE THE ADEQUACY OF

1	2	3
PHASED BASELINE REQUIREMENTS DEFINITION	TECHNICAL PROGRAM PLANS	COST, SCHEDULE, AND WORK PACKAGE PLANS
DOCUMENT MISSION, FUNCTION, ALLOCATED, & PRODUCT BASELINES	IDENTIFY ACTIVITIES THAT ARE CRITICAL TO ACHIEVING REQUIREMENTS	ESTABLISH SCHEDULES BUDGETS & PERFORMANCE MEASUREMENT CRITERIA

4	5	6
REQUIREMENTS COMMUNICATION	WORK PACKAGE PERFORMANCE TRACKING	BASELINE REQUIREMENTS ACHIEVEMENT TRACKING
COMMAND AND MOTIVATE TO ACHIEVE REQUIREMENT BY DOING ACTIVITIES	AUDIT WORK PACKAGE ACCOMPLISHMENTS VERSUS PERFORMANCE CRITERIA	ASSESS CONFIDENCE REQUIREMENTS ARE BEING OR WILL BE ACHIEVED

Fig. 44-5 Development risk management model.

Figure 44-5 shows the same six additional disciplines as shown in Figure 44-4, but in the form of a management model. This figure states that the supra-assurance function that we call program management must assure control over the cost, schedule, and technical risks that threaten fitness for use by assuring the adequacy of the six types of disciplines represented by the six segments of the Development Risk Management Model.

The first three segments of the model provide for highly integrated planning of (1) all the products that must be developed and (2) all the activities that must be performed. The fourth segment links the planning activities with the actual doing of the planned work. The fifth and sixth segments provide for management control to be based on two distinct but supplementary types of control data.

Each of the six segments of the management model now will be discussed in more detail.

Phased Baseline Requirements Definition In the development of a complex system, it is a standard practice for a customer or a company board of directors to limit their financial risks by authorizing just one phase of the development at a time. At the end of each phase the results are evaluated, and if satisfactory, the money to support the next phase is authorized.

There are two major aspects to the phasing process. The first aspect is the step-by-step evolution and documentation of system requirements. The second aspect, which will be discussed later, is the preparation and execution of phased program plans.

The step-by-step evolution and documentation of system requirements is done through what often is called the "System Engineering Process." Figure 44-5, Segment 1, corresponds with this process. However, the term "Phased Baseline Requirements Definition Process" is preferred because it is more definitive and because it concentrates attention on the tangible outputs of the process. These outputs are the Phased Baseline Requirements Documents. They range from the initial descriptions of the objectives of the development program to the specifications for manufacturing individual parts and procedures for maintaining and using the system equipments. These documents lend themselves to performance of a quality assurance function based on agreed standards for their format, scope, and content.

The words "Mission," "Function," "Allocated," and "Product" are abbreviations for the following baselines:

Mission Baseline
Functional Baseline
Allocated Baseline
Product Baseline

The Mission Baseline is a complete documentation of all the Missions that the system must perform or, for a consumer product, a complete definition of all the markets that the product must satisfy.

The last three terms are defined in detail in MIL-STD-490, "Specification Practices." Briefly, the Functional Baseline is a complete definition of all the functions that must be performed in order to fulfill the missions. For example, in the case of an automobile, one of the missions would be to transport people from their home to their place of work. One of the functions required to accomplish this mission would be "Control Direction." This term illustrates one of the most basic principles of the system engineering process. This principle is that functions must be defined in a way that does not constrain the design solution. For example, "provide steering wheel" would be an unacceptable definition of the control direction function.

The Allocated Baseline is sometimes called the "system specification" or the "configuration item specification part I." It sets forth all the performance requirements that the product must meet. An earlier term "design-to-baseline" was appropriate and descriptive in that each of the allocated requirements establishes a target that the designer must meet. For example, if the system reliability has been allocated in the form of a subsystem requirement of 1,000 hours mean time between failures, then the designer must design to meet this level of reliability.

The Product Baseline consists of the familiar drawings and specifications by which the engineering function communicates to the purchasing and manufacturing functions the actual form, fit, and results that must be achieved in the manufactured product. An earlier term "make to baseline" is still appropriate to this type of documentation. The product baseline includes all the written procedures that are required for testing, installation, maintenance, and operation of the system.

Another aspect of the first segment of the management model is "Risk Study Reports." Experience has shown that in the development of complex systems, top management attention must be focused on the risks that are inherent in the cost, schedule, and technical commitments that have been made. For example, in the development of a commercial aircraft, it is customary for the manufacturer to make firm commitments to the airline customers in regard to all the significant performance characteristics of the aircraft as well as in regard to the sale price and delivery schedule.   A thorough identification of development risks is essential so that development program funds and manpower may be concentrated on the most significant development problems and not dissipated on relatively trivial problems. For example, if aerodynamic stability is a major threat to achieving fitness for use, then a development program must provide for adequate development funds to be allocated to aerodynamic analysis and to wind tunnel testing.

Technical Program Plans   After product requirements have been set forth in a set of baseline requirements documents, the next step is to identify those activities which people must perform in order to give confidence that the requirement will be met.

	NASA A	NASA B	NASA C	NASA D	
PHASED ACTIVITIES	CONCEPT FORMULATION	CONTRACT DEFINITION	ENGINEERING DEVELOPMENT	HARDWARE PRODUCTION	OPERATIONAL DEPLOYMENT
PRIMARY PRODUCTS (OUTPUTS)	MISSION REQUIREMENTS FEASIBLE BASELINE DESIGN	DESIGN-TO REQUIREMENTS TEST-TO AND USE-TO REQUIREMENTS	MAKE-TO REQUIREMENTS TEST AND EVALUATION HARDWARE	OPERATIONAL HARDWARE INTEGRATED LOGISTIC SUPPORT	READY SYSTEMS OPERATIONAL MISSION RESULTS
NEXT PHASE PROGRAM PLANS	FOR DEFINITION	FOR DEVELOPMENT	FOR PRODUCTION	FOR OPERATION	
PRELIMINARY PLANS FOR LATER PHASES	FOR DEVELOPMENT FOR PRODUCTION FOR OPERATION	FOR PRODUCTION FOR OPERATION	FOR OPERATION		

Fig. 44-6   Phased activities, products, and plans.

This is done by writing technical program plans.   Segment 2 in the Development Risk Management Model covers this step.

Figure 44-6 illustrates the relationship of program plans to development phases and to the primary products or outputs of these phases.   Phased development is discussed in Section 8 of the Handbook.   Also, in that Section the Department of Defense (DOD) terms "concept formulation," "contract definition," "engineering development," "hardware production," and "operational deployment" are discussed. The DOD system for dividing the total life cycle of a complex engineering system into five phases is well suited to mass produced items such as missiles.   In some cases a sixth phase covering "obsolescence and disposal" may be needed.

For NASA (National Aeronautics and Space Administration) development programs only four phases are required.   This is so because each spacecraft is different and even the boosters are produced only in small numbers.   Consequently, there is no need for a distinct production phase.   The NASA Phases A, B, C, and D are defined in the Policy Directive NPD 7121.1A, "Phased Project Planning."   Briefly, Phase A (Preliminary Analysis) covers studies and definitions of potential space missions, together with conceptual designs for their accomplishment.   Phase B (Definition) covers extensive trade studies of design alternatives and the establishment of a baseline system, including functional baseline and allocated baseline documentation at the system level (system specifications). Phase C (Design) covers the development of most of the lower level specifications including the manufacturing, drawings, and support documentation that constitute the product baselines. Phase D (Development Operations) covers the final design details, system fabrication, check-out, and launch and mission operations.

The above paragraph discusses what Figure 44-6 identifies as "primary products" or "outputs" for each phase. In addition, the work done in each phase must include preparation of program plans for the following phases and preliminary plans for the later phases. The solid arrows indicate that the final program plans define the activities to be performed in the next phase. The dashed arrows indicate that the preliminary plans form the basis for final plans.

In this Section of the Handbook we are concerned with establishment of standards for the writing of phased program plans and the use of these standards as a factor in achieving the quality assurance objective of fitness for use in the development of complex systems.

The Development Risk Management Model indicates that the purpose of program plans is to identify only those activities which are critical to controlling risks. "Critical Activities" may be defined as "those program management, procurement, design, test, manufacturing, quality control, and product support activities that experience has shown must be subject to formal discipline to assure that products will accomplish their missions." It would be both economically and technically impractical to require, at the very beginning of each phase, complete planning of all activities. However, it is important to set standards for the planning of the critical activities.

In present-day engineering management practice, critical activities are grouped into areas of technology, such as reliability, maintainability, quality control, and product support. In each of these areas there are professional groups whose collective experience has provided the ability to write program-type specifications. It is program-type specifications, such as DOD's reliability program specification MIL-STD-785A, "Reliability Program for Systems and Equipment Development and Production," and NASA's NHB 5300.4(1A), "The Reliability Program Provisions for Aeronautical and Space System Contractors," that provide basic standards for quality assurance of development program plans. However, any government agency, industrial company, or professional society can develop its own program standards, either by writing an appropriate program-type specification or by developing checklists of the critical activities that should be included in development program plans.

Cost-Schedule Work Package Plans   The third segment in the Development Risk Management Model is concerned with quality assurance of the business management aspects of complex system development.

In Figure 44-4 the "Business" column shows the sequence of terms "work breakdown structure," "cost accounts," and "work packages." Experience in the development of complex systems has shown that management discipline based on work breakdown structures, cost accounts, and work packages can be extremely helpful in the control of cost, schedule, and technical development risks and therefore in the achievement of the objective of fitness for use. We will call this type of discipline "Work Package Program Planning."

The first step is to establish a work breakdown structure. The primary objective of a work breakdown structure is to delineate in a graphic and practical form all the products that must be produced and all the activities that must be performed throughout the development program. It provides a single, highly integrated, foundation for requiring, scheduling, and funding all the products and all the activities. The concept and mechanics of establishing a work breakdown structure for development programs are described in MIL-STD-881, "Work Breakdown Structures for Material Items." This program-type specification also provides a standard that can be used for quality assurance of this step in the development program business management system.

Figure 44-7 illustrates how cost accounts are formed by matrixing the items in a breakdown structure with the organizational units in a development company. A cost account covers all the work that a particular organization will do, on a particular work breakdown structure item, during one complete phase.

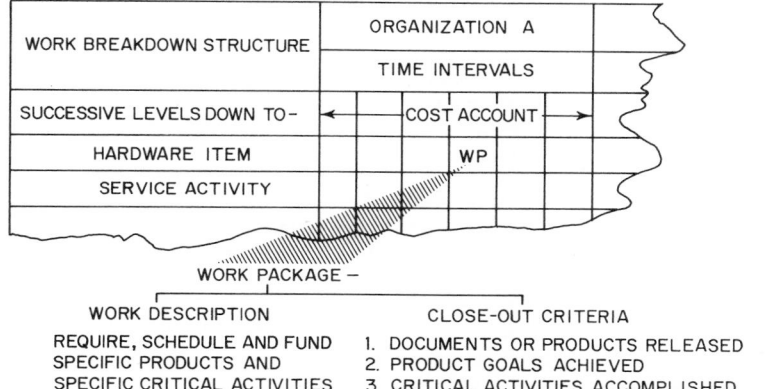

Fig. 44-7 Technical assurance through an integrated cost/schedule/technical control system.

Department of Defense Instruction 7000.2, "Performance Measurement for Selected Acquisitions," defines the term work package as a "delineation of work required to complete a particular job, assignable to a single organizational element and covering a relatively short span of time."

There are several logical ways for dividing each cost account into small, manageable, short-duration work packages. Figure 44-7 illustrates the simple procedure of dividing a cost account into a series of time intervals, each of which becomes a work package. The two aspects of work packages that are vital to quality assurance in the development of complex systems are shown in Figure 44-7 as "Work Package Work Description" and "Work Package Close-out Criteria." The work description for each work package must specifically require, schedule, and fund specific products and the performance of specific critical activities. In particular, the critical activities set forth in the technical program plans, such as the reliability program plan, must be specifically required, scheduled, and funded through the work package work description.

A very basic management principle is that confidence that the uncertainties in developing a complex system are being controlled and reduced depends on assurance that the planned development activities are being performed. For example, confidence that safety margins are being built into a structure depends on assuring that the critical activity of stress analysis actually is being performed and will be completed before design drawings are released to manufacturing. Likewise, confidence that reliability is being built into an electronic component depends on assuring that all the planned circuit analyses will be completed before the drawings are released. Consequently, it is vital that a work package not be closed out until its planned contribution to risk control actually has been achieved.

Figure 44-7 shows the criteria that are intended to implement this management quality assurance objective. Item 1, "Documents or Products Released," covers items such as the release of a drawing during the design phase or the completion of a manufacturing step during the production phase. Item 2, "Product Goals Achieved," requires establishment of time phased performance goals and demonstration by quantitative analysis or test that these goals have been achieved. For example, if a mean time between failures of 1,000 hours must be achieved at the end of a 4-year development period, quantitative goals must be established to correspond with the close-out date of appropriate work packages.

This is the way in which the traditional techniques, such as predicting reliability growth and auditing its accomplishment, are integrated into the business management system. During design, quantitative analyses or tests are required to prove that time phased performance goals have been achieved. During manufacturing, in-process measurements or inspections provide the evidence that this type of close-out criterion is being achieved.

The third item, "Critical Activities Accomplished," implements the principle that critical activities such as stress analysis of a structural design must be accomplished before the management system approves close-out of the corresponding work package. This requirement for tracking the accomplishment of critical activities is important for all characteristics, but it is particularly important in relation to intangible characteristics, such as safety, for which it is too difficult or impossible to track progress through quantitative analyses or tests.

Segment 3 of the Development Risk Management Model covers only assurance that the *planning* of work packages, together with their work descriptions and close-out criteria, is adequate. Segments 4, 5, and 6 deal with the *control* of the development program in accordance with this planning.

Requirements Communication   The fourth segment in the Development Risk Management Model is concerned with the responsibility of every supervisor in a line organization to communicate to the working level people their responsibilities for achieving the requirements set forth in the phased baseline requirements definition documents, by performing the activities set forth in technical program plans and in accordance with the cost and schedule criteria set forth in the work package program plan.

Figure 44-5 indicates that the responsibility of the supervisor includes not only communicating by command but also motivation of his subordinates to achieve specified requirements by performing planned critical activities in accordance with specified disciplines.

This inclusion of Segment 4 in the Development Risk Management Model does not indicate a need for vague, generalized motivational programs or for programs with unreasonable objectives. It does call for command and motivation of specific people, to perform specific activities, with the technical excellence required to achieve reasonable and specified quality objectives.

Work Package Performance Tracking   DOD Instruction 7000.2, "Performance Measurement for Selected Acquisitions," calls for development contractors to have a management system which provides simultaneous cost performance and technical performance measurements. It states or implies that this type of status data is essential for quality assurance of program management decisions during all phases of a complex system development program.

The Development Risk Management Model makes an intentional and important distinction between two types of performance measurement. Segment 5 covers "Work Package Performance Tracking" and Segment 6 covers "System Requirements Achievement Tracking." Although both types of tracking have the same objective of assuring that planned results are being achieved, there are important differences between them, and both are essential to controlling complex system development program risks.

In general, Work Package Tracking provides detailed and integrated information on cost, schedule, and technical performance. By contrast, Requirements Achievement Tracking is used only to check on a relatively few critical system characteristics, such as the payload on an airplane, and it does not integrate cost and schedule performance data with technical performance data. Another important difference is that the work package method is applicable from the beginning of a development program but the requirements achievement method is dependent on quantitative test and analysis data that may not be available until late in the development cycle.

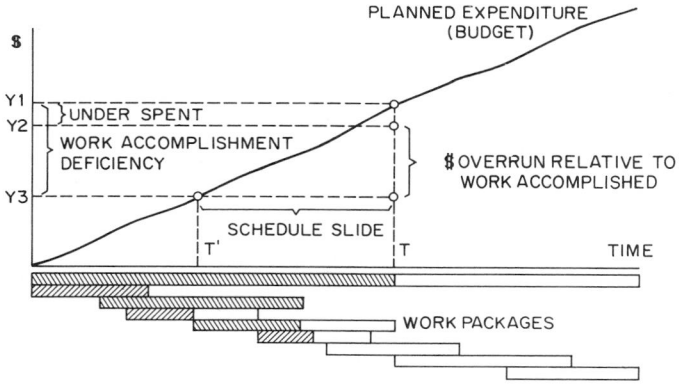

Y1 PLANNED VALUE WORK PLANNED TO BE COMPLETED AT TIME T
Y2 ACTUAL EXPENDITURE AT TIME T
Y3 PLANNED VALUE OF WORK ACTUALLY ACCOMPLISHED AT TIME T
    (SUM OF $ VALUES REPRESENTED BY CROSS HATCHING)

Fig. 44-8 Early warning of cost/schedule risks.

Work Package Performance Tracking starts at the individual work package level. It calls for a quality assurance function to track the achievement of the work package close-out criteria and to assure that close-out does not happen until the criteria have been met. The development of a complex system may involve several thousand work packages; therefore, a method is required for summing the information from individual work packages into charts that indicate the overall status of the program and also the status of each cost account. Figure 44-8 illustrates how this summation is achieved. The heavy black line represents traditional budgeting or planning of expenditures as a function of time. At the point in time represented by T, the chart shows a planned expenditure of $Y1$ and an actual expenditure of $Y2$.

$Y3$ represents the "planned value of work actually accomplished" at time T. The concept of "planned value" is really quite simple, but it is extraordinarily difficult to explain. The general objective is clear enough. It is to provide a simultaneous presentation of cost, schedule, and technical status data in a form that facilitates early recognition of problems that will result in development cost overruns. Two such problems are:

1. Planned work has been accomplished but at a cost that exceeds the budgeted or planned value.

2. Budgeted money has been spent but planned work has not been accomplished or planned technical objectives have not been met.

The first problem can be recognized very easily simply by noting that actual expenditures exceed the planned values or budgets. It is the second problem that is not revealed simply by comparing actual expenditures with a budget curve.

Note that in Figure 44-8 the fact that Y2 is less than Y1 indicates a favorable condition of underexpenditure relative to the planned expenditure at time T. However, the fact that Y3 is less than Y1 indicates that the actual work accomplished is far less than planned. The fact that Y3 is less than Y2 indicates a dollar overrun relative to work accomplished. The fact that T is later than T' shows that the work that has been accomplished at time T should have been accomplished at time T'.

Obviously, dependence on the traditional cost and schedule data provided by the values of Y1 and Y2 is dangerously deceptive. Every complex system program manager needs the kind of information that results from determining the value of Y3. It follows that the challenge to the total quality control system is how to provide an objective value of Y3.

The current practice for providing an answer to this challenge is illustrated by the work package blocks in the middle of Figure 44-8. Each rectangle represents a work package. For each rectangle, the left-hand edge is at the scheduled starting time and the right-hand edge is at the scheduled completion time. As work gets accomplished, the rectangle is crosshatched in so that the crosshatched area represents work done. The ratio of the crosshatched area to the total area represents the percent completion of that work package. Moreover, the height of each rectangle is on a vertical scale of dollars, so that the areas are proportional to dollars as well. The value of Y3 is obtained by summing up the $ values of all the crosshatched areas.

To understand the whole chart, it is necessary to realize that the horizontal time scale is used to represent three types of data. These types of data are:

1. Scheduling data (relating to budgets and work package starts and stops)
2. Actual time data (relating to actual expenditure)
3. Work accomplishment data (as a percentage of work planned)

Also it is necessary to realize that the credit assigned to work accomplished and represented by the crosshatching is expressed as a dollar value equal to the original budget corresponding with the percentage of the work package accomplished and irrespective of the actual expenditure.

Note that the top block represents a continuous "level of effort" type of work package. It has no start or stop dates and the credit represented by the crosshatching is assigned automatically with the passage of time. Level of effort work packages provide no information on achievement of technical objectives and no warning of potential cost overruns or schedule slippage. Consequently, DOD and NASA performance measurement specifications require that use of this type of work package be minimized.

Now consider the lower work packages in Figure 44-8. They are called "discrete work packages" because they have specifically planned start and stop dates. Also, as illustrated by Figure 44-7, they have specific work descriptions and close-out criteria. Figure 44-8 shows that at time T five work packages were planned for completion and one more for commencement. The crosshatching shows that actually only two work packages had been completed and three others started. In the figure, the started but not completed work packages are 50% crosshatched. This means that, in the absence of more specific evaluation of the planned value of the work accomplished, they were credited with 50% accomplishment. Again, note that the value of Y3 is obtained by summation of the $ values of the crosshatched areas for both the "level of effort" and the "discrete" work packages.

It is the type of information illustrated by Figure 44-8 and based on work package data that justifies the message presented by Figure 44-9. Warning of a potential cost overrun is provided by comparing actual expenditures with the budgeted cost of the work that actually has been performed.[5] Schedule warning is provided by comparing the revised completion dates for work packages or cost accounts with the original completion dates. Technical warning is provided by comparing current assessments of technical achievements with time phased achievement goals.

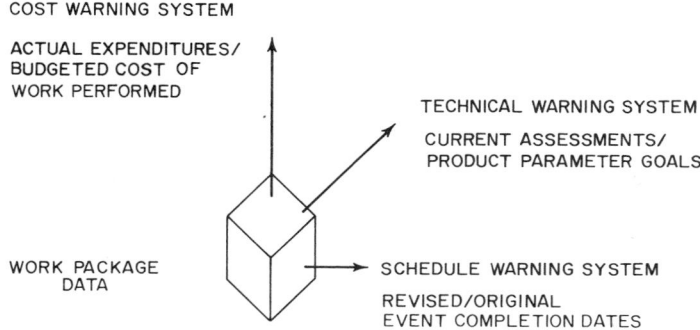

COST WARNING SYSTEM

ACTUAL EXPENDITURES/
BUDGETED COST OF
WORK PERFORMED

TECHNICAL WARNING SYSTEM

CURRENT ASSESSMENTS/
PRODUCT PARAMETER GOALS

WORK PACKAGE
DATA

SCHEDULE WARNING SYSTEM

REVISED/ORIGINAL
EVENT COMPLETION DATES

Fig. 44-9 Three warning systems.

System Requirements Achievement Tracking Segment 6 of the Development Risk Management Model relates directly to the system characteristics requirements set forth in Segment 1, "Phased Baseline Requirements Definition." For example, if a mean time between failures of 1,000 hours was specified in Segment 1, Segment 6 would include tracking achievement of this characteristic.

The traditional practice of qualification testing provides for verifying by test that all the characteristics required by design specifications actually have been achieved by the design solution. The traditional practice of acceptance testing provides for checking that these same characteristics are being achieved in the production units. However, qualification testing and acceptance testing are performed only at the end of a development program. In the case of a complex system, the development program may average a duration of 4 years and may take as much as 10 years. Obviously, at least in the case of critical characteristics, something more must be done to provide assessment of the degree to which requirements are being achieved.

There are three basic approaches to System Requirements Achievement Tracking during a development program. They may be called:

1. The Time-Phased-Goal Method
2. The Predicted Value-at-Completion-Method
3. The Probability Requirement-Will-Be-Achieved Method

Figure 44-10 illustrates the first two methods. The acronym PAE stands for Performance Achievement Event. A performance achievement event occurs at a point

---

[5] For a technique of reporting cost based on schedule accomplishment see Block, Ellery B., Accomplishment/Cost: Better Project Control, *Harvard Business Review*, May–June 1971, pp. 110–124.

in time when a meaningful assessment of a required characteristic can be made by quantitative analysis or by test or by a design review of all the analysis and test information that is available at the time of the review.   The dashed line at the top of Figure 44-10 represents a specified requirement for reliability, expressed as a mean time between failures.   The series of five circles represents a sequence of five predictions of the value that will be achieved at the end of the development period. The coincidence between the circles and the requirement line indicates that, throughout the development, it was always predicted that the requirement eventu-

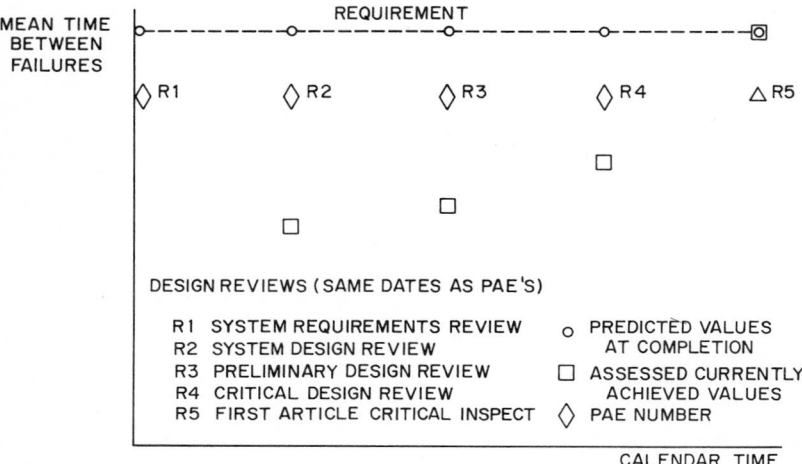

Fig. 44-10   PAE tracking chart.

ally would be achieved.   The five diamonds represent five performance achievement events corresponding with five design reviews.   The four squares represent an assessment of the value of mean time between failures that had been achieved at the point in time when the design review was held and the assessment was made.

Figure 44-11 represents the third method of tracking.   It illustrates that, throughout a development period, the predicted most probable value for the operational reliability was always the same and corresponded with a specified requirement. In addition, it shows that the confidence that the required and predicted value would be achieved improved steadily throughout the development period.   This in turn indicates that those activities which were planned to reduce uncertainty in the achievement of the required value actually were taking place.   This chart is only a conceptual illustration of the principle that the performance of development activities reduces uncertainty about the achievement of intangible characteristics such as safety.   It should not be confused with valid demonstrations of confidence levels based on statistical analysis of test data.

SUMMARY

The overall objective of the quality assurance function in relation to the development of a complex system is the same as for a simple product.   It is to assure achievement of fitness for use.   However, the scope of the assurance program must be broader. It must provide for assuring the quality of program management and for assuring the quality of development engineering as well as providing for the more familiar types of manufacturing and support quality assurance. To achieve all these objectives through basic quality assurance methods it is necessary to establish standards or criteria for the program management and development engineering functions and then to compare the execution of an actual development program with these standards. This Section of the Handbook presents a general standard in the form of a six-segment "Development Risk Management Model" (Figure 44-5). Various Department of Defense and National Aeronautics and Space Administration docu-

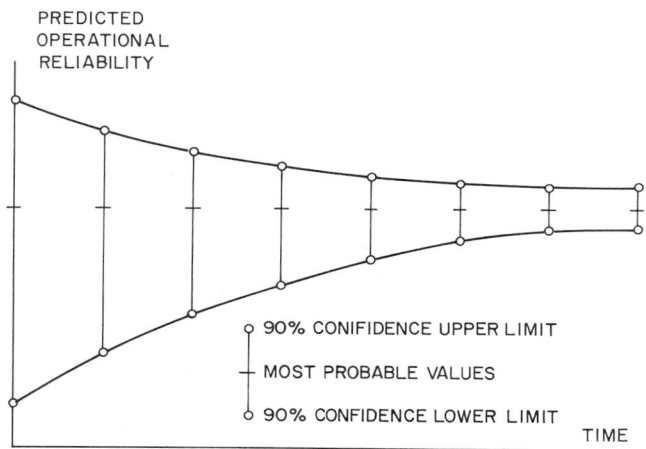

Fig. 44-11 Probability requirement will be achieved.

ments provide detailed standards or criteria for each segment of the model. To apply the model to the development of a new complex system, a program management type of organization (Figures 44-2 and 44-3) is needed. Such an organization should include a "technical program assurance" and a "design assurance function" as well as "manufacturing quality assurance" and a "support quality assurance" function. The usefulness of the model and the supporting techniques is not limited to the development of complex systems. Whenever development of any product involves cost, schedule, or technical risk, some of these techniques can be used to help control the risk. The degree of implementation should be related to the degree of risk. It is because complex systems require the orchestration of many technologies, many functions, and many organizations that the whole of the highly integrated total quality assurance systems represented by the model is necessary to control the risks that are inherent in their development.

Job Shop Quality

LEONARD A. SEDER

Leonard A. Seder and Associates, Malden, Massachusetts

WHAT IS A JOB SHOP?

The terms "job shop" and "mass production shop," though widely used, are loosely defined. Managers who use these terms are well aware that industrial life as lived in the job shop differs considerably from that prevailing in the mass production shop. This difference extends to the problems of creating, controlling, and improving quality. This Section undertakes to define the nature of the job shop and to explain the methods in use for dealing with job shop quality.

There is no single parameter which distinguishes the job shop from the mass production shop. Job shops vary in size from very small to very large. Some are captive; others are independent. Some serve sophisticated industrial customers; others serve relatively naive consumers. Their products range from one-of-a-kind non-repeating items to large lots of frequently reordered stock items. Some make proprietary products of their own design. Others develop designs jointly with customers' designs. Many cannot even be classified neatly in the foregoing terms, since their product mix spreads across the whole spectrum of customer sophistication, design responsibility, lot sizes, repeat rate, etc.

Despite this difficulty of classification, it is possible to identify certain basic common types of job shops and to recognize among them differences and commonality that affect the fashioning of a quality control program to suit their individual needs. Table 45-1 identifies four common types of job shop, and shows some typical products or operations which exemplify each type.

Percent Repeat Jobs. This term, which appears in the headings of Table 45-1, is one of the universal parameters of job shop operation. Percent repeat jobs is

TABLE 45-1   Types of Job Shops

		Typical products — or operations	
Type	Description	Percent repeat jobs low to moderate	Percent repeat jobs moderate to high
I	Large complex equipment	Locomotives Chemical plants Buildings Automated production equipment Radar sets	Farm equipment Aircraft Machine Tools Printing presses
II	Small, simple end products and components	Fashion fabrics Industrial adhesives Circuit boards Fabricated metals Books	Tires Shoes Garments Wall covering Small appliances Metal shapes Automotive components Electronic components Private-label foods Furniture
III	Custom parts	Machined parts Forgings Weldments	Stampings Castings Molded plastics Screw-machine parts Molded rubber Extruded parts Containers
IV	Subcontracted services	Toolmaking Diemaking Moldmaking Printing Machining Testing	Heat treating Welding Plating Packaging

defined as the percentage, out of the total number of jobs in the factory in any one month, which are identical repeats of job orders run previously.

The classification of low, moderate, and high percent repeat jobs have the following approximate values: "low" = under 35%; "moderate" = 35 to 80%; "high" = over 80%.

Large Complex Equipment.   Companies in Type I (Table 45-1) produce large complex units, each made up of thousands of different parts and components, each of these in turn being defined by its own "drawing number." These companies call themselves job shops because an individual job order or contract usually calls for a very small number of such large units, often only one. Only if the percent repeat jobs is moderate to high are they able to justify manufacturing these units as stock items and making (or buying) the input parts in economic quantities. Lacking a stock of finished units or components, it is necessary to produce from "scratch," and the time pressure becomes severe.

Small End Products and Components.   The Type II companies usually produce large quantities on any one order. However, they regard themselves as job shops because of the endless variations of size, shape, color, style, or configuration typically involved in their product lines. Even those with "standard" product lines frequently show hundreds of different "model numbers" in their catalogs. Those who make "specials" for the various customers' unique requirements have thousands of drawing numbers in their engineering files.

Custom Parts. These Type III companies are mainly in business as suppliers to Type I and II companies. They specialize in one or more of the processes listed and fill their shops with customer-designed parts of thousands of different configurations and compositions. Often they can satisfy a customer's annual requirements for a particular part number in just a few hours of production running time.

Subcontracted Services. Type IV companies differ from Type III only in that they tend to be small, independent shops specializing in particular operations, often working on customer-furnished material. Captive shops of this type are often in-house departments within a large Type I, II, or III company. Variety of jobs is again the rule, each job usually requiring only a few hours of production time.

Jobs per Operator per Week. All these four types of job shop exhibit two recurring themes of commonality:

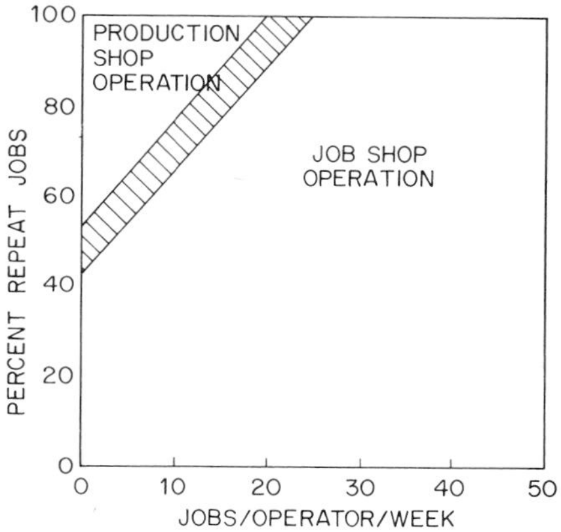

Fig. 45-1   The job shop grid.

1. Wide *variety of designs* (due to myriad different configurations, colors, sizes, shapes, models)

2. *Short production time* for any individual production task on any one "job"

These two factors may be conveniently combined into a single parameter of "jobs per operator per week," reflecting the average number of different orders, or different setups, or setup changes that will be handled by each operator over a week's time. Whatever the type of job shop, this number is generally much higher in the job shop than in the mass production shop. This fact has a direct bearing on the nature of the job shop quality program.

The "percent repeat jobs" (defined above) also varies in size among job shop types and within types.[1] However, the percent repeat jobs is generally much lower for job shops as a class than for mass production shops.

Job Shop Grid. When the two parameters of jobs per operator per week and percent repeat jobs are related to each other on the same diagram, there emerges a convenient way to quantify the distinction between the production shop and the job shop. The "job shop grid" in Figure 45-1 is designed to show this relationship.

The job shop grid opens the way to design and apply quality control methods which are keyed to the quantified parameters. At the outset it is evident that production shops are generally those with a small number of jobs per operator per week and a high percentage of repeat jobs. Above the level of 20 jobs per operator per week, we consider it a job shop regardless of the percentage of repeat jobs. Also, below a 50% repeat job rate, we consider it a job shop even though the jobs per operator per week is low.

[1]As implied in Table 45-1, the percent repeat jobs tends to be higher for some job shop types than others, e.g., Type II vs. Type I. However, the rate varies over the whole range, and for individual shops within one type.

THE JOB SHOP QUALITY PROGRAM

In a broad sense, the problems of job shop quality management are the same as for any other shop:

1. Planning of quality for new or modified products and processes
2. Controlling the quality during manufacture
3. Improving quality levels to reduce quality losses

Similarly, in a broad sense, the concepts and principles of solution of quality problems are the same as presented elsewhere in this Handbook, i.e., Planning, Sections 6, 8, and 9; Controlling, Sections 11 and 23; Improving, Sections 16 and 18. However, the numerous job orders (which create high jobs per operator per week and low percent repeat jobs) greatly influence the job shop approach to quality.

The impact of these numerous job orders is not on the materials, processes, or people; these generally remain common to all jobs. Neither is the impact on the systems, practices, and procedures; these likewise remain common to all jobs.[2] Rather, the impact is similar to that involved in launching many "new products" every week. For each of these "new products" there is need to discover (1) what is "new," (2) how this affects product design, plan of manufacture, special tools, quality requirements, etc., and (3) what needs to be done to assure that the "newness" is correctly identified and complied with by all departments.

Stated another way, the impact of the numerous job orders is primarily on preproduction planning, and especially on *manufacturing planning.* This planning creates a considerable problem of communicating, to all concerned, what is "different" about each order so that responsive action can be taken.[3] The amount of such communication can rise to enormous proportions because of the multiplying effect of (1) the number of job orders, (2) the number of ways in which each order is different, and (3) the number of processes, tools, etc., affected by each of these differences. A consequence of this great volume of communication is that the problem of quality control is a problem in *quality of communication* as much as a problem in conventional process and product quality control. As a corollary, when product nonconformance is detected, the correction to be made is very frequently in some detail of the job plan rather than in the product or manufacturing process.

In the light of the foregoing, the quality program for the job shop must include special provisions for:

Planning to communicate essential quality information to all concerned
Controlling the errors and inadequacies in this communication
Improving not merely the processes and products but also the planning and communication

THE JOB NUMERICS

As noted, preproduction planning is a major job shop activity, and involves every job. Since each job differs from all others in *design,* each requires its own *product specifications,* spelling out in detail the materials, formulation, configuration, end-product physical properties, quality and reliability requirements, and the rest. (Simplification is often possible in instances where a single specification can be used to

---

[2]These common "ingredients" may, however, contain the root cause of chronic quality problems. See Challenging the Basic Premises, below.

[3]Even at higher percent repeat jobs, reorders are seldom processed without a planning review for modifications initiated by customers, or dictated by internal experience from previous runs.

specify a whole "family" of items largely resembling each other but differing only in specific detail of size or color, etc.)

Since jobs also differ in the exact manufacturing process to be followed, each requires its own *manufacturing plan,* to communicate to Production and Inspection the necessary details of input materials, operation sequence, inspection or laboratory release points, special or unique tooling, in-process properties required, mandatory processing restrictions, and the like.

TABLE 45-2   Primary Job Numerics

Aspect of definition	Typical examples
To Define the Product	
Materials	Material specification numbers for metals, chemicals, agricultural products, etc.
Formulation	Specific proportions of various materials to be used
Configuration	Drawing or sketch showing dimensions, component parts, assembly details, etc.
End-product acceptability	Dimensional, physical, chemical, optical, metallurgical, electrical, visual, etc., tolerances
	Functional test requirements
Reliability	Maximum failure rate, or degree of degradation in specified endurance test
To Define the Manufacturing Plan	
Input materials	Sources, subcontractors
Operation sequence	Exact order of primary, secondary, finishing, packaging, etc., operations
	Specific machines, baths, ovens (when restricted)
Inspection points	Location of inspection stations or laboratory release points
Unique tooling	Design of specific form tools, molds, dies, assembly fixtures, artwork, etc.
In-process properties	Dimensions, thicknesses, densities, colors, electrical outputs, chemical values, strengths, etc., needed at specific operations
Mandatory processing restrictions	Temperatures and times for bakes, heat treatments, reactions, drying, curing, pasteurizing, etc.
	Hold times between operations

There appears to be no accepted generic term to represent, for a specific job order, all the details of product and manufacturing process.[4]   Hence the author has coined the term "Primary Job Numerics" to serve as such a generic term.   Table 45-2 summarizes and gives typical examples of these primary job numerics.   Obviously, mass production shops must also have these same numerics.   However, in the mass production shop the numerics are few in number, tend to become stabilized, and are easily remembered by shop personnel.   In the job shop they are many in number, are frequently changed, and require constant reference to the written documents.

Not all job shops have responsibility for preparing the numerics to define *both* product and manufacturing plan.   Types III and IV (Table 45-1) ordinarily receive product specifications from their customers and hence prepare only the manufacturing plan.   Types I and II prepare both sets of numerics for their own products, but only product specifications for those materials and components which they purchase.

---

[4]"Job Documentation" comes close, but it sometimes is used to include the recorded quality data, which is not part of our definition.

TABLE 45-3   Supplementary Job Numerics (To Prevent Product Deficiencies and Losses)

Aspect of definition	Typical examples
Materials	Special vendor instructions
	Special gages or test methods
	Classification of characteristics
	AQLs
Operation sequence	Special work instructions
	Exact details of important hand operations
	Permissible deviations from sequence
Inspection points	Special gages or test methods
	Classification of characteristics
	AQLs
Unique tooling	Identification numbers
	Tool inspection details
	Permissible tool deviations
In-process properties	Optimum settings of process variables
	Special gages or test methods
	Plans of control for operations with setup approval criteria, running approval criteria
Mandatory processing	Tolerances for times, temperatures, etc.
	Certifications required
End-product acceptability	Special gages or test methods
	Special customer "idiosyncrasies"
	Classification of characteristics
	AQLs
	Customer data submittals or certifications
	Visible defect acceptability limits
	Customer sampling plan impositions
Reliability	Testing details

The primary job numerics have long been recognized as essential and have found expression in various types of "legitimate" documentation in the shop. The product specification, manufacturing drawing, material specification, formulation or batching sheet, tool drawings, exploded assembly view, route card, operation sheet, inspection detail sheet, test procedure, and job order card are the more common names for the various means of communicating the needed numerics to shop personnel.

The primary job numerics outlined in Table 45-2 are the minimum details necessary to define and make the product. However, they are seldom sufficient to assure the quality of the end product or to attain economic operation. To make up for these deficiencies, there are additional numerics which provide the added information needed to minimize product deficiencies, rejections, repairs, yield losses, and customer complaints.

Some of these "Supplementary Job Numerics" are shown in Table 45-3. For each aspect of product and process definition, there are special details, unique to the individual job, which are of value to the shop personnel. Communicating these details to the shop personnel (through the documentation) provides the advance knowledge which can often spell the difference between success and failure to meet end-product requirements or between high and low "quality costs." Not all these supplementary job numerics are needed for all jobs. Indeed, one of the real dilemmas faced by job shop managers is the decision of how far to go in this direction (see below).

JOB PLANNING

To generate, communicate, and comply with all these job numerics requires that a major element of the job shop quality program must be concerned with individual job planning. This involves (1) organizing for job planning, (2) detecting and correcting job planning errors, (3) improving the job planning.

Organizing for Job Planning A major question is how far to go in completeness of planning. It is usual to carry out planning of the *primary* job numerics in total (or to leave only minor details to be worked out during the production run). However, the *supplementary* job numerics present a problem in striking the proper balance between overplanning and underplanning. Establishment of the numerics beforehand will work to avoid errors and misjudgments during the production run. However, the volume of detail and the lack of adequate information of some aspects (e.g., the expected rate of occurrence of specific defects, sequence deviations, or tool deviations; knowledge of the optimum settings of process variables, etc.) make it uneconomic or impossible to fill in all the details.

A major consideration in this decision is the "percent repeat jobs." A shop with a low percent repeat jobs must necessarily devote a major effort to planning the supplementary job numerics, since there is no "second chance." A shop with a high percent repeat jobs can place its major effort in control, at the sacrifice of planning, since the control activities will, over a period of time, influence the evolution of the correct numerics. Figure 45-2 shows this contrast diagrammatically.

A further consideration in extent of planning is the time schedule. Planning can be less than complete when the manufacturing cycle permits a trial lot to be piloted through ahead of the job order (to pin down many of the supplementary job numerics) or when the job running time is long enough to use data feedback and corrective action for the same purpose. (See Job Shop Control, below.)

Responsibility for job planning varies widely among job shops. In all but the smallest shops, the primary numerics are commonly developed and issued by a staff group, separate from line production. This group is variously designated as Research and Development, Engineering or Technical (especially when definition of product is part of the work), or as Manufacturing Engineering, Process Engineering, Production Engineering, Estimating, Planning or Industrial Engineering (when the planning is mostly limited to definition of manufacturing plan). However, there is no universal pattern of responsibility for generating the supplementary numerics. In some instances, staff Quality Control Engineers or Process Engineers have this responsibility. In other shops, line

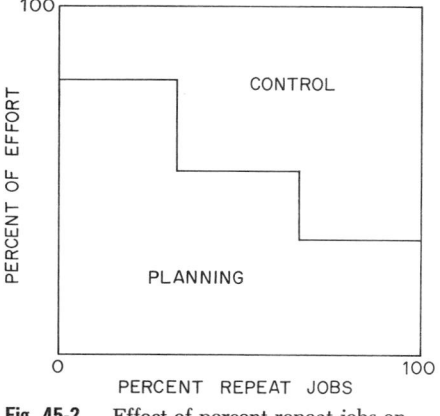

Fig. 45-2 Effect of percent repeat jobs on allocation of planning effort.

foremen, inspection supervisors, and even workmen and inspectors have the assignment. In still other cases, the supplementary inspection numerics are prepared by staff specialists, while the foreman is left to his own devices to develop and convey information on tools, setups, settings of process variables, etc.

As is usual in matters of organizing, it is more important to be clear than to be logical or uniform.   There is a need for providing the supplementary numerics, and the responsibility for doing so should be clear.   The job shop which has left this question vague would do well to face it cleanly.   As a general rule, if the generation and maintenance of any portion of the supplementary job numerics is to be delegated to Production, the responsibility and method should be made clear. Otherwise, in the author's experience, it tends to be neglected, poorly maintained, and ineffective.

Often the variety of work makes it necessary and possible to do the planning selectively based on the size or complexity of the job.   Jobs over a certain size, or involving new manufacturing techniques, or expected to become new standard products, are planned by the staff group, whereas small jobs, or those which involve only minor changes from "standard items" or previously run jobs, are planned by the line production people.[5]

Detecting and Correcting Job Planning Errors   The sheer number of details involved in the primary and supplementary numerics makes it inevitable that errors will occur in job planning.   Some will be the inadvertent errors of misplaced decimal points, transposed digits, incorrect arithmetic, and the like[6]   Others will arise from lack of sufficient knowledge, by the planner, of processes, economics of manufacture, capabilities, and reliabilities.

To minimize planning errors, it is useful to review the planning in some appropriate way.   For large jobs, this review tends to be elaborate and formal.   The planning documents are circulated to the key departments, after which there is a formal review meeting.   This meeting not only goes over errors and refinements; it also identifies possible problem areas.[7]   In addition, it may determine whether there is need to provide "sample" or "trial lot" evaluation before full production.   The review meeting also may establish the guidelines for delegating development of the supplementary numerics to lower levels of organization.

For smaller, low repeat rate jobs, the planning documents are likewise circulated to the key departments.   However, the review and sign-off usually take place without formal review meetings.

For high percent repeat jobs, reliance is largely placed on the control system. (See Job Shop Control, below.)

Improving Job Planning   Improvement of this planning, as applied to manufacture, involves preparation and use of machine and process capability knowledge in establishing tolerances, choosing processes, classifying characteristics, etc.   The approach is generally conventional, and is discussed in Section 9.

A concept known as "Group Technology" involves planning of jobbing work by identifying "families" of parts based on commonality of operations.   This commonality then is used as a basis for standardization of drawings, tooling, etc., with an obvious residual effect on quality planning.   As of the early 1970s, this concept had received some adoption in Europe, but very little in the United States.[8]

For improving the planning of the nonmanufacturing aspects of the job numerics, see generally Section 46.

---

[5] See generally Section 6 and especially Section 9.

[6] See generally Section 46.

[7] For some examples, see Kilduff, Francis B., For Small Shops: Low Cost Q.C., *Quality Assurance,* March 1965, p. 20.

[8] See generally, A Way to Make Diversity Pay Off, *Business Week,* Oct. 18, 1969, pp. 152, 154.   For a technical discussion, see Knayer, Manfred, Group Technology, *Industrial Engineering,* September 1970, pp. 23–27.   See also Hikichi, Tozo, Management Information and Control System in a Job Shop.   *Reports of Statistical Applications Research, JUSE,* vol. 19, No. 3, 1972, pp. 32–38.

JOB SHOP CONTROL

The "jobbing" nature of the job shop is derived from the diversity of products. However, the manufacturing processes which turn out these diverse products exhibit a high degree of commonality in materials, machines, instruments, and people. As a result, the job shop systems for quality control of manufacture closely parallel the systems in use in the mass production shops, but scaled to the size and needs of the company. In addition, the large number of jobs per operator per week and the mass of detail contained in the job numerics make it important to have special approaches to data feedback and corrective action.

Overall Control System Those minimal job shop systems which parallel the mass production systems are listed below, including reference to the conventional approach:

Control System	Section Reference
Vendor material	10
Identity and flow.	11, 46
Process control decision making	11
Tool and equipment qualification and maintenance	9, 11
Calibration and maintenance of measuring equipment . . .	13
Disposition of rejected material	12
Analysis and follow-up of customer complaints.	15

To formalize these systems, it is convenient to document them in a quality control manual which is then distributed to those concerned (see Section 6, under Quality Control Manual).

In the job shop it is uncommonly important to provide a sound plan for making decisions on whether the process should run or stop, and to make clear delegation of responsibility for decision making on the factory floor.[9] With limited manpower to spread over a multitude of jobs, it is also important that the job shop understand and make use of the concept of dominance[10] in order to maximize the effectiveness of that manpower. Setup dominance is the prevailing mode for most quality characteristics in the small-lot job shop, especially those of Types III and IV. The main reason[11] is that the running time is usually so short that the "time-to-time" variation of the process is minimal. Hence "if the setup is right, the lot is right." Accordingly, the job setup is a vital control station, and demands use of statistically valid plans for setup approval, e.g., narrow limit gaging, precontrol, control charts, etc.[12] These plans are needed whether the setup approval decision is assigned to operators or to inspectors.

Because of the importance of the setup, many job shops have made use of redundancy in the setup approval by requiring inspectors to check the setup before the lot is run off. This has not been merely a check on the operator (or setup man); it has also been a means of checking against vague specifications, special measuring equipment, etc. However, as skills have been upgraded and statistical plans have gained wider acceptance, there has been a trend toward establishing a state of self-control by the operator and turning the setup acceptance over to him.[13]

In one machine tool company where machine shop lot quantities were normally

---

[9] See Section 11, under Quality Responsibilities on the Factory Floor.
[10] See Section 9, under Concept of Dominance.
[11] Another reason is the prevalence of special tooling.
[12] See Section 23, under the respective headings.
[13] See generally Section 11, under Product Acceptance by Operators.

15 pieces or less, the setup acceptance responsibility was transferred from inspectors to experienced operators. Following the changeover, inspectors performed random audits of completed lots and reported the results for immediate manufacturing action. In addition, the summarized data were fed back in chart form to "rate" the various departments (lathe, milling, grinding, etc.)[14]

Data Feedback and Corrective Action   Many job shop managers have fallen into the trap of believing that once they have established an inspection system (even if, in a small shop, it means the hiring of the first inspector), they now have "quality control" and can relax. Now "quality control" will protect them against bad purchased materials, stop defects from being manufactured, and guard the outgoing product. It may well do these things, but an essential added need is to use the *information* gained from performing the inspection to *improve* quality. It can do this in several ways if appropriate feedback mechanisms are established:

1. For preventing defects in the unmanufactured portion of a job
2. For preventing defects in repeat orders of a job
3. For preventing defects in future orders for other jobs in the same "family"
4. For correcting problems in the "ingredients" (i.e., policies, systems, procedures, practices) common to all jobs

The extent of these benefits available to a particular job shop depends on the "jobs per operators per week," the "percent repeat jobs," and other factors. Consideration of these factors leads to the "Current Job Approach" and the "Repeat Job Approach" as two basic ways of achieving feedback and corrective action.

The Current Job Approach   This is a means of preventing defects in the unmanu-

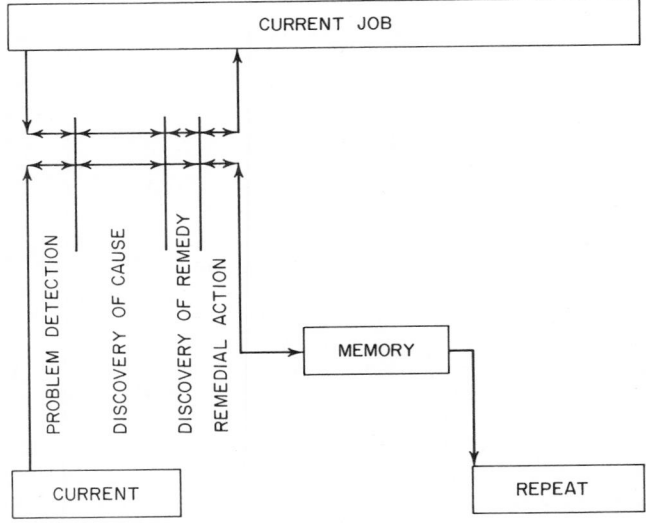

Fig. 45-3   Current job vs. repeat job correction.

[14] Ingle, Sudhaker R., Job Shop Sampling, *Quality Assurance*, September 1968, pp. 28–30.

INSPECTION REPORT		INSTRUMENT DEVELOPMENT LABORATORIES, INC. 67 MECHANIC ST., ATTLEBORO, MASS.		REPORT NUMBER	
FORM #164 REV.				DATE: 11/5/59	

LOT QUANTITY		PART NUMBER:		DESCRIPTION:				VENDOR:	
154		401185		Barrel				IDL	

ACC.	REJ.	INSPECTOR	P.O.	R.R.	W.O.	A.O.	DATE REC'D IN INSP.
0	All	J. Couchie	⋈ ⋈ ⋈	⋈ ⋈ ⋈	0801B	0502	11/3/59

CERTIFICATION REQUIRED				OPERATION NO. 150 – Complete	

CLASS	A. Q. L.	SAMPLE SIZE	REJECTION NO.	NO. IN SAMPLE DEFECTIVE	ACCEPTED PCS. RECEIVED BY: M. Taylor – Stockroom
MAJOR	1.5%	35	2	2	DATE:
MINOR	4.0%	25	3	4	REJECTED PCS. RECEIVED BY: W. Pendergast – Prod. Control
OTHER					DATE:

REJECTIONS			DISPOSITION	

REASONS FOR:	LIST BY ITEM:	LIST BY ITEM:
1. 1.595 + 001 is 1.5947 to 1.5956 −000		1. Sort for undersize 1.595 diameter and return defectives for rework
2. 0.125 ± 005 holes are 0.126 − 0.133		2. Defective 0.125 hole sizes do not affect function or fit – accept as is.
		Results of sorting: 143 accepted 11 rejected.

CORRECTIVE ACTION

Tooling correction promised by Industrial Engineering.

File for follow - up on 12/2/60

MATERIAL REVIEW BOARD

QUALITY CONTROL: W. Wold	DATE: 11/7/59
PRODUCT ENGINEER: C. Logan	DATE: 11/7/59
GOVERNMENT: L. Thuotte - AFQCR	DATE: 11/7/59

Fig. 45-4 Approach to corrective action.

factured portion of a job through feedback of information from the manufactured portion of the same job. It can be used whenever the running time of the job is longer than the time necessary to give the feedback signal, diagnose the cause, and determine and implement the corrective action. See, schematically, the top part of Figure 45-3. The value of such prevention is so obvious as to provide an incentive to prompt feedback of data on quality troubles, and prompt corrective action on the feedback.

Figure 45-4 shows the mechanism used in one electronics assembly plant to secure such prompt feedback and corrective action. The results of subunit, unit, and systems test are recorded by serial number, as to the item and the nature of the discrepancy. Copies of the test records are reviewed daily by a quality control engineer who determines the nature of each deficiency and initiates a "corrective-action request" (Figure 45-4) to the design engineer, manufacturing engineer, components engineer, test supervisor, test-set maintenance man, vendor liaison man, or other individual who can take the necessary action. The quality control engineer follows up each of the requests and the associated replies until the matter is disposed of by action, or by decision that no action is necessary.

Corrective action that will benefit the unmanufactured product may either involve a change in the *job numerics* or correction of an error in *complying* with the job numerics.

This current job approach is most applicable when the following combination of circumstances is present:

1. The economic gain through preventing defects in the unmanufactured units is obviously greater than the cost of the feedback and prevention machinery; i.e., large lots or expensive items are involved.

2. The causes of the defects are obvious enough to permit prompt diagnosis.

3. The organization for feedback and follow-up can be kept simple, e.g., one man with a clear assignment.

In the job shop with a low percent repeat job rate, it is often desirable to create deliberately the opportunity to use the current job approach even when the normal running time would be too short to use it. Instead of processing the entire order as a lot, a small "pilot" lot or single item precedes the main lot, and time is allowed for the feedback and correction to take place.

The pilot lot idea has long been used in job shops. However, in its early form the pilot lot was processed like any other lot. Then the final results were scanned, and if no trouble was reported in production, everything was assumed to be satisfactory; i.e., the tentative job numerics could be made permanent. Often the pilot lot was considered to be solely the means of making samples for customer approval. Experience has shown that there is much value in expending extra effort in planning the trial lot, collecting special data, analyzing the data, and using the results to modify the job numerics.

For example, when a mechanical piece part moves through a series of operations, all of which can influence a critical dimension, the fact that 9 of the 10 pieces in the pilot lot conform to final specifications might seem to be adequate to firm up the numerics; yet the full job order could easily run 30% defective as a result of inadequate process capability or wrong process centering. By requiring measurements of the 10 pieces after each operation, and treating the means and ranges statistically, the alert analyst would easily discover the problem and, moreover, would be able to identify the operation responsible, thus preventing a large loss when the remainder of the order is run.

The Repeat Job Approach For many jobs the running time is so short that the job is completed before the sequence of "analysis, feedback, and corrective action" can be completed. In such cases the knowledge gained from the analysis cannot be put to use on the "current" job. However, this same knowledge can be put to use on a repeat order *provided there is a memory system* which can:

1. Store the knowledge

2. Provide ready recall when repeat orders are received.

The lower half of Figure 45-3 shows diagrammatically the time relationship which permits this "repeat job approach" to give to future orders the benefit of the knowledge gained from previous orders. Since this approach involves the costs of maintaining a memory system, it is most applicable when the percent repeat jobs is relatively high, of the order of 75% or more. It probably cannot be justified economically if the percent is low, say 25% or lower. In between, the economics of the specific situation must be examined to determine whether it is less costly to provide protection for all potential repeat orders or suffer the losses of repeating the error for that smaller number of jobs which will be reordered. In addition, there are special situations which may warrant a memory system, as in the case of small first runs of development work on complex equipment, for it is generally important to "debug" the job numerics in the event that production orders are received later.

As in the current job approach, the scheme applies not only to manufacturing processes, but also to all job numerics or to the compliance therewith.

Memory Systems for Job Numerics. An astonishing variety of memory systems have been invented in different job shops to utilize this approach. In a medium-sized plant manufacturing custom aircraft parts (Type III), a "job history file" is maintained on each job by the manufacturing planning staff group. Into this file go the specifications, the job order copy, the job numerics, in-process and final inspection data on each run, foreman's comments on problems encountered and actions taken, results of troubleshooter's investigations, recommendations, and any formal change requests. When a repeat order is received, the planner must refer to this file to obtain the drawings, operation sequence, and other numerics. Thereby he "automatically" reviews the data and notes before issuing the new manufacturing order. Similar planning memories are in use in other plants with respect to items purchased from vendors, or for subcontracted operations. In other instances, designers maintain job files to accumulate suggested and/or confirmed design changes. Upon receipt of a repeat order, the designer is able to incorporate the accumulation into a reissue of the specifications.

Such memory systems for designers and planners often contain a mixture of raw quality data, unconfirmed "theories" as to the reasons for production difficulties, suggested changes in the job numerics, results of actual on-the-spot investigations, and solidly confirmed corrective actions. Experience has shown that these bits and pieces should be "digested," and that a plan of corrective action should be prepared during or immediately after the completion of the current job. If preparation of the plan of corrective action is delayed until the arrival of the repeat order, it is commonly found that the "undigested" information has deteriorated badly with the passing of time (since it relies so heavily on the fallible memories of human beings). In addition, the arrival of the new order is commonly accompanied by such considerable time pressure that digestion and analysis may be bypassed. However, while preparation of a plan of correction action should not be delayed, making the corrective changes effective can properly be delayed until the reorder has in fact been received from the customer. Such is the usual practice in the Type III shops. On the other hand, Type II shops usually issue the changes for standard items as soon as the analysis is complete.

"Digestion" requires establishing the discipline of corrective action investigation and follow-up, *even though the current job may already be completed.* The organization for investigation may, as in the case of the current job approach, be limited to one analyst when simple technology is involved. However, where the causes of defects and the needed corrections are not obvious, more talents are needed. In any event, responsibility for the investigation and decision should be clearly allocated. It may be a material review board, corrective action board, factory service group, quality engineering, or other specially designated team. The agreed-on corrective actions are ordinarily recorded, and the responsible department designated, together with the expected date of accomplishment (see Figure 45-4). Diligent follow-up by a systematic routine is then needed to assure that these intentions are executed during the interval between orders. Someone must therefore be given the job of "keeping a book" on pending corrective actions until completion.[15]

Memory Systems for Manufacture. These systems are created, usually by Production departments, to alert personnel to the hazards of known prior errors of execution, and to evolve more optimum supplementary numerics. For operator-controllable defects, for example, special "warning" or "caution" slips are often attached to the blueprints or instructions in the job file maintained in the factory. The operator assigned to the repeat order is thereby "flagged" to exercise special care on a particular job.

A further example is the job "setup card" file maintained for some processes. Each card is a record for a single job order. On the card are posted the conditions which prevailed in the process while that job was being run, as well as the results of inspection and test. For example, in calendering plastic film, the setup involves such numerics as roll speeds, roll temperatures, roll spacing, material feed rate, and many others. Often some of these are altered (and duly recorded) during the run to improve the quality of film being produced, based on the judgment of the foreman. The subsequent inspection and test results are likewise posted to the card.

When this same plastic film is reordered, the setup man consults the card file to identify the lots which showed the best test results. He then tries to reproduce the process conditions which prevailed during the manufacture of this best product.

As the card file builds up, a further step can be taken by analyzing the data through more sophisticated statistical methods, e.g., regression analysis.[16]

Memory Systems for Inspection. Such memory systems usually consist of job history cards to which inspection results are posted. The resulting knowledge of job quality levels and frequencies of specific defects can be used for a variety of improvement purposes. It can warn of inspection errors, lead to revision of defect classifications and AQLs, promote changes in inspection or test methods or gages, provide additional vendor instructions or notifications, furnish Pareto summaries of the vital few defects of each job, identify jobs where inspection or testing can be reduced, etc.

In addition, the memory system concept offers the job shop a way to diagnose the causes of "mysterious" defects, to determine process capabilities, to discover dominance, and to perform other statistical analyses. For example, in mass production, a few days or even hours may produce enough defects to provide the data needed for conclusive analysis. Job shop managers ordinarily are envious at these opportunities to collect and analyze data in such short order, and they often give up trying to apply such techniques to jobbing work. However, repeated small lots, plus a memory system, plus patience, will likewise furnish the data, analyses, and solutions, as will be discussed under Quality Improvement, below.[17]

QUALITY IMPROVEMENT

To remain competitive, the job shop must constantly engage in improvement or "breakthrough,"[18] quite aside from its day-to-day problems of enforcing quality compliance. The mass production shop must likewise engage in breakthrough,

[15] See, for example, Section 11, under Inspection Feedback to Production.
[16] See Section 26.
[17] When the data are organized by machine center rather than by defect type, the economics of analysis may be more favorable. The various ways of organizing the data are discussed below, under Quality Improvement.
[18] See Section 2, under Chronic Troubles; Breakthrough.

and the conceptual approach to breakthrough[19] is identical for these two forms of industrial organization. Where they differ is mainly in the nature of the improvement "project." Because of sheer volume, the mass production shop quality improvement project usually involves a specific defect on a specific product; e.g., the 3KL cylinders are out of round on the 2.500-inch dimension. In contrast, the job shop quality improvement project is usually concerned with remedy of some common cause which cuts across a variety of jobs.

(These "usual" projects are not universal. A mass production shop may have an ineffective system of maintaining instrument accuracy, so that many products are affected. In like manner, a job shop project may involve some high-volume production amid numerous low-volume jobs.)

The preoccupation with individual jobs is often a detriment to organizing for job shop improvement. A given common cause may adversely affect, say 5% of the jobs (see, for example, the case of "inductance out of specification" below). Preoccupation with looking for "blame" in each of the jobs affected may blind the managers to the existence of a common cause, and thereby to the opportunity for improvement.

Identification of logical job shop improvement projects is largely a matter of ingenious use of the Pareto principle.[20] The need is to identify those common causes which are at the root of the greatest amount of job shop trouble, and thereby will result in the greatest value of improvement for the least cost of analysis. Once a project has been chosen, the usual limitation to solution is more a matter of management than technology; someone must be liberated from the daily, job-to-job problems and given a license to diagnose the improvement projects.

Three approaches for project identification in job shops are presented below:

The Chronic Offenders approach
The Product Family approach
The Non-Job approach

The Chronic Offenders Approach In this approach, the Pareto analysis is first one of identifying the few jobs which result in the bulk of the quality losses. (The term "chronic offenders" refers to these few jobs.)

For example, a manufacturer of a line of floor polishers found that punch-press scrap was an important quality cost. A Pareto analysis of this scrap by part number (Figure 45-5) established that five of the parts accounted for half of the punch-press scrap. It became a logical project to reduce scrap on these chronic offenders, since the "percent repeat jobs" was high.[21]

In the complex assembly job shop, interest centers on individual assembly defects rather than on jobs *per se*. Defects are so numerous and varied on each job that corrective action must be concentrated on those recurring defects which account for the greatest dollar loss, or are the most serious to the customer, or both. A "chronic offender" chart is then made for each major job, indicating the predominant defects. When high losses and seriousness are both involved, the list can be a composite of "five top dollar-loss defects," plus all the serious ones.

Corrective action for chronic offenders follows the general methods discussed under the Repeat Job Approach, above. In addition, the list of chronic offenders is publicized for the attention and priority of all: managers, supervisors, analysts, production operators, inspectors, etc. (In one plant where the defects were mainly

---

[19] See generally, Juran, J. M., "Managerial Breakthrough," McGraw-Hill Book Company, New York, 1964.

[20] See Section 2, under the Pareto Principle; see also Section 16, under Pareto Analysis.

[21] The detailed approach to analysis of causes and discovery of remedy is discussed in Section 16 (for management controllable defects) and Section 18 (for operator controllable defects).

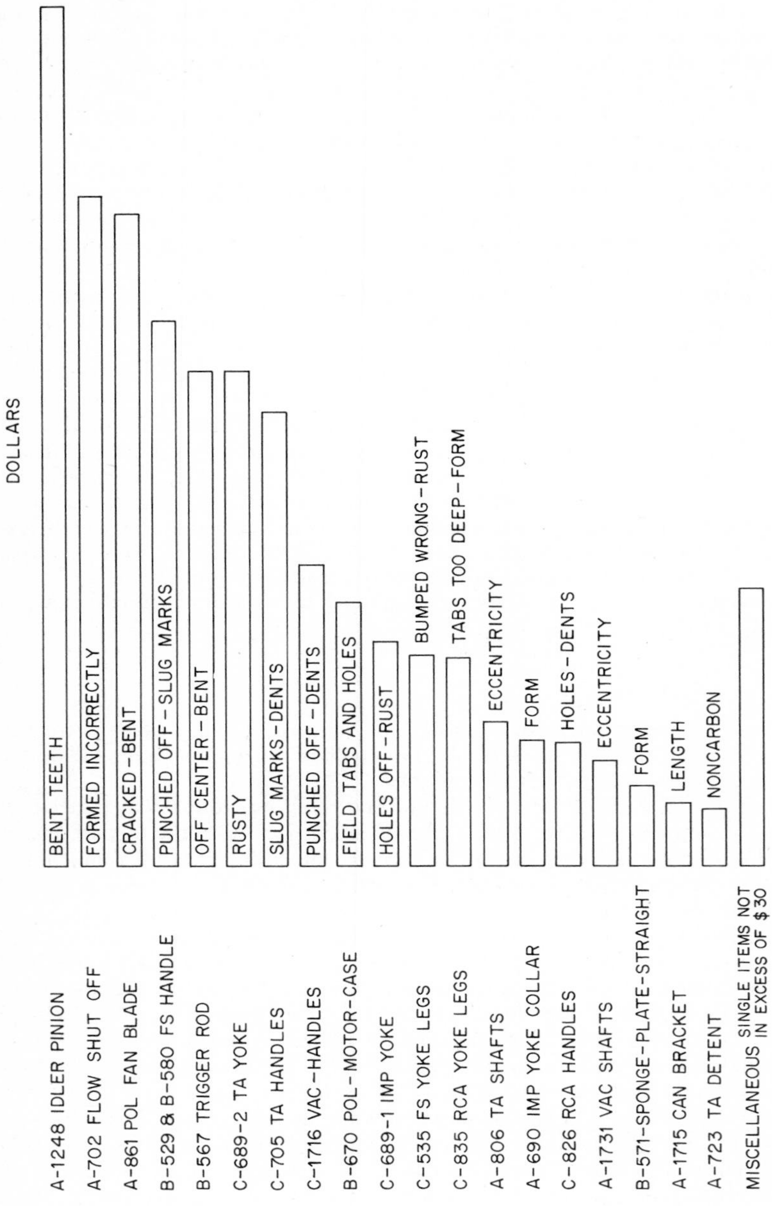

Fig. 45-5 Pareto analysis by part number.

operator controllable, good results were achieved by posting the chronic offenders list in each production department.) Along with this, the plant manager receives a weekly bulletin of progress in tackling these high dollar-loss items.

The chronic offenders list is never static. Some projects are removed from the list because they have been solved. New projects are added to the list as the result of new customer demands or competitor practice. Accordingly, it is necessary to revise the list of the "worst" offenders periodically (in the same manner that law-enforcement officers revise the list of the Ten Most Wanted Criminals.).

The Product Family Approach   This approach utilizes the fact that all jobs in a product family have similar customer requirements, design specifications, sequence of operations, process variables, inspection instructions, or other job numerics. Under such conditions, any job is a "repeat" for any other job in the same product family. Through this relationship, the "percent repeat jobs" is greatly increased. In consequence, the effort of diagnosis and remedy is amortized over a greater number of jobs. This amortization tends to make this approach economic for moderate and even low percent repeat job rates.

The instances of "families" are legion. Tire manufacturers have hundreds of job specifications to cover all the permutations of brand, size, fabric, construction, grade, wall color, tread design, etc. Yet, most of the numerics for, say, a 4-ply nylon tire are alike (allowing for size scaling) for all members of that family. In the calendered vinyl plastics business, myriads of artistic printing and embossing patterns are applied to only a dozen or so basic families of laminated, unsupported, or coated films. Again, the job numerics for each of these families prior to printing and embossing are largely alike.

The product family approach directs its efforts toward improving the job numerics for the entire family. This may come about in several ways:

1. By extending to all members of the family the knowledge gained when using the "Current Job" control plan. Once corrective action has become known for one job, such knowledge can be used to benefit other members of the family.

2. By utilizing the product family concept in setting up the memory system for the "Repeat Job" approach. Such usage supplies more data in a shorter time, and facilitates the identification of chronic offenders or defect concentrations. In turn, diagnosis of these "vital few" family problems leads to remedies which can be extended to the whole family.

3. By setting up a special project, in the absence of a memory system, to furnish the information in item 2 above and tackle the "vital few."

The Non-Job Approach   "Non-job" is used here in the sense of an approach to chronic defect reduction through discovery and elimination of common causes which are not job-related; i.e., the causes cut across many jobs. Because the causes common to many jobs are quite numerous, the first step in the non-job approach is to use the Pareto analysis to identify those common causes which might warrant further analysis. The Pareto study is conducted in various ways: by defect type, failure mode, process, department, discrepancy, "basic cause," etc. Out of these studies emerges the most promising avenue for further study, usually that Pareto distribution in which the fewest number of defect types (or whatever) account for the greatest proportion of the trouble.

The usual starting point is to study the distribution of rejects or losses by *common symptoms,* on the normally valid premise that common symptoms will be found to have common causes when further analyzed.

For example, an electronics assembly shop found (at subassembly) that a Pareto distribution by defect provided a good basis for further study, since one defect (solder) accounted for about 37% of all defects (Figure 45-6). Studies by failure mode, error type, discrepancy, etc., are similar in nature.

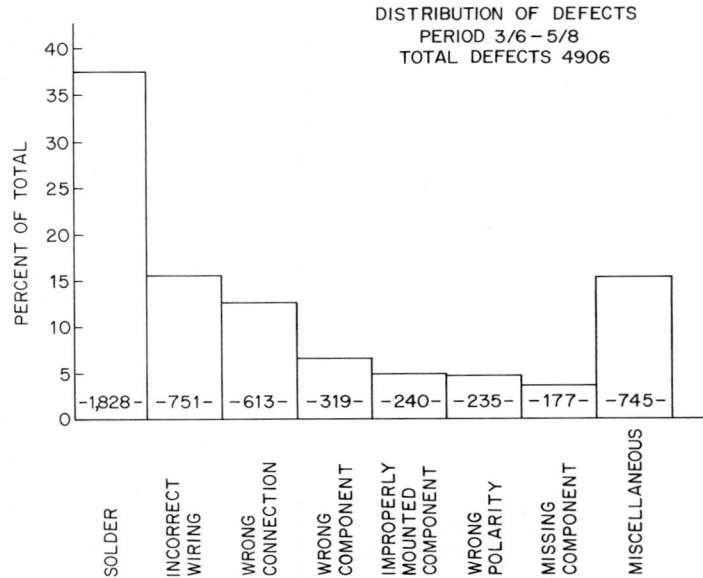

Fig. 45-6 Pareto analysis by common symptoms.

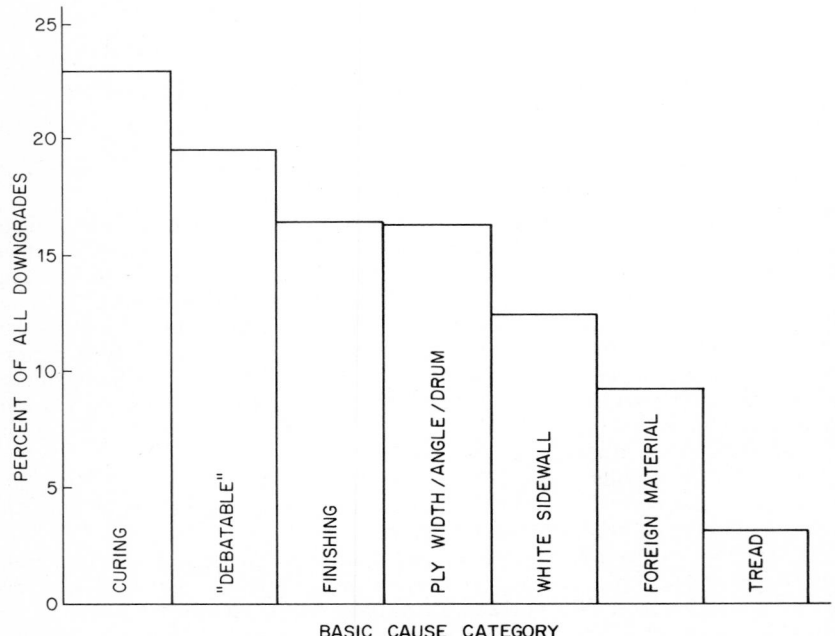

Fig. 45-7 Auto tire downgrades by basic causes.

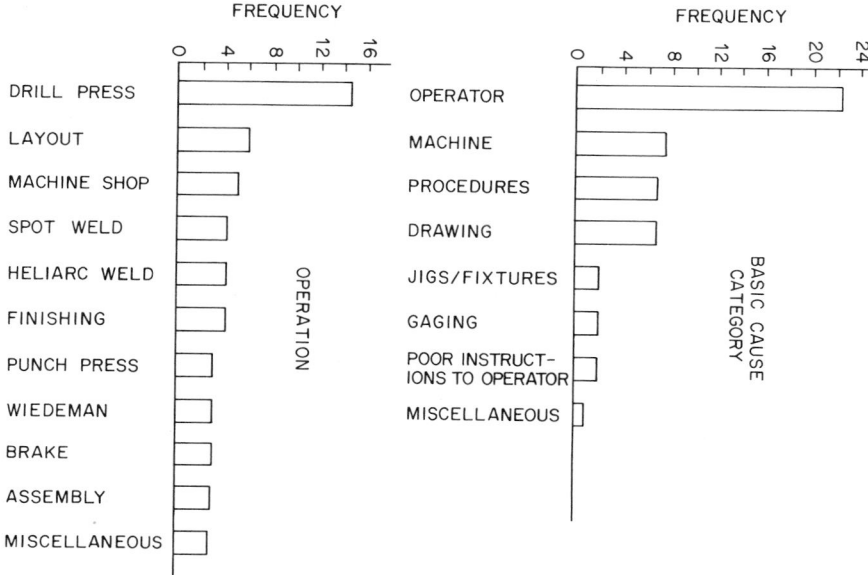

Fig. 45-8   Pareto analysis by basic cause category.

For many products, the study can usefully go one step further, even at the exploratory stage.   Whenever the causes for the principal symptoms categories are "obvious" (i.e., all knowledgeable hands agree) from the nature of the symptoms, then an analysis can be made by *basic cause categories.*   (Such obvious causes are so well recognized that they often find their way into the very name of the defect, such as "toolmarks," "incompletely lapped," "undercured," or "double-knurled.")

In an automobile tire plant, a Pareto distribution by defects was of no avail, since there was not sufficient concentration among the 85 identifiable defect types to justify study projects for each of about 20 principal defects.   However, by regrouping the 85 defect types into 7 basic cause categories (Figure 45-7), it became evident that one operation (curing) required better control systems.   It also became evident that the relationship of ply angle to width required a more complete planning of the supplementary job numerics.

In still other cases where defects might be the result of any of several possible causes, it is nevertheless instructive to attempt to classify by basic cause categories in the job shop.   This can be done by setting up a special study for a limited period (e.g., a week or a month), during which time each rejection or error is carefully traced to its origin by a task force representing Engineering, Production, and Inspection.   Based on the facts unearthed, they try to agree on the cause classification.

For example, a sheet metal fabricating shop studied its rejections in this way and obtained the Pareto distributions shown in Figure 45-8.   The most promising direction for study was the basic cause category "operator error," since operator errors (acknowledged as such by the operator in each case) were by a wide margin the biggest single class.

One machine tool builder prepared a check sheet to assist foremen in analysis of causes of defects.   The check sheet required each foreman to:

Describe the defect in terms of the specification, and of the effect on assembly or customer

Identify the source of process dominance[22]
Identify the plan in use for detecting nonconformance
Identify where the defect occurred and where it was found
Determine the extent to which operator self-control was present[23]
Determine the basic cause for the defect (Figure 45-9)[24]

WHAT WAS THE BASIC CAUSE FOR THE DEFECT ?

_____ SPECIFICATION NOT CLEAR   _____ TOOL WEAR

_____ SPEC MISINTERPRETED BY OPERATOR   _____ OPERATOR LOADING WRONG

_____ ROUTING ERROR   _____ OPERATOR REPEATABILITY

_____ MACHINING SKETCH ERROR   _____ MACHINE REPEATABILITY

_____ TAPE ERROR   _____ MEASUREMENT METHOD

_____ TOOLING ERROR   _____ MEASUREMENT ERROR

_____ FIXTURE WRONG   _____ DEVIATION FROM ROUTING SEQUENCE

_____ OPERATOR SET UP ERROR   _____ VENDOR MATERIAL DEFECTIVE

_____ LAYOUT ERROR   _____ MACHINE MALFUNCTION

_____ PRIOR OPERATION WRONG   _____ WRONG FEEDS & SPEEDS

_____ OTHER (DESCRIBE BELOW)   _____ OPERATOR INATTENTION

Fig. 45-9   Check sheet for defect cause analysis.

In an interesting analysis, Friedlander[25] studied the relationship of job shop lot rejections to (1) fabricating shop origin, (2) lot size, and (3) percent of waivered rejections, i.e., percent of nonconforming lots accepted as usable. Figure 45-10 shows, for the lathe shop and press shop:

1. The proportion of all factory lots made in that department. For example, of lots ranging from 1 to 20 pieces, the lathe shop processed 10%, whereas the press shop processed 21% (solid lines on the charts).

2. The proportion of all factory lot rejections occurring in that department. For example, of all rejected lots ranging from 1 to 20 pieces, 6.6% occurred in the lathe shop, while 34% occurred in the press shop. In addition, press shop rejections were nearly constant for all lot sizes, implying causation beyond that of operator. Figure 45-11 shows the press shop study extended to all lot sizes and includes data on percent of waivered rejections. The chart suggests that:

1. Since a clear drop-off in rejection rate is not evident until lot sizes attain 2,500 or more pieces, some well-tooled jobs were being found defective. This brought into question an earlier decision to permit press jobs to run without independent setup inspection if the inspector was not immediately available.

[22] See Section 9, under Concept of Dominance.
[23] See Section 11, under Concept of Operator Self-Control.
[24] Figure 45-9 is a portion of the two-page check sheet.
[25] Friedlander, Walter H., Process Control for Reliability, *Ninth Annual Symposium on Reliability,* pp. 524–528, IEEE, 1963. In the large job shop under study, 70% of the volume consisted of lots with 100 parts or less.

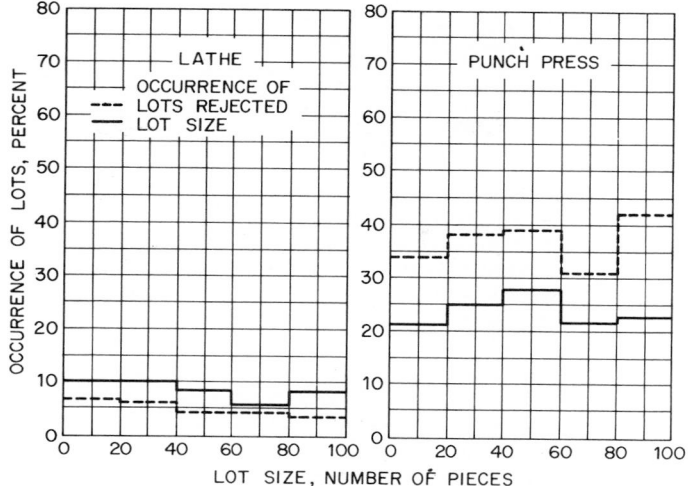

Fig. 45-10 Analysis of departmental contribution to job shop rejections.

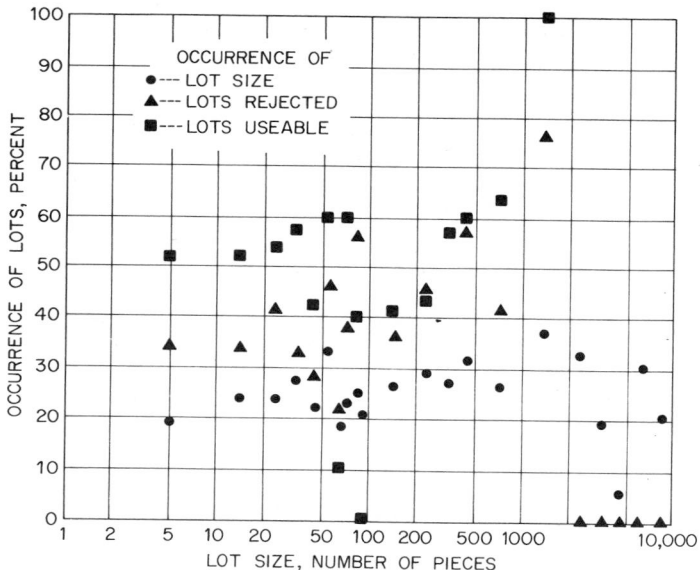

Fig. 45-11 Effect of lot size on rejection rate and on waiver rate.

2. The fact that about 50% of press shop rejections were waivered brought into question the adequacy of engineering tolerances.

The foregoing examples are "office" studies of a "macro" nature; i.e., they make use of past data to draw broad conclusions about common causes and to narrow the range of suspects. As the suspected common cause is analyzed, the need may be to go beyond past data and out of the office.

In a company making electrical inductors, "inductance out of specification" was by far the most frequent defect. Frequency distributions of a dozen high-reject lots showed two different symptoms patterns:

1. Some lots had adequate within-lot variability, but had poor centering of the mean of the distribution, resulting in rejects all beyond one of the limits.

2. Other lots had excessive within-lot variability, resulting in defects outside of both limits.

The common cause in this case was in the Engineering Department "sample shop" which established product tolerances as well as manufacturing instructions for wire size and number of turns. The practice of the sample shop was to make a single trial coil to the customer's specifications. Then, the wire size and number of turns which had been used to make this trial coil were incorporated in the manufacturing instructions. The system was defective because it failed to consider the effect of production variability. In consequence, it was unlikely that the results of the one trial coil would provide the Production Department with adequate within-lot variability, or with centering at the mean of the specification range. When the sample shop procedure was changed to making three coils, with calculated consideration for expected variability, there soon was a substantial reduction in the rejections.

It is evident from such cases, especially the last one, that job shop quality improvement is not confined to changing the job numerics or to providing a warning to Production the next time the job is run. The "common cause" often interacts randomly with jobs; it can affect any job at any time. Once tracking of such a common cause gets under way, the diagnostic trail frequently leads back to the fundamentals of the very system of preparing specifications, of assigning tolerances, of bidding or estimating, of controlling processes, etc.

Diagnostic Techniques   The techniques for diagnosis and remedy of the chronic problems in the job shop are similar to those in any shop; they are covered in detail in Section 16, Quality Improvement. However, the job shop diagnostician is seldom able to collect large quantities of data at will; his lot sizes are too small. This calls for ingenuity by the diagnostician in collecting the needed data from repeat orders of a job or from several members of a family. Often a variant of the "memory system" (see under The Repeat Job Approach, above) provides the answer by accumulating the data gradually over a period of time.

For example, machine capabilities in a job shop can be determined from an accumulation of measurements of 5 to 10 pieces per job over a series of jobs. As the data accumulate, a statistically adequate basis for estimating machine capability emerges from the "within-job range."[26]

Similarly, dominance can be identified by recording 5 or 10 "first piece" and "last piece" measurements on a series of jobs in the memory system. If, for a given machine or process, the series of jobs show no significant change between the two sets of measurements, setup dominance is indicated; otherwise, time dominance. In the latter event, the accumulated data give important quantified information on whether the time-to-time variation is steady or erratic from run to run. Recording of operator identity is the key to identifying operator dominance.

Even "within-piece" or position patterns of concentration of defects can be discovered by accumulation of data from small lots. In a plant making large castings for pumps and air compressors, a condition of leaks in castings was remedied only after patient recording of the location of the leaks, month by month. In this case the castings were made a few at a time, repaired, and shipped out. The memory device was a drawing copy on which the diagnostician accumulated all leak locations.

[26] See Section 9, under Process Capability.

REMEDIES FOR JOB SHOP PROBLEMS

When the identified problems are job-related, so are the remedies. In the chronic offenders and product family approaches, the remedies indicated by the diagnoses are usually changes in the job numerics. When the identified problems are not job-related, as in the non-job approach, the remedies must go deeper, e.g., modification of the overall system of specification, planning, control, etc.

Challenging the Basic Premises   The most difficult remedies are those for which it is necessary to question the basic premises or axioms on which management thinking has been erected. These premises are often of such long standing that little effort is being devoted toward changing them or even questioning them. These premises are further entrenched because their effect is interdepartmental; i.e., several major company departments are involved. In consequence, a change requires acquiescence or formal approval from the upper management of the company.

Some widespread examples of need for challenging basic premises are listed below. In studying these examples, it is well to keep in mind that these premises were very likely well founded in years gone by but have meanwhile become obsolete by the slow, undetected movement of events.

Unrealistic Specifications.   The large number of jobs per operator per week (so usual in the job shop) exposes the production and inspection personnel to a very large number of quality characteristics. Under such conditions, systems of "unrealistic specifications loosely enforced" become unmanageable because the shop people must carry in their heads so much detail of how loosely to enforce the specifications.

For job shops engaged in custom work, the way to avoid recurring violation of specifications (by operators who conclude that the tolerance is unrealistic or unimportant) seems, on the face of it, to give binding force to the specifications. However, no amount of criticizing, threatening, or pleading will assure compliance. The trouble is that the system is founded on a defective premise. The remedy lies not in more intense use of the present system; the remedy lies in change of the basic system.

This is not as easy as it sounds, since the system is logical once the basic premise is accepted. It is common for men to discuss enforcement of tolerances without questioning the basic premise itself. Such discussions may settle the specific instance without settling the broad question. It is only when the question "tight tolerances loosely enforced vs. realistic tolerances rigidly enforced" appears on some important agenda as a topic in its own right that the question has been brought out in the open.[27]

Informal Communication.   In very small model shops and specialty shops the communication from designer and planner to mechanic is highly informal and includes much oral communication. As the shop grows, this close relationship is gradually eroded by sheer size and complexity, and the need is for greater formality and greater reliance on written communication. However, in some job shops this communication retains many aspects of the informality of the model shop or specialty shop despite the fact that these have long since been outgrown. As discussed under Job Numerics, above, the communication of the supplementary job numerics is a necessary response in the modern industrial world of multiplicity of requirements.

Quotation Review.   The prevailing practice in quoting prices to customers is to

[27] See generally Section 8, under Unrealistic Tolerances Loosely Enforced.

base them on cost estimates prepared by an estimator who makes use of cost standards based on historical data.

In some types of product, the precision demanded has become such that the decisive factor in meeting cost and delivery standards is the ability to hold tolerances. Yet seldom is the estimator provided with adequate standard data (on the cost of precision) to enable him to come up with quotations which reflect the realities of holding the precision demanded.

Of course, adequate standard data should be prepared and made available to the estimators who, in turn, should be trained in how to use them. Until this is done, the job shop is well advised to bring Quality Control into the quotation procedure so that available quality capability knowledge is utilized. Use of this knowledge can aid in identifying unrealistic tolerances, predicting costs, anticipating gaging problems, defining vague characteristics, and improving inspection planning.

The basic premise here is that the estimator should be able to prepare the quotation. The premise is sound only if the estimator is equipped with the data on which a sound quotation can be built up.

Quality Planning. The "basic premise" question here is primarily one of separation of planning from execution. However, the question extends to numerous facets—choice of methods, tool control, gage control, definition of responsibilities, feedback systems, etc. The really decisive question is whether to formalize or not. Once there is a decision to formalize, the people involved can usually find ways appropriate to their needs.

An example of combined quality planning and execution is the Engineering Department model shop. These shops are manned by skilled model makers working directly with the engineering designers. The atmosphere is highly informal, with little reliance on drawings, tolerances, methods sheets, or other written communication. The model maker is expected to make the model by utilizing general-use machinery, to create ingenious setups so as to avoid expenditure for tools, to consult freely with the designer on open questions, and even to contribute ideas to the design itself. In such an organization form, reliance for quality is on the man (the model maker) rather than on some formal system.

As the job shop grows, the need arises for a greater degree of separation of planning from execution. This need is met by the creation of separate planners and a Planning Department. (The quality counterpart of this is separate quality control engineers and a Quality Control Engineering Department.) The planners soon find (as did the model makers before them) that the planning should not be uniformly applied to all jobs or functions. Some jobs are more defect-prone, more expensive, more unstable than others. Hence there arises the need for a rationale or logic to determine which part of the planning is to be done by the planners and which is to remain with the shop personnel.

Outdated Factory Organization. Many job shops organize their machinery on the colony plan; e.g., all lathes are in one room, all presses in another, etc. The intention is to reduce investment in machinery and to develop skills in the respective processes. This colony form of machine organization multiplies greatly the problem of preparing the job numerics and increases the opportunities for error. (It also increases process inventories, overall manufacturing intervals, and the complexities of process control.)

Here the basic premise is that as the job shop grows, the colony organization must be retained. This premise has been questioned on the grounds that growth should be through creation of "cellular" groupings which use special machine designs to minimize the preparation of extensive job numerics, increase machine utilization, improve coordination, etc.

For example, a manufacturer of cigarette making machinery embarked on a program of:

1. Use of light alloys to increase speed of metal cutting
2. Design of special machines on the Numerical Control principle to perform multiple operations during a single setup
3. Design of special inspection machines to verify the setups
4. Organization of the shop into small, compact crews [28]

Multiple Vendors.   For the small job shop, material usage is so modest that when an adequate source of supply has been established for any specific material, there is little point in looking for a second source.   As the shop grows, material usage grows with it, and there may be a need to shift from single to multiple vendors for some materials.   However, the basic premise of single vendors may meanwhile have become so rooted that it blocks consideration of multiple vendors. [29]

Operator Motivation.   The economics of job shop planning favor a higher degree of delegation to the work force than is readily feasible in the mass production shop. This delegation reduces the prevalence of operator monotony and boredom, but also increases the extent of operator controllability of defects. [30]   As these defects are brought to light, the managers conclude that since operator inattention, blunder, etc., created these defects (which is often true), it follows that better operator attention, etc., will eliminate all defects.   An extension of this logic is that the way to improve quality is to penalize operators for defects.   However, the logic is based on a defective premise, since even if operator errors can be eliminated, there still remain the management controllable defects (which usually are about 80% of all defects).

Actually, the wide delegation of duties to shop personnel, so prevalent in job shops, creates a favorable climate for new approaches to increasing job interest and improving worker motivation.   The job shop is thereby a good laboratory for testing out some of the modern ways being evolved to improve motivation. [31]

THE SMALL JOB SHOP

The approaches discussed in this Section for planning, controlling, and improving quality require much technique and effort beyond that needed for the basic "line" activities of designing and producing the product.   In the large job shop this additional work is mostly performed by staff specialists in a "Quality Control Engineering" department.   However, the small job shop seldom can justify use of such full-time specialists.   Neither can this small shop endure high quality losses.   The answer to this dilemma is universal for all small enterprises: everyone wears several hats.   The necessary quality "staff" activities do get carried out, but as part-time tasks for a man who is busy with many other part-time tasks.

---

[28] Williamson, D. T. N., A Better Way of Making Things, *Science Journal*, June 1968, pp. 53–59.   See also the discussion of "Group Technology" under Improving Job Planning, above.

[29] See Section 10, under Multiple Vendors.

[30] See generally Section 18, and especially, under Operator Controllable Errors, *et seq.* See also Section 11, under Concept of Operator Self-Control.

[31] See Section 18, under Job Enrichment.

TABLE 45-4   Assignment of Quality Control Tasks in a Small Job Shop

Tasks	Assigned to
Receiving inspection, in process inspection and test	Line inspectors and testers
Gage control and gage procurement	One full-time technician
Reliability test and evaluation, inspection planning, test equipment design, statistical methods	One quality control engineer
Quality control laboratory, special process controls	One laboratory technician
Vendor control, troubleshooting	Laboratory technician and quality control manager
New design review	Quality control manager
Command of the department	Quality control manager

For example, in one small job shop[32] a wide array of quality control tasks was assigned as shown in Table 45-4.

For the very smallest job shops, even the idea of a separate Quality Control Department may be too expensive. Instead, all the quality control tasks are distributed among other departments. In one small punch-press shop:

The raw materials inspector is the receiving clerk; the process inspectors are a collection of foremen or toolmakers; and the tool and gage inspector is one of the draftsmen. Records are kept by a production control clerk. Actually, the only formal inspector in the bunch is the last man to look at the product.[33]

[32] Kilduff, Francis B., For Small Shops: Low Cost QC, *Quality Assurance*, March 1965, p. 20.
[33] Kilduff, *op. cit.*

Section **46**

Support Operations

DR. SIGMUND P. ZOBEL

Canisius College, Buffalo, New York

CONTRIBUTION OF SUPPORT OPERATIONS TO PRODUCT QUALITY

The quality function involves numerous activities through which we achieve fitness for use. Those activities which directly influence the nature of the product (e.g., design, purchase of materials, fabrication, inspection) have received much attention from the quality control "movement." However, there are other activities, e.g., order filling, transportation, and counting, which though indirectly influencing quality of product, have largely escaped the attention of the quality control movement. This Section examines the ways in which quality control of these "indirect" activities can be used to improve product fitness for use.

The literature has not created a generic term which can embrace all these indirect activities. The author and the editors propose the term "Support Operations" as a broad term to designate these indirect activities.[1]

The manufacturing company's mission is to produce a product which is fit for use, can create a market, and can thereby generate the company's income. Awareness of the interrelation between fitness for use and income has led the companies to the familiar product quality controls. These controls have been most highly developed on those aspects of product progression which are obvious to the user, i.e., materials, processes, products. The effect of the support operations on fitness for use has been less obvious, and may account for the underdevelopment of quality controls in these "indirect" activities.

This split in emphasis extends to the study of the performance of the human beings as well. Traditionally, the most intense studies of quality performance and of motivation for quality have been devoted to those people who have an obvious connection with the physical product, i.e., the inspectors and the production operators. Extension of this study to the "indirect" personnel has been a comparatively recent phenomenon. The number (and variety) of these support personnel is considerable. Improvement of their contribution to the company's overall quality mission is a major opportunity which in most companies is still waiting to be realized.[2] This opportunity is present in several forms, each of value to the company and its clientele:

Improvement of manufacturing floor quality through reduction in paper work errors and through improved logistic support

Improvement of field quality through improved packaging, reduction of shipping errors, improved warehousing, better training of field service men, etc.

Improvement of cost effectiveness through reducing errors and redundancies, improving personnel efficiency, and reducing the total time span.

SUPPORT TASKS AND THEIR QUALITY PROBLEMS

Support operations are conducted through the performance of a variety of tasks which are described below.[3]

Document Preparation   A number of documents contain quality oriented information, and the accuracy of this information affects fitness for use. To illustrate:

Document	Potential Effect of Errors on Fitness for Use
Customer's order, as edited.	Shipment of wrong product, in wrong amounts, etc.
Quality specifications*	Product conforms to specification but is not fit for use
Instrument control documents	Measurement errors
Inspection and test reports	Failure to take corrective action
Formulation records	Improper batch formulation
Shipping documents	Improper delivery to the user

*A major problem in documentation is "drawing change control." When a specification is changed, the latest version must be supplied to all departments who need such information. The activities necessary to disseminate the changes are in the nature of support operations. In some industries, some very rigorous procedures are in force to provide assurance that the documents in use are of the latest issue. See generally Section 19, under Configuration Management.

Control of quality of document preparation is accomplished by one or more of the following:

1. Simple reliance on well-designed forms plus the competence of the personnel.

2. Redundancy in the form of supervisory or checker sign-off. The theory is that two independent activities (the original document preparation and the subsequent

(footnotes on p. 46-3)

checking) will not each make the same error. (See, in this connection, Errorless Proofreading, in Section 12, under Remedy for Inadvertent Inspector Errors.)

3. Sample checking of work done by the document preparation personnel, and analysis of the results to discover error patterns and to make improvements. This is done through construction of a matrix of errors vs. clerks as described in Section 18, under Operator Controllable Errors.

Figure 46-1 shows such a matrix as applied to preparing production orders. It is evident that errors are concentrated in certain error types, in certain clerks, and in certain combinations.

Error type	Production clerks				Total
	A	B	C	D	
Customer Order No.	1	0	0	2	3
Controlling specifications	0	3	10	6	19
Grade of product.	1	1	2	0	4
Quantity.	1	4	6	0	11
Special instructions	0	2	4	1	7
Shipping date	0	3	5	0	8
Etc.	•	•	•	•	•
	•	•	•	•	•
	•	•	•	•	•
	7	20	35	10	72

Fig. 46-1   Matrix of error types in preparing production orders.

4. Foolproofing the operation. A widely used example is the internal check of payroll documents through block summaries; e.g., each block of 50 documents is added vertically (by account) and horizontally (by payee), and the grand totals are then checked against each other.

In transmission of messages by coded language it is common to make use of "two-letter differences" to minimize error. For example, if two groups are defined as

BUMIN = shipment accepted
BUMAN = shipment rejected

a transmission error of "a" for "i" will reverse the meaning. (In the telegraphic codes the transmission for these letters is by the similar forms·–and··respectively, an easy source of error.)

If, however, two-letter differences are used, the groups would be defined, for example, by

BUMIN = shipment accepted
BOMAN = shipment rejected

Now it takes two simultaneous errors in transmission to reverse the meaning,

---

[1] Support Operations which serve manufacturing companies are not to be confused with "Service Industries," e.g., Insurance, Communication, Entertainment, etc. See Section 47 for an elaboration of this distinction. However, many of the studies made (and solutions evolved) in these service industries have application to support operations in manufacturing companies. In addition, the support operations discussed in this Section (46) have wide application in the service industries.

[2] For broader discussion, see Zobel, S. P., Quality Control from Front Door to Back Door, *Industrial Quality Control*, December 1960, pp. 9–11.

[3] The order of listing is not necessarily the order of importance.

and the odds against this are much higher because of the operation of redundancy mathematics.[4]

In a related example, use of two languages in the drafting room was found to be a source of error in product quality. In specifying a length of 122 inches, some draftsmen used the designation 122", while others used the designation 10'2". The latter was sometimes misinterpreted as 102". (Sometimes the reproduction process contributed to the error by dimming or obliterating the "foot" mark.)[5]

Transportation The transport of products affects product quality in several ways: correct identity of material, correct destination, and avoidance of damage. Some of these effects lend themselves to control by conventional methods similar to those used above in document preparation. However, an important limitation is that the transport function is often outside the orbit of Quality Control audits and thereby is less rigorously regulated than the activities which more directly affect the product.

For example, the fork lift truck system of transport makes wide use of wooden pallets. The quality of these pallets affects the amount of product damage done during product transport and storage. One study, involving multiple manufacturers and users, disclosed a general condition of wooden pallets not conforming to specification, and being widely unfit for use. Some large companies were abandoning the use of wooden pallets. An important contributing factor was the fact that the pallets were purchased as "supplies" rather than as "material." In the companies buying these pallets, quality of purchased "material" (going into products) was rigorously checked, against specification, by the Quality Control Department. However, quality of purchased "supplies," i.e., things which did not go into making the company's products, was outside the jurisdiction of the Quality Control Department. It was not even clear who had responsibility for assuring quality of supplies (which included pallets). The lack of these quality controls resulted in a collapse of quality, on an industry-wide basis, since there were no teeth in the procedure for enforcing the specification.[6]

Order Filling The "order" may be an internal requisition for material, supplies, etc., prepared by any of numerous departments (e.g., Production, Shipping, Laboratory) and sent to a storeroom to be filled. Alternatively, the order may be from external sources, mainly from customers. Either way, the prompt and correct filling of the order is important in achieving fitness for use (as well as efficient operation, productivity, customer goodwill, etc.). The errors which can degrade fitness for use include incorrect identity, inadequate rotation of stocks, improper labeling of perishable materials, etc.

Control of order filling is usually done by redundancy. A common form is the checker who verifies the selected material against the order or requisition. Sometimes the packer performs this verification. In still other cases, the stock selector himself checks the material against the order as a separate "countdown." The order form is often specially designed to provide space for the "checks" to be made.

For improvement of order filling, the use of sampling checks plus a matrix analysis[7] is again effective.

Measurement of Amount of Product Measurement of *quantity* of product (as distinguished from quality of product) is widely done. While most of this is for reasons of inventory control and the like, much of such measurement affects fitness for use.

---

[4]See, in this connection, Konz, Stephan, E. Braun, K. Jachindra, and D. Wichlan, Human Transmission of Numbers and Letters, *Industrial Engineering*, May 1968, pp. 219–224. See also Section 12, under Inspector Errors.
[5]Consulting experience of J. M. Juran.
[6]Personal communication from J. M. Juran, who conducted this study.
[7]See Section 18, under Operator Controllable Errors.

Weighing out ingredients affects the quality of the resulting batch. Improper counts can be harmful either in the plant or in the field. Two examples in the author's experience can be widely paralleled by others. In one case, a sand molding operation in a foundry was subjected to deterioration of the sand mix and to costly non-productive delay time because the core room miscounted the number of cores supplied to the molding room.[8] In another case the author purchased a large swing and slide set for home use. Before assembling it, he carefully inventoried all components against the packing list and instructions. It all seemed to be there, including the bag which contained the fasteners and small hardware. However, he did not count the number of nuts, bolts, bushings, etc. When assembly was nearly complete, it became apparent that several critical fasteners were not included. The advice of the merchant was either to buy the missing pieces or to dismantle and repack the entire set for return, whereupon a replacement set would be provided.

Control of errors of counting includes supervisory and audit checks as discussed above. In addition, there is wide use of aids to good counting. Scales are often used to estimate count by weight. Some of these scales are of proportionate design, e.g., 99 to 1. When the scales balance, the count is 100 times the contents of the small pan, plus the number of leftovers.[9] Machine counting is widely used for valuable products, e.g., coins in banks.

Foolproofing is also used to reduce errors in counts. A common form is a system of accountability in which the original quantity, the additions, withdrawals, and remainder on hand must check out against each other. The technique of stoichiometry in chemical processes is to the same effect. For packaging small parts, there is use of compartmented containers which permit counting at a glance, and which make any missing parts obvious.

Computation   This widely used operation includes manual addition or calculation, use of desk calculators (which involves manual manipulation of keys), and preparation of calibration curves, e.g., for colorimetric analyses or for calculation of regression curves (as in nondestructive testing to approximate a destructive test).

Control of computation includes redundant checking (self-checking by the individual making the computation, as well as by supervision and by independent checkers). In addition, there is a wide array of foolproofing built into modern computing devices. Computer programs are designed for self-checking the inputs and rejecting any anomalies.

For example, a public utility supplying gas to many users foolproofs the billing both as to computation of gas consumed and as to rates charged. Gas consumed is the difference between last month's meter reading and the new meter reading. All three figures are inserted by the billing operator. The computer is programmed to lock if, for example, the billed consumption does not equal the difference. In like manner, the rates charged are variable for different levels of consumption. These calculations are likewise checked by the computer, with provisions for bringing matters to a halt if an error has crept in.

Estimation   There is a surprising extent of estimation done, and much of it affects quality of product. Product designers estimate factors of safety, tolerances, and other product parameters. Reliability and maintainability are estimated, and plans for logistic support (inventory of spare parts, etc.) are prepared based on these es-

---

[8]Molds cannot be completed without the appropriate cores, resulting in loss of moisture (important to the finish quality of the steel casting) in the facing sand batch while it is in a "hold" state. See Zobel, S. P., Some Foundry Applications of Statistical Quality Control, *National Convention Transactions, ASQC,* 1959, pp. 79–87.

[9]If precision is needed, it must be established that the parts being counted by weight are uniform enough to permit use of this approximation.

timates. Environmental and life tests are made to provide estimates on failure rates, deterioration rates, etc. Subsequent field performance data are analyzed to provide a basis for reestimation.

Control of estimation is done in part by restricting such work to those who have the training and experience needed as a basis for making such judgments. A further control is the review of the judgments actually made to see whether subsequent data and events bear out the estimates made. In addition, there is available the concept of the ·"jury of opinion," i.e., the awareness that in important matters of judgment, a group review is less likely to overlook an error of judgment than is an individual. Design reviews, task forces, committees, and other team devices are all cases which include the concept of a jury of opinion. In all these instances the reviewers should be on the alert to identify the estimates and to concentrate their reviews on these estimates rather than on the subsequent calculations. The latter are much easier to verify than the former.

The foregoing categories are not an exhaustive list of support tasks. However, they do exemplify the principal types of problems encountered, and the usual approaches to their solution. While the supervisors of the departments involved are very much concerned with performing the tasks well, the extent of control achieved has not reached the levels attained for the tasks which have more obvious effects on product quality.

A principal reason for this gap in levels of control is the fact that the support tasks have not been brought into the orbit of any of the various disciplines which have arisen to study managerial processes. As noted, the Quality Control specialists have concentrated on those tasks which are more dramatic in their effect on product quality. Industrial engineers have emphasized the study of major systems; only incidentally have they studied the effect of the support tasks on product quality.

Another line of specialization has been that exemplified by the Administrative Applications Division of the American Society for Quality Control (ASQC). This specialty is importantly concerned with the concept that the statistical tools evolved to improve product quality have a wide range of application to many other fields of human endeavor. This concept is entirely valid, as demonstrated by many examples of application, historically as well as currently.[10] Some of the early papers published by this school of thought are listed in a Bibliography which appears at the end of this Section. It will be noted that some of the papers deal with quality-oriented tasks, while others deal with tasks which have no clear linkage with product quality. It will also be noted that some authors used a terminology such as "Application of Quality Control to Administrative Processes." Such terminology was commonly chosen to take advantage of the then favorable publicity surrounding the application of statistical methods to problems of quality control. However, it is a misnomer to use such terminology, since the common concept involved is statistical methods, not quality control.

The statistical tools utilized in analyzing support tasks (and in the papers cited in the Bibliography) are highly standardized and are discussed in Sections 22 through 28 of this Handbook.[11]

For further insight into applications of statistical methods to other than manufacturing support operations, the reader is referred to the work of the Administrative

---

[10] The earliest "practical" applications of probability theory were in gambling and in biometrics, not in product quality.

[11] The reader is reminded that "quality control" is not limited to the problem of holding the status quo through some continuing system of controls. "Quality control" also includes the studies for quality improvement. These studies make use of the entire array of managerial, engineering, and statistical tools of analysis. See generally Sections 16 and 18.

Applications Division of the American Society for Quality Control (ASQC) and the publications of both the Division and the Society.[12]

THE CONTROL LOOP FOR SUPPORT OPERATIONS

The support tasks discussed above are carried out, in various combinations, to perform support "operations," e.g., order editing, packaging. These operations combine, in turn, to constitute the support "systems," i.e., the networks of material flow, information flow, financial flow, etc. Through these systems the enterprise manages its internal affairs, and carries out its interfaces with the outside world, e.g., customers, vendors. The material flow network will be used to illustrate the problems and solutions inherent in control of support operations and systems.[13]

Figure 46-2 is a matrix showing the usual methods of control applicable to the principal operations which contribute to the material flow network.[14] For each operation there is shown the usual control subject, unit of measure, standard of performance, method of sensing, and method of comparing actual performance to standard.[15] Some supplemental explanation of Figure 46-2 is presented below.

Order Entry and Editing   There are really two major control subjects here:

1. The original order as prepared by the customer, the salesman, or the order clerk. This order is inspected (prior to entry or acceptance) for completeness, accuracy, inconsistencies, duplication with other orders, etc. Inspection may be done by a clerk or by a computer.

2. The order inspecting, editing, and processing. This work is checked by a sampling performed by the supervisor, by a departmental checker, or by an internal auditor.

Purchasing   Normally the departmental check of purchase orders is by supervisory review. However, certain errors of purchasing become evident during receiving inspection and at still other stations. In this way, the usual control of Purchasing's support activity is carried out not as a matter of routine, but under the exception principle. Figure 46-2 shows the approach used when routine checking is added.

Material Inventory and Stock Status   Here the control subjects are well defined by the parameters used in the basic control scheme, e.g., lead time for reorder. In addition, standards are commonly set for inventory levels, order size, etc. The control procedure is quite conventional.[16]

Stock Rotation   This subactivity can seriously influence product quality in special situations of time-related decay or degradation. Examples are oxidation or segregation of chemicals, crystallization of metals, evaporation of solvents, decay of radioactive or organic materials, and fading of colors. While positive programs of date

---

[12] For an uncommonly good example, see *Administrative Applications Division Conference Transactions, ASQC,* Arlington, Va., Mar. 12–13, 1970. This is a collection of 32 papers under the general heading "Statistical Science in Management," and devoted mainly to use of sampling and related techniques for quality control of support operations.

[13] For a more general discussion of systems analysis, see Section 20, under Planning — Computer Systems Design Specifications.

[14] For a more detailed analysis of this network, see Hopeman, Richard J., "Systems Analysis and Operations Management," Charles E. Merrill Books, Inc., Columbus, Ohio, 1969. The development in this Section is adapted from Hopeman's Figure 1-3, p. 9, and Figure 7-1, p. 157.

[15] These elements of the control feedback loop are derived from J. M. Juran, "Managerial Breakthrough," chap. 12, McGraw-Hill Book Company, New York, 1964.

[16] See, for example, Starr, Martin A., and David W. Miller, "Inventory Control: Theory and Practice," Prentice-Hall, Inc., Englewood Cliffs, N.J., 1962, or any other standard text on the subject.

Elements of control feedback loop	Operations in material flow network				
	Order entry and order editing		Purchasing	Material inventory and stock status	Stock rotation
Typical control subjects	Customer's order Product identity Shipping mode Date for shipping Etc.	Edited order (control subjects similar to customer's order)	Purchase order	Inventory level Order size Etc.	Date coding Storage conditions Etc.
Typical unit of measure	Errors per 100 orders	Errors per 100 orders	Errors per 100 orders	Various; usually in natural units	Percent of stock improperly rotated Percent discrepancies per 100 items stored
Typical standards of performance	Past history	Past history	Past history	Management objectives for parameters	Past history; management objectives
Sensing typically done by	Order clerk examining order; computer query	Sampling check by supervisor, checker, or auditor	Supervisor or checker; receiving inspector and others (by exception principle)	Sampling by internal auditor	Sampling by internal auditor
Typical method of comparing actual performance with standard	Periodic reports on error rate	Periodic reports on error rate	Periodic reports on error rate, consequences of errors	Status reports; periodic audit reports	Audit reports

Fig. 46-2 Matrix of control methods in material flow network. See p. 46-9 for horizontal continuation.

Operations in material flow network			
Material handling and protection	Material delivery	Packing for shipment to customers	Field servicing
Equipment design Equipment maintenance Protection of materials	Material identity Correctness of destination Timeliness	Package design Adequacy of procedures Conformance to procedures Padding, marking, sealing, etc.	Timeliness of service Adequacy of repairs Availability of spare parts
Percent of equipment in bad order Percent of product damaged	Percent of errors per 100 shipments Downtime due to lack of material	Errors per 100 packages	Time required to restore service Percent of recalls due to inadequate repair User downtime
Past history	Past history; budgeted goals	Management objectives; past history	Management objectives; past history
Internal audit; Quality Control (under exception principle)	Feedback of troubles from shop and field	Testing in packaging laboratory Quality Control check of outgoing product Field complaints and returns	Sampling check made by contacting users
Audit reports	Periodic reports	Complaint and other quality reports	Periodic reports

Fig. 46-2 (Continued) Matrix of control methods in material flow network.

coding and stock rotation are often in force, adherence to the procedures is notoriously poor, especially in the marketing chain. In consequence, audit procedures should be correspondingly strict.

Material Protection and Handling This activity is highly relevant to the integrity of the product. The equipment design (trucks, tote bins, pallets, etc.) must be appropriate to the nature of the product. Some products require adequate protection against moisture or airborne contaminants. Unitized pallets must be able to withstand the vertical loads as well as being strapped sufficiently to prevent damage by shifting of the load. For example, the writer has observed wide variation in the rigidity of unitized pallets of carbonated beverage bottles from different vendors. (One large, quality conscious bottler accepts or rejects truckloads of pallets based on the appearance of the first few pallet loads examined.)

Material Delivery This aspect of the broader materials management function concerns control subjects such as timeliness of arrival, correctness of destination, and correctness of identity. Achievement of good performance is a resultant of good control of paper work as well as good controls on the physical product by dispatchers, loaders, truckmen, etc.

Packaging for Shipment to Customers The increased complexity of products has influenced packaging to so great an extent that in some industries it is no longer a support operation. In such industries, e.g., frozen foods, the package design is an essential part of the product design. The packaging materials are not treated as "supplies" for quality control purposes but are placed entirely within the orbit of the Quality Control Department. This department checks the incoming packaging materials, the packaging process, and the final packaged product.

In industries where packaging is regarded as a support activity, there is usually need for quality controls anyway. In response to this need the support department prepares specifications both for the package and for the packaging process.[17] For fragile consumer products it is usual to conduct tests in a package testing laboratory to establish fitness for use. For products such as industrial machines, the packaging specification sets out requirements for protection, method of loading, and related parameters to guard against shock and environmental damage during transit.

It is a widespread practice for the Quality Control Department to check for compliance to these packaging requirements, even where packaging is classed as a support activity. Inspectors examine the finished package for adequate closure, markings, etc. Samplings are conducted to check for presence of product instruction manuals, accessories, and spare parts as well as for protective paddings and other product protection devices.

Field Servicing This support activity is commonly a Marketing Department responsibility.[18] However, field service performance is so vital to customer relations and to company income that it should be regarded as one of the most important of the control subjects in the entire spectrum of fitness for use.[19]

CASE EXAMPLES OF QUALITY IMPROVEMENT AND QUALITY CONTROL IN SUPPORT OPERATIONS

The tools used for quality improvement and control of support operations are quite similar to those used in direct operations. The cases which follow are intended not to explain the tools in detail but rather to exemplify their use in support operations.

[17] See generally Section 36B.

[18] See generally Section 15.

[19] See, for example, Section 43 (Household Appliances), under Measures of Service Performance.

For details on use of these tools generally, the reader is referred to those Sections which elaborate on the general nature and application of the respective tools.

Frequency Analysis and Pareto Analysis   Figure 46-3 shows the frequency of errors of various types found by Connell[20] in a sampling of high-volume claim documents. Figure 46-4 shows the same data arranged according to the Pareto analysis.

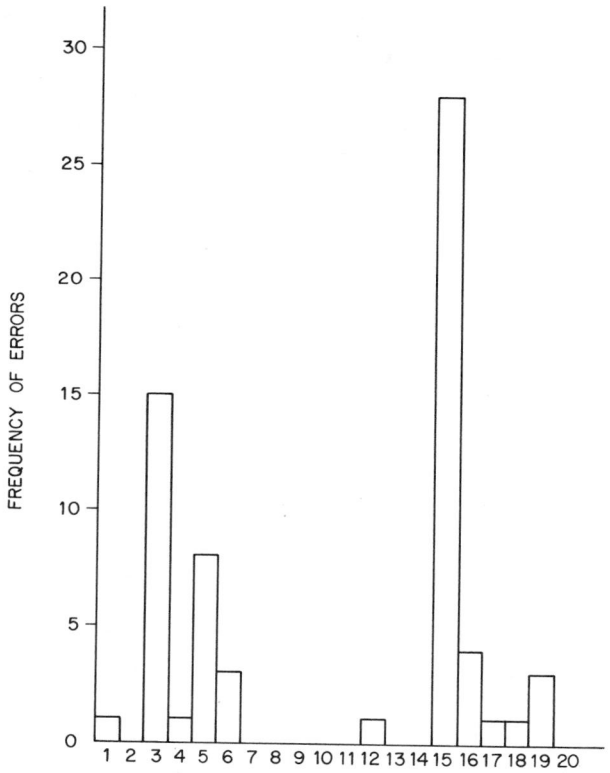

ERROR TYPES

Fig. 46-3   Frequency of error types in claim documents.

Design of Experiment and Analysis of Variance   A study was made to determine the causes of errors in recording production data in machine readable form.   Field observations and a controlled laboratory experiment were used to determine the effects of individuals, shifts, and location (continuous assembly line vs. job shop) on input errors.   Analysis of variance was among the statistical techniques used to isolate the principal sources of error.[21]

[20] Connell, F. M., Jr., Statistical Quality Control of Clerical Operations, *Industrial Quality Control,* September 1967, pp. 154–162.   Connell's study included use of sampling tables, control charts, and still other statistical tools.

[21] Smith, William A., Jr., Data Collection Systems—Part II, Environmental Effects on Accuracy, *Industrial Engineering,* January 1968, pp. 24–31.

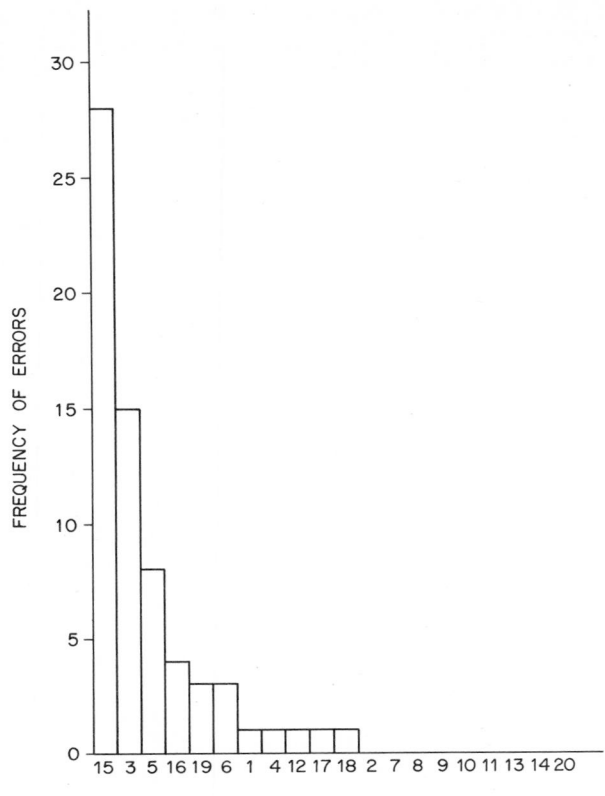

Fig. 46-4   Pareto analysis of error types in claim documents.

Bayesian Analysis   The Bayesian approach is to use historical sampling data plus the economic implications of available alternatives to assist in inspection decision making.   In an example given by Sorensen[22] the prior error rates of invoices were as follows:

Errors per 1,000 invoices	Proportion of time this error rate has occurred	Extension
10	0.10	1.0
50	0.25	12.5
100	0.50	50.0
200	0.15	30.0
	1.00	93.5

The "process average" for errors per 1,000 invoices is seen to be 93.5, or 9.35% defective.

[22] Sorensen, James E., Bayesian Analysis in Auditing, *The Accounting Review,* July 1969, pp. 555–561.

A sample of 20 invoices taken from a lot of 1,000 disclosed two errors in the sample. The economic data were as follows:

Cost to inspect one invoice = $0.45
"Rework" cost to correct one invoice = $4.00

The economic consequences of 100% inspection vs. lot acceptance without inspection now depend on whether one uses conventional statistical theory or Bayesian analysis, as follows:

Theory used	Cost to inspect 100%	Cost to accept without further inspection
Conventional statistical theory* . . .	$450	$374
Excess cost resulting from wrong decision	128	52
Bayesian analysis	450	402
Excess cost resulting from wrong decision	90	41

* See, for example, Spurr, William A., and Charles P. Bonini, "Statistical Analysis for Business Decisions," Chap. 15, Richard D. Irwin, Inc., Homewood, Ill., 1967.

The difference in the two approaches results from the fact that under Bayes' theorem, the findings in the sample are used to modify the historical distribution data. Omitting the mathematical derivations, the prior error rate distribution (after being modified by the findings in the sample) becomes a post (sample) distribution as follows:

Errors per 1,000 Invoices	Proportion of Occurrences
10	0.007
50	0.218
100	0.657
200	0.118
	1.000

The proportions of occurrences are used as weights to obtain weighted averages of the costs and excess costs (of wrong decisions) associated with each error rate. This is done independently for both the prior and post distributions, using a "payoff table" which shows the cost of a wrong decision at each rate of errors per 1,000 invoices.

Probability and Statistical Inference   Support operations frequently require use of sampling as a basis for statistical inference and for decision making. The "lot" from which the sample is drawn varies remarkably in form. An early paper by A. C. Rosander[23] states it well:

The accountant has to make an inference about a finite number of business transactions conducted during a fixed period of time such as one year. The population or universe which he samples may take one of many different forms. It may be books, or pages within books, or items on a page. It may be pieces of paper such as invoices, checks, vouchers, bills. It may be record cards such as are contained in an index file or a punch card file. In a large business, it may even be departments, stores, or warehouses. It may be physical assets in one form or another. In a company engaged in mining or selling precious ores, the accountant may be very much interested in how these ores are sampled and tested. In all of these situations a population or universe does exist, it can be defined, it can be circumscribed, and it can be sampled according to the principles of probability statistics.

[23] See the Bibliography at the end of this Section.

Applications of probability principles have been made in a wide variety of such situations: inventory valuation, credit reporting,[24] appraisal of property values,[25] aging of accounts receivable, etc.

Sampling for Auditing   In auditing the inventories of a large Maintenance storeroom, Kunz[26] found that:

72% of the audit checks verified the count on the books.

28% of the checks showed differences in count.   The value of these differences was distributed as follows:

Group	Value	Proportion of differences in this group
1	Over $100	5%
2	$15 through 99	15%
3	Under $15	80%

This Pareto analysis resulted in a decision to recheck the counts of all items in group 1, but to conduct only sampling checks of the items in groups 2 and 3.

Sampling of Quantity of Production   Measures of quantities of product are widely used for product formulation, measures of cost and productivity, inventory control, invoicing, etc.   In many cases, the practice is to "measure" 100% of the product; i.e., discrete units of product are counted 100%, while fungible products are weighed 100%.

For example, one company which sells large quantities of cotton retains a practice of determining, for each bale of cotton, the weight and moisture content.   The resulting dry weights are computed and entered, bale by bale, on the customer's bill.

In such cases it is often feasible to sample the weight and moisture content, since product uniformity often permits billing (or other action) based on sample averages times number of units of product.[27]

An early published example[28] concerned the average weight of rolls of paper. The paper mill recorded the weights of all rolls to the nearest ⅛ pound, and a clerk summarized these data.   It was found that a sampling of 20% of the rolls and a weighing to the nearest ¼ pound yielded equivalent results at a saving in clerical time.

Cumulative Sums and Other Tools for Forecasting Control   These tools are used to signal significant departures from forecast, or from budgeted figures, e.g., scrap, material usage, labor usage, and sales.

The author[29] has used a double error control in setting up an automatic procedure (e.g., self-contained and self-triggering by the forecasting computer program) for changing the parameters in a set of forecasting equations for weekly data.   From these equations (which were of the exponential smoothing form) forecasts were made for each of the next 52 weeks.   Each week the datum for the week was compared with forecast, and the sign and percentage of the error noted.   A running count was made of the last 13 signs and of proportions of error.   If 10 or more of the

[24] See Melvin J. Brown (Bibliography at the end of this Section).

[25] See John I. Boggs (Bibliography at the end of this Section).

[26] E. J. Kunz (Bibliography at the end of this Section).

[27] See generally Section 25A on Bulk Sampling.

[28] See Carl E. Noble (Bibliography at the end of this Section).

[29] Zobel, S. P., and R. Scamurra, "Development of an Adaptive Forecasting Procedure for Selected Unemployment Insurance Series," Cornell Aeronautical Laboratory, Inc., Jan. 31, 1967; Cal. No. XM-2306-G-I, New York State Department of Labor, Division of Employment Contract MS-3154.

last 13 errors were greater than 5% and had the same sign (+ or −), the forecasts were considered to be out of control, and the forecasting parameters were changed.[30]

A second error control was independently used. The actual data for the last 13 weeks were summed and compared with the sum of the forecasts for those weeks. If the 13 weeks' cumulative sum of actual data differed from the corresponding sum of forecasts by more than 10%, the forecasting was judged to be unsatisfactory, and new parameters were obtained for the forecasting equations.[31] (An out of control state could be indicated by either or both of the decision rules.)

A modification of the cumulative 13 weeks' error (as described above) would be to adapt the Cumulative Sum control chart (see Section 23) for control over forecasts.

Management Reports[32] These have wide application in support operations. An example given by Wilkinson[33] concerned management of the maintenance function. The principal control subjects proposed were dollars spent for maintenance, performance of maintenance personnel, and downtime. The proposed standard was in all cases the historical level of performance. Subsidiary control reports included backlog, costs per standard hour, emergency nonscheduled maintenance labor costs, scheduled and preventive maintenance activities.

Subjective Rating This tool plays a role in quality control, as, for example, in sensory testing.[34] The same tool of subjective rating is widely used in other applications, and the experience gained has significance for the applications to quality control.

An example is the problem of self-rating errors in training programs. In one study,[35] three types of self-rating errors were defined:

1. Failure to recognize standard performance, resulting in an overall upward or downward rating bias

2. General inconsistency around the trainee's own scale of rating

3. A tendency to rate "flatly," i.e., to overrate slow performance and to underrate fast performance

Regression analysis and control charts (based on regression lines) were used to improve performances of individuals.

ORGANIZING THE SUPPORT QUALITY ACTIVITIES

The support quality activities are carried out by a variety of company departments, vendors, and after-sales service companies. These organizations pursue their departmental or company goals, including the effectiveness of the quality support activities under discussion. However, these pursuits do not necessarily provide effective quality support activities because of some obvious weaknesses in organization and technique. Some of these weaknesses and their likely remedy are listed below.

Lack of Orchestration The support organizations seldom participate in the broad planning of quality. More usually they conduct departmental planning of their own affairs. Any quality failures become after the fact crises.

[30] This is an application of the sign test, one of several nonparametric tests useful in analyzing runs on control charts.

[31] The author is not aware of other applications of this approach.

[32] See generally Section 21, under Executive Reports on Quality.

[33] Wilkinson, John J., How to Manage Maintenance, *Harvard Business Review*, March–April 1968, pp. 100–111.

[34] See Section 12, under Sensory Qualities.

[35] Tahemach, J. B., and F. Wharton, Control Charts Aid Work Study Training, *Industrial Engineering*, vol. 2, No. 2, February 1970, pp. 29–32.

An organized approach to orchestration can consist of:

1. Identification of those aspects of the work of the support operations which significantly affect product quality. This identification can logically be done by a study team which includes the support department and the Quality Control Department.

2. Coordination of these significant operations with the mainstream of quality control through a well-known table of delegation:

Activity	Role of	
	Support organization	Quality control department
Quality planning	X	X
Execution of plan	X	
Audit of execution vs. plan . .		X

Such an approach retains for the support operations their jurisdiction over their day-to-day operations. Orchestration is provided through the joint planning and through the audit.

Inadequate Attention to Quality Improvement In part this results from failure of a support department to put chronic quality problems on its priority list for a breakthrough study. (Its "own" problems get priority.) Two examples can be cited.

1 . A manufacturer of large mechanical apparatus used a good deal of steel. Because of a shortage of covered storage, much steel was stored in an uncovered yard. Before being placed in open storage, the steel was treated with a rust preservative. However, there was much rusting since the materials handlers had no way of applying a first-in first-out method of stock rotation. The support department (Materials Management) met all criticisms with a demand for more covered storage space. However, an improvement project uncovered an alternative solution by periodically changing the color of the rust preservative to enable the materials handlers to rotate the stock.

2. A team study of causes of poor customer service established that a prime cause of loss of product identification was the pulling off, in transit, of the tickets which were wired to the pans. Following tryout of several alternatives, this long-standing method was replaced by use of self-adhesive clear plastic envelopes.

Inadequate Provision for Diagnosis The support departments commonly lack specialists in problem analysis. Hence this analysis must be done by the supervision or by outside staff specialists. A progressive step is to enlist the service of the quality staff specialists for diagnosis of chronic quality troubles.

Inadequate Measures of Quality Performance The support departments do measure their performance. However, these measures commonly concern the main performance measures by which the department is judged, e.g., cost or productivity.

A team study of support activities will commonly identify the needed measures of quality performance, and can set up appropriate scoreboards.

An exhaustive list of "Suggested Measurement Characteristics for Various Functional Groups" appears in the government manual on Zero Defects. [36] Many of these characteristics are quality-oriented. Some of the technical papers contained in this manual also suggest control subjects and units of measure applicable to some support operations. [37]

[36] "Zero Defects, Quest for Quality," pp. 220–232, Government Printing Office, Washington, D.C., 1968.

[37] See also Halpin, James F., "Zero Defects," pp. 130–155, McGraw-Hill Book Company, New York, 1966.

CONCLUSION

The boundary line between "direct" and "support" quality activities has undergone considerable change in the twentieth century. The Chief Inspectors who emerged in the reorganizations following World War I tended to regard inspection, test, and metrology as the core quality activities. The rise of the Quality Control Engineer expanded this core through the concept of organized quality planning and defect prevention. The rise of the Reliability Engineer expanded the core further to include some vital activities inherent in the launching of new designs. In some industries (e.g., drug, food) the core now includes product packaging and storage. In all regulated industries the core now includes much of the documentation activity.

These changes underscore the dynamic nature of the boundary between direct and support quality activities. However, the direction of change has been essentially one-way. The core has kept increasing, so that the support quality activities of today are all candidates to become the direct quality activities of tomorrow. At the same time, the growing complexity of industry has been creating new support activities which require new plans and controls to make them effective in control of quality.

The support activities are not unique to manufacturing industries. The service industries (see Section 47) likewise employ a wide array of support quality activities, many of which are identical to those used in the manufacturing industries. The tasks, the operations, and the tools are largely alike; what is different is the application and the emphasis.

The commonality of support activities as between Manufacture and Service industries can be extended to activities of a nonquality nature. For example, every company makes use of financial statements, and it is essential that these statements be "fit for use." To this end, an elaborate system of quality controls has sprung up to ensure that:

1. The accounting system, if followed, will accurately reflect the financial status of the company.

2. The system is actually being followed.

Because this Handbook is concerned with fitness for use of products and services sold by the company to its clientele, the discussions of Sections 46 and 47 do not extend to quality of such things as financial statements. (The users of these statements are managers, owners, creditors, etc., but not the clientele from whom the company derives its income.)

Despite this self-imposed boundary of this Handbook, the commonalities noted are of interest to many readers. The methods used in direct and support quality control activities actually have universal application to quality of human affairs in the broadest sense of the term.

BIBLIOGRAPHY OF EARLY PAPERS RELATING TO CONTROL OF SUPPORT AND SIMILAR OPERATIONS

Bicking, Charles A., "The Control Chart as a Tool in Management," presented at the 104th Annual Meeting of the American Statistical Association, Dec. 24, 1944. Bicking presented 10 case studies of use of control charts in such problems as clerical work improvement and merit rating of employees.

Conference Papers, First Annual Convention, ASQC, Chicago, June 5–6, 1947. Pertinent papers include Bolanovitch, D. J., Control Chart Treatment of Personnel Statistics; Wilson, R. H., "Scientific Control of Stockroom Inventories;" Parkin, Guy G., "Statistical Quality Concepts Applied to Waste and Personnel Efficiency."

Deming, W. E., and Leon Geoffrey, Sample Inspection in the Processing of Census Returns, *Journal of the American Statistical Association*, vol. 36, pp. 351–360, 1941; also Deming,

W. E., Benjamin J. Tepping, and Leon Geoffrey, Errors in Card Punching, *Journal of the American Statistical Association,* vol. 37, pp. 525–536, 1942.

Noble, Carl E., Statistical Cost Control in the Paper Industry, *Industrial Quality Control,* vol. 9, No. 6, pp. 42–46, May 1953.

Murdock, Bennett B., Some Aspects of Quality Control as Applied to Clerical Operations, *Industrial Quality Control,* vol. 7, No. 6, May 1951.

Byrne, James T., "Quality Control of Clerical Operations," paper presented at Industrial Seminar, Life Office Management Association, Cincinnati, Sept. 22, 1953.

Rosander, A. C., Probability Statistics in Accounting, *Industrial Quality Control,* vol. 11, No. 8, p. 27, May 1955.

Brown, Melvin J., "Applying Quality Control to Credit Reporting," paper presented at the Middle Atlantic Regional Conference, ASQC, New York, Mar. 28–29, 1952.

Boggs, John I., "Use of Sampling in the Appraisal of Property," paper presented at the Sixth Midwest Quality Control Conference, ASQC, Chicago, Nov. 15–16, 1951.

Kunz, E. J, (a paper dealing with application of sampling techniques to auditing of inventory values), presentation to San Francisco Chapter of the Internal Auditors' Institute, December 1955.

Noble, Carl E., Cost Accounting Potentials of Statistical Methods, *NACA Bulletin,* August 1952.

Trueblood, R. M., and R. M. Cyert, Statistical Sampling Applied to Aging of Accounts Receivable, *Journal of Accountancy,* March 1954, pp. 293–298.

Parkin, Guy G., Statistical Technique for Forecasting Sales, *Industrial Quality Control,* vol. 12, No. 5, November 1955.

Section **47**

Service Industries

J. M. JURAN

R. S. BINGHAM, JR.

INTRODUCTION

In this Section, the authors undertake to expound, for the service industries generally, the universal principles and common approaches through which these industries attain quality of service. The authors have examined the methods used by a number of service industries to carry out their respective quality missions. From these examinations, and from their personal experience with still other service industries, the authors have proposed a collection of universals and commonalities applicable to all service industries. The early part of the Section presents these universals, and the rest of the Section presents the industry cases studied.

Because the terms "service," "service industry," and still others are not yet standardized as to meaning, the authors will define these terms as they go along. These definitions are not proposed as standards; they are made only to clarify what the authors mean when they use the terms.

What Is Service?   Service is work performed for someone else.   The recipient of the service may be a consumer, e.g., haircutting, or an institution, e.g., computer leasing, or both, e.g., energy service.

Service work exists because it can outperform the client in meeting his own needs. For some of these needs (e.g., distant voice communication) only large centralized organizations are able to assemble the technology and investment required.   Without them the needs would not be met at all. Other service work exists because it offers alternatives which are superior in cost, time, convenience, etc. (e.g., mass transportation).   Still other service work exists to meet a wide variety of human psychological and physiological needs: amusement, freedom from disagreeable chores, opportunity for learning and for creativity.

Service work may include sale of a product, e.g., food in restaurants, spare parts used during automobile repair.   However, such sale of a product is normally incidental to the work performed for the client.

The Service Industries   Conventional classification of a national economy into "industries" commences by a subdivision into:

A. Manufacture, meaning mainly the processing of materials into finished durable and nondurable goods.

B. Nonmanufacture, which is all else.

In turn, nonmanufacture is divided into:

B1. Service industries (see below).

B2. Nonservice industries such as mining, agriculture, and construction.   From a quality control viewpoint, such industries have much in common with manufacture.   They engage in processing of materials, and (often) end up with finished products.   ("Manufacture" usually bears a connotation of being performed in factories.)

The category "Service Industries" includes principally:

Transportation (railroads, subways, airlines, bus lines, common carrier trucking, pipelines)

Public utilities (telephone communication, energy services, sanitation services)

Restaurants, hotels, and motels

Marketing (retail food, apparel, automotive, wholesale trade, department stores)[1]

Finance (commercial banks, insurance, sales finance, investment)

Real estate

News media

Personal services (amusements, laundry and cleaning, barber and beauty shops)

Professional services (lawyers, doctors)

Government (defense, health, education, welfare, municipal services)

It is evident that the term "service industry" is given multiple meanings such as nonmanufacture, utilities, or personal services.[2]   The meaning given by the authors is an industry which generally meets the criteria set out below, under Characteristics of a Service Company.

Collectively, the service industries are believed to account for over 50% of the national economy of the United States.   Some are highly automated, e.g., electrical

---

[1] Marketing is generally regarded as a service industry.   Although it sells manufactured products, the basic function it performs is one of distribution, which clearly meets the criteria of "service."   For a discussion of the relationship of marketing to quality, see Section 14.

[2] To make matters more complex, both manufactuing and service industries engage in "support operations" (document preparation, order filling, computation, estimation, etc.)   See Section 46, under Contributions of Support Operations to Product Quality, for an exposition.

energy supply. However, many are labor-intensive (e.g., restaurants). For such industries, wages may represent about 70% of total costs, as compared with 30% for manufacture. These labor-intensive industries face severe problems in recruitment, training, and motivation of employees, as well as intense pressures to increase their (usually) low wages. A major consequence is a trend toward increased use of new technology to improve both productivity and quality.[3]

Characteristics of a Service Company[4] A service company is an organized system of special skills and facilities. It sells the benefits of this system to its clients in a variety of ways, for example:

Lease of facilities, e.g., apartments, rental automobiles
Use of facilities, e.g., bus rides, telephone calls
Professional advice, e.g., medical, legal
Health maintenance, e.g., hospital service
Product maintenance, e.g., automobile repairs
Relief from self-service, e.g., restaurant service

In carrying out its mission the service company sells direct to the user. This is true not only for large industrial users but for numerous small users as well. In this latter respect, the service company differs sharply from the manufacturing company.[5]

These direct sales bring the service company into multiple contact with large numbers of consumers. For example, the telephone company contacts all its customers through order clerks, installers, billing service, repair office, repairmen. The hotel has multiple contact with the traveler: doorman, reception office, bellman, chambermaid, dining room, room service, telephone operator, cashier. Every single one of such multiple contacts is an opportunity for good quality of service, or bad quality.

These multiple contacts give rise to huge numbers of individual transactions. An electric power company serving a million customers may send out over 5 million invoices annually, receive over a million telephone calls, and be involved in hundreds of thousands of moves by these customers. All these transactions have their impacts on human beings, many highly articulate.

A favorable aspect of these direct contacts with the consumer is the opportunity for good feedback as to fitness for use. In this respect, the service company has an easier job than the manufacturing company, which is comparatively insulated from the consumer, and must resort to special studies to secure adequate feedback.

The extensive personal contact also sets up some relationships which are inherently uncomfortable for the consumer. To secure some services he surrenders his property into the custody of the service company, e.g., baggage for transport, or clothes to be cleaned. The service company holds this property in captivity, and a failure or a delay in returning it can greatly inconvenience the consumer. In other cases it is the consumer himself who feels he is held captive. The most usual form of this is waiting in a queue, or waiting for service when there are no effective alternatives.

---

[3] See, for example, Theodore Levitt, Production-Line Approach to Service, *Harvard Business Review*, September–October 1972, pp. 41–52.

[4] "Company" is used here in a generic sense. It may include governmental bodies and still other institutions created for service.

[5] This is not 100% true. Some service companies (e.g., in the insurance industry) sell extensively through independent agents. Also, some manufacturing companies sell direct to the consumer, e.g., through mail orders or through house-to-house selling. However, the service companies exhibit a very high proportion of direct sales to the consumer, whereas this proportion is very low for the manufacturing companies.

For some service failures the consumer can make a direct complaint and claim. He may be compensated for loss of property, but he is seldom compensated for loss of time or for his annoyance. What he can do is to turn to competing services. He can also do damage to the company by publicizing the trouble he has had. If the service is a monopoly, he can join other disgruntled consumers in collective efforts to block rate increases or legislation sought by the company.

SERVICE QUALITY DESIGN

In establishing their quality of design, the service industries are bound by the same broad considerations as are the manufacturing companies: identification of what constitutes fitness for use, choice of a design concept which is responsive to the identified needs of the user, translation of this concept into specifications.[6]

Design for Many Consumers   Beyond these basic needs, the service industries must give special emphasis to several added aspects of design which are inherent in dealing with a clientele of many consumers.

"Made to Order" Designs.   Human beings exhibit a wide spectrum of needs and likes, all stemming from differences in status, personal taste, etc. The service industries respond to this spectrum by such methods as:

1. Creating a range of choice for the client, e.g., the restaurant menu.

2. Providing a modular system design which permits the user to direct the system in accordance with his special needs. The classic example is the automated telephone system which permits the consumer to reach millions of destinations, unaided by human intervention. The humble vending machine is another example.

3. Providing assistance to meet that residue of "to order" needs which the engineered system cannot provide directly to the consumer. Examples are variations in cooking of meals to personal taste, or setting up conference telephone calls.

While these made to order designs are an essential aspect of service quality design, they are also a breeding ground for errors, i.e., in interpreting the special needs and in conforming to them. In addition, the special designs require special pricing, again multiplying the chances of error.

Technical Assistance.   The consumer has extensive need for such assistance. In some cases his technological ignorance requires that qualified specialists be available to diagnose his needs, e.g., human illness or a television set which is out of service. In other cases, the need is mainly for explanation, e.g., insurance policy provisions, airline timetables.

Simplicity.   In offering a design of service to thousands or millions of clients, the need for simplicity is absolute. Many consumers are unable to understand complex rules, variations, effects, etc. Still more consumers are unwilling to take the time to learn. (The unwillingness of consumers to read the "fine print" gets some of them into trouble.)

Auxiliary Services.   The service industries teem with "free" services which are provided to clients as part of the quality of design. An automobile service station will clean the client's windshield and check the status of oil, batteries, and tires while the pump is filling the gasoline tank. It also provides washroom facilities for the travelers. Motel chains offer free calls to a distant city to provide reservations for a future night's lodging. Airlines provide reading material for travelers who desire it. Fuel oil companies provide free oil burner maintenance service during the summer to avoid emergency calls during the busy winter heating season.

These auxiliary services are designed partly to meet competition and partly to meet a special need of consumers for "well-being." (See below.)

---

[6] For elaboration, see Section 2, under Quality of Design: Grade.

Time as a Service Parameter   A striking feature of the service industries is that the time required to provide service is regarded as an element of quality.[7]

Some service industries distinguish sharply between different subdivisions of time:

1. *Access Time.*   This is the length of time which elapses from the client's first effort to gain the service company's attention until he has that attention.   The standard for this "accessibility"[8] is expressed, for example, in the form:

80% of the incoming telephone calls should be answered within 15 seconds after the first ring.

Measurement of telephone access time can usually be done by automated recorders actuated by the telephone equipment.   Other forms of access time require sampling studies by observers.

2. *Queuing Time.*   Some services involve a queuing of clients due to variable loads or to considerations of economy.   In such cases the consumer is concerned with:

a. The length of the queue and therefore the waiting time.   The service company is in a position to plan this based on past history and probability considerations ("queuing theory").

b. The integrity of the queue, i.e., adherence to the principle of first come first served.   Some companies organize this by use of assigned serial numbers.   This also permits the clients to sit while they wait, and to occupy themselves with reading material provided for the purpose.   This may be embellished by a playroom and toys for children.

3. *Action Time.*   This is commonly defined as the interval between taking the customer's order and providing him with the service requested.

In designing the time aspect of service, it is important to stress the *customer's viewpoint* of elapsed time.   To a railroad or an airline, the emphasis on travel time may be from terminal to terminal, and this is clearly important.   To the shipper or passenger, the emphasis is from dock to dock or from point of origin to point of final destination.   The customer will make his decisions on this point-to-point basis, no matter what the carrier thinks.

In many situations the time taken to provide service is the decisive factor in marketing that service.   One category of such cases arises from the limited time available to the client.   The segment of the food service industry known as "Fast Food" has emerged to meet just such a need.

A second major reason for the critical importance of service time is the cumulative effect of delays.   A by-product of organizing human affairs around complex systems is that when those systems fail, a great deal of human activity is disrupted.   For example, a vital machine tool is delayed 8 days during railroad shipment.   Because the machine is critical to a factory production line, the entire factory is delayed for 8 days.   Some or all of this delay may extend to the factory's customers, and to *their* customers, etc.

As a corollary of the critical nature of service time, the service industries should:

1. Establish standards for the various components of service time, and set up controls to enforce these standards.

2. Improve present service time by studying enough cases of service to

---

[7] In manufacturing companies, delivery time is certainly regarded as a vital parameter of customer relations.   However, delivery time is not regarded as a part of "quality"; it is a wholly separate parameter.   The organization setup reflects this.   A separate department (Production Control, Materials Management, etc.) is designated to establish standards (schedules), measure performance, and report on results.

[8] See below, under Telephone Service Quality Control.

find out just where the time is being consumed (see below, under Quality Improvement).

3. Make service time a major parameter in design of future systems. For example, through design of special pallets and support equipment, the air freight industry has reduced to 30 minutes the time required to load 40 tons of cargo on a jet airplane.[9] In like manner, rental car leasing companies have shortened the time required to serve certain "regular" customers. This is done by conducting a credit investigation of these customers and creating a special file for them so that they bypass future credit checks and related paper work.

Design for Consumer "Well-Being" A further parameter of service quality is consumer well-being. This parameter is difficult to define, but some examples will make clear what is meant.

1. A serviceman repairs a household appliance. He does so promptly and with competence. His charges are fair. What the housewife remembers is that he tracked mud into her kitchen and smoked a vile-smelling cigar.

2. A housewife phones a utility company to question the invoice she has received. The service clerk straightens it out to the customer's satisfaction. What the housewife tells her husband and friends is that the service clerk was rude to her.

The service industries recognize that there are positive and negative aspects which affect consumer well-being. On the positive side are such matters as:

Atmosphere. Some service industries take active steps to create an "atmosphere" which will meet the tastes of their clientele. Obvious examples are seen in the industries devoted to travel, leisure, and entertainment. The clients may be predominantly commercial travelers, senior citizens, young unmarrieds, couples with young children, etc. These categories differ in their tastes to an extent such that the service industries design differences in decorations, furnishings, refreshments, provisions for leisure time, etc.

Feeling of Importance. Because service is work done for someone else, many consumers view the relationship between client and service company as one akin to master and servant. This viewpoint is flattering to the ego of the consumer and leads him to expect attention, courtesy, respect, and still other elements common to a master-servant relationship.

Service companies are well aware of this viewpoint, and stress to their employees the importance of courtesy, etc. Some go further, and design into their plan of customer relations some elements which enforce the consumers' feeling of importance: formal "welcome" symbols, various forms of continuing attention, free souvenirs, "thank you" letters, etc.

Information. Still another element of well-being is to know what to expect. For example, when a train is late, the passengers waiting in the station to board that train want to be informed as to the expected departure time. This "need to know" is not for the purpose of enabling the traveler to change plans depending on the length of delay. (Unless the delay is overwhelming, virtually all the passengers will wait it out anyway.) Instead, the need to know is based on an instinctive human desire for mastery over the environment. The consumer who knows what to expect derives a feeling of well-being from this knowledge, since he has the information needed for predictability and, at his option, for choice of alternatives. Lacking knowledge of what to expect, he is at the mercy of rumors and surprises, with the result that his anxiety rises.

---

[9] Cornwall, L.P., "Quality Control in International Air Freight," "Quality Control in Rail Transportation," August 1964. Available from Railroad Systems and Management Association, Chicago, Ill. (This collection of papers deals with the quality problems of several service industries.)

Increasingly, service companies are showing awareness of this consumer need to know, and are making provision, in their system design, to take the initiative in keeping the consumer informed on matters he regards as important to his well-being.[10]

Safety.   Because the user entrusts his person, property, and well-being to the custody of the service industries, "service safety" becomes as vital as product safety. The hotel, the restaurant, the carrier, etc., all have responsibilities for this safety, and these responsibilities were on the statute books for centuries before the current wave of activity in product liability.

The discussion of Product Liability (Section 14) has a good deal of application to the service industries, and the reader is urged to study the material presented, particularly under the heading Defensive Action.

Design for Continuity of Service   Many designs include provisions for maintaining continuity of service despite failures.   Telephone companies and airlines make use of alternative routings in the event of unavailability of standard routings.   Professional service groups (doctors, lawyers) organize their work in a way which permits continuity in the absence of any member.   Sometimes the alternative is provided through upgrading; i.e., the hotel or car rental service will meet the client's guaranteed reservation by giving him a higher-grade room or car at the guaranteed price. Still another form is that used by those repair shops which provide a "loan" of a piece of equipment while the client's equipment is undergoing repair.

CONFORMANCE TO DESIGN

In the service industries it is necessary to distinguish clearly between two very different problems in control of conformance:

1. The conformance of the "internal" process to the process standards.   This will be referred to as "internal conformance."

2. The conformance to the service design as seen by the clients.   This will be referred to as "external conformance."

Internal Conformance.   This relates to those aspects of the service company's operations which cannot be sensed by the clientele.   For example, the power company establishes standards for quality of fuel bought, for energy yield per ton of fuel, maintenance of equipment, etc.

Generally, the service industries' approach to internal conformance is similar to that used in the manufacturing industries for process control, cost control, etc. In addition, because of the large number of small clients, many service companies are heavily involved in processing invoices, checks, and related paper work carrying direct financial connotation to the consumer.   Control of quality of this data processing follows closely the methods discussed in Sections 20 and 46.

Some other aspects of internal conformance also have an impact on external conformance.   Maintenance of the equipment and process conditions influences strongly the ability of the company to achieve quality as seen by the user.   For example, the control of hospital medication errors is, on the face of it, squarely up to the personnel, notably the nurses.   On closer examination, the "system" is seen to be a major contributor to these errors.   (See below, under Control of Hospital Medication Errors.)

This interrelation between internal and external conformance requires that the review of internal conformance not be limited to that carried out by the departmen-

[10] For example, response to customer inquiries as to the status of their orders has been greatly speeded up through use of microfilm plus electronic retrieval methods.   See Instant Answers to Customer Order Inquiries, *Management Review,* November 1969, pp. 67–69.

tal supervision. Many service companies recognize this need, and set up audits which are all-pervasive. (See below.)

External Conformance. This is conformance to those features of service quality which can be sensed by the consumer. These features are by no means limited to the obvious, *sine qua non* elements of the design, e.g., wholesome restaurant food, clean hotel beds, correct telephone connections. They include also the features which contribute to timeliness and well-being.[11]

Measures of Service Quality For internal conformance, the measures of quality have much in common with the well-known measures widely used in control of manufacturing processes. Measure of external conformance is more complex, owing to the abstract nature of some of the qualities and the subjective reactions of consumers.

	Yes	No
Was your reservation handled courteously?	☐	☐
On your arrival, did you receive friendly courteous service from		
Doorman	☐	☐
Reservation clerk	☐	☐
Bellman	☐	☐
During your stay, did you receive friendly courteous service from		
Maid	☐	☐
Telephone operator	☐	☐
Room service	☐	☐
Valet service	☐	☐
Cashier	☐	☐

Fig. 47-1 Typical consumer comment form—hotel.

An obvious source of data on external conformance is the cross section of consumer complaints and claims. These reactions do not reflect the *amount* of annoyance suffered by consumers, since most of the annoyed consumers will not take the trouble to complain. (See Section 15, under Quality Complaints—General.) However, the complaints received do represent a sample of the *types* of annoyance to which all consumers are subject.

	Yes	No
Was the food quality satisfactory?	☐	☐
Was the service prompt?	☐	☐
Was the service friendly?	☐	☐
Were the prices reasonable?	☐	☐
Was the restaurant clean?	☐	☐
Was the washroom clean?	☐	☐

Fig. 47-2 Typical consumer comment form—restaurant.

A second method of measure of external performance is through solicitation of consumer comments. A typical form of this is the appraisal card made available to consumers in hotel rooms and restaurants (Figures 47-1 and 47-2). Some companies use the summaries of these cards as the basis for a regular executive report. (See the Howard Johnson case below.)

[11] Obviously, the manufacturing companies also have customers who are concerned with well-being. However, most of the impact of failure to conform to standards of well-being falls on "corporate customers," i.e., industrial employees, rather than on independent consumers. The response of these industrial employees is quite different from that of the consumer.

Additionally, companies design special surveys of customer reaction, through letter questionnaires, telephone contacts, and personal interview. The techniques used follow generally the principles discussed in Sections 4 and 14.

Optimum for Conformance   Adherence to service specifications poses the universal problem of finding the optimum level of conformance.[12]   In their approach to finding this optimum, the service industries are handicapped by the absence of data showing the relationship between quality of service and sales income, as well as by the absence of quality cost data.   Their studies of quality costs[13] have lagged considerably behind those of the manufacturing industries.   Lacking these cost and sales income data, the service industries must resort to other bases for establishing economic levels of conformance.

One approach is to use a "market" standard based on analysis of performance attained by multiple members of the same large service organization.

For example, standards for telephone service are based on a combination of past history and a "market" made up of numerous telephone exchanges within the Bell System.   (See below, under Telephone Service Quality Control.)   The comparison of performance of various airlines establishes a form of market standard.   (See below, under Airline Service Quality.)   A similar concept is used in the National Service Index of the U.S. Postal Service.   (See below, under Postal Service.)

A second approach is to study the performance of competitors.   It is common practice for executives of service companies to use competitors' services with an incidental purpose of appraising quality.   In addition, there are periodic special studies which follow generally the principles discussed in Section 14, under Competitive Evaluations.   In those cases where a large customer also buys from competitors, it may be feasible to acquire his data on competitive performance.

One form of standard which carries hidden risks to service quality is the conventional array of ratios used in managerial and financial control.   For example, when the manufacturing industries undertook to automate, their traditional ratios of support personnel to production personnel became meaningless.   A similar trend is evident in some service industries.   As an example, efforts to reduce the maintenance force to a level which holds a constant ratio to a production force (in process of automating) can result in deterioration of timeliness of service.

In like manner, improvements in other forms of operating performance can affect quality of service, as seen by the consumer.   For example, in the hospital, the traditional method used by a bed patient to call for service is to press a call button which is then answered, in person, by a nurse.   The trend has been to centralize the response to these patient calls by directing them to a switchboard operator. The operator answers this call via a loudspeaker located behind the patient's bed. In turn, the patient makes his wants known to the operator via a microphone located "somewhere" near his bed.   The system achieves some needed improvement in hospital manpower productivity, and may well reduce the "access time" for the patient.   However, some patients feel that the anonymous voice response represents a severe drop in well-being when compared with a response through the personal appearance of a nurse.

In virtually every service industry the literature includes studies of quality of service.   In some cases, e.g., medical care, these studies have been extensive, and mainly on a professional level.   In other industries the published studies have included "exposes" which, while presenting instances of quality failures, are seriously biased in their conclusions.

For the foreseeable future, the approach to par must remain on an industry-by-industry basis.   The practitioner will do well to seek out and review the published

---

[12] See Section 5, under Discovering the Optimum.
[13] See below, under Quality Improvement.   See also Section 5 generally.

studies, keeping in mind the risk of bias. In addition, he must compile his own past data, along with securing such competitive information as he can find.[14]

Audit for Assurance[15]   An example of a formalized audit in a service company is seen in the Howard Johnson Case (see below). The audit is all-pervasive, covering both internal and external aspects of quality.

As is common in formal audit plans, the service industry audit covers many incidents, observations, documents, etc. To reduce these findings to a simple score suitable for executive reports (or for motivation plans) requires systems of summary, weighting, demerit values, ratings, etc. Examples of these are seen below.

Audit or review of the work of professional categories of personnel (e.g., researchers, physicians) runs into a special obstacle. These professional categories tend to feel that the review must be by a "peer group"; e.g., only physicians should review the work of physicians. When audit of such professional work is done by administrative personnel, the findings are not accepted wholeheartedly. Many of these professionals regard their career as bound up with their profession rather than with the company (or hospital, etc.), which may be only the current habitat.

ORGANIZATION FOR QUALITY

Service industry organization for quality differs considerably from that used by manufacturing industries. There are also extensive differences among the service industries themselves. However, in general, the service industry organization exhibits the following features:

1. The day-to-day regulation and decision making on conformance to standards are largely in the hands of the line departments, without the presence of independent inspection and test personnel who have powers to hold up the delivery of nonconforming "product."

2. The concept of a separate staff of specialists in quality control has only a minority acceptance.

3. The concept of a high-level executive devoting full time to the quality function likewise has only minority acceptance. Where this organization form is used, the title of the executive is usually something other than Quality Manager.

4. Organized coordination of the quality function seldom exists in continuing form. For specific projects or crises, coordination may be set up through committees of departmental heads.

These differences from the forms prevailing in manufacturing industries do not mean that the service industries are poorly organized. As is evident from the cases discussed below, the service companies do succeed in establishing specifications for "products" and processes. They also succeed in establishing control procedures for adhering to specification. In addition they make some use of the concept of audit for assurance.

It may be concluded that the service industries are adequately organized for establishing specifications and standards, for planning of day-to-day controls, and for executing those controls. In addition, their approach to coordination appears to be adequate for dealing with crises and with specific agreed-on projects. However, their organization forms do not appear to be well suited for programs of quality improvement, since:

The concept of an organized approach to quality improvement has not been fully grasped.

[14] See generally Juran, J. M., "Managerial Breakthrough," chap. 15, The Standard, McGraw-Hill Book Company, New York, 1964.

[15] See generally Section 21, under Audit of Execution vs. Plan.

Their basic training in the nature of the quality function has been limited. There is a lack of trained specialists to carry out the details of diagnosis for quality improvement.

QUALITY IMPROVEMENT

The service industries abound in chronic quality problems, and thereby in opportunities for quality improvement. The general approach to such improvement, as set out in Section 16, can be applied to the service industries if they can be organized for such improvement. As noted above, the service industries are generally not well organized for this purpose.

These weaknesses in organization form do not preclude quality improvements if top management provides the leadership. For example, the Howard Johnson restaurant chain (see below) has engaged in massive programs for improving quality through:

1. Transferring most of the food processing to centralized factories
2. Shifting from franchised restaurants to owned restaurants

Additional improvement projects are the result of vendor initiative. Equipment manufacturers and materials men are active in studying the problems of the service industries as a source of ideas for new equipment or materials which will improve productivity, quality, etc. Purchase of such new equipment usually involves substantial investments for the service company, and thereby requires the approval of top management.

Large service companies maintain a staff of full-time technologists, particularly with respect to facilities and equipment. These technologists are active in studying ways to make improvements in productivity, quality, etc., through changes in facilities and equipment.[16]

Where top management does not provide the leadership for quality improvement,[17] the initiative, if any, must come from the middle management. However, in the absence of a manager devoted full time to the quality function, it is difficult and unusual for the line managers to evolve programs for quality improvement.

Study of Quality Costs In manufacturing companies, study of quality costs is a fruitful technique for identifying promising projects and for proving their promise to upper management (see Section 5). This technique is applicable to the service industries.

The standardized quality cost categories are likewise applicable to the service industries, especially with respect to internal conformance. The quality cost category "external failures" includes customer claims such as those discussed below under Airline Service Quality.

While the quality cost concept is clearly applicable to the service industries, the published cases of application have been too few to permit sound conclusions as to whether the potential benefits to the service industries would match those experienced by manufacturing industries. The likelihood is that in the service industries, the main benefit from quality improvement is increased income rather than reduced

---

[16] See, for example, Dixon, William J., Economic Benefits from a Quality Control and Reliability Program for Railroad Operations, published in "Quality and Reliability Engineering for Railroad Operations," pp. 5–10, 1966. Available from Railway Systems and Management Association, Chicago, Ill.

[17] This can be the result of preoccupation with the income producing aspects of the business. For example, bank managements traditionally have focused their attention on the loan making functions, with a resulting low priority on the "back room" functions of paper work and data processing. See Reed, John, Sure It's a Bank, But I Think of It as a Factory, *Innovation*, August 1971, pp. 26–35.

quality costs. In view of this, the service companies should be wary of overemphasis on quality costs.

Effect of Quality on Income   Studies to relate quality of service to income follow generally the approaches discussed in Section 4, especially under Quality and Share of Market. However, the great importance of time in the service industries has stimulated numerous improvements in income through shortening the time required to provide service.

In those cases where competition has equalized service performance as to other parameters, the residual inequality in the time parameter can become the decisive factor in share of market. For example, ". . . a number of studies have shown that consumers do not pick a brand of gasoline. Instead, they pick a service station, . . . and they do this in such a way as to minimize the time required to make a purchase. If the producer understands the consumer's preoccupation with service time, he has a basis for effectively planning his distribution and sales, as well as his product."[18]

One widespread form of study of service time is "Route Engineering," i.e., the planning of delivery operations amid a complex interrelationship of vehicles, drivers, customer needs, product types, alternative routes, delivery frequencies, etc. Aside from the effect on customer relations, these deliveries are a major factor in cost of service; e.g., in some industries, delivery costs run to about 20% of sales. Because of the complexity and importance of the overall problem, the tools of operations research have been widely used in route engineering.[19]

In some industries, elapsed time, even in internal operations, has an effect on income. For example, a modern bank cashes large numbers of checks drawn against other banks. To receive credit from these other banks, the cashing bank must meet strict deadlines. Even a few percent of delays in meeting deadlines can run into millions of dollars in annual earnings.[20]

One way of translating service quality improvements into income is through making the sales contract contingent on prompt delivery. Such contract provisions, e.g., penalty clauses, give a competitive advantage to the service company which has the firmest grip on its delivery interval.[21]

An imaginative approach aimed at increasing income is a bank's study of quality of investment advice, i.e., a form of vendor quality. The bank in question puts its securities brokers into competition through management of "paper portfolios." The participating competitors provide the bank with their investment judgments and the supporting reasons. The bank rewards the superior competitors with higher shares of the securities brokerage purchased by the bank.[22]

---

[18] Ackoff, R. L., The Meaning of Strategic Planning, *McKinsey Quarterly Summary,* vol. 3, No. 1, p. 54, 1966.

[19] See, for example, Benjamin, J. F., and R. J. Frock, The Application of Route Engineering Principles in the Beer Wholesaling Industry, *Beer Wholesaler,* April–June 1969, pp. 20–25. See also Frock, R. J., and J. E. Morehouse, Computer Shows How to Reduce Delivery Costs, *Linen Supply News,* vol. 52, No., 5, pp. 38–40.

A similar problem is that of programming bus transportation for school children. See *Data Processor XII,* December 1969, pp. 5:20–21. (The same article discusses delivery of bakery ingredients to customers in an industrial area.)

[20] See, for a case example, Reed, *op. cit.*

[21] An example of such penalty provisions in service to consumers is the breakfast shop which offers to provide breakfast free if the service takes longer than 10 minutes.

[22] Firms Eager to Play the Big Money Game For Chase Manhattan, *The Wall Street Journal,* Mar. 31, 1971, p. 15.

MOTIVATION FOR QUALITY

To a considerable degree, the approaches to motivation discussed in Section 18 are applicable to the service industries. There is the same need for observing the principles and implications of self-control, controllability, subspecies of error, etc.

In the service industries the problems of quality motivation for nonsupervisory employees differ in some ways from those found in manufacturing industries:

Service employees have extensive direct contact with consumers, and can thereby directly affect the company's customer relations.

This same direct contact gives many service employees a prompt, useful feedback of the effect of their actions on fitness for use. This direct feedback is in sharp contrast to the "meaningless" features of many factory jobs.

The fact that service employees do have extensive contacts with customers requires that the company develop the means of appraising the quality of this contact through sampling observation, customer feedback, etc. Sometimes, as in the Hospital Medication case (see below) it is quite difficult to establish such appraisals.

Despite the manpower problems inherent in a labor-intensive and (often) low-wage industry, service companies have evolved ways of establishing successful motivational programs. Some of these are highly formalized, being based on a comprehensive system of data feedback. (See the North American Van Lines case, below.) At the other extreme are the rather informal systems of employee rating, employee of the month award, etc.

COMMONALITY IN SERVICE INDUSTRIES

To discuss this commonality, it is useful first to look sideways at the parallel problem of commonality in manufacturing industries. Sections 29 through 46 of this Handbook discuss the quality problems of specific manufacturing industries. These differ remarkably in products, processes, materials, and underlying technology. Despite such diversity, the manufacturing industries have evolved an extensive commonality in their approach to the quality function. The "management" Sections of this Handbook (Sections 2 to 21) make this commonality abundantly clear.

(A major reason for this evolution of commonality has been the traditional gregariousness of manufacturing executives, plus their willingness to participate in expositions, conferences, seminars, etc., and to contribute papers, discussions, and exchanges of experience and ideas.)

This evolution of commonality has been of great assistance to all manufacturing industries. As the universals have become identified, and as the case histories of application have been published, it has become possible to:

1. Understand the nature of the quality function as something universal, and distinct from the specialized technology of each industry.

2. Structure seminars and training programs related to these universals.

3. Develop quality specialists and quality managers who can make themselves effective in any manufacturing situation.

Individual service industries also hold expositions, conferences, etc., in which their executives and specialists participate. However, these are insular in nature, being oriented to the problems of that industry and not to the universal problems of the quality function. In contrast, conferences to deal with quality problems which are common to all service industries are a rarity. As a result, while all service industries are keenly aware of the need for quality, and have evolved programs specially suited to their respective needs, these programs are likewise insular, i.e., every industry on its own. There has been no significant movement to identify what are the common problems of service industry quality, and what are the common solutions.

One of the professional society groups[23] has chosen as its mission ". . . the application of scientific methods for the quality of operations other than those directly connected with the manufacturing phases of operation." (An interpretation of this mission specifically includes the service industries.)[24] The professional base for this group has consisted of "management science" techniques such as statistical quality control, operations research, and probability sampling.

Summary on Commonality   The manufacturing industries have based their commonality on:

1. Universal elements of the managerial process, i.e., policies, objectives, plans, organization, manning, motivation, etc.   These universals apply fully to the service industries.

2. Universal parameters of quality (fitness for use).   These have extensive application to service industries as well.   However, the service industries make use of additional, important parameters, and these need to be studied in depth to evolve the universals which underlie them.

3. Universal functional activities through which fitness for use is achieved: product development, manufacturing planning, vendor relations, process control, test, sale, use, field maintenance, feedback, etc. (This is merely a restatement of the "Spiral," Figure 2-2.)   These activities are common to service industries as well, but with important differences in emphasis.

4. Universal skills, tools, and techniques.   These have extensive application to the service industries, but it is likely that there will need to be some new inventions to meet the special problems of the service industries.

In the judgment of the authors, the service industries would be well advised to take steps to evolve the universals and commonalities which underly quality of service.   These steps would parallel those taken in the manufacturing industries:

Conferences, seminars, and training courses on service quality, with attendance by managers and specialists from a variety of service industries.[25]

A professional society which structures its activities around service industry quality.

Journals, books, and other publications to exchange experiences and expound principles.

In all likelihood, all these activities can be set up under the programs of existing institutions, without the need for creating new ones.

CONTROL OF HOSPITAL MEDICATION ERRORS

During the last several centuries, the health industry has been spectacularly successful in increasing the human life span.   Maintaining the benefits of this breakthrough has required setting up numerous quality controls on a wide variety of activities, products, and systems, all relating to human health.   One of these systems is that of providing medication[26] to sick people.

[23] The Administrative Applications Division of the American Society for Quality Control.
[24] *ASQC Administrative Applications Division Newsletter*, October 1970, p. 5.
[25] When attendance is restricted to one industry, inhibitions arise since competitors are asked to learn from each other.   When attendance is from a variety of industries, these inhibitions are minimal.
[26] The terminology used here is that of the layman and is therefore not precise.   Medication may include remedies which are not "drugs" and which are obtainable from sources other than registered pharmacies.

Outside the hospital the procedure for medication is comparatively simple and direct:

The physician "prescribes" the medication by writing out a "prescription" in longhand and giving the prescription to the patient.

The patient takes the prescription to a pharmacist who "dispenses" the medication; i.e., he gives the patient the pills, capsules, etc., called for by the prescription. He also labels the container with a reference number and with the physician's instructions as to dose size and frequency.

The patient "administers" the medication himself and so bears the responsibility for following the medication program.

This procedure involves minimal record keeping. The original longhand prescription is filed by the pharmacist. He assigns a serial number and he also imprints this serial number on the label attached to the container given to the patient. If the pharmacist encounters problems in interpreting the prescription (e.g., legibility, abbreviations, units of measure), he contacts the physician direct.

The Hospital Procedure   In the hospital, the medication procedure becomes far more complex, partly because of sheer size and partly because of the intervention of the nurse. The traditional procedure has involved the following basic steps:

The physician writes out an order for a medication program (along with other orders) for the patient.

The nurse transcribes this order onto a form, a copy of which goes to the pharmacist.

The pharmacist dispenses the drugs, which are then delivered to the nurse.

The nurse administers the medication to the patient.

In a large hospital the resulting procedural network becomes formidable. The "pharmacist" becomes a central pharmacy with numerous branches. The "nurse" becomes numerous people in many departments, requiring nursing supervisors, floor clerks, etc. The "drug" is not merely a simple pill which a patient can take unaided; the drug now involves specialized technique for dilutions, measurement, injection, etc. The need to keep adequate histories and to fix responsibility creates added paper work. In due course the "system" reaches a state of size and complexity which itself becomes a part of the problem.

Attempts to change this procedure must take account of the vested interests of the "professional" groups involved. Each has jurisdictional rights which are rooted in tradition and are backed up by legislation. The physician may prescribe, dispense, and administer. The pharmacist may only dispense. The nurse may only administer.[27]

The Medication Error   The hospitals define a medication error as "a deviation from the physician's order." In quality control dialect, such an error is a "nonconformance," i.e., a failure to conform to specification.

It does not follow that in the absence of medication errors (as defined above) the medication will be fit for use. From the patient's viewpoint, an error is any state of affairs in which he is not cured, whether the medication does or does not conform to

[27] In the background are still other vested interests which can aid or resist procedural change:

The drug manufacturers, who develop, manufacture, and market the drugs which are the basis of so much modern therapy

The equipment and instrument makers who contribute extensively to placing diagnosis and remedy on a scientific basis

The numerous categories of laboratory specialists and technicians whose skills are vital to the use of the diagnostic and remedial tools

the physician's order. The patient's viewpoint broadens the concept of error to include "quality of design," i.e., the validity of the physician's order. This, in turn, depends on such factors as the adequacy of the diagnostic equipment, the competence of the physician, and the completeness of the research program behind the development of the prescribed drugs.

In the discussion which follows, the studies of "medication error" have been limited to studies of nonconformance, i.e., the hospital's definition. Obviously, the patient's definition is the most fundamental.

The Extent of Medication Errors   The annual number of medications ("dosages") administered to patients is fantastically high. Yet, until the 1960s, there existed only *mis*information on how many of these medications were failing to conform to the orders of the physician. The reasons behind this misinformation are informative in themselves:

1. Some medication errors are inadvertent; i.e., their existence is not known to the persons who made the error. Most of these errors then go undetected because the adverse effect falls on hospitalized sick people. The "alarm signal" created by the adverse effect cannot readily be recognized; it is drowned out by other, numerous alarms already present. The person most qualified to detect the new alarms is the physician, but he is seldom there.

2. Other errors are detected by the person committing them, but there is a reluctance to report this to the hospital authorities since historically the response of these authorities has often been one of criticism rather than one of analysis to look for ways of minimizing the error rate through foolproofing the system.

3. Even when errors are detected by persons other than those who committed them, the hospitals have traditionally been reluctant to put the incidents on record for fear of publicity or of lawsuits. (Thereafter, lacking such records, analysis for repetitive causes is effectively blocked.)

The foregoing (and other) forces had long combined to create a false sense of security as to medication errors. The actual studies made "showed" that these errors were rare occurrences.[28] Some practitioners were openly skeptical of these findings but lacked the data to make an adequate challenge.

A breakthrough came with the "disguised observation technique" developed by Kenneth N. Barker. This technique involves observation of hospital personnel and of the circumstances involved in medication in a way which could reconstruct (1) what should have happened and (2) what did happen. The first such study,[29] conducted at the University of Florida Teaching Hospital (in 1959), secured data on 572 doses administered by 9 nurses. It was found that one dose in every six involved some kind of error. This incidence was remarkably higher than that suggested by earlier studies purporting to be quantitative.

An elaboration of the disguised observation technique was the classic study by Barker, Kimbrough, and Heller.[30] (This will be referred to as the BKH study.) The BKH study was made at a non-University hospital to see whether such a service

[28] For example, A. Kruger (*Hospitals,* vol. II, p. 80, October 1937) identified only two medication errors in a 3,000-bed hospital over a period of 17 months.

[29] Barker, K., A Study of the Problem of Detecting Medication Errors in a Hospital, Master's Thesis, University of Florida, 1961. Abstracted (with W. McConnell) as How To Detect Medication Errors, *Modern Hospital,* vol. 99, pp. 95–105, July 1962, and in *American Journal of Hospital Pharmacy,* vol. 19, p. 360, August 1962.

[30] Barker, Kenneth N., Wilson W. Kimbrough, and William M. Heller, "A Study of Medication Errors in a Hospital." Original publication, University of Arkansas, 1966. Reprinted, University of Mississippi, 1968.

oriented hospital was as subject to error as a University hospital, with its strong orientation to teaching and research.

The BKH study confirmed the results of earlier disguised[31] observation studies. Of 9,789 "opportunities for error," a total of 1,461 actual errors were detected.[32] This is one error for every 6.7 opportunities. It also figures out to about one error per patient-day. Table 47-1 shows the error pattern in detail.

Causes of Medication Errors   The BKH study undertook also to analyze causes of the observed errors. To a surprising extent, the study found that procedural and technological problems dominated the error causes.

Dose Administered at Wrong Time.   Of the 808 errors, only 15 were categorized as "cause probably found." The real problem seemed to be one of "unrealistic tolerances loosely enforced."

TABLE 47-1   Medication Errors in a Hospital

Error type	No. of errors	Percent Of opportunities for errors	Percent Of all errors
Dose administered at wrong time. .	808	8.3	55
Wrong amount administered	253	2.6	17
Dose omitted	188	1.9	13
Extra dose	113	1.2	8
Unordered drug	88	0.9	6
Wrong dosage form.	11	0.1	1
Totals.	1,461	15.0	100

To elaborate, the hospital establishes standard schedules for administering drugs. For example, drugs to be given four times each day[33] may be scheduled for 9 A.M., 12 noon, 3 P.M., and 6 P.M. These published schedules, though uniform within one department, can vary from one department to another. However, the tolerances around these standard schedules are not clear. The BKH investigators established an arbitrary tolerance of 30 minutes, but found that the schedules were not being followed with any precision. In consequence, the investigators backed off and changed their concept of standard to one of timeliness based on the dose being "due at the time the nurse recorded (in the chart) that she had given it." However, the practice of the nurses (evidently with the sanction of the supervision) was to record the scheduled time rather than the actual time of administration.

There is evidence that the standardized schedule is regarded not as a firm specification, but rather as a target. It is obvious that some tolerance is needed around the scheduled time in any event, because of the sheer impossibility of the nurses' giving

[31] The "disguised" aspect of the observation lies in the fact that some subterfuge is used. The hospital personnel are given a plausible reason for the need for a team of observers during the period of study. However, the main reason is to study the error rate. For elaboration, see the BKH study, pp. 31–33, and pp. 291–298.

[32] "Opportunities for error" equals doses ordered plus doses ordered but not administered. An additional 868 doses were excluded from the study for the reason that the nurses under observation did not conduct the entire sequence of preparing and administering the dose; i.e., other nurses prepared the dose, or others (including the patient) administered the dose. Evidently many of these instances would be regarded as procedural errors; i.e., there are schools of thought which urge that a nurse should not administer a dose prepared by someone else and should not chart any dose she does not herself observe to have been administered.

[33] The medical abbreviation is "q.i.d.," from the Latin *quater in die.*

all the medications at precisely the time scheduled. However, the tolerance as evolved by the nurses and the supervision appears to be much wider than that regarded as reasonable by a set of investigators. For the same reason, many of the 808 "wrong time" errors listed by the investigators would probably not be regarded as a serious matter by the hospital staff.

Wrong Amount Administered. The BKH study found 253 instances of "wrong dose." By a wide margin, the "outstanding characteristic" behind the error was determined to be "Nurse mismeasured or miscalculated," 150 being categorized in this way. (Since about 25% of the errors lacked clues as to cause, these 150 probably account for about two-thirds of those wrong dose errors for which clues were available.)

However, a look at the details of the "mismeasured or miscalculated" soon makes clear that both calculation and measurement involve some technical obstacles. Only 15 errors of the 150 cases involved simple count of capsules or tablets; the rest required various manipulations, i.e., dilution, measurement, injection, etc.

Calculation consists of simple arithmetic, but this is complicated by multiple units of measure. Young physicians prescribe in metric units, but some older physicians retain the apothecary units, with obvious opportunities for error.[34] An official teaspoon is 5 milliliters. However, physicians commonly use the apothecary notation for one dram to prescribe one teaspoonful. The U.S. Pharmacopeia equates one dram with 3.7 milliliters, but this may be rounded off to 4.0 milliliters. Less frequent is the problem posed by the use of Fahrenheit and Centigrade scales for temperature.

Measurement also seems simple on the face of it, but on the nursing floor it is complicated by the variables inherent in the materials, tools, and measuring instruments used. In theory, the nurse has the last chance to avoid the error, or to make up, by human resourcefulness, for the deficiencies in the engineering of the system. (Some nurses do exactly that.) However, others are defeated by the problems of getting the right number of drops (again, how to measure a drop) into a wriggling patient's nose, or by liquids which are viscous or which foam, or by measuring 8 milliliters in a cup which has graduations only at 5 and 10 milliliters.

(It is interesting to contrast the precision of measurement in the hospital with that used in the drug manufacturing companies. Typical tolerances for active ingredient in tablets or capsules are plus and minus 10% on averages, with individual tablets limited to 85 to 115. Federal regulators have no hesitance in ordering mass recalls if these tolerances are exceeded. In addition, there are those who urge tightening of these tolerances to plus and minus 5%.)

Unordered Drug; Omission. The BKH study reported 188 omissions and 88 instances of unordered drug. In the former, the patient failed to receive an ordered drug. In the latter, the patient received a drug not ordered by the physician. Both these errors can and do occur in cases where "Nurse Selected and Used Wrong Drug," i.e., she omitted the right drug and administered an unordered drug. Of the 66 such cases, involving 91 errors, a majority (52 of the 91 errors) involved the phenomenon of similarity in names of drugs. An example (involving 9 cases) is a group of drugs all containing the name Darvon (the generic word is propoxyphene).

---

[34] Seemingly, no hospital has gone to the drastic step of refusing to accept prescriptions in apothecary terms. However, some have structured positive programs for complete conversion to metric measurement. See Bellafiore, Ignatius J., Using Two Measuring Systems Together Adds Another Source of Error, *Hospitals,* vol. 40, No. 22, pp. 116–120, November 1966.

At the time of the BKH study the manufacturer had four forms on the market:

Name	*Contents*
Darvon	32 mg propoxyphene
Darvon 65	65 mg propoxyphene
Darvon Compound	32 mg propoxyphene in combination with aspirin, phenacetin, and caffein
Darvon Compound-65 . . .	65 mg propoxyphene in combination with aspirin, phenacetin, and caffein

In like manner there are other drugs involving variations on some basic name, e.g., Hystadyl and Hystadyl EC; Lextron and Lextron Ferrous; Dimetane Expectorant and Dimetane Expectorant DC. So long as such similarities prevail, the nurses have the responsibility of keeping them straight. However, the question may be asked— why should the industry endure a system of names which, on the record, makes confusion easy?

Extra Dose. There were 113 extra doses given in the BKH study. In 75 of these cases the investigators found evidence of the cause, and of these 53 resulted from resumption of medication after surgery in the absence of known orders. A major contributing factor was the widespread confusion owing to the simultaneous presence of:

Published hospital procedure relative to automatic stopping of medication for patients "going to surgery"

Vague definitions of what constitutes "surgery," i.e., is going to remove a cast in the category of surgery?

Physicians' "standing verbal orders" countermanding the hospitals' published procedures

Inconsistency in practice among hospital departments and from physician to physician

Controllability of Medication Errors The foregoing analysis makes clear that the hospital medication system has quite a distance to go if it is to put the nurse in a state of self-control.[35] None of the criteria for self-control is fully met, so that the system abounds in "management-controllability."

Knowledge of "Supposed to Do." The basic "specification" is the physician's order for medication, and the prime job of the nurse is to assist the physician by executing that order. She must interpret and (usually) copy the order despite problems of handwriting legibility, abbreviations, private shorthand systems, etc. (Of course, it all should be standardized, but it is not standardized.)

Moreover, the nurse receives orders from a number of other sources:

1. The hospital procedural manual includes some impersonal orders on medication, e.g., automatic stop orders for patients going to surgery, or after 72 hours.

2. Jurisdictional rules governing the interfaces with the other professions and skills assembled in the hospital.

3. Overriding legislation on some matters, e.g., handling of narcotics.

4. An extensive work load which includes activities not related to medication.

---

[35] To be in a state of self-control, the nurse (or anyone else) must have:
Knowledge of what she is supposed to do
Knowledge of what she is doing
Means to regulate what she is doing
See generally Section 2, under Self-Control. See also Section 11, under Concept of Operator Self-Control.

These activities have standards of their own, and compete for the time and attention of the nurse.

5. The special cultural pattern of each hospital, which, as a continuing human community, evolves its own regulations, habits, dialect, etc. These cultural patterns are unique to each hospital so that a nurse moving from one hospital to another requires time to assimilate the local rules and dialect.

These multiple sources of orders converging on the nurse are obvious breeding grounds for "error."

Knowledge of "Is Doing." The nurse has a good deal of this knowledge through direct observation, supplemented by some instrumentation.[36] However, as compared with the factory operator, the nurse gets only limited "feedback" from the patient to whom she administers the medication. This limitation is inherent in the complex biological reactions which abound in the hospital.

Ability to "Regulate." To meet this criterion requires that the nurse be able to take some remedial action in the event that what she is doing fails to comply with what she is supposed to be doing.

The nurse has access to the physician or to a supervisor to secure answers to conflicts in orders, to get action on inadequate instruments, etc. In practice, the nurse does make good use of these sources of assistance and reference. But there are also numerous situations in which the work loads, the congestion, the emergencies, the oral orders, and the need for decisiveness in times of stress may force the nurse to act promptly because there seems to be no time to investigate, or no one to consult.

Reduction of Medication Error Rate   The incidence of hospital medication errors is simply shocking. In the experience of the authors, no other industry so critical to human life, and under the supervision of professionals, exhibits so high an error rate.[37] Only the error rate of outpatients is worse (and it is much worse).[38]

Successful reduction of this error rate has involved programs which require contributions from all the disciplines present in the hospital, including administration.

The Team Approach. All the comprehensive studies of medication error have made clear that the root causes of most errors go beyond the simplistic concepts of blaming this or that department. In consequence, resort is had to an interdepartmental study. To this end, a team is organized, consisting of key people from the cognizant hospital departments, with perhaps a respected outsider or two. This team identifies all activities involved in the medication procedure, and structures a flow diagram to aid all members in understanding the overall procedure. As the team broadens its understanding, it identifies "trouble spots," and these become the focal points for joint effort at improvement.[39, 40]

Quantifying the Error Rates. This fundamental step not only establishes the

---

[36] As noted in Causes of Medication Errors, above, there remains a residue of unsolved problems in measurement.

[37] All this coexists with a concept of studying thoroughly, by autopsy and by "peer review" the cases in which human beings die, or are threatened by contagion. Some of these investigations are carried out with an astonishing degree of persistence and resourcefulness. See, for example, Roueche, Berton, The Annals of Medicine; The Santa Claus Culture, *The New Yorker,* Sept, 4, 1971, pp. 66–81.

[38] Latiolais, Clifton J., and Charles C. Berry, Misuse of Prescription Medications by Outpatients, *Drug Intelligence and Clinical Pharmacy,* October 1969, pp. 270–277.

[39] For an excellent discussion, see Conley, Dean, A Management Team Approach to Hospital Systems Analysis, *Hospital Administration,* vol. 15, No. 1, pp. 1–21, Winter 1969–1970.

[40] See also "Hospital Medication Systems Study Guide," American College of Hospital Administrators, 840 N. Lake Shore Drive, Chicago, Ill., 1969.

overall frequency of error; it also identifies the main components of the error rate, i.e., the vital few types of errors which result in the bulk of the overall problem. Lacking knowledge of what are these vital few types of error, the remedial steps are like blind therapy—a remedy is applied without knowledge of the precise nature of the disease.

The methodology exemplified in the BKH study is a proved way of quantifying the error rates.

A similar approach was adopted by a British study team.[41] They also quantified the prevailing error rates and the main contributing components. (the overall error rate was comparable with that found in the BKH study.)

Remedying the Major Causes of Error. As the team identifies the vital few causes of error, it also evolves potential solutions. These can then be tested out to see whether the error rate actually goes down.

The British team structured several experiments to test out various potential improvements. (For example, in one experiment, physicians were asked to prescribe in metric units, using only official or approved names, writing in block capitals and abandoning most abbreviations, Latin, and ambiguous direction.) Some drastic reductions in error rate were observed, e.g., 15.3% down to 4.2%.[42]

To an increasing extent, the teams can find assistance from the results of studies reported in the literature.[43] For example, the nurse's transcription of the physician's order is a breeding ground for errors, and there is a broad school of thought which proposes to abolish this transcription. A related school of thought proposes to restore the direct linkage between physician and pharmacist on the ground that the pharmacist is professionally qualified to interpret the physician's order, whereas the nurses, aides, clerks, and other paramedical personnel assigned to transcription lack this qualification, in varying degrees. Practitioners have found ways to meet both these needs by providing the pharmacist with a copy of the prescription in the physician's own handwriting.[44]

Restructuring the Hospitals' Internal Procedures. This restructuring is needed to hold the gains resulting from the team efforts and to guard against sporadic errors. It is essential that this restructuring likewise be done by a team rather than leaving it for "each department on its own," because of the high degree of mutual interdependence.

Some of this restructuring consists of clarifying some long-standing ambiguities and tightening up some loose practices.[45] Mainly, however, the restructuring relates to assuring that the new practices designed to minimize the major causes of error are actually made effective and that they will remain in effect.

A mistake to be avoided is that of restructuring the procedure in the absence of quantified knowledge of what are the main error types. Lacking this knowledge,

[41] Hill, Peter A., and Hazel M. Wigmore, Measurement and Control of Drug Administration Incidents, *The Lancet,* Mar. 25, 1967, pp. 671–674.

[42] Hill and Wigmore, *op. cit.*

[43] See, for example, Barker, Kenneth N., The Effects of an Experimental Medication System on Medication Errors and Costs, *American Journal of Hospital Pharmacy,* June 1969, pp. 324–333 (Part One, Introduction and Error Study); also July 1969, pp. 388–397 (Part Two, The Cost Study).

See also Price, Elmina M., A Nurse Looks at Hospital Drug Distribution Systems, *American Journal of Hospital Pharmacy,* March 1967, pp. 104–111.

[44] See, for example, Dimmit, Deanna M., and Robert L. Lantos, Development of a Revised Manual Medication System in a Community Hospital, *American Journal of Hospital Pharmacy,* November 1967, pp. 617–624.

[45] Eckel, Fred M., Ten Traps in Drug Systems Cause Most Medication Errors, *Modern Hospital,* November 1968, pp. 104, 106, 108.

any revision of procedures may benefit only the minor causes of error, and may actually "lock in" some of the major causes.

Broad "Systems Revision." Remedies for causes are in some cases beyond the ability of the hospital "industry." In such cases the hospital must enlist the aid of the support industries which collaborate in the overall objective of health.

In many instances, it is these support industries which have taken the initiative (e.g., development of new drugs, instruments, equipment). An example closely related to medication error is the development of the "unit-dose" concept. Under this concept, drugs are identified at the factory in a way which preserves the identity to the bedside; i.e., the drug dosages are individually packaged, and labeled as to name, dosage, and expiration date. Despite the higher price of the unit-dose product, the concern over medication errors may turn out to be decisive.[46]

There are other instances in which the need to reduce hospital medication errors is in conflict with vested interests of support industries or disciplines. Older physicians cling to their habitual use of antiquated units of measure and terminology. Drug manufacturers may well resist eliminating "similar name" drugs (some of these have their origin in the marketing technique of deliberately using similar names to secure an association with an already accepted product).

In such cases of cultural or economic resistance, the hospital may choose to be circumspect, but it has a good deal of economic power it can bring to bear, and this power is on the increase.

TELEPHONE SERVICE QUALITY CONTROL

The bulk of telephone service in the United States is provided by American Telephone and Telegraph Company (AT&T), popularly known as the Bell System. This is a highly integrated service organization comprising not only the various regional operating telephone companes (e.g., Southern Bell) but also a research and development arm (Bell Telephone Laboratories), a manufacturing arm (Western Electric Company), and still other support organizations, notably the Long Lines Department, which operates the long-distance networks.

On matters of telephone service, the Bell System's direct contact with its customers is through the operating telephone companies. The consuming public makes up the great majority of these customers. However, a significant number of customers are organizations of various sorts, some very large, and collectively of great economic and political significance.

The telephone companies have for many years conducted formal programs for control of service quality. These programs extend to all areas of operation which directly contact the customer, and to the supporting services[47] as well.

Direct contact with the customers is maintained by three departments:

Traffic, which manages the networks through which telephone calls are completed

Commercial, which markets the company's services and receives service complaints

Controller, which bills customers and makes collections

---

[46] Barker, Kenneth N., Unit-Dose Injectables and the Hospital Medication Error Problem, *Bulletin, Parenteral Drug Association,* September–October 1966, pp. 157–165. See also "Unit Dose Distribution Systems," American Society of Hospital Pharmacists, Washington, D.C., 1972, for a collection of 74 papers plus 75 abstracts on the subject.

[47] An example of a support department is Plant, which maintains the physical facilities.

Control Subjects and Units of Measure   The telephone companies define "service" in terms of several control subjects:

1. *Accessibility*, i.e., the extent to which the company establishes prompt communication with the customer once he has signaled that he wants attention.   Examples would be:

Nature of Signal	Communication Is Established When
Customer removes instrument from cradle	The dial tone sounds
Customer dials "O"	The telephone company operator replies
Customer dials 611 (in New York City)	The repair office replies

The basic measure of accessibility is in the quantitative form:

X percent of responses in Y seconds

Measurement is made by sampling of operations.   Some of this is done by automated devices, triggered by customers' signals.   Where human responses are involved, random samplings of other sorts are conducted.

2. *Conformance to order*, i.e., the extent to which the customer's needs are met. Once communication has been established, the customer's order may take many forms.   He may:

Dial the number of another subscriber to whom he wishes to be connected.

Request a change in form of service, e.g., added lines, change of address.

Request assistance, e.g., setting up a conference call.

The unit of measure for conformance to order is partly quantitative and partly qualitative.   Percent of correct responses to the order can often be quantified, but interpretation, discussion, courtesy, etc., must be rated qualitatively.

3. *Customer Complaints.*   This includes all forms of negative customer reaction, e.g., wrong billing, failures of apparatus, improper directory listing.   These are quantified and structured into indexes.   In addition, samplings are used to secure added information on customer dissatisfaction with service.

All control subjects are broken down into elements which can be evaluated in natural units of measure.   For example, billing service is evaluated as in Table 47-2.

Actual measurement is done by the various operating telephone companies. However, the parent AT&T company employs staff specialists who aid in setting up systems of measurement, in analyzing summaries, in interpreting results, and in establishing standards.

Standards   Standards of service are largely historical; i.e., current performance is compared with past performance.   However, there does exist a considerable array

TABLE 47-2   Evaluation of Telephone Billing Service

	Median performance	Weight in composite index, %
Toll errors per 1,000 calls billed.................	2.3	45
Other errors per 1,000 bills	1.2	25
Percent of monthly bills not issued in 6 workdays	8.5	15
Percent collect charges not forwarded to billing office in 5 days...............................	1.5	5
Percent collect charges received too late to include on next bill	5.5	5
Other delayed charges per 1,000 calls*	2.8	5

* Hartman, W.C., Bell System Performance Measurements, *ASQC Annual Technical Conference Transactions,* 1965, pp. 626–628.

of "market" data on service performance because there are numerous telephone exchanges, commercial offices, and billing offices. Publication of the results attained by all these organizations makes clear where lies the central tendency, i.e., "the market." This same publication acts to stimulate lagging performances, while at the same time serving as a stabilizer to discourage uneconomical levels of performance.

Executive Reports While the basic measurements are made mainly in natural units, the executive reports include use of indexes, seriousness classification, and ratings. For example, one widely used method converts natural units into ratings through the following sequence of steps:

1. The frequency distribution of performances is calculated in natural units, e.g., errors per 1,000 calls billed.
2. The median performance is arbitrarily assigned a score of 97.
3. Any performance at 2.5 percentiles or better is assigned a score of 100.
4. Any performance at 97.5 percentiles or worse is assigned a score of 90.
5. These scores are then converted into ratings under the following standardized interpretations:

100–99   Excellent (or superexcellent)—may be at an uneconomical level
98–96   Fully satisfactory—within the economical performance range
95–90   Fair to mediocre—requires attention
Below 90   Definitely unsatisfactory[48]

Conversion of natural units to ratings makes it possible to prepare weighted ratings for all organization levels: exchanges, districts, regions, telephone companies, and Bell System. Table 47-3 shows, for a number of principal cities, the service ratings during January 1970[49] for:

Switching (mainly delays in getting dial tone)
Installation (mainly delays in filling customer orders for new or changed service)
Maintenance (mainly customer reports of troubles)

RESTAURANT QUALITY CONTROL

The restaurant is widely regarded as selling a "service" despite the fact that it delivers a "product" to the customer. The product is part of a broader service concept which usually provides the client with a range of choice of meals, and space in which to eat his chosen meal in comfort. The restaurant relieves him of the work of preparation and cleanup. Beyond these fundamentals, the restaurant may provide decor, relaxation, entertainment, a scenic view, and still other features which vary greatly from one establishment to another.

Restaurants compete not only with each other but also with alternative sources of food service: clients' homes, delicatessen shops, vending machines, etc. A major element of this competition is "quality." The significance of quality in this competition is evident in some ratings of restaurant quality. In some countries an independent judge of restaurant quality has attained a substantial following (e.g., the Guide Michelin or Duncan Hines). In such cases, changes in the ratings have been known to make significant changes in the fortunes of the restaurant involved.

---

[48] Hartman, W. C., Bell System Performance Measurements, *ASQC Annual Technical Conference Transactions,* 1965, pp. 626–628.

[49] At the time, the New York Telephone Company was struggling to regain its historically high levels of performance following a serious decline presumably due to underestimating the growth in demand. For added discussion, see A New Voice at New York Telephone, *Business Week,* Sept. 5, 1970, pp. 60–64.

TABLE 47-3   Ratings of Telephone Service, January 1970*

City	Ratings for		
	Switching	Installation	Maintenance
Boston	U	G	G
Chicago.	F	F	G
Cleveland	F	G	G
Dallas	G	G	G
Detroit	G	G	G
Los Angeles.	G	G	G
Miami.	F	G	P
New York City	P	P	P
Philadelphia	U	G	G
Pittsburgh	U	F	G
San Francisco	G	G	G
St. Louis	G	G	G
Washington, D.C.. . .	U	G	G
Bell System	F	G	G

G = Good/excellent
F = Fair
U = Unsatisfactory
P = Poor

*Derived from *Fortune*, May 1970, p. 266. Original data supplied by the Bell System to the Federal Communication Commission.

In small restaurants the control of quality is accomplished through the personal supervision of the proprietor, who is usually the chef as well. As the restaurant grows into a multiple unit organization located in multiple cities, the need arises to structure a formal system of controls. The system which is discussed below is that evolved by a large chain of restaurants operating in all parts of the United States.

The Company Howard Johnson Company is engaged primarily in serving the motoring public. There are over 800 Howard Johnson restaurants.[50] Somewhat over half of these are owned by the company, the rest being owned by franchisees. (In addition, some franchised locations are operated by Howard Johnson Company under a management contract.)

The restaurants, under the command of an operations vice-president, are organized into six geographic Regions which subdivide further into Districts. The Districts, in turn, subdivide into Areas, each of which consists of a number of restaurants. Each restaurant manager has full command of the personnel stationed at that restaurant. The chain of command then continues on to Area office, District office, Division office, and Operations office.

Manning these restaurants is a severe problem which is virtually industry-wide. In the United States there are relatively few restaurants in which the chef or manager can attain the social status or economic opportunity accorded to his counterpart in a number of European and other countries. The resulting modest career opportunities, coupled with traditional industry pay scales and working conditions, make it difficult to recruit a high-grade, stable work force. The high turnover rate nullifies the training already invested. With each new recruit the same old mistakes

[50] As of early 1970s. There were also over 400 Howard Johnson Motor Lodges, which are not discussed here.

can be repeated, and the turnover makes this go on and on. All this has had a profound effect on the approach to quality, as will be seen.[51]

The Process   The menus of the restaurants offer their clients a choice from about 900 different items of food. Historically, restaurant practice had been to process all food on the restaurant premises. The company's experience has been that this traditional approach results in too much variability in quality, largely because of the manpower problems. In consequence, the company has transferred most of the processing to four large factories created specially for the purpose of supplying the restaurants with processed or semiprocessed food. These plants process about 90% of the food used, and ship it (usually in frozen form) to the restaurants. The exceptions are such items as fresh vegetables and fruit, which the restaurants purchase locally.

The main reason for this drastic departure from industry tradition has been to minimize the quality problems. It has been found easier to control food processing quality in several large centralized plants than in hundreds of widely dispersed restaurants.

The Quality Control Plan   The company's approach is highly formalized, using organization and procedural methods quite similar to those employed by manufacturing companies.

Specifications.   Through extensive collaboration, the line operations people and the quality control staff[52] have worked up, for each food item, a complete specification setting out:

1. Product formulation, i.e., what types and quantities of materials are to be used as ingredients.

2. Processing instructions, both for mass reconstitution of factory processed foods and for preparation of individual servings. These instructions, in uniform format, cover the various operations performed at the restaurant (defrost, slice, fill, stir, add, etc.), along with the specified sizes of portions, temperatures, time cycles, protection criteria, etc.

All these specifications are collected, along with some related material, into a Manual of Procedure which is the company's fundamental instruction on restaurant food preparation.

Organization for Control.   At each restaurant the supervision needed to achieve day-to-day quality is done by the restaurant manager as part of his command responsibility. This direct supervision is supplemented by some staff controls as well:

1. Each Area has a staff Service Supervisor and a staff Food Supervisor. These staff supervisors exercise a form of surveillance over the restaurants in their Area, each with respect to his specialty. These staff specialists report to the Area manager.

2. At company headquarters there is a corporate quality control staff which is responsible to the Vice President and Executive Chef.[53] Most of the members of this staff carry the title of Supervising Chef. Each of these Supervising Chefs is

---

[51] An interesting contrast is seen in a study made by a QC Circle team in another culture. See Kojima, Yukie, How We Improved Our Services to Offer Refreshments and Lunches for Visitors to Our Company, *Reports of Statistical Application Research,* vol. 17, No. 2, pp. 31–35. 1970. This paper, originally published (in Japanese) in *Gemba To QC,* vol. 65, pp. 27–31, 1969, was awarded the 1969 Nihon Keizai Shimbun prize for Quality Control Literature.

[52] The company does not use this terminology; it has a special dialect of its own. See below.

[53] The company does not use the term corporate quality control staff. However, the duties have much in common with those carried out in manufacturing companies by corporate staff departments called Quality Assurance, Quality Control, etc. See Section 7, under The Corporate Quality Manager; also Section 21, under Quality Assurance.

assigned to carry out surveillance, on food matters, of the restaurants in a specific Division. These Supervising Chefs travel extensively, visting each assigned restaurant several times each year. The report of the Supervising Chef covers 47 different checkpoints relating to all aspects of food service: purchased materials, storage conditions, food preparation, kitchen stations, cooking, equipment, housekeeping.

Franchised Restaurants. These are subject to the same standards and surveillance as are the owned restaurants. The Supervising Chef visits franchised restaurants as well as owned restaurants, and conducts a review of the same subjects.

Franchised restaurants cannot be compelled to purchase their processed food solely from Howard Johnson. In consequence, the Supervising Chef extends his review to include the processed foods purchased by the franchisees.

The company's experience has been that while some of the franchisees are very competent, the range of variation in quality is greater among franchisees than among owned restaurants. As a result, the company faces special problems of enforcement in its dealings with some of the franchisees. [54]

Customer Feedback   The company makes extensive use of customer comment cards as a source of customer feedback. These cards are set out at the restaurant tables, and customers are invited to fill them in. The cards [55] provide for customer rating of "excellent," "satisfactory," or "unsatisfactory" on several aspects of restaurant service:

Quality
Service (Promptness)
Restaurant Cleanliness
Rest Room Cleanliness

Those comment cards which are executed by customers go to company headquarters, where they are processed by computer. The resulting executive report summarizes the data for the company and by the various subordinate organization units. Attention is concentrated on the percent "unsatisfactory" ratings for quality and promptness, for current month and year to date. These summaries are regarded by the company managers as an important measure of restaurant performance.

Other Companies   The basic concept of the Howard Johnson chain of restaurants is one of establishing company-wide standards for quality and then enforcing these standards through the line supervision plus surveillance from upper echelons, including company headquarters. This is also the basic concept followed by most chains of restaurants. [56] In like manner, the concept of transferring the bulk of food processing from many restaurants to a few central plants (in which Howard Johnson pioneered) is increasingly being adopted by other chains, although there are differences in the technology employed. [57,58]

[54] One consequence has been a long-range program to acquire more of the franchised restaurants. Whereas in 1960, about 80% of the restaurants were franchised, in 1970 only about 40% of the restaurants were franchised.

[55] See also Figures 47-1 and 47-2.

[56] See, for a related example, Whitworth, William, Profiles: Kentucky-Fried, *The New Yorker,* Feb. 14, 1970, pp. 40–52.

[57] *Business Week,* Oct. 30, 1971, p. 55.

[58] For an example of an elaboratedly engineered process of food preparation at the restaurant level (actually, at each member of a chain of "fast food" hamburger stands) see Levitt, Theodore, Production-Line Approach to Service, *Harvard Business Review,* September–October 1972, pp. 41–52.

TRANSPORTATION SERVICE QUALITY

Transportation is a huge service industry involving physical transport of people and goods by railroads, airlines, ocean shipping, motor vehicles, pipelines, and still other forms. This Section confines itself to a sampling of cases involving motor vehicle and air transport.

North American Van Lines (NA)   This company engages in transporting specialized goods, on an international scale. A substantial portion of its operations are those of a motor carrier within the United States. In this capacity the company transports household goods, residential, institutional, and commercial furniture, fixtures and related items, plus certain other sophisticated products such as computers, exhibits, and displays. Customers include the government, individual householders, and commercial companies.

North American's domestic service is provided through a system composed of company terminals, company drivers, and contract truckmen as well as agency locations and agents' drivers and employees. Only about 10% of the 10,000 or more persons in the system are direct employees of North American. The remainder are (1) independent businessmen who perform services under agency or contract truckmen agreements and (2) employees of these independent businessmen.

In such a widespread system, a continuing program to measure, control, and stimulate quality of performance is imperative. In part, the need arises from the regulated nature of the business. Almost every aspect of North American's service is subject to the jurisdiction of the Interstate Commerce Commission or other federal and state agencies. These regulations are highly formalized, and require a systematic approach to assure compliance.

Of equal significance is the economic motivation. Moving of household goods is a highly personalized service, and the moving industry is extremely competitive in terms of number of carriers. Only through superior service can one carrier stand out from the rest. An effective program to measure and promote quality of service is one of the management tools available for attaining such superior service.

In response to this need, North American has developed a program of quality measurement which it applies to all segments of its system. Under this program, the performance of all agents, contract truckmen, and company drivers is measured on a continuing basis. As will be seen, this measured performance is the decisive element in the operation of a collateral program for quality motivation.

The program for agents includes measurement in the following elements of the overall performance:

1. *Full Value Protection Sales.* This is measured by the effectiveness of the agent in selling the customer protection (for cargo loss and damage) beyond that provided by minimum tariff liability. Such a sale maximizes customer satisfaction in the case of claims, since such payment may then cover the loss to the extent incurred.

2. *Accuracy of Estimate.* This is measured by the effectiveness of the agent in estimating what will be the charges for the move. Customer satisfaction is importantly affected by the extent to which the actual charges conform to the estimate.

3. *Packing Efficiency.* This is measured by the extent to which shipments packed by the agent are free from complaints or claims for damaged goods.

4. *Storage Efficiency.* This is measured by the extent to which shipments stored by the agent are free from complaints or claims.

5. *Hauling Efficiency.* This is measured by the extent to which the shipments

transported by the agents' drivers are free from complaints or claims. The freedom from traffic accidents or safety violations also enters this measurement, as does proper completion of manifests and other shipment paper work.

6. *Destination Agent Calls.* This is measured by the extent to which an agent makes personal calls on NA customers who move into his territory. These calls are considered important because they provide the company with good-will contacts and with opportunities to give assistance to customers in getting settled.

7. *Paper work.* This is measured by the accuracy of the agent's completion of shipment bills of lading and other paper work according to Interstate Commerce Commission (ICC) requirements.

NA also measures the performance of the drivers in its independent contract truckmen fleets (household, new products, electronics) in the same manner as it does its agents' drivers. The same factors are included as in element 5, Hauling Efficiency, above.

The inputs available for measuring agency and contract truckmen performance include the following:

1. An information reporting system for collecting shipment-by-shipment data and then processing and summarizing these data into standardized reports. These reports are sent to agents and contract truckmen monthly along with details of deficiencies.

2. Feedback from (a) commercial organizations and military installations who engage NA to move the goods of transferred employees and service members, (b) those individuals who are moved, and (c) those persons who pay for their own moves.

3. The results of NA's surveillance of agencies. In addition to review of performance, this surveillance involves inspection of facilities and equipment, and appraisal of business methods. Some of the elements of this surveillance relate to quality control.

4. The results of surveillance of drivers by NA and by government bodies such as the ICC and Department of Transportation. This involves vehicle maintenance and safety factors, vehicle appearance, logs, and manifests.

Beyond measurement of performance, NA engages in programs to assist agents, contract truckmen, and employees in achieving results. A major element in these programs is the conduct of training and development through conferences, instruction manuals, training, films, etc.

Coupled with the measurement program, NA conducts annual motivational programs to stimulate high-quality performance and to secure suggestions for improvement. Provision is made for universal participation in these programs: agents, drivers, agency personnel, and NA personnel, both exempt and nonexempt.

In the operation of these motivational programs, "credits" are awarded for accepted suggestions and for superior performance in accordance with publicized standards and rules. The total of credits earned becomes the basis for awards of merchandise, trips, etc., some of considerable value. These programs recognize achievements in several different forms:

1. Measure of agency and driver performance, as discussed above.

2. Suggestions accepted. (The eligibility is universal.)

3. Ratings by customers. Customers are provided with forms to be used in rating the performance of packers, drivers, unpackers, and agents on an 11 point report. These ratings enter the achievement scores of the fleets and agents.

4. Ratings of NA area and home office personnel by agents, agency personnel, drivers, and fellow employees. These ratings enter the achievement scores of NA area and home office employees.

The results achieved have demonstrated the effectiveness of these programs.[59]

Postal Service   The U.S. Post Office is a huge organization engaged mainly in moving mail. (During 1969 it moved 84 billion, i.e., 84×10^9 pieces of mail, with a high degree of accuracy and with little damage to contents.) However, the service runs at a low level of productivity because of centuries of technological backwardness and other handicaps. These shortcomings are largely traceable to its history as a government department subject to political decisions which determined its income and which strongly influenced its expenditures.[60]

A major aspect of quality of postal service is the time required to deliver the mail. This "service time" consists of three major segments of time:

1. From point of drop (i.e., the point at which custody of the piece of mail passes from the sender to the Post Office) to cancellation

2. From cancellation to the "exit point," i.e., carrier, rental boxes, general delivery stations, etc.

3. From exit point to the patron

The time to deliver mail is defined as segment 2, specifically the difference in calendar days between the date of postmark and the date the sample is taken at the exit point.

The formal approach for measuring the time to deliver mail is through sampling of "live" mail at the exit points. This sampling is also used to secure other data, i.e., volume of mail, distances traveled, etc., for various categories of mail and services. Collectively, the measurement system and reports constitute the National Service Index of the Post Office.

Figure 47-3 shows one of the charts from the report.[61]

United Parcel Service (UPS)   This is a surface transportation company engaged in the delivery of parcels which have a maximum weight of 50 pounds and a combined length and girth not exceeding 108 inches. Its customers consist largely of manufacturers, wholesalers, distributors, and other commercial shippers. The company delivers some 2 million packages each business day and has as its main competitor the U.S. Postal Service's parcel post system. It is owned almost entirely by managers and supervisors active in operating the business, and by former employees, their estates and heirs, totaling some 4,500 stockholders. The company is regulated as a common carrier by the Interstate Commerce Commission, by various federal agencies such as the Department of Transportation, and by the regulatory bodies of the individual states.

In its operations the company uses some 20,000 drivers who pick up and deliver parcels, plus some 28,000 other people who sort packages, maintain vehicles, handle customer service duties, and provide all supporting services for the package delivery operations. Among these supporting services is a broad-based Industrial Engineering department which sets criteria, such as schedules, for efficient operation. Adherence to these criteria has a direct bearing on the ability of the company to

---

[59] "Since 1960, when the programs commenced, our quality measurements have indicated a steady improvement in quality of performance of about 10% per year." Quoted from Smith, Richard K., Quality Incentives at North American Van Lines, *ASQC Technical Conference Transactions,* pp. 910–913, 1966.

[60] A historic break with tradition followed the 1968 landmark study "Toward Postal Excellence. The Report of the President's Commission on Postal Organization" (available from the Superintendent of Documents, Washington, D.C.) A reform bill was subsequently enacted to give the postal service an autonomous status under a phased program.

[61] The Quality of Postal Service, National Service Index, Postal Quarter IV, Postal Fiscal Year 1969, Office of Statistical Programs and Standards, Bureau of Finance and Administration, U.S. Post Office.

control the quality of service provided to customers, but the whole system engaged in the movement of packages is expected to function efficiently as a matter of course.

Primary control of quality of service rests on the basic plan of operations. Under this plan:

A driver stops at a shipper's place of business each day to pick up packages. He appears automatically, without regard to the size of the shipper's business or the volume of the packages which can be expected from the account.

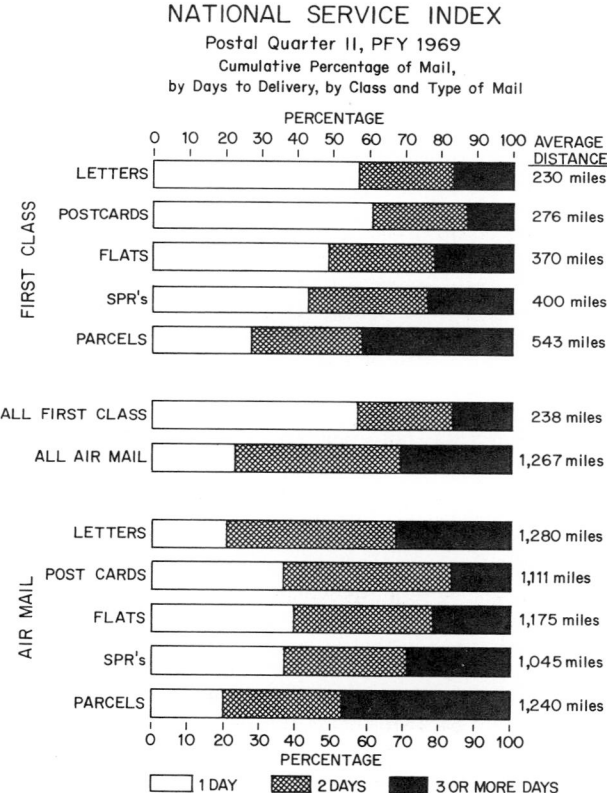

Fig. 47-3 Postal Service report.

Deliveries are made directly to the premises of the consignee whether he is located on the upper floor of an office building or at the end of a remote country lane.

Both delivery and pickup services are provided to all addresses within the area the company is authorized to serve.

If for any reason a delivery cannot be completed on first call, the driver makes a second, and if necessary, a third attempt at delivery. If the package still cannot be delivered, or if it is refused by the consignee, it is returned to the shipper without additional charge.

All packages sent via United Parcel Service are protected automatically for up to $100 against loss or damage without extra charge.

Specially designed records permit prompt answering of queries about the delivery of a package. The company maintains a teletype network to trace parcels, and any shipper may receive, upon request, proof that his package has been delivered. The proof is in the form of a signature which is obtained when the package is delivered.

United Parcel Service also provides an address search service to minimize delivery delays for incorrectly addressed parcels, and offers a C.O.D. service.

One of the basic methods of monitoring performance on these service features is the operating report. Every operating unit in the company fills out a daily report which includes columns for reporting on missed deliveries, missed pickup stops, missorted packages, and packages sent out a second or third day for delivery. These reports are reviewed daily by managers to identify patterns of service failure requiring correction.

A further control on quality is vested in the Customer Service department, which as a part of its responsibility, makes regular calls on customers to ferret out difficulties. These customer service people also conduct audits of customers' shipments to determine if packages are properly wrapped, if addresses are adequate, and if the shipping records submitted with the packages picked up coincide with the actual packages picked up. The audits are designed to spot trouble before it results in a service failure.

The Customer Service people also act as consultants when packaging problems arise which might cause loss of or damage to the customer's shipments. The company maintains package testing laboratories which will test a customer's proposed new package for compliance with National Safe Transit Standards to see if it is adequate for use in the UPS system. The Customer Service people enter into discussions with the customer about any matters which cause customer dissatisfaction so that quality of service is not impaired.

United Parcel Service also maintains a Delivery Information Department which is responsible for making prompt payment of claims and for providing customers with information about packages which they want traced. Control of quality of this phase of the service is maintained through daily reports in which the Delivery Information people tally the number and age of claims pending for settlement, and the number and age of tracing requests which have not been fulfilled. This report is presented to appropriate managers who oversee the quality of work in this area. The prevailing standards provide that all routine claims should be settled within 15 days.

A further technique used by the company to monitor and maintain quality is the insertion of data cards into packages being shipped. The consignee makes entries on the card, noting such things as the date the package was received, and returns the card to United Parcel Service, where it is assessed for quality of service. This technique is of value in determining the "dependability" of the service in terms of the time between pickup and delivery. The company has learned from its customers that this dependability is one of the most desirable elements of the service. The company does not guarantee that service between points A and B will take a given number of days, because storms or other external factors may disrupt the system, but the company considers any lapse from normal, consistent delivery time to be a service failure for which someone is held accountable.

Still another technique used to monitor service quality is a questionnaire which is given to national traffic managers of major companies to distribute at regional shipping locations. The questionnaire ostensibly comes from the traffic manager, not UPS, and asks for a frank assessment of UPS service. This approach reduces the risk that the local shipper will be biased by any feeling of friendship he has for the UPS driver who appears daily at his shipping dock. These questionnaires are examined by UPS for any service weaknesses which might be attributed to some segment of the operation.

The company also supplies shippers with training and reminder materials in an attempt to foster desirable shipping practices. It distributes a manual for use by shipping room personnel to brief them on how to keep records and perform other tasks required for shipment through the UPS system. It also distributes posters which contain packaging tips, which serve as reminders about package weight and size limits, and which urge care in the printing of addresses on labels.

Under the UPS system, every person in the organization is held accountable for that portion of the service job which he performs. Service is stressed constantly in meetings and through company publications so that everyone is kept constantly aware of the need to give the best possible service.

In addition, the company operates a profit-sharing plan which is linked to operating revenue. This plan is designed as a broad motivation to everyone in the company to adhere to and improve on standards of performance, including quality of service.

Airline Service Quality   The discussion which follows is included here mainly because of the availability of some data compilations on airline safety and on some other aspects of airline service quality as it affects directly the airline passenger. (Beyond this consumer aspect of airline service quality are some formidable quality problems involving complex technology and extreme demands for equipment reliability. These will not be discussed.)

Few forms of public safety are as closely regulated and analyzed as aviation safety. The cumulative results of years of this attention are evident in the trends of aviation fatalities. For scheduled air transport, the death rate per 100 million person-miles,[62] both domestic and international, has declined from a level of about 8.0 (during the decade of the 1930s) down to a level of about 0.2 during the last half of the 1960s.

More recently there have begun to appear published data compilations on non-safety aspects of quality as it affects consumers. What follows is an analysis of some elements of a Civil Aeronautics Board (CAB) report[63] on the performance of 22 United States airlines. The elements analyzed are:

Total complaints per 100,000 emplanements (Table 47-4)
Baggage complaints per 100,000 emplanements (Table 47-4)
Boardings denied because of oversales, in number of boardings per 1,000 emplanements (Table 47-5)
Percent of flights arriving on time (Table 47-6)

The CAB report makes clear that the data may not be fully comparable because of lack of standardization of criteria for defining what is a complaint, etc. (Evidently steps will be taken to standardize the meanings of these terms.) Despite this present limitation, the frequency distributions make evident the wide range of quality of service prevailing among the airlines. Except for the percentage of on-time arrivals, the differences between the best and the worst performances span an order of magnitude or more. The existence of such differences demonstrates also the potentialities inherent in the publication of performance data, for the benefit of both consumers and airlines.

---

[62] "Person" here includes passengers and crew.
[63] Consumer Complaint Survey Report, 1969, Civil Aeronautics Board, Washington, D.C. The report covers the fiscal year ending June 30, 1969, and compares the results with those of the calendar year 1966, which had been published in an earlier report.

TABLE 47-4   Airline Customer Complaints, Fiscal Year Ended June 30, 1969

Complaint rate per 100,000 emplanements	Number of airlines at this complaint rate	
	Total complaints	Baggage complaints
325 and over	4*	3†
300–324		
275–299		1
250–274	2	
225–249	2	
200–224	1	1
175–199	2	2
150–174	2	1
125–149	3	2
100–124	1	
75–99	2	2
50–74	2	2
25–49	1	4
0–24		3

*Values are 332, 462, 600, 779.
† Values are 403, 510, 579.

TABLE 47-5   Boardings Denied because of Oversales

Rate per 1,000 emplanements	Number of airlines at this rate
3.5–3.9	2
3.0–3.4	
2.5–2.9	3
2.0–2.4	4
1.5–1.9	5
1.0–1.4	1
0.5–0.9	7
0–0.4	

TABLE 47-6   Airline On-time Arrivals

Percentage of on-time arrivals	Number of airlines at this percentage
85–89	
80–84	2
75–79	4
70–74	3
65–69	5
60–64	4
55–59	
50–54	1
45–49	2
40–44	

All airlines maintain a formal system for recording and answering customer complaints. The trend has been to establish special departments (Customer Relations or similar name) to receive and process these complaints. (Letters acknowledging or answering customer complaints are usually signed by some high company official.)

Complaints deal with a wide variety of customer grievances, including such matters as discourtesy. However, about two-thirds of the complaints concern baggage lost or damaged. These baggage complaints are accompanied by claims, and the annual totals of these claims are formidable, averaging over a million dollars for each of the major airlines. Some airlines make provision to pay small claims then and there at the airport.

A further source of claims is "Boarding Denied." These are cases in which the space on the plane has been oversold, so that some passengers must be turned away despite the fact that they hold tickets for the flight. Under the rules of the Civil

Aeronautics Board, an airline which cannot get such passengers out promptly on another flight must offer them free transportation.

While some airlines have placed their emphasis on complaints which result in claims, the prevailing industry practice is to take all complaints seriously. Some airlines go further and make use of customer comment letters. These are placed in the seat pockets in front of the passengers, and they are invited to fill them in. The airlines which use these comment letters feel that the returns give them early warning of weaknesses in the service system.

The airlines are quite aware that there are multiple programs of action inherent in complaint investigation.[64] For the widely recurring complaints they establish committees which can attack the root causes as a project along the lines discussed in Section 16.

[64] See Section 15, under Processing of Complaints.

Quality Control and the National Culture

J. M. JURAN

INTRODUCTION

The goal of high quality is common to all countries. This common goal must compete with other national goals amid the massive national forces — political, economic, and social — which determine the national priorities. This Section examines these national forces and their effect on the problems of attaining quality.

Because of the complexity of the subject, the discussion is structured under several main headings involving the approach to quality in:

1. The capitalistic forms of national economy. These exhibit some important similarities, as discussed under Quality Control in Capitalistic Economies, below. In addition, these forms exhibit important differences as well. These differences are discussed under separate headings as follows:

   a. The United States of America, the largest capitalistic economy

   b. Japan, the second largest, and the one with the greatest growth rate

   c. Western European countries, which constitute most of the remainder of the highly industrialized capitalistic economies

   d. The "developing" countries, industrially speaking

2. The socialistic forms of national economy. (See Section 48A.)

In all types of national economy there are natural resources and limitations which influence the priority of goals. However, an even greater force is that of human leadership and determination. Historically, these human forces have been more significant than natural resources in determining whether goals are attained.

The words "capitalistic," "socialistic," and "developing" are simple labels for some very complex concepts. The broad definition of capitalism is private ownership of the means of production and distribution, as contrasted with state ownership under socialism. Yet all self-styled capitalistic countries include a degree of state ownership, e.g., in matters of health, education, transport, and communication. Similarly, the self-styled socialistic countries contain, in varying degrees, some private ownership of enterprises for production of goods and services. In like manner, countries which are "developing" in the industrial sense may be highly developed in terms of other aspects of national maturity, e.g., political or social. The reader is urged to keep in mind that the words "capitalistic," "socialistic," and "developing" are used in a relative sense and cannot be considered as absolutes.

The subject matter of this Section and of the companion Section 48A are of obvious interest and importance to those engaged (or contemplating engagement) in operations of an international nature. Such operations are becoming ever more extensive as trade barriers are progressively removed. However, removal of governmental barriers has little effect on cultural barriers. These remain as a continuing problem until the cultural patterns (and the reasons behind them) are understood, appreciated, and taken into account.

QUALITY CONTROL IN CAPITALISTIC ECONOMIES

All capitalistic economies exhibit some basic similarities which influence the importance of quality in relation to other goals in the economy.

Competition in Quality Capitalistic societies permit and even encourage competition among enterprises. One form of this competition is in quality. This competition in quality takes several different forms:

Creation of New Enterprises. A frequent reason for the birth of new enterprises is poor quality of goods or services. For example, a neighborhood has outgrown the capacity of the local food shop or restaurant, so that the clients must wait in long queues before they can receive service. In such cases, entrepreneurs will sense a market opportunity and will create a new enterprise which attracts clients by offering superior service.

The ease of creating new enterprises is a far greater force in quality improvement than is generally realized. All economies, whether capitalistic or socialistic, suffer poor quality during shortages of goods. Creation of new enterprises is one means of alleviating shortages, and thereby of eliminating an invariable cause of poor quality.

Product Improvement. A very common form of competition in quality is through improving products so that they have more appeal to the users and can therefore be sold successfully in the face of competition from existing products. These product improvements come mainly from internal product development carried on by existing companies. In addition, some product improvements are made by independents who either launch new enterprises or sell their ideas to existing companies.

New Products. These may be "products" or even new systems approaches, e.g., self-lubricating bearings to minimize user maintenance. The industrial giants of today include many members founded on new systems concepts. As with product improvements, the new products may originate through development from within or through acquisition from without.

While the capitalistic economies also include some limitations on competition, the general effect is one of great benefit to the user, as he has a range of choice available to him not only as among the competing domestic manufacturers, but usually as to foreign manufacturers as well.

Some aspects of competition are detrimental to quality. Attempts to secure momentary marketing advantages by unneeded perfectionism may force all manufacturers to follow, and reduce the income for all. Competition by emphasizing original price may actually increase the life cycle cost of the product. The mortality rate of companies unable to survive the competition may reduce the users' range of choice. In a number of important industries, the surviving companies consist of three or four very large manufacturers, resulting in an "oligopoly," i.e., competition by a few.

Direct Access to Marketplace Feedback   In the capitalistic economies, the income of the enterprise is determined by its ability to sell its products, whether directly to users or through an intermediate merchant chain. If poor quality results in excessive returns, claims, or inability to sell the product, the manufacturer stops production until he is able to remedy the poor quality.

This severe and direct impact of poor quality on the manufacturer's income has the useful by-product of forcing manufacturers to keep improving their market research and early warning signals, so as to be able to respond promptly in case of trouble.

Direct access to the marketplace is not merely a matter of receiving complaints and other information about bad quality, important though that is. Even more important is the access to the marketplace before products are launched and sales programs are prepared. In the capitalistic economies, the autonomous companies all make their own forecasts on how much they expect to sell. Their ability to thrive depends on how well they are able to realize their forecasts. The potential benefits and detriments force the companies to pay careful attention to the needs of the marketplace, which is the source of their income.

Standardization   All capitalistic countries make extensive use of the concept of product standardization. Some of this is done by the State for reasons of human health and safety, e.g., food, drugs, product safety. For such standards, compliance is mandatory. Other State standards, involving metrology and national interchangeability, while voluntary in theory, are mandatory through economic necessity. Still other standardization is done by professional societies, industry associations, independent standardization bodies, etc., on matters of technological definition, e.g., standards for tests or for materials.

A minority of the capitalistic countries make use of mandatory standards for control of quality of exported product, Japan being the outstanding example. More usually, there are no controls on quality of exports, or controls only on those few products which are symbolic of the country's reputation for excellence.

For a more extensive discussion, see Section 4, under Government Regulation of Quality; also Section 14, under Labeling.

Consumer Protection   The autonomy of the capitalist enterprises makes it possible for them to misrepresent their products, to sell poor quality products, and to fail to live up to their product warranties. While the extent of such bad practice is small in relation to the total economy, the amount of product involved is still substantial. The resulting consumer irritation breeds publicity, and this has been building up under the consumerism movement. (See Section 4, under Consumerism.)

All capitalistic countries maintain laws to help consumers. Some of these laws are of a criminal nature; i.e., if the products in a package fail to conform to the statements on the label, the State will take action against the manufacturer to force him to comply. Other laws are of a civil nature; i.e., if a consumer feels he has been given inadequate value, or has been damaged, he may resort to the courts to recover his loss. However, the costs and delays inherent in lawsuits discourage consumers from trying to secure remedies through the courts.

A useful consequence of the consumerism movement has been a growing awareness that (1) the individual consumer is at a considerable disadvantage when faced with product quality deficiencies, and (2) consumer organization for collective action is not on a scale or level of effectiveness comparable with that attained by other large categories of individuals, e.g., political parties for voters, labor Unions for workers, etc.

As of the beginning of the 1970s a good many experiments were in progress to find new and better ways for helping consumers to secure satisfaction in the event of product quality problems, and to help consumers to avoid getting into trouble in the first place. (See Section 4, under Consumerism.)

National Differences   Within the general framework of the capitalistic concept, there are nevertheless important differences in the approaches used to achieve good quality. As will be seen below, these differences have their origin in numerous elements of the national cultural patterns. These patterns are so deeply rooted that the main approach to quality must be designed to fit these patterns, and not the other way about. Only when things become so bad that a revolution is needed is there any serious effort to alter the cultural pattern.

QUALITY CONTROL IN THE UNITED STATES OF AMERICA

The American economy rests mainly on a base of numerous autonomous producers and marketers of goods and services. These autonomous companies are characterized by:

1. A high concentration of industry in relatively few companies; e.g., the number of manufacturing companies runs to over a million, but the top 500 manufacturing companies account for most of the national manufacture.

2. A high degree of private ownership of these large companies; i.e., normally a large company will have thousands of owners no one of whom owns more than a few percent of the company.

3. A "professional" management; i.e., the company is run by men who consider their lifetime career to be that of managing. These men become the real power in the company, since the owners are too numerous and since the established legal system of boards of directors usually results in the managers' dominating the board of directors.[1] The American managers and their highly developed concept of professional management are one of the main strengths of the American economy.

The features of autonomous companies and professional managers to run them have a considerable impact on the conduct of the quality function. Within the flexibility permitted by the "anarchy of the marketplace," each company determines what it will make or stop making; what quality policies it will employ, etc. Innovation plays an important role throughout, owing to the rather unique industrial history of the country.

The early European settlers of America faced the problems and opportunities associated with exploiting the immense natural resources of a large geographic area. Self-reliance and risk taking emerged as major traditions. An innovative spirit was developed in the early agricultural days, and remained a driving force when the new nation undertook to industrialize.

---

[1] This situation prevails only as long as the managers do an acceptable job of running the company.

The manufacturing industries at the outset followed the European tradition of placing much reliance for quality on the foremen and workmen. As the shops expanded in size, and as machinery began to replace laborers, the Americans broke sharply with European tradition by adopting what came to be known as the Taylor system[2] of "Scientific Management."

While the Taylor system was mainly intended to improve productivity by separating manufacturing planning from execution, the effect on the quality function was profound. The narrowing of the delegation to workmen required increasing emphasis on use of inspectors. The narrowing of the delegation to foremen required, in due course, that the inspectors be organized into a central inspection department. Then, when there arose a need for more emphasis on inspection and test planning, on quality improvement, and on reliability improvement, the concept of separating planning from execution was extended by the creation of new staff specialists in the form of the Quality Control Engineer and the Reliability Engineer.[3]

These new specialists, well trained and strongly oriented to the quality function, have played a useful and important role in supplying, to their respective companies, the new techniques demanded by emerging quality problems. In addition, these same specialists play an essential role in the work of the national professional societies associated with the quality function, notably the American Society for Quality Control.

Despite the stresses arising from the continuing use of the obsolete Taylor system and from the overemphasis on staff specialists, the Americans have given a good account of themselves as to quality of product. They have done this through:

1. Willingness to invest in additional production capacity (or new enterprises) in order to secure the sales inherent in shortages of goods. Elimination of such shortages also eliminates an inevitable cause of poor quality.

2. Willingness to invest in precise machinery, tools, and measuring instruments, all of which improve quality as well as productivity.

3. Responsiveness to the needs of the marketplace, both in the original market research and in the after-sales feedback.

4. A "professional" approach to management, with great willingness to provide for continuing training of managers and specialists.[4]

Beyond the foregoing contributions to their product quality, which have been evolutionary in nature, the Americans have also undergone several twentieth century "revolutions" which have had important consequences as to quality:

1. The Taylor system as noted above. This reduced the useful contribution of the foremen and workers, and this contribution has yet to be recaptured.

2. The emergence of Inspection Departments and Quality Control Departments which are centralized to a degree greater than those in any other large capitalistic economy.

3. The creation of many thousands of quality specialists, again to a degree more extensive than that prevailing anywhere else.[5, 6]

[2] See Section 18, under Role of Motivation—The Taylor System.

[3] The evolution of these organization forms is traced in detail in Section 7, under Evolution of the Quality Control Hierarchy; also in Section 7, under Staff Quality Control Departments.

[4] The training is unbalanced, since the "line" specialists and supervisors are generally not adequately trained in these techniques. See Section 17, under various training headings.

[5] These specialists are largely confined to the large mass production industries and the high-reliability industries. Small companies and jobbing industries have generally retained the tradition of placing full responsibility on line supervisors and line department specialists.

[6] These specialists have also exhibited an urge for "professionalism." See Section 17, under Quality Engineers and Other Specialists—Professionalism for Quality Specialists.

To this might be added the rise of industrial Unionism in the 1930s, with its sweeping effects on the nature of worker motivational programs.[7]

At the beginning of the 1970s, American managerial concern over quality was primarily a concern over such problems as product safety, threats of liability suits, and threats of new government regulation. Generally the managers felt that their quality was competitive in the marketplace; i.e., they were not losing business because of inferior quality, whether to domestic or foreign competitors. They had genuine concern over foreign competition, but their concern was one of meeting the prices rather than one of competing successfully in quality.

QUALITY CONTROL IN JAPAN

The Japanese approach to quality control is the most spectacular quality success story of our time, and deserves careful study by all who have an interest in national quality control programs.

As in the United States, much of Japanese industry is concentrated in a comparatively few large companies, though there are many small companies as well. There is a good deal of private ownership of industry, but Japanese companies operate with a higher ratio of debt to owned capital than do the American companies. As a result, the lending organizations exert substantial influence, as does the government, which has close relationships with the lending organizations.

Prior to World War II, the Japanese conducted substantial export of consumer products. These were sold at very low prices, but their quality was so poor that the name "Made in Japan" became a symbol of shoddy goods. The quality reputation of Japan was probably the worst of any of the industrialized nations.

At the end of World War II, the former military and political leaders of Japan were no longer in power, and the leadership vacuum was filled, in large part, by the industrialists. These men wanted Japan to advance as an industrial power, and not to decline back into an agricultural economy of the type so prevalent in mainland Asia. They faced a difficult road on which product quality was a principal obstacle.

At this point it is pertinent to observe the parallel between the problem faced by Japan in the post World War II period and that faced by Great Britain in the eighteenth century. Both nations consisted of a small set of islands, densely populated, with limited natural resources. The real resources were the energy and competence of the people. Great Britain's approach was to import cheap materials, process these through technological skills into products of high quality, export the finished products, use the resulting exchange to buy more materials, etc. This same approach was open to the Japanese if they could solve the problem of making the high-quality products needed to compete in the international market. Since the Japanese tradition on quality of exports had been the precise opposite, the Japanese set out to create a revolution in their approach. They did this in a variety of ways.

Study of Foreign Practice   Since World War II, the Japanese have carried on a continuing program of study of foreign practice in quality control. Some of this study has consisted of translation of foreign books and papers for dissemination among Japanese. In addition, numerous teams have been organized to go abroad, observe practice in foreign companies, discuss problems with foreign managers and specialists, and bring back reports on their findings. These teams are of several varieties:

1. *QC Study Teams.* This was the original form, and consisted primarily of upper managers of enterprises, quality managers, and leading professors and specialists.

---

[7] See Section 18, under Incentives for Defect Reduction by Operators; see also Section 18, under Role of the Labor Union.

2. *Foremen's Teams.* These have been created to enable foremen to see how quality is controlled in foreign countries and what is the role of their counterparts abroad. Membership on such a team is also one of the high awards open to foremen for outstanding work in product quality.

3. *QC Circle Teams.* The membership of these teams consists primarily of members and leaders of QC Circles. Here again, there is a twofold purpose: *(a)* to study the practice prevailing abroad and *(b)* to serve as a high award for outstanding attainment in the work of QC Circles.

Training [8] No nation has so extensively trained its people in quality control as have the Japanese. What is significant is that their training programs *started at the top* of the company and progressed downward, level by level, until finally the training extended to millions of nonsupervisors. In addition, their training was *all-pervasive*; e.g., it was given to all company departments and has dealt with all aspects of the quality function.

Statistical Methodology. While Japanese specialists were aware of the growing development of statistical methods prior to 1950, they date their formal training programs from 1950, the year in which Dr. W. E. Deming, a noted statistician then on the staff of the U.S. Occupation Forces, presented courses in statistical methods for quality control. The Japanese Union of Scientists and Engineers proceeded to structure follow-on courses, and mobilized a faculty of teachers to conduct them. These courses have become well standardized at several levels of sophistication and have been given to many thousands of people at various company levels. [9]

Management of Quality Control. Formal training dates from the author's courses conducted during the summer of 1954 for the top leaders of the economy and for several hundred upper managers. As with statistical methodology, the Japanese organized follow-on courses, created a faculty, and proceeded to extend these courses through the hierarchies to middle managers and superintendents.

Other Techniques. As the courses grew in number, they also widened in variety. The Japanese created added courses in related topics such as standardization, reliability, new product development, operations research, market research, sensory testing, computer programming, and inspection. Various professional organizations offer these courses: Japanese Union of Scientists and Engineers (JUSE), Japan Standards Association, Japan Management Association, and others.

Foreman Training. When the Japanese faced the problem of foreman training in quality control, they concluded that there should be an alternative to organizing out-of-company courses for so many thousands of men. The alternative they designed was to give the courses over the national radio network (later the TV network). These courses were given during the summer months, 6 days a week, 15 minutes a day. The textbooks used for the courses were sold in numbers exceeding 100,000.

Worker Training. Beyond the conventional on the job training, the Japanese have done an enormous amount of supplemental training through their unique QC Circle concept (see Section 18, under International Motivational Methods — The Japanese QC Circle).

Organization Japanese tradition has been to place responsibility on line managers, with minimal use of staff specialists. The extensive, company-wide training in

[8] For a detailed, authoritative presentation, see Ishikawa, Kaoru, Education and Training of Quality Control in Japanese Industry, *Reports of Statistical Applications Research*, vol. 16, No. 3, pp. 21–40, 1969.

[9] For an analysis of the extent of application, see Kogure, Masao, A Review of Application of Statistical Techniques in Japanese Industry, *Reports of Statistical Application Research*, vol. 16, No. 3, pp. 66–80, 1969.

quality control has permitted this tradition to be retained in the quality function in several major ways.

Upper Management. Japanese upper management takes personal leadership of the quality function through the concept of the "President's Audit," which is really an annual quality plan.[10] Through its prior training in quality control, through its direct participation in the quality planning, and through the subsequent reports on quality performance against plan, the upper management is able to exercise effective leadership of the quality function.

Middle Management. By virtue of prior training, and under the committee systems widely used in Japan, the middle managers carry out most of the interdepartmental planning and coordination of quality activities, with only limited use of staff specialists. The Japanese do have staff quality specialists, but their role is mainly one of consulting and training rather than one of direct involvement in planning, project direction, analysis, or coordination.

Foremen. The Taylor system of separating manufacturing planning from execution has had little adoption in Japan. Instead, Japanese practice has been to give foremen an important role in product and process planning, control, and improvement. Through his own training and that of the QC Circles, the foreman has been able to play this role effectively as applied to quality.[11]

Workers. Through the unique QC Circle concept, millions of Japanese workers have received training in quality control methodology, enabling them to participate in solution of quality problems. Quite aside from the benefits of this concept, in results achieved and in worker motivation,[12] the training and experience of the workers make them better qualified to assume foremen's duties. The evidence is that the former QC Circle members do in fact give superior performance when they become foremen. Since there are millions of QC Circle members, and since in due course they will dominate the ranks of foremen and managers, the implications for the caliber of future Japanese management are profound.

Promotion of Quality Control[13] Japanese promotion of quality control rests mainly on training, publications, and conferences, with an annual "quality month" as an opportunity for organized propaganda and showmanship.

Quality Month; Conferences. Starting in 1960, November has been the annual quality month. A good deal of conference activity is timed to take place during November, when thousands of "Q" flags fly all over the country. The conferences include:

Top Management QC Conference
Staff and Middle Management QC Conference
Foreman QC Conference
Consumer QC Conference

Still other conferences and symposia take place at other times of the year.

Conference programs typically include presentation of papers, discussions, ceremonial award of prizes, factory inspection tours, etc. Attendance at conferences reaches high levels, those for the foremen having exceeded 3,000.

Publications. Japanese specialists and managers have published numerous books

[10] See generally Section 6, under The Annual Quality Program. See also Mizuno, Shigeru, Company-wide Quality Control Activities in Japan, *Reports of Statistical Application Research,* vol. 16, No. 3, pp. 2–13.

[11] See Imaizumi, Masumasa, Foremen's Role in Quality Control in Japan, *Industrial Quality Control,* July 1966, pp. 14–15.

[12] See Section 18, under International Motivational Methods — The Japanese QC Circle.

[13] For a detailed analysis, see Mizuno, Shigeru, Nation-wide Quality Control Promotion Activities, *Reports of Statistical Application Research,* vol. 16, No. 3, pp. 81–88, 1969.

and papers on quality control, the most widely distributed being the "QC Handbook for Foremen" (see Section 17, under Production Foremen). In addition, there are several regular journals, as follows (the first three are in Japanese):

1. *Statistical Quality Control.* This monthly journal presents technique and practice, as well as reports of a newsworthy nature.

2. *Quality Control for the Foreman.* This lively monthly journal is devoted largely to case histories of quality improvement. As of the early 1970s it had neared the astounding circulation of 100,000 copies per month.

3. *Standardization and Quality Control* is also a monthly journal, emphasizing problems of standardization.

4. In addition, the English language quarterly journal *Reports of Statistical Application Research* offers theoretical papers with occasional summaries of general progress in Japanese quality control.[14]

The Deming Prizes[15]   These awards consist of:

1. The Deming Application Prize, awarded to *enterprises* for outstanding improvement in performance. (There are some subdivisions by company size.) In the first 18 years of the award (1951–1968) a total of 48 such prizes were awarded.

For industrial companies these prizes are more than mere welcome recognition of achievement in quality; they may be used in advertising and public relations as well. It is common for companies to make the award a high ceremonial occasion, and thereafter to refer to the Prize in some of its company and product publicity.

2. The Deming Prize, awarded to *individuals* for outstanding theoretical work in the field of quality control. One prize is awarded per annum usually to one person, but sometimes to a team.

3. The Nikkei Quality Control Literature Prize. This award, established in 1954 by *Nippon Keizai Shimbun (Japan Economic Journal)*, is also awarded to *individuals*.

All these prizes are awarded by a Deming Prize Award Committee consisting of authorities in quality control, plus representatives from the press, the cognizant Ministries, the managers of prior award winning companies, and still others. Subcommittees are appointed to establish criteria and regulations for making the awards, as well as to conduct the detailed examination of the work done by persons or organizations nominated for prizes.

The administration work for the award processes is carried out by the Japanese Union of Scientists and Engineers (JUSE), which has played a leading role in these awards from the outset.

Standardization   In addition to the conventional national organization, the Japanese provide for product certification, on a voluntary basis. This is done under the

[14] Additional bibliography on quality control in Japan:

Proceedings, International Conference on Quality Control, Japanese Union of Scientists and Engineers, Tokyo. This 876-page volume contains 231 papers, about half of them by Japanese. A valuable source of detail on actual practice.

Quality Control in Japan, *Reports of Statistical Application Research*, vol. 10, No. 1, March 1963. This issue of a journal normally devoted to statistical applications gives a 121-page summary of events from 1958 to 1962, including histories of quality developments in 15 specific industry groups.

Japan's Management, Bedreigung of Stimulans, Netherlands Institute for Efficiency, *Publication 502*, 1970. This is a report by a Dutch team which visited Japan to study Japanese quality control methods. The 122-page report is mainly in Dutch, but the summary, conclusions, and appendixes are in English.

"Quality Control in Japan," published by The Japan Commercial Gazette, Ltd., in commemoration of the 1969 International Conference. This 115-page volume includes case histories of QC in seven leading Japanese companies.

[15] For a detailed description, see QC in Japan Series, No. 3, Deming Prize, Japanese Union of Scientists and Engineers, 10 Sendagaya, Shibuyaku, Tokyo, Japan.

Industrial Standardization Law which sets up government machinery, supported by widely based committees, to:

Designate commodities for which standards are to be established
Establish standards for these "designated commodities"

Once a standard has been established, the way is open for any manufacturer to make application for authorization to use the official Japan Industrial Standards (JIS) mark on his product. The application procedure requires that the manufacturer provide a good deal of quality data on product and process (in addition to conventional documentation and payment of fees). A team of inspectors then reviews data and documents, visits the manufacturer's plant, and makes recommendations, all in accordance with an established examination procedure.[16] A successful manufacturer is then authorized to use the JIS mark. (This authority is subject to being rescinded under conditions set out in the law and the procedures.)

The JIS mark is mandatory for certain products involving consumer safety, e.g., electrical apparatus. On general products, the JIS mark is on a voluntary basis, and as of early 1970s only a minority of such products carried the mark.

Export Inspection Law   In the early postwar years, some Japanese exporters found that they could not sell their products abroad unless the quality was first certified by an independent test laboratory. In response to this situation, the various Japanese industry associations began to create independent laboratories, the first being for the cotton textile industry. Exporters' use of these laboratories was voluntary; i.e., an exporter who felt the need for the certificate would request an inspection and would pay the fee for it.

As experience was gained, the national government enacted an Export Inspection Law which made mandatory the prior voluntary certification. This law was made effective in 1958[17] and stated as its purpose ". . . the sound development of Japan's export trade, to maintain and enhance the good reputation of export commodities by carrying out inspection of her export goods."

Under the provisions of the law, the Cabinet may, by order, designate products which are to be subject to export inspection. The cognizant Minister is then required to establish quality standards for these designated products, including standards for packing, components, etc. The law then demands that the designated products shall not be exported unless they have been inspected and approved by qualified laboratories in accordance with prescribed methods. The cognizant Minister has flexibility in choice of methods, and may require inspection of designs, materials, processes, etc., as well as finished products.

The list of designated products has grown until by the early 1970s it comprised over 500 specific articles and commodities which accounted for nearly half of the value of goods exported. A total of 39 private laboratories and 6 government laboratories had been qualified to carry out the inspections. These laboratories are specialized by industry, e.g., cotton textiles, cameras, pottery.[18]

Supporting Organizations   While the basic action to improve quality has been taken by the industrial companies, these have received a good deal of support from various other bodies. These have included:

[16] For details, see Asaka, Tetsuichi, Quality Control Audit, *Reports of Statistical Application Research*, vol. 16, No. 3, pp. 14–20. Evidently both the product and the company's quality control system must pass the examination.

[17] Predecessor legislation, for silk and later for agricultural products, goes back to 1895. For some history, as well as discussion of problems of carrying out export controls, see Tano, Masahiro, Problems of Export Inspection, *Proceedings, International Conference on Quality Control*, pp. 723–726, JUSE, Tokyo, 1969.

[18] For a complete list, see "Quality Control in Japan," available from Japan Trade Center, 393 Fifth Ave., New York 10016.

Professional Societies. The major contributor has been the Japanese Union of Scientists and Engineers (JUSE), which was founded in 1946. The first Managing Director of JUSE, K. Koyanagi, sensed the importance of quality to the Japanese economy, and was a driving force in developing training courses, conferences, publications, and aids to the successful Japanese revolution in product quality.

Other professional societies active in the field have included Japan Standards Association and Japan Management Association.

A Japanese Society for Quality Control was not formed until 1971. It is intended to concentrate in the academic field.

Universities. Japanese University professors have contributed importantly to application of quality control in the companies as well as to theoretical development. The professors have been a principal source of training textbooks and articles for journals. They have done much of the training in courses and seminars. In addition, they have been a source of consulting manpower. (Japan has not developed independent consultants to the extent prevailing in the United States and Europe.)

Other Organizations. The quality control movement has been strongly supported by industrial companies, trade associations, the prestigious Federation of Economic Organizations, government Ministries, and still others. This support was essential to the launching of JUSE and is still highly visible on special occasions such as the 1969 International Conference on Quality Control.

QUALITY CONTROL IN WESTERN EUROPE

Despite extensive national and industry differences, the economies of Western Europe do exhibit some commonalities:[19]

1. Their enterprises are mainly capitalistic, and operate with a high degree of autonomy.

2. They have some very large enterprises, but the concentration of industry into a relatively few companies is not as extreme as is the case in the United States or in Japan. Small industries are very numerous, are quite important to the national economy, and carry a good deal of political weight.

3. Ownership of the companies, and especially the small companies, is mainly in the hands of few people, usually members of one or a few families. It is quite usual, in such cases of closely held ownership, for most or even all of the appointments to the important managerial posts to be made from the ranks of the owning families. Many of these owner-managers make wide use of the tools of modern management, and their approach is not distinguishable from that used by "professional" managers. In many other cases the approach of the owner-managers is based mainly on empiricism coupled with close personal supervision of all phases of the enterprise—the approach of the "dedicated amateur."

4. Government regulation of quality is widely applied to products which strongly affect health and safety. Consumer protection laws, originally limited to product description and to short weights or measures, are being extended into other areas. There has been some standardization of consumer products by the national Standards Institutions, and the official mark is available to manufacturers who wish to submit their products to be tested against the standard. This arrangement is voluntary and has as yet been extended to only a small minority of products. There are

[19] Generalizations about "Western Europe" are difficult and can be misleading. There is a good deal of communication, travel, trade, etc., among these countries, as well as numerous international commissions and organizations of many kinds. Nevertheless, each country retains a uniqueness derived from its cultural origins, and strengthened by the fierce sense of nationalism which still prevails.

also various voluntary or private consumer organizations some of which conduct product tests and publish journals to advise consumers on the relative merits of competing products.[20]

In earlier centuries of industrialization it was the Western Europeans who were the leaders in quality of manufactured product. The leadership tended to be specialized along product lines; i.e., one country was the generally acknowledged leader in precision measuring equipment, another in heavy engineering, a third in fine chemicals, etc.

A good deal of this leadership was the result of advances in technology. The Europeans exhibited great ingenuity in developing new products, processes, measuring instruments, and other improvements in technology. They also were among the leaders in adopting national and international standardization of metrology, materials, tests, and still other forms. The pace of all this technological change was considerable, and may well be regarded as a revolutionary pace.

In contrast, the approach of the Europeans to changes in their managerial direction has been to use evolution, not revolution. Their industrial and quality leadership grew out of the organization forms inherent in small, owner-managed companies. The personal interest and personal coordination supplied by the owner-manager was well designed to sense marketplace quality problems and to act on them, including, in some notable cases, a positive passion for product excellence. The results attained under these organization forms were long-standing positions of competitiveness and leadership in marketplace quality. As of the early 1970s, the European top managers saw no evidence (of a challenge to their quality) sufficient to demand a revolutionary revision in their managerial approach.

When the Americans adopted the Taylor system, the Europeans did not follow on a comparable scale. Instead, the Europeans retained a good deal of the delegation given to the foremen and workmen. As a result, the Europeans have placed less reliance on independent Inspection and Test Departments, or on creation of strong, centralized Quality Control Departments. The Europeans also made less use of quality specialists than the Americans, again preferring to rely more on the line managers and on the "line" engineers, e.g., design engineers, process engineers.[21]

The preference for using line rather than staff specialists means that the "staff" quality activities are largely done by line engineers.[22] For example, in France there are courses in reliability engineering and there are over a thousand men who are engaged in that activity. However, no one calls himself a Reliability Engineer. They remain Electronic Engineer, Mechanical Engineer, etc.[23]

The Europeans were among the first to make use of statistical methods for dealing with quality problems. (A number of their specialists preceded W. A. Shewhart, though their work was not as well publicized.) As these statistical methods began to be applied more widely to industrial processes, the European specialists were prompt in responding to the movement. In virtually all European countries, capable specialists emerged who prepared the necessary books and papers on the subject,

---

[20] See, for example, Lock, J. M., The Consumer Protection Movement in Great Britain, *1972 Technical Conference Transactions, ASQC,* pp. 283–287.

[21] Here again, it is difficult to generalize. Some large European companies *have* adopted many of the elements of the Taylor system, have reaped the benefits, and have created the associated problems.

[22] Note that even in the United States, what is "staff" work today becomes "line" work tomorrow. See Section 7, under Staff Quality Control Departments.

[23] Eldin, Jaques, Reliability Engineering in France, *Proceedings, 14th Annual Symposium on Reliability,* 1968, IEEE, pp. 254–257,

In a similar vein, see also van der Weiden, H., Status of Reliability in the Netherlands, *ibid.,* pp. 258–264.

organized training courses, and otherwise made the techniques available for use. Self-sufficiency in statistical methodology is universal among the European countries.

The Europeans have also addressed themselves to the subject of quality costs, though in this respect they have lagged somewhat behind the Americans. A significant European contribution was the British Productivity Council's film "Right First Time" produced in 1963, and emphasizing the opportunities to reduce quality costs. [24]

There have also been attempts to mount a national effort through well-organized sponsorship and propaganda. An early example of this was the Quality and Reliability Year conducted in Great Britain starting in October 1966. This program, sponsored by the National Council on Quality and Reliability, received endorsement from virtually all important national figures. In the propaganda sense, it was well done. At the action level, it was left to the individual companies to make use of the unusually favorable propaganda by organizing programs suited to their specific purposes. [25] The British concept of a Quality and Reliability Year has since been undertaken by other countries, e.g., Czechoslovakia and Yugoslavia.

The Europeans have followed a mixed pattern in the matter of creating a professional society dedicated to the quality function. Some countries, e.g., Italy, Spain, have organized a membership-type society along the lines of the American Society for Quality Control. Other countries, e.g., Great Britain, have established coordinating committees or councils whose members are professional and industrial societies with an interest in quality. Still other countries, e.g., the Soviet Union and Poland, have established a special office within the organization of a related discipline such as standardization or metrology.

The fact that Europe is multinational means that quality problems are international in their scope. A design may originate in country A, to be assembled in country B, with components made in C and D, to be used in all these countries, including E and F. The language problem alone is formidable. [26] Differences in cultural practices, technological standards, quality levels, etc., can further complicate these multinational arrangements. The growing unity of the markets will intensify these problems until solutions are evolved.

A useful major step toward international cooperation in quality was the organization of the European Organization for Quality Control (EOQC). Full membership in EOQC is limited to *organizations* designated by their respective countries. From its inception in 1957, EOQC grew steadily until, by the early 1970s, virtually all European countries, both Western and Eastern, were members.

The activities of EOQC have likewise undergone expansion, roughly in the following sequence:

1. Organization of annual European Conferences on Quality Control. These have been held since 1957, the location being in a different country each year.

2. Publication of a technical journal and a newsletter.

3. Establishment of European Committees to study specific problems in quality. The nature of these problems can be judged from the subject matter of the resulting Committee reports: [27] Glossary of Terms; General Guide to the Preparation of Speci-

---

[24] See Rolfs, B. G., Quality and Reliability, *Quality Engineer,* May–June 1964, pp. 81–89.

[25] For an example of a large-scale response to the British Quality and Reliability Year, see Groocock, J. M., "Quality Cost Control in ITT (Europe)," Paper presented at ASQC Annual Technical Conference, Pittsburgh, 1970. (Not published in the advance *Proceedings.*)

[26] For a discussion of the problems of language translation, see McLachlan, Hugh, Specification as a Product for Export, *IEEE Transactions on Reliability,* May 1971, pp. 70–73.

[27] Available from European Organization for Quality Control, P.O. Box 1976, Rotterdam 3005, Netherlands.

fications; Survey of Quality Reporting, Quality Auditing, and Quality Achievements in European Countries.

4. Establishment of Industry-oriented Sections, the first being the Automotive Section. These Sections become active in organizing special conferences, publishing special reports, etc.

QUALITY CONTROL IN DEVELOPING COUNTRIES

Most of the countries on our planet are "developing" in the industrial sense. They occupy most of the land surface, and include most of the human population. They are found on all continents, and in all climatic regions. They vary greatly in size and especially in cultural structure and history. Despite all this variation, their roads to attaining product quality exhibit a good deal of commonality. The discussion which follows is based on the author's personal observations in numerous developing countries, supplemented by the material available in the literature. An uncommonly valuable source is the collection of papers presented at the first International Conference on Quality Control (Tokyo, 1969). The *Proceedings* of this conference include about 40 papers from developing countries. Some of these papers provide excellent overviews of the quality problems faced by developing countries. Of special interest are the following papers in the *Proceedings*:[28]

Author	Country	Proceedings Page No.
Srinagabhushana and Sundara Raju.	India	457
Huey and Wong.	Hong Kong	771
del Valle.	Spain	775
Vashrangsi	Thailand	779
Müller.	Israel	795
Kao	Taiwan	813
Cho	Korea	(Supplement) 46

The following papers, though from countries usually no longer regarded as "developing," are also of special interest:

Shilkin	Australia	763
De Fremery.	Netherlands	801
Kofoed	Denmark	817

Industrial development usually follows some recognizable phases, from a primitive agricultural subsistence economy to sophisticated manufacture for export. The discussion which follows will elaborate the nature of these phases and the steps taken to enable progress in quality to keep pace with progress in national development.

Export of Raw Materials   The most primitive industrial form is the subsistence economy, barely able to feed its population through labor-intensive agriculture, fishing, etc. Consumption of these products is entirely domestic. Quality is poor because of inferiority or lack of quality standards, technology, equipment, instruments, consumer purchasing power, consumer education, quality control know-how, etc.

In countries possessed of natural resources beyond those needed for domestic

---

[28] Available from Japanese Union of Scientists and Engineers, 5-10 Sendagaya, Shibuyaku, Tokyo, Japan.

purposes (e.g., farmland, forests, energy, minerals, marine life) the first step toward industrialization is through export of the raw materials derived from these resources. Selling these resources in the world market requires that they meet international quality standards, which are usually much higher than domestic standards. Meeting these international standards becomes a major first step in evolution of the national program to improve quality.

Usually the contracts for export of raw materials incorporate the quality specifications to be met and the tests to be used, along with related criteria for sampling, etc. In addition, the foreign importer may provide assistance in the form of technical know-how.

In the early stages of such export contracts, it is common for some exporting companies to fail to meet the export quality standards. A usual response of the government (which is actively involved in such international contracts) is to enact legislation to protect the quality reputation of the country. These laws provide for independent laboratory approval of quality of such exported products as are regarded as critical to the national economy. These difficulties in early export quality may also give birth to new laboratories for the purpose of doing the necessary testing, and new organizations for establishing product standards.

The publicized quality problems also stimulate various specialists (e.g., statisticians, metrologists, standards specialists) to look for ways to make their specialty more useful to the economy. However, the concept of a quality function has not matured sufficiently to enable the company managements to make a coordinated use of these specialties.

The main reaction of the exporting companies is to establish product inspection on a scale which is responsive to the export quality needs. In due course, inspectors are appointed, equipped with instruments, and trained to use the instruments, specifications, and sampling methods in a way that will keep the company out of trouble with the government inspectors and the customers.

Export of Processed Materials A major advance in industrialization takes place when the developing country sets up to do local processing of materials, so that what is now exported is metals rather than ore, plywood or pulp rather than logs, "canned" fruit rather than raw fruit. This phase requires that sophisticated processes be built, operated, and maintained, with all the quality control implications.

Normally, the developing country requires technical assistance throughout the building and startup of such processes. This assistance may be provided by the customer, who also may provide some of the capital needed to build the plant. Alternatively, the assistance may come from an engineering company engaged for the purpose. Either way, the developing country acquires a good deal of the know-how needed to operate and maintain the process thereafter. However, the developing country faces the formidable task of training the personnel needed for operation, maintenance, and quality control.

For such export of processed materials, the quality controls multiply rapidly. The raw materials previously exported must now be quality controlled anyhow, since they are inputs to the process. Other raw materials must be bought locally, or imported. The process must now be controlled, with all the complexities of data feedback, cause and effect relationships, etc. The "final" product is more critical and complex than its predecessor. Collectively, these quality control needs are of a much higher order of complexity than those associated with mere export of raw materials.

The usual response of the developing countries to this phase is multiple in nature:

Extension of government export controls, not only to the processed goods being exported, but to surveillance over the process itself.

Extension of national standardization to include the principal processed products.

Invitation of foreign experts to train local personnel. In this phase the men invited are usually industry experts rather than quality control experts.

Sending personnel abroad to be trained, again on an industry basis.

Aside from these steps, which are on a process-by-process basis, there is a gathering awareness that something more is needed for industry generally. The response to this awareness is the creating of new aids to industry such as consulting assistance, training assistance generally, and professional development. Details of these forms of aid are discussed below.

Integrated Manufacture for Domestic Use   A third phase of industrial development is to undertake local manufacture of modern industrial and consumer products. This phase brings the economy into the entire life cycle of product development through product "wear out in use," and the associated quality problems. At the same time, the climate for quality is poor, since these products are in short supply, so that the resulting sellers' market gives priority to volume of production rather than to quality. In addition, the habits which take root during the period of shortages must later be uprooted one by one.

The methods and techniques for dealing with these problems are discussed throughout this Handbook, and will not be enumerated here. Instead, what is pertinent here is how the developing economy goes about it to be able to convert its practices so that it can successfully deal with the new problems.

The enterprises which undertake this new manufacture are two broad types. (1) subsidiaries of foreign companies and (2) domestic companies.

Foreign Subsidiaries.   These are branches of foreign companies who are already carrying out such manufacture in their home country and elsewhere. These companies supply the capital and skilled manpower needed to build the factory and to get it into operation. They provide key managers and specialists to hire and train local managers and supervisors who, in turn, hire and train the local work force. The array of know-how is very wide.

The factory is started up with a quality control system which is itself an import. It has been designed based on experience with manufacture and marketing in other countries, and has been in successful operation in those countries. It does not follow that it will continue in successful operation here.

Domestic Companies.   The great majority of these companies are very small, and they become suppliers to the large companies. The quality performance of these small suppliers is universally a subject of criticism, and the reasons for this poor performance are quite similar throughout developing countries generally: lack of top management awareness of needs and opportunities inherent in good quality control; reliance on inspection instead of prevention; lack of controls on incoming materials; inadequate operation standards; inadequate documentation; lack of qualified quality control personnel and of quality control know-how.

Despite these limitations, the numerous small manufacturers are an essential part of the economy, and the need is to upgrade their performance. This is done by propagandizing the need to improve, by providing consulting assistance, and by training programs.[29]

Government Quality Controls.   These tend to expand as industrialization grows. There are several usual areas of expansion:

1. Extension of Standardization. The official Standards Institution undertakes to establish standards for key products.

---

[29] For a more detailed case discussion (Hong Kong), see Huey, C. T., and A. S. C. Wong, Introducing Quality Control into Small and Medium Manufacturing Industries, *Proceedings, International Conference on Quality Control*, pp. 771–774, JUSE, Tokyo, 1969.

2. Extension of Certification. Independent Laboratories are designated (or created) to provide certification that products conform to standards. This certification is made mandatory for products involving human health and safety. For other products, the certification is voluntary.

3. Import Quality Controls. These controls are sometimes instituted both for quality reasons and to protect use of scarce foreign exchange.

4. Government Audit of Company Quality Control Practice. This form of control also exists,[30] but appears to be a minority practice.

Government Currency Controls. On the face of it, these controls are merely fiscal in nature. Actually, they can have a major impact on the ability to achieve quality.

A widespread practice is the use of currency controls to restrict import of products which compete with those of domestic manufacture or which could be made locally. The resulting monopoly conferred on established local manufacturers can act to reduce the priority they would otherwise give to quality improvement (to meet competition).[31, 32]

In cases where manufacturers need to import high-quality components because local quality is inadequate, the currency control office may deny the applications.[33] In like manner, an essential piece of test equipment may fail, and require a replacement component which is available only through import. Yet the currency control procedure may take 1 or 2 years to clear the request, during which time the product is being shipped without the test.[34]

Education and Training. In this phase there also arises full awareness of the new needs for education and training in an industrial society. The programs undertaken include:

1. General Education. The long-range plan for increasing literacy and education is opened up to include education in science and engineering.

2. Training in Technological Skills. Courses are established in various schools and institutions to provide training in the numerous technological skills needed by an industrial society. For the quality function this includes courses in inspection, testing of all kinds, and numerous quality control courses. (See generally Section 17.)

3. Training of quality managers and specialists. At the outset, this training must be done by outsiders. Either foreign experts are invited to give lecture courses, or local men are sent abroad to take established courses. These trainees later become the trainers.

Service to Industry. To assist companies in converting to the needs of an industrial society, new institutions are created. A widely used form is that of consulting assistance. This is often provided by a government Productivity Center. In the case of consulting in quality control, the alternatives may be to establish a specialized consulting service within the Productivity Center (e.g., Hong Kong, Taiwan), within

---

[30] Kao, S. C., National Quality Control in the Republic of China, *Proceedings, International Conference on Quality Control,* pp. 813–816, JUSE, Tokyo, 1969.

[31] See, for example, Vashrangsi, Charven, The History and Current State of Quality Control in Thailand, *Proceedings, International Conference on Quality Control,* pp. 779–782, JUSE, Tokyo, 1969.

[32] See also del Valle, Garcia, Problems of Quality Control in a Developing Country, *Quality,* vol. 10, No. 4, pp. 43–47, Winter 1966.

[33] For an extensive, illuminating analysis of a case history of undertaking manufacture of a complex product in a developing country, see Baranson, Jack, "Manufacturing Problems in India—The Cummins Diesel Experience," Syracuse University Press, 1967.

[34] Personal observation of J. M. Juran.

the Standards Institution (e.g., Israel), within the Statistical Institute (e.g., India), or as a separate service.[35]

Another form of service to industry is through the organized quality control "movement." (Here the initiative may come from volunteers rather than from the government.) This organized movement usually includes:

1. Formation of a national Quality Control Society
2. Conferences, seminars, and other meetings to permit exchange of experiences and discussion of problems
3. Publication of journals, books, films, and other forms for dissemination of know-how
4. Establishment of national or industry committees to conduct specific researches and studies
5. Contact with other countries to exchange experience and know-how

Consumerism.   In the early stages of manufacture for domestic consumption, the shortage of goods tends to hold down complaints about quality. (Some dealers avoid making complaints for fear that they will jeopardize their delivery quota.) As the shortages are alleviated, the weaknesses in quality become publicized, and forces arise in the economy to help the consumers deal with manufacturers on quality matters. (See Section 4, under Consumerism.) There may well be an overcorrection, resulting in new legislation to protect the consumer.

Export of Manufactured Product   This stage of development is reached in one of two major ways:

1. As a logical extension of manufacture for domestic use; i.e., as the manufacturers improve their competence, their quality improves until they are able to meet international standards in open competition.
2. As a method for industrial development despite lack of natural resources. In such cases the main resource of the nation is its manpower. It uses this resource by inviting foreign capital to establish factories on its soil and to employ this manpower to run these factories. An obvious example is Hong Kong, which has virtually no natural resources in the usual sense, yet which has an extensive manufacturing economy strongly oriented to export. In such economies, the manufacture "for export" is mainly as a source of supply for others, i.e., as a source of manufacturing capacity for a foreign owner, or as a subcontractor. Either way, the quality standards are at a sophisticated level.

Meeting these international standards requires further extension of the various approaches set out under the previous heading Integrated Manufacture for Domestic Use. In addition, there must be further training to understand and deal with the more exacting levels demanded by international standards. The home office or the contractor are important sources for this added know-how.

Cultural Resistance to Change   Throughout all phases of industrial development, numerous technological changes must be introduced into deeply rooted cultural patterns. Each of these technological changes has accompanying social effects; i.e., each has some effect on the beliefs, habits, status, etc., of those exposed to the change. These social effects are often resisted by those whose habits, etc., are threatened, and it is this "resistance to change" (really resistance to the social effect

[35] For some good case examples of such consulting service, see Srinagabhushana and S. M. Sundara Raju, Assessment of Quality Programmes in Developing Countries, *Proceedings, International Conference on Quality Control*, pp. 457–460, JUSE, Tokyo, 1969. See also Sreenivasan, N. S., and C. A. Setty, Quality on the Spot—India, *Quality*, vol. 15, no. 2, pp. 40–43, Summer 1971; see also Sreenivasan, N. S., and C. A. Setty, Organization for Quality Planning and Maintenance, *Quality Progress*, June 1972, pp. 22–23.

of technological change) which is the most difficult and elusive obstacle in the way of the development process.

For details of the nature of this cultural resistance, and for methods of dealing with it, see Section 7, under Administration of the Quality Staff Specialty; Introducing Change. See also Juran, J. M., "Managerial Breakthrough," Chapter 9, Resistance to Change—Cultural Patterns, McGraw-Hill Book Company, New York, 1964.

Section 48A

Quality Control in Socialist Countries

PROFESSOR F. EGERMAYER, RN DR., DR. SC.

Head of Department of Statistics and Quality Control,
Czech Technical College,
Prague, Czechoslovakia

Relevancy of Quality in Socialist Economies All industrially developed countries, irrespective of social system, place major emphasis on the problems of quality. In the Socialist countries, the basic aim is to meet the increasing material and cultural needs of the people. The central planning which is characteristic of socialist economies includes special provisions for the growth of product quality, and quality is a major determining element of the effectiveness of the national economy.

Planning must balance the contending needs of an economy, and the priorities must be shifted as required. Currently the socialist economy gives quality a position preferable to quantity. There is also awareness that improvement in quality can aid the economy substantially as much as increase in volume of production, and at an economy in production capacity. Thereby, quality improvement represents a significant reserve for increase in productivity and in national income.

Since 1963, the Socialist countries of the CMEA (Council for Mutual Economic Assistance) have been carrying out economic reforms aimed at increasing the management effectiveness of the national economies and especially of the central planning methods. The resulting process of reform has devoted attention to the planning mechanisms, to limiting undue rigidity in the role of the directive economy indexes, and to extending the competence, responsibility, and material interests of the industrial enterprises. These reforms emphasize the continuing role of the central political and economic authorities in conceptual decisions on policies of the economy, while providing more favorable conditions for the industrial enterprises and their production activity.

The reforms are also directed toward support of the state's policy on scientific technical progress, including product quality improvement, since product quality is a limiting factor in modern development. This is especially true for some of the highly industrially developed countries of the CMEA [e.g., the German Democratic Republic (GDR) and Czechoslovakia]. The economy of such countries includes extensive requirements for import of materials and energy, for carrying out processes employing advanced technology, and for substantial export of products.

The problems of quality control have broad relevance to national planning in several ways:

1. The need to manufacture products necessary to the development of the national economies

2. Elimination of products no longer responsive to market needs

3. Balance of the demand for technical development against the capacity of the economy

To help solve these problems on both the macroeconomic and microeconomic levels, the governments of Socialist countries have constituted special authorities which they use as aids to the government within the area of State Quality Control.

State Organization Forms   Within all Socialist countries of the CMEA there exist certain central government institutions which are responsible for the execution of State policies in the field of quality control (QC). Most of these institutions had their origin as the State Standardization and Metrology Service, and their scope has gradually become more extensive. For example, the USSR State Committee on Standards was established in 1925 and "was entrusted with the general supervision of the work in this field in all industries as well as the approval of standards that are obligatory for all branches of national economy."[1]

Following World War II all Socialist countries established State Boards of Standardization with functions similar to that of the USSR State Committee. In addition, the growing problems of product quality demanded creation of some State authority to conduct the necessary State supervision of industrial product quality. Two main organization forms emerged for this purpose:

1. Broadening the scope of the State Committee for Standards. For example, in the Soviet Union this Committee became responsible for problems of measuring and testing, and later for State evaluation and certification of quality of manufactured products. These broader duties were reflected in a broader title, i.e., State Committee for Standards, Measures and Measuring Instruments under the Council of Ministers of the USSR (since 1970 the State Committee of USSR for Standards).

A similar form was adopted by Czechoslovakia. Under a 1968 statute the Office for Standardization and Measurements became responsible for the following functions of State QC:

a. Quality evaluation of selected products for awarding (or withholding) the Quality Mark

b. Approval of selected products prior to distribution, as an added preventive protection for the user

c. Supervision of evaluated and approved products during usage

This office also determines which products are to be subjected to compulsory quality evaluation. The evaluations and certifications are carried out by State Test-

---

[1]Boitsov, V. V., Role of Standardization in Quality Improvement, *Proceedings, International Conference on Quality Control* (Supplement), pp. 5–11, Tokyo, 1969. Similarly, the Czechoslovak Society for Standards (nongovernmental) was created in 1922 and was active in founding the International Standards Organization (ISO), which held its first Congress in Prague in 1928.

ing Laboratories and Evaluation Committees which are manned by outstanding specialists. These Laboratories also review the drafts of National Quality Standards.

In Hungary, the Office of Standardization includes a Department for Quality Supervision which is responsible for the State QC.

2. The second form used is that of creating a new organization. For example, in 1964, the GDR established the German Board for Measuring and Goods Testing (DAMW)[2] by fusion with the State Metrological Service. DAMW participates in the national approach to quality in several ways:

 a. Detailed design of the nationwide system for QC

 b. Assisting the attainment of national quality goals and plans by checking them in the research and development stages, as well as in the production stage

 c. Creation of models of QC Systems for industrial plants

 d. Reporting the results of quality achievements to the Government and the Central Economic Authorities

Similar organization forms have been established in Poland,[3] Bulgaria, and Romania through the creation of State Boards or Committees. Their duties involve one or more of the following:

Establishment of a system of quality evaluation of products

Evaluation of products for adequacy of quality

Award of Quality "Marks," i.e., symbols of conformance to standards

In addition to the foregoing central authorities, there are some additional organizations for State QC. Mainly these are State Inspection organizations concerned with control of quality of exported goods, and are carried out within the scope of the Ministry of Foreign Trade. Such State inspections are found in the Soviet Union, Czechoslovakia, Hungary, and Romania.[4]

Quality Evaluation and Quality Marks   The most widely practiced concept of State QC in the Socialist countries is quality evaluation, and certification through the so-called "Quality Mark." Details of carrying out this concept vary somewhat from country to country,[5] but the following are common features:

1. The evaluation compares the characteristics of the product with the State standard for such products.

2. The result of the evaluation is expressed in a system of grades, usually in three levels:

[2] The scope of DAMW can be judged from some of the high points of a report given by the President of the DAMW to the EOQC Board. As of January 1970, DAMW employed 3,000 persons, 2,000 in the State QC and 1,000 in metrology. Testing to award the Quality Mark was done in about 70 laboratories located in various industrial centers and adapted to the structure of industry. The DAMW cooperates with numerous experts from industrial plants, Research Institutes, Universities, and Engineering Associations. (The DAMW and the Office of Standardization merged in 1973.)

[3] For details, see Ostrowski, Z., History of Actual Conditions of Quality Control in Poland, *Proceedings, International Conference on Quality Control* (Supplement), pp. 54–57, Tokyo, 1969. (Since then, in 1972, the Polish National Board for Quality Control and Measures was replaced by the State Committee for Standards and Measures.)

[4] For elaboration, see Dolyakov, V., The Quality Mark in the USSR, *Quality*, vol. 11, No. 4, pp. 106, 107, Winter 1967.

[5] For details of some approaches see Derbisher, A. V., Total Quality Control in the USSR, *Proceedings, International Conference on Quality Control* (Supplement), pp. 37–45, Tokyo, 1969; also Wagenfuhr, L., National Quality Control and National Mark System in the GDR, *ibid.*, pp. 821–824.

Of course, all Socialist countries have worked out and published (in their own language) detailed procedures for conducting the evaluations and certifications.

a. Highest quality, usually denoting quality which is competitive with the world quality level. This "grade" is awarded the highest mark, e.g., "Q," and this mark is displayed on the product.

b. "Good" quality, usually meaning that there is full compliance with the standard. This grade also merits a mark, e.g., "1."

c. All other, meaning less than full compliance with the Standard. This product receives no mark.

3. Provision is made for delegating to the factory the right to use the mark for some limited time, e.g., 1 to 3 years. Grant of such a right is based on review of the QC system of the plant as well as on product evaluation. Before the term expires, a reevaluation must be made.

4. The grades attained influence product prices and company profits (see below).

5. The results of grading are one of the measures of progress in product quality. For example, in Czechoslovakia, the State Quality Evaluation and Certification of Products began in 1966. During the first 6 years, the results were as given in Table 48A-1.[6]

TABLE 48A-1

Year	Number of products evaluated	Percent in grades			Percent not classified
		1	2	3	
1966	472	7.8	57.9	34.3	
1967	1,687	13.1	73.7	13.2	
1968	1,913	12.9	72.0	14.8	0.3
1969	2,828	20.9	64.2	14.2	0.7
1970	3,715	11.7	71.3	13.6	3.4
1971	5,999	13.8	71.5	12.6	2.1

Price, Profit, and Quality   The State Quality Evaluation and Certification serves to provide some important economic incentives to enterprises and workers in any of several ways:

1. In the form of variable wholesale prices depending on the product grade. For example, in the Soviet Union, provision is made for paying higher than normal prices to manufacturers whose products attain certification.[7] These price increases are calculated to:

a. Repay the manufacturer for added costs shown to have been justified to attain the certification level

b. Provide increased profit margins as an incentive for having met the certification criteria

The established procedures provide for granting these price increases based on submission of proof to the cognizant State committees.[8]

2. Profit sharing for employees who have taken part in the production of certified products. Provision is made for paying premiums to these employees in amounts up to 35% of standard rate of the increased profitability resulting from certified products.

---

[6]Data from the Office for Standards and Measurements. See Egermayer, F., Experiences from the Czechoslovak Quality Year, *Proceedings of the Prague Conference,* April 1970, p. 34, CSVTS (in Czech).

[7]A similar principle is applied in the GDR.

[8]For details, see Tkachenko, A. A., Price and Quality in Production, *Standards and Quality,* No. 9, September 1969, pp. 66, 67 (in Russian).

3. Price reduction in the event that the quality of certified products is not sustained.

4. Penalties levied on manufacturers for product which is classified into the lowest degree (no Quality Mark). In Czechoslovakia the charge for this is 5% of the wholesale price, payable directly into the State Budget. If this repeats itself, the manufacturer pays a classification fee amounting to 20% of the wholesale price of the products involved.

5. Variable profit margins for products in accordance with such factors as:

Strictness of the quality parameters (requiring intensive added effort)

Age of the design; i.e., older products can be made at lower cost because of acquired experience but have decreasing value to users owing to growing obsolescence

Optimal quality from the point of view of the needs of the national economy[9]

This latter concept (5) of varying profit margin in accordance with the optimum needs of the economy is under active study and presents many interesting potentialities.[10]

Further Elements of State QC   The State Quality Evaluation and Certification is based at the outset on verification of finished product quality, i.e., a form of finished goods inspection. As the list of evaluated products expands, it becomes increasingly evident that mere verification is neither economic nor of optimum effectiveness. As a result, the center of gravity of State QC shifts to preventive forms. As a major example, in the GDR over 20,000 types of product, representing about 60% of the industrial production, have been subject to evaluation. At one time the verification activity occupied 80% of the activity of the DAMW. Now a good deal of the labor capacity of the DAMW has been transferred to other forms of State QC. A similar tendency is in progress in the Soviet Union.

Evaluation in Preproduction Stages.   Under this concept the participation of the State QC is extended into the earlier phases of the product life cycle:

1. Study of the merits of the new product project, i.e., market potential, technological concept, standardization and reliability grade, cost estimate, price estimate, etc.

2. Design review for reliability, economic use of material, cost, and price measures

3. Test and evaluation of prototype samples

4. Appraisal of the "Zero Series" (the first or preproduction series of product units made)

5. Review of tolerances, process control methods, inspection and test methods

6. Application for the State Quality Evaluation, award of the Quality Mark, pricing of the new product, disposition of obsolete products, etc.

Participation in these phases includes an active role in the decisions which are made whether and how to proceed further with the project. Through all this participation the DAMW assures that the State policies on product quality are carried out, and that the effect on the national economy is constructive.

Standardization.   The standardization concept so widely used in the Socialist countries is likewise being extended, from the traditional emphasis on establishing and publishing standards, into more elaborate concepts:

[9]Note by the Editor (Juran). This would appear to be related to the concept of "life cycle costing." See Section 4, under Life Cycle Costing.

[10] See Wagenfuhr, L. P., New Methods for Stimulation of Technical Progress in GDR, *Proceedings, Second Conference of CSVTS on QC*, vol. 1, pp. 131–135, 1967 (in Czech); see also Quality Control and Quality Assurance, edited by DAMW, *Wirtschaft*, p. 163; also Heuer, R., Quality, Costs and Profit, *Wirtschaft*, p. 61, Berlin, 1967 (in German).

1. Integrated Standards.   This term is used to describe the effort to coordinate the interests of numerous manufacturers and consumers through optimizing standards for the related materials, semifinished and finished products.   For example, to improve the quality of electrical transformers, 36 standards are being developed on quality of transformer steel, insulating materials, oil, etc.[11]

2. Perspective Standards.   This term refers to multiple grades within a standard, each grade being associated with a specified target date for reaching it.   The intent is to avoid the static character of standards by building in a dynamic rate of improvement.[12]

Metrology.   The State QC is unthinkable without metrology development.   In every Socialist state there is a State Metrology Service engaged in production of primary reference standards, improvement of measuring instruments, and calibration of secondary standards.   These activities in metrology are closely related to the State QC.[13]

State QC in Industrial Plants   In the Socialist countries the State QC operates not only in the macroeconomic sphere; it extends also into the activities of the enterprises (microeconomic sphere), as these two areas are closely interwoven.

Enterprises in the Socialist countries operate under organized systems of quality assurance.   These systems at one time emphasized technical product conformance.   However, the current system includes assurance of the adequacy of the preproduction phases of a new product project, as well as the planning for manufacture.[14]

A key connecting link between the State QC and the enterprises is the Quality Manager of the enterprise.   This link is established by giving this Quality Manager a dual responsibility (1) to the Plant Director and (2) to the State QC.

In the first of these capacities, the Quality Manager supervises the plant QC Organization and is responsible to the Plant Manager for proper direction of this organization.

In the second of these capacities, the Quality Manager has responsibilities running to the State QC.   These responsibilities are both material and personal in nature; i.e., they are of a public responsibility character.   For example, in the GDR, each of about 1,200 Quality Managers of important plants and integrated works is required, as the chief of his QC Organization (TKO) to:

1. Call the prompt attention of his Plant Manager to inadequacies in quality
2. Recommend (where warranted) that production be halted and even that product already shipped be recalled.
3. Attend those managers' conferences in his plant involving product quality
4. Make recommendations on bonuses to be awarded to key plant personnel for quality level achievements

Despite the fact that the TKO Chief is subordinate to the Plant Manager, the Plant Manager is not competent to give orders to the TKO Chief on matters subject to the State QC, which is under control of the DAMW.   This Authority also provides for

[11] Boitsov, V. V., Role of Standardization in Quality Improvement, *Proceedings, International Conference on Quality Control* (Supplement), pp. 5–11, Tokyo, 1969.

[12] Boitsov, *op.cit.*

[13] See Ostrowski, Z., and T. Plebanski, "Modern Metrology Concept and Its Impact on the Quality Control System in the Example of Poland," *Contributed Paper No. 510, EOQC Conference*, Lausanne, June 1970.

[14] See, for example, Derbisher, A. V., Total Quality Control in the USSR, *Proceedings, International Conference on Quality Control* (Supplement), pp. 37–45, Tokyo, 1969.   The reader is cautioned that the term "total quality control" has a meaning different from that used in nonsocialist countries, since it arises from an entirely different social system.

the training of TKO Chiefs for the function of Commissioners of the DAMW, i.e., for the State QC tasks.[15]

Other Socialist countries, in varying degrees, likewise provide for integrated systems of QC in the industrial plants, and for a form of direct linkage between the State QC and the principal plants.[16]

Motivational Programs for Quality Improvement In the Socialist countries there has been a clear trend toward establishing a status of self-control[17] among the entire work force. Since defects are management controllable as well as operator controllable,[17] the establishment of worker self-control has required extensive technological preparation as well as political-ideological preparation.

The specific systems used in the Socialist countries to motivate quality improvement are the Saratov System[18] of defectless production and related systems using different names, e.g., the Polish DO-RO, the German Ohne Fehler. The details of these systems are described in Section 18, under the heading International Motivational Methods, and hence are not repeated here. Instead, the discussion which now follows will amplify the cultural origin and evolution of these systems.

For the production force to accept the responsibilities associated with defect prevention and self-control has required programs of training as well as motivation. An outstanding arrangement for this purpose is the so-called "Days of Quality" or also "Schools of Quality." This concerns regular weekly conferences attended by both managers and workers, to evaluate results as presented by the inspection department representatives. These results center on indexes of the quality performance achieved by workers, foremen, designers, technologists, and inspectors. In addition, the evaluations cover the progress made in fulfilling various objectives, the state of plant housekeeping, etc. The "Days of Quality" have become a very good form of training for all employees on matters of personal responsibility and work habits.

The Saratov System has also required broad changes in the role of the inspection department. During the early years of emphasis on quantity of production, the role of the inspection force was one of sorting the product to remove the defects. Under the Saratov System, with its emphasis on defect prevention, this role has changed to one of sampling inspection, feedback of quality data, and other assistance in defect prevention. (Product sorting is performed by the production force.)

The results achieved in the Soviet Union and other Socialist countries have been most impressive. In the Saratov region alone, the decrease of product claims between 1963 and 1965 was over 70%. There were also large decreases in the amount of work scrapped.

In the Soviet Union, there has been wide adoption of the Saratov System, in

[15] In the GDR, these matters are formalized by the Decree of DAMW on Assurance and Advancement of Product Quality in Industrial Plants and Integrated Works (Dec. 18, 1969), and by the respective Provisions for the execution of this Decree (Jan. 15, 1970).

[16] In Czechoslovakia, the Integrated QC System had been introduced since the years 1963–1965 under a Governmental Decree assigning this task to the Industrial Ministries.

[17] See Section 11, under Concept of Operator Self-Control; see also Section 16, under Controllability Quantification.

[18] The Saratov movement was initiated in 1955 by Professor B. Dubovikov, then director of a machinery plant in the Saratov region. His experiences were published in his book "Principles of Scientific Organization of Quality Control," Ekonomika, Moscow, 1966 (in Russian). See also *Ekonomicheskaya Gazeta*, No. 48, pp. 18–19, 1967 (in Russian). A summary of the development and results of the Saratov System is in the brochure by Y. M. Sorin, System of Organization of Defectless Production in the USSR and Abroad, *Znanye*, Moscow, 1967 (in Russian).

the manufacturing industries. By 1967, some 5,000 industrial plants had introduced this system. There were additional applications in other sectors of the national economy, especially in the building industry and in transportation, and further in the design organizations and research institutes. In total, the employees involved exceeded 5 million.

The Saratov System was also extended to other Socialist countries. In the GDR the performance of work according to the Saratov System became a principle for realization of the QC Assurance System in industrial plants and integrated works. This principle was even authorized legally.[19]

During 1969–1970, there was established in Bulgaria a number of special offices called "Bureau for Quality" to introduce and propagate the Saratov System.

In Poland the Saratov System was based on scientific premises elaborated by Professor T. Kotarbinski. His "Treatise on Good Working" inspired the pioneers of the Polish method of defectless working (called DO-RO, after Dobra Robota = Good Work). This program was launched under a national competition, initiated by the National Board for Quality and Measures, with the cooperation of the press, radio, and television media.[20]

In Czechoslovakia, the Saratov System has also been applied, especially within the machine tool industry. The system was popularized by being included in the National Quality Year, in a manner analogous to that used in Poland.[21]

Quality Education and Training   Sophisticated programs such as Integrated QC and the Saratov System[22] require extensive education and training for those who are called on to make these programs work. The growth of these new systems has been so dynamic that the schools within the formal education system have been unable to keep up with them and have therefore lagged behind the development of theory and practice in the QC area, as well as in education of the specialized personnel required. As a result, there has been a shift to institutions outside the formal education system in order to provide the needed education and training.[23]

Coincidental with these specific needs, there has emerged in the Socialist countries an intense pressure asking for the education and culture of the general public toward quality mindedness. This pressure has resulted in creation of special nongovernment institutions of a social character which:

1. Provide training courses for plant and other organization personnel. These courses are of both short- and long-term nature, and are conducted both internally and externally.

2. Inform the public about product quality and QC through the press, radio and TV broadcast, films, conferences, and exhibitions.

3. Stimulate public interest in nationwide actions, e.g., the Quality Year in Czechoslovakia.

These institutions cooperate closely with the official State QC organizations, the Economic Ministries, the Trade Unions, and other types of social organizations.

---

[19] See Decree of DAMW of Dec. 18, 1969, on Assurance and Advancement of Product Quality, paragraph 3.

[20] See Ostrowski, Z., History of Actual Conditions of Quality Control in Poland, *Proceedings, International Conference on Quality Control*, (Supplement), p. 57, Tokyo, 1969.

[21] See Egermayer, F., The Czechoslovak Quality Year, *Quality* (EOQC), vol. 13, No. 1, pp. 6–8, 1969; also in *Quality Progress*, September 1969, pp. 15, 41–42. For the experiences and results see the table of product grading under Quality Evaluation and Quality Marks, above. Also, see Egermayer, F., Experiences from the Czechoslovak Quality Year, *Proceedings of the Prague Conference, CSVTS*, April 1970, p. 34 (in Czech).

[22] See Section 18, under International Motivation Methods.

[23] Egermayer, F., Basic Problems in Education and Training for Quality, *Proceedings, 13th EOQC Conference*, Prague 1969, pp. 13-18.

They also exert pressure toward bringing modern ideas about quality control and reliability into the official school curricula at all grade levels.

In the Socialist countries this new education and training function is usually carried out by scientific-technical societies which have a wide, voluntary membership base. Such societies have established special committees consisting of experts and responsible personnel concerned with the interrelated problems of QC, reliability assurance, standardization, and metrology.

In the Soviet Union there was founded in 1959 a Committee for Reliability and Quality Control which functions within the All-Union Council of Scientific-Technical Societies. This Committee develops means for exchange of experiences and for propagation of the latest methods and forms of work (e.g., Saratov method), as well as for specific training in the areas of QC and Reliability Assurance.

To carry out these activities, the Committee arranges consultations, lectures, courses, and exhibitions in Moscow at the so-called "Cabinet" for Standardization and Reliability. This Cabinet has become a central social club where the prominent scientists, technical specialists, and economists meet with plant personnel. In addition, the Moscow Cabinet functions at the Polytechnical Museum of "Znanye," the All-Union Society for the propagation and extension of scientific knowledge. Aside from the Moscow Cabinet, there are at present some 250 smaller Cabinets throughout the whole of the Soviet Union.

A major activity of the Committee and of the Cabinet in Moscow is the program of regular seminars and lecture courses which are attended by some 1,500 to 2,000 participants who, at the same time, acquire the published textbooks and training manuals. Additional Committee activities include:

Conferences and symposia on questions of quality and reliability. During 1969 there were about 40 such conferences.

Technical publications and brochures, and technical films.

Management of radio and TV training and courses.

Preparation of displays for the Cabinets. (Most of these Cabinets are equipped with information libraries, documentary materials, and reading rooms.)[24]

Similar Committees, with similar objectives and activities, are found in other Socialist countries.[25]

There has also been progress in establishing programs within the regular school system. An outstanding example is the offering of study programs at the Technical University in Karl-Marx-Stadt (GDR), for preparation of inspection engineers and technicians. These programs, established in cooperation with the DAMW and the Kammer der Technik, include principles of organization and management of QC in industrial plants; quality problems in Socialist economies; the State QC; the

---

[24] Shor, Y. B., Forms and Education for Quality Control and Reliability Assurance Organized by Scientific-Technical Societies in the USSR, *Proceedings, 13th EOQC Conference*, pp. 144–145, Prague, 1969 (in German).

[25] See the papers related to this problem in the *Proceedings, 13th EOQC Conference*, Prague 1969. (The theme of this Conference was Education and Training for Quality and Reliability.) See also related papers in the *Proceedings of the International Conference on Quality Control*, JUSE, Session 13, Tokyo, 1969.

[26] See Trumpold, H., Education System for Quality Control in the GDR, *Proceedings, 13th EOQC Conference*, pp. 165–167, Prague, 1969 (in German).

With reference to educational programs in statistical methods for QC, see Schindowski, E., and K. Manteuffel, Development of Statistical Quality Control in the GDR, *Quality*, vol. 11, No. 3, pp. 77–39, 1967 (in German); see also Heene, E., and K. Manteuffel, Some Problems of Training in Statistical Methods for Quality Control, *Proceedings, 13th EOQC Conference*, pp. 45–48 Prague 1969 (in German).

problems of prices, profit, and quality costs; computer techniques; the latest testing and control methods for evaluation of quality; measurement technology, etc.[26]

Another example of programs within the regular school system is the program of postgraduate studies organized, for key personnel of the QC Departments at engineering firms, by the Department for Quality Control of the Czech College of Technology in Prague.[27]

The formation of a Committee for Education and Training within EOQC is a further favorable development for training in quality and reliability in the Socialist countries.

Qualimetry   This term has been coined as a label for the concept of measuring quality on a scientific basis.   A strong advocate of studying this concept has been the USSR Committee on Standards, Measures, and Measuring Instruments.

Because of its close association with the problem of executive reports on quality, the discussion of Qualimetry is, in this Handbook, given in Section 21, under the heading Qualimetry.

[27] Egermayer, F., Training for Quality and Reliability in Czechoslovakia, *Proceedings, 13th EOQC Conference,* pp. 153–155, Prague, 1969.

Appendix I
Glossary of Symbols

a = combination of factors A, B, C, . . . , n in a 2^n experiment in which only A occurs at the high level; similarly for b, c, . . . , n.

A = unit cost of acceptance (damage done by a defective piece which slips through inspection).

A = a multiplier of σ' used to locate the 3-sigma control limits above and below the central line on an X chart. $A = 3/\sqrt{n}$.

A = in maintenance time prediction, a rating for product design features.

A_1 = a multiplier of $\bar{\sigma}$ used to locate the 3-sigma control limits above and below the central line on an $\bar{X}$ chart. $A_1 = 3/c_2\sqrt{n}$.

A_2 = a multiplier of $\bar{R}$ used to locate the 3-sigma control limits above and below the central line of an $\bar{X}$ chart. $A_2 = 3/d_2\sqrt{n}$.

A_c = in sampling acceptance schemes, the acceptance number, i.e., the maximum allowable number of defective pieces in a sample of size n.

ACL = acceptance control limit, i.e., a distance d from APL in the direction of the RPL.

ANOVA = analysis of variance.

AOQ = average outgoing quality, i.e., the quality of product leaving the inspection department after acceptance sampling and any detailing found necessary.

AOQL = average outgoing quality limit, i.e., the worst quality, on the average, after acceptance sampling and any detailing found necessary.

APL = acceptance process level, i.e., a process level which is acceptable and should be accepted most of the time by the plan.

AQL = acceptable quality level, i.e., the lowest quality of incoming product which is to be accepted regularly.

ARL = average run length.

ASN = average sample number, i.e., the average number of units inspected per lot in sampling inspection, ignoring the 100% inspection of rejected lots.

ATI = Average total inspection, i.e., average number of items inspected in a lot under a specified acceptance procedure.

b = number of blocks in a randomized block experimental design.

b = number of good units rejected by the inspector.

$b_1, b_2, \ldots$ = estimates of regression coefficients β_1, β_2, ...

b_{10}, b_{50} = life by which 10% (or 50%) of a population would have failed.

B = in maintenance time prediction, a rating for design dictates for maintenance personnel.

B_1 = a multiplier of σ' used to locate the 3-sigma lower control limit on a chart for σ. β_1 is approximately $c_2 - 3/\sqrt{2n}$.

B_2 = a multiplier of σ' used to locate the 3-sigma upper control limit on a chart for σ. B_2 is approximately $c_2 + 3/\sqrt{2n}$.

B_3 = a multiplier of $\bar{\sigma}$ used to locate the 3-sigma lower control limit on a chart for σ. B_3 is approximately $1 - 3/c_2\sqrt{2n}$.

1

B_4 = a multiplier of $\bar{\sigma}$ used to locate the 3-sigma upper control limit on a chart for σ. B_4 is approximately $1 + 3/c_2\sqrt{2n}$.

c = number of defects, usually in a sample of stated size.

c = in sampling acceptance schemes, the acceptance number, i.e., the maximum allowable number of defective pieces in a sample of size n. (In government sampling tables the symbol Ac is used.)

c = a scale factor given in MIL-STD-414.

c = number of columns in an experimental design.

$\bar{c}$ = average number of defects per sample in a series of samples.

c' = standard or aimed-at average number of defects in a sample of stated size. c' may also refer to the population average number of defects per sample.

c_2 = ratio between the expected value of $\bar{\sigma}$ in a long series of samples and the σ' of the population from which they were drawn. $c_2 = \dfrac{\sqrt{2}}{n}\left(\dfrac{n-2}{2}\right)!\left(\dfrac{n-3}{2}\right)!$

c_{ij} = element in the ith row and jth column of a matrix C.

C = cost of repairing or replacing a defective once found.

C = in maintenance time prediction, a rating for design dictates for support facilities.

C_1 = the allowable number of defectives in the cumulative results of k_1 or fewer samples in the first stage.

C_2 = the allowable number of defectives in the cumulative results of $k_1 + 1$ to k_2 or fewer samples or the last k_2 samples.

ChSP = chain sampling plan.

CIM = change-in-mean-effect in Evolutionary Operations.

CRC = cumulative results criterion in acceptance sampling.

CSCC = cumulative sum control chart.

CSP = continuous sampling plan.

d = ratio of the difference to be detected in a test divided by the measure of variability.

d = the difference in readings in a paired sample.

d = the number of defectives in a sample.

d = number of defects reported by the inspector.

d_i = the signed differences in a Youden two-sample interlaboratory test.

$\bar{d}$ = the average difference in readings in a paired sample.

d' = deviation, in cells, from the assumed origin of a frequency distribution.

d_2 = ratio of the expected value of $\bar{R}$ (in samples of size n) to the s of the population.

D = the cumulative number of defectives in a series of samples.

D = largest deviation of actual percent cumulative frequency from theoretical percent cumulative frequency.

D = in a cumulative sum control chart, the least amount of change in the average that it is desired to detect.

D_1 = a multiplier of σ' used to locate the 3-sigma lower control limit on a chart for R. $D_1 = d_2 - 3\sigma_R/\sigma'$.

D_2 = a multiplier of σ used to locate the 3-sigma upper control limit on a chart for R. $D_2 = d_2 + 3\sigma_R/\sigma'$.

D_3 = a multiplier of $\bar{R}$ used to locate the 3-sigma lower control limit on a chart for R. $D_3 = 1 - 3\sigma_R/d_2\sigma'$.

D_4 = a multiplier of $\bar{R}$ used to locate the 3-sigma lower control limit on a chart for R. $D_4 = 1 + 3\sigma_R/d_2\sigma'$.

DA = double sampling AOQL tables of the Dodge-Romig sampling tables.

DF = degrees of freedom, the number of independent comparisons possible with a given set of observations (also called f).

DL = double sampling lot tolerance tables of the Dodge-Romig sampling tables.

DPH = defects per hundred.

DPU = defects per unit.

e = the constant 2.71828+.

e_{ij} = the experimental error associated with the measurement Y_{ij}.

E = maximum allowable error in estimate (desired precision).

E = the effect being estimated (difference between averages).

E_1 = a multiplier of $\bar{\sigma}$ to determine the 3-sigma control limits on a chart for individuals.

E_2 = a multiplier of $\bar{R}$ to determine the 3-sigma control limits on a chart for individuals.

EVOP = evolutionary operation.

f = frequency; generally, the number of observed values in a given cell of a frequency distribution.

f = sampling rate in continuous sampling.

f = in Skip Lot sampling, the fraction of lots to be inspected after the initial criteria have been satisfied.

f = degrees of freedom, the number of independent comparisons possible with a given set of observations (also called DF).

f = severity effect of the occurrence of an unsafe event.

F = ratio of two estimates of variance or the distribution of this ratio.

F' = ratio of two sample ranges or the distribution of this ratio.

$F(t)$ = proportion of population failing before time t.

FR = failure rate, i.e., the percentage of failures per unit time.

g = number of groups in a group screening experimental design.

g = a numerical factor used in calculations for the Weibull distribution.

h = a parameter of cumulative sum sampling plans.

h' = a parameter of cumulative sum sampling plans.

h_1, h_2 = intercept values in a sequential sampling plan for process parameter.

H = an index calculated in the Kruskal-Wallis ranks test.

i = cell interval; for grouped data, the distance from a point in one cell to a similar point in the next cell.

i = in Skip Lot sampling, the number of successive lots to be found conforming to qualify for skipping lots either at the start or after detecting a nonconforming lot.

i = number of successive acceptable units in continuous sampling.

I = cost of inspecting one piece.

I_m = minimum inspection per lot.

I = the square identity matrix.

k = number of sampling levels in continuous sampling plans.

k = a parameter of cumulative sum sampling plans.

k = number of treatments or levels of the factor to be investigated.

k = number of good units rejected by the inspector.

k_1 = the maximum number of samples for cumulation of defectives in the first stage.

k_2 = the maximum number of samples for cumulation of defectives in the second stage and in the "normal" period following the second stage.

K = the difference between a particular value and the average of the curve in units of standard deviation. $K = \dfrac{X - \mu}{\sigma}$. Also called z.

K = in Evolutionary Operation, a factor used in determining the error term. Converts range into estimated standard deviation.

K = factor for adjusting failure rate data.

L = lower specification limit for a quality characteristic X.

L = limiting values in table for continuous sampling plans.

L = a numerical factor used in calculations for Evolutionary Operations.

LACL = in variables sampling plans, the lower acceptance control limit.

LC = lot calculation.

LCL = lower control limit on a control chart.

LLL = lower lot limit.

LQ = limiting quality.

LR = lot rating.

LTPD = lot tolerance percent defective, i.e., the level of defectiveness that is unsatisfactory and therefore should be rejected by the sampling plan.

M = in MIL-STD-414, an acceptance limit.

$M =$ the mean square successive difference.

$M =$ a numerical factor used in calculations for Evolutionary Operation.

MAR $=$ maximum allowable range.

ML $=$ mean life.

MS $=$ mean square; e.g., MS_E is mean square for error.

MSD $=$ maximum standard deviation.

MTBF $=$ mean time between failures.

MTBHE $=$ mean time between human errors.

MTTR $=$ mean time to repair.

$M(t) =$ cumulative hazard rate for period 0 to t.

$n =$ number of articles or observed values in a sample or subgroup. Also, the number of trials of some event.

$n_0 =$ in a response surface experimental design, the number of center points.

$n_1 =$ in double sampling, the number of pieces in the first sample.

$n_2 =$ in double sampling, the number of pieces in the second sample.

$\bar{n} =$ average sample size.

$np =$ number of defective articles in a sample of size n.

$n\bar{p} =$ average value of np in a set of sample size n.

$N =$ number of articles in a lot or population.

OC $=$ operating characteristic, a plot describing the risks in a sampling plan.

$p =$ fraction defective, i.e., the ratio of the number of defective units to the total number of defective and nondefective units.

$p =$ probability of occurrence of an unsafe event.

$p =$ in sensory tests, the fraction correct identification of the unknown with standard.

$p_1 =$ in variables sampling plans, the acceptable fraction defective.

$p_2 =$ in variables sampling plans, the rejectable fraction defective.

$p' =$ aimed-at or standard values of the fraction of defective articles; also, the true value of p in a lot or population being sampled.

$\bar{p} =$ average fraction defective, i.e., the total number of defective units found in a set of samples divided by the total number of units in the samples.

$p_b =$ break-even value of fraction defective for which cost of inspection of $1/p_b$ units is equal to cost of damage done by one defective.

p_L (%) $=$ in variables sampling plans, estimate of percent defective below the lower specification limit.

p_U (%) $=$ in variables sampling plans, estimate of percent defective.

$P =$ the population percentage included between statistical tolerance limits.

$P_a =$ probability of accepting a given lot. Also, the probability of accepting a hypothesis.

$P (A) =$ probability of occurrence of event A.

$P_0, P_1, P_2, \ldots =$ probability of finding exactly $0, 1, 2, \ldots$ defectives in a sample.

$P_r =$ the probability of lot rejection.

PC $=$ PRE-Control.

$P_s =$ probability of survival. The probability of failure-free operation for a time period equal to or greater than t. (This is identical with R, reliability.)

$q = 1 - p$, the probability that a particular event will not happen in a single trial.

$q =$ in experimental design, number of components in a mixture.

$q =$ a test statistic for testing a hypothesis concerning means.

$Q_L, Q_U =$ quality indices used in MIL-STD-414.

$r =$ the number of occurrences of some event, e.g., the number of defectives in a sample, the number of occurrences of the less frequent sign in a test of hypothesis. Also, the distribution of this statistic.

$r =$ the sample correlation coefficient.

$R =$ range of a set of n numbers, i.e., the difference between the largest number and the smallest number.

$R =$ reliability. The probability of failure-free operation for a time period equal to or greater than t. (This is identical with P_s, the probability of survival.)

$R =$ unit cost of rejection (cost of finding a defective in a rejected lot, plus expense of correcting it).

$\bar{R}$ = mean of several ranges.

R_e = the rejection number, i.e., the number of defective pieces in a sample of size n which causes rejection of the lot.

$R(t)$ = proportion of population surviving to time t.

RL = reference level or reference quality level, i.e., engineering estimate of what the quality at delivery should be.

RPL = rejectable process level, i.e., a process level which is rejectable and should be rejected most of the time by the plan.

RQL = rejectable quality level.

RSM = response surface methodology, an experimental approach used to optimize many different kinds of industrial unit processes, and systems.

R^2 = the proportion of variation explained by a regression model. Also the square of the sample multiple correlation coefficient.

s = sample estimate of σ (standard deviation of population); e.g., s is the sample estimate of the standard deviation of individual values, $s_{\bar{x}}$ is the sample estimate of the standard deviation of sample means. Also called $\hat{\sigma}$.

s = in sequential sampling plans, a constant computed from the values of the APL and the RPL.

s = for the negative binomial, the difference between number of trials and number of occurrences.

s^2 = sample estimate of σ^2 (variance of a population); e.g., s^2 is the sample estimate of the variance of individual values, $s_{\bar{x}}^2$ is the sample estimate of the variance of sample means.

S = safeness of the system.

SA = single-sampling AOQL tables of the Dodge-Romig tables.

S.E. = standard error.

SL = single-sampling lot tolerance tables of Dodge-Romig tables.

SS = sum of squares; e.g., SS_E is sum of squares for error.

t = a specified period of failure-free operation.

t = treatment in a randomized block design.

t = statistic used to compare sample means or the distribution of the statistic.

t' = statistic used to compare sample means when the population standard deviations cannot be assumed equal. $t' = \dfrac{\bar{X}_1 - \bar{X}_2}{\sqrt{s_1^2/n_1 + s_2^2/n_2}}$

T = in sequential sampling, the cumulative sum of an appropriate statistic against the sample number n.

T = in cumulative sum control charts, the permissible average time before a process shift of D is detected.

T = total test time on all units.

T = maintenance time.

T = a preassigned termination time.

$T_L = (\bar{X} - L)/s$, a statistic used in MIL-STD-414.

$T_U = (U - \bar{X})/s$, a statistic used in MIL-STD-414.

T^2 = a statistic used to test population means on two characteristics (called Hotelling's T^2).

TBF = time between failures.

T_r = time of rth failure in sample of n.

u = defects per unit.

$\bar{u}$ = total number of defects in all samples divided by the total number of units in all samples, i.e., the defects per unit.

U = symbol used for statistics (for testing hypotheses) that follow a normal distribution.

U = upper specification limit for a quality characteristic X.

UACL = upper acceptance control limit.

UCL = upper control limit on a control chart.

ULL = upper lot limit ($\bar{\bar{X}} + 3\sigma$).

w = cell width.

w = the ranges of the n observations on each treatment.

$W =$ the weight of the bulk material that makes up on an increment.

$x =$ a vector of elements.

$x' =$ the transpose of the x vector.

$X_1, X_2, \ldots =$ observed value of some variable, usually a quality characteristic.

$X =$ arithmetic mean, the average of a set of numbers $X_1, X_2, X_3, \ldots, X_n$ is the sum of the numbers divided by n.

$\bar{X}' =$ an aimed-at or standard value of a quality characteristic. Also used to represent the true but often unknown mean of a universe being sampled.

$\bar{X} =$ mean of several $\bar{X}$ values. Often called the grand average.

$\bar{X}_{c(h)} =$ the mean of the h composite measurements.

$X =$ a matrix of elements.

$X' =$ inverse of matrix X.

$Y =$ observed value of a second variable.

$Y_i =$ the yield for run number i.

$Y_{ij} =$ the observation on the ith treatment in the jth block.

$\bar{Y} =$ average of values of Y variable.

$\bar{Y}_0 =$ in response surface methodology, the average of the center points.

$\hat{Y} =$ the predicted value for Y.

$z =$ normal distribution coefficient.

$Z_i =$ the ith values after a canonical analysis of the original X_i axis.

$Z(t) =$ hazard rate, i.e., instantaneous failure rate at time t.

α (alpha) $=$ probability of rejecting the hypothesis under test when it is true. (Called the type I error or level of significance.) In acceptance sampling, $\alpha =$ the producer's risk.

$\alpha =$ scaling parameter of the Weibull distribution.

β (beta) $=$ probability of accepting the hypothesis under test when it is false. (Called the type II error.) In acceptance sampling, β is the consumer's risk.

$\beta_1, \beta_2, \ldots =$ in regression the unknown parameters of the model.

$\beta =$ shaping parameter of the Weibull distribution.

$\beta_j =$ a term peculiar to a given block. It is the amount by which the response of a given treatment in the jth block differs from the response of the same treatment averaged over all blocks, assuming no experimental error.

γ (gamma) $=$ confidence level.

$\gamma =$ location parameter of the Weibull distribution.

Γ (gamma) $=$ the gamma function.

δ (delta) $=$ width of confidence interval.

$\delta_0 =$ in analysis of variance, an acceptably small value of the ratio σ_b/σ_w, the ratio of between-group variability to within-group variability.

$\delta_1 =$ in analysis of variance, an unacceptably large value for the ratio σ_b/σ_w, the ratio of between-group variability to within-group variability.

ϵ (epsilon) $=$ a random error term of a linear function.

η (eta) $=$ scale parameter of the Weibull distribution.

θ (theta) $=$ mean life: θ_0 is the acceptable mean life and θ_1 is the unacceptable mean life. (Also called μ.)

$\theta =$ in cumulative sum control charts, an angle on the mask used in the chart.

λ (lambda) $=$ failure rate, i.e., the percentage of failures per unit time.

μ (mu) $=$ the population mean (average), e.g., the mean of a lot, the mean time between failures, or the mean life. (μ_0 is the acceptable mean life and μ_1 is the unacceptable mean life.)

π (pi) $=$ the constant $3.14159+$.

ρ (rho) $=$ in bulk sampling, the intraclass correlation coefficient between test-units in the same increment.

ρ_r (rho$_r$) $=$ reliable life, i.e., life beyond which some specified proportion r of the items will survive.

σ (sigma) $=$ the population standard deviation; e.g., σ is the standard deviation of individual values, $\sigma_{\bar{X}}$ is the standard deviation of sample means. (Some literature uses σ' in place of σ.)

$\hat{\sigma} =$ sample estimate of σ (standard deviation of a population). Also called s.

$\bar{\sigma} =$ mean of several standard deviations.

Σ (sigma) $=$ a mathematical sign meaning "take the algebraic sum of the quantities which follow."

τ_d (tau$_d$) $= \dfrac{\overline{X}_1 - \overline{X}_2}{1/2(R_1 + R_2)}$, a statistic used to test the hypothesis about μ_1 and μ_2. Also, the distribution of the statistic.

$\tau_1 = \dfrac{\overline{X} - \mu_0}{R}$, a statistic used to test the hypothesis about μ_0. Also the distribution of the statistic.

ϕ_i (phi$_i$) $=$ in a randomized block experimental design, a term peculiar to the ith treatment, constant for all blocks regardless of the block in which the treatment occurs.

Φ (p) $=$ distribution function of process average.

χ^2 (chi^2) $=$ ratio of $\dfrac{(n-1)\,s^2}{\sigma_0{}^2}$ or the distribution of this ratio.

$!$ $=$ factorial sign $n!$ means "take the product of the integers from 1 through n." (Note: either $0!$ or $1! = 1$.)

Note: Three standards covering symbols and other matters are ASQC Std. A1-1971/ANSI Std. Z1.5-1971: Definitions, Symbols, Formulas and Tables for Control Charts; ASQC Std. A2-1971/ANSI Std. Z1.6-1971: Definitions and Symbols for Acceptance Sampling by Attributes; ASQC Std. A3-1971/ANSI Std. Z1.7-1971: Glossary of General Terms Used in Quality Control. These are published by the American Society for Quality Control, 161 W. Wisconsin Ave., Milwaukee, Wisconsin 53203.

Appendix II

Tables and Charts

For more extensive tables see Owen, D. B., "Handbook of Statistical Tables," Addison-Wesley Publishing Company, Inc., Reading, Mass., 1962.

TABLE A* Factors for Estimating σ' from $\bar{R}$ or $\bar{\sigma}$

Estimate of $\sigma' = \bar{R}/d_2$ or $\bar{\sigma}/c_2$ where $\bar{R}$ is the average of sample ranges and $\bar{\sigma}$ is the average of sample standard deviations.

Number of observations in subgroup n	d_2 factor for estimating σ' from $\bar{R}$ $(\sigma' = \bar{R}/d_2)$	c_2 factor for estimating σ' from $\bar{\sigma}$ $(\sigma' = \bar{\sigma}/c_2)$	Number of observations in subgroup n	d_2 factor for estimating σ' from $\bar{R}$ $(\sigma' = \bar{R}/d_2)$	c_2 factor for estimating σ' from $\bar{\sigma}$ $(\sigma' = \bar{\sigma}/c_2)$
2	1.128	0.5642	21	3.778	0.9638
3	1.693	0.7236	22	3.819	0.9655
4	2.059	0.7979	23	3.858	0.9670
5	2.326	0.8407	24	3.895	0.9684
			25	3.931	0.9697
6	2.534	0.8686	30	4.086	0.9748
7	2.704	0.8882	35	4.213	0.9784
8	2.847	0.9027	40	4.322	0.9811
9	2.970	0.9139	45	4.415	0.9832
10	3.078	0.9227	50	4.498	0.9849
11	3.173	0.9300	55	4.572	0.9863
12	3.258	0.9359	60	4.639	0.9874
13	3.336	0.9410	65	4.699	0.9884
14	3.407	0.9453	70	4.755	0.9892
15	3.472	0.9490	75	4.806	0.9900
16	3.532	0.9523	80	4.854	0.9906
17	3.588	0.9551	85	4.898	0.9912
18	3.640	0.9577	90	4.939	0.9916
19	3.689	0.9599	95	4.978	0.9921
20	3.735	0.9619	100	5.015	0.9925

*Reproduced by permission from "ASTM Manual on Presentation of Data," American Society for Testing and Materials, Philadelphia, Pa., 1945.

TABLE B Normal Distribution*

Proportion of total area under the curve from $-\infty$ to $K = \dfrac{X - \mu}{\sigma}$. To illustrate: when $K = 2$, the probability is 0.9773 of obtaining a value equal to or less than X.

K	0.00	0.01	0.02	0.03	0.04	0.05	0.06	0.07	0.08	0.09
−3.5	0.00023	0.00022	0.00022	0.00021	0.00020	0.00019	0.00019	0.00018	0.00017	0.00017
−3.4	0.00034	0.00033	0.00031	0.00030	0.00029	0.00028	0.00027	0.00026	0.00025	0.00024
−3.3	0.00048	0.00047	0.00045	0.00043	0.00042	0.00040	0.00039	0.00038	0.00036	0.00035
−3.2	0.00069	0.00066	0.00064	0.00062	0.00060	0.00058	0.00056	0.00054	0.00052	0.00050
−3.1	0.00097	0.00094	0.00090	0.00087	0.00085	0.00082	0.00079	0.00076	0.00074	0.00071
−3.0	0.00135	0.00131	0.00126	0.00122	0.00118	0.00114	0.00111	0.00107	0.00104	0.00100
−2.9	0.0019	0.0018	0.0017	0.0017	0.0016	0.0016	0.0015	0.0015	0.0014	0.0014
−2.8	0.0026	0.0025	0.0024	0.0023	0.0023	0.0022	0.0021	0.0021	0.0020	0.0019
−2.7	0.0035	0.0034	0.0033	0.0032	0.0031	0.0030	0.0029	0.0028	0.0027	0.0026
−2.6	0.0047	0.0045	0.0044	0.0043	0.0041	0.0040	0.0039	0.0038	0.0037	0.0036
−2.5	0.0062	0.0060	0.0059	0.0057	0.0055	0.0054	0.0052	0.0051	0.0049	0.0048
−2.4	0.0082	0.0080	0.0078	0.0075	0.0073	0.0071	0.0069	0.0068	0.0066	0.0064
−2.3	0.0107	0.0104	0.0102	0.0099	0.0096	0.0094	0.0091	0.0089	0.0087	0.0084
−2.2	0.0139	0.0136	0.0132	0.0129	0.0125	0.0122	0.0119	0.0116	0.0113	0.0110
−2.1	0.0179	0.0174	0.0170	0.0166	0.0162	0.0158	0.0154	0.0150	0.0146	0.0143
−2.0	0.0228	0.0222	0.0217	0.0212	0.0207	0.0202	0.0197	0.0192	0.0188	0.0183
−1.9	0.0287	0.0281	0.0274	0.0268	0.0262	0.0256	0.0250	0.0244	0.0239	0.0233
−1.8	0.0359	0.0351	0.0344	0.0336	0.0329	0.0322	0.0314	0.0307	0.0301	0.0294
−1.7	0.0446	0.0436	0.0427	0.0418	0.0409	0.0401	0.0392	0.0384	0.0375	0.0367
−1.6	0.0548	0.0537	0.0526	0.0516	0.0505	0.0495	0.0485	0.0475	0.0465	0.0455
−1.5	0.0668	0.0655	0.0643	0.0630	0.0618	0.0606	0.0594	0.0582	0.0571	0.0559
−1.4	0.0808	0.0793	0.0778	0.0764	0.0749	0.0735	0.0721	0.0708	0.0694	0.0681
−1.3	0.0968	0.0951	0.0934	0.0918	0.0901	0.0885	0.0869	0.0853	0.0838	0.0823
−1.2	0.1151	0.1131	0.1112	0.1093	0.1075	0.1057	0.1038	0.1020	0.1003	0.0985
−1.1	0.1357	0.1335	0.1314	0.1292	0.1271	0.1251	0.1230	0.1210	0.1190	0.1170

TABLE B   Normal Distribution *(Continued)*

K	0.00	0.01	0.02	0.03	0.04	0.05	0.06	0.07	0.08	0.09
−1.0	0.1587	0.1562	0.1539	0.1515	0.1492	0.1469	0.1446	0.1423	0.1401	0.1379
−0.9	0.1841	0.1814	0.1788	0.1762	0.1736	0.1711	0.1685	0.1660	0.1635	0.1611
−0.8	0.2119	0.2090	0.2061	0.2033	0.2005	0.1977	0.1949	0.1922	0.1894	0.1867
−0.7	0.2420	0.2389	0.2358	0.2327	0.2297	0.2266	0.2236	0.2207	0.2177	0.2148
−0.6	0.2743	0.2709	0.2676	0.2643	0.2611	0.2578	0.2546	0.2514	0.2483	0.2451
−0.5	0.3085	0.3050	0.3015	0.2981	0.2946	0.2912	0.2877	0.2843	0.2810	0.2776
−0.4	0.3446	0.3409	0.3372	0.3336	0.3300	0.3264	0.3228	0.3192	0.3156	0.3121
−0.3	0.3821	0.3783	0.3745	0.3707	0.3669	0.3632	0.3594	0.3557	0.3520	0.3483
−0.2	0.4207	0.4168	0.4129	0.4090	0.4052	0.4013	0.3974	0.3936	0.3897	0.3859
−0.1	0.4602	0.4562	0.4522	0.4483	0.4443	0.4404	0.4364	0.4325	0.4286	0.4247
−0.0	0.5000	0.4960	0.4920	0.4880	0.4840	0.4801	0.4761	0.4721	0.4681	0.4641

K	0.09	0.08	0.07	0.06	0.05	0.04	0.03	0.02	0.01	0.00
+0.0	0.5359	0.5319	0.5279	0.5239	0.5199	0.5160	0.5120	0.5080	0.5040	0.5000
+0.1	0.5753	0.5714	0.5675	0.5636	0.5596	0.5557	0.5517	0.5478	0.5438	0.5398
+0.2	0.6141	0.6103	0.6064	0.6026	0.5987	0.5948	0.5910	0.5871	0.5832	0.5793
+0.3	0.6517	0.6480	0.6443	0.6406	0.6368	0.6331	0.6293	0.6255	0.6217	0.6179
+0.4	0.6879	0.6844	0.6808	0.6772	0.6736	0.6700	0.6664	0.6628	0.6591	0.6554
+0.5	0.7224	0.7190	0.7157	0.7123	0.7088	0.7054	0.7019	0.6985	0.6950	0.6915
+0.6	0.7549	0.7517	0.7486	0.7454	0.7422	0.7389	0.7357	0.7324	0.7291	0.7257
+0.7	0.7852	0.7823	0.7794	0.7764	0.7734	0.7704	0.7673	0.7642	0.7611	0.7580
+0.8	0.8133	0.8106	0.8079	0.8051	0.8023	0.7995	0.7967	0.7939	0.7910	0.7881
+0.9	0.8389	0.8365	0.8340	0.8315	0.8289	0.8264	0.8238	0.8212	0.8186	0.8159
+1.0	0.8621	0.8599	0.8577	0.8554	0.8531	0.8508	0.8485	0.8461	0.8438	0.8413
+1.1	0.8830	0.8810	0.8790	0.8770	0.8749	0.8729	0.8708	0.8686	0.8665	0.8643
+1.2	0.9015	0.8997	0.8980	0.8962	0.8944	0.8925	0.8907	0.8888	0.8869	0.8849
+1.3	0.9177	0.9162	0.9147	0.9131	0.9115	0.9099	0.9082	0.9066	0.9049	0.9032
+1.4	0.9319	0.9306	0.9292	0.9279	0.9265	0.9251	0.9236	0.9222	0.9207	0.9192
+1.5	0.9441	0.9429	0.9418	0.9406	0.9394	0.9382	0.9370	0.9357	0.9345	0.9332

z	.00	.01	.02	.03	.04	.05	.06	.07	.08	.09
+1.6	0.9452	0.9463	0.9474	0.9484	0.9495	0.9505	0.9515	0.9525	0.9535	0.9545
+1.7	0.9554	0.9564	0.9573	0.9582	0.9591	0.9599	0.9608	0.9616	0.9625	0.9633
+1.8	0.9641	0.9649	0.9656	0.9664	0.9671	0.9678	0.9686	0.9693	0.9699	0.9706
+1.9	0.9713	0.9719	0.9726	0.9732	0.9738	0.9744	0.9750	0.9756	0.9761	0.9767
+2.0	0.9773	0.9778	0.9783	0.9788	0.9793	0.9798	0.9803	0.9808	0.9812	0.9817
+2.1	0.9821	0.9826	0.9830	0.9834	0.9838	0.9842	0.9846	0.9850	0.9854	0.9857
+2.2	0.9861	0.9864	0.9868	0.9871	0.9875	0.9878	0.9881	0.9884	0.9887	0.9890
+2.3	0.9893	0.9896	0.9898	0.9901	0.9904	0.9906	0.9909	0.9911	0.9913	0.9916
+2.4	0.9918	0.9920	0.9922	0.9925	0.9927	0.9929	0.9931	0.9932	0.9934	0.9936
+2.5	0.9938	0.9940	0.9941	0.9943	0.9945	0.9946	0.9948	0.9949	0.9951	0.9952
+2.6	0.9953	0.9955	0.9956	0.9957	0.9959	0.9960	0.9961	0.9962	0.9963	0.9964
+2.7	0.9965	0.9966	0.9967	0.9968	0.9969	0.9970	0.9971	0.9972	0.9973	0.9974
+2.8	0.9974	0.9975	0.9976	0.9977	0.9977	0.9978	0.9979	0.9979	0.9980	0.9981
+2.9	0.9981	0.9982	0.9983	0.9983	0.9984	0.9984	0.9985	0.9985	0.9986	0.9986
+3.0	0.99865	0.99869	0.99874	0.99878	0.99882	0.99886	0.99889	0.99893	0.99896	0.99900
+3.1	0.99903	0.99906	0.99910	0.99913	0.99915	0.99918	0.99921	0.99924	0.99926	0.99929
+3.2	0.99931	0.99934	0.99936	0.99938	0.99940	0.99942	0.99944	0.99946	0.99948	0.99950
+3.3	0.99952	0.99953	0.99955	0.99957	0.99958	0.99960	0.99961	0.99962	0.99964	0.99965
+3.4	0.99966	0.99967	0.99969	0.99970	0.99971	0.99972	0.99973	0.99974	0.99975	0.99976
+3.5	0.99977	0.99978	0.99978	0.99979	0.99980	0.99981	0.99981	0.99982	0.99983	0.99983

* Adapted with permission from Eugene L. Grant and Richard S. Leavenworth, "Statistical Quality Control," 4th ed. pp. 642–643, McGraw-Hill Book Company, New York, 1972.

TABLE C   Exponential Distribution*

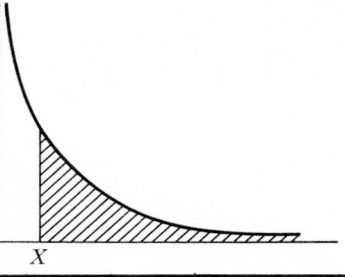

X

$\dfrac{X}{\mu}$	0.00	0.01	0.02	0.03	0.04	0.05	0.06	0.07	0.08	0.09
0.0	1.000	0.9900	0.9802	0.9704	0.9608	0.9512	0.9418	0.9324	0.9231	0.9139
0.1	0.9048	0.8958	0.8860	0.8781	0.8694	0.8607	0.8521	0.8437	0.8353	0.8270
0.2	0.8187	0.8106	0.8025	0.7945	0.7866	0.7788	0.7711	0.7634	0.7758	0.7483
0.3	0.7408	0.7334	0.7261	0.7189	0.7118	0.7047	0.6977	0.6907	0.6839	0.6771
0.4	0.6703	0.6637	0.6570	0.6505	0.6440	0.6376	0.6313	0.6250	0.6188	0.6126
0.5	0.6065	0.6005	0.5945	0.5886	0.5827	0.5769	0.5712	0.5655	0.5599	0.5543
0.6	0.5488	0.5434	0.5379	0.5326	0.5273	0.5220	0.5169	0.5117	0.5066	0.5016
0.7	0.4966	0.4916	0.4868	0.4819	0.4771	0.4724	0.4677	0.4630	0.4584	0.4538
0.8	0.4493	0.4449	0.4404	0.4360	0.4317	0.4274	0.4232	0.4190	0.4148	0.4107
0.9	0.4066	0.4025	0.3985	0.3946	0.3906	0.3867	0.3829	0.3791	0.3753	0.3716

	0.0	0.1	0.2	0.3	0.4	0.5	0.6	0.7	0.8	0.9
1.0	0.3679	0.3329	0.3012	0.2725	0.2466	0.2231	0.2019	0.1827	0.1653	0.1496
2.0	0.1353	0.1225	0.1108	0.1003	0.0907	0.0821	0.0743	0.0672	0.0608	0.0550
3.0	0.0498	0.0450	0.0408	0.0369	0.0334	0.0302	0.0273	0.0247	0.0224	0.0202
4.0	0.0183	0.0166	0.0150	0.0130	0.0123	0.0111	0.0101	0.0091	0.0082	0.0074
5.0	0.0067	0.0061	0.0055	0.0050	0.0045	0.0041	0.0037	0.0033	0.0030	0.0027
6.0	0.0025	0.0022	0.0020	0.0018	0.0017	0.0015	0.0014	0.0012	0.0011	0.0010

*Adapted with permission from S. M. Selby (ed.), "CRC Standard Mathematical Tables," 17th ed., pp. 201–207, The Chemical Rubber Co., 1969.

**TABLE D   Median Ranks*

Sample size $= n$

	1	2	3	4	5	6	7	8	9	10	11	12	13	14	15	16	17	18	19	20
1	.5000	.2929	.2063	.1591	.1294	.1091	.0943	.0830	.0741	.0670	.0611	.0561	.0519	.0483	.0452	.0424	.0400	.0378	.0358	.0341
2		.7071	.5000	.3864	.3147	.2655	.2295	.2021	.1806	.1632	.1489	.1368	.1266	.1178	.1101	.1034	.0975	.0922	.0874	.0831
3			.7937	.6136	.5000	.4218	.3648	.3213	.2871	.2594	.2366	.2175	.2013	.1873	.1751	.1644	.1550	.1465	.1390	.1322
4				.8409	.6853	.5782	.5000	.4404	.3935	.3557	.3244	.2982	.2760	.2568	.2401	.2254	.2125	.2009	.1905	.1812
5					.8706	.7345	.6352	.5596	.5000	.4519	.4122	.3789	.3506	.3263	.3051	.2865	.2700	.2553	.2421	.2302
6						.8909	.7705	.6787	.6065	.5481	.5000	.4596	.4253	.3958	.3700	.3475	.3275	.3097	.2937	.2793
7							.9057	.7979	.7129	.6443	.5878	.5404	.5000	.4653	.4350	.4085	.3850	.3641	.3453	.3283
8								.9170	.8194	.7406	.6756	.6211	.5747	.5347	.5000	.4695	.4425	.4184	.3968	.3774
9									.9259	.8368	.7634	.7018	.6494	.6042	.5650	.5305	.5000	.4728	.4484	.4264
10										.9330	.8511	.7825	.7240	.6737	.6300	.5915	.5575	.5272	.5000	.4755
11											.9389	.8632	.7987	.7432	.6949	.6525	.6150	.5816	.5516	.5245
12												.9439	.8734	.8127	.7599	.7135	.6725	.6359	.6032	.5736
13													.9481	.8822	.8249	.7746	.7300	.6903	.6547	.6226
14														.9517	.8899	.8356	.7875	.7447	.7063	.6717
15															.9548	.8966	.8450	.7991	.7579	.7207
16																.9576	.9025	.8535	.8095	.7698
17																	.9600	.9078	.8610	.8188
18																		.9622	.9126	.8678
19																			.9642	.9169
20																				.9659

* Adapted with permission from The Table of Median Ranks of Sample Values on Their Population with an Application to Certain Fatigue Studies, *Industrial Mathematics*, No. 2, p. 7, 1951.

TABLE E   Poisson Distribution*

1,000 $\times$ probability of c or fewer occurrences of event that has average number of occurrences equal to np.

np \ c	0	1	2	3	4	5	6	7	8	9
0.02	980	1,000								
0.04	961	999	1,000							
0.06	942	998	1,000							
0.08	923	997	1,000							
0.10	905	995	1,000							
0.15	861	990	999	1,000						
0.20	819	982	999	1,000						
0.25	779	974	998	1,000						
0.30	741	963	996	1,000						
0.35	705	951	994	1,000						
0.40	670	938	992	999	1,000					
0.45	638	925	989	999	1,000					
0.50	607	910	986	998	1,000					
0.55	577	894	982	998	1,000					
0.60	549	878	977	997	1,000					
0.65	522	861	972	996	999	1,000				
0.70	497	844	966	994	999	1,000				
0.75	472	827	959	993	999	1,000				
0.80	449	809	953	991	999	1,000				
0.85	427	791	945	989	998	1,000				
0.90	407	772	937	987	998	1,000				
0.95	387	754	929	984	997	1,000				
1.00	368	736	920	981	996	999	1,000			
1.1	333	699	900	974	995	999	1,000			
1.2	301	663	879	966	992	998	1,000			
1.3	273	627	857	957	989	998	1,000			
1.4	247	592	833	946	986	997	999	1,000		
1.5	223	558	809	934	981	996	999	1,000		
1.6	202	525	783	921	976	994	999	1,000		
1.7	183	493	757	907	970	992	998	1,000		
1.8	165	463	731	891	964	990	997	999	1,000	
1.9	150	434	704	875	956	987	997	999	1,000	
2.0	135	406	677	857	947	983	995	999	1,000	

TABLE E **Poisson Distribution** *(Continued)*

np \ c	0	1	2	3	4	5	6	7	8	9
2.2	111	355	623	819	928	975	993	998	1,000	
2.4	091	308	570	779	904	964	988	997	999	1,000
2.6	074	267	518	736	877	951	983	995	999	1,000
2.8	061	231	469	692	848	935	976	992	998	999
3.0	050	199	423	647	815	916	966	988	996	999
3.2	041	171	380	603	781	895	955	983	994	998
3.4	033	147	340	558	744	871	942	977	992	997
3.6	027	126	303	515	706	844	927	969	988	996
3.8	022	107	269	473	668	816	909	960	984	994
4.0	018	092	238	433	629	785	889	949	979	992
4.2	015	078	210	395	590	753	867	936	972	989
4.4	012	066	185	359	551	720	844	921	964	985
4.6	010	056	163	326	513	686	818	905	955	980
4.8	008	048	143	294	476	651	791	887	944	975
5.0	007	040	125	265	440	616	762	867	932	968
5.2	006	034	109	238	406	581	732	845	918	960
5.4	005	029	095	213	373	546	702	822	903	951
5.6	004	024	082	191	342	512	670	797	886	941
5.8	003	021	072	170	313	478	638	771	867	929
6.0	002	017	062	151	285	446	606	744	847	916

np \ c	10	11	12	13	14	15	16
2.8	1,000						
3.0	1,000						
3.2	1,000						
3.4	999	1,000					
3.6	999	1,000					
3.8	998	999	1,000				
4.0	997	999	1,000				
4.2	996	999	1,000				
4.4	994	998	999	1,000			
4.6	992	997	999	1,000			
4.8	990	996	999	1,000			
5.0	986	995	998	999	1,000		
5.2	982	993	997	999	1,000		
5.4	977	990	996	999	1,000		
5.6	972	988	995	998	999	1,000	
5.8	965	984	993	997	999	1,000	
6.0	957	980	991	996	999	999	1,000

TABLE E   Poisson Distribution *(Continued)*

np \ c	0	1	2	3	4	5	6	7	8	9
6.2	002	015	054	134	259	414	574	716	826	902
6.4	002	012	046	119	235	384	542	687	803	886
6.6	001	010	040	105	213	355	511	658	780	869
6.8	001	009	034	093	192	327	480	628	755	850
7.0	001	007	030	082	173	301	450	599	729	830
7.2	001	006	025	072	156	276	420	569	703	810
7.4	001	005	022	063	140	253	392	539	676	788
7.6	001	004	019	055	125	231	365	510	648	765
7.8	000	004	016	048	112	210	338	481	620	741
8.0	000	003	014	042	100	191	313	453	593	717
8.5	000	002	009	030	074	150	256	386	523	653
9.0	000	001	006	021	055	116	207	324	456	587
9.5	000	001	004	015	040	089	165	269	392	522
10.0	000	000	003	010	029	067	130	220	333	458

np \ c	10	11	12	13	14	15	16	17	18	19
6.2	949	975	989	995	998	999	1,000			
6.4	939	969	986	994	997	999	1,000			
6.6	927	963	982	992	997	999	999	1,000		
6.8	915	955	978	990	996	998	999	1,000		
7.0	901	947	973	987	994	998	999	1,000		
7.2	887	937	967	984	993	997	999	999	1,000	
7.4	871	926	961	980	991	996	998	999	1,000	
7.6	854	915	954	976	989	995	998	999	1,000	
7.8	835	902	945	971	986	993	997	999	1,000	
8.0	816	888	936	966	983	992	996	998	999	1,000
8.5	763	849	909	949	973	986	993	997	999	999
9.0	706	803	876	926	959	978	989	995	998	999
9.5	645	752	836	898	940	967	982	991	996	998
10.0	583	697	792	864	917	951	973	986	993	997

np \ c	20	21	22
8.5	1,000		
9.0	1,000		
9.5	999	1,000	
10.0	998	999	1,000

TABLE E   Poisson Distribution *(Continued)*

np \ c	0	1	2	3	4	5	6	7	8	9
10.5	000	000	002	007	021	050	102	179	279	397
11.0	000	000	001	005	015	038	079	143	232	341
11.5	000	000	001	003	011	028	060	114	191	289
12.0	000	000	001	002	008	020	046	090	155	242
12.5	000	000	000	002	005	015	035	070	125	201
13.0	000	000	000	001	004	011	026	054	100	166
13.5	000	000	000	001	003	008	019	041	079	135
14.0	000	000	000	000	002	006	014	032	062	109
14.5	000	000	000	000	001	004	010	024	048	088
15.0	000	000	000	000	001	003	008	018	037	070

np \ c	10	11	12	13	14	15	16	17	18	19
10.5	521	639	742	825	888	932	960	978	988	994
11.0	460	579	689	781	854	907	944	968	982	991
11.5	402	520	633	733	815	878	924	954	974	986
12.0	347	462	576	682	772	844	899	937	963	979
12.5	297	406	519	628	725	806	869	916	948	969
13.0	252	353	463	573	675	764	835	890	930	957
13.5	211	304	409	518	623	718	798	861	908	942
14.0	176	260	358	464	570	669	756	827	883	923
14.5	145	220	311	413	518	619	711	790	853	901
15.0	118	185	268	363	466	568	664	749	819	875

np \ c	20	21	22	23	24	25	26	27	28	29
10.5	997	999	999	1,000						
11.0	995	998	999	1,000						
11.5	992	996	998	999	1,000					
12.0	988	994	997	999	999	1,000				
12.5	983	991	995	998	999	999	1,000			
13.0	975	986	992	996	998	999	1,000			
13.5	965	980	989	994	997	998	999	1,000		
14.0	952	971	983	991	995	997	999	999	1,000	
14.5	936	960	976	986	992	996	998	999	999	1,000
15.0	917	947	967	981	989	994	997	998	999	1,000

*Adapted with permission from E. L. Grant and Richard S. Leavenworth, "Statistical Quality Control," 4th ed., McGraw-Hill Book Company, New York, 1972.

CHART E   Poisson Chart*

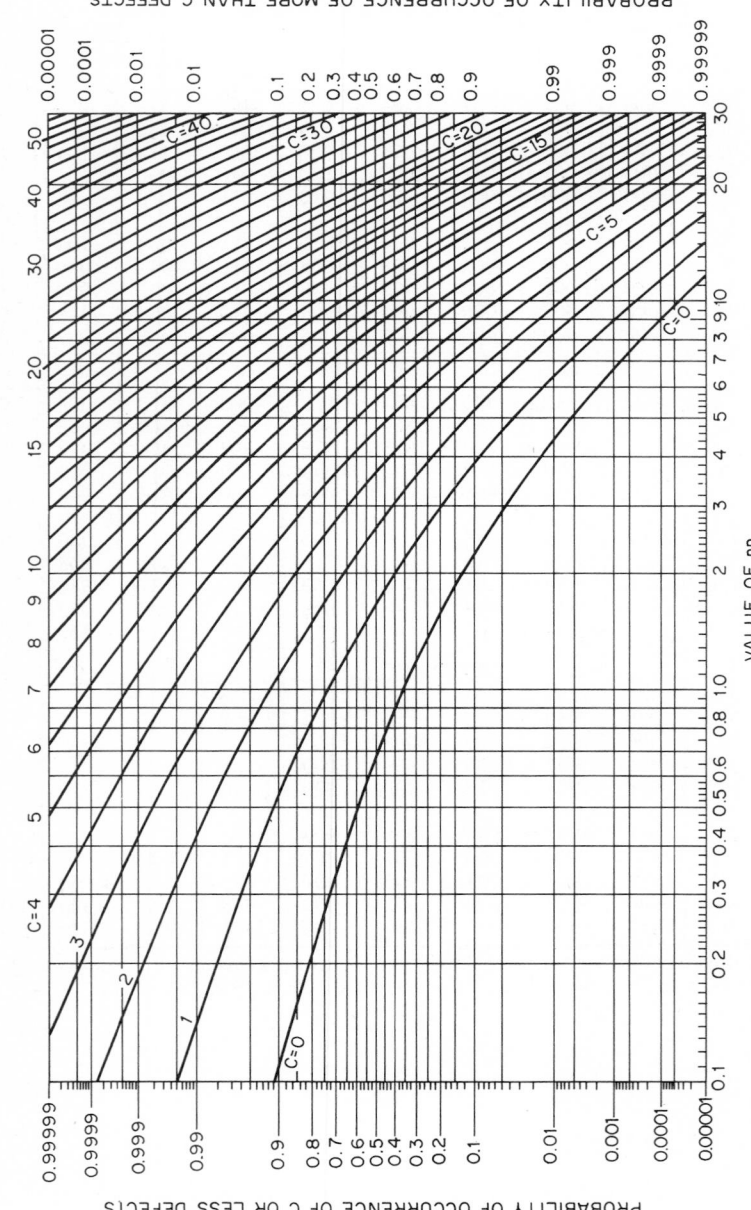

* Reproduced with permission from Harold F. Dodge and Harry G. Romig, "Sampling Inspection Tables," 2d ed., John Wiley & Sons, Inc., New York, 1959.

TABLE F Binomial Distribution*

Probability of r or fewer occurrences of an event in n trials, where p is the probability of occurrence on each trial.

n	r	p									
		0.05	0.10	0.15	0.20	0.25	0.30	0.35	0.40	0.45	0.50
2	0	0.9025	0.8100	0.7225	0.6400	0.5625	0.4900	0.4225	0.3600	0.3025	0.2500
	1	0.9975	0.9900	0.9775	0.9600	0.9375	0.9100	0.8775	0.8400	0.7975	0.7500
3	0	0.8574	0.7290	0.6141	0.5120	0.4219	0.3430	0.2746	0.2160	0.1664	0.1250
	1	0.9928	0.9720	0.9392	0.8960	0.8438	0.7840	0.7182	0.6480	0.5748	0.5000
	2	0.9999	0.9990	0.9966	0.9920	0.9844	0.9730	0.9571	0.9360	0.9089	0.8750
4	0	0.8145	0.6561	0.5220	0.4096	0.3164	0.2401	0.1785	0.1296	0.0915	0.0625
	1	0.9860	0.9477	0.8905	0.8192	0.7383	0.6517	0.5630	0.4752	0.3910	0.3125
	2	0.9995	0.9963	0.9880	0.9728	0.9492	0.9163	0.8735	0.8208	0.7585	0.6875
	3	1.0000	0.9999	0.9995	0.9984	0.9961	0.9919	0.9850	0.9744	0.9590	0.9375
5	0	0.7738	0.5905	0.4437	0.3277	0.2373	0.1681	0.1160	0.0778	0.0503	0.0312
	1	0.9774	0.9185	0.8352	0.7373	0.6328	0.5282	0.4284	0.3370	0.2562	0.1875
	2	0.9988	0.9914	0.9734	0.9421	0.8965	0.8369	0.7648	0.6826	0.5931	0.5000
	3	1.0000	0.9995	0.9978	0.9933	0.9844	0.9692	0.9460	0.9130	0.8688	0.8125
	4	1.0000	1.0000	0.9999	0.9997	0.9990	0.9976	0.9947	0.9898	0.9815	0.9688
6	0	0.7351	0.5314	0.3771	0.2621	0.1780	0.1176	0.0754	0.0467	0.0277	0.0156
	1	0.9672	0.8857	0.7765	0.6554	0.5339	0.4202	0.3191	0.2333	0.1636	0.1094
	2	0.9978	0.9842	0.9527	0.9011	0.8306	0.7443	0.6471	0.5443	0.4415	0.3438
	3	0.9999	0.9987	0.9941	0.9830	0.9624	0.9295	0.8826	0.8208	0.7447	0.6562
	4	1.0000	0.9999	0.9996	0.9984	0.9954	0.9891	0.9777	0.9590	0.9308	0.8906
	5	1.0000	1.0000	1.0000	0.9999	0.9998	0.9993	0.9982	0.9959	0.9917	0.9844

TABLE F Binomial Distribution *(Continued)*

n	r						p					
		0.05	0.10	0.15	0.20	0.25	0.30	0.35	0.40	0.45	0.50
7	0	0.6983	0.4783	0.3206	0.2097	0.1335	0.0824	0.0490	0.0280	0.0152	0.0078
	1	0.9556	0.8503	0.7166	0.5767	0.4449	0.3294	0.2338	0.1586	0.1024	0.0625
	2	0.9962	0.9743	0.9262	0.8520	0.7564	0.6471	0.5323	0.4199	0.3164	0.2266
	3	0.9998	0.9973	0.9879	0.9667	0.9294	0.8740	0.8002	0.7102	0.6083	0.5000
	4	1.0000	0.9998	0.9988	0.9953	0.9871	0.9712	0.9444	0.9037	0.8471	0.7734
	5	1.0000	1.0000	0.9999	0.9996	0.9987	0.9962	0.9910	0.9812	0.9643	0.9375
	6	1.0000	1.0000	1.0000	1.0000	0.9999	0.9998	0.9994	0.9984	0.9963	0.9922
8	0	0.6634	0.4305	0.2725	0.1678	0.1001	0.0576	0.0319	0.0168	0.0084	0.0039
	1	0.9428	0.8131	0.6572	0.5033	0.3671	0.2553	0.1691	0.1064	0.0632	0.0352
	2	0.9942	0.9619	0.8948	0.7969	0.6785	0.5518	0.4278	0.3154	0.2201	0.1445
	3	0.9996	0.9950	0.9786	0.9437	0.8862	0.8059	0.7064	0.5941	0.4770	0.3633
	4	1.0000	0.9996	0.9971	0.9896	0.9727	0.9420	0.8939	0.8263	0.7396	0.6367
	5	1.0000	1.0000	0.9998	0.9988	0.9958	0.9887	0.9747	0.9502	0.9115	0.8555
	6	1.0000	1.0000	1.0000	0.9999	0.9996	0.9987	0.9964	0.9915	0.9819	0.9648
	7	1.0000	1.0000	1.0000	1.0000	1.0000	0.9999	0.9998	0.9993	0.9983	0.9961
9	0	0.6302	0.3874	0.2316	0.1342	0.0751	0.0404	0.0207	0.0101	0.0046	0.0020
	1	0.9288	0.7748	0.5995	0.4362	0.3003	0.1960	0.1211	0.0705	0.0385	0.0195
	2	0.9916	0.9470	0.8591	0.7382	0.6007	0.4628	0.3373	0.2318	0.1495	0.0898
	3	0.9994	0.9917	0.9661	0.9144	0.8343	0.7297	0.6089	0.4826	0.3614	0.2539
	4	1.0000	0.9991	0.9944	0.9804	0.9511	0.9012	0.8283	0.7334	0.6214	0.5000
	5	1.0000	0.9999	0.9994	0.9969	0.9900	0.9747	0.9464	0.9006	0.8342	0.7461
	6	1.0000	1.0000	1.0000	0.9997	0.9987	0.9957	0.9888	0.9750	0.9502	0.9102
	7	1.0000	1.0000	1.0000	1.0000	0.9999	0.9996	0.9986	0.9962	0.9909	0.9805
	8	1.0000	1.0000	1.0000	1.0000	1.0000	1.0000	0.9999	0.9997	0.9992	0.9980

n	x										
10	0	0.5987	0.3487	0.1969	0.1074	0.0563	0.0282	0.0135	0.0060	0.0025	0.0010
	1	0.9139	0.7361	0.5443	0.3758	0.2440	0.1493	0.0860	0.0464	0.0232	0.0107
	2	0.9885	0.9298	0.8202	0.6778	0.5256	0.3828	0.2616	0.1673	0.0996	0.0547
	3	0.9990	0.9872	0.9500	0.8791	0.7759	0.6496	0.5138	0.3823	0.2660	0.1719
	4	0.9999	0.9984	0.9901	0.9672	0.9219	0.8497	0.7515	0.6331	0.5044	0.3770
	5	1.0000	0.9999	0.9986	0.9936	0.9803	0.9527	0.9051	0.8338	0.7384	0.6230
	6	1.0000	1.0000	0.9999	0.9991	0.9965	0.9894	0.9740	0.9452	0.8980	0.8281
	7	1.0000	1.0000	1.0000	0.9999	0.9996	0.9984	0.9952	0.9877	0.9726	0.9453
	8	1.0000	1.0000	1.0000	1.0000	1.0000	0.9999	0.9995	0.9983	0.9955	0.9893
	9	1.0000	1.0000	1.0000	1.0000	1.0000	1.0000	1.0000	0.9999	0.9997	0.9990

* Adapted with permission from Irwin Miller and John E. Freund, "Probability and Statistics for Engineers," Prentice-Hall, Inc., Englewood Cliffs, N.J., copyright © 1965, pp. 388–389.

For more extensive tables see The Staff of the Harvard University Computation Laboratory, "Tables of the Cumulative Binomial Probability Distribution," Harvard University Press, Cambridge, Mass., 1955, or W. H. Robertson, "Tables of the Binomial Distribution Function for Small Value of p," Sandia Corporation Monograph, January 1960, Available from the Office of Technical Services, Department of Commerce, Washington, D.C.

TABLE G * Distribution of t

Value of t corresponding to certain selected probabilities (i.e., tail areas under the curve). To illustrate: the probability is 0.95 that a sample with 20 degrees of freedom would have $t = +2.086$ or smaller.

DF	$t_{.60}$	$t_{.70}$	$t_{.80}$	$t_{.90}$	$t_{.95}$	$t_{.975}$	$t_{.99}$	$t_{.995}$
1	0.325	0.727	1.376	3.078	6.314	12.706	31.821	63.657
2	0.289	0.617	1.061	1.886	2.920	4.303	6.965	9.925
3	0.277	0.584	0.978	1.638	2.353	3.182	4.541	5.841
4	0.271	0.569	0.941	1.533	2.132	2.776	3.747	4.604
5	0.267	0.559	0.920	1.476	2.015	2.571	3.365	4.032
6	0.265	0.553	0.906	1.440	1.943	2.447	3.143	3.707
7	0.263	0.549	0.896	1.415	1.895	2.365	2.998	3.499
8	0.262	0.546	0.889	1.397	1.860	2.306	2.896	3.355
9	0.261	0.543	0.883	1.383	1.833	2.262	2.821	3.250
10	0.260	0.542	0.879	1.372	1.812	2.228	2.764	3.169
11	0.260	0.540	0.876	1.363	1.796	2.201	2.718	3.106
12	0.259	0.539	0.873	1.356	1.782	2.179	2.681	3.055
13	0.259	0.538	0.870	1.350	1.771	2.160	2.650	3.012
14	0.258	0.537	0.868	1.345	1.761	2.145	2.624	2.977
15	0.258	0.536	0.866	1.341	1.753	2.131	2.602	2.947
16	0.258	0.535	0.865	1.337	1.746	2.120	2.583	2.921
17	0.257	0.534	0.863	1.333	1.740	2.110	2.567	2.898
18	0.257	0.534	0.862	1.330	1.734	2.101	2.552	2.878
19	0.257	0.533	0.861	1.328	1.729	2.093	2.539	2.861
20	0.257	0.533	0.860	1.325	1.725	2.086	2.528	2.845
21	0.257	0.532	0.859	1.323	1.721	2.080	2.518	2.831
22	0.256	0.532	0.858	1.321	1.717	2.074	2.508	2.819
23	0.256	0.532	0.858	1.319	1.714	2.069	2.500	2.807
24	0.256	0.531	0.857	1.318	1.711	2.064	2.492	2.797
25	0.256	0.531	0.856	1.316	1.708	2.060	2.485	2.787
26	0.256	0.531	0.856	1.315	1.706	2.056	2.479	2.779
27	0.256	0.531	0.855	1.314	1.703	2.052	2.473	2.771
28	0.256	0.530	0.855	1.313	1.701	2.048	2.467	2.763
29	0.256	0.530	0.854	1.311	1.699	2.045	2.462	2.756
30	0.256	0.530	0.854	1.310	1.697	2.042	2.457	2.750
40	0.255	0.529	0.851	1.303	1.684	2.021	2.423	2.704
60	0.254	0.527	0.848	1.296	1.671	2.000	2.390	2.660
120	0.254	0.526	0.845	1.289	1.658	1.980	2.358	2.617
∞	0.253	0.524	0.842	1.282	1.645	1.960	2.326	2.576

* Adapted by permission from W. J. Dixon and F. J. Massey, Jr., "Introduction to Statistical Analysis," 3d ed., McGraw-Hill Book Company, New York, copyright © 1969. Entries originally from Table III of R. A. Fisher and F. Yates, "Statistical Tables," Oliver & Boyd, Ltd., London.

TABLE H* Percentile for $\tau_1 = \dfrac{\overline{X} - \mu_0}{R}$

Sample size	$\phi_{.95}$	$\phi_{.975}$	$\phi_{.99}$
2	3.175	6.353	15.910
3	0.885	1.304	2.111
4	0.529	0.717	1.023
5	0.388	0.507	0.685
6	0.312	0.399	0.523
7	0.263	0.333	0.429
8	0.230	0.288	0.366
9	0.205	0.255	0.322
10	0.186	0.230	0.288
11	0.170	0.210	0.262
12	0.158	0.194	0.241
13	0.147	0.181	0.224
14	0.138	0.170	0.209
15	0.131	0.160	0.197
16	0.124	0.151	0.186
17	0.118	0.144	0.177
18	0.113	0.137	0.168
19	0.108	0.131	0.161
20	0.104	0.126	0.154

* Adapted with permission from E. Lord, The Use of the Range in Place of the Standard Deviation in the *t* Test, *Biometrika,* vol. 34, 1957.

TABLE I Critical Values of *r* for the Sign Test*

Percentages are values for α for a two-tail
test. (Two-tail percentage points are given
for the binomial for $p = 0.05$.)

N	1%	5%	10%	25%
1				
2				
3				0
4				0
5			0	0
6		0	0	1
7		0	0	1
8	0	0	1	1
9	0	1	1	2
10	0	1	1	2
11	0	1	2	3
12	1	2	2	3
13	1	2	3	3
14	1	2	3	4
15	2	3	3	4
16	2	3	4	5
17	2	4	4	5
18	3	4	5	6
19	3	4	5	6
20	3	5	5	6
21	4	5	6	7
22	4	5	6	7
23	4	6	7	8
24	5	6	7	8
25	5	7	7	9
26	6	7	8	9
27	6	7	8	10
28	6	8	9	10
29	7	8	9	10
30	7	9	10	11
31	7	9	10	11
32	8	9	10	12
33	8	10	11	12
34	9	10	11	13
35	9	11	12	13
36	9	11	12	14
37	10	12	13	14
38	10	12	13	14
39	11	12	13	15
40	11	13	14	15
41	11	13	14	16
42	12	14	15	16
43	12	14	15	17
44	13	15	16	17
45	13	15	16	18
46	13	15	16	18
47	14	16	17	19
48	14	16	17	19
49	15	17	18	19
50	15	17	18	20

* Adapted with permission from W. J. Dixon and F. J. Massey, Jr., "Introduction to Statistical Analysis," 3d ed., McGraw-Hill Book Company, New York, copyright © 1969.

TABLE J* Percentiles for $\tau_d = \dfrac{\bar{X}_1 - \bar{X}_2}{\frac{1}{2}(R_1 + R_2)}$

$n = n_A = n_B$	$\phi'_{.95}$	$\phi'_{.975}$	$\phi'_{.99}$
2	2.322	3.427	5.553
3	0.974	1.272	1.715
4	0.644	0.813	1.047
5	0.493	0.613	0.772
6	0.405	0.499	0.621
7	0.347	0.426	0.525
8	0.306	0.373	0.459
9	0.275	0.334	0.409
10	0.250	0.304	0.371
11	0.233	0.280	0.340
12	0.214	0.260	0.315
13	0.201	0.243	0.294
14	0.189	0.189	0.276
15	0.179	0.216	0.261
16	0.170	0.205	0.247
17	0.162	0.195	0.236
18	0.155	0.187	0.225
19	0.149	0.179	0.216
20	0.143	0.172	0.207

* Adapted with permission from E. Lord, The Use of the Range in Place of the Standard Deviation in the t Test, *Biometrika*, vol. 34, 1947.

TABLE K[*] Distribution of F

Values of F corresponding to certain selected probabilities (i.e., tail areas under the curve). To illustrate: the probability is 0.05 that the ratio of two sample variances obtained with 20 and 10 degrees of freedom in numerator and denominator, respectively, would have $F = 2.77$ or larger. For a two-sided test, a lower limit is found by taking the reciprocal of the tabulated F value for the degrees of freedom in reverse. For the above example, with 10 and 20 degrees of freedom in numerator and denominator respectively, F is 2.35 and $1/F$ is $1/2.35$, or 0.43. The probability is 0.10 that F is 0.43 or smaller or 2.77 or larger.

n_2 \ n_1	1	2	3	4	5	6	7	8	9
					$F_{.95}$ (n_1, n_2)				
1	161.4	199.5	215.7	224.6	230.2	234.0	236.8	238.9	240.5
2	18.51	19.00	19.16	19.25	19.30	19.33	19.35	19.37	19.38
3	10.13	9.55	9.28	9.12	9.01	8.94	8.89	8.85	8.81
4	7.71	6.94	6.59	6.39	6.26	6.16	6.09	6.04	6.00
5	6.61	5.79	5.41	5.19	5.05	4.95	4.88	4.82	4.77
6	5.99	5.14	4.76	4.53	4.39	4.28	4.21	4.15	4.10
7	5.59	4.74	4.35	4.12	3.97	3.87	3.79	3.73	3.68
8	5.32	4.46	4.07	3.84	3.69	3.58	3.50	3.44	3.39
9	5.12	4.26	3.86	3.63	3.48	3.37	3.29	3.23	3.18
10	4.96	4.10	3.71	3.48	3.33	3.22	3.14	3.07	3.02
11	4.84	3.98	3.59	3.36	3.20	3.09	3.01	2.95	2.90
12	4.75	3.89	3.49	3.26	3.11	3.00	2.91	2.85	2.80
13	4.67	3.81	3.41	3.18	3.03	2.92	2.83	2.77	2.71
14	4.60	3.74	3.34	3.11	2.96	2.85	2.76	2.70	2.65
15	4.54	3.68	3.29	3.06	2.90	2.79	2.71	2.64	2.59
16	4.49	3.63	3.24	3.01	2.85	2.74	2.66	2.59	2.54
17	4.45	3.59	3.20	2.96	2.81	2.70	2.61	2.55	2.49
18	4.41	3.55	3.16	2.93	2.77	2.66	2.58	2.51	2.46
19	4.38	3.52	3.13	2.90	2.74	2.63	2.54	2.48	2.42
20	4.35	3.49	3.10	2.87	2.71	2.60	2.51	2.45	2.39
21	4.32	3.47	3.07	2.84	2.68	2.57	2.49	2.42	2.37
22	4.30	3.44	3.05	2.82	2.66	2.55	2.46	2.40	2.34
23	4.28	3.42	3.03	2.80	2.64	2.53	2.44	2.37	2.32
24	4.26	3.40	3.01	2.78	2.62	2.51	2.42	2.36	2.30
25	4.24	3.39	2.99	2.76	2.60	2.49	2.40	2.34	2.28
26	4.23	3.37	2.98	2.74	2.59	2.47	2.39	2.32	2.27
27	4.21	3.35	2.96	2.73	2.57	2.46	2.37	2.31	2.25
28	4.20	3.34	2.95	2.71	2.56	2.45	2.36	2.29	2.24
29	4.18	3.33	2.93	2.70	2.55	2.43	2.35	2.28	2.22
30	4.17	3.32	2.92	2.69	2.53	2.42	2.33	2.27	2.21
40	4.08	3.23	2.84	2.61	2.45	2.34	2.25	2.18	2.12
60	4.00	3.15	2.76	2.53	2.37	2.25	2.17	2.10	2.04
120	3.92	3.07	2.68	2.45	2.29	2.17	2.09	2.02	1.96
∞	3.84	3.00	2.60	2.37	2.21	2.10	2.01	1.94	1.88

n_1 = degrees of freedom for numerator. n_2 = degrees of freedom for denominator.

[*] Adapted with permission from E. S. Pearson and H. O. Hartley (eds.), "Biometrika Tables for Statisticians," 2d ed., vol. I, Cambridge University Press, New York, 1958.

10	12	15	20	24	30	40	60	120	∞
				$F_{.95}\ (n_1, n_2)$					
241.9	243.9	245.9	248.0	249.1	250.1	251.1	252.2	253.3	254.3
19.40	19.41	19.43	19.45	19.45	19.46	19.47	19.48	19.49	19.50
8.79	8.74	8.70	8.66	8.64	8.62	8.59	8.57	8.55	8.53
5.96	5.91	5.86	5.80	5.77	5.75	5.72	5.69	5.66	5.63
4.74	4.68	4.62	4.56	4.53	4.50	4.46	4.43	4.40	4.36
4.06	4.00	3.94	3.87	3.84	3.81	3.77	3.74	3.70	3.67
3.64	3.57	3.51	3.44	3.41	3.38	3.34	3.30	3.27	3.23
3.35	3.28	3.22	3.15	3.12	3.08	3.04	3.01	2.97	2.93
3.14	3.07	3.01	2.94	2.90	2.86	2.83	2.79	2.75	2.71
2.98	2.91	2.85	2.77	2.74	2.70	2.66	2.62	2.58	2.54
2.85	2.79	2.72	2.65	2.61	2.57	2.53	2.49	2.45	2.40
2.75	2.69	2.62	2.54	2.51	2.47	2.43	2.38	2.34	2.30
2.67	2.60	2.53	2.46	2.42	2.38	2.34	2.30	2.25	2.21
2.60	2.53	2.46	2.39	2.35	2.31	2.27	2.22	2.18	2.13
2.54	2.48	2.40	2.33	2.29	2.25	2.20	2.16	2.11	2.07
2.49	2.42	2.35	2.28	2.24	2.19	2.15	2.11	2.06	2.01
2.45	2.38	2.31	2.23	2.19	2.15	2.10	2.06	2.01	1.96
2.41	2.34	2.27	2.19	2.15	2.11	2.06	2.02	1.97	1.92
2.38	2.31	2.23	2.16	2.11	2.07	2.03	1.98	1.93	1.88
2.35	2.28	2.20	2.12	2.08	2.04	1.99	1.95	1.90	1.84
2.32	2.25	2.18	2.10	2.05	2.01	1.96	1.92	1.87	1.81
2.30	2.23	2.15	2.07	2.03	1.98	1.94	1.89	1.84	1.78
2.27	2.20	2.13	2.05	2.01	1.96	1.91	1.86	1.81	1.76
2.25	2.18	2.11	2.03	1.98	1.94	1.89	1.84	1.79	1.73
2.24	2.16	2.09	2.01	1.96	1.92	1.87	1.82	1.77	1.71
2.22	2.15	2.07	1.99	1.95	1.90	1.85	1.80	1.75	1.69
2.20	2.13	2.06	1.97	1.93	1.88	1.84	1.79	1.73	1.67
2.19	2.12	2.04	1.96	1.91	1.87	1.82	1.77	1.71	1.65
2.18	2.10	2.03	1.94	1.90	1.85	1.81	1.75	1.70	1.64
2.16	2.09	2.01	1.93	1.89	1.84	1.79	1.74	1.68	1.62
2.08	2.00	1.92	1.84	1.79	1.74	1.69	1.64	1.58	1.51
1.99	1.92	1.84	1.75	1.70	1.65	1.59	1.53	1.47	1.39
1.91	1.83	1.75	1.66	1.61	1.55	1.50	1.43	1.35	1.25
1.83	1.75	1.67	1.57	1.52	1.46	1.39	1.32	1.22	1.00

TABLE K   Distribution of F *(Continued)*

n_2 \ n_1	1	2	3	4	5	6	7	8	9
					$F_{.975}(n_1, n_2)$				
1	647.8	799.5	864.2	899.6	921.8	937.1	948.2	956.7	963.3
2	38.51	39.00	39.17	39.25	39.30	39.33	39.36	39.37	39.39
3	17.44	16.04	15.44	15.10	14.88	14.73	14.62	14.54	14.47
4	12.22	10.65	9.98	9.60	9.36	9.20	9.07	8.98	8.90
5	10.01	8.43	7.76	7.39	7.15	6.98	6.85	6.76	6.68
6	8.81	7.26	6.60	6.23	5.99	5.82	5.70	5.60	5.52
7	8.07	6.54	5.89	5.52	5.29	5.12	4.99	4.90	4.82
8	7.57	6.06	5.42	5.05	4.82	4.65	4.53	4.43	4.36
9	7.21	5.71	5.08	4.72	4.48	4.32	4.20	4.10	4.03
10	6.94	5.46	4.83	4.47	4.24	4.07	3.95	3.85	3.78
11	6.72	5.26	4.63	4.28	4.04	3.88	3.76	3.66	3.59
12	6.55	5.10	4.47	4.12	3.89	3.73	3.61	3.51	3.44
13	6.41	4.97	4.35	4.00	3.77	3.60	3.48	3.39	3.31
14	6.30	4.86	4.24	3.89	3.66	3.50	3.38	3.29	3.21
15	6.20	4.77	4.15	3.80	3.58	3.41	3.29	3.20	3.12
16	6.12	4.69	4.08	3.73	3.50	3.34	3.22	3.12	3.05
17	6.04	4.62	4.01	3.66	3.44	3.28	3.16	3.06	2.98
18	5.98	4.56	3.95	3.61	3.38	3.22	3.10	3.01	2.93
19	5.92	4.51	3.90	3.56	3.33	3.17	3.05	2.96	2.88
20	5.87	4.46	3.86	3.51	3.29	3.13	3.01	2.91	2.84
21	5.83	4.42	3.82	3.48	3.25	3.09	2.97	2.87	2.80
22	5.79	4.38	3.78	3.44	3.22	3.05	2.93	2.84	2.76
23	5.75	4.35	3.75	3.41	3.18	3.02	2.90	2.81	2.73
24	5.72	4.32	3.72	3.38	3.15	2.99	2.87	2.78	2.70
25	5.69	4.29	3.69	3.35	3.13	2.97	2.85	2.75	2.68
26	5.66	4.27	3.67	3.33	3.10	2.94	2.82	2.73	2.65
27	5.63	4.24	3.65	3.31	3.08	2.92	2.80	2.71	2.63
28	5.61	4.22	3.63	3.29	3.06	2.90	2.78	2.69	2.61
29	5.59	4.20	3.61	3.27	3.04	2.88	2.76	2.67	2.59
30	5.57	4.18	3.59	3.25	3.03	2.87	2.75	2.65	2.57
40	5.42	4.05	3.46	3.13	2.90	2.74	2.62	2.53	2.45
60	5.29	3.93	3.34	3.01	2.79	2.63	2.51	2.41	2.33
120	5.15	3.80	3.23	2.89	2.67	2.52	2.39	2.30	2.22
∞	5.02	3.69	3.12	2.79	2.57	2.41	2.29	2.19	2.11

$F_{.975}\ (n_1, n_2)$

10	12	15	20	24	30	40	60	120	∞
968.6	976.7	984.9	993.1	997.2	1,001	1,006	1,010	1,014	1,018
39.40	39.41	39.43	39.45	39.46	39.46	39:47	39.48	39.49	39.50
14.42	14.34	14.25	14.17	14.12	14.08	14.04	13.99	13.95	13.90
8.84	8.75	8.66	8.56	8.51	8.46	8.41	8.36	8.31	8.26
6.62	6.52	6.43	6.33	6.28	6.23	6.18	6.12	6.07	6.02
5.46	5.37	5.27	5.17	5.12	5.07	5.01	4.96	4.90	4.85
4.76	4.67	4.57	4.47	4.42	4.36	4.31	4.25	4.20	4.14
4.30	4.20	4.10	4.00	3.95	3.89	3.84	3.78	3.73	3.67
3.96	3.87	3.77	3.67	3.61	3.56	3.51	3.45	3.39	3.33
3.72	3.62	3.52	3.42	3.37	3.31	3.26	3.20	3.14	3.08
3.53	3.43	3.33	3.23	3.17	3.12	3.06	3.00	2.94	2.88
3.37	3.28	3.18	3.07	3.02	2.96	2.91	2.85	2.79	2.72
3.25	3.15	3.05	2.95	2.89	2.84	2.78	2.72	2.66	2.60
3.15	3.05	2.95	2.84	2.79	2.73	2.67	2.61	2.55	2.49
3.06	2.96	2.86	2.76	2.70	2.64	2.59	2.52	2.46	2.40
2.99	2.89	2.79	2.68	2.63	2.57	2.51	2.45	2.38	2.32
2.92	2.82	2.72	2.62	2.56	2.50	2.44	2.38	2.32	2.25
2.87	2.77	2.67	2.56	2.50	2.44	2.38	2.32	2.26	2.19
2.82	2.72	2.62	2.51	2.45	2.39	2.33	2.27	2.20	2.13
2.77	2.68	2.57	2.46	2.41	2.35	2.29	2.22	2.16	2.09
2.73	2.64	2.53	2.42	2.37	2.31	2.25	2.18	2.11	2.04
2.70	2.60	2.50	2.39	2.33	2.27	2.21	2.14	2.08	2.00
2.67	2.57	2.47	2.36	2.30	2.24	2.18	2.11	2.04	1.97
2.64	2.54	2.44	2.33	2.27	2.21	2.15	2.08	2.01	1.94
2.61	2.51	2.41	2.30	2.24	2.18	2.12	2.05	1.98	1.91
2.59	2.49	2.39	2.28	2.22	2.16	2.09	2.03	1.95	1.88
2.57	2.47	2.36	2.25	2.19	2.13	2.07	2.00	1.93	1.85
2.55	2.45	2.34	2.23	2.17	2.11	2.05	1.98	1.91	1.83
2.53	2.43	2.32	2.21	2.15	2.09	2.03	1.96	1.89	1.81
2.51	2.41	2.31	2.20	2.14	2.07	2.01	1.94	1.87	1.79
2.39	2.29	2.18	2.07	2.01	1.94	1.88	1.80	1.72	1.64
2.27	2.17	2.06	1.94	1.88	1.82	1.74	1.67	1.58	1.48
2.16	2.05	1.94	1.82	1.76	1.69	1.61	1.53	1.43	1.31
2.05	1.94	1.83	1.71	1.64	1.57	1.48	1.39	1.27	1.00

TABLE K   Distribution of F *(Continued)*

n_2 \ n_1	1	2	3	4	5	6	7	8	9
					$F_{.99}(n_1, n_2)$				
1	4,052	4,999.5	5,403	5,625	5,764	5,859	5,928	5,982	6,022
2	98.50	99.00	99.17	99.25	99.30	99.33	99.36	99.37	99.39
3	34.12	30.82	29.46	28.71	28.24	27.91	27.67	27.49	27.35
4	21.20	18.00	16.69	15.98	15.52	15.21	14.98	14.80	14.66
5	16.26	13.27	12.06	11.39	10.97	10.67	10.46	10.29	10.16
6	13.75	10.92	9.78	9.15	8.75	8.47	8.26	8.10	7.98
7	12.25	9.55	8.45	7.85	7.46	7.19	6.99	6.84	6.72
8	11.26	8.65	7.59	7.01	6.63	6.37	6.18	6.03	5.91
9	10.56	8.02	6.99	6.42	6.06	5.80	5.61	5.47	5.35
10	10.04	7.56	6.55	5.99	5.64	5.39	5.20	5.06	4.94
11	9.65	7.21	6.22	5.67	5.32	5.07	4.89	4.74	4.63
12	9.33	6.93	5.95	5.41	5.06	4.82	4.64	4.50	4.39
13	9.07	6.70	5.74	5.21	4.86	4.62	4.44	4.30	4.19
14	8.86	6.51	5.56	5.04	4.69	4.46	4.28	4.14	4.03
15	8.68	6.36	5.42	4.89	4.56	4.32	4.14	4.00	3.89
16	8.53	6.23	5.29	4.77	4.44	4.20	4.03	3.89	3.78
17	8.40	6.11	5.18	4.67	4.34	4.10	3.93	3.79	3.68
18	8.29	6.01	5.09	4.58	4.25	4.01	3.84	3.71	3.60
19	8.18	5.93	5.01	4.50	4.17	3.94	3.77	3.63	3.52
20	8.10	5.85	4.94	4.43	4.10	3.87	3.70	3.56	3.46
21	8.02	5.78	4.87	4.37	4.04	3.81	3.64	3.51	3.40
22	7.95	5.72	4.82	4.31	3.99	3.76	3.59	3.45	3.35
23	7.88	5.66	4.76	4.26	3.94	3.71	3.54	3.41	3.30
24	7.82	5.61	4.72	4.22	3.90	3.67	3.50	3.36	3.26
25	7.77	5.57	4.68	4.18	3.85	3.63	3.46	3.32	3.22
26	7.72	5.53	4.64	4.14	3.82	3.59	3.42	3.29	3.18
27	7.68	5.49	4.60	4.11	3.78	3.56	3.39	3.26	3.15
28	7.64	5.45	4.57	4.07	3.75	3.53	3.36	3.23	3.12
29	7.60	5.42	4.54	4.04	3.73	3.50	3.33	3.20	3.09
30	7.56	5.39	4.51	4.02	3.70	3.47	3.30	3.17	3.07
40	7.31	5.18	4.31	3.83	3.51	3.29	3.12	2.99	2.89
60	7.08	4.98	4.13	3.65	3.34	3.12	2.95	2.82	2.72
120	6.85	4.79	3.95	3.48	3.17	2.96	2.79	2.66	2.56
∞	6.63	4.61	3.78	3.32	3.02	2.80	2.64	2.51	2.41

$F_{.99}(n_1, n_2)$

10	12	15	20	24	30	40	60	120	∞
6,056	6,106	6,157	6,209	6,235	6,261	6,287	6,313	6,339	6,366
99.40	99.42	99.43	99.45	99.46	99.47	99.47	99.48	99.49	99.50
27.23	27.05	26.87	26.69	26.60	26.50	26.41	26.32	26.22	26.13
14.55	14.37	14.20	14.02	13.93	13.84	13.75	13.65	13.56	13.46
10.05	9.89	9.72	9.55	9.47	9.38	9.29	9.20	9.11	9.02
7.87	7.72	7.56	7.40	7.31	7.23	7.14	7.06	6.97	6.88
6.62	6.47	6.31	6.16	6.07	5.99	5.91	5.82	5.74	5.65
5.81	5.67	5.52	5.36	5.28	5.20	5.12	5.03	4.95	4.86
5.26	5.11	4.96	4.81	4.73	4.65	4.57	4.48	4.40	4.31
4.85	4.71	4.56	4.41	4.33	4.25	4.17	4.08	4.00	3.91
4.54	4.40	4.25	4.10	4.02	3.94	3.86	3.78	3.69	3.60
4.30	4.16	4.01	3.86	3.78	3.70	3.62	3.54	3.45	3.36
4.10	3.96	3.82	3.66	3.59	3.51	3.43	3.34	3.25	3.17
3.94	3.80	3.66	3.51	3.43	3.35	3.27	3.18	3.09	3.00
3.80	3.67	3.52	3.37	3.29	3.21	3.13	3.05	2.96	2.87
3.69	3.55	3.41	3.26	3.18	3.10	3.02	2.93	2.84	2.75
3.59	3.46	3.31	3.16	3.08	3.00	2.92	2.83	2.75	2.65
3.51	3.37	3.23	3.08	3.00	2.92	2.84	2.75	2.66	2.57
3.43	3.30	3.15	3.00	2.92	2.84	2.76	2.67	2.58	2.49
3.37	3.23	3.09	2.94	2.86	2.78	2.69	2.61	2.52	2.42
3.31	3.17	3.03	2.88	2.80	2.72	2.64	2.55	2.46	2.36
3.26	3.12	2.98	2.83	2.75	2.67	2.58	2.50	2.40	2.31
3.21	3.07	2.93	2.78	2.70	2.62	2.54	2.45	2.35	2.26
3.17	3.03	2.89	2.74	2.66	2.58	2.49	2.40	2.31	2.21
3.13	2.99	2.85	2.70	2.62	2.54	2.45	2.36	2.27	2.17
3.09	2.96	2.81	2.66	2.58	2.50	2.42	2.33	2.23	2.13
3.06	2.93	2.78	2.63	2.55	2.47	2.38	2.29	2.20	2.10
3.03	2.90	2.75	2.60	2.52	2.44	2.35	2.26	2.17	2.06
3.00	2.87	2.73	2.57	2.49	2.41	2.33	2.23	2.14	2.03
2.98	2.84	2.70	2.55	2.47	2.39	2.30	2.21	2.11	2.01
2.80	2.66	2.52	2.37	2.29	2.20	2.11	2.02	1.92	1.80
2.63	2.50	2.35	2.20	2.12	2.03	1.94	1.84	1.73	1.60
2.47	2.34	2.19	2.03	1.95	1.86	1.76	1.66	1.53	1.38
2.32	2.18	2.04	1.88	1.79	1.70	1.59	1.47	1.32	1.00

TABLE L* Distribution of χ^2

Values of χ^2 corresponding to certain selected probabilities (i.e., tail areas under the curve). To illustrate; the probability is 0.95 that a sample with 20 degrees of freedom, taken from a normal distribution, would have $\chi^2 = 31.41$ or smaller.

VALUES OF χ^2_p CORRESPONDING TO P

DF	$\chi^2_{.005}$	$\chi^2_{.01}$	$\chi^2_{.025}$	$\chi^2_{.05}$	$\chi^2_{.10}$	$\chi^2_{.90}$	$\chi^2_{.95}$	$\chi^2_{.975}$	$\chi^2_{.99}$	$\chi^2_{.995}$
1	0.000039	0.00016	0.00098	0.0039	0.0158	2.71	3.84	5.02	6.63	7.88
2	0.0100	0.0201	0.0506	0.1026	0.2107	4.61	5.99	7.38	9.21	10.60
3	0.0717	0.115	0.216	0.352	0.584	6.25	7.81	9.35	11.34	12.84
4	0.207	0.297	0.484	0.711	1.064	7.78	9.49	11.14	13.28	14.86
5	0.412	0.554	0.831	1.15	1.61	9.24	11.07	12.83	15.09	16.75
6	0.676	0.872	1.24	1.64	2.20	10.64	12.59	14.45	16.81	18.55
7	0.989	1.24	1.69	2.17	2.83	12.02	14.07	16.01	18.48	20.28
8	1.34	1.65	2.18	2.73	3.49	13.36	15.51	17.53	20.09	21.96
9	1.73	2.09	2.70	3.33	4.17	14.68	16.92	19.02	21.67	23.59
10	2.16	2.56	3.25	3.94	4.87	15.99	18.31	20.48	23.21	25.19
11	2.60	3.05	3.82	4.57	5.58	17.28	19.68	21.92	24.73	26.76
12	3.07	3.57	4.40	5.23	6.30	18.55	21.03	23.34	26.22	28.30
13	3.57	4.11	5.01	5.89	7.04	19.81	22.36	24.74	27.69	29.82
14	4.07	4.66	5.63	6.57	7.79	21.06	23.68	26.12	29.14	31.32
15	4.60	5.23	6.26	7.26	8.55	22.31	25.00	27.49	30.58	32.80
16	5.14	5.81	6.91	7.96	9.31	23.54	26.30	28.85	32.00	34.27
18	6.26	7.01	8.23	9.39	10.86	25.99	28.87	31.53	34.81	37.16
20	7.43	8.26	9.59	10.85	12.44	28.41	31.41	34.17	37.57	40.00
24	9.89	10.86	12.40	13.85	15.66	33.20	36.42	39.36	42.98	45.56
30	13.79	14.95	16.79	18.49	20.60	40.26	43.77	46.98	50.89	53.67
40	20.71	22.16	24.43	26.51	29.05	51.81	55.76	59.34	63.69	66.77
60	35.53	37.48	40.48	43.19	46.46	74.40	79.08	83.30	88.38	91.95
120	83.85	86.92	91.58	95.70	100.62	140.23	146.57	152.21	158.95	163.64

* Adapted with permission from W. J. Dixon and F. J. Massey, Jr., "Introduction to Statistical Analysis," 3d ed., McGraw-Hill Book Company, New York, copyright © 1969.

TABLE M* Percentiles of $F' = \dfrac{R_1}{R_2}$

Values of F' corresponding to certain selected cumulative probabilities. To illustrate: the probability is 0.95 that the ratio of sample ranges R_1/R_2 is 2.6 or less when $n_1 = n_2 = 5$

n_2	Cumulative probability	n_1								
		2	3	4	5	6	7	8	9	10
2	0.025	0.039	0.217	0.37	0.50	0.60	0.68	0.74	0.79	0.83
	0.05	0.079	0.31	0.50	0.62	0.74	0.80	0.86	0.91	0.95
	0.95	12.7	19.1	23	26	29	30	32	34	35
	0.975	25.5	38.2	52	57	60	62	64	67	68
3	0.025	0.026	0.160	0.28	0.39	0.47	0.54	0.59	0.64	0.68
	0.05	0.052	0.23	0.37	0.49	0.57	0.64	0.70	0.75	0.80
	0.95	3.19	4.4	5.0	5.7	6.2	6.6	6.9	7.2	7.4
	0.975	4.61	6.3	7.3	8.0	8.7	9.3	9.8	10.2	10.5
4	0.025	0.019	0.137	0.25	0.34	0.42	0.48	0.53	0.57	0.61
	0.05	0.043	0.20	0.32	0.42	0.50	0.57	0.62	0.67	0.70
	0.95	2.02	2.7	3.1	3.4	3.6	3.8	4.0	4.2	4.4
	0.975	2.72	3.5	4.0	4.4	4.7	5.0	5.2	5.4	5.6
5	0.025	0.018	0.124	0.23	0.32	0.38	0.44	0.49	0.53	0.57
	0.05	0.038	0.18	0.29	0.40	0.46	0.52	0.57	0.61	0.65
	0.95	1.61	2.1	2.4	2.6	2.8	2.9	3.0	3.1	3.2
	0.975	2.01	2.6	2.9	3.2	3.4	3.6	3.7	3.8	3.9
6	0.025	0.017	0.115	0.21	0.30	0.36	0.42	0.46	0.50	0.54
	0.05	0.035	0.16	0.27	0.36	0.43	0.49	0.54	0.58	0.61
	0.95	1.36	1.8	2.0	2.2	2.3	2.4	2.5	2.6	2.7
	0.975	1.67	2.1	2.4	2.6	2.8	2.9	3.0	3.1	3.2
7	0.025	0.016	0.107	0.20	0.28	0.34	0.40	0.44	0.48	0.52
	0.05	0.032	0.15	0.26	0.35	0.41	0.47	0.51	0.55	0.59
	0.95	1.26	1.6	1.8	1.9	2.0	2.1	2.2	2.3	2.4
	0.975	1.48	1.9	2.1	2.3	2.4	2.5	2.6	2.7	2.8
8	0.025	0.016	0.102	0.19	0.27	0.33	0.38	0.43	0.47	0.50
	0.05	0.031	0.14	0.25	0.33	0.40	0.45	0.50	0.53	0.57
	0.95	1.17	1.4	1.6	1.8	1.9	1.9	2.0	2.1	2.1
	0.975	1.36	1.7	1.9	2.0	2.2	2.3	2.3	2.4	2.5
9	0.025	0.015	0.098	0.18	0.26	0.32	0.37	0.42	0.46	0.49
	0.05	0.030	0.14	0.24	0.32	0.38	0.44	0.48	0.52	0.55
	0.95	1.10	1.3	1.5	1.6	1.7	1.8	1.9	1.9	2.0
	0.975	1.27	1.6	1.8	1.9	2.0	2.1	2.1	2.2	2.3
10	0.025	0.015	0.095	0.18	0.25	0.31	0.36	0.41	0.44	0.48
	0.05	0.029	0.13	0.23	0.31	0.37	0.43	0.47	0.51	0.54
	0.95	1.05	1.3	1.4	1.5	1.6	1.7	1.8	1.8	1.9
	0.975	1.21	1.5	1.6	1.8	1.9	1.9	2.0	2.0	2.1

* Adapted with permission from W. J. Dixon and F. J. Massey, Jr., "Introduction to Statistical Analysis," 3d ed., McGraw-Hill Book Company, New York, copyright © 1969.

CHART N   Confidence Limits for Fraction Defective*

Enter the horizontal scale with the sample fraction defective.   Rise vertically to the upper and lower curves for the stated sample size.   Read the corresponding upper and lower confidence limits on the vertical scale.   To illustrate: if a sample of 50 is 20% defective, the 95% confidence limits on the population fraction defective are 10 and 35%.

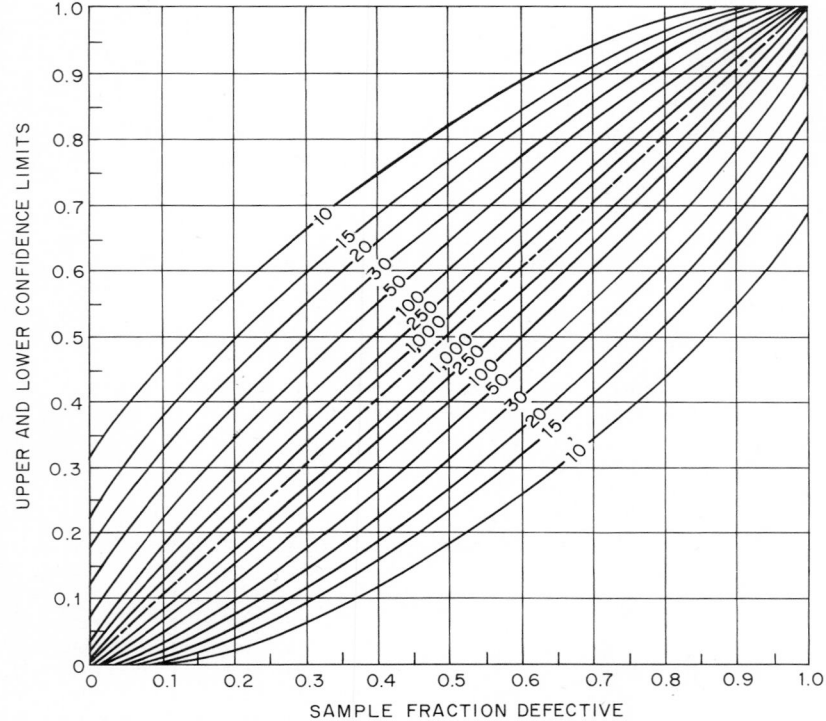

* By permission of Prof. E. S. Pearson from C. J. Clopper and E. S. Pearson, The Use of Confidence or Fiducial Limits Illustrated in the Case of the Binomial, *Biometrika,* vol. 26, p. 404, 1934.

TABLE O   Critical Values of Smaller Rank Sum for the Wilcoxon-Mann-Whitney Test*

n_2	α for 2-sided test	α for 1-sided test	n_1 (smaller sample)											
			1	2	3	4	5	6	7	8	9	10	11	12
3	0.20	0.10		3	7									
	0.10	0.05			6									
	0.05	0.025												
	0.01	0.005												
4	0.20	0.10		3	7	13								
	0.10	0.05			6	11								
	0.05	0.025				10								
	0.01	0.005												
5	0.20	0.10		4	8	14	20							
	0.10	0.05		3	7	12	19							
	0.05	0.025			6	11	17							
	0.01	0.005					15							
6	0.20	0.10		4	9	15	22	30						
	0.10	0.05		3	8	13	20	28						
	0.05	0.025			7	12	18	26						
	0.01	0.005				10	16	23						
7	0.20	0.10		4	10	16	23	32	41					
	0.10	0.05		3	8	14	21	29	39					
	0.05	0.025			7	13	20	27	36					
	0.01	0.005				10	16	24	32					
8	0.20	0.10		5	11	17	25	34	44	55				
	0.10	0.05		4	9	15	23	31	41	51				
	0.05	0.025		3	8	14	21	29	38	49				
	0.01	0.005				11	17	25	34	43				
9	0.20	0.10	1	5	11	19	27	36	46	58	70			
	0.10	0.05		4	9	16	24	33	43	54	66			
	0.05	0.025		3	8	14	22	31	40	51	62			
	0.01	0.005			6	11	18	26	35	45	56			
10	0.20	0.10	1	6	12	20	28	38	49	60	73	87		
	0.10	0.05		4	10	17	26	35	45	56	69	82		
	0.05	0.025		3	9	15	23	32	42	53	65	78		
	0.01	0.005			6	12	19	27	37	47	58	71		
11	0.20	0.10	1	6	13	21	30	40	51	63	76	91	106	
	0.10	0.05		4	11	18	27	37	47	59	72	86	100	
	0.05	0.025		3	9	16	24	34	44	55	68	81	96	
	0.01	0.005			6	12	20	28	38	49	61	73	87	
12	0.20	0.10	1	7	14	22	32	42	54	66	80	94	110	127
	0.10	0.05		5	11	19	28	38	49	62	75	89	104	120
	0.05	0.025		4	10	17	26	35	46	58	71	84	99	115
	0.01	0.005			7	13	21	30	40	51	63	76	90	105

*Reproduced by permission from M. W. Tate and R. C. Clelland, "Non-parametric and Shortcut Statistics," The Interstate Printers & Publishers, Inc., Danville, Ill., 1957.

TABLE P   Limiting Values for Number of Runs Above and Below the Median of a Set of Values*

(n_1 = number of values above the median and n_2 = number of values below the median)

$m = n_1 = n_2$	Probability of an equal or smaller number of runs		Probability of an equal or larger number of runs	
	$\alpha = 0.05$	$\alpha = 0.01$	$\alpha = 0.05$	$\alpha = 0.01$
5	3	2	9	10
6	3	2	11	12
7	4	3	12	13
8	5	4	13	14
9	6	4	14	16
10	6	5	16	17
11	7	6	17	18
12	8	7	18	19
13	9	7	19	21
14	10	8	20	22
15	11	9	21	23
16	11	10	23	24
17	12	10	24	26
18	13	11	25	27
19	14	12	26	28
20	15	13	27	29
21	16	14	28	30
22	17	14	29	32
23	17	15	31	33
24	18	16	32	34
25	19	17	33	35
26	20	18	34	36
27	21	19	35	37
28	22	19	36	39
29	23	20	37	40
30	24	21	38	41

* Reproduced by permission from Tables II and III of Freda S. Swed and C. Eisenhart, Tables for Testing Randomness of Grouping in a Sequence of Alternatives, *Annals of Mathematical Statistics,* vol. XIV, pp. 66, 87, 1943.

TABLE Q   Criteria for Testing for Extreme Mean*

Statistic	No. of observations	P_{90}	P_{95}	P_{98}	P_{99}
$r_{10} = \dfrac{X_2 - X_1}{X_n - X_1}$	3	0.886	0.941	0.976	0.988
	4	0.679	0.765	0.846	0.889
	5	0.557	0.642	0.729	0.780
	6	0.482	0.560	0.644	0.698
	7	0.434	0.507	0.586	0.637
$r_{11} = \dfrac{X_2 - X_1}{X_{n-1} - X_1}$	8	0.479	0.554	0.631	0.683
	9	0.441	0.512	0.587	0.635
	10	0.409	0.477	0.551	0.597
$r_{21} = \dfrac{X_3 - X_1}{X_{n-1} - X_1}$	11	0.517	0.576	0.638	0.679
	12	0.490	0.546	0.605	0.642
	13	0.467	0.521	0.578	0.615
$r_{22} = \dfrac{X_3 - X_1}{X_{n-2} - X_1}$	14	0.492	0.546	0.602	0.641
	15	0.472	0.525	0.579	0.616
	16	0.454	0.507	0.559	0.595
	17	0.438	0.490	0.542	0.577
	18	0.424	0.475	0.527	0.561
	19	0.412	0.462	0.514	0.547
	20	0.401	0.450	0.502	0.535
	21	0.391	0.440	0.491	0.524
	22	0.382	0.430	0.481	0.514
	23	0.374	0.421	0.472	0.505
	24	0.367	0.413	0.464	0.497
	25	0.360	0.406	0.457	0.489

* Adapted with permission from W. J. Dixon and F. J. Massey, Jr., "Introduction to Statistical Analysis," 3d ed., McGraw-Hill Book Company, New York, copyright © 1969.

CHART R Operating Characteristics of the Two-sided Normal Test for a Level of Significance equal to 0.05*

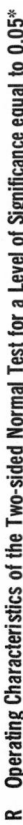

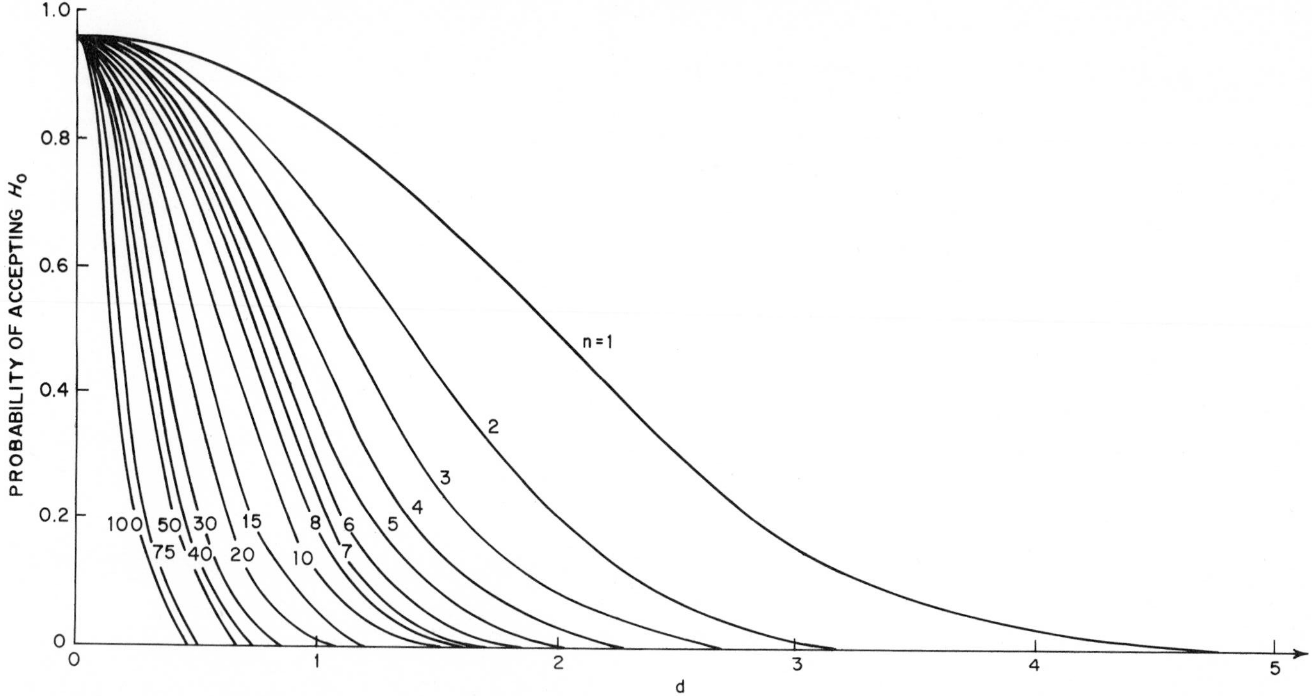
1.0
0.8
0.6
0.4
0.2
0
PROBABILITY OF ACCEPTING H_0
0
1
2
3
4
5
d
n = 1
2
3
4
5
6
7
8
10
15
20
30
40
50
75
100

* Adapted with permission from Charles D. Ferris, Frank E. Grubbs, and Chalmers L. Weaver, Operating Characteristics for the Common Statistical Tests of Significance, *Annals of Mathematical Statistics,* June 1946.

CHART S   Size of Sample for Arithmetic Mean When σ Is Unknown*

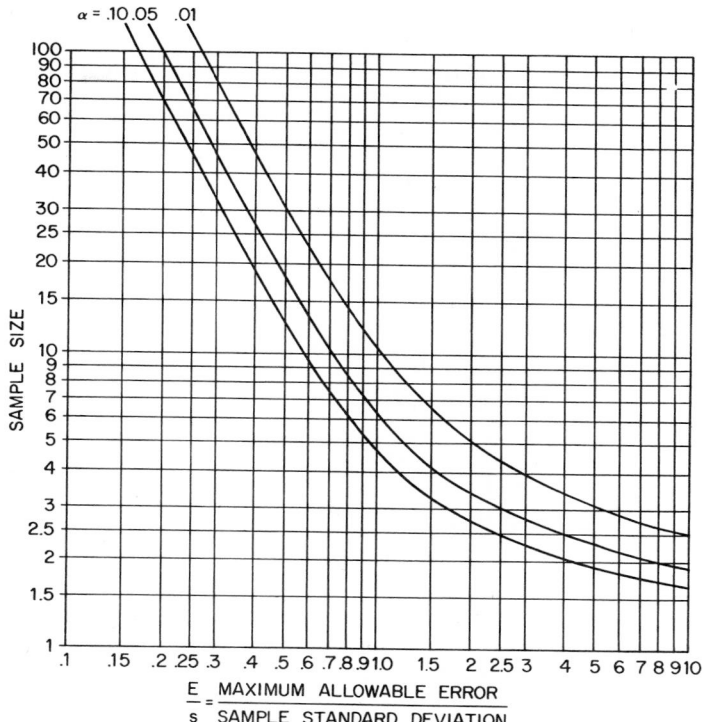

*Reproduced with permission from Frank M. Weida and Mary D. Lum, Statistical Inference, Reliability, and Significance, *WADC Technical Report* 53-149, U.S. Air Force, July 1953.

CHART T   Number of Degrees of Freedom Required to Estimate the Standard Deviation within P% of Its True Value with Confidence Coefficient γ

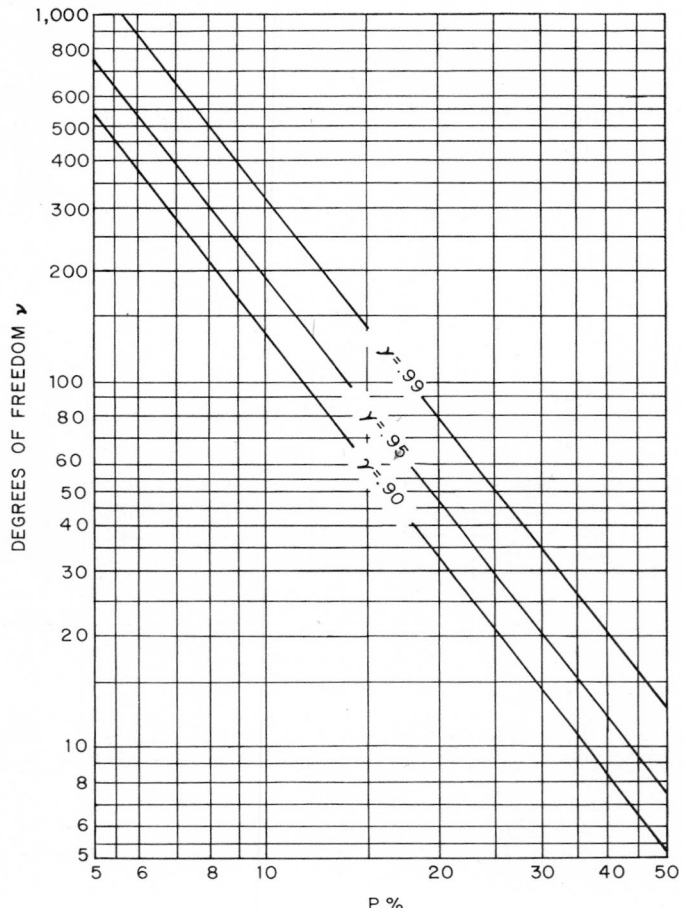

*Adapted with permission from J. A. Greenwood and M. M. Sandomire, Statistics Manual, Sample Size Required for Estimating the Standard Deviation as a Percent of its True Value, *Journal of the American Statistical Association,* vol. 45, p. 258, 1950. The manner of graphing is adapted with permission from E. L. Crow, F. A. Davis, and M. W. Maxfield, *NAVORD Report* 3369, NOTS 948, U.S. Naval Ordnance Test Station, China Lake, Calif., 1955. (Reprinted by Dover Publications, Inc., New York, 1960.)

TABLE U Tolerance Factors for Normal Distribution

Factors K_1 such that the probability is γ that at least a proportion P of the distribution will be included between $\bar{X} \pm K_1 R$ where $\bar{X}$ is the mean and R is the range in a sample of size n

P	$\gamma = 0.90$				$\gamma = 0.95$				$\gamma = 0.99$			
n	0.90	0.95	0.99	0.999	0.90	0.95	0.99	0.999	0.90	0.95	0.99	0.999
2	11.298	13.294	17.090	21.374	22.635	26.634	34.238	42.821	113.429	133.469	171.576	214.588
3	3.069	3.631	4.711	5.936	4.399	5.206	6.752	8.509	9.951	11.776	15.275	19.249
4	1.877	2.227	2.902	3.672	2.422	2.873	3.744	4.737	4.233	5.021	6.543	8.279
5	1.428	1.697	2.216	2.812	1.749	2.078	2.715	3.444	2.709	3.219	4.205	5.335
6	1.194	1.420	1.857	2.360	1.418	1.686	2.206	2.803	2.042	2.429	3.178	4.038
7	1.050	1.248	1.635	2.080	1.222	1.453	1.903	2.420	1.678	1.996	2.615	3.325
8	0.951	1.131	1.483	1.888	1.090	1.297	1.700	2.165	1.449	1.724	2.261	2.878
9	0.879	1.046	1.372	1.747	0.997	1.187	1.556	1.981	1.290	1.536	2.014	2.565
10	0.824	0.981	1.286	1.639	0.926	1.103	1.446	1.843	1.176	1.400	1.836	2.340
11	0.780	0.929	1.219	1.554	0.871	1.037	1.361	1.735	1.088	1.296	1.701	2.168
12	0.745	0.887	1.164	1.484	0.827	0.985	1.292	1.648	1.020	1.215	1.594	2.033
13	0.715	0.852	1.118	1.426	0.790	0.940	1.235	1.575	0.964	1.148	1.507	1.922
14	0.690	0.822	1.079	1.377	0.759	0.904	1.187	1.514	0.917	1.093	1.435	1.830
15	0.669	0.797	1.046	1.334	0.733	0.873	1.146	1.462	0.878	1.046	1.373	1.753
16	0.650	0.774	1.016	1.297	0.710	0.845	1.110	1.417	0.845	1.007	1.322	1.687
17	0.633	0.755	0.991	1.265	0.690	0.822	1.109	1.377	0.816	0.972	1.277	1.630
18	0.619	0.737	0.968	1.235	0.672	0.801	1.051	1.342	0.790	0.941	1.236	1.578
19	0.605	0.721	0.947	1.209	0.656	0.782	1.027	1.311	0.768	0.916	1.203	1.535
20	0.594	0.707	0.929	1.186	0.642	0.765	1.005	1.282	0.748	0.892	1.171	1.495

* Adapted with permission from S. K. Mitra, Tables for Tolerance Limits for a Normal Population Based on Sample Mean and Range on Mean Range, *Journal of the American Statistical Association*, vol. 52, No. 277, p. 92, March 1957.

TABLE V   One-sided and Two-sided Statistical Tolerance Limit Factors k for a Normal Distribution

Factors k such that the probability is γ that at least a proportion P of the distribution will be less than $\overline{X} + ks$ (or greater than $\overline{X} - ks$) where $\overline{X}$ and s are estimates of the mean and standard deviation computed from a sample size of n. Two-sided factors cover $\overline{X} \pm ks$.

One-sided Factors[a]

P → n ↓	$\gamma = 0.90$				$\gamma = 0.95$				$\gamma = 0.99$			
	0.90	0.95	0.99	0.999	0.90	0.95	0.99	0.999	0.90	0.95	0.99	0.999
3	4.258	5.310	7.340	9.651	6.158	7.655	10.552	13.857				
4	3.187	3.957	5.437	7.128	4.163	5.145	7.042	9.215				
5	2.742	3.400	4.666	6.112	3.407	4.202	5.741	7.501				
6	2.494	3.091	4.242	5.556	3.006	3.707	5.062	6.612	4.408	5.409	7.334	9.540
7	2.333	2.894	3.972	5.201	2.755	3.399	4.641	6.061	3.856	4.730	6.411	8.348
8	2.219	2.755	3.783	4.955	2.582	3.188	4.353	5.686	3.496	4.287	5.811	7.566
9	2.133	2.649	3.641	4.772	2.454	3.031	4.143	5.414	3.242	3.971	5.389	7.014
10	2.065	2.568	3.532	4.629	2.355	2.911	3.981	5.203	3.048	3.739	5.075	6.603
11	2.012	2.503	3.444	4.515	2.275	2.815	3.852	5.036	2.897	3.557	4.828	6.284
12	1.966	2.448	3.371	4.420	2.210	2.736	3.747	4.900	2.773	3.410	4.633	6.032
13	1.928	2.403	3.310	4.341	2.155	2.670	3.659	4.787	2.677	3.290	4.472	5.826
14	1.895	2.363	3.257	4.274	2.108	2.614	3.585	4.690	2.592	3.189	4.336	5.651
15	1.866	2.329	3.212	4.215	2.068	2.566	3.520	4.607	2.521	3.102	4.224	5.507
16	1.842	2.299	3.172	4.164	2.032	2.523	3.463	4.534	2.458	3.028	4.124	5.374
17	1.820	2.272	3.136	4.118	2.001	2.486	3.415	4.471	2.405	2.962	4.038	5.268
18	1.800	2.249	3.106	4.078	1.974	2.453	3.370	4.415	2.357	2.906	3.961	5.167
19	1.781	2.228	3.078	4.041	1.949	2.423	3.331	4.364	2.315	2.855	3.893	5.078
20	1.765	2.208	3.052	4.009	1.926	2.396	3.295	4.319	2.275	2.807	3.832	5.003
21	1.750	2.190	3.028	3.979	1.905	2.371	3.262	4.276	2.241	2.768	3.776	4.932
22	1.736	2.174	3.007	3.952	1.887	2.350	3.233	4.238	2.208	2.729	3.727	4.866
23	1.724	2.159	2.987	3.927	1.869	2.329	3.206	4.204	2.179	2.693	3.680	4.806
24	1.712	2.145	2.969	3.904	1.853	2.309	3.181	4.171	2.154	2.663	3.638	4.755
25	1.702	2.132	2.952	3.882	1.838	2.292	3.158	4.143	2.129	2.632	3.601	4.706
30	1.657	2.080	2.884	3.794	1.778	2.220	3.064	4.022	2.029	2.516	3.446	4.508
35	1.623	2.041	2.833	3.730	1.732	2.166	2.994	3.934	1.957	2.431	3.334	4.364
40	1.598	2.010	2.793	3.679	1.697	2.126	2.941	3.866	1.902	2.365	3.250	4.255
45	1.577	1.986	2.762	3.638	1.669	2.092	2.897	3.811	1.857	2.313	3.181	4.168
50	1.560	1.965	2.735	3.604	1.646	2.065	2.863	3.766	1.821	2.296	3.124	4.096

Two-sided Factors†

n												
2	15.978	18.800	24.167	30.227	32.019	37.674	48.430	60.573	160.193	188.491	242.300	303.054
3	5.847	6.919	8.974	11.309	8.380	9.916	12.861	16.208	18.930	22.401	29.055	36.616
4	4.166	4.943	6.440	8.149	5.380	6.370	8.299	10.502	9.398	11.150	14.527	18.383
5	3.494	4.152	5.423	6.879	4.275	5.079	6.634	8.415	6.612	7.855	10.260	13.015
6	3.131	3.723	4.870	6.188	3.712	4.414	5.775	7.337	5.337	6.345	8.301	10.548
7	2.902	3.452	4.521	5.750	3.369	4.007	5.248	6.676	4.613	5.488	7.187	9.142
8	2.743	3.264	4.278	5.446	3.136	3.732	4.891	6.226	4.147	4.936	6.468	8.234
9	2.626	3.125	4.098	5.220	2.967	3.532	4.631	5.899	3.822	4.550	5.966	7.600
10	2.535	3.018	3.959	5.046	2.839	3.379	4.433	5.649	3.582	4.265	5.594	7.129
11	2.463	2.933	3.849	4.906	2.737	3.259	4.277	5.452	3.397	4.045	5.308	6.766
12	2.404	2.863	3.758	4.792	2.655	3.162	4.150	5.291	3.250	3.870	5.079	6.477
13	2.355	2.805	3.682	4.697	2.587	3.081	4.044	5.158	3.130	3.727	4.893	6.240
14	2.314	2.756	3.618	4.615	2.529	3.012	3.955	5.045	3.029	3.608	4.737	6.043
15	2.278	2.713	3.562	4.545	2.480	2.954	3.878	4.949	2.945	3.507	4.605	5.876
16	2.246	2.676	3.514	4.484	2.437	2.903	3.812	4.865	2.872	3.421	4.492	5.732
17	2.219	2.643	3.471	4.430	2.400	2.858	3.754	4.791	2.808	3.345	4.393	5.607
18	2.194	2.614	3.433	4.382	2.366	2.819	3.702	4.725	2.753	3.279	4.307	5.497
19	2.172	2.588	3.399	4.339	2.337	2.784	3.656	4.667	2.703	3.221	4.230	5.399
20	2.152	2.564	3.368	4.300	2.310	2.752	3.615	4.614	2.659	3.168	4.161	5.312
21	2.135	2.543	3.340	4.264	2.286	2.723	3.577	4.567	2.620	3.121	4.100	5.234
22	2.118	2.524	3.315	4.232	2.264	2.697	3.543	4.523	2.584	3.078	4.044	5.163
23	2.103	2.506	3.292	4.203	2.244	2.673	3.512	4.484	2.551	3.040	3.993	5.098
24	2.089	2.480	3.270	4.176	2.225	2.651	3.483	4.447	2.522	3.004	3.947	5.039
25	2.077	2.474	3.251	4.151	2.208	2.631	3.457	4.413	2.494	2.972	3.904	4.985
26	2.065	2.460	3.232	4.127	2.193	2.612	3.432	4.382	2.460	2.941	3.865	4.935
27	2.054	2.447	3.215	4.106	2.178	2.595	3.409	4.353	2.446	2.914	3.828	4.888
30	2.025	2.413	3.170	4.049	2.140	2.549	3.350	4.278	2.385	2.841	3.733	4.768
35	1.988	2.368	3.112	3.974	2.090	2.490	3.272	4.179	2.306	2.748	3.611	4.611
40	1.959	2.334	3.066	3.917	2.052	2.445	3.213	4.104	2.247	2.677	3.518	4.493
45	1.935	2.306	3.030	3.871	2.021	2.408	3.165	4.042	2.200	2.621	3.444	4.399
50	1.916	2.284	3.001	3.833	1.996	2.379	3.126	3.993	2.162	2.576	3.385	4.323

* Adapted from Gerald J. Lieberman, Tables for One-sided Tolerance Limits, *Industrial Quality Control*, vol. XIV, No. 10, p. 8, April 1958, with the permission of the American Society for Quality Control.

† Adapted with permission from C. Eisenhart, M. W. Hastay, W. A. Wallis, "Techniques of Statistical Analysis," McGraw-Hill Book Company, New York, 1947.

TABLE W P for Interval between Sample Extremes*

γ is the probability that an interval will cover a proportion P of the population with a random sample of size N.

N \ γ	0.5	0.7	0.9	0.95	0.99	0.995
2	0.293	0.164	0.052	0.026	0.006	0.003
4	0.615	0.492	0.321	0.249	0.141	0.111
6	0.736	0.640	0.490	0.419	0.295	0.254
10	0.838	0.774	0.664	0.606	0.496	0.456
20	0.918	0.883	0.820	0.784	0.712	0.683
40	0.959	0.941	0.907	0.887	0.846	0.829
60	0.973	0.960	0.937	0.924	0.895	0.883
80	0.980	0.970	0.953	0.943	0.920	0.911
100	0.984	0.976	0.962	0.954	0.936	0.929
150	0.990	0.984	0.975	0.969	0.957	0.952
200	0.992	0.988	0.981	0.977	0.968	0.961
500	0.997	0.996	0.993	0.991	0.987	0.986
1,000	0.999	0.998	0.997	0.996	0.994	0.993

* Adapted with permission from W. J. Dixon and F. J. Massey, Jr., "Introduction to Statistical Analysis," 3d ed., McGraw-Hill Book Company, New York, copyright © 1969.

TABLE X N for Interval between Sample Extremes*

P \ γ	0.50	0.70	0.90	0.95	0.99	0.995
0.995	336	488	777	947	1,325	1,483
0.99	168	244	388	473	662	740
0.95	34	49	77	93	130	146
0.90	17	24	38	46	64	72
0.85	11	16	25	30	42	47
0.80	9	12	18	22	31	34
0.75	7	10	15	18	24	27
0.70	6	8	12	14	20	22
0.60	4	6	9	10	14	16
0.50	3	5	7	8	11	12

* Adapted with permission from W. J. Dixon and F. J. Massey, Jr., "Introduction to Statistical Analysis," 3d ed., McGraw-Hill Book Company, New York, copyright © 1969.

TABLE Y Factors for $\bar{X}$, R, σ, and X Control Charts—Trial Control Limits.*

$$\begin{cases} \text{Upper control limit for } \bar{X} = UCL_{\bar{X}} = \bar{\bar{X}} + A_2\bar{R} \\ \text{Lower control limit for } \bar{X} = LCL_{\bar{X}} = \bar{\bar{X}} - A_2\bar{R} \\ \qquad\qquad\qquad or \\ \text{Upper control limit for } \bar{X} = UCL_{\bar{X}} = \bar{\bar{X}} + A_1\bar{\sigma} \\ \text{Lower control limit for } \bar{X} = LCL_{\bar{X}} = \bar{\bar{X}} - A_1\bar{\sigma} \end{cases}$$

$$\begin{cases} \text{Upper control limit for } R = UCL_R = D_4\bar{R} \\ \text{Lower control limit for } R = LCL_R = D_3\bar{R} \end{cases}$$

$$\begin{cases} \text{Upper control limit for } \sigma = UCL_\sigma = B_4\bar{\sigma} \\ \text{Lower control limit for } \sigma = LCL_\sigma = B_3\bar{\sigma} \end{cases}$$

$$\begin{cases} \text{Upper control limit for } X = \bar{\bar{X}} + E_2\bar{R} \\ \text{Lower control limit for } X = \bar{\bar{X}} - E_2\bar{R} \\ \qquad\qquad\qquad or \\ \text{Upper control limit for } X = \bar{X} + E_1\bar{\sigma} \\ \text{Lower control limit for } X = \bar{X} - E_1\bar{\sigma} \end{cases}$$

Number of observations in subgroup	Factors for $\bar{X}$ chart		Factors for R chart		Factors for σ chart		Factors for X chart	
	From $\bar{R}$ A_2	From $\bar{\sigma}$ A_1	Lower D_3	Upper D_4	Lower B_3	Upper B_4	From $\bar{R}$ E_2	From $\bar{\sigma}$ E_1
2	1.880	3.759	0	3.268	0	3.267	2.660	5.318
3	1.023	2.394	0	2.574	0	2.568	1.772	4.146
4	0.729	1.880	0	2.282	0	2.266	1.457	3.760
5	0.577	1.596	0	2.114	0	2.089	1.290	3.568
6	0.483	1.410	0	2.004	0.030	1.970	1.184	3.454
7	0.419	1.277	0.076	1.924	0.118	1.882	1.109	3.378
8	0.373	1.175	0.136	1.864	0.185	1.815	1.054	3.323
9	0.337	1.094	0.184	1.816	0.239	1.761	0.010	3.283
10	0.308	1.028	0.223	1.777	0.284	1.716	0.975	3.251
11	0.285	0.973	0.256	1.744	0.321	1.679	0.946	3.226
12	0.266	0.925	0.284	1.717	0.354	1.646	0.921	3.205
13	0.249	0.884	0.308	1.692	0.382	1.618	0.899	3.188
14	0.235	0.848	0.329	1.671	0.406	1.594	0.881	3.174
15	0.223	0.817	0.348	1.652	0.428	1.572	0.864	3.161
16	0.212	0.788			0.448	1.552		
17	0.203	0.762			0.466	1.534		
18	0.194	0.738			0.482	1.518		
19	0.187	0.717			0.497	1.503		
20	0.180	0.698			0.510	1.490		
21	0.173	0.680			0.523	1.477		
22	0.167	0.662			0.534	1.466		
23	0.162	0.647			0.545	1.455		
24	0.157	0.632			0.555	1.445		
25	0.153	0.619			0.565	1.435		
Over 25	†	†			†	†		

*Factors reproduced from "1950 ASTM Manual on Quality Control of Materials" by permission of the American Society for Testing and Materials, Philadelphia, Pa. All factors in Table Y are based on a normal distribution.

†Values of these constants may be determined for larger sample sizes from the formulas given in the Glossary of Symbols.

CHART Z   Control Limits for p Charts

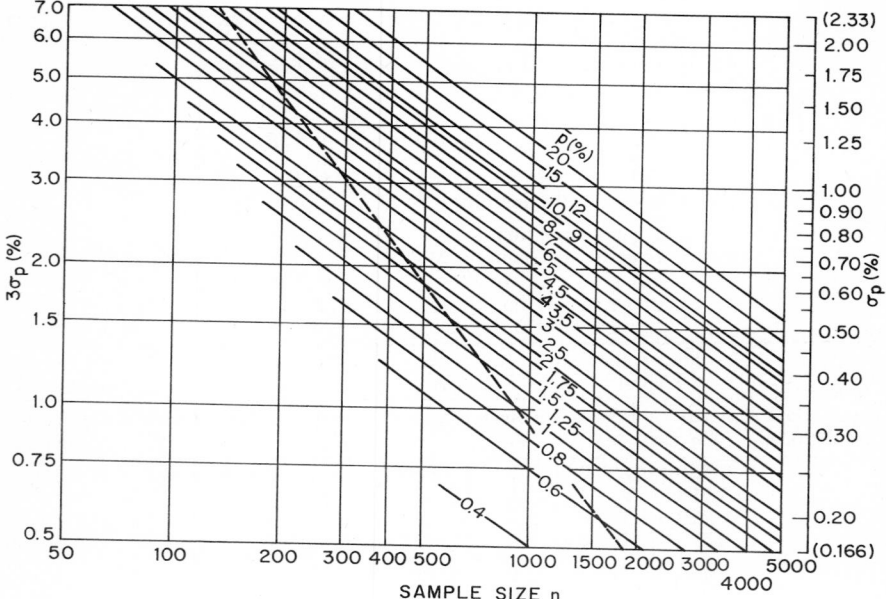

SAMPLE SIZE n

CHART AA   Control Limits for c, Number of Defects per Sample*

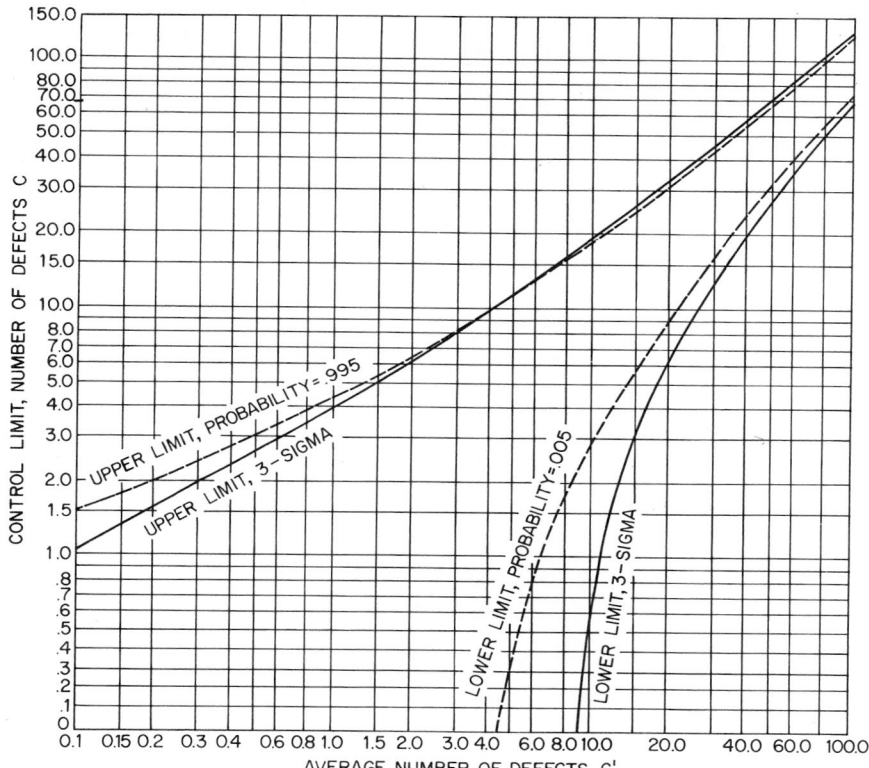

*Reproduced by permission from American War Standard Z1.3-1942, American Standards Association, New York.

TABLE BB   Factors for Cumulative Sum Control Chart*

$$2\,\alpha_0 = 0.0027$$
$$\alpha_0 = 0.00135\dagger$$

δ	θ	d
0.2	5°43′	330.4
0.4	11°19′	82.6
0.5	14°00′	52.9
0.6	16°42′	36.7
0.8	21°48′	20.6
1.0	26°34′	13.2
1.2	30°58′	9.2
1.3	32°59′	7.8
1.4	35°00′	6.7
1.6	38°40′	5.2
1.8	41°59′	4.1
2.0	45°00′	3.3
2.2	47°44′	2.7
2.4	50°12′	2.3
2.6	52°26′	2.0
2.8	54°28′	1.7
3.0	56°19′	1.5

† For limits comparable with the 3-sigma limits used in the Shewhart control chart.

*Adapted with permission from Norman L. Johnson and Fred C. Leone, "Statistics and Experimental Design in Engineering and Physical Sciences," vol. I, p. 322, John Wiley & Sons, Inc. New York, 1964.

TABLE CC Factors for $\bar{X}$, R, and σ Control Charts—Control to Selected Standards*

$$\begin{cases} UCL_{\bar{X}} = \bar{X}' + A\sigma' \\ LCL_{\bar{X}} = \bar{X}' - A\sigma' \end{cases}$$

(If actual average is to be used rather than standard or aimed-at average, $\bar{\bar{X}}$ should be substituted for $\bar{X}'$ in the preceeding formulas.)

$$\begin{cases} UCL_R = D_2\sigma' \\ \text{Central line }_R = d_2\sigma' \\ LCL_R = D_1\sigma' \end{cases}$$

$$\begin{cases} UCL_\sigma = B_2\sigma' \\ \text{Central line}_\sigma = c_2\sigma' \\ LCL_\sigma = B_1\sigma' \end{cases}$$

Number of observations in subgroup	Factor for $\bar{X}$ chart A	Factors for R chart		Factors for σ chart	
		Lower limit D_1	Upper limit D_2	Lower limit B_1	Upper limit B_2
2	2.121	0	3.686	0	1.843
3	1.732	0	4.358	0	1.858
4	1.500	0	4.698	0	1.808
5	1.342	0	4.918	0	1.756
6	1.225	0	5.078	0.026	1.711
7	1.134	0.205	5.203	0.105	1.672
8	1.061	0.387	5.307	0.167	1.638
9	1.000	0.546	5.394	0.219	1.609
10	0.949	0.687	5.469	0.262	1.584
11	0.905	0.812	5.534	0.299	1.561
12	0.866	0.925	5.593	0.331	1.541
13	0.832	1.026	5.646	0.359	1.523
14	0.802	1.121	5.693	0.384	1.507
15	0.775	1.207	5.737	0.406	1.492
16	0.750			0.427	1.478
17	0.728			0.445	1.465
18	0.707			0.461	1.454
19	0.688			0.477	1.443
20	0.671			0.491	1.433
21	0.655			0.504	1.424
22	0.639			0.516	1.415
23	0.626			0.527	1.407
24	0.612			0.538	1.399
25	0.600			0.548	1.392
Over 25	†			†	†

* Factors reproduced from "1950 ASTM Manual on Quality Control of Materials" by permission of the American Society for Testing and Materials, Philadelphia, Pa.

† Values of these factors may be determined for larger sample sizes from the formulas given in the Glossary of Symbols. All factors in Table CC are based on a normal distribution.

TABLE DD   Random Numbers*

1306	1189	5731	3968	5606	5084	8947	3897	1636	7810
0422	2431	0649	8085	5053	4722	6598	5044	9040	5121
6597	2022	6168	5060	8656	6733	6364	7649	1871	4328
7965	6541	5645	6243	7658	6903	9911	5740	7824	8520
7695	6937	0406	8894	0441	8135	9797	7285	5905	9539
5160	7851	8464	6789	3938	4197	6511	0407	9239	2232
2961	0551	0539	8288	7478	7565	5581	5771	5442	8761
1428	4183	4312	5445	4854	9157	9158	5218	1464	3634
3666	5642	4539	1561	7849	7520	2547	0756	1206	2033
6543	6799	7454	9052	6689	1946	2574	9386	0304	7945
9975	6080	7423	3175	9377	6951	6519	8287	8994	5532
4866	0956	7545	7723	8085	4948	2228	9583	4415	7065
8239	7068	6694	5168	3117	1586	0237	6160	9585	1133
8722	9191	3386	3443	0434	4586	4150	1224	6204	0937
1330	9120	8785	8382	2929	7089	3109	6742	2468	7025
2296	2952	4764	9070	6356	9192	4012	0618	2219	1109
3582	7052	3132	4519	9250	2486	0830	8472	2160	7046
5872	9207	7222	6494	8973	3545	6967	8490	5264	9821
1134	6324	6201	3792	5651	0538	4676	2064	0584	7996
1403	4497	7390	8503	8239	4236	8022	2914	4368	4529
3393	7025	3381	3553	2128	1021	8353	6413	5161	8583
1137	7896	3602	0060	7850	7626	0854	6565	4260	6220
7437	5198	8772	6927	8527	6851	2709	5992	7383	1071
8414	8820	3917	7238	9821	6073	6658	1280	9643	7761
8398	5224	2749	7311	5740	9771	7826	9533	3800	4553
0995	8935	2939	3092	2496	0359	0318	4697	7181	4035
6657	0755	9685	4017	6581	7292	5643	5064	1142	1297
8875	8369	7868	0190	9278	1709	4253	9346	4335	3769
8399	6702	0586	6428	7985	2979	4513	1970	1989	3105
6703	1024	2064	0393	6815	8502	1375	4171	6970	1201
4730	1653	9032	9855	0957	7366	0325	5178	7959	5371
8400	6834	3187	8688	1079	1480	6776	9888	7585	9998
3647	8002	6726	0877	4552	3238	7542	7804	3933	9475
6789	5197	8037	2354	9262	5497	0005	3986	1767	7981
2630	2721	2810	2185	6323	5679	4931	8336	6662	3566
1374	8625	1644	3342	1587	0762	6057	8011	2666	3759
1572	7625	9110	4409	0239	7059	3415	5537	2250	7292
9678	2877	7579	4935	0449	8119	6969	5383	1717	6719
0882	6781	3538	4090	3092	2365	6001	3446	9985	6007
0006	4205	2389	4365	1981	8158	7784	6256	3842	5603
4611	9861	7916	9305	2074	9462	0254	4827	9198	3974
1093	3784	4190	6332	1175	8599	9735	8584	6581	7194
3374	3545	6865	8819	3342	1676	2264	6014	5012	2458
3650	9676	1436	4374	4716	5548	8276	6235	6742	2154
7292	5749	7977	7602	9205	3599	3880	9537	4423	2330
2353	8319	2850	4026	3027	1708	3518	7034	7132	6903
1094	2009	8919	5676	7283	4982	9642	7235	8167	3366
0568	4002	0587	7165	1094	2006	7471	0940	4366	9554
5606	4070	5233	4339	6543	6695	5799	5821	3953	9458
8285	7537	1181	2300	5294	6892	1627	3372	1952	3028

* Adapted with permission from Donald B. Owen, "Handbook of Statistical Tables," Addison-Wesley Publishing Company, Inc., Reading, Mass., 1962. Courtesy of U.S. Atomic Energy Commission.

TABLE EE* Percentiles of the Studentized Range q

Values of q corresponding to a probability of 0.95. To illustrate: the probability is 0.95 that q (the range per standard deviation) is 4.59 or less when the number of treatments t is 6 and the degrees of freedom v is 15.

v \ t	2	3	4	5	6	7	8	9	10	11	12	13	14	15	20
1	17.97	26.98	32.82	37.08	40.41	43.12	45.40	47.36	49.07	50.59	51.96	53.20	54.33	55.36	59.56
2	6.08	8.33	9.80	10.88	11.74	12.44	13.03	13.54	13.99	14.39	14.75	15.08	15.38	15.65	16.77
3	4.50	5.91	6.82	7.50	8.04	8.48	8.85	9.18	9.46	9.72	9.95	10.15	10.35	10.52	11.24
4	3.93	5.04	5.76	6.29	6.71	7.05	7.35	7.60	7.83	8.03	8.21	8.37	8.52	8.66	9.23
5	3.64	4.60	5.22	5.67	6.03	6.33	6.58	6.80	6.99	7.17	7.32	7.47	7.60	7.72	8.21
6	3.46	4.34	4.90	5.30	5.63	5.90	6.12	6.32	6.49	6.65	6.79	6.92	7.03	7.14	7.59
7	3.34	4.16	4.68	5.06	5.36	5.61	5.82	6.00	6.16	6.30	6.43	6.55	6.66	6.76	7.17
8	3.26	4.04	4.53	4.89	5.17	5.40	5.60	5.77	5.92	6.05	6.18	6.29	6.39	6.48	6.87
9	3.20	3.95	4.41	4.76	5.02	5.24	5.43	5.59	5.74	5.87	5.98	6.09	6.19	6.28	6.64
10	3.15	3.88	4.33	4.65	4.91	5.12	5.30	5.46	5.60	5.72	5.83	5.93	6.03	6.11	6.47
11	3.11	3.82	4.26	4.57	4.82	5.03	5.20	5.35	5.49	5.61	5.71	5.81	5.90	5.98	6.33
12	3.08	3.77	4.20	4.51	4.75	4.95	5.12	5.27	5.39	5.51	5.61	5.71	5.80	5.88	6.21
13	3.06	3.73	4.15	4.45	4.69	4.88	5.05	5.19	5.32	5.43	5.53	5.63	5.71	5.79	6.11
14	3.03	3.70	4.11	4.41	4.64	4.83	4.99	5.13	5.25	5.36	5.46	5.55	5.64	5.71	6.03
15	3.01	3.67	4.08	4.37	4.59	4.78	4.94	5.08	5.20	5.31	5.40	5.49	5.57	5.65	5.96
20	2.95	3.58	3.96	4.23	4.45	4.62	4.77	4.90	5.01	5.11	5.20	5.28	5.36	5.43	5.71
∞	2.77	3.31	3.63	3.86	4.03	4.17	4.29	4.39	4.47	4.55	4.62	4.68	4.74	4.80	5.01

* Adapted by permission from James Pachares, Tables of the Upper 10% Points of the Studentized Range (Accompanied by Revised Tables of 5% and 1% Points), *Biometrika*, vol. 46, December 1959.

TABLE FF   Values of ϕ^2 for Determining Sample Size in Analysis of Variance*

$\alpha = 0.01; \ \beta = 0.2$

DF$_2$ \ DF$_1$	1	2	3	4	5	6	7	8	9	
2	80.37	106.63	119.75	127.62	132.87	136.63	139.45	141.63	143.38	
4	17.28	18.58	18.95	19.11	19.18	19.21	19.23	19.24	19.24	
6	11.36	11.12	10.77	10.49	10.27	10.11	9.97	9.86	9.77	
8	9.41	8.76	8.21	7.83	7.54	7.32	7.15	7.01	6.89	
10	8.47	7.63	7.02	6.58	6.26	6.03	5.84	5.68	5.56	
12	7.91	6.98	6.33	5.87	5.54	5.29	5.09	4.93	4.80	
14	7.55	6.56	5.88	5.41	5.07	4.81	4.61	4.45	4.31	
16	7.30	6.26	5.56	5.09	4.75	4.49	4.28	4.11	3.98	
18	7.11	6.05	5.35	4.86	4.51	4.24	4.04	3.87	3.73	
20	6.96	5.89	5.17	4.68	4.33	4.06	3.85	3.68	3.54	
24	6.76	5.66	4.93	4.41	4.08	3.80	3.57	3.42	3.28	
30	6.55	5.42	4.68	4.19	3.82	3.55	3.33	3.16	3.02	
40	6.35	5.20	4.45	3.96	3.57	3.31	3.10	2.92	2.79	
60	6.18	5.00	4.25	3.74	3.37	3.10	2.88	2.70	2.55	
80	6.10	4.88	4.16	3.65	3.28	2.99	2.76	2.59	2.43	
120	6.00	4.80	4.04	3.53	3.17	2.89	2.66	2.50	2.34	
240	5.90	4.71	3.96	3.46	3.06	2.79	2.56	2.40	2.25	
∞	5.84	4.62	3.87	3.35	2.98	2.70	2.47	2.29	2.14	

* These tables are computed from Emma Lehmer, Inverse Tables of Probabilities of Errors of Second Kind, *Annals of Mathematical Statistics,* vol. 15, p. 390, 1944.   Reproduced from W. J. Dixon and F. J. Massey, Jr., "Introduction to Statistical Analysis," 1st ed., p. 330, McGraw-Hill Book Company, New York.

10	12	15	20	24	30	40	60	120	∞
144.82	147.02	149.30	151.63	152.84	154.06	155.30	156.55	157.83	159.09
19.24	19.24	19.24	19.22	19.21	19.21	19.19	19.18	19.18	19.17
9.69	9.57	9.44	9.30	9.22	9.14	9.07	8.99	8.90	8.81
6.80	6.64	6.48	6.31	6.21	6.12	6.02	5.91	5.81	5.70
5.45	5.29	5.11	4.92	4.82	4.71	4.61	4.49	4.38	4.26
4.69	4.52	4.33	4.13	4.02	3.91	3.80	3.68	3.56	3.43
4.20	4.02	3.83	3.63	3.52	3.40	3.28	3.16	3.03	2.89
3.86	3.68	3.48	3.27	3.16	3.04	2.92	2.80	2.66	2.52
3.61	3.43	3.23	3.01	2.90	2.78	2.66	2.53	2.39	2.24
3.42	3.23	3.03	2.82	2.70	2.58	2.46	2.32	2.18	2.03
3.13	2.96	2.76	2.53	2.43	2.31	2.16	2.02	1.88	1.72
2.90	2.70	2.50	2.27	2.16	2.02	1.88	1.74	1.59	1.42
2.66	2.46	2.25	2.02	1.90	1.77	1.61	1.46	1.30	1.13
2.43	2.23	2.02	1.78	1.66	1.52	1.37	1.21	1.04	0.841
2.31	2.13	1.90	1.66	1.54	1.39	1.25	1.08	0.902	0.689
2.22	2.02	1.80	1.56	1.44	1.28	1.12	0.960	0.766	0.528
2.13	1.90	1.69	1.44	1.32	1.17	1.00	0.828	0.624	0.345
2.02	1.81	1.58	1.34	1.21	1.05	0.884	0.704	0.472	0.000

TABLE GG Critical Values of L for Link-Wallace Test*

n \ k	2	3	4	5	6	7	8	9	10	11	12	13	14	15	16	17	18	19	20
2	3.43	2.37	1.78	1.40	1.16	1.00	0.87	0.78	0.70	0.66	0.63	0.58	0.50	0.47	0.44	0.42	0.40	0.38	0.36
3	1.91	1.44	1.13	0.94	0.80	0.70	0.62	0.56	0.51	0.47	0.43	0.40	0.38	0.36	0.33	0.32	0.30	0.29	0.27
4	1.63	1.25	1.01	0.84	0.72	0.63	0.57	0.51	0.47	0.43	0.40	0.37	0.35	0.33	0.31	0.29	0.28	0.27	0.25
5	1.53	1.19	0.96	0.81	0.70	0.61	0.55	0.50	0.45	0.42	0.39	0.36	0.34	0.32	0.30	0.29	0.27	0.26	0.25
6	1.50	1.18	0.95	0.80	0.69	0.61	0.55	0.49	0.45	0.42	0.39	0.36	0.34	0.32	0.30	0.29	0.27	0.26	0.25
7	1.49	1.17	0.95	0.80	0.69	0.61	0.55	0.50	0.45	0.42	0.39	0.36	0.34	0.32	0.30	0.29	0.28	0.26	0.25
8	1.49	1.17	0.96	0.81	0.70	0.62	0.55	0.50	0.46	0.42	0.39	0.37	0.35	0.33	0.31	0.29	0.28	0.27	0.25
9	1.50	1.18	0.97	0.82	0.71	0.62	0.56	0.51	0.47	0.43	0.40	0.37	0.35	0.33	0.31	0.30	0.28	0.27	0.26
10	1.52	1.20	0.98	0.83	0.72	0.63	0.57	0.52	0.47	0.44	0.41	0.38	0.35	0.34	0.32	0.30	0.29	0.27	0.26
11	1.54	1.21	0.99	0.84	0.73	0.64	0.58	0.52	0.48	0.44	0.41	0.38	0.36	0.34	0.32	0.31	0.29	0.28	0.27
12	1.56	1.23	1.00	0.85	0.74	0.65	0.59	0.53	0.49	0.45	0.42	0.39	0.37	0.35	0.33	0.31	0.30	0.28	0.27
13	1.58	1.25	1.02	0.86	0.75	0.66	0.59	0.54	0.49	0.46	0.42	0.40	0.37	0.35	0.33	0.32	0.30	0.29	0.27
14	1.60	1.26	1.03	0.87	0.76	0.67	0.60	0.55	0.50	0.46	0.43	0.40	0.38	0.36	0.34	0.32	0.31	0.29	0.28
15	1.62	1.28	1.05	0.89	0.77	0.68	0.61	0.56	0.51	0.47	0.44	0.41	0.38	0.36	0.34	0.33	0.31	0.30	0.28
16	1.64	1.30	1.06	0.90	0.78	0.69	0.62	0.56	0.52	0.48	0.44	0.41	0.39	0.37	0.35	0.33	0.31	0.30	0.29
17	1.66	1.31	1.08	0.91	0.79	0.70	0.63	0.57	0.52	0.48	0.45	0.42	0.39	0.37	0.35	0.33	0.32	0.30	0.29
18	1.68	1.33	1.09	0.92	0.80	0.71	0.64	0.58	0.53	0.49	0.46	0.43	0.40	0.38	0.36	0.34	0.32	0.31	0.30
19	1.70	1.34	1.10	0.93	0.81	0.72	0.65	0.59	0.54	0.50	0.46	0.43	0.40	0.38	0.36	0.34	0.33	0.31	0.30
20	1.72	1.36	1.11	0.95	0.82	0.73	0.65	0.59	0.54	0.50	0.47	0.44	0.41	0.39	0.37	0.35	0.33	0.32	0.30

* Adapted by permission from T. E. Kurtz, B. F. Link, J. W. Tukey, and D. L. Wallace, Short-Cut Multiple Comparisons for Balanced, Single and Double Classifications: Part 1, Results, *Technometrics*, vol. 6, No. 2, pp. 106–107, May 1965.
  k = number of groups = number of ranges.   n = number in group = number per range.

Name Index

Abbe, Robert C., 13-19n.
Abramowitz, M., 20-39n., 20-40n.
Abrams, Harry N., 14-27n.
Ackley, Robert A., 13-3n.
Ackoff, R. L., 47-12n.
Acton, F. S., 26-4, 26-26
Adams, S. K., 33-17n.
Addelman, Sidney, 27-24, 27-25, 27-48
Adkins, L. A., Jr., 8-30n.
Adler, Lee, 14-12n.
Agnew, P. G., 4-22n.
Ahlborg, Kurt, 15-25n.
Alaimo, A. P., 21-8n.
Allen, G. C., 30-33
Allen, Paul E., 12-20n., 12-78
Allen, T. H., 8-4n.
Alopondis, James, 41-13
Amidon, E. H., 42-35
Anderson, L. E., 29-5n.
Anderson, Norman G., 12-19n.
Anderson, P. L., 40-7n.
Anderson, V. L., 27-40, 27-48
Andrews, D. L., 20-56
Angelo, N. B., 20-56
Anthony, R. N., 19-2n.
Antle, C. E., 22-50, 22-69
Arnold, W. E., 23-34, 23-35
Aroian, Leo A., 38-12
Aron, J. S., 20-47n.
Artim, Edward, 39-34
Asaka, Tetsuichi, 21-7n., 48-10n.
Asay, K. C., 17-10n.
Asgari, M., 20-56
Aspley, J. C., 14-32n.
Astrachan, Max, 17-24n.
Atkinson, A. C., 29-6n.
Aubin, Albert E., 41-1n.
Azgaldov, G. G., 21-33n.

Baba, Motomu, 16-44n.
Babakitis, J., 30-17
Backus, Fred F., 12-74n.
Bagley, J. M., 30-22
Bailey, Earl L., 4-15n.
Bailey, Larry E., 23-9, 23-35
Bailey, R. N., 30-22
Bain, L. J., 22-50, 22-69
Bainbridge, T. R., 27-36 to 27-38, 27-48, 29-13n.

Baker, Bronson B., 15-3n.
Bakunts, G., 31-25
Baldwin, J. G., 30-24n.
Ball, Leslie W., 8-16n., 44-1
Bar, Alfredo, 6-7n.
Baranson, Jack, 48-17n.
Barefoot, A. C., 30-3n.
Barish, Norman N., 23-13, 23-35
Barker, Kenneth N., 47-16, 47-21n., 47-22n.
Barlow, T. E., 34-24n.
Barnes, J. E., 31-26
Barneson, R. A., 27A-14
Barnett, E. Harvey, 27A-1, 27A-14
Barr, Donald R., 22-53, 22-69
Barr, Phil I., 7-8n.
Barrabee, James M., 5-17n.
Barrett, Gerald V., 18-33n.
Barrett, J. E., 30-36
Barry, Elmer N., 12-74n.
Bartlett, R. P., Jr., 31-26
Bayer, Harmon S., 9-29n.
Bayer, Lad J., 9-7n.
Bayes, Thomas, 22-61
Bazell, Robert J., 14-12n.
Bazovsky, Igor, 38-23
Beadon, J. A., 8-35n.
Beames, R. E., 5-16
Beamish, J. R., 31-26
Beaton, G. N., 8-13
Beattie, D. W., 24-44
Beaver, R. C., 15-14n.
Beazley, C. C., 31-25
Becker, F., 31-25
Beer, Michael, 18-42n., 18-43n.
Bell, Lawrence F., 2-5, 2-6
Bell, T. E., 20-27n.
Bellafiore, Ignatius J., 47-18n.
Benedict, Ruth, 7-27n.
Benjamin, J. F., 47-12n.
Bennett, Carl A., 22-43, 22-69, 29-21n., 29-34n., 29-51
Bennett, H. W., 30-36
Bennett, W. E., 30-25n.
Bensing, Phyllis L., 39-29n., 39-34
Benya, V. R., 30-9n.
Benzing, J. A., 30-37
Benzinger, Raymond B., 40-3n.
Bergere, Orland F., 15-12n.
Berkwitt, George, 18-33n.

See also Glossary of Symbols, Appendix I; Subject Index.

Subject Index

See also Glossary of Symbols, Appendix I; Name Index.